ICACT 2008

Proceedings of International Conference on Advanced Computing Technologies

ICACT 2008

Proceedings of International Conference on Advanced Computing Technologies

Chief Editor

Prof. P.S. Raju

Editor

Dr. S. Viswanadha Raju

BSP **BS Publications**

4-4-309, Giriraj Lane, Sultan Bazar,
Hyderabad - 500 095 - A.P.
Phone : 040 – 23445688, 23445605

This volume is collection of papers presented at the 'International Conference on Advanced Computing Technologies', held on 26-27 December 2008 at Gokaraju Rangaraju Institute of Engineering & Technology, Hyderabad, Andhra Pradesh, India.

Published by:

BSP BS Publications

4-4-309, Giriraj Lane, Sultan Bazar, Hyderabad - 500 095 - A.P.
Phone : 040 – 23445688; Fax : 91+40-23445611
e-mail : contactus@bspublications.net
website : www.bspublications.net

Note: The Editors does not claim any responsibility, liability for statements made and opinions expressed by authors.

ISBN: 978-81-7800-188-3

Preface

ICACT 2008 is a major international platform for research reports, case studies and discussions on advanced computing technologies. The Conference includes multi-path debates on theory and implementation of advanced computing techniques in engineering and other related fields. The conference provided a forum for research in development and application on computing technologies. The purpose of the conference is to combine basic research with application in the field of advanced computing. ICACT 2008 conference consists of invited papers and regular paper presentation.

We hope that the papers in these proceedings will serve as stepping stones towards future achievements.

- Editors

Contents

Session – 1

System Softwares and Algorithms

Session – 2

Advance Computer Architecture and Object Oriented Analysis

Session – 3

Databases and Data Mining

Session – 4
Distributed and Parallel Computing

Session – 5

Image and Speech Processing

Session – 6

Information Retrieval System

Session – 7

Networking, Cryptography and Mobile Computing

Session – 8

Applications of Science and Engineering

Session – 1

System Softwares and Algorithms

A Modified Differential Evolution using Non-linear Simplex Method to Initialize the Population

Millie Pant, Musrrat Ali and V. P. Singh,
Department of Paper Technology,
Indian Institute of Technology Roorkee, Saharanpur Campus, Saharanpur – 247001, India.
millifpt@iitr.ernet.in, musrrat.iitr@gmail.com, singhvp2@yahoo.co.in.

Abstract

The performance of population based search techniques like Differential Evolution (DE) depends largely on the selection of initial population. A good initialization scheme not only helps in giving a better final solution but also helps in improving the convergence rate of the algorithm. In the present study we propose a novel initialization scheme which uses the concept of Non Linear Simplex Method (NLSM) to generate the initial population. The proposed DE called NSDE is validated on a test bed of **10** benchmark problems with varying dimensions and the results are compared with the classical DE using random initialization and DE using opposition based learning. The numerical results show that the proposed algorithm using NLSM for generating the initial population accelerates the convergence speed quite considerably.

Keywords: *Stochastic optimization, differential evolution, crossover.*

1. Introduction

DE is comparatively a recent addition to class of population based search techniques. Nevertheless, it has emerged as one of the techniques most favored by engineers for solving continuous optimization problems. DE [1, 2] has several attractive features. Besides being an exceptionally simple evolutionary strategy, it is significantly faster and robust for solving numerical optimization problems and is more likely to find the functions true global optimum. Also, it is worth mentioning that DE has a compact structure with a small computer code and has fewer control parameters in comparison to other evolutionary algorithms. Originally Price and Storn proposed a single strategy for DE, which they later modified as ten different strategies [3].

DE has been successfully applied to a wide range of problems [4] – [**8**] etc.

Despite having several striking features and successful applications to various fields DE is sometimes criticized for its slow convergence rate for computationally expensive functions. By varying the control parameters the convergence rate of DE may be increased but it should be noted that it do not affect the quality of solution. Generally, in population based search techniques like DE an acceptable trade-off should be maintained between convergence and type of solution, which even if not a global optimal solution should be satisfactory rather than converging to a suboptimal solution which may not even be a local solution. Several attempts have been made in this direction to fortify DE with suitable mechanisms to improve its performance. Most of the studies involve the tuning or controlling of the parameters of algorithm and improving the mutation, crossover and selection mechanism. For details the interested reader may please refer to [9] – [14]. All the modified versions have shown that a slight change in the structure of DE can help in improving its performance. However, the role of the initial population, which is the topic of this paper, is widely ignored. Often, the whole area of research is set aside by a statement "generate an initial population," without implying how it should be done. There is only few literature is available on this topic. Shahryar Rahnamayan et al have introduced opposition based population initialization method [15]. To further continue the research in this direction, in this paper we propose a modified versions of DE to improve its performance in terms of convergence rate. The modified versions presented in this paper is the non linear simplex method embedded with uniform random number generator to initialize the population and is referred to as NSDE. Here we will show that initial populations may have effects, on the best objective function value found and number of function evaluation. Our motivation is to encourage discussion on whether one should pay more attention to the generation of initial populations. Performances of the proposed algorithms are compared with Basic DE and differential evolution initialized by opposition based learning (ODE), which is recently modified version of differential evolution [16], on a set of ten unconstrained benchmark problems.

Remaining of the paper is organized in following manner; in Section 2, we give a brief description of DE. In section 3, we explain the proposed NSDE algorithm. Section 4 deals with experimental settings and parameter selection. Benchmark problems are given in section 5. Section 6 makes comparison of algorithms. The paper finally concludes with section 7.

2. Differential Evolution (DE)

As mentioned earlier in the previous section, there are several variants of the DE-algorithm. Throughout the present study we shall follow the version *DE/rand/1/bin*, which is apparently the most commonly used version and shall refer to it as basic version.

This particular scheme is briefly described as follows:

DE starts with a population of NP candidate solutions which may be represented as $X_{i,G}$, $i = 1, \ldots,$ NP, where i index denotes the population and G denotes the generation to which the population belongs. The working of DE depends on the manipulation and efficiency of three main operators; mutation, reproduction and selection which briefly described in this section.

Mutation: Mutation operator is the prime operator of DE and it is the implementation of this operation that makes DE different from other Evolutionary algorithms. The mutation operation of DE applies the vector differentials between the existing population members for determining both the degree and direction of perturbation applied to the individual subject of the mutation operation. The mutation process at each generation begins by randomly selecting three individuals in the population. The ith perturbed individual, $V_{i,G+1}$, is then generated based on the three chosen individuals as follows:

$$V_{i,G+1} = X_{r3,G} + F * (X_{r1,G} - X_{r2,G}) \quad (1)$$

Where, $i = 1, \ldots,$ NP, $r_1, r_2, r_3 \in \{1, \ldots, NP\}$ are randomly selected and satisfy:

$r_1 \neq r_2 \neq r_3 \neq i$, $F \in [0, 1+]$, F is the control parameter proposed by Storn and Price [1].

Crossover: The perturbed individual, $V_{i,G+1} = (v_{1,i,G+1}, \ldots, v_{n,i,G+1})$, and the current population member, $X_{i,G} = (x_{1,i,G}, \ldots, x_{n,i,G})$, are then subject to the crossover operation, that finally generates the population of candidates, or "trial" vectors, $U_{i,G+1} = (u_{1,i,G+1}, \ldots, u_{n,i,G+1})$, as follows:

$$u_{j,i,G+1} = \begin{cases} v_{j,i,G+1} & \text{if } rand_j \leq C_r \vee j = k \\ x_{j,i,G} & \text{otherwise} \end{cases} \quad (2)$$

Where, $j = 1 \ldots n$, $k \in \{1, \ldots, n\}$ is a random parameter's index, chosen once for each i, and the crossover rate, $Cr \in [0, 1]$, the other control parameter of DE, is set by the user.

Selection: The selection scheme of DE also differs from that of other EAs. The population for the next generation is selected from the individual in current population and its corresponding trial vector according to the following rule:

$$X_{i,G+1} = \begin{cases} U_{i,G+1} & \text{if } f(U_{i,G+1}) \leq f(X_{i,G}) \\ X_{i,G} & \text{otherwise} \end{cases} \quad (3)$$

Thus, each individual of the temporary (trial) population is compared with its counterpart in the current population. The one with the lower objective function value will survive from the tournament selection to the population of the next generation. As a result, all the individuals of the next generation are as good or better than their counterparts in the current generation. In DE trial vector is not compared against all the individuals in the current generation, but only against one individual, its counterpart, in the current generation. The psuedocode and flow chart of algorithm is given here.

DE pseudo code:

Step 1: *Initialization:* The first step is the random initialization of the parent population. Generate randomly NP vectors, each of n dimensions:
$x_{i,j} = x_{min,j} + rand(0, 1)(x_{max,j} - x_{min,j})$, where $x_{min,j}$ and x_{max} are lower and upper bound for j^{th} component respectively, rand(0,1) uniform random number between 0 and 1.

Step 2: Calculate the objective function value $f(x_i)$ for all x_i.

Step 3: Select three points from population and generate perturbed individual v_i using equation (1).

Step 4: Recombine the each target vector x_i with perturbed individual generated in step 3 to generate a trial vector u_i using equation (2).

Step 5: Check whether each variable of the trial vector is within range. If not keep it within range using $u_{i,j} = 2 * x_{min,j} - u_{i,j}$, if $u_{i,j} < x_{min,j}$ and $u_{i,j} = 2 * x_{max,j} - u_{i,j}$, if $u_{i,j} > x_{max,j}$, otherwise go to step 6.

Step6: Calculate the objective function value for vector u_i.

Step 7: Choose better of the two (function value at target and trial point) using equation (3) for next generation.

Step 8: Check whether convergence criterion is met. if yes, stop; otherwise go to step 3.

3. Proposed algorithm NSDE

In this section we describe the proposed modified NSDE, which uses non linear simplex method in conjugation with uniform random number generator in initialization step.

3.1 NSDE

Providing the initial population with some extra information of search space is generally considered as important help for the DE algorithm, since it may lead to faster convergence and better quality of the solutions provided by the algorithm. The main idea presented in this study is that, nonlinear simplex method (NSM) developed by J.A. Nelder and R. Mead [16], is embedded with uniform random number generator for the generation of the initial population. The procedure of this is outlined as follows:

1. Generate a population P of size NP uniformly as in step 1 of DE and set k=1.
2. Generate a point by NSM Method, which has the following main operations.
   - 2.1 Select n+ 1 point from population P randomly and evaluate function at these points.
   - 2.2 Calculate the centroid of these points excluding the point X_{max} at which function is maximum.
   - 2.3 *Reflection*: Reflect X_{max} through the centroid to a new point X_1. And calculate the function value at this point.
   - 2.4 *Expansion:* If $f(X_1)<=f(X_{min})$ then expansion is performed and generate a new point X_2 in expanded region and evaluate function at this point. If $f(X_2)<f(X_{min})$ then point X_2 add to population Q and continue from step 2.1 with k=k+1. Otherwise add point X_1 to the population Q and continue from step 2.1 with k=k+1.
   - 2.5 *Contractions:* If $f(X_1)<f(X_{max})$ then contraction step is in walked to produce a new point X_3 add this point to population Q and go to step 2.1 with k=k+1.
   - 2.6 *Reduction:* This step we have replaced by uniform distribution. If $f(X_1)>f(X_{max})$ then generate point uniformly within range and add to Q. If k<NP go to step 2.1 else stop.

At the completion of NSM process select NP fittest point from the union of P and Q as initial population. After initialization step, NSDE algorithm works like the basic DE.

Thus, the initial population is provided with the information of the good regions that possess each particle as a vertex of the NSM simplex in each step. The algorithm is not computationally expensive, since for each particle of the initial population one function evaluation is done, which is inevitable even if we use a randomly distributed initial population.

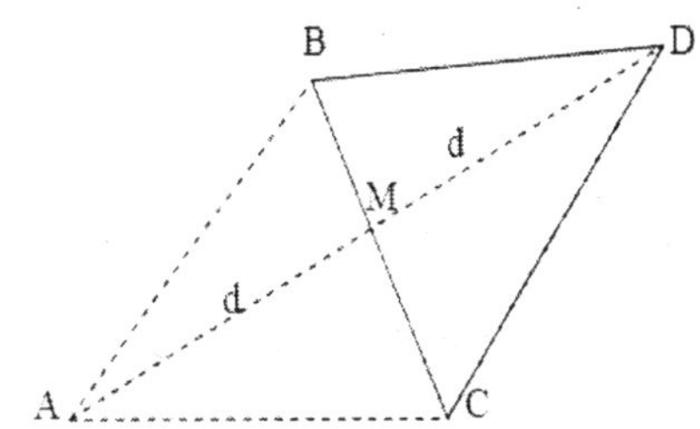

Fig. 1(a) Reflection of A to D

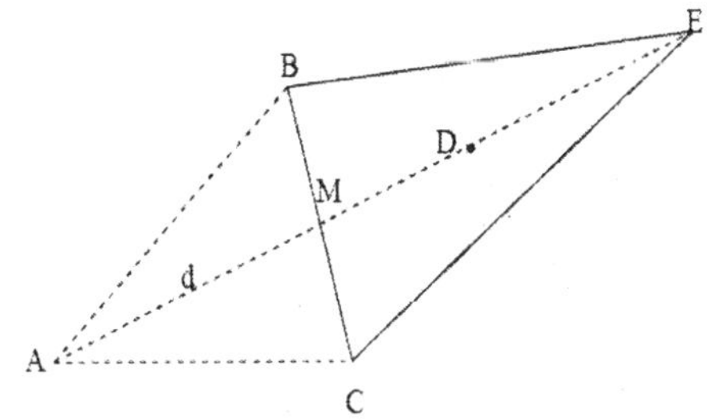

Fig. 1(b) Expansion of D to E

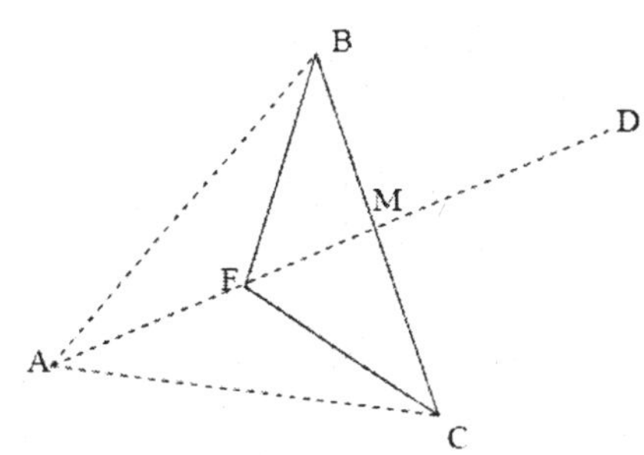

Fig. 1(c) Contraction of D to F

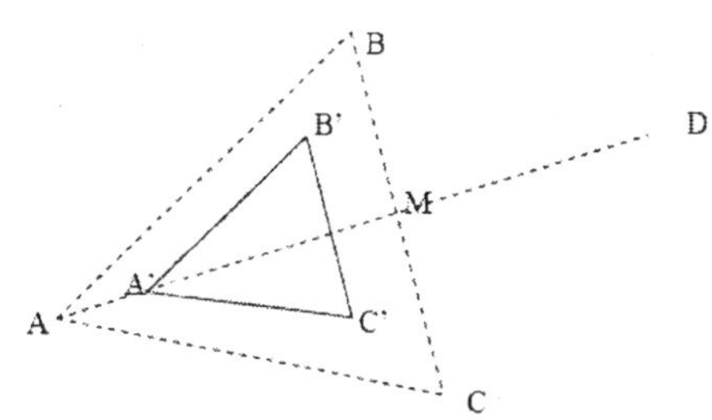

Fig. 1(d) Reduction of ABC to A'B'C'

4. Experimental Setup

With DE, the lower limit for NP is 4 since the mutation process requires at least three other chromosomes for each parent. While testing the algorithms, we began by using the optimized control settings of DE. Population size, NP can always be increased to help maintain population diversity. As a general rule, an effective NP is between 3 * n and 5 * n, but can often be reduced to minimize the NFE. For the present study we performed various experiments with the population size as well as with the crossover rate and mutation probability rate and observed that for problems up to dimension 30 a population size of 3*n is sufficient. But here we have taken fixed population size NP=100, which is slightly large than 3*n. Values of F scale outside the range of 0.4 to 1.2 are rarely effective, so F=0.5 is usually a good initial choice. In general C_r should be as large as possible to speedup the convergence so in this study we have taken C_r =0.9. All the algorithms are executed on a PIV PC, using DEV C++, thirty times for each problem. Random numbers are generated using the inbuilt random number generator *rand ( ) function* available in DEVC++. Over all acceleration AR is defined as

$$AR = \left(1 - \frac{\sum_{j=1}^{\mu} NFE(\text{by one algo})_j}{\sum_{j=1}^{\mu} NFE(\text{by other algo})_j} \right) \times 100$$

Where μ number of functions. In every case, a run was terminated when the best function value obtained is less than a threshold for the given function or when the maximum number of function evaluation ($NFE=10^6$) was reached. In order to have a fair comparison, these settings are kept the same for all algorithms over all benchmark functions during the simulations.

5. Benchmark Problems

The performance of proposed algorithms is evaluated on a test bed of ten standard, unconstrained benchmark problems taken from the literature [16]. The dimension of the problems varies from 2 to 30. Here we have taken both functions unimodal and highly multimodal in nature. The degree of multimodality for functions, keeps on increasing with the increase in the number of variables thereby, increasing the complexity of the problem. Benchmark problems are given in the Appendix.

6. Numerical results and comparisons

Comparisons of the algorithms is done in terms of average fitness function value, standard deviation and the corresponding t-test value; average number of function evaluations and the average time taken by every algorithm to solve a particular problem. The results are given in Table 1, Table 2 and Table 3. From these Table 3, which gives the average fitness function value, standard deviation and t values it can be observed that in terms of average fitness function value all the algorithms gave more or less similar results which are comparable to true function value. However when we do the comparison in terms of average time taken and average number of function evaluations then the proposed NSDE emerges as a clear winner. It converges to the optimum at a faster rate in comparison to the basic DE and ODE. This fact is also evident from the overall acceleration rate.

Table 1 Average Function Evaluations for 30 runs and overall acceleration rate

Fun.	Dim	Mean function		
		DE	ODE	NSDE
f_1	30	28020	26912	**26220**
f_2	30	37312	36639	**35500**
f_3	30	295232	**295112**	332860
f_4	10	382454	361234	**265420**
f_5	30	54503	53305	**52240**
f_6	30	52476	51589	**49170**
f_7	2	3845	3740	**3520**
f_8	4	7902	7934	**6780**
f_9	30	44034	41455	**35330**
f_{10}	10	220356	196871	**172200**
Total		1126134	1074791	979240
AR			4.559227	13.0441

Table 2: Average time of 30 runs

Fun.	Dim.	Average Time (Sec)		
		DE	ODE	NSDE
f_1	30	0.60	0.54	**0.51**
f_2	30	0.60	0.57	**0.55**
f_3	30	11.30	**11.10**	13.40
f_4	10	2.41	2.34	**2.13**
f_5	30	1.80	1.79	**1.70**
f_6	30	1.50	1.45	**1.41**
f_7	2	0.31	0.29	**0.23**
f_8	4	0.10	0.11	**0.09**
f_9	30	1.20	1.11	1.11
f_{10}	10	3.02	2.93	**2.67**

Table 3: Mean fitness, standard deviation of functions in 30 runs and t-valve

Function	Dim.	Mean fitness, (Standard deviation) and t-value		
		DE	ODE	NSDE
f_1	30	**0.0546854** (0.0131867) --	0.0901626 (0.0077778) 12.48	0.0916686 (0.00721253) 13.25
f_2	30	**0.0560517** (0.0116127) --	0.0918435 (0.00565233) 14.92	0.0866163 (0.00666531) 12.29
f_3	30	0.0957513 (0.00293408) --	0.0952397 (0.00499586) 0.48	**0.0951172** (0.00405255) 0.68
f_4	10	0.0931511 (0.0145175) --	0.0874112 (0.00699322) 1.92	0.0851945 (0.0121355) 2.26
f_5	30	0.0915561 (0.012111) --	**0.0885065** (0.00711877) 1.17	0.0916412 (0.00860403) 0.03
f_6	30	0.0942648 (0.00478545) --	0.0933845 (0.00620528) 0.60	**0.0926704** (0.00735851) 0.98
f_7	2	**4.26112e-008** (2.5783e-008) --	6.23824e-008 (2.75612e-008) 2.82	4.9999e-008 (2.95279e-008) 1.01
f_8	4	0.0620131 (0.0239495) --	**0.0528597** (0.0276657) 1.35	0.0591064 (0.0123711) 0.58
f_9	30	0.088998 (0.00880246) --	0.092875 (0.00487147) 2.08	0.0882776 (0.0103789) 0.29
f_{10}	10	-7.91444 (3.40729) --	-9.61563 (0.024986) 2.69	**-9.62952** (0.0238362) 2.71

7. Discussion and conclusions

This paper proposes a nonlinear simplex method for generating the initial population of points in a Differential evolution algorithm and compares its performance with basic DE and with opposition based DE which is a recently developed method. The numerical results show that the proposed version helps in improving the convergence rate of DE without compromising with its ability to produce a good fitness function value. In future we shall extend our algorithm for solving constrained optimization problems and also we will see the effect of having a modified mutation or crossover operator.

8. References

[1] R.Storn, and K.Price, "DE-a simple and efficient adaptive scheme for global optimization over continuous space", *Technical Report TR-95-012, ICSI, March 1995. Available via the Internet: ftp.icsi.berkeley.edu/pub/techreports/ 1995/tr-95-012.ps.Z,* 1995.

[2] R.Storn, and K.Price, "DE-a simple and efficient heuristic for global optimization over continuous space", *Journal of Global Optimization* 11(4), 1997 pp 41-359.

[3] K.Price, "An introduction to DE", *In: Corne, D., Marco, D. and Glover, F. (eds.), New Ideas in Optimization, McGraw-Hill, London (UK),* 1999 pp 78–108.

[4] F.S.Wang, W.M.Cheng, "Simultaneous optimization of feeding rate and operation parameters for fed-batch fermentation processes", *Biotechnology Progress* 15, 1999 pp 949–952.

[5] B.V.Babu, S.A. Munawar, "Differential Evolution for the Optimal Design of Heat Exchangers", *In: Proceedings of All-India seminar on Chemical Engineering Progress on Resource Development: A Vision 2010 and Beyond, Bhuvaneshwar,* 2000.

[6] B.V.Babu, R.P.Singh, "Synthesis & optimization of Heat Integrated Distillation Systems Using Differential Evolution", *In: Proceedings of All-India seminar on Chemical Engineering Progress on Resource Development: A Vision 2010 and Beyond, Bhuvaneshwar,* 2000.

[7] R.Angira, B.V.Babu, "Optimization of Non-Linear Chemical Processes Using Modified Differential Evolution (MDE)", *In: Proceedings of the 2nd Indian International Conference on Artificial Intelligence, Pune, India,* 2005a pp. 911–923.

[8] R.Angira, B.V.Babu, "Optimization of Process Synthesis and Design Problems: A Modified Differential Evolution Approach", *Chemical Engineering Science* 61, 2006a pp 4707–4721.

[9] P.K Bergey, C. Rgsdale, "Modified differential evolution: a greedy random strategy for genetic recombination", *omega* 33, 2005 pp 255-265.

[10] P.Kaleo, M.M.Ali, "A numerical study of some modified differential evolution algorithms", *European journal of operational research* 169, 2006 pp 1176-1184,.

[11] M.M.Ali, "Differential evolution with preferential crossover", *European journal of operational research* 181, 2007 pp 1137-1147.

[12] N.Noman, H. Iba, "Enhancing differential evolution performance with local search for high dimensional function optimization", *GECCO'05 Washington, DC, USA*, 2005 pp 967-974.

[13] A.K. Qin, P.N. Suganthan, "Self adaptive differential evolution algorithm for numerical optimization", *IEEE*, 2005 pp 1785-1791

[14] H.Y Fan, J.Lampinen, G.S.Dulikravich, "Improvements to mutation donor formulation of differential evolution", *International Congress on Evolutionary Methods for Design, Optimization and Control with Applications to Industrial Problems,* EUROGEN, 2003 pp 1-12.

[15] S.Rahnamayan, H.R. Tizhoosh, M.A Salman, "Opposition based-differential evolution", *IEEE transaction on evolutionary computation* 12(1), 2008 pp 64-79.

[16] J.A.Nelder, R Mead, "A simplex method for function minimization", *computer journal*, vol 7, 1965 pp 308-313.

Appendix

1. Sphere function:

$$f_1(x) = \sum_{i=1}^{n} x_i^2 \text{, with } -5.12 \le x_i \le 5.12 \text{, min } f_1(0,...,0) = 0$$

2. Axis parallel hyper-ellipsoid:

$$f_2(x) = \sum_{i=1}^{n} ix_i^2 \text{, with } -5.12 \le x_i \le 5.12 \text{, min } f_2(0,...,0) = 0$$

3. Rosenbrock's valley:

$$f_3(x) = \sum_{i=1}^{n-1}[100(x_{i+1}^2 - x_i^2) + (1 - x_i^2)] \text{ with } -2 \le x_i \le 2 \text{, min } f_3(1,...,1) = 0$$

4. Restrigin's function:

$$f_4(x) = 10n + \sum_{i=1}^{n}(x_i^2 - 10\cos(2\pi x_i)) \text{ with } -5.12 \le x_i \le 5.12 \text{, min } f_4(0,...,0) = 0$$

5. Griewenk function:

$$f_5(x) = \frac{1}{4000}\sum_{i=1}^{n} x_i^2 - \prod_{i=1}^{n}\cos(\frac{x_i}{\sqrt{i}}) + 1 \text{ with } -600 \le x_i \le 600 \text{, min } f_5(0,...,0) = 0$$

6. Ackley's function:

$$f_6(X) = -20 * \exp\left(-.2\sqrt{1/\text{n}\sum_{\text{i=1}}^{\text{n}} \text{x}_\text{i}^2}\right) - \exp\left(1/\text{n}\sum_{\text{i=1}}^{\text{n}} \cos(2\pi \text{x}_\text{i})\right) + 20 + e \text{, with } -32 \le x_i \le 32 \text{,}$$

$$\text{min } f_6(0,...,0) = 0$$

7. Beale function:

$$f_7(x) = [1.5 - x_1(1 - x_2)]^2 + [2.25 - x_1(1 - x_2^2)]^2 + [2.625 - x_1(1 - x_2^3)]^2 \text{ with } -4.5 \le x_i \le 4.5 \text{,}$$

$$\text{min } f_7(3, 0.5) = 0$$

8. Colville function:

$$f_8(x) = 100(x_2 - x_1^2)^2 + (1 - x_1)^2 + 90(x_4 - x_3^2)^2 + (1 - x_3)^2 + 10.1((x_2 - 1)^2 + (x_4 - 1)^2)$$

$$19.8(x_2 - 1)(x_4 - 1) \text{, with } -10 \le x_i \le 10 \text{, min } f_8(1,1,1,1) = 0$$

9. Levy function:

$$f_9(x) = \sin^2(3\pi x_1) + \sum_{i=1}^{n-1}(x_i - 1)(1 + \sin^2(3\pi x_{i+1})) + (x_n - 1)(1 + \sin^2(2\pi x_n))$$

$$\text{with } -10 \le x_i \le 10 \text{, min } f_9(1,...,1) = 0$$

10. Michalewicz function:

$$f_{10}(x) = -\sum_{i=1}^{n}\sin(x_i)(\sin(ix_i^2/\pi))^{2m} \text{ with } 0 \le x_i \le \pi \text{, m=10, min } f_{10(n=10)} = -9.66015$$

A Survey on Scalable CPU Scheduling in Real Time Database

Sadanand S. Patil[1] and Gajendra R.Bamnote[2]
[1]Lecturer, Priyadarshani College of Engineering, Nagpur, Maharashtra
[2]Assistant Professor, Prof. Ram Meghe Institute of Technology & Research, Bandera-Amaravati
sadanand.in@gmail.com grbamnote@rediffmail.com

Abstract

A new scalable priority table CPU scheduling algorithm in real time database RTDBS is presented. It is applicable in environments where data requests arrive with different requirements such as real-time deadline, and user priority. Previous work on CPU scheduling is based on traditional CPU scheduler for meeting the real-time deadlines. The general idea is based on modeling the CPU scheduler in RTDBS requests as points in the multi-dimensional space, where each of the dimensions represents one of the parameters (e.g., one dimension represents the deadline of task , another represents the criticalness or value and a third dimension represents the priority of the request, etc.). Then the CPU scheduling problem reduces to the problem of finding a linear order to scheduling these multi-dimensional points. Space-filling curves are adopted to define a linear order for sorting and scheduling objects that lie in the multi-dimensional space. This generalizes the one-dimensional CPU scheduling algorithms (e.g., EDF, MCF). Several techniques are presented to show how a CPU scheduler deals with the progressive arrival of task over time. In this paper we study and investigate of the alternative techniques of CPU scheduling algorithm over other traditional approaches.

1. Introduction

RTDBS can be viewed as an extension to conventional real-time systems. Therefore, there are subtle differences between the two systems as shown in figure (1). Conventional real-time systems can be perceived as the left side of the dashed line in figure (1), where a scheduled task might experience a preempt-resume behavior until termination. Whereas RTDB systems also include the right side of the graph where a transaction does not only experience the preempt-resume behavior, but rather is also subject to concurrency control, which causes transactions to block. After a transaction blocks, it might resume its previous execution, rollback and restart its previous execution, or get aborted and terminate its execution. Note that tasks in a conventional real-time system also block on synchronization protocols. However, the blocking period is for the duration of a critical region, whereas blocking in RTDBS is for the duration of the lifetime of the blocking transaction(s). Thus, in order to enhance the performance of RTDBS systems, we must reduce (minimize) the interaction between the CPU scheduler and the concurrency control module. The interaction between the two modules can be mainly the result of preemption, and partially, I/O operations. Both preemption and I/O operations cause transactions to wait while holding some resources[14].

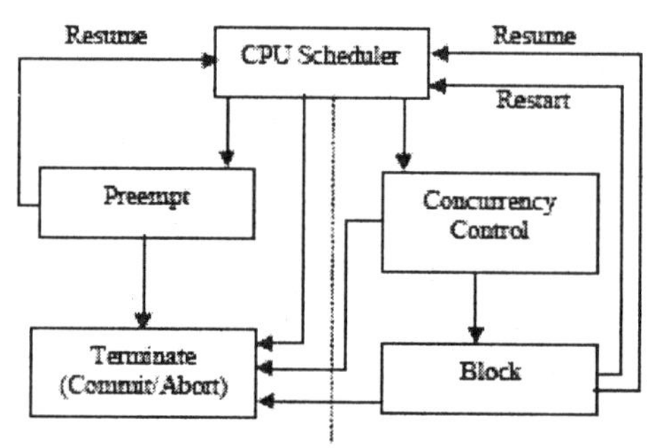

Fig. 1 CPU Scheduler

Priority-based scheduling algorithms have widely applied In real time database systems. These algorithms include Rate-Monotonic Scheduling (RM), Earliest Deadline First (EDF), Highest Value First (HVF) and Highest Value Density First (HVDF). In these algorithms, priorities of tasks are all calculated based on some characteristics of tasks, such as deadline, slack time, criticalness (i.e., the importance or value of a task). However, it is insufficient if the priority of a task is only determined by using a characteristic [6][9]. For example, EDF policy assigns the highest priority to the task with the earliest deadline. However, it is not most critical whether the deadline or the slack time is shorter or not. Simulation experiments show that priority-based scheduling algorithms should integrate two deadline constraints of the CPU requests, independent characteristics of criticalness and deadline, presented a kind of on-line scheduling algorithm, called as Criticalness-Deadline First (CDF). Every task is assigned priority based on the ratio of the relative deadline with criticalness as it arrives. Tests show that, based on the CPU scheduling of CDF, the performance of systems could be greatly increased compared to the algorithms of only using deadline or criticality as the characteristic parameter. [4,5]

The drawbacks of above algorithms are as follows:

1. Because the deadline and value of a task are different concepts completely, and their measure units are different also, so we cannot simply make arithmetic operation on them. For example, in CDF algorithm, We must restrict ranges of deadline and value of a task.
2. The problem of choosing parameter of integrating the value and deadline of a task, e.g., the choice of parameter a in MIX algorithm is very sensitive to ranges of parameters of a task. Different tasks are likely to have the same priorities in CDF or MIX algorithm.

Building reliable and efficient CPU schedulers in RTDBS has always been a very challenging task. It has become even more so with today's complex systems and demanding applications. As applications grow in complexity, more requirements are imposed on CPU schedulers in RTDBS, for example, the problem of CPU scheduling in multimedia servers. For overcoming these problems, we present a new real-time scheduling scheme based on scalable priority table design

2. Space-Filling Curves (SFC)

An optimal space-filling curve is one that sorts points in space in ascending order for all dimensions. In reality, when a space-filling curve attempts to sort the points in ascending order according to one dimension, it fails to do the same for the other dimensions. A good space-filling curve for one dimension is not necessarily good for the other dimensions. irregularity as a measure of goodness of space-filling curves [10]. The irregularity can be used as an indicator for the practical performance measures, e.g., CPU utilization, priority inversion, and deadline losses.

3. Scalable Priority Table Based Scheduling Algorithms

The general idea is based on modeling the CPU requests by the transaction of RTDBS as points in the multi-dimensional space where each dimension represents one of the parameters (e.g., one dimension represents the task deadline, another represents the criticalness and the third dimension represents the priority of the request, etc.). Then the scheduler problem reduces to finding a linear order to scheduling the task by traversing these multidimensional points.

The underlying CPU scheduling in RTDBS is based on space-filling curves (SFC). A space-filling curve maps the multi-dimensional space into the one dimensional space. It acts like a thread that passes through every cell element (or pixel) in the multi-dimensional space so that every cell is visited exactly once. Thus, space-filling curves are adopted to define a linear order for sorting and scheduling task that lie in the multi-dimensional space.

First, some principles should be of definitude in scheduling:

The earlier the deadline of a task is or the larger the value is, the higher the priority of the task is.

For tasks with the same deadline and same value, the earlier the arrival time of a task is, the higher the priority of the task is.

Figure (2) gives a kind of priority scheme table based on dead line value, where the arrow denotes the sequence of task priority. In this assignment method of priority, the deadline list of tasks sorts in ascending order, i.e., the earlier the deadline of a task is, the more the task locates at the front. However, the value list of tasks sorts in descending order such that the task with greater value

In the priority table in given below every task has a priority level:

$$P = i + j$$

Where, i and j denote positions of deadline and value of the task in their corresponding task lists respectively. The smaller the value of P is, the higher the priority level of tasks is. The tasks on an inclined line belong to the same priority level, but each task has a unique priority, which is assigned according to the following formula:

$$p = (i + j - 1) * (i + j - 2) / 2 + j \quad [8]$$

The smaller the value of p is, the higher the priority of a task. For tasks with the same priority level, this scheme prefers to executing tasks with earlier deadlines, i.e., the sequence of scheduling must execute according to the direction pointed by the arrow as shown in Figure.

This kind of design scheme of priority table on deadline (di) and value (vi) results in a scheduling algorithm called as Value first with Earliest Deadline (sweep) [8].

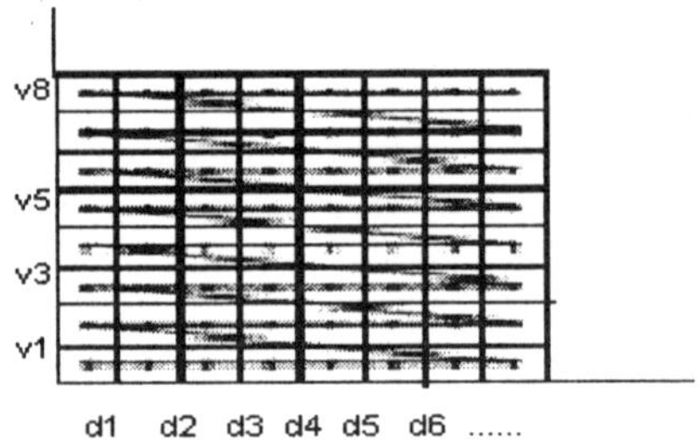

Fig. 2 SFC sweep Priority Table

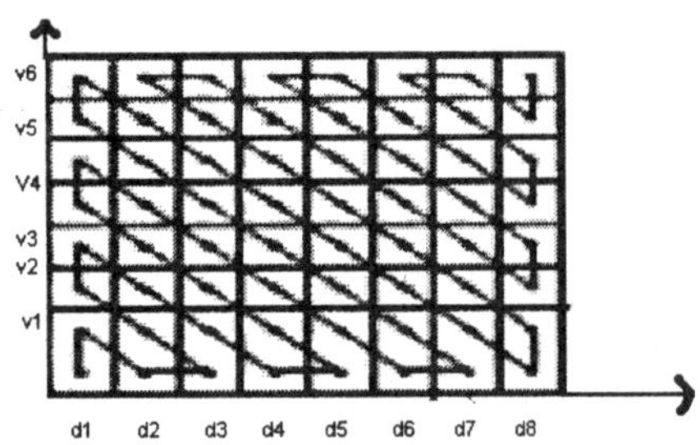

Fig. 3 SFC Diagonal Priority Table

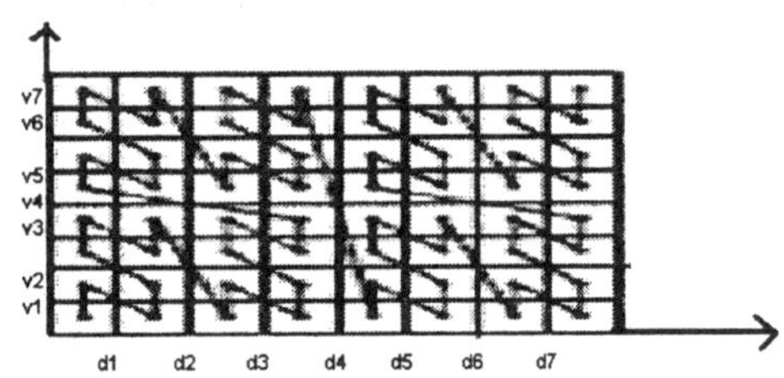

Fig. 4 SFC Pea no priority Table

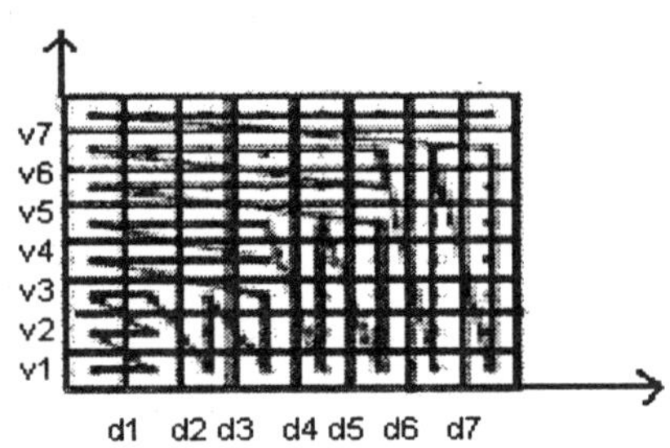

Fig. 5 SFC Spiral priority Table

In this scheduler, a CPU scheduler for RTDBS is modeled by multiple parameters, (e.g., real-time deadline, the criticalness etc.) and represented as a point in the multi-dimensional space where each parameter corresponds to one dimension. Using a space-filling curve (SFC), the multi-dimensional CPU request is converted to a one dimensional value. Then, CPU in RTDBS requests are inserted into a priority queue according to their one-dimensional value with a lower value indicating a higher priority.

3.1 The Non-Preemptive SFC CPU Scheduler

In this approach, once the CPU scheduler starts to walk through a full cycle of a space-filling curve, the cycle is never preempted. A newly arrived request for scheduling is inserted in the queue. If and only if it will not preempt the current cycle. If new task needs to preempt the cycle (i.e., New task has higher priority than current task), then it is inserted in a waiting queue. The cycle is finished when the execution of lowest priority task is completed, then, all requests from queue are moved to queue and a new cycle is generated.

3.2 The Fully-Preemptive SFC CPU Scheduler

This is the simplest approach. All tasks are inserted into a single CPU scheduler queue according to their space-filling curve priority. This scheduler is fully-preemptive in the sense that any incoming new task with higher priority than current task preempts the current cycle and starts a new one However, when has lower priority than, it is inserted in without affecting the current cycle.

The fully-preemptive CPU scheduler serves all tasks schedule according to their priority. Low priority requests may starve due to the continuous arrival of high priority requests. On the other hand, the non-preemptive CPU scheduler does not lead to starvation since it guarantees that lower priority disk requests in a certain cycle will be served before starting a new cycle. However, a priority inversion takes place where higher priority task may wait for lower priority task to be served. The drawbacks of the two approaches raise the motivation for having a combined CPU scheduler that has the merits of both schedulers.

3.3 Scalability of SFC CPU Schedulers in RTDBS

In this section, we address the issue of scalability of SFC CPU Schedulers in RTDBS, e.g., when the number of dimensions (schedule parameters) increases or when the number of priority levels per dimension increases.

Where each dimension has 16 priority levels. The Diagonal SFC CPU scheduler gives the best performance especially with higher dimensions. The Sweep, Pea no, and Spiral CPU scheduler have almost the same performance. [10]

4. Conclusions

This kind of design method of priority table can be used to integrate other two different characteristics of tasks, even be extended to integrate three different characteristics of tasks. we have proposed a new scalable priority table design for CPU scheduling algorithm in RTDBS for serving requests that require parameters (i.e., deadline, priority, etc.). The idea is to map the multiple parameters into the one-dimensional space. Then, we use the ordering imposed by space-filling curves to serve the CPU requests. Moreover, using EDF and HVF algorithms as the basclinc, Especially, under overload situations, these algorithms degrade graceful, and provide differentiated service for tasks of different criticalness levels.

5. References

[1] C.L. Liu and J.W. Layland. Scheduling Algorithms for Multiprogramming' in a Hard Real-Time Environment. Journal of the ACM, 20(1), 46-61, 1973.

[2] E.D. Jensen, C.D. Locke and H. Toduda. A Time-Driven Scheduling Model for Real-Time Operating Systems. Proceedings of Real-Time Systems Symposium, I pp.112-122, 1985.

[3] R. Abbott and H. Garcia-Molina. Scheduling Real-Time Transactions. SIGMOD Record, Vol. 17, No. 1, March 1988.

[4] J. Huang, J. Stankovic, D. Towesly and K. Ramamritham. Experimental Evaluation of Real-Time Transaction Processing. Proceedings of the 10th Real-Time Systems Symposium, pp. 144-153, 1989.

[5] R. K. Abbot and H. Garcia-Molina. Scheduling i/o requests with deadlines: A performance evaluation. In *Proc. Of the IEEE Real-Time Systems Symp., RTSS*, pages 113–125, Florida, Dec. 1990.

[6] W. G. Aref, I. Kamel, and S. Ghandeharizadeh. Disk scheduling in video editing systems. *IEEE Trans. on Knowledge and Data Engineering, TKDE*, 13(6):933–950, 2001.

[7] T. Asano, D. Ranjan, T. Roos, E. Welzl, and P. Widmayer. Space-filling curves and their use in the design of geometric data structures. *Theoretical Computer Science, TCS*, 181(1):3–15, 1997

[8] Qiang Wang, Hong-an Wang, Hong Jin, Guo-zhong Dai," Design and Evaluation of Priority Table Based Real-Time Scheduling Algorithms", Proceedings of the 2003 IEEE Changsha, China - October 2003 International Conference on Robotics Intelligent Systems and Signal Processing

[9] Y. Kim and S. H. Son, "An Approach Towards Predictable Real-Time Transaction Processing", *Proceedings of the 5th Euromicro Workshop on Real-Time Systems*, IEEE Computer Society Press, 1993.

[10] Walid G. Aref Khaled El-Bassyouni Ibrahim Kamel, Mohamed F. Mokbel, "Scalable QoS-Aware Disk-Scheduling" Department of Computer Sciences, Purdue University, West Lafayette, IN 47907-1398

[11] Y. Kim and S. H. Son, "Supporting Predictability in Real-Time Database Systems", *IEEE Real-Time Technology and Application Symposium (RTAS' 96)*, Boston, MA, June 1996.

[12] C. L. Liu, and J. W. Layland, "Scheduling Algorithms for Multiprogramming in Hard-Real Time Environments", *Journal of the ACM*, Vol. 20, No. 1, January 1973.

[13] C. D. Locke, "Best-effort Decision Making for Real-time Scheduling", Ph.D. thesis, Computer Science Department, Carnegie Mellon University, 1986.

[14] *Saud A. Aldarmi* and *Alan Burns,"* Dynamic CPU Scheduling with Imprecise Knowledge of Computation-Time", Real-Time Systems Group Department of Computer Science The University of York York, YO10 5DD, U.K.

Decision Support System for Jobshop Scheduling

Dr. A. Jawahar Babu[1], Dr. G. Janardhana Raju[2] and Dr. S. Viswanadha Raju[3]
[1]Professor & Head of Mech. Engg., Gudlavalleru Engineering College, Krishna Dist.
[2]Professor of Mechanical, Gurunanak Engineering College, Hyderabad
[3]Professor of CSE and HOD of MCA, Gokaraju Rangaraju Institute of Technology, Hyderabad

Abstract

Scheduling consists of planning and prioritizing activities that need to be performed in an orderly sequence of operation. A Decision Support System(DSS) for job shop scheduling which deals with prioritizing jobs while sequencing is developed. It is based on Analytical Hierarchical Process and some selected dispatching rules. The DSS is tested on a bench mark problem and results are presented.

1. Introduction

A Decision Support System (DSS) refers to a class of systems which support the process of making decisions. The emphasis is on 'support' rather than on automation of decisions [1]. Scheduling is a tool that optimizes use of available resources. Scheduling leads to increased efficiency and capacity utilization, reducing time required to complete jobs and consequently increasing the profitability of an organization [11]. In the present work, job shop scheduling is considered for the development of DSS. The job shop problem is considered important because it reflects the actual operation of several industries. In a job shop on any given day several jobs may require scheduling, each with a different processing sequence and different processing times on the machine. Job may or may not have promised delivery dates and the solution procedures differ as the objective of scheduling changes.

For n job, m machine scheduling problem, even though number of sequences are possible, the best sequence must satisfy the following conditions:

1. It must be technologically feasible (i.e., satisfy the machine precedence constraints).
2. It must optimize the effectiveness measure.

Evaluation of all possible combinations is an impossible task even for a problem of moderate size [5].

Many job shop scheduling approaches are reported in the literature. Most of these

Approaches are non-analytical in nature. Even for a simple problem, scheduling becomes extremely complex when dynamical uncertainties, e.g. machine breakdowns and uncertain arrival of jobs are taken into consideration [3]. Analytical results obtained are usually for special cases, and most real-life job shop scheduling problems do not fall into this class of special cases [2].The most preferred approach to job shop scheduling in the industry is using dispatching rules [4]. Many heuristic rules have been developed by various researchers to determine the priority by which a job should be processed. These rules can be classified as either static or dynamic, based on when the decisions referred to are made. With a static rule job priorities are determined in advance of processing jobs. The priorities remain the same throughout job processing.

Dispatching rules are attractive in terms of their simplicity and ease of application. However there are some shortcomings to usage of dispatching rules [6, 10]. They are:

1. Dispatching rules do not consider all of the available resources at the same time. The common practice is to employ an additional rule to first select a resource and then apply the dispatching rule. This contaminates effectiveness of dispatching rule.
2. Dispatching rules do not allow for the use of multiple criteria in the scheduling process. Dispatching rules often influence only one performance measure, whereas scheduling in the industry usually requires the meeting of several objectives simultaneously.
3. The rigid structure of the dispatching rules excludes the use of other useful information that may be available for scheduling.
4. There is no single universal dispatching rule. The choice of a suitable dispatching rule depends on the nature of the scheduling problem and the performance measure of the interest.

But the scheduling environment is dynamic, and hence dispatching rules also need to change over time [10]. In the dynamic rule on the other hand the job priorities change from machine to machine based on the status of a predefined condition that is examined before a job is assigned to the machine. This dynamic selection of dispatching rules is very attractive as now the scheduler is not constrained to just one dispatching rule or to any specific job shop conditions .The information available in the various job shop conditions may now be utilized to make better decisions.

2. Problem definition and assumptions

Present study deals with the development of a DSS for scheduling of a formal job shop problem [7] which is defined as follows:

"n jobs are to be processed on m machines. Each job consists of a set of m operations, one operation uniquely associated with each of the M machines. The processing time for an operation cannot be split. Technological constraints demand that the operations within each job must be processed in a unique order. The scheduling problem involves determining the sequence and timing of each operation on each machine, such that some given performance criterion is maximized or minimized".

A DSS using Analytical Hierarchy Process is proposed for the scheduling of the formal job shop problem with following assumptions:

(i) Each machine can perform only one operation at a time on any job.
(ii) A job, once taken up for processing, should be completed before another job can be taken up i.e. job preemption is not allowed.
(iii) No two successive operations of a job can be performed on the same machine.
(iv) An operation of any job cannot be performed until all previous operations of the job are completed.
(v) There are no alternative routings.
(vi) There are no interruptions in the shop floor i.e. machine breakdowns, shortage of raw materials etc.
(vii) The jobs are independent of each other, no assembly is involved.
(viii) There are no parallel machines.

3. Analytic hierarchy process (AHP)

As complex decision-making problems have many related factors or criteria, the traditional logical thinking process leads to a sequence of ideas so tangled that the original solution is often overlooked. In the AHP, the whole task of the decision maker is made simpler by constructing a hierarchy and developing a mathematical model that calculates the priority values for different criteria and sub-criteria present in the problem. The application procedure of AHP can be divided into the following three steps: 1. Representation of the problem in a hierarchical structure where the levels of the hierarchy show the overall goal, criteria, sub-criteria and alternatives of the given problem. 2. Making the pair wise comparisons and 3. Deriving the priority or preference values for the alternatives. The AHP helps to pair wise compare the criteria at a particular level of hierarchy to find out which criteria the decision maker wants to set with the highest priority. While comparing those criteria qualitatively, some corresponding scale values have to be assigned to them. These comparison values are generally used to develop a near consistent positive reciprocal matrix [8, 9].

4. Development of AHP model for job shop scheduling

The AHP serves as frame work to structure problems by providing judgments based on knowledge, reason or feelings and to derive a set of priorities considered as an optimal solution to a decision problem [8]. The adaptation of AHP technique leads to following three step hierarchical model for solving the job shop problem.

1. The criteria to evaluate the job shop schedule.
2. The performance metrics which will influence the criteria of step 1.
3. Based on the performance metrics of step 2 what scheduling rule to employ?

At the first hierarchical step the scheduling criteria required for the evaluation of the performance of the job shop are stated. In the present study make span has been considered as the scheduling criteria.

In the next hierarchical step suitable performance metrics are identified. These metrics are chosen such that they would significantly influence the performance criteria of step 1.These performance metrics also reflect the conditions existing at the jobshop.For the make span criteria, the following performance metrics are identified.

* Availability of machines.
* Number of jobs in the queue.
* Amount of work remaining.
* Number of operations remaining.

The 'availability of machines' performance metric is defined as the queue length of the next machine to which the job would go to after the present task is completed. Jobs going to machines with shorter queue length are preferred to other jobs.

The 'number of jobs in the queue' performance metric refers to the queue length of the present machine in which the task is to be processed. If this queue length is large it indicates that the machine has become a bottleneck and the jobs in its queue must be expeditiously processed. In this connection the jobs having least processing times are preferred to reduce queue length.

The 'amount of work remaining" performance metric refers to the total amount of time required for the job to complete all its operations in its route from the decision point. The job having the most work remaining is preferred.

The "number of operations remaining" performance metric refers to how many number of operations still be required by the job from the decision point. The job having more number of operations is preferred.

Finally in the last hierarchical step, the various candidate dispatching rules for scheduling are listed. The following figure shows the AHP model for a job shop problem with make span as the sole performance criteria.

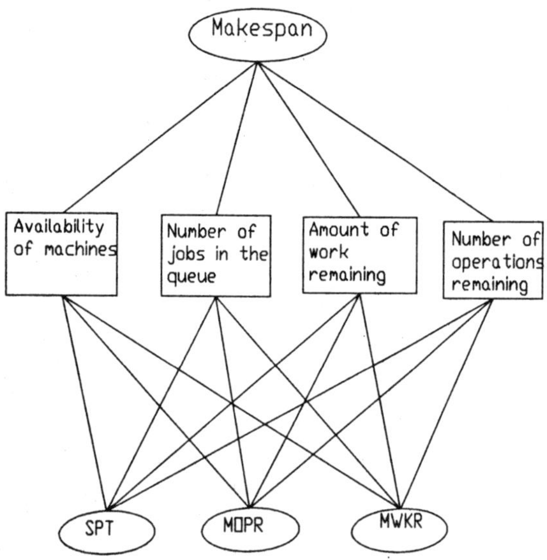

AHP model for job shop problem

SPT-Shortest processing Time

MOPR-Most Operations Remaining

MWKR-Most Work Remaining

For each performance metric, priority matrix for candidate dispatching job is computed. Then priority matrices have been combined. After that effect ratio of performance metrics on scheduling criteria is determined.

Final priority is determined using following formula:

Final priority = (Combined priority matrix)*effect ratio

Where effect ratio = Weight age given to each performance metric among themselves by considering 9-point scale.

9-point scale is a fundamental scale used to give importance of one activity over other. The preferences used in 9-point scale are from 1 to 9. Hence it is called so. In this scale the reciprocals to 9 integers are also used to impart preferences, i.e. an activity 'i' has one of the above numbers assigned to it when compared with an activity 'j', then 'j' has the reciprocal value when compared with 'i'. The job having the larger final priority is preferred.

4.1 Methodology for AHP – Example

Following section illustrates AHP approach described in the previous section using an example of a static job shop problem where the scheduling criterion is to minimize make span. The problem consists of six jobs all with three tasks and the job shop has three machines. The machine requirements, processing times of each task and precedence constraints are tabulated as shown below:

Job Number

1	2	3	4	5	6
1(4)	2(3)	1(5)	1(7)	3(3)	3(6)
2(5)	1(3)	3(3)	2(2)	2(5)	1(9)
3(3)	3(2)	2(7)	3(4)	1(5)	2(7)

Observing first job (reading column wise), 1(4) represents that the job 1 requires 4 units of time to complete its first task in machine1. Task 2 requires 5units of time on machine2. Task 3 requires 3 units of time on machine 3. Similar explanation holds good for other job.

Following steps have been followed to implement AHP to the above problem.

Step1: The criterion under consideration is 'make span'

Step2: The performance metrics that influence 'make span' are

1. Availability of machines
2. Number of jobs in the queue.
3. Total amount of work remaining.
4. Number of operations remaining.

1. **Availability of Machines :** Consider the first task for all the jobs from table. The following figure shows the present conditions in the job shop

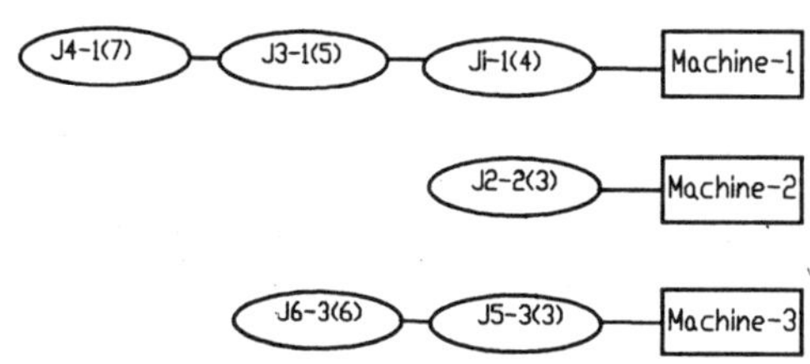

Consider machine1. There are three jobs waiting for machine1.After completion of present task job1 requires operation in machine2.After completion of present taskjob3 require operation in machine 3.

For job1, queue length at machine2 = 1

For job3, queue length at machine3 = 2

For job4, queue length at machine2 = 1

If the queue length decreases, the availab[illegible] machines for that job increases. Therefore jobs 1 and 4 have more availability of machines compared to that of job3. Hence job 1 and job4 are preferred to job3.

Correlating the preferences with choices of the jobs and normalizing it will result in the following observation matrix.

Job	QL	QL +1	Rec.	Pref.
1	1	2	7/2 = 3.5	3.5/9.33 = 0.375
3	2	3	7/3 = 2.333	2.333/9.33 = 0.25
4	1	2	7/2 = 3.5	3.5/9.33 = 0.375
		7	9.33	

QL = Queue Length, Rec = Reciprocal
Pref.= Preference.

Availability of machines is a performance metric which is generally used to reduce idle time of machines.

*In availability of machines the lesser the queue length, the higher the preference. Hence reciprocals are used.

2. **Number of jobs in the queue :** This performance metric is used to reduce queue length of jobs. In this case jobs having least processing times are preferred.
Processing time of job 1 = 4
Processing time of job3 = 5
Processing time of job4 = 7
Therefore job1 is preferred to other jobs and job3 is preferred to job4.
Correlating the preferences and normalizing will result in the following observation matrix:

Job	Processing Time	Reciprocals*	Preferences
1	4	16/4 = 4	4/9.486 = 0.422
3	5	16/5 = 3.2	3.2/9.486 = 0.3373
4	7	16/7 = 2.286	2.286/9.486 = 0.241

*In the second performance metric, the lesser the jobs in the queue, the higher the preference for that job. So the lesser the processing time, higher the preference for that job. Hence reciprocals are used here.

3. **Total Amount of work remaining :** In this criterion jobs having most work remaining are preferred. This is generally used to reduce make span.
Amount of work remaining for job 1 = 4 [illegible]
Amount of work remaining for job 3 = 5 + 3 + 7 =15
Amount of work remaining for job 4 = 7 + 2 + 4 = 13
Job3 has most work remaining. Hence it is preferred to other jobs.
Correlating the preferences and normalizing will result in the following observation matrix:

Job	Work Remaining	Preferences*
1	12	12/40 = 0.3
3	15	15/40 = 0.375
4	13	13/40 = 0.325
	40	

*Higher the amount of work remaining, higher the preference to the jobs.

4. **Number of operations remaining :** In this criterion jobs having most number of operations are preferred. It is generally used to reduce make span.
Number of operations remaining for job1 = 3
Number of operations remaining for job3 = 3
Number of operations remaining for job4 = 3
Correlating the preferences and normalizing will result in the following observation matrix:

Job	Operations Remaining	Preferences
1	3	3/9=0.333
3	3	3/9=0.333
4	3	3/9=0.333

After obtaining the observation matrix for each of the performance metric, a combined single matrix must be obtained which correlates preferences for all the performance metric as follows:

$$\begin{bmatrix} J1 \\ J3 \\ J4 \end{bmatrix} = \begin{bmatrix} 0.375 & 0.4217 & 0.300 & 0.333 \\ 0.25 & 0.3373 & 0.375 & 0.333 \\ 0.375 & 0.2410 & 0.325 & 0.333 \end{bmatrix}$$

In the next step of decision making process the effect of performance metrics on the scheduling criteria must be determined. Effect of performance metric means the weightings given to various criteria to meet the goal.

Keeping minimization of make span as the scheduling objective following weights have been assigned to performance metrics.

Availability of machines = 0.1
Number of jobs in the queue = 0.1
Amount of work remaining = 0.5
Number of operations remaining = 0.3

Here amount of work remaining and the number of operations remaining is given strong importance respectively over other two performance metrics.

As last step to identify the job having top priority final priority matrix must be obtained:

Final priority matrix = Combined preference matrix * Effect ratio matrix

$$= \begin{bmatrix} 0.375 & 0.4217 & 0.300 & 0.333 \\ 0.250 & 0.3373 & 0.375 & 0.333 \\ 0.375 & 0.2410 & 0.325 & 0.333 \end{bmatrix} \begin{bmatrix} 0.1 \\ 0.1 \\ 0.5 \\ 0.3 \end{bmatrix}$$

$$= \begin{bmatrix} 0.3297 \\ 0.3462 \\ 0.3241 \end{bmatrix}$$

Since Job3 has the largest priority, the scheduling decision for this problem is to allocate job3 to machine1.Job3 has most work remaining, compared to other two jobs. Hence at this decision point AHP selected 'most work remaining job.

This procedure is repeated for all the tasks and for all the jobs.

Results for the example problem are as shown below:

Priority Rule	MST	MFT	MMU	MTT	NTJ
SPT	40.00	23.00	0.34	5.33	3
LWR	41.00	23.50	0.33	5.83	2
MWR	38.00	30.17	0.36	10.17	6
FCFS	40.00	23.83	0.34	5.67	4
MOPR	35.00	25.17	0.39	5.83	4
AHP	35.00	29.83	0.39	9.83	6

MST – Make Span Time
MFT – Mean Flow Time
MMU – Mean Machine Utilization
MTT – Mean Tardy Time
NTF – Number of Tardy Jobs

The proposed DSS for job shop scheduling has been validated for a Bench mark problem and the results are presented.

Machine requirement (process times) for the Muth and Thompson six machine six job problem [10].

Task	Job number					
	1	2	3	4	5	6
no	Machine no(proc. time)					
1	3(1)	2(8)	3(5)	2(5)	3(9)	2(3)
2	1(3)	3(5)	4(4)	1(5)	2(3)	4(3)
3	2(6)	5(10)	6(8)	3(5)	5(5)	6(9)
4	4(7)	6(10)	1(9)	4(3)	6(4)	1(10)
5	6(3)	1(10)	2(1)	5(8)	1(3)	5(4)
6	5(6)	4(4)	5(7)	6(9)	4(1)	3(1)

The results obtained using single dispatching rules are inferior to scheduling method based on AHP.As the proposed DSS has incorporated both priority rules and AHP methodology for scheduling task, the manager is free to choose any option as regards to minimization of make span criteria. The scheduling method adopted in the present study can be modified to include multiple criteria.

Priority Rule	MST	MFT	MMU	MTT	NTJ
SPT	88.00	52.67	0.37	1.33	1
LWR	70.00	49.83	0.47	0.00	0
MWKR	61.00	55.83	0.54	0.00	0
FCFS	65.00	54.67	0.50	0.00	0
MOPR	59.00	52.17	0.55	0.00	0
AHP	55.00	51.50	0.59	0.00	0

5. Conclusions

In this paper attempt has been made to develop AHP based DSS to dynamically select the most appropriate dispatching rule from the several candidate rules, based on the existing job shop conditions. The developed DSS is implemented on the bench marking problem and results were compared with 'scheduling with some priority rules' with the objective of minimizing make span. Though it may not provide optimal solution, it does support the process of decision making as regards to scheduling task. One of the primary reasons for adopting a DSS is the many limitations of the cognitive processes of human decision makers. DSS gives the opportunity to overcome the cognitive limitations and offers effectiveness and efficiency in making decisions.

6. References

[1] S.L. Alter, "Decision Support Systems: Current Practices and continuing challenges", Addison-Wesley, Reading,M.A, 1980

[2] J.H.Blackstone, D.T Philips and G.L Hogg, "A State of the art Survey of Dispatching Rules for Manufacturing Job Shop Operations", International Journal of Production Research Vol.20,pp27-45,1982.

[3] G.Chryssolouris, "Manufacturing Systems: Theory and Practice", Newyork, Springer, 1992.

[4] K.N., Mc Kay, F.R.Safayeni and J.A. Bujacott, "Job Shop Scheduling Theory: What is relevant?" Interfaces, 18, pp84-90, 1988.

[5] P. Meller, "A review of Job Shop Scheduling", Operations Research Quarterly, 17(2), pp161-171, 1996

[6] Oliver Holthaus and Chandrasekharan Rajendran, "Efficient Job Shop Dispatching Rules: Further Developments", International Journal of Production Planning and Control, Vol. 11(2), pp171-178, 2000.

[7] F.A.Rodammer and K.P. White, "A Recent Survey of Production Scheduling", IEEE Transactions on Systems, Man and Cybernetics, 18, pp841-851, 1988.

[8] T.L.Saaty, "How to Make a Decision: The Analytic Hierarchy Process", European Journal of Operational Research, 48, pp9-26, 1990.

[9] T. L. Saaty, "Fundamentals of Decision Making and Priority Theory with the Analytic Hierarchy Process", The Analytic Hierarchy Process Series, 6, RWS Publications, Pittsburgh, 1994.

[10] V.Subramaniam, G.K.Lee, G.S.Hong, Y.S.Wong and T.Ramesh,"Dynamic Selection of Dispatching Rules for Job Shop Scheduling", International Journal of Production Planning and Control, Vol. 11(1), pp73-81.

[11] D.R.Sule, "Industrial Scheduling", PWS Publishing Company, An International Thompson Publishing Company, 1996.

An Architectural Approach on Distributed Multimedia Application Support in Operating Systems

Dr. V. Mahesh[1], M. Padma[2] and J. Durga[3]
[1]Professor, Dept of Computer Applications, St. Mary's School of Management Studies, Chennai -119.
[2]Asst.Prof, Dept of Computer Engineering, G. Pulla Reddy Engineering College, Kurnool, A.P
[3]Asst. Prof, Dept. of Computer Engineering, Kotam Tulasi Reddy Engineering College, Kurnool, A.P
meetvenmah@gmail.com, padma.m23@gmail.com

Abstract

In this paper we discuss some of the architectural principles which are useful to support the continuous media applications in a microkernel environment. In particular, we discuss (i) the principle of upcall-driven application structuring whereby communications events are system rather than application initiated, (ii) the principle of split-level system structuring whereby, key system .functions are carried out co-operatively between kernel and user level components and (iii) the principle of decoupling of control transfer and data transfer. Under these general headings a number of particular mechanisms and techniques are discussed.

1. Introduction

We are interested in both communications and processing support for distributed real-lime/multimedia applications in end systems, and believe that such applications.require *thread-to-thread* realtime support according to user supplied quality of service (QOS) parameters. Such support, depending on the level of QOS commitment required, may require dedicated, per-connection, resource allocation the CPU scheduler, virtual memory system and communication system. It may also require ongoing dynamic QOS management in all these areas[1]. Another important requirement we have imposed on ourselves is to support standard UNIX applications on the same machine as our real-time/ multimedia support infrastructure; we do not want to build a specialist real-time system that is isolated from the standard application environment. In our paper the prime consideration is the efficiency. In particular in minimizing system imposed overheads by reducing the cost and number of system calls, context switches and copy operation.

In this paper is structured as three main sections, each of which describes a key architectural principle of our design. The three principles are: (i) *up call driven application structuring* whereby communications events are system rather than application initiated, (ii) *split-level system structuring* whereby key system functions are carried out cooperatively between kernel and user level components and (iii) *decoupling of control transfer and data transfer* whereby the transfer of control is carried out asynchronously with respect to the transfer of data.

2. Upcall-driven Application Structuring

In conventional designs, system APIs are mostly *passive* and applications are mostly *active.* For example, when an application needs to send or receive data, it typically invokes a system call such send*()* or *recv().* It also provides the buffer from/to which data is to be sent/received. In contrast, our continuous media API is structured so that the system *infrastructure* is active and *applications* are passive. Application programmers attach *rthandlers,* which are C functions containing application code to process the real-time media, to *rtports,* which are globally unique units of addressing. Then, programmers establish *connections* with a given QOS between rtports. At connect time, the *system,* rather than the application, allocates buffers for connections ,and provides the thread on which the *rthandlers* will be executed. At data transfer time, the system decides to upcall the application to obtain/ deliver data at instants determined by the QOS specification (in terms of rate, jitter, delay etc.) provided by the application at connect time. When an application *rthandler* is upcalled, the address of the associated rtport's buffer is passed as an argument so that application code in the *rthandler* can access the buffer. Source *rthandlers* are expected to fill buffers with data to be sent, and sink *rthandlers* to use the data as provided.

There are three major benefits of style of an application/system interaction in our context. First, it relieves the application of the burden of explicitly creating threads and allocating buffers. Second, the *system*, rather than the application, can choose the timing of application code execution, and thus can optimally monitor and manage the Quality of Service (QOS) of the connection, *including the execution of application code*, to provide the required thread-to-thread QOS support. Third, the structuring of the API with the API *rthandlers* is a natural and effective model for real-time programming.

Real-time programming is considerably simplified when programmers can structure applications to react to events and delegate to the system the responsibility for initiating communication events. The programmer is still ultimately in control of event initiation but this control is expressed declaratively through the provision of QOS parameters at connect time and need not be explicitly programmed in a procedural style[2].

Along with these benefits, an *efficiency gain* potentially results from upcall-driven application structuring, because a single thread ca be used for both protocol and application processing. In conventional systems, application interface with communications by performing system calls which block and reschedule if the communications system is not ready to send or if data has not yet arrived. With infrastructure initiated communication, on the other hand, it is not necessary for the application and communications system to wait for each other, and thus no context switch is incurred, as the communication system always initiates the exchange and the application code is always be ready to run.

2.1 Split-level System Structuring

The distributed multimedia applications will require high degree of internal concurrency. For example, it is likely that each media stream will require at least one thread of execution and it is also likely that applications will be structured as *pipelines* of processing stages on streams of media.

Split-level structuring is used to maintain the merits of user space management while mitigating its demerits.

2.2 Split Level Scheduling

The above merits and demerits are particularly evident in the case of CPU resource management through user level threads. Here the benefits are cheap user level concurrency and the drawback is that the relative urgencies of threads in different address spaces are not visible to the kernel scheduler.

In split level scheduling, a small number of *virtual processors* (VPs) execute user threads in each address space. The split level scheduling schemes maintains the invariant that [5]:

- Each *user level scheduler (ULS)* always runs its most urgent user thread, and
- The *kernel level scheduler (KLS)* always runs the VP supporting the globally most urgent user thread.

Split level scheduling allows many contexts switches to take place cheaply in the same address space but also ensures that the relative urgencies of threads across the whole machine are appropriately taken into account.

Split Level Communication

The strategy of split level communication structuring is a leave the kernel responsible for multiplexing and demultiplexing network packets to application address spaces, but the application address spaces perform transport level processing. In this way, transport protocol processing can automatically take advantages of the split level scheduling infrastructure and thus exploit cheap user level context switches.

Split level communication structuring also allows meaningful deadlines to be placed on (transport level) protocol processing activities, as the ultimate deadline of the final packet delivery is easily available in the application context. Thus, the scheduling of protocol processing need not be performed 'blind' as it is in typical kernel implementation. Another advantage is that multiple transport protocols can easily be dynamically configured in and out of applications according to their particular requirements. This is important in a multimedia context where different protocols may be appropriate for different media types.

2.3 Split Level Buffer Management

The strategy of split level buffer management is for the kernel level manager to 'loan' physical, locked, buffers to per-address space managers, but to reserve the rights to reclaim the buffers if memory is urgently required or to retain the buffer longer than it has agreed to. The policy adopted in the design level is that the application is allowed to keep buffer for at least the normal duration of transport protocol processing time *plus* rthandlers execution time. If the period has elapsed and the application space has not returned ownership of the buffer to the kernel, the kernel may reclaim the buffer.

The semantic of 'reclaiming' locked buffers is to convert locked memory into standard swappable virtual memory. In this way, applications do not lose their data although they do lose guaranteed access latency to that data as the memory region is subject to being paged out. If the kernel does not need to reclaim buffers at the end of an rthandler execution, the user space manager may reuse buffers for other connections.

3. Decoupling of Control Transfer and Data Transfer

In traditional systems, the transfer of control and the transfer of data are usually tightly coupled. For example, the execution of a UNIX system calls passes data to the kernel and simultaneously transfers control to the kernel.

4. Direct Connections

In distributed multimedia applications it is often required to receive continuous media data from the network and directly play it out on a device such as an audio card or a frame buffer (which is probably managed by kernel level code). The application may or may not require keeping track of the transfer of individual buffers of data for synchronization purposes. The opposite scenario, where data from a local device is to be put directly onto the network, is equally common. In conventional operating system, the only way to achieve such a data flow is to route the data through an intermediate user process. But it involves significant per-buffer overheads [2].

In a *direct connection*, data that is to be passed directly between the network and a local device does not pass into user space at all; it is processed entirely within kernel space. When a direction connection is established, the infrastructure pre-maps the buffer associated with the connection into the output device's memory. Then, the data can be directly copied off the network card on to the device without leaving kernel space. The fragmentation/re-assembly functions of the in-kernel transport protocol.

If the user application does not need to synchronize with the delivery of buffers, no further overhead is incurred. However, if it is required to synchronize, the application can attach an rthandler to the rtport. This is up called on each buffer transfer with the usual rthandler semantic. The only difference in the API between this case and the normal case is that buffer pointer passed as an argument to the rthandler upcall will be a *null* pointer as the application context will not have the rights to directly access the kernel managed buffer.

5. Asynchronous System Calls

For continuous media connections *asynchronous system calls* exploit the *predictable periodicity* of the transfer of control and data between application address spaces and the kernel. To issue an asynchronous system call (e.g. an asynchronous version of *send()*), user level library code:

- Places an operation identifier and parameters in the shared KLS/ULS memory bulletin board area and then
- Sets an 'operation request' bit, also in the bulletin board area.

The KLS, when it runs at the next system clock tick, notices that an operation bit is consequently passes the user's parameters to a kernel server thread which carries out the system call on behalf of the ULS. This avoids a special domain crossing for the system call at the expense a bitmap on each clock interrupt.

5.1 Asynchronous software Interrupts

The implementation of software interrupts is similar to that of asynchronous system calls and similarly avoids a special domain crossing. The mechanism for kernel to VP control transfer is as follows:

- The KLS places an event identifier and parameters in the KLS/ULS bulletin board area
- The KLS alters the program counter field of the target VP's context structure points to a standard entry point in the ULS.

Thus, when the VP is next scheduled, the VP immediately enters its ULS, which picks up the event identifier and parameters, and schedules a user thread to deal with event. Asynchronous software interrupts are also provided as a service accessible from user level code. This service enables library code in one address space to cheaply notify an event to another address space on the same machine. The service also allows the sender to name a pre-existing memory segment shared between the sender and receiver address spaces so that data can be optionally transferred in the same call.

6. User Level Pipelines

The API for *pipelines* of processing stages is very similar to the connection abstraction. But rather than passing a *pair* of rtports as arguments to the *connect()* primitives, we pass a *list* of rtports. In the case of pipelines, the delay QOS parameter applies end-to-end over the entire chain of rtports.

Intermediate processing stages in pipelines are also realized in a similar way to that described above: When data arrives at an intermediate processing stage, the rthandler returns, it is assumed that the rthandler's application code has performed some appropriate processing on the buffer whose address was passed up to it, and the data can be passed on to the next page.

As the various stages of a pipeline form part of the same application, it is typically the case that pipelines are implemented in a single address space. The data transfer mechanism in this case is as follows: When an rthandler implementing one stage of a pipeline returns, having operated on a buffer, the next stage in the pipeline is simply passed the address of the same buffer. Meanwhile, the first stage sets of work on a second buffer; and so on. At the end of the pipeline, when buffers are finished with, they are returned to a user level pool from which that can be reused by the first pipeline stage. With this implementation, intra address space pipelines incur only user level control transfers between the threads dedicated to each pipeline stage, and zero copy operations between stages.

The API is the identical regardless of whether intra-address space, inter-address space or inter-machine connections or pipelines are used. Inter-address space communication on the same machine uses buffers that are statically mapped into both the source and sink address spaces for data transfer, and use asynchronous software interrupts.

7. Proposed Scenario

The integrated use of the principles and techniques described above, the scenario is illustrated in Fig. 1, involves the transfer of compressed video from a frame grabber card on a source machine to a decompress /display application on a sink machine. In figure 1, the large ovals represent user address spaces with library code below the horizontal line and application code above. The rectangles represent kernel space with the enclosed shaded regions representing devices.

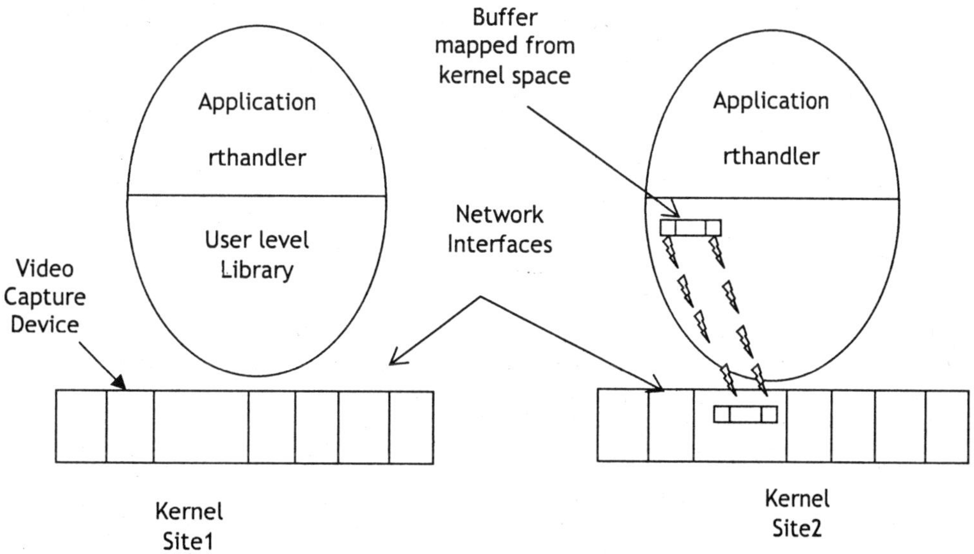

Fig. 1 An illustrative scenario

The send side features a *direct connection,* involves the video capture device and the network interface, which avoids the need for data to pass into user space. It also features the (optional) use of an *rthandler* to allow the sender, which is structured as an *upcall-driven application*, to monitor and synchronize with the progress of the connection.

On the receive side, the *split level buffer management system* allocates a physical buffer from the kernel buffer pool to hold incoming network packets associated with the connection. This buffer is statically mapped into both kernel space and the application address space.

In the *split level communication system*, when a complete network level packet has been received, the application address space's ULS is notified via the *conditional deadline* mechanism and initiates transport level processing.

This may involve the receipt of further network packets to build a complete user level buffer.

When a complete user buffer has been built, and the receiving thread has the globally earliest deadline, the ULS runs a thread which upcalls the application's rthandler with the address of the buffer as a parameter.

The receive side features a *user level pipeline* which involves one user thread performing decompressed and another displaying uncompressed video in a window. The display is achieved by means of *asynchronous system calls* to display device. Context switches between the two pipeline threads are achieved at user level costs and the transmission of data from the decompressor to the displayer does not involve data copying.

8. Conclusions

We discussed three architectural principles useful for the support of distributed real-time multimedia application in operating system. Firstly we contended that the principles of upcall-driven application structuring leads to well structural real-time applications, relieves applications of the burden of explicit thread creation and buffer allocation, and leads to potential efficiency gains because of reduced context switches.

Secondly we argued for the principles of split-level system structuring. We suggested that it can improve efficiency by exploiting application specific knowledge (e.g. scheduling deadline or buffer requirements) in a local, user level, context where application/manager interact6ion is cheap, while relying on a kernel level manager to 'bias' resources to application address spaces of the basis of their relative needs. Active co-operation of management information between user and kernel level managers is key, but as long as an asynchronous style of communication between managers is acceptable, this can be achieved cheaply by means of a shared memory 'bulletin board'.

Finally we discussed the three principles working together in this paper. They are capable of exploited in a range of operating system environments. Similarly many of individual techniques can be useful in a stand alone fashion. When it can be compared with the distributed level, the principles which we have discussed validated in terms of direct performance measurements.

9. References

[1] A.P. Black, 1983, 'An Asymmetric Stream Communication System', *Proceedings of 9th ACM Symposium in Operating System Principles'*, pp 4-10.

[2] M. Acceta, A. Tevanian and M. Young, 1986, 'Mach: A new Kernel Foundatiuon for UNIX Development', *Technical Report,* Camegie Mellon University.

[3] Geoff Coulson and Gordon Blair, 1995, 'Architectural Principles and Techniques for Distributed Multimedia Application Support in Operating Systems', ACM SIGOPS Operating Systems Review, Vol.29 (4), pp17-24.

[4] Geoff Coulson and Gordon Blair, 1994, 'Micro-kernel Support for Continuous Media in distributed Systems', *Computer Networks and ISDN Systems,* Vol 26 (10), pp 1323-1341.

[5] Geoff Coulson, Gordon Blair, P. Robin and D. Shepherd, 1994, 'Supporting Continuous Media Applications in a Micro-Kernel Environment', *Proceedings of the 1st International Workshop on Architecture and Protocols for High-Speed Networks,* pp 215-234.

[6] Ramesh Govindan, D.P. Anderson, 1991, 'Scheduling and IPC mechanisms for continuous media', *ACM SIGOPS Operating Systems Review,* Vol. 25 (5), pp 68-80.

[7] C.L. Liu and J.W. Layland, 1973, 'Scheduling Algorithms for Multiprogramming in a Hard-Real-Time Environment', *Journal of the ACM,* Vol. 20(1), pp 46-61.

[8] C.A. Thekkath, T.D. Nguyen, 1993, 'Implementing network protocols at user level', *Proceedings on Communications architectures, protocols and applications*, pp 64-73.

Modified Bacterial Foraging Optimization and its Application for the Design of a Nonlinear Taper

N. C. Chauhan, B. R. Vasista, M. Sandeep Reddy, M. V. Kartikeyan and A. Mittal
Dept. of Electronics and Computer Engineering,
Indian Institute of Technology Roorkee, Roorkee-247667, (UK), India
narendec@iitr.ernet.in

Abstract

This paper presents a modified bacterial foraging optimization (BFO) algorithm and its use for the design of a specific tapered transmission line. After discussing basic BFO technique, its modification is proposed which includes memory of the bacteria, swarming effects and variable swim length. The modified algorithm was tested on five test functions, which are commonly used for testing swarm intelligence based algorithms. Later on, the proposed modified BFO was used for the design of a nonlinear taper for use in a specific gyrotron. The paper also compares the results of modified BFO algorithm with the results obtained and earlier reported using standard particle swarm optimization algorithm.

1. Introduction

The living behaviors of natural creatures, such as ants, birds, bacteria are imitated to solve optimization and system identification problems [1]. A number of algorithms based on the behavior of biological populations, such as particle swarm optimization, ant colony optimization and bacterial foraging optimization are invented by different researchers. Passino introduced the bacterial foraging optimization method which is based on the imitation of the food-ingesting behaviors of E-coli bacteria, which are present in our intestines, in 2002 [2].

In this paper, we present a modified bacterial foraging method in which the bacteria can remember the direction which resulted in a better cost function, the swim length is varied according to fitness function such that bacteria closer to present global minima will have a smaller swim length while those far away will have a larger value and swarming effect by which all bacteria will move towards present global minimum. The results of modified BFO algorithm are tested on a test-bed of five functions. Finally, we apply the proposed BFO algorithm for the design of a specific nonlinear taper for output system of gyrotron. In this paper, we also compare the results of modified BFO with standard PSO.

2. Bacterial foraging algorithm

Bacterial foraging algorithm is inspired by the pattern exhibited by bacterial foraging behaviors. The algorithm proceeds by selecting bacteria with good foraging strategies and it eliminates bacteria with poor foraging strategies. This process either eliminates the poor strategies or refines them in to better ones. The foraging process in BFO algorithm involves the following steps – chemo taxis, reproduction and elimination-dispersion.

Chemo taxis: Bacteria have the tendency to gather to the nutrient-rich areas by an activity called "chemo taxis". It moves in a random direction ϕ (i), which is a random unit vector

$$\theta(i, j+1, k) = \theta(i, j, k) + C(i)\phi(i) \qquad (1)$$

where θ (i, j+1, k) indicates the position of the ith bacterium at the jth chemo tactic step in the kth reproductive loop, ϕ (i) is a random unit vector, and $C(i)$ is the length of run.

Reproduction: Successful bacteria reproduce while the others die, whose positions are occupied by the newly formed bacteria. For convenience, the total population is maintained constant by killing half the population with highest fitness values and remaining half reproduces and new bacterium occupies these vacant positions.

Elimination-dispersion: Some bacteria are dispersed to random locations due to factors like wind, etc. with some probability. The bacteria with probability p_{ed} are dispersed to random locations in the optimization domain.

The steps describing the classical BFO are shown in Fig. 1.

[Step 1:] Initialize parameters Dim, S, N_c, N_s, N_{re}, N_{ed}, $C(i)$ with $(i=1, 2... S)$, where,

Dim: Dimension of the search space, S: The number of bacteria in the population,

N_c: No. of Chemo-tactic steps, N_{re}: The number of reproduction steps,

N_{ed}: The number of elimination-dispersal events,

Ns:No. of swim steps,

$C(i)$: The size of the step taken in the random direction specified by the tumble.

$\theta(i, j, k)$: Position vector of the i-th bacterium, in j-th chemotactic step, and k-th reproduction.

[Step 2] Update cost or fitness value $J(i, j, k)$.

[Step 3] Elimination loop: l=l+1

[Step 4] Reproduction loop: $k=k+1$

[Step 5] Chemo taxis loop: $j=j+1$

[Sub-step a] For $i=1, 2... S$, take a chemo tactic step for bacterium i as follows.

[Sub-step b] Compute fitness function, $J(i, j, k)$.

[Sub-step c] Let J_{last}=J (i, j, k) to save this value since we may find a better cost via a run.

[Sub-step d] Tumble: generate a random unit vector φ (i) with each element $\varphi^m(i)$, $m=1, 2,..., $ Dim.

[Sub-step e] Move: follow the equation (1)

[Sub-step f] Compute $J(i, j+1, k)$.

[Sub-step g] Swim: we consider only the i-th bacterium is swimming while the others are not moving then.

i) Let m=0 (counter for swim length).

ii) While $m< N_s$ (if have not climbed down too long).

- Let $m=m+1$.
- If $J(i, j+1, k) < Jlast$ (if doing better), Let $J_{last} = J(i, j+1, k)$ and let

$$\theta(i, j+1, k) = \theta(i, j+1, k) + C(i) * \Phi(i)$$

and use this $\theta(i, j+1, k)$ to compute the new $J(i, j+1, k)$

Else, let m= Ns. This is the end of the while statement.

[Step 6] Update θ_g_best: Position vector of the best position found by all bacteria.

Jbest: Fitness of the best position found so far.

If $j < N_c$ go to step 5.

[Step 7] Let $S\_r=S/2$. The S_r bacteria with highest cost function (J) values die and the other half of bacteria population with best values split and the new bacteria will be at the same location as that of its parent.

[Step 8] If $k < N_{re}$, go to step 4. We have not reached the specified number of reproduction steps. So we start the next generation in the chemo-taxis loop.

[Step 9] If l < N_{ed}, for i= 1, 2.....S, with probability p_{ed} disperse bacterium to a random location on the optimization domain and go to step 3.

Fig. 1 Standard BFO algorithm

3. Modified bacterial foraging optimization

The above described algorithm when tested on multidimensional benchmark functions is observed to show a poor convergence. Classical BFO ignores the effects of swarming; all the bacteria are assumed to have same swim length, however varying swim length according fitness can have better convergence speed.

In order to improve the convergence we modify the standard BFO algorithm. The detailed flowchart for the modified BFO algorithm is shown in Fig. 2. The present algorithm includes four modifications:

- In classical BFO, we assumed that bacteria will move in a random direction in every chemo tactic loop but in nature bacteria can remember the previous direction in which there was increase in nutrient concentration [2]. This information is stored in a memory array which is an S×Dim -dimensional vector. So each time a bacteria encounters a favorable environment it remembers the direction in which it moved so that in the next swim step it can move in this direction since it is more probable to encounter a favorable condition, If at some point it reaches a toxic place (higher value of J^i) it moves back to previous position and from this point it generates a random direction (i.e., it tumbles) and moves in that direction. In this way the bacteria can reach richest nutrient concentration (minimum J^i) quickly.

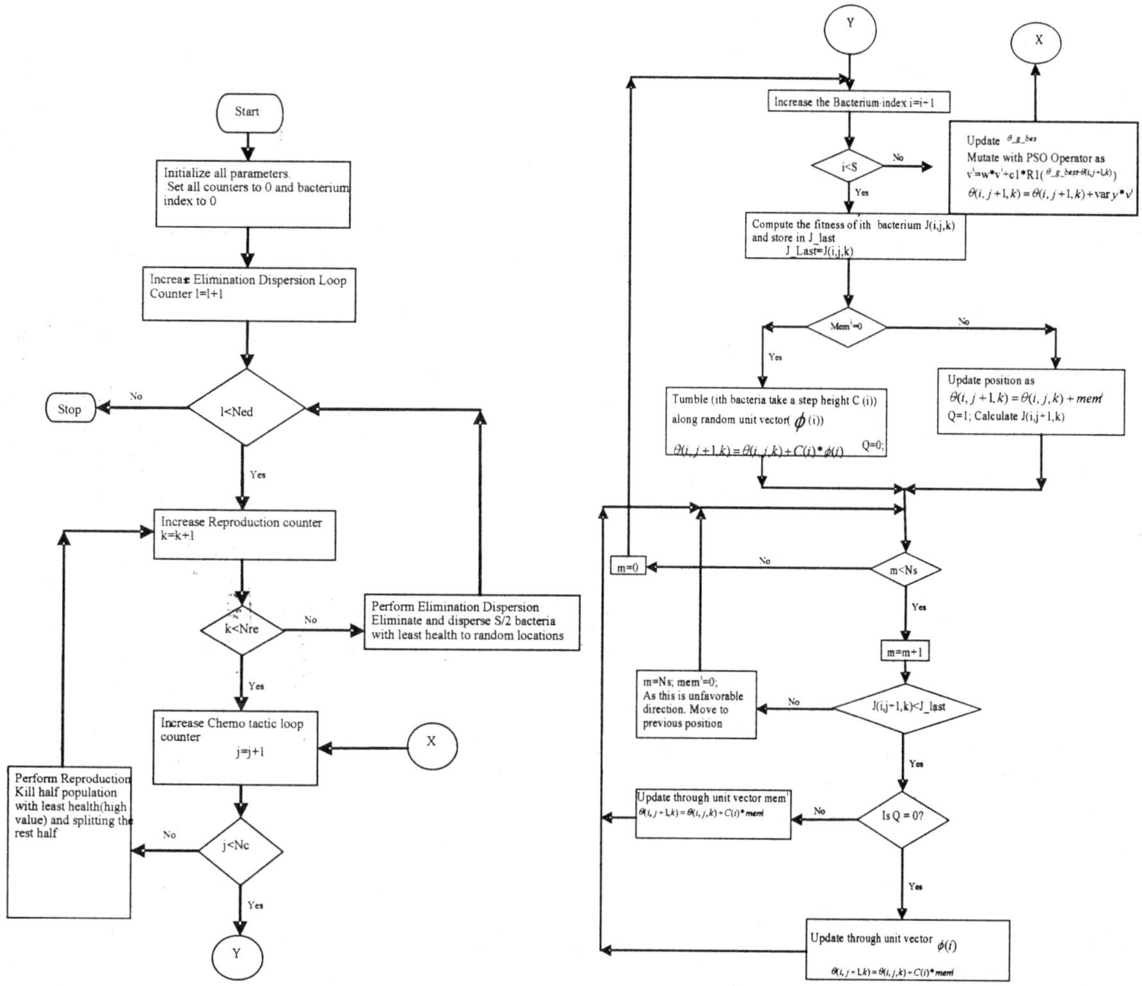

Fig. 2 Flowchart for modified BFO algorithm

- In the presented approach, after undergoing a chemo tactic step, each bacterium gets mutated by a PSO operator [3]. In this phase, the bacterium is stochastically attracted towards the globally best position found so far in the entire population at current time and also towards its previous heading direction. The PSO operator uses only the 'social' component and eliminates the 'cognitive' component as the local search in different regions of the search space is already taken care of by the chemo tactic steps of the BFOA algorithm.

$$v(i) = wv(i) + C_1 R_1 (\theta_{gbest} - \theta(i, j+1, k)) \quad (2)$$

$$\theta(i, j+1, k) = \theta(i, j+1, k) + v(i) * Vary \quad (3)$$

where $v(i)$ is the velocity of ith bacterium, w, C_1, $Vary$ are constants, R_1 is a uniformly generated random number.

In nature the bacteria has the tendency to release chemicals, through which it communicates with other bacteria.

- The chemo tactic step-size is varied in accordance with fitness [5] as:

$$A = \frac{K}{|Jbest - J(i, j+1, k)|} \quad (4)$$

$$C(i) = \frac{1}{1 + A} \quad (5)$$

where K is constant.

For bacteria far away from best C(i) ~1, so it results in a large step size

For bacteria close to *Jbest*, *C*(*i*) ~ 0, so that they can converge to global minima without any oscillations. However *C*(*i*) is varied according to following criteria:

If (C (i) <0.001) C (i) = 0.01,

If (C (i) >0.9) C (i) = 3.5.

- If bacteria during its chemo tactic step, if it encounters a unfavorable environment it returns to its previous position where there was a better concentration of nutrients.

4. Experiment on test functions

The performance of the BFO algorithm was evaluated on a test bed of five well-known benchmark functions [6] as shown in Table 1. The search range for these functions and the range of initializing bacteria positions are shown in Table 2. As the global optima for all these functions are at origin, asymmetric initializations are used for these functions in order to consider the practical situations. All these functions were tested with 10, 20 and 30 dimensions, except the last Schaffer f6 function which is two dimensional. The maximum number of iteration considered to stop the BFO algorithm were 1000, 2000 and 3000 for dimension 10, 20 and 30 respectively for De Jong's Sphere function, while they were considered to be 3000, 4000 and 5000 for 10, 20 and 30 dimensions for Generalized Rastrigin, Generalized Rosenbrock and Generalized Griewank functions respectively. The maximum iteration considered for Schaffer f6 function was 1000. The maximum error tolerance considered for all functions was 0.01 except Schaffer f6 function in which it was considered to be 0.00001. The BFO algorithm was stopped when either the error criterion was achieved or maximum iterations were reached.

Table 1 Benchmark functions

Function Name	Function
De Jongs's Sphere function	$f_1(x) = \sum_{i=1}^{n} x_i^2$
Rosenbrock function	$f_2(x) = \sum_{i=1}^{n-1} \left[100(x_{i+1} - x_i^2)^2 + (x_i - 1)^2\right]$
Generalized Rastrigin function	$f_3(x) = \sum_{i=1}^{n} \left[x_i^2 - 10\cos(2\pi x_i) + 10\right]$
Generalized Griewank function	$f_4(x) = \frac{1}{4000}\sum_{i=1}^{n} x_i^2 - \prod_{i=1}^{n} \cos\left(\frac{x_i}{\sqrt{i}}\right) + 1$
Schaffer's f6 function	$f_5(x) = 0.5 + \frac{(\sin\sqrt{x^2 + y^2})^2 - 0.5}{(1.0 + 0.001(x^2 + y^2))^2}$

Table 2 Initialization range and search range for test functions

Test Function	Range of search		Range of initializations	
	Lower	Upper	Lower	Upper
f_1	-100	100	50	100
f_2	-100	100	50	100
f_3	-10	10	2.56	5.12
f_4	-600	600	300	600
f_5	-100	100	15	30

The results of testing modified BFO (MBFO) on test functions are shown in Table 3. Due to probabilistic nature of evolutionary algorithms, the results shown here are the average of 50 runs of the algorithms on each test function for all dimensions. The table shows the average achieved optimum value with its standard deviation and number of successful runs with the count of average generation of success.

The comparison results of MBFO and PSO on test functions show that MBFO performed very well outperforming PSO on Rosenbrock's function and Generalized Griewank function, while the standard PSO performed well on Generalized Rastrigin and Schaffer f6 function. The total number of successes obtained with MBFO is higher than the total number of successes obtained with standard PSO algorithm.

5. Design of a tapered transmission line for a high power gyrotron

Gyrotron is a high power microwave tube that emits radiation at approximately electron cyclotron frequency [7]. The output system of gyrotron consists of a nonlinear output taper, a quasi-optical mode converter and an RF window. In this section, the design of a nonlinear taper of raised cosine type has been performed for a 42 GHz, 200 kW, and CW gyrotron. The requirement of a diameter taper in gyrotrons is to provide a good match between input and output sections of the taper with very low spurious mode content [7].

In this context, we considered four design parameters of the nonlinear taper namely - the length of the taper (L), the radius of the taper at the output end (r_2), the number of sections to be discredited (N), and a geometrical parameter gamma (γ) while keeping the radius of the taper at input end (r_1) constant. The range of design parameters considered for the design are summarized in Table 4. The objective for the design was to obtain a maximum transmission coefficient (i.e. S_{21}-parameter), operating with $TE_{0,3}$ mode with minimized spurious mode content. In this work, the analysis of the taper was carried out following [7, 8].

Table 3 Performance of Modified BFO (MBFO) on benchmark functions and its comparison with standard PSO

Fn.	Dim.	Average achieved optimum value (Standard deviation)		Number of successes (Average generation of success)	
		PSO	MBFO	PSO	MBFO
f_1	10	**0.01 (--)**	0.14 (1.28)	**50 (566)**	38 (374)
	20	0.01 (--)	**0.01 (--)**	50 (1291)	**50 (1274)**
	30	**0.01 (--)**	0.015 (--)	**50 (2081)**	49 (2338)
f_2	10	25.19 (62.34)	**0.13 (0.43)**	1 (2365)	**3 (1955)**
	20	131.94 (269.92)	**2.46 (6.62)**	0 (--)	0 (--)
	30	186.85 (370.73)	**3.88 (2.41)**	0 (--)	0 (--)
f_3	10	**2.30 (1.55)**	59.35 (41.44)	**4 (1904)**	0 (--)
	20	**14.20 (4.68)**	58.37 (24.73)	0 (--)	0 (---)
	30	**31.44 (7.15)**	82.26 (26.49)	0 (--)	0 (---)
f_4	10	0.075 (0.035)	**0.01 (--)**	0 (--)	**50 (875)**
	20	0.026 (0.026)	**0.01 (--)**	22 (2339)	**50 (2349)**
	30	0.02 (0.015)	**0.01 (--)**	27 (3222)	**50 (3790)**
f_5	2	**0.00097 (0.0029)**	0.27 (0.27)	**45 (532)**	0 (--)
Total successes (Total iterations)				249 (14300)	**290 (12955)**

A maximum transmission of 99.85% was obtained with modified BFO algorithm corresponding to output radius equal to 37.24 mm with the division of taper into 307 sections and the value of gamma parameter equal to 0.5042. The taper length was fixed at 350 mm in the experiment. The optimized taper plot obtained with these parameters is shown in Fig. 3. The result obtained here is found to be consistent with the same taper design result obtained with PSO algorithm and reported earlier by the authors in [9].

Table 4 Range of design parameters for nonlinear taper

Design Parameters	Range
Radius at output end of taper (R)	[35.0-45.0] mm
Number of sections (N)	[50-500]
Gamma (γ)	[0.1-1.0]

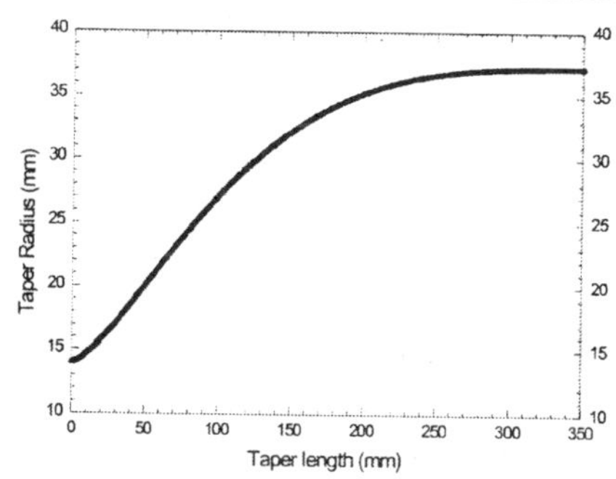

Fig. 3 Optimum geometry for taper design with transmission of 99.85% (Parameters: L = 350 mm, a_2 = 37.2427 mm, N = 307 and γ = 0.5042).

6. Conclusion

A modified Bacterial Foraging optimization algorithm is presented and it is used for the design of a nonlinear diameter tapered waveguide for output system of high power gyrotron as a case study. Although the presented algorithm is used for the design of only one component, it can be applied for design optimization of other high power microwave devices as well. The selection of BFO parameters was carried out in accordance with previous experimental investigations [5]. The results obtained with modified BFO algorithm were found to be efficient and comparable to with the standard PSO algorithm.

7. Acknowledgement

The authors gratefully acknowledge the financial support of the Department of Science and Technology (DST).

8. References

[1] L. Ljung, *System identication: Theory for the user.* Prentice- Hall Inc. Second Edition, YEAR.

[2] K. M. Passino, "Biomimicry of Bacterial Foraging for distributed Optimization and Control," *IEEE Control Systems Magazine*, vol. 22 pp.55-67, 2002.

[3] Synergy of PSO and Bacterial Foraging Optimization – A Comparative Study on Numerical Benchmarks Arijit Biswas1, Sambarta Dasgupta1, Swagatam Das1, and Ajith Abraham2

[4] J. Kennedy and R. Eberhart, "Particle Swarm Optimization," *Proc. IEEE International Conference on Neural Networks*, 1995.

[5] M. Tripathy, and S. Mishra, "Bacterial foraging based to optimize both real power loss and voltage stability limit," *IEEE Transactions on Power Systems*, 22(1), 240-408, 2007.

[6] D. W. Stephens, and J. R. Krebs, *Foraging theory.* Princeton University Press, Princeton, New Jersey, 1986.

[7] M. V. Kartikeyan, E.Borie and M. Thumm, *Gyrotrons – High Power Microwave and millimeter wave technology*, Springer – Verlag, Berlin Heidelberg, Germany, 2004.

[8] H.–U. Nickel. Hochfrequenztechnische Aspekte zur Entwicklung riickwirkungsarmer Ausgangsfenster fηr Millimeterwellen– gyrotrons hoher Leistung. Ph.D. Thesis, University of Karlsruhe, Germany, 1995.

[9] N. Chauhan, D. Wagner, M.V. Kartikeyan, A. Mittal and M. Thumm, "Design of nonlinear taper using particle swarm optimization," Int. J. Infrared Millimeter Waves, vol. no. 2008.

Sequence Alignment Algorithms using Dynamic Programming Technique

P.V. Lakshmi[1], Allam AppaRao[2] and G. AppaRao[1]
[1]GITAM University, Computer science & Engg Dept, Andhra Pradesh, India
pvl_7097@rediffmail.com,
[2]Jawaharlal Nehru Technological University, Andhra Pradesh, India
apparaoallam@gmail.com

Abstract

Sequence comparison plays a major role in bioinformatics and molecular biology. One of the most widely used techniques for sequence comparison is sequence alignment. Sequence alignment is a procedure of computing two or more sequences by searching for a series of individual characters or character pattern that are in the same order in the sequences. In this work, we introduce a novel interactive tool for aligning the nucleotide or protein sequences. The package supports three well-known algorithms: Smith-Waterman algorithm, Needleman-Wunsch algorithm and Progressive sequence alignment algorithm. It is implemented in Java and can be extended to include additional algorithms.

Keywords: *bioinformatics, pair-wise sequence alignment, multiple sequence alignment, biomolecules, dynamic programming.*

1. Introduction

Analyzing and comparing the string representations of sequences can reveal a lot of useful information about the sequences. As new biological sequences are being generated at exponential rates, sequence comparison is becoming increasingly important to draw functional and evolutionary inference of proteins. Numerous computer tools have been developed for alignment of nucleotide and protein sequences such as ClustalX [6], ClustalW [3], MEGA [5]. The algorithms implemented here use both pair-wise and Multiple sequence alignment techniques for building aligned sequences. The pair-wise sequence alignment techniques use two sequences for alignment while multiple sequence alignment algorithms aligns more than two sequences. Smith-Waterman algorithm, Needleman-Wunsch algorithm are pair-wise sequence alignment algorithm while progressive sequence alignment algorithm is multiple sequence alignment technique. In this work, we introduce a novel interactive tool for alignment of sequences like nucleotide or protein sequences. The package currently supports three well-known algorithms like Smith-Waterman algorithm, Needleman-Wunsch algorithm, Progressive sequence alignment algorithm. The reason behind our work is a lack of interactivity in existing tools. The existing packages, in contrast to our package, only visualize the resulting alignment. We strongly believe that this package can be extremely valuable to bioinformaticians.

2. Needleman-Wunsch algorithm

The Needleman-Wunsch algorithm [1], published in 1970, provides a method of finding the optimal global alignment of two sequences by maximizing the number of amino acid matches and minimizing the number of gaps necessary to align the two sequences. Because the Needleman-Wunsch algorithm finds the optimal alignment of the entire sequence of both proteins, it is a global alignment technique, and cannot be used to find local regions of high similarity. Needleman-Wunsch algorithm achieves, solves optimization problems by dividing the problem into independent sub problems. With sequence alignment the sub-problem can be thought of as the alignment of the 'prefixes' of two sequences to a certain point. Therefore dynamic programming matrix is computed. Dynamic programming technique align two sequences by beginning at the end of two sequences and attempting to align all possible pairs of characters(one from each sequence) using the scoring schemes for matches, mismatches and gaps. The highest set of scores defines the optimal alignment between two sequences. Dynamic programming approaches guarantee to provide the optimal alignment given a particular score scheme. For a given two sequences $x = x_1\ x_2\ x_3 \ldots x_i \ldots x_n$ and $y = y_1\ y_2\ y_3 \ldots y_j \ldots y_m$. Construct an $(n+1) \times (m + 1)$ matrix F. Its (i, j)th element F (i,j) for $i = 1,\ldots,n$, $j = 1,\ldots,m$ is equal to the score of an optimal alignment between $x_1\ x_2\ x_3 \ldots x_i$ and $y_1\ y_2\ y_3 \ldots y_j$. The element F (i, 0) for $i = 1,\ldots,n$ is the score of aligning $y_1\ y_2\ y_3 \ldots y_j$ to a gap region of length j. Build F recursively initializing it by the condition F (0,0) = 0 and then proceeding to fill the matrix from the top left corner to the bottom right corner. If F (i – 1,j-1),

F(i-1, j) and F(i , j-1) are known, F (i ,j) is clearly calculated as follows

$$F(i,j) = \max \begin{cases} F(i-1, j-1) + s(xi,yj) \\ F(i-1,j) - d \\ F(i, j-1) - d \end{cases}$$

where s(xi,yj) is the value obtained from substitution matrix such as BLOSUM, PAM. There are three possible ways to obtain the best score F (i ,j): x_i can be aligned to y_j, or x_i is aligned to gap or y_j is aligned to a gap. Calculating F(i ,j) we keep a pointer to the option from which F(n,m) we trace back the pointers to recover the optimal alignments. The value F (n,m) is exactly their score.

3. Smith-Waterman algorithm

The Smith-Waterman algorithm was published in 1981 [2] and is very similar to the Needleman-Wunsch algorithm. Yet, the Smith-Waterman algorithm is different in that it is a local sequence alignment algorithm. Instead of aligning the entire length of two protein sequences, this algorithm finds the region of highest similarity between two proteins. This is potentially more biologically relevant due to the fact that the ends of proteins tend to be less highly conserved than the middle portions, leading to higher mutation, deletion, and insertion rates at the ends of the protein. The Smith-Waterman algorithm allows us to align proteins more accurately without having to align the ends of related protein which may be highly different. The Smith-Waterman algorithm can be implemented by changing only a couple things in the Needleman-Wunsch algorithm. The algorithm can be written using the pseudo code below.

Initialization: F(0,j) = 0, F(i,0) = 0

Filling Matrix: foreachi, j = 0 to M,N

$$F(i,j) = \max \begin{cases} 0 \\ F(i-1, j-1) + s(xi,yj) \\ F(i-1,j) - d, \\ F(i,j-1) - d,) \end{cases}$$

Traceback:

$F_{opt} = \max(F(i,j))$

traceback(F_{opt})

where s(xi,yj) is the value obtained from substitution matrix such as BLOSUM, PAM. Only two things were changed in the Needleman-Wunsch algorithm to obtain the Smith-Waterman algorithm. When filling the matrix, we do not let any of the matrix values become negative, and thus we consider 0 as potentially being the maximum value of the three other cases (where $x_i = y_j$, or there is a gap in x or a gap in y). By not letting any of the values go below zero, we stop considering regions of high dissimilarity which have no good alignments. This allows the algorithm to focus on only those regions of the protein which are similar. The second change in the algorithm is in the traceback. Instead of starting at the n-terminus of both sequences, we start at the cell with the highest score in the entire matrix. This allows for the alignment of the similar subsequences of the proteins.

4. Progressive multiple sequence alignment algorithm

Progressive alignments are by far the most widely used multiple sequence alignment method. This approach has the great advantages of speed and simplicity combined with reasonable sensitivity. Among the progressive algorithms, Clustal-W [3] is the most popular program based on the improved algorithm presented by Feng and Doolittle [4]. Progressive alignment produces multiple alignments from number of pair wise alignments. First two sequences are chosen and aligned, then third sequence is chosen and aligned to alignment of first two sequences and the process continues until all the sequences have been used. We assumed same scoring scheme as pairwise alignment..

5. Results

We tested our method on two datasets of BChE sequences, mammals and bacteria. And all the experiments in this paper were performed on a PC with Pentium IV CPU (ZGHZ), 512KB Cache, and 256MB RAM. We chose our group of sequences from first and second data set obtained from http://www.ncbi.nlm.nih.gov/.Mammals:Human(homo sapiens,NP_000046), mouse (musmusculus, NP_033868), horse (Equuscaballus, NP_00075319), Sumatranorangutan (Pongoabe!i, NP_001127509), cattle (Bos taurus, NP_001070374), domestic cat (Felis catus, NP_001009364), Norwayrat (Rattusnorvegicus, NP_075231), chimpanzee (Pantroglodytes, XP_516857), BengalTiger (Pantheratigristigris, AAC06262), chicken (Gallusgallus, CAC37792). Bacteria: Thiocapsaroseopersicina, Chlorobium tepidum, Rhodobacter sphaeroides, Rhodobacter capsulatus, Synechocystis sp pcc6803, Rosebacter denitrificans, Heliobacillus mobilis, Bradyrhizobium japonicum, Rhodopseudomonas palustris, Rhizobium etli cFN42, Lawsonia intracellularis, Rubrivivax gelatinosus, Candidatus Kuenenia stuttgartiensis, Bradyrhizobium sp, Chloroflexus aggregans.

Sample aligned sequences of data set

```
[Human]0         :MVTEIHF-L LWILLL-C------MLFG--K-SH-T-EEDVI-ITTK-T
[Human]1         :M-------------------------------H-----S------KVT
[chimpanzee]2    :M--SVQSNLQAGAAAASCISPKYYMIFTPCKLYHLCCRESEINMHSKVT
[orangutan]3     :M------------------------------------R-S------KVT
(mouse)4         :MV-T-RSS-H-TE---DVI------I-TT-KNGRI--R-G-INL----P
[cow]5           :MQSRSTV-IYIRFVLWFL-LL---WV-LFE--K-SH-T-EE-DIIITTK
[horse]6         :M------QS-W--GTII--CI--RILLRF--L-LLWVLI--G--NSHTE
(horse)7         :EEDIIITTKNGKVR-G------MN-----L--P--V--L----G--G--
[cat]8           :MQSKGTIISIQFLLRF-LL----L---WVLI-G--K-SH-T-EE-DI-I
(mouse)9         :MQSKGTIISIQFLLRF-LL----L---WVLI-G--K-SH-T-EE-DIII
[dog]10          :MRSKGTILSIRL-L-LWFLL---L---WVLI-G--K-SHTEED
[mouse]11        :MQTQHTKVTQTHFL-LWILLL-CM-P-----FG--K-SH-T-EEDFII
[platypus]12     :MWSTGTSVPCQFLTWFL-LSCMLVSKSYMEEDF----V--I---TTKK
[brownrat]13     :MVTEIHFLLWILLLCMLFGKSHTEEDVIITTKTGRVRGLSMPILGGTV
[chicken]14      :MVWANGMSICARFLMWLLLLFMFIRKVVPEDNV-ITTE-K-GRV-RGT
human15          :E---------------------------------------------
[Human]0         :-G-R-VRG-LSM-PILG-G-T---VT-AF---LGIPYAQPPLGSLRFK
[Human]          :ICIRFLFWFLLLCMLIGKSHTEDDIIIATKNGKVRGMNLTVFGGTVTA
[chimpanzee]2    :ICIRFLFWFLLLCMLIGKSHTEDDIIIATKNGKVRGMNLTVLGGTVTA
[orangutan]3     :ICIRFLFWFLLLCMLIGKSHTEDDIIIATENGKVRGMNLTVLGGTVTA
(mouse)4         :-----VF---------G-G-T---V---T--AFL-GIPY-AQPPLGRL
[cow]5           :GKV--RGMH--LPV--L-G-G-T---V----TAFLGIPYAQPPL-G--
--
--
```

6. Conclusion

This work was started with pair-wise sequence alignment which includes calculating scores of those two sequences and aligning them with respect to each other. This is developed to Multiple Sequence Alignment in which we obtained a scoring matrix which represents all 'n' sequences and alignments from which we can observe similarities & mutations among different sequences. This work can be extended to develop an algorithm which can evaluate the relations among species evolved from common ancestor. We developed the package using the principle of Object Oriented Design and guidelines for developing effective algorithm visualization. It is developed in Java. The input can be read from a file. Output is aligned sequences and distance matrix. The key features of the package are: Can run on many hardware platforms and allows future developers to easily incorporate new algorithms into it.

7. References

[1] Needleman, S. B. and Wunsch, C. D. (1970). A general method applicable to the search for similarities in the amino acid sequence of two proteins. J. Mol Biol. 48, 443-453.

[2] Smith, T. F. and Waterman, M. (1981). Identification of common molecular subsequences. J. Mol. Biol. 147, 195- 197.

[3] Thompson, JD, Higgins, DG and Gibson, TJ (1994) CLUSTAL W: improving the sensitivity of progressive multiple sequence alignment through sequence weighting, position specific gap penalties and weight matrix choice. Nucleic Acids Research,(1994), vol.22,No.22.4673- 4680.

[4] Feng D-F, Doolittle RF: Progressive sequence Alignment as a prerequisite to correct phylogenetic trees. J. Mol. Evol. 25, (1987)

[5] Kumar S, Dudley J, Nei M & Tamura K (2008) MEGA: A biologist-centric software for evolutionary analysis of DNA and protein sequence 9: 299-306.

[6] ClustalXprogram. Thompson, J.D., Gibson, T.J., Plewniak, F., Jeanmougin, F. and Higgins, D.G. (1997). The ClustalX windows interface: flexible strategies for multiple sequence alignment aided by quality analysis tools. Nucleic Acids Research, 25:4876-4882.

Facilities Layout Optimization using Genetic Algorithm

Dr. K. Venkata Subbaiah[1], A.V.N. L. Sharma[2], Prof. G. V. S. Raju[3] and Altaf H. Basha[4]
[1]Andhra University, Waltair, [2&3]Swarnandhra College of Engg. & Tech
[4]Associate Professor in MCA, Gokaraju Rangaraju Institute of Technology, Hyderabad
avnls@hotmail.com rajugvst@rediffmail.com

Abstract

This paper presents Genetic Algorithm based model for facility layout. The flow between departments, distance between departments and their respective closeness relationship values are presented. Applications of Genetic Algorithm in recent years have been tried to solve plant layout design problem in real world. The approach to solve this problem is to add more constraints to make the situation closer to real world problems. The research finds that GA has good performance for finding solutions. In addition, Partially Match Crossover (PMX) and Reciprocal Exchange Mutation (REM) are prominent in finding solutions.

The present GA approach is compared with the previously published bench mark data of some of the heuristic approaches with some modifications, the existing data can be adapted to the newly designed GA model and the results indicate an average improvement of 87.32%.

Keywords: *Facilities Layout Design, Genetic Algorithm, CRAFT.*

1. Introduction

Plant layout deals with the arrangement of the most valuable assets of the enterprises, the facilities. A facilities in this context is a physical entity that facilities the performance of any job. It maybe a machine tool , a work-centre , a manufacturing cell, a machine shop, a department, a warehouse ,etc. Although the characteristics differ widely depending on the type of the facility, **Raoot** and **Rakshit(1993a)** state that area is the unique characteristic that is common for all facilities. The area which facilities occupy could be represented as:

(i) ***Single points*** where the facilities are assumed to be concentrated, (this way of modeling is suitable for location problems, where distances between facilities are quite large compared with dimensions of the facilities).

(ii) ***Distributed*** over a certain region. (In general this region is considered as a rectangle and the distribution is uniform for the sake of convenience),

(iii) ***Made up of finite elements*** (A planar site is divided into a grid of square blocks, for example 1 × 1 metres in dimension, as well known computer aided layout technique ***CRAFT*** is modeled. The space allocated to a facility is represented by a collection of adjacent blocks whose total area is equal to that of the facility. These squares are often called as cells, although they are not related to the integrated group of machines concept of cellular manufacturing that is also known as a cell).

Irrespective of the presentation type being used, it is essential that the location of machines / workstations be such that the distance travelled by personnel or material handling carriers between each pair of these facilities be minimized (**Heragu** 1992). **Immer** (1953), inform us of the fact that up to 40% of the wage bill in manufacturing is spent on material handling. **Matson** *et.al* (1992) declares the figure to be 60%. Cutting even 25% of this cost would lead to tremendous savings. Fitting and moving the facilities economically is the most effective way to cut these transportation costs. Fitting is placing the generally irregularly shaped facilities (small items) into available sites (Large objects) by optimizing some objectives while satisfying the restrictions. Moving the facilities means considering time as an additional dimension. The internal and external environment of the enterprise changes as time passes, so rearranging the facilities to maintain their fitness is necessary. **Rosenblatt** (1986) and **Conway** and **Venkataramanan** (1944), propose dynamic models to provide adaptation power against those changes in the long term. Nevertheless much of the research on the problem is devoted to the static case.

Domschke and Drexl (1985) note that over 2000 articles on the facility layout have been published in various journals. However, relatively few of these have been employed to multicriteria decision making techniques (Current *et al.*1990). Real life facility layout problems involve the selection of the most effective arrangement of physical facilities to allow greatest efficiency with a given combination of resources to produce a product or service.

At the same time it is necessary to satisfy multiple objectives such as the overall integration of all functions, minimum material movement, smooth work flow effective space utilization, employee satisfaction, safety, fiexibility, etc. (**Raoot** and **Rakshit** 1993b).

Although the type of facilities to be placed may vary in each context, steps to a solution remain largely the same. The area of each facility and the interconnection cost of every facility pair are estimated by using the data provided from production engineers. The interconnection cost may either be specified as a quantative measure (e.g. the weighted flow of materials) or a qualitative adjacency requirement. The goal is to minimize the total interconnection cost while satisfying all specified constraint (**Tam** and **Li** 1991).

2. Review of Past Approaches to the Plant Layout

(i) One of earliest attempts to formulate a multi-Objective facilities planning problem was done by **Meir J. Rosenblatt** in 1979. In the paper he formulated the problem as a Quadratic Assignment Problem. His approach was a combination of both Qualitative and Quantitative approaches to the layout problem. The two conflicting objectives were minimizing the material handling cost and maximizing the closeness rating measure.

(ii) In 1983, **Dutta** and **Sahu** proposed a heuristic, based on the same objective function as the one proposed by **Meir J. Rosenblatt.** The heuristic takes an initial layout and develops it step by step be pair- wise exchange routine in a single pass.

(iii) In 1985, **Fortenberry** and **Cox** proposed a new cost term. They also maintained it as multi pass algorithm. This yielded better results with further reduction in objective function value.

(iv) In 1987, **Urban** defined the cost term considering congruent objectives as

$$A_{ijkl=djl\,(fik+\,c\times\,rik)}$$

where c is constant weight that determines the importance of closeness rating to the work flow. The other terms having normal meanings.

(v) In 1992, **Harmonosky** and **Tothero** made considerable changes to the cost term. The facilities layout problem presented by Harmonosky and Tothero handles any number of factors in the objective function and it handles qualitative and qualitative factors in the same manner. They presented a heuristic which combines a construction and improvement procedure to quickly develop a good layout from the formulation.

3. Problem Formulation

The objective function depends on the flow between the departments and their relative locations. The formulation of the total cost of assignment of the facility layout problem can be given by

$$A_{ijkt} = \sum_{m=1}^{t} \propto_m T_{ikm} d_{ji}$$

Minimize

$$Z = \sum_{i}^{n}\sum_{j}^{n}\sum_{k}^{n}\sum_{l}^{n}\sum_{m=1}^{t} \propto_m T_{ikm} d_{ji} x_{ij} x_{kt}$$

Subject to:

$$\sum_{i}^{n}\sum_{k}^{n} T_{ikm} = 1 \qquad \text{for all m}$$

$$\sum_{i=1}^{n} X_{ij} = 1 \qquad j = 1,\ldots, n$$

$$\sum_{j=1}^{n} X_{ij} = 1 \qquad i = 1,\ldots,n$$

$X_{ij} = 0$ or 1 for all I,j

where

$\propto_m$ = weight for factor m

t = number of factors

n = number of departments

d_{ij} = distance between locations ***j*** and ***l***

$$X_{ij} = \begin{cases} 1 & \text{if department } i \text{ is assigned to location} \\ 0 & \text{Otherwise} \end{cases}$$

Otherwise in the final solution , each facility is assigned to a suitable site so that the total transportation cost (Z) is minimized without violating any imposed constraints i.e., each facility has to be assigned only once to a location on the floor plan and its area cannot be overlapped with one other.

4. Applying Genetic Algorithms for Solving Plant Layout Design

The facilities layout problem being the subject of the present work is solved by applying Genetic Algorithms. The various steps performed in applying Genetic Algorithms to the present problem is discussed below:

Step 1

The flow, Distance and the Closeness Relationship matrices are assumed to be symmetric. The values of the diagonal elements are assumed to be infinite. The values of the flow between the machines are represented by using a flow matrix. The distance between the machine locations are represented by the Distance matrix.

The intimacy of any department with its associated departments in the layout is represented by the parameter called Closeness Relationship value. The closeness relationship matrix might consist of either alphabets or their equivalent numerical value. In the present work the numerical value representation is considered.

Thus, the flow, distance and relationship matrices are entered by the user. Of these matrices, the distance matrix is kept as a global matrix in the program. But the flow and relationship matrices are maintained as local variables in the main program.

Step 2

However, the flow and the relationship between the departments don't claim 100% importance in all the cases. Here comes an important factor called the weight factor. The flow and relationship values are associated with particular weights (W1, W2) ranging from 0 and 1 .But the magnitude of the weights is maintained such that their sum is unity always.

i.e., W1+W2=1

The values of the weights W1 and W2 are entered by the user himself.

Step 3

Now we consider an important aspect in the application of the program. The chromosomes are entered by the user.

The chromosomes are the order in which the machines are arranged in the department locations. Consider chromosome 243165

This implied that six departments are arranged in the layout of six locations.

The actual may depend upon what the user enters.

2	4	3	1	6	5

Or

2	4	3
1	6	5

Or

Department/ Machine	Location in the layout
2	1
4	2
3	3
1	4
6	5
5	6

Or

2	4
3	1
6	5

Or

2
4
3
1
6
5

The actual layout, in which, the aspects of the number of rows and columns' present in the layout are to be decided by the user himself. It is like this that, when the user enters the distances between the locations, this aspect is automatically covered.

The present program simply decides the order in which the departments are arranged in the given layout. Obviously, this can be easily done for the case of small number of machines even manually. But as the number of department's increases, the calculations become more and more complex. Hence, programs like this are inevitable.

The user is free to decide the order of machines in the chromosomes. This introduces lot of randomness into the initial solution.

Step 4

(a) The total flow and total relationship values are calculated from the flow and closeness matrices entered earlier.

(b) By dividing each individual element of the flow and closeness matrices by the total flow and total relationship values respectively, we obtain the normalized flow and closeness matrices.

(c) Then the composite value comprising the normalized values of flow and closeness relationship between the individual department is calculated. In this calculation the weights for the flow and closeness matrices entered by the user are also considered. This is repeated for the entire feasible combinations of department in the layout. This way we obtain the composite matrix for all the departments in consideration.

(d) Now, we calculate the objective function value for each of the chromosomes entered by the user, by using the OBJCAL function.

Iteration no: 1

Step 5

(a) From the objective values of each chromosome, fitness of each chromosome using the formula,

Fitness of the chromosome =

(1+ objective function value of the associated chromosome)

Sum up all the fitness of all the chromosomes of all the individual chromosomes. It is called as total fitness.

(b) Calculate the selection probability of the chromosome using the formula.

Selection probability of the chromosome = (fitness of the chromosome/total fitness).

(c) Calculate the cumulative probability of each chromosome.

(d) Generate 10 random numbers between 0 and 1, corresponding to each chromosome

(e) In the present program we consider the crossover probability as 0.80 and mutation probability as 0.05
Now, If the corresponding random number of the chromosome is less than the crossover probability, then it is selected for crossover operation.
If the corresponding random number of the chromosome is less than the mutation probalibi proprobability, then it is selected for mutation operation

(f) If the corresponding random number of the chromosome is less than the mutation probability, then it is selected for mutation operation.

(g) Now the crossover and mutation operations are performed on the selected chromosomes by using the crossover and mutation functions described in the program.

(h) After the new offspring's are obtained as explained in the above steps they are added to the initial population and their respective objective function values are obtained by using the OBJCAL function described in the program.

(i) Now all the chromosomes' are arranged in the ascending order of their objective function values. Of these, the top ten chromosomes are selected as the population for the next iteration.

(j) Find the mean value of the objective function of all the chromosomes in the present iteration. It is meanprs

Step 6

Mean value of objective function of the chromosomes for previous iteration is given by meanprv.

If iteration no.$\neq 1$,

error = (meanprs-meanprv)/meanprv

else go to step 8.

Step 7

If iteration no.> 100 or error < 0.0005 terminate the program else increment iteration no. by 1

Step 8

go to step 5

Thus the program runs as mentioned above, till the loop terminates. At the end of each iteration, the chromosomes of the population and their objective function values are displayed. At the end we will be left with the best combination of arrangement of the facilities available

5. Results and Conclusions

The facilities layout design of six facilities is considered in the present work. The flow between the departments, (Table 1) the distance between the Departments (Table 2) and their respective closeness relationship values (Table 3) are represented in the matrices below.

Average improvement (Table 4) over the improvement heuristic approach = 6.113/7 = 87.32%

From the Table 4 it can be seen that the present Genetic Algorithm approach yields better results than the improved heuristic approach with positive average improvement of 87.32%

Table 1 The flow matrix (f_{ik})

	1	2	3	4	5	6
1	-	4	1	2	4	3
2	4	-	2	2	4	2
3	1	2	-	3	2	1
4	2	2	3	-	2	3
5	4	4	2	2	-	2
6	3	2	1	3	2	-

Table 2 Distance matrix (d_{jl})

	1	2	3	4	5	6
1	-	3	6	3	5	7
2	3	-	3	5	3	5
3	6	3	-	8	6	3
4	3	5	8	-	3	6
5	5	3	6	3	-	3
6	7	5	3	6	3	-

Table 3 Closeness Relationship matrix (r_{ij})

	1	2	3	4	5	6
1	-	3	4	3	3	4
2	3	-	0	5	2	3
3	4	0	-	4	4	3
4	3	5	4	-	4	3
5	3	2	4	4	-	5
6	4	3	3	3	5	-

Table 4 Comparison of Earlier Improvement Heuristic Approach and Genetic/Algorithm Approach.

W1	W2	EARLIER APPROCH	GENERIC ALGORITHM APPROACH	% improvement over
0	1	6 1 3 2 5 4 2.20	2 6 1 4 5 3 2.110	6.013
0.2	0.8	6 4 3 1 5 2 2.161	1 6 2 3 5 4 2.137	1.111
0.4	0.6	4 6 2 3 5 1 2.175	4 6 2 3 5 1 2.178	-0.138
0.5	0.5	1 5 3 2 6 4 2.192	4 5 2 3 6 1 2.185	0.319
0.6	0.4	5 4 2 3 6 1 2.044	1 5 3 2 6 4 2.161	-5.724
0.8	0.2	6 1 2 3 5 4 2.153	2 5 3 1 6 4 2.132	0.975
1	0	4 2 5 6 1 3 2.20	2 5 1 3 4 6 2.122	5.479

6.113

6. References

[1] Austin,s., 1989, Introduction of genetic algorithms. *Artificial Intelligence Expert, Mary 49-53.*

[2] Chutima,P., and Yiangkamolsing, C., Genetic Algorithms with improvement Heuristic for Plant Layout Problems. Research and Development *Journal of the Engineering Institute of Thailand, Vol10, No.2,62-72,1999.*

[3] Conway, D.G., and Venkataramanan, M.A., 1994 Genetic search and the dynamic facility layout problem. *Computers and Operations Research, 21, 955-960.*

[4] Current, J.. Min, H., and Schilling, D., 1990, Multiobjective analysis of facility location decisions. *European journal of Operational Research, 49 295-307.*

[5] Heragu, S.S., 1992, Recent models and techniques for solving the layout problems. *European Journal of Operational Research, 57,136-144.*

[6] Imam, M.H., and Mir, M., 1993, Automated Layout of Facilities of Unequal areas. *Journal of Computers and Industrial Engineering, 24,355-366.*

[7] Khare, V.K., Khare, M.K., and Neema, M.L., 1988 Combined computer aided approach for the facilities design problem and estimation of the distribution parameter in the case of Multigoal optimization. *Journal of computers and Industrial Engineering, 456-476.*

[8] Malakooti, B., 1989, Multiple objective facility layout: a heuristic to generate efficient alternatives. *International journal of Production Research, 27, 1225-1238.*

[9] Raoot, A.D., and Rakshit, A., 1993b, A linguistic pattern approach for multiple criteria facility layout problems. *International journal of Production Research, 31, 203-222*

[10] Rosenblatt, M.J., 1986, The dynamics of Plant Layout. Management Science, 32, 76-86.

[11] Tam, K.Y., and Li, S.G., 1991, A hierarchical approach to the facility layout problem. *International journal of Production Research,* 29, 165-184

Linear Polynomial Swarms for Aid to the Physicians Efforts in Proper Diagnosis of Breast Cancer

Sanat Mishra[1] and Bijan Bijari Misra[2]
[1]MKCG Medical College, Berhampur University, Berhampur, Orissa, India
sanatmisra.india@gmail.com
[2]Department of C S E A, Silicon Institute of Technology, Bhubaneswar, Orissa, India
misrabijan@gmail.com

Abstract

Breast cancer is one of the major tumor related cause of death in women. Various artificial intelligence techniques have been used to improve the diagnosis procedures and to aid the physician's efforts. In this paper, we propose Linear Polynomial Swarm to detect breast cancer. This method uses a linear Polynomial and the Particle Swarm Optimization technique to find the optimal set of polynomials that closely maps the input output relation. The performance of the approach is evaluated using the breast cancer data set. Simulation results show that the linear polynomial swarm model yields efficient result in comparison to many other methods.

1. Introduction

Breast cancer is the most common form of cancer in women in many countries. There are over 212,000 cases of breast cancer diagnosed in the USA each year. In Canada the figure is 20,500, Australia 13,000 and in the UK the figure is 41,000. Overall, one woman in every nine will get breast cancer at some time in her life. Breast cancer is overwhelmingly a female disease, but about 1% of cases occur in men (around 300 per year in the UK). Amongst women it becomes more common as age increases. More than 80% of cases occur in women over 50.

Most breast cancers are detected as a lump/mass on the breast, or through self examination or mammography [1]. Screening mammography is the best tool available for detecting cancerous lesions before clinical symptoms appear [2]. Surgery through a biopsy or lumpectomy has been the most common methods of removal. Fine needle aspiration (FNA) of breast masses is a cost effective, non-traumatic, and mostly invasive diagnostic test that obtains information needed to evaluate malignancy.

Recently, a new less invasive technique, which uses super-cooled nitrogen to freeze and shrink a non-cancerous tumor and destroys the blood vessels feeding the growth of the tumor, has been developed [3] in the USA.

Various artificial intelligence techniques have been used to improve the diagnoses procedures and to aid the physician's efforts [4, 5, 6, 7]. Fogel et al. [4] used evolutionary programming to train artificial neural networks to detect breast cancer using radiographic features and patient age. Results from 112 suspicious breast masses (63 malignant, 49 benign, biopsy proven) indicated that a significant probability of detecting malignancies can be achieved using simple neural architectures at the risk of a small percentage of false positives.

One of the most difficult problems for neural network modeling is selection of proper neural network structure. Usually single network fails to capture all the intricacy present in the data [8, 9, 10].

In this paper, we proposed the linear polynomial swarm (LPS) to detect breast-cancer. For this model, a linear polynomial is used and the Particle Swarm Optimization (PSO) is used to find the optimal coefficients for the polynomial that approximates the polynomial to the desired output. Simulation studies show the effectiveness of the proposed method.

The paper is organized as follows. The basic of the PSO technique is given in Section 2. Polynomial Neural Network (PNN) method is reviewed in Section 3. Section 4 describes the proposed LPS model. Section 5 presents the simulation results. Finally in Section 6 we present some concluding remarks.

2. Particle Swarm Optimization

The rules followed by the members of bird flocks and fish schools, that enable them to move synchronized, without colliding, resulting in an amazing choreography, was studied and simulated by several scientists. In simulations, the movement of the flock was an outcome of the individuals' (birds, fishes etc.) efforts to maintain an optimum distance from their neighboring individuals [11].

The social behavior of animals, and in some cases of humans, is governed by similar rules. However, human social behavior is more complex than a flock's movement. Besides physical motion, humans adjust their beliefs, moving, thus, in a belief space. Although two persons cannot occupy the same space of their physical environment, they can have the same beliefs, occupying the same position in the belief space, without collision. This abstractness in human social behavior is intriguing and has constituted the motivation for developing simulations of it. There is a general belief, and numerous examples coming from nature enforce the view, that social sharing of information among the individuals of a population may provide an evolutionary advantage. This was the core idea behind the development of PSO [11].

2.1 The PSO algorithm

PSO's precursor was a simulator of social behavior that was used to visualize the movement of a birds' flock. Several versions of the simulation model were developed, incorporating concepts such as nearest-neighbor velocity matching and acceleration by distance [11, 12]. When it was realized that the simulation could be used as an optimizer, several parameters were omitted, through a trial and error process, resulting in the first simple version of PSO [11].

PSO is similar to EC techniques in that, a population of potential solutions to the problem under consideration is used to probe the search space. However, in PSO, each individual of the population has an *adaptable velocity* (position change), according to which it moves in the search space. Moreover, each individual has a *memory*, remembering the best position of the search space it has ever visited [11]. Thus, its movement is an aggregated acceleration towards its best previously visited position and towards the best individual of a topological neighborhood. Since the "acceleration" term was mainly used for particle systems in Particle Physics, the pioneers of this technique decided to use the term *particle* for each individual, and the name *swarm* for the population, thus, coming up with the name *Particle Swarm* for their algorithm [12].

Two variants of the PSO algorithm were developed, one with a global neighborhood and other with a local neighborhood. According to the global variant, each particle moves towards its best previous position and towards the best particle in the whole swarm. On the other hand, according to the local variant, each particle moves towards its best previous position and towards the best particle in its restricted neighbourhood [11]. In the following paragraphs, the global variant is exposed (the local variant can be easily derived through minor changes).

Suppose that the search space is D-dimensional, then the i-th particle of the swarm can be represented by a D-dimensional vector, $X_i = (x_{i1}, x_{i2}, \ldots, x_{iD})$. The *velocity* (position change) of this particle can be represented by another D-dimensional vector $V_i = (v_{i1}, v_{i2}, \ldots, v_{iD})$. The best previously visited position of the i-th particle is denoted as $P_i = (p_{i1}, p_{i2}, \ldots, p_{iD})$. Defining g as the index of the best particle in the swarm (i.e., the g-th particle is the best), and let the superscripts denote the iteration number, then the swarm is manipulated according to the following two equations [9]:

$$v_{id}^{n+1} = v_{id}^{n} + cr_1^n\left(p_{id}^n - x_{id}^n\right) + cr_2^n\left(p_{gd}^n - x_{id}^n\right) \qquad (2)$$

$$x_{id}^{n+1} = x_{id}^{n} + v_{id}^{n+1} \qquad (3)$$

where $d = 1,2,\ldots,D$, $i = 1,2,\ldots,N$, and N is the size of the swarm; c is a positive constant, called *acceleration constant*; r_1, r_2 are random numbers, uniformly distributed in [0, 1]; and $n = 1, 2, \ldots$, determines the iteration number.

Equations (2) and (3) define the initial version of the PSO algorithm. Since there was no actual mechanism for controlling the velocity of a particle, it was necessary to impose a maximum value *Vmax* on it. If the velocity exceeded this threshold, it was set equal to *Vmax*. This parameter proved to be crucial, because large values could result in particles moving past good solutions, while small values could result in insufficient exploration of the search space. This lack of a control mechanism for the velocity resulted in low efficiency for PSO, compared to EC techniques [13]. Specifically, PSO located the area of the optimum faster than EC techniques, but once in the region of the optimum, it could not adjust its velocity stepsize to continue the search at a finer grain.

The aforementioned problem was addressed by incorporating a weight parameter for the previous velocity of the particle. Thus, in the latest versions of the PSO, Equations (2) and (3) are changed to the following ones [14, 15]:

$$v_{id}^{n+1} = \chi\left(wv_{id}^{n} + c_1r_1^n\left(p_{id}^n - x_{id}^n\right) + c_2r_2^n\left(p_{gd}^n - x_{id}^n\right)\right) \qquad (4)$$

$$x_{id}^{n+1} = x_{id}^{n} + v_{id}^{n+1} \qquad (5)$$

where w is called *inertia weight*; c_1, c_2 are two positive constants, called *cognitive* and *social* parameter respectively; and χ is a *constriction factor*, which is used, alternatively to w to limit velocity. The role of these parameters is discussed in the next section.

In the local variant of PSO, each particle moves towards the best particle of its neighborhood. For example, if the size of the neighborhood is 2, then the i-th particle moves towards the best particle among the $(i-1)^{th}$, the $(i+1)^{th}$ and itself.

The PSO method appears to adhere to the five basic principles of swarm intelligence, as defined by [11]:

1. *Proximity*: The swarm must be able to perform simple space and time computations.

2. *Quality*: The swarm should be a able to respond to quality factors in the environment.
3. *Diverse response*: The swarm should not commit its activities along excessively narrow channels.
4. *Stability*: The swarm should not change its behavior every time the environment alters.
5. *Adaptability*: The swarm must be able to change its behavior, when the computational cost is not prohibitive.

Indeed, the swarm in PSO performs space calculations for several time steps. It responds to the quality factors implied by each particle's best position and the best particle in the swarm, allocating the responses in a way that ensures diversity. Moreover, the swarm alters its behavior (state) only when the best particle in the swarm (or in the neighborhood, in the local variant of PSO) changes, thus, it is both adaptive and stable [11].

2.2 The parameters of PSO

The role of the *inertia weight* w, in Equation (4), is considered critical for the PSO's convergence behavior. The inertia weight is employed to control the impact of the previous history of velocities on the current one. Accordingly, the parameter w regulates the trade-off between the global (wide-ranging) and local (nearby) exploration abilities of the swarm. A large inertia weight facilitates global exploration (searching new areas), while a small one tends to facilitate local exploration, i.e., fine-tuning the current search area. A suitable value for the inertia weight w usually provides balance between global and local exploration abilities and consequently results in a reduction of the number of iterations required to locate the optimum solution. Initially, the inertia weight was constant. However, experimental results indicated that it is better to initially set the inertia to a large value, in order to promote global exploration of the search space, and gradually decrease it to get more refined solutions [15]. Thus, an initial value around 1.2 and a gradual decline towards 0 can be considered as a good choice for w.

The parameters c_1 and c_2, in Equation (4), are not critical for PSO's convergence. However, proper fine-tuning may result in faster convergence and alleviation of local minima. An extended study of the acceleration parameter in the first version of PSO, is given in [16]. As default values, $c_1 = c_2 = 2$ were proposed, but experimental results indicate that $c_1 = c_2 = 0.5$ might provide even better results. Recent work reports that it might be even better to choose a larger cognitive parameter, c_1, than a social parameter, c_2, but with $c_1 + c_2 <= 4$.

The parameters r_1 and r_2 are used to maintain the diversity of the population, and they are uniformly distributed in the range [0, 1]. The constriction factor χ controls on the magnitude of the velocities, in a way similar to the *Vmax* parameter, resulting in a variant of PSO, different from the one with the inertia weight.

3. Polynomial Neural Network

To improve the diagnoses procedure and to aid the physician's efforts, different artificial intelligence techniques have been used [17, 18, 19, 20]. Screening mammography is the best tool available for detecting cancerous lesions before clinical symptoms appear [21]. Out of the many different models, the models that inspired the most to design this model are Group Methods of Data Handling (GMDH) [22] and PNN [23]. The GMDH and PNN models are discussed below in brief to enlighten the background of our model.

Group Method of Data Handling is one of the methods of mathematical modeling, where we try to build an analytical function (called "model"), which behave in such a way that the predicted value of the output would be as close as possible to its actual value. Let us take first two input variables and let us combine a simple set of basis functions. For example if we denote input variables as x_1 and x_2, let the set of basis functions be $\{1, x_1, x_2, x_1*x_2\}$. (1 corresponds to constant bias and must be included in the set). Now we check 15 possible models, and choose one that is the best. (Each one of the tested models is called partial description, or PD). After that we take another pair of input variables and repeat operations resulting in one or more PD with its own value of criterion. Doing the same for each possible pair of n input variables, we obtain n(n-1)/2 PDs, each with its own value of the used criterion.

Then we compare those values and choose several PDs, which give better approximation for the output variables. Usually we select a predefined number F of best PDs that must be preserved at the next step of algorithm. The values predicted by the preserved PDs (called survivors), serve at the next iteration as input variables of the whole system. All the described actions are repeated again with the broadened set of input variables, and then the next iteration goes, etc.

PNN is a flexible neural network architecture whose structure (topology) is developed through learning. In particular, the number of layers of the PNN is not fixed in advance but becomes generated in fly. The essence of design procedure dwells on the GMDH. Each node of PNN exhibits a high level of flexibility and realized a polynomial type mapping (linear, quadratic and cubic) between input and output variables. By choosing the most significant input variables and polynomial order among these various types of forms available, we can obtain the best of the extracted partial descriptions according to both selecting nodes of each layer and generating additional layers until the best performance is reached. Such methodology leads to an optimal PNN structure. Let us take that the input–output data are given as

$$(X_i, y_i) = (x_{1i}, x_{2i}, \ldots\ldots, x_{ni}, y_i)$$

$i = 1, 2, 3, \ldots.., N$

The input–output relationship of the above data by PNN algorithm can be described in the following manner:

$$y = f(x_i, x_2, \ldots\ldots, x_N)$$

The estimated output $\hat{y}$ read as

$$\hat{y} = \hat{f}(x_1, x_2, \ldots\ldots, x_N)$$

$$= C_0 + \sum_{k1} C_{k1}x_{k1} + \sum_{k1k2} C_{k1k2}x_{k1}x_{k2} + \sum_{k1k2k3} C_{k1k2k3}x_{k1}x_{k2}x_{k3} + \ldots..$$

where C_k denotes the coefficients of the Kolmorgorov-Gabor polynomial.

To determine the estimated output, we construct a PD form for each pair of independent variables in the first iteration according to the number of the input variables. Here one determines the parameters of PD by the least square method by using given training data. Furthermore we choose the optimal model forming the first layer. In the sequel, we construct new PDs using intermediate variables being generated in the current iteration. Afterwards, we take another pair of new input variables, and repeat operation until the stopping criterion has been satisfied. Once the final layer has been constructed, the node characterized by the best performance is selected as the output node. The remaining nodes in that layer are discarded. Furthermore, all the nodes of previous layers that do not have influence on the estimated output node are also removed by tracing the data flow path of each iteration.

4. Linear Polynomial Swarm

This model is designed with an attempt to simplify the complexities of the methods we use in Group Methods of Data Handling (GMDH) [22] and Polynomial Neural Network (PNN) [23].

Let the input–output data are given as follows

$$(X_i, y_i) = (x_{1i}, x_{2i}, \ldots\ldots, x_{ni}, y_i)$$

$i = 1, 2, 3, \ldots.., N$

And the input–output relationship of the above data can be described in the following manner:

$$y = f(x_i, x_2, \ldots\ldots, x_N)$$

The estimated output $\hat{y}$ read as

$$\hat{y} = \hat{f}(x_1, x_2, \ldots\ldots, x_N) = C_0 + \sum_{k1} C_{k1}x_{k1}$$

where C_k denotes the coefficients of the polynomial.

To determine the estimated output, the PNN constructs PDs form each pair of independent features in each iteration. Here we have taken all the features at a time and used the particles of the swarm to construct PDs like the PNN. After constructing the first layer of PDs, we evaluate the PDs. We stop if they satisfy the stopping criteria; otherwise we preserve all the PDs or select a few out of it and proceed for the next layer. In a similar fashion, in our model after each iteration, we evaluate the PDs constructed by the swarm and stop if stopping criterion is met. Otherwise we proceed for the next iteration.

As a stopping criterion, we try to achieve zero level of error between the actual and estimated output as follows

$$\left(y - \hat{y}\right)^2 \approx 0$$

where y is the actual output and $\hat{y}$ is the estimated output. However to avoid infinite looping, we ensure that if it does not converges to zero level of error, we stop the simulation after a prefixed number of iterations. If the result is satisfactory, we develop the model; otherwise, we try with a different training set again. Further with a single training set, we may require several simulations to find one good result. All possible number of simulations with all possible training size may require infinite time to find the best possible solution. So a trade off between available time, training size, number of simulations, number of iterations in each simulation with the detection accuracy is required. However if it does not yields result to our expected level of accuracy we have to think of alternative tools. Again it has been observed that not only the simulation size and the training size, but the way the input data presented to the model, also affects a great deal to evolve a good model. Permutation of all possible ways of presenting the data with number of simulations and training size further complicates the task. However once the model is prepared, it can detect the cases in a real time environment.

5. Simulation and Result

The second and following pages should begin 1.0 inch (2.54 cm) from the top edge. On all pages, the bottom margin should be approximately 1-5/8 inches (4.13 cm) from the bottom edge of the page.

5.1 Dataset used

The breast cancer database [24] was created by Dr. William H. Wolberg, the University of Wisconsin

Hospitals, Madison. It contains nine different features such as

1. f1 = Clump Thickness,
2. f2 = Uniformity of Cell Size,
3. f3 = Uniformity of Cell Shape,
4. f4 = Marginal Adhesion,
5. f5 = Single Epithelial Cell Size,
6. f6 = Bare Nuclei,
7. f7 = Bland Chromatin,
8. f8 = Normal Nucleoli and
9. f9 = Mitoses.

All the features are continuous in nature and ranges from 1-10. Dr. Wolberg reported 699 clinical cases during the period from Jan-89 to Nov-91. These clinical cases are distributed over two classes: benign and malignant, where 458 (65.5%) cases belong to benign and the rest 241 (34.5%) belong to malignant.

5.2 Preprocessing the datasets

To use the data set for the model, Sample code number (id number of the patient) in the dataset is deactivated; the missing values are replaced with the mean value of the respective feature, the features of the dataset are normalized in the range from 0-1. Further for the purpose of mathematical evaluation, the class values has been represented as follows

(i) benign=1
(ii) malignant=2

5.3 Rule for input-output mapping

During simulation the estimated output does not converge exactly to 1 or 2 as per our representation of the classes taken above i.e. zero level of error for mapping the input to the output may not be feasible. So to distinguish the classes we have applied the following rule.

$$\hat{f}(x) = \begin{cases} < 1.5, \text{benign} \\ >= 1.5, \text{malignant} \end{cases}$$

5.4 Training set used for simulation

During simulation, we have verified the results with different training size. The standard rule speaks of 70% for training and 30% for testing. For this dataset 70% of 699 records i.e. 489 records is the suitable size for training. But in case of limited patients, whether this model can perform as good as that of a large dataset needs to be tested. During the process of testing we found that it gives very good results with only 60 records while considered for training. These 60 records have been taken randomly form the entire dataset and care has been taken to choose randomly 30 records form benign and rest 30 records from malignant. For different simulation, we have selected different training set and keep rest of the dataset for testing. Distribution data to train the model is kept alternately i.e. one from the class belonging to benign and the other form malignant. During simulation also we have taken care to present the records one from each class one after the other in the sequence of their arrival to train the model.

5.5 Parameters used for the simulation

The parameters considered to train the model using PSO are as follows:

1. Size of population of a swarm = 30
2. Maximum number of iterations = 500
3. First learning parameters, $c_1 = 1.4945$
4. Second learning parameters, $c_2 = 1.4945$
5. Inertia weight, w = 0.72984

5.6 Simulation with all the features

The effectiveness of this model can be judged from the error curve (Fig. 1) obtained during training of the model using the above parameters. The maximum number of iterations has been taken as 500, but from the error curve it reveals that the model get its optimum value hardly within 100 to 150 iterations.

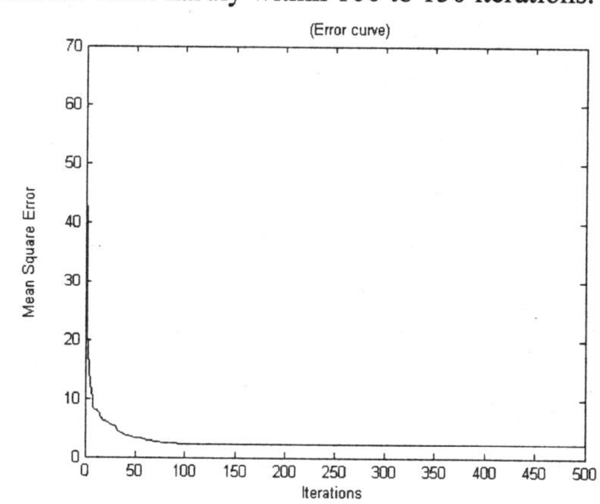

Fig. 1 Effectiveness of the model in decreasing error during training

The mathematical model generated is given below. It has got a detection accuracy of 97.139%. The result of this model is compared with other models as shown in Table 1. It is observed that the results are not the highest in comparison to all others, but the level of accuracy obtained is better than many others.

The mathematical model developed:

$$f(x) = 0.75859 + f_1 * 0.042096 + f_2 * 0.0073206 + f_3 * 0.0091884 - f_4 * 0.0076377 + f_5 * 0.0054761 + f_6 * 0.034036 + f_7 * 0.040397 + f_8 * 0.024775 + f_9 0.02373$$

Table 1 Comparison of detection accuracy with other existing methods

Method	Accuracy %	Reference
NB + kernel est	97.5±1.8	WD, WEKA, 10X10CV
SVM (5xCV)	97.2	Bennet and Blue
PSO	**97.139**	**LPS Model**
Naive MFT	97.1	Opper, Winther (with 683 examples), L-1-O est. 97.3
kNN with DVDM distance	97.1	our (KG)
GM k-NN, k = 3, raw, Manh	97.0±2.1	WD, 10X10CV
GM k-NN, k = opt, raw, Manh	97.0±1.7	WD, 10CV only
SVM (10xCV)	96.9	Opper, Winther (with 683 examples)
FSM - Feature Space Mapping	96.9±1.4	RA/WD, a=.99 Gaussian
Fisher linear discr. analysis	96.8	Ster, Dobnikar
MLP+BP	96.7	Ster, Dobnikar
MLP+BP (Tooldiag)	96.6	Rafał Adamczak
LVQ	96.6	Ster, Dobnikar
kNN, Euclidean/Manhattan f.	96.6	Ster, Dobnikar
SNB - semi-naive Bayes (pairwise dependent)	96.6	Ster, Dobnikar
GM IncNet	96.4±2.1	NJ/WD; FKF, max. 3 neurons
NB - naive Bayes (completly independent)	96.4	Ster, Dobnikar
SSV opt nodes, 3CV int	96.3±2.2	WD/GM; training 96.6±0.5
IB1	96.3±1.9	Zarndt
DB-CART (decision tree)	96.2	Shang, Breiman
GM SSV Tree, opt nodes BFS	96.0±2.9	WD/KG (beam search 94.0)
LDA - linear discriminant analysis	96.0	Ster, Dobnikar
OC1 DT (5xCV)	95.9	Bennet and Blue
RBF (Tooldiag)	95.9	Rafał Adamczak
GTO DT (5xCV)	95.7	Bennet and Blue
ASI - Assistant I tree	95.6	Ster, Dobnikar
MLP+BP (Weka)	95.4±0.2	TW/WD
Method	Accuracy %	Reference
OCN2	95.2±2.1	Zarndt
IB3	95.0±4.0	Zarndt
MML tree	94.8±1.8	Zarndt
ASR - Assistant R (RELIEF criterion) tree	94.7	Ster, Dobnikar
C 4.5 tree	94.7±2.0	Zarndt
LFC - Lookahead Feature Construction, binary tree	94.4	Ster, Dobnikar
CART tree	94.4±2.4	Zarndt
ID3	94.3±2.6	Zarndt
C4.5 (5xCV)	93.4	Bennet and Blue
C 4.5 rules	86.7±5.9	Zarndt
QDA - quadratic discriminant analysis	34.5	Ster, Dobnikar

5.7 Simulation with optimal set of features

From the above mathematical model it can be understood that all the features are not equally important in detection of breast cancer. Some of the features show less significance in comparison to others. To overcome the redundant features Swarm Intelligence is further used to select the optimal set of features for construction of LPS model to detect breast cancer. Mathematical model of the simulation is given below. It gives 96.9957% detection accuracy while using 6 features only out of total 9 features.

$$f_{optmal}(x) = 0.75206 + f_1 * 0.40535 + f_3 * 0.26265 + f_5 * 0.18637 + f_6 * 0.4272 + f_7 * 0.27781 + f_8 * 0.16853$$

5.8 Simulation with optimal set of features for different training set

In the above simulation we have the scope of considering 70% of the records of the entire dataset i.e. up to 489 records can be used for training the model. But in practice obtaining data from large number of patients may not be feasible always for different type of problems. To verify stability of this model with smaller training set we have tried to construct models starting with training set with size 10 up to 500 with a stepping of 10 each time. For each training set we have allowed LPS to select its suitable optimal set of features and to construct the model. 10 different simulations are performed for each training set and the mean value is presented in Fig. 2. It is observed that with 25 cases we can construct model with 90% detection accuracy. Considering cases beyond 100 does not influences the model any more in improvising its performance.

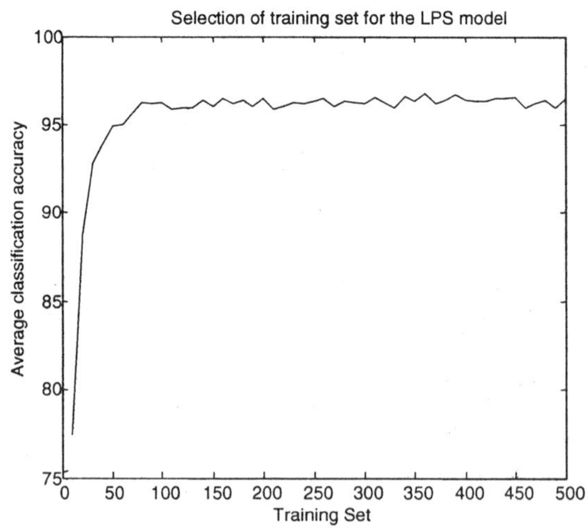

Fig. 2 Comparison of performance for different training set

5.9 Performance when limited features are available

Performing different tests with the patients are always expensive, time consuming and pain taking also. Here we have considered if only one feature is available then which one is the most important. Similarly if two or three features up to six features available then how it will affect the performance of the detection accuracy. For this simulation we have divided the data set to two almost equal halves i.e. set1 and set2. The distribution of the cases is done randomly, however care has been taken for uniform distribution of both classes. For each feature set size we have performed 10 different simulations and the best 3 results are presented in Table 2.

Table 2 Results of best 3 simulations while constructing the model by limiting the use of features from 1 to 6

Number features Selected	Training		Name of the features selected	Average detection accuracy	
	Dataset	Simulations		Training	Testing
1	Set1	Always same	f6	90	90.544
	Set2	Always same	f6	90.831	89
			Average	**90.415**	**89.772**
2	Set1	Sm1	f3,f1	90.286	95.702
		Sm2	f6,f7	92	93.123
		Sm3	f1,f2	91.714	92.264
	Set2	Sm1	f6,f2	95.129	94.286
		Sm2	f2,f6	95.415	93.143
		Sm3	f1,f6	92.837	90.571
			Average	**92.896**	**93.181**
3	Set1	Sm1	f4,f3,f6	93.714	95.129
		Sm2	f8,f7,f6	93.429	94.842
		Sm3	f7,f6,f1	92.571	94.556
	Set2	Sm1	f7,f1,f6	96.562	92.857
		Sm2	f8,f3,f6	95.702	92.857
		Sm3	f5,f6,f2	94.269	94
			Average	**94.374**	**94.040**
4	Set1	Sm1	f8,f6,f8,f3	93.429	95.702
		Sm2	f1,f6,f3,f2	93.143	94.842
		Sm3	f8,f2,f1,f5	92.571	95.415
	Set2	Sm1	f6,f5,f7,f1	95.702	92.857
		Sm2	f5,f4,f6,f1	95.415	91.714
		Sm3	f8,f6,f5,f6	93.983	91.429
			Average	**94.040**	**93.659**
5	Set1	Sm1	f1,f7,f6,f5,f6	91.714	93.983
		Sm2	f1,f8,f3,f6,f4	92	93.123
		Sm3	f9,f8,f4,f5,f6	90.286	93.41
	Set2	Sm1	f2,f2,f6,f5,f7	95.129	93.714
		Sm2	f6,f9,f7,f7,f5	93.123	92.857
		Sm3	f2,f6,f6,f9,f2	94.556	91.143
			Average	**92.801**	**93.038**
6	Set1	Sm1	f6,f6,f6,f2,f6,f8	94.286	96.275
		Sm2	f3,f3,f1,f1,f6,f3	93.429	96.848
		Sm3	f3,f2,f3,f1,f3,f6	94	95.989
	Set2	Sm1	f2,f2,f6,f1,f6,f2	97.135	95.429
		Sm2	f1,f1,f1,f6,f1,f3	97.135	93.714
		Sm3	f1,f6,f6,f1,f8,f6	95.702	94.571
			Average	**95.281**	**95.471**

The above table separately shows the results obtained for the training set and for the test set. Results of 3 simulations are presented by considering set1 as training set and similarly taking set2 as training set. Average of 6 simulations obtained in this process are presented in bold face has been taken for plotting of Fig. 3.

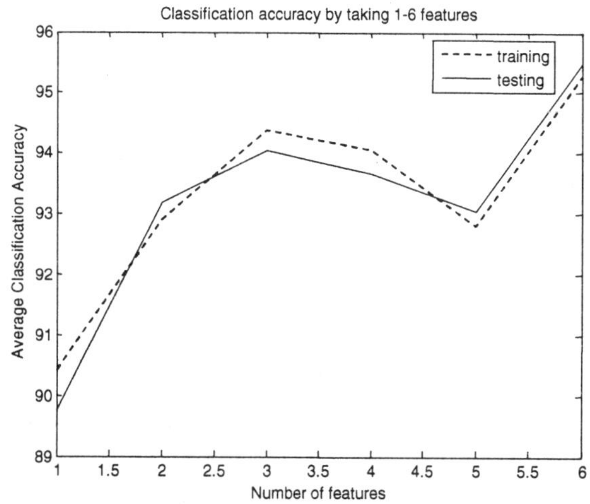

Fig. 3 Performance comparison for taking limited features

It is observed that if a single test is performed depending on our choice i.e. Bare Nuclei, then with 90% accuracy disease can be detected. Showing all combinations are not possible, few of them are shown as examples. In certain cases same feature has been selected multiple times, show its importance for the combination.

6. Conclusion

In this paper we have proposed linear polynomial swarm to help the physicians in diagnosis of breast cancer patients. Initial the PSO is used to optimize the coefficients. Then it is used to find the optimal set of features and drops the redundant features. We have also used this model to verify if less number of patients are available for any specific disease, whether this model can construct a model to support the physician. Further we have also used this approach to verify if reports on all the tests are not available or can this method suggest fewer tests that can equally help the diagnosis procedure. We have found suitable result in all the experiments, which can certainly aid to the physicians efforts.

7. References

[1] C. J. S. DeSilva, P. L. Choong, and Y. Attikiouzel, "Artificial Neural networks and Breast Cancer Prognosis," The Australian Computer Journal, Vol. 26, No. 1, pp. 78-81. 1994.

[2] R. Jain, and A. Abraham, "A Comparative Study of Fuzzy Classifiers on Breast Cancer Data, Australiasian Physical And Engineering Sciences in Medicine,' Australia, Vol. 27, No. 4, pp. 147-152, 2004.

[3] The Weekend Australia, 2002, Health Section, pp. 13-14.

[4] B. F. David, C. W. Eugene, M. B. Edward, and W. P. Vincent, "A step toward computer assisted mammography using evolutionary programming and neural networks," Cancer Letters, Vol. 119, No. 1, pp. 93-97, 1997.

[5] E. K. J. Charles, M. R. Linda, A. S. Katherine, and H. Peter, "Construction of a Bayesian network for mammographic diagnosis of breast cancer," Computers in Biology and Medicine, Vol. 27, No. 1, pp. 19-29, 1997.

[6] M. Shinsuke, K. Satoru, O. Naoyuki, S. Tadao, O. Takashi, H. Masatoshi, and S. Akio, "An expert system for early detection of cancer of the breast," Computers in Biology and Medicine, Vol. 19, No. 5, pp. 295-305, 1989.

[7] S. H. Barbara and G. M. Patricia, "Breast Cancer: Hormones and Other Risk Factors," Maturitas, Vol. 38, No. 1, pp. 103-113, 2001.

[8] P. Ramasubramanian and A. Kannan, "Quickprop Neural Network Ensemble Forecasting Framework for a Database Intrusion Prediction System," Neural Information Processing, Vol. 5, No. 1, pp. 9-18, 2004.

[9] Z. H. Zhou, J. X. Wu, W. Tang, "Ensembling Neural Networks: Many Could Be Better Than All," Artificial Intelligence, Vol. 137, No.1-2, pp. 239-263, 2002.

[10] P. M. Granitto, P. F. Verdes, H. A. Ceccatto, "Neural network ensembles: evaluation of aggregation algorithms," Artificial Intelligence, Vol.163, No. 2, pp. 139-162, 2005.

[11] R. C. Eberhart, P. Simpson, and R. Dobbins, Computational Intelligence PC Tools, Academic Press, 1996.

[12] J. Kennedy, and R. C. Eberhart, "Particle Swarm Optimization," Proceedings IEEE International Conference on Neural Networks, IV: pp. 1942–1948, IEEE Service Center, Piscataway, NJ, 1995.

[13] P. J. Angeline,"Evolutionary optimization versus Particle Swarm Optimization: Philosophy and performance differences," In: Porto VW, Saravanan N,Waagen D and Eiben AE(eds) Evolutionary Programming VII, pp. 601–610. Springer, 1998

[14] R. C. Eberhart, and Y. Shi, Comparison between genetic algorithms and Particle Swarm Optimization, In: Porto VW, Saravanan N, Waagen D and Eiben AE (eds) Evolutionary Programming VII, pp. 611-616. Springer, 1998.

[15] Y. Shi, and R. C. Eberhart, Parameter selection in Particle Swarm Optimization. In: Porto VW, Saravanan N, Waagen D and Eiben AE (eds) Evolutionary Programming VII, pp.611–616. Springer, 1998.

[16] J. Kennedy, The behavior of particles. In: Porto VW, Saravanan N, Waagen D and Eiben AE (eds) Evolutionary Programming VII, pp. 581–590. Springer, 1998.

[17] D. B. Fogel , E. C. Wasson , E. M. Boughton, and V. W. Porto," A step toward computer-assisted mammography using evolutionary programming and neural networks," Cancer Letters, Volume 119, Issue 1, pp. 93-97, 1997.

[18] C. E. Kahn, J. L. M. Roberts, K. A. Shaffer, and P. Haddawy, "Construction of a Bayesian network for mammographic diagnosis of breast cancer," Computers in Biology and Medicine, Volume 27, Issue 1, pp. 19-29, 1997.

[19] S. Morio, S. Kawahara, N. Okamoto, T. Suzuki, T. Okamoto, M. Haradas, and A. Shimizu, "An expert system for early detection of cancer of the breast," Computers in Biology and Medici-new, Volume 19, Issue 5, pp. 295-305, 1989.

[20] B. S. Hulka, and P. G. Moorman, "Breast Cancer: Hormones and Other Risk Factors," Maturitas, Volume 38, Issue 1, pp. 103-113, 2001.

[21] R. Jain, and A. Abraham, " A Comparative Study of Fuzzy Classifiers on Breast Cancer Data," Australiasian Physical And Engineering Sciences in Medicine, Australia, Volume 27, No.4, pp. 147-152, 2004.

[22] A. G. Ivahnenko, "Polynomial theory of complex systems," IEEE Trans. Syst., Man Cybern. SMC-1 (1971) 364–378.

[23] K. H. Sung, W. Pedrycz, B.J. Park, "Polynomial Neural Networks Architecture: Analysis and Design," Computers and Electrical Engineers 29 (2003) 703-725.

[24] J. Merz, and P. M. Murphy, UCI repository of machine learning databases. http://www.ics. uci.edu/-learn/MLRepository.html, (1996).

An Improved Harmony Search Algorithm with Differential Mutation Operator

Prithwish Chakraborty, Gourab Ghosh Roy and Swagatam Das
Dept. of Electronics and Telecommunication Engg., Jadavpur University, Kolkata, India
prithwish1611@gmail.com myself_gourab@yahoo.co.in swagatamdas19@yahoo.co.in

Abstract

The harmony search (HS) is a recently developed stochastic algorithm which imitates the music improvisation process. In this process the musicians improvise their instrument pitches searching for the perfect state of harmony. Practical experiences however suggest that the algorithm suffers from the problems of slow and/or premature convergence over multimodal and rough fitness landscape. This paper presents an attempt to improve the search performance of HS by hybridizing it with another very powerful optimization algorithm of current interest, well known as Differential Evolution (DE). The performance of the resulting hybrid algorithm has been compared with classical HS, the global best HS, and a very popular variant of DE over a testsuite of six well known benchmark functions and one interesting practical optimization problem. The comparison is based on the following performance indices– (i) accuracy of final result, (ii) computational speed, and (iii) frequency of hitting the optima.

1. Introduction

Search and optimization problems are ubiquitous through various domains of science and engineering. Researchers come up, at a regular basis, with new optimization algorithms, in order to meet the demand of the complex real-life problems. Recently, Geem *et al.* [1] developed a meta-heuristic optimization technique that emulates the jazz improvisation process. Unlike traditional gradient based optimization technique HS does not require complex x calculations, is free from divergence, and can handle discrete variables as well. It also does not require initial value settings for decision variables and thus may escape local optima. The HS has successfully been applied to various benchmark as well as real world optimization problems including the traveling salesman problem, the Rosenbrock's function, the hydrologic parameter calibration, two loop network design, and stress structure design etc. [2-6].

The performance of classical HS over numerical benchmark functions like those used in [7] suffers from stagnation and/or false convergence. Mahdavi *et al.* proposed an improved HS algorithm (IHS) that employs a novel method generating new solution vectors with enhanced accuracy and convergence speed. Recently, Omran and Mahdavi tried to improve the performance of HS by incorporating some techniques from swarm intelligence [8, 9] into the algorithm. The new variant called by them as GHS (Global best Harmony Search) reportedly outperformed three other HS variant over the benchmark problems. Fesanghary *et al.* tried to improve the local search behavior of HS by hybridizing it with Sequential Quadratic Program (SQP) [10]. In the pitch adjustment phase of classical HS each vector is probabilistically perturbed in random step size of fixed maximum amplitude. This step is quite similar to the mutation process employed for perturbing the search agents in Evolutionary Strategy (ES) [11]. This article proposes a new strategy for changing, for perturbing each vector with a differential mutation operator borrowed form the realm of Differential Evolution (DE) [12, 13]. The new mutation strategy is inspired by D. Zaharie's seminal works [14], where she theoretically showed that the differential mutation scheme has greater exploration power than the ES type mutation schemes. The new algorithm termed DHS (Differential Harmony Search), has been extensively compared with classical HS, GHS, and HIS. The rest of the paper is organized in the following way; section 2 briefly outlines the classical HS, section 3 introduces the hybrid GHS algorithm in sufficient details, the experimental and numerical results have been presented and discussed in section 4 and finally the paper is concluded in section 5.

2. The Classical Harmony Search Algorithm

Harmony search (HS) is a meta-heuristic algorithm (also known as soft computing algorithm or evolutionary algorithm) mimicking the improvisation process of musicians. In the process, each musician plays a note for finding a best harmony all together. Likewise, each decision variable in optimization process has a value for finding a best vector all together.

Algorithm

Harmony search tries to find a vector x that minimizes some cost function.

The algorithm as given by [2] is:

1. Initialize the harmony memory: pick k random vectors. $\vec{x}_1, \ldots\ldots\ldots \vec{x}_k$
2. Make a new vector $\overline{x'}$
   For each component
   (a) with probability *hmcr p* pick the component from memory, $x_i = x_i^{\text{rand}(\,)}$
   (b) with probability 1 − P_{hmcr} pick a new random value in the allowed range.
3. Pitch adjustment: For each component x_i' :
   (a) with probability P_{par} change x_i' by a small amount,
   $$x_i' = x_i' \pm bw.\, rand(\,)$$
   (b) with probability 1 − P_{par} do nothing.
4. If $\vec{x}_i$ is better than the worst $\vec{x}$ in the memory, then replace $\vec{x}$ by $\vec{x}_i$.
5. Repeat from step 2 until a maximum number of iterations has been performed.
   The parameters of the search are
   - k, the size of the memory. A typical value is in the order of 4 to 10.
   - P_{hmcr}, the rate of choosing from memory. A typical value is 0.95.
   - P_{par}, the 'pitch adjustment rate'. Typical values range from 0.3 to 0.99.
   - BW, the 'distance bandwidth', the amount of change for pitch adjustments.

3. The Differential Harmony Search (DHS) Algorithm

Experiments with the classical HS meta-heuristics over the standard numerical benchmarks suggest that the algorithm does suffer from the problem of premature and /or false convergence, slow convergence especially over multimodal fitness landscape. Also the performance of the classical HS algorithm deteriorates with the growth of search space dimensionality. To circumvent this problems, in the present work we replace the pitch adjustment operation in classical HS with a mutation strategy borrowed from the realm of the DE algorithms. After experimenting with the members of the classical DE family of Storn and Price [13], we find that the mutation strategy employed by DE/rand/1 produces best result when hybridized with classical HS. DE/rand/1 actually mutates the target vector two randomly selected population members. The process has been presented in equation 1.

$$\vec{x}_i' = \vec{x}_i' + F_1(\vec{x}_{r_1} - \vec{x}_{r_2}) \qquad (1)$$

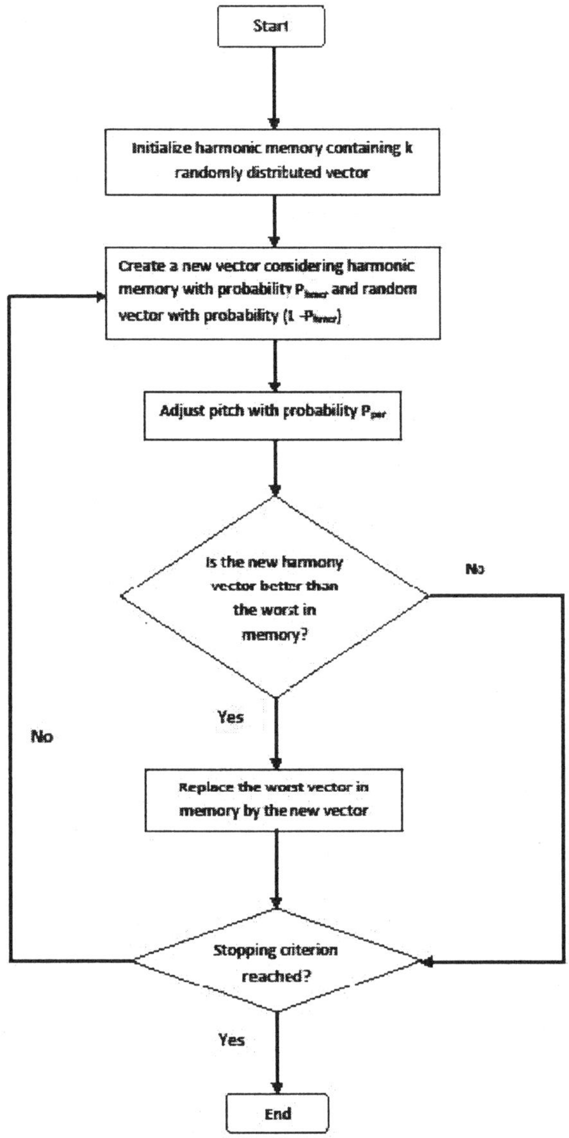

Fig. 1 Flow-chart of classical HS

From now onwards this modified HS equipped with a DE type mutation will be referred to as Differential Harmony Search (DHS). In what follows we undertake a simple mathematical analysis which shows that the DHS, under certain conditions, posses an increasing population variance (with generation) as compared to its classical counterpart. This ensures that the explorative power of DHS is on average greater than that of classical HS, which in turn results into better accuracy of the DHS algorithm. A flow-chart of the algorithm has been provided in Fig. 2.

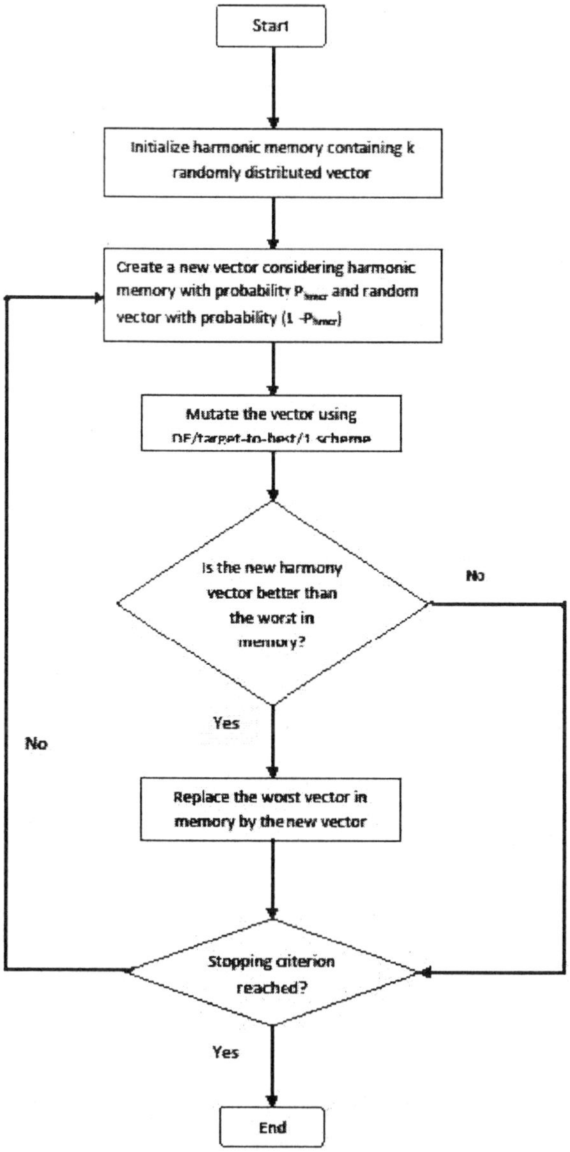

Fig. 2 Flow-chart of DHS

Performance analysis

Performance of any optimization algorithm is generally analyzed to determine its explorative power so that the algorithm can avoid local optima and converge at the global optima position. Greater is its explorative power, greater is the probability of finding near optimal solution as, it can escape premature convergence. Expected value of population variance form one generation to another generation is a good estimate of the algorithms explorative power. In this paper an effort is made to compute the population variance of Differential Harmony Search (DHS) algorithm and, a comparison is made with that of Harmony Search (HS) algorithm.

In DHS the perturbations are made independently for each component. As such, without loss of generality, we may conduct the analysis on one-dimensional elements. Let us consider a population of scalars $x = \{x_1, x_2, \ldots\ldots, x_m\}$ with elements $x_1 \in R$. The variance of this population is given by:

$$\mathrm{var}(x) = \frac{1}{m}\sum_{i=1}^{m}(x_i - \bar{x})^2 = \overline{x^2} - \bar{x}^2 \tag{2}$$

where, $\bar{x}$ = population mean and $\overline{x^2}$ = quadratic population mean.

If the elements of the population are affected by some random elements, var(x) will be a random variable and E[var(x)] will be the measure of the explorative power.

Variance of DHS is calculated below with the following assumptions.

Theorem 1. *Let $x = \{x_1, x_2, \ldots\ldots, x_m\}$ be the current population, $y = \{y_1, y_2, \ldots\ldots, y_m\}$ the intermediate population obtained after random selection and harmony memory consideration and $z = \{z_1, z_2, \ldots.., z_m\}$ the population obtained after pitch adjusting Y. If P_{HMCR} Harmonic Memory Consideration Probability and we consider the allowable range for the new values of x is $\{x_{min}, x_{max}\}$ where $x_{max} = a$, $x_{max} = -a$ and the required random numbers are continuously uniformly distributed between 0 and 1, then*

$$E[\mathrm{var}(x)] = \frac{2}{3}V(x) + \frac{m-1}{m}\{\bar{x}^2 P_{HMCR} - (\bar{x}P_{HMCR})^2\} + \frac{m-1}{m}\cdot\frac{a^2}{3}(1 - P_{HMCR})$$

Proof: Here $x = \{x_1, x_2, \ldots\ldots, x_m\}$ is the current population. So the population mean $\bar{x}$ is given by

$$\bar{x} = \frac{1}{m}\sum_{i=1}^{m} x_i \tag{3}$$

And, quadratic population mean $\overline{x^2}$ as

$$\overline{x^2} = \frac{1}{m}\sum_{i=1}^{m} x_i^2 \tag{4}$$

$y = \{y_1, y_2, \ldots\ldots, y_m\}$ is the intermediate population obtained after random selection and harmony memory consideration. Each element y_k of the population Y is obtained as:

$$y_k = \begin{cases} x_l & \text{with probability } P_{HMCR} \\ x_r & \text{with probability } (1 - P_{HMCR}) \end{cases} \tag{5}$$

where l and k are two elements of $\{1,2,\ldots.., m\}$ and is a x_r new random number in the allowable range $\{x_{min}, x_{max}\}$ or $\{-a\ a\}$ and the index k being a random variable with values in $\{1,2,\ldots.., m\}$

the probability $P_k = P\ (i = k) = \frac{1}{m}$.

$$\therefore E(x_l) = \sum_l x_l P_l = \frac{1}{m}\sum_l x_l = \bar{x} \quad (6)$$

$$E(x_l^2) = \sum_l x_l^2 P_l = \frac{1}{m}\sum_l x_l^2 = \overline{x^2} \quad (7)$$

In order to find $E(x_r)$ and $E(x_r^2)$, x_r may be initialized as follows:

$$x_r = -a + 2Ra :$$

where, R is a particular instantiation of a continuously uniformly distributed random number, lying between 0 and 1, while a and $-a$ represents the upper and lower bound of the allowable initialization range.

The probability distribution of R is given in the Fig. 3.

Fig. 3 $f(x)$=Continuous probability distribution function In this case, p=0, q=1 and x=R.

$$\therefore x_r^2 = a^2(4R^2 - 4R + 1)$$

So,

$$E(x_r) = -a + 2aE(R)$$

$$E(x_r^2) = a^2\{4E(R^2) - 4E(R) + 1\}$$

Now, $E(R) = \int_0^1 Rf(R)dR = \int_0^1 RdR = \left[R^2/2\right]_0^1 = \frac{1}{2}$

And, $E(R^2) = \int_0^1 R^2 f(R)dR = \int_0^1 R^2 dR = \frac{1}{3}$

Putting these values

$$E(x_r) = 0$$

$$E(x_r^2) = \frac{a^2}{3}$$

$$\therefore E(y_k) = E(x_l)P_{HMCR} + E(x_r)(1 - P_{HMCR}) = P_{HMCR}\bar{x} \quad (8)$$

$$E(y_k^2) = E(x_l^2)P_{HMCR} + E(x_r^2)(1 - P_{HMCR})$$

$$= \overline{x^2}P_{HMCR} + \frac{a^2}{3}(1 - P_{HMCR}) \quad (9)$$

Now $z = \{z_1, z_2, \ldots\ldots, z_m\}$ is the population obtained after mutating Y. Each element of the population Z has the following structure:

$$z_k = y_k + F(x_{\beta_1} - x_{\beta_2})$$

$$\therefore \overline{F} = E(F) = \frac{1}{2}$$

$$\overline{F^2} = E(F^2) = \frac{1}{3} \quad (10)$$

x_{β_1} and x_{β_2} are two randomly chosen members from x such that $\beta_1 \neq \beta_2$

$$so, E(x_{\beta_1}) = E(x_{\beta_2})$$

$$\therefore E(z_k) = E(y_k) + E(F)E(x_{\beta_1} - x_{\beta_2})$$

$$= E(y_k) + \overline{F}[E(x_{\beta_1}) - E(x_{\beta_2})]$$

$$= \bar{x}P_{HMCR}$$

$$E(z_k^2) = E(y_k + F(x_{\beta_1} - x_{\beta_2})^2)$$

$$= E(y_k^2 + F^2(x_{\beta_1}^2 + x_{\beta_2}^2 - 2x_{\beta_1}x_{\beta_2}) + 2Fy_k(x_{\beta_1} - x_{\beta_2}))$$

$$= E[y_k^2] + \overline{F^2}(E[x_{\beta_1}^2] + E[x_{\beta_2}^2] - 2E[x_{\beta_1}x_{\beta_2}])$$

$$+ 2\overline{F}E[y_k](E[x_{\beta_1}] - E[x_{\beta_2}]) \quad (11)$$

Now,

$$E[x_{\beta_1}x_{\beta_2}] = \sum_{\substack{\beta_1 \\ \beta_1 \neq \beta_2}} \sum_{\beta_2} x_{\beta_1}.x_{\beta_2} P(x_{\beta_1}, x_{\beta_2})$$

$$= \frac{1}{m(m-1)} \sum_{\substack{\beta_1 \\ \beta_1 \neq \beta_2}} \sum_{\beta_2} x_{\beta_1}.x_{\beta_2}$$

$$= \frac{1}{m(m-1)} \left\{ \left(\sum x_{\beta_1}\right)^2 - \sum x_{\beta_1}^2 \right\}$$

$$= \frac{1}{m(m-1)} \left\{ (m\bar{x})^2 - m\overline{x^2} \right\}$$

Also, $E[x_{\beta_1}^2] = E[x_{\beta_2}^2] = \overline{x^2}$

And, $E[x_{\beta_1}] = E[x_{\beta_2}] = \bar{x}$

Putting these in equation no.11, we get

$$E(z_k^2) = E[y_k^2] + 2\overline{F^2}\frac{m}{m-1}\left(\overline{x^2} - \bar{x}^2\right) \quad (12)$$

To calculate $E[\mathrm{var}(z)]$

$$E[\bar{z}] = E\left[\frac{1}{m}\sum z_k\right] = \frac{1}{m}\sum E[z_k]$$

$$= \frac{1}{m}\sum(\bar{x}P_{HMCR}) \quad (13)$$

$$= \bar{x}P_{HMCR}$$

$$E(\bar{z}^2) = E\left[\frac{1}{m^2}\left(\sum z_k\right)^2\right]$$

$$= \frac{1}{m^2}\{E(\sum z_k^2 + \sum_k \sum_{\substack{l \\ k \neq l}} z_k z_l)\}$$

$$= \frac{1}{m^2}(\sum E(z_k^2) + m(m-1)E^2(z_k))$$

$$= \frac{1}{m^2}(m\sum E(z_k^2) + m(m-1)E^2(z_k))$$

$$= \frac{1}{m}E(z_k^2) + \frac{m-1}{m}E^2(z_k)$$

$$E(\overline{z^2}) = E\left(\frac{1}{m}\sum z_k^2\right)$$

$$= \frac{1}{m}\sum E(z_k^2) = E(z_k^2)$$

$$\mathrm{var}(z) = \overline{z^2} - \bar{z}^2$$

$$\therefore E[\mathrm{var}(z)] = E[\overline{z^2} - \bar{z}^2]$$

$$= E(\overline{z^2}) - E(\bar{z}^2)$$

$$= E(z_k^2) - \frac{1}{m}E(z_k^2) + \frac{m-1}{m}E^2(z_k)$$

$$= \frac{m-1}{m}\left[E(z_k^2) - E^2(z_k)\right]$$

$$= \frac{m-1}{m}(E[y_k^2] + 2\overline{F^2}\frac{m}{m-1}V(x) - (\bar{x}P_{HMVCR})^2)$$

$$= \frac{m-1}{m}[\{\overline{x^2}P_{HMCR} + \frac{a^2}{3}(1-P_{HMCR})\} +$$

$$2\overline{F^2}\frac{m}{m-1}V(x) - (\bar{x}P_{HMCR})^2]$$

$$= \frac{m-1}{m}[\{\overline{x}^2 P_{HMCR} - (\bar{x}P_{HMCR})^2\} + \frac{a^2}{3}(1-P_{HMCR})$$

$$+ \frac{2m}{3(m-1)}V(x)]$$

$$= \frac{2}{3}V(x) + \frac{m-1}{m}\{\overline{x}^2 P_{HMCR} - (\bar{x}P_{HMCR})^2\}$$

$$+ \frac{m-1}{m}\cdot\frac{a^2}{3}(1-P_{HMCR}) \tag{14}$$

Proved

Lemma1. *Considering typical values of BW* (= 0.25) *and* P_{PAR} (= 0.63) *and assuming* P_{HMCR} *and* $m=8$, *intergeneration variance of DHS algorithm is greater than HS.*

Proof

For HS the inter-generation variance was given by [] a

$$E[\mathrm{var}(z)] = \frac{m-1}{m}(P_{HMCR}\overline{x^2} - (\bar{x}P_{HMCR})^2$$

$$+ \frac{a^2}{3}(1-P_{HMCR}) + BW^2\left(\frac{1}{3}P_{PAR} - \frac{1}{4}P_{PAR}^2\right))$$

Putting typical values of BW (= 0.25) and P_{PAR} (= 0.63) and assuming P_{HMCR} = 1 and $m=8$

$$E[\mathrm{var}(z)]_{HS} = 0.85V(x) + 0.0059 \tag{15}$$

And, for DHS putting P_{HMCR} and $m=8$ we get,

$$E[\mathrm{var}(z)]_{DHS} = 1.542V(x) \tag{16}$$

$$\therefore E[\mathrm{var}(z)]_{DHS} - E[\mathrm{var}(z)]_{HS} > 0 \tag{17}$$

Note that the analysis was performed ignoring the selection process. As such the actual value of variance of the function is slightly lesser than the computed one. Nevertheless, it serves to give a value for variance and proves superiority of DHS than the HS algorithm.

4. The Experimental Setup

4.1 Benchmark Functions Used

The performance of the DHS algorithm has been evaluated on a test suite of seven well-known benchmarks (Table 1) [25]. In Table 1, n represents the number of dimensions (we used n = 10, 20, and 30). The first two test functions are unimodal, having only one minimum. The others are multimodal, with a considerable number of local minima in the region of interest. All benchmark functions have the global minimum at the origin or very near to the origin [25]. Table 2 summarizes the initialization and search ranges used for these functions. An asymmetrical initialization procedure has been used here following the work reported in [15].

Table 1 Benchmark functions used

Function	Mathematical Representation
Sphere function	$f_1(\vec{X}) = \sum_{i=1}^{n} x_i^2$
Rosenbrock	$f_2(\vec{X}) = \sum_{i=1}^{n-1}[100(x_{i+1} - x_i^2)^2 + (x_i - 1)^2]$
Rastrigin	$f_3(\vec{X}) = \sum_{i=1}^{n}[x_i^2 - 10\cos(2\pi x_i) + 10]$
Griewank	$f_4(\vec{X}) = \frac{1}{4000}\sum_{i=1}^{n} x_i^2 - \prod_{i=1}^{n}\cos(\frac{x_i}{\sqrt{i}}) + 1$
Ackley	$f_5(\vec{X}) = -20\exp(-0.2\sqrt{(\frac{1}{n}\sum_{i=1}^{n} x_i^2)}) - \exp(\frac{1}{n}\sum_{i=1}^{n}\cos 2\pi x_i) + 20 + e$

Table 2 Search Ranges of Benchmark Functions

f	Global Optimum	Range of search	Range of Initialization
f_1	$f_1(\vec{0}) = 0$	$(-100, 100)^n$	$(50, 100)^n$
f_2	$f_2(\vec{1}) = 0$	$(-100, 100)^n$	$(15, 30)^n$
f_3	$f_3(\vec{0}) = 0$	$(-10, 10)^n$	$(2.56, 5.12)^n$
f_4	$f_4(\vec{0}) = 0$	$(-600, 600)^n$	$(300, 600)^n$
f_5	$f_5(\vec{0}) = 0$	$(-32, 32)^n$	$(15, 32)^n$

4.2 Simulation Strategy

Simulations were carried out to obtain a comparative performance analysis of the proposed method with respect to: (a) HS [2] (b) IHS [7] and (c) GHS [9].

For all the four algorithms we used the same population size for harmonic memory. To make the comparison fair, the populations for all the competitor algorithms (for all problems tested) were initialized using the same random seeds. We choose the number of fitness evaluations (FE) as a measure of computation time instead of 'generations' or 'iterations'. Thirty independent runs of each of the four algorithms were carried out and the average and the standard deviation of the best-ofrun values were recorded. Different maximum number of FEs were used according to the complexity of the problem. For all benchmarks the stopping criterion was set as reaching a fitness of 1.00e-05. However, for Shekel's Foxholes function (*f6*) it was fixed at 0.998.

5. Results

Table 3 compares the algorithms on the quality of the optimum solution. The mean and the standard deviation (within parentheses) of the best-of-run values for 30 independent runs of each of the four algorithms are presented. Each algorithm was run up to a predetermined maximum number of FEs (depending upon the complexity of the problem). Missing values of standard deviation indicate a zero standard deviation. The best solution in each case has been shown in bold.

Table 4 shows results of unpaired t-tests between DHS and the best of the three competing algorithms in each case (standard error of difference of the two means, 95% confidence interval of this difference, the t value, and the two-tailed P value). For all cases in Table 4, sample size = 30 and degrees of freedom = 58. It is interesting to see from Tables 3 and 4 that the proposed method meets or beats the nearest competitor in a statistically significant way.

Table 3 Average and the standard deviation of the best-of-run solution for 30 runs tested on seven benchmark functions

Fun	D	Max^m FE	Mean Best Value (Standard Deviation)			
			DHS	IHS	HS	GHS
f_1	10	50,000	5.884900e-002 (6.646400e-002)	1.639500e-002 (6.708000e-003)	2.171200e-002 (4.732000e-003)	6.318541e+000 (3.035200e+000)
	20	1×10^5	6.429200e-002 (8.725800e-002)	2.893210e-001 (4.892000e-002)	1.426900e-001 (2.220100e-002)	9.618317e+000 (3.994490e+000)
	30	5×10^5	9.389000e-003 (6.520000e-003)	9.990920e-001 (1.238010e-001)	2.542532e-001 (3.055009e-002)	1.769400e+000 (8.803482e-001)
f_2	10	50,000	1.568433e+001 (2.357514e+001)	9.753570e+000 (1.082548e+000)	1.031847e+001 (4.172880e-001)	2.254647e+003 (2.179374e+003)
	20	1×10^5	1.864111e+002 (8.497365e+001)	5.959299e+001 (2.589792e+001)	4.663445e+001 (2.596948e+001)	4.468664e+003 (3.825431e+003)
	30	5×10^5	1.045937e+002 (3.721272e+001)	6.15397e+001 (1.100124e+001)	5.553776e+001 (1.161574e+001)	6.355397e+002 (3.543231e+002)
f_3	10	50,000	4.927550e-001 (7.426300e-001)	2.173265e+001 (6.210750e+000)	2.306190e+001 (6.695788e+000)	5.189726e+000 (1.308674e+000)
	20	1×10^5	6.262530e-001 (5.226480e-001)	8.543985e+001 (1.381052e+001)	6.930525e+001 (1.343840e+001)	8.764900e+000 (3.102358e+000)
	30	5×10^5	2.309900e-002 (1.693000e-002)	1.853878e+002 (1.964701e+001)	1.166632e+002 (1.370221e+001)	3.512368e+000 (1.055009e+000)
f_4	10	50,000	2.701000e-002 (9.005000e-003)	9.035700e-002 (1.298720e-001)	6.340700e-002 (7.265900e-002)	2.266825e-001 (1.400353e-001)
	20	1×10^5	4.959500e-002 (5.200000e-004)	7.612600e-002 (9.901100e-002)	6.228300e-002 (1.311900e-002)	2.117310e-001 (1.109799e-001)
	30	5×10^5	7.316900e-002 (3.560000e-004)	7.334800e-002 (8.200000e-005)	7.301747e-002 (1.297544e-005)	9.785366e-002 (1.295663e-002)
f_5	10	50,000	7.467352e+000 (1.041000e-002)	1.083798e+001 (8.340050e-001)	1.036288e+001 (6.978520e-001)	8.643679e+000 (4.795448e-001)
	20	1×10^5	7.474070e+000 (1.598600e-002)	1.259577e+001 (7.375590e-001)	1.163075e+001 (7.591900e-001)	8.297712e+000 (2.890263e-001)
	30	5×10^5	8.297712e+000 (2.890263e-001)	1.337918e+001 (5.676430e-001)	1.142695e+001 (5.157850e-001)	7.598800e+000 (5.788477e-002)

Table 4 Results of unpaired t-tests on the data of Table 3

Fn, Dim	Std. Err	t	95% Conf. Intvl	Two-tailed P	Signifioanoe
f_1, 20	.016	4.7691	-0.11130337 to -0.04549263	< 0.0001	**Extremely significant**
f_1, 30	0.006	43.008	-0.25620711 to -0.23341489	< 0.0001	**Extremely significant**
f_3, 10	0.275	17.067	-5.237055 to -4.137545	< 0.0001	**Extremely significant**
f_3, 20	0.575	14.201	-9.311759 to -7.011041	< 0.0001	**Extremely significant**
f_3, 30	0.567	6.1563	-4.6233206 to -2.3544994	<0.0001	**Extremely Significant**
f_4, 10	0.013	2.7723	-0.06381928 to -0.01030072	0.0075	**very statistically significant**
f_5, 10	0.090	13.198	-1.361613 to -1.002987	< 0.0001	**Extremely significant**
f_4, 20	0.055	15.059	-0.9323926 to -0.7136074	< 0.0001	**Extremely significant**

Table 5 shows, for all test functions and all algorithms, the number of runs (out of 30) that managed to find the optimum solution within a given tolerance or cutoff value. In Fig. 4 we have graphically presented the rate of convergence of all the methods for all the functions (in 10 dimensions). These results show that the proposed method leads to significant improvements in most cases.

Table 5 Number of runs converging to the cut off fitness value for six benchmark functions

Function	Dim	No. of runs converging to the cut off			
		DHS	IHS	HS	GHS
f_1	10	30	30	30	14
	20	30	30	30	10
	30	30	30	30	4
f_2	10	30	30	30	6
	20	30	30	30	13
	30	30	30	30	30
f_3	10	30	25	22	30
	20	30	21	28	30
	30	30	18	30	30
f_4	10	30	26	22	4
	20	30	25	27	14
	30	30	30	30	11
f_5	10	30	21	26	30
	20	30	24	30	30
	30	30	30	30	30

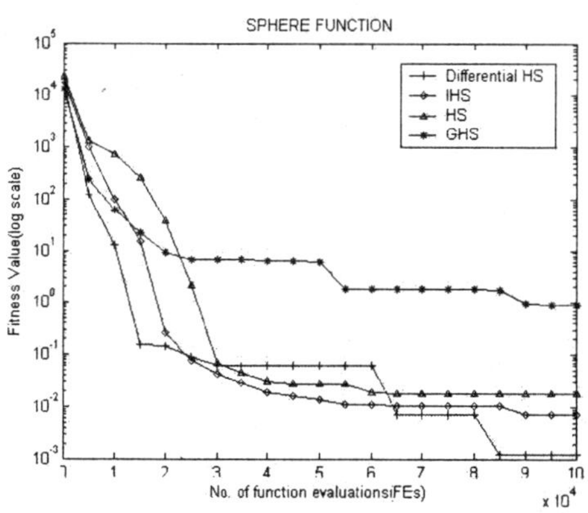

(a) Sphere (f_1)

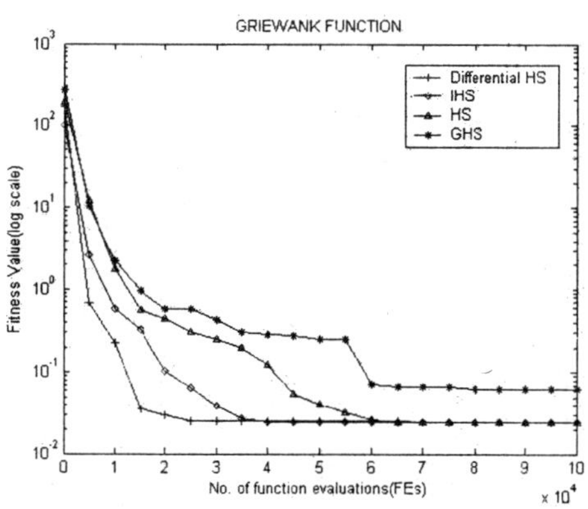

(b) Rosenbrock (f_2)

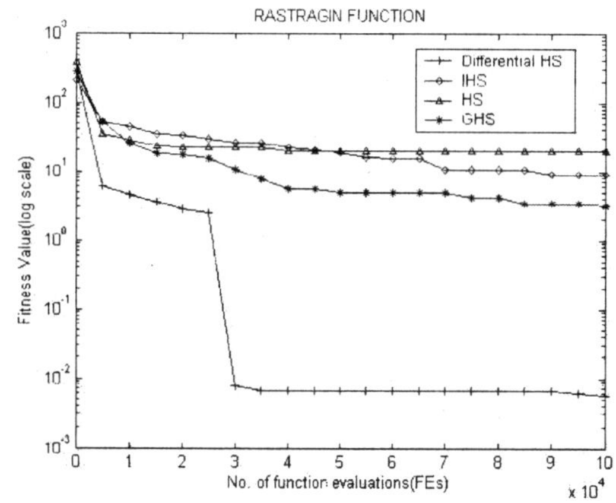

(c) Rastringin (f_2)

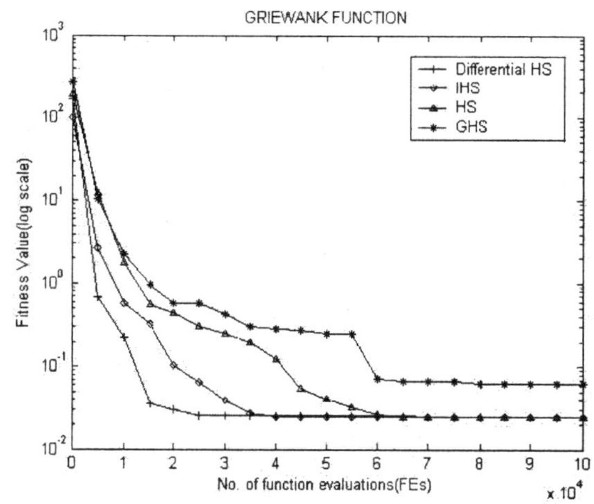

(d) Griewank (f_4)

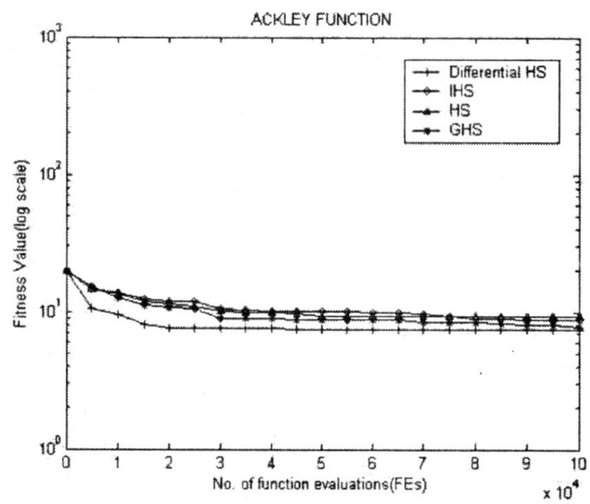

(e) Ackley (f_5)

Fig. 4 Progress to the optimum solution

6. Conclusions

This paper has presented an improved variant of the classical Harmony Search metaheuristic by blending with it a difference vector-based mutation operator borrowed from the DE family of algorithms. A theoretical analysis indicates that the population-variance of HS can be enhanced by the incorporation of the differential mutation operator. This intensifies the explorative power of HS and the algorithm, modified in this way, is able to beat the state-of-the-art variants of HS over popular benchmark functions in a statistically meaningful way. The Differential HS (DHS) was found to outperform the classical HS and its two variants namely GHS and HIS in terms of final accuracy, convergence speed and robustness. Future works will focus on studying the applications of DHS on engineering optimization problems.

7. References

[1] Z.W. Geem, J.H. Kim, and G.V. Loganathan, A new heuristic optimization algorithm: harmony search, Simulation 76 (2)60–68, 2002.

[2] Z.W. Geem, J.H. Kim, and G.V. Loganathan, Harmony search optimization: application to pipe network design, Int. J. Model. Simul. 22, (2)125–133, 2002.

[3] S.L. Kang, Z.W. Geem, A new structural optimization method based on the harmony search algorithm, Comput. Struct. 82 (9–10), 781–798, 2004.

[4] Z. W. Geem, K. S. Lee, and Y. Park, "Application of Harmony Search to Vehicle Routing", *American Journal of Applied Sciences*, 2005.

[5] A. Vasebi, M. Fesanghary, S. M. T. Bathaeea, "Combined heat and power economic dispatch by Harmony Search Algorithm", *International Journal of Electrical Power and Energy Systems*, 2007.

[6] Z. W. Geem, "Optimal Scheduling of Multiple Dam System using Harmony Search Algorithm", *Lecture Notes in Computer Science*, 2007.

[7] M. Mahdavi, M. Fesanghary., and E. Damangir, "An improved Harmony Search Algorithm for Solving Optimization Problems", *Applied Mathematics and Computation*, 2007.

[8] J. Kennedy and R. C. Eberhart, *Swarm Intelligence*. Morgan Kaufmann. 2001.

[9] M.G. H. Omran, and M. Mahdavi, "Global-Best Harmony Search", *Applied Mathematics and Computation*, In Press.

[10] M. Fesanghary, M. Mahdavi, M. Minary-Jolandan, and Y. Alizadeh, "Hybridizing Harmony Search Algorithm with Sequential Quadratic Programming for Engineering Optimization Problems", *Computer Methods in Applied Mechanics and Engineering*, 2008.

[11] H-G Beyer, *The Theory of Evolution Strategies*, Springer April 27, 2001.

[12] R. Storn and K. V. Price, "Differential evolution - a simple and efficient adaptive scheme for global optimization over continuous spaces", *Technical Report TR-95-012, ICSI*, http://http.icsi.berkeley.edu/~storn/litera.html, 1995.

[13] R. Storn, K. V. Price, and J. Lampinen, *Differential Evolution – A Practical Approach to Global Optimization*, Springer, Berlin, 2005.

[14] D. Zaharie, "On the explorative power of Differential Evolution", *3rd International Workshop on Symbolic and Numerical Algorithms on Scientific Computing, SYNASC-2001*, Timisoara, Romania, October 2 – 4, 2001.

[15] X. Yao, Y. Liu, and G. Lin, "Evolutionary programming made faster", *IEEE Transactions on Evolutionary Computation*, vol 3, No 2, (1999) 82-102.

[16] P. J. Angeline, Evolutionary optimization versus particle swarm optimization: Philosophy and the performance difference, Lecture Notes in Computer Science (vol. 1447), Proceedings of 7th International Conference on Evolutionary Programming – Evolutionary Programming VII (1998) 84-89.

Session – 2

Advance Computer Architecture and Object Oriented Analysis

A Memory Efficient Architecture for Diamond Search Block Matching Algorithm

Sumit K Chatterjee, Indrajit Chakrabarti
Dept of Electronics and Electrical Communications Engineering
Indian Institute of Technology, Kharagpur - 721 302, India
sumit2702@rediffmail.com *indrajit@ece.iitkgp.ernet.in*

Abstract

This paper proposes a parallel architecture for the Unconstrained Center Biased Diamond Search (UCBDS) algorithm, which is used in block-based motion estimation with reduced motion estimation complexity. The UCBDS algorithm gives better results as compared with Three Step Search (TSS) algorithm in terms of Peak Signal to Noise Ratio (PSNR), and is also faster due to its center-biased approach. However, owing to the irregular data access of the UCBDS algorithm, an efficient hardware architecture was formulated for its implementation. In the present paper, an architecture based on intelligent memory configuration has been proposed for the implementation of UCBDS. The proposed architecture is based upon nine processing elements (PEs) accompanied with the use of intelligent data arrangement and memory configuration. A technique for reducing external memory accesses has also been exploited. A register transfer level implementation as well as the simulation results on benchmark video clips are presented. Both TSS and UCBDS have been implemented using the proposed architecture and relevant design statistics on area and power have been provided for the same. The architectures, which have been synthesized under Synopsys Design Vision environment, can work at a frequency up to 100 MHz while consuming a power of approximately 459 mW. The proposed architecture provides the solution for realtime low bit rate video applications.

1. Introduction

Due to the stringent requirements of the real time video playback systems, video coding is the most essential part of any visual application. Furthermore, due to the limited channel capacity, these applications require a very high Compression ratio as well. Motion Estimation (ME) is the most essential part of any video coding technique [1-4]. ME exploits the temporal redundancy present between successive frames and removes the same. ME, which is very much computationally intensive, involves about 80% of the total computational power of the encoder [5]. Block Matching Motion Estimation (BMME) is one of the most efficient and popular technique to remove the temporal redundancy present between frames [6,7]. In this technique, the current frame is divided into blocks (candidate blocks), and for each block one searches for the best matched block (within a search range) in an available previous frame. Motion Vector (MV) is defined as the displacement between the candidate block (CB) position, and that of the best matched one in the previous (stored) frame. In Full Search (FS) method, one tries to find the best match by evaluating all possible candidate motion vectors.
However as this method typically computes the MV for all possible candidate macro-blocks (MB), the computational cost is very high.

This method is therefore, not much popular from the VLSI implementation point of view. Due to this, a large number of fast block matching algorithms have been proposed [5-9]. These algorithms reduce the computational time as well as the hardware overhead to a great extent. The major drawback associated with these fast algorithms is that there is always a chance that they may be trapped in some local minima and hence these algorithms give suboptimal results.

The Three Step Search (TSS) is one such sub-optimal BMA. TSS is one of the most popular BMAs, because of its faster estimation time. It consists of only three evaluation steps. Because of its fewer checking points, this algorithm is preferred from the implementation point of view [10 11].

The search space of TSS is reduced, due to which the reconstructed image yields a very high level of distortion. Furthermore, the first step of TSS has a relatively larger search pattern, due to which TSS is inefficient for finding blocks with smaller amounts of motion. This algorithm reduces the computational load and power, but at the cost of the quality of the reconstructed image. The Unconstrained Center Biased Diamond Search (UCBDS) algorithm proposed by J. Y. Tham *et al* [5] yields improvement in PSNR of the reconstructed image as compared to that of the TSS. This is because of the fact that unlike TSS, here the number of checking points are not fixed. Also, as this is highly center biased, it has a very compact diamond search point configuration, which gives fewer number of checking points as compared with TSS.

Although, software implementation for these fast search algorithms are very much suitable, a low power VLSI implementation is needed for the real time video application. As the search points for UCBDS are arranged in a diamond like shape, the memory access arrangement has to be completely different from that of the Exhaustive Search. The present work is concerned with developing an architecture for the implementation of the UCBDS algorithm based on nine processing elements (PEs). The architecture makes use of intelligent data reuse. This, coupled with low area requirement, makes the proposed architecture efficient and suitable for low power low bit rate video processing applications.

The rest of the paper is organized as follows. The next section briefly presents the UCBDS algorithm. A detailed description of the nine PEs architecture for implementing the UCBDS algorithm is given in section III. Results are provided in section IV. Finally, conclusions are drawn in section V

2. UCBDS Algorithm

The aim of motion estimation is to find the best matching block for the current block in the previous block. Various objective functions are suggested for block matching criterion [3,6]. The sum of absolute difference (SAD) criterion is the simplest one to be implemented in VLSI. This is why SAD is chosen as the block distortion measure (BDM). The SAD is calculated for each search point (u, v) as follows:

$$SAD(u,v)=\sum_{i=0}^{N-1}|F_t(x+i,y+j)-F_{t-1}(x+i+u,y+j+v)|...(i)$$

where F_t and F_{t-1} refer to the blocks in a current and the previous frames which are to be compared, (x,y) is the coordinate of the left-top pixel of the current block in F_t, and N is the size of the MB. Note that the values of u and v are limited between $-p$ and p, as the search area is a square of side $2p + 1$.

2.1 Unconstrained Center Biased Diamond Search (UCBDS) method

The study of MV distribution for most of the real world sequences reveals the fact that 80% to 99% of the blocks are stationary or quasi-stationary (within a radius of one pixel distance) [5]. In order to exploit the center biased MV distribution, a new search algorithm namely the New Three Step Search (NTSS) was introduced [9]. It is center biased and checks for eight extra points around the center. It provides a speed improvement of about ±18% as compared to TSS, but at the cost of additional hardware for checking eight extra points. Also, the number of steps in NTSS is fixed as before and no improvement is there with respect to TSS as far as the quality of the reconstructed image is concerned.

UCBDS algorithm is based on the assumption that although block displacement can occur in any direction, it mostly takes place vertically and horizontally. In this algorithm, two search patterns are employed. The first pattern called Long Diamond Search Pattern (LDSP) consists of nine checking points, from which eight points surround the center to compose a diamond like pattern. The second type of pattern called Small Diamond Search Pattern (SDSP) consists of four checking points, with a distance equal to one from the center. Firstly, LDSP is repeatedly used until the minimum SAD occurs at the center point. The search pattern is then switched from LDSP to SDSP which is the final stage. In this stage, five points are checked, and the position that yields the minimum BDM provides the MV. UCBDS is equally suitable for blocks with small as well as large motion vector. Another advantage of UCBDS from the implementation point of view is that it requires lesser number of checking points as compared with NTSS.

2.2 UCBDS algorithm

Fig. 1 gives an example of search procedure exploiting UCBDS. The search strategy now can be summarized as:

begin   */* UCBDS procedure */*

First step:

begin   */* First Step */*

1. Place LDSP with its center at the origin (0,0).
2. Compute SAD values at each of the nine search locations as indicated by solid spheres in Fig. 1.
3. Compare all SAD values and get the minimum.
4. **if** (minimum is at the center)
   then go to *Final Step*
   else
   go to *Middle Step*
   end */* First Step */*

Middle step:

begin /* *Middle Step* */

1. Create a new LDSP with the center coinciding with the location of the lowest SAD.
2. Ignore any search point that extends beyond the area of the search window.
3. Compute SAD values at each of the nine search locations.
4. Compare all SAD values and get the minimum.
5. **if** (minimum is at the present center)
   then go to *Final Step*
   else
   go to *Middle Step*

end /* *Middle Step* */

Final step:

begin /* *Final Step* */

1. Create a SDSP with the center same as the location of the current minimum SAD.
2. Evaluate SAD values at each of the five search locations as indicated by solid squares in Fig. 1.
3. Compare all SAD values and get the minimum.
4. Read the point giving the minimum SAD value as the motion vector.

End /* *Final Step* */

End /* *UCBDS procedure* */

3. Proposed Architecture

During block matching, most of the search pixels are used several times for calculating the SAD values at different candidate locations. In order to avoid extremely high memory bandwidth requirement, some intelligent data arrangement scheme is required. The data flow is regular and continuous for the full search block matching algorithm. But the same is not the case for the UCBDS algorithm due to the variable distance between the candidate locations. In the following section, we propose a novel architecture which has an on-chip buffer configuration for reducing the number of the external memory accesses. In this architecture, an intelligent memory arrangement [10] technique has been exploited which supports the parallel data access. The proposed 9 PE architecture for UCBDS consists of a memory unit, a control unit, a comparator tree and an address generator as depicted in Fig. 2. The operation of each unit is briefly described in the following subsections.

3.1 Memory unit

Random-access on-chip buffers have been used in the proposed architecture and have been utilized the characteristics of UCBDS to reduce the addressing and control overheads. The search area pixels are stored in on-chip buffers so that they are internally available whenever

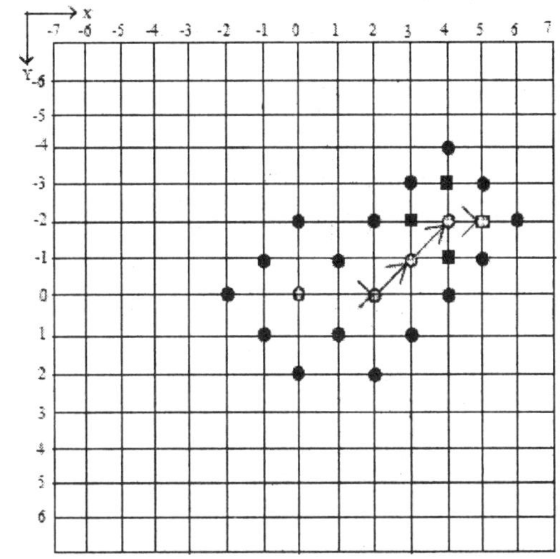

Fig. 1 Example of UCBDS strategy to locate a motion vector (+5,-2). The solid spheres indicate the location for the search points for LDSP. The solid squares indicate the location for the search points for SDSP. The location of the minimum SAD points is indicated by transparent sphere/square for LDSP/SDSP

necessary. In general, a double sized buffer is required for simultaneous I/O and computation.

For further I/O bandwidth reduction, we exploit the overlap between search areas of adjacent current blocks (as shown in Figure 3) and utilized the scheme of three half-search-areas (HSA), which has been introduced in [10]. An HSA buffer stores an HSA block (30×16 pixels), which is larger than the real half search area (30×15 pixels). The extra column is for filling the gap between the search areas of different tasks.

The memory unit consists of three half search area buffers, which are used to read and store the search blocks from an external memory. Two out of the three buffers are used for the purpose of reading and the third one is used for writing at

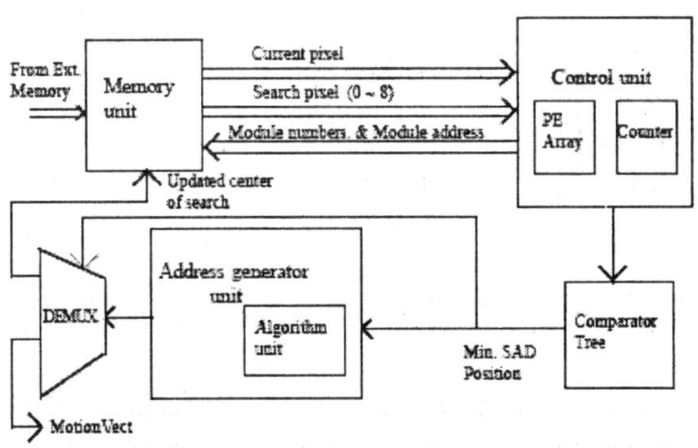

Fig. 2 Black diagram of the proposed architecture for UCBDS

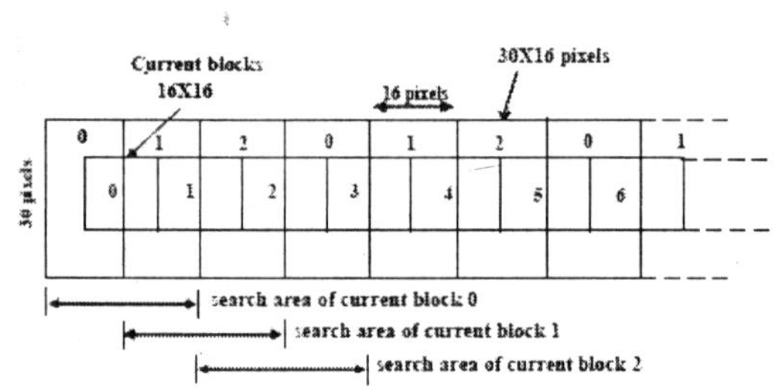

Fig. 3 Search areas of the adjacent current blocks

any point of operation. The operation of these can be understood with the aid of Fig. 4. During the execution of task 0 (matching current block 0), the search area pixels from HSA buffers 0 and 1 are accessed (read), at the same time, HSA buffer 2 is being filled by the right-half (HSA block 2) of the search area for task 1 (memory write). In the next stage, search area pixels are accessed from buffer 1 and 2 for the execution of task 1, and the new data (HSA block 3) is filled in buffer 0. The above process is repeated for the entire search process. These buffers are further divided into nine memory modules to enhance the memory bandwidth. Memory interleaving technique [10] is used for parallel data access. The search area pixels are interleaved among these nine memory modules. Figures 5 and 6 show the distribution of search area pixels into nine memory modules. The labels (from 0 to 8) indicate the index of the module that stores the pixel.

Fig. 5 and Fig. 6 clearly depict the fact that the search pixels corresponding to all candidate search locations will always lie at the different modules for both the LDSP as well as SDSP.

Therefore, it is possible to calculate the SAD valued at all the candidate positions simultaneously.

3.2 Control unit

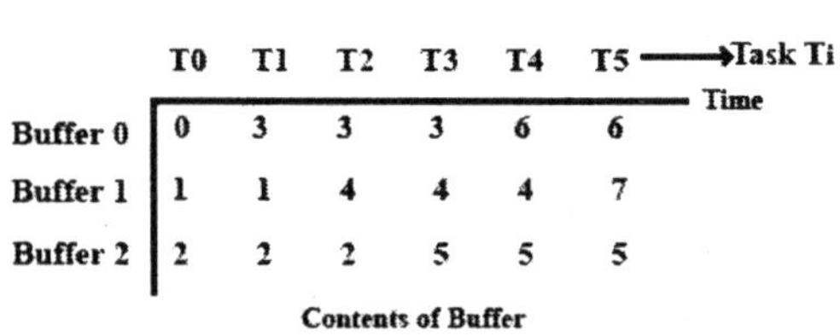

Fig. 4 Contents of the three Half Search Area Buffers

The control unit is a finite state machine (FSM). It receives the search point center at its input. It consists of a counter and a processing element (PE) array. The counter generates the control signals at proper count values. The PE array consists of nine processing elements (PEs). The current block pixels are simultaneously broadcast to all the PEs in a raster scanned order. Each PE takes a search pixel and a current pixel as input from memory unit and finds the mean absolute difference (MAD) for the same. The differences are cumulatively added to produce the SAD value for each 16X16 blocks in 256 clock cycles. The structure of a PE is shown in Fig. 7. These nine SAD values are then sent to the comparator tree.

3.3 Comparator tree

This accepts nine SAD values at its input and searches for the minimum SAD value amongst them. It also searches for the location of the current minimum SAD position. Thereafter, it sends the location to the next unit namely the address generator unit. The block diagram of the comparator tree has been shown in Fig. 8.

3.4 Address generator unit

The address generator unit (AGU) is the last and the most important part of the present architecture. It reads the location of the current minimum SAD position. If it is found to be at the center of LDSP, then the AGU initiates SDSP search procedure, which is the last stage of the search. The location at which the minimum SAD value is found corresponds to the final displacement vector, which is used to generate the motion vector (MV).

On the other hand, if the location of the current minimum SAD value is not at the center, then the AGU updates the center of the search by the location of the minimum and again goes for LDSP with the updated center of search.

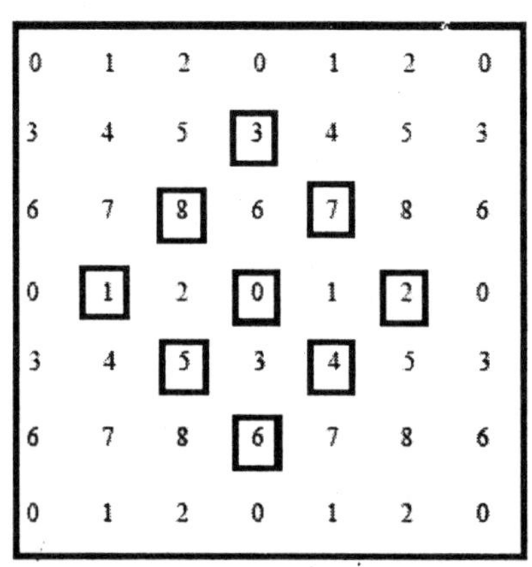

Fig. 5 Memory interleaving of LDSP

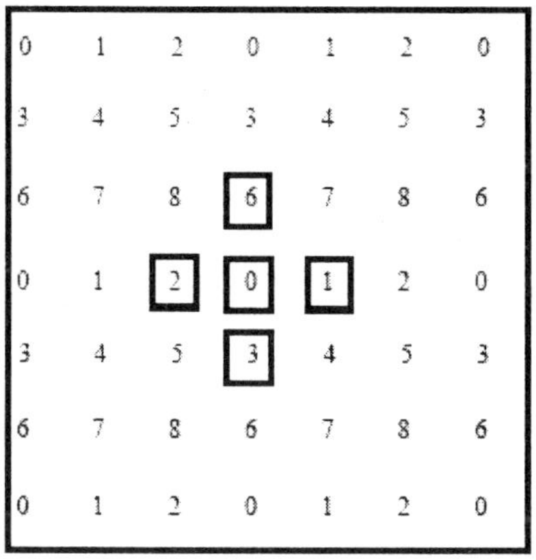

Fig. 6 Memory interleaving of SDSP

The procedure followed by the proposed architecture can now be enumerated as:

1. Read the center of search area.
2. Compute the SAD values at all the nine candidate search positions for LDSP.
3. Check for the location of the minimum SAD value.
4. **if** (location is at the center of search pattern (LDSP))
   then go to step 6
   else
   go to step 5.
5. Update the center of search by the current minimum location and go to step 2.

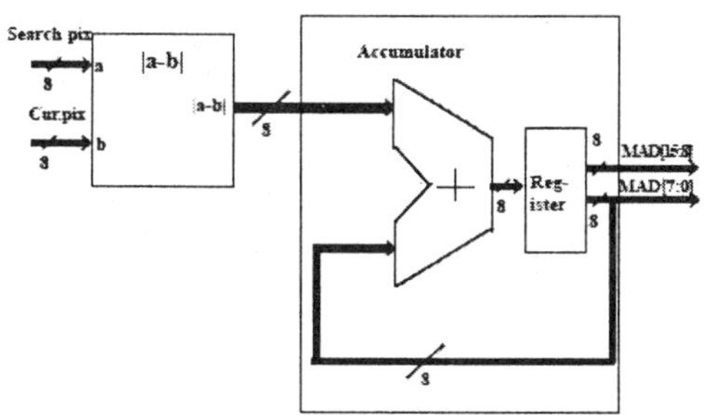

Fig. 7 Structure of the processing element (PE)

6. Find SAD values at five candidate positions for SDSP.
7. Check for the location of the minimum SAD value.
8. Calculate MV.

In contrast to the ROM based approach [12], where the duplicated search positions are skipped, in the proposed architecture all the nine PEs are used to evaluate the SAD values for both LDSP as well as SDSP to maintain the continuity as well as the simplicity of the algorithm. For SDSP, only five points are required for evaluation. Four outputs are simply ignored at this stage.

4. Results

4.1 Simulation results

The proposed architecture has been simulated for both the UCBDS and TSS algorithms in Xilinx-ISE 8.1i platform [13], using virtex4 device family. The synthesis simulaton tools used were XST(VHDL/Verilog) and Modelsim-XE(verilog) [14] respectively. The functionality of the proposed architecture has been tested for both the algorithms on two benchmark video clips, namely 'Foreman.qcif' and 'Newsreader.qcif'. Each frame is of size 176X144 pixels. Both of the frames contain 11X9 = 99 reference blocks each of size 16X16 pixels. The reconstructed images due to UCBDS and TSS are also provided. Table I provides the performance evaluation of UCBDS and TSS algorithm both of which have been implemented with the proposed architecture.

4.2 Synthesis results

The proposed architecture for TSS as well as UCBDS has been modeled using Verilog HDL language [15,16]. The behavioral Veilog model is then used for logic circuit synthesis executed by invoking the Synopsys design vision synthesis tool [17]. The logic circuit that implements the proposed architecture has been

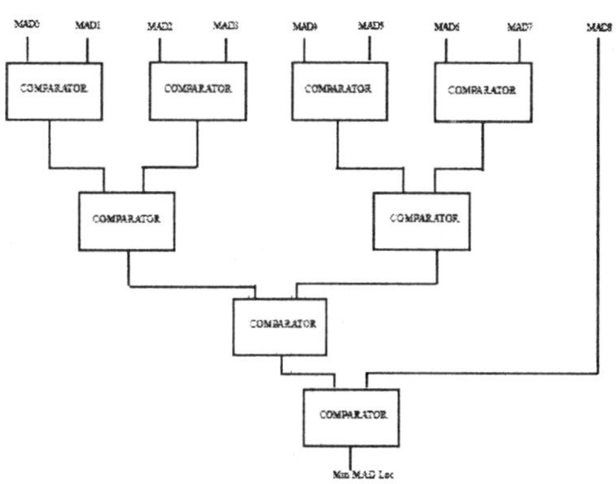

Fig. 8 Block diagram for the Comparator Tree

obtained. Table II shows the area required for the 9PEs UCBDS and 9PEs TSS architecture. The area is shown in terms of the standard unit which is equal to the area required by a 2-input NAND gate. Table II depicts the fact that UCBDS will consume approximately 20% more area than its TSS counterpart. The increase in the area may be ascribed to the additional hardware required for AGU which was not present in the architecture for TSS algorithm as the number of steps are fixed for the same. The decision regarding the LDSP/SDSP is taken in this additional unit. Table III presents the power consumption for the proposed 9PEs architecture for UCBDS and that of 9PEs TSS architecture. It is clear form the above table that the power requirements are more or less the same for both the architectures. The maximum operating frequency for the proposed architecture implementing UCBDS and TSS are found to be 100 MHz and 67 MHz respectively as obtained from invoking the Synopsys design vision synthesis tool.

Table 1 Performance comparison between 9 PEs UCBDS and 9 PEs TSS in terms of PSNR

Image Type	(9PEs) TSS	(9PEs) UCBDS
Foreman	35.8120dB	38.1750dB
News reader	34.5927dB	39.5578dB

Table 2 Area comparison between proposed 9 PEs UCBDS and 9 PEs TSS architecture.

Unit Name	UCBDS (9PEs)	TSS (9PEs)
Memory Unit	18887	18887
Control Unit	1806528	1807408
Comparator Tree	793	793
Address Generator Unit	348026	---
Total	2174234	1827088

Table 3 Power comparison between the proposed 9PEs UCBDS and 9PEs TSS Architecture.

Unit Name	UCBDS (9PEs)	TSS (9PEs)
Memory Unit	12.05 mW	11.89 mW
Control Unit	398.86 mW	432.77 mW
Comparator Tree	5.89 mW	5.86 mW
Address Generator Unit	41.69 mW	---
Total	458.49 mW	450.51 mW

5. Conclusion

The work described in the present paper is concerned with design and development of a parallel architecture for implementing a block matching motion estimation algorithm known as the Unconstrained Center Biased Diamond Search (UCBDS) algorithm, which performs better (provides higher PSNR) and faster compared to the Three Step Search (TSS) algorithm. The proposed parallel architecture is based on nine processing elements (PEs) coupled with the use of intelligent data arrangement and memory configuration. Moreover, external memory access has been reduced to enhance the overall speed of operation. A register transfer level implementation as well as simulation results of applying the UCBDS and TSS algorithms on benchmark video clips have been provided.

Comparison regarding area, speed and power between the UCBDS and TSS hardware implementation is also included. While the UCBDS architecture compares favorably with TSS architecture in speed and performance, its area is somewhat higher on account of the relatively complex address generator unit. The proposed architecture for UCBDS can work up to a frequency of 100 MHz. Therefore, the proposed architecture can find its application in low bit rate real time video applications.

Fig. 9 Reconstructed image of Foreman using TSS.

Fig. 10 Reconstructed image of Foreman using UCBDS.

6. References

[1] R. Srinivasan and K. R. Rao,"*Motion-compensated coder for videoconferencing,*" IEEE Trans. Commun,. Vol. COM-35, pp. 297-304, March 1987.

[2] Y. Ninomiya and Y. Ohtsuka *"A motion compensated interframe scheme for television pictures,"* IEEE Trans. Commun,. Vol. COM-30, pp. 201-211, Jan 1982.

[3] J. R. jain and A. K. Jain *"Displacement measurement and its application in interfarame image coding,"* IEEE Trans. Commun,. Vol COM-29, pp. 1799-1808, Dec 1981.

[4] C. H. Hsieh and T. P. Lin *"VLSI acrhitecture for block-matching motion estimation algorithm,"* IEEE Transactions on Circuits and systems for Video Technology,Vol.2, no.2, pp.169-175, June 1992.

[5] J. Y. Tham, S. Ranganath, M. Ranganath and A. A. Kassim *"A Novel unrestricted center-biased diamond search algorithm for block motion estimation,"* IEEE Transactions on Circuits and systems for Video Technology, Vol.8, no.4, pp.369-377, Aug 1998.

[6] R. Srinivasan and K. R. Rao, *"Predictive coding based on efficient motion estimation,"* IEEE Trans. Commun,. Vol. COM-33, pp. 888-895, Aug 1985.

[7] C. H. Hsich, P. C. Lu, J. S. Shyn and E. H. Lu, *"Motion Estimation algorithm using interblock correlation,"* IEE Electron. Lett., Vol. 26, no. 5, pp. 276-277, Mar. 1990.

[8] Jong-Nam Kim and Tae-Sun Choi, *"A Fast Three Step Search Algorithm with Minimum Checking Points,"* Proc. of IEEE conference on Consumer Electronics, pp.132-133, 2-4 June 1998.

[9] Renxiang Li, Bing Zeng, and Ming L. Liou, *"A New Three-Step Search Algorithm for Block Motion Estimation,"*IEEE Transactions on Circuits and systems for Video Technology, Vol.4, no.4, pp.438-442, August 1994.

[10] Her-Ming Jong, Liang-Gee Chen, and Tzi-Dar Chiueh, *"Parallel Architecture for 3-Step Hierarchical Search Block-Matching algorithm,"* IEEE Transactions on circuit and systems for video technology, Vol.4. No.4, pp.407-416, August 1994.

[11] Seth.K, Rangarajan.P, Srinivasan.S, Kamakoti.V, Bala Kuteshwar.V *"A Parallel Architectural Implementation of The New Three-Step Search Algorithm For Block Motion Estimation,"* Proc. of IEEE conference on VLSI Design, pp.1071-1076, august 2004.

[12] W. M. Chao, C. W. Hsu, Y. C. Chang and L. G. Chen *"A novel hybrid motion estimator supporting diamond search and fast full search,"*, Proc. of IEEE Symposium on Circuits and Systems ISCAS, pp.492-495, august 2002.

[13] http://toolbox.xilinx.com/docsan/xilinx8/ books/ data/docs/qst/qst0002;2.html

[14] http://www.model.com/resources/resources; manuals.asp

[15] Samir Palnitkar, *"Verilog HDL: A Guide to Digital Design and Synthesis,"* second edition, Prentice Hall publication, February 2003.

[16] J. Bhasker, *"Verilog HDL Synthesis: A Practical Primer,"*Star Galaxy Publication, November 1998.

[17] Synopsys reference manual 'synopsys/SOLD-2006.06' synopsys corporation, version 06.

Design and Implementation of Microcontroller Based Automatic ON/OFF Genset

S. Balamurugan[1], G. Arunprasath[2] and R. Karthikeyan[3]
[1]Department of Information Technology, Anna University, Coimbatore, India -641 013
[2&3]Department of Computer Science & Engg, Anna University, Coimbatore, India -641 013
sbnbala@gmail.com babblu.arun@gmail.com karthiaucs@gmail.com

Abstract

The recent crush is on managing the power failure prevailing on-date. This paper focuses mainly on the microcontroller implementation aspects in the event of power failure. In our paper, when power supply fails or if anyone of the phase is being cut off the microcontroller senses that and automatically turns on the genset and delivers power to the bus bar. if power supply resumes the microcontroller senses that and automatically cut off the genset supply to bus bar by using voltage sensing device.

1. Introduction

The microcontroller consists of a powerful CPU tightly coupled with memory RAM, ROM, EPROM [2] [3], various I/O features such as serial ports, timer/counter, interrupt controller, data acquisition interfaces-analog to digital converter (ADC),digital to analog converter (DAC),everything integrated on to a single silicon chip.

It does not mean that only microcontroller should have all the above said features on chip, depending on the need and area application for which it is designed, the on chip features, present in it may or may not include all the individual section said above.

Any microcomputer system requires memory to store a sequence of instructions making up a program, parallel port or serial port for communicating with an external system,

Timer/counter for control purposes like generating time delays, baud rate for the serial port, apart from the controlling unit called the Central Processing Unit.

If a system is developed with a microprocessor, the designer has to go for external memory such as RAM, ROM or EPROM and peripherals. But the micro controller has got all these peripheral facilities on a single ship so development of a similar system with a micro controller reduces PCB size and cost of the design.

One of the major differences between a micro controller and a microprocessor is that a controller often deals with bits, not bytes as in the real world application, for example switch contacts can only be open or close, indicators should be lit or dark and motors can be either turned on or off and so forth

ATMEL Microcontroller

Series: 89C51 Family, Technology: CMOS.
The major features of 8-bit microcontroller ATMEL 89C51:

- 8 Bit CPU optimized for control applications.
- Extensive Boolean processing (Single - bit logic) Capabilities.
- On – Chip Flash Program Memory.
- On – Chip Data RAM.
- Bi-directional and Individually Addressable I/O Lines
- Multiple 16-Bit Timer/Counters
- Full Duplex UART
- Multiple Source / Vector / Priority Interrupt Structure
- On – Chip Oscillator and Clock circuitry.
- On – Chip EEPROM.
- SPI Serial Bus Interface.
- Watch Dog Timer.

Would intend to counterfeit the password by replacing the photo, it would be possible to detect the change by scanning the passport and verifying the password hidden in the photo, does not match any more with the user login password. If it matches then user can view the message.

2. Hardware Components

We use the following components for developing the virtual keyboard.
Microcontroller:
Salient Features:

* 8- bit CPU optimized for control applications
* Extensive Boolean processing capabilities
* 64 k program memory address space
* 64 k program memory data space
* 4 k bytes of on- chip program memory

* 128 bytes of on- chip data RAM
* 32 bi-directional and individually addressable i/o lines
* Two sixteen bit timers/counters
* Full duplex UART
* 6- source/5- vector interrupt structure with two priority levels
* On- chip clock oscillator

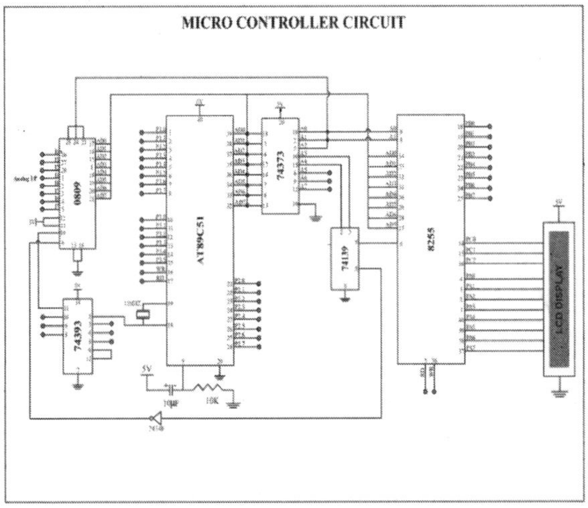

Fig. 1 Microcontroller Circuit

A. Memory Organization

The 8031 have separate spaces for program and data Memory. The program memory can only be read and not written to. The read strobe for external program memory is the *PSEN (program Store Enable).

The data memory allows up to 64 k bytes of external RAM to be addressed. The CPU generates *RD and *WR signals as needed during external memory access. The external program and Applying RD and PSEN signals may combine data memory.

Executing from external program memory:

During external program memory fetches 16 I/O lines (port 0 and port 2) are dedicated for bus functions. Port 0 serves as a multiplexed address / data bus. Port 0 emits the lower byte of the program counter while port 2 emits the higher byte.

Program status word (PSW):

CY PSW7: Carry flag receives carry out from bit 1 of ALU operands.

AC PSW6: Auxiliary carry flag receives carry out from bit 1 of addition operands.

F0 PSW 5: General-purpose status flag

RS1 PSW4: Resister bank select bit 1

RS0 PSW3: Resister bank select bit 0

OV PSW2: Overflow flag set by arithmetic operations

PSW1: User definable flag

P PSW0: Parity flag set by hardware to 1 if it contains an odd number of 1's, otherwise it is reset to 0

Addressing Modes: The following addressing modes are available in the 8031 instruction set.

The difference between Microprocessor and microcontroller is Microprocessor can only process with the data, Microcontroller can control external device. That is if you want switch" ON" or "OFF" a device, you need peripheral ICs
to do this work with microcontroller you can directly control the device.

Like Microprocessor, Microcontroller is available with different features. It is available with inbuilt memory, I/O lines, timer and ADC. The Microcontroller, which we are going to use, is 89C51 it is manufactured by ATMEL, MC, USA. This is advanced version of 8031. this Microcontroller have inbuilt 4K bytes of flash ROM, 256 bytes of RAM, 32 I/O lines(4 bit ports)and 6 vectored interrupts.

B. Flash Rom

4-kilobyte ROM is available in the Micro controller. It can be erased and reporogramed.If the available memory is not enough for your program, you can interface the external ROM with this IC, it has 16 address lines, so maximum of (2^16) i.e.,, 64 bytes of ROM can be interface with this microcontroller. Both internal and external ROM cannot be used simultaneously.

For external accessing of ROM, A pin is provided in microcontroller itself. EA should be high to use internal ROM, low to use external ROM.

Fig. 2 Memory module

C. Input/output Ports

There are four I/O ports available in AT89C51.They are port0, portl, port2, port3.All these ports are eight bit ports. All these ports can be controlled as eight-bit port or it can be controlled individually. One of the main feature of this microcontroller is it can control the port pins individually. For example to control a LED we need to use one I/O line in Micro processor with 8255 we have to use an eight bit port. In 89C51 port 1 is available for users port 3 is combined with interrupts. This can be used as interrupts (or) I/O ports, ports 2 & port 0 is combined with address bus data bus.

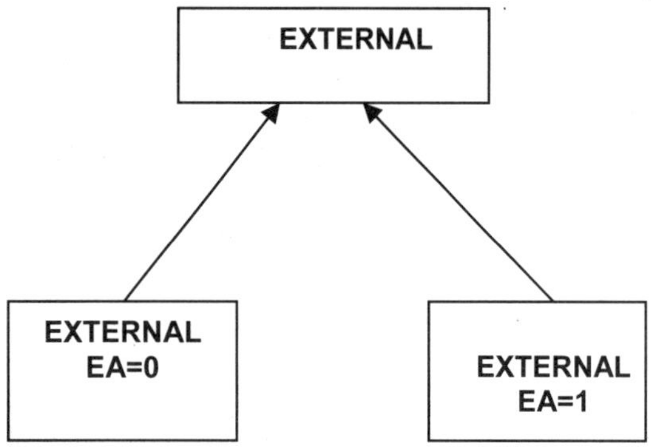

Fig. 3 I/O ports

3. System Architecture

- ADC 0808\0809
- 74393 COUNTER IC
- INVERTING IC 74139
- ADDRESS LATCH 74373
- 8255 IC

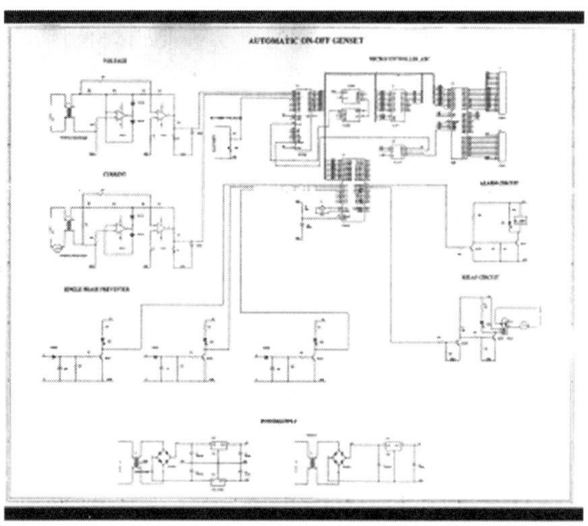

Fig. 4 Full system structure

A. ADC

The ADC 0808\0809 IC [4] is an analog to digital converter in the family of ADC 800 series from national semiconductor. it works with +5v and has a resolution of 8 bits. in addition to resolution, conversion time is another major factor in judging an ADC .conversion time is defined as the time it takes the ADC to convert analog to binary number. in the ADC the conversion time varies depending on the clocking signal applied to the clock pins, conversion time for ADC 0808\0809 is 100 microsecond an d the power consumption is 15mV and it has 8 number of analog inputs. The output of the ADC is connected to 8255 and LCD display.

B. 8255

The 8255 is peripheral interface connectıııg the LCD and microcontroller. The out put digital signals from the ADC is connected to the 8255. The 8255 is connected to the LCD display to show the digital out put of ADC.

C. Address Latch

74373 are used as address latch between the microcontroller and 8255. AD7–AD0 of the microcontroller is latched with the AD7-AD0 of 8255 through address latch IC 74373.

D. 89C51 Microcontrollers

It is programmed IC .The out put from the single phase indicator is 000. E.B devices supply to the load if anyone of the phase cut off. The out put of the single phase indicator out put will be 001. This is given as input to the microcontroller. As per the program the microcontroller turns ON the genset the voltage current ,battery are displayed as per the program in the IC.

E. Iinverting IC

IC 74139 is used to invert the low value into high value. This high value is applied to ADC. Active low signal is used for 8255 in CS. But ADC is worked with active high signal. By using IC 74139 the low value is converted into high value.

4. Design Methods

A. Instruction Set

The 8031 instruction set is optimized for 8 bit control applications. It provides extensive support for one-bit variables as separate data type, allowing direct manipulations in control and Control logic systems that require Boolean processing. The various instructions available can be categorized as follows.

- Arithmetic operation
- Logical operations
- Data transfer
- Boolean variable manipulations
- Program branching

B. CPU Timing

The 8031 have an on-chip oscillator that can be used if desired as a clock source for CPU. To use the on-chip oscillator, a crystal or a ceramic resonator is connected between pins XTAL1 and XTAL2.

C. Machine Cycle

The machine cycle consists of a sequence of 6-state time lasting for two oscillator periods.

D. Interrupt Structure

The 8031 provide five interrupt sources two external interrupts, two-timer interrupts and a serial port interrupt. Each of the interrupt.

Sources can be individually enabled or disabled by setting or clearing a bit in the SFR named IE (Interrupt Enable). All the interrupts can be.

Cleared at once to one of the priority levels by setting or clearing a bit in the SFR named IP. There is also an internal polling sequence that is made use of when interrupt requests of the same priority level occur simultaneously.

E. Timer/Counters

The 8031 has two 16-bit timer/counter registers. These can be configured to operate either as timers or as event counters. These timer/counters have four operating modes which are selected by the bits M1, M0 in TMOD.

F. Memory Configuration

Memory is an integral part of the microprocessor system. While executing a program the processor needs to access memory quite frequently to read instruction codes and data stored in the memory. Memory has certain signal requirements to write into and read from its registers. Similarly microprocessor initiates a set of signals when it wants to read from write in to memory. The required signals are generated using an interfacing circuit.

In interfacing any memory with the microprocessor, first the address and the data lines must be connected to the memory chip. The number of address lines connected to the memory depends on its capacity. The remaining address lines are used to generate the chip select signal for the memory chip using decoder circuits.

G. EPROM Configuration

In our design we used 8K EPROM 2764. This is the Erasable Programmable Read Only Memory. In this you can store data up to 8K using an EPROM programmer. The stored data can be erased using an ultra violet eraser. By passing the ultraviolet rays through the windows provided in the EPROM the stored data will be lost even if the power goes off. Generally this is used to store the monitor program of any system.

In this design the address lines A0 - A12 of the micro controller are connected to the address lines of the EPROM 2764. The data lines of DO - D7 of the EPROM are connected to data lines of the processor. All these lines from the processor is connected to the EPROM through a latch. The RD line of the processor is connected to the OE line of the EPROM. The CS line of the EPROM is connected to the decoder output (ESEL) of the select the logic circuit. The address range for the EPROM is 2002 - 3FFF.

H. RAM Configuration

The Random Access Memory [5] is also called as Read and Write Memory. In this memory one can read the stored data as well as he can write the data to the memory. This mainly used for temporary storage of data and programmers. The user can have access to memory.

In our design configuration we use 8K RAM 6264. All the address and the data line of the microprocessor are connected to the RAM through a latch because of the demultiplexing nature of the address and data lines of 8051. Address lines AO-A12 are connected to the 13 address lines of the RAM 6264. The 8 data line DO-D7 are connected to the data lines (multiplexed lower order address lines AO-A7) of the processor through a latch IC 74LS373. The same design is followed in the EPROM also.

I. Key Board Display Control

In our system design we used 8279 for keyboard and display control. The key board contains 20 keys and the display has 6 number of seven segment displays. The 8279 is a hardware approach to interfacing a matrix key board and a multiplexed display.

J. Configuration of 8279

The 8279 are a 40-pin device with four major sections: keyboard, data, display and processor interface. Keyboard section - this section has eight lions (RL0-RL1) that can be connected to eight columns of a keyboard.

K. Scan Section

This section has a scan counter and four scan lines (SLO-SL3). These sections are connected to rows of a matrix keyboard and the digit drives of multiplexed display.

L. Display Section

The display section has 8 output lines divided in to two graphs (OAO-OA3) and (OB0-OB3). These lines are used along with the scan lines for multiplexed display.

M. Processor Section

This system includes eight data lines (DO - D7) and other interfacing lines AO, RD, WR, CLK etc. The RD and WR signals are connected to RD and WR signals of the 8051. The AO line of the 8051 is connected to AO address line of 8051. When AO is high the signals are interpreted as control words or status and when it is low signals are interpreted as data. The CS line of 6279 is USED line of 74LS138.The clock input to 8279 is 1 MHz signal. The 3 MHz clock derived from 8051 is divided by the counter and then given to the 8279 clock input.

N. Configuration of keyboard:

The keyboard is organized in matrix form. The scan lines s0, s1 and s2 form the row of the matrix. The eight return lines from 8279 (RL0-RL7) form the 8 columns of the matrix.

Normally the return lines are in high state. The scan lines s0,

O. Configuration of Seven Segment Display

This output lines OAO-OA3 and OBO-OB3 of 8279 are used to glow the 8 segments of SSDS. The outputs of the 8279 are connected to the transistor BC158. Those transistor act as a power transistor, since the output from 8279 can't drive the SSDS. The transistors are of PNP type and the conduct only when the outputs OAO-OB3 are low. In our design the 6 SSDS ae connected in parallel. The data is sending to display in multiplexed mode. So to select the displays the 8279 has three output lines SLO-SL2 called multiplexed scan lines.

P. Example of Latch

Typical example of the latches is the 74LS373 and the 8282. Both are functionally, similar; however, they are not pin compactable. These octal latches are suitable to latch 8-bit data here we use 74LS373 D LATCH. The devices include eight D latches with tri-state buffers. It requires two input signals, enables (G) and output control (OC). The enable is an active high signal connected to the clock input of the flip-flop. When the signal goes low, data are latched from the data bus. The output controls signal is active low, enable the tri-state buffers to output data to display devices.

5. Working Principle

A. Power supply

The present chapter introduces the operation of power supply circuits built using filters, rectifiers, and then voltage regulators. Starting with an ac voltage, a steady dc voltage is obtained by rectifying the ac voltage, then filtering to a dc level, and finally, regulating to obtain a desired fixed dc voltage. The regulation is usually obtained from an IC voltage regulator unit, which takes a dc voltage and provides a somewhat lower dc voltage, which remains the same even if the input dc voltage varies, or the output load connected to the dc voltage changes.

A block diagram containing the parts of a typical power supply and the voltage at various points in the unit is shown in Fig. 6. The ac voltage, typically 120 V rms, is connected to a transformer, which steps that ac voltage down to the level for the desired dc output. A diode rectifier then provides a full-wave rectified voltage that is initially filtered by a simple capacitor filter to produce a dc voltage.

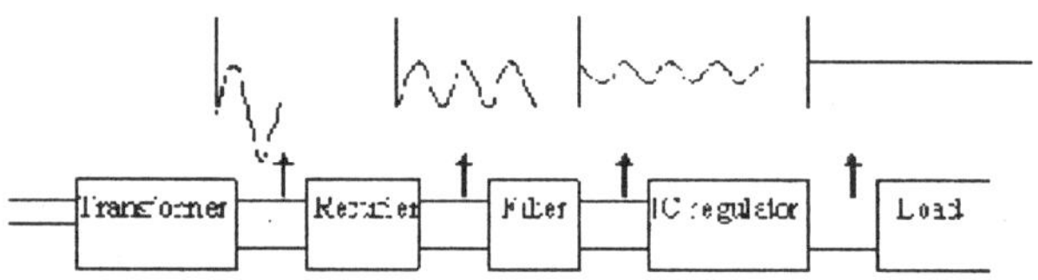

Fig. 5

IC Voltage Regulators

Voltage regulators comprise a class of widely used ICs. Regulator IC units contain the circuitry for reference source, comparator amplifier, control device, and overload protection all in a single IC. Although the internal construction of the IC is somewhat different from that described for discrete voltage regulator circuits A power supply can be built using a transformer connected to the ac supply line to step the ac voltage to desired amplitude, then rectifying that ac voltage, filtering with a capacitor and RC filter, if desired, and finally regulating the dc voltage using an IC regulator.

Positive Voltage Regulators in 7800 series:

IC Part	Output Voltage (V)	Minimum Vi (V)
7805	+5	7.3
7806	+6	8.3
7808	+8	10.5
7810	+10	12.5
7812	+12	14.6
7815	+15	17.7
7818	+18	21.0
7824	+24	27.1

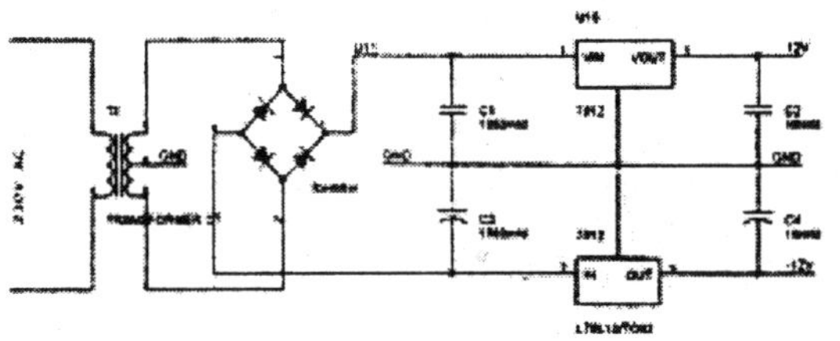

+5V Power Supply

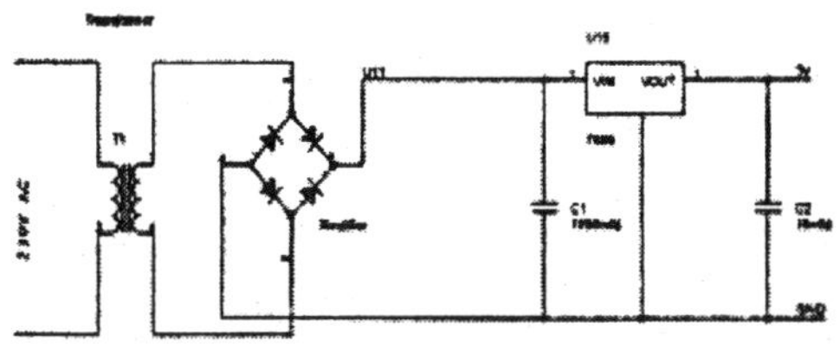

+12V and 12V Power Supply

Fig. 6 Power supply unit

B. Current Measurement

The Ac current it can be measured with the help of current transformer. The primary winding carries the load current. The product of several amperes and few turns in primary is equal to the product of several current will be less. The principle of CT is quite different from a converted power transformer. The load on secondary of a CT is small and so we may say the CT work under short circuited.

The AC Current measurement can be done with the help of a current Transformer across with a shunt resistor and rectifiers, which is based on diodes. When we use diodes rectification to measure the current, we get only RMS value of the current. Normally in digital millimeters also used to get RMS current only. But the measurement must be on the peak current, by using the precision rectifiers and shunt resistor we can achieve this, the circuit and the description for precision rectifier.

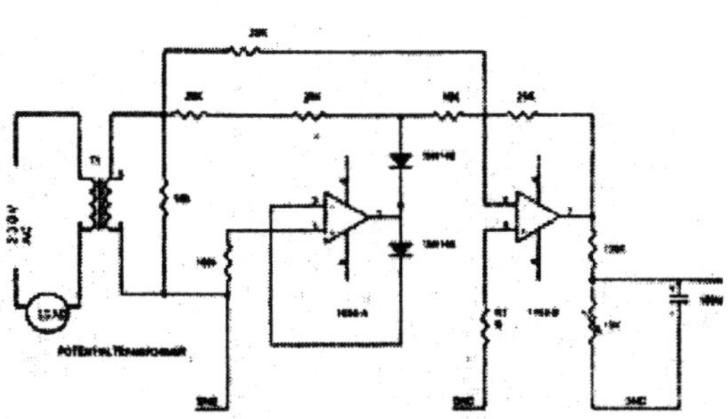

Fig. 7 Current measurement unit

C. Voltage Measurements

A potential transformer is similar to a conventional two winding transformer in two respects. there are some difference also one major difference is that in a PT the secondary load is only a volt meter and hence the secondary current is very small. In power transformer the magnetizing current is negligible compared to secondary rated current or secondary current is much higher than magnetizing current.

The AC voltage measurement is normally done with the help of rectifiers, which is based on diodes. When we use diode rectification to measure the voltage, we get only RMS voltage. Normally in digital multimeters also we used to get RMS voltage only. But the measurement must be on the peak voltage, by using the precision rectifiers we can achieve this, the circuit and the description for precision rectifiers as follows. An absolute-value circuit, or full-wave precision rectifier, can be implemented by summing the output of a half-wave rectifier and its input with the proper phase and amplitude relations. In this circuit, first we use one operational amplifier as an inverting rectifier similar to that of the normal diode rectifier. The output from the amplifier is added to the original input signal in the next operational amplifier with the signal amplitude and phase relations. Negative alterations of the amplitude result in no output at the output of the op-amp due to the rectification. The original input feeds to the second op-amp through a 20-kohm resistor, and the output of the first op-amp feeds A2 through a 10-kohm resistor.

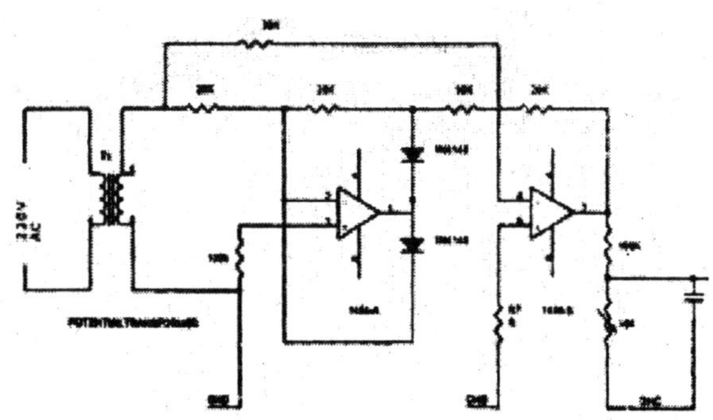

Fig. 8 Voltage measurement Unit

D. Single Phase Inverting

If E.B supply fails or any one of the phase cut out, then the microcontroller senses and automatically turn ON the genset.

The microcontroller sensed through single phase indicator each phase supply is given to 6v/500mA transformer. The output of the transformer is rectified and connected to the base of the transistor. The transistor will conduct if the base current is above 0.7v .the out put voltage of the transformer is 6v.since emitter is grounded so collector current is 0.Each collector current is 0.each collector terminal is connected microcontroller if any one of them fails a base current is 0 and the collector current is 0.the high value is given to the microcontroller the microcontroller turn ON the genset through start relay at the same time the buzzer alarm is activated to indicate that E.B supply fails. When the genset is turned ON and connected to the bus bar then the alarm is de-activated.

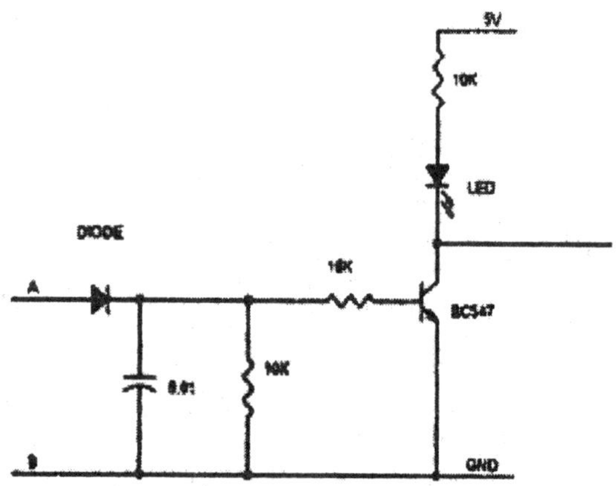

Fig. 9 Single Phase inverter Unit

E. Bridge Rectifier

When four diodes are connected as shown in the fig the circuit is called the bridge rectifier the power supply is given to step down transformer. The output of the step down transformer is connected to bridge rectifier.

The input of the circuit is applied diagonally opposite currents of the network and the output is taken from the remaining two corners. The output from the bridge rectifier has some ripple. The ripple can be filtered by using capacitor for constant DC output voltage. Voltage regulator ic are used

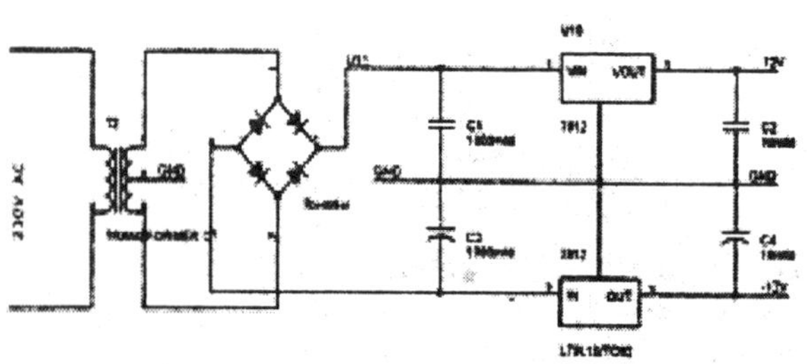

Fig. 10 Bridge Rectifier Unit

F. Precision Rectifier

The AC current measurement can be done with the help of current transformer across with a shunt resistors and rectifiers which is based on diodes. When we use diodes rectification to measure the current, we get only Rms value of current. But the measurement most be on the peak current by using the precision rectifiers and shunt resistors.

The current transformer will step down the high current to lower value, that is if the input current is 15A output of the current transformer will be 5A to convert from the current to voltage we are using a shunt resistor.

To the original input signal in next op-amp with the signal amplitude and phase relations. Negative alteration of the amplitude result in no output of the op-amp through a 20 k ohm resistor, and the output of the first op-amp feed A2 through a10 k ohm resistor.

G. Alarm Circuit

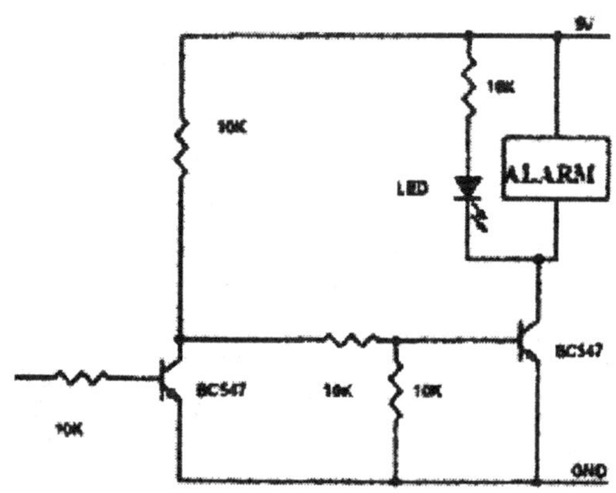

Fig. 11 Alarm unit

H. Relay Circuit

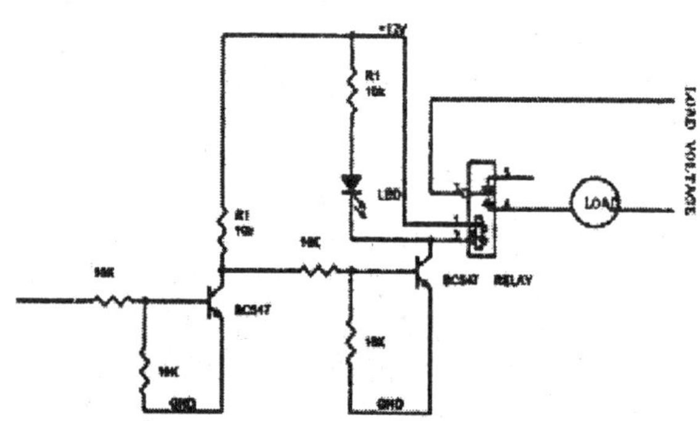

Fig. 12 Relay Unit

6. Conclusion

Our paper involves microcontroller to supply uninterrupted power to load through genset when E.B. supply fails. Here we have used microcontroller IC89C51 to sense the E.B.supply when fails and when supply returns. In this voltage, current, battery voltage is displayed with the help of LCD.

7. References

[1] Mohamed Ali Mazidi, Janice Gillispie Mazidi, "The 8051 microcontroller and embedded system", Pearson education, 2004

[2] A K Ray, K M Bhurchandi, "Advanced microprocessors and peripherals "TATA Mc GRAWHILL PUBLISHING. Second edition

[3] Myke Predko "Programming and Customizing The 8051Microcontroller"

[4] David Calcutt, Fred Cowan, Hassan Parchizadeh "8051 Microcontrollers"

[5] Programming 16-bit Microcontrollers in C by Lucio Di Jasi

Software Metrics Based Evaluation of Web Services

D. Rajaguru and P. Dhavachelvan
Department of Computer Science, Pondicherry University, Puducherry, India.
raja.guru42@gmail.com, dhavachelvan@gmail.com

Abstract

A Web service is a software system designed to support interoperable machine-to-machine interaction over a network. It has an interface described in a machine-process able format. A simple web service is designed and used for performance testing with a variety of web services polices and message sizes. The performance of web service is evaluated with the implementations of web services and comparing them with a number of alternative technologies. Metrics can be used to improve software productivity and quality and also for measurement purposes. Software metrics evaluating the caching efficiency for a given services. It focuses on three aspects of web service metrics – usage, evaluation, and performance. Usage metrics measure various aspects of the frequency and types of uses of agency web sites. Evaluation metrics focus on the customer utility, usability, and satisfaction. Performance metrics measure the speed and efficiency of providing the information. This paper presents the analysis of software metrics based evaluation on web services. The model is implemented in Web Service Evaluation System, which can provide more accurate, and reasonable results to end-user.

1. Introduction

Web services have been widely accepted as platform-independent services-oriented technology. By applying text-based transport protocols, web services enable applications to interact with each other across heterogeneous systems. A Web service is a software system designed to support interoperable machine-to-machine interaction over a network. It has an interface described in a machine-process able format.

Web services are software components that communicate using pervasive, standards-based Web technologies including HTTP and XML-based messaging. Web services are designed to be accessed by other applications and vary in complexity from simple operations. A simple web service is designed and used for performance testing with a variety of web services polices and message sizes. The web services performance for evaluating the current implementations of web services and comparing them with a number of alternative technologies. It is used to measure the performance and the efficiency of the system [13].

Metrics can be used to improve software productivity and quality and also for measurement purposes. Software metric based evaluation of web services is Metrics approximating the end-to-end response time. It provides a means to calculate the overall response time. Software metrics evaluating the caching efficiency for a given web service. It focuses on three aspects of web service metrics – usage, evaluation, and performance. Usage metrics measure various aspects of the frequency and types of uses of agency web sites. Evaluation metrics focus on the customer utility, usability, and satisfaction. Performance metrics measure the speed and efficiency of providing the information.

This paper presents the analysis of software metrics based evaluation on Web Services. Depending on the web services it based on the performance and evaluation. The model is implemented in Web Service Evaluation System, which can provide more accurate, reasonable results to end user [2].

Different domains have different evaluation factors; domain experts have to customize evaluation factors set for the domain based on their experience. Therefore the evaluation model for Web Services uses reasonable factors to evaluate Web Services, which provides a more practical, accurate evaluation mechanism compared with common attributes of Web Services.

Section 2 presents the survey of well-known evaluation of web services and Section 3 concludes the work.

2. Survey on Available Techniques

In this section, we provide a survey of software metrics based evaluation of web services.

Celine Boutrous-Saab, Tarek Melliti, Lynda Mokdad [1] given the performance evaluation of mobile access to web services considering the gateway scenario. The model takes into account the gateway message processing strategies and the complexity of the web services. The evaluation of requests process is made by Markov chain. Thus the performances measures can be deduced easily. This model is that it is a product-form queuing network. and it has a product form solution. So, it can be solved easily and several performance measures can be deduced

HUANG Baohua, HU Heping t, LU Zhengding, YAO Hanbing, LI Ruixuan [3] proposed the evaluating trust degree of Web services with the method of neural network from the aspect of trust history sequence. The applicable neural network structure, neural network constructing, input standardization, training sample constructing, and the procedure of evaluating trust degree of Web services with trained neural network.

Jianting Zhang, Deana D. Pennington, William K. Michener [4] developed a prototype for performance evaluation. The geospatial modeling using the Web Services technologies remains effective in the wired LAN computation environment for data volume as large as 10000 points. The same data volume level incurs significant response lags under the wireless WAN computation environment. The results are used as a guideline for geospatial modeling using the Web Services technologies when performances need to be taken into considerations.

Kezhe Tang, Shiping Chen, David Levy, John Zic and Bo Yan [5] designed a simple web service and used for performance testing with a variety of WSS polices and message sizes. The test results are categorized, compared and analyzed to work out the overheads for individual security setting. Web Services Security (WSS) provides message-level protection between two ends (clients and web services) through message integrity, message confidentiality and message authentications.

Kyriakos Kritikos and Dimitris Plexousakis [6] given two Constraint Programming (CP) QoS-based WS discovery algorithms for unary constrained WS specifications that produce accurate results with good performance. They also evaluated these algorithms on matchmaking time, precision and recall in different settings in order to demonstrate their efficiency and accuracy.

There are two main approaches for QoS-based WS matchmaking: a) Ontology-based b) Constraint Programming (CP) based. The first approach suffers from performance problems due to the use of ontology reasoners. The second approach was fast but the two research works adopting it return inaccurate results and do not provide advanced categorization of results. This both approaches do not provide useful matchmaking results for over-constrained QoS demands. For these, they had devised a semantic QoS metric matching algorithm and two complementary CP-based and QoS-based WS discovery approaches exploiting it: one with unary and one with n-ary constraints. These two approaches are accurate, provide advanced categorization of results and produce results even for over constrained demands but they had not been evaluated.

Laszlo Gonczy, Silvano Chiaradonna, Felicita Di Giandomenico, András Pataricza, Andrea Bondavalli, and Tamás Bartha [7] applied the methodologies and tools for dependability analysis of Multiple Phased Systems (MPS) to this emerging category of dependability critical systems. This dependability analysis constitutes a very useful support to the service provider in choosing the most appropriate service alternatives to build up its own composite service.

LIU Ji-bo, XIANG Zhan-hong, ZHU Pei-dong [8] proposed a trust evolvement method of the macro self-organization for Web service combination. The control rule of the trust degree in the Dempster-Shafer (D-S) rule was utilized based on the entity network interactive behavior, and a proportion trust control rule was put up. The control rule makes the Web service self-adaptively study and gradually form a proper trust connection with its cooperative entities and to improve the security performance of the whole system. By using this method we can greatly improve the reliability and success rate of Web service combination.

N.W. Lo, Chia-Hao Wang [9] proposed a architecture and reputation appraisal model to monitor, store and evaluate the physical usage and post-condition of requested Web services in a requester-located network to better support service requesters such that they can select suitable Web services based on their QoS requirements, trustworthiness of Web services, and effect of network connection requesters and providers. CosmosQoS that expands the current Web services architecture to take the network condition factor into account with a robust monitoring mechanism, a customizable QoS description scheme, and a proxy-oriented QoS evaluation method.

Ricardo Lemos Vianna, Maria Janilce Bosquiroli Almeida, Liane Margarida Rockenbach Tarouco, Lisandro Zambenedetti Granville [10] offers the Web services to the network management to established management protocols and Web based applications. The possibility of using Web services composition for network management considering two approaches: (i) a single device needs to be contacted and its information composed, (ii) many devices need to be contacted and the information retrieved from them need to be composed. The performance of Web services compositions for network management considering response time and network traffic. Performance investigations are crucial because Web services protocols are based on plain text XML documents and impose a processing overhead, which may prevent their adoption depending on the requirements and limitations of the management environment

Web services composition is that it reduces the network bandwidth consumption near to the management interface once the manager always needs exchanging only two messages with the aggregator, independent of the amount of information aggregated. The heavy interactions between gateways and devices and between aggregators and gateways can be confined near devices neighborhood.

Stephen J. H. Yang James S.F. Hsieh Blue C. W. Lan Jen-Yao, Chung [11] proposed an evaluation method for trustworthy service compositions. The trustworthiness of involved Web Services will be evaluated by analyzing past experiences so that the trustworthiness of the composite service could be estimated from the evaluation of each Web Service and aggregation topology of the composite service.

Shiping Chen, John Zic, Kezhe Tang, David Levy [12] conducted a quantitative performance evaluation of WSS overhead. Based on the evaluation, they extend our existing web services performance model by taking the extra WSS overheads. A simple benchmark is designed and used to test the performance of the web service against a variety of message sizes with/without applying the basic WS-Security policies. They introduced different metrics like Latency Increment Percentage, WSS Performance Modeling.

Shiping Chen, Bo Yan, John Zic, Ren Liu, Alex Ng [13] evaluated the performance of the web services and comparing them with a number of alternative technologies. The web services performance behaviors and performance model can be used to estimate web services latencies.

A number of leading web services products and a well-known SOAP open source were selected to see how much difference there was between the implementations and configurations. The designed data structures and sizes to mimic realistic applications of web services. A number of observations were obtained by extensively benchmarking the selected web services implementations, and these insights lead to a simple performance model that can be used for web services performance prediction.

Vassileios Tsetsos, Christos Anagnostopoulos, Stathes Hadjiefthymiades [14] addressed the issues related to the evaluation of the retrieval effectiveness of semantic matchmaking systems. The conventional evaluation schemes do not fully capture the added value of service semantics nor do they take into account the assigned degrees of match, supported by the majority of discovery engines. The generalization of the evaluation process based on fuzzy set theory techniques can lead to more accurate and meaningful evaluation results.

Wenlong Huang, Taoying Liu, Yi Zhao [15] implemented a community data sharing system based on Web Services, Honeycomb. In Honeycomb, Web Services invocation is the main performance bottleneck of query execution and cache technique is utilized to improve query performance. It's based on the query evaluation, cache design and implementation in Honeycomb. Community data sharing is an emerging paradigm of data sharing.

Walter Binder, Samuel Spycher, Ion Constantinescu, Boi Faltings [16] evaluated the performance and scalability of the MVGiST and compare it with a traditional, locking-based concurrency control mechanism. The efficient web service directory that is based on the Multiversion Generalized Search Tree (MVGiST), an integration of a multidimensional index structure with multiversion concurrency control. The MVGiST is able to index web services according to their input and output parameters, supports a high level of concurrent read requests.

MVGiST is particularly well suited as index structure for our service directory: Web service descriptions can be considered multidimensional data (input and output parameters), Read access is far more frequent than updates, the process of automated service composition requires a long-term, constant view of the directory data, therefore calling for consistency over multiple reads and queries generated by service composition algorithms can be complex and a high number of concurrent accesses is to be expected (the directory is a shared resource), overhead for read concurrency has to be as small as possible.

Xu Meng, Chen Junliang, and Mei Xiang [17] have given an FQoS (Feeling of QoS) Model to the quality of web services in the view of users. The evaluation mechanism is to automate measurement of the quality of web services and maintain this information to provide them. FQoS provision system is implemented for a prototype. FQoS provision system is similar to the client's real feeling.

Feeling of QoS (FQoS) model and the FQoS evaluation mechanism which could measure, estimate, and provide quality metrics for users. In the FQoS model, the relation between web service and its quality metrics was no longer one-to-one but one-to-more, so each user group had its own QoS result. A user could put forward his sensitive metrics of QoS, and according to which, the FQoS Provision System could provide the proper QoS results. FQoS could enhance the rightness of all works based on quality such as web service selection.

Angela Stoof. Rob L. Martens. Jeroen J. G. Van Merrienboer [18] given the Competence maps of final attainment levels of educational programs in terms of interrelated competencies. Key requirements for the competence-mapping tool were validity and practicality. Validity refers to internal consistency and meaningful links to the external realities represented. Practicality refers to a design approach of evolutionary prototyping, in which feedback from intended users and domain experts is collected throughout the development process.

Grace A. Lewis, Lutz Wrage [19] describes a process for evaluating the fitness of a technology within its anticipated specific context. This process includes hands-on experimentation with the technology to achieve a greater understanding of its implications as well as early competence development. It use narrowly focused model problems to sustain or refute hypotheses about the examined technologies.

Hossein Saiedian, Shawn Mulkey [20] developed a Web services application technology in distributed real-time data delivery systems; determine the appropriate contexts in which such a design can be considered. Focus on distributed real-time systems and more specifically, on distributed soft real-time systems, which stand to benefit most from the use of Web services technology.

3. Conclusion

In this theoretical analysis, we have reviewed and discussed some of the web services evaluation based on the software metrics approach. The different models of metric based evaluation on web services are analyzed with the goal to identify the impact over the quality and performance of the web services. The mechanism that customizes evaluation factor for Web Services in different domains which obtains more accurate and reasonable results to end user.

4. References

[1] Celine Boutrous-Saab, Tarek Melliti, Lynda Mokdad, "Performance Evaluation For Mobile Access To Composite web Services", International Conference on Internet and Web Applications and Services, 2006.

[2] Han Tao, Guo He-qing, Guo He-qing, "An Evaluation Model for Web Services", IEEE, 2005.

[3] HUANG Baohua, HU Heping, LU Zhengding, YAO Hanbing, LI Ruixuan, "Trust Degree of Web Services and Its Evaluation with Neural Network", Wuhan University Journal of Natural Sciences, Vol. 11 No. 5, PP-1302-1305, 2006.

[4] Jianting Zhang, Deana D. Pennington, William K. Michener, "Performance Evaluations Of Geospatial Web Services Composition And Invocation", IEEE International Conference on Web Services (ICWS 2007), 2007.

[5] Kezhe Tang, Shiping Chen, David Levy, John Zic and Bo Yan, "A Performance Evaluation of Web Services Security", Proceedings of the 10th IEEE International Conference, 2007.

[6] Kyriakos Kritikos and Dimitris Plexousakis, "Evaluation Of QoS-Based Web Service Matchmaking Algorithms", IEEE Congress on Services, PP-567-574, 2008.

[7] Laszlo Gonczy, Silvano Chiaradonna, Felicita Di Giandomenico, András Pataricza, Andrea Bondavalli, and Tamás Bartha, "Dependability Evaluation of Web Service-Based Processes", Springer-Verlag Berlin Heidelberg, pp. 166 – 180, 2006.

[8] LIU Ji-bo, XIANG Zhan-hong, ZHU Pei-dong, "Trust Evolvement Method of Web Service Combination Based on Network Behavior", Springer, PP-558–563, 2008.

[9] N.W. Lo, Chia-Hao Wang, "Web Services QoS Evaluation and Service Selection Framework - A Proxy-oriented Approach", 2007.

[10] Ricardo Lemos Vianna, Maria Janilce Bosquiroli Almeida, Liane Margarida Rockenbach Tarouco, Lisandro Zambenedetti Granville, "Evaluating The Performance Of Web Services Composition For Network Management", IEEE Communications Society,2007.

[11] Stephen J. H. Yang James S.F. Hsieh Blue C. W. Lan Jen-Yao, Chung, "Composition and Evaluation of Trustworthy Web Services", 2006.

[12] Shiping Chen, John Zic, Kezhe Tang, David Levy, "Performance Evaluation and Modeling of Web Services Security", IEEE Intl. Conf. on Web Services, 2007.

[13] Shiping Chen, Bo Yan, John Zic, Ren Liu, Alex Ng, "Evaluation and Modeling of Web Services Performance", IEEE International Conference on Web Services, 2006.

[14] Vassileios Tsetsos, Christos Anagnostopoulos, Stathes Hadjiefthymiades, "On the Evaluation of Semantic Web Service Matchmaking Systems", Proceedings of the European Conference on Web Services (ECOWS'06), 2006.

[15] Wenlong Huang, Taoying Liu, Yi Zhao, "Query Evaluation And Performance Optimization In Distributed Community Data Sharing System Based On Web Services", IEEE International Conference on Services Computing, 2008.

[16] Walter Binder, Samuel Spycher, Ion Constantinescu, Boi Faltings, "An Evaluation of Multiversion Concurrency Control for Web Service Directories," IEEE International Conference on Web Services, 2007.

[17] Xu Meng, Chen Junliang, and Mei Xiang, "The Evaluation And Provision Mechanism For FQOS Of Web Services", Proceedings of the Fifth International Conference on Grid and Cooperative Computing, IEEE, 2006.

[18] Angela Stoof. Rob L. Martens. Jeroen J. G. Van Merrienboer, "Web-based support for constructing competence maps: design and formative evaluation", 2006.

[19] Grace A. Lewis, Lutz Wrage [19], "A Process for Context-Based Technology Evaluation: Examples for the Evaluation of Web Services Technology", Proceedings of the Fifth International Conference on Commercial-off-the-Shelf (COTS)-Based Software Systems (ICCBSS 2006), IEEE, 2006.

[20] Hossein Saiedian, Shawn Mulkey, "Performance Evaluation Of Eventing Web Services In Real-Time Applications", IEEE Communications Magazine, 2008.

Optimizing Techniques for noise in IC Layout Design

Jitesh R. Shinde[1] and Dr.S.B.Pokle[2]
[1]Electrical / Electronics Engg. Dept., G.H.Raisoni Institute of Engg. & technology for Women, Nagpur
[2]HOD Electronics & Comm., G.H. Raisoni College of Engg.,Nagpur

Abstract

In an integrated circuit, achieving timing closure on design is the process of creating a design implementation that is free from logical, physical and design rule violations and meets or exceeds the timing specification for the design [3].

Just as noise beyond certain level is hazardous to human beings and environment, in the same way noise is one of the major performance limiting factors in chip design that may affect signal integrity, functionality and hence may even lead to chip malfunctioning or even failure. "Today one in five chips fails because of this" (Source: Collett International Research, Inc. 2000). Noise becomes very painful to deal with; particularly in mixed signal chips. Mixed signal circuitry has the most problems with noise because analog and digital circuits operate at very different noise levels.

So, in this paper we had mainly concentrated on optimizing strategies for noise in IC Layout Design specially related to ASIC in deep sub-micron technology.

1. Introduction

Suppose in a digital circuitry, we have two transistors that connect across a power rail. Every time this two transistors switch, there is possibility of dead short across power rail. Multiply this short circuit current by 10000 or million even. This short circuit current manifests itself as current spike which is nothing but noise. Thus, noise in an integrated circuit can be a very pretty big problem, particularly when in our circuitry we are having some sensitive block that is trying to pick up some very low value signals, located next to noisy circuitry that doing all sort of computations, control logic and noisy switching. Hence, we have to pay special attention to our layout and floor plan and need to understand where the signals are wiring to and from. We need to be very careful.

2. Optimizing Techniques

A. Signal swing

This implies that reduce the value of voltage or amplitude that is being wired around the chip. In a digital circuit, for instance, zero state is representated by zero volts, whereas one state can be representated by 5 volt. Thus, there is voltage swing of 5 volts. Now, if we reduce voltage swing to only 2 volt, we would be switching less energy each time a flip flop flips.

So while designing a layout, it will be good choice (if possible) to use digital logic family that has very small swings so that overall noise level will be low from start.

B. Insulation Strategy

Second technique to reduce noise is to wrap noisy block as shown in Fig. 1. There are various layout techniques to make that wall viz.

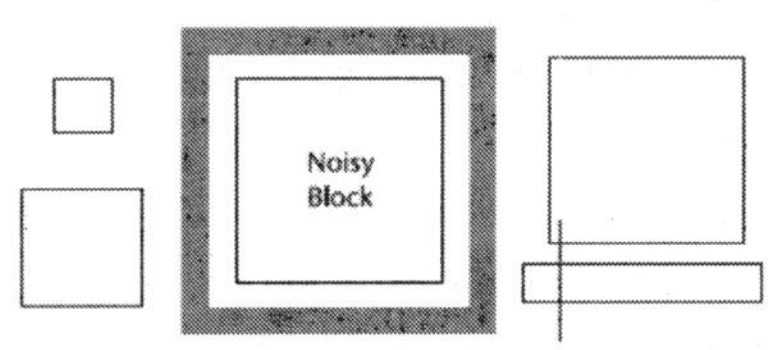

Fig. 1

1. Wrap a big ring of ground substrate contacts around the whole block.

   Noise travels through substrate very easily (minimum resistance path).

   As noise tries to escape the block through substrate, it first encounters a ground substrate contact. Since ground substrate contact is grounded path.

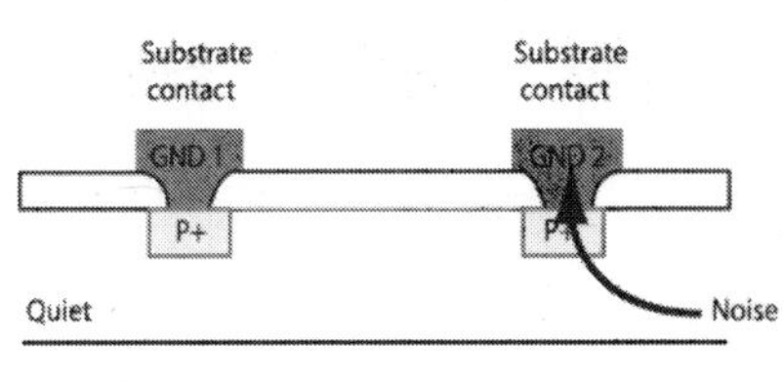

Fig. 2

Hence any noise voltage or noise currents will be attracted to the contact (Fig. 2).

2. Use big fat piece of wire hard tied to ground.

   Resistance is inversely proportional to cross-sectional area of wire. Hence increasing thickness of wire implies reduction in resistance of wire. This concept is illustrated in Fig. 3 and 4.

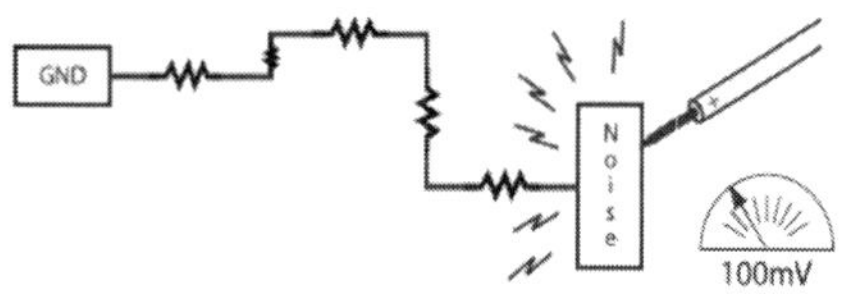

Fig. 3 Use of thin skinny wire (Not well grounded)

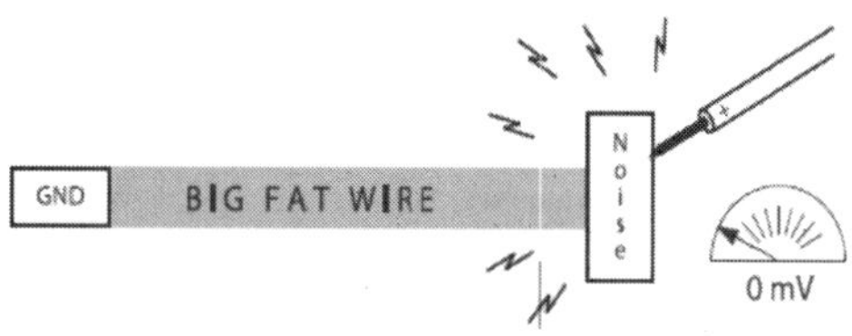

Fig. 4 Use of big fat piece of wire (well grounded)

3. Insulation structure or guard band

   Such structures are often provided by manufacturing people to keep noise leakage optimum.

   Putting a solid guard band around the whole noisy block is effectively like putting the noise generating circuitry inside the house with all windows closed. If we have any gaps in the guard band its like having some windows open and hence some noise can leak out [4].

C. Alternate Operational Period

This implies that having noisy and quiet circuitry doing their operation in separate time periods as shown Fig. 5. This will greatly minimize noise problem [4].

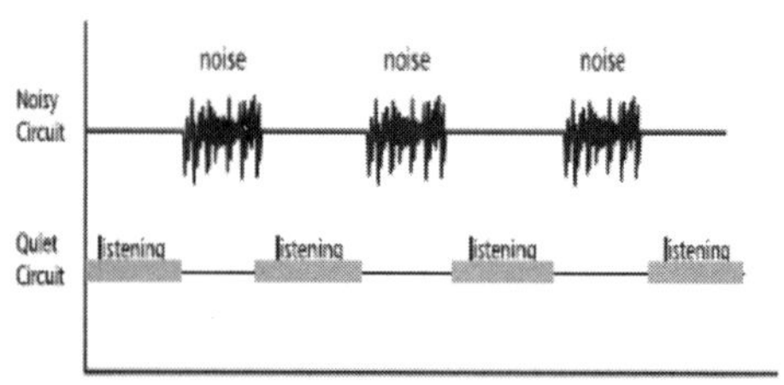

Fig. 5

D. Placement

Placing noisy and quiet blocks as far as away from each other will minimize possibility of noisy block affecting quiet block. This placement technique is illustrated in floor plan shown in Fig. 6.

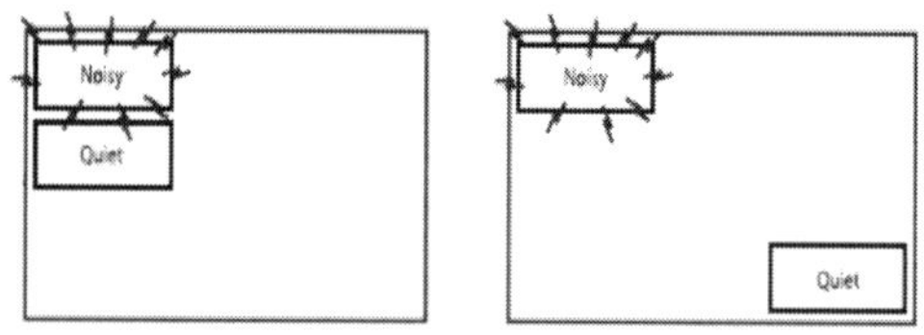

Fig. 6

E. Crosstalk Noise Reduction

"Crosstalk due to coupling capacitance between adjacent interconnect lines, in 0.18 micron and below, has become a major performance limiting factor that can cause both noise injection and signal timing deviation."

- ***Bruno Franzini, STMicroelectronics, SNUG Europe 2001-***

Crosstalk is the interaction between signals on two different electrical nets. The one creating crosstalk is called an aggressor, and the one receiving it is called a victim. Often, a net is both an aggressor and a victim. When the signals in the neighboring wires switch, the coupling capacitors cause transfer of charge between them. Depending on the relative rate of switching (rise and fall times of the signals) and the amount of mutual capacitance, there can be significant crosstalk noise [1, 2].

Crosstalk noise between neighboring signal wires can cause two major problems that affect the operational integrity of IC designs:

Crosstalk delay and Crosstalk glitch.

- Crosstalk delay changes the signal propagation on some of the nets, reducing achievable clock speed.

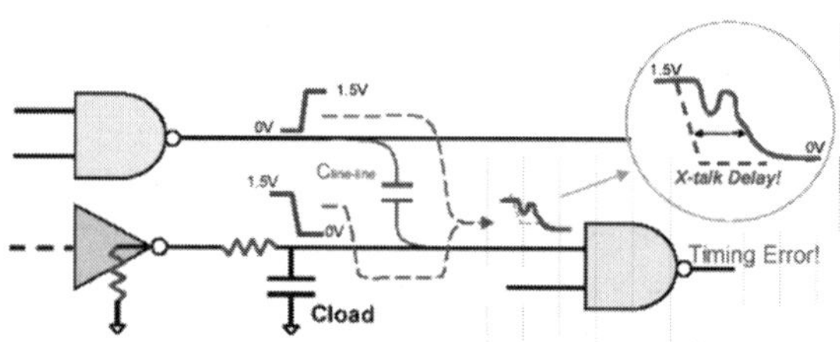

Fig. 7

- Crosstalk glitch causes voltage spikes on some nets, resulting in false logic states being captured in the registers.

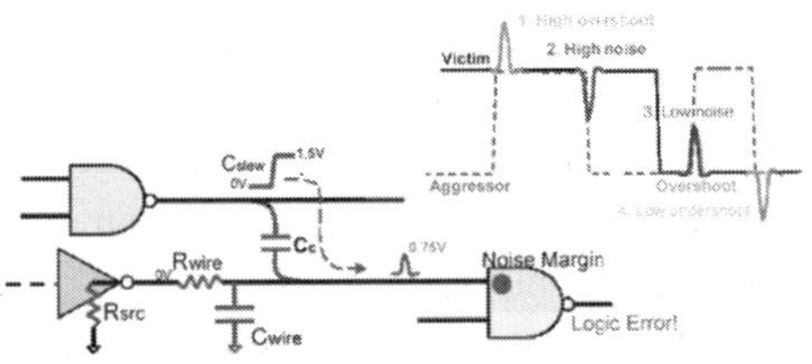

Fig. 8

Ways of reducing or eliminating crosstalk:-

1. Crosstalk decrease with interconnect spacing [1,4].

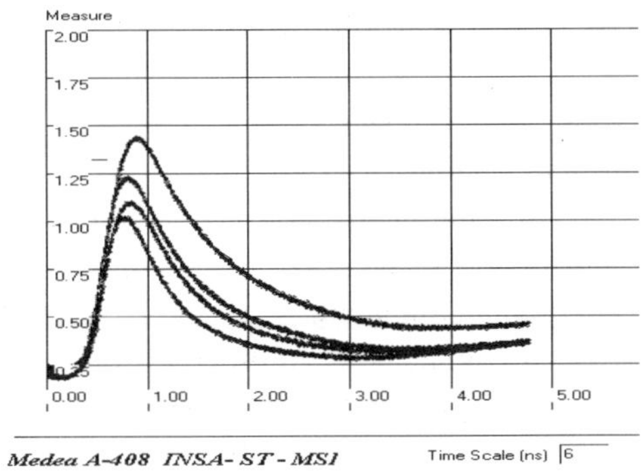

Fig. 9

2. Significant reduction of crosstalk by Low-K dielectrics between signals.
3. Do not route more than 2200μm!

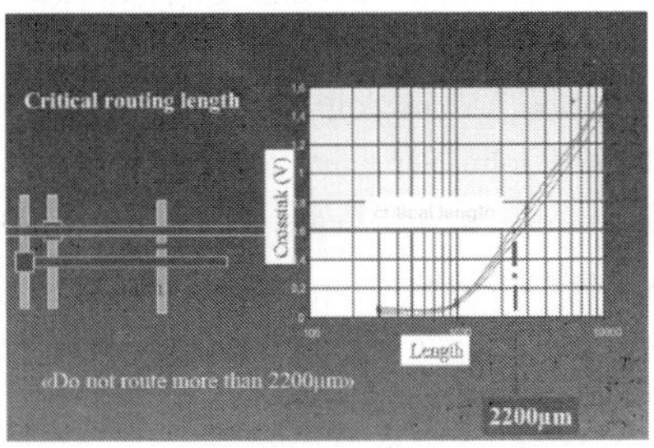

Fig. 10

4. Insert Repeaters if distance is too Long.

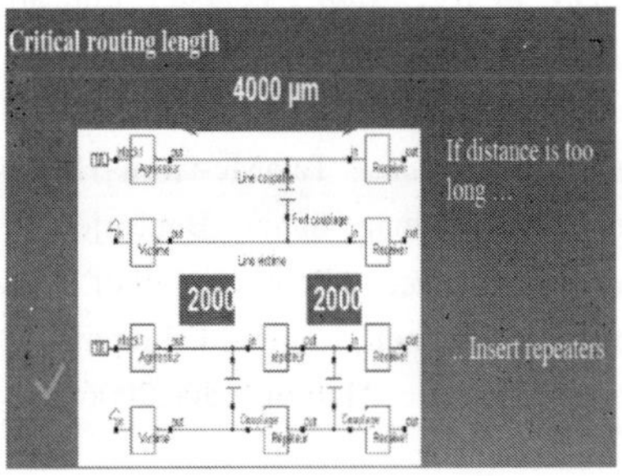

Fig. 11

5. Smart Routing.

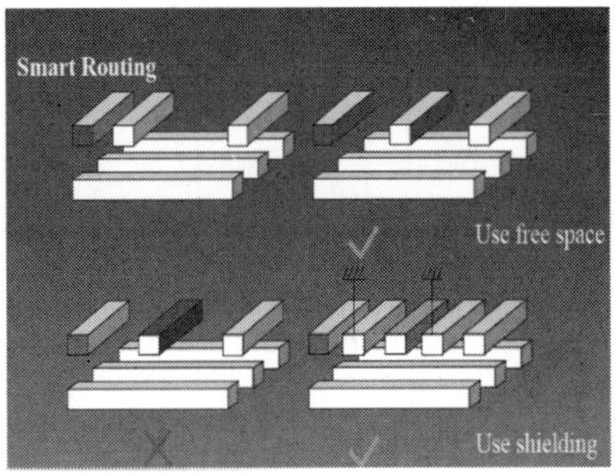

Fig. 12

To explain concept of shielding as shown in above figure, consider an example of coaxial cable. In coaxial cable, outer shielded wire is connected to ground. If any noise happens outside, it will be picked up by the grounded signal not the inner wire where our required signal is, and thus saves our required signal from unwanted noise signal from outside.

The same approach is use to shield desired signal from noise signal as explain below:

Let's have an area on metal one that we connect to ground. Then we will run our signal on metal2. Effectively, now we have grounded shield on one side. Any noise that comes from below is picked up by the ground and not by the signal wire (See Figure given below).

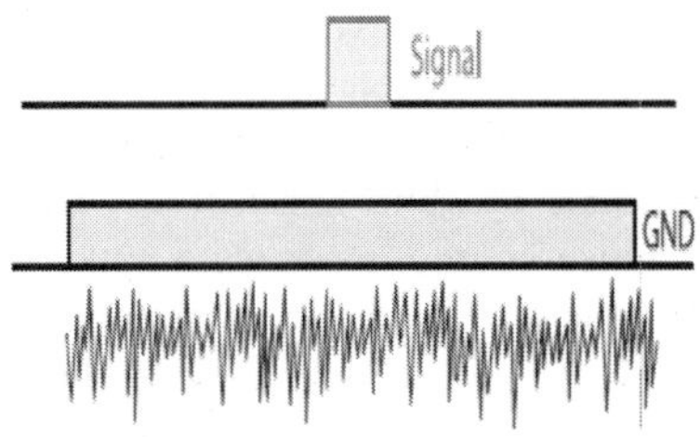

Fig. 13

F. Decoupled Capacitor

Higher the frequency of the signal, easier it will pass through capacitor. This is basic function of capacitor. Based on this function of capacitor, so in our circuit if we have circuit block with one of these big capacitors across its power rails, then any noise that gets zapped into the power rail will preferentially be sucked down to ground. Very little will pass the capacitor into the circuit.

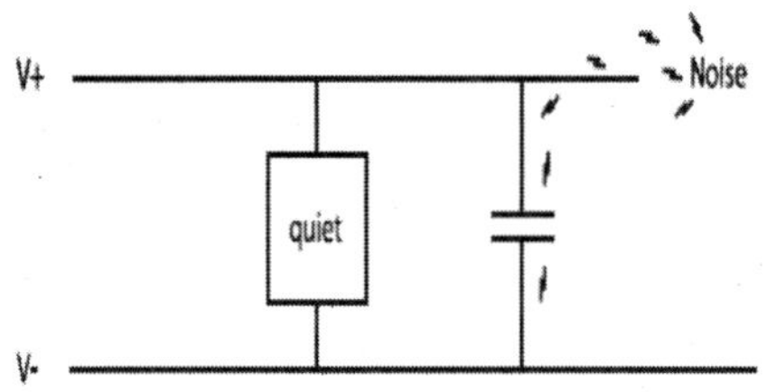

Fig. 14

G. Differential signals

Another design technique that affects layout design is using differential signals.

A differential circuit is a design technique that examines the difference between two specially run signals emanating from same source. Two wires are laid out next to each other throughout their entire rail. Each wire carries the same information, but in an inverted state from the information in the other wire.

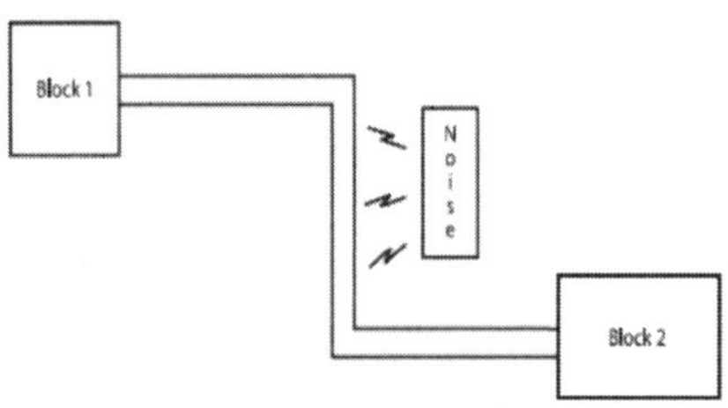

Fig. 15

As shown in above figure, pair of lines runs parallel and in close proximity to each other.

Here it might happen that this paired signal may pass fairly close by third noise block. Every once in while this noise source generates a spike of noise. A noise spike could originate from someone turning on switch or any of hundred of causes. Because these two wires are very close to each other, it is very likely that noise peak will occur at the very same time and at the same amplitude on both wires. The spikes have been coupled on both the wires at the same time.

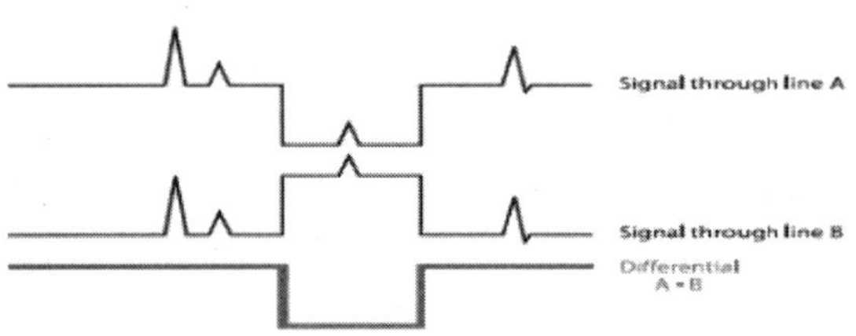

Fig. 16

As shown in figure, if we look at wires independently, we would see the spikes in each of the wire. However, when we do our calculations looking at two wires differentially, we do not see any spikes in the result. Spike minus spike equals zero.

Thus differential signal scheme is very noise immune. But it should be noted that use of this scheme depend on what the circuit does.

2. Closure on Noise Issues

Here in this paper we have gone through various techniques to optimize noise issues in IC layout design viz.

a. Using lower voltage swings.
b. Guard banding.
c. Time scheduling to alternate circuit operation.
d. Shielding.
e. Differential Signaling.
f. Decoupling the power rails, etc.

But today, since this field is growing at very fast rate there may be many more such other techniques to optimize noise issues in IC layout design which are yet to be explored.

3. References

[1] Jan M. Rabaey, Anantha Chandrakasan, Borivoje Nikolic, "*Digital Integrated Circuits*" Pearson Education, second edition.

[2] Michael John Sebestian Smith, "*Appliction Specific Integrated Circuit*" Pearson Education, 2008.

[3] Cadence website.

[4] *IC Mask Design Essential Layout Techniques Book,* Mc-Graw-Hill.

[5] Neil H. E. Weste, David Harris, Ayan Banerjee, "*CMOS VLSI Design*"Pearson Education, third edition.

[6] Neil Weste, Kamran Eshraghian, "*Principles of CMOS VLSI Design*" Pearson Education, second edition.

[7] Sung-Mo Kang, Yusuf Leblebici, "*CMOS Digital Integrated Circuits*" TataMc-Graw-Hill.

[8] Ben G. Streetman, Sanjay Baneerjee, "*Solid State Electronic Devices*" Prentice Hall of India ,2005.

[9] Doughlas Pucknell, Kamran Eshraghian, "*Basic VLSI Design*", Prentice Hall of India ,2006.

Performance Analysis of Web Service Architecture

Jijun Lu and Swapna S. Gokhale
Department of Computer Science and Engineering, University of Connecticut Storrs, CT 06269, USA
jijun.lu, ssg@engr.uconn.edu

Abstract

This paper proposes a *M/G/m* queue to analyze the performance of the web service architecture. The choice of the *M/G/m* queuing model is motivated by two observations. First, the multi-threaded application server, which performs a bulk of the processing constitutes a bottleneck resource in the web service architecture. Second, for systems with a bottleneck, the performance approximation introduced by modeling only the bottleneck resource while ignoring the rest may be reasonable. Experimental validation of the *M/G/m* model using deterministic and heavy-tailed workloads confirms that the model provides a reasonable estimate of the service response time for low to moderate traffic intensities. The model is conceptually simple, requires the estimation of very few parameters and is hence easy to apply.

1. Introduction and Motivation

A web service is a software system designed to support interoperable interaction between computers over a network [25]. Web services allow developers to create open applications that are compatible with different programming languages, operating systems, hardware platforms, and are accessible from any geographic location. Web services eliminate many of the complexities that have been required for applications to interactwith each other. Due to its decentralized, loosely coupled, and highly interoperable architecture, web service technology has become the primary solution for business integration and collaboration problems [5].

This widespread use of web service technology in business and critical applications necessitates that these services be offered with superior performance. The performance of a service can also be used as a criteria in service composition to select appropriate web services that satisfy the overall QoS requirements [10]. When a web service is provisioned, it is essential that an estimate of its performance be obtained for a particular hardware and software configuration. Hardware configuration options may include the capacity and the number of processors and caching strategies. Software configuration options may include the number of server threads/processes to serve client requests. For an expected load it may also be necessary to determine the appropriate hardware and software configuration options during provisioning to ensure acceptable service performance.

One of the ways of analyzing the performance of a web service is by conducting actual measurements. While the measurement-based approachmay be viable to estimate service performance for a given set of configuration options, it is cumbersome and expensive to do predictive or "what-if" analysis and to explore a set of alternative configurations using this approach. Model-based analysis, which consists of capturing the relevant aspects of the web service architecture into a model, experimentally validating the model and then using the validated model to predict service performance for different settings is an attractive alternative to the measurement-based approach.

In this paper, we present a model-based approach to analyze the performance of the web service architecture. Our approach is based on the following two key observations. The first observation indicates that in a web service a bulk of the processing occurs in the application tier, and hence, this tier constitutes a bottleneck resource [14]. Additionally, prior research suggests that for systems with a bottleneck, approximation in the performance estimates introduced by modeling only the bottleneck resource and abstracting the other details may be acceptable [22]. The second observation suggests thatmostmodern application servers deployed in the application tier of the web service architecture possess concurrent processing capabilities. Considering these two observations together, we hypothesize that the performance of the web service architecture may be modeled using a multi-server queuing station. In particular, we propose the use of a *M/G/m* queue to model the web service architecture. The performance metric of interest is the response time of a client request. In the absence of an analytical or a computationally tractable method to obtain an exact solution for the response time of a *M/G/m* queue, we use an approximation proposed by Sakasegawa [21]. We validate the model for deterministic and heavy-tailed workloads experimentally. Our results indicate that the *M/G/m* model provides a reasonably approximate estimate of the response time of the web service architecture for low to moderate traffic intensities. The model is conceptually simple, requires the estimation of a few parameters, and is hence easy to apply.

The balance of the paper is organized as follows: Section 2 presents an overview of the web service architecture, the rationale for modeling it as a *M/G/m* queue and the expression to compute the approximate response time. Section 3 describes the workload characteristics used for validation. Section 4 describes the experimental testbed. Section 5 summarizes and discusses the experimental results. Section 6 summarizes the related research and places our work in context. Conclusions and future research directions are offered in Section 7.

2. Performance Analysis Methodology

In this section, we describe our methodology to analyze the performance of the web service architecture. Towards this end, we first provide an overview of the web service architecture and then discuss the rationale for modeling it using a *M/G/m* queue. Finally, we present an expression to compute the approximate response time.

2.1 Web service architecture

The web service architecture typically consists of three tiers, namely, the web tier, business tier and data tier as shown in Fig. 1. The web tier consists of a front-end web server, the application server resides in the business tier where the business logic is implemented and the back-end database resides in the data tier. The clients consume services by using high-level and platform-independent calls. The web server intercepts and redirects the calls to the application server which performs the processing. The application server makes calls as needed to the back-end database, and responds to the client as appropriate.

Popular web servers include Microsoft IIS [17] and Apache HTTP [15], whereas popular application servers include Microsoft IIS [17] and Apache Tomcat [16]. Both the web and application servers are capable of concurrent processing, implemented using a thread-based, processbased or a hybrid strategy. Under these strategies, a limited number of threads/processes can be forked a priori to process incoming requests. If all these threads/processes are busy, either additional threads/processes can be forked or the incoming request waits in a queue. We assume the latter in this paper, that is the size of the thread/process pool is static and no additional threads/processes are forked.

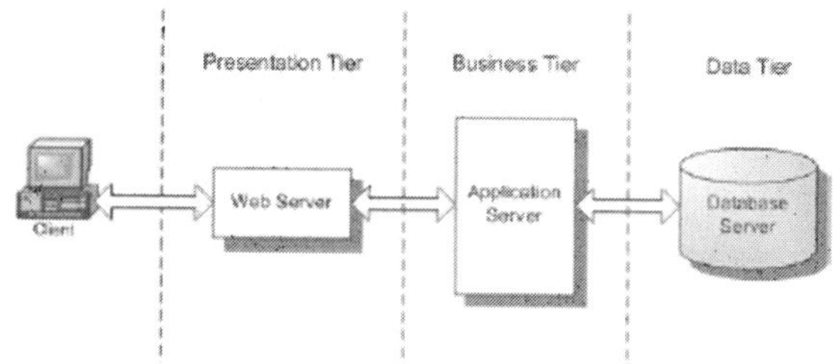

Fig. 1 Threetiered web service architecture

2.2 Queuing model

An elaborate model of the multi-tiered web service architecture may be built using a queuing network, with a multi-station queuing center used to model each multithreaded server (web, application, database) [14]. The resulting model is complex, and has several parameters. Extensive data needs to be collected to estimate these parameters. Previous work [14] and our observations suggest that in the web service architecture, a negligible amount of processing occurs in the web and database tiers, while a bulk of the processing occurs in the application tier where the business logic resides [14]. The application tier is thus the bottleneck resource and it dominates the response time.

With the existence of a bottleneck tier in the web service architecture, the approximation resulting from modeling only the bottleneck resource, while ignoring the rest is acceptable [22]. Furthermore, since the application server in the bottleneck tier will invariably possess the capability to process multiple requests concurrently, it is appropriate to model the bottleneck tier of the web service architecture using a multi-station queuing model. Thus, we propose the use of a *M/G/m* queue to model the bottleneck tier, and hence, the entire web service architecture.

We assume that the bottleneck resource, which is the application server, consists of multiple threads, with a thread pool size of m. Client requests arrive according to a Poisson distribution with rate λ. Request service times are independent and identically distributed random variables following a general distribution with finite mean μ^{-1} and finite coefficient of variance c_s (the ratio of standard deviation to the mean). Specifically, for deterministic service times, $c_s = 0$; for exponential service times, $c_s = 1$; and for heavy-tailed service times, $c_s \rightarrow \infty$ [13]. Let $\rho = \lambda/(m\mu)$ denote the traffic intensity (also known as utilization factor [13]). For a stable system $\rho < 1$ and the queuing discipline is first-come-first-served (FCFS). Table 1 summarizes the parameters of the *M/G/m* model. For most web applications, the capacity of the queue to hold requests when all the resources are busy is typically very large to ensure that the probability of denying a service request is very low. Thus, for the purposes of modeling we assume the queue size to be infinite. Fig. 2 provides a pictorial depiction of the *M/G/m* queue, and Table 1 summarizes the parameters of the *M/G/m* queuing model.

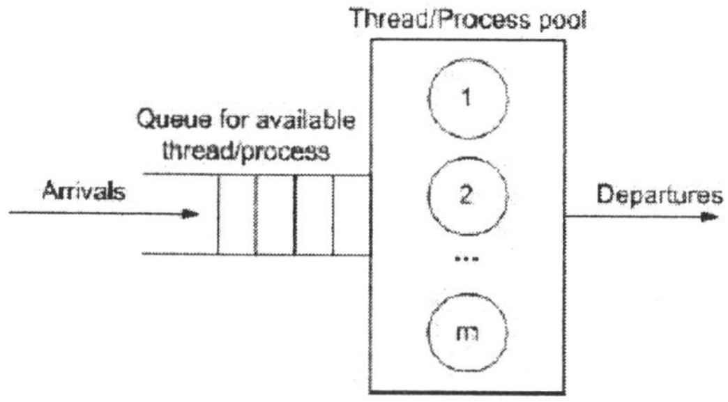

Fig. 2 M/G/m queuing model

Table 1 Parameters of the *M/G/m* queue

Symbol	Meaning
N	Number of jobs in queue and system
R	Response time
T	Service time
m	Number of servers
λ	Arrival rate
μ	Service rate
c_s	Coefficient of variance of service time (standard deviation divided by the mean)
ρ	Traffic intensity $\rho = \lambda/(m\mu)$

The performance metric we consider is the mean response time of a client request, denoted *R*. Except in certain special cases, there is no known analytical or computationally tractable solution for the response time of a *M/G/m* queue. We thus consider an approximation [21] to first obtain the mean number of requests in the queue, given by Equation (1). From Equation (1), the mean response time for the *M/G/m* queue following Little's law [13] is given by Equation (2).

$$L_q \approx \frac{(1+c_s^2)}{2}\frac{\rho^{\sqrt{2(m+1)}}}{1-\rho} \qquad (1)$$

$$R_{M/G/m} \approx 1/\mu + \frac{(1+c_s^2)}{2\lambda}\frac{\rho^{\sqrt{2(m+1)}}}{1-\rho} \qquad (2)$$

3. Workload Characteristics

In this section, we describe the workload characteristics used for experimental validation. We consider service scenarios where each client request is for a static file, and the web service responds with the file. To the best of our knowledge, very little is known about the workload properties of a web service. However, as indicated in [4], the distribution of file sizes requested from a web server is heavy-tailed. We thus consider two types of workloads, namely, deterministic and heavy-tailed as described below.

3.1 Deterministic Workload

For a deterministic workload, all the requests in a single experiment are for the same file size. We consider four deterministic workloads with file sizes of 64 KB, 128 KB, 256 KB and 512 KB. The smallest size is 64 KB due to the measurement granularity, which is 10 msec for our test bed (described in Section 4). We note that even for a deterministic workload, with the same file size in every request, the service time on an experimental test bed/real system will fluctuate [13], implying that $c_s \neq 0$ in Equation (1). However, since these fluctuations are expected to be small in magnitude, we use the term deterministic workload to indicate relatively stable workload compared to the heavy-tailed workload.

3.2 Heavy-tailed workload

We generated the heavy-tailed workload based on the Pareto distribution, which has been widely used to model such characteristics in Internet workloads [4]. The Pareto distribution is characterized by a shape parameter α and a scale parameter k. The cumulative distribution function (CDF) of the Pareto distribution is given by Equation (3), where $\alpha, k > 0$ and $x > k$.

$$F(x) = 1 - k^{\alpha}x^{-\alpha} \qquad (3)$$

When $\alpha > 1$, the Pareto distribution has a finite mean which is given by:

$$E[X] = \frac{\alpha k}{\alpha - 1} \qquad (4)$$

A series of numbers following the Pareto distribution can be generated by computing the inverse of the CDF presented in Equation (3) as below [11]:

$$x = F^{-1}(u) = k(1-u)^{-\frac{1}{\alpha}} \qquad (5)$$

In Equation (5), if α and k are known, then for random variates u_i's generated from the uniform distribution $U(0, 1)$ we can generate values $\{x_i\}$'s following the Pareto distribution. Note here $x_i > k$ for every i. It is expected that most $\{x_i\}$'s will have values that are close to k and a small number of $\{x_i\}$'s will be extraordinary high.

When the shape parameter α is fixed, the scale parameter k for a given mean $E[X]$ can be obtained as:

$$k = E[X] \cdot (1 - 1/\alpha) \quad (6)$$

We set the value α to 1.36, based on prior research [4]. For four different mean file sizes, namely, 120 KB, 150 KB, 180 KB and 200 KB, using the pre-selected α, k was computed from Equation (6). Using the (α, k) pair, the CDF Fs_i of file size S_i is obtained. Then the probability of each file size is computed as:

$$Ps_i = Fs_i - Fs_{i-1} \quad (7)$$

The distribution of individual file sizes 64 KB, 128 KB, 256 KB, 512 KB, 1 MB and 2 MB which make up the heavy-tailed workload, for the four mean file sizes considered above is reported in Table 2.

Table 2 File size distribution (Ps_i) in heavytailed workload

File size (S_i)	Mean file size S_i			
	120KB	150KB	180KB	200KB
64 KB	0.6099	0.4776	0.3305	0.2274
128 KB	0.2381	0.3189	0.4086	0.4716
256 KB	0.0928	0.1242	0.1592	0.1837
512 KB	0.0361	0.0484	0.0620	0.0716
1 MB	0.0141	0.0189	0.0242	0.0279
2 MB	0.0055	0.0073	0.0094	0.0109

Table 3 Hardware and software configuration

Machine	Hardware	Software
Server	Dell OptiPlex GX260 (Intel Pentium 4 processor at 2.4GHz, 1GB of RAM, 40GB hard driver and Intel PRO 1000 MT network adapter)	Microsoft Windows XP Professional SP2, Microsoft IIS 5.1
Client	IBM ThinkPad T40 (Intel Pentium-M processor at 1.5GHz, 1GB of RAM, 40GB hard driver and Intel PRO 100 VE network adaptor)	Microsoft Windows XP Professional SP2

4. Experimental Infrastructure

In this section, we describe the experimental infrastructure used for model validation. We also describe the process used to estimate the mean service time for each file size.

4.1 Testbed description

The hardware platform consists of one sever and one client. The hardware and software configurations of the experimental testbed are summarized in Table 3. Both computers are connected via a 100M Ethernet LAN. A simple web service is deployed on the server machine. In a multi-threaded server, as the size of the thread pool increases, each thread may experience some performance degradation. However, when the thread pool size remains below a threshold, the performance degradation is negligible. As a rule of thumb, to ensure negligible degradation, the size of the thread pool should be two times of the number of CPUs on the host machine [20]. Thus, for the single processor server in our testbed, the size of the thread pool is chosen to be 2. The default maximum queue length used in IIS (3000) is very large as compared to the number of threads, thus the assumption of infinite queue length needed to apply the *M/G/m* model is reasonable.

4.2 Service time estimation

To compute the mean response time based on the *M/G/m* model for a given workload using Equation (2), the mean service time for the workload needs to be obtained. For a workload, its mean service time will depend on the distribution of the file sizes in the workload and the mean service times of each of those file sizes. Thus, to estimate the service time of a workload, the mean service time of each file size in the workload needs to be obtained.

To estimate the mean service time for a single file size, client requests at a very low arrival rate were presented to the server. The chosen arrival rate ensured that the resulting traffic intensity was very low (less than 0.4%). The measured response time for 200 such requests was used to compute the average. Since the traffic intensity is very low, queuing delay is negligible and the response time is dominated by the service time. As a result, the mean service time was approximated using these response time measurements under very low load which are in Table 4.

Table 4 Mean service time for each file size

File size (S_i)	Service time ($\overline{T}_{S_i}$) (msec.)
64 KB	9.77
128 KB	15.10
256 KB	25.02
512 KB	52.71
1 MB	105.85
2 MB	208.95

Using the service times of each file size, the average service time for a given heavy-tailed workload is computed using Equation (8). S_i denotes the file size, $\overline{T}s_i$ denotes the mean service time of file size S_i and Ps_i denotes the probability of requesting a file of size S_i in the workload. The average service times for different heavy-tailed workloads computed using Equation (8) are summarized in Table 5.

Table 5 Mean service times of heavytailed workload

Mean file size ($\overline{S}_i$)	Mean service time ($T_{\overline{S}_i}$) (msec.)
120 KB	15.12
150 KB	17.70
180 KB	21.18
200 KB	22.94

$$T_{\overline{S}_i} = \sum_i T_{S_i} P_{S_i} \quad (8)$$

5. Results and discussion

Several scenarios, each with a single deterministic or a heavy-tailed workload were considered during experimentation. For the deterministic workload, all the client requests were for the same file size. For the heavy-tailed workload, requests were generated according to the file size distribution for a given mean file size. In each scenario, request arrivals were generated according to a Poisson distribution with varying rates. The arrival rates are chosen to maintain the condition necessary for a stable system. Due to the high variability in the Poisson arrival process and for the file size distributions considered, the steady state mean queue length given by Equation (1) increases with ρ [13]. The traffic intensity is considered to be low for $\rho < 0.3$, medium for $0.3 \leq \rho < 0.5$, and high for $\rho \geq 0.5$ [13]. For each arrival rate, using the measured response times of 200 requests, the average response time was obtained. The mean response times were computed for the *M/G/m* model from Equation (2). For each workload, the traffic intensity for each arrival rate is also reported.

The measured and the computed average response times along with the traffic intensities for deterministic workloads are reported in Table 6. The results indicate that the response times predicted by the model are very close to the measured response time for low to moderate loads, where ρ is around 50%. The predicted response time is lower than the measured response time, with deviations within 10% for moderate traffic intensities. For higher traffic intensities, however, significant deviations occur. However, for the file sizes considered, the system is already heavily loaded when $\rho > 0.5$ [19], which cause these deviations.

The measured and the computed response times for Heavy-tailed workloads are reported in Table 7. The trends in the deviations between the computed and measured times are similar to that of the deterministic workload.

Thus, in summary, the above experimental results suggest that the *M/G/m* queuing model provides a reasonably approximate estimate of the response time for the web service architecture for low to moderate traffic intensities.

6. Related Research

Most of the existing work in web service performance focuses mainly on the enabling technologies and standards such as XML extensions and SOAP. Andreozzi *et al.* [2] present a model for rigorous representation of service characteristics. Gouscos *et al.* [8] present a simple approach to model certain web service management attributes such as QoS and provisioning price, and discuss how this information can be accommodated within basic specification standards such as WSDL. Thomas *et al.* [23] represent distributed web services by modeling the flow of messages and methods in a web service transaction. Such a model can assist in ensuring the correctness of web flows in terms of deadlock and correct termination of the web services transaction. Tu *et al.* [24] discuss design strategies to improve the performance of GIS web services. Dabous *et al.* [6] benchmark the performance of a capital market legacy system and investigate the associated overheads of using SOAP as a wire format for web services. Aghdaie *et al.* [1] present two performance optimizations which reduce the overhead of a client-transparent fault-tolerant scheme. McGregor *et al.* [18] introduce an approach to reclaim and improve the performance knowledge for organizations to establish a framework that enables the definition of web services from a performance measurement perspective. Levy *et al.* [12] present an architecture and prototype implementation of a performancemanagement system for cluster-based web services. Elfwing *et al.* [7] conduct experiments with SOAP in a web service environment to determine the response time when using SOAP and compare it to the response time when using CORBA. Their results indicate that a direct and naïve use of SOAP would result in a response time degradation by a factor of 400. Cardellini *et al.* [3] consider different categories of web applications, and evaluate how static, dynamic and secure web service requests affect performance and quality of service of distributed web sites. Ho *et al.* [9] describe a conceptual framework for building a software tool to record the behavior of a web service.

Very few efforts have focused on the performance modeling of web service architectures. The work closest to the research reported in this paper is by Liu *et al.* [14], where each of the three tiers of the web service architecture is modeled by a multi-station queuing center. A closed queuing network model is then used to represent the three-tiered web service architecture. This elaborate model has several parameters and requires instrumentation and extensive data collection at each tier. In comparison, the *M/G/m* queue is conceptually much simpler, requires the estimation of very few parameters and still provides a reasonable estimate of the response time for moderately high traffic intensities.

Table 6 Measured and computed response times (Deterministic workload)

$1/\lambda$ (msec.)		2000	1000	500	200	150	100	50	40	30	20
S_i = 64KB	ρ	0.0024	0.0050	0.0103	0.0255	0.0371	0.0554	0.1502	0.1927	0.3171	0.5198
	R_{meas}	9.78	10.00	10.13	10.26	11.15	11.30	12.86	15.21	16.15	22.09
	$R_{M/G/m}$	9.77	10.03	10.10	10.22	11.13	11.17	12.40	14.00	14.70	19.69
S_i = 128KB	ρ	0.0040	0.0078	0.0160	0.0398	0.0589	0.0995	0.2576	0.3478	0.5250	-
	R_{meas}	15.12	15.33	15.41	15.84	16.30	17.32	19.39	21.00	27.31	-
	$R_{M/G/m}$	15.10	15.27	15.35	15.78	16.25	17.12	18.32	19.69	24.28	-
	$R_{M/G/1}$	15.15	15.32	15.42	15.88	16.37	17.53	19.11	23.81	-	-
S_i = 256KB	ρ	0.0064	0.0125	0.0263	0.0760	0.1147	0.1962	0.6068	-	-	-
	R_{meas}	25.10	25.15	26.24	28.10	29.53	31.18	48.19	-	-	-
	$R_{M/G/m}$	25.02	25.08	26.15	27.60	28.87	29.59	42.26	-	-	-
S_i = 512KB	ρ	0.0132	0.0265	0.0571	0.1669	0.2569	0.4718	-	-	-	-
	R_{meas}	53.09	55.21	56.42	61.11	65.10	71.43	-	-	-	-
	$R_{M/G/m}$	52.73	53.15	54.31	58.46	61.34	66.49	-	-	-	-

Table 7 Measured and computed response times (Heavytailed workload)

$1/\lambda$ (msec.)		2000	1000	500	200	150	100	50	40
$\overline{S}_i$ = 120KB	ρ	0.0038	0.008[illegible]	0.0190	0.0560	0.0783	0.1201	0.3992	0.5373
	R_{meas}	15.15	15.20	16.55	17.03	18.20	18.51	21.13	28.19
	$R_{M/G/m}$	15.12	15.12	16.00	16.66	17.10	17.27	19.64	24.04
$\overline{S}_i$ = 150KB	ρ	0.0044	0.0094	0.0181	0.0554	0.0787	0.1268	0.3584	0.5528
	R_{meas}	17.68	17.91	18.25	19.10	20.10	21.81	24.07	36.63
	$R_{M/G/m}$	17.71	17.92	18.12	18.32	18.67	19.00	21.88	30.79
$\overline{S}_i$ = 180KB	ρ	0.0055	0.0111	0.0243	0.0709	0.0991	0.1596	0.4529	0.6345
	R_{meas}	21.24	21.69	23.88	25.49	26.20	27.69	34.72	47.81
	$R_{M/G/m}$	21.21	21.44	23.33	24.76	25.44	26.14	30.69	39.78
$\overline{S}_i$ = 200KB	ρ	0.0063	0.0131	0.0231	0.0754	0.1115	0.1843	0.4909	0.7327
	R_{meas}	23.00	23.50	25.04	27.15	30.20	31.31	40.63	55.81
	$R_{M/G/m}$	22.94	23.21	24.09	26.80	28.43	29.60	35.76	45.51

7. Conclusions and future research

In this paper, we hypothesize that the performance of the web service architecture can be modeled using the *M/G/m* queue. Our hypothesis is based on the observation that a multi-threaded application server usually constitutes a bottleneck resource in a web service, because it performs a bulk of the processing and modeling only the bottleneck tier can provide a reasonably approximate estimate of performance. We confirm our hypothesis by experimentally validating the *M/G/m* model with deterministic and heavy-tailed workloads. The proposed model is conceptually simple, requires the estimation of very few parameters and is hence easy to apply.

Our future research directions include extending the methodology to consider QoS provisioning and overload control. Developing techniques to use the performance estimates obtained from the model for composing web services and clustering/partitioning strategies is also a direction of future research.

8. References

[1] N. Aghdaie and Y. Tamir. Performance optimization for transparent fault-tolerant Web service. In *Proc.IEEE Pacific Rim Conference on Communications,Computers and Signal Processing (PACRIM'03)*, pages 29–32, 2003.

[2] S. Andreozzi, P. Ciancarini, D. Montesi, and R. Moretti. Towards a model for quality of Web and grid services. In *Proc. 13th IEEE Int'l Workshops on Enabling Technologies: Infrastructure for Collaborative Enterprises (WET ICE'04)*, pages 271–276, 2004.

[3] V. Cardellini, E. Casalicchio, and M. Colajanni. A performance study of distributed architectures for the quality of Web services. In *Proc. 34th Annual Hawaii Int'l Conference on System Sciences (CDROM)*, 2001.

[4] M. Crovella, M. S. Taqqu, and A. Bestavros. *Heavy-Tailed Probability Distributions in the World Wide Web*. A practical Guide To Heavy Tails: Statistical Techniques and Application. Birkhauser, Boston, 1998.

[5] D. Cunningham, J. Anderson, and B. Medairy. Network-centric architecture to enable secure communications and discovery. In *Proc. IEEE Aerospace Conference*, 2004.

[6] F. T. Dabous, F. A. Rabhi, and H. Yu. Performance issues in integrating a capital market surveillance system using Web services. In *Proc. 3rd Int'l Conference on Web Information Systems Engineering (WISE'03)*, pages 287–290, 2003.

[7] R. Elfwing, U. Paulsson, and L. Lundberg. Performance of SOAP in Web service environment compared to CORBA. In *Proc. 9th Asia-Pacific Software Engineering Conference*, pages 84–93, 2002.

[8] D. Gouscos, M. Kalikakis, and P. Georgiadis. An approach to modeling Web service QoS and provision price. In *Proc. 3rd Int'l Conference on Web Information Systems Engineering Workshops*, pages 121–130, 2003.

[9] S. Ho, W. M. Loucks, and A. Singh. Monitoring the performance of a Web service. In *Proc. IEEE Canadian Conference on Electrical and Computer Engineering*, pages 109–112, 1998.

[10] M. C. Jaeger, G. Rojec-Goldmann, and G. Muhl. QoS aggregation for Web service composition using work-flow patterns. In *Proc. 8th IEEE Int'l Enterprise Distributed Object Computing Conference (EDOC'04)*, pages 149–159, 2004.

[11] S. Jin and A. Bestavros. *Generating Internet Streaming Media Objects and Workloads*, chapter 1. Recent Advances on Web Content Delivery. Kluwer Academic Publishers, 2005.

[12] R. Levy, J. Nagarajarao, G. Pacifici, M. Spreitzer, A. Tantawi, and A. Youssef. Performance management for cluster based Web services. In *Proc. IFIP/IEEE 8th Int'l Symp. on Integrated Network Management*, pages 247–261, 2003.

[13] L. Lipsky. *Queueing theory: A Linear Algebraic Approach*. McMillan and Company, New York, 1992.

[14] X. Liu, J. Heo, and L. Sha. Modeling 3-tiered Web applications. In *Proc. 13th IEEE Int'l Symp. on Modeling, Analysis and Simulation of Computer Telecommunications Systems (MASCOTS'05)*, pages 307–310, 2005.

[15] Apache Software Foundation. Apache HTTP server project. http://httpd.apache.org/.

[16] Apache Software Foundation. Apache Tomcat. http://tomcat.apache.org/.

[17] Microsoft Corporation. Internet information services (IIS). http://www.microsoft.com/ WindowsServer2003/iis/default.mspx.

[18] C. McGregor and J. Scheifer. A framework for analyzing and measuring business performance with Web services. In *Proc. IEEE Int'l Conference on Ecommerce (CEC'03)*, pages 405–412, 2003.

[19] R. Nossenson and H. Attiya. Evaluating self-similar processes for modeling Web servers. In *Proc. Int'l Symp. on Performance Evaluation of Computer and Telecommunication Systems (SPECTS'04)*, pages 805–812, 2004.

[20] Jeffrey Richter. The CLR's thread pool. http://msdn.microsoft.com/msdnmag/issues/03/06/NET/default.aspx.

[21] H. Sakasegawa. An approximation formula Lq.= $\alpha\rho^{\beta}/(1-\rho)$. *Annals of the Institute of Statistical Mathematics*, 29(1):67–75, 1977.

[22] L. Sha, X. Liu, Y. Lu, and T. Abdelzaher. Queueing model based network server performance control. In *Proc. 23rd IEEE Real-Time Systems Symp. (RTSS'02)*, pages 81–90, 2002.

[23] J. P. Thomas, M. Thomas, and G. Ghinea. Modeling of Web services flow. In *Proc. IEEE Int'l Conference on E-Commerce (CEC'03)*, pages 391–398, 2003.

[24] S. Tu, M. Flanagin Y. Wu, M. Abdelguerfi, E. Normand, and V. Mahadevan. Design strategies to improve performance of GISWeb services. In *Proc. Int'l Conference on Information Technology: Coding and Computing (ITCC'04)*, pages 444–448, 2004.

[25] World Wide Web Consortium (W3C). Web services glossary. http://www.w3.org/TR/ ws-gloss/.

Design Issues of Reconfigurable Embedded System Architectures

Prof. Sunil Kr. Singh[1], Dr. M. P. S. Bhatia[2], Dr. Rajni Jindal[3]
[1]Asst. Professor, CSE Department, Bharati Vidyapeeth's College of Engineering, New Delhi, INDIA
[2]Professor, CSE Department, Netaji Subhash Institute of Technology (NSIT), New Delhi. INDIA
[3]Asst. Professor, CSE Department, Delhi College of Engineering, Delhi, INDIA
anujsunilsingh@yahoo.co.in, sksingh@bvcoend.ac.in bhatia.mps@gmail.com rajnijindal@dce.ac.in

Abstract

Modern high-performance embedded systems face many challenges, due to availability of several classes of modern applications in present technolology era and they are demanding very high performance from system with minimum resource. Reconfigurable computing system is emerging technology as an important for system design for present and future computation requirement of application in flexibility and performance aspect. In this paper, we discuss the design issue of Reconfigurable Embedded System (RES) by using reconfigurable computing. High performance with limited resources needs application-specific architectures (ASIC), while flexibility requires adaptive capabilities. Reconfigurable computing devices promise to meet both needs i.e. flexibility and performance. We identified some major key step in RES design as system hardware and software partitioning, architecture design space analysis, application analyses, different reconfigurable method tool, libraries, compilation & scheduling of process/task, use of FPGA and some other programmable devices in designing of reconfigurable computing system, and the state-of-the art of RESs . Reconfigurable computing using FPGAs (Field Programmable Gate Array) is emerging as an alternative to conventional ASICs (Application Specific Integration circuit) and general purpose processors. While these devices are currently available but the issue of how to design these systems is unresolved. Finally, in this paper, we try to solve some of above design issue and method for designing of Reconfigurable Embedded System.

Keywords: Reconfigurable Computing, ASIC, FPGA, HW/SW partitioning, Design Environment, Dynamic Reconfiguration, Scheduling.

1. Introdution

Many emerging application in the fields of multi-media, (mobile) communication, networking, computing, consumer electronics etc. require high performance, flexibility and wide variety of functionalities after the system utilization. That's why we try to present in this paper that system architecture has been an emerging topic for research and development and much has change over last few years of the history of modern high-performance embedded system. Flexible system must function in rapidly changing environment in multiple mode of operation. For such system, efficient hardware architecture must mach with algorithm to maximize performance and minimize resource. So that structurally adaptive reconfigurable architecture can meet both these need, achieving high performance with changing algorithm. Reconfigurable computing device, like FPGA (Field programmable Gate Array) allow the implementation of architecture that change in response to the changing environment. These reconfigurable hardware components are already being used in combination with traditional processor to deliver novel ways of implementing application. So FPGA technology shows great promise computational system. Thus the target systems are built on a heterogeneous computing platform: including reconfigurable H/W, ASIC and general purpose processor.

2. Related Research Work

Research related area in the field of Reconfigurable Computing is rapidly advancing for scientific and high performance multimedia applications. While today's Field Programmable Gate Array (FPGA) technology shows great promise for implementing reconfigurable computational systems, their capabilities in certain areas (such as floating point arithmetic) cannot equal other technologies. For this reason, efficient system architectures must encompass an heterogeneous mix of the best technologies. The target systems are built on a heterogeneous computing platform: including configurable hardware, ASIC and general purpose processors and FPGA based upon partial reconfigurable SRAM. The primary difficulty in this approach lies in system design. A designer must now maintain a set of different system architectures, which exist at different times in the system's lifetime, and map these architectures onto the same group of resources. The designers must manage the behavior of the system, determining the operational modes of the system, the rules for transitioning between operational modes, and the functional properties within each operational mode. In addition, the system must make efficient use of the resources, enabling the designer to minimize the envelope of hardware required to support the union of all operational modes. Currently system design tools are insufficient to manage this complexity. In this paper, we try to propose some basic tool for designing RES

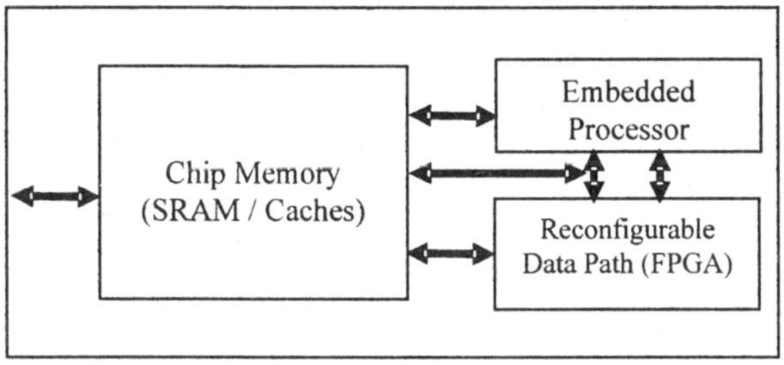

Fig. 1 Target structure ofDynamic Reconfigurable Embedded System

3. Reconfigurable Computing System

Conventional computing for the execution of algorithm have primary two methods, one is using Von-neumann computing in which programming of microprocessor/microcontroller using S/W, the second method is making application specific processor or integrated circuits. The first one is more flexible solution with performance degradation in the later method the system has been designed for particular application , may not be cost effective to modify to add more feature. So the use of reconfigurable computing system (RCS) which fill the gap between H/W(ASIC/ASIP) & S/W(Microprocessor) approaches. Because conventional computing system have fixed H/W and variable algorithm (S/W) to implement a system but in RCS, it has both H/W as well as algorithm(S/W) are variables have some basic.

With this approach, reconfigurable computing system have some basic properties and model which are given as:

Properties of RCS

Reconfigurable configurable computing system normally consisting of a matrix of programmable computational units with a programmable interconnection network superimposed on the computational matrix. The main characteristics that have in RCS are

1. Distributed computation,
2. Configurable data path
3. Spatial computation
4. Distributed control and scheduling

Designe Models of Reconfigurable Computing

There are some basic model can be used for simulating the architecture of RCS, so that a designer carefully analyze the need of method and component used in design of target system. Some are given as:

1. Behavioral modeling
2. Algorithm / Structural Modeling Mesh model
3. Resource Modeling
4. Partially Reconfigurable model
5. Multi-context modeling
6. Constraint modeling
7. Parallel Model

4. Need of Tools & Compilers for RES

One important observation of typical embedded system application show that 80 % or more execution time is spent on 20% or less of the code. If all the code is to placed on an FPGA using RES, it is unlikely to generate an efficient application in term of performance & cost.

Developing RES devices on the basis of high capacity FPGAs requires many tools, such as FPGA-based boards for rapid prototyping, computer-aided design (CAD) systems, libraries, IP (intellectual property) cores, etc. we try to suggest and describe such tools targeted to the design of reconfigurable embedded systems, whose specifications may change continuously . Some developed tools are given as:

- Software tools for configuring the FPGA, debugging hardware, interactions with the board and providing the required experiments.
- Core Xilinx Spartan 3 FPGA-based prototyping board with an external USB interface.
- Extension boards for connecting typical peripheral equipment and solving application-specific problems, such as implementation of interfaces, communication with standard devices (like memories), etc.
- Hardware/software tools for data compression and decompression that enable the volume of data transmitted from/to FPGA to be reduced size.
- Hardware/software support for reconfiguration of FPGA-based circuits through reloading reconfiguration bits, which have to be preliminary stored in a flash memory available on the board.
- Hardware/software tools for executing operations over binary/ternary vectors and matrices.
- VHDL templates and IP cores for application specific circuits.

- Useful VHDL and Handel-C projects providing essential support for developing reconfigurable embedded systems.
- For dynamic nature of the target applications, use Real-time operating systems, such as VxWorks.
- Use SystemC as simulating language for H/W & S/W simulation and verification in same environment.

5. Reconfigurable Embedded System Configuration & Synthesis:

A basic model configuration process generates hardware architecture specifications, software modules, process/schedule tables, communications maps, synthesizable hardware specifications, and a run-time Configuration Manger for dynamic adaptation to changing environments. The synthesis process attempts to optimize hardware/software architectures for user-cost such as weight, power, algorithmic accuracy and flexibility.

At this point, the synthesis procedure can generate the actual runtime artifacts. From the behavioral models, a set of tables is produced for the Configuration Manager. The state based behavior is defined in the Behavior Models. These models are transformed into a compact state table. The table contains next state equations for each operational mode. The interfaces to internal and external events are generated to provide the state transition variables to the state machine. These tables and variable interfaces are executed directly by the configuration manager. The synthesis process for hardware, software and both are given as:

A. Hardware Synthesis

For each configurable component (FPGA), a design specification is generated. This design specification includes a hardware design file for each component for each mode. The design for a component*mode is specified in structural VHDL. The VHDL design incorporates computational components from the design library, which can contain user defined VHDL behavioral descriptions and vendor-supplied Intellectual Property (IP) modules. These modules are glued together using components from a standard interface runtime library, which is part of the Runtime Environment described later. These interfaces connect computational components on the same chip with simple FIFO's and asynchronous handshaking interfaces. These interface components manage the physical hardware resources (pins and wires), buffer data, and multiplex multiple logical communications across a single set of wires. When required, data format conversions are also supplied.

B. Software Synthesis

For the general-purpose RISC/DSP components, a set of software specifications is generated. These specifications provide the information needed by the Runtime Environment to enact the desired computational behavior. The Runtime Environment requires several categories of design files:

- Software Load Modules contain executable modules that are downloaded to the processors in the system. The system can generate a common load module that contains the superset of all executable functions (if memory is sufficient) or it will generate a customized module for each of the processors in the system. The customized module is clearly more memory-efficient.
- Real-time schedules contain the list of processes and their priorities. A unique schedule is generated for each processor and for each mode of operation.
- Communication maps describe the information flow between processes. These "streams" can perform communication between two modules on the same processor, or they can transport data across the network, through intermediate processors, and to a remote process anywhere in the system.

C. H/W & S/W Synthesis

Interfaces between software modules and hardware modules/data sources/sinks are automatically inserted during the synthesis process. These interfaces perform the "care and feeding" of hardware interfaces, converting complex communication protocols into simpler hardware compatible protocols. The interfaces also multiplex multiple logical streams over a single physical port and perform data conversion functions.

The result of the synthesis and post processing is a complete executable system, ready for deployment. The deployment is performed in concert with the Runtime Environment.

6. Dynamic Runtime Reconfiguration

The dynamic runtime reconfiguration must support implementation platforms with the following attributes:

- **Heterogeneity:** Optimizing the architecture for performance, size, and power requires that the most appropriate implementation techniques be used. Implementations will require software (implemented on RISC and DSP processors), configurable hardware on FPGAs, and a mix of ASIC components.
- **Low overhead / High Performance:** the runtime environment must minimize overhead, since overhead results in extra hardware requirements.

- **Hard Real-Time:** The target systems have significant real-time constraints.
- **Reconfiguration:** The execution environment must allow hardware and software resources to be reallocated dynamically. During reconfiguration, the application data must remain consistent and real-time constraints must be satisfied.

All the above issues must be addressed at multiple levels. At the lowest level, the hardware must be capable of reconfiguration. Software-programmable components, such as DSP's and RISC processors, have excellent inherent hardware support for reconfiguration, since software has the ability to change system function by changing memory contents. Internal CPU hardware structures are designed to restrict dangerous conditions that could damage hardware. FPGA's are an unrestricted collection of gates, switches, and connectors. This process must be provided by a cooperation of the design process and the runtime infrastructure.

7. Target Architecture and Application Optimization

A. Traget Architecure Optimization

Reconfigurable system is a promising alternative to deliver both flexibility and performance at the same time. Technology-dependent tools and high-level abstract supporting tools have been proposed to solve the various design problems at different abstraction levels. However, a complete overview of how to integrate them into a single design flow is missing. In this work, we use a real case study to demonstrate our design target architecture optimization flow of Run Time Reconfigurable (RTR) systems.

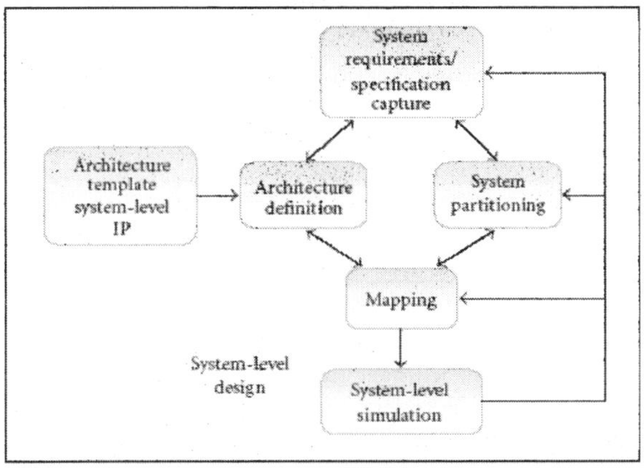

Fig. 2 A general View of system-level design flow

The above design flow is divided into some basic system-level design and implementation-level design. The process at system-level design is to make various partitioning decisions and evaluate system performance. At implementation level, executable code and HW net list are generated using technology-dependent tools. A general view of the system-level design flow is given in Fig. 2. The some basic following new features are identified in each phase when reconfigurability is taken into account.

(i) ***System requirements/specification capture*** needs to identify requirements and goals of reconfigurability (e.g., flexibility for specification changes and performance scalability).

(ii) ***Architecture definition*** needs to model the reconfigurable technologies of different types and vendors at abstract level and include them in the architecture mode.

(iii) ***System partitioning*** needs to analyze and estimate the functions of the application for SW, fixed HW, and reconfigurable HW. The parts of the targeted system that will be realized on reconfigurable HW must be identified. There are some rules of thumb that can be applied. If an application has roughly several same sized hardware accelerators that are not used at the same time, these accelerators can be implemented onto DRHW. If an application has some parts in which specification changes are foreseeable or there are foreseeable plans for new generations of the applications, it may be beneficial to implement it onto DRHW.

(iv) ***Mapping needs*** to map functions allocated to *reconfigurable* hardware onto the respective architecture model. The special concerns at this step are the temporal allocation and the scheduling problem. Allocation and scheduling algorithms need to be made either online or offline.

(v) ***System-level simulation*** needs to observe the performance impacts using reconfigurable resources for a particular system function. The effect of configuration overhead should be highlighted in order to support designers to perform system analysis or design space exploration.

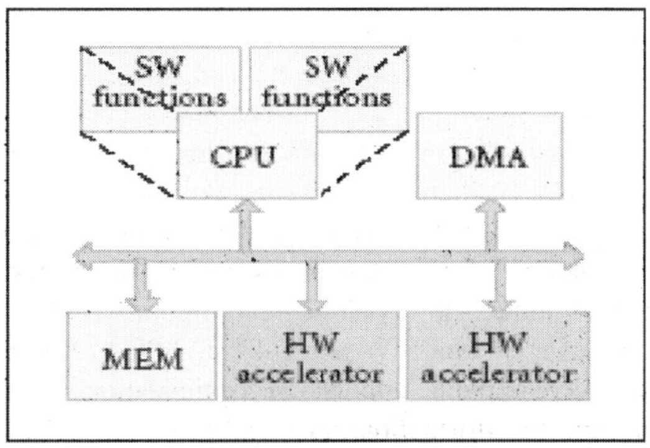

Fig. 3 A general view of initial fixed architecture

The reconfigurable components are mainly used as coprocessors in System on Chips. The new architecture is redefined partly based on the existing architecture and partly using the system specification as input. The initial architecture is often dependent on many things not directly resulting from the requirements of the application. Therefore, the initial architecture and the HW/SW partition are often given at the beginning of system-level design (Fig. 4).

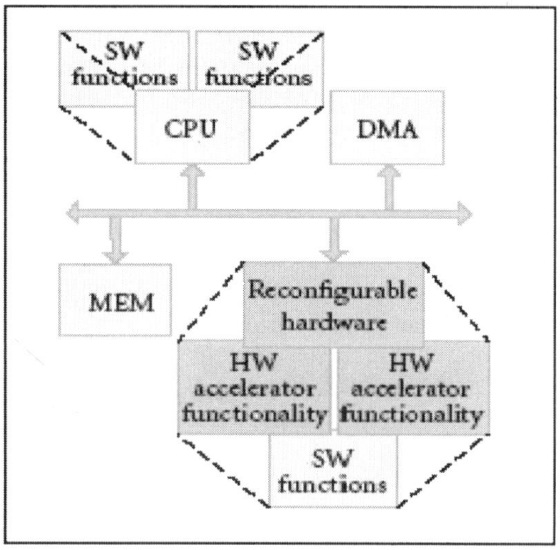

Fig. 4 A modified view of reconfigurable system level design flow

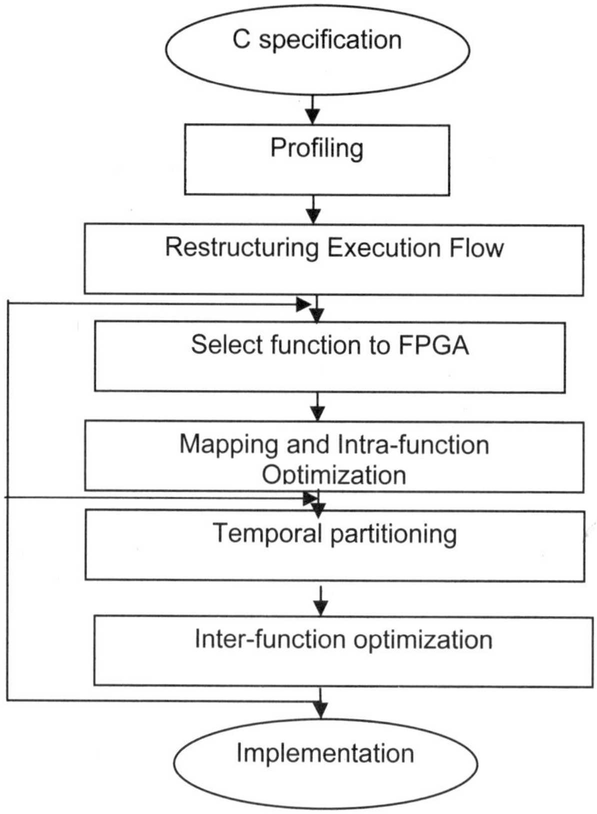

Fig. 5 Application optimization Design flow in reconfigurable embedded system.

B. Application Optimization

Generally FPGA has used over the ASIC design flow for the embedded system because run- time or dynamic reconfiguration is of special interest among all the researcher because it provides a performance and cost advantage over a load-time configuration. The processor can be an embedded RISC like ARM or MIPS, generally such configuration use an open-source processor LEON, which is compatible with SPARC V8 and has same performance as RISC. The main advantage of an open source core is that to provide design flexibility, i.e. provide interface between FPGA and processor. The FPGA has direct access to main memory. It compile C code to the FPGA easier the other communication models.

Generally, there is a particular border between H/W and S/W design. Software is generally programmed in a sequential mode but hardware is developed in parallel mode. In dynamic reconfiguration, the gap between H/W and S/W is burned by FPGA. We try to manually explain application optimization in RES through transformation on C source code. For this purpose we make use of FPGA features to improve performance and reduce area.

Due to dynamic reconfiguration, the optimization is divided into two stages. The first stage in intra-function optimization. Main techniques include specify word length, simple SIMD etc. the intra-function optimization will not affect other parts of the system. In the second stage, after the temporal partitioning, we get the knowledge of different functions that how they are grouped into one configuration and how they are perform inter-function optimization Fig. 5. The main technique includes resource, localizing memory access, pipelining and parallelizing among functions. So by using two stage optimization, we get more performance and use small area than a sequentially written C program can provide. As a c based methodology, various design steps are performed on c level, like, profiling, mapping, optimization and restructuring execution flow. Its also reduce the debugging and verification work.

8. Conclusion

The main advantage of Reconfigurable Embedded System is the combined flexibility and performance. However, implementing RES does require extra efforts in the various design stages, from the general view of system-level design flow to modified view of reconfigurable system level design flow. In this paper, we discuss the design issue of Reconfigurable Embedded System (RES) by using reconfigurable computing. High performance with limited resources needs application-specific architectures (ASIC), while flexibility requires adaptive capabilities. We also present a design flow of application optimization for Reconfigurable Systems. However, some key step of our design issue, tools and method for designing of Reconfigurable Embedded System are still done manually, and the demonstrator is under development. We are going to concentrate on different design issue. The main challenge is to develop such system also to develop a compiler which compile the selected and optimize application code for the target reconfigurable embedded system. Our goal is to provide the basic design issue for reconfigurable embedded system architecture.

9. References

[1] Villasenor, J., Mangione—Smith, W., "Configurable Computing", Scientific American, June, 1997.

[2] S. Edwards, L. Lavagno, E.A. Lee, A. Sangiovanny-Vincentelli, "Design of Embedded Systems: Formal Models, Validation, and Synthesis", *Proc. of the IEEE*, vol. 85, no. 3, March, 1997, pp. 366-390.

[3] www.gaisler.com

[4] Xilinx, Inc., Virtex- E 1.8V field programmable Gate Array, Feb 2001.

[5] R. Ernst, J. Henkel, and T. Benner, "Hardware–software cosynthesis for microcontrollers," IEEE design Test Comput., vol. 10, pp. 64–75, Dec.1993.

[6] K. M. GajjalaPurna and D. Bhatia, "Temporal partitioning and scheduling for reconfigurable computing," Proc. IEEE Symp. FPGAs for Custom Computing Machines, pp. 329–330, 1998.

[7] K. Bondalapati and V. Prasanna. "Reconfigurable Computing systems in Proc. IEEE, vol.90, no.7, July 2002, pp.1201-1217

[8] K. Chatta and R.Vemuri, "Hardware–software codesign for dynamically reconfigurable architectures," in Proc. of FPL'99, Glasgow, Scotland, Sept. 1999.

[9] Juanjo Noguera and Rosa M. Badia, "HW/SW Codesign Techniques for Dynamically Reconfigurable Architectures", IEEE Transactions on VLSI Systems, Vol. 10, NO. 4, august 2002, pp 399-415.

[10] Xilinx, "Virtex platform datasheet," May 2007, http://www.xilinx.com. ,Septembe 1999.

[11] K. Bondalapati and V. Prasanna. "Reconfigurable Computing systems in Proc. IEEE, vol.90, no.7, July 2002, pp.1201-1217

[12] Juanjo Noguera and Rosa M. Badia, "HW/SW Codesign Techniques for Dynamically Reconfigurable Architectures", IEEE Transactions on VLSI Systems, Vol. 10, NO. 4, August 2002, pp 399-415.

[13] Andr'e DeHon and John Wawrzynek, "Reconfigurable Computing: What, Why, and Implications for Design Automation", technical report.

[14] Sandeep Neema: "Constraint based System Synthesis", Technical Report, Department of Electrical and Computer Engineering, Vanderbilt University, 1999.

Timing Driven Physical Implementation of USB 2.0 Core using SoC Encounter

L.Basavaraj[1] and R.D Sudhaker Samuel[2]
[1]Research Scholar,SJCE,JSS Research Foundation Mysore, Karnataka-570002
[2]Department of Electronics and comm. Sri Jayachamarajendra college of engg, Mysore, Karnataka-570004
basavaraj.vvce@gmail.com *sudhakersamuel@yahoo.com*

Abstract

In today's modern computing era, high-speed communication needs to happen between computer and its peripherals combined with minimum power consumption. Universal Serial Bus helps to achieve this objective by providing high data throughput with utilization of minimum bandwidth. USB is a serial bus standard to interface devices by allowing it to be connected and disconnected without rebooting the computer. With new USB 2.0 specifications, data rates of over 480 Mb/s are possible. The intent of this paper is to perform net list to Geometric Data Stream implementation of USB 2.0 functional core. The system is implemented using ASIC Semi Custom methodology with timing driven approach, which aims to achieve maximum frequency of operation. This paper proposes a physical implementation of USB core i.e. starting from gate level net list, the design flow includes highly optimized placement and routing using Cadence SoC Encounter. Various placements, Clock Tree Synthesis and routing approaches are tried out during the design cycle to achieve maximum operating frequency.

Keywords: USB, ASIC, placement and routing, Cadence, SoC Encounter.

1. Introduction

Current peripheral products do not require any changes to operate in a USB 2.0 system. Many Human Interface Devices, such as mouse, keyboards and game pads will not require the additional performance that USB 2.0 offers and will remain as full or low speed peripherals as defined by USB 1.1. The higher data rate of USB 2.0 will, however, open up the possibilities of exciting new peripherals. Video-conferencing cameras will perform better with access to higher bandwidth. Next-generation, higher-speed and higher resolution printer and scanner devices will be enabled at the high-end. High density storage devices such as R/W DVD will also be enabled by USB 2.0. These devices require minor changes to the peripheral interface, as defined in the USB 2.0 specification. Overall, the additional cost to support USB 2.0 is expected to be minimal to the peripheral. The version 2.0 specification that is under development is an evolutionary step that increases performance capabilities at low cost for USB peripherals in a backwards compatible fashion. The Cadence Encounter® digital design platform accurately converts the high-level logical specification of a digital integrated circuit into a detailed physical blueprint [4] [5] and then detailed design information showing how the IC will be physically implemented [1].

2. USB 2.0 Core

The Universal Serial Bus has evolved to the standard interconnect between computers and peripherals. Everything from a mouse to a camera can be connected via USB. With the new USB 2.0 specification, data rates of over 480 Mb/s are possible. The Universal Serial Bus is a point-to-point interface. Multiple peripherals are attached through a hub to the host. This core provides a function for the peripheral device to interface. It can be used to interface almost any peripheral to a computer via USB. This core fully complies with the USB 2.0 specification and can operate at USB full and high speed rates at 12 and 480 Mb/s. The overall architecture of the core is shown in Fig. 1.

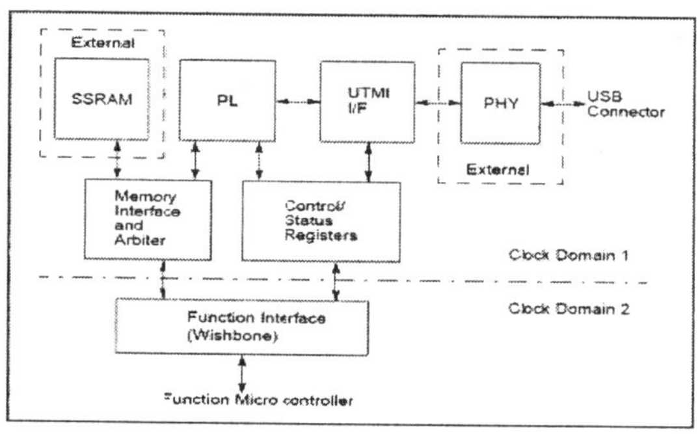

Fig. 1 Core Architecture Overview

The host interface provides a bridge between the internal data memory and control registers to the function controller. The data memory and control registers interface to the protocol layer. The protocol layer interfaces to UTMI interface block. The UTMI block interfaces to the PHY.

3. Physical Implementation of USB 2.0 Core

The SoC Encounter provides a full-chip, hierarchical physical prototyping system that validates the physical feasibility of the net list. Physical information is used to partition the design into hierarchical modules, while simultaneously creating timing budgets that are realistic. This approach achieves timing closure without long design iterations because the timing results produced by the physical prototype correlate with those produced by the chip's final implementation. The Cadence SoC Encounter is a versatile tool, which takes a design from the RTL sign-off stage to the GDSII format.

Design Inputs: To implement the design it is necessary to import LEF files, DEF files, SDC files, and LIB files.

Library Exchange Format: LEF defines the elements of an IC process technology and associated library of cell models. It is an ASCII data format from Cadence, used to describe a standard cell library. It includes the design rules for routing and the Abstract Layout of the cells, no information about the internal netlist of the cells.

Design Exchange Format: A Design Exchange Format file contains the design-specific information of a circuit and is a representation of the design at any point during the layout process. DEF conveys logical design data to, and physical design data from, place-and-route tools. Logical design data can include internal connectivity that is represented by a net list, grouping information, and physical constraints. Physical data includes placement locations and orientations, routing geometry data, and logical design changes for back annotation. Place and route tools also can read physical design data, for example, to perform ECO changes.

Synopsys Design Constraints: The Synopsys widely used design constraints format, known as SDC, describes the design intent and surrounding constraints for synthesis, clocking, timing, power, test and environmental and operating conditions. A complete list of the constraints available in SDC is available through request of a license.

USB netlist: Most netlists either contain or refer to descriptions of the parts or devices used. Each time a part is used in a netlist, this is called an instance. Thus, each instance has a master, or definition. These definitions will usually list the connections that can be made to that kind of device, and some basic properties of that device. These connection points are called ports or pins, among several other names.

CTS for the core: The goal of CTS is to minimize skew and insertion delay. Clock is not propagated before CTS. Large complex designs can contain hundreds of clocked elements. The clock tree has to be designed to minimize clock skew.

CTS can be operated in two modes. They are

1. Manual CTS, which controls the number of clock levels and control the number and type of clock buffers.
2. Automatic CTS, which is based on timing constraints in specification file.

Timing Analysis

The static timing analysis is an important step in analyzing the performance of a design. It is possible to have both pre-layout and post-layout static timing analysis and constraints setting. It is a thorough and efficient way to determine if the logic being designed will result in the hardware functioning within its timing specifications and constraints. The following analysis can be done using STA.

1. Do the signals arrive at pins in time.
2. Do the signals stay long enough at the required state to be useful.
3. Will the signals propagate with proper slew or slope.
4. Are clock/data signals wide enough.
5. Will the hardware run at a specified clock frequency.
6. Identify parts of the path, which need attention.
7. Clock distribution and correctness.

Generally, static timing analysis is much faster than timing-driven gate-level simulation and does not require stimulus vector generation. Therefore, unlike dynamic analysis, the quality of the static approach is independent of the quality of stimulus vectors. However, proper functionality of the design cannot be checked in static analysis. An accurate and efficient static timing analysis has many benefits, such as providing quick and efficient information to enhance the design performance and easing the design debugging procedure. This application note presents the most important concepts and techniques of static timing analysis and contains practical examples.

The different options for timing analysis can be divided as Pre Place, Pre CTS, Post CTS and Post Route.

Pre-Place analysis generates timing reports before the design is placed. In this mode, the software ignores the net load while building the timing graph and runs FE timing analysis for generating timing reports. The DRV report files are not generated in this mode.

Pre-CTS analysis generates timing reports for a design whose clock tree has been created. By default, in this mode the software runs trial Route, native default extraction, and FE timing analysis for generating timing reports.

Post-CTS analysis generates timing reports for a design whose clock tree has been created. By default, in this mode the software runs trial Route, native default extraction, and FE timing analysis for generating timing reports.

Post-Route analysis generates timing reports for a design whose routing is complete. By default, in this mode the software runs native detailed extraction, and FE timing analysis for generating timing reports.

4. Results

The following figures show the results obtained after synthesis and implementation of the design. Fig. 2. shows the schematic with the modules, which are used in encounter for placement and routing.

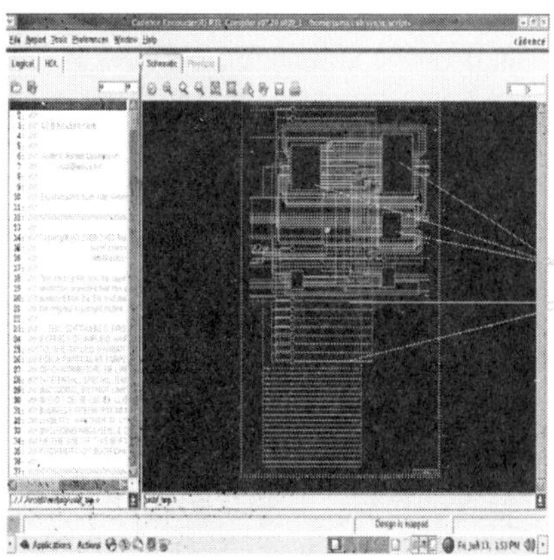

Fig. 2 Schematic of the design after RTL compiler

Fig. 3 shows the floor area selected for the design. The die area is selected by specifying the height and width of the die. It should be selected such that aspect ratio should be less than 1 and core utilization below 70%.

Fig. 4 shows the standard cell placement for the design in the defined die area. After placing the standard cells filler cells and spare cells are need to be added. These cells get placed in the empty places, which are not filled by standard cells. These empty places can be seen in the Fig. 4. After placing the cells clock has to be added. Once clock is added it does the trial routing. The design after this phase is shown in Fig. 5.

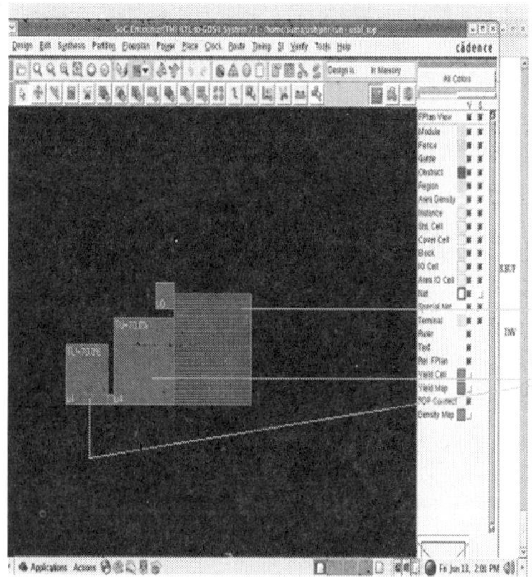

Fig. 3 Die area and modules of the design

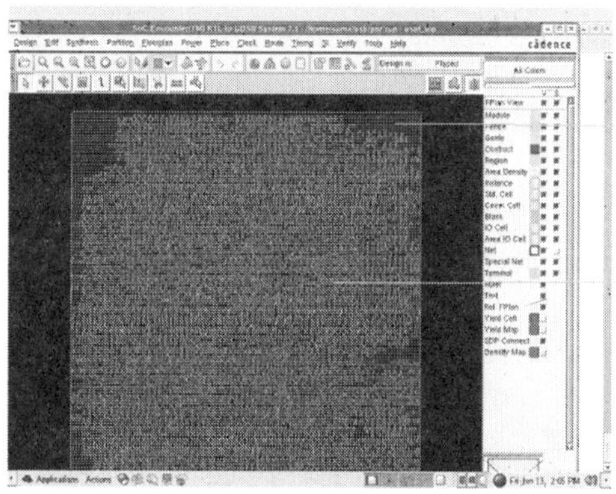

Fig. 4 Standard cell placement in the design

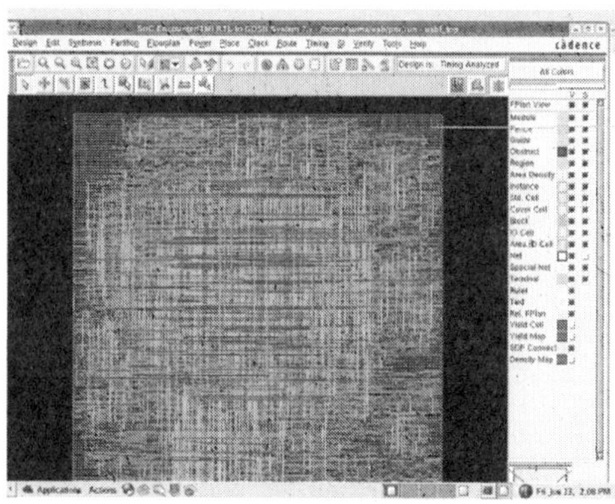

Fig. 5 Design after Clock Tree Synthesis

Once the cells are placed the design has to be routed. Routing is done in two phases of detailed and global routing. Fig. 6 shows the design after routing. Red color shows the congestion in the design after routing. Fig. 7 shows the enlarged portion of a point of the design. It shows the wire connection of the point enlarged.

Fig. 8 shows the details of a point on the design. It tells about the type of net, wire direction, bounding box and the routed layer. It also gives the status of the net.

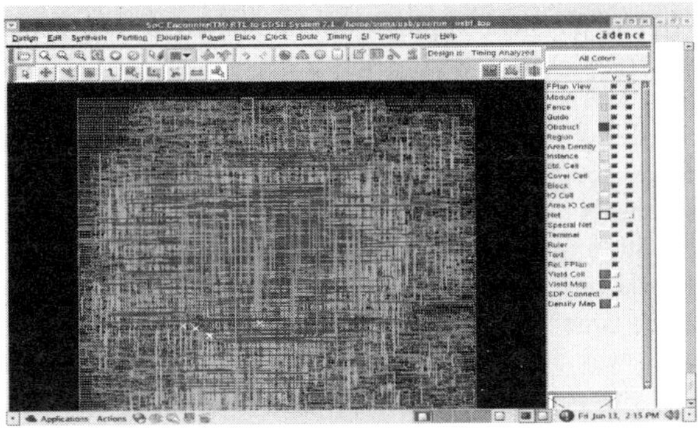

Fig. 6 Design after routing

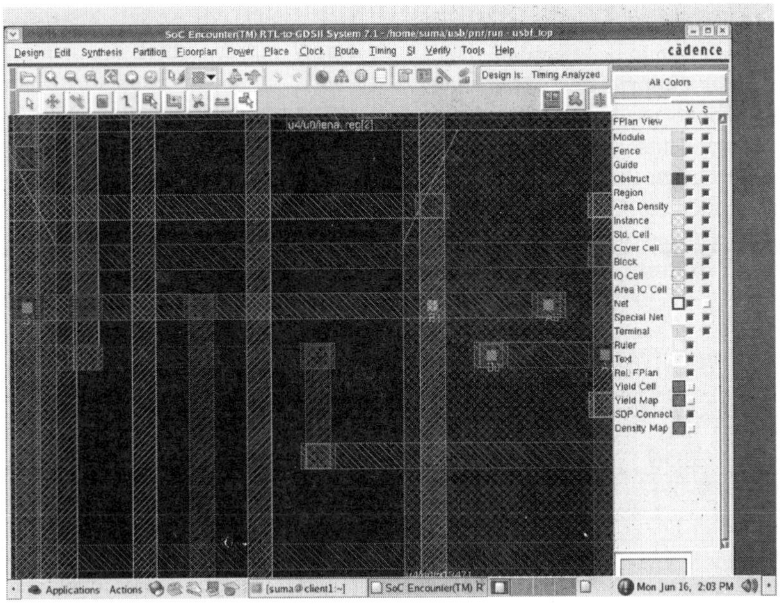

Fig. 9 Enlarged view of a part of the design

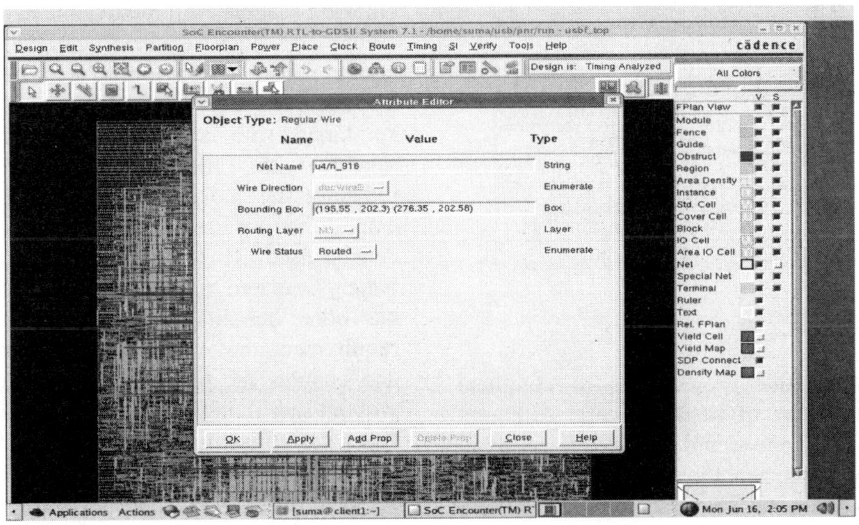

Fig. 10 Description of a cell on the design

5. Timing Reports

The timing reports of the USB 2.0 core implemented on SoC shown gives the slack time for 2 paths for 5 ns time period and are grouped as pre CTS, post CTS, post Route. The time period was first selected as 33 ns and then it was reduced to 10 ns, 8 ns and finally to 5 ns. The timing report for clock period of 33 ns, 10 ns, 8 ns for pre CTS, post CTS and post Route is shown in Appendix A.

Table 1 shows the various slack time obtained for different paths after routing for time period of 33 ns, 10 ns, 8 ns and finally for 5 ns.The timing analysis was done for 50 paths. From the table it can be seen that the slack time has reduced to 0.050 for 5 ns.The slack time should be positive for the design to be effective.

Table.2 shows the design comparison obtained for the Artisan library components used in the design with the Hitachi library components. By using Artisan library components in the design and optimizing it, the die area used has been reduced to 422500mm^2 and the core utilization is also reduced to 46%. The clock period was reduced to 5 ns from 33 ns for positive slack time.

Table 1 Slack time after routing

Time period/path	33ns	10ns	8ns	5ns
Path1	26.074	3.156	1.156	0.050
Path2	26.182	3.234	1.234	0.353
Path3	26.300	3.352	1.352	0.405
Path4	26.330	3.383	1.383	0.521
Path5	26.841	3.905	1.905	0.544
.....	......	......	.....	.....
......	....	......	......	.....
Path 50	29.094	6.072	4.072	1.353

Table 2 Comparison of two libraries

Library	Hitachi	Artisan
Technology	0.18 micron	0.18 micron
Metal layers	5	6
Core utilization	71%	46%
Clock period	33ns	33ns/10ns/8ns/5ns
Die area	580503mm2	422500mm2

6. Conclusion

The requirement of this project was to complete physical implementation of USB 2.0 core. Although optimization of speed, power and area are the common objectives during implementation of any VLSI chip, the designers have to settle for a trade off among these common guiding factors. Hence this project was concentrated on the time driven implementation and optimization.

The physical implementation started with a netlist generated using RTL compiler. The LEF, .LIB and SDC were the other inputs to this project. After taking the design through several iterations, a well-optimized clock specification file was developed for clock tree synthesis

Starting from the clock period of 33 ns the time period has been optimized upto 5 ns with a positive slack time period. Placement of standard cells, filler cells was done by selecting the desired die area such that the core density does not exceed 70% utilization. Several routing techniques were tried to achieve minimum parasitics on nets.

After placing the standard cells, filler cells and spare cells are added. These cells get placed in the empty places, which are not filled by standard cells. Clock is added after the placement of cells. Trial routing is done once the clock gets added. Routing of the core is done in global as well as detailed phases. The timing reports of the USB 2.0 core implemented on SoC gives the slack time for 50 paths which are obtained for pre CTS, post CTS, post Route. The time period was first selected as 33 ns and then it was reduced to 10 ns, 8 ns and finally to 5 ns.

7. Future Scope

An implementation of the USB core was done for timing driven, future it can be implemented for power driven and area constraints and optimising the same. The scan chain insertion can be done to improve the testability of the design. A holistic approach to low power design can drastically cut the power requirements for the USB 2.0 core. The power can be reduced in both the digital and analog blocks of the PHY. The redesigned PLL/DLL, with optimized clocking scheme, will remove the need for a significant amount of high-frequency clocking circuitry. The active power consumption will be further reduced through the use of a new transmit architecture, combined with an extensively optimized clocking scheme within the receive and transmit paths. By reducing the power demands up to 50% not only extends battery life but also a lower cost power supply can be used. This is an important issue in portable, battery-operated products. The low-power architecture has other benefits. By reducing the supply current requirement, the overall power consumption is lowered and enables the pin count to be minimized by half without sacrificing any functionality. The ultra-low pin count design is a major advantage in terms of enabling the use of lower-cost packaging. Alternatively, package pins can be made available for other signals. The need for fewer pins also reduces the cost of production test, as well as considerably easing SoC-integration

The current-generation USB 2.0 designs are typically in the region of $1mm^2$ to $1.2mm^2$ in area. Depending on the specific foundry process, this size barrier can be reduced to by approximately 50%. This significant area reduction can be achieved through a combination of architectural and implementation optimizations. For example, a redesigned PLL/DLL architecture can eliminate the need for complex clocking circuitry, which contributes significantly to the overall reduction in area. The PHY can be floorplanned in such a way that as the digital block scales with the smaller process geometries, the overall macro area is allowed to shrink this is not always the case with mixed-signal designs.

8. References

[1] Naveed Sherwani, "Algorithms for VLSI Physical Design Automation," third edition by Springer (India) Private Limited.

[2] LEF/DEF Language Reference Product Version 5.5 January 2003

[3] Narayanan Thondugulam, P.A.Semi, "Using Cadence Chip Optimizer with SoC Encounter GXL for Design" by Cadence designer network.

[4] Sabih H. Gerez, "Algorithms for VLSI Design Automation," edition 2006 by John Wiley & Sons Ltd.

[4] Cadence Encounter Conformal Support, Quartus II 8.0 Handbook, Volume 3

[5] CADENCE "ENCOUNTER RTL COMPILER" Publication: CAD/CAM Update (Newsletter) Volume: 17 Issue: 9 by: Worldwide Videotex

[6] M. Sarrafzadeh, C. K. Wong, "An Introduction to VLSI Physical Design", McGraw-Hill Book Company, 1996.

[7] Sadiq M. Sait and Habib Youssef ,"VLSI Physical Design Automation: Theory and Practice" 1st edition (November 15, 1999) by World Scientific Publishing Company.

[8] Ahmed Aminc Jcrraya, Sungjoo Yoo, Norbert When and Diederik Verkest, "Embedded Software for SoC ," 1 edition (September 30, 2003) Springer.

[9] SAN JOSE, "Cadence and TSMC Announce Digital Flow Based On Cadence SoC Encounter; Cadence Platform Validated for Hierarchical SoC Design of 0.18-Micron and Below Process Technologies" JUN-02 by Business Wire

[10] Himanshu Bhatnagar, "Advanced ASIC Chip Synthesis" second edition, Kluwer Academic Publishers.

[11] Jan Axelson," USB Complete," Third Edition by Lakeview Research

[12] http://www.synopsys.com

[13] http://www.cadence.com

An Open Source Methodology to Increase Observability in Verilog Programs

L.Swarna jyothi[1] and Dr.A.S.Manjunath[2]
[1]Professor, Research Scholar Dr. MGR university, JSS Academy of Tech Education Bangalore
[2]CEO & MD Manvish eTech Pvt. Ltd., Bangalore
swarna_jy@yahoo.com asmanju@gmail.com

Abstract

This paper presents an approach for the static analysis of verilog programs and adding assertions, documentation statements and monitor statements at required points, using Lex, Yacc, CC, Parser Tree, etc. The method mainly concentrates on control structures of verilog to add on assertions and monitor statements. It also observes deviation from coding standards. Once these constructs are identified, suitable actions will be taken in order to optimize the program. An analysis report is produced indicating the location where the violations occurred and the list of rules violated. The parsing is accomplished by using Lex and Yacc. This approach is proposed to use command line interface, i.e., accept user input about the file to be parsed, the pattern to be looked for in the source file and the action to be taken. The input is then redirected to a file which is in turn fed to the parser. In the parser, the source file is scanned line by line and action is taken according to users options. This methodology will help programmers adopt proper coding practice apart from reducing design verification gap.

1. Introduction

Many articles cite the fact that 70% of the time is spent in verification [1]. The traditional black box approach to verification is to provide a set of input test vectors to a design simulation and monitor the actual output against the intended output. The test bench consists of a combination of cases that reflect the specification, worry cases and random inputs. Unfortunately, even rather simple designs can require an enormous number of test vectors and therefore simulation time to exhaustively test for all possible combination of inputs. Lastly, in certain types of implementations errors are difficult to stimulate with functional tests. These are referred to as verification hot spots. There is a lack of control, i.e. an inability to activate, stimulate or sensitizes a specific point within the design. The consequence of these observability and controllability limitations is that a chip may require an expensive – approximately $1M re-spin or worse a field recall due to design flaws undetected during the verification stage.

The basic ABV (Assertion based verification) method compares the implementation of a design against its specified assertions by embedding assertions in a design and having them monitor design activities. Assertions are placed wherever the protocols may be misused, assumptions violated, or design intent incorrectly implemented. Whenever an assertion is violated, it is reported immediately without the requirement for the problem to the design's outputs. Assertions play a big role in embedded software development [9], paper proposes a model-based design flow for assertions and assumptions that together ensure the correctness, both functional and non-functional, of a complex embedded system.

Assertion-Based Verification provides benefit to users by: Increasing observability of bugs, Increasing controllability, facilitating the diagnosis of bugs by identifying bugs at or near their cause, finding bugs earlier in the design cycle, uncovering bugs that would have otherwise remained undetected, enabling the use of formal and semi-formal verification techniques, preventing wasted simulation cycles, improving verification productivity, lowering risk of bugs avoiding discovery, facilitating the integration of work from multiple designers, supporting design reuse and third part IP. The roles of controllability and observability in design for test [10] has been well discussed in the paper

Static analysis tools can serve an important role in raising the awareness of developers about subtle correctness issues and prevent future bugs. Identifying and eliminating errors which may lead to error in the future and to maintain a standard coding style has always been a tedious process requiring lot of time and energy.

FOSS software is often the basis for innovations and for evolving open and commercial closed source solutions in the market. Openness is a benefit in customization and flexibility of solutions. Result is quality, reliable and secure code. Some FOSS innovations in education are OLPC, MIT OpenCourseWare, Wikipedia and California Open Source Textbook etc.

There are many open source tools for parser generation [3-6], verilog parsing [2] and source navigation for verilog [8]. Source Navigator [8] for Verilog is full featured tool for editing and navigating through large projects with many verilog files. It parses verilog code into a database that can be used to navigate files, trace connectivity, and find modules and signals in the design. Veritak [7] is a commertial Verilog HDL Compiler/Simulator that supports the major Verilog 2001 HDL features. It provides an integrated environment, which includes a VHDL to Verilog translator, a syntax highlighting editor. There are some open source parser generators [3-6]. Icarus Verilog [2] is a FREE Verilog simulation and synthesis tool with VPI. It operates as a compiler, compiling source code written in Verilog -IEEE-1364- into some target format.

The proposed tool basically suggested to run from the command line. This would enable the tool to be seamlessly integrated as a backend to other tools. The tool requires as input the input file, the options and the actions. This is specified at the command prompt. Extensive use of C libraries is made to achieve reusability. CC is used as a parser generator and a lexical analyzer generator. Parser Tree which is a preprocessor for CC that inserts parse tree building actions at various places in the CC source is used. The output of Parse Tree is run through CC to create the parser.

The document is organized as follows: Section 2 describes requirements analysis to determine the requirements of the system. Section 3 presents proposed overall system architecture. Sections 4 display the design aspect of proposed architecture and performance of the system. Finally, Section 6 presents the conclusions drawn from the entire work.

2. Analysis

Requirements analysis is critical to the success of a project. Requirements must be measurable, testable, related to identified business needs or opportunities, and defined to a level of detail sufficient for system design. The activities in analysis are to understand the verification domain and its components, interacting with the system to discover the hardware and software requirements.

The proposed system incorporates open source softwares such as Lex, Yaac, CC and parse tree which further enhance verification activities. CC is a parser generator and a lexical analyzer generator, Parse Tree is a preprocessor for CC, Lex is used to provide the Pattern Matching Description, Yacc is used to provide the set of Grammar Rules.

This tool is estimated to consume maximum of 100 kb of disk space. This includes the space taken by the source code along with the libraries used. The application can run either on a single threaded or multi threaded environment. The tool can be run on only Linux platform as Lex and Yacc are required. The tool can run either on single or multi processor environment

The working environment of the project is Linux. The code is portable on any flavor of Linux which supports AT & T Lex and Yacc. For the code to be portable on other platforms such as Windows or Mac, some level of tuning has to be done to ensure easy portability. This could be a Future Enhancement.

Overall system architecture

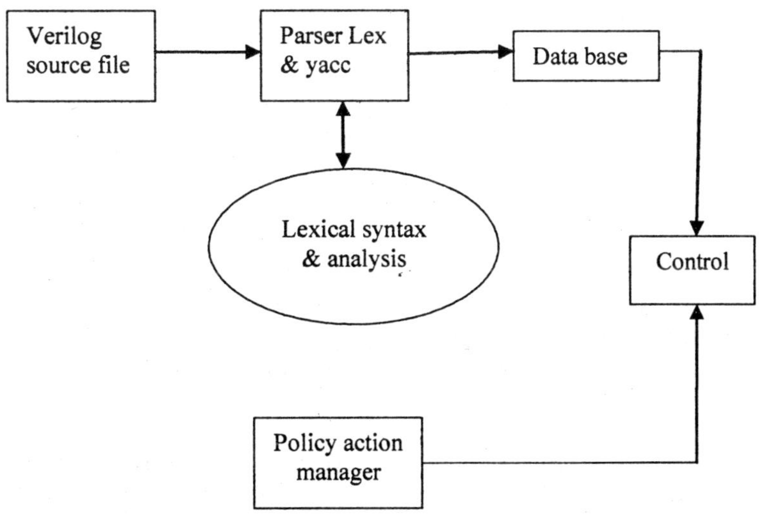

Fig.1 System architecture

Verilog source file

The File contains the Source Code which needs to abide to a set of Policies determined by the Programmer. This forms the Input to the Parser, which is **Verilog source file** responsible for obtaining the most Granular Unit of the Code on which the Policy is applied.

Parser

A Parser breaks data into smaller elements, according to a Set of Rules that describe its Structure or Syntax. These Rules together form a Grammar. Each Rule in the Grammar, known as a Production Rule, describes the composition of a named symbol. Once the syntax of a data source has been described by the Grammar Rules, a Parser can use the Grammar to parse the data source. Parsing is the process of matching grammar symbols to elements in the Input Data, according to the Rules of the Grammar.

The Output of the Parser is a Parse Tree. The Parse Tree expresses the Hierarchical structure of the Input data. Each node in the tree has a Label, which is the name of a Grammar symbol; and a Value, which is an element from the Input Data. This Output forms a Data Block, which is the most Granular unit of the Code.

Parsers are used in the construction of Compilers, in routine Programming tasks, such as reading comma-delimited files, extracting data from formatted reports, and Verifying the Correctness of data formats.

CC (Compiler Compiler) is a parser generator for the C++ programming language. It constructs bottom-up parsers in conjunction with its preprocessor, Parse Tree. CC tutorials on the web helped us in understanding finer details about CC and Parse Tree. It is a parser generator and a lexical analyzer generator. Here CC is used to parse the verilog Source Code Input.

Parse Tree – It is a preprocessor for CC that inserts parse tree building actions at various places in the CC source. The output of Parse Tree will run through CC to create the parser.

Lex and Yaac

Lex is used to provide the Pattern Matching Description for all the constructs of verilog language. The lexer can be used to scan the input text extremely fast, independent of the number of expressions that it is trying to match. A lex lexer is almost always faster than a lexer that you might write in C by hand. Lex is a tool for building lexical analyzers or lexers. A lexer takes an arbitrary input stream and tokenizes it, i.e., divides it up into lexical tokens. This tokenized output can then be processed further, usually by yacc, or it can be the "end product. When you write a lex specification, you create a set of patterns which lex matches against the input. Each time one of the patterns matches, the lex program invokes C code that you provide which does something with the matched text. In this way a lex program divides the input into strings which we call tokens. Lex itself doesn't produce an executable program; instead it translates the lex specification into a file containing a C routine called yylex(). Your program calls yylex() to run the lexer.

Yacc is used to provide the set of Grammar Rules which defines the relationships among the various patterns returned by Lex. You code a grammar and input it to yacc. Yacc will read your grammar and generate C code for a syntax analyzer or parser. The syntax analyzer uses grammar rules that allow it to analyze tokens from the lexical analyzer and create a syntax tree. The syntax tree imposes a hierarchical structure for the tokens.

Where lex recognizes regular expressions, yacc recognizes entire grammars. Lex divides the input stream into pieces (tokens) and then yacc takes these pieces and groups them together logically

Figure 2 illustrates the file naming conventions used by lex and yacc. We'll assume our goal is to write a BASIC compiler. First, we need to specify all pattern matching rules for lex (**bas.l**) and grammar rules for yacc (**bas.y**). Commands to create our compiler, **bas.exe**, are listed below:

```
yacc –d bas.y                 # create y.tab.h, y.tab.c
lex bas.l                     # create lex.yy.c
cc lex.yy.c y.tab.c –obas.exe # compile/link
```

Yacc reads the grammar descriptions in **bas.y** and generates a syntax analyzer (parser), that includes function **yyparse**, in file **y.tab.c.** Included in file **bas.y** are token declarations. The **–d** option causes yacc to generate definitions for tokens and place them in file **y.tab.h**. Lex reads the pattern descriptions in **bas.l**, includes file **y.tab.h**, and generates a lexical analyzer that includes function **yylex**, in file **lex.yy.c**.

Finally, the lexer and parser are compiled and linked together to form the executable, **bas.exe**. From **main**, we call **yyparse** to run the compiler. Function **yyparse** automatically calls **yylex** to obtain each token.

Database

The Output of the Parser which comprises of Data Blocks of the Code, on which the Policies are applied are stored in a component called Database. This method of storing the Data Blocks in a Database proves to be more efficient for the application of Policies than applying them directly on the Output of the Parser. This is because the Policies need not be applied on All the Data Blocks resulting from the Parser.

Policy and action manager

A Policy is a deliberate plan of action to guide decisions and achieve rational outcome. Policy differs from Rules. While Rules can compel or prohibit behaviors, Policy merely guides actions toward those that are most likely to achieve a desired outcome. An Action is a Measure that needs to be taken when a Policy is encountered. Every Policy can have a Single Action or Multiple Actions to be carried out on the Code

Control unit

The Control Unit is responsible for applying the Policies, each having a single or multiple Actions on the Data Blocks retrieved from the Database.

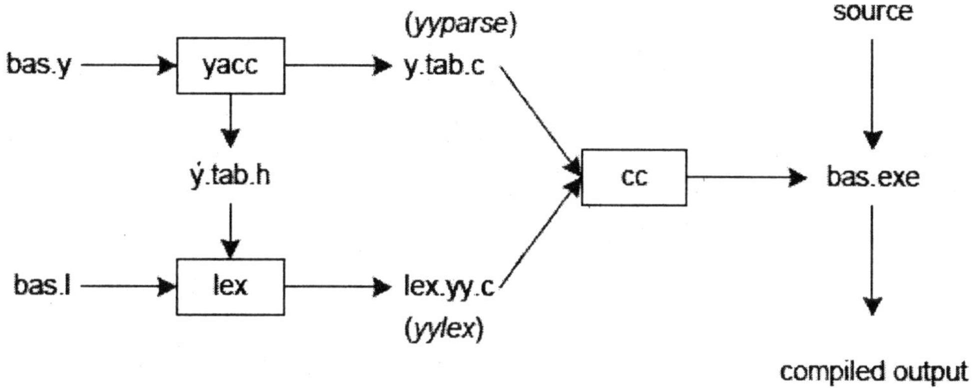

Fig. 2 Naming conventions

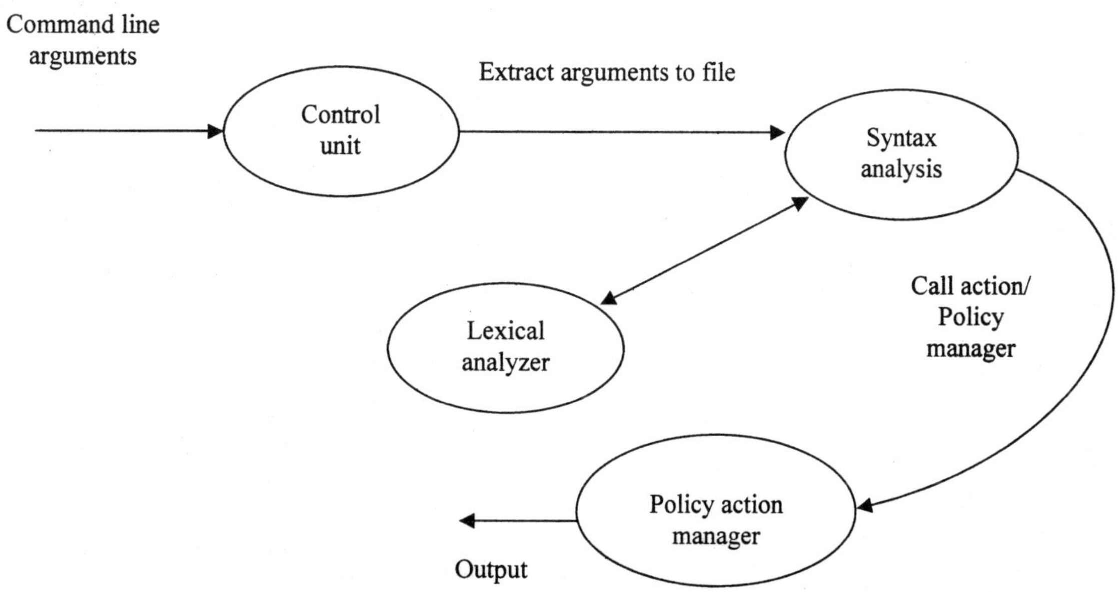

Fig. 3 Data Flow Diagram

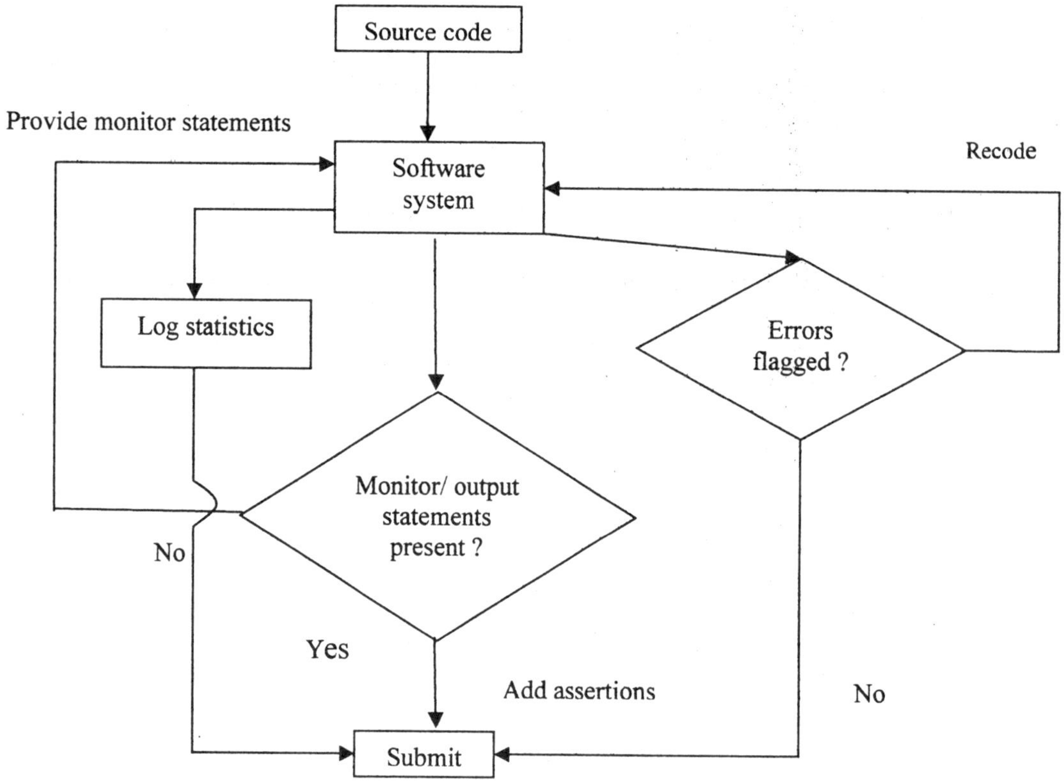

Fig. 4 Working of the system

The input source file (Fig. 3) is given to the control unit which in turn feeds it to the parser. In the parser, control is first given to the syntax analyzer which reads the input file one line at a time and then passes the control to the lexical analyzer which returns appropriate tokens back to the syntax analyzer. Upon the successful recognition of a grammar rule the syntax analyzer calls the policy and action manager to take the corresponding actions based on the options given by the user and hence the output is produced.

Fig. 4 displays the integration of different functional modules of the system. Errors are flagged when the programmer does not follow the standard coding practices and the syntax of the language. Programmer re-looks the code for proper implementation of the logic when the errors are flagged. Monitor and output statements will help the person trace the flow of signals and the logic. Adding assertions in the program will help reach the point of error and corner cases.

Algorithms

Algorithms for Parser:
Algorithm lexer.l

```
%{
/* Verilog Declaration Section – Literal Block */
%}

/* Lexeme Definition Section –
   Syntax for Constructs to be parsed */ %%
 /* Translation Rules Section – Regular
    Expressions followed by Action */
 %%
 /* Auxiliary Procedures Section – Program
    Fragments needed by the Actions*/
```

Algorithm parser.y

```
%{
/* Verilog declaration Section – Literal Block
*/
%}
/* Token Definition Section – Tokens returned
   by the Lexical Analyser */
%%
/* Rules Section – Definition of Grammar
rules */
%%
/* Subroutine Section – includes routines to
handle errors and EOF conditions along with a
"main" */
```

Algorithm for control_unit.c

```
/* Preprocessor Declaration Section */
/* Function Definition Section – */
```

main()

Step 1: Extraction of Command Line Arguments to a File

Step 2: File containing the Policies to be applied is passed to the Policy/Action Manager

Step 3: Accepted Input File fed to the Parser

Algorithm for policy_actionmgr.c

/* Preprocessor Declaration Section */

/* Global Declaration Section – Arrays to keep Track of Policies and Actions */

/* Function Definition Section –

Specific functions ()

Implementation of the Actions

manager ()

Step 1: Set the Arrays based on the Policies encountered

Step 2: Call specific Functions to execute Actions corresponding to policies

3. Conclusion

The suggested methodology is quite promising as it achieves improvement in observability and readability of the program. This also helps the programmers to adopt proper coding standards. The overall effort is to reduce design verification gap and filtering of errors from reaching implementation stage. The added advantage of this methodology is the use open source softwares and the Linux environment. This will further increase verification activities.

4. Acknowledgements

We thank Niveditha, Pooja, and Gajendra for the timely help. We also thank JSSATE Management for providing facilities and AICTE for research funding.

5. References

[1] Assertion based verification, October 18 - 22, 2004 by Jack Horgan, EDACafe

[2] http://icarus.com/eda/verilog/index.html -- Free Verilog simulation and synthesis tool/ parser.

[3] http://en.wikipedia.org/wiki/Yacc -- AT&T Yacc is the classical parser generator that comes with Unix

[4] http://accent.compilertools.net/ -- A parser generator that works for all grammars without any restrictions.

[5] http://www.ics.uci.edu/~arcadia/Aflex-Ayacc/aflex-ayacc.html -- Aflex and Ayacc are similar to the Unix tools Lex and Yacc, but they are written in Ada and generate Ada output.

[6] http://invisible-island.net/byacc/byacc.htm -- Berkeley Yacc is a public domain LALR(1) parser generator

[7] http://www.sugawara-systems.com/ -- Veritak is a commertial Verilog HDL Compiler/Simulator that supports the major Verilog 2001 HDL features.

[8] http://snverilog.sourceforge.net/ -- It parses verilog code into a database that can be used to navigate files, trace connectivity, and find modules and signals in the design.

[9] Jean-Yves Brunel, Marco Di Natale, Alberto Ferrari Paolo Giusto, Luciano Lavagno SoftContract: an Assertion-Based Software Development Process that Enables Design-by-Contract- Proceedings of the Design, Automation and Test in Europe Conference and Exhibition (DATE'04) 1530-1591/04 $20.00 © 2004 IEEE-- - This paper discusses a model-based design flow for requirements in distributed embedded software development.

[10] Kenneth M. Butler, Rohit KapurS, M. Ray Mercer, Doli E. Ross - The roles of controllability and observability in design for test- - IEEE VLSI Test Simposium 1992

Extraction of MOS Device Parameters from C-V Measurement, using VEE Pro Software

Viranjay M. Srivastava
Jaypee University of Information Technology, Solan, H.P., India
viranjaymohan@gmail.com

Abstract

A procedure to characterize oxide and conductor layers that are grown or deposited on semiconductor is by studying the characteristics of a MOS capacitor, that is formed of the conductor (Metal) – insulator - semiconductor layers. For a capacitor formed of Metal-silicon dioxide-silicon layers with an oxide thickness of 528 Å (measured optically), some of the material parameters were found from the curve drawn through Visual Engineering Environment Programming (VEE Pro) software. In this research, to find good result i.e. for recalibration of the probes, vary the voltage with smaller increments and perform the measurements by varying the voltage from +5V to -5V and then back to +5V again. All these experiments completed in BEL Laboratory.

1. Introduction

The real importance of capacitance-voltage curve (C-V) measurement techniques is that, a large number of device parameters can be extracted from two seemingly simple curves: high frequency C-V curve and quasistatic C-V curve. These parameters can provide critical device and process information.

We can divide the parameters into three groups.

1. Includes typical MOS device parameters such as flatband voltage, threshold voltage, etc.
2. Oxide charge parameters, includes interface trap charge density, mobile ion charge density, etc.
3. Consists of doping-related parameters.

Also using C-t data, carrier generation lifetime and recombination lifetime can be extracted

This research addresses the following parameters that can be extracted from a high-frequency C-V (HF-CV) curve:

1. Oxide thickness
2. Flat band capacitance and flat band voltage
3. Threshold voltage
4. Calculating the metal-semiconductor work function difference [1].

Using the VEE Pro Software with my programming to stores data on Excel sheet parameters can be automatically calculated from data at the end of the C-V test, and then be automatically entered into the Data worksheet for the test.

2. Experiment

For the calculation of above four parameters, I have to go through the following processes.

2.1 Extracting the Oxide Thickness

For a relatively thick oxide (>200 Å), extracting the oxide thickness is fairly simple. The oxide capacitance (C_{OX}) is the high-frequency capacitance when the device is biased for strong accumulation. In the strong accumulation region, the MOS-Capacitor acts like a parallel plate capacitor and the oxide thickness may be calculated from C_{OX} and the gate area using the following equation:

$$Tox = A.\epsilon ox/Cox \quad (1)$$

Here I have,

A is area of metal= $10^{-2}cm^2$,

$\epsilon ox = 34.515*10^{-14}$ F-cm^{-1},

Cox is Oxide capacitance measured by C-V curve(Accumulation Region) = 6.5 pF

So by calculation of above equation (1), I got the value of T_{OX} = 531 Å

2.2 Extracting the Flatband Capacitance and Flatband Voltage

Application of a certain gate voltage, the flatband voltage (V_{FB}) results in the disappearance of band bending. At this point, known as the flatband condition, the semiconductor band is said to become flat. Because the band is flat, the surface potential is zero (with the reference potential being taken as the bulk potential deep in the semiconductor). Flatband voltage and its shift are widely used to extract other device parameters, such as oxide charges.

I can identify V_{FB} from the C-V curve. One way is to use the flatband capacitance method. In this method, the ideal value of the flatband capacitance (C_{FB}) is calculated using equations (2) and (3). Once the value of C_{FB} is known, the value of V_{FB} can be obtained from the C-V curve data, by interpolating between the closest gate-to-substrate (V_{GS}) values ([1] Page no.487–488)

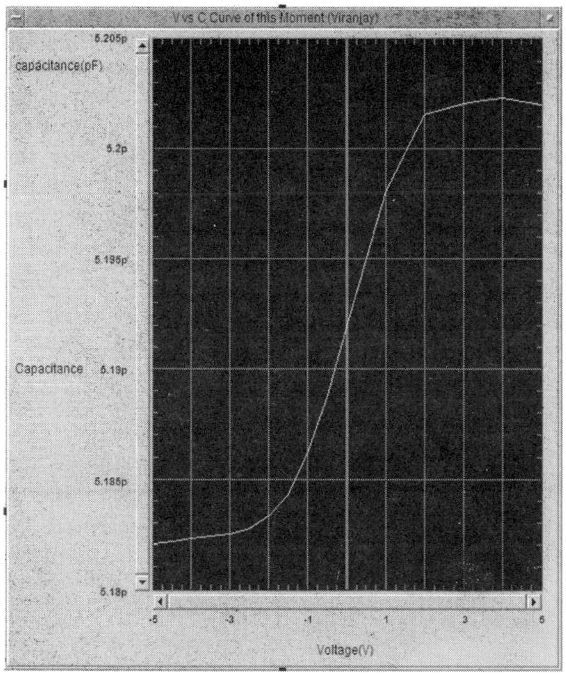

Fig. 1 Capacitance vs Gate voltage for a 1m.m. x 1m.m. capacitor

Equation (2) calculates the Debye length parameter (λ) that is used in equation (3). Based on the doping profile, the calculation of λ requires one of the following doping concentrations: N at 90% of W_{MAX} [1], I can put N_A (bulk doping concentration for a p-type, acceptor, material), or a N_D (bulk doping concentration for an n-type, donor, material).

The flatband capacitance method is invalid when the interfaces trap charge density (D_{IT}) becomes very large (10^{12}– 10^{13} per cm^2 or greater).

$$\lambda_D = \sqrt{\frac{\varepsilon_S kT}{q^2 N_x}} \qquad (2)$$

where kT is the thermal energy at room temperature= 4.046×10^{-21} J, and $N_X = N_A$ or $N_X = N_D$ and λ_D is the extrinsic Debye length.

Now for flatband condition,

$$C_{FB} = \frac{C_{OX} \cdot \varepsilon_S . A / \lambda_D}{C_{OX} + \varepsilon_S . A / \lambda_D} \qquad (3)$$

where C_{FB} is the flatband capacitance (pF), C_{OX} is the oxide capacitance (pF),

ϵ_S is the permittivity of the substrate material (F/cm), $\epsilon_S = 11.7*8.85*10^{-14}$ Fcm^{-2} and A is the gate area (cm^2), so by solving the equation (2) and (3), I got the value of $\lambda_D=1.19*10^{-5}$ cm as well as C_{FB}= 3.8433 pF.

The extrinsic Debye length is an idea borrowed from plasma physics [2]. In semiconductors, majority carriers can move freely. The motion is similar to plasma. Any electrical interaction has a limited range. The Debye length is used to represent this interaction range. Essentially, the Debye length indicates how far an electrical event can be sensed within a semiconductor.

2.3 Extracting the Threshold Voltage

The turn-on region for a MOSFET corresponds to the inversion region on its C-V plot. When a MOSFET is turned on, the channel formed corresponds to strong generation of inversion charges. It is these inversion charges that conduct current. When a source and drain are added to a MOS- Capacitor to form a MOSFET, a p-type MOS- Capacitor becomes an n-type MOSFET (n-channel MOSFET). Conversely, an n-type MOS-Capacitor becomes a p channel MOSFET [3].

The threshold voltage (V_{TH}) is the point on the C-V curve where the surface potential ($\O_S$) equals twice the bulk potential ($\O_S = 2\O_B$). This curve point corresponds to the onset of strong inversion.

For an enhancement-mode MOSFET, V_{TH} corresponds to the point where the device begins to conduct. The physical meaning of the threshold voltage is the same for both a MOS-C C-V curve and a MOSFET I-V curve. However, in practice, the numeric V_{TH} value for a MOSFET may be slightly different, due to the particular method used to extract the threshold voltage. I can calculate V_{TH} from a C-V curve by following formula:

$$V_{TH} = \left[\pm \frac{A}{C_{OX}} \sqrt{4\varepsilon_S q |N_{BULK}| |\phi_B|} + 2|\phi_B| \right] + V_{FB} \qquad (4)$$

where N_{BULK} is the bulk doping $10^{16}cm^{-3}$, $\O_B$ is the bulk potential= –0.344V,

V_{FB} is the flatband potential= –0.954–(–0.09846) V = –0.86V.

After calculation by formula, I got V_{TH}= 0.37V

2.4 Calculation of Metal-Semiconductor Work Function Difference

The metal-semiconductor work function difference ($\O_{MS}$) is commonly referred to as simply the work function. It contributes to the shift in V_{FB} from the ideal zero value, along with the effective oxide charge ([2] pp. 395–402 and [3] pp. 462–477).

The work function represents the difference in work necessary to remove an electron from the gate and from the substrate.

$Ø_{MS}$ is needed in the next subsection, "Extracting Effective and Total Bulk Oxide Charge." Therefore, it is derived here as follows:

$$Ø_{MS} = Ø_M - [Ø_S + (E_G/2) - Ø_B] \quad (5)$$

where $Ø_M$ is the metal work function= 4.1V,

$Ø_S$ is the substrate material work function (electron affinity) = 4.15V,

E_G is the substrate material bandgap = 1.12V,

$Ø_B$ is the bulk potential = –0.344V.

For silicon, silicon dioxide, and aluminum (for p type Si)

$$Ø_{MS} = 4.1 - [4.15 + (1.12/2) - (-0.344)] \quad (6)$$

Therefore,

$$Ø_{MS} = -0.954V \quad (7)$$

Similarly we can get for n type Si, $Ø_{MS}$ = -0.27V and

$$Ø_{MS} = -0.61 - (kT/q).\ln (N_{BULK}/n_I). \text{ (Doped Type)} \quad (8)$$

where n_I is the intrinsic carrier concentration $=1.2*10^6*C_{MAX}*\Delta V_{FB}/D^2.\text{ions/cm}^2$ $=1.2*10^6*5*0.6*25^2= 2.15*10^{10}\ cm^{-3}$ and Dope Type is +1 for **p-type** materials and –1 for **n-type** materials.

For example, for an MOS capacitor with an Al gate and **p-type** silicon (N_{BULK} = $10^{16}\ cm^{-3}$) which gives $Ø_{MS}$ = –0.95V [4].

Also, for the same gate and **n-type** silicon (N_{BULK} = $10^{16}\ cm^{-3}$), $Ø_{MS}$ = –0.27V. The supply voltage of modern CMOS devices is decreasing.

3. Result

The readings & calculation of the above said four parameters oxide thickness, Flat band capacitance and flat band voltage, Threshold voltage and metal-semiconductor work function difference are shown in the experiment details with readings which is taken from the data stored in sheet, produced after the execution of VEE Pro software for the wafer of MOS fabrication of 528 Å thick oxide layer [5]. This result is also verified by the SUPREM simulator.

4. Conclusion

The goal is to achieve a minimal work-function difference between the gate and the semiconductor, while maintaining the conductive properties of the gate. Based on the C-V characterization of a MOS capacitor with VEE Pro software in BEL lab [6], which resulted in erroneous values of material parameters mainly the substrate dopant concentration, on which most of the other parameters are based. The readings stored in excel sheet can be used for further processing. In this experiment I can also identified the improper contact of the probes with the wafer surface as the most probable cause of that along with the possibility of going unintentionally into deep depletion or having the equipment improperly calibrated.

This experiment can be used in future for measuring its sanitation of pipes, furnaces and to calibrate the parameters in fabrication Lab before the fabrication of a device.

5. References

[1] Thamos J. Mego" Guidelines for Interpreting CV data" *Solid State Technology*, p.p. 159-163, May'1990

[2] Sze, S.M., "*Physics of Semiconductor Devices*", 2nd edition. Wiley, New York (1985)

[3] Nicollian, E.H. and Brews, J.R., "*MOS Physics and Technology*", Wiley, New York (1982).

[4] Thamos J. Mego" On line C-V doping profile measurement of low dose ion implant"*IEEE trans. on electron devices*, vol. 27, no. 12, pp. 2268-1173, Dec'1980.

[5] "MOS Application note-1", *MSI electronics*, woodside, N.Y.-1137(Manual).

[6] "Agilent VEE pro user's Guide", Agilent Company.

Intelligent Model for Agent Based Secure Web Services Discovery

V.Prasath, D. Kiran Kumar Reddy and M. Thirumaran
Dept. of Computer Science, Pondicherry Engg.College
prasathvijayan@gmail.com *kirankumarpec@gmail.com* *thirumaran.pec@gmail.com*

Abstract

Web services are becoming increasingly important in the enterprise sector and as a result, the security of web services will become paramount. A web service security requires authentication, confidentiality, integrity and Non-reputation. The Universal Description, Discovery and Integration (UDDI) registries do not have the ability to publish the security related information. However the defined web services security can only detect known threats but in the internet resources new threats has become challenging to the service provider and consumer in order to consume the services in secure way. In this paper we describe the architecture of our agent based secure workflow system that can apply security to web services environment to protect against unknown threats and vulnerabilities based on security diagnose of each transaction..

1. Introduction

Web services are relatively new technologies that allow a client to communicate with a server by sending messages using the HTTP protocol[3]. However, most organizations are still hesitating to deploy Web services in a WAN. One important reason is the security of Web services. Currently, the society of Web services have produced a series of specifications in order to enhance the security of Web services from basic WS-Security that aims at end-to-end security to WS-Trust, WS-Secure Conversation and WS-Secure Policy that aim at securing exchange of multiple messages in multiple trust domains with different local policies[8]. In principle, Web services can run on many geographically distributed computers, and thus raise many security-related issues[6]. We concentrate here on one key issue, providing security for web services in dynamic nature. In particular we are interested in focusing on web service security. This concept is implemented in ASWSD through the aggregation of several intelligent agents to tackle future threats, and through specialisations of intelligent agent capabilities to deal with known threats or risks. Such a mechanism is unlike a rule-based detection mechanism which can not detect unforeseen attacks.

In this paper we explain the architecture of integration of web services security with our secure workflow system and also, explain how to enhance security against future risks and threats of web service is achieved. We believe that security diagnose can be used to improve the secure web service applications. A brief description of our agent-based framework system overview is given in Section 2. In Section 3 we explain intelligent architecture for agent based secure web service discovery. In Section 4 we explain the architecture evaluation of our architecture using SAAM. An example of secure searching the web services will be illustrated in Section 5. The concluding remarks are presented in Section 6.

2. System Overview

Fig.1 shows a conceptual view of the proposed system architecture. The design of secure web services discovery is the key for web services security. The technique facilitates the security diagnose between agents [2]. Therefore it is feasible to realize the automatic system of secure web services based on the agent. Fig.1 explains how to achieve automated secure web service discovery, retrieval and to update new threats.

- Automatic Web service discovery involves automatically locating the web services required by consumers. We should check results satisfy the security requirements.
- Automatic Web service execution involves an agent automatically executing an identified web service threats.
- Automatic Web service security diagnose involves execution of existing threats test case to match, if request is not return to the consumer then security diagnose will be verified for each transaction.

3. Agent Based Secure Web Services Discovery (ASWSD)

We propose a model called ASWD for secure web services discovery. Most business communication needs secure transaction over network path. Our architecture is based on the two phase access model.

During the first phase services provider need to register their services should accomplish the security requirements given by the UDDI registry. In this phase UDDI has to execute web service test case to find out the provider services has threat that are vulnerable to the consumer. If security requirements fail to met, then it will inform to the web service provider to support security requirements that needs to register their service into the registry. Web service provider provides permission to UDDI that introduce new add on security features into service during registration. Web service consumers are able to retrieve web services from the UDDI registry, according to their retrieval conditions, and subsequently perform the services with required security needs. During the second phase when user sends web request to the target service with the session

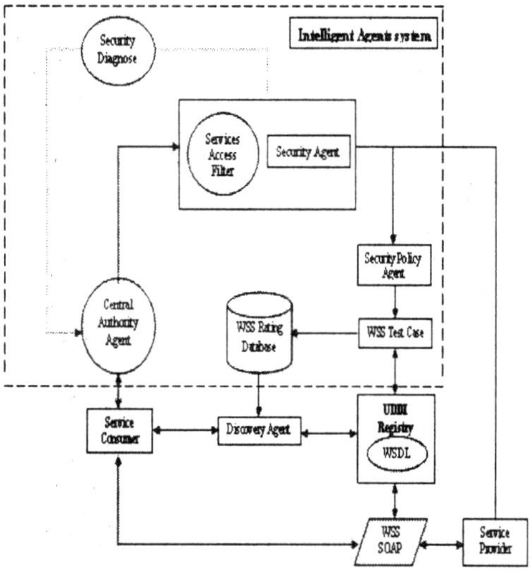

Fig. 1 Architecture of ASWSD

information in the target address, the security agent will trace the user name from the target address. Based on the current information services access filter will allow or deny the user to access the web service. For each transaction, security agent will process an information regarding new threat diagnose. Security diagnose will inform to the central authority agent to deny the access to particular transaction without required authority certificate processing. This will reduce new threats attack to the registry and provide successful access to the service consumer to avoid any misuse.

3.1 Security Policy Manager

The Security Manager describes the security requirement that service provider needs to be registering their WSDL into the registry. WSS test case(Fig. 2) describe a testing methodology for web services security and outline a process that can be adopted to evaluate web services security rating. WSS Test Case can be classified according to different categories of threat faced by web services. WSS security rating should be calculated based on the specific security mechanisms that incorporated into web services, latency of the web service with and without the above WSS settings. Based on these setting non functional requirements for web services providing similar functionalities should be calculated and ranked.

3.2 Discovery Agent

A discovery agent receives service requests containing specifications for functional, security requirements from the service consumer, finds the services that meet the specified criteria, and then returns a list of services to the consumer. Discovery should be based on WSS security rating for concerned request. The list of available services will be return to the service consumer with order priority. This avoids the overhead of discovery mechanism to search secure web services over UDDI registry for consumers needs.

3.3 Security Agent

The proposal system is based on the technique of web services security threats that are faced by the consumer during transaction. It also requires for UDDI services to prevent from new threats that can affect the user transaction. It will monitor the user transaction and has to maintain the transaction database for security traffic. Any new security symptoms will be observed or existing threat has been detected then it will inform to security diagnose for further notification to the central authority agent deny the particular user transaction. Once Central Authority Agent will revised the new threat and apply to test case model with proper permission from security manager.

3.4 Security Diagnose

It need to observe and analyse the behaviour of each transaction, they also need to be able to recognise unusual or uncommon activities/conditions of both user and provider applications by analysing the previous and common transaction activities. The aggregation of components in a system can protect against unknown errors while separated functionalities of the components can only detect known errors. This concept is implemented in ASWSD through the aggregation of several intelligent agents to tackle future threats, and through specialisations of intelligent agent capabilities to deal with known threats or risks. Such a mechanism is unlike a rule-based detection mechanism which can not detect unforeseen attacks.

3.5 Web Services Access Filter

Now we describe the filtering algorithm towards the above objective.

Input: User request with Security Token
Output: Allow/Deny User Request against threat action

Incoming Request (Req)

{ if (Request Id is in Threat List)

{ deny the request

if (check whether malicious user)}

else

{verify the central authority agent

certificate for access}

}

else if (incoming access will make load

to server (dos attack) || perform malicious

action against security agent test case)

{deny service temporarily and check

authority}

else
{allow access to service that available in the registry}

Fig. 2 Filtering Algorithm

3.6 Ranking and Selection Algorithm

When the discovery agent receives a discovery request, it executes Func_Match which returns a list of services that meet the functional requirements. If a security requirement has been specified then Sec_Search is executed next on the set of services and it returns a subset of services that meet the security requirements in accordance with the WSS rating scores.

Input: User request with specified security criteria
Output: Secure match set of services from UDDI

U (H): Select all available services that exists in UDDI
WSS (H): Select services that web security policy applied

1. for each web services WS_i in U (H)
   //find services that meet functional Requirements
2. Fun_Search = Functional_Match(functional Requirements);
3. if WSS(H) requirements specified then
4. Sec_Search=Secuirty_Match(Fun_Search ,WSS(H) specified);
5. if WSS(H) ratings specified then
   //select all available services in U(H) that matches with security information
6. return output of S ec_Search available services in WSS_i in U (H)
7. else
8. return o utput of Sec_Search available services WS_i in U (H)

Fig. 3 Ranking and Selection Algorithm

4. Evaluation of Architecture

The proposed architecture is evaluated by the Software Architecture Analysis Method (SAAM). All the scenarios corresponding to each application of the agent based secure web services discovery are listed and evaluated. The steps corresponding to SAAM for evaluating the agent web services security are described as follows:

4.1 Scenario Development

The Scenarios chosen for evaluation of the architecture are given below:
Scenario 1: Authentication and Access Control
Scenario 2: Integration with existing security environment
Scenario3: Automated threat response
Scenario 4: Ability to retrieve related domain services
Scenario 5: Language neutral
Scenario 6: Support for easy up gradation
Scenario 7: Support for security standards
Scenario 8: Malicious attack protection
Scenario 9: Data collection
Scenario 10: Encrypted Data
Scenario 11: Service virtualization

Scenario 12: Ability to incorporate other functional behaviors that rely on secure service discovery.

Scenario 13: Fail negatively

4.2 Scenario Classification

The Scenarios are classified as direct or indirect with respect to the supportability of the scenario in the abstract architecture shown in Fig. 4.

Scenario 1	Direct
Scenario 2	Indirect
Scenario 3	Indirect
Scenario 4	Direct
Scenario 5	Indirect
Scenario 6	Indirect
Scenario 7	Indirect
Scenario 8	Indirect
Scenario 9	Indirect
Scenario 10	Direct
Scenario 11	Indirect
Scenario 12	Indirect

Fig. 4 Scenario Interaction

4.3 Scenario Evaluation

To evaluate the architecture based on scenarios, neglecting direct scenarios, indirect scenarios has to be considered for calculating number of components affected in architecture. Each of the indirect and direct scenarios is evaluated as follows:

Scenario 1: This scenario requires that the user should get the authentication and access rights to their request before accessing the web services that present in the registry. To provide for this central authority agent has to provide security token to the user to establish a connection to access the web services the web services instead of contacting to the UDDI registry.

Scenario 2: This scenario is supported in architecture; it can be easily integrated with other security environment

Scenario 3: This scenario needs updated web services security test case database for frequently access the new threat issues while user queries the web services.

Scenario 4: This scenario requires discovery agent component to use efficient selection algorithm to retrieve the security services from related domain based on wss rating information.

Scenario 5: The proposed architecture should support for implementation in any language.

Scenario 6: This scenario demands the proposed architecture to support for adding new components or subcomponents within a component.

Scenario 7: This scenario needs standards security format for transferring messages in secured manner, where there is possibility of getting unknown or non-standard security format.

Scenario 8: This scenario requires the architecture to possess the security properties to protect the web services and registry from serious attack. It supports protection against the latest Web Services and XML-based attacks.

Scenario 9: This scenario requires architecture to be risks assessment to protect the service from fault and failure from attacks. An audit data is crucial for identifying and diagnosing attack as well as proving compliance.

Scenario 10: This scenario reveals that if any data bit is missed or error bit is occurred in encryption of messages in communication.

Scenario 11: This scenario requires the architecture to be used in secure environment. Since it hiding details on back end resources.

Scenario 12: The interfaces provided between the components are more flexible and hence this architecture requires only minimal changes for the support of this scenario.

Scenario 13: This scenario requires the architecture to possess the security properties across all Web services traffic and must be applied in a consistent manner regardless of the different types of technologies being connected in the web service network.

4.4 Scenario Interaction

Scenario interaction is to reveal changes in components when two or more scenarios affect components in architecture. Table: 1 shows the list of scenarios which affects the component description.

Components	**Scenario affecting the component**
Service Consumer	Scenario 2,Scenario 9
Security Diagnose	Scenario 2,Scenario 7, Scenario 9
Central Authority Agent	Scenario 1,Scenario9
Security Policy Agent	Scenario 1,Scenario 2
WSS Rating	Scenario 2
Discovery Agent	Scenario 8,Scenario 9
Service Provider	Scenario 11
Security Agent	Scenario 7, Scenario 8
WSS Test Case	Scenario 3, Scenario9, Scenario13

The Fig. 5 shows scenario interaction chart corresponds to table 1, in which x- axis contains components in architecture and y-axis contains scenarios which are indirectly affecting the components.

4.5 Overall Evaluation

The Software Architecture Analysis Method (SAAM) reveals that proposed architecture for agent based secure web services discovery is flexible and maintainability is also high since in scenario interaction table shows components which are not affected by more than three scenarios. Hence the proposed architecture proved it possesses high quality attributes in it.

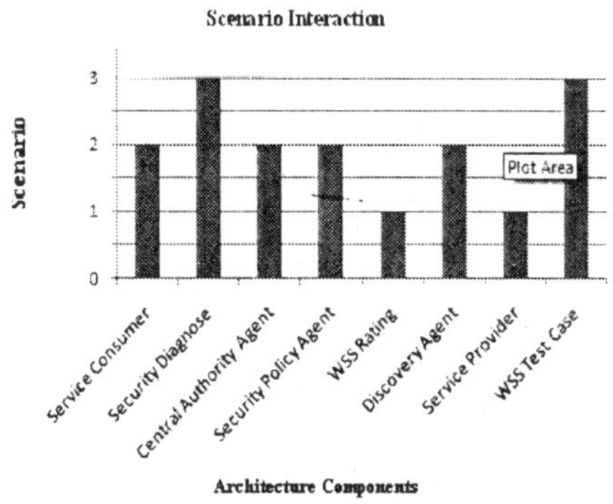

Fig. 5. Scenario Interaction Chart

5. Example

In this section, we give an example that involves threat dos attack from valid user. We assumed that the consumer want to access the web services that available in the UDDI. The feature here is session based filter. In the current implementation, we do not focus on who can login and retrieve a WSDL file. This is important as well because if some attackers can easily register and get many user names, they can retrieve many valid session identities by themselves directly. We take a session based approach that each valid Web service request have to present its session identity with it. We designed a services access based filtering algorithm that can allocate the processing capability of a service among different users using the recorded session information. This filtering algorithm can guarantee that when the working load is high, the requests from DoS will be discarded, so the normal request can still come in and get processed with a reasonable response time.

6. Conclusion

With an increasing number of web services providing similar functionalities, security has become one of the most critical issues. UDDI has no way to identify the secure web services when multiple service providers are now providing similar services. We proposed an architecture called ASWSD to automate agent based secure web service discovery and retrieval for aggregation of several intelligent agents to tackle future threats, and risks for both consumer and provider that allow efficient access to web services present in the registry with dynamic nature. This paper also identifies and details an approach to web services security testing techniques and diagnose processes. It aims to standardized process for evaluating security mechanisms in web services. A discovery agent helps finding services that meet the functional and security requirements specified by the consumers. It also presents the WSS rating algorithm to match the consumer security needs based on rating attributes and top ranked services are returned to the service consumers.

7. References

[1] Kassem Saleh and Maryam Habil, "The Security Requirements Behavior Model for Trustworthy Software", International MCETECH Conference on e-Technologies 2008 pp 235 - 238.

[2] Janette Hicks, Madhusudhan Govindaraju, Weiyi Meng, "Enhancing Discovery of Web Services through Optimized Algorithms" IEEE International Conference on Granular Computing 2007 pp 685 - 698.

[3] Colin Atkinson, Philipp Bostan, Oliver Hummel and Dietmar Stoll, "A Practical Approach to Web Service Discovery and Retrieval", IEEE International Conference on Web Services (ICWS 2007).

[4] Janette Hicks, Madhusudhan Govindaraju, Weiyi Meng, "Search Algorithms for Discovery of Web Services", IEEE International Conference on Web Services (ICWS 2007).

[5] Artem Vorobiev and Jun Han, "Specifying Dynamic Security Properties of Web Service Based Systems", IEEE Computer Society 2006.

[6] Jie Xu, Erica Y. Yang, and Keith H. Bennett, "A Practical Approach to Secure Web Services", Proceedings of the Ninth IEEE International Symposium on Object and Component-Oriented Real-Time Distributed Computing 2006.

[7] Slim Trabelsi Jean-Christphe Pazzaglia Yves Roudier, "Secure Web service discovery: overcoming challenges of ubiquitous computing", Proceedings of the European Conference on Web Services (ECOWS'06).

[8] David Geer, "Taking Steps to Secure Web Services", Technology News, October 2003.

[9] Tiantian Zhang, Junzhou Luo, Weining Kong "An Agent-based Web Service Searching Model", 9th International Conference on Computer Supported Cooperative Work in Design Proceedings pp 390 – 295.

A Comparative Study of Various Techniques Implemented to Improve the Performance of Flash ADC

Prof.S.S.Khot[1], Ms R.P. Ghugardare[2] and Dr.M.S.Sutaone[3]
[1]Asst Prof, Dept of E&TC Sinhgad Academy of Engg, Kondhwa, Pune-411048
[2]Lecturer, Dept of E&TC KN College of Engg, Vadgaon, Pune-411041
[3]Professor, Dept of E&TC Government College of Engg, Pune-411005
khotsir@yahoo.co.in rakhi_g_14@yahoo.co.in mssutaone@gmail.com

Abstract

There are various architectures of the ADC; out of these architectures FLASH ADC architecture which is also known as parallel architecture is fastest of all. This paper represents the basic architecture of the flash ADC, advantages of this architecture over other architectures and different techniques to improve the performance of flash ADC.

1. Architecture

Flash ADCs (sometimes called parallel ADCs) are the fastest type of ADC and use large numbers of comparators. An N-bit flash ADC consists of 2N resistors and 2^N-1 comparators arranged as in Fig. 1.

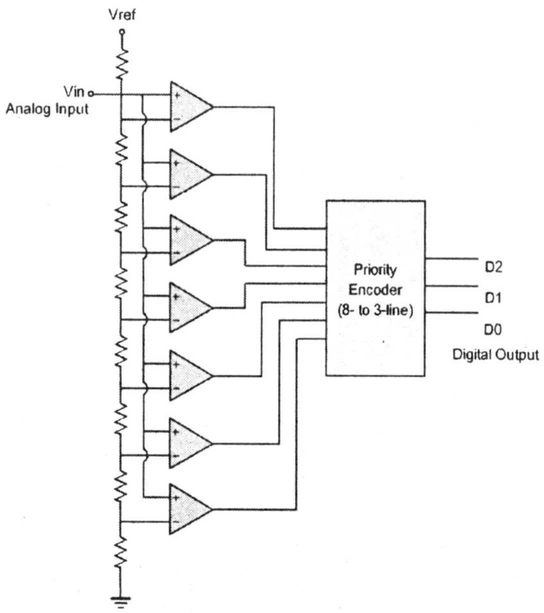

Fig. 1 Flash ADC

Each comparator has a reference voltage from the resistor string which is 1 LSB higher than that of the one below it in the chain. For a given input voltage, all the comparators below a certain point will have their input voltage larger than their reference voltage and a "1" logic output, and all the comparators above that point will have a reference voltage larger than the input voltage and a "0" logic output. The 2^N-1 comparator outputs therefore behave in a way analogous to a mercury thermometer, and the output code at this point is sometimes called a *thermometer* code. Since 2^N-1 data outputs are not really practical, they are processed by a decoder to generate an N-bit binary output.

The input signal is applied to all the comparators at once, so the thermometer output is delayed by only one comparator delay from the input, and the encoder N-bit output by only a few gate delays on top of that, so the process is very fast. However, the architecture uses large numbers of resistors and comparators and is limited to low resolutions, and if it is to be fast, each comparator must run at relatively high power levels. Hence, the problems of flash ADCs include limited resolution, high power dissipation because of the large number of high speed comparators (especially at sampling rates greater than 50 MSPS), and relatively large (and therefore expensive) chip sizes. In addition, the resistance of the reference resistor chain must be kept low to supply adequate bias current to the fast comparators, so the voltage reference has to source quite large currents. [1]

2. Flash Vs Other ADC Architectures

A. Flash vs. Successive Approximation Register (SAR) ADCs

In a SAR converter, the bits are decided by a single high-speed, high-accuracy comparator one bit at a time (from the MSB down to the LSB), by comparing the analog input with a DAC whose output is updated by previously decided bits and thus successively approximates the analog input. This serial nature of the SAR limits its speed to no more than a few Msps, while flash ADCs exceed giga-sample per second (Gsps) conversion rates. SAR converters are available in resolutions up to 16-bits. Flash ADCs are typically limited to around 8-bits. The slower speed also allows the SAR ADC to be much lower in power. For example, the MAX1106, an 8-bit SAR converter, uses 100 μA at 3.3 V with a conversion rate of 25 ksps. The MAX104 dissipates 5.25 W. This is about 16,000 times higher power consumption compared to the MAX1106; but also 40,000 times faster in terms of its maximum sampling rate.[2]

B. Flash vs. Pipelined ADCs

A pipelined ADC employs a parallel structure in which each stage works on one to a few bits of successive samples concurrently. This improves speed at the expense of power and latency. However, each pipelined stage is much slower than a flash section. The pipelined ADC requires accurate amplification in the DACs and interstage amplifiers, and these stages have to settle to the desired linearity level. By contrast, in a flash ADC, the comparator only needs to be low offset and be able to resolve its inputs to a digital level (i.e., there is no linear settling time involved). However, some flash converters require preamplifiers to drive the Comparators. Gain linearity needs to be carefully specified.

Pipelined converters are capable of conversion speeds of around 100 Msps at 8 to 14-bit resolutions. An example of a pipelined converter is the MAX1449, a 105 MHz, 10-bit ADC. For a given resolution, pipelined ADCs are around 10 times slower compared to flash converters of similar resolution. Pipelined converters are possibly the optimal architecture for ADCs that need to sample at rates up to around 100Msps with resolution at 10-bits and above. At resolutions of up to 10-bits, and conversion rates above a few hundred Msps, flash ADCs dominate. Interestingly, there are some situations where flash ADCs are hidden inside a converter employing architecture to increase its speed. This is the case, for example, in the MAX1200; a 16-bit pipelined ADC that includes an internal 5-bit flash ADC. [2]

C. Flash vs. Integrating ADCs

Single, dual and multi-slope ADCs can achieve high resolutions of 16-bits or more are relatively inexpensive and dissipate materially less power. These devices support very low conversion rates, typically less than a few hundred samples per second. Most applications are for monitoring DC signals in the instrumentation and industrial markets. This architecture competes with sigma-delta converters. [2]

D. Flash vs. Sigma-Delta ADCs

Flash ADCs do not compete with this architecture because currently the achievable conversion rates differ by up to two orders of magnitude. The sigma-delta architecture is suitable for applications with much lower bandwidth, typically less than 1 MHz, with resolutions in the 12 to 16-bit range. These converters are capable of the highest resolution possible in ADCs. They require simpler anti-alias filters (if needed) to bandlimit the signal prior to conversion. They trade speed for resolution by over sampling, followed by filtering to reduce noise. However, these devices are not always efficient for multi-channel applications. This architecture can be implemented by using sampled data filters (also known as modulators) or continuous time filters. For higher frequency conversion rates the continuous time architecture is potentially capable of reaching conversion rates in the hundreds of Msps range with low resolution of 6 to 8-bits. This approach is still in the early research and development stage and offers competition to flash alternatives in the lower conversion rate range. Another interesting use of a flash ADC is as a building block inside a sigma-delta circuit to increase the conversion rate of the ADC.

3. Different Techniques used to Improve the Performance of Flash ADC

1. A circuit design using an integrating resistor network to improve DNL (differential nonlinearity). Two resistors connected in series between comparator cells average error sources. While significantly improving the DNL, the extra resistors are low-tolerance and do not affect power dissipation or input capacitance. The resistors are minimum-width and are placed in the empty spaces between comparator cells in an existing 8b flash converter and have no impact on die size. [3]
2. To reduce the large number of comparators, A/D conversion is done in two steps (i.e. sub ranging) for an example 8-bit ADC. The result of the first 4-bit conversion (coarse step) is converted back to analog via an ultra-fast 4-bit D/A converter (DAC), and then applied to a difference amplifier (with gain K). The residue (with K = 1 [3]) or the amplified residue (with k=24[4]) is then converted by the second Chit conversion stage (fine step). The two sets of data are accumulated in the 8-bit output register. Since the two steps of this class of flash ADC's require two clock cycles, it is called "half-flash". Reducing the conversion speed to one half k the price for reducing the number of comparators from (2^n-1) to $2(2^{n/2}-1)$ for an n-bit ADC. [4]
3. Flash-type analog-to-digital converters (ADC's) presenting a nonlinear behavior, i.e., having nonequally spaced threshold levels, may introduce harmonic distortion that can be reduced by employing large-amplitude dither-based conversion

techniques. However, large-scale dithering is difficult to implement and, in addition, severely reduces the ADC input dynamic range. a new ADC architecture is presented based on ordinary flash conversion and dynamic element matching, that strongly reduces nonlinear distortion. It eliminates the need for large-scale dither signals by randomizing the resistor positions in the resistor string used to generate the voltage references. [5]

4. The resistive ladder divides the converter reference voltages in a set of 2^n reference voltages (with n the number of bits of the A/D converter), which are compared in parallel with the analog input signal. A logic encoder converts the thermometer code generated by the comparators into a Gray code. are the output-drivers after the dynamic latches slices of the implemented 6 bit ADC. The schematic has been divided into three parts: the pre-amplifier, the comparator and the nand-gate. The output Si selects one of the 63 ROM-lines. [6]
5. A signal processing algorithm called dynamic element matching (DEM) can be used to reduce the effects of component mismatches in DACs [3] and ADCs thereby improving their performances. DEM algorithms dynamically rearrange the interconnections of mismatched components so that the time averages of the equivalent components at each of the component positions are nearly equal. Consequently, if the appropriate DEM algorithms are applied to the mismatched components that cause comparator mismatches and to the mismatched components that cause reference signal errors, the time averages of the ADC's comparator offsets and the time averages of the ADC's reference signals would be near their ideal values. Therefore, the time average of the ADC's transfer characteristics would be nearly ideal, and the ADC's output distortion could be reduced.[7]
6. The thermometer code-to-binary code encoder has become the bottleneck of the ultra-high speed flash ADCs. In this paper, the authors presented the fat tree thermometer codeto-binary code encoder that is highly suitable for the ultrahigh speed flash ADCs. The simulation and the implementation results show that the fat tree encoder outperforms the commonly used ROM encoder in terms of speed and power for the 6 bit CMOS flash ADC case. The speed is improved by almost a factor of 2 when using the fat tree encoder, which in fact demonstrates the fat tree encoder is an effective solution for the bottleneck problem in ultra-high speed ADCs.[8]

4. Conclusion

Thus we have seen the architecture of Flash ADC and compared it with other ADCs architectures and found that it's the fastest ADC as compared to others. But also found the disadvantages like high power consumption as well as low resolution etc. We have also seen different Design methods to improve the performance of the flash ADC's like minimizing the number of comparators, dealing with nonlinearities, preventing thermometer code from being bottle neck etc.

In some designs DNL is improved by using integrating resistors network. Large use of comparators can be avoided by doing the conversions in two steps. Harmonic distortion introduced due to non linear behaviour can be eliminated by employing large amplitude dither based conversion techniques. The resistive ladder divides the converter reference voltages in a set of 2^n reference voltages. The schematic has been divided into three parts: the pre-amplifier, the comparator and the nand-gate. The output Si selects one of the 63 ROM-lines. A signal processing algorithm called dynamic element matching (DEM) can be used to reduce the effects of component mismatches in ADCs. fat tree thermometer codeto-binary code encoder that is highly suitable for the ultrahigh speed flash ADCs.

5. References

[1] Kevin Kattrnann and Jeff Barrow "A Technique for Reducing Differential Non-Linearity Errors in Flash A/D Converters" Analog Devices Computer Labs Division, Greensboro, NC.1991IEEE

[2] Dr. Mahmoud Fawzy Wagdy Qiong Xie "Comparative ADC Performance Evaluation Using a New Emulation Model for Flash ADC Architectures", Department of Electrical Engineering. 1995 IEEE

[3] Paolo Carbone and Maurizio Caciotta "Stochastic-Flash Analog-to-Digital Conversion" 1998 IEEE.

[4] Correction K. Uyttenhove, A. Marques' and M. Steyaert "A 6-bit 1 GHz Acquisition Speed CMOS Flash ADC with Digital Error" IEEE 2000.

[5] P. Stubberud and J. W. Bruce, "An analysis of flash dynamic element matching analog to digital converters," in *IEEE Midwest Symposium on Circuits and Systems*, vol. 2, Aug. 2000, pp. 684–687.

[6] Daegyu Lee, Jincheol Yoo, Kyusun Choi, Jahan Ghaznavi "Fat tree ancoder design for ultra high speed flash ADC"

[7] Michael Choi and Asad A. Abidi, *Fellow* "A 6-b 1.3-Gsample/s A/D Converter in 0.35 um CMOS", *IEEE.*

[8] M. P, Flynn, C. Donovan, and L. Sattler, "Digital calibration incorporating redundancy of flash ADCs," *ZEEE Trum. Circuits Syst. II,* vol. *50,* no. 5, pp. 205-213, May 2003.

[9] Venkata Srinivas, Shanthi Pavan, Ashish Lachhwani, and Naga Sasidhar " A Distortion Compensating Flash Analog-to-Digital Conversion Technique", IEEE Journal of Solid-State Circuits, VOL. 41, NO. 9, pp. 1959- 1969, September 2006.

[10] K. A. Shehata, and H. F. Ragai H. Husien "design and implementation of high speed 4 bit flash ADC" Arab Academy for Science and Technology, Cairo, Egypt. 2006.

[11] www.hardwaresecrets.com.

[12] http://www.maxim-ic.com

Design and Development of Smart Card Based Quick Charger for an Electric Car

Robert Prabhakar M., Sanket Dessai, and S.G. Shivaprasad Yadav
Embedded System Design Centre,
M S Ramaiah School of Advanced Studies, Bangalore
In Collaboration with Coventry University (UK)
roby205@hotmail.com sanketdessai0808@gmail.com shivaspy@gmail.com

Abstract

The Electric vehicles (EVs) are one way of reducing vehicle emissions that contribute two-thirds of all air pollution in most cities. In order to increasingly use the electric cars there is a need to develop a smart charging station, which can charge the batteries quickly. At present, electric car companies in India do not have a smart charging station. All it has is the conventional type of charging method which takes hours to recharge the batteries.

To counter the above mentioned problems a smart card based quick charging station for electric cars has been designed. The charging station consists of a microcontroller-based system that includes a smart card RFID (Radio Frequency Identification) reader, pilot circuit, 16x2 LCD (Liquid Crystal Display) screen and 4x3 keypad. The charging station consists of six chargers. Each charger gives 35A current and 42V voltage. There are two modes of charging to be selected – min and max. In min mode, only 3 chargers are switched on giving 20-40 % charge. In max mode, 6 chargers are switched on, giving 70-90% charge. The RFID reader module plays a vital role in identification of the user, and provides better flexibility for the selection of chargers with a control algorithm implemented in MikroC. Pilot circuit is a means of control between the EVSE (Electric Vehicle Supply Equipment) and the Electric Car. The role played by the pilot circuit is important because it selects number of chargers and energizes the system. The selection of chargers is done through relays. There are two relays used for opening and closing. One relay is to switch on 3 chargers and the second relay switches on the remaining 3 chargers. The microcontroller is used in the operating of the relays. Various test cases for correctness have been executed. The system is tested for performance with minimum and maximum charging choice to the user.

1. Introduction

Electric Vehicle (EV) runs on the chemical energy stored in the rechargeable battery packs. EV doesn't have an Internal Combustion Engine (ICE) like the gasoline vehicles but rather electric motors. So, an EV receives its power from the rechargeable battery packs. But it is the electric motor, which causes the EV to move i.e., the wheels are set in motion by the power delivered by the electric motor. Unlike a gasoline-powered vehicle, an EV doesn't need gears to match power curves because the electric motor in EV has the ability to provide a high torque when the vehicle is stopped. This is the reason why an EV doesn't have a gearbox or a torque converter. [1]

EV has a technique called 'regenerative braking' in which every time the vehicle slows down when the user applies the brake, the energy created is sent to the batteries and thus recharging the batteries. This function is carried out by the electric motor, which has the ability to convert movement energy back into electricity. In general EVs can be classified into two types, namely, battery electric vehicles and hybrid vehicles. Battery EVs convert chemical energy in to electrical energy in the batteries. HEV (hybrid electric vehicle) converts chemical energy in to electric energy through an ICE (internal combustion engine) and a generator.

EV has a few advantages over a gasoline-powered vehicle,

- → More energy efficient than all gasoline powered vehicles
- → Produces no exhaust fumes
- → Reduces dependence on petroleum
- → May mitigate global warming by alleviating the green house effect
- → Quieter than gasoline powered vehicles there by reducing the noise pollution

2. Charging

Batteries in BEVs (Battery Electric Vehicle) must be periodically recharged. BEVs most commonly charge from the power grid (at home or using a street or shop recharging point), which is in turn generated from a variety of domestic resources; such as coal, hydroelectricity, nuclear and others. Home power such as roof top photovoltaic solar cell panels, micro hydro or wind may also be used. Electricity can also be supplied with a portable fueled generator. Although not strictly a BEV, the Ford Reflex concept car incorporates photovoltaics into its exterior to help provide power to its lights, slightly reducing drain on its hybrid power train. Charging time is limited primarily by the capacity of the grid connection. A normal household outlet is between 1.5 kilowatts (in the US, Canada, Japan, and other countries with 110 Volt supply) to 3 kilowatts (in countries with 240 V supply). The main connection to a house might be able to sustain 10 kilowatts, and special wiring can be installed to use this. At this higher power level charging even a small, 7 kilowatt-hour (14–28 mi) pack, would probably require one hour. This is small compared to the effective power delivery rate of an average petrol pump, about 5,000 kilowatts. Even if the supply power can be increased, most batteries do not accept charge at greater than their charge rate ("C1".)

The charging power can be connected to the car in two ways:

The first is a direct electrical connection known as conductive coupling. This might be as simple as a mains lead into a weatherproof socket through to special high capacity cables with connectors to protect the user from high voltages. The second approach is known as inductive coupling. A special 'paddle' is inserted into a slot on the car. The paddle is one winding of a transformer, while the other is built into the car. When the paddle is inserted it completes a magnetic circuit, which provides power to the battery pack. The major advantage of this approach is that there is no possibility of electrocution as there are no exposed conductors although interlocks can make conductive coupling nearly as safe. Conductive coupling equipment is lower in cost and much more efficient due to a vastly lower component count. In 1995, some charging stations charged BEVs in one hour. In November 1997, Ford purchased a fast-charge system produced by AeroVironment called "PosiCharge" for testing its fleets of Ranger EVs, which charged their lead-acid batteries in between six and fifteen minutes. In February 1998, General Motors announced a version of its "Magne Charge" system which could recharge NiMH batteries in about ten minutes, providing a range of sixty to one hundred miles. In 2005, handheld device battery designs by Toshiba were claimed to be able to accept an 80% charge in as little as 60 seconds. Scaling this specific power characteristic up to the same 7 kilowatt-hour EV pack would result in the need for a peak of 336 kilowatts of power from some source for those 60 seconds. It is not clear that such batteries will work directly in BEVs as heat build-up may make them unsafe. In 2007, Altairnano's NanoSafe batteries are rechargeable in a few minutes, versus hours required for other rechargeable batteries. A NanoSafe cell can be charged to over 80% charge capacity in about one minute. [9]

3. RFID Reader Module

RFID Reader Module, are also called as interrogators. They convert radio waves returned from the RFID tag into a form that can be passed on to Controllers, which can make use of it. RFID tags and readers have to be tuned to the same frequency in order to communicate. RFID systems use many different frequencies, but the most common and widely used & supported by the Reader is 125 KHz. The designed reader had been used which is available in the market as a Plug & Play module. The following function as the reader supports:

Supports reading of 64 Bit Manchester Encoded cards

1. Pins for External Antenna connection
2. Serial Interface (TTL)
3. Wiegand Interface also available
4. Customer application on request

Note: The TTL RS-232 Interface cannot be connected directly to a PC COM port. Therefore the signal must be converted to RS 232 level for PC connection.

This Firmware has the following Functions:

- Read Tag-ID
- Send Tag-ID in ASCII Format through the Serial/ Wiegand Interface. [20]

4. Design of the Charging Station

The Fig. 1 shows the design of the charging station. The charging station console consists of the above devices such as the 16x2 LCD screen, 4x3 keypad, and MAX232 circuit used as a voltage converter, RFID reader and a circuit to select the number of chargers based on the requirement of the user. There are totally 6 chargers present in the station. 3 chargers are used for minimum charge where as 6 for maximum charge. PIC16F877A microcontroller is used to control the entire system. 4 ports (Port B, Port C, Port D and Port E) of the microcontroller have been used for the interfacing and building of the circuit to select the number of chargers. Port C is for the 3 control lines of the LCD, Port D is for the 8 data lines of the LCD (D0-D7), Port B for the interfacing of the keypad and Port E for the building up of the circuit to select the number of chargers.

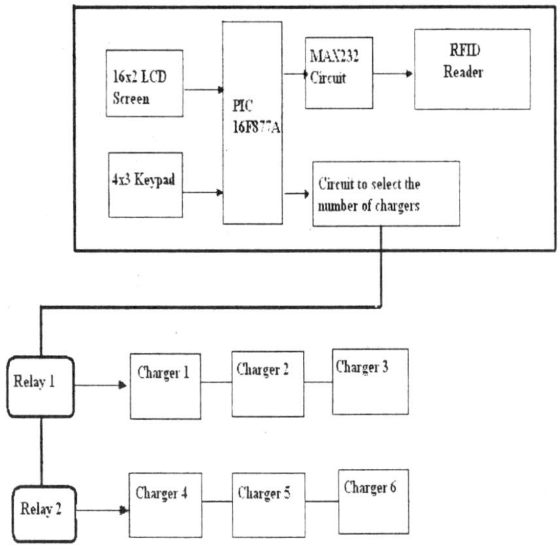

Fig. 1 Design of charging station

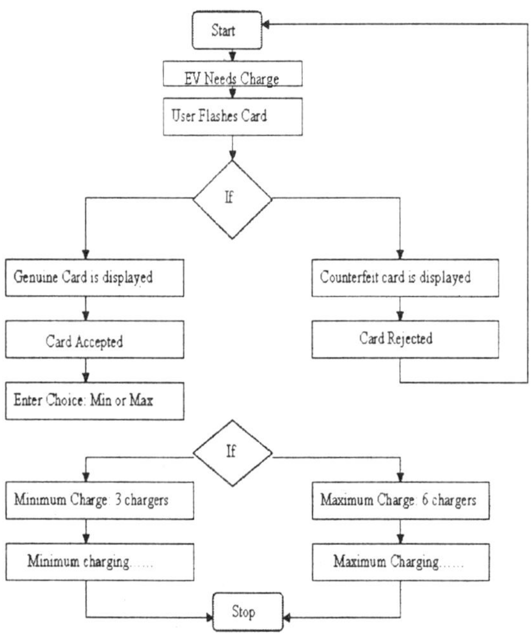

Fig. 2 Algorithm for system design

The algorithm in the Fig. 2 as follows: The user comes with the EV to charging station for charging batteries. The user flashes the card over the reader module, which has an antenna. The reader should receive the ASCII code from the reader module and should display it on the LCD screen through the microcontroller. The reader module is interfaced to the microcontroller. If the correct code is displayed, then the card is accepted and asks for the choice, whether maximum or minimum charge. If the user opts for minimum charge only 3 chargers are selected whereas 6 for maximum charge. If the ASCII code is not a correct code, then it asks the user to flash the genuine card.

4.1 Selection of the charge module Design for the Charging Station

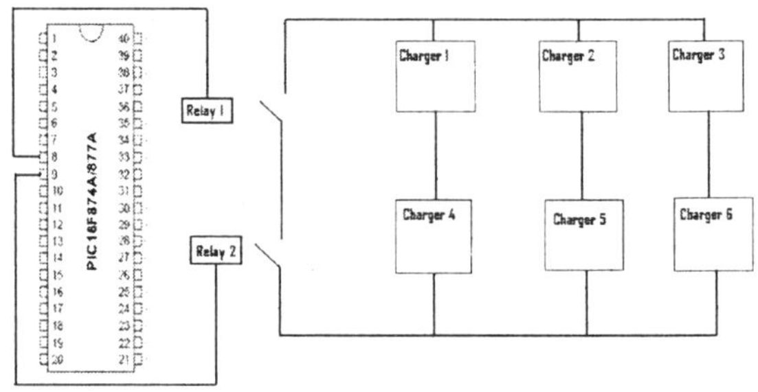

Fig. 3 Selection of charge for the system

The Fig. 3 shows how a microcontroller is used to select chargers. When relay 1 is closed, chargers 1, 2 and 3 are activated. In the same way, when relay 2 is closed the next 3 chargers are activated. First relay is connected to the 8th pin of Port E and the second relay is connected to 9th pin of Port E.

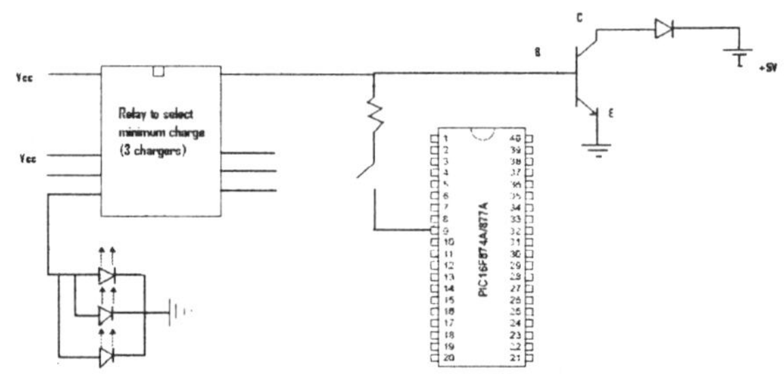

Fig. 4 Selection of charge for the system

The Fig. 4 has been designed to select the number of chargers in order to charge the batteries based on the user's requirement. The user has two options for charging. The first one is minimum charge, where only 3 chargers are activated and the second option is maximum charge, where all the 6 are activated. The selection of chargers is done through the closing/opening of relays.

The Fig. 5 shows about the selection of the next 3 chargers. Closing of a relay means activation of the chargers and opening of the relay means deactivation of the chargers. It is the function of microcontroller to open and close the relays. But, a microcontroller cannot drive a relay directly. Therefore, a driver circuit is used as a control means between the microcontroller and the relays. Through the driver circuit microcontroller can operate the relays.

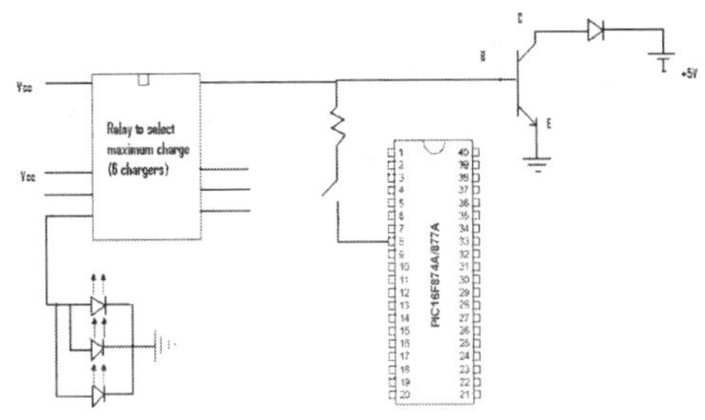

Fig. 5 Selection of charge for the system

5. Experimental Setup with Validation of Discussion of results

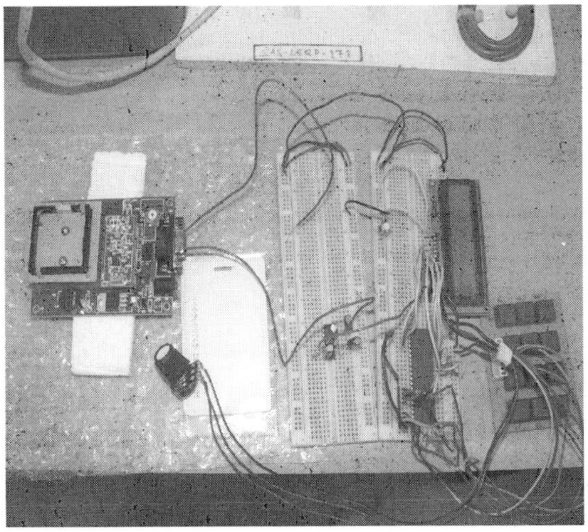

Fig. 6 Experimental setup of charging station control circuit

The Fig. 6 shows experimental set up with 4x3 keypad and LCD interface to the PIC16F877A microcontroller. The 8 data lines (D0-D7) of the LCD are connected to Port C of the microcontroller and the 3 control lines (RS, R/W, E) are connected to Port D. The crystal oscillator frequency is 20 MHz. The 4x3 keypad is connected to Port B of the microcontroller. 11, 32 pins of the microcontroller are connected to +5v supply and 12, 31 pins are grounded. The RFID reader interface to the microcontroller along with the MAX232 circuit is used as a voltage converter between the reader and the microcontroller. The suitable single layer PCB had been fabricated with the integration of all the modules of the system.

6. Test Cases

The following test cases had been studied keeping in mind about the Reva Electric car, which is a major leader in electric cars.

6.1 Initial Stage When Vehicle is Connected

Fig. 7 Initial stage of the charging station

The Fig. 7 shows the initial stage soon after the vehicle is connected to the charging station. The LCD displays "RevaSmartCharger FlashCard." The red LED represents +12v supply exclusively for the s-cube relays and green LED is for the rest of the system which represents +5v supply. The square shaped metal on the extreme right hand side outside the PCB board is the transformer which converts incoming alternating current into direct current. This is the very first stage that occurs among many other stages.

6.2 Second Stage Where the Genuine Card Number is Displayed

Fig. 8 Shows next state when the card is flashed

The above Fig. 8 shows the next stage soon after the card is flashed over the antenna of the reader. Once the card is read, the buzzer beeps and LED glows and displays the number on the LCD screen for the user to see. The LCD displays "RevaSmartCharger 350899." This is the second stage that occurs.

6.3 Third Stage: Card Accepted with full charging

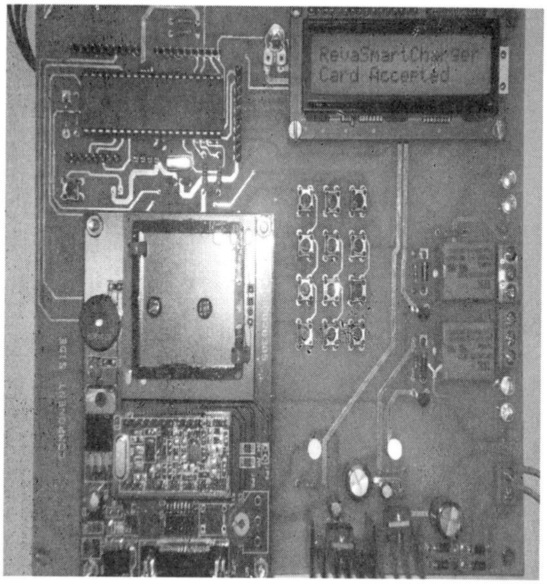

Fig. 9 Shows regarding the card accepted

The above Fig. 9 shows the third stage soon after the card number is flashed on the LCD screen. Since the card displayed is a genuine card, the LCD displays "Card Accepted." This is the third stage that occurs. Soon after the card is accepted the fourth stage in which the LCD displays "Min or Max", allowing the user to choose whether he wants minimum charge or maximum charge.

6.4 Sixth Stage: Maximum Charging Selected (all the LED's are glowing)

Fig. 10 Shows about the maximum charging

The Fig. 10 shows the sixth stage. If the user opts for maximum charging then the user should press '#' key on the keypad. Now the LCD displays "Max Charging", which means maximum charging is taking place. This is the sixth stage that occurs. The fifth state had tested for minimum charging where the user opts for minimum charging user should press '*' key on the keypad. Now the LCD displays "Min Charging", which means minimum charging is taking place. This is the fifth stage that occurs.

6.7 Eighth Stage: Card Rejected

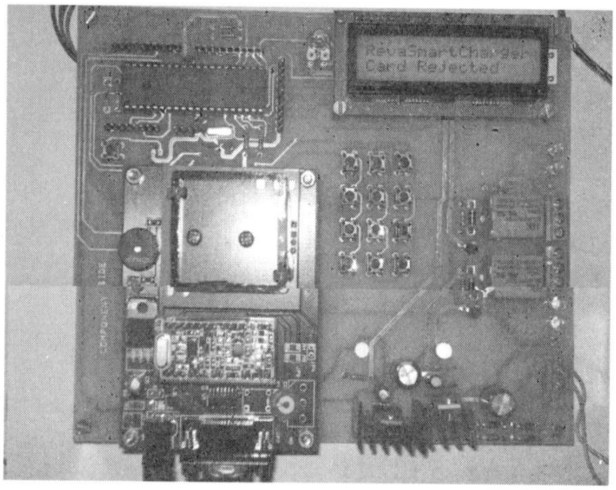

Fig. 11 Shows regarding the card rejected

The above Fig. 11 shows the eighth stage soon after an unauthorized card is flashed over the antenna of the reader where the LCD displays "Card Rejected".

7. Conclusions

It can be concluded that with the use of the microcontroller the controlling of the charging station becomes very simple and easy. Since the microcontroller controls the entire system, there is no need of a human being to keep checking the system. Also it is very important to realize that the EV industry cannot progress if they do not have a proper quick charging station. The use of the RFID reader module plays a vital role in the identification of the user. The charging scheme designed here is flexible for the user. The user can opt for either maximum charge or minimum charge. It can be concluded that the fast charging station makes the charging quicker than the conventional type.

8. Future Work

It can further be developed by designing a system in addition to it where can make the vehicle not to move while the charging is going on. Further development is needed to check whether the vehicle is properly connected to the charging station or not. Also there is need to develop where an advanced smart card with an embedded IC and reader could be used in which the user can hold currency in the smart card to charge the car. The system which can sense the over heating of the batteries, and provide the necessary cooling.

9. References

[1] Macro S.W. Chan, K.T. Chau and C.C. Chan, "*Modeling of Electric Vehicle Chargers*", Department of Electrical & Electronic Engineering, The University of Hong Kong, Pokfulam, Hong Kong, China, IECON'98 Proceedings of 24th Annual Conference of the IEEE, Published Date 31st Aug-4th Sep'98, Volume1, Ps.433-438.

[2] Timothy M.Jurgensen, Scott B.Guthery, *"Smart Cards The developers Toolkit*", Pearson Education,Inc., 2002.

[3] Michael H.Westbrook,"*The Electric Car*",The Institution Electrical Engineers, London, UK, 2005.

[4] Proposed Amendments to the California Zero Emission Vehicle Regulations: Date of Release: May 11, 2001 Scheduled of Consideration: June 28, 2001.

[5] PIC16F877A Datasheet (June 2007)

[6] http://evproduction.org/wiki/index.php?title=Battery_electric_vehicle (June-December 2007)

[7] www.http://en.wikipedia.org/wiki/Battery_electric_vehicle (June-December 2007)

[8] Bellis, M. (2006) "The History of Electric Vehicles: The Early Years" *About.com* article at inventors.about.com accessed on 6 July 2006.

[9] http://www.personal.leeds.ac.uk/~pscbrwm/cbev/about.html (June-December 2007)

[10] Anderson, C.D. and Anderson, J. (2005) "New Charging Systems" *Electric and Hybrid Cars: a History* (North Carolina: McFarland & Co., Inc.) ISBN 0-7864-1872-9, p. 121.

[11] John G.Hayes (General Motors), "Battery Charging Systems For Electric Vehicles", pp.4/1-4/7, Printed and Published by the IEE, The Institute of Electrical Engineers, 1998.

[12] Craig B. Toepfer (Ford Motor Co.), "Charge! EVs power up for the long haul", pp.41-47, Printed and Published by the IEE, The Institute of Electrical Engineers, 1998.

[13] Thomas L. Quinn, Bor Yann Liaw, "Electric Vehicle Rapid Charging Infrastructure In Hawaii", pp.1719-1725, 2000-01-1606, Society of Automotive Engineers (SAE), 2000.

[14] Guan-ChyunHsieh, Jung-ChienLi, Jia-ChwenHwang, "Design and Implementation of A Novel Ni-Cd Battery Charger", pp.1163-1167,IEEE.1992.

[15] Hae-Woo Park, Chang-Seok Han, Chui-Soo Kim, Bong-Ho Lee, and Young-Woo Kim,Paul R. Gifford , "Ni-MH Battery Charger with a Compensator for Electric Vehicles", pp. 412-420, 960447, Society of Automotive Engineers (SAE), 1996.

[16] "Toshiba's New Rechargeable Lithium-Ion Battery Recharges in Only One Minute", (http://www.technologyreview.com/read_article.aspx?id=17250&ch=biztech&a=f), (October, 2007)

[17] Muhammad Ali Mazidi, Janice Gillespie Mazidi, "The 8051 Microcontroller and Embedded System", Pearson Education Inc., 2000.

[18] Yunyan Wang, Jingxin Li, Jiuchun Jiang, Liyong Niu, "Management Information System of Charging Station for Electric Vehicle (EV)", School of Electrical Engineering, Beijing JiaoTong University, Beijing 100044, China.

[19] http://www.pge.com/about_us/environment/electric_vehicles/ (June-December 2007)

[20] http://www.sparrl.com/download/rfid.pdf (November 2007)

A Novel Method in Datapath Operator Cell Design

Manikandan Raju
Senior Lecturer, MIT, Meerut,
vlsimani@gmail.com

Abstract

I present a new design for a 1-b full adder featuring hybrid-CMOS design style. The quest to achieve a good-drivability, noise robustness, and low-energy operations for deep submicrometer guided my research to explore hybrid-CMOS style design. Hybrid-CMOS design style utilizes various CMOS logic style circuits to build new full adders with desired performance. This provides the designer a higher degree of design freedom to target a wide range of applications, thus significantly reducing design efforts. I also classify hybrid-CMOS full adders into three broad categories based upon their structure. Using this categorization, many full-adder designs can be conceived. I will present a new full-adder design belonging to one of the proposed categories. The new full adder is based on a novel XOR–XNOR circuit that generates XOR and XNOR full-swing outputs simultaneously. This circuit outperforms its counterparts showing 5%–37% improvement in the power-delay product (PDP).

1. Introduction

The Demand and popularity of portable electronics is driving designers to strive for smaller silicon area, higher speeds, longer battery life, and more reliability. Power is one of the premium resources a designer tries to save when designing a system. Full adders are fundamental units in various circuits, especially in circuits used for performing arithmetic operations such as compressors, comparators, parity checkers, and so on [1]. Several logic styles have been used in the past to design full adder cells. Each design style has its own merits and demerits.

A hybrid-CMOS full adder can be broken down into three modules [3]. Module I comprises of either a XOR or XNOR circuit or both. This module produces intermediate signals that are passed onto Module II and Module III that generate Sum and outputs, respectively.

There are several circuits available in [1] and [3] for each module and several studies have been conducted in the past using different combinations to obtain many adders [1], [3], [5]. In this paper, I broadly categorize hybrid-CMOS adder designs in three categories based on their structure. I then present a new improved circuit for the simultaneous generation of the XOR and XNOR outputs to be used in module I. The new circuit is based on CPL style.

I also propose a new output unit. This unit is used in module III. Using the new circuits in module I and III, I build a new hybrid-CMOS full-adder cell. The new adder is optimized for low PDP and is compared with the classical static-CMOS, CPL, TFA, TGA, NEW14T, HPSC, and NEW-HPSC full-adder cells. The proposed full-adder design exhibits low PDP, full-swing operation, and excellent driving capabilities without trading off area and reliability. To evaluate the performance of the new full adder in a real circuit, I embedded it in a 4- and 8-b, 4-operand carry-save array adder with final carry-propagate adder. The new adder displayed better performance as compared to the standard full adders and can be cascaded without the need of buffer insertion.

2. Proposed Circuits for Module I and III

Hybrid-CMOS full adders can be divided into three modules [3]. Module I consists of either an XOR or XNOR circuit. Module II and module III generate Sum and Cout. I present two new circuits, one for each module I and module III.

2.1 Module I

In recent times, simultaneous generation of XOR and XNOR has been widely used for module I [4], [2]. This feature is highly desirable as non skewed outputs are generated that are used for driving the select lines of the multiplexer inside the full adder. Fig. 1(a) shows a configuration using only six transistors and is presented in [4]. This circuit has been widely used to build full-adder cells [4], [2]. The circuit has a feedback connection between XOR and XNOR function eliminating the non-full-swing operation. The existence of and connections give good driving capability to the circuit and the elimination of direct connections between them avoids the short circuit currents component.

However, when there is an input transition that leads to the input vector *AB: XX-11* or *AB: XX-00*, there is a delay in switching the feedback transistors. This occurs because one of the feedback transistors is switched ON by a weak signal and the other signal is at high impedance state. Consider the case when the input vector AB changes from "01" to "00." Initially, when the input AB is in state "01," logic "0" is passed through the nMOS transistor N1 and logic "1" is passed through the pMOS transistor P2. However, when the next input state "00" arrives, a weak "0" is passed through two pMOS transistors P1 and P2 to XOR output, and XNOR output is at high impedance state since N1 and N2 are OFF. This weak "0" switches ON the feedback transistor , present in the feedback loop, so that the XNOR output is pulled up to logic "1," which switches ON the feedback transistor to discharge the output node XOR to logic "0." This causes the increase in delay. As the supply voltage is scaled down, this delay tends to increase tremendously. This also causes the short circuit current to rise and causes the short circuit power dissipation to increase and eventually increase the power-delay product. To reduce this problem careful transistor sizing needs to be done to quickly switch the feedback transistors.

An improved version of the circuit in [2] is presented in [6].Two pull-up pMOS-transistors and two pull-down nMOS-transistors are added to the circuit to restore full-swing operation [see Fig. 1(b)]. The improved circuit performs successfully at low supply voltages but this comes at the expense of increased area and number of transistors. Another disadvantage of the new circuit is that each of the inputs drives four gates instead of two gates doubling the input load. This will cause slow response when this circuit is cascaded. I propose a novel XOR–XNOR circuit using eight transistors that generates XOR and XNOR outputs simultaneously. This circuit provides a full-swing operation and can operate at low voltages. The proposed XOR–XNOR circuit is based on complementary pass-transistor logic using only one static inverter instead of two static inverters as in the regular CPL style XOR circuit. The proposed circuit is shown in Fig. 1(c). The first half of the circuit utilizes only nMOS pass transistors for the generation of the outputs. The cross-coupled pMOS transistors

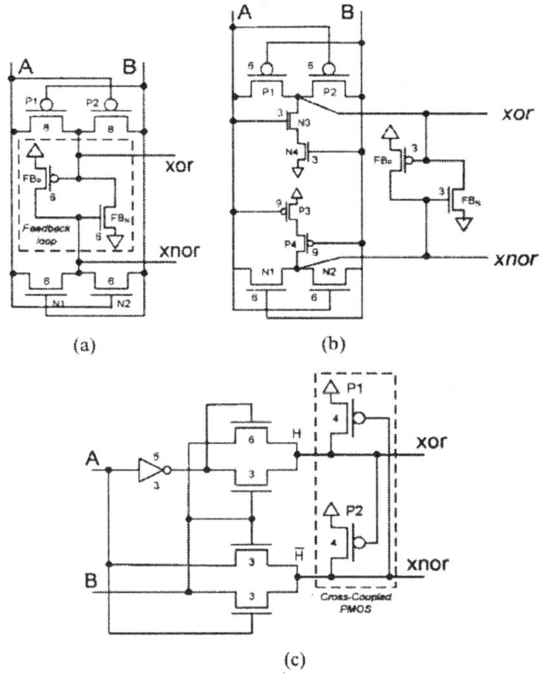

Fig. 1 (a) Circuit in [4]. (b) Circuit in [6]. (c) Proposed circuit.

Table 1 Operation of the Proposed XOR-XNOR Circuit

A	B	H	H'	Function
0	0	Good 0	NOP	P2 turns ON and pulls H' to VDD
0	1	Bad 1	Good 0	P1 turns ON and pulls H to VDD
1	0	NOP	Good 0	P1 turns ON and pulls H to VDD
1	1	Good 0	Bad 1	P2 turns ON and pulls H' to VDD

guarantee full-swing operation for all possible input combinations and reduce short-circuit power dissipation. The circuit is inherently fast due to the high mobility nMOS transistors and the fast differential stage of cross-coupled pMOS transistors. Table I indicates the functioning of the proposed circuit more clearly. For any input vector, the pMOS transistors are switched ON by a good and, therefore, avoid any static power dissipation. Owing to the lower *Vthn* and high electron mobility of the nMOS transistors, the circuit has a faster response as compared to the previous circuit.

The proposed XOR–XNOR circuit was compared to circuits in Fig. 1(a) and (b).Fig. 2 shows the input pattern used. I consider all the possible input transitions with an output transition at every input transition. The circuit in [6] and the proposed circuit consume almost the same power but my circuit is 10% faster. Owing to the higher speed of my circuit, there is almost 5%–37.5% saving in PDP in this module. The proposed circuit uses only 2% more area when compared to the circuit in [4] but the circuit in [6] uses 43% more area. The increase in area is due to the addition of four more transistors, particularly the two pMOS pull-up transistors.

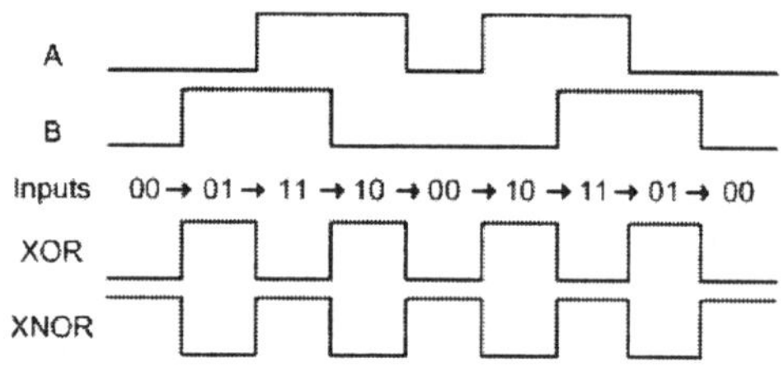

Fig. 2 Input test pattern for XOR–XNOR circuits.

2.2 Module III

The output of module III can be expressed as

$$C_{\text{out}} = A \cdot H' + C_{\text{in}} \cdot H.$$

This expression can be realized with a 2-to-1 multiplexer with and as the select lines. The most common implementation of the previous expression is using transmission gates (TG). Fig. 3(a) shows the circuit for a 2-to-1 multiplexer. The problem with the TG multiplexer is that it cannot provide the required driving capability to drive cascaded adder stages. One solution to this problem is to have an output buffer as shown in Fig. 3(a). This would incur extra delay and an overhead of four transistors. Another possibility is to use the complement of the expression, i.e,

$$\overline{C_{\text{out}}} = \overline{A} \cdot H' + \overline{C_{\text{in}}} \cdot H.$$

In this case, two inverters will be required to invert the inputs and one inverter at the output. This will result in unbalanced and output switching times and extra delay.

A circuit based on the static-CMOS logic style is presented in [2]. This circuit overcomes the problems of the TG multiplexer design. It uses ten transistors and is shown in Fig. 3(b). This circuit possesses all the features of static CMOS logic style such as robustness to voltage scaling and good noise margins. I propose a hybrid design for module III. I use the inherently low power consuming TG logic style and the robust static-CMOS logic style to create a new hybrid-CMOS circuit. The proposed circuit is shown in Fig. 3(c). The new circuit also utilizes ten transistors and possesses the properties of both static-CMOS and TG logic styles. The carry is evaluated using the following logic expression:

$$C_{\text{out}} = \overline{(A \oplus B)\overline{C_{\text{in}}} + \overline{A} \cdot \overline{B}}.$$

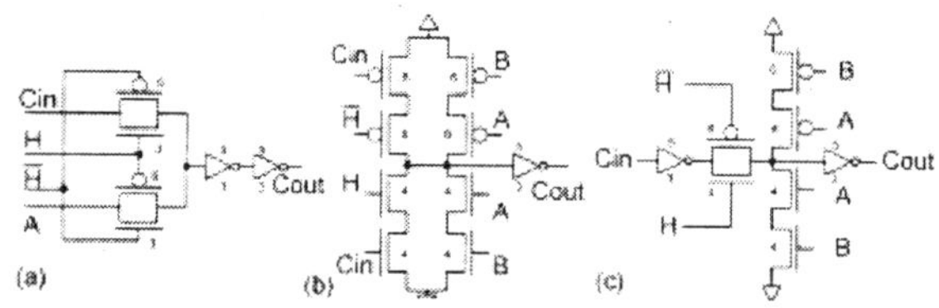

Fig. 3 Circuits for module III.

A transmission gate preceded by a static inverter is used to implement, and are the complementary gate signals to this TG. This unit propagates the signal to the output when is at logic "1" and is at logic "0." Two pMOS pull-up transistors in series with two nMOS pull-down transistors are used to generate. Complementary and signals are not required. When and are at logic "0" they switch ON both the pMOS transistors to generate and assign it logic "1." When and are at logic "1" they switch ON both the nMOS transistors to generate and assign logic "0." At all other times, this section remains OFF. The static inverter at the output produces the desired output. Table III shows the results of proposed circuit when compared to the circuit in [2]. Due to the additional inverter in the proposed design, it consumes slightly more power as compared to the circuit in [2]. There is redundant switching at the input since the complement of is generated even if it is not propagated to the output. This can be avoided by placing the inverter after the TG but this causes a problem as charge can leak through the closed TG and cause a reversal of voltage level at the output. This tradeoff has to be made but this guarantees excellent signal integrity without any glitches. The proposed circuit is 1.5 faster than the compared one and requires slightly lesser area for the layout despite the same number of transistors. Transistor sizes for both the circuits are shown in the figure. There is an overall 40% reduction in the PDP achieved by the proposed circuit. I use the proposed circuit for module III in the proposed hybrid-CMOS full-adder design.

3. Proposed Hybrid-CMOS Full adder

In this section, I will present the new full-adder design based on the new circuits proposed in the Sections I–III. Before I present the new adder, I review some of the existing and most frequently used circuits that can be used in the different modules of the full adder. By using these circuits many different hybrid-CMOS full adders can be conceived.

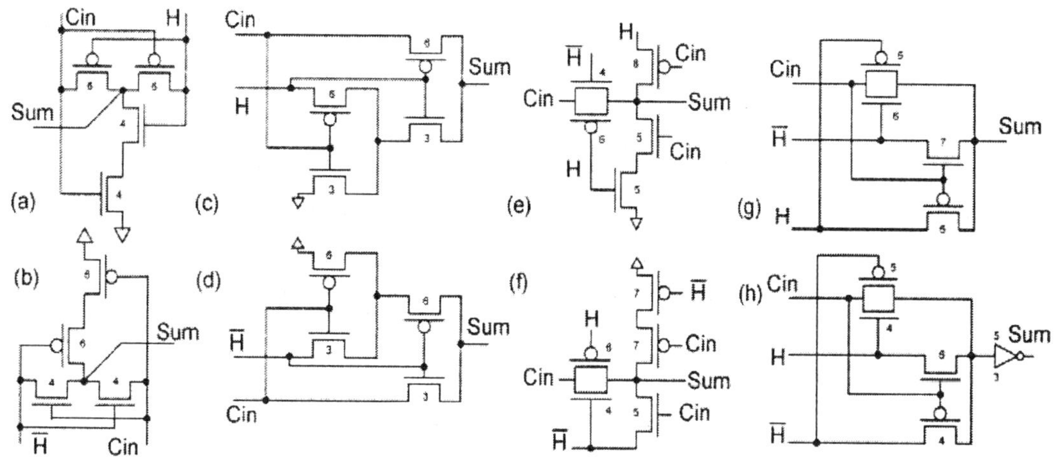

Fig. 4 Circuits for module II

Since I have already discussed different circuits for module I and module III, I will restrict my discussion to circuits for module II here. These circuits that can be used in module II are shown in Fig. 3. These circuits are required to generate the Sum output given inputs, and. These circuits essentially perform the XOR or the XNOR function and can be used in the first module of the adder too. Fig. 4(a) and (b) [8] uses four transistors each and generate the output using and or inputs. These circuits have been used in many adders for both module I [3], [7] and module II [7]. These circuits, however, have some threshold-loss problems. In circuit (a), for an input vector "00," it produces a bad logic "0" as the pMOS pass transistors pass a poor logic "0" through them. Similarly, for circuit (b) for an input vector "11" the output is at a poor logic "1." The output signal, when given to the following gate, can cause a functional failure or cause long delay in switching a transistor. This may lead to redundant power consumption and possible glitches. Fig.4(c) and (d) are powerless/groundless XOR and XNOR circuits [9], respectively, each requiring four transistors. These circuits use the and or inputs to generate the output. These circuits are used to build 41 ten-transistor adders and are presented in [1]. Again, these circuits also suffer from threshold-loss problems. For example in circuit (c), for the input vector "00" and "01," the circuit produces poor voltage levels. Circuits with this problem have very poor driving capabilities and cause significant glitches. Fig. 4(e) and (f) [17] require five transistors each and provide full-swing outputs. These circuits use all the three inputs (i.e., and) to generate the Sum output signal. They do not suffer from threshold loss and are good candidates for module II. Several authors have previously used this circuit in their adders [3], [5].

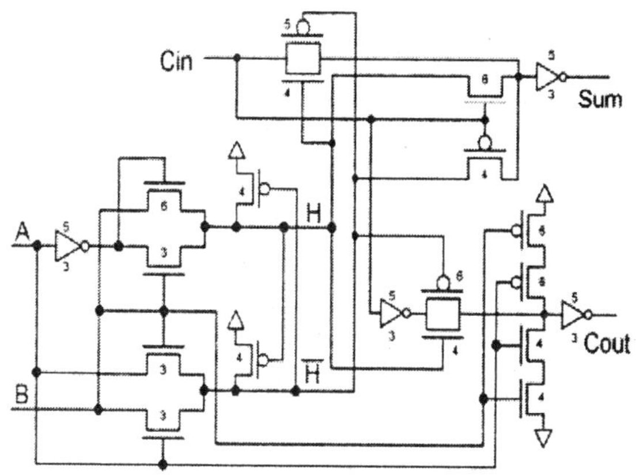

Fig. 5 Proposed hybrid-CMOS full adder

I classify this circuit as a hybrid-CMOS design style circuit due to the presence of a TG, pass-transistor, and static pull-down network. All these modules have either ground or power supply connections thereby eliminating direct path between ground and power supply. Fig. 4(g) has transmission-function implementation of XOR and XNOR functions. This circuit does not have supply rails thereby eliminating short circuit current. Fig. 4(h) is essentially the complement and has an inverter to produce Sum. This provides good driving capability due to the presence of the static inverter. This circuit is one of the best performers among all the circuits mentioned before in terms of signal integrity and average power-delay product [3]. Both the circuits avoid the problem of threshold loss and have been widely used in adder implementation [2]. I employ this circuit for My full-adder design.

3.1 Proposed Full Adder

As mentioned earlier in Section II, the centralized full adders, both XOR and XNOR circuits are present (both in module I) that generate the intermediate signals and, these signals are passed on to module II and III along with the carry from the previous stage and the other inputs and to produce the and one existing circuit in the three modules. The proposed adder is shown in Fig. 5. In module I, the proposed XOR–XNOR circuit produces balanced full-swing outputs. It has high-speed operation due to the cross-coupled pMOS pull-up transistors providing the intermediate signals quickly. Since the other two modules rely heavily on the intermediate signal and to produce the final outputs, the delay response of module I is critical. The proposed XOR–XNOR circuit is 1.7 faster than the best available XOR–XNOR circuits. Due to this reason, the new adder is faster than the compared adders. Module II is a transmission-function implementation of XNOR function to generate the followed by an inverter to generate. This provides good driving capability to the circuit. Due to the absence of supply rails there are no short circuit currents. The circuit is free from the problem of threshold loss and has the lowest PDP amongst all circuits that are used for moduleII [3].

Module III employs the proposed hybrid-CMOS output stage with a static inverter at the output. This circuit has a lower PDP as compared to the other existing designs. The static inverter provides good driving capabilities as the inputs are decoupled from the output. The structure of the circuit is very symmetric and, therefore, the layout is regular. Due to the low PDP of module II and module III, the new adder is expected to have low power consumption. In Sections V and VI, the simulation environment and experimental results will be discussed.

4. Simulation Results and Discussion

All the circuits are implemented using MAGIC 7.1 layout editor and extracted using TSMC 0.18- m technology. Simulations are carried out using HSPICE. Parasitic capacitances are also considered in the results. To simulate a real environment, input buffers for all inputs of the test circuit are used. The transistor sizes of these buffers are chosen such that there is sufficient signal distortion as expected in an actual circuit. A minimum output load of fan-out of four inverters (FO4) is used for power and delay measurements, the value of which amounts to 5.6 fF (1.4 fF for each inverter in 0.18- m technology). The generic simulation test bench used along with the transistor sizes of each buffer. The circuit performance of the test circuits is evaluated in terms of worst-case delay, power consumption, and power-delay product for a range of supply voltages (0.8–1.8 V) at 50-MHz frequency. The delay is calculated from 50% of voltage level of input to 50% of voltage level of resulting output all the rise and fall output transitions.

By optimizing the transistor sizes of the full adders considered, it is possible to reduce the delay of all adders without significantly increasing the power consumption, and transistor sizes can be set to achieve minimum PDP. All adders were designed with minimum transistor sizes initially and then simulated. To achieve minimum PDP, an iterative process of redesigning and transistor sizing after post-layout simulations was carried out. Comparison of full adders designed to achieve minimum PDP is discussed below. In particular, three subsections refer to delay, power, and PDP, respectively. In each subsection, effects of varying supply voltage and load are considered.

5. Conclusion

Hybrid-CMOS design style gives more freedom to the designer to select different modules in a circuit depending upon the application. Using the adder categorization and hybrid- CMOS design style, many full adders can be conceived. As an example, a novel full adder designed using hybrid-CMOS design style is presented in this paper that targets low PDP. The proposed hybrid-CMOS full adder has better performance than most of the standard full-adder cells owing to the novels design modules proposed in this paper. It performs well with supply voltage scaling and under different load conditions. When embedded in a four-operand CSA, it outperforms all the other adders making it suitable for larger adders. The proposed adder has better noise immunity as compared to the standard adder such as static CMOS, making it suitable for deep-submicrometer operation. I recommend the use of hybrid-CMOS design style for the design of high-performance circuits.

6. References

[1] H. T. Bui, Y. Wang, and Y. Jiang, "Design and analysis of low-power 10-transistor full adders using XOR–XNOR gates," *IEEE Trans. CircuitsSyst. II, Analog Digit. Signal Process.*, vol. 49, no. 1, pp. 25–30, Jan.2002.

[2] M. Zhang, J. Gu, and C. H. Chang, "A novel hybrid pass logic with static CMOS output drive full-adder cell," in *Proc. IEEE Int. Symp. Circuits Syst.*, May 2003, pp. 317–320.

[3] A. M. Shams, T. K. Darwish, and M. A. Bayoumi, "Performance analysis of low-power 1-bit CMOS full adder cells," *IEEE Trans. Ver Large Scale Integr. (VLSI) Syst.*, vol. 10, no. 1, pp. 20–29, Feb. 2002.

[4] D. Radhakrishnan, "Low-voltage low-power CMOS full adder," *IEEE Proc. Circuits Devices Syst.*, vol. 148, no. 1, pp. 19–24, Feb. 2001.

[5] M. Sayed and W. Badawy, "Performance analysis of single-bit full adder cells using 0.18, 0.25, and 0.35_m CMOS technologies," in *Proc. Int. Symp. Circuits Syst.*, 2002, pp. III-559–III-562.

[6] C.-H. Chang, J. Gu, and M. Zhang, "A review of 0.18-_m full adder performances for tree structured arithmetic circuits," *IEEE Trans. Very Large Scale Integr. (VLSI) Syst.*, vol. 13, no. 6, pp. 686–695, Jun. 2005.

[7] R. Shalem, L. K. John, and E. John, "A novel low power energy recovery full adder cell," in *Proc. Great Lake Symp. VLSI*, 1999, pp.380–380.

[8] J. Wang, S. Fang, and W. Feng, "New efficient designs for XOR and XNOR functions on the transistor level," *IEEE J. Solid-State Circuits*, vol. 29, no. 7, pp. 780–786, Jul. 1994.

[9] H. T. Bui, A. K. Al-Sheraidah, and Y. Wang, "New 4-transistor XOR and XNOR designs," in *Proc. 2nd IEEE Asia Pacific Conf. ASICs*, 2000, pp. 25–28.

[10] H. Lee and G. E. Sobelman, "New low-voltage circuits for XOR and XNOR," *IEEE Proc. Southeastcon.*, pp. 225–229, 1997.

A Review of ADC Architectures and their Design Implementations

Prof.S.S.Khot[1], Ms R.P. Ghugardare[2] and Dr.M.S.Sutaone[3]
[1]Asst Prof, Dept of E&TC Sinhgad Academy of Engg, Kondhwa, Pune-411048
[2]Lecturer, Dept of E&TC SKN College of Engg. Vadgaon, Pune-411041
[3]Professor, Dept of E&TC Govt College of Engg, Pune-411005
khotsir@yahoo.co.in rakhi_g_14@yahoo.co.in mssutaone@gmail.com

Abstract

The analog to digital converters is the key components in modern electronic systems. As the digital signal processing industry grows the ADC design becomes more and more challenging for researchers. In these days an ADC becomes a part of the system on chip instead of standalone circuit for data converters. This increases the requirements on ADC design concerning for example speed, power, area, resolution, noise etc. New techniques and methods are going to develop day by day to achieve high performance ADCs. There are 5 types of ADC. Each ADC has its own feature. This paper gives the exact features of all types of ADC and its applications in various fields like communication, military applications, biomedical, control applications.

1. Introduction

Signals in the real world are analog: light, sound, you name it. So, real-world signals must be converted into digital, using a circuit called ADC (Analog-to-Digital Converter), before they can be manipulated by digital equipment. When you scan a picture with a scanner what the scanner is doing is an analog-to-digital conversion: it is taking the analog information provided by the picture (light) and converting into digital. When you record your voice or use a VoIP solution on your computer, you are using an analog-to-digital converter to convert your voice, which is analog, into digital information. Digital information isn't only restricted to computers. When you talk on the phone, for example, your voice is converted into digital (at the central office switch, if you use an analog line, or at you home, if you use a digital line like ISDN or DSL), since your voice is analog and the communication between the phone switches is done digitally. When an audio CD is recorded at a studio, once again analog-to-digital is taking place, converting sounds into digital numbers that will be stored on the disc. Whenever we need the analog signal back, the opposite conversion – digital-to-analog, which is done by a circuit called DAC, Digital-to-Analog Converter – is needed.

2. Working of ADC

2.1 Sampling

For our explanations, consider the analog signal found on Fig. 1. Let's assume that it is an audio signal, since this the most popular applications for analog-to-digital and digital-to-analog conversions. The "y" axis represents voltage while the "x" axis represents time.

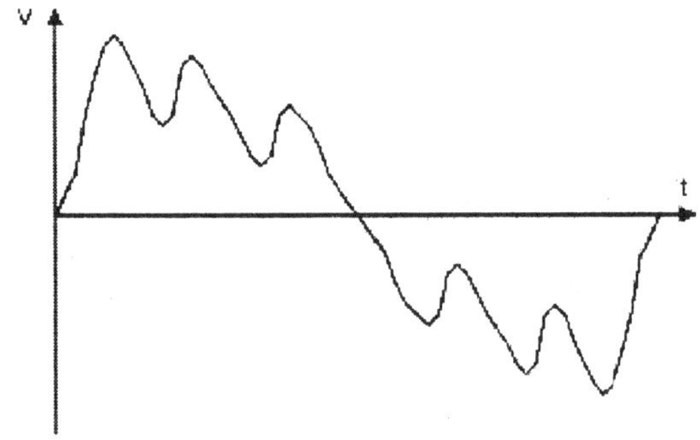

Fig. 1 An analog signal

What the ADC circuit does is to take samples from the analog signal from time to time. Each sample will be converted into a number, based on its voltage level. On Fig. 2 you see an example of some sampling points on our analog signal.

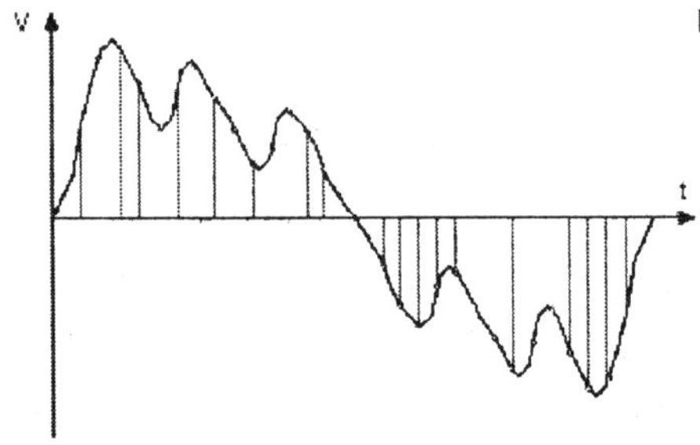

Fig. 2 Sampling points

The frequency on which the sampling will occur is called sampling rate. If a sampling rate of 22,050 Hz is used, for example, this means that in one second 22,050 points will be sampled. Thus, the distance of each sampling point will be of 1 / 22,050 second (45.35 µs, in this case). If a sampling rate of 44,100 Hz is used, it means that 44,100 points will be captured per second. In this case the distance of each point will be of 1 / 44,100 second or 22.675 µs. And so on.

You can see an example on Fig. 3, where we show how the signal would be after being converted to digital and back to analog. As you can see, the original waveform is more "rounded".

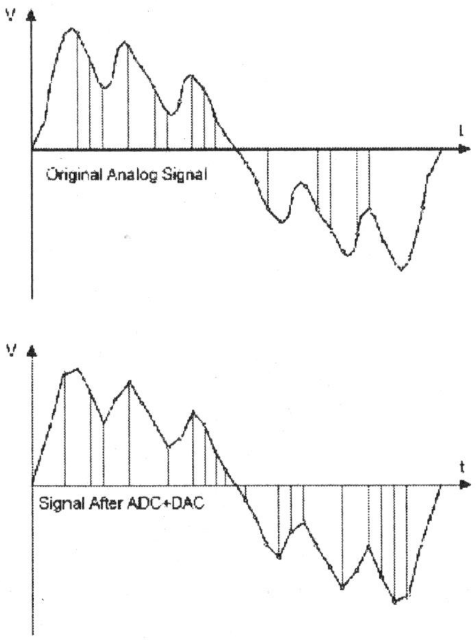

Fig. 3 Signal after being converted to digital and back to analog

So, the more sampling points we use – i.e. the higher the sampling rate –, the more perfect will be the analog signal produced by the digital-to-analog converter (DAC). However, the more samples we capture more storage space is necessary to store the resulting digital data. For example, an analog-to-digital conversion using a 44,100 Hz sampling rate will generate twice the number of data as a conversion using a 22,050 Hz sampling rate, as it will capture twice the samples from the original waveform.

Nyquist theorem states that the sampling rate on analog-to-digital conversions must be at least two times the value of the highest frequency you want to capture.

2.2 Resolution

The value of each sampled point will be stored on a fixed-length variable. If this variable uses eight bits, this means it can hold values from 0 to 255 (2^8 = 256). If this variable uses 16 bits, this means it can hold values from 0 to 65,535 (2^16 = 65,536). And so on.

So, if you are using an 8-bit analog-to-digital converter, the lowest value will be zero and the highest value will be 255. If a 16-bit analog-to-digital converter is used, the lowest value will be zero and the highest value will be 65,535. See Figure 4

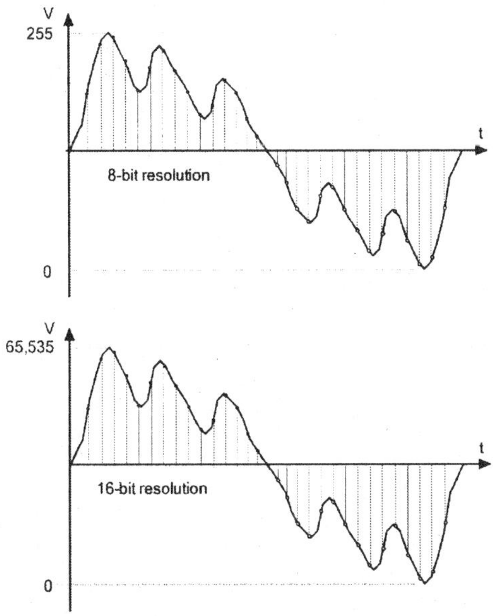

Fig. 4 8- and 16-bit resolutions comparison

One of the ways to know the necessary number of bits for an ADC is by calculating the desired noise level. Since the values sampled from the original analog signal will several times need to be "rounded" to the nearest possible digital equivalent, this provides what is called quantization noise. The tolerable noise level depends on the application. The phone system can have a higher noise level than an audio CD, for example, since we want to hear our CDs with the best possible quality.

The signal-to-noise ratio (SNR), which measures the noise level, can be easily calculated thru this formula, where n is the number of bits used on the ADC:

$$\text{SNR} = 6.02 \times n + 1.76 \text{ dB} \quad (1)$$

In summary, while the sampling rate give us the analog-to-digital "x" axis resolution, the variable size gives us the "y" axis resolution.

3. Design of ADCs

There are several ways to build an ADC. We can divide ADC design into four main groups:

- Parallel design (also known as Flash ADC);
- Digital-to-Analog Converter-based design (e.g. ramp counter, successive approximation, tracking);
- Integrator-based design (e.g. single-slope, dual-slope);
- Sigma-delta design (also known as delta-sigma, 1-bit ADC or oversampling ADC).

Each one of these main groups can have several different implementations. We are going to talk about each one of these groups individually.

3.1 Parallel Design

Flash ADC

The Flash ADC, also called parallel ADC, is very easy to understand. It works by comparing the input voltage – i.e. the analog signal – to a reference voltage, which would be the maximum value achieved by the analog signal. For example, if the reference voltage is of 5 volts, this means that the peak of the analog signal would be 5 volts. On an 8-bit ADC when the input signal reached 5 volts we would find a 255 (11111111) value on the ADC output, i.e. the maximum value possible. Then the voltage reference is lowered thru a resistor network and other comparators added, so the input voltage (analog signal) can be compared to other values. On Figure 5 you can see a 3-bit Flash ADC. The comparison is done thru an op amp. All resistors have the same value.

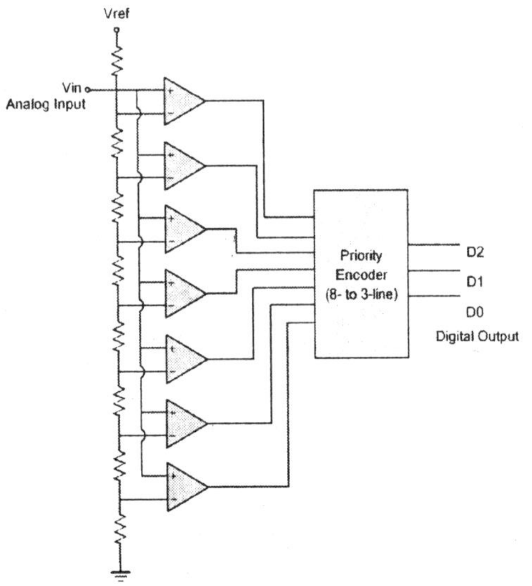

Fig. 5 Flash ADC.

Even though Flash ADC uses a very simple design, it requires a lot of components. The number of required comparators is 2^n-1, where n is the number of output bits. Thus for an eight-bit Flash ADC 255 comparators would be necessary, and for a 16-bit Flash ADC, 65,535!

On the other hand, Flash ADC is the fastest ADC type available. The digital equivalent of the analog signal will be available right away at it output (it will only have the propagation delay inserted by the logic gates) – hence the name "flash".

Another advantage of Flash ADC is that you can create an ADC with non-linear output. Usually ADCs have a linear output, i.e. each digital number corresponds to a fixed voltage increase on the analog input. For example, on the 3-bit ADC shown above with a Vref of 5 V, each digital number would represent 625 mV (5 V / 2^3). So 0 V = 000, 0.625 V = 001, 1.250 V = 010 and so on up to 5 V = 111.

Since Flash ADC comparisons are set by a set of resistors, one could set different values for the resistors in order to obtain a non-linear output, i.e. one value would represent a different voltage step from the other values.

Design Methods

1. A flash analog-to-digital converter is proposed that employs a new dynamic element matching architecture. The architecture uses a new strategy of incorporating switches in the voltage reference generator that allows lower hardware complexity and higher conversion speed than comparable converters. If DEM is used the current sources to turn on is chosen randomly each sample, causing the frequency domain distortion to be spread out over the frequency range as approximate white noise. Hence, the spurious tones are removed, but the noise floor is raised. This can be compensated for by applying oversampling, thereby getting a higher SFDR compared with not using DEM. In the DEM is introduced by adding three switches at each reference level of the reference generator. [1]
2. A common approach to decode the thermometer code is to use a gray or binary-encoded ROM. The appropriate row *m* in the ROM is selected by using a circuit that has the output of comparator *m* and the inverse of comparator *m*+1 as inputs. The output is one if the output of comparator *m* is one and the output of comparator *m*+1 is zero. This may be realized by, e.g., a 2-input AND gate, where one input is inverted. However, this solution selects multiple rows if bubble errors occur, which introduces large errors in the output of the decoder. If only single bubble errors occur, this can be corrected for by using 3-input NAND gates. This solution removes all bubble errors if they are separated by at least three bits in the thermometer scale. The main advantage of this ROM decoder approach is that it is simple and straightforward to

design. It is, however, a slow and power consuming solution. Another disadvantage is that as the speed increases, more bubble errors are introduced and a more advanced bubble error correction scheme than the 3-input NAND is required. This further reduces the speed of the decoder as well as adds to the overall power consumption. [2]

3. The output of a thermometer-to-binary decoder is the number of ones on the input, represented in, e.g., gray or binary code. This is utilized when using an ones-counter as a decoder and gives the same result as the bit swapping technique. However, the bit swapping technique also requires a thermometer decoder, since the output is a bubble error corrected thermometer code. Using the ones-counter the output is the decoded binary code and it also applies global bubble error correction/suppression. Another benefit of the approach of using the ones-counter as a decoder is that, depending on the speed requirement on the ADC, a suitable ones-counter topology may be selected by trading speed for power. we are looking for a decoder to be used in high-speed applications. This implies that a high-speed ones counter is suitable, which makes the Wallace tree topology. [2]

3.2 DAC-Based Designs

Ramp Counter ADC

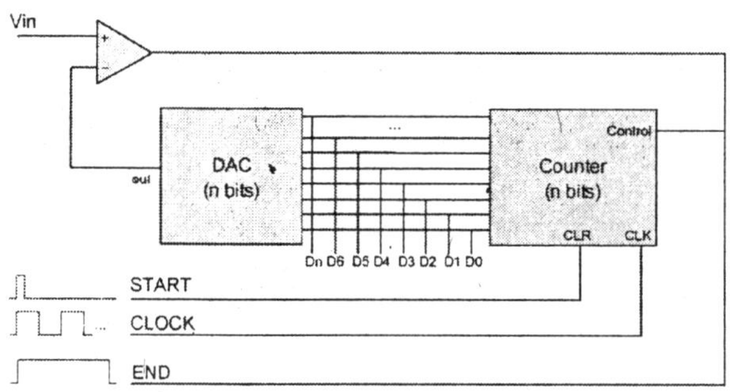

Fig. 6 Ramp counter ADC

Ramp counter ADC, also called digital ramp ADC, is shown on Fig. 6. Vin is the analog input and Dn thru D0 are the digital outputs. The control line found on the counter turns on the counter when it is low and stops the counter when it is high.

The basic idea is to increase the counter until the value found on the counter matches the value of the analog signal. When this condition is met, the value on the counter is the digital equivalent of the analog signal.

It requires a START pulse for each analog voltage you want to convert into digital. The END signal represents the end of the conversion for each individual voltage (each sample), and not for the entire analog signal. Each clock pulse moves the counter. Supposing an 8-bit ADC, for converting the analog value for "128" into digital, for example, it would take 128 clock cycles.

It works by counting from 0 to the maximum possible value (2^n-1) until it "finds" the correct digital value for the analog voltage present at Vin. When this is true, the END signal is given and the digital value for Vin is for at Dn thru D0.

So the main problem with this circuit is that it is very slow, as it would require up to 2^n-1 clock cycles to convert each sample. For an eight-bit ADC, it would take up to 255 clock cycles to convert a single sample. For a 16-bit ADC it would take up to 65,535 clock cycles to convert one sample.

Successive Approximation ADC

The second classical ADC circuit using DAC design is called successive approximation, which is the most used one, shown on Figure 7. Vin is the analog input and Dn thru D0 are the digital outputs. As you can see, it uses a buffer, so the digital data is still available while the converter is processing the next sample. SAR stands for Successive Approximation Register. It has the same control signals as the ramp counter ADC: START, which commands the ADC to start the conversion, CLOCK and END, which tells us that the conversion of that particular sample has finished.

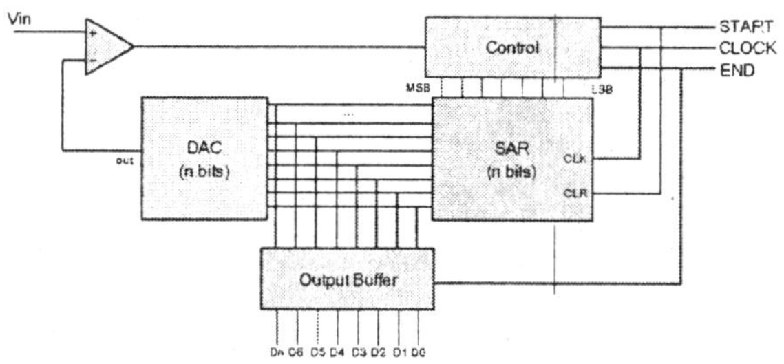

Fig. 7 Successive approximation ADC

While the ramp counter ADC does the analog-to-digital conversion counting from 0 to the maximum possible value (2^n-1) until it "finds" the correct digital value for Vin, the successive approximation ADC starts first setting the MSB (most significant bit, on an eight-bit ADC it would be D7). In order to facilitate the explanations below, consider an eight-bit ADC.

The comparison between Vin and the DAC output will tell the control unit if this bit should remain set at 1 or should be set at 0, as the op amp will tell right away the control unit if the sample value is greater or lower than 128 (2^7). Then D6 is set to one, and from the comparison done by the op amp, the control unit will know if this bit should remain set or not. And so on.

The good thing about the successive approximation ADC is its speed. At the worst case it will find the correct digital value for the sample at n clock cycles, where n is the number of bits used. For an eight-bit ADC, the digital value for each sample can be found in up to eight clock cycles (compare to 255 on the ramp counter), and for a 16-bit ADC the digital value for each sample can be found in up to 16 clock cycles (compare to 65,535 on the previous circuit).

And, as we mentioned, another great advantage of this circuit is the use of an output buffer, which allows the circuit that is fed by the ADC to read the digital data while the ADC is already working on the next sample.

Design methods

The proposed architecture of a successive approximation ADC based on the capacitor-array.The ADC includes a capacitor-array DAC, a successive approximation register (SAR), a latched comparator and a SH circuit. The N bit DAC implemented by a binary weighted capacitor-array consists of Ci's: $C_{i+1} = 2C_i$ (i = 0 ~N-1), and C_N as a hold capacitor. The grounded switches SD i (i = 0 ~ N-1), which controlled by the SAR, connect these capacitors and the power supply line of Vdd or that of ground. The SH circuit is composed of the switched op-amp configured as voltage follower and the hold capacitor C_N, as shown in Fig. 1. The operation of proposed ADC is as follows. In the first step, the comparator input nodes are shorted to a reference voltage Vrefc (Vrefc < Vdd - Vth) by S1, and the capacitors $C_0 \sim C_{N-1}$ are connected to the power supply line of ground. Since S2 is OFF, S3 and S4 are ON; the C_N is charged to an input voltage Vin through the switched op-amp. In the next step, the states of S1 and S2 are flipped, S3 and S4 are OFF; the switched op-amp output changes to a high-impedance, thereby the Vin is held on the C_N. This causes a change of the common node voltage of DAC Vcin, from Vrefc to Vrefc - (C_N / Ctotal) × Vin, where Ctotal = $C_0 + C_1 + \ldots + C_N$. Then, the SAR operates the N-bit DAC with the successive approximation algorithm. Since the Vcin is always compared with the constant reference voltage Vrefc, the latched comparator having a narrow input common mode range can be employed with low power dissipation. In this architecture, since the offset voltage of the comparator is constant, it does not cause non-linearity error of the ADC. Although the parasitic capacitor of the DAC output node gives the attenuation of Vcin, it does not decrease the input voltage range of ADC, and does not cause any offset error and nonlinearity error. Other advantage of the ADC is that the input impedance keeps a high because of the SH circuit implemented by the switched op-amp.[3]

3.3 Integrator-Based Designs

There are a few ways of designing analog-to-digital converters using an integrator. Let's take a look on two of them, single-slope ADC and delta-sigma ADC.

Single-Slope ADC

On Fig. 8 you can see a single-slope ADC. If you pay close attention, you will see that it is very similar to a ramp counter ADC, as it uses a counter, but instead of using a DAC for generating the comparison voltage, it uses a circuit called integrator, which is basically formed by a capacitor, a resistor and an operational amplifier (op amp). The MOSFET transistor makes the necessary control circuit.

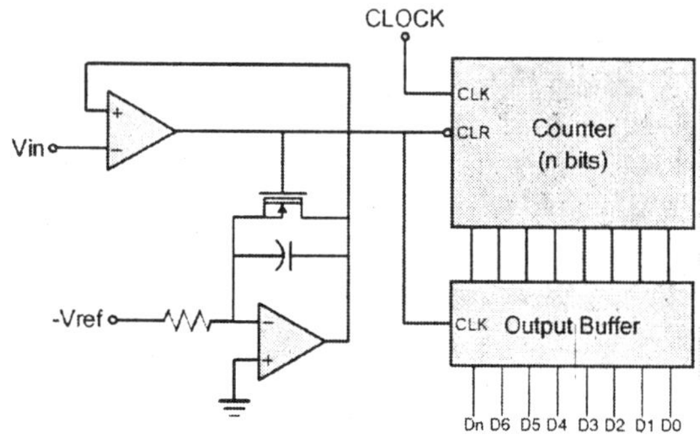

Fig. 8 Single-slope ADC

The integrator produces a sawtooth waveform on its output, from zero to the maximum possible analog voltage to be sampled, set by -Vref. The minute the waveform is started, the counter starts counting from 0 to 2^n-1, where n is the number of bits implemented by the ADC. When the voltage found at Vin (the analog signal) is equal to the voltage achieved by the triangle waveform generated by the integrator, the control circuit captures the last value produced by the counter (by triggering the output buffer clock pin), which will be the digital correspondent of the analog sample being converted. At the same time, it resets the counter and the integrator, starting the conversion of the next sample.

Like the successive approximation ADC, this circuit uses an output buffer, meaning that the last converted value can be read while the ADC is converting the current value.

It requires up to 2^n-1 clock cycles to convert each sample. For an eight-bit ADC, it would take up to 255 clock cycles to convert a single sample. For a 16-bit ADC it would take up to 65,535 clock cycles to convert one sample.

Dual-Slope ADC

Another popular design based on this one is called dual-slope ADC, which solves an inherent single-slop problem called calibration drift, which leads to inaccuracy over time because the integrator isn't linked to the clock signal (i.e., the sawtooth waveform isn't synchronized with the counter clock).

A classic dual-slope ADC can be seen on Fig. 9.

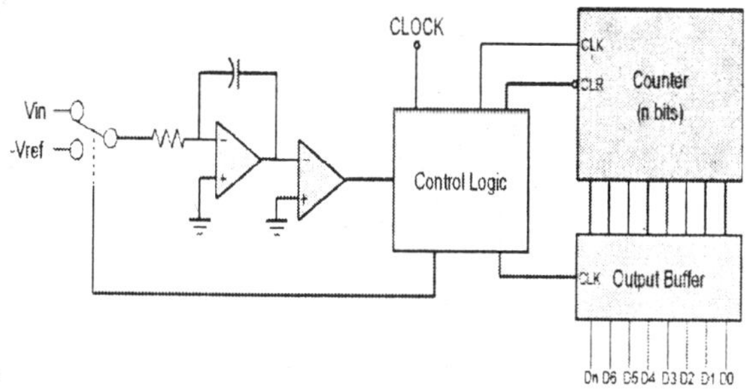

Fig. 9 Dual-slope ADC

Sigma-Delta ADC

The sigma-delta ADC – also called delta-sigma, 1-bit ADC or oversampling ADC – uses a different approach. We can divide it into two major blocks: analog modulator, which takes the analog signal and converts it into a stream of bits, and digital filter, which converts the serial stream from the modulator into an "usable" digital number.

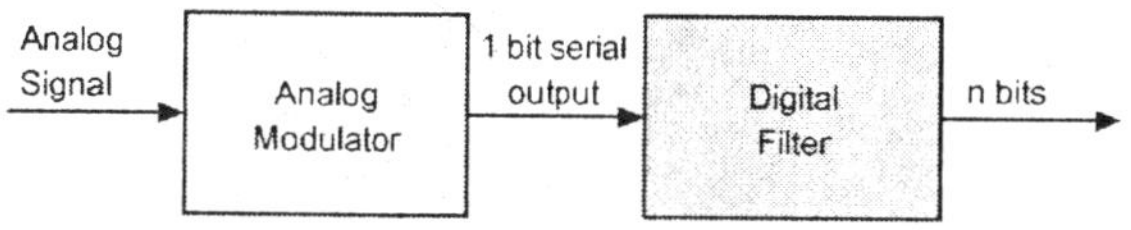

Fig. 11 Block diagram of a sigma-delta ADC

The analog modulator is somewhat similar to a dual-slope ADC, however using a 1-bit DAC as a feedback loop. The basic sigma-delta modulator design can be found on Fig. 12.

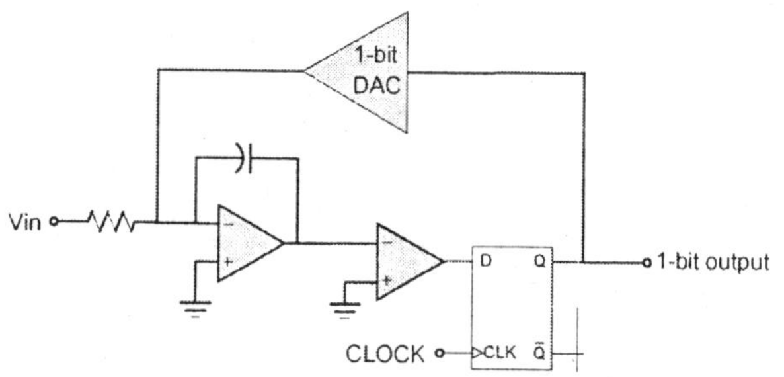

Fig. 12 Sigma-delta ADC analog modulator basic design

The analog signal will make the first op amp, which is a summing integrator, to create a sawtooth waveform proportional to the analog signal voltage. This sawtooth waveform found on the integrator output is then compared with zero volts by the second op amp, which is a comparator. It can be considered a 1-bit ADC, since its output will have only two states, high or low, depending whether the integrator output is positive or negative. The comparator output is stored on the D-type flip-flop, which is a one-bit static memory. This flip-flop is clocked at a very high frequency.

Then the flip-flop output is used to feedback the circuit thru a one-bit DAC. This one-bit DAC will basically convert the "0" or "1" stored at the flip-flop into a positive or negative reference voltage to be added to the input of the summing integrator.

So the summing integrator will sum the next sample with the result of the previous sample (a positive or a negative voltage), aiming to maintain zero at the integrator output.

The result is that at the flip-flop output we will have a series of zeros and ones that correspond the sampled data: the bitstream average level represents the analog input signal average voltage.

The problem with sigma-delta ADCs would be that with using just one bit the SNR would be too low. If you remember our formula SNR = 6.02 x n + 1.76 dB, sigma-delta ADCs would have a SNR of only 7.78 dB.

However, due to oversampling, the quantization noise is thrown to the high frequencies of the spectrum, and not spread all over the spectrum as it occurs with other designs. This effect is called shaped noise. With all the noise concentrated in a specific portion of the spectrum – on a frequency range above the sampled data –, is quite easy to construct a filter to remove it, thus improving SNR. This kind of filter is known as low pass filter (which allows only frequencies below a certain trigger frequency to pass thru it) and this filtering is done on the digital filtering stage.

The next step is to know what digital number the bitstream found at the analog modulator represents, what is done by the digital filtering block, which does also the low pass filtering already explained.

Since the bitstream is oversampled (i.e. its clock is higher than the sampling rate), this stage also "reduces" its clock rate to the sampling rate. This process is known as decimation.

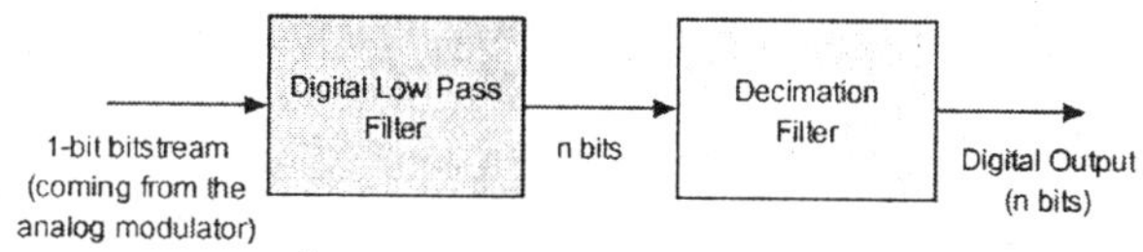

Fig. 13 Block diagram of the sigma-delta digital filter.

Design Methods

A two stage pipelined delta sigma modulator (PDSM) ADC is presented for broadband, high-resolution applications, which incorporate a first, order delta sigma modulator in each stage and combines the most significant bits of the first stage with the second stage output. A key feature of the PDSM ADC architecture is a SINC filter residue averaging technique, which results in mitigating the effect of track/hold and analog, subtract circuit errors, DAC non-linearity, and component mismatch. The input bandwidth of 62.5 MHz and the sampling frequency of 1 GHz result in an over sampling ratio of 8 for the first order modulators. MATLAB simulations for the two stages ADC show 13–15 bit resolution. A transistor level design in 0.18 um CMOS for the two stage ADC was captured with Cadence tools and simulations show 12 bit resolution with a 50 MHz input. [4]

4. Conclusion

From this study we can conclude that Flash ADC is the fastest way to convert an analog signal to a digital signal. They are suitable for applications requiring very large bandwidths. However, flash converters consume a lot of power, have relatively low resolution, and can be quite expensive. This limits them to high frequency applications that typically cannot be addressed any other way. Examples include data acquisition, satellite communication, radar processing, sampling oscilloscopes, and high-density disk drives.

The DAC based analog-to-digital converter (ADC) has become the most popular ADC architecture for sampling rates from a few megasamples per second (MS/s) up to 100MS/s+, with resolutions from 8 to 16 bits. They offer the resolution and sampling rate to cover a wide range of applications, including CCD imaging, ultrasonic medical imaging, digital receiver, base station, digital video (for example, HDTV), xDSL, cable modem, and fast Ethernet.

Successive-approximation-register (SAR) analog-to-digital converters (ADCs) are frequently the architecture of choice for medium-to-high-resolution applications, typically with sample rates fewer than 5 megasamples per second (Msps). SAR ADCs most commonly range in resolution from 8 to 16 bits and provide low power consumption as well as a small form factor. This combination makes them ideal for a wide variety of applications, such as portable/battery-powered instruments, pen digitizers, industrial controls, and data/signal acquisition.

Integrating ADCs provide high resolution and can provide good line frequency and noise rejection. These converters have been around for quite some time. The integrating architecture provides a novel yet straightforward approach to converting a low bandwidth analog signal into its digital representation. These types of converters often include built-in drivers for LCD or LED displays and are found in many portable instrument applications, including digital panel meters and digital multi-meters.

Sigma Delta analog-to-digital converters (ADCs) are used predominately in lower speed applications requiring a trade off of speed for resolution by oversampling, followed by filtering to reduce noise. 24 bit Sigma Delta converters are common in Audio designs, instrumentation and Sonar. Bandwidths are typically less than 1MHz with a range of 12 to 18 true bits. [18]

References

1. E. S¨all, K. O. Andersson, and M. Vesterbacka, "A dynamic element matching technique for flash analog-to-digital converters," in *Nordic Signal Processing Symposium*, June 2004, pp. 137–140.
2. Erik Säll, Mark Vesterbacka and K. Ola Andersson "a study of digital decoder in flash ADC" by 2004 IEEE.
3. Takeshi Yoshida, Miho Akagi, Mamoru Sasaki and Atsushi Iwata "A 1V supply successive approximation ADC with rail-to-rail input voltage range" 2005 IEEE.
4. Kevin Kattmann and Jeff Barrow "A Technique for Reducing Differential Non-Linearity Errors in Flash A/D Converters" Analog Devices Computer Labs Division, Greensboro, NC.1991IEEE
5. Dr. Mahmoud Fawzy Wagdy Qiong Xie "Comparative ADC Performance Evaluation Using a New Emulation Model for Flash ADC Architectures" Department of Electrical Engineering. 1995 IEEE
6. Paolo Carbone and Maurizio Caciotta "Stochastic-Flash Analog-to-Digital Conversion" by 1998 IEEE.
7. K. Uyttenhove, A. Marques' and M. Steyaert "A 6-bit 1 GHz Acquisition Speed CMOS Flash ADC with Digital Error Correction" IEEE 2000.
8. P. Stubberud and J. W. Bruce, "An analysis of flash dynamic element matching analog to digital converters," in *IEEE Midwest Symposium on Circuits and Systems*, vol. 2, Aug. 2000, pp. 684–687.
9. Daegyu Lee, Jincheol Yoo, Kyusun Choi, Jahan Ghaznavi "fat tree encopder design for ultra high speed 4 bit flash ADC"
10. Michael Choi and Asad A. Abidi, *Fellow* "A 6-b 1.3-Gsample/s A/D Converter in 0.35 um CMOS", *IEEE.*

11. M. P, Flynn, C. Donovan, and L. Sattler, "Digiial calibration incorporating redundancy of flash ADCs," *ZEEE Trum. Circuits Syst. II,* vol. *50,* no. 5, pp. 205-213, May 2003.

12. Venkata Srinivas, Shanthi Pavan, Ashish Lachhwani, and Naga Sasidhar " A Distortion Compensating Flash Analog-to-Digital Conversion Technique", IEEE Journal of Solid-State Circuits, VOL. 41, NO. 9, pp. 1959- 1969, September 2006.

13. K. A. Shehata, and H. F. Ragai H. Husien "design and implementation of high speed low power 4 bit flash ADC, Arab Academy for Science and Technology, Cairo, Egypt. 2006.

14. Saiyu Ren Ray Siferd "1GS/s pipelined delta sigma modulator ADC using residue averaging technique" 2007 IEEE.

15. www.hardwaresecrets.com.

16. http://www.maxim-ic.com

Simulation of Digital Organisms using AI Techniques to Design Controllers

Raja Mohamed. S[1], Rajeswaran. N[2], RamaRaju V[3], Dr Madhu T[4]
[1]Dept of CSE/SVECW
[2]Dept of ECE/SVECW
[3]Dept of ECE/VIT
[4]Principal/GVIT
raja_delip@yahoo.com *rajeswarann@gmail.com* *tennetimadhu@yahoo.co.in*

Abstract

Real time modeling of characters/creatures is increasing day by day in developing various computer games. The real world simulation of digital organism in the virtual world is done using artificial life techniques like Co-evolution, Ecology and Learning during lifetime. Both the complex and noncomplex life techniques include for complex and non-complex digital organisms are represented by their genome through which properties like co-existence, altruism, mutation etc are tested and adapted to improve their surveillance. This paper deals with a new method to create real world AI engine that incorporates the above qualities.

1. Introduction

The realistic physical modeling of characters in games and virtual worlds is becoming a viable alternative to more traditional animation techniques. Physical modeling of characters and environments can enhance realism and allow users to interact with the virtual world much more freely. By modeling the forces and torques acting on bodies within a virtual environment, detecting and responding to collisions between bodies, respecting constraints arising from, for example, joints in articulated multi-body objects, etc., the system behaves in a believable manner in all situations, and the user can therefore be allowed to interact with it much more freely. The growing popularity of this approach is demonstrated by the appearance over the last couple of years of a number of off-the-shelf physics engines aimed at games programmers (e.g. MathEngine). While these engines handle the modeling of inanimate bodies, programmers are still left with the task of writing controllers for motile objects within the environment (e.g. cars, human characters, monsters, etc.). Writing a controller for a physically modeled character is a question of calculating the appropriate forces to apply to each body part at each point of time to achieve the desired movement (e.g. a realistic walking gait for a human character). This is generally a very hard task. Artificial life techniques can be useful in automating this task. For example, artificial evolution can generate suitable controllers for simple behaviors, given only a high level description of that behavior in terms of a fitness function. In this paper, the state of the art in evolving controllers, and also in evolving the characters' body shapes, is described. It is then suggested that current approaches will not be able to scale up to more complicated behaviors. A number of possible solutions to this problem are described. Finally, several routes for delivering this technology to the games industry are discussed.

2. Background

Several groups have employed techniques from the fields of artificial intelligence and artificial life to automate the generation of controllers for physically simulated characters. The use of genetic algorithms in this area generally falls into one of two categories: the evolution of controllers for characters with predefined, fixed body shape [1], [5]; and the evolution of both the controller and the body shape of the creature [2], [7], [8], [10], [13]. Karl Sims [10]. He used an artificial evolutionary process to generate both controllers and body shapes for creatures that could perform simple tasks such as crawling, swimming, jumping and following a target. However, the basic limitation of the model is that it cannot be used for more complex behaviors. Each creature is described by a "genome" that contains information about the body shape and controller. In Sims' work, the body shape was described by a directed graph, where each node represents an individual body part, and the connections between nodes describe how the parts are connected. Each node also describes an augmented neural network type controller for the corresponding body part. This representation provides modularity to the mapping from genotype (the description of the creature) to phenotype (the instantiation of the creature as a physical model and controller), and naturally leads to features such as duplication and recursion of body parts.

A run is started by randomly generating a population of genotypes. Each genotype in turn is translated into a physical creature, and then evaluated in a physically simulated environment for its performance at a given task. Sims used two basic environments, sea and land. The sea environment included a simplistic model of fluid drag, while the land environment included gravity, a ground plane, and frictional forces for ground contacts. A number of different criteria (or "fitness functions" in genetic algorithm jargon) were used for scoring the success of each creature in its environment. The evolutionary process can only get off the ground if the initial, randomly generated population of creatures contains at least one creature that can achieve a non-zero score on the fitness function. The more complicated the function is, the less likely this is to be the case. For example, consider an attempt to evolve a behavior whereby a creature needed to process complex visual data about the movement of another creature standing in front of it, and use this to decide whether that creature was a friend or foe. This enterprise would clearly have little chance of success if the evolutionary process was starting from scratch

The first, randomly generated population of creatures typically performed poorly at the designated task, although a few would, by chance, have some degree of success. Each creature was scored according to its performance, and when all creatures had been evaluated the population was ranked according to score. The best individuals were kept to form the basis of a new generation. This new population was filled up by adding mutated forms of these best genotypes and genetic crosses of pairs of genotypes. By repeating this process, efficient creatures evolved surprisingly quickly. Sims typically used populations of 300 individuals and the experiment for 50-100 generations. In a recent reimplementation of Sims' work, a single run of this size would take between 2-3 hours on a single 1GHz Pentium PC. Pictures and movies of a variety of creatures evolved using these systems are available online. One of the nice properties of systems such as these is that each run generally produces a very different result due to the stochastic nature of the evolutionary process. Sims only selected for high-level behaviors such as the ability to move forwards, but within the vast space of different creature designs describable with the genetic system used, there are countless forms, which can competently perform such behaviors. The evolutionary process is therefore a tool for exploring interesting regions of this immense landscape of creature designs; it is a creative machine for generating suitable and interesting forms and behaviors, not limited by the preconceptions of a human designer's imagination.

3. Proposed Models to achieve more Complex Behaviors

Researchers in the field of evolutionary robotics have considered various methods of overcoming the difficulties like selecting a non-zero fitness function, mutation etc. These generally involve either the incremental acquisition of increasingly complicated tasks [3], [9], or the decomposition of the task into a sequence of easier tasks together with some way of combining them [8]. A problem with many of these approaches is that the decomposition of the task into easier and/or incremental steps is something of an art in itself and there are no general guidelines to suggest the most appropriate way to do this sensible task. Decomposition from the designer's point of view may not be the best route by which one can evolve a complex behavior; in the worst case, it could even be a hindrance. Despite the problems described above with evolving single creatures to perform complex tasks, there are a number of alternative approaches that have shown some signs of success. Five such popular methods are given below:

3.1 Co-Evolution

Co-evolution is a very promising technique for developing complex behaviors, especially when there is a competition between two or more creatures. The idea is that rather than evolving a population against a fixed fitness function, two populations are used instead, with one evolving against the other. For example, Hillis evolved efficient number sorting algorithms by co-evolving a population of candidate algorithms against a population of numbers to be sorted [6]. As the sorting algorithms got improved, so are the population of numbers to be sorted evolved to present tougher challenges to the algorithms. Evolution in one population thereby catalyzed further evolution in the other. Sims has also used a similar technique to evolve interesting competitive behaviors in virtual creatures. In this work, rather than simulating a single creature at a time, he simulated a couple. These two creatures were opponents in a simple game where they had to fight for possession of a cube that was initially placed halfway between them. The creatures not only evolved behaviors to reach the cube quickly, but also to fend off their opponents. A wide variety of different behaviors were evolved in this way, and the resulting competitions were very engaging to watch.

3.2 Virtual Ecologies

Taking co-evolution to its logical conclusion, we could forget about defining some sort of high-level game (such as fighting for possession of a cube) altogether. Instead, we could simply concurrently simulate a large population of creatures that are competing with each other for basic resources such as food and space, and let the creatures reproduce "by themselves" according to, say, how much food they have managed to eat. That way we get away from the sort of "artificial selection" we have talked about up to now (a fitness function is really the virtual equivalent of the selection employed by livestock farmers when trying to improve a particular trait in their animals), towards a closer approximation to "natural selection". We would not be selecting for particular high-level behaviors, but rather creating a virtual ecology and letting it evolve in any way it likes. Some progress in this direction has been made [7], although because of the much larger drain on computational resources required to simulate large populations of creatures concurrently, these studies have used somewhat simplified physical simulations. As computers become increasingly powerful, as physics engines become more efficient, and, most importantly, with the opportunities for running massively parallel simulations afforded by the Internet, the size of the ecologies that can be modeled and the complexity of the physical simulation will certainly increase greatly over the coming months and years.

3.3 Lifetime Learning

The creatures' controllers improve by evolution, but they do not actually adapt whilst an individual creature is being simulated. Some recent results from evolutionary robotics suggest that combining an evolutionary algorithm with the ability of the controllers to adapt or learn over an individual creature's lifetime can lead to improved robustness and complexity of behaviors compared to evolution by itself [4]. Giving an individual creature the ability to adapt and learn during its lifetime effectively smoothes the search space over which evolution is happening, thereby helping the process to progress. It is reasonable to assume that adding these sorts of abilities to our artificial creatures will improve their ability to evolve complex behaviors just as it has done in evolutionary robotics.

3.4 Behavioral Primitives

The evolution of complex behaviors can in general be evolved by task decomposition. Rather than trying to evolve complex behaviors, another approach is to evolve a collection of primitive behaviors, and then use other, non-evolutionary techniques for combining these primitive into more complicated sequences. The task of programming a game character using this approach could now become somewhat like directing an actor in a film; the character has a certain degree of competence at autonomous behavior and the programmer/director issues high-level commands to it such as "jump from top" or "attack the target! ". Some have suggested that this is the most useful route by which this sort of technology may be harnessed by games programmers. Alternatively, rather than directing the creatures manually, other AI techniques could be used to co-ordinate the primitive behaviors to automatically generate more complex tasks [11].

3.5 User Guided Evolution

Another alternative to supplying a fixed fitness function to the genetic algorithm is to present the user with a variety of creatures from the evolving population at various intervals, and allow them to select their favorite creatures to be used as the foundation of the next generation. The user may select the creatures by any criteria they wish, and can therefore guide the path of evolution according to their own preferences without having to formally instruct the individual creatures.

4. Results and Discussion

Simulation and optimization of digital creatures was attempted by several researches. In this paper Framsticks software is used to simulate and evolve digital creatures. Framsticks virtual world is a system for simulation and optimization of three dimensional agent structures and their control systems. It allows users to perform pre-defined experiments. It is open and allows creating user-defined experiment setups, fitness functions, and neurons and is suitable for testing various research hypotheses where fast 3D simulation and evolutionary optimization is required.

The physical structure of Framsticks agents is made of parts (material points) and joints. The control system is made of neurons (including sensors and actuators) and their connections. In this work, only a subset of system features was used: physical structure was fixed (not optimized), and there was a homogeneous, fuzzy control system (ie. it was not composed of many heterogeneous neurons with changing topology). Framsticks supports multiple genetic representations and operators. These representations range from simple and direct descriptions of agents to the ones encoding developmental process in genotypes. In this work, the direct encoding was used, and special genetic operators were designed to provide mutation and crossing over of a fuzzy control system.

Licensing Characters from a Virtual Library

One possibility would be for a specialist artificial life company to develop this technology in-house, and build up a huge library, or virtual zoo, of different characters. Games companies could inspect these characters and license individual characters for specific games or other applications. This approach would be particularly appropriate for evolved body shapes as well as controllers, as characters evolved in this way often have very strange or unusual forms and behaviors. The virtual zoo could therefore act as a source of inspiration for new types of characters, as well as a source for directly licensable characters.

Online Evolution

At the other extreme, a consumer application could be written that allows users to evolve their own creatures, and to exchange them with other users over the Internet. Alternatively, a central server could oversee a genetic algorithm in which the evaluation of individual creatures was farmed out to end-users' PCs over the Internet. This could be achieved as a background process on the PC, while the user was playing a game or it could be run as a screen-saver. Users could also be allowed to guide evolution according to their own aesthetic tastes.

Co-Evolved Characters for Combat Games

Another example application would be to co-evolve twin populations of creatures competing in some sort of contest, such as a combat game. Having co-evolved creatures in this way, by allowing evolution in one population to catalyze evolution in the other, one of the creatures in the contest could simply be replaced by a human player. The difficulty is about designing a user interface that allows the player to control the creature in a suitable way.

Co- Existence

Fig1a represents the fitness parameters of five different genotypes that are generalist population and fig1b genotypes are of specialist population type. During the fitness test of genotypes only one out of 5 remains at end of the run. Here density dependent selection acts to create multiple niches. At one extreme, organisms could specialize, adapting to one resource at the expense of their competitiveness for others. The effect of this is to partition the environment such that as many species as there are resources are potentially able to coexist. Update function is O= (2/1+e-iβ). Where O is the activation variant, i denote synaptic weights and β denotes steepness parameter of Transfer function

Altruism and Mutation

The concept of unselfishness that takes place in digital organism evolution during the course of simulation gives interesting information that kin-cheaters eliminate kin-altruists very early. Same group of creatures will not allow it's brother creature to evolve over period of time in order to survive in the world. During this phase there is no sexual contact between organism A (DNA) and B (RNA). Creatures have achieved higher mutation rate when they were tested in an open environment.

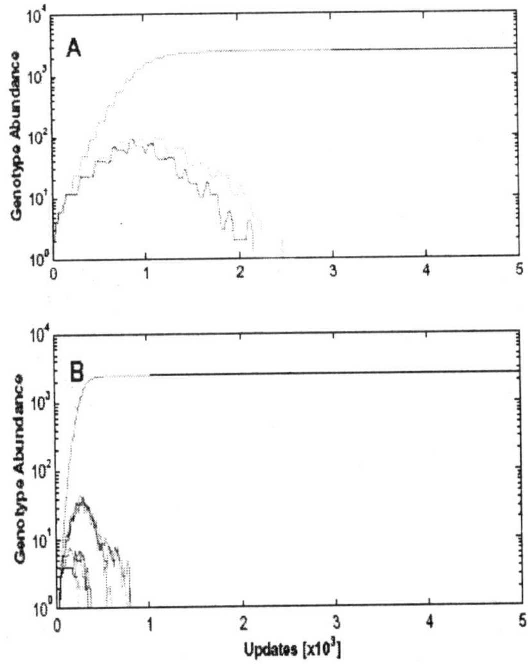

Fig. 1a & 1b Co-existence of genotypes during continued ecology phase with infinite resources

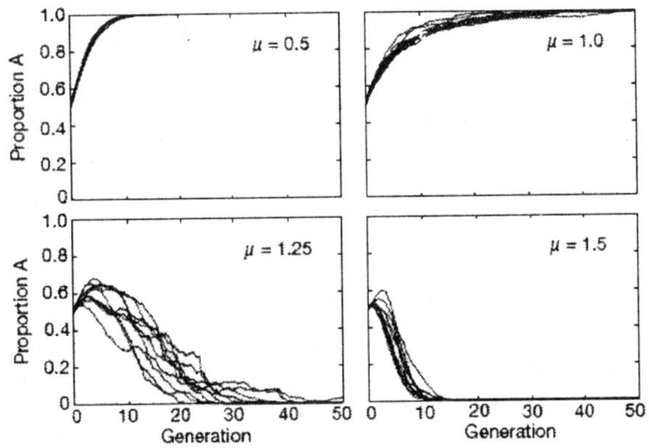

Fig. 2 Competitions for one pair of organisms at four different mutation rates

Organism A replicates 1.96 times faster than B. Genomic mutation rate Fidelity F=e-μ. Where μ=RL is the mutation rate per genome and R is the rate of error per evolving instruction sets, L is the length of the genomic sequence. To measure the actual growth rate of the population spawned from a single organism across a range of mutation rates. The decay in growth rate with increasing mutation rate was well described by

$$w(\mu) = w0 \exp(-a\mu-b\mu2)$$

w0 is the intrinsic replication rate, a and b are robust parameters estimated by fitting data concerned to the organism groups.

Complex Creatures (Bending, Rotating, Touching, Equilibrium)

To examine the evolutionary origin of a complex feature in much greater detail we have performed experiments with digital organisms—computer programs that self replicate, mutate and compete. Evolution will occur whenever and wherever three conditions are met: replication, variation (mutation), and differential fitness (competition). According to a case study of the genomic and phenotypic changes in a population that evolved an especially complex function, and then a functional-genomic analysis of the first genotype able to perform that function. Genetic encoding sequence of the digital organism comes with three types that are recurrent, simulated and developed. Genetic encoding has also got information on no of points, joints, and connections in the respective organism For example in framsticks world genome is represented using the following format X[T][G][S][-3:1,-2:1,-1:1] Where t denotes touch, G denotes gyroscope and S denotes smell all receptors or sensors mounted in one stick. Here the Brain of the system which is nothing but the neural network of that digital organism.

Table1 Rewards for performing nine one and two input logic functions

Function name	Logic operation	Computational merit
NOT	~A; ~B	2
NAND	~(A and B)	2
AND	A and B	4
OR_N	(A or ~B); (~A or B)	4
OR	A or B	8
AND_N	(A and ~B); (~A and B)	8
NOR	~A and ~B	16
XOR	(A and ~B) or (~A and B)	16
EQU	(A and B) or (~A and ~B)	32

The symbol (~) denotes negation. The reward for computational merit increases with 2n, where n is the minimum number of nand operations needed to perform the listed function. Symmetrical operations, shown separated by a semi-colon, are treated as the same function. No added benefit is obtained for performing any function multiple times. These functions include all one and two-input logic operations except ECHO, which requires no nand operations and was not rewarded. Trajectories of the two fitness components showing each genotype in the line of descent for different population. Replication efficiency which is the ratio of genome length to the energy used in an organism's lifetime and computational merit shown in log2 transformed which is the product of all the rewards obtained by the organism for logic functions performed during its lifetime.

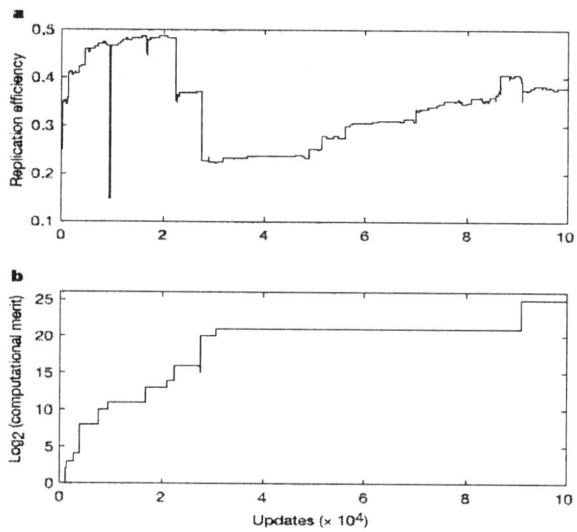

Fig. 3 Fitness function graph.

5. Conclusions

With the help of artificial evolution, body shapes of characters and creatures and creating one evolved genetic algorithm and used evolutionary details to capture the complex behaviors of digital organism with difficult fitness functions. This method helps capturing the finest details / movements of various creatures. Methods suggested in this paper vindicate that effective construction of digital creatures and evolving them in an artificial environment provides sufficient information to design the physical controllers in order to emulate them in a successful way.

6. References

[1] Arnold, D. (1997). Evolution of Legged Locomotion. MSc thesis, School of Computing Science, Simon Fraser University.

[2] Bongard, J.C. & Paul, C. (2000). Investigating MorphologicalSymmetryandLocomotive Efficiency Using Virtual Embodied Evolution. Meyer, J.-A. et al. (eds.) From Animals to Animats: The Sixth International Conference on the Simulation of Adaptive Behavior: MIT Press.

[3] Dorigo, M. & Colombetti, M. (1997). Robot Shaping: An Experiment in Behavior Engineering. MIT Press.

[4] Floreano, D. & Urzelai, J. (1999). Evolution of Neural Controllers with Adaptive Synapses and Compact Genetic Encoding. Floreano, D. et al. (eds.) Advances in Artificial Life: Proceedings of the Fifth European Conference on Artificial Life, pp.183-194: Springer Verlag.

[5] Gritz, L. & Hahn, J. K. (1997). Genetic Programming Evolution of Controllers for 3-D Character Animation. Koza, J.R. et al. (eds.) Genetic Programming 1997: Proceedings of the Second Annual Conference, pp.139-146: Morgan Kaufmann.

[6] Hillis, W. D. (1991). Co-evolving parasites improves simulated evolution as an optimization technique. Langton, C. G. et al. (eds.), Artificial Life II, pp.313-384: Addison-Wesley.

[7] Komosinski, M. & Ulatowski, S. (1999). Framsticks: Towards a Simulation of a Nature-Like World, Creatures and Evolution. Floreano, D. et al. (eds.) Advances in Artificial Life: Proceedings of the Fifth European Conference on Artificial Life, pp.261-265: Springer Verlag.

[8] Lee, W.-P. (1997). Evolving Robots: from Simple Behaviors to Complete Systems. Ph.D. thesis. Department of Artificial Intelligence. University of Edinburgh.

[9] Perkins, S. (1998). Incremental Acquisition of Complex Visual Behaviour using Genetic Programming and Shaping. PhD thesis, Division of Informatics, University of Edinburgh.

[10] Sims, K. (1994b). Evolving Virtual Creatures. Computer Graphics, (SIGGRAPH 94 Proceedings), pp.15-22: ACM SIGGRAPH.

[11] Terzopoulos, D., Tu, X. & Grzeszczuk, R. (1994). Artificial Fishes: Automomous Locomotion, Perception, Behavior, and Learning in a Simulated Physical World. Artificial Life 1, pp.327-351.

[12] Van de Panne, M. & Fiume, E. (1993). Sensor-ActuatorNetworks. ComputerGraphics (SIGGRAPH 93 Proceedings), pp.335-342: ACM SIGGRAPH.

[13] Ventrella, J. (1999). Animated Artificial Life. Chapter 3 in Heudin, J.-C. (ed.) Virtual Worlds: Synthetic Universes, Digital Life and Complexity: Perseus Books.

Design and Analysis of Object Oriented Software using UML in different perspectives

S. Balamurugan and P.Ganesh Kumar
Department of Information Technology, Anna University, Coimbatore, India
sbnbala@gmail.com *pganeshkumar_ms@yahoo.co.in*

Abstract

The paper aims to employ a modeling language aimed to provide a unified framework for representing online system personal finance management system. The proposed modeling methodology is based on the principle of object orientation [3], which allows describing both software and functionalities. Furthermore, it is illustrated how the well-known object-oriented specification language unified modeling language can be adopted, to provided an adequate formalization of its semantics, to describe structural and behavioral aspects of online personal finance management system related to both logical and physical parts. It is needed to implement the software on the basis of Object Oriented Model developed. Flaw in modeling process can substantially contribute to the development cost and time. The operational efficiency may be affected as well. Therefore special attention should be paid to the correctness of the models that are used at all planning levels and hence Unified Modeling Language (UML) [4] plays an important role.

1. Introduction

Most of the effort to date in object oriented community has been focused on programming language issues. Object-oriented programming languages are useful in removing restrictions due to the inflexibility of traditional programming languages. In a sense, however, this emphasis is a step backwards for software engineering by focusing excessively on implementation mechanisms, rather than the underlying thought process that they support.

The real pay-off comes from addressing front-end conceptual issues, rather than back-end implementation issues. Design flaws that surface during implementation are most costly to fix than those that are found earlier. Focusing on implementation issues too early restricts the design choices and often leads to inferior product. An object-oriented development approach encourages software developers to work and think in terms of application domain through most of the software engineering lifecycle.

Object-oriented development [5] is a conceptual process independent of programming language until final stages. Object-oriented programming is fundamentally a new way of thinking and not a programming technique. Its greatest benefits come from helping specifiers, developers, and customers express abstracts concepts clearly and communicate them to each other. It can serve as a medium for specification, analysis, documentation and interfacing as well as programming.

The Unified Modeling Language (UML) is a graphical language for visualizing, specifying, constructing, and documenting the artifacts of a software-intensive system. The Unified Modeling Language offers a standard way to write a system's blueprints, including conceptual things such as business processes and system functions as well as concrete things such as programming language statements, database schemas, and reusable software components. UML is officially defined by the Object Management Group (OMG) [3] as the UML metamodel, a Meta-Object Facility metamodel (MOF). Like other MOF-based specifications, UML has allowed software developers to concentrate more on design and architecture.

UML diagrams represent three different views of a system model:

- Functional requirements view: Emphasizes the functional requirements of the system from the user's point of view. And includes use case diagrams.
- Static structural view: Emphasizes the static structure of the system using objects, attributes, operations and relationships. And includes class diagrams and composite structure diagrams.
- Dynamic behavior view: Emphasizes the dynamic behavior of the system by showing collaborations among objects and changes to the internal states of objects. And includes sequence diagrams, activity diagrams and state machine diagrams.

2. Class diagram

UML class diagrams [3] are the mainstay of object-oriented analysis and design. UML class diagrams show the classes of the system, their interrelationships (including inheritance, aggregation, and association), [7] [8] [9] [21] and the operations and attributes of the classes. Class diagrams are used for a wide variety of purposes, including both conceptual/domain modeling and detailed design modeling.

Customer banks with the Financial Institution through its banking site via network. Both of them use computer for communication. Credit cards are issued to the customers via the credit card company, and they in turn aggregate to form credit unions. A customer can own many credit cards of different companies.

Financial Institution provides customer the facility to maintain an account. A customer can possess multiple accounts in various institutions. These accounts aggregate to form account aggregation, which is yet another facility provided by the financial institution. Students account and Retirement account are a kind of account (inherited from the account class). The customer can maintain these accounts if they possess proper eligibility. The customer can transfer funds to a creditor he wishes after the validation of the account numbers. The customer can perform transaction if he has a valid account in the institution. He can also perform foreign exchange transaction which is the inherited form of transaction. He can check the status of the transaction which he/she has performed (scheduled, processed or pending). From this status the customer can know about the completion of transaction. The customer is also provided with the facility of viewing the account history. The customer can make payments which can be of any type (multiple, recurring, email, electronic or cheque according to his wish. The customer can also pay bills (e-bills/ overdue bills) online. This is depicted in Fig. 1

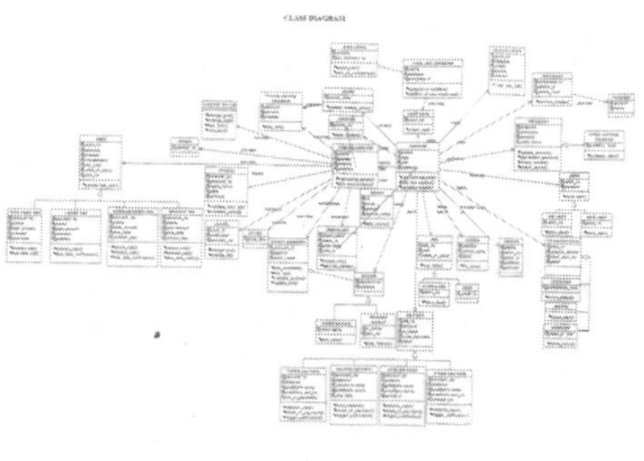

Fig. 1 Class Diagram Depicting the dependencies between various classes identified

3. Use Case Diagram

Use case diagrams [16] [19] [20] model the functionality of a system using actors and use cases. Use cases are services or functions provided by the system to its users.

A. Customer Signing in

The customer banks with the Financial Institution and the first step in this process is to sign up the respective institution. The financial institution checks for validity and the customer can perform transaction. After the financial institution has checked for validity, it can provide customer service like providing options for review, changing passwords. Etc and hence the stereotype "extend" is included.

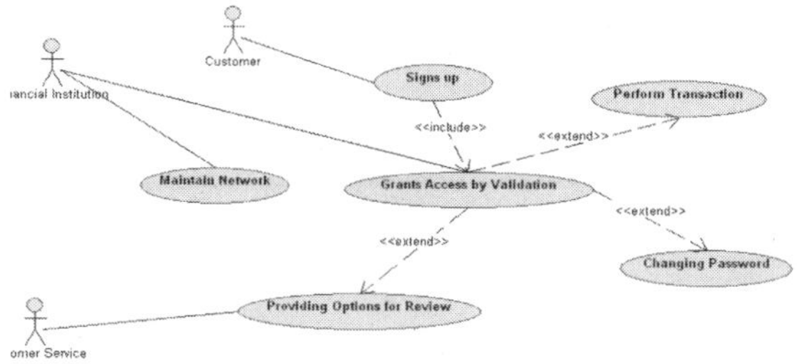

Fig. 2 Use Case Diagram for Signing in Process

B. Performing Transaction

The customer can transfer funds between accounts which he has in respective financial institution checks for minimum balance. So the stereotype "include" is specified here. The customer views the transaction status only after performing transactions and the same reason holds here as shown in Fig. The financial institution maintains the account of the payee and the latter makes the payment to the creditor he wishes. Then the creditor can receive the payment. After the payee/ customer makes the payment, the financial institution issues receipts and so the stereotype "extend" is used here. Issuing the receipts happens only after issuing bills for making the payment. Hence the stereotype "include" has been specified.

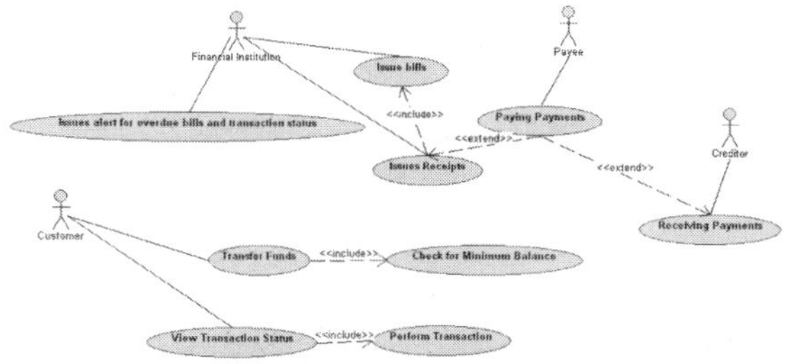

Fig. 3 Use Case Diagram for Transaction Process

C. Account Aggregation and Fund Transfer

The financial institution provides the option for performing transactions, checking for minimum balance, viewing account history and account aggregation to the customer. Money transfer, withdrawal and deposits are the options under transaction and it is done on the accounts of the customer as shown in Fig. 4. The stereotype "include" is used for the options because the options must include only the above mentioned things.

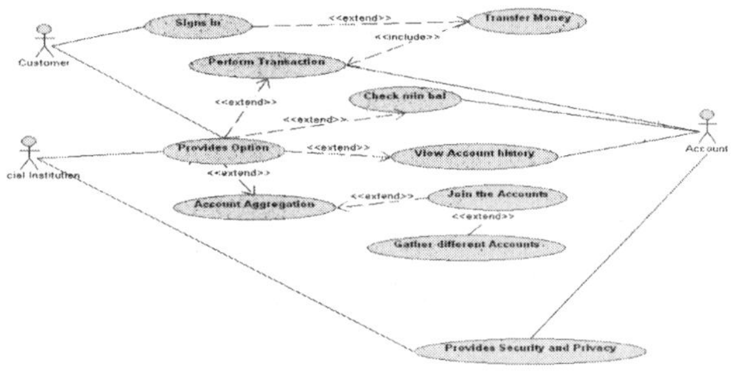

Fig. 4 Use Case Diagram for Account Aggregation and Fund Transfer

D. Credit Cards, Mortgages and Financial Planning Calculators

After the financial institution grants access to the customer by validation, it provides the option of getting loans, performing mortgages which in turn include involving brokerages, involving in auctions, performing financial planning calculations and the customer can choose any of these options shown in the Fig. 5. The stereotype "include" is used here. The customer maintains stock, and based on the value of the stock, the financial institution planning calculatos forecasts the amount of the customer after a certain period.

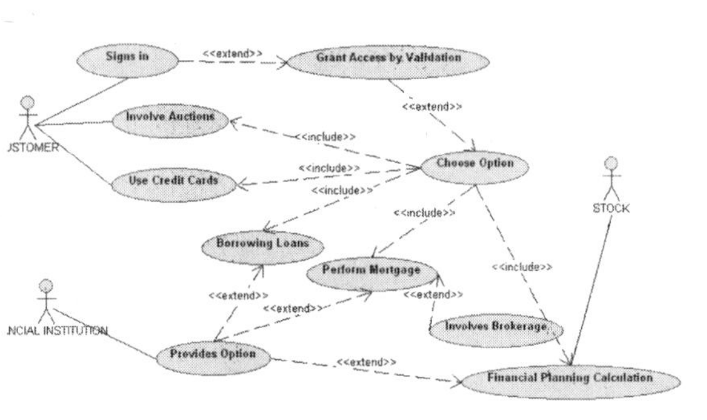

Fig. 5 Use Case Diagram for Credit Cards, Mortgages and Financial Planning Calculators

4. Interaction Diagram

Interaction diagrams [10] [11] [12] model the behavior of use cases by describing the way groups of objects interact to complete the task. The sequence diagram [3] [4] is used primarily to show the interactions between objects in the sequential order that those interactions occur.

A. Customer Signing in

The customer, in order to perform online banking, contacts the banking site. The banking site asks for the information of the customer's account like the account number and the account details. After the customer has given the correct information, the banking computer calls the customer service department of the bank and the latter checks for the validation of this information. Then it grants/denies customer. After customer has given required information, the customer service department stores the entered information in the bank's database. The message between the bank's central computer and the customer service is synchronous because only after the response from the customer service department, the computer can send the needed information to the customer. The messages between the customer and the computer are asynchronous between the latter can or cannot make use of the options offered.

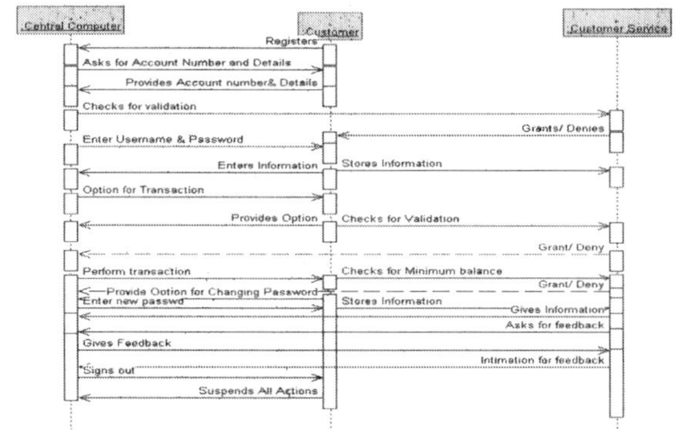

Fig. 6 Sequence Diagram for Signing in Process

B. Performing Transaction

After the customer chooses the option for transaction, the banking site provides the option for the customer to perform transaction. Again, the customer gives the user id and password for validation by the customer service department and access is granted/ denied.

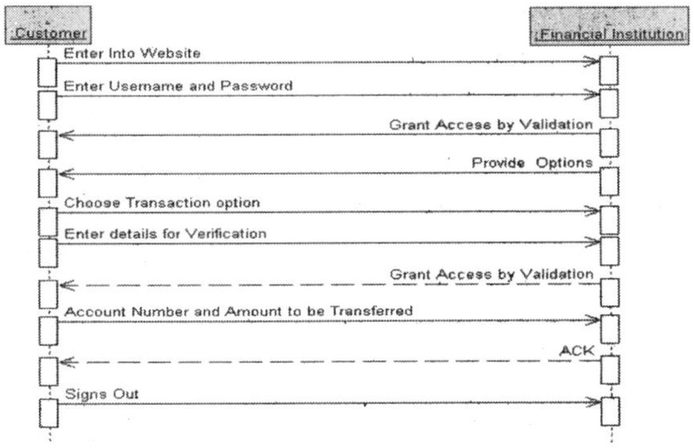

Fig. 7 Sequence Diagram for Performing Transaction

The customer service department checks for the minimum balance just in case if the customer wants to transfer funds between his account or making payments Always there will be an option for the customer to change his/her password in the banking site

The customer can or cannot use this facility and if he/she uses this facility the new information is stored in the bank's database. Also the option for the "feedback" from the customer is always an option in the banking site, which the customer can or cannot respond. The customer can sign out he wishes. This is depicted in the Fig. 7and Fig. 8

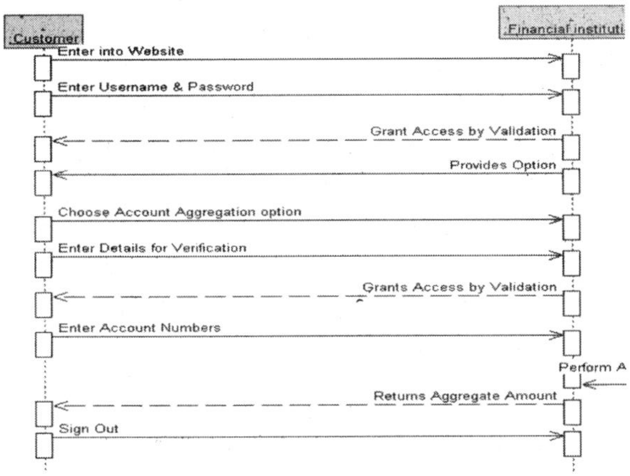

Fig. 8 Sequence Diagram for Account Aggregation

After the customer has signed out the customer service suspends all the actions in the account and closes it until the customer signs up again. The messages from the financial institution to the customer are asynchronous because the customer can or cannot choose the option offered. On the other hand the message from the customer to the financial institution is synchronous because only after the response from the customer the next activity is decided.

C. Making Payments

The customer signs up and the Financial Institution checks for validation. The bank issues a bill to the customer to their email id. The customer makes the payment to the creditor. After the creditor, receives the payment, the financial institution issues receipts to the customer. The customer can provide the option to view the transaction status. The customer can sign out at this point and the financial institution suspends all the activities corresponding to the account. This is depicted in Fig. 9and Fig.10

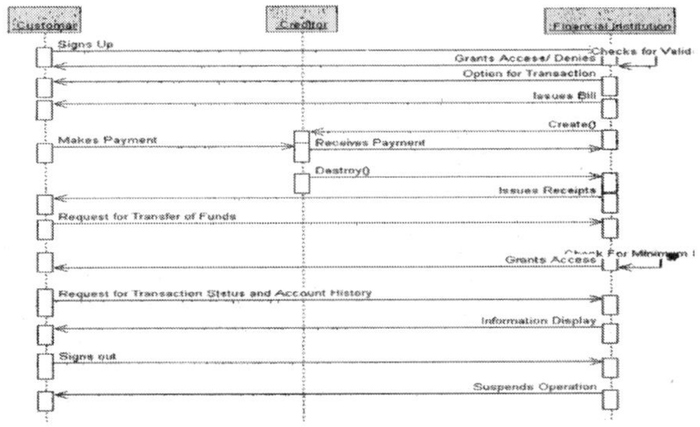

Fig. 9 Sequence Diagram for Issuing Bills and Fund Transfer

D. Providing Loans

After the customer has signed up and his validity has been checked, the customer can go for the option of providing loans from the financial institution. The customer enters the information regarding him/her and also his/her account details, after the validation of the information, the financial institution gives an option of loans that he/she can apply for. The financial institution also checks whether the customer has the privilege for having a particular loan which he wants to borrow. This is depicted in Fig. 11

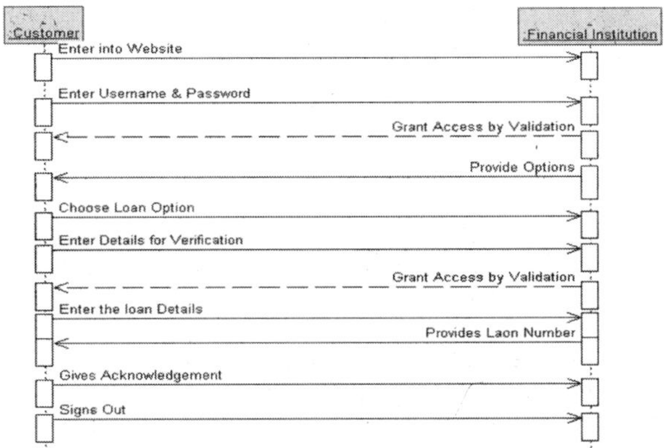

Fig. 10 Sequence Diagram for Providing Loans

The customer can pay the amount as per the bank's rules. The customer can sign out at this point and the financial institution suspends all the activities corresponding to the account. The messages from the customer to the financial institution are synchronous because only after the response from the customer the next activity is decided.

E. Stocks, Auctions, Credit Cards and Mortgages

After the customer has signed up and his validity has been checked, the customer can go for the option of maintaining stocks in the financial institution. The customer enters the information needed and it is stored in the bank's database. The Financial Planning Calculators calculate the amount that will be available in his/ her account periodically after number of years as per customer's wish.

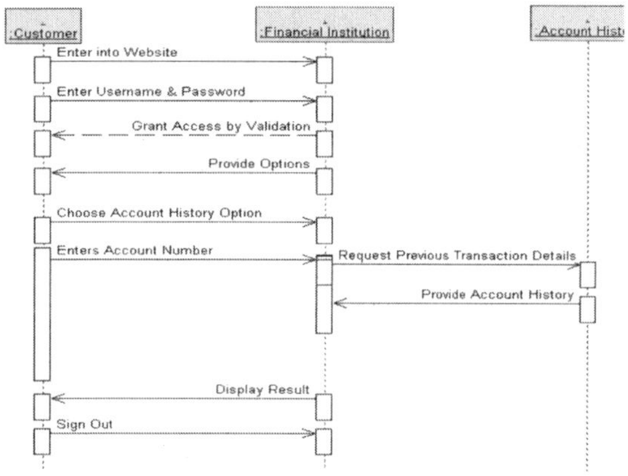

Fig. 11 Sequence Diagram for Viewing Account History

The customers can opt for the option of credit cards. After the validity of information, the credit card company issues the credit card to the customer. The customer can sign out at this point and the financial institution suspends all the activities corresponding to the account.

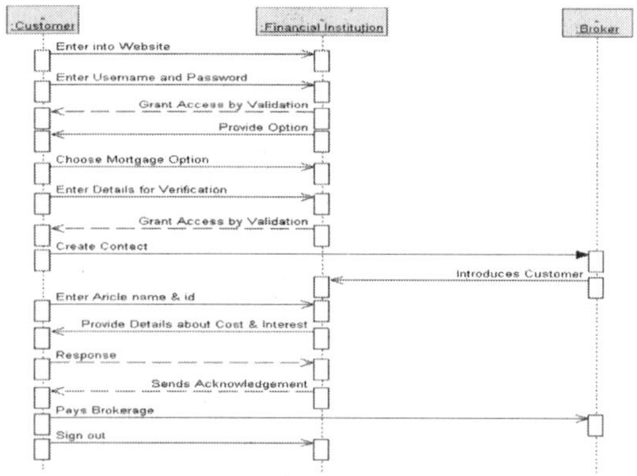

Fig. 12 Sequence Diagram for Mortgage System

The messages from the financial institution to the customer is asynchronous because the customer can or cannot choose the options offered. On the other hand the message from the customer to the financial institution is synchronous because only after the response from the customer, the next activity is decided.

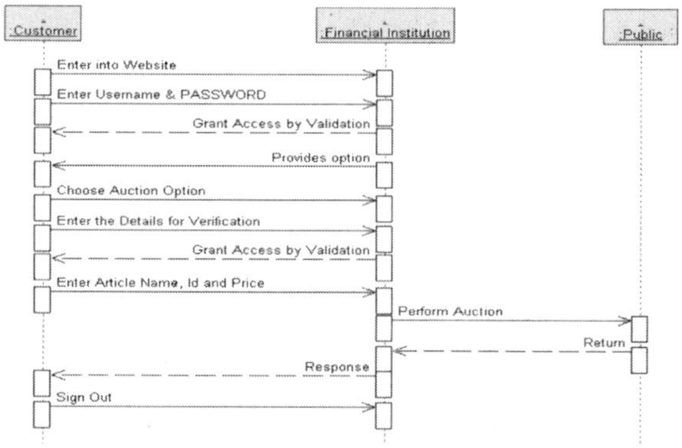

Fig. 13 System for Auction

The messages from the customer to the broker are synchronous for the same reason and the converse is asynchronous. The brokers are active only during the mortgage period and are destroyed later.

5. Activity Diagram

UML 2 activity diagrams [3] [14] [15] are typically used for business process modeling, for modeling the logic captured by a single use case or usage scenario, or for modeling the detailed logic of a business rule. Activity diagrams do not give detail about how objects behave or how objects collaborate.

A. Customer Signing in

The banking site requests for the information of the customer's account like the account number and account details. After the customer has given the correct information, the banking computer calls the customer service department of the bank and latter checks for validation of this information. Then the customer is either granted or denied access. This is depicted in Fig.14

B. Performing Transaction

The Financial Institution checks for minimum balance just in case if customer wants to transfer funds between his account or make payments. Always there will be an option for the customer to change his/ her password in the banking site depicted in Fig.16 The customer can or cannot use this facility and if he uses this facility, the new information will be stored in the bank's database.

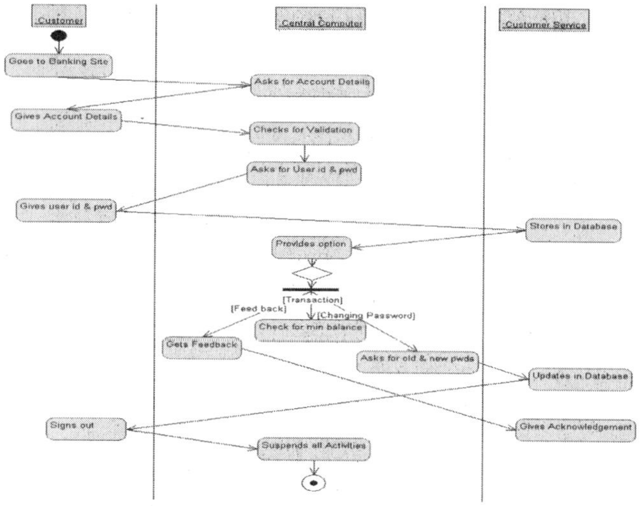

Fig. 14 Activity Diagram for Signing in Process

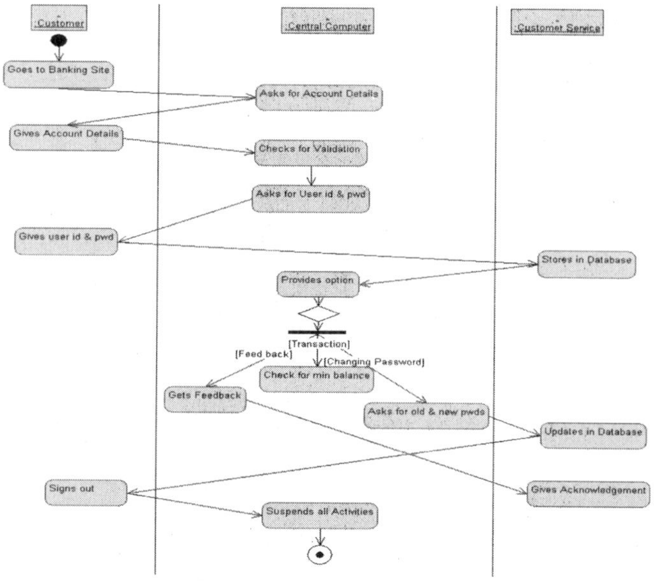

Fig. 15 Activity Diagram for Transaction Process

C. Making Payments

The bank issues a bill to the customer to his email id. The customer makes a payment to the creditor. After the creditor receives the payment, the financial institution issues receipts to the customer. If the customer chooses to transfer funds between accounts, the financial institution checks for minimum balance.

D. Stocks, Auctions, Credit Cards and Mortgages

After the customer has signed up and his validity has been checked, the customer can go for the option of maintaining stocks in the financial institution. The customer enters the information needed and it is stored in the bank's database. The Financial Planning Calculators calculate the amount that will be available in his/ her account periodically after number of years as per customer's wish. The customers can opt for the option of credit cards. After the validity of information, the credit card company issues the credit card to the customer. The customer can sign out at this point and the financial institution suspends all the activities corresponding to the account. The messages from the financial institution to the customer is asynchronous because the customer can or cannot choose the options offered. On the other hand the message from the customer to the financial institution is synchronous because only after the response from the customer, the next activity is decided. The messages from the customer to the broker is synchronous for the same reason and the converse is asynchronous. The brokers are active only during the mortgage period and are destroyed later.

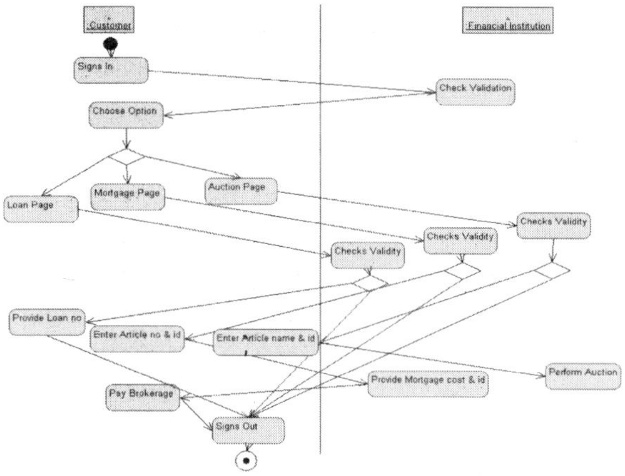

Fig.16 Activity Diagram for Auctions, Mortgages and Loans

6. State Chart Diagrams

State diagrams [3] [7] are used to describe the behavior of a system. State diagrams can describe the possible states of an object as events occur. Each diagram usually represents objects of a single class and tracks the different states of its objects through the system.

Payment

The customer can opt for the transaction option and thus the transaction is in active state. At this state, the customer receives bills, if he has to make payments. Then the customer is in the state of making payments and concurrently, the financial institution is in the state of checking the minimum balance in his account as depicted in Fig. 17 After the payment has been made by the customer, the Financial Institution sends receipts to the customer and he moves to the receiving state.

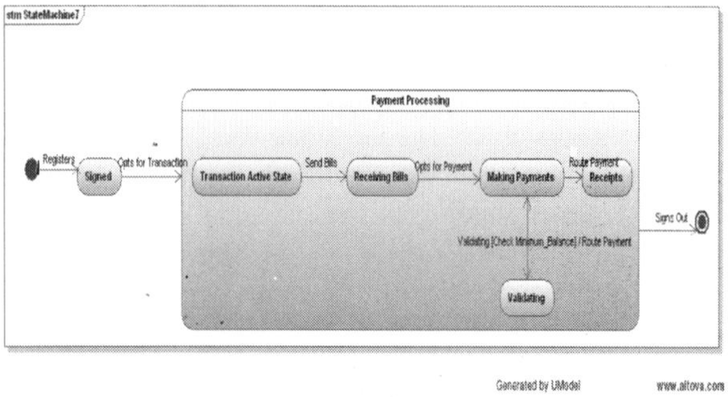

Fig. 17 State Machine Diagram for Payment Bills and Receipts

After the customer has preferred the option for transaction like payment making, then the bills are issued to the customer. Bills are initially in the un forwarded state and the financial institution sends bills, and hence moves to the forwarded state. After the payments have been made by the customer, the receipts which were in the unforwarded state initially, turns to forwarded state after the financial institution has sent them to the customer as a symbol of acknowledgement as in Fig. 22

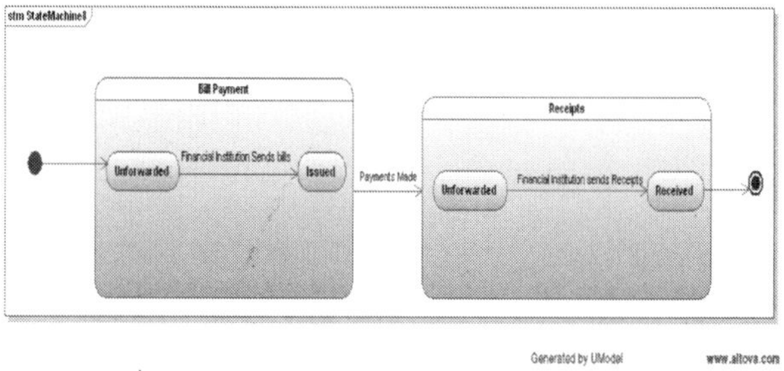

Fig. 18 State Machine model for Bills-Receipts Customer

Initially, the customer is in unsigned state, and after he has entered his name and password, the state switched to waiting. The customer provides an option for transaction and concurrently the financial institution is in the validating state and it checks for the minimum balance in his account. The customer after performing the transaction signs out and concurrently all the operations in the account is closed by the Financial Institution which is in closing state.

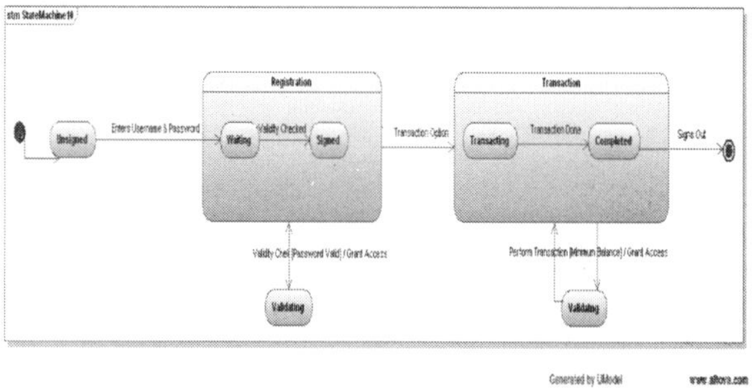

Fig. 19 State Machine Model for Customer

Transaction

Initially, the customer is in unsigned state, and after he has entered his name and password, the state switched to signed state. Then the customer may choose for options in transaction like transferring funds, making payments and viewing the transaction status as shown in Fig. 25 Concurrently the Financial Institution checks for minimum balance in his account when he is making payments and transferring funds, After the customer has finished performing transaction, he can exit and he is in the unsigned state and concurrently the account activities are maintained in the suspended state.

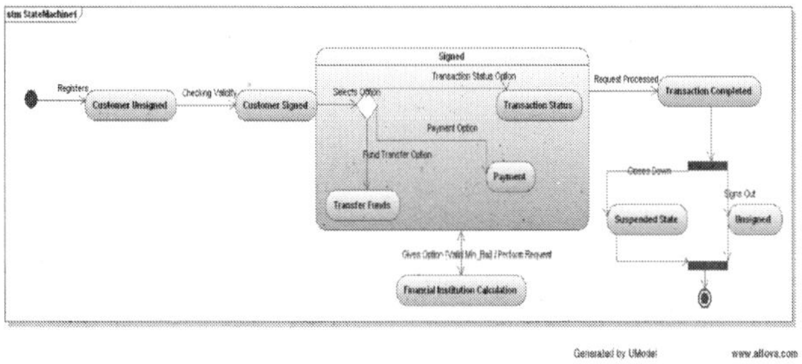

Fig. 20 State Machine Diagram for Transaction

7. Deployment Diagrams

The deployment diagram [22] [23] [24] captures the configuration of the runtime elements of the application. This diagram is by far more useful when a system is built and ready to be deployed. But, this does not mean that deployment diagram is started after the Online personal Finance Management System is built. On the contrary, the deployment diagram should start from the time the static design is being formalized using, say, class diagrams. This deployment diagram then evolves and is revised until the system is built.

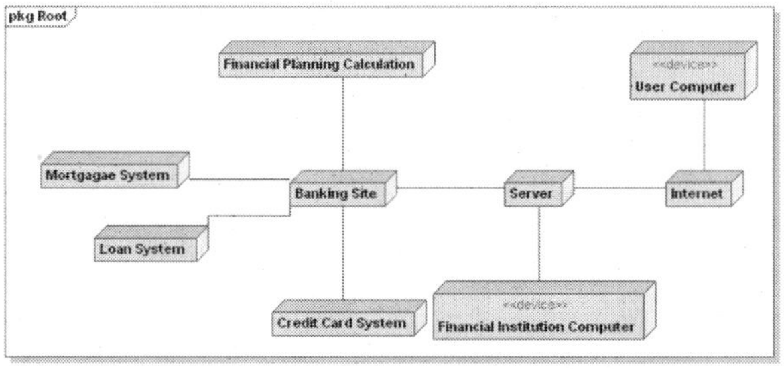

Fig. 21 Deployment Diagram depicting the Processors and Devices in an Online Personal Finance Management System

8. Conclusion and Future Work

The paper has focused on the essential and extended Object Oriented features of an Online Personal Finance Management System. Various models of UML have been employed to analyze the static, dynamic and functional view of the system. In spite of several user-friendly, time-saving, cost-effective, convenient and flexible options provided by banks in the virtual space, Online Personal Finance has not achieved a major break-through that it deserves. However if an Object Oriented approach is adopted while building the software, an explosive growth in Online Personal Finance arena could be traced. The paper depicts the structural and behavioral aspects of online personal finance management system related to both logical and physical parts.. It is a fact that design flaws that surface during implementation are most costly to fix than those that are found earlier. Focusing on implementation issues too early restricts the design choices and often leads to inferior product. Hence the developed object-oriented approach encourages software developers to work and think in terms of application domain through most of the software engineering lifecycle. Since flaw in modeling process can substantially contribute to the development cost and time and affect the operational efficiency special attention is paid to the correctness of the UML models that are used at all planning levels rather than focusing much on implementation issues.

9. References

[1] Conrad Bock, U.S. National Institute of Standards and Technology, "UML 2 Composition Model", Journal of Object Technology, Vol.3, No.10, 2007

[2] Thomas M.Atwood, "The Case for Object Oriented Databases" IEEE Spectrum, 0018-9235/91/ 0002-004, pp 44-48, 2007

[3] James Rumbaugh, Michael Blaha, William Premerlani, Frederick Eddy, William Lorensen "Object Oriented Modeling and Design", Prentice-Hall of India Private Limited.

[4] Grady Booch, "Object-Oriented Analysis & Design with Applications", Pearson Education

[5] Rogert.S.Pressman, "Software Engineering:A Practioner's Approach" Fifth Edition, McGraw-Hill Higher Education.

[6] Dionisis X. Adamopoulos and George Pavlou, University of Surrey, England Constantine A. Papandreou, Hellenic Telecommunications Organization (OTE) "Advanced Service Creation Using Distributed Object Technology", IEEE Communications Magazine 0163-6804/02, 2007

[7] http://atlas.kennesaw.edu/~dbraun/csis4650/A&D/UML_tutorial/state.htm

[8] http://www.agilemodeling.com/artifacts/stateMachineDiagram.htm

[9] http://www.agilemodeling.com/style/stateChartDiagram.htm

[10] http://www.informit.com/articles/article.aspx?p=360441&seqNum=5

[11] http://www.developer.com/design/article.php/3080941

[12] http://www.stickyminds.com/sitewide.asp?Function=edetail&ObjectType=ART&ObjectId=3718

[14] http://www.agilemodeling.com/artifacts/activityDiagram.htm
[15] http://www.sparxsystems.com.au/resources/uml2_tutorial/uml2_activitydiagram.html
[16] http://www.agilemodeling.com/artifacts/useCaseDiagram.htm
[17] http://www.developer.com/design/article.php/2109801
[18] http://www.andrew.cmu.edu/course/90-754/umlucdfaq.html
[19] http://atlas.kennesaw.edu/~dbraun/csis4650/A&D/UML_tutorial/use_case.htm
[20] http://www.objectmentor.com/resources/articles/usecases.pdf
[21] http://www.agilemodeling.com/artifacts/classDiagram.htm

Object Oriented Implementation of Grid Framework using .Net Technology

K. Mukherjee[1] and G. Sahoo[2]

[1]Dept. of Computer & Engg. B.I. T Mesra Extension Centre Lalpur, Ranchi

[2]Dept. of IT BIT Mesra, Ranchi

kmukherjee@bitmesra.ac.in gsahoo@bitmesra.ac.in

Abstract

It is difficult to analyze the performance of a dynamic environment like the Grid. It is a real time scenario to collect and analyze data in Grid environment. The Grid has to become more realistic by adapting to the changing resource usages scenario. The objective of this paper is to present an object oriented implementation of a hierarchical agent framework for performance tuning of different applications running on Grid environment. The result of the implementation is presented in order to demonstrate the effectiveness of agent Framework.

Keyword: Grid, Hierarchical Agent Framework, .NET Technology, C. L. R.

1. Introduction

Grid runs on the environment where availability of resources at any instant of time is not predictable. Hence it is very difficult to monitor any application running on Grid environment. This is why the performance analysis in Grid must be influenced by dynamic data collection, data reduction and low cost data capturing. In this paper, we propose a hierarchical agent framework which takes into account the above issues. The agenda of our proposed framework is to maintain the overall performance of a number of jobs that are concurrently running in Grid and support them to adapt to the changing resource usage scenario by enabling local tuning action or migrating onto a different useful node. In this paper, we have used the concept of performance properties used in APART project[2] and implementation of our proposed framework has been done using .NET Technology.

2. Related Work

A lot of research has been done in order to predict and monitor the different applications running on Grid Environment. In this regard, a lot of performance and tuning tools came into existence like PABLO[1], PARADYN[11], PAMELA [], PACE [12] , SCALEA[17] , EXPERT [19], SCALEA-G ,GRADS etc. The main lack in many of these tools is that they address only traditional parallel architecture. But out of the above mentioned tools, some like SCALEA –G is based on the concept of the architecture of Grid. Some projects are based on the concept of component framework and improvement of scheduling decisions. Again the GRADS project highlights on building a framework which consists of an application manager that monitors the performance of different applications running on Grid environment. In this paper, like GRADS project, we have used a hierarchical analysis agent framework which is capable to analyze the performance of applications and tuning the applications that are running on Grid environment. Our proposed framework consists of sub framework with different agenda like analyzing the performance, tuning the application etc.

3. Framework of Agent

Agent Framework consists of layers and each layer has different job assignment. Within the system, a group of interacting, autonomous agents work together towards a common goal – to set up and maintain the service level agreement between a client of computational services and the owners of the computational resources. Each agent is responsible for pursuing these autonomously. Altogether six agents are used, these are: Broker Agent, Resource Provider Agent, JobController Agent, JobExecutionManager Agent, Analysis Agent, and Tuning Agent. The functions of these agents and the interactions among them have been thoroughly discussed in [0]. We make use of multiple Analysis Agents in our multi-agent system and organize these agents in a hierarchy. The environment that has been selected for the implementation of our framework is described in [0] and includes different types of Grid resources like clusters, SMPs and even workstations of dissimilar configurations. All of these are tied together through a Grid middleware layer. A Grid site comprises a collection of all these local resources, which are geographically located in a single site. All these Grid sites, which mutually agree to share resources located in several sites, form a global Grid. Global Grid provides support for multiple Grid resource registries and Grid security services through mutually distrustful administrative domains.

On top of the above environment, we propose to build a hierarchical analysis agent framework, where agents are divided into the following four logical levels of deployment in descending order: (1) Grid Agent (GA), (2) Grid Site Agent (GSA), (3) Resource Agent (RA) and (4) Node Agent (NA). These agents interact with each other and perform teamwork to analyze the performance of large compute-intensive applications. At the four levels of agent hierarchy(4), each agent has some specific responsibilities.

At level 1, individual workstations, SMP nodes and each individual node in the clusters are considered as computational resources. Node Agents (NA)work on these computational resources and their responsibility is to analyze the performance of the resources. Each agent plays a specific role and has a well-defined set of responsibilities or sub goals in the context of the overall system. When a job is submitted onto a host, a JobExecutionManager Agent (JEM Agent), which is essentially a mobile agent is associated with it and is deployed on the same host [0]. In case, the execution performance of a job degrades due to a performance problem, which can be solved locally, the NA informs JEM Agent by raising a 'Warning' message immediately. Also NA invokes a Tuning Agent (discussed later) for local tuning of the job.

At the next level, a *Resource Agent (RA)* is deployed which analyses the overall performance of the nodes in a cluster. Thus, when a collection of cluster nodes (each node can be an SMP or workstation or a desktop PC) acts as the resource provider, the RA is responsible for looking after the performance at the cluster level (such as cluster level load balancing). Cluster configuration can be homogeneous or heterogeneous. RAs also interact with the JEM Agents and keep them informed about the current status of the resources and execution performance of each job running on the resources. At a higher level, a *Grid Site Agent (GSA)* is deployed. This agent is responsible for the entire Grid resources located at a particular geographical site. The resource providers at a particular Grid site may be under single administrative domain and may have different policies regarding resource availability and usage. The GSA must be able to interact with all these resource providers. A GSA is also useful to identify any fault in any of the resources and also to check whether any of the resources is overloaded. The GSAs (at the local site or at a remote site) are consulted at the time of migration of a job, in order to find the next suitable resource.

Finally, at the highest level, a *Grid Agent (GA)* is associated with the global Grid and looks after the health of the entire Grid. There is only a single GA, which liaises with all the GSAs and analyzes the overall performance of the resources at each Grid site. This analysis is based on the data collected from the GSAs and other agents. Thus GA must be regularly updated by other agents in the system. Among all the agents at different levels, the current work concentrates on the lowest level agents, i.e. on the agents at the node level. The remaining part of the paper presents the design and implementation of the *Node Agents*.

4. Analysis of Effectiveness

The construction of a Node Agent depends on its availability, efficiency and usability.

A performance property characterizes specific performance behavior of a program and can be checked by a set of conditions. Every performance property is associated with a severity figure, which shows how important the performance property is in the context of the performance of an application. When the severity figure crosses a pre-defined threshold value, the property becomes a performance problem and the performance property with highest severity value is considered to be a performance bottleneck. In our system, the resource provider publishes the policies and defines the specific performance properties to be checked for detecting any kind of performance bottleneck at the time of execution of a job. For each performance property, the evaluation process is also defined and stored for later use by the NA. At the time of allocating a job onto a specific resource provider, an SLA is established between the resource provider and the client. During this process, first the client sends Task Service Level Agreement (TSLA) to the Resource Broker and the Resource Provider sends Resource Service Level Agreement (RSLA) to the Resource Broker. When a specific resource provider is selected for a job [0], the SLA is finalized and the client sends Binding Service Level Agreement (BSLA) to the Resource Provider. The NA in this environment uses the BSLA and the job metadata, which also comes as a part of the BSLA. BSLA provides detailed information about the job and the resources, while job metadata contains the information regarding significant parts of the job. The specific information can be obtained with the help of historical data or domain knowledge of the client. When execution of a job starts,

NA begins collecting monitoring data. On the basis of this data and the performance property specifications (defines the condition, confidence and severity for each property), it evaluates the severities of specified performance properties (using the process specifications) and generates *Performance Details Report.* A Tuning Agent (TA), which is invoked by the NA, is responsible for performing any local tuning action, so that any performance bottleneck or performance problem can be removed. The TA accepts the *Performance Details Report* from the NA, and decides what actions to be taken after consulting the *Performance Property Specification* and the *Performance Tuning Process Specification. Performance Tuning Process Specification* stores recommendations regarding actions, which may be taken for every performance problem depending upon their severity. The process specifications are basically an expert's knowledge base, which may be created and stored on a particular resource provider. The TA generates a *Performance Tuning Report.* We create subclasses of the process specifications for every subclass of performance property. Thus, in our current implementation, InsufficientParallelism ProcessSpecification is a subclass of the classPerformancePropertyProcessSpecification, which specifies the analysis process of the Insufficient Parallelism property, and LoadImbalanceProcessSpecification is another subclass, which specifies the analysis process of the Load Imbalance property.Similarly,InsufficientParallelismTuningProcessSpecification is a subclass of theclassPerformanceTuningProcessSpecification that specifies the tuning process for the property Insufficient Parallelism, and LoadImbalanceTuningProcessSpecification is another subclass of the same class that specifies the tuning process for the property Load Imbalance.

5. .NET Implementation

The entire multi-agent framework [0] has been implemented using C# technology. A part of our hierarchical analysis agent framework has been implemented using .NET Framework [20]. .NET Framework is a C# Agent Development Environment, built with C# registry facilities. It provides standard agent technologies. The agent platform can be distributed on several hosts, each one of them executes one C# Common Language Runtime (CLR). .NET Framework follows FIPA standard, thus its agent communication platform is FIPA-compliant. It uses Agent Communication Language (ACL) for efficient communication in distributed environment. .NET Framework supports agent's mobility and agents can execute independently and parallel on different network hosts. .NET Framework uses one thread per agent. Agent tasks or agent interactions are implemented through the logical execution threads. These threads or behaviors of the agents can be initialized, suspended and spawned at any given time.
In .NET Framework, multiple agents can interact with each other using their own containers [16]. Containers are the actual environments for each agent. Typically multiple agents can be active at same time on different nodes with various containers. But there is only one central agent, and it needs to start first. In our implementation, the NA is first initiated as central agent, which coordinates with other agents. In a Grid environment, it is important that the performance analysis be done at run-time and tuning action is taken at run-time without incurring much overhead. Thus, the active .NET Framework agents on a Grid resource cooperate with each other and interact in order to detect performance problems in real time.

Initially, a job is instrumented depending on the types of data the Analysis Agent requires to collect. As soon as the job starts its execution, JEM Agent communicates with the corresponding NA sitting at that particular node. NA receives the BSLA and the job metadata from the JEM Agent along with a 'Ready' message. It then sends a 'Query' message to the JEM Agent with a fraction value (e.g. 0.05) indicating the portion of a significant block of the job (in the current implementation, a significant loop) to be executed before collecting any performance data. The job starts and continues its execution up to the specified percentage or fraction of the significant part. After completing this portion, JEM Agent sends execution performance data to the NA and suspends the job. NA immediately starts analyzing the data on the basis of the commitment included in the BSLA. If NA finds some indication regarding degradation in execution performance of the job, it sends a 'Warning' message to the JEM Agent and invokes TA. NA also sends 'Performance Details' message to TA mentioning the identified performance property and its severity along with other details. TA decides some tuning action for executing the remaining part of the block and directs the JEM Agent to resume job after applying the tuning action. If no performance problem is detected by the NA, the job resumes and the remaining part (e.g. 0.95) of the significant block continues its execution as before. It is often possible that multiple jobs are executing on the same host (particularly on an SMP system). Consequently multiple JEM Agents are associated with these jobs, although there is only one NA. However, in our system communication between the JEM Agents and sole NA continues until the NA starts analysis of data for a particular job. As a job remains suspended during the analysis, it is desirable that the analysis time remains as less as possible. So the NA does not entertain any communication during this time. Communication starts again when the analysis is finished. Interactions among the agents during the analysis and local tuning process are depicted in the sequence diagram in Fig. 1.

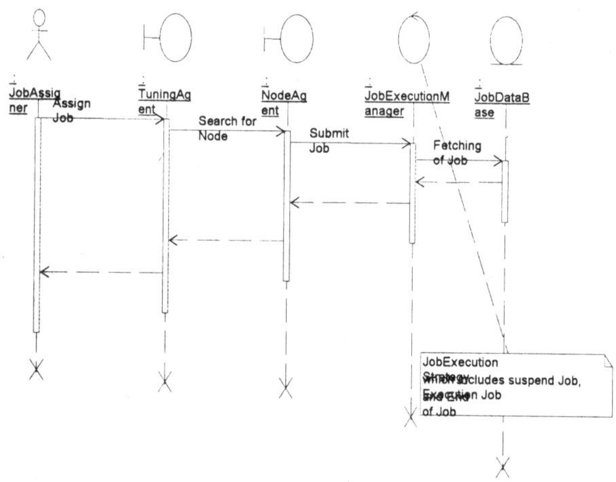

Fig. 1

In the current implementation, we have implemented the specifications, computations and tuning related to Insufficient Parallelism Property. Analysis of this property and tuning the job to avoid a performance problem related to this property has been discussed in [16].

6. Experiment

The experiment is done on Windows XP and Enterprise Linux platform of version 4.

The computational nodes of the test bed include HP NetServer LH 6000, HP ProLiant ML570 G4 with 4 Intel core2 Duo processors, Intel core2 Duo PCs and Intel Pentium-4 PCs. The nodes communicate through a fast local area network. The Grid test bed is built with Globus Toolkit 4.0 (GT4) [0]. The multi-agent system (which includes the hierarchical analysis agent framework) is implemented on top of GT4. The agents (NA, JEM Agent and TA) are deployed on every node. This paper demonstrates the results of local performance tuning of multiple applications running on the same node. Exclusively one NA is responsible for analyzing the performance of multiple jobs submitted to the same node and running simultaneously. Experiments have been carried out on a HP ProLiant ML570 G4 with 4 Intel core2 Duo processors (referred as *HPserver*) in the Grid environment. As test codes, we have used C# codes directives and executed in .NET Framework. It has already been mentioned that the current work presents the results related to analysis and tuning of *Insufficient Parallelism* problem observed in the test codes. When identified by the NA, TA decides that additional processors are required to overcome this performance problem. For example, if the job initially executes on p (>=1) processors, performance enhancement may be achieved by providing more processors (q>p) at run-time. TA decides whether the job will continue either with p processors or with additional processors q (>p) and resumes job after allocating additional resources to the job. The framework supports multiple jobs running on the same node. Thus, multiple parallel C# codes start executing using single processor on the *HPserver* and an NA monitors performances of all of them by profiling and analyzing the performance data. We use simple timer routines for profiling. After completing a part of the computation, the NA analyses the data, identifies that performance needs to be improved (the BSLA is consulted for this purpose – not within the scope of this paper) and recognizes that performance can be improved by adding more processors to the execution environment. Thus the local Tuning Agent (TA) is invoked and the number of processors is increased at run-time. Hence, the remaining part of the application is executed on the same server with more processors.

7. Result

We have experimented with two different test codes. However, in order to demonstrate the effectiveness of our system, we submitted multiple images of the same code as separate jobs. The jobs have been initiated at different times. Thus, in case I, two Matrix Multiplication (jMM1 and jMM2) and two Gauss

Elimination (jGE1 and jGE2) jobs started at different times, but a major portions of them were executed concurrently. Data sizes varied from 1000 to 2000 for both jobs. In the second case (Case II), again four jobs were started on the same resource provider and executed concurrently. In this case, data sizes varied from 3000 to 4000. In both cases, experimental data were collected in the following three scenarios.*Scenario 1*: Test codes execute on the *HPserver* with one processor without any interaction with the NA and TA. *Scenario 2*: Test codes execute initially on one processor and interact with NA. After computing a certain fraction of the significant loop (here 0.05), NA detects InsufficientParallelism problem and the TA tunes each job to run (remaining part) on four processors of the *HPserver*.

Scenario 3: Test code executes entirely on four processors of the *HPserver* without interaction with NA and TA.

Fig. 2 (a) and (b) compare the execution times of the Matrix Multiplication test codes in the above three scenarios. The results demonstrate that performances obtained in Scenario 2 and Scenario 3 are almost same, which signify that the overhead for run-time analysis and tuning is nominal. In case of Gauss Elimination, we obtained similar results.

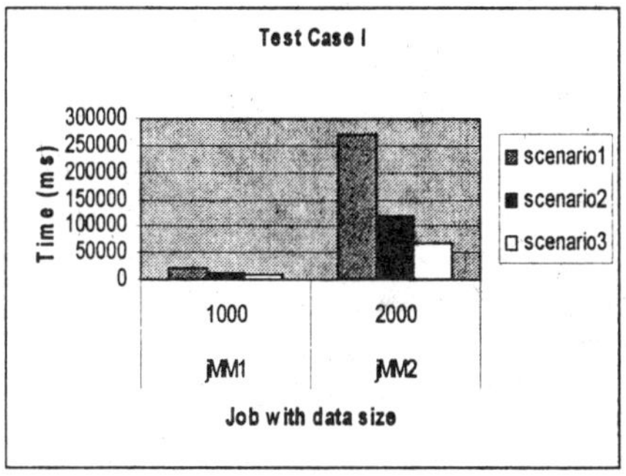

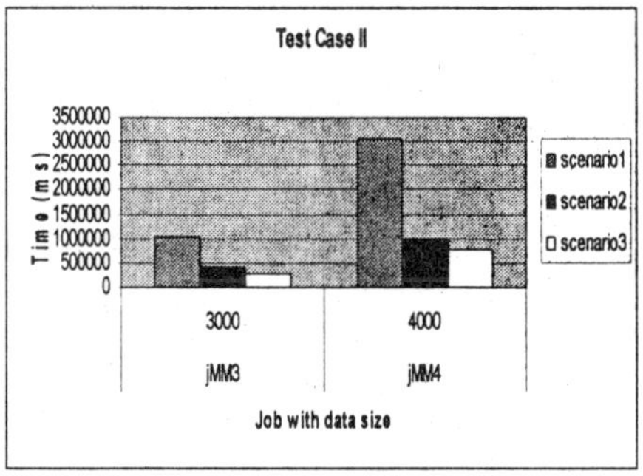

Fig. 2(a) Performance Improvement Fig. 2(b) Performance Improvement for Test Case I for Test Case II

Fig. 3(a) and 3(b) shows the overheads associated with execution of these jobs in Scenario 2. The times required for run-time analysis, tuning and communication among the agents are measured and shown. These overheads are negligible compared to the performance improvement of the jobs even though when multiple jobs are running concurrently on the same resource and only one NA is responsible for performance analysis of these multiple concurrent jobs.

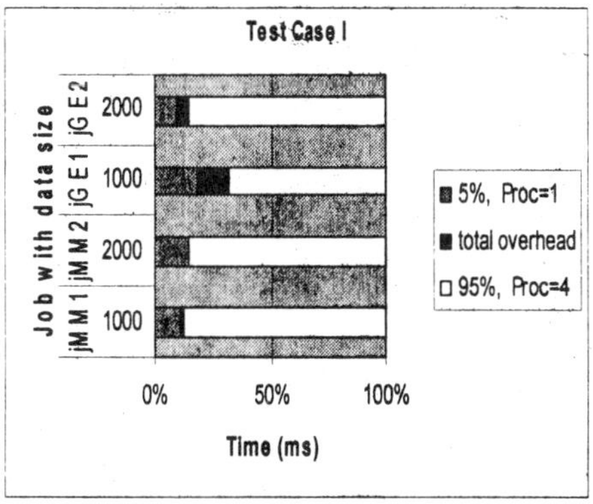

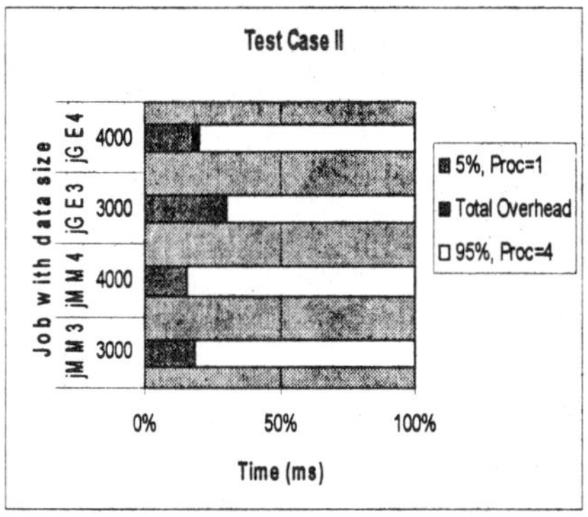

Fig. 3(a) Overhead Calculation Fig. 3(b) Overhead Calculation for Test Case I for Test Case II

8. Conclusion

In this paper, we have presented an object-oriented specification for implementation of Node Agent in a hierarchical Analysis Agent framework for Grid environment. This framework is actually used for performance analysis of applications executing concurrently on distributed systems (like Grid) and also for dynamically improving their execution performances. This paper highlights the interaction and exchange of information among the agents for collecting data, analyzing and improving the performance by application of local tuning actions. It also discusses the implementation of some of them. The results presented in this paper highlight the effectiveness of the framework by demonstrating the performance improvement through tuning and showing that the agent control overheads are negligible even when multiple jobs are submitted concurrently onto the same

10. References

1 DeRose, L., Y. Zhang, D.A. Reed, "SvPablo: A Multi-Language Performance Analysis system", in Proceedings of 10th Internal Conference on Computer performance, pp. 352-355, Spain, 1998.

2 Fahringer, T., Gerndt, M., Riley, G.D., and Traiff, J. L., "Formalizing OpenMP Performance Properties with ASL", In Proceedings of the Third International Symposium on High Performance Computing (October 16-18, 2000), ISHPC, pp. 428-439.

3 Foster I., C. Kesselman, J. Nick, and S. Tuecke, "Grid Services for Distributed System Integration", IEEE Computer, pp. 37-46, June 2002.

4 Furlinger K., "Scalable Automated Online Performance Analysis of Applications using Performance Properties", PhD. Thesis, 2006 in Technical University of Munich, Germany.

5 Furlinger K., M. Gerndt, "A Lightweight Dynamic Application Monitor for SMP Clusters", HLRB and KONWIHR joint Reviewing Workshop 2004, March 2004.

6 Furmento N., A. Mayer, S. McGough, S. Newhouse, T. field, and J. Darlington, "ICENI: Optimization of Component Applications within a Grid environment", Parallel Computing, 28(12): 1753-1772, 2002.

7 Globus Toolkit 4.0 – available in www.globus.org/toolkit.

8 GrADS: Grid Application Development Software Project, http://www.hipersoft.rice.edu/grads/.

9 Kennedy K., et al, "Toward a Framework for Preparing and Executing Adaptive Grid Programs", Proceedings of the International Parallel and Distributed Processing Symposium Workshop (IPDPS NGS), IEEE Computer Society Press, April 2002.

10 Kesler J. Charles, "Overview of Grid Computing", MCNC, April 2003.

11 Miller, B.P., M. D. Callaghan, J.M. Cargille, J.K. Hollingsworth, R.B. Irvin, K. L. Karavanic, , K. Kunchithapadam, T. Newhall, "The Paradyn Parallel Performance Measurement tools", IEEE Computer 28 (11), pp. 37-46, 1995.

12 Nudd, g.R., Papaefstathiou, E., et. Al., "A layered Approach to the Characterization of Parallel Systems for Performance Prediction", in Proceedings of Performance Evaluation of Parallel Systems, pp. 26-34, Warwick, 1993.

13 Ribler R.L, H. Sinitchi, D. A. Reed, "The Autopilot Performance-Directed Adaptive Control system", Future Generation Computer Systems 18(1), pp. 175-187, September 2001.

14 Roy S., M. Sarkar and N. Mukherjee – "Optimizing Resource Allocation for Multiple Concurrent Jobs in Grid Environment", Accepted for publication, In Proceedings of Third International Workshop on scheduling and Resource Management for Parallel and Distributed systems, SRMPDS '07, Hsinchu, Taiwan, December 5-7, 2007.

15 Roy S., N. Mukherjee, "Utilizing Jini Features to Implement a Multiagent Framework for Performance-based Resource Allocation in Grid Environment" Proceedings of GCA'06 – The 2006 International Conference on Grid Computing and Applications, pp-52 58.

16 Truong H.-L., T. Fahringer, "SCALEA- G: A Unified Monitoring and Performance Analysis System for the Grid", Scientific Programming, 12(4): 225-237, IOS Press, 2004

17 Truong H.-L., T. Fahringer. "SCALEA: A Performance Analysis Tool for Distributed and Parallel Programs", Published in Proc. Of the 8th International Euro-Par Conference (Euro-Par 2002), Paderborn, Germany, August 2002.

18 taglione G., F. Quarta, E. Cortese, "Scalability and performance of .NET FRAMEWORK message transport system", AAMAS Workshop on AgentCities, Bologna, 2002. Available from: http://sharon.cselt.it/projects/.NET Framework/papers/Final-ScalPerfMess.NET FRAMEWORK.pdf>.

19 Wolf F., B. Mohr. "Automatic Performance Analysis for SMP Cluster applications", Technical Report, Germany, August 2001.

20 Wolski, R., N.T. Spring and J. Hayes, "The Network Weather service: A distributed performance forecasting service for metacomputing", Future Generation Computer Systems 15(5), pp. 757-768, October 1999.

A Multitier High-level Mechanism for Secure Object Oriented Design

K. Mustafa and S. Rehman
Department of Computer Science Jamia Millia Islamia (Central University), New Delhi-110025, INDIA
kmfarooki@yahoo.com *shabana.infosec@gmail.com*

Abstract

Security has been largely considered as an hazardous component of networking, apart from an undesirable maintenance artifact, it now stands a proven myth and advocated as an integral SDLC activity. In this paper, we propose to integrate security by using a established design practices, early in the design phase itself. Object oriented software development, is a relatively new approach which is most common among software developers. Moreover it is easier for a designers to integrate security in object oriented software than procedural methods. Thereby, secure design of OOS is addressed at a higher level apart from issues concerning the same.

1. Introduction

Software's security features are affected by the decisions taken at the design phase[1].Recent research studies indicates that software must be designed with security in mind *'right from the beginning'* [2] [3]. At the design phase, a system must present unified security design that takes into account security principles. Many security properties cannot be verified by the testing activity alone; however verification through analysis and modeling at the design stage can increase the confidence that provides a sound basis for developing a secure software[4].It is not advisable to design software without any concern for security, and then attempt to fit a security solution on top of the existing design [5].Although most security defects are born during implementation, the most expensive are one of those, introduced in the design phase[20]. A proactive approach of paying close attention to security during the design phase prevents expensive redesign and yields substantial benefits during all later phases of the SDLC. Falk at el conducted in 2008 for examination of the prevalence of user-visible security design flaws by looking at the sites from 214 U.S financial institutions, it was revealed that 76% of the sites in their survey suffered from at least one design flaw [28].Design considerations include architectural issues at the system level as well as individual component level.

The change in the programming paradigm from structured programming to object-oriented technology has migrated to several application areas. Security awareness has become a topic of interest in object oriented software because of the differences in programming paradigms. In an object-oriented software, analysts should take security requirements into consideration when they start designing of an object model. The method, component of an object model can be a crucial part that contributes much to the success of the implementation of an application system with security requirements [15].Recently UML has become a standard for object-oriented modeling in the field of software engineering. Specification of the security policies using UML provides the understanding of security requirements, so the developer acceptance for security aspects will grow. This paper focuses on integration of security aspects of object oriented software development process in design phase.

The rest of the paper is structured as follows: Section 2 describes the 'software security' and Section 3 describes the purposed stages of the integrating security in object oriented software design. Section 4 is about the various problems and issues in the secure software development, and section 5 summarizes the paper.

2. Software Security

Software security—the process of designing, building, and testing software for security—identifies and expunges problems in the software itself. In this way, software security practitioners attempt to build software that can withstand attacks proactively [19].The goal of software security is to produce software that is able to (i) Resist or withstand many anticipated attacks, (ii) Recover rapidly, with minimum damage, from attacks that cannot be resisted or withstood [7]. Secure software cannot be intentionally subverted or forced to fail. In short, software that remains correct and predictable in spite of intentional efforts to compromise that dependability is referred as secure software [8]. Security may be added explicitly at the requirements level. Security requirements may include the abuse cases. While describe the system's behavior under attack. At the design level, designers, architects, and analysts must clearly document assumptions and identify possible attacks.

At the specifications based architecture stage and at the class-hierarchy design stage—security analysts may uncover and rank risks so that some mitigation mechanism can be initiated, this can be done by risk analysis. Disregarding risk analysis at this level lead to cost problems. At the code level, programmer should focus on implementation flaws, especially those that static analysis tools, which can scan source code for common vulnerabilities; and discover lack of security features. Security assessment encompass two strategies: testing security functionality with standard functional testing techniques, and risk-based security testing based on attack patterns and threat models. A good security test plan uses both strategies. Security problems aren't always apparent, even when user probe a system simply put attacks will happen, regardless of the strength of design and implementation, so monitoring software behavior is an excellent defensive technique. Knowledge gained by understanding attacks and exploits should be cycled back into the development organization. As design phase of software lifecycle is one of the most important phases, the knowledge of organized best practices of producing secure design based on the existing methodology make the task of producing secure software easier.

3. Securing Object Oriented Design

Designing secure software is more straightforward when security is integrated in the requirement phase. However, the process is still far from over. Even with the best requirements, software design is a challenging activity and must be performed with great care and clear goals. A critical review of related literature reveals various practices being adapted by experts/developers for secure design. Such practices can be easily traced to certain category/process that are integrated to design of object oriented design.. The Fig 1. depicts the step wise process of the secure design practices at each level of the object oriented design. Moreover, a logical integration of so called a 'selection of best practices' results in the following multitier high level mechanism; which is explained in the following sections

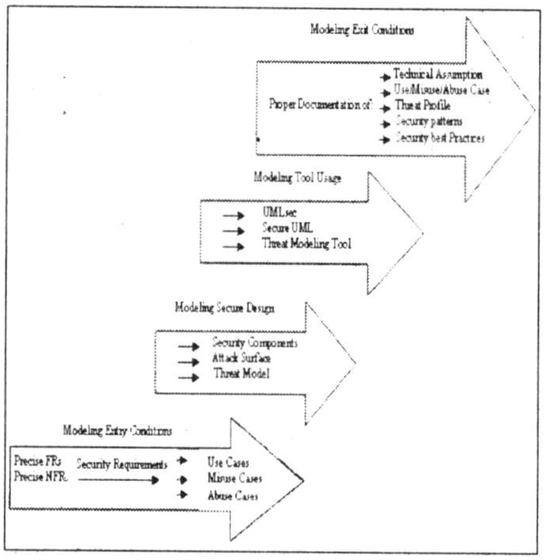

Fig. 1 Securing object oriented design modeling

A. Modeling Entry Conditions

The entry condition includes those process that need to be satisfied in order to enter the design phase. Before entering the design phase the process of gathering functional requirements should be fully completed, the necessary steps that should be included in the requirement gathering are discussed as follows:

- **Precise Functional Requirements**
  As defined in requirements engineering, functional requirements specify particular behaviors of a system [22]. Functional requirements may be calculations, technical details, data manipulation and processing and other specific functionality that show 'how a use case is to be fulfilled' [22].
- **Precise Non Functional Requirements**
  A Non-Functional Requirement is usually some form of constraint or restriction that must be considered when designing the solution. A system constraint is a constraint imposed by the system and not dictated by a Business Need. Since system constraints are part of a "solution", they should be documented in the System Specifications document.

  Further classification of the Non-Functional Requirements can also be done by classifying them into categories such as "Performance Constraints, Design Constraints, Quality Constraints, etc. This classification can be used if there is deemed to be a benefit. Security itself is one of the Non Functional Requirements but other Non-Functional Requirements also needs a security, therefore here we are emphasizing on the security of non functional requirements.

- **Precise Security Requirements**
  Security requirements are user-oriented quality requirements that specifies a minimum required amount of a quality subfactor of the security quality factor[23]. The typical objectives of security requirements are shown in Table 1.

Table 1 Objctives of security requirements

Objectives
Ensure proper access control to the user of the software.
Ensure proper identification of the user of the software.
Ensure proper verification of the identities.
Ensure that authorization of the user is in place.
Detect attempted intrusions by unauthorized persons.
Ensure that user of the software cannot later repudiate their interactions.
Ensure that confidential data are properly protected from unauthorized users.
Ensure that software can survive attack.
Ensure proper backup for the data stored in the software.
Ensure that system maintenance does not unintentionally disrupt the security mechanisms of the application, component, or center.

- **Sample Use Cases**
  A use case is a specific way of using a system using some part of functionality[21].Use cases are a best practice for analysis of functional requirements and understanding 'how they impact the system'[20].In order to start the designing of the software, use cases and their description should be finished and properly documented.
- **Sample Misuse Cases**
  A misuse case is the opposite of use case. Its sole purpose is to identify how a use case should not behave [20]. A misuse case should capture the type of attacks that can be made on the system and how the system should behave in such situations. This is a relatively new approach, but it helps in addressing the security requirements of software. A misuse case can also help in designing of the test cases purely to test the security strength of the system.
- **Sample Abuse Cases**
  The abuse cases are much the same as misuse cases. Conceptual distinction between use and abuse which is not present in the definition of misuse cases is that, an abuse case is a "A family of complete transactions between one or more actors and the system that results in harm" [27].

B. Modeling Secure Design

In this part, the main focus is on the secure design activities that could be included in the design phase of SDLC. These activities are given as under:

- **Identify components responsible for security functions**
  Designing the overall component structure of a system is a key activity in the design phase. Each component identified in the design must be carefully analyzed for its security needs. Some components will require protection. Other components will provide protection in the form of input validation, authentication, or cryptographic routines. These latter components must be the focus of extra attention from security engineers.
- **Document Attack Surface**
  When developers know early 'what the attack surface looks like' they can design and code accordingly from the starting, rather than waiting for a big, nasty surprise at the end[24].Some of the most common attack surface are listed in Table 2.

Table 2 Attack surfaces

Attack Surface
The networking protocols enabled by default.
The endpoints that should support authentication and authorization. Focus on other anonymous endpoints.
The off-by-default features. Look for code that auto-starts or will execute when accessed, such as services, daemons, ISAPI filters and applications, SOAP services, and Web roots.
Reusable components (ActiveX® controls, COM objects, and .NET Framework assemblies, especially those marked with the Allow Partially Trusted Callers Attribute).
The networking protocols enabled by default.

- **Create threat model**
  Threat modeling is an engineering technique used to describe threats to the software. Threat models are developed in order to understand the risk to software from malicious users or applications. Threat modeling allows development teams to anticipate attacks by understanding how an adversary chooses targets (assets), locates entry points and conducts an attack [18].A well-implemented threat model will profile the assets

that need to be protected, how the threats to these assets, the attacks that could be used to realize a threat, and the conditions under which the attack may be successful. A threat model shows how adversaries view the system, its components, and where they are likely to attempt its exploitation. Not only is this important for identifying potential threats, but also in understanding what application defenses must be defeated in order for a threat or series of threats to be realized. Microsoft has defined a structured method for threat modeling, consisting of steps that are listed in Table 3:

Table 3 Threat modeling steps

S. No.	Threat Modeling Steps
1.	Identify assets.
2.	Create an architecture overview.
3.	Decompose the application.
4.	Identify the threats.
5.	Categorize the threats using the STRIDE model (Spoofing, Tampering, Repudiation, Information disclosure, Denial of service, and Elevation of privilege).
6.	Rank the threats using the DREAD categories (Damage potential, Reproducibility, Exploitability, Affected users, and Discoverability).
7.	Develop threat mitigation strategies for the highest ranking threats.

Once threats are identified, and responses determined, a cost-benefit analysis must be performed to assess the impact of implementing those responses. This analysis is called risk management.

C. Modeling Tools Usage

During the design phase, tools can support the creation of a secure design, the linking of design elements to requirements and the creation of a security test plan. Tool support offers several benefits when undertaking secure software design. Some of the tools that can helping the development of secure design are as follows:

- **UMLsec**
  UMLsec is an extension to the unified modeling language (UML) in order to include security considerations as early as possible into the development. An extension to UML was chosen because UML is a standardized language and many developers are trained to use it. This makes it easier for many developers to learn UMLsec. Additionally there are many software-development-tools for UML that could also be extended and then be used for automatic analysis of a Model with respect to security weaknesses[25].
- **Secure UML**
  SecureUML extends UML to support authorization constraints. The capability of specifying significant information related to access control, and of deriving complete access control infrastructures (using EJB components), is presented in [5]. Basically, SecureUML defines a set of stereotypes and uses them to automatically produce the code that controls how users can access the different parts of the software. These stereotypes consider the static parts of UML only .
- **Threat Modeling Tools**
  There are various threat modeling tools that are freely available in the market. Some threat modeling tools are meant for the threat evaluation of the organization and not particularly for software, but they can be used for software threat evaluation as well. Some of these tools are listed in Table 4

Table 4 Threat modeling tools

Threat Modeling Tools
MTMA(Microsoft Threat Modeling tool)
Microsoft Threat Modeling and Analysis V2.1
PTA(Practical Threat Analysis)
Corporate Threat Analysis
Trike (Threat Modeling Framework)

D. Modeling Exit Conditions

The exit conditions of secure design process depends on the time and resources available but the most common task that should be completed before the exit from the design phase are listed in Table 5.

Table 5. Exit conditions

Exits Conditions
A complete documentation of all the technical assumptions
Proper counter measure or alternatives for every misuse case
Documentation of each and every threat profile
Documentation of security patterns in such a way that it

encapsulates security expertise in the form of identified solutions and present issues and trade-offs in the usage of the pattern
Integrated data backup strategies in the design documentation
Proper documentation of identified trust boundaries, trust levels, entitlements, encryption requirements.
Identified extra security controls where trust level is low
Included encryption details such as encryption algorithm, hashing algorithm, and key length in the design document
Properly documented log retention strategy
Documentation of infrastructure security best practices addressing operating system, Web server, application server, database, FTP, e-mail[26]

4. Issues

When we speaks of "secure software" it means that there is high confidence but no guarantee that the software is secure, because there are many issues that make 'security integration process in SDLC' more difficult and complex. Therefore software developers should prepare themselves for incoming difficulties in their path of secure software production. Here we have listed out some of these difficulties.

- As there is advancement in the software development process, the numbers of threats are also increasing. What may appear to be secure software today could be shown to be insecure tomorrow [5,17].
- Now-a-days, software applications are large and complicated. It is common for any software to have hundreds of thousands of lines of code. The complexity makes it difficult to develop a systematic approach for assessing security of such applications.[17,18]
- Even if secure software had been initially developed, it is very difficult to say that it will remain secure even at the time of enhancement, repair, and remediation.[5]
- To consistently follow such processes and practices, all producers and maintainers of such software must be adequately trained and so managed, supported, and coached, so that they can consistently maintain the required level of personal and team discipline[5,6]. But unfortunately, there are very few people who are well trained in this area.
- The methods for qualifying the capabilities of the likely number of required processes and organizations would necessarily be time consuming and expensive [5]. Therefore most organization prefer to exclude security, in order to produce their software on time and under budget.
- It is important to identify the class of software applications to which particular security assessment approach can be applied. The wide variety of existing software applications and their diverse set of characteristics make this task extremely difficult.[17]
- Because there are numerous known vulnerabilities, and a number of them can be present in a software application, it is impractical to list them all and test for their presence in a software application. Furthermore, some vulnerabilities are so complicated in nature that testing for their presence or absence becomes a monumental task.[17]
- There is no single security assessment approach that can address all existing vulnerabilities. This is difficult to do however, because there is no clear and established definition of vulnerability. This ambiguity also limits the ability to bound the set of vulnerabilities that a security assessment covers or should cover [17].
- As software security is continued to gain the attention of security experts and organizations, the tools and techniques used by attackers are becoming increasingly sophisticated and invasive.[9]
- Many security models are still not adequate for producing secure software products. Implementing some of them is complex and difficult to realize.[9]

The issues stated above, clarifies the need of prescriptive design of the security assessment framework, because framework are found quite handy and fruitful for these purposes. A work in this area may reduce some of the current problems/issues in the secure software development.

5. Conclusion

Due to the fast growing importance of security in the information systems, security should not be an afterthought in software development process. Here we have described a stage wise process for the incorporation of security into the design phase of software development process. Issues were also discussed so that software developers could prepare themselves for the existing difficulties in this area. Our work covers the importance of security in software design.

In future we are trying to develop a security assessment framework for object orientated software in which we will use the same strategy for coding and testing phase. This work will help programmers as well as security experts for building secure software.

6. References

[1] Pankaj Goyal, "Security Engineering and Software Engineering,"Department of Computer Science & Engineering, IIT Kanpur, report repository-2005.

[2] J. J¨urjens, "UMLsec: Extending UML for Secure Systems Development" In Proc. of 5th Int.Conf. on the Unified Modeling Language number 2460 in LNCS.Springer, 2002, pp 412–425.

[3] T. Lodderstedt, D. Basin, and J. Doser "SecureUML:A UML Based Modeling Language for Model-Driven Security",In Proc. of 5th Int.Conf. on the Unified Modeling Language number 2460 in LNCS.Springer, 2002, pp 426-441.

[4] David P. Gilliam, John C. Kelly, John D. Powell, Matt Bishop: "Development of a Software Security Assessment Instrument to Reduce Software Security Risk", WETICE, 2001,pp.144-149.

[5] Information Technology Bulletin, Commonwealth of Pennsylvania, Governor's Office of Administration/Office for Information Technology Business Solutions, Center of Excellence, Application Security Standards and Policies , 2005.

[6] Samuel T. Redwine, Jr. and Noopur Davis, "Processes to Produce Secure Software", Software Process Subgroup of the Task Force on Security across the Software Development Lifecycle, National Cyber Security Summit, March 2004.

[7] Samuel T. Redwine, "Software Assurance: A Guide to the Common Body of Knowledge to Produce, Acquire, and Sustain Secure Software Version 1.0.", US Department of Homeland Security, May 2006.

[8] Software Security Assurance, State-of-the-Art Report (SOAR,) July 31, 2007.

[9] S. Sodiya, S. A. Onashoga, and O. B. Ajayi "Towards Building Secure Software Systems", University of Agriculture, Issues in Informing Science and Information Technology Volume 3, Abeokuta, Nigeria, 2006.

[10] Chenxi Wang, William A. Wulf, "Towards A Framework For Security Measurement", Department of computer science, University of Virginia, proceedings of NISSC,1997.

[11] Daniel Guinier, "Object-oriented software for auditing information systems security following methodology for IS risk analysis and optimization per level", ACM, SIGSAC, 1992, pp.22 -30.

[12] Marianne Swanson, "Security Self-Assessment Guide for Information Technology Systems", NIST, Nov 2001.

[13] Tim Grance, Joan Hash, Marc Stevens, "Guide to Information Technology Security Services", NIST, Special Publication 800-35, 2003.

[14] CNSS Instruction No. 4009, Revised June 2006.

[15] Sureerut Inmor, Dr. Vatcharaporn Esichaikul, "A Security Model for an Object-Oriented Information System", Computer science, dissertation, 2002.

[16] Security in the Software Lifecycle, Department of Homeland Security, Making Software Development Processes and Software Produced by Them More Secure, DRAFT Version 1.2 ,2006.

[17] Anil Bazaz, "A Framework for Deriving Verification and Validation Strategies to Assess Software Security", Dissertation submitted to the faculty of Virginia Polytechnic Institute and State,University, Blacksburg, VA, 2006.

[18] James McCurley,Dave Zubrow,Carol Dekkers, "Measures and Measurement for Secure Software Development ",Carnegie Mellon University, 2007.

[19] Gary McGraw, "Software Security: Building Security In", Addison Wesley 2006.

[20] Security Innovation Inc., "The Application Security", Wilmington, MA10887, ww.securityinnovation.com, 2005

[21] Ivar Jacobson, "Object-Oriented Software Engineering", Addison Wesley Professional, 1992

[22] Wiegers, Karl E,"Software Requirements 2:Practical techniques for gathering and anaging requirements throughout the product development cycle", 2nd ed., Redmond: Microsoft Press, 2003

[23] http://opfro.org/index.html?Components/Work Product/requirementsSet/Requirements/Security ruirements.html~ ontents.

[24] Frank Swiderski, Window Snyder, "Threat Modeling" Microsoft Press, 2005.

[25] Jan Jurjens, "Secure Systems Development with UML",Springer, 2005.

[26] Anurag Agarwal, "Secure SDLC: Integrating security into your software development life cycle" Techtarget, The IT Media Experts, 2006.

[27] McDermott J, Fox C. Using Abuse Case Models for Security Requirements Analysis. In: Proc. 15th Annual Computer Security Applications Conference (ACSAC'99), IEEE Computer Society Press, 1999.

[28] Laura Falk, Atul Prakash and Kevin Borders, "Analyzing Websites for User-Visible Security Design Flaws" Symposium on Usable Privacy and Security, 2008

A Case Study on Estimation of Software Development Effort

Vandana Bhattacherjee[1], Sanjay Kumar[2] and Ekbal Rashid[3]
vbhattacharya@bitmesra.ac.in[1] *k_sanjay71@yahoo.co.in*[2]
[3]Dept. of Comp. Sc. & Engg. Birla Institute of Technology, Mesra, Ranchi
ekbalrashid2004@yahoo.com

Abstract

Accurate project effort estimation is an important goal for the software engineering community. Till date most work has focused upon building algorithmic models of effort estimation for example COCOMO. We describe an alternative approach to estimation based upon the use of analogy. The objective is to estimate the development effort of student programs based on the values of certain attributes. We have developed a case based reasoning model and have validated it upon student data. Due to the nature of the software engineering domain, it is important that software cost estimation models should be able to deal with imprecision and uncertainty associated with such values. It is to serve this purpose that we propose our case based model for software cost estimation. We feel that case based models are particularly useful when it is difficult to define concrete rules about a problem domain in addition to this, expert advice may be used to supplement the existing stored knowledge.

Keywords: *Effort estimation, case based reasoning, Analogy.*

1. Introduction

Estimation models in software engineering are used to predict some important attributes of future entities such as software development effort, software reliability, and productivity of programmers. Among such models, those estimating software effort have motivated considerable research in recent years [21]. Accurate and timely prediction of the development or maintain a software system is one of the most critical activates in managing software project, and has come to be known as '*Software Cost Estimation'*. Due to the nature of the software engineering domain, it is important that software cost estimation models should be able to deal with imprecision and uncertainty associated with such values. It is to serve this purpose that we propose our case based model for software cost estimation. We feel that case based models are particularly useful when it is difficult to define concrete rules about a problem domain in addition to this, expert advice may be used to supplement the existing stored knowledge. The rest of the paper is organized as follows: section 2 gives a brief overview of the various software cost estimation method, section 3 describes the case based reasoning approach in general. In section 4 we present Methodology Overview, section 5 presents the Results and in section 6 conclusion is presented.

2. Overview of software cost estimation Methods

There are many software cost estimation methods, and we give a brief overview of some of the more popular ones, namely, algorithmic method, analogy based estimation, expert judgment method, top down estimation and bottom up estimation method.

The algorithmic methods are designed to provide some mathematical equation to perform software estimation. The various software cost estimation models based on algorithmic method are the COCOMO & COCOMO II, Putnam, ESTIMACS and SPQR/20 [7]. Even though these methods are repeatable and modifiable, the disadvantages are that they do not deal with interrelationship between management constraints, such as cost versus quality. Poor sizing inputs and inaccurate cost drive rating will result in inaccurate estimation, since some experience and factors cannot be easily quantified. Estimating by analogy means comparing the proposed project to previously completed similar project where the project development information is known. This method is based on actual experience of projects but it is difficult to ensure the degree of similarity between previous projects and new one. We shall discuss more about this method later in our paper. Expert judgment techniques involve consulting with software cost estimation experts to use their experience and understanding of the proposed project to arrive at an estimate of its cost. Delphi technique and group consensus techniques are the most widely used expert judgment methods. It is an empirical method but also a subjective one. Top-down estimating method is also called Macro Model. Using it, cost estimation is derived from the global properties of the software project, and then the project is partitioned into various low-level components. The advantage of this method are, it is efficient and given system level view but it is too rough. In Bottom-up estimating method, the cost of each software components is estimated and then result are combined to arrive at an estimated cost of overall project. It is a detailed and stable method but it may overlook many of the system-level costs, and may be inaccurate and more time-consuming.

Several researchers have used soft computing approaches to estimate software cost. Idri et al have implemented the COCOMO cost model using fuzzy logic in [2] and also a fuzzy logic based analogy estimation approach in [3-5]. Case based reasoning has also been used by Kadoda et al in [9], Myrtveit et al in [10] and Ganesan et al in [12]. Bhattacharjee et al have proposed Expert Case Based Models in [19-22] [24-25].

3. Case based Reasoning

Case-based reasoning (CBR) is a problem solving paradigm that is fundamentally different from other major AI approaches, in that instead of relying solely on general knowledge of a problem domain it uses specific cases [1]. Instead of making association along generalized relationships between problem descriptors and conclusion, CBR utilizes the specific knowledge of previously experienced, concrete problem situation (cases). Finding a similar past case, and reusing it in the new problem situation: this is the technique of CBR to solve a new problem. A second important difference is that CBR is also an approach to incremental, sustained learning since a new experience is retained each time a problem has been solved, making it available for future problems.

Thus, the notion of case-based reasoning does not only denote a particular reasoning method, irrespective of how the cases are acquired, it also denotes a machine learning paradigm that enables sustained learning by updating the case base after a problem has been solved. Learning in CBR occurs as a natural by-product of problem solving. When a problem is successfully solved, the experience is retained in order to solve similar problems in the future. When an attempt to solve a problem fails, the reason for the failure is identified and remembered in order to avoid the same mistake in the future. Case based reasoning prefers learning form experience, since it is usually easier to earn by retaining a concrete problem solving experience then to generalize from it.

Case-based estimation is one of the more attractive techniques in the software effort estimation field. Central tasks that all case-based reasoning methods have to deal with are to identify the current problem situation, find a past case similar to the new one, use that case to suggest a solution to the current problem. Evaluate the proposed solution, and update the system by learning form this experience. How this is done, what part of the process that is focused, what type of problems that drives the methods, etc. varies considerably. We can thus broadly categorize the four primary steps comprising a CBR estimation system as:

- Retrieve the most similar case or cases, i.e., previously developed projects.
- Reuse the information and knowledge represented by the case (s) to solve the estimation problems.
- Revise the proposed solution.
- Retain the parts of this experience likely to be useful for future problem solving.

Case based estimation comes in handy when limited, domain knowledge is available and optimum solution is difficult to define. In cost estimation we use analogy by stating, "Similar Projects will have similar costs". An advantage of case- based cost estimation is that it is easy to comprehend and explains its process to practitioners. In addition, it can model a complex set of relationship between the dependent variable (such as, cost or effort) and the independent variables or cost drivers. However, its deployment in software cost estimation needs improvements. The best working example of case-based reasoning is the complex human intelligence. However, our (human) reasoning by analogy is more then always approximate and vague rather then precise and certain.

We present here an approach to software cost estimation based on Case Based Reasoning.

4. Methodology Overview

The environment of our study is the university campus and students of computer science and engineering are our target group. All students are provided with same level of guidance by instructors, support by the laboratory staffs, resources like computers, software etc., so for the students, development effort is the development time.

The parameter chosen for the model were based upon certain assumptions [23]. These are as follows:

- The final lines of code produced affects the development time.
- The number of methods is a predictor of how much effort is required to develop a program.
- The programming language exposure / experience of a programmer affects the development time.
- The inherent program difficulty level also affects the development time.

The values for lines of code, number of functions, level of difficulty, experience of the programming language and development time were collected from programs developed by post-graduate students of the institute over a period of six months. We have considered only post-graduate students in our study.

5. Results

We present the results obtained when applying the Case Based Reasoning model to the data set. The accuracy of estimates is evaluated by using the magnitude of relative error MRE.

Prediction level *Pred* is also used to test the performance of the model. It is defined as:

Pred (p) = K/N

Where, N is the total size of the data set and K is the number of programs with MRE less than or equal to p. We calculate *Pred (0.25)*, mean of MRE called MMRE and minimum of MRE called minMRE.

Table 1 Prediction Error Analysis (Manhattan Distance)

Parameters	Development time (minutes)
MMRE	1.02
MinMRE	0.00
Pred (0.25)%	46.66

Table 2 Prediction Error Analysis (Euclidean Distance)

Parameters	Development time (minutes)
MMRE	0.198
MinMRE	0.00
Pred (0.25)%	95.0

6. Conclusion

We developed the case based reasoning model using two similarity measures: Manhattan Distance and Euclidean Distance. The prediction in 46.66% of the cases is within 25% error for the Manhattan Distance based model while the prediction in 95% of the cases was within 25% error for the Euclidean Distance based model. The results may be considered good considering the fact that development time is a very complex attribute since it is dependent on human behavior. As part of our ongoing work, we are collecting data from different categories of students and with more parameters. Developing Case Based Reasoning models with different parameters and varying similarity measures and comparing their performance is part of our future work. We are also planning to incorporate weight measures with the various attributes.

7. References

[1] A. Abran and P.N.. Robillard. (1996), "Function Points Analysis: An Empirical Study of its Measurement Processes", IEEE Transactions on Software Engineering, 22(12): pp. 895-909.

[2] A. Idri, L.Kjiri, and A Abran. (2000), "COCOMO Cost Model Using Fuzzy Logic", *In Proceedings of the 7th International Conference on Fuzzytheory and Technology*, pp.219-223. Atlantic City, NJ, USA.

[3] A. Idri and A Abran. (2000b), "Towards A Fuzzy Logic Based Measures for Software Project Similarity", *In Proceedings of the 6th Maghrebian Conference on Computer Sciences*, pp. 9-18, Fes Morroco.

[4] A. Idri and A. Abran. (2001), "A Fuzzy Logic Based Measures For Software Project similarity: Validation and Possible Improvements", In *Proceedings of the 7th International Symposium on Software Metrics*, pp. 85-96, England, UK, IEEE.

[5] A. Idri , A. Abran and T.M. Khoshgoftaar .(2001c), " Fuzzy Analogy: Anew Approach for Software Cost Estimation", *In Proceedings of the 11th International workshop on software Measurements*, pp.93-101, Montreal, Canada.

[6] A. Aamodt and E. Plaza. (1994), "Case-Based Reasoning: Foundational Issues, Methodological Variations. and System Approaches", *AI Communication*, IOS Press, vol. 7:1, pp.39-59.

[7] B.W.Boehm.(1981), "Software Engineering Economic", Prentice –Hall.

[8] B.W.Boehm et al. (1995), "Cost Models for Future Software Life Cycle Processes: COCOMO II". *Annals of Software Engineering: Software Process and Product Measurement, Amsterdam.*

[9] G.Kadoda, M Cartwright, L Chen, and M.shepperd.(2000), "Experiences Using Case- Based Reasoning to Predict Software Project Effort", In *Proceeding of EASE*, p.23-28, Keele,UK.

[10] I. Myrtveit and E. Stensrud. (1999), "A Controlled Experiment to Assess the Benefits of Estimating with Analogy and Regression Models", IEEE *transactions on software Engineering*, vol 25,no. 4, pp. 510-525.

[11] J.Matson, E.B.E.Barrett, J.M. Mellichamp. (1994), Software Development Cost Estimation Using Function Points", Tran*saction on Software Engineering*, vol. 20, no 4, pp. 275-287, IEEE Computer Society.

[12] K. Ganeasn, T.M. Khoshgoftaar, and E. Allen. (2002), "Case-based Software Quality Prediction", *International journal of Software Engineering and Knowledge Engineering*, 10 (2), pp. 139-152.

[13] L. Angelis and I Stamelos. (2000), "A Simulation Tool for Efficient Analogy Based Cost Estimation", *Empirical software Engineering*, vol. 5, no. 1, pp.25-68.

[14] L. Angelis, I. Stamelos, and M. Morisio. (2001), "Building a Software Cost Estimation Model Based on Categorical Data", *in Proceedings of the 7th international software Metrics Symposium*, pp. 4-15, London, UK, IEEE Computer Society.

[15] M. Shepperd C. Schofield, and B. Kitchenham. (1996), "Effort Estimation using Analogy", In *Proceeding of the 18th International Conference on Software Engineering,* pp.170-178, Berlin.

[16] M. Shepperd and C. Schofield. (1997), "Estimating Software Project Effort Using Analogies", IEEE Transactions on Software Engineering, vol. 23, no 12, pp. 736-743, November 1997.

[17] R. Gulezian. (1991), "Reformulating and Calibrating COCOMO", *Journal Systems Software,* vol. 16, pp.235-242.

[18] S. Vicinanza and M.J. Prietulla. (1990), "Case-Based Reasoning in Software Effort Estimation", In *Proceeding of the 11th International Conference on Information System.*

[19] S. Kumar and V.Bhattacharjee,(2005),"Fuzz logic based Model for Software cost Estimation ",*In Proceedings of the international Conference on information Technology, Nov'05,* PCTE, Ludhiana India.

[20] S. Kumar and V.Bhattacharjee,(2007),"Analogy and Expert Judgment: A Hybrid Approach to Software Cost Estimation", *In Proceedings of the National Conference on information Technology: Present practice and Challenge, Sep'07,* New-Delhi, India.

[21] V. Bhattacherjee and S. Kumar,(2004),"Software cost estimation and its relevance in the Indian software Industry", *In Proceedings of the International Conference on Emerging Technologies IT Industry, Nov'05,* PCTE, Ludhiana India..

[22] V. Bhattacherjee and S .Kumar,(2006),"An Expert-Case Based Frame work for Software Cost Estimation", *In Proceedings of the* National Conference on Soft Computing Techniques for Engineering Application (SCT-2006), NIT Rourkela.

[23] V. Bhattacherjee,(2006),"The Soft Computing Approach to Program Development Time Estimation In *Proceeding of the International Conference on Information Technology, ICIT 06, Dec'06, Bhubneshwar, India, IEEE Computer Society.*

[24] V. Bhattacherjee, S .Kumar and Ekbal Rashid (2008), "Estimation of Software Development Effort in University Setting: A Case Study", *Accepted for Presentation at* National Conference on Architecturing Future IT Systems (NCAFIS '08), Indore, October 2008.

[25] V. Bhattacherjee, S .Kumar and Ekbal Rashid (2008), "Case Based Estimation Model using Project Feature Weights", Communicated to C3IT, 2009 Hooghly, Kolkata

A Study of the ongoing Research and Industrial Adoption of AOSD

Rupali Ahuja[1] and Anita Goel[2]
[1]Maitreyi College, University of Delhi, New Delhi-110003
[2]Dyal Singh College, University of Delhi, New Delhi-110003
rupali_ahuja1@yahoo.com agoel@dsc.du.ac.in

Abstract

Software development involves building of software systems that manipulate both the functional requirements and the non-functional requirements (like security, authentication, etc.) of the system. Aspect oriented software development (AOSD) is an emerging software development technology that focuses on modularizing the non-functional requirements of the software system. During the last decade, intensive research has been undertaken for the development of methods, tools and languages to support AOSD. Several research projects have been initiated that use AOSD techniques for software development. Moreover, AOSD has penetrated into several commercial applications, and prototypes have been developed in areas such as application server, operating system kernel, real-time embedded system, engineering design, distributed middleware, software visualization, and data processing.

In this paper, we perform a study on the ongoing research in AOSD under three categories - (1) tools, languages and frameworks to support AOSD, (2) research project initiatives for using AOSD during software development, and (3) industry-level adoption of AOSD in software development projects. Our study suggests that advantages of AOSD have been widely recognized by the software development community. New tools are being developed and the existing ones are being adapted to facilitate the use of AOSD for software development in different areas.

1. Introduction

The increase in size and complexity of the software systems and the need to achieve better quality of the software has resulted in software development to be an increasingly complex discipline. In addition to the basic functionality of the system, the software has to deal simultaneously with many non-functional concerns of the system. The non-functional concerns include the functionalities required for logging, error handling, standard enforcement, feature variation, performance management, performance optimization, caching and performance monitoring. The non-functional concerns do not fit naturally into a single software module or related modules and are made subparts of many software modules. Such concerns that cut orthogonally through a system are referred to as *crosscutting concerns* 0.

Aspect Oriented Software Development (AOSD) 0 is an emerging software development technology that enables developers' to capture and modularize the crosscutting concerns of a system. It provides means for the systematic identification, separation, representation and composition of crosscutting concerns. Aspect-Oriented Programming (AOP) languages provide abstractions for the modular implementation of crosscutting concerns in code, known as *Aspects*. Aspects are similar to classes, but implement the crosscutting concerns. At compile time, the classes and the aspects are combined into a final executable form using an aspect weaver.

The non-intrusive and the modular approach of AOP to handle crosscutting concerns has resulted in reducing costs involved in the development, maintenance and evolution of the software system. Gattani 0 highlights the benefits of AOSD as – (1) increased modularity, (2) centralization of aspect code, (3) handling of crosscutting concerns non-intrusively, (4) increased cohesiveness of modules, (5) reduced redundancy, (6) easy extensibility, and (7) increased maintainability.

AOSD is a rapidly evolving area and has constantly gained in popularity both in academia and industry alike. Steps are being taken to include AOSD in curricula of universities as a subject. Brichau et al. 2005 0 suggests a model curricula consisting of six modules for training software engineers, and introducing AOSD in teaching at post graduate level. Several major corporations like Siemens, IBM, Xerox, and Boeing have undertaken projects involving AOSD.

Bradley 0 examines the uses and problems associated with AOSD. He states that AOP has met with problems that affect the understandability, readability, testability and correctness of software in the real world software projects. He also stresses that AOP has the potential to increase the quality of software and to improve the method of software development. Zaidman et al. 0 describe their experiences with applying dynamic analysis solutions with the help of Aspect Orientation (AO) on an industrial legacy application written in C. Duck 0 investigates the benefits and pitfalls encountered while using AOP in commercial applications. He examined the experience of eleven programmers in five countries who used AOP in their role as project manager, lead architect or programmer.

Here, our study focuses on three different aspects of AOSD – (1) the steps and initiatives taken for the development of AOSD, (2) the using of AOSD in several research-level projects by academicians, and (3) adoption of AOSD at the industry level. We briefly describe the AOP terminology, the common languages, and the tools that are available for AOSD. AOSD is now being adopted for mainstream project development both at the research-level and industry-level. The paper lists some of the key projects that have adopted AOSD for software development.

In this paper, Section 2 gives an overview of AOP, and the tools and languages that support AOP. Section 3 discusses the research level initiatives taken for AOSD. Section 4 presents a report on adoption of AOSD at the industry level. Section 5 states the conclusion.

2. Aspect Oriented Programming

AOP 0 is a programming paradigm based on identification and separation of core concerns from crosscutting concerns of the software. The core concerns or the functional requirements of the software are implemented using an object oriented language (for example, Java) and the non-functional requirements or crosscutting concerns are implemented separately in an aspect oriented way. Some examples 0 of crosscutting concerns are - logging, tracing, security, design patterns, performance optimization, performance monitoring, profiling, caching, persistence, transaction management, authorization and authentication, exception handling, synchronization, quality of service etc.

AOP facilitates the separation of concerns by modularizing the crosscutting concerns in an *aspect*.

2.1 AOP Terminology

AOP follows a *join point* model. Join points represent well defined points in a program's execution. A join point defines an event in a system where a crosscutting concern can be joined with the core concern at compile time or run time. Many points in the execution flow of the program act as join points. Some of the join points are constructor/ method call/execution, field set and get points, object /class initialization and exception handling points. Join points may contain other join points, as a method call may invoke other method calls before returning 0.

The set of join points where weaving rules have to be merged with the main program are specified using a language construct called *point cut*. A point cut picks out a set of join points based on a defined criterion specified using an expression. AOP has a construct called as *advice*, which indicates the code that should run at each join point. Advice is similar to the methods that we implement in a class in object -oriented programming. There are three types of advice *before(), after() and around(),* which are used depending on whether the crosscutting code is inserted before, after or around a join point, respectively.

Aspect is a program unit similar to the "class" of OOP but is specifically meant to implement the functionality of a required crosscutting concern. An aspect is built from *pointcut* that defines the location where an aspect modifies an application program and *advice* which defines the modifications to be applied. The aspect is weaved at appropriate points in the application program using *aspect weaver*, during pre-compilation, leading to logical separation of the aspect from the core code.

2.2 AOP Languages

AOP is gaining momentum in the software community and the enterprise space at large. Several AOP languages exist today, and most are extensions of existing languages. Here we list some of the commonly used aspect oriented languages.

AspectJ 0 is a general purpose aspect oriented extension for Java. AspectJ 0 is sponsored by BEA Systems and IBM and is considered as the de-facto standard for AOP in Java. ***AspectC++*** 0 is a set of C++ language extensions to facilitate Aspect Oriented Programming with C++. ***AspectC*** 0 is a simple aspect oriented extension to C, intended to support programming for operating system and embedded system. ***AspectWerkz*** 0 is a framework targeted towards dynamic AOP in real world commercial applications. It supports an alternate XML-based aspect declaration style.

AspectXML 0 is an Aspect Oriented XML Weaving Engine (AXLE) which is accessible to applications inside of both Java and .NET. The AXLE is flexibly scaleable and can be implemented as a set of XSLT files or as a complex API built using Java or C#. ***Aspect#*** 0 is a framework for the CLI (.Net and Mono). ***Encase AOP*** 0 is a framework for the .NET Platform written in C#. ***The Orthogonal Weaving Model (OWM)*** is a dynamic framework by which .NET developers can implement aspect. ***Aspect.NET*** is a language-agnostic visual environment for developing aspect-oriented applications for Microsoft.NET.

2.3 AOP Tools

The adoption of a new technique at mainstream level is facilitated with the development of tool support. Several tools have been developed to provide support for AOSD. The Integrated Development Environment (IDE) for AOSD has advanced to the point where an organization can now safely use them. Some of the popular IDE for AOSD are as follows-

The ***AspectJ Development Tools (AJDT)*** 0 project provides Eclipse-platform based tool support for AOSD with AspectJ. AJDT also provides a crosscutting visualizer that displays modules as rectangles and uses color coded lines to show the crosscutting of concerns.

Aspect Mining Tool (AMT) 0 requires the user to run AMT analyzer to extract necessary line-oriented statistics about the software. It uses the collected statistics, aspects and a modified version of AspectJ compiler 0, for crosscutting depiction.

The ***Aspect Browser*** 0 is another mature visualizer which is more flexible as it does not rely on code compilation but instead on regular expressions which match aspects textually to the points of execution that they crosscut. It is capable of showing crosscutting information for more than just Java files. It can be used as a visualizer for other aspect-oriented languages such as AspectC.

3. Research Projects of AOSD

AOP introduced by Xerox back in the 1990s, has been getting more and more mature through several initiatives and innovations in the research community, the open-source community, and the enterprise arena. Research projects are actively being pursued to integrate AOP with other software development tools and techniques in areas like distributed quality-of-service, multi-agent system architectures, object databases, domain-specific visual modeling, workflow, e-commerce, and coordination protocols in middleware. Here, we describe some of the research projects being pursued with AOSD.

The ***Concurrent Programming research Groups at Illinois Institute of technology*** 0 dedicates itself to investigate research areas in the field of AOSD. The projects on which it is working are as follows-

- ***Dynamic Aspect C++ compiler*** (DAC++) represents an extension to the C++ compiler to provide support to dynamic aspects. Dynamic aspects allow application to evolve easily over time. DAC++ represents the first Dynamic Aspect Oriented system that supports a rich feature set of aspect oriented capabilities for C++ language. Some of the features supported by DAC++ are - dynamic aspect, dynamic pointcut expression, class-based aspect, three types of advices support, strong context exposure, two weaving modes and multiple aspects interaction.
- ***Network Dynamic Aspect C++*** (NDAC++) represents extending C++ toward the support of inter-process and network aspects. NDAC++ allows easy implementation and evolution of network applications and network designs. Additionally, it helps in implementing network applications that can be managed easily.
- ***Dynamic Weaver Framework*** is a language independent framework for Dynamic Aspect-Oriented Programming.
- ***Aspect-Oriented Statechart Framework*** allows specifying behavior for an object via Harel's statecharts. The framework is capable of taking individual objects and composing them in orthogonal regions to achieve the weaving of individual concerns. Events generated in one orthogonal region are broadcast to the other orthogonal regions, providing a communication mechanism between the regions. The framework introduces determinism by allowing one orthogonal region to handle an event before or after another region.
- The ***Executable Choreography Framework*** provides support architecture for the incremental development of applications that target highly dynamic service-oriented environments. Contextual Aspect-Sensitive Services (CASS) is a service-oriented support architecture that exploits dynamic AOP. It is introduced as the services whose instance interfaces can dynamically be adapted by Service Refinement Layers, using aspect weaving. It modularizes the structure and the collaborative behavior of composite services. Service refinement layers can be used to compose and choreograph Web Services.
- ***Mailslots*** is an Aspect-Oriented IPC technique for UNIX Winner of the IBM Linux Scholar Challenge, 2002.
- ***Requirements based*** automated aspect verification supports automated aspect testing.

The ***CiAO project*** 0 is implemented using AspectC++. It is an aspect-aware embedded operating system that provides easy configurability of fundamental architectural properties by aspects. Interrupt synchronization is implemented using aspects as a configurable strategy, providing a good separation of synchronization issues. CiAO is aimed to support a variety of 8-32 bit architectures.

The computing laboratory of ***Oxford University*** is working on a project that aims to construct a framework based on AOP for constructing better refactoring tools. The researchers at this university are also working to improve the AspectJ language by identifying its deficiencies, and proposing new language features to overcome them.

The ***Aspect-Oriented Software Engineering Group of Lancaster University*** 0 aims to develop systematic means for identification, modularization, representation and composition of crosscutting concerns (the aspects) throughout the software life cycle. This group is working on several projects of AOP such as -

- ***Aspect Oriented databases*** to extend existing database technology with aspects.
- ***AspOEv - An Aspect Oriented Evolution Framework for object-oriented databases.*** The project aims at employing an aspect-oriented approach to facilitate customization, extension and exchange of the schema modification, structural and behavioral consistency strategies in an object database evolution framework.
- ***PROBE - Proof Obligations for Aspect-Oriented Systems*** is a project that aims to establish concrete connections between aspectual requirements, UML design specification of aspects and the code implementing these specifications.
- ***VERA - Verifiable Aspect Models for Middleware Product Lines.*** The overall aim of the VERA project is to develop a modeling framework for verifiable composition of aspect models pertaining to middleware families.

XASPECTS 0 is a project undertaken by ***Demeter Center of Software Sciences***. The goal of the project is to explore ways of integrating domain-specific aspect-oriented solutions into general purpose AOP. The key idea behind this integration is to translate domain-specific aspects at compile time into general AspectJ source code. AspectJ serves as a base language from which other aspects can be defined.

David et al. 0 use AOP to evolve the ***Mckoi Database Server,*** to change the functionality of the database without altering the source code of the database, separate the original source code from the added source code, modularize the feature of monitoring the database, substitute the monitoring feature for a different monitoring feature (try different strategies), adopting monitoring feature late in the life cycle as it is well modularized.

The ***C-SAW*** 0 project is currently sponsored by ***NSF*** (2005-2007). Initial support (2002-2005) was provided by DARPA. The research is being conducted by members of the Software Composition and Modeling Laboratory (SOFTCOM) at the University of Alabama at Birmingham (UAB). C-SAW (Constraint Specification Aspect Weaver) provides Two-Level Aspect Weaving to Support Model-Driven Program Transformation. The C-SAW weaver framework serves as a generalized transformation engine for manipulating models. It is a plug-in for Generic Modeling Environment (GME).

Tarim 0 is a research project on testing aspect-oriented programs written using AspectJ. The project focuses on automated tool supports for generating, selecting, and inspecting generated tests for units in AspectJ programs. The project adapts the existing testing techniques for object-oriented programs (developed in the Straw project). The project is led by ***Tao Xie at North Carolina State University***.

ASTA 0 is a research project undertaken by ***University of Helsinki*** for developing tools and methodology to facilitate systematic testing of aspect-oriented software. The project builds on the results of the previous RITA project that developed an environment for testing framework-based software product lines.

European Network of Excellence on Aspect-Oriented Software Development (AOSD-Europe) - 0 network of excellence aims to establish a premier virtual European research centre on AOSD. The virtual research centre will synthesize collective viewpoint, expertise, research agenda and commercial foci of its member organizations. It plans to create a vision and pragmatic realization of the application of AOSD technologies to improve fundamental quality attributes of software systems, especially those critical to the information society. It will also act as an interface and a centralized source of information for other national and international research groups, industrial organizations and governmental bodies to access their work and enter collaborative initiatives.

The strategic basic research project ***AspectLab*** 0 addresses the development of complex, distributed software systems using AOSD methods, languages and techniques. It proposes collaboration between the current AOSD actors in ***Flanders***. Its aim is to strengthen generic research in this field and demonstrate the power and advantages of AOSD to Flemish software industry for a range of non-trivial and representative applications.

4. Industrial projects of AOSD

AOP has reached a decent maturity level due to several initiatives from different companies with different priorities and goals (IBM, BEA, Motorola, Seimens JBoss, Spring, and Microsoft to name a few). Here, we list some of the industrial projects that have adopted AOP for software development.

Aquarium project 0 undertaken by ***Object Mentor Incorporated,*** implements AOP for *Ruby*. Ruby is an open source, object-oriented scripting language that is used like *Perl* to process text files and to do system management tasks. Aquarium provides an intuitive syntax, supports runtime addition and removal of advice, advises Java through *JRuby*, and demonstrates value of dynamically typed languages for AOP.

Phoenix.NET is a research project for AOP on .NET, initiated by Microsoft.

Motorola 0 reported on the successful initial adoption of AOSD technologies within one of the core business units at Motorola - the Networks and Enterprise Business Unit. The Motorola *WEAVR* is an industrial strength AOSD tool that supports weaving of UML 2.0 behavioral models. The WEAVR tool includes an aspect oriented simulation engine. The simulator executes aspect oriented models in such a way that the modular structure of connectors is maintained. The models execute in a semantically equivalent way to the woven model The Motorola WEAVR supports a classic joinpoint model based on objects and methods for UML 2.0, but also introduces a novel joinpoint model for state machine diagrams.

The ***Siemens Aspect Manager*** 0 is an Eclipse plug-in that makes the configuration task much easier and supports the reuse of predefined aspect libraries effectively. The Aspect Manager uses an aspect repository server from which aspects can be queried and imported. This aspect repository hosts several aspects in form of JARs. The Aspect Manager contacts the server and gets knowledge of all available reusable aspects.

NearInfinity have used AspectJ to build a product for enterprise compliance auditing. They note that most projects add auditing as an afterthought and it shows in the poor quality results. One key benefit of separating out the auditing implementation is that it allows consistent policy implementation. The system uses load-time weaving with AspectWerkz.

JBoss is using AOP to provide transparent middleware software. It is promoting the message of annotations for ease of use and aspects for ease of extension. Aspects are the basis of its EJB3 container (log, security, transactions, locks, remoting, etc). Interestingly, JBoss is using aspects to build product line variation. Using aspect provides pluggable eviction, persistence, replication, and transactional support without tangling the core cache code.

AOP for the ***Spring framework*** 0 integrates coarse-grained proxy-based AOP into the core framework and uses it for transaction management, security, remoting, performance monitoring, tracing and logging, and framework internals.

BEA JRockit JVM Support for AOP includes AOP API that replaces current bytecode instrumentation techniques to a world of plain Java API. It provides complete runtime control for hot deployment and undeployment, agnostic from the programming model you like for your aspects. By using JRockit JMAPI capabilities, AspectWerkz brings AOP one step ahead by officially supporting all major JVM (Sun, IBM, BEA). This allows hooking AspectWerkz in a seamless way to provide dynamic on the fly weaving of Aspects no matter your environment.

YAPB AOP 1.2.3.4 is Yet Another Proxy Based AOP for Java. It is proxy-based (AspectWerkz proxy), pure java, no language extensions, no external tools needed, simple and intuitive. It provides programmatic configuration and un-configuration, supports AOP Alliance API for MethodInterception.

BEA WebLogic domain wizard makes it possible to install a WebLogic server with AspectWerkz AOP in a minute.

AO4BPEL uses AOP for Business Process Management, by extending IBM's BPEL engine - BPWS4J. It allows aspects to interact with business processes, in areas such as adding promotions, performance monitoring etc. across processes. It also provides middleware aspects like reliability and security for SOAP messaging.

The ***Glassbox Troubleshooter*** builds on the Glassbox Inspector's AspectJ and JMX monitoring technology. The Troubleshooter adds root cause analysis and a focused GUI client that dramatically simplifies the process of Java troubleshooting. It provides flexible and modular approach to monitor performance for enterprise systems. It can capture statistics such as total count, total time, and worst-case performance for requests.

ASML is currently investigating the use of AOP within their development process. They are working on the Ideals project 0 with four major research institutions. The project aims at identifying crosscutting concerns at both implementation and architecture level, and modularizing of these crosscutting concerns using AOP techniques.

The ***Houspanossian et al.*** 0 have extended an open-source software system using AOP. They have introduced the new functionality as aspects of the base system in a flexible and maintainable way. The base system is an open-source BPEL engine called ActiveBPEL. The system to extend is a BPEL engine and the new functionality deals with the publication of the status of engine using a pub/sub mechanism.

Hewlett Packard (HP) is using AOP with frameworks.

InfraRED is a tool for monitoring performance of a J2EE application and diagnosing performance problems. It collects metrics about various aspects of an application's performance and makes it available for quantitative analysis of the application.

Design by Contract (DbC) is a way of describing the contract of a component interface in a programmatically testable way. Contract4J 0 is an open-source tool that supports Design by Contract (DbC) in Java, using AspectJ for the implementation. It demonstrates an alternative approach to aspect-aware interface design with two syntax forms supporting a common protocol.

Oracle is working on a project to provide integrated support for AOP in their JDeveloper IDE. The focus of the project is to integrate AspectJ Design Time Environment (ADJT) into JDeveloper.

5. Conclusion

AOSD is an emerging paradigm that provides explicit abstractions for crosscutting concerns. AOSD improves modularity of the system leading to a reduced complexity and easier maintainability of the system. Crosscutting concerns are represented as aspects which may arise during requirements specification, design, implementation, testing etc.

AOSD community has recently received a great deal of interest and importance both in academics and the industry. The study aims to explore the growing interest of the software development community in integrating aspect oriented techniques for software development. The paper also presents the initiatives taken and the advancements made by research community using aspect oriented software development. We find that AOSD is rapidly gaining acceptance among the software developers for use during the development of the software.

6. References

[1] A. Duck, "Implementation of AOP in non-academic projects", In the Industry Track proceedings of the 5th international conference on AOSD, 2006.

[2] A. Houspanossian and M. Cilia, "Extending an Open-Source BPEL Engine with Aspect-Oriented Programming". In the Proceedings of the Argentinean Symposium on Software, 2005.

[3] A. Zaidman, B. Adams, K.D. Schutter, "Applying Dynamic Analysis in a Legacy Context: An Industrial Experience Report". In Proceedings of the 1st International Workshop on Program Comprehension through Dynamic Analysis (PCODA), pp 6-10, 2005.

[4] AJDT: http://www.eclipse.org/ajdt/

[5] AOSD: http://www.aosd.net

[6] AOSD Europe: http://www.narcis.info/research/

[7] AOSD Engineering Group of Lancaster University: http://www.comp.lancs.ac.uk/computing/aop/

[8] Aspect#: http://aspectsharp.sourceforge.net/

[9] Aspect Browser, http://www-cse.ucsd.edu/~wgg

[10] AspectC: http://www.cs.ubc.ca/labs/spl/projects

[11] AspectJ5: http://www.eclipse.org/aspectj

[12] AspectJ compiler 1.2. http://eclipse.org/aspectj/

[13] AspectLab: http://ssel.vub.ac.be/aspectlab/

[14] Aspect Mining Tool: http://www.cs.ubc.ca/labs/spl

[15] AspectWerkz: http://aspectwerkz.codehaus.org/

[16] ASTA : http://www.cs.helsinki.fi/group/roosa/asta/

[17] Concurrent Programming research group of Illinois Institute of Technology, http://www.iit.edu/~concur/

[18] C-SAW: http://www.cis.uab.edu/gray/Research

[19] D. Lohmann, J. Streicher, O. Spinczyk and W. Schröder-Preikschat, "Interrupt Synchronization in the CiAO Operating System: Experiences from Implementing Low-Level System Policies by AOP", Workshop ACP4IS, Vancouver, Canada, Mar, 2007.

[20] D. Shepherd, T. Roper, L. Pollock, "Using AOP to Ease Evolution", In proceedings of International Conference on Software Maintenance (ICSM), 2005.

[21] D. Wampler, "Contract4J for Design by Contract in Java: Design Pattern-Like Protocols and Aspect Interfaces". In proceedings of the 5th AOSD workshop on ACP4IS, 2006.

[22] D. Wiese, U. Hohenstein, R. Meunier, "How to Convince Industry of AOP", Siemens AG, CT SE 2. In the proceedings of the industry track, AOSD, 2007.

[23] Encase AOP: http://theagiledeveloper.com/

[24] Kiczales, J. Lamping, A. Mendhekar, C. Maeda, C. Lopes, J.M. Loingtier, J. Irwin, "Aspect-Oriented Programming". In proc. 11th European Conference on Object-Oriented Programming (ECOOP), LNCS 1241, Springer Verlag, Finland, pp 220–242, 1997.

[25] G. Kiczales, E. Hilsdale, J. Hugunin, M. Kersen, J. Palm, W. G. Griswold, "An overview of AspectJ". In Proceedings European Conference on Object-Oriented Programming, LNCS 2072, Springer-Verlag, Berlin, Heidelberg, pp 327–353, 2001.

[26] J. Brichau, R. Chitchyan, S. Clarke, E. D'Hondt, A. Garcia, M. Haupt, W. Joosen, S. Katz, J. Noyé, A. Rashid, M. Südholt, "A Model Curriculum for Aspect-Oriented Software Development", IEEE computer Society, Vol. 23, No. 6, Dec. 2006.

[27] J. Gattani. "An Analysis of Aspect Oriented Programming with AspectJ", Technical report, University of Houston, www2.cs.uh.edu/~jayg/AOP.

[28] J.T. Bradley, "An Examination of Aspect-Oriented Programming in Industry", A thesis submitted to the Colorado State University Honors Program, 2003.

[29] O. Spinczyk, D. Lohmann, and M. Urban, "Advances in AOP with AspectC++", Software Methodologies, Tools and Techniques (SoMeT), IOS Press, Tokyo, Japan, Sept., 2005.

[30] P. Durr, R.V. Engelen, "Applying AOP in an Industrial Context: An Experience Paper". In Proc. Workshop on Best Practices in Applying Aspect-oriented Software Development. Aspect-Oriented Software Association, 2006.

[31] R. Ahuja, A. Goel, "A study of Applications of Aspect Oriented programming", In proceedings of National Conference on Challenges and Opportunities in Information Technology, COIT'08. India, pp 9-13, March, 2008.

[32] R. Ahuja, A. Goel, "Aspect Oriented programming: A programming paradigm". In proceedings of National Conference on Information Technology (NCIT'07), India, pp 375-380, Sept., 2007.

[33] Ruby: http://aquarium.rubyforge.org

[34] Russell Miles, "An Introduction to the AspectXML Concept", www.aspectXML.org.

[35] Spring framework:http://www.springframework.org/

[36] T. Cottenier, T. Elrad, "The Motorola WEAVR: Model Weaving in a Large Industrial Context". In Proceedings of the International Conference on Aspect-Oriented Software Development, Industry Track, Vancouver, Canada, 2006.

[37] TARIM: http://people.engr.ncsu.edu/txie/tarim/

[38] XAspects: http://www.ccs.neu.edu/research

An Approach to Support QoS in Composite Web Service Environment

Lalit Purohit[1] and Amit Kumar Vyas[2]
[1]Lecturer, Deptt. of I.T., Shri.G.S.Instt. of Tech & Sc., road, Indore (M.P.)
[2]Software Engineer, Impetus Infotech (India) Pvt Ltd., 23, park 14 B, Palasia AB road, Indore (M.P.)
lpurohit@sgsits.ac.in amitk.vyas@impetus.co.in

Abstract

In this paper, we propose an approach to support QoS in composite web service environment. This approach includes an extension to UDDI for publishing QoS parameters of the web services. We also propose an approach to dynamically discover and compose the participating web services, based on the QoS parameters specified.

In the present scenario, many service providers' offer web services for same functional requirements. Consumers of offered web services have many options available to choose the web service for same business needs and require some way to prioritize the services available. QoS may be one of the ways to prioritize these web services. Current specifications of UDDI do not support QoS based publishing and discovery of web services. To support QoS based publishing and discovery of web services, the UDDI schema is extended to store QoS parameters of web services. Moreover, in conformance with this extension, the UDDI publish and search API's are also modified.

For dynamic discovery of web services based on QoS parameters, we propose architecture to search the web services meeting QoS requirements and invoke them using web service contract (WSDL). Further, the architecture uses dynamically invoked web services to accomplish a business process by composing them together.

The example implemented in the paper is order processing system of automobile company. BPEL is used as composition language. Web Services are developed in JAVA and services QoS requirements are exposed through WS-policy.

Keywords: *Business process Execution Language, Quality of Service (QoS), UDDI, WS-policy.*

1. Introduction

As more and more web services for same functional requirements are increasing, the web service consumers need some mechanism to prioritize the web services. One of the mechanisms for selecting the web services may be based on QoS parameters. The QoS parameters such as cost, response time, security, reliable messaging etc. may be considered for selecting the web services [3]. Current UDDI specification [13] does not provide support for publishing QoS parameters of the web services. Moreover, from the view point of service registry, to provide QoS support for the web services, three things are required. First, registry schema should have provision to store QoS parameters of web services. Secondly, the service provider should be able to publish QoS parameters of web services. Also, the web service consumer should be able to discover the web services on the basis of QoS parameters. Lastly, the web service contract (WSDL) should describe the way to invoke the web service based on QoS requirements.

In order to store QoS parameters of the web services, we need to provide some support in the registry. One of the ways to provide this support is by extending the schema of the registry. Accordingly, we need to modify publish and search API's of UDDI to support QoS based publishing and discovery of web services.

To consume the QoS enabled web services, the web service consumers need a way to know the QoS requirements of the web service. The above QoS requirements can be advertised in the WSDL using WS-Policy [14]. The policy may include elements for specifying QoS such as secure and reliable web services. WS-SecurityPolicy is one such web services specification which provides the means of achieving QoS (security) for the web services.

Once the QoS parameters of the web services are published in the registry and QoS requirements are advertised in the WSDL using WS-policy, the web service consumer can invoke the web service in conformance of the QoS requirements of the web service. In the real business scenario such as online order processing system of four wheeler automobile company, the business tasks may be performed by composing various web services. In such composite environment, QoS based web service discovery and composition is more complex, e.g., the online order processing system of four wheeler automobile company requires the composition of various services from parts manufacturers, banks, transporters etc. to process the order. Here, various web service providers may offer web services for same functional requirements, e.g., web services from different wheel manufacturers, transporters etc. Therefore, we need some mechanism to chose one web service from the set of web services for same business needs and compose them to process the order.

2. Related Work

Most research concerning QoS support for web services has been about specifying and measuring the QoS parameter of web services. Some researchers [1][2][4] have developed framework to measuring the QoS parameters for web service. In the research done by Daniel A. Menascé, et al. [4], the current system suggest the mechanism to compose web services based on the QoS attribute of services. The system docs not support the mechanism to specify QoS parameters of web services being registered by service providers. Also, research done by Demian Antony D'Mello, et al. [1], the system specify the way to rank the web services to be composed but system do not specify any support for registering QoS enabled web services in the UDDI. However, in our system we are extending the UDDI such that the QoS parameters of web services can be stored alongwith the service details. Further, the UDDI API's are extended to support searching and publishing QoS based web services.

3. Emerging Technologies

In this section we have presented the emerging technologies used to demonstrate our work.

3.1 Web Services

A Web service can be defined as a software component, which provides a specific service, and which can be described, advertised, discovered and invoked over the Web, by using standard technologies and protocols [5]. Also, web service is a new way of distributed computing, which is based on standard technologies such as XML, WSDL [12], and UDDI [13]. Web service has an interface described in a machine-processable format called WSDL. Other systems interact with the Web service in a manner prescribed by its description using SOAP over HTTP [17]. The basic architecture of Web services includes three components as shown in Fig. 1.

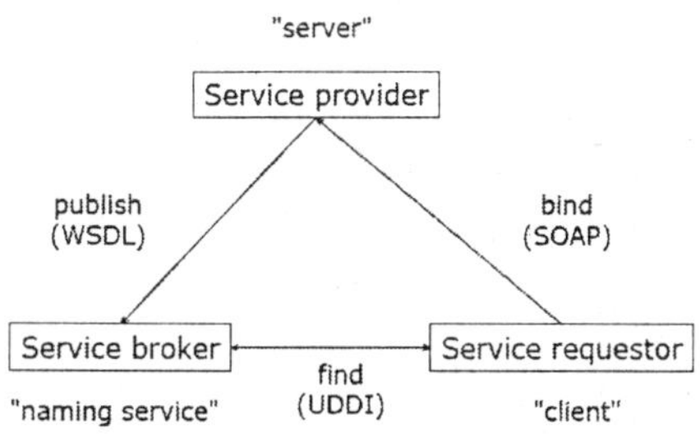

Fig. 1 Web Service Architecture

The service provider implements the service and use service broker to publish it. The service requester finds the service from service broker by providing key value pair as input. The service broker returns the address of service interface called WSDL. The details of service invocation are obtained from the WSDL file. Once all the details are fetched, the service is accessed at the specified address.

3.2 UDDI

UDDI stands for universal description, discovery, and integration, and it defines a way to store and retrieve information about a business and its technical interfaces, in our case Web services. A UDDI registry makes it possible to discover what technical programming interfaces are provided for interacting with a business [13, 19]. There are several types of information that have to be stored in such a registry, including information about the company (business entity) that offers services, as well as the description of each service including interface specifications and pointers to servers where those services can be invoked. The data to be stored can be divided into six types of entities that build up the data model of the registry. Figure 2 shows the data model of UDDI with entities. It also shows their relationships and the link to the WSDL documents.

The business entity at the top of containment hierarchy contains one or more business service entities. The services in turn contain binding template entities. The tModel instances (service types) are referenced by the binding template entities. A binding template points to an access point URL where the service can be accessed. The binding template could point to a mobile number as a contact point. A service type entity (tModel) has a reference to a Web service type specification, which typically is a WSDL document. The UDDI registry merely contains a URL pointing to the URL of service providers end where the document can be found, not the WSDL document itself.

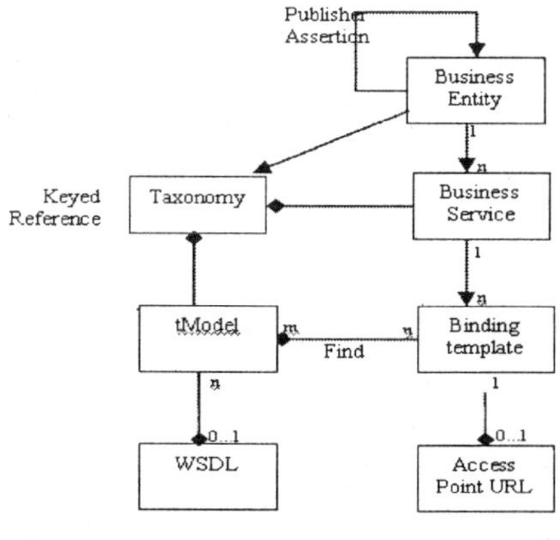

Fig. 2 UDDI Data Model

Businesses, services and tModels can contain zero to many references to taxonomy entries to categorize their content. WSDL references are implemented as URLs; therefore, any other specification format can easily be supported as well. UDDI is not bound to WSDL. There is an m:n relationship between the binding template and the tModel. A tModel is just a technical fingerprint containing quite abstract metadata. Even if a service points to several tModels, it does not necessarily have to implement multiple interfaces on a technical level.

3.3 Web Service Composition

Web service composition refers to the task of integrating two or more web service to perform a task. The integration of web services is possible in two ways. When the services to be composed are known before the composition, it is called static composition. Whereas, when services to be composed are not known before the composition and are determined at the time of composition is called dynamic composition [7, 8]. When different web services are composed the individual services can be invoked in different manner [4]:

- (i) **Parallel:** Two or more services can be invoked in parallel.
- (ii) **Sequential:** Services are invoked one after the other.
- (iii) **Join:** The web service is activated only when all of its predecessor web services are completed.
- (iv) **Probabilistic Invocation:** The successor services are invoked with a probability value p.
- (v) **Fastest Predecessor triggered invocation:** The first predecessor to complete activates a web service.

3.4 Quality of Service (QoS)

The QoS requirements for web services refer to quality aspect of a web service. It may include performance, reliability, scalability, availability, interoperability, capacity, robustness, exception handling, accuracy, integrity, accessibility, availability, interoperability, security etc. [16]. Among these the most widely used QoS are performance, scalability, reliability and security.

Performance: The performance of a web service represents how fast a service request can be completed. It can be measured in terms of throughput, response time, latency, execution time, and transaction time, and so on.

Reliability: Web services should be provided with high reliability. Reliability here represents the ability of a web service to perform its required functions under stated conditions for a specified time interval.

Scalability: Web services should be provided with high scalability. Scalability represents the capability of increasing the computing capacity of service provider's computer system and system's ability to process more users' requests, operations or transactions in a given time interval.

Security: Web services should be provided with the required security. With the increase in the use of web services which are delivered over the public Internet, there is a growing concern about security. The web service provider may apply different approaches and levels of providing security policy depending on the service requestor.

3.5 Business Process Execution Language (BPEL or BPEL4WS)

Business Process Execution Language for Web Services (BPEL or BPEL4WS) is a language used for the definition and execution of business processes using Web services. BPEL enables the top-down realization of Service Oriented Architecture (SOA) through composition, orchestration, and coordination of Web services. BPEL provides a relatively easy and straightforward way to compose several Web services into new composite services called *business processes* [18]. The business process is the collection of one or more tasks, which performs a particular goal. The BPEL is used to model a business process composed of number of web services. The BPEL supports static composition of web services. Further, BPEL statements are executed by BPEL engine which in-turn calls/invokes different web services to collectively perform a task. BPEL is an XML language that supports process oriented service composition [6, 15].

3.6 WS-Policy

WS-policy specifications enable web service based applications to specify policy information. The Web service specifications (WS*) are designed to be composed with each other to provide a rich set of tools for secure, reliable, and/or transacted Web services. WS-Policy by itself does not provide a negotiation solution for Web services. WS-Policy is a building block that is used in conjunction with other Web service and application-specific protocols to accommodate a wide variety of policy exchange models. WS-Policy provides a flexible and extensible grammar for expressing the capabilities, requirements, and general characteristics of entities in an XML Web services-based system. WS-Policy defines a framework and a model for the expression of these properties as policies [14, 15].

WS-Policy defines a policy to be a collection of policy alternatives, where each policy alternative is a collection of policy assertions. Some policy assertions specify traditional requirements and capabilities that will ultimately manifest on the wire (e.g., authentication scheme, transport protocol selection). Other policy assertions have no wire manifestation yet are critical to proper service selection and usage (e.g., privacy policy, QoS characteristics). WS-Policy provides a single policy grammar to allow both kinds of assertions to be reasoned about in a consistent manner [14, 15].

4. QoS support in composite web service environment

Any web service based system may require many web services to be composed together to perform a composite task. The web services selected for composition should satisfy not only functional requirements but also non-functional requirements such as cost, time, reliability, security etc. The QoS parameters corresponding to non functional requirements of the web services are to be stored in the UDDI. The QoS parameters are to be published by the publisher in the registry and service consumer searches appropriate web services based on QoS parameters, from the registry. The QoS requirements of the web services are advertised in the WSDL of web service, using WS-policy specifications. The support is required at two places for QoS enabled web services – at broker end (UDDI) and in service contact (WSDL).

4.1 QoS Support at Broker End

UDDI is a registry to store information for web services. UDDI provides API's to publish and search the web services in the registry. Save_service API is used by publisher to publish the web service details in the UDDI and find_service API is used by web service consumer to search the web service in the UDDI. In order to support web services with QoS we need to modify save_service and find_service API's of UDDI. In the UDDI, category for group of web services is represented by tModel. Therefore, we may use tModel to represent a category for group of web services using a particular QoS. To realize this, we can extend UDDI schema to store parameters supported for a particular QoS as well as values of parameters with reference to web services.

Extension to save_service API includes - adding the extra parameter that specify QoS parameter and its value. QoS parameter measures the QoS associated with the web service and value specify its value. Here, value is any float value in the range 0 & 1. We can define certain QoS that are associated with particular category of web services. All the web services in the same category have same set of QoS parameters, e.g., web services identified with same tModel of QoS.

The current UDDI API provides support for searching web services on the basis of service_key, service_category etc.. With the addition of QoS support in UDDI registry, the find_service API is required to incorporate QoS parameters. The modified find_service API can be used for searching web services with or without QoS support.

4.2 QoS Support at Service Provider End

When web service is searched from the UDDI, the web service client needs a way to invoke it. WSDL is the interface providing information about web service invocation. Since the service is QoS enabled, therefore QoS requirements of the web service is to be specified in the WSDL. The web service consumer will look for the service requirements and will invoke the web service accordingly. In order to specify service QoS requirements the WS-Policy elements can be used in the WSDL [12].

4.3 Web Service composition

Any real world business process may be comprises of various business tasks. Each of these business tasks may be performed using web services. The business process can be performed by selecting various web services from a web service pool and composing them together. Composition of web services can be achieved by defining execution path using BPEL language specifications. The web services participating in the business process can be selected dynamically on the basis of QoS supported and the value of various QoS parameters. Fig. 3 shows one such web service composition corresponding to the business process of automobile company. The mathematical model to select the web services based on QoS requirements of web service using probabilistic analysis approach can be derived as follows:

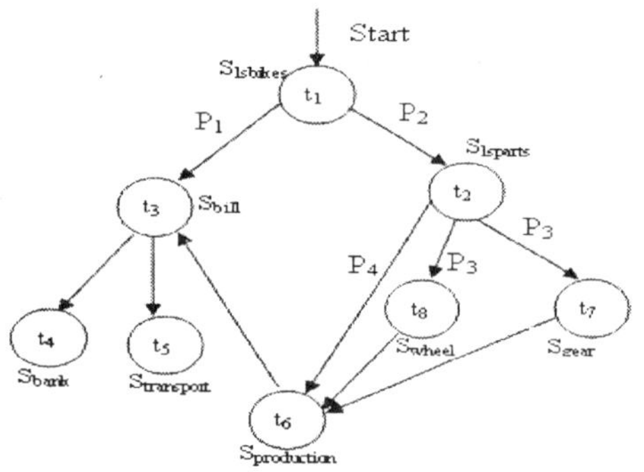

Fig. 3 Web Service Composition

In Fig. 3 the circle represents web services and arrow represents the order of service invocation. Services S_{bill} and $S_{lsparts}$ are invoked in parallel with probability P_1 and P_2 ($P_1 + P_2 = 1$), respectively. $S_{lsparts}$ invokes the service S_{wheel} & S_{gear} with probability P_3 and $S_{production}$ with the probability of P_4 ($P_3 + P_4 = 1$), respectively. Let t_i and c_i be the execution time of Web service *i* and the cost to execute that service, respectively. If *T* and *C* are the total execution time and total cost of the composite web service, then for Fig. 3.1,

$$T = t_1 + P_1 t_3 + P_2[t_2 + P_3\{\max(t_7, t_8) + t_6\} + P_4 t_6 + t_3] + \max(t_4, t_5)$$

$$C = c_1 + P_1 c_3 + P_2[c_2 + P_3\{\max(c_7, c_8) + c_6\} + P_4 c_6 + c_3] + \max(c_4, c_5)$$

The total execution time *T* and cost *C* is to be minimized therefore, services with minimum value of t_i and c_i will be selected from UDDI registry for composition. The t_i and c_i information about web services are already publish by publishers in the UDDI and used for selecting optimal web service composition.

5. System Architecture

The online order processing system of four wheeler automobile company is using web services from various service providers such as wheel manufacturers, gear manufacturers, banks, transporters etc. Many web service providers offers services for each of wheel manufacturing, gear manufacturing, transportation etc. When order is placed from any showroom, different services are to be selected to process the order. Web services participating in the composition are selected to optimize the value of composition based on QoS. Fig. 4 shows system architecture diagram.

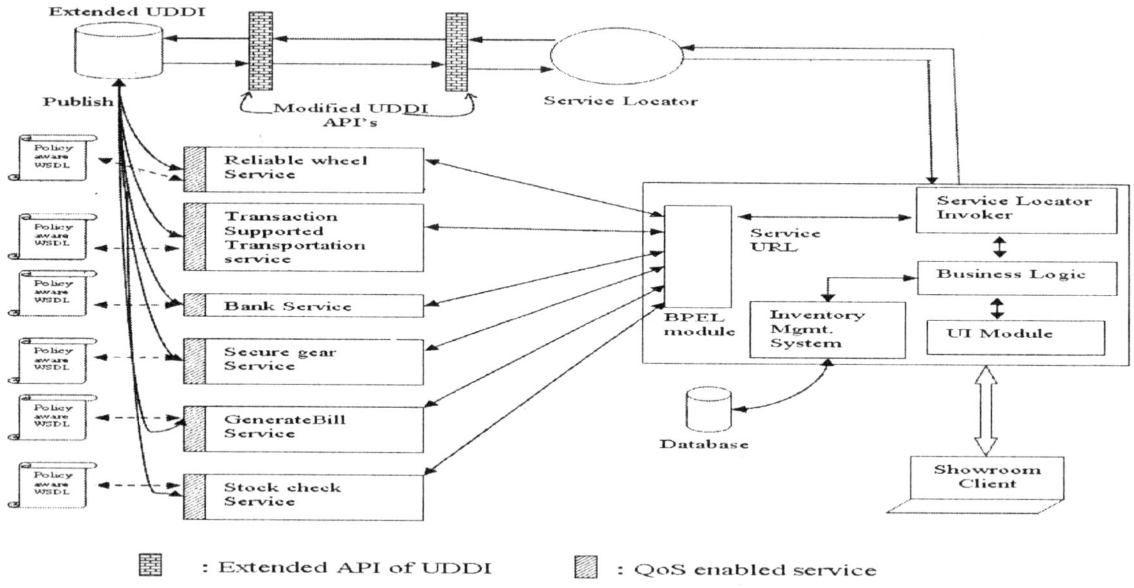

Fig. 4 System Architecture Diagram

The showroom owner places the online order for vehicle. As soon as order is placed, the inventory of company is checked for the availability of required number of vehicles. If order can be fulfilled, the bill web service generates the bill and transportation & bank web services are used to process the order. If sufficient numbers of vehicles are not found in the inventory, the parts manufacturers are to be contacted.

Therefore, service locator module searches the web services of parts manufacturers in the UDDI based on the QoS requirements of web services. The UDDI returns the URL of WSDL of web service. The service locator invoker module parses the WSDL and extracts the web service details to invoke the web service. URLs of all the web services are given as input to BPEL module.

The order processing system of a four wheeler automobile company is consisting of six web services: Stock check service, Wheel service, Bank service, transportation service, gear service and bill service. The values for the QoS parameter are assumed to be float values and lies in the range 0 to 1. Values closer to one are assumed to have better QoS. Table 1 shows the QoS requirements of each web service.

Table 1 QoS requirements of services

Service	QoS requirement
Stock Check service	Reliability
Bill service	Performance
Transportation service	Security
Wheel Service	Reliability
Gear Service	Security
Bank Service	Reliability

6. System Implementation

The system consists of multiple web services implemented using JAVA and deployed on apache AXIS 1.4 (SOAP processor). Service locator module is written in JAVA. WS-policy specifications are used to specify service QoS requirements in the WSDL interface. Web services are composed by using BPEL. Active BPEL engine 3.1 is used as BPEL processing engine. jUDDI is used as UDDI implementation. The jUDDI schema and API's are extended/modified to support QoS based web services. Following modifications/extension in jUDDI is done.

6.1 Extension to the jUDDI database

Database is extended by adding two new tables to store QoS parameters associated with the web service.

QoS_category : This table stores the category of QoS. The QoS is identified by tModel key in the schema. Various columns for the table are shown in Fig. 5.

tModel_key	QoS_Parameter

Fig. 5 QoS_category

Service_QoS : The table gives the association between QoS and web services. The touple in the table represents QoS parameter for the web service identified by service key. Various columns for the table are shown in Fig. 6.

Service_key	QoS_Parameter	QoS_Parameter _Value

Fig. 6 Service_QoS

6.2 Extensions to the UDDI API's

Various UDDI API's are modified to support QoS based service publishing and discovery. Interfaces that are extended or added are as follows:

Interfaces, IRegistry, RegistryObject, IFuction, DataStore, IHandler, Inquiry and Publish.

6.3 WS-policy for advertising QoS requirements

The service contract (WSDL) of web service contains WS-policy element to advertise the QoS requirements of web service, e.g., for online order processing system of automobile company has gear web service using secure communication. In order to advertise security requirements of the gear web service following WS-policy element is added in its WSDL. It shows the requirements of encrypting and signing message parts.

6.4 Web Service composition:

The service locator module searches for various web services in the UDDI and give them as one of the input to BPEL process. The composition of web services is achieved using BPEL specifications. The BPEL process formed is deployed as web service. This leads to dynamic discovery and composition of web services based on QoS requirements. The services meeting QoS requirements are selected to participate in composition. The composition is shown in the Fig. 7.

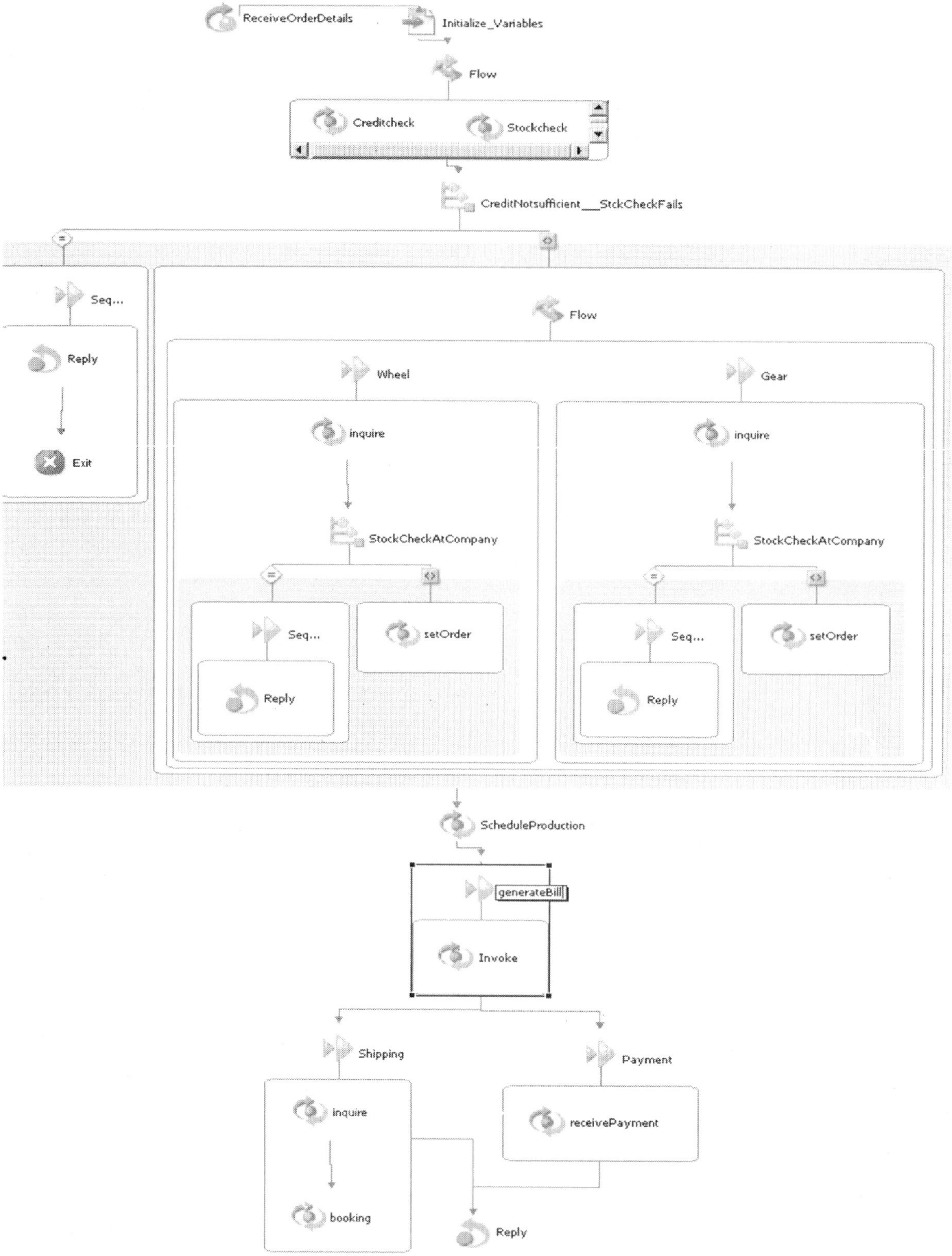

Fig. 7 BPEL based composition

7. Conclusions and Future work

In this paper we have presented a possible extension in the UDDI schema to store the QoS parameters. We have presented the extension to the UDDI API's for publishing and searching the web services based on their non functional requirements (QoS). Further, this paper also gives an approach to dynamically discovery and composition of web services based on the QoS. Future modifications in the system can be thought of as follows:

(i) A mechanism for measuring the QoS parameter associated with web services and a Feedback system for updation of QoS values stored, from web service consumer can be implemented. This mechanism can be implemented as part of UDDI registry.

(ii) Fuzzy rule based composition of the web services can be thought of to make the composition dynamic.

8. References

[1] Demian Antony D'Mello, V. S. Ananthanarayana "Quality Driven Web Service Selection and Ranking" IEEE computer society, © 2008.

[2] Jianqiang Hu, Changguo Guo, Huaimin Wang, Peng Zou "Quality Driven Web Services Selection" IEEE International Conference on e-Business Engineering (ICEBE'05)-2005.

[3] M. Tian, A. Gramm, T. Naumowicz, H. Ritter, J. Schiller, "A Concept for QoS Integration in Web Services" IEEE International Conference on Web Information Systems Engineering Workshops (WISEW'03) – 2004.

[4] Daniel A. Menascé, "Composing Web Services: A QoS View" IEEE INTERNET COMPUTING – 2004

[5] Rachid Anane, Behzad Bordbar, Fanyu Deng & Robert J. Hendley, "A Web Services Approach to Learning Path Composition",IEEE International Conference on Advanced Learning Technologies, 2005.

[6] Nikola Milanovic, Miroslaw Malek, "Current Solutions for Web Service Composition", IEEE Computer Society, 2004.

[7] Jinghai Rao and Xiaomeng Su, "A Survey of Automated Web Service Composition Methods", N-7491, Trondheim, Norway, 2005.

[8] Bastin Tony Roy Savarimuthu, Maryam Purvis, Martin Purvis, "Agent Based Web Service Composition in the Context of a Supply-Chain Based Workflow" The Information Science Discussion Paper Series, Number 2006/04, February 2006, ISSN 1172-6024

[9] Jie Xu, Erica Y. Yang, and Keith H. Bennett, "A Practical Approach to Secure Web Services ", IEEE international symposium, 2006.

[10] Patrick C. K. Hung, Haifei Li, Jun-Jang Jeng, "WS-Negotiation: An Overview of Research Issues ",IEEE, HICSS 2004.

[11] Active BPEL engine & designer, at http://www.**active**vos.com/

[12] W3, Web Services Definition Language (WSDL) 2.0, at http://www.w3.org/

[13] OASIS, Universal Description, Discovery, and Integration(UDDI), at http://uddi.org/pubs/uddi_v3.htm

[14] W3C, Web Services Policy Framework, at http://www.w3.org/Submission

[15] IBM, Web Services Policy Framework, at www.ibm.com/

[16] W3C, QoS for Web Services: Requirements and Possible Approaches, at http://www.w3c.or.kr/

[17] W3C, Web Services Architecture, at http://www.w3.org/

[18] Business Process Execution Language (BPEL) , at http://www.oracle.com/

[19] Universal Description, Discovery, and Integration(UDDI), at http://www.ws.apache.org

SS1.0 – A New Novel Software Solution to control Shoulder Surfing

Divyans Mahansaria[1] and Karthik.S[2]
[1]B.Tech (CSE), SRM University
[2]Lecturer (Comp. Sc. & Engg.), SRM University
divyansmahansaria@srmuniversity.co.in *shivkaar@hotmail.com*

Abstract

Shoulder surfing uses direct observation techniques, such as looking over someone's shoulder, to get information. Shoulder surfing is an effective way to get information because it's relatively easy to stand next to someone and watch as the user types in information to authenticate himself/herself to enter into a particular system. Often users are unaware of the presence of any external device, such as, a camera, which may be placed in order to trap the user and obtain valuable information, such as, passwords, while the user types through. In order to control shoulder surfing we have constructed a software (SS1.0) which can play a major role in culminating shoulder surfing. It could be used in different types of devices, such as computers, ATM's etc. According to our survey, it is has a high user acceptance with many people readily agreeing to use it in electronic devices, mainly computers. This paper deals with an overview of Shoulder Surfing with a direct plunge into the various aspects related to SS1.0.

1. Introduction

[7] The notion of shoulder surfing is something many find a little bizarre. It is something that each of us does at one point of time in our lives and sometimes without even realizing we do it. But there are those among us who do it all the time in the hope of learning vital pieces of information about us. Authentication is indeed at the heart of any secure system; a user has to be authenticated before he/she involves in online transactions, enters a secured vault, opens a safe or reach his/her email account and many other things. If sensitive information or unauthorized access is given to a wrong identity, the security of the entire system will collapse. [8] Identity theft refers to fraudulence that involves stealing money or getting other benefits by pretending to be someone else. The person whose identity is used faces various consequences when held responsible for the perpetrator's actions. In many countries, specific laws make it a crime to use another person's identity for personal gain. We must remain cautious while revealing our personal information in any form. Anyone who is truly concerned about identity should certainly make themselves familiar with shoulder surfing.

Shoulder surfing has become a major concept in present world scenario. In reality, this terminology is used to describe one of the many ways criminals obtain the personal information they need, to commit identity theft.

1.1 What is Shoulder Surfing?

[8] Shoulder surfing is using direct observation techniques, such as, looking over someone's shoulder, to get information. Shoulder surfing is an effective way to get information be it in a user's home while he works on his personal computer or in a public place which is more prone to shoulder surfing attack. [8] Shoulder surfing can also be done long distance with the aid of binoculars or other vision-enhancing devices. Inexpensive, miniature closed-circuit television cameras could also be concealed in ceilings, walls or fixtures to observe data entry. From a business point of view, the most dangerous form of shoulder surfing is when someone breezes up to talk to someone just as he/she may be entering his/her password. [3] The proliferation of laptop and personal digital assistant (PDA) usage, especially on now ubiquitous wireless networks, has greatly increased the danger of unauthorized observation of authentication procedures and even theft of password information. Mobile computing users in a public place are not aware of all the activity in their surroundings, and are vulnerable to persons visually observing or even recording their authentication session, with the intent of extracting login information. Similar considerations apply to access points (security doors) where the user is expected to authenticate by entering a PIN. Most authentication methods involve pressing keys on a keyboard or selecting objects on a screen, and both the screen and the keyboard are visible to the authorized user and the shoulder surfer, as well.

One should remain cautious of his/her surroundings if he/she is authentication by the traditional authentication methods prone to Shoulder Surfing.

1.2 Shoulder Surfing as a planned activity

[7] It is important to note that the process of shoulder surfing is not as straight forward as it may sound. It really isn't simply a case of peering over someone's shoulder and then writing down the information. There is a lot more to it. Most gangs who operate using this process operate two-fold. One half of the gang is responsible for following individuals who have been selected as targets and the other half is charged with the task of getting the details for their credit or debit cards.

One common way of doing this is as follows:

- One member of the team starts following a person.
- This continues until the person stops at, say, an ATM transaction machine to make a transaction.
- The member of the gang who has been following him could stand behind the person.
- At this point he makes a note of the person's PIN number.
- When the person moves away another member of the gang takes up the pursuit
- When the opportunity presents itself, they steal the handbag or rob him, thus gaining the money already drawn from the cash machine, in addition to card and PIN number

Once the gang is in possession of the card and the PIN number, they then proceed to empty money out of the victim's bank account before the card can be frozen.

2. Few tips to reduce Shoulder Surfing on a small scale

[9] Shoulder surfing certainly is not the most technical form of identity theft, but many have used this method to commit major fraud. The first step in the prevention of it is in understanding that this problem does exist. There are certain precautions which may be taken by the user on a small scale while authenticating in any system, that are not using any prevention techniques to control the havoc of Shoulder Surfing. Shielding keypad from view by using body or cupping by hand while typing passwords - is obviously one such method. One should experiment and create best password. It is advisable to use mixtures of numbers and letters rather than single, simple words for passwords. [7] One should never carry important letters or statements from banks or building societies. These documents, along with credit or debit card, can be a treat to any, would-be robber. One could invest in two factor authentication methods, such as, tokens. One should always remember to dispose of the receipts carefully after completing an ATM transaction. It is not a solution to Shoulder Surfing, but doing so can be a bit handy when it comes to protecting customers from revealing their personal information to strangers (probably a Shoulder Surfer).

3. Our Brainchild – SS1.0 – A software solution to Shoulder Surfing

The Beta Version of SS1.0 has been developed using Dot Net Platform and the programming language C#. In this software solution, users create an authentication account initially. Information regarding a particular user such as his/her User Name and Password is taken. This information is, then, stored in a Database using SQL. Any number of users can register in the system and a complete database which contains the entire information about the user along with their Usernames & Passwords can be formed. Most importantly, this database is hidden from the user and only accessible to the system programmer or administrator of the particular system.

Let us suppose that, at a later point of time, someone wants to logon to a system which has SS1.0 installed and which contains the information about several users who have already registered and have the right to use the system. The incoming user will be asked to enter his authentication information, Username & Password as is usually done for a secured system. Now SS1.0 comes into the picture. We have an interactive screen where, as usual, the username & password need to be entered. The username will be entered in the usual fashion as is done in most computer systems. But the trick lies while entering the password. The software uses an inbuilt novel technique to make the users enter their password.

As the cursor is clicked on the password field a popup box appears. It contains a 3*12 order matrix (i.e. 3 rows and 12 columns). The rows are numbered using the numbers 1, 2 & 3, while the columns are numbered using numbers from 1 to 12. The elements of the matrix will be a randomly generated set of alphabets & numerals without repetition of any alphabet or numerals in the matrix. Thus all 26 letters in the alphabet & 10 numerals (0-9) fill the matrix. Now instead of entering the actual password in the 'password field', the user is going to enter the positions of the constituent characters (alphabets or numerals) of his password in the 'password field'.

Let us suppose, for example, a password corresponding to a username "HELLO" is "HI5". In this case, the user enters "HELLO" in the 'username field'. In the password field, the user will enter the position of the character 'H' followed by 'I' and then the position of '5'. As the position, the user will enter first the row number of a particular element, then just after that the column number of that particular element. Let us assume we have the matrix for a particular iteration as:-

	1	2	3	4	5	6	7	8	9	10	11	12
1	a	c	g	Y	z	x	5	4	3	1	j	k
2	b	e	f	7	6	8	0	P	q	r	u	v
3	d	s	t	2	9	h	i	L	m	n	o	w

Fig. 1 SS1.0 concept

In this matrix, the position that the user has to enter corresponding to the password "HI5" can be calculated as:-

For 'H' – position is 36 (i.e. 3rd row & 6th column), for 'I' – position is 37 (i.e. 3rd row & 7th column) and for '5' – position is 17 (i.e. 1st row & 7th column).
Thus, the user will enter "36 37 17" as his password instead of "HI5".

The Matrix will generate random elements for each new login (i.e. for every subsequent authentication the matrix elements are going to dynamically change).
Now, let us suppose that the matrix for new login changes to the one as show in fig.2.

	1	2	3	4	5	6	7	8	9	10	11	12
1	a	c	g	y	z	x	7	6	8	1	j	k
2	b	e	f	3	4	5	0	P	q	r	u	v
3	d	s	t	2	9	h	n	L	m	i	o	w

Fig. 2 SS1.0 concept

In this matrix the position for the same password "HI5" can be calculated as:-

For 'H' – position is 36 (i.e. 3rd row & 6th column), for 'I' – position is 310 (i.e. 3rd row & 10th column) and for '5' – position is 26 (i.e. 2st row & 6th column).
Thus, the user will enter "36 310 26" as his new password instead of "HI5".

3.1 Demonstration of SS1.0

Step 1: A user starts the system to logon.

Fig. 3 User Logon

Step 2: Let us assume the user wants to personalize his settings and so creates an authentication account before login. He has to fill in a registration form and is free to choose a user id and password not present in the database of the system. If the user id and password chosen is unique, a new account is being set.

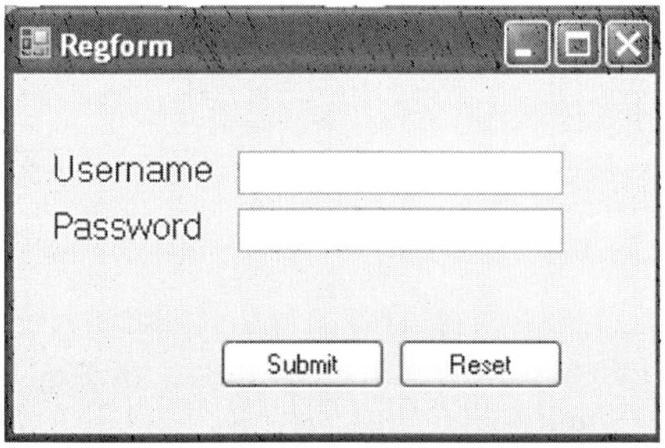

Fig. 4 SS1.0 registration form snapshot

Step 3: Suppose a user wants to login to the system. He initially requires an authentication. There will be two fields': one containing user name & the other containing password. The user name is entered, as usual. While entering the password, a new scheme is being applied. As is evident from fig.5, a randomized matrix of alphanumeric elements is present. The user has to find out the corresponding position of his/her password and provide the positions as his/her password in the password field. Then 'Submit' is clicked for verification of the correctness of the provided username & password.

Fig. 5 SS1.0 form snapshot

Step 4: A comparison between the entered information for authentication and the already existing user names & passwords in the database (to which SS1.0 is linked) is made. If there exits such an account, then the login becomes successful. However, if the authentication information is incorrect, then the login fails & authentication information may again be retaken from the user.

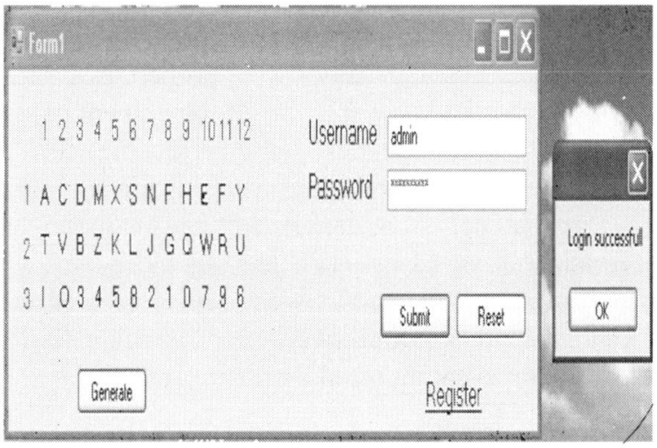

Fig. 6 SS1.0 login snapshot

4. Utility of using SS1.0

Let there exits a sneaker who tries to figure out the authentication details of a user through Shoulder Surfing. On using this software by the user, his/her efforts will go in vain. A sneaker can either look onto the keyboard or look at the screen at a time. If he looks onto the keyboard then what he will get to see is a false authentication password of the user. Suppose the one who sees the password tries to keep the password in mind and waits for the user to leave the system and then try to get the actual password through positions entered by the user, his effort will also go in vain because after each login the positions in the matrix are dynamically changed. Let us consider another possibility when the user just gazes at the screen and tries to memorize the positions of each corresponding alphabets & numerals present on the screen. But that would prove futile, by the time the user authenticates and logins without the sneaker knowing any of the typed entity.

Using SS1.0, we can also avoid the loss of passwords which could have been obtained otherwise through the use of binoculars, closed-circuit television cameras or other vision-enhancing devices that a shoulder attacker may use in order to trap a user. The keyboard and monitor of a computer are usually present at an angle of around 90□. Now a single external device such as a camera can generally focus in only one direction (i.e. either a monitor or keyboard). In both cases, our method is resistant to the trap laid by the shoulder attacker.

Yet another effective advantage of using SS1.0 is that it involves figuring out positions. It has been biologically proven that such type of mental exercise improves one's cognition. [10] It does not involve cases like the one shown in figure-7 which is highly unprofessional, more time consuming as well as dangerous.

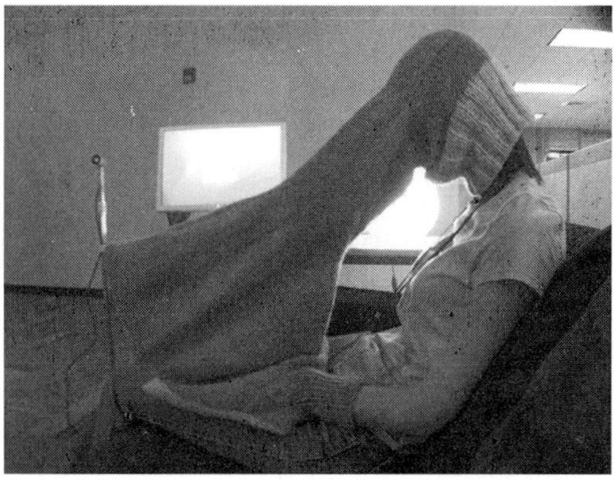

Fig. 7 Futile way to control Shoulder Surfing

From the discussions we can see that the software solution SS1.0 could be a Novel solution in controlling Shoulder Surfing.

5. Certain constraints in using this software

While SS1.0 is by far suitable in controlling Shoulder Surfing, it does suffer certain drawbacks. The mechanism is new so users need to be aware of the use of the new software (although the use is very simple). The login time will increase than usual. But keeping the high performance and other benefits in mind, we can compensate on the time taken for initial logon.

6. Alphanumeric vs. graphical passwords

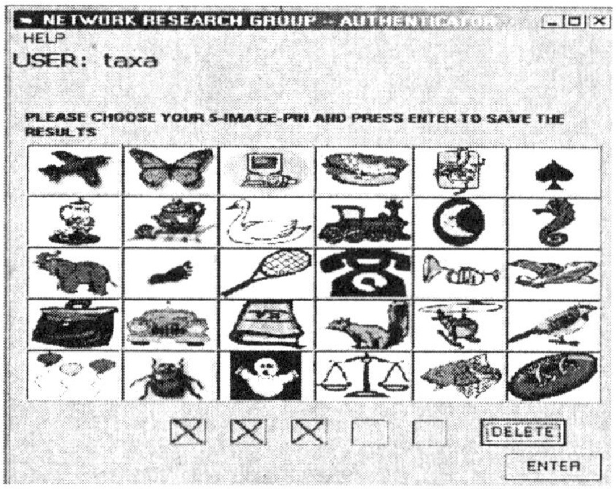

Fig. 8 An image based scheme to control Shoulder Surfing

[4] Graphical password schemes are believed to be more secure and more resilient to dictionary attacks than textual passwords, but more vulnerable to shoulder surfing attacks. Several researches have been conducted in various parts of the world regarding this. These surveys showed that it is easy to remember face passwords & easy to figure out the password from a set of images. This shows that it is more prone to shoulder surfing attack. In fig.8, we see an image - based scheme in which a user chooses certain images as his authentication information. While choosing a particular image a sneaker can easily view the image being chosen and thus steal the valuable authentication information of a user. Images could also be replaced instead of alphanumeric elements in the matrix of SS1.0. But that would increase the complexity of the system. The space required for display would be more with limited options of choosing password. Most importantly, using alphanumeric password is a general scheme which could be used worldwide on any networked machine. Sticking onto particular sets of pictures for each machine would be too restrictive. Generally different schemes of images are applied to different machines which make them more restrictive to a particular machine which in turn cannot be used as a common password worldwide to all the machines connected over a network.

7. Survey Analysis

Maybe people aren't just being nosey when they look over one's shoulder. They could also be doing it to get a glimpse at one's corporate data. Users of laptops and Smartphone in public places need to be more aware of the risk of being 'shoulder surfed' by strangers spying on their private business communications, suggests new research.

A Britain based technology company has just released a survey that suggests 80 per cent of British people admit to having read over a stranger's shoulder while on public transport, in coffee shops and in shared work places. Some 56 per cent of those who admitted to shoulder surfing are attracted to their neighbors' laptop, says business development manager of the technological company.

In order to further prove the utility of SS1.0 we undertook a survey. The result of the survey was encouraging. A large majority of the people thought that SS1.0 could be very useful in reducing shoulder surfing. During our survey we found out that initially it took a bit more time to login using this method but as the user became more accustomed to the software the time taken to login reduced considerably.

8. Conclusions

[5] Passwords possess many useful properties as well as widespread legacy deployment; consequently we can expect their use for the foreseeable future. Unfortunately, today's standard methods for password input are subject to a variety of attacks based on observation, from casual sneaking (shoulder surfing), to more exotic methods. We have presented an alternative approach to password entry, which can go a long way in preventing shoulder surfing attacks.

9. Future Work

Although this software has been well tested and accepted, in the future we propose to enhance the capabilities of the present version & overcome the few limitations that it presently poses. Security is becoming all the more important in the present world scenario. Proper research work needs to done with the invention of new techniques to solve the problem related to various aspects of security. We are carrying out research work to embed features in SS1.0 which could control other forms of authentication hacking attacks as well.

10. References

[1] Divyans Mahansaria, Ashish Kalsi, "E-Learning", *Proceedings TISC 2007*, Chennai, December, 2007.

[2] S.Bindu etal, "A Novel Cognition based graphical Authentication Scheme which is resistant to shoulder surfing attack", *Proceedings ICIP 08*, I.K. International, Bangalore, August, 2008.

[3] Bogdan Hoanca, Kenrick Mock, "Screen Oriented technique for reducing the incidence of shoulder surfing".

[4] Behzad Malek etal, "Novel Shoulder – Surfing Resistant haptic – based graphical password".

[5] Manu Kumar, Tal Garfinkel, Dan Boneh, Terry Winograd, "Reducing Shoulder-surfing by Using Gaze-based Password Entry".

[6] Paul Dunphy, "The Realities of graphical passwords".

[7] Website - www.aboutidentitytheft.co.uk

[8] Website - www.wikipedia.com

[9] Website – www.spamlaws.com

[10] Website – www.notechhacking.com

Web 3.0: Emerging Applications for Internet Generation

Navneet Bhardwaj[1] and Priyanka Bhutani[2]
[1]M.Tech (IT) 11th Semester, University School of Information Technology, GGS Indraprastha University, Delhi
[2]Lecturer, University School of Information Technology, GGS Indraprastha University, Delhi
navneet.it@gmail.com priyabhutani@yahoo.com

Abstract

With more than 10 years of work on semantic web foundations and more than five years when the phrase becomes highly popular in Internet Generations. It's an ultimate opportunity for the innovators to develop some own idea to classify Internet enabled Technologies that would help us common man's life become more comfortable. Following the introduction of the phrase "Web 2.0" as a description of the recent evolution of the Web, the term "Web 3.0" has been introduced to hypothesize about a future wave of Internet innovation. Views on the next stage of the World Wide Web's evolution vary greatly, from the concept of emerging technologies such as the Semantic Web transforming the way the Web is used (and leading to new possibilities inartificial intelligence) to the observation that increases in Internet connection speeds, modular web applications, and advances in computer graphics will play the key role in the evolution of the World Wide Web. However the emerging applications of Web 3.0 help easier accessibility for new internet generation.

Keywords: *Semantic Web, Web 2.0, Web 3.0, RDF, Piggybank, SPARQL, XML, Open ID, Layers*

1. Introduction

In a short span of time the WWW has revolutionized information, which is transferred between computer applications. That information is not necessary for humans to explore its syntax and make parsers for flow of information transfer when modern technological languages like XHTML, XML and other related languages are used [1]. Web 3.0 is one of the terms used to describe the evolutionary stage of the Web that follows Web 2.0. Given that technical and social possibilities identified in this latter term are yet to be fully realized the nature of defining Web 3.0 is highly speculative. In general it refers to aspects of the internet which, though potentially possible, are not technically or practically feasible at this time.

The term "Web 3.0" has been introduced to hypothesize about a future wave of Internet innovation. Views on the next stage of the World Wide Web's evolution vary greatly, from the concept of emerging technologies such as the Semantic Web transforming the way the Web is used (and leading to new possibilities inartificial intelligence) to the observation that increases in Internet connection speeds, modular web applications, and advances in computer graphics will play the key role in the evolution of the World Wide Web [2].

2. Major trends of Web 3.0

There are various complementary technologies embodied with important trends, these are:

- **Transformation** of the Web from a network of separately provided applications and content repositories to a more seamless and interoperable whole.
- **Ubiquitous connectivity**, broadband adoption, mobile Internet access and mobile devices which help better utilization resources;
- **Network computing**, software-as-a-service business models, Web services interoperability, distributed computing, grid computing and cloud computing;
- **Open technologies**, open APIs and protocols, open data formats, open-source software platforms and open data (e.g. Creative Commons,Open Data License);
- **Open identity**, OpenID, open reputation, roaming portable identity and personal data; It is a decentralized, free and open standard that lets users control the amount of personal information they provide.
- **The Intelligent Web**, Semantic Web technologies such as RDF, OWL, SWRL, SPARQL, GRDDL, semantic application platforms, and statement-based data stores;
- **Distributed databases**, the "World Wide Database" (enabled by Semantic Web technologies); and
- **Intelligent applications**, natural language processing [3], machine learning, machine reasoning, autonomous agents [4].

- **Widgets and other embedded application:** Widgets and other embedded applications provide easier comfort and accessibility and faster loading of web pages in nanoseconds.

3. Layer Topology of Web 3.0

The layer topology of web 3.0 is described below:

1. **Api Services:** It forms the foundation layer in which there are raw hosted services that have powered in Web 2.0 will become engines of Web 3.0. Google's search and AdWords APIs, Amazon's affiliate APIs, a seemingly infinite ocean of RSS feeds, a multitude of functional services, such as those included in the multipurpose Web Services Marketplace, and many other examples.
2. **Aggregation Services:** It forms the middle layer of Web 3.0 layer topology. These are the intermediaries that take some of the hassle out of locating all those raw API services by bundling them together in useful ways. Obvious examples today are the various RSS aggregators, and emerging web services
3. **Application Services:** It forms the top layer of Web 3.0. These will not be like the established application categories we are used to, such as CRM, ERP or office, but a new class of composite applications that bring together functionality from multiple services to help users achieve their objectives in a flexible, intuitive and self-evident way.
4. **Serviced Clients:** It is a half layer in which there is role for client-side logic in the Web 3.0 landscape, but users will expect it to be maintained and managed on their behalf, which is why it is chosen to call these clients 'serviced'. Whether those clients are based on browser technology or on Windows technology is moot point that I shall also be returning to [5].

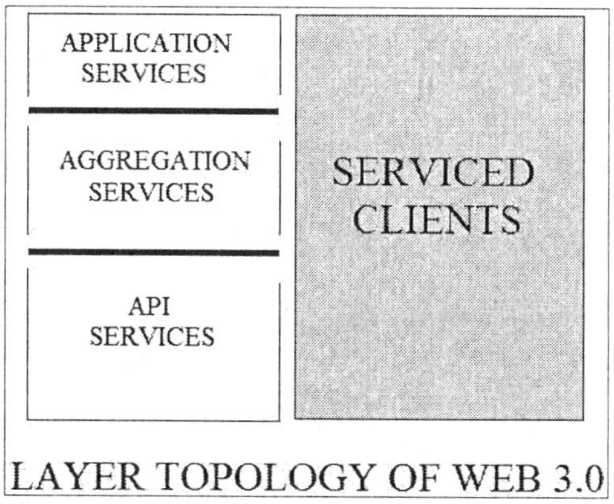

Fig. 1 Layer topology of Web 3.0

4. Emerging Web Development Languages Employed

(a) **XML:** XML is the syntactic foundation layer of the Semantic Web. All other technologies providing features for the Semantic Web will be built on top of XML. Requiring other Semantic Web technologies (like the Resource Description Framework) to be layered on top of XML guarantees a base level of interoperability. The technologies that XML is built upon are Unicode characters and Uniform Resource Identifiers (URIs). The Unicode characters allow XML to be authored using international characters. URIs are used as unique identifiers for concepts in the Semantic Web. XML is not a language; it is actually a set of syntax rules for creating semantically rich markup languages in a particular domain. In other words, you apply XML to create new languages. Any language created via the rules of XML, like the Math Markup Language (MathML), is called an application of XML. A markup language is primary concern is how to add semantic information about the raw content in a document; thus, the vocabulary of a markup language is the external "marks" to be attached or embedded in a document. This concept of adding marks, or semantic instructions, to a document has been done manually in the text publishing industry for years .the first key principle of XML is markup is separate from content.[6] A corollary to that principle is that markup can surround or contain content. Thus, a markup language is a set of words, or marks, that surround, or 'tag,' a portion of a document is content in order to attach additional meaning to the tagged content. The mechanism invented to mark content was to enclose each word of the language is vocabulary in a less-than sign (<) and a greater-than sign (>). To use the < and > characters as part of a tag, these characters cannot be used in content, and therefore they are replaced by the special codes (called entities).

(b) **RDF:** RDF is the machine process able document, now the computer (of course) can't actually "understand" what you said, but it can deal with it in a way that seems like it does. Then, they could put that information back on the Web. At the simplest level, the Resource Description Framework is an XML-based language to describe resources. Such a resource is accessed via a Uniform Resource Locator (URL). This mechanism for describing resources is a major component in what is proposed by the W3C's Semantic Web activity:

an evolutionary stage of the World Wide Web in which automated software can store, exchange, and use machine-readable information distributed throughout the web, in turn enabling users to deal with the information with greater efficiency and certainty [6]. RDF's simple data model and ability to model disparate, abstract concepts has also led to its increasing use in knowledge management applications unrelated to Semantic Web activity.

While XML documents attach Meta data to parts of a document, one use of RDF is to create Meta- data about the document as a standalone entity. The RDF model is also called as triple, because it contains three parts viz. Subject, Predicate and Object.RDF is a directed, labeled graph data format for representing information in the Web. RDF is often used to represent, among other things, personal information, social networks, metadata about digital artifacts, as well as to provide a means of integration over disparate sources of information. This specification defines the syntax and semantics of the SPARQL query language for RDF.

(c) AJAX:

Ajax (asynchronous JavaScript and XML), or AJAX, is a group of interrelated web development techniques used for creating interactive web applications or rich Internet applications. Despite the name, the use of JavaScript, XML, or its asynchronous use is not required. In traditional JavaScript coding, if you want to get any information from a database or a file on the server, or send user information to a server, you will have to make an HTML form and GET or POST data to the server. The user will have to click the "Submit" button to send/get the information, wait for the server to respond, then a new page will load with the results.Because the server returns a new page each time the user submits input, traditional web applications can run slowly and tend to be less user-friendly.With AJAX, your JavaScript communicates directly with the server, through the JavaScript **XML Http Request** objectWith an HTTP request, a web page can make a request to, and get a response from a web server - without reloading the page. The user will stay on the same page, and he or she will not notice that scripts request pages, or send data to a server in the background [7].

Advantages

In many cases, the pages on a website consist of much content that is common between them. Using traditional methods, that content would have to be reloaded on every request. However, using Ajax, a web application can request only the content that needs to be updated, thus drastically reducing bandwidth usage and load time.

- The use of asynchronous requests allows the client's Web browser UI to be more interactive and to respond quickly to inputs, and sections of pages can also be reloaded individually. Users may perceive the application to be faster or more responsive, even if the application has not changed on the server side.
- The use of Ajax can reduce connections to the server, since scripts and style sheets only have to be requested once [8][9].

Disadvantages

- Dynamically created pages do not register themselves with the browser's history engine, so clicking the browser's "back" button would not return the user to an earlier state of the Ajax-enabled page, but would instead return them to the last page visited before it. Workarounds include the use of invisible IFrames to trigger changes in the browser's history and changing the anchor portion of the URL (following a #) when AJAX is run and monitoring it for changes.
- Dynamic web page updates also make it difficult for a user to bookmark a particular state of the application. Solutions to this problem exist, many of which use the URL fragment identifier (the portion of a URL after the '#') to keep track of, and allow users to return to, the application in a given state.
- Because most web crawlers do not execute JavaScript code, web applications should provide an alternative means of accessing the content that would normally be retrieved with Ajax, to allow search engines to index it
- Any user whose browser does not support Ajax or JavaScript, or simply has JavaScript disabled, will not be able to use its functionality. Similarly, devices such as mobile phones, PDAs, and screen readers may not have support for JavaScript or the XMLHttpRequest object. Also, screen readers that are able to use Ajax may still not be able to properly read the dynamically generated content.

- The same origin policy prevents Ajax from being used across domains, although the W3C has a draft that would enable this functionality.
- The lack of a standards body behind Ajax means there is no widely adopted best practice to test Ajax applications. Testing tools for Ajax often do not understand Ajax event models, data models, and protocols [10].

(d) Other Small Web Development Languages:

Other Web Development languages are:

- JSON
- JSAN
- JSDoc [11]

5. Major Applications and Web Portal languages developed for Web 3.0

1. **Timeline:** A timeline contains one or more *bands*, which can be panned infinitely by dragging with the mouse pointer. A band can be configured to synchronize with another band such that panning one band also scrolls the other.

   A timeline is implemented as a div element that contains inner div elements as its bands (right). The banddivs are cropped and positioned relative to the timeline div.

   A band div itself contains several inner elements that implements various parts of the band. For example, the two timelines above show labels for days, weeks, months, and years. The bands also have different background colors, and the weekly band of the second timeline has weekend markings. All of these visual elements are "painted" by adding HTML elements to the band divs at the appropriate positions.

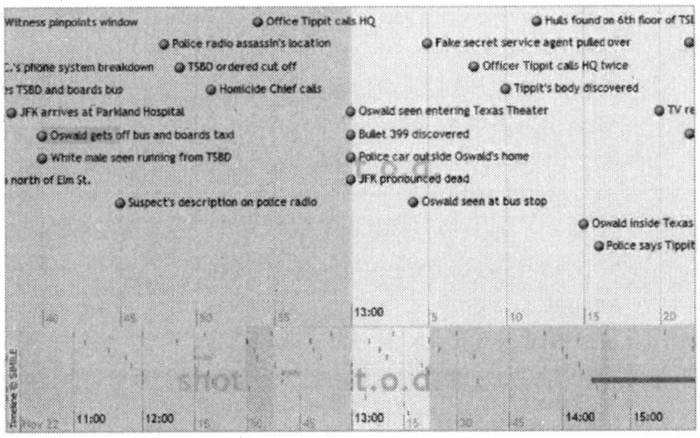

Fig. 2 Timeline Description

As a band is panned, its div is shifted horizontally or vertically, carrying all of its visual elements along. When either end of the band div approaches the visible (non-cropped) area, the band div is re-centered, its coordinate origin is changed, and then its various visual elements are re-"painted" relative to the new coordinate origin. All of this "paging" is done as seamlessly as possible so that the user experiences smooth, *infinite* panning.

A band is responsible for supporting panning as well as coordinating its various sub-components:

- an ether, whose sole responsibility is mapping between pixel coordinates and dates/times;
- an ether painter, which paints date/time labels and the background of the band as well as the highlight (the lighter part of the lower band in the first timeline above);
- zero or more decorators, which further decorate the background of the band; and
- an *event painter*, which paints the events.

The band also takes an *event source* which provides events to be displayed in that band. Different bands can have different event sources. This flexibility allows for *timeline mashups*, as exemplified here. Various sub-components that do painting take a theme, which stores default visual and behavioral settings [12].

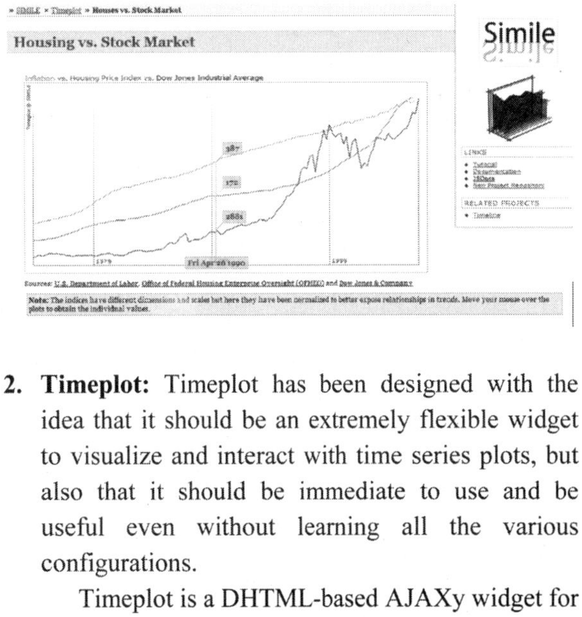

2. **Timeplot:** Timeplot has been designed with the idea that it should be an extremely flexible widget to visualize and interact with time series plots, but also that it should be immediate to use and be useful even without learning all the various configurations.

   Timeplot is a DHTML-based AJAXy widget for plotting time series and overlay time-based events over them (with the same data formats that Timeline supports) [13].
3. **EXHIBIT 2.0:** Exhibit is a three-tier web application framework written in Javascript, which you can include like you would include Google Maps.

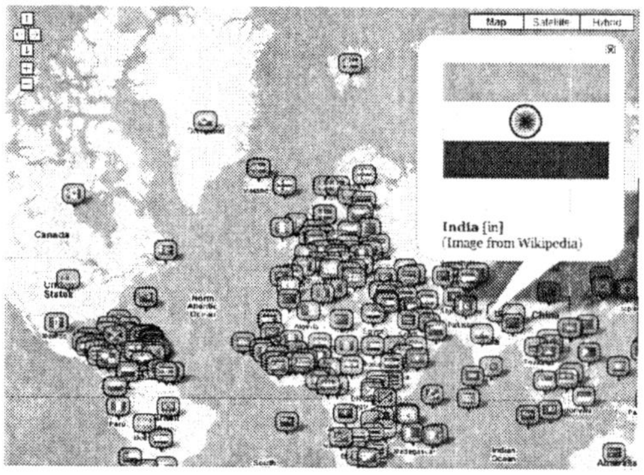

Fig. 3 Exhibit 2.0 Description

If you just want to show a few hundred records of data on maps, timelines, scatter plots, interactive tables, etc., why bother learning SQL, ASP, PHP, and CGI.

To use Exhibit, you write: a simple data file, and an HTML file in which you specify how the data should be shown.

4. **Piggybank:** The Semantic Web initiative has defined a standard data model called RDF in which information on the Web can be recorded. Using this W3C standard for representing data, one can describe information independent of formatting. And such data represented in RDF (e.g. "pure" information) is much more conducive to mixing, reusing and re-purposing.

   Piggy Bank is an extension to the Firefox Web browser that extracts information from existing Web pages and stores it in RDF. If a Web page already links to RDF information, extraction simply means retrieving that information. Otherwise, Piggy Bank employs custom software code that untangles the "pure" information from the Web page' formatting.

   Having extracted the "pure" information and stored it on your computer, Piggy Bank can now apply its own user interface to let you browse through that information independent of the original Web sites. For example, Piggy Bank can call upon Google Maps to display geographical information even if the original Web sites do not offer cartographic views of their data.

5. **Freebase.Com:** Freebase is a highly structured collaborative online database and website developed by Metaweb. Freebase contains data harvested from sources such as Wikipedia and MusicBrainz, as well as individually contributed data from its users. Freebase runs on a database infrastructure created in-house by Metaweb that utilizes a graph model. Queries to the database are made in "Metaweb Query Language" (MQL).

6. Summary and Conclusions

This research paper explains the Emerging Internet Generation of Web 3.0, first of all this paper covers the major trends of web 3.0 and its topology layers. In the next part we have explained the programming language of web services and its factors responsible for generating newer range of information and database accessible applications. We have also explained new applications and website that are under development.

Our further research development includes mass utilization of these programming languages and develops newer range of applications that would enable us easier connectivity of applications and web browser. Embedded applications such as widgets and plugins will also be defined. Our new dream is to integrate all platforms into one unique application which consumes fewer resources. We also plan to introduce Scalable Vector Graphics (SVG) with three dimensional Web Browser which would likely to be named WebCube. Such is the Miracle of Web.

7. References

[1] Ian Horrocks, Peter Schneider, "Three Theses of Representation in the Semantic web", WWW 2003, May 20-24 2003, Hungary, ACM 1-58113-680-3/03/0005

[2] Dean Giustini. http://student.bmj.com/issues/08/03/editorials/095.php

[3] Demonstration of Web 3.0 Cortex Intelligence. Cortex Intelligence (December 6, 2007) "http://www.cortex-intelligence.com/tech/"

[4] Nova Spivack, "The third generation Internet is coming http://www.kurzweilai.net/meme/frame.html?main=/articles/art0689.html?m%3D3

[5] Phil Wainewright, "What to expect on Web 3.0" http://blogs.zdnet.com/SAAS/?p=68

[6] Navneet Bhardwaj, Sanjay Kumar Malik "Meeting the challenges of various layers of Semantic Web Architecture", ETIT'07 National Conference, Bhopal

[7] AJAX tutorial: http://www.w3schools.com/Ajax/ajax_httprequest.asp

[8] Merrill, Christopher: http://www.webperformanceinc.com/library/reports/AjaxBandwidth/

[9] The Advantages of using AJAX: http://ajaxwebhosting.lunarpages.com/ajax-advantages.php

[10] The disadvantages of using AJAX: http://ajaxwebhosting.lunarpages.com/ajax-disadvantages.php

[11] Kevin Kelly - "Web 3.0" http://in.youtube.com/watch?v=J132shgIiuY

[12] www.simile.mit.edu/timeline/

[13] www.simile.mit.edu/timeplot/

[14] http://simile.mit.edu/wiki/Piggy_Bank_Introduction

A New Dynamic Cohesion Metric for Object Oriented Design

Vandana Bhattacherjee[1], Vinay Singh[2], Kumar Rajnish[3]
[1]Department of CS & E *Birla Institute of Technology*
[2]Usha Martin Academy, Ranchi
[3]Birla Institute of Technology Muscat, Oman
vbhattacherjee@ieee.org *mailtovsingh@yahoo.co.in*

Abstract

The complex dynamic behaviour of many real world applications motivates the development of dynamic metrics. While static metrics can satisfactorily predict the quantity of software like size and complexity, and can predict the resource requirement for development and maintenance of software, nevertheless quality attributes like maintainability, efficiency, reliability, and changeability need to be judged more on the basis of runtime behaviour of the system rather than on the basis of static analysis of code. This paper presents a proposal for a dynamic cohesion metric. Cohesion is the degree to which the elements of a class or object belong together and is an important attribute of a class in Object-Oriented (OO) design. OO Cohesion metrics have been proposed in literature and are based on parameters of the class like pairwise variable access by various methods of the class. The objective of this work is to propose a dynamic cohesion metric. The proposed metric is illustrated with examples.

***Keywords*:** Object-Oriented, Static Metrics, Cohesion, Dynamic Metrics, Object-Oriented Modeling.

1. Introduction

Software metrics help developers and managers to assess the quantity and quality of software. Static metrics can satisfactorily predict the quantity of software like size and complexity, and can predict the resource requirement for development and maintenance of software. However, quality attributes like maintainability, efficiency, reliability, and changeability need to be judged more on the basis of runtime behaviour of the system rather than on the basis of static analysis of code. The objective of this work is to study existing static cohesion metrics and propose a dynamic cohesion metric.

The metrics suite proposed by Chidamber and Kemerer is one of the best-known OO metrics [10-11]. Various researchers have conducted empirical studies to validate the OO metrics for their effects upon program attributes and quality factors such as development or maintenance effort [12-13]. Alshayeb and Li predict that OO metrics are effective (at least in some cases) in predicting design efforts [14]. Chae, Kwon and Bae investigated the effects of dependence variables on cohesion metrics for OO programs [15]. Several other researchers have validated OO metrics for effects of class size and with the change proneness of classes [16-18]. Li [19] theoretically validated Chidamber and Kemerer metrics using a metric evaluation framework proposed by Kitchenham et al [20] and discovered some of the deficiencies of Chidamber and Kemerer metrics in the evaluation process and proposed a new suite of OO metrics that overcome these deficiencies. Rajnish and Bhattacherjee have conducted research on class complexity and class inheritance metrics [21-24] [29-33].

Munson et al [34] obtained dynamic complexity based on the complexity of the component and its frequency of execution. Ammar et al [35] extended dynamic complexity definitions to incorporate concurrency complexity of dynamic specifications. Yacoub et al [36] proposed a suite of dynamic complexity and coupling metrics based on the execution of simulation models for systems modeled using Real Time Object Oriented Modeling (ROOM). Arisholm and Cho et al have worked on dynamic coupling metrics [37] [38].

The rest of the paper is organized as follows- In Section 2 we present the static cohesion metric which is the basis of our dynamic cohesion metric and the corresponding dynamic metric. In Section 3 we present an example for illustration of proposed metric and comparison with static metric. Section 4 presents the discussion and future scope.

2. Static and dynamic cohesion metric

Chidamber and Kemerer proposed the Lack of Cohesion (LCOM) metric which is a measure of the number of different methods within a class that reference a given instance variable. Kenneth L. Morris defined cohesion as Total Fan-in for all objects divided by the total number of objects. Li and Henry redefined LCOM as the number of disjoint sets of local methods such that no two sets intersect and any two methods in a set share at least one local instance variable. Other researchers like Hitz and Montazeri have provided a graph theoretic definition of Li and Henry's definition. Bieman and Kang have considered Tight Class Cohesion and Light Class Cohesion based on direct or indirect usage of a variable. Rajnish and Bhattacherjee have proposed cohesion metrics for Object-Oriented design on the basis of common variable access by a pair of methods in a class as in [25-28] [39]. We give a brief overview of the μ metric as it will be the basis of our proposed dynamic metric.

2.1 Static Cohesion Metric

The static cohesion metric μ proposed in [25] for measuring cohesion of a class satisfies the following two requirements, viz., first, it gives values that can be uniquely interpreted in terms of cohesion, and, second, the values would be within a range of 0 to 1. The value 0 would signify maximum cohesion and 1 the minimum cohesion [25-28]. Let I_1 and I_2 be the sets of instance variables used by methods M_1 and M_2. To evaluate μ, first calculate LOCA (Level Of Common Access) between a pair of methods M_1 and M_2, defined as:

$$LOCA\ (M_1, M_2) = \frac{I_1 \cap I_2}{I_1 \cup I_2}$$

LOCA thus gives the ratio of common variables accessed by any two methods to the total number of variables jointly accessed by those two methods.

Next define the mean LOCA, EOC for any pair of methods in a class C that is calculated as,

$$\text{EOC} = \frac{\sum_{allpairs} LOCA(M_i\ M_j)}{\binom{n}{2}}$$

Thus, EOC measures the average level of common access for any method pair of Class C, and the lack of cohesion between methods of class C would be measured by proposed cohesion metric μ defined as follows. The static metric for cohesion of a class C (having *n* methods) called μ is:

$$\mu = 1 - \text{EOC} \in [0,1].$$

It is obvious that in a class in which all methods access all variables, the LOCA value for all pairs would be 1. Hence, EOC would also be 1 giving a metric value of 0. This is the case of perfect (or, maximum) cohesion. On the other extreme, consider a class in which no two methods access a common variable-in which case, LOCA value for all the pairs would be 0. EOC would also be 0 giving a metric value of 1. This is the case of minimum cohesion.

2.2 Dynamic Cohesion Metric

In this section we propose the Dynamic cohesion metric named Dμ as the counterpart of the above static cohesion metric μ. It is defined as follows:

I_j: set of variables accessed by method M_j $\{x \mid x$ is a variable accessed by $M_j\}$.

$ID_j = \{(x, n_{xj}) \mid x$ is a variable accessed n_x number of times by method $M_j\}$.

$ID_i \cap ID_j = \{(x, n_x) \mid [(x, n_{xi}) \in ID_i \land (x, n_{xj}) \in ID_j] \land n_x = \min(n_{xi}, n_{xj})\}$.

$ID_i \cup ID_j = \{(x, n_x) \mid [(x, n_{xi}) \in ID_i \lor (x, n_{xj}) \in ID_j] \land n_x = \max(\{n_{xi}, n_{xj}\})\}$.

$|ID_i|$= sum of all n_{xi} where $(x, n_{xi}) \in ID_i$

We now define the Dynamic Level Of Common Access, DLOCA which measures the actual fraction of variables which have been accessed by both methods.

$$\text{DLOCA (Mi, Mj)} = \frac{|ID_i \cap ID_j|}{|ID_i \cup ID_j|}$$

The mean Dynamic Existence Of Cohesion (DEOC) is now calculated as follows,

$$\text{DEOC} = \frac{\sum_{allpairs} DLOCA(M_i\ M_j)}{\binom{n}{2}}$$

Finally, the Dynamic cohesion metric is calculated as $D\mu = 1 - DEOC \in [0,1]$.

3. Illustration of static and dynamic cohesion metric

A sample Java program is used to illustrate the computation of μ and Dμ metric. For the Java program given in the Text box above, the static access of variables by methods is given in Figure 1. For the given example μ and Dμ is calculated as follows:

Calculation of Static Cohesion Metric

As shown if Fig. 1, Method *m1* accesses instance variables {*x, y, z, f1, f2*}; Method *m2* accesses instance variables {*x, y*}; Method *m3*accesses instance variables {*x, y, z*}; and Method *m4* accesses instance variables {*f1, f2*}.

LOCA (m1, m2) =2/5=0.4;
LOCA (m1, m3) =3/5=0.6;
LOCA (m1, m4) =2/5=0.4;
LOCA (m2, m3) =2/3=0.67;
LOCA (m2, m4) =0;
LOCA (m3, m4) =0;
EOC= (0.4+0.6+0.4+0.67)/6=0.345;
μ=1-EOC=1-0.345=0.655;

Calculation of Dynamic Cohesion Metric

We will calculate Dμ for different values of inputs. Since input "*N*" plays an important role in deciding which method is executed, we will consider N as our dynamic parameter.

```
import java.util.*;
class m1{
  int x;int y;int z;double f1; double f2;
  m1(int x, int y, int z, double f1, double f2)  {
    this.x=x;
    this.y=y;
    this.z=z;
    this.f1=f1;
    this.f2=f2;
    System.out.println("Method        m1(      )
      invoked"); }
  void m2( )  {x=x+5; y=y+10;
     System.out.println("Method        m2(      )
      invoked"); }
  void m3( ) {x=x+15; y=y+20; z=z-10;
      System.out.println("Method        m3(      )
      invoked");}
  void m4( ){double y=(f1+ f2)/10;
    System.out.println("Method        m4(      )
      invoked");}
 Public class my1test {
  public static void main(String args[])  {
    Scanner inp = new Scanner(System.in);
    System.out.println("Enter     three     integer
      values");
         int x=inp.nextInt();
         int y=inp.nextInt();
         int z=inp.nextInt();
         System.out.println("Enter two double
      values");
         double f1=inp.nextDouble();
          double f2=inp.nextDouble();
     m1 o1 = new m1(x, y, z, f1, f2);
     System.out.println("Enter value for n");
     int n=inp.nextInt();
     for(int i=2;i<=n;i++)  {
          if(i%2 == 0){
    o1.m3( ); o1.m4( );}
else     { o1.m2( );}}}}
}
```

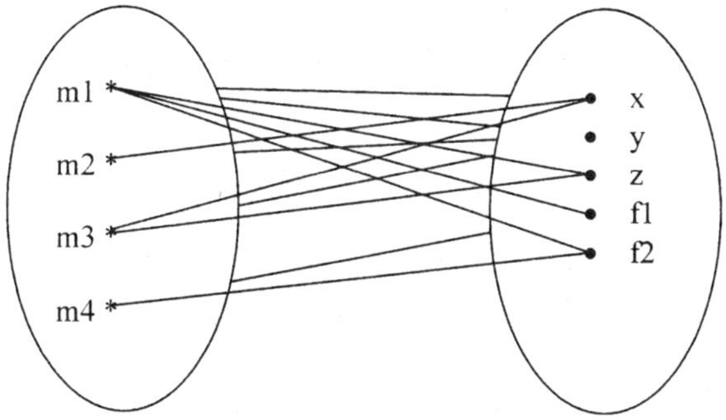

Fig. 1 Static access of variables by methods

First run: inputs N = 100 (other inputs are irrelevant in this toy application).

ID_1= {(*x, 1*), (*y, 1*), (*z, 1*), (*f1, 1*), (*f2, 1*)}; ID_2= {(*x, 49*), (*y, 49*)}; ID_3= {(*x, 50*), (*y, 50*), (*z, 50*)}; ID_4= {(*f1, 50*), (*f2, 50*)};

$ID_1 \cap ID_2$= {(*x, 1*), (*y, 1*)}; ID1$\cup ID_2$= {(*x, 49*), (*y, 49*), (*z, 1*), (*f1, 1*), (*f2, 1*)};

$ID_1 \cap ID_3$= {(*x, 1*), (*y, 1*), (*z, 1*)}; $ID_1 \cup ID_3$= {(*x, 50*), (*y, 50*), (*z, 50*), (*f1, 1*), (*f2, 1*)}; $ID_1 \cap ID_4$= {(*f1, 1*), (*f2, 1*)}; $ID_1 \cup ID_4$= {(*x, 1*), (*y, 1*), (*z, 1*), (*f1, 50*), (*f2, 50*)};

$ID_2 \cap ID_3$= {(*x, 49*), (*y, 49*)}, $ID_2 \cup ID_3$= {(*x, 50*), (*y, 50*), (*z, 50*)}; $ID_2 \cap ID_4$= {}; $ID_2 \cup ID_4$= {(*x, 49*), (*y, 49*), (*f1, 50*), (*f2, 50*)}; $ID_3 \cap ID_4$= { }; $ID_3 \cup ID_4$= {(*x, 50*), (*y, 50*), (*z, 50*), (*f1, 50*), (*f2, 50*)};

DLOCA (ID_1, ID_2) =2/101 = 0.0198
DLOCA (ID_1, ID_3) =3/152 = 0.0197
DLOCA (ID_1, ID_4) =2/103 = 0.0194
DLOCA (ID_2, ID_3) =98/150 = 0.6533
DLOCA (ID_2, ID_4) = 0
DLOCA (ID_3, ID_4) = 0

The mean Dynamic Existence of Cohesion (DEOC) is now calculated as

DEOC= (0.0198+0.0197+0.0194+0.6533+0+0)/6= 0.1187

Dμ=1-DEOC= 1-0.1187 = 0.8812

3.1 Example with Variations

In addition, a slight change was incorporated in the *for loop* of the Java program and changed as follows:

```
for(int i=2;i<=n;i++)  {
if(i%2 == 0){
o1.m2( ); o1.m3( );}
else  { o1.m4( );}}
```

It was seen that the Dμ value for N = 100 now became 0.875, which means the Dynamic Cohesion had increased. The Dμ values were calculated for both the programs. Table 1 presents the values for both the variations of the program.

From Table 1 it is observed that Dμ can be used to measure the actual runtime properties of an application or program as compared to the expected properties measured by μ i.e. μ is same for every run because it is measured at the class level and Dμ is different for different runs because it is concerned with frequently invoked and frequently executing objects methods of an application or program.

Table 1 Comparison between Dμ for different runs (Value of μ = 0.655 was same for all cases)

Input values of N for different runs	Dμ (Sample Program)	Dμ (Sample Program with the changed For Loop)
4	0.767	0.712
6	0.832	0.758
8	0.813	0.787
10	0.825	0.804
20	0.854	0.843
50	0.874	0.869
100	0.881	0.875
200	0.901	0.883
300	0.886	0.886
400	0.886	0.886
1000	0.888	0.888

In addition, when we changed the For Loop, calls to method *m2* and *m4* were interchanged, Dynamic Cohesion values improved slightly.

4. Discussion and future scope

In this paper, we have proposed a dynamic cohesion metric based on an existing cohesion metric μ. From the illustration in Section 3 and subsequent Table 1 reporting the findings, it is clear that our dynamic cohesion metric is able to measure the runtime property of an application or program. It has been observed that active objects are sources of errors because they execute more frequently and experience several state changes. Hence we are motivated to assess the dynamic cohesive behavior of objects at run time.

Static and dynamic metrics are both important in that they give different indications. Dynamic metrics are concerned with frequently invoked and frequently executing objects while static metrics measure the static behavior of a program.

Our future work includes exploring the dependency between static and dynamic metrics. We are working on the validation of the proposed dynamic cohesion metric on a bigger and more representative data set.

5. Acknowledgement

This research work has been partially funded by UGC [F. No.: 33 – 61/ 2007 (SR)] under financial grants for Major Research Project.

6. References

[1] G.Booch, Object-*Oriented Design and Application*, Benjamin/Cummings, Mento Park, CA, 1991.

[2] J.M.Bieman and B.K.Kang, "Cohesion and Reuse in an Object-Oriented System", in *Proc. Symp. Software Reliability*, (1995) 259-26.

[3] L.C.Briand, J.W.Daly and J.K.Wust, "*A Unified Framework for Cohesion Measurement in Object-Oriented Systems*", Empirical Software Eng., 1, 1 (1998), 65-117.

[4] F.Brotoeabreu, "The MOOD Metrics Set", in *Proc. ECOOP'95 Workshop Metrics*, 1995.

[5] H.S.Chae, Y.R.Kwon and D.H.Bae, "*A Cohesion Measures for Object-Oriented Classes*", Software practice and Experiences, 30, 12 (2000), 1405-1431.

[6] N.I.Churcher and M.J.Sheppered, Comments on "A Metric Suite for Object-Oriented Design", *IEEE Trans. on Software Engineering.*,21 (1995), 263-265.

[7] B.Henderson-Sellers and J.M.Edwards, "*Books Two of Object-Oriented Knowledge: The Working Object*", Prentice Hall, Sydney, 1994.

[8] M.Hitz, and B.Montazeri, Correspondence, Chidamber and Kemerer's Metrics Suite: "A Measurement Theory Perspective", *IEEE Trans. on Software Engineering*, 22, 4(1996), 267-271.

[9] M.Lorenz, and J.Kidd, "Object-Oriented Software Metrics": A Practical Guide, 1994.

[10] S.R.Chidamber and C.F.Kemerer, "Towards a Metric Suite for Object-Oriented Design", in *Proc. Sixth OOPSLA Conf.*, (1991), 197-211.

[11] S. R. Chidamber and C.F.Kemerer, "A Metric Suite for Object-Oriented Design", *IEEE Trans. on Software Engineering*, 20, 6(1994), 476-493.

[12] L.C.Briand and J.K.Wust,"Modeling Development Effort in Object-Oriented Systems Using Design Properties", *IEEE Trans. on Software Engineering.* , 27, 11(2001), 963-986.

[13] H.Kabaili, R.K.Keller and F.Lustman, "Cohesion as Changeability Indicator in Object-Oriented System", in *Proc. Fifth European Conf. Software Maintenance and Reengineering*, 2001.

[14] M.Alshayeb and Li. W. "An Empirical Validation of Object-Oriented Metrics in Two Different Iterative Software Processes", *IEEE Trans. on Software Engineering*, 29, 11 (2003) 1043-1049.

[15] H.S.Chae, Y.R.Kwon and D.H.Bae, "Improving Cohesion Metrics for Classes by considering Dependent Instance Variables", *IEEE Trans. on Software Engineering*, 20, 6 (1994), 476-493.

[16] E.Arisholm, L.C.Briand., and Foyen, "A Dynamic coupling measures for Object-Oriented Software", *IEEE Trans. on Software Engineering*, 30, 8 (2004) 491-506.

[17] K.EL.Emam, S.Benlarbi, N.Goel, and S.N.Rai, "The Confounding Effect of the Class Size on the Validity of Object-Oriented Metrics", *IEEE Trans. on Software Engineering*, 27, 7(2001), 630-650.

[18] W. M. Evanco, Comments on ""The Confounding Effect of the Class Size on the Validity of Object-Oriented Metrics", *IEEE Trans. on Software Engineering*, 29, 7 (2003), 670-672.

[19] W.Li,"Another metric suite for object-oriented programming", *The Journal of Systems and Software* 1998; 44(2): 155-162.

[20] B.Kitchenham, SL.Pfleeger, and NE. Fenton, "Towards a framework for software measurement validation", *IEEE Trans. On Software Engineering* 1995; 21(12):929-944.

[21] K. Rajnish and V.Bhattacherjee, "Maintenance of Metrics through class Inheritance hierarchy", *proceedings of International conference on Challenges and Opportunities in IT Industry"*, PCTE, Ludhiana, 2005, pp.83.

[22] K. Rajnish and V.Bhattacherjee," A New Metric for Class Inheritance Hierarchy: An Illustration*", proceedings of National Conference on Emerging Principles and Practices of Computer Science & Information Technology"*, GNDEC, Ludhiana, 2006, pp 321-325.

[23] V.Bhattacherjee and K.Rajnish, "Class Complexity-A Case Study", *Proceedings of First International Conference on Emerging Application of Information Technology(EAIT-2006),* Elsevier publication, Science City, Kolkata, India, 2006, pp. 253-258.

[24] K. Rajnish and V.Bhattacherjee. "Complexity of Class and Development Time: A Study", Journal of Theoretical and Applied Information Technology (JATIT-2K6), Asian Research Publication Network, Islamabad, Pakistan, Vol. 3, No.1, June-Dec-2006, pp. 63-70.

[25] K. Rajnish and V.Bhattacherjee. "Cohesion Metric for Object-Oriented Design". *Proceedings of Second National on Innovation in Information and Communication Technology(NCIICT-2006)*, July 7-8, PSG College of Technology, Coimbatore, India, pp. 73-78.

[26] P.K.Mahanti, K.Rajnish and V.Bhattacherjee. "Measuring Class Cohesion: An Empirical Approach", *Proceedings of ISCA 19th International Conference on Computer Applications in Industry and Engineering (CAINE-2006),* November 13-15, Las Vegas, Nevada, USA, pp. 193-198.

[27] K. Rajnish and V.Bhattacherjee. " Class Cohesion and development Time : A Study", *Proceedings of National Conference on Methods and Models in Computing(NCM2C-2006)*, Macmillan Advanced Research Series, December 18-19, School of Computer and Systems Sciences, JNU, New Delhi, India, 2006, pp. 26-34.

[28] K. Rajnish and V.Bhattacherjee. "Class Cohesion: An Empirical and Analytical Approach" *International Journal of Science and Research (IJSR),* Victoria, Australia, Vol.2, No.2, 2007, pp. 53-62.

[29] K. Rajnish and V. Bhattacherjee, "Class Inheritance Metrics and development Time: A Study", *International Journal Titled as "PCTE Journal of Computer Science",* Vol.2, Issue 2, July-Dec-06, Punjab, pp. 22-28.

[30] K. Rajnish and V. Bhattacherjee, "Object-Oriented Class Complexity Metric- A Case Study", *Proceedings of 5th Annual International Conference on Information Science Technology and Management (CISTM)*, 2020 Pennsylvania Ave NW, Ste 904, Washington DC, the Information Institute, USA, July 16-18, Hyderabad, 2007, pp. 36-45.

[31] K. Rajnish and V. Bhattacherjee, "Class Inheritance Metrics-An analytical and Empirical Approach", *Accepted for publication in INFOCOMP- Journal of Computer Science*, Federal University of Lavras, Brazilian Computer of Society, Brazil [Acceptance Date- 13-09-2007], 2007.

[32] K. Rajnish and V. Bhattacherjee, "Applicability of Weyuker Property 9 to Object-Oriented Inheritance Tree Metric" *proceedings of IEEE 10th International Conf. on Information Technology (ICIT-2007),* published by IEEE Computer Society Press, Conf. Venue: 17th to 20th December, NIT, Rourkela, 2007,pp.234-236.

[33] K. Rajnish, V. Bhattacherjee and S. K. Singh, "An Empirical Approach to Object-Oriented Inheritance Tree Metric*", Published in the proceedings of National Level Technical Conference (Techno Vision 2007),* Department of MCA, Sri Shankaracharya College of Engineering and Technology, Bhillai, 2007, pp.145-150.

[34] J.C.Munson, T. M. Khoshgoftaar, "Meauring Dynamic Program Complexity", *IEEE Software*, Nov. 1992, Vol. 9, No.6, pp. 48-55.

[35] H. H. Ammar, T. Nikzadeh, J. Dugan", A Methodology for Risk Assessment of Functional Specification of Software Systems Using colored PetriNets", *Proceedings of the 4th International Software Metrics Symposium, Metrics'97*, Albuquerque, New Mexico, Nov. 1977, pp.108-117.

[36] S. Yacoub, HJ. Ammar, T.Robinson, "Dynamic Metrics for Object-Oriented Design", *Proceedings of the 6th Int. Symposium on Software Metrics, Metrics'99*, Boca Raton, Florida USA, Nov. 99, pp. 50-61.

[37] E. Arisholm, "Dynamic Coupling measures for Object-Oriented Software", *8th IEEE Symposuim on Software Metrics (Metrics'2002)*, Canada, June 2002, pp.33-42.

[38] E.S. Cho, C.J. Kim, S.D. Kim, Y.S. Rhew, "Static and Dynamic Metrics for effective object clustering", *Proceedings of Asia Pacific Software Engg. Conf.*, IEEE Computer Society, Taiwan, Dec. 1998, pp. 78-85.

[39] K.Rajnish, V.Bhattacherjee, "Interaction among classes and its effect on Cohesion Metric", *proceedings of Second National Conference on methods and Models in Computing(NCM2C-2007)*, School of Computer and System Sciences, JNU, New Delhi, 2007, pp.17-26.

[40] Internal Repots, *"Department of Computer Science and Engineering"*, Birla Institute of Technology, Ranchi, Jharkhand, India.

[41] R. Pratap, *"Gettign started with MATLAB VI"*, Oxford University Press, 1998.

On Line Visual Inspection System (OLVIS) Schemes for Process Industries

Ashwani Kumar Dubey[1] and Dr. R.P.Singh[2]
[1]Sr. Lecturer, Deptt. of E&CE, Applied College of Management and Engineering (MDU) Mitrol, Distt- Palwal, India
[2]Principal, Applied College of Management and Engineering (MDU) Mitrol, Distt- Palwal, India
dubey1ak@yahoo.co.in *ravindra10765@gmail.com*

Abstract

With an emerging requirement for improved quality control within the manufacturing industry, the use of Visual Inspection of the manufactured product becomes a necessity, especially to fulfill the ISO 9000 industrial quality standard and also the application of Visual Inspection System is feasible when the application has large part volumes, demands precise measurements, requires consistent or 100% inspection, or is in a hazardous environment. It improves the overall effect on the product guaranteeing a predictable quality, yielding greater customer satisfaction and thus increased market share, while lowering production costs".

1. Introduction

In mass-production manufacturing facilities, an attempt is often made to achieve 100% quality assurance of all finished products. One of the most difficult tasks in this process is that of inspecting for visual appearance - an inspection that seeks to identify both functional and cosmetic defects.

Technical reasons for installing an OLVIS are given by the increasing complexity of designs, as a result of miniaturization, increases of machine speed, controls, and tooling in the inspection area. Manual systems cannot always contain these designs, because the resolution, operational and reaction speeds are too slow. In fact, the human visual inspection is at best between 70% and 90% effective and furthermore, this effectiveness can only be achieved if a rigidly structured set of inspection checks is implemented. However, in some critical applications, such as aerospace and medicine, even a single faulty product is unacceptable and may cause disasters **[0]-[3]**.

Therefore, inspection systems should monitor all manufacturing steps and report defects as soon as possible. Non-visual automated inspection tasks using contact inspection devices like *coordinate measuring machines* (CMM) are slow in operation because a single touch probe is used to take individual readings from the object. The programming of the CMM is based on engineering drawings. An operator, who carefully guides the tactile probe to these points, indicates the location of the reference points. In the inspection, the CMM is unable to proceed until the locations of the reference points have been established. Thus, the CMM approach is not suited to a totally automated method of inspection, since the use of a tactile probe is not always possible due to the nature of the object. Since OLVI operations are non-contact, there is also a lower risk of product damage during inspection.

2. Visual Inspection System

It is a system having capability of acquiring one or more images of an object, capable of processing, analyzing and measuring various characteristics of the acquired images, and interpreting the results of measuring in such a way that some useful decisions can be made about the object

2.1 Hierarchies of Vision Terms

The following hierarchical subdivision of machine vision tasks can be enumerated: -

2.1.1 Location Specific coordinates for the a priori known physical position of the object should be determined.

2.1.2 Recognition and Identification Characters, parts, components, etc. should be recognized, identified, classified, categorized, or sorted by assigning them to some category from the set of given categories. In some applications there is a further distinction between recognition and identification; identification is said to be a sub-process of recognition.

2.1.3 Measurement or Gauging Specific positions or dimensions of objects should be measured by one-or two-dimensional non-contact light sensitive sensors and in 3D applications by structured light or other triangulation techniques.

2.1.4 Motion Estimation Moving objects should be detected and their position, velocity and moving direction should be determined. Equivalently, if the camera is moving, position, velocity and trajectory of the camera should be determined.

2.1.5 Guidance and Control Mobile or static robots, robot arms, vehicles, etc. should interact with their environment in combination with a vision system. This includes tracking, navigation and control, which are often also called Robot Vision, too.

2.1.6 Inspection (Visual) Objects should be checked if they have been manufactured within permitted tolerances conforming to a given standard, functional or cosmetic defects should be detected, comparing measurements or images to pre-selected tolerance limits for quality inspection and/or sorting decisions. Motion estimation applications for instance may also use recognition and identification techniques, measurement operations will often result in an accept/reject decision, which can be considered as inspection. However, there are applications that use only a limited number of pattern recognition techniques. Figure1 shows the hierarchy of vision terms in a simplified diagram; all terms are embedded in pattern recognition, since all use its methods **[3]-[4]**. Currently the main application of machine vision lies in the On Line Visual Inspection System (OLVIS) of industrial products and to a lesser extent in robot vision, because these applications increase productivity and improve product quality in the manufacturing process.

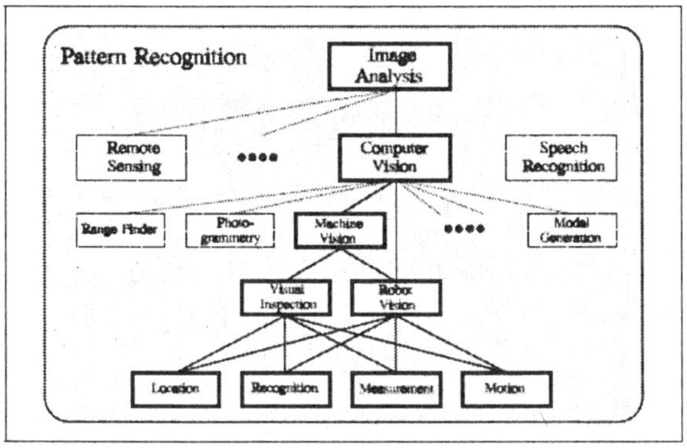

Fig. 1 Hierarchies of vision terms

The electronics industry is the most active one in applying computer vision techniques for OLVIS of their products like printed circuit boards, integrated circuit chips, photo masks etc., since significant technological advances in design and production of electronic assemblies have increased the speed of production while reducing physical size. Such production advances have complicated the existing human visual inspection process. Inspection systems have been retrofitted onto existing production lines and generally OLVI systems now appear in every major industrial sector.

2.2 Constraints of OLVIS

In the manufacturing industry, human operators in the very beginning always carried out tasks that require visual inspection. The continuing development of machine vision and especially OLVIS, so that it now provides a competitively priced, robust solution to inspection problems, is initiating a change from human to machine vision for inspection purposes **[4]**.

For OLVIS, machine vision techniques have both advantages and disadvantages compared with human vision. Humans have integrated vision systems that are interdependent on various sensors, using adaptive coupling with the brain and other sensory organs. In addition, the level of fatigue, previous training, and knowledge all affect the performance of the human visual system in quantifiable ways. Therefore, comparisons can only be made between the two visual systems on a functional basis, as shown in Table 1. **[5]-[6]**. The constraints, which impinge on automated visual inspection, may be described as economical, operational, environmental, and intrinsic constraints:

2.2.1 Economical Since development costs can be as high as Rs 1, 00, 000 or more (there are OLVIS systems with development costs of several million dollars) all available commercial OLVI systems are high priced. Therefore, prior to any installation or development of an OLVI system, it should be determined whether the economic expense is justified.

2.2.2 Operational Management has a logistic duty to provide cover in the event of a breakdown in the availability of the OLVI system. The speed with which assistance from specialist personnel can be obtained and the need for personnel to ensure the day-to-day operation of the system must be taken into account.

2.2.3 Environmental Industrial plants present a very hostile environment for vision hardware. There are a variety of different causes of problems for vision systems, such as distorted products due to essential clamping, machine and tools vibration that interferes with the sensor, mist and sprays that partially obliterate products, grime and dirt that obscure information for inspecting the product, thermal changes which disturb measurements, electrical noise that influences sensors, starting and stopping of adjacent machines (leads to voltage surges), to name only a few. Summing up all constraints, one can see that the automation of a visual inspection task is related to different sub-problems. Thus the tradeoff between different constraint parameters is difficult to evaluate. Thus, all of the constraints have to be considered before an automation of a visual inspection task is undertaken **[5]-[7]**.

Table 1 Comparison of human and machine vision

Topic	Human Vision	Machine Vision
Flexibility	Very adaptable and flexible as to task and type of input	Very rigid as to task, requires quantized data
Ability	Makes accurate estimates on subjective matters	Can make dimensional measurements based on pre-determined data inputs
Color	Subjective in color	Measures magnitude of chromatic parameters
Sensitivity	Adaptive to lighting conditions, physical characteristics of surface of the object and distance to the object. Limited ability to distinguish between shades of gray, varies as function of individual from day to day	Sensitive to level and frequency of illumination as well as physical nature of surface and distance to object. Ability to quantize is high and fixed by sensor, environment and system characteristic
Response	Speed is slow - in the order of 1/10 second	Speed is very high - in the order of 1/1000 second and higher, depending on hardware
Perception	Perceives brightness on logarithmic scale. Affected by surroundings (background)	Perceives brightness in either linear or logarithmic scale
Spectrum	Limited to visual spectrum (380-700nm)	Uses entire spectrum, from X-rays to Infrared

3. State of The Art of Automated Visual Inspection

Visual inspection of an object may be simply formulated as follows "Given an object, determine if the object satisfies given conditions of acceptability".

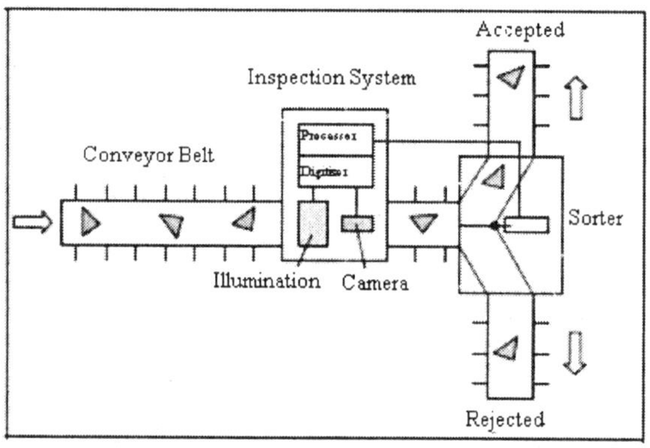

Fig. 2 An on line visual inspection system

3.1 Abstract Version of an OLVI System

3.1.1 Transport system The transport system, for instance a conveyor belt, moves the object to be inspected to the inspection station.

3.1.2 Inspection system A visual system, usually consisting of an illumination device, camera, digitizer, and processor system analyses the object if it is within the specifications. The processing includes the sensing of the visual data, digitizing, and image processing to enhance relevant features, and matching of the detected features with the specified features.

3.1.3 Sorter Following the matching a decision is made whether the object has passed the inspection or not and the processor directs the sorter to accept or to reject the object.

3.1.4 Input Inspection This refers to testing incoming materials whether their quality is acceptable for further use.

3.1.5 Process inspection It is the intermediate control of the output between two working stages, controlling the product as well as the production machines.

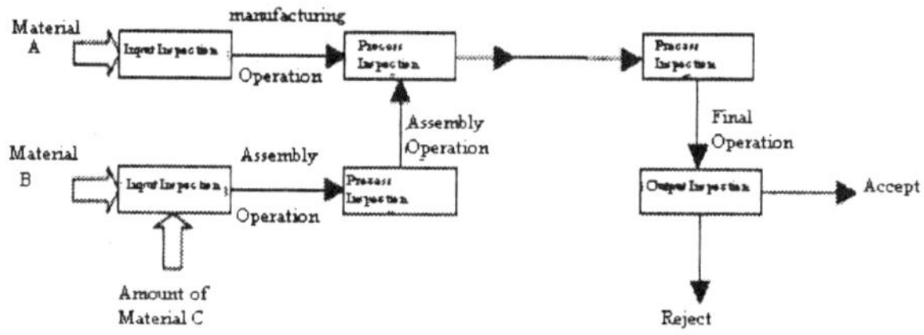

Fig. 3 Inspection stages in a production line

3.1.6 utput Inspection It is the final quality control of products finished in an assembly or manufacturing stage to determine if the product has reached a predefined quality standard.

4. Model Based Visual Inspection

A prior knowledge is used implicitly or explicitly by all visual inspection systems, since inspection can only be performed by matching the object under inspection with a set of predefined conditions of acceptability. Image Features are priori known specifications described by an explicit object model. Figure4 shows the relation between feature detection, image features and object features schematically, and the object model is used for representing inspection-relevant data.

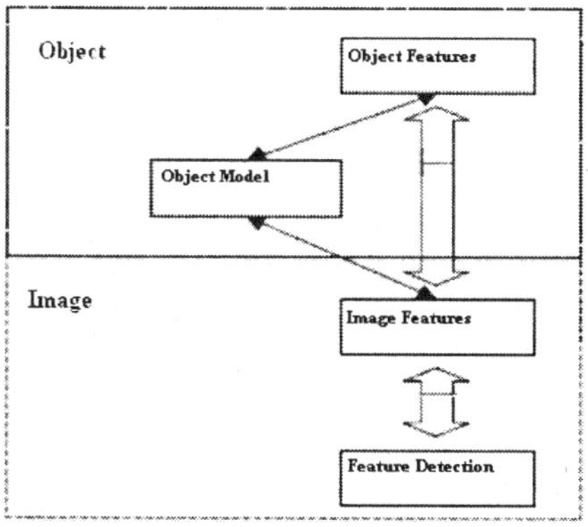

Fig. 4 Relation between object and image features

4.1 Component of an OLVI System

In general, the design of an OLVI system is divided into two stages: the modeling or training phase and the inspection phase as shown in Figure 5. Thus, the major components of an OLVI system are:

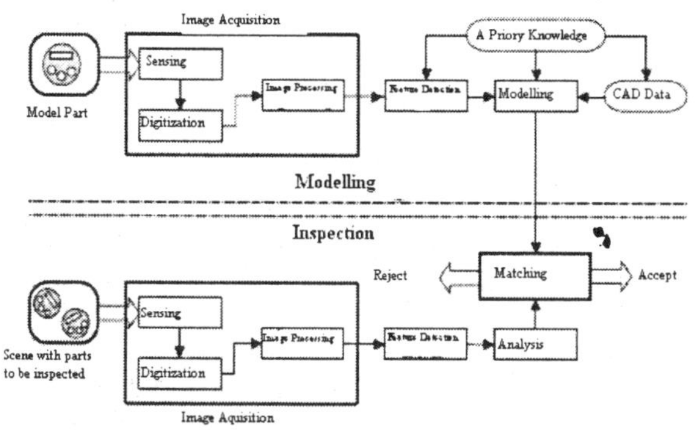

Fig. 5 Components of a visual inspection system

4.1.1 Image Acquisition It consists of sensing, digitization and image preprocessing, providing the spatial representation of the object. One of the most important aspects in OLVI systems is image acquisition, because the image quality strongly influences the quality of the result. Therefore, image acquisition involves the design and placement of the illumination device, the choice and placement of sensors and optics and the choice of digitizers and image processing algorithms to provide high quality basis data of the part under examination [7].

4.1.2 Feature detection The process by which an initial image is transformed to features, containing a high amount of information to be used for inspection.

4.1.3 Modeling Selected features together with predefined specifications are used to generate an explicit object model, represented in a model data structure.

4.1.4 Analysis In the inspection stage (in contrast to modeling) the detected features are selected by a filtering process to reduce the feature set. A feature is said to be detected, if a certain decision rule is able to assign it as belonging to a given subset of object features.

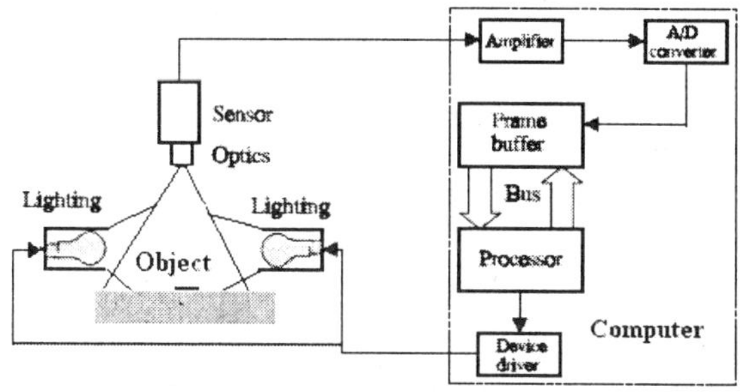

Fig. 6 Schematics of OLVIS Hardware

4.1.5 Matching Inspection proceeds by matching the data structure inferred from the observed image to the model data structure. Usually this step is not separated from the analysis.

4.2 Inspection Features

Before an inspection can take place, it must be determined which object features should be taken as inspection features represented as features in the input images. Some geometric features are corners, holes, lines, curves, and the like. There are innumerable techniques for feature detection, ranging from simple binary image segmentation by thresholding to edge detection and line-tracing to more sophisticated algorithms capable of extracting features from complex industrial scenes considering physical surface properties such as reflectance, surface orientation and complex textures as well.

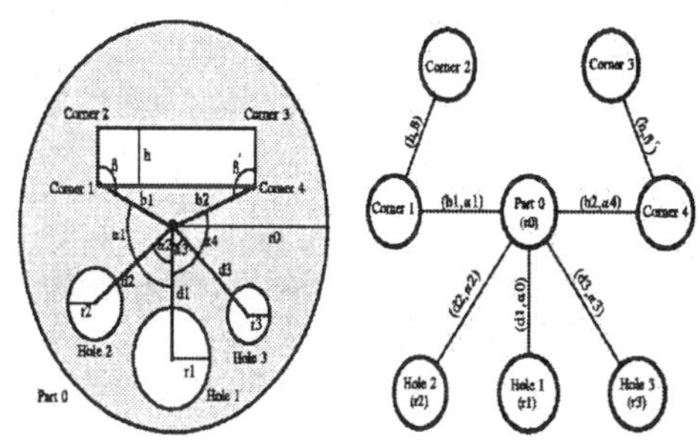

Fig. 7 Object and its model based on features

4.3 Feature Matching

The decision whether the object can be accepted or not, is made by matching the detected features with the object features described in the inspection model. There are several techniques for doing this matching. Some matching methods use the total image by subtracting the actual image from the reference image. Others use similarity measures (such as correlation or cross-correlation), applied to the image and reference intensity values or coefficients of some mathematical transforms (such as the Fourier Transform), and computed to determine the similarity between the actual object and the inspection model. If all measurements correspond to a certain measure with the model, the object passes the inspection. Feature based OLVI systems are invariant to translation and rotation and are not very sensitive to noise and image distortion. They depend on the quality of the algorithms used to detect the relevant features, their processing order, and the quality of the inspection model.

4.4 Inspection using Binary Images

A binary image is of class logical. Binary images contain only 0's and 1's. Pixels with the value 0 are displayed as black; pixels with the value 1 are displayed as white. Binary images are sufficient to inspect silhouettes of industrial objects (like flat objects without surface characteristics).

(a) **(b)**

Fig. 8 Binary images

Fig. 8(b) shows an example of Fuel Gauge to be inspected. These systems usually perform only simple coarse verifications, such as testing for the presence of an object. Binary images have the advantage that inexpensive sensors in conjunction with simple lighting arrangements can acquire them, which eliminate shadows and highlights for the purpose of binary representation. The lighting constraint is the main reason why this technique is only usable for flat objects, since all other objects will introduce severe lighting problems due to shadows and highlights **[2]-[6]**.

Therefore, this method cannot be used if surface reflectance, texture or surface orientation information is needed. Binary images are used in the inspection of Printed Circuit Boards (PCB's), since the pre soldered bare boards have only two types of surface, metal and substrate; both surfaces are flat and the inspection does not require surface reflectance or surface orientation information. Figure 8(a) shows a thresholded binary image of a PCB detail. Binary OLVI systems use only simple detection schemes such as pixel counting or boundary examination, which can be executed very rapidly. A simple thresholding scheme reduces the gray level PCB image to a binary one, or the sensor itself, providing a variable, controllable threshold, performs this conversion.

4.5 Inspection Using Gray-Level Images

At present there are only a few systems capable of performing visual inspection on gray-level (intensity) images in complex industrial environments with dirt and unfavorable lighting conditions. To adhere to the speed constraint these systems use special hardware for the image processing and the defect detection, thus increasing the hardware costs. For dimensional verification new systems are in development, since hardware costs are decreasing. Some inspection tasks can only be performed using gray-level images since they are based on inspecting surface properties of objects like glass panels, coated sheet steel, bottoms of bottles, and thin film heads of magnetic disks.

Furthermore, agricultural inspection applications like fish quality control, where black skin and blood spots should be detected, chicken grading systems and the detection of water core damage to apples were developed.

(a) **(b)**

Fig. 9(a) Gray level image **(b)** Complemented image of fuel gauge dial casing

Fig. 9 shows the gray-level image & its complemented image of the Fuel Gauge casing **[7]**. Most of the applications using gray level images are reported in the field of the inspection of electronic devices, especially the inspection of solder joints, since they are volumetric objects (Figure 10). Therefore, binary processing is not adequate for the description of the 3-D surface of the joint. The surface geometry is used as inspection criterion, associating solder joint features with brightness, size, volume, surface area and surface curvature. Statistical decision rules are then used to classify joints into various types of defects.

This method is based on the assumption that the physical solder joint surface can be approximated by the surface reflectance, if fixed illumination is used **[5]**, **[7]**. Texture inspection can only be done with the help of gray-level or color images. In industry several textures need to be inspected prior to the delivery of the product, especially if inspection is the last step before selling it to the consumer.

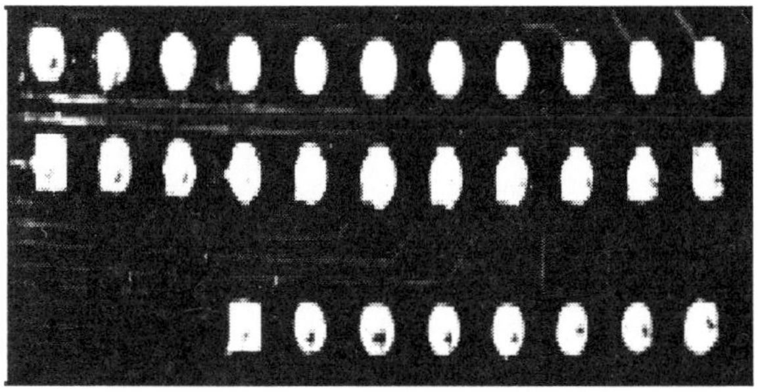

Fig. 10 Gray level image of solder joints

Therefore, the packaging of products like cigarettes and videocassettes is inspected before leaving the factory. Other products like silk, woven textile, carpet wear and lace produced by the textile industry are also inspected.

5. Results

It is hard to decide which type of data should be used for a specific inspection task, since it strongly depends on the constraints given by the environment, lighting conditions, imaging constraints, inspection speed, development cost and the like.

Table 2 Different data used for different applications

Application Type	Example	Data Type
Electric/ Electronic	Printed Wiring Boards, IC chip patterns (photo masks), CRT-photo masks	Binary, Intensity, X-Ray
	Solder joints	Intensity, X-Ray
	IC wafer, semiconductors, thin film heads of magnetic disks	Intensity
	Color CRT displays	Color
Metalwork	Casings, drill holes	Binary, Intensity
	Bolts, screws, welding, machine parts, aluminum and railcar wheels, Automobile parts (bumpers, body, motor castings, etc.)	Binary, X-Ray
	(Hot) steel and aluminum	Intensity
Glass & plastic	Bottle caps	Intensity
	CRT faceplates, glass panels, bottles, lamps	Intensity
Food	Industrial food (instant meals), Agricultural products, meat, fruits	Intensity, Color
	Industrial food, food packages	X-ray
Letterings	Labels and packaging	Binary, Intensity
	Printings, painted surfaces	Intensity, Color
Miscellaneous	Web, woven textiles, apparel, Wood, lumber, kitchen cabinets	Intensity, Color
	Break shoes	Binary

However, due to the development for more than 35 years, commonly used data types can be identified for specific applications listed in Table 2. In relation to the data, different inspection algorithms have to be used, where the amount of data per object influences the complexity of the algorithm, ranging from simple algorithms in the binary data computation to complex, time consuming strategies in color and range image computing. A comparison of characteristics of different data types is shown in Table 3.

Table 3 Characteristics of different data type

Input data	Binary	Intensity	Color	X-ray
Amount of Data Bit/pixel	Small 1	Medium Typical 8	Large Typical 24	Medium - large Typical 8-16
Algorithms Used	Simple	Sophisticated	Complex	Sophisticated
Speed	High, Real time without Special hardware	Slow, Due to time consuming Algorithms	Very slow	High, Real time poss-ible
Surface Reflectance/ Texture	No	Good	Very good	No
Hardware Costs	Inexpensive Orientation Necessary For simple tasks only	Moderate, Special Hardware for real time applications	High, Exact calibration Necessary Inspection, Color Classification Possible	Very high Inspection table, High contrast Images, Safety risks

6. Conclusion

This innovative approach to inspect various product flaws is quite reliable and satisfactory. OLVIS definitely improves the quality of products as well as it enhances the productivity with less manufacturing costs. This inspection system is not limited only to the process industries but also can be extended to electronics and automobile industries.

7. References

[0] A. Barr, E.A. Feigenbaum, "The Handbook of Artificial Intelligence", Vol.1, Vol.2, Pitmann Books, London, 1981."Automated Visual Inspection", IFS, Bedford, UK and North-Holland, The Netherlands, 1985-1986.

[1] A. Na, D. Zhao, M. Shridhar, "Vision-based Defect Detection Method for Fine-pitch Surface-mounted Devices", Proc. of the IS&T/SPIE Symposium on Machine Vision Applications.

[2] A. Rosenfeld, and A.C. Kak, "Digital Image Processing (Academic Press Inc.) 2nd. Ed.", Text Book, 1993.

[3] B.G. Batchelor, P.F. Whelan, "Ethical, Environmental and Social Issues for Machine Vision in Manufacturing Industry", Proc. of Conf. on Machine Vision Applications, Architectures and Systems IV, Philadelphia, Proc. Vol.SPIE-2597, pp.2-17, 1995.

[4] C.K. Cowan, A. Bergman, "Determining the Camera and Light Source Location for a C.R. Dyer, "Gauge Inspection Using Hough Transforms", IEEE Trans. Pattern Anal. Mach.

[5] D. Poussart, D. Laurendeau, "3-D Sensing for Industrial Computer Vision", in: J. Sanz(Ed.), "Advances in Machine Vision", Springer Verlag, New York, pp.122-159, 1989.

[6] I.E. Abdou, W.K. Pratt, "Quantitative Design and Evaluation of Enhancement Thresholding Edge Detectors", Proc. IEEE, Vol.67, No.5, pp.753-763, 1979.

[7] www.Mathswork.com

Session – 3

Databases and Data Mining

An Efficient Queue Structure Model for Mining Frequent Patterns in Large Databases

Divya Bhatnagar[1], Neeru Adlakha[2], K. R. Pardasani[3]
[1]Department of MCA, MPCT, Gwalior–474006, India
divyabbb@yahoo.co.in
[2]Department of Mathematics, JIET, Raghogarh, Guna, India
neeru.adlakha@jiet.ac.in
[3]Department of Mathematics, MANIT, Bhopal–462003, India
kamalrajp@hotmail.com

Abstract

This paper proposes a model for mining frequent patterns in large databases by implementing queue data structure. The whole database is scanned only once and the data is compressed in the form of queue and performed on queue data structure to achieve this efficiency.

Keywords: *Intersect, Queue, Transactions, Rowsets, Frequent Patterns, Data Mining.*

1. Introduction

Data mining has been recognized as promising field of database research due to its wide and significant applications in industry. It is a key step in the knowledge discovery process in large databases [1]. It consists of applying data analysis and discovery algorithms that under limitation of acceptable computational efficiency, produce a particular enumeration of patterns over the data[6]. Due to massive amount of data generated from business transactions, there arose a need for an efficient algorithm to discover new interesting patterns from these databases in order to derive new information and knowledge for effective decision making. One of the important problems of data mining is to discover association rules from the database. A key component in association rule mining problem is to find all frequent itemsets.

Many algorithms have been implemented for finding frequent patterns for data mining. In large databases the problem of mining frequent patterns gets multifold. Since the database needs to be scanned several times, efficient algorithms are required for mining frequent patterns. One of the important development in area of association rule mining was development of Apriori [7] algorithm. It was improved structure. The frequent patterns are mined from this compressed database of queue structure. This approach brings efficiency in data mining as the number of database scans is effectively less than two. Appropriate mathematical operations are designed by partition [8] and sampling [9], but both of these approaches were inefficient when the database was dense. PASCAL[2] is an optimization of Apriori but when all the candidate patterns are candidate key patterns, then the algorithm behaves exactly like Apriori. The queue structure model proposes the most optimized approach with only one database scan and fewer of support counts as compared to others. Many algorithms have been implemented for finding frequent patterns for data mining. The proposed queue structure model further proposes the most optimized approach with fewer efforts as compared to others. It increases the efficiency by generating the frequent patterns by just intersecting the transactions containing the items and further using queues in order to make optimal use of resources. Thus, the algorithm mines the frequent patterns by accessing the database only once.

2. Proposed Model

The approach has been proposed for mining frequent patterns in large databases. Here, a model has been developed using a queue. A queue is an ordered collection of items from which items may be deleted at one end called the front of the queue and into which items may be inserted at the other end called the rear of the queue[4]. One queue is created for each item and the transaction ids containing each of the items are inserted in the nodes of the queue. In this way, the whole database is compressed in the form of queues. The mathematical operations like intersection and union are performed to calculate the frequency of itemsets. The apriori property is used to prune the number of processing operations i.e., if a set is not frequent then all of its supersets will also be infrequent. To find a frequent pattern, the queues associated with the items are intersected and the result, i.e., the common transaction_ids are stored into the queues for that pattern. If the number of items in queue >= minsup, the pattern is considered frequent, otherwise it is discarded and the queue is deleted. The proposed algorithm IQ frees the memory space by deleting the structures when they are no more required. Patterns with infrequent sub-patterns are also infrequent [1]. But since the algorithm generates the patterns from the frequent sub-patterns only, it highly reduces the possibility of generating infrequent patterns. Unlike PASCAL algorithm we do not need to keep track of support counts for the sub-patterns [2]. Also it reduces the efforts as we generate up to k-1 patterns only.

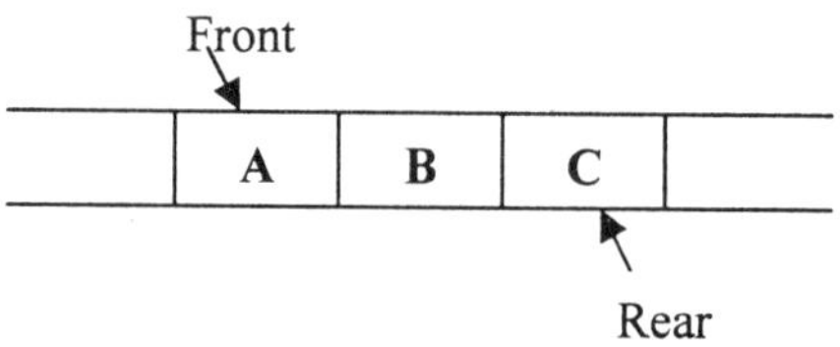

Let α, $\beta \in$ Fk i.e., α and β be two frequent k-itemsets with α = (i1,........ , ik_1, ik), β = (i1,..., ik_1, i^*k) and ik < i^*k. Now, $\alpha \cup \beta$ = (i1,..,ik_1,ik,i^*k) is the candidate frequent k+1-itemset. Now, $\alpha \cup \beta$ has a subset $\gamma = (\alpha\text{-}\beta) \cup (\beta\text{-}\alpha)$ i.e., {ik, i^*k} whose support was not taken into consideration while calculating the supports for α or β. Therefore, its support is to be fetched from the reference matrix. Hence, sup($\alpha \cup \beta$)=min[sup {α}, sup {β}, sup {γ}] is the support of $\alpha \cup \beta$. For example, let α={B,C,E} and β={B,C,F} be the two frequent 3-itemsets. Then (α-β)={E} and (β-α)={F}. Then α and β forms the candidate 4-itemset {B,C,E,F}. In this process, the newly formed subset γ is{E,F}. The support of {E,F} is read from the reference matrix R and the support of {B,C,E,F}=min [{B,C,E},{B,C,F},{E,F}].

3. The Algorithm

Algorithm: Q-Model Find frequent patterns using queues.
Input: Database, T, transaction_ids;
minimum support threshold, *min_sup*.
Output: L, frequent itemsets in T.
Method:

(1) L_1 = List_of_all-frequent-1_itemsets(T);
(2) min_sup = minimum support threshold;
(3) L = L_1;
(4) L_2 = Freq2(L_1, min_sup); free Q;
(5) for (k=3; L_{k-1}<>ϕ; k++) FreqK(L_{k-1}, L_2);
(6) L= $\cup_k L_k$;
(7) return L;

Procedure Freq2Q (L_1: frequent 1-itemsets; minsup)
(1) for (i=1;i<=n-1;i++) // n=dimensions
(2) {for (j=i+1;j<=n;j++)
(3) {sup = (intersectQ (L_{iq},L_{jq}));
(4) if sup>=minsup add(L_2, sup, join (L_1[i,j]));}
(5) free qi;}
(6) free q_n;
(7) return L_2;

Procedure FreqK (L_k: frequent k-itemsets; minsup)
(1) sizeK=size-of(L_k);
(2) for (i=1;i< sizeK;i++) // n=dimensions
(3) {for (j=i+1;j<=n;j++)
(4) {if (l_i [1] = l_j [12])$\wedge$(l_i [2] = l_j [2]) $\wedge$.....$\wedge$ (l_i [k-2] = l_j [k-2]) $\wedge$ (l_i [k-1] < l_j [k-1])
(5) if (min(sup[L_i],sup[Lj], sup[L2[l_i [k-1], l_j [k-1]]>=minsup)
addQ(Lk,supK,join (L_k[i,j]);}
(6) return L_k;

Procedure intersectQ (q_i, q_j);
(1) create q_t; //temp. Q for resultant Q
(2) count=0;
(3) for each item $\in$ q_I
(4) for each item $\in$ q_j
(5) if q_I .item = q_j .item then
(6) add q_I .item to q_t;
(7) count++;
(8) if count>=min_sup then
(9) return address of q_t
(10) else delete q_t;
(11) return 0;

4. Running Example

D

T-id	Items
T1	A C D F
T2	B C E F
T3	A B C E F
T4	B E F
T5	A B C E F

T

Item	Rowsets
A	1, 3, 5
B	2, 3, 4, 5
C	1, 2, 3, 5
D	1
E	2, 3, 4, 5
F	1, 2, 3, 4, 5

We illustrate Q-Model on the database [2] for minsup = 3/5. The transaction database is read once and the transaction-ids of the items are stored in queues. From here on, the database will not be accessed anymore. The size of the queue gives the support count of all frequent-1 items and the pointers to their corresponding queues are stored in Q1.

L1

Item Sup ptr-q

Item	Sup	ptr-q		Queue				
A	3	*qa	→	T1	T3	T5		
B	4	*qb	→	T2	T3	T4	T5	
C	4	*qc	→	T1	T2	T3	T5	
E	4	*qe	→	T2	T3	T4	T5	
F	5	*qf	→	T1	T2	T3	T4	T5

Apply freq_gen to L1 to generate L2. As the size of qa ∩ qb and qa ∩ qe is less than min_sup, AB and AC are not added to L2. After all the 2-itemsets generating from an item are mined, the queue of that item is freed.

C2	Sup
AB	2
AC	3
AE	2
AF	3
BC	3
BE	4
BF	4
CE	3
CF	4
EF	4

→

L2	Sup
AC	3
AF	3
BC	3
BE	4
BF	4
CE	3
CF	4
EF	4

Now, to determine the support of 3-itemset {ACF}, L2 is searched for itemset {CF} and if found the minimum of the supports of all the predecessors of {ACF}, i.e., min[sup{AC}, sup{AF}, sup{CF}] becomes the support of {ACF}. In this way all the frequent 3-itemsets are mined and stored in L3.

L3	Sup
ACF	3
BCE	3
BCF	3
BEF	4
CEF	3

Further we mine for all 4-itemsets. The only 4-itemset is {BCEF} here. {BCE}, {BCF} are combined to form {BCEF}. The supports of {BCE} and {BCF} indicate the support of all the proper subsets of {BCEF},except that of {EF}. So, sup(EF) is taken from L2 and min[sup(BCE), sup(BCF), sup(EF)] gives the support of {BCEF}. Therefore, sup(BCEF) = min[3,3,4]=3. This frequent 4-itemset and its support is then stored in L4.

L4	Sup
BCEF	3

5. Conclusion

We evaluate Q-model against Apriori and PASCAL. Apriori and PASCAL have to count all their support by a pass over the database. But the proposed model accesses the database only once to store the transaction–ids in the queues and count the support of all 1-itemsets only. Like Apriori, number of patterns generated are same in Q-model i.e., 10 (2-items) + 6 (3-items) +6 (4-items) = 22. Like PASCAL, the Q-model counts the support from the supports of its predecessors. But in PASCAL where at least two database passes are required (it behaves like apriori with weakly correlated data), Q-model requires only a single database pass. Also the queues for the corresponding items are freed after their job is over thus consuming storage space for a limited period of time only.

	Apriori	PASCAL	Q-Model
Number of Database Pass	4	2	1
Support counts From Database	28	17	6

For fast discovery of patterns, Q-Model is both effective and easy to implement. It can be implemented on distributed databases and parallel processing to make it faster. Partitioning can improve the algorithm further. Another important area where this algorithm can be applied are data stream mining and incremental data mining.

6. References

[1] Han, J., Kamber, M.: Data mining: *Concepts and Techniques*. Morgan Kaufmann Publishers, San Francisco (2001)

[2] Bastide, Y., Taouil, R., Pasquier, N., Stumme, G., Lakhal, L.:Mining frequent patterns with Counting Inference, SIGKDD Explorations Vol. 2 , Issue 2

[3] Hongyan Liu, Jiawei Han, Dong Xin, Zheng Shao: Top-Down Mining of Frequent Patterns from Very High Dimensional Data

[4] Tenanbaum M., Augenstein M.J., Langsam Y.: Data Structures using C and C++ : Prentice-Hall India, Ed. 2.

[5] Pujari A.K. : Data Mining:*Techniques*: Universities Press.

[6] Fayyad U.,Piatetsky-Shapiro G., Smyth P., and Uthrusamy R 9Eds.). Advances in Knowledge Discovery and Data Mining. AAAI press, Menlo Park,CA, ISBN:0-262-56097-6, pages:611,1996.

[7] Agarwal R. and Srikant R. : Fast algorithms for mining association rules in large databases. In Proc. 20th VLDB, pages 478-499, Sept. 1994.

[8] Sarasere A.,Omiecinsky E., and Navathe S. : an efficient algorithm for mining association rules in latge databases. In Proc. 21st VLDB, pages 432-444, Sept. 1995.

[9] Toivonen H. L sampling large databases for association mining rules . In Proc. 22nd VLDB, pages 134-145, Sept. 1996.

Automatic Clustering with the Bacterial Evolutionary Algorithm

Archana Chowdhury[1] and Swagatam Das[2]
[1]M.P.C.C.E & T,Bhilai, Chattisgarh, India.
[2]Dept. of Electronics and Telecommunication Engg,
Jadavpur University, Kolkata, India
archana81077@yahoo.com, swagatamdas19@yahoo.co.in

Abstract

This paper describes an evolutionary clustering algorithm, which can partition a given dataset automatically into the optimal number of groups through one shot of optimization. The proposed method is based on a recently developed evolutionary computing technique known as the Bacterial Evolutionary Algorithm (BEA). The BEA draws inspiration from a biological phenomenon of microbial evolution. Unlike the conventional mutation, crossover and selection operaions in a GA (Genetic Algorithm), BEA incorporates two special operations for evolving its population, namely the bacterial mutation and the gene transfer operation. In the present context, these operations have been modified so as to handle the variable lengths of the chromosomes that encode different cluster groupings. Experiments were done with several synthetic as well as real life data sets including a remote sensing satellite image data. The results estabish the superiority of the proposed approach in terms of final accuracy.

Keywords: *Clustering, Pattern Recognition, genetic Algorithm, Bacterial Evolution, Metaheuristics.*

1. Introduction

The objective of clustering is to partition unlabeled data [1] into groups of identical objects. Each group, called a 'cluster', consists of objects that are similar between themselves and dissimilar to objects belonging to other groups. Clustering, or cluster analysis, is prevalent in any discipline that involves analysis of multivariate data. In the past few decades, cluster analysis has played a central role in diverse domains of science and engineering [1-3].

Clustering algorithms can be *hierarchical* or *partitional* [2]. In hierarchical clustering, the output is a tree showing a sequence of clustering with each cluster being a partition of the data set [2]. Partitional clustering algorithms, on the other hand, attempts to decompose the data set directly into a set of disjoint clusters. They try to optimize certain criteria (e.g. a Squared-error function).

The problem of partitional clustering has been approached from the diverse fields of knowledge like statistics (multivariate analysis) [4], graph theory [5], expectation maximization algorithms [6], artificial neural networks [7], evolutionary computing [8], swarm intelligence [9] and so on. While there remains a plethora of clustering algorithms, the important issue of determining the correct number of clusters in a virgin dataset is rarely touched upon. Finding the exact number of clusters is difficult because, unlike in supervised learning, there are no class labels for the data and, thus, no obvious criteria to guide the search. An account of the works undertaken in this direction can be found in [8].

In this work, the problem of automatic clustering has been approached from a framework of the Bacterial Evolutionary Algorithm (BEA) [10]. The BEA is a relatively new addition to the vast family of evolutionary computing techniques. Nature has served as an endless resource of ideas and metaphors for building the variations of the basic GA scheme [11]. Instead of using the conventional crossover, mutation and selection cycles of a GA, BEA employs two special operations to evolve its population of chromosomes (each of which encodes one trial solution of the optimization problem). The first of these is *bacterial mutation*, which mimics a process occurring in the bacterial genetics level and aims at improving the parts within the chromosomes. The second one, called *gene transfer operation*, is employed for the exchange of information between chromosomes in the population. It is motivated by the phenomenon of transfer of strands of genes through a population of bacteria. By means of this mechanism, one bacterium can rapidly spread its genetic information to the other cells without any crossover operation. Previously there have been only a few applications of the BEA mainly to model identification and fuzzy system parameters discovery [9]. This, to the best of our knowledge is the first paper that employs BEA to a pattern recognition problem.

The proposed algorithm, called by us the ACBEA (Automatic Clustering with BEA), encodes one complete partitioning of the data in a chromosome such that each part or gene in the chromosome represents a cluster. Since the number of clusters is not known a priori, the chromosomes come with variable lengths, each encoding a different number of classes in the data. We have incorporated a new operation called *chromosome repair* and also have modified both the mutation and gene transfer operations slightly to handle these variable-size chromosomes.

2. The Crisp Clustering Problem

A *pattern* is a physical or abstract structure of objects. It is distinguished from others by a collective set of attributes called *features*, which together represent a pattern [8]. Let P = {P_1, P_2... P_n} be a set of *n* patterns or data points, each having d features. These patterns can also be represented by a profile data matrix $\mathbf{X}_{n\times d}$ having *n* *d*-dimensional row vectors. The *i*-th row vector $\vec{X}_i$ characterizes the *i*-th object from the set P and each element $X_{i,j}$ in $\vec{X}_i$ corresponds to the j-th real value feature (j = 1, 2, ...,d) of the *i*-th pattern (i = 1, 2,. ...., n). Given such an $\mathbf{X}_{n\times d}$, a partitional clustering algorithm tries to find a partition C = {C_1, C_2,......, C_K}of *K* classes, such that the similarity of the patterns in the same cluster is maximum and patterns from different clusters differ as far as possible. The partitions should maintain the following properties:

1. $C_i \neq \Phi \ \forall i \in \{1,2,\ldots,K\}$.
2. $C_i \cap C_j = \Phi, \forall i \neq j$ and $i, j \in \{1,2,\ldots,K\}$.
3. $\bigcup_{j=1}^{K} C_j = P$

Since the given dataset can be partitioned in a number of ways maintaining all of the above properties, a fitness function (some measure of the adequacy of the partitioning) must be defined. The problem then turns out to be one of finding a partition $\mathbf{C}^*$ of optimal or near-optimal adequacy as compared to all other feasible solutions $\mathbf{C}$ = { C^1, C^2,........, $C^{N(n,K)}$} where,

$$N(n,K) = \frac{1}{K!}\sum_{i=1}^{K}(-1)^i \binom{K}{i}^i (K-i)^i \qquad (1)$$

is the number of feasible partitions. This is same as,

$$\underset{C}{Optimize}\ f(X_{n\times d}, C) \qquad (2)$$

where *C* is a single partition from the set **C** and *f* is a statistical-mathematical function that quantifies the goodness of a partition on the basis of the distance measure of the patterns. It has been shown in [28] that the clustering problem is NP-hard when the number of clusters exceeds 3.

3. Automatic Clustering with BEA

In this section we describe the automatic clustering algorithm based on the BEA. The ACBEA starts with a population of variable length chromosomes, each of which encodes an entire grouping of the data. To measure the compactness, we first define the mean spread of the *i*-th cluster by taking the mean pair wise distance between the objects belonging to a cluster. This can be done by adding the elements of the upper or lower triangular portion of the adjacency matrix constructed for each cluster and dividing the sum by the total number of elements added i.e. $n_i(n_i - 1)/2$ where n_i is the number of objects belonging to the cluster under test. The mean spread of the i-th cluster can be mathematically formalized as:

$$MS_i = \frac{1}{n_i(n_i-1)}\sum_{k=1}^{n_i}\sum_{j=1}^{n_i} d(\vec{X}_k, \vec{X}_j) \qquad (3)$$

where $\vec{X}_k$ and $\vec{X}_j$ are two data points belonging to the same cluster C_i and $d(\vec{X}_i, \vec{X}_q)$ denotes their distance (similarity measure) in the feature space. At this point please note that we do not use here the popular criterion of intra-cluster variance, which squares the distance value and is more strongly biased towards the spherically shaped clusters around the cluster centroid. The compactness is defined as the reciprocal of the mean spread:

$$Com_i = \frac{1}{MS_i} \qquad (4)$$

3.1 Encoding the Chromosomes and Population Initialization

In order to make room for several possible choices of the number of clusters, ACBEA encodes an entire partitioning of the data in a single chromosome or bacterium cell. In each such chromosome, a gene encodes one cluster [12]. Thus if the *r*-th chromosome contains *K* genes $\{G_1^r, \ldots\ldots, G_i^r, \ldots\ldots, G_K^r\}$, it actually encodes a partitioning of the dataset into *K* clusters. Each such group or cluster G_i^r of the *r*-th chromosome contains n_i^r number of data points such that $\sum_{i=1}^{K} n_i^r = n$ where *n* is the total number of data points in the given dataset. Each gene encoding a cluster actually consists of the integral labels of those data points, which belong to that cluster. For example, the *i*-th gene G_i^r of the *r*-th chromosome contains n_i^r integers $\{l_{i1}^r, l_{i2}^r, \ldots, l_{ij}^r, \ldots, l_{n_i^r}^r\}$ such that $l_{ij}^r \in \{1,\ldots,n\}$ and l_{ij}^r physically means that the j-th object from the data set P = {P_1, P_2... P_n} under test, belongs to the *i*-th cluster encoded by the *r*-th chromosome. This representation scheme has been shown diagrammatically in Fig.1.

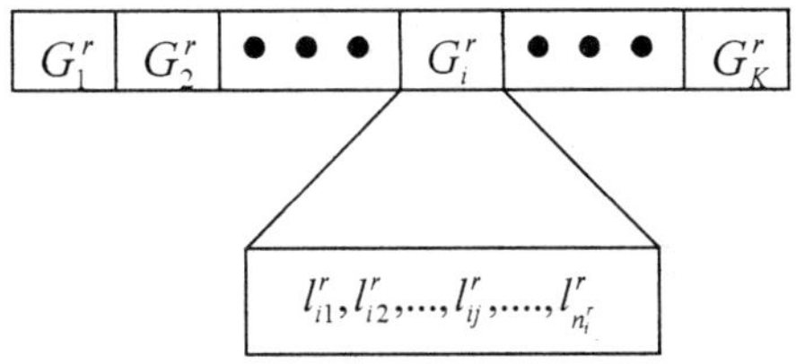

Fig 1. Chromosome representation scheme for ACBEA

In this work we have refrained from using an encoding based on cluster centers even though these have been the most commonly found encoding scheme in the EA clustering literature. Initially each chromosome is generated in such a fashion that the number of clusters to be encoded by it is chosen randomly from the set of integers {2, 3..., K_{MAX}}. Hence the possible number of clusters may vary between 2 and K_{MAX} which may be supplied by the user.

3.2 Genetic Operators

1. **Bacterial Mutation** After the generation of the initial population, the bacterial mutation is applied to each chromosome one by one. The mutation operators of the ACBEA differ to some extent from those of the classical BEA reported in [10]. They are specifically designed to allow the length of the chromosomes to be changed dynamically as the evolutionary learning process progresses. In bacterial mutation, the first chromosome is chosen and then it is reproduced in m – 1 clone. Each clone is then mutated probabilistically with the one of the following three operators:
   1. The *random replacement* mutation which occurs with a probability P_{rr}.
   2. The *Split-gene* mutation occurring with a probability P_{sg}.
   3. The *Merge-gene* mutation occurring with a probability of P_{mg}.

The clones are next evaluated according to some fitness function (to be discussed in the next section). The best chromosome from the m individuals is selected to remain in the population and the other m–1 individuals are deleted. This genetic operation is applied to all the chromosomes in the current population. Below we elaborate each mutation operator.

1. **The random replacement mutation:** In this operation, the *i*-th gene of a chromosome is selected randomly. A new one, not previously contained in the cluster encoded by that gene, with a probability P_{dr}, replaces each data label of the selected gene. This operation for the *j*-th data label of the *i*-th gene in *r*-th chromosome may be expressed as:
   1. *Replace with* l_k, *if rand (0, 1)* $< P_{dr}$
   2. Where l_k is an integer and $l_k \in \{1,...,n\}$ but $l_k \notin \{ l_{i1}^r, l_{i2}^r, ..., l_{ij}^r, ..., l_{n_i^r}^r \}$, $\{l_{i1}^r, l_{i2}^r, ..., l_{ij}^r, ..., l_{n_i^r}^r\}$ is the set of data labels contained in the *i*-th gene and *rand* (0, 1) is a uniformly distributed random number in [0, 1].Thus the cluster encoded by the mutated gene is reconfigured, although the number of data points belonging to it remains unaltered.
2. **The Split-gene mutation:** In this case, we first rank the genes of a target chromosome in the ascending order of their cohesiveness. Next we set a gene selection probability P_{gs}. Based on P_{gs}, s_j number of genes with relatively low cohesion are selected for splitting where $S_j < K/2$ and the minimum value of S_j is 1. Those selected may be represented as: $\{G_{s1}^r,...G_{si}^r...,G_{sj}^r\}$ and $G_{si}^r \in \{G_1^r,...,G_i^r,...,G_K^r\}$. Finally we randomly split each gene in $\{G_{s1}^r,...G_{si}^r...,G_{sj}^r\}$ into two clusters. The resulting number of genes in the chromosome becomes $K+2.S_j$ and this number has to be smaller than K_{MAX}, otherwise the mutation operator terminates.
3. **The Merge-gene mutation:** Like the previous case, we first set a gene selection probability P_{gm}. Based on P_{gm}, m_j number of genes with relatively low cohesion are selected for merging where $m_j < K/2$ and the minimum value of m_j is 2. The selected genes in this way form a *merging pool*: $\{G_{m1}^r,...G_{mi}^r...,G_{mj}^r\}$ where $m_j<K$ and $G_{mi}^r \in \{G_1^r,...,G_i^r,...,G_K^r\}$. Finally the genes in $\{G_{m1}^r,...G_{mi}^r...,G_{mj}^r\}$ are merged together into a single gene and is returned to a random location of the chromosome. In this way the length of the chromosome becomes $K - m_j + 1$ and this length must be greater than 2 (the minimum number of possible clusters) or otherwise the mutation operator terminates.

After mutating the *i*-th gene, ACBEA calls for a procedure for repairing the chromosomes. During the repairing procedure, all the genes of a mutated chromosome are scanned to remove duplicates in such a way that if a data label is found in another gene, it is removed. For those record labels that have not been assigned to any of the genes after their removal, they are randomly assigned to one of the genes (except the one from which they were removed).

4. **The Gene Transfer Operation:** The gene transfer operation is schematically illustrated in Fig.2. It takes place through the following steps:
   a) The population is sorted in two halves: the half with individuals with better fitness is called the *superior half* while the other half is called the *inferior half*.
   b) One chromosome is randomly picked up from the superior half and named *source chromosome*, while another one is selected at random from the inferior half and is named *destination chromosome*. Now according to some given criteria a 'good' part or gene from the source chromosome is to be transferred to the destination chromosome. Here, in context to the clustering problem, goodness of a cluster encoded by each gene is synonymous to its cohesiveness given by equations (3) and (4).
   c) In ACBEA, the gene with highest compactness value is transferred from the source chromosome to the destination chromosome. In the destination chromosome, the coming gene overwrites a randomly selected gene with lower compactness value.
   d) Steps 1 through 3 are repeated N_{inf} times where N_{inf} stands for the number of *infections* per generation.

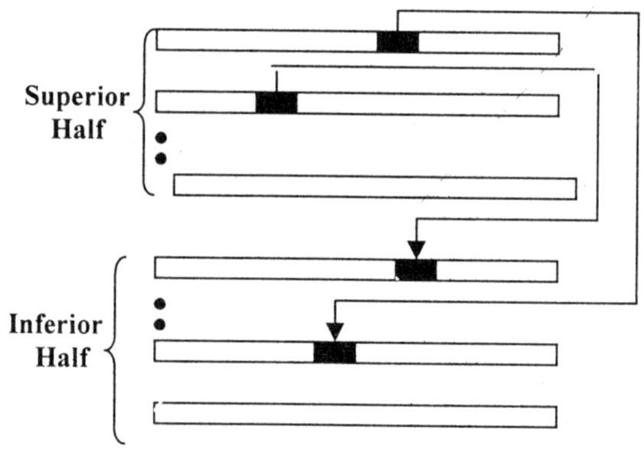

Fig. 2 Scheme for the gene transfer operation

After the transfer of the gene to an inferior chromosome, it goes through a repairing mechanism, where all the genes of the chromosomes are thoroughly scanned to remove any duplicate data-label that occurs in more than one gene. The mutation and gene transfer operations are looped until a maximum number of generations have been exceeded.

3.3 Designing the Fitness Function

Selection of a suitable fitness function acts as a major driving force behind any evolutionary computing technique. The fitness function of the ACBEA is based on a recently developed *clustering validity index*. Cluster validity indices correspond to the statistical-mathematical functions used to evaluate the results of a clustering algorithm on a quantitative basis.

The fitness function of the ACBEA is based on the CS measure, recently proposed by Chou *et al.* [13]. Before applying the CS measure; centroid of a cluster is computed by averaging the data vectors belonging to that cluster using the formula

$$\vec{m}_i = \frac{1}{N_i} \sum_{\vec{X}_j \in C_i} \vec{X}_j \tag{5}$$

A distance metric between any two data points $\vec{X}_i$ and $\vec{X}_j$ is denoted by $d(\vec{X}_i, \vec{X}_j)$. Then the CS measure can be defined as,

$$CS(K) = \frac{\frac{1}{K}\sum_{i=1}^{K}\left[\frac{1}{N_i}\sum_{\vec{X}_i \in C_i} \max_{\vec{X}_q \in C_i}\{d(\vec{X}_i, \vec{X}_q)\}\right]}{\frac{1}{K}\sum_{i=1}^{K}\left[\min_{j \in K, j \neq i}\{d(\vec{m}_i, \vec{m}_j)\}\right]}$$
$$= \frac{\sum_{i=1}^{K}\left[\frac{1}{N_i}\sum_{\vec{X}_i \in C_i} \max_{\vec{X}_q \in C_i}\{d(\vec{X}_i, \vec{X}_q)\}\right]}{\sum_{i=1}^{K}\left[\min_{j \in K, j \neq i}\{d(\vec{m}_i, \vec{m}_j)\}\right]} \tag{6}$$

A lower value of CS (K) indicates the better quality of the partitioning. As can easily be perceived, this measure is a function of the ratio of the sum of within-cluster scatter to between-cluster separation. The CS measure based fitness function (to be maximized) for the i-th chromosome encoding K classes may be described as:

$$f_1 = \frac{1}{CS_i(K) + eps} \tag{7}$$

where *eps* is a small bias term equal to 0.002 and it prevents the fitness function from moving up to infinity if somehow CS_i (K) becomes zero for a chromosome. We choose CS measure as the basis of the fitness evaluation mechanism, as according to the authors, it is more efficient in tackling clusters of different densities and/or sizes than the other popular validity measures, the price being paid in terms of high computational load with increasing K and n.

4. Experimental Setup

In this section we compare performance of the ACBEA algorithm with two recently developed partitional clustering algorithms. The former two algorithms are well-known as the GCUK (Genetic Clustering with an Unknown number of clusters *K*) [14] and the DCPSO (Dynamic Clustering PSO) [15].

4.1 The Datasets Used

We have used six real life datasets to compare the contestant clustering methods.

The following real-life datasets [16] are used in this study. Here n = number of data points, d = number of features and K = number of clusters.

1. Iris plants database (n =150, d = 4, K = 3)
2. Glass (n =214, d = 9, K = 6)
3. Breast cancer data set (n = 683, d = 9, K = 2)
4. Wine (n = 178, d = 13, K = 3)
5. Vowel Dataset (n = 871, d = 3, K = 6)

4.2 The Competitive Algorithms

In order to evaluate the performance of BEA, we compare it with two recently developed automatic clustering algorithms known as the DCPSO (Dynamic Clustering with Particle Swarm Optimization) [15] and GCUK (Genetic Clustering with an Unknown *K*). We also take into account the classical k-means algorithm [17] for the comparative study.

4.3 Algorithmic Settings

This paper uses the "usual" parameter settings for the three search techniques. Table 1 summarizes these settings. In addition, the same parameter settings have been used for all the clustering problems to make the comparison fair. In Table 1, Popsize indicates the size of the population.

Table 1: Parameters for competitive clustering algorithms

GCUK		DCPSO		BEA	
Parameter	Value	Parameter	Value	Parameter	Value
Pop size	50	Pop size	100	Pop size	20
Crossover Probability μ_c	0.8	Inertia Weight	0.72	P_{rr}	0.54
				P_{sg}	0.31
Mutation probability μ_m	0.001	C_1, C_2	1.494	P_{mg}	0.23
		P_{ini}	0.75	P_{dr}	0.30
				P_{gm}	0.44
K_{max}	20	K_{max}	20	K_{max}	20
K_{min}	2	K_{min}	2	K_{min}	2

4.4 Simulation Strategy

All the three optimization algorithms are stochastic in nature. Hence, for each problem they have been run several times. Since the algorithms have been made to work on the same framework as described in section 4, the actual number of classes has not been supplied to any of them for any of the problems detailed in section 5.Out of multiple runs for a given algorithm for a given problem, only those were considered successful in which the algorithm could determine the true number of classes. The results have been stated in terms of the mean values and standard deviations over 50 successful runs in each case. Since the population size for DCPSO, PSO and GA are markedly different; the present authors choose number of fitness evaluations as a measure of computation time instead of 'generations' or 'iterations'. Number of fitness evaluations roughly equals the product of the population size and the number of generations. In this study, all the competitor algorithms except the K-means were allowed to run for 2×10^5 function evaluations. The algorithms were compared based on:

1) The *CS measure* as defined in equation (6);
2) The *intra-cluster distances*, i.e. the distance between data vectors within a cluster, where the objective is to minimize the intra-cluster distances.
3) The *inter-cluster distances*, i.e. the distance between the centroids of the clusters, where the objective is to maximize the distance between clusters.
4) The *robustness,* i.e. the number of times an automatic clustering algorithm can find out the correct number of clusters.

The latter two objectives respectively correspond to crisp, compact clusters that are well separated. All the algorithms discussed here have been developed from scratch in Visual C++ platform on a Pentium IV, 2.2 GHz PC, with 512 KB cache and 2 GB of main memory in Windows Server 2003 environment. The graphs and figures have been obtained using MATLAB 6.5.

5. Results

Table 2 summarizes the clustering result over five public domain datasets in terms of the final CS-measure value, mean inter-cluster, and intra-cluster distances. For the population based search algorithms, the mean best value and the standard deviation over 50 successful runs have been reported. Except for the K-means algorithm, no method has been supplied with the exact number of classes. Only a maximum number of clusters (20 for all cases) has been specified for all of them. Figure 4 provides a visual feel of the performance of four clustering methods over the iris dataset. The actual four-dimensional dataset has been plotted in 3 dimensions using the first three features only.

Row 1 of Table 2 and Figure 3 indicate the fact that Fisher's iris dataset is not sufficiently challenging to compare the performance between advanced clustering algorithms despite its great popularity in the clustering community. All the three methods performed equally well on this dataset whereas K-means algorithm frequently got stuck in local minima. Substantial performance differences occur for challenging clustering problems with a large number of data-items and clusters as well as overlapping cluster shapes. Over the wine dataset, accuracy of K-means and the new method where comparable, however this was the only case where PSO based clustering yielded best results. Over the rest three datasets and especially for the vowel data, that has strongly overlapping classes associated with it, the BEA method gives best results in terms of robustness and accuracy. It can be seen that in almost all the cases BEA based method gives a greater number of successful runs.

Since all the datasets used here have their nominal partitions known to the user, the present work also computes the mean number of misclassified data-points. This is the average number of objects that were assigned to clusters other than according to the nominal classification. Table 4 reports the corresponding mean values and standard deviations over 50 successful runs for all the three population based algorithms. One can easily see that the DCPSO based dynamic clustering algorithm yields lowest number of misclassified items in most of the cases. However, for breast cancer dataset, performance of the K-means is comparable to the new method.

Table 2 Clustering result over five real life datasets (For alalgorithms, mean and standard deviation over 50 successful runs and equal number of Function Evaluations 2×10^5 has been used for the last three Algorithms)

Dataset	Algorithm	successful runs %	CS measure	Intra cluster Distance	Inter cluster Distance
Iris	K-means	NA	0.9562±0.06021	3.542±0.056	1.726±0.052
	BEA	**88%**	**0.1735±0.029**	**3.125±0.068**	**2.487±0.063**
	DCPSO	40%	0.6508±0.673	3.144±0.056	2.0144±0.0474
	GCUK	48%	0.9081±0.8267	3.274±1.72	2.0058±0.561
Wine	K-means	NA	1.2645±0.0021	3.975±0.0026	0.7113±0.00054
	BEA	**86%**	**0.8065±0.0037**	**3.112±0.02573**	**0.8915±0.00663**
	DCPSO	60%	0.7721±0.046	3.851±0.0173	0.9613±0.00054
	GCUK	54%	1.3945±0.0281	3.065±0.1226	0.7563±0.0078
Breast-Cancer	K-means	NA	0.6445±0.041	6.975±0.0026	1.7113±0.00054
	BEA	**68%**	**0.4265±0.0035**	**5.0212±0.02573**	**1.2215±0.03663**
	DCPSO	22%	0.6021±0.32	5.851±0.0173	2.9613±0.00054
	GCUK	30%	0.548±0.0478	6.851±1.0161	2.4413±0.0194
Vowel	K-means	NA	2.32±0.0047	149962.75±0.0026	1898.7113±0.0054
	BEA	**74%**	**0.9265±0.075**	**142809.12±0.02573**	**2982.8215±0.0663**
	DCPSO	56%	1.1321±0.231	15002.51±0.0173	1932.9613±0.00054
	GCUK	26%	2.8921±0.62	149987.34±0.0923	2009.903±0.0173
Glass	K-means	NA	0.92±0.68	11054.561±309.4	1053.890±22.14
	BEA	**80%**	**0.7065±0.0062**	**10974.644±210.1**	**954.672±19.04**
	DCPSO	66%	1.1089±0.29	11088.546±333.9	1031.872±34.95
	GCUK	48%	1.0977±0.112	11109.302±435.6	1077.929±18.77

Table 3 Results of Unpaired *t*-Tests on the Data of fourth column of Table 2

Dataset	Std. Err	*t*	95% Conf. Intvl	Two-tailed *P*	Significance
Iris	0.095	5.0274	-0.665 to -0.288	< 0.0001	**Extremely significant**
Wine	0.097	0.3542	-0.227 to 0.158	0.7240	Not Significant
Breast Cancer	0.007	18.1905	-0.134 to -0.108	< 0.0001	**Extremely significant**
Vowel	0.034	5.9860	-0.273 to -0.137	< 0.0001	**Extremely Significant**
Glass	0.002	130.182	-0.216 to -0.210	< 0.0001	**Extremely Significant**

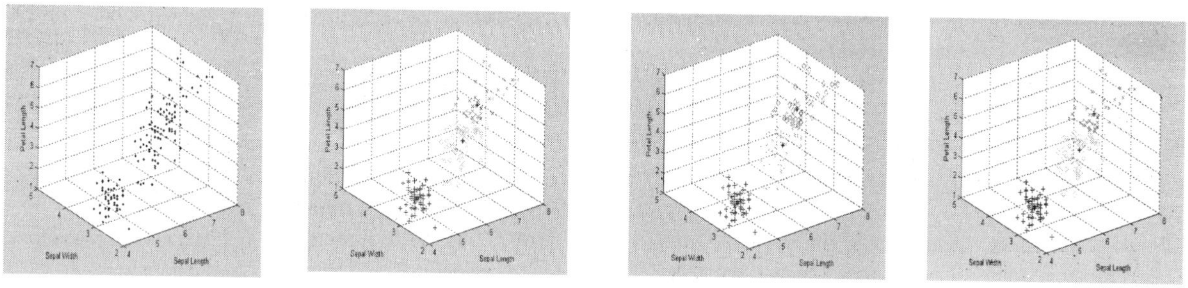

(a) Unlabelled 3-D plot of (b) Clustering with BEA Iris data (c) Clustering with GCU (d) Clustering with DCPSO

Fig. 3 performance of four clustering methods over the iris dataset

Table 4 Mean Classification Error over nominal partition and standard deviation over the 50 successful runs on the real world datasets for the four algorithms compared

Dataset	Mean Classification Error			
	BEA	DCPSO	GCUK	k-means
Iris	**2.35±0.00**	4.15±0.0	5.00±0.00	3.96±0.00
Wine	**36.65±0.0**	99.4±1.09	100.24±1.05	114.50±1.53
Breast Cancer	**22.25±0.28**	27.01±1.25	29.00±1.55	29.15±0.50
Vowel	**418.75±3.10**	453.58±6.61	476.42±6.92	473.72±4.25
Glass	**92.55±0.19**	102.1±0.68	98.21±0.08	105.36±0.54

6. Conclusion

This paper has presented a new, Bacterial Evolutionary Algorithm-based strategy for crisp clustering of real world datasets. An important feature of the proposed technique is that it is able to find the optimal number of clusters automatically (that is, the number of clusters does not have to be known in advance) even for very high dimensional datasets where tracking of the number of clusters may be well nigh impossible. The proposed ACBEA algorithm has been shown to meet or beat two other state-of-the-art clustering algorithms in a statistically meaningful way over majority of the benchmark datasets discussed here. This certainly does not lead us to claim that ACBEA may outperform DCPSO or GCUK over every dataset since it is impossible to model all the possible complexities of a real life data with the limited test-suit that we used for testing the algorithms. In addition, the performance of DCPSO and GCUK may also be enhanced with a judicious parameter tuning, which renders itself to further research with these algorithms. However, the only conclusion we can draw at this point is that BEA with the suggested modifications can serve as an attractive alternative for dynamic clustering of completely unknown datasets.

7. References

[1] R. O. Duda , P. E. Hart., Pattern Classification and Scene Analysis. John Wiley and Sons, 1973.

[2] A. K. Jain, M. N. Murty, P. J. Flynn, Data clustering, a review, ACM Computing Surveys, vol. 31, no.3, 264—323, (1999).

[3] B.S. Everitt, Cluster Analysis. Halsted Press, third edition (1993).

[4] E.W. Forgy, Cluster Analysis of Multivariate Data: Efficiency versus Interpretability of classification, Biometrics, 21, (1965) 768-9.

[5] C. T. Zahn, Graph-theoretical methods for detecting and describing gestalt clusters. IEEE Transactions on Computers C-20 (1971), 68–86.

[6] M.H. Law, M.A.T. Figueiredo, and A.K. Jain, Simultaneous Feature Selection and Clustering Using Mixture Models, IEEE Transactions Pattern Analysis and Machine Intelligence, vol. 26, no. 9, pp. 1154-1166, Sept. 2004.

[7] N. R. Pal, J. C. Bezdek, E. C.-K. Tsao, Generalized clustering networks and Kohonen's self-organizing scheme, IEEE Trans. Neural Networks, Vol 4, (1993) 549–557.

[8] S. Das, A. Abraham, and A. Konar, Metaheuristic Clustering, Studies in Computational Intelligence, Springer Verlag, Germany, 2009.

[9] A. Abraham, S. Das, and S. Roy, Swarm Intelligence Algorithms for Data Clustering, Soft Computing for Knowledge Discovery and Data Mining, Oded Maimon and Lior Rokach (Eds.), Springer Verlag, Germany, pp. 279-313, 2007.

[10] N. E. Nawa, T. Furuhashi, Fuzzy System Parameters Discovery by Bacterial Evolutionary Algorithm, in IEEE Transactions on Fuzzy Systems (vol. 7, no. 5, pp.608-616, October 1999).

[11] J.H. Holland, Adaptation in Natural and Artificial Systems. University of Michigan Press, Ann Harbor (1975).

[12] E. Falkenauer, Genetic Algorithms and Grouping Problems, John Wiley and Son, Chichester (1998).

[13] C.H. Chou, M.C. Su, E. Lai, A new cluster validity measure and its application to image compression. Pattern Analysis and Applications 7(2), (2004) 205-220.

[14] S. Bandyopadhyay, U. Maulik, Genetic clustering for automatic evolution of clusters and application to image classification, Pattern Recognition, 35, (2002) 1197-1208.

[15] M. Omran, A. Salman and A. Engelbrecht. Dynamic Clustering using Particle Swarm Optimization with Application in Unsupervised Image Classification. Fifth World Enformatika Conference (ICCI 2005), Prague, Czech Republic, 2005.

[16] C. Blake, E.Keough and C.J.Merz, UCI repository of machine learning database (1998). http://www.ics.uci.edu/~mlearn/MLrepository.html

[17] J. MacQueen, Some methods for classification and analysis of multivariate observations, Proceedings of the Fifth Berkely Symposium on Mathematical Statistics and Probability, 281-297 (1967).

Clustering Algorithms in Microarray Spot Detection – A comparative study

Karteeka Pavan K[1] and Appa Rao Allam[2]
[1]R.V.R & J.C. College of Engineering, Guntur
karteeka@yahoo.com
[2]J.N.J.U., Kakinada, Andhra Pradesh
apparaoallam@gmail.com

Abstract

The DNA microarrays are emerging technologies in Bioinformatics, which are used to analyze the expression level of DNA, and have many applications in Pharmacology, Medical diagnosis, Environmental engineering and Biological sciences. A Microarray consists of thousands of spots that must be scanned and digitized for further analysis. Image analysis is an important aspect for microarray experiments that can affect subsequent analysis such as identification of differentially expressed genes, coexpressed genes. A major issue in gene microarray image analysis is to accurately quantify spot shapes and intensities of microarray image. In this paper, we present an overview of the methods for microarray image segmentation and showed experimentally the multiple feature k-means clustering method performs more accurately than single feature k-means clustering method

1. Introduction

The recent development of DNA array technology, or DNA arrays – also called Microarrays , genechips, DNA chips and bio chips - has enabled researchers to monitor simultaneously levels of thousands of genes as they are expressed in tissues , cell lines, patient samples etc., at particular times and under a variety of different conditions The use of microarrays in measuring gene expression levels in variable conditions provides biologists with a better understanding of gene functions, and has many applications in life sciences [1][2].

A DNA micro array is a glass slide, in which DNA molecules are attached at fixed locations, which are called spots , each related to a single gene In a microarray experiment, the hybridized arrays are imaged to measure the red (Cy5) and green fluorescence (Cy3) intensities for each spot on the glass slide. The input microarray images consists of a pair of 16- bit images in TIFF format. For image analysis purpose, a composite 8-bit gray – scale image is computed.

A microarray image consists of arrays of spots arranged in the form of a grid. All of the grids contain the same number of rows and columns of spots. These grids , called subgrids, are arranged so as to maintain a relatively equal distance from each other and together they form a complete array [3]. Figure 1 shows an example of subgrid in a microarray image. The process of extracting features for further analysis from a microarray image can be categorized into three main steps: gridding, segmentation and quantification. Gridding is to assign each spot with individual coordinates. Segmentation is to classify the pixels into foreground, background and others [4]. Quantification is to compute unique intensity values for each spot, which are related to the quantity of mRNA present in the solution that hybridize at the particular location of a microarray substrate.

Subgrid gridding and spot segmentation are the most important steps in microarray image processing. These steps are necessary inorder to map each spot to its gene information and to determine the preliminary location of the spots, before a precise segmentation and subsequent intensity measurement are performed. All In the past few years, more than twenty commercial software and free packages have been devised to extract the intensities of each gene and conduct further analysis. Some well-known tools are ScanAlyze [17], GenePix [16], ScanArray Express [15], GenePix Pro6, Spot [14] and QuantArray [15].

In this paper, we compare k-means clustering method with optimized clustering method and experimentally showed that optimized clustering method capture a large no of true foreground pixels.

Following this introduction , Section 2 introduces the Gridding , Section 3 we present the Segmentation methods. Clustering based segmentation methods in section 4, Experimental results are given in Section 5. Conclusions and future work are provided in Section 6.

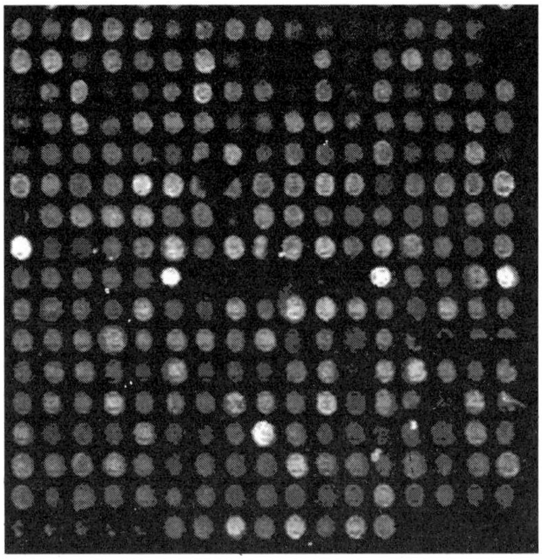

Fig. 1 A portion of a sample microarray image

2. Gridding

The process Gridding, which is also called addressing, assigns the coordinates to each Microarray spot. A microarray image includes the number of sub-grids , the number of rows and columns in each sub-grid, and often, the coordinate of a marker position. In Figure 2, we show a gridded microarray image. The issues need to be addressed when processing the image are the misregistration of the red and green channels, the skew ness of the sub-grids in the image, and the rotation of the grid axes relative to the image. The Gridding phase is carried out manually or automatically. Automatic addressing increases the speed of the analysis, but only few softwares offer this option. For the automatic addressing the problems need to be considered are the contamination of the slide surface, the variety of the spot shape and size, and the highly dynamic signal intensities. Usually, an initial guess of such parameters is given as input for an automatic addressing techniques to start the process. Sample parameters include the number of sub-grids, columns and rows in a sub-grid, row spacing, row and column resolution, tip spacing, and spot width and height. A few recent studies focus on automatic microarray image analysis[7, 8, 9]. A reliable addressing procedure is desirable to ensure the accuracy of the subsequent process discussed below.

3. Segmentation

Segmentation classifies pixels in (spot signal) foreground or background. Automatic segmentation performances are strongly affected by defects due to the "source" acquisition system problems. Existing methods for Microarray spots segmentation can be classified in four groups[10]: Fixed Circle, Adaptive circle, Aaptive Shape, Histogram Based Methods are discussed below

Fixed Circle Segmentation

Fixed circle segmentation was first used in ScanAlyze. It assigns the same size (diameter) and shape(circle) to all the spots. It uses a constant-diameter circle as the shape of all the spots in the image. GenePix and ScanArray Express also provide the option for fixed circle method. Fixed circle method is simple to implement, and works well when all the spots are circular and have approximately the same size. However, the shape and size of spots vary in practice, and hence circular segmentation clearly cannot satisfy the needs.

Adaptive Circle Segmentation

Adaptive circle segmentation considers the shape of each spot as a circle, where the center and diameter of the circle are estimated for each spot. An implementation of this approach can be found in GenePix, ScanAlyze, ScanArray Express, Imagene, and Dapple [18]. The main drawback of the adaptive circle segmentation algorithm is that it restricts the shape of the spots to be circles. However, the spots in a microarray image can take shapes including ellipses, donuts, and other irregular shapes.

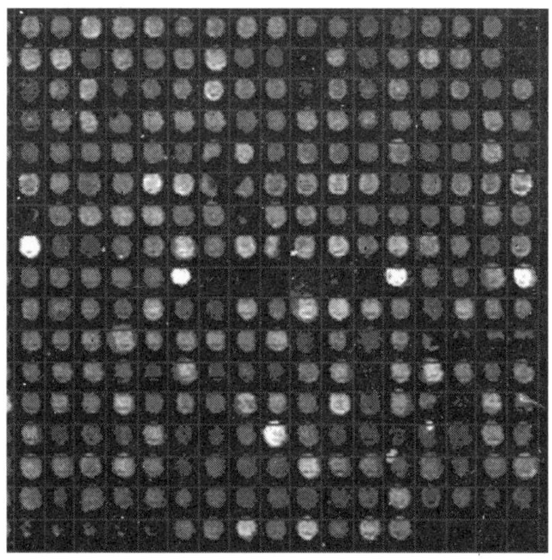

Fig. 2 Gridded microarray image

Adaptive Shape Segmentation

Seeded region growing[13] (SRG) and Watershed [12] are common techniques that deal with different shapes in image segmentation. In SRG, the regions grow outwards from the seed points, preferentially, based on the difference between the pixel value and the running mean of values in an adjoining region. These two methods require an initial point to be known, which is called the seed. One of the advantages of using SRG in microarray image processing is that the location of foreground pixels and background pixels can be estimated. SRG has been implemented in microarray processing package Spot [14]. Although SRG can be applied to microarray images containing spots of any shape and size, it has the disadvantage that the spots generated are generally smaller than the actual size.

Histogram-based Segmentation

Using histograms to classify a pixel into either foreground or background is a simple and intuitive idea. In (Chen et al. 1997), a new segmentation method is introduced, which uses a circular target mask to cover all the foreground pixels, and computes a threshold using Mann-Whitney test. If the pixel intensity is greater than a certain threshold, it is assigned to the foreground region; otherwise it is assigned to the background region. They use a statistical test to find sets of signal pixels with intensities significantly different from the local background. The application of Chen's method can be found in ScanArray Express Histogram methods are simple in concept, but a suitable size of the mask is difficult to choose in comparison with the spot size. When the mask is too small, it may not cover all the foreground pixels. In contrary, when the mask is too large, it may overlap with neighboring spots. According to *Yang et al.*, Chen's method is not as accurate as other recently introduced segmentation methods [10].

4. Clustering-based Segmentation

Clustering is one of the pioneering approaches in image segmentation. Clustering methods have some advantages when applied for microarray image segmentation, since they are not restricted to a particular shape and size for the spot.

k-means Clustering

A clustering method has been recently proposed in microarray image analysis [4], *Wu et al.* used a k-means clustering algorithm in microarray image segmentation. They attempt to cluster the pixels into two groups, one for foreground, and the other for background. Let { Spot (i, j) | i=1,..m; j=1,.n},RG be the spot image that will be segmented. *Wu et al* used to indicate the type of the cluster that a pixel in Spot belongs to and the definition of SpotType(i,j) is as follows:

$$\text{SpotType}(i,j) = \left.\begin{cases} 0, & \text{back ground pixel} \\ 1, & \text{fore ground pixel} \\ 2, & \text{noise} \end{cases}\right\} \quad (1)$$

i=1,..m; j=1,.n

The type of SpotType(i,j) will be used for the foreground and background corrections. The center of two clusters that represent background and foreground is the mean of intensities that belongs to background and foreground, respectively. *Wu et al* denoted MeanBack and MeanFore as background and foreground, the numbers of the pixels *NumberBack* and *NumberFore* for background and foreground, respectively. The segmentation algorithm based K-means clustering can be described as follows:

Step 1: Initial clustering. Let *MinPixel* and *MaxPixel* be the minimum and maximum value of intensity in the spot that will be segmented and *NumberFore*=0, *NumberBack*=0.

If |Spot(i, j) - *MinPixel*| > |Spot(i, j) - *MaxPixel*|, Then Spot(i, j) belongs to foreground, let SpotType(i, j) = 1, *NumberFore* = *NumberFore* + 1; Otherwise, it belongs to background and let

SpotType(i, j) = 0, *Numberback* = *Numberback* + 1. After this process, calculate the center as follows:

$$\left.\begin{aligned} \text{MeanFore} &= \sum_{SpotType(i,j)=1} Spot(i,j) \,/ NumberFore \\ \text{MeanBack} &= \sum_{SpotType(i,j)=0} Spot(i,j) \,/ NumberBack \end{aligned}\right\} \quad (2)$$

Step 2: For the Spot(i, j), SpotType(i, j) = 0,

$$\text{if } \frac{(NumberBack*|\text{Spot}(i,j)-\text{MeanBack}|)}{(\text{NumberBack}-1)} > \frac{(NumberFore*|\text{Spot}(i,j)-\text{MeanFore}|)}{(\text{NumberFore}+1)} \quad (3)$$

Then move *Spot*(i,j) from the background cluster to the foreground cluster, i.e. let *SpotType*(i, j) = 1,

NumberFore = *NumberFore* + 1 and

Numberback = *Numberback* –1 and adjust the cluster means of two clusters according to (2). The similar calculations can be applied to the Spot(i, j) for which SpotType(i, j) = 1

Step 3: If there is no movement between two clusters representing background and foreground, stop. Otherwise, repeat Step 2.

Optimized k-means Clustering

Image processing algorithms have been developed based on the information about the intensities of the pixels only. In the microarray image segmentation, the problem encountered that the position of the pixel also influences the result of the clustering, and subsequently that of segmentation. Based on this observation, *Luis Rueda* and *Li Qin* [5,6] propose an optimized k-means microarray image segmentation (OKMIS) method, which perform two main stages: a multiple feature clustering process discussed below, followed by a post processing noise removal procedure, To apply the k-means algorithm on a single spot, they take all the pixels contained in the spot region (a single spot region at a time is taken), which are obtained from the gridding process, and create a dataset D={x1,x2..xn} where

xi =[xi(1), xi(2) , xi(3),... xi(d)]^t is a d-dimensional vector that represents the ith pixel in the spot region (from left to right, and from top to bottom). In our model, we use two features, i.e. d = 2. The features of *xi* are obtained as follows:

$xi^{(1)}$: It corresponds to the pixel intensity (an integer value).

$xi^{(2)}$: It represents the distance from the center of the spot region to the pixel. Thus, assuming that the coordinates of the ith pixel are represented by the two-dimensional vector $p_i=[p_{ix},,p_{iy}]^t$, $xi^{(2)}$ is computed as follows :

$$xi^{(2)} = ||pi-c||$$

where c =[cx ,cy] tis a two-dimensional vector that represents the "weighted" center of the spot region, and is obtained as:

$$c = \frac{1}{\sum_{i=1}^{n} x_i^{(1)}} \sum_{i=1}^{n} x_i^{(1)} p_i$$

5. Experimental Results

We have implemented the two methods on Stanford microarrays (Diabetes category).The results are shown in the following figures. We experimentally shown that the optimized k-means clustering method captures more foreground pixels .We are providing the original spots in the 1st column and corresponding results after implementing k-means in the second column and optimized k-means in the third column.

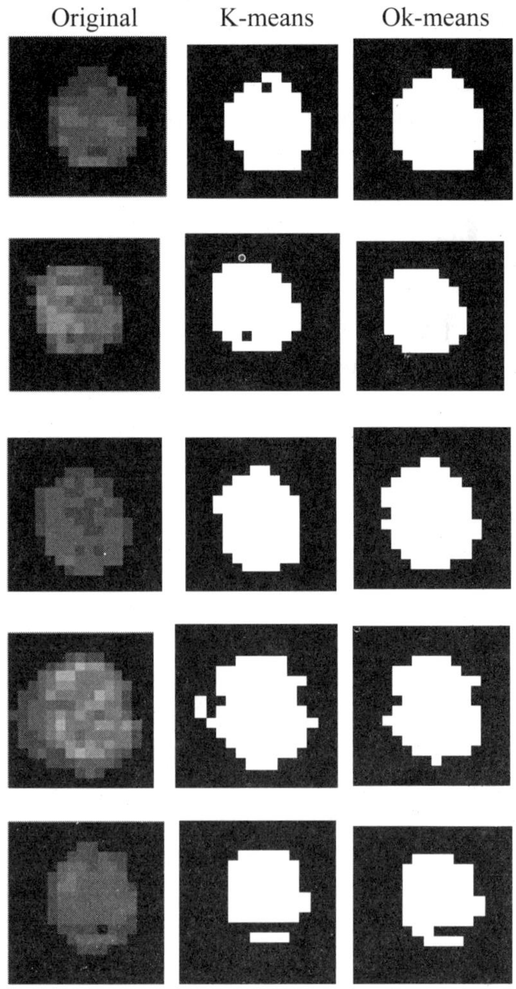

6. Conclusion

In this paper, we experimentally shown that optimized k-means method more accurately captures the pixels than in the k –means method. In the microarray image segmentation, it is not enough to just group the pixels into foreground and background, the noisy pixels also need to be identified to quantify spot intensity correctly. Therefore, detecting noise pixels is our future endeavor.

7. References

[1] S.Draghici, Data Analysis Tools for DNA Microarrays Chapman & Hall /CRC, 2003

[2] M.schena, Microarray Analysis , John Wiley & sons , 2002

[3] H.Y.Jung and H.G. Cho, An automatic block and spot indexing with k – nearest neighbors graph for microarray image analysis , Bioinformatics, vol.18, 2002 pp 141-151

[4] S.Wu and H.Yan. "Micro array image Processing based on clustering and morphological analysis ",Proceedings of the First Asia – Pcific Bioinformatics Conference on Bioinformatics 2003, vol.19.pp.111-118,2003

[5] Luis Rueda and Li Qin ,An Unsupervised Learning Scheme for DNA Microarray Image Spot Detection

[6] Li Qin, Luis Rueda , Spot Detection and Image Segmentation in DNA Microarray Data .

[7] M.Katzer, F.Kummert, and G.Sagerer, "A markov random field model of microarray gridding" Symposium on Applied Computing, pp72-77,March 9-12,2003

[8] Angulo, Serra , Automatic analysis of DNA Microarray images using Mathematical Morphology, Bioinformatics, Vol.19, No.5,2003,pp.553-562

[9] Luis Rueda and Vidya Vijayadharan, A New approach to Automatically Detecting Grids in DNA Microarray Images, ICIAR 2005, LNCS3656, pp.982-989

[10] Y.H.Yang, M.J.Buckley, S. Dudoit, T.P.Speed, Comparison of Methods for Image Analysis on cDNA Microarray data, Journal of Computational and Graphical Statistics, Vol.11,No.1,2002, pp.108-136

[11] Chen Y, Dougherty E, and Bittner M. Ratio – based decisions and the quantitative analysis of cDNA microarray images. Journal of Biomedical Optics, 2: 364- 374 ,1997

[12] S.Beucher, F.Meyer, The Morphological Approach to Segmentation: The Watershed Transformation, Mathematical Morphology in Image Processing, Vol.34 of Ptical Engineering, pp 433-481

[13] R. Adams, L.Bischof, Seeded Region Growing, IEEE Trans.on Pattern analysis and Machine Intelligence Vol.16, No6.pp.641-647,1994

[14] Buckly M. The Spot user's guide.CSIRO Mathematical and Information Sciences, 2000

[15] GSI Lumonics Quant Array Analysis Software, Operator,s Manual, 1999

[16] Axon Instruments, GenePix 4000A : User's manual, 1999

[17] Eisen M ScanAlyze Uses Manual, 1999

[18] Buhler J.,Idekar T, and Haynor D. Dapple:Improved Techniques for Finding Spots on DNA Microarrays. Technical Report UWTR 2000-08-05,University Of Washington

Design and Implementation of Scalable Sequential Pattern Mining Algorithm for Sequence of Transaction

Aruna Tiwari and Puneet Vyas
SGSITS, 23, park road, indore
atiwari@sgsits.ac.in *vyas.puneet@hotmail.com*

Abstract

In this paper, a result on Scalable Sequential Pattern Mining Algorithm for Sequence of Transactions (S^2PMST) is presented. This algorithm is analyzed and implemented. The implementation is being tested on different datasets. The experiment is being conducted on sequence database containing large number of sequences with large number of items in the transaction and the algorithm shows fast execution time against varying number of sequences.

Keywords: *Sequence database, Sequence, Item set, Items.*

1. Introduction

Discovering sequential patterns from a large database of sequences is an important problem in the field of knowledge discovery and data mining. Briefly, given a set of data sequences, the problem is to discover subsequences that are frequent, in the sense that the percentage of data sequences containing them exceeds a user-specified minimum support.

Mining frequent sequential patterns has found a host of potential application domains, including retailing (i.e. market-basket data), telecommunications, and, more recently, the World Wide Web (WWW). In market-basket databases, each data sequence corresponds to items bought by an individual customer over time and frequent patterns can be useful for predicting future customer behavior. In telecommunications, frequent sequences of alarms output by network switches capture important relationships between alarm signals that can then be employed for online prediction, analysis and correction of network faults.

Finally in the context of the WWW, server sites typically generate huge volumes of daily log data capturing the sequences of page accesses for thousands or millions of users. Discovering frequent access patterns in WWW logs can help improve system design (e.g., better hyperlinked structure between correlated pages) and lead to better marketing decisions (e.g. strategic advertisement placement).

Sequential Pattern Mining is a technique used to discover frequent subsequences as patterns in a sequence database. Given a set of sequences called a sequence database, where each sequence consists of a list of item set, and given a user specified support threshold called MinSup, sequential pattern mining is to find all the frequent subsequences, i.e., the subsequences whose occurrence frequency in the sequence database is not less than MinSup (Minimum support threshold).

Most of the earlier algorithms for sequential pattern mining are based on the Apriori property [1] that any sub pattern of a frequent pattern must be frequent. Based on this heuristic, a series of Apriori-based algorithms such as AprioriAll[1] and GSP [1] were proposed. This series of algorithms are characterized by the candidate generate and test that they first generate a set of candidate patterns and then test whether each candidate is supported sufficiently. Zaki in [1] proposed another approach for mining frequent sequential patterns, called SPADE [1]. Unlike Apriori based algorithms, this approach does not make multiple scans of the sequence database, and it can mine all the frequent sequences in three database scans. Another series of sequential pattern mining algorithms is the pattern growth algorithms such as, Web access pattern mining algorithms based on WAP-Tree [8] and Prefix Span [2]. Pattern growth algorithms are said to be more effective. Prefix Span is a well-known pattern growth algorithm with high performance. For Prefix Span there is no need for candidate generation, and only recursive projections of databases according to their prefixes are created. The first step of Prefix Span is to scan the sequence database to get the length-1 sequence, which is the frequent 1-itemsets. Then the sequence database is divided into different partitions according to the number of length-1 sequence, each partition is the projection of the sequence database that take the corresponding length-1 sequences as prefix. The projected databases only contain the postfix of these sequences. By scanning the projected database all the length-2 sequential patterns that have the parent length-1 sequential patterns as prefix can be generated. Then the projected database is partitioned again by those length-2 sequential patterns. The same process are executed recursively until the projected database is empty or no more frequent length-k sequential patterns can be generated. Although Prefix Span has excellent performance, we found that Prefix Span suffers from the cost of multiple scanning of same data. Assume that the frequent 1-itemsets are {a, b, c, d, e}, and an access sequence S = bafdecg. For the first step, Prefix Span divides the search space into five subsets according to the five prefixes: (1) the ones with prefix a, (2) the ones with prefix b,..., and (5) the ones with prefix e. While generating the patterns with prefix, say a, starting from a Prefix Span scans S once; and while generating the patterns with prefix b, starting from b Prefix Span scans S once more. The subsequences containing a are checked two times. Considering that at the same time as generating the patterns with prefix a, we can also generate all that containing a, the waste of work really exists. For the mining of access patterns longer than 1, the same kind of waste exists too. These costs add to the overhead. It is found that existing algorithms can be responsive for a small scale of sequence database i.e. sequence database containing small number of sequences, but cannot be responsive for a large scale of sequence database. Therefore in this paper we consider the responsiveness of sequential pattern mining algorithm in large scale of sequence database i.e. Sequence Database containing large number of sequences, therefore we focus on scalability.

2. Basic Concepts

Sequential pattern mining is being done on the records of type <Sid, sequence>containing patterns in the form of sequences. Sequential pattern mining is done to identify the frequency of occurrence of patterns above a minimum integer value called minimum support threshold which is a user specified value.

There is no simple rule to decide what should be this value. In general, it seems like the guidelines can be what is the intended usage of the results, how many frequent patterns are hoped to be found, what sequence length is expected of a useful result.

Table 1 Sequence Database Containing Customer Purchase

Sequence Id	Sequence
1	<{Bred} {Bred, cake, milk} {Bred, Milk}{Chips} {Milk, Sugar} >
2	<{Bred, Chips} {Milk} {Cake, Milk} {Bred, Eggs}>
3	<{Eggs, Sugar} {Bred, Milk} {Chips, Sugar}{Milk}{Cake} >
4	<{Eggs} {Butter} {Bred, Sugar}{Milk}{Cake}{Milk}>

A frequent sequential pattern is a sequence whose statistical significance in the database is above user-specified threshold. Sequential Pattern Mining is about finding the complete set of frequent subsequences called sequential pattern, given a set of sequences and a user specified minimum threshold. Table 1, shows above a sequence database taken over a customer purchase analysis with an item set = {Bred, Milk, Cake, Chips, Sugar, Butter}. An item set is also called transaction or element, contains a set of items, items within an element are unordered and we list them alphabetically, < {Bred, Milk} {Milk}> is a subsequence of Sequences with sequence id 1 and 3, given a minimum support threshold, min_sup=2, < {Bred, Milk} {Milk}> is a sequential pattern. Sequential pattern mining algorithm is necessary for numerous applications such as the analysis of web access patterns in electronic commerce, customer purchasing patterns in supermarkets, hard disk access patterns in computer systems, and so on. The basic concepts related to sequential pattern mining are given below:

- Sequence: a sequence is an ordered list of events, a sequence S is denoted as $<e_1e_2 e_3 \ldots e_l>$, where event e_1 occurs before e_2 which occurs before e_3 and so on. Event e_j is also called an element of sequence S. In the case of customer purchase data, an event refers to a shopping trip in which a customer bought items at a certain store. The event is thus an itemset that is an unordered list of items that the customer purchased during the trip to certain store. Thus a sequence is an ordered list of item sets.
- Item set: let I = $\{i_1, i_2, i_3, i_4 \ldots, ip\}$, be the set of items ,an item set is a nonempty set of items taken from I.
- Sequence database: a sequence database is a set of tuples, <SID,s>,where SID is a sequence_id and s is a sequence. The table 1 shows a sequence database for all the customers of the store.
- Support Count: the support count of a Sequence s in a sequence database is the number of sequences in the sequence database containing sequence s.
- Minimum Support Threshold: It is a positive integer which is used for testing whether a sequence is frequent or not, also called min_sup in short
- Sequential Pattern: a sequence s is frequent in sequence database S if support count of sequence s is >= min_sup,i.e for a sequence s to be frequent, it must occur at least min_sup times in S. A frequent sequence is called a sequential pattern.

- Subsequence: a sequence $s=<e_1,e_2,e_3,\dots,e_l>$ is called a subsequence of another sequence $s'=<e_1',e_2',e_3',e_4',\dots,e_l'>$,where $e_1,e_2,\dots,e_l$ and $e_1',e_2',e_3',\dots,e_l'$ are item sets, if each $e_1,e_2,e_3,\dots,e_l$ are subsets of $e_1',e_2',e_3',\dots,e_l'$. For example s=<(ab)c> is a subsequence of s'=<(abcd)(ce)>, where a,b,c,d,e are items.
- Apriori: The method of generating candidates before testing them during a scan over the database, insuring that if a candidate may be frequent then it will be generated.
- Transactional Database: Transactional database refers to the collection of Transaction records; in most cases they are sales records. With the popularity of computer and e-commerce, massive transactional databases are available now.

3. Sequential pattern mining algorithm

The following and subsequent pages discusses sequential pattern mining algorithm that mine sequential pattern given the sequence database and a fixed minimum support threshold integer called Minsup, the algorithm is based on the following properties:

Property 1: Sequential pattern growth

Given a sequence $S = I_1\ I_2\ I_kI_{k+1} \dots I_m$. Let $G = i_1i_2i_3\dots i_k$ be a ξ-pattern and be a subsequence of sequence, where $i_k=I_k$, we call an item i which belongs to set $\{I_{k+1},I_{k+2},\dots,I_m\}$ a suffix candidates of G with respect to S.

Let SD be a sequence database containing sequence of sets of items, G be a ξ-pattern of SD .For an item e, the sequence Ge is a ξ-pattern of SD if item e is a ξ-pattern, i.e., item *e* is frequent, in the set of suffix candidates of G.

Property 2: Sequential pattern apriori

Let SD be a sequence Database containing sequence of sets of items. If a sequence G is not a ξ-pattern of SD, any sequences containing *G* cannot be a ξ-pattern of SD.

The first property is used to grow sequential patterns. For example, assume that d is a 75%-pattern, a frequent length-1 subsequence of SD. The set of suffix candidates of d is {a, b, c}, {a, c} are 75%-patterns in the set of suffix candidates of *d*, then da and dc are 75%-patterns of SD. Furthermore for the 75%-pattern da, assume that the set of its suffix candidates is {b,c}, and c is a 75%-pattern in the set of its suffix candidates, then dac is 75%-pattern of SD.

The second property is the sequential pattern version of Apriori heuristic according to which all subsequences of a frequent sequence are frequent, and is used to terminate a searching process of a path of the search space. According to this property, for example, if item *b* is not a 75%-pattern of SD, then any sequences containing *b* cannot be a 75%- pattern and we need not search the search space beginning with *b*. Similarly, if it has been known that the sequence *ac* is not 75%-pattern of SD, then any sequences containing *a* and c after *a* cannot be a 75%-pattern, and we need not search the search space beginning with c occurring after a.

The algorithm [10] is presented below, the inputs to it are the sequence database and a support threshold and the output is all the sequential patterns with support not less than this support threshold (Minsup).

Algorithm 1

SSPM (SD, Minsup) begin

Step 1.Remove all infrequent items:

- 1.1 SD' ←*SD* sorted in ItemId;
- 1.2 Scan SD' to calculate support counts of every item, and accordingly remove the items which supports are less than Minsup;
- 1.3 SD ← SD' restored to the original order;

Step 2.Construct data structure by following steps

- 2.1 Enter into Header all the frequent items and their support counts;
- 2.2 Sort Header in support ascending order;
- 2.3 For each item in Header construct a list that contains all the instances of that item;

Step 3. For each item e in the Header do

- 3.1 Find the set of all such items that begin the Sequential patterns that contain item e, and Store the results in set *L*1;
- 3.2 For each e belonging to L1 (denoted by first) do

  Repeat

  Grow the sub tree beginning with efirst to the next level (denoted by Li of the search space in the Preorder):

  (1) For the root item (i.e., the node Being visited in this preorder traversal), scan the sequences Containing this root and all its ancestor items to find all its frequent Successors, and store the results in set Li;

  (2) The pointer to each instance of a successor item is buffered so as to be used in the next iteration; until the search space beginning with efirst cannot grow furthermore

End

4. Illustrative examples of Sequential pattern mining

4.1 Example of Web Access Patterns

In mining sequential patterns, the input data is a set of sequences, called data-sequences. Each data-sequence is a list of transactions, where each transaction is a set of literals, called items. A sequential pattern also consists of a list of sets of items. The problem is to find all sequential patterns with a user specified Minimum support, where the support of a sequential pattern is the percentage of data-sequences that contain the pattern. Discovering sequential patterns is an important problem in data mining with a host of application domains including medicine, telecommunications, and the World Wide Web. As a more concrete example, the Yahoo! Internet directory (www.yahoo.com) enables users to locate interesting WWW documents by navigating through large topic hierarchies consisting of thousands of different document classes. These hierarchies provide an effective way of dealing with the abundance problem present in today's keyword-based WWW search engines. The idea is to allow users to progressively refine their search by following specific topic paths (i.e., sequences of hyperlinks) along a (predefined) hierarchy. Given the wide variety of topics and the inherently fuzzy nature of document classification, there are numerous cases in which distinct topic paths lead to different document collections on very similar topics. For example, starting from Yahoo's home page users can locate information on hotels in New York City by following either Travel - Yahoo!Travel- North America – United States – New York – New York City – Lodging - Hotels or Travel – Lodging - Yahoo! Lodging – New York - New York Cities - New York City - Hotels and Motels, where "-" denotes a parent-child link in the topic hierarchy. Mining user access logs to determine the most frequently accessed topic paths is a task of immense marketing value, e.g., for a hotel or restaurant business in New York City trying to select a strategic set of WWW locations for its advertising campaign.

4.2 Example of Hard Disk Access Patterns

Another example can be a computer consists of essentially three components: CPU, Memory, and Hard disk. It is well known that hard disks are far slower than CPU and memory. Specially, the speed of CPU and memory has been being improved rapidly; the speed of hard disks, however, has been improved Little, and could not be expected to have a great improvement in the future due to its mechanical mechanism. The hard disk has become a bottleneck of modern computers.

A solution is to discover the sequences of accesses to a hard disk, which are pursued frequently by users of an operating system (i.e., the hard disk access patterns), and to implement a perfecting cache based on those patterns. This gives rise to the necessity of the technology used to mine frequent sequential access patterns in user access log, which is a sequential pattern-mining problem. A hard disk can be modeled as an array of data blocks. For current standards its elements are generally numbered with four-byte integers, ranging from 0 to 232.Users read data blocks from a hard disk by using block numbers (Note that we consider the read operation only). Then a log of accesses from a user is a sequence of block numbers, and can be modeled as < BlkNol, BlkNo2, . . . , BlkNon >. A log of accesses from all users forms a sequence database, each item of which is a block number. User access patterns can be mined in this sequence database. In the following we measure the size of a sequence database by using the number of different items in that database. The size of a sequence database in the above example would be very large. Specially, different operating systems have different sizes of sequence databases. Thus a Sequential Pattern Mining algorithm is required to be responsive for any size of the sequence databases.

5. Experiments and Results

The system has been tested against having hardware Pentium® 4 CPU 3.00GHz & 248 MB RAM and software platforms having OS Microsoft Windows XP Professional Version 2002, service pack 2 , JDK 1.6.0, JCreator an Editor of java.

5.1 Synthetic Data set Description

The dataset mimics the retail organization, which is often referred as basket data having 26 items, the item-set consisting of any of the items of these 26 forms the sequence database. The sequence database consisting of text file with following format of each row of text file:

<Itemset><blank space><itemset><blank space><itemset> ....
<Itemset><blank space><itemset><blank space><itemset> ....
....

We have used very simple dataset format for testing sequential pattern mining algorithm, this is easily understandable to naive users. The experiment is being conducted on this sequence database containing large number of sequences. The execution time is used as a performance metric, which is defined as the time interval from the time when the mining process is started to the time when the mining process is completed. The test cases consists of sequence database of varying sequences like sequence database consisting of 1000 sequence, 6000 sequence etc, we measure the time of execution of the mining algorithm in different test cases we observed fast responsiveness against varying number of sequences which shows scalability of the algorithm the time of execution varies only by a small amount against varying size of the sequence database and thus shows responsiveness of the algorithm against large sequence database.

5.2 Synthetic Data Set Results

To test scalability of the sequential pattern-mining algorithm we vary the number of sequences in the sequence database and measure the mining execution time.

The system has been tested for different number of sequences and mining execution time required for mining sequential pattern is measured as shown by Table 2 below.

Table 2 Result showing mining execution in seconds against varying number of sequences

Total number of sequences	Execution time in seconds
1000	7
6000	32
11000	62
16000	88
20000	112
25000	152
30000	184
40000	203

5.3 Real Life Data Set

The real life sequence database contains sequence of itemsets bought by user. We know each item has a unique id. Therefore, the set of all items over a retail domain can be viewed as a finite set from the alphabet Σ. When user's purchases itemsets within this domain, then each user trip corresponds to a string over alphabet Σ. Different trips correspond to different strings over the alphabet Σ. The history of all user purchase can be considered a sequential database of such strings. We consider mapping of alphabet to item name such that each item corresponds to an alphabet. Thus this is being assumed that alphabet "a" represents item milk, "b" represents item bread, "c" represents item rise, "d" represents item sugar, "e" represents item eggs, "f" represents item biscuits, "g" represents item bean and so on. Thus the sequence database consists of the following sequences of items; its contents are described as follows:

abcde bcf geab
def bca ade

The sequence database file having the above content contains multiple lines of sequences. Each line represents one user's purchase history during various trips. The first sequence abcde bcf geab ,consists of multiple transactions each representing users purchase history during a particular trip to grocery shop, like the first sequence has three transactions abcde, bcf and geab, representing itemset bought by the customers during various visits to store ,for example abcde represents sequence milk bread rise sugar eggs.

Given a sequence database of such a purchase history; we want to determine the sequences of itemsets called sequential patterns: that is, the most frequently accessed sequence of item sets and how they are accessed together.

These patterns can be used to analyze the utility and interrelatedness of these itemsets. Using the above sequential database representing the user purchase history, what we really need to find are frequent substring called sequential patterns over the sequential database.

5.4 Real Life Data Set Results

The sequential pattern mining algorithm when executed for real life dataset as described by section 5.3, algorithm outputs the result as shown by fig 1 which gives advice, in terms of frequency of occurrence of sequential patterns, so as to promote sell of the goods by identifying what sequence of item sets is mostly purchased by the user.

The output <b e> indicates that the user as per the convention discussed in section 5.3 mostly purchases sequence <bread eggs>.

The manager of a goods company can identify what sequential patterns are occurring frequently in the sequence database and can take appropriate marketing actions to better structure his goods shop. The manager of the grocery company can learn more about the buying habits of your customers. The results may be used to plan marketing or advertising strategies, as well as catalog design. For instance, sequential pattern mining results analysis may help managers design different store layouts. In one strategy, items that are frequently purchased together can be placed in close proximity in order to further encourage the sale of such items together. If customers who purchase computers also tend to buy financial management software at the same time, then placing the hardware display close to the software display may help to increase the sales of both of these items. In an alternative strategy, placing hardware and software at opposite ends of the store may entice customers who purchase such items to pick up other items along the way.

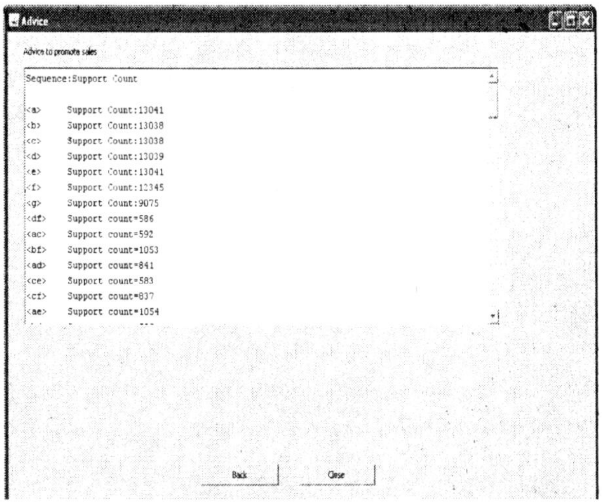

Fig. 1 Result of the sequential pattern mining algorithm is executed, Advice to promote sell of goods is <b f> i.e. <bred biscuits > sequence is purchased frequently.

For instance, after deciding on an expensive computer, a customer may observe security systems for sale while heading towards the software display to purchase financial management software, and may decide to purchase a home security system as well. Sequential pattern analysis can also help retailers to plan which items to put on sale at reduced prices. If customers tend to purchase computers and printers together, then having a sale on printers may encourage the sale of printers as well as computers. Thus manager of the company will be interested in finding sequential patterns embedded in a sequence database of item sets. The discovered sequential pattern plays an essential role in mining associations, correlations and many other interesting relationships among data. The manager can make rules for inventory by seeing the sequential pattern frequency so as to enhance catalog design and cross marketing. Thus sequential pattern can lead to increased sales by helping manager of the goods company do selective marketing and plan their shelf space.

6. Conclusion

The S^2PMST addresses the scalability issue in solving sequential pattern mining problem; it shows responsiveness against large number of sequences. The algorithm is being tested for sequence database on two different datasets synthetic and real life data sets that mimics retail organization data set where a customer buys a set of items in one transaction then another set of items in second transaction and so on. The algorithm addresses the scalability issue in solving sequential pattern mining problem. To ensure scalability the algorithm uses mining execution time as the performance metric and measures it against varying number of sequences. The algorithm can be extended so that it could be integrated directly with DBMS.

Acknowledgements: We would like to thank Mr. Mitesh Singh Jat, IISC Bangalore, India for their encouragement, direction and motivation.

7. References

[1] Zaki M., SPADE: "An Efficient Algorithm for Mining Frequent Sequences",Machine Learning,vol. 42,no. 1-2,pp. 31-60, 2001.

[2] Jian Pei Jiawei Han Behzad Mortazavi-Asl Helen Pinto, "Prefix Span: Mining Sequential Patterns Efficiently by Prefix-Projected Pattern", Proceedings of the 17th International Conference on Data Engineering, page 215, 2001.

[3] Srikant and Agrawal,GSP: "Generalized Sequential Pattern Mining",IEEE ,1996.

[4] Pei, J., Han, J., & Wang, "Mining Sequential Patterns with Constraints in Large Databases", Conference on Information and Knowledge Management, Proceedings of the eleventh international conference on Information and knowledge management, pp 18 - 25,2002.

[5] R.Agrawal , R.Srikant, "Mining Sequential Patterns", IEEE, 1995.

[6] Minos, Garofalakis, Rajeevrästogi and kyuseokshim, SPIRIT: "Sequential Pattern Mining with Regular Expression",Proceedings of the 25th International Conference on Very Large Data Bases,pp,223-224,1999.

[7] C.Romero Morales,A.R Porras Perez,S.ventura Soto,C.Hervas Martinez and Zafra Gomez, "Using sequential pattern mining for links recommendation in adaptive hypermedia educational systems", current Developments in Technology-Assisted Education,2006.

[8] Jian pei,jiaweihan,behzad martazavi,hua zhu, "Mining access patterns efficiently from web logs",Proceedings of the 4th Pacific-Asia Conference on Knowledge Discovery and Data Mining, Current Issues and New Applications, pp 396 - 407,2000.

[9] Jay Ayres, Johannes Gehrke, Tomi Yiu, and Jason Flannick, "Sequential Pattern Mining using A Bitmap Representation", Conference on Knowledge Discovery in Data Proceedings of the eighth ACM SIGKDD international conference on Knowledge discovery and data mining,pp 429 - 435 ,2002.

[10] Jiahong wang,Yoshiaki Asanuma,Eiichiro Kodama,and Toyoo Takata, "A scalable sequential pattern mining algorithm",Proceedings of the IEEE International Conference on Computer Systems and Applications - Volume 00,pp 437-444,2006.

[11] Pei-Hsin Wu,Wen-Chih Peng and Ming-Syan Chen,"Mining Sequential Alarm Patterns in a Telecommunication Database", Proceedings of the VLDB 2001 International Workshop on Databases in Telecommunications II,ACM ,pp 37-51,2001.

[12] J. Han, M. Kamber: Data Mining: Concepts and Techniques, Academic Press, 2001.

[13] I.H.Witten, E.Frank, Data Mining: Practical Machine Learning Tools and Techniques, Morgan Kaufmann, 2005.

Clustering with Multi-objective Differential Evolution Algorithms – A Comparative Study

Debarati Kundu, Sayan Ghosh, Kaushik Suresh, Swagatam Das and Ankur Mondal
Dept. of Electronics and Telecommunication Engg, Jadavpur University, Kolkata, India
kundu.debarati@gmail.com sayan88tito@gmail.com kaushik_s1988@yahoo.com swagatamdas19@yahoo.co.in mondal.ankur@gmail.com

Abstract

This paper considers the task of fuzzy clustering in a multi-objective optimization (MO) framework. It compares the performances of four recently developed multi-objective variants of DE over the fuzzy clustering problem, where two conflicting fuzzy validity indices are simultaneously optimized. The resultant Pareto optimal set of solutions from each algorithm consists of a number of non-dominated solutions, from which the user can choose the most promising ones according to the problem specifications.The performances of four DE variants have also been contrasted to that of two most well-known schemes of MO clustering namely the NSGA II (Non Dominated Sorting GA) and MOCK (Multi-Objective Clustering with an unknown number of clusters K). Experimental results over four artificial and four real life datasets (including a microarray dataset of budding yeast) of varying range of complexities indicates that DE holds immense promise as a candidate algorithm for devising MO clustering schemes.

Keywords: *Differential Evolution, multi-objective optimization, fuzzy clustering, micro-array data clustering.*

1. Introduction

Optimization-based automatic clustering algorithms greatly rely on a cluster validity function (optimization criterion) the optima of which appear as proxies for the unknown "correct classification" in a previously unhandled dataset. Different formulations of the clustering problem vary in the optimization criterion used. Most existing clustering methods, however, attempt to optimize just one such clustering criterion modeled by a single cluster validity index. This often results into considerable discrepancies observable between the solutions produced by different algorithms on the same data. A single cluster validity measure is hardly able to judge the correctness of clustering for a wide variety of real life datasets. A wrong choice of the validity measure may lead to poor clustering results. Thus, the singleobjective clustering method may prove futile (as judged by means of expert's knowledge) in a context where the criterion employed is inappropriate. In situations where the best solution corresponds to a tradeoff between different conflicting objectives, common sense advocates a multi-objective framework for clustering. In the case of iterative optimization algorithms, it is possible that a singleobjective approach would visit such tradeoff solutions during a run, but would not recognize them as good and discard them.

Although there has been a plethora of papers reporting several single-objective evolutionary clustering techniques (a comprehensive survey of which can be found in [1]), very few research works have so far been undertaken towards the application of evolutionary multi-objective optimization algorithms (EMOA) for pattern clustering. A state-of-the-art literature survey indicates that the Differential Evolution (DE) [3, 4] has already proved itself as a promising candidate in the field of evolutionary multi-objective optimization (EMO) [5 – 8]. Unlike NSGA II or PESA II, however, the multi-objective variants of DE have not been applied to the general data clustering problems till date, to the best of our knowledge. This paper primarily compares the performances of four most representative multi-objective DE algorithms [9 – 12] on the multi-objective fuzzy clustering problem. Since DE, by nature, is a real-coded population-based optimization algorithm, we here resort to centroidbased representation scheme for the search variables. Note that in contrast to single objective optimization that yields a single best solution, in MOO, a number of, often conflicting, objective functions are optimized simultaneously and thus an MOO algorithm, in general, ends up with a number of Pareto optimal solutions. None of these Pareto optimal solutions can be improved upon an objective any further without degrading it on another. Here we consider the Xie-Beni index [13] and the Fuzzy C Means (FCM) measure (J_m) [14] as the objective functions. Note that any other and any number of objective functions could be used in the proposed MOO clustering framework. The performance of the multi-objective DE-variants have also been contrasted with two best-known EMOA-based clustering methods till date. The first one of these is MOCK by Handl and Knowles [15] while the second one is based on NSGA II and was used by Bandyopadhyay *et al.* for pixel clustering in remote sensing satellite image data [16]. Although we experimented with a large variety of datasets, here we report the results for ten representative datasets including the microarray Yeast sporulation data [17].

2. Multi-objective Optimization with DE

In this section we outline four most frequently used variants of DE, specially devised for tackling the MOO problems.

2.1 The MO Problem

In many practical or real life problems, there are many (possibly conflicting) objectives that need to be optimized simultaneously. Under such circumstances there no longer exists a single optimal solution but rather a whole set of possible solutions of equivalent quality. The field of Multi-objective Optimization (MO) deals with simultaneous optimization of multiple, possibly competing, objective functions. The MO problems tend to be characterized by a family of alternatives, which must be considered equivalent in the absence of information concerning the relevance of each objective relative to the others. The family of solutions of an MO problem is composed of the parameter vectors, which cannot be improved in any objective without causing degradation in at least one of the other objectives. This forms the central idea of *Pareto-optimality*. The concepts of *dominance* and *Pareto-optimality* [18, 4] may be presented more formally in the following way:

Definition 1: Consider without loss of generality the following multi-objective optimization problem with m decision variables x (parameters) and n objectives y:

Maximize:

$$\vec{Y} = f(\vec{X}) = (f_1(x_1,\dots,x_m),\dots,f_n(x_1,\dots,x_m))$$

Where

$\vec{x} = [x_1,\dots,x_m]^T \in P$ and $\vec{y} = [y_1,\dots,y_m]^T \in O$ and

where $\vec{x}$ is called decision (parameter) vector, P is the parameter space, $\vec{y}$ is the objective vector, and O is the objective space. A decision vector $\vec{A} \in P$ is said to dominate another decision vector $\vec{B} \in P$ (also written as $\vec{A} \succ \vec{B}$) if and only if:

$$\forall i \in \{1,\dots,n\}: \quad f_i(\vec{A}) \geq f_i(\vec{B})$$
$$\wedge \ \exists j \in \{1,\dots,n\}: \quad f_j(\vec{A}) > f_j(\vec{B}) \qquad (2)$$

Based on this convention, we can define nondominated, *Pareto-optimal* solutions as follows:

Definition 2: Let P $\vec{A} \in P$ be an arbitrary decision vector.

(a) The decision vector $\vec{A}$ *is said to be* non-dominated regarding the set $P' \subseteq P$ if and only if there is no vector in P' which can dominate $\vec{A}$. Formally,

$$\nexists \quad \vec{A}' \in P' : P' \succ P \qquad (3)$$

(b) The decision (parameter) vector $\vec{A}$ r is called Pareto-optimal if and only if $\vec{A}$ is non-dominated regarding the whole parameter space P.

2.2 The Differential Evolution (DE) Algorithm

DE is a population-based global optimization algorithm that uses a floating-point (real-coded) representation. The i-th individual (parameter vector or *chromosome*) of the population at generation (time) t is a D-dimensional vector containing a set of D optimization parameters:

$$\vec{Z}_i(t) = [Z_{i,1}(t), Z_{i,2}(t),\dots Z_{i,D}(t)] \qquad (4)$$

Now, in each generation, a donor $\vec{y}_i$ (t) is created. The method of creating this donor vector demarcates between the various DE schemes. In one of the earliest variants of DE, now called DE/rand/1 scheme, to create $\vec{y}_i(t)$ Y r for each i-th member, three other parameter vectors (say the r_1, r_2, and r_3-th vectors such that r_1, r_2, r_3 $\in$ $[1, NP]$ and $r_1 \neq r_2 \neq r_3$ are chosen at random from the current population.

Next the difference of any two of the three vectors is multiplied by a scalar number F and the scaled for j = 1, 2, ..., D and $rand_j$ (0, 1) $\in$ [0, 1] is the j-th evaluation of a uniform random number generator. $m(i)$ $\in$ [1, 2,...., D] is a randomly chosen index which ensures that $\vec{R}_i(t)$ gets at least one component from $\vec{Z}_i(t)$. To keep the population size constant over subsequent generations, the next step of the algorithm calls for 'selection' in order to determine which one between the target vector and trial vector will survive in the next generation i.e. at time t = t+1. If the trial vector yields a better value of the fitness function, it replaces its target vector in the next generation; otherwise the parent is retained in the population:

$$\vec{Z}_i(t+1) = \begin{cases} \vec{R}_i(t) & \text{if } f(\vec{R}_i(t)) \leq f(\vec{Z}_i(t)) \\ = \vec{Z}_i(t) & \text{if } f(\vec{R}_i(t)) > f(\vec{Z}_i(t)) \end{cases} \qquad (7)$$

where $f(.)$ is the function to be minimized.

2.3 The Multi-objective Variants of DE

In this comparative study, we have used four significant multi-objective variants of the DE algorithm, namely the Pareto DE (PDE) [9], the multi-objective DE (MODE) [10], The DE for Multi-objective Optimization (DEMO) 11], and the Non-dominated Sorting DE (NSDE) [12]. We do not provide a detailed description of these algorithms here for the sake of space economy.

3. Multi-objective Clustering Scheme

3.1 Search-variable Representation

To search for the globally optimal solution to a problem using DE, parameters of the problem have to be represented by real numbers. In the proposed method, if there are n document vectors, each D-dimensional, and if the user-specified maximum number of clusters is k then each chromosome is a vector of real numbers of dimension $k \times D$. The entries are reserved for k number of p-dimensional cluster centers. A single chromosome can be shown as $\vec{Z}_i(t)$ =

$\vec{m}_1$	$\vec{m}_2$	....	$\vec{m}_k$

3.2 Selecting the Objective Functions

The performance of a multi-objective clustering algorithm critically depends upon the clustering objectives it tries to optimize simultaneously. Conflict among the objective functions is often beneficial since it guides to globally optimal solutions. It also ensures that no single clustering objective is optimized leaving other probable significant objectives unnoticed.

In this work we choose the Xie-Beni index XBq and the FCM objective function Jq as the two objectives. The FCM measure Jq may be defined as:

$$J_q = \sum_{j=1}^{n}\sum_{i=1}^{k} u_{ij}^q \cdot d^2(\vec{Z}_j, \vec{m}_i), \quad 1 \le q \le \infty \qquad (8)$$

where q is the fuzzy exponent, d indicates a distance measure between the j-th pattern vector and i-th cluster centroid, and u_{ij} denotes the membership of j-th pattern in the i-th cluster. The XB index is defined as a function of the ratio of the total variation σ to the minimum separation sep of the clusters. Here σ and sep may be written as:

$$\sigma = \sum_{i=1}^{k}\sum_{p=1}^{n} u_{ip}^2 \cdot d(\vec{m}_i, \vec{Z}_p) \qquad (9)$$

$$\text{and} \quad sep(Z) = \min_{i \ne j}\{d^2(\vec{m}_i, \vec{m}_j)\} \qquad (10)$$

The XB index is then written as:

$$XB_q = \frac{\sigma}{n \times sep(Z)} = \frac{\sum_{i=1}^{k}\sum_{p=1}^{n} u_{ip}^q \cdot d^2(\vec{m}_i, \vec{Z}_p)}{n \times \min_{i=j}\{d^2(\vec{Z}_i, \vec{Z}_j)\}} \qquad (11)$$

Note that when the partitioning is compact and the individual clusters are well separated, value of σ should be low while sep should be high, thereby yielding lower values of XB_q index. The objective therefore is to minimize the XB index. For computing the measures described in equations (8) and (11), the centers encoded in a DE vector are first extracted. Let the set of centers be denoted by $\{\vec{m}_1, \vec{m}_2, \ldots, \vec{m}_k\}$. The membership value of the j-th pattern in i-th cluster u_{ij}, I = 1,2,…., k and j = 1,2,…., n are computed as:

$$u_{ij} = \frac{1}{\sum_{p=1}^{k}\left(\frac{d(\vec{m}_i, \vec{Z}_j)}{d(\vec{m}_p, \vec{Z}_j)}\right)^{\frac{2}{q-1}}} \qquad (12)$$

and the cluster membership values are recomputed. Note that the XB_q index is a combination of global (numerator) and particular (denominator) situations. The numerator is similar to J_m but the denominator has a factor that gives the separation between to minimum distant clusters. Hence this factor only considers the worst case, i.e. which two clusters are closest to each other and forgets about the other partitions. Here, greater value of the denominator (lower value of whole index) signifies a better partitioning. Thus it is evident that J_m and XB_q indices should be simultaneously minimized in order to get good solutions. The two terms at the numerator and the denominator of XB_q may not attain their best values for the same partitioning when the data has complex and overlapping clusters, such as remote sensing image data.

3.3 Selecting the Best Solution from Pareto-front

Multi-objective clustering does not return a single solution, but a set of solutions corresponding to tradeoffs between the two objectives. In our work, we choose the solution on the Pareto front with the best value of crowding distance as the optimal solution.

3.4 Evaluating the Clustering Quality

In this work, the final clustering quality is evaluated using two external measures. Specifically we choose the Adjusted Rand Index [19] (which is a generalization of the Rand index [20]) and the Silhouette index. Silhouette width reflects the compactness and separation of the clusters. Given a set of data points $Z = \{\vec{Z}_1, \ldots, \vec{Z}_n\}$ and a given clustering solution $C = \{C_1, C_2, \ldots, C_k\}$, the silhouette width $s\{\vec{Z}_j\}$ for each data $\vec{Z}_j$ belonging to cluster C_i indicates a measure of the confidence of belongingness, and it is defined as:

$$s(\vec{Z}_j) = \frac{b(\vec{Z}_j) - a(\vec{Z}_j)}{\max(a(\vec{Z}_j), b(\vec{Z}_j))}. \quad (14)$$

Here $a(\vec{Z}_j)$ denotes the average distance of data point $\vec{Z}_j$ from the other data points of the cluster to which the data point $\vec{Z}_j$ is assigned (i. e. cluster C_i). On the other hand, $b(\vec{Z}_j)$ represents the minimum of the average distances of data point $\vec{Z}_j$ from the data points belonging to clusters C_r, $r = 1,2,\ldots k$, and $r \neq i$. The value of $s(\vec{Z}_j)$ lies between -1 and $+1$. Large values of $s(\vec{Z}_j)$ (near to 1) indicate that the data point $\vec{Z}_j$ is well clustered. Value of $s(\vec{Z}_j)$ around 0 means that the data point lies between two clusters and a negative value of $s(\vec{Z}_j)$ indicates that the data point $\vec{Z}_j$ is probably placed in a wrong cluster. Overall silhouette index $S(C)$ of a clustering solution $C = \{C_1, C_2, \ldots, C_k\}$ is defined as the mean silhouette width over all the data points:

$$s(C) = \frac{1}{n}\sum_{j=1}^{n} s(\vec{Z}_j) \quad (15)$$

Greater values of $s(C)$ (near to 1) reflect that most of the data points are correctly clustered and this in turn indicates a better clustering solution. Silhouette index can be evaluated for any distance measure.

4. Experimental Results

4.1 Datasets used

The experimental results showing the effectiveness of multi-objective DE based clustering has been provided for six artificial and four real life datasets. The artificial datasets are named as Dataset_1 to Dataset_6 with number of clusters varying from 3 to 10. Table 1 presents the number of objects, dimensionality and the number of clusters for each data. The real-life datasets are iris, wine, breast-cancer [21] and the yeast sporulation data. We consider here the microarray data on the transcriptional program of sporulation in budding yeast, the collection and analysis of which have been described in [17]. The sporulation dataset is available publicly from the website: http://cmgm.stanford.edu/pbrown/sporulation. This dataset consists of 6118 genes measured across 7 time points (0, 0.5, 2, 5, 7, 9 and 11.5 h) during the sporulation process of budding yeast. The data are then log-transformed. Among the 6118 genes, the genes, whose expression levels did not change significantly during the harvesting, have been ignored from further analysis. This is determined with a threshold level of 1.6 for the root mean squares of the log2-transformed ratios. The resulting set consists of 474 genes. Please note that for the yeast sporulation dataset, we have used the Pearson correlation coefficient based distance measure [22], instead of the conventional Euclidean distance (which has been used for the rest of the datasets), as it has been shown to be more effective for clustering microarray datasets [22].

Table 1 Average Silhouette index and number of clusters found and standard deviations (in parentheses) by six contestant algorithms over 30 independent runs on ten datasets.

Dataset	Silhouette Index					
	MODE	DEMO	PDE	NSDE	NSGA2	MOCK
Dataset_1	**0.670726 (0.0321)**	0.670523 (0.08263)	0.656594 (0.05372)	0.661661 (0.00493)	0.669317 (0.0892)	0.66342 (0.0736)
Dataset_2	0.678734 (0.03716)	0.670530 (0.05381)	0.663812 (0.00366)	**0.683382 (0.00082)**	0.674393 (0.00927)	0.658921 (0.004731)
Dataset_3	0.771363 (0.00938)	**0.774611 (0.002376)**	0.766945 (0.04824)	0.767333 (0.004712)	0.765691 (0.005686)	0.768419 (0.006721)
Dataset_4	**0.849184 (0.00472)**	0.838303 (0.056741)	0.824910 (0.00721)	0.840613 (0.04752)	0.827618 (0.02871)	0.832527 (0.007825)
Dataset_5	0.778102 (0.04363)	**0.778736 (0.008125)**	0.746241 (0.00673)	0.777406 (0.05345)	0.768379 (0.005384)	0.769342 (0.006208)
Dataset_6	0.643316 (0.00381)	0.637986 (0.008112)	**0.645446 (0.05524)**	0.640832 (0.004983)	0.642091 (0.002833)	0.640957 (0.008349)
Iris	0.606353 (0.03483)	**0.606864 (0.03234)**	0.569675 (0.04752)	0.600304 (0.004618)	0.566613 (0.082651)	0.6003725 (0.005129)
Wine	**0.582197 (0.00427)**	0.568391 (0.007473)	0.525840 (0.01213)	0.5457383 (0.009497)	0.5767342 (0.009415)	0.576834 (0.000812)
Breast Cancer	**0.648297 (0.00734)**	0.609123 (0.57813)	0.619219 (0.00567)	0.628352 (0.006782)	0.6004642 (0.004561)	0.626719 (0.01094)
Yeast Sporulation	**0.676434 (0.00072)**	0.558619 (0.057832)	0.595367 (0.00721)	0.604513 (0.005728)	0.641306 (0.04813)	0.613567 (0.005738)

4.2 Parameters for the Algorithms

All the multi-objective DE variants have been used with 40 parameter vectors in each generation and each run of each algorithm was continued for 100 generations. The value of scale factor F is a random value between 0.5 and 1. The other parameters for the multi-objective GA (NSGA II) based clustering are fixed as follows: number of generations = 100, population size = 50, crossover probability = 0.8, mutation probability = $\frac{1}{\text{Chromosome\_length}}$ Please note that the four DE variants and the NSGA II use the same parameter representation scheme. Clustering with MOCK was performed with the source codes available from http://dbkgroup.org/handl/mock/.

4.3 Presentation of Results

The mean Silhouette index values of the best-of-run solutions provided by six contestant algorithms over the 10 datasets have been provided in Table 2. The best entries have been marked in boldface in each row. Table 3 enlists the adjusted rand index values except for Yeast sporulation data as no standard nominal classification is known for this dataset. Tables 3 and 4 show the results of unpaired t tests (standard error of difference of the two means, 95% confidence interval of this difference, the t value, and the two-tailed P value) between the best and second best algorithms in terms of both average Silhouette index and adjusted rand index. For all cases in Tables 3 and 4, sample size = 30 and number of degrees of freedom = 58. The results listed in Tables 2 to 4 indicate that there is always one or more multiobjective DE variant that beats the NSGA II or MOCK in terms of mean Silhouette index and adjusted rand index in a statistically significant fashion.

Table 3 Mean value of adjusted rand index found and standard deviations (in parentheses) by six contestant algorithms over 30 independent runs on nine datasets.

Dataset	Algorithms					
	MODE	DEMO	PDE	NSDE	NSGA2	MOCK
Dataset_1	**0.846199 (0.031257)**	0.828437 (0.046182)	0.719584 (0.00563741)	0.819794 (0.035285)	0.802180 (0.004782)	0.810934 (0.0059348)
Dataset_2	0.847621 (0.006312)	0.9273464 (0.0008573)	0.9372649 (0.036451)	**1.000000**	0.9378123 (0.006821)	0.946547 (0.004536)
Dataset_3	0.951786 (0.004827)	**1.000000**	0.9758732 (0.05736)	0.894635 (0.005736)	0.963841 (0.0046719)	0.878732 (0.0712523)
Dataset_4	**1.000000**	0.857463 (0.065639)	0.840953 (0.076829)	0.919843 (0.0121436)	0.957818 (0.004678)	0.978761 (0.006734)
Dataset_5	0.983785 (0.076764)	**0.993173 (0.089371)**	0.876710 (0.023376)	0.982013 (0.084372)	0.947641 (0.006646)	0.9454568 (0.0012043)
Dataset_6	0.881413 (0.05983)	0.881136 (0.078348)	**0.884930 (0.007846)**	0.880265 (0.056347)	0.881395 (0.056483)	0.910294 (0.016743)
Iris	0.738626 (0.0756779)	**0.748784 (0.067457)**	0.709036 (0.025739)	0.738960 (0.001436)	0.715898 (0.005739)	0.786574 (0.075763)
Wine	**0.875849 (0.0087642)**	0.858876 (0.0035287)	0.8265764 (0.0032429)	0.845365 (0.0065761)	0.828645 (0.0074653)	0.864764 (0.0034398)
Breast Cancer	0.956456 (0.0056453)	0.912173 (0.0043247)	0.937857 (0.0087743)	**0.950965 (0.0065682)**	0.944236 (0.006521)	0.9465731 (0.006748)

Table 4 Unpaired t-test results for silhouette index

Dataset	Std. Err	t	95% Conf. Intvl	Two-tailed P	Significance
Dataset_1	0.001	7.1968	-0.0121 to -0.0068	< 0.0001	**Extremely Significant**
Dataset_2	0.002	3.8990	-0.0129 to -0.0040	< 0.0001	**Extremely Significant**
Dataset_3	0.007	34.9267	-0.2665 to -0.2373	< 0.0001	**Extremely Significant**
Dataset_4	0.001	3.0961	-0.0051 to -0.0010	0.0037	**Very Significant**
Dataset_5	0.003	3.0684	-0.0156 to -0.0032	0.0040	**Very Significant**
Dataset_6	0.002	3.0584	-0.0109 to -0.0022	0.0041	**Very Significant**
Iris	0.009	1.3744	-0.0309 to 0.0059	0.1774	Not Significant
Wine	0.003	2.3999	-0.0118 to -0.0010	0.0214	**Significant**
Breast Cancer	0.009	1.3744	-0.0309 to 0.0059	0.1774	Not Significant
Yeast Sporulation	0.003	2.3999	-0.0118 to -0.0010	0.0214	**Significant**

Table 5 Unpaired *t*-test Results for adjusted rand index

Dataset	Std. Err	*t*	95% Conf. Intvl	Two-tailed *P*	Significance
Dataset_1	0.021	2.9201	-0.1050 to -0.0189	0.0059	Very significant
Dataset_2	0.013	5.0453	-0.0922 to -0.0394	< 0.0001	Extremely Significant
Dataset_3	0.002	17.965	-0.0452 to -0.0360	< 0.0001	Extremely Significant
Dataset_4	0.005	6.4431	-0.0419 to -0.0219	< 0.0001	Extremely Significant
Dataset_5	0.009	1.3744	-0.0309 to 0.0059	0.1774	Not Significant
Dataset_6	0.003	2.3999	-0.0118 to -0.0010	0.0214	Significant
Iris	0.009	1.3744	-0.0309 to 0.0059	0.1774	Not Significant
Wine	0.003	2.3999	-0.0118 to -0.0010	0.0214	Significant
Breast Cancer	0.009	1.3744	-0.0309 to 0.0059	0.1774	Not Significant

4.4 Significance and Validation of Microarray Data Clustering Results

In this section the best clustering solution provided by different algorithms on the sporulation data of yeast has been visualized using the cluster profile plot (in parallel coordinates) and the heatmap plot in MATLAB 7.0.4 version. Parallel coordinates [23] is a common way of visualizing high-dimensional geometry. A point in *n*-dimensional space is represented as a polyline with vertices on the parallel axes; the position of the vertex on the *i*-th axis corresponds to the *i*-th coordinate of the point. Cluster profile plots (in parallel coordinates) of seven clusters for the best clustering result (provided by MODE) on yeast sporulation data has been shown in Fig. 1. The blue polylines indicate the member genes within a cluster while the black polyline indicates the centroid of that gene. Cluster profile plots (Fig. 1) also demonstrate how the cluster profiles for the different groups of genes differ from each other, while the profiles within a group are reasonably similar.

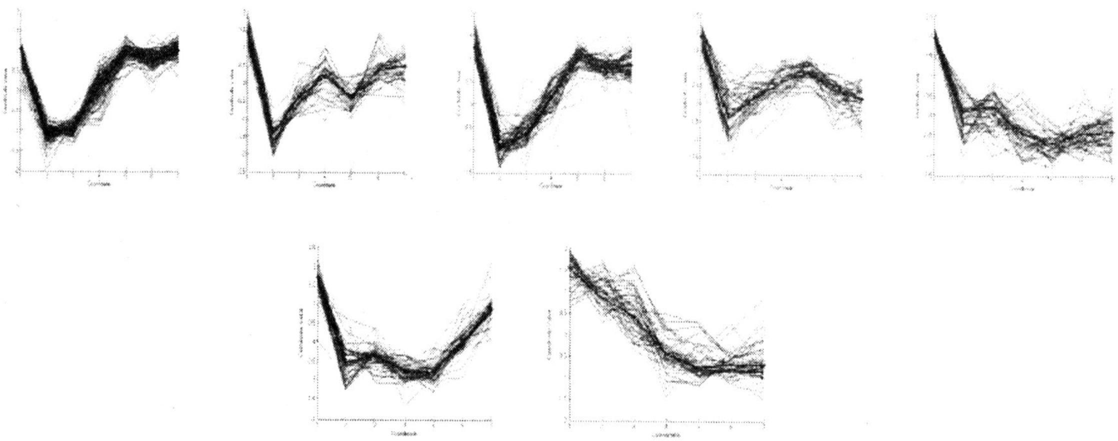

Fig. 1 Parallelcoords plots and heatmap of cluster 1 to 5 (from left to right on top), and for clusters 6 and 7 below

Genes within the same cluster are expected to exhibit similar expressions as they should have similar functionality or contribute to the same biological processes. Here we attempt to determine the biological meanings of the clusters by using Gene Ontology (GO) terms using the popular web-based tool FatiGO [24] (www.fatigo.org) FatiGO extracts the GO terms for a query and a reference set of genes and further computes various statistics for the query set. In our experiment, a query is the set of genes of a cluster and union of the genes from the other clusters is taken as the reference set. The GO level is fixed at three. It is not possible to evaluate each cluster of the final solutions provided by all the algorithms here. SO, two interesting clusters from the clustering results obtained on Yeast Sporulation data set by the best performing algorithm (MODE in this case) is examined. Fig. 2 shows a part of the FatiGO results of cluster 2 and 6 of multi-objective clustering on the sporulation data. It can be observed that the percentage of genes in the query cluster is considerably different from that of the reference cluster in almost all the functionalities. This implies that the correct genes are selected to remain in the same cluster.

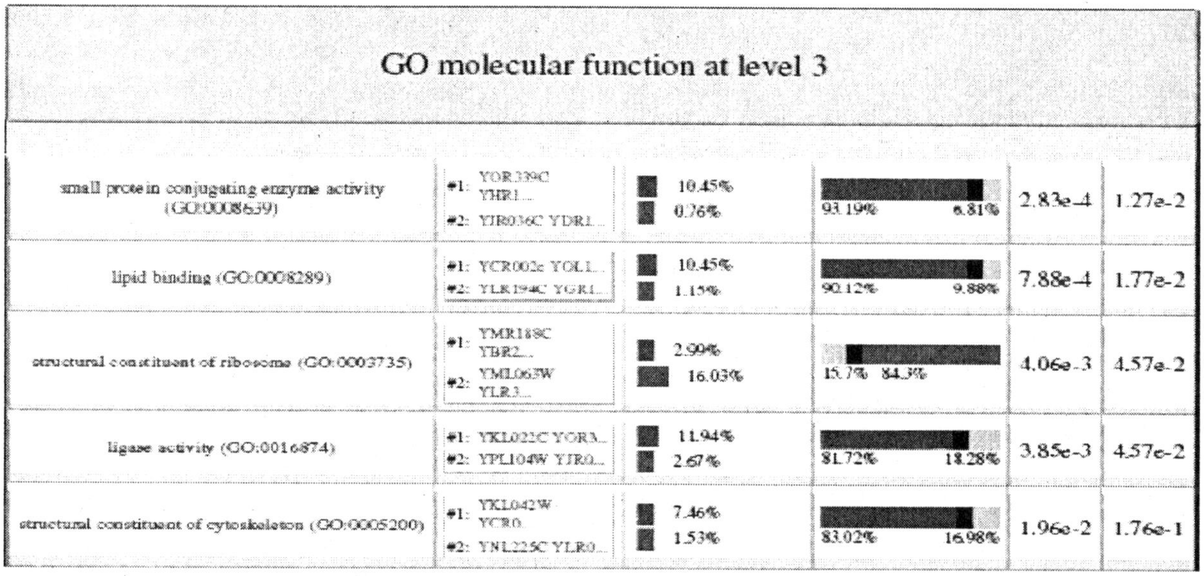

Fig. 2 Part of FatiGO result for cluster 2 of the best multi-objective clustering algorithm on yeast sporulation dataset

5. Conclusions

This paper compared and contrasted the performances of four state-of-the-art multi-objective variants of DE with two other prominent multiobjective clustering algorithms. The multi-objective DE-variants used the same chromosome representation scheme. Tables 2 to 4 indicate that one or more multi-objective DE variants were always able to produce better final clustering solutions as compared to MOCK or NSGA II in terms of both adjusted Rand index and Sillhouette index when all the algorithms were let run for an equal number of generations. Visualization of the yeast sporulation data clustering results indicate that the MODE yielded compact and well separated clusters. Our experimental results indicate that DE holds immense promise as a candidate optimization technique for multi-objective clustering. Future research may extend the multi-objective DE-based clustering schemes to handle discrete chromosome representation schemes that no longer depend on cluster centroids and thus are not biased in any sense towards spherical clusters. As a scope of further research, the technique of multi-objective optimization with other cluster validity indices needs to be studied. Moreover, new ways of comparing the performance of multi-objective solutions have to be defined.

6. References

[1] K. Deb, A. Pratap, S. Agarwal, and T. Meyarivan, "A fast and elitist multiobjective genetic algorithm: NSGA-II", *IEEE Transactions on Evolutionary Computation*, vol. 6, no. 2, 2002.

[2] J. D. Knowles and D. W. Corne, "Approxmating the nondominated front using the pareto archived evolution strategy", *Evolutionary Computation*, vol. 8, no. 2, pp. 149.172, 2000.

[3] R. Storn and K. V. Price, "Differential evolution – a simple and efficient adaptive scheme for global optimization over continuous spaces", *Technical Report TR-95-012, ICSI*, http://http.icsi.berkeley.edu/~storn/litera.html, 1995.

[4] R. Storn, K. V. Price, and J. Lampinen, *Differential Evolution - A Practical Approach to Global Optimization*, Springer, Berlin, 2005.

[5] Y. Sawaragi, H. Nakayama, and T. Tanino, "Theory of multiobjective optimization" (vol. 176 of *Mathematics in Science and Engineering*). Orlando, FL: Academic Press Inc., 1985.

[6] K. Deb, *Multi-Objective Optimization using Evolutionary Algorithms*, John Wiley & Sons, 2001.

[7] C. A. Coello Coello, G. B. Lamont, and D. A. Van Veldhuizen, *Evolutionary Algorithms for Solving Multi-Objective Problems*, Springer, 2007.

[8] A. Abraham, L. C. Jain and R. Goldberg (Eds.), *Evolutionary Multiobjective Optimization: Theoretical Advances and Applications*, Springer Verlag, London, 2005.

[9] H. A. Abbass and R. Sarker, "The pareto differential evolution algorithm", *International Journal on Artificial Intelligence Tools*, 11(4):531-552, 2002.

[10] F. Xue, A. C. Sanderson, and R. J. Graves, "Paretobased multi-objective differential evolution", in *Proceedings of the 2003 Congress on Evolutionary Computation (CEC'2003)*, volume 2, pages 862–869, Canberra, Australia, 2003, IEEE Press.

[11] T. Robic and B. Filipic, "DEMO: Differential Evolution for Multiobjective Optimization", In C. A. Coello Coello, A. H. Aguirre, and E. Zitzler, editors, *Evolutionary Multi-Criterion Optimization, Third International Conference, EMO 2005*, pages 520–533, Guanajuato, Mexico, 2005, Springer. Lecture Notes in Computer Science Vol. 3410, 2005.

[12] A. W. Iorio and X. Li, "Solving rotated multiobjective optimization problems using differential evolution", in *AI 2004: Advances in Artificial Intelligence, Proceedings*, pages 861–872, Springer- Verlag, Lecture Notes in Artificial Intelligence Vol. 3339, 2004.

[13] X. Xie and G. Beni, "Validity measure for fuzzy clustering", *IEEE Trans. Pattern Anal. Machine Learning*, Vol. 3, pp. 841–846, (1991).

[14] J. C. Bezdek, "Cluster validity with fuzzy sets", *Journal of Cybernetics*, (3) 58–72, (1974).

[15] J. Handl and J. Knowles, "An evolutionary approach to multiobjective clustering", *IEEE Transactions on Evolutionary Computation*, 11(1):56-76, 2007.

[16] S. Bandyopadhyay, U. Maulik, and A. Mukhopadhyay, .Multiobjective genetic clustering for pixel classification in remote sensing imagery, *IEEE Transactions Geoscience and Remote Sensing*, 2006.

[17] S. Chu *et al.* "The transcriptional program of sporulation in budding yeast", *Science*, 282, 699–705, 1998.

[18] R.E. Steuer, Multiple Criteria Optimization: Theory, Computations, and Application. New York: John Wiley & Sons, Inc., 1986.

[19] L. Hubert and P. Arabie, "Comparing partitions", *Journal of Classification*, 193–218, 1985.

[20] W. M. Rand, "Objective criteria for the evaluation of clustering methods", *Journal of the American Statistical Association*, 66, 846–850, 1971.

[21] C. Blake, E.Keough and C.J.Merz, UCI repository of machine learning database (1998). http://www.ics.uci.edu/~mlearn/MLrepository.html

[22] Theodoridis and K. Koutroumbas, *Pattern Recognition*, Second Edition, Elsevier Academic Press, 2003.

[23] D. A. Keim and H.-P. Kriegel, "Visualization techniques for mining large databases: a comparison", *IEEE Transactions on Knowledge and Data Engineering*, v.8 n.6, p.923-938, December 1996.

[24] F. Al-Shahrour, R. Díaz-Uriarte, and J. Dopazo, "FatiGO: a web tool for finding significant associations of Gene Ontology terms with groups of genes", *Bioinformatics*, 20, 578-580, 2004.

Exploring Random Forest Classifier in Parallel Computing Environment

Vrushali Y Kulkarni[1], Vineet Krishnan[2] and Deep Shah[3]
[1]Professor, Computer Engineering, MIT, Pune *vykulkarni@mitpune.com*
[2]Associate Software Engineer, Sungard, Pune

Abstract

The aim of this paper is to present the research work done in exploring the Random Forest technique for classification which is a recent development in the field of data mining. Random Forest is an ensemble classifier and works efficiently and accurately on large data sets. By nature, Random Forest is a suitable candidate for parallel processing and the study work is based on implementing random forest in parallel computing environment which is a less focused area till now.

1. Introduction

The aim of the research work was to explore random forest classifier. It is one of the techniques for data mining. Data mining is broadly classified as descriptive data mining and predictive data mining. Descriptive concentrates more on describing the data, grouping into categories, and summarizing the data. Predictive data mining concentrates on analyzing past data and generating trends for future. Descriptive tends more towards unsupervised machine learning while predictive tends towards supervised machine learning. The classification technique is a part of predictive data mining.

The predictive data mining can be carried out by generating a predictive model. A model is an abstraction of a real life problem. It concentrates on the key features, and produces output for a given set of inputs which are statistical inferences. Analysing data is often the process of building an appropriate model for data. Predictive data mining has its root in the classical model building process of statistics. The predictive model works on the basis of feature analysis of predictor variables. One or more features or inputs are considered as predictors. The output is some function of predictors which is called hypothesis. The generated hypotheses are tested for their acceptance or rejection. Ideally a model has to provide a high accuracy of prediction but it can be accepted with allowable tolerance. Since there are different error estimation techniques to decide the error tolerance, this model always works successfully with estimated error.

Random Forest is one of the techniques to implement the predictive model. Random Forest generates many decision (classification) trees. To classify new data set, the input vector (combination of predictors) is tested across each tree in the forest. Each tree gives a classification for new data records, these classifications are called as votes. The new data is identified to be of the class for which there are maximum votes.

For generating Random Forest, if the size of training data is N, then n cases (rows) are sampled at random with replacement from the original data set. If there are M input variables (predictors), then a number k << M is chosen. At each node k, variables are selected at random out of M and the best split on the k is used to split the node. This value of k is kept constant during the entire forest growing process. Each tree is grown to the full extent, there is no pruning. Usually k is selected as k = square root of M for near optimal results. Features of Random Forest are

- The methodology is general and not restricted to particular metrics or research objectives.
- It runs efficiently on large data sets, Fast algorithm (can be faster than growing/pruning a single tree), easily parallelized
- It is more robust to outliers and noise compared to other classifiers
- It has an efficient method for estimating missing data and retains accuracy when a large portion of data is missing.
- It gives estimates of which attributes are important in the classification.
- Built-in cross validation via the use of Out-Of-Bag (OOB) samples to estimate test error rate Good accuracy without over-fitting

As Random Forest generates many classification trees, and generation of each tree is independent of each other, Random Forest is by nature a natural candidate for parallel processing. As data mining is usually done on very large data sets, also Random Forest has ability to work on the data with a large number of predictors, the research work was carried out in a parallel processing environment. An asymmetric cluster of computers was established. The mechanism for communication among the nodes was message passing using the MPICH library.

2. Literature Survey

Random Forest technique is recent development in the field of machine learning developed by Leo Breiman and Adled Cutler. [1] Random Forest uses an ensemble of trees as their constituent models. While each of the constituent trees is trained on a bootstrap sample of the data, the final outputs are the aggregation of the outputs of the individual classifiers. Random Forests are good for both classification and prediction and have shown superior performance over other machine learning techniques for a variety of applications.

For complex problems, it is generally accepted that it is difficult to design a single classifier to achieve the desired performance [3]. For such complex problems, both theoretical and empirical studies have proved that using an ensemble of individual classifiers is more effective in achieving improved classification performance. In classifier ensemble, outputs of individual classifiers are combined to arrive at the final classification decision. Such combination strategically utilizes the information provided by the constitute classifiers, thus achieves higher classification performance.

Random Forest has an internal mechanism for doing unbiased estimate of the generalization error as the forest building process progresses [3]. As per Breiman, each tree is trained on bootstrap samples (randomly drawn, with replacement) of the training set. On average, about one-third of samples are not in the bootstrap set, which are called as "out-of-bag" (OOB) samples. The OOB samples are used to estimate the generalization error of the forest. The classification accuracy is depending on the strength of the individual tree and the correlation among the individual trees. Minimizing the correlation increases the classification accuracy.

There is comparatively less work on parallel implementation of Random Forest. The original Random Forest algorithm is implemented using Fortran 77. The parallel version called PARF is implemented using Fortran 90. Though by nature Random Forest can be implemented in parallel, very few applications have taken advantage of it. The packages like R and Weka have support for Random Forest but there is no parallel implementation.

One challenge is how to design classifiers for ultra-high dimensional classification problems [9]. There is a strong need now to build useful classifiers with hundreds of millions or billions of features, for applications such as text mining and drug safety analysis.

Parallel computing is a need for recent data mining applications involving huge amount of data. Broadly speaking, techniques for scaling data mining algorithms can be divided into five basic categories: 1)Manipulating the data so that it fits into memory, 2)Using specialized data structures, 3)distributing the computation so that it exploits several processors, 4)pre-computing intermediate quantities, 5)reducing the amount of data mined [10].

Random Forest classifiers are inherently flexible for both binary and multiclass classification problems.

Parallel Computing supports characteristics as improved performance, high availability, scalability, and economical implementation. Parallel computing is achieved by installing a cluster of computers.

Cluster of computers - Cluster computing provides a platform for performing a computationally intensive application in parallel. Many commonly used search engines are implemented using clusters for load balancing. A cluster is a network of computers that can work together to solve a problem. To facilitate working together, the computers that make up a cluster (often called nodes) may share disk resources, use fast network hardware, and use special software for control and communication. Additionally, to reduce time and expense for cabling and maintenance, clusters are often built in a physically compact form using rack-mounted hardware.

3. Design and Algorithm

As mentioned earlier in the introduction part, Random Forest is generated by building different classification trees. "mtry" is the number of attributes (features) selected randomly for generating individual tress. Other parameters are the number of trees to be generated in the forest, which is usually kept constant, and the node-size. This number indicates that there will be no split of node after node-size records. Usually node-size is kept as one. The algorithm for classification tree is not discussed here as standard versions of decision tree algorithm are readily available.

Below given is the algorithm for working of Random Forest in parallel processing environment.

Logic implemented at master node

1. For each node

    Verify if specified number of trees has been generated

    if yes, then send kill signal to worker nodes

    else continue

2. Select any node in the cluster
    Randomly choose "mtry" number of attributes for tree building. This is the attribute set for that tree.
    Send attribute set to worker node
    Select training data set (depending on the method specified by the user), this is the record set for building the tree.
    Send record set to tree building process
3. end of for in step 1
4. for each node in cluster
    Receive maximum accuracy tree for that particular node
5. end for
6. Display maximum accuracy for all nodes in the cluster
7. Exit

Logic implemented at worker node

1. for each tree
    Receive attribute set from master
    Check for kill signal
        If yes then exit loop
        Else continue
    Receive record set
    Build tree
    Test tree
    Save accuracy
2. end for
3. return accuracy of best tree to master node
4. exit

4. Experimentation and Results

Following experimentation were done-

1. Testing Random Forest algorithm on standalone processors.
2. Testing Random Forest algorithm on cluster of computers
3. Testing Random Forest algorithm for binary class problem as well as multiclass problem.
4. Comparing Random Forest implementation against decision tree implementation.
5. Comparing Random Forest algorithm against ANN (Back-propagation algorithm), but it is out of scope of this paper.
6. Testing performance of Random Forest by using different sampling techniques.

In all the experimentation, the configurable parameter was mtry (number of attributes selected at a time for building of individual trees) which was varied by keeping the number of trees and number of nodes as fixed parameters.

The database used for binary classification was a small subset of the US 1990 Census database. It consists of 10282 instances (rows) and 29 input variables and 2 classification classes.
The database used for multiclass classification was Nursery database with 12960 instances (rows), 9 input variables and 5 classification classes.

A 4 node cluster was setup with Sunfire X2100 servers each of 2.6 GHz and 4 MB RAM. The Operating system was Rocks 4.5 with SGE scheduler, MPI parallelizer and Ganglia monitoring tool.

The measurements were initially carried out on 4 different CPUs (standalone) and the graph in Fig 1 shows the time required to generate 10 trees for the specified mtry values.

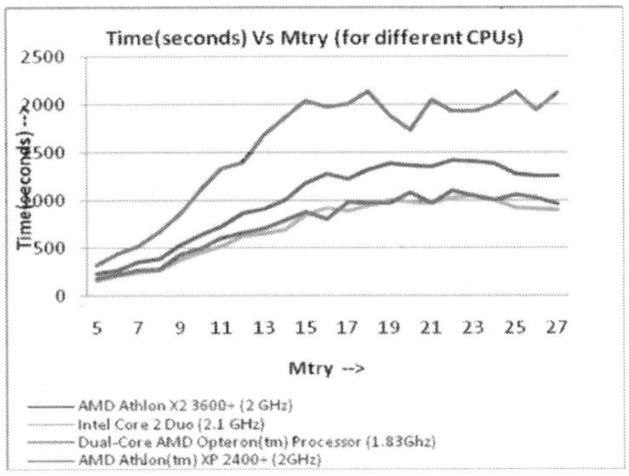

Fig. 1 Time (seconds) Vs Mtry (for different CPUs)

The two graphs in Fig 2 show the effect of mtry value on the time required for tree generation and the accuracy of the generated forest.

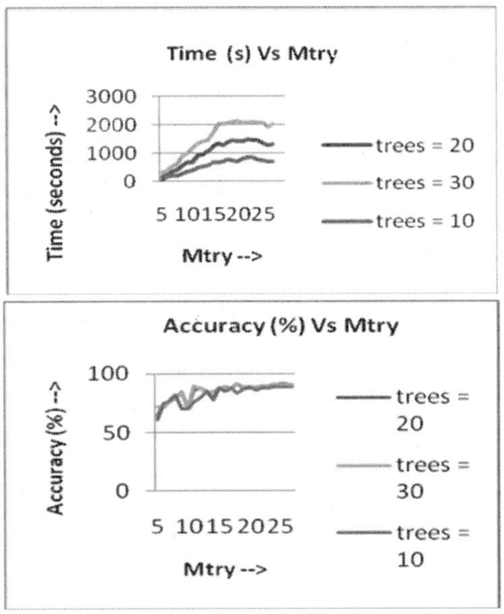

Fig. 2 Graph of Time Vs Mtry and Accuracy Vs Mtry

From the above graph, we can see that as the value of mtry increases, after a particular value of mtry, the accuracy of classification of the database gradually stabilizes. This 'stability value' for accuracy has been observed to half the total number of input variables (M/2), for most datasets.

The different sampling techniques used for experimentation were –

1. Fixed-Interval sampling – This refers to the type of sampling in which every 'n-th' record is considered from the training dataset.
2. Block Sampling – In this sampling technique, starting from a random record, the required number of instances are chosen in a continuous fashion from the training dataset.
3. Simple Random Sampling – In this technique, random instances from the training dataset are chosen.

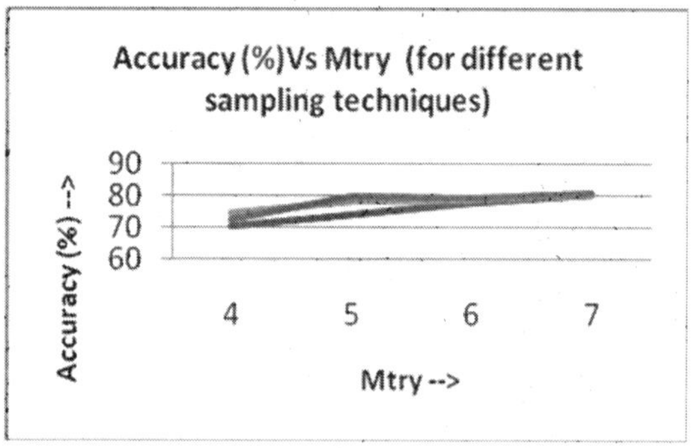

Red-Fixed interval, Green- Block, Blue –Simple Random

Fig. 3 Graph of Accuracy Vs Mtry for different sampling techniques

From the graph in Fig 3, we can conclude that for datasets where the class distribution is uniform, simple random sampling has the least error rate. This is also a proven fact in Statistics where it is generally accepted that random sampling is the best estimate for any sort of survey or classification attempts.

The graph in Fig 4 shows the comparison between the Random forest generator and decision tree generator, with respect to classification accuracy for different datasets.

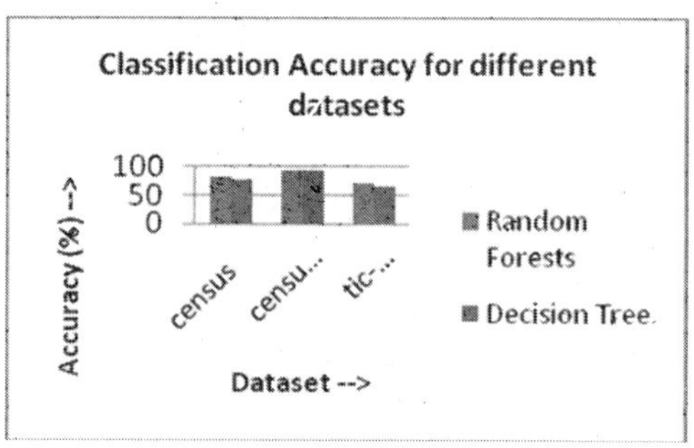

Fig. 4 Comparative study (accuracy for different datasets)

The datasets used in the above comparison are

1. Census – This is a tiny subset of the US 1990 Census database. It contains 30162 instances, 9 variables and 2 classification classes.
2. Census-medium – This is another subset of the US 1990 Census database. It contains 10282 instances, 29 variables and 2 classification classes.
3. Tic-tac-toe – This is the tic-tac-toe database, which shows the possible outcomes in a game of tic-tac-toe after a certain number of moves.

From the above graph, we can conclude that for most datasets, Random Forests outperform decision trees in terms of classification accuracy. However, the difference of classification accuracy varies between datasets.

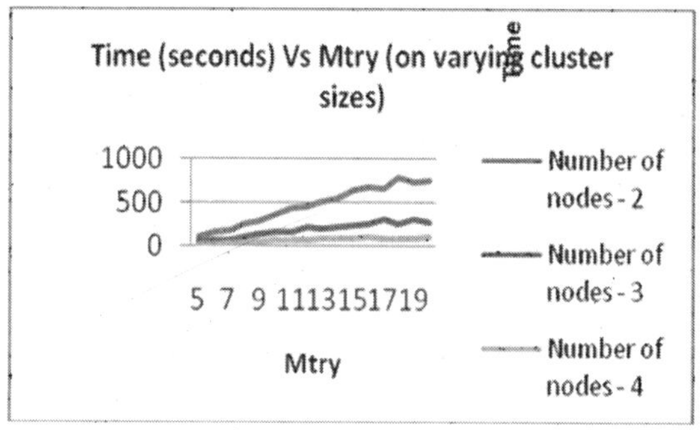

Fig. 5 Graph of Time Vs Mtry on varying cluster size

In the graph of Fig 5, we notice that there is a large difference between the results on a cluster of 2 nodes and a cluster of 3 nodes. This is because, the master node does not carry out any computation itself; however, it just supplies the attribute set and training dataset to each of the worker nodes. Thus, for a cluster of two nodes, there is just one node and hence the effective speedup with respect to a single machine is relatively negligible.

5. Discussion and Summary

Random Forest is a newly evolved technique for classification and prediction which works satisfactorily over very large datasets having more features. It is simple to implement and has a natural advantage of parallel implementation which enhances its performance and applicability.

6. Future Enhancements

In this research work, less stress was given on general error estimation of Random Forest, effect of correlation among individual trees on the forest error rate. In future work we are trying to do in-depth study of these features of Random Forest. For study purpose, no specific application was selected. We are now concentrating on seismic data and analyzing seismic data using Random Forest in parallel processing environment.

Acknowledgements – The above mentioned research work was possible due to the financial grant provided by BCUD, University of Pune, India and RCFC, MIT, Pune, India.

7. References

[1] Leo Breiman, Random Forests, Machine Learning, 45, 5-32,2001

[2] Lan Guo, Yan Ma, Bojan Cukic, Hashinder Singh, Robust Prediction of Fault-Proneness by Random Forests, ISSRE'04, 1071-9458/04, IEEE

[3] Weizhong Yan, Application of Random Forest to Aircraft Engine Fault Diagnosis, CESA, October 4-6, 2006, Beijing, China

[4] Ingrid Zukerman, David W Albrecht, Predictive Statistical Models for User Modeling, School of Computer Science and Software Engineering, Monash University, Clayton, Victoria 3800, Australia

[5] C V Apte, S J Hong, R Natrajan, E P D Pednault, F A Tipu, S M Weiss, Data-intensive analytics for predictive modelling,

[6] John Shafer, Rakesh Agarwal, Manish Mehta, SPRINT: A Scalable Parallel Classifier for Data Mining, IBM Almaden Research Center, 650 Harry Road, San Jose, CA 95120

[7] Johannes Gehrke, Raghu Ramakrishnan, Venkatesh Ganti, RainForest – A Framework for Fast Decision Tree Construction of Large Datasets, Department of Computer Sciences, University of Wisconsin-Madison

[8] Mahesh Pal, Random Forests for land cover classification, 0-7803-7929-2, 2003 (IEEE)

[9] Qiang Yang, Xindong Wu, 10 Challanging problems in Data Mining Research, Internal Journal of Information Technology and Decision making Vol 5 No 4 (2006) 597-604

[10] Robert Grossman, Yike Guo, Parallel Methods for Scaling Data Mining Algorithms to Large Datasets, Handbook of Data Mining and Knowledge Discovery, Oxford University Press, 2002

Some Interesting Knowledge Structures for Discovery of Decision Rules with Exceptions and Hierarchies – A Review

Saroj[1] and Yogita[2]
[1]Department of Computer Science and Engineering,
Guru Jambheshwar University of Science and Technology, Hisar – 125001, India
ratnoo_saroj@gmail.com
[2]Department of Computer Science and Engineering, Amity School of Engineering and Technology, Delhi.
thakranyogita@yahoo.co.in

Abstract

Discovering exceptions and hierarchies is an important data mining task. Exceptions are deviations from the commonsense/general rules. Exceptions are interesting as they exhibit unexpectedness and contradict prior knowledge about the domain. Discovering exceptions along with the decision rules increases the quality of decision making even in rare circumstances. Discovering knowledge in hierarchical form allows us to organize complex concepts in a comprehensible manner. The discovered knowledge in data mining is usually represented in the form of 'If-Then' Production Rules (PRs). PRs ignore exceptions as machine noise and are not suitable for the discovery of the hierarchical relationship among the classes of the data being mined. They fail to support approximate reasoning. This paper attempts to describe and review some interesting and innovative knowledge structures for the discovery of decision rules that accommodate exceptions and hierarchies. The knowledge structures taken in this paper support many other paradigms of good knowledge structures.

Keywords: *Decision Rules, Rule Triplet, Censored Production Rules, Exception Directed Acyclic Graphs, Ripple Down Rules, Hierarchical Censored Production Rule, Censored Production Rules with Fuzzy Hierarchy.*

1. Introduction

The decision rules in data mining are usually represented in the form of '*If-Then*' Production Rules (PRs). PRs, being high level and symbolic representation of knowledge, have been the predominant knowledge structure for the discovery of decision rules. Though, PRs are easy to implement, they fail to capture some of the vital aspects of the real world knowledge due to the rigidity in their structure. Production Rules (PRs) are confined to commonsense knowledge focusing on high generality and support. For example the rule '*If* bird *Then* fly' is of high regularity because almost all birds fly. However there are few exceptions like the Kiwi and Penguin, which do not fly. These birds are exceptions/deviations to the general rule for birds. Though exceptions cover a very small portion (low support) of data and are very often ignored as machine noise, it has always been challenging to discover exceptions because they are interesting and valuable pieces of knowledge that help decision makers to opt for correct actions in exceptional circumstances[1, 6].

PRs discover knowledge at a single conceptual level, hence, fragmenting the knowledge into a large number of rules. A large number of rules are not comprehensible to people as meaningful knowledge from which they can gain insights into the basis of decision making. Mining of rules at multiple concept level leads to discovery of more comprehensible, informative and refined knowledge. Hierarchies provide comprehensible knowledge that carries much more information than a collection of simple flat rules. Taxonomic structures with inheritance relations between concepts based on meaningful properties are probably most easily grasped by people. Therefore, discovery of decision rules at multiple concept level has been another important issue and various hierarchical decision rule structures have been tried [11, 12, 14, 15, 17].

Variable precision logic is concerned with the problem of reasoning with incomplete information and resource constraints. The certainty and specificity are two aspect of variable precision logic. Certainty refers to the degree of belief in a conclusion while specificity refers to the degree of detail of a description. A system that gives more certain answers given more time is called a variable certainty system. A system that gives more specific answers given more time is called a variable specificity system. PRs are not suitable for approximate reasoning under resource constraints and are unable to exhibit variable precision logic [12, 13].

Researchers in the field of data mining have tried more flexible and dynamic knowledge structures that remove the above deficiencies of PRs. In fact, the contemplation of knowledge structures that are more comprehensible, can accommodate exceptions, discover knowledge at multiple concept level and are suitable for approximate reasoning, has been an imperative issue for the research in data mining[14, 15]. This paper brings together such interesting knowledge structures in the hope to motivate further research in this area of significant importance. The survey attempts to examine those knowledge structures in details that have noteworthy contribution in the discovery of exceptions and hierarchies.

The remaining of this paper is organized as below. Section 2 presents a description of some novel and interesting knowledge structures which have been used for the discovery of decision rules that accommodate exceptions and hierarchies. Section 3 is devoted to the work related to discovery of exceptions and hierarchies using the knowledge structures described in this paper. Section 4 concludes the paper.

2. Knowledge Structures for the Discovery of Exceptions and Hierarchies

Researchers have used various innovative knowledge structures for the discovery of exceptions or/and hierarchies like Rule Triplet, Censored Production Rules (CPRs), Exception Directed Acyclic Graphs (EDAGs), Ripple Down Rules (RDRs), Hierarchical Ripple Down Rules (HRDRs), Hierarchical Production Rules (HPRs), Hierarchical Censored Production Rules (HCPR) and Censored Production Rules with Fuzzy Hierarchy (CPRFH). A brief description of each of the above knowledge structure is given below.

2.1 Rule Triplet

Suzuki has defined a rule triplet as a vehicle for the discovery of exceptions [1-5]. A Rule Triplet is collection of commonsense rule, exception rule and reference rule. Both commonsense rule and reference rule provide base for exception. Reference rule is rule of low support and/ or low confidence.

$r(x, x', Y, Z) \equiv (Y \rightarrow x,\ Y \wedge Z \rightarrow x',\ Z \rightarrow x')$

In the above rule, each of Y and Z represents a conjunction of atoms, an atom being an event representing a value assignment or a range assignment to an attribute. Here x and x′ have the same attribute but different values. We call $Y \rightarrow x$ a commonsense rule and $Y \wedge Z \rightarrow x'$ an exception rule and $Z \rightarrow x'$ a reference rule [2, 3]. Suzuki further argues that if $Z \rightarrow x'$ holds with high accuracy and support then the exception rule $Y \wedge Z \rightarrow x'$ exhibits low unexpectedness and the obtained pattern is often uninteresting. His approach assumes that $Z \rightarrow x'$ is a weak/negative rule i.e. x' seldom occurs given Z. The reference rule is given the representation as Z $\not\rightarrow$ x'. An example of such a rule triplet is given below Figure 1.

Commonsense rule: antibiotics → recovery
Exception rule: antibiotics ∧ staphylococci → death
Reference rule: staphylococci--/> death

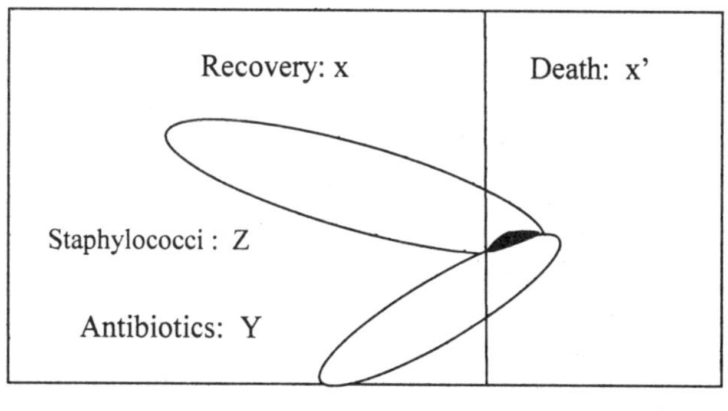

Fig. 1 Rule triplet

The interpretation of above rule is that most of the patients on antibiotics recover. Most of the patients on staphylococci also recover and there are very few counter examples. A combination of the antibiotics and staphylococci leads to certain death. Such rules are not only highly unexpected but are life saving also.

2.2 Exception Directed Acyclic Graphs (EDAGs)

EDAG is a knowledge structure that generalizes and subsumes production rules, decision trees, and rules with exceptions [6]. The structure is a directed acyclic graph with the semantics that nodes are premises, some of which have attached conclusions, and the arcs are inheritance links with disjunctive multiple inheritances. These generalizations allow substantially smaller knowledge structures to be generated than either rules or trees alone, and overcome problems of trees in dealing with disjunctive concepts involving replication of sub-trees. EDAG inference is computationally simple, even under conditions of partial information, and its simplicity should make it easily understood by people. A complexity measure has also been developed to analyze and compare EDAGs on uniform basis. The reader may refer to [6] for the detail operational interpretation of an EDAG.

A part of EDAG for the lens dataset is shown in Figure 2. Lenses are none is default decision but if astigmatic is 'not astigmatic' then soft lenses; and if astigmatic is 'astigmatic' then hard lens. Further down the lens is none if prescription is 'hypermetrope'. Please note that the conclusion changes as new attributes appears in the premise.

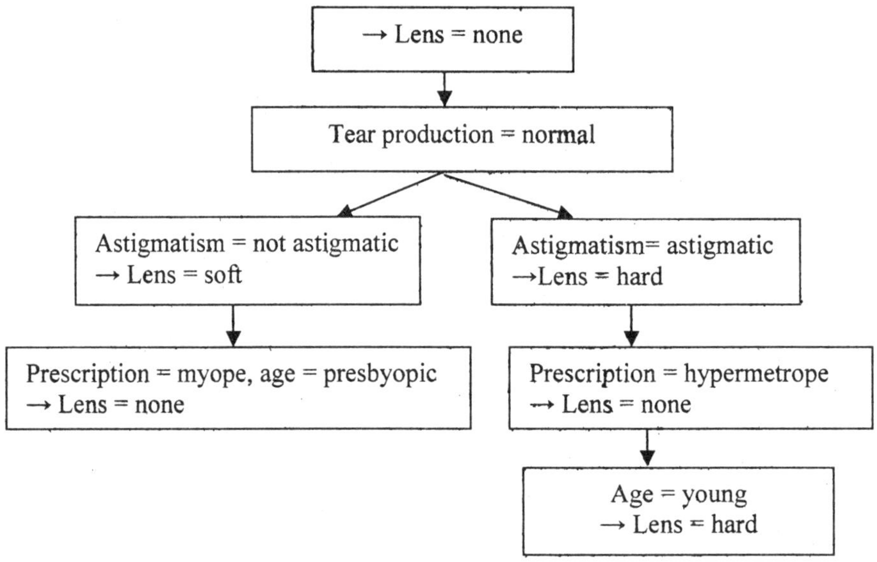

Fig. 2 EDAG for lens dataset

2.3 Ripple- Down Rule

Ripple Down Rules (RDRs) represent the exception rules in a concise manner in order to keep all general rules consistent. RDRs have exactly the same representational and deductive capabilities as standard production rules. RDR is a rule with hierarchical exceptions and has the following structure [7].

If condition *Then* conclusion *Except*

If ..*Then*..*Except*

If.....

Else if

If premise is true then conclusion is taken only if *Except* part is not true. If premise part of a RDR is true and the condition in the *Except* part is also true then the decision will be made on the basis of *Except* part. If premise is false then *Else* part will be considered for decision.

An example of a simple RDR is given in Figure 3. RDRs provide a well intelligible and modifiable representation even for very large expert systems and allow for very simple and rapid knowledge acquisition [8]. A RDR is unable to capture taxonomical structure inherent in the classes involved and hence not able to impart control over the specificity part of a precision in decision making [9].The rules and exception are nested and, nesting beyond a level compromises the comprehensibility of the rule compared to a CPR which accommodates all exceptions at one level.

If Bird *Then* Fly *Except*
If Young Bird *Then* Not Fly *Except*
If Penguin *Then* Not Fly *Except*
If penguin-in-plain *Then* fly
Else If Airplane *Then* Fly *Except*
If Engine failure Then Not Fly *Except*
If Airplane has more engines *Then* Fly *Except*

Fig. 3 Ripple down rules

2.4 Censored Production Rule

Censored Production Rules (CPRs) are PRs augmented with exception(s)/censors and were proposed by Michalski and Winston [10]. A Censored Production Rule (CPR) is of the form: *If* P *Then* D *Unless* C. In this rule P is the premise part and is a conjunction of attribute-value pairs. C may contain a single exception/censor or it may be disjunction of exceptions/censors. The '*If* P *Then* D' part of a CPR holds frequently and the censor C holds rarely. Therefore the *Unless* operator acts like an exclusive OR operator between decision and censor but it has an expositive aspect which is not commutative. To capture this asymmetry precisely, two parameters are associated with this kind of rule structure

$$\textit{If}\ P \rightarrow D\ \textit{Unless}\ C: \gamma_1: \gamma_2$$

$\gamma_1 = \Pr[P,D]/\Pr[P] = \Pr[D|P] = \Omega_{PD}/\Omega_P$

$\gamma_2 = \Pr[P,C]/\Pr[P] = \Pr[C|P] = \Omega_{PC}/\Omega_P$

Where Ω_{PD} is subset of events for which both P and D hold, Ω_{PC} is subset of events for which both P and C hold and Ω_P is the subset of the events for which P holds. The main constraints on CPR are that $\Omega_{PD} \cap \Omega_{PC} = \varphi$, $\Omega_{PD} \cup \Omega_{PC} = \Omega_P$, $\gamma_1 + \gamma_2 <= 1$ and $\gamma_1 >> \gamma_2$. The example of such a CPR is as follows:

If bird → fly (0.99) □ penguin (0.002) □ kiwi (0.001) □ emu (0.0005). Here $\gamma_1 = 0.99$ and $\gamma_2 = 0.002$, 0.001 and 0.0005 and $\gamma_1 >> \gamma_2$. $\gamma_1 + \gamma_2$ is slightly less than 1 because some of the censors may not be present in this rule. A CPR of above type enables us to express the assertion that most of the birds fly but there are exceptional birds that don't. It is to be noted that *If* bird → penguin □ fly is not a CPR.

'*If* P *Then* D' part of the CPR expresses commonsense rule and the Unless C part acts as a switch and changes the polarity of D to ~D whenever it holds true. We are free to ignore a censor/exception condition if the resources are scarce to establish its presence or simply no information is available as to whether the censor holds true or not. Given more time, the censor condition is evaluated lending more certainty to the high speed decision if the censor does not hold, or negating the decision if the censor holds true. Take another example of the following CPR:

If [X lives_in_city Y)] *Then* X is_in_city Y (0.9) *Unless* on_tour (0.05)

Now, consider a query "where is X?" The quickest possible answer is that 'X is_in_city Y' with a confidence level of 90 percent. By taking into account that X is not on tour, we can conclude with more certainty that 'X is_in_city Y' as the confidence factor increases up to a level of 95 percent. There are hardly any rules that shall hold universally. Usually, there exist exceptional cases where a rule that has worked well in past is not applicable. Whenever a new exception is discovered, it can be incorporated in a CPR easily. Thus, a CPR is a comprehensible and dynamic knowledge structure to accommodate exceptions as and when they are discovered. A CPR as an underlying knowledge representation for a reasoning system is capable of exhibiting variable precision logic in which certainty varies while specificity remains constant. However, a CPR is unable to capture the hierarchical structure inherent in the real world knowledge and hence would not impart control over the specificity part of precision in the decision making. To address this shortcoming of the CPR Bharadwaj and Jain have introduced Hierarchical Censored Production Rules [11, 12].

2.5 Hierarchical Censored Production Rule

A Hierarchical Censored Production Rule (HCPR) is a Censored Production rule augmented with specificity information which can be made to exhibit variable precision in the reasoning such that both certainty of belief in a conclusion and its specificity may be controlled by the reasoning process [11, 12].

< Decision> *If* (precondition)
Unless (censor-conditions)
Generality (general-information)
Specificity (specific-information)

A HCPR has the above form:

The generality gives the clue about the next general concept in hierarchy and specificity gives the specific concept related to the decision class under consideration. Figure 4 shows an example set of HCPRs:

X is_in_city Y *If* [X lives_in_city Y] (0.9) *Unless* on_tour (0.05)
Generality[ ]
Specificity[X is_at_home, X is_outside_home]
X is_at_home *If* [time_is_night] (0.95) *Unless* doing_overtime (0.005)
Generality[X is_in_city Y]
Specificity[ ]
X is_outside_home if [time_is_day] (0.96) *Unless* is_ill (0.002)
Generality[X is_in_city Y]
Specificity[ ]

Fig. 4 A set of HCPRs

Assuming 'X is_in_city Y' is true we can consider the additional fact that the 'time_is_night' to reach a more specific conclusion 'X is_at_home'.

It is clear from above example that HCPRs can be used to handle trade-offs between the precision of an inference and its computational efficiency leading to control of the certainty of conclusion and its specificity. A HCPR based system provides a general framework for intelligent systems that supports variable precision logic, excellent mechanism for handling exceptions, various machine learning paradigms and various inference mechanisms [12]. HCPR based systems would have applications where decisions must be taken under resource constraints (time/space) with uncertain information.

The related HCPRs can further be fused together to generate a HCPRs tree. A HCPR tree is a collective and systematic representation of all the related HCPRs about a given problem domain [11, 13]. Here, the term collective means the set of all rules or definitions related to a most generalized concept in the knowledge base. A HCPR in a HCPR's tree is the smallest chunk of knowledge that may be created modified or removed without directly affecting the other HCPRs in the HCPR-tree. A HCPRs-tree about the domain 'where is X' is depicted in Figure 5. Only the decision classes are shown in the tree and, the precondition and censor parts are left out for the sake of simplicity. In HCPRs-tree any HCPR is a more specific case of its parent HCPR. The root represents the most generalized concept.

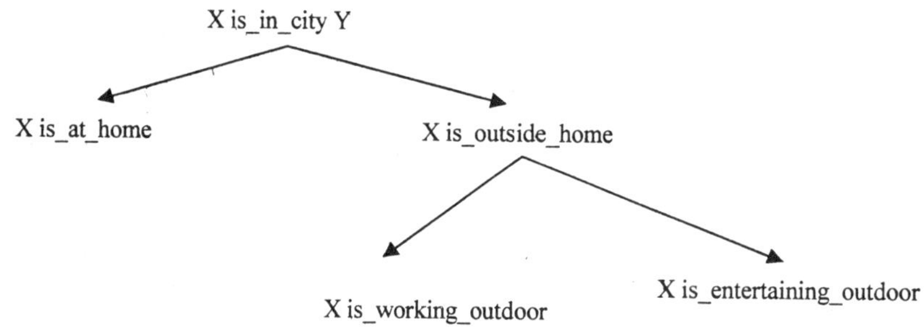

Fig. 5 HCPRs-tree HCPRs tree

Once this is verified we can descend to its children for more specific information depending upon our requirement and resources. If a HCPRs gets blocked by any of its preconditions being false or any of the censors/exceptions being true then all the HCPRs below it are also blocked and no further search of its children is necessary. HCPRs trees related to common concept can be fused together using fusion and fission algorithms for dynamic restructuring of the rule base. During the process of dynamic restructuring HCPRs systems are capable of learning new concepts [12].

2.6 Censored Production Rules with Fuzzy Hierarchy

In a HCPR, if D_1 is the general class of D_2 then the set of properties in the premise of D_1 is a proper subset of the set of properties in the premise of D_2. Censored Production Rules with Fuzzy Hierarchy (CPRFHs) include the possibility of fuzzy hierarchies where the general and specific classes share quite some number of properties but neither is a proper subset of the other[14, 15]. Degree of subsumption and coefficient of similarity have been used as quantitative measures for the fuzzy hierarchical relationships among the classes. Degree of subsumption decides the relationship of generality and specificity keeping in view the coverage of the common properties in the classes under consideration [14, 15]. Coefficient of similarity decides the relationship of generality and specificity keeping in view the matching and non-matching properties in the classes under consideration [15]. A typical CPRFH is given below:

D_1 *If* [Premise(0.8)]
Unless [C_1 □ C_2 □...]
Generality[D_2(0.8, 0.54)]
Specificity[D_3 (0.8, 0.61), D_5(0.75, 0.62)]

The number next to the premise is the confidence of the rule (*If* P *Then* D). The numbers in the generality part show the degree of subsumption and coefficient of similarity respectively between the general class D_2 and the class under consideration D_1. The numbers in the specificity part are degree of subsumption and coefficient of similarity between D_1 and its specific classes D_3 and D_5 respectively. . The corresponding tree structure for above CPRFH is given in figure 6. CPRFHs trees can be generated on the same pattern as HCPRs and have all the properties of HCPRs systems in addition to fuzzy hierarchies.

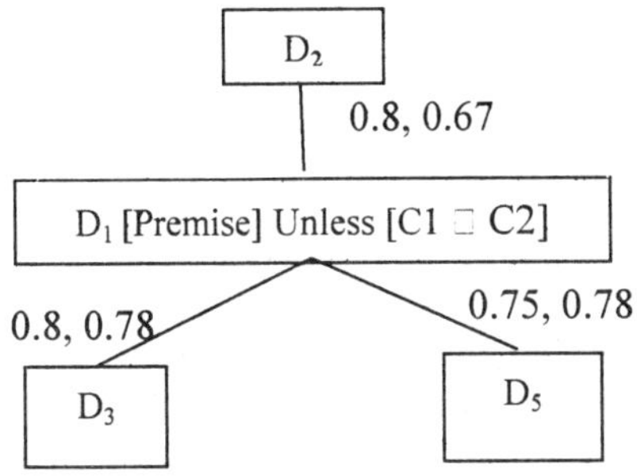

Fig. 6 Tree structure of a CPRFH

A lot of work has been done in the field of exception discovery. Discovery methods for exceptions fall into two categories from the view point of background knowledge. In a directed approach the user provides the commonsense rule from his experience/knowledge of domain and then the discovery method obtains exceptions that deviate from the user specified rules [18, 19, 20, 21]. Silberschatz and Tuzhilin proposed evaluation functions for subjective interestingness of discovered pattern [18]. Their evaluation function mainly considers unexpectedness of the discovered pattern as compared to a set of user's belief. Tuzhilin and Padmanabhan have proposed a method for exception discovery that defines the unexpectedness as a logical contradiction of a rule to a set of beliefs (commonsense rules) [19]. Liu et al. have proposed a language in which the user can express domain knowledge as impressions, and an algorithm that discovers exceptions on the basis of input impressions [20]. Directed methods are useful in discovering rules each of which is unexpected from the user point of beliefs and obviously suffer from users' subjective biases or their lack of expertise about the domain. In undirected approach no background knowledge is provided and the data mining algorithm itself discovers rule pairs each of which consists of a commonsense rule and its corresponding exception rules [1, 2, 4, 22, 23]. Exceptions have low support and high confidence. That is why exceptions can only be discovered at a low threshold for support. However a low threshold for support results into discovery of a huge number of other rules that may not be interesting. In this context, Hussain and Suzuki have provided the objective and unbiased (from users' belief point of view) measure of the interestingness of a newly discovered rule in relation to already mined commonsense rules [24]. Many other studies in interesting rule discovery focus on unexpectedness by finding exception rules, each of which represents a different regularity from domain knowledge or a set of strong rules [25]. Suzuki and Shimura [26] have given an undirected discovery method MEPRO that discover rule pair and is based on rule discovery system ITRULE [27]. In this method, several undirected methods are proposed, each of which obtains rule pairs [1, 2, 22, 23, 26]. Discovery of pairs of commonsense and exception rules under threshold scheduling has been successful in the efficient discovery of interesting rules from financial data which has been provided as a benchmark dataset for data mining methods [28].Though the undirected approach for the exception discovery is free from users' biases its complexity is higher than the directed approach as it suffers from extra search for strong rules.

Zytkow and Suzuki have further proposed a meta-pattern representation of rule triplet and a unified algorithm for systematic generation of all types of exceptions [2, 3]. Its effectiveness is proved with 15 real world datasets form UCI machine learning data repository [3].

Gaines (1991) shows that ripple-down rules are a particular case of rules with exceptions that can encode some knowledge structures more compactly [7, 8]. A key feature of RDR is that rules are never modified or deleted, but locally patched. Suryanto, Richards and Compton have worked on removing the redundancy from the RDR knowledge base. They experimented on a pathology knowledge base and the algorithm is applicable to any multiple classification RDR knowledge based system [29]. Two knowledge structures, Ripple Down Rules and HCPRs are combined and a new knowledge structure Hierarchical Ripple Down Rules (HRDRs) is proposed by Fadl and Bharadwaj [9]. HRDRs join the best features of RDR and HCPR. A Censored Production Rule (CPR) is an excellent knowledge structure that supports an efficient mechanism for handling exceptions and exhibit variable precision logic with regard to certainty [10]. Basheer and Bharadwaj have proposed an evolutionary approach to discover CPRs [30]. A parallel genetic algorithm approach has been suggested for discovery of exceptions in the form of CPRs by Saroj and Bharadwaj [31, 32]. Bharadwaj and Kandwal have successfully applied a post processing scheme to combine the discovered PRs into CPRs. They have been able to reduce the size of rule sets increasing its comprehensibility [33].

A Hierarchical Censored Production Rule (HCPR), suggested by Bharadwaj and Jain, is a Censored Production rule augmented with specificity information. A HCPR not only accommodates exceptions but it also contains the general and specific concepts related to the class under consideration. Fusion and fission algorithms to facilitate automatic restructuring of the HCPRs to ensure consistency and minimum redundancy have also been devised. Many features that are related to good quality knowledge structures namely general control scheme, variable precision logic, dynamic restructuring and small rule repair have already been addressed for the HCPRs systems [12, 13]. Bharadwaj and Hewahi have given a genetic algorithm approach for adaptive HCPRs based systems [34]. A parallel reasoning approach using HCPRs as underlying knowledge structure has also been depicted [35, 36]. Recently evolutionary approaches have been productively implemented for the discovery of CPRs, HPRs, HCPRs and CPRFHs [14, 15, 30, 31, 35, 36]. The rule sets discovered in the above works have been of smaller size and more comprehensible with exceptions and hierarchies inbuilt in the discovered knowledge. A HCPR is particularly suitable knowledge structure for discovery of knowledge form data streams as a dynamic restructuring of the discovered knowledge is required to address the issue of concept drift [32]

4. Conclusions

This paper contains a comprehensible description of various interesting knowledge structure like Rule Triplet, CPRs, EDAGS, RDRs, HCPRs and CPRFHs for the discovery of exception as well as hierarchies. We have fruitfully offered a one place package to have a good deal of information about some interesting knowledge structures that accommodate hierarchies and exceptions. We have stressed not only the theoretical description of various knowledge structures but have also explained them with the help of examples so that this work becomes more comprehensible and useful. We have also reviewed research work carried out on various knowledge structures. Rule Triplet and CPRs are effective knowledge structures for exception discovery. RDR has been in use in some of the most prominent rule based systems like ConveyIT, Oncology Decision Support Tool and expert systems. HCPRs and CPRFHs are sound and intelligent knowledge structures that hold promises for approximate reasoning and reasoning under resource constraints.

5. References

[1] E. Suzuki, "Undirected Discovery of Interesting Exception Rules", International Journal of Pattern Recognition and Artificial Intelligence, vol. 16, august,pp. 1065-1086, 2002.

[2] E. Suzuki, and J.M. Zytkow, "Unified Algorithm for Undirected Discovery of Exception Rules", Principles of Data Mining and Knowledge Discovery LNAI 1910 (PKDD), Springer, Berlin, pp. 169-180, 2000.

[3] E. Suzuki, and J.M. Zytkow, "Unified Algorithm for Undirected Discovery of Exception Rules", International Journal of Intelligent Systems, vol. 20, July, pp. 673-691, 2005.

[4] E. Suzuki, and M. Shimura, "Exceptional Knowledge Discovery in Databases Based on Information Theory", Proc. Second Int'l Conf. Knowledge Discovery and Data Mining (KDD), Portland, august 2-4, pp. 275-278, 1996.

[5] E. Suzuki, "Data Mining Methods for Discovering Interesting Exceptions from an Unsupervised Table", Journal of Universal Computer Science, vol. 12, June, pp. 627-653, 2006.

[6] B.R. Gaines, "Transforming Rules and Trees into Comprehensible Knowledge Structures", Advances in Knowledge Discovery and Data mining, American Association for Artificial Intelligence, Menlo Park, CA, pp. 205-226, 1996.

[7] B.R. Gains, and P. Compton, "Induction of Ripple Down Rules Applied to Modeling Large Database", Journal of Intelligent Information System, vol. 5, pp. 211- 228, 1995.

[8] T. Scheffer, "Algebraic Foundation and Improved Methods of Induction of Ripple Down Rules", Second Pacific Knowledge Acquisition Workshop, Sydney, pp. 279-292, 1996.

[9] M. Fadl, Ba-Alwi, and K. K. Bharadwaj, "Automated Discovery of Hierarchical Ripple Down Rules (HRDRs)", Proceedings of the 23rd IASTED, Innsbruck, Austria, 2005.

[10] R.S. Michalski, and P.H. Winston, "Variable Precision Logic", Artificial Intelligence, vol. 29, pp. 121-146, 1986.

[11] K.K. Bharadwaj, and N.K. Jain, "Hierarchical Censored Production Rules (HCPRs) System", Data and Knowledge Engineering, vol. 8, pp. 19-34, 1992.

[12] K.K. Bharadwaj, and N. K. Jain, "Some Learning Techniques in Hierarchical Censored Production Rules (HCPRs) System", International Journal of Intelligent Systems, vol. 13, pp. 319-344, 1997.

[13] N. K. Jain, K. K. Bharadwaj, and N. Marranghello, "Extended Hierarchical Censored Production Rules (EHCPRs) System: An approach towards generalized knowledge representation", Journal of Intelligent Systems, pp. 259-295, 1999.

[14] K.K. Bharadwaj, B. M. AlMaqaleh, and M. Basheer, "Evolutionary Approach for Automated Discovery of Censored Production Rules with Fuzzy Hierarchy", International Multi-conference of Engineers and Computer Scientists, Hong Kong, pp. 716-721, 2007.

[15] Saroj, and K. K. Bharadwaj, "A Parallel Genetic Programming Approach for Automated Discovery of Censored Production Rules with Fuzzy Hierarchy", International Conference on Information processing, Bangalore, India, 2008.

[16] H. Suryanto, and P. Compton, "Learning Classification Taxonomies from a Classification Knowledge Based System", Proceedings of the First Workshop on Ontology Learning in Conjunction with ECAI, Berlin, pp. 1-6, 2000.

[17] S. Tsumoto, "Mining Diagnostic Rules from Clinical Databases Using Rough Set and Medical Diagnostic Model", Information Science, vol. 162, pp. 65-80, 2004.

[18] A. Silberschatz, and A. Tuzhilin, "What Makes Patterns Interesting in Knowledge Discovery Systems", IEEE Trans. Knowledge Discovery and Data Engineering, vol. 8, June, pp. 970-974, 1996.

[19] B. Padmanabhan, and A. Tuzhilin, "A Belief-Driven Method for Discovering Unexpected Patterns", Proc. Fourth Int'l Conf. Knowledge Discovery and Data Mining (KDD), New York, august 27-31, pp. 94-100, 1998.

[20] B. Liu, W. Hsu, and S. Chen, "Using General Impressions to Analyze Discovered Classification Rules", 3rd International Conference on Knowledge Discovery and Data Mining (KDD), Newport Beach, California, august 14-17, pp. 31-36,1997.

[21] A. Silberschatz, and A.Tuzhilin, "On Subjective Measures of Interestingness in Knowledge Discovery", Proceedings of the First International Conference on Knowledge Discovery and Data Mining, Montreal, august 20-21, pp. 275-281, 1995.

[22] E. Suzuki, "Autonomous Discovery of Reliable Exceptions Rules", In Proc. Of the 3rd International Conference on Knowledge Discovery and Data Mining, Newport Beach, California, august 14-17, pp. 259-262, 1997.

[23] E. Suzuki, "Discovering Unexpected Exceptions: A Stochastic Approach", Fourth International Workshop on Rough Sets, Fuzzy Sets, and Machine Discovery (RSFD), Tokyo, Japan, November 6-8, pp. 225-232,1996.

[24] F. Hussain, H. Liu, E. Suzuki, and H. Lu, "Exception Rule Mining with a Relative Interestingness Measure", Knowledge Discovery and Data Mining (PAKDD), LNAI 1805, Springer, pp. 86-97, 2000.

[25] H. Liu, H. Lu, L. Feng, and F. Hussain, "Efficient Search of Reliable Exceptions", In Proc. Third Pacific- Asia Conference on Knowledge Discovery and Data Mining(PAKDD), Berlin, pp. 194-203, 1999.

[26] E. Suzuki, and M. Shimura, "Exceptional Knowledge Discovery in Databases Based on Information Theory", Proc. Second Int'l Conf. Knowledge Discovery and Data Mining (KDD), Portland, august 2-4, pp. 275-278, 1996.

[27] P. Smyth, and R.M. Goodman, "An Information Theoretic Approach to Rule Induction from Databases", IEEE Trans .Knowledge and Data Engineering, vol. 4, pp. 301-316, 1992.

[28] E. Suzuki, "Mining Financial Data with Scheduled Discovery of Exception rules", Proc. Discovery Challenge 2000, September, 2000.

[29] H. Suryanto, D. Richards, and P. Compton, "The Automatic Compression of Multiple Classification Ripple Down Rule Knowledge Based Systems: Preliminary Experiments", 3rd International Conference Knowledge-Based Intelligent Information Engineering Systems, Adelaide, South Australia, pp. 203-206, 1999.

[30] K.K. Bharadwaj, and B. M. Almaqaleh, "Evolutionary Approach for Automated Discovery of Censored Production Rules", Proc. of World Academy of Science, Engineering and Technology, vol. 10, ISSN 1307- 6884, 2005.

[31] Saroj, and K.K. Bharadwaj, "A Parallel Genetic Algorithm Approach for Automated Discovery of Censored Production Rules", Proc. Artificial Intelligence and Application, 2007.

[32] Saroj, and K.K Bharadwaj, " Distributed Mining of Censored Production Rules in Data Streams", Proceedings of the 7th WSEAS International conference on Artificial Intelligence, Knowledge Engineering and databases (AIKED'08)", University of Cambridge, UK, 2008.

[33] R. Kandwal, and K.K. Bharadwaj, "A Cumulative Learning Approach to Data Mining Employing Censored Production Rules (CPRs)", Enformatika 7, 2005.

[34] K.K. Bharadwaj, N.K. Jain, and N. M. Hawai, "Adaptive Hierarchical Censored Production Rules system: A Genetic Algorithm Approach", Advances in Artificial Intelligence SBIA'96', Curitiba, pp. 81-90, 1996.

[35] K.K. Bharadwaj, and R. Varshneya, "Parallelisation of Hierarchical Censored Production Rules", Information and Software Technology, vol. 37(8), pp. 453-460, 1995.

[36] Saroj, and K.K Bharadwaj, "A Parallel Genetic Algorithm Approach to Automated Discovery of Hierarchical Production Rules", Accepted for World Online Conference on Soft Computing, November, 2008.

Analysis of Human Face through Fuzzy Based Simulated Model

R. Ramya[1] and R.Priya[2]

[1]Senior Lecturer, Dept of CSE, Bharathiyar College of Engineering and Technology, Karaikal, (Pondicherry State).
(Research scholar Dr. MGR Educational And Research Institute Chennai)
ramyamagesh25@rediffmail.com

[2]Lecturer, Department of Software Engineering and Information Technology,
A.V.C College of Engineering, Mayiladuthurai,
Mannampandal–609305, Nagapattinam District, Tamil Nadu, S. India.
priyaraji_2002@yahoo.co.in

Abstract

In the present paper we define the extraction of appropriate facial features and consequent recognition that can be robust to facial expression variations among different samples. Facial features and expressions are critical to everyday communication. Besides speaker recognition, face assists a number of cognitive tasks. Extracting and validating emotional cues through fuzzy analysis of users' facial expressions is of high importance for improving the level of interaction of man and machine communication systems. Facial animation with various parameters. A novel Neuro fuzzy system is then created, based on rules that have been defined through analysis of FAP variations both at the discrete emotional space, as well as in the 2D and 3D continuous activation–evaluation one. The Neuro fuzzy system allows for further learning and adaptation to specific users' facial expression characteristics, measured though FAP estimation in real life application of the system, using analysis by clustering of the obtained FAP values.

Keywords: *Facial expression analysis; MPEG-4 facial animation parameters; Activation evaluation emotion representation; Neuro fuzzy network; Rule extraction; Adaptation, Back Propagation Algorithm.*

1. Introduction

Human face is tells about the human being and so many communication and prediction can be done through the face such as via lip reading and etc various expressions come on to the face of human being in different situations. Interpersonal communication is for the most part completed via the face. Facial expressions are generated by contractions of facial muscles. Facial features such as eyelids, eyebrows and lips, often indicated by wrinkles. Hence, one can model a particular expression as a set of given concurrent deformations, facial expression intensities may be measured by determining the geometric deformation of the particular facial features and examining their relation to the ones depicted in the priori represented expressions; barring situations of extreme or acted expressions, in most circumstances more than one of these representations may be close enough to the actual measurements. An overview of the methodologies used for automatic analysis of facial expression representation, an important parameter of this approach is the effectiveness of the image processing procedures. In actual situations, such as processing visual data from talk shows, many kinds of noise may hinder feature extraction. The easiest (and safest) way for an expression recognizers to get around would be to provide no label for the given sequence. However, the lack of evidence for a particular feature being deformed, when this feature is used in the representation of an expression, should not always be considered as absence of this feature: it may be attributed to a mistake of the image processing algorithms. A flexible recognizers should be able to handle the absence of information or evidence and incorporate it into the final estimate. In this paper, we describe the .uncertainty generated during the image processing for feature extraction phase through validation of the results against a set of anthropometric criteria and propose a methodology based on which fuzzy rules containing knowledge on expression analysis and estimation can be evaluated in an uncertain environment. the evaluation of the fuzzy rules representing the mapping between measure features and estimated expression, given the uncertainty contained in the input provided by the image processing.

2. Preliminaries

Activation–emotion space is a representation that is both simple and capable of capturing a wide range of significant issues in expression. It rests on a simplified treatment of two key themes.

1. **Valence:** The clearest common element of emotional and expressional states is that the person is materially influenced by feelings that

are 'valence', i.e., they are centrally concerned with positive or negative evaluations of people, or things or events; the link between emotion, expression and valence is widely agreed.

2. **Activation level:** Research has recognized that emotional and expressional states involve dispositions to act in certain ways. A basic way of reflecting that theme turnout to be surprisingly useful. States are simply rated in terms of the associated activation level, i.e., the strength of the person's disposition to take some action rather than none. The axes of the activation–evaluation space reflect those themes. The vertical axis shows activation level, the horizontal axis evaluation. A basic attraction of that arrangement is that it provides a way of describing emotional and expressional states which is more tractable than using words, but which can be translated into and out of verbal descriptions. Translation is possible because emotion-related words can be understood, at least to a first approximation, as referring to positions in activation–emotion space. A surprising amount of emotional discourse can be captured in terms of activation–emotion space circular pattern. From that and related evidence, work presented in which shows that there is a circular structure inherent in emotionality. In this framework, identifying the centre as a natural origin has several implications. Emotional strength can be measured as the distance from the origin to a given point in activation–evaluation space. The concept of a full-blown expression can then be translated roughly as a state where emotional and expressional strength has passed a certain limit. An interesting implication is that strong expressions are more sharply distinct from each other than weaker expressions with the same emotional orientation. A related extension is to think of primary or basic expressions as cardinal points on the periphery of an expression circle.

Plutchik has offered a useful formulation of that idea, the 'emotion wheel'; the emotion wheel is presented in.

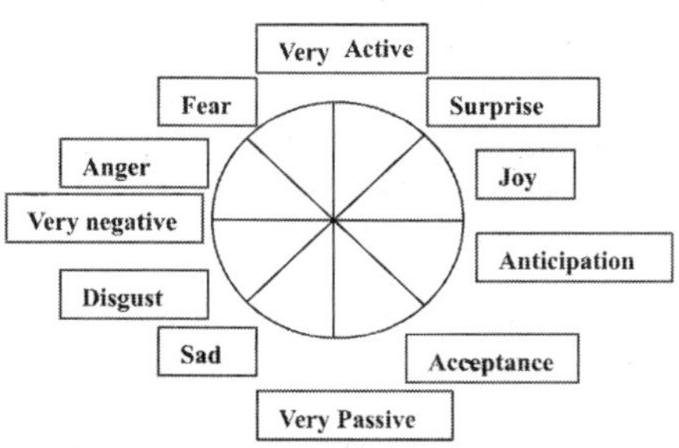

Fig. 1 The activation–emotion space

3. Facial Expression Recognition

Ekman and Friesen find six universal facial expressions that are expressed and interpreted in the same way by humans of any origin all over the world. They do not depend on the cultural background or the country of origin. Figure shows one example of each facial expression. The Facial Action Coding System (FACS) precisely describes the muscle activity within a human face .So-called Action Units denote the motion of particular facial parts and state the involved facial muscles. Combinations of AUs assemble facial expressions. Extended systems such as the Emotional FACS specify the relation between facial expressions and emotions.

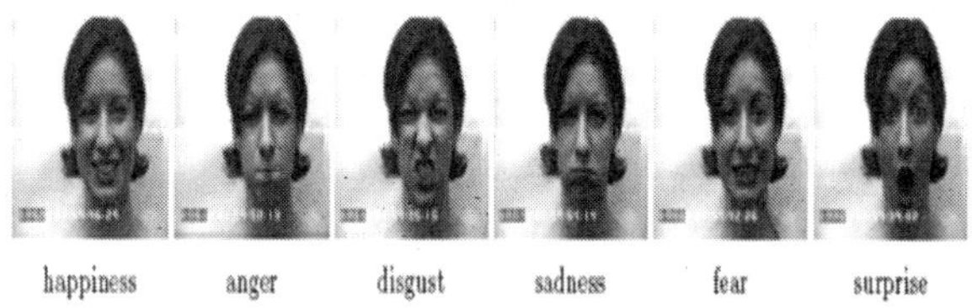

Fig. 2 Different Facial Expression

The Cohn–Kanade Facial Expression Database (CKDB) contains a number of 488 short image sequences of 97 different persons showing the six universal facial expressions. It provides researchers with a large dataset for experiment and benchmarking. Each sequence shows a neutral face at the beginning and then happiness anger disgust sadness fear surprise.

Procedure for recognizing facial expressions according to Pantic develops into the peak expression. Furthermore, a set of AUs has been manually specified by licensed FACS experts for each sequence. Note that this database does not contain natural facial expressions, but volunteers were asked to act them. Furthermore, the image sequences are taken in a laboratory environment with predefined illumination conditions, solid background and frontal face views. Algorithms that perform well with these image sequences are not necessarily appropriate for real-world scenes.

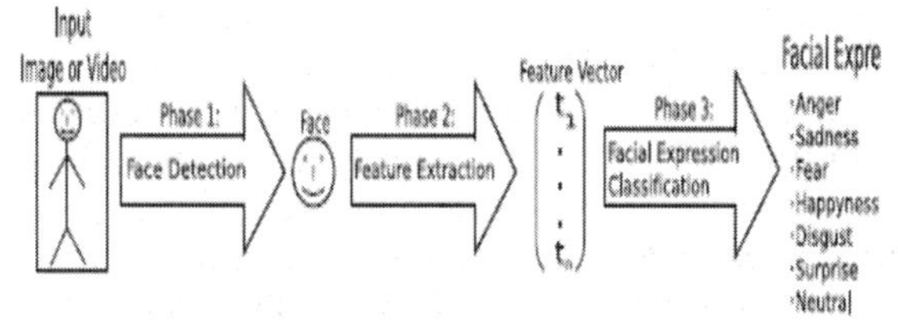

Fig. 3 The six universal facial expressions as they occur in

4. Model-based Interpretation of Facial Expressions

Our approach makes use of model-based techniques, which exploit a priori knowledge about objects, such as their shape or texture. Reducing the large amount of image data to a small set of model parameters facilitates and accelerates the subsequent facial expression interpretation, which mitigates the computational problems often associated with model–based approaches to FER. According to the usual configuration [4], our model-based approach consist of seven components, which are illustrated in Figure This approach fits well into the three-phase procedure of Pantic where skin color extraction represents a pre-processing step, mentioned by Chibelushi . Phase 1 is contains by the core of model-based techniques: the model, localization, the fitting algorithm, and the objective function. Phase 2 consists of the facial feature extraction, and Phase 3 is the final step of facial expression classification

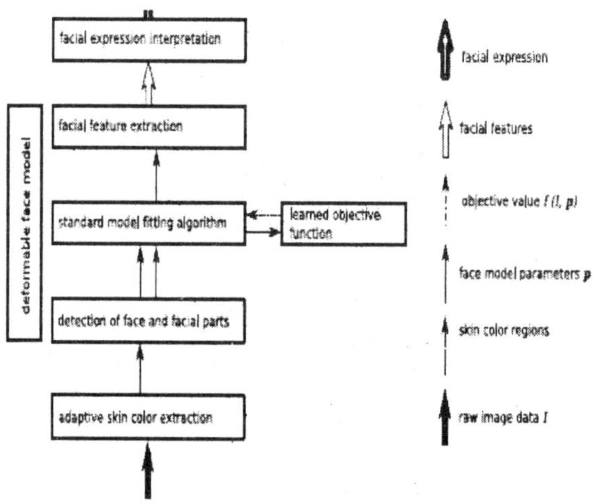

Fig. 4 Model-based image interpretation splits the challenge of image interpretation into computationally independent modules

5. Feature extraction

Feature expression representation, an important parameter of the expression analysis process is the effectiveness of the image processing procedures. Automatic analysis systems usually require good input to avoid errors, which is often ensured by the use of specific environment conditions In actual situations, such as processing visual data from talk shows, many kinds of noise may hinder feature extraction: subjects turning their heads, or moving their hands may lead to feature occlusion or bad and uneven lighting may hamper edge-or color-based feature extraction algorithms. The appearance and deformation of one or more features may not be available for a given frame of a picture, feature extraction is performed resulting in a set of masks, i.e., binary maps indicating the position and extent of each facial feature. The left, right, top and bottom-most coordinates of the eye and mouth masks, the left right and top coordinates of the eyebrow masks as well as the nose coordinates, are used to define the feature points. For the nose and each of the eyebrows, a single mask is created. On the other hand, since the detection of eyes and mouth can be problematic in low-quality images, a variety of methods is used, each resulting in a different mask. In total, we have four masks for each eye, three for the mouth and one for each one of the eyebrows. The methodologies applied in the extraction of following can be consider. A feed-forward back propagation neural network trained to identify eye and non-eye facial area. The network has 13 inputs; for each pixel on the facial region the NN inputs are luminance Y, chrominance values Cr and Cb and the ten most important DCT coefficients (with zigzag selection) of the neighboring 8 × 8 pixel area.

1. A second neural network, with similar architecture to the first one, trained to identify mouth regions.
2. Luminance based masks, which identify eyelid and sclera regions.
3. Edge-based masks.
4. A region growing approach based on standard deviation.

All detected masks have to be validated against a set of criteria; of course, different criteria are applied to masks of different facial features. Each one of the criteria verify the masks in order and decide whether they have acceptable size and position for the feature they represent. This set of criteria consist of relative anthropometric measurements, such as the relation of the eye and eyebrow vertical positions, which when applied to the corresponding masks produce a value in range [0,1] with zero denoting a totally invalid mask(false membership grade) in this manner, a validity confidence degree is generated for each one of the initial feature masks(true membership grade). For example, two criteria that can be used for the validation of the eye masks are the following:

$$M_{eye}^{1c} = 1 - \left| 1 - \frac{d_2/d_6}{0.49} \right| \quad (1)$$

$$M_{eye}^{2c} = 1 - \frac{|d_4|}{d_5} \quad (2)$$

where 1 2 Meyce and Meyce are the confidence degrees acquired through the application of each validation criterion on an eye mask. The former of the two criteria is based on where the ration of eye width over bipupil breadth is reported as constant and equal to 0.49. In almost all cases these validation criteria, as well as the other criteria utilized in mask validation, produce confidence values in the [0,1] range. In the rare cases that the estimated value exceeds the limits, it is set to the closest extreme value, 0 for negative values and one for values exceeding one. The features measured for the application of the two example criteria are explained in Table FAPs vocabulary for archetypal expression description

Joy F3, F4, F5, F6, F7, F12, F13, F19, F20, F21, F22, F33, F34, F41, F42, F53, F54

Sadness F19, F20, F21, F22, F31, F32, F33, F34, F35, F36

Anger F4, F5, F16, F18, F19, F20, F21, F22, F31, F32, F33, F34 , F35, F36, F37, F38

Fear F3, F4, F5, F8, F9, F10, F11, F19, F20, F21, F22, F31, F32, F33, F34, F35, F36, F37, F38

Disgust F3, F4, F5, F8, F9, F10, F11, F19, F20, F21, F22, F33, F34, F55, F56, F57, F58, F59, F60

Surprise F3, F5, F6, F7, F10, F11, F19, F20, F21, F22, F31, F32, F33, F34, F35, F36, F37, F38, F53, F54

Eye mask features used in the process of mask validation

d6- Bipupil breadth

d2- Eye width

d4- Distance of eye's middle vertical coordinate and eyebrow's middle vertical coordinate

d5 -Eyebrow width

The fusion algorithm is based on a Dynamic Committee Machine structure that combines the masks based on their validity confidence, thus producing a final mask together with the corresponding estimated confidence, and the confidence degree is always higher than the degree of any of the considered initial masks. Confidence for each feature mask is based on three parameters, absolute anthropometric measurements, face symmetry exploitation and examination of the facial feature size constancy over a period of ten frames. A way to evaluate our feature extraction performance is Williams' Index (WI), which compares the agreement of an observer with the joint agreement of other observers. An extended version of WI, which deals with multivariate data, can be found in Chalana and Kim. The modified Williams' Index I' divides the average number of agreements (inverse disagreements, Dj,j') between the computer (observer 0) and n – 1 human observers (j) by the average number of agreements between human observers:

$$WI = \frac{\frac{1}{n}\sum_{j=1}^{n}(1/D_{0,j})}{\frac{2}{n(n-1)}\sum_{j}\sum_{j':j'>j}(1/D_{j,j'})} \qquad (3)$$

and in our case we define the average disagreement between two observers j, j' as:

$$D_{j,j'} = \frac{1}{D_{bp}} \| M_j^x \veebar M_{j'}^x \| \qquad (4)$$

where ⊏ denotes the pixel-wise xor operator, || || xj M denotes the cardinality of feature mask x constructed by observer j, and Dbp (bipupil breadth) is used as a normalization factor to compensate for camera zoom on video sequences.

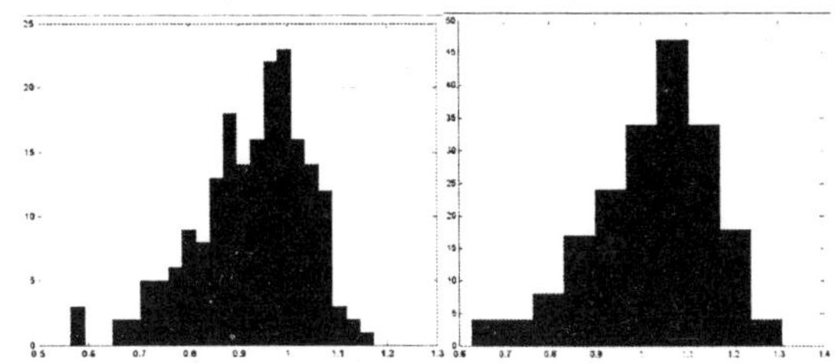

Fig. 5 Williams index distribution (average on eyes and mouth)

These feature masks are used to extract the Feature Points (FPs) considered in the definition of the FAPs used in this work. Each FP inherits the confidence level of the final mask from which it derives; the four FPs (top, bottom, left and right) of the left eye share the same confidence as the left eye final mask. As consider both sources of information for the estimation of the value of the FAP alleviates some of the initial uncertainty in the output. Thus, for cases in which two distinct definitions exist for an FAP, the final value and confidence for the FAP are as follows:

$Fi=Fi^1+ Fi^2/2$ (5)

The amount of uncertainty contained in each one of the distinct initial FAP calculations can be estimated by

$Ei^1 =1- Fi^{1c}$ (6)

The amount of uncertainty contained in each one of the distinct initial FAP calculations can be estimated by

$Ei^1 =1- Fi^{1c}$ (7)

for the first FAP and similarly for the other. The uncertainty present after combining the two can be given by some t-norm operation on the two:

$Ei^1 =t(Fi^{1c}.Ei^2)$ (8)

The Yager t-norm with parameter w = 5 gives reasonable results for this operation

$Ei= 1-\min\{(1,((1-Ei^1)^w +(1-Ei^2)^w))^w)\}$ (9)

The overall confidence value for the final estimation of the FAP is then acquired as

$Fi^c=1-Ei$ (10)

FAP measurements are transformed to antecedent values xj for the fuzzy rules using the fuzzy numbers defined for each FAP, and confidence degrees cj ,x are inherited from the FAP

$$x_j^{\ c} = Fi^c \quad (11)$$

where Fi is the FAP based on which antecedent xj is defined.

6. Possibilistic rule evaluation

In the process of exploiting the knowledge contained in the fuzzy rule base and the information extracted from each frame in the form of FAP measurements, with the aim to analyze and classify facial expressions, a series of issues has to be tackled

1. FAP degrees need to be considered in the estimation of the overall result
2. The case of FAPs that cannot be estimated, or equivalently are estimated with a low degree of confidence, needs to be considered.
3. The activation of contradicting rules needs to be considered.

A conventional approach to the evaluation of fuzzy rules of the form

IF $x_1, x_2, \ldots, x_n$ THEN y

is as follows

$$y = t(x_1, x_2, \ldots, x_n)$$

where t is a fuzzy t-norm, such as the minimum

$$t(x_1, x_2, \ldots, x_n) = \min(x_1, x_2, \ldots, x_n)$$

the algebraic product

$$t(x_1, x_2, \ldots, x_n) = x_1, x_2, \ldots, x_n$$

the bounded sum

$$t(x_1, x_2, \ldots, x_n) = x_1 + x_2 + \ldots + x_n$$

and so on. Another well-known approach in rule evaluation is described in Lee and Takagi and utilises a weighted sum instead of a t-norm in order to combine information from different rule antecedents.

$$y = w_1 x_1 + w_2 x_2 + \ldots\ldots\ldots + w_n x_n.$$

Both approaches are well studied and established in the field of fuzzy automatic control. Still, they are not adequate for the case of facial expression estimation: their main disadvantage is that they assume that all antecedents are known, i.e., that all features arem measured successfully and precisely. where the non-activation of an FAP automatically implies that the expression profiles that require it are not activated either. Therefore, the flexible rule evaluation scheme that we propose is in fact a generalizations of the t-norm based conventional approach. In the t-norm operation described in equation (16), antecedents with lower values affect most the resulting value of y, while antecedents with values close to 1 have trivial and negligible affect on the value of y. Having that in mind, we can demand that only antecedents that are known with a high confidence will be allowed to have low values in that operation. More formally, we demand that the degree k(x) to which antecedent x is considered in the operation is low, i.e., its complement c(k(x)) is high, only when the confidence xc with which the value of x is known is high and the value of x is low. This can be expressed as

$$c(\ k(x)) = t\ x_c\ c(x))$$

where c is a fuzzy complement. Applying De Morgan's law we have that the degree to which antecedent x is considered is

$$k(x) = u(c(x_c), x)$$

where u is a fuzzy s-norm. It is easy to see that equation (22) satisfies the desired marginal conditions (1) when $x_c \rightarrow 1$, then $c(x_c) \rightarrow 0$ and $k(x) \rightarrow x$, i.e., the antecedent is considered normally, $x_c \rightarrow 0$, then $c(x_c) \rightarrow 1$ and $k(x) \rightarrow 1$, i.e., the antecedent is not allowed to affect the overall evaluation of the rule. The formula that provides the overall evaluation assumed in this discussion is the one followed by the conventional approach, with the exception that antecedents participate with their considered values

$$y = t(k(x_1), k(x_2), \ldots, k(x_n)).$$

Thus, the activation level of a rule with this approach can be interpreted in a possibilistic manner, i.e., it can be interpreted as the degree to which the corresponding output is possible, according to the available information; in the literature, this possibilistic degree is referred to as plausibility. Dealing with feature uncertainty in facial expression recognition 13 The confidence is determined by the confidence values of the utilized inputs, i.e., by the confidence values of the rule antecedents, as follows The definition of y_c in this manner has the desired effect that $y_c = 0$ is equivalent to the complete lack of information, as it can only happen when all inputs are known with confidence zero; this property is essential in possibilistic reasoning. The complete possibilistic representation of the calculated output is provided as Bel = $t(y, y_c)$ Pl = y

The extreme cases are:

1. Bel = P_l = 1, which occurs when y = yc = 1 and implies absolute confidence that the specific profile is the one perfectly matching the observed face
2. Bel = P_l = 0, which occurs when y = 0 and implies absolute confidence that the specific profile is not one matching the observed face
3. Bel = 0, P_l = 1 which occurs when y = 1, $y_c = 0$ and implies absolute ignorance.

7. Experimental results

Facial expressions observed on real faces. As far as the knowledge of the system is concerned, facial expression information is coded using MPEG-4 FAPs and expressed through conventional fuzzy rules The evaluation of the fuzzy rules is also performed in the conventional manner. Figure presents frame A, one of the frames that lead the original prototype to failure. As we can see in Figure where the masks for the eyes detected using the various implemented approaches are presented, the utilized methodologies do not provide reliable eye region detection. As a consequence, the FAP specifications acquired using any of these approaches are unreliable and lead to poor performance of the expression classification component. When, on the other hand, we combine these masks, considering at the same time the confidence in their validity, which, as expected, allows The most important feature points detected on frame A, using the feature masks that resulted from the process of the fusion of multiple masks, are presented in Figure. The original prototype did not provide any output owing to the asymmetry in the detection of the eye related points, whereas the proposed methodology activates (to a high degree) the following three rules, all corresponding to profiles of the archetypal expression of joy.

Fig. 6 Original frame A

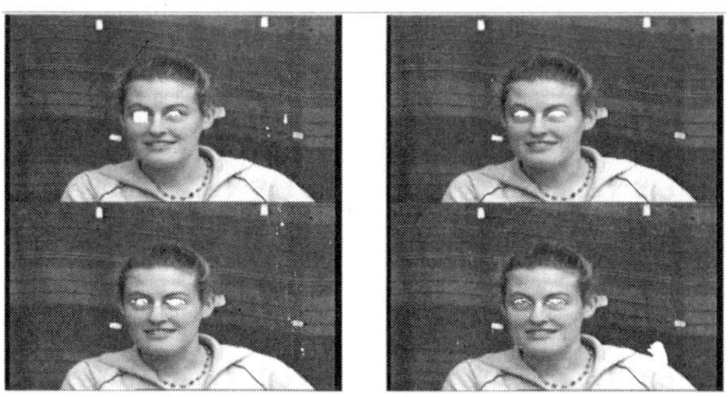

Fig. 7 Mask of Eyes In Frame A

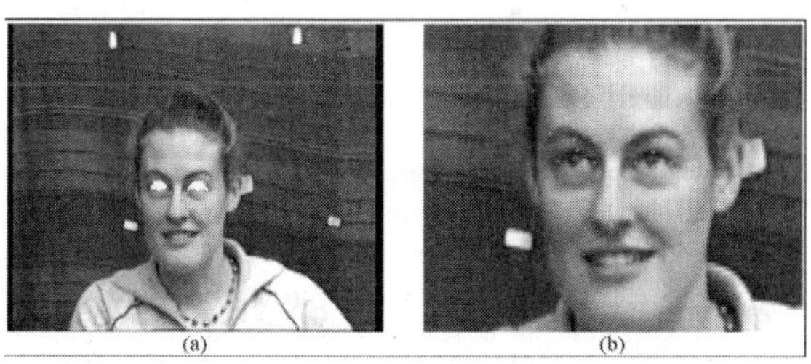

Fig. 8(a) Final mask for the eyes in frame A and (b) detected feature points on frame A

The overall results of the two evaluation approaches are defined by Table. We can see that although the conventional approach totally fails to provide any output, the proposed possibilistic approach both identifies quadrant one as the correct output and incorporates the inputs' uncertainty in the output.

Table 1 Summary of results Quadrant Ground truth Conventional Belief Plausibility

Quadrant	True value	Convent ional	Belief	Plausibility
1	1	0	0.21608	0.3015
2	0	0	0.06160	0.09135
3	0	0	.00238	0.00352
Neutral	0	0	<0.00001	<0.00001

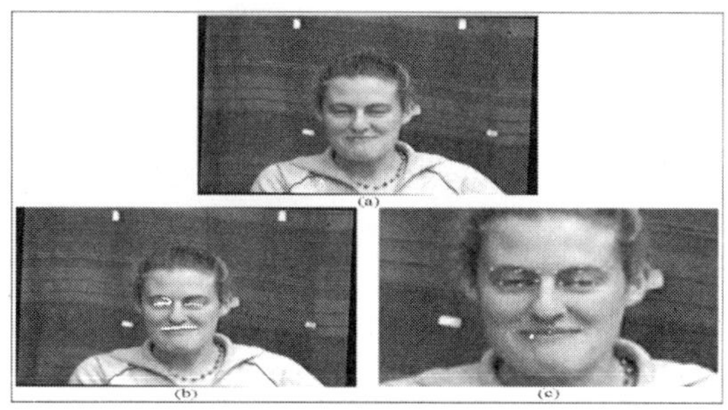

Fig. 9(a) Original frame B; (b) mouth and eyes mask for frame B and (c) detected feature points on frame B

As a last example, let us consider frame C, presented in Figure 9(a). The original prototype fails to provide any output in this frame as well, owing to the poor performance of the mouth detection algorithms. As can be seen in Figure (b) and (d) none of the utilized methodologies can lead to the successful estimation of the mouth region in frame C. Moreover, even fusion of the masks cannot overcome the problem, as is made evident in Figure (a), where the final mask for the mouth is presented. Main feature points detected in frame C are presented in Figure (b). Owing to the fact that in the considered frame sequence the observed person is speaking throughout the recording, all rules have been edited as to make all FAPs that are defined using the mouth as optional. Thus, even if the detected mask had proper size, shape and location in order to be validated against anthropometric criteria (which is not the case of the mask in Figure (a)), the unreliable FAP estimations it would provide would not be allowed to characterize a profile as definitely not present; during speech, all FAPs that are defined using the mouth are considered as unreliable owing to the fact that mouth feature point positions are determined by phonemes rather than disposition. Rules activated in this case correspond to profiles of the disgust, fear and anger archetypal expressions.

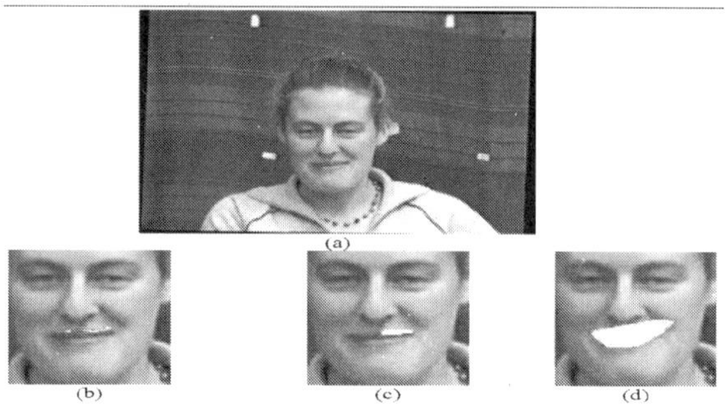

Fig. 10(a) Original frame and (b) and (d) mouth masks detected in frame C

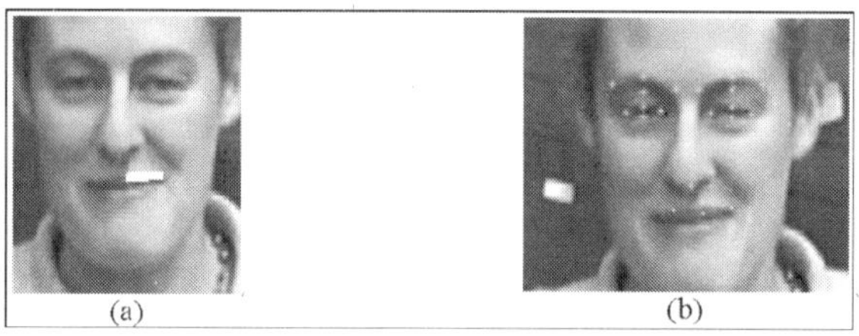

Fig. 11(a) Final mask for the mouth in frame C and (b) main feature points detected in frame C

So, we can see that by the proposed approach, where imprecision as well as failure of the image processing process are considered, quantified and incorporated as information in the evaluation process, and optional antecedents are permitted in the rule base, a number of situations can be dealt with; these situations were not tractable by an otherwise successful system that did not have these characteristics. As a result, even in cases where insufficient information is available for the determination of the observed expression, the system is able to provide useful information by at least ruling out improbable cases.

8. Conclusions

Facial expression analysis and classification systems based fuzzy rules for the representation of the knowledge utilized by the expert system. On the other hand, fuzzy rules and fuzzy expert systems are designed for problems where the input is provided in a constant and accurate manner by a set of sensors. In the case of facial expression analysis, where fuzzy inputs are the output of the imperfect process of feature extraction via image processing, conventional fuzzy rules and conventional rule evaluation methodologies are often inadequate and lead to extremely poor performance. In this paper, we have chosen to independently apply multiple image processing methodologies and fuse their results, by minimizing the uncertainty that is inherent in this process.. A combination of rule activation and confidence corresponds to the belief, thus indicating the degree to which available knowledge supports the rule. This is a reasonable feature of a system that aims to incorporate uncertainty and lack of confidence in its operation; probabilistic systems cannot provide meaningful or even reliable output in the case where insufficient input information is available. Experimental application of extended fuzzy rules, consideration of confidence in the process of feature extraction and flexible rule evaluation provide for more robust operation in an uncertain environment. Thus, the resulting system outperforms its conventional predecessor in cases where the image-processing component fails or the observed facial expression does not strictly comply to the specified rules by missing some optional characteristic.

9. References

[1] Black, M. and Yacoob, Y. (1997) "Recognizing facial expressions in image sequences using local parameterized models of image motion", International Journal of Computer Vision, Vol. 25, No. 1, pp.23–48.

[2] Chalana, V. and Kim, Y. (1997) "A methodology for evaluation of boundary detection algorithms on medical images", IEEE Transactions on Medical Imaging, October, Vol. 16, No. 5, pp.642–652.

[3] Cowie, R., Douglas-Cowie, E., Tsapatsoulis, N., Votsis, G., Kollias, S., Fellenz, W. and Taylor, J. (2001) "Emotion recognition in human-computer interaction", IEEE Signal Processing Magazine.

[4] Dietterich, T.G. (2000) 'Ensemble methods in machine learning', in Kittler, J. and Roli, F. (Eds.): First International Workshop on Multiple Classifier Systems, Lecture Notes in Computer Science, Springer-Verlag, New York, pp.1–15.

[5] Donato, G., Bartlett, S., Hager, C., Ekman, P. and Sejnowski, J. (1999) "Classifying facial actions", IEEE Transactions on Pattern Analysis and Machine Intelligence, Vol. 21, No, 10, pp.974–989.

[6] Fasel, B. and Luettin, J. (2003) "Automatic facial expression analysis: a survey", Pattern Recognition, Pergamon–Elsevier, Vol. 36, pp.259–275.

[7] Ioannou, S., Raouzaiou, A., Karpouzis, K., Pertselakis, M., Tsapatsoulis, N. and Kollias, S. (2004) "Adaptive rule-based facial expression recognition", in Vouros, G. and Panayiotopoulos, T. (Eds.): Lecture Notes in Artificial Intelligence, Springer-Verlag, SETN 2004, Samos, Greece,Vol. 3025, pp.466–475.

[8] Klir, G. and Yuan, B. (1995) ,"Fuzzy Sets and Fuzzy Logic, Theory and Applications", Prentice-Hall, New Jersey.

[9] Krog, A. and Vedelsby, J. (1995) "Neural network ensembles, cross validation and active learning",

[10] Tesauro, G., Touretzky, D. and Leen, T. (Eds.): Advances in Neural Information Processing Systems, MIT Press, Cambridge, MA, Vol. 7, pp.231–238.

[11] Lanitis, A., Taylor, C. and Cootes, T. (1997) "Automatic interpretation and coding of face images using flexible models", IEEE Transactions on Pattern Analysis and Machine Intelligence, Vol. 19, No. 7, pp.743–756.

[12] Lee, M.A. and Takagi, H. (1993) "Integrating design stages of fuzzy systems using genetic algorithms", Proceedings of IEEE International Conference on Fuzzy Systems, San Francisco, CA, Vol. 1, pp.612–617.

[13] Mase, K. and Pentland, A. (1991) 'Recognition of facial expression from optical flow', IEICE Transactions, Vol. E74, No. 10, pp.3474–3483.

[14] Mehrabian, A. (1968) "Communication without words", Psychology Today, Vol. 2, No. 4,pp. 53–56.NoE: (2004) Human-Machine Interaction Network on Emotion (HUMAINE) http://emotionresearch.net

[15] Oliver, N., Pentland, A.P. and Berard, F. (1997) "LAFTER: lips and face real time tracker", IEEE Computer Society Conference on Computer Vision and Pattern Recognition, June, San Juan, pp.123–129.

[16] Pantic, M. and Rothkrantz, L.J.M. (2000a) "Expert system for automatic analysis of facial expressions", Image and Vision Computing, Vol. 18, pp.881–905.

[17] Plutchik, R. (1980) Emotion : A Psychoevolutionary Synthesis, Harper and Row, NY, USA.

[18] Raouzaiou, A., Tsapatsoulis, N., Karpouzis, K. and Kollias, S. (2002) "Parameterized facial expression synthesis based on MPEG-4", Eurasip Journal on Applied Signal Processing, Vol. 2002, No. 10, pp.1021–1038.

[19] Rosenblum, M., Yacoob, Y. and Davis, L. (1996) "Human expression recognition from motion using a radial basis function network architecture", IEEE Transactions on Neural Networks, Vol. 7, No. 5, pp.1121–1138.

Extension of Clustering Algorithms and their Application in Cancer dataset

R. Kavitha Kumar[1], Dr. R. M Chandrasekar[2], E. Ilavarasan A.Athirai[3], K.P Mafina[4], and C. Sahiti [5]
[1]Programmer, Pondicherry Engineering College,
Puducherry.rkavikumar@yahoo.com.
[2]Registrar, Trichy Anna University.
[3]Assistant Proffesor, Pondicherry Engineering College, Puducherry,
[4]Student, Pondicherry Engineering College,
Puducherry.smileathii@yahoo.co.in

Abstract

Clustering is one of the most important research areas in the field of data mining. Since data to be processed is rapidly growing larger, clustering is very important to mine and to find meaningful knowledge among the huge datasets. Clustering means creating groups of objects based on their features in such a way that the objects belonging to the same group are similar and those belonging to different groups are different. In this paper, we describe clustering algorithms K-means, K-modes and show how they are efficiently used to cluster cancer data. As cancer classification has become one of the most important criteria for cancer treatment, we have chosen the cancer dataset which consist of gene expressions of various genes. We cluster the genes into groups showing to which cancer type they belong.

1. Introduction

The most distinct characteristic of data mining is that it deals with very large and complex datasets. .ie datasets often contain millions of objects described by tens, hundreds of various types of attributes. This requires data mining to be scalable and capable of dealing with different types of attributes. Thus we choose clustering to efficiently partition these large datasets containing all types of attributes.

However, the K-means algorithm only works on numeric data. It uses the Euclidean distance for calculation of means, this prohibits it from being used in applications where categorical data is involved. Though categorical data can be converted into numeric values for clustering, it does not give good results.

Ralambondrainy's method of K-means clustering involves conversion of categorical values into binary attributes but this involves high computational and space costs which makes it ineffective. So, we go in for an extension of K-means algorithm which is the K-modes algorithm. The K-modes algorithm eliminates the drawback of the k-means algorithm and clusters categorical values by the use of dissimilarity measure instead of Euclidean distance but there are certain drawbacks in this algorithm also. This K-modes algorithm is strongly dependant on the selection of modes during the clustering process and the non-uniqueness of the modes also make it more unstable. To remove this problem of initialization, we introduce a method for initial selection of the modes making the clustering more efficient.

In this paper, we cluster the cancer dataset using the K-modes algorithm, as this dataset involves categorical attributes. This dataset consist of gene expressions of various genes. Cancer classification is of great importance in today's world. Cancer classification has been based primarily on morphological appearance but this has serious limitations in identifying the cancer types. So, we go in for Gene expression monitoring by DNA micro arrays which efficiently help us in identifying the cancer types. In this dataset, we have gene expression of genes, by which we cluster them into groups and identify the cancer types with the previously discovered results. Thus, we identify which type of genes cause which type of cancer and further new classes of cancer can be determined by identifying new gene classes. In our dataset, we found that majority of the gene types belonged to AML (acute myeloid leukemia) or ALL (acute lymphoblastic leukemia). We were able to classify the gene types according to the different types of cancer.

2. K-means algorithm

The K-means algorithm is classified as a partitional clustering method. It is useful in partitioning large datasets with numeric attributes. Given a set of numeric objects X and integer number k (<=n) where n is the number of object in X, the K-means algorithm searches for a partition of X into k clusters. The objective of this algorithm is that, it has to partition the k clusters in such a way that the sum of squared errors is the minimum. It uses the Euclidean distance for measurement. We calculate the mean of the objects as the cluster centers using this Euclidean distance. The algorithm is formulated so that it minimizes the problem,

$$P(W,Q)= \sum_{l=1}^{k} \sum_{i=1}^{n} w_{i,l}\, d(X_i,Q_l)$$

Subject to

$$\sum_{l=1}^{k} w_{i,l} = 1, 1 \leq i \leq n$$

$$W_{i,l} \in \{0,1\}, 1 \leq i \leq n, 1 \leq l \leq k$$

Where W is an n×k partition matrix, Q represents the means of the data points and the other data points are clustered with these means as the reference, $Q=\{Q_1,Q_2....Q_k\}$.Here, as the Euclidean distance is used for measuring the distance, we are not able to cluster categorical attributes. This is the major drawback of the K-means algorithm.

3. K-modes algorithm

K-modes algorithm is an extension of the K-means algorithm. The drawback of the K-means are removed by introducing the following modifications

1. Using a simple matching dissimilarity measure for categorical objects.
2. Replacing means of the clusters by modes.

As the dissimilarity measure is used, we are able to cluster categorical data removing the drawback of K-means.

3.1 Dissimilarity measure

Let X, Y be two categorical objects described by m categorical attributes. The dissimilarity measure between X and Y can be defined by the total mismatches of the corresponding attribute categories of the two objects.

$$D(x,y) = \sum_{J=1}^{m} \delta(x_j,y_j)$$

Where

$$\delta(x_j,y_j)=\{ 0, (x_j=y_j) \quad 1, (x_j \neq y_j)\}$$

3.2 Mode of a set

The mode of $X= \{X_1, X2....X_n\}$ is $Q=\{q_1, q_2,...q_m\}$ that minimizes

$$D(X,Q) = \sum_{I=1}^{n} d(Xi,Q)$$

Here, Q need not necessarily be element of X.

The major drawback of the k-modes algorithm is the initialization and the non-uniqueness of the modes.

We follow the below mentioned approach to minimize the problem of initialization and this method has proved fairly efficient in selecting the modes.

1. Calculate the frequencies of all the categories for all attributes and store them in a category array in descending order of frequency. Here, $c_{i,j}$ denotes category i of attribute j and $f(c_{i,j}) \geq f(c_{i+1,j})$ where $f(c_{i,j})$ is the frequency of category $c_{i,j}$
2. Assign the most frequent categories equally to the initial k modes. For E.g. assume k=3.
3. we assign,
   $Q_1=[q_{1,1}=c_{1,1},q_{1,2}=c_{2,2},q_{1,3}=c_{3,3},q_{1,4}=c_{1,4}]$
   $Q_2=[q_{2,1}=c_{2,1},q_{2,2}=c_{1,2},q_{2,3}=c_{4,3},q_{2,4}=c_{2,4}]$and
   $Q_3=[q_{3,1}=c_{3,1},q_{3,2}=c_{2,2},q_{3,3}=c_{1,3},q_{3,4}=c_{3,4}]$
4. Start with Q_1. Select the record most similar to Q_1 and replace Q_1 with the record as the first initial mode. Select the record which is the most similar to Q_2 as the second initial mode. Continue the process until Q_k is replaced. This step is taken so that empty clusters are avoid.

4. Data set

We apply the k-modes algorithm to the cancer data set. This dataset contains gene expressions for 100 instances of genes across 62 attributes. We cluster the genes based on these attributes, this clustering identifies which types of gene belongs to which type of cancer.

This dataset shown below contains gene attribute values and we use the proposed initialization method to select the k initial modes for this dataset, we then assign the data points to the closest modes and recalculate the modes. By repeatedly doing this we cluster this dataset.

Gene	Att-1	C	Att-2	C	.	Att-62
AFFX-BioB-5_at	-342	A	-87	A	..	-176
AFFX-BioB-M_at	-200	A	248	A	..	-284
AFFX-BioB-3_at	41	A	262	A	. .	-81
AFFX-BioC-5_at	328	A	295	A	..	9 .

5. Experimental results

This gene dataset consist of 100 gene samples across 62 attributes, we clustered these genes using the k-modes algorithm along with the above mentioned technique for initialization. We were able to obtain 3 classes of genes from the clustering. These classes of genes were correlated with the previously obtained results and it was found that the genes belonged to AML (Acute myeloid leukemia), ALL (acute Lymphoblastic leukemia), that is either T-lineage ALL or B-lineage ALL. Thus we were able to distinguish which types of genes cause which type of cancer.

6. Conclusion

The k-means algorithm clusters only numeric data as it uses Euclidean distance for measurement. As an extension, we use k-modes for clustering categorical data. It uses dissimilarity measure instead of Euclidean distance. The cancer dataset taken is clustered into 3 classes using this k-modes algorithm and we were able to identify which genes caused which type of cancer.

7. Comparison

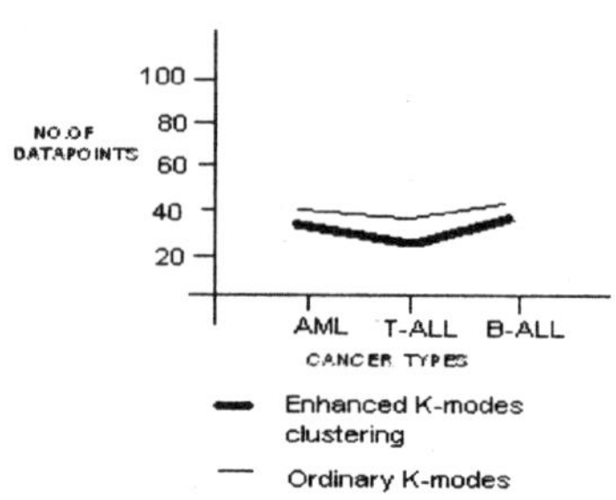

8. References

[1] Ming Lei, Pilian He, Zhichao Li, "An Improved K-Means algorithm for Clustering Categorical Data", Aug 2006, Volume 3 'Journal of Communication and Computer.

[2] T. R. Golub, D. K. Slonim, "Molecular Classification of Cancer: Class Discovery and Class Prediction by Gene Expression". 15 Oct, 1999, Volume 286 Science www.sciencemag.org.

[3] Ohn Mar San, Van-Nam Hyung, "An Alternative Extension of K-means Algorithm for Clustering Categorical Data", Int. J. Appl. Math. Computer. Science. 2004, Vol. 14, No. 2, 241–247.

[4] Zhexue Huang, "Extensions to the K-Means Algorithm for Clustering Large Data Sets with Categorical Values", Data Mining and Knowledge Discovery 2, 283–304 (1998).

[5] Shehroz S Khan, Dr. Shri Kant, "Computation of Initial Modes for K-modes Clustering Algorithm using Evidence Accumulation", IJCAI-07, 2784.

The Role of Data Mining in CRM for Efficient Campaign Management

Sai Hanuman A[1], Sesham Anand[2], Dr. Vinaybabu A[3], Dr. Govardhan A[3] and Dr. Padmanabham P[4]

[1] School of Computing, GRIET, Hyderabad, A P, India, *a_saihanuman@hotmail.com*

[2]Department of CSE, MVSREC, Hyderabad, A P, India, *sesham_anand@hotmail.com*

[3]Department of CSE, JNTU, Hyderabad, A P, India

[4]Principal, Bharat Eng College, Hyderabad, A P, India

Abstract

Data Mining plays a crucial role in science, technology and management, especially in Customer relationship management (CRM). CRM is a process that manages the interaction between a company and its customers. In the light of the advances made in the modern Industry there is a need to extract the information in an efficient manner from the existing Databases. Data Mining is a process of identifying valid, potential, useful and understandable pattern from the Database. In this paper ,we tried to analyze the role of Data Mining in CRM by taking a real time dataset of a US based Insurance Company. Some useful inferences have been drawn using Data Mining Algorithms such as C4.5 Decision tree for a better Campaign Management.

1. Introduction

1.1 Customer relationship management

CRM is a set of strategies, processes, and associated technology enablers designed to improve the interactions and engagement of customers. It involves not only the use of these systems, but also corporate cultural transformation and ongoing programs with the appropriate organizational framework. Sales force automation (SFA), customer service and support, and enterprise marketing management are among the main CRM areas.

Customer relationship management (CRM) is a process that manages the interactions between a company and its customers. The primary users of CRM software applications are database marketers who are looking to automate the process of interacting with customers.

Customer Relationship Management (CRM) emerged in the last decade to reflect the central role of the customer for the strategic positioning of a company. CRM takes a holistic view over customers. It encompasses all measures for understanding the customers and for exploiting this knowledge to design and implement marketing activities, align production and coordinate the supply-chain. CRM puts emphasis on the coordination of such measures, also implying the integration of customer-related data, meta-data and knowledge and the centralized planning and evaluation of measures to increase customer lifetime value.

CRM gains in importance for companies that serve multiple groups of customers and exploit different interaction channels for them. This is due to the fact that information about the customers, which can be acquired for each group and across any channel, should be integrated with existing knowledge and exploited in a coordinated fashion.

Customer Relationship Management (CRM) as a product/market segment was first introduced by companies such as Siebel and Oracle, with many other players, including SAP, PeopleSoft and Microsoft joining subsequently. The initial set of products mostly support easy management of information for customer facing functions, including *contact management, sales force automation,* etc.

1.2 Objective of CRM

The maximization of lifetime values of the (entire) customer base in the context of a company's strategy is a key objective of CRM. Various processes and personnel in an organization must adopt CRM practices that are aligned with corporate goals. For each institution, corporate strategies such as diversification, coverage of market niches or minimization of operative costs are implemented by "measures", such as mass customization, segment-specific product configurations etc. The role of CRM is in supporting customer-related strategic measures.

Customer understanding is the core of CRM. It is the basis for maximizing customer lifetime value, which in turn encompasses customer segmentation and actions to maximize customer conversion, retention, loyalty and profitability. Proper customer understanding and actionability lead to increased customer lifetime value. Incorrect customer understanding can lead to hazardous actions. Similarly, unfocused actions such as unbounded attempts to access or retain all customers, can lead to decrease of customer lifetime value (law of diminishing return). Hence, emphasis should be put on correct customer understanding and concerted actions derived from it.

1.3 Data Mining

Data Mining is a process of identifying valid, novel, potentially useful and understandable pattern from the Database.

1.3.1 Knowledge Discovery in Databases

The term Knowledge Discovery in Databases, or KDD for short, refers to the broad process of finding knowledge in data, and emphasizes the "high-level" application of particular data mining methods. It involves the evaluation and possibly interpretation of the patterns to make the decision of what qualifies as knowledge. It also includes the choice of encoding schemes, preprocessing, sampling, and projections of the data prior to the data mining step. KDD [6],[11] refers to the overall process of discovering useful knowledge from data.

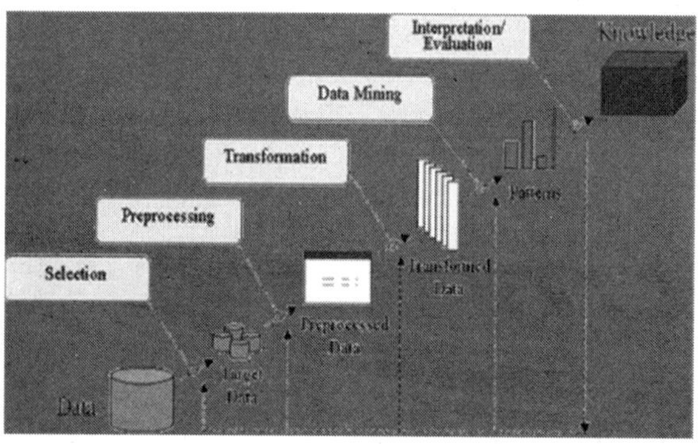

Fig. 1 KDD Process

The overall process of finding and interpreting patterns from data involves the repeated application of the following steps:

1. Learning the application domain
2. Creating a target dataset
3. Data cleaning and preprocessing
4. Data reduction and projection
5. Choosing the function of data mining
6. Choosing the data mining algorithm(s)
7. Data mining
8. Interpretation
9. Using discovered knowledge

1.3.2 KDD Techniques

There are many different approaches that are classified as KDD techniques. Some of them discussed in [6],[11]are:

- Probabilistic Approach
- Statistical Approach
- Classification Approach
- The Bayesian Approach to KDD
- Pattern Discovery and Data Cleaning
- The Decision Tree Approach
- Deviation and Trend Analysis
- Neural networks
- Hybrid Approach

Before applying any of these techniques the data is to be properly organized and cleaned. Real world databases and data available in files contain a lot of noisy, missing and inconsistent data because of huge size and often errors occurred during data entry. In order to improve the quality of data and also the quality of data mining results, we need to preprocess the data by applying various techniques. There are a number of data pre processing tasks available [11]. They are:

a) Data cleaning
b) Data integration and transformation
c) Data reduction
d) Discretization and concept hierarchy generation

2. Role of Data Mining for CRM

Data mining, by its simplest definition, automates the detection of relevant patterns in a database. Data mining uses well-established statistical and machine learning techniques to build models that predict customer behavior. Today, technology automates the mining process, integrates it with commercial data warehouses, and presents it in a relevant way for business users.

Data mining, on the other hand, extracts information from a database that the user did not know existed. Relationships between variables and customer behaviors that are non-intuitive are the jewels that data mining hopes to find. And because the user does not know beforehand what the data mining process has discovered, it is a much bigger leap to take the output of the system and translate it into a solution to a business problem.

Data mining helps marketing users to target marketing campaigns more accurately; and also to align campaigns more closely with the needs, wants, and attitudes of customers and prospects.

2.1 Campaign management

The goal of CRM is to allow marketing organizations to tune the customer interaction strategies to the specific needs of individual, giving customers what they want. Instead of interacting with large number of customers, the new role of marketing is to interact with individual customers. This involves identifying and understanding unique customer patterns as well as being able to create customized offers for small customer groups that correspond to the patterns.

As a result of the complex interactions that are now possible, the function of marketing is increasingly becoming tied to technology, ranging from complex data mining algorithms to campaign management software applications. Campaign management software allows marketing professionals to segment groups of customers into smaller groups and specify the interaction that should take place with those individuals.

A user of campaign management software would define these segments by selecting customers in the data base that have the desired characteristics. The current trend is to integrate tightly data mining and campaign management technologies. The past few years have been significant improvements by CRM vendors with respect to integrating data mining into the CRM process. This trend is expected to continue resulting in CRM applications driving more and more marketing activities based on data mining results.

3. Data Mining for an Insurance Company

In this exploration the case study we have chosen is mainly related to financial plan/Insurance Company. When an Insurance company starts any new policy it needs to campaign the policy to the customers. Customers can be divided into 2 types i.e., existing and new. To campaign the policy to existing customers we need to take the existing data of previous policies taken by the existing customer. To analyze this data Data Mining algorithms are highly useful. When the policy we are starting is of higher premium, campaigning this to all customers is of no use. At some times we need to spend more money on each customer for efficient campaign.

So there is a need of categorizing the existing customers in to different types. In this study we divided the customers in to the categories Gold, Silver and Normal depending upon the amount of their existing Insurance. We need to analyze about various factors affecting a client to choose any Insurance Policy type. At this stage the Data Mining algorithms are helpful to analyze the data. After training the present customers data, when new customers are added the Data Mining Algorithms can categorize the new customer's status.

For this exploration we have taken the real time data set of a US based Insurance Company as a part of Finance Plan.

3.1 Objective of the Analysis

Mainly this analysis is useful for the Campaign Management of Insurance Company. The Inferences drawn through this analysis will direct the marketing people to know about the loyal customers. When there is a high Quality Policy (more premium), through this knowledge discovery Market people can easily create the list of the target group.

3.2 Description of the Data

In this the data is spread across various data bases like Insurance, Personal Information, and Events. We have taken a few important attributes for use in the Algorithms.

Table 1 The available client variables

Client Name	Category
Client Age	Spouse Age
Client Profession	Spouse Profession
Client Income	Spouse Income
Client Assets	Spouse Assets
Client Insurance Amount	Spouse Insurance Amount
Client DOB	Events Present

In the available client variables, Client Age, Client Insurance Amount categories are supposed to be the high priority variables for our exploration. Depending upon the total Insurance Amount of the clients, the clients are divided into three categories Gold, Silver and Normal. In the total package of insurance while gold occupies the highest position , silver and normal occupy the second and third positions.

3.3 Exploratory Data Analysis

For analyzing the data and to work on the Data Mining Algorithm, client age client Insurance Amount and category have been identified as important variables. As the number of records are comparatively less we used 10 fold cross validation techniques for this analysis.

Table 2 Data Analysis

Variable	Statistics	Values
Age	Min	28
	Max	60
	Mean	38.115
	Standard Deviation	5.711
Amount	Min	$2000
	Max	$1,0000000
	Mean	896996.701
	Standard Deviation	1503073.034
Category	G: Gold Customer S: Silver Customer N: Normal Customer	

3.4 WEKA Data Mining Software

Fig. 2 WEKA software Logo[12]

In this paper we have chosen WEKA software to perform data mining tasks. WEKA stands for "Waikato Environment for Knowledge Analysis". It was developed at the University of Waikato, New Zealand. It is a data mining workbench having facilities to observe data files, pre-process them and perform knowledge analysis using various data mining algorithms implemented including classification, clustering, regression analysis, association rules etc. All these activities can be performed in a single interface. One of the strengths of WEKA lies in its ability to recognize common file types which can be created using commonly available spreadsheet programs like Microsoft Excel or Notepad etc. WEKA can be installed and used in almost all platforms as it is written in Java language. The native format of data to be submitted to WEKA is described in [10]. Details of the software can be found in [12].

3.5 Classification using C4.5 Decision tree algorithm

Decision Tree approach is most useful in classification problems. In this technique, a tree is constructed to model the classification process. Once the tree is built, it is applied to each data in the data base which results in classifying that data. In other words there are two steps involved, one step is to build the tree, and the other applying the tree to the data base. Algorithms differ on how to build effective trees. The C4.5 algorithm is an improvement over the Induction algorithm ID3 technique, which builds decision tree based on information theory and attempts to minimize the expected number of comparisons. The basic idea is to formulate questions whose answers provide most information. The concept used to quantify information is called entropy. The objective of decision tree classification is to iteratively partition the given data set into sub sets where all elements in each final subset, belong the same class. It is basically a Divide and Conquer approach. The division results in multiple probabilities whose sum is one. The algorithm chooses the splitting attribute with highest gain in information, where gain is defined as the difference between how much information is needed to make a correct classification before the split versus how much information is needed after the split.

In C4.5, the missing data is ignored, the continuous data can be divided into ranges, it allows classification via either decision trees or ruled generated from them. For splitting purposes it uses largest gain ratio to ensure larger than average information gain.

Partial Decision Tree (PART) is a rule generator that uses J48 to generate pruned decision trees from which rules are extracted. To make a single rule a pruned decision tree is built for current set of instances, the leaf with largest coverage is, made into a rule, and the tree is discarded.

3.6 Partial Output of C4.5 Algorithm

```
=== Run information ===
Scheme   :     weka.classifiers.trees.J48 -C 0.25 -M 2
Relation  :   CRM_data-
weka.filters.unsupervised.attribute.Remove-R2
Instances :   82
Attributes :  2 (age, category)
Test mode:   10-fold cross-validation
=== Classifier model (full training set) ===
J48 pruned tree
------------------
age <= 35: g (28.0/8.0)
age > 35
|  age <= 37: s (6.0/1.0)
|  age > 37: n (48.0/21.0)
Number of Leaves  :  3
Size of the tree :  5
Time taken to build model: 0 seconds
=== Stratified cross-validation ===
=== Summary ===
Correctly Classified Instances          44                53.6585
%
Incorrectly Classified Instances        38
46.3415 %
Kappa statistic                         0.287
Mean absolute error                     0.2649
Root mean squared error                 0.3808
Relative absolute error                 79.5635 %
Root relative squared error             93.5543 %
=== Detailed Accuracy By Class ===
TP Rate  FP Rate  Precision  Recall  F-Measure  ROC
Area  Class
 0     0      0      0      0      0.315    s
```

```
0.792   0.155   0.679   0.792   0.731   0.779   g
0.514   0.426   0.474   0.514   0.493   0.554   n
0.318   0.15    0.438   0.318   0.368   0.678   s
=== Confusion Matrix ===
 a  b  c  d   <-- classified as
 0  0  1  0 | a = s
 0 19  5  0 | b = g
 0  8 18  9 | c = n
 0  1 14  7 | d = s
```

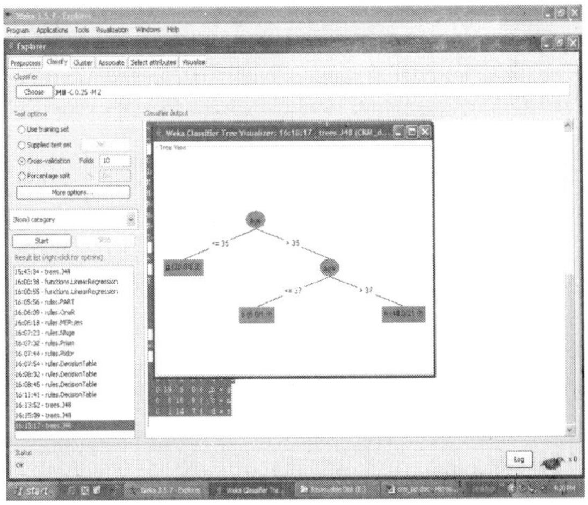

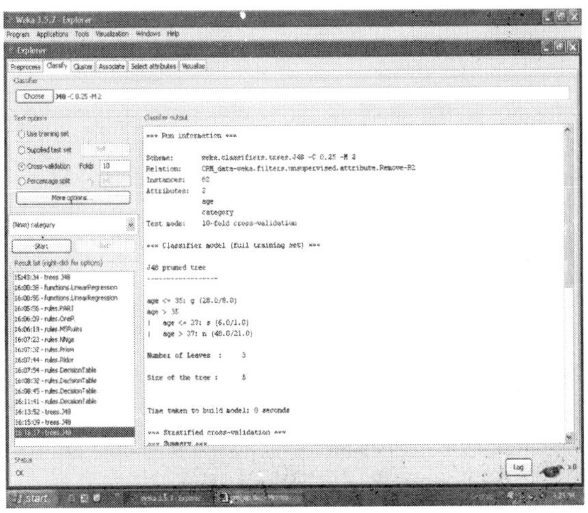

3.7 Inferences Drawn

1. If the age is less than or equal to 35 they are likely to be a Gold customer (G). For a New Insurance policy if the premium is high, this age group should be the target group. For efficient Campaign Management even we can afford to spend something on this group.
2. If the age is in between 35 to 37, the category is Silver Customer(s). Even the percentage of customers in this category is less. So, Campaigning Medium or less premium policies to this group is better.
3. If the age is more than 37, they will come under Normal group (N). Percentage of Customers in this group are likely to be more. Campaigning less premium policies to the group will give good results.

4. Conclusion

The role of Data Mining in various fields is thus well evident. We have explored and analyzed the role of Data Mining in the field of Customer Relationship Management (CRM). For this study we have taken the real time data set of a US-based Insurance Company. We have made an attempt to discover the knowledge using various Mining Algorithms such as C4.5 Decision tree algorithm . The inferences drawn from the output of various Data Mining Algorithms are essential for efficient Campaign Management.

5. Future Scope

For better Campaign Management there is a need for discovering more knowledge from the existing databases. There are various Algorithms and techniques available in Data Mining. By applying other techniques and Algorithms on this data set will definitely increase the efficiency of Campaign Management.

6. Acknowledgements

We wish to place on record my gratitude to the management and staff of GRIET for their invaluable help throughout this project. I am indebted to prof. P.S.Raju, Director, and Dr Jandhyala N Murthy, Principal, of GRIET for their continuous encouragement and patronage. I wish to thank Dr P. Eliah for Editorial help.

7. References

[1] Polo Giudici, Applied Data Mining, c2003, John Wiley and Sons Ltd, ISBN-0-470-84679-8

[2] Kurt Thearling, Building Data Mining Applications for CRM, Tata Mcgrawhill

[3] Fayyad, Piatetsky -Shapiro, Smyth, "From Data Mining to Knowledge Discovery: An Overview",. *Advances in Knowledge Discovery and Data Mining,* AAAI Press / The MIT Press, Menlo Park, CA

[4] Ian H. Witten and Eibe Frank (2005) "Data Mining: Practical machine learning tools and techniques", 2nd Edition, Morgan Kaufmann, 2005

[5] Margaret H. Dunham, Data Mining, Introductory and Advanced Topics 2005, Pearson Education, India. ISBN 81-7808-996-3

[6] Peggy Wright, Knowledge Discovery In Databases: Tools and Techniques, http://0-www.acm.org.library.vu.edu.au/crossroads/xrds5-2/kdd.html

[7] Pyle, Dorian (1999) Data Preparation for Data Mining. Morgan Kaufmann publishers

[8] Quinlan, J. R(1993). C4.5: Programs for Machine Learning. Morgan Kaufmann Publishers, 1993

[9] T. Kanungo, D. M. Mount, N. Netanyahu, C. Piatko, R. Silverman, and A. Y. Wu, An efficient k-means clustering algorithm: Analysis and implementation, IEEE Trans. Pattern Analysis and Machine Intelligence, 24 (2002), 881-892

[10] ARFF file format, http://www.cs.waikato.ac.nz/~ml/weka/arff.html

[11] Overview of the KDD process http://www2.cs.uregina.ca/~hamilton/courses/831/notes/kdd/1_kdd.html

[12] http://www.cs.waikato.ac.nz/ml/weka/

Generation of Clusters for Duplicate Records using Union-Find Algorithm

K. Prasanna Lakshmi, K.R. Madhavi, T.Anitha
Dept of IT, GRIET

Abstract

An algorithm for grouping of duplicate records of large databases into clusters for the purpose of integration of information is proposed. The clustering technique is applied for the newly arrived record in order to place it in an appropriate cluster. It also facilitates retrieval of data corresponding to duplicate records. The clustering is based on union algorithm which tends to assign similar records to a cluster.

1. Introduction

The advancement in technology, the world has witnessed an exponential growth in data being stored in electronic form. More so due to the introduction of the world wide web, where there is exchange of heavy amounts of information. The storage and retrieval of data in an efficient way by the relational databases contributed significantly to this exponential increase of data. In addition to databases there are other sources of information such as files and other legacy systems of data storage.

These storage sources facilitate not only the storage of huge volume of data but also a variety of data and quality of data. This feature of storage sources results in number of problems, one of which is identification of duplicate records or approximately duplicate records within a single database or among multiple data sources. In the context of the foresaid situation, it is necessary to integrate the information from various sources for all practical purposes. The outcome of such integration should be the consolidation of all the information into a single data warehouse. The challenge that arises for doing so is the management of duplicate records which refer to the same real world entity. The present work aims at addressing the above problem of data integration, the approach towards it being a *clustering* perspective.

In this approach, first the duplicate records are identified. The identification of duplicate records is made difficult as real world data are generally incomplete and noisy. Such problems are resolved by *data cleaning*[1]. Data cleaning is one of the methods in data preprocessing which transforms data to a readable form. After cleaning, data is arranged in an order based upon a set of fields selected in order to identify duplicate records successfully. Once the data is arranged in an order they are formed into clusters using union algorithm

In section 2 data pre-processing is discussed. Section 3 reviews the system for detecting pair-wise approximate duplicates and the technique of clustering. In section 4 conclusions are presented.

2. Data Preprocessing

In preprocessing, data entries are stored in a uniform manner in the database, resolving the problems. The steps that are involved in preprocessing are data cleaning, data transformation etc., and these steps format the input data and make data comparable and more usable. A comprehensive collection of papers related to various data preparation approaches are found in [2]. After this process, the data is stored in tables with comparable fields. The next section identifies which fields should be used for comparison.

3. Duplicates Detection

Identification of duplicate records, multiple records referring to the same entity, has been known since many years as *record linkage* or *record matching problem* [3] and has been studied by many researchers under different names such as Merge/Purge [4], record linkage, Name matching [5], etc. There are multiple techniques for duplicate record detection. We can divide these techniques broadly into 2 categories :

(i) ad hoc techniques which work quickly on existing relational databases and
(ii) principled techniques that are based on probabilistic inference models [6].

The probabilistic methods are better in terms of accuracy and ad hoc are better in terms of fastness. The focus of these techniques is on quality of comparison and not the efficiency of duplicate detection process which improves the speed of duplicate detection.

The naïve algorithm for duplicate detection in tables A and B is to execute a nested loop comparison, which requires a total of |m|.|n| comparisons where |m| is the number of records in A and |n| is the number of records in B. The cost of following this method is very expensive even for moderately sized tables, which makes it economically non viable. Hence supportive techniques to reduce the number of comparisons must be made use of. In the following section we discuss the technique for reducing the number of comparisons.

3.1 Transitivity Law

The well known and standard method of detecting exact duplicates in a table is to sort the table and then to check if consecutive records are identical. Similarly the approximate records may not be situated next to each other but will be found nearby after sorting in best case. In other case they will be scattered making it difficult to identify the duplicates or approximate duplicates. Such results depend on the choice of fields to sort. The idea of sorting is to achieve preliminary clustering, and then to do pair-wise comparison.

While comparing the records the transitivity property holds.

Transitive law states that
If a R b and b R c, then a R c

Transitivity property may be explained as follows. If a record α is a duplicate of record β and in turn if β is a duplicate of record γ, then by transitivity α is a duplicate of γ. So the number of comparisons is reduced.

3.2 Efficient duplicate detection

The system scans the sorted database for approximate duplicates and if found, they are clustered using union algorithm The algorithm used provides a general method for keeping track of disjoint sets. It allows performing set-union operations on sets which are in some way equivalent, while ensuring that the end product of such a union is disjoint from any other set. A tree structures is used to represent these sets. Two objects x and y are members of the same set if and only if x and y are nodes of the same tree, which is equivalent to saying that they share the same root. There are four important operations.

- Makeset(x): Create a new singleton set {x}.
- Find(x): Return the root element of the set containing x.
- Union(x,y): Compute the union of the two sets containing x and y.
- Equiv(x,y): determine whether x and y satisfy some equivalence criterion.
- Update( ) : Details of

For level component labeling the algorithm becomes:

```
for records p do
{
MakeSet(p);
for all neighbors n < p do
if ( Equiv( n, p ) )
Union( n, p );
Update();
    }
```

In this context the condition n < p means that n is a record which is approximate to p. In this case Equiv(n,p) is true if selected fields of the records n , p are equivalent. Union calls Find internally to determine the root nodes of the trees containing n and p and generates clusters. The details of clusters which are parent information and selected field names are stored in a table called set for further processing.

The pseudo code for MakeSet(p), Equiv(n, p) and Union(n, p) are

```
MakeSet(p)
begin
   parent(p) = -1
end

Equiv(n, p)
begin
  if selected fields for records n and p are
  same then return True
  else return False
     end

update()
begin
   make an entry into the set table
end

Union(n, p)
begin
     t = parent(n) +parent(p)
     if(parent(n) > parent(p)
       then
          parent(n)=p
          parent(p)=t
     else
          parent(p)=n
          parent(n)=t
     end

     Find(n)
     begin
        while(parent(n) >= 0 )
          do n=parent(n)
             return n
     end
```

Suppose that record R1 is the record of consideration. The algorithm first tests whether R1 is already known to be a member of one of the clusters represented in the set table. This test is done by comparing the cluster representation of R1 to each representation of clusters R2 in the table. If this comparison is success then *find* algorithm is used to get the address of the parent and an insertion of R1 is done into the same cluster. If not matched then union algorithm is called and a new cluster is generated. For finding approximate duplicates entire database need not be searched which reduces the time of search and space needed for searching. The idea behind this approach is that, if a record R1 is not similar to a record R2 already in cluster, then it will not match the other members of the cluster either. The integration of different databases is also followed using union algorithm. The time complexity is approximately O(log N). All experiments show that the algorithm is as accurate as the standard method while significantly performing many fewer record comparisons as much as 75 % savings.

4. Conclusion

In this paper, we addressed the problem of recognizing approximate duplicate data detection. To integrate data from multiple sources, one must first identify the information which is common in these sources.

The core of the proposed approach is a clustering algorithm, which aims at discovering clusters of duplicate records based on union-find algorithm on sorted data. The integration of information sources is an important area research. There is much to be gained from integrating multiple information sources. It is desirable for record matching algorithms to be as domain-independent as possible and also for the algorithms to indicate the strength of the match between records.

5. References

[1] IEEE Data Eng. Bull., S. Sarawagi, ed., special issue on data cleaning, vol 23, no. 4 , Dec 2000.

[2] IEEE Data Eng. Bull., E. Rundensteiner, ed., special issue on date transformation, vol. 22, no. 1, Jan. 1999.

[3] H.B. Newcombe, Handbook of Record Linkage. Oxford Univ. Press, 1988.

[4] M.A. Herna´ndez and S.J. Stolfo, "Real-World Data Is Dirty: Data Cleansing and the Merge/Purge Problem," Data Mining and Knowledge Discovery, vol. 2, no. 1, pp. 9-37, Jan. 1998.

[5] M. Bilenko, R.J. Mooney, W.W. Cohen, P. Ravikumar, and S.E. Fienberg, "Adaptive Name Matching in Information Integration," IEEE Intelligent Systems, vol. 18, no. 5, pp. 16-23, Sept./Oct. 2003.

[6] W.E. Winkler, "Methods for Record Linkage and Bayesian Networks," Technical Report Statistical Research Report Series RRS2002/05, US Bureau of the Census, Washington, D.C., 2002.

Comparative Study of Hierarchical Clustering Algorithms Suitable for Video Data Mining

D. Saravanan and Dr. G. Geetha
Department of Computer Applications, Sathyabama University, Chennai
sa_roin@yahoo.com *gitaskumar@yahoo.com*

Abstract

The amount of information produced every year is rapidly growing due to many factors among all media. Video is a particular media embedding visual, motion, audio and textual information. Given this huge amount of information, the indexing process must be automated in order to build a dictionary of image region. This process is carried out in various steps. One such important step is clustering. There are many clustering techniques available today. In this paper, we attempt to give a comparative study of existing algorithms suitable for video data mining.
Keywords: Hierarchical, clustering, video, datamining, image processing, BIRCH, CURE, CHAMELEON

1. Introduction

Clustering is an unsupervised machine learning process that creates clusters such that data points inside a cluster are close to each other, and also far apart from data points in other clusters. Clustering in data mining [SADC93, CHY96] is a discovery process that groups a set of data such that the intracluster similarity is maximized and the intercluster similarity is minimized [JD88, KR90, PAS96, CHY96].

Clustering is used in many applications, as a stand-alone tool to get insight into data distribution and as a preprocessing step for other algorithms. Specifically it is used in Pattern Recognition, Spatial Data Analysis, Image Processing, Economic Science, document classification etc.

2. Categories of Clustering Algorithms

There are four main categories of clustering algorithms: partitioning, density-based, grid-based, and hierarchical.

2.1 Clustering Approaches

2.1.1 Partitioning algorithms

Construct various partitions and then evaluate them by some criterion (k-means, k-medoids)

2.1.2 Hierarchical algorithms

Create a hierarchical decomposition of the set of data (or objects) using some criterion (AGNES, DIANA)

2.1.3 Density-based

Based on connectivity and density functions – grow a cluster as long as density in the neighborhood exceeds a threshold (DBSCAN, CLIQUE)

2.1.4 Grid-based

Based on a multiple-level grid structure (i.e., quantized space) (STING, CLIQUE)

2.1.5 Model-based

A model is hypothesized for each of the clusters and the idea is to find the best fit of the data to the given model (EM)

3. Clustering Algorithms Suitable for Video Data Mining

Current Video data mining techniques emphasize on pattern discovery. We require content-adaptive pattern discovery techniques that would adapt to variations in content, and make the event-search tractable. Clustering in data mining is a discovery process that groups a set of data.

Out of the four clustering approaches, Hierarchical algorithms are best suited for video data mining due to its simplicity and efficiency[1]. They produce a nested sequence of clusters, with a single all-inclusive cluster at the top a single point clusters at the bottom.

Hierarchical clustering algorithms are classified as agglomerative or divisive. The agglomerative (bottom up) approach repeatedly merges two clusters, while the divisive (top down) approach repeatedly splits a cluster into two.

Agglomerative clustering method does not suit video data mining application due to following reasons – they do not scale well, time complexity of at least $O(n^2)$, where n is the number of total objects, can never undo (backtrack) what was done previously and do not give rise to dead-end solutions. [2]

Divisive clustering method is suitable for statistical analysis [3]. This method cannot be used for video data mining as they can never undo.

Hence a best suited clustering algorithm for video data mining would be to integrate Hierarchical clustering with another clustering technique.

Many algorithms were proposed like BIRCH[4], CURE[5], CHAMELEON[6] etc. integrating Hierarchical and distance based clustering methods.

In the following table, we bring out the comparative study of various clustering algorithms that are suitable for video data mining. For our purpose, we have considered BIRCH, CURE and CHAMELEON.

4. Comparative study of Hierarchical clustering Algorithms

BIRCH	CURE	CHAMELEON
Uses tree structure and incrementally adjusts the quality of sub clusters	Selects well scattered points from cluster and then shrinks them towards the centre of the cluster by a specific fraction	Uses dynamic modeling
BIRCH employs Clustering Feature and Clustering Features tree	Cure employs combinations of random sampling and partitioning	CHAMELEON employs finding initial sub cluster and merging sub clusters using dynamic framework
Clusters multi-dimensional metric data points	Clusters metric space dataset	Can be applied to any data set
Algorithm Incrementally construct a CF (Clustering Feature) tree, a hierarchical data structure for multiphase clustering Phase 1: scan DB to build an initial in-memory CF tree (a multi-level compression of the data that tries to preserve the inherent clustering structure of the data) Phase 2: use an arbitrary clustering algorithm to cluster the leaf nodes of the CF-tree	Algorithm Draw random sample *s*. Partition sample to *p* partitions with size *s/p* Partially cluster partitions into *s/pq* clusters Eliminate outliers By random sampling If a cluster grows too slow, eliminate it. Cluster partial clusters. Label data in disk	Algorithm 1. Use a graph partitioning algorithm: cluster objects into a large number of relatively small sub-clusters 2. Use an agglomerative hierarchical clustering algorithm: find the genuine clusters by repeatedly combining these sub-clusters
Improvements required: 1. Way of increasing the threshold dynamically 2. The dynamic adjustment of outlier criteria 3. more accurate quality measurements 4. Handles only numeric data and sensitive to the order of the data record 5. A new architecture to propose a parallel execution as well as interactive learnings.	Improvements required: Cure performs multiple mistakes for which remedy is sought. The following were some of the mistakes: 1. CURE failed to find the right clusters for a given data set 2. It produces a dendogram of possible clustering solution at different levels of granularity 3. It merges together sub-clusters that belong to two different genuine clusters.	Improvements required: 1. It should support static model also. 2. Processing cost should be reduced 3. It should be applied to different applications domain and tested.

5. Conclusion

We have made an attempt to compare the existing clustering algorithms that are suitable for video data mining. This study brings out the characteristics of BIRCH, CURE and CHAMELEON and focuses on the improvements needed in each algorithm. This would definitely aid in the development of new algorithms suitable for video data mining.

6. References

[1] JngHwan Oh, Babitha Bandi 'Multimedia Data Mining Framework for Raw Video Sequences' In Proc. MDM/KDD 2002: International Workshop on Multimedia Data Mining(with ACM SIGKDD 2002)

[2] Ian Davindson and S.S Ravi 'Agglomerative Hierarchical Clustering with Constraints: Theoretical and Empirical Results ' 4th SIAM Data Mining Conf .2004

[3] L. Kaufman and P. J. Rousseeuw. *Finding Groups in Data: An Introduction to Cluster Analysis*, John Wiley & Sons, 1990.

[4] T. Zhang, R.Ramakrishnan, and M.Livny, "BRICH: An Efficient data clustering method for very large databases ," in Proceedings of 1996 ACM SIGMOD International Conference on Management of Data (SIGMOD '96) (Monteral , Canada) PP 103-114 , June 1996.

[5] S.Guha, R.Rastogi, and .Shim, "An efficient clustering algorithm for large database," in proceedings of 1998 ACM_SIGMOD International conference on Management of Data (SIGMOD'98) (Seattle, WA), pp 73-84, June 1998.

[6] G.Karypis,E.H.Han and V.Kumar "CHAMELEON: A hierarchical clustering algorithm using dynamic modeling," Computer ,Vol 32pp 68-75,1999.

[7] M.Stonebaker,R.Agrawa, U.Dayal, E.J Neuhold, and A.Reuter, DBMS research at a crssroads:The Vienna update. In proc .of the 19th VLDB Conference, pages 688-692, Dublin, Ireland,1993.

[8] M.S .Chen, J.Han, and P.S.Yu. Data mining: An overview from database perspective. IEEE Transactions on Knowledge and Data Eng., 8(6):866-883 ,December 1996.

[9] A.K. Jain and R.C.Dubes. Algorithms for Clustering Data ,Prentice Hall,1998.

[10] L.Kaufman and P.J Rousseeus, Finding Groups in Data : an Introduction to Cluster Analysis, John Wiley & sons, 1990.

[11] L.J Hubert P.Arabie and G.De Soete, Clustering and Classification, World Scientific,1996.

Analysis and Design of a Comprehensive Text Categorization Approach for English Language

Dr. R.V. Dharaskar[1], Dr. V.M. Thakre[2], Prof. M.B. Chandak[3] and Mr. Shantanu A. Lohi[4]
[1]Professor & Coordinator, PG Dept. of Computer Sci. & Engg, GH Raisoni College of Engg., Nagpur
[2]Professor, PG Dept. of Computer Sci. & IT, SGB Amravati University, Amravati
[3]Asst. Prof. & Head, Dept. of Computer Sci. & Engg., SRKN Engg. College, Nagpur
[4]M.Tech. III Semester, PG Dept. of Computer Sci. & Engg, GH Raisoni College of Engg., Nagpur

Abstract

The important aspect of automatically sorting and classifying a set of documents into any category by incorporating a predefined set is Text categorization. Automated text classification is gaining notability since it frees organizations from the hectic and time consuming need of manually organizing documents, which can be too expensive, or simply not feasible given the time constraints of the application or the number of documents involved. In terms of accuracy, modern text classification systems proves better than that of trained human professionals, which is made possible by a combination of information retrieval technology and machine learning technology in text classification approach. There are numerable useful applications of this approach spanning various scientific and general fields of work. This paper deals in depth the feasibility of text categorization pertaining to various domains along with making substantial use of techniques like document indexing, text filtering and classifier learning technique. Also the approaches of standard input and tokenization is considered for a better output which shall be devoid of any complexity for text classification.

1. Introduction

The automated categorization (or classification) of texts into predefined categories has witnessed a booming interest in the last 10 years, due to the increased availability of documents in digital form and the ensuing need to organize them. In the research community the dominant approach to this problem is based on machine learning techniques: a general inductive process automatically builds a classifier by learning, from a set of preclassified documents, the characteristics of the categories. The advantages of this approach over the knowledge engineering approach are a very good effectiveness, considerable savings in terms of expert labor power, and straightforward portability to different domains. This paper discusses the main approaches to text categorization in terms of the standard input taken in the form of textual documents or direct entries made through keyboard. The prospect of this research does not get into details of any printed textual format as an input.

The Text Categorization methods we are discussing are completely general, and do not depend on the availability of special-purpose resources that might be unavailable or costly to develop. These assumptions need not be verified in operational settings, where it is legitimate to use any source of information that might be available or deemed worth developing. Relying only on endogenous knowledge means classifying a document based solely on its semantics, and given that the semantics of a document is a *subjective* notion.

For application developers, this interest is mainly due to the enormously increased need to handle larger and larger quantities of documents, a need emphasized by increased connectivity and availability of document bases of all types at all levels in the information chain. But this interest is also due to the fact that TC techniques have reached accuracy levels that rival the performance of trained professionals, and these accuracy levels can be achieved with high levels of efficiency on standard hw/sw resources. This means that more and more organizations are automating all their activities that can be cast as Text Categorization tasks. This paper thus embarks on to take a closer look at a simplified text categorization approach by describing the standard methodology through which a Text Categorization system is built.

The categories are just symbolic labels: no additional knowledge (of a procedural or declarative nature) of their meaning is usually available, and it is often the case that no metadata (such as e.g. publication date, document type, publication source) is available either. In these cases, classification must be accomplished only on the basis of knowledge extracted from the documents themselves. Text Categorization is a *subjective* task: when two experts (human or artificial) decide whether or not to classify document *dj* under category *ci*, they may disagree, and this in fact happens with relatively high frequency. A news article on Aamir Khan selling raising money from his shows and giving it to prime minister fund for children be filed under Politics or under Finance or under Entertainment, or under any combination of the three, or even under neither, depending on the subjective judgment of the system.

Proposed Plan of Work

- Document Organization
  Indexing with a controlled vocabulary is an instance of the general problem of document base organization. In general, many other issues pertaining to document organization and filing, be it for purposes of personal organization or structuring of a corporate document base, may be addressed by Text Categorization techniques.
- Text Filtering
  Text filtering is the activity of classifying a stream of incoming documents dispatched in an asynchronous way by an information producer to an information consumer. A typical case is a news feed, where the producer is a news agency and the consumer is a newspaper. In this case, the filtering system should block the delivery of the documents the consumer is likely not interested in (e.g., all news not concerning sports, in the case of a sports newspaper).

Research Methodology to be Employed

- Document Indexing Techniques
  The Text Categorization community has not displayed much creativity in devising document weighting techniques specific to TC. In fact, most of the works reported in the TC literature so far use the standard document weighting techniques, either of a statistical or of a probabilistic nature, which are used in all other subfields of IR, including text search. The only exception to this we know is , where the *idf* component in *tfidf* is replaced by a function learnt from training data, and aimed at assessing how good a term is at discriminating categories from each other. Also in TC, as in other subfields of IR, the use of larger indexing units, such as frequently adjacent pairs or syntactically determined phrases, has not shown systematic patterns of improvement, which means that terms are usually made to coincide with single words, stemmed or not.
- Classifier Learning Techniques
  The number of classes of classifier learning techniques that have been used in TC is bewildering. These include at the very least probabilistic methods, regression methods, decision tree and decision rule learners, neural networks, batch and incremental learners of linear classifiers, example-based methods, support vector machines, genetic algorithms, hidden Markov models, and classifier committees (which include boosting methods).
  Rather than attempting to say even a few words about each of them, we will introduce in some detail two of them, namely support vector machines and boosting. The reasons for this choice are twofold. First, these are the two methods that have unquestionably shown the best performance in comparative TC experiments so far. Second, these are the newest methods in the classifier learning arena, and the ones with the strongest justifications from computational learning theory.

Proposed Solutions

The proposed system shall have two major phases of execution where the first phase deals with the input to the system and the second phase deals with the actual categorization.

Phase 1: System can accept data in pdf, RTF, word format. So in this phase the system converts the data into proper format i.e., ASCII format.

Phase 2: Here system will parse the data and this process is called as Tokenization. After which system will match each word with different word set and decide its category.

Applications

- The need to handle and organize documents in which the textual component is either the unique, or dominant, or simplest to interpret, component.
- The need to handle and organize *large* quantities of such documents, i.e. large enough that their manual organization into classes is either too expensive or not feasible within the time constraints imposed by the application.
- The fact that the set of categories is known in advance, and its variation over time is small.

2. Bibliography

[1] Crammer, K. & Singer, Y., On the algorithmic implementation of multiclass kernel-based vector machines. *Journal of Machine Learning Research*, **2**, pp. 265–292, 2001.

[2] Sebastiani, F.,Machine learning in automated text categorization. *ACM Computing Surveys*, **34(1)**, pp. 1–47, 2002.

[3] Frakes, W.B., Stemming algorithms. *Information Retrieval: Data Structures and Algorithms*, eds. W.B. Frakes & R. Baeza-Yates, Prentice Hall: Englewood Cliffs, US, pp. 131–160, 1992.

[4] Caropreso, M.F., Matwin, S. & Sebastiani, F., A learner-independent evaluation of the usefulness of statistical phrases for automated text categorization. *Text Databases and Document Management: Theory and Practice*, ed. A.G. Chin, Idea Group Publishing: Hershey, US, pp. 78–102, 2001.

[5] Zobel, J. & Moffat, A., Exploring the similarity space. *SIGIR Forum*, **32(1)**, pp. 18–34, 1998.

[6] Salton, G. & Buckley, C., Term-weighting approaches in automatic text retrieval. *Information Processing and Management*, **24(5)**, pp. 513–523, 1988. Also reprinted in [63], pp. 323–328.

[7] Yang, Y., A study on thresholding strategies for text categorization. *Proceedings of SIGIR-01, 24th ACM International Conference on Research and Development in Information Retrieval*, eds. W.B. Croft, D.J. Harper, D.H. Kraft & J. Zobel, ACM Press, New York, US: New Orleans, US, pp. 137– 145, 2001.

[8] Debole, F. & Sebastiani, F., Supervised term weighting for automated text categorization. *Proceedings of SAC-03, 18th ACM Symposium on Applied Computing*, ACM Press, New York, US: Melbourne, US, pp. 784–788, 2003. An extended version appears as [64].

[9] Lewis, D.D., An evaluation of phrasal and clustered representations on a text categorization task. *Proceedings of SIGIR-92, 15th ACM International Conference on Research and Development in Information Retrieval*, eds. N.J. Belkin, P. Ingwersen & A.M. Pejtersen, ACM Press, New York, US: Ko

Semi-Supervised Learning for Text Classification

Prof. Nitin N. Pise
Asst. Professor (Computer Engineering),
Maharashtra Institute of Technology,
Sr. No. 124, Paud Road, Kothrud, Pune – 411038, INDIA.
nnpise@yahoo.com, nnpise@rediffmail.com

Abstract

Automatic text classification is an important research area due to current growth of Internet, which has resulted in huge amount of information that has become a challenge to access efficiently. In the modern world, there is a growing need for text classification, because the sources of information to be managed, such as web pages, news sources, and database management, are increasing rapidly.

The paper discusses basic text classification process, existing supervised and un-supervised learning methods, Then how the use of unlabeled data increases classifier performance is explained. Semi-supervised learning addresses the problem of labelled data by using large amount of unlabeled data, together with the labelled data, to build better classifiers. Because semi-supervised learning requires less human effort and gives higher accuracy, it is of great interest both in theory and in practice. The paper discusses various important approaches to semi-supervised learning such as self-training, co-training(CO), expectation maximization (EM) ,CO-EM, Then the use of graph-based methods is explained.

Then the limitations of existing learning methods are explained. Finally a new adaptive learning methodology is proposed where learning can be either supervised, unsupervised or semi-supervised and it can switch from supervised to unsupervised or semi-supervised as per the scenario.

Index Terms – Semi-Supervised, Learning, Text Classification, Classifier, Training

1. Introduction

Information retrieval (IR) [12] deals with the representation, storage, organization of and access to information items. The representation and organization of the information items should provide the user with easy access to the information in which he is interested. The user must first translate this information need into a query which can be processed by the search engine (or IR system). In its most common form, this translation yields a set of keywords (or index terms) which summarizes the description of the user information need. Given the user query, the key goal of an IR system is to retrieve information which might be useful or relevant to the user. The emphasis is on the retrieval of information.

The aim of text classification is to assign a new document to one or more categories based on their content. Text classification is a multi-label classification problem because a document might be relevant to several categories. The process of automatic text classification is to analyze the content of training document, build some classification schemes (i.e. classifiers) and then classify test documents using these classification schemes. Automated text classification has been used in a number of different applications: automatic indexing, content management, filtering, and routing, word sense disambiguation, and Yahoo!- style search space categorization. A plethora of techniques have been developed for text classification, including Nearest-Neighbors, Neural Networks, Naïve Bayes, Decision Trees, and Support Vector Machines (SVMs). In most cases, the classification algorithms require sufficient training data in order to generalize well on unseen documents.

In recent years we have seen a tremendous growth in the number of text document collections available on the Internet. As a result, there is an overriding need to provide effective content-based text retrieval, search and querying capabilities. Automatic text categorization, the process of assigning unseen documents to user-defined categories, is an important task that can help in the organization and querying of such collections. Using automatic text categorization, one can rapidly enable such retrieval and querying capabilities on a large scale.

2. Text Operations

Not all words are equally significant for representing the semantics of a document. In written language, some words carry more meaning than others. Usually, noun words (or groups of noun words) are the ones which are most representative of document content. Therefore, it is usually considered worthwhile to pre-process the text of the documents in the collection to determine the terms to be used as index terms. During this pre-processing phase other useful text operations can be performed such as elimination of stop words, stemming (reduction of a word to its grammatical root), the building of a thesaurus, and compression.

We say that using the set of all words in a collection to index its documents generates too much noise for the retrieval task. One way to reduce this noise is to reduce the set of words which can be used to refer to (i.e. to index) documents. Thus, the pre-processing of the documents in the collection might be viewed simply as a process of controlling the size of the vocabulary (i.e. the number of distinct words used as index terms). It is expected that the use of a controlled vocabulary leads to an improvement in retrieval performance.

3. Related Work

K-nearest neighbour (KNN) [19] is a statistical and most accurate method of classifying documents. Given a document, KNN selects k most similar documents from the training set and uses the categories of these documents to determine categories of the document being classified. Even with optimized k, it performs poorly in comparison with other methods. Also required classification time is long. Also it is difficult to find optimal value of k.

SVM uses decision surfaces to divide data points into classes. Simply training documents are represented as vectors and algorithm determines hyper planes that separate different classes of training documents. Test documents are classified according to their positions with respect to the hyper planes. But SVM has some drawbacks. It requires high computations to train the data. It needs a good kernel function. Also, SVM is sensitive to noisy data and hence prone to over fitting. Parameter tuning is difficult.

Decision Tree Learning [19] is one of the most widely used techniques. Its accuracy is competitive with other methods, and it is very efficient. Here the classification model is a tree, called decision tree. There are some disadvantages of decision tree learning. Training-time is relatively expensive. A document is only connected with one branch. Once a mistake is made at a higher level, any sub tree is wrong. It does not handle continuous variable well. A a "fully grown" tree may be prone to over fitting, as some branches may be too specific to the training data.

Naïve Bayes (NB) Learning [19] is widely used because of its simplicity and computational efficiency. NB uses relative frequencies of words in a document as words probabilities and uses these probabilities to assign a category to the document. But it needs several training papers for each topic to classify an unknown paper. Introducing intelligence is difficult. Also it performs very poorly when features are highly correlated.

Figure.1 shows the overall flow diagram of the text categorization task. Consider a set of labeled documents from a source $D = [d1, d2, K dn]$ belonging to a set of classes $C = [c1, c2, K, cp]$. The text categorization task is to train the classifier using these documents, and assign categories to new documents. In the training phase, the n documents are arranged in p separate folders, where each folder corresponds to one class. In the next step, the training data set is prepared via a feature selection process.

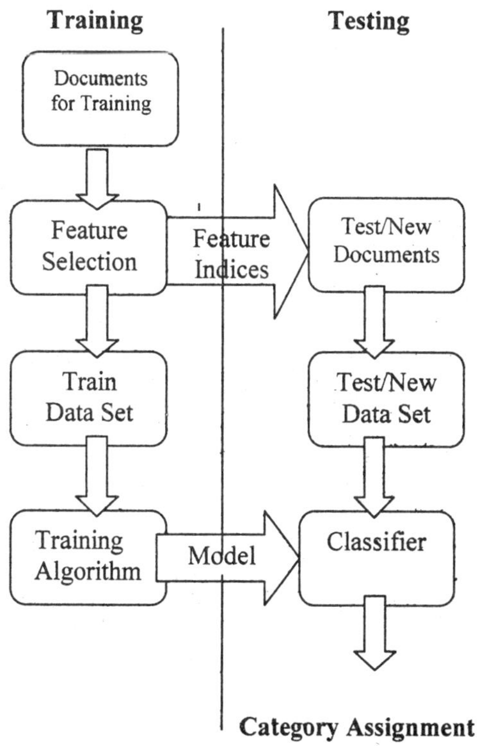

Fig. 1 Flow Diagram of Text Classification

It is observed from previous research that words work well as features for many text categorization tasks. In the feature space representation, the sequences of characters of text documents are represented as sequence of words. Feature selection involves tokenising the text, indexing and feature space reduction. Text can be tokenised using term frequency (TF), inverse document frequency (IDF), term frequency inverse document frequency (TFIDF) or using binary representation.

Many supervised learning methods have been applied to text classification problem. K-nearest neighbour classification compares testing document with training documents, and determines the categories of testing document according to k-nearest neighbour's categories. Linear Least Squares Fit described by Shi Hong Bo (2002) estimates the likelihood of the association between document terms and categories via a linear parametric model. Naïve Bayes classification by Y.C. Fang assumes all features of document are independent of each other given a category. Under such assumption, learning scheme estimates the conditional probability of each feature given a category, and then determines the category to which testing document belongs according to these conditional probabilities. The Naïve Bayes classifier described by (Baoyi Wang, 2005 ; Y.C. Fang) is a popular machine learning method for text classification because it is fast and easy to implement and performs well. Its severe assumption that each feature word is independent with other feature words in a document makes higher efficiency possible but also adversely affects the quality of its results because some of feature words are interrelated.

Use of Self- Organizing Maps (SOM), Growing Hierarchical SOM (GHSOM) described by Andres Rauber, Nitin Pise(2005, 2006) [1, 8, 9] [which are the architectures of neural networks can be used for document classification.

Xiaojin Zhu (2005) describes support vector machines which select a small number of critical boundary documents from each category and build a discriminant function that separates them widely as possible. Tree- Augmented Naïve Bayes (TAN) is a tree like structure Bayesian network proposed by Friedman, which is the natural extend of Naive Bayesian model. Its main idea is to combine the simplicity of Naïve Bayesian classifier with the ability to express the dependence among attributes in Bayesian network, which can enhance the classification performance of the classifier.

4. Supervised and Unsupervised Learning

In supervised learning, generally target values are given. The data are labeled with pre-defined classes. It Is like that a "teacher" that gives the classes. Test data are classified into these classes. These require a large amount of labeled data to achieve high performance by accurately labeling new instances in the future. These samples have to be manually labeled by a human annotator, which requires expert who is knowledgeable in the application domain. The process itself is expensive and can be very slow and error-prone.

Richard Duda et al. (2006) [13] investigate a number of unsupervised procedures, which use unlabelled samples. There are at least five reasons for interest in unsupervised procedures. First collecting and labeling a large set of sample patterns can be costly. Second, one might wish to proceed in the reverse direction: Train with large amounts of less expensive unlabeled data, and only then use supervision to label the groupings found.

Richard Duda et al. (2006) give detailed description of k-means clustering, unsupervised Bayesian Learning, where the training samples are used to compute the posterior density p (Θ | D). Y.C. Fang explains one strategy based on Principle Direction Divisive Partitioning; [27], an unsupervised document clustering algorithm and how it improves classifier performance is explained.

In the unsupervised case the solution suffers from the usual problems associated with parametric assumptions without providing any of the benefits of computational simplicity.

5. Need for Semi-Supervised Learning

As very large data is involved with some applications, if supervised Learning is carried out, it will take very long time for training the system with labelled samples. So the labelled samples or categories are not available, unsupervised learning i.e. clustering techniques have to be applied so that given input patterns are classified into nearest matching classes. So the study involves the mixed approach, i.e. semi-supervised learning which can be applied to various fields. E.g. web filtering where a very large number of unseen documents are involved and intrusion detection using text classification.

Semi supervised learning refers to the use of both labeled and unlabeled data for training. It contrasts supervised learning (data all labeled) or unsupervised learning (data all unlabeled). In many learning tasks, unlabeled data is plentiful but labeled data is limited and expensive to generate. Because it requires less human effort and gives higher accuracy, it is of great interest.

In many practical learning domains e.g. text processing, there is a large supply of unlabeled data but limited labelled data, and in most cases it can be expensive to generate that labelled data.

6. Survey of Semi-Supervised Learning Methods

Recently, there has been a lot of interest in the continuum between completely supervised and unsupervised learning (Nigam, 2001; Ghani, Jones, &Rosenberg, 2003). Classification described by Sugato Basu et al., (2004) is a supervised task, where supervision is provided in the form of a set of labelled training data, each data point having a class label selected from a fixed set of classes (Mitchell, 1997). The goal in classification is to learn a function from the training data that gives the best prediction of the class label of unseen (test) data points. Generative models for classification learn the joint distribution of the data and class variables by assuming a particular parametric form of the underlying distribution that generated the data points in each class.

The framework of semi-supervised learning is applicable to both classification and clustering defined by Sugato Basu et al. (2004) Supervised classification has a fixed known set of categories, and category-labelled training data is used to induce a classification function. In this setting, the training can also exploit additional unlabeled data, frequently resulting in a more accurate classification function. Several semi-supervised classification algorithms that use unlabeled data to improve classification accuracy have become popular in the past few years, which include co-training (Blum & Mitchell, 1998), transductive support vector machines (Joachims, 1999), and using Expectation Maximization to incorporate unlabeled data into training (Ghahramani & Jordan, 1994; Nigam et al., 2000). Unlabeled data have also been used to learn good distance measures in the classification setting (Hastie & Tibshirani,1996). A good review of semi-supervised classification methods is given by Xiaojin Zhu, 2007; Pavan Kumar Mallapragada.

A variety of semi-supervised techniques have been developed for both generative and discriminative models. A straightforward, generative semi-supervised method is the expectation maximization (EM) algorithm. The EM approach for naïve Bayes text classification models is discussed by Nigam et al. (2000) proposed two augmentations to the basic EM to improve classifier accuracy. The first extension introduces a weighting factor which dynamically adjusts the strength of the unlabeled data.

Generative semi-supervised methods rely on a model for the distribution of the input data, and can fail either when this model is wrong, or when the structure of the input data is not correlated with the classification task Discriminative semi-supervised methods, including probabilistic and non-probabilistic approaches, such as transductive or semi-supervised support vector machines (TSVMs, S3VMs) and a variety of other graph based methods assume high density within class and low density between classes, and can fail when the classes are strongly overlapping.

6.1 Self-Training

Self-training is a commonly used technique for semi-supervised learning. In self-training a classifier is first trained with the small amount of labelled data. The classifier is then used to classify the unlabeled data. Typically the most confident unlabelled points, together with their predicted labels, are added to the training set. The classifier is re-trained and the procedure repeated. Note the classifier uses its own predictions to teach itself. The procedure is also called self-teaching. The generative model and EM approach can be viewed as a special case of 'soft' self-training. One can imagine that a classification mistake can reinforce itself. Some algorithms try to avoid this by 'unlearn' unlabeled points if the prediction confidence drops below a threshold. .Self-training has been applied to several natural language processing tasks.

6.2 Co-Training and Expectation Maximization (EM)

Co-training (Blum & Mitchell, 1998) (Mitchell, 1999) assumes that (i) features can be split into two sets; (ii) each sub-feature set is sufficient to train a good classifier; (iii) the two sets are conditionally independent given the class. Initially two separate classifiers are trained with the labelled data, on the two sub-feature sets respectively. Each classifier then classifies the unlabeled data, and 'teaches' the other classifier with the few unlabeled examples (and the predicted labels) they feel most confident. Each classifier is retrained with the additional training examples given by the other classifier, and the process repeats.

In co-training, unlabeled data helps by reducing the version space size. In other words, the two classifiers (or hypotheses) must agree on the much larger unlabeled data as well as the labelled data.

Nigam and Ghani (2000) perform extensive empirical experiments to compare co-training with generative mixture models and EM. The use of EM [11] for semi-supervised learning has been proposed in (Miller & Uyar, 1997).

6.3 Transductive SVMs

Transductive support vector machine (TSVM) is an extension of standard support vector machines with unlabeled data. In a standard SVM only the labelled data is used, and the goal is to find a maximum margin linear boundary in the Reproducing Kernel Hilbert Space. In a TSVM the unlabeled data is also used. The goal is to find a labelling of the unlabeled data, so that a linear boundary has the maximum margin on both the original labelled data and the (now labelled) unlabeled data. The decision boundary has the smallest generalization error bound on unlabeled data (Vapnik, 1998). Intuitively, unlabeled data guides the linear boundary away from dense regions.

However finding the exact transductive SVM solution is NP-hard. Major effort has focused on efficient approximation algorithms. Early algorithms

(Bennett & Demiriz, 1999) (Demirez & Bennett, 2000) (Fung & Mangasarian, 1999) either cannot handle more than a few hundred unlabeled examples, or did not do so in experiments. The SVM-light TSVM implementation (Joachims, 1999) is the first widely used software.

6.4 Graph-Based Methods

Rouhollah Rahmani and Sally A. Goldman (2006) defined graph-based semi-supervised methods [22] where the nodes are labelled and unlabeled examples in the dataset, and edges (may be weighted) reflect the similarity of examples. Graph methods are nonparametric, discriminative, and transductive in nature. Some of the graph-based methods like mincut, harmonic, local and global consistency, manifold regularization are discussed by Xiaojin Zhu (2006).

MISSL (Multiple-Instance Semi-Supervised Learning) [14] that transforms any MI problem into an input for a graph-based single-instance semi-supervised learning method that encodes the MI aspects of the problem simultaneously working at both the bag and point levels is described by Rouhollah Rahmani and Sally A. Goldman (2006). MISSL makes use of the unlabeled data.

Many of these graph based methods discussed by Marko Grobelnik and Dunja Mladenic (2007) do not scale well since the cost is cubic in the size of the graph.

6.5 Multi-view Learning

Co-training by K. Nigam et al., (2000) and related multi-view learning methods by Gregory Druck et al., (2007) assume that multiple classifiers are trained over multiple feature views (splits) of the same labelled examples. As capacity control, these classifiers are encouraged to make the same prediction on any unlabeled example. However, multiple feature views often do not naturally exist in practice, and these methods resort to artificially creating random feature splits.

6.6 Generative Discriminitive Hybrids

In many approaches, parameters are separated into two subsets, one of which is trained discriminatively and the other generatively. Raina, present a model for document classification in which documents are split into multiple regions. For a newsgroup message, regions might include the header and the body. In this model, each region has its own set parameters that are trained generatively, while the parameters that weight the importance of each region in the final classification are trained discriminatively. Experimental results show that this hybrid algorithm gives better classification accuracy than either naïve Bayes or logistic regression alone.

6.7 Semi-supervised subspace learning

Semi-supervised subspace learning algorithm [20] by Xiaofei He (2004) incrementally learns an adaptive subspace by preserving the semantic structure of the image space, based on user interactions in a relevance feedback driven query-by-example system. The algorithm is capable of accumulating knowledge from users, which could result in new feature representations for images in the database so that the system's future retrieval performance can be enhanced. Experiments on a large collection of images have shown the effectiveness and efficiency of the algorithm.

6.8 Semi-Supervised Classification with Markov Random Fields

Xiaojin Zhu and Zoubin Ghahramani, 2002) describe the use of Boltzmann machines in semi-supervised classification. It treats the labelled / unlabeled dataset as a Markov random field, and derive a Boltmann machine learning algorithm for it to learn the feature weights, label noise and labels for unlabeled data at all once.

6.9 With Label Propagation

Xiaojin Zhu and Zoubin Ghahramani (2002) give a simple iterative algorithm, label propagation [24], to propagate labels through the dataset along with high density areas defined by unlabeled data. The problem is formulated as a particular form of label propagation, where a node's labels propagate to neighbouring nodes according to their proximity.

6.10 Combining Active Learning with Gaussian Fields and Harmonic Functions

Active learning and semi-supervised learning are combined under a Gaussian random field model. Labelled and unlabeled data are represented as vertices in a weighted graph, with edge weights encoding the similarity between instances. The semi-supervised learning problem is then formulated in terms of a Gaussian random field on this graph, the mean of which is characterized in terms of harmonic functions. Active learning is performed on top of the semi supervised learning scheme by greedily selecting queries from the unlabeled data to minimize the estimated expected classification error (risk); in the case of Gaussian fields the risk is efficiently computed using matrix methods. Xiaojin Zhu et al. (2005) presents experimental results on synthetic data, hand written digit recognition, and text classification tasks. Maria-Florina Balcan et al. (2005) explains the use of simple Gaussian field and harmonic function algorithm on the FreeFoodCam dataset.

6.11 Other Methods

Xiaojin Zhu et al. presents an algorithm based on convex optimization for constructing kernels for semi-supervised learning. The kernel matrices are derived from the spectral decomposition of graph Laplacians, and combine labelled and unlabeled data in a systematic fashion. A nonparametric kernel approach is presented that incorporates order constraints during optimization.

7. Evaluation using Machine Learning Datasets

To evaluate structure learning methods with labelled and unlabeled data, Ira Cohen,et al., (2004) started with an empirical study involving simulated data. They artificially generated data to investigate: 1) whether the structure stochastic search (SSS) algorithm finds a structure that is close to the structure that generated the data and 2) whether the algorithm uses unlabeled data to improve the classification performance. A typical result is as follows: They generated data from a TAN structure with 10 features. The data set consisted of 300 labelled and 30,000 unlabeled records. They first estimated the Bayes error rate by learning with the correct structure and with a very large fully labelled data set. They obtained a classification accuracy of 92:49 percent. They learned one Naive Bayes classifier with only the labelled records and another with both labelled and unlabeled records. Finally, they learned a Bayesian network classifier with SSS algorithm using both labelled and unlabeled records. The results are presented in the first row of Table 1. With the correct structure, adding unlabeled data improves performance significantly (columns TAN-L and EM-TAN). Note that adding unlabeled data degraded the performance from 16 percent error to 40 percent error when they learned the Naive Bayes classifier.

Table 1 Classification Results (in %) for Naive Bayes, TAN

Dataset	Train #lab	Train #unlab	Test	NB-L	SSS
TAN Aritificial	300	30000	500 00	83.4	91.1

8. Proposed Learning Methodology

8.1 Limitations of existing learning methods

If new examples are given for classification, new learning is required. So incremental learning is not possible. Learning process is time consuming. If new features are considered for the learning, again training is required. There are flaws in learning methodologies, feature set selection. Also there are limitations in learning due to optimal feature set selection and their inter-relations. So distinguishing factors must be surfaced.

There is bias in the semi-supervised learning methods. Either first supervised learning takes place and then unsupervised learning is done or vice versa but not simultaneously. Incremental learning is not possible. Many semi-supervised learning methods scale as badly as $O(n^3)$ as they were originally proposed. Because semi-supervised learning is interesting when the size of unlabeled data is large, this is clearly a problem.

8.2 Adaptive Learning Methodology

The authors propose a new framework for learning to overcome the drawbacks of existing learning methods. The proposed learning methodology will be intelligent. Focus will be on adaptive learning based on perspective from experience. It can be a supervised or unsupervised or semi-supervised. There will be switching among these learning methods as per the requirement. Figure 2 shows the proposed adaptive learning methodology.

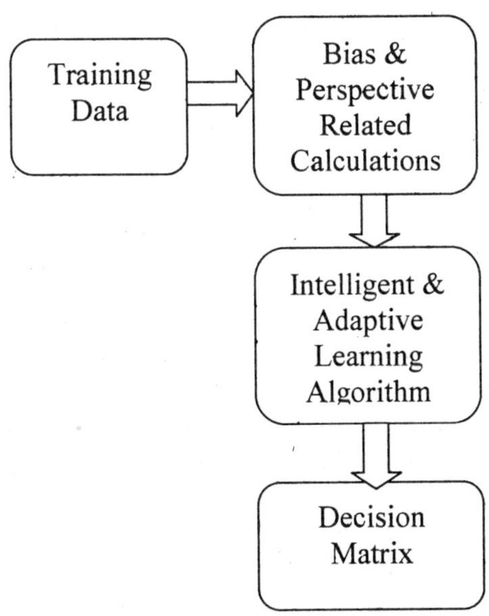

Fig. 2 Proposed Adaptive Learning

9. Conclusion and Future Work

Nowadays, text classification on large-scale real documents has become a popular problem in many fields, such as natural language processing, information retrieval, artificial intelligence, and distributed computing.

To fully utilize the potential of unlabeled data, the abilities and limitations of existing methods must be understood. Semi-supervised learning is still a very young discipline; more work is needed to develop the field.

The authors propose a new adaptive learning methodology where learning can be either supervised, unsupervised or semi-supervised and it can switch from supervised to unsupervised or semi-supervised as per the scenario by considering all perspectives.

10. Acknowledgment

I would like to acknowledge BCUD, University of Pune for granting Rs. 1.5 lakhs for this research. Also I would like to thank the management of MIT, Pune for providing all facilities for the research.

11. References

[1] Andres Rauber, The GHSOM Architecture and Training Process, http://www.ifs.tuwien.ac.at/~andi/ghsom/description.htm

[2] Baoyi Wang, Shaomin Zhang, 2005, A Novel Text Classification Algorithm Based on Naïve Bayes and KLdivergence, Proceedings of the Sixth IEEE International Conference on Parallel and Distributed Computing, Applications and Technologies.

[3] Gregory Druck, Chris Pal, Xiaojin Zhu, Andrew McCallum, 2007, Semi-Supervised Classification with Hybrid Generative/Discriminative Methods, KDD, San Jose, California, USA.

[4] Ira Cohen, Fabio G. Cozman, Nicu Sebe, Marcelo C. Cirelo,Thomas S. Huang, 2004, Semi Supervised Learning of Classifiers: Theory, Algorithms, and Their Application to Human-Computer Interaction", IEEE Transactions On Pattern Analysis And Machine Intelligence, Vol. 26, No. 12, pp 1553-1567.

[5] Kamal Nigam, A. McCallum, S. Thrun, and T. Mitchell, 2000, Text classification from labelled and unlabeled documents using EM", Machine Learning, 1–34, Kluwer Academic Publishers, Boston.

[6] Maria-Florina Balcan, Avrim Blum, Patrick Pakyan Choi, John Lafferty, Mugizi Robert Rwebangira, Xiaojin Zhu, 2005, Person Identification in Webcam Images: An Application of Semi-Supervised Learning", Proc. of the ICML Workshop on Learning with Partially Classified Training Data, Bonn, Germany.

[7] Marko Grobelnik, Dunja Mladenic, 2007, Text Mining, Link Analysis and Semantic Web, Jozef Stefan Institute Ljubljana, Slovenia, KDD.

[8] Nitin Pise, 2005 Document Classification using Neural Networks, Proceedings of International Conference on Cognitive Systems, New Delhi, India.

[9] Nitin Pise, 2006, Application of Neural Network in Information Retrieval", Proceedings of National Conference on Artificial Intelligence, Baramati, India.

[10] Pavan Kumar Mallapragada, Rong Jin, Anil K. Jain, and Yi Liu, "SemiBoost: Boosting for Semi-supervised Learning", Department of Computer Science and Engineering, Michigan State University.

[11] Pedro J. Moreno, Shivani Agarwal, 2003, An Experimental Study of EM-Based Algorithms for Semi-Supervised Learning in Audio Classification, Proceedings of the ICML-2003 Workshop on The Continuum from Labelled to Unlabeled Data, Washington DC.

[12] Ricardo Bacza-Yates, Berthier Ribeiro Neto,2004, Modern Information Retrieval, Pearson Education.

[13] Richard Duda, Peter Hart, David Stork, 2006, Pattern Classificaion", John Wiley & Sons (Asia) Pte Ltd.

[14] Rouhollah Rahmani, Sally A. Goldman, 2006, "MISSL: Multiple-Instance Semi-Supervised Learning", 23 rd International Conference on Machine Learning, Pittsburgh, PA.

[15] S. Mohanty, P. K. Santi, Ranjeeta Mishra, R.N. Mohapatra, Sabyasachi Swain, 2006, "Semantic Based Text Classification Using WordNets: Indian Language Perspective", in Proceedings of GWC, Masaryk University, pp. 321–324.

[16] Setu Madhavi Namburu, Haiying Tu, Jianhui Luo and Krishna R. Pattipati, "Experiments on Supervised Learning Algorithms for Text Categorization", Dept. of ECE, University of Connecticut, USA.

[17] Shi Hong Bo, Wang Zhi-Hai, Hunag, Hau-Kuan, Jing-li-Ping, 2002, "Text Classification Based on the TAN Model", Proceedings of IEEE Region 10 Conference on Computers, Communications, Control and Power Engineering, pp 43-46.

[18] Sugato Basu, Mikhail Bilenko, Raymond J. Mooney, 2004, "A Probabilistic Framework for Semi-supervised Clustering", Proceedings of the Tenth ACM SIGKDD International Conference on Knowledge Discovery and Data Mining.

[19] Tom Mitchell, Machine Learning. McGraw Hill, 1997.

[20] Xiaofei He, 2004, Incremental Semi-Supervised Subspace Learning for Image Retrieval ACM MM.

[21] Xiaojin Zhu, 2007, Semi-Supervised Learning Literature Survey, Computer Sciences TR 1530, University of Wisconsin – Madison.

[22] Xiaojin Zhu, 2005, Semi-Supervised Learning with Graphs", Doctoral Thesis, Carnegie Mellon University.

[23] Xiaojin Zhu, Zoubin Ghahramani, Towards Semi-Supervised Classification with Markov Random Field, School of Computer Science, Carnegie Mellon University, USA.

[24] Xiaojin Zhu, Zoubin Ghahramani, 2002, Learning from Labeled ans Unlabeled Data with Label Propogation",m Field", School of Computer Science, Carnegie Mellon University, USA.

[25] Xiaojin Zhu, 2007, Semi-Supervised Learning Tutorial, International Conference on Machine Learning.

[26] Xiaojin Zhu, Z. Ghahramani and J. Lafferty, 2003, Semi-supervised learning using Gaussian fields and harmonic functions, 20th International Conference on Machine Learning.

[27] Y.C. Fang, S. Parthasarathy, F. Schwartz, "Using Clustering to Boost Text Classification", Ohio State University.

Spatial Databases Emerging New Type of Databases

Swati S. Sabnis (MCA, M.Phil (CS))
JSPM's ABACUS Institute of Computer Application, Hadapsar, Pune
swatisabnis7@gmail.com

Abstract

Spatial databases are used in geography, biology, statistics, geographic information science, remote sensing, computer science, mathematics, and scientific modeling. In this paper initially information about the spatial data is mentioned followed by spatial data model consisting of elements, geometries, and layers. It is followed by fundamental database elements. Introduction spatial queries consisting of range query, adjacency and overlays with analysis on spatial databases. It is followed by Database Content and an organization mission. We will conclude this paper with the requirement of spatial techniques for spatial indexing.

Keywords: *Element, geometry, layer, range query, proximity query, adjacency, overlays.*

1. Introduction

Spatial databases provide concepts for databases that keep track of objects in a multidimensional space. Spatial database is a database that is optimized to store and query data related to objects in space, including points, lines and polygons. Typical databases can understand various numeric and character types of data, additional functionality need to be added for databases to process spatial data types. These are typically called geometry or feature.

2. Spatial Data

A common example of spatial data can be in a road map. A road map is a 2-dimensional object that contains points, lines and polygons that represent cities roads and political boundaries as states or provinces. A road map is a visualization of geographic information. The location of cities, roads and political boundaries that exist on surface of the Earth are projected onto a 2 dimensional display or piece of paper preserving the relative positions and relative distances of the rendered objects.

The data that indicates the Earth location (latitude and longitude or height and depth) of these rendered objects is the spatial data. When the map is rendered, this spatial data is used to project the locations of the objects on a 2-dimensional piece of paper. A GIS (Geographic Information System) is often used to store, retrieve and render this Earth-relative spatial data.

Other types of spatial data include data from computer-aided design (CAD) and computer aided manufacturing (CAM) systems. Instead of operating on objects on a geographic scale CAD/CAM systems work on a smaller scale such as for an automobile or much smaller scale as for printed circuit boards.

The differences among these systems GIS and CAD/CAM are only in the scale of the data, not its complexity. They might all actually involve the same number of data points. On a geographic scale, the location of a bridge can vary by a few tenths of an inch without causing any noticeable problems to the road builders. But if diameter of an engine's piston is off by a few tenths of an inch, the engine will not run. A printed circuit board is likely to have many thousands of objects etched on its surface that are no bigger than the smallest detail shown on a road builder's blueprints.

3. Spatial Databases

The Spatial Data Management Systems are designed to make the storage, retrieval and manipulation of spatial data easier and more natural to users such as a GIS. Once this data is stored in a spatial database, it can be easily and meaningfully manipulated and retrieved as it relates to all the other data stored in the database. Spatial databases provide concepts for databases that keep track of objects in a multi dimensional space. e.g. cartographic database and GIS databases that store maps include two-dimensional spatial descriptions of their objects. These databases are used in many applications, such as environmental, logistic management and war strategies. Other databases such as meteorological databases for weather information are three-dimensional. In general a spatial database stores objects that have spatial characteristics that describe them. The spatial relationships among objects are important and they are needed when querying the database. A spatial database can refer to an n-dimensional space for any 'n'.

The main extensions that are needed for spatial databases are models that can interpret spatial characteristics. In addition, spatial indexing and storage structures are often needed to improve performance. The basic extensions needed are to include 2-D geometric concepts such as points, lines, segments, circles, polygons, arcs etc., in order to specify the spatial characteristics of objects. In addition spatial operations are needed to operate on the objects' spatial characteristics. For example, we need spatial operations to compare the distance between two objects and other such operations. We also need spatial Boolean conditions to check whether two objects spatially overlap and perform other similar operations e.g. a geographic information system will contain description of the spatial positions of many types of objects. Some objects such as highways, buildings, and other landmarks have static spatial characteristics. Other objects like vehicles, temporary building etc. have dynamic spatial characteristics that change over time.

4. Spatial Data Model

The spatial data model is a hierarchical structure consisting of elements, geometries and layers which correspond to representations of spatial data. Layers are composed of geometries, which in turn are made up of elements. e.g. a point might represent a building location, a line string might be a road or flight path, and a polygon could be a state, city, zoning district or city block.

4.1 Element

An element is the basic building block of a geometric feature for the Spatial Data Option. The supported spatial element types are points, line strings and polygons. e.g. elements might be modeled to historic markers (point clusters), roads (line strings) and country boundaries (Polygon). Each coordinate in an element is stored as an x, y pair. [1]

Point data consists of one coordinate and the sequence number is 0. Line data consists of two coordinates representing a line segment of the element, starting with sequence number 0. Polygon data consists of coordinate pair values. One vertex pair for each line segment of the polygon. The first coordinate pair (with sequence number 0), represents the first line segment. With coordinates defined in either a clockwise or counter clockwise order around the polygon with successive sequence numbers. Each layer's geometric objects and their associated spatial index are stored in the database in tables.

4.2 Geometry

A geometry or geometric object is the representation of a user's spatial feature modeled as an ordered set of primitive elements. Each geometric object is required to be uniquely identified by a numeric geometry identifier (GID), associating the object with its corresponding attribute set.

A complex geometric feature such as a polygon with holes would be stored as a sequence of polygon elements. In a multi element polygonal geometry, all sub elements are wholly contained within the outermost element, thus building a more complex geometry from simpler pieces e.g. geometry might describe the fertile land in a village. This could be represented as a polygon with holes that represent buildings or objects that prevent cultivation.

4.3 Layer

A layer is a heterogeneous collection of geometries having the same attribute set e.g. one layer in a GIS might include topographical features, while another describes population density, and a third describes the network of roads and bridges in the area (lines and points).

5. Fundamental Database elements

Elements of reality modeled in a GIS database have two identities:

1. The element in reality - entity
2. The element as it is represented in the database - object

A third identity that is important in cartographic applications is the symbol that is used to depict the object/entity as a feature on a map or other graphic display

These definitions and the following concepts are based on those defined by the DCDSTF, (Digital Cartographic Data Standards Task Force) [2]

5.1 Entity

- An entity is "a phenomenon of interest in reality that is not further subdivided into phenomena of the same kind"
    - e.g. a city could be considered an entity and subdivided into component parts but these parts would not be called cities, they would be districts, neighborhoods or the like
    - e.g. a forest could be subdivided into smaller forests

5.2 Object

- An object is "a digital representation of all or part of an entity"

- The method of digital representation of a phenomenon varies according to scale, purpose and other factors
  - e.g. a city could be represented geographically as a point if the area under consideration were continental in scale
  - The same city could be geographically represented as an area if we are dealing with a geographic database for a state or a county

5.3 Entity types

- Similar phenomena to be stored in a database are identified as entity types
- An entity type is any grouping of similar phenomena that should eventually get represented and stored in a uniform way, e.g. roads, rivers, elevations, vegetation
  - Provides convenient conceptual framework for describing phenomena at a general level
  - Organizational perspective influences this interpretation to a large degree
- Precise definitions should be generated for each entity type
  - Helps with identifying overlapping categories of information
  - Aids in clarifying the content of the database [2]
- The first step in database development is the selection and definition of entity types to be included
  - This is guided by the organization's mandate and purpose of the database
  - This framework can be as important as the actual database because it guides the development
- The second step of database design is to choose an appropriate method of spatial representation for each of the entity types

5.4 Spatial object type

- The digital representation of entity types in a spatial database requires the selection of appropriate spatial object types
- The National Standard for Digital Cartographic Databases specifies a basic list of spatial objects and their characteristics
- This classification is based on the following definition of spatial dimensions: 0-D - an object that has a position in space, but no length
  - A point 1-D - an object having a length
  - Composed of two or more 0-D objects
  - A line 2-D - an object having a length and width
  - Bounded by at least three 1-D line segment objects
    - An area 3-D - an object having a length, width and height/depth
  - Bounded by at least four 2-D objects
  - A volume
    - note very specific definitions for line segment, string, link, chain

5.5 Object classes

An object class is the set of objects which represent the set of entities

- e.g. the set of points representing the set of wells

5.6 Attributes

- An attribute is a characteristic of an entity selected for representation
- Usually non-spatial
  - Though some may be related to the spatial character of the phenomena under study
    - e.g. area, perimeter

5.7 Attribute value

- The actual value of the attribute that has been measured (sampled) and stored in the database
- An entity type is almost always labeled and known by attributes
- e.g. a road usually has a name and is identified according to its class - e.g. alley, freeway
- Attributes values often are conceptually organized in attribute tables which list individual entities in the rows and attributes in the column
  - Entries in each cell of the table represent the attribute value of a specific attribute for a specific entity
  - Note: attribute table is not an official DCDSTF term

5.8 Database model

- It is a conceptual description of a database defining entity type and associated attributes
  - Each entity type is represented by specific spatial objects
- After the database is constructed, the database model is a view of the database which the system can present to the user
  - Other views can be presented, but this one is likely useful because it was important in the conceptual design
    - e.g. the system can model the data in vector form but generate a raster for purposes of display to the user

- Need not be related directly to the way the data are actually stored in the database
  - e.g. census zones may be defined as being represented by polygons, but the program may actually represent the polygon as a series of line segments
- Examples of database models can be grouped by application area
  - e.g. Transportation applications require different database models than do natural resource applications

6. Spatial Queries

Spatial query is the process of selecting features based on their geographic (or spatial) relationship to other features. e.g. you might be interested in finding out which features lie within a certain distance of other features. Which are adjacent to other features? Which are contained inside other features, or which intersect other features.

In spatial databases, you can perform spatial queries using features from different themes. The process of overlaying one theme with another in order to determine their geographic relationships is called spatial overlay. In this way we can analyze the relationships between themes. Let us imagine we are new to a city and want to find a good hotel. Where is the hotel closest to your location? Suppose you are standing at the airport. Two of your themes (airport & hotels) can be analyzed to determine the spatial relationship between them.

Spatial query is part of a larger process called spatial analysis. Spatial analysis combines the various spatial querying techniques into a series of steps, which help to solve problems such as:

- Locating areas of economic deprivation
- Analyzing the proximity of areas of long term illness to industrial regions
- Analyzing flooding patterns and determining the areas and types of land use affected.
- Determining potentially hazardous areas in landslide prone areas
- Determining the relationship between population density and number of schools.

We can categorize the spatial queries into the following types – Range query, nearest neighbor query and spatial query.

6.1 Range Query or Proximity Query

A range query finds objects of a particular type that are within a given a given spatial area or within a particular distance from a given location e.g. find all schools with the Pune city area or find all hospitals within 2 kilometers of the accident etc. are all range queries.

6.2 Nearest Neighbor Query or Adjacency

Nearest neighbor query finds an object of a particular type that is closer to a given location. Adjacency as a special case of proximity query, because you are finding features that are zero distance away from the selected features. Adjacent linear features must be connected and adjacent polygon features must share a common boundary. e.g. find the school that is closest to your house or find the hospital nearest to the accident place etc. are nearest neighbor queries.

6.3 Spatial Joins or Overlays

Overlays join the objects of two types based on some spatial condition, such as the objects intersecting or being within a certain distance of one another e.g. find all the hotels that are on the highway from Pune to Mumbai or find all police stations within 2km of the riot site etc. are spatial joins

7. Spatial Analysis

In statistics, **spatial analysis** or **spatial statistics** includes any of the formal techniques which study entities using their topological, geometric, or geographic properties. The phrase properly refers to a variety of techniques, many still in their early development, using different analytic approaches and applied in fields as diverse as astronomy, with its studies of the placement of galaxies in the cosmos, to chip fabrication engineering, with its use of 'place and route' algorithms to build complex wiring structures. The phrase is often used in a more restricted sense to describe techniques applied to structures at the human scale, most notably in the analysis of geographic data. The phrase is even sometimes used to refer to a specific technique in a single area of research, for example, to describe geostatistics. [3]

Modern spatial analysis focuses on computer based techniques because of the large amount of data, the power of modern statistical and geographic information science (GIS) software, and the complexity of the computational modeling. Spatial analytic techniques have been developed in geography, biology, epidemiology, statistics, geographic information science, remote sensing, computer science, mathematics, and scientific modeling.[4]

8. Database Content and an organization mission

8.1 Organization Mandates

- Organizations have mandates to perform certain tasks that carry out their missions
  - Mandates are the reasons they exist as organizations
- Organizations have different needs for data depending on their mandates and the activities required to carry out these mandates
  - Mandates often help identify and define entities of interest, requiring a certain view of the world
  - What might seem at first glance to be the same data need in two different organizations can actually be quite different when we look at a more detailed level
    - e.g. wildlife and forestry departments both need information on vegetation but the detail needed is different

8.2 Database contents

Example: Transportation

- Highway data from the different points of view of a natural resources organization and a highway transportation organization
  - A natural resource organization might only need logging roads and the connecting access to state highways
  - The transportation organization's main interest is in characterizing highways used by the public
    - The database might also be used to store detailed highway condition and maintenance information
  - We would expect their need for highway data to be more detailed than would the natural resource organization's

Example: wetlands

- Wetlands data from the different points of view of an ecological organization and a taxing authority
  - Ecological organization might define wetlands as a natural resource to be preserved and restricted from development
    - That perspective might require considerable detail for describing the area's biology and physical resources
  - A taxing authority might define a wetland to be a "wasteland" and of very little value to society
    - That description might require only the boundary of the "wasteland" in the database

8.3 Database design

- In each organization only certain phenomena are important enough to collect and represent in a database
  - The data collection process involves a sampling of geographic reality, to determine the status of that reality (whether past, present or future)
- Identifying the phenomena and then choosing an appropriate data representation for them is part of a process called database design
- Almost all entities of geographic reality have at least a 3-dimensional spatial character, but not all dimensions may be needed
  - e.g. highway pavement actually has a depth which might be important, but is not as important as the width, which is not as important as the length
- Representation should be based on the types of manipulations that might be undertaken
- Map-scale of the source document is important in constraining the level of detail represented in a database
  - e.g. on a 1:100,000 map individual houses or fields are not visible

8.3.1 Steps in database design

1. Conceptual

- Software and hardware independent
- Describes and defines included entities
- Identifies how entities will be represented in the database
  - i.e. selection of spatial objects - points, lines, areas, raster cells
- Requires decisions about how real-world dimensionality and relationships will be represented
  - These can be based on the processing that will be done on these objects
  - e.g. should a building be represented as an area or a point?
  - e.g. should highway segments be explicitly linked in the database?

2. **Logical**
    - Software specific but hardware independent
    - Sets out the logical structure of the database elements, determined by the data base management system used by the software
3. **Physical**
    - Both hardware and software specific
    - Requires consideration of how files will be structured for access from the disk

8.3.2 Desirable database characteristics

- Database should be:
    - Contemporaneous - should contain information of the same vintage for all its measured variables
    - As detailed as necessary for the intended applications
        - The categories of information and subcategories within them should contain all of the data needed to analyze or model the behavior of the resource using conventional methods and models
    - Positionally accurate
    - Exactly compatible with other information that may be overlain with it
    - Internally accurate, portraying the nature of phenomena without error - requires clear definitions of phenomena that are included
    - Readily updated on a regular schedule
    - Accessible to whoever needs it

8.3.3 Issues in database design

- Almost all entities of geographic reality have at least 3-dimensional spatial character, but not all dimensions may be needed
    - e.g. highway pavement has a depth which might be important, but is not as important as the width, which is not as important as the length
- Representation should be based on types of manipulations that might be undertaken
- Map-scale of the source document is important in constraining the level of detail represented in a database
    - e.g. on a 1:100,000 map individual houses or fields are not visible

9. Conclusion

For spatial queries to be answered efficiently, spatial techniques for spatial indexing are needed. Complex issues arise in spatial analysis, many of which are neither clearly defined nor completely resolved, but form the basis for current research. The most fundamental of these is the problem of defining the spatial location of the entities being studied. For example, a study on human health could describe the spatial position of humans with a point placed where they live, or with a point located where they work, each choice has dramatic effects on the techniques which can be used for the analysis.

10. References

[1] "Advanced Topics in Computer Science", Study material, Revathy Pub, Madurai, 2005.

[2] Robinson, A., R. Sale, J. Morrison, and P. Muehrcke, "The Elements of Cartography, (5th ed.)", John Wiley and Sons, New York. 1984.

[3] Benenson, I. and P. M. Torrens, "*Geosimulation: Automata-Based Modeling of Urban Phenomena*", Wiley, 2004.

[4] Abler, R., J. Adams, and P. Gould, "*Spatial Organization--The Geographer's View of the World*", Englewood Cliffs, NJ: Prentice-Hall, 1971.

The Need, use and Efficiency of Mining in Spatial Databases

M. Satish, B. Kishore and P. Srinivasa Rao
IT Dept., GMRIT, Rajam
satish.m@gmrit.org *kishore.gmr@gmail.com* *psr.sri@gmail.com*

Abstract

Today world of computing, software are experiencing the renaissance. In this software renaissance mining of Spatial Database plays crucial role.

Spatial mining refers to extraction of knowledge, spatial relationship or other interesting patterns not explicitly stored in spatial databases.

This paper mainly emphasize on Spatial Data Cube Construction and Spatial OLAP, Spatial Association of Analysis, Spatial trends with different issues, Spatial Clustering methods, at last Mining Raster Databases. In overall this paper explains the use and efficiency of mining of Spatial Databases.

Keywords: *RasterDatabases, Renaissance, Extracting, OLAP.*

1. Introduction

A spatial database stores large amount of space-related data, such as maps, preprocessed remote sensing or medical imaging data, VLSI chip layout data. Spatial databases have many features distinguishing them from relational databases. They carry topological and/or distance information, usually organized by sophisticated, multidimensional spatial indexing structures that are accessed by spatial data access methods and often require spatial reasoning, geometric computation, and spatial knowledge representation techniques.

Spatial data mining refers to the extraction of knowledge, spatial relationships, or other interesting patterns not explicitly stored in spatial databases. Such mining demands an integration of data mining with spatial database technologies. It can be used for understanding spatial data, discovering spatial relationships and relationships between spatial and non-spatial data, constructing spatial knowledge bases, reorganizing spatial databases, and optimizing spatial queries. It is expected to have wide applications in geographic information systems, geo-marketing, remote sensing, image database exploration, medical imaging, navigation, traffic control, environmental studies, and many other areas where spatial data are used. A crucial challenge to spatial data mining is the exploration of efficient spatial data mining techniques due to the huge amount of spatial data and the complexity of spatial data types and spatial access methods.

Statistical spatial data analysis has been a popular approach to analyzing spatial data. The approach handles numerical data well and usually proposes realistic models of spatial phenomena. However, it typically assumes statistical independence among the spatially distributed data, although in reality, spatial objects are often inter-related. Moreover, experts having a fair amount of domain knowledge and statistical expertise can only perform most statistical modeling. Furthermore, statistical methods do not work well with symbolic values, or incomplete or inconclusive data, and are computationally expensive in large databases. Spatial data allows the extension of traditional spatial analysis methods by placing minimum emphasis on efficiency, scalability, cooperation with database systems, improved interaction with the user, and the discovery of new types of knowledge.

2. Spatial Data Cube Construction and Spatial OLAP

As with relational data, we can integrate spatial data to construct a data warehouse that facilitates spatial data mining. A spatial data warehouse is a subject-oriented, integrated, time-variant, and nonvolatile collection of both spatial and non-spatial data in support of spatial data mining and spatial-data-related decision-making processes. Let's have a look at the following example,

Example There are about 3000 weather probes distributed in British Columbia (BC), each recording daily temperature and precipitation for a designated small area and transmitting signals to a provincial weather station. With a spatial data warehouse that supports spatial OLAP, a user can view weather patterns on a map by month by region, and by different combinations of temperature and precipitation, and can dynamically drill down or roll up along any dimension to explore desire patterns, such as "wet and hot regions in the Fraser Valley in Summer 1999".

There are several challenging issues regarding the construction and utilization of spatial data warehouses. The first challenge is the integration of spatial data from heterogeneous sources and systems. Spatial data are usually stored in different industry firms and government agencies using various data formats. Data formats are not only structure-specific (e.g., raster- vs. vector-based spatial data object-oriented vs. relational models, different spatial storage and indexing structures, etc.), but also vendor-specific (e.g., ESRI, MapInfo, Intergraph, etc.). There has been a great deal of work on the integration and exchange of heterogeneous spatial data, which has paved the way for spatial data integration and spatial data warehouse construction.

The second challenge is the realization of fast and flexible on-line analytic processing in spatial data warehouses. The star schema model is a good choice for modeling spatial data warehouses since it provided a concise and organized warehouse structure and facilitates OLAP operation However, in a spatial warehouse, both dimensions and measures may contain spatial components.

There are three types of dimensions in a spatial data cube:

- A non-spatial dimension contains only non-spatial data. Non-spatial dimensions temperature and precipitation can be constructed for the warehouse since each contains non-spatial data whose generalizations are non-spatial (such as "hot" for temperature and "wet" for precipitation).
- A spatial-to-non-spatial dimension is a dimension whose primitive-level data are spatial but whose generalization, starting at a certain high level, become non-spatial. For example, the spatial dimension City relays geographic data fit the U.S. map. Suppose that the dimension's spatial representation of, say, Seattle is generalized to the string "pacific-northwest". Although "Pacific-northwest" a spatial concept, its representation is not spatial (since, in our example, it if string).It therefore plays the role of a non-spatial dimension.
- A spatial-to-spatial dimension is a dimension whose primitive level and all its high-level generalized data are spatial. For example, the dimension equ_temperature_region contains spatial data, as do all of its generalizations, such as with regions covering 0-5 degrees (Celsius), 5-10 degrees, and so on.

We distinguish two types of measures in a spatial data cube.

A non-spatial data cube contains only non-spatial dimensions and numerical measures. If a spatial data cube contains spatial dimensions but no spatial measures, its OLAP operations, such as drilling or pivoting, can be implemented in a manner similar to that for non-spatial data cubes.

Of the three measures, area and count are numerical measures that can be computed similarly to that for non-spatial data cubes; regions-map is a spatial measure that represents a collection of spatial pointers to the corresponding regions. Since different spatial OLAP operations result in different collections of spatial objects in region map, it is a major challenge to compute the merges of a large number of regions flexibly and dynamically.

There are at least three possible choices in regard to the computation of spatial measures in spatial data cube construction.

Collect and store the corresponding spatial object pointers but do not perform pre-computation of spatial measures in the spatial data cube. This can be implemented by storing, in the corresponding cube cell, a pointer to a collection of spatial object pointers, and invoking and performing the spatial merge (or other computation) of the corresponding spatial objects, when necessary, on- the-fly. This method is a good choice if only spatial display is required (i.e., no real spatial merge has to be performed), or if there are not many regions to be merged in any pointer collection (so that the on-line merge is not very costly), or if on-line spatial merge computation is fast (recently, some efficient spatial merge methods have been developed for fast spatial OLAP). Since OLAP results are often used for on-line spatial analysis and mining, it is still recommended to pre-compute some of the spatially connected regions to speed up such analysis.

Pre-compute and store a rough approximation of the spatial measures in the spatial data cube. These choices good for a rough view or coarse estimation of spatial merge results under the assumption that it requires little storage space. For example, a minimum bounding rectangle (MBR), represented by two points can be taken as a rough estimate of a merged region. Such a pre-computed result is small and can be presented quickly to users. If higher precision is needed for specific cells, the application can either fetch pre-computed high-quality results, if available, or compute them on-the-fly.

Selectively pre-compute some spatial measures in the spatial data cube. This can be a smart choice. The selection can be performed at the cuboid level, that is, either pre-compute and store each set of mergeable spatial regions for each cell of a selected cuboid, or pre-compute none if the cuboid is not selected. Since a cuboid usually consists of a large number of spatial objects, it may involve pre-computation and storage of a large number of mergeable spatial objects, some of which may be rarely used. Therefore, it is recommended to perform selection at a finer granularity level examining each group of mergeable spatial objects in a cuboid to determine whether such a merge should be pre-computed. Decision should be based on the utility (such as access frequency or access priority), sharability of merged regions, and the balanced overall cost of space and on-line computation.

With efficient implementation of spatial data cubes and spatial OLAP, generalization-based descriptive spatial mining, such as spatial characterization and discrimination, can be performed efficiently.

3. Spatial Association Analysis

Similar to the mining of association rules in transactional and relational databases, spatial association rules can be mined in spatial databases. A spatial association rule is of the form

A => B [s%, c%].

Where A and B are sets of spatial or non-spatial predicates, s% is the support of the rule, and c% is the confidence of the rule. For example, the following is a spatial association rule: is a (X, "school") A close to(X, "sports center") => close to(X, "park") [0.5%, 80%]. This rule states that 80% of schools that are close to sports centers are also close to parks and 0.5% of the data belongs to such a case.

Various kinds of spatial predicates can constitute a spatial association rule. Examples include distance information (such as close to and far-away) topological relations (like intersect, overlap, and disjoint), and spatial orientations (like left of and west of).

Since spatial association mining needs to evaluate multiple spatial relationships among a large number of spatial objects, the process could be quite costly. An interesting mining optimization method called progressive refinement can be adopted in spatial association analysis. The method first mines large data sets roughly using a fast algorithm and then improves the quality of mining in a pruned data set using a more expensive algorithm.

To ensure that the pruned data set covers the complete set of answers when applying the high-quality data mining algorithms at a later stage, an important requirement for the rough mining algorithm applied in the early stage is the superset coverage property: that is, it preserves all of the potential answers. In other words, it should allow a false positive test, which might include some data sets that do not belong to the answer sets, but it should not allow a false negative test, which might exclude some potential answers.

For mining spatial associations related to the spatial predicate close to, we can first collect the candidates that pass the minimum support threshold by applying certain rough spatial evaluation algorithm for example, using a minimum bounding rectangle structure (which registers only two spatial points rather than a set of complex polygons). Then evaluating the relaxed spatial predicate, g close to, which is a generalized c close to covering a broader context that includes close to, touch, and intersect.

If two spatial objects are closely located, their enclosing minimum bounding rectangles must be closely located, matching g close to. However, the reverse is not always true: it the enclosing minimum bounding rectangles are closely located, the two spatial objects may or nay not be located so closely. Thus, the minimum bounding rectangle pruning is a false positive testing tool for closeness: only those that pass the rough test need to be further examined using more expensive spatial computation algorithms. With this preprocessing, only the patterns that are frequent at the approximation level will need to be examined by more detailed and finer, yet more expensive, spatial computation.

4. Spatial Clustering Methods

Spatial data clustering identifies clusters, or densely populated regions, according to some distance measurement in a large, multidimensional data set.

5. Spatial Classification and Spatial Trend Analysis

Spatial classification analyzes spatial objects to derive classification schemes in relevance to certain spatial properties, such as the neighborhood of a district, highway, or river.

Spatial classification:
Suppose that you would like to classify regions in a province into rich versus poor according to the average family income. In doing so, you would like to identify the important spatial-related factors that determine a region's classification. There are many properties associated with spatial objects, such as hosting a university, containing interstate highways, being near a lake or ocean, and so on. These properties can be used for relevance analysis and to find interesting classification schemes. Such classification schemes may be represented in the form of decision trees or rules.

Spatial trend analysis deals with another issue: the detection of changes and trends along a spatial dimension. Typically, trend analysis detects changes with time, such as the changes of temporal patterns in time-series data. Spatial trend analysis replaces time with space and studies the trend of non spatial or spatial data changing with space. For example, we may observe the trend of changes in economic situation when moving away from the center of a city, or the trend of changes of the climate or vegetation with the increasing distance from an ocean. For such analyses, regression and correlation analysis methods are often applied by utilization of spatial data structures and spatial access methods.

There are also many applications where patterns are changing with both space and time. For example, traffic flows on highways and in cities are both time and space related. Weather patterns are also closely related to both time and space. Although there have been a few interesting studies on spatial classification and spatial trend analysis, the investigation of spatiotemporal data mining is still in its infancy. More methods and applications of spatial classification and trend analysis, especially those associated with time, need to be explored in the future.

6. Mining Raster Databases

Spatial database systems usually handle vector data that consist of points, lines, polygons (regions), and their compositions, such as networks or partitions. Typical examples of such data include maps, design graphs, and 3-D representations of the arrangement of the chains of protein molecules. However, a huge amount of space-related data are in digital raster (image) forms, such as satellite images, remote sensing data, and computer tomography It is important to explore data mining in raster image databases. Methods for mining raster and image data are examined in the following section regarding the mining of multimedia data.

7. Conclusion

Database is a computerized record keeping system. Data Base Management System is nothing but which allows the users to perform Insertion, Deletion and other operations. Mining means extract of the required or essential data, even though most of advanced data base concepts exists Data Mining have been introduced.

In Data Mining OLAP, MOLAP, ROLAP Servers, Spatial, Multimedia Databases are more popular. Spatial Database mining is a hard task if we are aware of it. Spatial database mining extracts the knowledge information. This is the way how mining takes place in Spatial Databases of real world applications.

8. References

[1] Data Mining Techniques, Arun k pujari 1st Edition

[2] Data warehousung,Data Mining and OLAP, Alex Berson, smith.j. Stephen

[3] Data Mining Concepts and Techniques, Jiawei Han and MichelineKamber

[4] Data Mining Introductory and Advanced topics, Margaret H Dunham PEA

[5] The Data Warehouse lifecycle toolkit, Ralph Kimball Wiley student Edition

Privacy Preserving Data Mining Using Randomized Perturbation Technique

P.Kamakshi[1] and Dr.A.Vinaya Babu[2]
[1]Asst.Professor Dept. Of C.S.E. Kakatiya Institute Of Technology and Science, Warangal
[2]Professor Dept. Of C.S.E. J.N.T.U., Hyderabad
Kamakshi_chiku@yahoo.co.in

Abstract

With the rapid growth in database, networking, and computing technologies, there is tremendous growth in the amount of private data collected about individuals. Huge volumes of detailed personal data are regularly collected from government, educational, business organizations; medical history, credit records and shopping habits. Such data can be integrated and analyzed digitally. Data mining successfully extracts knowledge from such large collection of data. On one hand, this has led to the development of data mining tools that aim to infer useful trends from this data and the extracted knowledge support a variety of domains like marketing, weather forecasting, and medical diagnosis. But, on the other hand, easy access to personal data poses a threat to individual privacy. The output obtained after executing data mining algorithms reveals something about the contents of other databases, which are considered to be private. A large amount of such information is often specific to individual users or contains confidential information. There has been growing concern about the chance of misusing personal information extracted from such data. The true problem is not data mining, but the way data mining is done. Privacy is becoming an increasingly important issue in many data mining applications. Privacy preserving data mining techniques provides solution for this Problem. PPDM gives valid data mining results without learning the underlying data values .The benefits of data mining can be enjoyed, without compromising the privacy of concerned individuals. The main objective of privacy preserving data mining is to develop algorithms and models for modifying the original data in some way, so that the private data and private knowledge remain private even after the mining process. This paper presents randomized data perturbation privacy preserving data mining technique which protects user's privacy and still produces accurate results.
Keywords: Data mining, knowledge, privacy

1. Introduction

Data mining technology has been developed with the goal of providing tools for automatically and intelligently transforming large amount of data into knowledge relevant to users. Data mining, with its promise to efficiently discover valuable non-obvious information from large databases, is particularly sensitive to privacy concerns. Privacy is becoming an increasingly important issue in many data mining applications that deal with health care, security, financial and other types of sensitive data. Data including sensitive data is generally stored by a number of entities, ranging from individuals and small businesses to national governments. Business and scientific databases typically contain confidential information.

1.1 Privacy Issues in Data Mining

Data mining and knowledge discovery in databases investigate the automatic extraction of previously unknown patterns from large amounts of data. It is obvious that if a data mining algorithm is run against the union of databases, its output becomes known to one or more of the parties. It reveals something about the contents of the other databases. For example, if a researcher from a medical institution learns that the overall a percentage of patients that have certain symptom is 50%, while he knows that this percentage in his population of patients is 40%, then he also learns that more than 50% of the patients of the other institutions have this symptom. In another case in which two or more parties owning confidential databases wish to run a data mining algorithm on the union of their databases without revealing any unnecessary information. For example, when two separate medical institutions wish to conduct a joint research on their databases but still want to preserve the privacy of their patient's sensitive information. The parties realize that combining their data will provide some mutual benefit, but none of them is willing to reveal its database to any other party. In this scenario it is required to protect privileged information, but it is also required to enable its use for research or for other purposes. Another interesting example is the research center which has the database of DNA sequences of a group of people. Personal medical histories are often stored in databases of hospitals. Hospitals cannot provide any information about individual medical history to the research center due to privacy regulations. In many situations, individual variables are inherently sensitive and people are reluctant to divulge them to a data miner. In some cases, although the variables themselves are not sensitive, it will help identify confidential information through links between databases. Those variables that can help identify confidential information should also be paid attention. The following is the example to illustrate re-identification by linking: Figure1 provides a demonstration of re-identification by directly linking or matching of shared attributes. The example gives us an idea of how privacy breaches can happen if only those inherent sensitive variables are considered and privacy problem cannot be solved by only removing personal identification numbers of data records. Due to privacy and confidentiality concerns discussed above, application of data mining technologies is largely constrained. PPDM has emerged to address the privacy issue in data mining.

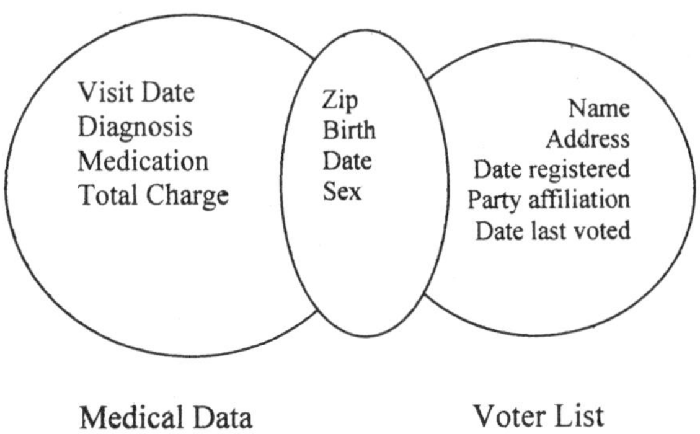

Fig. 1 Example of re-identification by links

Privacy preserving data mining has been studied during the past several years. Several techniques ranging from perturbation to secure multi-party computation have been explored. In this paper a technique of privacy preserving data mining is discussed which perturb randomly the sensitive data and preserve the underlying probabilistic properties. When the confidential data is numerical, one important technique than can be used is data perturbation. Randomization perturbation is one of the promising approaches in privacy-preserving data mining. In randomization approach privacy of the data can be obtained by perturbing sensitive attributes with randomization algorithms and submitting the randomized version to the data miner. The algorithm is so chosen that aggregate properties of the data can be recovered with sufficient precision while individual entries are significantly distorted. Randomization method disguises data by probabilistically changing the value of a sensitive attribute to another value. Statistical databases often use random data perturbation (RDP) methods to protect against disclosure of confidential numerical attributes. One of the key requirements of RDP methods is that they provide the appropriate level of security against snoopers, who attempt to obtain information on confidential attributes through statistical inference. Database administrators have to balance requirements for confidentiality against the needs of legitimate users for easy access and analysis of organizational data. Using statistical databases, database administrators can allow users access to aggregate statistical information, but not the information regarding a specific entity. However, even in statistical databases, a snooper may be able to infer confidential information associated with a particular individual through a clever choice of queries, leading to disclosure of information. Random data perturbation (RDP) involves the addition of random noise to confidential numerical attributes. Thus, even if a snooper is able to isolate an individual value of a confidential attribute, the true value is not disclosed. While perturbation methods guarantee that complete or exact disclosure will never occur, they are susceptible to partial disclosure. Partial disclosure occurs when the amount of information that a snooper is able to obtain about a confidential attribute through queries and statistical analysis, exceeds the amount that the database administrator intended to provide to users .In other words, the value of the perturbed attribute is "closer" to the true value of the attribute than intended. When a database administrator specifies a certain level of security, he/she is simultaneously specifying the maximum amount of disclosure about confidential attributes that should be available to any user, devious or otherwise. This, in turn, also means that the database administrator should be able to correctly *evaluate* the amount of disclosure The basic idea behind this technique is to scramble the data in such a way that the central place cannot tell with probabilities better than a pre-defined threshold whether the data from a customer contain truthful information or false information.

2. Randomized data perturbation technique

In randomization approach the privacy of the data is obtained by perturbing it with randomization algorithms and submitting the randomized version, thus hiding the data and guaranteeing protection against the reconstruction of the data[5]. In this scheme, a random number is added to the value of a sensitive attribute. For example, if X is the value of a sensitive attribute than, Xi+r will appear in the database, where r is a random value drawn from some distribution. This method is known as additive data perturbation. Most commonly used distributions are the uniform distribution over an interval $[-\alpha, \alpha]$ and Gaussian distribution with mean equal to zero and standard deviation σ. The algorithm is so chosen that aggregate properties of the data can be recovered with sufficient precision while individual entries are significantly distorted. The server has a complete and precise database with information from its clients, and it has to make a version of this database public, for others to work with. One important example is census data; the government of a country collects private data for research and economic planning. However, it is assumed that private records of any given person should not be released nor be recoverable from what is released. In particular, a company should not be able to match up records in the publicly released database with the corresponding records in the company's own database of its customers. The method of randomization can be described as follows. Consider a set of data records denoted by $X = \{x1 \ldots xN\}$. For record $xi \in X$, we add a noise component which is drawn from the probability distribution $fY(y)$. These noise components are drawn independently, and are denoted $y1 \ldots yN$. Thus, the new set of distorted records are denoted by $x1+y1 \ldots xN+yN$. We denote this new set of records by $z1 \ldots zN$. In general, it is assumed that the variance of the added noise is large enough, so that the original record values cannot be easily guessed from the distorted data. Thus, if X be the random variable denoting the data distribution for the original record, Y is the random variable describing the noise distribution, and Z is the random variable denoting the final record, we have:

$$Z = X + Y$$

$$X = Z - Y$$

By subtracting Y from the approximated distribution of Z, it is possible to approximate the original probability distribution X. At the end of the process, we only have a distribution containing the behavior of X. Figure.2 gives the block diagram of data perturbation technique to preserve privacy of sensitive data .One key advantage of the randomization method is that it is relatively simple, and does not require knowledge of the distribution of other records in the data. One important feature of this method is that it does not require costly cryptographic operations or sophisticated protocols to maintain the privacy of sensitive information [10]. Our experiment was performed on numerical database by applying Gaussian technique to all the attributes in a given database. The same technique can be applied to selected attributes, which the database administrator considers as more sensitive.

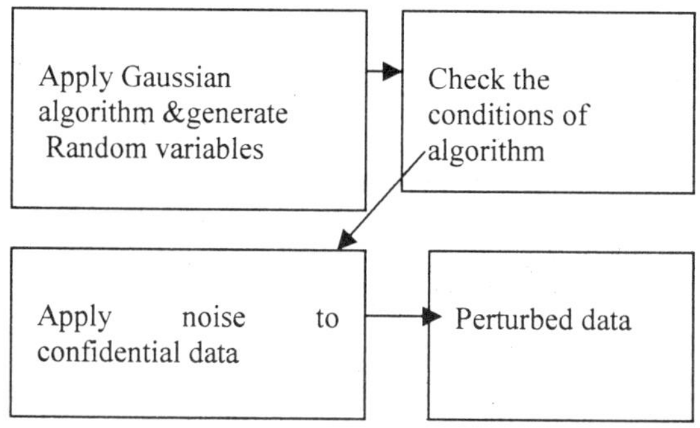

Fig. 2 Block diagram for implementing perturbation technique

Example: Table 1 gives a sample database of student marks and noise is added to the values of attributes Subject1 and Subject2 marks. Table 2 gives the perturbed values after adding noise .The observed results are shown as graph in Figure3.

Table 1 Student_marks table

Sno.	Rollno	Subject1	Subject2	total
1	1801	56	89	145
2	1802	58	56	114
3	1803	78	23	101
4	1804	98	45	143
5	1805	25	12	37
6	1806	45	78	113
7	1807	47	15	62
8	1808	74	47	121
9	1809	15	78	93
10	1810	99	65	164

Table 2 Student_marks after perturbing the data

Sno.	Rollno	Subject1	Subject2	total
1	1801	57	90	147
2	1802	57	56	113
3	1803	78	23	101
4	1804	98	47	145
5	1805	25	12	37
6	1806	47	78	125
7	1807	47	15	62
8	1808	74	47	121
9	1809	15	77	92
10	1810	98	65	163

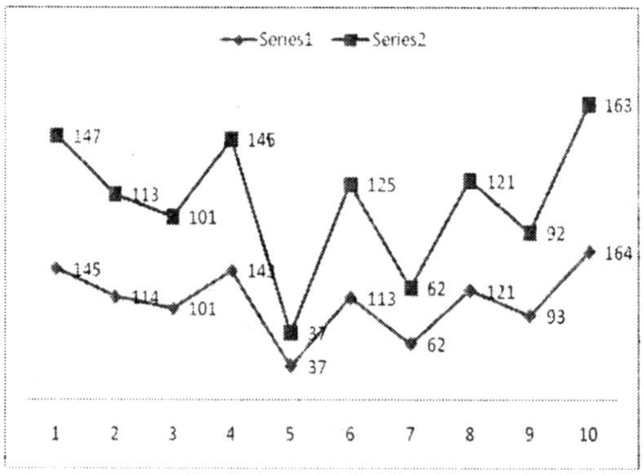

Fig. 3 Graph shows the difference between original and perturbed values

3. Conclusion

Data mining technology has emerged as a means of identifying patterns and trends from large quantities of data. Data mining uses data warehousing model for gathering all data into a central site, then running an algorithm against that data. Privacy considerations may prevent this approach because extracted knowledge after data mining process may also contain private and personal information. There has been growing concern about the chance of misusing personal information extracted from such data. It is a challenge to mine data without violating the data owners' privacy. The sticking point is how to protect privacy while preserving the usefulness of data mining results. If the privacy is associated with the identity of an individual then sometimes removing identification information from the data solves the problem. However, there exist many applications where such simple solutions do not work. The data set may still reveal certain information that violates the privacy of different entities associated with the data. In this paper we discussed privacy preserving data mining technique using random data perturbation method. In randomization techniques privacy can be obtained by randomly perturbing the data while preserving the underlying probabilistic properties. This approach tries to preserve data privacy by adding random noise from a known distribution to the privacy sensitive data. This paper gives a theoretical and a practical approach for perturbing numerical data. While our discussion was limited to numerical confidential variables, it is possible to extend the theoretical methodology to develop new perturbation technique for categorical data.

4. References

[1] D. Agarwal and C.C.Aggarwal, " On the design and quantification of privacy preserving data mining algorithms", *In the proceedings of the 20th sysmposium on principles of database systems* Santabarbara,California,USA, May2001.

[2] R.Agarwal and R.Srikant, "Privacy preserving data mining", *In Proceedings of the 19th ACM SIGMOD conference on Management of Data* ,Dallas,Texas,USA, May2000

[3] J. Canny, "Collaborative filtering with privacy". *In IEEE Symposium on security and privacy* , pages 45-57 Oakland, May 2002.

[4] M. Kantarcioglu and C. Clifton, "Privacy-preserving distributed mining of association rules on horizontally partitioned data", *In the ACM SIGMOD Workshop on Research Issues on Data Mining and Knowledge Discovery (DMKD'02),* pp. 24–31,Madison, June 2002,

[5] K. Muralidhar, R. Sarathy, and R. A. Parsa, "A general additive perturbation method for database security," Management Science, vol. 45, no. 10, pp. 1399–1415, 1999.

[6] R.Agrawal, A.Evfimievski, R.Srikant, "Information sharing across private databases", *In Proc.of ACM SIGMOD*, 2003.

[7] J. Han and M. Kamber, Data Mining: Concepts and Techniques. Morgan Kaufmann Publlshers, 2000.

[8] H. Kargupta, S. Datta, Q. Wang, and K. Sivakumar, "On the privacy preserving properties of random data perturbation techniques" *In Proc. of 3rd IEEE Int. Conf. on Data Mining,* Washington, DC, USA,, pages99–106, 2003.

[9] K. Muralidhar, R. Parsa, and R. Sarathy, " A general additive data perturbation method for database security",*Management Science,* 19:1399–1415, 1999.

[10] B. Pinkas, "Cryptographic techniques for privacy preserving data mining " *SIGKDD Explorations,* 12–19, 2002

[11] A. Evfimievski, "Randomization in privacy preserving data mining", *In ACM SIGKDD Explorations Newsletter*, volume 4, pages 43–48, 2002.

[12] Vaidya, J, Clifton, C., " Privacy-Preserving Data Mining: Why, How, and When", *IEEE Security and Privacy,* 2, 19-27, 2004.

[13] Clifton, C, Kantarcioglu, M, Vaidya,J Lin, X, Zhu, M Y. , "Tools for privacy preserving distributed data mining" , *SIGKDD Explor. Newsl.*, 28-34, 2002

[14] Weiss G M, "Data Mining in Telecommunications", *In Data Mining and Knowledge Discovery Handbook,* A Complete Guide for Practitioners and Researchers. Kluwer Academic Publishers, 1189-1201, 2005.

[15] H. Kargupta, S. Datta, Q. Wang, and K. Sivakumar, "On the privacy preserving properties of random data perturbation techniques", *In Proceedings of the 3rd IEEE International Conference on Data Mining,* pages 99–106, Melbourne, Florida, November 19-22, 2003.

Web Mininig: Integration of Semantic Web and Web Usage mining

D. Vasumathi[1], Dr. A. Govardhan[2], and K. Suresh[3]
[1]Asso.Professor CSE, JNTUCEH, [2]Professor CSE, JNTUCEH and [3]Asst.Professor I.T, VCE, Hyderabad
devara_vasukumar@yahoo.co.in govardhan_cse@yahoo.co.in kallamsuresh@yahoo.co.in

Abstract

The main idea of the Semantic Web is to enrich the current Web by machine-processable information in order to allow for semantic-based tools supporting the human user. Semantic web Mining aims at combining the two fast developing research areas Semantic Web and Web Mining .Web Mining aims at discovering insights about the meaning of Web resources and their usage. Given the primarily syntactical nature of data Web Mining operates on, the discovery of meaning is impossible based on these data only. In this paper, we discuss the interplay of the Semantic Web with Web Mining, with a specific focus on usage mining.

1. Introduction

Web Usage Mining is the application of data mining methods to the analysis of recordings of Web usage, most often in the form Of Web server logs .One of its central problems is the large number of patterns that are usually found: among these, how can the interesting patterns be identified? For example, an application of association rule analysis to a Web log will typically return many patterns like the observation that 90% of the users who made a purchase in an online shop also visited the homepage- a pattern that is trivial because the homepage is the site's main entry point. Statistical measures of pattern quality like support and confidence, and measures of interestingness based on the divergence from prior beliefs are a primarily syntactical approach to this problem. They need to be complemented by an understanding of what a site and its usage patterns are about i.e. a semantic approach. A popular approach for modeling sites and their usage is related to OLAP techniques: a modeling of the pages in terms (possibly multiple) concept hierarchies, and an investigation of patterns at different levels of abstraction, i.e. Knowledge discovery Cycle which iterates over various "roll- ups" and "drill-downs". Concept Hierarchies conceptualize a domain in terms of taxonomies such as product catalogs, topical thesauri, Etc. The expressive power of this form of knowledge representation is limited to be a relationship. However, for many applications, a more expressive form of knowledge representation is desirable, for example *ontologies* that allow arbitrary relations between concepts.

A second problem facing many current analyses that take semantics into account is that the conceptualizations often have to be hand-crafted to represent a site that has grown independently of an overall conceptual design, and that the mapping of individual pages to this conceptualization may have to be established. It would thus be desirable to have a rich semantic model of a site, of its content and its (hyperlink) structure, a model that captures the complexity of the manifold relationships between the concepts covered in a site, and a model that is "built into" the site in the sense that the pages requested by visitors are directly associated with the concepts and relations treated by it.

The *Semantic Web* is just this: today's Web enriched by a formal semantics in form of ontologies that captures the meaning of pages and links in a machine-understandable form. The main idea of the Semantic Web is to enrich the current Web by machine-processable information in order to allow for semantic-based tools supporting the human user. In this paper, we discuss on one hand how the Semantic Web can improve Web usage mining, and on the other hand how usage mining can be used to built up the Semantic Web..

2. Web Usage Mining

Web mining is the application of data mining techniques to the content, structure, and usage of Web resources. This can help to discover global as well as local structure within and between Web pages. Like other data mining applications, Web mining can profit from given structure on data (as in database tables), but it can also be applied to semi structured or unstructured data like free-form text. This means that Web mining is an invaluable help in the transformation from human understandable content to machine understandable semantics. A distinction is generally made between Web mining that operates on the Web resources themselves (often further differentiated into *content* and *structure* mining), and mining that operates on visitors' *usage* of these resources.

These techniques, and their application for understanding Web usage, will be discussed in more detail in section 5.In *Web usage mining*, the primary Web resource that is being mined is a record of the requests made by visitors to a Web site, most often collected in a Web server log [5].The content and structure of Web pages, and in particular those of one Web site, reflect the intentions of the authors and designers of the pages and the underlying information architecture. The actual behavior of the users of these resources may reveal additional structure.

First, relationships may be induced by usage where no particular structure was designed. For example, in an online catalog of products, there is usually either no inherent structure (different products are simply viewed as a set), or one or several hierarchical structures given by product categories, manufacturers, etc. Mining the visits to that site, however, one may find that many of the users who were interested in product A were also interested in product B. Here, "interest" may be measured by requests for product description pages, or by the placement of that product into the shopping cart (indicated by the request for the respective pages). The identified association rules are at the center of cross-selling and up-selling strategies in E-commerce sites: When a new user shows interest in product A, she will receive a recommendation for product B (cf. [3, 4]).

Second, relationships may be induced by usage where a different relationship was intended. For example, sequence mining may show that many of the users who visited page C later went to page D, along paths that indicate a prolonged search (frequent visits to help and index pages, frequent backtracking, etc.) [1, 2]. This can be interpreted to mean that visitors wish to reach D from C, but that this was not foreseen in the information architecture, hence that there is at present no hyperlink from C to D. This insight can be used for static site improvement for all users (adding a link from C to D), or for dynamic recommendations personalized for the subset of users who go to C ("you may wish to also look at D").It is useful to combine Web usage mining with contentand structure analysis in order to "make sense" of observed frequent paths and the pages on these paths. This can be done using a variety of methods. Many of these methods rely on a mapping of pages into ontology. And underlying ontology and the mapping of pages into it may already be available, the mapping of pages into an existing ontology may need to be learned, and/or the ontology itself may have to be inferred first. In the following sections, we will first investigate the notions of semantics (as used in the Semantic Web) and ontologies in more detail. We will then look at how the use of ontologies, and other ways of identifying the meaning of pages, can help to make Web Mining go semantic. Lastly, we will investigate how ontologies and their instances can be learned.

3. Semantic Web

The Semantic Web is based on a vision of Tim Berners-Lee, the inventor of the WWW. The great success of the current WWW leads to a new challenge: a huge amount of data is interpretable by humans only; machine support is limited. Berners-Lee suggests to enrich the Web by machine-processable information which supports the user in his tasks. For instance, today's search engines are already quite powerful, but still return too often too large or inadequate lists of hits. Machine-processable information can point the search engine to the relevant pages and can thus improve both precision and recall. For instance, it is today almost impossible to retrieve information with a keyword search when the information is spread over several pages. The process of building the Semantic Web is today still heavily going on. Its structure has to be defined, and this structure has then to be filled with life. In order to make this task feasible, one should start with the simpler tasks first. The following steps show the direction where the Semantic Web is heading:

1. Providing a common syntax for machine understandable statements.
2. Establishing common vocabularies.
3. Agreeing on a logical language.
4. Using the language for exchanging proofs.

Berners-Lee suggested a layer structure for the Semantic

Web: (i) Unicode/URI, (ii) XML/Name Spaces/ XML Schema, (iii) RDF/RDF Schema, (iv) Ontology vocabulary, (v) Logic, (vi) Proof, (vii) Trust.

1 This structure reflects the steps listed above. It follows the understanding that each step alone will already provide added value, so that the Semantic Web can be realized in an incremental fashion. On the first two layers, a common syntax is provided. *Uniform resource identifiers (URIs)* provide a standard way to refer to entities,2 while *Unicode* is a standard for exchanging symbols. The *Extensible Markup Language (XML)* fixes a notation for describing labeled trees, and XML Schema allows to define grammars for valid XML documents. XML documents can refer to different *namespaces* to make explicit the context (and therefore meaning) of different tags. The formalizations on these two layers are nowadays widely accepted, and the number of XML documents is increasing rapidly.

The *Resource Description Framework (RDF)* can be seen as the first layer which is part of the Semantic Web. According to the W3C recommendation [4],

RDF "is a foundation for processing metadata; it provides interoperability between applications that exchange machine understandable information on the Web." RDF documents consist of three types of entities: resources, properties, and statements. Today the Semantic Web community considers these levels rather as one single level as most ontologies allow for logical axioms. Following [2], ontology is "an explicit formalization of a shared understanding of a conceptualization". This high-level definition is realized differently by different research communities. However, most of them have a certain understanding in common, as most of them include a set of concepts, a hierarchy on them, and relations between concepts. Most of them also include axioms in some specific logic. To give a flavor, we present here just the core of our own definition [3], as it is reflected by the Karlsruhe Ontology framework KAON.3 It is built in a modular way, so that different needs can be fulfilled by combining parts.

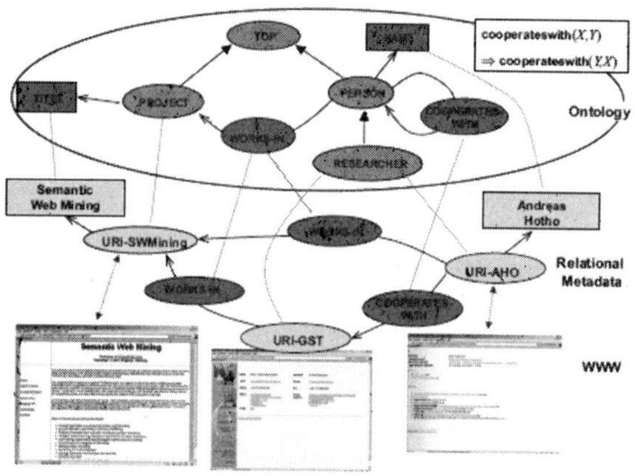

Fig. 1 The relation between the WWW, relational metadata, and ontologies

Definition 1 *A* core ontology with axioms *is a tuple* O :=(C;_C;R; _;_R;A) *consisting of _ two disjoint sets* C *and* R *whose elements are called* concept identifiers *and* relation identifiers, *resp.,*
_ a partial order _C on C, *called* concept hierarchy *or* taxonomy,*_ a function _*:R ! C+ *called* signature *(where* C+ *is the set of all finite tuples of elements in* C*),_ a partial order _*R *on* R, *called* relation hierarchy, *where* r1 _R r2 *implies* j_(r1)j = j_(r2)j *and* _i(_(r1)) _C _i(_(r2)), *for each* 1 _ i _ j_(r1)j, *with* _i *being the projection on the* i*th component, and _ a set* A *of logical axioms in some logical language* L.

This definition constitutes a core structure that is quite straightforward, well-agreed upon, and that may easily be mapped onto most existing ontology representation languages. Step by step the definition can be extended by taking into account axioms, lexicons, and knowledge bases [1].As an example, have a look at the top of Figure 1. The set C of concepts is the set fTop, Project, Person, Researcher, Literalg, and the concept hierarchy _C is indicated by the arrows with a bold head. The set R of relations is the set fworks-in, researcher, cooperates-with, nameg. The relation 'worksin' has (Person, Project) as signature, the relation 'name' has (Person, Literal) as signature.4 In this example, the hierarchy on the relations is flat, i. e., _R is just the identity relation. For an example of a non-flat relation, have a look at Fig. 2.

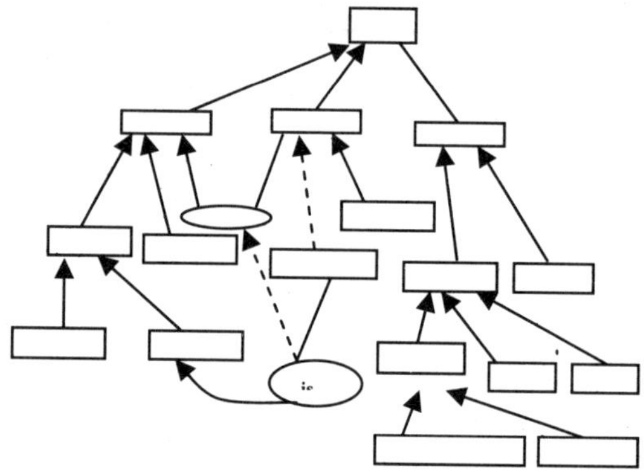

Fig. 2 Parts of the ontology of the content of a fictitious tourism Web site

The objects of the metadata level can be seen as instances of the ontology concepts. For example, 'URI-SWMining' is an instance of the concept 'Project', and thus by inheritance also of the concept 'Top'. Up to here, RDF Schema would be sufficient for formalizing the ontology. Often ontologies contain also logical axioms. By applying logical deduction, one can then infer new knowledge from the information which is stated implicitly. The axiom in Figure 1 states for instance that the 'cooperates-with' relation is symmetric. From it, one can logically infer that the person addressed by 'URI-AHO' is cooperating with the person addressed by 'URI-GST' (and not only the other way around). A priori, any knowledge representation mechanism5 can play the role of a Semantic Web language. *Frame Logic* (or *F–Logic*; [2]), for instance, provides a semantically founded knowledge representation based on the frame and slot metaphor. Probably the most popular framework at the moment are Description Logics (DL). DLs are subsets of first order logic which aim at being as expressive as possible while still being decidable. The description logic SHIQ provides the basis for the web language DAML+OIL.6 Its latest version is currently established by the W3C Web Ontology Working Group (WebOnt)7 under the name OWL. Several tools are in use for the creation and maintenance of ontologies and metadata, as well as for reasoning within them. Our group has developed *OntoEdit* [4, 5], an ontology editor which is connected to *Ontobroker* [1], an inference engine for F–Logic. It provides means for semantic based query handling over distributed resources. In this paper, we will focus our interest on the XML, RDF, ontology and logic layers.

4. Using Semantics for Usage Mining and Mining the Usage of the Semantic Web

Semantics can be utilized for Web Mining for different purposes Some of the approaches presented in this section rely on a comparatively *ad hoc* formalization of semantics, while others exploit the full power of the Semantic Web. The Semantic Web offers a good basis to enrich Web Mining: The types of (hyper)links are now described explicitly, allowing the knowledge engineer to gain deeper insights in Web structure mining; and the contents of the pages come along with a formal semantics, allowing her to apply mining techniques which require more structured input. Because the distinction between the use of semantics for Web mining and the mining of the Semantic Web itself is all but sharp, we will discuss both in an integrated fashion. Web usage mining benefits from including semantics into the mining process for the simple reason that the application expert as the end user of mining results is interested in *events in the application domain*, in particular user behavior, while the data available—Web server logs—are technically oriented sequences of *HTTP requests*. A central aim is therefore to map HTTP requests to meaningful units of application events. *Application events* are defined with respect to the application domain and the site, a non-trivial task that amounts to a detailed formalization of the site's business model. For example, relevant E-business events include product views and product click-throughs in which a user shows specific interest in a specific product by requesting more detailed information (e.g., from the Beach Hotel to a listing of its prices in the various seasons). Web server logs generally contain at least some information on an event that was marked by the user's request for a specific Web page, or the system's generating a page to acknowledge the successful completion of a transaction. For example, consider a tourism Web site that allows visitors to search hotels according to different criteria, to look at detailed descriptions of these hotels, to make reservations, and so on. In the Web site, a hotel room reservation event may be identified by the recorded delivery of the page reserve. php?-user=12345&hotel=Beach Hotel people=2&-arrive=01May&depart=04 May, which was generated after the user chose "room for 2 persons" in the "Beach Hotel" and typed in the arrival and departure dates of his desired stay. What information the log contains, and whether this is sufficient, will depend on the technical set-up of the site as well as on the purposes of the analysis.So what are the aspects of application events that need to be reconstructed using semantics? In the following sections, we will show that a requested Web page is, first, about some *content*, second, the request for a specific *service* concerning that content, and third, usually part of a larger sequence of events. We will refer to the first two as *atomic application events*, and to the third as *complex application event*.

4.1 Atomic application events: Content

A requested Web page is about something, usually a product or other object described in the page. For example, search hotel.html?facilities=tennis may be a page about hotels, more specifically a·listing of hotels, with special attention given to a detailed indication of their sports facilities. To describe content in this way,URLs are generally mapped to concepts. The concepts are usually organized in taxonomies (also called "concept hierarchies", see [1] and the definition in Section 3). For example, a tennis court is a facility. Introducing relations, we note that a facility belongs-to an accommodation, etc. (see Fig. 2).

4.2 Atomic application events: Service

A requested Web page reflects a purposeful user activity, often the request for a specific service. For example, search hotel.html?facilities=tennis was generated after the user had initiated a search by hotel facilities (stating tennis as the desired value). This way of analyzing requests gives a better sense of what users wanted and expected from the site, as opposed to what they received in terms of the eventual content of the page. To a certain extent, the requested service is associated with the request's URL stem and the delivered page's content (e.g., the URL search hotel.html says that the page was a result of a search request). However, the delivered page's content may also be meaningless for the understanding of user intentions, as is the case when the delivered page was a "404 File not found". More information is usually contained in the specifics of the user query that led to the creation of the page. This information may be contained in the URL query string, which is recorded in the Web server log if the common request method GET is used. The query string may also be recorded by the application server in a separate log. As an example, we have used ontology to describe a Web site which operates on relational databases and also contains a number of static pages, together with an automated classification scheme that relies on mapping the query strings for dynamic page generation to concepts [5]. Pages are classified according to multiple concept hierarchies that reflect content (type of object that the page describes), structure (function of pages in object search), and service (type of search functionality chosen by the user). A path can then be regarded as a sequence of (more or less abstract) concepts in a concept hierarchy, allowing the analyst to identify strategies of search.

This classification can make Web usage mining results more comprehensible and actionable for Web site redesign or personalization: The semantic analysis has helped to improve the design of search options in the site, and to identify behavioral patterns that indicate whether a user is likely to successfully complete a search process, or whether he is likely to abandon the site . The latter insights could be used to dynamically generate help messages for new users.Oberle [4] develops a scheme for application server logging of user queries with respect to a full-blown ontology (a "knowledge portal" in the sense of [2]). This allows the analyst to utilize the full expressiveness of the ontology language, which enables a wide range of inferences going beyond the use of taxonomy-based generalizations. He gives examples of possible inferences on queries to a community portal, which can help support researchers in finding potential cooperation partners and projects. A largescale evaluation of the proposal is under development.

The ontologies of content and services of a Web site as well as the mapping of pages into them may be obtained in various ways. At one extreme, ontologies may be handcrafted ex post; at the other extreme, they may be the generating structure of the Web site (in which case also the mapping of pages to ontology elements is already available). In most cases, mining methods themselves must be called upon to establish the ontology (*ontology learning*) and/or the mapping (*instance learning*), for example by using methods of learning relations (e.g., [3]) and information extraction (e.g., [1, 3]).

4.3 Complex application events

A requested Web page, or rather, the activity/ies behind it, is generally part of a more extended behavior. This may be a problem-solving strategy consciously pursued by the user (e.g., to narrow down search by iteratively refining search terms), a canonical activity sequence pertaining to the site type (e.g., catalog search/browse, choose, add-to cart, pay in an E-commerce setting [3]), or a description of behavior identified by application experts in exploratory data analysis. An example of the latter is the distinction of four kinds of online shopping strategies by [4]: *directed buying* earch/*deliberation*, *hedonic browsing*, and *knowledge building*. The first group is characterized by focused search patterns and immediate purchase. The second is more motivated by a future purchase and therefore tends to browse through a particular category of products rather than directly proceed to the purchase of a specific product. The third is entertainment- and stimulus-driven, which occasionally results in spontaneous purchases. The fourth also shows exploratory behavior, but for the primary goal of information acquisition as a basis for future purchasing decisions. Moe characterized these browsing patterns in terms of product and category pages visited on a Web site. Spiliopoulou, Pohle, and Teltzrow [4] transferred this conceptualization to the analysis of a non-commercial information site. They formulated regular expressions that capture the behavior of search/deliberation and knowledge building, and used sequence mining to identify these behaviors in the site's logs.

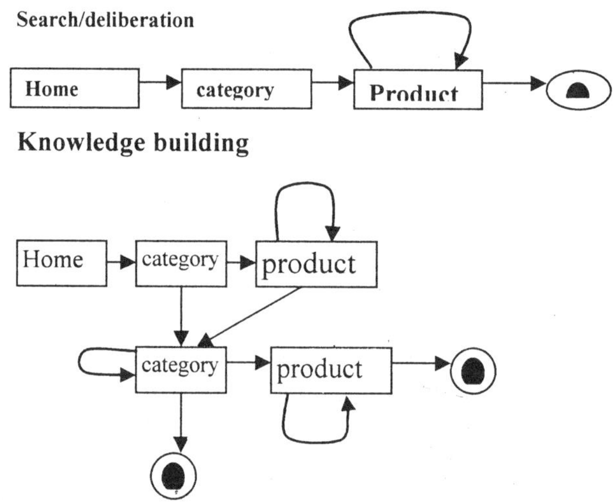

Fig. 3 Parts of the ontology of the complex application events of the example site.

4.4 How is knowledge about application events used in mining?

Once requests have been mapped to concepts, the question arises how knowledge is gained from these transformed data. We will investigate the treatment of atomic and of complex application events in turn. Mining using multiple taxonomies is related to OLAP data cube techniques: objects (in this case, requests or requested URLs) are described along a number of dimensions, and concept hierarchies or lattices are formulated along each dimension to allow more abstract views.

The analysis of data abstracted using taxonomies is crucial for many mining applications to generate meaningful results: In a site with dynamically generated pages, each individual page will be requested so infrequently that no regularities may be found in an analysis of navigation behavior. Rather, regularities may exist at a more abstract level, leading to rules like "visitors who stay in Wellness Hotels also tend to eat in restaurants". Second, patterns mined in past data are not helpful for applications like recommender systems when new items are introduced into product catalog and/or site structure: The new Pier Hotel cannot be recommended simply because it was not in the tourism site before and thus could not co-occur with any other item, be recommended by another user, etc. A knowledge of regularities at a more abstract level could help to derive a recommendation of the Pier Hotel because it too is wellness Hotel (and there are criteria for recommending Wellness Hotels).After the preprocessing steps in which access data have been mapped into taxonomies, two main approaches are taken in subsequent mining steps. In many cases, mining operates on concepts at a chosen level of abstraction. For example, the sessions are transformed into points in a feature space [3], or on the sessions transformed into sequences of content units at a given level of description (for example, association rules can be sought between abstract concepts such as Wellness Hotels, tennis courts, and restaurants).This approach is usually combined with interactive control of the software, so that the analyst can re-adjust the chosen level of abstraction after viewing the results (e.g., in the miner WUM; see [5] for a case study).Alternatively to this 'static' approach, other algorithms identify the most specific level of relationships by choosing concepts dynamically. This may lead to rules like "People who stay at Wellness Hotels tend to eat at vegetarian only Indian restaurants"—linking hotel-choice behavior at a comparatively high level of abstraction with restaurant choice behavior at a comparatively detailed level of description. For example, Srikant and Agrawal [4] search for associations in given taxonomies, using support and confidence thresholds to guide the choice of level of abstraction. Daiand Mobasher [1] present a scheme for aggregating towards more general concepts when an explicit taxonomy is missing. They apply clustering to sets of sessions; this clustering identifies related concepts at different levels of abstraction. Semantic Web Usage Mining for complex application events involves two steps of mapping requests to events. As discussed in Section 4.3 above, complex application events are usually defined by regular expressions in atomic application events (at some given level of abstraction in their respective hierarchies). Therefore, in a first step, URLs are mapped to atomic application events at the required level of abstraction. In a second step, a sequence miner can then be used to discover sequential patterns in the transformed data.

The shapes of sequential patterns sought, and the mining tool used, determine how much prior knowledge can be used to constrain the patterns identified: They range from largely unconstrained first-order or k-th order Markov chains [7], to regular expressions that specify the atomic activities completely (the name of the concept) or partially (a variable matching a set of concepts) [4, 2]. Examples of the use of regular expressions describing application-relevant courses of events include search strategies [5], a segmentation of visitors into customers and non-customers [7], and a segmentation of visitors into different interest groups based on the customer buying cycle model from marketing [4].To date, few commonly agreed-upon models of Semantic Web behavior exist. The still largely exploratory nature of the field implies that highly interactive data preparation and mining tools are of paramount importance: They give the best support for domain experts working with analysts to contribute their background knowledge in an iterative mining cycle.

5. Extracting Semantics from Web Usage

The effort behind the Semantic Web is to add semantic annotation to Web documents in order to access knowledge instead of unstructured material. The purpose is to allow knowledge to be managed in an automatic way. Web Mining can help to learn definitions of structures for knowledge organization (e. g., ontologies) and to provide the population of such knowledge structures. All approaches discussed here are semi-automatic. They assist the knowledge engineer in extracting the semantics, but cannot completely replace her. In order to obtain high quality results, one cannot replace the human in the loop, as there is always a lot of tacit knowledge involved in the modeling process [5]. A computer will never be able to fully consider background knowledge, experience, or social conventions. If this were the case, the Semantic Web would be superfluous, since then machines like search engines or agents could operate directly on conventional Web pages. The overall aim of our research is thus not to replace the human, but rather to provide him with more and more support. In [6], we have discussed how content, structure, and usage mining can be used for creating Semantics. Here we focus on the contribution of usage mining. In the World Wide Web as in other places, much knowledge is socially constructed. This social behavior is reflected by the usage of the Web. One tenet related to this view is that navigation is not only driven by formalized relationships or the underlying logic of the available Web resources, but that it "is an information browsing strategy that takes advantage of the behavior of like-minded people Recommender systems based on "collaborative filtering" have been the most popular application of this idea. In recent years, the idea has been extended to consider not only ratings, but also Web usage as a basis for the identification of like-mindedness ("People who liked/bought this book also looked at ..."); see [3] for a recent mining-based system; see also [6] for a classic, although not mining-based, application. Web usage mining by its definition always creates patterns that structure pages in some way. The basic idea is (a) to offer terms that are shown in the hierarchy as related, and (b) to infer from terms that occurred frequently in previous search histories a relative weighting on the set of pages that are described only coarsely by the few terms of the inltial current query. To sum up, these examples show various ways of how the Semantic Web can be built up using techniques of Web (usage) mining.

6. Conclusions and Outlook

In this paper, we have studied the combination of the two fast-developing research areas Semantic Web and Web Mining, especially usage mining. We discussed how Semantic Web Usage Mining can improve the results of 'classical' usage mining by exploiting the new semantic structures in the Web; and how the construction of the Semantic Web can make use of Web Mining techniques. A truly semantic understanding of Web usage needs to take into account not only the information stored in server logs, but also the *meaning* that is constituted by the sets and sequences of Web page accesses. The examples provided show the potential benefits of further research in this integration attempt. One important focus is to make search engines and other programs able to better understand the content of Web pages and sites. This is reflected in the wealth of research efforts that model pages in terms of an ontology of the content. Overall, three important directions for further interdisciplinary cooperation between mining and application experts in Semantic Web Usage Mining have been identified:

1. the development of ontologies of complex behavior,
2. the deployment of these ontologies in Semantic Web description and mining tools and
3. continued research into methods and tools that allow the integration of both experts' and users' background knowledge into the mining cycle. Web mining methods should increasingly treat content, structure, and usage in an integrated fashion in iterated cycles of *extracting* and *utilizing* semantics, to be able to understand and (re)shape the Web.

7. References

[1] C.C. Aggarwal. Collaborative crawling: Mining user experiences for topical resource discovery. In *KDD - 2002– Proceedings of the Eighth ACM SIGKDD International Conference on Knowledge Discovery and Data Mining, Edmonton, CA, July 23-26, 2002*, pages 423–428, New York,2002. ACM.

[2] M. Baumgarten, A.G. B¨uchner, S.S. Anand, M.D. Mulvenna, and J.G. Hughes. User-driven navigation pattern discovery from internet data. In M. Spiliopoulou and B. Masand, editors, *Advances in Web Usage Analysis and User Profiling*, pages 74–91. Springer, Berlin, 2000.

[3] B. Berendt. Detail and context in web usage mining:Coarsening and visualizing sequences. In R. Kohavi, B.M.Masand, M. Spiliopoulou, and J. Srivastava, editors, *WEBKDD2001 – Mining Web Log Data Across All Customer Touch Points*, pages 1–24. Springer-Verlag, Berlin Heidelberg,2002b.

[4] B. Berendt, B. Mobasher, M. Nakagawa, and M. Spiliopoulou. The impact of site structure and user environment on session reconstruction in web usage analysis. In *Workshop Notes of Fourth WEBKDD Web Mining for Usage Patterns & User Profiles at KDD - 2002,July 23, 2002*, pages 115–129, 2002.

[5] B. Berendt and M. Spiliopoulou. Analysing navigation behavior in web sites integrating multiple information systems. *The VLDB Journal*, 9(1):56–75, 2000.

[6] Bettina Berendt, Andreas Hotho, and Gerd Stumme. Towards semantic web mining. In *[22]*, pages 264–278.

[7] J. L. Borges and M. Levene. Data mining of user navigation patterns. In M. Spiliopoulou and B. Masand, editors,*Advances in Web Usage Analysis*.

Analysis of Assorted Bioinformatics Tools and its Metrics

P. Dhavachelvan and Jayanthi Manicassamy
Department of Computer Science, Pondicherry University, Pondicherry, India.
dhavachelvan@gmail.com *jmanic2@yahoo.com*

Abstract

Bioinformatics is a field of computational molecular biology which merging with few other sciences which entails statistics techniques, database creation for solving biological problems by means of biological data analysis and interpretation of accurate result. Since biological data's can be predicted in an unpredictable rate. There is a need for managing and interoperating this data for real time environment for which various tools, techniques, algorithms, databases has been developed. Assorted tools have been developed in this area of bioinformatics for diverse analysis processes like sequence analysis, functional analysis, structural analysis and similarity and homology analysis. Factors that are to be considered in the designing of bioinformatics tools are software should be made globally available and the tools developed should be flexible to the users since mostly the users are of biologists. It is significant to evaluate these tools by identifying bioinformatics methods with optimal sensitivity, predictive and other capabilities since there is need for high-throughput techniques or computational tools are required that can be effectively and efficiently utilized by researchers, developers and novice's users. This paper provides an analysis made on various bioinformatics tools of which twenty five tools are taken for details study. The survey is made on these tools based on the study and classification like sequence analysis tools, pattern matching tools and textmining tools with features and the associated metrics are identified for each tool. This helps us to proceed in the development of new tool with the common features that are required for the development of bioinformatics tools, enhancement of existing tools or utilization of better existing tools.

Keywords: *Pattern Matching, Sequence Analysis, Text Mining, Bioinformatics, Evaluation, Software Metrics.*

1. Introduction

Bioinformatics aim to solve biological problems using related information, using mathematical, statistical and computing methods. The definition of bioinformatics varies based on the usage. Many tools have been developed which has been categorized based on the functionalities are Homology and Similarity Tools like 3D spatial homology search tool [1] for gene expression for finding genes with a similar spatial expression pattern which could potentially reveal novel or unknown genes involved in similar processes or pathways. Protein Function Analysis Tools like GOFFA tool [2] is Gene Ontology for Functional Analysis allows the user to interactively select GO terms according to their significance and specific biological complexity within the hierarchical structure. Structural Analysis Tools like PREDICTOR tool [3] for DNA structure prediction which allows the calculation of atomic structures of double-helical DNA with up to 150 Watson-Crick base pairs and sequence analysis tools have been developed or adapted to deal with the experimental riches of complex and multivariate data in biological problem solutions. Sequence Analysis Tools which includes "Database search" like text based search, sequence based search, motif based search and structure based search. "Analysis Tools" like DNA, RNA and protein sequence analysis, "Function analysis" like phylogeny, microarray analysis tools and various tools have also been developed.

Since biological resources are real entity that should be kept updated based on the researches that requires vast space, it could not be build by one so database like NCBI, PDB, EMBDL, Medline etc... has made to share its resources. Most of the bioinformatics related applications and tools utilities these Databases. The study made on various tools that falls in this category as mentioned above have made a deep analysis for identifying features and functionalities for each tools.

Software metrics quantifies some characteristics or attributes of a product or process by means of measurement using numerical ratings, Since quantitative have been proven very powerful in computer science and other sciences Statistical analysis is also being made to identifying the qualifying levels. There is no standard terminology for defining software metrics it depends on the requirements. Identification of features and functionalities are not only considered, we have also identified various metrics on each tools which has been represented in this paper since metrics based evaluation is used to represent the retrieval ability and performance of the tool like identity metrics, error rate, error report, precision, recall for bioinformatics tools.

Based on the classification made by us for tools web have explained each tool under that category like Pattern matching tools, Sequence analysis tools and Text mining tools.

2. Survey on Bioinformatics Tools

The survey made on the bioinformatics tools for which a detailed analysis has been made has been explained in this section. These tools have been categorized based on their features and functionalizes that have explained below by means of categories.

Pattern Matching Tools

Pattern matching is the act of checking for the presence of the constituents of a given pattern. a pattern concerns conventionally either sequences or tree structures. There are various tools that have been developed in pattern matching, in the area of bioinformatics for various analysis processes like sequence analysis, functional analysis, structural analysis and similarity analysis. The following are pattern match tools that have taken for the study in bioinformatics tools.

David He et. al [4] developed a new web-tool which uses graphical visualization methods borrowed from protein interaction studies to identify and characterize repetitive elements in low-complexity sequences where repetitive protein sequences with a limited amino acid palette are abundant in nature and many of them play an important role in the structure and function of certain types of proteins. However, such repetitive sequences often do not have rigidly defined motifs. This tool is license free, which is flexible following an algorithm based approach that is navigateable.

Richard J. Edwards et. al [5] developed tool for making motif-motif comparisons which is a GUI based, license free, open source. It identifying and describing similarities between regular expression motifs. It can identify a number of different relationships between motifs, including exact matches, variants of degenerate motifs and complex overlapping motifs. Motif relationships are scored using shared information content, allowing the best matches to be easily identified in large comparisons. Many input and search options are available, enabling a list of motifs to be compared to within itself to identify recurring motifs or to datasets of known motifs. This tool is a computational approach with online help facilities.

Marti A et. al [6] developed a web-based search engine that provides biologists with new ways to access the scientific literature. One of the features is the ability to search and browse article figures and their captions with a grid view and many different figures associated with the same keywords, providing new insight into the literature. An abstract/title search and list view shows at a glance many of the figures associated with each article. The interface is carefully designed according to usability principles and techniques.

Anne Laure et. al [7] has developed tool which associates with GUI web server with license free for finding internal repeats at three levels which quickly identifies statistically significant internal repeats in DNA and amino acid sequences and in 3D structures using dynamic programming. The associated web server also shows the relationships between repeats at each level and facilitates visualization of the results. This tool is a computational based supported by any browser type which is flexible and user friendly.

Dietrich et. al [8] has developed a web service tool for researchers in the biomedical research community for literature search that analyze text for contained information and then link them to the corresponding entries in bioinformatics databases such as Swiss-Prot, PubMed data entries and gene ontology concepts. The tool automatically integrates links to database concepts to offer additional support to readers and to authors will be extended in the future with novel modules for information extraction. All services are preloaded to avoid startup overhead. All documents are processed in a single stream right upon submission, i.e. no preprocessing is performed to store intermediary information. Any contained query is passed to the index service for document retrieval. As soon as a request reaches the central Whatizit server, the requested modules are activated and the stream of text is passed through all required components in a single stream. Tool provides a text input area where user can submit any kind of Unicode-encoded text or retrieve Medline abstracts for subsequent analysis which is license free and platform independent. Which is a computational based, with online help following a computational approach.

Sequence Analysis Tools

There are various sequences analysis tool that have been created in this field of bioinformatics for various processes like functional analysis, structural analysis and similarity analysis. The following are the sequence analysis tools that have been taken for study that have been explained below.

Xiang et. al [9] has developed a web interface for comparative genomics and phylogenetic analysis of Plasmodium gene families which causes malaria by the intercellular protozoan parasite. Gene families were clustered and could be searched using keywords, gene-family information, domain composition, Gene Ontology and BLAST. This tool contained 8980 sets of gene families derived from six malaria parasite genomes like Plasmodium falciparum, Plasmodium berghei, Plasmodium knowlesi, Plasmodium chabaudi, Plasmodium vivax and Plasmodium Yoelii which is helpful for researchers working on malaria parasite phylogenomics. The technology used here is PHP and Perl which is fully web tool based on computational approach.

Mario Falchi et. al [10] an efficient tool for mining complex inbred genealogies that identify clusters of individuals sharing the same expected amount of relatedness. It also allows reconstruction of sub-pedigrees suitable for genetic mapping in a systematic way. The tool is developed in Java which is platform independent, GUI based user friendly tool followed a computational approach for tool development.

Jacques Oberto et. al [11] has developed a web service of platform independent, license free to facilitate extraction, by molecular geneticists and phylogeneticists, of specific gene and protein sequences from completely determined prokaryotic genomes. Upon selection of a particular prokaryotic organism and gene, two levels of visual gene context information are provided on a single dynamic page. The amino acid sequence is provided for protein-coding query genes. Query results can be exported as a rich text format word processor file for printing, archival or further analysis.

Jimin Pei et. al [12] has developed a web server which is user friendly that constructs multiple proteins sequence alignments using PROMALS, a progressive method that improves alignment quality by using additional homologs from PSI-BLAST searches and In addition to alignment construction, this server outputs useful information about predicted secondary structures, sequence grouping and positional conservation for target sequences. The tool is license free with GUI based which follows algorithm based approach.

Shaun Mahony et. al [13] has developed a web server that is designed to support the study of DNA-binding motifs which is a GUI based developed using C++ of license free and platform independent. This tool may be used to query motifs against databases of known motifs, the software aligns input motifs against the chosen database and lists of the highest-scoring matches are returned. Such similarity-search functionality facilitates the identification of transcription factors that potentially interact with newly discovered motifs. This tool is a highly flexible, allowing user to 'mix-and-match' between various alignment methods, multiple alignment strategies and tree-building methods. This is a computational approach tool with help facility provided.

Text Mining Tools

In this area of bioinformatics various mining tools have been developed which involves common evolutionary relationship, structure identification and identifying biological proprieties that has specific functionalities. The following are the text mining tools that have been made in this study have been explained below

Jung-jae Kim et. al [14] Developed a ontology based, novel search engine supporting any browser type that imposes positional restriction on occurrences matching multi-term queries, based on the observation that terms with semantic relations which are explicitly stated in text are not found too far from each other. For better results MedEvi further identifies additional keywords of biological and statistical significance from local context of matching occurrences in order to help users reformulate their queries.

Arek Gladki et. al [15] has developed a web tool is a bio-linguistic method used to identify biologically relevant information with true correlation which is significance in crucial for any bio-medical research, literature mining with no exception which can discover biomedically meaningful, overrepresented and specific words using a statistical approach. It is especially useful for detecting low-frequency associations between user query and keywords such as drugs and genes or less obvious correlations between diseases. It also aims at providing information directly and specifically linked with user provided context. This also supports the feature of ontology of fully web-based supported by any type of browser.

Dean Cheng et. al [16] has developed a web server which is used for biomedical text mining and information retrieval which includes an extensive set of category specific thesauruses and also integration of many well annotated databases like OMIM, DrugBank, SwissProt, HMDB, HPRD and GAD as supplementary text resources which is customizable. This tool uses simple dictionary approach to identify biological or biomedical associations and could not identify novel or newly named diseases, genes, cell types, drugs or metabolites. Another limitation lies in its inability to extract context or meaning from sentences or terms.

Mounir Errami et. al [17] has developed a web tool for problems that persist for duplicated publications, this tool detects duplicate via analysis of citations at submission time can be performed by journals, this tool is combined with this database, which makes detection of duplicate for authors, editor and reviewers and it is resources can be customized to perform on any text-based database. This is fully computational supporting any type of browser.

Yoshimasa et. al [18] has developed a platform independent web-based GUI based search engine for MEDLINE abstracts, which is designed particularly to help users browse biomedical concepts appearing in the documents retrieved by the query. The concepts are presented to the user in a tabular format and ranked based on the co-occurrence statistics. The concept collected from several biomedical databases and thesauri such as UniProt, BioThesaurus, UMLS and DrugBank. This follows an algorithm based computational approach supporting any browser type.

3. Metrics Based Survey

In this section we have described below some of the metrics that are applicable for bioinformatics tools that we have taken for survey made. Evaluating a tool is done by means of metrics evaluation. Here below we have give a general survey chart for metrics for bioinformatics tools. The metrics which are applicable for a particular tool has been represented as follows

Specificity (Sp):
Specificity [19] in general is a standard evaluation metrics that measures the proportion of negative patterns correctly recognized as being negative.

$$\text{Specificity (Sp)} = TN / (TN + FP) \quad (1)$$

where, TN – number of True Negative, FP – number of False Positive. This metrics are applicable for the tools BAGET, PlasmoGF, Jenti, PROMALS, STAMP, SubSeqer, CompariMotif, Biotext, Swelfe, Whatizit, MedEvi, PolySearch, etBlast, e-Lise and FACTA.

Expected Value (E-Value):
E-value (Expected value) [20] is a statistical measure that reflects the expected number of alignments between the text and the pattern that have the same or even better similarity score. E-value is also said to be the number of hits one can expect to get from a search in a database of random sequence with the same distribution of amino acids as the real database. This metric is applicable for the tool CompariMotif.

Lexical Precision (LPrecision):
LPrecision [21] is the extraction precision metrics that measure the performance of the extraction modules through syntactic analyzes and pattern based extraction from the corpus which is calculated as

$$\text{LPrecision} = \text{Correct}_{\text{Extracted}} / \text{all}_{\text{Extracted}} \quad (2)$$

where, $\text{all}_{\text{Extracted}}$ – all the information that are being extracted and $\text{Correct}_{\text{Extracted}}$ are the correct information that are extracted from all the information that are being extracted. This metrics are applicable for the tools Biotext and Whatizit.

Lexical Overall (LO) Metrics:
Lexical Overlap [21] denotes the shared concepts between the manual and extracted ontology which is calculated as LO = Correct / all (3)

Let Lo be the set of all domain relevant extracted concepts. This metrics are applicable for the tools Biotext, Swelfe and Whatizit.

Structural Root Mean Square Deviations RMSD:
RMSD [22] makes an approximate estimation of the average protein structure match difference of random related structures. The RMSD of two structures (A and B) of identical length of L_N, is written as

$$\text{RMSD} = \sqrt{R^2_A + R^2_B - 2\frac{\sum r_{Ai} * r_{Bi}}{\sum r^2_{Ai} \sum r^2_{Bi}} R_A R_B} \quad (4)$$

where, R_A (R_B) is the radius of gyration for protein structure A (B), r_{Ai} (r_{Bi}) is the coordinate vector after global superposition. This metrics are applicable for the tool Swelfe.

Motif Score:
Motif score [4] of a motif and a sequence is defined as the maximum match score over all positions in the sequence where the motif would fit without overhanging the ends of the sequence.

$$\text{Motif Score} = IC * \text{Number of matched positions} \quad (5)$$

where, IC is Information Content. This metrics are applicable for the tool Swelfe.

Relative RMSD:
rRMSD [22] used to eliminate the dependencies in protein structures which is calculated as

$$\text{rRMSD} = \text{RMSD} / \sqrt{R^2_A + R^2_B - 2CR_A R_B} \quad (6)$$

This metrics is applicable for Swelfe tool

Pattern Match:
Pattern match metrics [19] is the universal standard metrics that are applicable for all applications, tools or techniques that are involved in pattern matching which is calculated as Pattern Match =Total number of matches /Number of matches correctly predicted (7)

This metrics are applicable for the tools PlasmoGF, Jenti, PROMALS, STAMP, SubSeqer, CompariMotif, Biotext, Swelfe, Whatizit, MedEvi, PolySearch, etBlast, e-Lise and FACTA.

Density of the Alignment:
Alignment is used most probably done while going for pattern match where we define Density of alignment [19] as Density of Alignment = Alignment Score / Alignment Length (8)

This metrics are applicable for the tool Swelfe.

Lexical Recall:
To measure the performance of the extraction modules through syntactic analyzes and pattern based extraction we calculated Lexical Recall [21] as

$$\text{LRecall} = \text{Correct}_{\text{Extracted}} / \text{all}_{\text{Corpus}} \quad (9)$$

where, $\text{Correct}_{\text{Extracted}}$ are the correct information that are extracted and $\text{all}_{\text{Corpus}}$ is all the information extracted. This metrics are applicable for the tools Biotext and Swelfe.

Length of repeats:
Length of the repeats [4] is the total size of the repeat that are been considered for pattern matching in motif comparison. This metrics are applicable for the tools SubSeqer, CompariMotif and Biotext.

Information Content Rank:
IC_m matches are ranked [5] by the total number of matching positions and then by the number of exactly matching fixed positions which are used in motifs.

Information Content Match (IC_m):
IC_m [5] is simply the sum of the component IC_i values which is used in motif comparison of protein sequences, where IC is the Information Content at position i. This metrics are applicable for the tools CompariMotif, Biotext, Swelfe, Whatizit, MedEvi, PolySearch, e-Lise and FACTA.

Match Positions:
This Match Position [4] metrics is the total number of match positions that are found in the whole sequence to which it is compared with other sequence. This metrics are applicable for the tools Jenti and etBlast.

Match score:
The match score [23] for a sequence is defined as

$$M_i = \sum_{j=1}^{n}(h_j + d_j g) \qquad (10)$$

where, n is the number of hits in the match, h_j is the score of the j th hit in the match, d_j is the length of the gap between hit $j - 1$ and hit j ($d_1 = 0$), and g is a 'gap penalty'. This metrics are applicable for the tool Biotext.

Number of nodes:
Global metrics for Cell graph. Number of nodes [24] in a graph is defined as the degree of a node is defined as the number of its edges. This metrics are applicable for the tools Jenti, STAMP and SubSeqer.

Clustering Coefficient:
Clustering coefficient [24] is one of the Computes quantitative metrics for tissue characterization and classification

$$C_i = (2E_i) = (k(k + 1)) \qquad (11)$$

where, k is the number of neighbors of the node i and E_i is the number of existing links between its neighbors. This metrics are applicable for the tool Jenti.

Error rate:
Error rate for NLP in mutation evaluation metrics [25] could be defined a Error rate = 1 / Precision (12)

Global metrics for Error rate = total entities detected / number of entities correctly detected. This metrics are applicable for the tools Jenti, PROMALS, Biotext, Swelfe, Whatizit, MedEvi, PolySearch, etBlast, e-Lise and FACTA.

Accuracy:
Accuracy that classifies catalytic protein structures [26] which is one of the performance metrics is calculated as

Accuracy = (TP + TN) / (TP + TN + FP + FN) (13)

where, TP – True Positive, TN – True Negative, FP- False Positive, FN – False Negative. This metrics are applicable for the tools BAGET, PlasmoGF, Jenti, PROMALS and STAMP.

Number of vertices:
Number of vertices [24] in a graph is defined as

$$V(G) = e - n + 2 \qquad (14)$$

where, e is the number of edges and n is the number of nodes. This metrics are applicable for the tools Jenti, and SubSeqer.

Identity Metrics:
Identity metrics [19] identifies similarity between amino acid pairs used in Protein analysis. This metrics are applicable for the tools PlasmoGF, Jenti and PROMALS.

Molecular weight: (10) (10
The molecular weight [22] is the mass of a protein or molecule which is calculated as the sum of the atomic mass of all the atoms in the molecule.

Sensitivity (Sn):
Sensitivity (Sn) metrics [19] measures the proportion of positive patterns correctly recognized genes in a sequence of DNA in general or in a string of DNA which can be calculated as

Sn = TP / (TP + FN) (15)

where, TP – True Positive and FN – False Negative.

F-Score:
F-score [10] is an evaluation metrics to measure the performance of the tool. It combines precision metrics and recall metrics used for Named entity recognition is defined as

F-Score = (2*precision*recall)/(precision + recall) (16)

This metrics are applicable for the tools Whatizit, MedEvi, PolySearch, etBlast, e-Lise and FACTA.

Precision Metrics:
Precision is one of the metrics that evaluates the tool performance. Precision evaluation is for NLP [28] then it is calculated as

Precision = (correct + (α. partial)) / (correct + spurious + (α. partial)) (17)

If precision evaluation is for named entity recognition it is expressed as

Precision [27] = (number of NE's a system correctly detected) / (total number of NE's identified by the system) (18)

Precision [10] is evaluated as the measure that measures the proportion of samples correctly classified.

P = (TP + TN) / (TP + TN + FP + FN) (19)

where, TN, TP – True Negative, True Positive and FN, FP – False Negative, False Positive.

This metrics are applicable for the tools BAGET, PlasmoGF, Jenti, PROMALS, STAMP, SubSeqer, CompariMotif, PolySearch, etBlast, e-Lise and FACTA.

Recall Metrics:

Recall Metrics is also another metrics that are involved in the performance of the tool. Recall for named entity recognition [27] is defined as

Recall = number of NE's a system correctly detected / total number of NE's contained in the input text. Commonly used Recall evaluation in NLP [10] is the rate of correctly detected entities over all correct entities is defined as Recall = (correct + (α·partial)) / (correct + missing + (α·partial)) (20)

This metrics are applicable for the tools BAGET, PlasmoGF, Jenti, PROMALS, STAMP, SubSeqer, CompariMotif, MedEvi, PolySearch, etBlast, e-Lise and FACTA.

Error Report:

Error report [28] as a global metric which is defined as, Error report = Percentage of wrong results in a system's output. (21)

This metrics are applicable for the tools PlasmoGF, STAMP, Biotext, Swelfe, Whatizit, MedEvi, PolySearch, etBlast, e-Lise and FACTA.

Relative number of hits :

Relative number of hits (RelHit) [14] denotes the shared concepts between the manual and extracted ontology. $LO(O_1, O_2) = | Lo_1 \cap Lo_2| / | Lo_2 |$ = Correct / all (22)

Let Lo_1 be the set of all domain relevant extracted concepts and Lo_2 the set of concepts of the Gold Standard. This metrics are applicable for the tools Biotext, Swelfe, Whatizit, MedEvi, PolySearch, etBlast, e-Lise and FACTA.

Positive Predictive Value (PPV):

Positive Predictive value (PPV) [29] is the percentage of true positive to the total number of positives recognized by the system, which can be calculated as

PPV = TP / (TP + FP) (23)

where, TP – True Positive and FP – False Positive. This metrics are applicable for the tools BAGET, PlasmoGF, Jenti, PROMALS, STAMP, SubSeqer, CompariMotif, MedEvi, PolySearch, etBlast, e-Lise and FACTA.

Negative Predictive Value:

Negative Prediction Value (NPV) [29] is the percentage of true negatives to the total number of negatives recognized by the system, which can be calculated as NPV = TN / (FN + TN) (24)

This metrics are applicable for the tools BAGET, PlasmoGF, Jenti, PROMALS, STAMP, SubSeqer, CompariMotif, MedEvi, PolySearch, etBlast, e-Lise and FACTA.

Information Retrieval (IR) Metrics:

Information retrieval (IR) Metrics [27] used in the evaluation of information retrieval for named entity recognition which is calculated as IR Metrics = Number of data's correctly retrieved / total number of data's retrieved (25)

This metrics are applicable for the tools PolySearch, e-Lise and FACTA.

4. Conclusion

Since, bioinformatics tools are increasingly important at present for real-time decision making for solving biological problems. In this paper we have given made a survey on various bioinformatics tools which has been discussed theoretically about its features, functionalities and metrics. The study carried out made a way for classifying of tools that we have taken for survey on the bases of analyzed features and functionalities like GUI, algorithm based, search, automatic detection, browser type etc. Metrics identification for a tool can provide us a means for evaluating this tool which qualifies a tool which is followed as one of the methods. The main reason behind for carrying out this evaluation on the bioinformatics tools is for the quality implications that could be enhanced on the developed tools or in the development of new tools for the developers in addition to new functionalities. Another important reason behind this survey carried out to represent how to carry out quality measures by experimenting on the developed bioinformatics tools for better utilizing of better existing tools.

5. References

[1] Lydia Ng, Chris Lau, Rob Young, Sayan Pathak, Leonard Kuan, Andrew Sodt, Madhavi Sutram, Chang-Kyu Lee, Chinh Dang and Michael Hawrylycz, "NeuroBlast: a 3D spatial homology search tool for gene expression", BioMed, July 2007.

[2] Hongmei Sun, Hong Fang, Tao Chen, Roger Perkins, and Weida Tong, "GOFFA: Gene Ontology for Functional Analysis – A FDA Gene Ontology Tool for Analysis of Genomic and Proteomic Data", BioMed, March 2006.

[3] Jochen Farwer, Martin J. Packer, Christopher A. Hunter, "PREDICTOR: A Web-Based Tool for the Prediction of Atomic Structure from Sequence for Double Helical DNA with up to 150 Base Pairs", ISO Press, 2007.

[4] David He and John Parkinson, "SubSeqer: a graph-based approach for the detection and identification of repetitive elements in low-complexity sequences", ACM Portal, pp 1016–1017, Feb 2008.

[5] Richard J. Edwards, Norman E. Davey and Denis C. Shields, "CompariMotif: quick and easy comparisons of sequence motifs ", ACM Portal, pp 1307–1309, March 2008.

[6] Marti A. Hearst, Anna Divoli, Harendra Guturu, Alex Ksikes, Preslav Nakov, Michael A. Wooldridge and Jerry Ye, "BioText Search Engine: beyond abstract search", ACM Portal, pp 2196–2197, June 2007.

[7] Anne-Laure Abraham, Eduardo P. C. Rocha and Joel Pothier, "Swelfe: a detector of internal repeats in sequences and structures", ACM Portal, pp 1536–1537, May 2008.

[8] Dietrich Rebholz-Schuhmann, Miguel Arregui, Sylvain Gaudan, Harald Kirsch and Antonio Jimeno, "Text processing through Web services: calling Whatizit", ACM Portal, pp 296–298, November 2007.

[9] Xiang Xu, Jinyu Wu, Jian Xiao, Yi Tan, Qiyu Bao, Fangqing Zhao and Xiaokun Li, "PlasmoGF: an integrated system for comparative genomics and phylogenetic analysis of Plasmodium gene families", ACM Portal, pp 1217–1220, March 2008.

[10] Mario Falchi and Christian Fuchsberger, "Jenti: an efficient tool for mining complex inbred genealogies", ACM Portal, pp 724–726, January 2008.

[11] Jacques Oberto, "BAGET: a web server for the effortless retrieval of prokaryotic gene context and sequence", ACM Portal, pp 424–425, December 2007.

[12] Jimin Pei, Bong-Hyun Kim, Ming Tang and Nick V. Grishin, "PROMALS web server for accurate multiple protein sequence alignments", Oxford Journal, pp 649-652, April 2007.

[13] Shaun Mahony and Panayiotis V. Benos, "STAMP: a web tool for exploring DNA-binding motif similarities", Oxford Journal, W253–W258, April 2007.

[14] Jung-jae Kim, Piotr Pezik and Dietrich Rebholz-Schuhmann, "MedEvi: Retrieving textual evidence of relations between biomedical concepts from Medline", ACM portal, pp 1410–1412, March 2008.

[15] Arek Gladki, Pawel Siedlecki, Szymon Kaczanowski and Piotr Zielenkiewicz, "e-LiSe—an online tool for finding needles in the '(Medline) haystack", ACM Portal, pp 1115–1117, March 2008.

[16] Dean Cheng, Craig Knox, Nelson Young, Paul Stothard, "PolySearch: a web-based text mining system for extracting relationships between human diseases, genes, mutations, drugs and metabolites", Oxford Journals, pp 399-405, May 2008.

[17] Mounir Errami, Justin M. Hicks, Wayne Fisher, David Trusty, Jonathan D. Wren, Tara C. Long and Harold R. Garner, "De´ja`vu—A study of duplicate citations in Medline", ACM Portal, pp 243–249, December 2007.

[18] Yoshimasa Tsuruoka, Junichi Tsujii and Sophia Ananiadou, "FACTA: a text search engine for finding associated biomedical concepts", Oxford Journal, September 2008.

[19] Scott Coull, Joel Branch, Boleslaw Szymanski and Eric Breimer, "Intrusion Detection: A Bioinformatics Approach", IEEE, pp 24- 33, December 2003.

[20] Yong Huang, Lingdi Ping, Xuezeng Pan, Guoyong Cai, "A Fast Exact Pattern Matching Algorithm for Biological Sequences", IEEE digital library, pp 8-12, 2008.

[21] Marta Sabou, Chris Wroe, Carole Goble, Gilad Mishne, "Learning domain ontologies for web service descriptions: An experiment in bioinformatics", ACM, pp 10-14, May 2005.

[22] Yang Zhang and Jeffrey Skolnick, "Scoring Function for Automated Assessment of Protein Structure Template Quality ", ACM Portal, pp 702–710, 2004.

[23] Timothy L. Baile and William Stafford Noble,"Searching for statistically significant regulatory modules",ACM Portal, pp16–25, June 2003.

[24] Cigdem Demir. b. ,Chandandeep Nagi. c. , Bulent Yener, "Cell-Graph Mining for Breast Tissue Modeling and Classification ", PubMed, pp 5311-4, December 2007.

[25] Witte R, Baker CJ., "Towards A Systematic Evaluation Of Protein Mutation Extraction Systems ", Pubmed, pp 1339-59, December 2006.

[26] Ian M. Overton, Gianandrea Padovani, Mark A. Girolami2 and Geoffrey J. Barton, "ParCrys: a Parzen window density estimation approach to protein crystallization propensity prediction", ACM Portal, pp 901–907, February 2008.

[27] Yang Jin, Ryan T McDonald, Kevin Lerman, Mark A Mandel,Steven Carroll, Mark Y Liberman, Fernando C. Pereira, Raymond S Winters and Peter S White, "Automated recognition of malignancy mentions in biomedical literature ",BMC Bioinformatics, pp7-492, November 2006.

[28] Witte R, Baker CJ., "Towards A Systematic Evaluation Of Protein Mutation Extraction Systems", Pubmed, December 2006.

[29] Cigdem Demir. b.Chandandeep Nagi. c. Bulent Yener, "Cell-Graph Mining for Breast Tissue Modeling and Classification", pp 5311-4, PubMed, 2007.

A Review on Open Source and Free Expert System Shells

G. N. R. Prasad[1], Dr. A. Vinaya Babu[2], B. Sasidhar[3] and P. M. Yohan[4]
[1]Sr. Asst. Professor, Dept. of MCA, CBIT, Gandipet, Hyderabad
gnrp@yahoo.com
[2]Director, SCDE, Prof. of CSE, JNTU, Hyderabad.
dravinayababu@yahoo.com
[3]Assoc. Professor, Dept. of MCA,CMEC, Maisammaguda, Secunderabad
buddigasasi@yahoo.com
[4]Assoc. Professor, Dept. of MCA, Wesley P.G. College, Secunderabad

Abstract

A shell is a complete development environment for building and maintaining knowledge-based applications. It provides a step-by-step methodology for a knowledge engineer that allows the domain experts themselves to be directly involved in structuring and encoding the knowledge. Use of shells reduces development time up to 50%. Open source is a set of principles and practices that promote access to the design and production of goods and knowledge. Free software is a matter of freedom: people should be free to use software in all the ways that are socially useful. Software differs from material objects—such as chairs, sandwiches, and gasoline—in that it can be copied and changed much more easily. These possibilities make software as useful as it is. In this paper we are discussing the various Open source and free software related to Expert System Shells. Many expert system shells are compared and discussed in this paper. In this paper, we are discussing about Open and free expert system shells.

1. Introduction

Knowledge-based expert systems, or simply expert systems, use human knowledge to solve problems that normally would require human intelligence. These expert systems represent the expertise knowledge as data or rules within the computer. These rules and data can be called upon when needed to solve problems. Books and manuals have a tremendous amount of knowledge but a human has to read and interpret the knowledge for it to be used. Conventional computer programs perform tasks using conventional decision-making logic -- containing little knowledge other than the basic algorithm for solving that specific problem and the necessary boundary conditions.

Most expert systems are developed via specialized software tools called shells. These shells come equipped with an inference mechanism (backward chaining, forward chaining, or both), and require knowledge to be entered according to a specified format (all of which might lead some to categorize OPS5 as a shell). They typically come with a number of other features, such as tools for writing hypertext, for constructing friendly user interfaces, for manipulating lists, strings, and objects, and for interfacing with external programs and databases. These shells qualify as languages, although certainly with a narrower range of application than most programming languages.

2. Expert System Shells

While any conventional programming language can be used to build a knowledge base, the expert system shell simplifies the process of creating a knowledge base. It is the shell that actually processes the information entered by a user; relates it to the concepts contained in the knowledge base; and provides an assessment or solution for a particular problem. Thus, an expert system shell provides a layer between the user interface and computer operating system to manage the input and output of data. It also manipulates the information provided by the user in conjunction with the knowledge base to arrive at a particular conclusion. The structure of the shell is very similar to that of an interpreter or a front-end to a database program. The shell also manages the user interface, performing functions that range from the validation of numeric values entered on the screen to management of the mouse and the representation of graphical objects. The shell is often sold as an end-product, allowing the purchaser to encode a knowledge base from scratch the same way a user would purchase a database management system. On the other hand, knowledge bases can be sold as products--where a shell or interpreter may be an incidental part of the package--in the same way a user might buy data.

2.1 Jess

The Java Expert System Shell is a portable, extensible, fast reasoning engine written in Sun Microsystem's Java language. It was developed at Sandia National Laboratories (USA) and is distributed free of charge for academic use. Jess has a large, worldwide user community. Jess is commonly used in agent research, as it provides a convenient way to integrate complex reasoning capabilities into Java-based software. Jess users have developed many software extensions, including ones for fuzzy logic, database access, blackboards, and language understanding. Jess has been used to deploy many real systems, including some based on a multiagent paradigm.

Jess is a rule engine and scripting environment written entirely in Sun's Java language by Ernest Friedman-Hill at Sandia National Laboratories in Livermore, CA. Using ***Jess***, you can build Java software that has the capacity to "reason" using knowledge you supply in the form of declarative rules. ***Jess*** is small, light, and one of the fastest rule engines available. Its powerful scripting language gives you access to all of Java's APIs. ***Jess*** includes a full-featured development environment based on the award-winning Eclipse platform.

2.2 Jboss drools

Drools is a business rule management system (BRMS) and an enhanced Rules Engine implementation, ReteOO, based on Charles Forgy's Rete algorithm tailored for the Java language. More importantly, Drools provides for Declarative Programming and is flexible enough to match the semantics of your problem domain with Domain Specific Languages, graphical editing tools, web based tools and developer productivity tools

2.3 Euler Proof Mechanism

Euler is an inference engine supporting logic based proofs. It is a backward-chaining reasoner enhanced with Euler path detection. It has implementations in Java, C#, Python, Javascript and Prolog.

2.4 InfoSapient

It is a rules engine that allows members of the business community to enter and maintain business rules using everyday language. The resulting automated decision-making is similar to the way informed human make decisions. Many variables may be considered simultaneously and used to weigh risks and opportunities in order to arrive at the best course of action. Given ambiguous situations that are typically found in business processes, InfoSapient will always arrive at a 'best' course of action. This allows complex decision-making to take place at the precise moment it is needed without depending on the skill and experience of a highly distributed workforce.

2.5 Jena

It is a Java framework for building Semantic Web applications. It provides a programmatic environment for RDF, RDFS and OWL, SPARQL and includes a rule-based inference engine. Jena is open source and grown out of work with the HP Labs Semantic Web Programme.

2.6 Jlog

It is an implementation of a Prolog interpreter, written in Java. It's primary benefit is that can be run on almost any platform supporting Java (such as a web browser), and as such it is well suited for educational purposes. It works as both an application and as an applet.

It includes built-in source editor, query panels, online help, animation primitives, and a GUI debugger. It can open and save files when running as an application, but not as an applet (because of the security model for web browsers; however it is possible to copy and paste Prolog source between JLog and a local text editor).

JLog is also suitable for developers who need an embedded Prolog engine in Java. JLog make is easy to consult, construct queries, and evaluate query results. It also includes translation facilities to map between Prolog terms and standard Java objects.

2.7 Jeops

The Java Embedded Object Production System is a project intended to give Java the power of production systems. JEOPS adds forward chaining, first-order production rules to Java through a set of classes designed to provide this language with some kind of declarative programming. With that, the development of intelligent applications, such as software agents or expert systems is facilitated. JEOPS is a Java based forward chaining RULE ENGINE. This Rule Engine is used to power up the business process by rules in Java Application Servers, client applications, and Servlets

2.8 Focl

It is an expert system shell and machine learning program written in Common Lisp. The machine learning program extends Quinlan's FOIL program by containing a compatible explanation-based learning component. FOCL learns Horn Clause programs from examples and (optionally) background knowledge. The expert system includes a backward-chaining rule interpreter and a graphical interface to the rule and fact base.

2.9 Babylon

It is a development environment for expert systems. It includes frames, constraints, a prolog-like logic formalism, and a description language for diagnostic applications. It is implemented in Common Lisp and has been ported to a wide range of hardware platforms.

2.10 Mike

The Micro Interpreter for Knowledge Engineering is a full-featured, free, and portable software environment designed for teaching purposes at the UK's Open University. It includes forward and backward chaining rules with user-definable conflict resolution strategies, and a frame representation language with inheritance and 'demons' (code triggered by frame access or change), plus user-settable inheritance strategies. Automatic 'how' explanations (proof histories) are provided for rule execution, as are user-specified 'why' explanations. Coarse-grained and fine-grained rule tracing facilities are provided, along with a novel 'rule graph' display which concisely shows the history of rule execution. MIKE, which forms the kernel of an Open University course on Knowledge Engineering, is written in a conservative and portable subset of Edinburgh-syntax Prolog, and is distributed as non-copy-protected source code. MIKE version 1 was described in the October/November 1990 issue of BYTE. MIKE v1.50, which was formerly available from a range of ftp servers, has been superseded by two newer versions: MIKEv2.03, a full Prolog source code version, incorporating a RETE algorithm for fast forward chaining, a truth maintenance system, uncertainty handling, and hypothetical worlds, and MIKEv2.50, a turnkey DOS version with menu-driven interface and frame- and rule-browsing tools, fully compatible with MIKEv2.03, but without source code.

2.11 Wind ExS

The Windows Expert System is a fully functional Windows-based forward chaining expert system. Its modular architecture allows the user to substitute new modules as required to enhance the capabilities of the system. WindExS sports Natural Language Rule Processor, Inference Engine, File Manager, User Interface, Message Manager and Knowledge Base modules. It supports forward chaining, and graphical knowledge base representation.

2.12 RT-Expert

It is a shareware expert system that lets C programmers integrate expert systems rules into their C or C++ applications. RT-Expert consists of a rule-compiler that compiles rules into C code, and a library containing the rule execution engine. RT-Expert for DOS works with Borland Turbo C, Borland C++, and Microsoft C/C++ compilers. The personal edition is licensed for educational, research, and hobby use. Applications created with RT-Expert personal edition are not licensed for commercial purposes. Professional editions are available for commercial applications using DOS, Windows, and Unix environments.

2.13 Clips 6.0

It is C Language Integrated Production System is an OPS-like forward chaining production system written in ANSI C by NASA. The CLIPS inference engine includes truth maintenance, dynamic rule addition, and customizable conflict resolution strategies. CLIPS, including the runtime version, is easily embeddable in other applications. CLIPS includes an object-oriented language called COOL (CLIPS Object-Oriented Language) which is directly integrated with the inference engine. CLIPS runs on many platforms including IBM PC compatibles (including Windows 3.1 and MS-DOS 386 versions), Macintosh, VAX 11/780, Sun 3/260, and HP9000/500.

2.14 Fuzzy CLIPS

It is a version of the CLIPS rule-based expert system shell with extensions for representing and manipulating fuzzy facts and rules. In addition to the CLIPS functionality, FuzzyCLIPS can deal with exact, fuzzy (or inexact), and combined reasoning, allowing fuzzy and normal terms to be freely mixed in the rules and facts of an expert system. The system uses two basic inexact concepts, fuzziness and uncertainty. Versions are available for UNIX systems, Macintosh systems and PC systems. There is no cost for the software, but please read the terms for use in the FuzzyCLIPS documentation. FuzzyCLIPS is available via WWW (World Wide Web).

3. Conclusion

The word free means not free, it is freedom. You are freedom to use the software and to modify the code.

The open and free software provide the similar functions of commercial or proprietary GIS software. The lack of awareness among on us is moving towards proprietary software. The GNU licensed software supports free software.

4. References

[1] Alberico, Ralph. (1990). AI/expert systems: The library connection. In Nancy Melin Nelson (Ed.), Technology for the '90s: Microcomputers in Libraries (pp. 65-95). Westport, CT: Meckler.

[2] Carrington, Bessie M. (1990, April). Expert systems: Power to the experts. Database, 13(2), 47-50. EJ 408 971.

[3] Davies, Jim. (1987). Artificial Intelligence, Expert Systems, Natural Language Interfaces, Knowledge Engineering, and the Librarian. Paper presented at the First Pacific Conference on New Information Technology for Library and Information Professionals, Bangkok, Thailand, June 16-17, 1987. 13pp. ED 318 428.

[4] Knox-Quinn, Carolyn. (1988, November). A simple application and a powerful idea: Using expert system shells in the classroom. Computing Teacher, 16(3), 12-15. EJ 385 838.

[5] Quinn, Kenneth. (1990). Expert systems shells: What to look for. Reference Services Review, 18(1), 83-86.

[6] Ruyle, Kim E. (1988, August). Artificial Intelligence in Education. 5pp. ED 306 945.

[7] Shaoul, Jean, & Smith, P.J. (1987). Expert Systems A Competent Tool for Training? 6pp. ED 317 173.

[8] Wilson, Harold O., & Burford, Anna Marie. (1990, March). Artificial intelligence and expert systems. Journal of Education for Business, 65(6), 275-79. EJ 408 060.

[9] Bruce G. Buchanan and Edward H. Shortliffe, "Rule-Based Expert Systems: The MYCIN Experiments of the Stanford Heuristic Programming Project", Addison-Wesley, Reading, MA, 1985.

[10] Frederick Hayes-Roth, "The knowledge based ex pert system: A tutorial", IEEE Computer 17(9):11-28, 1984.

[11] Bruce G. Buchanan and R.O. Duda, "Principles of Rule-Based Systems", Tech Report HPP-82-14, 1982. (Discusses the design of expert systems, including representation, inference, and uncertainty management. Examples from numerous specific systems, and discusses which problems are suitable for attack by rule-based systems.)

[12] Bruce Buchanan and Reid Smith, "Fundamentals of Expert Systems", Annual Review of Computer Science 3, 23-58, 1988.

[13] Joseph Giarratano and Gary Riley, "Expert Systems Principles and Practice", PWS Publishing (20 Park Plaza, Boston, MA

[14] James P. Ignizio, "Introduction to Expert Systems: The Development and Implementation of Rule-Based Expert Systems", McGraw-Hill, 1991.

[15] Samuel J. Biondo, "Fundamentals of Expert Systems Technology: Principles and Concepts", Ablex, Norwood, NJ, 1990. 160 pages

[16] Dennis Merritt, "Building Expert Systems in Prolog", Springer-Verlag, 1989.

[17] David Hu, "C/C++ for Expert Systems", Management Information Source, Portland, OR

[18] Firebaugh, Morris W., "Artificial Intelligence: A Knowledge-Based Approach", PWS-Kent, Massachusetts

[19] Charles L. Forgy, "OPS5 User's Manual", Technical Report,Carnegie Mellon University, School of Computer Science, Pittsburgh

[20] Thomas Cooper and Nancy Wogrin, "Rule-based Programming with OPS5", Morgan Kaufmann Publishers, 1988

[21] Charles L. Forgy, "RETE: A fast algorithm for the many pattern/many object pattern match problem", Artificial Intelligence 19(1):17-37, September 1982.

[22] Daniel P. Miranker, "TREAT: A better match algorithm for AI production systems". In Proceedings of the Sixth National Conference on Artificial Intelligence (AAAI-87), pages 42-47, August 1987.

[23] Daniel P. Miranker, "TREAT: A New and Efficient Match Algorithm for AI Production Systems", Morgan Kaufmann Publishers, 1990,143 pages.

[24] Mark Perlin, "The match box algorithm for parallel production system match", Technical Report CMU-CS-89-163, Carnegie Mellon University, School of Computer Science, Pittsburgh, Pennsylvania, May 1989.

[25] Michael A. Kelly and Rudolph E. Seviora, "An evaluation of DRETE on CUPID for OPS5 matching", in Proceedings of the Eleventh International Joint Conference on Artificial Intelligence (IJCAI-89), pages 84-90, Detroit MI, August 1989, Morgan Kaufmann Publishers.

[26] http://www.cs.cmu.edu/Groups/AI/html/faqs /ai/expert/part1/faq-doc-6.html

Using Kalman Filter and Velocity Renovation to Improved GPS Location Tracking

Mohammad Zahaby[1], Prof. Ganesh D. Bhutkar[2] and Prof. M. L. Dhore[3]
Vishwakarma Institute of Technology, Pune, India
mohammad_zahaby@yahoo.co.uk ganesh.bhutkar@vit.edu manikrao.dhore@vit.edu

Abstract

We present algorithms for estimating location of users based on Global Positioning System (GPS) technology. We propose two algorithms, Kalman Filter and Velocity Renovation, which can be used in conjunction with GPS location tracking.

GPS is a satellite-based navigation system made up of a network of 24 satellites placed into orbit by United States (US) Department of Defense (DoD). GPS was originally intended for military applications, but in 1980s, government made a system available for civilian use. GPS can show you your exact position on the Earth in any weather conditions, anywhere in the world, 24 hours a day. There are no subscription fees or setup charges to use GPS[5].

Improved location tracking algorithm which uses Kalman filter with velocity renovation process is proposed. Velocity renovation process consists of a velocity estimator and direction finder. By this process, proposed algorithm can use accurately estimated velocity in location estimation.

1. Introduction

Location tracking plays an important role in many applications such as location-based services and radio resource management.

In Kalman filtering method, smoothing procedure by linear regression makes estimated location more accurate than that of GPS method. Kalman filtering method estimates velocity as well as location and uses them in the next estimation process. However, estimated velocity has a large error of estimation.

By recursive process of Kalman filtering, error of estimated velocity induces inaccuracy of location tracking. Moreover, Kalman filtering method needs transient time to reach a reliable estimation, so big location error is generated at first part of location tracking until enough data come to filter.

An improved location tracking algorithm which uses velocity renovation process with Kalman filter is proposed in this paper. By velocity renovation process, more accurately estimated velocity can be used in Kalman filtering. Accurately estimated velocity will be able to increase the performance of location estimation and shorten transient time of estimation.

2. Analysis of Location Estimation

Tracking Service based on geographic and location information are expanding business area gradually. This service collects location of moving object and presents it on a geographic map.

Global Positioning System (GPS) is a widely-used and very useful system for position location and tracking but GPS relies on radio signals from orbiting satellites that cannot penetrate structures generally. Moreover, fifteen meter location accuracy of GPS is not entirely sufficient for close area training purposes. Alternative position tracking technologies known in art are also generally unable to deliver performance features required for close area training exercises.

GPS satellite signals can be detected by GPS receivers, which calculate their locations anywhere on the Earth at any time.

To reduce error in GPS and get better accuracy from GPS signal, we used Kalman filter and velocity estimation.

Implementation of Kalman filter has these stages [2,3]. $S(k)$ is contains location data is defined as

$$S(k) = (X(k), Y(k), V_x(k), V_y(k))^T \quad (1)$$

where $X(k)$ and $Y(k)$ are coordinates (x and y) of a GPS's location at time instant k, respectively. $V_x(k)$ and $V_y(k)$ in equation (1) denote x-axis and y-axis directional velocities of a GPS receiver at time instant k, respectively. State model of Kalman filter is

$$S(k) = AS(k) \quad (2)$$

where A is a transformation matrix between first and next measurement

$$A = \begin{bmatrix} 1 & 0 & d & 0 \\ 0 & 1 & 0 & d \\ 0 & 0 & 1 & 0 \\ 0 & 0 & 0 & 1 \end{bmatrix}$$

and d is time increasing unit. Based on equation (1) and (2), process of Kalman filtering method can be summarized like this: At first, predict $S(k|k-1)$ and minimum predicted Mean Square Error (MSE) $M(k|k-1)$ can be obtained by

$$S(k|k-1) = AS(k-1|k-1)$$

$$M(k|k\text{-}1) = AM(k\text{-}1|k\text{-}1)A^T + BQB^T \quad (3)$$

where B is an optional control input to current state

$$B = \begin{bmatrix} 0 & 0 \\ 0 & 0 \\ d & 0 \\ 0 & d \end{bmatrix}$$

and Q is system dynamic noise. By (3), Kalman gain can be described as

$$K(k|k\text{-}1) = M(k|k\text{-}1)H^T.\{R + HM(k\text{-}1|k\text{-}1)H^T\}^{-1} \quad (4)$$

where R is receiver noise and H is measurement sensitivity matrix

$$H = \begin{bmatrix} 1 & 0 & 0 & 0 \\ 0 & 1 & 0 & 0 \end{bmatrix}$$

Finally, estimated vectors by Kalman filtering can be updated by

$$S(k|k) = AS(k|k\text{-}1) + K(k)\{L(k) - H(k)AS(k|k\text{-}1)\} \quad (5)$$

$L(k)$ in (5) is defined as

$$L(k) = (l_1(k), l_2(k))^T \quad (6)$$

where $l_1(k)$ and $l_2(k)$ are coordinates (x and y) of estimated location by GPS.

Process of Kalman filtering method progresses recursively whenever new estimated location $L(k)$ of GPS comes to Kalman filter.

Kalman filtering method estimates velocity as well as location of a GPS receiver and uses them estimation at next time. Kalman filtering method uses 0 m/s as initial velocity and approaches to original velocity of GPS receiver by recursive process of Kalman filter. By reason of this, first part of estimated velocity has big error and transient time is needed to reach to reliable estimation. This also occurs when velocity of GPS receiver is changed. Estimated location and velocity data affect next estimation, so inaccurately estimated velocity induces location estimation error of Kalman filtering method. To reduce error, an improved location tracking algorithm is proposed in following section.

3. Location Tracking with Velocity Estimation

Block diagram of proposed location tracking algorithm which uses velocity renovation process with Kalman filter is shown in Fig. 1. Velocity renovation process is to use accurately estimated velocity in Kalman filter for increasing accuracy of location estimation. It consists of two parts. One is velocity estimator and other is direction finder. By estimated velocity and direction in velocity renovation process, x-axis and y-axis directional velocities can be estimated. Estimated velocities are passed to Kalman filter. After that, estimated velocities in (5) of Kalman filtering method are replaced by estimated velocities of velocity renovation process.

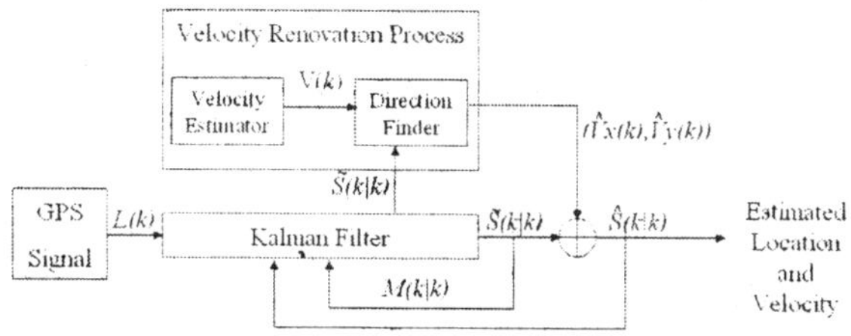

Fig. 1 Block diagram of proposed location tracking algorithm.

3.1 Velocity Estimator

There are many conventional methods for velocity estimation, but they require SNR information to remove noise and interference which affect estimation. SNR-independent velocity estimation methods which eliminate effect of noise and interference without SNR information are proposed in [1,4]. IQ-based ACF estimation method in [4], which is one of SNR-independent velocity estimation methods, is used as a velocity estimator in velocity renovation process.

Auto-correlation function of in-phase component of channel is defined as

$$\Phi_d = E[x(i).x(i+d)]$$

and ratio $\Phi 1$ to $\Phi 0$ and ratio of $\Phi 2$ to $\Phi 0$

$$R1 = \frac{\Phi 1}{\Phi 0} \qquad R2 = \frac{\Phi 2}{\Phi 0}$$

where $\Phi 0$, $\Phi 1$ and $\Phi 2$ are estimated via [1]

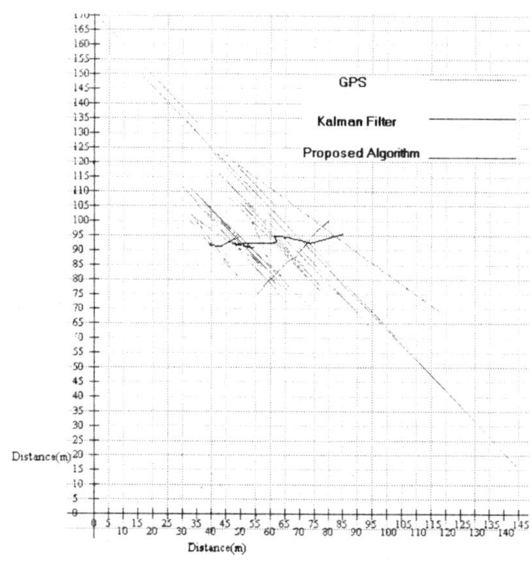

Fig. 2 Estimated location by GPS method, Kalman filtering method and proposed algorithm.

$$\begin{aligned} \phi 0 &= \frac{1}{N}\sum_{i=1}^{N} E[x_i.x_i] \\ \phi 1 &= \frac{1}{N-1}\sum_{i=1}^{N-1} E[x_i.x_{i+1}] \\ \phi 2 &= \frac{1}{N-2}\sum_{i=1}^{N-2} E[x_i.x_{i+2}] \end{aligned} \quad (8)$$

Maximum Doppler frequency estimated by IQ-based ACF estimation method can be defined by

$$f_m \approx \sqrt{\frac{D_1 - D_2 - D_3}{\pi^2(4D_1 - D_2)}} \qquad (9)$$

where D_1,D_2 and D_3 are

$$D_1 = sinc(B.T_s) - R_1$$
$$D_2 = sinc(2B.T_s) - R_2 \qquad (10)$$
$$D_3 = R_2 \,.\, sinc(B.T_s) - R_1\, sinc(2B.T_s)$$

and

$$\sin c(x) = \frac{\sin(\pi x)}{\pi x}$$

B and T_s, are bandwidth of receiver and sampling period, respectively. By estimated maximum Doppler frequency, velocity of a GPS receiver can be estimated as

$$V = \frac{c.f_m}{f_c} \qquad (11)$$

where c and f_c are speed of propagation and carrier frequency, respectively.

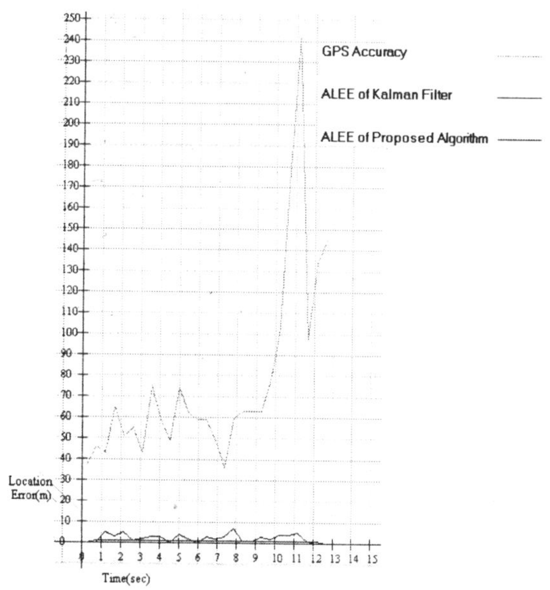

Fig. 3 Comparison of ALEE graph for Kalman filter and average GPS accuracy

3.2 Direction finder

Direction finder in velocity renovation process is simply designed using differences of estimated locations. Estimated direction of GPS receiver can be obtained by

$$\theta_k = \begin{cases} tan^{-1}(D_k), & when \tilde{X}(k) > \hat{X}(k-1) \\ tan^{-1}(D(k)) + \pi, & when \tilde{X}(k) < \hat{X}(k-1)) \end{cases} \qquad (12)$$

where $D(k)$ is $\{Y(k)-Y(k-1)/X(k)-X(k-1)\}$. $(X(k),Y(k))$ is estimated location coordinates by Kalman filtering at time instant k, and $(X(k-1),Y(k-1))$ is estimated location coordinates by proposed algorithm at time instant $k-1$. Estimated direction θ_k has big variation because estimated location coordinates which are used in (12) are not accurate, especially $(X(k), Y(k))$. Instead of just taking estimated data, smoothing method is applied for reducing variation of θ_k.

Smoothed value of direction θ_k can be calculated by taking average of estimated directions within window size as follows

$$\theta_k = \frac{1}{W} \sum_{i=k-(W-1)}^{k} \theta_k, \quad when \quad k \geq W \qquad (13)$$

where W is size of window.

3.3 Replacement of estimated velocity

By (11) and (13), x-axis and y-axis directional velocities in velocity renovation process at time instant k can be obtained by

$$(V_x(k),\ V_y(k))^T = (V\cos\theta_k\, , V\sin\theta_k)^T \qquad (14)$$

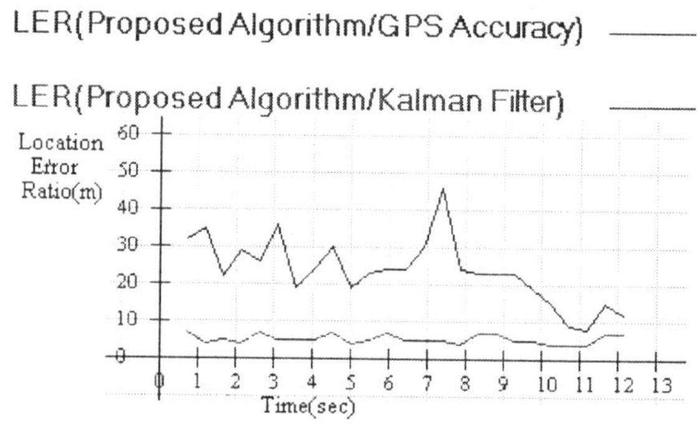

Fig. 4 Comparison of ALEE graph for Kalman filter and average GPS accuracy.

x-axis and y-axis directional velocities in estimated vector $S(k|k)$ by Kalman filtering method is replaced by $(V_x(k),\ V_y(k))^T$ in (14). Finally, estimated vector $S(k|k)$ by proposed algorithm is represented by

$$S(k|k) = [X(k),\ Y(k),\ V_x(k),\ V_y(k)]^T$$

3.4 Calculate ALEE and LER

Average Location Estimation Error (ALEE) is defined as

$$ALEE = \frac{1}{N} \sum_{k=1}^{N} \sqrt{\{X(k) - X'(k)\}^2 + \{Y(k) - Y'(k)\}^2} \qquad (15)$$

where $(X(k),Y(k))$ and $(X'(k),Y'(k))$ are original location coordinates and estimated location coordinates, respectively.

Location Error Ratio (LER) is defined as

$$LER(\alpha/\beta) = \frac{ALEE\ of\ \alpha}{ALEE\ of\ \beta} \quad (16)$$

where α and β are algorithms for comparing.

4. Practical experience

Practically we moved GPS receiver in six different places in Pune City in India. In Table 1, we can see different GPS location tracking with Kalman filter and velocity estimation in these places.

Figure 2 shows and compares estimated GPS location tracking by Kalman filtering method and velocity renovation in first location of those six locations when we moved GPS receiver in straight line. Estimated location by velocity renovation has smallest error among others. This result can be shown by average location estimation error (ALEE) that is shown in Fig. 3 and location error ratio (LER) is shown in Fig. 4.

Table1 Average results of location tracking for six different places (All numbers are in meter).

	GPS accuracy	ALEE of Kalman filter	ALEE of velocity renovation
Location 1	68.86	2.26	0.61
Location 2	98.64	5.37	0.49
Location 3	24.49	3.17	0.53
Location 4	97.38	5.49	0.75
Location 5	95.02	2.64	0.45
Location 6	41.31	3.14	0.24
Average	70.95	3.68	0.51

5. Conclusion

Location tracking algorithm with velocity renovation process has been proposed in this paper. Velocity renovation process consists of velocity estimator and direction finder, and it is to use more accurately estimated velocity in Kalman filtering. Proposed algorithm reduces location estimation error into 0.51 meter. In addition, differently from Kalman filtering method, proposed algorithm estimates location of a GPS receiver reliably without transient time by velocity renovation process which works independently of Kalman filter. Proposed algorithm improves ability of location tracking and it is verified by outage probability and LER.

6. References

[1] Hyunkyu Yu, Student Member, IEEE, Goohyun Park, Student Member, IEEE, Hangyu Cho, Student Member, IEEE,Changeon Kang, Senior Member, IEEE, and Daesik Hong, Member, IEEE, "SNR-Independent Methods for Estimating Maximum Doppler Frequency", IEEE SIGNAL PROCESSING LETTERS, VOL. 12, NO. 5, MAY 2005

[2] Jemin Lee, Hyungjoon Song, Sungmok Oh and Daesik Hong, "An Improved Location Tracking Algorithm with Velocity Estimation in Cellular Radio Networks", Information and Telecommunication Lab. (B715), Dept. of Electrical and Electronic Eng., Yonsei Univ. 2006 IEEE, pg 618 - 622

[3] MOHINDER S. GREWAL, LAWRENCE R. WEILL, ANGUS P. ANDREWS, "GLOBAL POSITIONING SYSTEMS, INERTIAL NAVIGATION, AND INTEGRATION", SECOND EDITION, WILEY-INTERSCIENCE A John Wiley & Sons, Inc., Publication, 2007

[4] Wei Sheng and Steven D. Blostein, Department of Electrical and Computer Engineering Queen's University, Kingston, Ontario, CANADA K7L 3N6, "SNR-INDEPENDENT VELOCITY ESTIMATION FOR MOBILE CELLULAR COMMUNICATIONS SYSTEMS", IEEE International Conference on Acoustics, Speech, and Signal Processing (ICASSP '02), vol.3, May 2002, pp.III-2469 - III-2472.

[5] http://www8.garmin.com, "What is GPS?"

Source Code Plagiarism Detection Using Back-Propagation Neural Network

Kalindi Sinha, Ruchira Barik, Shubhra, Sindhura T and Ch. Aswani Kumar
School of Computing Sciences, VIT University, Vellore, India
aswanis@gmail.com

Abstract

Plagiarism is a prevalent problem which is affecting all the people worldwide, specially the academic institutions and research organizations. Our goal is to detect plagiarism using neural network techniques. We train the backpropagation neural network with seven different plagiarism parameters and test the network to get the optimal or desired result. The experimental results on a set of programs prove the ability of the proposed approach.

1. Introduction

Plagiarism is the presentation of thoughts or work of someone else, as one's own, i.e., plagiarism is to use another person's idea or a part of their work and pretend that it is one's own [1]. With the easy availability of information from sources such as the Internet, there no longer seems to be a need to write codes from scratch. This has proved to be a great pain for academic establishments, whose aim is to award qualifications to those who have achieved a certain level of proficiency in some areas, and not just to those who have recorded acceptable marks. A good discussion on the need for plagiarism prevention can be found in [2] .

This paper proposes an approach to detect plagiarism that could occur between pairs of source code and thus offers a simple solution to a complex problem. In this paper, we implement a backpropagation neural network with parameters like Keyword-Operator Sequence Matching, Operator Matching, Operand Matching, Comment Line Matching, Program Order Matching, Source Line Matching and Halstead's Metric and Cyclomatic Complexity for plagiarism detection. The organisation of this paper is as follows: In Section 2, we deal with the related work in the field of plagiarism prevention and detection. Section 3 describes the neural network features. In Section 4, we propose a backpropagation based neural network model for plagiarism detection. We discuss the implementation issues of the backpropagation neural network in Section 5, followed by conclustion and acknowledgements.

2. Related Work

Faidhi and Robinson characterized six levels of program modification in a plagiarism spectrum [3]. Every higher level inherits the lower level representation. Level 0 denotes the original program without modifications. In Level 1 only comments and indentation are changed. Level 2 plagiarism represents the changes in identifiers. Plagiarism at Level 3 represents changes in declarations. Level 4 plagiarism represents changes in program modules. Level 5 represents the changes in program statements. At Level 6 plagiarism is done by making changes in the decision logic. As the level of modification increases, the similarity in the code becomes less recognizable. Some of the earlier tools for detecting plagiarism use attribute counting techniques but are not popular, as they did not prove to be very effective. The following is a brief description of some of the widely used tools for plagiarism detection.

2.1 JPLAG

JPlag relies on structure comparison alone. It takes as input a set of programs and compares these programs pair wise (computing for each pair a total similarity value and a set of similarity regions). The output is a set of HTML pages that allow for exploring and understanding the similarities found in detail [4].

2.2 MOSS

Moss (for a Measure of Software Similarity) removes all white space and punctuation from each source-code file and converts all characters to lowercase. Then it divides the remaining nonwhite space characters of each file into k- grams, which are contiguous substrings of length k. Each k-gram is hashed and a subset of all k-grams to be the fingerprint of the document is selected. The fingerprint includes information about the position of each selected k-gram in the document and the fingerprints are compared to find similar files [5].

2.3 YAP

Source texts are used to generate token sequences. Each token string is (non-redundantly) compared with all the others using Running-Karp-Rabin Greedy-String-Tiling (RKR-GST) algorithm [6]. In [7], an index based approach is used for detecting plagiarism. A good survey and implementation of various plagiarism algorithms is discussed in [8].

2.4 TurnitIn

TurnitIn is an internet based plagiarism detection service. TurnitIn checks for possible plagiarism by comparing submitted papers to several databases using a proprietary algorithm. It scans its own database(s) and also has licensing agreements with large academic proprietary databases.

3. Neural networks

Neural networks are simplified models of the biological nervous system and therefore have drawn their motivation from the kind of computing performed by a human brain. A neural network is a highly interconnected network of a large number of processing elements called *neurons* in an architecture inspired by the brain. A neural network can be massively parallel and therefore is said to exhibit *parallel distributed processing* [9, 10].

Neural networks are a collection of processing units that interact through weighted links. Each unit calculates a weighted sum of its input signals, which is then processed by an activation function to produce the output. A supervised training stage determines the weight of each link. The neural network processes set of inputs, and each output is compared to the desired output.

3.1 Advantage of using neural networks

Neural networks are the most appropriate method to implement a plagiarism detector because they categorize data automatically by learning classification boundaries from patterns in training data. Various learning rules can be used to train the network (i.e. modify the weights) in order to make the network reach a desired output in case of supervised learning. Neural networks have been successfully applied to problems in the fields of pattern recognition, image processing, data compression, forecasting, and optimization, to quote a few.

4. Design

A feedforward back propagation neural network is used for the implementation. The scores from the algorithms discussed in the first section are given as inputs to the input layers of the neural network. The proposed neural network architecture is shown in Fig 1. There are 7 nodes in the input layer which take the scores from the 7 comparison algorithms as inputs. There are 5 nodes in the hidden layer and one in the output layer. The number of hidden and output layers is decided after a large number of trials. Then a back-propagation algorithm is used to train the network. Here, we use the multilayer perceptron model to dynamically modify the weights in order to reach the desired output.

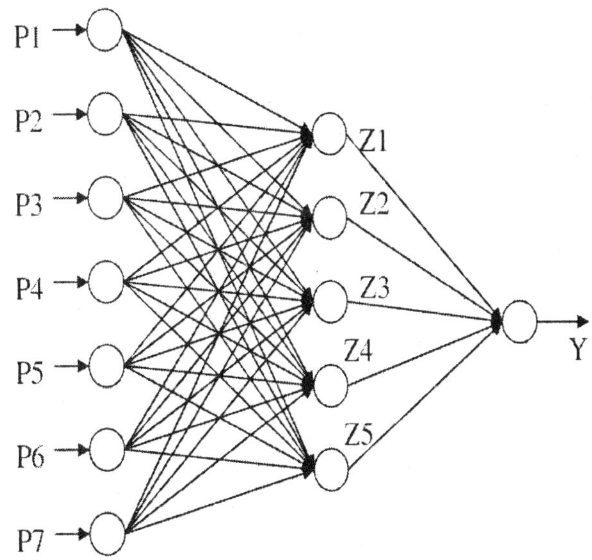

P1: Keyword-Operator Sequence Matching
P2: Operator Matching
P3: Operand Matching
P4: Comment Line Matching
P5: Program Order Matching
P6: Source Line Matching
P7: Halstead's Metric and Cyclomatic Complexity
Z1, Z2, Z3, Z4, Z5: Outputs of hidden layer nodes
Y: Output of output node

Fig. 1 Proposed neural network architecture.

4.1 Parameters comparison

In this paper, different plagiarizing transformations are analyzed with following algorithms:

1. Keyword-Operator Sequence Matching
2. Operator Matching
3. Operand Matching

4. Comment Line Matching
5. Program Order Matching
6. Source Line Matching
7. Halstead's Metric and Cyclomatic Complexity Computing

In Keyword-Operator Sequence Matching, keywords of each file are extracted initially and they are matched with keyword of another file [11]. On the basis of number of keywords matched in each file matching score is computed. The Operator and Operand Matching determine the total number of matching operators and identifiers in source code. In identifier matching, variable names as well as function names both are considered. Comment Line Matching algorithm compares each line of comments from both files. The entire comment is compared regardless of whether they are keywords in the comment or not. For Program Order Matching we find sequence of code that appears to perform the same functions despite changes in comments and identifiers name. We have used Greedy String Tiling algorithm [6] for Program Order Matching. Source Line Matching compares each line of source code from both files. But it excludes comment lines and sequences of white space are converted to single white space. A line of source code may have a comment at the end. The comment is stripped off for this comparison. We have used Halstead's metric for finding the program effort matching. McCabe's Cyclomatic complexity calculates the number of execution paths through a program and thus gives an indication of program's complexity. Each algorithm is useful in finding different clues to plagiarism that the other algorithms do not cover.

4.2 Input values

The input values to be given to each of the seven input layer nodes are obtained by comparing the source codes on the basis of the seven parameters. Twenty sets of C++ source codes are used for the purpose of training. An initial set of small random weights are assigned to all the connections of the neural network. A target value is given to the neural network based on the prior knowledge of whether the source codes being compared are plagiarised or not and according to it the network is trained. 500 iterations are used to get the optimal set of weights. After training the network, a source file and a sample file, which is suspected of plagiarism, are compared on the basis of the seven parameters mentioned in section 4.1 and a set of values as percentages is obtained. The percentages are expressed as decimal values after dividing by hundred. These decimal values are given as input to the neural network. For the purpose of testing the network ten pairs of C++ source codes were used.

4.3 Output values

For each node we use the linear activation function in the output layer and tanh function in the hidden layer, such that the output is scaled to lie in the range [0, 1]. The output gives the confidence of the system whether plagiarism has occurred or not. Thus a more accurate result of plagiarism is obtained.

5. Implementation Details

The design of the system described above has been implemented using Java. The system uses back-propagation learning to train the neural network for detecting the extent of plagiarism between any two selected programs.

We initially take twenty sets of programs, about which we have prior knowledge of the ones which are plagiarised and the ones which are not. Pairs of programs from this set are compared, and the scores of comparison between the programs, on the basis of seven parameters previously mentioned, are obtained. Thus for each pair of programs, we get a set of seven scores. These are given as inputs to our system. The desired output for the pair is 1, if plagiarism has been done, otherwise it is 0. With a number of such pairs of programs, the neural network is trained until the RMS error is minimised. The inputs as given to the Neural Network can be seen in Fig 2.

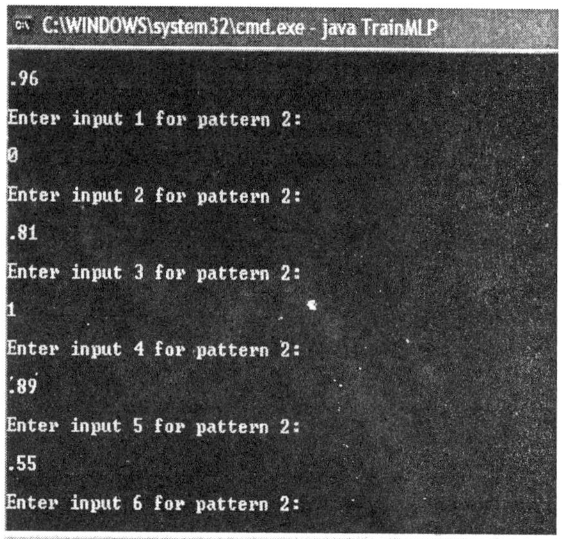

Fig 2 Training the Network

After the training phase is over, the network is ready to be used to give an extent of plagiarism between any two suspected programs. The source program and the suspected target program are compared to get the levels of matching for the seven parameters. These are given as input to the network, as shown in Fig. 3, which then gives an output in the range 0 to 1, showing the extent of plagiarism between the files as shown in Fig. 4.

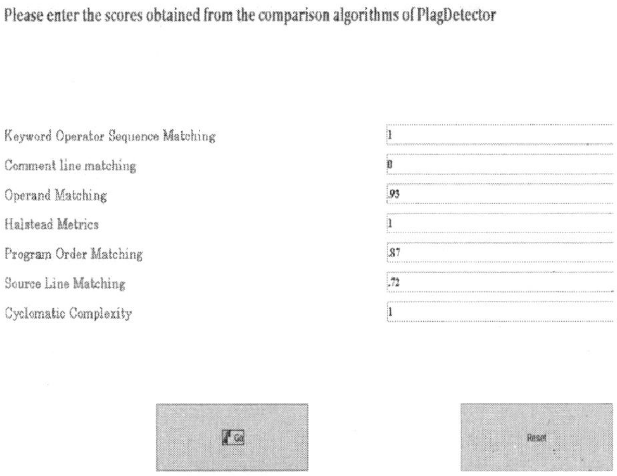

Fig. 3 Testing the Network

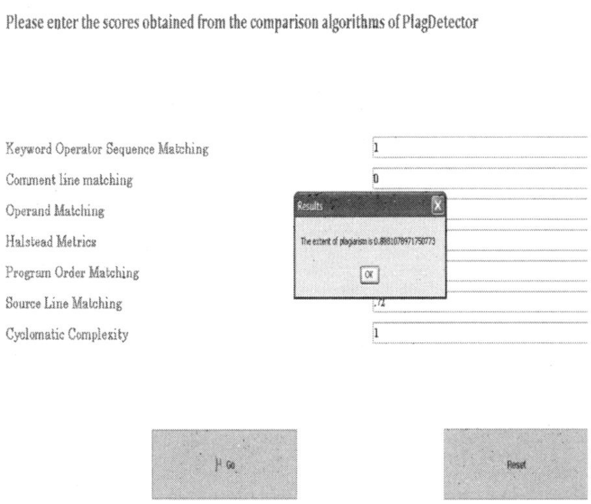

Fig. 4 Result of Plagiarism

We perform 500 iterations of the training algorithm to train the network so that the final result is almost equal to the desired target output value. This implies that the RMS Error will gradually decrease as the number of iterations increase. The RMS Error pattern for the various iterations, shown in Fig. 5, depicts the gradual decrease in the error with increasing number of iterations. The error values for the corresponding iterations can be seen in the following Table:

In future, techniques should be investigated to perform plagiarism detection with sources from the Internet. Also the proposed method should be tested on some benchmark datasets and compare the results with available plagiarism tools. Design of a natural language tokenizer as well as the integration of it with Internet based searches should be explored.

Table 1 RMS Error values

Iterations	RMS Error
0	1.00528
10	.996390
20	.758377
30	.358197
40	.133356
50	.029997
60	.009628
70	.002623
80	4.53263E-4
90	1.07475E-4
100	2.80786E-5

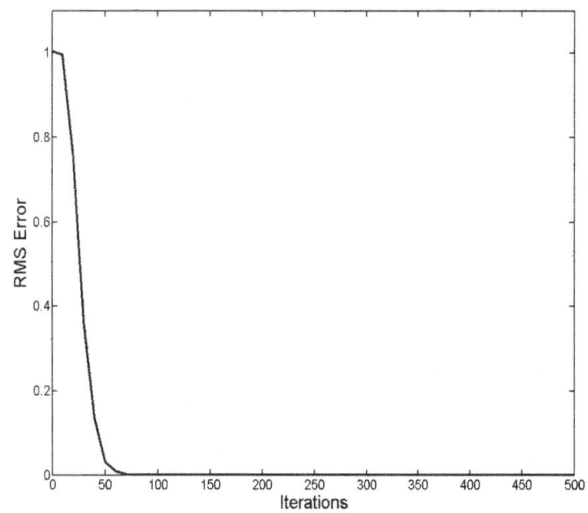

Fig. 5 Graph Showing Decrease in RMS Error

6. Conclusion

In this paper, our aim is to recognise cases of plagiarism. This is achieved by training the neural network by a back propagation algorithm. The source codes of programs are evaluated using seven different plagiarism transformations and using these results, the proposed neural network is trained. The preliminary experimental results are promising. Potential future work in this direction is also indicated.

7. Acknowledgement

One of the authors Ch. Aswani Kumar gratefully acknowledges the financial support from Dept. of Science and Technology, Govt. of India under the grant number SR/S3/EECE/25/2005.

8. References

[1] Steve Engels, Vivek Lakshmanan, Michelle Craig, Plagiarism Detection Using Feature-Based Neural Networks, SIGCSE '07, March 7-10 2007, Covington, Kentucky, USA.

[2] Edward L. Jones, " Plagiarism Monitoring and Detection – Towards an Open Discussion", Journal of Computing Science in Colleges, Vol. 16, No. 3, 2001, pp. 191-196.

[3] J.A. Faidhi and S.K. Robinson, "An Empirical Approach for Detecting Program Similarity and Plagiarism within a university Program Environment", Vol. 11, 1987, pp. 11-19.

[4] Cho Liu, Chen Chen, Jiawei Han and Philip S. Yu, "JPlag: Detection of Software Plagiarism by Program Dependence Graph Analysis", Proc. of 12th ACM SIGKDD International Conference on Knowledge Discovery and Data Mining, 2006, pp. 872-881.

[5] Kevin W. Bowyer and Lawrence O. Hall, "Experience using MOSS to detect cheating in Programming Assignments", Proc. of 29th ASEE/ IEEE Frontier in Education Conference, 1999, pp. 18-22.

[6] Finton Culwin, Anna Machead and Thomas Lancaster, "Source Code Plagiarism in UK HE Computing Schools, Issues, Attitudes and Tools", Technical Report SBU-CISM-01-01, 2001.

[7] Steven Burrows, Seyed M.M. Tahaghoghi and Justin Zobel, "Efficient and Effective Plagiarism Detection for Large Scale Repositories", Proc. of the 2nd Australian Undergraduate Students Conference, 2004, pp. 9-16.

[8] Alan Parker and James O. Hamblen, "Computer Algorithms for Plagiarism Detection", IEEE Transactions on Education, Vol. 32, No. 2, 1999, pp. 94-99.

[9] S. Rajasekaran and G.A. Vijayalakshmi Pai, Neural networks, Fuzzy logic, and Genetic algorithms synthesis and application, Prentice Hall of India Pvt Ltd, 2004.

[10] Sathish Kumar, Artificial Neural Networks-A Classroom Approach. Tata McGraw Hill, 2004.

[11] Shauna D. Stephans, "Using Metrics to Detect Plagiarism", Journal of Computing Science, Vol. 16, No. 3, 2001, pp. 191-196.

Handwritten Hindi Character Recognition: A New Approach

Dayashankar Singh[1] Dr. (Mr.) Maitreyee Dutta[2] and Sarvpal H. Singh[3]
[1&3]Lecturer (CSE), M.M.M. Engg. College, Gorakhpur(UP)
dss_mec@yahoo.co.in spsingh@mmmec.net
[2]Asst. Prof. & Head (CSE), NITTTR, Chandigarh
d_maitreyee@yahoo.co.in

Abstract

In this paper we have proposed an approach to recognize handwritten Hindi characters using multilayer perceptron (MLP) with two hidden layer. The Gradient Feature extraction technique has been implemented for Handwritten Hindi Character recognition. The HCR system was trained by backpropagation feed-forward neural network using several different forms of handwritings provided by both male and female faculty members of different age groups The feed-forward neural network with two hidden layers and one output layer has been used for training the network. The features extracted from characters are gradients calculated by Sobel operator. Horizontal and vertical templates of Sobel operator have been used for gradient calculation. Experimental result shows that Gradient Feature extraction technique with MLP network provides good recognition accuracy around 94% for handwritten Hindi characters and requires small training time.

Keywords: *Neural Network, Feature Extraction, Handwritten character Recognition, Multilayer Perceptron (MLP), Hindi Character Recognition (HCR).*

1. Introduction

Recognition of handwritten characters is a challenging task because of the variability involved in the writing styles of different individuals. Neural Network has become very popular research area for many years because of its various application potentials. Many works towards handwritten character recognition of Chinese, Arabic, Farsi, Japanese etc have been reported by researchers but a very little attention has been given to handwritten character recognition of Indian languages. Hindi is a second official language in India and it is widely spoken in northern India. Hindi and English are used in many offices of India such as railway, embassy, Sales-tax, passport etc. Therefore it becomes very important to develop automatic Hindi character recognition (HCR) system. For recognition of handwritten Hindi characters, selection of feature extraction technique becomes very important in order to enhance the recognition accuracy.

In this paper, we have developed an automatic Hindi character recognition system using Gradient feature extraction technique. The backpropagation feed-forward neural network has been used to train the network. An analysis has been performed by considering 221 samples of Handwritten Hindi characters acquired by various male and female faculty members of different age groups. Out of 221 samples, 151 samples have been used for training (train set) the network and remaining 70 samples have been used for testing (test set) the network. Experimental result shows that this gradient feature extraction technique provides high accuracy and less training time. The overview of the paper is as follows: In section 2, Hindi characters are discussed. In section 3, Gradient Feature extraction is described. In Section 4, a brief review of MLP for handwritten Hindi character recognition is introduced and training algorithm has also been discussed. In Section 5, experimental results and discussion are provided. Section 6 concludes the paper with future scope.

2. Hindi Language

The Hindi language is second official language in India. Approximately five hundred million people use this language all over the world. It is widely spoken in northern region of India and also used in many offices in India.

The Hindi language consists of 49 characters. Out of which 13 are vowels and remaining 36 characters are consonants. It is written from left to right. A set of Hindi characters are shown in Fig. 1.

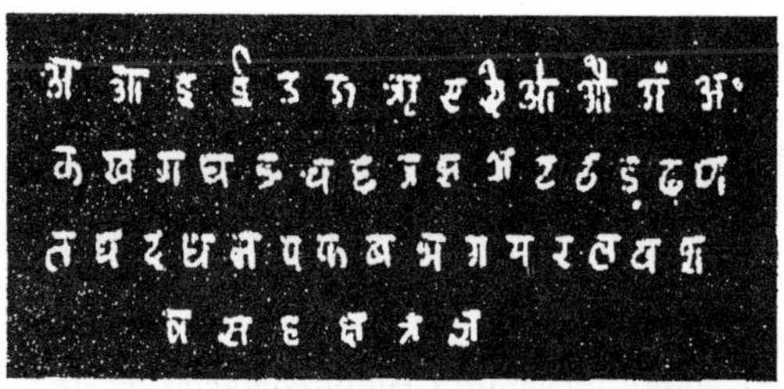

Fig. 1 A set of Handwritten Hindi Characters [1]

3. Feature Extraction

Feature extraction plays an important role in the success of handwritten character recognition system. Selection of robust feature extraction is very important in order to get high recognition accuracy. In this paper, Gradient feature extraction technique has been successfully implemented for handwritten Hindi character recognition.

3.1 Gradient Feature Extraction

Each image of character is normalized into 32×32 size. The gradient operator, named Sobel operator is used to calculate the gradients. The Sobel operator is used for edge detection. The Sobel operator uses two templates to compute the gradient components in horizontal and vertical directions, respectively [3, 4, and 5]. The horizontal template computes the gradients in vertical direction while vertical template computes the gradients in horizontal direction. The templates are shown in Fig. 2.

-1	0	1
-2	0	2
-1	0	1

Vertical Template

1	2	1
0	0	0
-1	-2	-1

Horizontal Template

Fig. 2 Sobel operator templates

The two gradient components at location (i, j) are calculated by [5, 6]:

$Gx = gv(i, j) = f(i-1, j+1) + 2f(i, j+1) + f(i+1, j+1) - f(i-1, j-1) - 2f(i, j-1) - f(i+1, j-1)$ ---(1)

$Gy = gh(i, j) = f(i-1, j-1) + 2f(i-1, j) + f(i-1, j+1) - f(i+1, j-1) - 2f(i+1, j) - f(i+1, j+1)$ ---(2)

The gradient strength and the direction are calculated as follows:

$$G(i,j) = \sqrt{gv^2(i,j) + gh^2(i,j)} \quad (3)$$

$$\theta = \arctan(Gy / Gx) \quad (4)$$

3.1 Procedure

The procedure for Gradient Feature extraction for handwritten Hindi character recognition is given below.

- Capture image of a Hindi character in 30 × 30 pixels
- Binarization of 30 × 30 pixel character into 32 × 32 matrixes by imposing boundary of zeros.
- Implementation of Sobel operator on 32x32 matrixes for gradient calculation.
- Gradient values are in a 30 × 30 matrix with values ranges between 0 to 2π and gradient is set to -1 where a pixel is surrounded by 8 black pixels.

4. Backpropagation Neural Network

The feed forward backpropagation network is a very popular model in neural networks. It does not have feedback connections, but errors are backpropagated during training. Many applications can be formulated by using a feed forward backpropagation network, and the methodology has been a model for most multilayer neural networks. Errors in the output layer determine the measures of hidden layer errors, which are used as a basis for adjustment of connection weights between the input and hidden layer. Adjusting the two sets of weights between the pair of layers and recalculating the output is an iterative process that is carried on until the error falls below a tolerance level. Learning rate parameters scale the adjustments to weights [6,7, 8]. A MLPN with one hidden layer and one output layer is shown in Fig. 3.

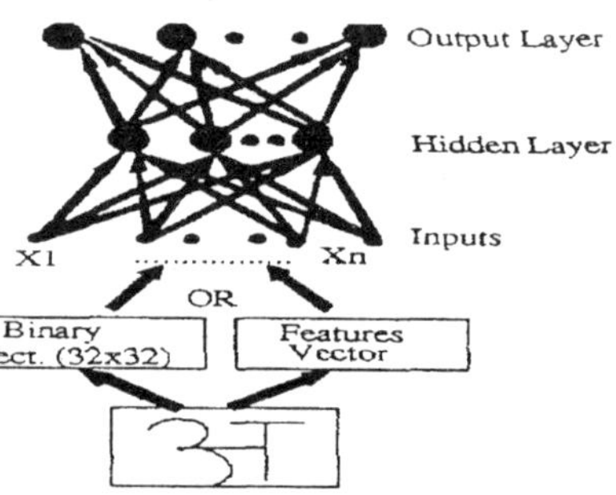

Fig. 3 Multilayer Perceptron Network [1]

4.1 Backpropagation Training Algorithms

We have implemented Gradient feature extraction technique in matlab v7. There are many variations of the backpropagation algorithm. The simplest implementation of backpropagation learning updates the network weights and biases in the direction in which the performance function decreases most rapidly - the negative of the gradient. One iteration of this algorithm can be written as,

$$W_{k+1} = W_k - \alpha_k . g_k$$

Where W_k is a vector of current weights, g_k is the current gradient, and α_k is the learning rate. Gradient is calculated after every iteration and compared with threshold gradient value 1e-10. If gradient is greater than the threshold value then it performs next iteration.

There are two different ways in which this gradient descent algorithm can be implemented:

- ✓ Incremental mode
- ✓ Batch mode

In the incremental mode, the gradient is computed and the weights are updated after each input is applied to the network. In the batch mode all of the inputs are applied to the network before the weights are updated.

Batch Gradient Descent (traingd)

The batch steepest descent training function is traingd. The weights and biases are updated in the direction of the negative gradient of the performance function. There is only one training function associated with a given network. There are various training parameters associated with traingd: epochs, show, goal, time, min_grad, and lr. The learning rate lr is multiplied with the negative of the gradient to determine the changes to the weights and biases. The larger the learning rate, the bigger is the step. If the learning rate is made too large, the algorithm becomes unstable. If the learning rate is set too small, the algorithm takes a long time to converge. The training status is displayed for every iteration of the algorithm. (If show is set to NaN, then the training status never displayed.) The other parameters determine when the training stops. The training stops if the number of iterations exceeds epochs, if the performance function drops below goal, if the magnitude of the gradient is less than mingrad, or if the training time is longer.

5. Experimental Result

We have initialized the mouse in graphics mode and created a 30x30 box on screen so that samples could be written directly on screen. We have made a C++ program through which character written by a person directly on screen is converted first into binary. For this, as mouse writes in 30 × 30 box then that portion is converted into 1 and the portion which is untouched with mouse pointer in the box is taken as 0. In this way we convert the handwritten character into binary values. After converting the character into binary, we apply the Sobel operator on the binary values of character that calculates the gradient values of character. The flow chart of gradient feature extraction technique has been given in Fig. 4.

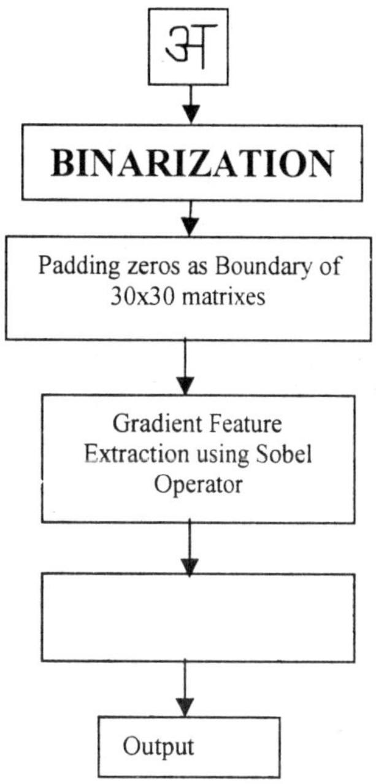

Fig. 4 Flowchart for Hindi Character Recognition

5.1 Character Recognition by MLP network

In this paper, MLP network uses three layer feed-forward neural networks. There are two hidden layer and one output layer. We have taken 12 neurons at hidden layer and two neurons at output layer. Since we have trained the network for two Hindi characters, therefore we have taken only two neurons at output layer. We have taken tan sigmoid function (tansig) at hidden layer and pure linear (purelin) function at output layer. Learning rate has been considered as 0.05. Experiment has been carried out on 151 samples of training set and 70 samples for test set and result of this experiment is given below in Table 1.

Table 1 Results for handwritten Hindi character recognition using Gradient Feature and MLPN

Input to MLPN	No of hidden units	No of iterations	Training time (sec)	Classification time (ms)	Performance on training set (%)	Performance on test set (%)
30×30 gradient input	12	50	255.31	74.30	100	94

5.2 Discussion

The experimental result shows that Gradient Feature extraction technique with MLPN provides very good recognition accuracy. It also requires small training time and classification time. The training time can be further minimized by performing integer calculation. In Gradient Feature extraction, floating point operations have been performed and there are large variations in gradients that can be further minimized in order to improve recognition accuracy.

6. Conclusions

Although we have tried our best to complete a great deal of work but still we feel tremendous scope for improving/enhancing this work further. In future, we would like to improve the recognition accuracy of the network for Hindi characters by using more training samples and by making advancements in our feature extraction system. The efforts can be made to develop an automatic system for recognizing all handwritten Hindi characters.

A brief outline about the future scope of this work can be given as follows.

- It can be extended for Hindi word recognition by including regular expressions.
- It can also be extended for Hindi to English translation by including regular expressions and grammar.

7. References

[1] Verma B.K, "Handwritten Hindi Character Recognition Using Multilayer Perceptron and Radial Basis Function Neural Network", IEEE International Conference on Neural Network, vol.4, pp. 2111-2115, 1995.

[2] Sutha.J. Ramraj.N, "Neural Network Based Offline Tamil Handwritten Character Recognition System", IEEE International Conference on Computational Intelligence and Multimedia Application, 2007 Volume 2, 13-15, Dec.2007, Page(s): 446-450, 2007.

[3] Weipeng Zhang; Yuan Yan Tang; Yun Xue, "Handwritten Character Recognition Using Combined Gradient and Wavelet Feature" IEEE International Conference on Computational Intelligence and Security, Volume 1, Page(s) 662-667, Nov. 2006.

[4] Hailong Liu, Xiaoqing Ding, " Handwritten Character Recognition using gradient feature and quadratic classifier with multiple discrimination schemes" Eighth IEEE International Conference on Document Analysis and Recognition, Vol.1, Page(s) : 19-23, August 29-1 Sept. 2005.

[5] Cheng-Lin Liu, "Normalization-Cooperated Gradient Feature Extraction for Handwritten Character Recognition" IEEE Transactions on Pattern Analysis and Machine Intelligence, Volume 29, Issue 8, Aug. 2007 Page(s) 1465-1469.

[6] Dayashankar Singh, Dr.(Mrs.) Maitreyee Dutta, Sarvpal H. Singh, " Hindi Character Recognition using Directional Gradient Feature Extraction", International Journal of Computer Application for Engineering, Technology and Sciences (IJ-CA-ETS), C.U.Shah College of Engineering and Technology, Wadhwan city, Gujrat,India.

[7] Neural Computing Theory and Practices by Philip D. Wasserman.

[8] Neural Networks, Fuzzy Logic, and Genetic Algorithms by S. Rajasekaran and G.A. Vijaylakshmi Pai.

A Genetic Algorithm Optimized Neural Net for Classification based on NOFM Algorithm

Kumar Saurabh Bisht and Sanjay Chaudhary
Dhirubhai Ambani Institute of Information and Communication Technology, Gandhinagar, 382007, India
kumar_bisht sanjay_chaudhary@daiict.ac.in

Abstract

Classification is one of the major data-mining problems where a dataset is divided into mutually exclusive groups such that the members of a group are as similar as possible and of different groups as dissimilar. This paper presents an approach to classification using rule extraction through neural network, based on NOFM algorithm. The result shows the effectiveness of the proposed approach.
Keywords: Classification, NOFM, Genetic Algorithm, Neural Network

1. Introduction

Classification is one of a major data mining problem. Various classification algorithms have been designed, one of them popular approach is based on decision trees. Neural networks, despite their empirically proven abilities, have been little used for classification, as the classification was not explicitly stated as symbol rules that are suitable for verification. Classification approaches based on neural network are not very common due to following reasons:

1. Neural Network training session may fall into local minima trap and learning time can be usually long
2. Articulating classification rules in the layered structure of neural network is considered difficult.
3. Hence, it is also difficult to incorporate domain knowledge into a neural network.

However the merits of neural network cannot be ignored on account of their ability to learn and improve. Infact some research cases [1] [2] have shown those neural networks are superior choice in comparison to decision trees on account of low error rate.

In this paper we propose a classification approach based on genetic algorithm optimized neural network that uses NOFM algorithm [3] for rule extraction. The approach consist of three steps:

1. **Neural Net construction and training**: In this phase a neural network is constructed and trained.
2. **Network tuning:** A genetic algorithm based module fine tunes the neural net by modifying the weight of links between nodes and removing redundant links.
3. **Rule Extraction:** In this phase classification rules are extracted from the neural network. The rules generated are in the form

If (N of the following M antecedents are true) then...

This method of form is used as from experiments that indicate neural networks are good at learning **N-of-M** concepts (Fisher & McKusick, 1989). It is to note that purely conjunctive rules result if N = M, while a set of disjunctive rules results when N = 1 hence using **N-of-M** rules does not restrict generality.

In the following sections a brief background on neural net, genetic algorithm and NOFM algorithm is given. Subsequently the proposed algorithm and approach has been discussed followed by results and conclusion.

2. Neural Network

Neural Networks [4][5][6] or NNs are algorithms for optimization and learning, based on concepts of working of brain. A neural network is a highly parallelized dynamic system that consists of directed graphs. The topology is such that it generates the output by means of a reaction of its state on the given input data.

Generally a neural network consists of following component:

1. A directed graph of set of nodes.
2. A weight associated with each link/arcs interconnecting the nodes.
3. A transfer function associated with each node. The transfer function can be expressed as:

$$f(\Sigma w^{*}l, \Theta)$$

where "w" is associated with each link "l" connecting the node with other nodes and Θ is the activation function of the node. The nodes received inputs from previous layers and applied the weighted sum of these inputs to this activation function.

Mathematically the output a node in neural network can be represented as a weighted sum of the activation functions. For example the output of f_3 node in second layer can be expressed as:

$$f_3 \text{ output} = w_{13}\, f_1(x_1) + w_{23} f_2(x_2)$$

w_{13} = weight of link connecting nodes f_1, f_3.

w_{23} = weight of link connecting nodes f_2, f_3.

Similarly the output of other nodes can be calculated and perpetrated in the network till the output layer.

3. Genetic Algorithm

Genetic algorithms [7][8][9] or GAs are adaptive search algorithms. GAs are based upon the principles of evolution and natural selection. They are adept at searching large, nonlinear search spaces. Genetic algorithms search large and complex search spaces to efficiently determine near optimal solutions in reasonable time frames by simulating biological evolution.

In general, genetic algorithms consist of following components:

1. Encoding of problem into chromosomes
2. A fitness function that evaluates chromosome
3. Operators to generate new population: mutation, crossover

A genetic algorithm operates according to the following steps:

1. Population initialization: sets of initial chromosomes are generated
2. Evaluation: Each member of the population is evaluated
3. Reproduction: Generation of new sets of chromosomes.

When a genetic algorithm has appropriate encoded solutions of a problem and operators that can generate better new chromosomes from parent chromosomes, the algorithm generates population of better and better chromosomes resulting in the convergence to global optimum. As genetic algorithm can improve the current best candidate monotonically they do not have the problem of local minima trap.

Local minima traps are a common problem associated with Neural Network. It happens when the learning phase of the network keeps oscillating between two error peaks and therefore fails to converge to optimal solution in learning phase.

4. NOFM Algorithm

The idea behind NOFM [3] algorithm is that individual antecedents (links) do not have unique importance. groups of antecedents form equivalence classes in which each antecedent has the same importance as, and is interchangeable with, other members of the class. However training using back propagation does not naturally bunch links into equivalence classes; rather link weights are distributed across a range of real numbers. Hence in the first step of the NOFM algorithm links are grouped into equivalence classes using a standard clustering method (Hartigan,1975). This enables to consider link as a group and not follow any particular link. After the formation of groups those groups are identified and eliminated that does not effect calculation. These groups are generally with low link weights and few members. The biases of the unit are optimized using backpropagation. After the optimization rules are formed, these rules are further simplified by eliminating the weights and the biases resulting in N-of–M style rules.

NOFM algorithm

1. With each hidden and output unit form groups of similarly weighted links.
2. Set link weights of all group members to the average of the group.
3. Eliminate any groups that do not significantly affect whether the unit will be active or inactive.
4. Holding all links weights constant, optimize biases of all hidden and output units using the backpropagation algorithm.
5. Form a single rule for each hidden and output unit. The rule consists of a threshold given by the bias and weighted antecedents specified by remaining links.
6. Where possible simplify rules to eliminate superfluous weights and thresholds.

Fig. 1,2 and 3 shows example of rule extraction using NOFM algorithm

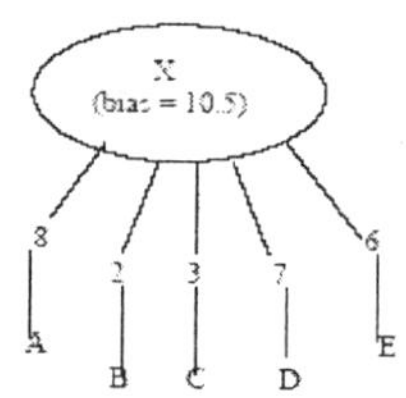

Fig. 1 Initial Unit

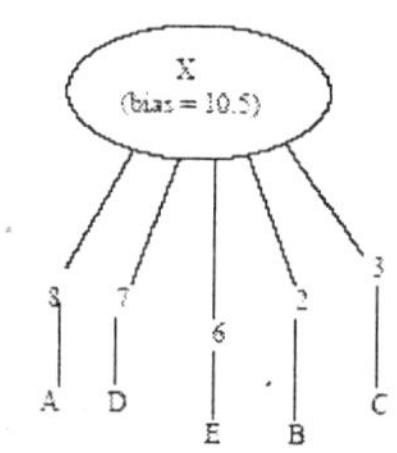

Fig. 2 Unit after step 1 and step 2 of

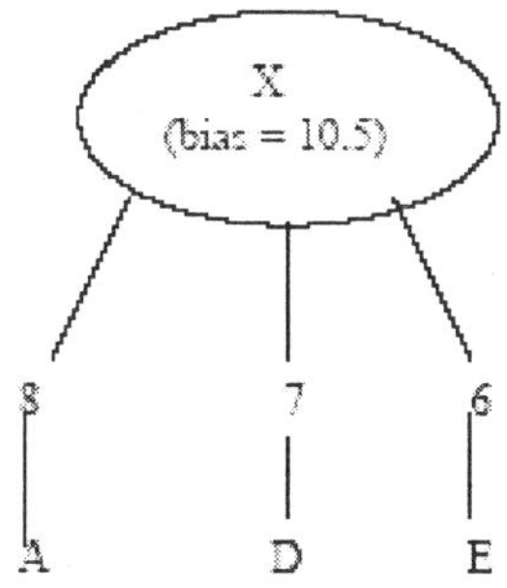

Fig. 3 Unit after step 3

After Step 4 & 5: If 7* *NumberReturn* (A, D, E) >10.5 then X

Where NumberReturn returns the number of true antecedent

After Step 6: if 2 of {A, D, E) then X

5. NOFM Based Algorithm

We propose an algorithm based on NOFM algorithm. In our approach we optimize the neural net with genetic algorithm and try to reduce the learning time of the neural net. The algorithm is as follows:

1. Apply a cluster algorithms to find cluster of hidden node activation values.
2. Enumerate and discretize activation values and compute network output.
3. Use backpropogation to modify the weights depending upon the error
4. Repeat Step 2 and 3 for different sample and generate a vector of weights
5. After generating a sizable number of weight vectors use genetic algorithm to find suitable combination of weights. Each chromosome of the genetic pool is constituted by weight vector. Genetic operators like mutation and cross over is used to generate superior combination of weight vector.
6. Now that the network is trained, for each hidden unit enumerate the input value that lead to them and generate a set of rules to describe the hidden unit's discretized value in terms of input.
7. Merge two sets of rules obtained in previous two steps to obtain rule relating input and output.

In step 1 the algorithm used to cluster hidden nodes activation value, is a simple cluster algorithm as follows:

1. Determine smallest integer "d" such that if all the activation values re approximated to "d" decimal place the network accuracy remains unaffected.
2. Each activation value (β) is represented by the integer nearest to $\beta * 10^d$. The set of these discreet values is (say):
   $$\omega = \{\omega_1, \omega_2, \omega_3, \ldots\ldots \omega_n\}$$
3. Sort ω_i where i<=n, such that they are in increasing order.
4. Find pair of adjacent values $\omega_{i,j}$ $\omega_{i,j+1}$ in ω such that if they are replaced then no conflicting data is generated.
5. If such values are present then swap them and repeat step 4m else set i =i+1 and start over from step 3.

This algorithm tries to merge as possible values into one interval as possible, as long as it does not compromise the data generation. It is to note that this algorithm is order sensitive and resulting cluster depends on the order in which hidden units are clustered.

6. Results

We define 5 classification problems on dataset having attributes age, salary, years of job experience.

We classify the data tuples into two groups: Group A and Group B as per the following definition.

(Age < 35) ^ (years of job experience ε [0,1]) (Age > 35) ^ (years of job experience ε [1,4]) v (Age > 35) ^ (years of job experience ε [4,5])

All the tuples that satisfy this condition are labeled as Group A and others as Group B.

Following was the result for the 5 classification problem

Table 1 Average accuracy rate, number of rules generated

Classification problem number	Accuracy	Number of Rules (average)
1	92%	7.04
2	98%	3.1
3	57%	12
4	89%	5.6
5	82%	7.67

Table 2 Coding of attribute for neural net

Attribute	No. of inputs	Subintervals
age	4	(20,30) (30,35) (35,40) (40,60)
salary	6	(10k, 20k), (20k, 30k)(30k, 40k)(40k, 50k)(50k, 60k), (60k, 70k)
Years of experience	4	(0,1), (1,3), (3,4), (4,5)

8. Conclusion and Future Work

In this paper we have presented a genetic algorithm optimization for classification using neural net based on NOFM algorithm The experimental results show that approach is successful in obtaining high quality rules from given data set. Except for one case (classification problem 2) every other case had accuracy of above 80%. This fairly validates our attempt to apply the connectionist approach to classification to generate rules that are similar in order of quality as generally observed for decision trees.

For future work there are various areas in this approach where further improvement can be achieved like to induce a mechanism of reducing input units of network by feature selection or to reduce the time of training so that the rule deduction is faster.

9. References

[1] J. R. Quinlan, "Comparing Connectionist and Symbolic learning Methods," in *Computational Learning Theory and Natural Learning Systems,* vol. 1, S.J. Hanson, G.A Darstall and R.L Rivest Eds. , A Bradford Book, MIT Press, 1994, pp. 445-456.

[2] J.W Shavlik, R.J Mooney and G.G Towell, "Symbolic and Neural Learning Algorithms : An Experimental Comparison", *Machine Learning,* vol. 6, no.2, pp. 111-143,1991

[3] Geoffrey G. Towell, Jude W. Shavlik, "The Extraction of Refined Rules from Knowledge Based Neural Networks", *Machine Learning*

[4] Hand David, Mannila Heikki and Smyth Padhraic, "Principles of Data Mining", MIT Press.

[5] Dunham, Margaret H, *Data mining Introductory and Advance Topics*, PHI,

[6] Kai Fu and Wenhua Xu, "Training Neural Network", *IEEE Computer Society Press, 1997*

[7] Rajshekhran S,Pai VijayLakshmi, Neural Networks, Fuzzy Logic and Genetic Algorithm, PHI,2003

[8] Yang Lei, Dai Yu, Zhang Bin, Gao Yan, "A Genetic Algorithm Optimized New Structured Neural Network for Multistage Decision-Making Problem", Proceedings of the Sixth International Conference on Parallel and Distributed Computing, Applications and Technologies (PDCAT'05), IEEE, Computer Society, 2005

[9] Yan Zhu, Jian Chen, "Studies on Genetic Multilayer Feedforward Neural Networks and the Development of GMNN", IEEE, 1999.

Evaluation of Feature Selection Methods for Predictive Modeling Using Neural Networks in Credit Scoring

Raghavendra and Jay B.Simha
Dr. M.G.R. Educational and Research Institute, Chennai, Abiba Systems, Bengaluru – 560 085
raghavendra_bk@rediffmail.com jay.b.simha@abibasystems.com

Abstract

A credit-risk evaluation decision involves processing huge volumes of raw data, and hence requires powerful data mining tools. Several techniques that were developed in machine learning have been used for financial credit-risk evaluation decisions. Data mining is the process of finding patterns and relations in large databases. Neural networks are one of the popular tools for building predictive models in data mining. The major drawback of neural network is the curse of dimensionality which requires optimal feature sub set. Feature selection is an important topic of research in data mining. Feature selection is the problem of choosing a small subset of features that optimally is necessary and sufficient to describe the target concept.

In this research an attempt has been made to investigate the preprocessing framework for feature selection in credit scoring using neural network. Feature selection techniques like best first search, info gain etc method have been evaluated for the effectiveness of the classification of the risk groups on publicly available data sets. In particular, German, Australian and Japanese credit rating data sets have been used for evaluation. The results have been conclusive about the effectiveness of feature selection for neural networks and validate the hypothesis of the research. The work is under progress to select the optimal feature selection method for the given data profile.

Keywords : *Data Mining, Neural Networks, Credit Scoring, Feature Selection.*

1. Introduction

With the rapid growth in the credit industry, credit scoring models have been extensively used for credit admission evaluation [1]. Several quantitative methods have been developed for the credit admission decision. The credit scoring models are developed to categorize applicants as either accepted or rejected with respect to the applicant's characteristics such as age, income, and marital condition. Credit officers are faced with the problem of trying to increase credit volume without excessively increasing this exposure to default. The benefits of credit scoring involve reducing the credit analysis cost, enabling faster credit decisions, closer monitoring of existing accounts.

Practitioners and researchers have developed a variety of traditional statistical models and data mining tools for credit scoring which involves linear discriminant models, logistic models, k-nearest neighbor models, decision tree models, neural network models, and genetic programming models. Empirical research results from the available literature suggests that neural network models for credit scoring gives more accurate, adaptive, and robust results followed by linear discriminant analysis, logistic regression, decision trees, and k-neatest neighbor. The major drawback of a neural network approach is that neural network becomes computationally expensive with increase in number of features. In this research work an attempt has been made to evaluate various feature selection methods for credit risk classification using neural network.

The rest of the paper is organized as follows: Section 2 reviews the prior literature. Neural Network technique is discussed is Section 3. In Section 4 Feature Selection methods are discussed. Experimental methodology is discussed in Section 5. Section 6 includes Results and discussions followed by conclusion.

2. Literature survey

Recent advances in computing technology in terms of speed, cost, as well as access to tremendous amounts of computing power and the ability to process huge amounts of data in reasonable time has spurred increased interest in data mining applications. Machine learning has been one of the methods used in most of these data mining applications. The data used as input to any of these learning systems are the primary source of knowledge in terms of what is learned by these systems. There have been relatively few studies on preprocessing of data for use in these data mining systems as input [5].

In another research the optimal parameters, the comparative efficiency and accuracy of three models:

Multi Layer Perception, Ensemble Averaging and Boosting by Filtering have been investigated in the light of credit loan application classification. The objective of the research was to find the best tool among the three neural network models for this kind of decision context. The experimental results indicate that Committee Machine models were superior to a single Multi Layer Perception model, and that Boosting by Filtering outperformed Ensemble Averaging [6].

The prediction of corporate bankruptcies is an important and widely studied topic since it can have significant impact on bank lending decisions and profitability [2]. Author's present two contributions: First, the review topic of bankruptcy prediction with emphasis on neural-network (NN) models. Second, the NN bankruptcy prediction model. Inspired by one of the traditional credit risk models developed by Merton, the novel indicators for the NN system has been proposed and shows that the use of these indicators in addition to traditional financial ratio indicators provides a significant improvement in the prediction accuracy (from 81.46% to 85.5%).

Huanng et al [3] used back propagation neural network (BNN) as a benchmark and obtained prediction accuracy around 80% for both BNN and artificial neural network (ANN) methods for the United States and Taiwan markets. However, only slight improvement of SVM was observed. Another direction of the research was to improve the interpretability of the AI-based models. Then they applied recent research results in neural network model interpretation and obtained relative importance of the input financial variables from the neural network models. Based on these results, they conducted a market comparative analysis on the differences of determining factors in the United States and Taiwan markets.

There is an approach to solve a classification problem by combining feature selection and neural networks. The main idea is to use techniques from the field of information theory to select a set of important attributes that can be used to classify tuples. A neural network is trained using these attributes; the neural network is then used to classify tuples [4].

3. Neural Networks

Practitioners and researchers have developed a variety of traditional statistical models and data mining tools for credit scoring which involve linear discriminant models, logistic models, k-nearest neighbor models, decision tree models, neural network models, and genetic programming models. Neural network approach is outlined below.

Neural networks a form of sub symbolic computation and are based on the workings of the brain. A neural network comprises a set of weighted edges and nodes. Learning is achieved by modification of these weights. Most networks contain a number of layers, the first layer being the input layer, the final layer being the output layer. Other internal layers (hidden layers) are often required to ensure sufficient computational power in the network [4].

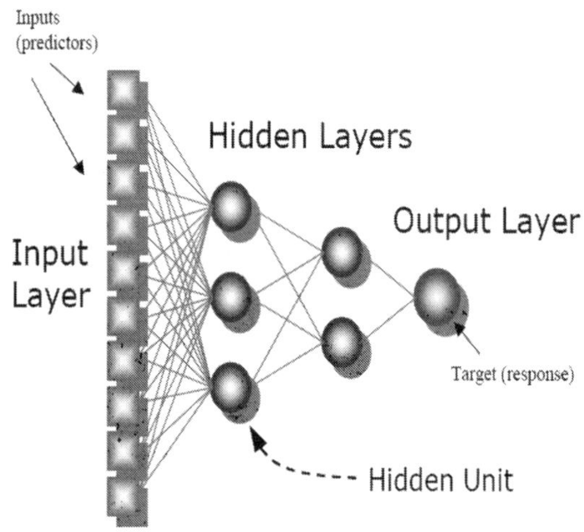

Fig. 1 Multilayer perceptron (MLP)

A network can be trained to map input values to corresponding output values by providing a training set. The network is repeatedly tested and modified to produce the correct output.

The generation of output by a neural network is accomplished via firing values from nodes. An input is passed to the input layer which in turn can activate the internal layers, which in turn activated the output layer, finally resulting in an output.

Given 'n' links feeding into a node, each link has an input value X_j and a weight W_j. The nodes have an associated threshold, τ. If, according to some activation function, the node has a sufficiently high activation level, the node fires a value onto the next layer. Commonly used activation functions include:

$$f(a) = \begin{cases} 1 & \text{if } a > \tau \\ 0 & \text{otherwise} \end{cases} \quad (1)$$

$$f(a) = \frac{e^{a} - e^{-a}}{e^{a} + e^{-a}}$$

Where a, the activation of a node, is $\sum_{j=1}^{n} X_j W_j$ and τ is a threshold. The initial input vector is fed into the network; sets of nodes are fired which finally results in an output vector.

To train the network, any errors in the output are fed back through the network causing a modification of the weights on the nodes. Errors can be calculated at the output layer. For internal nodes, the error is a function of all nodes that use the node's output and the output from that node.

The error at the output layer is used to re-modify the weights coming to the output layer. This allows the calculation of errors at the last hidden layer etc. The error is back-propagated through the network.

The major criticism of a neural network approach include the fact that because neural networks learn the classification rules by multiple passes over the training data set, the learning time, or the training time needed for a neural network to obtain a high classification rate, is usually long[7]. In addition, there is difficulty in understanding the rules generated by neural networks as they are buried in the network architecture and the weights assigned to the links between the nodes. Also, there is difficulty in incorporating any available domain knowledge. Final and important drawback of neural network is curse of dimensionality, which will affect all the factors which are discussed above. The limitation can be minimized to some extent by proper selection of features as discussed in later sections.

4. Feature selection methods

Feature selection is often an essential data preprocessing step prior to applying a classification algorithm such as Multi Layer Perception (MLP). The term feature selection is taken to refer to algorithms that output a subset of the input feature set. One factor that plagues classification algorithms is the quality of the data. If information is irrelevant or redundant or the data is noisy and unreliable then knowledge discovery using training is more difficult [10]. Regardless of whether a learner attempts to select features itself or ignores the noise, feature selection prior to learning can be beneficial. Reducing the dimensionality of the data reduces the size of the hypothesis space and allows algorithm to operate faster and more effectively. In some cases accuracy on classification can be improved [10]. Feature Selection methods are outlined below.

BFS

This method searches the space of attribute subsets by greedy hill climbing augmented with a backtracking facility. Setting the number of consecutive non-improving nodes allowed controls the level of backtracking done. Best first may start with the empty set of attributes and search forward, or start with the full set of attributes and search backward, or start at any point and search in both directions (by considering all possible single attribute additions and deletions at a given point) [9].

InfoGainAttributeEval

This method evaluates the worth of an attribute by measuring the information gain with respect to the class [9]. InfoGain is calculated using the following equation,

InfoGain(Class,Attribute) = H(Class) - H(Class | Attribute)

WrapperSubsetEval

This method evaluates attribute sets by using a learning scheme and cross validation is used to estimate the accuracy of the learning scheme for a set of attributes [9].

GainRatioAttributeEval

This method evaluates the worth of an attribute by measuring the gain ratio with respect to the class [9]. GainRatio is calculated using the following equation, GainR(Class, Attribute)=(H(Class)-H(Class | Attribute)) / H(Attribute)

RandomSearch

This method performs a Random search in the space of attribute subsets. If no start set is supplied, random search starts from a random point and reports the best subset found. If a start set is supplied, random search searches randomly for subsets that are as good as or better than the start point with the same or fewer attributes [9].

ChiSquaredAttributeEval

This method evaluates the worth of an attribute by computing the value of the chi-squared statistic with respect to the class [9].

ConsistencySubsetEval

This method evaluates the worth of a subset of attributes by the level of consistency in the class values when the training instances are projected onto the subset of attributes. Consistency of any subset can never be lower than that of the full set of attributes; hence the usual practice is to use this subset evaluator in conjunction with a Random or Exhaustive search which looks for the smallest subset with consistency equal to that of the full set of attributes [9].

PrincipalComponents

This method performs a principal components analysis and transformation of the data. Use in conjunction with a Ranker search. Dimensionality reduction is accomplished by choosing enough eigenvectors to account for some percentage of the variance in the original data-default 0.95 (95%). Attribute noise can be filtered by transforming to the PC space, eliminating some of the worst eigenvectors, and then transforming back to the original space [9].

ReliefFAttributeEval
This method evaluates the worth of an attribute by repeatedly sampling an instance and considering the value of the given attribute for the nearest instance of the same and different class and this can operate on both discrete and continuous class data [9].

SVMAttributeEval
This method evaluates the worth of an attribute by using an SVM classifier. Attributes are ranked by the square of the weight assigned by the SVM. Attribute selection for multiclass problems is handled by ranking attributes for each class separately using a one-vs-all method and then "dealing" from the top of each pile to give a final ranking [9].

5. Experimental methodology

The framework for feature selection in credit scoring is shown in Fig. 2. The process of evaluation is as follows. The feature selection algorithms are applied on the data set and the selected features from each of the algorithm are used to develop a predictive model for risk classification using a neural network. A ten fold cross validation has been used for evaluation.

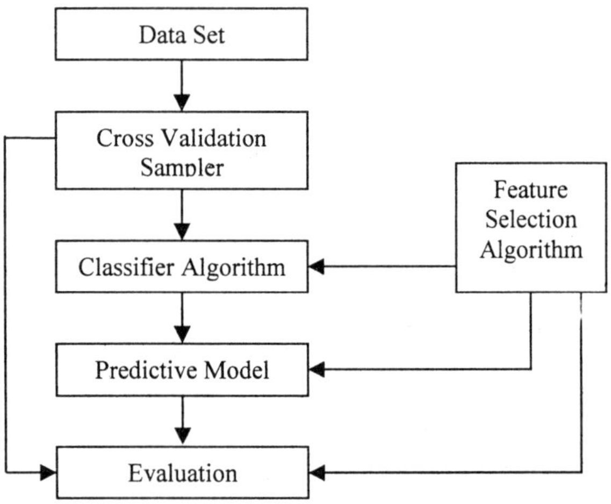

Fig. 2 Feature selection framework.

In 10-fold cross validation, the original sample is partitioned into 10 sub samples, of the 10 sub samples, a single sub sample is retained as the validation data for testing the model, and the remaining 9 sub samples are used as training data. The cross-validation process is then repeated 10 times (the folds), with each of the 10 sub samples used exactly once as the validation data. The 10 results from the folds then can be averaged (or otherwise combined) to produce a single estimation. The advantage of this method over repeated random sub sampling is that all observations are used for both training and validation and each observation is used for validation exactly once.

6. Results and discussions

Three publicly available datasets-Australian, German, and Japanese credit data are used. In the evaluation different feature selection methods have been evaluated for the effectiveness of the classification of the risk groups using neural network.

The classification accuracy, number of features selected and average true positive rate are used to measure the performance of the predictive model with the neural network. Table 1 gives the specifications for the datasets and classification accuracy before pre processing. The results of the evaluation are given in the Table 2. From the results it can be observed that the classification accuracy and number of features selected by BFS, wrapperSubsetEval, and RandomSearch methods with neural network are more efficient when compared with other methods. The classification accuracy and number of features selected are almost similar. Figure 3 gives feature dimensionality reduction, and Figure 4 gives classification accuracy details after evaluation process.

Table 1 Specifications for the datasets

Sl. No	Dataset	No of instances	Total no. of attributes	No of classes	CA
1	Australian	690	15	2	79.4
2	German	1000	21	2	71.6
3	Japanese	690	16	2	84.2

Table 2 Neural network specification for the Australian, German, and Japanese datasets

Feature Selection Methods	Australian Data Set		German Data Set		Japanese Data Set	
	NFS	CA	NFS	CA	NFS	CA
All Features	15	79.42	21	71.6	16	84.20
BFS	6	88.08	3	72.9	7	81.27
InfoGain	14	80.42	20	73.8	15	80.85
WrapperSubsetEval	7	66.38	1	68.8	8	71.91
GainRatio	14	85.3	20	73.8	15	80.85
RandomSearch	6	79.42	6	71.5	7	84.78
ChiSquared	14	79.42	20	71.6	15	84.20
Consistencysubset	12	84.78	14	71.8	13	83.3
PrincipalComponent	12	84.78	20	71.6	15	84.20
ReliefAttributeEval	14	79.42	20	71.6	15	84.20
SVMArrtibuteEval	14	79.42	20	71.6	15	84.20

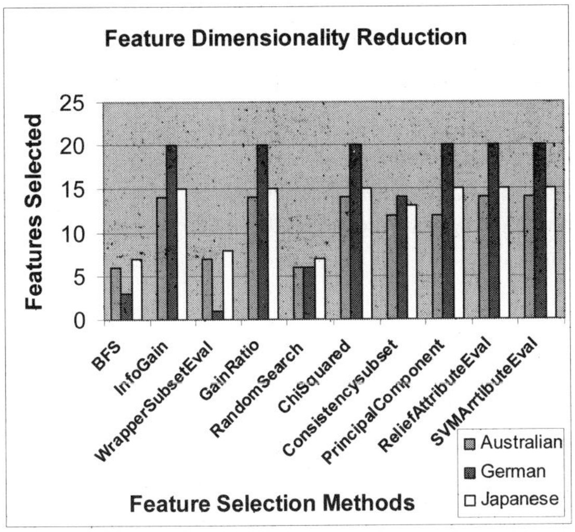

Fig. 3 Feature dimensionality reduction

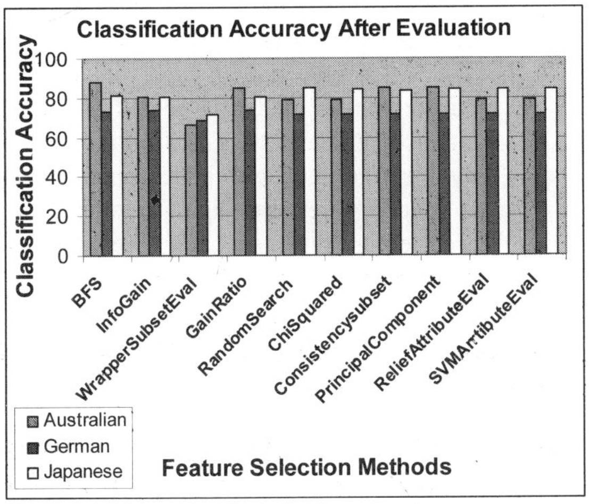

Fig. 4 Classification accuracy after evaluation

7. Conclusion

In this research work an attempt has been made to evaluate feature selection algorithms on the data sets and the selected features from each of the algorithm are used to develop a predictive model for risk classification using a neural network. The results have been conclusive about the effectiveness of feature selection for neural networks and validate the hypothesis of the research. The work is under progress to select the optimal classifier for the given data profile.

8. References

[1] Cheng –Lung Huang, Mu-Chen Chen, Chieh-Jen Wang, "Credit scoring with a data mining approach based on support vector machines", Expert Systems with Applications, vol 33, No. 4, pp 847-856, November 2007.

[2] Amir F. Atiya , Senior member, IEEE, "Bankruptcy Prediction for Credit Risk Using Neural Networks: A Survey and New Results", IEEE Transactions on Neural Networks, Vol. 12, No. 4, July 2001.

[3] Zan Huanng, Hsinchun Chen, Chia-Jung hou, Wun-Hwa Chen, Soushan Wu, "Credit rating analysis with Support Vector Machines and neural network: a market comparative study, Decision Support Systems", v 37, no 4, pp 543-558, September 2004.

[4] P.O'Dea, J.Griffith, C.O'Riordan, "Combining Feature Selection and Neural Networks for Solving Classification Problems", Technical Report of the Dept. of IT, NUI, Galway, 2001.

[5] Piramuthu S., "Evaluation Feature Selection Methods for Learning in Data Mining Applications", 31st Hawaii International Conference on System Sciences, vol 5, pp 294-301, Jan 1998.

[6] Meliha Handzic, Felix Tjandrawibawa and Julia Yeo, "How Neural Networks Can Help Loan Officers to Make Better Informed Application Decesins", Information Science And Information Technology Education Joint Conference, pp 97-108, Jun 2003.

[7] H. Lu, R. Setiono, and H. Liu. Nuerorule: A connectionist approach to data mining. In Proceedings of the 21st VLDB Conference, pages 478-489, 1995.

[8] P.S.Yu C.C. Aggrawal. Data mining techniques for associations, clustering and classification. In Proceedings of the 3rd Pacific-Asia Conference on Methodologies for Knowledge Discovery and Data Mining, pp 13-23, 1999.

[9] http://www.cs.waikato.ac.nz/ml/weka/

[10] Liu H., Sentino R, "Some issues on scalable Feature Selection, Expert Systems with Application", vol 15, pp 333-339, 1998.

Predicting the Class Labels of the Given Training Tuples through Backpropagation Algorithm

Dr. C. V. Guru Rao and V.Shankar
Principal, kits-wgl Asst. professor, Department of Information Technology
Kakatiya Institute of Technology & Science, Warangal, Andhra Pradesh, India – 506 015
vuppu.shankar@gmail.com

Abstract

In this paper we presented the predicted class labels of the given training tuples or datasets using neural network algorithm. i.e., the trained network is found. Databases are rich with hidden information that can be used for intelligent decision making. Classification and prediction are two forms of data analysis that can be used to extract models describing important data classes or to predict future data trends. Recent data mining research has built scalable classification and prediction techniques capable of handling large disk-resident data. One of such classification is by back propagation. This is a neural network algorithm for classification that employs a method of gradient descent. It searches for a set of weights that can model the data so as to minimize the mean squared distance between the networks class prediction and the actual class label of data tuples. Rules may be extracted from trained neural networks in order to help improve the interopabilty of the learned network.

Keywords: *Database, classification, Neural Network, Network Topology, Back-propagation.*

1. Introduction

There are many different kinds of neural networks and neural network algorithms. The most popular neural network algorithm is backpropagation which gained repute in the 1980s̄. In this paper we learn about multilayer feed-forward networks, the type of neural network on which the backpropagation algorithm performs.

What is backpropagation?

Backpropagation is a neural network learning algorithm. The field of neural networks was originally classified by psychologists and neuron biolysis who sought to develop and test computational analogues of neurons. Roughly speaking: a neural network is a set-of connected input/output units in which each connection has a weight associated with it. During the learning phase, the network learns by adjusting the weights so as to be able to predict the class label of the input types.

A sample Neural Network: A multilayer-feed forward N-N consists of an input, one or more hidden layers and an out-put layer.

- Each layer is made up of units.
- The inputs (attributes measured for each training tuple) are fed simultaneously into the units making up the input layer.
- These inputs pass through the input layer and are than weighted and fed simultaneously to a second layer known as hidden layer.
- The outputs of the hidden layer units can be input to another hidden layer and so on. The number of hidden layers is arbitrary, usually only one is used. The weighted outputs of the last hidden layer are input to output layer which emits the network's prediction for given tuples.

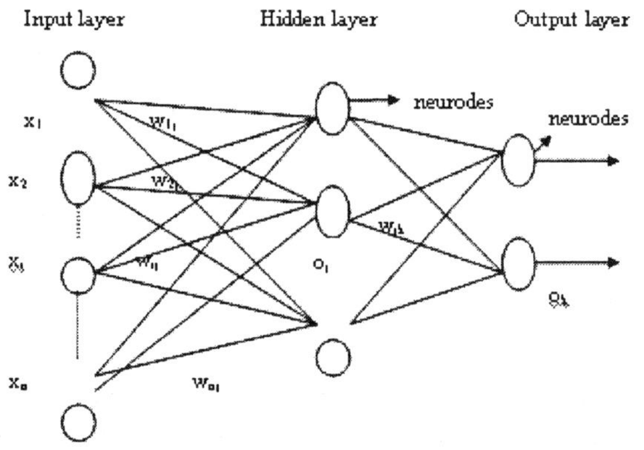

Fig. 1 A Multi Layer Feed-Forward Neural Network

Defining a Network topology

How can I design the topology of the neural network?

- Before training can begin, the user must decide on the network topology by specifying the
    1. No. of units in the input layer
    2. No. of units in each hidden layers (if more than one)
    3. No. of units in the output layer.

- Normalizing the input values for each attribute measured in the training tuples will help speed up the learning phase. Typically fall between 0.0 and 1.0.
- Discrete valued attributes may be encoded such that there is one input unit per domain value. For ex: If an attribute A has 3 possible or known values, namely {a0, a1, a2}, then we may assign 3 input units to represent A that is we may have, say I_0, I_1 ,I_2 as input units. Each unit is initialized to 0. If $A=a_0$ then I_0 is set to 1. If $A=a_1$, I_1 is set to 1, and so on.
- For classification, one output unit may be used to represent two classes (where the value 1 represent one class and the value 0 represents the other).

  If there are more than two classes, then one output unit per class is used.

BackPropagation

How does backpropagation work?

- Backpropagation learns by iteratively processing a data set of training tuples, comparing the network's prediction for each tuple with the actual known target value. The target value may be the known class label of the training tuple (for classification problems) or a continuous values (for prediction)
- For each training tuple, the weights are modified so as to minimize the mean squared error between the network's prediction and the actual target value. These modifications are made in the "Backwards" direction, that is, from the output layer, through each hidden layer down to the first hidden layer (hence the name backpropagation). Although it is not guaranteed, in general the weights will eventually converge, and the learning process stops.

Algorithm: Back propagation. Neural Network learning for classification or prediction

Input:

1. D, a data set consisting of training tuples and their associated target values.
2. l, the learning rate.
3. Network, a multi layer feed-forward network.

Output: A trained neural network.

Method:

1. Initialize all weights and biases in network
2. While terminating condition is not satisfied{
3. For each training tuple x in D{
4. // Propagate the inputs forward:
5. For each input layer unit j {
6. Oj=Ij //output of an input unit is its actual input value.
7. For each hidden or output layer unit j{
8. Ij; $=\sum wijOi+\theta_j$;//compute net input of unit j w.r.t to the previous layer, i
9. $Oj = \dfrac{1}{1+e^{-Ij}}$; } //compute output of each unit j
10. back propagate the errors;
11. for each unit j in the output layer
12. Errj=Oj (1-0j) (Tj-Oj); // compute the error
13. for each unit j in the hidden layers, from the last to the first hidden layer
14. Errj= Oj (1-Oj) $\sum_k$ Errk wjk;// compute the error w.r.t to the next high layer, k
15. For each weight wij, in network {
16. Δwij=(l) Errj O_i;//weight increment
17. wij=wij+Δ wij;}//weight update
18. for each bias θj in network{
19. $\Delta\theta$j= (l) Errj; //bias increment
20. }
21. }

Step 1 Initialize the weights and biases

- The weights in the network are initialized to small random numbers ranging from -1.o to 1.0 or -0.5 to 0.5.

  Each unit has a bias associated with it and initialized to small random numbers.

  Each training tuple X is processed by the following steps.

Step 2 Propagate the inputs forward

- First, the training tuple is fed to the input layer of the network. The inputs pass through the input units, unchanged. That is for an input unit, j, its output, Oj=Ij (input value)
- Next, the net input and output of each unit in the hidden and output layers are computed. This is a linear combination of its inputs. To help illustrate this point, a hidden or output layer is shown in the Fig.

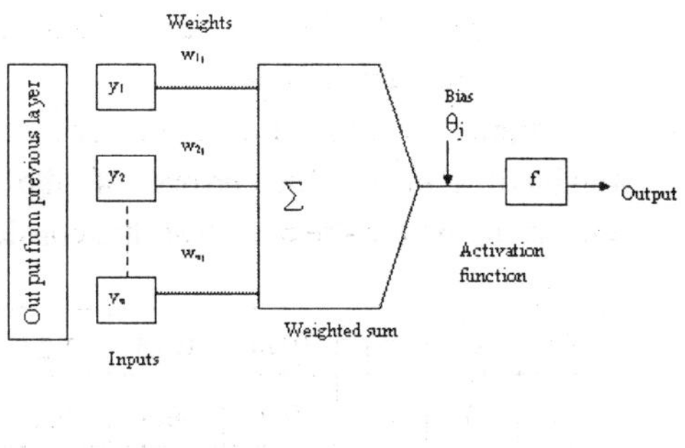

Fig. 2 A hidden or output layer unit j

Each connection has a weight. To compute the net input to the unit, each input connected to the unit is multiplied by its corresponding weight, and this is summed.

Given a unit j in a hidden or output layer, the net input, Ij, to unit j is

$$I_j = \sum_k w_{ij} o_i + \theta_j \quad (1)$$

where wij => weight of the connection from unit i in the previous layer to unit j;

Oi =>output of unit I from the previous layer

θj => bias of the unit.

Bias acts as a threshold in that it serves to vary the activity of the unit.

- Each unit in the hidden and output layers takes its net input and then applies an activation function to it. The logistic or sigmoid function is used.

  Given the net input Ij to unit j, then Oj,

  The output of unit j, is computed as

  $$O_j = \frac{1}{1+e^{-I_j}}$$

- We compute the output values, oj, for each hidden layer upto and including the oi layer which gives the network's prediction. In practice it is good idea to save all the intermediate values at each unit as they are required again later when backpropagating error. This can reduce the amount of computation required.

Step 3 Back propagate the error

- The error is propagated backward by updating the weights and biases to reflect the error of the network's prediction.

  For a unit j in the output layer the error

  Err j is computed by

  $$Err_j = o_j (1-o_j) (T_j-o_j)$$

  Where Oj => is the actual output of unit j

  Tj=> is the known target value of the given training tuple.

- To compute the error of hidden layer unit j, the weighted sum of the errors of the units connected unit j in the next layer are considered.

The error of a hidden layer unit j is

$$Err_j = o_j (1-o_j) \sum_k Err_k w_{jk},$$

Where wjk = weight of the connection from unit j to a unit k in the next higher layer.

Errk = error of unit k.

- The weights and biases are updated to reflect the propagated errors.

  Weights are updated by the following equations, where △ wij is the change is weight wij:

  $$\triangle w_{ij} = (l)\, Err_j\, o_i$$

  $$w_{ij} = w_{ij} + \triangle w_{ij}$$

  Where l is learning rate.

  Constant, typically value between 0 and 1

- Biases updated:

  $$\triangle\theta_j = (l)\, Err_j$$

  $$\theta_j = \theta_j + \triangle\theta_j$$

- Note that here we are updating the weights and biases after the presentation of each tuple. This is referred to as case updating. Alternatively, the weight and bias increments could be accumulated invariables, so that the weights and biases are updated after all of the tuples in the training set have been presented. This is known as epoch updating.

Step 4 Terminating Condition: i.e Training stops when.

- All wij in the previous epoch were so

Unit j	Net i/p, Ij	Output, oj
4	0.2+0-0.5-0.4=-0.7	$\frac{1}{1+e^{0.7}} = 0.332$
5	-0.3+0+0.2+0.2=0.1	$\frac{1}{1+e^{-0.1}} = 0.525$
6	(-0.3) (0.332)-(0.2) (0.525)+0.1=-0.105	$\frac{1}{1+e^{0.105}} = 0.474$

small as to be below some specified threshold.

X1	X2	X3	W14	W15	W24	W25	W34	W35	W46	W56	θ 4	θ 5	θ 6
1	0	1	0.2	-0.3	0.4	0.1	-0.5	0.2	-0.3	-0.2	-0.4	0.2	0.1

(OR)

- The percentage of tuples misclassified in the previous epoch is below some threshold.

(OR)

- A prespecified number of epochs has expired.

Sample Calculations for learning by the backpropagation algorithm:

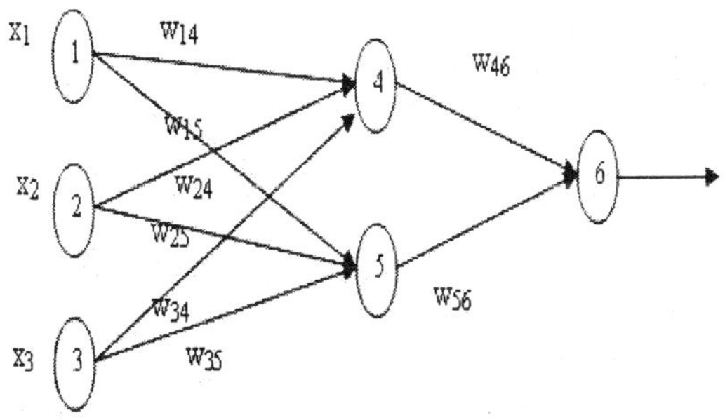

Fig. 3 An example of multi layer feed-forward neural network.

Let the learning rate be (l) = 0.9.

The initial weight and bias values of the network are given in the following table along with the first training tuple,

X = (1,0,1), whose class label is 1.

The net input and output calculations:

Calculation of the error at each node

Unit j	Errj
6	(0.474) (1-0474) (1-0.474)=0.1311
5	(0.525) (1-0.525) (0.1311) (-0.2)=-0.0065
4	(0.332) (1-0.332) (0.1311) (-0.3)=-0.0087

Weight or bias	New Value
W46	-0.3+(0.9) (0.1311) (0.332)=-0.261
W56	-0.2+(0.9) (0.1311) (0.525)=-0.138
W14	0.2+(0.9) (-0.0087) (1)=0.192
W15	-0.3+(0.9) (-0.065) (1)=-0.306
W24	0.4+(0.9) (-0.0087) (0)=0.4
W25	0.1+(0.9) (-0.0065) (0)=0.1
W34	-0.5+(0.9) (-0.0087) (1)=-0.508
W35	0.2+(0.9) (0.0065) (1)=0.194
θ6	0.1+(0.9) (0.1311)=0.218
θ5	0.2+(0.9) (-0065)=0.194
θ4	-0.4+(0.9) (-0087)=-0.408

2. Conclusion

We predicted the class labels of the given training tuples or datasets i.e the trained network is found. From these classes we will generate the useful rules to mine the important patterns from the databases.

3. References

[1] Simple neural networks by Rosen blatt[Ros58].

[2] Learning concepts by Minsky and Papert[Mp69]

[3] Backpropagation Algorithm by Rumelhart, Hinton and Williams[RHW86]

[4] Variations for Backpropagation by Hanson and Burr[HB88].

[5] Dynamic adjustment of the learning rate and momentum parameters by Jacobs[JAC88].

[6] Dynamic adjustment of the network topology by Mezard and Nadal[MN89].

[7] An extensive survey of applications of Neural networks in industry, business and science by widrow,Rumelhart and Lehar [WRL94].

[8] Variations in Backpropagations by Chauvin and Rumelhart[CR95].

[9] Critiques of techniques for rule extraction from neural networks by Cravan and Shavlik[CS97].

[10] Theoretical foundations of Neural networks by Roy [ROY00].

[11] Data Mining and concepts by Han and Kamber[HK04].

Data Mining in a Regression Framework

Sesham Anand[1], Sai Hanuman A[2], Dr. Govardhan A[3], Dr. Vinaybabu A[3] and Dr. Padmanabham P[4]

[1] Department of CSE, MVSREC, Hyderabad, A P, India,
sesham_anand@hotmail.com
[2] School of Computing, GRIET, Hyderabad, A P, India,
a_saihanuman@hotmail.com
[3]Department of CSE, JNTU, Hyderabad, A P, India
[4]Principal, Bharat Eng College, Hyderabad, A P, India

Abstract

Rapid progress in data collection methods and technology has made it possible to acquire huge quantities of data available for various organizations and for researchers. This amount of data will be of little use unless it enables to get required information. Statistical summary methods for data analysis are to some extent useful but cannot be used for large amount of data. Hence the field of Data mining has emerged recently which is an amalgamation of various disciplines like statistics, machine learning, mathematics etc which is used for extraction of hidden or hitherto unknown information from large amount of data.

Cross Industry Standard Process for Data Mining (CRISP-DM) is an industry standard process which helps in doing data Mining. It defines the following stages Problem Understanding, Data Understanding, Data Preparation, Modeling, Evaluation, and Deployment. Modeling techniques come from fields of machine learning, signal processing, evolutionary computing and statistics etc. There are many modeling techniques like regression, neural networks, decision trees, rule induction methods, association rules, clustering, classification, etc.

The aim of this paper is to make a preliminary study of various regression based data mining techniques. Initially the component-based views of data mining algorithms are introduced followed by an introduction to regression techniques and its variants.

1. Introduction

Data Mining is an analysis of (often large) observational data sets to find unsuspected relationships and to summarize the data in novel ways that are both understandable and useful to the data owner [1]. The result of any data mining process is usually a model or pattern involving relationships and summaries derived from data. A data mining algorithm is a well defined procedure that takes data as input and produces output in the form of models or patterns. Any data mining algorithm contains the following components as explained by Hand et al[1,2] the task, the structure of the model or pattern to fit the data, the score function to judge the quality of the fitted model, the search or optimization method to optimize the score function, the data management technique to be used for storing, indexing and retrieving the data. This particular component-based view of data mining algorithms has the advantage of providing a general high-level framework for analysis and synthesis.

2. Modeling phase

A model is a high level description of data, or an abstract representation of a real world process. It can be descriptive in nature or inferential i.e. to infer about the population from which the data was drawn or about future data values [1]. These models will usually have a functional form. There are various forms like regression, hidden-markov models etc. Each model will have a set of parameters for which appropriate values are chosen by estimation. This is done by maximizing or minimizing a score function which measures the fit of the model to the data. This paper discusses about the regression models. A good-fitting model has several benefits. The structural form of the model describes the patterns of association and interaction. The sizes of the model parameters determine the strength and importance of the effects. Inferences about the parameters evaluate which explanatory variables affect the response variable, while controlling effects of possible confounding variables. Finally, the model's predicted values smooth the data and provide improved estimates of the mean of response variable, at possible explanatory variable values [8].

3. Regression Models

One important mode of statistical reasoning of data mining is to predict the value of a variable from the known values of one or more other variables. Such predictions are necessary when some variable cannot be observed directly and need to be estimated from other variables. The variable to be predicted is called 'dependent (criterion) variable' or 'response variable', and the variables used as predictors are called 'independent variables (predictor)' or 'stimulus variables' 'explanatory' or 'causal variables'.

Regression analysis is one of the most widely used form of analysis of dependence. It is used to explore the relationship between a set of independent variables and a single dependent variable. A regression model is a weighted combination of independent variables that corresponds as closely as possible to the dependent variable. Regression is used for description, inference and prediction purposes [3]. Regression methods fall into two categories [10]: parametric regression, which assumes that the nature of the relationships (but not the specific parameters) between the dependent and independent variables is known a priori (e.g., is linear), and nonparametric regression like neural networks which does not make any such assumption as to how the dependent variables are related to the predictors. Instead it allows the regression function to be driven directly from data. There are various parametric regression models available in the literature. Some of them are the classical linear models, generalized linear models and logit models etc. These are briefly reviewed in the next section.

3.1 Classical Linear Models

In the linear regression model [6], each 'y' in a sample of 'n' observations is expressed as a linear function of the x's plus a random error, 'ε':

$$y_1 = \beta_0 + \beta_1 x_{11} + \beta_2 x_{12} + \ldots \beta_q x_{1p} + \varepsilon_1$$
$$y_2 = \beta_0 + \beta_1 x_{21} + \beta_2 x_{22} + \ldots \beta_q x_{2p} + \varepsilon_2 \ldots$$
$$y_n = \beta_0 + \beta_1 x_{n1} + \beta_2 x_{n2} + \ldots \beta_p x_{np} + \varepsilon_n.$$

The number of x's is denoted by 'p'. The β's are called regression coefficients.

This is also expressed in matrix terms as

$$\mathbf{y} = \mathbf{Xb} + \epsilon$$

where **y** and ϵ are vectors of order (n x 1), **b** is a vector of order [(p+1) x 1] and **X** is a matrix of order [n x (p +1)].

The classical linear model is the simplest model that can be used to relate the response variable to the explanatory variables. It is assumed that the response variable is normally distributed. The independent variables are truly independent, are uncorrelated and the regression weights are estimated using the least squares method.

Table 1 Linear model characteristics

$Y_i \sim N(\mu_i, \sigma^2)$ Observations Normally distributed and independent.	$\mu = \eta$, identity link	$\eta = \sum_{1}^{p} x_j \beta_j$, Linear predictor based on covariates $x_1, \ldots, x_p$

The main assumption that is made in this technique is the Linearity of the phenomenon measured. It represents the degree to which the change in dependent variable is associated with the independent variable. If such a linear relationship is not observed, transforming the data values, through logarithm, square root etc, of one or more independent variables is done to achieve linearity.

Additional assumptions that accompany the equations of the model are as follows:

1. $E(\varepsilon_i) = 0$ **for all** $i = 1, 2, \ldots, n$.
2. $\mathrm{var}(\varepsilon_i) = \sigma 2$ **for all** $i = 1, 2, \ldots, n$.
3. $\mathrm{cov}(\varepsilon_i, \varepsilon_j) = 0$ **for all** $i \_= j$.

Assumption 1 states that the model is linear and that no additional terms are needed to predict 'y'; all remaining variation in 'y' is purely random and unpredictable. Thus if $E(\varepsilon i) = 0$ and the x's are fixed, then $E(y_i) = \beta_0 + \beta_1 x_{i1} + \beta_2 x_{i2} + \ldots + \beta p\ x_{ip}$, and the mean of '$y$' is expressible in terms of these 'p' number of x's with no others needed. In assumption 2, the variance of each εi is the same, which also implies that $\mathrm{var}(y_i) = \sigma 2$, since the x's are fixed. Assumption 3 imposes the condition that the error terms are uncorrelated, from which it follows that the y's are also uncorrelated, that is, $\mathrm{cov}(y_i, y_j) = 0$. [4].

The method of least squares, which minimizes the squared difference between the predicted value and the actual value of the dependent variable, lies at the heart of regression. When more than one predictor variable is involved, the process is known as multiple regression. In most cases the problem arises in having to choose appropriate number of independent variables out of several, for inclusion in the model. There are several approaches for this task. The most demanding of course is for the researcher to specify exact set of independent variables called Confirmatory specification. In another method called Sequential search, a set of variables are defined and then selectively adding or deleting among these variables until some overall criterion measure is achieved. Stepwise regression is the most popular procedure in this category. In another technique termed as combinatorial approach, in which all possible combinations are examined.

3.2 Generalized Regression Models (GLM)

The generalized regression model is a more general form of the classical linear model. Given a set of explanatory variables, the response variable besides following a normal distribution, can also follow other distributions like poisson, binomial, bernoulli etc. An important aspect of these models is that they assume independent observations as in linear models. Such models which have different distribution patterns cannot be calibrated using least squares analysis. A method known as Maximum Likelihood Estimation (MLE) is therefore used. This procedure searches for coefficients which, when multiplied by appropriate independent variables, are most likely to produce the desired distribution of the dependent variable.

Supposing that a random sample y_i , $i = 1,\ldots,n$ from a density Pr_θ (y) indexed by some parameter θ. The log probability of the observed sample is

$$L(\theta) = \pi_{I=1}^{n} \log Pr_\theta (y_i)$$

The principle of maximum likelihood assumes the most reasonable values of θ are those for which the probability of the observed sample is largest. Generalized Regression Models allow two extensions; first the distribution of the random component can be other than normal and second some other link functions are used.

3.2.1 Logistic regression model

One of the most important kinds of generalized linear model for data mining is logistic regression model [5]. While dealing with individual choice models the dependent variable is a probability, which cannot be observed. What can be observed are the actual choices made by individuals when they are faced with two or more alternatives. In the two choice case, the choice of an individual could either be 0 or 1. Linear regression models cannot be used for binary response variables, because a linear function is unlimited, so the model could predict values for the response variable outside the interval [0,1], which is meaningless. Instead we use logistic regression. It is one of the most important predictive data mining methods. Let y_i (i=1,2,3,....n) be the observed values of a binary response variable, which can take only the values 0 or 1. The level 1 usually represents the occurrence of an event of interest called success.

$$\Pi_i = P(Y_i = 1), \text{ for } i=1,2,\ldots.n$$

A logistic regression model specifies that an appropriate function of the fitted probability of the event is a linear function of the observed values of the explanatory variables. This is usually a logit function

$$\text{logit}(\Pi_i) = \log [\Pi_i / 1 - \Pi_i].$$

The logit function implies that the dependence of Π_i on the explanatory variables is described by a sigmoid function. Hence

$$\Pi_i = e^{(a+bx_i+b_2x_{i2}\ldots+b_ix_{ip})} / 1 + e^{(a+bx_i+b_2x_{i2}\ldots+b_ix_{ip})}.$$

This relationship corresponds to the function known as a logistic curve. Once Π_i is calculated on the basis of the data, a fitted value for each binary observation for y_i can be obtained, where y_i=1 above Π_i and y_i=0 below Π_i.

3.2.2 Multinomial Logit (MNL) models

If the response variable has several choices, each with some probability of occurrence, then the probability of occurrence of any one event is obtained by the following Multinomial Logit (MNL) formulation.

$$P(j: J_i) = e^{(a+bxj+b2xj2\ldots+bjxjp)} / \Sigma^{Ji}_{i=1} e^{(a+bxi+b2xi2\ldots+bixip)}.$$

The P(j: J_i) is the probability of occurrence of event j, out of J events, (a+bxi+b2xi2...+bixip) is the stimulus function associated with each of the J events. The functional form ensures that sumof probabilities of all the choices is always 1.

3.2.3 Poisson Regression Model

Many discrete response variables have counts as possible outcomes [8]. Counts also occur in summarizing categorical variables with contingency tables. The simplest GLM for count data assumes a poisson distribution for the random component. Like counts, poisson variates can take any nonnegative integer value. The basic model formulation is that the mean of the poisson random variable is a function of predictor information,

$$E(Y) = \mu = \lambda = \exp\{\alpha + \beta_1 x_1 + \ldots + \beta_p x_p\}.$$

Because the log of this function produces a linear combination of the predictors, this model is said to have a log link function. Here the function that links the mean to the linearized predictor is the log function.

3.2.4 Log-Linear Models

These models are also called as symmetric generalized linear models. They are used to describe the associative structure among the explanatory variables. They are basically used for count data which follow poisson distribution [5].

3.2.5 Generalized Additive Model (GAM)

Although linear models like simple regression are very attractive because of their simplicity, they often fail in many situations where the effects are non-linear [15]. GAM are statistical methods that are used to identify and characterize nonlinear regression effects. A GAM model is of the form:

$$E(Y \mid X_1, X_2, \ldots X_P) = \alpha + f_1(X_1) + f_2(X_2) + \ldots + f_p(X_p).$$

where f_j's are unspecified smooth functions.

Each function is fit using scatter plot smoothers like cubic smoothing spline or kernel smoother etc. All linear terms are usually replaced by a more general functional form. An example of a GAM would be an additive logistic regression. Similar to a GLM, GAM will have various link functions like identity, logit, probit, log etc for gaussian, poisson, binomial response data. Here one point is to be remembered that the functions f's can be non linear. An example could be (a semi parametric form). $g(\mu) = X^T \beta + \alpha_k + f(Z)$

An algorithm for fitting additive models can be found in [15].

3.3 Regression Splines

Multivariate Adaptive Regression Splines (MARSplines) [10] [15] is an implementation of techniques popularized by [14] for solving regression-type problems, with the main purpose to predict the values of a continuous dependent or outcome variable from a set of independent or predictor variables. Models such as a linear regression [e.g., Multiple Regression, General Linear Model (GLM)], nonlinear regression (Generalized Linear/Nonlinear Models),and regression trees assume some form of functional relationship between dependent and independent variables. Multivariate Adaptive Regression Splines (MARSplines) on the other hand is a nonparametric regression procedure that makes no assumption about the underlying functional relationship between the dependent and independent variables. Instead, MARSplines constructs this relation from a set of coefficients and basis functions that are entirely determined from the regression data. The MARS model is as follows:

$$Y = f(X) = \beta_0 + \Sigma\, \beta_m H_{km}(X_{v(k,m)}),$$

Where $H_{km}(X_{v(k,m)}) = \Pi\, h_{km}$ and

$X_{v(k,m)}$ is the predictor in the m'th product.

MARSplines constructs this relation from a set of coefficients and basis functions that are entirely driven from the regression data. The methods are based on the divide and conquer strategy, which partitions the input space into regions, each with its own regression equation. This makes MARSplines particularly suitable for problems with higher input dimensions (i.e., with more than 2 variables), where the curse of dimensionality would likely create problems for other techniques.

The MARSplines technique has become particularly popular in the area of data mining because it does not assume or impose any particular type or class of relationship (e.g., linear, logistic, etc.) between the predictor variables and the dependent (outcome) variable of interest.

3.4 Classification and regression trees (CART)

There are many tree based data mining algorithms like CART, ID3, C4.5, C5.0 etc[15]. If the target is prediction, regression trees are employed and for classification purposes classification trees are used. Tree based methods usually partition the feature space into a set of rectangles, and then fit a simple model in each rectangle. CART provides a general framework that can be instantiated in various ways to produce different trees. In this method one needs to decide upon the splits at each node, which property to test at each node, how to prune the tree, how to handle the missing data etc. More details on CART can be found in [16] [17]. First of all the space is split into two regions, and the response is modeled to get the best fit. These regions are further split into sub regions and the process goes on. The split regions are displayed using a recursive binary tree. The resulting tree might be very large and hence a pruning strategy like cost-complexity pruning is usually chosen. The advantage of using a tree based approach is its interpretability. [18] CART regression trees fit a constant regression model at each leaf node of the tree.

4. Neural Networks

A neural network is a very general term which includes a number of models and learning methods. Neural networks produce continuous output; and are suitable to be used for estimation and prediction. One of the advantages of using neural networks is that they are quite robust with respect to noisy data. No prior assumption is made with respect to the distribution of the data unlike other regression techniques [12].

The term 'neural network' has its origins in attempts to find mathematical representations of information processing in biological systems. A neural network consists of a layered, feed forward, completely connected network of artificial neurons, or nodes [19]. The feed forward nature of the network restricts the network to a single direction of flow and does not allow looping or cycling. The neural network is composed of two or more layers, although most networks consist of three layers: an input layer, a hidden layer, and an output layer. There may be more than one hidden layer, although most networks contain only one, which is sufficient for most purposes. The neural network is completely connected, meaning that every node in a given layer is connected to every node in the next layer, although not to other nodes in the same layer. Each connection between nodes has a weight (e.g., W_{1A}) associated with it. At initialization, these weights are randomly assigned to values between zero and 1. They take nonlinear functions of the linear combinations of the inputs. In general they are non linear statistical models. They can be treated as a two stage regression model with one output class to predict. A neural network model can be represented as follows:

$$Z_m = \sigma(\alpha_{0m} + \alpha^T_m X), \quad m = 1,\dots M,$$
$$T_k = \beta_{0k} + \beta^T_k Z, \quad k = 1,\dots K,$$
$$f_k(X) = g_k(T), \quad k = 1,\dots,K$$

where $Z = (Z_1, Z_2, \dots Z_M)$ and $T = (T_1, T_2, \dots T_k)$. and σ is the activation function. It is usually chosen as a sigmoid function. Z_m are the derived features created from linear combinations of inputs and Y_k, $k=1\dots K$ are the target measurements for the kth class. T_k are the target outputs.

The output function $g_k(T)$, allows the transformation of outputs. If $g_k(T)$ is chosen as an identity function ie $g_k(T)=T$, then this method becomes regression. The neural network model consists of unknown parameters called as weights, whose values are chosen to fit the model to the training data well. For regression, we use the sum-of-squared errors as the error function. There are many neural network models mentioned in the literature like back propagation networks, radial basis functions etc.

5. Open Source Software Package

There are a number of computer packages available in open source. One such package called "R" can be used for implementing and working with above discussed methods. "R" is a language [7] and environment for statistical computing and graphics. "R" provides a wide variety of statistical (linear and nonlinear modelling, classical statistical tests, time-series analysis, classification, clustering,) and graphical techniques, and is highly extensible. One of R's strengths is the ease with which well-designed publication-quality plots can be produced, including mathematical symbols and formulae where needed. R is available as Free Software and is open source.

6. Summary and Conclusion

Regression analysis is most widely used technique in statistical data mining for application of prediction and explanation. Prediction involves the extent to which the one or more independent variables can predict their dependent variable. In explanation, the regression coefficient for each independent variable provides substantive reason for the effects of the independent variables.

There are various methods of regression such as Linear, Multiple, Non linear, Logit, Multinomial, MARSplines, Neural Networks and other non parametric methods. Many problems can be solved by linear regression, and by applying transformation of variables a non linear problem can also be converted to linear one. Linear regression models are used to model the relationship between a continuous response variable and a set of predictor variables.

If the response data consists of count data, Poisson regression is employed. Logit models are most suitable when the responses are dichotomous, in the form of yes or no (0 or 1) and the out put is probability. When more than one predictor is used, such as an individual having several choices but need to choose any one, and the output is probability, Multi Nomial Logit is appropriate. These models however assume that the relationship between the predictor and response is non linear. Regression trees such as CART are adapted to predict continuous or ordered values rather than class labels.

There are two important methods of fitting models to data, the method of Least Squares and the Maximum Likelihood method. In the method of least squares, the regression weights are so obtained that the squared difference between the predicted value and the actual value of the dependent variable is minimized, while in the maximum likelihood method the procedure searches for coefficients which, when multiplied by appropriate independent variables, are most likely to produce the desired distribution of the dependent variable. The latter method is most appropriate for non linear response and predictor variables are involved.

Table 2 Summary of regression methods

Regression model	Linear	Multiple	Logistic	Multinomial	Poisson	Log-Linear	MARS	Neural
Response Type	Continuous	Continuous	Binary	Multinomial Mixed	Count	Count	Continuous	No assumption is made
Response Distribution	Normal	Normal	Bernoulli		Poisson	Poisson	-------	NA
Link Function	Identity $g(\mu_i) = \mu_i = \beta_0 + \beta_1 x_{i1}$	Identity $g(\mu_i) = \mu_i = \beta_0 + \beta_1 x_{i1} + \ldots + \beta_p x_{ip}$	Logit $g(\mu_i) = \log(\Pi_i / 1 - \Pi_i)$	Generalized logit	Log $g(\mu_i) = \log \mu_i$	Log $g(\mu_i) = \Sigma \beta_j x_{ij}$	No assumption is made	No assumption is made
Score Function(Goodness of fit)	$\Sigma(y-\mu)^2$	$\Sigma(y-\mu)^2$	$G^2 = 2 \Sigma\{y \log(y/\mu) - (y-\mu)\}$	Pseudo R square	$2\Sigma\{y \log(y/\mu + (m-y) \log[(m-y)/(m-\mu)]\}$	$G^2 = 2 \Sigma n_{ijk} \log(n_{ijk}/\mu_{ijk})$	$GCV = \Sigma(y_i - f(x_i))^2 / (1 - c/N)^2$	$\Sigma(y-\mu)^2$
Pearson's statistic(X^2)	$\Sigma(y-\mu)^2$	$X^2 = \Sigma(y-\mu)^2 / V(\mu)$	$X^2 = \Sigma(y-\mu)^2 / V(\mu)$	$2 \Sigma \Sigma y_{ij} \log(y_{ij} / \mu_{ij})$	$\log L(\beta) = \{y_i \log(\mu_i) - \mu_i\}$	$2\{y_i \log(y_i/\mu_i) - (y_i - \mu_i)$	--------	------

7. References

[1] David Hand, Heikki Mannila, Padhraic Smyth, *Principles of Data Mining*, MIT Press Cambridge CA (2001).

[2] Wray Buntine, Bernd Fischer, Thomas Pressburger, *Towards automated synthesis of data mining programs*,

[3] James Lattin, J.Douglas Carroll, Paul E. Green, *Analyzing multivariate data*, Thomson Asia Pte Ltd, 2003

[4] Alvin C. Rencher , *Methods of multivariate Analysis*, 2nd Edition 2002 , John Wiley & Sons

[5] Paolo Giudici, *Applied Data Mining*, Statistical *Methodsa for Business and Industry*, John Wiley and Sons, 2003

[6] P. McCullagh, and J.A Nelder, *Generalized Linear Models*, 2nd Edition, Chapman and Hall London

[7] R Development Core Team (2008). *R: A language and environment for statistical computing. R Foundation for Statistical Computing,* Vienna, Austria. ISBN 3-900051-07-0, URL http://www.R-project.org.

[8] Agresti, Alan, *An Introduction to categorical analysis Second Edition,* John Wiley & Sons.

[9] Agresti, Alan,, *Categorical Analysis, Second Edition,* John Wiley & Sons

[10] *Multivariate Adaptive Regression Splines (MARSplines)* http://www.statsoft.com/textbook/stmars.html

[11] Richard Berk, *Data Mining Within a Regression Framework*, University of California, Los Angeles, http://repositories.cdlib.org/uclastat/papers/2004010101.

[12] Thomas C. M. Lee, *On Algorithms for ordinary least squares regression spline fitting: a comparative study*, Department of Statistics, Colorado State University, Fort Collins, Journal of Statistics, Comput. Simul., 2002, Vol. 72(8), pp. 647–663

[13] http://cran.r-project.org/web/views/Multivariate.html

[14] Trevor Hastie, Robert Tibshirani, Jerome Friedman, *The elements of statistical learning, Data Mining, Inference and Prediction* by Springer.

[15] Breiman L., Friedman, J., Olshen, R., and Stone, *Classification and Regression Trees.* (1994).

[16] Richard O. Duda, Peter E. Hart, David G. Stork, *Pattern Classification,* Second Edition, Wiley Interscience

[17] Nong Ye, *The Handbook of data Mining,* 2003, Lawrence Erlbaum Associates publishers, London

Classifying the Human Chromosomes using Neural Networks

G. Shyama Chandra Prasad[1] and B.Satyanarayana[2]
[1]Associate Professor [2]Professor,
SLC'sIET, Hyderabad, A.P., India

Abstract

This study aimed to represent an advanced software tool assists in analyzing and classifying the human chromosomes. Our new software handles both classifying and analyzing the medical image of human chromosomes according to the following steps: 1-we use the image processing utilities in Matlab to analyze the image; where we provide a new filter to remove the noise depending on the objects that exists in the image. 2-The filtered image enters to a segmentation algorithm to segment this image to the most acceptable one. 3-The segments will enter two tracks for classifying the chromosomes that are contained in the segment: the first one depends on using the image processing for measuring the length of each chromosome; while the second one deals with initiating the neural network to classify the chromosomes according to the chromosomes characteristics. There is a noticeable enhancement in the image processing approach as a result of using our filter which improve the image quality by a factor equal to 91.7%.

Key words: *Multi-layer feed forward neural network, back propagation, image profile, metaphase, Matlab*

1. Introduction

Chromosomes are tightly coiled microscopic rod-like structures of DNA and protein that are found in the nuclei of Eukaryotic cells. Each chromosome consists of two sets of genetic material connected at the centromere. The human body chromosomes are 46 chromosomes, arranged into 23 pairs, 22 for body chromosomes and one pair for sexual chromosomes.

This study got its idea from a problem that faces the technicians in the cytogenetics labs in analyzing the human chromosomes. Such problem can be summarized in: counting the number of chromosomes (taking into consideration overlapping and touching chromosomes), studying the banding patterns in each one and determining the possible genetic disease, if there is any. So, instead of doing the classification process manually by a microscope with the naked eye, our software can do this task using both Image processing approach and Neural Networks. Our software package can be characterized by minimizing the consuming time needed to classify the chromosomes and gain reliable results.

To accomplish the objective, we use a digital camera and microscope to capture the metaphase image. Also, we adapt the capabilities of Matlab tool to build our software. As a final conclusion to our works, we implement two tracks to classify human chromosomes: using length of the chromosome and Neural network, each one gives us some types of results.

There exists many trials have been done in order to classify the human chromosomes; we will focus on the one that uses AI especially Neural Network. In these trails, the Neural Network handles the image segmentation, chromosomes classification and rearranges them into pairs.

Seung *et al.* selected some features of the chromosome like: relative length, normalized density profile (d.p) and centromeric index to be used in identification of human chromosomes. They trained neural network classifier by changing the number of samples which used to get (d.p.) to classify the chromosomes.

Boaz covered all aspects of human chromosome analysis: segmentation using separation of clusters of partially occluded chromosomes, feature description, selection and extraction and classification by Multi-Layer Perceptron (MLP) Neural Network.

In our study, we create a connection between image processing and Neural Network, i.e. the image segmentation is done by image processing techniques and the classification is done by Neural Network.

Problem formulation

When technicians in the cytogenetics labs want to examine the human cell to see if there is any genetic disorder, they take a cell sample from the patient and prepare the slide to: study it with a very high magnifying power microscope, count the chromosomes and study the banding pattern in each one of them. In order to get correct results, this process might be repeated many times with different types of cells. Both the time and effort to accomplish these tasks are relatively long which implies that there is a necessary demand for a new approach. So, we present this work to implement the above tasks using an advanced software tool.

Proposed software approach

The process of human chromosome classification executed by our proposed software passes through two main stages given by the following:

1. Image processing; this phase is concerned with analyzing the image which is taken from the microscope via digital camera and examine this image if it is in RGB form or not. If it was in that form, we should convert it into gray scale image to make it easier to be handled by Matlab. After that, we apply an advanced filtering technique (since we don't use the built-in filters in Matlab) to remove the noise which is exists in the image. We create our own filter because all types of prefabricated filters are used to remove creation types of noise. But in the treated images, the object which we considered it as noise and must be removed is in fact an object in the image. Several of the built in filters (that exist in Matlab) use the value of an output pixel that is determined by the median of the neighborhood pixels rather than the mean, but in our image we want to separate some pixels from its neighborhood. Our filtering algorithm removed 91.7% of the noise in the image. After that, the segmentation process begins with cutting the image into the most likely segments which usually contain one chromosome. However; some critical segments could contain the overlapping or touching chromosomes.

   As a new track in chromosome classification, we calculate the length of each chromosome in a single segment to classify the chromosome according to the length using "Skeletonization / Medial Axis Transformation" technique. According to this calculated length, we can classify the chromosome.
2. Neural Network; it is the second stage of chromosome classification that begins with initiation of the Multi-Layer Neural Network with Back-Propagation algorithm and the suitable architecture form, train and transfer functions.

   After creating the Neural Network, the typical chromosomes have been inserted in it to be the target in the training process. The output of the segmentation algorithm, which will be an array of objects, will be converted from matrix form into vector form. This vector represents the new input to the Neural Network. This Neural Network uses Back Propagation algorithm

Our work will classify the chromosomes, which means that the neural network will be trained to distinguish them and rearrange them into pairs. Each pair must have two identical chromosomes. If there is any extra or lost or defected chromosome, the neural network will show it through its decision. Also the network will separate the noise which the filter algorithm could not remove and still in the image after segmentation (our proposed flowchart that illustrates these procedures is shown in Fig.1).

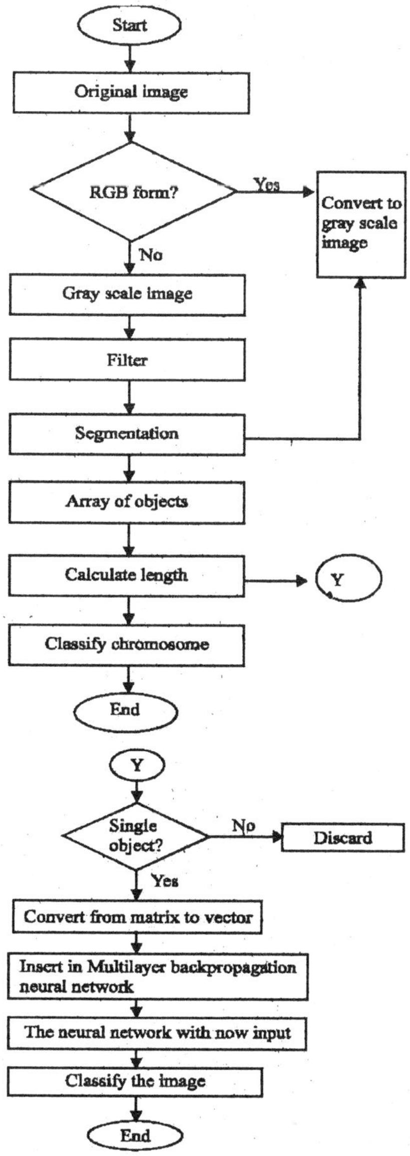

Fig. 1 Flowchart of human chromosome classification

Medical image preprocessing and acquisitions

To calculate the chromosome length using Skeletonization /Medial Axis Transformation approach, we apply some Matlab functions to reduce foreground regions in a binary image to skeletal remnant that largely preserves the extent and connectivity of the original region. Each point on the skeleton has an intensity which represents its distance to boundary in the original object. Calculating the length of each object depends on the depth and recursion principle. The calculation proceed as follows: the first phase calculates the number of paths which we have in each object. The second phase takes the tallest path from which we take the length.

Since traditionally the calculated chromosome length was measured by base pair, but we have not this unit in Matlab tool, so we adapt some mathematical transformation to substitute pixel instead of base pair.

Applied matlab tools and output results

In this study, we use Matlab as a programming language since Matlab is widely used in all areas of applied mathematics in education and research. Matlab stands for MATrix LABoratory and the software is built up around vectors and matrices[7]. This makes the software particularly useful and great tool for solving algebraic and differential equations and for numerical integration. Matlab also has some toolboxes useful for signal processing, image processing, Neural Network, Database, Wavelet... etc, which have ready built-in functions.

Matlab Image Processing Toolbox contains many powerful tools for image processing. It extends the basic capabilities of Matlab by providing a number of specialized I/O, display and processing functions for image and image processing. When working with images in Matlab, there are many things to keep in mind such as: loading images, using the right format, saving the data as different data types, how to display an image and conversion between different image formats. The following image formats are supported by Matlab: BMP, HDF, JPEG, PCX, TIFF, XWB...etc. The image is stored as matrix using standard Matlab matrix conventions. There are five basic types of image supported by Matlab: Indexed images, Intensity images, Binary images, RGB images and 8-bit images.

Artificial Neural Networks (ANNs) as a tool in Matlab are networks of interconnected simple units that are based on a greatly simplified model of the brain. ANNs are useful learning tools by being able to compute results quickly interpolating data well. ANNs are composed of units (also called nodes) that are modeled after neurons, with weighted links interconnecting the units together (Fig. 2). The main difference between ANNs and other learning mechanisms is that it is composed of these simple units and they work together in a highly parallel manner. The Neural Networks have many algorithms that specify how this network should works.

Back-propagation algorithm is the most popular approach to implement learning in neural networks (also called generalized gradient descent and generalized delta rule). This algorithm is a multi-layer network using a weight adjustment based on the sigmoid function (Fig. 3). This method of training is an example of a supervised learning, where the target of the function is known.

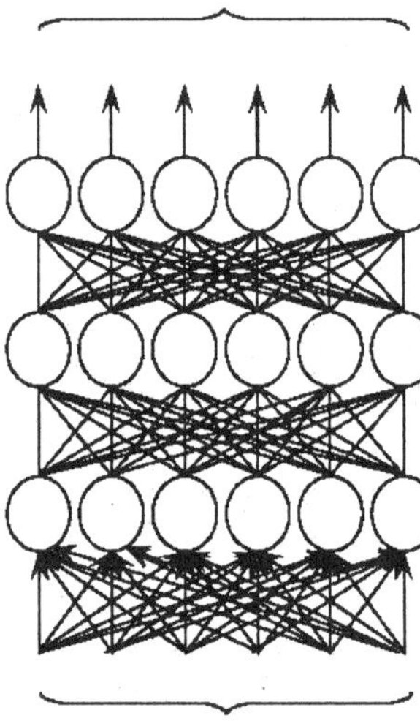

Inputs

Fig. 2 Neural network architecture

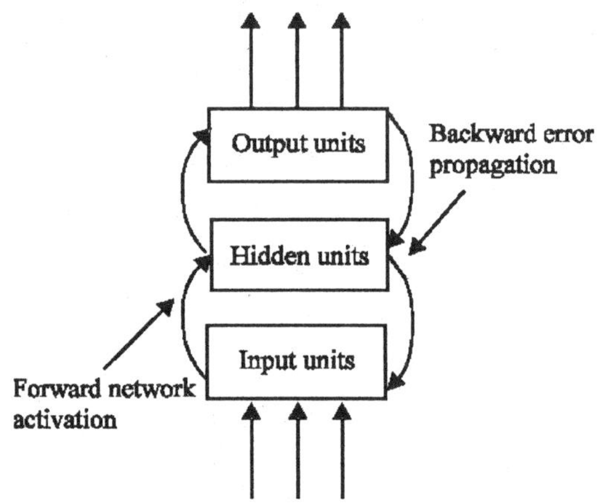

Fig. 3 Back-propagation algorithm

As a result of applying our proposed software in human chromosome classification, we reach to the following results:

1. The medical image was filtered by 91.7% using our filter.
2. Classifying the chromosomes can be done through calculating the chromosome length.
3. Using the Neural Network as another track enables us to distinguish the human chromosomes.

2. Conclusion

The medical image of human chromosome is treated by our software. It is entered in filter algorithm to remove the noise of the image that it can contain with cleaning percentage reach to 91.7%. Then this filtered image entered to segmentation algorithm, which cuts the original image into most likely segments which can contain one object (one chromosome) or in some bad cases it can contain more than one object (overlapping or touching chromosomes). One of the tracks to classify the human chromosomes is concerned with the length of each chromosome (by converting the image into skeletonization form). Another track of classifying the chromosomes is entering the images after segmentation into the Neural Network to study each segment and classify the chromosome that is contained in it.

Research Focus: As a future works, we recommend using an expert system to achieve the goals mentioned in this study and compare its performance with that obtained in our results.

Also, as a tutorial tool, we suggest that the medicine students study this software tool and try to apply it in the classification approach comparing its results with that obtained by their traditional techniques.

3. References

[1] http://www.ornl.gov/sci/techresources/HumanGenome/posters/chromosome/faqs.shtml

[2] Mader, Sylvia S., 1993. Biology (Part 2: Genetic Basics of Life). 4th Edn. Dubuque, Wm. C. Brown Publishers.

[3] Barch, Margarent J., 1997. The AGT Cytogenetics. 3rd Edn. Cambridge, Peter Collin Publishing.

[4] Ryu, Seung Y., M. Cho, M. Jong and H. Woo, Seung. A study for the feature selection to identify giemsa-stained human chromosomes Based on Artificial Neural Network http://bsent.inje.ac.kr/bmetest/bmehtml/boardlink/research/re4_3.pdf

[5] Boaz, L., 1998. Toward a completely automatic neural network based human chromosome analysis. http://www.ee.bgu.ac.il/~boaz/IEEESMCLerner1998.pdf

[6] Hanselman, Duane and Littlefield Bruce, 1996. Mastering Matlab. Prentice-Hall.

[7] The Image Processing Toolbox (Version 3) of MatLab 6.5

[8] Gonzalez, Rafael C., 2002. Digital Image Processing. 2nd Edn. Prentice-Hall, Inc.

[9] http://www.cs.sfu.ca/~oschulte/king.pdf

[10] Sandberg, Kristian. Introduction to Image Processing in Matlab. http://amath. colorado.edu/scico/tutorials/matlab/Image Process. html

Session – 4

Distributed and Parallel Computing

IDA: Contributing towards Reliable and Secure Distributed Storage

Tarang Gupta and Anshul Malik
University School of Information Technology
Guru Gobind Singh Indraprastha University, Kashmere Gate, New Delhi – 110006
tarang127@gmail.com anshulmalik1987@gmail.com

Abstract

Distributed Storage is a methodology that allows us to store the data in slices at different locations, thereby rendering our data more secure against natural calamities, human error and unauthorized human intervention.

Conventional storage techniques like RAID systems are reliable but do not ensure confidentiality of data being stored for a long time. Moreover, space requirements are also more, to store the multiple copies of the data.

Also, there are two potential security weak spots; first, if the attacker breaks into even a single location he/she will be able to access the entire data. Secondly, with the illimitable computing capabilities of the computers available today, the block cipher encryption can be broken easily.

This paper proposes a Distributed Storage scheme to solve these problems. This scheme will make use of Information Dispersal Algorithm to first slice the data, encrypt these slices, and store each encoded slice at a different location.

1. Introduction

Technological developments have affected all facets of life, computer files have become larger, storage is more critical and security breaches have unfortunately become inevitable. There is an ever increasing demand for the reliability and privacy of the information storage system. Many innovative systems have been designed for effective data storage like RAID, tape backups etc., which have reduced the catastrophic impact of natural and man-made intrusions, for sure, but each has its own shortcomings and a trade-off exists between the cost and the security. IDA or Information Dispersal Algorithm allows us to store the data as small slices in geographically distributed systems.

IDA allows for the reconstruction of entire information desired, even when some of the storage machines are not available or the data in them has been corrupted due to some reason.

The paper begins by delineating the problems faced in the storage system used at present. This discussion is followed by description of concept behind information dispersal algorithm and its working. Section 4 onwards, we proceed with the explanation of the system intended to provide Distributed Storage implementing IDA and Reed Solomon Coding [4]. In the end we compare and contrast the prevalent technology with the proposed technology and analyze the pros and cons of the two.

2. Where is the Fault?

The methods currently being used by majority of the storage systems make use of Duplication or Mirroring, but these methods force one to make a difficult compromise between security, reliability and cost-effectiveness.

RAID setups with their susceptibility to power spikes, natural calamities or other system-level problems have caused losses. Even with disk mirroring data can be lost in events of natural disasters. Then we have tape backups, which are all the more susceptible to physical destruction. Even more, unauthorized people can easily gain access to them [1].

All these problems are being faced by professional storage services and organizations irrespective of their size on a global level.

To some Mirroring, might seem to be a good technique but the maintenance cost involved is way too high. One might say that data redundancy is another option because more the copies of data, it is less likely that all of them will be damaged or corrupted at the same time. But then the tradeoffs like duplication cost, risk of a copy being stolen exists. An even bigger limitation that poses some serious threats to the effectiveness of the system is the bandwidth requirement which increases leading to high costs of data transfer over the network.

3. Information Dispersal

The roots of Distributed Storage can be traced to "The Cauchy Reed-Solomon Information Dispersal Algorithm" (IDA), which explains how data can be divided into unrecognizable slices, which are then distributed to various geographically separated storage locations. Distributed Storage has been designed keeping in mind the key design goals: privacy, security and cost effectiveness.

The biggest advantage of Distributed Storage lies in the fact that there is no single location, which stores entire data at a time. Moreover, in order to retrieve the entire data correctly and securely only few locations are required at a time [2].

Even in case of natural calamities or failures like hardware, connection, facility etc. our data remains safe because pieces of it are scattered at different places (the probability of a calamity at each of the storage location is very less) and individual slices don't carry enough information to allow the notorious viewer to get gist of the content

4. How does it work?

A general block diagram of such a system will be as shown in Fig. 1. The client or the user's computer is connected to a network gateway. The network gateway then employs IDA [3], and distributes the slices to various storage servers through the network. A client is connected to many gateways but only one serves it at a time. Moreover, the storage systems are not capable of communicating with the client directly.

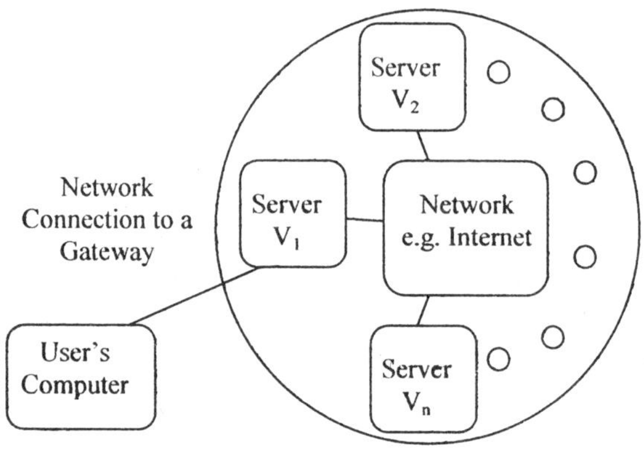

Fig. 1 Illustrating the working of a Distributed Storage System

Since the system employs IDA it can thus reliably store and reconstruct information even if a minority of servers fail or are compromised.

5. Operating Procedure

The clients or users interact with a single designated processor or machine called the gateway. The gateway receives request to store information and also distributes information to all other storage servers called the Internal Servers. The clients can communicate only with the gateway and not with the Internal Servers. In turn, these servers can interact with the gateway and not with the client directly.

On getting a storage request, the gateway slices the information and forwards these slices to the Internal Servers for storage, which store the IDA slice along with some extra information (the hash digest of the slice). To retrieve, gateway contacts required number of servers to reconstruct the original data.

In order to guarantee, that adequate number of servers have received correct information, distributed.

Digital signatures are used where each server contributes a partial signature on the (hash of the) information received from the gateway.

Gateway combines partial signatures from servers receiving information and sends the combined signature to the client for verification.

When the client requests retrieval, gateway contacts sufficient number of Internal Servers. While depositing the slices, each server computes and stores hash digests for all IDA slices which later help to detect and discard corrupt IDA. When the gateway demands for the slices the Internal Servers return not just the IDA slice but also this hash digest. The gateway determines the correctness of the slices by applying hash function to the received slices and compares the result with hash digests returned by their respective servers. The clients either calculate the hash digest or receive the hash digest from the gateway of the information that they wish to be stored at the distributed servers, which they compare with the digest value of the information received to ensure integrity of data.

6. Reed Solomon Coding

We use erasure codes to divide a data object into m fragments and then encode them into n fragments, where all the fragments have the same size and $n \geq m$, hence, Redundancy Rate

$$r = n/m \quad (n \geq m) \tag{1}$$

Now while decoding erasure codes need only any t ($t \geq m$) fragments out of the n encoded fragments to reconstruct the data.

We can take the original data fragments as a vector $D = (D_1, D_2, \ldots, D_3)$, and the encoding function ENC maps the original data fragments onto the encoded fragments

$$ENC(D)=E, \quad E=(E1, E_2, \ldots, E_n). \tag{2}$$

We have a decoding function DEC, which maps a subset of E back to the original data D, i.e.

$$DEC(E_{i1}, E_{i2}, \ldots, E_{it}) = D \tag{3}$$

Reed Solomon (RS) codes form a subclass of erasure codes. RS Codes are *linear codes*, meaning the encoding function is linear. Hence the encoding function of a RS Code can be described by a vector-matrix multiplication,

$$ENC(D) = DG \quad (4)$$

where, G = Generator matrix $(m \times n)$,

D = Original data fragments vector.

RS codes are also *Maximum Distance Separable* (MDS) codes [4], meaning that any m encoded data fragments can be used to and are sufficient to recover the data. This requires that any m × m square sub-matrix of G is non-singular. Decoding function can be described as

$$DEC(E') = E'G'^{-1} \quad (5)$$

where, E′ = m elements sub vector of E,

G′ = the sub-matrix with m corresponding Rows of G

7. Implementation details

The communication between the Client and the system happens via an SSL enabled browser. SSL or Secure Socket Layer is a cryptographic protocol which enables secure communication on the Internet for things like web surfing, email, Instant Messaging and various other kinds of data transfers. SSL has recently been succeeded by Transport Layer Security (TLS) which is based on SSL itself with few differences.

The server applications are invoked by the gateway via the Common Gateway Interface, when requested by the client for deposit or retrieval. The information between the Client and the server is encrypted using SSL which in turn uses the public-and-private key encryption system from RSA, including the use of a digital certificate. The communication between the Internal Servers and the gateway is monitored by a protocol. We have processes known as daemons that run on each internal server and listen for communication from gateway. We can implement the functionality of these daemons using web servers. These daemons also have less overhead than web servers as the gateway can make a single open connection with a daemon and make several transactions with an internal server over this single connection, whereas the web servers often result in multiple connections for multiple transactions which seriously affect the performance. The protocol which the gateway uses to communicate with internal servers requires less overhead to process than standard http protocol.

A short compendium of the process can be written as follows. The Client sends the data to the Gateway to get it deposited. The Gateway performs the job of slicing the data using the IDA, and forwards these slices to the Internal Servers. At these servers the data with its encrypted digest is stored. The encoding scheme allows for the fingerprinting of the slices using one way hash function. MD5 encoding scheme is an example of the many available schemes to choose from.

These fingerprints are used to verify which IDA slices are correct. Gateway reconstructs the data using IDA sends it to client. The client can optionally verify the validity of the data received by hashing it and comparing the hash value to the one stored when document was deposited.

8. IDA v/s Copy Based System

8.1 Reliability

Very high reliability is offered by Copy based systems, where if data is mirrored to n devices, simultaneous failure of up to n-1 devices would not cause data loss. But this reliability comes with a price that is n times a single copy.

RAID systems employ Parity for reliability and allow at most two devices to fail at a time thereby avoiding data loss. Hence, RAID systems are not as expensive as Copy Based Systems but they are not so reliable as well. Although, RAID systems can be configured for more reliability but such systems would be much more expensive since they are both Copy and Parity based systems. IDA takes care of all these drawbacks, for example, you may have IDA system in which data is backed up to 16 separate devices of which any 4 can fail, thereby reducing the storage overhead and increasing the reliability.

8.2 Security

Spreading of information is an important achievement by IDAs. Slices of data are stored, which constitute a small fraction of the complete data. Each of these slices is unique. We can then disperse the data to 'p' devices and the data can be successfully recovered if p-m devices are available. ('p' and 'm' are positive integers set by the IDA). So even if an attacker breaks into multiple devices he/she will not be able to access the data until p-m devices are gained access of. Whereas, in a copy-based system even if a single device falls prey into the hands of an attacker, whole data will be yielded. Since a copy-based system creates multiple copies hence the chances of attack increase.

8.3 Efficiency

Efficiency of IDAs is the biggest benefit they offer, [1].

$$\text{Storage Overhead} = p / (p-m) \quad (6)$$

There is also some storage overhead associated with the block file device of around 12%. Now suppose, data of 1 GB is to be stored with a toleration of maximum 4 simultaneous failures and over 16 locations, then the total storage required across all the 16 locations is:

$$[p / (p-m)]*1 + 12\% \text{ of } 1 \quad (7)$$
$$= 16/12 + .12$$
$$= 1.45 \text{ GB}$$

As opposed to this, we would require % GB of storage in case of a copy-based system. In case of a parity-based system the same efficiency as of IDA can be achieved by using four storage devices, including one used exclusively for parity data. Even though the storage requirements of such a parity system will be same but it can only support one failure without data loss.

Hence, IDAs combine the best of both: High reliability of copy-based storage and the high efficiency of parity-based systems.

By using Distributed storage system we can detect and correct data on a device if it becomes corrupted or is destroyed. As the hash value of the slices are being stored in the internal server along with the data, we can easily run timely checks to see which server's data has been corrupted. Correction can be done by recalculating all the data contained in the missing slice by inspecting the available slices.

9. Advantages of Distributed Storage System

9.1 Exemplary Security and Privacy

In copy-based system we have to trade reliability for security. An additional copy creates and additional attack site from where the data could be stolen. Whereas, with information dispersal more the slices produced, more secure and reliable the system becomes, because then more number of servers would be required to get access of the information.

9.2 Cost-Effective

This concept bolsters the need for cutting down the high costs involved in storage by immensely reducing the size of data stored at each location resulting in to a meager storage overhead of 30-100 percent Whereas, in copy based systems making n copies results into n*100 percent expansion which increases the cost of storage and congestion problems stupendously.

9.3 Extensively Scalable and Robust

IDAs transfer the processing responsibilities from centralized servers to gateways. The gateway slices the data and forwards it to the Internal Servers after calculating the hash digests. The Internal Digests also store the slices after calculating the Hash digests. This Distributed Storage Network can be easily expanded by adding as many Internal Servers or gateways as desired and by modifying the IDA to increase or decrease the number of slices depending upon the criticality of the information.

One may say that the unavailability of a gateway may crash the entire system. To circumvent this limitation we can use multiple gateways connected with each other and to the same storage servers. The client is connected to many gateways at a time but only one system is designated as the principal or acting gateway for the client. Each time principal gateway receives a request to store the data it slices the information and stores the hash value of the received information. This hash value is then stored in all the connected gateways. In case of failure another gateway is immediately designated to the client, for its use hence preventing the system from dysfunction.

Scalability of IDAs can also be attributed to addition of as many slices of data as per the requirement. Contrary to this, RAID systems scale by adding disks, making copies and adding parity which increases the cost manifold.

9.4 Long Lasting Storage

Distributed storage enables to store data for ad infinitum as integrity checks can be run on data to keep the data valid throughout and by rebuilding the data in case of discrepancies.

The Hash Digests provides a mechanism to detect incongruity among the actual data and the slices stored on distributed servers. As mentioned above, in case of discrepancies the data can be rebuilt.

9.5 Performance-Oriented

This Distributed Storage system stands out because of its efficiency, which doesn't allow bottlenecks in our storage process.

The only additional overhead in Distributed Storage is the redundancy of the slices that can be configured as per the requirements. Unlike RAID based systems, where creating multiple copies took toll of not only the storage space but also the bandwidth.

We can also choose the locations to retrieve data from depending on geographical closeness, traffic or physical constraints.

9.6 Easy to Configure

Since Distributed Storage Systems are based on software and minimal amount of hardware, almost all aspects of a Distributed Storage can be configured on the fly.

9.7 Easy to Manage and Monitor

A malfunctioning gateway can be detected by the corresponding client in which case another gateway connected to it is designated as the principal gateway. Only a small subset of the internal servers is required to reconstruct the entire data, which compensates the unavailability of some internal servers. We have often seen that the solutions are not tailor made for a specific industry and this locks you into a particular architecture and a specific vendor thereby obscuring the flexibility that may be required time and again. With Distributed Storage systems one can design solutions which are industry specific, yet easy to implement and flexible to suit the varying needs invariably.

Distributed Storage Systems can be used in Media, Entertainment, Web, Telecommunication, Sciences and Energy, Health Care and Government etc. Such kind of a system gives a lot of power in the hands of the client.

10. Conclusion

Taking into account all the aspects of Distributed Storage System (IDAs) over Copy based systems and parity based systems both positive and negative, it can be said that Distributed Storage or IDA has all the promise and arsenal to become a major breakthrough. Its success is attributed to its adeptness at enforcing the most important determinants of the data storage scenario : Security, Reliability and Cost Effectiveness.

11. References

[1] Michael O. Rabin, "Efficient dispersal of information for security, load balancing, and fault tolerance", Journal of the ACM (JACM), New York, Volume 36, April pp. 335 – 348, 1989

[2] Ned Dimitrov. "Information Dispersal" February 2008

[3] Azer Bestavros, "An adaptive information dispersal algorithm for time critical reliable communication", Boston, pp. 423- 438, 1994

[4] Bernard Sklar, "Reed Solomon Codes", 2001

[5] Christian Cachin, Stefano Tessaro, "Asynchronous Verifiable Information Dispersal", November 2004.

Distributed Rogue Access Point Detection in IEEE 802.11 Wireless LAN using Mobile Agent

A. V. Dhaygude[1], M. S. Karyakarte[2], Prof. S. B. Vanjale[3] and Prof. M. S. Vanjale[4]
[1 & 3]Bharati Vidyapeeth University's College of Engineering, Pune 43
atul.dhaygude@gmail.com svanjale@rediffmail.com
[2]Vishwakarma Institute of Information Technology, Pune
karyakarte.ms@gmail.com
[4]AISSMS IOIT, Pune 01
msvanjale@rediffmail.com

Abstract

With rise in popularity if IEEE 802.11 wireless LAN, there is tremendous rise in attacks on wireless LAN. Therefore security of wireless LAN is poses serious challenge before research community. One such serious challenge in wireless security domain is detection is rogue access points. Plenty of work has been done in detecting rogue access point in IEEE 802.11 wireless LAN. In spite of this many solutions are far from satisfactory.

In this paper we propose a new method of detecting rogue access point using mobile agent. Mobile agent technology is best suited for remote information retrieval making it an ideal choice for detecting rogue access points.

1. Introduction

Because of the flexibility, affordability, and ease of installation, the use of wireless local area networks (WLANs and Wi-Fi) are increasing at a tremendous rate. There are currently more than 75 million wireless LANs in use worldwide. As wireless LAN deployments increase, so does the challenge to provide these networks with security. Wireless LANs face the same security challenges as their wired counterparts, and more. Because the medium for wireless is air, wireless LANs has the added issue of securing data that travels the airwaves. Wireless LAN signals can travel through the walls, ceilings, and windows of buildings up to thousands of feet outside of the building walls. That's why wireless local area networks are subject to a variety of threats. [1]

One of those threats is illegal access points. Having illegal access points is serious threat to security of WLAN (wireless LAN). As WLANs are increasingly getting popular in last mile networks where ERP (Enterprise Resource Planning), SCM (Supply Chain Management), CRM (Customer Relationship Management) etc. software are deployed, threat to security of WLAN will lead to huge loss for an organization. Therefore comprehensive analysis of vulnerabilities of WLAN must be done and steps must be taken to strengthen security.

2. Related work

Although fair amount of work has been done in investigating efficient methods of detecting rogue access point in wireless LAN, this area still offers plenty of opportunity for further investigation in this regards as most of the solutions available today are far from satisfactory. The brief information of related work has been mentioned below.

Monitoring RF waves and IP traffic are two broad classes of approaches to detecting rogue APs. Most existing commercial products take the first approach they either manually scan the RF waves using sniffers e.g., AirMagnet [2], NetStumbler [3]) or automate the process using sensors ([4],[5],[6]).

Three recent research efforts [7, 8, 9] also use RF sensing to detect rogue APsIn [7], wireless clients are instrumented to collect information about nearby APs and send the information to a centralized server for rogue AP detection. The main idea of [8] is to enable dense RF monitoring through wireless devices attached to desktop machines. The focus of [9] is on detecting protected layer- 3 rogue APs. The studies of [10, 11] detect rogue APs by monitoring IP traffic. The authors of [10] demonstrated from experiments in a local testbed that wired and wireless connections can be separated by visually inspecting the timing in the packet traces of traffic generated by the clients. The technique in [11] requires segmenting large packets into smaller ones. In the technique [12]. Wei Wei, and his associates have done their work to detect rogue access point by passive method.

3. Drawbacks of existing works

1. Manual RF scanning is very time consuming and detects rogue AP only when scanning is applied. This leaves ample scope for an attacker to launch attack and finish its work before he gets detected. This is severe loophole of this method.
2. RF scanning approach also suffers from problem of scaling of network as it is not easily scalable.
3. RF scanning method has considerable deployment cost, and also scores low marks when it comes to effectiveness and accuracy.
4. Manual RF scanning is high power consuming method. Consumption of power is an important parameter in mobile computing. Methods used in mobile computing should consume less power.
5. Automatic scanning using sensors is less time consuming than manual scanning and provides a continuous vigilance to rogue APs. However, it may require a large number of sensors for good coverage, which leads to a high deployment cost.
6. Automatic scanning depends on signatures of APs (e.g., MAC address, SSID, etc.), it becomes ineffective when a rogue AP spoofs signatures.
7. Sometimes wireless clients are instrumented to collect information about nearby APs and send the information to a centralized server for rogue AP detection. This approach is not resilient to spoofing. Secondly, it assumes that rogue APs use standard beacon messages inIEEE 802.11 and respond to probes from the clients, which may not hold in practice. Last, all unknown APs (including those in the vicinity networks) are flagged as rogue APs, which may lead to a large number of false positives.
8. Sometimes dense RF scanning is used for more accurate access point detection. However, it relies on proper operation of a large number of wireless devices, which can be difficult to manage.
9. Most of the existing works detect either layer-2 or layer-3 rogue access point.
10. The authors of [10] demonstrated from experiments in a local testbed that wired and wireless connections can be separated by visually inspecting the timing in the packet traces of traffic generated by the clients. The settings of their experiments are very restrictive. Furthermore, the visual inspection method cannot be carried out automatically.
11. The method used in [12] has passive method of detecting rogue access points but works with only TCP protocol. Furthermore it detects rogue access point only if computer behind rogue access point access central server where application which implements this method is deployed.

4. Our approach

4.1 Introduction of mobile agent

Mobile agents are computer programs, which are autonomous, proactive and reactive, and have ability to learn. They move from one node to another node and interact with each other, sharing information to better carry out their goals. Mobile agents spread intelligence across the network, while they move in a network. The mobility of mobile agents allows them to be created, deployed, and terminated without disrupting the network configuration. [13] Mobile agents are programs being sent across the network from the client to the server or vice versa. An agent that can be executed after being transferred over the network will be called an agent host [13]. A software agent is a common name and describes a software entity that computerizes some of the regular or difficult tasks on behalf of human or other agents. Mobile agents can travel in network following their itinerary and carrying logic and data to perform a set of management tasks at each of the visited nodes in order to meet their designed objectives [13].

The concept of remote programming using mobile agents is considered as an alternative to the traditional client-server programming based on the remote procedure call or the static distributed object paradigm (e.g. CORBA).A software agent is recognized by a life-cycle model, a computational model, a security model, and a communication model. But a mobile agent is additionally identified by a basic agent model and navigation model.

4.2 Why mobile agent?

After initial euphoria of mobile agent, now expectations of research community from mobile agent are more realistic. After decade of first introduction of mobile agents, it is now clear that mobile are best suited for remote information retrieval. Considering nature of mobile computing where computing hosts are away from each other and in such scenario if we want to know what is happening on remote host, use of mobile agent become unavoidable. Therefore detection of presence of rogue access point in wired, wireless or hybrid (wired as well as wireless mixed) type of network is a fit case for use of mobile agent for such detection. [14]

5. Architecture of Rogue access point detection using mobile agent

Here we propose 2 architectures to detect rogue access point using mobile agent. Below are abbreviations used in these architectures.

SA- Server Application
CA- Client Application
MAS- Mobile Agent System
MA- Mobile Agent

Case-I Proposed mobile agent based architecture for rogue access point detection.

5.1 Initial Set-up

As shown in Fig. 1, consider a hybrid network (wired + wireless). Wired network is established with the help of layer-2 switch. Authorized access point is connected this layer-2 switch. We will develop client-server software where server part(SA) will keep generating sufficient long alpha numeric string after every 2 minutes and will broadcast this string over entire network (wired as well as wireless). Here in this architecture we will deploy SA on central server. CA will be deployed on each authorized computer in the network. CA will send acknowledgement to SA, every time it receives alpha-numeric string from SA. CA when receives string from SA, stores it in text file on client computer on which it is deployed. MAS will be deployed on all authorized computers in network. As and when new computers will come in network, system administrator is supposed to deploy CA and MAS on these new computers. Only after such deployment these new computers will be allowed to operate in network. As shown in Fig. 1 in case-I attacker installs rogue access point either in NIC (Network Interface Card) port or in switch port. Our target is to detect this rogue access point. Behind this rogue access point there will be unauthorized computer i.e., computer 7. This computer 7 will not have MAS and CA installed on it.

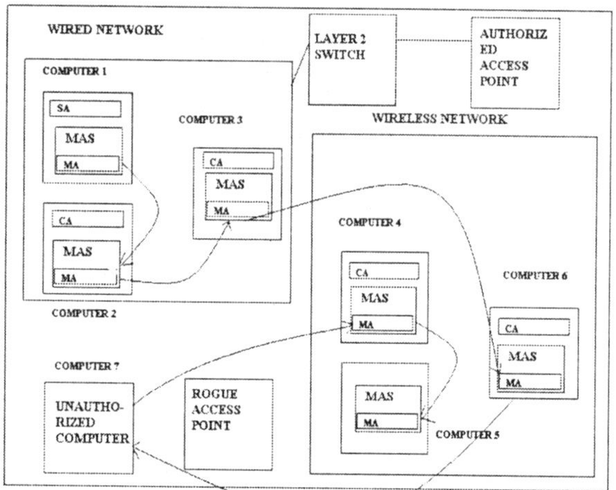

HYBRID NETWORK (WIRED – WIRELESS)

Fig. 1 Proposed mobile agent based architecture for rogue access point detection case-I

5.2 Detection Methodology

Initially SA will start generating alpha-numeric strings after every 2 minutes and subsequently will broadcast them over entire network. Computers which will be active at that time will record these strings and will acknowledge them. Mean time MA will start from central server. SA with itself will have file containing so far generated alpha-numeric strings. MA will take this file from SA. MA will select any active computer from network randomly and will visit that computer. Say computer 2 as shown in Fig. 1. After reaching there MA will ask computer 2 to produce any past generated alpha-numeric string. This selection of past-generated, to be asked, alpha-numeric key will be totally random in manner so that attacker will find it difficult in guessing the pattern of selection. As computer 2 is an authorized computer, it will have that alpha-numeric key with it and computer 2 will produce it and will get authenticated. After this MA will head for another new computer by using random computer selection method. Say computer 3 as shown in Fig. 1. Just like computer 2, as computer 3 is also authorized computer it will also get authenticated by MA. After this MA will again run random algorithm and will select next computer to visit. Say computer 6. Computer 6 will also get authenticated as it is also authorized computer. After this let us assume MA tries to visit computer 7 which is unauthorized computer. As computer 7 will not have MAS and CA deployed on it, MA will not get executed on computer 7. As MA is not getting executed on one of computers of your network, this will be considered as serious offence and access point connected that computer will be declared as rogue access point. In this way we managed to detect rogue access point. After visiting all computers MA will return to central server and will take newly updated file of alpha-numeric strings from SA. After that it will again keep visiting computers in network in above mentioned manner.

Case-II Proposed mobile agent based architecture for rogue access point detection

5.3 Initial Set-up

Set up for case-II will be slightly different from set-up of case-I. As shown in Fig. 2 most of part of setup will be same as of case-I. In case-II we will assume that unauthorized computer i.e. in our case computer 7 will have MAS and CA deployed on it. This might happen if an attacker is from inside of network. Although an attacker from outside of network can also obtain MAS and CA on its computer. In this case attacker will copy file containing past generated alpha-numeric strings, from any one of computers from your network. In this case this unauthorized computer might get authenticated by MA wrongly. To overcome this problem following methodology is used.

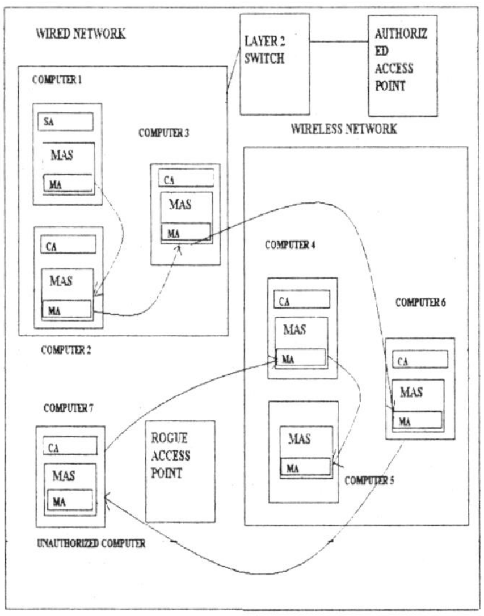

HYBRID NETWORK (WIRED + WIRELESS)

Fig. 2 Proposed mobile agent based architecture for rogue access point detection case-II

5.4 Detection Methodology

Just like case-I, here again MA will visit computer 7(unauthorized computer with MAS, CA and copied database file which contains past generated alpha-numeric strings). Here computer 7 will have database file with its created date as date on which it has got copied. MA here can check entries in file. If file has alpha-numeric strings of past few days and has recent date as its date of creation then this will be marked as suspicion by MA as this will never happen i.e. recent file creation date and past alpha-numeric string entries. In this way even if attacker manages to copy database file, corresponding rogue access point can be detected.

6. Advantages of mobile agent method

1. As it does not use any signature checking, it is free from spoofing attacks.
2. Can be used in any type LAN i.e. wired, wireless or both.
3. Because of increase in processing power of client, overhead generated by MA will much less.
4. With progress in time, database file will have more entries resulting into stronger authentication.
5. Detection is protocol neutral
6. Can detect layer-2 as well as layer-3 access points.
7. Will generate less false alarms.
8. Mobile agents add fault-tolerance. The network is not vulnerable to a single-point of failure.
9. It is extremely difficult for an intruder to disrupt working of mobile agent based system.
10. Mobile agents can take advantage of the inherent parallelism of large networks to offer performance improvements over conventional centralized security monitoring by distributing the workload over the network.
11. Distributed rogue access detection using mobile agent scales well as more agents can be added when new computers are added to the network. Maintaining and upgrading the mobile agent based system can be accomplished by dispatching or cloning new agents and retracting or disposing of old agents.
12. Agents can be adaptively assigned to different tasks spanning a range of responsibilities from intrusion detection and diagnosis, to reconfiguration and recovery.
13. Agents can be developed to run on heterogeneous computer systems and take advantage of the built-in agent communication capabilities.

7. Conclusion

In this paper we have proposed architecture for detecting rogue access point in IEEE 802.11 networks using mobile agent. Our method overcomes various drawbacks of existing methods available for said purpose. Further research on issues like after how many minutes alpha-numeric strings can be generated, total number of mobile agents to be used, strengthening string generation etc. can be done.

8. References

[1] "Threats to Wireless Local Area Network (WLAN) and Countermeasures", A. V. Dhaygude, K.R. Patil, A. A. Sawant, ICONS' 07, January 27-29, 2007, Erode, Tamilnadu, India.

[2] AirMagnet. http://www.airmagnet.com.

[3] NetStumbler. http://www.netstumbler.com.

[4] AirDefense, Wireless LAN Security. http://airdefense.net.

[5] Rogue Access Point Detection: Automatically Detect and Manage Wireless Threats to Your Network. http://www.proxim.com.

[6] Cisco Wireless LAN Solution Engine (WLSE). http://www.cisco.com/en/US/products/sw/cscowork/ps3915/.

[7] A. Adya, V. Bahl, R. Chandra, and L. Qiu. Architecture and techniques for diagnosing faults in IEEE 802.11 infrastructure networks. In Proc. ACM MOBICOM, September 2004.

[8] P. Bahl, R. Chandra, J. Padhye, L. Ravindranath, M. Singh, A. Wolman, and B. Zill. Enhancing the security of corporate Wi-Fi networks using DAIR. In Proc. ACM MOBISYS, 2006.

[9] H. Yin, G. Chen, and J. Wang. Detecting Protected Layer-3 Rogue APs. In Proceedings of the Fourth IEEE International Conference on Broadband Communications, Networks, and Systems (BROADNETS), Raleigh, NC, September 2007.

[10] R. Beyah, S. Kangude, G. Yu, B. Strickland, and J. Copeland. Rogue access point detection using temporal traffic characteristics. In Proc. IEEE GLOBECOM, Dec 2004.

[11] C. Mano, A. Blaich, Q. Liao, Y. Jiang, D. Salyers, D. Cieslak, and A. Striegel. RIPPS: Rogue identifying packet payload slicer detecting unauthorized wireless hosts through network traffic conditioning. ACM Transactions on Information Systems and Security

[12] Wei Wei, Kyoungwon Suh,Bing Wang, "Passive Online Rogue Access Point Detection Using Sequential Hypothesis Testing with TCP ACK-Pairs" IMC'07, October 24-26, 2007, San Diego, California, USA.

[13] Shamila Makki, Subbarao V. Wunnava, "Application of Mobile Agents in Managing the Traffic in the Network and Improving the Reliability and Quality of Service" IAENG International Journal of Computer Science, 32:4, IJCS_32_4_16, 12 November 2006

[14] Antonio Carzaniga, Gian Pietro Picco, Giovanni Vigna, "Is Code Still Moving Around? Looking Back at a Decade of Code Mobility",

A Game-Theoretic Model for Dynamic Load Balancing in Distributed Systems

Shailendra S. Aote[1] and Dr. M. U. Kharat[2]
[1]III Sem., M. Tech., PG Dept. of CSE, G.H.R.C.E., Nagpur
[2]Professor, PG Dept. of CSE, G.H.R.C.E., Nagpur

Abstract

Load balancing is the process of improving the performance of a parallel and distributed system through a redistribution of load among the processors. In this paper we present the framework for obtaining a user optimal load balancing scheme in distributed system. We formulate the Dynamic load balancing problem in distributed systems as a noncooperative game among users. The system model considers various parameters and accordingly the load balancing algorithm is defined. For the proposed noncooperative load balancing game, we consider the structure of the Nash equilibrium. Based on this structure we derive a new distributed load balancing algorithm. Our focus is to define the load balancing problem and the scheme to overcome it, by using new area called game theory.

Keywords : *Game theory, Distributed System, Dynamic load balancing*

1. Introduction

A distributed system can be viewed as a collection of computing and communication resources shared by active users. When the demand for computing power increases the load balancing problem becomes important. A general formulation of this problem is as follows: given a large number of jobs, find the allocation of jobs to computers optimizing a given objective function (e.g. total execution time). Load balancing is to ensure that every processor in the system does approximately the same amount of work at any point of time. Processes may migrate from one node to another even in the middle of execution to ensure equal workload. Algorithms for load balancing have to rely on the assumption that the on hand information at each node is accurate to prevent processes from being continuously circulated about the system without any progress. Load balancing is one of prerequisites to utilize the full resources of parallel and distributed systems. Load balancing may be centralized in a single processor or distributed among all the processing elements that participate in the load balancing process.

There are three typical approaches to load balancing problem in distributed systems:

1. *Cooperative approach*: In this case there are several decision makers (e.g. jobs, computers) that cooperate in making the decisions.
2. *Noncooperative approach*: In this case there are several decision makers (e.g. users, jobs) that are not allowed to cooperate in making decisions. Each decision maker optimizes its own response time independently of the others and they all eventually reach equilibrium.
3. *Global approach*: In this case there is only one decision maker that optimizes the response time of the entire system.

Load balancing algorithms can also be classified as static and dynamic.

1. *Static*: Static load-balancing algorithms assume that all information governing load-balancing decisions that can include the characteristics of the jobs, the computing nodes, and the communication network are known in advance. Load-balancing decisions are made deterministically or probabilistically at compile time and remain constant during runtime. The static algorithms have one major disadvantage – it assumes that the characteristics of the computing resources and communication network are all known in advance and remain constant.
2. *Dynamic*: Dynamic load-balancing algorithms attempt to use the runtime state information to make more informative load-balancing decisions. Undoubtedly, the static approach is easier to implement and has minimal runtime overhead. However, dynamic approaches may result in better performance.

2. Working Strategy

Daniel Grosu and Anthony T. Chronopoulos [2] presented the static load balancing scheme in distributed system. They found a formal framework for characterizing user-optimal allocation schemes in distributed systems. They gave a characterization of the Nash equilibrium and a distributed algorithm for computing it. They also compare the performance of noncooperative load balancing scheme with that of other existing schemes. Daniel Grosu, Anthony T. Chronopoulos and Ming-Ying Leung [5] also found the solution for load balancing problem by considering cooperative approach. They have shown fairness index is one. As the game theory is the promising area, Eitan Altman, Hisao Kameda and Yoshihisa Hosokawa [10] found the existence and uniqueness of Nash equilibria for routing games that arises in load balancing in distributed system. Riky Subrata, Albert Y. Zomaya, Bjorn Landfeldt [6] generates the game theoretic model and algorithm to solve the grid load balancing problem. For that they combine the merits of both the load balancing schemes to generate the new hybrid one. Finally Sandeep Sharma, Sarabjit Singh, and Meenakshi Sharma [4] have studied various load balancing schemes with the parameters overload rejection, fault tolerance, stability, dynamic or static, cooperative and resource utilization, where they found static load balancing algorithms are more stable in compare to dynamic and it is also ease to predict the behavior of static, but at a same time dynamic distributed algorithms are always considered better than static algorithms.

3. System Modeling

The parameters involved in modeling are defined and presented as below with m number of nodes and n numbers of users.

X_i = Processing rate of the node i

φ_j = Job generating rate

Sji = Fraction assign to the node i by user j

μ_i = Capacity of the node i to carry the weight

where i = 1, 2, 3,......, m

j = 1, 2, 3,.......,n

$\varphi = \sum_{j=1}^{n} \phi_j$ is the total job arrival rate in the system.

The system model is presented in Figure.

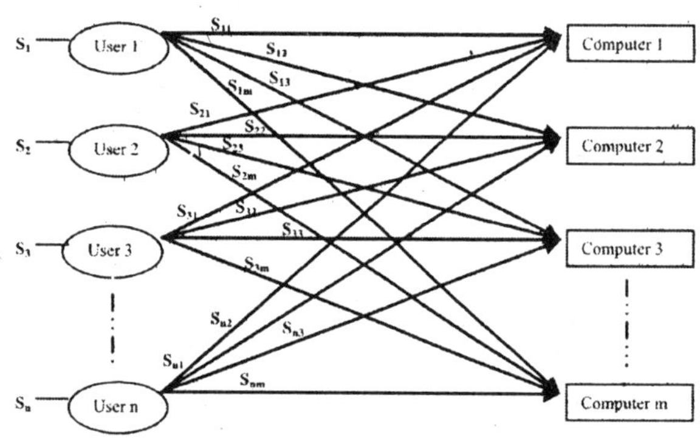

Fig. 1 The Distributed System Model

The users have to decide, how to distribute their jobs to computers such that they will operate optimally. Thus user j (j = 1,.......,n) must find the fraction S_{ji} of all its jobs that are assigned to computer i

$(\sum_{i=1}^{m} s_{ji} = 1$ and $0 \le Sji \le 1$, i =1,....., m) such that the expected execution time of its jobs is minimized.

Let S_{ji} be the fraction of jobs that user j sends to computer i. The vector Sj = (S_{j1}, S_{j2}, ..., S_{jn}) is called the *load balancing strategy* of user j. The vector S = (S1, S2,..., Sn) is called the *strategy profile* of the load balancing game.

Definition 3.1 A *Nash equilibrium* of the load balancing game defined above is a strategy profile S such that for every user j

$$Sj \ \varepsilon \ \arg \min_{Sj} Dj\,(S1, S_2,...., Sj,......S_n)$$

A strategy profile S is a Nash equilibrium if no user can benefit by deviating unilaterally from its load balancing strategy to another feasible one.

At each node i

$$\sum_{j=1}^{n} \phi_j \le X_i$$

and $$\sum_{j=1}^{n} s_{ji} \le \mu_i$$

should satisfy.

Algorithm for determining the condition, that is, when to execute the algorithm for load balancing is as follows.

1. if $Xi < \sum_{j=1}^{n} \phi_j$

   Respond to user j and block the incoming process

   Go to step 4.

2. if $\mu_i < \sum_{j=1}^{n} s_{ji}$

   Calculate

   $$P = \sum_{j=1}^{n} s_{ji} - \mu_i$$

3. Select S_{ji} such that

   $S_{ji} > 0$ and

   S_{ji} has a value nearer to P.

4. Change the strategy of user j for which value of P satisfies.

At the step 4 execution of Nash Equilibrium algorithm begins which is use to change the strategy of user j. The computation of Nash equilibrium might require some coordination between the users. From the practical point of view we need decentralization and this can be obtained by using distributed greedy best response algorithms. In these algorithms each user updates from time to time its load balancing strategy by computing the best response against the existing load balancing strategies of the other users.

The execution of this algorithm is initiated periodically or when the system parameters are changed. Once the Nash equilibrium is reached, the users will continue to use the same strategies and the system remains in equilibrium. This equilibrium is maintained until a new execution of the algorithm is initiated.

4. Expected Outcome

The physical model of system is simulated along with various parameters. We will check the system under various parameters like overload rejection, fault tolerance, resource utilization and process migration. Outcome involves various outputs regarding to mentioned parameters. The deliberation of these parameters plays important role for proper execution of load balancing algorithm.

When the overload situation occurs then first the overload rejection measures causes to execute the algorithm. Fault tolerance parameter enables an algorithm to continue operating properly in the event of some failure. If the performance of algorithm decreases, the decrease is proportional to the seriousness of the failure, even a small failure can cause total failure in load balancing. Process migration parameter provides when does a system decide to export a process? It decides whether to create it locally or create it on a remote processing element. The algorithm should be capable to decide that it should make changes of load distribution during execution of process or not. Resource utilization include automatic load balancing A distributed system may have unexpected number of processes that demand more processing power. If the algorithm is capable to utilize resources, they can be moved to under load processors more efficiently

5. Conclusion

Load balancing ensures the proper utilization of system resources. Here we have studied the essentials for load balancing by considering the mathematical model. Existence and uniqueness of Nash Equilibria enables us to redistribute the load among the system. Also we have discussed about the expected outcome after simulation carried out. The parameters like overload rejection, fault tolerance, resource utilization and process migration are suggested to study for optimal utilization of load.

6. References

[1] www.gametheory.net

[2] Daniel Grosu and Anthony T. Chronopoulos. *"A Game-Theoretic Model and Algorithm for Load Balancing in Distributed Systems", 2002*

[3] Penmatsa, S.; Chronopoulos, A.T. *"Dynamic Multi-User Load Balancing in Distributed Systems", 2007.*

[4] *Sandeep Sharma, Sarabjit Singh, and Meenakshi Sharma. "Performance Analysis of Load Balancing Algorithms", 2008.*

[5] *Daniel Grosu, Anthony T. Chronopoulos and Ming-Ying Leung. "Load Balancing in Distributed Systems: An Approach Using Cooperative Games", 2002.*

[6] *Riky Subrata, Albert Y. Zomaya, Bjorn Landfeldt. "Game-Theoretic Approach for Load Balancing in Computational Grids", 2008.*

[7] Neeraj Nehra, R.B. Patel, V.K. Bhat, *"A Framework for Distributed Dynamic Load Balancing in Heterogeneous Cluster", 2007*

[8] *Erol Gelenbe and Rakesh Kushwaha. "Dynamic Load Balancing in Distributed Systems", 1994.*

[9] Subhash Suri, Csaba Toth, Yunhong Zhou, *"Uncoordinated Load Balancing and Congestion Games in P2P Systems".*

[10] *Eitan Altman, Hisao Kameda and Yoshihisa Hosokawa, "Nash Equilibria in Load Balancing In Distributed Computer Systems", 2002.*

[11] *Subhash Suri, Csaba Toth, Yunhong Zhou, "Selfish Load Balancing and Atomic Congestion Games", 2004.*

[12] H. Ammar and Su Deng, "A simple Dynamic Load Balancing Algorithm for Homogeneous Distributed Systems", 1988.

A Unified Framework for Distributed Shared Memory Consistency Models

Prof. Bal Gopal[1] and Pankaj Kumar[2]
[1]Dept. of Computer Application, Integral University, Lucknow
pan79jan@yahoomail.com
[2]Research Scholar, Computer Application, Integral University, Lucknow
pk79jan@rediffmail.com

Abstract

Distributed Shared Memory (DSM) is an architectural approach that allows processors to support a single shared address space that is implemented with physically distributed memory. The consistency model of a DSM system specifies the ordering constraints on concurrent memory accesses by multiple processors. Lots of Consistency Model are defined by a wide variety of source including architecture system, application programmer etc.

The paper reviews and discusses the different Distributed Shared Memory Consistency Models and presents a Unified Framework. This paper considers only the 'read' and 'write' memory operation to define the unified framework.

Keywords: *DSM, MCM*

1. Introduction

A Distributed Shared Memory (DSM) system provides application programmers the illusion of shared memory on top of massage passing distributed system, which facilitates the task of parallel programming in distributed system. DSM is technique for making multicomputers easier to program by simulating a shared address space on them. In simple way we can say that DSM represents a successful hybrid of two parallel computer classes i.e. shared memory and distributed memory. It provides the shared memory abstraction in system with physically distributed memories and consequently combine the advantages of both approaches [3, 4, 6, 9, 16].

A memory consistency model, or memory model, for a multiprocessor specifies how memory behaves with respect to read and write operations from multiple processors [3, 5]. With respect to the programmer's point of view, the model enables correct reasoning about the memory operations in a program. From the system designer's point of view, the model specifies acceptable memory behaviors for the system. As such, the memory consistency model influences many aspects of system design, including the design of programming languages, compilers, and the underlying hardware. In order to enhance performance, multiprocessors tend to implement sophisticated memory structures. These memories may replicate data through constructs such as caches and write buffers. Furthermore, the time required to access a data object may vary between processes and between objects. Any of these architectural features allow processes to have inconsistent views of memory, which, in turn, can result in unexpected program outcomes [5, 10, 15].

A memory consistency model is a set of guarantees describing constraints on the outcome of sequences of interleaved and simultaneous operations. Fewer guarantees allow more performance optimizations but yield machines that are very complex to understand and program. It is thus essential to provide multiprocessor programmers with a precise description of the memory model of the underlying machine. Several memory consistency models have been described in the literature. These descriptions arise from a wide variety of sources including architecture, system, and database designers, application programmers, and theoreticians. These descriptions use different types and degrees of formalism and hence are difficult to compare. Others are informal and sometimes ambiguous. There is no single unified formalization that describes the memory models addressed in the literature or provided by several existing machines.

2. Memory Consistency in DSM

The consistency model of a DSM system specifies the ordering constraints on concurrent memory accesses by multiple processors, and hence has fundamental impact on DSM systems' programming convenience and implementation efficiency [18].

DSM allows processes to assume a globally shared virtual memory even though they execute on nodes that do not physically share memory. The DSM software provide the abstraction of a globally shared memory in which each processor can access any data item without the programmer having to worry about where the data is or how to obtain its value In contrast in the native programming model on networks of workstations message passing the programmer must decide when a processor needs to communicate with whom to communicate and what data to be send. For programs with complex data structures and sophisticated parallelization strategies this can become a daunting task [7, 19].

On a DSM system the programmer can focus on algorithmic development rather than on managing partitioned data sets and communicating values. The programming interfaces to DSM systems may differ in a variety of respects. The memory model refers to how updates to distributed shared memory are rejected to the processes in the system. The most intuitive model of distributed shared memory is that a read should always return the last value written unfortunately the notion of the last value written is not well defined in a distributed system. [3, 18, 19].

The memory consistency model can be categorized into parts one which is based on read and write memory operation called as uniform model and the other which is based on synchronization operation also called hybrid model. The synchronization operations are mapped to corresponding operations provided by concurrency control [2, 6, 12].

3. Proposed Framework

The main component of our framework is the consistency models which considers only read and write memory operation to define consistency condition. We identify the characteristics that are inherent to all memory consistency models and the characteristics that are model-specific. The framework is the combination of strong and relaxed memory model which proposes a simple and general definition of memory consistency models.

The proposed framework is based on the models which come in to the category of uniform model. The unified framework is categorized by four properties, order of access; concurrency; atomicity and scope. The order of access defines the sequence in which accesses are seen by interested parties. The concurrency of access defines if nodes can concurrently access the data and the modes in which they can access it. The scope determines the set of data that is to be kept consistent and atomicity defines whether the propagation of updates is done on per access basis or whether several local updates can be done before a batched update is sent out [2]. We have taken Atomic consistency (AC), Sequential consistency (SC), Causal consistency (CC), Processor consistency (PC), PRAM, Cache consistency and Slow memory consistency models for our unified framework which is shown in Fig. 1

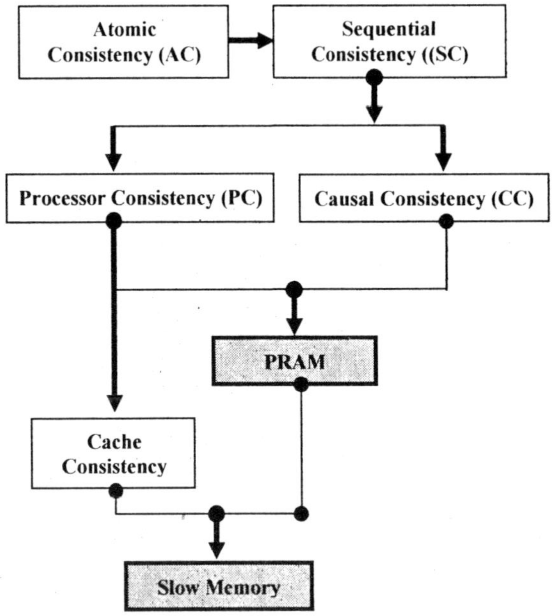

Fig. 1 Structure of uniform Frameworks

The first two AC & SC is the strong consistency whereas the other one are relaxed consistency. Atomic Consistency is the strict consistency among all the models of framework. If we follow the path from Top to Bottom, The sequential consistency is evolved from the atomic consistency so it inherits some property of atomic consistency. The processor consistency and the causal consistency i.e. defined by the sequential consistency. The PRAM model is evolved by combining the processor consistency as well as causal consistency. The cache consistency is defined by processor consistency and based on cache coherency. Slow memory model is the combination of PRAM and Cache Consistency. But if follow the path from Bottom to Top, the Sequential Consistency is the combination of Processor and Causal consistency and Processor Consistency is the combination of Pram and Cache consistency.

3.1 Atomic Consistency (AC)

This is the strictest of all consistency models. With atomic consistency, operations take effect at some point in an operation interval. It is easiest to think of operation intervals as dividing time into non-overlapping, consecutive slots [12, 18].

Tanenbaum describes atomic consistency as that in which, "any read to a memory location x returns the value stored by the most recent write operation to x". For example, the clock cycle of a memory bus could serve as an operation interval. Multiple accesses during the same operation interval are allowed, which causes a problem if reads and rites to the same location occur in the same operation interval. One solution is to define read operations to take effect at read-begin time and write operations to take effect at write-end time. This is called static atomic consistency. With dynamic AC, operations can take effect at any point in the operation interval; as long as the resulting history is equivalent to some serial execution [12, 20]. Atomic consistency is often used as a base model when evaluating the performance of an MCM.

3.2 Sequential Consistency (SC)

Sequential consistency was first defined by Lamport in 1979. He defined a memory system to be sequentially consistent if the result of any execution is the same as if the operations of all the processors were executed in some sequential order, and the operations of each individual processor appear in this sequence in the order specified by its program [1]. This is equivalent to the one-copy serializability concept found in work on concurrency control for database systems. In a sequentially consistent system, all processors must agree on the order of observed effects [3, 12, 17]. The following is a legal execution history for SC but not for AC [17, 18]:

P1	W(x)1				
P2			W(y)2		
P3		R(y)2		R(x)0	R(x)1

Note that R(y)2 by processor P3 reads a value that has not been written yet! Of course, this is not possible in any real physical system. However, it shows a surprising flexibility of the SC model. Another reason why this is not a legal history for atomic consistency is that the write operations W(x)1 and W(y)2 appear commuted at processor P3. Sequential consistency has been the canonical memory consistency model for a long time. However, many multi-processor machines actually implement a slightly weaker model called processor consistency [4].

3.3 Causal Consistency (CC)

Causal Consistency means that all processor see all causally related shared access in the same order [6]. Mosberger describes Causal consistency as "A memory is causally consistent if all machines agree on the order of causally related events. Causally unrelated events (concurrent events) can be observed in different orders" [18].

A memory is causally consistent if all processors agree on the order of causally related events. Causally unrelated events (concurrent events) can be observed in different orders [1, 6, 10].

For example: the following is a legal execution history under CC but not under SC.

P1	W(x)1		W(x)3		
P2	R(x)1	W(x)2			
P3	R(x)1			R(x)3	R(x)2
P4	R(x)1			R(x)2	R(x)3

Note that W(x)1 and W(x)2 are causally related as P2 observed the first write by P1. Furthermore, P3 and P4 observe the accesses W(x)2 and W(x)3 in different orders, which would not be legal under SC

3.4 Processor Consistency (PC)

Processor Consistency is perhaps the clearest example of the problem that can arise if it is not defined the consistency model in formal way. In fact it is a family of memory consistency models that are based on the same idea but have small difference. These differences led to different memory behavior and consequently to different memory consistency models. The basic idea of these memory consistency models is to relax some conditions imposed by sequential consistency and to require only that write operation issued by the same processor are observed by all processor in the order they were issued [12]. Goodman defined PC to be stronger than coherence but weaker than SC. PC can be interpreted as a combination of coherence and PRAM. Thus, every PC history is also coherent and PRAM. However, for a history to be PC it not only has to be coherent and PRAM but those two conditions also must be satisfiable in a mutually consistent way. It is easiest to think of PC as a consistency model that requires a history to be coherent and PRAM simultaneously, rather than individually. That is, processors must agree on the order of writes from each processor but can disagree on the order of writes by different processors, as long as those writes are to different locations [6, 17, 18]. For example

P1	W(x)1	W(c)1	R(y)0
P2	W(y)1	W(c)1	R(x)0

Notice that P1 observes accesses in the order:
W(x)1, W(c)1, R(y)0 , W(y)1 , W(c)1
While P2 observes accesses in the order:
W(y)1, W(c)1, R(x)0, W(x)1, W(c)1

That is, P1 and P2 disagree on the order of writes to location c. As there is no consistent ordering that would remove this disagreement, the history fails to be PC. The differences between PC and SC are subtle enough that Goodman claims most applications give the same results under these two models.

3.5 Pipelined RAM (PRAM)

The acronym PRAM is often used as a shorthand for Parallel Random Access Machine which has nothing in common with the Pipelined RAM consistency model. The reasoning that led to this model was as follows: consider a multi-processor where each processor has a local copy of the shared memory. Mosberger describes PRAM consistency is consistency in which ".all processors (machines) observe the writes from a single processor (machine) in the same order while they may disagree on the writes by different processors (machines)" [18].

For the memory to be scalable, an access should be independent of the time it takes to access the other processors' memories. On a read, a PRAM would simply return the value stored in the local copy of the memory. On a write, it would update the local copy first and broadcast the new value to the other processors [6, 12, 18].

Assuming a constant time for initiating a broadcast operation, the goal of making the cost for a read or write constant is thus achieved. In terms of ordering constraints, this is equivalent to requiring that all processors observe the writes from a single processor in the same order while they may disagree on the order of writes by different processors. For example

P1	W(x)1		W(x)3		
P2		R(x)1	W(x)2		
P3				R(x)1	R(x)2
P4				R(x)2	R(x)1

P3 and P4 observe the writes by P1 and P2 in different orders, although W(x)1 and W(x)2 are potentially causally related.

3.6 Cache Consistency (Coherence)

Cache consistency and coherence are synonymous. Coherence is a location-relative weakening of SC. Recall that under SC, all processors have to agree on some sequential order of execution for all accesses. Coherence only requires that accesses are sequentially consistent on a per-location basis. Clearly, SC implies coherence but not vice versa. Thus, coherence is strictly weaker than SC [3, 6, 17, 18]. The example below is a history that is coherent but not sequentially consistent:

P1	W(x)1	R(y)0
P2	W(y)1	R(x)0

Clearly, any serial execution that respects program order starts with writing 1 into either x or y. It is therefore impossible that both read accesses return 0. However, the accesses to x can be linearized into R(x)0, W(x)1 and so can the accesses to y: R(y)0, W(y)1. The history is therefore coherent, but not SC. In essence, coherence removes the ordering constraints that program order imposes on accesses to different memory locations.

3.7 Slow Memory

Slow memory is a location relative weakening of PRAM. It requires that all processors agree on the order of observed writes to each location by a single processor. Furthermore, local writes must be visible immediately (as in the PRAM model). The name for this model was chosen because writes propagate slowly through the system. Slow memory is probably one of the weakest uniform consistency models that can still be used for intercrosses communication. m. However, this algorithm guarantees physical exclusion only. There is no guarantee of logical exclusion [6,18]. For example, after two processes P1 and P2 were subsequently granted access to a critical section and both wrote two variables a and b, then a third processP3may enter the critical region and read the value of as written by P1 and the value of b as written by P2. Thus, for P3 it looks like P1 and P2 had had simultaneous access to the critical section. This problem is inherent to slow memory because the knowledge that an access to one location has performed cannot be used to infer that accesses to other locations have also performed. Slow memory does not appear to be of any practical significance.

4. Relating Memory Models of Unified Framework

Defining memory consistency models formally makes it easier to compare and relate them. The Fig. 2 shows the relationship among the different models of uniform model.

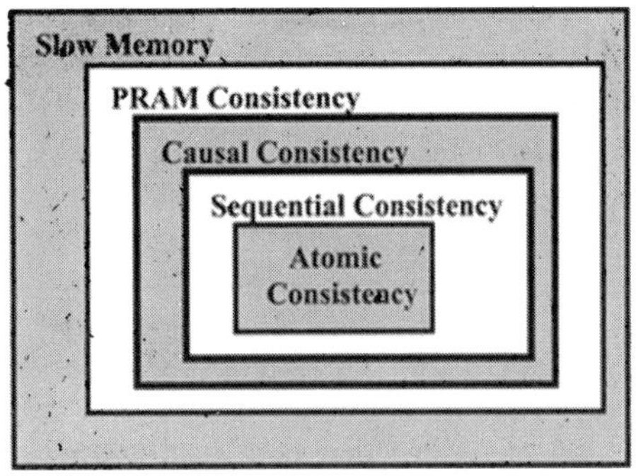

Fig. 2 Relation b/w models of unified framework

Each rectangle shows the possible results that can be produced under the unified framework. As the figure shows that the strongest model is Atomic consistency model because it imposes a total order on execution and requires real time order to be preserved. Sequential consistency imposes only a total order on execution. So atomic consistency is strictly stronger than the sequential consistency.

Causal consistency is strictly stronger than the PRAM consistency. Both memory models require that program order on running process. Causal model requires also that all processors must respect the read by order. PRAM consistency is strictly stronger than Slow memory since slow memory only requires programmers order.

5. Conclusion

In this paper we presented a Unified Framework to describe different memory consistency models. The proposed framework considered only the read and write operation and it is not depend upon the synchronization operation so the models taken for defining the framework shows the uniformity property. The Atomic Consistency and Sequential Consistency is the strong consistency. The Atomic Consistency is also the strict consistency. Relations between different consistency models are also defined. A framework can also be designed by using the read and write memory operation as well as synchronization operation.

6. References

[1] L. Lamport, "How to Make a Multiprocessor Computer That Correctly Executes Multiprocess Programs", IEEE Transaction Computers, vol. C-28, no. 9, pp. 690-691 September 1979

[2] S. Weber, P.A. Nixon and B Tangney," A flexible Frame work for Consistency Management in Object Oriented Distributed Shared Memory", Department of Computer Science, Trinity College, Ireland, Oct. 13, 1998.

[3] Paul Krzyzanowski "Distributed Shared Memory and Memory Consistency Models" Rutgers University – CS 417: Distributed Systems ©1998, 2001.

[4] Z. Huang, C. Sun and M. Purvis "Selection-based Weak Sequential Consistency Models for Distributed Shared Memory" Departments of Computer & Information Science University of Otago, Dunedin, New Zealand , School of Computing & Information Technology Griffith University, Brisbane, Australia.

[5] Lisa Higham, Jalal Kawash and Nathaly Verwaal, "Define and Comparing Memory Consistency Model" 1997 ISCA, Proceeding of PDCS'97.

[6] Abdelfatah Aref Yahya and Rana Mohamad Idrees Bader "Distributed Shared Memory Consistency Object-based Model", Journal of Computer Science 3 (1): 57-61, 2007 ISSN1549-3636© 2007 Science Publications.

[7] J. Silcock "A Consistency Model for Distributed Shared Memory on RHODOS among Shared Memory Consistency Models" Deakin University, 1997.

[8] John B.Carter, John K. Bennett and Willy Zwaenepoel "Techniques for Reducing Consistency-Related Communication in Distributed Shared Memory Systems, "Rice University, TOCS95.

[9] Changhun Lee "Distributed Shared Memory" Proceedings on the 15th CISL Winter Workshop Kushu, Japan ¢ February 2002.

[10] Sarita V. Adve, Member, IEEE, Vijay S. Pai, Student Member, IEEE, and Parthasarathy Ranganathan, Student Member, IEEE "Recent Advances in Memory Consistency Models for Hardware Shared Memory Systems" proceedings Of The Ieee, Vol. 87, No. 3, March 1999.

[11] Albert Meixner and Daniel J. Sorin "Dynamic Verification of Memory Consistency in Cache-Coherent Multithreaded Computer Architectures" Duke University, Department of Electrical and Computer Engineering, Technical Report #2006-1, April 18, 2006.

[12] Alba Cristina Magalhães Alves de Melo "Defining Uniform and Hybrid Memory Consistency Models on a Unified Framework" Proceedings of the 32nd Hawaii International Conference on System Sciences -1999 IEEE.

[13] Jason F. Cantin, Student Member, IEEE, Mikko H. Lipasti, Member, IEEE, and James E. Smith, Member, IEEE "The Complexity of Verifying Memory Coherence and Consistency" IEEE Transactions On Parallel And Distributed Systems, Vol. 16, No. 7, July 2005.

[14] Robert C. Steinke and Gary J. Nutt "A Unified Theory of Shared Memory Consistency" Journal of the ACM, Vol. V, No. N, Month 20YY, Pages 1–47 2002.

[15] Z. Huang, C. Sun and M. Purvis "A View-based Consistency Model based on Transparent Data Selection in Distributed Shared Memory" Technical Report OUCS-2004-03.

[16] Ing. Thomes Seidmann," Distributed Shared memory in Modern Operating System" Ph.D. Thesis, Slovak University of Technology, January, 2004.

[17] Jalal Y. Kawash" Limitations and Capabilities of Weak Memory Consistency Systems" Ph.D. Thesis Calgary, Alberta January, 2000.

[18] D. Mosberger: "Memory consistency models", Operating Systems Review, 17(1):18-26, Jan. 1993.

[19] Benny Wang-Leung Cheung, Cho-Li Wang and Francis Chimoon Lau, "Migrating-Home Protocol for Software Distributed Shared Memory", Journal of Information Science and Engineering, 2000.

[20] Jerzy Brzezinski, Michal Szychowick, "Replication of Checkpoints in Recoverable DSM System", Proceedings of 21 IASTED, Feb 2003.

Resource Discovery and Task Assignment for Distributed System using Semantic Service

Sudhir G. Shikalpure and Laxman D. Netak
Dr. Babasaheb Ambedkar Technological, University, Lonere. India
shikalpure@rediffmail.com ldnetak@yahoo.com

Abstract

Distributed Systems (DS) offer mechanism to share dynamic, heterogeneous resources, which are spread across various multiple organizational domains. The key issue in DS to discover and locate resources. A time efficient along with location and Resource Discovery (RD) is very important. In the past research, scientist proposed several approaches to discover and locate resources such as syntax based resources discovery. In this paper Semantic approach is studied that use ontology knowledge base framework which provide vocabularies with explicitly defined and automatically machine-interpretable meanings to discover and locate resources. An experimental result of task parallelism shows that Semantic approach is performing well as compared to other approaches.

1. Introduction

Desktops and workstations are becoming more powerful and more ubiquitous. These powerful machines are usually not utilized to their full capabilities and have enough idle cycles available for use. There has been significant effort to build high throughput delivering systems out of such workstations. These high throughput systems are gaining popularity among scientists who need to run large simulations. The systems are growing to accommodate larger numbers of workstations with growing demand. Discovery of available resources in such environments is a challenging problem.

Distributed computing environment supporting scientific applications that require high throughput computation. The resources are contributed to the system by a number of different autonomous entities. Applications have different requirements for the number and capabilities of the resources they need in order to complete their execution. Building such distributed systems that provide high throughput computing involve challenges like resource discovery, resource scheduling and resource allocation. In this paper we will be concentrating on RD, which is a fundamental problem in large-scale, distributed high throughput computing systems.

RD is the efficient process of determining which resources are best for completion of the task with most effective using the resources in shortest amount of time. Due to the heterogeneous environments resource discovery becomes difficult for the specific request and in distributed system existing resource discovery is highly constrained. [1,2,3].

Therefore semantics can be considered to improve res- ource discovery, while enabling users to state high-level expressive queries. The module can be implem- ented in the knowledge layer of semantic architecture. So information must be described in such way that computer can interpret it and develop its meaning. Computer understandable information is one that is annotated with semantics, which describes the mean- ing of the information. A collection of annotations where their meanings are described is called ontology. Ontology describes the concepts in the domain and also the relationship that hold the concepts. To realize such system a prescribed of the domain knowledge in ontology is needed.

2. Review of Resource Discovery Mechanisms

Different operating system, different organizational domain, lack of portability between platform depe- ndent applications make resource discovery more diff- cult. RD is the process by which a node can become aware of the attribute and the capabilities of other nodes in the network, so a job can complete with most efficient use of resources within shortest amount of time. There are two approaches for resource discovery that can be classified as query based approach and agent based approach in distributed systems. In a query based discovery the resource information store is queried for resource availability. Most of the system follows this approach. Query based system are further differentiate whether the query is perform against centralized database or distributed database. Resource discovery can be categorized in two forms query based resource discovery and agent based resource discovery [4].

In Agent based approach, agents running at individual nodes learn about the existence of each other using a mechanism called distributed awareness.

Each agent maintains information about the other agents periodically and exchanges this information among them. Whenever an agent needs detailed information about individual components of the system we use the information gathered by the distributed awareness mechanism and then assemble dynamically agents capable of reporting the state of remote resources and to negotiate the use of these resources.

In summary, these discovery mechanisms performs on keyword based matching queries from the user requests and poorly in result and allows just simple queries based on the presence or absence of word but with restricted expressive description mechanism. Therefore it is necessary to explicitly, precisely and unambiguously describe resources and specify various resource description and these description should be automatically interpretable and understandable by middleware components.

3. Semantic Approach for Resource Discovery

Distributed systems are heterogeneous environments and metadata themselves are also heterogeneous. In such heterogeneous and dynamic environments key word matching is insufficient to achieve high correct ness resource discovery. In order to improve the correctness of a discovery mechanism, resources must be given well defined meaning carried by semantic information added to the resource descriptions. For example, different virtual organizations may be making use of different terminologies to describe the same resources in system. As a result, the integration of related system resources are difficult task. A Semantic approach can solve this problem enabling the common ontologies facilitate communication between resource providers and users. Semantic serv- ice, as semantic web technologies, enables combination of applications, data, resources, and users specific domain on the system and straight forwardness automation of middleware tasks such as selecting distributed resource for application based on their requirements [5,6]. When a user requests an applic- ation execution for resource discovery, middleware find the set of resources for performing the applic- ation. A semantic appro ach can achieve better resour- ce matching than an attribute based on exact matching of attributes.

4. Exploring the Ontologies

Ontology originate in Greek language, meaning 'the study of being.' In the beginning they developed in Artificial Intelligence for knowledge sharing and reuse. Recently it is used in information retrieval, knowledge management and e-commerce. They provide machine process able semantics of information source that can be communicated between entities.

Ontology can be defined as "a formal, explicit definit- ion of a shared conceptualization". A conceptualiz- ation can be referring an abstract model of some phenomenon in the world that identifies the relevant concepts of that phenomenon. Explicit means that the used concepts and their constraints should be explicitly described and formal means that the ontology should be machine-readable.

According to Karlsruhe Ontology model [8], an ontology with datatypes is a structure O: = (C, T, ≤C, R, A, σR, σA, ≤R, ≤A, I, V, tC, tT, tR, tA) consisting of

- Six disjoint sets C, T, R, A, I and V called concepts, datatypes, relations, attributes, instances and data values respectively.
- Partial orders ≤C on C called concept hierarchy or taxonomy and ≤T on T called type hierarchy.
- Functions mapping σR: R→ C2 called relation signature and σA: A→CxT called attribute signature.
- Partial orders ≤R on R called relation hierarchy and ≤A on A called attribute hierarchy, respectively.
- A function tC: C→ 2I called concept instantiation.
- A function tT: T→ 2V called datatype instantiation.
- A function tR: R→ 2IxI called relation instantiation.
- A function tA: A→ 2IxV called attribute instantiation

The logical model allows the use of reasoner that can check whether the statements and definitions in the ontology are mutually reliable, which concepts cascade under which definitions. The reasoner can therefore help to maintain the hierarchy correctly.

4.1 Knowledge Base

Once we have the entity types, relations, and attributes encoded in ontology, the next feature of the semantic annotation representation are the entity descriptions. It should be possible to identify, describe, and interconn ect the entities in a general, flexible and standard fashion. We call a body of formal knowledge about entities a knowledge base although a bit old-fashion, this term best reflects the representation of non-ontological formal knowledge. A knowledge base is expected to contain mostly instance knowledge data, so other names can also make a good match for such a database. We consider that the ontology (defining all classes, relations, and attributes, together with additional constraints and dependencies) is a sort of schema for the knowledge base and so both should be kept into a semantic any sort of a system for formal knowledge reasoning and management, which provi- des the basic operations: storage and retrieval accor- ding to the syntax and semantics of the selected formalism.

4.2 Matchmaking Module

Matchmaking performs semantic resource matchmaking and ontology based matchmaker service as shown in the figure 1. This architecture comprises three modules: matchmaking, request handling and resource discovery.

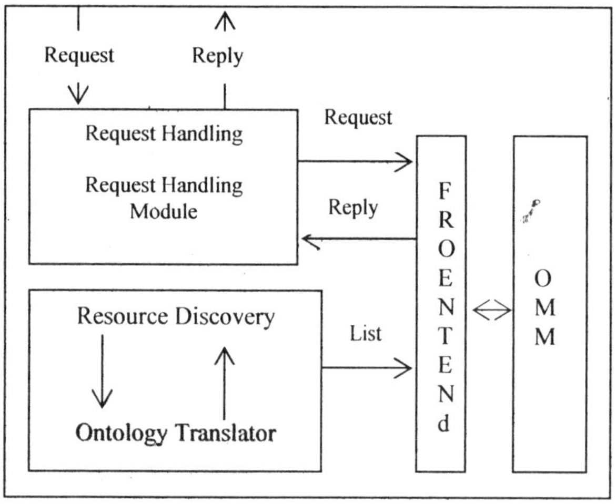

Fig. 1 Architecture of Ontology based Resource Matchmaker service (OMMS)

A. Matchmaking Module

Matchmaking module uses query and inference system written in java. This module performs matchmaking and return the result as java object as allows us to process the results and return a list which matching resources to the user query.

B. Request Handling

In this module the request is expressed using request ontology. User submit request in RDF and receive a list of matching resources then user can express their preference for matching resources by using ranking function and user indicate the number of returned resources that are sorted according to the ranking value.

C. Resource Discovery

This module is the key part of OMMS, which dynamically collects resource information from multiple resources. Different resource providers may express their resources using different schema so ontology translator is developed to translate the various formats used in heterogeneous environment into resource ontology [9].

4.3 Resource Description Ontology

Different Ontology languages provide different facilities, most recent development in standard ontology language is Web Ontology Language (OWL) from the World Wide Web Consortium.

Defining Classes: The first step is to group together related resources in order to create ontology.

Defining Properties: Ontology classes are created to group together similar resources. As the class hierar chy does not give any information about the classes themselves, so we define various meaningful properties for each class of the ontology.

Ontology Creation: Using RDF schema, ontology defines objects, properties of objects, and relation ship among objects. We use Protégé, an ontology editor that supports the RDF schema, to develop our ontologies. Protégé provides an integrated environment for editing ontology and instances. Also it hides ontology language from the ontology developers allowing developer to work with high-level concepts, which as a result leads to rapid ontology development.

Protégé-OWL APIs is used to dynamically create instance of a particular concept and also to assign values to appropriate properties in the resource ontology template. With these features, the resource information of the entire system can be described semantically, which in turn bring about semantic based discovery of distributed resources. [11,12].

5. Experimental Results

The performance of the resource discovery module has been designed to run using Java program on distributed servers with using Jena semantic web framework. Using Java, for client we designed four modules as communication client, server detector, task runner and main class. Using communication model we connect to the server with socket programming. Task runner module was used to execute the task assigned by the server. Server side we used the system information, task assignment and communication modules. Using ontology API and inference engine, server detects the peer(s) along with the peer resources information. Results are as shown in the following figures.

Here we focus on task parallelism distributing execution processes (threads) across different distributed computing nodes i.e. each processor executes a different thread (or process) on the same or different data. The threads may execute the same or different task. We are calculating One-way hashing function that takes input streams, called pre-text, and map them to hash values using MD5. We assign the maximum set size and the calculating the total possible combination from the given key set.

As shown in the Fig. 2 and Fig. 3, we obtain the list of available resources like CPU speed, CPU Architecture has X86, CPU cycles, free of maximum CPU cycles, available Memory and operating system details. By using this resource information server choose the peers for task execution. It shows which task is running along with task set number with progress bar of running task assigned to that peer. Finally it gives the information of task completed with task name.

We obtain the list of peers with its resources as shown in the Fig. 3. When you select the peer from the list, the resources are shown. Which display the CPU used, CPU free in percentage, total RAM of that system and how much it is used and also shows free RAM in percentage. Now for assigning the task we select the peer(s) as per client resource request from the peer list. Suppose you are select the five peers from the list and start the task then it will execute among five peers simultaneously. It checks for task, which is running currently and completed. Meanwhile suppose one of the peer was failed or disconnect then the task assign for that peer will be discarded completely and that task will assign among other peer. After task executed successfully log files are created. We compare time taken for executing the same task on a single standalone machine and in distributed computing system by using log files as shown in the Fig. 4. In the Fig. 4, on x-axis, we are having different systems like standalone and distributed. On y-axis, we are having the time in milliseconds. The figure shows that Distributed System takes less time for the completion of task as compared to standalone system.

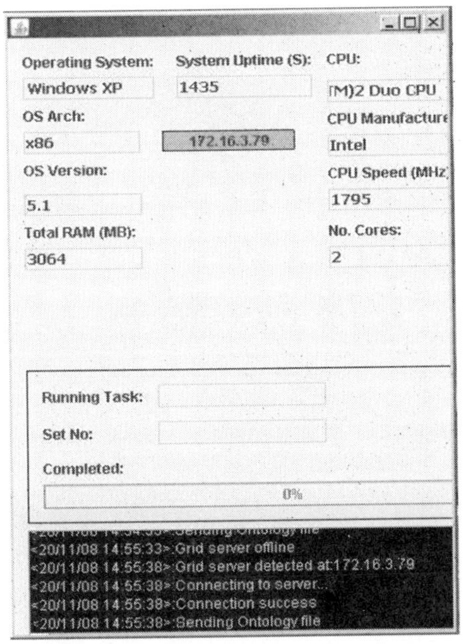

Fig. 2 Showing the client resources and task performance

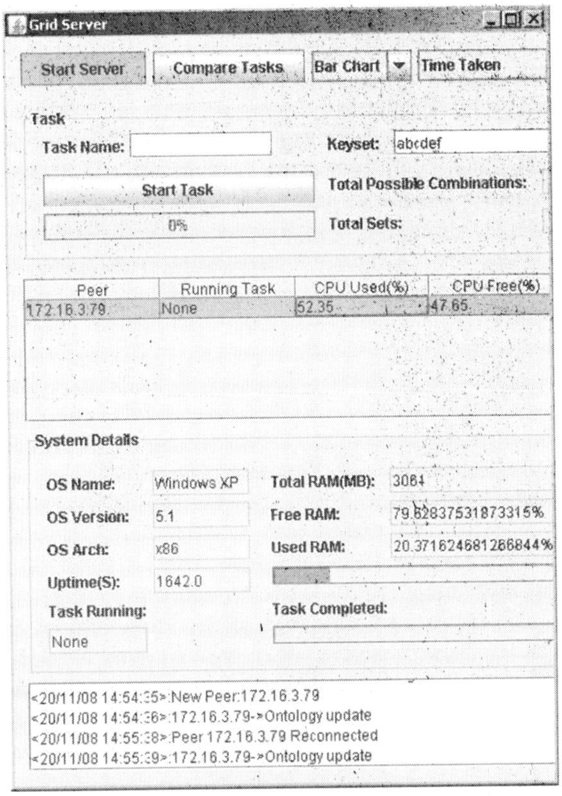

Fig. 3 Server showing peers connected and running completed tasks with available and used resources

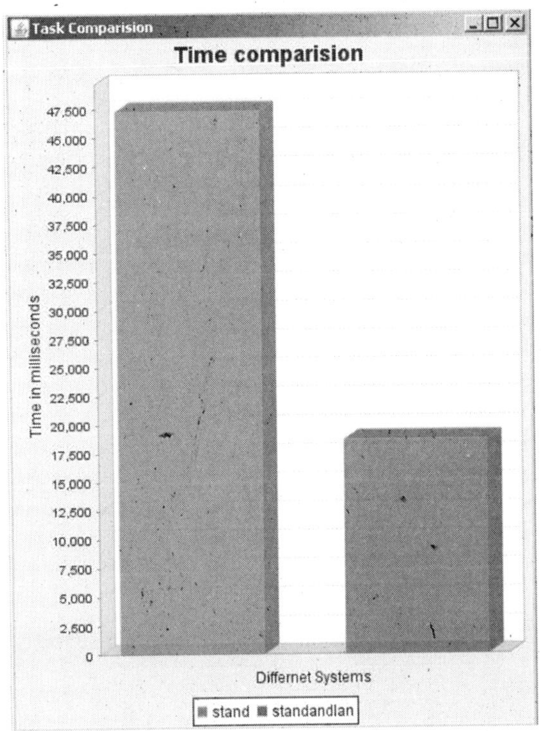

Fig. 4 Graph shows comparison of task executing as time between standalone machine and distributed system

6. Conclusion and Future Work

In this paper, we explore the knowledge base that can be constructed through the use of proposed ontologies and inference mechanism that can be improve the performance of discovery results in Distributed System. Ontology use centralized approach for resource discovery, which reduces the scalability. In the future, we will explore the scalability of this design to the larger system with thousands of peer.

7. References

[1] Iamnitchi A., Foster I., Nurmi D. C., "A Peer-to-Peer Approach to Resource Discovery in Grid Environments", Proc. of the 11th Symposium on High Performance Distributed Computing, Edinburgh, UK, 2002.

[2] C. Kesselman, I. Foster., "Computational grids", In The Grid: Blueprint for a New Computing Infrastructure, chapter 2, Morgan-kaufman edition, 1999.

[3] R. Raman, M. Livny, and M. Solomon. "Matchmaking: Distributed resource management for high throughput computing.", In Proceedings of the 7th IEEE High Performance Distributed computing(HPDC).

[4] Klaus Krauter, Rajkumar Buyya, and Muthucum aru Maheswaran, "A Taxonomy and Survey of Grid Resource Management Systems", School of Computer Science and Software Engineering, Monash University, Melbourne, Australia. http://www. buyya.com /papers/gridtaxonomy-report .pdf

[5] Brooke J., Fellows D., Garwood K. and Goble C., "Semantic matching of Grid Resource Descriptions," In Proceedings of the European Across Grids Conference, 2004. http://www.Grid-interoperability.org/semres.pdf

[6] Jinguang Gu, Heping Chen, Xinmeng Chen and Yi Huang, "An Ontology-based Knowledge Repository Model on the Grid", 2006. *www.semgrid.net/CitationBefore2006.1/KGGI04-79 .pdf*

[7] Foster I., Kesselman C. and Tuecke S., "The Anatomy of the Grid: Enabling Scalable Virtual Organizations," International Journal of High Performance Computing Applications, 15 (3). 200-222. 2001. *http://www.globus.org/research /papers/anatom .pdf*

[8] G.Stumme, M. Ethrig et., "The Karlsruhe view on ontologies", Technical report, University of Karlsruhe Institute 2003.

[9] Andreas Harth, Yu He, Hongsuda Tangmunarun-kit, Steafan Decker., "A Semantic Matchmaker Service on the Grid", ACM 2004.

[9] Adriana Iamnitchi and Ian Foster, "A Peer-to-Peer Approach to Resource Location in Grid Environments ," University of Chicago.

[10] W. Hoschek, "A Unified Peer-to-Peer Database Framework for Scalable Service and Resource Discovery", Proceeding of Third International Workshop on Grid Computing: GRID 2002

[11] *http://www.protege.stanford.edu/overview/* protege-owl.html

[12] OWL Web Ontology Language Overview, W3C Recommendation, 10 February 2004 http://www.w3.org/TR/owl-features/

DRDS: Dynamic Resource Discovery System – An Approach to Resource Discovery in a Grid Computing Environment using Dynamic Agents

D. Sudheer Kumar Reddy[1] and Dr. Arun Agarwal[2]
[1]Senior Software Engineer, Motorola India Private Ltd., Hyderabad, India.
sudheer@motorola.com
[2]Professor, University of Hyderabad, Hyderabad, India.
aruncs@uohyd.ernet.in

Abstract

Grid computing technology is an emerging technology where computational and information resources are shared and managed by diverse organizations in widespread locations. These locations are usually referred as virtual organizations. In such scenarios, challenges are encountered in scaling the existing Grid Services like Discovery of resources due to geographical distribution and dynamic behavior of resources. Managing Grid infrastructure plays a vital role in effectively utilizing the capabilities provided by Grid computing technology.

Resource discovery is an essential service that is required in any resource sharing environments like Grid Computing. It is used to search information about resources available in the Grid network. This paper discusses a new solution called Dynamic Resource Discovery System (DRDS) by using dynamic agents. This solution is based on agents that cooperate in the Grid environment. The proposed system is fully decentralized; therefore it easily scales with the number of resources, and can work in environments with irregular resource participation.

1. Introduction

Grid computing [1] is distributed computing [2] taken to the next evolutionary level. The goal is to create the illusion of a simple yet large and powerful self-managing virtual computer out of a large collection of connected heterogeneous systems sharing various combinations of resources. The Grid is a new approach to high-performance and large scale networked computing that has the potential to alter how computing resources are allocated for large projects. Built on the Internet and the World Wide Web, it is a new class of infrastructure comprising a set of high-speed computers, storage systems and networks, plus a set of Grid services (or middleware) to coordinate the ensemble of resources. By providing scalable, secure, high-performance mechanisms for discovering and negotiating access to remote resources, the Grid promises to make it possible for scientific collaborations to share resources on an unprecedented scale, and for geographically distributed groups to work together in ways that were previously impossible [3].

A Grid in reference to Grid computing [4] refers to loose resources and users that may be geographically separated and may be under different administrative domains. A Grid uses the resources of many separate computers connected by a network (usually the Internet) to solve large scale computation problems and use most of the idle time on many resources throughout the world. Such arrangements permit handling of data that would otherwise require the power of expensive supercomputers or would have been impossible to analyze.

A resource on a Grid could be any entity that provides access to a service. This could range from compute servers to databases, scientific instruments and applications. In a heterogeneous environment like a Grid, resources are generally owned by different people, communities or organizations with varied administration policies, and capabilities. Naturally obtaining and managing access to these resources is not a simple task. The aim of resource management is to simplify this process to users who just want to get their work done. In the Grid computing environment resource management is collection of software components that let users to access heterogeneous resources transparently, without having to worry about availability, access methods, security issues and other policies.

Resource discovery is an important task of every resource-sharing system like Grid computing environment. The challenge lies in providing a robust, flexible and secure design of resource discovery. Existing technologies [5] [6] [7] try to address a limited set of requirements with varied capabilities. The information provided by the existing systems is required but not sufficient because they lack in the topology information and integrated way of looking at various tasks involved in management of Grid resources.

Grid Management Information Server (GMIS) [8] framework is developed with the aim of addressing these requirements. In GMIS framework one of key components is Discovery Server. Discovery server will discover all resources dynamically in a Grid network using dynamic agents. Discovering resources on a Grid is an automated process which keeps track of addition and deletion of resources from the Grid. To gather the information about resources, dynamic agents are used. Resource details will be stored in relational database on GMIS. The next section discusses GMIS architecture briefly.

2. GMIS Architecture

The GMIS framework provides dynamic discovery of resources and maintains status information of the available resources in a Grid network. This information will be provided to all the registered entities on need basis. The registered entity can be another GMIS or a viewer that displays resource information. It includes distributed network management architecture by employing the remote monitoring of dispersed resources. This architecture distributes the information services functionality across the network using GMIS-GMIS communication.

The GMIS framework provides services for discovery, monitoring and brokerage of resources in a Grid network. Discovering resources on a Grid is an automated process which keeps track of addition and deletion of resources from the Grid. To gather the information about resources, communicator server is used. Resources details will be stored in a relational database on GMIS.

Monitoring service is used to monitor resources on grid level, cluster level and node level. Using this service, Grid resources are visually represented as icons on a viewer with resource status. GMIS framework allows the user to display summary information and summary view of cluster which is comparable and analyzable.

Brokerage service allocates the best possible resource or a combination of resources for the job execution based on set of attributes given by the users.

The Fig. shows the architecture of GMIS.

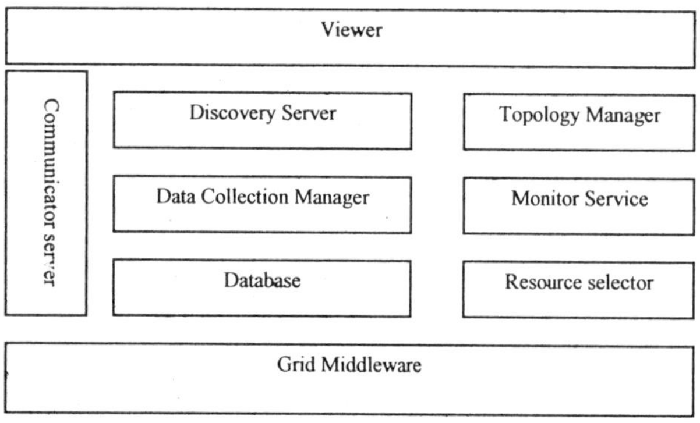

Fig. 1 GMIS Architecture

There are nine components in GMIS architecture:

1. ***Discovery Server:*** Discovery Server discovers resources on a Grid. Resource discovery is at three levels: (1) Node level (2) Cluster level and (3) Grid level. In node level, an internet protocol address or Fully Qualified Domain Name (FQDN) is used to discovery resource information. In Cluster level and Grid level, a range of internet protocol addresses are used to discover resources. User provides the information on internet protocol addresses or FQDN, using user interface on Viewer. Discovery Server sends a request to resource agent software using communicator server. Upon receiving the request, resource discovery agents on resources gather resource information and sends to Discovery Server. The resource information is stored in the relational database through Topology Manager.
2. ***Data Collection Manager:*** Data Collection Manager provides the procedures to communicate with the agent software for information about the resources. It receives notifications from agents, and initiates actions accordingly. It polls resources for current status of resources and parses the poll responses. It updates the Topology Manager with the current resource information. It also handles events like addition of resource, deletion of resource and modification of resource.
3. ***Database:*** Database contains information about the resources on Grid. The data will get updated by Topology Manager and retrieved by other services like Monitor Service and Resource Selector.
4. ***Topology Manager:*** Topology Manager maintains all resources information in a tree structure called Management Information Tree (MIT) as managed objects. Managed objects will be created when there is a notification from the Discovery Manager. Managed objects will be modified or deleted based on the messages from Data Collection Manager. It also updates Database when ever there is a change in resource information.
5. ***Monitor Service:*** Monitor Service provides information to the viewer by retrieving the resource information from Database. It controls and maintains the various users' access levels. The access information is persistently stored in the database. Each Grid can have different or same access levels for the same user. Viewer will provide interface for 'user access' configuration.

6. ***Resource Selector:*** Resource Selector is responsible for generating a set of best possible resources for the given set of resource attributes. The entire resources information is in database and Topology manager updates the information. Resource Selector takes inputs from user and searches in the database. If appropriate resources data is available in the database, those details will be provided to the user. Users can use these resources for their job execution. A user interface is provided on viewer to submit jobs. Key features of Resource Selector are:
    - Providing Brokerage Service
    - Generate Activation Graph
    - Job execution
7. ***Communicator Server:*** Communicator server establishes and maintains communication between the GMIS and resources agent software.
8. ***Grid Middleware:*** Grid Middleware like schedulers, resource allocation managers interact with the GMIS services using Application Programming Interfaces (APIs). For instance, when a scheduler needs a resource for a particular application, it interacts with the topology manager through the resource selector, and a suitable resource is provided.
9. ***Viewer:*** Viewer interacts with the GMIS services through monitor service e.g., status information of resources. Viewer is a web based application uses Tomcat Apache as a Web Server. Icons are used to represent Grid, Cluster and Node. Resource information gets from database using Java Servlets. Viewer contains user interfaces for user management, Discovery of services, Monitoring Services, Resource Selection and Job submission.

The rest of the paper will discuss the Discovery Server architecture, design and development details, since the main objective of this paper is to present discovery server component of GMIS.

3. Discovery Server

A Grid is a collection of resources through which a virtual organization can be formed. A Grid resource could be any entity that provides access to a range of services like computation servers. Resource Discovery is required to find computational resources and services over Grid. Discovery server records the identity and essential characteristics of services available to its users. This would help Grid users in determining additional resources available in Grid.

Discovery of resources is a vital function in a distributed system, particularly when that system spans multiple locations as in that context no one is likely to have detailed knowledge of all components. Discovery of resources identifies resources or services with desired properties. This task requires the ability to collect information from multiple, perhaps distributed information sources.

To summarize, Resource discovery in Grid environment is required for the following main reasons:

- To get the information about resources health status of the resources
- To construct and execute applications
- To describe about Grid resources
- For resource scheduling and allocation

Import design considerations are:

- **Seamless and transparent user access to resource information** – all information related to resources in a Grid can be accessed by the user by selecting options in the viewer without any need of understanding of the Grid infrastructure.
- **Easy to use web-based interface** – the viewer is web based and platform independent. User can access the viewer from any operating system and web browser. The information and controls available in the viewer are presented to the user in an intuitive way, so that the user can perform all his activities with ease.
- **Collation of information from multiple resources** – The information of resources presented under various Grids or managed by different GMIS can be viewed by the user within a single Viewer.
- **Efficient resource management** - In order to gain maximum benefit from resources, the GMIS provides appropriate resources based on the job requirements. GMIS maintains latest resource information along with their status.
- **Scalable and Adaptable framework** - GMIS doesn't impose any kind of limitations on the Grid or Jobs submitted by the user. If large numbers of resources/jobs are to be managed then only hardware needs to be upgraded. GMIS can be integrated with other Grid technologies like Globus by agreeing on data exchange formats.

- **Poll and Event based information gathering mechanisms** – The information about resources will be gathered using poll mechanism where GMIS send a request to resource agent. In case of Events mechanism, the resources agents automatically send information to GMIS whenever there is change in resource status.

Discovery Server in GMIS is developed with the above design considerations. Discovery server will discover all resources dynamically in a Grid network using dynamic agents. Discovering resources on a Grid is an automated process which keeps track of addition and deletion of resources from the Grid. Resource details are stored in relational database on GMIS. The following figure shows how the resources are discovered and stored in a database and provides information to services like monitor.

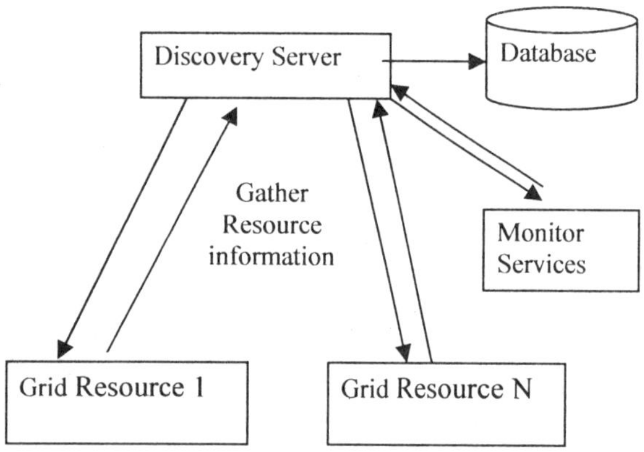

Fig. 2 Discovery Server

Two types of discoveries are supported in this system. One is hardware resources discovery and other one is Services discovery. Hardware resource discovery is at three levels: (1) Node level (2) Cluster level and (3) Grid level. In node level, an internet protocol address or Fully Qualified Domain Name (FQDN) is used to discovery resource information. In Cluster level and Grid level, a range of internet protocol addresses are used to discover resources. User provides the information on internet protocol addresses or FQDN, using user interface on Viewer. A resource discovery manager process Resource Discovery Manager (RDM) will be running at the server which is part of GMIS. This process requests for the hardware resource information. Resource discovery agents are dynamic agents; running on resources will gather the resource information and sends it to RDM. The resource information is stored in the relational database.

Similarly, hardware resource discovery methodology has been used for services also. How ever, there is one limitation i.e., services should be in a particular directory, which is configurable, or services name should start with "UH_".

In general, computing resources have two types of attributes: (i) static attributes such as the type of operating system installed, network bandwidth, processor speed and storage capacity (including physical and secondary memory) and (ii) dynamic attributes such as processor utilization, physical memory utilization, free secondary memory size, and network bandwidth utilization; and application resources have many types of attributes. All these attributes (both computing and application resources) will be maintained in an XML file which is stored in a GMIS Database.

4. Design and Implementation of Discovery Server

Discovering resources on Grid network is an automated process which keeps track of resources as they are added or removed from a Grid network. Dynamic agents are used to gather information about a wide variety of Grid resources. These resource details are stored in relational database.

The Dynamic Resource Discovery System mainly consists of four modules, namely Resource Discovery Agent (RDA), Resource Discovery Manager (RDM), Critical Information Agent (CIA) and Resource Description Factory (RDF). Three modules RDA, CIA, and RDF are running at every node as Agents. All the four modules are running on server node where GMIS is running. All these autonomous modules coordinate to transfer information between them at periodic time intervals, ensuring that GMIS will get the latest resource information dynamically and instantly. Descriptions of these four modules are given below:

- RDA – collects the information and forwards to RDM when RDM request for resource information or when RDA receives alerts from CIA.
- CIA – collects the information periodically and forwards to RDA, when there is a critical change in the resource.
- RDM – collects the information from all RDAs in a Grid Network.
- RDF – this module is used for communication between the above three modules. This generates XML file where the resource information is stored.

Communication between these modules is shown in the following figure.

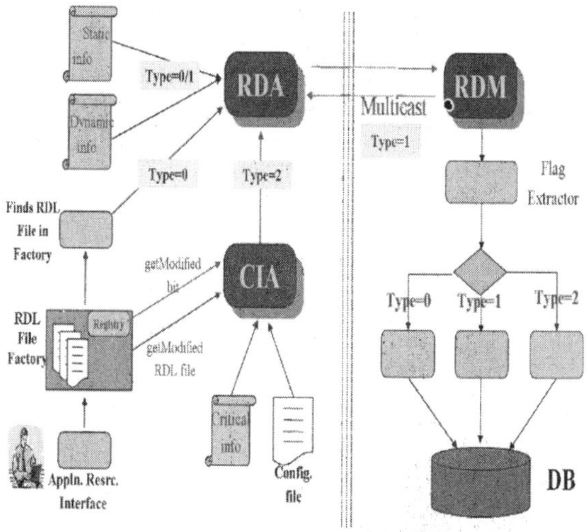

Fig. 3 Dynamic Resource Discovery System

4.1 Dynamic Resource Discovery Algorithm

1. For every new resource,
   (a) Register the resource through Application Resource Interface.
   (b) Generate a Resource Description Language (RDL) message and add this to RDL file.
   (c) Send message to RDA with message type as 0.
2. At CIA, check for the critical information by using configuration file. If any difference os found then send a message to RDA with message type as 2.
3. At RDA, listen for the messages and act upon the message type.
   (a) If message type is 0 means, it is for the new resource. Collect both static and dynamic resource information and forward the information to RDM.
   (b) If message type is 1 then it is for the dynamic resource information request from RDM. Collect the dynamic resource information and send to RDM.
   (c) If message type is 2 then it is from CIA. Forward the message to RDM.
4. At RDM,
   (a) Periodically send a request to all RDAs with message type as 1.
   (b) Listen to the messages coming from RDAs.
   (c) If message type is 0, then insert the new resource information into Database.
   (d) If message type is either 1 or 2, then update the database with the latest information.

4.2 Data flow diagram of Dynamic Grid Network Discovery process

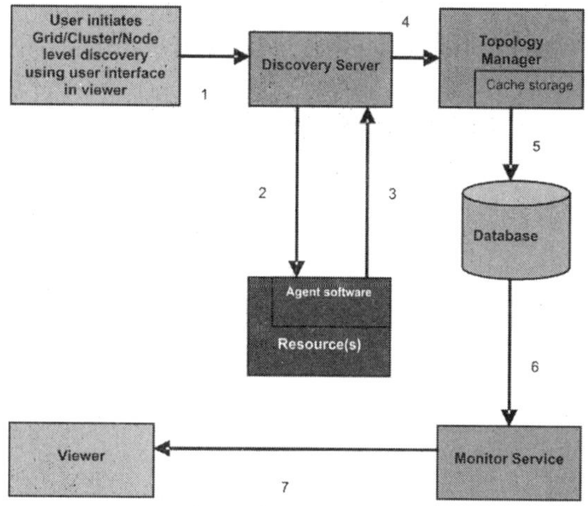

Fig. 4 Dynamic Grid Network Resource Discovery process

1. To discover resources on Grid, user initiates Grid/Cluster/Node level discovery using the interface provided in the viewer. To discover node level resources user has to provide either internet protocol address or Fully Qualified Domain Name (FQDN). To discover cluster level or grid level, a range of internet protocol addresses need to be provided by the user. Viewer forwards this request to Discovery Server.
2. Discovery server sends a broadcast message to all the resources using the communicator server.
3. Agent software which runs at resources responds to the message sent by the Discovery server with resource information.
4. Discovery server forwards resource information to Topology Manager. Topology Manager constructs hierarchical MIT and stores in cache storage.
5. Topology Manager updates the database with resource information.
6. Monitor service retrieves the resource information by using relational database queries.
7. Monitor service updates the viewer with resource information retrieved from the database.

4.3 Data flow diagram of Dynamic Event based Resource Discovery Process

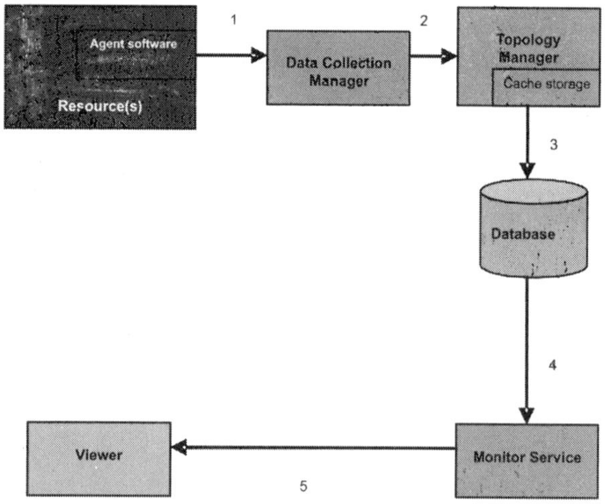

Fig. 5 Dynamic Event based Resource Discovery Process

1. When a new resource or application is added/deleted/modified an event sent by the agent software which is runs on resources to Data Collection Manager.
2. Data Collection Manager passes resource information to Topology Manager. Topology Manager constructs/updates hierarchical MIT and stores in cache storage.
3. Topology Manager updates the database with resource information.
4. Monitor service retrieves resource information by using relational database queries.
5. Monitor service updates the viewer with resource information retrieved from the database.

5. Conclusions and Future Enhancements

The resource management used in Grid Computing environments need to be adaptive so that they can handle dynamic changes in availability of resources and user requirements. At the same time, they need to provide scalable, controllable, measurable, and easily enforceable policies for management of the resources. GMIS framework is developed to address these requirements. This paper describes the Dynamic Resource Discover System which is used in GMIS for discovery of resources.

Future enhancements will involve simulation of this system to show that Dynamic Resource Discovery System performs extremely well and to be used for resource discovery in many Grid environments.

6. References

[1] IBM Red Book, Introduction to Grid Computing with Globus, September, 2003.

[2] Distributed Computing, http://e-comm.webopedia.com/TERM/D/distributed_computing.html

[3] Arun Agarwal, "Development of Grid Middleware for Integration of Dispersed Resources", A technical report by Prof. Arun Agarwal, Department Of Computer and Information Sciences, School of Mathematics & Computer/Information Sciences, University of Hyderabad, Hyderabad 500046, INDIA, September 2004.

[4] Foster, I., Kesselman, C. and Tuecke, S. The Anatomy of the Grid: Enabling Scalable Virtual Organizations. International Journal of High Performance Computing Applications, 15 (3). 200-222.2001.

[5] Czajkowski, K., S. Fitzgerald, I. Foster, and C. Kesselman, "Grid Information Services for Distributed Resource Sharing". In Proc. 10th IEEE International Symposium on High Performance Distributed Computing (HPDC-10), IEEE Press, 2001.

[6] Fisher, S., "Relational Model for Information and Monitoring". Technical Report GWD-Perf-7-1, GGF, 2001.

[7] "Data Grid Information and Monitoring Services Architecture: Design, Requirements and Evaluation Criteria", Technical Report, DataGrid, 2002.

[8] D. Sudheer Kumar Reddy and Arun Agarwal, "GMIS : Grid Management Information Services – Design of a Framework for Monitoring, Discovering, and Brokeraging in a Grid Computing environment", in proceedings of International Conference on Advanced Computing and Communication Technologies for High Performance Applications, Cochin, India, September, 2008.

Microcontroller Hybrid Network for Distributed Embedded Applications

Trupti Nagrare[1] and Dr. V M. Thakare[2]
[1]Research scholar, Embedded System and computing, G.H. Raisoni College of Engineering, CRPF gate, Digdoh Hills, Nagpur(M.S.), India
gladiolus_trupti@yahoo.com
[2]Professor, Department of Computer science & Information Technology, Amravati University, Amravati(M.S.), India
vilthakare@yahoo.co.in

Abstract

A distributed system is a collection of individual computing devices that can communicate with each other. In this work proposal of an hybrid microcontroller network is presented whose main application is oriented toward the implementation of a functionally distributed system which can be commanded from the main node called master node, where a programmed is develop for user interface and act as system monitor supervising the events related to the indebted operation of the network. Individual node can perform their own function for which they are designed with care of network protocol. From the information that handles to node level and the present status of the network[1]. The network was implemented under the common bus topology and the application including the physical layer handling under the RS232 standard used in the connection between each considered microcontroller node , as well as we can extent the network with different microcontroller from different families such as Motorola, microchip, AVR and Atmel[2].

1. Introduction

There are many systems where more than two processing elements take part' which introduces the need of such a specific mechanisms and proposals that satisfy the different applications that appear in the instrumentation and control areas. For the purpose of controlling, distributed instrumentation play important role, as the system allows solution for the problem, which is not solved by its own nature with a single device processing. Hence that is segmented into a number of tasks which are processed by different units but as a whole solves unique problem. The following description suggests the technique for the connection between different elements that composes the distributed system at both physical and logical levels. Each element of the system consists of microcontroller circuit which acts as a specialized system that internally contains some peripheral resources that facilitate their relation with the outer world. Thus here we design a circuit to solve the problem of network and to provide a advantage of using microcontroller in each element of the network element Thus the exposition of a microcontroller network applied to the functionally distributed instrumentation arises. Starting from the fact that not all the work loads, that results from dividing the problem, are homogenous, it is interesting to combine different technologies where the diversity of microcontrollers and the potentialities that each manufacturer implements in its different models allow choosing the most appropriate device according to the requirements that the application demands. From the last propositions, is important to think in an hybrid network (different types from microcontroller) that works in transparent way to the user.

2. Distributed system concept

Here we consider each one of the units that constitute the network as a node. The diversification of the microcontroller's nodes that compose the network derives from the fact that the assigned service load for each node demands that the associated microcontroller counts on with sufficient peripheral resources to carry out the functions that have been distributed to it, and that they are usually of different nature for each node. Furthermore all of them have the obligation to take care of the communication events that are generated in the network in an opportune and efficient way, and without reduction of excluding communication load [duties that are carrying out].

A system is *centralized* if its components are restricted to one site, *decentralized* if its components are at different sites with no or limited or close coordination. When a decentralized system has no or limited coordination, it is called *networked*; otherwise, it is termed *distributed* indicating a close coordination among components at different sites. Among models that give specific definitions of a distributed system, distributed systems can be examined using these three dimensions of hardware, control, and data[2][3].

The design of the network also incorporates schemes of fault tolerance, definition of the data format that is being handled, generic adaptability, synchronization, scalability and generic functions, among them those of the system initialization in remote way via main node, and those that correspond to every node in individual form[4]. The proposal includes the protocol definition and the commutation between the half and full duplex communication way, as well as some variations that help the communication at electrical level[5].

Distributed system = distributed hardware + distributed control + distributed data

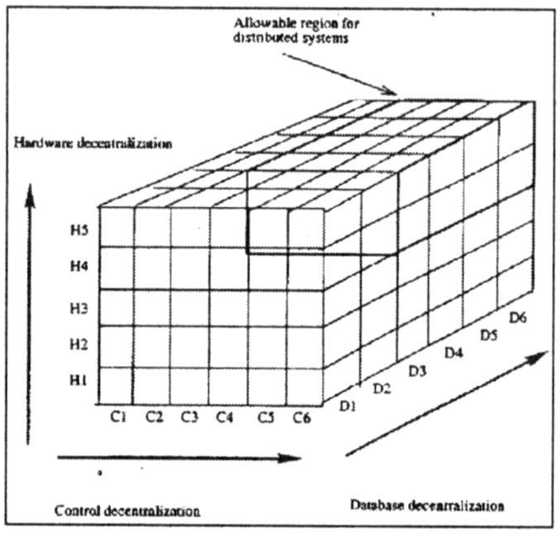

Fig. 1 Distributed System

3. Network topology

When one speaks of microcontroller networks, the topologies that have a more reliable operation are daisy chain and common bus. Fig. 2 shows a basic network that uses a topology of common bus. Common bus topology is easy to wire, troubleshoot, program. All the nodes required to have a USART so that communication is possible with all the nodes.

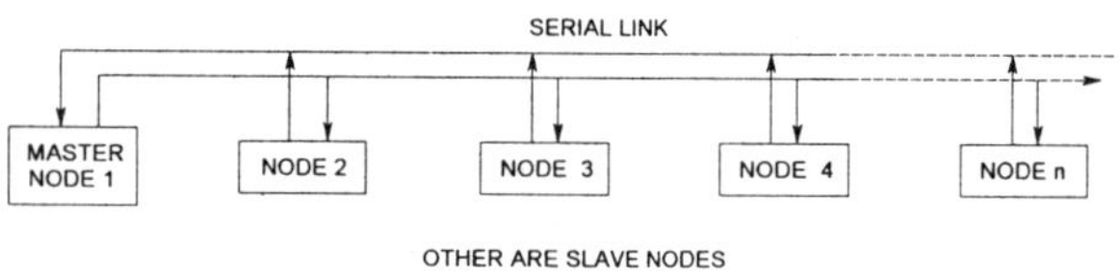

Fig. 2 Common Bus Topology for the Microcontrollers Network

4. Scope of problem

As the problem related to communication between various types of microcontrollers, its scope is very vast. In many of the automotive application like industrial automation, home/office automation this distributive application is use. As well as in the automotive applications this network is beneficial.

The distributive embedded system provides various advantages like-

- The parallelism of distributed systems reduces processing bottlenecks and provides improved all-around performance
- Distributed systems can efficiently support information and resource (hardware and software) sharing for users at different locations.
- Distributed systems are capable of incremental growth and have the added advantage of facilitating modification or extension of a system to adapt to a changing environment without disrupting its operations.
- With the multiplicity of storage units and processing elements, distributed systems have the potential ability to continue operation in the presence of failures in the system.
- Distributed systems can be easily scaled to include additional resources (both hardware and software)[9].

5. Aspects of associate circuitry

For the communication among the nodes of the network (Fig. 3), the RS-232 standard is used. The use of this format presents the advantage that the nodes can be microcontrollers, PC's or any device that has serial asynchronous communication capabilities. The main advantages of the RS-232 are that the protocol and circuitry requirements are simpler and cheaper than other alternatives.

Here is the simple circuitry which shows the microcontroller network

5.1 Analysis of the Microcontrollers which Participate in the Hybrid Network

For the implementation of the microcontrollers network is not required that all nodes conforming it be of the same mark or model. The only requirement is that the microcontroller is able to communicate on RS-232 standard and fulfils the requirements of the chosen communication protocol.

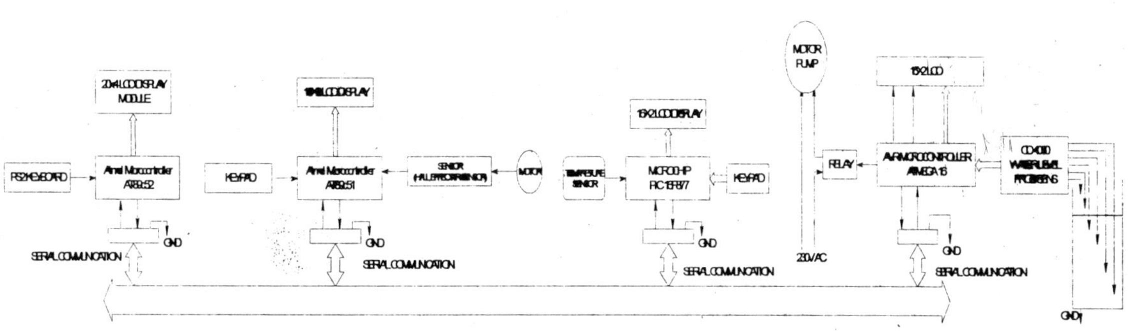

Fig. 3 Network Electrical Block Diagram

It is important to point out that if a network is implemented entirely with equal microcontrollers, it is enough to configure one node for the communications system and the result could be extensive for the remaining nodes. The difference among them will be at code level only, based on the activities that have been assigned to them. With such a network an efficient coding can be done which causes reduction in time making for code.

On the other hand, there are cases when all the nodes are not necessarily equal in their reference, as in the case of this work, although in some situation they can be from the same manufacturer as it happens with the Atmel AVR devices, where 4 different microcontroller models were used. A microcontroller of the Microchip company and one more from the Motorola company were included as well.

The manufacture implementation technology of the several microcontrollers used presents important differences. In the internal architecture, a contrast exist between the Von Neumann Technology implemented in the 68HC11, and the typical Harvard architecture in the PIC's and the AVR's.

Another important difference is directly related to the communication in the network and it refers to the fact that all the microcontrollers listed in table 1 include, inside their internal available peripheral modules, one for the asynchronous communication series, typically represented by a UART. This is not an indispensable requirement and it can be used, for example, a PIC16F84 microcontroller that implements the functions of a UART by means of software techniques and where two of their Input / Output pins can be used as transmitter and receiver.

Each one of the microcontrollers has its operation philosophy for the handling of the pins in charge of the serial communication and its own configuration registries for information transfer. For the 68HC11, the SCI (Serial Communication Interface) is used, that is a powerful UART with superior capacities to those of the other microcontrollers in the communications line. The PIC16F877 in turn, contains a USART that should be configured in asynchronous operation. The ATMEL AVR's participates with their own blocks of asynchronous communication series (UART's) [9] [10] [11]

For the serial communications events in the RS-232 bus, the synchronization aspect becomes a very important factor to consider. Certain time delays should be introduced during their data transmission and reception process that will depend on each microcontroller node to assure that these events happen successfully.

5.2 Standards of RS232

In RS-232, user data is sent as a time-series of bits. Both synchronous and asynchronous transmissions are supported by the standard. In addition to the data circuits, the standard defines a number of control circuits used to manage the connection between the DTE and DCE. Each data or control circuit only operates in one direction that is, signalling from a DTE to the attached DCE or the reverse. Since transmit data and receive data are separate circuits, the interface can operate in a full duplex manner, supporting concurrent data flow in both directions. The standard does not define character framing within the data stream, or character encoding.

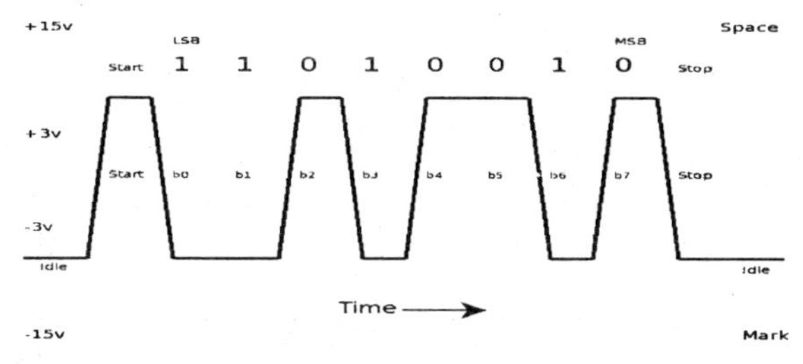

Fig. 4 Voltage Levels at RS232

Diagrammatic oscilloscope trace of voltage levels for ASCII "K" character (0x4b) with 1 start bit, 8 data bits, 1 stop bit.

The RS-232 standard defines the voltage levels that correspond to logical one and logical zero levels. Valid signals are plus or minus 3 to 15 volts. The range near zero volts is not a valid RS-232 level; logic one is defined as a negative voltage, the signal condition is called marking, and has the functional significance of OFF. RS232 is used mainly for longer distance communication or for more number of nodes[14].

6. Communication Protocol

The communication protocol defines the rules for the transmission and reception of information between the nodes of the network. Thus for two or more nodes to be able to communicate to each other, it is necessary that both use the same protocol.

Due to concerns on protocols that govern network behavior, rehearsals have been made in Master - Slave configuration where all the actions are commanded from a main node and can be directed towards a specific node or to all the elements that compose the network. Also the "token Passing" protocol has been used to allow a "multi – master" scheme in which each node (in a exclusive way) can behave like Master in the time interval when it has all the faculties to transmit through the bus if required, then yielding the control to another node in a predefined sequence.

The transference of information, independently of the network topology, is made by means of messages that can be of a predetermined fixed length or of variable size. For the distributed network both options were developed.

In Fig. 5 a basic example of the variable length protocol used is shown. The first message byte corresponds to the identification number of the node to which the message goes to, and the second is the number of the node that is sending the message. The third byte corresponds to the length of the present message. Normally the microcontrollers are taking care of the activities that have been delegated to them in the distribution of tasks. The moment that a message is sent to the bus, all the nodes listen to it, but they must have the capacity to discriminate if the present message is for them or not[12][13].

Fig. 6 shows the flow chart of the subroutine that takes place when the interruption by the arrival of data in the serial channel appears in the microcontrollers. At the moment that the third byte is received, each node verifies if the message is for it. If its ID corresponds, then it will be in charge to receive the number of bytes of the message, indicated at the third locality, where the length of the message is deposited[16]

6.1 Master-Slave Protocol

This protocol was the first one implemented for the distributed network and it consists basically of a centralized system where the master node was represented by master controller and the other microcontrollers acted as slaves nodes. The sequence of events initiated when the user accessed the network elements arming a variable message of fixed size or as the one previously described thus running consultation functions or exercising some of the functions implemented for some specific node. Working like this, the communication between the slave nodes does not exist and none of them can send information to the master node without previous authorization.

6.2 Token Passing Protocol

This appears like a multi - master scheme, where all the network nodes can be master (but not all simultaneously) during a determined time interval, when they can transmit or require information on the bus. When their management as main node ends, they will give to the following node the control of the network, in a sequence defined previously. This alternative presents the problem that, if one (or several nodes) for whatever reason are disabled, and the node that at such time behaves as master must yield the control to one of the elements that are inactive, then a blockade of the activities takes place, neutralizing the system with it. It is in these cases where the schemes of faults tolerance have relevance. For the previously described situation, the solution is that before yielding the control to a node, the master must make a verification of the existence of the microcontroller who will take its place. The master node verifies that exist a candidate to take charge of the network. Once the message is sent, the master will wait for an answer. If an answer does not exist once a predefined counter has expired, the master node will send a new verification message to the node that follows in a sequence, doing that until it finds the next operative node[16][17].

Destiny node	Source node	Message lenght	Function	Parameters		......		Checksum

Fig. 5 Messages of Variable Length

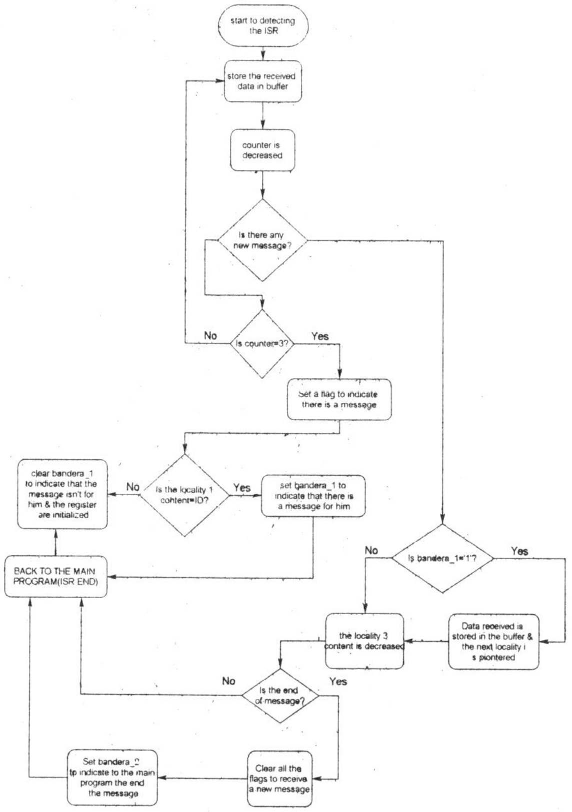

Fig. 6 Algorithm to attend to the ISR

7. Conclusion

The most interesting benefit that the implementation of a hybrid network offers is the enrichment of the potentialities of a network of microcontroller elements, that combining different technologies, allow the development of distributed systems in accordance to the necessities specified for diverse applications.

8. References

[1] Goscinski A. "Distributed Operating Systems: The Logical Design", Editorial Addison-Wesley, 1991.

[2] Nutt, G. J. "Centralized and Distributed Operating Systems., New Jersey Editorial Prentice Hall Int.,pp 418

[3] Laplante, P. "Real-Time Systems Design and Analysis: an Engineer's Handbook , IEEE Press. 1993.

[4] Jie Wu. "Distributed System Design".

[5] Tanenbaum and Van Steen "Distributed Systems".

[6] Weijia Jia "Distributed Network Systems".

[7] Ceballos Sierra, F. J. "Enciclopedia de Microsoft Visual Basic 6.0", Editorial Addison-Wesley Iberoamericana.

[8] "AVR RISC Microcontroller", Atmel Corporation, 1999.

[9] "Microchip PIC16F87X ", Microchip Technology Inc., 1999.

[10] "A Distributed Coordination Protocol for a Heterogeneous Group of Peer Processes", Aikebaier Ailixier ,hayashibara, Naohiro; Enokido, Tomoya; Takizawa, Makoto; Advanced Networking and Applications, 2007. AINA '07. 21st International Conference on 21-23 May 2007 Page(s):565 - 572 Digital Object Identifiers 10.1109/AINA.2007.12

[11] "Controlling Distributed Hyperbolic Plants with Adaptive Nonlinear Model Predictive Control", Jos´e M. Igrejay, Jo˜ao M. Lemosz and Rui Neves da Silva.

[12] "Distributed reservation CDMA for wireless LAN Sung", Won Lee; Dong Ho Cho; Global Telecommunications Conference, 1995. GLOBECOM '95, IEEE Volume 1, 13-17 Nov. 1995 Page(s):360 - 364 vol.1 Digital Object Identifier 10.1109/GLOCOM.1995.500381.

[13] "Distributed learning in wireless sensor networks" IEEE Signal Processing Magazine 2006.

[14] "Distributed fusion in sensor networks", IEEE Signal Processing Magazine 2006.

[15] E. Catmull. A tutorial on compensation tables. In *Computer Graphics*, volume 13, pages 1–7. ACM SIGGRAPH, 1979.

Session – 5

Image and Speech Processing

Facial Expression Classification using Multilayer Perceptron

Praseeda Lekshmi V[1], Dr.M.Sasikumar[2] and Reena Sathyan[3]
[1]Assistant Professor, College of Engineering Kidangoor
vplekshmi@rediffmail.com,
[2]Professor, Marian Engineering College, Trivandrum
drmsasikumar@yahoo.com,
[3]Lecturer, University College of Engineering Kariavattom
reenauck@gmail.com

Abstract

Face exhibits different facial expressions which can be instantly recognized by human eyes. But it is very difficult for a computer to extract and use the information content from these expressions. In this paper we present a method to analyze facial expression from video images by using Gabor Wavelets and classified using a neural network classifier. The key frames from video images are extracted. Gabor filtering is done on face images and the resulting vectors are projected on to feature space. The weight vectors are classified using a neural network classifier. Our method reliably works even with faces, which carry heavy expressions.

1. Introduction

Face recognition has drawn considerable interest and attention from many researchers for the last two decades because of its potential applications, such as in the areas of surveillance, secure trading terminals, control and user authentication. The problem of face recognition is either to identify facial image from a picture or facial region from an image and recognize a person from set of images. A robust face recognition system has the capability of distinguishing among hundreds, may be even thousands of faces. A number of face recognition methods have been proposed.

Facial expressions play a significant role in our social and emotional lives. They are visually observable, conversational, and interactive signals that clarify our current focus of attention and regulate our interactions with the environment and other persons in our vicinity [17]. They are our direct and naturally preeminent means of communicating emotions [12], [17].Therefore, automated analyzers of facial expressions seem to have a natural place in various vision systems, including automated tools for behavioral research, lip reading, bimodal speech processing, videoconferencing, face/visual speech synthesis, affective computing, and perceptual man-machine interfaces. It is this wide range of principle driving applications that has lent a special impetus to the research problem of automatic facial expression analysis and produced a surge of interest in this research topic. Most approaches to automatic facial expression analysis attempt to recognize a small set of prototypic emotional facial expressions, i.e., fear, sadness, disgust, anger, surprise, and happiness (e.g., [2], [9], [13], [15]; for an exhaustive survey, see [16]).This practice may follow from the work of Darwin [4], and more recently Ekman [12], who suggested that basic emotions have corresponding prototypic expressions. In everyday life, how ever, such prototypic expressions occur relatively rarely; emotions are displayed more often by subtle changes in one or few discrete facial features, such as the raising of the eyebrows in surprise [14]. To detect such subtlety of human emotions and, in general, to make the information conveyed by facial expressions available for usage in the various applications mentioned above, automatic recognition of facial gestures (atomic facial signals) is needed.

2. Background and Related work

Most of current systems for analysis and tracking of facial motions from shape and appearances are based on linear models. Active shape models (ASM) [8] are well known linear models for facial motion analysis and tracking using point distribution models in linear subspace. By constraining deformation of point distributions into a linear subspace of the training shapes during local search, it achieves robust fitting of face models [8]. Active appearance models (AAM) combine the linear shape model of points distributions in ASM and the linear texture appearance model by aligning appearance models into a normalized shape using piecewise affine warping [7]. Iterative model refinement algorithms are proposed based on a prediction model, which is learned as a regression model using observations of linear shape and appearance model parameter variations after perturbations. Bilinear and multilinear models are applied to improve accuracy in modeling facial expression recognitions [1, 10] and facial expression synthesis [5]. All these models are based on linear shape and appearance models with extensions for multiple factors. In addition, any of these models do not count dynamics in facial expressions except [3]. Feature-based facial expression recognition system may overcome the limitation of linear subspace of templates by directly tracking features like facial action units [6]. Feature based approaches, however, are hard to model appearance variations in facial expression and may not be able to synthesize appearance of new facial expressions.

Rest of the paper is organized as follows. Section 3, 4, and 5 deals with Gabor wavelets, Principal Component Analysis and Multilayer Perceptron Neural Network. Section 6 gives the proposed approach. Results are discussed in section 7 and section 8 deals with conclusion.

3. Gabor wavelets

The main characteristics of wavelet are the possibility to provide a multiresolution analysis of the image in the form of coefficient matrices. Strong arguments for the use of multiresolution decomposition can be found in psycho visual research, which offers evidences that the human visual system processes the image in a multi scale way. Wavelets provide a time and frequency decomposition at the same time. Computational complexity of wavelets is linear with the number of computed coefficients. Thus the complexity is less compared to other fast transformations.

The Gabor wavelet representation of images allows description of spatial frequency structure in the image while preserving information about spatial relations. The response image of Gabor filter can be written as a correlation of input image $I(x)$ with Gabor kernel $P_k(x)$

$$a_k(x_0) = \iint I(x) P_k(x - x_0)\, dx \tag{1}$$

$$p_k(x) = \frac{k^2}{\sigma^2} \exp\left(-\frac{k^2}{2\sigma^2} x^2\right)\left(\exp(ikx) - \exp\left(-\frac{\sigma^2}{2}\right)\right) \tag{2}$$

where k is the characteristic vector.

$k = (k_x, k_y) = (k_v \cos\theta_w, k_v \sin\theta_w)$ and

$$k_v = 2^{-\frac{v+2}{2}} \pi \ ; \ \theta_w = w\frac{\pi}{8}$$

Here v is the discrete set of different frequencies and w is the orientation.

4. Principal Component Analysis

PCA is a useful statistical technique that has found applications in the fields such as face recognition, image compression etc. It is a common technique for finding patterns in the data of high dimensions. In PCA, face images are projected in to feature space or face space. Weight vector comparison was done to get the best match.

Let the training set of face images be X_1, X_2, $X_3 \ldots Xn$, then the average set or mean of faces be defined as

$$m = \frac{\sum_{i=1}^{n} X_i}{n} \tag{3}$$

Notice that the symbol m to indicate the mean of set X.

The average distance of each face from the mean of the data set is given by

$Q_1 = X_1 - m;\ Q_2 = X_2 - m \ldots\ Qn = Xn - m$

which is the standard deviation

The covariance matrix is given by

$C = A * A'$

where $A = [Q_1\ Q_2\ Q_3 \ldots\ldots\ldots Qn]$.

In order to reduce the dimensionality, co-variance can be calculated as

$C = A' * A$.

Eigen values and Eigen vectors are calculated for the covariance matrix.

All the face images in the database are projected in to Eigen space and weight for each image is calculated. Then image vectors for each face image is obtained as

$$\text{ImageVector} = \sum_{i=1}^{10} \text{weight}(i) * \text{Eigevector}(i) \tag{4}$$

5. Multilayer Perceptron Neural Network

Neural networks are predictive models loosely based on the action of biological neurons. A neural network is a network of weighted, additive values with nonlinear transfer functions. However, despite the name, neural networks are far from "thinking machines" or "artificial brains".

The following diagram (Fig.1) illustrates a perceptron network with three layers:

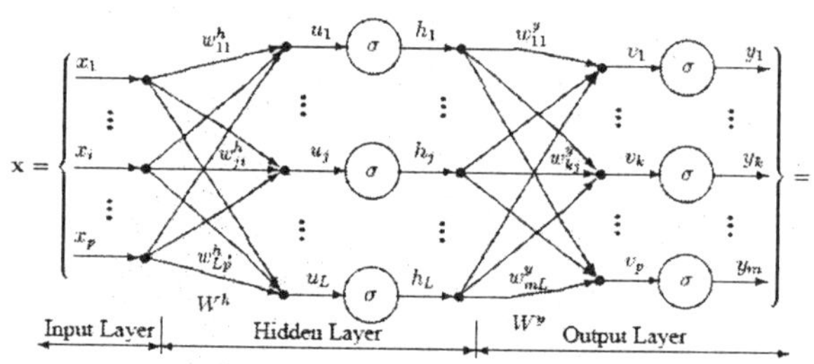

Fig. 1 Diagram illustrates a perceptron network with three layers

This network has an input layer (on the left) with three neurons, one hidden layer (in the middle) with three neurons and an output layer (on the right) with three neurons. There is one neuron in the input layer for each predictor variable. In the case of categorical variables, *N*-1 neurons are used to represent the *N* categories of the variable.

The goal of the training process is to find the set of weight values that will cause the output from the neural network to match the actual target values as closely as possible. There are several issues involved in designing and training a multilayer perceptron network:

- Selecting how many hidden layers to use in the network.
- Deciding how many neurons to use in each hidden layer.
- Finding a globally optimal solution that avoids local minima.
- Converging to an optimal solution in a reasonable period of time.

6. Proposed Approach

We have considered the video face image sequences with certain degree of orientation and large variations in the facial expressions. Fig. 2.shows an image sequence in the database. From the input video, the key frames with the peak expressions on the sequence are searched automatically by subtracting each frame from the normal image. There were 'K' face image sequences with 'M' frames and 'N'expressoins for each face so that 'K x M x N' face images are used as the database.

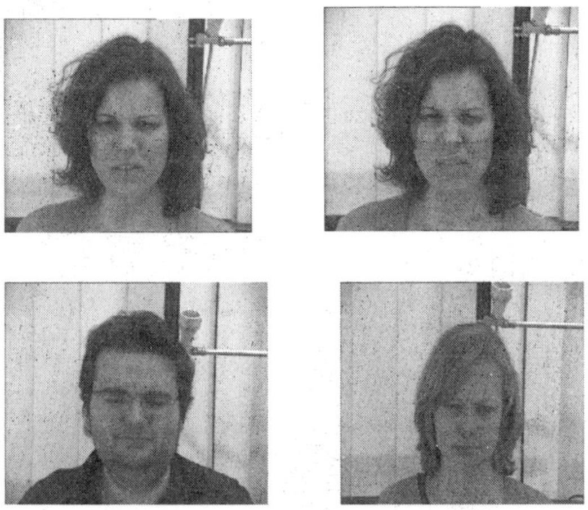

Fig. 2 Sample face Images

Normalization is done to make the images with uniform scale. The original images from the database are normalized to a size P x Q. Each N expressions from K x M images are grouped together to form different expression groups. The images are subjected to wavelet transformation. A window of size nxn is placed to the centre of the image. Every point is convolved with Gabor wavelets with v different frequencies and w different orientations. Convolution gives complex valued feature values. The magnitude of these complex values is selected for further processing.

The computational time for the feature vectors obtained from Gabor filters is very high due to its large size. To reduce the dimension of feature vectors Principal Component Analysis is performed.

The high dimensional feature vectors obtained from wavelets are projected to PCA spaces so that different groups of feature spaces namely 'Happy', 'Neutral,'Anger','Surprise' are obtained. The feature vectors are used to train a multilayer perceptron neural network.

The probe video image is also subjected to preprocessing steps before projecting it into feature space. The vector output from Gabor filters are projected to PCA spaces. The feature vectors of the test image are compared with that of each of the expression groups to find the best match between the testing face and all the prototypes. The multi layer neural network classifier tells us which person carries the expression and how far the expression on the testing face is from each type of expressions.

7. Results

We have selected face image sequences of five persons from FG-NET consortium [11] with variations in lighting conditions, small orientations, wearing glasses, heavy expressions etc. The expressions used were 'happy','normal','surprise', and 'anger'. Face images were normalized to a uniform size. Gabor wavelet filtering was done on the face images. The images were projected to separate PCA spaces to reduce the dimension. The PCA outputs are given to a multilayer perceptron neural network. The test image was also subjected to wavelet transform followed by PCA and neural network to identify the face and expression belongs to it. The average performance ratio is 91%. The efficiency plots for three sets of images are shown in Fig. 3.

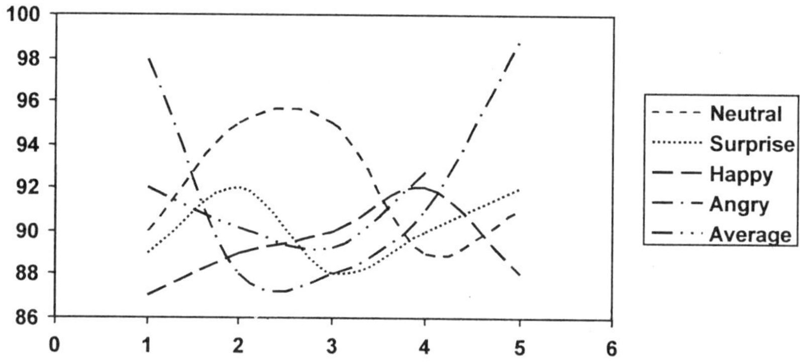

Fig. 3 Efficiency plot

8. Conclusion

In this paper, face recognition and expression classification from video face images are explained. Input video images with peak expressions are extracted and normalized to a uniform size.Gabor filtering is done on face images and the resulting high dimensional vectors are compressed using PCA.The expressions are classified using a multilayer perceptron neural network. The test image is also subjected to preprocessing steps and the output of Gabor filter is projected to PCA spaces followed by neural network classifier. The feature vector of the test image is matched against each of the expression groups to find the best match.

Our logic performs well for recognition of expressions from face sequences. The computational time and complexity is also very small. We have proposed a method to improve the efficiency and to increase the database by including more complex expressions as a future work.

9. References

[1] B. Abboud and F. Davoine. Bilinear factorisation for facial expression analysis and synthesis. *IEF Proc. Vis. Image Signal Proceess.* 152(3), 2005.

[2] M. Black and Y. Yacoob, "Recognizing facial expressions in image sequences using local parameterized models of image motion,Comput.Vis" vol. 25, no. 1, pp. 23–48, 1997.

[3] C.-S. Lee and A. Elgammal. Facial expression analysis using nonlinear decomposable generative models. In *AMFG*, pages 17–31, 2005.

[4] C. Darwin, *The Expression of the Emotions in Man and Animals*.Chicago, IL: Univ. of Chicago Press, 1872, 1965.

[5] E. S. Chuang, H. Deshpande, and C. Bregler. Facial expression space learning. In *Proc. of PG*, pages 68–76, 2002.

[6] Y. li Tian, T. Kanade, and J. F. Cohn. Recognizing action units for facial expression analysis. *IEEE Trans. PAMI*, 23(2), 2001.

[7] T. F. Cootes, G. J. Edwards, and C. J. Taylor. Active appearance models. In *Proc. of ECCV*, volume 2, pages 484 – 498, 1998.

[8] T. F. Cootes, C. J. Taylor, D. H. Cooper, and J. Graham. Active shape models: Their training and applications. *CVIU*, 61(1):38–59, 1995.

[9] I. Essa and A. Pentland, "Coding, analysis, interpretation and recognition of facial expressions," *IEEE Trans. Pattern Anal. Machine Intell.*, vol. 19, pp. 757–763, July 1997.

[10] H.Wang and N. Ahuja. Facial expression decomposition. In *Proceedings of the Ninth IEEE International Conference on Computer Vision*, volume 2, pages 958–965, 2003.

[11] Frank Wallhoff: Facial Expressions and Emotion Database *http://www.mmk.ei.tum.de/~waf/fgnet/feedtum.html*, Technische Universität München 2006

[12] *Handbook of Emotions*, M. Lewis and J. M. Haviland-Jones, Eds., Guilford Press, New York, 2000, pp. 236–249.

[13] K. Mase, "Recognition of facial expression from optical flow," *IEICE Trans.*, vol. E-74, no. 10, pp. 3474–3483, 1991.

[14] A. Ortony and T. J. Turner, "What is basic about basic emotions?," *Psychol.Rev.*, vol. 74, pp. 315–341, 1990.

[15] M. Pantic and L. J. M. Rothkrantz, "Expert system for automatic analysis of facial expression," *Image Vis. Comput. J.*, vol. 18, no. 11, pp. 881–905, 2000.

[16] "Toward an affect-sensitive multimodal human-computer interaction," in *Proc. IEEE*, vol. 91, pp. 1370–1390, Sept. 2003.

[17] J. Russell and J. Fernandez-Dols, *The Psychology of Facial Expression*. New York: Cambridge Univ. Press, 1997

Facial Expression by Feature Extraction

Praseeda Lekshmi V[1] and Dr. M. Sasikumar[2]
[1]Assistant Professor, CEK
vplekshmi@rediffmail.com
[2]Professor, MEC
drmsasikumar@yahoo.com

Abstract

Face recognition and expression analysis is one of the most challenging research areas in the field of pattern recognition. If we could identify a person irrespective of lighting condition, orientation, expression, color, pose etc, then it is possible for a computer too. But the automated face and expression recognition system is still a challenging task. In this work, different features like nose length, mouth location, inter eye distance and the areas of eye and mouth regions are extracted and used for identifying a particular face image from a database. Eye regions, nose, mouth, inter eye distance, and nose length are the distinct features. Expressions are identified by doing geometrical analysis on these features. These components are aligned horizontally, if they have any variation in orientation. It exhibits a good performance ratio.

1. Introduction

Face recognition is a task that humans perform routinely and effortlessly in their daily lives. It is a visual pattern recognition problem where a three-dimensional object is to be identified based on its two-dimensional image. In recent years, significant progress has been made in this area; owing to better face models and more powerful computers, face recognition system can achieve good results under constrained situations. Another, maybe more important motivation of facial expression recognition is that expression itself is an efficient way of communication: it's natural, non-intrusive, and has shown that, surprisingly, expression conveys more information than spoken words and voice tone. To build a friendlier Human Computer Interface, expression recognition is essential.

Recognizing faces and facial expressions are important abilities for many practical applications. Face expression recognition is useful for human-computer interaction, perceptual user interfaces, and interactive computer games [7] [6]. The face expression recognition problem is challenging because different individuals display the same expression differently. Selecting the most relevant features and ignoring unimportant features is a key step in solving this problem. Research in psychology [1] showed that facial expressions play a major role in human conversation coordination and have a greater influence on auditors than the textual content of a spoken message.

Facial expression recognition should not be confused with human emotion recognition as is often done in computer vision. Facial expression recognition deals with classification of facial motion and facial feature deformation in to abstract classes that are purely based on visual information. But emotions are result of many different factors such as emotional voice, pose, gestures, facial expressions etc. To analyze the facial expression, face regions have to be detected first. Next step is to extract and represent the facial changes caused by facial expressions. Geometric based and Appearance based methods are examples of feature extraction methods. In Geometric based method, the shape and location of facial features are extracted as feature vectors. In Appearance based method, image filters are applied either to whole face or to specific regions of facial image to extract facial features.

We present a method which makes use of the position of eye and mouth regions and length of the nose. Using the position of two eyes, some parameters are computed. These parameters are then used to identify the expression of the query image from a set of known images. Algorithm for correcting differences in orientation is applied to individual facial images using features such as eyes, nose and mouth. The proposed method is tested on Yale face database. The experimental results have demonstrated that the efficiency of the algorithm is good.

2. Background and related work

A lot of research has been going on in the area of human face detection and recognition [3]. Most face detection and recognition methods fall into two categories: Feature based and Holistic. In feature-based method, face recognition relies on localization and detection of facial features such as eyes, nose, mouth and their geometrical relationships. In holistic approach, entire facial image is encoded into a point on high dimensional space. Principal Component Analysis (PCA) and Active Appearance Model (AAM) [9] for recognizing faces are based on holistic approaches. In another approach, fast and accurate face detection is performed by skin color learning by neural network and segmentation technique [4]. Independent Component Analysis (ICA) was performed on face images under two different conditions [8]. In one condition, image is treated as a random variable and pixels are treated as outcomes and in the second condition pixels are treated as random variables and image as outcome. Facial expressions are extracted from the detailed analysis of eye region images is given in [2]. Large range of human facial behavior is handled by recognizing facial muscle actions that produce expressions is given in [10]. Video based face recognition is explained in [5].

Rest of the paper is organized as follows. Section 3 describes the proposed method. Results are discussed in section 4.Conclusion is given in section 5.

3. Method

We have considered the face images with certain degree of orientation and large variations in the facial expressions. Fig. 1.shows some images in the database.

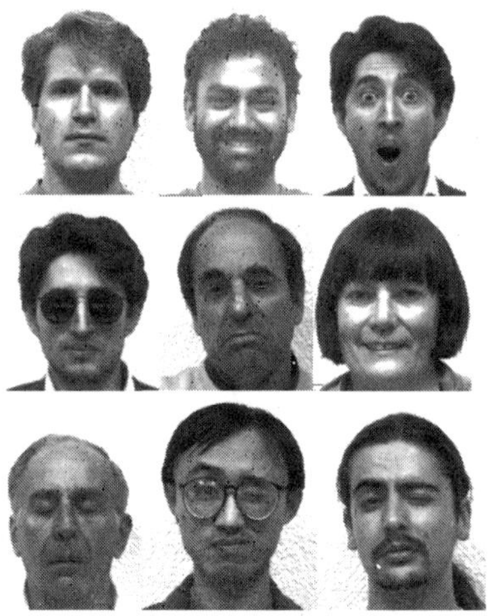

Fig. 1 Face Images in the database

Frontal looking faces with neutral expressions called normal faces and faces with set of non-neutral expressions form the database. The normal faces, also called reference faces form the face gallery.

Usually facial expressions are highly reflected in eyes and mouth regions. For analyzing the expressions with in the face, these regions are located first. Using the position of two eyes and the mouth, geometrical parameters are computed. These parameters are then used to identify the expression with in the face region.

Initially all the images in the database are preprocessed. As a preprocessing step, the images are normalized and cropped to get the eye region. Fig.2 shows the image obtained after cropping. The brightness of thic cropped image is enhanced to increase clarity and to reduce noise.

Fig. 2 Original image and cropped image

The vertical projection profile is calculated which is shown in Fig 3. The projection profile is searched for a large valley with an intervening peak. The peak area indicates the eye area in the image.

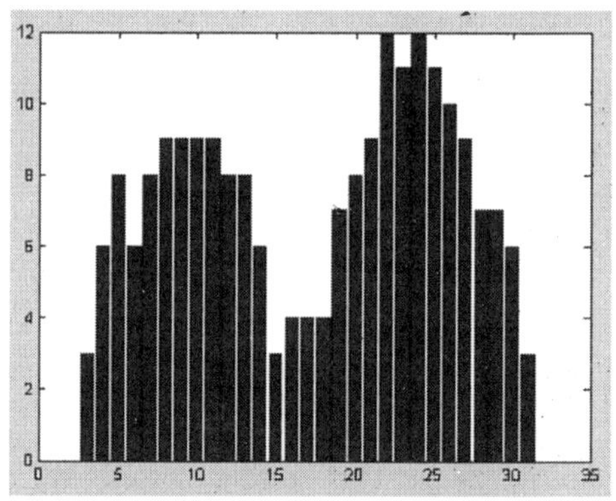

Fig. 3 Vertical Projection Profile

Using eyes, any orientation in the face image can be corrected. Orientation identified and corrected is shown in Fig. 4.

Fig. 4 Face Image and Orientation identified

After calculating the inter eye distance, nose and mouth are identified as they generally appear along the middle of two eyes in the lower half. The inter eye distance, nose length, eye and mouth area are computed for the analysis of facial expressions. Histogram for finding the nose length is given in Fig. 5.

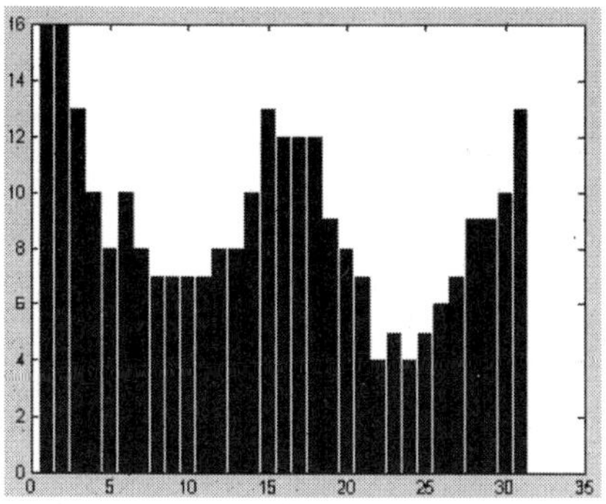

Fig. 5 Calculation of nose length

4. Results and Discussions

Experiments are conducted on set of 120 facial images taken from Yale face database. These images are 256 gray level images. The Yale [11] was taken from the Yale Center for Computational Vision and Control. It consists of images from 15 different people, using 11 images from each person, for a total of 165 images. The images contain variations with the following total expressions or configurations: center-light, with glasses, happy, left-light, without glasses, normal, right-light, sad, sleepy, surprised, and wink

The efficiency plot is given in figure 6.

The performance ratio for "happy "is 94%, for "sad" it is 89%, for "surprise" it is 91% and for "wink" 88%.

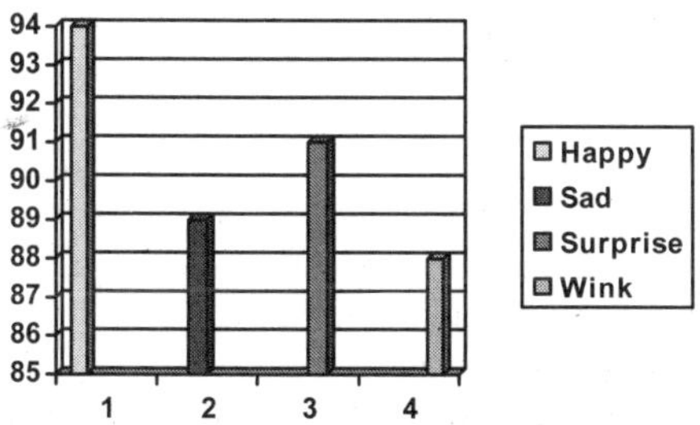

Fig. 6 Efficiency Plot

5. Conclusion

Here face recognition and facial expression analysis are performed. Four expressions namely "Happy, Sad, Surprise and Wink" are analysed.The method exhibits a better performance ratio. It is proposed to extend the work by including the challenging conditions of face recognition namely large variations in illumination and orientation.

6. References

[1] E. Boyle, A.H. Anderson, A. New lands, "The effects of visibility on dialogue performance in a cooperative problem solving task", *Language Speech* 37 (1) 1–20, 1994.

[2] Tsuyoshi Moriyama, Takeo Kanade, Jing Xiao and Jeffrey F. Cohn " Meticulously Detailed Eye region Model and It's Application to Analysis of Facial Images" , *IEEE Transactions in Pattern Analysis and Machine Intelligence*, Vol.28, No.5, May 2006

[3] Chellappa. R, Wilson and Sirohey.S, "Human and machine recognition of faces: A Survey" *In Proc.IEEE*, 83(5): 1995, 705-740

[4] Hichem Sahbi, Nozha, Boueimma, Tistarelli, J. Bigun, A.K.Jain (Eds), and "Biometric Authentication "LNCS2539, Springer Verlag Berlin Heidelberg, pp: 112-120, 2002.

[5] Dmitry O. Gorodnichy "Video-based framework for face recognition in video", Second Workshop on Face Processing in Video. *(FPiV'05) in Proceedings of Second Canadian Conference on Computer and Robot Vision (CRV'05),* Victoria, BC, Canada, 9-11, pp. 330-338,May, 2005.

[6] M. Pantie and L. J. M. Rothkrantz. "Automatic analysis of facial expressions: The state of the art". *IEEE Trans. Pattern Analysis and Machine Intelligence*, 22(12):1424–1445, 2000.

[7] A. Samal and P. A. Iyengar. Automatic recognition and analysis of human faces and facial expressions: A survey. *Pattern Recognition*, 25:65–77, 1992.

[8] Marian Stewrt Bartlett, Javier R, Movellan and Terrence J Seinowski , "Face Recognition by Independent Component Analysis", *IEEE Transactions on Neural Networks,* Vol.113, No.6, November 2002

[9] Nathan Faggian, Andrew Paplinski, Tat-Jun Chin, "Face Recognition from Video using Active Appearance Model Segmentation"

[10] Yan Tong, Weinhui Lio, Qiang Ji,"Facial Action Unit Recognition by Exploiting Their Dynamic and Semantic Relationships", *IEEE Trans. on Pattern Analysis and Machine Intelligence,* Vol.29, No.10, October 2007

[11] K. I. Chang, K. W. Bowyer, and P. J. Flynn, "An evaluation of multi-modal 2D+3D face biometrics," *IEEE Transactions on Pattern Analysis and Machine Intelligence*, , pp. 619–624.vol. 27, no. 4, 2005.

A Combine Approach for Skin Color Based Hand Gesture Extraction

Amresh Nikam, Poonam Kapade and Sonali Patil

Abstract

For many application like hand gesture recognition face detection, localization and tracking, skin color play an important role. In hand gesture recognition many times a power glove use for identifying hand and its shape. Some systems are uses pixel-based skin color detection techniques but they uses specific color space for identifying skin color. In this paper we are propose a method which is combination of different color space skin detection method. This approach gives very clear result for detecting hand.

1. Introduction

Man machine interface is currently an active research area in the human computer interaction (HCI). In hand gesture recognition system the first step is extraction hand from input frame. For detecting hand there are various methods which based on skin color. Skin color is an important feature for identifying hand because pixel color based method is much efficient than geometrical feature based method

In this paper first we explain the most commonly methods are used for skin color detection then we explain our approach for skin color detection.

2. Color-spaces used for skin modeling

Colorimetry, computer graphics and video signal transmission standards have stated many color-spaces with different properties. A wide variety of them have been applied to the problem of skin color modeling. The following sections briefly review the most popular color-spaces used for skin color detection [1].

2.1 RGB

RGB is a color-space originated from CRT (or similar) display application, when it was convenient to describe color as a combination of three colored rays (red, green and blue). It is one of the most widely used color-spaces for processing and storing of digital image data. However, high correlation between channels, significant perceptual non-uniformity, mixing of chrominance and luminance data makes RGB not a very favorable choice for color analysis and color-based recognition algorithms.

2.1.1 Normalized RGB

Normalized RGB is a representation that is easily obtained from the RGB values by a simple normalization procedure:

$$r = R/(R+G+B),\ g = G/(R+G+B),$$
$$b = B/(R+G+B)$$

As the sum of the three normalized components is known ($r + g + b = 1$), the third component does not hold any significant information and can be omitted, reducing the space dimensionality. The remaining components are often called "pure colors", for the dependence of r and g on the brightness of the source RGB color is diminished by the normalization. A remarkable property of this representation is that for matte surfaces, while ignoring ambient light, normalized RGB is invariant (under certain assumptions) to changes of surface orientation relatively to the light source. This, together with the transformation simplicity helped this color-space to gain popularity among the researchers

2.2 HSI, HSV, HSL - Hue Saturation Intensity (Value, Lightness)

Hue-saturation based color-spaces were introduced when there was a need for the user to specify color properties numerically. They describe color with intuitive values, based on the artist's idea of tint, saturation and tone. *Hue* defines the dominant color (such as red, green, purple and yellow) of an area; *saturation* measures the colorfulness of an area in proportion to its brightness. The "intensity", "lightness" or "value" is related to the color luminance. The intuitiveness of the color-space components and explicit discrimination between luminance and chrominance properties made these color-spaces popular in the works on skin color segmentation. Hue is invariant to highlights at white light sources, and also, for matte surfaces, to ambient light and surface orientation relative to the light source. However, points out several undesirable features of these color-spaces, including hue discontinuities and the computation of "brightness" (lightness, value), which conflicts badly with the properties of color vision.

$$h = \begin{cases} 0 & \text{if } max = min \\ (60^0 \times (g-b) / (max - min)) \bmod 360^0 & \text{if } max = r \\ 60^0 \times (b-r) / (max - min)) + 120^0 & \text{if } max = g \\ 60^0 \times (r-g) / (max - min)) + 240^0 & \text{if } max = b \end{cases}$$

$$
s = \begin{cases} 0 & \text{if } \max = \min \\ \dfrac{(\max - \min)}{(\max + \min)} = \dfrac{(\max - \min)}{2l} & \text{if } l \leq ½ \\ \dfrac{(\max - \min)}{2 - (\max + \min)} = \dfrac{(\max - \min)}{2 - 2l} & \text{if } l > ½ \end{cases}
$$

$$
l = ½ (\max + \min)
$$

2.3 YCrCb

YCrCb is an encoded nonlinear RGB signal, commonly used by European television studios and for image compression work. Color is represented by *luma* (which is luminance, computed from nonlinear RGB, constructed as a weighted sum of the RGB values, and two color difference values *Cr* and *Cb* that are formed by subtracting luma from RGB red and blue components.

$\boldsymbol{Y = 0.299R+0.587G+0.114B}$

$\boldsymbol{Cr = R-Y}$ (9)

$\boldsymbol{Cb = B-Y}$

The transformation simplicity and explicit separation of luminance and chrominance components makes this color-space attractive for skin color modeling.

3. Skin color identification in different color spaces

The RGB, HIS, and YCrCb color-spaces are mostly used for skin color modeling. In this section we see the how the skin tone is identifying in these color-spaces.

3.1 Skin color detection in RGB color space

Skin color detection in RGB color space is mention in the paper "15 Seconds of Fame". With the help of heuristic rules it is determined, whether a certain pixel of input image corresponds to the skin color. The skin color with the following rules [2], [3], which describe the skin cluster in the RGB colour space:

The skin colour at uniform daylight illumination

$R > 95$ AND$G > 40$ AND$B > 20$ AND

$\max\{R, G,B\} - \min\{R, G,B\} > 15$ AND

RGB components must not be close together greyness elimination

$|R - G| > 15$ AND

also R and G components must not be close together otherwise we are not dealing with the fair complexion

$R > G$ AND $R > B$ *R component must be the greatest component*

OR

The skin color under flashlight or (light) daylight lateral illumination

$R > 220$ AND $G > 210$ AND $B > 170$ AND $|R - G| \leq 15$ AND *R and G components must be close together*

$R > B$ AND$G > B$ B *component must be the smallest component*

3.2 Skin color detection in HSI color space

Kjeldson and Kender defined a color predicate in HSV color space to separate skin regions from background [4]. Skin color classification in HSI color space is very simple. Using threshold skim we easily find out the skin color. chosen the threshold as [*H1, S1*] and [*H2, S2*], and a pixel is classified to have skin tone if the values [*H,S*] fall within the threshold and this distribution gives the localized hand image. In our experiment we choose the threshold (10.0, -1.0) and (35.0, 1.0).

3.3 Skin color detection in YCrCb color space

The skin color region can be identified by the presence of a certain set of chrominance (i.e. Cr and Cb) values that is narrowly and consistently distributed in the YCrCb color space. The location of these chrominance values have been found and can be illustrated using the CIE chromaticity diagram as shown in Fig.-1. The RCr and RCb as the respective ranges of Cr and Cb values that correspond to skin color, which subsequently define our skin color reference map. The ranges that the most suitable for all the input images that tested are RCr = [133,173] and RCb =[77,127]. This map has been proven, in experiments, to be very robust against different types of skin color.
The skin color segmentation in YCrCb is as follow:

$$
I(x,y) = \begin{cases} 1. \text{ if } [Cr(x,y) \in R_{Cr}] \cap [Cb(x,y) \in R_{Cb}] \\ 0. \text{ Otherwise} \end{cases}
$$

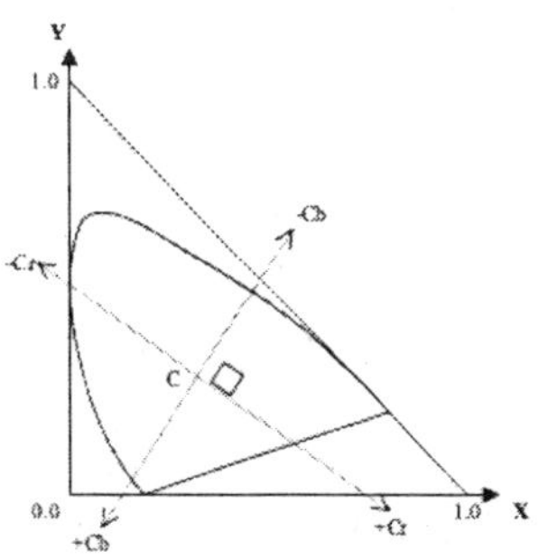

Fig. 1 Chrominance values found in facial region

The output pixel at point O(x, y) is classified as skin color and set to 1 if both the Cr and Cb values at that point fall inside their respective ranges, RCr and RCb. Otherwise the pixel is classified as non-skin color and set to 0.

4. Propose method

In our propose method first we find out the skin color of hand of the input image I. suppose I_1, I_2, and I_3 are the skin color segmented images of RGB, HSI, and YCrCb color space respectively as shown in Fig. 2.

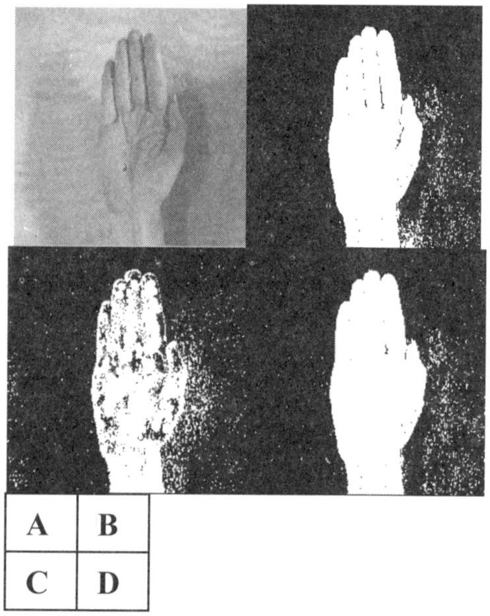

Fig. 2 (A) Original Image, (B) using RGB, (C) using HIS, (D) using YCrCb skin color.

In three images the hand region that is corrupted by noise. The noise may appear as small holes on the hand region due to undetected hand features such as nail, small hairs on hand or it may also appear as objects with skin color appearance in the background scene. Therefore we perform simple morphological operations such as dilation to fill in any small hole in the hand area and erosion to remove any small object in the background area [5]. The intention is not necessarily to remove entirely, but to reduce the amount and size of the noise.

After performing the morphological operation the segmented images look like as shown in Fig. 3.

Now the last stage is making the final hand segmented area using the following formula

I(x,y) = white if any two images of (I_1',I_2',I_3') have white pixel at x, y position other wise black. From this image reconstruct the image where the white pixel region replacing with skin color. Fig. 4 shows the result of this process.

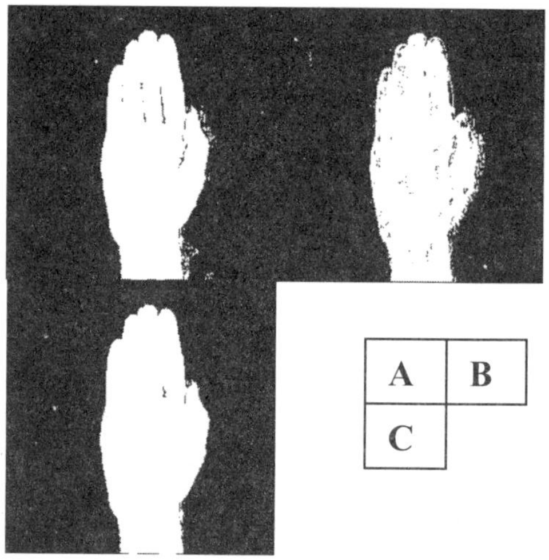

Fig. 3 Applying morphological operation on (A) 11, (B) I2, (C) I3

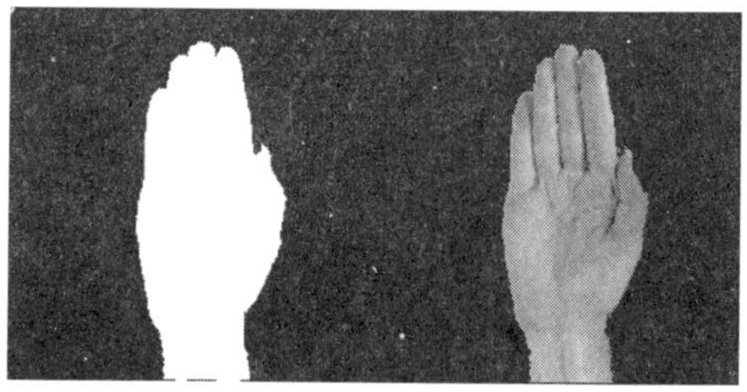

Fig. 4 Result of final segmented hand

5. Result

The following Table 1 show the result of our propose method. From this table our approach gives the better result in hand gesture segmentation.

Table 1 Comparison between different color space

	Real skin pixels detected	**Non-Real skin pixels detected**
RGB	89.23%	8.33%
HSI	84.63%	12.43%
YCrCb	92.37%	19.53%
Our propose method	96.17%	4.12%

6. References

[1] "Color space-Wikipedia, the free encyclopedia" http://en.wikipedia.org/wiki/Color_space

[2] J. Kova˘c, P. Peer, F. Solina. 2D vrrsus 3D color space face detection. Technical report, Computer Vision Laboratory, Faculty of Computer and Information Science, University of Ljubljana, 2003.

[3] P. Peer, F. Solina. An Automatic Human Face Detection Method, *Proceedings of Computer Vision Winter Workshop*, Ed. N. Br¨andle, pp. 122–130, Rastenfeld, Austria, 1999.

[4] Kjeldsen, R. and Kender., J., "Finding Skin in Color Images," *Proceedings of the Second International Conference onAutomatic Face and Gesture Recognition*, pp. 312-317 (1996).

[5] Rafael C. Gonzalez and Richard E. Woods. "Digital Image processing" Second edition 200, ISBN 81-7808-69-8, Page number 523.

A Novel Method for Linear Feature Extraction Based on Markov Random Fields and Morphological Operations

C. NagaRaju[1], S. Anusha Naidu[2] and A. Vijaya Lakshmi[3]
[1]Professor & Head of CSE
[2]Asst. Professor in CSE,
[3]MCA
VRS&YRN College of Engg. & Tech, Chirala-523155.

Abstract

In this paper we present a model-based approach to the automatic extraction of linear features, in the images. This method consists of two steps. The first step utilizes local information related to the geometry and radiometry of the structures to be extracted. It consists of a series of morphological filtering stages. The resulting image serves as input to a line-following algorithm, which produces a set of line segments. In the second step, a segment linking process is carried out incorporating contextual, a priori knowledge about the object shape, with the use of Markov Random Field (MRF) theory. In this approach the extracted line segments, produced by the morphological operators, are organized as a graph. The linking of these segments is then achieved through assigning labels to the nodes of the graph, using domain knowledge; extracted line segments measurements and spatial relationships between the various line segments. The interpretation labels are modeled as a MRF on the corresponding graph and the linear feature identification. This type of problem is formulated as a maximum a posteriori (MAP) estimation rule.

Keywords: *linear features, MAP, MRF, Gradient and Random field.*

1. Introduction

Several approaches for linear feature extraction have been proposed in the literature, most of them dealing with the problem of linear feature identification by using either synthetic aperture radar (SAR) images or optic (visible range) images. The paper is organized as follows: In paper a new proposed morphological approach for linear feature detection is described.

2. Local Analysis

The features we search for linear featured objects are characterized by their geometry and image appearance. The linear featured objects like roads appear on an optical airborne image as thin, elongated structures with a maximum width w_{max} .They are locally rectilinear, with each object pixel belonging to a line segment that is longer than a minimum length l_0 and each object segment is considered as a bright structure with respect to its surrounding. All this information can be integrated and extracted using mathematical morphology. A series of morphological operators, adapted to the geometrical characteristics of the objects we want to identify, are successively applied to the input image. A line-following algorithm is then applied to the resulting image in order to produce a set of line segments.

Step1: We want to remove dark structures from the image, without influencing the shape of the bright elongated structures of interest. For this reason, we apply a morphological closing by reconstruction, using a square flat structuring element (SE) of size equal to $w_{max}/4$.

Step2: Linear featured object segments correspond to elongated bright regions with a certain width. In order to eliminate bright structures that do not belong to any line segment with minimum length l_0 , we apply on the reconstructed image of step 1 a morphological opening by using l_0 pixels long linear structuring elements successively oriented in 32 possible directions. The resulting value at each pixel is the supremum of all these directional openings.

Step3: In this step, we eliminate very wide linear bright structures that correspond to objects larger than the specified objects. Initially, we perform a morphological closing operation with a square SE of size $w_{max}/4$, in order to remove remaining dark spots from the image. After this, we retain only bright structures with widths less than w_{max}, by applying an opening top-hat operator with a flat square SE of size w_{max}. The remaining structures correspond to the roads that we want to extract. Finally, we apply once again closing with a flat square SE of size $w_{max}/4$, in order to make the regions inside the roads more uniform.

Step4: The final result of step 3 gives a higher response at the points belonging to the roads compared with the surrounding background. An easy way to extract the road regions would be the application of a threshold to the resulting image as in [1].

Unfortunately, this leads to partial detection of the roads disconnected segments, together with some spurious results corresponding to false alarms. In order to overcome this problem, and to produce one pixel width line segments, we extract, from the resulting image of step 3, the pseudo-medial axis of the objects, over which we apply a line-following algorithm using the orientation of the SE which produces the supremum of the directional openings. The pseudo-medial axis of the objects is extracted by performing the watershed transformation on the response image I.

3. Global Analysis

The global analysis step of our approach is based on the earlier work of Tupin et al. [9] and is carried out on the level of the road segments. A graph is built, which contains all possible connected line segments that are created by using some connectivity criteria. The object identification process is then treated as an optimum graph labeling problem. This is carried out by associating an energy function to the line segments, based on a Markovian model of linear featured objects. Given the observation process, the minimization of this energy function will produce the best configuration of the line segments.

Step1: Graph creation

We will denote by S_{det} the set of the detected line segments. Each segment of S_{det} is defined by its endpoints. Two line segments of S_{det} can be connected if their distance is less than a fixed threshold, and if the angle between them is less than a specified value. We create a new set S_{con}, which corresponds to all possible connections between the elements of S_{det}. Let $S = \{S_{det}, S_{con}\}$, with its cardinality denoted by N.

For each line segment i ϵ S we assign a saliency measure R_i defined as:

$$R_i = I/(|\theta - \acute{\alpha}|+1) \quad (1)$$

where I is the mean value of the morphological object detection response, along the line segment is the line segment orientation, and ά is the mean value of the morphological object detection orientation response, along the line segment. We associate a graph structure (G) to the set S, each segment i belonging either to S_{det} or S_{con} being one of its nodes, and two nodes i and j being linked by an arc if they share a common endpoint. In order to introduce contextual knowledge with the use of a Markovian model, we must define a neighbourhood system. The neighbourhood N_i of each node i contains all the line segments that have a common endpoint with i. For each segment i□S_{det} we define cliques that correspond to both of its end points. Each of these cliques contains all the segments that share the specific extremity. If N_{det} denotes the number of elements of S_{det}, then the total number of cliques equals 2 xN_{det}. After the definition of our neighborhood system, we attach attributes to the nodes and arcs of G. The arc between nodes i and j is associated with a value $□_{ij}$ representing the angle between the two segments. For each node i□S, we associate a normalized length l_i and an observation value d_i, that reflects the probability of this segment belonging to the object. d_i should increase when, adjacent to it, segments belong also to the object, something that rises from the continuity that characterizes our region of interest. For this reason we express d_i as a function of the saliency measures r_k:

$$d_i = \max_{j \in V_i} \{(ri - rj)/2\} \quad (2)$$

The identification of the object will be carried out with an appropriate labeling of the graph. A label l_i is associated to each node i with $l_i = 1$ if i is a part of the object and $l_i = 0$ otherwise. The optimum configuration $L = (l_1; l_2; :::; l_N)$ of the segments of S, given the observation process $D = (d_1; d_2; :::; d_N)$, can be estimated with a MAP criterion that maximizes the posterior probability distribution given by:

$$P(l|d)=p(d|l)P(l)/p(d) \quad (3)$$

where P(l) is the prior probability of labelings l, p(d/l) is the conditional probability distribution function (p.d.f.) of the observations d, also called the likelihood function of l for d fixed, and p(d) is the density of d which is a constant when d is given.

Step2: Energy definition

We consider that the conditional probability distribution p(d/l) corresponds to a Gibbs distribution. By assuming independence between the different observations (d_i) and supposing that the conditional probability distribution of d_i only depends on the labelings l_i, we can write

$$p(d|\ l) = \Pi_{i=1}^{N} p(d_i/l_i) \ □ \ \exp(-□_{i=1}^{N} V(d_i/l_i)) \quad (4)$$

where $V(d_i/l_i)$ denotes the potential of segment i. This type of potential can be deduced from the observation field D and reflects the likelihood of every segment as belonging or not to a road.

The conditional probability distributions $p(d_i/l_i)$ are learned from an experiment after a manual segmentation of the objects, performed by a human observer. After this experiment, we notice that object segments may have almost any observation value d, while non-linear segments have observations with values greater than a threshold t. Based on this heuristic; the following linear conditional potentials have been chosen:

$$V(d\,|\,0) = \begin{cases} \frac{d}{t}\ if\ d < t \\ 1 \quad otherwise \end{cases} \text{ and } V(d\,|\,l) = 0, \forall d$$

In order for the potentials to correspond to a probability distribution, we normalize the values V (d|l) so that:

$$\int_0^1 p(d = x \mid 1)dx = \int_0^1 \exp^{[-V(d=x \mid 1)]}dx = 1$$

This condition holds for the potentials that correspond to object segments, as they are equal to zero. For the non-linear object segments, potentials of the form:

V $(d_i/0)$ + $\log Z_0$ are used; Z_0 denotes a normalization factor given by:

$Z_0 = (1\text{-}t)(1/e)\text{-}t(1/e\text{ -}1)$,with e = exp(1).

Step3: Prior Probability of Labeling

Our prior object model is based on the assumptions that objects like roads are long structures with low curvature and that intersections between them are rare. By considering the label field L as a MRF, we can use once again the MRF-Gibbs field equivalence in order to introduce a priori knowledge to the object identification task. The prior probability of labelings P(l) can be expressed in terms of an energy function U(l) as:

$$P(L=l)=1/Z_1\exp(-U(l)) \tag{5}$$

where Z1 is the partition function and $U(l) = \sum_{c \in C} V_c(l)$. The clique potentials $V_c(l)$ carry a priori information about the geometrical characteristics of the features to be extracted. Every clique c contains one segment belonging to S_{det}(with length l^{det}), along with the segments of S_{con} (with length l^{con}) that share the same extremity. Based on the main assumptions of our object model, we have chosen the following potentials for every clique c:

$$\forall i \in c, li = 0 \Rightarrow Vc(l) = 0 \tag{6}$$

$$\exists! i \in c/li = 1 \Rightarrow Vc(l) = K1 + 1 - l_i^{det} - \log Zo \tag{7}$$

$$\exists!(i,j) \in c^2/li = lj = 1$$

$$\Rightarrow Vc(l) = \sin(\theta ij) + 1 - l_i^{det} - l_j^{con} + 2\log Zo \tag{8}$$

in all other cases,

$$V_c(l) = K2\sum_{i/i \in c} li \tag{9}$$

Equation 6 describes a null situation, which does not have to be penalized or favored with respect to the a priori assumptions about the object structure. In equation 7, by choosing $K_1 > 0$ we penalize short objects: i.e. the clique potential is high for a clique with only one isolated segment, except when this isolated segment has a high normalized length l_i^{det} (close to 1). High values of K_1 favor more connected configurations. Equation 8 imposes the constraint of low curvature and at the same time penalizes configurations with short detected and long connecting segments. Finally, $K_2 > 0$, in equation 9, makes less probable the appearance of crossroads.

The additional factors $\log Z_0$ and $2\log Z_0$, in equations 8 and 9 respectively, facilitate the comparison between the clique potential values and the conditional potentials of the null configurations (where all the segments of the current clique are labeled as 0). In the case of a clique with one segment labeled as 1, the factor $K_1 + 1 - l_i^{det}$ in equation 6 is directly compared with the conditional potential component V $(d_i/0)$ of the current segment i. In the case of a Clique with two segments i, j labeled as 1, the factor $\sin(\theta_{ij})+1-l_i^{det}+l_j^{con}$ of equation 7 is compared with the sum of the conditional potential components $V(d_i|0)$, $V(d_j|0)$.

Step4: Posterior Probability

The posterior probability P(l/d) can be also expressed in terms of a global energy function U(l|d), which can be deduced from the potentials described in the previous two sections:

$$P(l|d)=\frac{1}{Z2}\exp(-U(l|d)),$$

$$U(l|d)=\sum_{i=1}^{N} V(di|li) - \sum_{c \in C} Vc(l) \tag{10}$$

The MAP configuration of the line segments can be estimated by minimizing the energy function U(l|d).

4. Results

Original

After morphological operations.

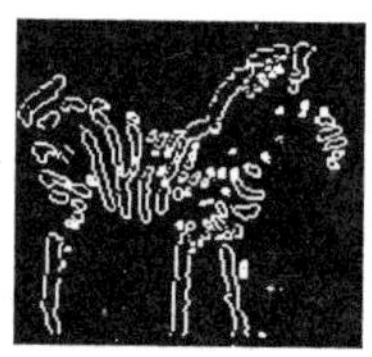

After Markov Random Field Model

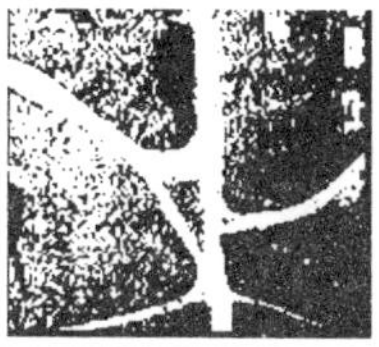

Original.

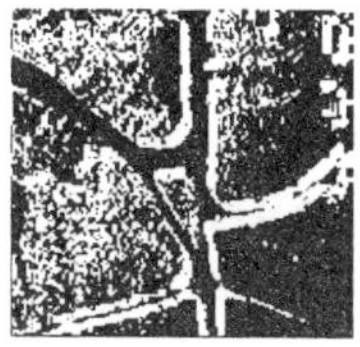

After Morphological operations.

After Markov Random Field Model

5. Discussion and Conclusions

The model-based technique for linear feature extraction, in digitized images, which combines both local and global criteria; its main advantage is the high detection performance in heavily textured environments along with its ability of identifying elongated structures independently of their size. Concerning the local analysis step, we utilized the morphological operators proposed by Chanussot et. al.[1], in order to identify linear structures with specific geometrical properties. Additionally, we extracted the linear feature main axis and applied a line-following algorithm. This process produced a set of line segments with meaningful orientation properties and eliminated a sufficient number of false alarms. In the next step of our work, we created a Markovian linear model; similar to the one proposed by Tupin et.al[6.] in order to introduce contextual knowledge to our analysis. At the same time, we proposed some necessary modifications in order to incorporate additional information about the nature of the line segment candidates. These include a discrimination between the initially detected segments (S_{det}) and the ones corresponding to the possible connections (S_{con}), the introduction of a new observation measure (d_i) that reflects more efficiently the likelihood value of each segment and the use of fewer number of potential parameters (t, K_1, K_2). One of the most important limitations of our method is that it is not entirely unsupervised, due to the setting of five parameters, two of them concerning the local analysis step (w_{max}, l_0) and three (t, K_1, K_2) influencing the linking process. The parameters w_{max}, l_0 are based on a priori knowledge about the size of the object. On the other hand, the proposed ranges of the parameters t, K_1, K_2, give optimal results for this type of environments, independently of the size of the linear features of interest. Further analysis should be carried out towards the problem of identifying segments with high curvature, especially when this is higher that the maximum object width found in the image and in the choice of a more efficient skeletonization process for the extraction of the object main axis. Finally, improvements could be obtained during the connection step, by searching for the best path between extremities of the segments we want to connect, instead of assuming that all objects may be found by connecting a set of initially detected segments. Even the modified version of this method could not produced accurate result for noise Images.

6. References

[1] R. Adams and L. Bischof, "Seeded region growing" *Pattern Anal. Much. Intell,* vol. 16, no. 6, pp. 641-647, Jun. 1994.

[2] S. Beucher and F. Meyer, 'The morphological approach to segmentation: The watershed transformation," in *Mathematical Morphology in Image Processing,* E. Dougherty, Ed. New York: Marcel Dekker, 3992.

[3] A. Bleau and L. J. Leon, "Watershed-based segmentation and region merging," *CV/U,* vol. 77, no. 3, pp. 317-370, Mar. 2000.

[4] J. S. De Bonet and P. A. Viola, "A non-parametric multi-scale statistical model for natural images," in *Advances in Neural Information Processing Systems,* M. I. Jordan, M. J. Keams, and S. A. Solla, Eds. Cambridge, MA: MIT Press, 1998, vol. 10.

[5] L. Breiman, "Bagging predictors," *Mach. Learn.,* vol. 24, no. 2, pp. 123-140, 1996.

[6] H. Cheng and C. A. Bouman, "Multiscale bayesian segmentation using a trainahle context model," *IEEE Trans. Image Process.,* voj. 10, no. 4, pp. 511-525, Apr. 2001-

[7] F. S. Cohen, Z. Fan, and M. A. Patel, "Classifcation of rotated and scaled textured images using gaussian markov random field models," *IEEE Tram- Pattern Anal. Mach. Inteli,* vol.13, no. 2, pp. 192-202, Feb. 1991.

[8] F. Dornaika and H. Zhang, "Granulometry using mathematical inor-*plicaiions,* Tokyo, Japan, Nov. 2000, pp. 51-54.

[9] B. Draper, J. Bins, and K. Baek, "ADORE: Adaptive object recognition," *Videre,* vol. 1, no. 4. pp. 86-99. 2000.

Analysis of Rolling Shutter Effect and Compensation in Image Databases

R. Sinduja and R. Thenmalar
II M.E Computer Science,
V.L.B Janakiammal College of Engineering & Technology, Coimbatore, Tamil Nadu, India.
Sinduja_VLB @ rediffmail.com thenmalar_atm@yahoo.com

Abstract

Due to the sequential-readout structure of complementary metal-oxide semiconductor image sensor array, each scanline of the acquired image is exposed at a different time, resulting in the so-called electronic rolling shutter that induces geometric image distortion when the object or the video camera moves during image capture. In this paper, we propose an image processing technique using a planar motion model to address the problem. Unlike previous methods that involve complex 3-D feature correspondences, a simple approach to the analysis of inter- and intraframe distortions is presented. The high-resolution velocity estimates used for restoring the image are obtained by global motion estimation, Bezier curve fitting and local motion estimation without resort to correspondence identification. This is conducted in image databases.

Keywords: *Complementary metal-oxide semi-conductor (CMOS) sensor array, motion analysis, rolling shutter.*

1. Introduction

The demand for image sensors is growing rapidly due to the increasing popularity of digital video cameras in surveillance, personal communications, consumer electronics, etc. Although the charge-coupled device (CCD) has been the dominant technology for image sensors, the complementary metal-oxide semiconductor (CMOS) technology is becoming a popular alternative because CMOS sensors can directly integrate with image processing or communication circuits, providing low cost, low power solutions for various applications.

However, due to the sequential-readout nature of CMOS sensor array, each row (scanline) of the sensor array is exposed at a different time, resulting in the so-called rolling shutter that induces geometric distortion to the image if the video camera or the object moves during image acquisition. As a result, the object may appear slanted, sheared, elongated, shrunk, or even arbitrarily deformed. Such undesirable effect seriously degrades the visual quality of the image.

We are primarily concerned with correcting the image deformation caused by rolling shutter by means of image processing. Although the rolling shutter effect of CMOS sensors is well known, little work has been found in the image processing literature that can effectively address the problem. A mathematical model for rolling-shutter cameras has been developed; however, the estimation of model parameters requires 3-D correspondences and even object shapes that are difficult to obtain from the kind of image dealt with in this work. In contrast, the approach presented here is much simpler and more tractable.

The contributions of this paper are twofold. First, the modeling of the rolling shutter effect is accomplished without resort to 3-D analysis. The planar motion assumption of the model, which is commonly made in many image processing problems, greatly reduces the complexity of the problem. Second, the rolling shutter compensation algorithm provides scanline realignment at high resolution that even works for blurry image sequences with moderate depth range or large motion. The above procedure is applied to image databases.

The rest of this paper is organized as follows. Section II explains how the rolling shutter is formed, and Section III reviews solutions for the rolling shutter problem. Section IV presents the modeling of the rolling shutter effect, and Section V describes the rolling shutter compensation algorithm. The setup and results of the experiment for testing the algorithm are presented in Section VI. The conclusion in Section VII.

2. Rolling Shutter Effect

The internal structure of a common 3-transistor active photon sensor is as follows. The photodiode collects the photons and converts them to photocurrent. The charges are integrated in the photodiode capacitor, and the expose time of the photocurrent integration is controlled by the rest signal. Up to this point, the CMOS sensor is similar to the CCD sensor.

However, the sequential-readout structure distinguishes the CMOSE sensor array from the CCD sensor array. In a typical CMOS sensor array architecture, there is only one row of readout elements so that only one row of sensors is selected by the row select signal in each readout operation. The accumulated charges are transferred to the column amplifiers, where the signals are amplified. Then a row of analog to digital converters (ADCs) converts the signal to digital form. In this structure the sampling time of each row is different, so is the reset time of integration.

The timing of readout and exposure is sketched in Fig 3. Because there is only one row of readout circuits, the readout time of different rows cannot overlap. Alsom the exposure of each row cannot begin until the readout of the corresponding scanline of the previous frame is completed. Since the exposure of each row is triggered at a different time, a rolling shutter is in effect and causes image deformation if the object or the camera moves during image capture.

The extent of the rolling shutter effect depends on the exposure time and the readout time. When the imaging chip has a standalone frame buffer, the readout process simply transfers the pixel data to the frame buffer. This operation can be done in a few clock cycles, allowing the total readout time per frame to be less than a few thousand cycles. The readout time in this case is much smaller than the exposure time; therefore, there is little rolling shutter effect unless the object moves extremely fast (more than one pixel in a single readout operation).

However, in cases where there is no on-chip frame buffer, which is a common design choice to save cost, the rolling shutter has a profound effect on image quality. Webcams, for instance, normally have no or very small local buffer and have to transfer via USB oir Firewire the recorded image data to the host computer, where the image is processed. The readout time of such devices is limited by the transmission rate. In this case, the readout time is comparable to the exposure time and may dominate the whole imaging process, making the rolling shutter effect profoundly noticeable.

3. Related Work

The rolling shutter effect can be prevented by using a mechanical shutter. Alternatively, one can design a new circuit with a local sample-and-hold for each photo sensor so that the whole sensor array experiences a single exposure. However, this method reduces the fill factor of the photo sensor and degrades the efficiency of photo collection. As a result, the readout rate is still limited by the transmission rate.

Approaches that address the rolling shutter effect by image analysis have been proposed. One approach is to derive a time-de-pendent perspective model for the rolling-shutter camera by assuming that the perspective transformation of each scanline is a function of the relative location and velocity between the object and the camera. The condition under which the rolling shutter effect becomes negligible was also derived. Aider et al. further applied the model to estimate the camera parameters and the object dynamics, but the shape of the object and the correspondences, of the object between frames must be known a priori.

Wilburn et al pointed out that the rolling shutter effect is not always undesirable and built a 2-D array of rolling-shutter cameras to achieve high-speed imaging. The final image was constructed by stitching the scanlines acquired by different cameras at the same exposure time.

4. Modeling of Rolling Shutter Effect

We focus on the scenario in which the camera undergoes with respect to the object a translational motion parallel (or nearly parallel) to the image plane. The planar motion model is based on two observations. First, the rolling shutter effect is notice able when the camera or the object moves rapidly in a single direction. It is less noticeable for complex motions such as rotating and zooming. Second, the difference in image distortion is hardly noticeable when depth range of the objects in the scene is moderate. Such a planar motion model has been commonly adopted for many image processing problems, such as image deblurring, motion-compensated video coding, and video stabilization.

For simplicity, the image with rolling shutter effect is referred to as the distorted image throughout the remaining paper, whereas the image without rolling shutter effect is referred to as the normal image. With the planar motion model, the distorted image due to rolling shutter can be modeled as a transformation of the normal image solely dependent on the relative motion between the camera and the scene. Without loss of generality, we assume the scene is static and only the camera moves.

In the following, n denotes the frame number, s = (sx, sy) denotes the coordinates of a pixel in the distorted image, and p = (px, py) denotes the coordinates of a pixel in the normal image. Furthermore, let v(t) = (vx(t), vy(t)) denote the camera motion at time t, and T the time interval between two successive images of the normal image sequence. For simplicity, we assume that the nth normal image is sampled at (n+0.5)T and the pixels in the nth frame of the distorted image sequence is sampled at $nT+s_y$. Each scanline of a distorted image is sampled at a specific instant during the exposure, and the interval between the sampling instants of two successive scanlines is defined as the unit time.

Interframe and intraframe distortions are discussed separately. The intraframe distortion refers to the shape deformation of objects in a video frame, whereas the interframe distortion refers to the deformation of object shape between successive frames of an image sequence.

A. Interframe Distortion

Assume p1 in the n – 1th frame and p2 in the nth frame of a normal image sequence correspond to the same scene point. Since the two frames are sampled at (n-0.5)T and (n + 0.5)T, respectively, the image displacement of the point can be described by

$$p2 = p1 + \int_{(n-0.5)T}^{(n+0.5)T} V(t)dt \tag{1}$$

Likewise, the image displacement between a point s1 in the n-1th frame and the corresponding point s2 in the nth frame of a distorted image sequence can be described by

$$s2 = s1 + \int_{(n-1)T+s_{1y}}^{nT+s_{2y}} V(t)dt \tag{2}$$

Note that because the sampling time of a scene depends on the scanline on which it is projected, the integration interval is controlled by the vertical position of the scanline. If there is no camera motion between (n-1)T+s_{1y} and nT+s_{2y}, s2=s1 and the image displacement (or geometric distortion) is zero, there is no rolling shutter effect. This matches with intuition. On the other hand, if $v_y(t)$ =0 during the integration interval, the point remains on the same scanline, but its horizontal displacement is a function of $v_x(t)$. In general, v(t) can be an arbitrary function. Note that (2) cannot be solved because it is a self-dependent function of s_2y. One of the contributions of this paper is to make this equation tractable, as presented in Section V.

B. Intraframe Distortion

Let p1 and p2 be two points in the nth frame of a normal image sequence, and n a time instant at which the camera is still. Denote the corresponding points of p1 and p2 at this time instant r1 and r2, respectively. Note that r1 and r2 are auxiliary points for mathematical derivation. Generalizing (1) yields

$$p_1 = r_1 + \int_{n}^{(n+0.5)T} v(t)dt \tag{3}$$

$$p_2 = r_2 + \int_{n}^{(n+0.5)T} v(t)dt \tag{4}$$

Subtracting (3) from (4), we have

$$p_2 - p_1 = r_2 - r_1 \tag{5}$$

Similarly, considering two points s1 and s2 in the nth frame of the distorted image sequence that correspond to r1 and r2 respectively, we have

$$s_1 = r_1 + \int_{n}^{nT+s_1t} v(t)dt \tag{6}$$

$$p_2 = r_2 + \int_{n}^{nT+s_{2y}} v(t)dt \tag{7}$$

Subtracting (6) from (7) yields

$$s_2 - s_1 = r_2 - r_1 + \int_{nT+s_2y}^{nT+s_1y} v(t)dt$$

$$= p_2 - p_1 + \int_{nT+s_2y}^{nT+s_1y} v(t)dt \tag{8}$$

By rearranging the above equation, we have

$$p_2 = p_1 + s_2 - s_1 - \int_{nT+s_2y}^{nT+s_1y} v(t)dt \tag{9}$$

Which has two implications. First, if the camera does not move during the time interval (nT+s_{1y}, nT+S_{2y}), p_2-p_1 = s_2-s_1 and, as we expect, there is no rolling shutter effect. Second, if s2 and s1 are on the same scanline, the integration interval in (9) is zero, and, thus, the distance between pixels of a scanline is not affected by the rolling shutter.

The analysis presented above forms the theoretical basis of the rolling shutter compensation algorithm described in the next section. Before moving on, we present another useful equation. In (2), the displacement from s1 to s2 is obtained by an integration of v(t). If v(t) is continuous, according to the mean value theorem, e can find some T in the interval ((n-1)T+s_{1y},nT+s_{2y}) such that

$$v(T) = \frac{1}{T + s_2y - s_1y}(s_2 - s_1). \tag{10}$$

This imposes a constraint on the velocity v(t) of a point between two successive frames.

5. Distortion Correction Algorithm

Undoing the rolling shutter effect is a challenging task. There are three primary problems to be addressed. First, from (9), we know that if s1 and p1 are identified and the velocity v(t) is known, the displacement between s2 and p2 can be derived and corrected. However, a pair of s1 and p1 need be identified first. Second, because the input sequence is geometrically distorted and motion blurred, velocity estimation by feature detection and matching is difficult. An alternative solution has to be sought. Third, the temporal sampling of v(t) must be at the scanline level, which is much higher than the frame rate. However, traditional motion analysis methods can only produce motion information at frame rate.

Most video sequences begin with a fixed scene and camera. If the camera is still at the beginning of a distorted image sequence so that the first frame is a normal image, the first problem can be solved. Specifically, when $v(t) = 0$ for $0 < t \leq T$ so that $s = p$ for any point in the first frame, the center pixel $s_m = (s_{mx}, s_{my})$ of the nth distorted frame is at the same location as its corresponding point $pm = (p_{mx}, P_{my})$ of the normal image. This relationship can be derived from (1) and (2) by noting that

$$s_m = r + \int_{nT+s_{my}}^{nT+s_{my}} v(t)dt$$

$$= r + \int_{0.5T}^{nT+0.5T} v(t)dt = P_m \qquad (11)$$

where r represents the location of s_m (and p_m) in the first frame. We can choose the middle scanline of the image as the references for compensation.

The second problem can be solved by determining the global motion of the entire frame first and estimating the velocity of each scanline from the resulting global motion. Note that it is easier to obtain robust global motion estimate than corresponding points. Also note that no identification of correspondences is needed in this approach.

The third problem is solved by using parametric curve fitting to interpolate the velocity and achieve fine-granularity velocity estimation. Unlike the deterministic interpolation, the parametric curve fitting can effectively generate smooth data and adapt to local samples.

The strength of the algorithm comes from the novel combination of several techniques. The overall flowchart of the proposed system is shown in Fig. 1. First, global motion estimation is performed per frame to obtain the initial velocity estimate. The resulting global motions are interpolated using Bezier curve to estimate the velocity per scanline. Then local motion refinement is performed to improve the velocity estimate. In this step, two constraints based on the analysis described in the previous section are imposed to detect outliers. Local motion refinement and velocity estimation are performed iteratively. Finally, the image is restored by religning the scanlines.

Each component of the algorithm is detailed in the following. We use v'(t) to denote the estimated velocity and v(t) the true velocity.

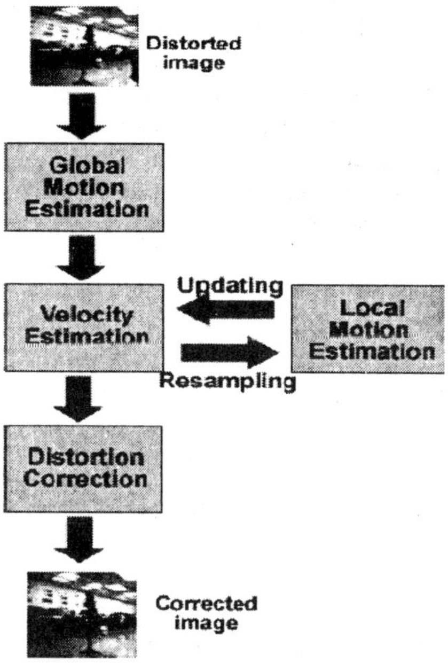

Fig. 1 Block diagram of the proposed system

A. Global Motion Estimation

The block-based motion clustering method described in is adopted to compute the global motion vector frame by frame. Although a simple block matching instead of complex correspondence matching is used for global motion estimation, it is found that the overall system performance is not affected.

First, the current n^{th} image is segmented into blocks (16 x 16 in our implementation). Second, for each block, a matched block in the previous frame with minimal sum of absolute difference is determined. The displacement between the current block and its matched block is the motion vector. Then, the 2-D histogram of the motion vectors of all blocks of the current frame is generated and low-lass filtered to reduce the estimation noise. Finally, the peak in the filtered histogram is chosen as the global motion vector g(n) of the current frame.

The exact relation between g(n) ad v(t) is unknown. However, we observe empirically that g(n) of distorted image sequence is pretty close to the global motion vector of the normal image sequence. Therefore, from (1) we have

$$g(n) \cong \int_{(n-0.5)T}^{(n+0.5)T} v(t)dt \qquad (12)$$

By setting T= (n + 0.5)T in (10), we get the initial estimate of the velocity of the middle scanline.

$$v'((n+0.5)T) = f(n)/T. \qquad (13)$$

B. Velocity Estimation

The global motion estimation generates a rough estimate of the velocity v'(t) at t=(n+0.5)T. However, the temporal resolution of the velocity required for the scanline is hundred times higher. For a VGA-size frame, for example, the velocity of each of the 640 scanlines of the frame has to be determined. Thus, an interpolation scheme is needed to meet the resolution requirement.

If piecewise linear interpolation is applied, discontinuities at frame instants would occur and result in over compensation. Such overcompensation makes the video look worse than the rolling shutter effect itself.

Smooth parametric curves, specified by control points, are known for producing smooth representation of camera or object trajectory in film and computer graphics. We adopt this approach and choose Bezier curve to represent the velocity. A Bezier curve $q(\lambda)=(qx(\lambda), qy(\lambda))$ is *a* 3-degree polynomial. The x component of $q(\lambda)$ is described by

$$q_x(\lambda)=(1-\lambda)^3c_1+3\lambda(1-\lambda)^2c_2+3\lambda_2)(1-\lambda)c_3+\lambda_3c^4 \tag{14}$$

where $0 \leq \lambda \leq 1$ and c_1, c_2, c_3 *and* c_4 are the control points. The exact formula applies to the *y* component *qy(i)*.

The control points of the nth frame can be determined from four samples on the curve. We obtain four nearby velocity samples from (13) and solve for the control points by imposing the following conditions:

$$qx(0)=v_x'((n-1.5)T) \tag{15}$$

$$qx(1/3)=v_x'((n-0.5)T) \tag{16}$$

$$qx(2/3)=v_x'((n+0.5)T) \tag{17}$$

$$qx(1)=v_x'((n+1.5)T) \tag{18}$$

The same set of conditions is imposed on *qy(i)* except that *v'x* is replaced by *v'y*. Once the control points are obtained, the velocity of the ith scanline in the nth distorted image is computed by

$$v'(nT+i)=q\left(\frac{(i/T+1.5}{3}\right) \tag{19}$$

This is an important equation since it can be applied to convert sample on the Bezier curve to a velocity estimate and reversely a velocity estimate to a sample on the Bezier curve. The velocity estimate thus obtained is smooth and free of overcompensation.

C. Local Motion refinement

Further improvement of the velocity estimate is needed because 1) not all blocks have true matching in the global motion estimation due to limited field of view and 2) the Bezier curve is continuous and cannot handle the case where *v(t)* experiences a sudden change.

We adopt an iterative scheme in which the outliers are detected first and then local refinement of the velocity estimate is performed. Consider a point s in the current frame. Is corresponding point in th previous frame must locate inside the frame. According to (10) and letting *T=nT+sy*, the following two constraints can be established.

$$0 \leq s_x + \frac{v_x(nT+s_y)}{v_y(nT+s_y)+1}h \leq w \tag{20}$$

$$0 \leq s_y + \frac{v_y(nT+s_y)}{v_y(nT+s_y)+1}h \leq h \tag{21}$$

where w and h, respectively are the width and height of the video frame. When any of the constraint is violated,m the true correspondence of s is outside the previous frame; thus, the velocity estlmate *v'(nT+Sy)* is unreliable. In practice, because *v(t)* is unknown, we approximate (20) and (21) by using the estimated velocity *v'(t)* and adding the safety margins ε_x and ε_y

$$\varepsilon_x \leq s_x + \frac{v'_x(nT+s_y)}{v'_y(nT+s_y)+1}h \leq w-\varepsilon_x \tag{22}$$

$$\varepsilon_y \leq s_y + \frac{v'_y(nT+s_y)}{v'_y(nT+s_y)+1}h \leq h-\varepsilon_x \tag{23}$$

These two constraints are used for outlier detection. If a point *s1* and its velocity estimate satisfy (22) and (23), we perform local motion estimation to refine the velocity estimate, in a way similar to global motion estimation except that only a small region around s1 insteead of the entire frame is considered. After the local motion *1(s1,n) = (lx(s1,n), ly(s1,n))* of *s1* in the nth frame is found, the corresponding *s2* in the previous frame is located using (2)

$$s_2 = s_1 - 1(s_1,n) = s_1 - \int_{(n-1)T+s_{2y}}^{nT+s_{1y}} v(t)dt. \tag{24}$$

Applying (24) and substituting *T = NT+Sly* into (10), we obtain the refined velocity of *s1*

$$v'(nT+s_1y)=\frac{1(s_1,n)}{T-(s_1y-s_2y)}=\frac{1(s_1,n)}{T-ly(s_1,n)} \tag{25}$$

The local motion refinement and velocity estimation are performed iteratively. More precisely if the residual in the local motion estimation is lower than a threshold, the velocity estimate obtained from (25) and converted through (19) is used to impose a new constraint on the control points, in addition to the four constraints (15)-(18), for new velocity estimation. Then, for each scanline, the closest four velocity samples are used to compute the control points in (14).

D. Scanline Realignment

Image correction is done by re-aligning the scanlines after the velocity estimate $v'(t)$ is obtained. According to (8), the corresponding point p of s can be obtained by

$$p = s - \int_{(n+0.5T}^{nT+sy} v'(t)dt. \qquad (26)$$

Because (26) does not depend on S_x, all pixels in the same scanline are moved by the same displacement. Since $v'(t)$ is in floating point precision, p does not necessarily fall on the image sampling grid. In our algorithm, the intensity of s is as signed to the four samples nearest to p, and each is weighed inversely proportional to its distance to p. The intensity of the sample is normalized by the sum of the weights it receives. Finally, the missing pixels in the image are filled by averaging the near by pixels. The scanline realignment algorithm described here is similar to the free-form deformation used in image metamorphosis .

6. Experimental Results

The Fig. 2 shows the illustration of the rolling shutter effect. This is the sample image taken from the digital camera. Fig. 3 shows the compensation of rolling shutter effect. Similarly figure 4 shows the illustration of the rolling shutter effect and Fig. 5 shows the compensation of rolling shutter effect.

Fig. 2 Illustration of rolling shutter effect

Fig. 3 Compensation of rolling shutter effect

Fig. 4 Illustration of rolling shutter effect

Fig. 5 compensation of rolling shutter effect

7. Conclusion

In this paper we have described about the image domain analysis of the rolling shutter effect and developed a distortion correction algorithm to undo the rolling shutter effect.

Instead of finding the exact correspondence between successive frames of the distorted image sequence, the algorithm uses global motion estimation, parametric curve fitting and scanline realignment to compensate the distortion. The algorithm is simple and effective.

8. References

[1] C.Geyer, M.Meingast and S.Sastry, "Geomentric models of rolling-shutter cameras," in Proc. Omnidirectional Vision, Camera Networks and Non-classical Cameras, Oct.2005,pp.12-19.

[2] O.Ait-Aider, N.Andreff, J.M.Lavest and P.Martinet, "Exploiting rolling shutter distortions for simultaneous object pose and velocity computation using a single view", in Proc 4th IEEE Int.Conf. Computer Vision Systems, Jan 2006,pp,35-41.

[3] S. Lauxtermann et al., "A mega-pixel high speed CMOS imager with sustainable gigapixel/sec readout rate," in Proc. 2001 IEEE Workshop on Charge-Coupled Devices and Advanced Image Sensors, Lake Tahoe, NV, June 7-9, 2001, pp. 48-51.

[4] M. Wäny and G. Paul, "CMOS image sensor with NMOS only global shutter and enhanced responsivity," in IEEE Transactions on Electron Devices, Vol. 50, No. 1, January, 2003, pp. 57-62.

[5] Chia-Kai Liang, Yu-Chun Peng, Hung-Au Chang, Che-Chun Su and Homer H. Chen, "The effect of digital image stabilization on coding performance," International Symposium on Intelligent Multimedia, Video and SpeechProcessing, October, 2004.

Classification of Images Using SVMs

M. Raja Sekar[1], Prof P. Prem Chand[2] and Prof I.V. Muralikrishna[3]
[1]DRK College of Engineering and Technology,
Department of Computer Science and Engineering, Hyderabad, India
rmummalaneni@yahoo.com
[2]Dept.of CSE ,College of Engineering,
Osmania University, Hyd, India-500007
drpremchand_p@yahoo.com
[3] Director (Research and Development)
Jawaharlal Nehru Technological University, Kukatpally, Hyderabad-500072-India
ivm@ieee.org

Abstract

We introduce a method of feature selection for Support Vector Machines. The method is based upon finding those features which minimize bounds. In many supervised learning problems feature selection is important for a variety of reasons. This paper describes the design of multi-category Support Vector Machines (SVMs) for classification of cars. To train and test the SVMs a collection of yste5 images of different types of cars were used. As it is well known that SVMs are sensitive to the number of features in pattern classification applications, the performance of the SVMs as a function of the number and type of features was also studied. Our goal here, in feature selection is to obtain a smaller set of features that accurately represent the original set. A K-fold cross validation procedure with three subsets was applied to assure reliability. In a kernel optimization experiment using five popular shape features.

Keywords: *support vector machines, multi-category classification, feature selection*

1. Introduction

We perform a systematic evaluation of feature selection (FS) methods for Support Vector Machines (SVMs). The Support Vector Machine is a theoretically superior machine learning methodology with great results in classification of high dimensional datasets and has been found competitive with the best machine learning algorithms. In the past, SVMs have been tested and evaluated only as pixel-based image classifiers. Moving from pixel-based techniques towards object-based representation, the dimensions of remote sensing imagery feature space increases significantly. This results increasing complexity of the classification process, and causes problems to traditional sample-based classification schemes. The objective of this study is to evaluate SVMs for effectiveness and prospects for object-based image classification as a modern computational intelligence method. An SVM approach for multi-class classification was followed, based on primitive image objects produces by a multi-resolution segmentation algorithm. The segmentation algorithm produced primitive objects of variable sizes and shapes. Then, a feature selection step took place in order to provide the features for classification which involved spectral, texture and shape information. For training the SVM, sample image objects, derived from the segmentation procedure were used. The SVM approach seems very promising for Object Based Image Analysis and the future work will focus on the integration of SVM classifiers with rule-based classifiers.

2. Classification Approach

Recently, Support Vector Machines (SVMs) have been a promising tool for image classification. When is the solution to the support vector training problem global, and when is it unique? By "global", we mean that there exists no other point in the feasible region at which the objective function takes a lower value SVMs belong to the class of maximum margin classifiers (Heisele et al. 2003). The goal of maximum margin classification in binary SVM classification (Vapnik 1998) is to separate the two classes by a hyper plane such that the distance to the support vectors is maximized. SVMs perform pattern recognition between two classes by finding a decision surface that has maximum distance to the closest points in the training set which are termed support vectors. The procedure starts with a training set of points where each point x_i belongs to one of the two classes identified by the label y_i *belongs to* {-1, 1}. This hyper plane is called the optimal separating hyperplane (OSH). The OSH has the form:

$$\mathbf{h(y)=\sum\alpha_i\, y_i\, x_i\ \ x+c;} \qquad \mathbf{(1)}$$

The coefficients α_i and b in (1) are the solutions of a quadratic programming problem (Vapnik, 1998). Classification of a new data point x is performed by computing the sign of the right side of (1). For multicategory classification, (2) is employed:

$$\mathbf{d(y)= h(x) \div norm\ of} \sum \alpha_i\, x_i\, y_i\ x+c; \qquad (2)$$

The sign of d is the classification result for x, and $|d|$ is the distance from x to the hyperplane. Intuitively, the farther away a point is from the decision surface, i.e., the larger $|d|$, the more reliable the classification result. The entire construction can be extended to the case of nonlinear separating surfaces. Each point x in the input space is mapped to a point $z = \Omega(x)$ of a higher dimensional space, called the feature space, where the data is separated by a hyper plane. The key property in this construction is that the mapping $\Omega(x)$ is subject to the condition that the dot product of two points in the feature space $\Omega(x)$. $\Omega(y)$ can be rewritten as a kernel function $K(x, y)$. The decision surface has the equation:

$$\mathbf{h(y)} = \sum \alpha_i\, x_i\, y_i\ y+c; \qquad (3)$$

where, the coefficients _i and b are the solutions of a quadratic programming problem. Note that $g(x)$ does not depend on the dimensionality of the feature space. Kernel functions commonly used for pattern recognition problems are

$$\mathbf{L(x,y)=(1+x.y)^e} \qquad (4)$$

which results in a classifier that is a polynomial of degree d and There are two basic strategies for solving q-class problems with SVMs. In the One-vs-all approach, q SVMs is trained. Each of the SVMs separates a single class from all remaining classes (Schölkopf et al. 1995, Cortes and Vapnik 1995). In the pairwise approach (used in this work), $q(q-1)/2$ machines are trained. Each SVM separates a pair of classes. The pair wise classifiers are arranged in trees, where each tree node represents a SVM. Regarding the training effort, the one-vs-all approach is preferable since only q SVMs have to be trained compared to $q(q-1)/2$ SVMs in the pairwise approach. The runtime complexity of the two strategies is similar: the one-vs-all approach requires the evaluation of q, the pairwise approach the evaluation of q-1 SVMs. Recent experiments on person recognition indicate similar classification performances for the two strategies (Nakajima et al. 2000). The input to the SVMs is a set of features obtained from the car image. The image processing feature extraction methods used are described in the next section.

3. Image Processing

Image processing starts with a 24-bit color image of the robotic scene that contains a car located on a platform. Ten different types of cars are considered. Image processing operations used are (Kartoun 2003). conversion to gray-scale,thresholding using the Otsu method (Otsu 1979), removal of noise from the image due to optical lens distortion, adaptation to ambient and external lighting conditions, and segmentation of the car from the background. The end result is an image of segmented bag from which features are extracted. Using the MATLAB's Image Processing Toolbox (MathWorks 1998), eight popular shape features were extracted from each car image:

- Area: actual number of pixels in the region
- Bwarea: the area of the objects in a binary image
- Bounding Box : the ratio of the height and width of the smallest rectangle that can contain the region.
- Equivalent Diameter: the diameter of a circle with the same area as the region. Computed as $(4 \cdot Area/\prod)^{0.5}$.
- Entropy: E = entropy(I) returns E, a scalar value representing the entropy of intensity image I.
- Centroid: Each cluster in the partition is defined by its member objects and by its centroid, or center.
- FilledArea: Scalar the number of on pixels in FilledImage.
- FilledImage Binary image (logical) of the same size as the bounding box of the region. The on pixels correspond to the region, with all holes filled in.

Fig. 1

Fig. 2

Fig. 3

Fig. 4

Fig. 5

	C1	C2	C3	C4	C5
Area	168	25	343	66	98
BW Area	89.8750	1.6103e+003	312.8750	3.8614e+3	2.9216e+003
Bounding Box.	[9.5000 53.5000 0.5000 184 54 3]	[27.5000 36.5000 0.5000 61 21 3]	[0.5000 0.5000 0.5000 100 56 3]	[4.5000 19.5000 0.5000 84 37 3]	[0.5000 0.5000 0.5000 100 62 3]
Equivalent Diameter	33.7360	45.2795	19.951	70.1174	60.9912
Entropy	7.3420	7.5540	6.2918	7.6128	7.5330
Centroid	[99.5060 83.6012 1.9286]	[53.1200 49.0400 1.9200]	[53.0058 38.2332 2.0845]	[49.6515 38.3485 2.2727]	[51.4592 15.2653 1.9694]
Filled Image	[54x184x3 logical]	[21x61x3 logical]	[56x100x3 logical]	[37x84x3 logical]	[62x100x3 logical]
Pixel List	[168x3 double]	[25x3 double]	[343x3 double]	[66x3 double]	[98x3 double]

The heart of the support vector machine design is the kernel selection. Kernels project the data into a high dimensional feature space and thereby increase the computational power of the linear learning machines The kernels chosen for the car classification problem are the most common ones used in support vector machines, i.e., the polynomial and the Gaussian RBF kernels. The SVMs procedure was implemented in the "OSU SVM MATLAB Toolbox" (Ma and Ahalt 2003). Optimization procedure was conducted, using the eight car features.

4. Conclusions

Multi-category car classification for five cars was performed using SVMs. In future the SVMs procedure will be tested using polynomial and RBF kernels. In this work we analyzed eight popular shape features for ten cars. We also observed that entropy is not suitable for image classification. From this results we can say that equivalent diameter, bounding box are important features in image classification.

5. References

[1] Argialas D. and V.Goudoula 2003. Knowledge-based Land Use Classification from IKONOS Imagery for Arkadi, Crete, Greece. Remote Sensing for Environmental Monitoring, GIS Applications, and Geology II, Proceedings of SPIE Vol. 4886. Argialas, D., and C. Harlow 1990.

[2] Computational Image Interpretation Models: An Overview and a Perspective. *Photogrammetric Engineering and Remote Sensing*, Vol. 56, No 6, June, pp. 871. Baatz, M. & Schäpe, A. 2000. Multiresolution Segmentation – an optimization approach for high quality multi-scale image segmentation. *In: Strobl, J. et al. (eds.): Angewandte Geographische Information sverarbeitung XII. wichmann, Heidelberg, pp. 12-23.*

[3] Benz U., Hoffman P., Willhauck G., Lingenfelder I. and M. Heynen, 2004. Multi-resolution, object-oriented fuzzy analysis of remote sensing data for GIS-ready information. *ISPRS Journal of Photogrammetry and Remote Sensing 58* pp. 239

[4] Biederman, I. 1985. Human image understanding: Recent research and a theory. Computer Vision, Graphics, and Image Processing, 32, 29–73. 5.Binaghi E., Gallo I. and M. Pepe 2003. A Neural Adaptive Model for Feature Extraction and Recognition in High Resolution Remote Sensing Imagery Int. J. Remote Sensing.

[5] Cortes C. and V. Vapnik. Support-vector network. Machine Learning.

[6] De Moraes R.M. 2004. An Analysis of The Fuzzy Expert Systems Architecture for Multispectral Image Classification

[7] Using Mathematical Morphology Operators (Invited Paper)

[8] International Journal of Computational Cognition.

Detection of Pupil and Iris for Personal Identification

C. M. Patil and SudarshanPatil Kulkarani
JSS Research Foundation
Dept of Electronics & Communications Engg., S J College of Engg, Mysore-06
patilcm@gmail.com *pk.sudarshan@gmail.com*

Abstract

Biometric systems are getting more attention in the present era. Iris recognition is one of the most secure and authentic among the other biometrics and this field demands more authentic, reliable and fast algorithms to implement these biometric systems in real time. In this paper we propose an efficient algorithm to detect the inner and outer boundary of the iris. The inner boundary is accurately located by applying an edge detection and Circular Hough Transform (CHT) in an extracted region from the coarse center. The presented method further proposes a process of extracting the outer boundary of the iris. The achieved results are compared with the published algorithms and evaluated. Experimental results show promising performance on iris images captured in ideal and non-ideal conditions from the CASIA Iris Database with two different image sizes.

1. Introduction

The term "Biometrics" refers to a science involving the statistical analysis of biological characteristics. Here biometrics is used in a context of analyzing human characteristics for security purposes. This measurable characteristic, Biometric, can be physical, such as face, eye, iris, fingerprint, and voice or behavioral, like signature and typing rhythm. Nowadays, security is one of the important factors in the field of information, business, e-commerce, military and etc. For this reason, personal identification has become a significant topic. Some previous methods of identification such as PIN (personal Identification Number), password, ID card and signatures that are used widely, have some drawbacks. ID card or PIN can be stolen, password may be forgotten and signatures can be imitated. Biometric characteristics are used to overcome these problems. Fingerprints, voiceprints, retinal blood vessel patterns can be substituted instead of non-biometric methods for more safety and reliability. Among the physiological characteristics, iris patterns (Fig. 1) have a wonderful and abundant structure and full of complex textures. These patterns are well protected from the external environment and can not be stolen, copied, stored or imitated. The iris texture is unique from one person to other ones. Also we can easily capture iris image from distance without physical contact and these features are stable during the life [1]. Each iris is a unique structure, featuring a complex system which is stable and unchanging throughout life.

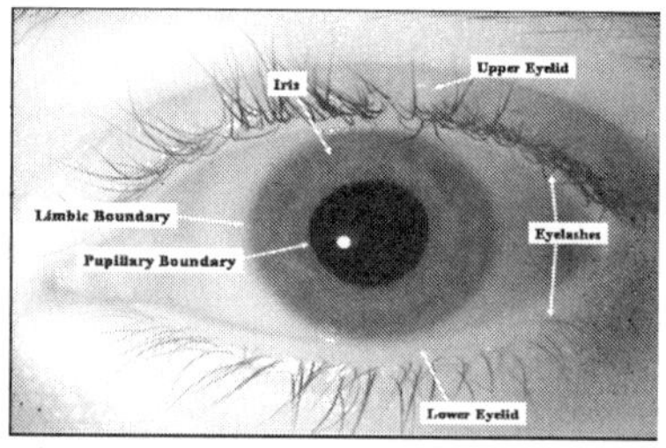

Fig. 1 Image of an eye showing the Iris patterns

The iris is formed in the beginning of the pregnancy during the first three months of gestation; its structure is completed in the eighth month and then it goes through some texture changes, but in the second and third years of age it stops to change. Each person has different iris, even if they are identical twins. Each person also has different irises in each eye. The pupil diameter of human eyes fluctuates either to adapt the amount of light to the retina or when a subject is gazing at a fixed object in absence of light stimulation and/or visual accommodation. A crucial point is represented by a reliable estimation of the pupil edge. Most of the methods require some knowledge about the degradation parameters, typically the blur and the additive noise; the relevant procedure to identify these parameters depends on the adopted model of the image. The purpose of this paper is detecting the edge of the pupil and iris.

2. Iris localization

This paper proposes an algorithm to locate the boundaries of the iris and the pupil. The proposed method is applied to binary image to search for a coarse circle of the pupil using canny edge detection and Circular Hough Transform [3] to accurately find the inner and outer boundary of the image then knowing exactly where the pupil and iris. This procedure is essential particularly on automated recognition system as shown in Fig. 2.

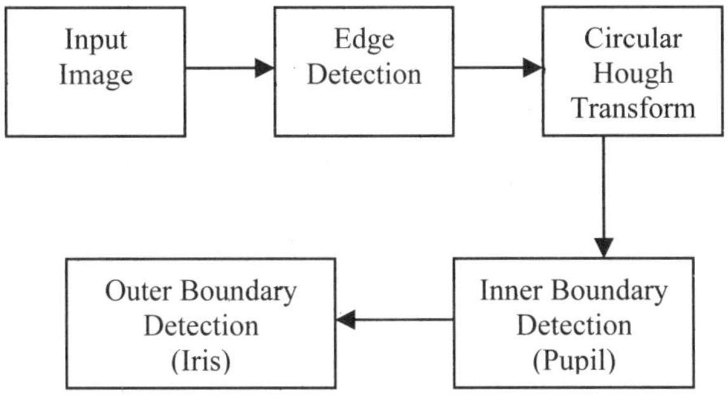

Fig. 2 Diagram showing processing steps, from image capture to iris boundary detection

3. Advantage and disadvantage of Hough Transform

Hough transform directly detects the object's edges using image global features; it can link every point to form a closed edge in image field. If the shape or edges of objects is known, using Hough transform edges can be detected and points can be linked together easily. The main advantage of the Hough transform technique is its tolerance to the presence of gaps in feature boundary descriptions and is relatively unaffected by image noise. Also the Hough transform provides parameters to reduce the search time for finding lines based on a set of edge points, and that these parameters can be adjusted based on application requirements. The disadvantage of Hough transform is that the calculation quantity is very large. With image size increasing, the quantity of data will become too large and the processing quantity of data will be slow. However, there are two major drawbacks from the Hough transform; these drawbacks are the requirements for a large amount of storage and high cost in computation.

4. Proposed Method

Both iris and pupil have circular shape. In our approach Hough transform will be prominently used to isolate these circular shapes. The equation of a circle is

$$r^2 = (x-a)^2 + (y-b)^2 \quad (1)$$

Where a and b are the center of the circle in the x and y direction respectively and where r is the radius. The parametric representation of the circle is

$$x = a + r\cos(\theta) \quad (2)$$
$$y = b + r\sin(\theta)$$

Step 1. Edge Detection

The first step is to filter (Median) out any noise in the original image, and trying to locate and detecting any edges using canny edge detection. The purpose of edge detection is to decrease the number of points in the search space for the objects.

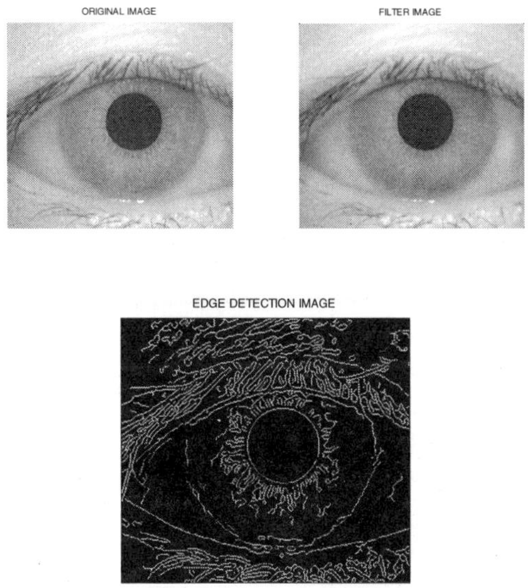

Fig. 3 Diagram shows the original image, filtered image and edge detection image

Step 2. Circular Hough Transform

The same procedure for line detection using Hough transform would follow to find the circle, but with an increased dimensionality to the search space, it is now a three dimensional parameter space (a, b, r). For detecting circles in images, the circular Hough transform provides good detection. For each edge point draw the circle with center in the point with the desired radius. When every edge point and every desired radius is used, the accumulator will now contain numbers corresponding to the number of circles passing through the individual coordinates. The discrete space constructed through accumulator and detection of parameters of curves by detecting the peak in the Hough space [5]. Thus the highest numbers correspond to the center of the circles in the image. Therefore, a number of circular filters of different radii are tried and the best fit one is picked out. The center of the pupil and iris as detected by the circular filter becomes a coarse center and the coarse radius of the pupil and iris is the radius of the chosen filter.

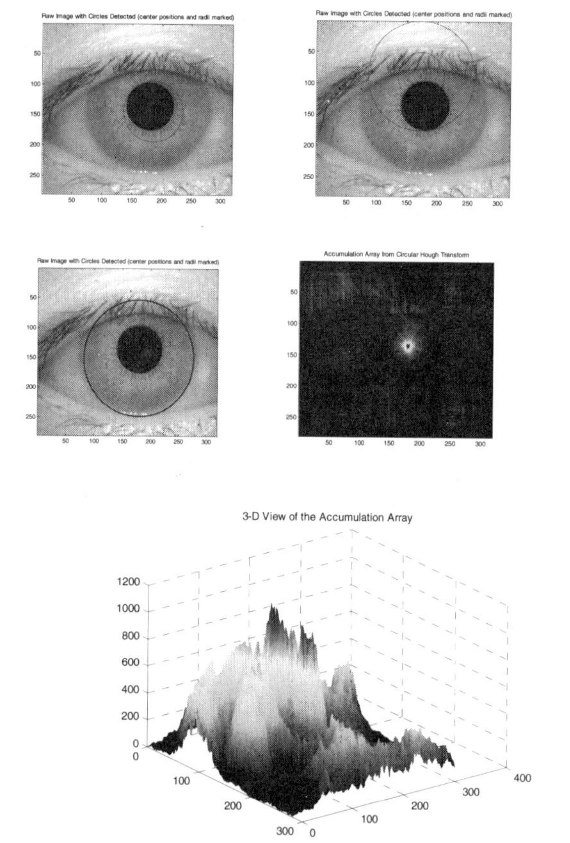

Fig. 4 Diagram shows the detection of edge points with different radii circles and accumulation of array

5. Performance evaluation

The algorithm is implemented to evaluate the performance on the whole CASIA iris database [8], with two different sizes, using MATLAB. Version 2 of CASIA is better for evaluating the robustness of iris segmentation algorithms as it includes many poor quality images as a result of factors such as occlusion, illumination, reflection, off-focus, the use of make-up, etc. The experimental results demonstrate the robustness of the proposed method against influential factors. Fig. 5 shows some experimental results from the CASIA database where the robustness of the proposed method to pupil dilation, hair presence, bad illumination, and occlusion is demonstrated. The overall performance is summarized in Table 1. Canny edge detector used with threshold 0.48 to remove most of the noise due to the texture and leave the edges of the image. The Hough transform has been applied on these images after canny edge detection, and then marked the circles of image. The computational complexity highly depends on the number of edge pixel and the number of radii to be matched.

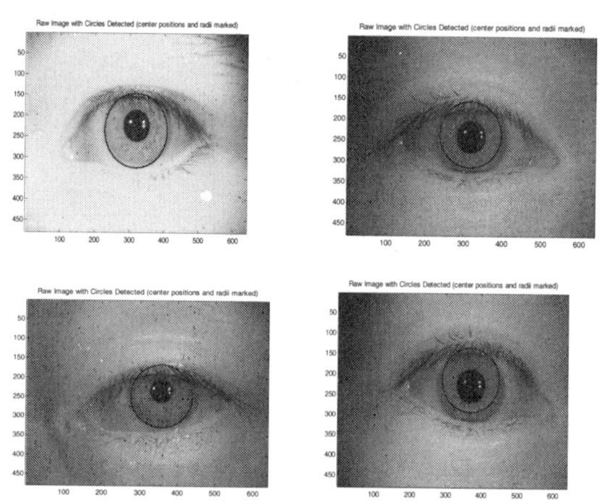

Fig. 5 Examples of experimental results

Table 1 Overall performance summary on CASIA iris database.

Ver	Image size	No. of images	Successful rate
1	320× 280	756	99.22 %
2	640× 480	1200	99.12%

6. Conclusions

In this paper, a boundary detection of iris and pupil location method is presented using proposed circular filters. The proposed circular filter allows us to coarsely detect the circle of the pupil region in an iris image, and then accurately located by using a circular Hough transform. The segmentation is done in a coarse-to-fine manner. Furthermore, the proposed approach considerably reduces the time load for detecting the boundaries. The future works will be about modifying to shorten the runtime and evaluating the proposed method on more iris databases.

7. References

[1] E. *Wolff*, "Anatomy of the Eye and Orbit."

[2] Pupil edge detection and morphological identification from blurred noisy images. D. Iacoviello', M. Lucchetti', G. Calcagnini2, F. Censi

[3] Object Detection using Circular Hough Transform, Mohamed Rizon, Haniza Yazid, Puteh Saad, Ali Yeon Md Shakaff,2Abdul Rahman Saad

[4] Process of Recognition of Human Iris: Fast Segmentation of the Iris Roger, F. Larico Chavez, Yuzo Iano, Member IEEE, and Vicente B. Sablón

[5] M. Schulze (2003, July 23). *Circular Hough Transform: A Java applet demonstration*, [Online]. Available: http://markschulze.net/java/hough

[6] Detecting Coins with Different Radii based on Hough Transform in Noisy and Deformed Image, Mohamed Roushdy

[7] Circle Detection Using Hough Transforms Documentation, Jaroslav Borovi_cka

[8] CASIA Iris Image Database. http://www.sinobiometrics.com

Image Watermarking Encoder for FPGA Devices

S. China Venkateswarlu, B. Y. David Solomon Raju and C. M. Renu Babu
Asst. Professor, Dept of ECE, HITS College of Engg, Bogaram, Hyderabad-501 301
cvenkateswarlus@gmail.com davidesolomonraju@gmail.com renubabu.m2001@gmail.com

Abstract

Both encryption and digital watermarking techniques need to be incorporated in a digital rights management framework to address different aspects of content management. While encryption transforms original multimedia object into another form, digital watermarking leaves the original object intact and recognizable. The objective is to develop low power, real time, reliable and secure watermarking systems, which can be achieved through hardware implementations. In this paper, we present an FPGA based implementation of an invisible spatial domain watermarking encoder. The watermarking encoder consists of a watermark generator, watermark insertion module, and a controller. Most of the invisible watermarking algorithms available in the literature and also the algorithm implemented in this paper insert pseudorandom numbers to host data. Therefore, we focus on the structural design aspects of watermarking generator using linear feedback shift register. We synthesized the prototype watermarking encoder chip in a Xilinx 8.2i using Vertex technology, which can be operated at 50MHZ frequency.

1. Introduction

Unauthorized access of digital content is being prevented by implementing encryption technologies. However, it doesn't prevent an authorized user from illegally replicating the decrypted content. Hence, encryption alone does not address all the IP issues related to DRM. Issues related to ownership rights of digital content are addressed by digital rights management (DRM) systems [1, 2]. Various aspects of content management namely, content identification, storage, representation, and distribution and intellectual property rights management is highlighted in DRM. Digital watermarking is one of the key technologies that can be used for establishing ownership rights, tracking usage, ensuring authorized access, preventing illegal replication and facilitating content authentication. Therefore, a two layer protection mechanism utilizing both watermarking and encryption is needed [3].

Digital watermarking is the process of embedding data called a watermark into a multimedia object such that watermark can be detected whenever necessary for DRM. The digital watermarking system essentially consists of a watermark embedder and a watermark detector [4, 5]. The embedder inserts a watermark onto the host object and the detector detects the presence of the watermark. An entity called watermark key is also used during the process of embedding and detecting the watermark. This watermark key is unique and exhibits a one-to-one correspondence with every watermark. The key is private and known to only authorized parties, eliminating the possibility of illegal usage of digital content.Short for ***Field-Programmable Gate Array,*** a type of logic chip that can be programmed. An FPGA is similar to a PLD, but whereas PLDs are generally limited to hundreds of gates, FPGAs support thousands of gates. They are especially popular for prototyping integrated circuit designs. Once the design is set, hardwired chips are produced for faster performance.Short for ***programmable logic device***, a generic term for an integrated circuit that can be programmed in a laboratory to perform complex functions. A PLD consists of arrays of AND and OR gates.

A system designer implements a logic design with a device programmer that blows fuses on the PLD to control gate operation.

System designers can use development software that converts basic code into instructions a device programmer needs to implement a design.

PLD types can classified into the following groups

- PROMs (Programmable Read Only Memory) - offer high speed and low cost for relatively small designs
    - **PLAs (Programmable Logic Array)** - offer flexible features for more complex designs
    - **PAL/GALs (Programmable Array Logic/Generic Array Logic)** - offer good flexibility and are faster and less expensive than PLAs

The goal is to develop low power, real-time, reliable and, secure watermarking systems [16, 17]. VLSI implementation of the watermarking algorithms is not yet significantly explored. A hardware based watermarking system can be designed on a field programmable gate array (FPGA) board, Trimedia processor board [7], or custom IC. The choice between the FPGA and cell based IC is a trade-off between cost, power, and performance [15, 18]. Invisible Robust algorithm is chosen as it is simple yet robust against geometric attack and is tested using Stir mark benchmark [20].

2. Watermarking Algorithm

In this section, we describe the invisible-robust algorithm [19] chosen for VLSI implementation. Let us assume the following notations: I – original gray scale image, W – binary or ternary watermark image, I* – watermarked image, (i, j) – pixel location, E1,E2 – watermark embedding functions, D – watermark detection function, r – neighborhood radius, IN – neighborhood image, K - digital watermark key, and α1, α2 – scaling constants.

The watermark insertion process consists of the following: First, the watermark W Which is a ternary image having pixel values {0,1 or 2} is generated using the digital Key K. Then, altering the pixels of original image performs watermark insertion. Using watermark-embedding functions.

$$
\begin{aligned}
& I^*(i,j) = I(i,j) && \\
\textit{if} \quad & W(i,j) = 0; && \\
& = E_1(I(i,j), I_N(i,j)) && \\
\textit{if} \quad & W(i,j) = 1; && (1) \\
& = E_2(I(i,j), I_N(i,j)) && \\
\textit{if} \quad & W(i,j) = 2; &&
\end{aligned}
$$

The encoding functions E_1 and E_2 are defined as follows.

$$E_1(I, I_N) = (1 - \alpha_1) I_N(i,j) + \alpha_1 I(i,j)$$

$$E_1(I, I_N) = (1 - \alpha_1) I_N(i,j) + \alpha_1 I(i,j) \qquad (2)$$

$$E_2(I, I_N) = (1 - \alpha_1) I_N(i,j) + \alpha_2 I(i,j) \qquad (3)$$

The signs of α1 and α2 are used for the detection function and their actual values determine the watermark strength. The neighborhood image pixel gray value IN is calculated as the average gray value of the neighboring pixels of the original image for a neighborhood radius r. For example, for neighborhood radius r = 1, it is [13]:

$$I_N(i,j) = \left(\left(I(i+1,j) + I(i+1,j+1)/2 \right) + I(i,j+1) \right)/2 \qquad (4)$$

The scaling (1 – α1) is used to scale IN to ensure that watermarked image gray value I* never exceeds the maximum gray value for 8-bit image representation corresponding to pure white pixel. The neighborhood radius determines the upper bound of the watermarked pixels in an image.The first step of detection process is the generation of watermark W using the watermark key K. Next, the watermark is extracted from the test (watermarked) image using the detection function given below, for α1 > 0 and α2 < 0.

$$
\begin{aligned}
W^*(i,j) &= 1 \textit{ if } I^*(i,j) - I_N(i,j) > 0. \qquad (5) \\
&= 2 \textit{ if } I^*(i,j) - I_N(i,j) < 0.
\end{aligned}
$$

By comparing the original ternary watermark image W and the extracted binary watermark image W*, the ownership can be established when the detection ratio is larger than a predefined threshold. The value of the threshold determines the minimum acceptable level of watermark detection.

Table 1 Performance of already proposed watermarking chips

	Design Type	Watermarking	Multimedia	Domain	Chip Features
Hsiao [6]	Custom IC	Invisible-Robust	Image	Wavelet	NA
Maes [7]	FPGA board/IC	Invisible-Robust	Video	Spatial	17/14 kG Logic
Tsai [8]	Custom IC-0.35μ	Invisible-Robust	Image	DCT	3.3V, 50MHz
Petitjean [9]	FPGA board	Invisible-Robust	Image	Fractal	50MHz
Garimella [10]	Custom IC-0.13μ	Invisible-Fragile	Image	Spatial	1.2V
Mathai [11]	Custom IC-0.18μ	Invisible	Video	Wavelet	1.8V
Tsai [12]	Custom IC	Invisible-Robust	Video	Spatial	NA
Mohanty [13]	Custom IC-0.35μ	Robust-Fragile	Image	Spatial	3.3V, 545MHz
Seo [14]	FPGA board	Invisible-Robust	Image	Wavelet	82MHz
Mohanty [15]	Custom IC-0.35μ	Visible	Image	Spatial	3.3V, 292MHz

3. Architectural Design of Watermarking Encoder

In this section, the architecture of the invisible-robust watermarking encoder algorithm described in the previous section, is elaborated. We first provide high-level description of the encoder, followed by their architectural details.

3.1 Watermarking Encoder

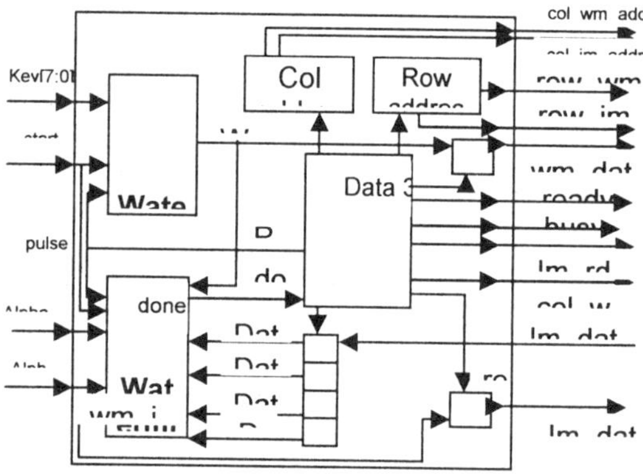

Fig. 1 Watermarking Encoder

The high-level view of the proposed chip is shown in Fig. 1. The encoder includes the units, such as watermark generation, watermark insertion, control, row and column address decoder, and registers. The generation unit is used to produce the watermark, and insertion unit is used to insert the watermark into the host image. The control unit controls the operation of the above two modules and the data flow in encoder. The address decoders are used to decode the memory address where the image and watermark are stored. The registers are used for buffering purpose. We assume that there are two external RAMs, one to store the original image and other to serve as a storage space for watermark data available. The watermarked image is written back to the RAM storing the original image.

3.2 Watermark Generation Unit

Pseudorandom sequence generator generates the ternary watermark. The watermark generation unit consists of linear feedback shift register (LFSR). LFSR is a very crucial unit in watermark security and detection. It is a sequential shift register with combinational feedback logic around it that causes it to cycle pseudo randomly through a sequence of binary values. Therefore, we have studied the difficulties of a LFSR and have taken appropriate measures to ensure quality design [21–23]. The LFSR consists of flip-flops (FFs) as sequential elements with feedback loops. The feedback around a LFSR comes from a selected set of points called taps in the FF chain and these taps are fed back to FFs after either XORing or XNORing.

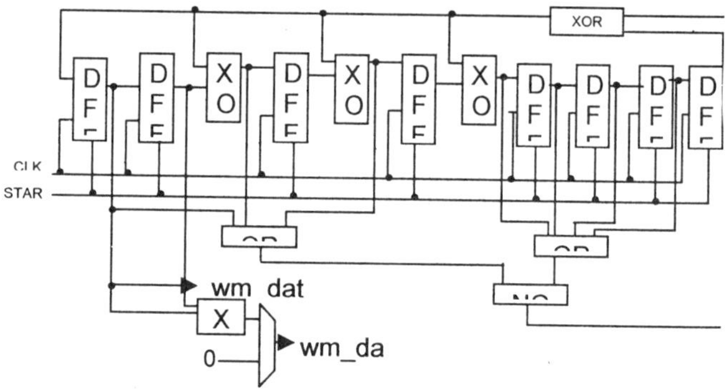

Fig. 2 Watermark Generation Unit

The design aspects considered when modeling LFSRs are as follows [21–23].

- **XOR or XNOR Feed Back Gates:** The feedback path may consist of either all XOR Gates or all XNOR gates; LFSR will produce same number of values with different Sequence for a particular tap setting.
- **One-to-Many or Many-to-One Feedback Structure:** Both one-to-many or many-to-one feedback structures can be implemented using same number of gates. However, a one-to-many feedback structure will have a shorter worst case delay.
- **Prohibited or Lockup State:** Special care should be placed on the design aspect such that LFSR avoids the prohibited or lockup state. In the case of XOR gates, the LFSR will not sequence through the binary value when all bits are at logic zero. Similarly, for XNOR gates the LFSR will not sequence through the binary values if all bits are at logic one. Thus, the LFSR should bypass these initializations during power up.
- **Ensuring a Sequence of All 2n Values:** If taps provided for a maximal length sequence are used, the LFSR configurations described so far will sequence through (2n − 1) binary values. The feedback path can be modified with extra circuitry to ensure that all 2n binary values are included in the sequence. Fig. 2 shows the LFSR we designed adopting the above-discussed facts. The 8-bit LFSR is modeled so as to use one-to-many feedback structure and has been modified for a 2n looping sequence. It calculates and holds the next value of the LFSR, which is then assigned to the output signal WM DATA after each clock edge. The NOR of all

LFSR bits minus the most significant bit that is LFSR REG (6:0) generates the extra circuitry needed for all 2n sequence values.

3.3 Watermarking Insertion Unit

Figure 3 shows the architecture of the watermark insertion unit designed to perform the watermarking insertion. The invisible-robust watermarking involves adding or subtracting a constant times the pixel value to be watermarked to or from a constant times the neighborhood function as described in the watermark encoder function in the previous section. The four data lines provide the pixels I(i, j), I(i + 1, j), I(i, j + 1), and I(i + 1, j + 1) for the row-column address pair (i, j). First, the I(i, j + 1) and I(i + 1, j + 1) are given to the adder1 as input. Then, the resulting sum and carry out from adder1 are fed to the adder2 along with I(i+1, j). The resulting sum of the adder2 is the neighborhood function value. The division by two is performed by shifting the results bit to the right by one bit, consequently discarding the rightmost bit (LSB). The scaling of the neighborhood function is achieved by multiplying it with ($1 - \alpha 1$) using the multiplier2. At the same time, the scaling of the image pixel gray values is performed in multiplier1 by multiplying I (i, j) with $\alpha 1$ or $\alpha 2$. The eight high order bits of the multipliers are fed to the adder/subtract unit to perform watermark insertion. Since, we are concerned only with the integer values of the pixels, the lower eight bits of the multiplier results are discarded, which represent the values after the decimal point.

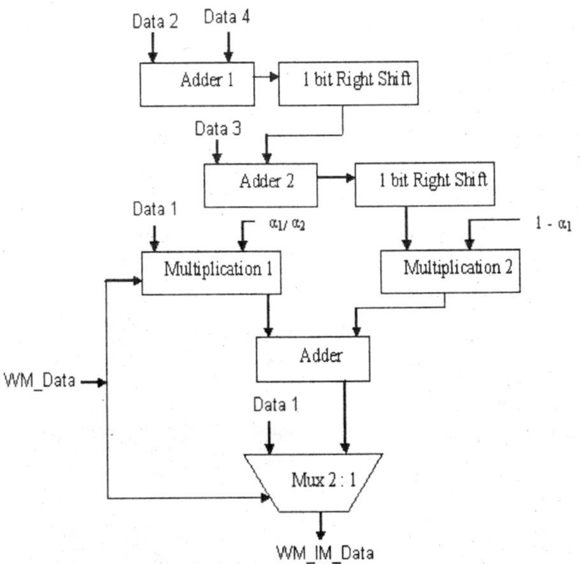

Fig. 3(a) Watermark Insertion Unit

The output of the adder/subtract unit(watermarked image pixels) and the original image pixel values are multiplexed based on the watermark values and are driven on to signal WM IM Data if the watermark value is "1" or "2" as per watermark encoding function in the previous section.

3.4 The Control Unit as a Finite State Machine (FSM)

Figure 3(b) shows the control unit implemented as FSM. Following are the control signals: ***Start*** – active high signal used to activate all the modules, ***Alpha1*** – 8-bit input scaling constants for watermark insertion algorithm, ***Alpha2*** – 8-bit input scaling constants for watermark insertion algorithm, ***Key*** – 8-bit Digital watermark key. Following are the output control signals: ***Ready*** – signal to indicate the insertion process is completed. ***Busy*** – signal to indicate the watermarking process is in progress.

The FSM has six states as defined below. At each state certain events take place and the FSM moves to the next state on the next positive edge of the clock.

- **S0:** When the signal start is reset the control jumps to the state S0. In this state the I(i, j) is read from the image RAM. The column and row addresses are registered in row var and col var.
- **S1:** The second data I(i, j + 1) is read from the image RAM. In this state the column address is incremented to (Col IM addr = col var + 1).
- **S2:** The data I(i+1, j) is read from the image RAM. The row address is increased to (row IM addr = row var +1).
- **S3:** In this state fourth data I(i + 1, j + 1) is read from the image RAM. The row address is incremented to (row IM addr = row var +1). The column address is incremented to (Col IM addr = col var + 1).

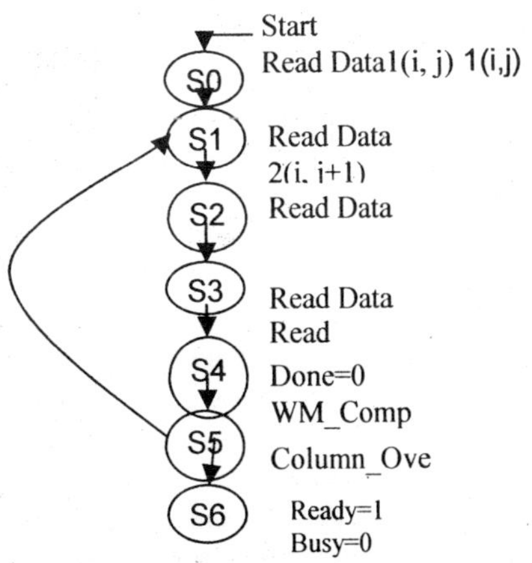

Fig. 3(b) Control Unit Structural Design

- **S4:** The signal Read done is set, indicating that all the four pixels are read from image RAM for an address pair (i, j). The control will be in this state until done signal from the watermark insert module is set. The watermarked image pixel value and watermark pixel value are stored in respective RAM at address (i, j).
- **S5:** The column address and row address are is incremented (Col_var = Col_var+1) and (Row_var = Row_var + 1). In this state he control checks for the possibility of column overflow, i.e., the column address reached its right most pixel address or not. If Col_var is equal to the right most address then the control moves to state S6 else to state S0. As well as the control checks for row overflow, i.e. the column address reached its right most pixel address or not. If Row_var is equal to the lower most address then the control moves to state S6, else to state S0.
- **S6:** In state S6, the busy signal is reset and ready signal is set indicating that the input image is watermarked.

4. Implementation, Conclusions and Futurescope

The Watermarking Encoder was modeled using Verilog HDL and functional simulation was performed. The three modules created are watermark insertion, watermark generator, and watermark control unit. The watermark control unit is the main module which instantiates the other two components. The synthesis of the chip is carried out using Synplify Pro™ tool targeting Xilinx VIRTEX-E technology with xcv50e-8cs144 target device. The simulations are done using the ModelSim. Figure 4 shows the RTL schematic of the synthesized encoder. The timing simulation is presented in Fig. 5. From the synthesis results we provide the macro statistics and timing report of the units in Table 2.The minimum period is reported for both generation unit and encoder, whereas the critical path delay is reported for the insertion unit which is fully combinational. The cell usage indicates all the logical cells that are basic elements of the technology.

This paper presented an architecture and FPGA implementation of a Image watermarking encoder. An Unauthorized User, in order to use our watermarked image, should know the following: 1) The 8-Bit Digital Key. 2) Watermarking Algorithm. 3) Pseudorandom Number Generator. This way, we are achieving security. The disadvantage of the watermarking algorithms implemented is that the processing needs to be done pixel-by-pixel. In future, we are aiming to investigate block-by-block processing. Since DRM systems need both encryption and watermarking, we think that combining both the hardware along with data compression hardware would be beneficial. Moreover, the on-chip encryptor can be used in storing the watermarking generator key in encrypted form, thus enhancing the watermark security.

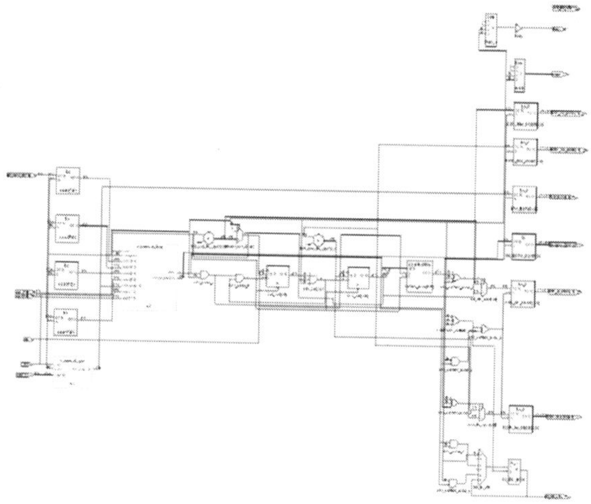

Fig. 4 RTL schematic of Watermarking Encoder

Table 2 Summary of Synthesis Report

Units	Clock/ Delay	Cell Usage(BELs)
Watermark Generation	3.684	43
Watermark Insertion	19.415	122
Overall Encoder	19.569	838

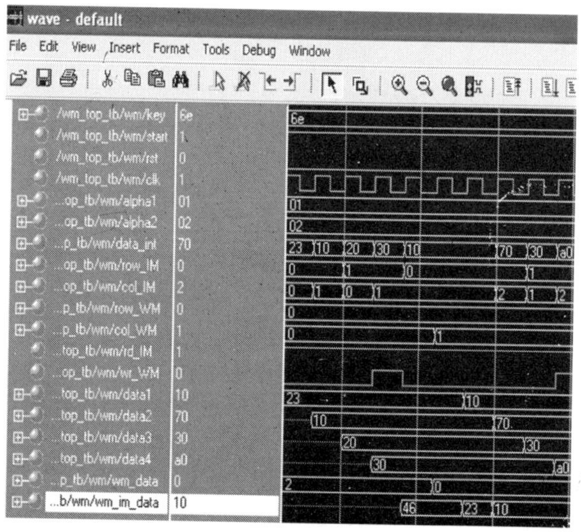

Fig. 5 Simulation Results of Watermarking Encoder

5. References

[1] Emmanuel,S.,Kankanhalli, M.S.: A Digital Rights Management Scheme for Broadcast Video. ACM-Springer Verlag Multimedia Systems Journal 8 (2003)

[2] Kundur,D.,Karthik,K.:DigitalFingerprinting and Encryption Principles for Digital Rights Management. Proceedings of the IEEE 52 (2004)

[3] Eskicioglu, A.M., Delp, E.J.: An Overview of Multimedia Content Protection in Consumer Electronics Devices. Elsevier Signal Processing: Image Comm. 16 (2001)

[4] Memon, N., Wong, P.W.: Protecting Digital Media Content. Communications of the ACM 41 (1998) 35–43

[5] Mohanty, S.P.: Digital Watamerking of Images. Master's thesis, Department of Electrical Engineering, Indian Institute of Science, Bangalore, India (1999)

[6] Hsiao, S.F., Tai, Y.C., Chang, K.H.: VLSI Design of an Efficient Embedded Zero tree Wavelet Coder with Function of Digital Watermarking. IEEE Transactions on Consumer Electronics 46 (2000) 628–636

[7] Maes, M., Kalker, T., Linnartz, J.P.M.G., Talstra, J., Depovere, G.F.G., Haitsma, J.: Digital Watamarking for DVD Video Copyright Protection. IEEE Signal Processing Magazine 17 (2000) 47–57

[8] Tsai, T.H., Lu, C.Y.: A Systems Level Design for Embedded Watermark Technique using DSC Systems. In: Proceedings of the IEEE International Workshop on Intelligent Signal Processing and Communication Systems. (2001)

[9] Petitjean, G., Dugelay, J.L., Gabriele, S., Rey, C., Nicolai, J.: Towards Real-time Video Watermarking for Systems-On-Chip. In: Proceedings of the IEEE International Conference on Multimedia and Expo (Vol. 1). (2002) 597–600

[10] Garimella, A., Satyanarayan, M.V.V., Kumar, R.S., Murugesh, P.S., Niranjan, U.C.: VLSI Impementation of Online Digital Watermarking Techniques with Difference Encoding for the 8-bit Gray Scale Images. In: Proc. of the Intl. Conf. on VLSI Design. (2003) 283–288

[11] Mathai, N.J., Sheikholeslami, A., Kundur, D.: VLSI Implementation of a Real-Time Video Watermark Embedder and Detector. In: Proceedings of the IEEE International Symposisum on Circuits and Systems (Vol. 2). (2003) 772–775

[12] Tsai, T.H., Wu, C.Y.: An Implementation of Configurable Digital Watermarking Systems in MPEG Video Encoder. In: Proc. of Intl. Conf. on Consumer Electronics. (2003) 216–217

[13] Mohanty,S.P.,RanganathanN., Namballa, R.K.: VLSI Implementation of Invisible Digital Watermarking Algorithms Towards the Development of a Secure JPEG Encoder. In:Proceedings of the IEEE Workshop on Signal Processing Systems. (2003) 183–188

[14] Seo, Y.H., Kim, D.W.: Real-Time Blind Watermarking Algorithm and its Hardware Implementation for Motion JPEG2000 Image Codec. In: Proceedings of the 1st Workshop on Embedded Systems for Real-Time Multimedia. (2003) 88–93

[15] Mohanty, S.P., Rangnathan, N., Namballa, R.K.: VLSI Implementation of Visible Watermarking for a Secure Digital Still Camera Design. In: Proceedings of the 17th International Conference on VLSI Design. (2004) 1063–1068

[16] Petitcolas, F.A.P., Anderson, R.J., Kuhn, M.G.: Information Hiding - A Survey. Proceedings of the IEEE 87 (1999) 1062–1078

[17]. Voloshynovskiy, S., Pereira, S., Pun, T., Eggers, J., Su, J.: Attacks on Digital Watermarks: clasification, Estimation-based Attacks Benchmarks. IEEE Communications Magazine 39(2001)118–126

[18]. Mathai,N.J., Kundur, D., Sheikholeslami, A.: Hardware Implementation Perspectives of Digital Video Watermarking Algortithms. IEEE Transanctions on Signal Processing 51 (2003) 925–938

[19] Petitcolas,F.A.P.:Watermarking Schemes Evaluation. IEEE Signal Processing 17 (2000) 58–64

[20] Petitcolas, F.A.P.: Watermarking Schemes Evaluation. IEEE Signal Processing **17** (2000) 58–64

[21] Nelson, V.P., Nagle, H.T., Irwin, J.D., Caroll, B.D.: Digial Logic Analysis and Design. Prentice Hall, Upper Saddle River, New Jersey, USA (1995)

[22] Smith, D.J.: HDL Chip Design: A Practical Guide for Designing, Synthesizing and Simulating ASICs and FPGAs Using VHDL or Verilog. Doone Publications, USA (1998)

[23] Smith, M.J.S.: Application-Specific Integrated Circuits. Addison-Wesley Publishing Company, MA `01867, USA (1997)

SDMS – An Image Processing Application

Mr. Bhushan V. Patil[1], Mr. Kalpesh V. Joshi[2], Mr. Kiran H.Sonawane[3]
[1]M.Tech, Bhopal, 49, Gayatri Colony, Shirpur,
patilbhushan007@gmail.com
[2](M.E) Amravati, 7, Shivaji Nagar, Wadibhokar Road, Dhule,
kalpesh_vj@rediffmail.com)
[3](M.E) Aurangabad, 16, Wankhedkar Nagar, Deopur, Dhule,
khsona2007@rediffmail.com)

Abstract

Lights! Camera! Action! constitute the basic fundamentals of Digital image processing. Digital image processing is a rapidly evolving field with growing applications in science and engineering. Image processing holds the possibility of developing the ultimate machine that could perform the visual functions of all living beings. Digital image processing has a broad spectrum of applications such as remote sensing via satellites, medical processing, radar, sonar, and automated inspection of industrial parts. Simple Digital Metrology System abbreviated as SDMS is a digital image processing application involving the field of measurement and calibration. The principal idea of this system is to automate the inspection process of sheet metal components manufactured by small and medium scale industries. The motive behind developing SDMS is to reduce the time and labor spent by the industries for inspection of components. This paper shall throw light upon various aspects of image processing and will focus mainly on the details of SDMS as an application of digital image processing.

1. Introduction

Modern digital technology has made it possible to manipulate multi-dimensional signals with systems that range from simple digital circuits to advanced parallel computers. The goal of this manipulation can be divided into three categories:

Image Processing image in -> image out.

Image Analysis image in -> measurements out.

Image Understanding image in -> high-level description out.

The term digital image processing generally refers to the processing of a two dimensional picture by a digital computer. It is the use of computer algorithms to perform image processing on digital images. Digital image processing has the same advantages (over analog image processing) as digital signal processing has (over analog signal processing) -- it allows a much wider range of algorithms to be applied to the input data, and can avoid problems such as the build-up of noise and signal distortion during processing. Digital image.

Digital image processing, either as an enhancement for human observers or performing autonomous analysis, offers advantages in cost, speed, and flexibility, and with the rapidly falling price and rising performance of personal computers it has become the dominant method in use.

Images are produced by a variety of physical devices including still and video cameras, x-ray devices, electron microscopes, radar, and ultrasound. The goal in each case for an observer, human or machine, is to extract useful information about the scene being imaged.

Metrology is the science of calibration, extraction and measurement of physical quantities. Measurement is the determination of the size or magnitude of something. Accuracy of the measurement taken is dependent on the type of the object, which is to be measured. The need of accuracy is directly proportional to the resources it uses. An ideal measurement system should be efficient, accurate and its cost of operation should be modest. The idea of developing the Simple Digital Metrology System (SDMS) was born with the same intention.

2. Fundamentals of Digital Image Processing

Firstly, we shall introduce the basic terms associated with digital image processing.

Digital Image: A digital image is an array of real or complex numbers represented by a finite number of bits. An image given in the form of a transparency, slide, photograph, or chart is first digitized and stored as a matrix of binary digits in computer memory. The digitized image can then be processed and/or displayed on a high resolution display device.

Digital Compression: It involves reducing the amount of memory needed to store a digital image. The amount of data associated with visual information is so large that its storage would require enormous storage capacity. Storage and/or transmission of such data require large capacity or bandwidth which could be very expensive. Image data compression techniques are concerned with the reduction of number of bits required to store or transmit image without any appreciable loss of information and thus reducing the storage requirement. Popular compressed formats used today are *.jpg, *.gif, etc.

Digital Decompression: This process involves the restoration of the compressed image to its original format. It is essential to convert the compressed image back to its original format before performing analysis of the image. This decompression is achieved by reversing the technique used for encoding the image and converting it into the compressed format. For example – we will use Inverse JPEG-DCT to uncompress the image in *.jpg format. This retrieval of the image data may result in data loss.

Image Enhancement: Image defects, which could be caused by the digitization process or by faults in the imaging set-up, can be corrected using Image Enhancement techniques. The main goal is to accentuate certain image features for subsequent analysis or for image display. The enhancement process itself does not increase the inherent information content in the data. It simply emphasizes certain specified image characteristics. Enhancement algorithms are generally interactive and application-development.

Measurement Extraction: Also known as image analysis, can be used to obtain useful information from the image. It is concerned with making quantitative measurements from an image to produce a description of it. Simplest applications are like reading a label on a grocery item, sorting parts on an asembly line and so on. Advanced image analysis systems measure quantitative information and use it to make sophisticated decisions with the aid of information acquired. Image analysis techniques require extraction of certain features that aid in the identification of the object.

3. Simple Digital Metrology System (SDMS)

Simple Digital Metrology System is a system developed with a view of automating the inspection of sheet metal components in the industry. Using techniques of digital image processing, SDMS calculates the dimensions of the component, compares them with a given standard set of dimensions and records the result. If the calculated and standard dimensions do not match then the user is informed about the mismatch.SDMS is an automated system wherein the only manual task is to place the component on the work surface and click the measure button. Thus, this system has many advantages over the manual inspection techniques that are widely popular today.

Services provided: The following services are provided by SDMS to the end user:

- Provides automation of manual inspection process.
- Provides facility to measure any sheet metal components -of any shape and geometry.
- Provides facility to identify the faulty components.
- Each dimension of the component is recorded and checked for accuracy.
- Functionality to inspect any component within the dimension 3"x 3".
- Facility to print reports of the inspection.
- Facility to program the system to measure any component by the user

The Manual Inspection Procedure: The manual process has an Inspector who measures each and every dimension of the component with specialized instruments like Vernier Calipers and notes the results in an Inspection Report. The following figure (See "Fig. 1") summarizes the manual inspection procedure:

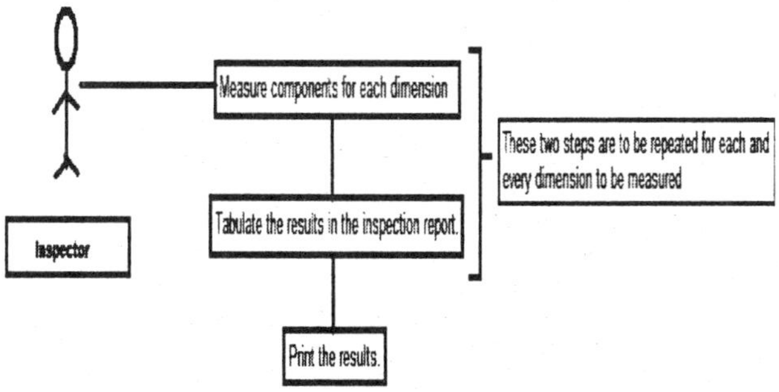

Fig. 1 Manual inspection Process

Drawbacks of the manual process: Consider the component to be a plain washer. It has geometric characteristics like concentricity, ovality, taper, and angularity. These characteristics cannot be accurately measured using the manual process.

System Scope: The target component size is 3" x 3". Target tolerance: +/- 0.05mm. This system is intended to work for any sheet metal component, which is; flat in nature, of any shape and geometry, component material should be opaque and can be of any composition. Height of the component is pre-defined. Maximum height of the component should not exceed 5mm. The camera used should be easily available in the market.

Block Diagram: Entire SDMS is divided into 4 major modules, which then are further divided into sub modules. The basic block representation of the system is as shown in the Fig. 2.

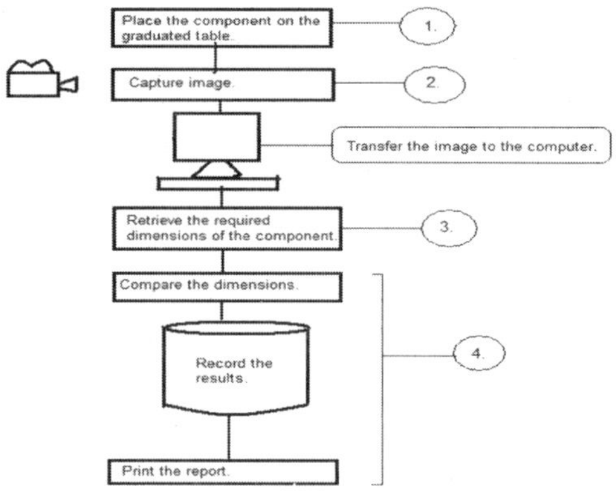

Fig. 2 Basic Block Diagram

The work space of the system comprises of a graduated monochrome table. The component to be inspected is place on this grid. Then using a high resolution digital camera, the image of the component is acquired. This image is then transferred to the computer using USB connectors. Various image processing operations are then performed on this image and dimensions are extracted. These extracted dimensions are then compared with the standard set of dimensions provided by the end user. If there is a mismatch such that tolerance bounds are not satisfied then the user is informed about the mismatch and is advised to reject the component. Also a timely inspection report generation facility is also provided.

Placement of the component: The set up required for the placement of the component should be such that a clear, sharp image is obtained. The image should lack shadows and other distortions. The main objective of the set up should be that the methodology employed must be independent of the height of the component. The reason for this being a geometrical error termed as height compensation is encountered. In the "Fig. 3" below, let 'e' denote the error introduced.

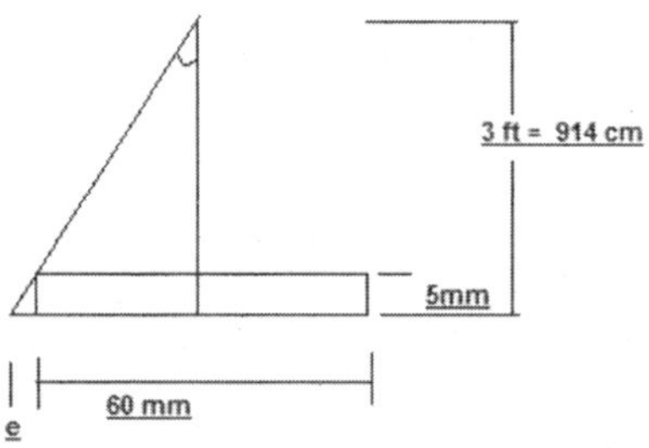

Fig. 3 Height Compensation

Using basic laws of trigonometry the error (e) thus obtained in the image does not satisfy the accuracy requirement of the system thus leading to system failure.

To overcome this problem the set up used is as shown below:

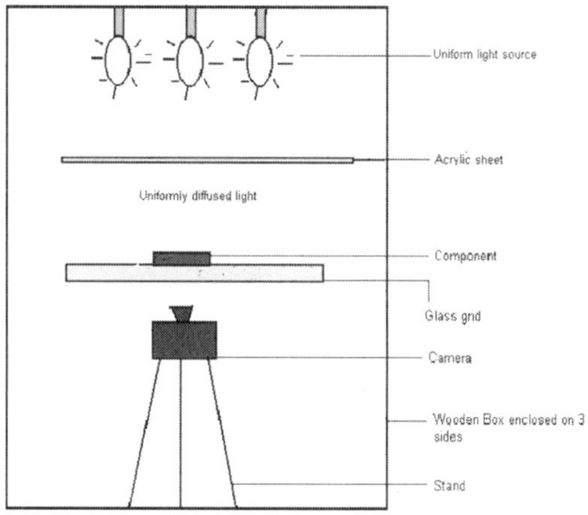

Fig. 4 Placement Set Up

Here, we have placed the camera below the graduated glass surface. The component is placed over the grid. To avoid shadows and other noise in capturing the image we are using a uniformly diffused light source. The image thus obtained is clear, sharp and void of shadows (See "Fig. 5"). The resolution of the camera ranges from 6-8 mega pixel depending upon market availability.

Fig. 5 Sample Image

Capture and transfer of image: The viewing plane of the camera must coincide with the work area of the system. The distance of the camera from that of the work space is fixed. The image is transferred to the computer as soon as it is captured. This transfer takes place using USB. Also, the camera is controlled by the user via the computer.

Processing of image and retrieval of dimensions: This module deals with the actual processing of the image to extract desired information. Various image processing algorithms like edge detection, corner detection, curve detection, and format conversions are implemented so as to acquire the required dimensions from the image. This module will be discussed in detail in the next section.

Compare and Store result: When the desired dimensions are extracted from the fresh image, they are compared with a standard set already available.

The result of the comparison is provided to the user. The information about the components, their standard dimensions, the required tolerance, and the result of comparison are all stored in the database. Facility to print inspection reports is available.

Operating environment: Ideal Requirements: 256 MB primary memory, 20 GB secondary memory, 40x CD-ROM, Pentium 4 1.8 GHz CPU, 17” monitor.

Minimum requirements: 128 MB primary memory, 10 GB secondary memory, 40x CD-ROM, Pentium 3.633 MHz CPU, 15” monitor.

Other Hardware/Software Requirements

Hardware required: Additional hardware required is a high resolution digital camera, a sufficiently bright monochromatic light source, and cords to connect camera to computer.

Operating System Support: The OS version should be ideally Windows XP but compatible with all Win 98 and above versions. The resolution supported by the monitor should be 800 x 600 pixels.

4. SDMS and Image Processing.

As mentioned earlier, SDMS employs various algorithms like edge detection, corner detection, et al. In this section we will highlight the details about these algorithms and the various software modules developed to carry out the processing of the component. The modules are: Image conversion, Inspect component, New component entry, Printing inspection report, and deleting a component.Image Conversion: In this module the image which is in .jpg format is converted to monochrome bitmap (*.bmp) format. A BMP computer image is the easiest to understand because it does not use compression, making pixel data retrieval much easier. The main reason for using monochrome bitmap is so as to reduce the image processing time as the values to be processed are either 0 or 255. Also, we are interested only in the boundary characteristics of the image so monochrome bitmap is highly suitable for this application. Currently, we are using Image Magick, a free image processing tool available on the Internet to carry out this format conversion. The resulting image is an image in the threshold monochrome bitmap format. (The threshold is chosen such that the unnecessary greys are eliminated).

Inspect Component: In this module, all the image processing algorithms come into play. The basic principle followed in this part is to acquire the boundary of the component, extract corners, calculate slopes using these corners and in case of error these slopes will not match with those of the standard set.

Getting pixel data:Input to this function are the x and y co-ordinates of the pixel

Output: pixel data value, 0 if black and 255 if white.

In this module, the bitmap file is manipulated such that the data value of the desired pixel is obtained. In terms of image processing, the most important information is the following:

Number of columns – byte #18, Number of rows - byte #22 Raster data – byte #(4 x number of colors) to byte #1078 + (number of columns x number of rows) -1.

All this information is stored in the bitmap header which contains all the essential information of the file. On analyzing this file with the help of the available information, the pixel data value can be obtained.

Edge Identification: The captured image of the component will appear as shown in the “Fig. 6”.

The image will be scanned from the left corner in the diagonal direction. When the scanner encounters a black pixel the image will be then scanned in the left or the right direction. The pixels around that being scanned will be checked. If the pixel above the scanner is white and the one below is black then that implies that we are tracing the edge. Thus the boundary can be extracted. Next we extract the corners using these boundary pixels.

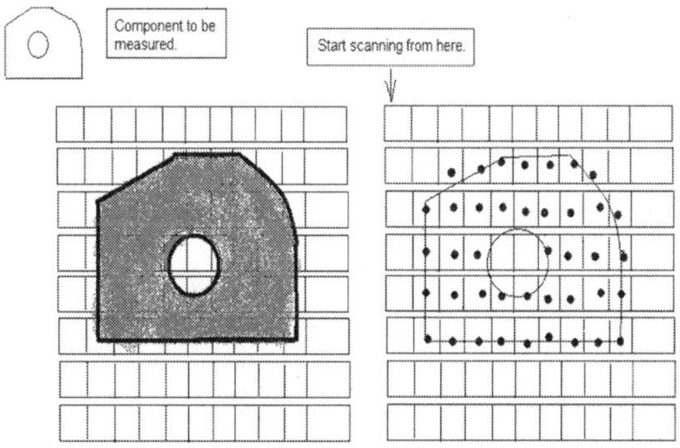

Fig. 6 Edge Detection

Corner Detection: For corner a 5x5 Moore matrix method is employed. A threshold (T) is fixed. Consider a matrix M[5,5] to be the Moore matrix. In this method, each and every pixel on the boundary is considered as the pixel under focus and its value is stored at M[3,3]. The data value for all surrounding pixels (i.e. all the pixels which constitute the matrix) is acquired. These values will be either 0 or 255. Next, we calculate the number of pixels having data value as zero in the matrix. Let this value be stored in Black Sum. Then, using the relation

Black sum >= Threshold (1)

It is determined whether the pixel constitutes a corner pixel.

If the relation stated above holds then the pixel uner focus is considered as a corner pixel.

Extracting dimensions: Here we calculate the slope of each edge using the corner pixel positions. If there is a mismatch in the number of corners or the slope value, then there is an error in the component. Using relation,

1mm== 'x' pixels (2)

(x depends upon the resolution of the camera)

We can calculate the dimension value in millimeters of a particular edge. If this value does not satisfy the tolerance constraints even then the component is rejected.

New component entry: This module stores the information of the new component in the system. The image of the new component is captured. Next, the corners of this template image are extracted,(using corner detection discussed above). As soon as the corners are detected, the user is prompted to enter the dimension value in millimeter. He is also to enter various aspects like tolerance, 'max' value of the dimension, and the 'min' value of the dimension. Thus all the necessary information about the component is acquired and store in the database.

Printing inspection report: For each component, when the inspection is conducted, the inspection report s to be printed. This report houses the result of the inspection and the name of the inspector. This module provides facility to print the inspection report.

Deleting a component: This module provides the user with the option of deleting a component. If the user wishes to use this option then the component selected by the user will be permanently deleted from the system.

5. Behavior of the System

The following State Transition Diagram illustrates the core behavior of SDMS (See "Fig7").

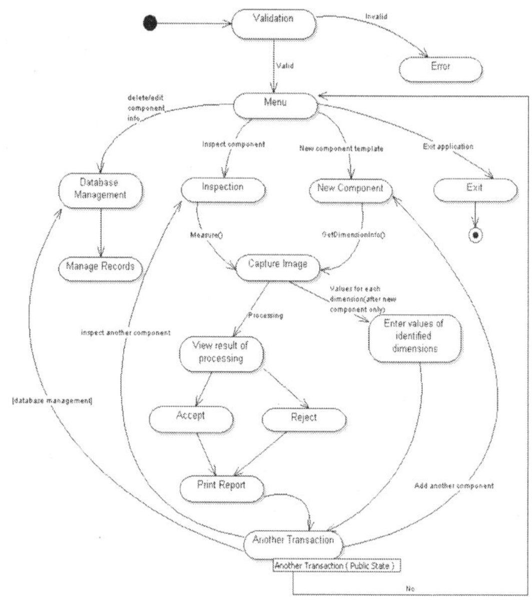

Fig. 7 State Transition diagram of SDMS

6. Development Paradigms

The software development paradigms that are followed in SDMS are:

1. Object Oriented Design.
2. Structural Design.

The following modules will follow an object-oriented approach:

-Module for entry of new object.
-Validation of User.
-Placement of the component.
-Capturing the Image.
-Transferring the image to PC.
-Entry for new object.

The module comprising of the actual image processing algorithm and comparison of dimensions will be structural in nature. The structured paradigm is employed so as to reduce the processing time (time complexity) of the algorithm.

This system is implemented using Microsoft Visual Basic v6.0 and C. The database is designed in Microsoft Access. The GUI is developed using VB v6.0 and the core image processing modules are developed using C.

6. Advantages of SDMS

The following are the major advantages of this system:

Reduction in time for inspection up to 60-80%:

The graph (See "Fig. 8") shown below emphasizes the fact that SDMS is more efficient with respect to time.

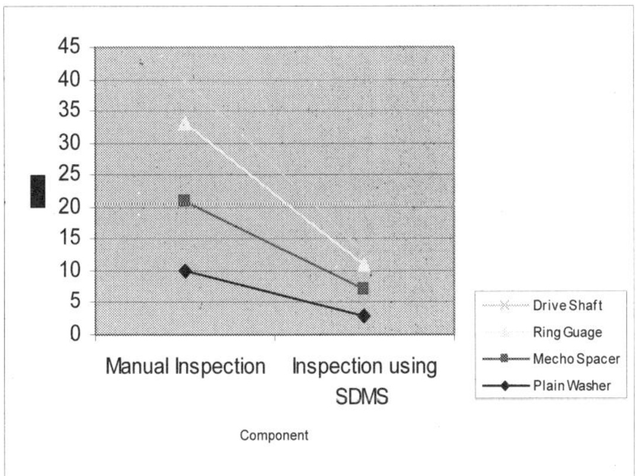

Fig. 8 Performance Analysis

Reduced cost of the system: SDMS is a very cost efficient system. The existing systems available in the market today are extremely expensive and are not affordable by small or medium scale industries. On the contrary, in SDMS the only major cost is that of a digital camera and the computer. The following 'Cost Vs Benefit Analysis' gives the profitability of using SDMS.

Time required to measure one dimension ~ 10 to 15 sec.

Assume that each component has approximately 10 dimensions

Thus total time to measure one component = 10 x 15 = 150sec.

Ideally, SDMS takes approximately 100 sec. Thus 50 sec saved!!!

Say, an inspector earns Rs.200/day...approximately 1.44paise/sec. 86.4 paise/component.

If there are 200 inspections per day then Rs.172.80 saved in a day!

Assume the cost of the system to be Rs.5000, and then the entire cost of the system is recovered in 29 days only!

Other advantages of SDMS include:

-Manual errors are reduced.

-Manual labor is reduced.

-Automation of recording and printing reports.

7. Challenges Faced In Digital Image Processing

An image is not a direct measurement of the properties of physical objects being viewed. Rather it is a complex interaction among several physical processes. The challenge is often underappreciated by novice users due to the seeming effortlessness with which their own visual system extracts information from scenes. Human vision is enormously more sophisticated than anything we can engineer at present and for the foreseeable future. Thus one must be careful not to evaluate the difficulty of a digital image processing application on the basis of how it looks to humans.

If teasing useful information out of the soup that is an image isn't challenging enough, the problem is further complicated by often severe time budgets. Few users care if a spreadsheet takes 300 milliseconds to update rather than 200, but most industrial applications must operate within hard constraints imposed by machine cycle times.

On top of this many digital image processing applications are constrained by severe cost targets. Thus we often face the engineer's dreaded triple curse, the need to design something good, fast, and cheap all at once.

8. Other Existing Applications

These are a few applications similar to the SDMS:

a) Fabric Drape Measurement System using Digital Image Processing. Developed at North Carolina State University.
b) Measurement of particle shape using Digital Image Processing. Developed at the University of Kent.
c) Robust Pose Determination for Autonomous Docking. Developed at Oakridge National Laboratory
d) Measurement of fatigue crack using Digital Image Processing.
e) Foot scan, Hand scan, dimension scan systems by visImage Systems.
f) Non Contact Wound Measurement system. Developed at Baylor College of Medicine.

Many more applications involving Digital Image Processing are available like plasma TVs, Camcorders, etc.

10. Future Scope

Currently, Simple Digital Metrology System is developed for 2 dimensional manipulations and measurements. This system can be further expanded to work in a 3 dimensional work plane. An integrated MIS can be provided along with this system thus automating the various domains of the industry, for example Customer Information System or a Materials Inventory System can be integrated with SDMS to provide greater functionality.

11. References

[1] Anil K. Jain, "*Fundamentals of Digital Image Processing*", Pearson Education Inc.

[2] Allan Hanbury, "Short Introduction to Digital Image Processing".

[3] Gonzalez, Rafel C., Woods, Richard C., Digital Image Processing, Addison-Wesley 1992 www.wikipedia.com,*Digital Image Processing.*

[4] Gamedev,"*An introduction to Digital Image Processing"*

[5] Bill Green, "*Raster Data Tutorial*".

Adaptive Motion Estimation with Artifact Reduction for Video Compression

Mrs. K. Sivakami Sundari[1] and Mr. P. Senthil Kumar[2]
[1] Professor & Head, Department of Information Technology
[2] Lecturer, Department of Information Technology,
Velammal College of Engineering and Technology, Viraganoor, Madurai

Abstract

An efficient and fast motion vector estimation algorithm suitable for video compression is devised. Existing Block matching algorithms (BMA), use the origin as initial search center, which may not track the motion very well. To improve the accuracy of the fast BMA's, a new adaptive motion tracking search algorithm nominated as center biased BMA is proposed in this paper. Based on the spatial correlation of motion blocks available in the search region, a predicted starting search point, which reflects the motion trend of the current block, is adaptively chosen. This predicted search center is found closer to the global minimum compensation, and thus the center biased BMA's can be used to find the motion vector more efficiently. This Exhaustive Search is the simplest algorithm, but computationally most expensive block matching process. Cost function is computed with all possible neighbors around the search window. As a result of which it finds the best possible match and gives the highest PSNR amongst any block-matching algorithm. The coarse-to-fine approach with logarithmic decrease in step size was the salient feature of 3SS method. In a video sequence where the motion vector distribution is highly centre biased, an additional 8 neighbor checking points are searched in the first step of N3SS Proposed algorithm computes the inter block correlation with the help of four spatial neighbors. The inter block motion correlation is defined by the displacement between the current block's motion vector and the mean motion vector of its four neighbors. When the magnitude of displacement vector is small, the current block's motion vector should highly correlate with its neighbors. This simple measure for the inter block correlation can track the current block's motion and provide a robust initial search center prediction. Still the quantization and motion compensation leads to losses whereby there come artifacts. Significant progress has recently been made in enhancing the artifacts affected MPEG images. This novel image enhancement algorithm was developed with the application as suitable for low vision viewers. Capturing and rendering an image that fulfils the observer expectation is a difficult task. The current work sharpens the compressed images in the Discrete Cosine Transform domain with cycle shifting applied both in forward and reverse directions. Algorithm is devised for those with reduced visual acuity. This in turn eliminates the difficulty of reading the text and viewing the images with low bit rates. The proposed enhancement algorithm consists of two stages: firstly these high-frequency characteristics of the image are enhanced by suitably weighing each element of the encoding quantization table to suppress the block artifacts, secondly, a post processing technique is applied on the received images which in turn shifts the image sub blocks and reapplies the JPEG in order to remove the ringing effects For ease of application the mathematical mode of the modified table is to be kept at the receiver, Experimental results show that the proposed algorithm enhances the image quality metrics like SNR, PSNR and MSE with improved compression ratio. Also it reduces the computational requirements

Keywords: *Motion Analysis, Motion Estimation, Motion Compensation, Video tracking, etc.,*

1. Introduction

Recently, due to the fast development of communication techniques, transmission of a video sequence has been emphasized for the near future. Considering limited channel bandwidth and real-time processing requirement, it is necessary to apply efficient video source coding with very high compression ratio. To achieve this objective, the temporal redundancy between adjacent frames in a video sequence has to be properly identified and eliminated. Block matching algorithm (BMA), an efficient and popular method, has been widely adopted to decrease the temporal redundancy in many video compression standards, such as ITU-T H.263, ITU-T H.264, ISO/IEC MPEG-1, MPEG-2 and MPEG-4.

The motion estimation and compensation technique is widely used for video coding applications but the real-time motion estimation is not easy due to its enormous computations. Block-matching motion estimation is a key process in video coding technology that reduces the temporal redundancy between adjacent frames. It is a way of locating matching blocks in a sequence of digital video frames for the purposes of motion estimation. The purpose of a block matching algorithm is to find a matching block from a frame i in some other frame j, which may appear before or after i. This can be used to discover temporal redundancy in the video sequence, increasing the effectiveness of inter frame video compression. Block matching algorithms make use of criteria to determine whether a given block in frame j matches the search block in frame i. The 3GPP/ 3GPP2 mandatory video codec's with MPEG-4 Simple Profile or H.263 Baseline have adopted this technology extensively.

The overwhelming complexity of motion estimation (ME), using a full search based brute-force approach has led to explosive research in ME. The research has led to myriad fast algorithms, and yet finding the "most efficient" algorithm remains an open research problem. Most ME algorithms exhibit trade-offs between quality and speed. Since ME is highly scene dependent, and, no one technique can be fully relied to generate good visual quality for all kinds of video scenes. Instead, it is the quint essence of a variety of techniques, such as motion starting point, motion search patterns, and adaptive control to curb the search, avoidance of search stationary regions, etc., that makes an ME algorithm robust and efficient across the board. Block-matching motion estimation is quite computationally intensive if the Full Search (FS) algorithm is used which exhaustively checks all possible candidate motion vectors within the search window. Therefore, fast block- matching algorithms (BMAs) are useful for accelerating the process without serious distortion, and are especially suitable for the current 3G real-time video applications. Fundamentally speaking, search methods with different shapes or sizes in the fast BMAs can determine not only their search speeds but also resulted performance. Statistical experiments have showed that the motion field of real-world video sequences is usually stationary or quasi-stationary, which results in a center biased motion vector distribution instead of a uniform motion vector distribution. Furthermore, about 50% to 95% of the motion vectors are enclosed in a circular area with radius of two pixels and centered on the position of zero.

A vast number of block matching algorithms (BMAs) have been proposed [10]. Some of the well known algorithms are: block pixel decimation [11], three step search algorithm (TSS),two dimensional logarithmic search algorithm (2D-LOG) as well as their variations [1], new three step search algorithm (NTSS) [2.], four step search algorithm [3], conjugate directional search [4], [5], [6.], orthogonal direction search algorithm (OSA), dynamic search window adjustment (DSWA) [7.], cross search [8.], diamond search [9], gradient-based search, zone-based search, refined zone-based search , parallel hierarchical one-dimensional search algorithm (PHODS), and candidate vector-based four step search algorithm (CV4SS).[9]. Multi resolution algorithms perform ME at multiple levels successively, starting with the lowest resolution level using low-pass filtering or sub sampling. Considering the merits of the diamond search and hexagon search, our block-matching process mainly comprises three phases: (1) the big diamond search to fit the directional centre-biased characteristics of the real-world video sequence; (2) the directional hexagon search to identify a small region where the best motion vector is expected to locate; (3) the small diamond search to select the best motion vector in the located small region. of real-world video sequences can be mainly in horizontal and vertical directions, the VSS algorithm adopts two kinds of asymmetrical hexagonal search shapes with different directionality separately, i.e., horizontal hexagon and vertical hexagon. . The Mean Absolute Difference (MAD), rather than Mean Square Error (MSE), is used as the matching criterion to reduce the block-matching

A computationally efficient post processing technique to reduce compression artifacts in low-bit-rate video coding is proposed in this paper. Blocking and ringing effects are two majors artifacts observed in block DCT-based codec, such as H.263, when coding at very low bit rates. Reduction of these artifacts can significantly improve the overall visual quality of decoded video. Spatial filtering [12,13], iterative reconstruction techniques [14,15,16] and stochastic reconstruction techniques [17, 18,19] are among the blocking artifact reduction methods that have been proposed for still images. For video coding the strength of the filter depends on the type of the frame. Few filters optimize the performance based on certain criteria. Schematic diagram of video Compression with Block matching is in Fig. 1.

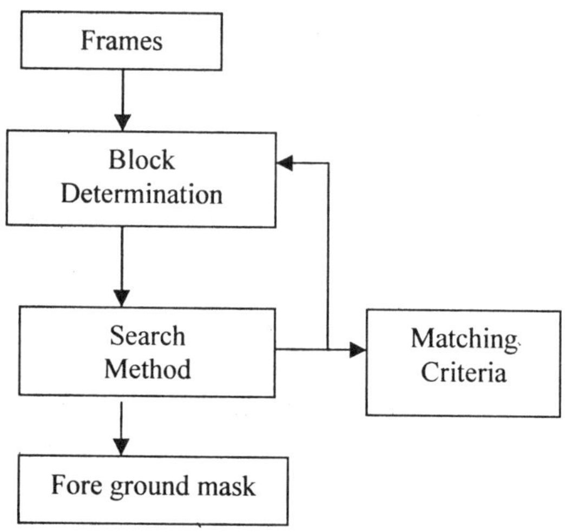

Fig. 1 Representation of Block matching

2. Search Algorithms

This section discusses few block-based search algorithms. A lot of variations of this algorithm exist and they differ mainly in the way in which the step size is changed. Some people argue that the step size should be halved at every stage. Some people believe that the step size should also be halved if an edge of the search space is reached. However, this last idea has been found to fail sometimes.

Three Step Search **(TSS)** was introduced by Koga et al in 1981. It became very popular because of its simplicity and also robust with near optimal performance. It searches for the best motion vectors in a course to fine search pattern. The algorithm may be described as: An initial step size is picked. Eight blocks at a distance of step_size from the centre (around the centre block) are picked for comparison. The step size is halved. The centre is moved to the point with the minimum distortion.

These steps are repeated till the step size becomes smaller than 1. A particular path for the convergence of this algorithm is shown below. Major problem with the Three Step Search is a uniformly allocated checking point pattern in the first step, which becomes inefficient for small motion estimation.

Two Dimensional Logarithmic Search algorithms were introduced by Jain & Jain around the same time that the Three Step Search was introduced and is closely related to it, although this algorithm requires more steps than the Three Step. Pick an initial step size. Look at the block at the Centro the search are and the four blocks at a distance of s from this on the X and Y axes. If the position of best match is at the centre, halve the step size. If however, one of the other four points is the best match, then it becomes the centre and step 1 is repeated. When the step size becomes 1, all the nine blocks around the centre are chosen for the search and the best among them is picked as the required block.

Binary Search algorithm is very popular for motion estimation and in fact it is used for motion estimation by MPEG-Tool. The basic idea behind this algorithm is to divide the search window into a number of regions and do a full search only in one of these regions. It may be described as :The MAD is evaluated on a grid evaluated on a grid of 9 pixels that includes the centre, the four corners of the search window and four pixels at the boundaries. The search window is divided into regions based on these points. A full search is performed in the region corresponding to the point with the smallest MAD.

Four Step Search (FSS) algorithm was proposed in 1996 by Lai-Man Po and Wing-Chung Ma. It is based on the real world image sequence's characteristic of centre-biased motion. The algorithm starts with a nine point comparison and then the other points for comparison are selected based on the following algorithm.

Step1: Start with a step size of 2. Pick nine points around the search window centre. Calculate the distortion and find the point with the smallest distortion. If this point is found to be the centre of the searching area go to step 4, otherwise go to step 3.

Step 2: Move the centre to the point with the smallest distortion. The step size is maintained at 2. The search pattern however depends on the position of the previous minimum distortion. a) If the previous minimum point is located at the corner of the previous search area, five points are picked ,.b) If the previous minimum distortion point is located at the middle of the horizon

Step 3: The search pattern strategy is the same, however it will finally go to step 4.

Step 4: The step size is reduced to 1 and all nine points around the centre of the search are examined.

The computational complexity of the four step search is less than that of the three step search, while the performance in terms of quality is as good. It is also more robust than the three step search and it maintains its performance for image sequences with complex movements like camera zooming and fast motion. Hence it is a very attractive strategy for motion estimation. Below figure bestows few searching pattern of block matching algorithm

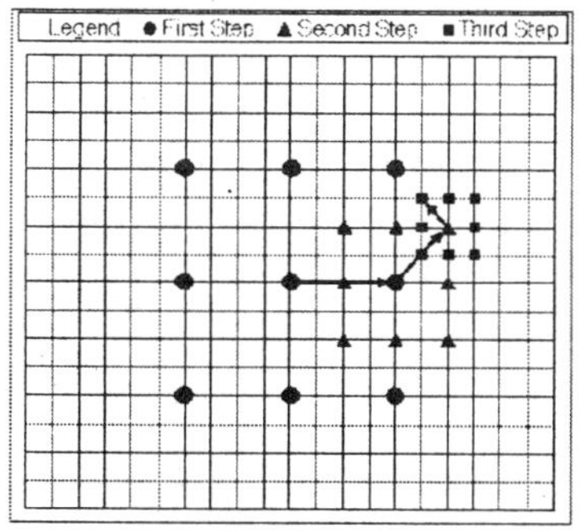

Fig. 2 Path for convergence of TSS

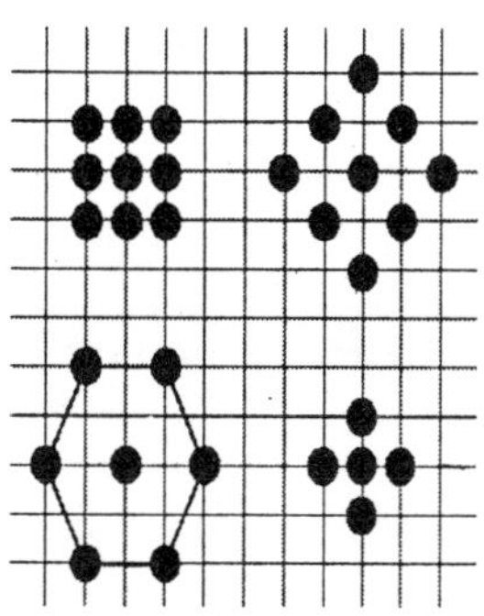

Fig. 3 Conventional search algorithms–pattern

3. Adaptive Motion Estimation

To improve the conventional diamond search (DS) method in terms of both coding efficiency and speed, several modified algorithms have been introduced. One of these algorithms uses a different initial search point and search patterns with selective application of large diamond search (LDS) and small diamond search (SDS) according to the characteristics of motion activity assessed by the similarity of motion vector field among contiguous blocks. In the LDS case, the LDSP (Large Diamond Search Pattern) is centered at the search center, and all the checking points of LDS pattern are tested at the first step. If the minimum SAD occurs at the search center of LDSP, then the search pattern is switched from LDSP to SDSP (Small Diamond Search Pattern), and the position having the minimum SAD in SDSP is decided as the motion vector. Otherwise, a new center of LDSP is placed at the point that yields the minimum SAD in the previous step, and all points on the new LDSP are tested again. This process is iteratively repeated until the minimum SAD falls on the search center. The LDS is exactly the same as the conventional diamond search. The proposed method is distinct from other algorithms in that the search pattern depends on how much the motion vectors are scattered

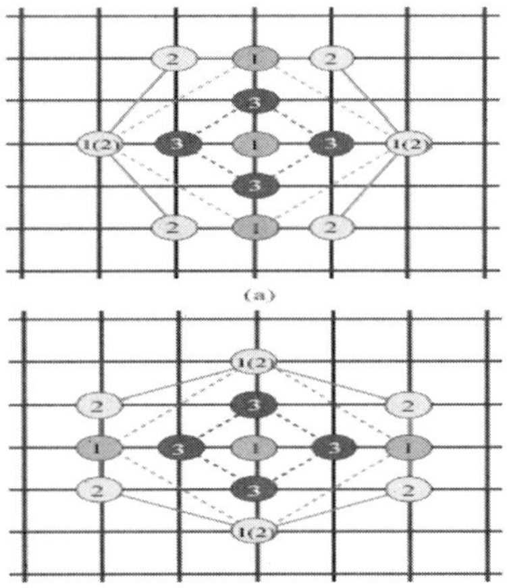

Fig. 4 Schematic representation of Adaptive motion estimation

4. Artifacts with video frames

In order to consider why flicker artifacts occur in periodically inserted I-pictures, let us first define reconstructed image R as, $R(O,P) = W(O-P) + P$, where O denotes the original image and P denotes a predicted image. $W(X)$ is $T^{-1}Q^{-1}QT(X)$. T represents a transform and Q refers to quantization. Inter-frame predicted images in static and panning regions in successive frames tend to be almost the same. Reconstructed images in such regions are, therefore, also almost the same. Hence, coding noise patterns will be continuous in the video coding structure. However, coding noise patterns will be discontinuous with periodically inserted I-pictures in the video coding structure. Since intra predicted images in periodically inserted I-pictures differ from inter-frame predicted images in previous P-pictures, reconstructed I-picture images will differ from previously reconstructed P-picture images even if their original images were identical. When, as a result of quantization, this discontinuity has been increased, it comes to be perceived as flicker and ringing artifacts.

5. Artifact reduction

Proposed algorithm applies a non linear transfer function to the difference between co-located pixels in two consecutive frames in addition to the shifting and averaging algorithms. Flicker artifacts are removed with NL filtering and the ringing artifacts are suppressed with the other part. The output of the nonlinear characteristic is then added to the pixel located in the current frame. This filter can be seen as a mechanism which cuts off the filtered pixel if its difference with the previous pixel exceeds a given threshold. The filter interprets the excess of signal in the current pixel as noise.

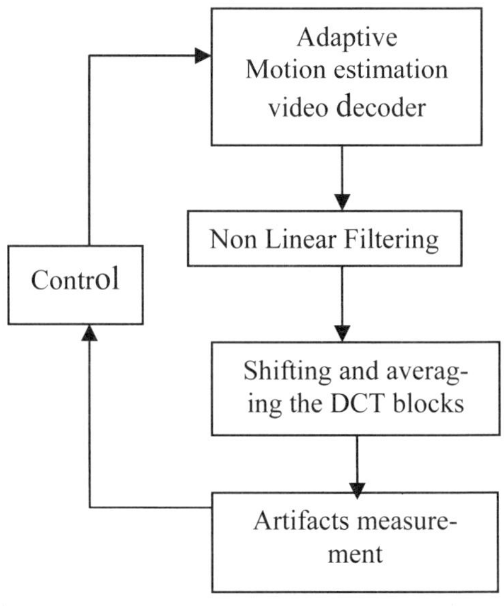

Fig. 5 Artifact reduction process

6. Experimental Results

Table 1 shows the results of the proposed adaptive motion estimation. For the performance comparison of the proposed method, we tested not only the adaptive motion method but also additionally the three step search and four step search methods with artifact reduction algorithms. For the evaluation of coding efficiency, of the search method the number of search points are computed and found to be minimum. The amount of artifacts are computed with PSNR vs bit rate.

Algorithms	PSNR	Average search points
TSS	29.9875	23.6545
FSS	30.3323	18.5109
Adaptive search	31.7543	15.5909

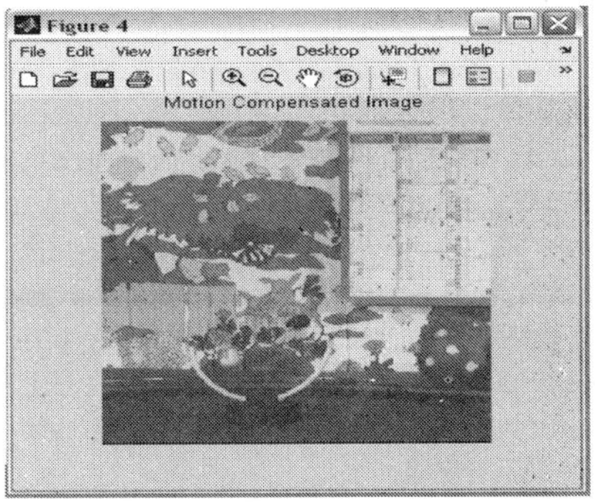

Fig. 6a Three Step Search

Fig. 6b Four Step Search

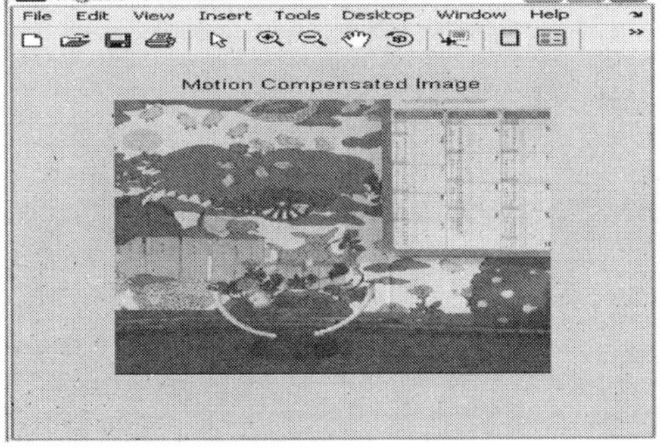

Fig. 6c Adaptive Search Method

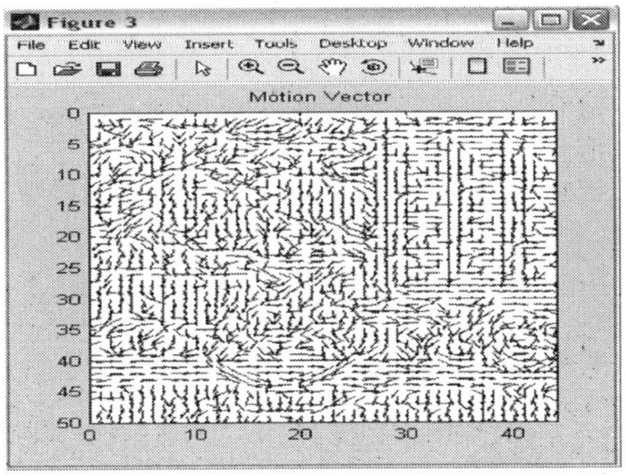

Fig. 6d Search pattern

7. Conclusion

The proposed algorithm of the hybridization of adaptive motion estimation with artifact reduction was tested on different scene contents at various bit rates. To illustrate the performance, the simulation result of few image frame sequence are projected. The proposed method has reduced the coding artifacts while improving the sharpness of the up-converted picture. A unified metric for digital video processing referred as BME is computed to detect the errors. The proposed method outperforms the other compression method. Fig. 6 bestows the improvement of the visual quality of the proposed algorithm over the other algorithms. Fig. 7 illustrates the quantitative analysis.

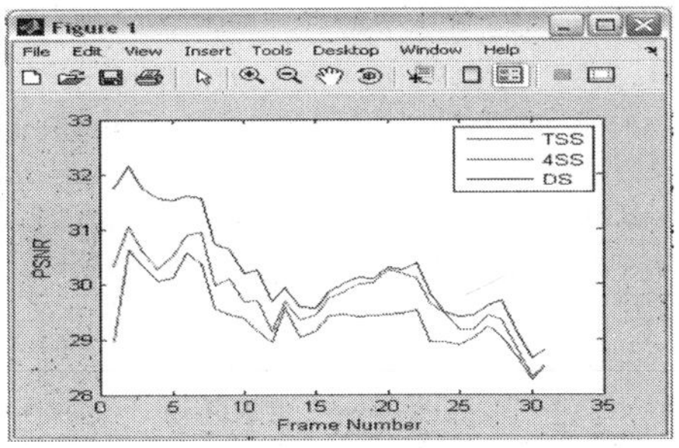

Fig. 7a Frame performance Vs PSNR

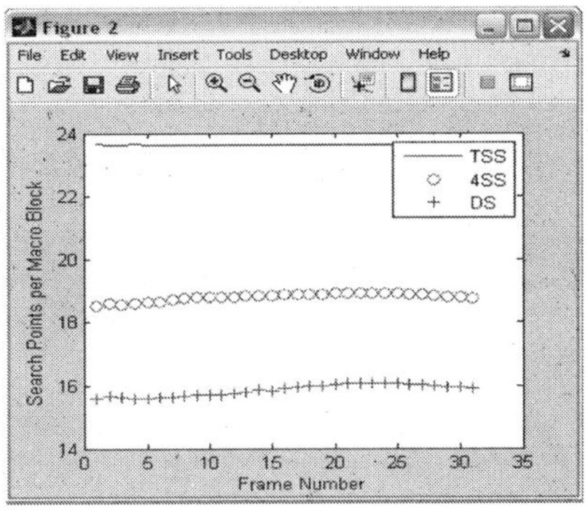

Fig. 7b Frame performance with search path

8. References

[1] X. Lee and Y. Q. Zhang, "A fast hierarchical motion-compensation scheme for video coding using block-feature matching," IEEE Trans. Circuits Syst. Video Technol., vol. 6, no. 6, pp. 627–635, Dec. 1996.

[2] R. Li, B. Zeng, and M. L. Liou, "A new three-step search algorithm for fast motion estimation," IEEE Trans. Circuits Syst. Video Technol., vol. 4, no. 4, pp. 438–442, Aug. 1994.

[3] L. M. Po and W. C. Ma, "A novel four-step search algorithm for fast blockmatching," IEEE Trans. Circuits Syst. Video Technol., vol. 6, no.3, pp. 313–317, Jun. 1996.26

[4] Liu and A. Zaccartin, "New fast algorithms for estimation of block motion vectors," IEEE Trans. Circuits Syst. Video Technol., vol. 3, no. 2, pp. 148–157, Apr. 1993.

[5] R. Srinivasan and K. R. Rao, "Predictive coding based on efficient motion estimation," IEEE Trans. Circuits Syst. Video Technol., vol. Com-33, no. 8, pp. 888–896, Aug. 1985

[6] B. Zeng, R. Li, and M. L. Liou, "Optimization of fast block motion estimation algorithms," IEEE Trans. Circuits Syst. Video Technol., vol. 7, no. 6, pp. 833–844, Dec. 1997.

[7] L. W. Lee, J. F. Wang, J. Y. Lee, and J. D. Shie, "Dynamic search window adjustment and interlaced search block-matching algorithm," IEEE Trans. Circuits Syst. Video Technol., vol. 3, no. 1, pp. 85–87, Feb.1993.

[8] M. Ghanbari, "The cross-search algorithm for motion estimation," IEEE Trans. Commun., vol. 38, no. 7, pp. 950–953, Jul. 1990.

[9] S. Zhu and K. K. Ma, "A new diamond search algorithm for fast block matching," IEEE Trans. Circuits Syst. Video Technol., vol. 9, no. 2, pp. 287–290, Feb. 2000.

[10] T. Koga, K. Ilinuma, A. Hirano, Y. Iijima, and T. Ishiguro, "Motion compensated interframe coding for video conferencing," in Proc. Nat. Telecommun. Conf., New Orleans, LA, Nov. 1981, pp. G5.3.1–G5.3.5.

[11] J. R. Jain and A. K. Jain, "Displacement measurement and its application in inter frame image coding," IEEE Trans. Commun., vol. COM-29, no. 12, pp. 1799–1808, Dec. 1981.

[12] H.C.Reeves and J.S.Lim, Reduction of blocking effects in image coding," Opt. Eng., vol. 23, pp. 34–37, 1984.

[13] G.Ramamurthi and A.Gersho, "Nonlinear space-variant post processing of block coded images," IEEE Trans. Acoust., Speech Signal processing, vol. ASSP-34, pp. 1258–1269, 1986.

[14] A.Zakhor, "Iterative procedures for reduction of blocking effects in transform image coding," IEEE Trans. Circuits Sys. Video Technology, vol. 2, pp. 91–95, 199

[15] Y.Yang, N.P.Galatsanos, and A.K.Katsaggelos, "Regularized reconstruction to reduce blocking artifacts of block discrete cosine transform compressed images," IEEE Trans. Circuits Sys. Video Technology, vol. 3, pp. 421–432, 1993.

[16] H.Paek, R.Kim, and S.Lee, "On the pocs-based post processing technique to reduce blocking artifacts in transform coded images," IEEE Trans. Circuits Sys. Video Technology, vol. 8, pp. 358–367, 1998.

[17] R.L.Stevenson, "Reduction of coding artifacts in transform image coding," Proc. Int. Conf. Acoustics, Speech, Signal Processing, vol. 5, pp. 401–404, 1993.

[18] Luo, C.W.Chen; K.J.Parker, and T.S.Huang, "Artifact reduction in low bit-rate dct-based image compression," IEEE Trans. Image Processing, vol. 5, pp. 1363–1368, 1999.

[19] Ozcelik, J.C.Brailean, and A.K.Katsaggelos, "Image and video compression algorithms based on recovery techniques using mean field annealing," Proc. IEEE, vol. 83, pp. 304–316, 1995/s)

[20] A. Netravali and B. Haskell, Digital Pictures Representation and Compression, of Science and Technology (HKUST), Hong Kong

Classification of Facial Images using FFNN

Shubhangi D. Sapkal[1], Mahananda D. Malkauthekar[2] and Sangeeta N. Kakarwal[3]
[1]Lecturer CSE Dept., Govt. College of Engg., Aurangabad
shubhangi_parde@yahoo.com
[2]Asstt. Professor in CSE Dept., MIT Engg. College, Aurangabad
nandamalkauthekar@yahoo.co.in
[3]Asstt. Professor in CSE Dept., P.E.S. College of Engg., Aurangabad
s_kakarwal@yahoo.com

Abstract

We present in this paper, Fourier descriptor and feedforward neural network for face recognition. Analysis is done for various number of iterations. Comparison shows that faces are recognized with FFNN more accurately with 50000 iterations. For experiment, FERET database is used.

1. Introduction

Face recognition involves computer recognition of personal identity based on geometric or statistical features derived from face images. Even though humans can detect and identify faces with little or no effort, building an automated system that accomplishes such objective is, however very challenging. The challenges are even more profound when one considers the large variations in the visual stimulus due to illumination conditions, viewing directions or poses, facial expression, aging, and disguises such as facial hair, glasses or cosmetics.

Face recognition research provides the cutting edge technologies in commercial, law enforcement, and military applications. An automated vision system that performs the functions of face detection, verification and recognition will find countless unobtrusive applications, such as airport security, and access control, building surveillance and monitoring, human-computer intelligent interaction and perceptual interfaces.[1]

2. Fourier Descriptor

Location and description of substantial variations in the first derivative of object boundaries often yield suitable information. A typical mathematical technique is shape description based on the Fourier transform.

We are dealing with two-dimensional images, but our world is three-dimensional and the same objects, if seen from different angles, may form very different 2D projections.

If $x(k)=x_k$ and $y(k)=y_k$ are the coordinates expressed notation for the boundary of an image can be represented as the sequence of coordinates $s(k)=[x(k),y(k)]$, for k=0,1,2….,k-1. Each coordinates pair can be treated as a complex number so that

$$s(k)=x(k)+jy(k)$$

The discrete fourier transform (DFT) of s(k) is $a(u)=\sum s(k)e^{-j2\Pi uk/K}$ for k= 0 to k-1 and u=0,1,2,….., k-1.

The complex coefficients a(u) are called the Fourier descriptors of the boundary.

The inverse fourier transform of these coefficients restores s(k).

$$s_k(u)=\sum a(u)e^{j2\Pi uk/K}$$

Suppose, instead of all the fourier coefficients , only the first P coefficients are used . This is equivalent to setting a(u)=0 for u>p-1.the result is the following approximation to s(k):

$s_i(k)=\sum a(u)e^{j2\Pi uk/k}$ for k=0,1,…,k-1 and for u=0 to p-1.

Although only P terms are used to obtain each component of s(k) , k still ranges for 0 to k-1. [2]

3. Feedforward Neural Network

A Feed forward artificial neural network consists of layers of processing units, each layer feeding input to the next layer in a Feed forward manner through a set of connection weights or strengths. The weights are adjusted using the back propagation learning law. The patterns have to be applied for several training cycles to obtain the output error to an acceptable low value. Once the network is trained, it can be used to recall the appropriate pattern for a new input pattern. The computation for recall is straightforward, in the sense that the weights and the output functions of the units in different layers are used to compute the activation values and the output signals. The signals from the output layer correspond to the output.

Back propagation learning emerged as the most significant result in the field of artificial neural networks. The back propagation learning involves propagation of the error backwards from the input training pattern, is determined by computing the outputs of units for each hidden layer in the forward pass of the input data. The error in the output is propagated backwards only to determine the weight updates. [3]

4. Analysis of Image Recognition with Fd

In Fourier descriptor method, images are first converted to binary images. Using labeling, all regions in the image are found and take boundaries of each region in the image. These boundary values are used to find fourier descriptors, which are imaginary values in the form of (x + iy). Inverse Fourier descriptors using different values of Fourier descriptors such as 100%, 50%, 30% and 20% are obtained and analyze the recognition results with different values. Instead of using FD images, mean values of each row of the image are used for classification.

p_mean = mean(vi)

where, vi is the ith vector in the image.

5. Result Analysis

1. FFNN is trained for front face images with 100%, 50%. 30%, 20%, 10% FD (350 images of 70 persons, 70*5=350) and following network architecture is used.
   Number of layers=3
   Neurons in first layer=48
   Neurons in second layer=192
   Neurons in third layer=350
   Transfer function for all layers is 'tansig'.
   Test results for different face images and different percentages of reconstructed images with Epochs=50000 are shown in Table1 and Graph1.
2. FFNN is trained front face images with 100%, 50%. 30%, 20%, 10% FD (350 images of 70 persons, 70*5=350) and following network architecture is used.
   Number of layers=3, Neurons in first layer=48
   Neurons in second layer=240
   Neurons in third layer=350
   Transfer function for all layers is 'tansig'
   Test results for different face images and different percentages of reconstructed images with Epochs=60000 are shown in Graph2 and Table2.
3. Comparison between recognition rate with two architectures given below of FFNN and using all (100%, 50%, 30%, 20%, 10%) FDs is shown in Table3 and Graph3:
   (i) 3-layer (48-192-350) FFNN, epochs=50000
   (ii) 3-layer (48-240-350) FFNN, epochs=60000

Graph3 shows the difference between recognition rate of two network architectures. When number of neurons in hidden layer are increased above some limit, the result is inverse. Generally, up to some limit, increasing number of neurons in hidden layers and/or number of iterations improves recognition rate.

6. Conclusions

Classification of facial images by Neural Network is done and is compared with Nearest neighbor method. Statistical approach is used for feature extraction.

FFNN is a multilayer Neural Network, which uses back propagation for learning. From the obtained results, it can be said that, three layers are sufficient for classification. As number of layers increased more than three, it does not improve the recognition rate, but instead of that, if number of epochs and neurons in hidden layers are increased upto some limit, it improves the recognition rate.

Reconstructed images are obtained which reduces dimensions of database. Instead of training network for one image of each person with some reduced dimensions, images with different dimensionality reduction (i.e. more than one feature vectors of each person) gives recognition rate more than others. Here, 5 feature vectors for each person with different dimensions i.e. 100%, 50%, 30%, 20%, 10% dimensions, (70*5=350 feature vectors for 70 persons) are used.

Table 1 Recognition rate by 3-layer (48-192-350) FFNN (50000 epochs) with all (100%, 50%, 30%, 20%, 10%) FD values

% of FD used for testing	No. of images for		Front faces	Alternate expression	Quarter left	Quarter right	Half right
	Training	Testing					
100	350	70	98.57	62.85	32.85	27.14	15.71
50	350	70	100	62.85	25.71	24.28	12.85
30	350	70	100	65.71	28.57	25.71	11.42
20	350	70	100	64.28	21.42	28.57	10.00
10	350	70	100	58.57	24.28	21.42	7.14

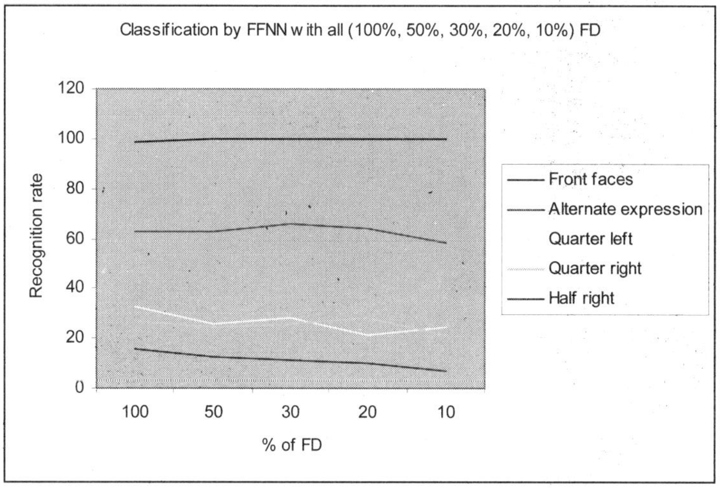

Graph 1 Recognition rate by 3-layer (48-192-350) FFNN (50000 epochs) with all (100%, 50%, 30%, 20%, 10%) FD values

Table 2 Recognition rate by 3-layer (48-240-350) FFNN (60000 epochs) with all (100%, 50%, 30%, 20%, 10%) FD values

% of FD used for testing	No. of images for		Front faces	Alternate expression	Quarter left	Quarter right	Half right
	Training	Testing					
100	350	70	100	64.28	31.42	21.42	8.57
50	350	70	100	64.28	27.14	20.00	11.42
30	350	70	100	61.42	22.85	21.42	11.42
20	350	70	100	61.42	27.14	11.42	7.14
10	350	70	100	52.85	27.14	12.85	7.14

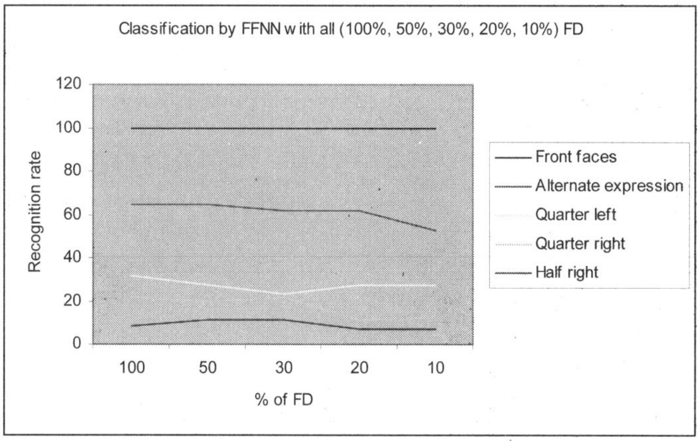

Graph 2 Recognition rate by 3-layer (48-240-350) FFNN (60000 epochs) with all (100%, 50%, 30%, 20%, 10%) FD values

Table 3 Comparison between recognition rate by two FFNNs

Layers of FFNN	Front faces	Alternate expression	Quarter left	Quarter right	Half right
48-192-350 (50000 epochs)	99.71	62.85	26.56	25.42	11.42
48-240-350 (60000 epochs)	100	60.85	21.71	17.42	9.13

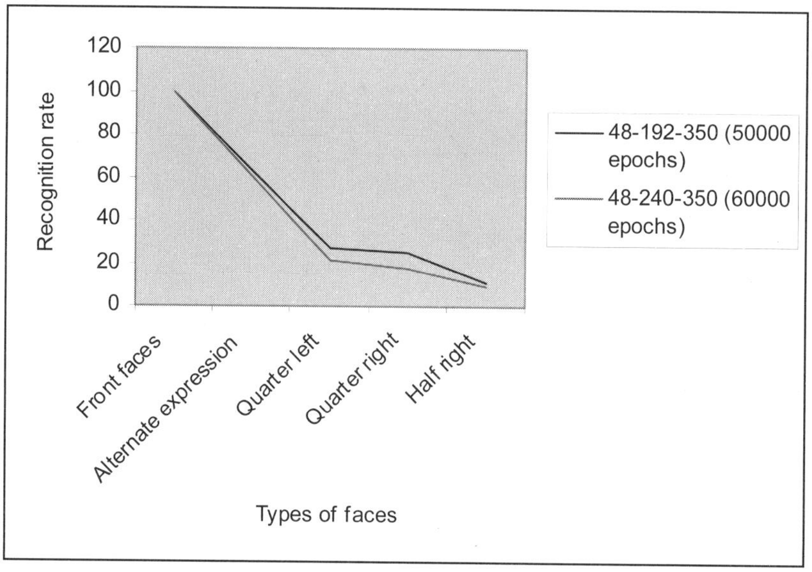

Graph 3 Recognition rate by two FFNNs

7. References

[1] Kevin Bowyer, "Face Recognition Technology: Security versus Privacy", IEEE Technology And Society Magazine | SPRING 2004

[2] Gonzalez and Woods, "Digital Image Processing",2nd edition

[3] B. Yegnanarayana, "Artificial Neural Networks"

[4] Milan Sonka, Vacloc Hlavac-Ronger,Boyle, "Image Processing, analysis and Machine Vision"

[5] Steve, C. Giles, Ah Tsoi, Andrew, "Face recognition: A hybrid neural network approach"

[6] Gonzalez, Woods and Eddins, "Digital Image Processing using MATLAB"

[7] Gonzalez and Woods, "Digital Image Processing",2nd edition

[8] Raphael Feraud, "A Fast and Accurate Face Detector Based on Neural Networks", IEEE on Pattern Analysis and Machine Intelligence, Vol. 23, No. 1, Jan 2001.

[9] Elzbieta Pekalska, "Classifiers for dissimilarity-based pattern recognition", International Conference on Pattern Recognition (ICPR'00), 2000 IEEE

[10] Terrillon, McReynolds, Sadek, "Invariant Neural-Network based Face Detection with Orthogonal Fourier-Mellin Moments", Proceedings of the International Conference on Pattern Recognition (ICPR'00), 2000 IEEE

[11] Blanz and Vetter, "Face Recognition Based on Fitting a 3D Morphable Model", IEEE Transactions on Pattern Analysis and Machine Intelligence, Vol. 25, No. 9, September 2003

[12] Haiyuan WU, Ryutaro KIDO and Shioyama, "Improvement of Continuous Dynamic Programming for Human Gesture Recognition", Proceedings of the International Conference on Pattern Recognition (ICPR'00), 2000 IEEE

[13] O. Sukmarg, "Combined Shape Descriptors of Face Region and Contour of Human Object in MPEG Compressed Domain"

[14] Website: www.icgst.com

[15] Website: http://www.statsoft.com/textbook/glosn.html

[16] Website: http://www.cs.ut.ee/~toomas_1/linalg/lin1/node16.html

[17] Website http://rkb.home.cern.ch/rkb/AN16pp/node215.html

[18] Website: http://www.fon.hum.uva.nl/praat/manual/Principal_component_analysis.html

[19] Website: http://www.attrasoft.com/imagefinder42/imageverification.html

A New Biometric Watermarking Algorithm for Color Images using DWT and SVD

Mrs.V.Santhi[1], G.Manikandan[2], and M.M.Eugene[2]
[1]Faculty in School of computing Sciences
[2]Students in School of computing Sciences
School of Computing Sciences, VIT University – 632 014
vsanthi@vit.ac.in

Abstract

As usage of internet is increasing tremendously the volume of multimedia data floating around is also increasing. Thus it requires a new mechanism to protect multimedia data from unauthorized access. Watermarking is one among many security mechanisms, by which a piece of secret information could be hidden into protect copyrights of multimedia data. In the proposed algorithm, biometric data iris is used as watermark for copyright protection of digital image, since it is a well protected organ with unique and rich set of features, while offering good stability over time. The iris part is extracted from the image using segmentation and converted into template through normalization process. Transformed RGB color spaces of input image is converted into wavelet coefficients using discrete wavelet transformation technique (DWT) followed by singular value decomposition (SVD) to hide watermark in singular elements of wavelet coefficients. Robustness of proposed algorithm is tested through various image manipulation functions and it is observed that the proposed algorithm is robust against transformation and geometric attacks.

Keywords: *Biometric Watermarking, Image Watermarking, Discrete Wavelet Transformation, Singular Value Decomposition.*

1. Introduction

Biometric is the science of verifying one's identity using face recognitions, behavioural traits like signature and voice. Biometric identifiers remain with the concerned person throughout their life time rather than the identification cards which can be lost or can go to a third person who can misuse it [1]. Biometric data can be used as watermark for copyright protection as it brings uniqueness in an individual's identity. Among many techniques watermarking is one which is used to protect copyrights of multimedia data which includes image, audio, video and text [2][3]. Watermarking technique is not only used for copyright protection but also used for ownership verification, authentication, finger printing and broadcast monitoring.

In section II review of related works given and in section III the basics of singular value decomposition technique is discussed in detail. Basics of discrete wavelet transformation and feature extraction of biometric data is given is section IV and V respectively. Proposed algorithm is in given elaborately in section VI. Finally performance evaluation is added in section VII.

2. Review of Related Works

Many papers with different techniques are available to hide watermark into a cover data. Among them few papers which are related to proposed algorithm are selected for review.

In [4] DWT technique is used to decompose image into four band of frequency in which a visual watermark is embedded in all band of frequency. The scaling factor for the LL sub band is 0.05, and the scaling factor for the other three sub bands is 0.005. The magnitude of the singular values are also calculated and found that wavelet coefficients with the highest magnitude are found in the LL band, and those with the lowest coefficients are found in the HH band. Robustness of image is tested against Gaussian blur, Gaussian noise, JPEG compression, sharpening, rescaling, rotation, cropping, contrast adjustment, histogram equalization, and gamma correction. Result shows that information hidden in LL band is resistant to attacks including Gaussian noise, JPEG compression, and scaling. HH band is resistant to sharpening, cropping, contrast adjustment, histogram equalization, and gamma correction. LH band is resistant to the rotation attack. In [5] SVD technique is combined with 3-scale Distributed Discrete Wavelet Transformation (DDWT) technique to hide watermark in the frequency domain. PSNR values and the Pearson's correlation is calculated and found that the watermarking scheme is resistant to both geometry and non-geometry attacks such as cropping, rotation, sharpening, Gaussian noise, Gaussian blur, contrast adjustment, waveform, fish eye, histogram equalization and rescale. In [6] the biometric watermark is embedded three times in the details of the highest level DWT of the host image. This redundancy of embedding watermark increases the correct extraction rate of the hidden data. Various attacks were done on the test images and found that this watermarking scheme is robust to compression and additive noise and quite resilient to moderate linear mean filtering.

Iris part of an eye image is extracted using segmentation and normalized process to extract feature as template which is used as biometric watermark as unique biometric identifier. Input image or cover image is third level decomposed using biorthogonal spline 9-7 filter. Then all the coefficients in third level of wavelet decomposition with magnitude greater than "T1" and less than "T2" are selected to embed biometric watermark. Using quantization approach watermark is embedded [7].

In proposed algorithm instead of using quantization technique as in [7] to hide biometric watermark SVD technique is combined with DWT technique to hide biometric data.

3. Singular Value Decomposition

Singular value decomposition is a linear algebra technique used widely in image processing applications due to its following features [8].

(a) The Singular Values (SVs) of an image has very good stability, which means that when a small value is added to an image, this does not affect the quality with great variation.

(b) An image matrix has many small singular values compared with the first singular value. Even ignoring these small singular values in the reconstruction of the image does not affect the quality of the reconstructed image

The main purpose of choosing SVD is that the singular values generated remains the same even after attacks such as rotation, scaling and translation is performed on an image data. This is the reason behind for the selection of SVD technique to combine with DWT technique in proposed algorithm. The SVD belongs to orthogonal transform which decompose the given matrix into three matrices of same size [9]. SVD technique can be applied to matrix of any size. Any image can be considered as a matrix without loss of generality. So SVD technique can be applied to any kind of images.

Let A be an image matrix then the SVD decomposition of matrix A is defined as follows.

$$A = U\Sigma V^T \quad (1)$$

U and V are unitary matrices where U matrix is called left singular values and V matrix is called right singular values.

$$U \Sigma V^T = \text{SVD}(A) \quad (2)$$

such that Σ= diagonal($\lambda_1, \lambda_2, \ldots$).

Where Σ is the diagonal matrix having as its main diagonal all positive singular values of A. Rank of the matrix is equal to number of nonzero values in singular matrix. The order of singular matrix is equal to order of input matrix. To get the original matrix back singular matrix is multiplied with unitary matrices as in (3).

$$A= \lambda_1 U_1 V_1^T + \lambda_2 U_2 V_2^T + \ldots + \lambda_r U_r V_r^T, \quad (3)$$

4. Discrete Wavelet Transform

Wavelets are a mathematical tool for hierarchically decomposing functions. They allow a function to be described in terms of a coarse (overall shape) and details that range from broad to narrow. Regardless of whether the function of interest is an image, a curve, or a surface, wavelets offer an elegant technique for representing the levels of detail present. If function is an image the wavelet tool decompose it into coarse level of overall image, broad details and narrow details. It is currently used in wide variety of applications such as audio and video compression and image compression [10]. Discrete Wavelet Transformation DWT-based watermarking argues that embedding a watermark in its sub-bands results in robust scheme that can resist to different kinds of attack. The four bands of DWT are of different frequency by which LL is low frequency band which shows overall coarse structure and HH ,LH and HL bands are high frequency band which shows detail of an image.

5. Feature Extraction

In the proposed system iris is used as watermark, so it is required to extract region of interest by segmentation. The upper and lower radius of the pupil is obtained from centre of the pupil. The canny edge detector is used to detect edge and convolved with the 2D Gaussian filter which performs the smoothing function [11] [12].

Gradient of the smoothed image is approximated by (4),The orientations of the edges are obtained to get the edges of the eyelids and iris by (5).

$$\nabla_f \approx |G_x| + |G_y| \quad (4)$$

$$\alpha(x,y)=\tan^{-1}(G_x/G_y) \quad (5)$$

Due to the light illumination during the image capture there will be contraction (or) dilation of the pupil and hence changes in the shape of the iris. By normalization technique the correct features of the iris is extracted by converting the Cartesian coordinates of the iris part into polar coordinates to make the iris part rectangular in shape. Feature Encoding transforms the normalized iris features into a unique biometric template. Gabor filter is used to encode normalized iris pattern. Fig. 1 shows the process of extracting feature from an eye image.

Fig. 3 The process of extracting template from biometric data

6. Proposed Method

In the proposed method RGB values of cover image are extracted and transformed into RGB color spaces to decorrelate. Discrete wavelet transformation technique is applied on input image and converted into wavelet coefficients. Singular value decomposition technique is applied on selected band of wavelet coefficients to get significant singular values in which watermark is to be embedded. The iris part is extracted from eye image using segmentation process and converted into template which is called watermark to be hidden in a cover image. Proposed algorithm is divided into two modules namely embedding algorithm and extraction algorithm. Diagrammatic representation of both embedding and extraction process is shown in Fig.3 and Fig.4 respectively.

A. Embedding process

During embedding process the RGB components are retrieved from a color image and converted into RGB color spaces as shown in Fig. 2. The color spaces are decomposed to get different level of frequency present in an image using DWT. Frequency coefficients of middle frequency bands (LH, HL) are SVD transformed to get significant singular values to embed watermark. The embedding process is given below.

(a) R-component (b) G-component (c) B-component

Fig. 2 RGB components of the original image

1. Apply DWT on color spaces of cover image. One level of decomposition produces four band of frequency namely LL, HL, LH and HH.
2. Apply SVD on middle frequency band HL and LH band on the cover image using(6).
   $$U^k \Sigma^k V^{kT} = SVD(A^k) \quad (6)$$
   where k=1,2 and it denotes LH and HL band and λ^k_i, i=1,....,n are the singular values of Σ^k
3. Apply SVD using(7) on the template which is segmented part of iris and separate them into two halves one half is to be hidden in HL band and other half in LH band.
   $$U_w \Sigma_w V^T_w = SVD(W) \quad (7)$$
   where λ_{wi}, i=1,...,n are the singular values of Σ_w.
4. Modify the singular values of the cover image in HL and LH with the singular values of the watermark by (8).
   $$\lambda^{*k}_i=\lambda^k_i+\alpha_k\lambda_{wi}, i=1,....,n, k=1,2 \quad (8)$$
5. Now obtain the modified DWT coefficients by(9)
   $$A^{*k}=U^k_a\Sigma^{*k}_a V^{kT}_a, k=1,2 \quad (9)$$
6. Apply inverse SVD followed by inverse DWT with modified LH and HL coefficients to get watermarked image.

As the size of watermark template extracted from biometric data is quite large, the middle frequency bands HL and LH are used to hide watermark. Watermark can be hidden in one or more number of bands of one level of composition or multilevel of decomposition of cover data.

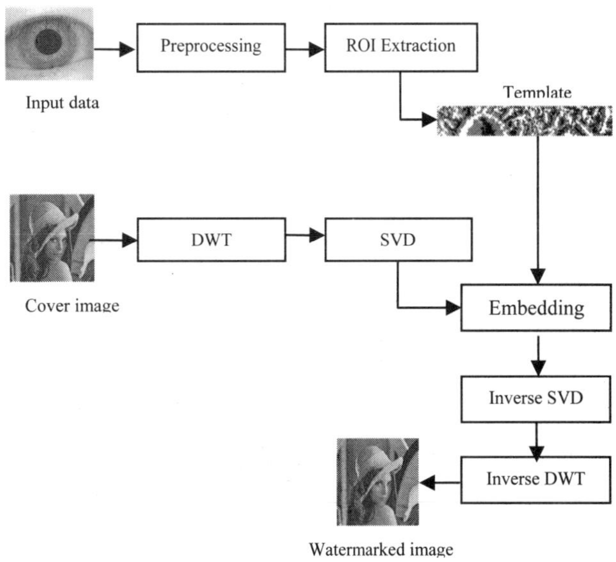

Fig. 3 Watermark embedding

B. Extraction process

1. By applying DWT, watermarked image is decomposed into four subbands of LL, LH, HL and HH.
2. Apply SVD on HL, LH band on the cover image.
   $$U^k_a\Sigma^{*k}_a V^{kT}_a=A^{*k} \quad (10)$$
   where k=1,2 and it denotes LH and HL band selection.
3. Extract the watermark using singular values from HL and LH band,
   $$\lambda^k_{wi}=(\lambda^{*k}_i-\lambda^k_i)/\alpha_k, i=1,....,n, k=1,2 \quad (11)$$

4. Construct the watermarks by applying inverse SVD using(12)

$$W^k=U_w\Sigma^k_w V^T_w, k=1,2 \quad (12)$$

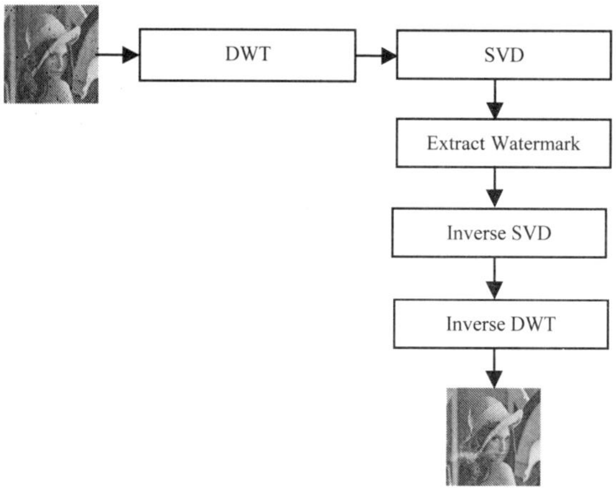

Fig. 4 Watermark embedding process

7. Performance Evaluation

The performance of our proposed algorithm is analyzed using Lena test image of size 512x512 and watermark size of 20x480. It is observed that watermark can be hidden in all the three color channels or in any one of the three channels. In this proposed method watermark is hidden in one color space of RGB color spaces. The quality of the watermarked image can be measured either subjectively or objectively and it is observed that both subjective and objective quality of watermarked image is good. The PSNR is the objective criteria used to measure the quality of the watermarked image. The Equation for measuring PSNR and NC are shown in (14) and (15) respectively.

$$MSE = \frac{1}{mn}\sum_{i=1}^{m}\sum_{j=1}^{n}(f(i,j) - f'(i,j))2 \quad (13)$$

$$PSNR=10\log_{10}\left(\frac{255^2}{MSE}\right) \quad (14)$$

$$NC = \frac{\sum_{i=1}^{n}\sum_{j=1}^{m} w(i,j)*w_e(i,j)}{\sqrt{\sum_{i=1}^{n}\sum_{j=1}^{m} w^2(i,j)}\ \sqrt{\sum_{i=1}^{n}\sum_{j=1}^{m} w_e^2(i,j)}} \quad (15)$$

where W and W_e are original and extracted watermark.

$f(i,j)$ and $f'(i,j)$ represent the pixel values of original host image and the watermarked image respectively and parameters *m,n* specifies row and column size of images respectively. The quality of the extracted watermark is obtained through normalized correlations (NC) using (15), which is used to measure the similarity between original watermark and extracted watermark. Original image and watermark used in proposed algorithm is shown in Fig. 5. Watermarked image in red color space after it undergone various attacks are shown in Fig. 7. Similarly watermark hidden in green and blue components and its variations after attacks are shown in Fig.8 respectively.

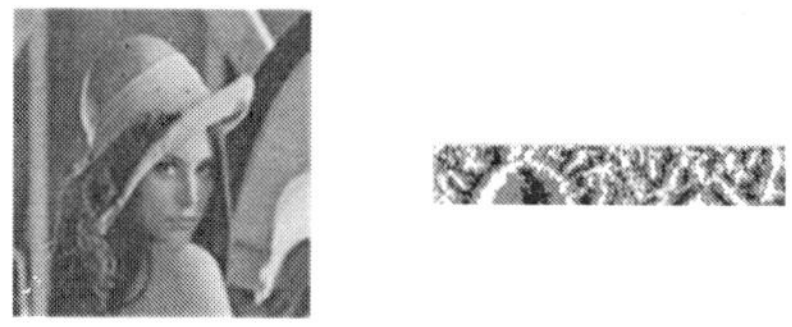

Fig. 5 (a) original image (b) watermark

Proposed algorithm is tested against attacks such as rotation, addition of pepper and salt, gamma correction, histogram equalization, intensity adjustment and blurring using Lena test image. When watermark is hidden into red color space the quality of watermarked image is not degraded and after various attack, the similarity of extracted watermark and original is shown in Table1. Similarly watermark extracted from green and blue components after attacks are compared with original watermark by calculating normalized correlation coefficients which are shown in Table 2 and Table 3.

PSNR values of R and B component while Gamma correction attack is made found low. When Histogram attack is made the PSNR values of R, G and B component are all low and hence the system is not robust to this attack. The PSNR value of G component is low when Intensity adjustment attack is made. Hence hiding the watermark in G and B component for this system shows more robustness for various kinds of attacks. Calculated normalized correlation of extracted watermark after various attacks from RGB color spaces are shown in Fig. 6a and Fig. 9

Table 1 Watermark extracted from Red color space

Attacks	NC	PSNR
Rotation	0.9999	37.4928
Pepper and salt	0.9179	24.5955
Gamma correction	0.8806	22.4976
Histogram equalization	0.7055	12.0473
Intensity adjustment	0.8558	37.3976
Blurring	0.9986	33.9593

Table 2 Watermark extracted from G component

Attacks	NC	PSNR
Rotation	0.9999	37.6475
Pepper and salt	0.9470	24.9238
Gamma correction	0.3518	37.4918
Histogram equalization	0.9186	16.7055
Intensity adjustment	0.8833	14.9976
Blurring	0.9954	32.8279

Table 3 Watermark extracted from B component

Attacks	NC	PSNR
Rotation	0.3348	35.4082
Pepper and salt	0.6500	25.4450
Gamma correction	0.8312	19.1914
Histogram equalization	0.5367	13.6740
Intensity adjustment	0.3530	37.3598
Blurring	0.9928	33.3760

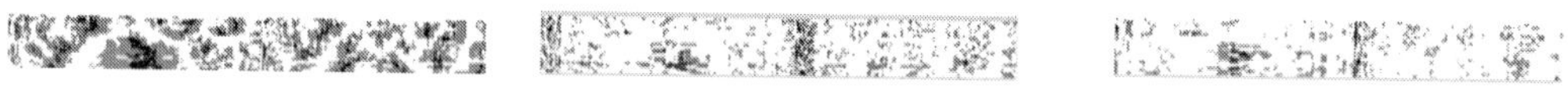

NC = 0.8806 (Red) NC = 0.3518 (Green) NC = 0.8312 (Blue)

(a) Gamma correction

NC = 0.8806 (Red) NC = 0.3518 (Green) NC = 0.8312 (Blue)

(b) Intensity adjustments

Fig. 6 Extracted watermark after attacks from red, green and blue color space watermarked image

(a) Pepper & salt

(b) Gamma corrections

(c) Rotation

(d) Histogram equalization

(e) Intensity adjustments

(f) Blurring

Fig. 7 Watermarked image in green color space after various attacks

(a) Pepper & salt

(b) Gamma correction

(c) Rotation

(d) Histogram equalization

(e) Intensity adjustments

(f) Blurring

Fig. 8 Watermarked image in blue color space after

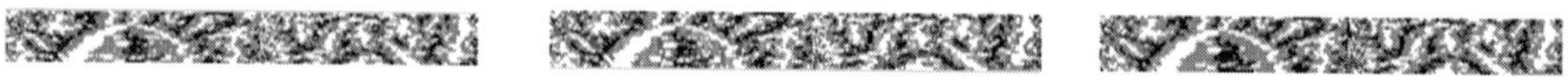

NC = 0.9179 (Red) NC = 0.9470 (Green) NC = 0.6500 (Blue)

(c) salt and pepper

NC = 0.8806 NC = 0.3518 NC 0.8312

(d) Gamma correction

NC = 0.9999 NC = 0.9999 NC = 0.3348

(e) Rotation

NC = 0.7055 NC = 0.9186 NC = 0.5367

(f)Histogram Equalization

Fig. 9 Extracted watermark after attacks from red, green and blue color space watermarked image

8. Conclusion

- In proposed algorithm the features of DWT-SVD techniques are combined.
- Embedding can be carried out in all frequencies without visible distortion in cove image
- Algorithm is found to be robust against many attacks as per the results, classified as non-blind watermarking algorithm, which can be used for copyright protection application where robustness is very important.
- Watermark inserted in red color space performs well than green and blue color spaces.
- Proposed algorithm is not robust to rotation attack in RGB color spaces, thus our future work is to make algorithm robust to rotation attack in RGB color space.

9. References

[1] J. Daugman, "How iris recognition works", IEEE *Trans. CSVT,* 14(1), 2004, pp 21-30

[2] I. J. Cox, M. L. Miller, and J. A. Bloom, "Digital Watermarking", Morgan Kaufmann Publishers, 2002.

[3] E. T. Lin, A. M. Eskicioglu, R. L. Lagendijk and E. J. Delp, " Advances in Digital Video Content Protection", Proceedings of the IEEE, Special Issue on Advances in Video Coding and Delivery, 2004.

[4] Emir Ganic, and Ahmet M. Eskicioglu, "Robust DWT-SVD Domain Image Watermarking: Embedding Data in All Frequencies", MM&SE'04, 2004.

[5] Chu-Hsing Lin, Jung-Chun Liu, Chih-Hsiong Shih, Yan-Wei Lee, " A Robust Wateramrking Scheme for Copyright Protection", Proceedings of IEEE, International Conference on Multimedia and Ubiquitous Engineering, 2008.

[6] Khalil Zebbiche, Lahouari Ghouti, Fouad Khelifi and Ahmed Bouridane, "Protecting Fingerprint Data using Watermarking", IEEE, Proceedings of the First NASA/ESA Conference on Adaptive Hardware and Systems (AHS'06), 2006.

[7] Shiraz Ahmad, and Zhe-Ming Lu, " A Joint Biometrics and Watermarking Based Framework for Fingerprinting, Copyright Protection, Proof of Ownership, and Security Applications", Proceedings of IEEE, International Conference on Computational Intelligence and Security Workshops, P. R. China, 2007.

[8] Liu Liang and Sun Qi,"A new SVD-DWT composite watermarking",ICSP2006 proceedings

[9] Zhe-Ming Lu, Hong-Yi Zheng, Ji-Wu Huang, "A Digital Watermarking Scheme Based on DCT and SVD".

[10] Eric J. Stollnitz, Tony D. DeRose, and David H. Salesin. Wavelets for computer graphics: A primer, part 1. *IEEE Computer Graphics and Applications*, 15(3):76–84, May 1995.

[11] W. Boles, B. Bonashash, "A Human Identifiaction Technique using Images of the Iris and Wavelet Transform", IEEE *Trans.* on Signal Processing, 46(4), 1998.

[12] R. Wildes, "Iris recognition: an emerging biometric technology", Proceedings of IEEE, 85(9), 1997.

Analysis of Classification Methods of Face Images using PCA and Fisher-Based Algorithms

Mrs. Mahananda D. Malkauthekar[1] and Mrs. Shubhangi D. Sapkal[2]
[1]Assistant Professor, Department of C. S. E., MIT (E), Aurangabad, Maharashtra, India
nandamalkauthekar@yahoo.co.in
[2]Lecturer, Department of C. S. E., Govt. College of Engg., Aurangabad, Maharashtra, India
Shubhangi_parde@yahoo.com

Abstract

This paper presented results of performance test of face recognition algorithms. Here two algorithms Principal Component Analysis (PCA) and Fisher Discriminant Analysis (FDA) have been analyzed. Recognition process comprises the two steps: training and testing. In the training phase a set of the eigenvectors of the covariance matrix of the images used for training. In testing phase, firstly all the training images are used for the testing. Test image will be compared with all the images in the eigenspace and measures the Euclidean distance. The image with the lowest Euclidean distance is the matched image. These two algorithms are evaluated experimentally on FERET database face images each with the moderate subject size.

Keywords: *Principal Component Analysis, Nearest Neighbor classification, Fisher Discrimination Analysis, FERET.*

1. Introduction

Face recognition is something that humans are exemplarily accurate at. Face recognition in general is recognition of moving people in natural scenes, in particular requires a basic set of visual tasks to be performed robustly.

Face recognition can be defined as the identification of a person from an image of his face. It falls into a bracket of technology aptly named biometrics. We, as humans, have an innate ability to recognize faces and take for granted our abilities that allow us to quickly identify a person often with very limited information. Creating a computer system to try and compete with the human visual system is extremely complex and so far unsolved.

The basic objective of this work is to determine the ability of using pattern recognition methods in detecting face correctly. Author has used here two methods, one is statistical and other is an experimental. A comparison is made on the two methods used to analyze results.

2. Feature Extraction by PCA

2.1 Overview

Let a face image X_i be a two-dimensional m by m array of intensity values. Thus, an image may also be considered as a vector of m^2 dimension. Denote the training set of n face images by $X=(X_1,X_2,\cdots X_n)\subset R^{m^2\times n}$ and we assume that each image belongs to one of c classes.

Thus defines covariance matrix as follows

$$\Gamma=\frac{1}{n}\sum_{i=1}^{n}(X_i-\overline{X})(X_i-\overline{X})^T=\Phi\Phi^T$$

where

$$\Phi=(\Phi_1,\Phi_2,\cdots,\Phi_n)\subset R^{m^2\times n} \text{ and } \overline{X}=\frac{1}{n}\sum_{i=1}^{n}X_i$$

Then, the eigenvalues and eigenvectors of the covariance can be calculated. Let $U=(U_1,U_2,\cdots U_r)\subset R^{m^2\times n}$ $(r\prec n)$ be the r eigenvectors corresponding to the r largest eigenvalues. Thus, for a set of original face images $X\subset R^{m^2\times n}$, their corresponding eigenface-based feature $Y\subset R^{r\times n}$ can be obtained by projecting X into the Eigenface space as follows:

$$Y=U^TX.$$

The eigenvectors corresponding to non-zero eigenvalues of the covariance matrix form an orthonormal basis that rotates and/or reflects the images in the N-dimensional space [6][7][9].

2.2 Results

The FERET dataset face images are used for classification.

2.2.1 Resizing

Size of the images is fixed. Original image size is (768*512*3), which is changed to (60*60). RGB images are converted to grayscale images.

Facial images of 3 subjects (9 images for each person, 9*3=27 images) with different expression and angles are used for classification shown in Fig. 2.1.

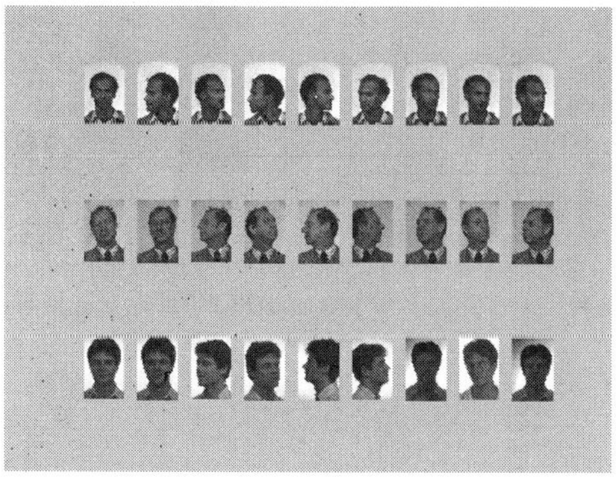

Fig. 2.1 Training images from FERET database

Three different persons are used and 9 images of each person. Front face for each class are used for training and all images of faces with different angles and expressions are used for testing.

2.2.2 Class1

The Euclidian distance of front face of class1 (Person1) with all images of three classes is shown in Table 2.1, Where I1,…In are the images and P1,P2,P3 are the persons.

Table 2.1 Euclidian distance of front face of class-1 with all images

	I1	I2	I3	I4	I5	I6	I7	I8	I9
P1	0	2.20	1.67	3.23	1.41	1..56	1.04	1.51	1.60
P2	0.99	1.61	0.79	2.30	1.00	0.87	1.07	0.61	2.44
P3	1.41	1.83	1.45	2.60	1.57	1.23	1.29	1.45	2.64

2.2.3 Class2

The Euclidian distance of front face class2 (Person2) with all images of three classes is calculated and shown in Table 2.2

Table 2.2 Euclidian distance of front face of class-2 with all images

	I1	I2	I3	I4	I5	I6	I7	I8	I9
P1	0.99	1.57	3.30	0.74	1.97	1.75	1.90	1.91	1.30
P2	0.	2.46	3.38	1.50	1.03	2.65	1.14	1.05	1.23
P3	1.29	2.55	2.75	1.71	1.69	2.65	1.19	2.15	2.32

2.2.4 Class3

The Euclidian distance of front face of class3 (Person3) with all images of three classes is calculated and shown in Table 2.3.

Table 2.3 Euclidian distance of front face of class3 with all remaining images

	I1	I2	I3	I4	I5	I6	I7	I8	I9
P1	1.42	1.11	1.17	1.07	1.20	1.05	1.22	0.73	0.99
P2	1.29	0.35	0.53	0.50	0.54	0.74	0.47	0.71	0.30
P3	0	1.48	1.05	1.23	1.28	1.22	9.99	1.20	1.16

Recognition rate with Euclidian distance given in the Table 2.4.

Table 2.4 Recognition rate with euclidian distance

PCA	**Recognition rate by Euclidean distance with dimensionality reduction**		
	Front faces	Changed angle	Changed Expressions
No. of images	6	18	3
Recognition rate	100	44.44	32.33

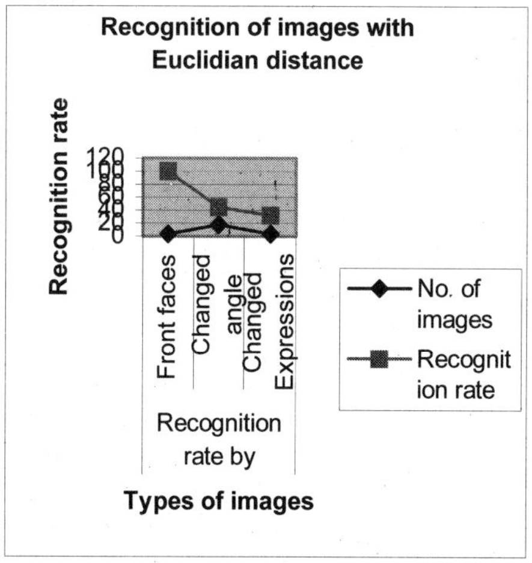

Fig. 2.2 Recognition rate of different images

3. Fisher Descriminant

3.1 Overview

The Fisher's linear discriminant (FLD) is used to find an optimal subspace for classification in which the ratio of the between-class scatter and the within-class scatter is maximized.

Fisher Discriminant algorithm steps are as follows:

Training images are projected into a subspace. The test images are projected into the same subspace and identified using a similarity measure. What differs is how the subspace is calculated? Following are the steps to find the Fisher discriminants for a set of images

Step 1 The within class scatter matrix

The within class scatter matrix measures the amount of scatter between items in the same class. For the ith *class*, a scatter matrix (S_i) is calculated as the sum of the covariance matrices of the centered images in that class.

$$S_i = \sum_{x \in X_i} (x - m_i)(x - m_i)^T$$

where m_i is the mean of the images in the class. The within class scatter matrix (S_W) is the sum of all the scatter matrices.

$$S_W = \sum_{i=1}^{C} S_i$$

Where C is the number of classes.

Step 2 The between class scatter matrix

The between class scatter matrix (S_B) measures the amount of scatter between classes. It is calculated as the sum of the covariance matrices of the difference between the total mean and

$$S_B = \sum_{i=1}^{C} n_i (m_i - m)(m_i - m)^T$$

mean of each class.

Where n_i *is* the number of images in the class, m_i is the mean of the images in the class and m is the mean of all the images.

Step 3 The generalized eigenvalue problem

Solve for the generalized eigenvectors (*V*) and eigenvalues (□) of the within class and between class scatter matrices.

$$S_B V = \Lambda S_W V$$

Step 4 Keep first C-l eigenvectors

Sort the eigenvectors by their associated eigenvalues from high to low and keep the first C -1 eigenvectors. These eigenvectors form the Fisher basis vectors.

Step 5 Project images onto Fisher basis vectors

Project all the original (i.e. not centered) images onto the Fisher basis vectors by calculating the dot product of the image with each of the Fisher basis vectors. The original images are projected onto this line because these are the points that the line has been created to discriminate, not the centered images [5].

3. 2 RESULTS

3.2.1 Fisher Discriminant Test for Two Classes

Following is an example of calculating the Fisher discriminants for a set of images. Let the twelve images in Fig. 3 be training images. There are two classes; images x^1 - x^6 are in the first class and images x^7 – x^{12} are in the second class. The training images viewed as vectors are

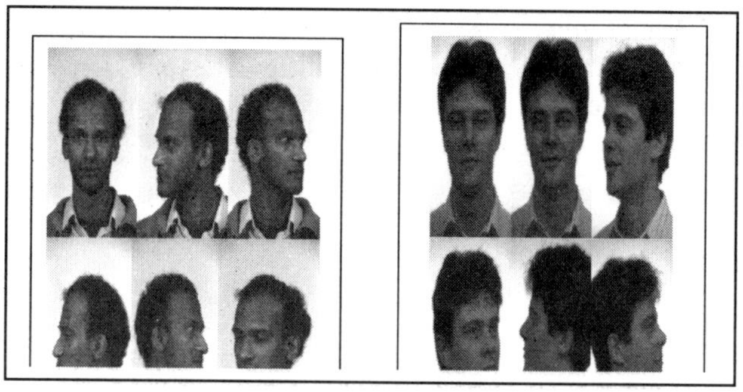

Fig. 3.1 Training images used for fisher discriminant

The within class scatter matrix is calculated as:

SW = S1+S2

Table 3.1 Within class scatter matrix

	C1	C2	c3	c4	c5	c6	c7	c8	c9
r1	1.9	1	0.2	0.4	-0.1	1.6	0	-1	0.8
r2	1	7.3	4.5	1.1	-1.7	0.7	-0	-4	-2
r3	0.2	4.5	4.6	1.3	-0.5	0.2	0.2	-3	-2
r4	0.4	1.1	1.3	1.8	-0	0.5	0.3	-2	-0
r5	-0	-1	-0	0	1	-0.4	0.2	1.2	0.1
r6	1.6	0.7	0.2	0.5	-0.4	0.2	0.1	-1	1
r7	0	-0	0.2	0.3	0.2	0.1	0.5	0.3	-0
r8	-1	-4	-3	-1.7	1.2	-1	0.3	8.2	-1
r9	0.8	-2	-2	-0.2	0.1	1	-0	-1	4.3

Within class scatter matrix shows the distances of the images within the class. Our aim is to minimize the within class scatter matrix. The graph 1 shows the graph for the matrix. Each bubble in the graph shows the values in that region. It is clear from the graph that the images within the class are closer.

The between class scatter matrix is:

Table 3.2 Between class scatter matrix

C	X1	X2	X3	X4	X5	X6
1	186	235	225	221	243	235
C	X7	X8	X9	X10	X11	X12
2	168	105	129	169	116	105
C 3	X13	X14	X15	X16	X17	X18
	29	1	42	46	7	4

Between class scatter matrix shows the distances of the images between the two classes. Our aim is to maximize the between class scatter matrix. Graph 3.2 shows the matrix. Each bubble in the graph shows the values in that region. It is clear from the graph that the images between the two classes are not closer.

Since there are two classes, only one eigenvector is kept. The non-zero eigenvector and the values of the images projected onto the first eigenvector are shown in Table .

Table 3.3 Values of the images projected onto the first eigenvector

Graph 3.3 shows a plot of the points, clearly illustrating the separation between the two classes.

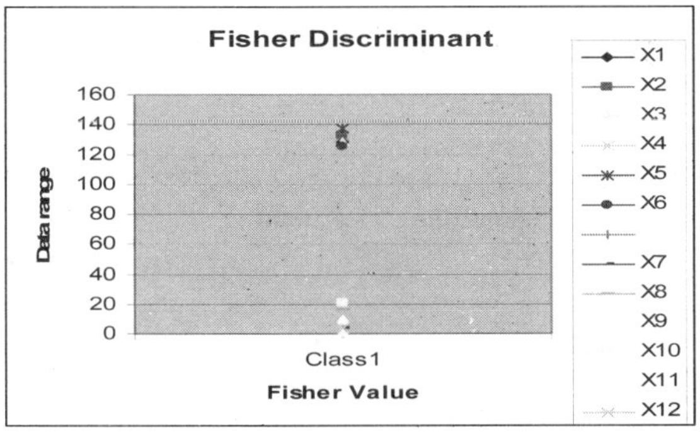

Graph 3.3 Plot of the images projected onto fisher basis vectors.

For classifying face images with Euclidean distance, images are trained for each subject (of 2 persons) and all images of two classes are used for testing. Euclidean distance is used as a classifier. Dimensions are reduced. Here all the images are recognized correctly as shown in the Table 3.4.

Table 3.4 Euclidian distance of each image of 2 persons with all training images

0	5	0	11	9	3	124	112	127	107	119	124
5	**0**	5	6	4	8	129	117	132	112	124	129
0	5	**0**	11	9	3	124	112	127	107	119	124
11	6	11	**0**	2	14	135	123	138	118	130	135
9	4	9	2	**0**	12	133	121	136	116	128	133
3	8	3	14	12	**0**	121	109	124	104	116	121
124	129	124	135	133	121	**0**	12	3	17	5	0
112	117	112	123	121	109	12	**0**	15	5	7	12
127	132	127	138	136	124	3	15	**0**	20	8	3
107	112	107	118	116	104	17	5	20	**0**	12	17
119	124	119	130	128	116	5	7	8	12	**0**	5
124	129	124	135	133	121	0	12	3	17	5	**0**

Here the diagonal of the matrix shows the minimum distance between the images. Since we have used all the training images for testing, the distance of each image with itself is minimum, which is zero as shown in the diagonal of the matrix.

3.2.2 Fisher Discriminant Test for Three Classes

Following is an example of calculating the Fisher discriminants for a set of images. There are three classes; images x^1 - x^6 are in the first class, images x^7 – x^{12} and images x^{13} – x^{18} are in the third class.

The within class scatter matrix is calculated as:

SW=S1+S2+S3

Table 3.5 Within class scatter matrix SW

	c1	c2	c3	c4	c5	c6	c7	c8
r1	0.6	0.2	0.1	0	-0	0.1	-0.1	-0
r2	0.2	1.1	0.3	0.1	-0.1	0	-0.1	-0
r3	0.1	0.3	0.7	0.1	0	0.1	-0.1	-1
r4	0	0.1	0.1	0.2	-0	0.1	0	-0
r5	-0	-0	0	-0	0.2	-0	-0.1	0
r6	0.1	0	0.1	0.1	-0	0.2	0	-0
r7	-0	-0	-0	0	-0.1	0	0.3	0.1
r8	-0	-0	-1	-0	0	-0.1	0.1	1.1
r9	0	-0	-0	-0	-0.1	0.1	0.1	-0

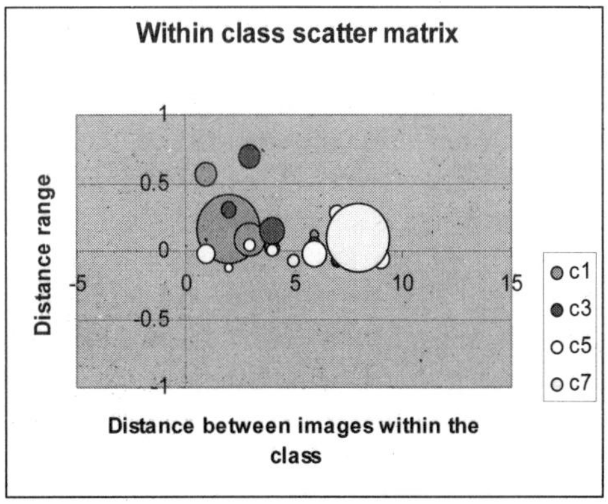

Graph 3.4 Distance between the images within the class.

Within class scatter matrix shows the distances of the images within the class. Our aim is to minimize the within class scatter matrix. The graph 3.4 shows the graph for the SW. Each bubble in the graph shows the values in that region. It is clear from the graph that the images within the class are closer.

The between class scatter matrix is calculated as:

SB = SB1+SB2+SB3

Table 3.6 The between class scatter matrix SB

	C1	C2	C3	C4	C5	C6	C7	C9
R1	5.9	0	-1	7.2	0.7	-0	7	-1
R2	0	0	-0	0	0	0	0	-0
R3	-1	-0	3	-0.6	-1	-2.1	-2	1.2
R4	7.2	0	-1	8.9	0.7	-0.4	8.5	-1
R5	0.7	0	-1	0.7	0.3	0.6	1	-0
R6	-0	0	-2	-0.4	0.6	1.5	0.4	-1
R7	7	0	-2	8.5	1	0.4	8.5	-1
R8	1.2	0	-0	1.4	0.2	0.1	1.4	-0
R9	-1	-0	1.2	-0.8	-0.4	-0.8	-1	0.5

The values of the images projected onto the first eigenvector are shown in Table 3.7. Where X1...X18 are the images and C1, C2 and C3 are the classes.

Table 3.7 Values of the images projected onto the first eigenvector

Fisher Discriminant		Recognition rate by Euclidean distance with dimensionality reduction		
		Front faces	Changed angle	Changed Expressions
Fisher test on two classes		2	8	2
Fisher test on three classes		3	12	3
Recognition rate	All faces used for training	100	100	100
	Only front faces are used for training.	100	100	100

For classifying face images with Euclidean distance, images are trained for each subject (of 3 persons) and all images of three classes are used for testing. Euclidean distance is used as a classifier. Dimensions are reduced. Here all the images are recognized correctly as shown in the table 3.8.

Table 3.8 Euclidian Distance of Each Image of 3 Persons with All Training Images.

Here the diagonal of the matrix shows the minimum distance between the images. Since we have used all the training images for testing, the distance of each image with itself is minimum, which is zero as shown in the diagonal of the matrix.

Three different persons are used and 6 images of each person. Front face images are trained for each subject (of 3 persons) and all images of faces with different angles and expressions of three classes are used for testing. Euclidean distance is used as a classifier. Dimensions are reduced .The results of the images, which are recognized correctly, are shown below.

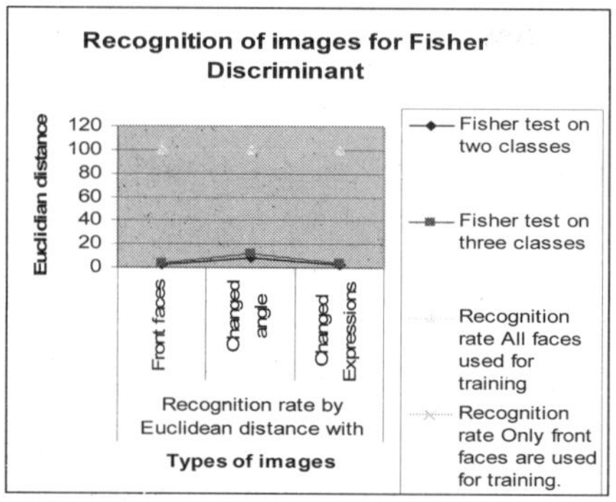

Graph 3.7 Recognition rate for fisher discriminant

The graph 3.7 shows that the recognition rate for Fisher Discriminant for both the cases 1) When all images are used for training and 2) When only front faces are used for training. The recognition rate is 100% for two classes as well as for three classes.

The comparative study as shown in the following Table 3.9 and in the graph 3.8 shows that the results are improved in FLDA for the different types of images.

Table 3.9 Comparative study of statistical method and experimental method

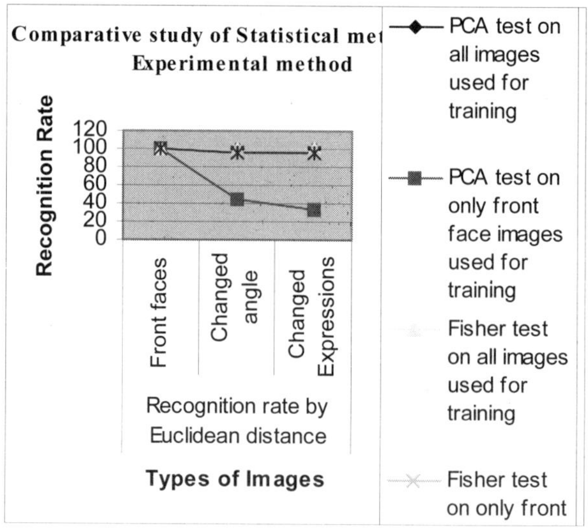

Graph 3.8 Comparative study

The above graph 3.8 shows that the result of Fisher test for changed expressions is 100% while the result of PCA test for changed expression is 32.33%.

4. Conclusions

PCA Algorithm is easy to implement because of its simplicity. There is a high correlation between the training data and testing data so the accuracy of PCA algorithm depends on many things. PCA has better accuracy with frontal faces. Scale and orientation of an image will affect the accuracy greatly. PCA takes less processing time, and is efficient in storage. The accuracy of Eigenface is satisfactory (Over 90%).

FDA has better accuracy with face expression. Calculation of ratio of between-class scatter to within-class scatter requires a lot of processing time.

The accuracy of Fisher face is good (100%). The FDA is tested for two sets of experiments, first set of experiment is for two classes and the second is for three classes. It is seen that there is no change in the performance of the algorithm if we increase the number of classes. It has also been seen that as the size of an image increases, the efficiency of our algorithm decreases gradually and even it becomes impossible to calculate the covariance matrix of images of large sizes. This problem can be resolved by using images of smaller size instead of large size. This will not only fix the size of the covariance matrix but also become independent of the database size. This not only decreases our computational cost but also improves the performance.

Table 3.3 The Values of the Images Projected onto the First Eigenvector

	c1	c2	c3	c4	c5	c6	c7	c8	c9
r1	1.79	-0.0116	1.6433	2.5133	-0.3441	-1.3881	1.7361	0.2552	0.4872
r2	-0.01	0.0001	-0.0106	-0.0163	0.0022	0.009	-0.0112	-0.0017	-0.0031
r3	1.64	-0.0106	1.5052	2.3021	-0.3152	-1.2715	1.5902	0.2338	0.4462
r4	2.51	-0.0163	2.3021	3.5208	-0.4821	-1.9446	2.4321	0.3575	0.6825
r5	-0.34	0.0022	-0.3152	-0.4821	0.066	0.2663	-0.333	-0.0489	-0.0984
r6	-1.38	0.009	-1.2715	-1.9446	0.2663	1.074	-1.3433	-0.1975	-0.3769
r7	1.73	-0.0112	1.5902	2.4321	-0.333	-1.3433	1.68	0.247	0.4714
r8	0.25	-0.0017	0.2338	0.3575	-0.0489	-0.1975	0.247	0.0363	0.0693
r9	0.48	-0.0031	0.4462	0.6825	-0.0984	-0.3769	0.4714	0.0693.	0.1323

Table 3.8 Euclidian Distance of Each Image of 3 Persons with All Training Images

0	49	39	35	57	49	18	81	57	17	70	81	157	185	144	140	179	182
49	**0**	10	14	8	0	67	130	106	66	119	130	206	234	193	189	228	231
39	10	**0**	4	18	10	57	120	96	56	109	120	196	224	183	179	218	221
35	14	4	**0**	22	14	53	116	92	52	105	116	192	220	179	175	214	217
57	8	18	22	**0**	8	75	138	114	74	127	138	214	242	201	197	236	239
49	0	10	14	8	**0**	67	130	106	66	119	130	206	234	193	189	228	231
18	67	57	53	75	67	**0**	63	39	1	52	63	139	167	126	122	161	164
81	130	120	116	138	130	63	**0**	24	64	11	0	76	104	63	59	98	101
57	106	96	92	114	106	39	24	**0**	40	13	24	100	128	87	83	122	125
17	66	56	52	74	66	1	64	40	**0**	53	64	140	168	127	123	162	165
70	119	109	105	127	119	52	11	13	53	**0**	11	87	115	74	70	109	112
81	130	120	116	138	130	63	0	24	64	11	**0**	76	104	63	59	98	101
157	206	196	192	214	206	139	76	100	140	87	76	**0**	28	13	17	22	25
185	234	224	220	242	234	167	104	128	168	115	104	28	**0**	41	45	6	3
144	193	183	179	201	193	126	63	87	127	74	63	13	41	**0**	4	35	38
140	189	179	175	197	189	122	59	83	123	70	59	17	45	4	**0**	39	42
179	228	218	214	236	228	161	98	122	162	109	98	22	6	35	39	**0**	3
182	231	221	217	239	231	164	101	125	165	112	101	25	3	38	42	3	**0**

Table 3.9 Comparative Study of Statistical Method and experimental Method

Fisher Discriminant	**Recognition rate by Euclidean distance with dimensionality reduction**		
	Front faces	Changed angle	Changed Expressions
PCA test on all images used for training	100	100	100
PCA test on only front face images used for training	95	44.44	32.33
Fisher test on all images used for training	100	100	100
Fisher test on only front face images used for training	100	100	100
Fisher test on two classes	100	100	100

4.1 Future Scope

The recognition rate can be improved by increasing the no. of images. Further one can use the illumination variations face images for testing. This is important because in the real world, face detectors will detect partial faces either due to occlusion or other factors.

Another approach is to localize the face first and then extract the features. This will defiantly improve the performance because the localization of face will remove the background of the face image and it doesn't matter the different hair styles, head cap etc.

5. References

[1] Dr. Despina Polemi, Final Report On "Biometric techniques: Review and evaluation of Biometric techniques for identification and Authentication"at Institute Of Communication And Computer Systems, National Technical University Of Athens, April 1997, pp no. 01-20

[2] Gregory Williams, "More than pretty face, Biometrics and smart card Tokens" at GSEC, on 24th December 2001, pg. No. 1- 25

[3] Uday Banerjee "Enforcing Security with Biometrics" on 18th May 2002, Pg. No. 12.

[4] http://www.frvt.org/DLs/FERET7.pdf

[5] An introduction to evaluating biometric systems, P. Jonathan Phillips, Alvin Martin, C.L. Wilson, Mark, Przybocki 2000 IEEE}

[6] A Novel Method Of Face Recognition Based On The Fusion Of Classifiers Ming Li, Zhi-Yun Liu School of Computer and Communication, Lanzhou University of Technology, Lanzhou, 730050, China.

[7] A Novel Incremental Principal Component Analysis and It Application for Face Recognition Haitao Zhao, Pong Chi Yuen, Member, IEEE, and James T. Kwok, Member IEEE

[8] Face Recognition by Using Neural Networks Classifiers Based on PCA and LDA, Byung-Joo Oh , Dept. of Electronics Engineering, Hannam University, Korea.

[9] Appearance–based Statistical Methods for Face Recognition, Kresimir Delac Mislav Grgic, Panos Liatsis

Facial Expression Recognition

Mr Sachin Ruikar[1], Mr. Atul Ingole[2] and Mr. Chittaranjan Mahajan[3]
ruikarsachin@gmail.com ingoleatulb@gmail.com chittaranjan_m1@yahoo.co.in

Abstract

For good human computer interaction it is sometimes necessary to evaluate the state of emotion of the human being sitting in front of the machine. Scientists have earlier used voice for this purpose. Another technique is to use the facial images to obtain facial expressions. For the later approach different methods have been used. Mainly are Knowledge-based methods, Feature invariant methods, Template matching methods, Appearance-based methods. These come under geometrical methods and statistical methods. Statistical methods are posing invariant and require a learning algorithm. Hence it requires using of an appearance based method. It uses haar based features which are reminiscent of haar basis functions to train our feature classifier which uses Multi Class Adaboost Algorithm for learning. It again uses Lookup Table based weak classifier instead of using the ordinary threshold based weak classifier because it is a multi class problem.

1. Introduction

1.1 Brief Description

In our paper the facial expression is extracted from human faces by an expression classifier that is learned from boosting Haar feature based Look-Up-Table type weak classifiers. The expression recognition system consists of three modules, face detection, facial feature landmark extraction and facial expression recognition. Out of the three modules we have implemented only the facial expression recognition. The implemented system can automatically recognize seven expressions in real time that include anger, disgust, fear, happiness, neutral, sadness and surprise. Experimental results are reported to show its potential applications in human computer interaction.

1.2 System Training Block

This stage involves the training of the expression classifier. We make use of the multi class Adaboost algorithm for seven classes of expression viz., anger, disgust, fear, happiness, neutral, sadness and surprise. The training database consists of 36X36 pixels cropped frontal face images of different Japanese female portraying different expressions. The system training diagram as shown in Fig.1.

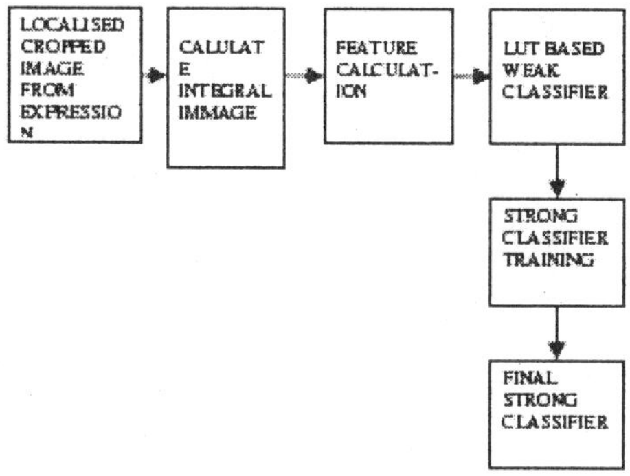

Fig. 1 System Training Block Diagram

1.3 System Working Block

The cropped and localized face image output from a face detector is given as an input to the expression classifier. The output of classifier is one of the seven possibilities from the expression class of the face. This output can be used as an input for running entertainment applications like media players. The system working block diagram as shown in figure 2.

1.4 System Overview

The proposed facial expression recognition system consists of three modules, face detection, facial feature landmark extraction and facial expression classification. In our work we implement only the third and the last module i.e., facial expression classification. Expressions are divided into seven categories that include anger, disgust, fear, happiness, neutral, sadness and surprise. Here we only consider the problem of frontal facial expression recognition. A classifier for facial expression recognition is learned by boosting Haar feature based Look-Up Table type weak classifiers.

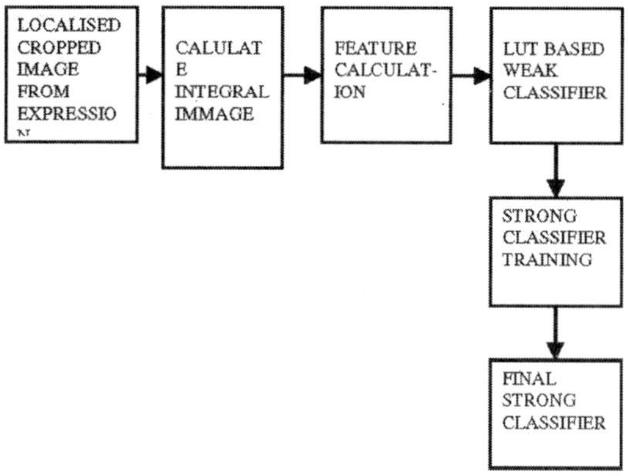

Fig. 2 System working Block Diagram

2. Design/Manufacturing

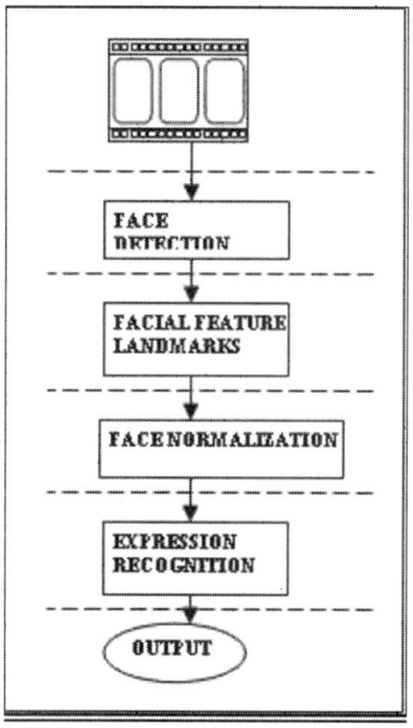

Fig. 3 An Automatic Expression Recognition System

2.1 Integral Images

In order to be successful, a detection algorithm must posses two key features; accuracy and speed. There is generally a trade-off between the two. Through the use of a new image representation, the integral image, Viola & Jones described a means for the fast feature evaluation that proves to be an effective way to speed up the classification task.

$$ii(x, y) = \sum_{x' \leq x, y' \leq y} i(x', y')$$

Where ii(x, y) is the integral image and i(x, y) is the original image. Using the following pair of recurrences:

s(x ,y) = s(x,y-1)+i(x, y) (1)
ii(x ,y) = ii(x-1,y)+s(x , y) (2)

(Where s(x, y) is the cumulative row sum, s(x,-1) = 0, and ii (-1, y) =0) the integral image can be computed in one pass over the original image.

Using the integral image any rectangular sum can be computed in four array references). Clearly the difference between two rectangular sums can be computed in eight references. Since the two rectangle features defined above involve adjacent rectangular sums they can be computed in six array references, eight in the case of the three-rectangle features, and nine for four-rectangle features.

2.2 Feature Extraction: Haar-Like Features

Our object detection procedure classifies images based on the value of simple features. There are many motivations for using features rather than the pixels directly. The most common reason is that features can act to encode ad-hoc domain knowledge that is difficult to learn using a finite quantity of training data. For this system there is also a second critical motivation for features: the feature-based system operates much faster than a pixel-based system. The simple features used are reminiscent of Haar basis functions which have been used by Papa Georgiou et al. More specifically, we use three kinds of features. The value of a *two-rectangle feature* is the difference between the sums of the pixels within two rectangular regions. The regions have the same size and shape and are horizontally or vertically adjacent. A *three-rectangle feature* computes the sum within two outside rectangles subtracted from the sum in a center rectangle. Finally a *four-rectangle feature* computes the difference between diagonal pairs of rectangles. The automatic expression recognition system is shown in Fig. 3.

2.3 Weak Classifiers

For the AdaBoost algorithm to work, several weak classifiers are needed. To achieve this, *features*, that can be seen as simple geometric shapes are generated. The rectangles of the simple geometric shapes are the areas that the positive and negative sums are calculated over, to produce the scalar function that is the actual feature. Each feature is combined with a simple decision rule and trained to form the weak classifiers needed for the boosting. There are three types of weak classifiers used. Two-, three- and four-rectangle features. The rectangles are of equal sizes and adjacent. The two rectangle feature is used in horizontal as well as vertical orientation The weak classifier is applied to a sub-image region of the image. The sub-image is here shown by the rectangle around Uncle Fester's head. The darker and lighter rectangles show the rectangles of the feature.

The pixels under the feature's dark rectangles are summed and subtracted from the sum under its white rectangle, and the result is compared to a value determined during training. Thus each weak classifier uses a simple step function to determine if the sub-image depicts the object:

2.3.1 Threshold based weak classifiers for face Detector

The weak learner used in the paper is based on a single feature. For all the training data, Labeled as faces and non-faces, all the possible features are computed, along with their corresponding optimal thresholds that minimize their individual misclassification errors. Among all these features, the one that has the least error is selected as a "good" feature and its threshold acts as the separating boundary between faces and non-faces. Thus, a weak classifier consists of a feature (*f*), its threshold (_), polarity (*p*), and the following hypothesis (*h*):

$$h_j(x) = \begin{cases} 1, & p_j f_j(x) < p_j \theta_j \\ 0 & otherwise \end{cases}$$

2.3.2 LUT (lookup table) weak classifiers for expression classifiers

Above a threshold-type weak classifier, whose output is Boolean value, is used, that is, where is the Haar feature and *b* is a threshold, see Fig.3a. The main disadvantage of this threshold model is that it is too simple to fit complex distributions, such as a multi-Gaussian model. For a multi-class problem, $\varpi_1,\ldots,\varpi_k$, therefore a real-valued 2D Look-Up-Table (LUT) type weak classifier, Assuming *fHaar* has been normalized to [0, 1], the range is divided into *n* sub-ranges: *binj* = [(*j*-1)/*n*, *j*/*n*), *j* = 1,…,*n*

The weak classifier h(x,l) is defined as:-

If fHaar(x) _ binj then h(x,l)=2Pl

(j)-1,

Where Pl

(j)=P(x__l | fHaar(x) _ binj).

Given the characteristic function

If u_[(j-1)/n,j/n] and y=l

Bj,l

n(u,y)=1,

Otherwise

Bj,l

n(u,y)=0,

The LUT weak classifier can be formally expressed as:

hLUT(x,y)=_n

j=1_k

l=1(2Pl

(j)-1) Bj,l n(fHaar(x),y).

2.5 Multi class Adaboost Algorithm

The two-class Adaboost algorithm has been successfully used in face detection, gender classification, etc. However, many problems such as expression recognition are multi-class in nature. Fortunately, based on a measure of Hamming loss, Schapire and Singer have extended Adaboost to a multi-class multi-label version.

Algorithm

Given: the sample set $S=\{(x_1,Y_1),\ldots,(x_m,Y_m)\}$, and the size of the final strong classifier T.

Initialize: D1(i,l)=1/(mk), i=1…m, l=1…k, where k=|Y|.

For t =1…T

Step 1. Under the distribution D_t, select a weak classifier ht:XxY_[-1,1] from the weak classifier pool to maximize the absolute value of

$$R_t=\sum_{i,l} D_t(i,l) Y_i(l) h_t(x_i,l).$$

Step 2. Let,

$\alpha t = \ln\{(1+r_1)/(1-r_2)\}/_2$.

Step 3. Update the distribution:

$D_{t+1}(i,l)$=[Dt(i,l)exp(-_tYi[l]ht(xi,l))]/Zt,

Where Zt is a normalization factor so that D_=1 is a p.d.f.

Output the final strong classifier:

H(x,l)=sign(_t_tht(x,l))

2.6 Final Strong Classifier

The final strong classifier is given by:

H(x) = arg max *t* { *_t _t ht(x,l)* }

Where arg max *l* means the value of *l*(expression class) for which the term under the sign of summation becomes highest.

This value of *l* gives the expression class of the input image.

1 -> ANGER
2 -> DISGUST
3 -> FEAR
4 -> HAPPINESS
5 -> NEUTRAL
6 -> SADNESS
7 -> SURPRISE

3. Results

Implementation Details

Expression classifier

Form The Resized Database

1. Resize the given JAFE (Japanese female expression) database from 256X256 to 36X36 pixels. The database contains 213 images of 7 facial expressions (6 basic facial expressions + 1 neutral) posed by 10 Japanesefemale models. Each image has been rated on 6 emotion adjectives by 60 Japanese subjects. Read the list of subjects from the names in file "list1.txt" and image directory "JAFE" and after resizing store the images into new directory "njafe". Perform any post processing of the resized images to reduce the noise generated during resampling (aliasing).e.g., "KA.AN1.39. tiff" where KA stands for the name of the person, AN belongs to the expression class {(AN) anger, (DI)disgust, (FE)fear, (HA)happiness, (NE)neutral, (SA)sadness and (SU)surprise}.

Create The Integral Images

2. Read the file names from the file "list1.txt". For every image name read from the file, read the corresponding "tiff" image file from the directory "njafe" and store it into the matlab workspace. Create a 36X36 zero matrix "ii" of type uint32. Calculate the integral image and store it in the directory "intimage" as the variable "ii" itself as ".mat" files and file names in a sequence. e.g., "37SU", where 37 indicate the image index and "SU" indicates the expression.
   Calculate Features Within A 36 × 36 Window And Store Them
3. Calculate the FEATURE ONE (vertically lateral 2 rectangles). Total number of possible features here are 1240 considering minimum size of the window as 8X8 and delta=2 pixels. Read the names of the images in the database from the file "f_list.txt". For every file name read load the corresponding integral image from the "intimage" directory into the matlab workspace using the variable "ii". Create a "feature_one" matrix of all zeros containing 1240 elements of type double. Set the scaling size of feature to delta=2 pixels per scale, starting with an 8X8 feature. Calculate the coordinates of sub windows and find the "feature_one" for every possible feature after scanning and scaling using the given formula. After all the feature responses have been calculated store the "feature_one" matrix as ".mat" file in the directory "store_feature\feature_one".e.g.," 1NE.mat", where 1 is the index of the image and can vary from 1 to 213.
4. Calculate the FEATURE two (horizontally lateral 2 rectangles). Repeat the same procedure as described in step 3. Use the name "feature_two" as the name of the matr while storing, store it in the directory "store_feature\feature_two".
5. Calculate the FEATURE three (horizontally lateral 3 rectangles). Total number of possible features in this case is 385. Repeat the same procedure as described in step 3. Use the name "feature_three" as the name of the matrix. And while storing, store it in the directory "store_feature\feature_three".
6. Calculate the FEATURE four(four rectangles). Total number of possible features in this case is 1240. Repeat the same procedure as described in step 3. Use the name "feature_four" as the name of the matrix. And while storing, store it in the directory "store_feature\feature_four".
7. Rewrite the feature database as 3D array where one dimension is the total number of features i.e., (1240 + 1240 + 385 + 1240 = 4105), other dimension is the total number of images in database and third dimension is thevalue which consists of two elements. First element is the feature value which is a normalized value [0, 1] and second is the numeric value of class viz., (1-7)
   1. AN -> ANGER
   2. DI -> DISGUST
   3. FE -> FEAR
   4. HA -> HAPPINESS
   5. NE -> NEUTRAL
   6. SA -> SADNESS
   7. SU -> SURPRISE

   Store this array as "feature" in the directory "training_database(feature+class) as a "feature.mat" file.

   LUT(lookup table) FORMATION
8. The weak classifier used here is a 2D LUT type weak classifier instead of the regular threshold based weak classifier because expression classification is a multi class problem. The columns of the LUT are the numbered bins into which the Fhaar has been divided and the rows are the 7 classes into which expression is to be classified. First read the image names from the "f_list.txt" and then for each name select one of the features (1, 2, 3 or 4) say feature 1 and for all varying in scale and position, find the bin position into which the feature value falls. Now add a value 1 to the location corresponding to the found bin and the given class. Repeat this for rest of the 1239

features of feature 1 category. Similarly do for feature 2, feature 3 and feature 4. Now add another column and row to the LUT in the end and calculate the row sum ad store it in the last element of the row. Do the same for column sum. Store this LUT into the directory "LUT\prob_looup_table" as "Prob_class_bin.mat" file.

Weak Classifier

9. Load the variable "Prob_class_bin" from the file "Prob_class_bin.mat". During training compare the bin of the feature value of the tagged image with the LUT bins and find the probability that the sample belongs to a particular class given a particular bin from the Lookup

Table. Below is shown the Lookup Table for 8 bins

Table 1

	Bin 1	Bin 2	Bin 3	Bin 4	Bin 5	Bin 6	Bin 7	Bin 8	Total
Anger	111092	9224	1574	662	368	165	59	6	123150
Disgust	107531	8888	1456	650	277	151	75	17	119045
Fear	119796	8673	1486	716	412	173	79	25	131360
Happiness	115528	8713	1447	743	458	234	112	20	127255
Neutral	111736	8581	1399	710	422	193	86	22	123149
Sadness	114654	9547	1522	717	419	262	117	17	127255
Surprise	111687	8434	1483	687	446	244	129	40	123150
Total	792024	62060	10367	4885	2802	1422	657	147	874364

4. Conclusion

In our paper we have used a novel facial expression recognition method in which the expression classifier is learned by boosting Haar feature based Look-Up-Table weak classifiers. The training is done on JAFE database consisting of 213 facial expression photos of different Japanese women. The Lookup Table used is (7X8), where 7 are the number of expression classes and 8 is the number of bins into which normalized feature response is divided. Final classifier selects 1400 different weak classifiers out of a pool of weak classifiers. Experimental results on a database of 213 mirror images show an average recognition rate of 20 percent. The low accuracy is due to the use of less number of images during training stage, which can be improved with increased size of training database. Also the training error converges to zero with increase in number of training images. Furthermore the developed automatic real time facial expression recognition system may be useful in future humanoid toy robot. Also this paper focuses on facial expression recognition problems; our framework can be used in other two-class or multi-class pattern recognition problems too.

5. References

[1] L. Chen, L. Zhang, L. Zhu, M. Li, and H. Zhang, "A novel facial feature point localization algorithm using probabilisticlike output," presented at the Asian Conf. Computer Vision, 2004.

[2] T. Cootes, G. Edwards, and C. Taylor, "Comparing active shape models with active appearance models.," in *Proc. Brit. Machine Vision Conf.*, 1999, vol. 1, pp. 173–182.

[3] P. Jensen and J. Bard, *Operations Research Models and Methods*. New York: Wiley, 2003, ch. 5–6, pp. 146–222.

[4] X. Li, S. Lin, S. Yan, and D. Xu, "Discriminant locally linear embedding with high order tensor data," *IEEE Trans. Syst., Man, Cybern. B, Cybern.*, vol. 38, no. 2, pp. 342–352, Apr. 2008.

[5] Q. Liu, R. Huang, H. Lu, and S. Ma, "Face recognition using kernel based fisher discriminant analysis," presented at the IEEE Int. Conf. Automatic Face and Gesture Recognition, 2002.

[6] Q. Liu, H. Lu, and S. Ma, "Improving kernel fisher discriminant analysis for face recognition," *IEEE Trans. Circuits Syst. Video Technol.* vol. 14, no. 1, pp. 42–49, Jan. 2004.

[7] S. Lucey and T. Chen, "A GMM parts based face representation for improved verification through relevance adaptation," in *Proc. IEEE Int. Conf. Computer Vision and Pattern Recognition*, 2004, pp. 855–861.

[8] S. Lucey and T. Chen, "Using overlapping distributions to deal with face pose mismatch," presented at the Brit. Machine Vision Conf., 2005.

[9] K. Mtiller, S. Mika, G. Riitsch, K. Tsuda, and B. Scholkopf, "An introduction to kernel based learning algorithms," *IEEE Trans. Neural Netw.*, vol. 12, no. 2, pp. 181–201, Mar. 2001.

[10] G. Nemhauser and L. Wolsey, *Integer and Combinatorial Optimization*. New York: Wiley, 1988.

[11] F. Jing, M. Li, H. Zhang, and B. Zhang, "An efficient and effective region-based image retrieval framework," *IEEE Trans. Image Process.*, vol. 13, no. 5, pp. 699–709, May 2004.

[12] Y. Pang, Y. Yuan, and X. Li, "Gabor-based region covariance matrices for face recognition," *IEEE Trans. Circuits Syst. Video Technol.*, vol. 18, no. 7, pp. 989–993, Jul. 2008.

[13] Y. Pang, D. Tao, Y. Yuan, and X. Li, "Binary twodimensional PCA," *IEEE Trans. Syst., Man, Cybern. B, Cybern.*, vol. 38, no. 4, pp. 1176–1180, 2008.

[14] P. Philips, H. Moon, S. Rizvi, and P. Rauss, "The feret evaluation methodology for face recognition algorithms," *IEEE Trans. Pattern Anal. Mach. Intell.*, vol. 22, no. 10, pp. 1090–1104, Oct. 2000.

[15] P. Phillips, P. J. Flynn, T. Scruggs, K. W. Bowyer, J. Chang, K. Hoffman, J. Marques, M. Jaesik, and W. Worek, "Overview of the face recognition grand challenge," in *Proc. IEEE Int. Conf. Computer Vision and Pattern Recognition*, 2005, pp. 947–954.

[16] A. Qamra, Y. Meng, and E. Y. Chang, "Enhanced perceptual distance functions and indexing for image replica recognition," *IEEE Trans. Pattern Anal. Mach. Intell.*, vol. 27, no. 3, pp. 379–391, Mar. 2005.

[17] Y. Rubner, C. Tomasi, and L. Guibas, "The earth mover's distance as a metric for image retrieval," *Int. J. Comput. Vis.*, vol. 40, no. 2, pp. 99–121, Nov. 2000.

[18] S. Shan, Y. Chang, W. Gao, B. Cao, and P. Yang, "Curse of mis-alignment in face recognition: Problem and a novel misalignment learning solution," in *Proc. IEEE Int. Conf. Automatic Face and Gesture Recognition*, 2004, pp. 314–320.

[19] T. Sim and S. Baker, "The CMU pose, illumination, and expression database," *IEEE Trans. Pattern Anal. Mach. Intell.*, vol. 25, no. 12, pp. 1615–1617, Dec. 2003.

[20] L.Wang, Y. Zhang, and J. Feng, "On the Euclidean distance of images," *IEEE Trans. Pattern Anal.Mach. Intell.*, vol. 27, no. 8, pp. 1334–1339, Aug. 2005.

[21] J. Zhang, M. Marszalek, S. Lazebnik, and C. Schmid, "Local features and Kernels for classification of texture and object categories: An in-depth study," *Int. J. Comput. Vis.*, vol.73, no. 2, pp. 213–238, Jun. 2007.

[22] S. Zhou and R. Chellappa, "From sample similarity to ensemble similarity: Probabilistic distance measures in reproducing kernel Hilbert space," *IEEE Trans. Patter Anal.Mach. Intell.*, vol. 28, no. 6, pp. 917–929, Jun. 2006.

[22] Maja Pantic, and Leon J.M. Rothkrantz, "Automatic Analysis of Facial Expressions: The State of Art", *IEEE Trans. on PAMI*, VOL. 22, NO. 12, 2000, pp. 1424-1445.

[23] C. Padgett and G.W. Cottrell, "Representing Face Images for Emotion Classification", *in Proc. Conf. Advances in Neural Information Processing Systems*, Denver, USA, 1996, pp. 894-900.

[24] M. S. Bartlett, G. Littlewort, I. Fasel, et al., "Real Time Face Detection and Facial Expression Recognition: Development and Applications to Human Computer Interaction", *in IEEE CVPR Workshop on Computer Vision and Pattern Recognition for Human-Computer Interaction*, Wisconsin, USA, 2003.

[25] T. Kanade, J. F. Cohn, and Y. L. Tian, "A comprehensive database for facial expression analysis", *in IEEE Proc. Int'l Conf. on FG*, Grenoble, France, 2000, pp 46-53.

[26] R. E. Schapire and Y. Singer, "Improved boosting algorithms using confidence-rated predictions", *Machine Learning*, VOL. 37, NO. 3, 1999, pp. 297-336.

[27] P. Viola and M. Jones, "Rapid Object Detection using a Boosted Cascade of Simple Features", *in IEEE Proc. Int'l Conf. on CVPR*, Hawaii, USA, 2001, pp. 511-518.

[28] Tong WANG, Haizhou AI, Gaofeng HUANG, A Two-Stage Approach to Automatic Face Alignment, *in Proc. SPIE International Symposium on Multispectral Image Processing and Pattern Recognition*, Beijing, China, 2003, pp. 558-563.

[29] Yubo WANG, Haizhou AI, Bo WU, Chang HUANG "Real Time Facial Expression Recognition with aboost" by Dept. of Computer Science and technology, singhua university, State Key Laboratory of Intelligent Technology and Systems, Beijing

Machine Readable Blood Group Analyzer

Dr. A S Arvind[1], Dr. K Sugendran[2], H.N. Suma[3], K. Vijayalakshmi[4], Manswi. M .Gundi[5],
[1]Professor & Head, Department of Bio-Medical Engineering, IAM, Bangalore.
[2]Professor & Head, Department of Bio-Chemistry, IAM, Bangalore.
[3]Assistant Professor, Department of Medical Electronics, BMSCE, Bangalore,
hnsuma@yahoo.co.in
[4]Sl Grade Lecturer, Department of Medical Electronics, BMSCE, Bangalore,
vijubms_bms@yahoo.co.in
[5]Department of Medical Electronics, BMSCE, Bangalore.

Abstract

Screening and reading manually from an image to arrive at certain conclusions is an activity which involves subjectivity and is tedious for the operator. So image analysis using a computer-based application could demonstrate great precision and efficiency as opposed to the tedious and error-prone human eye analyzing and measuring hundreds to thousands of reactions in one sample image. In this paper an attempt is made towards an automated technique for the analyzing of multiple reactions from real-time color images containing them, in the frame work of statistical modeling, based on mathematical morphology tools operated on the grayscale image. The proposed system results in locating each of the area, identifying and analyzing them individually in the given image.
Keywords : *Color image processing analysis, reactions in real-time images, averaging technique, connected component analysis.*

1. Introduction

It is essential that everyone know their own blood group and that of their family members. There are many occasions when knowing your blood group could be important, for example, if you or a member of your family, require an urgent blood transfusion it would be useful to know your blood group in advance. If it was an uncommon group it would allow the hospital valuable time to ensure adequate supplies. If you travel overseas carrying a blood group card could prove invaluable. Accidents and other emergencies can often be dealt with more efficiently knowing the blood group of the person or persons involved.

The Machine Readable blood group analyzer is one of the many automated systems that have been created for the purpose of scanning accurately the objects present in the given image. The accuracy of any scanning depends on the method used to arrive at the scan. Typically, averaging followed by connected component mean analysis will do the job. But, different scanning techniques yield different results. Various segmentation techniques can be used for the purpose like, clustering, edge detection, thresholding, water shedding etc. Also the application of various morphological operations like erosion, adaptive filtering etc., gives the result more clarity.

One of the biggest challenges that is faced in the analysis of this image was the uniqueness in the way all the reactions were aligned and the proximity of adjacent image created a lot of initial hurdles in separating them after a few steps of processing.

A large amount of literature has been dedicated to the automatic or semiautomatic analyzer and scanning of objects, in particular the BLOOD GROUP and classifying blood cell Rh-factor.

In previous grayscale methods of separation and classification, images of blood groups are in RGB format. Similarly, in this case, the images had varying color within itself. This is partially overcome by the use of morphological illumination correction. Morphological correction is a non-linear filtering based on:

a) objects in the scene are smaller than a given size and
b) The shading correction.

Utilizing previous research, "Automation of blood group", as a starting point, the philosophy is expanded to optimize the analysis methodology. The goal is to enhance the accuracy of statistical results. In this method, color clustering is used to perform image averaging. We have replaced color clustering by grayscale conversion from RGB to gray function. This is done by obtaining a digital picture of the image containing the reactions by means of a flat-bed scanner and then by converting the picture to grayscale (divided into 256 shades of gray), for computation efficiency. Since the areas of interest are the reactions, which appear darker than the background, the focus is only on the averaging and finding the mean.

A Machine readable ABO Blood Grouping Card has an advantage; all the three antisera are in a dried dot form on a single card, which on addition of water droplets can be brought back to solution phase, which on further addition of blood drop gives the agglutination reaction that can be read for knowing the blood group and Rh factor.

2. Methodology

The given tested Blood grouping card is acquired into the system by high resolution scanning and converted to RGB format. The RGB image is converted to its grey scale equivalent. The image components are selected for further processing giving more importance to the most distinguishing features, where the reaction is denser. In the first step, the entire image is divided into sub-images and processed individually to make effective use of the memory and hasten the analyzing process. Then, ROI (Region of interest) is performed locally on each of these sub-images after scanning the cards. This results in partitioning of the image into 3 distinct regions of background and foreground. The clustered foreground image (grayscale) is then converted to a binary image. Finally, we arrive at the total average values after calculating mean and matrix on each of the binary sub-images. In addition, it was required that the density of the reactions region wise over the entire image be displayed, so the reaction being a direct measure of density, was shown regionally. The circular images were analyzed using our algorithm and successful segmentation and averaging of reactions contained in these images was achieved using IMAGE PROCESSING TOOL of MATLAB. The most important feature of this technique is that there are no parameters to be tuned by the user. GUI was created by the use of the guide toolbox present in matlab. The same allows the user to save, print and retrieve the data stored.

3. Algorithm

Step1: Read the RGB image of the card in '.jpg' format from the file.
Step2: Resize the image for the standard size [569X789] that has been fixed by the program.
Step3: Define the row and column coordinates for the region of interest (ROI).
Step4: Obtain the mask according to the coordinates defined and segment the region interest (ROI).
Step5: Convert RGB image segment to binary through conversion from RGB to gray and then using threshold of gray scale.
Step6: Crop the image to adjust the region of interest (ROI).
Step7: Obtain the mean of the binary image and store it in a variable.
Step8: Increment the column coordinates to obtain the next region of interest (ROI).
Step9: Repeat the steps 4-7 and increment column coordinates.
Step10: Repeat step 4-6 and obtain a matrix of ONES to the same size as cropped image.
Step11: Perform logical operation 'AND' between the matrix of ONES and the cropped image.
Step12: Check the resultant matrix with the use of 'ALL' function in the MATLAB.
Step13: Compare the result of 'ALL' with the given options to compute the Rh factor.
Step14: Display the main blood group by comparing the mean calculated earlier with preset limits and threshold values.
Step15: Create a GUI to enter the details of the subject with interactive fields such as print, refresh, scan, save, and open.

4. Result

ABO fan blood grouping card was designed, developed, evaluated and exhibited for the detection of blood grouping and Rh typing as a permanent record proof on blood group identity which can be used for the military and paramilitary forces and the society at large.

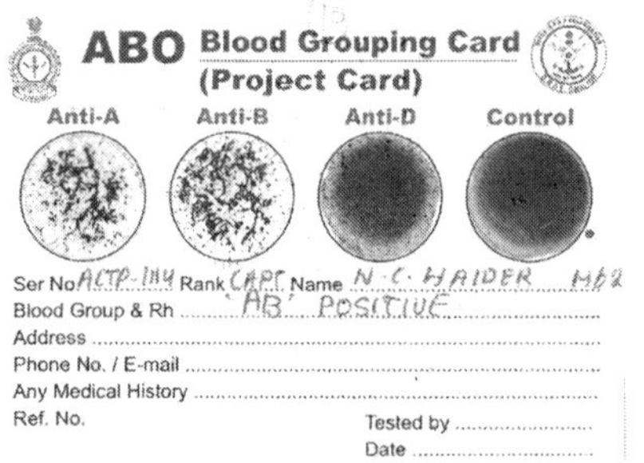

Fig. 1 Original Image

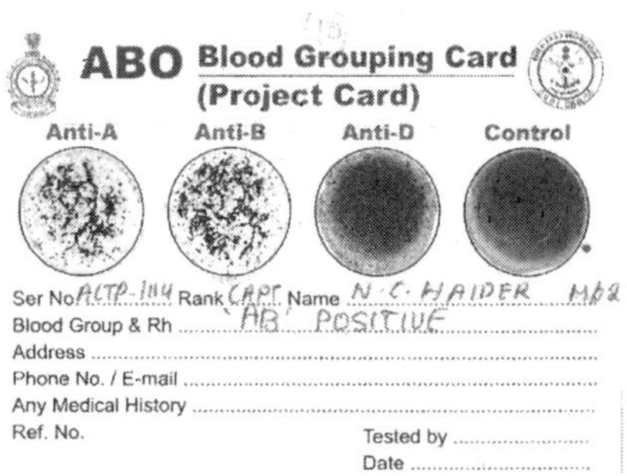

Fig. 2 Pre-processed Image

Table 1 The Accuracy values

No. of samples tested.	No. of positive identification.	NO. of errors	Accuracy	Distribution of blood group cards.							
				A+	A-	B+	B-	AB+	AB-	O+	O-
50	50	0	100%	21	00	16	00	03	00	09	01

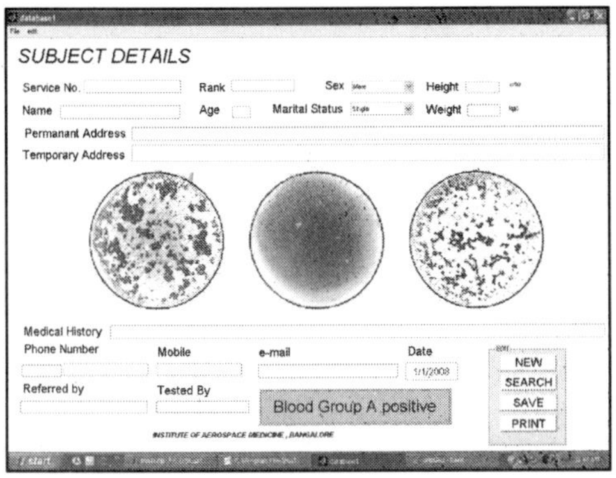

Fig. 3 Final Image

5. Conclusion

The Machine readable blood grouping cards have an edge over other existing system as they are stable and active even at room temperature for prolonged period of time, avoiding the need of refrigerator during storage.

Above this, the developed Machine readable ABO-blood grouping card can be transported to villages and remote areas at room temperature without much careful handling thereby facilitating transportation.

The algorithm was tested on 50 samples for detection. The algorithm returned 100% correct results and no false positive or false negative results were reported.

Single test that is not economical with liquid antisera is quiet possible economically with this system as one test requires only one card and there is no need to purchase the whole set containing three different antisera bottles of minimum 5 ml each in conventional system.

Also, after performing the test, these cards can be preserved as I-card for future medical references and identifications.

It is one among the life saving system which has low price, very economical, simple and handy.

These cards can be used for HBDI (Human biological data interchange) whenever it's required.

This system, as of now, is restricted to the type of images worked upon, but it can be easily adapted for other images by modifying the features taken into consideration for averaging. Hopefully, in the near future, this work can be expanded to develop a more robust scanner that can scan any objects from any given image.

6. References

[1] Cecilia Di Ruberto, Andrew Dempster, Shahid Khan and Bill JarraJ, "Analysis of infected blood cell images using morphological operators", Image and Vision Computing, Volume 20, no.2, February 2002, Pages 133-146.

[2] J. Angulo and G. Flandrin. "Automated detection of working area of peripheral blood smears using mathematical morphology". Analytical Cellular Pathology, Vol. 25, no. 1, 2003, pgs. 37-49

[3] Lifeng Liu; S. Sclaroff, "Medical image segmentation and retrieval via deformable models" Proceedings of International Conference on Image Processing, 7-10 October 2001, 1071-1074.

[4] "A novel white blood cell segmentation scheme based on feature space clustering", Springer Berlin / Heidelberg, 1432-7643 (Print) 1433-7479 (Online), Volume 10, Number 1 / January, 2006.

[5] Juan D. Garcia, PhD student, Universitat Politècnica de Catalunya, Barcelona, Spain. "Use of Morphological Operations for Blood Smear Processing".

[6] Luis Hernandez, Paula Gothreaux, Liwen Shih,Computer Engineering, University of Houston - Clear Lake (UHCL) and Gerald Campbell Neuropathology, University of Texas Medical Branch – Galveston (UTMB), "Toward Real-Time Biopsy Image Analysis and Cell Segmentation".

[7] Mathworks MATLAB® Reference Manuals with IMAGE PROCESSING TOOLBOX.

[8] Gonzalez, Rafel C., Woods, Richard C., Digital Image Processing, Addison-Wesley 1992.

[9] AABB Blood Bank Operations Manual (1990) American association of blood banks, Maryland, USA (10th Edn).

[10] Arslan O (2006), Electronic cross matching. Transfusion Med Rev 20:75-79.

A Robust Invariant Curvature Scale Space Based Recognition Algorithm for Shape Based Image Recognition

Vivek M Gulhane[1] and Dr. V M Thakare[2]
[1]Prof. COEIT, Jalgaon, [2]Prof. Amravati University, Amravati
viprogulhane@rediffmail.com vilthakare@yahoo.co.in

Abstract

Retrieval efficiency and accuracy are two important issues in designing a content-based database retrieval system. The efficient retrieval of the data base image is dependent on various factors such as the environment considered for query image, the reading source and the channel for communication. These factors affect the recognition of any given query image. To overcome the effect of environmental noises and rotation affect an image recognition algorithm based on curvature scale space for contour based approach is proposed. Database retrieval method based on shape information using curvature feature is proposed. The method evaluates the closed counter and process on the curvature smoothening using different level of Gaussian values. The proposed CSS based recognition algorithm found to be efficient in recognition for invariant features such as rotation and noise level for trademark image recognition.

Keywords: *Image recognition, contour, curvature space scale, rotational invariance, and Gaussian noise.*

1. Introduction

Information is basically represented in multimodal features. Humans can efficiently and effectively process information simultaneously in multiple dimensions. These multiple media that aid effective communication can be characterized into speech, audio, image, video, and textual data. Advances in computing and networking are generating a significant amount of interest in multimedia services and applications. Powerful processors, high-speed networking, high-capacity storage devices, improvements in compression algorithms, and advances in processing of audio, speech, image, and video signals are making image systems technically and economically feasible in image recognition.

Various applications in image recognition and image databases have been described in the literature. Much of the past research in image retrieval has concentrated on the feature extraction stage. For each database image, a feature vector which describes various visual cues [1], such as shape, texture, or color [1, 3] is computed. Given a query image, its feature vector is calculated and those images, which are most similar to this query based on an appropriate distance measure in the feature space, are retrieved. The traditional image matching methods based on image distance or correlations of pixel values are in general too expensive and not meaningful for such an application. The methods proposed in past for image recognition can be broadly classified into two categories on the basis of the approach used for extracting the image attributes. The spatial information preserving methods [4, 8] derive features that preserve the spatial information in the image. It is possible to reconstruct the image on the basis of these feature sets. Representative techniques include polygonal approximation of the object of interest [5, 6], physics-based modeling, and principal component analysis (PCA). The non-spatial information [7] preserving methods extract statistical features that are used to discriminate among objects of interest. These include heuristics based on edge angle histograms, and other ad hoc shape measures [10, 12]. These techniques were suggested for greater accuracy at a cost of heavy computation or faster operation with lesser accuracy. In the following sections, we briefly review the existing invariant moment based recognition method. In this paper, we address the problem of an efficient and accurate retrieval from a large image database based on image content of its shape. Since we desire a system that has both high speed and high accuracy of retrievals a curvature based recognition algorithm for image recognition is proposed. The proposed hierarchical content-based image retrieval algorithm is applied to a trademark image database with 1100 images for the evaluation of the proposed recognition algorithm under different querying condition.

2. Image retrieval system

Digital images are a convenient media for describing and storing spatial, temporal, spectral, and physical components of information contained in a variety of domains e.g. aerial/satellite images in remote sensing, medical images in telemedicine, Fingerprints in forensics, museum collections in art history, registration of trademarks and logos. These databases typically consist of thousands of images, taking up gigabytes of memory space. While advances in image compression algorithms have alleviated the storage requirement to some extent, the large volume of these images makes it difficult for a user to browse through the entire database. Therefore, an efficient and automatic procedure is required for indexing and retrieving images from databases.

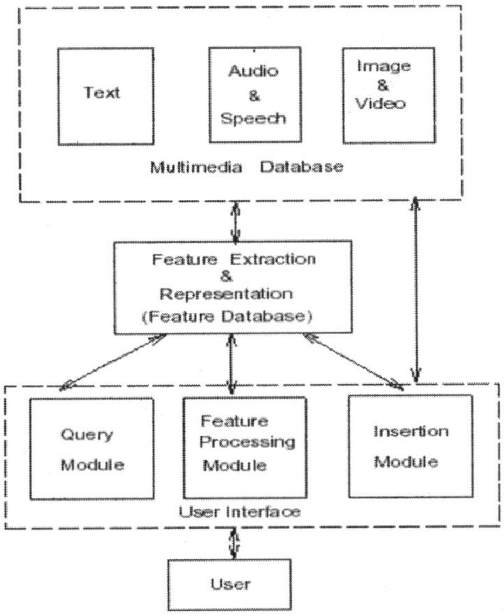

Fig. 1 General Image retrieval system

Traditionally, textual features, such as filenames, caption and keywords have been used to annotate and retrieve images. But, there are several problems with these methods. First of all, human intervention is required to describe and tag the contents of the images in terms of a selected set of captions and keywords. In most of the images there are several objects that could be referenced, each having its own set of attributes.

3. Invariant Moment based recognition

It is desirable to have an image retrieval system which is insensitive to large variations in image scale, rotation, and translation. Hence, the pruning stage has to be not only fast but should also extract invariant features for matching. We use the following features to represent the shape of an image.

Edge Angles: A histogram of the edge directions is used to describe global shape information.

Invariant Moments: The global image shape is also described in terms of seven invariant moments.

(a) Edge Directions

A histogram of the edge directions is used to represent the shape attribute. The edge information contained in the database images is generated in the preprocessing stage using the canny edge operator. Euclidean distance is used to compute the dissimilarity value between two histograms.

There are many advantages and limitations in representing an image with its edge directions.

Use of edge directions captures the general shape information.

Histogram of the edge directions is invariant to translations in the image. Thus, the positions of the objects in the image have no effect on the edge directions. This may also turn out to be a limitation, as two totally different images may yield similar edge direction histograms.

The use of edge directions is inherently not scale invariant. Two images identical in every respect except their size will yield different numbers of edge points and hence different histograms. In order to have invariance to scale, we normalize the histograms with respect to the number of edge points in the image. A drawback of normalized histograms is its inability to match parts of images. If an image, Q is a part of another image. I, then the histogram of Q is contained within the histogram of I. Normalized histograms do not satisfy this property.

(a) (b) (c)

Fig. 2 Example of shape representation using edge directions; (a) database image,(b) corresponding edge images, and (c) corresponding edge direction histograms

A histogram of the edge directions is also not invariant to rotation. A shift of the histogram bins during matching partially takes into account image rotations. A rotation of the image shifts each of the edge directions by the amount of rotation. But, due to quantization effects in binning the edge directions, the effect of rotation is more than a simple shift in the bins. Rotation also affects the bin memberships. For example, if a quantization of 45° (bin size = 45°) is used, then two edge points with directions of 30° and 40° will fall into the same bin. But, if the same image is rotated by 10° then these two points will fall into adjacent bins. We note that for a rotation of 45°, there is no such effect. To reduce this effect of rotation, we smooth the histograms. A histogram can be treated as a 1-D discrete signal. Smoothing can then be defined as

$$I_s[i] = \frac{\sum_{j=i-k}^{i+k} I[j]}{2k+1},$$

where $I[j]$ is the original histogram, I_s is the smoothed histogram, and the parameter k determines the degree of smoothing. In our experiments we have used k = 1.

The matching results depend on the bin size. By choosing a larger bin size, the matching speed is increased. But, this also reduces the accuracy in case of an arbitrary rotation of the image. A rotation not only causes a shift in the histogram bins but also affects the bin membership. Use of a very small bin size reduces the matching speed (since the number of bins increases). Use of a small bin size also requires that the edge directions be found to a very high degree of accuracy.

(b) Invariant Moments

The shape of an image in terms of 7 invariant, moments. These features are invariant under rotation, scale, translation, and reflection of images and have been widely used in a number of applications due to their in variance properties. For a 2-D image, f(x, y), the central moment of order (p + q) is given by

$$\mu_{pq} = \sum_x \sum_y (x-\bar{x})^p (y-\bar{y})^q f(x,y).$$

Moment invariants based on the 2nd- and 3rd-order moments are given as:

$$\begin{aligned}
M_1 &= (\mu_{20} + \mu_{02}),\\
M_2 &= (\mu_{20} - \mu_{02})^2 + 4\mu_{11}^2,\\
M_3 &= (\mu_{30} - 3\mu_{12})^2 + (3\mu_{21} - \mu_{03})^2,\\
M_4 &= (\mu_{30} + \mu_{12})^2 + (\mu_{21} + \mu_{03})^2,\\
M_5 &= (\mu_{30} + \mu_{12})(\mu_{30} - 3\mu_{12})[(\mu_{30} + \mu_{12})^2 - 3(\mu_{21} + \mu_{03})^2]\\
&\quad + (3\mu_{21} - \mu_{03})(\mu_{21} + 3\mu_{03})[3(\mu_{03} + \mu_{21})^2 - (\mu_{21} - \mu_{03})^2],\\
M_6 &= (\mu_{20} - \mu_{02})[(\mu_{30} + \mu_{12})^2 - (\mu_{21} + \mu_{03})^2\\
&\quad + 4\mu_{11}(\mu_{30} + \mu_{12})(\mu_{21} + \mu_{03}),\\
M_7 &= (3\mu_{21} - \mu_{03})(\mu_{30} + \mu_{12})[(\mu_{30} + \mu_{12})^2 - 3(\mu_{21} + \mu_{03})^2]\\
&\quad - (\mu_{30} - 3\mu_{12})(\mu_{21} + \mu_{03})[3(\mu_{03} + \mu_{21})^2 - (\mu_{21} - \mu_{03})^2].
\end{aligned}$$

M1 through M6 are invariant under rotation and reflection. M-j is invariant only in its absolute magnitude under a reflection. Scale invariance is achieved through the following transform.

$$M_1' = M_1/n, \quad M_2' = M_2/r^4, \quad M_3' = M_3/r^6, \quad M_4' = M_4/r^6,$$
$$M_5' = M_5/r^{12}, \quad M_6' = M_6/r^8, \quad M_7' = M_7/r^{12},$$

where n is the number of object points and r is the radius of gyration of the object:

$$r = (\mu_{20} + \mu_{02})^{1/2}.$$

4. Curvature scale space representation

(a) Corner Detection

The algorithm of edge and boundary interpretation is based on operating with object's vertices, where each vertex is a corner with the line segments that are connected to it. Each vertex of the object according to the definition is located in corner. This is the reason we first needed to detect all the corners of the object. Corner detection is an important task in various computer vision and image-understanding systems [1]. Corner detection should satisfy a number of important criteria:

(i) All the true corners should be detected
(ii) No false corners should be detected
(iii) Corner points should be well localized
(iv) Corner detector should be robust with respect to noise
(v) Corner detector should be efficient

There are different methods for corner detection in literature. Each one is based on different principle. Each method addresses different problem in corner detection. For example, [2] uses a generalized Hough transform for edge detection, where the transform is needed to detect the edge lines (boundaries) of the object and the generalization is performed to cope with the corners that are not sharp. On the other hand [1] analyses the curvature scale of object's contour and extracts the points with the maxima of absolute curvature. The method is based on CSS (The Curvature Scale-Space Technique) method.

(b) Curvature Scale Space

The CSS technique is suitable for recovering invariant geometric features (curvature zero crossing points and/or extrema) of a planar curve at multiple scales. To compute it, the curve G is first parameterized by the arc length parameter u:

$$\Gamma(u) = (x(u), y(u))$$

An evolved version Gs of G can then be computed.

$$\Gamma_\sigma = (X(u,\sigma), Y(u,\sigma))$$

Where $X(u,\sigma) = x(u) \otimes g(u,\sigma) \quad Y(u,\sigma) = y(u) \otimes g(u,\sigma)$

Where $\otimes$ is the convolution operator and $g(u,\sigma)$ denotes a Gaussian of width σ. In order to find curvature zero – crossings or extreme from evolved versions of the input curve, one needs to compute curvature:

$$\kappa(u,\sigma) = \frac{X_u(u,\sigma)Y_{uu}(u,\sigma) - X_{uu}(u,\sigma)Y_u(u,\sigma)}{\left(X_u(u,\sigma)^2 + Y_u(u,\sigma)^2\right)^{1.5}}$$

where,

$$X_u(u,\sigma) = x(u) \otimes g_u(u,\sigma) \qquad X_{uu}(u,\sigma) = x(u) \otimes g_{uu}(u,\sigma)$$
$$Y_u(u,\sigma) = y(u) \otimes g_u(u,\sigma) \qquad Y_{uu}(u,\sigma) = y(u) \otimes g_{uu}(u,\sigma).$$

The corners are defined as the local maxima of the absolute value of curvature. At a very fine scale, there exist many such maxima due to noise and the digital contour. As the scale is increased, the noise is smoothed away and only the maxima corresponding to the real corners remain. The CSS corner-detection method finds the corners at these local maxima

The process of CSS image corner detection is as follows:

Utilize the canny edge detector to extract edges from the original image.

Extract the edge contours from the image:

(i) Fill the gaps in the edge contours.
(ii) Find the T – junctions and mark them as T – corners.
(iii) Compute the curvature at highest scale σ_{high} and determine the corner candidates by comparing the neighboring minima.
(iv) Track the corners to the lowest scale to improve localization.
(v) Compare the T – corners to the corners found using the curvature procedure and remove corners which are very close.

The following is an explanation of each stage of the CSS corner detector.

Steps description:

1. Here canny edge detection was used, but it may be replaced by any other edge detector
2. The canny edge detector can cause gaps at T-junctions and the corners may not be found with the CSS method.
   (i) If the endpoint is nearly connected to another endpoint, fill the gap and continue the extraction
   (ii) If the endpoint is nearly connected to an edge contour, but not to another endpoint, mark this point as a T-junction corner.

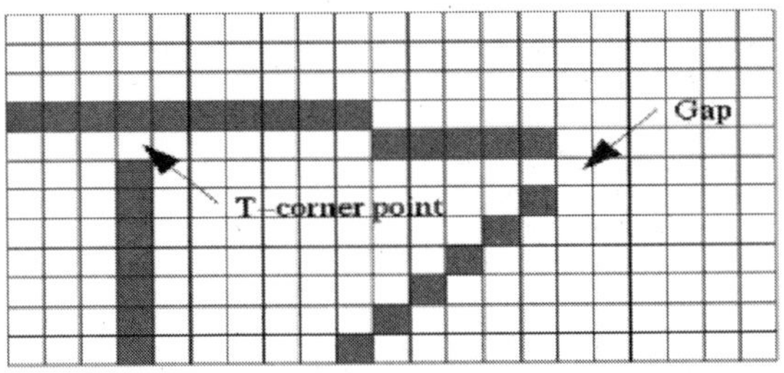

Fig. 3 Two cases of gaps in the edge contours

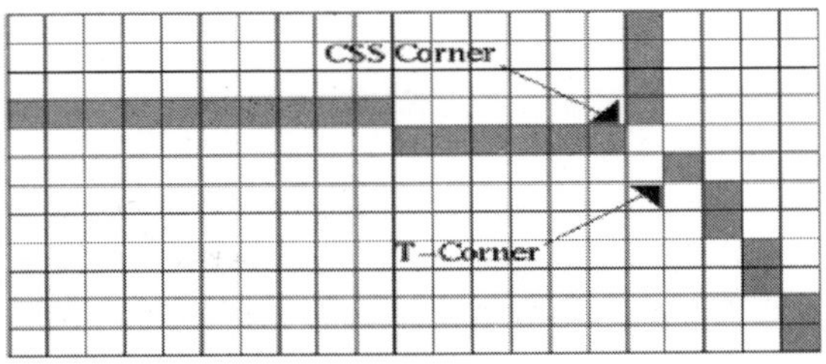

Fig. 4 case where one corner is marked twice

3. The edge contours are extracted from the edge image and the absolute value of curvature is computed at the initial scale sigma (high). The local maxima of absolute curvature are the possible candidates for corner points. A local maximum is either a corner, the top value of a rounded corner or a peak due to noise. The latter two should not be detected as corners. The curvature of a real corner point has a higher value than that of a rounded corner or noise. The corner points are also compared to the two neighboring local minima. The curvature of a corner should be twice that of one of the neighboring local minima. This is because when the shape of the contour is very round, contour curvature can be above the threshold t. The threshold t depends on sigma (high) used and it is set according to it.
4. After the initial corner points are located, tracking is introduced to the detection. As the corners were detected at scale sigma (high), the corner localization might not be good.
   The curvature is computed at a lower scale and the corner candidates examined in a small neighborhood of the previous corners. Corner locations are updated, if needed, in this neighborhood. Tracking is continued until scale is very low. This process gives very good localization. No threshold is needed in the tracking. The number of corners is determined at the initial sigma (high), and tracking only changes the localization, not the number of corners. Tracking improves the localization of the corners. Corners do not move dramatically during tracking and only a few other curvature values need to be computed.
5. As described before, corners are declared using two methods and, in some cases, the two methods mark the same corner. In Fig 3, the case where one corner is marked twice is shown. The edge extraction algorithm examines a small neighborhood when it arrives at the end of a contour. The corner in Fig 4 is a Y junction and it is marked twice. The CSS method finds a corner on the continuous contour and the edge extraction algorithm marks a T-corner at the end of the other contour as it is nearly connected to a continuous edge contour. The final part of the algorithm is to examine the points marked by the edge-extraction algorithm. These T-junction corners are compared to the corner points found with the CSS method and if they are very close to each other, the T-junction Corners are removed.

4. Results observation

1. CSS based Recognition

(i) Orientation: '0 Degree' , Noise level: 0

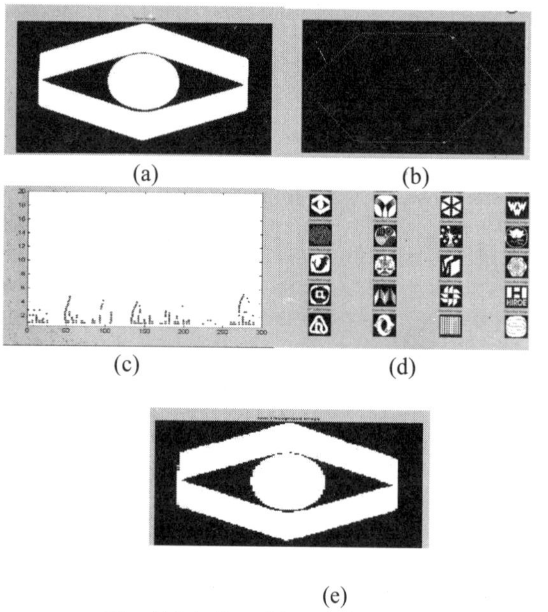

Fig. 5 (a) Considered Query Image
(b) Extracted Contour for given Query Image
(c) Curvature Scale space (CSS) plot for the given Query Image (d) Classified Image samples
(e) Recognized Image

(ii) **Orientation: '30 Degree', Noise level: 0**

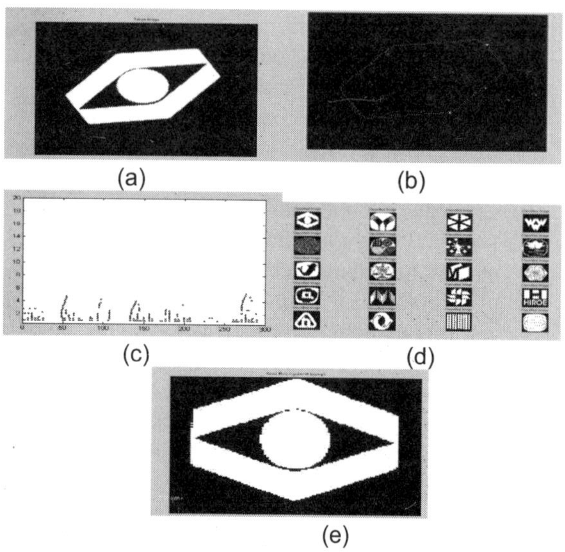

Fig 6 (a) Considered Query Image
(b) Extracted Contour for given Query Image
(c) Curvature Scale space (CSS) plot for the given Query Image (d) Classified Image samples
(e) Recognized Image

(iii) **Orientation: '0 Degree', Noise Level: mean = 0.1, Variance = 0.2, Noise Type: Gaussian**

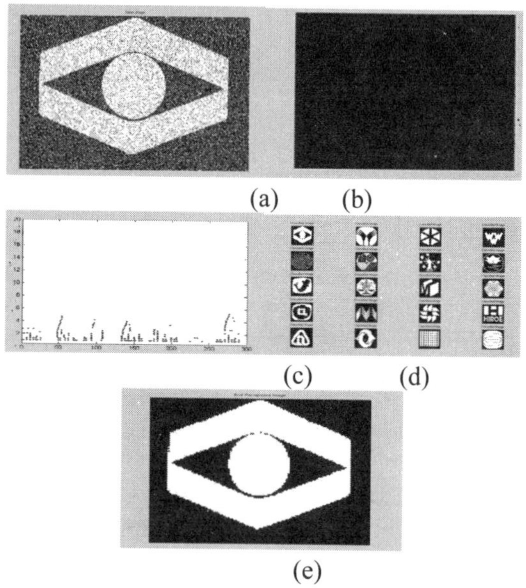

Fig. 7 (a) Considered Query Image
(b) Extracted Contour for given Query Image
(c) Curvature Scale space (CSS) plot for the given Query Image
(d) Classified Image samples
(e) Recognized Image

2. Invariant-moment based method

(i) Orientation: '0 Degree', Noise level: 0

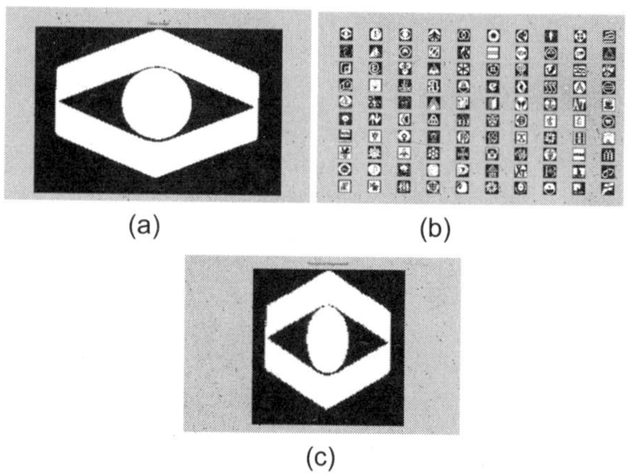

Fig 8. (a) Taken image for testing the Implementation
(b) Classified Images for Given Query Image
(c) Recognized image based on Invariant-Moment method

(ii) **Orientation: '30 Degree', Noise level: 0**

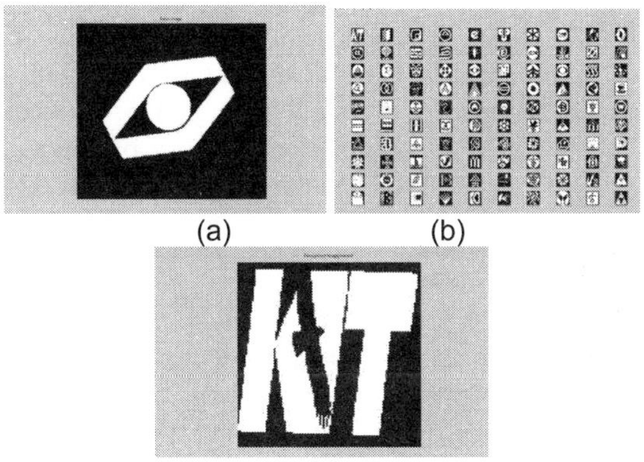

(a) (b) (c)

Fig. 9 (a) Taken image for testing the Implementation (b) Classified Images for Given Query Image (c) Recognized image based on Invariant-Moment method

(iii) Orientation: '0 Degree' ,Noise Level: mean = 0.1, Variance = 0.2, Noise Type: Gaussian

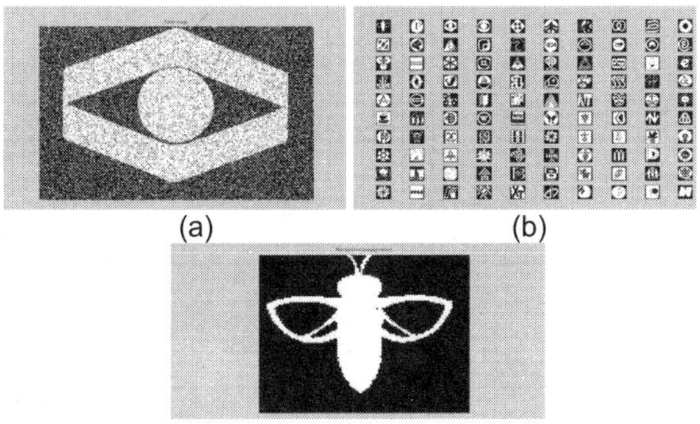

(a) (b) (c)

Fig. 10 (a) Taken image for testing the Implementation (b) Classified Images for Given Query Image (c) Recognized image based on Invariant-Moment method

Fig. 11 Computation Time plot for the two methods

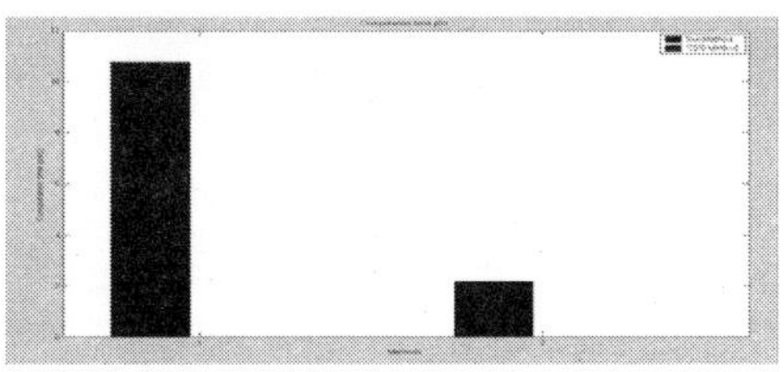

Fig. 12 Classification plot for the two systems

5. Conclusion

An efficient shape-based retrieval algorithm has been developed to retrieve trademark images. Efficiency and accuracy of retrievals are achieved by designing a two stage hierarchical retrieval system. The proposed CSS based method shows promising technique for shape–based image database retrieval. The technique is robust under rotation, and noisy versions of the input images. It is observed that the CSS based estimation outperforms the estimation with less classified symbols and accurate retreveation of trademark image as compared to the Invariant based method. The proposed pruning strategy is robust under noisy raw trademark images and faded master-marks, arbitrarily oriented images and scaled images multiple trademarks in database with different scales as well as scale difference in master-marks in database.

6. References

[1] H. Asada and M. Brady, "The curvature primal sketch," IEEE Trans, Pat, Anal. Machine Intell, vol, PAMI-8 pp. 2-14, 1986.

[2] D.H. Ballard, "Generating the Hough Transform to detect arbitary shapes" Patt Recogn., vol. 13 pp. 111-122, 1981.

[3] D.H. Ballard and C.M. Brown, Computer Vision. Engle Cliffs, NI: Prentice –Hall, 1982.

[4] H. Bluem, "Biological shape and visual science (part I)," J. Theoretical Biol., vol. 38, pp. 205-287, 1973.

[5] P. E. Danielsson, "A new shape factor," CGIP, vol. 7, pp. 292-299, 1978.

[6] L. S. Davis, "Understanding shape: Angles and sides," IEEE Trans. Comput., vol. C-26, pp. 236-242, 1977.

[7] R. O. Duda and P.E. Hart, "Use of the Hough transformation to detect lines and curves in pictures," Comm.ACM, vol.15, pp. 11-15, 1972.

[8] H. Freeman, "Computer processing of line-drawing images," Comput Surveys, vol, 6, 1974.

[9] M. Gage and R.S. Hamilton, "The heat equation shrinking convex phanc curves," J. Differential Geometry, vol. 23, pp.69-96, 1986.

[10] A. Goetz, Introduction to Differential Geometry. Reading, MA:Addison-Wesley, 1970.

[11] R. M. Haralick, A. K. Mackworth, and S. L. Tanimoto, "Computer Vision update," Tech.Rep, 89-12, Dept. Comput. Sci. Univ. British Columbia, Vancouver , 1989.

[12] J. Hong and X. Tan, "Recognize the similarity between shapes under affine transformation," in Proc. ICCV(Tampa, FL), 1988, pp. 489-493.

[13] B. K. P. Horn and E. J. Weldon, "Filtering closed curves," IEEE Trans Patt. Anal. Machine Intell., vol. PAMI-8, pp. 665-668, 1986.

[14] P. V. C. Hough, "Method and means for recognizing complex patterns," U.S. patent 3 069 654, 1962.

[15] R. A. Hummel, B. Kissia, and S. W. Zucker, "Debluring Gaussian blur,"CVGIP, vol. 38, pp. 66-80, 1987.

[16] W. Kecs, The Convolution Product and Some Applications. Boston, MA: D. Reidel, 1982.

[17] B. Kimia, A. Tannenbaum, and S.W. Zucker, "Toward a computational theory of shape: An overview," TR-CIM-89013, McGill Univ., 1989

Application of Haptics Technology in Virtual Reality

Ms Shubhangi H. Patil[1], Mr. Patil B.S[2], Mr. Patil A. D[3] and Ms. Tejashri H. Mohite[4]
[1]Asst.prof. & Co-ordinator, FD cell, Electronics dept., Dr. J.J.M.C.O.E
[2]H.O.D., IT dept, P.V.P.I.T.
[3]Sr. Lecturer, Mech. Dept, D.K.T.E Dr.J.J.M.C.O.E
Lecturer, Electronics Dept, Dr.J.J.M.C.O.E
sbp_jjm2004@yahoo.co.in

Abstract

In the real world of technology, we rely on our sense of touch, resistance, pressure or force to do everyday task. New technologies from area of virtual reality now allow computer users to use their sense of touch to feel virtual objects. This is named as "Haptics". This paper describes various devices for haptic interface. these devices allow users to feel and touch virtual objects with a high degree of realism. The haptics laboratory works on the engineering design of haptic interfaces, that is of systems which comprises software and hardware components that concern the sense of touch. More generally ,haptics is used today in the science of touch in real and virtual environments.
Keywords: Haptics, Virtual reality

1. Introduction

Haptics is a technology related to sense of touch and derived from the Greek word "haptesthai" that is science of touch. It is an application which allows a user to feel simulated 3D objects in a virtual environment. In real word we heavily rely upon the tectile and kinesthetic cues we receive. Tactile cues are sensations like textures, vibrations and bumps where as kinesthetic cues are contours, shapes and sensations like weight of stone etc.

Typical user interface devices are input only; tracking physical manipulations but providing no physical feedback representing the results of manipulations .haptics interface allow users to interact directly with data structure also. It transforming the computing world and human machine interfaces into reality experienced in daily world.

In 1965 the computer graphics pioneer Ivan Sutherland envisioned the building of an "ultimate display", a multimodal synthetic environment, which included force and touch feedback. He was one of th first researcher to realize the significance of the sense of the touch. By using special input output devices like joystiks, data gloves etc., users can receive feedback from the computer applications in the form of felt sensations in the hand or other part of the body. In combination with visual display ,haptics technology can be used to train people for tasks requiring hand eye coordination., such as surgery and space ship maneuvers. It can also be used in games you fell as well as see your interactions with images.

2. How do humans "feel"?

We use our hands to explore and manipulate objects in our environment. While exploring an object we actively scan out our fingers across its surface and squeeze or palpate it to sense its physical properties to manipulate an object we apply force to make it,while simultaneously sensing the results of these actions. Thus almost all of the hand activities we use both the sensory and motor part of the haptic system.[2]

When we touch the object in real world, it imposes forces on our skin. These net forces, plus the posture and the motion of the arms are transmitted to the brain as kinesthetic information.This is how we sense coarse properties of the objects. there is large section of brain called primary sensory cortex that is responsible for processing all the rich information flowing in from mechanoreceptors in fingers , face ,and all of the body These have names like pacinian and meissner's disks. They are what allow us to feel things like touch, pressure, stretching, motion. When these stops functioning, the listed tasks will become impossible.

3. How "feel" of object can be created?

Receptors embedded in skin convey tactile information such as spatial and temporal variations of the force distribution on the skin, within the contact region of an object. Slipping of surface fine textures, small shapes and softness are felt through our tactile sensors. In addition the skin temperature ,which relates to the temperature and thermal properties of an object ,is also sensed through specialized tactile sensor.

Haptic images seem quite complex compared to visual auditory information .To be successful ,however VE does not have to perfectly replicate reality, it only need to match the abilities and limitations of human sensory motor and cognitive system. For example because of ,limitation human vision ,graphic images displayed at about 30 frames per second seem continuous and can even convey a sense of telepresense.

To envoke sense of touching object we must first model the geometric ,material kinethestic and dynamic properties of the world we wish to represent .we must then device computational methods to determine the forces that results when we interact with objects.[1] The rely on the model used and must be considered carefully to meet the real time needs .Due to high serve rates required to generate smooth transition and distinct sensations it is important that the rendering algorithms must be efficient.

The basic diagram is shown bellow, in Fig 1.

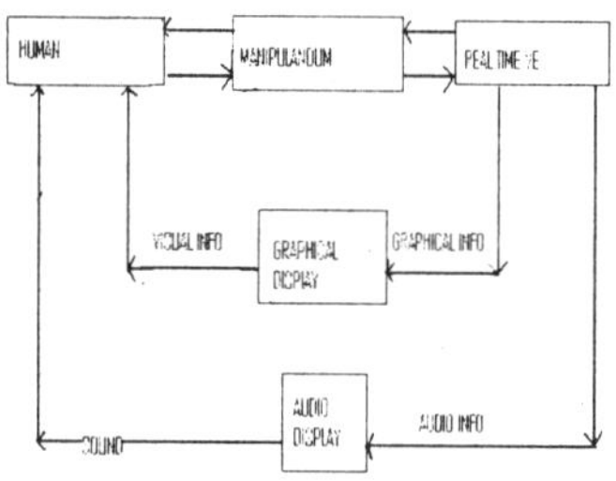

Fig. 1 Basic diagram of haptics system

4. Haptic interface devices

Haptic interaction between a person and a computer requires a special device that can convert motion of the person to meaningful quantities that can be input to the computer, and at the same time, convert computed quantities to physical forces and torques that can be felt by the person. Many different kinds of devices have been invented that enable haptic interaction with the whole hand, or arm, or even the whole body. We consider here only the type of device that can be engaged by the hand. Haptic devices can have several degrees of freedom (DOF). For example ,an ordinary mouse device has two DOFs; that is, it can be moved left/right, and also moved forward/backward, yielding two independent position measurements for input to the computer. Similarly, the familiar joystick gaming device can be tilted left/right or forward/backward, yielding two independent angles. Neither the mouse nor the joystick are haptic devices, since they provide only input to the computer. Adding motors or other actuators to these devices would permit haptic interaction, since they could then serve not only as input devices, but also as output devices. Haptic devices with 3 DOFs allow translation in 3D, and those with 6 DOFs allow both translation and rotation in 3D. Haptic devices usually employ either serial or parallel linkages whose joint positions are measured with encoders and whose joint torques are affected by motors. One may recognize that the preceding description also applies to robot arms; in fact, many early haptic interface devices were based on robot arms. In the case of a robot arm, the computer commands the arm's joint motors to move the arm tip to a particular position and orientation in space. As a haptic device, the user holds the arm tip, moving it to a particular position/orientation as the computer monitors the joint angles. When the computed position of the tip reaches a place where motion is no longer wanted (according to the virtual environment model), the motors are turned on to provide stiff resistance to further motion.

For this scheme to work, the arm must be back-drivable, or else the user's hand force and torque must be measured at the tip and used to control motion. Critical considerations for haptic interface devices include degrees of freedom, bandwidth, resolution, and stiffness range. First of all, haptic interaction with a realistic 3D virtual environment has proven difficult with devices having fewer than 6 DOFs, but providing six-DOF capability often implies high mechanical complexity and cost. Second, the response of the device should be as "lively" as possible; otherwise interaction with the virtual environment will feel sluggish. The hand is capable of feeling frequencies of several hundred Hz, but achieving the highest possible bandwidth in an elctromechanical device is challenging. [5]Third, for the hand to feel small nuances of the virtual environment (e.g., fine texture or stick-slip friction) the device must be able to resolve extremely small changes in position and force. Finally, when the user moves through free space, nothing should be felt; when a hard virtual surface is contacted, it should feel perfectly rigid. In practical systems, neither of these objectives is achieved ,however the range of possible stiffness felt by the hand should be maximized. Haptic devices primarily engage the proprioceptive senses in the hand and arm, but also involve the discriminative touch sensors, chiefly through high frequency effects. Collectively, bandwidth, resolution, and impedance range determine the fidelity of the haptic device. The ideal haptic interface device has yet to be invented. One popular commercial device is a small cable driven highly back-drivable 3-DOF arm with three encoders and three motors. A new approach uses magnetic levitation to provide 6-DOF interactions over limited ranges of motion with a single moving part.

5. Applications of Haptics technology:

5.1 The MicroTactus Tactile Enhancement System.

The MicroTactus is a family of instruments that we have designed to detect signals arising from the interaction of a tip with soft or hard objects and to magnify them for haptic and auditory reproduction, as shown in Fig 2; all in a hand-held single-unit system as shown in Fig 2. To date the MicroTactus principle was tested in the form of an enhanced arthroscopic surgical probe used to detect small cuts in cartilage-like materials and other tissue anomalies.

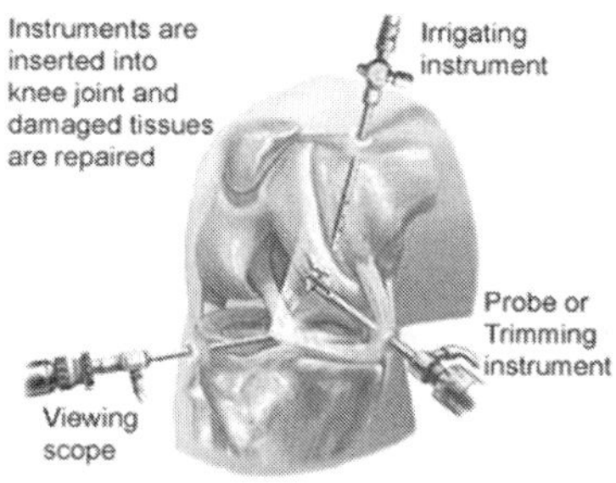

Fig. 2 Handheld single unit system

Hand-Held MicroTactus-Enhanced Probe is shown in Fig.3 and 4.

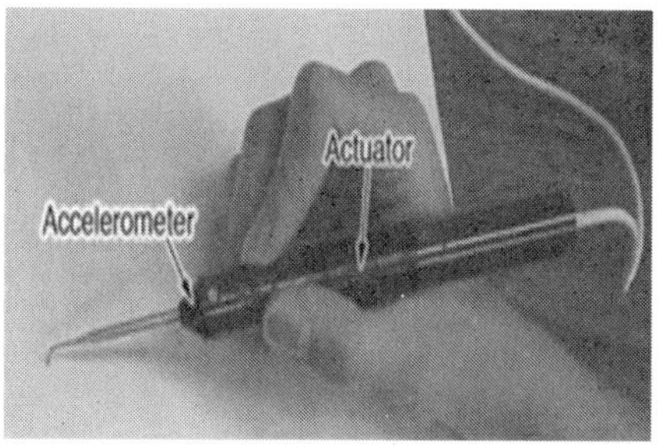

Fig. 3 Hand-Held MicroTactus-Enhanced Probe

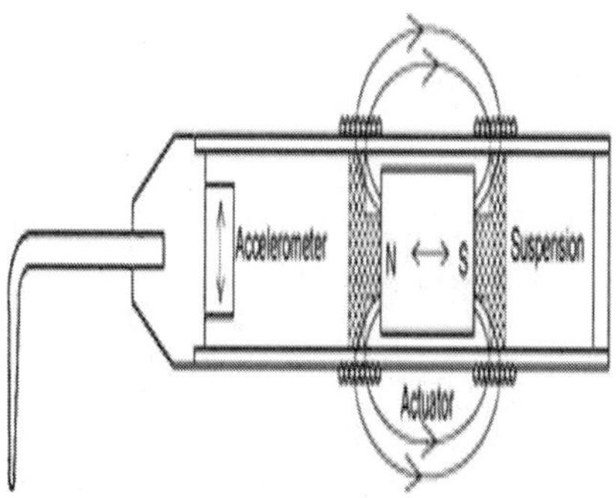

Fig. 4 Internal Structure

5.2 The Morpheotron Haptic Shape Display.

The Morpheotron is a 2-DOF, servo controlled, spherical mechanism. It functions by rolling a plate around a center of rotation that is located inside of the operators finger pad, causing local deformation at the contact area to mimic the deforming action that is normally present during the exploration of a physical surface. This has been shown to result in a strong sensation of experiencing shape[4]. The Morpheotron may be mounted on top of a lightweight gantry allowing it to be rolled on a table under the control of the operator along the x and y directions thereby providing an additional two degrees of freedom. It is shown in Fig 5.and 6

5.3 3G iPhone

When iPhone was lunched, though quite expensive, it was sold in the market like hotcake. Nowadays, where 3G capability on smart phones is a must (esp. outside the US market, EU, Japan, Asia), despite iPhones' sleek design and sophisticated multi-touch screen, 3G capability is the one thing that missing.

Fig. 5 Shape Display: The Morpheotron

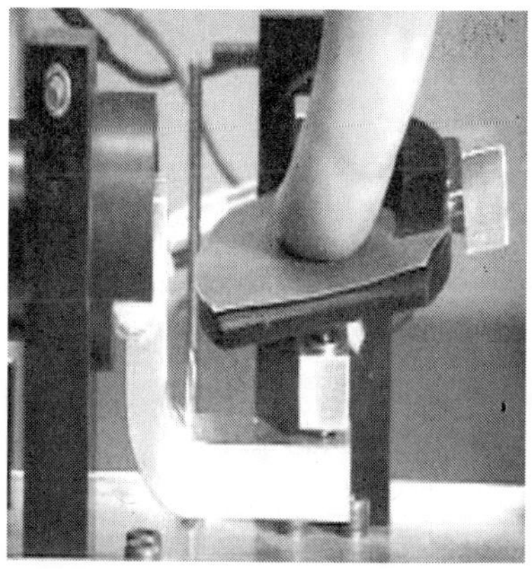

Fig. 6 Exploring a virtual shape

As PC World writes, the new iPhone features a GPS (Global Positioning System) service. And if it seems that it's quite too big for your pocket (specs here), then this is good news, the new iPhone now comes with a thinner casing, not to mention the "improved virtual keyboards with heptics", like multitouch technology .

Fig. 7 3G iPhone

Further, with iPhone 2.0 software, this 3G iPhone provides enterprise applications, including push e-mail support through the Microsoft Exchange Mail Server. It also includes an SDK (software development kit) for developers to write iPhone applications.

6. Conclusion

Haptics technologies are made available that let users to consider realism and usefullness.They allow the the visual displays to be extended to make them more realistic ,useful and engaging for visitors and scholers . The success of haptic interface can be attributed to its simplicity and high performance.It is safe,convinient to use.

7. References

[1] Force and touch feedback for virtual reality, Grigore C. Burdea, John Wiley and Sons, Inc., New York, 1996.

[2] Touch in virtual environments, M. L. McLaughlin, J. P. Hespanha, and G. S. Sukhatme, Eds., Pentice Hall IMSC Press Multimedia Series, New Jersey, 2002.

[3] Force and touch feedback for virtual reality, Grigore C. Burdea, John Wiley and Sons, Inc., New York, 1996.

[4] Lorentz magnetic levitation for haptic interaction, Device design, performance, and integration with physical simulations,P. J. Berkelman and R. L. Hollis, *Int'l. J. of* Robotics Research, vol. 19, no. 7, July 2000,

[5] Sensing and displaying spatially distributed fingertip forces in haptic interfaces for teleoperator and virtual environment systems," S. J. Lederman and R. L. Klatzky, Presence, vol. 8, no. 1, 1999.

Research on DNA Matching and Classification

Ms. Priti C. Golar[1] and Ms. U. Shravankar[2]
[1]M. Tech. C.S.&E, G.H. Raisoni College of Engineering. Nagpur.
psuparkar@yahoo.co.in
[2]G.H.Raisoni College of Engineering, Nagpur, Department of CSE.

Abstract

DNA is short for the scientific words, 'Deoxyribonucleic Acid'. DNA looks like a ladder that is curled around continuously and features about 3 billion rungs that attached to the ladder .The rungs are made up of simple natural base chemicals known as guanine, cytosine, thiamin and adenine. The order in which these chemicals are arranged on a strand of DNA is unique to every individual person, making DNA a very efficient tool for a identification of a person as well.

In our project the aim is that initially the sequence of different DNA like human, animal and other sequence of DNA will be stored in the database.

After getting the DNA sequence by our project, it will be matched with the sequence that is stored in the database and then it will be used to check whether it belong same human or same animal.

After that the sequence can also be used to predict the diseases in the human, with the help of existing sequence relating to that particular DNA.

Keywords: Deoxyribonucleic Acid, Matching & Classification.

1. Introduction

To develop an efficient DNA matching and classification software for the development of the genetic. DNA plays an important for studying history, human evolution and other field. DNA is an unbeatable code of human being that can be retrieved form any part of his body or even a drop of blood. The aim is to develop an efficient database and the database matching software for the development genetic science. The project will be used well trained to receive the disease , species from the previous database available .

The research will be used many purpose the scope of the research is almost unlimited but still it can be used of following purpose. The **basic** purpose will be to get the current sample and match it with the existing one and then get the result

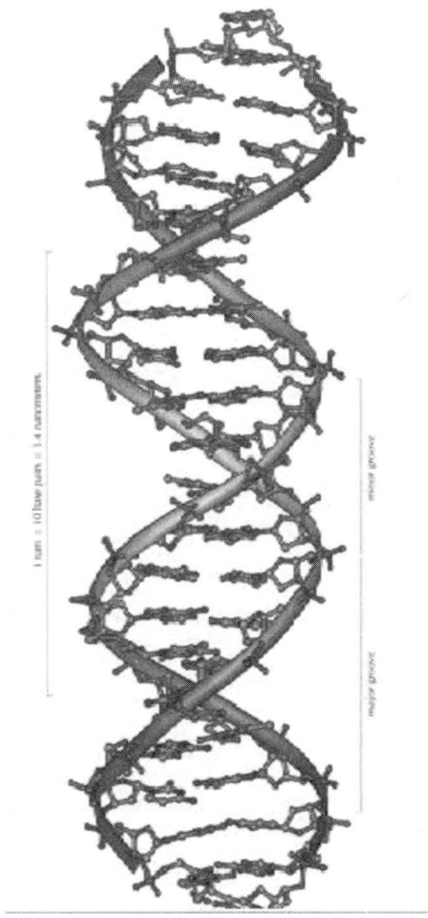

Fig. 1

The result so obtained could be used for following purpose.

1. Medical Research
2. Basic life science research
3. Forensics
4. Animal Husbandry
5. Agriculture

Reason for selection the problem

The DNA helps a lot for detecting much disease. In India the development of DNA is quiet less. In country like INDIA where majority of population is below the poverty line, spread of disease is very high low to low sanity and high cost of prevention measure. With agriculture our main aim the result could be use to increase the productivity. The principle can be applied for self identification and can increase the security.

2. Plan of Work

To collect the basic sample and study the methods of comparison. After wards digitations of the collected data (sample) and atomize the process for the comparison.

Then collect the sample database already available in the net and then compare it the sample and then get the result.

Use this result for finding disease and other research required.

1. **Fragment Sequencing:** DNA sequencing depends on breaking up the DNA strand into smaller subsets for which bse pair sequences can be determined. In addition, the methodology used to sequence a given DNA fragment requires many copies of the fragment in question. A key biochemical procedure called the polymerase chain reaction, or PCR, meets both needs. The DNA fragment for replication is selected between two DNA markers called primers that match unique regions a few dozen bases long in the DNA. Hundreds of primers for interesting areas of DNA are available commercially from biotechnology companies, as are machines that let researchers create their own primers for any desired ATGC sequence.

   A set of four special fluorescent markers are attached to the A, T, G, and C nucleotides, each responding with a different wavelength of light, typically red, yellow, green, and blue. Each labeled nucleotide is also modified so that it will terminate DNA replication once it attaches at one end of a growing strand. Adding the four fluorescent markers into a PCR process results in copies of the DNA fragment truncated at every possible base position along its length, with a fluorescent label identifying the terminating nucleotide. The sample is then **run** through an electrophoresis gel, which sorts fragments by size, resulting in a defining fluorescent marker for each nucleotide **Sequence Assembly.** The next problem is to position.

   This gel are scanned with a laser optical system, resulting in an overlapping graphs with **the** trace **peaks** inheriting the color at each position

   Sequence Assembly

   The next problem is to take *many* overlapping DNA fragment sequences a few hundred bases long and assemble them into longer segments of interest, such **as** genes spanning thousands of bases. Thousands of **fragments** must be sequenced and pieced together a long jigsaw puzzle by matching random overlapping ends.
2. **Database processing:** Initially the sequence of difference DNA like humans, animal and other sequence of DNA will be stored in the database initially while registering and also huge database of DNA sequence is available for free. After getting the DNA sequence by our project, it will be matched with the sequence that is stored in the database and then it will be used to cheque whether its belong same human or some animal. The sequence can also be used to predict the disease in the human, with the help of existing sequence relating to that particular DNA.
3. **Genotyping and linkage analysis**

   DNA sequencing by itself only yields abstract data in the form of nucleotide codes. To use this data, researchers must relate it to biologically relevant properties and individual traits. The ultimate goal is to identify dong the whole DNA gene not just the nucleotide sequence but also the, traits and conditions controlled by particular genes and the proteins they encode.

3. Methodology

STEP 1- Shearing of DNA

DNA to be sequenced is usually received from collaborators as large (150-200 kb) fragments of purified genomic DNA on ice. We keep the DNA in a very cold freezer (-80°C) until we're ready to start.

The first step is shearing the large fragments. Since DNA sequencing machines can only sequence small strands of DNA, the strands are sheared into many little pieces by a HydroShear machine.

The HydroShear uses hydrodynamic (water jet) shearing forces to fragment DNA strands

STEP 2- Insertion of Fragments into a Plasmid

All the small random fragments generated by shearing are inserted, or "ligated," into a plasmid (a loop of nonessential bacterial DNA) called pUC18. The pUC18 vector allows for propagation and replication in Escherichia coli bacteria (E. coli). Each plasmid has a gene for antibiotic resistance (green in the diagram below) as well as a LacZ gene (blue) that produces blue pigment. These two genes will be important later. The fragments, shown here in various colors, are inserted in the middle of the LacZ gene.

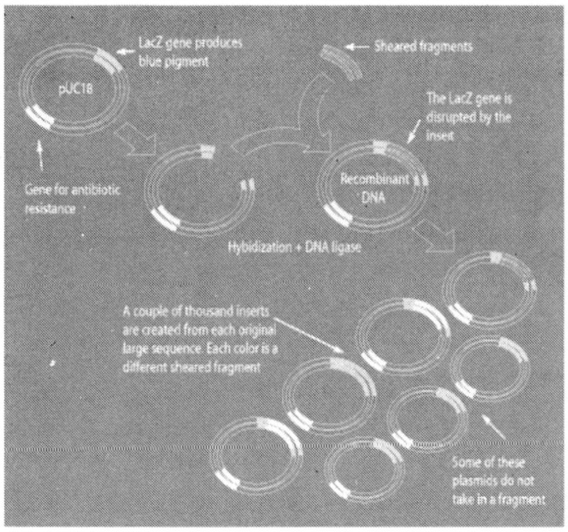

Fig. 2

STEP 3- Transformation

The plasmids are mixed into a solution containing E. coli. (E. coli normally lives in the intestines of healthy humans and other animals.) This solution is placed in a cuvette that fits into an "electroporation" machine.

Fig. 3

A cuvette for use in the electroporation machine.

In this machine, the plasmids are encouraged (not very gently!) to enter the bacteria cells. An electric shock is sent through the cuvette, and this opens the cell pores wide enough for the plasmids to enter. Think of it as a bacterial torture chamber ;^).

Some of the bacterial cells become "transformed" when they incorporate recombinant DNA. The recombinant DNA, in this case, is the 2-4-kb fragment previously sheared and ligated into the pUC18 plasmid.

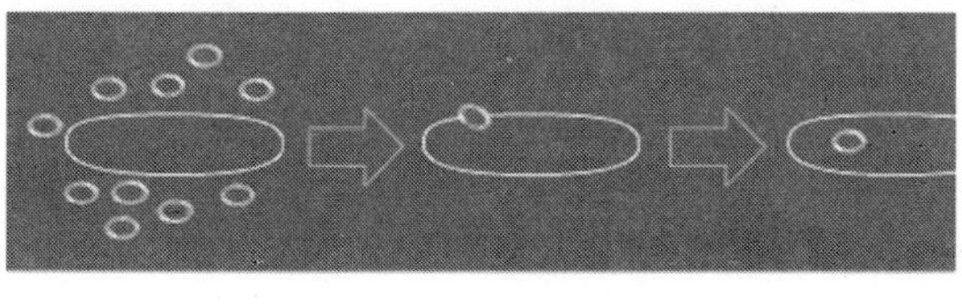

Fig. 4

STEP 4- Sub-Cloning the Sheared Fragment

STEP 5- Colony Picking

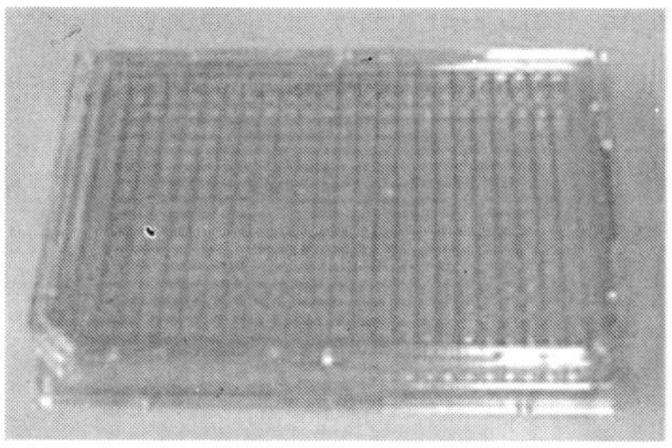

Fig. 5 A 384-well culture stock plate.

Believe it or not, millions of copies of the DNA fragments are just not enough; we need billions! So each colony needs to be cultured again. This entails picking the good colonies from the agar plates and transferring each one to a well on a 384-well plate.

Instead of taking a chance that a technician might go blind picking colonies all day, we use a robot called the Genetix Q-Pix. JGI has four pickers that operate 24 hours a day. The robots' imaging system can discriminate between white and blue colonies. Each colony is put into a separate well that contains 70 μl of a nutrient-rich liquid medium.

All together, JGI can produce 500 384-well plates in a day (but we average 240). That's 192,000 colonies! The plates are incubated for 18-20 hours at 37°C. After incubating, they can be stored at -80°C until they are ready for production Sequencing.

Fig. 6

STEP 6- Lysing the Cell

At this point, our plasmids are still trapped inside the bacterial cell. To get to our original fragment, we need to isolate the plasmid from the rest of the cell. This starts with the PlateMate Plus robot (shown below). The robot takes 2 μl from the 384-well culture stock plate and puts it onto a new 384-well plate. Each well on the new plate also contains 8 μl of Amersham denature buffer.

STEP 7- Rolling-Circle Amplification

Now that the plasmid is free of the cell, we need to amplify (make many, many copies of) just the fragment-containing pUC18 plasmid. This is achieved by a reaction called rolling-circle amplification, or RCA. If you are familiar with PCR (the polymerase chain reaction), then it may help you to know that RCA is very similar. The end result of RCA will be millions of snowflake-like structures, each containing several copies of the plasmid DNA.

Fig. 7

New strands of DNA matching the DNA in the plasmid are formed in connected arcs as polymerase "rolls" around the circular plasmid (center ring).

To prepare the reaction, 10 µl of Amersham TempliPhi reagent is added to each of the 384 wells containing only 2 µl of the plasmid. The TemliPhi reagent consists of

- dNTPs (the four nucleotides, A, T, G, and C)
- phi29 polymerase (an enzyme that adds nucleotides to a strand of DNA)
- random primers (which give polymerase a place to start building)

The reaction is incubated for 18 hours at a constant 30°C.

STEP 8-Sequencing Chemistry

The plate with the chemicals for the sequencing reaction is loaded onto a thermal cycler, which goes through a three-part heating cycle 30 times. In each cycle, the DNA is "unzipped" (denaturation, 1 minute at 94°C), the primers attach to one strand of the DNA (annealing, 15 seconds at 50°C), and then the primer sequence is extended by adding dNTPs (elongation, 4 minutes at 60°C) that complement the sequence on that strand. Because all four normal nucleotides are present, chain elongation proceeds normally until, by chance, DNA polymerase inserts a fluorescently tagged ddNTP instead of the normal dNTP. This halts the elongation process, leaving a DNA sequence that ends with one of the four colored ddNTPs.

STEP 9- Post-Sequencing-Reaction Cleanup

We're almost ready to read the bases by capillary electrophoresis. But first the reaction must be cleaned up. To remove the unused product of the sequencing reaction,

1. Beads (magnetic microparticles) are added to the sequencing reaction solution. DNA, but not the excess dye terminators, is induced to attach to the beads.
2. Magnets draw down the DNA and beads so the waste solution can be aspirated.
3. The beads are washed with ethanol and then dried.
4. Water is then added to the beads, and the DNA strands detach from the beads and reenter solution because they have higher affinity for water than for the beads.
5. Magnets are then used to secure the beads while the pipettor removes the clean DNA/water solution to a new plate.

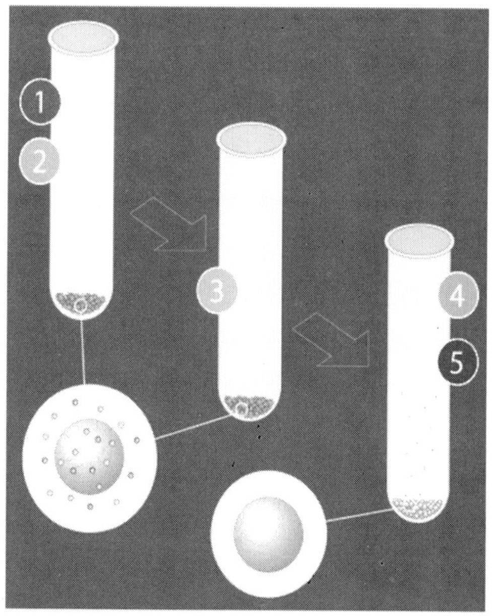

Fig. 8

STEP 10- Capillary Sequencing

Ten µl from each well is transferred to a new 384-well PCR plate to be loaded onto a MegaBACE 4000 or ABI 3730xl sequencer. Each plate i Bar codes are used to track plates to be sequenced.

Our wells now contain billions of copies of our original fragment, but they are all different lengths and each ends with a dye terminator. The fragments, which have a negative charge, move through the capillaries of the sequencing machine toward the positively charged pole. Shorter fragments move faster than longer ones. At the detection window, a laser excites the dyes. A detector "reads" the colors, one at a time, to determine the sequence of the tagged As, Ts, Gs, and Cs.

STEP 11- Assembly

The fragments are finally re-aligned based on overlaps in their sequences. To make the job challenging, only about 1 kb at the end of each fragment is actually sequenced. The computer has to figure out where each fragment fits, based on the sequences of these ends (known as "reads") along with information about the fragment size.

JGI uses a program called Phrap, which was developed by Phil Green from the University of Washington. It is a program for finding the best-fit alignment for small genomes. A similar program called JAZZ was developed here at JGI by Dan Rohksar and is used for larger genomes.

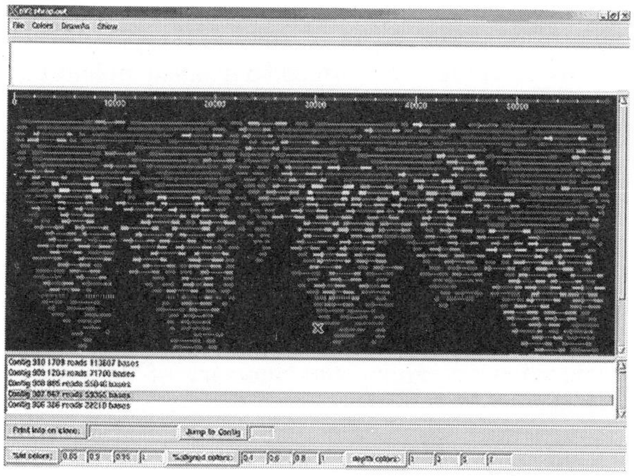

Fig. 9

STEP 12- Quality Assessment

The consensus sequences determined by Phrap are viewed in another program called Consed. This program makes it easy to find bases with low Phred scores.

Phred scores are denoted with upper-case (high quality) or lower-case (low quality) letters. More precise scoring is highlighted with a background color gradient from white to black, white being high quality. Mismatches with the consensus are highlighted in red, and inserted bases are noted with an asterisk

In addition to the quality of the assembly, the possibility of contamination of the source DNA is checked. Since every organism has a unique percentage of its genome that is made up of Gs and Cs (G+C content), contamination can be identified by plotting this distribution.

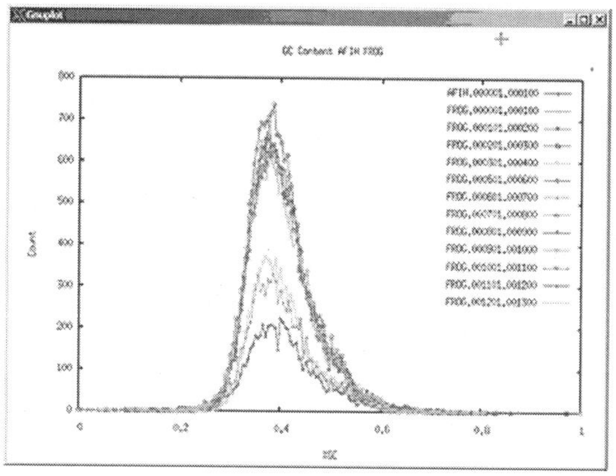

Fig. 10

4. References

[1] Williams C.E. and St. Clair D.A., Phenetic relationships and levels of variability detected by restriction fragment length polymorphism and random amplified polymorphic DNA analysis of cultivated and wild accessions of Lycopersicon esculentum. Genome, 36:619-630. (1993).

[2] Shapiro A.L., Vineula E., Maizel J. V. Molecular weight estimation of polypeptide chains by electrophoresis in SDSpolyacrylamide gels. Biochem. and Biophysical Research Communications **28**:815-20 (1967).

[3] Weber K. and Osborne M. The reliability of molecular weight determinations by dodecyl sulphate-polyacrylamide gel electrophoresis. Journal of Biological Chemistry 244:4406-12 (1969)

[4] Aaij C. and Borst P. The gel electrophoresis of DNA. Biochimica et Biophysica Acta 269:192-200 (1972) .

[5] Meyer J.A., Sanchez D., Elwell L.P. and Falkow S. Simple agarose gel electrophoretic method for the identification and characterisation of plasmid deoxyribonucleic acid. Journal of Bacteriology 127:1529-37 (1976).

[6] Southern E.M. Measurement of DNA length by gel electrophoresis. Analytical Biochemistry 100:319-23 (1979)

[7] Plikaytis B.D., Carlone G.M., Edmonds P. and Mayer L.W. Robust standard estimation of standard curves for protein molecular weight and linear duplex DNA base pair number after gel electrophoresis. Analytical Biochemistry **152**:346-64 (1986).

[8] Owen R.J. and Beck A. Evaluation of three procedures using a laser densitometer and microcomputer for estimating molecular sizes of restriction endonuclease digest fragments and application to Campylobacter jejuni chromosomal DNA. Letters in Applied Microbiology 4:5-8 (1987).

A New Image Encryption Approch with Dual Carrier Images

Panduranga H.T[1], and Aravind B.N[2]
[1]Lecturer, Dept. of Electronics and Communication Engineering, Govt. Engineering College, Hassan
ht_pandu@yahoo.co.in
[2]Lecturer, Dept of Telecommunication Engineering, Kalpatharu Institute of Technology, Tiptur.
aravin_bn@yahoo.com

Abstract

In recent years secret permutations have been widely used for protecting different types of multimedia data, including speech files, digital images and videos. In this paper we describe a new method for image encryption which employs dual secrete carrier images. The main idea behind the present work is that an image can be viewed as an arrangement of pixels of binary code and try to change the weight of this binary code. Encryption process includes XOR operation of each pixel of original image with the newly generated pixels from keyword and carrier images, resulting in encrypted pixels.

1. Introduction

In the digital world today, the security of digital images becomes more and more important, since the communications of digital products over networks occur more and more frequently. Furthermore, special and reliable security in storage and transmission of digital images is needed in many applications, such as pay-TV, medical imaging systems, military image database and communications as well as confidential video conferencing, etc. In recent years, some consumer electronic devices, especially mobile phones and hand-held devices have also started to provide the function of saving and exchanging digital images via the support of multimedia messaging services over wireless networks.

However there are several image encryption methods, each of them having their own strength and weakness. Ismet Ozturk and Ibrahim Sogukpinaar [1] have discussed the analysis and comparison of image encryption algorithms. And they classify the image encryption methods in to three major types: position permutation, value transformation and visual transformation. A Mitra et al [2] have presented a new approach for image encryption using combination of different permutation techniques. The intelligible information present in an image is due to the correlations among the bits, pixels and blocks in a given arrangement. This perceivable information can be reduced by decreasing the correlation among the bits, pixels and blocks using certain permutation techniques. S. R. M. Prasanna et. el [3] have presented an image encryption method with magnitude and phase manipulation using carrier images. Here they used the concept of carrier images and one dimensional Discrete Fourier Transform for encryption purpose and it deals with private key cryptosystem, works in the frequency domain. S.S. Maniccam and N.G. Bourbakis [4] have presented a new methodology which performs both lossless compression and encryption of binary and gray-scale images. The compression and encryption schemes are based on SCAN patterns generated by the SCAN methodology. The SCAN is a formal language-based two-dimensional spatial-accessing methodology which can efficiently specify and generate a wide range of scanning paths or space filling curves. C. Kachris et. el [5] have designed a detailed architecture for SCAN algorithm. N. K. Pareek et. el [7] and Xiaojun Tong et. el [8] have used chaotic sequence for image encryption.

The rest of this paper is organized as follows: Section 2 explains the basics of secrete dual carrier images and a 16 character alphanumeric keyword. The proposed image encryption method using keyword and carrier images is described in Section 3. This paper is concluded by providing the summary of the present work in Section 4.

2. The idea behind the proposed work

In many of the existing image encryption process they use only text string as a encrypting keyword. Very few image encryption processes discuss the concept of carrier images. In this paper we made an attempt to club these two concepts to generate a new image encryption process. Here the carrier image refers to a secrete image which is used as similar to secrete keyword for encryption purpose. In our proposed encryption process we used only two carrier image as a secrete images hence the name dual carrier image for encryption. Instead of dual carrier image we can also user multiple carrier images. For sake of simplicity we used only two carrier images.

Here alphanumeric keyword consisting of sixteen characters is used as encrypting key consisting of eight character combination of A and B and eight numerals Between 1 to 8. Here the character A and B represents the carrier image one and carrier image two respectively and a numeral between 1 to 8 represents the bit position of a pixel from Most Significant Bit (MSB) to Least Significant bit (LSB) respectively.

3. The proposed scheme for image encryption

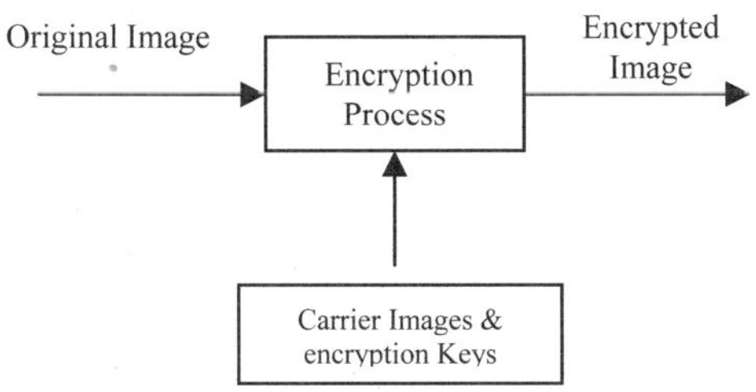

Fig. 1 Block diagram of proposed image encryption scheme

Figure 1 shows the block diagram of the proposed technique consisting of encryption process block and a carrier image and encryption key block. When the image to be encrypted is given as input to encryption process block then it performs XOR operation between each pixels of original image and newly generated pixels from the combination of carrier images and encryption key to result an encrypted image at the output. For better understanding let consider an example.

'A' represents a carrier image-1, 'B' represents a carrier image-2 and "a1a2a3a4b1b2b3b4" represents an alphanumerical keyword consisting of character followed by a number. Where character represents an 8-bit pixel of corresponding carrier image and numbers represents the bit position in that pixel. Each time a new pixel is generated using keyword information and the corresponding pixel values of carrier images.

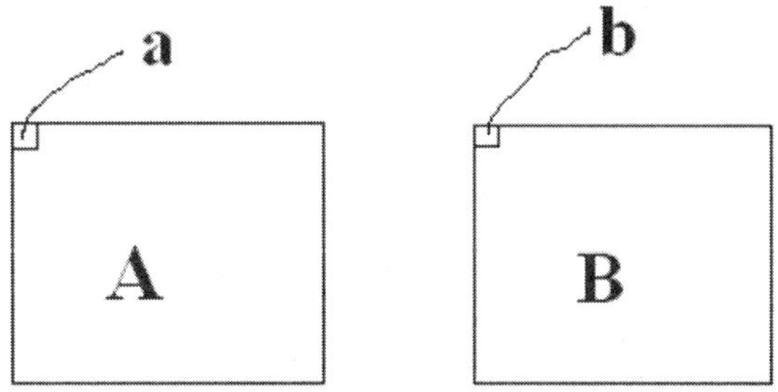

Fig. 2 Carrier image1 – image A and Carrier image 2 – image B

a =

a1	a2	a3	a4	a5	a6	a7	a8

b =

b1	b2	b3	b4	b5	b6	b7	b8

New pixel =

a1	a2	a3	a4	b1	b2	b3	b4

New pixels are generated depending on the encrypting keyword. This process of generation of new pixels is continued for entire image and these newly generated pixels are used for encryption by performing XOR operation with the corresponding pixel of original image.

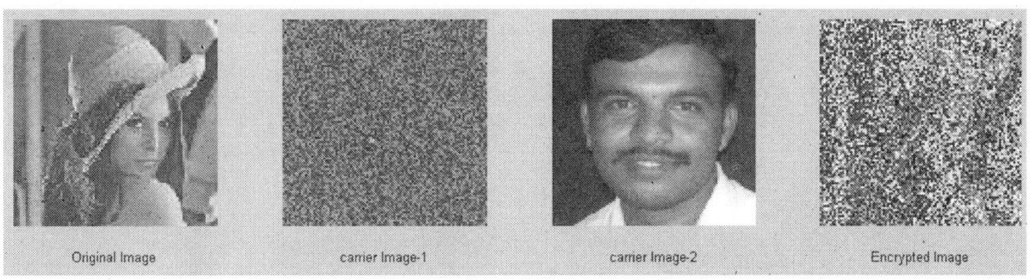

Keyword = 'a1a2a3a4b1b2b3b4'

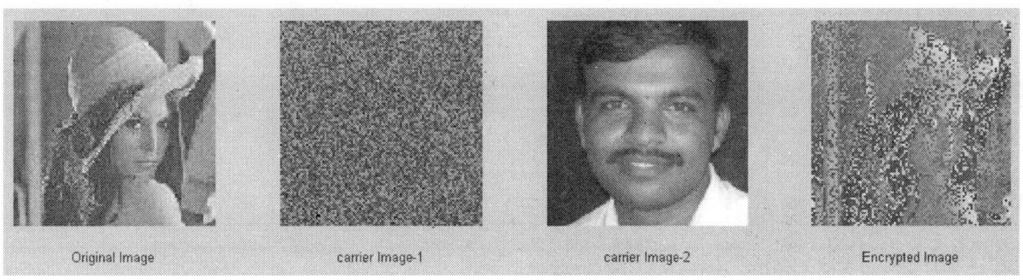

Keyword = 'a1a1a1a1a1a1a1a1'

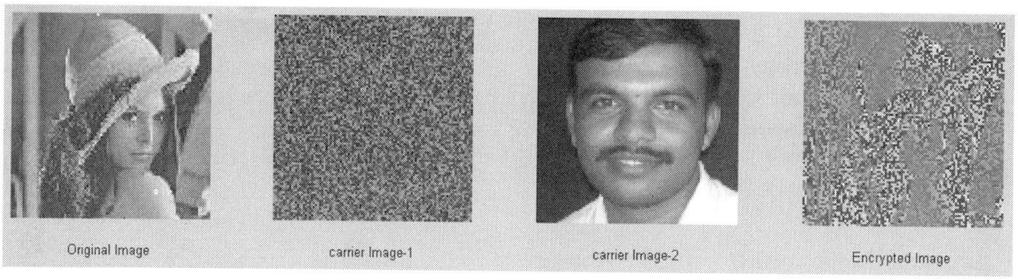

Keyword = 'a8a8a8a8a8a8a8a8'

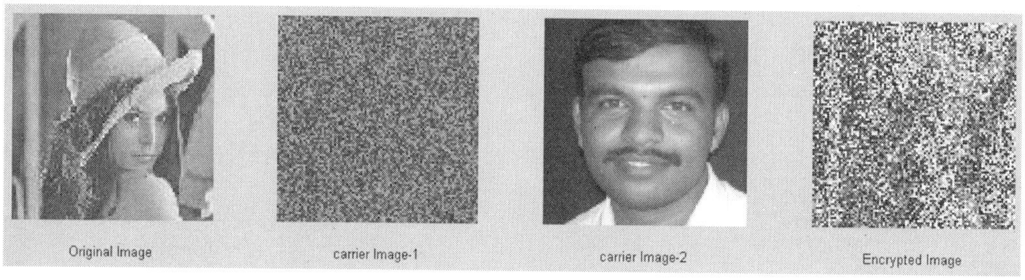

Keyword = 'a1a2a3a4a5a6a7a8'

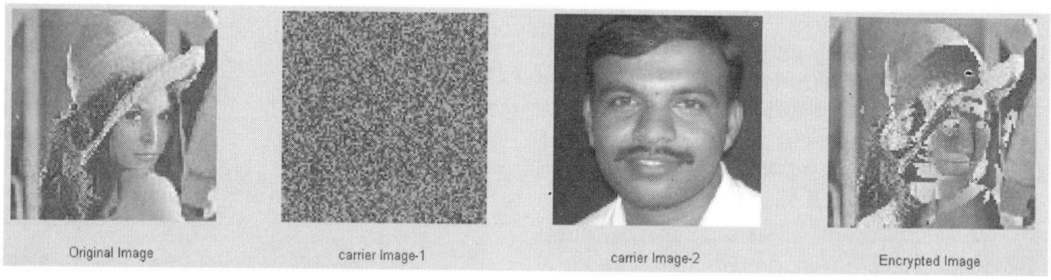

Keyword = 'b1b1b1b1b1b1b1b1'

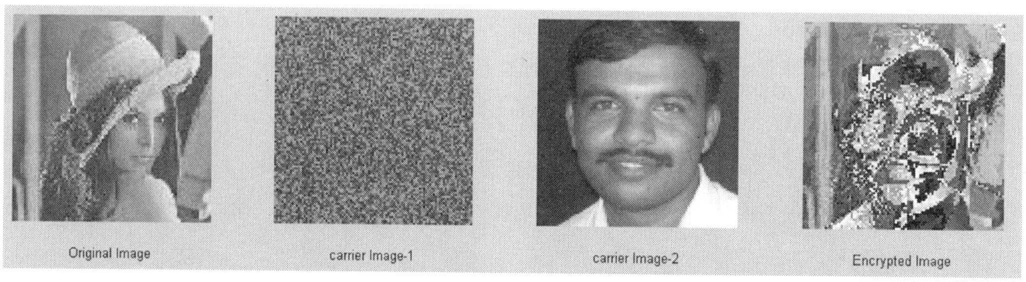

Keyword = 'b1b2b3b4b5b6b7b8'

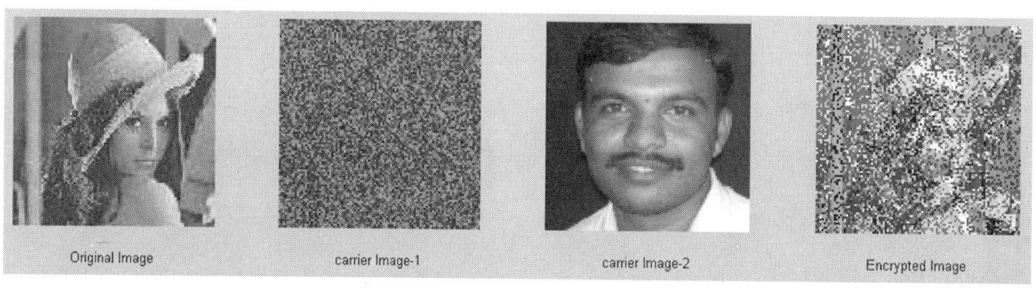

Keyword = 'a1b1a1b1a1b1a1b1'

4. Conclusion

Simple and effective method has been proposed in this paper for image encryption using dual carrier image and encryption keyword. This paper has presented a concept of combining dual carrier image and keyword. Since the keyword consists of 16 character including two characters and eight numbers more than one million combination of keyword can be generated. From the experimental result we can inform that the combined dual carrier images for encryption is better than single carrier image.

5. References

[1] Ismet Ozturk and Ibrahim Sogukpinaar, "Analysis and Comparison of Image Encryption Algorithms," *Transaction on engineering, Computer and Technology*, 2004, vol.3, pp.38-42.

[2] Mitra et. el., " A New Image Encryption Approach using Combinational Permutation Techniques," *IJCS*, 2006, vol. 1, No 2, pp.127-131.

[3] S. R. M. Prasanna et. el., "An Image Encryption Method with Magnitude and Phase Manipulation using Carrier Images," *IJCS*, 2006, vol. 1, No 2, pp.132-137.

[4] S.S. Maniccam and N.G. Bourbakis, "Image and video encryption using SCAN patterns," *Pattern Recognition*, 2004, vol. 37, pp. 725-737.

[5] C. Kachris et. el., " A reconfigurable logic based processor for the SCAN image and video encryption algorithm," *IJPP*, vol. 31, no. 6, Dec 2003, pp. 489-506.

[6] Chao Shen Chen and Rong Jian Chen, "Image encryption and decryption using SCAN methodology," *Proc. PDCAT*, 2006.

[7] N. K. Pareek et. el., "Image encryption using chaotic logistic map," *Image and vision computing*, 24, 2006, pp.926-934.

[8] Xiaojun Tong and Minggen Cui, "Image encryption with composed chaotic sequence cipher shifting dynamically," *Image and vision computing*, 26, 2008, pp.843-850.

[9] Dominik Engel et. el., "An Analysis of Lightweight Encryption Schemes for Fingerprint Images," *IEEE Trans. Information forensic and security*, vol. 3, no. 2, June 2008.

Image Retrieval on Parallel Multicomputers

T. Venu Gopal[1], B. Ramesh Naik[2] and Dr V.Kamakshi Prasad[3]
[1]Asst professor, Department of Computer Science & Engg, JNTU Kakinada, AP, India
t_vgopal @rediffmail.com
[2]Asst professor, Department of Computer Science & Engg, KIET, Kakinada, AP, India
rameshnaik3@gmail.com
[3]Professor in CSE, SIT, JNTU Hyderabad, AP, INDIA.
kamakshiprasad@yahoo.com

Abstract

This paper presents an overview of parallel architectures for the efficient and fast retrieval of images. The state of the art approach for image retrieval uses a priori extracted features i.e. Fourier descriptors and limits the applicability of the retrieval techniques. Image retrieval system is an online application which requires a large number of computations especially for large image database (ex more than 10000 images). Most of the researchers focus on sequential approaches for image retrieval. For the retrieval from a large image database a huge amount of calculation in matching and recognition process are required. A computer with limited computational power can hardly perform this task. Hence parallel computing is needed in this system.

Keywords: *Feature Database, Fourier Descriptors, Grid Multicomputer, Hypercube Multicomputer, Image Retrieval.*

1. Introduction

Recent researches on image retrieval focus on content based image retrieval (CBIR), which utilizes low level image features such as color, texture and shape. Several commercial and academic prototypes of CBIR systems have been developed recently to allow searching through image databases by image content. These include QBIC, Photo book, Virage and Visual SEEK.

Content based retrieval (CBR) has gained considerable attention recently. In general, shape representations are classified into two categories, boundary-based and region-based [1]. The first one describes the considered region by using its external characteristics (i.e. the pixels along the object boundary) while the second one represents the considered region by using its internal characteristics (i.e. the pixels contained in the region). Several shape description approaches were developed in the two categories. For example, area, compactness for the region-based category, and perimeter, curvature for the boundary-based category may be cited [1, 5, 12]. In our paper we focus on contour based methods.

One of the key issues raised in the online retrieval and object recognition, is the efficient, accurate and fast retrieval of the objects. Accurate recognition of a shape depends on its representation. Therefore an efficient representation of shape information is the basic task of computer vision. Many representation techniques exists among them, methods based on Fourier Descriptors (FD) achieve both well representation and normalization [11,13,15].

A practical image retrieval system based on Parallel Multicomputers is presented in this paper. By reason of large amount of calculation in matching and recognition process, huge image database, one computer with limited performance can hardly competent. So parallel computing is needed in this system. The focus is on switched multi-computers and they are of three types Grid based, Hypercube and BCC Multicomputers.

In this paper the performance of retrieval system is studied for the above three interconnection networks and their performance is compared.

The rest of the paper is organized as following. Section 2, describes Fourier descriptors and Section 3 describes Grid, hypercube and BCC interconnection topologies that exists in parallel distributed system, Section 4 describes about existing system and its drawbacks. Section 5 describes about proposed system and its implementation issues. Section 6 gives our experimental results and Section 7 concludes the paper with future work.

2. Fourier descriptors

Starting at arbitrary point (x_0,y_0) in the boundary, coordinates pairs (x_0,y_0), (x_1,y_1), (x_2,y_2),.....,(x_{k-1},y_{k-1}) are encountered in the traversing boundary, say ,in clockwise direction. These coordinates can be expressed in the form $x(k)= x_k$, $y(k)= y_k$. With this notation the boundary itself can be represented as sequence of coordinates $z(k)=[x(k),y(k)]$, for $k=0,1,2,,\ldots\ldots.K-1$. Each coordinate point can be treated as complex number $z(k)=x(k)+jy(k)$, $k = 0,1,\ldots,.K-1$ be the boundary sequence. The FD is defined as the Discrete Fourier Transform of $Z(k)$

$$Z(k) = \frac{1}{K}\sum_{n=0}^{K-1} z(k).e^{-2\pi ink/K} \qquad 2.1$$

where $k = 0,1,\ldots\ldots..K-1$.

The reason why Fourier descriptors are used for the feature matching are FD describe the shape in terms of its spatial frequency content.[2, 9, 14] Begin by representing the boundary of the shape as a periodic function (in one of a few possible ways). Expand this in a Fourier series; obtain a set of coefficients that capture shape information [6]. These coefficients are called as Fourier descriptors using eq 2.1.

The Fourier descriptors are obtained from the sequence Z_k by truncating elements Z_0 and Z_1, than by taking the absolute value of the remaining elements and dividing every element of thusly obtained array by $|Z_1|$. To summarize, the Fourier descriptors are

$$C_k - 2 = |Z_k| / |Z_1|, k = 2,3,\ldots..N-1 \qquad 2.2$$

3. Parallel distributed system

There are two main classifications of multiprocessor 'supercomputers' today with respect to the programming model, namely shared memory and distributed memory architectures. The two architectures are suited to solving different kinds of problems. Shared memory machines are best suited to so-called 'fine-grained' parallel computing, where all of the pieces of the problem are dependent on the results of the other processes. Distributed memory machines on the other hand are best suited to 'coarse-grained' problems, where each node can compute its piece of the problem with less frequent communication. Another issue with distributed memory clusters is message passing. Since each node can only access its own memory space, there has to be a way for nodes to communicate with each other. Beowulf clusters use MPI [4, 16] to define how nodes communicate.

Based on the architecture of interconnection network the distributed system is classified into Bus and Switched. In Bus based architecture there is a single network that connects all the machines. In switched systems there are individual wires from machine to machine with different wiring patterns. Switched multi-computers are best suited to problems that have an inherent 2-dimensional nature [17].

Switched multi computers are of three types

(i) Grid based Multicomputers.
(ii) Hypercube Multicomputers.
(iii) BCC Multicomputers.

Grid based Multicomputers are easy to understand and lay out on printed circuit boards. The longest possible path grows as square root of the number of CPU's. In this if we have 100 nodes then the longest distance between two nodes is about 10 hops[8].

Hyper cube multi computers are an n- dimensional cube. In n-dimensional hyper cube each CPU has n connections to other CPU's. Thus the complexity of the wiring increases only logarithmically with the size. Since only nearest neighbors are connected, messages have to make several hops to reach their destinations. The longest possible path grows logarithmically with size [7, 8]. In our system all the images are stored in image database and their features are stored in feature database across all the nodes. Each node contains a part of images in image database and features in feature database.

Query image is given to a master node, which extracts its features and broadcasts these features to all the nodes in the form of message. Each node receives this message in several hops as master node is not directly connected to all the nodes. If we employ Hyper cube Multi computers the message will take less hops compare to the Grid Multicomputers.

Body Center Cube is a type of interconnection networks, which is an improved version of Hypercube model, master node is placed at the centroid of the cube which is equidistant to all the nodes.

In BCC Structure each vertex is CPU and each edge is a connection between CPUs. In our system the strategy used is to distribute features, images and computations over an ensemble of 'n' processing and storage nodes.

4. Existing System

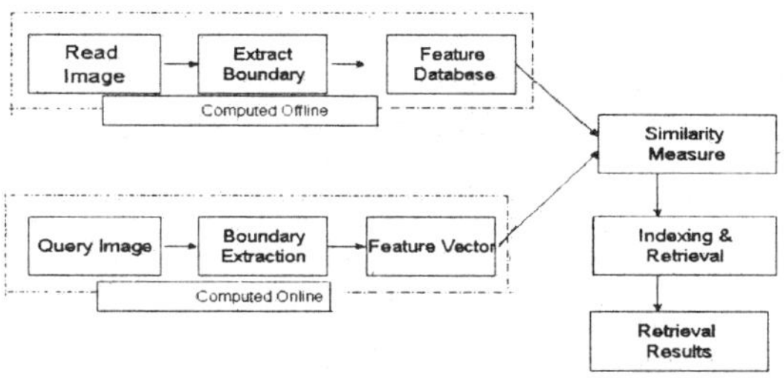

Fig. 4.1 Image Retrieval System

Fig 4.1 shows a block diagram of image retrieval model[2,13,15]. The input images are taken from MPEG-7 part B Shape database [18]. Image retrieval model consists of two major modules i) Feature database creation, it is explained in section 4.1 and ii) Query image Retrieval, it is explained in section 4.2. MPEG-7 shape database consists of 1400 images in 70 different categories, each image shape category in turn consists of 20 related images. Among 70 classes few classes are given in Fig 4.2

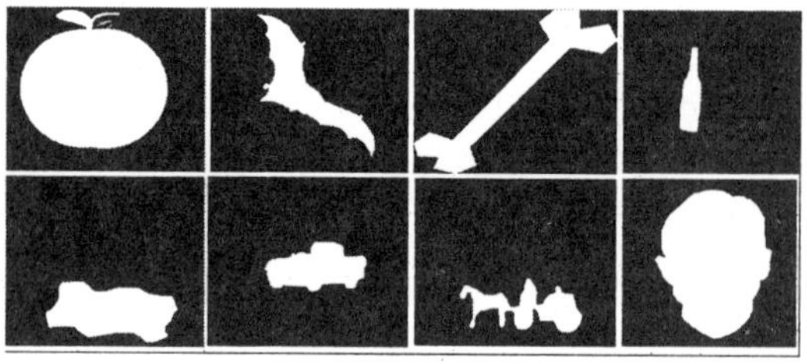

Fig. 4.2 Image samples from MPEG-7 database

4.1 Steps for creating Feature database from large image database

(i) Read image
(ii) Boundary extraction
(iii) Extract the shape features.
(iv) Store the extracted features in the
(v) feature database with an index
(vi) Repeat the above steps for all the
(vii) images present in the image database.

(i) Read an image : An image is loaded by giving its URL address in the image retrieval system interface.

(ii) Boundary extraction: In this procedure we are using Contour based method which requires only external characteristics such as boundary. Internal characteristics of the shape are ignored as shown in figure 4.1.1 and Figure 4.1.2 to extract the Boundary we used morphological Boundary extraction procedure [12]. X = A-(AΘB) where A is input image, B is the structuring element, X is the extracted boundary of A. A is the image shown in fig 4.1.1 and X is the boundary extracted image as shown in Fig 4.1.2.

Fig. 4.1.1 original shape Fig 4.1.2 boundary of shape

(iii) Feature Extraction: Features of image are extracted by applying Discrete Fourier Transforms given in Eq 2.1 on shape boundary and they are called as Fourier descriptors. These Fourier descriptors are used as features of images.

(iv) Feature Database: All the extracted features (FD's) of the image are stored in the separate database Known as Feature Database.

(v) All the above 5 steps are repeated for all the images and their features are stored in the feature database with indexing.

Feature Database is created offline and it is one time process as shown in fig 4.1

4.2 Algorithm for shape retrieval

(i) Read query image
(ii) Boundary extraction.
(iii) iii) Extract the shape features of query image.
(iv) Similarity Measure.

Step i) to step iii) are same as given in section 4.1.

iv) Similarity Measure: In the proposed methodology Euclidian distance given in equation 4.1 is used as measure of similarity. The difference d between Query features (FD^Q) and target features in database (FD^T) are stored. Features of the Images having less difference are more similar.

$$d = (\sum_{i=1}^{N} | FD_i^Q - FD_i^T |^2)^{\frac{1}{2}} \qquad 4.1$$

Feature database is created offline and similarity measure of query image with feature database is performed online. As explained in Fig 4.1 Feature database consists of a very large number of image features in our example it is 1400 images derived from MPEG-7 shape database. A snapshot of the image database is given in Fig 4.2 Each image has approximately 1000 to 5500 features. These features are Fourier Descriptors computed from eq 2.1. When ever a query image is given its features are extracted as given in equation 2.1 on a Java online indexing & retrieval framework, and they are compared with all the features of images stored in feature database. Euclidian distance given in equation 4.1 is used as measure of similarity. Number of features are not constant for all the images, they vary with the image. To calculate Euclidian distance between query image and image in database we consider only first N features, where N is the minimum of features among query image and image in database. In the best case considering only first 1000 features to calculate the distance between query image and image in database, 1000 subtractions, 1000 additions, 1000 multiplications and one square root. Approximately 3000 operations are to be performed for one distance calculation as given in equation 4.1. Like this it is to be calculated for all the images in the database i.e. 1400 images in this case. If each image has N features and for M images to calculate Euclidian distance 3*M*N operations are to be performed, approximately 40 X 10^5 operations.

Above number of operations will slow down the retrieval performance of the system. one computer with limited performance can hardly competent. So parallel computing is needed in this image retrieval system[3].

5. Proposed method

In this paper we are proposing an algorithm to distribute the workload, image database and feature database which works on all the three different interconnection topologies stated below. The algorithm contains two parts, first part will run on master node, while the second part will run on all the slave nodes. After processing master node, has to retrieve top 'p' similar images as its counterpart in sequential system.

Initially the image database as well as the feature database is distributed among slave nodes. Query image is given to a master node, which extracts its features and broadcasts these features to all the nodes in the form of message. After receiving query features each slave node will extract 'p' most similar features using Eq 4.1 from its feature database and forward them to master node. In fig 5.1 the functionalities of master node and the generalized connection between master and slave nodes are shown.

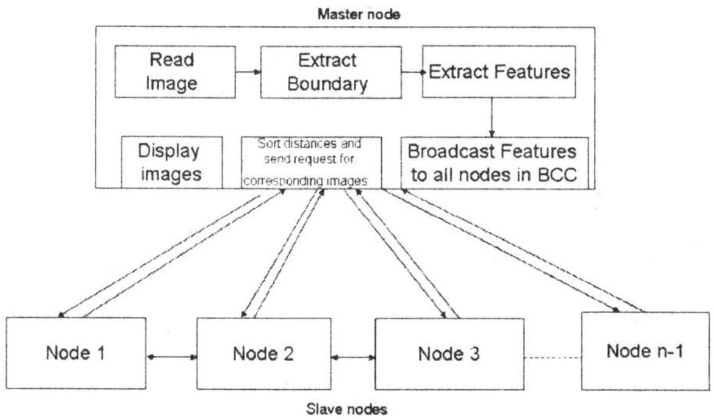

Fig. 5.1 generalized connection between master and slave nodes.

Master node collects the similarity results obtained from each of the 'n' slave nodes and sorts the n*p similarity distances of image samples by using m-way merge sort technique. Truncate the sorting approach so as to include the best 'p' results. The signatures of best 'p' images are sent to the corresponding slave nodes requesting for the related images. After receiving all the 'p' images the master node will display them. Algorithmic steps for image retrieval on parallel architecture.

Master node

(i) Read query image
(ii) Boundary extraction
(iii) Extract the shape features of query image using Eq 2.1.
(iv) Broadcast features to all 'n' slave nodes using MPI_BCAST () primitive.
(v) Receive the results of 'n' slave process using MPI_RECV() primitive.
(vi) Sort n*p results and select most similar 'p' results.
(vii) send request 'p' more similar images to the 'n' slave nodes where the corresponding images stored.
(viii) Receive the 'p' most similar images from the nodes containing them using MPI_REC () primitive.
(ix) Display the 'p' most similar images.

Slave node

(i) Receive the feature of the Query Image using MPI_REC().
(ii) Compare the query features with features in feature database using Eq 4.1called distance stored them in an array.
(iii) Sort the array containing distances.
(iv) Forward 'p' most distances to Master node.
(v) Forward the images after getting the request from the master.

Size of each image is approximately 20KB. Query image features are extracted in the master and approximately there are about 1000 features each feature is of double data type (8 bytes). In our experiment top 20 images are to be extracted (p=20). Slave nodes will compute similarity measure and sends a vector of top 20 distances and their indexes stored in the form of signature. Size of signature is 8 bytes. The size of the data corresponding to each one of the 'p' best results that are transferred from every slave to the master is 8 bytes as we are sending distances which are of double data type. Therefore each slave process transfers 8*p bytes per query.

5.1. Grid Multicomputers

Let the squared grid contain N X N processors. If the whole grid is viewed as one hierarchy (one-level), then choosing the center node as the master node (i.e., the group leader with the entire grid as the group) would obviously minimize the total communication cost. Depending on whether N is an odd or even number, the cost can be calculated as follows. When N is odd, there exists a true central node, and it will be taken as the master node. When N is even, there is no true central node. Any one of the four nodes in the central "area" can be picked as the master, as shown in Fig 5.2. the total communication cost for an N X N grid using a central master node is

$$\begin{cases} \dfrac{N^3 - N}{2} & \text{for } N = \text{ODD} \\ \dfrac{N^3}{2} & \text{for } N = \text{EVEN} \end{cases}$$

It can be shown that using any non-central monitor would cost more, with the monitor at corner costing most.

Traffic involved in the retrieval process of a Grid Multicomputer. By considering a grid of 33X33 consisting of 1089 nodes, where *n* is the dimension of the interconnection network.

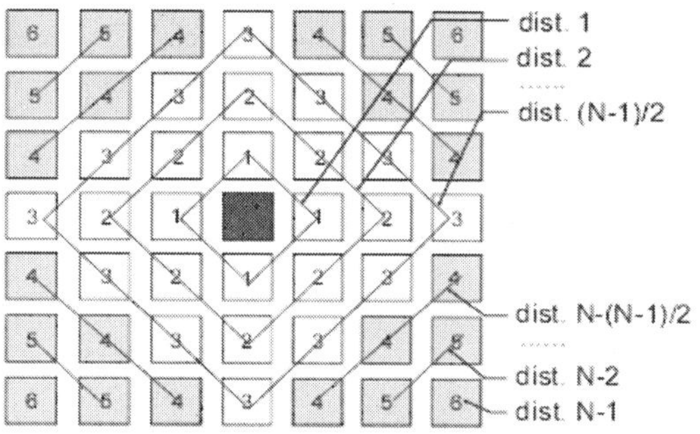

Fig. 5.2 Grid multi computer

(i) Message consisting of features of query image broadcast from master to all slave nodes. $((n^3-n)/2*1000*8)$
i.e 17952 *1000*8 =143.616MB

(ii) Each slave node forwards best p image signature's (p*8) Total signatures received by master node is $(n^3-n)/2*p*8$
i.e 17952*20*8=2.872MB

(iii) Master node sorts all the distances which are received from slaves and select best p signatures of images from n*p signatures and forward it to corresponding slave nodes. Total messages forwarded is 20*p*8(in worst case)
i.e 30*20*8=4.8KB

(iv) After receiving the request, total messages forwarded by slaves are 30*20*20KB i.e 12MB.

Total traffic involved in this retrieval process is 158.48MB.

5.2 Hypercube Multicomputer

An n-cube consists of 2^n nodes[10], addressed (numbered) from 0000...00 to 1111....1. A link exists between two nodes if their addresses differ in one and only one bit.

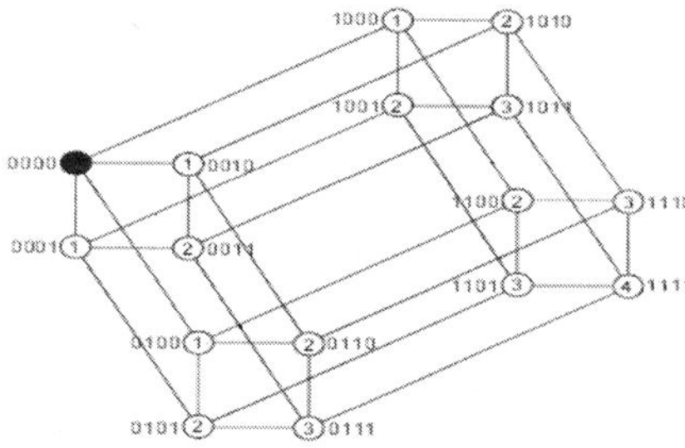

Fig. 5.3 Hypercube multi computer

The n-dimensional cube is completely symmetric structure, in which any node can be selected as master node the total communication cost is same. In Fig 5.3 node 0000 is selected as master node, the number inside node represents its communication cost. The total communication cost

$$=1.\binom{n}{1}+2.\binom{n}{2}+.............+n.\binom{n}{n}$$

$$=n*2^{n-1}$$

Traffic involved in the retrieval process of a Hyper Cube Multicomputer. By considering hypercube of 10-dimension (n) consisting of 1024 nodes,

(i) Message consisting of features of query image that broadcast from master to all slave nodes, communication cost is
$n*2^{n-1}*1000*8.$
i.e 5120*1000*8 =40.96MB

(ii) Each slave node forwards best p image signature's (p*8). Communication cost for receiving signatures by master node is $n*2^{n-1}*p*8$.
i.e 5120*20*8=0.819MB

(iii) Master node sorts all the distances which are received from slaves and select best p signatures of images from n*p signatures and forward it to corresponding slave nodes. Communication cost for forwarded messages (in worst case) is 20* p*8
i.e 8*20*8=1.28KB

(iv) After receiving the request, cost for messages forwarded by slaves is 8*20*20KB
i.e 3.2MB.

Total traffic involved in this entire retrieval process is 44.98MB.

5.3 BCC Multicomputer

In each BCC there are 9 nodes one master and 8 slave nodes as shown in fig 5.4 which is a 3-dimensional. In 4-D there are 36 nodes, 6-Dimesion BCC has 73 nodes as shown in fig 5.4. Let us consider a 9-dimensional BCC having 1170 Nodes [10].

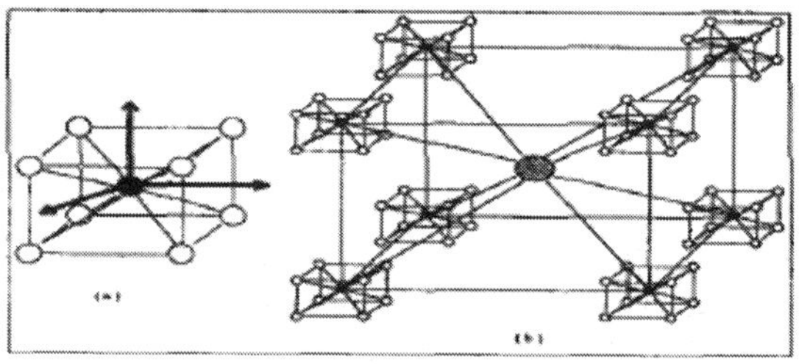

Fig. 5.4 3-and 6- Dimensional BCC

Traffic involved in the retrieval process of a BCC Multicomputer is

(i) Message consisting of features of query image broadcast from master to all slave nodes.
3*(n*1000*8)
3*1170*1000*8 =28.08MB

(ii) Each slave node forwards best p image signature's (p*8)
Total signatures received by master node is
3*n*p*8 i.e 3*1170*20*8 =561.6 KB

(iii) Master node extracts best p signatures of images from n*p signatures and forward it to corresponding slave nodes
3*20*8=480 bytes

(iv) Slave nodes after receiving request from master forwards the requested image. Like this p images are forwarded to the master from slave nodes
3*20 *20KB =1.2MB

Total Traffic Involved Approximately is 29.84MB.

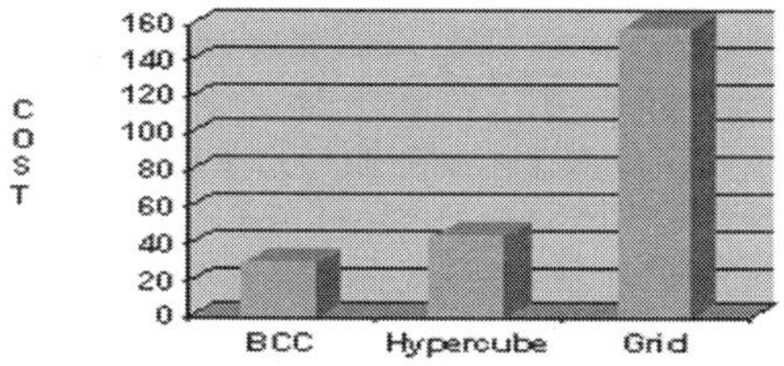

Fig. 5.5 Communication cost of multi-computers

From the above analysis and fig 5.5 it is clear that BCC has very less communication cost in comparison with other two interconnection topologies even though it has less number of slave nodes.

6. Experimental Results

In this paper, performance of Multicomputers with three different interconnection topologies for image retrieval using MPEG-7 database is given. The configurations for the master and slave nodes are same for all the three interconnections.

The slave node is a PC with an Intel Pentium 4, 2GHz Processor and 512MB of RAM memory, the operating system used is windows XP. The master node is an IBM server with an Intel Pentium 4, 2GHz Processor and 2 GB of RAM memory, the operating system used is windows server 2003.

Our experimental setup has been programmed under java retrieval frame work for retrieval of images with standalone system, GRID, Hypercube and BCC Multicomputer systems separately and compared the results of above interconnection topologies. The image database used is MPEG-7 shape database which consists of 1400 images in 70 different categories, each image shape category in turn consists of 20 related images.

We have conducted the first experiment on a standalone system and results are obtained in 246 seconds. The second experiment has been conducted using 24 slave nodes and one master node placed in the center in Grid fashion and results are obtained in 61.8 seconds. The third experiment has been conducted using 15 slave nodes and one master node in Hypercube fashion and results are obtained in 45.3 seconds. The fourth experiment has been conducted using 8 slave nodes and one master node placed at the centroid in BCC fashion and results are obtained in 39.6 seconds.

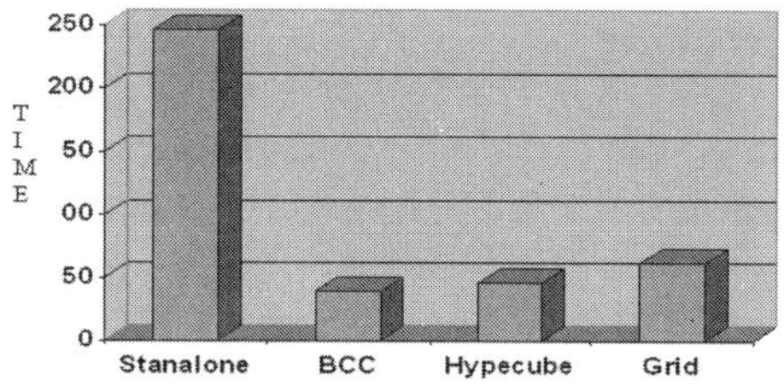

Fig. 6.1 Execution times of multi -computers

From the above results BCC way of interconnection topology is efficient parallel architecture in terms of execution time as shown in Fig. 6.1.

Speed up: In parallel computing, speedup refers to how much a parallel algorithm is faster than a corresponding sequential algorithm. Speedup is defined by the following formula: $S_p = T_s/T_p$ Where T_s is the execution time of the sequential algorithm T_p is the execution time of the parallel algorithm. From our experimental results it is shown that BCC exhibits a speed up of 6.21 which is better than its remaining counterparts as shown in fig 6.2.

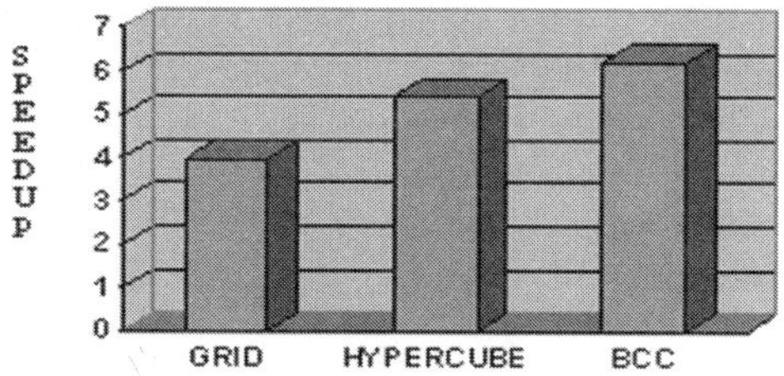

Fig. 6.2 speedup of multi-computers

7. Conclusion and Future work

In this Paper, a parallel implementation of image retrieval system has been presented. Both the algorithm and the parallel implementation have been tested with a java retrieval framework, shown a remarkable performance improvement over standalone implementation.

The proposed parallel implementation works on the experimental system of interconnection topologies, Grid, Hypercube and BCC Multicomputers for image retrieval system.

It is concluded that BCC interconnection topology has better performance than Grid and Hypercube Multicomputers with a speedup of 6.21 over standalone systems.

Future work will introduce strategies for dynamic load balancing within the retrieval system. an additional aspect that will be taken into consideration in future implementations is fault tolerance, inorder to tolerate system degradations produced by faulty nodes.

8. References

[1] Dengsheng Zhang and Guojun Lu, "Review of shape representation and description techniques, Pattern recognition 37,pp 1-19, 2004.

[2] Venu Gopal.T , Kamakshiprasad.V, " A Novel approach to Shape Based Image Retrieval Integrating Adapted Fourier descriptors and Freeman Code", IJCSNS Vol-8 No6, June 2008.

[3] O. Kao, "SMP and Cluster Architectures for Retrieval of Images in Digital Libraries" ERCIM Workshop Proceedings - No. 01/W001, Zurich, Switzerland, December, 11-12, 2000.

[4] MPI A: " Message-Passing Interface Standard", Message Passing

[5] Jahne B. "Digital Image Processing - Concepts, Algorithms, and Scientific applications". 4th Edition, Springer, 1997.

[6] Persoon, E., and Fu, KS. "Shape Discrimination Using Fourier Descriptors". IEEE Transactions on Systems, Man, and Cybernetics, March 1977, Vol. SMC-21, No 3, 170-179.

[7] Kyung-Hwa Ok, "The Design of A Hierarchical Body-Centered Cube Interconnection Network," Feb. 1992

[8] Dajin Wang; Jiannong Cao "On optimal hierarchical configuration of distributed systems on mesh and hypercube" Parallel and Distributed Processing Symposium, 2003. Proceedings. International 22-26 April 2003 Page(s):8 pp.

[9] Zahn C.T., and Roskies, R.Z. Fourier Descriptors for Plane Closed Curves. IEEE Transactions on Computers, March 1972, Vol. C-21(3).

[10] Sanjay Ranka, Sartaj Sahni "Image Template Matching on MIMD Hypercube Multicomputers" Proc. of the 1988 International Conference on Parallel Processing.

[11] Dengsheng Zhang and Guojun Lu . "A Comparative Study of Fourier Descriptors for Shape Representation and Retrieval", 5th Asian conference on computer vision, Melbourne, Australia. ACCV2002.

[12] Gonzalez, R.C., and Wintz, P. "Digital Image Processing. 2nd Edition", Addison-Wesley, 1987.

[13] T.Venu Gopal , Dr. V.Kamakshi Prasad and B.RameshNaik "Modified Approach to Shape Representation and Retrieval" First National conference 65-72,CCCA-2008, Coimbatore, India.

[14] Dengsheng Zhang and Guojun Lu. "An integrated approach to shape based retrieval", 5th Asian conference on computer vision, Melbourne, Australia. ACCV2002.

[15] Dengsheng Zhang and Guojun Lu . "A Comparative Study on Shape Retrieval Using Fourier Descriptors with Different Shape Signatures", ICME01.

[16] Bosque, J.L.; Robles, O.D.; Rodriguez, A.; Pastor, L. "Study of a parallel CBIR implementation using MPI" Computer Architectures for Machine Perception, 2000. Proceedings. Fifth IEEE International Workshop Volume, Issue, 2000 Page(s):195 - 204.

[17] Andrew S. Tanenbaum "Distributed Operating Systems" pearson education 2001

[18] www.imageprocessingplace.com/root_files_ v3/image_databases.htm

Recognition of Continuously Spoken Bangla Numbers

Mohammad Ali Moni[1], Md. Mijanur Rahman[1], Md. Farukuzzaman Khan[2]
[1]Dept. of CSE, Jatiya Kabi Kazi Nazrul Islam University, Trishal, Mymensingh, Bangladesh.
[2]Dept. of CSE, Islamic University, Kushtia, Bangladesh.
moni_cse1@yahoo.com mijan_cse@yahoo.com mfkhan_bd@yahoo.com

Abstract

This research work is concerned with the design and development of a software system to recognize continuously spoken Bangla numbers. In the proposed system, the speech samples were recorded by window's default sound recorder and stored as RIFF (.wav) format. Then by End Detection Technique, the individual word segments were separated from continuously spoken numbers. The Mel Frequency Cepstrum Coefficients (MFCCs) were used to extract features from the word segments for recognition. The distance between reference and test patterns was measured by Euclidean distance measurement technique and finally the decision was taken by minimum distance. Since Bangla number system includes different words in the utterances of all numbers from 0 to 99, utterances of all the hundred numbers were included in the reference database. In addition other four words are required to utter Bangla numbers e.g. Shoto (kZ - hundred), Hazar (nvRvi - thousand), Lakkho (j¶ - 0.1 million) and koti (‡KvwU - 10 million). Thus reference database was made by 104 distinct speech patterns. The utterances of 200 numbers originating from five speakers were recorded as test database. Thus 1000 spoken Bangla numbers were recorded and included in the test database. The developed system achieved segmentation accuracy at about 98.30% on average and recognition accuracy at about 95% for single speaker and about 82% for multiple speakers.

Keywords: *MFCC, Feature Extraction, Speech Segmentation, Speech Recognition, End Point Detection, Euclidean distance.*

1. Introduction

Speech is the most versatile medium for communication among people in the world and one of the most natural means of exchanging information for humans. With the advances of technology, an increasing demand of communication between man and machine led scientist to develop effective and reliable tools to use with speech signals. In this prospect, various laboratories and industries throughout the world are working to recognize human speech by machine. The aim of a continuous speech recognition system to provide an efficient and accurate mechanism to transcribe human speech into text or numbers [1, 2].

Bangla speech recognition is the newest theme as software implementation. But unfortunately the progress of such research with Bangla language is not satisfactory yet [3]. In our country, research works in this field have achieved a limited success so far as compared to the other foreign languages. Early researchers have developed Bangla speech recognition system for phonemes [4,5], letters [6], words [7], small vocabulary continuous speech [8] and medium vocabulary continuous speech [2] with a limited performance. In this paper, we have presented a Bangla speech recognition system that works with continuously spoken Bangla numbers and gives output as printed Bangla numbers.

2. Bangla number system

Bangla number system is a decimal system, which is composed of 10 digits or symbols. These 10 symbols are 0,1,2,3,4,5,6,7,8,9 and are used as the digits of any number. This number system is actually a positional-valued system in which the value of a digit depends on its position. For example consider a Bangla number: Ak koti teish lakkho poitallish hazar soi shoto atattur (12345678 = 12345678).

The digits in the number carry positional values as follows:

Ak (1) actually represents 1koti (1 Koti=10 million)

Dui (2) actually represents 2 Nijut (2 Nijut = 2 millions = 20 lakkho)

Tin (3) actually represents 3 Lakkho (3 lakkho = 0.3 million)

Char (4) actually represents 4 Ajut (4 Ajut = 40 thousands)

Pach (5) actually represents 5 Hazar (5 Hazar = 5 thousands)

Soi (6) actually represents 6 Shoto (6 Shoto = 6 hundreds)

Shat (7) actually represents 7 Doshok (7 Doshok = 7 tens)

Aat (8) actually represents 8 Akok (8 Akok = 8 units)

In practice, ajut and nijut are usually not uttered in Bangla language. For examples, the utterance of the number 101112113 (101112113) will be Dosh koti agaro lakkho baro hazar ak shoto tero (`k †KvwU GMvi j¶ ev‡iv nvRvi GK kZ ‡Zi).

In English number system, there are also 10 (0, 1, 2, 3, …, 9) digits and using 34 words we can utter any English number. They are zero to twenty, thirty, forty, fifty, sixty, seventy, eighty, ninety, hundred, thousand, million, Billion, Trillion, and And. Now out of this 34, 28 numbers e.g. zero to twenty, thirty, forty, fifty, sixty, seventy, eighty, and ninety can be called ***Single word numbers*** because only one word is required in their utterances and all other numbers can be called ***multiple word numbers***. Similarly in Bangla number system 99 numbers Shunno(0) to niranobboi (99) can be called ***Single word numbers*** and all other numbers can be called ***multiple word numbers***. Some examples are given in Table 1.

Table 1 Single and Multiple word numbers

Number Type	Bangla	English
Single word numbers	Tin (3), Shat (7), Shotero (17), Baish (22), Titallish (43), Atanno (58), Niranobboi (99)	Three, Seven, eleven, fifteen, thirty, sixty, Ninety
Multiple word numbers	Dui shoto tero (213), Nobboi hazar baro (90012), Tin Lakkho Ponchash hazar shat shoto pach (350705), Bish koti akush lakkho baish hazar dui shoto teish (202122223), Shat shoto ashi koti pachish lakkho birashi hazar tin shoto nobboi (7802582390).	Twenty-Two, Sixty-eight, Ninety-nine, Thirteen hundreds and sixty, Three thousands and fifty, Four Millions and sixteen thousands and eight hundreds and fifty seven.

From above, we observed that English numbers could be uttered using only 34 words, but in Bangla, 104 words are required to utter any number. They are Shunno (ïb¨) to niranobboi (wbivbeŸB), Shoto, Hazar, Lakkho, and Koti.

3. System development

The complete recognition system for continuously spoken Bangla numbers is shown in Figure-1 as object/process diagram. The individual objects/processes are discussed in following sub-sections.

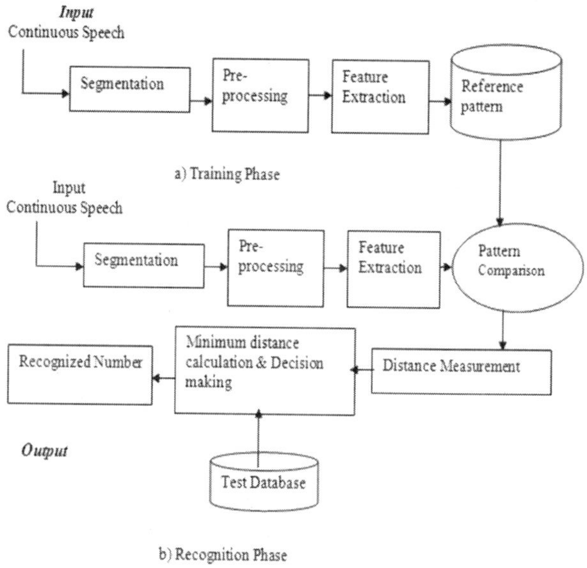

Fig. 1 Object or process diagram of the system for continuously spoken Bangla numbers

3.1 Sample collection and preprocessing

The recording of continuously spoken Bangla numbers was made in laboratory environment. In this process, Creative Vibra 128 sound card, a quality microphone and windows default sound recording system were used. As human speech signal contains significant amount of energy within 2.5 KHz, system setting was made in 8 KHz - 8 bit - mono mode, which was sufficient for representing signals up to 4 KHz without aliasing [9] effect. The spoken numbers was stored as the PCM (.wav) sound file format. For the ease of next processing, discarding 58 bytes file header, data was extracted and stored in a buffer as integers. Sometimes recorded speech contains noise or long-time silence at the beginning or the end as shown in Figure-2 that becomes very harmful for segmentation. For this reason, the time spectrum of every spoken number was checked and manually removed these noises from the speech.

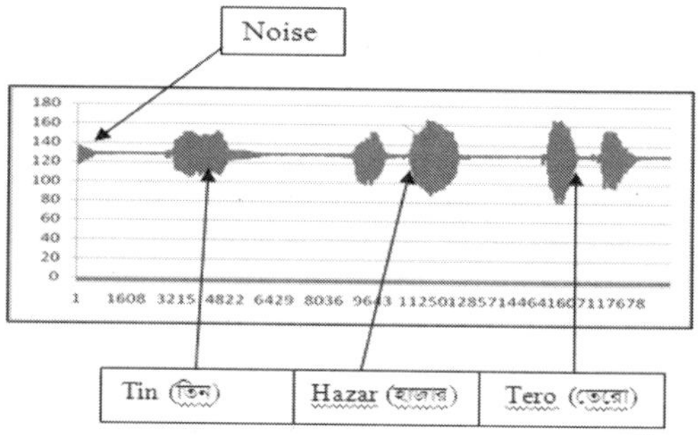

Fig. 2 Speech that contains noise at the beginning

3.2 Segmentation of Continuous Speech

The important requirement for recognition is to segment the continuous speech into uniquely recognizable and meaningful units (words in this work). In this research, End Point detection Technique [10] was implemented to segment continuous speech.
In this method, segmentation was done by detecting the proper start and end points of the speech events and then separated into different pieces containing the audio signals on the basis of the detected start and end points. To make the segmentation process easy, the threshold technique was used. It detects start and end points by tracing abrupt change of the data sequence that is greater than or less than a given threshold. Each segmented number-unit was stored in a separated buffer file. For better understanding, consider a multiword Bangla number "Dosh koti agaro lakkho baro hazar ak shoto tero (101112113)". The time spectrum of this number is shown in the figure 3, where S1, S2, S3, ..., S9 and E1, E2, E3, ... ,E9 indicate the starting points and ending points of each unique word respectively.

After segmentation, it was segmented into 9 number-units "Dosh" "koti" "agaro" "lakkho" "baro" "hazar" "ak" "shoto" and "tero". The time spectrums of each segment are shown in Fig. 4. The resulting segments may have unvoiced portion in both sides of each segment. Therefore an additional program module was developed to select the proper starting and end point of voice portion of each segment.

3.3 Preprocessing

In this work, preprocessing of the signal includes frame blocking, preemphasis, and windowing as shown in Fig. 5. At first, speech samples were grouped in a set of samples, called a frame representing typically between 16 to 32 ms of speech. Then, a preemphasis was applied as below:

$$y(n) = s(n) - C \times s(n-1)$$

where the constant C falls generally between 0.9 and 1.0 [11]. This was followed by windowing that involves multiplying a speech signal by a finite-duration window. The most popular hamming window is defined by the following equation:

$$h(n) = 0.54 - 0.46\cos\left(2\pi\frac{n}{N-1}\right), \quad (0 \le n \le N-1)$$

$$= 0, \text{ otherwise}$$

where N is the window length [11]

3.4 Feature Extraction

Feature extraction is the common part of all recognition systems and signal processing front-end, which converts the speech waveform to some type of parametric representation for further analysis and processing. This parametric representation is used for the collection of meaningful features. MFCC is the stronger feature for Bangla speech recognition [12] and was used in this research. Computation of MFCC includes a series of operations e.g. Fast Fourier Transform (FFT), Mel frequency warping, Discrete Cosine Transform (DCT) and finally the computation of Mel Frequency Cepstrum Coefficient (MFCC). The sequence is shown in Fig.5.

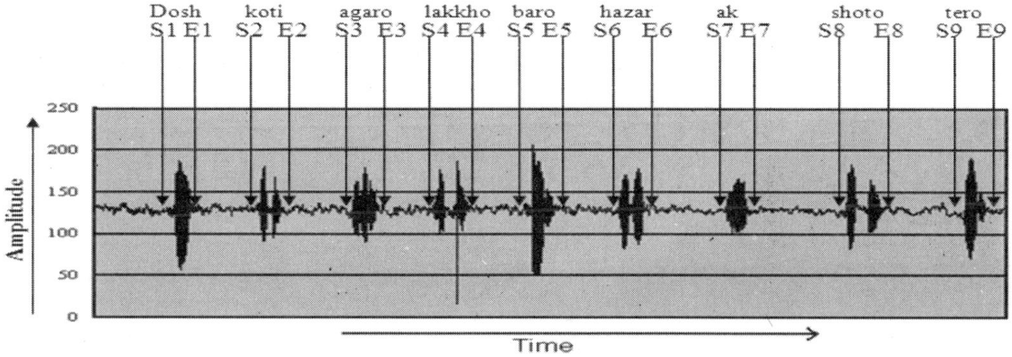

Fig. 3 Time spectrum of Dosh koti agaro lakkho baro hazar ak shoto tero **(`k †KvwU GMv‡iv j¶ ev‡iv nvRvi GK kZ †Z‡iv).**

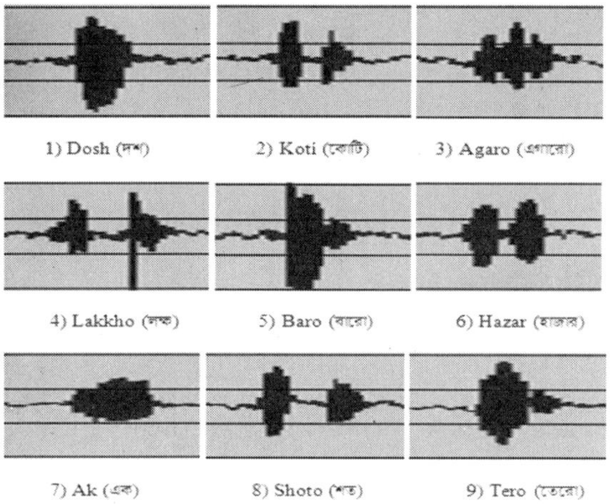

Fig. 4 Time spectrum of each segment

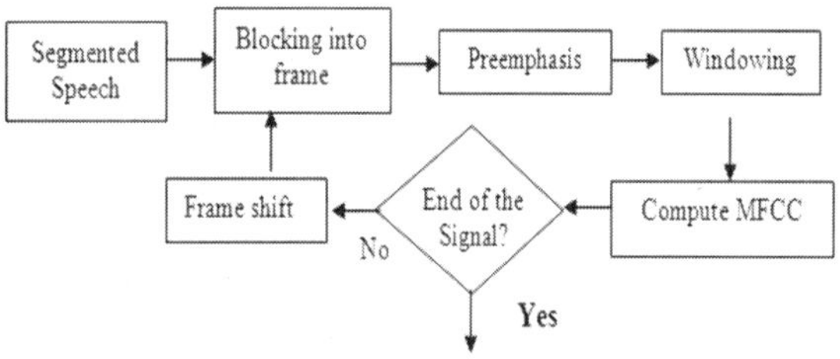

Fig. 5 The sequence of operations for Preprocessing and Feature extraction

3.5 Recognition

This is the final step that requires automatic detection or classification of objects or events. Features collected in the previous step were used to compare pattern. This can be done in a wide variety of ways. For its simplicity in computation, Euclidian distance measurement technique was used to compare the patterns in this work. Unknown speech patterns are identified by comparing the feature of an unknown pattern to each member of the stored reference patterns. The reference pattern matches the best with the unknown test pattern was the result. Details of this process are shown Fig. 6.

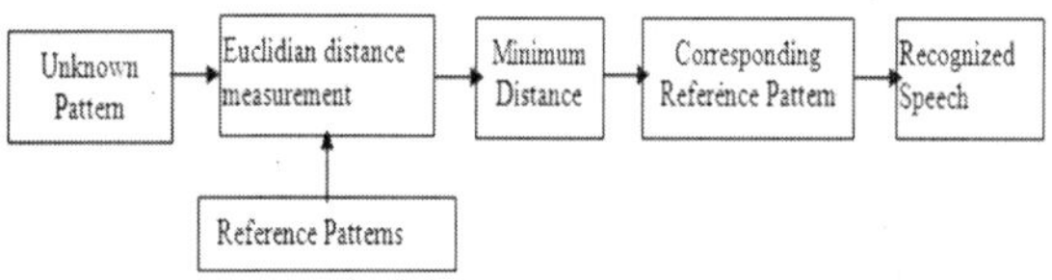

Fig. 6 Spoken number recognition system

4. Experimental results

The system was tested with prerecorded continuously spoken numbers. A total of 200 numbers originated from five speakers were constituted the test database. Both single and multiple word numbers were included in test database. For better result, multiple word numbers were segmented into individual number-units (words).

During segmentation, different threshold values were tested to fit the system. In our experiment, a threshold of 50 was produced good result and was selected as standard for all speakers.

4.1 Segmentation Results

Segmentation is needed for the multi words number to segment into unique meaningful words. Each of these segments must be one of the 104 patterns stored in reference database. The percentage of accuracy rate of segmentation has been calculated using the following equation:

$$Segment\ Accuracy(\%) = \frac{No.\ of\ correct\ segment\ obtained}{No.\ of\ correct\ segment\ expected} \times 100$$

(For single speaker)

$$\text{Average Segmentation accuracy}\ (\%) = \frac{1}{N}\sum_{i=1}^{N} accuracy(i)$$

Where, i is a speakers' identification number and N is the total number of speakers.

The detailed segmentation results are shown in Table 2.

Table 2 Segmentation Results

No. of Speakers	Expected No. of Correct Segmented Numbers	Obtained No. of Correct Segmented Numbers	No. of failure	Segmentation Accuracy (%)	Segmentation Failure (%)
1	200	195	5	97.50	2.50
2	200	197	3	98.50	1.50
3	200	198	2	**99.00**	1.00
4	200	197	3	98.50	1.50
5	200	196	4	98.00	2.00
Average Rate (%)				98.30	1.70

4.2 Recognition Results

The success rate was calculated by the following equations:

$$Success\ Rate(\%) = \frac{Total\ number\ of\ success}{Total\ number\ of\ samples} X\,100$$

$$\text{Average Success Rate } (\%) = \frac{1}{N}\sum_{i=1}^{N} Success(i)$$

Where, i is a speaker number and N is the total number of speakers.

The detailed recognition results are shown in Table 3 and the graphical representation of the recognition result for different speakers is shown in Fig. 7.

Table 3 Recognition Results

Speaker Number	Expected No. of Correct Recognition	Obtained No. of Correct Recognition	Recognition Accuracy (%)	Recognition Failure (%)
1	200	190	**95.00**	5.00
2	400	353	89.25	11.75
3	600	502	83.67	16.33
4	800	642	80.25	19.75
5	1000	771	77.10	22.90
Total	3000	2458	81.93	18.07

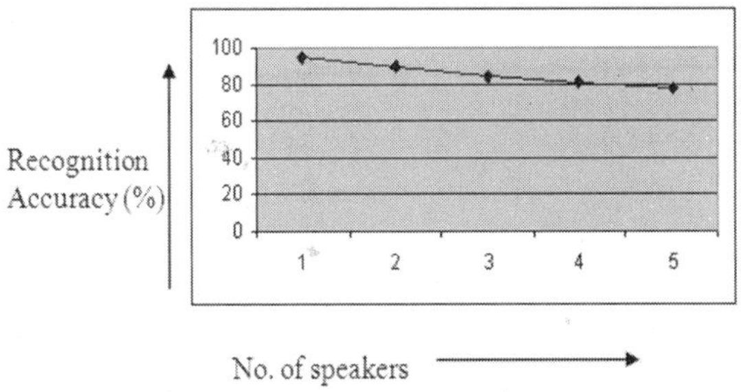

Fig. 7 Graphical representation of the recognition result for different speakers

5. Discussion

In this research the main objective was to develop a system for recognition of continuously spoken bangla numbers. So far, we have described all system modules and how they interact with each other in order to make the entire system more reliable. The performance of the system depends on two conditions: proper segmentation of the numbers and efficient recognition of each individual number. Both the average segmentation and recognition accuracy rates are quite satisfactory as given in table 1 & 2. To the best of our knowledge, as compared to the concurrent work in the similar field, this success is a new advancement for Bangla language. Due to very common problems in the continuous speech recognition system, the recognition accuracy was not better as segmentation accuracy. The main observation in this case is that the non-uniform articulation of speech. Even for a single speaker, it is difficult to maintain the uniformity in articulation for the same speech. In addition to that, the pauses between the numbers were not identical in all cases because of the variability nature of the speech signals. The speed of utterance, loudness variation, speaker's emotion was also the common source of errors.

6. Conclusion

In this paper, a novel approach for the recognition continuously spoken Bangla numbers has been introduced. Several new algorithms have been developed and proved efficient by a number of experiments. From the experimental results as discussed above, the developed system may be used in Data entry operation, as Voice calculator, in numerical computation, in Voice dialing and like other fields. Future systems should employ knowledge (syntactic or semantic) of linguistics and more powerful recognition tools like Gaussion Mixture Models (GMMs), Time-Delay Neural Networks (TDNNs) and the Hidden Markov Model (HMM).

7. References

[1] Holmes, John N and Holmes, Wendy J "*Speech synthesis and recognition*", Taylor & Francis Books Ltd, 1999.

[2] Pelton, Gordon E., "*Voice Processing*", McGraw-Hill International Edition, 1993.

[3] Md. Rabiul Huq, M. Sc. Thesis, "*A medium vocabulary speech to text system*", Dept. of Computer Science & Engineering, Islamic University, Kushtia-7003, February-2005.

[4] Karim, A. H. M. Rezaul, "*Bangla Phoneme Recognition*", Graduation Thesis Report, Shahajalal University of Science & Tech., Sylhet, 2002

[5] S. M. Jahangir Alam, M.Sc. Thesis "*System Development for Bangla Phoneme Recognition*", Dept. of Computer Science & Engineering, Islamic University, Kushtia-7003, July-2004.

[6] Abul Hasanat, Md. Rezaul Karim, Md. Shahidur Rahman and Md. Zafar Iqbal, "*Recognition of Spoken letters in Bangla*", 5th ICCIT 2002, East West University, Dhaka, Bangladesh, 27-28 December 2002.

[7] Kaushik Roy, Dipankar Das and M. Ganjer Ali, "*Development of the Speech Recognition System using Artificial Neural Network*", 5th ICCIT 2002, East West University, Dhaka, Bangladesh, 27-28 December 2002.

[8] Md. Saidur Rahman, M.Sc. Thesis, "*Small Vocabulary Speech Recognition in Bangla Language*", Dept. of Computer Science & Engineering, Islamic University, Kushtia-7003, July-2004.

[9] ED Laboratory, "*Computer Application Trainer Manual*", Seul, South Korea, 1997.

[10] Md. Farukuzzaman Khan and Dr. Ramesh Chandra Debnath, "*Bangla Sentence Recognition Using End-Point Detection Technique*", Rajshahi University Studies : Part B, Journal of Science, Vol 32, 2004.

[11] Jean-Claude Junqua & Jean-Paul Haton, "*Robustness in Automatic Speech Recognition: Fundamentals and Applications*", Kluwer Academic Publishers, Dordrecht, The Netherlands, 1997. 7003, July-2004.

[12] Md. Farukuzzaman Khan and Ramesh Chandra Debnath, "*Comparative Study of Feature Extraction Methods for Bangla Phoneme Recognition*", 5th ICCIT 2002, East West University, Dhaka, Bangladesh, 27-28 December 2002.

Open Domain Real Time Lecture Translation System

Sonal Sharma and A.K.Dubey
[1]Lecturer, Deptt of Electronics & Communication Engineering,
Applied College of Management & Engineering
Palwal (Haryana), India.
[2]Sr. Lecturer in the Deptt of Electronics & Communication Engineering,
Applied College of Management & Engineering (ACME)
sonal_87_Sharma@yahoo.co.in dubey1ak@yahoo.co.in

Abstract

This paper describes our work in open domain speech translation. We describe how we developed a lecture translation system by moving from speech translation of European Parliament Plenary Sessions and seminar talks to the open domain of lectures. Many persons had started with speech recognition and statistical machine translation. The paper presents the speech translation performance of these systems on lectures and gives an overview of final real-time lecture translation system with proposed block diagram.

Keywords: SST, ASR, SLT, TTS, and SMT.

1. Introduction

Growing international information structures and decreasing travel costs could make the dissemination of knowledge in this globalize world very easy – if only the language barrier could be overcome. Lectures are a very effective method of knowledge dissemination. Such personalized talks are the preferred method since they allow the speakers to tailor their presentation toward a specific audience, and in return allow the listeners to get the most relevant information through interaction with the speaker. In addition, personal communication fosters the exchange of ideas, allows for collaboration, and forms ties between distant units, e.g. scientific laboratories or companies. At the same time it is desirable to allow the presenters of talks and lectures to speak in their native language, since, no matter how proficient in a foreign language, one will always feel more confident in the native tongue. To overcome this obstacle human translators are currently the only solution. Unfortunately, translation services are often prohibitively expensive such that many lectures are not given at all as a result of the language barrier **[1]-[2]**. The use of modern machine translation techniques have the potential to provide translation services at no costs to a wide audience, making it possible to overcome the language barrier and bring the people closer together.

This paper describes our ongoing work in unlimited domain speech translation of lectures starting from systems built within the framework of CHIL and TC-STAR. CHIL (Waibel et al., 2004), *Computers in the Human Interaction Loop*, aims at making significant advances in the fields of speaker localization and tracking, speech activity detection and distant-talking automatic speech recognition. The long-term goal is the ability to recognize speech in a real reverberant environment, without any constraint on the number or distribution of microphones neither in the room nor on the number of sound sources active at the same time. TC-STAR (TC-Star, 2004), *Technologies and Corpora for Speech-to-Speech-Translation*, is envisaged as a long-term effort to advance research in all core technologies for Speech-to-Speech Translation (SST) which is a combination of Automatic Speech Recognition (ASR), Spoken Language Translation (SLT) and Text to Speech (TTS). The objective of the project is to make a breakthrough in SST that significantly reduces the gap between human and machine translation performance. The focus hereby is on the development of new algorithms and methods. So far the project targets a selection of unconstrained conversational speech domains – speeches and broadcast news – and three languages: European English, European Spanish, and Mandarin Chinese. The paper is organized as follows: The developmental work started from ASR and SMT evaluation systems for European Parliament Plenary Session (EPPS, TCSTAR) (St¨uker et al., 2006) and the NIST Rich Transcription evaluation RT-06S on seminars (CHIL) (F¨ugen et al., 2006b)**[5]-[7]**. In section -3 we first compare the different ASR systems of both domains and show how we merged these systems for lecture recognition. Furthermore, we present first results of acoustic and language model adaptation on the lecture domain. In section 4 we give Statistical Machine Translation(SMT) results on text and ASR input for lectures of our 2006 SMT evaluation system for EPPS. In addition, we explain in detail how we adapted our EPPS SMT system towards the more conversational style of lectures and present the corresponding machine translation results. Section-5 provides an overview of our real-time lecture translation system, Section-6 conclude this paper.

2. Development and Evaluation Data

For Auto speech recognition (ASR) and statistical machine translation (SMT) experiments on lectures, we selected three different lectures from Cristian Fugen(ISL) as development and evaluation data. These lectures were held in non-native English by the same speaker on different topics and were recorded with close talking microphones (F¨ugen et al., 2006a). Dev: This 24min talk was held to give a broad overview of current research projects in our lab. t035: A 35min talk held as a conference key-note, which is only partly covered by the Dev talk. t036+: A 31min talk on the same topic as t035, but held in a different environment and situation[4]. For the ASR experiments We used the seminar part of the NIST RT-06S development data and the 2006 EPPS development Data as additional data sources.

3. Speech Recognition

In this section we first compare the 2006 evaluation systems for European Parliament Plenary Sessions (St¨uker et al., 2006) and CHIL seminars (F¨ugen et al., 2006b) and show how we developed a single system, which performs almost as good as the evaluation systems on both domains. This is followed by the presentation of the system's performance on the lecture domain. All speech recognition experiments were done using the Janus Recognition Toolkit (JRTk) featuring the Ibis decoder (Soltau et al., 2001) [8]. For language modeling, we used the SRI Language Modeling Toolkit (SRILM) (Stolcke, 2002).

A. Data

For acoustic model training, we selected the following corpora: ICSI and NIST meeting recordings (Janin et al., 2004; (LDC), 2004), TED lectures (Lamel et al., 1994), CHIL seminars (Waibel et al., 2004), and European Parliament Plenary Sessions (EPPS) (Gollan et al., 2005). Given the results in (F¨ugen et al., 2006b) we have not used the ISL meeting corpus as well as the Hub4 Broadcast News corpus due to their channel mismatch: both corpora were recorded with lapel microphones.

Table 1 Comparison Table

	ICSI	NIST	TED	CHIL	EPPS
SPEAKER	463	77	52	67	1894
DURATION	72h	13h	13h	13h	80H

Table 1 gives an overview of the total amount of speech in the different corpora. This table 1 represents the number of speakers and total amount of speech for the acoustic model training data. For language model training, some additional text data was used on top of the 2006 evaluation systems' (F¨ugen et al., 2006b; St¨uker et al., 2006) language model training data.

B. System Description

The acoustic model used for the experiments below were al trained in the same way , resulting in a size of 16,000 distributions over 4,000 models , with a maximum of 64 Gaussian per model. These models were all based on same quint-phone context decision tree and phoneme set that was used for the RT-06S evaluation system. Furthermore, also the acoustic model training setup was taken from the RT-06S system: (1) a first incremental growing of Gaussians, (2) estimation of the global STC transform (Gales, 1998), (3) a second incremental growing of Gaussians. To train the distributions for the semi-continuous system and to compensate for the occasionally worse fixed-state alignments, 2 iterations of Viterbi training were performed (4). For the SAT models, 4 additional iterations of SAT Viterbi training by using constrained MLLR in the feature space (FSA) (Gales, 1997) were applied (5). We use an MFCC FFT front-end with a 42-dimensional feature space after linear discriminant analysis (LDA) and a global STC transform with utterance-based cepstral mean subtraction (CMS). More details can be found in (F¨ugen et al., 2006b).

C. Baseline Experiments and Comparisons

The goal is to build a single acoustic model for domains, EPPS and CHIL seminars and to finally use this acoustic model on the lecture data. For this, we compared different acoustic models trained on different subsets of the acoustic training material described in Section 3.1.. All subsets contain the CHIL corpus, which is therefore not explicitly mentioned in the table rows below. We were used a three pass decoding setup to be comparable with other evaluation systems. The first pass uses incremental speaker based vocal tract length normalization (VTLN) and constrained MLLR estimation and is decoded with the semi continuous models (4) using tight search beams. The second pass uses the same semi continuous acoustic models as pass one, but before decoding, MLLR (Leggetter and Woodland, 1995) adaptation together with estimation of fixed VTLN and constrained MLLR parameters is performed. For this, the confidence weighted hypotheses of the previous pass are being used. For the third pass, the FSASAT acoustic models (5) are used together with the same adaptation scheme applied in pass two. After that, confusion network combination (CNC) (Mangu et al., 1999) is being performed, using the lattices of the third pass only. We used exactly the same decoding dictionaries and language models as for the EPPS and RT-06S evaluation systems.

CHIL Seminars

For the CHIL seminars we used the same language models and dictionaries as described in (F¨ugen et al., 2006b). The 4-gram language model was trained on AMI and non-AMI meetings, TED, some CHIL data, BN, proceedings and web data related to meetings and CHIL lectures. The interpolation weights, which were tuned on held-out CHIL data are shown in Table 2. The language model has a perplexity of 130 on the RT-06S development data, while 16% 4-grams, 41% 3-grams, 39% 2-grams, and 4% 1-grams were used. The dictionary consists of around 59k pronunciation variants over a vocabulary of 52k. It has an OOV-Rate of 0.65 on the RT-06S development data. As can be seen in Table 2, acoustic models trained on EPPS alone or additionally including TED are significant worse than the other two systems. The performance of the two other systems is nearly identical, which means that adding the EPPS data to the acoustic model training data used in RT-06 (ICSI+NIST+TED) does not hurt (but also does not improve the results).

European Parliament Plenary

Session For the European Parliament Plenary Sessions we used the language models and dictionaries as described in (St¨uker et al., 2006)[3]. The 4-gram language model was trained on EPPS transcriptions and final text editions, BN, and UN and reached a perplexity of 93 on the 2006 EPPS development data, whereas 29% 4-grams, 36% 3-grams, 32% 2-grams, The CHIL data was used in all systems for AM training. and 4% 1-grams were used. The interpolation weights were tuned on the 2005 EPPS development data. The dictionary for EPPS consists of 45k pronunciations over a vocabulary of 40k and has an OOV-Rate of 0.43 on the 2006 EPPS development data. As can be seen in Table 3 the last system trained without EPPS performs worst.

Table 2 Results on the RT06 development data

CHIL	1st	2nd	3rd	cnc
EPPS	40.3	-.-	-.-	-.-
TED+EPPS	38.7	-.-	-.-	-.-
ICSI+NIST+TED+EPPS	34.1	27.5	26.2	25.5
ICSI+NIST+TED	34.0	27.1	26.0	25.5

Furthermore, compared to the acoustic model used for the 2006 EPPS evaluation (MS23, (St¨uker et al., 2006))[3],The acoustic model training setup developed for RT-06S is significantly better (MS23 vs. EPPS rows). An additional gain can be seen by adding TED, which is also a corpus containing European English. By adding the meeting data, the system improves not further, instead it is in between the EPPS and TED+EPPS systems. Nevertheless, after doing confusion network combination, it performs identical to the TED+EPPS system. Compared to the CHIL seminars, the EPPS results are much better.

The reason for that lies in the huge available amount of acoustic and language model in-domain training data for EPPS compared to CHIL, where only a very small amount of in-domain data is available. Furthermore, the language used in the European Parliament is more formal and therefore less spontaneous.

Table 3 Results on the 2006 EPPS Development Data

	1st	2nd	3rd	cnc
MS23	22.6	-.-	-.-	-.-
EPPS	20.8	15.4	14.7	14.5
TED+EPPS	20.1	14.8	14.3	14.1
ICSI+NIST+TED+EPPS	20.6	15.1	14.6	14.1
ICSI+NIST+TED	29.1	-.-	-.-	-.-

This leads also to a better OOV-rate and language model perplexity with higher n-gram coverage for larger n-grams.

D. Lecture Domain

Based on the perplexities and OOV-Rates on Dev shown in Table 4 we selected the language model and dictionary built for the CHIL seminars for our baseline experiments. Not surprisingly, this selection holds also for the evaluation talks. The EPPS language model and vocabulary is, due to the large amount of in-domain data, too specific. The OOV-rates of the RT-06S (CHIL) vocabulary and for t036+ are surprisingly low – the only explanation for that is that this talk is not very specific.

Table 4 Perplexities (PPL) and OOV-Rates of the CHIL and EPPS language models and vocabularies

	Dev		t035		t036+	
	PPL	OOV	PPL	OOV	PPL	OOV
CHIL	173	0.22	117	0.27	186	0.09
EPPS	205	1.29	230	1.83	229	1.72

As can be seen in Table 5, the acoustic model trained on all data performs significantly better than the other models. For this reason we selected this model for our further experiments. The baseline results on the lecture evaluation talks are shown in Table 6. With the training setup developed for RT-06S we were significantly improved our results compared to the acoustic models developed in (F¨ugen et al., 2006a) (MS11 column in Table 6). Furthermore, it can be seen that the system performs quite well on unseen domains (t035) and different environments (t036+).

Model adaptation experiments

Lectures are an ideal domain for doing adaptation, because the lecturer and also the topic might be known in advance (Cettolo et al., 2004)[1]. Therefore, we give first acoustic and language model adaptation results. As can be seen, this allows us to reduce the decoding setup from three to only a single decoding pass without any loss in WER and is the first step towards a real-time lecture recognition and translation system. For acoustic model adaptation an additional amount of around 7 hours of speech for the same speaker was available. For the adaptation experiments subsets of this data with different durations were used to compute VTLN and constrained MLLR (FSA) parameters and to perform model based MLLR adaptation. The results can be seen in Table 8.

Table 5 Baseline results on Dev with the CHIL dictionary and language model

	1st	2nd	3rd	cnc
EPPS	23.9	-.-	-.-	-.-
TED+EPPS	23.4	-.-	-.-	-.-
ICSI+NIST+TED+EPPS	21.4	16.2	15.0	15.5
ICSI+NIST+TED	24.3	-.-	-.-	-.-

Table 6 Baseline results on the evaluation talks t035 and t036+

	1st	2nd	3rd	cnc	MS11
t035	17.3	12.6	12.1	12.2	12.7
t036+	16.7	12.0	11.6	11.5	12.4

The MS11 column contains the final (CNC) results with the acoustic model trained in (F¨ugen et al., 2006a).

Table 7 Acoustic model adaptation results with different amounts of adaptation data

	0.5hrs	1.5hrs	3.5hrs	7hrs	sup
Dev	20.9	20.0	19.5	18.9	12.0
t035	14.2	13.1	12.6	12.1	10.1
t036+	13.3	12.3	11.5	10.7	9.3

In the column 'sup', supervised adaptation would performed on the particular talk itself CNC with the baseline systems. The results on the Dev talk are significantly worse. This is due to a large channel mismatch between the adaptation material and the Dev talk. To confirm this, we adapted on the particular talk itself and reached for all talks reasonable results (see column sup in Table 7). It can also be seen, that doubling the adaptation data results in a relative gain of around 0.5% in WER. For language model adaptation we only did a first experiment by tuning the interpolation weights and reselecting the different corpora with respect to the lecture domain. The perplexity on the Dev talk could only be reduced slightly from 173 to 168. Nevertheless we saw significant gains in WER on all lectures, which are reported in Table 8.

4. Statistical Machine Translation

In this section, we describe the statistical machine translation (SMT) component in our lecture translator that was used to translate the lectures in Section 2. from English to Spanish and German. The underlying phrase-based SMT system was originally developed within TC-STAR for translating speeches from the European Parliament Plenary Sessions (EPPS). In these experiments, we used loose coupling, passing the first-best hypothesis from the recognizer to the translation component. Translation results are reported using the well known evaluation metrics BLEU (Papineni et al., 2002) and NIST (NIST, 2004). All MT scores were calculated using case-insensitive scoring and one reference translation per test set.

A. Phrase alignment

To find a translation for a source phrase ˜ f = f1...fl we restrict the general word alignment: Words inside the source phrase align to words inside the target phrase and Words outside the source phrase. The Language model adaptation results on top of the acoustic model adaptation on 7hrs of speech. Perplexities should be compared with Table 4.align outside the target phrase.

Table 8 Language model adaptation results

	Unadapted	adapted	PPL
Dev	18.9	16.1	168
t035	12.1	10.5	165
t036+	10.7	9.1	193

This constrained alignment probability is calculated using the well-known IBM1 word alignment model, but the summation of the target words is restricted to the appropriate regions in the target sentence **[9]**. Also, the position alignment probabilities are adjusted accordingly (Vogel, 2005). Optimization is over the target side boundaries i1 and i2. Similar to pi1,i2 (f|e) we can calculate pi1,i2 (e|f), now summing over the

$$p_{i_1,i_2}(f|e) = \prod_{j=1}^{j_1-1} \sum_{i \notin (i_1..i_2)} \frac{1}{I-k} p(f_j|e_i) \times \prod_{j=j_1}^{j_2} \sum_{i=i_1}^{i_2} \frac{1}{k} p(f_j|e_i) \times \prod_{j=j_2+1}^{J} \sum_{i \notin (i_1..i_2)} \frac{1}{I-k} p(f_j|e_i) \quad (1)$$

source words and multiplying along the target words. To find the optimal target phrase we interpolate the log probabilities and take the pair (i1, i2) that gives the highest probability. The interpolation factor c can be estimated on a development test set. The scores calculated in the phrase alignment are alignment scores for the entire sentence. As phrase translation probabilities we use the second term in above equation.

B. Decoder

The beam search decoder combines all model scores to find the best translation. In these experiments, the different models used were:

1. The translation model, i.e. the word-to-word and phrase-to-phrase translations extracted from the bilingual corpus according to the new alignment method described in this paper.
2. A trigram language model. The SRI language model toolkit was used to train the models (Stolcke,2002) **[11]**.
3. A word-reordering model, which assigns higher costs to longer distance reordering. We use the jump probabilities p(j|j0) of the HMM word alignment model (Vogel et al., 1996) where j is the current position in the source sentence and j0 is the previous position.
4. Simple word and phrase count models. The former is essentially used to compensate for the tendency of the language model to prefer shorter translations, while the latter can be used to give preference to longer phrases.

For each model a scaling factor can be used to modify the contribution of this model to the overall score. The decoding process is organized into two stages: First, the word-to-word and phrase-to-phrase translations and, if available, other specific information like named entity translation tables are inserted into a translation lattice. In the second step, we find the best combinations of these partial translations, such that every word in the source sentence is covered exactly once. This amounts to doing a best path search through the translation lattice, which is extended to allow for word reordering: Decoding proceeds essentially along the source sentence. At each step, however, the next word or phrase to be translated may be selected from all words laying or phrases starting within a given look-ahead window from the current position (Vogel, 2003).

C. Training Data

For training the baseline translation systems, the parallel EPPS corpus was used. For English-Spanish, a version was created by RWTH Aachen within TC-STAR (Gollan et al., 2005). The English-to-German models were trained on the EPPS data as provided by Philipp Koehn (Koehn, 2003) **[10]**. In addition, a small number of lectures similar in style to our development and evaluation data was collected, transcribed, and translated into Spanish and German. Altogether, parallel lecture corpora of about 12,000 words were available in each language.

Table 9 English-Spanish lecture translation system on t036+. Results on manual transcripts are shown in brackets

system	NIST	Bleu
baseline (EPPS)	4.71 (5.61)	15.41 (20.54)
TM-adaptation	4.78 (5.67)	16.05 (21.43)
LM-adaptation	5.10 (5.99)	17.58 (22.90)
final system	5.22 (6.11)	18.57 (24.00)

Table 10 English-German lecture translation system on t036+

system	NIST	Bleu
baseline (EPPS)	4.00 (4.71)	09.32 (12.53)
TM-adaptation	4.29 (5.06)	11.01 (14.95)
LM-adaptation	4.37 (5.12)	11.67 (14.96)
final system	4.67 (5.47)	13.22 (17.25)

5. Real-time lecture translation system

For our current version of a real-time lecture translation system, which simultaneously translates lectures given in English into Spanish and German, we integrated the above described speech recognition and machine translation systems together with a sentence segmentation component and a speech synthesis into a client-server framework similar to the one described in (F¨ugen et al., 2001)**[2]** as shown in **Fig. 1.** To reach real-time end-to-end performance, we had to tune the above described single pass speech recognizer to run faster than real-time, by further restricting the beam search, which resulted in an increase in WER to about 13% on the evaluation talks. The other system components did not need further tuning. To keep the latency of the system as short as possible, the speech recognizer already starts to decode, while the speaker is talking and continuously returns partial back traces with first best hypotheses. Since the machine translation awaits complete sentences as input, we merged the partial hypotheses together, and resegmented them to sentence like segments. This means, that different from other speech transcription systems no speech segmentation was performed before processing it by the speech recognizer, instead it was done afterwards, to have the ability to tune the segmentation boundaries with respect to optimal machine translation performance. Currently, the segmentation is done at silence regions only, whereby additional thresholds are defined to produce segments with a length of about five to ten words. Thereby, the latency of the system could be limited to a maximum of about five seconds. We plan for more sophisticated segmentation algorithms in the future.. As can be seen, the system can deliver the output in different ways: **Subtitles:** Simultaneous translations can be projected to the wall as subtitles. This is suitable if the number of output languages is small. *Targeted Audio* Another solution for providing the simultaneous translation without disturbing others is the so called targeted audio device. The targeted audio device is a beam-steered loudspeaker, consisting of several small ultrasound loudspeakers. It outputs audio in a beam with a width of about 1-2 meters. People sitting within the beam are able to hear everything; people outside the beam do not. In future applications, several such targeted audio devices could be assigned in various languages to accommodate each participant in the lecture room.

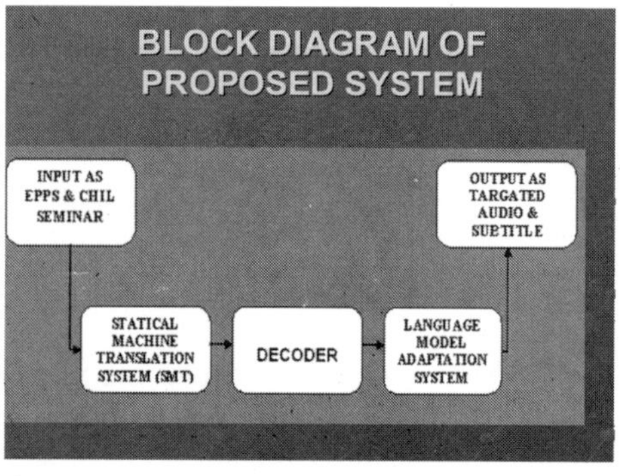

Fig. 1 Proposed system of real time lecture translation system

6. Conclusion

In this paper, we try to present our work in taking first steps towards building open domain speech translation systems. We try to developed an ASR system for lectures by merging the evaluation systems for European Parliament Plenary Sessions and CHIL seminars. Furthermore, we combined the resulting system with the translation system used in TC-STAR to translate lectures on a new domain from English to Spanish and German. For Translation, lectures still pose a significant challenge.

We are researching on further aspect of RTLTS and are trying to develop a device by wearing that device on eyes the text written on lecture board is converted in to our native script.

7. References

[1] Cettolo, F. Brugnara, and M. Federico. . "Advances in the Automatic Transcription of Lectures". In ICASSP, Montreal, Canada. . 2004.

[2] F¨ugen, M. Westphal, M. Schneider, T. Schultz, and A. Waibel.. "LingWear: A Mobile Tourist Information System". In Proc. of the Human Language Technology Conf. (HLT), San Diego, California, March. NIST. 2001.

[3] F¨ugen, M. Kolss, D. Bernreuther, M. Paulik, S. St¨uker, S. Vogel, and A. Waibel. "Open Domain Speech Recognition & Translation: Lectures and Speeche"s. In ICASSP, Toulouse, France. 2006a.

[4] F¨ugen, M. W¨olfel, J. W. McDonough, S. Ikbal, F. Kraft, K. Laskowski, M. Ostendorf, S. St¨uker, and K. Kumatani.. "Advances in Lecture Recognition: The ISL RT-06S Evaluation System". In To be published at Interspeech, Pittsburgh, PA, USA, September. 2006b, 2006.

[5] J. F. Gales. Maximum Likelihood Linear Transformations for HMM-based Speech Recognition. Technical report, Cambridge University, Cambridge, United Kingdom. . 1997

[6] J. F. Gales. Semi-tie covariance matrices. In ICASSP. C. Gollan, M. Bisani, S. Kanthak, R. Schl¨uter, and H. NeyCross Domain Automatic Transcription on the TC-STAR EPPS Corpus. ICASSP. 1998, 2005.

[7] Janin, J. Ang, S. Bhagat, R. Dhillon, J. Edwards, N. Morgan, B. Peskin, E. Shriberg, A. Stolcke, C. Wooters, and B. Wrede. The ICSI Meeting Project: Ressources and Research. In Proc. of the ICASSP Meeting Recognition Workshop, Montreal, Canada, May. NIST. 2004.

[8] Koehn.. "Europarl: A Multilingual Corpus for Evaluation of Machine Translation." 2003 http://people.csail.mit.edu/koehn/publications/europarl.

[9] L.F. Lamel, F. Schiel, A. Fourcin, J. Mariani, and H. Tillman.. "The Translanguage English Database TED". In ICSLP, volume LDC2002S04, Yokohama, September. LDC. Linguistic Data Consortium (LDC).. ICSI, ISL and NIST Meeting Speech Coprora at LDC. http://www.ldc.upenn.edu catalog IDs LDC2004S02, LDC2004S05, LDC2004S09. 1994, 2004.

[10] Stolcke, "Modeling linguistic segment and turn boundaries for N- ... gration", in Proc. ICASSP, Orlando, FL, May 2002.

[11] Philip Koehn, Franz Josef Och, and Daniel Marcu. Statistical Phrase-Based Translation. In NAACL/HLT 2003.

Pattern Recognition using a Hybrid Model based on Genetic Algorithm and Neural Network

Satish Chandra[1] and D.S. Chauhan[2]
[1]Department of Computer Science & IT
[2]Department of Electronics & Comn.
Jaypee University of Information Technology, Waknaghat, Solan , HP, India
satish.chandra@juit.ac.in

Abstract

The use of genetic algorithms to design neural networks for brain-tumor pattern recognition is discussed. In many control applications, standard supervised learning techniques (such as back-propagation) cannot be used due to lack of training data. Reinforcement learning techniques, such as genetic algorithms, are a computationally-expensive but viable alternative if a simulator is available for the pattern recognition purposes. This paper briefly describes how Genetic Algorithm is used to learn the most appropriate inputs to a Multi Layer Neuranl Network (MLP).

Keywords: Neural Networks (NN), Pattern recognition, Digital Image Processing (DIP), Genetic Algorithm (GA), Magnetic resonance imaging(MRI)

1. Introduction

In recent years there has been increasing interest in the use of Neural Networks (NN) in the diagnosis of various types of cancers. It is found that a Neural Ensemble based Detection system gives not only a high rate of overall identification but also a low rate of false negative identification. The incidence of primary malignant brain tumours is already 8/100000 persons per year and is still increasing. In spite of aggressive conventional and advanced treatments, the prognosis remains uniformly fatal. The reason is not only the rapid tumour growth but especially the fact that, long before the neoplasm can be diagnosed; it has already grossly invaded the surrounding brain parenchyma, rendering surgical removal virtually ineffective [5]. Here we present a model based on Genetic Algorithms and Neural Network (NN) which can be used to identify the tumour pattern from MRI.

This paper discusses first, the basic image processing technique used for MRI, followed by a pattern recognition model based on Genetic Algorithms and Neural Network. Finally a brief report on the performance of model is given.

2. Image Preprocessing

Pattern recognition is the sequence of steps that must be performed after appropriate features have been detected. Classification is the most widely used strategy used for recognizing the objects based on its features. It is assumed that N features have been detected in images and these features have been normalized so that they can be represented in the same metric space[6]. As an MRI gives the finer details of brain tumors, we have taken the Brain Images obtained from the MRI as the input to the model being developed.

First of all, the MRI image obtained is processed to get a graph representation. This is necessary as it involves a reduction in the dimensionality of the input data. For example if we take a 256 x 256 image and we input each pixel to the ANN we would need 65537 adaptive weight for every unit in the first hidden layer. This implies that a very large training set would be needed to ensure that the weights are well determined. So, huge computation resources will be required making the ANN impractical. The technique used to overcome this problem is dimensionality reduction by pixel averaging and consequent feature extraction. Feature extraction can be viewed as a preprocessing step which removes distracting variance from a dataset, so that downstream classifiers or regression estimators perform better [7]. Preprocessing involves the techniques of smoothing, enhancement, and segmentation. It also involves removal of noise and elimination of unnecessary information.

3. Proposed model

Genetic Algorithm is used to select optimal inputs and also to find optimal weights for the neural network. The block diagram of the model used is given in Fig.1.

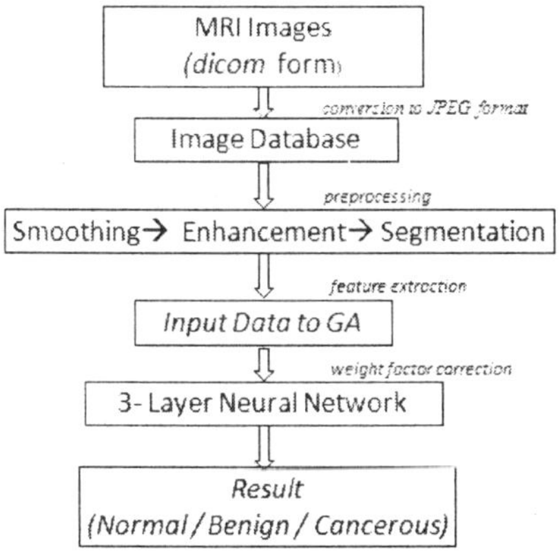

Fig. 1

3.1 Genetic Algorithm

A genetic algorithm is a stochastic based beam search in which successor states are generated by combining two parent states, rather by modifying a single state[1]. It takes its inspiration from natural selection and survival of the fittest in the biological world. GA differs from more traditional optimization techniques in that they involve a search from a "population" of solutions, not from a single point. Each iteration of a GA involves a competitive selection that weeds out poor solutions. The solutions with high "fitness" are "recombined" with other solutions by swapping parts of a solution with another. Solutions are also "mutated" by making a small change to a single element of the solution[2]. Recombination and mutation are used to generate new solutions that are biased towards regions of the space for which good solutions have already been seen. Pseudo-code for a genetic algorithm is as follows:

1. Initialize the population
2. Evaluate each chromosome of the initial population
3. Generate new chromosome of the mating current chromosomes, by performing Mutation and Crossover.
4. Remove numbers of population for new chromosomes.
5. Evaluate new population
6. Repeat through Step 3 until some convergence criteria is satisfied (stopping criteria)

The block diagram of GA is given in Fig.2

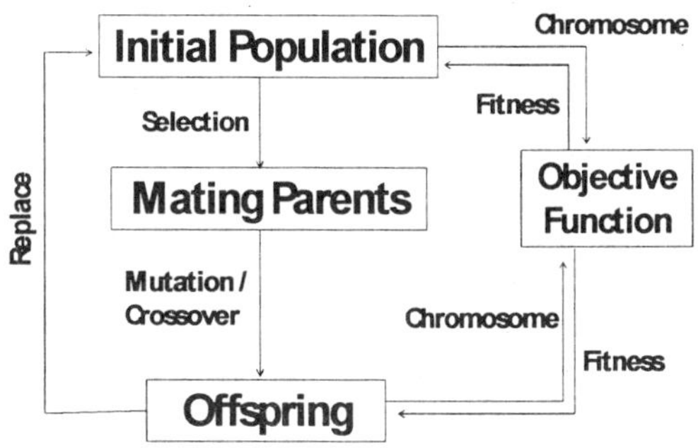

Fig. 2

3.2 Neural Network Design

A neural network (NN) is an interconnected group of artificial neurons that uses a mathematical or computational model for information processing based on a connectionist approach to computation. In most cases a NN is an adaptive system that changes its structure based on external or internal information that flows through the network. In a NN model simple nodes, which can be called "neurons" or "Processing Elements" (PE) are connected together to form a network of nodes.

Most NN algorithms are designed to alter the strength (weights) of the connections in the network to produce a desired signal flow. NNs have been applied successfully in many medical images interpretation problems where there input layer presented the relevant descriptions of the various healthy or suspected areas of the image (which present anomalies), and its output layer gives a decision on the nature of those areas (benign or malign tumors)[4].

Neural Networks fall in this category. The non-interpretability aspect of NN layers makes the design of this NN a difficult and non evident task. This fact could degrade the NN capacities of generalization and prevents any attempt at modeling the knowledge previously acquired by an expert human (doctor) [4]. A block diagram of the NN used in the proposed model is shown in the Fig.3.

The three layer NN proposed here is capable of producing a decision function with enough hidden units. Sigmoid function is used as the transfer function. The NN uses the best chromosome obtained from the GA as the initial weight vector. It consists of following steps:

1. Create weight vector from the most suitable chromosome obtained from GA.
2. Compute output of the feed-forward NN.
3. Compute Error between desired output and actual output.
4. Update weight using back-propagation

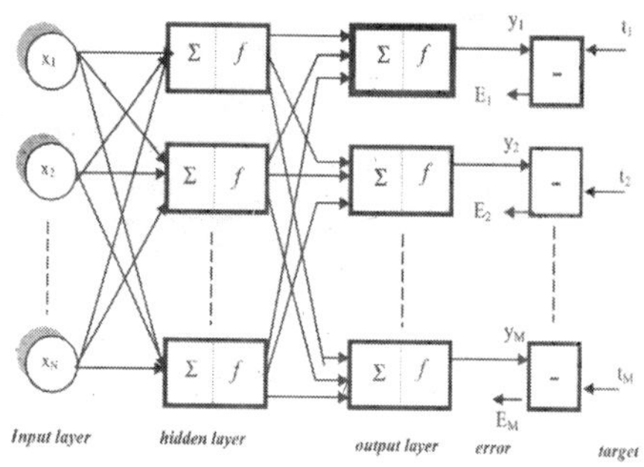

Fig. 3

4. Implementation

Images of size 80 X 80 pixels were used to train the NNs. These images represent the smallest sized images of brain tumor. The number of hidden nodes and input coding are predefined. Fig. 4 shows some of the images used to train the NN.

Failure Rate (FR) is computed as

$FR = (N_T - N_C) / N_T X 100$

Where N_T = Total number of tested images

N_C = Number of cancerous images

Phase 1: Training

Image size = 80X80 pixels

Number of Images = 20

Number of Hidden nodes = 60

Phase 2: Testing

Population size = 15

Chromosome length=6400

Number of Iteration = 300

Accuracy required =80%

5. Test Results

After 16 generations the GA met the stopping criteria. The error after 220 iterations is of the order 0.006 and the algorithm achieves the desired accuracy. Fig.5 shows the performance of the algorithm for the test data. As the required accuracy was increased, the number of iterations also grew.

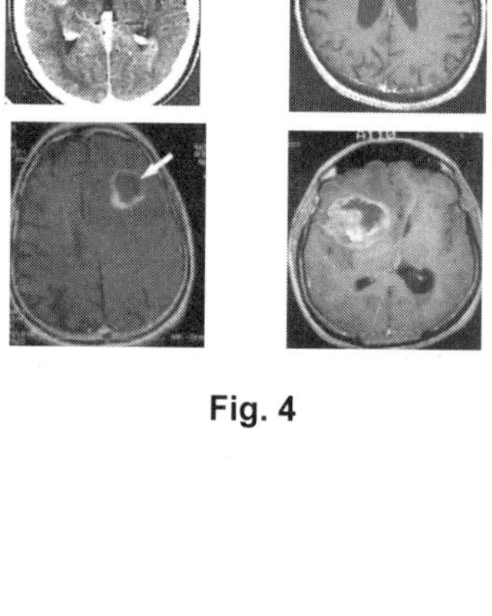

Fig. 4

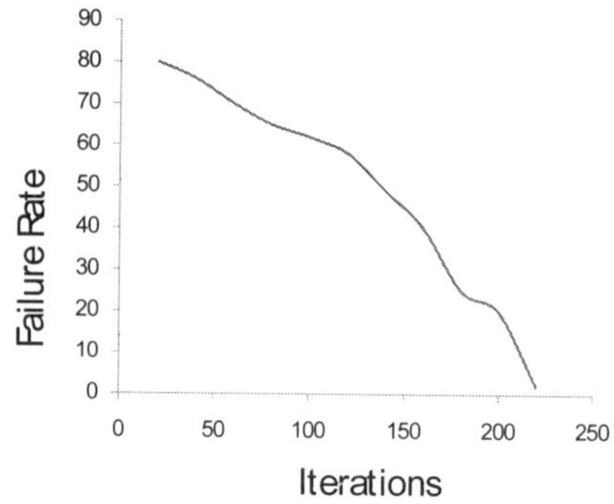

Fig. 5

6. Conclusion

The hybrid of GA and NN is capable of recognizing the tumor pattern present in brain. The results of NN learning are sensitive to the initial weights. GA is used to find a good starting weight vector for input to the NN. The GA adversely affects the computation time but the same is compensated in the NN. This technique can be used to detect anomalies present in the brain, which cannot be detected by naked eyes. When genetic algorithms are used to train multilayer networks they may exhibit poor convergence due to a fundamental problem called the structural/functional mapping problem [8]. This problem arises, regardless of whether a binary encoding or a real-valued encoding is used, because genetic algorithms operate on a population of solution strings and at any given generation it is possible to have multiple representations of functionally equivalent networks within the population. So, methods must be devised to overcome this problem.

The overall efficiency and accuracy depends, of course, on many factors such as resolution of images, number of hidden nodes etc.

7. References

[1] S. Russel ,P.Norwig , Artificial Intelligence – a modern approach, Prentice Hall of India 2006, 116-117

[2] D.E.Goldberg, Genetic algorithms in search, Optimazation and Machine Learning, Addision-Wesley Pub. Comp. Inc., Reading, MA, 1992

[3] R.C.Gonzalez , R.E. Woods ,Digital Image Processing, Pearson Education

[4] N.Benamrane, A. Aribi, L.Kraoula, Fuzzy Neural Networks and Genetic Algorithms for Medical Images Interpretation ,Vision and Medical Imagery group, SIMPA Laboratory, Oran, Algeria

[5] A.R.Kansal, S.Torquato, G.R.Harshiva, T.S.Deisboeckeb , Simulated Brain Tumour Growth Dynamics Using a 3-D Cellular Automata.

[6] S. Levialdi, V. Cantoni, V. Roberto, Artificial Intelligence Visionm: Image Description, Recognition and Communication, Academic Press, 1996

[7] Christopher J.C. Burges, Geometric Methods for Feature Extraction and Dimensionality Reduction

[8] Whitley, D., & Hanson, T. "Optimizing Neural Networks Using Faster, More Accurate Genetic Search", Proc. of the 3rd Int. Conf. on Genetic Algorithm, Morgan
Kauffman, pp 391-396, 1089

Voice Biometrics: An Identification Engine for Information Security

Safia Yasmeen and Jameela Bano
Assistant Professors, Muffakham Jah College of Engineering and Technology (Osmania University)
Road # 3, Banjara Hills, Hyderabad
safia.yasmeen@gmail.com *jameela7862002@yahoo.co.in*

Abstract

Authentication plays a very critical role in security-related applications like E-commerce. There are a number of methods and techniques for accomplishing this key process. In this regard, biometrics is gaining increasing attention these days. Security systems, having realized the value of biometrics, use biometrics for two basic purposes: to verify or identify users. There are number of biometrics and different applications need different biometrics.

This paper presents the different methods of biometrics based on the user verification for e-commerce. In this paper we present some biometrics-based methods for authenticating a user. Since there are as such many biometrics techniques having there advantages as well as disadvantages. we will further emphasize the indispensable mechanism for establishing one such system based on Voice Biometrics and then enlighten how this approach can be used for providing a non-permeable environment for e-Commerce activities.

Key words: *MFCC: Mel frequency Cepstral coefficients. FFT/DCT: Fourier Transform or the Discrete Cosine Transform.*

1. Introduction

In today's time virtually all the business activities are being done online (E-commerce). In the present era of information technology all the business activities are being done online. E-commerce has become an progressively important. As it refers to the communication over the computer mediated network which involves the transfer of right or ownership to service. There are seven unique features of E-commerce like global reach, universal standards, Ubiquity, richness, interactivity, information density and personalization/customization. [1]. E-Commerce has made access to information easier and faster but this easiness comes with an overhead of maintaining security because information can be modified or deleted by unauthorized access. In every major function of society, information security is becoming increasingly important. Information systems require a method to launch the credentials that define a user's identity. Today, the greater part of information systems use passwords as certificate to authenticate the user's identity. The major problem with this type of identification mechanism is that given a password can we confirm that it belongs to the person who presents it. Many passwords based, online signature based and token based (Smart Card) commonly referred to as access cards based identification and verification systems [2] have been proposed and implemented but such kind of systems do no provide a high degree of security and user convenience. To provide secure information operating environments, a faithful authentication system must be developed to prevent illicit users from gaining access to secret or sensitive data. A strong authentication can be gained by combining different verification features. This is especially important when legally signing a user into a secure system and allowing access to secure or sensitive data. Therefore there should be a system of preventing unauthorized access to the resources by having reliable means of user or client verification.

Let us consider a typical scenario in which a user has three saving bank accounts, one demit account, three credit cards with different banks and he also has web accounts for E-banking, reserving railway tickets, air tickets, hotel reservations, E-billings etc. In a typical E-verification scenario for accessing each of these accounts user is given a unique username and password or in some cases may be given an access card like an ATM card, Member ship card and he is required to provide his Network ID, a valid combination of a username and password to the authentication server, each time he wants to access each of these services, thus a user is required to remember multiple usernames and passwords, which is highly tiresome. If he chooses to keep same network ID's for all these accounts then with one correct hacking effort, all of his assets are uncovered. Moreover, passwords can be easily guessed, access cards can be stolen and online signatures can be forged. Thus, new methods of user verification and identification are required which will provide a high degree of safety and security measures and even higher degree of user convenience for carrying out online transactions. Protection of information resources must involve a process that unambiguously identifies and authenticates users. Some unique, unchangeable aspect of the user must be used to verify his or her identity namely a biometric. A simple solution is to use some unique physical attribute of a person for user authentication, such as biometrics. Biometric technology is one area that no segment of the IT industry can afford to ignore. Biometrics provides security benefits across the spectrum, from IT vendors to end users, and from security system developers to security system users. Here we discuss a number of critical applications that are in need of biometrics. For decades, many highly secure environments have used biometric technology for entry access.

2. Biometrics

Biometric is the most secure and convenient authentication tool. It can not be borrowed, stolen, or forgotten and forging one is practically impossible. Biometrics measure individual's unique physical or behavioral characteristics to recognize or authenticate their identity. Common physical biometrics includes fingerprints, hand or palm geometry, retina, iris, and facial characteristics. Behavioral characters characteristics include signature, voice, keystroke pattern, and gait. Of this class of biometrics, technologies for signature and voice are the most developed. Biometrics can be defined as

"Biometric identifying an individual based on his or her distinguishing Physiological and/or behavioral characteristics called a biometric identifier "[7].

It tries to associate/disassociate an individual with previously determined identity or features. Because many physiological or behavioral characteristics are distinctive to each person called one-to-one mapping, biometric identifiers are inherently more reliable and more competent than knowledge-based and token-based techniques in differentiating between an authorized person and a fraudulent impostor. Common physiological biometrics includes fingerprints, hand geometry, iris and retina, DNA and vein, and facial images, while common behavioral biometrics includes signature, voice recordings and keystroke rhythms, any one of these biometric measurements is sufficient to positively identify an authorized person from among hundreds of others. These features are extracted by using appropriate recording devices, are processed and then stored as an identification template for the user. Some enabling biometric technologies include:

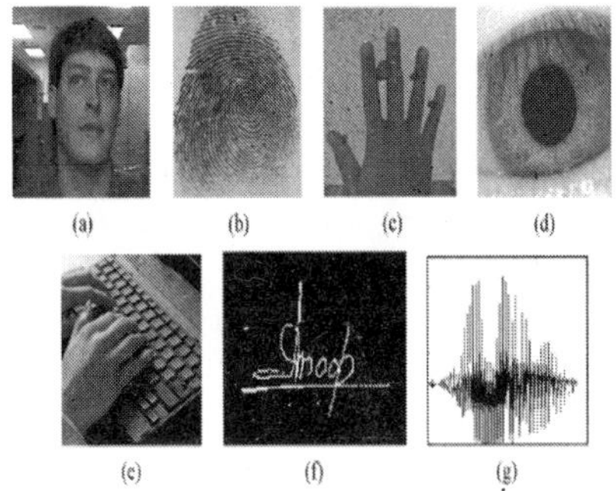

Examples of biometric characteristics: (a) face, (b) fingerprint, (c) hand geometry, (d) iris, (e) keystroke, (f) signature, and (g) voice.

Fig. 1 Examples of Biometric Characteristics [17]

2.1 Fingerprinting

One of the oldest ways to verify a person's identity is fingerprinting. With Fingerprinting a user gently places fingers against a small reader device. Characteristics such as whorls, arches, and loops are recorded along with the patterns of ridges, furrows, and minutiae. Depending on the security level in the organization [8]. There are a variety of approaches to fingerprint verification, such as traditional police method, using pattern-matching devices, and things like moiré fringe patterns and ultrasonic's. This seems to be a very good choice for in-house systems.

2.2 Hand Geometry

A biometric modality that uses the physical structure of an individual's hand for recognition purposes. This involves analyzing and measuring the shape of the hand. It might be suitable where there are more users or where user accesses the system infrequently. Accuracy can be very high if desired and flexible performance tuning and configuration can accommodate a wide range of applications. Organizations are using hand geometry readers in various scenarios, including time and attendance recording.

2.3 Iris and Retina based recognition

Human eyes are very unique and hard to fake and based on these two methods are used: Retinal scanning analyzes the layer of blood vessels at the back of the eye. Retina is scanned using a low-intensity light source and an optical coupler. A person is required to look closely in the device and focus on a green light while scanning is performed. The whole process takes about 10-15 seconds. Since there is no known way to reproduce or fake a retina, no additional attempt is made to check false acceptance. Another method of eye recognition is Iris- scan of more than 200 points in the highlighted tissue surrounding the pupil. In this case user can be either close to the video camera or some distance away, depending on the device. The verification is done in less than 5 seconds and the process involves focusing a beam of light on the eye to watch for pupil dilation. This is to prevent users from fooling the system. Both methods do not necessitate users to take out glasses and are not at all harmful to eyes

2.4 Vein Biometric

Face or hand vein thickness and their locations are considered being unique enough to make out a person. An infrared scan from a curved reader device performs a vascular scanning process and then compares it to the database records to find a match. A user places a hand on the metal plate with guides on it to take more than 90 measurements of the length, width, thickness and surface of the hand and a number of fingers with hand geometry scan. It is a simple, fast and accurate procedure, but unable to tell the difference between a living and a fake or a dead hand, if pressure is properly applied. Unfortunately, human hand geometry is not unique, although if a way will be developed to combine hand geometry with any other method, the authentication process can be successfully used.

2.5 Face Recognition.

Digital cameras are used to capture the images and then the captured image is matched to the image/picture stored in a database where critical attributes such as the overall facial structure, distances between eyes, nose, mouth, and jaw edges are matched for comparison. A user usually stands within some distance from the camera and is required to perform some human facial movement, like smiling. This is to enable the system to identify a mould or fake face. In this method the decision is typically made in less than 5 seconds.

2.6 Signature verification

People have used signature for centuries to authenticate paper documents. Signature verification systems usually include a special pen and tablets. The verification can be accomplished by analyzing characteristics such as position, speed, velocity, and pressure of pen strokes [2]. Two approaches utilized in this field are static and dynamic signature verification. The static approach only analyzes the geometric features (shape) of a signature, while the dynamic approach analyzes both static and dynamic features such as speed, velocity etc. Each person has a unique style of signature and no two signatures of a person are the same. Despite the variations in an individual's signature, there have been relatively few successful signature-based applications to date in comparison with other biometric methodologies.

2.7 Voice recognition

It is a process of validating speech (some phrase spoken by user) through the microphone. The entire process takes 5 to 10 seconds authentication requires a user to reproduce low and high sound frequencies.

2.8 Vascular Pattern

Vascular pattern technology is very similar to Retinal Scan technology in that it uses infrared light to produce an image of the vein pattern in the face, in the back of a hand, or on the wrist. Vascular pattern technology is generally acceptable to users except that some users still object to any biometric method that uses infrared.

Biometric is an enabling technology that can make our society safer, reduce frauds and lead to user convenience. For a particular biometric to be acceptable it should adhere to following requirements:

Accuracy and Performance: It should offer a correct decision by providing positive identification, it verifies the input biometric sample based on the claimed enrolled identity of a particular user and the result is either accept or reject based on a single match just like network logins and any e-commerce activity carried out using our credit cards.

Security: A good biometric system should not expose the data or accept fraud data. This can be achieved by either using aliveness detection [5] or by making use of multi-model use of biometric [4].

Privacy: It should provide an irrefutable proof of identity of a person.

Acceptance: The extent people are willing to accept for a particular biometric in their daily lives.

This is probably the most critical issue concerned with the use of biometrics The proposed system uses voice biometrics for providing user authentication.

3. Voice Biometrics

One of the most natural biometric technology that is being used after fingerprinting is the voice biometrics,. As every human being is blessed with the voice which is unique and distinct from one another. The voice characteristics of human speech are determined by

speech pattern, which is unique for each individual [15]. These speech patterns are formed by a combination of both behavioral and physiological factors. Voice recognition systems are either text-dependent or text-independent, depending on whether specific worlds must be spoken in a fixed order or not.
A voice template needs 2K to 8K of memory storage varied from different applications. Generally, people are willing to accept voice-based biometric systems. However, poor quality and ambient noise, as well as the emotional and physical state of the speaker can affect the accuracy of voice recognition. The words we speak are broken down into individual components called phonemes and each phoneme is delivered with some pitch, tempo and inflection. These three aspects of voice give each of us our unique sound. For using voice as a biometric parameter, we need to capture voice sample through a microphone attached to a computer, a microphone of good quality is capable of noise reduction as well and thus it provides better voice components being extracted, after capturing the voice and the components captured are then converted into digital signals and these signals are transmitted to the destination (e-commerce server) using Voice Over Internet Protocol (VOIP)[7] where authentication is done using authentication technique. Reference template (voice sample with a sample ID), also called reference voiceprint, of every user is taken and stored at the server. During the user identification phase as shown in figure 2 input speech is compared against all the templates and a match is made to find the appropriate sample ID, this can be used for providing a user with a new user ID if he forgets his existing User ID as in case of forgotten user names and passwords in network ID based systems.

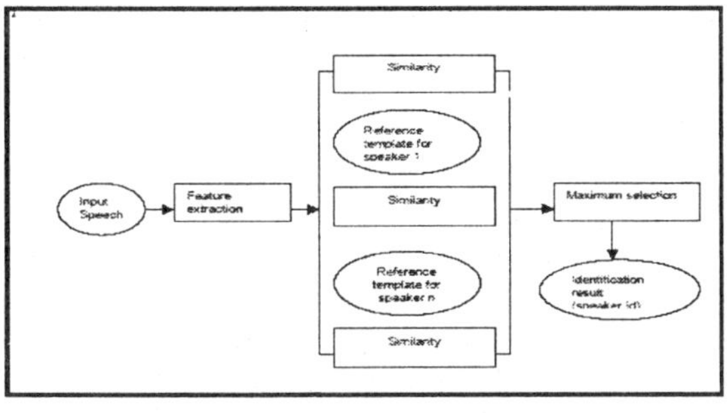

Fig. 2 Speaker Identification Model [18]

In verification phase as shown in Fig. 3 features are extracted from the sample and it is compared against the template of the user and if the result is equal or more than the threshold value then the users claim is accepted otherwise it is rejected.

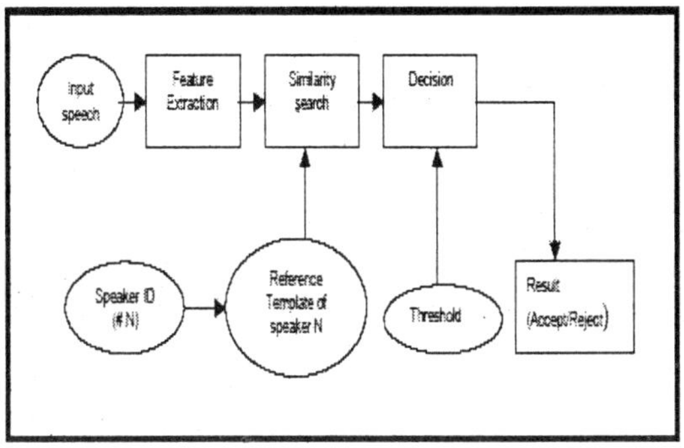

Fig. 3 Speaker Verification Model [18]

3.1 Text-independent

It accepts any spoken input, making it possible to design non-porous verification applications that examine the ongoing speech of an individual. The ability of text independent technology to operate unobtrusively and in the background makes it attractive for customer related applications, because customers need not pause for a security check before moving on to their primary business objective. Text independent technology is most secure but it is more difficult to implement than text-dependent or text prompted technology because it requires longer samples of speech and is more sensitive to the acoustic quality of the input [9] This approach is most suitable for biometric applications for providing network security for ecommerce applications.

3.2 Text-dependents

Here user is required to log-on to the system using his login ID and then he is asked to speak out his password into the microphone if it is correct, user is authenticated. Text-dependent systems provide "strong authentication [7].

3.3 Text-dependent with speech recognition

User is only required to speak out his login Id in the microphone and Speech recognition decodes the input, and speaker verification uses the same input as the biometric sample it compares to the reference voiceprint.

3.4 Text Prompted

It is challenge-response kind of system, Text-prompted systems ask the speaker to repeat a series of randomly selected digit strings, word sequences, or phrases. Text prompting requires longer enrollment than text-dependent technology. The proposed system uses text-independent verification because it offers a high degree of protection and security.

4. Speaker verification and identification

A speaker verification system is composed of two distinct phases, a training phase and a test phase. Each of them can be seen as a succession of independent modules. The first step consists in extracting parameters from the speech signal to obtain a representation suitable for statistical modeling as such models are extensively used in most state-of-the-art speaker verification systems. The second step consists in obtaining a statistical model from the parameters. A speaker identification system gets a test utterance as input. The task of the system is to find out which of the training speakers made the test utterance. So, the output of the system is the name of the training speaker, or possibly a rejection if an unknown person has made the utterance. For verification of an utterance, the input is the speech signal to be verified against the name of the speaker whom it is identified as. The expected result is a either accept or reject decision, the acceptance of the test utterance if it does originate from the proclaimed speaker, or a rejection [9].

4.1 Feature extraction

Here the objective is to reduce the amount of data available as sample to information which is essentially required. Mel frequency cepstral coefficients (MFCC) are used for feature extraction

MFCC: These are coefficients that represent audio, based on perception. It is derived from the Fourier Transform or the Discrete Cosine Transform of the audio clip. The basic difference between the FFT/DCT and the MFCC frequency bands are positioned logarithmically on the Mel scale which approximates the human auditory system's response more closely than the linearly spaced frequency bands of FFT or DCT. Experiments show that the parameterization of the MFCC coefficients, which is best for discriminating speakers is different from the one usually, used for speech recognition applications. For example, speaker recognition error rates might be reduced if the "standard" MFCC feature dimension for speech recognition is increased. Feature recognition process cuts the digitized audio signal, which is the sequence of sample values, into overlapping windows of equal length. The cut-out portions of the signal are called "frames", they are extracted out of the original signal every 10 or 20 ms The length of a frame is about 30 ms For speaker recognition tasks, sometimes longer frames are used in comparison to the feature extraction method used for speech recognition in order to increase spectral resolution. Each frame in the time domain is transformed to a MFCC vector called feature vectors; each vector represents cepstral properties of the signal within the corresponding window.

4.2 Vector quantization

Vector quantization is a speaker modeling technique used for coding the feature vector extracted from MFCC. For recognition systems it is important to be able to estimate probability distributions of the computed feature vectors. Because these distributions are defined over a high-dimensional space, it is often easier to start by quantizing each feature vector to one of a relatively small number of template vectors, which together comprise what is called a codebook. A typical codebook would contain about 256 or 512 template vectors. Estimating probability distributions over this finite set of templates then becomes a much simpler task. The process of quantizing a feature vector into a finite number of template vectors is known as vector quantization. The process takes a feature vector as input and finds the template vector in the codebook that is closest in distance. The identity of that template is then used in the recognition system. [10]. in the training phase, reference templates are generated and verification thresholds are computed for each phonetic category. In the verification phase, after the phonetic categorization, a comparison with the reference template for each particular category provides verification score for that category [11] The final verification score is a weighted linear combination of the scores from each category.

5. Voice Biometric: User's viewpoint

Technology acceptance and its use is an issue that has received the attention of researchers and practitioners for many decades, successful investment in technology can lead to enhanced productivity of the system, while failed system can lead to undesirable consequences [12]. For successful deployment of any technology it is crucial to do a feasibility study in advance. Technology Acceptance Model [13], best explains how a user reacts to a particular technology. Technology Acceptance Model proposes that factors like perceived usefulness, perceived ease-of-use, perceived strength of control are critical antecedents to technology acceptance decision [13]. We will refer to this model to explain why voice biometric is good candidate for possible integration to E-commerce systems.

- *Perceived Usefulness*: It is the extent to which a person believes that using a particular system would enhance his job performance [13], it is directly proportional to increase in the use of a particular technology (E-commerce is our case). Biometric based methods as already discussed are more efficient and more reliable as compared to existing system based on Network ID's, PKI and digital signatures.

- *Perceived ease-of-use*: The degree to which a person feels that using a system would be free from efforts [13], again an important parameter in acceptance of a particular system. Voice biometric requires a single sign-on parameter (voice print of the user) for authentication and this is something user inherently posses, he just need to utter few words in the microphone attached to his PC and soon he is logged into the network, if he is an authentic user, it is definitely better then any of the previously implemented user verification methods like Network ID's, Access Cards plus PIN, Digital Signatures etc., where user is required to remember passwords, PIN's and keys respectively.
- *Perceived Strength of Control*: Users perception about the security that a system offers, is a major factor that leads to acceptance of a particular system. Biometrics-based technologies are applied most often in security, monitoring, and fraud prevention where they positively identify individuals and distinguish one person from another. This characteristic differentiates biometrics from all other forms of automated security. An access card system can, at most, determine only whether a person has a viable access card, and password can determine only whether the person knows the proper password. None of them verify that the person presenting the card or entering the password is the individual authorized to do so. Biometric systems determine whether a biometric sample, such as a fingerprint or voiceprint such as spoken password, comes from a specific individual by comparing that sample with a reference biometric.
- *Feasibility*: Another factor that plays a vital role in the acceptance of any technology is its feasibility in terms of availability of resources and economy for implementation of a particular system. E-commerce is basically defined as an act of carrying out online transactions with a PC. A higher percentage of E-commerce users make use of PC for online transaction and a small percentage of users use mobile devices for doing so (M-Commerce). Unlike any other biometric based technology like fingerprint based verification, users are required to either purchase new devices enabled with fingerprint reader modules like PDA's or to integrate a finger print reader, drivers and backend fingerprint handling algorithms with the existing PC. It turns out to be much more expensive than using voice biometric wherein the recording device for collecting the voiceprint of the user is just a microphone, which most of home PC users already have [Table 1].

Table 1 Comparison of technologies with reference to TAM.

Factors → / Biometric identifier ↓	Perceived usefulness	Perceived Ease of use	Perceived Strength	Feasibility
Network ID's	M	L	L	H
Access cards	M	M	L	M
Signature	L	M	L	M
Face	M	L	M	L
Iris	H	L	H	L
Finger	H	M	H	L
Voice	H	H	M	H

As shown in table 1, [17] voice biometric emerges as the best candidate for possible integration as a user verification tool for E-commerce provided it provides a high degree of security and strength of control. Fingerprint biometric, has been in market for quite sometime and it has already been integrated into smart cards and PDA's, the scope of usage of fingerprint technology is limited to its use in an access card or carrying out transactions using PDA's or computers which have inbuilt fingerprint reading modules. Whereas most of the E-commerce activities are carried out by users using their home or office PC's thus any new technology that we want to incorporate to enhance the performance of the system should be integral with the existing system without incurring much effort and expenditure.

5. A Case study - Voice Biometrics

Two major components of voice biometric based user verification system are Instruction phase and Verification phase During Instruction phase (figure 3(a)), input speech is provided for feature extraction for enrollment and a voiceprint (template) is obtained and it is identified with a sample ID within the sample store. Each user ID maps to one sample ID. During Instruction phase (Fig. 3(b)), user provides his User ID and speech model to the system, from the sample store; voiceprint of the concerned user is obtained for comparison against speech and the template in store.

one-to-one mapping of sample is provided for verification and a keep count is generated by counter which is normalize by taking into account consideration of various parameters like background noise, loudness, strength, and pitch verification etc. If the obtained normalized count is above a threshold level which is set by the system, user is acknowledged otherwise he is discarded.

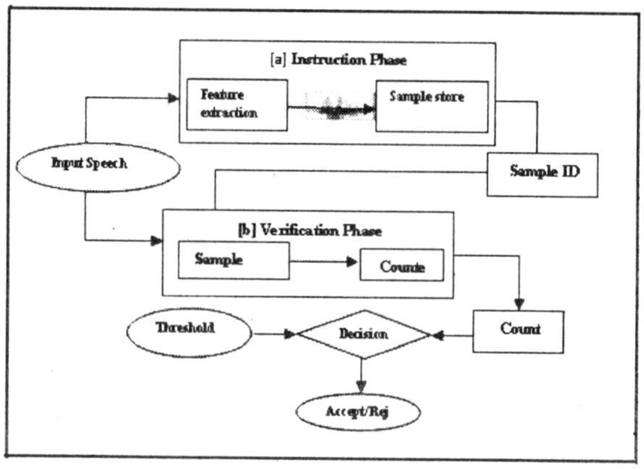

Fig. 4 User verification system

While any biometric authentication returns a probability based measurement a physical trait Authentify has honed the use of voice biometrics to provide a robust authentication tool that strap up the inherent advantages of voice biometrics such as ease of use, reliability, feasibility and information delivery capabilities

6. Conclusion

Users are turning towards the various biometric systems to improve there information security. As all the biometric solutions are capable enough for coping up with the problem of security in E commerce.

In this paper we have tried to look at the biometrics and its types and on the wider perspective of voice biometrics and its exercise to enforce security of information in E-commerce. With the progress E-commerce and network technology, the technology of user authentication must be improved to secure sensitive information high levels of security technologies are required in our anxious world. This main aim of this paper is to study the basic concepts of biometric technologies to highlight different techniques and authentication benefits using human voice as a tool so as to enhance future requirements to establish identity and reinforce security.

7. References

[1] Laudon. C, Traver. C, *E-commerce: Business, Technology, Society,* Second Edition, Addison Wesley,2003,ISBN:0321-10056

[2] J Yi, C Lee and J. Kim, "*Online signature verification using temporal shift estimated by phase shift gabor filter*", in IEEE Trans. On Signal Processing Vol. 53 pp, 776-783 , Feb. 2005.

[3] Irvind S. Ghai "*VOIP enabled e-commerce* ", Internet telephony, The Top 10 trends in VOIP, May 2003.

[4] A.K. Jain and A. Ross , "*Multibiometrics systems*" Communications of The ACM, special issue on Multimodal Interfaces, Vol 47,No 1,pp 34-40, Jan 2004.

[5] R, Derakuchani et al,"*Determination of Vitality from A non-invasive Biomedical Measurement for use of fingerprint Scanners*", Pattern recognition, No 12, pp 383-396,2003.

[6] Furui, S . "*Recent Advances in Speaker Recognition"*. Pattern recognition letters 18(1997) 859 –872.

[7] Jain, A.K. Bolle, R. and Pankanti S. (eds.). *Biometrics: Personal Identification in Networked Society.* Kluwer, New York, 1999.

[8] Jain, A.K., Prabhakar, S., and Pankanti, S. "*On the similarity of identical twin fingerprints*", Pattern Recog. 35 (2002), 2653–2663.

[9] Markowitz, J. Ieri, Oggi, domani: "*Speaker recognition yesterday, today, and tomorrow*". In Proceedings of COST250 Workshop on Speaker Recognition in Telephony (Rome, Italy, Nov. 10). European Co-operation in the Field of Scientific and Technical Research, 1999.

[10] J. Makhoul, S. Roucos, and H. Gish. "*Vector quantization in speech coding*". Proceedings of the IEEE, 73(11): 1551--1588, November 1985.

[11] D. A. Reynolds, "*Speaker identification and verification using Gaussian mixture speaker models,*" Speech Communication, vol. 17, no. 1-2, pp. 91–108, 1995.

[12] Gupta M.P, Kumar P. and Bhattacharya J.(2004) , "*Government Online: Opportunity and challenges*", TMH , New Delhi.

[13] Davis, F.D (1989),"*Perceived Usefulness, Perceived Ease of Use, and User Acceptance of Information Technology*", MIS Quarterly, Vol. 13, No 3, pp 318-340

[14] A Performance Evaluation of Biometric Identification Devices, J. Holmes, L. Wright, R. Maxwell (Sandia National Laboratories, SAND91-0278/UC-906, June 1997).

[15] Daugman, J. G. (1993) High confidence visual recognition of persons by a test of statistical independence. *IEEE Trans. Pattern Anal. and Mach. Intell.*, 15, 1148-116.

[16] Jain, A. K., Hong, L., and Pankanti, S. Biometrics: promising frontiers for emerging identification market. (Online) Connecticut Department of Social Services.http://www.cse.msu.edu/cgi-ser/web/tech/document?ID=436 (Feb.2000)

[17] Anil K. . Jain, Arun Ross,Sharath Pankanti," Biometrics: a tool for Information security", IEEE transactions on Information Forensics and security,Vol 1,No 2,June 2006

[18] Simon Liu and Mark Silverman," A Practical Guide to Biometric Security Technology", Security,IT Pro, IEEE, January | February 2001

[19] Human interface laboratories, Japan.

Development of a Procedure for the Automatic Recognition of Disfluencies in the Speech of People Who Stutter

K.M Ravikumar[1], Sachin Kudva[2], Dr.R.Rajagopal[3] and Dr.H.C.Nagaraj[4]
[1] Asst.Professor, Dept. of ECE. Ghousia college of Engg.,Ramanagara,
[2]Embedded Software Engg., Toshiba Embedded Systems, Bangalore,
[3]CTO, L&T, Bangalore,
[4]Principal, NMIT, Bangalore
kmravikumar@rediffmail.com sachinkudva@gmail.com rrcrl@yahoo.co.in principal@nmit.co.in

Abstract

Automatic Recognition of disfluencies is an important task to identify the severity of stuttering. The approach is to develop an automatic speech recognition (ASR) system which provides the transcription of the uttered sentences. The existing method which uses artificial neural network (ANN) requires high levels of agreement as prerequisite before attempting to train and test ANNs to separate fluent and nonfluent. In the present work the designed system is able to give the output in terms of uttered phonemes, the recognition of disfluencies is made as easy as recognition of repetition of group of phonemes as a repetition disfluency (R) and repetition of single phonemes as a prolongation disfluency (P). Hidden Markov Models(HMM's) were used for recognition of the different phonemes. Out of 80 files 55 were used for training and 25 for testing. Recognition results were 100 % with given training data and 80.78% for testing data.
Keywords: *ASR, HMM, phoneme, prolongation, repetition, Stuttering.*

1. Introduction

1.1 Stuttering

Stuttering, also known as stammering in the United Kingdom is a speech disorder. The type of disfluencies that employed are: 1.interjections (extraneous sounds and words such as "uh" and "well"); 2.revisions(the change in content or grammatical structure of a phrase or pronunciation of a word as in " there was a young dog , no , a young rat named Arthur"); 3.incomplete phrases (the content not completed); 4.phrase–repetitions; 5.word-repetitions; 6.part-word-repetitions; 7.prolonged sounds(sounds judged to be unduly prolonged); 8.broken words(words not completely pronounced)[10].

Conventional way of making stuttering assessments are to count the occurrence of these types of disfluencies and express them either as the number of disfluent words as a proportion of all words in a passage or measure the time the disfluencies take compared with the duration of the entire passage. The main difficulty in making such counts are that 1.they are time consuming to make and 2. there are poor agreements when different judges make counts on the same material[1]

The following area of research concerns finding automatically, the extent of stuttering in the person, thus making the work of the speech-language pathologist easier. This is done using ASR systems. HMM based ASR systems have been used here for the study.

1.2 HMM Based ASR Systems

Speech recognition field is one of the most challenging fields that have faced the researchers from a long time. The enormous applications using speech recognizers are still waiting for the one which are free from the constraints of speakers, vocabularies and environment. This task is not an easy one due to the interdisciplinary nature of the problem and as it requires speech perception to be implied in the recognizer, thus making them speech understanding. There exist different techniques of recognizers with different claims of success by their researchers. However, the sole technique that gains the acceptance of the researchers to be the state of the art is Hidden Markov Model (HMM) technique[8]. It is agreed to be the most promising one. It might be used successfully with other techniques to improve the performance, but the results and the potential of this algorithm is reliable. The systems based on HMM mainly develop a Gaussian model for every unit of speech which can be phonemes, syllables etc. During recognition, pattern matching algorithms such as Dynamic Time Warping (DTW) are used with these models as reference[2,4].

1.3 Phonemes

In human language, a phoneme is the smallest structural unit that distinguishes meaning. Phonemes are not the physical segments themselves, but, in theoretical terms, cognitive abstractions or categorizations of them. An example of a phoneme is the /t/ sound in the words tip, stand, water, and cat. These instances of /t/ are considered to be the same sound despite the fact that in each word they are pronounced somewhat differently. The difference may not even be audible to native speakers. That is, a phoneme may encompass several recognizably different speech sounds, called phones. In our example, the /t/ in tip is aspirated, [t^h], while the /t/ in stand is not, [t]. In the English language there exist about 44 distinguishable standard phonemes[7]. The ASR system we have used recognizes speech at the phoneme level, which means that a Gaussian model is built for each phoneme individually. The output of the system is thus obtained as a phoneme level transcription, which we process and conclude if stuttering has occurred or not.

A standard HTK based ASR developing software, HTK or HMM toolkit is used. The transcription is processed using C++ which outputs the result

1.4 The Fundamentals of HTK & Speech Recognition

HTK is a toolkit for building Hidden Markov Models (HMMs). HMMs can be used to model any time series and the core of HTK is similarly general-purpose. However, HTK is primarily designed for building HMM-based speech processing tools, in particular recognizers. Thus, much of the infrastructure support in HTK is dedicated to this task. As shown in the Fig. 1, there are two major processing stages involved. Firstly, the HTK training tools are used to estimate the parameters of a set of HMMs using training utterances and their associated transcriptions. Secondly, unknown utterances are transcribed using the HTK recognition tools.

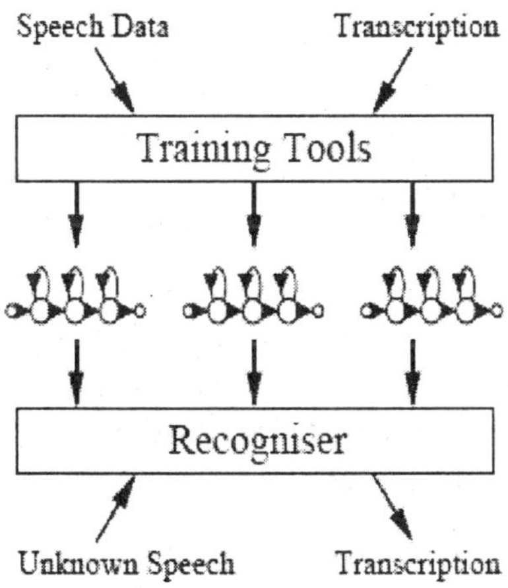

Fig. 1 HTK Fundamentals

Let each spoken word be represented by a sequence of speech vectors or observations O, defined as

$$O = o_1, o_2, \ldots\ldots o_T$$

where o_T is the speech vector observed at time t. The isolated word recognition problem can then be regarded as that of computing

$$\arg\max_i \{p(\omega_i \mid o)\}$$

where ω_i is the ith vocabulary word. This probability is not computable directly but using Bayes' Rule gives

$$p(\omega_{ij} o) = \frac{p(o \mid \omega_i) p(\omega_i)}{p(o)}$$

Thus, for a given set of prior probabilities $p(\omega_i)$, the most probable spoken word depends only on the likelihood $p(o \mid \omega_i)$. Given the dimensionality of the observation sequence O, the direct estimation of the joint conditional probability $p(o_{1,} o_2, \cdots \mid \omega_i)$ from examples of spoken words is not practicable. However, if a parametric model of word production such as a Markov model is assumed, then estimation from data is possible since the problem of estimating the class conditional observation densities $p(o \mid \omega_i)$ is replaced by the much simpler problem of estimating the Markov model parameters.

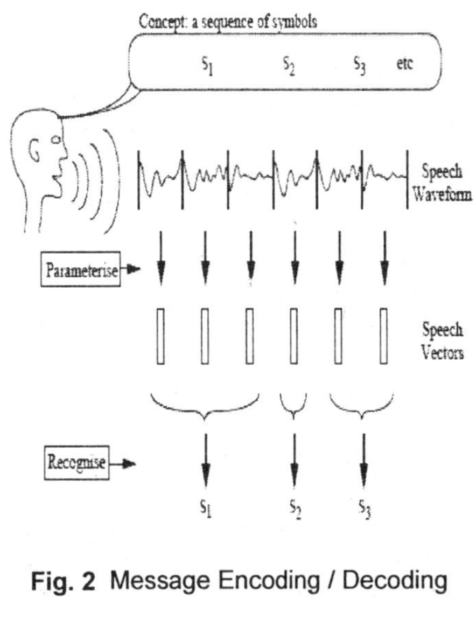

Fig. 2 Message Encoding / Decoding

In HMM based speech recognition, it is assumed that the sequence of observed speech vectors corresponding to each word is generated by a Markov model as shown in Fig. 2.

On decoding the output transcription can be obtained as shown in Fig. 3.

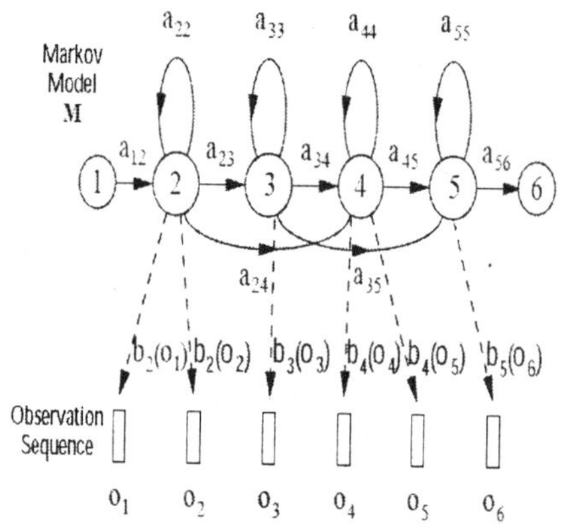

Fig. 3 The Markov Generation Model

Given that X is unknown, the required likelihood is computed by summing over all possible state sequences $X = x(1), x(2), x(3), \cdots x(T)$, that is

$$P(O \mid M) = \sum_X a_{x(0)x(1)} \prod_{t=1}^{T} b_{x(t)}(o_t) a_{x(t)x(t+1)}$$

where $x(o)$ is constrained to be the model entry state and $x(t+1)$ is constrained to be the model exit state.

As an alternative to equation, the likelihood can be approximated by only considering the most likely state sequence, that is

$$\hat{P}(O \mid M) = \max_X \left\{ a_{x(0)x(1)} \prod_{t=1}^{T} b_{x(t)}(o_t) a_{x(t)x(t+1)} \right\}$$

Although the direct computation of these equations is not tractable, simple recursive procedures exist which allow both quantities to be calculated very efficiently.

Given a set of training examples corresponding to a particular model, the parameters of that model can be determined automatically by a robust and efficient re-estimation procedure. Thus, provided that a sufficient number of representative examples of each word can be collected then a HMM can be constructed which implicitly models all of the many sources of variability inherent in real speech. Fig. 4 summarizes the use of HMMs for isolated word recognition. Firstly, a HMM is trained for each vocabulary word using a number of examples of that word. In this case, the vocabulary consists of just three words: "i", "split" and "it". Secondly, to recognize some unknown word, the likelihood of each model generating that word is calculated and the most likely model identifies the word.

1.5 Recognition and Viterbi Decoding

Using recursive formulae as discussed earlier the total likelihood $p(o \mid M)$ can be found out. Thus, this algorithm could also be used to find the model which yields the maximum value of $p(o \mid M_i)$, and hence, it could be used for recognition. In practice, however, it is preferable to base recognition on the maximum likelihood state sequence since this generalizes easily to the continuous speech case whereas the use of the

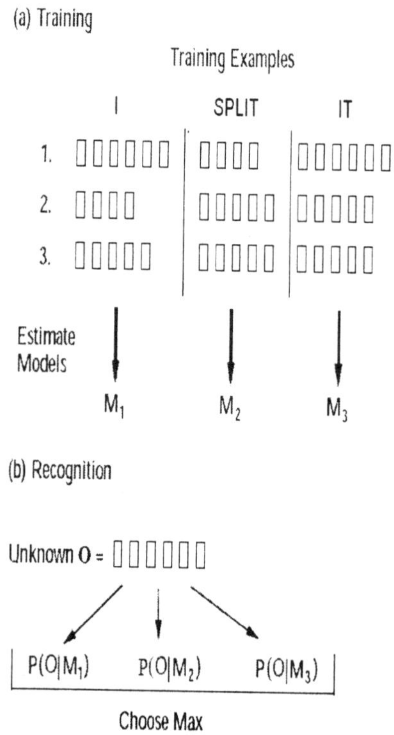

Fig. 4 Using HMMs for Isolated Word Recognition

total probability does not. This likelihood is computed using essentially the same algorithm as the forward probability calculation except that the summation is replaced by a maximum operation. For a given model M, let $\Phi_j(t)$ represent the maximum likelihood of observing speech vectors o_1 *to* o_t and being in state j at time t. This partial likelihood can be computed efficiently using the following recursion

$$\phi_j(t) = \max\{\phi_i(t \mid 1) a_{ij}\} b_j(ot)$$

Where, $\phi_1(1) = 1$ and

$$\phi_j(1) = a_{1j} b_j(o_1) \quad for \quad 1 < j < N$$

The maximum likelihood $p(o \mid M)$ is then given by

$$\phi_N(T) = \max\{\phi_i(T) a_{iN}\}$$

As for the re-estimation case, the direct computation of likelihoods leads to underflow; hence, log likelihoods are used instead. The recursion then becomes

$$\Psi_j(t) = \max_i\{\Psi_i(t-1) + \log(a_{ij})\} + \log(b_j(o_t))$$

This recursion forms the basis of the so-called Viterbi algorithm. As shown in Fig. 5, this algorithm can be visualized as finding the best path through a matrix where the vertical dimension represents the states of the HMM and the horizontal dimension represents the frames of speech (i.e. time). Each large dot in the figure represents the log probability of observing that frame at that time and each arc between dots corresponds to a log transition probability. The log probability of any path is computed simply by summing the log transition probabilities and the log output probabilities along that path. The paths are grown from left-to-right column-by-column. The same concept can be extended for continuous speech recognition.

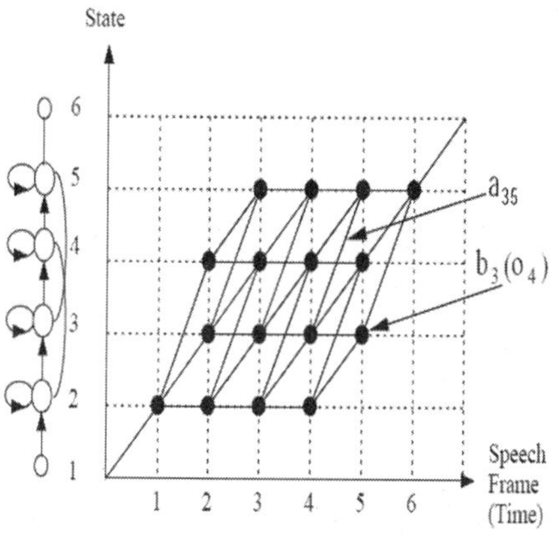

Fig. 5 The Viterb Algorithm for Isolated Word Recognition

2. Approach to the problem

2.1 The Problem Statement

HTK is widely used software for speech recognition. Whether the software could be used for identification of disfluency in speech was the problem in hand. The recognition was done on phoneme level.

We started with a recognizer which could recognize "I SPLIT IT". R's could be of the form "I I split it" and P's of the form "I S-S-S-SPLIT IT"

2.2 Approach

The Phonetic Transcription used here was

I – ay
SPLIT – s p l ih t
IT – ih t

(i) Model used

The model used for recognition is shown in Fig. 6. Recognition is to be done in order I - SPLIT – IT. (start – I – split – it)
Words may be repeated (R)
Words may be missed (through the null 1)
Phrases may be repeated (through null 2)
Starting phonemes of each word may repeat (P)

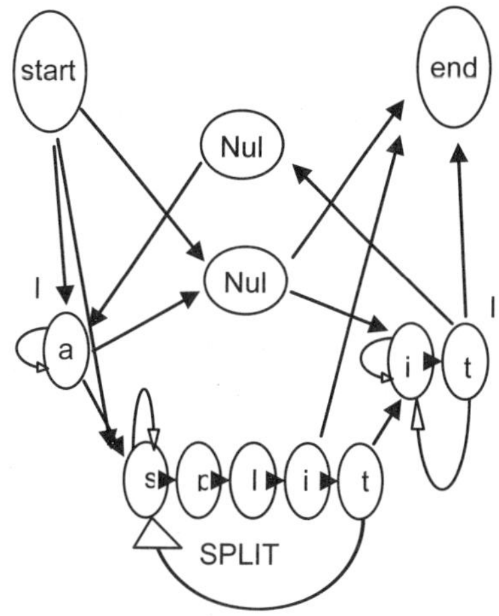

Fig. 6 Recognition Model

(ii) Training data

Various instances of the "I SPLIT IT" were recorder using WaveSurfer software. Typical waveforms is shown in Fig. 7.

(iii) Phoneme Labeling.

The transcription was applied to the recorded data and the phonemes were aligned approximately using WaveSurfer. Fig. 8 helps in labeling.

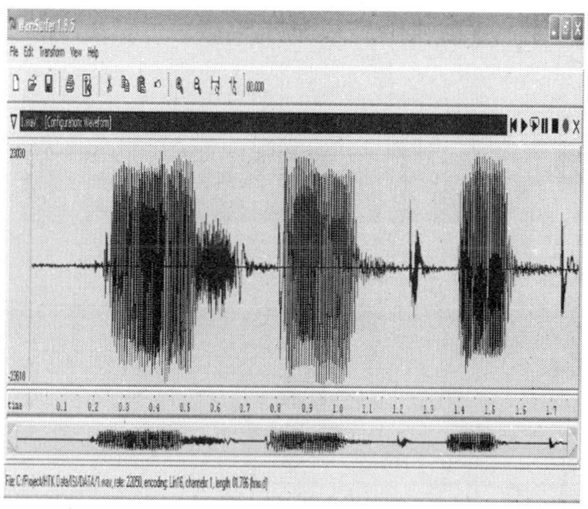

Fig. 7 Waveform of "I SPLIT IT"

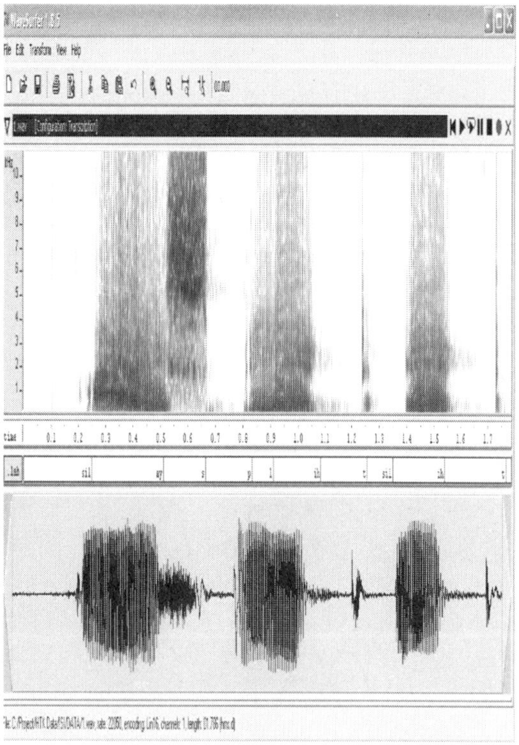

Fig. 8 Labeling of phonemes to recorded data

(iv) Train using HTK

The various training utterances were used to build models for recognition. Double mixture Gaussians were used to model each of the 6 phonemes in question.

(v) Recognition results

Output transcriptions were provided to HTK to obtain recognition accuracy and the result were shown in Fig. 9.

Fig. 9 Recognition accuracy

Recognition results were 100 % with given training data.

(vi) Stuttering data

Fig. 10 shows the Simulated stuttered data for the sentence I Spilt It.

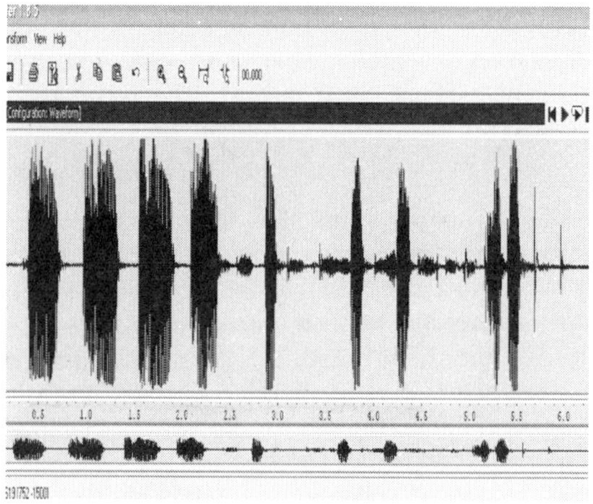

Fig. 10 Stuttered Waveform of "I SPLIT IT"

(vii) Final Output

The output phoneme level transcription was converted to word level transcription using HTK and processed in C++ to pin point where R occurred and where P occurred. Output obtained is shown in Fig. 11.

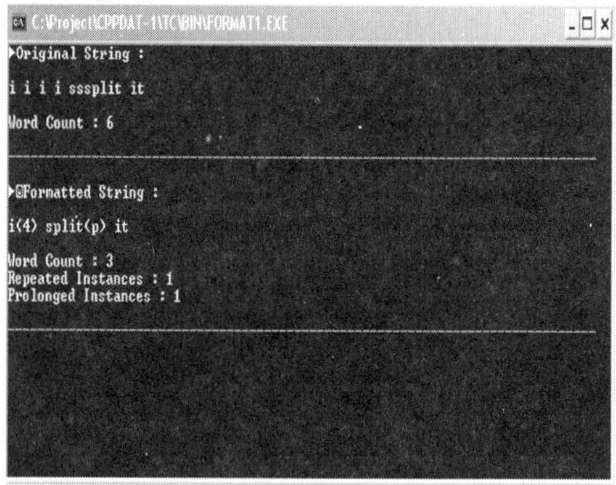

Fig. 11 Final Output

(viii) Extended to Paragraph

An all Phoneme passage was selected and speech of 40 speakers was recorded twice. The mean age of speaker was 20. The passage contained 132 words and approximately 457 phonemes each. The model was trained for all 44 standard phonemes. Out of the 80 files 55 were used for training and 25 for testing.

(ix) Pre-processing on recorded data

The recorded data was pre-processed to remove background noise and silence using GoldWave application for better performance of recognizer.

3. Result

The Recognition was carried out on test files and the accuracy was 80.78%, which is a improvement from the existing method which uses ANNs with 78.01% [5, 6].The accuracy may be improved by using more training data and checking with alternate method ,like using syllable segmentation instead of phoneme level segmentation.[11]

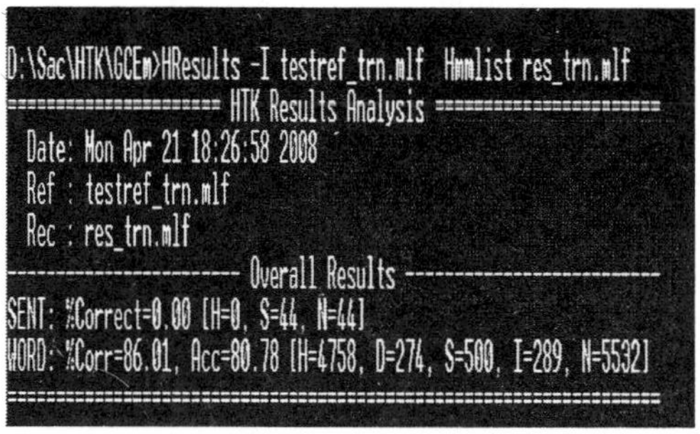

Fig. 12 Recognition result on Test data

4. Acknowledgment

The Authors would like to thank *itie Knowledge Solutions* for providing technical support and timely guidance.

5. References

[1] D.Kully and E.Boerg, "An investigation of inter_clinic agreemet in the identification of fluent and stuttered syllables,"Journal of fluency disorders, vol.13, pp.309_318, 1988.

[2] E.Keogh, "Exact indexing of dynamic time warping,".In VLDB. pp. 406-417. Hong Kong, china 2002.

[3] H. Silverman & D.morgan, "the application of dynamic programming to connected speech segmentation," IEEE ASSP Mag.7,no.3,7-25,1990.

[4] Neeta Awasthy, J.P.Saini and D.S.Chauhan, "Spectral Analaysis of Speech: Anew Technique" Internatioal Journal of Signal Processing ,Vol 2, No.1, pp.19-29.

[5] Peter Howell, Stevie Sackin, and Kazan Glen, "Development of a Two-stage procedure for the Automatic Recognition of Dysfluencies in the speech of children who stutter: I. Psychometric Procedure Appropriate for selection of Training Material for Lexical Dysfluency Classifiers," JSLHR, vol.40, pp.1073-1084,October 1997.

[6] Peter Howell, Stevie Sackin, and Kazan Glen, "Development of a Two-stage procedure for the Automatic Recognition of Dysfluencies in the speech of children who stutter: II. ANN Recognition of Repetitions and Prolongations with supplied word segment markers," JSLHR, vol.40, pp.1085-1096,October 1997.

[7] Praveen Kumar Yettapu "Phoneme Segmentation and Alignment for TTS" Project Report submitted in partial fulfillment of the requirement for the Degree of Master of Engg., in Signal Processing,June 2005.

[8] P. Kenny, M. lenning, and P. Mermelstein, " A linear predictive HMM for vector-valued observation with application to speech recognition," IEEE Trans. Acoust., speech processing , vol.38, No.2, pp.220-225,Feb.1990.

[9] Sandipan Chakroborthy and Goutam Saha, "Improved Text-Indepent Speaker Identification Using Fused MFCC & IMFCC Feature Sets Based on Gaussian Filter," Internatioal Journal of Signal Processing ,Vol 5, No.1, pp.11-19.

[10] W.Johnson et al., "The onset of stuttering, minneapolies : university of minnesata press,"1959.

[11] W.Reichl and G.Ruske, "syllable segmentation of continuous speech with Artificial Neural Networks," In Processing of Eurospeech, Berlin, vol.3, pp.1771-1774, 1993.

Real Time Automatic Speech Recognition System Blind People

P. Laxminarayana, Mythilisharan and A.V.Ramana
Department of ECE, Research and Training Unit for Navigational Electronics, Osmania University – Hyderabad
laxminarayana@osmania.ac.in

Abstract

Automatic speech recognitions (ASR) and synthesis systems are very much useful for blind people in many ways. An ASR system can be used in real time for applications like enquiry of cost and availability of various items in the super market, or any other shop. Of course it will be also useful to find out the location of an item where it is available in the big super market. Outstanding research work in speech recognition, synthesis and computing has produced the development of commercial speech recognition systems for voice-driven computing and word-processing systems in English and European Languages. Though significant research work is being carried out in Indian languages too, like in Hindi, Tamil, Bengali and Telugu, ASR systems are not yet launched into the Indian market. An application for manipulating the student database using real time speech recognition system in Telugu is developed to enhance the ASR usage in Indian languages. Similarly an ASR based application specific dialogue system can be developed easily to help the blind people. Of course the developed ASR system is in the native language, it will be very much useful for the local people.

Keywords: Automatic Speech Recognition, Spectrum, Segmentation, Training, IWR, CSR

1. Introduction

Automatic Speech Recognition (ASR)

Speech is a natural mode of communication for people. Yet people are so comfortable with speech, they would also like to interact with the computers via speech, rather than having confined to interfaces such as keyboards and pointing devices. Since the 1950's, great progress has been made so far in ASR for different languages. A speech interface can support many applications for example, telephone directory assistance, spoken database querying, "hands-busy and eyes-busy" applications, and office dictation and voice (language) translation devices. It will be very much useful for the blind people at enquiry or dialogue related applications.

Significant research is happening in Indian languages like in Hindi, Tamil, Bengali, Oriya and Telugu languages, to make the ASR systems available for special applications like Railway enquiry systems, Language translation systems. Still there is lot of scope for further enhancements and sophistication to expand into various other applications.

To start with, we have selected few names and numbers for developing an ASR system. The system is developed using Matlab and GUI, it can be used by any non technical person, who doesn't know much about ASR technology, to enter the data of the objects available in shop or market. Of course the blind person can only speak and talk to the machine to know the details required item in his own language. Therefore he doesn't need any knowledge about the ASR.

The shop person will feed the of item like cost, availability in to the system. Just the person entering the shop will enquire through a microphone with ASR system to know the details of interested item. The system will listen to the person and give the complete details.

The procedure of design and development of the system with a block diagram is explained in the next section. The specific techniques, algorithms and the parameters used in the presently developed application are explained in the following sections. Later the results of the developed system are analyzed.

ASR Development using HMM word models

The task of the ASR is to take input as an acoustic waveform (O) and produce output as a string of words (W). As shown in Fig.1 in the Feature Extraction stage, the acoustic waveform is sampled into frames which are transformed into spectral features. Models are trained from known examples of what we expect to see in the future. In the Acoustic Modeling (AM) stage, we compute the likelihood of the observed spectral feature vectors given linguistic units (words, phones, subparts of phones). Finally, in the decoding phase, we take the acoustic model (AM), which consists of this sequence of acoustic likelihoods, plus a dictionary of word pronunciations, combined with the language model (LM) (generally an *N*-gram grammar), and output the most likely sequence of words by comparing the test pattern to be recognized with all models and choose the closest model based on certain criteria.

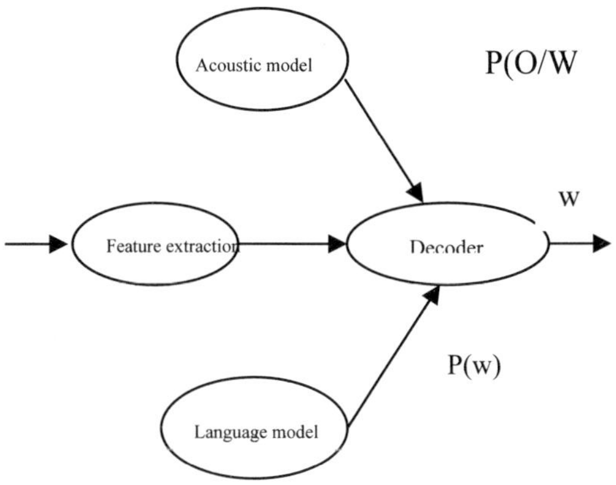

Fig. 1 block diagram of a speech recognizer

An ASR system can be developed in the following phases.

- *Data acquisition*: Real time data collection in the form of sentences (numbers and names with silence in between the words) pronounced by various speakers.
- *Segmentation*: The speech sentence is segmented into words (numbers and names without silence at the ends) and silence as a separate word.
- *Training*: Development of Word models using HMM.
- *Recognition and Testing*: Real time acoustic data collected should be given to the ASR to recognize the spoken words using the developed Word models.

Therefore the developed ASR system consists of Data Acquisition/collection, segmentation of collected speech data in to Words i.e. silent or non silent segments, Training the data for generating the HMM word models for the collected data. Then we can use the system for entering marks and any other data of the students using these HMM models. This complete system of data collection, segmentation, training and recognition is developed using Matlab and GUI. This ASR system can be used by any one to enter the data easily because it is fully developed with GUI. For the user of the system he doesn't need any knowledge of the HMM or ASR.

When we execute the main program from the MATLAB command window the first window (GUI) appears as shown in Fig.2. It contains different tabs, like "Data Collection", "Segmentation", "Training", and "IWR" and "CSR" for recognition which are different subsections of ASR.

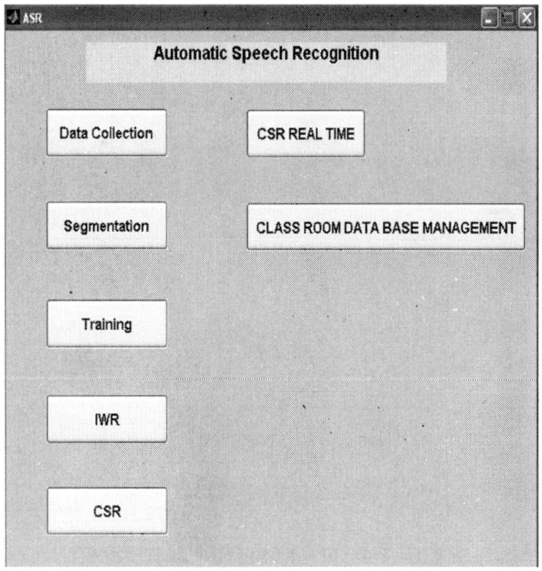

Fig. 2 Main GUI window for ASR system

The ASR system development is explained in the following sub-sections.

2. ASR Implementation

Real-time data collection

The speech samples are collected in real-time using the microphone connected to the computer through the data acquisition tool box in matlab. The data is sampled at 16-kHz and quantized with 16 bits/sample. For building the word models, we have considered the speech frames of 25-ms duration with 15-ms overlap and 10-ms step size for the frame. One frame of samples is processed before collecting the next frame of samples to keep the system working in real-time.

The user of this system has to click the button "Data Collection" in the first window and we will see the other GUI window of data collection as shown in Fig.3. It contains tabs for "Name" of the person (whose speech is to be recorded, which should be typed by user) and the "Category" (men, women, boy or girl). As the "Data Type" is divided into numbers and names, the "Text to be Read" will appear on the window according to the selection of the "Data Type". Click the tab "Start Recording" and speak the text for recording. After the text is read, click the button to "Stop Recording" for stopping the recording. It also contains the tabs like "Play Back" the recorded speech (for verification) and "Save" the recoded speech file under the selected "File Name" which automatically generated using "Category", "Name", "Data Type" and "Iteration" selection.

E.g. Men\PLN\PLN_Names_1.wav

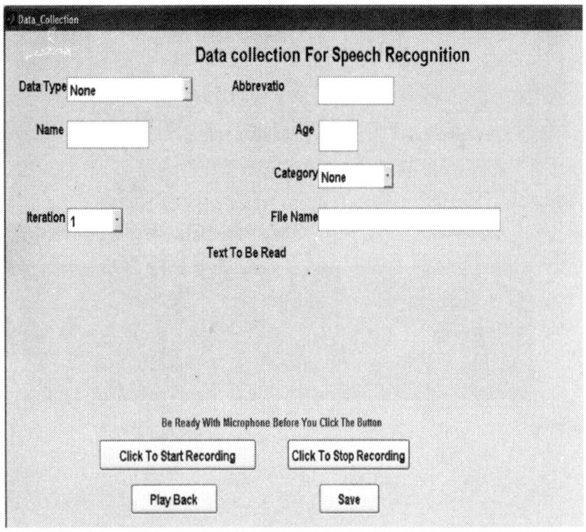

Fig. 3 Data collection GUI window

Segmentation of the Recorded Speech Data

For segmentation of the speech into silence and non-silence parts, the properties of speech like energy and spectrum are used. Silence frames will have less energy and flat (approximately white) amplitude spectrum, whereas the non-silence frames may be of voiced or unvoiced sounds will have some peaks in the spectrum. These peaks may represent the pitch or formants. Energy of the frame and the normalized amplitude spectrum vector of the frame are used to decide a frame as silent or non-silent using certain thresholds. For calculating thresholds, we assumed that the first 20 frames of the recorded speech data as silence.

To open the sub-window of the segmentation, click segmentation tab in the main GUI/ window (Fig.2). Then the following GUI menu as shown in Fig.4 appears. Then select the file to be segmented from the list, and click here for "Automatic Segmentation of Words". It will generate the different segmented files for each word.

ASR Training

Training contains basically two steps. Initially we will extract the features of the speech data frame by frame. Later the HMM word model parameters for each word will be found using the features of that word data. The (different) parameters of the word HMM model are mean, variance of each state, State Transition Probabilities, initial probabilities of each state. The accuracy of the system depends upon how much training data is used

To open the training windows click the "Training" tab in the main ASR window.

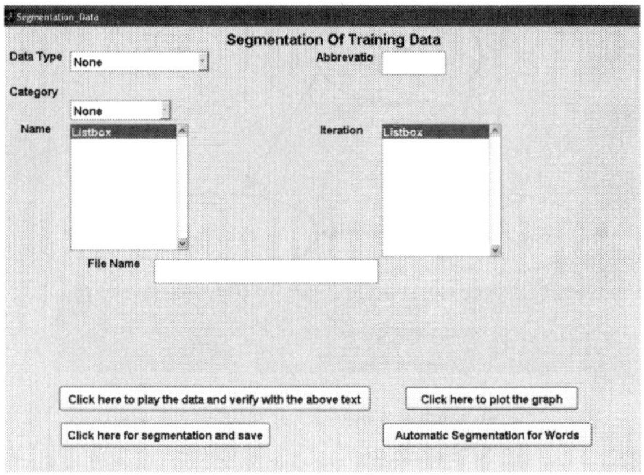

Fig. 4 Segmentation GUI window

In the training window as shown in Fig.5, user can select either all the words or few interested words for training. Click for "Training" tab for training the selected speech data.

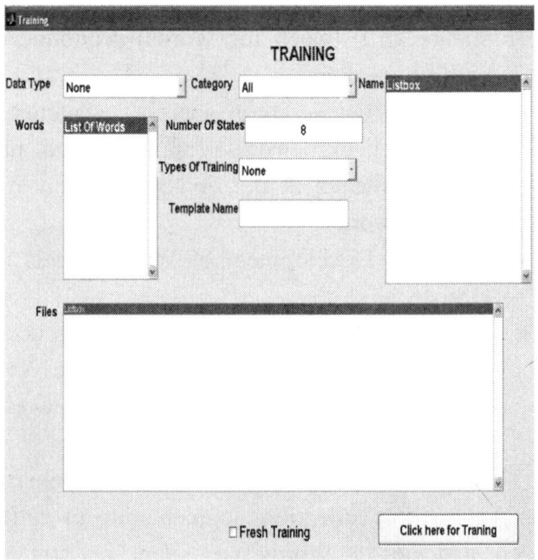

Fig. 5 Training GUI window

Feature Extraction

Extraction of Features is required for both training and recognition. Once the digitized and quantized speech is available in frames, we transform each frame into a sequence of acoustic feature vectors. The raw speech signal is analyzed in a small time window of 25-ms duration and it is repeated for every 10-ms making the frame rate for feature extraction of about 100 frames/sec. In this ASR application, Mel Frequency Cepstrum (MFCC) is used. There is no separate window for feature extraction. This feature extraction will be done in the backend. Therefore user doesn't have any GUI for this task. However the present GUI will give the MFCC graphs of the speech during recognition only for technical analysis for engineers.

HMM Word Models

Each state of the word template (HMM model) is represented by two parameters: mean and variance vector for that state. The states are interpreted as acoustic models of a sound. While the transition probabilities will provide the temporal constraints, indicating, how the states may follow each other in sequence. Because, speech always goes forward in time, transitions in a speech application always go forward (or make a self-loop, allowing a state to have arbitrary duration). Mean indicates the approximate cepstral frequencies of a sound and variance will indicate the permissible variations in the frequencies for the same sound/state.

For all of the numbers and names considered in this project, to start with, left-right HMM model with 8 (by default) states per word are considered i.e. we are assuming eight sounds in a sequence for any word. There can be different number of states for different words also. There is an option in the GUI to choose the number of states depending upon the number of sounds in that word.

In our *project*, we considered 49 different words (names and numbers) and 1 silence model i.e. treating silence also as a separate word model, totaling 50 words. Since the words HMMs do not include any silence, we need a separate silence HMM.

Calculation of HMM parameters

First each example of the given word, the number of frames in each example will be equally divided in to number of states for that word model. The fames of each state of all examples will be combined to calculate the mean and variance vectors for that state. Then the transition probabilities will be calculated using the [3]. Initial probabilities for all states are zero except first state of any word. Forward and backward (viterbi) algorithms are used iteratively to find out correct number of frames in each state [1]. Again compute mean and variance vectors of the states. Repeat the process for convergence. Then calculate the STP.

State Transition Probabilities (STP)

In our exercise, we are considering 49 different words (names and numbers) and 1 silence model i.e. treating silence also as a separate word model, totaling 50 words.

Hence the probabilities for different words are calculated as follows:

- STP (Individual final state of any word, by considering equal prob. to all 8 states) 1/8 = 0.125. This is considered only for final state. STP for other states is calculated based on HMM training for words i.e. based upon the number of vectors falling in to a state.

ASR Recognition

The best match of a template to the input speech is measured in two steps.

- For a given input utterance, measure its minimum distance to each template.
- Choose the template that delivers the smallest distance.

The search trellis concepts are used here for calculating the minimum edit distance. For this project we have chosen the back tracing method.

3. Simulations and Results

Training was done on data collected by the 9 people (3 women and 6 men) with five examples (iterations) each per speaker are trained.

Total number of different words considered = 29 numbers + 20 names + 1 silences = 50

- 9 speakers * 5 time/speaker= 45 examples of each word are taken to train and get a Word HMM model.
- In total as 50 words are considered, 50 HMM word models are available in the developed ASR.
- To obtain the HMM model parameters of each word, 5 iterations are used for training the system using forward and backward algorithm for convergence.

Isolated Word Recognition

Once the training is completed for about 2250 words for 9 different speakers to create a dictionary of 50 words (including silence), then each segmented isolated word is verified against the dictionary of words for matching. The recognition algorithm detects and verifies each isolated word for its correctness as shown in Fig.6.

- When the training and recognition is performed for only one individual speaker at a time, the word recognition success rate is 100% for the 50 word dictionary.
- When the training is performed on 9 speakers' data together to form 50 word dictionaries and then the recognition is performed for only one individual speaker at a time, the word recognition success rate is more than 96%.

Table 1 IWR Results

<table>
<tr><td colspan="4">Trained with 5 men data and tested for one man data individually (test data not included in training)</td></tr>
<tr><td>Total words</td><td>Words detected correctly</td><td>Words detected wrongly</td><td>WER (%)</td></tr>
<tr><td>245</td><td>228</td><td>17</td><td>7</td></tr>
<tr><td colspan="4">Trained with 6 men data and tested for one man data individually (test data included in training)</td></tr>
<tr><td>Total words</td><td>Words detected correctly</td><td>Words detected wrongly</td><td>WER (%)</td></tr>
<tr><td>1470</td><td>1411</td><td>59</td><td>4</td></tr>
<tr><td colspan="4">Trained with 2 women data and tested for one woman data individually (test data not included in training)</td></tr>
<tr><td>Total words</td><td>Words detected correctly</td><td>Words detected wrongly</td><td>WER (%)</td></tr>
<tr><td>245</td><td>221</td><td>24</td><td>10</td></tr>
<tr><td colspan="4">Trained with 3 women data and tested for one woman data individually (test data included in training)</td></tr>
<tr><td>Total words</td><td>Words detected correctly</td><td>Words detected wrongly</td><td>WER (%)</td></tr>
<tr><td>735</td><td>691</td><td>44</td><td>6</td></tr>
<tr><td colspan="4">Trained with 6men 3 women data and tested individual(test data included in training)</td></tr>
<tr><td>Total words</td><td>Words detected correctly</td><td>Words detected wrongly</td><td>WER (%)</td></tr>
<tr><td>2205</td><td>2119</td><td>86</td><td>4</td></tr>
</table>

4. Conclusions

From the results we can conclude that the developed system can be easily used for a dialogue system using Speaker dependent ASR.

- Presently, the number of states for each word is taken as 8 only. But we have to choose the number of states based on the number of sounds in the words.
- Since the silence is detected as a word in the continuous speech recognition, refined segmentation algorithms is required to detect the boundaries properly. Further, analysis is to be done why, sometimes the silence is detected as a word.
- The trained and tested data is same in the present results. However it should be tested for separate data for which it is not trained.

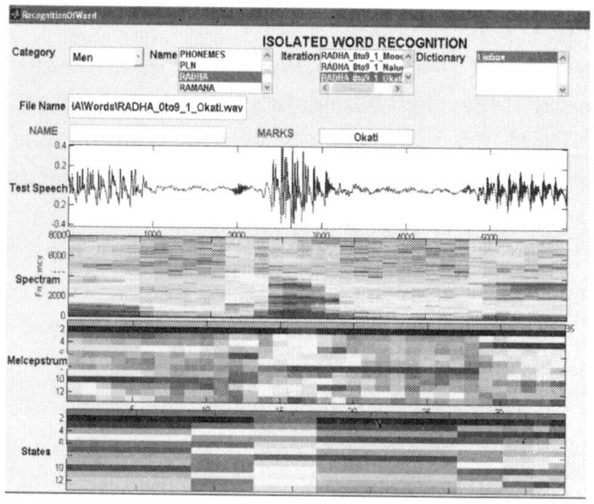

Fig. 6 GUI window for IWR (shows the spectrum for recognition of the word "Okati")

- At present the system is trained only for 9 people including both men and women with 5 iterations each. The accuracy will be more if it is trained for individual only. i.e. Speaker dependent system. We can also have separate template for each word for category: Men, Women, Boys and Girls.
- This system can also be improved to speaker independent ASR by considering more number of speakers.
- The success rate for recognition may be improved further by considering phoneme models in place of word models.
- The present system is developed using MATLAB only for research and experimental analysis. But same thing can be developed without using MATLAB may be in 'C' or any assembly programming also. Just a simple computer is enough. Of course for mass production we can go for Digital signal processor for reducing the size and cost of the system

5. References

[1] Rabiner, L.R. and Juang, B.H. (2003), *Fundamentals of Speech Recognition*, Pearson Education, Daniel Jurafsky and James H. Martin (2002), *Speech and Language Processing,* Pearson Education Asia

[2] L. R. Rabiner, "*A tutorial on hidden Markov models and selected applications in speech recognition,*" Proc. IEEE, vol. 77, no. 2, pp. 257–286, 1989.

[3] *Lecture Notes of Summer School on ASR (2007),* 16th - 25th July 2007, IIIT, Bangalore, Organized IEEE Signal Processing Society, Bangalore.

[4] Rabiner and M.R. Sambur, "An Algorithm for determining End-points of Isolated Utterances", *Bell Technical Journal,* Feb 1975, pp 297-315

Designed Generalized Code for Real Time Image Processing of Welding Process

Er. Pradeep N. Fale[1] and Prof. S. A. Raut[2]
[1]PG Student
[2]Asst. Professor
PG Departement of Computer Science & Engg, G.H.Raisoni College of Engineering, Nagpur, INDIA.
pradeep_fale@rediffmail.com *rautsa@gmail.com*

Abstract

In early days the welding process will be done manually and there is more time consuming task, and also the welding will be done on object is not be fine weld with right angle. The most of the work is done on arc welding using laser sensors techniques. Welding process is one of the most important processes in manufacturing units. The Quality of welded output completely depends on the control of the process parameters, but still the conventional Manual welding, is used where there is no suitable control on the process parameters. Hence Quality of welded output is not satisfactory and manufactured goods do not meet International export standards. The large manufacturing units have automated welding by means of WELDING ROBOS, but they are very costly, high power and maintenance requirement equipments not affordable by small and medium scale entrepreneurs.

This paper describes, to design a generalized code for real time image processing on welding process with different object to identify the object and apply the different algorithms for image tracing and find the space between the two objects. The proposed generalized code is used for different applications in which there is need to find the distance between two objects and to take the action depends on the minimal distance between them. If the distance is in the range then find the distance between the objects and the torch tip that is fixed in robotic arm for welding. If the threshold gap is in the range then the robotic arm is ready for welding. Our task is to make a cost efficient, human free automatic welding process in which the welding parameters are controlled suitably so as to ensure a high quality output, which meets the international export standards.

1. Introduction

Welding is one of the widely used methods for joining metals. In spite of the numerous advances in the science and technology of welding, failures do occur and weld is still considered to be the weakest portion. Conventionally, the quality of the weld is ascertained only after the welding has been completed through the use of Non Destructive Testing (NDT) such as ultrasonic or radiography. Since each of these techniques is applied only after the welding is completed, a lot of time, material and manpower are wasted before one comes to know about the soundness of the weld. Inherent Limitations in conventional welding processes can be overcome if the weld is continuously monitored in real time for the assessment of defects and their automatic elimination by on-line control of the welding parameters. Moreover, the defective weld can be repaired immediately without continuing the Process further. This strategy to monitor, control and maintain quality of welds is commonly known as adaptive welding or intelligent welding. Intelligent welding, as the name implies, combines welding equipment with intelligent sensing and control, knowledge of human experts, and Artificial Intelligence (AI) to improve joining efficiency and reduce the weld in homogeneities and defect. [1]

As welding and inspection of weld are complicated tasks, it has been said to be difficult to automate completely them. With various sensors have been developed with increasing speed and some applications of intelligent system to these tasks have been tried. Recent status of automatic inspection of weld and robot welding by intelligent robot applied artificial vision and image processing are reviewed.

In developed countries, some form of welding is used in more than 50% of manufactured products. Acceptable welding requires fine-tuning and exact conditions. Even minute variations in conditions and control can cause a weld to be unacceptable. Thus, there has been a need for robust, reliable, real-time welding fault detection, especially in safety-critical applications in automotive manufacture.

Design generalized code for real time image processing on welding process is to design a generalized code for any type of object that will be welding by robotic arm, That code detect which type of object is weld and find out the main threshold gap between the two objects. we will provide some default threshold gap between two objects if the gap is not match then there is no permission for the robotic arm to weld the object if it is in limit then passing the image parameter of the two objects and by using that configuration check the object type and applying the different algorithms.

2. Literature Survey

Traditional welding robots are playback ones, which cannot adapt environment and weld distortion. Especially in the more and more extensive arc-welding course, the deficiency and limitation of playback welding technology becomes more prominent because of changeable welding condition. It becomes one of the key technologies influencing the development of modern robotic welding technology to eliminate or decrease uncertain influence on quality of welding such as changing welding condition etc. [2].

With the development of advanced manufacturing technology, it becomes an inexorable trend to realize the automatic, flexible and intelligent welding product manufacture. With the advantage of interchangeability and reliability, robotic welding can boost productivity, improve work condition, stabilize and guarantee weld quality, and realize welding automation of the short run products.

Robotic welding should become more widely available to smaller job shops. New technology enables robotics for fabrication projects that were never considered for automation because they were very low volume or just making parts for custom fabrication [12].

The most significant change in robotic welding over the past few years has been the increased power of Off-Line Programming (OLP). Off-line programming allows integrators to create programs without cutting into production time. OLP is now becoming viable for robotics make robots essential in the fabrication industry.

There has been an increase in the digital communication between the robot and its controller. Making faster and more reliable transfer of data and power input flowing from the controller to the welding robot. Digital communication and faster processing speeds between the robot, the power source and the wire feeder have expanded the capabilities for robotic welding.

Digital welding is becoming the basic power supply for robotic welding systems. Digital communication, coupled with improved software in digital image processing, made welding robotics more user-friendly. With technology developments, today's flexible welding robots successfully address material and process-based issues. Welding robots will always be in demand. Assisting with dull, dangerous and dirty jobs, flexible robotic welding fills the needs of a growing application [12].

As superpower laser transmitter or plane-laser transmitter is very expensive, currently; it is difficult to apply them to industry. While single-stripe laser with low power is relatively cheap, it can be widely used. Therefore, it is necessary to research on the image processing based on single stripe laser. Though the seam image based on laser is much better than that based on other common light sources, it will still be disturbed by welding spatter, fume and voltaic arc, that how to eliminate these noises as quick as possible is the key to realize precise seam tracking and real-time control. In this paper, according to the characteristic of laser image, some technologies include wavelet transform are used for image processing and good result is gotten [7].

The Automated Welding Manufacturing System (AWMS) is a research and development testbed for automated gas metal arc welding technology. Its activities are aimed at developing and validating standards that will contribute to increased use of automated welding technology by manufacturers. The National Institute of Standards and Technology (NIST) plans to work with technology suppliers and manufacturing users to test systems in the AWMS. Our experiments and control system designs will test the feasibility of interface standards and intelligent control technology to increase productivity, improves quality, and reduce the cost of system integration. Further, the integration techniques that make multi-vendor system solutions more effective and easier to build, program, and operate [9].

Seam tracking and weld penetration control are two fundamental issues in automated welding. A number of approaches, including pool oscillation, infrared sensing, ultrasonic sensing, and radiography, have been proposed to sense the weld penetration from the weld-face. [10]. Whereas the seam tracking technology has matured, however, accurate Penetration control still remains an unresolved problem due to the limitations associated with each individual sensing method. New sensing principles are strongly needed [l0]. It is known that the sag depression is directly determined by the geometry of the pool bottom surface. Thus, we proposed to monitor the full penetration state, which is specified by the backside bead width, using the geometry of the sag behind the pool rear. Experimentation showed that despite variations in the welding conditions and parameters, the backside bead width can be accurately determined from the sag depression using a simple linear model [l0]. This reflects the inherent dependence of the sag geometry on the backside opening. It is known that the weld penetration status is essential in the root pass. To acquire high quality joints, the root pass is frequently gas tungsten arc (GTA) welded. The above correlation was acquired based on GTA welding without filler. Thus, this correlation can be used to develop a practical penetration control method, with a weld-face sensor that can be attached to and move with the torch [11].

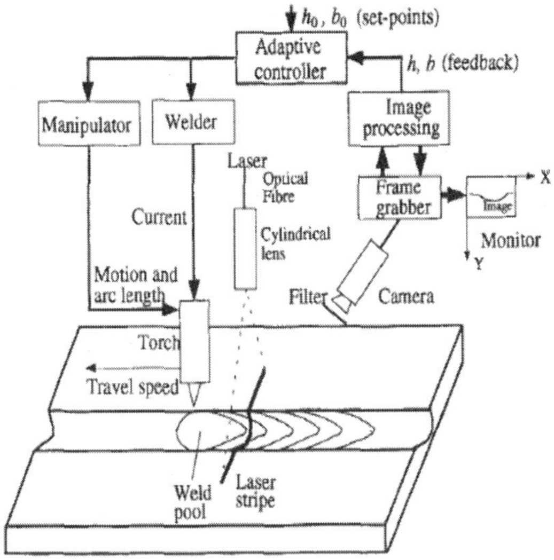

Fig. 1 Experimental System Design. The sensor, which consists of the laser, lens, and camera, is attached to and moves with the torch

3. Proposed Work

First of all, the image capture camera capture the image of the objects in the different angle, and passing that images to the PC by using an USB interface device as shown in Fig. 3.1.

Fig. 2 Captured image of welding objects

Applying the different techniques for finding the object for that particular image. Then calculate the distance between two objects by using standard algorithms or by applying the MATLAB function or tools.

After finding the gap if it is in between the threshold that is given to the system then the object is ready for welding. Otherwise to adjust the gap between the object manually.

Then the robotic arm is ready for welding again the second web camera finds the distance between the objects and welding robotic arm. It is not in range then moving the arm in the definite range if it is the range then the object is ready to weld and that information is pass to the LABVIEW Application that application is passing some signals to the micro controller then micro controller take the action for welding.

4. System Design

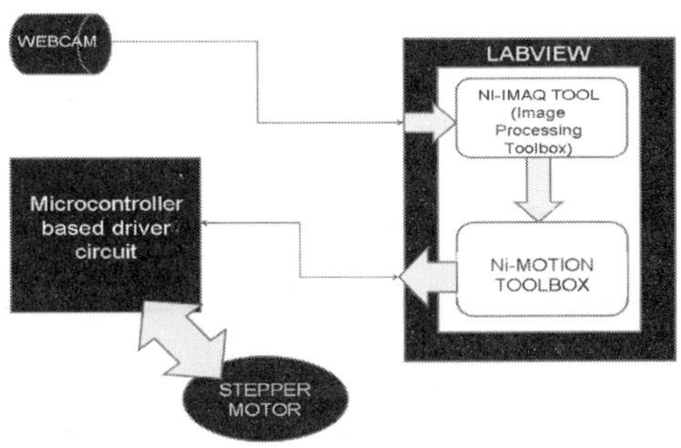

NI-IMAQ tool is used for interfacing between the DIP based tools to LABVIEW Application.

5. Control Flow Design

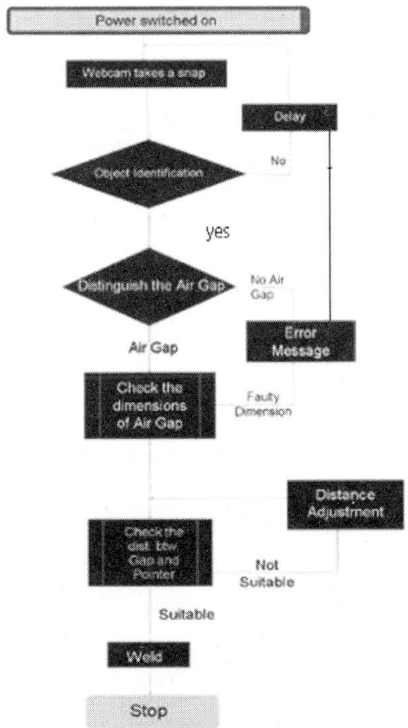

6. How We Solve the Problem

The design is further divided into two parts. Image sampling unit and Image-processing unit. The former is responsible for gathering the image information of the welding area in real time, and the latter finishes high-speed processing and transmitting of the gathered data.

6.1 Image sampling unit

The position between welding objects is fixed and can be calibrated ahead of time. Thus the depth information of welding object can be calculated out according to the position of the welding object. The position relation between the coordinate and the tool coordinate so that the coordinate of this spot also can be figured out under the tool coordinate.

Fig. 3.1 Dimenational

Fig. 4.2 Dimenational

Fig. 5.3 Dimenational

6.2 Image processing unit

Fast speed of measurement is needed to realize real-time guidance in the course of welding, thus image-processing speed becomes the key influence on the speed of measuring. For that we are using specific Image process algorithms.

6.3. Action undertaken for welding area recognition

Image processing unit needs to get the position of the welding area in each object, so the area of welding should be recognized at first. According to the picture that outputs; actually, the output values of elements corresponding to the area of welding are not exactly same. Through choosing certain threshold value for screen, the welding area can be figured out. After that the work of robotic arm is done, moving the arm towards the objects and if threshold value i.e. air gap between objects and the arm is the fixed (2 mm) then the arm is ready for welding by using code give the command to the arm and the object is weld.

7. Conclusion

In literature, we found that most of the existing methods to form the objects are based on the image depth calculations. Some methods deal with the formation of the image model, where the object model is formed first and then the model is post processed. Our proposed model is the basic simple model, which is constrained by image processing. Presented work is only the preliminary work consist of the basic idea and mathematics behind it. Presently we are working on our said procedures. In future, we will go for more number of algorithms and the tools, which will be better for image processing. In addition to this, development of the robotic arm mechanism and algorithm will be another tasks.

8. Acknowledgement

This is my industry based PG project. Presented work consisting of the basic idea and the implementations where we have been reached so far. In future, we will go for more number of DIP based MATLAB tools as well as other views which will be from better for moving the robotic arm based control. Implementation is in progress and will be completed in a due course.

9. References

[1] N.M.Nandhitha, N.Manoharan, B.Sheela Rani1, B.Venkataraman, Baldev Raj "A Comparative Study On The Performance Of The Classical And Wavelet Based Edge Detection For Image Denoising On Defective Weld Thermographs" 12th A-PCNDT 2006 – Asia-Pacific Conference on NDT, 5th – 10th Nov 2006, Auckland, New Zealand

[2] C. J. Liu, Y B Li, J G Zhu and S H Ye "Study On Sensor Design Technique For Real Time Robotics Welding Tracking System" International Symposium on Instrumentation Science and Technology, Journal of physics: Conference Series 48 (2006) 811-816.

[3] Lin ShangYang and Chen ShanBen. Welding robot and application. The press of the mechanical industry, 2000, 8.

[4] Cobos P., Monasterio F., "Fpga implementation of the Horn & Shunk Optical Flow Algorithm for Motion Detection in real time Images". Dcis'98 Proceedings, XIII Design of circuits and integrated systems conference, pp: 616- 621. (1998).

[5] Chen ShanBen, Wu Lin. The robot welds the intellectual control technology of welding seam quality of space and system research. The technological final report of key item of the national natural science fund, 2001. 6.

[6] Du ZhiJun The application of the industrial robot and development trend Mechanical engineer.2002 (5). -8-10

[7] Xiwen Liu, Guorong Wang and Yonghua Shi "Image Processing of Welding Seam Based on Single-stripe Laser Vision System" IEEE proceeding of the sixth International Conference on Intelligent System Design and Application.ISDA'06. 0-7695-2528-8/06, 2006

[8] Simpson SW and Gillespie P (1998) 'In-process monitoring of welding processes—a commercial success', Australasian Welding Journal, 43, 16–17.

[9] W.G. Rippey, J.A. Falco "The NIST automated Arc Welding Testbed", Proceedings of 7th International Conference on Computer Technology in Welding San Francisco, CA, July 8-11, 1997.

[10] Y. M. Zhang et al., "Determining joint penetration using weld-face geometry," Welding J., vol. 72, pp. 463s469s, 1993.

[11] Yu M. Zhang, Radovan Kovacevic, and Lin Li "Adaptive Control of Full Penetration Gas Tungsten Arc Welding" IEEE Transactions on Control Systems Technology, Vol. 4, No. 4, July 1996

[12] http://www.roboticsonline.com/public/articles/articlesdetails.cfm

[13] http://robots.surrey.ac.uk/People/mes3sl/mes3sl.htm

[14] Rafael C. Gonzalez and Richard E. Woods "Digital Image Processing".

[15] Rafael C. Gonzalez, Richard E. Woods and Steven L. Eddins "Digital Image Processing using MATLAB".

[16] Stephen J. Chapman "MATLAB Programming for Engineers" 2nd edition Thomson bookware Companion Series.

Session – 6

Information Retrieval System

An Adaptive Technique to Categorize Indic Language Documents

D. A. Meedeniya and A. S. Perera
Department of Computer Science and Engineering, Faculty of Engineering, University of Moratuwa, Sri Lanka.
dulanim@uom.lk shehan@uom.lk

Abstract

The significant growth of the electronic media to store and exchange text documents has led to the use of tools, which analyses and categorizes documents based on their content. The availability of full-text documents in electronic form emphasizes the need for intelligent information retrieval techniques. In Sri Lanka most of the public services use text documents written in Sinhala to provide their services. As a result, there is an essential need for a system which can be used to analyze and process documents in Sinhala. The main techniques examined in this study include data pre-processing and data clustering. The approach makes use of a transformation based on the text frequency and the inverse document frequency, which enhance the clustering performance. This research provides an approach based on Latent Semantic Analysis to process text documents written in Sinhala, and empower citizens and organizations to do their daily work easily.

1. Introduction

The development of Information Communication Technology (ICT) extracts the knowledge from all over the world and creates new changes in the human life. As a result, information has a strategic importance for most of the organizations as well as for every citizen. In the modern world digitized textual information is becoming a common repository for most of the organizations [1]. Although text documents are only a small portion of an organization's repository, it is one of the most readily available and easily accessible resources. Text documents can range from simple structures such as table of contents, chapters, paragraphs, headings, indexes to more complex and automated content such as automatic indexing, concept space, hypertext links. It enables the users to browse, search and retrieve knowledge stored as information. Knowledge extraction and transformation of the information into a format that can be easily shared and stored are some of the important components of an organization. Today most of the companies having problems in categorizing and organizing their huge volume of text documents [1].

Sri Lanka mainly uses three languages, English, Sinhala and Tamil, in day to-day life. Each of these languages has their own scripts, and sometimes it cause difficulties to utilize information technology in Sri Lanka. Sri Lankan people have a high literacy rate, but only 10% of them utilize English. As a result, most of the organizations use documents written in indigenous languages, to deliver their public services. Therefore for better governance in Sri Lanka, it is essential to communicate in both Sinhala and Tamil languages. To provide a better service, there is a need for non-English based document analyzing and categorizing systems, as it is currently available for English text documents.

Traditionally, text categorization is carried out by human experts as it requires a certain level of vocabulary recognition and knowledge processing. However with the rapidly increasing of the text documents, automatic ways of assigning labels to documents is required. Automated text classifier relieves the burdens of reading full-text documents and memorizes every class definition in a knowledge structure. But how well can a machine classifier perform? It is a research interest and in fact there is a great need to evaluate the effectiveness of automated text classification, to justify its advantages.

Text processing allows to combine, to summarize and to categorize text documents without affecting the original content [1]. Text categorization automatically assigns category labels to free text documents. It is possible to assign one or many categories to a given document depending on the application domain. These categories can be predefined or defined at the time of categorization [2]. The task of assigning the appropriate category label can be ambiguous even for a human analyst. When a machine imitates the human behaviour, the algorithm has to deal with a large collection of uncertainty coming from various sources. Human language is ambiguous even on the pure lexicon level, which contains words and word combinations with multiple senses [3]. Moreover this is a complex task to perform as it requires heuristics to approximate the human behaviour.

Human text analysts are familiar with the techniques used to organize, access, and extract knowledge in textual format. They make use of brainstorming sessions, activity organization, creativity freethinking, critical analysis and restriction considerations to achieve these tasks. In the text analysis task, the experience level is not a good predictor. The skills such as analytic ability, pattern recognition ability and cognitive style have to be considered in the categorization task [4]. A perfect text categorization tool should be capable of doing these tasks automatically and efficiently. With the growth of the non-English based documents, the value of the text categorization systems can be enhanced by expanding it to categorize non English text [5].

This research project is mainly focused on finding an approach and developing a tool to cluster documents, based on the content in the documents, written in Indic languages. An important goal of this text mining application is to examine a large collection of text to extract patterns and models and incorporate it in a text categorizer. This study narrows the focus to a specific form of textual documents, which is based on categorizing Sinhala newspaper articles. The finding of this study can be successfully apply to applications such as news dispatching and spam email filtering which require to label bulk messages in a short period of time according to the message content, which is a task that is not easily done with human efforts [6].

This paper provides an account of the most prominent features of the text categorizing, including data pre-processing and clustering algorithms. This paper is organized as follows. Section 2 discusses the research problem which is focused to examine. Section 3 details the data sets used in this study. Section 4 includes the review of the referred literature, which covers core areas of the study. Section 5 explains the experiment methodology. Section 6 consists with the summaries of the test results. Then the conclusion, presents the concluded remarks and the possible future work as an extension of this study. Finally the reference section is included as a proof of the study and it will compile the paper.

2. Research Problem

In the modern world electronically accessible text documents play an important role in many organizations. Most of the documents are written in the native language of a country. Therefore the systems used to analyze and process textual data, should be able to work with documents, irrespective of the language used. This motivated the researchers, to research on text analysis systems based on non-English based languages. Most of the developed approaches are focused on only the text data written in English. It is important to see whether these approaches are scalable to domains with non-English text documents or to domains with very short or long documents. Text Categorization is an active research area focused on non-English text and multilingual approaches.

Data repositories and data warehouses contain a large collection of unstructured data which makes it difficult to retrieve information and navigate on the documents. Most of the documents written in Indic languages have mainly focused for human interpretation with no semantic structure. Therefore it is difficult to retrieve information automatically, from large data sets. Although existing search engines are capable of querying and finding the relevant documents; they are not capable enough to identify the exact semantics of the document.

Most of the text categorization systems generate categories with different levels of abstraction, which makes it difficult to compare and integrate. For example the phase, 'layered architecture of a software design' can be incorrectly categorized in both 'Architecture' and 'Software' categories [1]. However this is a trivial process for a human facilitator. Although a large collection of documents afford useful information for the people, it is a challenge to find out the useful information from a large collection of documents.

Existing systems and algorithms are capable of grouping documents into categories. However most of them have limitations which cause noise and irrelevant results [7]. Traditional text processing systems are not capable enough to formulate suitable results by extracting only the relevant documents, without processing lists of irrelevant documents. Even with clear information it is difficult to extract all the suitable key terms in a large collection of data set [8]. Most of the text categorization systems are based on the English text and they do not pay more attention to the significant features of the languages, which are absent or unimportant in the English language [5]. For a country like Sri Lanka, there is an essential need for a system, which can be used to analyze and process documents written in Sinhala. Considering all the above facts, there is a requirement for finding an appropriate approach to analyze and categorize Sinhala text documents, based on their content.

3. Literature Review

3.1 Overview

Over the years, there had been a variety of state-of-the-art methodologies which were involved with text mining tasks. Text categorization is the process of grouping documents into classes based on their content [9].Clustering is the process of partitioning the data sets into subsets, so that the data in each cluster is sharing the common characteristics. [9]. Clustering identifies interesting distribution in the underlying data by maximizing the intra-cluster similarity and minimizing the inter-cluster similarity. Some algorithms identify common features among the data set using the attributes and their correlations. These algorithms belong to the class of unsupervised learning [3].

3.2 Latent Semantic Analysis

Latent Semantic Indexing is a popular, powerful vector space information retrieval model for concept based searching. It compresses document vector into vectors of a lower-dimensional space, whose dimensions are obtained as combinations of the original dimensions by looking at their patterns of co-occurrence [10]. This is done by producing a set of concepts related to the documents and terms.This technique uses SVD process to decompose the input text document matrix into a low dimensional triplet [11, 12, and 13].

3.3 Gaussian Mixture Model

A Gaussian Mixture Model is an automatic cluster detection method which used to recognize patterns. They model the probability density function of observed variables using a multivariate Gaussian mixture density. This technique identifies the clusters by combining the multivariate normal density components. Given a series of inputs, it refines the weights of each distribution through expectation-maximization algorithms [14, 15].

3.4 K-Means Clustering Algorithm

The K-means algorithm is a widely used central clustering technique that minimizes the average distance between an observation and its cluster center. The algorithm first selects the number of clusters and determines the cluster centers. It assigns each collection of words to the nearest cluster center by minimizing the average squared Euclidean distance between the words and its cluster center and re-computes the new cluster centers. This procedure is repeated until some convergence criterion is met. This method allows texts to be classified quickly [16, 9].

4. Methodology

The research methodology was conducted mainly in two phases, where the data pre-processing was applied on the data set to remove noise and clean the data as the first phase. In the second phase, data clustering techniques were applied to identify the grouping of documents. The research methodology was based on the following manner, which is shown in Figure 1.

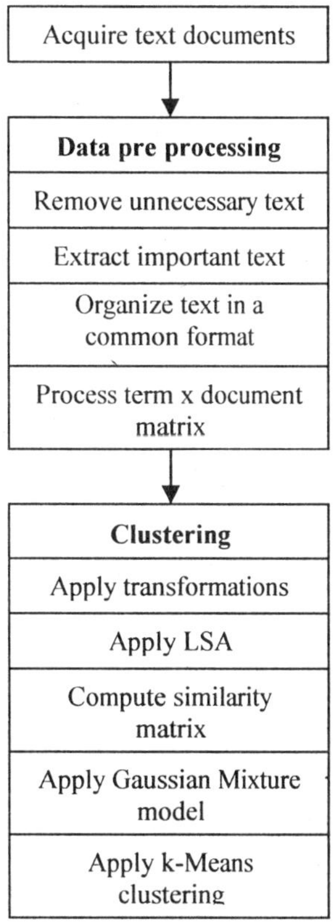

Figure 1. Main steps of the implementation procedure

4.1 Data Pre-processing

Data consists of textual data with noise; hence some attributes may be irrelevant to the clustering task. Therefore relevance analysis on data has to be performed to remove redundant attributes from the learning process. For this experiment we selected only 9 documents. We used a data cleaning and preprocessing algorithms to extract remove noise and clean the textual data. It used to avoid the interference of irrelevant words during the clustering. We have identified the common words which are not affecting to the categorizing process. Based on the identified common words, we used a word filtering process to eliminate predefined words such as prepositions, commonly used words and non-alphabetic words [17]. This helps to recognize and classify significant vocabulary items from the text. As the main part in data pre-processing, each data file which contains the newspaper articles, was compared with the words in the common file and eliminated the unnecessary words. Then it extracted only the important first 100 words from each data file and stored all the data elements in a one file, in such a way that each row in the created file is corresponded to a term in a given news article and each column is corresponded to a given article. This single file was used for further processing on text categorization. In this study we considered the first 100 words in each document because, most of the time the main idea of an article includes in the first paragraph of the text. Normally the last paragraph concludes the things in the article and the remaining paragraphs contain the supporting text [17]. Moreover this helps to reduce the dimensionality of the word matrices and reduce the processing time. Also this solves the problem of having different number of words in an article.

As the next step we calculated the frequency of each unique term in all files, in file wise and put it in a matrix. In this phase we considered the terms appear in more than one document to improve the performance of clustering. This stage converted all the data items into a term-by-document matrix, in which each element indicates the frequency with which each term (row) occurs in each document (column). This is the basis for Latent Semantic Analysis. A sample term x document frequency matrix is shown in the Figure 2.

Next we applied term frequency x document frequency transformation to the term x document matrix using the following expressions.

$$tf[i][j] = \frac{\text{Frequency of the word i in document j}}{\text{Frequency of all words in document j}} \quad (1)$$

$$idf[i][j] = \log \frac{[\text{ abs (total number of documents) }]}{[\text{ abs (\# of documents with the word i) }]} \quad (2)$$

$$X = tf \times idf \quad (3)$$

Documents

Unique terms

$$\begin{pmatrix} 1\,0\,2\,0\,0\,0\,0\ldots\ldots \\ 0\,2\,0\,0\,4\,0\,0\ldots\ldots \\ 0\,0\,0\,3\,1\,0\ldots\ldots \\ 0\,1\ldots\ldots\ldots\ldots \\ \ldots\ldots\ldots\ldots\ldots\ldots \end{pmatrix}$$

Figure 2. Sample of term x document frequency matrix

4.2 Text Clustering

To analyze the relationship between documents, we started with applying Latent Semantic Analysis (LSA) with the singular value decomposition (SVD), to the transformed matrix to reduces the vector space. SVD constructs an n dimensional abstract space, where each term and document is presented as vectors. SVD is used to get the associations among terms. SVD decomposes a term-by-document matrix into the product of three matrices as (3) follows.

$$X = U \times S \times V' \text{ ------ } (3)$$

X – Original matrix with p rows and r columns

U – Ortho-normal matrix, with linearly independent column vectors

S – Diagonal matrix, with singular values.

V – Ortho-normal matrix

A large singular value indicates a large effect of the dimension on the sum squared error of the approximation. We selected only the important dimensions with highest singular values, n, in the diagonal matrix and the corresponding singular vectors of the other two matrices, to reduce the dimensionality. The number of terms, n, should be large enough to fit the real structure in the data as well as small enough to eliminate unimportant data. The reduced dimensionality matrix contains 2 real values to represent the important data in each document. It corresponds to a least squares best approximation to the original matrix. This gives the best approximation in least square sense, to matrix X with k parameters. The rows of U_k represents the word vectors and the rows of V_k represents the document vectors in the LSA space.

As the next step in categorization we computed the document-by-document similarity matrix by getting the inner product of the matrices with the selected values, where the dot product between the i and j rows of the matrix US gives the i,j cell of XX'.

$$XX' = U S^2 V \quad (4)$$

Then we calculate the correlation of the similarity matrix in column wise, to describe the degree of relationship among documents. Since the words and documents are represented as vectors, it is easy to find the similarity between the documents. The coefficient of determination is computed for further categorization.

$$Correl(X,Y) = \frac{\sum (x-\bar{x})(y-\bar{y})}{\sqrt{\sum (x-\bar{x})^2 \sum (y-\bar{y})^2}} \quad (5)$$

Since there can be clusters with different sizes and correlations, first we applied Gaussian mixture model to cluster data. It assigns the clusters by selecting the components which maximize the posterior probability. This algorithm iteratively finds the local optimum results. We identified the number of clusters the data set can be divided, the class mean and class covariance for each document. In the second mode of operation, we applied the k-means algorithm with the identified number of clusters, to prove the association of each data point to an appropriate cluster and display the result. Additionally a diagram is drawn to have a better clue about the cluster separations.

5. Data Set

Data sets are rich with hidden information that can be used to make intelligent decisions. A large collection of annotated, homogeneous document set is needed to experiment the categorization ability of a system. To ensure that the method works in realistic situations, we have selected news articles as the data set for this study. It is sufficiently enough from the textual analysis point of view, as they are short documents with a title, which can be used to organize information properly.

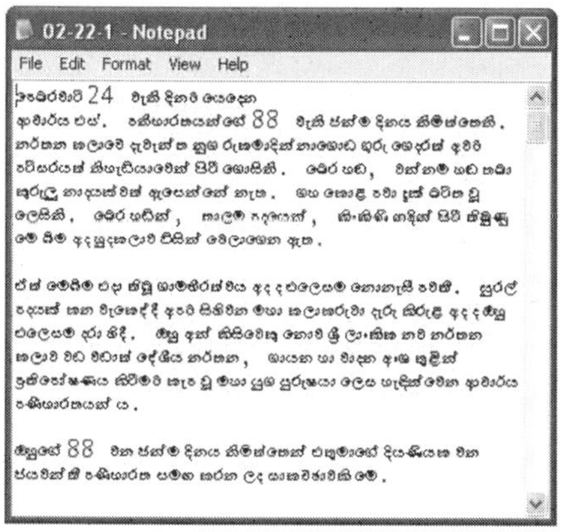

Figure 3. Sample of a data file

The source of the text collection for this study comes from the Sinhala newspaper articles which are available in UNICODE font. This collection consists of articles that have appeared in the 'Dinamina' newspaper during the month March, 2008. These articles consist with a title and a document body. The total number of documents in the corpus is 1200. These documents contain different number of words ranging from 100 to 1500.

6. Experimental Results

This study considered several criteria such as LSA, GMM, k-Means to find relationships between documents. According to our experiment with nine documents, Table 1 shows the similarity matrix between documents obtained by calculating the correlations among documents. This matrix clearly shows that the first five documents can be group into one cluster and the next four documents can be group into another cluster.

Table 2-1 Document similarity matrix 1

	1	2	3	4	5
1	1	0.9105	1	0.9982	0.8422
2	0.9105	1	0.9121	0.8843	0.9898
3	1	0.9121	1	0.998	0.8442
4	0.9982	0.8843	0.998	1	0.8087
5	0.8422	0.9898	0.8442	0.8087	1
6	-0.8575	-0.568	-0.8556	-0.8866	-0.4448
7	-0.8535	-0.5615	-0.8515	-0.8829	-0.4378
8	-0.8517	-0.5587	-0.8497	-0.8813	-0.4347
9	-0.8112	-0.4967	-0.809	-0.8445	-0.3679

Table 2-2. Document similarity matrix 2

	6	7	8	9
1	-0.8575	-0.8535	-0.8517	-0.8112
2	-0.568	-0.5615	-0.5587	-0.4967
3	-0.8556	-0.8515	-0.8497	-0.809
4	-0.8866	-0.8829	-0.8813	-0.8445
5	-0.4448	-0.4378	-0.4347	-0.3679
6	1	1	0.9999	0.9965
7	1	1	1	0.9971
8	0.9999	1	1	0.9973
9	0.9965	0.9971	0.9973	1

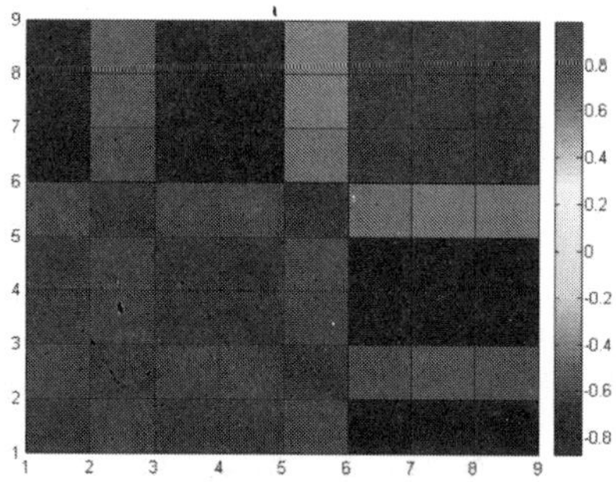

Figure 4. Graph of the similarity matrix

The results can be further proven by considering the graph shown in Fig. 4 which is based on the similarity matrix. Fig. 5 clearly illustrates the 2 clusters resulting from the k-means algorithm. This is used to identify the documents with a relationship.

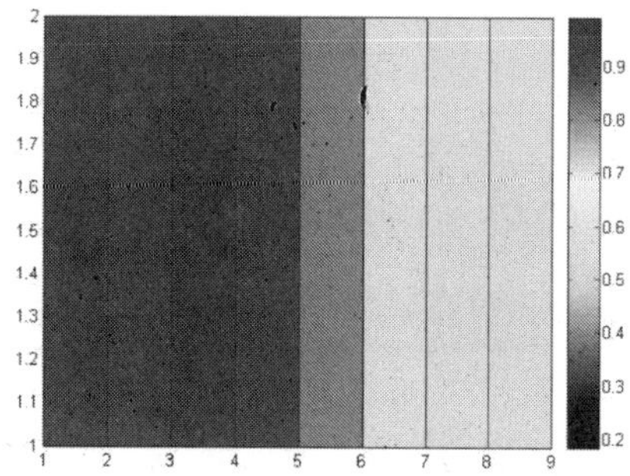

Figure 5. Graph obtained by k-means clustering

7. Conclusion

The bloom of information era has brought the wide collection of textual data that are generated, propagated, exchanged, stored and accessed through electronic media across the world. The recent advances in text processing have made text a candidate for computer assisted exploration and retrieval of information. The constant growth of text documents widens the document storage scope and makes it difficult to retrieve information. Today Sinhala text documents in electronic format are widely used in the

Sri Lanka, especially in offices and organizations. Therefore there is a requirement for advance analysis of those documents to group them according to the content and document comparisons. Patterns are found when there are relationships among data sets. Careful studies of the correlation of the data sets have to be considered, to discover a pattern, within the text data.

With the use of text-frequency, inverse document frequency, transform matrices, latent semantic analysis, singular value decomposition, Gaussian mixture model and k-means clustering this study precisely identify the clusters of data files. This research would provide an efficient way to analyze text documents written in Sinhala, and empower citizens and organizations to do their daily work with a great degree of ease. By using an automatic text categorizing system, it is possible to group the documents based on their content, within a short period of time. This approach can be practically applied to group news articles according to their subject such as political, economic, art, etc. This approach can be further extended to applications such as analyzing insurance claims, automatic fax processing, e-mail filtering and many more text mining applications. This study can be extended to measure the scalability and performance of this approach when the number of documents increases to a large number. Findings of such research can be used to fine tune this approach to an optimum usage.

8. Acknowledgement

We would like to thank for all, who extended their support to make this research a success.

10. References

[1] Andrea L. Houston, Kenneth R. Walsh, "Using an AI-Based Tool to Categorize Digitized Textual Forms of Organizational Memory", *Proceedings of the 29th Ann& Hawaii International Conference on System Sciences (HICSS-29)* – 1996, 1060-3425/96 IEEE.

[2] Ji He, Ah-Hwee Tan, Chew-Lim Tan, "*A Comparative Study on Chinese Text Categorization Methods*", A-H. Tan, P.Yu (Eds), PRICAI 2000 workshop on text and web mining, Melbourne, pp. 24-35, August 2000.

[3] "Sinhala hodiya", available at http://www.LANandWAN.com/Sinhala/hoodiya.htm

[4] Bled, Slovenia, "*Machine Learning in Text Data Analysis*", ICML-99 Workshop, June 30, 1999. Available at http://atlas-conferences.com.

[5] Fotis Lazarinis, Jesus Vilares Ferro, John Tait, "*Improving Non-English Web Searching*" (iNEWS07), SIGIR 2007 workshop report, ACM SIGIR Forum, Vol. 41 No. 2, December 2007.

[6] Yuen-Hsien Tseng , "*FJU Test Collection for Evaluation of Chinese Text Categorization*", 2004 , available at http://www.lins.fju.edu.tw/~tseng/ Collections/ Chinese_TC.html

[7] Text mining tool, Magenta Technology text understanding approach, available at http://www.magenta-technology.com/en/technology.

[8] Honkela, T., Kaski, S., Lagus, K., and Kohonen, T.: *Newsgroup Exploration with WEBSOM Method and Browsing Interface.* Helsinki University of Technology, Laboratory of Computer and Information Science, Report A32, 1996.

[9] Sameh H. Ghwanmeh, "Applying Clustering of Hierarchical K-means-like Algorithm on Arabic Language", *International Journal Of Information Technology,* Volume 3 Number 1 2006 Issn 1305-2403.

[10] Helena Ahonen-Myka, "*Processing of Large Document Collections*", University of Helsinki.

[11] Chung-Hong Lee, Hsin-Chang Yang, Sheng-Min Ma , "A Novel Multilingual Text Categorization System using Latent Semantic Indexing", *First International Conference on Innovative Computing, Information and Contro,* Volume II (ICICIC'06), pp. 503-506.

[12] Pavel Praks, Jiri Dvorsky, Vaclav Snasel, "Latent Semantic Indexing for Image Retrieval Systems".

[13] Landauer, T. K., Foltz, P. W., & Laham, D. ," Introduction to Latent Semantic Analysis, *Discourse Processes,* 25, 259-284, (1998).

[14] Yogesh Raja - Shaogang Gong, "Gaussian Mixture Model (GMM)", Queen Mary and Westfield College, England.

[15] Andrew W. Moore, "Clustering with Gaussian Mixtures", Carnegie Mellon University. Available at www.cs.cmu.edu/~awm.

[16] Jiawei Han and Micheline Kamber, *Data Mining: Concepts and Techniques*, Second Edition, Morgan Kaufmann publications, United States of America, 2006.

[17] D.A.Meedeniya, A.S.Perera, "A Comparative Study on Data Representation to Categorize Text Documents", *20th International Conference on Software Engineering and Knowledge Engineering (SEKE'08)*, 2008.

[18] Daniel t. Larose, *Data mining methods and models*, John Wiley & Sons, Inc, United States of America, 2006.

[19] Wesley Chu, Tsau Young Lin (Eds.), *Foundations and Advances in Data Mining*, vol 180, Springer-Verlag Berlin Heidelberg, 2005.

[20] David Taniar, *Research and Trends in Data Mining Technologies and Applications*, Idiea Group publication, 2007.

[21] Bei Yu, John Unsworth , "An Evaluation of Text Classification Methods for Literary Study", University of Illinois at Urbana-Champaign, http://www.digitalhumanities.org/dh2007/abstracts/xhtml.xq?id=157

[22] Gair, James W. Selected and Edited by Barbara C. Lust, Studies in South Asian Linguistics. Sinhala and Other South Asian Languages, New York / Oxford: Oxford University, 1998.

[23] Gair, James W., Sinhala - The Indo-Aryan Languages, George Cardona & Dhanesh Jain (eds.), London / New York: Routledge (Routledge Language Family Series), 2003.

[24] Chid Apte, Fred Damerau, Sholom Weiss, "Text Mining with Decision Rules and Decision Trees" , IBM Research Division, T.J. Watson Research Center, Yorktown Heights, NY 10598.

[25] Samaranayake, V. K., Nandasara, S. T., Dissanayake, J. B., Weerasinghe, A.R., Wijayawardhana, H., "*An Introduction to UNICODE for Sinhala Characters*", University of Colombo School of Computing, 2003.

[26] Heikki Hyötyniemi, "Text Document Classification with Self-Organizing Maps", *Proceedings of STeP'96.* Jarmo Alander, Timo Honkela and Matti Jakobsson (eds.), Publications of the Finnish Artificial Intelligence Society, pp. 64-72.

[27] Kanoksri Sarinnapakorn and Miroslav Kubat, "Combining Sub classifiers in Text Categorization: A DST-Based Solution and A Case Study", *IEEE transactions on knowledge and data engineering*, vol. 19, no. 12, December 2007.

[28] White paper on "*Natural Language Computing*", Available at http://research.microsoft.com/research /pub/China-Natural Language Computing-Home.mht.

[29] Guo D., Berry M.W., Thompson B.B., Bailin S., "Knowledge Enhanced Latent Semantic Indexing", *Information Retrieval*, Volume 6, Number 2, April 2003, pp.225-250(26).

[30] Dean Wright, "*Integrating Language Identification with Text Classification*", UMBC, 2004.

[31] Daniel Boley, Maria Gini, Kyle Hastings, Bamshad Mobasher, Jerry Moore, "A client-side Web agent for document categorization", *Internet Research: Electronic Networking Applications and Policy*, Volume 8 · Number 5 · 1998 · pp. 387 399, © MCB University Press · ISSN 1066-2243.

[32] David L. Olson Dursun Delen, *Advanced Data Mining Techniques,* Springer-Verlag Berlin Heidelberg, USA, 2008. ISBN: 978-3-540-76916-3

[33] Ian H.Witten, Eibe Frank, *Data Mining: Practical Machine Learning Tools and Techniques*, Second edition, Morgan Kaufmann Publishers, CA, 2005.

[34] Hichem Sahbi, "A Particular Gaussian Mixture Model for Clustering", Cambridge University, UK.

Automatic Document Classifier based on Statistical Machine Learning Techniques

Rajashree Shettar and Dr. Shobha G
Department of Computer Science, R.V. College of Engineering,
Bangalore, 560059, Karnataka, India
rajshri.shettar@gmail.com *shobhatilak@rediffmail.com*

Abstract

In this paper Document Classification (DC) based on statistical machine learning techniques has been implemented. DC based on the Naïve Bayes model involves representing the text document using probabilistic mode and DC based on Vector Space Model uses TFIDF (term frequency inverse document frequency). In this paper we present an automatic document classification technique using Naïve Bayes Classifier approach (NB) and Vector Space approach (VS) which classifies the text documents to pre-defined classes (topics or themes) of documents based on supervised machine learning techniques. A comparison of both these supervised machine learning techniques on the 20 Newsgroups corpora shows that for NB algorithm works better than VS algorithm for our implementation of document classifier.

1. Introduction

The task of document classification (DC) deals with automatically classifying text documents to predefined categories. The automatic text documents is of great practical importance given the massive volume of text available through the WWW, news feed, electronic mails, corporate databases and digital libraries. Document classification (DC) is known under a number of synonyms such as Text Categorization (TC), routing and topic identification. There are two main approaches to document classification namely *supervised* learning and *unsupervised* learning. In supervised leaning, the classifier is first trained with a set of training data in which documents are labeled with their categories and then the learned module is for classification of documents. The unsupervised is mainly based on clustering. In this paper we focus on supervised learning. Supervised document classifiers also known as statistical document classifier, are primarily based on probability model and statistics. The statistical occurrences of each concept in the example document are analyzed by the document classification and a model or classifier is constructed for each category that is used to classify subsequent documents automatically. The system refines its model by "learning" the categories as new documents are processed.

The approaches to supervised learning are through the Naïve Bayes model (NB) and Vector Space Models (VS). The document classification is done based on Naïve Bayes classifier algorithm and space vector algorithm. The naïve bayes algorithm uses probabilistic model and space .vector algorithm uses TFIDF concept (Term Frequency- Inverse Document Frequency). Many learning algorithms such as *k*-nearest neighbor (*k*-NN) [1, 2, 3], Support Vector Machines (SVM) [4], neural networks (NNet) [5, 6], linear least squares fit (LLSF) [7], and naive Bayes (NB) [8, 9] have been applied to document classification. A comparison of these techniques is presented by Yang and Liu in [7]. They conclude that all these techniques perform comparably when each category contains over 300 documents. However, when the number of positive training documents per category is less than 10, SVM, *k*-NN, and LLSF outperform significantly NNet and NB

In the problem of document classification we have a set D of documents and a set S of predefined categories. The aim is to assign a Boolean value to each $\langle di, cj \rangle$ pair, where $di \in D$ and $cj \in S$. A value true assigned to $\langle di, cj \rangle$ stands for the decision of assigning true for the document $di \;\; to \;\; cj$. A value of false assigned to $\langle di, cj \rangle$ stands for the decision of not assigning the document di to cj. The task is to approximate the unknown target function $f : D \times S -> \{true, false\}$ that describes the way the document should actually be classified by the classifier function $f' : D \times S -> \{true, false\}$ such that the number of decisions of f and f' that do not coincide is minimized.

2. Document Preprocessing and Representation

In order to classify text documents by applying machine learning techniques, documents should be preprocessed. In preprocessing step, the documents should be transformed into a suitable form to apply the learning algorithms. In this phase all the documents present in the input corpus are parsed and keywords containing alpha characters are extracted. The keywords are words that are obtained after eliminating the stop words, low frequency words and very high frequency words. Apart from this a document can have numbers and non-alphabetic characters, etc which is removed during preprocessing. All the HTML mark-up tags are removed from the documents. In order to define words that are in the same context with same term and consequently to reduce dimensionality, stemming of words has also been considered. A term in the document collection can stand for a distinct single-word, a stemmed word or a phrase. In vector space representation, defining terms as distinct single words is referred to as "bag of words" (BOW) representation. Some researchers state that using phrases rather than single words to define terms produce more accurate classification results [14, 15]; whereas others argue that using single words as terms does not produce worse results [16,17]. As BOW is more often used method for defining terms and it is computationally more efficient than the phrase representation, this representation is chosen to define terms of the feature space in this paper. A vocabulary list of corpus and also specific vocabulary list of each category (category keyword list) is created after the input training documents are preprocessed. The vocabulary list contains the occurrence count of each keyword in the training corpus. The category keyword list for each category contains the occurrence count of each keyword in the category. For dimensionality reduction document frequency (DF) of a term is used. Document frequency (DF) of a term is the number of documents that term appears. In this technique, the document frequency of each unique term is computed and terms whose document frequencies are less than a predetermined threshold are eliminated. The basic assumption behind this technique is that low frequency terms are either non-informative for document categorization or they do not have much weight in global performance. This technique also leads to improvement in categorization accuracy as low frequency terms are generally noise terms. However, DF is usually not used for aggressive term elimination because there is another widely accepted assumption in information retrieval that low-DF terms are distinctive and thus relatively informative and for this reason should not be removed aggressively [18].

3. Naïve Bayes Probabilistic Model

The Naive Bayes (NB) classifier is a probabilistic model that uses the joint probabilities of terms and categories to estimate the probabilities of categories given a test document [10]. The naive part of the classifier comes from the simplifying assumption that all terms are conditionally independent of each other given a category. Because of this independence assumption, the parameters for each term can be learned separately and this simplifies and speeds the computation operations compared to non-naive Bayes classifiers. Abstractly, the probability model for a classifier is a conditional model $p(C \mid F1, F2, \ldots Fn)$ over a dependent class variable C with a small number of outcomes or classes, conditional on several feature variables Fl through Fn. The problem is that if the number of features n is large or when a feature can take on a large number of values, then basing such a model on probability tables is infeasible [12]. We therefore reformulate the model to make it more tractable. The Bayes' theorem [3] relates the conditional and marginal probabilities of stochastic events C and F :

$$Pr(C|F) = \frac{Pr(F|C)Pr(C)}{Pr(F)} \qquad (1)$$

Where: $p(C)$ is the prior probability of hypothesis C; p(F) is the prior probability of training data F; $p(C \mid F)$ is the probability of C given F and; $p(F \mid C)$ is the probability of F given C. Using Bayes' theorem for several feature variables Fn , we can rewrite this as:

$$p(C|F_1, \ldots, F_n) = \frac{p(C)p(F_1, \ldots, F_n|C)}{p(F_1, \ldots, F_n)} \qquad (2)$$

In practice we are only interested in the numerator of that fraction, since the denominator does not depend on C and the values of the features Fi are given, so that the denominator is effectively constant. The numerator is equivalent to the joint probability model which can be rewritten using repeated applications of the definition of conditional probability as:

$$p(C, F_1, \ldots, F_n)$$

$$= p(C)p(F_1|C)p(F_2|C,F_1).p(F_3|C,F_1,F_2)...p(F_n|C,F_1,F_2,\ldots,F_{n-1}) \qquad (3)$$

This means: assuming that each feature Fi is conditionally independent of every other feature Fj for j≠i and $p(Fi \mid C, Fj) = p(Fi \mid C)$ the equation (1) can be expressed as:

$$p(C, F_1, \ldots, F_n) = p(C)p(F_1|C)p(F_2|C), \ldots = p(C)\prod p(F_i|C). \qquad (4)$$

Therefore by using the above derivation the Naïve Bayes Classifier can be given as:

$$classify(f_1, \ldots, f_n) = argmax_c P(C = c)\prod_{i=1}^{n} p(F_i = f_i|C = c). \qquad (5)$$

4. Naïve Bayes Model for Document Classification

Consider the problem of classifying documents by their content. The documents are drawn from a number of classes or categories which can be modeled as set of words where the independent probability that the $i\text{-}th$ word of a document occurs in a class C can be written as $p(wi \mid C)$. We assume that the probability of a word in a document is independent of the length of the document, or that all documents are of same length. Then the probability of a given document D given a class C, is

$$p(document \mid class) = \prod_i p(word_i \mid class) \tag{6}$$

From Equation (1)

$$p(class \mid document) = \frac{p(class)p(document \mid class)}{p(document)} \tag{7}$$

So: $p(class \mid document) = p(class)\prod_i p(word_i \mid class)$ (8)

$p(word_i \mid C)$: Probability that the $i\text{-}th$ word of a given document occurs in a document from class C, and this can be calculated as the follow:

$$p(word_i \mid C) = \frac{\text{Number of times the word occurs in the category } C + 1}{\text{Number of words in } C \text{ category} + \text{size of the vocabulary list}} \tag{9}$$

5. Vector Space TFIDF Model

The most widely used method for document representation is the Vector Space Model (VSM) introduced by Salton et al. [13], which has been used in this paper. In this model, each document is represented as a vector d. Each dimension in the vector d stands for a distinct term in the term space of the document collection.

Each document vector d is represented as

$$d = (w_1, w_2, w_3, \ldots, w_{|T|}) \tag{10}$$

where w_i is the weight of ith term of document d and $|T|$ is the number of distinct terms in the document collection.

We define tf_i as the raw frequency of term i in document d.

N as the total number of documents in the document corpus;

N_i as the number of documents in the corpus where term i appears; and

$|T|$ as the number of distinct terms in the document collection (after stop word removal and stemming is performed).

The weight of term i in document d is assigned proportionately to the number of times the term appears in the document, and in inverse proportion to the number of documents in the corpus in which the term appears.

$$wi = tf_i.\log\left(\frac{N}{N_i}\right) \tag{11}$$

TF×IDF weighting approach weights the frequency of a term in a document with a factor that discounts its importance if it appears in most of the documents.

6. Vector Space Model for Document Classification

When used for document classification, represents the text documents as vectors where distinct word is a separate term. It assigns some weight to each term (word) in the vector (document) depending on the importance of that term (word) in the vector (component). There are several approaches to assigning weights. One of the popular approaches is called TFIDF (Term Frequency / Inverse Document Frequency) which assigns a higher weight to a word which appears in relatively fewer documents but its frequency in those documents is high.

The second and following pages should begin 1.0 inch (2.54 cm) from the top edge. On all pages, the bottom margin should be approximately 1-5/8 inches (4.13 cm) from the bottom edge of the page.

7. Phases of Document Classification

In the following sections different phases of document classifier has been discussed. In section 7.2 and section 7.3 naïve bayes trainer and classifier algorithm has been discussed respectively. Section 7.4 and section 7.5 describes the vector space trainer and classifier algorithm respectively and finally the experimental results are presented in section 8 with conclusion in section 9.

7.1 Naïve Bayes Trainer Algorithm

Naïve Bayes is a supervised document classifier that is trained before it can be used to classify the documents. The vocabulary list of the corpus and the keywords list of each category are taken and prior probabilities for each category is calculated and the posterior probability given a word from the Vocabulary (Wk) that the category will be v is calculated.

Input: vocabulary list of the corpus, keyword list of each category.

Output: Calculates the prior probability of each category, posterior probability given a word from the vocabulary Wk that the category will be v.

```
1. Get the Vocabulary List, Wk.
2. Get the Category List, Nk.
3. Calculate prior probability p(v) for each category
   p(v) <- total_number_of_documents_category[v] / total_number_documents_corpus.
4. Calculate total word count n for each category in the document corpora.
   For each category in corpus
     For each keyword in category list
       Fetch the next keyword from the vocabulary list, Wk.
       Fetch the number of keyword occurrence Nk from the category list.
         Calculate the posterior probability.
         p(Wk | v) = (Nk + 1)/(n + size of vocabulary list)
     End For
   End For
5. Write the posterior probabilities of all the keywords of each category to a file.
6. Return
```

7.2 Naïve Bayes Classifier Algorithm

It classifies the given document based on training performed by the naïve bayes trainer i.e. by using prior probabilities of each categories and posterior probabilities of each keywords and the most relevant category the input document belongs to is calculated using the Naïve Bayes algorithm. It classifies the given document by tokenizing the given document, eliminating the stop words, extracting the keywords.

Input: text document to be classified, trained data of Naïve Bayes trainer.

Output: category to which the document belongs to, statistical information like classification accuracy, etc.

```
1. Get the prior probability p(v).
2. Get the posterior probability p(Wk | v) for each category.
3. Get the document to the classified.
4. Tokenize the document.
5. Eliminate stopwords.
6. Eliminate low and high frequency words.
7. For each category v in the corpus
      For each keyword Wk in document
            If keyword in vocabulary list
            Get keyword posterior probability p(Wk | v)
            Probability_class = probability_class * p(Wk | v)
      End For
            Probability_class[i] = probability_class[i] × p(v)
   End For
      For each category in corpus
         If (category < probability_class[i])
               Category = probability_class[i]
         End If
      End For
8. Return category
```

7.3 Vector Space Trainer Algorithm

This module trains the Space Vector classifier by taking the vocabulary list of corpus and keyword list of each category and calculating TFIDF weight of each word.

Input: vocabulary list of corpus, keyword list of each category.

Output: calculates the TFIDF weight of word in a given category and stores it in a file.

```
1. Get the vocabulary list
2. Get category list
3. Calculate total word count for each category 'n'
            N <- total word occurrences in a given category
4. For each category in corpus
            V <- next category
            For each keyword in category list
                  Wk <- next keyword
                  Nk <- no of keyword occurrences
                  Calculate the TFIDF weight for keyword
                     TFIDF = Nk / N
            End For
   End For
5. Write the TFIDF weight of all the keywords of each categories to a file.
6. Return
```

7.4 Vector Space Classifier

This module performs the classification of a given document using the training performed by the previous module. Classifies the given document by tokenizing the given document, eliminating the stop words, extracting the keywords and by using the TFIDF weight of each keyword calculates the most relevant category to a given category.

Input: text document to be classified, trained data of vector space trainer.

Output: category to which the document belongs, statistical information like classification accuracy, etc.

```
1. Get the TFIDF weight for each keyword in each category
2. Get the document to the classified
3. Tokenize the document
4. Eliminate stopwords
5. Eliminate low and high frequency words
6. For each category 'V' in corpus
         For each keyword 'Wk' in document
               If keyword in vocabulary list
                  Get keyword TFIDF weight of keyword
                  Category_weight = Category_weight + TFIDF
               End For
   End For
               For each category in corpus
                  If( category < Category_weight[i] )
                        Category = Category_Weight[i]
                  End If
               End For
7. Return category
```

8. Experimental Analysis and Results

In this paper the experimental evaluation of performance on supervised machine learning techniques using the naïve bayes and vector space approach for automatic classification of documents has been conducted. The standard 20 Newsgroup corpora has been used as the data set for training and testing purpose. The 20 Newsgroups data set is a collection of approximately 20,000 newsgroup documents, partitioned evenly across 20 different newsgroups. The data is organized into 20 different newsgroups, each corresponding to a different topic. Some of the newsgroups are very closely related to each other (e.g. comp.sys.ibm.pc.hardware / comp.sys.mac.hardware), while others are highly unrelated (e.g. misc.forsale / soc.religion.christian). Here is a list of the 20 newsgroups, partitioned (more or less) according to subject matter:

Table1 List of 20 different categories of 20_Newsgroups dataset.

comp.graphics comp.os.ms-windows.misc comp.sys.ibm.pc.hardware comp.sys.mac.hardware comp.windows.x	rec.autos rec.motorcycles rec.sport.baseball rec.sport.hockey	sci.crypt sci.electronics sci.med sci.space
misc.forsale	talk.politics.misc talk.politics.guns talk.politics.mideast	talk.religion.misc alt.atheism soc.religion.christian

The DC classifies both text and HTML files. It recursively descends directories, to find text files. In case of multiple documents per file, the document boundaries are found. Results have shown that the supervised (statistical) classifier using Naïve Bayes and vector space algorithm can classify documents into any one of the 20 categories present in the 20_newsgroup dataset. 80% of the documents (i.e. 16,000 documents) present in the 20_newsgroup dataset were used for training the classifiers and remaining 20% of the documents (i.e. 4000 documents) for testing the algorithms accuracy have been used. The Naïve Bayes algorithm has been found to give the best results for classification with accuracy over 86% on an average for 20 categories. Vector space accuracy was just above 73% for our implementation.

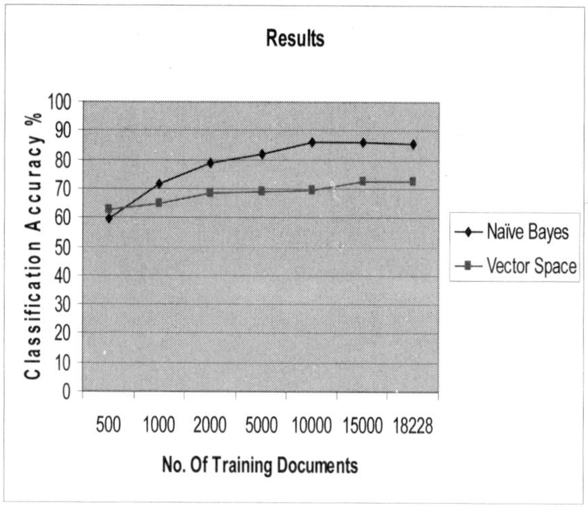

Graph 1 The classification accuracy of naïve bayes and vector space algorithm.

9. Conclusion

An automated document classification system has been implemented in this paper using the concept of statistical machine learning technique. Statistical algorithms require that the entire training set be pre-classified and tagged with their respective categories. The Naïve Bayes algorithm was found to give the best result for classification with accuracy over 86% on an average for 20 categories. Space vector accuracy was just above 73% for our implementation, but with more sophisticated methods of vectorization documents this can be improved further.

The document classification can be improved by considering key word phrases and collection of words rather than single terms for keywords. It can also be integrated with search engine to give category specific search result.

10. References

[1] Masand, B., G. Lino, and D. Waltz, "Classifying News Stories Using Memory Based Reasoning", *15th Ann Int ACM SIGIR Conference on Research and Development in Information Retrieval*, pp. 59–64, 1992.

[2] Yang, Y., "An Evaluation of Statistical Approaches to Text Categorization", *Journal of Information Retrieval*, Vol. 1, No. 1–2, pp. 69–90, 1999.

[3] Yang, Y. and J. P. Pedersen, "A Comparative Study on Feature Selection in Text Categorization", *The Fourteenth International Conference on Machine Learning*, pp. 412–420, 1997.

[4] Joachims, T., "Text Categorization with Support Vector Machines: Learning with Many Relevant Features", *European Conference on Machine Learning (ECML)*, 1998.

[5] Ng, H. T., W. B. Goh, and K. L. Low, "Feature Selection, Perceptron Learning, and a Usability Case Study for Text Categorization", *20th Ann Int ACM SIGIR Conference on Research and Development in Information Retrieval*, pp. 67–73, 1997.

[6] Wiener, E., J. O. Pedersen, and A. S. Weigend, "A Neural Network Approach to Topic Spotting", *Proceedings of the Fourth Annual Symposium on Document Analysis and Information Retrieval*, 1995.

[7] Yang, Y. and X. Liu, "A Re-examination of Text Categorization Methods", *Proceedings of SIGIR-99, 22nd ACM International Conference on Research and Development in Information Retrieval*, Berkeley, US, 1999.

[8] McCallum, A. and K. Nigam, "A Comparison of Event Models for Naive Bayes Text Classification", *AAAI-98 Workshop on Learning for Text Categorization*, 1998.

[9] Koller, D. and M. Sahami, "Hierarchically Classifying Documents Using Very Few Words", *Proceedings of 14th International Conference on Machine Learning*, pp. 170–178, Nashville, US, 1997.

[10] Mitchell, T.M., *Machine Learning*, McGraw Hill, 1997.

[11] Joachims, T., "A Probabilistic Analysis of the Rocchio Algorithm with TFIDF for Text Categorization", *ICML-97*, 1997.

[12] Ioan Pop, "An approach of the Naïve Bayes Classifier for the Document classifier", *Proceedings of the International Journal on Information Sciences and Computing, IJISAC* , General Mathematics, Vol. 14, No. 4 (2006), pp. 135-138.

[13] Salton, G., C. Yang, and A. Wong, "A Vector-Space Model for Automatic Indexing", Communications of the ACM , Vol. 18, No. 11, pp. 613–620, 1975.

[14] Cohen, W. W. and Y. Singer, "Context-Sensitive Learning Methods for Text Categorization", *Proceedings of the 19th Annual ACM SIGIR Conference,* 1996.

[15] Fuernkranz, J., T. Mitchell, and E. Riloff, "A Case Study in Using Linguistic Phrases for Text Categorization on the WWW", *Sahami, M., editor, In Learning for Text Categorization: Papers from the 1998 AAAI Workshop (Technical Report WS-98-05),* 1998.

[16] Dumais, S., T. Platt, D. Heckermann, and M. Sahami, "Inductive Learning Algorithms and Representations for Text Categorization", *Proceedings of the Seventh International Conference on Information and Knowledge Management,* 1998.

[17] Sahami, M., Using Machine Learning To Improve Information Access, Ph.D. Thesis, Stanford University, 1998.

[18] Yang, Y. and J. P. Pedersen, "A Comparative Study on Feature Selection in Text Categorization", *The Fourteenth International Conference on Machine Learning,* pp. 412–420, 1997.

Overall Operation of DNA Computer with Emphasis on Memory Operations

Mr. Subrata Sinha
Lecturer (Comp. Sc), Center for Bioinformatics Studies, Dibrugarh University, Dibrugarh, India
subratasinha@indiatimes.com

Abstract

DNA encodes information through the order, or sequence of the nucleotide along each strand. Organisms differ from one another because their DNA sequence differs. DNA has a huge storage and processing capacity. DNA computer is realized in laboratories. This paper describes an abstract model of a DNA Computer. The overall operation of a DNA Computer is presented along with the DNA data encoding Scheme. In this Paper the main focus is given on how the electronic input device/Output device interacts with the DNA memory Unit, followed by data encoding and storage in DNA memory. Above all an Operational Model has been sketched giving main emphasis on memory operations. The next generation computer will be DNA Computers with gigantic storage capacity and massive parallel processing capacity.

1. Introduction

DNA(Deoxyribo Nucleic Acid) is a molecule consists of two long polynucleotide chains(known as Complementary) strand composed four types of nucleotide subunit, viz.Adenine(A), Guanine(G), Thymine (T), Cytocine (C). Nucleotides are covalently linked together. Adenine of One strand makes two hydrogen bond with the corresponding Thymine of Complementary chain and Guanine makes three hydrogen bond with Cytocine. Each of these chains is known as a DNA Chain or a DNA strand. Structure of DNA provide an Mechanism for heredity in organisms. Structure of DNA is not described in details.

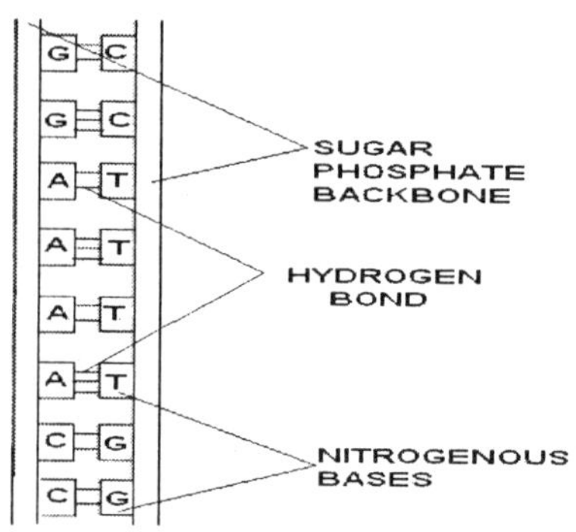

Fig. 1 Schematic Diagram of DNA

DNA encodes information through the order, or sequence of the nucleotide along each strand. Organisms differ from one another because their DNA sequence differs.

DNA pass on the information i.e., our IQ, aptitudes, physical appearance and even the skill of survival from one generation to the next generation. This signifies that DNA has a huge storage capacity and we are going to explore the storage capacity of DNA in this paper.

A. Operations of DNA : Denaturation : Separation of Complementary strands by breaking the hydrogen bonds among the complementary base pairs. Annealing: Binding of Complementary strands. Ligation: Joining linear DNA fragments together with covalent bonds is called ligation.Enzyme Ligase is responsible for ligation. Cleavage: breaking a DNA strand into two or more segments is known as cleavage. Restriction enzymes are responsible for cleaving.

All these operations can be used as basic operations of a DNA computer.

B. Motivating factors for choosing DNA for next generation computing: Huge memory: A small volume can contain a huge number of DNA molecules. 5 gms of DNA per one liter of water contains in a solution about 10^{21} bases. By considering 10 to 100 base pairs per byte. We can have 10^{19} to 10^{20} bytes, which comes around 10^7 to 10^8 tera bytes i.e 1 crore tera bytes.

High data density: Data density of DNA is highly impressive. As the nucleotides are spaced 0.35 nanometer apart, which gives 18 Mbit per inch and 1 Million Mbit per square inch, which is 1000000 times more than today's high performance hard drive which is 7Gbits per square inch.

Faster Data Access: In bacteria DNA can be replicated at a rate of about 500 bp a second. Which is only 1000 bits/Second but if we allow many copies of the replication enzymes to works on DNA is parallel. First of all, the replication enzymes can start on the second replicated strand of DNA even before they're finished copying the first one. So already the data rate jumps to 2000 bits/sec. But look what happens after each replication is finished- the number of DNA strands increases exponentially (2^n after n iterations). With each additional strand data rate increases by 1000 bits/sec. So after 10 iterations, the DNA is being replicated at a rate about 1 Mbit/sec after 30 iterations it increases to 1000 GBits /sec. This is beyond the sustained data rates of the fastest hard drives.

Another important property of DNA is its double stranded nature. The bases A and T, and C and G can bind together, forming base pairs. Therefore every DNA sequence has a natural complement. Complementary strands hybridize together to form a double stranded DNA. This complementary makes DNA a unique data structure for computation and can be exploited in many ways. Error Correction is one example. Errors in DNA happen due to many factors. Occasionally, DNA enzymes simply make mistakes, and cutting where they should not or inserting T for a G.DNA can also be damaged by thermal energy and UV energy from the sun. If the error occurs in one of strands of double stranded DNA, repair enzymes can restore the proper DNA sequence by using the complement strand as a reference. In this sense. double stranded DNA is similar to a **RAID 1 array,**

A wide range of character representation is possible with a a DNA sequence of length 8 nucleotide i.e., 4^8(65536) characters, which naturally means that a DNA sequence of length 10 or 100 can encode 4^{10}(1048576) or 4^{100}(1.6×10^{60}) characters which is beyond imagination. Considering a length of 8 nucleotide where only middle 4 nucleotide is used for encoding for some special designing issues explained later. In this paper I have shown an encoding of 4^4(256) characters.

Speed: A DNA strand of length 1000 bp can encode one processor state and so a liter of solution encodes the state of approximately 10^{18} distinct processors. It shows a massive parallelism as Recombinant DNA operations that act on all the DNA molecules at the same time.

Energy Requirements: Many recombinant DNA operations such as denaturing and annealing are reversible, so they require arbitrarily small energy.

2. Architecture of a DNA Computer

The concrete architecture of a DNA computer is yet to be designed, but a an model can be proposed based on the resent scenarios in Bio Molecular Computation (BMC). The present day DNA computer is a Laboratory with scientists working inside it with chemicals and test tubes, but the days are coming when we will have a DNA computer much similar to today's PC at our disposal but with a huge storage and massive processing capacity. In this paper I have proposed a model of such computer.

As the DNA computer will be used by general users, so Input and Output device will be as usual i.e., electronic component. Input device will be Keyboard and ouput device will be monitor.

My whole work revolves around the basic architecture as shown below. We have considered Input and output unit as electronic and Processing and storage as DNA, so a converter in both end is required which will convert user input in the form electronic instruction to a molecular form so that Recombinant DNA operations can be performed.

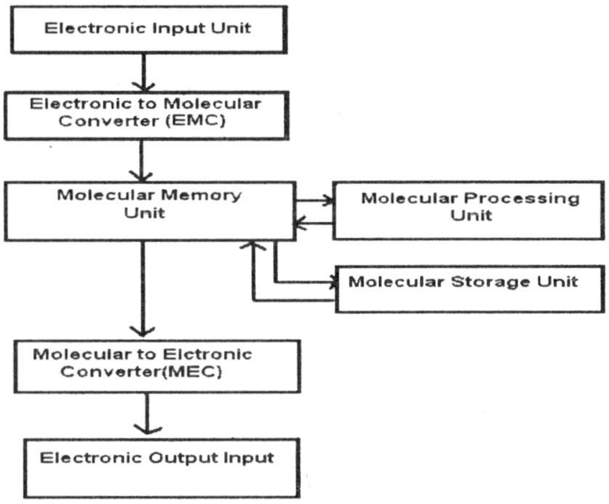

Fig. 2 Proposed Model of a DNA Computer

Input from a Keyboard will move to *DNA synthesizer* which will generate the required polymer based on the user input,Each character on the keyboard will have some specific corresponding DNA strand polymer-mer or 10-mer based on DNA encoding Scheme (Annex I).

A. DNA Memory Operations: Once the DNA strand is produced it should be stored temporarily for future reference in primary memory.

DNA memory can be formed using the hairpin DNA,as shown by Masahiro takinove and Akira Suyama of University of Tokyo and JST Agency , In their paper they have shown how molecular reactions can be used for a DNA molecular memory.

DNA molecular memory is composed of two types of DNA: a hairpin DNA which forms intramolecular base pairs and a linear DNA which does not. Let us take an example of the Hairpin DNA , with sequence 5'-TAMRA-GGACACGGTGCAGTGTAAGCAACTATTGTCTTCGTGTCC-Dabcyl-3' .TAMRA is a flurocent dye and Dabcyl is a quencher. Hairpin DNA acts as a memory molecule with a memory address,

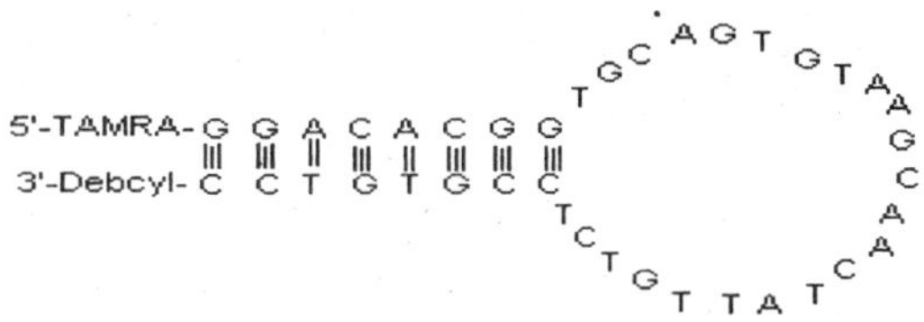

Fig. 3 Hairpin DNA

Hairpin DNA forms in a ssDNA only when opposite ends are having rich GC content, as G bind with C and viceversa. Here the loop region actually is used for memory address which is recognized by data DNA.

The linear DNA as a data molecule with a address tag of the memory. Here in our case we have taken a sequence

5'GACACGGAGACAATAGTTGCTTACACTGCA-3'

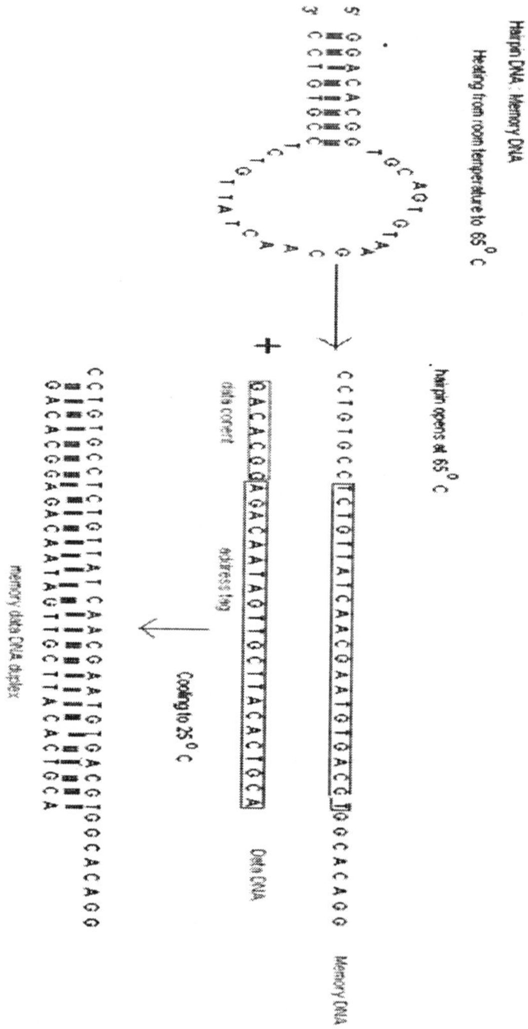

Fig. 4 Writing Data DNA to Memory DNA

The basic principle of erasing a Data from the memory is to separate the Data DNA from Memory DNA. Erasing operation consists for the following steps: Heating the Data memory DNA duple from room temperature to Erasing temperature i.e., upto 75° C and then cooling it quickly to room temperature, the duplex is denatured and memory DNA again forms the hairpin structure and Data DNA can not annealed to the hairpin DNA as intramolecular affinity is more than inter molecular affinity.

Writing operation make the data DNA bind with the memory DNA through a series of operations: heating up the solution from room temp^r (25° C) to writing temperature (65 °C). As the temperature is increased to 65 °C , the intra-molecular hydrogen bonding breaks and the hairpin DNA opens and hybridizes with the data DNA which has the address tag of the memory DNA, the cooling it to room temperature. At room temperature memory Data DNA duplex is stable

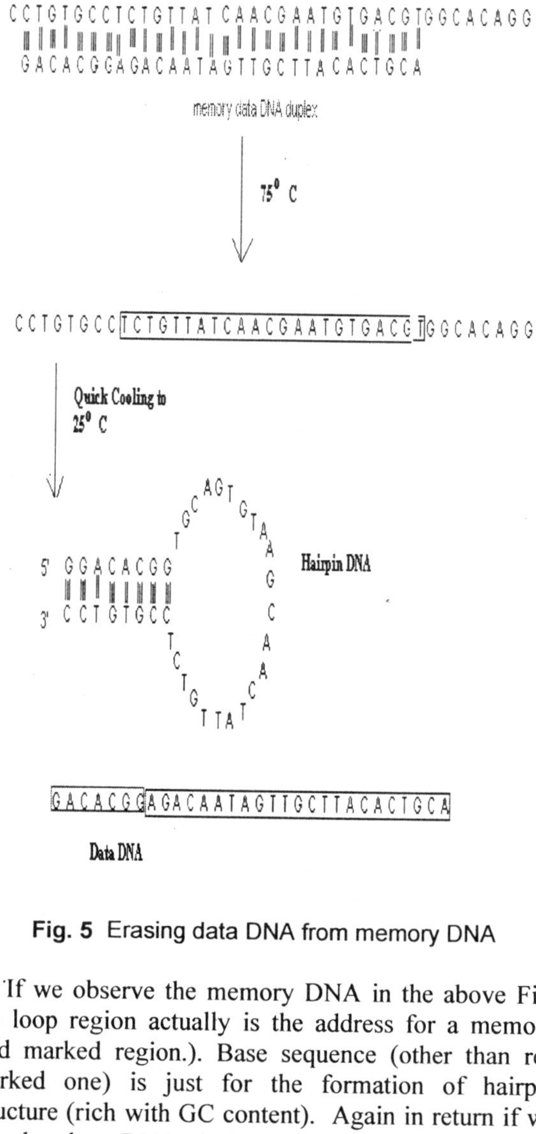

Fig. 5 Erasing data DNA from memory DNA

If we observe the memory DNA in the above Fig, the loop region actually is the address for a memory (red marked region.). Base sequence (other than red marked one) is just for the formation of hairpin structure (rich with GC content). Again in return if we see the data DNA, it has two parts the green one represents data content and red one represents address tag.

Now if we want to standardize the method of data encoding and memory addressing scheme, we have to fix the length of the data content sequence as well as memory address and memory address tag of data DNA. So if want to standardize memory address scheme, we need to study the memory DNA, i.e hairpin DNA very closely. We found that the hairpin DNA has a base sequence of length 8 nucleotides, now excluding 8 nucleotides in both hands which is solely responsible in the formation of hairpin DNA, we find a sequence of length 23 nucleotides, which actually forms the address of the memory. So the possible number of memory addresses are for a given sequence of length 23 is 4^{23}, i.e., 70368744177664 bytes which is approx 70 TB. Now if closely observe our data DNA sequence which is **GG**ACAC**GG**AGACAATAGTTGCTTACACT GCA, so first 8 nucleotide is data content part and the rest is address tag sequence. Among these 8 nucleotide we have to remember that these short sequence of length 8 nucleotides should be rich in GC content, so leave first two and last two nucleotide as G. Now we can have 4 nucleotides left for encoding 256 characters (as $4^4 = 256$).

As we know the data DNA has two parts i.e data content part and a address tag which will direct the data DNA to its memory location, so data content part should be ligated with the corresponding address tag, so that it can form a complete data DNA. The address sequence should be ligated with data content part based on the available address which are free and not occupied by a data DNA.

Synthesizing the address tag and data content part and then ligating them may take longer time than a technique where data content part and address sequence will be concatenated before we enter the codes in the synthesizer.

The molecular memory if present in the solution has only addresses at the loop of memory DNA , but DNA fixed on a solid surface shows higher ability.

While reading the sequence through a device, similar to automated DNA sequencer, we need to ignore the nucleotides after first 8 nucleotides.

3. Partial Operation of DNA Computer

A. The Overall operation of DNA computer in terms of memory access and retrieval can be visualized as follows:-

1. Character code is sent to Strand Code Converter- while user presses any key of keyboard a character code corresponding to the pressed character is generated and sent to the Converter.
2. Conversion of Character code to Strand Code:- Converter is an component which will accept the character code sent from keyboard and compares it with the strand code library(where for each character code one strand code entry will be there) and generates a corresponding strand code of length 8 (8-mer), the data content part of data DNA.
3. Concatenation of address tag with data Content part (before synthesizing)
   Allocation of address is an important issue, where the data DNA will be stored in the memory DNA. Address allocator is a component which will have a close look on the Memory Controlling Unit for the available memory addresses. Thus having a free address from MCU, allocator assigns a address to the newly generated data content part following Concatenation of Strand Code with the address tag.
4. Data DNA code is now sent to synthesizer for generation of actual data DNA strand. Which is a ssDNA.
5. DNA Synthesizer is a automated device used to custom-build DNA molecules to contain a particular sequence of nucleotides.
6. Data DNA with address tag is now sent to Memory Unit for temporary storage.
   Where three operations may occur
   1. Memory Write
   2. Memory Erase
   3. Memory Read

   All Operations are described before.
7. Memory Controlling Unit will have close look on DNA molecular memory and will maintain a list of free addresses and occupied addresses.
8. Memory Read : Once data is written to memory DNA we need to read the data in future that can be done by a unit. Can be termed as DNA Reader(Presently known as DNA Sequencer) The output will be in Strand Code.
9. Converter will work as Sequence Interpreter and will convert the Strand Code to Character Code taking the reference of Strand Code/Character Code Library.
10. Character Code will be Converted to human readable character and displayed in output device

B. Molecular Processing Unit

In the cell, DNA is modified biochemically by a variety of **enzymes** For example, there are enzymes that cut DNA and enzymes that paste it back together. Other enzymes function as copiers, and others as repair units. Molecular biology, Biochemistry, and Biotechnology have developed techniques that allow us to perform many of these cellular functions in the test tube. It's this cellular machinery, along with some synthetic chemistry, that makes up the palette of operations available for computation. Just like a CPU has a basic suite of operations like addition, bit-shifting, logical operators (AND, OR, NOT NOR), etc. that allow it to perform even the most complex calculations, DNA has cutting, copying, pasting, repairing, and many others. And note that in the test tube, enzymes do *not* function sequentially, working on one DNA at a time. Rather, many copies of the enzyme can work on many DNA molecules simultaneously. This is the power of DNA computing, that it can work in a massively parallel fashion.

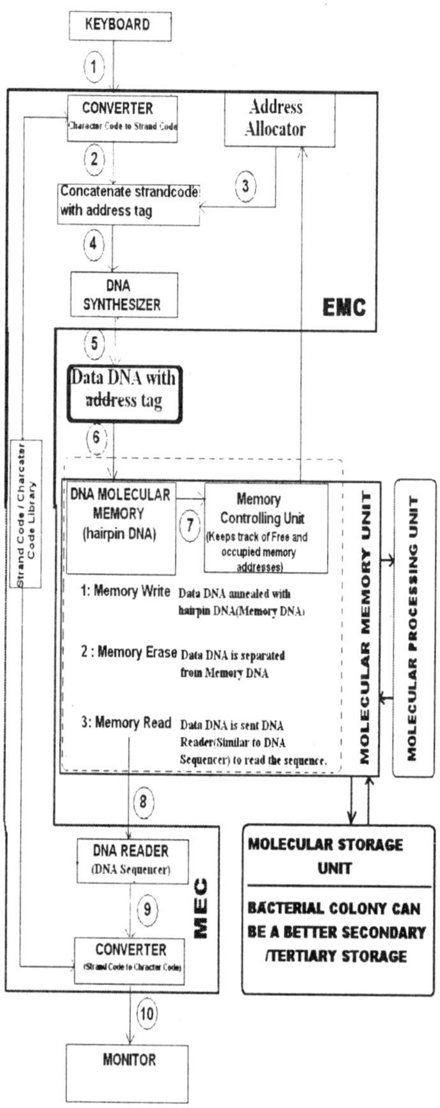

Fig. 6 Partial Operation of DNA Computer

The main power of DNA Processor will be massive parallelism. DNA Chips are something where DNA strands are attached to silicon substrate in large arrays(for example Affymetrix's genechip).Production technology of MEMS is advancing rapidly, allowing for novel integrated small scale DNA Processing devices.

C. Molecular Storage Unit

Molecular Storage Unit will mainly consists of bacteria, The organism should be strong enough to withstand all adverse condition. We can select E.Coli or Deinococcus Radiodurans in this regard, the latter is a better choice for data storage because it can withstand in high temperature, dessication, UV Light and Ionizing radiation doses 1000 time higher than humans.

4. Conclusion

Although we believe that there is greate potential for DNA Computing, the field is still at a very early stage. It is unlikely that DNA Computers will be used for tasks like word processing, but they may ultimately find a niche for solving large-scale intractable combinatorial problems. Although the basic operations required for DNA computers already exist, the problem of automating, miniaturizing and integrating them into a general purpose desktop DNA computer is future challenge.

The Major Challenges in DNA Computation is encoding Problem, Researchers use various encoding scheme for their experiments, but when we think for a complete general purpose computer, we must have a common encoding scheme, which in this paper I have tried to do.

Another Challenge on Constructing DNA Computer is to reduce the time and space necessary to perform a computation. A promising approach to this problem is to use automated miniaturized system that reduce the role of the slow human operator, by using a technique called MEMS micro flow device technology. Which will highly reduce the laboratory work done today to do computation out of DNA.Along with time it will be less error prone.

5. Acknowledgment

This work is done with the core support from the Scientists of Indian Council of Medical Research-Regional Medical Research Center, Lahoal, Dibrugarh.

6. References

[1] John H. Reif, "Paradigm for Biomolecular Computation", Unconventional Models of Computation, Newzealand. Springer Publishers, 1998, pp. 72–93.

[2] Masahiro takinoue, Akira Suyama," Molecular reactions for a Molecular memory based on hairpin DNA". *Chem Bioinformatics Journal*, Vol 4,No.3, pp. 93-100(2004).

[3] Martyn Amos, "DNA Computation", Phd Thesis, University of Warwick, 2008, pp. 9–11.

[4] T.A Brown," Genome 3", Garland Science Publishing, 2007, pp. 5-8.

Annexure I

DNA Encoding Scheme

A Sample ssDNA which can form a hairpin structure i.e a probable Memory DNA (in consideration with experiment of Takinoue and Suyama)

C C A A A A C C A A A A A A A A A A A A A A A A A A A A A A A G G T T T T G G

Hairpin base part ⟷ Memory Address Part ⟷ Hairpin base part

Annexure Fig. 1

If we need to store a character of Table 1 in the memory DNA then we have to concatenate the first entry of Table 2 with the corresponding entry of Table 1.

Table 1 (Character Set) **Table 2** (A set of possible Address Tag)

Table 1	Table 2
G G T T T T G G	T T T T T T T T T T T T T T T T T T T T T T T
G G T T T A G G	T T T T T T T T T T T T T T T T T T T T T T A
G G T T T G G G	T T T T T T T T T T T T T T T T T T T T T T G
G G T T T C G G	T T T T T T T T T T T T T T T T T T T T T T C
G G T T T T G G	T T T T T T T T T T T T T T T T T T T T T A T
G G T T T A G G	T T T T T T T T T T T T T T T T T T T T T A G
.	
.	
.	
G G G G G G G G	G G G G G G G G G G G G G G G G G G G G G G G
256 Possible Characters	4^{23} = 70368744177664 possible memory address tags

Annexure Fig. 2

Any of the possible 256 Characters (yet to be standardized) can be stored in any of 4^{23} possible addresses

For Example if we consider the first entry GGTTTTGG represents alphabet A and we need to store it to an memory address shown in annexure figure 1, then definitely we need to ligate the 8-mer with the address tag TTTTTTTTTTTTTTTTTTTTTTT.

So the data DNA will be G G T T T T G G T T T T T T T T T T T T T T T T T T T T T T T and it can form a memory data DNA duplex with above memory in Fig. 1

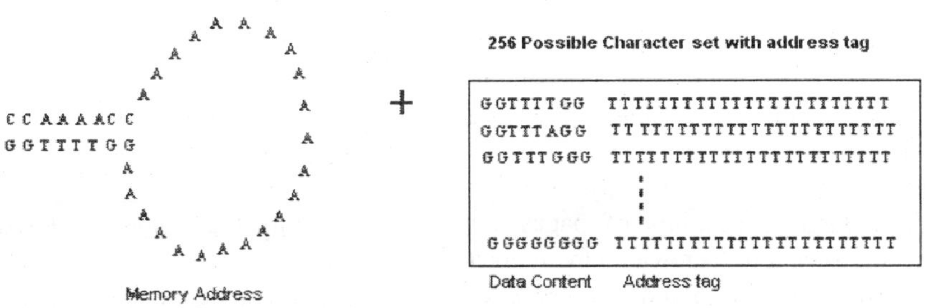

Annexure Fig. 3

So we can draw a conclusion that any of 256 characters can be stored in a memory address taken as an example.

Crawling the Web Using Graph Partitioning Models

Sahar Farajian[1], Ganesh Bhutkar[2] and Shraddhanand Pukale[3]
[1]PG Research Scholar, [2&3]Assistant Professor,
Department of Computer Engineering, Vishwakarma Institute of Technology, Pune - 411037, Maharashtra, India.
saharfarajian@gmail.com *ganesh.bhutkar@vit.edu* *shraddhanand.pukale@vit.edu*

Abstract

The large size and the dynamic nature of the web make it necessary to continually maintain web based information retrieval systems. Crawlers facilitate this process by following hyperlinks in web pages to automatically download new and updated web pages. However due to large size of the web, it is not possible for crawlers to search the entire web. Thus, we propose two models to first partition the web and then crawl each part separately.

In this paper we discuss the basic issues related to search engines and also web crawlers. In the next section, we explain our partitioning methods in details. This is then followed by the basic challenges faced by the crawlers.

Keywords: *Search Engine, Web crawler, Crawling Policy, Graph structure of the web, Web graph partitioning*

1. Introduction

The web has grown from a few thousands pages in 1993 to more than estimated size of 11.5 billion, at present. The consequence of the popularity of the web as a global information system is that it is flooded with a large amount of data and hence finding useful information on the web is often a tedious and frustrating experience. New tools and techniques are crucial for intelligently searching useful information on the web.

Web crawlers are an essential component of all search engines and are increasingly becoming important in data mining and other indexing applications [2]. Broad web search engines as well as many more specialized search tools rely on web crawlers to acquire large collections of pages for indexing and analysis. Such a web crawler may interact with millions of hosts over a period of weeks or months, and thus issues of robustness, flexibility, and manageability are of major importance. In addition, input/output performance, network resources, and operating system limits must be taken into account to achieve high performance at a reasonable cost.

2. Web Search Engine

Before the emergence of Internet search engine, people were confined traversing through sites they had already known of, in a hope to find useful links. This may have been adequate in the early days of the Internet, but as the Internet continued to grow exponentially, it became necessary to develop a means of locating desired content. Search services are now among the most frequently visited sites on the web with millions of hits every day. Without a search engine, no matter how well sites are designed and organized, finding information would be much tedious and time consuming. Fig. 1 illustrates the architecture of search engine [4]. In general, three major components of the search engine are: crawling system, indexing system and also searching system.

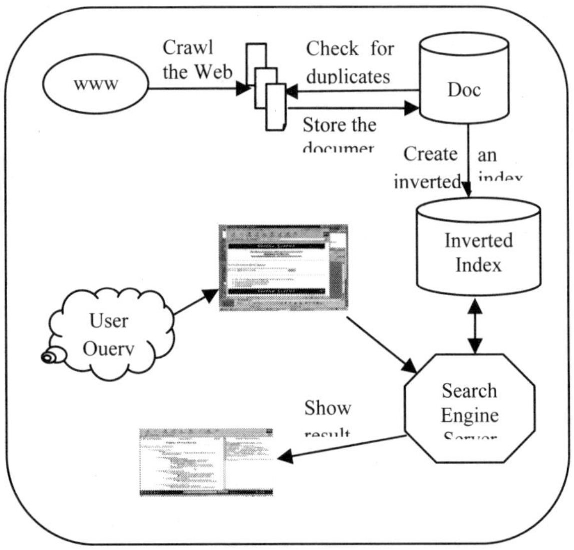

Fig. 1 Architecture of a Search Engine

The client specifies the query to the search engine. Search engine looks in the index file in database for matches. After search engine gathers matching pages, it will sort them by relevancy and sends the result pages back to the client.

Web crawler is a module aggregating data from the Internet in order to make them searchable. The indexer takes the collection of documents or data and builds list of words and notes where they were found and stores the indexed file into the database. Systems usually run the crawler and indexer sequentially in cycles. First the crawler retrieves the content, and then the indexer generates the searchable index. Based on the index, the page matching to the criteria specified will be return.

3. The Web Crawler

To find information on the hundreds of millions of web pages that exist, a search engine employs crawlers, to build lists of the links found on web sites. When a crawler is building its lists, the process is called web crawling. Fig. 2 shows the architecture of a web crawler. Downloader is a software program that downloads web pages. They are stored in the database for further processing with search engines. Through the downloaded pages, URLs are extracted and added to the queue. Scheduler specifies which URL to visit next.

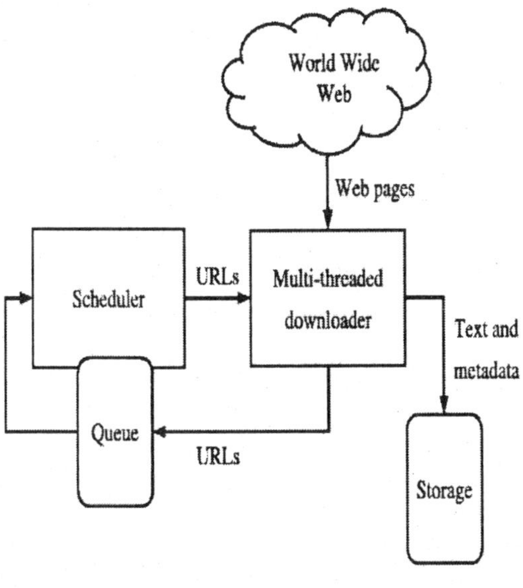

Fig. 2 Architecture of a Standard Web Crawler

As mentioned before, the crawler maintains a list of unvisited URLs called the frontier. The list is initialized with seed URL that may be provided by a user or another program. Each crawling loop involves picking the next URL to crawl from the frontier, fetching the page corresponding to the URL through HTTP, parsing the retrieved page to extract the URLs, and finally adding the unvisited URLs to the frontier. The crawling process may be terminated when a certain number of pages have been crawled.

4. Crawling Model

In a general sense, a crawler may be evaluated by its ability to retrieve good pages. From the beginning, a key motivation for designing web crawlers has been to retrieve web pages and add them to a local repository. Such a repository may then serve particular application needs such as those of a web search engine. Due to the size of the web and its constant change, it is important to fetch first relevant pages before the irrelevant ones in order to not to waste resources and time. Thus, this is the research question of study: How to follow the links as efficiently as possible in a crawler?

There are a number of algorithms that can be used while crawling, such as Breadth-First, Depth-First, Page-Rank [1] and many others. But because the web is large, it is not efficient to apply the algorithm on the web directly. Thus, the idea is to partition the web first and then apply the desired algorithm on each partition separately. There are two partitioning models that can be used: Page-Based partitioning model and Site-Based partitioning model. But before explaining them, we should know about graph structure of the web.

4.1 Graph Representation of the Web

A hyperlink is a reference of a web page B that is contained in a web page A [5]. When the hyperlink is clicked on in a web browser, the browser displays page B. This functionality alone is not helpful for web information retrieval. Typically, authors create links because they think they will be useful for the readers of the pages. Thus, links are usually either navigational aids, or they point to pages whose content augments the content of the current page. The second kind of links tends to point to high quality pages that might be on the same topic as the page containing the link.

Based on this motivation, link analysis makes the following simplifying assumptions:

- A link from page A to page B is a recommendation of page B by the author of page A.
- If page A and page B are connected by a link the probability that they are about the same topic is higher than if they are not connected.

According to the above idea, the web can be modeled as a set of nodes and vertices, where pages are as the nodes and hyperlinks as the vertices. This is explained in the following section.

4.2 Web Graph Partitioning

An undirected graph G = (V, E) is defined as a set of vertices V and a set of edges E. Every edge $e_{ij} \in E$ connects a pair of distinct vertices v_i and v_j. Multiple weights w^1_i, w^2_i, ..., w^M_i may be associated with a vertex $v_i \in V$. $\prod = \{v_1, v_2, \dots, v_k\}$ is said to be a K-way partition of G if each part V_k is a nonempty subset of V, parts are pairwise disjoint, and the union of the K parts is equal to V. A partition $\prod$ is said to be balanced if each part V_k satisfies the balance criteria:

$W^m_k \leq W^m_{avg}(1 + \varepsilon)$; k=1,2,...,K and m=1,2,..., M. (1)

In Eq. 1, each weight W^m_k of a part V_k is defined as the sum of the weights w^m_i of the vertices in that part. W^m_{avg} is the weight that each part should have in the case of perfect load balancing. The maximum imbalance ratio that is allowed is depicted by ε.

In a partition $\prod$ of G, an edge is said to be cut if its pair of vertices fall into two different parts and uncut otherwise. The cutsize definition for representing the cost $\chi(\prod)$ of a partition $\prod$ is

$$\sum_{e_{ij} \in \varepsilon} c_{ij} \qquad (2)$$

After these definitions, the K-way, multi-constraint graph partitioning problem can be stated as the problem of dividing a graph into two or more parts such that the cutsize is minimized (Eq. 2) while the balance criteria (Eq. 1) on the part weights is maintained.

4.2.1 Page-Based partitioning model

In page-based partitioning model, the link structure between the pages is represented by a page graph G_p=(Vp, Ep). In this representation, each page p_i corresponds to a vertex v_i. There exists an undirected edge e_{ij} between vertices v_i and v_j if and only if page p_i has a link to page p_j or vice versa. Multi-links between the pages are collapsed into a single edge. Two weights w^1_i and w^2_i are associated with each vertex v_i. The weight w^1_i of vertex v_i is equal to the size (in bytes) of page p_i, and represents the download and storage overhead for p_i. The weight w^2_i of vertex v_i is equal to 1, and represents the overhead for requesting p_i.

In this model, maintaining the balance criteria on part weights W^1_k and W^2_k (Eq. 1) in partitioning the page graph Gp, effectively balances the download and storage overhead of processor as well as the number of page download requests issued by processor.

4.2.2 Site-Based Partitioning Model

Due to the enormous size of the web, the constructed page graph may be huge, and hence it may be quite costly to partition it using Page-Based Partitioning Model. For efficiency purposes, Site-Based Partitioning Model is proposed, which considers sites instead of pages as the atomic tasks for assignment. In this model, the link structure between the pages is represented by a site graph $G^S = (V^S, E^S)$. All pages belonging to a site S_i are represented by a single vertex $v_i \in V^S$. The weights w^1_i and w^2_i of each vertex v_i are respectively equal to the total size of the pages (in bytes) and the number of pages hosted by site S_i. There is an edge e_{ij} between two vertices v_i and v_j if and only if there is at least one link between any pages $p_x \in S_i$ and $p_y \in S_j$. The cost c_{ij} of an edge $e_{ij} \in E^S$ is equal to the total string length of all links (p_x, p_y) and (p_y, p_x) between each pair of pages $p_x \in S_i$ and $p_y \in S_j$.

Balancing the part weights (Eq. 1) and minimizing the cost (Eq. 2) has the same effects with those explained in the Page-Based model.

5. Crawling Issues

Web crawlers are a central part of search engines, and details on their algorithms and architecture are kept as business secrets [6]. When crawler designs are published, there is often an important lack of detail that prevents other from reproducing the work. In order to build a high-performance web crawler, there are several issues that should be considered:

- URL
- Crawling Policies
- Robots Exclusion Standard
- Robot Traps
- Deep Web

5.1 The URL Itself

Links are written in many ways: relative, absolute, erroneously. The crawler should canonicalize the links in order to avoid fetching the same page many times. It should check to see whether the extracted URL has been fetched before and the belonged page has been visited or no. Also, it should check to see if it can fetch the page, due to restrictions of robot exclusion protocol that is described later.

5.2 The Crawling Policies

There are two important characteristics of the web that generate a scenario in which web crawling is very difficult: its large volume and its rate of change, as there are a huge number of pages being added, changed and removed every day. Also, network speed has improved less than current processing speeds and storage capacities.

The large volume implies that the crawler can only download a fraction of the web pages within a given time, so it needs to prioritize its downloads. The high rate of change implies that by the time the crawler is downloading the last pages from a site, it is very likely that new pages have been added to the site, or that pages have already been updated or even deleted.

The behavior of a web crawler is the outcome of a combination of several policies:

- Selection policy that states which pages to be downloaded.
- Re-visit policy that states when to check for changes to the pages.
- Politeness policy that states how to avoid overloading websites.

5.3 Robots Exclusion Standard

In 1993 and 1994, the early times of web, there were occasions that people found that they have been indexed by an indexing robot, or that a resource discovery robot has visited part of a site that for some reason shouldn't be visited by robots. In recognition of this problem, many web Robots offer facilities for web site administrators and content providers to limit what the robot does. This is achieved through two mechanisms, mentioned in Table 1.

Table 1 Mechanisms for Robot Exclusion Standard

Robots Exclusion Protocol	A web site administrator can indicate which parts of the site should not be visited by a robot, by providing a specially formatted file on their site, in http://.../robots.txt.
The Robots META Tag	A web author can indicate if a page may or may not be indexed, or analyzed for links, through the use of a special HTML META tag.

5.4 Robots Traps

A robot trap (or crawler trap) is a set of web pages that may intentionally or unintentionally be used to cause a web crawler to make an infinite number of requests or cause a poorly constructed crawler to crash. Robot traps may be created to catch Spambots or other crawlers that waste a website's bandwidth. They may also be created unintentionally by calendars that use dynamic pages with links that continually point to the next day or year.

At times, a crawler may encounter a spider trap that leads it to a large number of different URLs referring to the same page. One way to alleviate this problem is by limiting the number of pages that the crawler accesses from a given domain. There is no algorithm to detect all spider traps. Some classes of traps can be detected automatically, but new, unrecognized traps arise quickly.

5.5 The Deep Web

The deep web is the name given to pages on the web that are not part of the surface web that is indexed by common search engines. It consists of pages, which are not linked to by other pages. The deep web also includes sites that require registration or otherwise limit access to their pages, prohibiting search engines from browsing them and creating cached copies.

It is estimated that the deep web is several magnitudes larger than the surface web. Because a large amount of useful information resides in the deep web, search engines have begun exploring alternative methods to crawl the deep web.

6. Conclusion

Due to the dynamism of the web, crawling forms the backbone of applications that facilitate web information retrieval. While the typical use of crawlers has been for creating and maintaining indexes for general-purpose search engine, diverse usage of crawlers is emerging both for client and server based applications. Crawlers are becoming important tools to support applications such as web portals, online searching, and competitive intelligence. A number of crawling algorithms have been proposed in the literature. Often the evaluation of these crawlers is done by comparing a few crawlers on a limited number of queries/tasks without considerations of statistical significance. Anecdotal results while important do not suffice for thorough performance comparisons. As the web crawling field matures, the disparate crawling strategies will have to be evaluated and compared on common tasks through well-defined performance measures.

7. References

[1] B. Yate, C. Castillo, M. Marin, A. Rodriguez, "Crawling a Country: Better Strategies than BreadthFirst for Web Page Ordering", *International World Wide Web Conference Committee (IW3C2).*

[2] M. Buzzi, "Cooperative crawling", *Proceedings of the First Latin American Web Congress (LA-WEB 2003)*

[3] C. Chung, C. Clarke, "Topic-oriented collaborative crawling", *CIKM 2002*

[4] V. Shkapenyuk, T. Suel, "Design and Implementation of a High-Performance Distributed Web Crawler"

[5] M. Henzinger, Link Analysis in Web Information Retrieval, IEEE Computer Society Technical Committee on Data Engineering

[6] Sergey Brin and Lawrence Page. "The anatomy of a large-scale hypertextual Web search engine", *Computer Networks and ISDN Systems*, 30(1{7):107{117, 1998.

Ontology Based Information Extraction from Resume

Mhapasekar Darshan P.
S.S.P.M.'S College of Engineering, Sindhudurg, Maharastra, Pin 416602
darshan_mhapsekar@yahoo.co.uk

Abstract

A semi unstructured document lacks these structuring characteristics. There are no relations with associated predicates, no attribute-value pairs, no tags-value and no n- tuples. Consequently, there is no information asserted by any relation about the contents of an unstructured document. For some unstructured documents, it is possible and useful to impose structure by establishing XML file over the information contents of the document. This approach to extracting information from semi-unstructured documents and reformulating the information.

1. Introduction

We characterize our approach as being ontology based. Ontology is a branch of philosophy that attempts to model things as they exist in the world; it is particularly appropriate for modeling objects including their relationships and properties. We use an augmented semantic data model to provide an ontology that describes the view we wish to have over a domain of interest. The semantic data model lets us create an ontological model instance as sets of objects and constraints over these objects. Further, as augmented, it lets us done data representation and expected contextual keywords for each object set within the ontology. Based on application ontology with these characteristics, we apply a constant/keyword recognizer, and a structured-text generator to filter an unstructured document with respect to the ontology and populate a generated XML schema with tag-values associated as per XML format. We thus extract information of interest from an unstructured document and reformulate it as a structured document.

2. Extraction and Structuring Framework

Fig. 1 shows the framework we use to extract and structure the data in an unstructured document. Boxes represent files and ovals represent processes. As Figure shows, the input to our approach is an application ontology and an unstructured document, and the output is a filtered and structured document which is in XML file format.

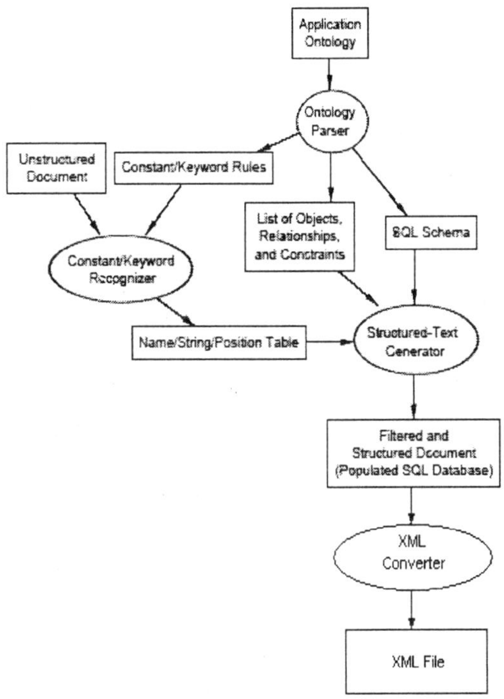

Fig. 1 Framework for ontology-based information extraction & converting

Since all the processes and intermediate file formats are fixed in advance, our framework in Figure constitutes a general procedure that takes as input any declared ontology for an application domain of interest and an unstructured document within the application's domain and produces as output structured data, filtered with respect to the ontology. The only step that requires significant human intervention is the initial creation of an application ontology. However, once such an application ontology is written, it can be applied to unstructured documents from a wide variety of sources, so long as these documents correspond to the given application domain

3. Process Description

The input to our system is application ontology and a set of unstructured documents. The semantic data model we use for the input ontology, augmented to allow regular expressions as descriptors for constants and context keywords. Constants are potential values in lexical object sets, while context keywords may be associated with any object set (lexical or non lexical).

Resume

Name: Bhore Ajay A.

Address: S.S.P.M. C.O.E.,
Harkul Budruk,
Kankavali,(E),
416402.

Email Id: sunnybhore@yahoo.co.in

Phone No: 9922231888

Date of Birth: 12,DEC 1984.

Qualification:

B.E. Computers	Distinction 72%	Mumbai University
H.S.C	Distinction 78%	Mumbai University
S.S.C.	Distinction 82%	Mumbai University

Fig. 2 Resume (Semi Unstructured Document)

Gi en the inputs as described above, the next step is to invoke the ontology parser. For a given application ontology, the parser creates an SQL schema as a sequence of create table statements. Object-set names from the ontology denote attributes in the generated SQL tables. Attributes are of type varchar for lexical object sets or type integer for nonlexical object sets. The parser includes a simple normalizer that produces its schema in an acceptable normal form assuming that the application ontology. Not all information in the ontology is needed by the structured-text generator, so the parser also extracts the list of objects and constraints to be used by the generator. Finally, the parser also creates a file of constant/keyword rules. This file is a list of regular expressions in Perl syntax, tagged with object-set names from the ontology.

After invoking the parser, the main program invokes the constant/keyword recognizer and then the structured-text generator for each unstructured document. The recognizer applies each regular expression to the unstructured document. When the Perl program recognizes a string S according to a regular expression E with tag T, it emits T as the name, S as the string, and the beginning and ending character numbers in the document as the position. We call this list the \name/string/position table. "The structured-text generator uses the object/relationship/constraint list and the SQL schema to match attributes (object-set names in the ontology) with values (constants described in the name/string/position table). Then the generator forms tuples for relations in the generated SQL schema. The generator forms tuples according to heuristics, applied in the following order.
Keyword Proximity: If the constraints in the ontology require at most one constant for an object set, and if there is a context keyword for the object set in the name/string/position table, we use keyword proximity to reject all but the closest constant tagged with the same object-set name as the keyword's object-set name. For constants that are equally close before and after a keyword, we favor the constant value that appears after the keyword. By \reject" we mean that we remove the entry from the name/string/position table.
Functional Relationships: If the ontology dictates that the database can accept one constant for an object set S and exactly one constant appears for S, we insert the constant in the database (regardless of keyword proximity).
Nonfunctional Relationships: If the ontology dictates that the database can accept many constants for an object set and if there are one or more constants, we insert them all.

Ontological structure is the model where we write the regular expression in perl language to extract the required information

4. Ontology Structure

Ontological structure is necessary for information extraction .We use an augmented semantic data model to provide an ontology that describes the view we wish to have over a domain of interest. The semantic data model lets us create an ontological model instance as sets of objects and constraints over these objects. Further, as augmented, it lets us done data representation and expected contextual keywords for each object set within the ontology. Based on application ontology with these characteristics, we apply a constant/keyword recognizer, and a structured-text generator to filter an unstructured document with respect to the ontology.

For creating the ontological structure we use the regular expression in PERL language. A regular expression is a special text string for describing a search pattern. You can think of regular expressions as wildcards on steroids. For example for searching the email id in the inputted document we will write the regular expression in such manner. For Example email regular expression will be

Email(Id)?[:]*|EMAIL(ID)?[:]*#[A-Za-z0-9_.]*+@[A-Za-z]*+.[A-Za-z]{2,4}+(.[A-Za-z]{ 2 ,4})?

Particular regular expression will search firstly for the word Email id / EMAIL ID/ Email / EMAIL then for the email id's such as

shashikantbsingh@yahoo.com or prasad_koyande19@yahoo.co.in

For finding the word Email we will write the regular expression and for finding the contents of that Email we will write an another regular expression to differentiate between both of these expressions we use the symbol #. [A-Za-z.] this syntax will accept name which contains all the capital and small letters then it will look for @ symbol then for the domain name, then for the word .co / .com

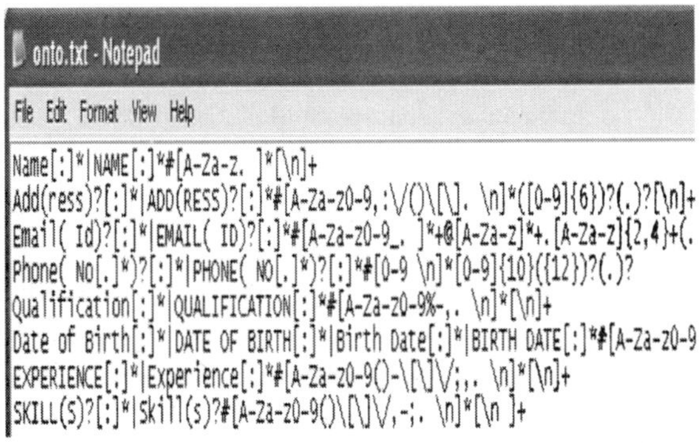

Fig. 3 Regular Expression for Resume

5. Implementation

The information extraction consist of three major tasks which are reading the RTF document which consist of unstructured information, reading of ontological structure and matching it with the unstructured document and save the extracted information in the MS ACCESS database. There are two inputs one is unstructured document which contains the information & second is the ontological structure which contains the Regular expression based on that useful information is extracted. RTF text editor kit is created and all the contents in the inputted RTF document are being placed in the new document known as doc and that doc content are considered as a single string and is put in the string variable s1 which is further used for processing.

The whole ontological structure file is being read and is buffered then the each line in the buffer content is being considered for processing. For example we are considering the resume in which name is the key word or we can say the field name for which we will find the name of the particular person. For finding the word name we will write the regular expression and for finding the contents of that name we will write another regular expression to differentiate between both of these expressions we use the symbol #. For this purpose we read the line character by character as soon as we find the # symbol we place all the regular expression before that symbol in the string variable pattern and the remaining part in the another string symbol pattern1. Then the pattern content is being matched with the unstructured document as soon as we found that required formatted content we divide that string s1 into two parts the second part is being placed in the another string named as "str" then the pattern1 is being matched with the str content and the required information is extracted according the format specified in the pattern1 regular expression. And that extracted content placed in the array ai[] sequentially to feed it into the intermediate database.

The second and following pages should begin 1.0 inch (2.54 cm) from the top edge. On all pages, the bottom margin should be approximately 1-5/8 inches (4.13 cm) from the bottom edge of the page.

6. Experimental Result

6.1 Extracted Information

The following Table 1 shows the extracted information from ten resumes which was given as an input to our project. Each field in the below table contain the respected extracted information.

6.2 Efficiency

According to the information extracted from the Ten Resumes we have calculated the efficiency of our project. The efficiency of our project is been calculated by following formula,

Table 1 Table of Extracted Information

Name	Address	Email	Phone	Qualification	DOB	Experienc	Skills
Bhore Ajay A.□	S.S.P.M. C.O.E., □Hakul	sunnybhore@yahoo	9922231888	□□B.E. ComputersDistinction 72%□Mumb	null	3years in	Mico-Control and Ha
Bhore Ajay A.□	S.S.P.M. C.O.E. □Hakul I	sunnybhore@yahoo	9922231888	□B.E. Computers 72% Distinction \	null	s :□	null
Bhore Ajay A.□	s C.O.E. □Hakul Budruk,(	sunnybhore@yahoo	9922231888	□ Mumbai University□B.E. Computers 72'	null	s :□	null
Bhore Ajay A.□	S.S.P.M. C.O.E. □Hakul	sunnybhore@yahoo	9922231888	□B.E. Computers 72% Distinction \	null	s :□	:□Good in communi
Bhore Ajay A.□	S.S.P.M. C.O.E. □Hakul	sunnybhore@yahoo	9922231888	□B.E. Computers 72% Distinction \	null	s :□	:□Good in communi
DINESH D CHO	A/23, Ekopa C.H.S, □	dineshdchougule12	9960601538	□B.E. Computers 78% Distinction \	1st June 1984□ null		:□Good in communi
DINESH D CHO	A/23, Ekopa C.H.S, □	dineshdchougule12	9960601538	□B.E. Computers 78% Distinction \	1st June 1984□ null		:□Good in communi
DINESH D CHO	A/23, Ekopa C.H.S, Gunsa	dineshdchougule12	9960601538	□B.E. Computers 78% Distinction \	1st June 1984□ null		:□Good in communi
DINESH D CHO	A/23, Ekopa C.H.S, Gunsa	dineshdchougule12	9960601538	□B.E. Computers 78% Distinction \	1st June 1984□ null		:□Good in communi
DINESH D CHO	A/23, Ekopa C.H.S, Gunsa	dineshdchougule12	9960601538	□B.E. Computers 78% Distinction \	1st June 1984□ null		:□Good in communi

$$\text{Efficiency} = \frac{\text{No. of right information extraced for particular Attribute}}{\text{No. of Documents}}$$

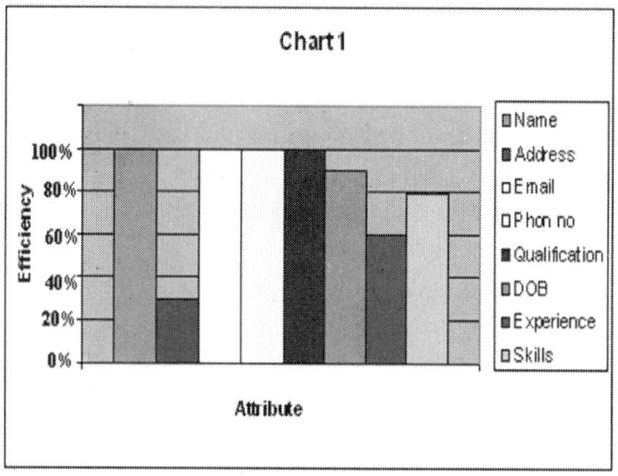

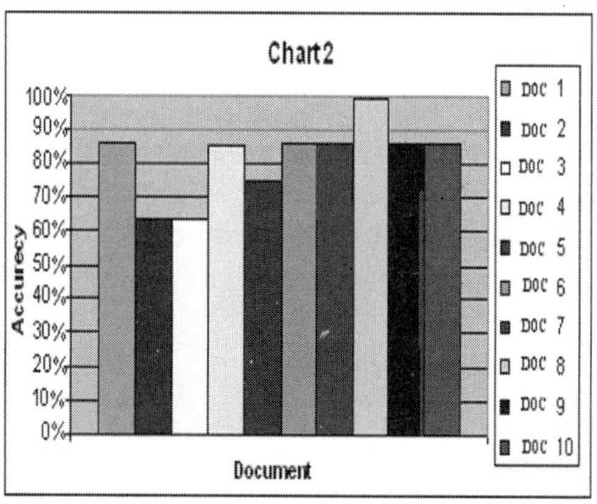

Fig. 4 Efficiency Graph for Extracted Information

6.3 Accuracy

According to the information extracted from the Ten Resumes we have calculated the Accuracy of our project. The Accuracy of our project is been calculated by following formula

$$\text{Accuracy} = \frac{\text{No. of right information extracted for single Document}}{\text{No. of Attributes}}$$

Fig. 5 Accuracy Graph for Extracted Information

7. References

[1] David W. Embley, Stephen W. Liddle.(1998). Ontology Based Extraction and Structuring of Information from Data-Rich Unstructured Documents. Proceedings of the Conference on Information and Knowledge Management (CIKM'98), Washington D.C, 52-59.

[2] Yihong Ding. "Semiautomatic Generation of Data-Extraction Ontologies", A Thesis Proposal Presented to the Department of Computer Science Brigham Young University, July 3, 2001.

[3] D.W. Embley, D.M. Campbell, Y.S. Jiang,(1998) .A Conceptual-Modeling Approach to Extracting Data from the Web. Proceedings of the 17th International Conference on Conceptual Modeling (ER'98). 78-91. Springer.

[4] Tina Eliassi-Rad. (2001). A system for building intelligent agents that learns to retrieve and extract information. International Journal on User Modeling and User-Adapted Interaction, Special Issue on User Modeling and Intelligent Agents. 13:35–88

[5] Kristina Lerman, Craig Knoblock, Steven Minton. (2001). Automatic Data Extraction from Lists and Tables in Web Sources. Proceedings of the workshop on Advances in Text Extraction and Mining (IJCAI-2001). AAAI Press

PageRank Computation Methods: A Text Mining Application Method for Information Retrieval

D. Saritha[1] and P. Parimala[2]
[1]Head of the Department, MCA, [2]Student, M. Tech II year
G.V.P. College of Engineering
saritravi@gmail.com parimala.rachem@gmail.com

Abstract

In this paper, we discuss the performance issues o. two models of PageRank algorithm, used by the Google, an effective search engine. The algorithm is developed in two different models which is constructed for a tiny 6-node web graph. This paper describes PageRank, a method for rating Web pages objectively and mechanically. We compare the general method of PageRank, a random surfer model with the power iteration method.

1. Introduction

Text mining finds interesting patterns from large databases also called Text data mining often. Text mining usually involves the process of structuring the input text, deriving patterns within the structured text and finally evaluation and interpretation of the output. Text mining tasks include text categorization,text clustering, concept/entity extraction, document summarization and entity relation modeling. Information Retrieval (IR), a field developed in parallel with database systems is a task, given a set of documents and a user query, of finding the relevant documents. The basic measures include Precision and Recall. Information Retrieval on the web is much more challenging than traditional IR systems. Web search engines are the most visible IR applications. Search engines are operated by entering query into the system. The search engines comprise of two ranking functions, similarity based on content or text and ranking based on link structure analysis. This paper focuses on the link structure analysis which is used by Google Search engine for ranking of pages using an algorithm called PageRank or Pigeonrank.

2. Search Engines

A Search Engine is the key for finding specific information on the vast expanse of the World Wide Web. Search Engines mine data available in databases, newsbooks and open directories. Search Engines operate algorithmically or a mixture of algorithm and human input. The three basic types of search engines are

(a) Crawler based - are those that use automated software agents (called crawlers) that visit a Web site, read the information on the actual site, read the site's meta tags and also follow the links that the site connects to perform indexing on all linked Web sites as well.

(b) Human powered - rely on humans to submit information that is subsequently indexed and catalogued. Only information that is submitted is put into the index.

(c) A hybrid of the above two

The same search on different search engines produce different results as not all indices are going to be exactly the same. It depends on what the spiders find or what the humans submitted. Not every search engine uses the same algorithm to search through the indices. The algorithm is what the search engines use to determine the relevance of the information in the index to what the user is searching for.

One of the elements that a search engine algorithm scans for is the frequency and location of keywords on a Web page. Those with higher frequency are typically considered more relevant. But search engine technology is becoming sophisticated in its attempt to discourage what is known as keyword stuffing, or spamdexing.

Another common element that algorithms analyze is the way that pages link to other pages in the Web. By analyzing how pages link to each other, an engine can both determine what a page is about (if the keywords of the linked pages are similar to the keywords on the original page) and whether that page is considered "important" and deserving of a boost in ranking. Just as the technology is becoming increasingly sophisticated to ignore keyword stuffing, it is also becoming more savvy to Web masters who build artificial links into their sites in order to build an artificial ranking.

3. PageRank

PageRank was developed at Stanford University by Larry Page (hence the name *Page*-Rank) and later Sergey Brin, as part of a research project about a new kind of search engine.

Google, the original employer of the Page Rank algorithm describes in its own words:
"PageRank relies on the uniquely democratic nature of the web by using its vast link structure as an indicator of an individual page's value. In essence, Google interprets a link from page A to page B as a vote, by page A, for page B. But, Google looks at more than the sheer volume of votes, or links a page receives; it also analyzes the page that casts the vote. Votes cast by pages that are themselves "important" weigh more heavily and help to make other pages "important".

PageRank is a ranking metric for hypertext documents. Google is an effective search engine for its major reason of PageRank algorithm. The idea behind the development of PageRank algorithm is the inherent hyperlink structure of the web which is used to generate an approximation of relevancy.

3.1 PageRank Explanation

Performing a user search requires two general steps.

(a) Perform text query ,which group and locally rank pages according to traditional IR methods and

(b) Merge the above results with the global PageRank scores to order the documents returned by a search.

Traditional IR methods involve a textual search of the pages in the web page which is then matched to the documents and a relevancy set is created. The relevancy set is the group of pages closely related to the query terms. Once a relevancy set is created containing documents relevant to the query terms, the Google system merges relevancy set rankings with the PageRank scores and displays the results. A search that returns the PageRank score is reporting the importance of hierarchy of pages containing the query terms.

3.2 PageRank Calculation

PageRank is defined as follows:
We assume page A has pages T1...Tn which point to it .The parameter d is the damping factor which can be set between 0 and 1. Also C(A) is defined as the number of links going out of page A.

The PageRank of a page A is given as:

$$PR(A) = (1-d) + d(PR(T1)/C(T1)+ \dots + PR(Tn)/C(Tn))$$

The PageRanks form a probability distribution over web pages, so the sum of all PageRanks is one.
PageRank or PR(A) can be calculated using a simple iterative algorithm, and corresponds to the principal Eigen vector of the normalized link matrix of the web.

The PageRank thesis constructs page importance hierarchies based upon the link structure of the web.

4. Applications of PageRank

4.1 Estimating Web Traffic

It is interesting to see how PageRank corresponds to actual usage because PageRank roughly corresponds to a random surfer.

4.2 Backlink Predictor

The system starts out with a single URL and no other information, and the goal is to try to crawl the pages close to the optimal order. The optimal order is to crawl pages exactly the order of their ranking according to an evaluation function. The evaluation function here is simply the number of citations, given complete information. PageRank is a more effective way to order the crawling than the number of known citations. In simple words, PageRank is a better predictor than citation counting even when the measure is number of citations.

This ability of predicting citations is a powerful justification for using Page Rank.

4.3 Other Uses

A version of PageRank is used to rank academic doctoral programs based on their records of placing their graduates in faculty positions.
PageRank can also help the user to decide if a site is trustworthy or not.

A Web Crawler may use PageRank as one of a number of importance metrics it uses to determine which URL to visit next during the crawl.

PageRank has been developed as a replacement of traditional ISI impact factor .Instead of counting the total citation to a journal, the importance of each citation is determined in a PageRank fashion.

5. Random Surfer Model

Assume a user surfing the web randomly walk from page to page to go to the next. During this walk, the user approaches to dead ends, pages with no outgoing links. This random walk is known as Markov chain or Markov process.

A Markov chain is a stochastic process with the Markov property. This property is given as "*given the present state, future states are independent of past states*". Markov chains are often described by a directed graph, where the edges are labeled by the probabilities of going from one state to the other states. The limiting probability that a infinite random surfer visits any particular page is its PageRank.

Consider W as a set of web page hyperlinks and n be the number of pages in W. Let G be the n by n connectivity matrix of thc portion of the web. These set of WebPages may be modeled as nodes in the directed graph.

$g_{ij} = 1$, if there exists a hyperlink to node i from node j

$g_{ij} = 0$, otherwise

The number of nonzeros in G is the total number of hyperlinks in W.

Let r_i and c_j be the row and column sums of G.

$$r_i = \sum_i g_{ij}, \quad c_j = \sum_j g_{ij}$$

Let d be the probability that the random walk follows a link, with a value of d =0.85.Then 1-d is the probability that some arbitrary page is chosen and y = (1-d)/n is the probability that a particular random page is chosen.

Let A be the n-by-n matrix whose elements are

$$a_{ij} = \begin{cases} d\, g_{ij} / c_j + y \;; & c_j \neq 0 \\ 1/n \;; & c_j \neq 0 \end{cases}$$

The jth column is the probability of jumping from the jth page to the other pages on the web. If the jth page is a dead end that is it has no out-links, then we assign a uniform probability of 1/n to all the elements in its column.

The matrix A is the transition probability matrix of the Markov chain. The elements of the above transition probability matrix are strictly between zero and one and the column sums of this matrix are all equal to one. A nonzero solution of the equation

$$x = Ax$$

exists and is unique with the scaling factor .If the scaling factor is chosen so that

$$\sum x_i = 1$$

Here x is the state vector of the Markov chain and is Google's PageRank.

6. Implementation

Consider a 6-node tiny web graph for the implementation of the above stated random surfer model, in Fig. 1. A set of pages in the web may be modeled as nodes in a directed graph. The edges between nodes represent links between pages.

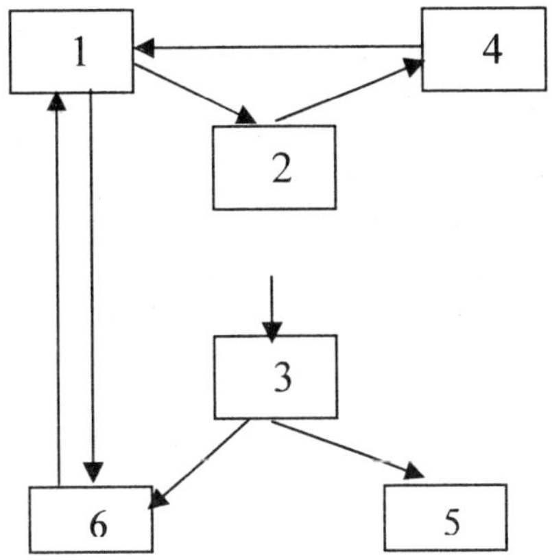

Fig. 1 A tiny 6 node web

To calculate PageRank, a mathematical model of the link structure of the web is built. An adjacency matrix G from the graph of the web in the figure mentioned above. All entries of G will be 0 and 1.

For the 6-node graph in Figure 1, the connectivity matrix G is

$$G = \begin{bmatrix} 0 & 0 & 0 & 1 & 0 & 1 \\ 1 & 0 & 0 & 0 & 0 & 0 \\ 0 & 1 & 0 & 0 & 0 & 0 \\ 0 & 1 & 1 & 0 & 0 & 0 \\ 0 & 0 & 1 & 0 & 0 & 0 \\ 1 & 0 & 1 & 0 & 0 & 0 \end{bmatrix}$$

An entry of 1 in the second row, first column indicate that page two links to page one.

Here for this 6-node web graph, n = 6, d = 0.85, so y = (1-0.85)/6 = 0.025

The nine connections are described by

i = [2 6 3 4 4 5 6 1 1]

j= [1 1 2 2 3 3 3 4 6]

PageRank can be computed in MATLAB by taking advantage of the particular structure of the Markov matrix.

The transition matrix can be written as $A = dGP + ez^T$

Where P is the diagonal matrix formed from the reciprocals of the outdegrees,

$$p_{jj} = \begin{cases} 1/c_j \;; & c_j \neq 0 \\ 0 \;; & c_j \neq 0 \end{cases}$$

e is the n-vector of all ones, and z is the vector with components.

$$z_j = \begin{cases} y \;; & c_j \neq 0 \\ 1/n \;; & c_j \neq 0 \end{cases}$$

The equation x = Ax can be written as (I – dGP)x = □e

Where □ = z^T x.

Let □=1, so the equation (1-d*GP*)x=e can be solved for x.

Then the resulting x can be rescaled so that

$$\sum_i x_i = 1$$

The following MATLAB statements implement the above approach,

c = full(sum(*G*)) computes the column sums

c = 2 2 3 1 0 1

and c(5) = 0 since page five is a dead end and has no out-links.

The statements

x= (I – d**G***P*)/e

x =x/sum(x)

Solve the linear system to produce

x =

0.3210
0.1705
0.1066
0.1368
0.0643
0.2007

The bar graph of the above values of x is shown in the Fig. 2.

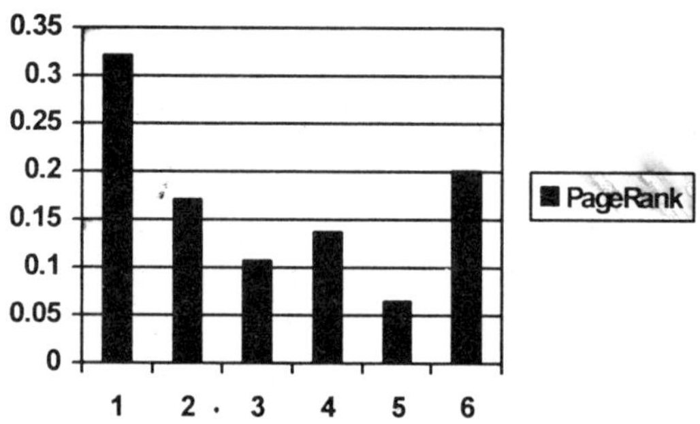

Fig. 2

If the URLs are sorted according to the PageRanks listed along with their in and out-degrees, the result is tabulated in Table 1 as follows:

Table 1

Page	PageRank	In	Out	URL
1	0.3210	2	2	http://www.1.com
6	0.2007	2	1	http://www.6.com
2	0.1705	1	2	http://www.2.com
4	0.1368	2	1	http://www.4.com
3	0.1066	1	3	http://www.3.com
5	0.0643	1	0	http://www.5.com

Page 1 has a higher PageRank than Page 4 and Page 6, even though they all have the same number of in-links.

7. Power Method

A matrix free method such as the power iteration method is required due to the size of the matrices and the vectors involved. The power method is cheap to implement.

The power method can also be implemented in a way that doesnot actually from the Markov matrix but preserves sparsity.

The properties of the power method are:

(a) Converges to unique vector
(b) Convergence rate
(c) Vectorizes
(d) Storage for only a single vector
(e) Matrix vector multiplication with very sparse matrix
(f) Accurate (no subtractions)
(g) Simple (few decisions)

The following statements in MATLAB are implemented to solve the PageRank problem by the Power method.

G = d**G***P*;

z = ((1-d)*(c=0) + (c==0))/n;

Begin with

x=e/n

Then repeat the statement until convergence

x = *G**x + e*(z*x)

The difference in the number of iterations can be seen when implementing the random surfer model and the power method. The size and sparsity of the web matrix create limitations on the solution methods and have caused the predominance of the power method. PageRank's thesis is that it is not the quantity of inlinks to a page but rather the quality of inlinks. The power method applied to the stochastic matrix is the predominant method for finding the important PageRank vector.

8. Pros and Cons of PageRank

One of the PageRank's strengths is query independence, since PageRank is calculated for all pages in the web, independent of any query. This facet is also considered as a weakness due to the volatile nature and vast size of the web. The web contains so many documents that performing PageRank calculations must be done utilizing distributed methods of computing, so that portions of the calculations are completed on separate computers. Prior to calculating PageRank for the known web, a web crawl must be done to build the transition probability matrix. Both of these tasks are extremely time consuming .Much of the research surrounding the PageRank algorithm today focuses on the issue of updating the PageRank vector, so that it may be updated more frequently at a lower computational cost.

PageRank is a recursive calculation in nature: the PageRank for page i depends on the PageRanks of all pages that link to page i .A page will receive high PageRank due to the high PageRank of an inlinking page. Spamming the search engine is also done by intentionally setting the pages with one inlink from a page with high PageRank.

Link farms are networks of pages that all link to one another, and link to a separate page .The PageRanks of the network of pages may then sum to the equivalent of an inlink from one page with a high PageRank.

9. Conclusion

The Search Engine, Google's success is for two reasons which are the quick response time and quality of results. A high quality of results is preferable to efficient retrieval, but an excessive response time will discourage the impatient end user. The ranking algorithms developed, will return the most relevant documents in the list of results for the user.

The basic mathematical model, the random surfer model is the basis for getting an idea of how the ranking is done for pages on the web. This model uses the Markov matrix for implementation which is a bit complex .The power method on the other hand lessens the number of iterations, but preserves sparsity.

Further research is being carried out on the PageRank algorithm .Several researchers including the originator of this algorithm, the Google is focusing on enhancing the efficiency of the algorithm as well as developing new algorithms.

10. References

[1] Sergey Brin and Lawrence Page "The Anatomy of a Large Scale Hypertextual Web Search Engine" Proceedings of the seventh International Conference on World Wide Web 7 :107-117

[2] Search Engine Watch : Up-to-date information on leading Search engines http://www.serachenginewatch.com/

[3] Amy N. Langville and Carl D. Meyer."Deeper Inside PageRank". February 2004.

[4] Lawrence Page, Sergey Brin, Rajeev Motwani and Terry Winograd. "The PageRank Citation Ranking: Bringing order to the Web". Technical Report, Computer Science Department, Stanford University, 1998.

[5] Google Technology: The Google Search Engine Commercial search engine founded by the originators of PageRank. http://www.google.com/technology.

Parallel Algorithms for String Matching on 2D Linear Array with Reconfigurable Pipelined Bus Systems

S. Viswanadha Raju[1], A.Vinaya Babu[2], Altaf.H.Basha[3], B. Sasidhar[4], A.Govardhan[2]
[1]Professor, Dept Computer Science and Engineering,
[2]Professor, Dept Computer Science and Engineering, JNTuniversity, Hyderabad.
[3]Assistant Professor, Dept of MCA,
Gokaraju Ranga Raju Institute of Engineering and Technology, Hyderabad.
[4]Asoc.Professor, CM Engineering College, Hyderabad

Abstract

We consider the string matching on 2D LARPBS. This has applications such as string databases, cellular automata and computational biology. The main use of this method is to reduce the time spent on comparisons in string matching by using LARPBS. We identified some disadvantages: Reconnecting the sub buses and shuffling the contents for string matching on 1D LARPBS. These problems can be solved by 2D LARPBS.

Keywords: *Hamming Distance, LARPBS, PRAM, Reconfigurability, string matching*

1. Introduction

String matching mainly deals with the problem of finding all the occurrences of a string in a given text. String matching had been one of the most extensive problems in computer technologies during the past two decades. Pattern matching is widely implemented in information retrieval, web search engine, DNA sequencing [et al. 13,14,16] artificial intelligence and several other fields. Two sub-problems for the string matching problem considered, the first is the exact string matching and the second is approximate string matching with k-mismatches. Experimental results of well known sequential algorithm can be found in [6,9]. Since the VLSI (Very Large Scale Integration) technology has been developed rapidly, hardware approaches have also been proposed [9,3]. But most of the algorithms that can be found in the literature multiphase algorithms; they need preprocessing phase in order to retrieve special structures in either the pattern or the reference string. It is then difficult to build special purpose hardware for just string matching tasks. We propose two kinds of parallel algorithms for both string matching problems without any preprocessing phase. First propose on-line solutions; it means that they process the inputs in turn, without knowledge of whole pattern at the beginning of the computation; its elements will be treated one by one. Then we give solutions that require a constant number of steps. Several computational models that have been considered for parallel string matching algorithms the PRAM model, mesh structure[15,17] and etc. The parallel string matching algorithm is often said to be optimal if its cost is O (nm). The first optimal O (log m) time string matching algorithm was introduced by Galil [3]

The text string of length n and a pattern of length m, Galil presented a optimal constant time complexity parallel algorithm with n processors for the exact string matching problem [3] on a conceptual CRCW PRAM model but this algorithm requires additional space and needs to preprocess the text string. Recently, on a linear systolic array, Park and George proposed an architecture based on data flow for both sub problems,[15] solving them in O $(n/k+ \alpha)$ where k is the number of streams and $1\leq \alpha \leq m$ with k*m processors. In this algorithm the approaches were based on the computation of the well-known Hamming distance. The string matching problem solving on the LARPBS model, introduced by Pan and Li in [7], it has known a growing success since the end of two thousands as well as all optical bus based models. Many authors have been discussed for sorting or matrix multiplication or selection[2,8,11]. The used pipelined optical bus, instead of an electrical one. The pipelined optical bus utilizes optical fibers to transmit information. When compared with naïve algorithm in $O(m^2)$ cycles with O(n+m) processors, string matching algorithm requires more processors and is much simpler in constant cycles. The present algorithm use m*(n-m+1) processors on LARPBS.In this identified three disadvantages: First, divide the bus into several sub-buses, second, reconnecting the buses, third when we need to move the processors but it is not possible that has been solving by just change their contents. For solving above problem, propose a 2D LARPBS

The rest of the paper organized as follows: In section 2, we provide brief description of LARPBS. In section 3, we introduce our approach for our parallel string matching algorithm. In section 4, we designed parallel string matching algorithm on 2DLARPBS. Conclusions reported in section 5.

2. LARPBS Model

The linear array with a reconfigurable pipelined bus system (LARPBS) consists of three waveguides. It is presented by Pan and Li in [7]. It is based on the ideas of using pipelined bus systems and processor array reconfiguration. This is called the one dimensional parallel processing optical model. In such model, a pipelined optical bus system uses optical waveguides instead of electrical signals to transfer the several messages which can circulate at the same time among processors through the bus in a pipelined fashion. The communication time for the LARPBS model is measured based on the number of bus cycles used. A bus cycle is the end-to-end propagation delay on the bus .The time complexity of an algorithm is determined in terms of time steps, where a single time step comprises one bus cycle and one local computation which is the time taken for an optical signal to propagate through the entire bus. The properties of optical bus as follows: Unidirectional propagation and predictable delay per unit length, in addition to the high propagation speed of light. These advantages of using waveguides enable synchronized concurrent access of an optical bus in a pipelined fashion.

The optical bus of a LARPBS processes three distinct waveguides. The message waveguide is used for sending data and the select and reference waveguides has been used for sending address information. The message waveguide is similar to reference waveguide. The shape of the bus is U structure, as per the structure of bus; the upper half of the bus is used for transmission and lower half for reception. Each processor is connected to the bus through the directional couplers, for transmitting and the other for receiving. Hence, the bus is divided into two segments, the transmitting segment and the receiving segment. The receiving segments of the reference and message waveguides have an extra segment of fiber between every pair of consecutive processors. The receiving segment is used to introduce one unit propagation delay in these two waveguides. Hence the propagation delays on the receiving segments of the reference and select waveguides not the same. In addition the select bus has switch controlled conditional delay between every pair of consecutive processors is placed on the transmitting segment segments of the select waveguide. The conditional delays can be implemented using 2x2 optical switches. The switch can function in two different states. If set to cross, a unit time delay is introduced On the other hand, if the switch is open the messages can pass-through without any delay. Hence many divide and conquer algorithms fit naturally into this model. The main features of the model is several basic data operations such as broadcast, multicast, split, binary prefix sum and minimum finding.

2.1 Reconfigurability

The importance of this model in fact that it can support dynamic reconfiguration facility on the bus. The separate set of optical switches exists on each waveguide of bus. That's why some more optical switches inserted on each segment of the bus. Half of the optical switches on both transmitting and receiving sides (one per waveguide). If all these switches set to straight, the bus system operates only the select and reference waveguide represented [4]. The message waveguide is similar to the reference waveguide. P_1 and P_4 have their switches set to cross. P_2, P_3, P_5 have their switches set to straight

A regular pipelined bus system connecting all the processors. However, if the switches at processors P_i set to cross, the bus is split into two separate buses, one connecting processors $P_1P_2...P_i$ and the other connecting processors $_{Pi+1...Pn}$. Thus the whole is split into two separate LARPBS structures These two sets can work independently as two LARPBS.

2.2 Addressing

An address technology is called coincident pulse technique. The coincident pulse technique is the most common and flexible way of communication among the many methods. That addressing is done using the coincident pulse technique [10]. The coincident pulse technique helps in addressing b manipulating the relative time delay of select and reference pulses on separate buses so that they will coincide only at the required receiver. The coincident pulse technique uses frames for writing and addressing information. Each processor processes a select and reference frame that has N slots for the N processors on the LARPBS. If processor P_i wants to send message to processor Pj, P_i transmits a message frame on the message waveguide and a pair of select and reference pulses on the select and reference waveguides. The technique requires the select and reference waveguides of delays between the select and reference waveguides in order to make the pulses coincide at processor P_j. With such method, it is possible to route messages or to broadcast messages on the optical bus. However when more than one message arrive at the same processor in the same bus cycle, it accepts only the first message, the others automatically ignored. It is due to the fact that an electrical processor cannot match the transmission speed of an optical bus [7]. Why the LARPBS is powerful model, and basic operations broadcasting , multicasting, binary prefix sum computation and compression [6,3]

3. 2D LARPBS

We propose a 2-D model in this section. See Fig 2.1 A 2-D LARPBS has two sets of switches at each row and column intersection: conditional delay switches and reconfigurable switches [10]. It has one extra pair of switches for the convenience of row bus reconfiguration and column bus reconfiguration. Actually, since we do not assume column communication be performed concurrently, each processor can use the same set of switches (including reconfigurable switch pairs and conditional delay switch) for its row bus and column bus if the switching between column bus and row bus can be done in a reasonable time. We classify a communication step into two types: a column communication step and a row communication step. The communication performance of an algorithm designed for this model is calculated by the total number of bus cycles for both row communication steps and column communication steps.

3.1 Basic operations on 2D LARPBS

2D LARPBS is more scalable than 1D LARPBS, but communication in a 2D LARPBS is more restrictive. One-to-one communication in LARPBS can be done in constant time, but not all permutation of the one-to-one communication can be done in 2D LARPBS in constant time: in this section some special permutation operations can be done in O(1) time matrix-transpose, 2D-integer-prefix-sums, and 2D compaction. These basic permutation operations will be used as blocks in the algorithms[10].

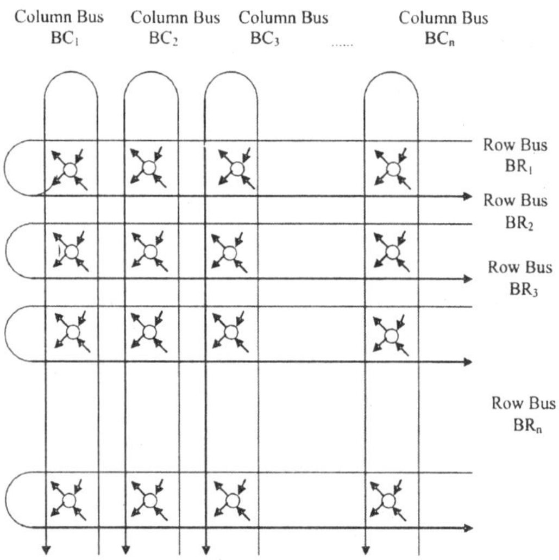

Fig 2.1 2D LARPBS Model

4. Results and Discussions

In this section, designing of algorithms for both problems, such as the exact string matching problem (Aho 1974) and the approximate string matching with k-mismatches. These algorithms designed based on the Hamming distance. Hamming distance is used for error correction. So it is best of known for finding of differences between two strings. The Hamming distance is a measure of distance between two strings equal is the number of positions for which the corresponding symbols may be different, that need to be changed to obtain one from the other, as per the definition for the following two strings: "rama" and "rimu" have a Hamming distance of 2.

Let $A=a_1, a_2..a_m$ and $B=b_1, b_2..b_m$ be two strings of length m. The Hamming distance of string A and string B, noted Ham(A,B), is the number of locations where A[i]!=B[i], $1\leq i\leq m$. How to use this definition in order to solve string matching problem as shown below:

Let us consider text(T)length of n and pattern(P) length of m. suppose there is an occurrence of P in T, it means the text string $t_i,t_{i+1}..t_{i+m-1}$ equal to P, so that $H(t_i,t_{i+1}..t_{i+m-1},P)=0$. It is used for exact string matching problem. Suppose that there is an occurrence of P in T. It means that a factor $t_i,t_{i+1}..t_{i+m-1}$ of R is equal to P with at most k mismatches , hence $Ham(t_i,t_{i+1}..t_{i+m-1},P) \leq k$. It is used for string matching with k-mismatches. A naïve algorithm for solving the string matching problem can proceed as follows: consider the first n-m+1 positions of the text string. Occurrences of the pattern can start only at these positions. The algorithm checks each of these positions for an occurrence of the pattern. The time complexity for the occurrence of pattern is O(mn)

At this point, it can easily deduce a naïve algorithm for both problems on a LARPBS.Comparing all subscripts $r_i r_{i+1}...r_{i+m-1}$ of the reference string ($1\leq i\leq n-m+1$) of length m with the pattern , let us denote those factors R_i. This solution requires the sending of m messages ($p_1 p_2...p_m$) to perform the comparisons for each ri $r_{i+1}....r_{i+m-1}$ of a R_i. As a processor can receive at most one message per cycle, it takes m cycles to compare the pattern with all the Ri . We must add m more cycles between them to make processor i know Ham (R_i, P) from the m next processors. As it requires to know the pattern, this solution is not on-line. To reduce the number cycles to O(m) and obtain the algorithm on a LARPBS with O(n) processors. First, describe the approach with the exact string matching problem, and will show later how to easily adapt it for the approximate string matching problem with k-mismatches.

Given a string $R=r_1 r_2...r_n$ of length n, it requires n-processors LARPBS that contains an element of R on each processor, i.e. processor I contains the ith element of R. for designing of an algorithm require one source processor that sends the elements of the pattern P one by one. The main aim of computation, for a pattern of length m, processor i ($1 \le i \le n-m+1$) has calculated Ham(Ri ,P) , i.e. Ham($r_i\ r_{i+1} \ldots r_{i+m-1}, p_1 p_2 \ldots p_m$).

4.1 Constant Time String Matching Algorithm on 2D LARPBS

The algorithm can be extended to 2D LARPBS; here is the 2D LARPBS algorithm. the data on processors have been organized such that they represent the m sets of length of n-m+1 of the text string with m* n-m+1 matrix plus, the first processor of each row segment holding the first element of each set also carries an element of pattern. The process is similar as per above for the remaining m-1 rows.

First show how to find the occurrences of pattern P in text string T on 2D LARPBS with m*(n-m+1) in constant time O (1).

Algorithm for string matching (pattern P, text T)

Begin

Initially: m elements of pattern initially distributed to the m processors on the first column, one processor and $L_{i,j}$ distributed to the m*(n-m+1) processors on the row and column. Where $1 \le i \le m$ and $m \le j \le m*(n-m+1)$

First processors broadcast elements on row buses: each first processor $p_{i,1}$, where $1 \le i \le m$, broadcasts the element $c_{i,1}$ to every processor in the ith row using only row buses .After this multiple row broadcast communication operations each processor $P_{i,j}$ saves received element as $r_{i,j}$.

Compare and Set results: Each processor $P_{i,j}$ compares $r_{i,j}$ with $X_{i,j}$, if $r_{i,j} = X_{i,j}$ if sets result=1 otherwise, result=0

Sum up 1's: perform a one-dimensional binary prefix sum operation on each column simultaneously for the value of result. Each processor $P_{i,j}$ where $1 \le (i,j) \le m$ stores the binary prefix sums to $b_{i,j}$.

Based on Hamming Distance: If $P_{m,j} = 0$ then the string matching(i.e. exact string matching) otherwise approximate string matching with k mismatches.

End.

Each step in the above algorithm runs in constant time. Thus we have the following theorem.

Fact 1: There is a constant time string matching algorithm on a 2D LARPBS that finds the occurrences of pattern in text using m*(n-m+1) processors

Example: Text string T(n)= abcbcd and Pattern string P(m)= bcb

L1 ={ abcb}, L2={bcbc} L3={cbcd}

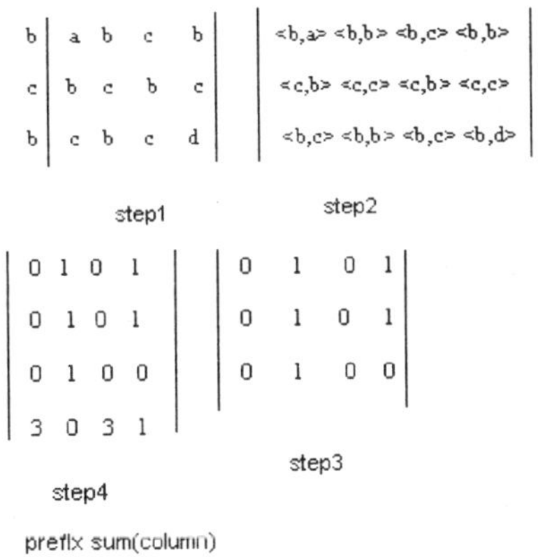

As per the given example, after step 4 in the matrix $M_{m+1,j}$ values useful for deciding the matching is exact string matching or approximate string matching with the k mismatches.

5. Conclusions

We studied both optical interconnection models and efficient algorithms for these models. Mainly we concentrated on a simple but powerful optical interconnection network model-LARPBS. This model extended to 2DLARPBS to improve the efficiency of the algorithm. We achieved a constant O(1) time algorithm for string matching on 2DLARPBS without any preprocessing the pattern string or text string. This is first known optimal algorithm for pattern matching on 2DLARPBS.Our future research on same problem with three dimensions or another mode, which contains minimum communication, and improve the performance.

6. Acknowledgements

We would like to thank our colleagues in the Department of Computer Science and Computer applications for their advice and helpful discussions. We thank Prof P.S.Raju, Director, and Dr.J.N.Murthy, Principal, and professor P.Eliah ,GRIET for his moral support and providing Laboratory. We grateful to the British Library, JNTUniversity Library for their services.

7. References

[1] Aho, A.V., Hopcroft, J.E., & Ullman, J.D. (1974). *The Design and Analysis of Computer Algorithms.* Addison Wesley Publishing Company.

[2] Datta, A., (2002). Efficient graph-theoretic algorithms on a linear array with a reconfigurable Pipelined bus system. *Journal of supercomputing,* 23, no.2, 193-211.

[3] Galil, Z. (1995). A constant-time optimal parallel string matching algorithm. *Journal of the ACM*, 42, no.4, 908-918.

[4] Guo, Z., Melhem, R., Hall, R., Chiarulli, D., & Levitan, S. (1991). Array processors with pipelined optical buses. *Journal of parallel and distributed computing*, 12, no3, 269-282.

[5] Isenman, M. & Shasha, D. (1990). Performance and architectural issues for string matching. *IEEE Transactions on computers*, vol.39, no.2, pp.238-250.

[6] Lecrop, T. (1995). Experimental result on string matching algorithms. *Software-practice and experience* vol.25, pp.727-767.

[7] Li, K., & Pan, Y. (1999). Linear array with a reconfigurable pipelined bus system: Concepts and applications. *Information sciences and international journal*, 11, no .7, 237- 258.

[8] Li, K., Pan,Y. & S.Zhen. (1998). Fast and processor efficient parallel matrix multiplication algorithm in a linear with a reconfigurable pipelined bus system. *IEEE Trans Parallel and Distributed systems* 9, no 8, 705-720.

[9] Michailidis, P.D, Margaritis, K.G. *(2002)* On-Line String Matching Algorithms: Survey and Experimental Results. *International journal of computer mathematics ,79, No.2,867-888.*

[10] Bourgeois, A.G, Trahan, J.L. (2000). Relating two dimensional reconfigurable meshes with optically pipelined buses. *International journal of foundations of computer science*, vol.11, 553-571.

[11] Trahan, Y.P.J.L, Bourgeois, A.G., & Vaidyanathan, R. (2000). Optimally scaling permutation routing on reconfigurable arrays with optically pipelined buses. *Journal of parallel on Distributed computing*, 60, no.9, 1125-1136.

[12] Viswanadha Raju, S., & Vinayababu, A. (2004). *Performance in the design of Parallel Programming. Proc ObComAPC-2004, Allied Publications*, pp.380 to 392.

[13] Viswanadha Raju, S., Vinayababu, A., & Mrudula, M. (2006). *Backend Engine for Parallel string Matching using Boolean Matrix.* Proc PARELEC-2006, IEEE Computer Society , 281-283.

[14] Viswanadha Raju, S., Mantena, S.R., Vinayababu, A., & Raju, G.V.S. (2006). *Efficient Parallel String Matching Using Partition Method.* Proc PDCAT-2006,IEEE Computer Society, 281-284.

[15] Viswanadha Raju, S., Vinayababu, A., Yanaiah, S.P., & G.V.S.Raju, (2006). *Parallel Approach for K String Matching. Proc NCIMDiL-2006,* Indian Institute Of Technology, Kharagpur , 5-10.

[16] Viswanadha Raju, S., Vinaya Babu, A. (2006). *Optimal Parallel String Matching Algorithm on Body Centered Hypercube.* International Journal of Mathematics and Computer Science,1 No.4, 473-484.

[17] Viswanadha Raju, S. & Vinaya Babu, A. (2006). Optimal Parallel algorithm for String Matching on Mesh Network Structure. *International Journal applied mathematical Sciences*, 3 No.2, 167-175

WSD Approaches for Information Retrieval

Dr. S. K. Dwivedi[1] and Parul Rastogi[2]
[1]Reader, BB Ambedkar Central University, Lucknow (India)
skd200@yahoo.com
[2]Research Scholar, BB Ambedkar Central University, Lucknow (India)
parul_rastogi@yahoo.com

Abstract

Information retrieval on web face various challenges, Word Sense Disambiguation (WSD) is one of them. Sense ambiguity has the detrimental effect on the performance of information retrieval. There are numerous approaches that the researchers have applied for the WSD in the field of Information Retrieval (IR). This paper first delineates this research and surveys the resulting efforts in information retrieval. We had given an analytical evaluation of the various WSD approaches for Information Retrieval. The paper will also discuss the drawbacks of the approaches and will conclude with the evaluation of the success rate of the numerous approaches.

Keywords: *word sense disambiguation, information retrieval, web information retrieval*

1. Introduction

The importance of IR is increasing day by day, but the quality of the results is still not 100% due to certain barriers. Sense ambiguity is one of them. An IR system is highly affected by the characteristics of text, one such characteristic is *word sense ambiguity*. Most words are ambiguous to some degree, what sense a word occurrence has depends on the context it appears in. For some words, their senses are unrelated, for example the word 'bank' could refer to a river bank or in could be in the context of financial organization. For most words however, their senses are related (e.g., through metaphor), the word 'crash' for example can refer to a physical event or the value of shares in a stock market dropping.

As IR systems process written text, they are affected by word sense ambiguity. IR systems are entirely different from a typical database system where retrieval of structured data is emphasized.

However IR focuses on less structured data/ document. If the IR is on the web then the degree of unstructured data will be quiet high.

In the field of computational linguistics, the problem is generally called word sense disambiguation (WSD), and is defined as the problem of computationally determining which "sense" of a word is activated by the use of the word in a particular context. WSD is essentially a task of classification of word senses in the classes, the context provides the evidence, and each occurrence of a word is assigned to one or more of its possible classes based on the evidence.

The remainder of the paper is organized as follows: in section 2, we discussed the various IR models, while in section 3 we surveyed the various approaches of WSD for IR and Web IR. In section 4 we had done overall comparison of all WSD approaches. A short conclusion finishes the paper.

2. Information Retrieval (IR) Models

An IR model is characterized by four parameters:

- representations for documents and queries,
- matching strategies for assessing the relevance of documents to a user query,
- methods for ranking query output, and
- Mechanisms for acquiring user-relevance feedback.

IR models can be classed into three types: set theoretic, algebraic and probabilistic models.

2.1 Set theoretic Model/Boolean Model

Boolean models are based on set theory. Sets can be thought of as any well-defined collection of things. The Boolean model represents documents by a set of index terms, each of which is viewed as a Boolean variable and valued as True if it is present in a document. No term weighting is allowed. Queries are specified as arbitrary Boolean expressions formed by linking terms through the standard logical operators: AND, OR, and NOT. Retrieval status value (RSV) is a measure of the query-document similarity. In the Boolean model, RSV equals 1 if the query expression evaluates to True otherwise it is 0. All documents whose RSV evaluates to 1 are considered relevant to the query.

For information retrieval, set theory is easily presented and was a natural choice for developing search models. In reality, Boolean information retrieval is more of a data model than an information model. Queries to the system can only be described in binary decisions a document is either relevant or not relevant.

2.2 Algebraic Model (AM)

Vector space models are built on the premise that the meaning of a document can be derived from its constituent terms. Put another way vector space model represents the documents and queries as vectors in a multidimensional space, whose dimensions are the terms used to build an index to represent the documents. The theory assumes that the underlying meaning of a document can be found from the terms used in the document itself. The creation of an index involves lexical scanning to identify the significant terms, where morphological analysis reduces different word forms to common "stems", and the occurrence of those stems is computed. Query and document surrogates are compared by comparing their vectors, using, for example, the cosine similarity measure. In this model, the terms of a query surrogate can be weighted to take into account their importance, and they are computed by using the statistical distributions of the terms in the collection and in the documents [Salton 1983]. The vector space model can assign a high ranking score to a document that contains only a few of the query terms if these terms occur infrequently in the collection but frequently in the document.

2.3 Probabilistic Model (PM)

The probabilistic retrieval model is based on the Probability Ranking Principle, which states that an information retrieval system is supposed to rank the documents based on their probability of relevance to the query, given all the evidence. The theory is that for every user's query there is a set of documents which contain exactly the relevant documents and no other. This idealized set does not know when the query is run, so the model has to make guesses at what could be the right answer to the query. A result set can be generated, proposed to the user, scored, and re-evaluated.

3. WSD approaches for Information Retrieval

Initial work on WSD in information retrieval does not returned positive results. The experiments of Krovetz and Croft [1] showed that there is considerable ambiguity even in a specialized database. Word senses provide a significant separation between relevant and irrelevant documents. He concluded that resolving lexical ambiguity have little impact on retrieval effectiveness for documents that have many words in common with the query.

Sanderson [2] concluded that word sense ambiguity is only problematic to an IR system when it is in context of very short queries. He also focused on the point that the disambiguator must resolve word senses to a high degree of accuracy.

Further various researchers used approaches which however returned positive results. The various approaches are as follows-

3.1 Indexing method

Gonzalo [3] experimented with a retrieval approach based on indexing in terms of WordNet synsets instead of Word forms. He performed numerous experiments using standard vector space model with different indexing spaces and found the improvement in the results. Again in 1999 he further concluded with their experiment that WSD is also beneficial to long queries in information retrieval. They concluded that –a) Part-Of-Speech tagging does not seem to help Improving retrieval, even if it is manually annotated, b) Using phrases as indexing terms is not a good strategy

3.2 Sense based vector space retrieval model

Christopher Stokoe[4] described a system that performs sense based information retrieval which, when used in a large scale IR experiment, demonstrated improved precision over the standard term based vector space model. Their disambiguation strategy used a combination of high precision techniques and sense frequency statistics in an attempt to reduce the impact of erroneous disambiguation on retrieval performance. It became clear from their work that an automated disambiguation system provides benefits in IR

3.3 Semantic Similarity Method

Semantic Similarity relates to computing the similarity between concepts which are not lexicographically similar. Semantic Similarity methods are classified into four Categories –

3.3.1 Edge Counting Methods

Measure the similarity between two terms (concepts) as a function of the length of the path linking the terms and on the position of the terms in the taxonomy [5,6].

3.3.2 Information Content Methods

Measure the difference in information content of the two terms as a function of their probability of occurrence in a corpus [7,8].

3.3.3. Feature based Methods

Measure the similarity between two terms as a function of their properties (e.g., their definitions or "glosses "in WordNet) or based on their relationships to other similar terms in the taxonomy [9].

Giannis Varela [10] experimented with several semantic similarity methods for computing the conceptual similarity between natural language terms using WordNet. He demonstrated that it is possible to exploit this information (as embedded in taxonomic ontologies and captured algorithmically by semantic similarity methods) for improving the performance of retrievals on the Web.

3.4 Relevance Feedback Model

Relevance feedback is an interactive approach that has been shown to work particularly well in classical information retrieval and more recently in Internet search settings. In this setting, after receiving results for a query the user is asked to rate the relevancy of some of them. This information is passed to the search engine, and the engine reranks the results to better suit the user's intent

Eric Brill [11] used web graph based reranker for the reranking of the retrieved results in response to the given query. They applied their approach for the WSD and found good results.

3.5 Phrase Recognition Method

In the phrase recognition method noun phrases in queries are identified and classified into four types: proper names, dictionary phrases, simple phrases and complex phrases. A document has a phrase if all content words in the phrase are within a window of a certain size. The window sizes for different types of phrases are different and are determined using a decision tree. Phrases are more important than individual terms. Consequently, documents in response to a query are ranked with matching phrases given a higher priority.

Shuang Liu [12] utilized the method and found major improvements in the document retrieval.

3.6 Language Sense Model

Each document has two different presentations: namely term representation and sense representation. The language model on term representations (LMTR) is the traditional approach. The language model on sense representations (LMSR) is similar to the one on term representations. The Language Sense Model (LSM) for information retrieval utilizes both term and sense representation. The model helps in relating the terms with its possible sense in easier way.

Shenghua Bao [13], used the LSM and found that it outperforms both vector space model and traditional language models significantly on both medium and long queries.

3.7 Term Expansion Method

It is an attempt to manage the information provided by a WSD system in order to overcome the problem of the mismatch between a concept in a query and in a document, and the problems derived from the natural language ambiguity. This method expands terms within the queries and the collection documents. To carry out the expansion, it first selects the most likely WordNet synset returned by the WSD system in the event of a tie it selects all the synsets with the maximum probability. And afterwards, it generates the term expansion using all synonyms belonging to the selected synsets. Sergio Navarro [14] used the method and found good results.

4. Discussion

Word Sense Disambiguation is one of the factors that deteriorate the performance of the Information Retrieval tasks. Various researchers have worked on to improve the performance of IR by using diversified methods and models as discussed in section 3.

Though all the methods showed improvements in the performance of Information retrieval but each method has some pitfalls.

Gonzalo used Indexing, from his work he identified that the information retrieval applications are benefited by the WSD. According to him taking phrases as indexing terms may decrease retrieval efficiency. Shuang Liu used the phrases in his method and found improvements in the document retrieval. Gonzalo pointed out that the phrase indexing works better with the long queries because in that case relevant document containing just one query term is ranked much higher with phrase indexing, because false partial matches with a phrase are not considered. This concludes to this fact that the indexing phrases techniques improved the performance of the IR web applications.

Shuang Liu used the phrase recognition for the query expansion and also concluded that the short queries are benefited by this method.

Sergio used the method of term expansion which is quiet similar to the Phrase recognition method of Shuang Liu. Both the researchers used the common concept of query expansion and made use of WordNet for the phrase/ term indexing purpose In their experiment of term expansion, Sergio was not confident about the performance of their method for all types of queries.

Giannis Varela, experimented various semantic similarity method based on various features like Information Content, Edge counting etc. and found that these method will improve the performance of retrieval on the web.

Christopher Stokoe found overall improvements in the precision results. They made use of sense based vector space model to show improvements in the performance of the IR. The IR techniques based on vector space model outperforms with small to long queries.

Eric Brill utilized the human intervention in another way just by getting the relevance feedback from the end user and reranking the results according to the relevance feedback.

Shenghua Bao used LSM and found that it outperforms the vector space model which redirects that their method is better then the Christoper Stokoe as they used sense based vector space model.

In general all the approaches discussed above are based on Algebraic or Probabilistic model. Set theoretic model can not be used as a base for WSD approaches as ranking of the retrieval output is not possible due to same RSV.

The overall comparison of all the methods illustrate that all the methods are Knowledge based methods and used WordNet (an electronic lexical database) as a knowledge source. To understand the success rate of all the approaches we can refer to Table1.

Table 1 Overall comparison of various WSD approaches

Approach	IR Model	Resource	Success Rate
Indexing approach	AM	WordNet	29% improvement over standard run
Sense based vector space retrieval model	AM	WordNet	absolute increase of 1.73% and a relative increase over TF*IDF of 45.9%.
Semantic Similarity Method	AM	WordNet	Promising performance improvements
Relevance Feedback Model	PM	WordNet	Improvement in overall recall by 30%
Phrase Recognition Method	PM	WordNet	Improvement in performance
Language Sense Model	PM	WordNet	Outperforms vector space and traditional model by 7.53% on medium queries and 16.09% in long queries.
Term Expansion Method	PM	WordNet	Good results for the SEMCOR test collection

The approaches we discussed in the paper are somehow related to each other, because all the approaches used WordNet as a common resource. Almost all approaches used the concept of measuring the similarity between the terms and the senses by creating indexes in some or other way.

The scope of IR applications is quiet wide. It is now obvious from the above survey that application of WSD has the positive impact on the Information Retrieval tasks.

5. Conclusion

Information Retrieval is a common NLP task. Performance of IR is hindered due to WSD. Various researchers have worked in this field and tried to find out the best resultset by applying WSD. In the beginning researchers failed to get success and they get negative results. But very soon various researchers noticed promising results of WSD application in Information Retrieval tasks.

6. References

[1] R. Krovetz & W.B. Croft , "Lexical Ambiguity and Information Retrieval", in ACM Transactions on Information Systems, Vol.10(2), April, pp. 115-141, 1992.

[2] M. Sanderson, "Word sense disambiguation and information retrieval", in Proceedings of 17th ACM SIGIR Conference, July, Dublin, Ireland, pp.142-151, 1994.

[3] J. Gonzalo, F. Verdejo, I. Chugur and J. Cigarran, "Indexing with WordNet synsets can improve Text Retrieval", in Proceedings of the COLING/ACL '98 Workshop on Usage of WordNet for NLP, Montreal, 1998.

[4] C. Stokoe, M. P. Oakes and J. Tait, "Word Sense Disambiguation in Information Retrieval Revisited", in Proceedings of SIGIR, 28 July - 1 August , Toronto, Canada, pp. 159-166, 2003

[5] Y.Qiu and H.Frei, "Concept Based Query Expansion. Z.Wu and M.Palmer.Verb Semantics and Lexical Selection." In Annual Meeting of the Associations for Computational Linguistics (ACL'94) Las Cruces, New Mexico, pp. 133 –138,1994.

[6] Y.Li, Z.A.Bandar and D.McLean. "An Approach for Measuring Semantic Similarity between Words Using Multiple Information Sources." IEEE Trans. On Knowledge and Data Engineering, Vol. 15(4), July/Aug., pp. 871 –882, 2003.

[7] D.Lin. "Principle-Based Parsing Without Overgeneration",. In Annual Meeting of the Association for Computational Linguistics (ACL'93) , Columbus, Ohio, pp 112 –120,1993.

[8] O.Resnik. "Semantic Similarity in a Taxonomy: An Information-Based Measure and its Application to Problems of Ambiguity and Natural Language.", Journal of Artificial Intelligence Research, Vol. 11 pp. 95 –130, 1999.

[9] P.Lord, R.Stevens, A.Brass and C.Goble. A.Tversky. "Features of Similarity", Psycological Review, Vol. 84(4) pp. 327 –352,1977.

[10] G. Varela, E. Voutsaki and P. Raftopoulou, "Semantic Similarity Methods in WordNet and their Application to Information Retrieval on the Web", in Proceedings of WIDM, November, Bremen, Germany, pp. 10-16, 2005.

[11] E. Brill and S. Vassilvitskii, "Using Web-Graph Distance for Relevance Feedback in Web Search" in Proceedings of SIGIR, August, Seattle, Washington, USA, pp. , 2006

[12] S Liu, F Liu, C Yu and W Meng, "An Effective Approach to Document Retrieval via Utilizing WordNet and Recognizing Phrases" in Proceedings of *SIGIR'04*, July 25–29, Sheffield, Yorkshire, UK, pp. 266-272, 2004

[13] S Bao, L Zhang, E Chen, M Long, R Li, and Y Yu, " LSM: Language Sense Model for Information Retrieval", Advances in Web-Age Information Management, Springer Berlin, Heidelberg, 2006.

[14] S Navarro, F Llopis and R Munoz, "IRn in the CLEF Robust WSD Task 2008", in· Cross Language Evaluation Forum (CLEF-2008), www.clef-ampaign.org/2008/working_notes/NavarroRobust-paperCLEF2008.pdf

Topical Crawlers Based on Mutual Information Feature Selection Method

N. V. G Sirisha Gadiraju[1] and G.V Padma Raju[2]
[1]Asst. Professor
[2]Professor
S.R.K.R. Engineering College, Bhimavaram,
siri_gnvg@yahoo.co.in gvpadmaraju@gmail.com

Abstract

Search Engines collect data from the Web by crawling it. In spite of consuming enormous amounts of hardware and network resources these general purpose crawlers end up fetching only large fraction of the visible web. When information need is only about a specific topic special type of crawlers called as Topical Crawlers complement Search Engines. In this paper we evaluate the performances of two topical crawlers called Traditional Focused Crawler and Accelerated Focused Crawler. Naive Bayesian Classifier guides these crawlers in fetching topic relevant documents. The features used in training the crawlers and in determining the relevancy of unvisited document to the specified topic are gathered using mutual information feature selection method. In determining the relevancy of unvisited URL to a specific topic, Traditional Focused Crawler uses the features of the parent page where as Accelerated Focused Crawler uses features around the link itself. The crawlers were evaluated using two methods. One based on the number of topic relevant target pages found and retrieved and the second based on the lexical similarity between crawled page and topic description for the topic provided by the editors of Dmoz.org. Due to the limited amount of resources consumed by these crawlers they have applications in web portals, niche search engines and business intelligence.

1. Introduction

Keyword search and surfing are the dominant ways of accessing hypertext on the Web. The size of the publicly indexable World-Wide-Web has exceeded 23.68 billion pages in the year 2008. This is very large compared to the one billion pages in the year 2000. Dynamic content on the web is also growing day by day. Search engines are therefore increasingly challenged when trying to maintain current indices using exhaustive crawling.

Making an educated guess about the worth of clicking on a link (u; v) without knowledge of the target v is central to the surfing activity. Automatic programs that can learn this capability would be of great value in personalized search domain.

Focused crawler [1] aim to search and retrieve only subset of the World-Wide Web that pertains to a specific topic of relevance. It is an automatic program that emulates the human behavior. It learns to predict the relevance of an unseen HREF target page with respect to an information need, based on information limited to the HREF source page. In contrast to giant, all-purpose crawlers which process large portions of the Web in a centralized manner, a distributed set of focused crawlers can cover specialized topics in more depth. Due to the limited resources used by a good focused crawler, users can make use of them in their PCs.

The major problem in focused crawling is that of properly assigning credit to all pages along a crawl route that yields highly relevant documents. A classifier can be used to assign credit (priority) to unvisited URLs. The classifier is trained with specific topic's positive and negative example pages. It is then used to predict the relevance of unvisited URL to the specific topic. Naive Bayesian Classifier is a popular classifier used to automatically tag documents [7]. It is based on the fact that if we know the probabilities of words (features) appearing in a certain category of document, given the set of words (features) in a new document, we can correctly predict the relevance of the new document to the given category or topic. Relevance can have any value between 0 and 1.

A major characteristic or difficulty of the text classification problem is the high dimensionality of the feature space. The native feature space consists of the unique terms (words or phrases) that occur in documents, which can be tens or hundreds or thousands of terms for even a moderate-sized text corpus. This is prohibitively high for the classification algorithm. It is highly desirable to reduce the number of features automatically without sacrificing classification accuracy. Stop word removal [5], stemming [4] and term goodness criterion helps in achieving a desired degree of term elimination from the full vocabulary of a document corpus. Mutual Information is the term goodness criterion used in this paper.

2. Topical Crawlers

While surfing, the user typically has topic-specific information need, and explores out from a few known relevant starting points in the Web graph to seek new pages relevant to the chosen topic. The topical crawlers discussed in this paper also start from a set of topic relevant URLs called seeds URLs. The documents represented by these seed URLs are fetched and the links embedded in these seed documents are collected. The relevancy of these links to target topic is found out by means of a classifier. The links are then added to a priority queue of unvisited links with a priority equal to the relevancy calculated above. Document representing the link present at the front of the queue is fetched and process repeats until a predefined goal is attained.

In determining the relevancy of a link to the target topic, Traditional Focused Crawler uses features of the parent page where as Accelerated Focused Crawler uses features around the link itself. Both the crawlers are trained on a set of topic relevant URLs called training URLs. The training URLs are nothing but the URLs used to seed the crawlers. Accelerated Focused Crawler is also trained on documents retrieved by Traditional Focused Crawler.

3. Mutual Information Based Feature Selection

Features are gathered from the DOM tree [2] representation of the document using a DOM parser. For extracting the features, first the HTML document is converted to XML document which is in turn converted to a DOM tree.

Of all the features gathered from the document corpus, good features are selected using mutual information criterion. Mutual Information [6] selects words that appear frequently in documents that are in the specified topic but are rare in documents not in the topic. Let $\{t_i\}_{i=1}^{m}$ denote the set of topics in the training space, $T=\bigcup_{i=1}^{m} t_i$ and $F=\{f,\bar{f}\}$ denote the set in which the feature f occurs or f does not occur. The topic specific feature scores can then be combined to measure the goodness of the term at a global level MI(f;T) as

$$MI(f;T)=\sum_{i=1}^{m} p(f\wedge t_i)\log_2\frac{p(f\wedge t_i)}{p(f)\times p(t_i)}+\sum_{i=1}^{m} p(\bar{f}\wedge t_i)\log_2\frac{p(\bar{f}\wedge t_i)}{p(\bar{f})\times p(t_i)}$$

where m is the number of topics considered in the training set. Let MI(f;T) = MI(f). The terms with highest MI(f) are only considered .

4. Experimental Study

4.1 Test Beds Creation

For evaluating the crawlers the topic relevant seed URLs, training URLs, target URLs and the topic descriptions are collected from content.rdf file of Open Directory Project (ODP). The topics Food_Service,Model_Aviation,Nonprofit_Resources,Database_Theory, Mutual_Funds, Roller_Skating are crawled. The ODP relevant set for a given topic was divided into two random subsets. The first set is the seeds. This set of URLs was used to initialize the crawl as well as provide the set of positive examples to train the classifiers. The second set is the targets. It is a holdout set that was neither used to train nor to seed the crawlers. These targets were used only for evaluating the crawlers. The topics were divided into two test beds. The crawlers have crawled all the topics present in the two test beds. The first test bed is Food_Service, Model_Aviation, Nonprofit_Resources. The second test bed is Mutual_Funds, Roller_Skating, Database_Theory. For training a classifier we need both positive and negative examples. The positive examples for a topic are the pages corresponding to the seed URLs for that topic in the test bed. The negative examples are the set of seed URLs of other two topics in the same test bed. The topic descriptions for the topics are written by DMoz editors and are not accessible by the crawlers directly. They are also used only to evaluate the crawlers.

4.2 Evaluation Schemes

The crawlers' effectiveness is found out using relevance measure called recall. Table 1 shows the assessments schemes used in this paper. It consists of two sets of crawler effectiveness measures differentiated mainly by the source of evidence to assess relevance.

Table 1 Evaluation Schemes

Relevance Assessments	*Recall*
Target Pages	$\lvert S_c^t \cap T_d \rvert / T_d$
Target Descriptions	$\sum_{p\in S_c^t} \sigma(p, D_d)$

S_c^t is the set of pages crawled by the crawler C at time t.

T_d is the target set

D_d,p are the vectors representing the topic description and crawled page respectively.

σ is the cosine similarity function

The first relevance measure called target recall focuses only on the target pages that have been identified for the topic. The second relevance measure called DMoz recall employs relevance assessments based on the lexical similarity between crawled pages (whether or not they are in target set) and the topic descriptions. Both the measures are dynamic in that they provide a temporal characterization of the crawl strategy.

The target pages are nothing but a set of pages relevant to the topic. These are specified by the user before the crawl starts. After the crawler has crawled for the topic, the intersection of set of crawled pages and target pages is found out. Target recall is obtained by dividing the size of the resultant set obtained by the size of the target set.

To find the cosine similarity between the crawled page and the topic description for the specific topic, both of them have to be represented in mutually compatible format. For this features and term frequency values of features are found from the crawled page as well as topic description of the topic and vectors D, p are constructed. Cosine similarity function ($\sigma()$) is given by

$$\sigma(p,D) = \frac{\sum_{i \in p \cap D} p_i D_i}{\sqrt{(\sum_{i \in p} p_i^2)(\sum_{i \in D} D_i^2)}}$$

where p_i and D_i are the term frequency weights of "term i" in page p and topic description D respectively. Recall for the full crawl is estimated by summing up the cosine similarity scores over all the crawled pages.

4.3 Results, Comparison and Discussion

Offline analysis is done after all the pages have been downloaded and the experiments are over. Recall is measured as shown in Table 1. The horizontal axis in all the plots is time approximated by the number of pages crawled. The vertical axis shows the performance metric i.e. target recall or DMoz recall. Nature of topic is said to have impact on crawler performance [1, 3]. From the Figures 1 and 2 we can see that the crawlers have fetched more number of topic relevant target pages when crawled for a co-operative topic like Nonprofit_Resources.

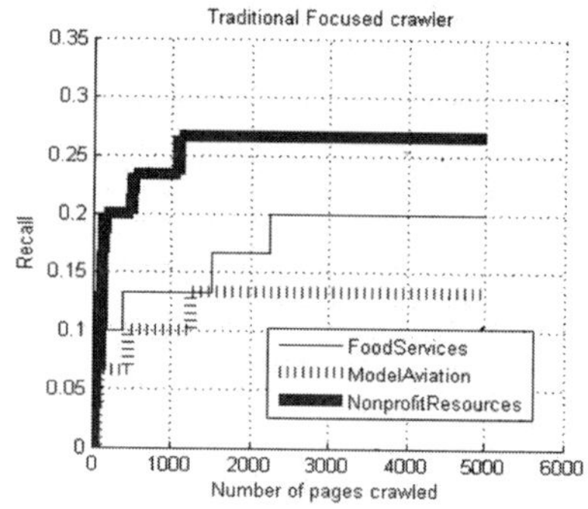

Fig. 1 Target recall of Traditional Focused Crawler

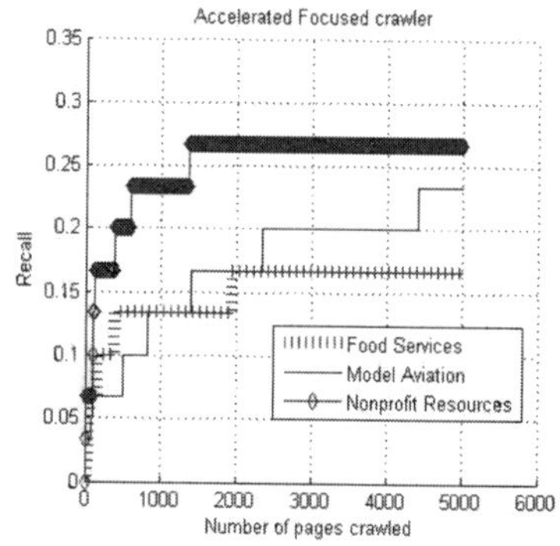

Fig. 2 Target recall of Accelerated Focused Crawler

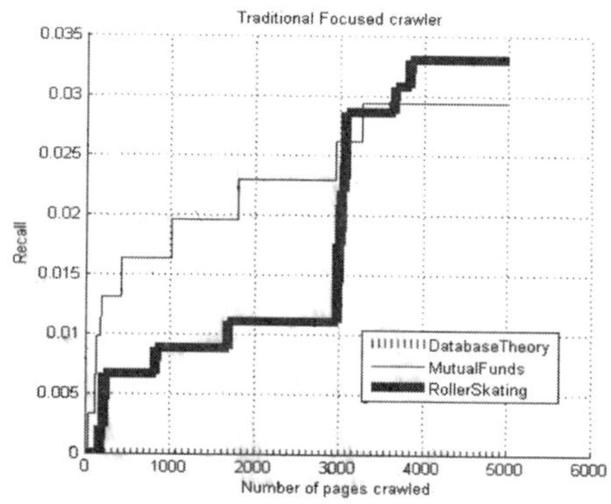

Fig. 3 Target recall of Traditional Focused Crawler

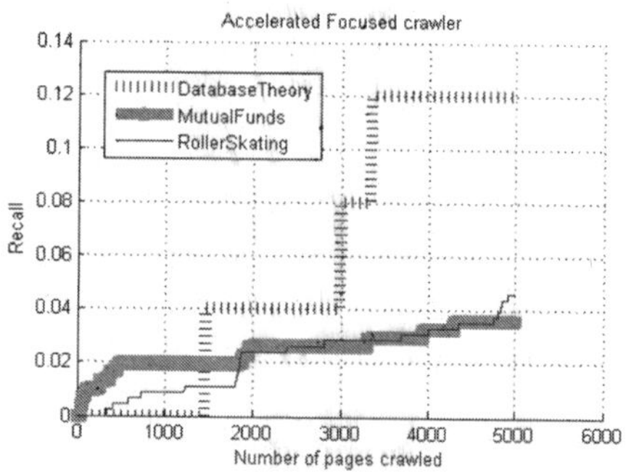

Fig. 4 Target recall of Accelerated Focused Crawler

The effect of the size of training data and test data on crawler performance is also studied. When crawled for the topics Food_Services, Model_Aviation and Nonprofit_Resources training data is large (nearly 200 to 300 documents relevant to topic). Crawlers were able to fetch more number of target pages as shown by recall values in Figures 1 and 2.The number of URLs specified as targets is only 30 for each of the topics in this test bed. When crawled for the topics Database_Theory, Mutual_Funds, Roller_Skating the crawlers were trained with only 75 documents relevant to the specified topic and the number of URLs specified as targets are 25 for Database_Theory, 306 for Mutual_Funds and 455 for Roller_Skating. Though the target set is large in the second test bed the crawlers were able to fetch only few of them as shown in Figs. 3 and 4.

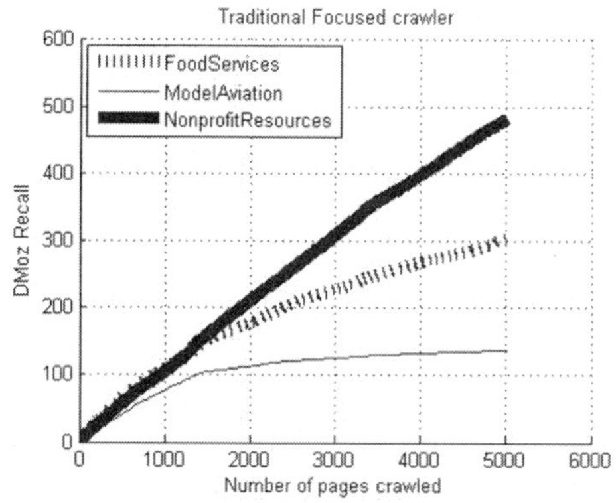

Fig. 5 DMoz recall for Traditional Focused Crawler

It shows that when classifier is used to guide the crawlers, good training (large set of training data) yields good crawler performance. Accelerated Focused Crawler is trained over the documents fetched by the Traditional Focused Crawler i.e. it has large training data set. This once again suggests the use of Accelerated Focused Crawler instead of Traditional Focused Crawler in fetching topic relevant documents

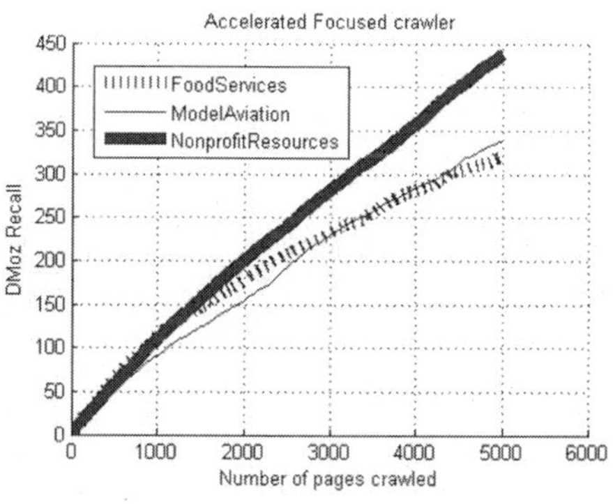

Fig. 6 DMoz recall for Accelerated Focused Crawler

When crawlers were evaluated using lexical similarity between the crawled page (whether are not they are in target set) and the topic descriptions Accelerated Focused Crawler has shown better Dmoz recall than Traditional Focused Crawler for all topics as shown in Figs 5,6,7,8.

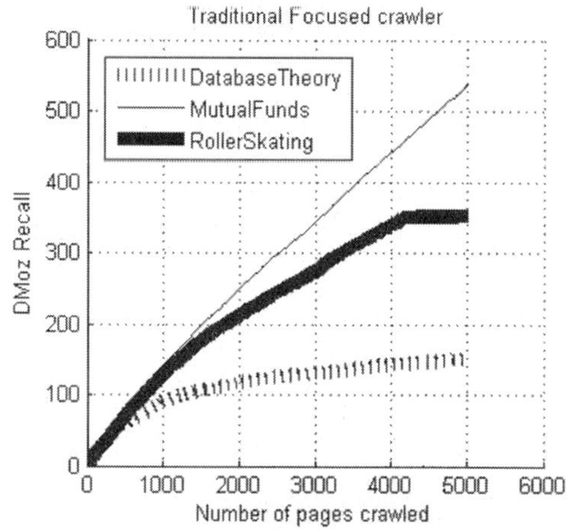

Fig. 7 DMoz recall of Traditional Focused Crawler

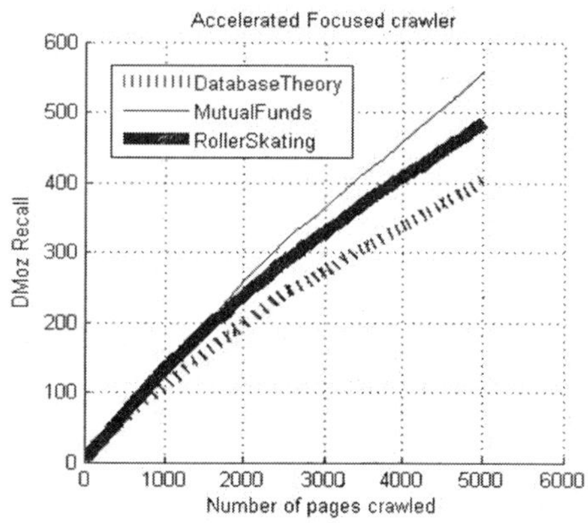

Fig. 8 DMoz recall of Accelerated Focused Crawler

In Figure 8 the DMoz recall values are in decending order of magnitude for the topics Mutual_Funds, Roller_Skating and Database_Theory. This is because Mutual_Funds was described briefly when compared to Roller_skating and Roller_Skating was described briefly when compared to Database_Theory by the Dmoz editors. This result suggests that when crawlers are driven by keyword queries or topic descriptions it is better to describe the topic or theme using only and all prominent terms of the topic. This results in collecting more number of pages relevant to the topic.

Figure 10 shows that when training set of documensts available is small (in the case of

Database_Theory, Mutual_Funds, Roller_Skating) Accelerated Focused Crawler has outperformed Traditional Focused crawler in average target recall. Figure 9 show us that the performance of Traditional Focused Crawler and Accelerated Focused Crawler are nearly the same when training data set is large. From Figure 3 we can see that Traditional Focused Crawler has found 0 targets for the topic Database_theory. This is because the target set size is only 27 for this topic. In the case of other two topics in the same test bed the number of targets is greater than 300.

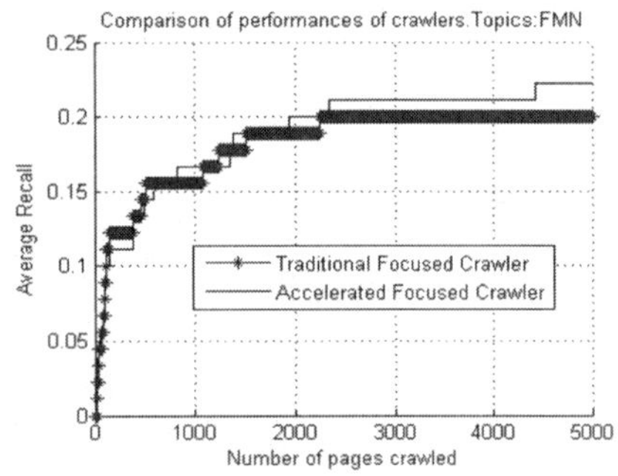

Fig. 9 Average target recall of crawlers. Topics-FMN

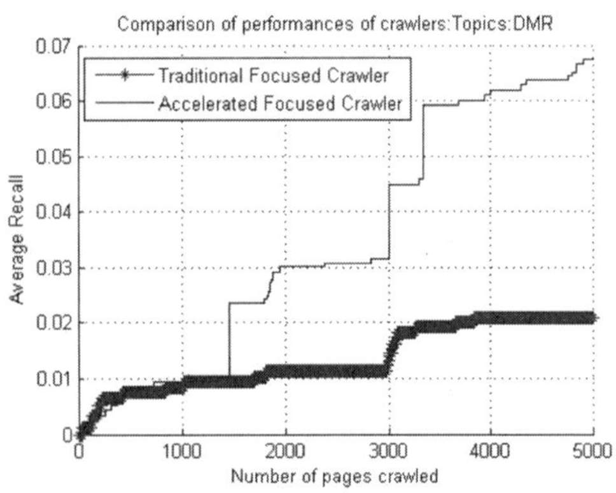

Fig. 10 Average target recall of crawlers. Topics-DMR

These target sets were not picked in that way intentionally but it was because the number of links specified as relevant by DMoz editors for the topic Database_theory was less compared to the other two topics. This result may indicate that Database_Theory is less popular topic in the Web. Accelerated Focused Crawler (Figure 4) has shown better performance in this case also. This shows that the popularity of topic also effects crawler performance

5. Conclusions

Accelerated Focused Crawler is a simple enhancement to Traditional Focused crawler. It assigns better priorities to the unvisited URLs in the crawl frontier. The crawlers were trained with documents relevant to the topic gathered from Dmoz.org. Features are extracted from the DOM representation of parent (source) page using mutual information feature selection method. When a small training data set is available, it is suggestive to use Traditional Focused Crawler only to train Accelerated Focused Crawler and not for fetching topic relevant documents. When training data is large we can make use of Traditional Focused Crawler for fetching topic relevant documents. In any case Accelerated Focused Crawler has performed well compared to Traditional Focused Crawler. Popularity of the topic as well as the nature of the topic i.e. whether it is competitive or collaborative also has effect on crawler performance. When crawlers are driven by keyword queries or topic descriptions, describing the topic or theme using only and all prominent terms of the topic enhances the performance of the crawl.

6. References

[1] S. Chakrabarti, M. vander Berg and B. Dom , "Focused crawling: a new approach to topic-specific web resource discovery". In the *Proceedings of the eighth international conference on World Wide Web,* Toronto, Canada, pp. 1623–1640, 1999.

[2] S. Chakrabarti, K. Punera, M. Subramanyam "Accelerated Focused Crawling through Online Relevance Feedback", In *the Proceedings. of the 11th international conference on World Wide Web, Honolulu*, Hawaii, USA, pp..148-159, 2002.

[3] F. Menczer, G. Pant, M. E. Ruiz, P. Srinivasan "Evaluating Topic-driven Web Crawlers", In the *Proceedings. of the 24th annual international ACM SIGIR conference on Research and development in information retrieval*, New Orleans, U.S, pp. 241–249 2001.

[4] M.F. Porter, "An algorithm for suffix stripping, *Program"*, Volume 14, Issue 3, pp. 130-137, 1980.

[5] J.W. Wilbur and K. Sirotkin, "The automatic identification of stop words", *Journal of Information Science*, Volume 18, Issue 1, pp. 45 – 55, 1992.

[6] Y. Yang, Jan O. Pedersen, "A Comparative Study on Feature Selection in Text Categorization", In the *Proceedings of the Fourteenth International Conference on Machine Learning*, Morgan Kaufmann Publishers Inc., San Francisco, CA, USA, pp. 412–420, 1997.

[7] Zhang H., "The Optimality of Naive Bayes" In *the Proceedings of 17th International FLAIRS conference*, Miami Beach, May 17-19, 2004.

Analysis of Assorted Bioinformatics Tools and its Metrics

P. Dhavachelvan and Jayanthi Manicassamy
Department of Computer Science, Pondicherry University, Pondicherry, India.
dhavachelvan@gmail.com jmanic2@yahoo.com

Abstract

Bioinformatics is a field of computational molecular biology which merging with few other sciences which entails statistics techniques, database creation for solving biological problems by means of biological data analysis and interpretation of accurate result. Since biological data's can be predicted in an unpredictable rate. There is a need for managing and interoperating this data for real time environment for which various tools, techniques, algorithms, databases has been developed. Assorted tools have been developed in this area of bioinformatics for diverse analysis processes like sequence analysis, functional analysis, structural analysis and similarity and homology analysis. Factors that are to be considered in the designing of bioinformatics tools are software should be made globally available and the tools developed should be flexible to the users since mostly the users are of biologists. It is significant to evaluate these tools by identifying bioinformatics methods with optimal sensitivity, predictive and other capabilities since there is need for high-throughput techniques or computational tools are required that can be effectively and efficiently utilized by researchers, developers and novice's users. This paper provides an analysis made on various bioinformatics tools of which twenty five tools are taken for details study. The survey is made on these tools based on the study and classification like sequence analysis tools, pattern matching tools and textmining tools with features and the associated metrics are identified for each tool. This helps us to proceed in the development of new tool with the common features that are required for the development of bioinformatics tools, enhancement of existing tools or utilization of better existing tools.

Keywords: Pattern Matching, Sequence Analysis, Text Mining, Bioinformatics, Evaluation, Software Metrics.

1. Introduction

Bioinformatics aim to solve biological problems using related information, using mathematical, statistical and computing methods. The definition of bioinformatics varies based on the usage. Many tools have been developed which has been categorized based on the functionalities are Homology and Similarity Tools like 3D spatial homology search tool [1] for gene expression for finding genes with a similar spatial expression pattern which could potentially reveal novel or unknown genes involved in similar processes or pathways. Protein Function Analysis Tools like GOFFA tool [2] is Gene Ontology for Functional Analysis allows the user to interactively select GO terms according to their significance and specific biological complexity within the hierarchical structure. Structural Analysis Tools like PREDICTOR tool [3] for DNA structure prediction which allows the calculation of atomic structures of double-helical DNA with up to 150 Watson-Crick base pairs and sequence analysis tools have been developed or adapted to deal with the experimental riches of complex and multivariate data in biological problem solutions. Sequence Analysis Tools which includes "Database search" like text based search, sequence based search, motif based search and structure based search. "Analysis Tools" like DNA, RNA and protein sequence analysis, "Function analysis" like phylogeny, microarray analysis tools and various tools have also been developed.

Since biological resources are real entity that should be kept updated based on the researches that requires vast space, it could not be build by one so database like NCBI, PDB, EMBDL, Medline etc... has made to share its resources. Most of the bioinformatics related applications and tools utilities these Databases. The study made on various tools that falls in this category as mentioned above have made a deep analysis for identifying features and functionalities for each tools.

Software metrics quantifies some characteristics or attributes of a product or process by means of measurement using numerical ratings, Since quantitative have been proven very powerful in computer science and other sciences Statistical analysis is also being made to identifying the qualifying levels. There is no standard terminology for defining software metrics it depends on the requirements. Identification of features and functionalities are not only considered, we have also identified various metrics on each tools which has been represented in this paper since metrics based evaluation is used to represent the retrieval ability and performance of the tool like identity metrics, error rate, error report, precision, recall for bioinformatics tools. Based on the classification made by us for tools web have explained each tool under that category like Pattern matching tools, Sequence analysis tools and Text mining tools.

2. Survey on Bioinformatics Tools

The survey made on the bioinformatics tools for which a detailed analysis has been made has been explained in this section. These tools have been categorized based on their features and functionalizes that have explained below by means of categories.

Pattern Matching Tools

Pattern matching is the act of checking for the presence of the constituents of a given pattern. a pattern concerns conventionally either sequences or tree structures. There are various tools that have been developed in pattern matching, in the area of bioinformatics for various analysis processes like sequence analysis, functional analysis, structural analysis and similarity analysis. The following are pattern match tools that have taken for the study in bioinformatics tools.

David He et. al [4] developed a new web-tool which uses graphical visualization methods borrowed from protein interaction studies to identify and characterize repetitive elements in low-complexity sequences where repetitive protein sequences with a limited amino acid palette are abundant in nature and many of them play an important role in the structure and function of certain types of proteins. However, such repetitive sequences often do not have rigidly defined motifs. This tool is license free, which is flexible following an algorithm based approach that is navigateable.

Richard J. Edwards et. al [5] developed tool for making motif-motif comparisons which is a GUI based, license free, open source. It identifying and describing similarities between regular expression motifs. It can identify a number of different relationships between motifs, including exact matches, variants of degenerate motifs and complex overlapping motifs. Motif relationships are scored using shared information content, allowing the best matches to be easily identified in large comparisons. Many input and search options are available, enabling a list of motifs to be compared to within itself to identify recurring motifs or to datasets of known motifs. This tool is a computational approach with online help facilities.

Marti A et. al [6] developed a web-based search engine that provides biologists with new ways to access the scientific literature. One of the features is the ability to search and browse article figures and their captions with a grid view and many different figures associated with the same keywords, providing new insight into the literature. An abstract/title search and list view shows at a glance many of the figures associated with each article. The interface is carefully designed according to usability principles and techniques.

Anne Laure et. al [7] has developed tool which associates with GUI web server with license free for finding internal repeats at three levels which quickly identifies statistically significant internal repeats in DNA and amino acid sequences and in 3D structures using dynamic programming. The associated web server also shows the relationships between repeats at each level and facilitates visualization of the results. This tool is a computational based supported by any browser type which is flexible and user friendly.

Dietrich et. al [8] has developed a web service tool for researchers in the biomedical research community for literature search that analyze text for contained information and then link them to the corresponding entries in bioinformatics databases such as Swiss-Prot, PubMed data entries and gene ontology concepts. The tool automatically integrates links to database concepts to offer additional support to readers and to authors will be extended in the future with novel modules for information extraction. All services are preloaded to avoid startup overhead. All documents are processed in a single stream right upon submission, i.e. no preprocessing is performed to store intermediary information. Any contained query is passed to the index service for document retrieval. As soon as a request reaches the central Whatizit server, the requested modules are activated and the stream of text is passed through all required components in a single stream. Tool provides a text input area where user can submit any kind of Unicode-encoded text or retrieve Medline abstracts for subsequent analysis which is license free and platform independent. Which is a computational based, with online help following a computational approach.

Sequence Analysis Tools

There are various sequences analysis tool that have been created in this field of bioinformatics for various processes like functional analysis, structural analysis and similarity analysis. The following are the sequence analysis tools that have been taken for study that have been explained below.

Xiang et. al [9] has developed a web interface for comparative genomics and phylogenetic analysis of Plasmodium gene families which causes malaria by the intercellular protozoan parasite. Gene families were clustered and could be searched using keywords, gene-family information, domain composition, Gene Ontology and BLAST. This tool contained 8980 sets of gene families derived from six malaria parasite genomes like Plasmodium falciparum, Plasmodium berghei, Plasmodium knowlesi, Plasmodium chabaudi, Plasmodium vivax and Plasmodium Yoelii which is helpful for researchers working on malaria parasite phylogenomics. The technology used here is PHP and Perl which is fully web tool based on computational approach.

Mario Falchi et. al [10] an efficient tool for mining complex inbred genealogies that identify clusters of individuals sharing the same expected amount of relatedness. It also allows reconstruction of sub-pedigrees suitable for genetic mapping in a systematic way. The tool is developed in Java which is platform independent, GUI based user friendly tool followed a computational approach for tool development.

Jacques Oberto et. al [11] has developed a web service of platform independent, license free to facilitate extraction, by molecular geneticists and phylogeneticists, of specific gene and protein sequences from completely determined prokaryotic genomes. Upon selection of a particular prokaryotic organism and gene, two levels of visual gene context information are provided on a single dynamic page. The amino acid sequence is provided for protein-coding query genes. Query results can be exported as a rich text format word processor file for printing, archival or further analysis.

Jimin Pei et. al [12] has developed a web server which is user friendly that constructs multiple proteins sequence alignments using PROMALS, a progressive method that improves alignment quality by using additional homologs from PSI-BLAST searches and In addition to alignment construction, this server outputs useful information about predicted secondary structures, sequence grouping and positional conservation for target sequences. The tool is license free with GUI based which follows algorithm based approach.

Shaun Mahony et. al [13] has developed a web server that is designed to support the study of DNA-binding motifs which is a GUI based developed using C++ of license free and platform independent. This tool may be used to query motifs against databases of known motifs, the software aligns input motifs against the chosen database and lists of the highest-scoring matches are returned. Such similarity-search functionality facilitates the identification of transcription factors that potentially interact with newly discovered motifs. This tool is a highly flexible, allowing user to 'mix-and-match' between various alignment methods, multiple alignment strategies and tree-building methods. This is a computational approach tool with help facility provided.

Text Mining Tools

In this area of bioinformatics various mining tools have been developed which involves common evolutionary relationship, structure identification and identifying biological proprieties that has specific functionalities. The following are the text mining tools that have been made in this study have been explained below

Jung-jae Kim et. al [14] Developed a ontology based, novel search engine supporting any browser type that imposes positional restriction on occurrences matching multi-term queries, based on the observation that terms with semantic relations which are explicitly stated in text are not found too far from each other. For better results MedEvi further identifies additional keywords of biological and statistical significance from local context of matching occurrences in order to help users reformulate their queries.

Arek Gladki et. al [15] has developed a web tool is a bio-linguistic method used to identify biologically relevant information with true correlation which is significance in crucial for any bio-medical research, literature mining with no exception which can discover biomedically meaningful, overrepresented and specific words using a statistical approach. It is especially useful for detecting low-frequency associations between user query and keywords such as drugs and genes or less obvious correlations between diseases. It also aims at providing information directly and specifically linked with user provided context. This also supports the feature of ontology of fully web-based supported by any type of browser.

Dean Cheng et. al [16] has developed a web server which is used for biomedical text mining and information retrieval which includes an extensive set of category specific thesauruses and also integration of many well annotated databases like OMIM, DrugBank, SwissProt, HMDB, HPRD and GAD as supplementary text resources which is customizable. This tool uses simple dictionary approach to identify biological or biomedical associations and could not identify novel or newly named diseases, genes, cell types, drugs or metabolites. Another limitation lies in its inability to extract context or meaning from sentences or terms.

Mounir Errami et. al [17] has developed a web tool for problems that persist for duplicated publications, this tool detects duplicate via analysis of citations at submission time can be performed by journals, this tool is combined with this database, which makes detection of duplicate for authors, editor and reviewers and it is resources can be customized to perform on any text-based database. This is fully computational supporting any type of browser.

Yoshimasa et. al [18] has developed a platform independent web-based GUI based search engine for MEDLINE abstracts, which is designed particularly to help users browse biomedical concepts appearing in the documents retrieved by the query. The concepts are presented to the user in a tabular format and ranked based on the co-occurrence statistics. The concept collected from several biomedical databases and thesauri such as UniProt, BioThesaurus, UMLS and DrugBank. This follows an algorithm based computational approach supporting any browser type.

3. Metrics Based Survey

In this section we have described below some of the metrics that are applicable for bioinformatics tools that we have taken for survey made. Evaluating a tool is done by means of metrics evaluation. Here below we have give a general survey chart for metrics for bioinformatics tools. The metrics which are applicable for a particular tool has been represented as follows

Specificity (Sp):

Specificity [19] in general is a standard evaluation metrics that measures the proportion of negative patterns correctly recognized as being negative.

$$\text{Specificity (Sp)} = TN / (TN + FP) \quad (1)$$

where, TN – number of True Negative, FP – number of False Positive. This metrics are applicable for the tools BAGET, PlasmoGF, Jenti, PROMALS, STAMP, SubSeqer, CompariMotif, Biotext, Swelfe, Whatizit, MedEvi, PolySearch, etBlast, e-Lise and FACTA.

Expected Value (E-Value):

E-value (Expected value) [20] is a statistical measure that reflects the expected number of alignments between the text and the pattern that have the same or even better similarity score. E-value is also said to be the number of hits one can expect to get from a search in a database of random sequence with the same distribution of amino acids as the real database. This metric is applicable for the tool CompariMotif.

Lexical Precision (LPrecision):

LPrecision [21] is the extraction precision metrics that measure the performance of the extraction modules through syntactic analyzes and pattern based extraction from the corpus which is calculated as

$$\text{LPrecision} = \text{Correct}_{\text{Extracted}} / \text{all}_{\text{Extracted}} \quad (2)$$

where, $\text{all}_{\text{Extracted}}$ – all the information that are being extracted and $\text{Correct}_{\text{Extracted}}$ are the correct information that are extracted from all the information that are being extracted. This metrics are applicable for the tools Biotext and Whatizit.

Lexical Overall (LO) Metrics

Lexical Overlap [21] denotes the shared concepts between the manual and extracted ontology which is calculated as

$$LO = \text{Correct} / \text{all} \quad (3)$$

Let Lo be the set of all domain relevant extracted concepts. This metrics are applicable for the tools Biotext, Swelfe and Whatizit.

Structural Root Mean Square Deviations RMSD:

RMSD [22] makes an approximate estimation of the average protein structure match difference of random related structures. The RMSD of two structures (A and B) of identical length of L_N, is written as

$$RMSD = \sqrt{R^2_A + R^2_B - 2\frac{\sum r_{Ai} * r_{Bi}}{\sum r^2_{Ai} \sum r^2_{Bi}} R_A R_B} \quad (4)$$

where, R_A (R_B) is the radius of gyration for protein structure A (B), r_{Ai} (r_{Bi}) is the coordinate vector after global superposition. This metrics are applicable for the tool Swelfe.

Motif Score:

Motif score [4] of a motif and a sequence is defined as the maximum match score over all positions in the sequence where the motif would fit without overhanging the ends of the sequence.

$$\text{Motif Score} = IC * \text{Number of matched positions} \quad (5)$$

where, IC is Information Content. This metrics are applicable for the tool Swelfe.

Relative RMSD:

rRMSD [22] used to eliminate the dependencies in protein structures which is calculated as

$$rRMSD = RMSD / \sqrt{R^2_A + R^2_B - 2CR_A R_B} \quad (6)$$

This metrics is applicable for Swelfe tool

Pattern Match:

Pattern match metrics [19] is the universal standard metrics that are applicable for all applications, tools or techniques that are involved in pattern matching which is calculated as Pattern Match = Total number of matches/Number of matches correctly predicted (7)

This metrics are applicable for the tools PlasmoGF, Jenti, PROMALS, STAMP, SubSeqer, CompariMotif, Biotext, Swelfe, Whatizit, MedEvi, PolySearch, etBlast, e-Lise and FACTA.

Density of the Alignment

Alignment is used most probably done while going for pattern match where we define Density of alignment [19] as Density of

Alignment = Alignment Score / Alignment Length (8)

This metrics are applicable for the tool Swelfe.

Lexical Recall:

To measure the performance of the extraction modules through syntactic analyzes and pattern based extraction we calculated Lexical Recall [21] as

$$LRecall = Correct_{Extracted} / all_{Corpus} \quad (9)$$

where, $Correct_{Extracted}$ are the correct information that are extracted and all_{Corpus} is all the information extracted. This metrics are applicable for the tools Biotext and Swelfe.

Length of repeats:

Length of the repeats [4] is the total size of the repeat that are been considered for pattern matching in motif comparison. This metrics are applicable for the tools SubSeqer, CompariMotif and Biotext.

Information Content Rank:

IC_m matches are ranked [5] by the total number of matching positions and then by the number of exactly matching fixed positions which are used in motifs.

Information Content Match (IC_m):

IC_m [5] is simply the sum of the component IC_i values which is used in motif comparison of protein sequences, where IC is the Information Content at position i. This metrics are applicable for the tools CompariMotif, Biotext, Swelfe, Whatizit, MedEvi, PolySearch, e-Lise and FACTA.

Match Positions:

This Match Position [4] metrics is the total number of match positions that are found in the whole sequence to which it is compared with other sequence. This metrics are applicable for the tools Jenti and etBlast.

Match score:

The match score [23] for a sequence is defined as

$$M_i = \sum_{j=1}^{n} (h_j + d_j g) \quad (10)$$

Where, n is the number of hits in the match, h_j is the score of the j th hit in the match, d_j is the length of the gap between hit $j - 1$ and hit j ($d_1 = 0$), and g is a 'gap penalty'. This metrics are applicable for the tool Biotext.

Number of nodes:

Global metrics for Cell graph. Number of nodes [24] in a graph is defined as the degree of a node is defined as the number of its edges. This metrics are applicable for the tools Jenti, STAMP and SubSeqer.

Clustering Coefficient:

Clustering coefficient [24] is one of the Computes quantitative metrics for tissue characterization and classification

$$C_i = (2E_i) = (k(k + 1)) \quad (11)$$

where, k is the number of neighbors of the node i and E_i is the number of existing links between its neighbors. This metrics are applicable for the tool Jenti.

Error rate:

Error rate for NLP in mutation evaluation metrics [25] could be defined as

$$\text{Error rate} = 1 / \text{Precision} \quad (12)$$

Global metrics for Error rate = total entities detected / number of entities correctly detected. This metrics are applicable for the tools Jenti, PROMALS, Biotext, Swelfe, Whatizit, MedEvi, PolySearch, etBlast, e-Lise and FACTA.

Accuracy:

Accuracy that classifies catalytic protein structures [26] which is one of the performance metrics is calculated as

$$\text{Accuracy} = (TP + TN) / (TP + TN + FP + FN) \quad (13)$$

where, TP – True Positive, TN – True Negative, FP- False Positive, FN – False Negative. This metrics are applicable for the tools BAGET, PlasmoGF, Jenti, PROMALS and STAMP.

Number of vertices:

Number of vertices [24] in a graph is defined as

$$V(G) = e - n + 2 \quad (14)$$

where, e is the number of edges and n is the number of nodes. This metrics are applicable for the tools Jenti, and SubSeqer.

Identity Metrics:

Identity metrics [19] identifies similarity between amino acid pairs used in Protein analysis. This metrics are applicable for the tools PlasmoGF, Jenti and PROMALS.

Molecular weight:

The molecular weight [22] is the mass of a protein or molecule which is calculated as the sum of the atomic mass of all the atoms in the molecule.

Sensitivity (Sn):

Sensitivity (Sn) metrics [19] measures the proportion of positive patterns correctly recognized genes in a sequence of DNA in general or in a string of DNA which can be calculated as

$$Sn = TP / (TP + FN) \quad (15)$$

where, TP – True Positive and FN – False Negative.

F-Score:
F-score [10] is an evaluation metrics to measure the performance of the tool. It combines precision metrics and recall metrics used for Named entity recognition is defined as

F-Score = (2*precision*recall)/(precision + recall) (16)

This metrics are applicable for the tools Whatizit, MedEvi, PolySearch, etBlast, e-Lise and FACTA.

Precision Metrics:
Precision is one of the metrics that evaluates the tool performance. Precision evaluation is for NLP [28] then it is calculated as

$$\text{Precision} = (\text{correct} + (\alpha.\ \text{partial})) / (\text{correct} + \text{spurious} + (\alpha\ .\ \text{partial})) \quad (17)$$

If precision evaluation is for named entity recognition it is expressed as

Precision [27] = (number of NE's a system correctly detected) / (total number of NE's identified by the system) (18)

Precision [10] is evaluated as the measure that measures the proportion of samples correctly classified.

$$P = (TP + TN) / (TP + TN + FP + FN) \quad (19)$$

where, TN, TP – True Negative, True Positive and FN, FP – False Negative, False Positive.

This metrics are applicable for the tools BAGET, PlasmoGF, Jenti, PROMALS, STAMP, SubSeqer, CompariMotif, PolySearch, etBlast, e-Lise and FACTA.

Recall Metrics:
Recall Metrics is also another metrics that are involved in the performance of the tool. Recall for named entity recognition [27] is defined as

Recall = number of NE's a system correctly detected / total number of NE's contained in the input text. Commonly used Recall evaluation in NLP [10] is the rate of correctly detected entities over all correct entities is defined as

$$\text{Recall} = (\text{correct} + (\alpha \cdot \text{partial})) / (\text{correct} + \text{missing} + (\alpha \cdot \text{partial})) \quad (20)$$

This metrics are applicable for the tools BAGET, PlasmoGF, Jenti, PROMALS, STAMP, SubSeqer, CompariMotif, MedEvi, PolySearch, etBlast, e-Lise and FACTA.

Error Report:
Error report [28] as a global metric which is defined as,

Error report = Percentage of wrong results in a system's output. (21)

This metrics are applicable for the tools PlasmoGF, STAMP, Biotext, Swelfe, Whatizit, MedEvi, PolySearch, etBlast, e-Lise and FACTA.

Relative number of hits :
Relative number of hits (RelHit) [14] denotes the shared concepts between the manual and extracted ontology.

$$LO(O_1, O_2) = | Lo_1 \cap Lo_2 | / | Lo_2 | = \text{Correct} / \text{all} \quad (22)$$

Let Lo_1 be the set of all domain relevant extracted concepts and Lo_2 the set of concepts of the Gold Standard. This metrics are applicable for the tools Biotext, Swelfe, Whatizit, MedEvi, PolySearch, etBlast, e-Lise and FACTA.

Positive Predictive Value (PPV):
Positive Predictive value (PPV) [29] is the percentage of true positive to the total number of positives recognized by the system, which can be calculated as

$$PPV = TP / (TP + FP) \quad (23)$$

where, TP – True Positive and FP – False Positive. This metrics are applicable for the tools BAGET, PlasmoGF, Jenti, PROMALS, STAMP, SubSeqer, CompariMotif, MedEvi, PolySearch, etBlast, e-Lise and FACTA.

Negative Predictive Value:
Negative Prediction Value (NPV) [29] is the percentage of true negatives to the total number of negatives recognized by the system, which can be calculated as

$$NPV = TN / (FN + TN) \quad (24)$$

This metrics are applicable for the tools BAGET, PlasmoGF, Jenti, PROMALS, STAMP, SubSeqer, CompariMotif, MedEvi, PolySearch, etBlast, e-Lise and FACTA.

Information Retrieval (IR) Metrics:
Information retrieval (IR) Metrics [27] used in the evaluation of information retrieval for named entity recognition which is calculated as

IR Metrics = Number of data's correctly retrieved / total number of data's retrieved (25)

This metrics are applicable for the tools PolySearch, e-Lise and FACTA.

4. Conclusion

Since, bioinformatics tools are increasingly important at present for real-time decision making for solving biological problems. In this paper we have given made a survey on various bioinformatics tools which has been discussed theoretically about its features, functionalities and metrics. The study carried out made a way for classifying of tools that we have taken for survey on the bases of analyzed features and functionalities like GUI, algorithm based, search, automatic detection, browser type etc. Metrics identification for a tool can provide us a means for evaluating this tool which qualifies a tool which is followed as one of the methods. The main reason behind for carrying out this evaluation on the bioinformatics tools is for the quality implications that could be enhanced on the developed tools or in the development of new tools for the developers in addition to new functionalities. Another important reason behind this survey carried out to represent how to carry out quality measures by experimenting on the developed bioinformatics tools for better utilizing of better existing tools.

5. References

[1] Lydia Ng, Chris Lau, Rob Young, Sayan Pathak, Leonard Kuan, Andrew Sodt, Madhavi Sutram, Chang-Kyu Lee, Chinh Dang and Michael Hawrylycz, "NeuroBlast: a 3D spatial homology search tool for gene expression", BioMed, July 2007.

[2] Hongmei Sun, Hong Fang, Tao Chen, Roger Perkins, and Weida Tong, "GOFFA: Gene Ontology for Functional Analysis – A FDA Gene Ontology Tool for Analysis of Genomic and Proteomic Data", BioMed, March 2006.

[3] Jochen Farwer, Martin J. Packer, Christopher A. Hunter, "PREDICTOR: A Web-Based Tool for the Prediction of Atomic Structure from Sequence for Double Helical DNA with up to 150 Base Pairs", ISO Press, 2007.

[4] David He and John Parkinson, "SubSeqer: a graph-based approach for the detection and identification of repetitive elements in low-complexity sequences", ACM Portal, pp 1016–1017, Feb 2008.

[5] Richard J. Edwards, Norman E. Davey and Denis C. Shields, "CompariMotif: quick and easy comparisons of sequence motifs ", ACM Portal, pp 1307–1309, March 2008.

[6] Marti A. Hearst, Anna Divoli, Harendra Guturu, Alex Ksikes, Preslav Nakov, Michael A. Wooldridge and Jerry Ye, "BioText Search Engine: beyond abstract search", ACM Portal, pp 2196–2197, June 2007.

[7] Anne-Laure Abraham, Eduardo P. C. Rocha and Joel Pothier, "Swelfe: a detector of internal repeats in sequences and structures", ACM Portal, pp 1536–1537, May 2008.

[8] Dietrich Rebholz-Schuhmann, Miguel Arregui, Sylvain Gaudan, Harald Kirsch and Antonio Jimeno, "Text processing through Web services: calling Whatizit", ACM Portal, pp 296–298, November 2007.

[9] Xiang Xu, Jinyu Wu, Jian Xiao, Yi Tan, Qiyu Bao, Fangqing Zhao and Xiaokun Li, "PlasmoGF: an integrated system for comparative genomics and phylogenetic analysis of Plasmodium gene families", ACM Portal, pp 1217–1220, March 2008.

[10] Mario Falchi and Christian Fuchsberger, "Jenti: an efficient tool for mining complex inbred genealogies", ACM Portal, pp 724–726, January 2008.

[11] Jacques Oberto, "BAGET: a web server for the effortless retrieval of prokaryotic gene context and sequence", ACM Portal, pp 424–425, December 2007.

[12] Jimin Pei, Bong-Hyun Kim, Ming Tang and Nick V. Grishin, "PROMALS web server for accurate multiple protein sequence alignments", Oxford Journal, pp 649-652, April 2007.

[13] Shaun Mahony and Panayiotis V. Benos, "STAMP: a web tool for exploring DNA-binding motif similarities", Oxford Journal, W253–W258, April 2007.

[14] Jung-jae Kim, Piotr Pezik and Dietrich Rebholz-Schuhmann, "MedEvi: Retrieving textual evidence of relations between biomedical concepts from Medline", ACM portal, pp 1410–1412, March 2008.

[15] Arek Gladki, Pawel Siedlecki, Szymon Kaczanowski and Piotr Zielenkiewicz, "e-LiSe—an online tool for finding needles in the '(Medline) haystack", ACM Portal, pp 1115–1117, March 2008.

[16] Dean Cheng, Craig Knox, Nelson Young, Paul Stothard, "PolySearch: a web-based text mining system for extracting relationships between human diseases, genes, mutations, drugs and metabolites", Oxford Journals, pp 399-405, May 2008.

[17] Mounir Errami, Justin M. Hicks, Wayne Fisher, David Trusty, Jonathan D. Wren, Tara C. Long and Harold R. Garner, "De'ja'vu—A study of duplicate citations in Medline", ACM Portal, pp 243–249, December 2007.

[18] Yoshimasa Tsuruoka, Junichi Tsujii and Sophia Ananiadou, "FACTA: a text search engine for finding associated biomedical concepts", Oxford Journal, September 2008.

[19] Scott Coull, Joel Branch, Boleslaw Szymanski and Eric Breimer, "Intrusion Detection: A Bioinformatics Approach", IEEE, pp 24- 33, December 2003.

[20] Yong Huang, Lingdi Ping, Xuezeng Pan, Guoyong Cai, "A Fast Exact Pattern Matching Algorithm for Biological Sequences", IEEE digital library, pp 8-12, 2008.

[21] Marta Sabou, Chris Wroe, Carole Goble, Gilad Mishne, "Learning domain ontologies for web service descriptions: An experiment in bioinformatics", ACM, pp 10-14, May 2005.

[22] Yang Zhang and Jeffrey Skolnick, "Scoring Function for Automated Assessment of Protein Structure Template Quality ", ACM Portal, pp 702–710, 2004.

[23] Timothy L. Baile and William Stafford Noble,"Searching for statistically significant regulatory modules",ACM Portal, pp16–25, June 2003.

[24] Cigdem Demir., Chandandeep Nagi., Bulent Yener, "Cell-Graph Mining for Breast Tissue Modeling and Classification ", PubMed, pp 5311-4, December 2007.

[25] Witte R, Baker CJ., "Towards A Systematic Evaluation Of Protein Mutation Extraction Systems ", Pubmed, pp 1339-59, December 2006.

[26] Ian M. Overton, Gianandrea Padovani, Mark A. Girolami2 and Geoffrey J. Barton, "ParCrys: a Parzen window density estimation approach to protein crystallization propensity prediction", ACM Portal, pp 901–907, February 2008.

[27] Yang Jin, Ryan T McDonald, Kevin Lerman, Mark A Mandel,Steven Carroll, Mark Y Liberman, Fernando C. Pereira, Raymond S Winters and Peter S White, "Automated recognition of malignancy mentions in biomedical literature", BMC Bioinformatics, pp7-492, November 2006.

[28] Witte R, Baker CJ., "Towards A Systematic Evaluation Of Protein Mutation Extraction Systems", Pubmed, December 2006.

[29] Cigdem Demir. Chandandeep Nagi. Bulent Yener, "Cell-Graph Mining for Breast Tissue Modeling and Classification", pp 5311-4, PubMed, 2007.

Fast and Efficient Web Page Classification Based on URL Features Oriented Metadata Generation Algorithm

K. Selvakuberan[1], M. Indra Devi[2] and Dr R Rajaram[3]
[1]Innovation Labs (Web 2.0), TATA Consultancy Services, Chennai,
[2]Senior Lecturer, Department of IT, TCE, Madurai and
[3]Dean, Department of CSE, TCE, Madurai
selvakuberan.k@tcs.com midit@tce.edu rrajaram@tce.edu

Abstract

Web page classification is the interesting research area and machine-learning techniques gain the most significance as manual classification of web pages becomes very difficult. As web pages contain more irrelevant words than relevant words, preprocessing of web pages is must before applying classification. For the classification purposes the relevant words in the web page called as features are used. There are so many feature extraction and feature selection algorithms discussed by many researchers for the classification purpose. In this paper we consider Uniform Resource Locators (URLs) and the words present in the URL are considered as features and in turn they are used for classification purposes. We propose an algorithm called Meta Data Generator which effectively generates the Meta data using the features that are extracted from URL. Our experimental results show that this algorithm definitely improves classification accuracy in the classification of web pages.

Keywords: *web page classification, Meta data generation, feature selection, Uniform Resource Locators, Machine Learning Classifiers*

1. Introduction

The World Wide Web is growing exponentially while at the same time number of users of Internet also becomes large. It is impossible for the users to remember the URL of all the web pages they need and so they rely on search engines to fetch the required web pages. The Internet is a powerful medium for communication between computers and for accessing online documents all over the world but it is not a tool for locating or organizing the mass of information. Tools like search engines assist users in locating information on the Internet. They perform excellently in locating but provide limited ability in organizing the web pages. Search engines also have a large repository of web pages and they need a better classification technique to retrieve the required information. Even though manual classification of web pages will be an excellent one, it is impractical for search engines to adopt it as the sheer size and dynamic nature of the web pages prevent this. So automatic methods are needed for the classification and most of the search engines use machine learning algorithms for automatic classification of web pages as these machine learning classifiers learns themselves from the examples and improve with experience. Internet users are now confronted with thousands of web pages returned by a search engine using simple keyword search. Searching through those web pages is in itself becoming impossible for users. Thus it has been of more interest in tools that can help make a relevant and quick selection of information that we are seeking. We find that HTML meta tags are a good source of text features, but are not in wide use despite their role in search engine rankings. But most of the pages may not contain meta data. [4][5]

Automatic Web-page classification by using hypertext is a major approach to categorizing large quantities of Web pages. Two major kinds of approaches have been studied for Web-page classification: content-based and context-based approaches.[8][9] Typical content-based classification methods utilize words or phrases of a target document in building the classifier and can achieve only limited accuracy. This is because very often a Web page contains no obvious clues textually for its category. For example, some pages contain only images and little text information [1][2]. By exploiting the hyper textual information, context-based approaches additionally exploit the relationships between the Web pages to build a classifier. As a consequence, they are found to be more accurate than pure content based classifiers.

The paper is organized as follows. Section 2 discusses the related work. Section 3 describes the web page structure. Section 4 describes the feature selection. Section 5 deals with our proposed approach. Section 6 focus on Experimental set up and results. Section 7 ends with conclusion and section 8 describe the references.

2. Related work

Luis Gravano , Panagiotis G. Ipeirotis and Mehran Sahami describe QProber, which automates the categorization of searchable Web databases into topic hierarchies. QProber uses a combination of machine learning and database querying techniques. They use machine learning techniques to initially build document classifiers. Rather than actually using these classifiers to categorize individual documents, they extract classification rules from the document classifiers, and transform these rules into a set of query probes that can be sent to the search interface of the available text databases. The algorithm then simply uses the number of matches reported for each query to make classification decisions, without having to retrieve and analyze any of the actual database documents. This makes the approach very efficient and scalable. [1]

Min-Yēn Kan and Hoang Oanh Nguyen Thi demonstrate the usefulness of the uniform resource locator (URL) alone in performing web page classification. This approach is faster than typical web page classification, as the pages do not have to be fetched and analyzed. Their approach segments the URL into meaningful chunks and adds component, sequential and orthographic features to model salient patterns. The resulting features are used in supervised maximum entropy modeling [2]

MinYen Kan explores the use of URLs for web page categorization via a two-phase pipeline of word segmentation/expansion and classification. SVM light machine learner is used to classify the web pages.[3]

Huan Liu and Rudy Setino propose an algorithm called Inductive Algorithm. It is a probabilistic wrapper model besides the exhaustic search and heuristic approach [6]

Huan Liu and Lei Yu proposed that feature selection algorithms for classification and clustering, groups and compares different algorithms with a categorizing framework based on search strategies, evaluation criteria, and data mining tasks, reveals unattempted combinations, and provides guidelines in selecting feature selection algorithms. With the categorizing framework, an integrated system for intelligent feature selection is built up. For employing feature selection, wrapper, filter and hybrid model are adopted.[7]

Our work differs from all of the above approaches in a way that we extract features from URL without applying segmentation/expansion and once extracted we store these features in the Meta tag of the source document, so that they can be used for classification.

3. Web page structure

Web pages are heterogeneous in nature. They may be unstructured documents like text document, semi structured documents like HTML files or fully structured documents like XML file. Web pages may also contain image files, audio files etc. There may not be any uniform structure or content in the related web pages or web pages under a same website. Some web pages may not contain a single word even in the home page itself. META tags are very useful for the classification of web pages but they are not properly defined in all the web pages. Most of the web pages do not contain this META tags and some provide TITLE and DESCRIPTION tags to aid classification of the web page. The web pages may vary in length and contain stop words, HTML tags, infrequent words, punctuation symbols, etc which decreases the classification accuracy and requires more storage and time for classification. So these less useful words may be removed while the web page is considered for classification. The terms more useful for classification are extracted from the web pages and these are called as features. There are so many well-defined feature extraction algorithms to extract relevant features from the page and these features are used for training the classifiers into categories. The web pages can be represented in various ways. The simplest form to represent a web page is to extract text found in the BODY element and stores it in matrix format. This representation does not exploit the peculiarities of web pages that is HTML structure and hyper textual nature of web pages.

3.1 HTML structure

For improving web page representation, exploiting HTML structure will help us identify where the more representative terms can be found. For example, we can consider that a term enclosed within the <title> and </title> tags is generally more representative for the topic of a web page than a term enclosed within the <body> and </body> tags.

For instance, several sources (elements) for web page representation are:

*BODY, the body part of a web page;

*TITLE, the title of a web page;

*H1~H6, section headings;

*EM, emphasized content;

*URL, hyperlinks that may contain descriptor for the linked web pages. If keywords can be extracted from an URL, these keywords are relatively important

*META describes the meta-description of a web page. It is invisible to users of webrowsing, but it may provide description, keywords, and date for a web page.[4][5]

4. Feature Selection

Feature extraction or selection is one of the most important steps in pattern recognition or pattern classification, data mining, machine learning and so on Data preprocessing is an indispensable step in effective data analysis. It prepares data for data mining and machine learning, which aim to turn data into business intelligence or knowledge. Feature selection is a preprocessing technique commonly used on high dimensional data. Feature selection studies how to select a subset or list of attributes or variables that are used to construct models describing data. Its purposes include reducing dimensionality, removing irrelevant and redundant features, reducing the amount of data needed for learning, improving algorithms' predictive accuracy, and increasing the constructed models' comprehensibility. Feature-selection methods are particularly welcome in interdisciplinary collaborations because the selected features retain the original meanings domain experts are familiar with. The rapid developments in computer science and engineering allow for data collection at an unprecedented speed and present new challenges to feature selection. Wide data sets, which have a huge number of features but relatively few instances, introduce a novel challenge to feature selection.[9]

5. Our Proposed Approach

Our approach is the classification of the web pages based on meta data generated using the URLs alone. With the level of current technology in web page indexing, automatically compiled indices only covers a fraction of the accessible web. Current webpage classification techniques use a variety of information to classify a target page - the text of the page itself, its hyperlink structure, the link structure and anchor text from pages pointing to the target page and its uniform resource locator (URL). Of this information, a web page's URL is the least expensive to obtain and one of the more informative sources with respect to classification. The URL itself is quite informative and the humans can attain a large amount of information from it without any need to examine the actual contents of the web page. As the URL is short, ubiquitous (all web pages, whether or not they are accessible or even exist, have URLs) and is largely content-bearing, it seems logical to expend more effort in making full use of this resource. Our implementation uses a two-step approach, in which a URL is first tokenized into meaningful tokens, which are then analyzed as features for classification. The features selected from URL are stored under meta tags and hence it is easy for future classification.

```
Algorithm Meta Data Generator
{
 Tokenization (URLs)
  Split the URL into words
  Apply stemming
  Store the resultant words as features from URLs;
 Meta Data generation (Features)
   Open the HTML file
   Check for Meta Tag / Meta data
   If (META Tag)
     Append URL features to the list
  Else
     Create Meta Tag
      Store the URL features
 Classification
      Get the Keyword from the user
      Stem the keyword
      Check if this stemmed keyword is in the meta tag
of the underlying web page
      If so, Classify this web page as positive
      Else
      classify this web page as negative .
}
```

6. Experimental Setup

6.1 Dataset Used

WEBKB dataset is a benchmark dataset in the UCI repository containing four universities web pages. There are seven categories of web pages in this data set. They are: course, project, department, university, staff, faculty and student. More than 8000 web pages are there in this dataset. For our experiment we select course and student categories. In the course category there are 930 web pages treated as positive examples and from other categories we select 66 web pages as negative examples. In the student category the number of web pages is 1341 and is treated as positive web pages and we randomly select 229 pages from other categories as negative examples. It is clearly described in Table 1

Table 1 Experimental Setup

S.No	Name of the category	No. of positive examples	No. of negative examples
1.	Course	930	66
2.	Student	1341	229

6.2 Results and Discussions

Experimental results show that 80% of the web pages are classified correctly. The results are displayed in Tables 2 and 3.Using the features available from URL, we perform meta data generation. This approach improves the classification accuracy.

Table 2 Classification performance before meta data generation

S.no	Name of the category	No. of web pages contain Meta data	Total no. of documents	Classification Performance
1.	Course	24	996	0.0240
2.	Student	48	1570	0.0305

Table 3 Classification performance after meta data generation

S.no	Name of the category	No. of web pages contain Meta data	Total no. of documents	Classifi cation Perfor mance
1.	Course	820	996	0.8232
2	Student	1064	1570	0.6777

Conclusion and Future work

Given that the URL is a ubiquitous feature of web pages, this paper shows how they can be maximally leveraged for classification tasks. In this paper, we have quantified the performance of web page classification using only the URL feature. We concentrate on URL feature extraction and web page classification using URL features. And also Meta tags are generated using the features extracted from URLs. Results indicate that these Meta data significantly improves classification accuracy. This feature of web pages, when treated correctly, exceeds the performance of some source document based features. We focus next on combining URL based classification with full text based classification to have a better machine learning classifier.

7. References

[1] Luis Gravano , Panagiotis G. Ipeirotis and Mehran Sahami, (2003) "QProber: A System for Automatic Classification of Hidden-Web Databases", *ACM Transactions on Information Systems, Vol. 21, No. 1, Pages 1–41*

[2] Min-Yen Kan and Hoang Oanh Nguyen Thi, (2005) "Fast Webpage Classification Using URL Features", *CIKM'05, Bremen, Germany. ACM*

[3] MinYen Kan(2004) "Web Page Categorization without the Web Page", *WWW2004, New York, USA.,pp262 – 263 ACM*

[4] John M.Pierre (2001) "On the Automated Classification of Web Sites", *Link¨oping Electronic Articles in Computer and Information Science, Vol. 6: nr 0. http://www.ep.liu.se/ea/cis/2001/000/.*

[5] Tom M.Mitchell (1999) "The Role of Unlabeled data in Supervised Learning", *Proceedings of the Sixth International Colloquium on Cognitive Science"1999*

[6] Huan Liu and Rudy Setino(1996) "Feature Selection and Classification–A probabilistic wrapper approach" *Proceedings of IEA-AIE 1996.*

[7] Huan Liu and Lei Yu "Towards Integrating Feature Selection Algorithm for Classification and Clustering" *IEEE Transactions on Knowledge and Data Engineering, Vol 17,Issue 4, 491-502*

[8] Gautam Pant, & Padmini Srinivasan(2006) "Link Contexts in Classifier-Guided Topical Crawlers", *IEEE Transactions on Knowledge and Data Engineering, Vol. 18, No. 1 pp 107 – 122*

[9] Arul Prakash Asirvatham, & Kiranthi Kumar Ravi (2001) "Web Page Categorization based on document structure" *Proceedings of ACM, 2001*

Web 2.0 Mapping Mashup Applications for Academic Universities – Comparative Case Study (Secure Google Maps API versus Microsoft Virtual Earth API)

D. Sravani[1], Dr. M. V. S. S. Giridhar[2], P.Praneeth[3], M.K. Rami Reddy[4] and Md.Ilyasuddin[5]
[1&2]CSE, JNTU, MIPGS, O.U., [3,4&5]B.Tech IV/IV, CSE, MGIT, Hyderabad
sravani.mummadi@yahoo.co.in mvssgiri@yahoo.com prani_9@yahoo.co.in
korare_2711@yahoo.com ilu4ever_32@yahoo.com

Abstract

Web Mapping is the process of designing, implementing, generating and delivering maps on the World Wide Web. A common challenge for many web developers is the creation of web applications that capture and describe geographical information. As a result of Web 2.0 technologies such as Asynchronous JavaScript and XML (Ajax) web-based mapping applications with rich contents can be developed with better interactivity, functionality, accuracy and usability. These applications (for example Academic Universities Web Mapping) provide users with maps to search and browse geographic information. The integration of information on maps as a layer is known as Mashups. The Value of a mashup lies in better user interface for that data or in combining data from a number of sources in an interesting way. In this paper we want to propose Web mapping strategies for Academic Universities, using robust Secure Google Maps API version 2, and Microsoft Virtual Earth API with a comparative study of API's involving tests on browser compatibility, performance, accuracy, functionality, usability, geocoding and development support etc. We explain how web-mapping works, Google Maps API motivation for such academic application, with our Microsoft Virtual Earth implementation of our Web mapping application of MGIT. We conclude with Map Abstraction Layer which improves interoperability of API's integrating development methodology. Finally issues pertaining to securing Google Maps API will be discussed.

Keywords: *Web mapping, Web GIS (Geographic Information System), Google Maps API version 2, Microsoft Virtual Earth, Map Abstraction Layer, Web 2.0 Mashups*

1. Introduction to Web Mapping

Web Mapping is the process of designing, implementing, generating and delivering maps on the World Wide Web.[8] It provides maps for users to search and browse spatial information, such as location and routes. Web cartography deals with usage of web maps, the evaluation and optimization of techniques and workflows, the usability of web maps, social aspects etc. Due to the change in technologies, with high bandwidth Internet connections and advanced web development techniques, nowadays geographic data can be provided and transferred across Internet at a low cost, making it possible for everyone to integrate and display a map in a website. Web GIS (Geographic Information System) emphasizes on analysis, processing of project specific geodata and exploratory aspects. Web maps are increasingly gaining analytical capabilities along with acting as presentation media for Web GIS. A special case of web maps are mobile maps, displayed on mobile computing devices, such as mobile phones, smart phones, PDA's, GPS and other devices. The maps on these devices are displayed by a mobile web browser or web user agent, are called mobile web maps which can display context and location sensitive information, points of interest etc.

The use of web as a dissemination medium of maps can be regarded as a major advancement in cartography and opens new opportunities, such as real-time maps, cheaper dissemination, more frequent and cheaper updates of data and software, personalized map content, distributed data sources and sharing of geographic information. Important research issues of web mapping are interactivity, usability, security, reliability etc. Classification web maps include static map, dynamic map, view-only map, interactive map etc. Common Web map functionality includes Viewing modes (Road map mode, Satellite/ aerial mode, Hybrid mode etc.), Navigation (Zooming and Panning), Controls, Overlays, Markers, Information Windows, Polylines, polygons and circles, Driving directions, Geocoding (the process by which information is associated with particular geographic points in the world often identified by degrees in latitude and longitude), Points of interest etc. Web-based mapping usability involves sophisticated Graphical User Interface (GUI) with the guidelines like: terminology should be clear and unambiguous and designers should avoid jargon; Professional designers should be used to improve the graphic design of the site. The design should enhance and complement the text and the maps, focusing the user's attention on the content; A meaningful legend should be presented as port of the default view of the map so that the map is self explanatory; A locator or context map, that shows where the map is being viewed in relation to a larger geographic data should be provided; Buttons should have text or icons with tool tips showing the name and describing the purpose or action. There should be large enough for users to accurately identify the text or image and to click with the mouse; Help should be provided and there must be a range of appropriate error messages.

1.1 Web Mapping Technology

To create or implement a web-based map, several techniques, any programming environment, programming language and server side framework, can be used. In any case of technology choice, both server and client side technologies have to be used to be able to provide and display dynamic and interactive maps.

1.1.1 Ajax (Asynchronous JavaScript and XML)

Ajax allows web applications to be loaded and updated through several micro requests instead of just one large macro request, which is a traditional model for web applications. Ajax is rather a collection of powerful technologies: standards-based presentation using XHTML and CSS; dynamic display and interaction using the Document Object Model (DOM); data interchange and manipulation using XML and XSLT; asynchronous data retrieval using XMLHttpRequest; and JavaScript binding everything together. [11, 13]. Below Fig. 1. Illustrates Ajax-based web Application model.

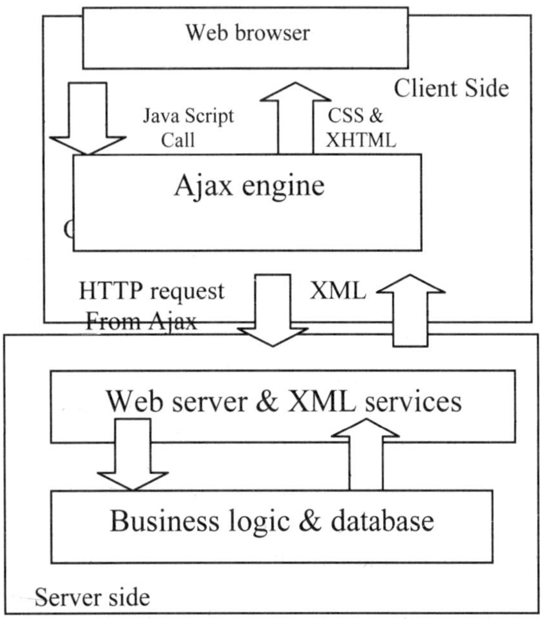

Fig. 1 Ajax based web application development

1.1.2 Web-based maps

When an integrated map is displayed in a user's browser window three parts (a 3-tier application framework) are involved: the user's browser, the web server hosting the site with the map, and the API system. A map system consists of several sets of servers, one set hosting static files, such as JavaScript's and images, one set used to calculate routes and other geographical information and two sets of servers hosting the road map and satellite tile images. On the client side Dynamic HTML (DHTML) and Ajax are used to display the map in the browser window. DHTML is a combination of using the JavaScript event model together with CSS positioning. That is what creates the possibility to drag objects, in this case the map, displayed in web pages. The map is broken up into a grip of images called tiles, which are absolutely positioned square formed images, normally 256 x 256 pixels, displaying the different parts of the map. When the map is dragged new images are fetched from the tile servers as soon as the area is visible and the no longer visible tiles are removed. This removing and adding process creates the maps infinite scrolling effect. [1, 2]. Consider Fig. 2 which depicts Google Maps Tiles.

Fig. 2 Google maps with tiles outlined

1.1.3 Geographical data

The geographical data used and displayed by the different web map APIs is in general coming from the same data vendors.[12] The majority of the API's use a combination of data from companies as NAVTEQ and TeleAtlas for the road maps. The satellite/aerial imagery is coming from companies like DigitalGlobe which is photographing the Earths surface with their QuickBird satellite. The satellite makes fifteen orbits around the Earth per day and photographs strips which measure 16.5 by 330 kilometers. The average resolution is 60 square centimeters per pixel but because of the huge competition for the camera most of the planet has only been photographed with a low resolution. In addition to the QuickBird satellite, low resolution imagery is also captured by others satellites as the Landsat-7, which has been taking images of the entire planet at a resolution of 15 meters. After the images have been taken they are sent to ground stations for post-processing. The differences in photographic angle are corrected and the images are resampled so that their pixels will be aligned with a latitude-longitude grid. Many areas of high interest, as cities, are also photographed by aircraft to get a higher resolution; clearly visible in the resulting photos are car sunroofs, lampposts, and even people.

1.2 Features of Web 2.0

The important feature of Web 2.0 over traditional Web 1.0 includes, [5] Creators: Thin line between contributors, developers, and users. In many cases, users themselves contribute and collaborate; User interface: The user interface can be more adaptive, customized and often like that of a desktop application; Content Serving: Using the semantic web (Web 3.0) markup that describes data specifically; Reading content: Using syndication such as RSS/Atom feeds; User experience: Rich; Applications: XML Web Services, example www.ebay.com; Navigation: Customized and let's the user navigate web pages; Presentation: XHTML, Ajax and CSS. The major building blocks of Web 2.0 include CSS, XML, Web Services; Web 2.0 tools include: Ruby on Rails, Turbo gears, and ASP.NET 3.0/3.5.

2. Overview of important features of Google Maps API version2 [1,2,3,14]

The functionality of robust Google Maps API version 2 supports three Viewing modes: Map view, Satellite view, and Hybrid view. It supports map controls in three sizes map-type control, scale control, overview map, and local search control. Its Overlays include Markers (or Pushpins, optional with a custom icon), InfoWindows associated with the marker and map. It supports Ploylines and polygons to display routes or a polygon highlighting a region, on top of the map. It supports development of custom controls by extending GControl class. It has Marker Manager Utility to provide solution to slow rendering of map and visual cluttering, if the map contains number of markers. It supports Route and driving directions with textual directions and current traffic situation using Mobile GPS receivers. It supports the KML (Keyhole Markup Language and GeoRSS data formats using GeoXML overlay. KML features include Place markers as GMarkers, Icons with a size of 32 x 32 px; Descriptive HTML displayed inside infowindows, Polygons / Polylines, Styles for Polylines/Polygons, Ground Overlays without rotation/opacity. It supports addition of event listeners for mouse movement and keystrokes. It supports the languages: Japanese, French, German, Italian, Spanish, Catalan, Basque, Dutch, and Galician. The major limitation of Google Maps API is that they work only within a browser; thereby embedding a Google Map application in a Windows (or other) application is not possible.

Our example motivation of Academic University Google Map application came from the below figure 3. [15].

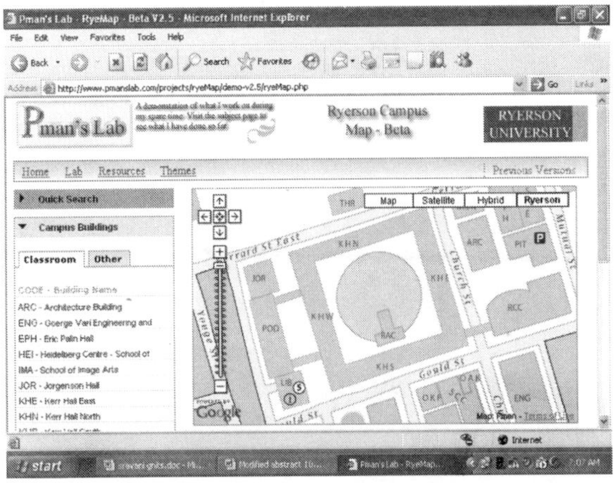

Fig. 3 Example of University Google Map application.[15]

3. Overview of important features of Microsoft Virtual Earth Control API [16]

The functionality provided by Microsoft's Virtual Earth Map Control API includes Viewing modes like Road, Aerial, Hybrid, Birds eye view and 3D view. Navigation control includes Dashboard control which comes in three sizes: Normal, Small, and tiny sizes. Controls include Find control and Minimap (overview map). Overlays / shapes include Pushpins with info boxes, Polylines and polygons, Shape layers, Messages, Route and driving directions, GeoRSS, VE Collection layer, and events.

The following plates snapshots depict our MGIT Virtual Earth implementations. Fig. 4 depicts pushpins on MGIT across India. Fig. 5 depicts pushpins customized over all blocks of MGIT. Fig. 6 depicts Route map from mehdipatnam to MGIT. Finally Fig. 7 and 8. depicts Route Map across road.

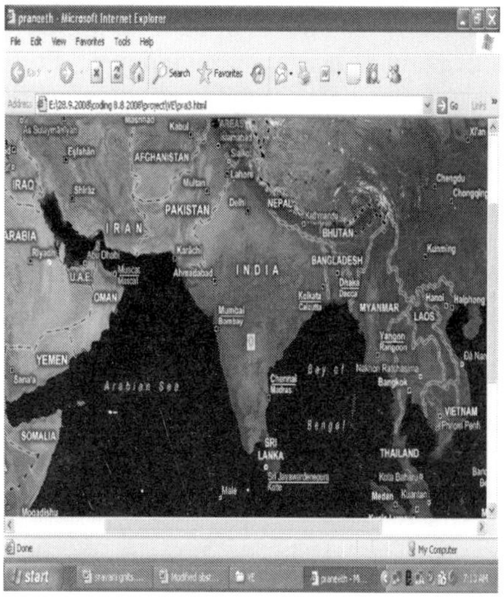

Fig. 4 Pushpins on MGIT across India

Fig. 7 Route map across road

Fig. 5 Pushpins customized over all blocks of MGIT

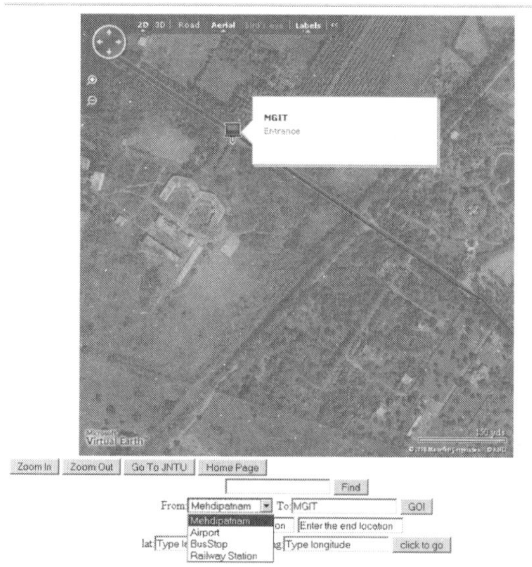

Fig. 8 Road map route

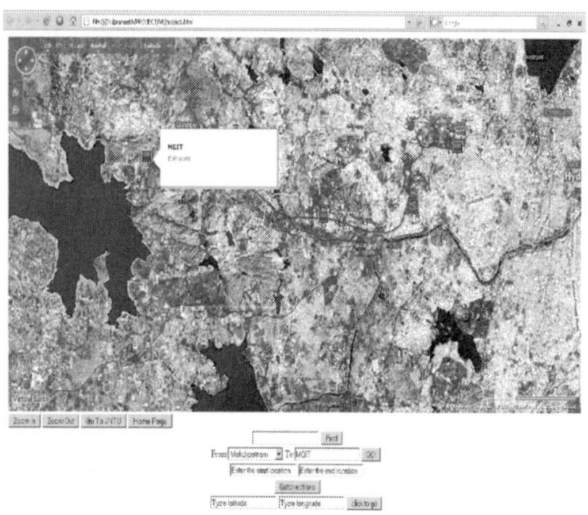

Fig. 6 Route map from Mehdipatnam to MGIT

4. API's Comparative Tests

4.1 Geocoder

Both Google Maps and Virtual Earth provide geocoding functionality for translation of postal addresses into geographical coordinates. Addresses can be sent either as unparsed texts containing all address information or as multiple address parts such as: street, zip code, city etc. Both API's support unparsed addresses only.

4.1.1 Spherical law of cosines

The distance calculation between two points on a spheres surface, using geographic coordinates, can be done in several ways: Haversine formula, the Spherical laws of cosines and the Vincenty formula. When geocoding tests were performed to measure the geocoder's accuracy the spherical laws of cosines were performed to calculate the distances between points. The formula is defined as:

$D = \arccos(\sin(lat_1).\sin(lat_2) + \cos(lat_1).\cos(lat_2).\cos(long_2 - long_1)).R$

where (lat_1, $long_1$) is one point's coordinates, (lat_2, $long_2$) the other points coordinates, d is the distance and R the spheres radius which in this case was the Earth's average radius, 6374 km. latitude, or lat, is the angle between any point on the earth's surface and the plane of the Equator. Each pole is 90 degrees: +90 degrees at the North Pole and -90 degrees at the South Pole and in-between the equator is placed at the 0-degree parallel of latitude longitude, or lang, is the angle east or west between any point on the earth's surface and the plane of an arbitrary north-south line between the two geographic poles. The line passing through Greenwich, UK, is the international zero-longitude reference line, the Prime Meridian. The Spherical law of cosines is less accurate than the haversine formula, but according to the company Movable Type Ltd, create of a JavaScript implementation of the Haversine and Spherical law of cosines formulas, the numeric precision of JavaScript is so good, 15 significant figures using IEEE 754 floating-point numbers, and that the simple Spherical law of cosines formula gives well-conditioned results down to distances as small as around 1 meter.

4.2 File Load test

To test the amount of data download when a web-map based map is viewed, the same area was displayed with the road map mode, at the same zoom level and with the same map size. The downloaded files were recorded to see sizes and hosting servers and below table shows the results, the amount of data downloaded. All file sizes are in kilobytes (KB) and Google Maps and Virtual Earth provide their API JavaScript files with compression. Table 1 shows Map API load test results.

Table1 Map API load test results

[KB]	Google Maps	Virtual Earth
JavaScript size	73	146
Tile image size	435	434
Total size	516	606
Tile Servers	4	4

4.3 Browser compatibility

Table 2 shows Map API browser compatibility. .

Table 2 API browser compatibility according to map API service providers

Browser	Google Maps	Virtual Earth
Internet Explorer	6.0+	5.5+
Fire fox	0.8+	0.9+
Mozilla	1.4+	-
Netscape	7.1+	-
Opera	8.02+	-
Safari	1.2.4+	-

Table 3 shows Browser compatibility test results.

Table 3 Browser compatibility test results: Working browsers are marked with X

Browser	Google Maps	Virtual Earth
Internet Explorer	X	X
Firefox	X	X
Netscape	X	X
Opera	X	-
Safari	X	-

4.4 API comparison

4.4.1 Viewing modes

Table 4 shows API Viewing Modes.

Table 4 API viewing mode. Supported nodes are marked with X.

Viewing Mode	Google Maps	Virtual Earth
Map/road	X	X
Satellite/Aerial	X	X
Hybrid	X	X
Birds eye	-	X
3D	-	X

4.4.2 Controls (Google Maps and Microsoft Virtual Earth)

Table 5 and Table 6 show Available controls with Google Maps and Microsoft Virtual Earth.

Table 5 Available controls with Google Maps

Control	Functionality
Map control in three sizes	Pan, return to start location and zoom
Map type control	Change map viewing mode
Scale control	Scale indicator
Overview map control	Small overview of the map
Local search control	Location search control(Google Ajax search API)
Custom controls	Yes, possibility to add HTML elements to map

Table 6 MS Virtual Earth controls

Control	Functionality
Dashboard in three sizes	Zoom and change viewing mode
Scale	Fixed scale indicator, not removable
Find control	Loction search control. Where and What search
Mini map	Small overview of the map
3D map control	Pan, rotate and tile the map in 3D mode
Custom controls	Yes, possibility to add HTML elements to map

4.4.3 API provided overlays

Table 7 shows API provided overlays.

Table 7 API provided overlays

Overlay	Google Maps	Virtual Earth
Pushpin/marker	Yes	Yes
Info Window/box	Yes	Yes
Detached info window/box	Yes	-
Tabbed Info Window/box	Yes	-
Message	-	Yes
Polyline	Yes	Yes
Polygon	Yes	Yes
Content Grouping	Marker Manager	Content Layer

4.4.4 Driving Directions

Table 8 shows API driving direction functionality.

Table 8 API driving direction functionality

Feature	Google Maps	Virtual Earth
Multiple Point	Yes	No, only two point direction
Textual descriptions	Collection of plain text directions or preformatted HTML	Collection of plain text directions
Options	-	Shortest or quickest route
Route Information	Distance and duration	Distance and Duration
Traffic information	Current traffic situation in some supported cities	-
Localization	9 Languages	1 Language

4.4.5 Customizability provided by API's

Table 9 shows customizability provided by API's.

Table 9 Customizability provided by API's

Element	Google Maps	Virtual Earth
Pushpin / Marker	Custom icons, changeable at any time	Fully customizable pushpins with HTML or icon image. Changeable at any time
Info window/box	Customizable with PdMarker extension	Customizable with CSS
Controls	Customizable with extensions	-

4.4.6 GeoXML Overlays and layers provided by API's

Table 10 shows GeoXML overlays and layers provided by API's.

Table 10 GeoXML Overlays and layers provided by API's

Data Format	Google Maps	Virtual Earth
GeoRSS	Yes	Yes
KML	Yes	-
VE collection	-	Yes

4.4.7 Usability

Table 11 shows API usability evaluation results.

Table 11 API usability evaluation results

Guide line	Google Maps	Virtual Earth
Draggable Map	Yes	Yes
Grouped pan buttons	Yes	No pan buttons
Pan buttons grouped according to directions	Yes	No pan buttons
Tool tips	Localized tool tips for all buttons	English tool tips for buttons tool tips without text
Default zoom	Original Center	Original center
Overview map	Yes, fully intractable	Yes, fully intractable

5. Map Abstraction Layer: [5]

Fig 9 depicts JavaScript abstraction layer in between web applications and map API's.

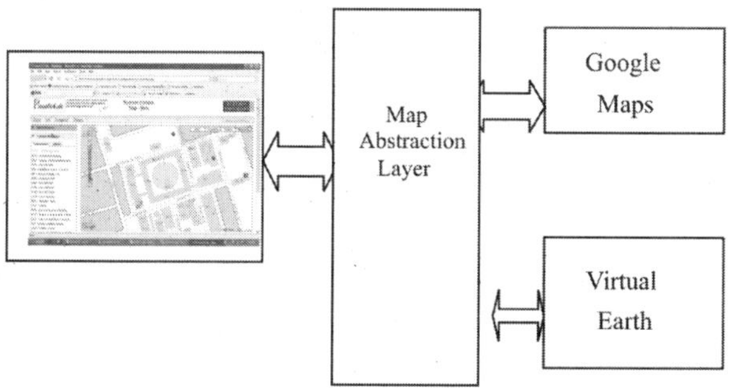

Fig. 9 Java Script abstraction layer in-between web applications and map API's

Web application

To eliminate too much dependability on application development API's, the need for a Map Abstraction layer is felt. This layer is placed between the web application and the Map API. It provides a common interface to all included map APIs at the same time and there fore the map used could easily be switched with a small work effort. Most of the methods implemented in the layer will be forwarding method calls from the application to the Map API's, creating a common interface, however since the API's are constructed differently, with different methods and different object types, some common objects have to be created. Latitude – longitude object has to be created for coordinates as well as objects for locations, markers, polylines and polygons. In addition to this some common objects have to be created, such as routes, parts and steps, to provide driving directions for all API's.

6. Securing Google Maps [6]

An enforceable solid security policy should serve as the foundation of any security effort. Without a policy, our safe guards could be insufficient or unenforceable. Google Attack Libraries are broken down into three main components: Socket initialization and establishment; Google Query requesting; and retrieving a Google query response. The steps involved in Psuedocoding include: Initializing socket; Send Google Request; Retrieve Google Response; Scrap Google Responses, and Return total hits. The Python language proved the most useful and efficient for creating Automated Google Query code. Its OOP style, easily accessible regular expression engine, and indexing methods made it easy to create, send, retrieve and scrape Google Information. The C# from Microsoft .NET library is the most extendable language implementation of our Google libraries because it can be merged into any program that's compatible with Microsoft Visual Studio .NET. Conducting Google Vulnerability tests scans is one of the easiest tasks that have hit the information security industry in the past few years. The key to automating such a task is the looping constructs that wrap around the library implementation. We can implement loopin constructs to automate searching and information retrieval for numerous purposes. Nearly all vulnerability scans utilizes the allinurl: advanced searching flag to search for strings stored within the Google cache.

7. Conclusions

In this paper, we proposed the technological issues of working on Web Mapping pertaining to Web 2.0 mashups. We are motivated that every academic university should have such an application which provides such geographic data. We compared the API's Google Maps and Microsoft Virtual Earth, about their strengths and Weaknesses. We provided the need for Map Abstraction: Layer. Finally issues pertaining to securing Google Web Maps from hackers are discussed.

8. References

[1] Christopher C.Miller, " A Beast in the Field: The Google Maps Mashups as GIS/2", Cartographica, The International Journal for Geographic Information and Geo Visualization, Volume 41, issue 3, pp. 187 – 199, 2005.

[2] "Is Google Maps GIS?" (http://highearthorbit.com), GIS India Journal, July 2008, page 8 – 10.

[3] Dionysius G. Synodinos, "Web Maps with the Google Map API", Dr.Dobbs Journal, December 2007 pp 36 - 41.

[4] Developer IQ Magazine Cover Story," Mashups", VOL 7 No. 9, September 2007.

[5] Laszlo Zentai, "Application of Web 2.0 in Cartographic education: Is it time for Cartography 2.0?" 2006.

[6] Johnny Long, "Google Hacking for penetration testers", SYNGRESS, 2005

[7] Richard Kendall Et. Al., "Development of a Weather Forecasting Code: A Case Study" IEEE Software, August 2008.

[8] Zng-Ren Peng, Ming-Hsiang Tsou, "INTERNET GIS Distributed Geographic Services for the Internet and Wireless Networks", Wiley, 2003.

[9] Ravindranath Jampani et. Al," Overlaying Multiple Maps Efficiently", International Institute of information Technology, Hyderabad 2001.

[10] Zao Liu et.al, "Implementing a Caching and Tiling Map Server: a Web 2.0 Case Study", 2006.

[11] Young Liu, Et. Al., "Leveraging Web 2.0 technologies in a cyber Environmental Research", OGF-19, Semantic Web 2.0 and Grid Workshop, January 29, 2007, NC, USA.

[12] A.M. Chandra, S.K.Ghosh, "Remote Sensing and Geographical Information Systems", Narosa Publications, 2006.

[13] Michael Purvis et. Al., "Beginning Google Maps Applications with PHP and Ajax", APress, 2006

[14] Manlai You, et. Al., "A Usability evaluation of Web Zoom and Pan functions, International Journal of Design, Vol. 1, No. 1, 2007.

[15] http://www.pmanslab.com/projects/rye Map/demo-v2.5/ryeMap.php

[16] Jon Arking, "Professional Windows Live Programming", Wrox Publication, 2008.

Sequence Arithmetic for Reducing the Search Space for Proteins Database

Y. RamaDevi[1] and C.R.Rao[2]
[1]Dept. of CSE, Chaitanya Bharathi Institute of Technology, Hyd-75
[2]DCIS, University of Hyderabad,
rdyellasiri@yahoo.co.in

Abstract

This paper presents intelligent sequence arithmetic, which is useful in reducing the search domain of protein sequences database. The arithmetic introduces typical characteristics of the protein sequence such as Alphabet set (A-Set), Prime Alphabet set of a Group (P-Set), Difference Set (D-Set) and Active Set (X-Set), Universal Alpha bet set (U-Set), etc. It also presents some of the mathematical elements such as Position Matrix (P-Matrix), Hash Key set (H-Set) for the sequences of a group. A sample of 500 sequences divided into 53 classes was tested, A-Set, P-Set, D-Set etc were generated for the sequence, classes and for system. When a new protein is given, we were able to reduce the search space by nearly 75% and on this reduced dataset; advanced classifying algorithm can be applied. A Software model is proposed for the automatic extraction of Sequence Knowledgebase from the sample sequence data warehouse and reducing the search space.

1. Introduction

With the massive inflow of new biological data, sequencing of the data has become a challenging for investigators throughout the world. Many sequencing projects have already uncovered nearly half a million-protein sequences, but 35- 50% of these proteins have not yet assigned a function yet and nearly 25,882 protein structures are mapped. Analysis of protein starts with its sequencing: it considers the basic function and analyzing its properties depends on pair wise comparisons with the sequence of other proteins whose properties are already known. Starting with pairwise alignment, we have multiple alignment techniques, profile analysis and pattern recognition methods.

2. Protein Sequences

Proteins are the molecules made of 20 Amino Acids with diverse chemical properties; they form functional and structural machinery of each cell in every organism. They are involved for giving biological signals, and act as catalyst for metabolic activities of the body. They have many levels of structure the primary structure, which is the1D sequence, the secondary structure, which is composed of the regular substructures that the protein polymer forms due to streric and hydrogen bond interactions the tertiary structure, which is the most complex protein structure, composed of multiple chains. Proteins are grouped not by functional families, but according to the secondary structure they have. The focus in protein classification is on finding proteins that have similar chemical architectures. SCOP, CATH, DALI, CE and CL, PROCHECK are some of protein classifier based on sequence identity, intermolecular interactions.

Sequence arithmetic for protein classification aims at finding the essential amino acids, which occur in a group and this information, is used to map the sequences which are already present in the protein database. Various sequence arithmetic operations can be used to reduce the search space and find the nearest neighbors to the group which sequence belongs [1].

2.1 Protein sequence identification

For a given set of sequences which belong to a class, we generate sets that play an important role in the identification of a novel sequence, these sets as shown in Table 1 help us in the sequence algebra.

2.2 Set

Sets are denoted by capital letters and lower case letters denotes its elements. We denote x as an element of A by $x \in A$ otherwise $x \notin A$.[2].

Given a group of sequences, the set of characters, which are used to construct them, is known as the Alphabet Set (A-Set). Prime Set (P-Set) is set of alphabets that are compulsory in every sequence of a group. Difference Set (D-Set) consists of alphabets, which are not present in any sequence of a group. Active Prime Alphabet Set (X- Set) contains set of alphabets, which are active in classification of sequences. Hash Set (H-set) is set of numbers representing attributes of all sequences, which belong to a group. U-Set contains set of permissible alphabets, which are used to construct the sequences. P-Matrix is the sparse matrix representing location of a given alphabet string in a sequence.

Table 1 Important sets to be generated that are used in sequence arithmetic

A-Set: Set of alphabets, those are used to construct the sequences of a group. P-Set: Set of alphabets, those are compulsory in every sequence of a group. D-Set: Set of alphabets, those are not present in any sequence of a group. X-Set: Set of alphabets, those are active in classification of sequences. H-Set: Set of numbers representing attributes of all sequences, which belong to a group. U-Set: Set of alphabets, those are used to construct the protein sequences P-Matrix: Sparse Matrix representing location of a given alphabet string in a sequence.

Given below are mathematically representations

A-Set = {x /x is valid character in the sequence}

U- Set = $\cup$ of sequences i

A-Set $\subseteq$ U-Set

P-Set = $\cap$ of sequences i

D- Set = (A-Set) – (P-Set)

The knowledge base is build in finding the U-Set, A-Set, D-Set, P-Set for each family of sequences colleting the sample data from Sequence Information system. They are used to determine the family of an unknown sequences using expert system techniques namely forward chaining and backward chaining.

2.3 Alphabet set (A-set)

A-Set for a Sequence: It consists of all the symbols, which appear in the sequence.

A-Set for a Group: It is the union of all A-Set of the sequences, which belong to a particular group.

A-Set for a System: It is the union of all A-Set of the Group that belongs to a particular System. This is also called Universal set (U-set)

U- Set = $\cup$ of sequences i

2.4 Prime set (P-set)

P-Set for a Sequence: It consists of all the symbols, those are compulsory in the sequence.

P-Set for a Group: It is the intersection of all P-Set of the sequences, which belong to a particular group.

P-Set for a System: It is the union of all P-Set of the Group that belongs to a particular System.

2.5 Difference set (D-set)

D-Set for a Sequence: It consists of all the symbols that are not present in the sequence.

D-Set for a Group: It is the intersection of all D-Set of the sequences, which belong to a particular group.

D-Set for a System: It is the union of all D-Set of the Group that belongs to a particular System.

3. Knowledge Extraction for Sequence Classification

Extraction of knowledge is possible, from the sample information of known sequences. This knowledge base can be used for the identification of unknown sequence. It is possible to identify an effective inference engine model that work on this knowledgebase for the classification of unknown sequences. This model has lot of impact on protein sequence classification.

The input for this process is sequence information. The following information about the sequence is required for the knowledge extraction.

1. Sequence String
2. Sequence Group ID

The following steps are followed in the process of extraction of knowledge base for the sequences [3].

1. Extract the distant Group IDs from the sequence samples
2. Compute Alphabet set for each sequence
3. Compute Alphabet set for each Group using the following rule
   The Union of alphabet set of all the sequence of a group generates the group alphabet set.
   Group A-Set = $\cup$ **A_i** where A_i is Alphabet set of ith sequence of the group
4. Compute Universal Alphabet set
   Universal Alphabet Set U-Set = $\cup$ A_i where A_i is Group Alphabet set of ith Group of the group
5. Compute the prime set of the group
   The Intersection of alphabet set of all the sequence of a group generates the Prime set of a group.
   Prime of Group P-Set = $\cap$ **A_i** where A_i is Alphabet set of ith sequence of the group
6. Compute D-Set of each group
   D- Set = (U-Set) – (A-Set of a group)

7. Compute Prime Alphabet Location Set (PL)of a group.
   Prime Alphabet Location set consists of all the locations in which the element of alphabet set occurs.
   $PL = \cap \mathbf{L}_i$ where L_i is location matrix of ith sequence of the group
8. Compute Prime alphabet frequency table

3.1 Inference Engine for Identification of Unknown Sequence

The knowledge base is build in finding the U-Set, A-Set, D-Set, P-Set for each family of sequences colleting the sample data from Sequence Information system. They are used to determine the family of an unknown sequences using expert system techniques namely forward chaining and backward chaining.

The inference engine follows the following algorithm for the classification of protein sequence.

1. Compute the Alphabet set of the given unknown sequence
2. Use the following conditions for deciding whether the sequence belong to a family or not using knowledgebase
   a. (A-Set of sequence) – (A-Set of family) = null
   b. (P-Set of Family) – (A-Set of sequence) = null
   c. (D-Set of Family) $\cap$ (A- Set of Sequence) = null

   If any of the following conditions are not satisfied the sequence will not belong to that family.
3. The step two will give a set of families closely related to the sequences. Find the location matrix of the sequence for the X- alphabet set. Family location matrix members are subset of the calculated location matrix of the sequences.
4. Another phase of tuning is with the alphabet count Intersection of alphabet count set of a family should be member of the alphabet count set of the sequence.

The above four steps will give a set of protein families which are very close to the sequence. We can perform minute operations for further classification for finding exact family.

4. Implementation Issues

4.1 Architecture of Model Expert System

The Architecture of a Model Expert System is shown in Fig. 1

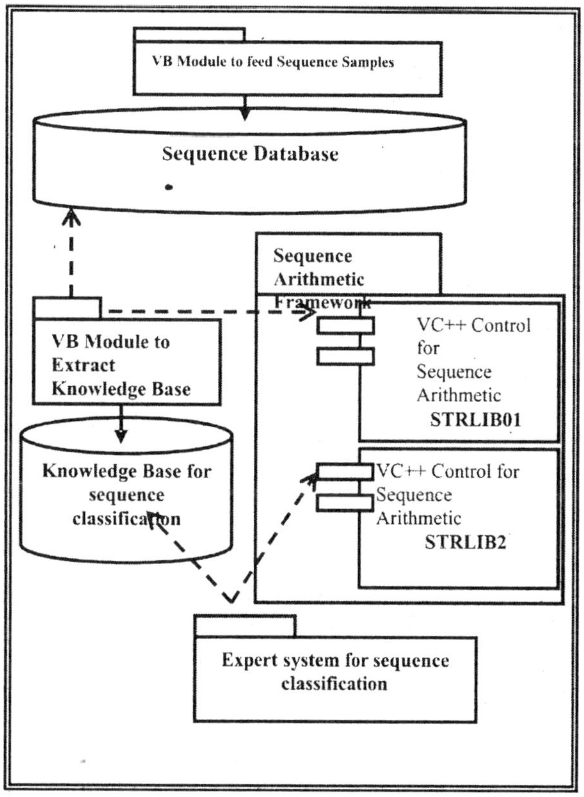

Fig. 1 Architecture of a Model Expert System

Sequence Arithmetic Framework: The different interface methods generated in this Framework is as shown in Table 2.

The sequence arithmetic is a computer based classification method, which tends to be faster and cheaper than other classifications. The arithmetic is totally depending on known protein samples for the classification. The accuracy of this method will depend on the protein sequence information system size and accuracy of the data in the sampling system. The disadvantage of the method is it cannot give assurance for finding exact protein family. But it will give probable set of families to which the protein sequence belongs to depending on the behavior of the sample protein sequence of the family.

Table 2 STRLIB01 interface methods

	Name/ Arguments	**Remarks /Samples**
01	BSTR **GetSet**(LPCTSTR str)	Returns Alphabet Set for given sequence
02	BSTR **GetUnionset**(LPCTSTR str1, LPCTSTR str2)	Gets Union Set
03	BSTR **GetSetInterSection**(LPCTSTR str1, LPCTSTR str2)	Returns Intersection set
04	BSTR **GetDiffSet** (LPCTSTR str1, LPCTSTR str2)	Returns difference set
05	short **IsEmpty**(LPCTSTR Str1)	Returns Whether a set is empty or not
06	Short **IsSubSet**(LPCTSTR Master, LPCTSTR Prime)	Returns whether a set is subset of other or not
07	Short **GetSLength**(LPCTSTR Str)	Returns length of a sequence
08	BSTR **GetLocationMatrix**(LPCTSTR Str, LPCTSTR bit)	Returns location matrix of a string
09	BSTR **InterLocMat**(LPCTSTR Str1, LPCTSTR Str2, LPCTSTR Bit, short L)	Finds Intersection of two location matrices up to given length of sequence
10	Short **ProcessString**(LPCTSTR Str, LPCTSTR bit)	To find number of occurrence of a given string
11	BSTR **TrimYRDString** (LPCTSTR Str)	Removes spaces

The GPCR family is considered as a sample database. They are divided into 5 classed as shown in Table 3

Table 3 GPCR data from GPCR database

Class	**Examples**	**No. of Entries**
A.Rhodopsin like	Rhodopsin and adrenergic receptors	3,519
B. Secretin like	Calcitonin receptors	217
C. Metabotropic glutamate/pheromone	Metabotropic receptors	131
D. Fungal pheromone	pheromone receptors	24
E. cAMP receptor (Dictyostelium)	cAMPreceptors	5

5. Conclusions

The search space has been considerably reduced both for conserved sequences (Myoglobin) about 75% and most diverged sequences about 70%. The generation of Alphabet set for the unknown sequence, prime set and Difference set in sequence reduced the domain search space. On these reduced space one can apply the BLAST Algorithm.

6. References

[1] RamaDevi Y "Intelligent Sequence Arithmetic for Protein Classification", International conference on human and machine Interaction, (ICHMI), Bangalore-India—2004.

[2] Tremblay J.P. Manohar R, Discrete Mathematical Structures with Applications to Computer Science, McGraw- Hill Pub, 1987.

[3] RamaDevi Yellasiri, C.R.Rao "Knowledge Discovery Using Sequence Arithmetic For GPCR Classification", MEPCONCT-06,Tamil Nadu, India-2006

[4] wordnet.princeton.edu/perl/webwn

[5] en.wikipedia.org/wiki/Sequence

[6] www.orafaq.com/glossary/faqgloss.htm

[7] library.thinkquest.org/2791/MDCTARY/S.htm

Session – 7

Networking, Cryptography and Mobile Computing

A Multiple Axis Key Shadowing Cipher Technique for Symmetric Key Cryptograph

K.Venkateswara Rao[1], S. Rama Krishna[2] and M.Srinivasarao[3]
[1]Associate professor J.N.T.U, C.E.H, Hyd.
[2]Assistant Professor VYCET, chirala.
[3]Professor SIT, J.N.T.U, Hyd.
askme4c@yahoo.com ramakrishna.ss@gmail.com

Abstract

Network security is a complicated subject, historically only tackled by well-trained and experienced experts. The most secure ciphering techniques use a mathematical algorithm and a variable value known as a 'key'. There are several ways of classifying cryptographic algorithms Secret Key Cryptography, which uses a single key for both encryption and decryption. The goal of cryptography extends beyond merely making data unreadable; it also extends into user authentication, Privacy/confidentiality, Integrity and Non-repudiation.

This paper explains a novel method in ciphering techniques ' a multiple axis key shadowing ' and offers practical guidelines you can put into place today to protect your critical data in the communication . SAKS (single axis key shadowing) ciphering is a simplified algorithm which gives a better performance than Caesar cipher by shadowing. But the technique is less immune to bruteforce attack. As an improvement to the SAKS we formulate MAKS ciphering technique. MAKS is a poly alphabetic cipher technique. This proposed method shown betterment to poly alphabetic caeser cipher 'vigenere' by disturbing the frequency histogram .Effectiveness of this paper laid by implementation of simple technique used in symmetric key cryptographic algorithm.

In this proposed method of ciphering same algorithm can be used for both encryption and decryption. MAKS is less complextic with playfair cipher technique which is betterment to the vigenere cipher technique. In this paper MAKS cipher technique compared with vingenere technique, SAKS and playfair cipher got satisfactory results for the various keys based on method [SIMM93].

Keywords: SAKS, MAKS, Shadowing, Reshadowing.

1. Introduction

Cryptography comes from the Greek words for – "**secret writing**". Cryptography is the science of enabling secure communications between a sender and one or more. It deals with a process associated with scrambling plain text (ordinary text, or clear text) into cipher text (a process called encryption) then back again (known as decryption).

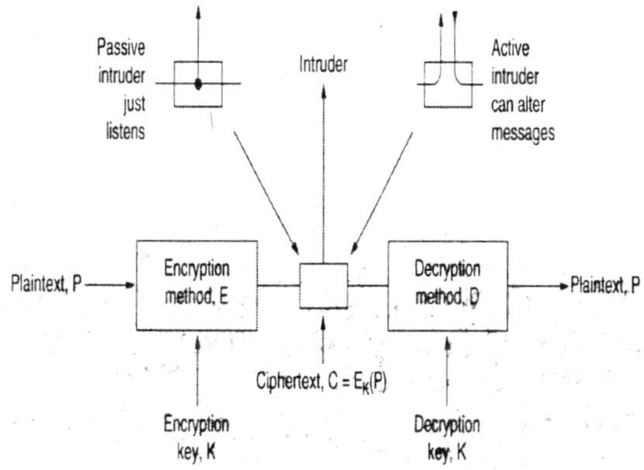

Fig. 1 The Encryption model

An intruder is hacker or cracker who hears and accurately copies down the complete cipher text. Passive intruder only listens to the communication channel. But, active intruder can also record messages and play them back later, inject his own messages, or modify legitimate messages before they get to the receiver.

Cryptography concerns itself with four objectives. Confidentiality (the information cannot be understood by any one for whom it was unintended).Integrity (the information cannot be altered in storage or transit between sender and intended receiver without the alteration being detected).Non-repudiation (the creator/sender of the information cannot deny at a later stage his or her intentions in the creation or transmission of the information).Authentication (the sender and receiver can confirm each others identity and the origin/destination of the information).

In symmetric encryption, same key is used for both encryption and decryption To maintain security and privacy, Alice and Bob need to ensure that the key remains private to them. Symmetric encryption can be implemented by **DES** – The Data Encryption Standard, **AES** – The Advanced Encryption Standard and Cipher modes. The earliest known use of a substitution cipher and the simples was by Julius Caesar. With only

25 possible keys the Caesar cipher is far from secure. A dramatic increase in the key space can be achieved by allowing an arbitrary substitution recall the assignment for Caesar cipher. This is 10 orders magnitude greater than the key space for DES and would seem to eliminate bruteforce techniques for cryptanalysis. There is how ever another line of attack. If the cryptanalyst knows the nature of the plain text, then the analyst can explicit the regularities of the language. Such a cryptanalysis might proceed in **[SINK66]**. Relative frequency of the letters can be determined and compared to a standard frequency distribution for English Fig. 2. and Table 1 Based on **[SEBE89].**

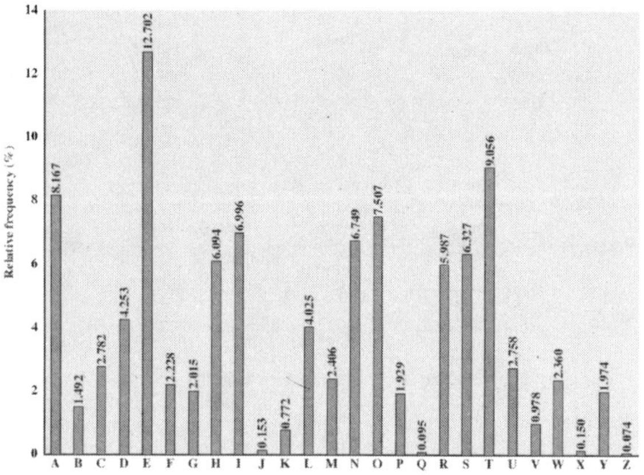

Fig. 2 The Encryption model

Table 1

Z 13.33	H 5.83	F 3.33	B 1.67	C 0.00
P 11.67	D 5.00	W 3.33	G 1.67	K 0.00
S 8.33	E 5.00	Q 2.50	Y 1.67	L 0.00
U 8.33	V 4.17	T 2.50	I 0.83	N 0.00
O 7.50	X 4.17	A 1.67	J 0.83	R 0.00
M 6.67				

Another way to improve on the simple mono alphabetic technique is to use different mono alphabetic substitutions as one proceeds through the plaintext message. The general name for this approach is poly alphabetic cipher. This is also called as vigenere cipher technique as the periodic nature of the keyword can be eliminated by using a non repeating keyword that is as long as the message itself. Vigenere proposed what is referred to as an auto key system. In which a key word is concatenated with the plaintext itself to provide a running key.

Even this scheme is vulnerable to cryptanalysis. Because the key and plain text share the same frequency distribution of letters, statistical technique can be applied. These regularities can be exploited to achieve successful cryptanalysis. Although the techniques for breaking a vigenere cipher are by no means complex, a 1917 issue of scientific American characterized this system as " impossible of translation" this is a point worth remembering when similar claims are made for modern algorithms. Gilbert vernam AT&T engineer in 1918 suggested vernam cipher, an army signal corp., officer, Joseph Mauborgne proposed improvement to vernam cipher. That yields the ultimate in security.

The best known multiple letter encryption cipher is the playfair and it is based on the use of 5 x 5 matrix of letters constructed using a keyword which is invented by british scientist sir Charles wheatstone in 1854, but it bears the name of his friend baron playfair of St.Andrews, who championed the cipher at the British foreign office.

As betterment to mono alphabetic substitution cipher SAKS has been formulated and discussed in section II. The SAKS is a simple technique a letter is substituted in its cipher with a shadow but the practical deficiencies in SAKS lead to the formulation of the next poly alphabetic cipher technique MAKS is having detailed study in section III. MAKS performance has been evaluated based on the model referred **[SIMM93]** with SAKS, vigenere and playfair techniques in section IV.

2. Single axis key shadowing technique

This is a simple technique in the ciphering as we are taking a plain text letter and an axis key. The cipher letter can be a shadow of the plain text letter with the axis key. Here axis key is fixed. The effectiveness of this technique is same algorithm can be used for encryption as well as decryption. If we take a object in front of a mirror we find its shadow with same distance as object to window the same way if we take shadow we can easily tell where is the original object. Basing on the same concept the algorithm works for encryption and decryption.

AK: AXIS KEY may be of any element where it takes on a value in range 1 to 26 .

P: plaintext letter p

SC: shadow cipher of plain text substituted in cipher text

A. Shadowing(encryption) Algorithm

If we numerical equivalent to each letter (a=1,b=2,etc.), then the encryption shadowing algorithm can be expressed as follows .

SC= E **(P)** = **AK**+ **(AK - P)**

IF **SC**<=0 THEN **SC**=26+**SC**

IF **SC**>26 THEN **SC**=**SC**-26

B. Re-shadowing (decryption) Algorithm

If we numerical equivalent to each letter (a=1,b=2,etc.), then the encryption shadowing algorithm can be expressed as follows .

P=D (SC) = AK+ (AK – SC)
IF P<=0 THEN P=26+P
IF P>26 THEN P=P-26

This algorithm gives better result when compare to the caeser cipher; as the elements are substituted with their shadows based on the axis key. Axis key reverses the frequency histogram. Cryptanalysts track out this algorithm by known plain text, and brute force attack. As betterment to this algorithm we can convex or concave the shadow. That is shadow with a shift. For the improvement in the basic concept of shadowing with single axis key we can increase number of axis keys where as the ciphering technique can be called as the multiple axis key shadowing technique.

Table 2

	A	**B**	**C**	**D**	**E**	**F**	**G**	**H**	**I**	**J**	**K**	**L**	**M**	**N**	**O**	**P**	**Q**	**R**	**S**	**T**	**U**	**V**	**W**	**X**	**Y**	**Z**
A	A	Z	Y	X	W	V	U	T	S	R	Q	P	O	N	M	L	K	J	I	H	G	F	E	D	C	B
B	C	B	A	Z	Y	X	W	V	U	T	S	R	Q	P	O	N	M	L	K	J	I	H	G	F	E	D
C	E	D	C	B	A	Z	Y	X	W	V	U	T	S	R	Q	P	O	N	M	L	K	J	I	H	G	F
D	G	F	E	D	C	B	A	Z	Y	X	W	V	U	T	S	R	Q	P	O	N	M	L	K	J	I	H
E	I	H	G	F	E	D	C	B	A	Z	Y	X	W	V	U	T	S	R	Q	P	O	N	M	L	K	J
F	K	J	I	H	G	F	E	D	C	B	A	Z	Y	X	W	V	U	T	S	R	Q	P	O	N	M	L
G	M	L	K	J	I	H	G	F	E	D	C	B	A	Z	Y	X	W	V	U	T	S	R	Q	P	O	N
H	O	N	M	L	K	J	I	H	G	F	E	D	C	B	A	Z	Y	X	W	V	U	T	S	R	Q	P
I	Q	P	O	N	M	L	K	J	I	H	G	F	E	D	C	B	A	Z	Y	X	W	V	U	T	S	R
J	S	R	Q	P	O	N	M	L	K	J	I	H	G	F	E	D	C	B	A	Z	Y	X	W	V	U	T
K	U	T	S	R	Q	P	O	N	M	L	K	J	I	H	G	F	E	D	C	B	A	Z	Y	X	W	V
L	W	V	U	T	S	R	Q	P	O	N	M	L	K	J	I	H	G	F	E	D	C	B	A	Z	Y	X
M	Y	X	W	V	U	T	S	R	Q	P	O	N	M	L	K	J	I	H	G	F	E	D	C	B	A	Z
N	A	Z	Y	X	W	V	U	T	S	R	Q	P	O	N	M	L	K	J	I	H	G	F	E	D	C	B
O	C	B	A	Z	Y	X	W	V	U	T	S	R	Q	P	O	N	M	L	K	J	I	H	G	F	E	D
P	E	D	C	B	A	Z	Y	X	W	V	U	T	S	R	Q	P	O	N	M	L	K	J	I	H	G	F
Q	G	F	E	D	C	B	A	Z	Y	X	W	V	U	T	S	R	Q	P	O	N	M	L	K	J	I	H
R	I	H	G	F	E	D	C	B	A	Z	Y	X	W	V	U	T	S	R	Q	P	O	N	M	L	K	J
S	K	J	I	H	G	F	E	D	C	B	A	Z	Y	X	W	V	U	T	S	R	Q	P	O	N	M	L
T	M	L	K	J	I	H	G	F	E	D	C	B	A	Z	Y	X	W	V	U	T	S	R	Q	P	O	N
U	O	N	M	L	K	J	I	H	G	F	E	D	C	B	A	Z	Y	X	W	V	U	T	S	R	Q	P
V	Q	P	O	N	M	L	K	J	I	H	G	F	E	D	C	B	A	Z	Y	X	W	V	U	T	S	R
W	S	R	Q	P	O	N	M	L	K	J	I	H	G	F	E	D	C	B	A	Z	Y	X	W	V	U	T
X	U	T	S	R	Q	P	O	N	M	L	K	J	I	H	G	F	E	D	C	B	A	Z	Y	X	W	V
Y	W	V	U	T	S	R	Q	P	O	N	M	L	K	J	I	H	G	F	E	D	C	B	A	Z	Y	X
Z	Y	X	W	V	U	T	S	R	Q	P	O	N	M	L	K	J	I	H	G	F	E	D	C	B	A	Z

3. Multiple axis keys shadowing technique

One of the simplest algorithms is referred as the multiple axis key shadowing technique. The set of single axis key shadowing rules consists of 26 axis keys, with shadow of 0 through 25.

Each shadow cipher is denoted by a key letter which is the cipher text letter that substitutes for the plaintext letter a, thus with axis key e is denoted by key value shadow cipher i. To aid in understanding the scheme and to aid in its use a matrix know as the shadow table is constructed as Table 2.

Each of 26 axis keys is laid out horizontally with the key letter for each cipher to its left. A normal alphabet for the plaintext runs across the top. The process of encryption is simple: given a axis key x an plain text letter y the cipher text letter is at intersection of the row labeled x and the column labeled y; in this case z.

To encrypt a message a key is needed that is as long as the message. Usually the key is repeating axis keyword. For example if the keyword

A. Shadowing (Encryption)

Plaintext: t h e r e a r e s e v e r a l v
MAK: m i s s o n i m p o s s i b l e
SHADOW: f j g t m c j m g a h g t q x b

Decryption is equally simple. The key letter again identifjes the row the position key o f the cipher text letter in that row determines the column, and the plaintext letter is at the top of that column.

B. Reshadowing (Decryption)

SHADOW: f j g t m c j m g a h g t q x b
MAK:m i s s o n i m p o s s i b l e
RESHADOW:t h e r e a r e s e v e r a l v

The strength of this cipher is that there are multiple cipher text letters for each plain text letter, one for each unique letter of the keyword. Thus, the letter frequency information is more obscured. However not all knowledge of the plaintext structure is lost. For example figure shows the frequency distribution for a vigenere cipher with a keyword of length nine. An improvement to that is achieved in this MAKS technique, but considerably frequency information remains.

It I instructive to sketch a method of breaking this cipher, because the method reveals some of the mathematical principles that apply in cryptanalysis. First suppose that the opponent believes that the cipher text was encrypted using either mono alphabetic substitution or a vingenere cipher. A simplest test can be made to make a determination. If mono alphabetic substitution is used then the plain text thus referring to there should be on cipher letter with a relative frequency occurrence of about 12.75%, once with about 9.25%, and so on. If only a single message is available for analysis, we would not expect an exact match of this small sample with a statistical profile of the plain text language. Nevertheless, if correspondence is close, we can assume` a mono alphabetic substitution.

4. Experimental results

one way of reavealing effictiveness of the MAKS and other ciphers is shown in figures, based on**[SIMM93]** . the line labeld plaintext plots the frequency distribution of a sample of 615 alphabetic characters. This is also frequency distribution of any monoalphabetic substitution cipher.

Frequency of the characters have been tabulated in Tables 3 and 4

Table 3

FREQUNCY	A	B	C	D	E	F	G	H	I	J	K	L	M
PLAINTEXT	**48.00**	**5.00**	**18.00**	**21.00**	**84.00**	**11.00**	**6.00**	**26.00**	**49.00**	**0.00**	**3.00**	**52.00**	**57.00**
MAKS	21.00	8.00	36.00	22.00	17.00	16.00	28.00	16.00	30.00	21.00	32.00	17.00	15.00
VIGENERE	1.00	18.00	1.00	5.00	9.00	30.00	6.00	12.00	22.00	31.00	15.00	24.00	35.00
PLAYFAIR	27.00	14.00	4.00	10.00	32.00	3.00	62.00	22.00	23.00	0.00	13.00	42.00	80.00
SAKS	1.00	5.00	6.00	7.00	14.00	93.00	45.00	19.00	0.00	7.00	57.00	22.00	3.00
PLAINTEXT	0.57	0.06	0.21	0.25	1.00	0.13	0.07	0.31	0.58	0.00	0.04	0.62	0.68
MAKS	0.25	0.10	0.43	0.26	0.20	0.19	0.33	0.19	0.36	0.25	0.38	0.20	0.18
VIGENERE	0.01	0.21	0.01	0.06	0.11	0.36	0.07	0.14	0.26	0.37	0.18	0.29	0.42
PLAYFAIR	0.32	0.17	0.05	0.12	0.38	0.04	0.74	0.26	0.27	0.00	0.15	0.50	0.95
SAKS	0.01	0.06	0.07	0.08	0.17	1.11	0.54	0.23	0.00	0.08	0.68	0.26	0.04

Table 4

FREQUENCY	N	O	P	Q	R	S	T	U	V	W	X	Y	Z
AINTEXT	**7.00**	**0.00**	**19.00**	**45.00**	**93.00**	**14.00**	**7.00**	**6.00**	**5.00**	**1.00**	**2.00**	**12.00**	**22.00**
MAKS	10.00	24.00	36.00	22.00	10.00	18.00	12.00	32.00	16.00	19.00	13.00	22.00	18.00
VIGENERE	45.00	19.00	7.00	16.00	41.00	32.00	19.00	16.00	17.00	8.00	4.00	20.00	35.00
PLAYFAIR	40.00	21.00	14.00	44.00	19.00	45.00	4.00	0.00	13.00	28.00	8.00	32.00	46.00
SAKS	0.00	49.00	26.00	7.00	11.00	84.00	21.00	18.00	5.00	48.00	0.00	12.00	53.00
PLAINTEXT	0.08	0.00	0.23	0.54	1.11	0.17	0.08	0.07	0.06	0.01	0.02	0.14	0.26
MAKS	0.12	0.29	0.43	0.26	0.12	0.21	0.14	0.38	0.19	0.23	0.15	0.26	0.21
VIGENERE	0.54	0.23	0.08	0.19	0.49	0.38	0.23	0.19	0.20	0.10	0.05	0.24	0.42
PLAYFAIR	0.48	0.25	0.17	0.52	0.23	0.54	0.05	0.00	0.15	0.33	0.10	0.38	0.55
SAKS	0.00	0.58	0.31	0.08	0.13	1.00	0.25	0.21	0.06	0.57	0.00	0.14	0.63

The plot was developed in the following way the number of occurences of the letter e (the most frequently used letter). As a result e has relative frequency of 1 a of 0.57 b of about 0.06 and so on. The point on horizontal axis correspond to the letters in order of decreasing frequency.

Fig. 3, also shows the frequncy distribution that results when the text is encrypted using the MAKS,playfair, vigenere and plain text.

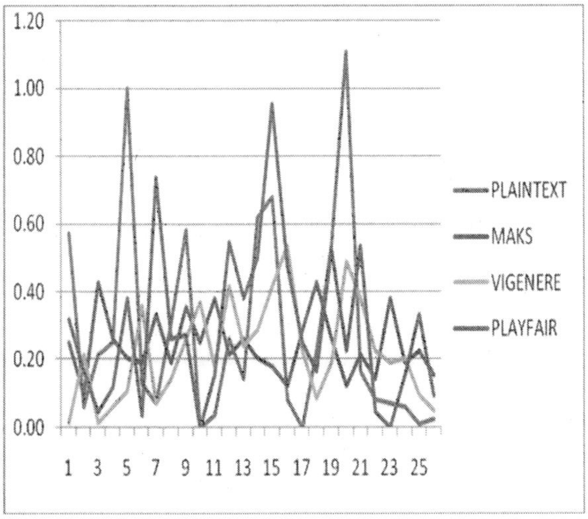

Fig. 3

Fig. 4 shows the frequncy distribution that results when the text is encrypted using the MAKS and plain text.

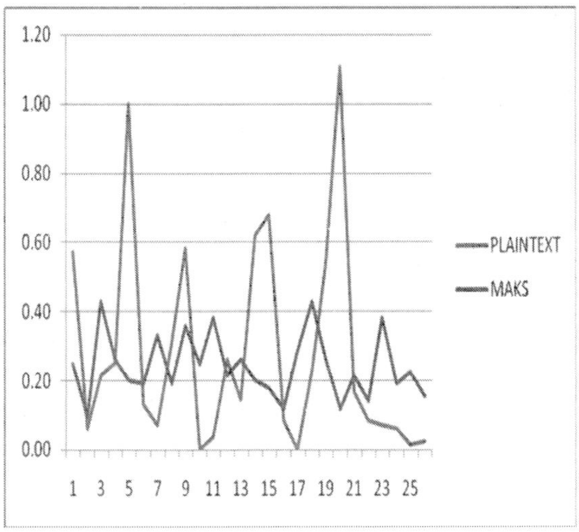

Fig. 4

Figure 5, 6 shows the frequncy distribution that results when the text is encrypted using the MAKS with vigenere cipher , playfair.

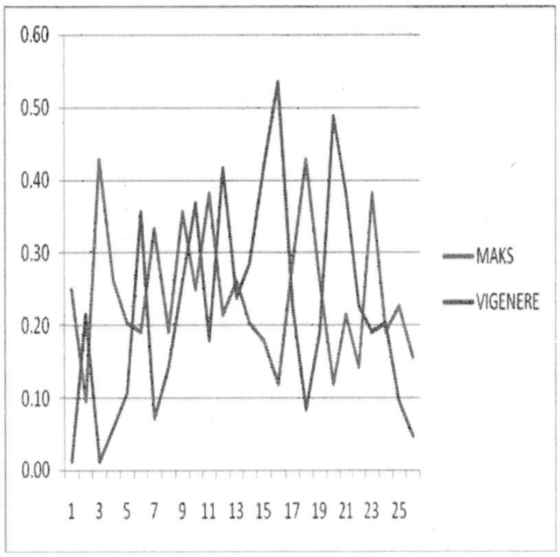

Fig. 5

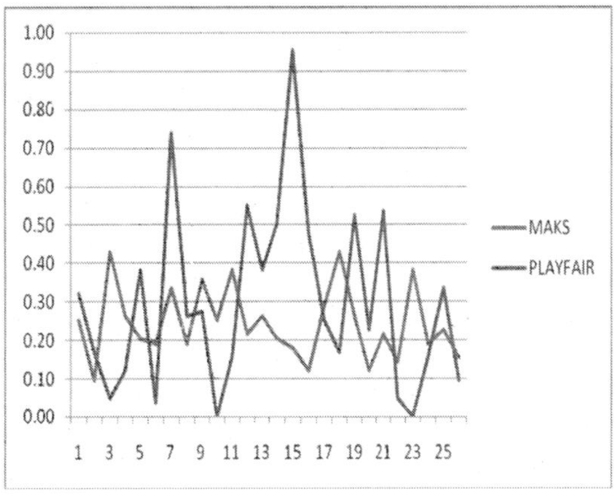

Fig. 6

Fig. 7, 8 shows the frequncy distribution that results when the text is encrypted using the MAKS with SAKS with shorter key length and longer.

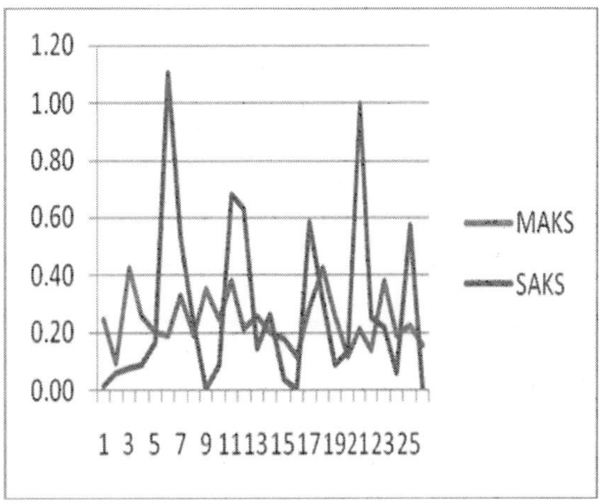

Fig. 7

To normalize the plot, the number of occurances of each letter in the ciphertext was again divided by the number of occurancess of e in the plaintext. the resulting plot therefore shows the extent to which the frequency distribution of letters, which makes it trivial to solve substituion ciphers, is masked by encryption. If the frequency distribution information were totally concealed in encryption process, the ciphertext plot of frequencies would be flat, and cryptanalysis using ciphertext only would be effectively impossible. As the figure shows , the MAKS has flatter distribution than does plain text,SAKS, poly alphabetic cipher and play fair but neverthless it reveals plenty of structure for a cryptanalyst to work with.

5. Conclusions

This paper explains a novel method in ciphering techniques 'a multiple axis key shadowing 'is a poly alphabetic cipher technique. SAKS ciphering is a simplified algorithm which gives a basic idea of shadowing its advantages and disadvantage. It is shown good results over Caeser cipher technique. But SAKS can be track out by bruteforce technique .Instead of using single key using more keys will improve cryptographic strength. That's why poly alphabetic cipher MAKS has been proposed. This proposed method shown betterment to poly alphabetic caeser cipher 'vigenere' by disturbing the frequency histogram .Effectiveness of this paper laid by implementation of simple technique used in symmetric key cryptographic algorithm. In this proposed method of ciphering same algorithm can be used for both encryption and decryption the complexity is also low when compared with playfair cipher technique which is an alternative betterment to the vigenere cipher technique and results are satisfactory.

Comparisons made between MAKS cipher technique, vingenere technique, SAKS and playfair cipher got satisfactory results for the various keys. Flatter curve has been observed than the plain text, vigenere, playfair and SAKS in MAKS as in the method encyclopedia Britannica cryptographic strength and proven a better method.

As a future scope we can modify model for single axis key shadowing technique by taking convex or concave shadows with a shift in shadow may get better result.

6. References

[1] **GARD72:**Gardner,M.Codes,Ciphers,and Secret Writing. Newyork:Dover 1972.

[2] **KAHN96** : Kahn, D. The Codebreakers; The story of Secret Writing. NewYork: Scribner,1996.

[3] **KOHN81**:Konheim, A.Cryptography:A Primer.New York:wiley, 1981,

[4] **KORN96:** Korner,T. The Plesures of Counting.Cambridge,England:Cambridge University Press, 1996.

[5] **SIMM93:** Simmons, G."Cryptology." Encyclopaedia Britannica, 1993.

[6] **SINK66:** Sinkov, A. Elementary Cryptanalysis: A mathematical Approach. Wasington DC: The Mathematical Association of America, 1966.

[7] **WAYN96:** Wayner, P. Disappearing Cryptography. Boston:APProfessional Books, 1996.

Achieving Better Contrast in Visual Cryptography Schemes

Thomas Monoth and Babu Anto P
Department of Information Technology, Kannur University, Kerala, India-670 567
isres@yahoo.com babu_anto_p@yahoo.com

Abstract

In this paper we present an improved method for the generation of shares is proposed using additional matrix. Visual cryptography method for encrypting printed texts, handwritten notes, and pictures are done in a perfectly secure way, and decoding these data with the human visual system. The contrast is the most important parameter in visual cryptography. Usually, the reconstructed secret image will be darker than the background of the original secret image. The proposed scheme achieves better contrast and reduces the noise in the reconstructed secret image without adding any computational complexity. In this technique the number of white pixels in the reconstructed secret image can be improve 20% or more compare to the existing method.

1. Visual Cryptography

Visual Cryptography (VC) was introduced by Naor and Shamir in 1994[1]. VC is a method for encrypting material such as printed texts, handwritten notes, and pictures in a perfectly secure way, and decoding the material with the human visual system is the basic idea behind this paper. This form of data encryption is called VC and it is relatively new in the area of computer science. In VC all documents are considered to be image. In this paper the secret information considered as binary image called secret image. While encrypting, the secret image is split into two or more separate images called shares. The shares are such that no information from the original image is revealed to the viewer. To decode the encrypted information, that is to get the original information back, the shares are stacked and the image pops out. These images are usually printed on transparencies and superimposing these transparencies will reveal the secret image. Fig. 1 depicts the concept behind VC (2 out of 2 scheme).

Fig. 1a Secret image

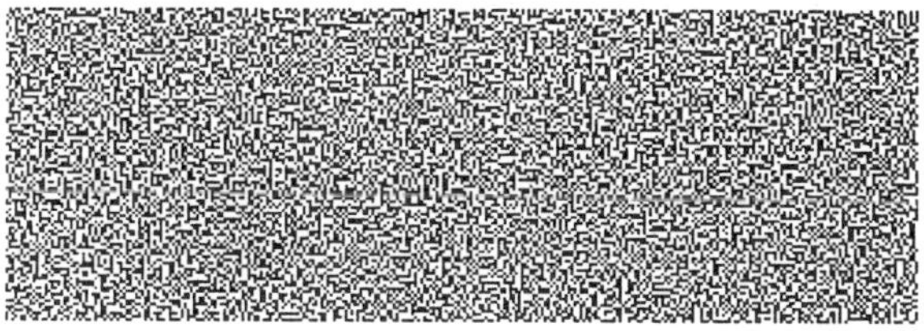

Fig. 1b Share1

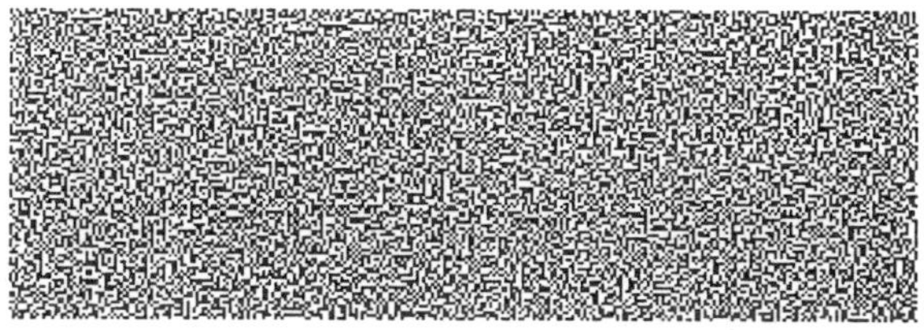

Fig. 1c Share2

Fig. 1d Retrieved image

2. Visual Cryptography Schemes

There are different types of Visual Cryptography Schemes (VCS). The VCS describes the way in which an image is encrypted and decrypted. For example, there is the '*k out of n*' scheme that says *n* shares will be produced to encrypt an image, and *k* shares must be stacked to decrypt the image. If the number of shares stacked is less than *k*, the original image is not revealed. Increasing the number of shares or participants will automatically increase the level of security of the encrypted message.

The message (secret data) consists of a collection of black and white pixels. Each pixel appears in n version called shares, one for each transparency. Each share is a collection of m black and white subpixels. The resulting structure can be described by an n x m Boolean matrix S = $[s_{ij}]$, where

$s_{ij} = 1 \Leftrightarrow$ the jth subpixel in the ith share is black.

$s_{ij} = 0 \Leftrightarrow$ the jth subpixel in the ith share is white.

A ‘k out of n’ VCS consists of two collections of n x m matrices C_0 and C_1. To share a white pixel, the dealer randomly chooses one of the matrices in C_0. Similarly to share a black pixel, the dealer randomly chooses one of the matrices in C_1. The chosen matrix defines the color of the m subpixels in each of the n shares [2][3]. The collections C_0 and C_1 must have the following properties:

1. For any S in C_0, the "OR" V of any k of n rows satisfies $H(V) \leq d - \alpha m$.
2. For any S in C_1 the "OR" V of any k of n rows satisfies $H(V) \geq d$.
3. For any subset $\{i_1, i_2, \ldots, i_q\}$ of $\{1, 2, \ldots, n\}$ with $q < k$, the two collections of q x m matrices obtained by restricting each n x m matrix in C_0 and C_1 to the rows $i_1, i_2, \ldots, i_q$ are indistinguishable in the sense that they contain the same matrices with the same frequencies.

The property (1) and (2) refers to the contrast of the scheme and (3) refers to the security of the scheme, guaranteeing that if there are less than k parties, they will not be able to obtain any information on the secret image[5].

The collections C_0 and C_1 are obtained by permuting the columns of the basis matrices S^0 and S^1 in all possible ways[4]. The size of the collections C_0 and C_1 is the same and it is denoted by r. The r is computed using the equation:

$$r = 2^{n-1}! \quad (1)$$

The contrast is the most important parameter for VCS. It determines how well the original image is recognizable. The relative difference α is calculated using the equation:

$$\alpha = |n_b - n_w|/m \quad (2)$$

Where n_b and n_w are the number of the black subpixels which are generated from a black and white pixel in the secret image, respectively and the m is pixel expansion. This is called the relative difference. The contrast β computed using the equation

$$\beta = \alpha . m \quad (3)$$

The value β is the contrast, which is to be as large as possible. The minimum contrast that required to ensure that the black and white area will be distinguishable is $\beta \geq 1$.

3. ‘n out of n’ VCS

The (n, n) VCS, the original message is visible if and only if all n shares are sacked together, if fewer than n shares are stacked together no information available to the viewer[5]. Let G be the ground set which is given by

$$G = \{ g1, g2, \ldots\ldots gn \} \text{ of n elements.}$$

Let $E = \{ \pi_1, \pi_2, \ldots\ldots\ldots\ldots \pi_{2^{n-1}} \}$ be the collection of all subsets with even cardinality and let $O = \{ \sigma_1, \sigma_2, \ldots\ldots \sigma_{2^{n-1}} \}$ be the collection of all subsets with odd cardinality. Each of them is defined by a matrix which is called by S^0 and S^1 with order n x 2^{n-1}. For $1 \leq i \leq n$ and $1 \leq j \leq 2^{n-1}$, all the matrices are obtained by permuting the columns of $S^0 = [sij^0]$ and $S^1 = [sij^1]$ in which

$$sij0 = 1 \Leftrightarrow gi \in \pi_j,$$

$$sij^1 = 1 \Leftrightarrow gi \in \sigma_j,$$

The pixel expansion m in (n, n) VCS can be computed as:

$$m = 2^{n-1} \quad (4)$$

3.1 ‘2 out of 2’ VCS

Let n = 2 . Then G = {1, 2},

$$E = \{ \theta, \{1,2\} \} \text{ and}$$

$$O = \{ \{1\}, \{2\} \}$$

For the (2, 2)-VCS, the basis matrices, S^0 and S^1 design as follows:

$$S^0 = \begin{bmatrix} 1 & 0 \\ 1 & 0 \end{bmatrix} \qquad S^1 = \begin{bmatrix} 1 & 0 \\ 0 & 1 \end{bmatrix}$$

Using the equation (2) and (3), for the basis matrices, the relative difference α and contrast β computed as :

$$\alpha = ½ \text{ and } \beta = 1 \quad (a)$$

There are two collections of matrices, C_0 for encoding white pixels and C_1 for encoding black pixel. The matrices C_0 and C_1 can be designed as:

$$C_0 = \left\{ 2 \text{ matrices obtained by permuting the columns of } \begin{bmatrix} 1 & 0 \\ 1 & 0 \end{bmatrix} \right\}$$

$$C_1 = \left\{ 2 \text{ matrices obtained by permuting the columns of } \begin{bmatrix} 1 & 0 \\ 0 & 1 \end{bmatrix} \right\}$$

The problem that arises with this scheme is that for every pixel encoded from the original image, two subpixels are placed on each share in a horizontal or vertical fashion. This results in a distorted image.

To solve this problem, for the (2, 2)-VCS with 4-subpixels, which has two basis matrices, S^0 and S^1 as follows:

$$S^0 = \begin{bmatrix} 1 & 0 & 1 & 0 \\ 1 & 0 & 1 & 0 \end{bmatrix} \qquad S^1 = \begin{bmatrix} 1 & 0 & 0 & 1 \\ 0 & 1 & 1 & 0 \end{bmatrix}$$

Using the equation (2) and (3), for the basis matrices, the relative difference α and contrast β computed as :

$$\alpha = ½ \text{ and } \beta = 2 \quad (b)$$

There are two collections of matrices, C_0 for encoding white pixels and C_1 for encoding black pixel. The matrices C_0 and C_1 can be designed as:

$$C_0 = \left\{ \text{24 matrices obtained by permuting the columns of } \begin{bmatrix} 1 & 0 & 1 & 0 \\ 1 & 0 & 1 & 0 \end{bmatrix} \right\}$$

$$C_1 = \left\{ \text{24 matrices obtained by permuting the columns of } \begin{bmatrix} 1 & 0 & 0 & 1 \\ 0 & 1 & 1 & 0 \end{bmatrix} \right\}$$

3.1.1 Example

Fig. 2a Secret image

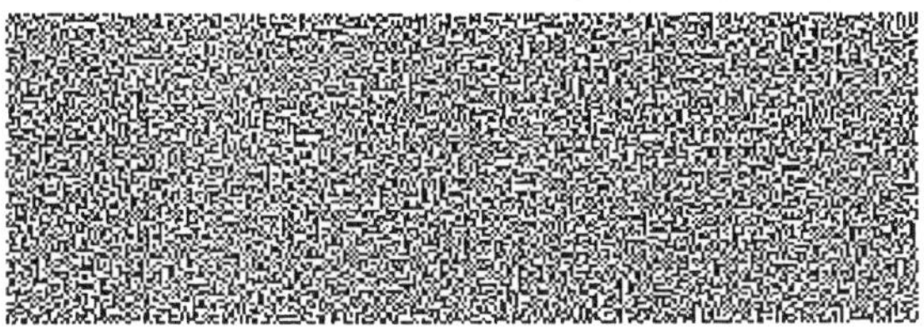

Fig. 2b Share1

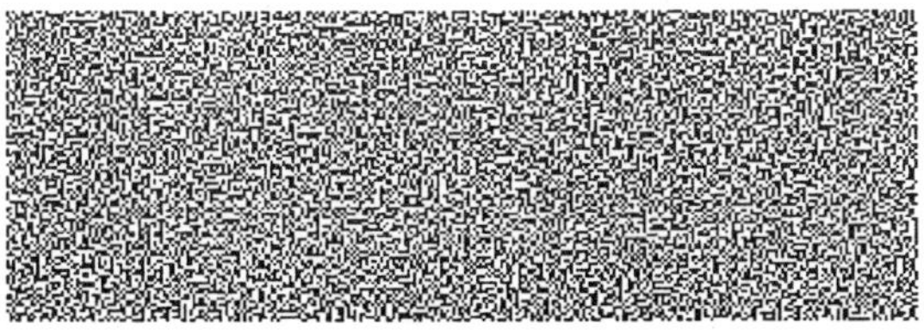

Fig. 2c Share2

Fig. 2d Retrieved image

The Fig. 2a, 2b and 2c are example of the '2 out of 2' scheme. The Figure 2d is the result of laying share1 over share2. The details of pixels in secret image, share1, share2 and reconstructed image (share1+share2) are shown in Table 1.

Table 1

Image	Total Columns	Total Rows	Total Black Pixels	Total white Pixels	Total Pixel
Secret image	150	50	2223	5277	7500
Share1	300	100	15000	15000	30000
Share 2	300	100	15000	15000	30000
Share1 + Share 2	300	100	19446	10554	30000

4. Proposed Method

In this section we propose a new method for improving the contrast of reconstructed secret image using additional basis matrix. The additional basis matrix, we call it as AS^0. The additional matrix AS^0 is used to share white pixels in the secret data. In the existing method, the black pixels are reconstructed exactly same as in the original data (secret data). But the reconstruction of white pixels in existing method causes loss of contrast in the reconstructed secret image. Using the additional matrix, we can improve the contrast of the reconstructed image, by increasing the number of white pixels in reconstructed image. The white pixels in the proposed method will increase 20% or more compare to the existing method. The additional matrix AS^0 can be designed as :

Let P be the set which is given by

$P = \{ p_1, p_2, \ldots\ldots p_n \}$ of n elements.

Each of them is defined by a matrix which is called by AS^0 with order $n \times 2^{n-1}$. For $1 \le i \le n$ and $1 \le j \le 2^{n-1}$, all the matrices are obtained by permuting the columns of $AS^0 = [as_{ij}^0]$ in which

$$as_{ij}^0 = 1 \iff 1 \le i \le n \text{ and } j=1,$$
$$as_{ij}^0 = 0 \iff 1 \le i \le n \text{ and } 2 \le j \le 2^{n-1}.$$

The (n, n) VCS has the parameters r, α and m. The parameters are computed using the equations (1), (2) and (4) respectively. The collection of matrices C_0 is obtained by permuting the columns of S^0 plus permuting the columns of AS^0 and the collection of matrices C_1 is obtained by permuting the columns of S^1.

4.1 Proposed '2 out of 2' VCS

For the (2,2)-VCS, the basis matrices, S^0 , AS^0 and S^1 designed using above results as follows:

$$S^0 = \begin{bmatrix} 1 & 0 & 1 & 0 \\ 1 & 0 & 1 & 0 \end{bmatrix} \quad AS^0 = \begin{bmatrix} 1 & 0 & 0 & 0 \\ 1 & 0 & 0 & 0 \end{bmatrix} \quad S^1 = \begin{bmatrix} 1 & 0 & 0 & 1 \\ 0 & 1 & 1 & 0 \end{bmatrix}$$

There are two collections of matrices, C_0 for encoding white pixels and C_1 for encoding black pixels. The matrices C_0 and C_1 can be designed as:

$C_0 = \{$24 matrices obtained by permuting the columns of $\begin{bmatrix} 1 & 0 & 1 & 0 \\ 1 & 0 & 1 & 0 \end{bmatrix}$ + 24 matrices obtained by permuting the columns of $\begin{bmatrix} 1 & 0 & 0 & 0 \\ 1 & 0 & 0 & 0 \end{bmatrix}$ $\}$

$C_1 = \{$24 matrices obtained by permuting the columns of $\begin{bmatrix} 1 & 0 & 0 & 1 \\ 0 & 1 & 1 & 0 \end{bmatrix}$ $\}$

Using the equation (2) and (3), for the basis matrices S^0 and S^1 the relative difference α and contrast β computed as :

$$\alpha = \tfrac{1}{2} \text{ and } \beta = 2 \qquad \text{(c)}$$

The α and β of reconstructed secret data are computed as α and β of the basis matrices S^0 and S^1 plus α and β of AS^0_5. Then

$$\alpha = {}^5/_8 \text{ and } \beta = 2.5 \qquad \text{(d)}$$

The results (c) and (d) shows the relative difference and contrast of proposed scheme are better compare to the existing scheme.

4.1.1 Example

Fig. 3a Secret image

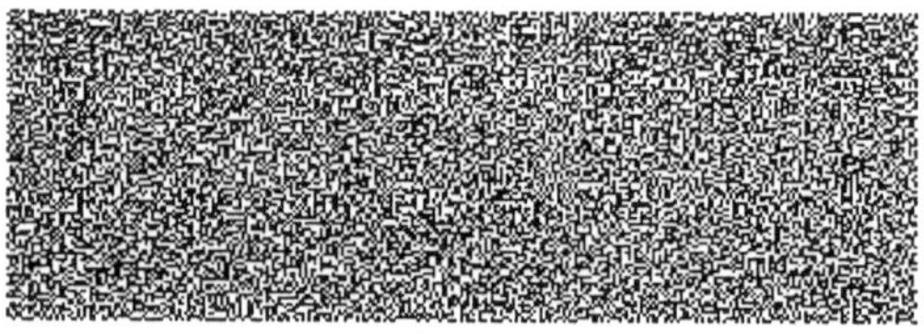

Fig. 3b Share1

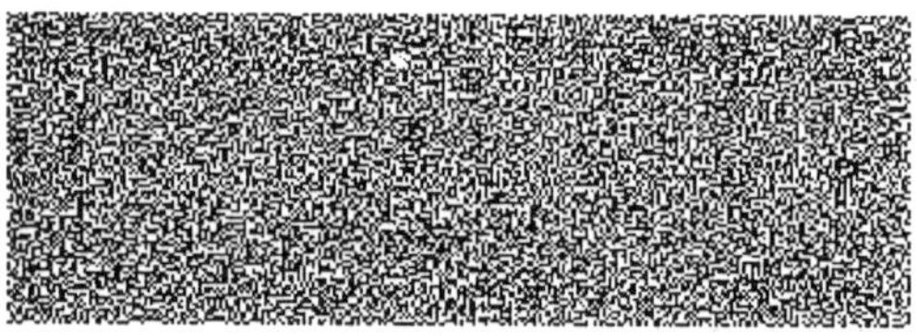

Fig. 3c Share2

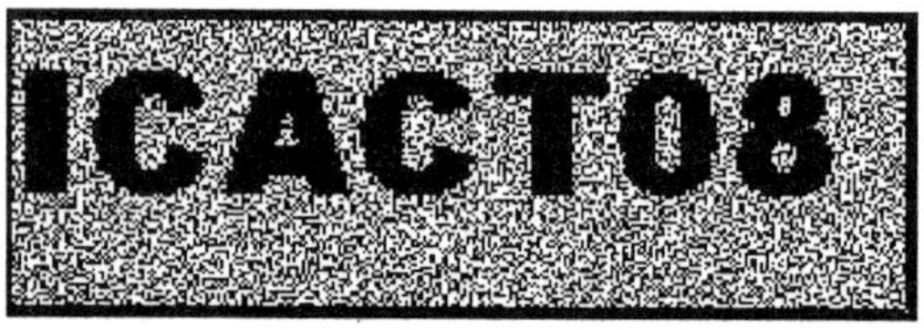

Fig. 3d Retrieved image

The Figs. 3a, 3b and 3c are example of the '2 out of 2' scheme using additional matrix. The Figure 3d is the result of laying share1 over share 2. The details of pixels in secret image, share1, share2 and reconstructed image (share1+share2) are shown in Table 2.

Table 2

Image	Total Columns	Total Rows	Total Black Pixels	Total white Pixels	Total Pixel
Secret image	150	50	2223	5277	7500
Share1	300	100	16058	13942	30000
Share 2	300	100	16058	13942	30000
Share1 + Share 2	300	100	18388	11612	30000

Comparing the Table1 with Table 2, the reconstructed image have more white pixel in the Table2 than Table1. The number of white pixels in the reconstructed image is improved 20% or more compare to the existing method. And also compare reconstructed images in Figure 2d with Figure 3d, we can see that proposed method achieved better contrast than existing ones.

5. Conclusions

In this paper we present an improved method for the generation of shares is proposed and proved using examples. The contrast is one of the most important parameter in visual cryptography scheme. The proposed method increases the number of white pixels and thus the contrast of the decrypted image compare to the conventional VCS. The proposed method can be extended to 'k out of n' and 'n out of n' visual cryptography schemes.

6. References

[1] M. Naor and A. Shamir. "Visual Cryptography" *Advances in Cryptology-Eurocrypt '94* Proceeding, LNCS vol. 950, Springer-Verlag, pp. 1-12, 1995 .

[2] Stinson,D, "Visual secret sharing and threshold schemes", Potentials, IEEE , Vol. 18 Issue: 1, pp. 13 -16, 1999.

[3] G. Ateniese, C. Blundo, A. D. Santis, and D. Stinson. "Constructions and bounds for visual cryptography", *Proc. 23rd International Colloquium on Automata, Languages,and Programming (ICALP '96)*, pp.416–428, 1996.

[4] G. Ateniese, C. Blundo, A. D. Santis, and D. Stinson. "Visual secret sharing for general access structures", *Information and Computation*, 129(2): pp. 86–106, 1996.

[5] G. Simmons, "How to (Really) Share a Secret", *Advances in Cryptology-CRYPTO'88*, vol. 403, pp. 390-448, 1989.

An Asymmetric Image Encryption and Decryption based on Jumbled Parallel Computing (IEJPC)

Karthik. T[1], Varalakshmi. R.S[1], Subburaj V[2] and Thavavel V[3]
[1]MCA dept, TSM, Madurai
[2]Lecturer, MCA Dept, TSM, Madurai
[3]Asst. Prof, MCA Dept, Karunya University

Abstract

Since the advent of data communication over networks, it has become imperative to ensure security of information. Cryptography is a technique that is being employed. In this paper, it is shown how to adapt certain matrix transformation to create a novel asymmetric block encryption scheme. The proposed scheme is especially useful for encryption of large amounts of data, like digital images. First, a pair of keys is given by using matrix transformation; second, the image is encrypted using private key in its transformation domain; finally the receiver uses the public key to decrypt the encrypted messages. This scheme satisfies the characters of convenient realization, less computation complexity and good security. As a step towards the systematic application of public key cryptography, this article proposes an extension to the JCA framework to integrate threshold cryptography. Under this extension, various TC providers implementing different TC primitives can be plugged into a security application at run-time. This extension also makes it easy for an existing JCA-aware application to be migrated to use threshold cryptography. An example provider of threshold ECC is implemented under this framework extension. It is our belief that such an extension would help speed up the adoption of threshold cryptography.
Keywords: Security in Military and Air force, Threshold cryptography, Image Encryption Elliptic curve Threshold Cryptography, and Java cryptography architecture

1. Introduction

Nowadays, communication networks such as mobile networks and the Internet are well developed. However, they are public networks and are not suitable for the direct transmission of confidential messages. To make use of the communication networks already developed and to keep the secrecy simultaneously, cryptographic techniques need to be applied. Traditional symmetric ciphers such as Data Encryption Standard (DES) are designed with good confusion and diffusion properties [1]. These two properties can also be found in this paper which are usually erotic and are sensitive to system parameters and initial conditions. For image encryption, two-dimensional (2D) or higher-dimensional chaotic maps are naturally employed as the image can be considered as a 2D array of pixels [2-9]. In [2], Fridrich suggested that a chaos based image encryption scheme should compose of two processes: chaotic confusion and pixel diffusion. The former permutes the pixels of a plain image with a 2D chaotic map while the latter alternates the value (gray-level) of each pixel in a sequential manner. By means of JCA we proposed the image into a 4 x 4 matrix transformations and then into grayscale image by means of ECC-TC. Although measures such as pre-computation of permutation mode and sine table were suggested to reduce the computational complexity, the relatively slow diffusion process still limits the performance of this cryptosystem. To accelerate the encryption speed of Lian's cryptosystem and other ciphers based on the iterative confusion-diffusion processes, we propose to introduce certain diffusion effect in the confusion process so that this effect is not solely contributed by the slow diffusion process. Simulation results show that the number of overall rounds and hence the number of time-consuming diffusion processes is reduced without sacrificing the security level. The overall encryption time is shortened although the time required in the confusion stage is increased slightly.

Also, **IEJPC** focuses to achieve the lower bound in terms of tIme necessary to perform authenticated encryption, and decryption as well, or

$$time(ll_{rl}\ Enc\ \&\ sgn) \approx max\ \{time(Enc), time(sgn)\}$$

and

$$time(ll_{rl}\ Dec\ \&\ ver) \approx max\ \{time(Dec), time(ver)\}$$

At best, the **IEJPC** would consume roughly the same time as the most time-consuming operation (either signing or encryption).

Furthermore, to meet the big gap between the state-of-the-art security research community and the state-of-the-art security practice. The paper proposes a 3-tier framework based on Java Cryptography Architecture (JCA) [10] for **IEJPC** services.

2. State of Art Research on AIEMT

Without loss of generality, we consider encrypting the grayscale image, named as IM×N (To RGB image, using its luminance space). The whole encryption process is described as follows:

Step-1: Creating the key pairs: private key for encryption, public key for decryption;

Step-2: Dividing original image into distinct P×P blocks and transforming them into DCT domain;

Step-3: Using the private key to encrypt the frontal K × K coefficients of P×P every block;

Step-4: Making the inverse DCT transformation and uniting all P × P blocks;

Step-5: Deal with the transformed coefficients and keep them between 0 and 1.

First, we create a set of orthonormal bases{ui, i = 1, 2, . . .K} of length P and an invertible matrix A of size P ×P by using the method of [11]. {ui} forms the column vector of U, defined as:

$$[A]=\begin{bmatrix} a1la12...a1p \\ a21k22...a2p \\ \vdots \;\vdots\;\vdots\;\vdots \\ ap1ap2...app \end{bmatrix} \quad [U]=\begin{bmatrix} u1la12...a1k \\ u21k22...a2k \\ \vdots\;\vdots\;\vdots\;\vdots \\ up1ap2...apk \end{bmatrix} \qquad (1)$$

The private key and public key are AU and A^{-t} U, respectively, where A^{-t} denotes the inverse transpose of A. The details of encryption and decryption are as following:

2.1 Encryption

Step-1: Dividing original image into distinct P × P blocks and transforming them into DCT domain, the corresponding DCT coefficients are named as $X_{M\times N}$.

$$X_{M\times N} = DCT\,(I, [P\ P]) \qquad (2)$$

Step-2: Encrypting the frontal K×K coefficients of every P×P block, respectively. Let X1 denotes the matrix composed by the frontal K ×K coefficients of certain P ×P block X0, the corresponding encryption formula by using the private key AU can be described as:

$$X_2 = AUX1 \qquad (3)$$

Step-3: Replacing the frontal P × K coefficients of X_0 with $X_2 \in R^{P\times K}$

If K is close to P, according to the characteristic of DCT coefficients, the rest (P − K) × (P − K) coefficients are all close to 0. So we can directly replace them and the decrypted image is almost not influenced.

$$X0\,(i, j) = X2\ \{1 \le i \le P,\ 1 \le j \le K\} \qquad (4)$$

Step-4: Making the inverse DCT transformation and uniting all P ×P blocks, the final result is defined as $X2_{M\times N}$.

$$X2_{M\times N} = IDCT\,(X_{M\times N}) \qquad (5)$$

Step 5: Keeping all the transformed coefficients between 0 and 1.

- Get the minimum of $X2_{M\times N}$
- Ensure all the coefficients of $X2_{M\times N} > 0$
- Get the maximum of updated $X2_{M\times N}$
- Ensure all the coefficients of $X2_{M\times N} < 1$

Step-6: Saving the encrypted image as bmp file.

2.2 Decryption

The decryption operation is a usual correlation process with five elements: (1) block length P; (2) encryption matrix dimension K; (3) public key A^{-t} U; (4) the coefficient minimum Min; (5) the coefficient maximum Max. Suppose $X3_{M\times N}$ denotes the encrypted image, the details of decryption are following:

Step-1: Recovering all coefficients of $X3_{M\times N}$

$$X3_{M\times N} = X3_{M\times N} \times Max - Min \qquad (6)$$

Step-2: Applying DCT transformation to each distinct P × P block of $X3_{M\times N}$

$$X4_{M\times N} = DCT\,(X3_{M\times N}, [P\ P]) \qquad (7)$$

Step-3: Decrypting the frontal P ×K coefficients of every P × P block, respectively. Let D1 denotes the matrix composed by P ×K coefficients of certain P×P block D0, the corresponding decryption data D2 € $R^{K\times K}$ by using the public key A^{-t} U can be given as following:

$$\begin{aligned} &\Rightarrow D2 = (A^{-t}U)^t D_1 \\ &\Rightarrow D2 = (U^t A^{-1})(AU)\, X_0 \\ &\Rightarrow D2 = (U^t U)\, X_0 \end{aligned} \qquad (8)$$

Because the column vector of U is a set of orthonormal bases, it is easily proved: $U^tU=E$. So, we can draw the conclusion:

$$\Rightarrow D_2 = X_0 \qquad (9)$$

Step-4: Replacing the frontal P × K coefficients of D_0 with D_2 and 0.

$$Do(i,j) = \begin{Bmatrix} D2\{1 \le t, j \le k\ \} \\ 0\{\ k \le i \le p, 1 \le j \le k\} \end{Bmatrix} \qquad (10)$$

Step-5: Making the inverse DCT transformation and uniting all P ×P blocks, the final result is defined as $X5_{M\times N}$.

$$X5_{M\times N} = IDCT\,(X4_{M\times N}) \qquad (11)$$

Step-6: Saving the decrypted image as bmp file.

3. Proposed Optimal IEJPC

The proposed scheme with the assumption that a private key group set Us= {u_1, u2, u3 ...un} exists with n signers, having equal authority to examine and sign, divides the whole message into t ($1 \leq t \leq n$) readable sub-message blocks. Each of these t participants needs only to examine and break the private key of their corresponding sub-message block. After receiving the block, the designated receiver first proceeds to recover the message by providing his own public key and verify it. The proposed scheme consists of the two phases as like the first scheme.

3.1 Encryption

There is a trusted SA responsible for selecting the following parameters and generating the users' private keys.

(i) A finite field defined as Fp elements, where p is a large prime number.
(ii) A secure elliptic curve $E(Fp)$ over Fp,
(iii) Generator point $G \in E(Fp)$ whose order is a large prime number, q within $p+1 \pm 2\sqrt{p}$;
(iv) A one-way hash function h whose output is an integer
(v) A secret polynomial:
$$f(x)= e_{t-2} x^{t-2} + e_{t-1} x^{t-1} +..+ e_0 + e_1 x \bmod q$$
where $e_i \in [1, q-1]$ and i=0,1,...t-1;
(vi) The group private key $f(0)=e_0$ and group public key $Y_s=f(0)G$ of the signer group;
(vii) The private keys $f(x_i)$ and the public keys $Y_i=f(x_i)G$ of all signers u_i (i=1,2...,n) in the signer group, where x_i is the public identification code of the signer u_i.. when $i \neq j$, $x_i \neq x_j$ the private key X_r and the public key $Y_r= X_r\,G$ of the specified receiver u_r.

The parameters p, E, q, G, h, Ys, y_i and Y_r are then declared publicly. By means of the secret polynomial function the public and private obtained from original image are shown in Fig. 1.

(A)

(B)

(C)

Fig. 1 Original image (A), public key image (B) and encrypted private key image (C)

3.2 Decryption

After receiving the group-private key block (r, s, r1, r2... rt), the receiver U_v performs the following procedure to recover the message blocks {$m_1,m_2,...m_t$}, as follows.

Step-1: Compute the common session key Z shared with U_s, using the received (r, s), the public key Y_s of the signer group Us, and the private key x_v, as follows.

$$Z= sY_v+(r.X_v)\, Y_s =(x_z,y_z) \qquad (12)$$

Step-2: Recover the message blocks according to the following equation.

i. Compute

$$ut_{i1} = r_i.h(i \,||\, x_z)^{-1} \bmod p$$
$$ut_{i2} = (y_z - s_i) \bmod q \qquad (13)$$

ii. Compute inverse transform

$$k_{i2}= ut_{i2} \oplus \wp(\,ut_1) \text{ and}$$
$$k_{i1}= ut_{i1} \oplus \partial(\,ik_2) \qquad (14)$$

iii. Knowing two points ($1,ik_1$) and ($2,ik_2$), use the Lagrange interpolation and find the polynomial

$$\widetilde{F}(x) = a_0 + a_1 x \bmod p$$

iv. Extract m_i from a_0 as follows $a_0=(m_i||l_i)$

By means of the breaking code of private key sent by the user and the public key known by the t users the image can be recovered.

4. JAC framework extension for IEJPC

JCA [10] and the Common Data Security Architecture (CDSA) are two cryptographic frameworks [12] for conventional public key cryptography. Neither of them supports group-oriented cryptography. Recently JCA has been extended to support RSA based group-oriented cryptography [13]. The present work extends the JCA architecture to integrate the ECC based threshold cryptography, one of the most important types of group-base public key cryptography. The UML class diagram of TC based ECC framework extension is depicted in Fig 2.

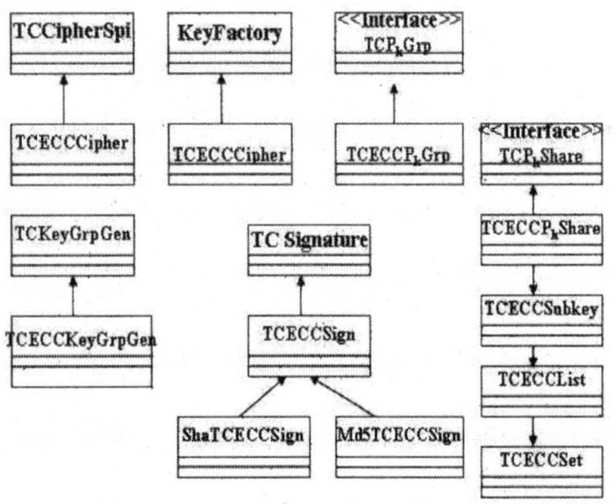

Fig. 2 UML class diagram of ECC-TC framework

Under this extension, various TC providers can be plugged into a security application at runtime. The extension also makes it easy for those JCA-based applications to easily be migrated to use threshold cryptography to enhance system security. It is our belief that this integration would speed up the adoption of threshold cryptography.

To test the above framework extension, we have implemented an example provider based on the threshold ECC algorithm [14], which can be used for threshold signcryption. The example provider has the following concrete classes:

- TCECCCipher inherits the TCCipherSpi and implements the threshold ECC algorithm.It is used in the threshold decryption and in the threshold co-signing as well.
- TCECCSgn extends the TCSgnSpi and provides the threshold signature service.
- TCECCGrpGen is defined to extend the TCKeyGrpGenSpi and used to generate key shares
- TCECCPvtKeyGroup extends the TCPvtKeyGroup and houses a collection of TCECCPvtKeyShr
- TCECCKeyFactory extends the KeyFactorySpi class

5. Conclusion

In large computer complexes, information security becomes a very pertinent issue. Furthermore in applying layers of security, it is also crucial to conserve network resources such as processor time and memory. This paper has attempted to propose a parallel scheme in terms for image threshold encryption which would be superior to well-studied sequential scheme in terms of their efficiency, since they allow parallel encryption as well as parallel decryption. Besides, an attempt is made to improve the efficiency of the proposed scheme by dividing the message into several sub-blocks. The paper has endeavored to integrate the features of ECC and TC to provide the best of both worlds in information security. To bridge gap between the state-of-the-art security research community and the state-of-the-art security practice, a layered framework is proposed for IEJPC extending the functionalities of JCA. In future, we would evaluate the performance of the new scheme for various attacks in comparison to the well-known the existing schemes.

6. References

[1] Schneier B. Cryptography: Theory and Practice. Boca Raton: CRC Press;

[2] Fridrich J. Symmetric Ciphers Based on Two-dimensional Chaotic Maps. *Int. J.Bifurcat Chaos,* 8(6):1259-84, 1998.

[3] Belkhouche F, Qidwai U, Gokcen I, Joachim D. "Binary image transformation using two-dimensional chaotic maps". *In: Proc ICPR 2004*, 823-6, Aug 2004.

[4] Guan ZH, Huang FJ, Guan WJ. "Chaos-based image encryption algorithm", *Phys Lett A* ,346:153-7, 2005.

[5] Lian SG, Sun J, Wang Z. "A block cipher based on a suitable use of chaotic standard map". *Chaos, Solitons and Fractals,* 26(1):117-29, 2005.

[6] Feng Y, Li LJ, Huang F. A "symmetric image encryption approach based on line maps". *In: Proc ISSCAA* 2006, 1362-67, Jan 2006.

[7] Chen G, Mao YB, Chui CK. 'A symmetric image encryption scheme based on 3D chaotic cat maps". *Chaos, Solitons & Fractals*, 12:749-761, 2004.

[8] Mao YB, Chen G, Lian SG, A novel fast image encryption scheme based on the 3D chaotic baker map. *Int. J. Bifurcat Chaos*, 14(10): 3613-24, 2004.

[9] Lian SG, Sun J, Wang Z. Security analysis of a chaos-based image encryption algorithm, *Physica A* 351:645-61, 2005.

[10] Sun Microsystem, "Java cryptography architecture API, specification & reference", http://java.sun.com/j2se/sdk/1.3/docs/guide/security/CryptoSpec.html, 1999.

[11] T. Chuang and J. Lin, "A new multiresolution approach to still image encryption," *Pattern Recognition Image Anal.*, Vol. 9, No. 3, pp. 431-436,1999.

[12] Y. M. Tseng and J. K. Jan, "An Efficient Authenticated Encryption Scheme with Message Linkages and Low Communication Costs", *Journal of Information Science and Engineering*, 41-46, 2002.

[13] The Open Group, "Common security:CDSA and CSSM, version 2", http://www.opengroup.org/publications/catalog/c914.htm.

[14] Y. Huang, D. Rine, and X. Wang, "A JCA-based implementation framework for threshold cryptography", *Computer Security Applications Conference, IEEE Proc.*, 85-91, 2001

Adaptive Nonlinear Channel Equaliser Using MLANN

Gunamani Jena[1], Dr. R Baliarsingh[2] and Dr G M V Prasad[3]
[1]Prof. CSE, BVC Engg Col. (JNTU)
[2]Prof.CSE, NIT, Rourkela
[3]Prof. ECE, BVCEC
g_jena@rediffmail.com rbsingh@nitrkl.ac.in

Abstract

In this paper a novel MLANN-based nonlinear channel equaliser structure using Back Propagation algorithm is proposed for adaptive nonlinear channels. The difficulties associated with channel nonlinearities can be overcome by equalisers employing ANN. Because of nonlinear processing of signals in an ANN it is capable of producing arbitrarily complex decision regions. For this reason the ANN has been utilized for the channel equalisation problems. Here the MLANN structure is used for developing an efficient equaliser for nonlinear channel. The performance of MLANN equaliser has been obtained through computer simulation for different nonlinear channels. The British Broadcasting channel is taken for experiment. The convergence characteristics and bit error rate (BER) are obtained through simulation study and results are analyzed. It is observed that non-linear channel equaliser offers superior performance in terms of BER compared to its LMS counterpart. The MLANN equaliser outperforms the LMS equaliser particularly for nonlinear channels with respect to higher convergence rate and lower mean square error (MSE).

Keywords: MLANN Multilayer Artificial Neural Network, LMS: Least Mean Square, BER: Bit Error Rate, MSE: Mean Square Error, BP: Back Propagation.

1. Introduction

In digital communication the channels deliver the corrupted and transform versions of their input waveforms at the receiver. The corruption of the waveform may be statistically additive and/or multiplicative, because of possible background thermal noise, impulse noise and fades. Transformations performed in the channel are frequency translation, non-linear or harmonic distortion and time dispersion. By using adaptive channel equaliser at the front end of the receiver, the noise introduced in the channel gets nullified and hence signal-to-noise ratio of the receiver improves. This paper deals with the design of an adaptive channel equaliser based on MLANN architecture and the study of its performance.

The performance of the linear channel equaliser employing a linear filter with FIR or lattice structure and using a least mean square (LMS) or recursive least square (RLS) algorithm is limited specially when the nonlinear distortion is severe. In such cases nonlinear equaliser structures may be conveniently employed with added advantages in terms of lower bit error rate (BER), lower mean square error (MSE) and higher convergence rate than those of a linear equaliser. Artificial neural network (ANNs) can perform complex mapping between its input and output space and are capable of forming complex decision boundaries. Further, because of nonlinear characteristics of ANNs these networks of different architecture have found successful application in channel equalisation problem. One of the earliest applications of ANN in digital communication channel equalisation is reported by Siu et. al [6]. They have proposed a multilayer perceptron (MLP) structure for channel equalisation with decision feedback and have shown that the performance of this network is superior to that of a linear equaliser trained with LMS algorithm. Using MLP structures in the problem of channel equalisation, quite satisfactory results have been reported for Pulse Amplitude Modulation (PAM) and Quadrature Amplitude Modulation (QAM) signals [1], [2], [4].

2. Data Transmission System

Consider a synchronous data communication link with 4-QAM signal constellation to transmit a sequence of complex-valued *symbols* $t(k) = x_{2\lambda} + jx_{2\lambda+1}$ at time kT, where 1/T denotes symbol rate, x_λ, $\lambda = 0, 1, ...$, represents the unmodulated information sequence having statistical independent and probable values {1, -1}. The transmitted symbols t(k) may be written in terms of its in-phase and quadrature components as $t(k) = t_{k,I} + jt_{k,Q}$. A discrete-time model for the digital transmission system with equaliser is shown in Fig.1.

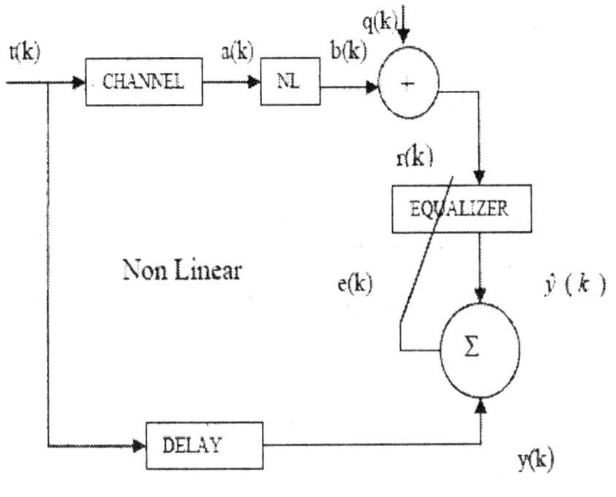

Fig. 1 Digital Transmission system with Equaliser

The combined effect of the transmitter filter, the transmission medium and other components are included in the "channel". A widely used model for a linear dispersive channel is a FIR model whose output at time k may be written as

$$a(k)=\sum_{i=0}^{N_h-1} h(i)\, t(k-i) \qquad (1)$$

Where h(i) are the channel tap values and N_h is the length of the FIR channel. If the nonlinear distortion caused by the channel is to be considered, then the channel model should be treated as nonlinear and its output may be expressed as

$$a'(k) = \varphi(t(k), t(k-1), \ldots, t(k-N_h+1); h(0), h(1), \ldots, h(N_h-1)) \qquad (2)$$

Where φ(.) is some nonlinear function generated by "NL" block. The channel output is corrupted with additive white Gaussian noise q(k) of variance σ^2 to produce r(k), the signal received at the receiver. The received signal r(k) may be represented by its in-phase and quadrature components as $r(k)= r_{k,I} + jr_{k,Q}$. The purpose of the equaliser is to recover the transmitted symbol t(k) or $t(k-\tau)$ from the knowledge of the received signal samples without any error, where τ is the transmitted delay associated with the physical channel.

3. Channel Equaliser As A Pattern Classifier

The channel output is passed through a time delay to produce the equaliser input vector as shown in Figure. 1.1. For this consider a K-ary PAM system with signal constellation given by $s_i = 2i - K - 1; 1 \le i \le K$. The arguments for the channel equaliser as pattern classifier may be extended for QAM signal constellation. The equaliser input at the k th time instant is denoted as U_k and is given by

$U_k = [u_1\ u_2 \ldots u_M]^T$ where $u_i = r(k-i+1)$

for $i = 1, 2, \ldots, M$, the equaliser order is denoted by m and $[.]^T$ denotes matrix transpose. The ANN utilize this information to produce an output, $\hat{y}(k)$ which is an estimate of the desired output $y(k) = t(k-\tau)$. The delay parameter of the equaliser is denoted by τ. Depending on channel output vector U_k, the equaliser tries to estimate an output which is close to one of the transmitted values, s_i, for $i = 1, 2, \ldots, K$. In other words, the equaliser seeks to classify the vector U_k into any one of the K classes. Depending on values of M and N_h, and current and past J – 1 transmitted symbol the classification decision of the equaliser is affected. The J-dimensional transmitted symbol vector at the time instant k is given by

$$\Gamma_k = [t(k)\ t(k-1) \ldots t(k-J+1)]^T \qquad (3)$$

Where $J = M + N_h - 1$. The total number of possible combinations of T_k is given by $N_t = K^J$. When the additive Gaussian noise q(k) is zero, let the M-dimensional channel output vector is given by

$$B_k = [b(k)\ b(k-1) \ldots b(k-M+1)]^T \qquad (4)$$

Corresponding to each transmitted symbol vector Γ_k there will be one channel output vector B_k. Thus, B_k will also have N_t number of possible combinations, called desired channel states. These N_t states are to be partitioned into K classes C_i, $i = 1, 2, \ldots, K$ depending on the value of the desired signal y(k). The states belonging to class C_i are given by $B_k \varepsilon C_i$ *if* $y(k) = s_i$. When the white Gaussian noise is added to the channel, B_k becomes equal to U_k, which is a stochastic vector. Since each of s_i is assumed to be equiprobable, the number of channel states in each class is given by N_t/K. The observation vectors form clusters around the desired channel states and thus, the statistical means of these data clusters are the desired states. Therefore, determining the transmitted symbol t(k) with knowledge of the observation vector U_k is basically a classification problem. For this purpose, a decision function may be formed as follows [7]:

$$DF(U_k) = w_0 + w_1u_1 + w_2u_2 + \ldots + w_Mu_M \qquad (5)$$

Here, w_i, i = 0, 1. M are the weight parameters. Ignoring the time index k, the decision function may be written as $DF(U) = W^T u$, where U is the current channel observation vector augmented by 1 and $W = [w_0\ w_1 \ldots w_M]^T$ is the weight parameter vector. For the K classes, K numbers of decision functions are found with the property

$$DF_i(U) = W_i^T U \ge 0 \text{ if } U \in C_i; \quad < 0 \text{ otherwise} \qquad (6)$$

for $i = 1, 2, \ldots, K$. Here, W_i is the weight vector associated with the i th decision function. A generalized nonlinear decision function is needed to take care of many practical linearly non-separable situations and this can be formed as

$$DF(U) = \sum_{i=0}^{N_f} w_i \phi_i(U) \qquad (7)$$

where the $\{\phi_i(U)\}$, $i = 1, 2, \ldots, N_f$ are real, single-valued functions of the input pattern U, $\phi_o(U) = 1$ and N_f is the number of terms used in the expansion of the decision function DF(U). Let us define a vector U^* with each of the components are the functions $\phi_i(U)$ and given by $U^* = [1 \phi_1(U) \phi_2(U) \ldots\ldots \phi_{Nf}(U)]^T$.

The decision function may be expressed as

$$DF(U) = W^T . U^* \qquad (8)$$

Thus using $\{\phi_i(U)\}$, the (M + 1)-dimensional augmented channel observation vector U may be transformed into a(N_f + 1)-dimensional vector U^*. Using this decision function, complex decision boundaries can be formed to carry out nonlinear classification problems. This may be achieved by employing different ANN structures for the channel equalisation problem, which is described in the following sections.

4. ANN Structures for Equalisation

In this paper MLANN structure and LMS structure have been discussed for nonlinear channel equalisation problem and their performance in terms of convergence speed, MSE level, and BER is compared by taking different linear and nonlinear channel models. Brief description of the MLANN structure is given below.

4.1 Multilayer Artificial Neural Network

The general architecture along with detail processing in a single node is depicted in Fig. 2 and Fig. 3.

Let $X^{(l)}$ be a a(n_l + 1)-dimensional vector representing l th layer output of the MLP for l = 0, 1, ..., L, where L is the number of layers and n_l is the number of nodes in the layer l. Let $X^{(0)}$ be the input pattern vector given by $X^{(0)} = U$, where $U = [1, u_1\ u_2 \ldots U_{n0}]^T$ is the input pattern applied to the MLP. Since no processing takes place in the input layer of the MLP, the input becomes equal to the output for this layer. At the k th instant, U(k) and its corresponding desired output pattern Y(k) are applied to the MLANN and the estimated output of the network $\hat{Y}$ (k) is computed.

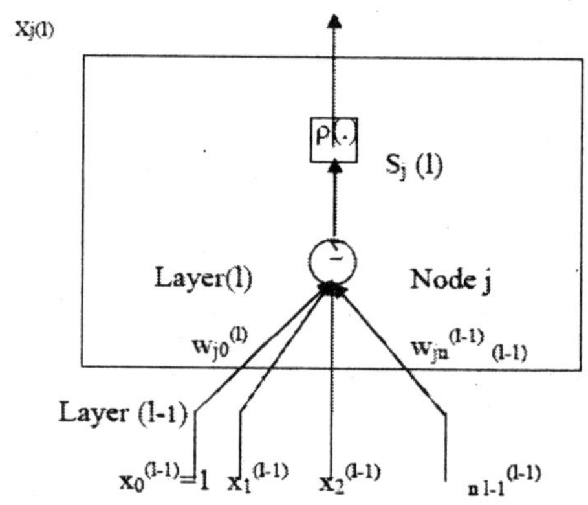

Fig. 2

Here, $\hat{Y}(k) = X^{(L)}$. The error vector at the k th instant is computed as $e(k) = Y(k) - \hat{Y}(k)$. The weights associated with the network are then updated using the most popular BP algorithm [5, 8]. This procedure is repeated till the mean square error (MSE) of the network approaches a minimum value. The MSE at time index k may be defined as $\eta(k) = (1/n_L)\sum_{j=1}^{n_L}[e_j(k)]^2$, where $e_j(k)$ is the error associated with the j th output node given by $e_j(k) = y_j(k) - \hat{y}_j(k)$.

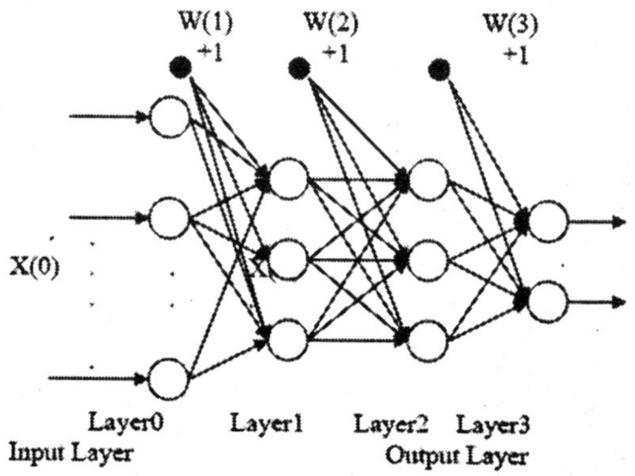

Fig. 3 MLANN Structure

Table 1

Operations	MLANN
Addition	$3\sum_{i=0}^{L-1} n_i n_{i+1} + 3n_L - n_0 n_1$
Multi	$4\sum_{i=0}^{L-1} n_i n_{i+1} + 3\sum_{i=1}^{L} n_i - n_0 n_1 + 2n_L$
Tanh(.)	$\sum_{i=1}^{L} n_i$
Cos(.)/sin(.)	-

$n_0^+ = n_0 + 1$

5. MLANN-Based Channel Equalisation

An equalisation scheme for 4-QAM signals is shown in Fig. 1.3. Each of the in-phase and the quadrature component of the received signal at time instant k, $r_{k,I}$ and $r_{k,Q}$ passes through a tapped delay line. These delay signals constitute the input pattern to the ANN and is given by $U(k) = [u_1\ u_2\ ...\ u_{M-1}]^T = [r_{k,I}\ r_{k,Q}\ r_{k-1,I}\ r_{k-1,Q}\ ...]^T$. At the time instant k, U(k) is applied to the ANN and the network produces two outputs $\hat{y}_1$ and $\hat{y}_2$ corresponding to estimated value of the in-phase and quadrature component of the transmitted symbol or its delayed version, respectively. For the equalisation problem, MLANN structure along with a linear one trained with LMS algorithm are employed for the simulation studies. The BP algorithm is employed for MLANN-based equalisers. Further, in all the MLANN structures, all the nodes except those of the input layer have tanh(.) nonlinearity, as activation function is basically a four-category classification problem. Since equalisation is basically four nonlinear boundaries can be formed by using an ANN, it may be conveniently employed to form discriminate functions to classify the input pattern

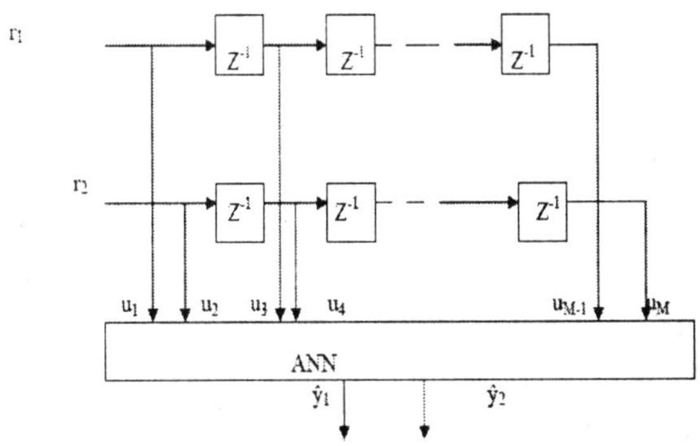

Fig. 4 Structure of an ANN-based equaliser

6. Simulation Studies

Extensive simulation studies have been carried out for the channel equalisation problem as described by Figure. 1.1. The MLANN structure with BP algorithm and a linear FIR equaliser with LMS algorithm are used. The channel impulse response [3] considered in this study is given by

$$h(i) = \begin{cases} \frac{1}{2}\left\{1 + \cos\left[\frac{2\pi}{\Lambda}(i - 2)\right]\right\}, & i = 1, 2, 3 \\ 0, & \text{otherwise} \end{cases} \quad (9)$$

The parameter Λ determines the eigen value ratio (EVR) of the input correlation matrix, $r = E[U(k)U^T(k)]$ where E is the expectation operator. The EVR is defined as $\lambda_{max}/\lambda_{min}$ where λ_{max} and λ_{min} is the largest and the smallest Eigen value of R, respectively. The digital message was with 4-QAM-signal constellation and in the form {±1 ±j1} in which each symbol was obtained from a uniform distribution. To the channel output a zero mean Gaussian noise was added, the received signal power is normalized to unity so as to make the SNR equal to the reciprocal of noise variance at the input of the equaliser. To study the performance of the equaliser under different EVR conditions of the channel, the parameter Λ was varied from 2.9 to 3.5 in steps of 0.2. The value of EVR is given by 6.08, 11.12, 21.71 and 46.82 for Λ value of 2.9, 3.1, 3.3 and 35 respectively. Selection of the detailed structure of MLANN, the various parameter values including the learning rate μ and the momentum rate γ were determined by numerous experiments to give the best results in the MLANN and LMS structures. In the MLANN based equaliser a two-layer structure was selected in which an output layer was six, eight and two, respectively. To have a fair comparison between the LMS and MLANN based equalisers, in both of the cases input pattern was expanded to a 18-dimensional pattern from r(k) and r(k – 1). Both μ and γ were set to a value of 0.02 for both LMS and MLANN structures. The MSE floor corresponds to the steady state value of the MSE, which was obtained after averaging over 500 independent runs each consisting of 3000 iterations. To study the BER performance, each of the equaliser structures was trained with 3000 iterations for optimal weight solution. After completion of the training, testing of the equaliser was carried out. The BER was calculated over 100 independent runs each consisting of 10^4 data samples. Six different channels were studied with the following normalized transfer function given in z-transform form:

$$\begin{aligned} &CH = 1:\ 1.0, \\ &CH = 2:\ 0.447 + 0.894z^{-1}, \\ &CH = 3:\ 0.209 + 0.995z^{-1} + 0.209z^{-2}, \\ &CH = 4:\ 0260 + 0.930z^{-1} + 0.260z^{-2}, \\ &CH = 5:\ 0.304 + 0.903z^{-1} + 0.304z^{-2}, \\ &CH = 6:\ 0.341 + 0.876z^{-1} + 0.341z^{-2}. \end{aligned} \quad (10)$$

CH = 1 corresponds to a channel without any ISI since it has a unity impulse response. CH = 2 corresponds to a non-minimum phase channel [1]. CH = 3, CH = 4, CH =5, and Ch = 6 corresponds to Λ values of 2.9, 3.1, 3.3 and 3.5 respectively. Three different nonlinear channel models with the following types of nonlinearity were introduced (refer to Fig. 2)

$$\begin{aligned} &NL = 0:\ b(k) = a(k), \\ &NL = 1:\ b(k) = \tanh(a(k)), \\ &NL = 2:\ b(k) = a(k) + 0.2a^2(k) - 0.1a^3(k), \\ &NL = 3:\ b(k) = a(k) + 0.2a^2(k) - 0.1a^3(k) + 0.5\cos(\pi a(k)). \end{aligned} \quad (11)$$

NL = 0 corresponds to a linear channel model. NL = 1 corresponds to a nonlinear channel which may occur in the channel due to saturation of amplifiers used in the transmitting system. NL = 2 and NL = 3 are two arbitrary nonlinear channels.

6.1 MSE Performance Study

The convergence characteristic and variation of MSE floor with SNR is described here. Here, the MSE performances of MLANN structures along with a linear LMS-based equaliser are reported considering different channels with linear as well as nonlinear channel models. The convergence characteristics for CH = 6 at SNR level of 15 dB are plotted in Fig. 5. It may be observed that the ANN-based equalisers show much better convergence rate and lower MSE floor than those of the linear equaliser for linear as well as nonlinear channel models. Out of the two the MLANN structures based equaliser maintains its superior performance over the LMS based structures in terms convergence speed and steady state MSE level for the linear and nonlinear channel models.

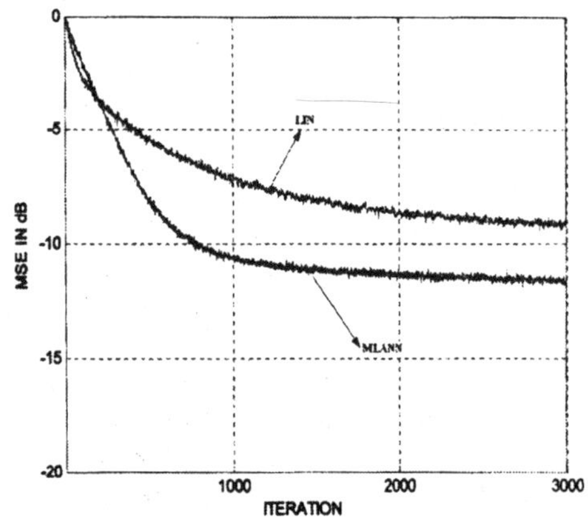

Fig. 5a NL = 0

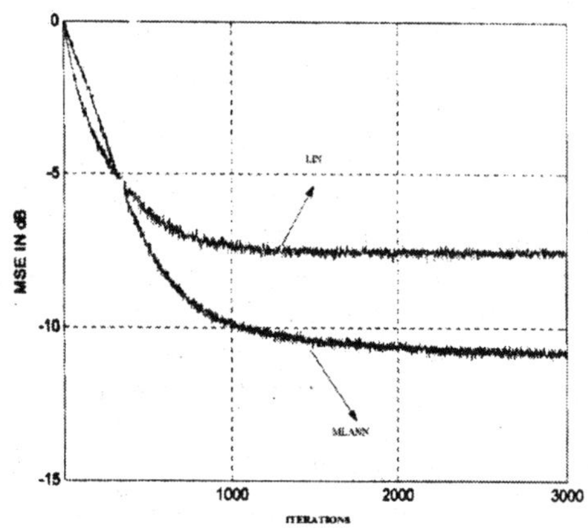

Fig. 5b NL = 1

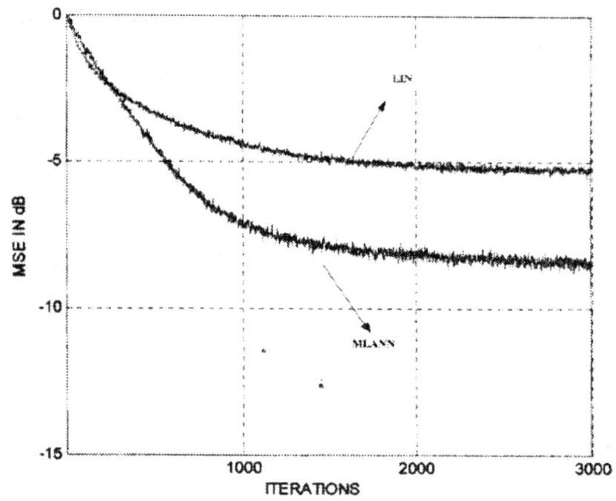

Fig. 5c NL = 2

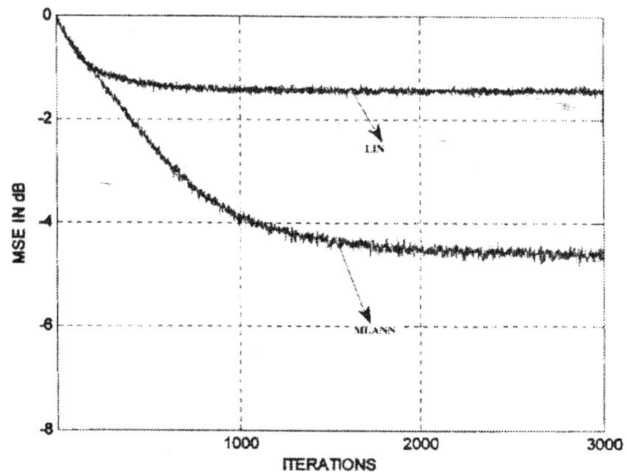

Fig. 5d NL = 3.

Fig. 5. Convergence characteristics of the three ANN-based and linear LMS-based equalisers for CH= 6 with different nonlinear models at SNR of 15 dB

6.2 BER Performance Study

The bit error rate (BER) provides the true picture of performance of an equaliser. The computation of BER was carried out for the channel equalisation with 4-QAM-signal constellation using the MLANN-based and the linear LMS-based structures.

6.3 Variation of BER with SNR

The BER performance for CH = 2 is plotted in Fig. 6. The performance of the MLANN-based equaliser is superior to that of LMS based linear and nonlinear channel models. The MLANN-based equaliser outperforms other structures.

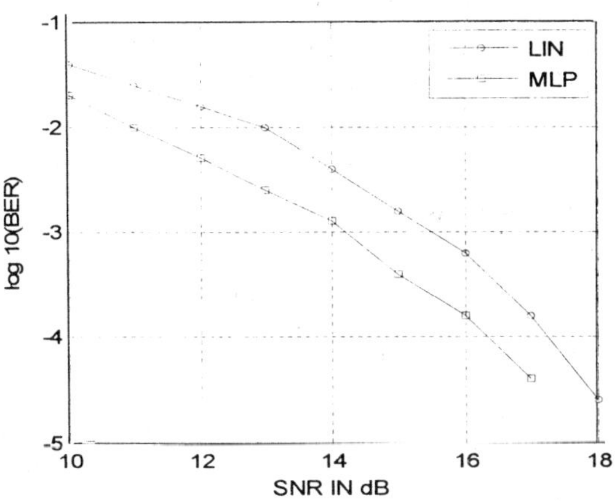

Fig. 6a

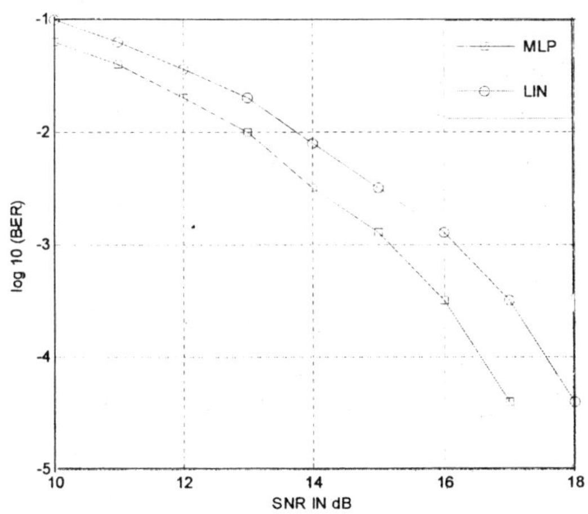

Fig. 6b

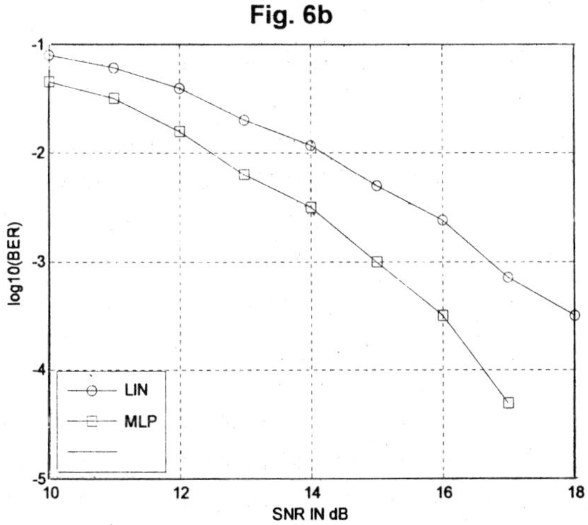

Fig. 6c

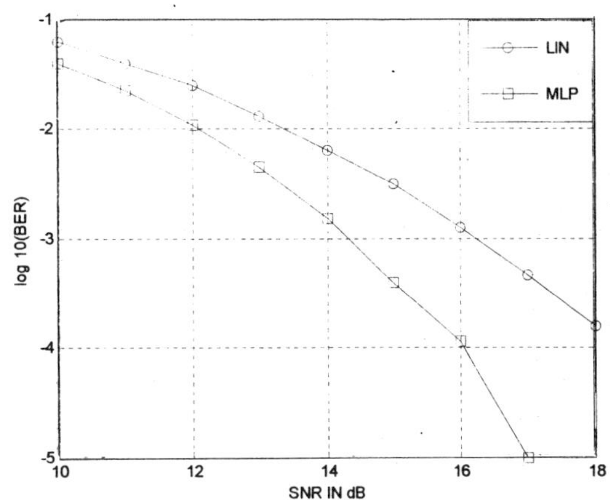

Fig. 6d

Fig. 6 BER performance of the three ANN based and linear LMS based equalisers for CH=2 with variation of SNR (a) NL=0, (b) NL=1, (c) NL=2, (d) NL=3.

6.4 Effect of EVR on BER performance

The BER was computed for channels with different EVR values for linear as well as nonlinear channel models at SNR value of 12 dB. The results obtained are plotted in Fig. 7. As EVR increases the BER performance of all the four equalisers degrades. However, the performance degradation due to increase the EVR is much less in the ANN-based equaliser with comparison to the linear LMS-based equaliser. The performance of the MLANN-based equaliser with linear and the three nonlinear channel models for a wide variation of EVR from 1 to 46.8.

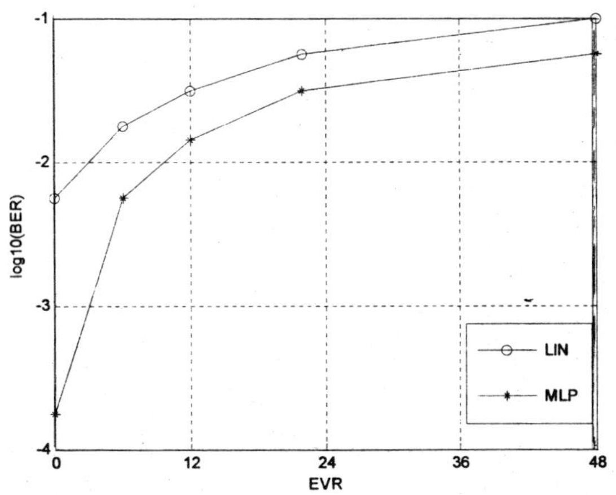

Fig. 7a

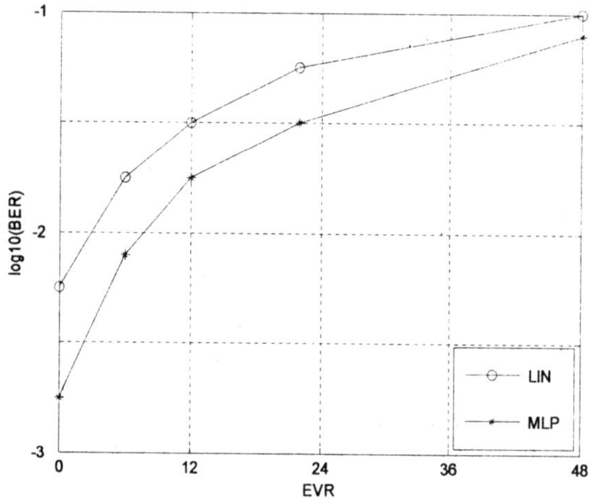

Fig. 7b

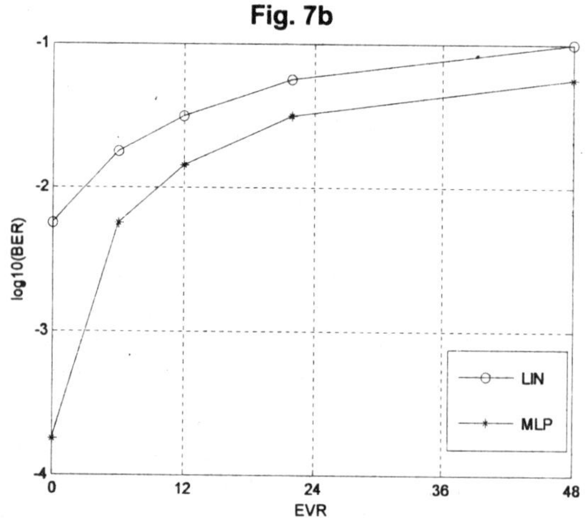

Fig. 7c

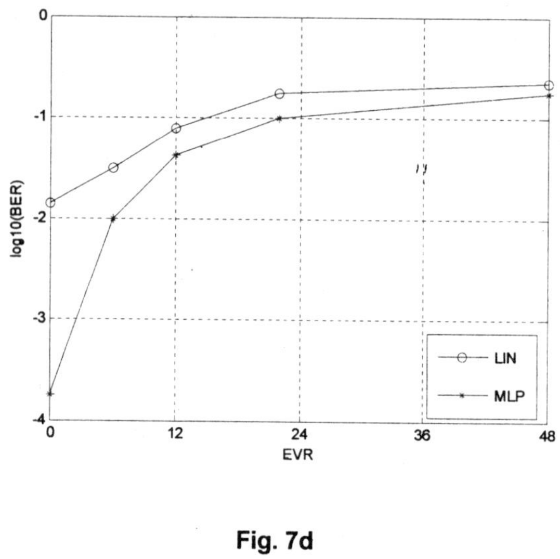

Fig. 7d

Fig.7 Effect of EVR on the BER performance of the three ANN based and linear LMS based equalisers for CH=2 with variation of SNR (a) NL=0, (b) NL=1, (c) NL=2, (d) NL=3

7. Conclusion

Considering channel equalisation as a multi-category classification problem, it is shown that performance of MLANN-based equalisers provide substantial improvement in terms of convergence rate, MSE floor level and BER. In a linear equaliser the performance degrades drastically with increase in EVR, especially when the channel is nonlinear. However, it is shown that, in the MLANN-based equaliser the performance degradation with increase in EVR is not so severe.

8. References

[1] S. Chen, G. J. Gibson, C. F. N. Cowan, and P. M. Grant, "Adaptive channel equalisation of finite nonlinear channels using multilayer perception," Signal Process, vol. 20, pp. 107-119, 1990.

[2] G.J. Gibson, S.Siu, and C.F.N. Cowan, "The application of nonlinear structures to the reconstruction of binary signals," IEEE Trans. Signal processing, vol.39 pp. 1877-1884, Aug.1991.

[3] S. Haykin, Adaptive Filter Theory, 2nd ed. Englewood Cliffs, NJ: Prentice –Hall, 1991.

[4] M. Meyer and G. Pfeiffer, "Multilayer Perceptron based decision feed–back equalisers for channels with inter symbol interference" Proc. IEE, vol. 140, pt. 1, pp. 420-424, Dec.1993.

[5] Y. H. Pao, "Adaptive Pattern Recognition and Neural Networks. Reading," M.A.: Addison –Wesley, 1989.

[6] S. Siu, G. J. Gibson, and C.F.N. Cowan, "Decision feedback equalisation using neural network structures and performance comparison with standard architecture," Proc. Inst. Elect. Engg, vol. 137, pt. 1, pp. 221-225, Aug. 1990.

[7] J. T. Tou and R.C. Gonzalez, Pattern Recognition Principles. Reading, MA: Addison –Wesley, 1981.

[8] B. Widrow and M.A. Lehr, "30 Years of adaptive neural networks: Perceptron, madaline and back propagation," Proc. IEEE, vol. 78, pp. 1415-1442, Sept. 1990.

Key Agreement Protocol for Dynamic Peer Group with Efficient Authentication

M.Sukanya
M.E Computer Science and Engineeering, Adhiyamaan College of Engineering, Hosur, TN
sukan_07@yahoo.co.in

Abstract

Many applications in Dynamic Peer Group are becoming increasing popular nowadays. In these group-oriented applications, it is important to establish the group key securely and efficiently. The members in Dynamic Peer Group are symmetrical and dynamic, so the contributory key agreement is more appropriate. In this project an efficient and authenticated key agreement scheme has been proposed in the Dynamic Peer Group. In this scheme, the members in the Dynamic Peer Group are divided into several clusters according to Linker Cluster Architecture. In each cluster, the members perform the BD protocol to establish the cluster key and the TGDH protocol to generate the group key among the clusters. This method can not only avoid the weakness of AKA (Auxiliary Key Agreement) of BD, but also reduce the computation cost of TGDH scheme. In this scheme the members have been authenticated by an ID-based signature, and the security is proved in Random Oracle Model.

Keywords: Dynamic Peer Group, Linker Cluster architecture, BD protocol, TGDH protocol, AKA (Auxiliary Key Agreement).

1. Introduction

Many multiparty key agreement protocols have been proposed in the latest twenty years. The first key agreement applied in multiparty was proposed by Ingemarsson et al. in 1982 which was named ING. BD protocol proposed by Burmester and Desmedt was the first constant round protocol. The scheme is proven secure provided the DH problem is sound. It needs only constant-round and the computation cost is not expensive. However, when membership events happen, in order to ensure the independence of group key, all the members in the group have to start the protocol at the first step again. If the dynamic events are frequent, the merits of BD are not noticeable. TGDH protocol was proposed by Kim et al. which based on binary tree. The hierarchical idea is applied in this scheme and it can reduce the communication cost when the membership events happen. But the computation cost of TGDH is expensive. When the tree is deeper, the number of exponentiation is more notable. The number of exponentiation is the main factor in the computational overhead.

In this paper, an efficient and authenticated key agreement scheme is proposed which can be applied in the DPG. In this scheme, the members in the group are divided into clusters, so that the members whose physical locations are nearby can be in a cluster . Members in a cluster arranged in a circle perform the BD protocol to establish the cluster key. All the clusters arranged in a tree perform the TGDH protocol to generate the group key. This method can not only avoid the weakness of AKA of BD protocol, but also reduce the computation cost of TGDH scheme. The performance of the new group key agreement is analyzed in section *4*. We also provide an ID-based signature scheme to authenticate all the members, and we prove the security of signature algorithm in Random Oracle Model.

2. Related Work

Signature Scheme: In this paper, ID-Based signature is used to authenticate the members in the key exchange and we prove the security of the signature scheme in Random Oracle Model. Now we introduce the ID-Based key setting using pairing (SK key setting for short) first. This scheme is proposed by Sakai and Kasahara in 2003. As Cheng said this kind of key setting has the potential to improve performance, where an identity string is mapped to an element h of the cyclic group $Z\square q$ instead of a point on an elliptic curve directly.

Hardness Assume: Boneh proposed a new complexity assumption called the Strong Diffie-Hellman (SDH) assumption. This assumption has similar properties to the Strong RSA assumption, hence the name.

Table 1 The Notation of Our Protocol

n	The number of group members
p, q	Prime number
α	The generator of Z_p^*
G	A cyclic group
P	The generator of G
M_i	The member of group
r_i	The random value chosen by member M_i
k_{C_i}	Cluster key of cluster C_i
bk_{C_i}	The blinded value of cluster key
$k_{<i,j>}$	The value of node $< i, j >$ in the tree
$bk_{<i,j>}$	The blinded value of $k_{<i,j>}$
$head_{C_i}$	The header of ClusterC_i
$sign_i(M)$	Signature algorithm
$veri_j(M)$	Verification algorithm
Key	The group key

3. "Our Scheme"

3.1 Notation

In this paper, we define the notation as **Table 1**:

3.2 Description of Our Scheme

In this scheme, the members of a group are split into clusters Ci. The members in the cluster are ranged as a ring; the relationship of each cluster is tree structure. We define the cluster in **Figure 1.** (A) As $C1$, there are six members nodes in $C1$, and node$M2$ is the header (denoted as $headC1$), who takes the charge of the communication with the headers of other clusters.

3.3 Initial Key Agreement (IKA)

3.3.1 Key Agreement in Cluster

BD protocol is performed in the cluster to establish the cluster key. We take $C1$ for example.

1. The member M_i chooses r_i randomly, computes $Y_i = \alpha^{ri} \bmod p$, and sends $signi\ (Y_i)$ to M_{i+1} and M_{i-1};
2. Each member M_i receives $sign_{i+1}(Yi+1)$ and $sign_{i-1}(Yi-1)$ and to verify the sender. If the verification equation in $veri_i(Yi+1)$ and $veri_i(Yi-1)$ is hold, then computes $Xi = (Yi+1/Yi-1)^{ri}$, and sends $sign_i(X_i)$ to everyone in the cluster;
3. After verifying the senders, M_i computes the cluster key:

$k_{c1} = Y^{tri}{}_{i-1} \cdot X^{t-1}{}_i \cdot X^{t-2}{}_{i+1} \cdot \ldots X_{i-2} \bmod p = \alpha^{r1r2+r2r3+\cdots+r6r1}$. Since there are 6 members in cluster $C1$, so the value of t is 6.

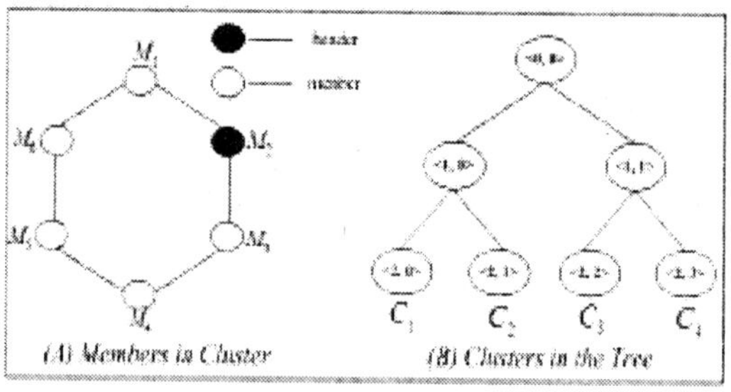

Fig. 1 The Logic Topology of Group

Table 2. Relationship between the Clusters

$S--Sender$

$R--Receiver$

$S \setminus R$	C_1	C_2	C_3	C_4
C_1	$--$	bk_{C_1}	$--$	$--$
C_2	bk_{C_2}	$--$	$bk_{<1,0>}$	$bk_{<1,0>}$
C_3	$--$	$--$	$--$	bk_{C_3}
C_4	$bk_{<1,1>}$	$bk_{<1,1>}$	bk_{C_4}	$--$

3.3.2 Group Key Agreement among Clusters

After the cluster key k_{Ci} being established, the structure among each cluster is a tree, and each cluster can be viewed as a leaf node in this tree. The TGDH protocol is performed among clusters. The header of each cluster takes charge of the communication with the other headers, such as broadcasts the blinded values of cluster key bk_{Ci}. In **Figure 1.**(B), there are four clusters in the group, we define the cluster keys of the four clusters is $k_{Ci}(i = 1, 2, 3, 4)$ respectively. When each member computers the group key, the leaf node of the tree needn't the blinded value of all the leaf nodes, *i.e.* the members in cluster C_2 compute the group key, only to know the blinded value of C_1 which is bk_{C1} and the blinded value of the non-leaf node $< 1, 1 >$ which is $bk_{<1,1>}$. Therefore, different from TGDH [3], we define that the blinded value of this non-leaf node is provided by the rightmost leaf node of the subtree rooted by this non-leaf node. For example, the blinded value $bk_{<1,1>}$ is sent by the header of cluster C_4 in the **Figure 1.**(B). In this method, the communication overhead is lower than TGDH protocol because not all the blinded values must be sent to the leaf node. Explicitly, we express the relationship as the **Table 2**: (if C_i does not need the blinded value sent by C_j, then the corresponding place is denoted as '$--$')

In **Table 2**, for C_1, we know that the members in cluster C_1 need the blinded value bk_{C2} sent by $headC2$ and the blinded value $bk_{<1,1>}$ sent by $head_{C4}$. $head_{C2}$ broadcasts $sign_{headC2}\ (bk_{C2})$ to members of C_1. After verifying the sender, the members in $C1$ can computer the shared value $k_{<1,0>} = (bk_{C2})^{kC1} \bmod p = \alpha^{kC1\ kC2}$

mod$p$. The $headC_4$ broadcasts $sign_{headC4}(bk_{1,1})$ to C_1, and all the members in $C1$ can compute the group key: $Key = (bk_{1,1})^{k_{1,0}} = (\alpha^{\alpha kC3\, kC4})\alpha^{kC1\, kC2}$ $= \alpha^{\alpha kC1 kC + kC kC4}$.

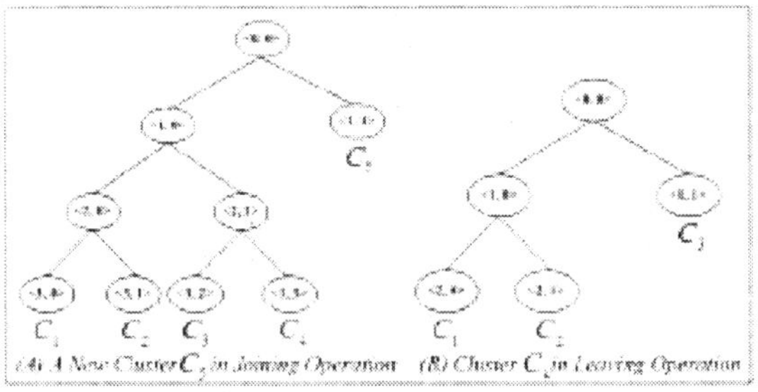

Fig. 2 Joining and Leaving Operation

3.4 Auxiliary Key Agreement (AKA)

BD protocol is efficient with only constant communication rounds to exchange the information, but it is short for tackling with the dynamic events. When a member joins /leaves the group, in order to guarantee the backward/ forward secrecy of the group key, the other members must choose the random value again, in other words, the BD protocol lacks of convenient AKA. In our scheme the group is split into several clusters, and when new members join in or old members leave, the group events will happen in some clusters instead of entire group. In this way, only these members in the changed cluster change the random values.

3.4.1 Join

If M_{n+1} join the group, we assume that M_{n+1} join C_i according to Linked Cluster Architecture . M_{n+1} multicast a join request message with its blinded value to C_i and $head_{Ci}$ responds. The members in C_i choose the random values again, establish the cluster key according to section *3.3.1*, and $head_{Ci}$ refreshes the blinded value bk_{Ci} in **Table 2**. All the members of group compute the group key according to section *3.3.2*.

3.4.2 Leave

Similar to section *3.4.1*, if M_i leaves the group, the other members of cluster of M_i choose the random values again and compute the new cluster key, and establish the new group key according to section *3.4.1*.

3.4.3 Multiple Members Join

a. If these members are discrete, they join one by one according to section *3.4.1*.

b. If these members form a cluster, they perform as section *3.4.5*.

3.4.4 Multiple Members Leave

A network fault may cause leave of multiple members at the same time. When this kind of case happens, it performs as section *3.4.2*.

3.4.5 Join and Leave as Cluster

If a new group as a cluster merges with original group, it joins in the tree according to TGDH. See **Figure 2.(A)**. In this case, $head_{C4}$ gives $bk_{<0,0>}$ (the blind value of original group key) to new cluster C_5, and $head_{C5}$ broadcasts their value bk_{C5} to group. When a cluster is split from original group, the operation is similar to the leaving of TGDH. According to **Figure 1.(B)**, if $C4$ leaves the group, cluster C_3 replaces the parent node of C_3 and C_4 (see **Figure 2.(B)**), and all the members refresh the value of the **Table 2** according to section *3.3.2* to compute the new group key.

3.5 ID-Based Signature

The members must communicate with each other to establish the group key, *i.e.* in the cluster C_1, M_1 and M_2 exchange the blinded value α^{r1} and α^{r2}, respectively. If members do not verify the identities of senders when receive these blinded values, it is vulnerable to man-in-middle attack.

In this section, a signature scheme is proposed: $signi(M)$ and $verij(M)$ to authenticate the members.

3.5.1 Setup

The system parameters are generated by Key Generation Center (KGC). $G1$ is an additive group and G_2 is a multiplicative group. The order of both the two groups is prime q and a bilinear map $e: G_1 \times G_1 \rightarrow G_2$. P is one of the generators of G_1; s is the master key of the KGC. H_1 and $H2$ are hash functions against collision, H_1: $\{0, 1\}^{\square} \rightarrow Z^{\square}_q$, H_2: $\{0, 1\} \square \times G_1 \rightarrow Z^{\square}_q$. The system parameters are $(G_1, G_2, e, q, P, sP, H_1, H_2)$, and they are public.

3.5.2 Extract

Our key extract scheme is based on the SK key setting [9]. For given identity IDA, the master key s and system parameters, $H_1(IDA) = a_A \varepsilon Z^{\square}_q$. The secret key of ID_A is $d_A = (s + a_A)-1P$ and $Q_A = a_AP + sP$ is the corresponding public key of ID_A.

3.5.3 Signature Algorithm: *signi* (*M*)

We assume the message is M, signer i chooses $r_i \varepsilon Z^{\square}_q$ randomly, and computers: $U = r_iP$, $h = H_2(M,U)$, $V = (r_i + h)(s + a_i)-1P$. The signature of M is (U, V).

3.5.4 Verification Algorithm: *verij(M)*

When receives (U, V), verifier j computes $h = H2\ (M, U)$ firstly, and verifies whether the following equation is hold or not: $e(V,Q) = e(P,U + hP)$.

4. "Performance Analysis"

4.1 Communication Overhead

The communication overhead is measured by the number of the messages. That is to say the overall communication overhead of the scheme is the summation of messages exchanged in cluster and messages exchanged among clusters. In order to compare these protocol conveniently, we assume the size of group is n, and the size of the each cluster is k. In IKA phase, members in cluster perform BD protocol and the message overhead is $C^1{}_b = n\ k\ [2k+k(k-1)] = n+nk$. Among clusters the members perform TGDH protocol. According to **Table 2**. we know that the message overhead which the leaf nodes need to send is $k \cdot \sum^{n/k}{}_{i=1} h_i$, where h_i is the height of leaf node i. So the message overhead in performing TGDH is

$C^1{}_t : K \cdot \sum_{i=1}{}^{n/k}\ h_i < K \cdot n/k \cdot \log n/k = n \cdot \log n/k$. Therefore, we can compute the overall communication overhead in IKA phase as

$C^1 = C^1{}_b + C^1{}_t = n + nk + n \cdot \log n/k.$

In AKA (we only discuss single member joining in for short), a new member join in a certain cluster, all the members in this cluster must choose the random value again, so the overhead of message in cluster is $C^2{}_b = 2(k + 1) + k\ (k + 1) = k^2 + 3k + 2$.When perform the TGDH, the header of cluster whose cluster key has been updated sends the blinded values of key path to the other members who need. The message overhead of this phase is

$C^2t = K(\sum_{i=0}{}^{\log n/k-1} 2^i + \log n/k)\ K(n/k - 1 + \log n/k - 1) = n + k \log n/k - 2k$.So we can compute the overall communication in AKA as: $C^2 = C^2{}_b + C^2{}_t = K^2 + 3K + 2 + n + K \log n/k - 2k = k^2 + k + n + k \log n/k + 2$.

To see **Table 3**, this is the performance comparison of these three kinds of protocols. It is said that, if the size of group is approximate seven the BD protocol is the most efficient. In order to compute conveniently, we define that $n = 100,\ k = 10$. Fig. 3 describes the performance of the three protocols in IKA and AKA.

Table 3 Comparison of the Three Kinds of Protocols

Protocols	Communication Overhead		Computation Overhead
	IKA	AKA	
BD	$n^2 + n$	$n^2 + n$	constant
TGDH	$2n^2 - 3n - n(logn - 1)$	$(n-1)\log n$	$\log n$
OUR	$n + nk + n\log\frac{n}{k}$	$k^2 + k + n + k\log\frac{n}{k} + 2$	$\log\frac{n}{k}$

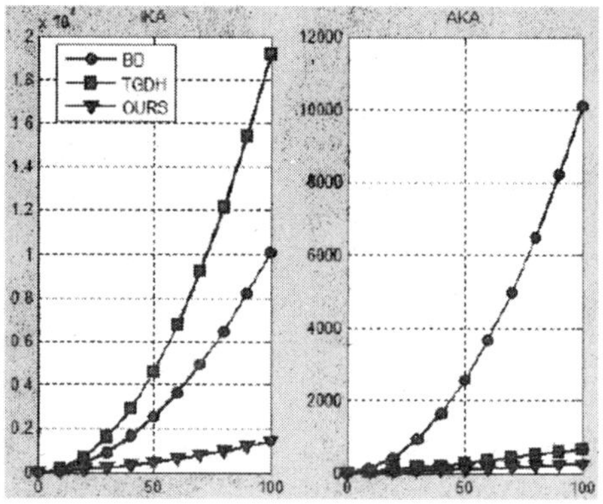

Fig. 3 Performance of IKA and AKA in the Three Protocols

4.2 Computation Overhead

When establish the group key, the exponential operation is used in our scheme, so we use the number of exponential operations to measure the computation overhead. It is constant of exponential operation in establishing the cluster key; the overhead of the TGDH protocol depends on the tree height and it means the number of exponential is log2 (n/k).

5. "Conclusions "

An authenticated key agreement protocol is proposed which can be adapted by the dynamic peer group. The group is split into several clusters, the BD protocol is performed in each cluster and the TGDH protocol is performed among clusters. My scheme combines the traits of BD and TGDH, therefore the performance of communication and computation is improved. The ID-based signature prevents the man-in- middle attack, and the security of signature algorithm which withstands existential forgery on adaptively chosen message attack is proved.

References

[1] New Efficient and Authenticated Key Agreement Protocol in Dynamic Peer Group, Shengke Zeng, Mingxing He and Weidong Luo, Xihua University, China,ARES,March 2008.

[2] J.B. Dennis and E. Anthony. The Architectural Organization of a Mobile Radio Network via a distributed Algorithm. IEEE Transactions on Communications, 29(11), 1694-1701, 1981.

[3] M. Burmester and Y. Desmedt. A Secure and Efficient Conference Key Distribution System. In: Proc.Eurocrpt'94, Berlin: Springer-Verlag, 275-286, 1994.

[4] Y. Kim, A. Perrig and G. Tsudik. Tree-based Group Key Agreement, ACMTransactions on Information and System Security (TISSEC), 60-96, 2004.

[5] I. Ingemarsson, D. Tang and C. Wong. A conference key distribution system. IEEE Trans. on Information Theory, 28(5), 714-720, 1982.

[6] W. Diffie and M.E. Hellman. New Directions in Cryptography. IEEE Transaction Information Theory, 22(6), 644-654, 1976.

[7] S.Hongsong and M.Mingxing. A Communication-Efficient Key Agreement Protocol in Ad hoc Networks. IEEE International Conference on Wireless Networks, Communications, and Mobile Computing, Vol.1, 285- 291, 2005.

[8] D. Boneh and M. Franklin. Identity-Based Encryption from the Weil Pairing. In: Proc. Crypto'01, 213-229, Berlin: Springer-Verlag, 2001.

[9] D. Boneh, B. Lynn and H. Shacham. Short Signatures from the Weil Pairing. In: Proc. Asiacrypt'01, 514- 532, Berlin: Springer-Verlag, 2001.

[10] Y.Amir, Y.Kim and C.N Rotaru. On the Performance of Group Key Agreement Protocols.ACM Transactions on Information and System Security, 7(3), 457-488, 2004.

[11] R.Sakai and M.Kasahara. ID based Crytosystems with Pairing on Elliptic Curve. Cryptology ePrint Archive, Report, PP.054, 2003.

[12] Z-Cheng and L.Chen. On security proof of McCullagh-Barreto's key agreement protocol and its variants. Cryptology ePrint Archive, Report, PP.201, 2005.

Implementation of Wi-Fi in Industrial Automation with Enhanced Security

Shankar Ganesh, Kamal Kumar Panta and Venkata Veeravalli
Cisco Offshore Development Center, HCL Technologies, Chennai.

Abstract

This white paper focuses on potential application of Wi-Fi in Industrial Automation and methods to implement by first converting the serial data of a machine to TCP/IP format the using Wi-Fi for communication.The paper also describes about the present Wi-Fi performances, Vulnerabilities of using Wi-Fi with several case studies and innovative method to enhance the security features.

1. Introduction

After a few years of small-scale pilot tests, Wireless LANs (WLANs) based on the IEEE 802.11 standards are now moving into the mainstream for enterprise customers. The good news is that overall the wireless LAN technology is maturing. The original crop of products ware designed for the requirements of home users and small-scale commercial installations. These solutions scale to support networks incorporating dozens or hundreds of access points with thousands of users. We are now witnessing the introduction of tools that will allow us to build and maintain those large-scale wireless LANs with features to address the security, performance, and manageability requirements of commercial users. That also means commercial buyers will have to be able to sift through the options and develop a solution that will provide solid foundation from which to grow.

The purpose of this white paper is to identify potential areas of future Wi-Fi application in Industries and suggesting a innovative method to improve security features. We will assume a basic understanding of WLAN fundamentals.

2. Expanding Wi-Fi Market from WLAN To Industrial Automation

As we all see Wi-Fi has a enormous growth in WLAN. After analyzing Wi-Fi performance, we did a market survey of Wi-Fi products. Today Wi-Fi products are mostly used for Wireless Data & Voice communication between wired & wireless products in WLAN only. From this survey we came to a wild idea of expanding Wi-Fi to industries.

3. Industrial Automation

With the development of network and telecommunication technologies, advanced communication infrastructure has rapidly spread to other sectors of the industry. As a result, various attempts to introduce Ethernet and TCP/IP with Wi-Fi to factory floors by combining industrial communication technologies used in controlling, monitoring or data acquisition, and IT (Information Technologies) characterized by voice/data/screen communication, can be found in various practical applications.

Traditionally, factory automation systems have been lead by manufacturers, and as a result, communication methods and protocols have tended to emphasize real-time control, stability and reliability rather than interoperability. However, as standard Ethernet and TCP/IP technologies were introduced to the scene of industry alongside rapid development and expansion of Ethernet technologies, such tendencies have begun to change.

The established industrial bus standards existing in various forms are reinforcing real-time adaptability and reliability and switching to Ethernet bases to Wi-Fi. The Ethernet based systems are also being improved upon to make them endure in harsh factory environments.

By introducing low-cost, standard Ethernet, Wi-Fi and TCP/IP technologies with an existing infrastructure to devices such as PLC, sensors and controllers in the factory floor, added value such as remote control, setup facilitation, lowered costs, system efficiency, as well as prospective added value resulting from interdisciplinary usage and integration of established business systems, is anticipated.

Application Areas

- Remote management of the various equipments on the factory floor
- Remote work program transfer for the PLC and the robot on the factory floor
- Sensor data acquisition and monitoring

Benefits

- Cost-reduction in the system development due to using low-cost, industry-standard Ethernet technologies
- Labor cost reduction and improved efficiency due to remote management
- Easier operation environment using various IT technologies such as Internet, Web, and Database
- Cost-reduction due to TCP/IP-oriented, simplified network hierarchy
- Easy to establish company ERP (Enterprise Resource Planning) system by connecting TCP/IP-based business system with manufacturing system

4. Case Studies

1. Factory Work Program Download: Hyundai Heavy Industries:

Hyundai Heavy Industries is one of the market leaders in the heavy industry. Their product line ranges from shipbuilding, engines, plant to various industrial electronic systems.

Target System: Industrial Robot:

For simple, repetitive, and dangerous tasks in manufacturing automation, various industrial robots have been widely used in the factory floor in machine, electronics and chemical industries.

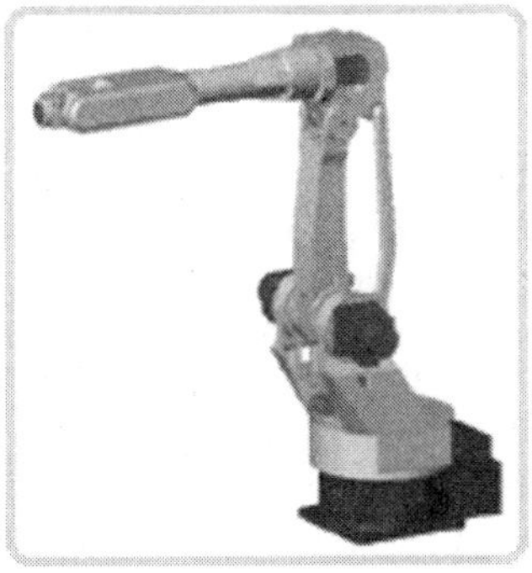

Hyundai Industrial Robot

Motive

There are multiple industrial robots operating in production lines for assembly and welding, the controller of which has a serial console port for work program downloads. In the factory floor, the robots are managed using PCs directly connected to the serial console port of the robot controller, and the work program is also downloaded to the robots through this connection. As a result, multiple PCs are required for the management of multiple robots and accordingly the situation prohibits efficient and systematic management due to the additional management layer from the PCs. Therefore, they decided to move to an Ethernet-based system in which the robot operation is directly managed from the central office through an Ethernet network and the work program is downloaded as such. So once converted into TCP/IP, we can also connect it with Wi-Fi devices for transferring data.

System Diagram:
Previous System

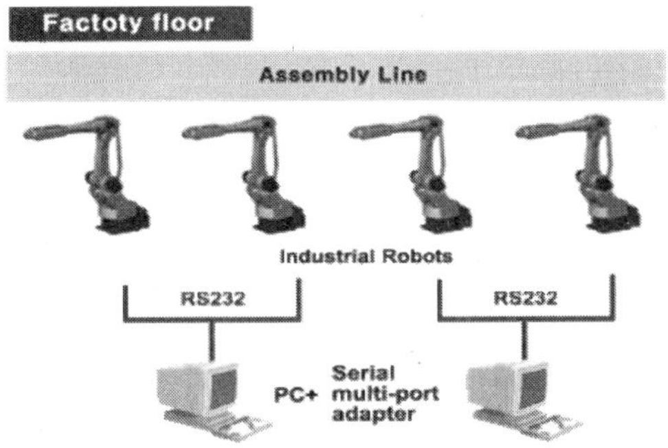

As you see here data to robots are given via wired serial connection, which can extend to a max of 100M.

New System

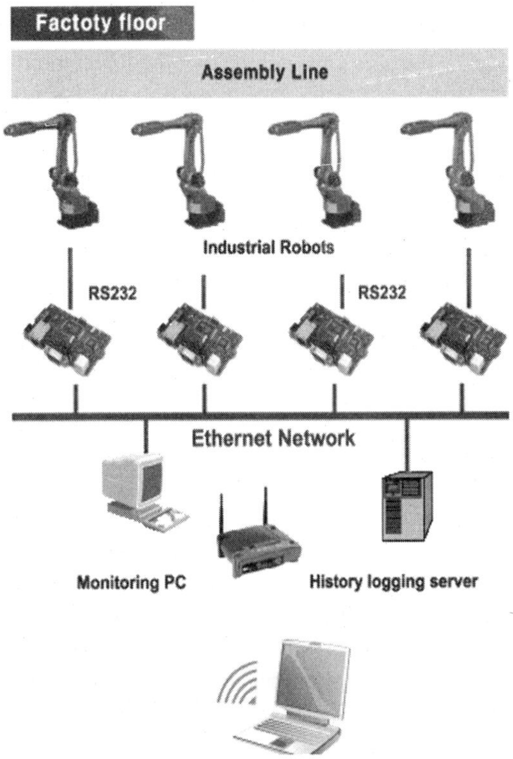

Here serial data is converted to TCP/IP first and once TCP/IP it can be sent by both wired connection for central monitoring and wireless for mobile monitoring.

Benefits

The original management system could control and monitor the onsite robot system from PCs on the local site. In the new system, any computers on the network including the central management office can manage the robots directly. As a result, it enables the production manager to download the work program directly to multiple robots simultaneously through the TCP/IP network, to make the whole system more efficient and flexible with the assistance of the database system.

5. Understanding Wi-Fi Performance

Now we will focus on Wi-Fi performance and security issues. Much has been said about the security of 802.11 wirelesses LAN (WLAN), or Wi-Fi. The weakness of the original encryption, Wired Equivalent Privacy (WEP), led to the adoption of Wi-Fi Protected Access (WPA), a standard that brings Wi-Fi up to the same level of security as Internet access. Less has been said about the true performance or capacity of Wi-Fi. Descriptions of the "maximum" throughput, either 11 Mbps (for 802.11b) or 54 Mbps (for 802.11a/g), are generally accompanied by a disclaimer about how your actual throughput will be less. Network managers and architects need to look seriously at Wi-Fi capacity because it will directly affect the user experience and network design, and it is not as easily fixed as security. Network managers and architects must understand the reality of Wi-Fi capacity for several important reasons:

- So that the network can be properly designed in the first place.
- Because the Wi-Fi network will more than likely have to be expanded in the future to meet growing user demands.
- Probably most importantly, so users have realistic expectations.

Users have become accustomed to high-speed wired networks. Generally, when response times are slow, it is because of applications, not the network. People have forgotten the days when the network itself could be the problem. Wi-Fi takes us back to those "bad" old days. How bad is a Wi-Fi network? It is not all doom and gloom—wireless LAN throughput is better than dial-up, which many telecommuters rely upon. Wi-Fi can provide adequate performance for most applications, but may not be the best fit for high-volume applications such as CAD/CAM. Users need to understand that the throughput is more like what they receive at home over DSL or cable modems than what they are used to having at the office. Most vendors in the Wi-Fi arena will readily admit that actual throughput is usually about 40- 60 percent of the "full" bandwidth. For 802.11b this means 4.4-6.6 Mbps, and for 802.11a/g, 21-32 Mbps. And that may be the best case.

It is important to understand the factors that affect capacity and performance in a Wi-Fi network to understand why getting 60 percent is something to be happy about, and to understand what actions you can take to reach that level. Reasons For Limitations The limitations of Wi-Fi's capacity are related to the nature of the underlying protocol and the limitation of the radio frequency (RF) technology. An RF signal loses power as you move farther from the source. (Like all electrical signals, radio waves lose power as they travel through any type of matter—a little loss through air, a big loss through concrete or metal.) Wi-Fi handles this loss of strength by decreasing the throughput available. The throughput does not decrease linearly but instead follows a defined step function. The speeds in Mbps are:

- 802.11b: 11, 5.5, 2 and 1
- 802.11g: 54, 48, 36, 24, 18 12, 9, 6, 2 and 1
- 802.11a: 54, 48, 36, 24, 18, 12, 9 and 6

The important capacity question is how far out you can count on a particular speed. This is not as clear-cut as you would think, and finding out the actual distance/throughput figure can be complicated. Several factors affect the throughput you can get at a particular distance, including:

- Power output from your Wi-Fi card. Not all Wi-Fi cards are equal; some are "stronger" than others.
- The power output from the access point. Though this is configurable, it's set at the maximum allowed level—whenever possible. But interference and environmental factors could prevent you from using this setting.
- Type of access point used. The maximum ranges vary from manufacturer to manufacturer; check with your particular vendors.
- The type of antenna used on the access point.
- The density of the building environment.

There are no standards or even generally agreed speed and distance points. Different vendors and sources will give different values, which is not very helpful to a capacity planner.

6. Understanding WLAN Vulnerabilities

Shunning wireless LANs now would be akin to banning Internet access a decade ago. Rather, companies should cautiously tap the rewards of Wi-Fi while taking appropriate steps to understand and mitigate associated risks. The first step in managing risk is to fully understand common wireless LAN vulnerabilities.

In a survey that I developed for INT Media Research, Wi-Fi users were asked to identify security incidents experienced by company WLANs over the past year. Not surprisingly, half the participants declined to respond to this sensitive question. Of the remainder, approximately one in six reported at least one incident of unauthorized APs, stations associating with the wrong AP, war driving and active intrusion on the WLAN (Figure 1). As expected, actual penetration into wireless APs, peer stations or adjacent wired networks proved much less common. Incidents like these illustrate several common WLAN vulnerabilities. To strengthen the security of future WLANs, let us consider the root causes.

Controlling WLAN Access

Undoubtedly, controlling access is more difficult in WLANs than with wireline Ethernet LANs. It's true that nearly every Wi-Fi AP supports Wired Equivalent Privacy (WEP), a link-layer security standard which is intended to make WLANs as "safe" as Ethernet. Yet WEP is relatively weak, and to facilitate plug-and-play networking, most Wi-Fi products default to open system mode. In this mode, there is no access control on the WLAN segment. Any station can join the party simply by sending an "associate" request to the WLAN's AP. WLANs operating in open system mode have the following vulnerabilities:

- **Unauthorized use of WLAN bandwidth**
  All stations sending to an AP eat into the shared bandwidth. Although one 802.11b channel can carry 11 Mbps, overhead typically reduces effective throughput to 6 Mbps or less. Signal strength drops with distance, bottoming out at 1 Mbps. Clearly, WLAN bandwidth is a precious commodity. Even stations without malicious intent that do no more than transmit to your AP still reduce the WLAN capacity available to others.
- **Unauthorized access to intranet services**
  Some companies make the mistake of treating WLANs just like Ethernet LANs, deploying APs inside the company firewall. Teleworkers using wireless gateways to reach DSL or cable connections at home often make a similar mistake. Without adequate access control on the WLAN, wireless gateways and APs should always be placed in untrusted territory. Failure to do so leaves the door wide open for unauthorized stations to access, attack and steal confidential data from intranet servers.
- **Unauthorized access to the Internet**
  Even if you firewall your intranet away from your WLAN, what stands between Wi-Fi squatters and your Internet uplink? If your answer is "nothing," unauthorized stations can compete with legitimate users for WAN bandwidth, and your enterprise could be liable for misdeeds launched from your WLAN. MAC- or user-level access controls, deployed on or between the AP and the Internet uplink, can address this vulnerability.
- **Wireless Station Compromise**
  Network access control is challenging enough, but what about end stations? Unless desktop security measures are applied, unauthorized wireless stations can hear Windows Network Neighborhood broadcasts, reach shared files or printers or launch denial-of-service attacks against other PCs on the WLAN. Wireless stations must be hardened against peer attack, just like wired PCs with always-on Internet connections.
- **AP Compromise**
  The most critical node on the WLAN is the AP itself. Many APs are installed with default parameters—easily-guessed administrator logins, SNMP community strings and HTTP/Telnet listening ports for remote administration. The same methods used to harden WAN access routers should be applied to wireless APs—disable unused services, configure strong passwords and community strings, employ secure management protocols and use access-control lists to narrow exposure. Beware that eliminating these vulnerabilities may not be possible in entry-level APs that lack enterprise-grade security knobs.

Alternatives to Open System Mode:

There are several alternatives to operating your AP in open system mode, ranging from simple-butvery- weak to complex-but-more-secure:

- **Closed System Mode**
  When associating with an AP, the wireless station supplies the name of the network, called a Service Set ID (SSID). Many APs will accept null or "ANY" SSIDs. Some vendors support an option requiring the station to supply the exact SSID. By configuring a hard-to-guess SSID, disabling AP beacons that broadcast SSID and enabling *closed system* mode, you can prevent visitors and neighbors from accidentally associating with your AP. However, this will not stop a determined war driver, because SSID values can still be learned by eavesdropping on other frames.

Confidentiality Concerns

Each company must determine its own requirement for data confidentiality. After the Best Buy incident, Security Focus participants debated whether credit-card numbers really require confidentiality. Public opinion aside, privacy legislation like the Health Insurance Portability and Accountability Act (HIPAA), the Gramm-Leach-Bliley (GLB) Act and the U.K. Data Protection Act, require companies to keep non-public personal information private and secure. These mandates must be considered when deploying any kind of network, but the risk of disclosure is higher in a broadcast radio network. When considering confidentiality, remember that operating a WLAN without encryption leaves it vulnerable to:

- **Traffic Analysis:** Attackers can learn quite a bit from the headers surrounding even non-confidential payload. Valid SSIDs, MAC addresses and IP addresses can all be obtained by analyzing captured frames, helping an attacker penetrate wireless and adjacent networks. Destination addresses, DHCP requests, DNS queries and NetBIOS broadcasts can help attackers breach intranet servers and file shares. The less information you give away on the WLAN, the lower your risk.
- **Disclosure of Private Data:** In my INT Media survey, privacy was the number-one security concern, important to 94 percent of those surveyed. Eavesdropping on wireless payload can disclose logins, passwords, file names, mail server addresses, database locations and more, depending upon the application. For example, capturing wireless inventory management traffic could reveal sales volumes, customer buying habits, and top-selling items. When assessing your own vulnerability to WLAN eavesdropping, consider visitors in your lobby and conference rooms, as well as neighboring offices above and below you. Careful antenna placement can reduce these vulnerabilities, but usually cannot eliminate them. There are many options for providing WLAN payload confidentiality, some unique to wireless and others commonly used to provide secure remote access:
- **WEP Encryption:** As previously noted, this weak link-level encryption is supported by most APs. Given enough traffic, a war driver can crack static WEP keys. However, WEP is still a good first step to eliminate casual eavesdropping, particularly in smaller WLANs where keys can be manually updated at regular intervals without difficulty.
- **Proprietary Wireless Encryption:** Several vendors offer non-standard solutions for wireless authentication and confidentiality. For example, Net Motion protects data transmitted between a Mobility Server and Client with DES, 3DES, At one out of five companies, employees may already have installed unauthorized access points Two fish or AES encryption, deriving unique session keys with Diffie-Hellman.
- **Temporal Key Integrity Protocol:** TKIP is a standard now under development to mend the most glaring WEP weaknesses. TKIP is expected to use 802.1X for authentication and key delivery, and to encrypt with short-lived "temporal" keys that are refreshed often enough to prevent key reuse (the event that leads to WEP key cracking). If the IEEE approves TKIP this summer, firmware upgrades may be available for existing Wi-Fi products by the end of 2002.
- **VPN Encryption:** WEP and TKIP encrypt frames on the wireless link only. PPTP, IPSec or L2TP-over-IPSec VPNs encrypt data all the way from remote access clients to security gateways at the private network edge. Wireless laptops and teleworker desktops already equipped with VPN clients for secure remote access over the Internet may reuse these clients to encrypt data over Wi-Fi. There are several alternatives for terminating the VPN tunnel:
- **Tunnel to the AP:** A few access points can operate as VPN gateways, terminating PPTP or IPSec tunnels at the edge of the WLAN—for example, the Colubris CN1050.
- **Tunnel to a VPN/Firewall:** Depending upon network size, traffic load and distribution, you may tunnel Wi-Fi to your existing VPN/firewall or deploy additional VPN/firewall(s).
- **Tunnel to a WLAN Access Concentrator:** In larger WLANs where greater mobility and scalability are required, consider tunneling to a special purpose wireless access appliance from Bluesocket, ReefEdge or Vernier Networks.
- **Upper-Layer Encryption:** Methods commonly used to encrypt Internet applications can be used to protect wireless traffic, too. For example, mail messages over Wi-Fi can be encrypted with PGP or S/MIME. Remote administration can be protected with Secure Shell. Secure remote desktop access can be accomplished with a service like Expert City's Go To My PC.

When choosing a solution, consider not only air link encryption, but end-to-end network security. Those who want to wait before making a long-term investment in wireless security can leverage measures already deployed for Internet-based remote access. Doing so will improve near-term security and help you better understand the unique challenges associated with protecting WLANs.

Data Integrity and Reliability

Many companies take data integrity and reliability for granted, but risk-averse industries know better. These vulnerabilities exist in wired networks, but again are greater in WLANs:

- **Replay:** According to INT Media survey results, wireless replay attacks are not very common— but they do happen. Unencrypted frames are easily captured and replayed. IPSec VPNs provide strong replay protection, but nothing prevents re-sending a captured frame that was encrypted with WEP. Ultimately, replay success depends on the application—for example, duplicate TCP data will usually be discarded.

- **Forgery:** WEP includes a CRC that detects corruption, but cannot prevent a frame from being modified such that the CRC still passes. TKIP includes a stronger Message Integrity Code (MIC) to prevent forgery. In the meantime, if your business cannot risk data forgery or requires no repudiation, use a VPN or higher-layer solution to ensure wireless data integrity.
- **Spoofing:** In Ethernet LANs, IP spoofing of inside addresses can be blocked at the perimeter firewall. And ARP cache poisoning—a LAN attack that exploits the Address Resolution Protocol to redirect frames—cannot reach beyond the local subnet. These attacks are therefore primarily insider threats. By contrast, on WLANs, outsider spoofing is much more likely. You can reduce this risk by using static ARP on the wired segment attached to your APs and avoiding unprotected DHCP—for example, bind IP addresses to known MAC addresses, or allow DHCP access only after 802.1X authentication.
- **Session Hijacking:** Man-in-the-middle (MitM) attacks like session hijacking are possible in WLANs. An attacker can use a high-powered AP to intercept associate requests, masquerade as the legitimate AP, relay WLAN traffic to intended destinations, and return responses to requesting stations. Stations and intranet servers may be unaware that sessions have been hijacked. To reduce MitM risk, monitor for rogue APs and use 802.1X with strong mutual authentication. To limit what the MitM can do with intercepted traffic, use end-to-end encryption and data integrity.
- **Packet Floods:** In recent years, on-line businesses have learned to protect Internet-facing servers from denial-of-service (DoS) attacks. Wireless APs and servers connected directly to the WLAN require similar protection. For example, if you place your APs on a firewall DMZ, use DoS thresholds to defeat TCP SYN or UDP packet floods generated by a war driver hoping to cripple your WLAN.
- **Jamming:** WLANs are also vulnerable to lowtech jamming, where an attacker generates RF signal (noise) on the same channel(s) occupied by your WLAN. A WLAN analyzer can be used to locate the source. When jamming is unintentional— for example, a 2.4 GHz phone system or microwave— the offending signal source can often be moved. Alternatively, change the channel used by your AP or move to a different band (i.e., 802.11a).

Security

With no cables to run around the house, wireless networks are convenient and easy to install, so homes with high-speed Internet access are adopting them at a rapid pace. Because wireless networking works by sending information over radio waves, it can be more vulnerable to intruders. Like signals from your cellular or cordless phones, signals from your wireless network can also be intercepted. Since you can't physically prevent someone from connecting to your wireless network, you need to take some additional steps to keep your network secure.

Securing your wireless network shouldn't be difficult or time consuming.

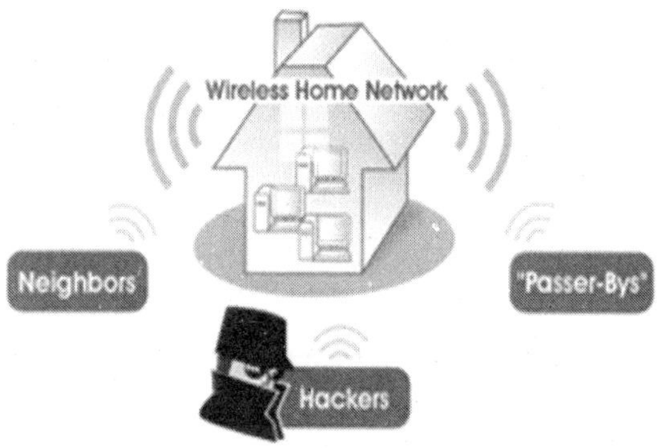

Radio waves from a wireless network can be intercepted by anyone around your house.

7. Innovative Method to Improve Security

We have designed an innovative solution to overcome wireless security issues by implementing Hardware Security Smart Antenna Balloon Connector.

The objective of the smart antenna system is to provide spatial filtering capability over a range of potential mobile station scans angles. This task is accomplished using a WLAN antenna array, a multichannel RF front end which can capture the full 80 MHz spectrum of the IEEE 802.11b WLAN standard, a multichannel digitization system, and a real-time processing engine. The above subsystems make it possible to provide digital samples of mobile station packet data which can be isolated according to the direction of origin.

Spatial isolation (filtering) is accomplished by performing a mathematical beamforming operation on the digital samples. This requires the use of a processing engine which, in this case, consists of a custom high-speed, high gate count field-programmable gate array (FPGA) printed circuit board. In addition to the beamforming operation, this processing engine can implement arbitrary direction finding algorithms as well as interference mitigation algorithms like null steering [4]. The smart antenna system is designed to coverall domestic and foreign direct sequence spread spectrum (DSSS) channels.

The smart antenna system described above is illustrated in Fig. 1. It consists primarily of four sections. The first section is an 8-channel antenna array with the front-end electronics. Each channel has a low noise amplifier (LNA) followed by filters, additional amplifiers, and a single mixing stage, where the 2.4 GHz RF is mixed down to a 300 MHz IF. The 8-element antenna array has a gain of 12 dB and the LNAs have a 1.5 dB noise figure. A 300 MHz IF was chosen so that the down conversion was kept to a single stage and also to ease the filtering requirements. Following the analog front-end are the analog-to-digital converters (ADCs), where 200 MSPS 8-bit ADCs are used to digitize each of the 8-channels. A direct band-pass sampling scheme is used to digitize the 300 MHz IF on each channel and the 200 MSPS ADC speed provides the 80 MHz of bandwidth required to receive all the DSSS channels. The outputs of the ADCs are demultiplexed by a factor of two in order to reduce the speed to 100 MSPS for the data collection and processing. The 8-channel, 200 MSPS 8-bit ADCs with the 1:2 demultiplexing produces 128 bits at 100 MSPS. The data collection and processing is done using an FPGA and additional memory storage. A Xilinx Virtex-II (XC2V6000-4), containing 6 million gates, is used to perform calibration, digital beamforming, and direction finding algorithms [5]. Following the beamforming process the digital output (corresponding to the data for a particular direction of interest) is fed to a digital-to-analog converter (DAC) where the data is then mixed back up to 2.4 GHz and directly inserted into a COTS access point and computer where the packet data is processed using commercial software tools. The user of interest is identified using the COTS hardware and software and associated control information is fed back to the FPGA in order to facilitate additional direction finding and tracking of the user of interest.

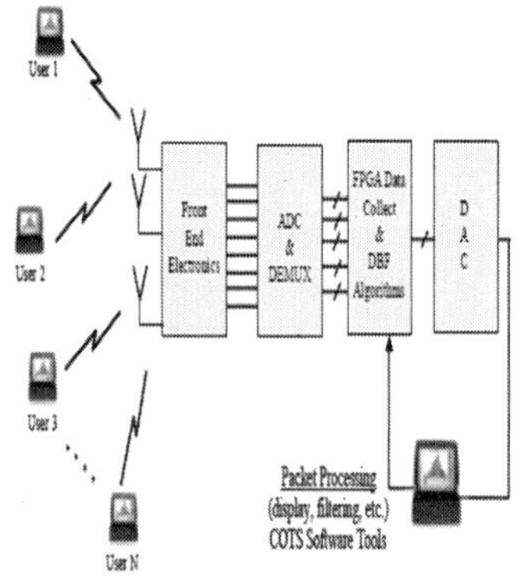

Figure 1. Smart antenna system configuration for WLAN surveillance and user tracking.

Fig. 1 Smart antenna System configuration for WLAN surveillance and user tracking

This concept provides a unique hardware security by following features:

- Allows owner to give his own encryption key,
- Scans the location of owner's Wi-Fi devices and automatically changes the amplitude levels of Wi-Fi signal, so he can obtain desired bandwidth at any location,
- Generates noise signal which will be acting as Wi-Fi jamming signal for the whole region covered and only that particular owner will have the filter in his connector of Wi-Fi device,

As per as software security is concerned we are implementing a time based encryption algorithm having encryption key which is obtained while syncing of those devices.

So by implementing this technology the owner doesn't need to change his access point for security issues and this doesn't affect future Access point upgrading also.

8. Conclusion

Thus we found few new applications for Wi-Fi to be introduced in Industries by first converting serial data to TCP/IP then implementing Wi-Fi devices to handle it. We have addressed potential problems of Wi-Fi and developed innovative solution to conquer those problems. So by implementing Wi-Fi in industries the rate of growth of Wi-Fi will increase and with minimal security issues.

9. References

Books

[1] R.T. Compton, Jr. *"Adaptive Antennas, Concepts and performance"*, Prentice Hall, NJ, 1988.

Magazine & Newspaper Articles

[2] E.G. Desautel, K. Dongsu, J.S. Kenney, and D. Kiesling, "Interference mitigation in WLAN networks using client-based smart antennas," *IEEE Radio and Wireless Conf., RAWCON*, pp. 63-66, 2002.

[3] D. Bartolome and A.I. Perez-Neira, "MMSE techniques for space diversity receivers in OFDM-based Wireless LANs," *IEEE Journal on Selected Areas in Comm.*, vol. 21, pp. 151-160, Feb. 2003.

[4] Robin Layland Posted 8/27/2004; Published 03/2004,

[5] Troubleshooting Wireless LANs to Improve Wi-Fi Uptime and Security By Fluke Networks Published 2005, Posted April 21, 2006 Abstract: IEEE 802.11-based wireless LANs

Website or Webpage

[6] searchMobileComputing.com, http://searchmobilecomputing.techtarget .com/sDefinition/0,,sid40_gci1025328,00.html Parani10 on Amazon website

Preventive Approaches for Web Application's Security Attacks

Dr.A.Damodaram[1], R.Sridevi[2], K. Venkateshwara Rao[3] and M.V.Ramaraju[4]
[1]Professor, [2&3]Associate Professor, [4]II Year M.Tech(CS),
Dept of CSE, JNTUCEH, Hyderabad

Abstract

Web application is most predominated application that is accessed over a network such as the Internet. web applications arc presentation-oriented that generates interactive web pages containing various types of markup language (HTML, XML, and so on) and dynamic content in response to requests. As there is heavy traffic in today's web world it is essential to maintain security concerns and prevention approaches in order to protect web applications from cyber culprits. There are modern tools and technologies such as AJAX technology are available to prepare web applications as simple as user friendly. Ajax web technology, by design makes number of calls to the web server to process a user request. As there is an increase in session management vulnerabilities and a greater risk of hackers gaining access to the many hidden URLs which are necessary for AJAX requests to be processed we need to provide high end web security measures to protect web sites from vulnerabilities.

In this presentation we addressed some of the most common web application attacks that are occurred frequently as 80% of web application threats. This paper suggests effective prevention approaches to provide some security aspects to web applications from attacking vectors like SQL injection and Cross Site Scripting vulnerabilities.

1. Introduction

The web has been embraced by millions of businesses as an inexpensive channel to communicate and exchange information with prospects and transactions with customers. In particular, the web provides a way for marketers to get to know the people visiting their sites and start communicating with them. All this data must be somehow captured, stored, processed and transmitted to be used immediately or at a later date. Web applications, in the form of submit fields, enquiry and login forms, shopping carts, and content management systems, are those website widgets that allow this to happen. The web is a highly programmable environment that allows mass customization through the immediate deployment of a large and diverse range of applications, to millions of global users. Modern web pages allow personalized dynamic content to be pulled down by users according to individual preferences and settings. Web applications are computer programs allowing website visitors to submit and retrieve data to/from a database over the Internet using their preferred web browser. The data is then presented to the user within their browser as information is generated dynamically (in a specific format, e.g. in HTML using CSS) by the web application through a web server. Web applications query the content server (essentially a content repository database) and dynamically generate web documents to serve to the client (people surfing the website). The documents are generated in a standard format to allow support by all browsers (e.g., HTML or XHTML). JavaScript is one form of client side script that permits dynamic elements on each page.

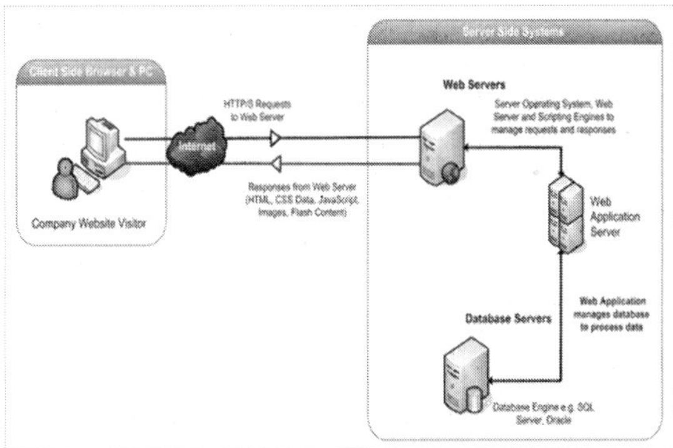

Fig. 1

AJAX (Asynchronous JavaScript Technology and XML) is modern technology that simplifies the data representation through the web which attracting the attention of businesses all around the globe. AJAX is the scripting language used – JavaScript (JS) which allows for a number of advantages including: dynamic forms to include built-in error checking, calculation areas on pages, user interaction for warnings and getting confirmations, dynamically changing background. It is a collection of technologies each providing robust foundations when designing and developing web applications. Web applications allow legitimate website visitors to submit and retrieve data to/from a database over the Internet using their preferred web browser. Databases are central to modern websites – they store data needed for websites to deliver specific content to visitors and render information to customers, suppliers, employees and a host of stakeholders. User credentials, financial and payment information, company statistics may all be resident within a database and accessed by legitimate users through off-the-shelf and custom web applications.

Despite their advantages, web applications do raise a number of security concerns stemming from improper coding. Serious weaknesses or vulnerabilities[8], allow hackers to gain direct and public access to databases in order to churn sensitive data. Many of these databases contain valuable information (e.g., personal and financial details) making them a frequent target of hackers. Although such acts of vandalism as defacing corporate websites are still commonplace, nowadays, hackers prefer gaining access to the sensitive data residing on the database server because of the immense pay-offs in selling the data. Websites depend on databases to deliver the required information to visitors. If web applications are not secure, i.e., vulnerable to, at least one of the various forms of hacking techniques, then the entire database of sensitive information is at serious risk. Some hackers, for example, will take advantage of web application vulnerabilities and may maliciously inject code within vulnerable web applications to trick users and redirect them towards phishing sites. This technique is called Cross-Site Scripting and may be used even when the web servers and database engine contain no vulnerabilities themselves. There is an increase in session management vulnerabilities and a greater risk of hackers gaining access to the many hidden URLs, which are necessary for AJAX requests to be processed. The advent of AJAX applications has raised considerable security issues due to a broadened threat window brought about by the very same technologies and complexities developed. With an increase in script execution and information exchanged in server/client requests and responses, hackers have greater opportunity to steal data.

2.1. SQL Injection: The most severe web application vulnerability

SQL Injection[1,5] is the hacking technique, which attempts to pass SQL commands (statements) through a web application for execution by the backend database. If not sanitized properly, web applications may result in SQL Injection attacks that allow hackers to view information from the database and/or even wipe it out. This technique allows an attacker to retrieve crucial information from a Web server's database. Depending on the application's security measures, the impact of this attack can vary from basic information disclosure to remote code execution and total system compromise. SQL Injection happens when a developer accepts user input that is directly placed into a SQL Statement and doesn't properly filter out dangerous characters. This can allow an attacker to not only steal data from your database, but also modify and delete it.

The vulnerability is present when user input is either incorrectly filtered for string literal escape characters embedded in SQL statements or user input is not strongly typed and thereby unexpectedly executed. Attackers commonly insert single quotes into a URL's query string, or into a forms input field to test for SQL Injection. Not all the SQL injection attacks are in the form of harmful codes like the one described earlier. They can be used to gain unauthorized access or to flood the server in order to cause a denial-of-service attack. The primary form of SQL injection consists of direct insertion of code into user-input variables that are concatenated with SQL commands and executed. A less direct attack injects malicious code into strings that are destined for storage in a table or as metadata. When the stored strings are subsequently concatenated into a dynamic SQL command, the malicious code is executed. The injection process works by prematurely terminating a text string and appending a new command. Because the inserted command may have additional strings appended to it before it is executed, the malefactor terminates the injected string with a comment mark "--". Subsequent text is ignored at execution time.

Any procedure that constructs SQL statements should be reviewed for injection vulnerabilities because SQL Server will execute all syntactically valid queries that it receives. A skilled and determined attacker can manipulate even parameterized data. Incorrectly validated or invalidated string literals are concatenated into a dynamic SQL statement, and interpreted as code by the SQL engine.

Let us take an example that illustrate how SQL injection threat can compromises user information which is retrieved by execution of dynamic SQL statement that is prepared form user input data such as search activity.

SELECT * from user_transactions where user_id is <current_authorized_user> and transaction_date > <start_date>;

The above sql statement retrieves all the user transaction details which belong to current authorized user and transactions made after the date which is given from user input form. But Attackers may be able to trick the back- end database of a Web application into executing malicious SQL code. The attacker supplies malicious data input which invalidates the sql statement conditions by providing SQL escape characters such as quotes as shown below.

SELECT * from user_transactions where user_id is <current_authorized_user> and transaction_date > <start_date> or 't'='t';

The above statement fetches all the transactional records and reveals secure information to an authorized person. Through SQL Injection, the hacker may input specifically crafted SQL commands with the intent of bypassing the login form barrier and seeing what lies behind it. This is only possible if the inputs are not properly sanitized and sent directly with the SQL query to the database. SQL Injection vulnerabilities provide the means for a hacker to communicate directly to the database. Once an attacker realizes that a system is vulnerable to SQL Injection, he is able to inject SQL Query / Commands through an input form field. This is equivalent to handing the attacker your database and allowing him to execute any SQL command including DROP TABLE to the database.

2.2 SQL Injection: Prevention approaches

Here are two approaches provided to prevent web application from SQL injection threat.

2.2.1 Approach 1: Preprocessing the user input

It is often the case that a web application will 'escape' the single quote character (and others), and otherwise 'massage' the data that is submitted by the user, such as by limiting its length. In this approach the user submitted data is submitted to a preprocessor before send data to sql execute statement. The motive of this approach is to invalidate malicious user input to some extent. In most of the cases the malicious user input contains single quotes that are embedded into user input data such as search string or username/password input strings. The preprocessor detects such escape characters and produces counter characters to invalidate input data which contains escape characters. It will works as follows

Input = replace ("' ", " ' ' ");

This preprocessing will effect in preventing certain SQL injection flaws as there is no direct access to database queries from user input directly. From the above example the after preprocessing the user input data the resultant SQL query will contains phrases as '' t '' = '' t ''. As it is violated SQL statement structure and returns SQL error for the given SQL statement execution. This is prevention mechanism there is no chance of obtaining secure data from an unauthorized access control.

Limitations: The preprocessing mechanism will works fine upto some extent where there is data sources (db) contains valid data. Valid data is in terms of it doesn't contains any SQL escape characters. SQL injection prevention by this approach will be failed when persistent data contains some special characters like the following cases.

If user provided his login name or password as

Username: admin'—

Password: password

And when attacker updates this password as follows

UPDATE users set password = 'password' where username = 'admin'--'.

This statement updates the admin role's password and leads to denial of service for admin user. The above approach doesn't prevent these types of attacks.

2.2.2 Approach 2: Use Encryption/Decryption of secure data

In this approach the secured data is kept in encrypted format in data resources such as in db. Using strong symmetric encryption such like DES it is highly impossible to generate malicious SQL statements. It is suggested to perform character oriented encryption to support db schema structures for all kinds of databases to support storage capability of encrypted user data.

Persistent_data = encrypt (Ek, user_data);

The persistent data will be saved into database. While retrieval of user data, decryption is going to perform to the resultant data obtained from the queries.

User_data = decrypt (Ek, persistent_data);

When attacker attempts to inject malicious code, the user input is subjected to encryption function before preparing SQL statement. The encryption function return invalidated output for the malicious data input. The SQL statement will looks like

UPDATE users set password = 'password' where username = +encrypt(Ek, 'admin'--'). This forms an invalidated SQL statement.

Limitations: Encryption and decryption of user data may leads to conserve some processor cycles but it is minor as per security concerns.

3.1 Cross Site Script attacks: A common attack against web applications

Cross Site Scripting is one of the most common application-layer web attacks. CSS[2] commonly targets scripts embedded in a page which are executed on the client-side rather than on the server-side. The concept of CSS is to manipulate client-side scripts of a web application to execute in the manner desired by the malicious user. When a malicious user injects a script in a legitimate shopping site URL which in turn redirects a user to a fake but identical page. The malicious page would run a script to capture the cookie of the user browsing the shopping site, and that cookie gets sent to the malicious user who can now hijack the legitimate user's session. Legitimate users have been frequently tricked into clicking a link, which redirects them to a malicious but legitimate-looking page which in turn captures all their details and sends them straight to the hacker.

A web page contains both text and HTML markup that is generated by the server and interpreted by the client browser. Web sites that generate only static pages are able to have full control over how the browser interprets these pages. Web sites that generate dynamic pages do not have complete control over how their outputs are interpreted by the client. The use of XSS might compromise private information, manipulate or steal cookies, create requests that can be mistaken for those of a valid user, or execute malicious code on the end-user systems. Exploited CSS is commonly used to achieve malicious results like Identity theft, gaining free access to a paid content, spying functionality etc.

The following input/output processing of web application provides the means for XSS attack.

- Injection points to the program: There are two ways by which the input is sent to the web server: GET and POST.
- All routines that returns data to the browser such as error messages, information to the users and warnings.

Asynchronous GET and POST is possible through Ajax-XMLHttpRequest (XHR) object. Application worms take advantage of this to attach themselves to the web pages and modify the functionality based on the input provided by the hacker. List of name/value pairs being sent to the server in the form of an http request. The request may contain their information such as a list of cookies, the referrer URL etc.

Cross Site Scripting is generally made possible where the user's input is displayed. Such type of malicious code injection may happen like the following invalid code injection into a dynamic web site content.

1.)http://hack.com/getInfo?name=<script>alert(document.cookie);</script>

2.)"<img src=http://hack.com/"+ document.cookie + ">"

3.2 Cross Site Script attacks: Prevention approaches

Here are few approaches that can prevent dynamic content sites from cross site scripting attacks.

3.2.1 Approach 1: Use HTML block elements.

In this process the dynamic site content is displayed with in some parent block elements such as HTML text areas and comment out blocks. HTML text area elements can be used to display the web contents which are obtained from the user as standard HTML format. It prevents execution of malicious code which is injected by the attacker.

HTML comment blocks are also useful to comment out the dangerous hacking code execution. It is implemented by surrounding user data by comment block as follows

<COMMENT><!-- code (NOT PARSED BY FILTER//-->
</COMMENT>

3.2.2 Approach 2: Use HTML Encoded characters

In this approach any non-validated user data is always encoded to the appropriate HTML characters as it is written back to the user. For instance the character "<" would be encoded as "&lt" and, although appearing to the user as the less-than character, would not be interpreted by the client application as the start of a HTML tag. As most of the CSS attacks are involved in injecting malicious HTML tag structures such as IMG and EMBED tags, these tags can easily invalidated using HTML encoded characters. The resulted content send to the client will be looks like

Original content: <IMG src="hack.org?s_cookie="+document.cookie/>

HTML encoded content: &ltIMG src="hack.org&cookie=document.cookie"&gt.

3.2.2 Approach 3: Use IP Binding for session stealing

This approach is effectively useful when attacker has stolen a legitimate user's session and when the culprit tries to access server from a remote place. In this approach the client IP address is captured in the server when the user authenticated to web application system. The client IP is stored in user session as long as user has valid session. In addition to checking of session Id of authorized user the client IP address also will be tested to check for a valid request.

3.3 Cross Site Request Forgery attacks

Cross Site Request Forgery attacks are special kind of CSS type attack where it acts as sleeping giant in web applications. CSRF vulnerabilities exist in web applications with a predictable action structure and whi ch use cookies, browser authentication or client side ce rtificates to authenticate users. The basic idea to CSRF is simple; an attacker tricks the user into performing an action of the attackers choosing by directing the victim's actions on the target application with a link or other content. The consequences of CSRF vulnerabilities include identity theft and cheats business transactions.

Most of the CSRF attacks are performed using hidden form elements as follows

```
<form action=http://www.bigbank.com/transfer.php>
<input type="hidden" name="to" value="hacker"/>
<input type="submit" value="Submit"/> <input type=
"hidden" name="amount" value="10000"/></form>
<script>document.forms[0].submit();</script>
```

This is hidden form post activity that is targeted to hack an online transaction site in victims browser and leads to illegal amount transactions with out user involvement.

3.4 Cross Site Request Forgery attacks: Prevention approaches

CSRF attacks can be prevented using special secret token for every form post activity, which identifies the legitimate form post activity. The lifetime of such secret token will be valid for single request and hence uncontrollable repeated malicious activities can be prevented. The secret token code is generated as follows

```
<form action="fundTransfer.do" method="POST">
<input type="hidden" name="xsrfSecretToken"
value="qiou3hkps986hn"/> <input type="text"
name="amount"/> <input type="submit"
value="Send"> </form>
```

When the web application formulates an action, the application includes a name value pair like name as secret code and the corresponding value generated as some cryptographic 128 bit code which is generated using session Id as base. When action is performed by the user namely form post action, before the action executed the secret token is validated from stored token provided valid for the corresponding request. If the value provided does not match, the action is going to be aborted.

4. Related work

The proposed solutions are strong enough to protect web applications from attacks like SQL injection, CSS and CSRF attacks. These protection approaches can be implemented as platform independent and can apply for any web 2.0 application building tools & technologies. It is also applicable for any type of client side scripting languages such as java script, ASP scripts etc... The server side overhead involved in this implementation is not much heavy and it doesn't degrade any network traffic parameters. We expect the attention paid to this class of attacks to reach more aspects of web security problems (such as CSS or SQL injections), and we hope that our solution will prove useful in protecting vulnerable web applications. We are going to implement all the above proposed approaches to make web applications most secured from attacks.

5. Conclusion

Many web servers have vulnerabilities that can result in unauthorized access to a system by means of submitting malicious requests. Given even a tiny hole in a web-application code, an experienced hacker can break into most commercial websites. The risk of poor application security must exceed our imagination. Unless a web application has a strong, centralized mechanism for validating all input from HTTP requests (and any other sources), vulnerabilities based on malicious input are very likely to exist.

In this work we addressed most common web application attacks and proposed a solution to prevent such attacks in real world. These prevention approaches are platform independent and can effectively reduces hacking culprit activities to some extent in the current internet world.

6. References

[1] Xiang Fu, *A Static Analysis Framework For Detecting SQL Injection Vulnerabilities,* IEEE, 31st Annual International Computer Software and Applications Conference, 2007.

[2] Jayamsakthi Shanmugam, M.Ponnavaikko, *XSS Application Worms,* IEEE, 8th ACIS International Conference on Software Engineering, 2007.

[3] Jessie Burns, *Cross Site Reference Forgery, http://www.isecpartners.com,* 2005

[4] Trend micro, *trend_micro_web_2.0_threats*

[5] Microsoft: Data security, *http://msdn .microsoft .com /en- us/magazine/cc163917.aspx*

[6] Shiuh-Jeng Wang, Yao-Han Chang1, *Investigations in Cross-Site Scripts,* 2007

[7] Jeremiah Grossman, Cross-Site Request Forgery "The sleeping giant". *www.whitehatsec.com,* July 2007

[8] http:*//www.webappsec.org/projects/statistics/*

Streaming Media Caching Algorithms for Transcoding Proxies (TeC & AMTrac)

M. NagaRatna[1], Dr.V.Kamakshi Prasad[2] and T.Y.J.Naga Malleswari[3]
[1]Asst.Professor, Dept.of CSE, JNTUCEH.
mratnajntu@gmail.com
[2]Additional Controller of Examination, JNTU.
kamakshiprasad@yahoo.com
[3]Asst.Professor, Dept.of CSE,SACET, Chirala.
malli_yamu@yahoo.co.in

Abstract

Streaming media is expected to become one of the most popular types of web content in the future. Due to increasing variety of client devices and the range of access speeds to the Internet, multimedia contents may be required to be transcoded to match the client's capability. The emergence of ubiquitous computing enables mobile users to access the Internet with their laptops, PDAs, or even cell phones which lead to high quality video transfer can be problematic due to long delay or size mismatch between the application display and the screen. Our proposed solution to this problem is to enable network proxies with the transcoding capability, and hence provide different, appropriate video quality to different network environment. The proxies in our transcoding-enabled caching (TeC) system perform transcoding as well as caching for efficient rich media delivery to heterogeneous network users.

We propose three different TeC caching strategies. We study the performance of TeC caching algorithms and compare them with other approaches. Since transcoding is a CPU-intensive task, the transcoded versions can be saved to reduce the CPU load for future requests. However, this can quickly exhaust cache space.

In this paper, we introduce the idea of meta-caching by looking into a transcoding procedure. Instead of caching certain selected transcoded versions in full, meta-caching identifies intermediate transcoding steps from which certain intermediate results (called metadata) can be cached so that a fully transcoded version can be easily produced from the metadata with a small amount of CPU cycles. We propose AMTrac, Adaptive Meta-caching for Transcoding, which adaptively applies meta-caching based on the client request pattern and available resources.

The results indicate that, TeC improves the cache effectiveness, decreases the user-perceived latency, and reduces the traffic between the proxy and the content origin server. Our proposed AMTrac can significantly improve the system throughput over existing approaches.

1. Introduction

Proxy caching is a popular approach to enhance the performance of web content delivery. The proxies are usually deployed much closer to the clients than the content servers. Frequently accessed objects are stored at the proxies so that client requests can be satisfied without having to contact the distant content servers.

Moreover, the characteristics of access links between the clients and the Internet also vary widely, ranging from narrowband wireless and modem connections (9.6 Kbps – 56 Kbps) to broadband connections (1 Mbps– 100 Mbps). Therefore, in the highly heterogeneous Internet environment, it is difficult to provide a single version of streaming media that can run satisfactorily on all clients. Multimedia contents may need to be converted to a form suitable for display on the target client depending on the availability of resources. This conversion process is called *transcoding*.

Since portable devices generally have different screen sizes, color depths or connection bandwidth from traditional desktop computers, a media object (e.g. a movie) that is good for desktop computers cannot be directly displayed on a PDA. It must be customized appropriately beforehand or at runtime. This type of customization for typical QoS support is often referred to as *content adaptation*.

Transcoding, offers on line real-time adaptation[5] support. Possible forms of Transcoding include lowering the bit rate of a media stream by reducing the image resolution, size and/or frame rate, and a combination of these. Transcoding can be performed at either the content servers or proxies. In server-based transcoding , transcodes done in an offline fashion to reduce processing cost when the objects are accessed. However, server-based transcoding is not as flexible as proxy-based transcoding. Proxy-based transcoding relieves content providers from the burden of having to keep track of client device characteristics and maintain multiple versions of the same object.

We introduce Transcoding-enabled Caching (TeC) proxies for streaming media distribution over the Internet. The proxies in our system perform transcoding as well as caching. Depending on the connection speed and processing capability of an end user, the proxy transcodes the requested (and possibly cached) video into an appropriate format and delivers it to the user. By putting the transcoding unit on the content delivery path, we perform content adaptation at the network edges[1].

We propose three caching strategies for TeC. The first two algorithms cache at most one version of a video object. They operate differently when a user requests a video version that is coded at a lower bit-rate than the one cached in the proxy. The third algorithm may cache multiple versions of the same video object and hence reduces the processing load at the transcoder.

The transcoded result for a request can be cached so that future identical requests can be served without transcoding. This kind of transcode-enabled caching designs has been investigated and the focus has been on efficient utilization of different resources (e.g., CPU, storage, bandwidth) to improve the throughput of the transcoding proxy[2, 6]. All of the existing designs treat the transcoding unit as a black box. The cached data is either the input and/or the output of the transcoder. Specifically, if a transcoded version is fully cached (*full-caching* scheme), identical future requests can be directly served without additional transcoding. However, to cache each transcoded version may quickly exhaust the cache space. On the other hand, if a transcoded version is not cached (*no-caching* scheme), identical requests will result in repetitive transcoding, consuming extensive CPU cycles.

In this paper, we propose a meta-caching scheme in which, intermediate transcoding steps are studied and identified so that appropriate intermediate results (called *metadata*) can be cached. With the cached metadata, the fully transcoded object can be easily produced with a small amount of CPU cycles. Since only metadata is cached, the required cache space is greatly reduced. The saved cache space can be used to store metadata for other transcoding sessions so that, in certain conditions, overall computing load can be reduced. It is better than the full-caching and no-caching schemes. AMTrac, which stands for *A*daptive *M*eta-caching for *Tr*anscoding. In AMTrac,the meta-caching scheme is adaptively used upon dynamic client accesses and available resources.

In the remaining paper we explained system architecture of TeC proxy, the pseudocode of Tec algorithms, principle of meta-caching, Design of AMTrac and analysis of their performance.

2. System Architecture of TeC proxy

Transcoding-enabled caching (TeC) proxy consists of the components shown in Figure 1. The proxy acts as a client to the content server. An RTP/RTSP client is built into the proxy to receive the streamed content from the origin server (server link). The received stream is put into the input buffer.

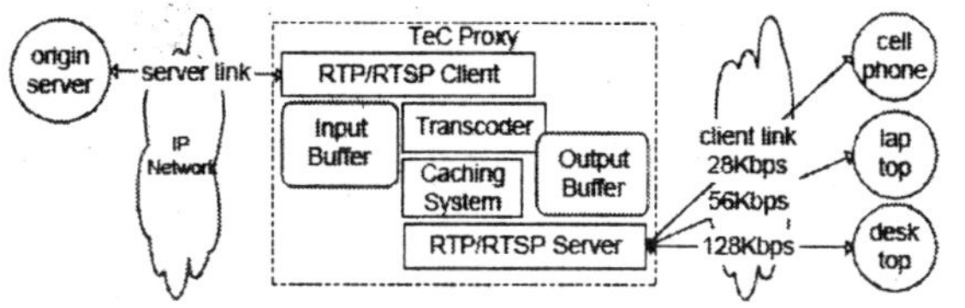

Figure 1. System and components for the Tec proxy.

The transcoder continuously pulls bit streams from the input buffer and subsequently pushes the transcoded bits out to the output buffer. The proxy caches the content either from the input buffer or the output buffer while the transcoder produces the content. Additionally, the proxy acts as a server to the end user. Hence, an RTP/RTSP server is built to stream the video to the end user (client link). The data in the output buffer is obtained either from the transcoder or the caching system. The size of the input and output buffers can be small given that the transcoder processes the video data in a streamlined fashion. The speed of the process, i.e., the transcoding bit-rate, is defined as the number of bits the transcoder generates per second. Given that the transcoding bit-rate is larger than the minimum of the server link and the client link bandwidths, the transcoding process does not significantly increase the end-toend delay. Given the real time transcoding capability, the TeC proxies dynamically transcode video objects to different variants to satisfy the end users in heterogeneous environments. Each variant is a version. If version x can be obtained from transcoding version y, we call version y *transcodable version* for x . Conversely, version x is the *transcoded version* of y . In video transcoding, a higher bit-rate version can be transcoded to a lower bit-rate version. The transcoded version may have fidelity degradation compared with the original version. For video transcoding, this loss is negligible when bit-rate reduction is coupled with resolution reduction. The reduction in the spatial resolution already yields the bit-rate reduction. The end user specifically asks for a certain version of an object based on the awareness of ones connection and display device. If there are packet losses in the server link due to congestion, the TeC proxy can choose not to cache for the session.

3. Transcoding-enabledCaching Algorithms:

We define the following events in a TeC proxy:
Exact hit: the requested version of the video object exists in the cache.
Transcode hit: the requested version does not exist in the cache, but a transcodable version of the video exists.
Miss: the requested or a transcodable version of the video does not exist in the cache.

Let us assume that the origin server has *n* versions at bitrates *b0,b1,b2.....bn-1* for each video object. The highest bitrate version is *b0* and the lowest is *bn-1*, i.e., *b0>b1>...>bn-1*. When version *bj* is requested from the end user and there is version *bi* (*bi>bj*, i.e., *bi* is a transcodable version for *bj*) in the cache, the TeC proxy transcodes *bi* to *bj* and sends the transcoded *bj* to the client instead of fetching *bj* from the content origin. Therefore, it is a cache hit (i.e.,a *transcode hit*) even though *bj* is not directly available from the cache at the time of request.

Note that when the origin server has only one bit-rate version of a video (possibly a high bit-rate) and a user with low-speed connectivity requests that object, our proxy transcodes the original video into an appropriate bit-rate object and streams it to the user. Hence, TeC works well regardless of whether the content origin supports various bit-rate versions of the videos or not.

We propose three different caching algorithms for the TeC system. TEC-11 and TEC-12 cache at most one version of a video object at the proxy at any time. These two algorithms operate differently when there is a *transcode hit*. On the other hand, TEC-2 may cache multiple versions of the same video and hence reduces the processing load on the transcoder.

3.1 Cache Single Version (TEC-11 and TEC-12):

This algorithm allows at most one version of a video object to be cached at the proxy at any single time. By caching only one version, we store more video objects and efficiently utilize the storage space. The main challenge of this algorithm is deciding which bit-rate version of the video to cache. When an exact cache hit occurs, the TeC proxy refreshes the access record of the object and streams it to the client. If a request leads to a cache miss, the TeC proxy fetches the video from the origin server, transcodes it if needed. streams it to the user and caches it. Remember that we consider each version of a video as an independent item; although a request is to a video that is cached, if the request had to be responded from the content origin (i.e., the user requests a higher bit-rate version than the cached one), then it is a cache miss.

When a user requests version *bi* of a video while *bj*, where *bi>bj*, exists in the cache, *bj* is removed before *bi* is fetched from origin server and subsequently cached at the proxy. Since we allow only one version of an object to be cached, the lower bit-rate version is evicted from the cache. If a request results in a transcode hit, the TeC proxy transcodes the cached object to an appropriate bit-rate and streams it to the user. In the mean time, the proxy chooses which version to cache in two different ways, which leads to two variations of the algorithm. For algorithm TEC-11, the proxy refreshes the access record of the already cached object (i.e., the higher bit-rate) without caching the newly transcoded version. For algorithm TEC-12 the proxy evicts the transcodable version from the cache and stores the newly transcoded version. In summary, if the client requests version *bj* of a video while *bi*, where *bi>bj* , exists in the cache, *bj* is transcoded from *bi* and streamed to the user. TEC-11 refreshes the access record of bi, but TEC-12 removes *bi* and caches *bj*.

Whenever the cache is full and requests to the un-cached video are received, certain files in the cache must be replaced. We use the existing popular cache replacement algorithms (e.g., LRU, LFU) for this purpose. The pseudocode of TEC-11 and TEC-12 is presented in Figure 2.

3.2 Cache Multiple Versions (TEC-2)

The motivation of caching multiple versions of the same video object is to reduce the processing load on the transcoder. For example, if *bi* and *bj* are both in the cache, a request to *bj* will lead to an exact hit and no transcoding is needed. In addition, if the accesses to a certain video object across its variants shows high temporal locality, TEC-2 may further improve the caching efficiency. When there is a cache miss, the TeC proxy fetches the video from the origin, transcodes it to the requested version if required, streams it to the client and caches it even when other bit-rate versions of the same video object are in the cache. Consequently, multiple versions of a popular video can be cached at a given time. If a transcode hit occurs, the transcoder generates the requested version. It is subsequently delivered to the end user and cached in the proxy. For

```
Version b_i of a video object is requested...

if b_i is already in the proxy cache
   stream b_i to the user from the cache
   update the access record of b_i
else if b_j of the same video is in the cache and b_j > b_i
   transcode b_j into b_i
   stream the transcoded b_i to the end user
   if TEC-11
      update the access record of b_j
   if TEC-12
      evict b_j from the cache
      store b_i in the cache
      update the access record of b_i
else if b_j is in the cache and b_j < b_i
   evict b_j from the cache
   fetch version b_i of the video from the origin
   stream b_i to the end user
   if the cache space is not enough for b_i
      evict victims using a replacement algorithm
   store b_i in the cache
   update the access record of b_i
else
   fetch version b_i of the video from the origin
   stream b_i to the end user
   if the cache space is not enough for b_i
      evict victims using a replacement algorithm
   store b_i in the cache
   update the access record of b_i
```

Figure 2. Cache single version algorithms TEC-11 and TEC-12

```
Version b_i of a video object is requested...

if b_i is already in the proxy cache
   stream b_i to the user from the cache
   update the access record of b_i
else if b_j is in the proxy cache and b_j > b_i
   transcode b_j into b_i
   stream the transcoded b_i to the end user
   if the cache space is not enough for b_i
      evict victims using a replacement algorithm
   store b_i in the cache
   update the access record of b_i and b_j
else
   fetch version b_i of the video from the origin
   stream b_i to the end user
   if the cache space is not enough for b_i
      evict victims using a replacement algorithm
   store b_i in the cache
   update the access record of b_i
```

Figure 3. Cache multiple versions, algorithm TEC-2

example, if the client requests version *bj* of a video while *bi (bi>bj)* exists in the cache, *bj* is transcoded from bi, delivered to the user, and cached. Note that both bi and bj now exist in the cache.

Similar to TEC-11 and TEC-12, when we need space to cache new objects, we use an existing cache replacement algorithm. Figure 3 shows the pseudocode of TEC-2 algorithm

4. Principle of Meta-caching

To illustrate the principle of meta-caching, we first define a storage versus computing space.

4.1 StorageComputing (SC) Space

Given any media adaptation process, meta-caching is defined as the caching of intermediate results that are created during the course of the adaptation process. As an example, Figure 4 defines the flow graph of a certain media adaptation process composed of four computing sub-modules. Caching the intermediate result from each of the four sub-modules leads to skipping that sub module in the next identical session so that the computing of that sub-module is saved. However, some storage space is required to store the intermediate result. In general, caching the output of each sub-module maps to one point in a space, called *Storage vs. Computing space*. Suppose Figure 4 illustrates such a mapping for this particular process. The vertical axis indicates the amount of storage required to store the intermediate results from any of the sub-modules, relative to storing the final processed results. The horizontal axis indicates the amount of computing load required to create the final result with the help of the intermediate results from any of the sub-modules. This computing load is relative to the computing load when the intermediate result is not available, i.e., the computing load of the full adaptation process.

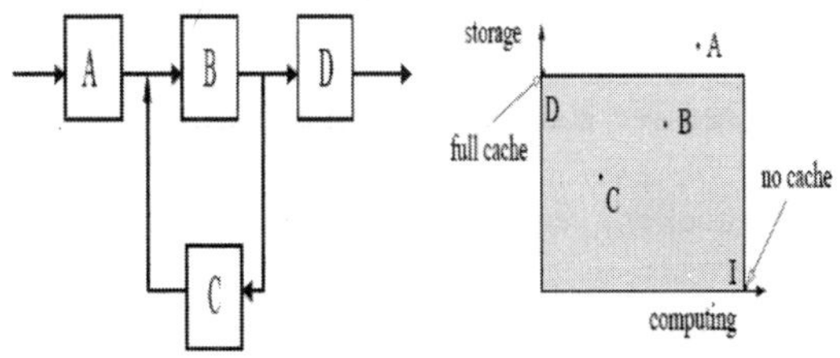

Figure 4: an example processing flow and the corresponding mapping in the SC space

Clearly, if the intermediate result of any sub-module is directly available (from a cache, for example) instead of computing it from the input, the computing load required to create the final output is smaller. Now we discuss some of the specific points within the SC space. If nothing from the flow is cached, the point I (no cache) indicates no storage requirement. But 100% of the CPU is required when a final adapted output is requested. On the other hand, if the final output is cached (full cache), 100% of the storage is required while no computing is needed. In MPEG transcoding, they can be mapped to the caching of sequence-level and pixel-level metadata, as the former requires less storage space and more computing than the latter.

5. Design of AMTrac

As aforementioned, AMTrac should work adaptively perform transcoding based on the client access pattern and available resources dynamically. Thus, it is important to monitor the dynamically changing system resource availability and the client access pattern. In this section, *Resource-driven Replacement Policy* and *Reactive Cache Adjustment* are designed to work with *Progressive Request Admission* for these purposes.Assume the proxy provides *v* different versions of an object to client requests in AMTrac. Each object version is either cached with its metadata only or cached with its fully transcoded result. Thus, in AMTrac, the cache space is logically split into two parts. One is for caching metadata of different object versions, and the other is to cache the fully transcoded object versions. The size of each part changes dynamically. AMTrac keeps track of the requested object version, even after an object version is evicted. We use the following data structure for each object to record important runtime information to assist the implementation of a proposed strategy. In this structure, *Ps* is calculated as the ratio of the *active disk size* over the *total disk size*. The *active disk size* is the sum of the size of all active (requested) cached objects at present. The *total disk size* is the total available cache size. Based on these, the following policies work together to implement AMTrac.

5.1 Progressive Request Admission:

Upon a client request for the *jth* version of an object, there are three cases as follows:

• If the requested object version *j* is fully cached, the request is directly served and the corresponding data item, *r*[*j*], is increased by 1.

• If the requested object version is cached with its metadata, the request is served with the online meta-transcoding (Transcoding based on metadata). The transcoded result is sent to the client. The corresponding data item, *r*[*j*], is increased by1. The reactive cache adjustment is activated to determine whether this fully transcoded object version should be cached or not.

• If the requested object version does not exist in the cache:

– If the object version is being accessed for the first time, the proxy performs online transcoding to produce the object version *j*. Correspondingly, the metadata is cached.The corresponding data item, *r*[*j*], is increased by 1.*ms*[*j*] gets updated. The status of this object version *s*[*j*] is set to 1. If there is insufficient cache space, the replacement policy is activated to make room for its caching.

– If the object version has been accessed and its status is replaced (*s*[*j*] = 0), the object version is transcoded again and sent to the client. *r*[*j*], is increased by 1.The reactive cache adjustment is activated to determine whether the corresponding metadata should get cached.

Table 1 Field of Data structures

field	information
α	storage for caching metadata (relative to full result)
β	CPU for producing the fully-transcoded object from metadata (relative to no cache)
v	the total number of versions of each object
$ms[1..v]$	an array to record the metadata size of each version
$fs[1..v]$	an array to record the full data size of each version
$r[1..v]$	an array to record the references to each version
$s[1..v]$	object status with 0 for being replaced, 1 for cached
$U[1..v]$	the utility value of the object version
P_s	current storage utilization (%)
P_c	current CPU utilization (%)

5.2 Resource drivenReplacement Policy

When there is not enough cache space, replacement is activated.To maximize cache performance, clearly, it is important to select the right victim.In our design, a utility based policy is used to select the right victim. The utility function is designed as follows:

$$U(i_j) = \begin{cases} \frac{r_j}{S_j} \times \frac{\alpha_j}{\alpha_j+\beta_j} & \text{if } P_c \geq P_s, \\ \frac{r_j}{S_j} \times \frac{\beta_j}{\alpha_j+\beta_j} & \text{if } P_c < P_s. \end{cases} \quad (1)$$

In equation 1, *Sj* indicates the occupied cache space of this object version, where *Sj* = *max*(*ms*[*j*], *fs*[*j*]); *rj* is the reference number to this object version; *αj* is the storage unit (in percentage) used for caching the metadata of version *j*, while *βj* is the CPU unit to transcode to the final version *j*; *Pc* represents the current CPU utilization, and *Ps* indicates the current storage utilization.

Thus, in this equation, *rj*/ *Sj* considers that if an object version is more popular with a unit storage, the object version should have a high utility value and has higher chance to be cached. If *Pc* > *Ps*, the current system is CPU constrained, so the utilization of the storage is encouraged. If *Pc* < *Ps*, the system is storage constrained, and the utilization of the CPU is encouraged.

Thus, the utility of an object version considers both the object popularity and the current available resources to find the least valuable object version. Each time the replacement policy is activated, all cached object versions must refresh their utility. Based on the utility function, we design the replacement policy as follows.

When the replacement policy is activated, it compares all the object versions in the cache based on their utility values. The one with the minimum value is selected as the victim and the following procedure loops until sufficient space is found.

- If the selected victim has its fully transcoded data cached in the proxy, the system selects to evict its fully cached data and caches its meta data (it consumes a bit more CPU and it is done when the next time a request is received for this object version). *fs*[*j*] is set to 0, while *ms*[*j*] is updated accordingly.
- If the selected victim has only metadata cached, the metadata is evicted, *ms*[*j*] is set to 0. *r*[*j*] is set to 0. The corresponding object version status, *s*[*j*], is also set to be replaced.

5.3 Reactive Cache Adjustment

According to our design, for each object version, there could be three possible cases, namely replaced, with metadata cached, or with fully transcoded result cached. To accommodate the dynamic client accesses and thus to maximize the system performance, we design the reactive cache adjustment policy upon diffᵉrent situations.This adjustment is passive since it is always invoked due to new client requests.

- If a currently replaced object version is accessed, the system starts to evaluate whether the current utility of this object version is increased and is large enough to get cached. The new utility is calculated assuming the object version consumes *ms*[*j*] for storage. If the utility is larger than the utility of any cached one, the metadata of this object version gets cached and *ms*[*j*] and *u*[*j*] are set accordingly. The replacement policy is activated if needed.
- If an object version is cached with metadata, the system starts to evaluate whether the fully transcoded data of this object version should be cached or not. Assuming the fully transcoded object version is cached using space *fs*[*j*], its corresponding utility value is compared with the current cached object versions. If the new utility of this object version is higher than that of any cached one, the fully transcoded object version gets cached. Its *fs*[*j*] and *u*[*j*] are updated accordingly. Correspondingly, its metadata gets evicted and *ms*[*j*] is set to 0. Additional space is reclaimed with the assistance of the replacement policy when necessary.

6. Performance Analysis

Algorithm TEC-11 that caches higher bit-rate versions shows better result than TEC-12. TEC-2 achieves less improvement over LRU compared with TEC-11 because TEC- 11 stores larger number of unique video objects .The Transcoding load is significantly lighter in TEC-2 since it caches multiple versions of the same object. We also observe that the transcoding load of FVO is much heavier than other algorithms. Compared with FVO, TEC-11 achieves similar overall byte hit ratio with less transcoding load.

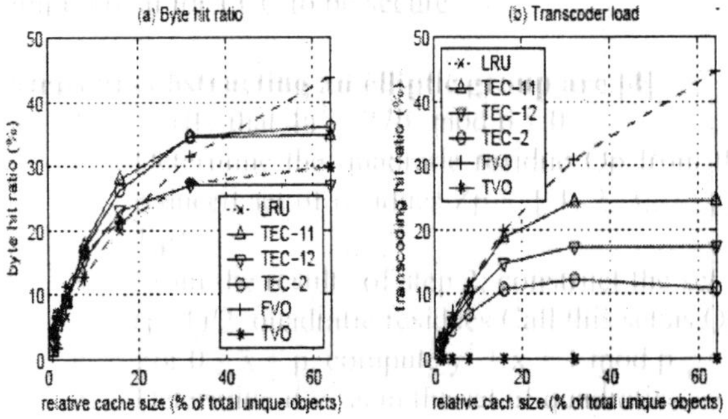

Figure 5: Performance Comparison

When compared with FVO and TVO, the TEC algorithms generally showed better performance with less Transcoding load. When the cache size is large or full versions are requested more often, FVO achieves the highest byte hit ratio as it stores more full version objects and serves requests to lower bit-rate versions by transcoding. However, it comes with the price of high transcoding load. TEC and TVO put less burden on the transcoder than FVO. The performance of TVO could not match that of TECs however, as it does not support transcoding from an already transcoded object in the cache. Hence TVO requires more traffic between the content origin and the transcoding proxy than TECs. In addition, TVO may cause the cache to store multiple versions of the same video in an undeterministic fashion. On the other hand, TEC-11 and TEC-12 store at most one version per object. Among TECs, TEC-2 gave good performances when the cache size is large, users are in heterogeneous environment, and the access pattern shows strong temporal locality.

Comparing full caching with no caching since full-caching is storage constrained, with larger cache space, more client requests could be served from cache without repetitive transcoding. although metacaching and AMTrac have a higher CPU load with the increase of cache size, throughput of these approaches is higher than that of full-caching.

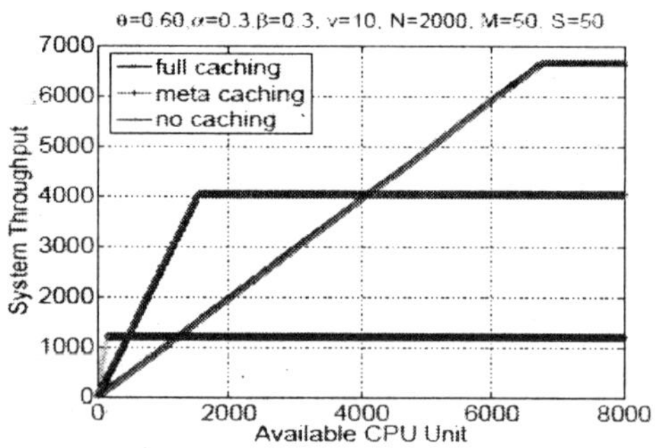

Figure 6: Comparisons between three methods: available CPU ranges up to 8000

7. Related Work

Some studies on transcoding proxy services for images and videos exist. However, little work has been done on exploring the impact of transcoding on proxy caching. Due to the large size of media objects, some research has examined the effectiveness of caching them partially (e.g., prefix caching and segment-based caching)[3,4].

Many researchers have contemplated with the idea of putting transcoders at network intermediaries. Transcoding of HTML and image contents is explored but they do not cover streaming media transcoding. MOWSER InfoPyramid data model allows mobile users to specify the QoS parameters.Although all of the above mentioned work investigates transcoding, none considers caching. There are several recent studies that propose caching algorithms for transcoding proxies. Soft caching , Net- Blitz , and TranSquid are transcoding enabled proxy systems that propose caching, but they focus only on web images and not streaming videos.

Several schemes for caching video streams from the Internet have been proposed. These schemes however, do not use transcoding at the local network proxies. Prefix caching stores the initial parts of popular videos on the proxy to reduce the playback latency. Selective caching stores only certain parts of the video. The selection of the frames depends on network environments. Partial caching with server scheduling is considered in for saving bandwidth from the origin server.

8. Summary & conclusions

We evaluated the performance of TEC algorithms and compared them with the traditional network caches without transcoding capability, and with FVO and TVO that also combine streaming media caching with transcoding. TeC improves the cache effectiveness, decreases the user perceived latency, and reduces the traffic between the proxy and the content origin server.

In this paper, We proposed the Transcoding-enabled Caching (TeC) system for streaming media distribution networks. By placing the transcoding service at the proxies, we perform content adaptation at the network intermediaries. We proposed various caching strategies for our TeC system. In an corporate environment where users show less heterogeneity, caching one version for each video object is desirable. When the users have heterogeneous environment and the access pattern has strong temporal locality, caching multiple versions of popular objects is beneficial.

A meta-caching scheme is proposed that offers a new point of control in the computing and storage space. With model-based analysis on the meta-caching scheme, we propose an adaptive meta-caching system, called AMTrac, which can adaptively use the meta-caching scheme based on client accesses and available resources in the system. Experiments show that it significantly outperforms existing strategies.

9. References

[1] J. Wang, "A survey of web caching schemes for the internet," *ACM Computer Communication Review*, vol. 29, no. 5, pp. 36–46, Oct. 1999.

[2] B. Shen, S. Lee, and S. Basu. Caching strategies in transcoding-enabled proxy systems for streaming media distribution networks. In *IEEE Transactions on Multimedia*, volume 6, pages 375–386, April 2004.

[3] S. Chen, B. Shen, S. Wee, and X. Zhang, "Adaptive and lazy segmentation based proxy caching for streaming media delivery," in *Proc. ACM NOSSDAV 2003*, Monterey, CA, June 2003, pp. 22–32.

[4] S. Sen, J. Rexford, and D. Towsley, "Proxy prefix caching for multimedia streams," in *Proc. IEEE INFOCOM'99*, New York, NY, Mar. 1999, pp. 1310–1319.

[5] C-W. Lin J. Xin and M-T. Sun. Digital video transcoding. In *Proceedings of IEEE*, volume 93(1), pages 84–97, Jan. 2005.

[6] X. Tang, F. Zhang, and S. T. Chanson. Streaming media caching algorithms for transcoding proxies. In *Proceedings of the 31st International Conference on Parallel Processing (ICPP)*, Vancouver, Canada, August 2002.

Cryptography using Elliptic Curve – Multiplication Issue

Ms. Yogita S. Pagar
Lecturer, Dept. of Information Technology, P.E.S. College of Engineering, Aurangabad
yspagar@yahoo.com

Abstract

Public key algorithms create a mechanism for sharing keys among large numbers of participants or entities in a complex information system. Unlike other popular algorithms such as RSA, ECC is based on discrete logarithms that much more difficult to challenge at equivalent key lengths. At the time of its discovery, the ECC algorithm was described and placed in the public domain. This paper explains the Montgomery Algorithm for large number multiplication and its use in Elliptic curve Cryptography. There are many forms of Montgomery Algorithm. We have studied software implementations. ECC is implemented over a prime field.

Keywords: *Elliptic Curve Cryptography (ECC), Elliptic Curve discrete logarithm problem (ECDLP), Montgomery Multiplication*

1. Introduction

At the foundation of every cryptosystem is a hard mathematical problem that is computationally infeasible to solve. The discrete logarithm problem is the basis for the security of many cryptosystems including the Elliptic Curve Cryptosystem. More specifically, the ECC relies upon the difficulty of the Elliptic Curve Discrete Logarithm Problem (ECDLP) [3].

The two geometrically defined operations over certain elliptic curve groups, point addition and point doubling form the core part in developing the ECC system. By selecting a point in an elliptic curve group, one can double it to obtain the point 2P. After that, one can add the point P to the point 2P to obtain the point 3P. The determination of a point kP in this manner is referred to as Scalar Multiplication of a point. The ECDLP is based upon the intractability of scalar multiplication products.

2. Logarithm Problem

In the multiplicative group Zp*, the discrete logarithm problem is: given elements r and q of the group, and a prime p, find a number k such that r = qk mod p. If the elliptic curve groups is described using multiplicative notation, then the elliptic curve discrete logarithm problem is: given points P and Q in the group, find a number that Pk = Q; k is called the discrete logarithm of Q to the base P. When the elliptic curve group is described using additive notation, the elliptic curve discrete logarithm problem is: given points P and Q in the group, find a number k such that Pk = Q. In a real application, k would be large enough such that it would be infeasible to determine k in this manner [3].

3. ECC Basics

3.1 Elliptic Curves

An elliptic curve over real numbers may be defined as the set of points (x,y) which satisfy an elliptic curve equation of the form:

$$\mathbf{y^2 = x^3 + ax + b,} \qquad \text{(i)}$$

where x, y, a and b are real numbers.

Each choice of the numbers a and b yields a different elliptic curve. For example, a = -4 and b = 0.67 gives the elliptic curve with equation $\mathbf{y^2 = x^3 - 4x + 0.67}$; If $x^3 + ax + b$ contains no repeated factors, or equivalently if

$$\mathbf{4a^3 + 27b^2 \neq 0} \qquad \text{(ii)}$$

then the elliptic curve $\mathbf{y^2 = x^3 + ax + b}$, can be used to form a group. To define the gtoup an operation called addition denoted by + is defined for the set E(a,b) where a and b satisfy equation (ii). In geometric terms the rules for addition can be stated as follows: If three points on an elliptic curve lie on a straight line, their sum is *O*. From this definition the rules of addition over an elliptic curve are defined as follows [3].

1. *O* serves as the additive identity. Thus *O*=- *O* ; for any point P on the elliptic curve , A+ *O*=A.
2. The negative of the point A is the point with the same x coordinate but the negative of the y coordinate i.e. A=(x,y) then –A=(x,-y). These points can be joined by vertical line(as shown in Fig. 1)
3. To add two points A and B with different x coordinate draw a straight line between them and find the third point of intersection C.
4. The geometric interpretation of the preceding item also applies to two points C & -C with same x coordinate. Therefore we have C + (-C) = *O*

5. To double a point A, draw the tangent line and find the other point of intersection C, then A + A= 2A = -C (as shown in Fig. 2).

With the preceding list of rules it can be shown that the set E(a,b) is an Abelian Group[3].

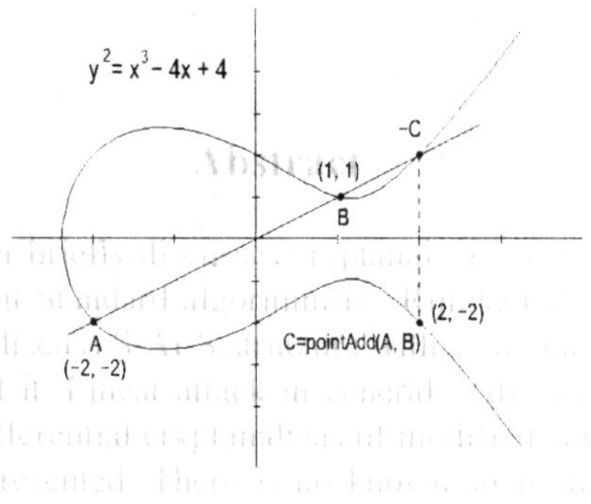

Fig. 1 Point Addition on Elliptic Curve

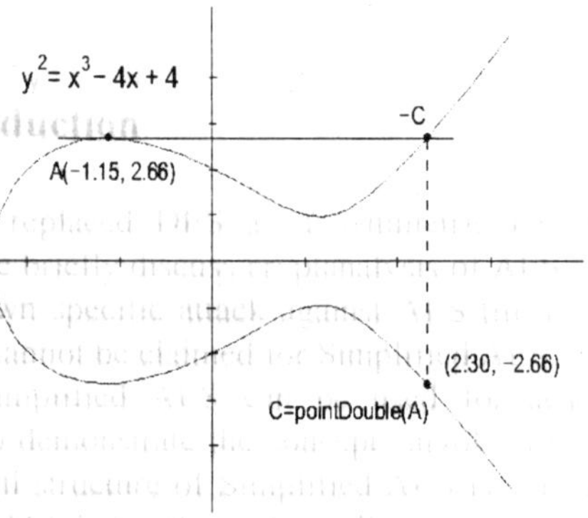

Fig. 2 Elliptic Curve Point Doubling

3.2 Elliptic Curves over F *p*

For a prime curve over Fp we use a cubic equation in which the variables and coefficients all take on values in the set of integers from 0 through P-1 and in which calculations are performed modulo P.

Prime curves are best for software applications because the extended bit-fiddling operations needed by binary curves are not required.

3.3 Elliptic Curves over $F2^m$

For a binary curve defined over $GF(2^m)$ the variables and coefficients all take on values in $GF(2^m)$ and in calculations are performed over $GF(2^m)$.

Binary curves are best for Hardware applications where it takes remarkably few logic gates to create a powerful fast cryptosystem.

4. Elliptic Curves Over Prime Field

Let the prime number p=23 and let us consider a=1 and b=1 ,$a^3+27b^2 \bmod p \neq 0$We then determine the quadratic residues Q_{23} from the reduced set of residues $Z_{23}=\{1,2,3,.....21,22\}$

Table 1 Modular Arithmetic

x^2 mod p	$(p-x)^2$ mod p	=
1^2 mod 23	22^2 mod 23	1
2^2 mod 23	21^2 mod 23	4
3^2 mod 23	20^2 mod 23	9
4^2 mod 23	19^2 mod 23	16
5^2 mod 23	18^2 mod 23	2
6^2 mod 23	17^2 mod 23	13
7^2 mod 23	16^2 mod 23	3
8^2 mod 23	15^2mod 23	18
9^2 mod 23	14^2 mod 23	12
10^2 mod 23	13^2 mod 23	8
11^2 mod 23	12^2 mod 23	6

Therefore the set of [(p-1)/2]-1 quadratic residues $Q_{23}=\{1,2,3,4,6,8,9,12,13,16,18\}$. Now for $0<=x<p$, compute $y^2=x^3+x+1 \bmod 23$ and determine if y^2 is in the set of quadratic residues Q_{23}: [2]

Table 2 Quadratic Residues

X	0	1	2	3	4	5	6	7	8	9	10	11
Y^2	1	3	11	8	0	16	16	6	15	3	22	9
$y^2 \in Q_{23}$	Y	Y	N	Y	N	Y	Y	Y	N	Y	N	Y
Y1	1	7		10	0	4	4	11		7		3
Y2	22	16		13	0	19	19	12		16		20

Contd...

x	12	13	14	15	16	17	18	19	20	21	22
y^2	16	3	22	10	19	9	9	2	17	14	22
$y^2 \in Q_{23}$	Y	Y	N	N	N	Y	Y	Y	N	N	N
y1	4	7				3	3	5			
y2	19	16				20	20	18			

The elliptic group Ep(a,b) = $E_{23}(1,1)$ thus include the points:

$E_{23}(1, 1)$ ={ (0,1) (0,22) (1,7) (1,16) (3,10) (3,13) (4 , 0) (5, 4) (5, 19) (6, 4) (6, 19) (7, 11) (7, 12) (9, 7) (9, 16) (11, 3) (11, 20) (12,4) (12,19) (13,7) (13,16) (17,3) (17, 20) (18, 3) (18, 20) (19,5) (19,18) }

Figure 3 shows a scatter plot of Elliptic group E_{23} (1,1) [2].

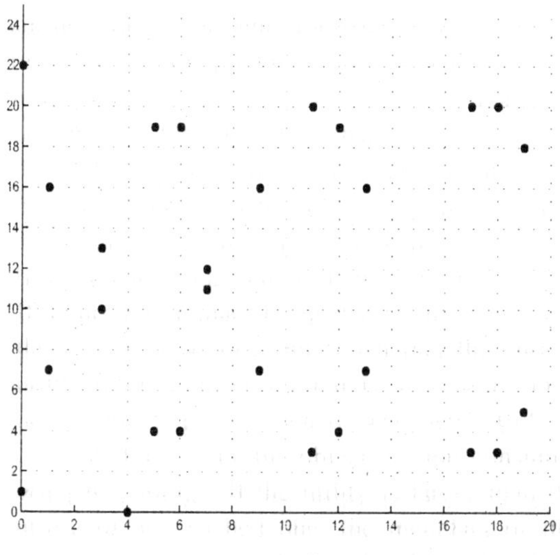

Fig. 3 Scatter plot of Elliptic curve $E_{23}(1,1)$

5. ECC Encryption and Decryption

Firstly plain text message m is encoded in an (x, y) point Pm. Pm point is encrypted and subsequently decrypted. When key exchange algorithm is used, an encryption/ decryption system requires a base point G and an elliptic group Ep (a, b) as parameters.

When a communication between the two users A and B is considered, user A selects a private key nA and generates a public key PA=nA*G. Similarly user B selects a private key nB and generates a public key PB=nB*G. To encrypt and send a message Pm to B, A chooses a random positive integer number k and produces the cipher text Cm that contains a pair of points: Cm = {kG, Pm + kPB}. Nobody except A knows the value of k and nobody except for B can remove the mask kPB. For an attacker to remove the message, the attacker would have to compute k, when k*G and the value of G. This calculation should be impractical for ECC to be secure.

Steps of constructing an elliptic group are [4]:

1. Verify that $4a^3 + 27b^2 \bmod p \neq 0$
2. Determine the quadratic residue Qp from the reduced set of residues Zp = { 1, 2, 3,,….., p-1,p}
3. From the results of step 2, construct the set of (p- 1)/2, quadratic residues Call this set as Qp
4. For $0 \leq x < p$, compute $y^2 + x + 1 \bmod p$
5. Determine if y^2 is in the set of quadratic
6. residues Q23.
7. The elliptic group Ep(a, b) is obtained form the results of step 5

6. Problem of Large Number Multiplication

The choice of multiplier configuration is an important one in large number multiplications. Since it is the building block used to perform the multiplications. The choice of using a symmetric multiplier vs. a non-symmetric one is analyzed. The non-symmetric multiplies has 3 intrinsic problems that make it unfavorable for performing large number multiplications [3].

1. The partial product configuration makes row carry propagate difficult.
2. The partial product configuration makes column accumulate difficult.
3. The size of the partial products is irregular.

For these reasons the Non-Symmetric multipliers are deemed inappropriate for large number multiplication. Other than the symmetry, the decision of the size of multiplier used is also important. There are several factors that play a role in the choice of multiplier, these factors include speed, size and power consumption. Smaller multipliers are faster, for larger numbers, the smaller multipliers will require a longer time to perform the total multiplication. A multiplication of number as large as 1024 bits requires a lot of computation.

Assuming we have an N * N multiplier, in order to multiply two numbers of lengths NM would require M2 multiplications. Each multiplication outputs a result of length 2 * N, this result is the partial product of the multiplication. These partial products have to be summed in an efficient manner to produce the final output. Carry follow and overflow prevention are the two methods available for large multiplication.

The advantage of the carry follow method is that it doesn't require a lot of additional resources, namely extra registers. The additions are performed in order, while some sub word permutations are required to properly align the partial products for additions. It can be clearly seen that this method does not provide the highest benefits in term of number of calculations. The advantage of the overflow prevention method is that it does not require following the overflow bit. This means that the additions do not need to be performed in order.

A much higher degree of instruction level parallelism can be achieved since additions can be performed in order.

Another advantage is that this method provides improved performance overt the carry follow method. This comes at the price of added resources, namely this method requires a larger number of registers.

Encryption methods such as RSA use modular arithmetic, specifically modular exponentiation.

Modular exponentiation requires performing large number multiplication as well as division to be able to represent numbers in modular form. The division, however, is extremely computationally intensive, much more so than multiplication. For this reason, a method used for efficient RSA encryption and decryption requires a technique to efficiently handle the division required in modular arithmetic [3].

7. Montgomery Algorithm for Large Number Multiplication

The Montgomery multiplication algorithm is the most efficient modular multiplication algorithm available. It replaces trial division by the modulus with a series of additions and divisions by a power of 2. Thus it is well suited for hardware implementation. Long carry propagation is the major problem in large number modular arithmetic. This can be avoided by using carry save adders CASs to perform the addition stages of Montgomery's algorithm [2].

The Montgomery algorithm for modular multiplication is considered to be the fastest algorithm to compute xy mod n in computers when the values of x, y, and n are large. Suppose we want to compute xy mod n in a computer. We first choose a positive integer, r, greater than n and relative prime to n. The value of r is usually 2m for some positive integer m. This is because multiplication, division and modulo by r can be done by shifting or logical operations in computers. Since gcd(r, n) = 1, there are two numbers r-1 and n0 with 0 < r-1 < n and 0 < n0 < r, satisfying rr-1 - nn0 = 1. The algorithm is based on the fact that the computation of xr-1 mod n can be done very efficiently by the algorithm reduce.

When the numbers X, Y and N are large, we can apply the above algorithm to compute XY mod N in an efficient way [5].

8. The Montgomery Algorithm for Fast Multiplication

Montgomery reduction

Montgomery reduction is an algorithm introduced by peter L. Montgomery.

Among other things, it is used in modular arithmetic as an efficient way of performing an exponentiation of two numbers modulo a large number, i.e.

C= a b (mod n), where a, b, and n are k-bit integers.

Formal statement

Let n be a positive integer, and let R and T be integers such that r > n, gcd (n, R) = 1 and 0 < T < nR. The Montgomery reduction of T modulo n with respect to R is defined as the value TR-1 (mod n), R-1 is the modular inverse of R The algorithm used to calculate this value is much more efficient than classical method of taking product over the integer and reducing the result modulo n.

9. Use in Cryptography

Many important cryptosystems such as RSA and DSA are based on arithmetic operations, such as multiplication, modulo a large number. The classical method of calculating a modular product involves first multiplying the numbers as if they were integers and taking modulo of the result. However, modular reduction is very expensive computationally equivalent to dividing two numbers. The situation is even worse when the algorithm requires modular exponentiation. Classically, a* b (mod n) is calculated repeatedly multiplying a by itself b times, each time reducing the result modulo n. Taking a single modulo at the end of calculation will result in increasingly larger intermediate products- infeasible if b is very large.

Using Montgomery representation of numbers allows calculating a * b (mod n) for any b with only two modular reductions. A rough outline of the algorithm is as follows:

1. Find suitable R
2. Using classical method calculate,
a0 = a * R (mod n) i.e. one modular reduction.
3. Using Montgomery reduction algorithm,
repeatedly calculate,
ai = a0 + ai-1 * R-1 (mod n) = ai+1 * R (mod n).
i.e no modular reductions.
The Montgomery reduction at each step prevents this from growing.
4. Using the classical method again calculate, ai-1 * R-1 = ak mod n

There are several optimizations for this algorithm, the most obvious of which being exponentiation by squaring. Another method for modular multiplication for the calculation of x * y mod n, when a, b and n are very large, using Montgomery algorithm. To calculate x * y mod n, first choose a positive integer r, greater than n and relatively prime to n. The value of r is usually 2m for some positive integer m. This is because multiplication, division and modulo by r can be done by shifting or logical operations in computers. The two numbers are relatively prime, so we have, gcd(r, n) =1, & there are two numbers, r-1 and n' with 0< r--1 < n and 0 < n' < r, satisfying rr-1 – nn'= 1.This algorithm makes use of reduce algorithm for computing x r-1 mod n. From the above explanation we see that it is possible to calculate x * y mod n using Montgomery algorithm when x, y and n are large quantities. This paper relies on the two variables namely n' and r-1. n' variable is one of that satisfies the equation rr-1 – nn' =1. The modular multiplication and exponentiation algorithms based on Montgomery reduction technique require that the number of modulus be an odd integer.

A modular multiplication algorithm invented by Montgomery is even stranger:

1. Now suppose that we want to compute: 789098 × 123456 ÷ 1000000 modulo 876543.
2. Separate last digit of 123456
3. Multiply 789098 by it. We have partial product.
4. Now we want to divide by 10, but we can't do it because this number isn't divisible by 10. So we add a multiple of 876543, which we're allowed to do because we're working modulo 876543.
5. Repeat steps 1,2 and 3 for all digits of 789098.
6. As per the method explained, multiplying it by 1000000 and checking that it equals 770211 modulo 876543. I could not find the mathematical relation between these two numbers, 770211 and 876543 [5].

10. Conclusion

ECC is a best solution for security.
Compared to RSA, ECC offers more security.
The good thing about this technique is that the decisions about what multiple of the modulus to add depend only on the last digit of the result, which is not affected by any carries. So carry-save architecture works very well here.

11. References

[1] William Stallings,"Cryptography and Network Security: Principles and Particles", Book, (4th Edition), Pearson Publication. pp. 259 - 314

[2] Ciaran McIvor, Maire McLoone, John V McCanny, " Fast Modular Multiplication and RSA Cryprographic Processor Architectures"

[3] www.certicom.com

[4] Prof. Jean-Yves Chouinard, "Design of Secure Computer Systems CSI 1438/ CEG4394"

[5] Prof. D.J. Gaun, "Montgomery Algorithm for Modular Multiplication", SCI 162 and CSCI 284/Vora/GWU.

Cryptanalysis of Simplified AES

S. J. Karale[1] and Prof. A.S. Alvi

[1]Sr. Lecturer, YCCE, Nagpur

[2]Asstt. Prof., PRMITR,, Badnera

sjkarale@in.com

Abstract

This paper briefly discusses cryptanalysis of Advanced Encryption Standard algorithm i.e. Rijndael algorithm. We then discuss S-AES structure with some interesting aspects of it. Linear attack in general is discussed and finally differential cryptanalysis of modified simplified AES is presented. There is no known such attack for AES, but using linear attack on modified simplified AES, it can be shown that simplified AES is vulnerable to cryptanalysis attack. Here we have considered modified Simplified AES differential cryptanalytic attack.

1. Introduction

AES has replaced DES as a symmetric key block cipher. We briefly discuss cryptanalysis of AES. There is no known specific attack against AES till date, but the same cannot be claimed for Simplified AES.

The Simplified AES can be used for academic purpose to demonstrate the concepts involved in AES. The overall structure of Simplified AES is very much similar to AES but with much smaller parameters.

Linear cryptanalysis of modified Simplified AES discussed here can be further extended to consider similar attack on AES in future.

2. Cryptanalysis of AES

Till date there is no known attack against the full version of AES, which can break it faster than an exhaustive key search.

The designers of AES claim that no 4-round differential characteristic holds with probability greater than 2^{-150}, and also no 4-round linear characteristic exist with a bias greater than 2^{-75}. An analysis of the propagation of activity patterns leads to the conclusion that any linear or differential characteristic activates at least 25 S-boxes. But to prove this there must exist at least a differential or a linear hull which hold with a probability of 2^{-128} or a bias equal to 2^{-64} , respectively. This demonstrates that the cumulative effect of characteristics is very large in AES. However, more recently, Keliher et al. obtained an upper bound on the maximum average linear hull probability and also on the maximum expected differential probability of 2^{-92} for 9 rounds or more. This result is computation based. Park et al. using theoretic arguments obtained an upper bound of 2^{-112} and of 2^{-105} on the maximum differential probability, and on the maximum linear hull probability for 4 rounds of AES, respectively. Several types of integral attacks have been designed and applied with success against reduced-round versions of AES. Gilbert and Minier propose one of the most significant one. Also since AES has a simple algebraic structure, several papers have demonstrated puzzling properties, which could be exploited in the future in an attack.

3. S-AES structure

We examine some interesting aspects of the structure of AES. Fist point is that encryption and decryption algorithms begin and ends with the add key function which is easily reversible without knowledge of the key and therefore adds no security. The second point is that round two does not include the mix column function. Third related point is that although decryption algorithm is the reverse of the encryption algorithm, it does not follow the same sequence of functions.

From implementation point of view, it is desirable that decryption follows the same function sequence as encryption. This permits decryption algorithm to be implemented in the same way as the encryption algorithm increasing space efficiency.

Now if are able to interchange the second and third functions, the fourth and fifth functions, and the sixth and the seventh functions in the decryption sequence, we can create the same structure as the encryption algorithm.

This is achieved in the S-AES structure and therefore both encryption and decryption follow the same sequence giving rise to more efficient implementation.

4. Linear Cryptanalysis Simplified

Any cryptosystem (e.g. AES) of the sort we are interested in cryptanalysing can be written as a "circuit" made of "wires," "XOR gates", and nonlinear multi-input, multi-output "Sboxes." The "input" bits are the key and plaintext, while the output bits are the ciphertext. Each S-box may be replaced by its best linear approximating circuit (which is made purely of wires, XOR gates, and "constant 1s") and "noise gates" attached to the outputs. By "best approximation" we mean, among all Boolean GF2-linear functions of the inputs, find the ones, which agrees with each output at the most possible input configurations. And then add a "noise gate" to that output. "Noise gates" are 1-input, 1-output gates, which with some probability p perform an inversion $x \to \neg x$, but with probability $1 - p$ just transmit the input unchanged. Actually, for this to be an equivalent circuit, these inversion decisions have to be nonrandom and in fact are governed by some nonlinear function of the S-box inputs (or outputs). The approximate probabilistic model is to model all the noise gates as actually making independent random decisions. That is a good model because cryptosystems are generally intentionally designed to "look random." We can either make this approximation, or not (i.e. be exact). We can be able to retain exactness all the way until the final cryptanalytic step 6. If we want to be approximate, then label each noise gate with its characteristic probability value p. In fact it will be more convenient not to deal with p, but rather with the unbalance defined by $u = |1 - 2p|$. Note $0 \leq p < ½$ and $0 < u \leq 1$. If we want to be exact, then label each noise gate with a description of exactly what nonlinear function of which bits tell it when to invert. Reversibility lemma: It is artificial to regard XOR gates as having two "inputs" and one "output." In fact all 3 wires are equivalent; any two of them determine the other's logical state and according to the same function in all cases. Also, is similarly is artificial to regard noise gates as having an "input" and an "output." Again both wires are equivalent and the thing is reversible.

Noise gate mobility lemma: If we slide a noise gate along a wire, through an XOR or other noise gate, and continue along the wire (either wire is OK, if we go through an XOR gate7) continuing as far as we want, then the new circuit will be entirely equivalent to the old one.

We (although this is not needed for attacking AES) can also slide XOR gates along wires and through each other in various ways.

Noise gate unbalance lemma: The unbalance of each noise gate will be at least 2–n assuming all S-boxes have ≤ 2n input bits. Specific S-boxes may involve even-more-unbalanced noise gates that these (worse S-box designs have larger u and lead to easier-to-crack cryptosystems) but every noise gate shall be at least this unbalanced.

Piling-up lemma: With n noise-gates in succession along a wire.

1. If the noise-gate inversion decisions are modeled as statistically independent, then the net effect is the same as a single noise gate with unbalance U = u1u2u3 · · · un , which is the product of the individual unbalances. (And again $0 < P < 1/2$.)
2. But if two noise-gate inversion decisions perhaps are dependent in a positively correlated manner, then this product is a lower bound: $U \geq u_1u_2u_3 \cdots u_n$.
3. To get minimum confidence that we know any particular key bit, it is sufficient to perform U–2 experiments (if that bit is attached to an unbalance-U noise gate and we only see the noise-corrupted bit each experiment).

Warning: The quadratic formula was designed to work over the complex field and will not necessarily work over finite fields since the square and cube roots it asks for, may not exist. (And really, polynomial equations over finite fields do not necessarily have solutions, although in our cases a solution must exist.) However, square and fourth roots of $GF(2^8)$-elements always exist and for random field elements, cube roots exist with probability > 1/3. So it will work with decent probability. It is not possible to prove secret-key cryptosystem security without first proving P6=NP. In the other direction, it currently usually is not possible to prove cryptanalysis will be successful without making heuristic probabilistic assumptions about the cryptosystem, which strictly speaking are false. Actually, exactness could be retained even then too, but at that point we apparently won't be able to do much useful unless you make an approximation. It may, however, be possible to retain exactness on just some noise gates but treating the rest probabilistically, thus improving over a pure-approximate approach. That might be a good focus for future research.

But we should not "go both ways" – the total number of noise gates is conserved! Also, it is not allowed to slide a noise gate past a "T-junction", where two wires are soldered together, but that need not be an obstacle because it is possible to slide the T-junctions themselves, including through XOR gates, provided appropriate duplicate XOR gates are then added to the circuit to generate the correct duplicate signals Or, we can duplicate the noise gate and "slide it both ways" through the T-junction and up both foreign arms. Either way, this costs more gates but enables further sliding.

We are now ready to explain linear cryptanalysis:

1. Write down the equivalent circuit of the cryptosystem.
2. Replace all nonlinear S-boxes by their equivalent circuits [best linear approx. followed by or preceded by noise gates] The

linear circuits all are to be written in terms of XOR gates and constant 1s only.

3. Use noise-gate mobility to slide all the noise gates along the wires until they reach key-bit inputs. (Note: the topology of the wire-interconnections may make this impossible for some cryptosystems, at least without enormous duplication requirements caused by "sliding through T-junctions"; but it is trivially possible for the AES cryptosystem, since each noise gate (we locate them at the S-box inputs) only needs to slide though a single XOR gate to reach a key-bit, at which point each and every bit of the [extended] key will talk to a totally-GF2-linear circuit through exactly one noise gate.)
4. We may now use reversibility to regard the plaintext and ciphertext bits as the "inputs" and the key bits as "outputs." If the number of key bits is less than or equal to the number of plaintext bits then (in general) the values of the key bits (although polluted by noise) will thus be determined. We then just do this over and over again with different random plaintext-ciphertext pairs each time to average out the noise and determine the key bits with confidence.
5. However, if the number of key bits is large enough then they will not actually be determined by the plaintext and ciphertext (underdetermined system, more unknowns than equations). But each pc-pair (for an n-bit plaintext) will always give a set of n GF2-linear equations satisfied by the set of noise-corrupted-key-bits.

5. Differential Cryptanalysis of modified S-AES

In order to use differential cryptanalysis to break 16-round, 56-bit DES an attacker needs 2^{47} chosen plaintexts (approx. 985 terabytes) and a computational effort on the order of 2^{47}. The number of chosen plaintexts needed is dependent on the ability of XOR differences to propagate through a block cipher algorithm (and therefore partly dependent on the number rounds) and the computational effort comes from the size of the subkey used for each round. The search space of differential cryptanalysis is the subkey of the last round and not the encryption key.

It's also interesting to know that the use of independent subkeys, in place of a 56-bit key and a subkey generation algorithm to produce 16 48-bit subkeys, is not of muchuse against differential cryptanalysis. Once an attacker has the subkey for the last round, they can attack the second-to-the last round. They can climb the rounds of your block cipher like a latter and recover all 16 independent subkeys without significantly more effort than if you had just used a subkey generation algorithm. Your 768-bit encryption key can be broken in 48-bit chunks independent of one another.

Given below is a step-by-step differential cryptanalysis on a modified version of SDES, which has three rounds, no initial or final permutation, and uses three independent subkeys.

Step 1: Choose an XOR difference for the plaintext pairs

We'll use an XOR difference of "10000000." This means that each of our plaintext pairs will differ in only the first bit. For example "00000000" will be paired with "10000000", "00000001" will be paired with "10000001", ..., "01100100" will be paired with "11100100", ..., and "01111111" will be paired with "11111111".

Step 2: Generate ciphertext pairs for some plaintext pairs

Differential cryptanalysis is a chosen plaintext attack, so we need access to the encryption equipment with the key installed. This doesn't mean we can see the key, though we just need to have access to the equipment.

We're going to encrypt 25 randomly chosen plaintext pairs from our plaintext pairs above, for a total of 50 encryptions. If our cipher had more rounds we would have to do a lot more work.

When we do these 50 encryptions we get 25 ciphertext pairs, paired by the fact that both ciphertexts in a pair came from one of the plaintexts of a plaintext pair.

Plaintext -> Ciphertext
One pair:
01111001 -> 11111001
11111001 -> 11111110
Second pair:
01000100 -> 10101100
11000100 -> 10011001
A third pair:
00000011 -> 01000010
10000011 -> 10110111
etc.

Step 3: Get 2 pieces of information out of each ciphertext pair

3.1) The first piece of information we want out of each ciphertext pair is what the input to E/P was for the last round. This is trivial. The right half of the ciphertext is what went into E/P. So, for the second pair, the two inputs to E/P were "1100" for the first ciphertext and "1001" for the second.

3.2) The second piece of information we need is not so trivial. We're going to have to find out what the expected XOR difference that came out of the S-boxes in the last round was. Let's do this for the second ciphertext pair. We already know that the left halves of our two ciphertexts for this pair are "1010" and "1001". Their XOR difference is "0011" then, because the second and third bits differ.

Now we want to know what kind of XOR difference went into the XOR4. Fortunately, differences propagate through XORs as if they themselves were being XORed. Let's say that A1, B1, C1, A2, B2, and C2 are all bits and that C1 = A1 XOR B1 and C2 = A2 XOR B2. If we know that A1 and A2 are different and B1 and B2 are the same, then we know that C1 and C2 are different. If A1 and A2 are different and B1 and B2 are also different, then we know that C1 and C2 are the same. Obviously, if A1 and A2 are the same and B1 and B2 are the same then C1 is the same as C2. So to know the XOR difference between C1 and C2 we just take the XOR difference between A1 and A2 and the XOR difference between B1 and B2 and XOR them.

We know that the left half of the plaintext was used as input to the XOR4 in the first round. The plaintext XOR difference for a pair is "10000000". The XOR difference of the output of the first round must also be "10000000" then. After the switch the XOR difference is "00001000". Round 2 doesn't touch the right half so the XOR output of round 2 is "00001000". After a switch we have the input to round 3 which is "10000000". So one input to the XOR4 was "1000" and the output was our "0011" from above. The XOR difference we would expect for the other input (the one coming out of P4) then is "1011".

P4 is not a problem, we just take its inverse to know what its input was.

$P4^{-1}$("1011") = "1110".

Step 4: Try all possible values for the subkey K3

There are 256 possible values for subkey K3, 0 through 255 or "00000000" through "11111111". We have to try all 256 of them.

For every subkey, what we have to do is recreate E/P, the 8-bit XOR after E/P, and the S-boxes for each ciphertext pair. The reason we have to use 25 ciphertext pairs instead of just one is that there is a chance a false input might get lucky and produce the right output, but this won't happen 25 times. The number 25 has nothing to do with the key size or block size so it does not add to our measure of complexity.

Let's try a subkey of "10101010" with our second ciphertext pair. The inputs to E/P were "1100" and "1001", so the E/P outputs are "01101001" and "11000011". Now we XOR both of these to get "11010111" and "01101001". Let's put the first one through the S-boxes. S0("1101") = (row 3, column 2) = "11". S1("0111") = (row 1, column 3) = "11". So the output of the S-boxes is "1111". Do the same for the second to get: "1010". So the S-box outputs with this subkey for this ciphertext pair have an XOR difference of "0101". But we were expecting to get an XOR difference of "1110" so we can throw this subkey out. The subkey that doesn't get thrown out is the one that was used during encryption for out chosen plaintext/ciphertext pairs.

In a block cipher with more rounds we wouldn't be so sure what our expected XOR difference should be, but we would have a pretty good idea and we could do this same sort of thing probabilistically and pick the subkey that produced bad XOR differences the least.

Let's try a subkey of "10101111" with our second ciphertext pair. The outputs of E/P are the same, but then the inputs to the S-boxes are different because the subkey is different. Our new S-box inputs are "11000110" and "01101100". If we put these through the S-boxes we get "0111" and "1001". The XOR difference is "1110". This is the same as our expected XOR difference. If this subkey passes several such tests then we can be pretty sure that it is the right subkey for K3 that was used in encryption, which it is.

6. Conclusion

To begin with we have discussed cryptanalysis of AES. Next we have seen that by using differential cryptanalysis that modified Simplified AES is vulnerable against differential attack. Using this as a foundation, a better cryptanalytic attack on AES can be designed or rather linear attack on AES can be understood in a better manner in future.

7. References

[1] H. Bizaki, S. Mansoori, A. Falahati, "Linear Cryptanalysis on Second Round Mini-AES", Second IEEE International Conference On Information Communication Technology ICTTA, April 2006.

[2] W. Smith, "1. AES seems weak 2. Linear time secure cryptography", Online works of Warren Smith, June 8,2007.

[3] Daniel Augot, Pascale Charpin, and Nicolas Sendrier: Studying the Locator Polynomials of Minimum Weight Codewords of BCH Codes, IEEE Trans. Info. Theory 38,3 (1992) 960-973.

[4] Alexander Barg & Gilles Zemor: Distance properties of expander codes, IEEE Trans. In-form. Theory 52,1 (Jan. 2006) 78-90.

[5] William Stallings, Cryptography and Network Security, EEE, New Delhi, 2008.

Magnetic Resonance Imaging Image Optimization using Stochastic Resonance

Vinay Kumar Shukla
National Brain Research Centre NH-08, Near NSG Campus, Manesar, Haryana 122050, India
vinay@nbrc.res.in

Abstract

Stochastic resonance is manifest in non-linear systems, where the response to a small periodic signal is enhanced by noise. In this paper, we propose a novel image optimization enhancement technique based on stochastic resonance (SR). The aim of this work is to optimize the image at different thresholds. Based on different threshold values the optimize image is more enhance. Since Gadolinium contrast agent is declare as a hazardous substance. The proposed technique is novel and have wider application in medical pathology.

Index Terms-Stochastic Resonance, Gadolinium.

1. INTRODUCTION

In the MR of molecules of brain, rapid return to the ground state from the excited state also requires stimulating Radio frequency matching the resonance condition. The lattice field provided by the surrounding nuclear environment must fluctuate to transform energy from the excited proton to the lattice. The spectral density of this field differs for different tissue types. The spread governs the 'energy content' in the frequency range appropriate for resonance condition. Therefore the lattice field must fluctuate neither too slowly nor too rapidly for effective relaxation. A contrast agent increases transition rate by increasing the energy content in the frequency range appropriate for resonance condition.

In the MR images contrast between different tissues is governed by the rate of transition (or inverse of the relaxation time $1/T_1$) of the tissue. Contrast agents increase the relaxation rate over pure solvent. Reducing T_1 amounts to affecting the amplitude and time scale variation of local magnetic fields experienced by water molecules. The increase in the relaxation rate leads to an enhancement in the MR images. Such an enhancement of signals to cross the threshold by an absorption of appropriate amount of 'noise' is a well established phenomena — The phenomena of stochastic resonance in threshold systems [1, 2].

In image processing SR effect is observed by considering the image pixel values as either dynamical or as non-dynamical (threshold) systems. Qinhua Ye et. al [3] have used the former formalism to extract weak lines from noisy images and for image enhancement as applied to sonar image processing. Marks et al [4] have applied the threshold detector model to retrieve the original image from a 'noised' image. T Ray et al [5] have applied a multithreshold formalism to selectively enhance a range of pixels (corresponding to the lesion).

Processed images for different parameters were obtained, wherein it was observed that there is indeed a stochastic resonance like effect occurring for a set of optimal parameters. However this requires the post contrast image. In order to select the processed image closest to the contrast enhanced image, an index quantifying the information content in the processed image needs to be determined or formulated. In the sections that follow a brief account of the action of a contrast agent followed by a presentation of the results of SR processed images using the formulation of Ray et al and the various approaches followed towards the search for a descriptor parameter to automatically determine the optimal parameters for the image that best matches the post contrast image without It , is given.

2. METHOD

Multi Threshold System

To adaptively select the threshold and noise strength depending on the value of the input signal(pixel) an image is assumed to be consisting of independent, distinguishable pixels x_i which can be taken as ID signal, each of them much below a threshold value. For such a system the output or measurement depends on the initial value xi (0).

$Y = g(x_i)$. So it can take the form

$$Y(t) = \mathrm{sgn}(x_i(t)) = \begin{cases} 0 & \text{if } x_i(t) < T_i, \\ 1 & x_i(t) \geq T_i \end{cases}$$

The pixels are made to cross the threshold by subjecting each of them to a Gaussian additive noise with mean zero and standard deviation σ_i

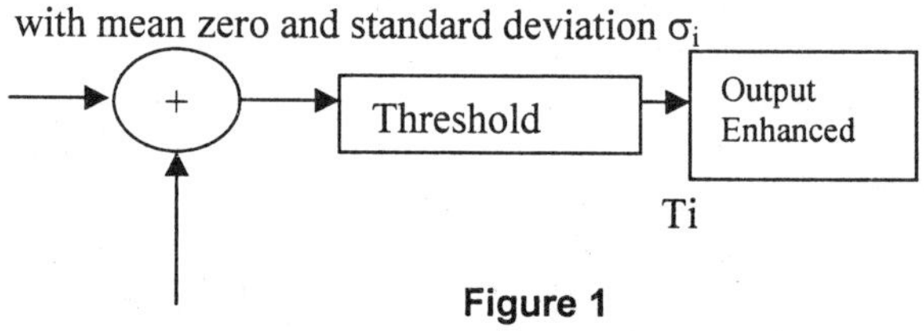

Figure 1

The optimal noise for x_i to cross T_i can be devised by maximizing the probability that ($x_i + \xi_i$) crosses T_i.
Consider $\Pr(x_i + \xi_i \ge T_i)$
$= \Pr(\xi_i \ge (T_i - x_i))$
$= \int f_\xi(x)\, dx$

where the subscripts are dropped for convenience

$$\Pr(xi + \xi_i \ge T_i) = 1 - \Pr(x_i + \xi_i \le T_i)$$

$$= 1 - \frac{1}{\sigma\sqrt{2\pi}} \int_{-\infty}^{z} e^{-t2/2\sigma 2} dt \qquad (1)$$

where the cdf is evaluated with mean zero.
Let

$$\phi(z) = 1 - \frac{1}{2\pi} \int_{-\infty}^{Z} e^{-x2/2} dx$$

$$= \frac{1}{2}\left[1 + erf(\frac{z}{\sqrt{2}})\right] \qquad (2)$$

Substituting $\frac{t^2}{\sigma^2} = t'^2$

Or $\frac{t}{\sigma} = t'$

$dt = \sigma dt$

Changing the variable t =T-x to t` = $\left(\frac{T-X}{\sigma}\right)$

and t = - ∞ to t` = - ∞ gives

$$\Pr(\xi i \ge Ti - Xi) = P = 1 - \frac{1}{\sigma\sqrt{2\pi}}.\sigma \int_{-\infty}^{T-x)/\sigma} e^{-t'2/2} dt$$

$$= 1 - \frac{1}{\sqrt{2\pi}}\left[\int_{-\infty}^{T-X/\sigma} e^{-t'2/2} dt \right] \qquad (3)$$

The term in the square bracket in (3) is $\phi\left(T - \frac{X}{\sigma}\right)$

$$\therefore p = 1 - \frac{1}{2} - \frac{1}{2} erf\left(\frac{T-X}{\sigma\sqrt{2}}\right)$$

$$\text{Or } P = \frac{1}{2}\left(1 - erf\left(\frac{T-X}{\sigma\sqrt{2}}\right)\right) \qquad (4)$$

For z <<1

$$erf(z) \cong \frac{2}{\sqrt{\pi}} e^{-Z^2} Z\left[1 + \frac{2.z^2}{1.3} + \frac{(2z^2)^2}{1.3.5} + \ldots\ldots\ldots\ldots\right]$$

and for z >>1
erf (z)

$$\mathrm{erf}(z) \cong 1 - \frac{e^{-z^2}}{\sqrt{\pi}}\left(Z^{-1} - \frac{1}{2}Z^{-3} + \frac{3}{4}Z^{-5} - \frac{15}{8}Z^{-7} + \frac{105}{16}Z^{-9} + \ldots\ldots\ldots\ldots\right)$$

Letting $Z = \frac{Ti - xi}{\sigma\sqrt{2}}$

$$\frac{Ti - Xi}{\sqrt{2}} \rangle\rangle \sigma \text{ i.e. } z >> 1 \qquad (5)$$

for low noise and threshold (say $Ti \cong 20\, x_i$)
Therefore

$$erf(z) \cong \left(1 - \frac{e^{-z^2}}{\sqrt{\pi}} Z^{-1} + \frac{1}{\sqrt[2]{\pi}} e^{-z^2} Z^{-3}\right)$$

Higher order terms can be neglected because of condition in (5)

Therefore

$$P \cong \frac{1}{2}\left(1 - erf\left(\frac{T-x}{\sigma\sqrt{2}}\right)\right)$$

$$= \tfrac{1}{2}\left(1 - \left(1 - \frac{z^{-1}e^{-Z^2}}{\sqrt{\pi}} + \frac{1}{\sqrt[2]{\pi}} Z^{-3} e^{-z^2}\right)\right)$$

or

$$P = \frac{1}{2}\left(\frac{Z^{-1}e^{-z^2}}{\sqrt{\pi}} - \frac{1}{\sqrt[2]{\pi}} Z^{-3} e^{-z^2}\right) \qquad (6)$$

where $Z = \frac{T-X}{\sigma\sqrt{2}}$. This gives the probability that the noise is greater than T-x .Maximizing the above w.r.t. σ.

i.e. $\frac{dp}{d\sigma} = 0$

gives $= Z^{-2} - 2 + \tfrac{3}{2} Z^{-4} + Z^{-2} = 0$

or $Z^4 = \tfrac{3}{4}$

or $\left(\frac{T-X}{\sigma\sqrt{2}}\right) = \left(\tfrac{3}{4}\right)^{1/4}$ simplifying further gives

$$\sigma = \left(\tfrac{2}{3}\right)^{1/4}(T - X)$$

$$\sigma \cong 0.17(T - X) \qquad (7)$$

Noise of standard deviation as given above is added to the pixel which has the maximum probability of taking x_i above the threshold T_i. However in order to avoid the process of requantising the gray levels so as to confine to the dynamic range [0 255], the expectation value of the noise calculated for each σ_i, x_i, Ti as

$$n_{ii}=\Sigma n_{ij}p_{ij} \quad (8)$$

where n_{ij} is the noise corresponding to the jth realization for the ith pixel is added to each of the corresponding pixel x_i. The pixel x_i is therefore transformed to

$$x_i = x_i + n_{ii} \quad (9)$$

This process gives nothing more than the usual spatial enhancement provided by other techniques like applying a logarithmic, polynomial, exponential etc. transformation Fig.2a, b, c and Fig.2d. However the applications of the formalism applied to pixel class rather than only the individual pixels is suggested. The results of applying such formalism are given below.

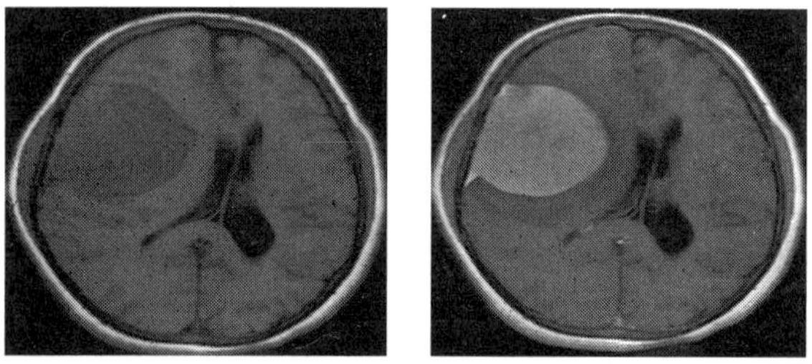

Fig. 2a. Pre Contrast b. Post Contrast

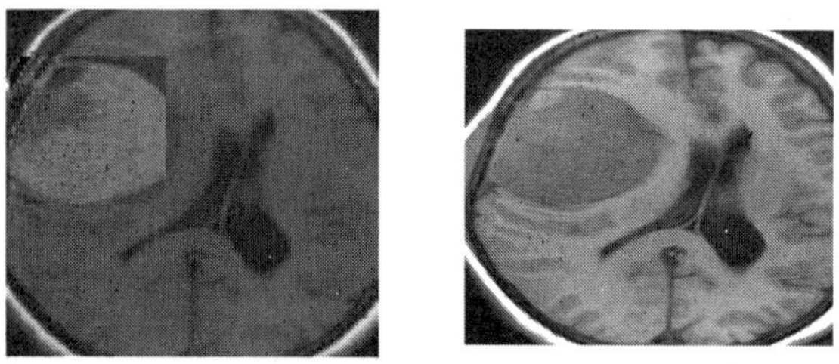

c. SR processed image d. Enhanced Image

3. Result

The proposed work is widely useful in medical pathology. The gadolinium enhanced image and normal enhanced image using stochastic resonance is much more different. Since gadolinium is declare as a hazardous element and it is no more useful in current medical pathology. But our stochastic resonance technique is absolutely enhance the image. Compare to pre-processing image and after post processing image we found that image are more enhanced.

4. Discussion

It can be said that Stochastic Resonance enhancement is a surrogate of the biochemical enhancement induced by contrast agents.

We are now in a position to explore the future scope and applications of stochastic resonance based image optimization of magnetic resonance images. As we know commonly used radiological software are not that much feasible for enhancing images containing noise. The stochastic resonance method also provides further improvement in the image appearance, and can also provide additional benefits in diagnostic accuracy. Stochastic resonance method has enough potential in clinical aspect to extract latent information in MR images without introducing unwanted artifacts. The proposed method is quite useful to improve noisy images, lower contrast image, region based enhancement, localization of tumors etc. Image Optimization based on Stochastic Resonance is also done in segmentation of Prostate. [6].

5. References

[1] Gammaitoni, P. Hanggi,P.jung. and F.Marchesoni, "Stochastic resonance," Reviews of Modern Physics, vol.70, No.1, pp223-287, 1998.

[2] V S Anishchenko, A B Neiman, F Moss, L Schimansky-Geier Physics- Uspekhi 42(1) 7 – 36(1999).

[3] Qinghua Ye, Haining Huang and Chunhua Zang, "Image Enhancement Using Stochastic Resonance", Proc.IEEE Int. Conf. Image Processing, 2004.

[4] Robert J. Marks II et al., 2002 IEEE International Symposium on Circuits and Systems, vol. 4, 521(2002).

[5] Tamaghna Ray and Prasun Roy, Technical Report: NBRC/CNS/2004/1407, Computational Neuroscience and Neuroimaging Laboratory, National Brain Research Centre, Manesar, Gurgaon, India.

[6] Klein S. et al "Automatic Segmentation of the prostate in 3D MR images by atlas matching using localized mutual information" Med Physics. 2008; 1407-1417

X-Server Database: An ADBMS for Secure Transmissions over all Networks

[1]Prof. Prakash Devale, [2]Pritesh Patil and [3]Amol Dhumane
[1]IT Department, Bharati Vidyapeeth, University College of Engineering, Pune-43
[2]Computer Engg Dept, Bharati Vidyapeeth, University College of Engineering, Pune-43
[3]Computer Engg Dept, Vishwakarma Institute of Information Tech. Pune- 47
prakash_ devale@yahoo.com p.patil.k@gmail.com amol.dhumane@gmail.com

Abstract

Nowadays XML is being used as an underlying technology for most of the transactions on the internet. XML is widely used for Database Storage. Most of the leading product developed companies use XML as their Metadata framework. This work started with a goal to manage XML data and to provide security to XML data while wired or wireless data transfer. It helps in storing, managing, publishing, retrieving data from Database in XML format and updating stored data in XML documents. The databases are normalized upto 3NF. There are different workspaces of this work. First is a SQL Manager, which helps to retrieve and manage data from XML documents, second is Relationship Builder which helps in establishing the relationship between the relations, and User Management and Security which helps in creating users or clients of the database and to assign security and privileges. Major feature of our database is its platform independence, which would help us to use this database with different environments which supports JAVA, for example we can install the database server on LINUX and on Windows or LINUX clients.

Keywords: *Query Analyzer, Relationship, Client-server based database, XML Encryption, Enterprise Manager*

1. Introduction

Making a cross-platform tool was a challenge some 10 years ago, but this has totally changed now. In 1993 when Sun Microsystems introduced the JAVA platform, making platform independent software's was a breeze. The slogan "Compile once, Run anywhere" could be heard, thanks to Java. Not only does Java provide the capabilities to make the software run on many platforms, but also as a programming language it is very superior to its contemporaries.

X-Server database is a Client – Server based Database. It is more user-friendly, easy to retrieve data and easy to access the database for both the programmer and the client or end user. It is used to create database, tables, query and the reports. User can view the database, create the tables and analyze the query and after all he can make reports on the basis of tables and with respect to their queries.

For Creating, accessing and maintaining the database, User should have permissions from the Server. Server granted the permissions and after that client (user) can do what he wants to do. Client can view only the encrypted form of data because of all the data are maintained in the XML database in Encrypted form what a client can never perceive. For the security point of view it has particular users with their passwords who are the authorized persons who can access the database. This is query analyzer database to which multiple users can access at the same time with no restrictions. It is a platform independent database and more economical than any other databases.

The database proposed in this paper is platform independent. XML Metadata framework is the key feature, by which one can deal with data within very less time and accurately [1]. At different level the security issues have been considered. In terms of putting the join between two tables or databases in proposed database which works on XML metadata framework means the XML files containing data, we have considered primary key and foreign key concepts [1,3,5].

Our database provides inbuilt GUI forms for handling different application which requires third party backend. It also provides auto report generation facility. For secure delivery of records on the network the database proposed in this paper, it provides the encryption strategy.

2. Future Scope

The future extent of this SQL Query Analyzer is too extensive to comprehend. Today the IT Industries demand for effective environment and efficient tools. They want to specify the following strategies before implementing the software needs. XML Database helps professionals and the Corporate to record and maintain the data into the database. Even Corporate uses the database like Oracle [12,13,14], MS – Access, SQL

Server and MySQL[8] for accessing, retrieving and maintaining data into the database, but for these databases user should have absolute knowledge about the Commands of Structured Query languages and should be well trained in accessing the granting permissions from the server. For using the above specified databases Corporate has to pay the respected amount as per the Company rules and regulations for getting the registration from the authorized Database Companies. Installation cost, maintenance cost and the implementation cost can affect the company's production cost. This database is a platform independent server database and can be used with free of cost platform provided by the Sun Microsystems.

Scope of X- Server application is to provide a XML based Data Server, which will have a provision to store data in XML format [2,4]. X- Server provides a tool for:

1. Storing metadata
2. SQL Manager to handle DDL and DML statements
3. Creating indexes on XML data
4. Handling XML data through Cache Mechanism
5. Middleware to act as an interface to SQL Manager to parse SQL statements and pick data from XML metadata.

The clients using X-Server database are assumed to have the knowledge of SQL to use Query analyzer of SQL Manager for accessing the data. No existing applications need to be modified on the client side. Users login to the system by providing the username and password and then interact with the system and other optional parameters.

3. Technology Overview

Java: Java language is used due to its powerful features such as it is simple to understand, highly object oriented, robust, secure, architecture neutral, portable, multithreaded and dynamic.

XML: XML stands for extensible Markup Language. The word "extensible" implies that a developer can extend his ability to describe a document, and define meaningful tags for his application XML is used to generate dynamic contents.

Databases: The study of databases like SQLSERVER, ORACLE [9,10,11], MySQL [6,7] are done in the aspect of manipulating the stored data by their respective query language.

Use of SAX: SAX is an interface that allows us to write applications to read the data held in an XML document. It is primarily a Java interface.

Use of JDOM: JDOM is an open source, treebased, pure Java API for parsing, creating, manipulating, and serializing XML documents.

4. System Architecture

This section describes the X-Server Database architecture defining major tiers comprising that architecture. The architecture of the database proposed in this paper is the very simple to understand and implement, fig. 1 shows the architecture of X-Server database.

Client connects to X-Server entering all necessary details such as Server Name, Login and password. After connecting Client sends or receive content of XML Documents via SQL Manager. Server fetches request made by Front End for processing, parses the request and then processed request is given back to Client in the form of Response. Administrator takes care of User Management by creating, editing and deleting users.

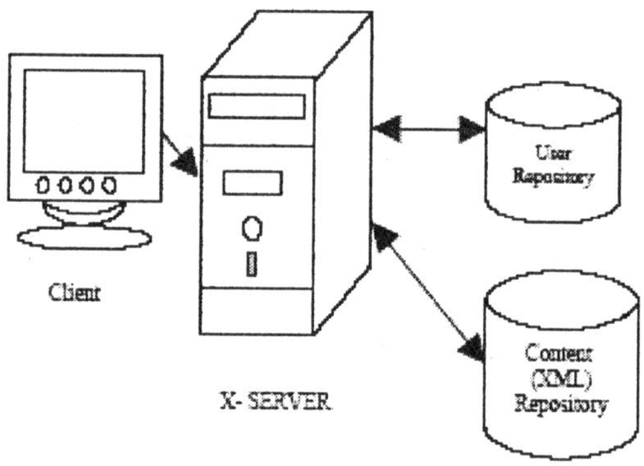

Fig. 1 Physical structure of X-Server Database

The detailed system design consists of different components of the system and the primary responsibilities and/or behavior of this component. All kinds of services it provides to its clients. The Client X- SERVER User Repository Content (XML) Repository connection module connects X-server Client to X Server. SQL manager accepts the options for building and executing the query. User module is at Client end. Responsibilities of this component are:

- Access to SQL Manager
- Save the Query
- Choose mode of result display i.e. Grid or file.

5. Database Design

X-server database design process includes the designing of SQL manager, Data storage section, Relationship builder, security, GUI design of database.

A. SQL MANAGER

- To establish the connection with respective database.
- Parse the query in proper syntax. (It contains "syntax.xml" which is used for syntax checking).
- Execute the query.
- Display the result in grid or in file format.
- Provide option for saving the query so formed.

All syntax's for DDL as well as DML Queries are stored in "syntax.xml" file.

Example syntax:

```
<select>
    <from/>
    <where/>
    </select>
```

B. Data Storage

With the popularity of XML, most of the servers need to work with and store XML data.

Example .xml file format

```
<sysDB>
    <sysDatabaseName>DatabaseName</
    sysDatabaseName >
    <table name="tbl_name">
    <col name="column_name"/>
    <value name="value"/>
    </table>
    </sysDB>
```

C. Relationship Manager

Relationship Builder of X-server builds relation between two XML documents, implementing the concepts of primary and foreign keys. It is a tool to facilitate joining two XML files based on attributes common in both files. The attribute in one xml file is a primary key and it gets related to some attribute in other xml file, which is a foreign key.

D. GUI Design

This section describes the X-Server architecture defining major layers comprising that architecture. Front End can be any Form Template Designer or application that sends or receive XML Documents. Like other Servers, X-Server also has Service Providers- Request and Response, which are implemented via Java Classes. Server fetches request made by Front End for processing and then processed request is given back to Client in the form of Response. X-server provides standard API for processing XML based information and way of passing XML documents and non-XML documents to and from Server. API will consist of different classes written in Java using OOPS concepts, which are used for connecting to database, executing queries and displaying the result. Figure 1 below explains the architecture of the project.

E. General constraints and Conditions

- **Availability or volatility of resources**
  Volatile resources such as main memory must conform to the current standard configuration. The software will be handling files occupying memory of the order of megabytes.
- **Security requirements**
  The system will be password protected. Since multi-user feature is disabled the sole purpose of the password is for security reasons.
- **Memory and other capacity limitations**
  The software will be handling files occupying memory of the order of megabytes. Sufficient volatile and non-volatile memory does become a constraint.

F. User Management and Authentication

This module helps in managing users by Creating users, Editing users, Deleting users, assigning/ editing their passwords.

G. Security: XML Encryption

Server will provide its own authentication features to authenticate users via facility of XML Encryption/Decryption, which ensures that, unauthorized individuals or intruders cannot access important documents. Figure 2 shows the detailed internal structure of X-server database of fig.1.

X-server database provides a complete GUI to handle all activities performed by the clients or users. Users can perform the activities according to the privileges they obtain. At the time of adding new users administrator can assign minimum to higher level privileges. The relations created by using X-server database are normalized upto higher level of normalization.

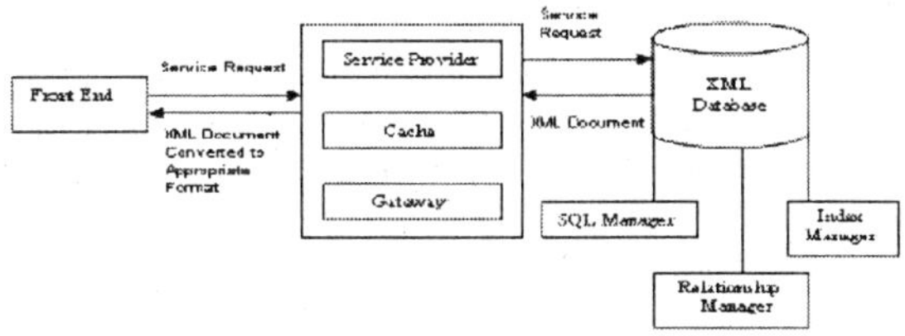

Fig. 2 X-Server Database internal architecture

6. Screen Shots and Results

Figs 3(a, b, c) shows some of the screens of the proposed database.

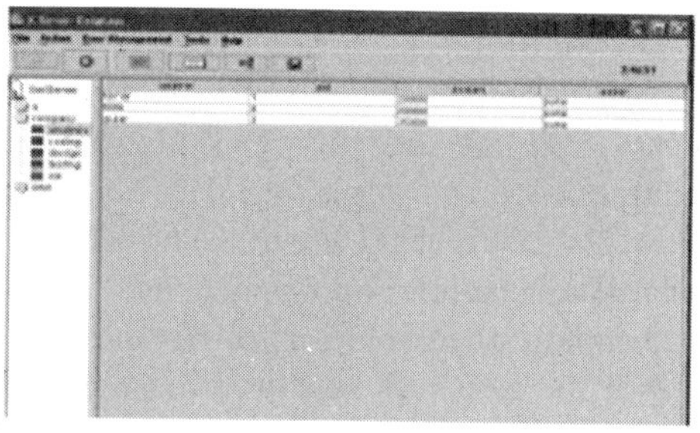

Fig. 3(a) Table View of Database

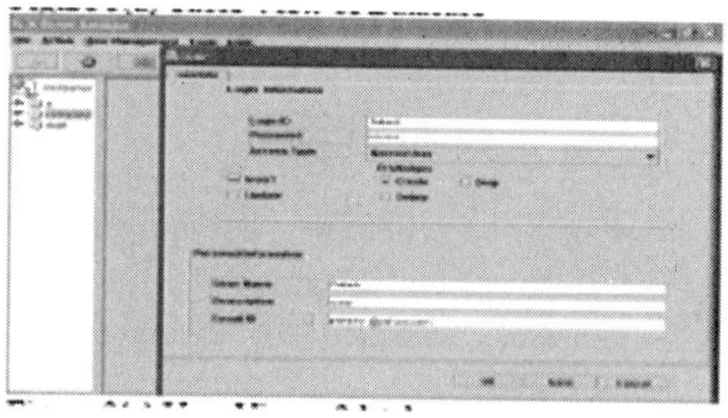

Fig. 3(c) User View of database

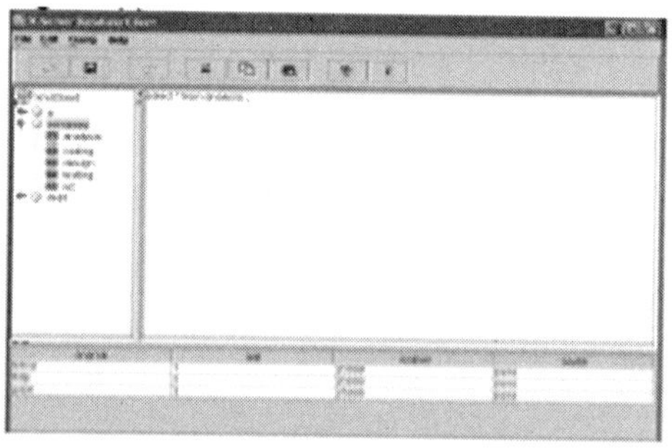

Fig. 3(b) SQL Manager view

7. Conclusion

XML has become very popular in various Web and platform independent applications. There is an increasing need to store XML documents. This XServer will provide an efficient way to store, maintain, publish and exchange XML documents. Although its possible to store XML in the form of text files, or to extract the data from structured XML and store it relationally, neither solution is as potential as X-Server Database. The X-server uses core XML services such as a SAX Parser and JDOM. These provide the core services for parsing the incoming document to determine the appropriate class and method to call, as well as getting the data out of the XML format for manipulation by the database. X-servers will provide an important building block for the next generation of Web applications.

8. References

[1] Using Stylus Studio to Deploy XML Data Services: A Zap Think.

[2] JOSHUA LUBELL , An XML Repository Architecture for Step Modules

[3] Umesh Kumar Rai, Realising XML benefits in Life Insurance, XML white paper Wipro.

[4] SQL/XML, XQuery, and Native XML Programming Languages White Paper.

[5] FIXML Tutorial: Working With Complex Message Sets Defined Using XML Schema.

[6] MySQL: The Best Choice for Modern Online Database Applications Enterprise White paper.

[7] A Guide to Database High Availability, White paper.

[8] MySQL High Availability Solutions, www.MySQL.com.

[9] http://docs.oraclewhitepapers.com/oraclewhitepapers/totalrecall.

[10] http://docs.oraclewhitepapers.com/oraclewhitepapers/nextgeneration-soa.

[11] http://docs.oraclewhitepapers.com/oraclewhitepapers/j developer

[12] http://docs.oraclewhitepapers.com/oraclewhitepapers/databa se10g_release2.

[13] http://docs.oraclewhitepapers.com/oraclewhitepapers/acade micenterprise.

[14] William Miles, Optimizing SQL Query Processing, White Paper, 2005.

Discovery of Objects through Radio Frequency

B.Sudhir, Dr.C. Nageswara Raju and R.Guruvaiah

Department of M.C.A., S.V.P.G. College, Balaji Nagar, Kadapa.

Abstract

If I don't safe guard what I have, it will be challenging thing. The safety of goods is common concept. From animals to ATM cards and even to systems protection privacy, is common thing. For this sole purpose RFID is used. The RFID device serves better than bar code or a magnetic strip. It provides a unique identifier for that object. To get information it must be scanned. This trend shows that we are moving from virtual side to real world. In this paper we discuss the challenges that are there with digital concepts in radio frequencies. It provides a means of communicating with the transponder (the RFID tag). RFID tags do not need to contain batteries, and can therefore remain usable for very long periods of time. RFID devices that are intended to be implanted inside a living by casing that will not irritate or react with the living tissues and harm the body.

The smallest tags that will likely be used for consumer items don't have enough computing power to do data encryption to protect your privacy. The most they can do is PIN-style or password-based protection. Advanced Digital Solutions intends to use its implanted RFID for payment. This can help the user from theft and make it impossible to lose your credit card. This paper deals with how RFID tags clarify the issues when they arise when objects and user are carelessly related. This can be done be each user setting private and temporary identification code to each object. This will solve the problems of object management to its maximum.

1. Introduction

Irrespective of distance from the scanner, product automatic identification was a remote concept in olden days. This phenomenon became real with the introduction of RFID (Radio frequency identification). This feature can be used for the living or non living. This is a method of remotely storing and retrieving data using devices called RFID tags (electronically programmed with unique information). An RFID tag is a small object, such as an adhesive sticker, that can be attached to or incorporated into a product.

RFID tags contain antennae to enable them to receive and respond to radio-frequency queries from an RFID transceiver. RFID is increasingly used with biometric technologies for security. Unlike ubiquitous UPC bar-code technology, RFID technology does not require contact or line of sight for communication. RFID data can be read through the human body, clothing and non-metallic materials. RFID is also called dedicated short range communication (DSRC).

2. Difference between RFID and Barcode

RFID eliminates the need for line-of-sight reading that bar coding depends on. RFID scanning can be done at greater distances than bar code scanning. High frequency RFID systems (850 MHz to 950 MHz and 2.4 GHz to 2.5 GHz) offer transmission ranges of more than 90 feet, although wavelengths in the 2.4 GHz range are absorbed by water (the human body) and therefore has limitations.

Types of RFID tags

1. Passive RFID tags

These tags don't have their own power supply, the minute electrical current induced in the antenna by the incoming radio-frequency scan provides enough power for the tag to send a response. Due to power and cost concerns, the response of a passive RFID tag is necessarily brief, typically just an ID number (GUID). Lack of its own power supply makes the device quite small: commercially available products exist that can be embedded under the skin. As of 2004, the smallest such devices commercially available measured 0.4 mm × 0.4 mm, and thinner than a sheet of paper; such devices are practically invisible. Passive tags have practical read ranges that vary from about 10 mm up to about 5 meters.

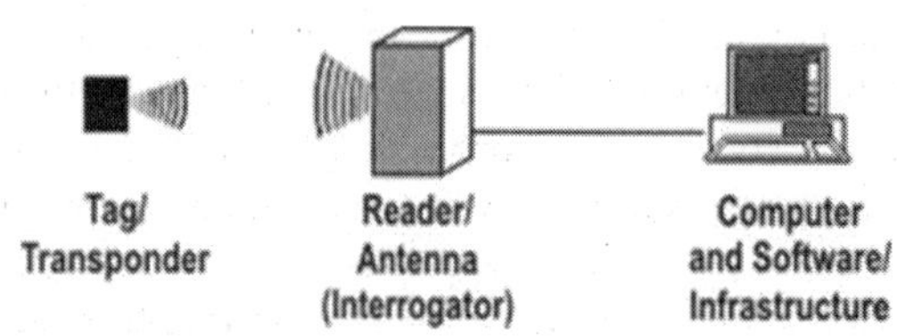

2. Active RFID tags:

These on the other hand, must have a power source, and may have longer ranges and larger memories than passive tags, as well as the ability to store additional information sent by the transceiver. At present, the smallest active tags are about the size of a coin. Many active tags have practical ranges of tens of meters, and a battery life of up to several years.

As passive tags are much cheaper to manufacture and do not depend on a battery, the vast majority of RFID tags in existence are of the passive variety. There are four different kinds of tags commonly in use. They are categorized by their radio frequency: Low frequency tags (between 125 to 134 kilohertz), High frequency tags (13.56 megahertz), UHF tags (868 to 956 megahertz), and Microwave tags (2.45 gigahertz). UHF tags cannot be used globally as there aren't any global regulations for its usage.

3. Semi-passive tags

Semi-passive tags are similar to active tags in that they have their own power source, but the battery only powers the microchip and does not power the broadcasting of a signal. The response is usually powered by means of backscattering the RF energy from the reader, where energy is reflected back to the reader as with passive tags. An additional application for the battery is to power data storage.

If energy from the reader is collected and stored to emit a response in the future, the tag is operating active.

Whereas in passive tags the power level to power up the circuitry must be 100 times stronger than with active or semi-active tags, also the time consumption for collecting the energy is omitted and the response comes with shorter latency time. The battery-assisted reception circuitry of semi-passive tags leads to greater sensitivity than passive tags, typically 100 times more. The enhanced sensitivity can be leveraged as increased range (by one magnitude) and/or as enhanced read reliability (by reducing bit error rate at least one magnitude).

The enhanced sensitivity of semi-passive tags places higher demands on the reader concerning separation in denser population of tags. Because an already weak signal is backscattered to the reader from a larger number of tags and from longer distances, the separation requires more sophisticated anti-collision concepts, better signal processing and some more intelligent assessment of which tag might be where. For passive tags, the reader-to-tag link usually fails first. For semi-passive tags, the reverse (tag-to-reader) link usually collides first.

Semi-passive tags have three main advantages: greater sensitivity than passive tags; longer battery powered life cycle than active tags; they can perform active functions (such as temperature logging) under their own power, even when no reader is present for powering the circuitry.

4. Beacon tags

Beacon tags blink the coded identity signal at a regular pattern. This may be a constant blink rate or a blink rate with stochastic shift or some triggered blinking. Not to activate the responder function in a tag first prevents from limiting the speed capabilities and improves the availability of the identification information under noisy conditions. Therefore the beacon concept appliers to very robust processes: The regular availability of the coded signal reduces latency and allows for low power levels, as with active tags. However, the permanent talk of many tags may pollute the frequency channel and therefore prevent from operating in denser populations. The design of the blinking scheme must take the battery life cycle into account. Currently (2008) none of the offered products follows any known line of international standardization. However, all blinking must obey the national wireless communications regulations concerning power level and channel occupation.

Applications of RFID

RFID is being used more frequently, and this trend of increasing usage is one that will continue. At present RFID is used in many different industries for various purposes. Bellow is a list of some the most common locations/uses of RFID tags and similar technology.

Passports

A biometric passport is a combined paper and electronic identity document that uses biometrics to authenticate the identity of travelers. The passport's critical information is stored on a tiny RFID computer chip, much like information stored on smartcards. Like some smartcards, the passport book design calls for an embedded contact less chip that is able to hold digital signature data to ensure the integrity of the passport and the biometric data.

The currently standardized biometrics used for this type of identification system are facial recognition, fingerprint recognition, and iris recognition. These were adopted after assessment of several different kinds of biometrics including retinal scan. The International Civil Aviation Organization defines the biometric file formats and communication protocols to be used in passports. Only the digital image (usually in JPEG) of each biometric feature is actually stored in the chip.

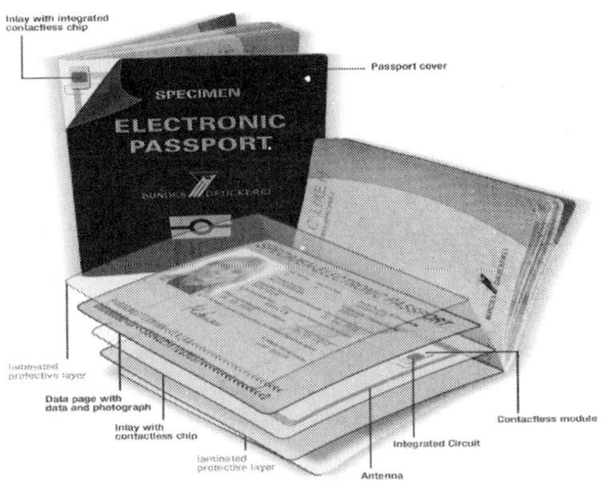

The comparison of biometric features is performed outside the passport chip by electronic border control systems (e-borders). To store biometric data on the contact less chip, it includes a minimum of 32 kilobytes of EEPROM storage memory, and runs on an interface in accordance with the ISO/IEC 14443 international standard, amongst others. These standards ensure interoperability between different countries and different manufacturers of passport books.

Electronic tolls

Enforcement is accomplished by a combination of a camera which takes a picture of the car and a radio frequency keyed computer which searches for a drivers window/bumper mounted transponder to verify and collect payment. The system sends a notice and fine to cars that pass through without having an active account or paying a toll.

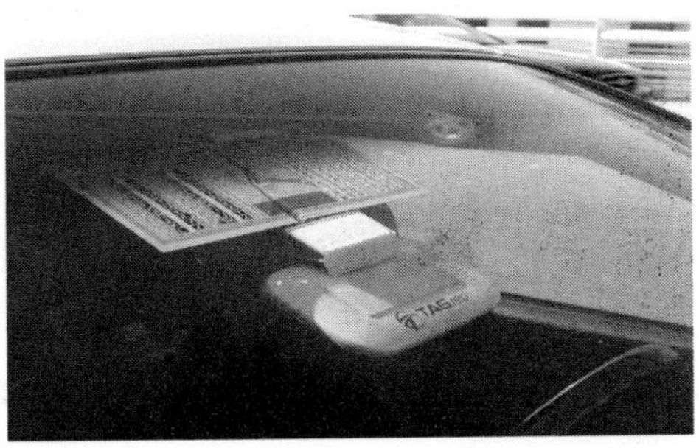

Animal Identification:

Texas Instruments RFID (TI-RFID™) low frequency (LF) RFID technology has been used to identify millions of livestock animals around the world. These systems track meat and dairy animals, valuable breeding stock and laboratory animals involved in lengthy and expensive research projects. The Australian National Livestock Identification System (NLIS) is the first and the largest implementation of RFID for animal tracking in the world.RFID transponders are worn as ear tags or as an inter-ruminal capsules. Farm management can be fully automated for such processes as feeding, weighing, disease management, and breeding practices.

Low frequency (LF) RFID, with an operating frequency of 134.2 kHz, has been adopted internationally for animal identification applications following many years of development, exhaustive testing and practical field evaluation. The International Standards Organization (ISO) and the Australian/New Zealand standards for the electronic identification of animals are based on LF 134.2 kHz RFID technology. (ISO11784/11785, AS5018/5019)

The Texas Instruments LF RFID technology was selected by the ISO as the basis for these standards. TI-RFID™ 134.2 kHz LF technology has been adopted by the NLIS in Australia after exhaustive field testing of all available technologies. Through these trials the TI-RFID half-duplex (HDX) technology was demonstrated to have superior performance under practical conditions. NLIS tags have now been in use for several years, with great success.

New Trends in RFID

Innovation around the design and manufacture of RFID tags is an ongoing process. Some of the most promising new designs are covered in the following sections.

Alternative Tag Designs

Many factors affect the readable range and accuracy of tags including those that are physical and environmental. Some examples are detection near metal or liquid and extreme weather conditions such as low temperature or high humidity. Besides simply improving on existing technology to overcome these limitations, alternative physics are being employed that can sidestep or leapfrog these limitations.

The majority of the work in the alternative physics area includes developments around chip less tags, introduced in Chapter 3, "Components of RFID Systems." Chip less tags promise to improve upon the physical limitations of radio frequency detection while potentially offering reduced costs due to the absence of integrated circuitry. Chip less tags can be more easily applied to metal and liquid or embedded in items like paper, thereby offering greater flexibility and functionality in connection with their use.

One chip less tag technology showing promise in supply chain applications uses Surface Acoustic Wave (SAW) technology. SAW technology involves the propagation of radio frequency acoustic waves on the surface of polished crystals. Other promising chipless technologies that have the potential to revolutionize RFID applications use nanotechnology, genomics, or even chemistry to achieve chipless tagging and unique identification of objects such as paper currency and product labels. CrossID, Inkode, Pharmaseq, RF SAW, and Tapemark are just a few developers and suppliers of chipless tag technologies and solutions.

When it comes to major advancements in IC-based tag design, Smart Active Label (SAL) technologies are gaining momentum in the market. SAL offers enhanced range and accuracy attributes while being less vulnerable to liquid or metal. With packaging similar to passive tags that are used in flexible mediums, such as labels, SAL is essentially a semi-active tag with a power source in the form of a thin, flexible battery. Using SAL labels, tagging and detecting cans of soda and bottles containing liquid can become more practical and economical.

Tag Packaging

Tag packaging plays a significant role in the applicability and practicality of specific uses of RFID. Expect to see tag and antenna packaging designs that will continue to push the envelope of creativity and ingenuity, much as injectable and ingestible tags have done in the past. Chip less tags based on nanotechnology will certainly be at the forefront of such developments.

Another entirely different approach to tag packaging that is very promising is related to printed electronics. This involves the process of "printing", antennae, transistors, or even integrated circuits using conductive ink and standard printing processes. The potential to inexpensively print a tag onto a box or the packaging of an item unlocks a new set of possibilities for the widespread application of RFID in everyday items. Already, a company called Precisia has designed a smart label RFID tag that uses conductive ink-instead of copper-for its antenna.

Sensory Tags

Tags whose packaging integrates them with sensors can monitor, record, and even react to all sorts of environmental conditions. Known as sensory tags, these tag types promote an entirely new set of applications. The major advancements here will be around the coupling or combining of RFID tag technology with sensor technology in very small form factors.

Smart Dust is one such combination that offers the functionality of tiny environmental sensors known as Micro Electro Mechanical Sensors (MEMS) with active RFID tag-like capabilities. Each such device is expected to be one cubic millimeter in size. The potential applications of this technology span a wide area, from monitoring battlefield activities in a military operation to tracking the facial movements of the disabled to control their wheelchairs.

Architecture for New Network

RFID systems generate mountains of new data that need to be synchronized, filtered, analyzed, managed, and acted upon, often in real-time or near real-time. Each tag is essentially a single computing device, albeit a very simple one, that acts as one node in a network of, eventually, billions or even trillions of such devices. This new network is dramatically different and in many ways more complex than even the Internet, the most complex network ever known.

This fact is due primarily to the number of nodes that could exist in the expanded model of a worldwide RFID network, which figures to be several orders of magnitude larger than the number of nodes on the Internet. This simply means that traditional computing architectures and infrastructures will not be adequate to handle the dramatically higher data volumes expected in such a network. Next, we discuss two different approaches under development that address these new requirements, from both the hardware and software viewpoints.

Microprocessor Design

Several computer giants are revising their microprocessor development roadmaps in favor of a new microprocessor architecture called Chip Multi-Threading (CMT). One of the pioneers in this area is Sun Microsystems which has already introduced the first design of this new architecture. This is just in time for the expected volume spike from RFID data as the US Department of Defense (DoD) and major retailers around the world go into full deployment mode with their RFID mandates.

Simply put, CMT architecture bucks the trend of traditional microprocessor design and architecture that primarily seeks to perform single tasks faster and faster. Instead, CMT is an architecture that allows the efficient execution of many tasks simultaneously. This is parallel computing taken all the way to the core of the microprocessor.

Peer-to-Peer Computing

Although the data generated by RFID systems can easily reach trillions of bytes that need to be processed almost instantaneously, in fact, much of the data is disbursed across one or more enterprises, and often, across the globe. This suggests that local processing of data, by RFID readers, before passing it along to a centralized computer can dramatically reduce the burden placed on centralized computing resources.

This is an excellent scenario in which to apply Peer-to-Peer (P2P) programming techniques to perform RFID-related data processing locally. P2P technology is a type of distributed computing technique that decentralizes computing tasks across several less powerful cooperating computers (peers) within a network. Expect RFID readers to become increasingly more intelligent. Readers will per-form many of the data processing, analysis, and management tasks within a local net-work of cooperating tags and readers. They will accomplish what today is mostly done by centralized computers.

3. Conclusion

Identification of different objects and its control is possible better by RFID. The new trends in this area will pave way for new areas where we can use RFID. Though they have some disadvantage still it will fulfill the required work without fail.

4. References

1. www.rfidtimes.org
2. www.strike-the-root.com
3. www.tech-faq.com
4. www.technologyreview.com

[1] How we are becoming a micro-chipped population, by Mika Belle, *Boise Weekly*,

[2] A Radio Chip in Every Consumer Product, by Claudia H. Deutsch and Barnaby J. Feder, NY Times, Feb. 25, 2003.

[3] RFID Revolution: Are we close?, by Matt Hines, *ZDNET.com*, March 3, 2004.

[4] School RFID Plan Gets an F, by Kim Zetter, *Wired*, Feb. 10, 2005.

[5] Radio Frequency ID: A New Era for Marketers?, by John Stermer, Consumer Insight, Winter 2001.

* sudhirkrupa@rediffmail.com

Design and Implementation of A Novel Stego Archiver

S.Balamurugan[1], C. Arul raj[2] and V. Harish[2]
[1]Department of Information Technology, Coimbatore, India -641 013
[2&3]Department of Computer Science & Engg, Anna University, Coimbatore,India-641 013
sbnbala@gmail.com *arulrajdce@gmail.com* *harish_vi@yahoo.co.in*

Abstract

The objective of the paper is to design and develop a novel model Stego Archiver that deals with 4 levels of security in terms of cryptography using RSA algorithm, Compression using Zip algorithm, CRC Checking and Steganography. In addition to these four levels of security we are using radix 30 methods also. Stego Archiver can hide the files in any image formatted file and other multimedia file formats including audio and video files. Stego Archiver is capable of hiding data in any kind of audio files including mp3 files and any kind of video files including mpg, dat etc. Since we are using CRC checking also, any attempt to make any changes in original data can be find out easily.

1. Introduction

STEGO ARCHIVER may help to provide solution for this problem. We developed the STEGO ARCHIVER by using jdk1.3 and we used Ms Access as the backend. We had implemented 4 levels of security in our application. Paper covers the steganographic method like hiding the information's under a cover text. It exploits the steganographic [2] [3] nature of white space. It conceals a secret message in ASCII cover text by appending spaces and tabs to the end of lines. Because spaces and tabs are invisible in most text viewers, the message is effectively hidden from casual observers.

Hiding arouses less suspicion to the users. Password embedded photo enforces ownership and also duplication of the card is prevented. This type of mark in a secret fashion to enforce ownership uses Watermarking system, another important part of information hiding.

We also provide CRC checking to find out if the original message is edited by some hackers or not. This provides another level of security. STEGO ARCHIVER report if any intruder tries to hack the document hidden inside the picture file. The paper focuses on concealing message in ASCII text by appending white space to the end of lines. Because spaces and tabs are generally not visible in text viewers, the messageis effectively hidden from casual observers if encryption is used, message cannot be read even if it is detected. Once a steganographic system is discovered, it is rendered useless. The problem can be recovered if the hidden data depends on some sort of key for extraction. Identity cards are given to selected users along with password (key).

In the field of data security, the password is hidden as an invisible watermark in the photo of the card. If any one would intend to counterfeit the password by replacing the photo, it would be possible to detect the change by scanning the passport and verifying the password hidden in the photo, does not match any more with the user login password. If it matches then user can view the message.

Survey of the Existing System

In today's dynamic and information rich environment, information systems have become vital for any organization to survive. With the increase in the dependence of the organization on the information system, there exists an opportunity for the competitive organizations and disruptive forces to gain access to other organizations information system. This hostile environment makes information systems security issues critical to an organization. Current information security literature either focuses on anecdotal information by describing the information security attacks taking place in the world or it comprises of the technical literature describing the types of security threats and the possible security systems. In order to secure the transmission of data, Cryptography has to be implemented. Cryptography is the science of devising methods that allow information to be sent in a secure form in such a way that the only person able to retrieve this information is intended recipient. The basic principle is this: A message being sent is known as plaintext. The message is then coded using a cryptographic algorithm. This process is called encryption, an encrypted message is known as cipher text, and is turned back into plaintext by the process of decryption. Encryption can be done using symmetric or asymmetric algorithms. In symmetric algorithms only one key is used both to encrypt and decrypt the message. In asymmetric algorithms, a key used to encrypt a message is different from the key that is used to decrypt the message. There are several algorithms present in the market for Cryptography. Some of the commonly used once are IdeaA, RSA and Blowfish [4] [5] thatl involves asymmetric or symmetric methods and also involves private and public keys. The analysis of the existing system has to be carried to learn the details of the existing system. System analysis is the process of gathering and interpreting facts, diagnosing problems and using the information to recommend improvements to the system.

2. Design and Analysis

The system deals with security during transmission of data. Commonly used technologies are cryptography. This system deals with implementing security using Steganography and cryptography. In this the end user identifies an image which is going to act as the carrier of data. The data file is also selected and then to achieve greater speed of transmission the data file and image file are compressed and sent. Prior to this the data is embedded into the image and then sent.

The image if hacked or interpreted by a third party user will open up in any image previewer but not displaying the data. This protects the data from being invisible and hence be secure during transmission. The user in the receiving end uses another piece of code to retrieve the data from the image.

The end goals of the system span a number of different audiences; these goals include the following:

1. Enabling users to sent secured data over a network
2. Find out if hacking occurs during the sending of data.
3. Uses a multithreaded powerful tool to send file over the LAN

A. Goals and Requirements

The system deals with security during transmission of data. Commonly used technology is cryptography. This system deals with implementing security-using Steganography. In this technology, the end user identifies an image which is going to act as the carrier of data. The data file is also selected and then to achieve greater speed of transmission the data file and image file are compressed and sent. Prior to this the data is embedded into the image and then sent. The image if hacked or interpreted by a third party user will open up in any image previewer but not displaying the data. This protects the data from being invisible and hence be secure during transmission. The user in the receiving end uses another piece of code to retrieve the data from the image. For JPEG images, Outguess preserves statistics based on frequency counts. As a result, statistical tests based on frequency counts are unable to detect the presence of steganographic content. Before embedding data into an image, Outguess can determine the maximum message size that can be hidden while still being able to maintain statistics based on frequency counts.

CRCSET is an anti-virus utility. Its purpose is to protect programs from third parties manipulation .CRC set is the most effective weapons against computer viruses. This the Cyclic Redundancy Check, or CRC, is an error-checking algorithm used in many types of computer operations, especially in data transfer.

Before transmitting the data, the utility want to calculatc thc CRC valuc and attach with data. In receiving end, the CRC recalculated and based on that calculated value, it will specify the acceptation or rejection.

B. Problem Definition

Stego Archiever enables the user to send data securely over various kinds of networks. Basically in this paper the users interact with the client software running on the client machine.

3. Module Description

This paper contains mainly six modules. They are

- Authentication Section
- Huffman Encoding and Decoding
- RSA Encryption and Decryption
- Compression and Decompression
- CRC generation and Verification
- Data Embed and De-Embed
- File Sending and Receiving

A. Authentication Section

This module deals with authentication. This module checks whether a particular user has the required authentication to access the software. Usernames and Corresponding Passwords are stored in the database with their private and public keys. While the user entering his username and password this module check to see whether the particular user existing or not. If the user has the administrative power then this module loads the corresponding administrative page for the user, else it authenticate the user and load the software.

Fig. 1 User Authentication

B. Huffman Encoding and Decoding

This module deals with Huffman encoding and decoding. This module accepts the input in text format and converts it into binary format. Converted binary formatted file will be saved into a file with the same name and its extension will be .huff. Huffman decoding is done by accepting the file with extension .huff and using the Huffman tree table the encoded data will be converted into original file.

C. RSA Encryption and Decryption

This Module has two sub modules: Encryption and Decryption. Encoded file using Huffman encoding technique will be given as input to the Encryption module and it will provide a corresponding output file with extension .enc. Decryption process is done by giving .enc file as input to the system and it will provide the output file with extension .huff.

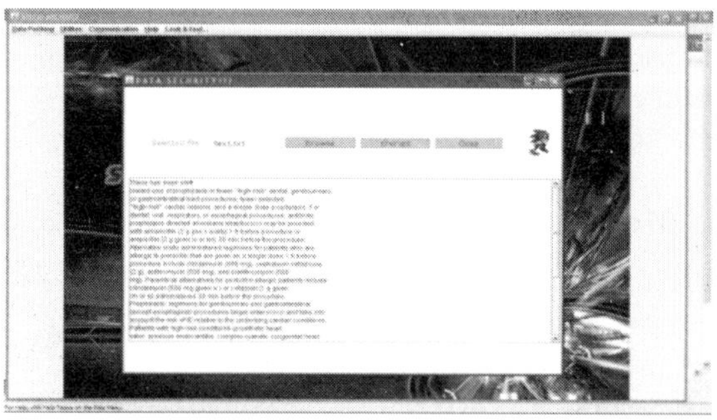

Fig. 2 RSA Encryption and Decryption

D. Compression and Decompression

Zip algorithm is used for the compression and decompression purpose. This technique maps arbitrary input into printable character output. The form of encoding has the following relevant characteristics. The range of the function is a character set that is universally re-presentable at all sites, not a specific binary encoding of that character set. Thus, the characters themselves can be encoded into whatever form is needed by a specific system. For instance, the character 'E' is represented in ASCII system as a hexadecimal 45 and in EDCDIC- based system as hexadecimal- c5.

E. CRC Generation and Verification

There are many utilities that perform CRC checks on other but most of these are external programs that are usually run only once, if at all. The CRC generated by these utilities must be compared to a value in an external file; if the values match, the program is not infected.

This approach has two problems: the first is that the CRC check is run only once when the user gets the program, if at all. Most people would never run the check a second time. The second problem is that the CRC is stored in an external file (e.g. the documentation). If someone wants to tack a virus onto the program, it becomes a simple matter to run the validation program, copy the CRC values to the documentation, and distribute the infected program. Anyone running the validation program would find the same CRC in the program as in the documentation, and in comes the virus.

F. Embedding and De-Embedding

This module deals with identifying the data and the image to embed the data into the image before it can be transmitted. This is then followed by compression to increase the rate of transfer of files between the networks..

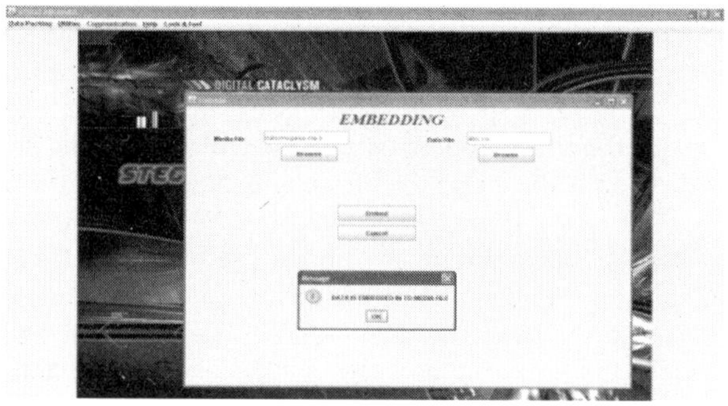

Fig. 3 Embedding and De-Embedding

The file is then selected using the GUI interface provided through Java. The module then prompts to identify the image file which needs to house the data file. The developed system will provide support to select and embed data into .bmp & .jpg files. The selected image file is then previewed before it can house the data. The data is then embedded into the image file in such a way that the image file is not corrupted, at the same time the data is secure. The image if hacked or interrupted by a third party can be viewed in any browser without actually displaying the data. The data on the receivers end is isolated and removed from the image. The module deals with identifying the hidden data in the image. The module receives the image file that is decompressed and decompresses it using Radix 64. The decompressed file is then previewed to view the image file. The image file is then browsed to remove the associated data. The data is then removed from the image file.

G. File Sending and Receiving

This module deals with file sending and receiving over the network. This module supports multithreaded socket programmed application.

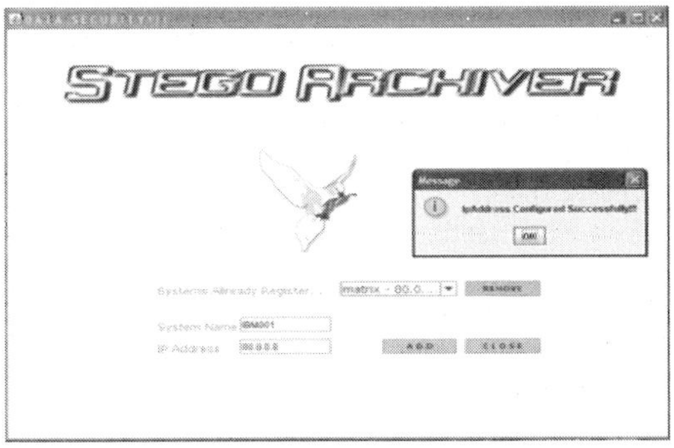

Fig. 4 File Sending and Receiving

It supports multiple file sending from different client machines to a particular system concurrently. It opens multiple ports for this purpose and it's an efficient tool for sending files over the network. The protocol used for this purpose is TCP I/P. Java's streaming package is used to develop this module.

4. Cryptography with Java

A. Encryption and Decryption

Encryption is the process of converting normal data or plaintext to something incomprehensible or cipher-text by applying mathematical transformations. These transformations are known as encryption algorithms and require an encryption key. Decryption is the reverse process of getting back the original data from the cipher-text using a decryption key. The encryption key and the decryption key could be the same as in symmetric or secret key cryptography, or different as in asymmetric or public key cryptography.

B. R.S.A Introduction

R.S.A. stands for Rivest, Shamir and Adleman - the three cryptographers who invented the first practical commercial public key cryptosystem. Today it is used in web browsers, email programs, mobile phones, virtual private networks, secure shells, and many other places. Exactly how much security it provides is debatable, but with sufficiently large keys you can be confident of foiling the vast majority of attackers. Until recently the use of RSA was very much restricted by patent and export laws. However, the patent has now expired and US export laws have been relaxed.

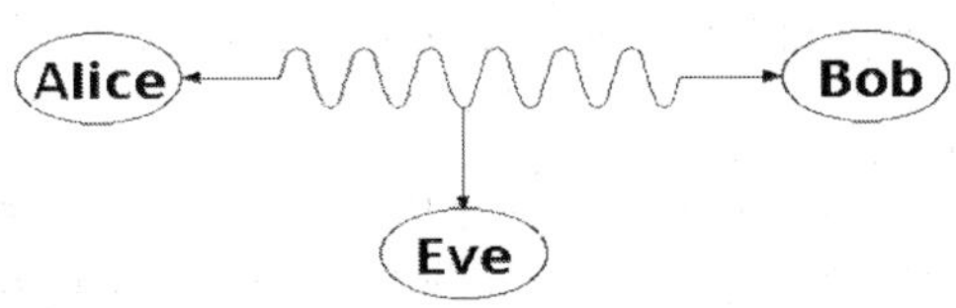

Fig. 4

Alice and Bob want to communicate in secret, while Eve wants to eavesdrop. Alice and Bob could be military jets, on-line businesses or just friends trying to have a private conversation. They can't stop Eve listening to their radio
signals (or tapping their phone line, or whatever), so what can they do to keep their communication secret?

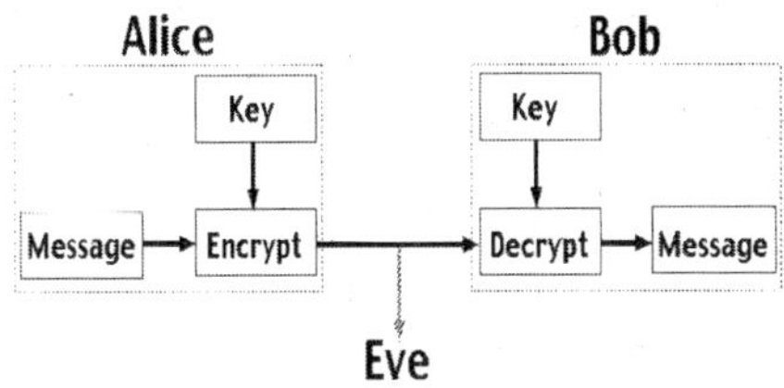

Fig. 5

One solution is for Alice and Bob to exchange a digital key, so they both know it, but it's otherwise secret. Alice uses this key to encrypt messages she sends, and Bob reconstructs the original messages by decrypting with the same key. The encrypted messages (cipher texts) are useless to Eve, who doesn't know the key, and so can't reconstruct the original messages. With a good encryption algorithm, this scheme can work well, but exchanging the key while keeping it secret from Eve is a problem. This really requires a face to face meeting, which is not always practical.

Public key encryption is different, because it splits the key up into a public key for encryption and a secret key for decryption. It's not possible to determine the secret key from the public key. In the diagram, Bob generates a pair of keys and tells everybody (including Eve) his public key, while only he knows his secret key. Anyone can use Bob's public key to send him an encrypted message, but only Bob knows the secret key to decrypt it. This scheme allows Alice and Bob to communicate in secret without having to meet.

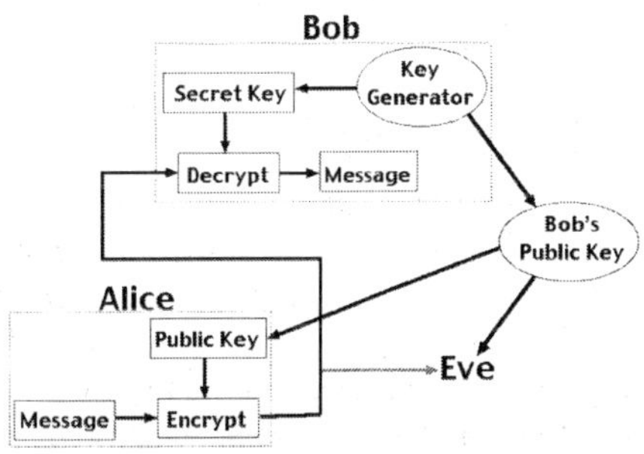

Fig. 6

However, if Eve can tamper with Alice and Bob's communication as well as passively listening, she could substitute her public key for Bob's, and then decrypt Alice's messages using her own private key.

Practicalities Encryption

The RSA algorithm itself only encrypts numbers. What usually happens is that RSA is used to encrypt a key for a symmetric cipher, such as Rijndael, and then the message is encrypted using this key. In interactive uses, the first step is called the 'key exchange' and after that, network traffic can flow in both directions using the same symmetric key. Often this will be combined with authentication of client.

All computer data is ultimately just binary numbers, so you could just break this into suitable chunks and apply RSA to each chunk. However, this puts you at some risk of being cryptanalysis, as plaintexts are often predicable to some extent. For example, if an attacker knows you will say either 'attack by land' or 'attack by sea', they can try encrypting both messages with the public key, and compare these cipher texts to the intercepted cipher text. You can mitigate this somewhat by including random junk in each encrypted chunk, but there are other attacks. Another reason is that RSA is slow compared to symmetric ciphers.

Digital Signatures

With RSA, the encryption and decryption techniques are very similar. In fact it is possible to reverse them - encrypt a message using the private key. The cipher text produced is a digital signature. When decrypted with the public key it reproduces the original message. This process is secure, because the only way to produce a something that decrypts to a chosen message is to know the private key. Like encryption, you don't in practice sign the whole message. The usual approach is to take a hash of the message, and sign that. The hash is a kind of fingerprint that is (almost) unique to that particular message. It is important to use a secure hash algorithm, so it's impractical for an attacker to find another message that produces the same hash. The chance of a collision occurring randomly is miniscule.

5. Java Networking

Java is the first programming language designed from the ground up with networking in mind. Most important—those are crucial to Internet applications, yet difficult to address in other languages. Together, these and other Java features allow web surfers to quickly download and execute untrusted programs from a web site without worrying that the program may spread a virus, steal their data, or crash their systems. Indeed, the intrinsic safety of a Java applet is far greater than that of shrink-wrapped software. One of the biggest secrets about Java is that it makes writing network programs easy.

Socket Class

A socket is a connection between two hosts. It can perform seven basic operations:

- Connect to a remote machine
- Send data
- Receive data
- Close a connection
- Bind to a port
- Listen for incoming data
- Accept connections from remote machines on the bound port

The Server Socket Class

The Server Socket class contains everything you need to write servers in Java. It has constructors that create new Server Socket objects, methods that listen for connections on a specified port, and methods that return a Socket object when a connection is made so that you can send and receive data.

1. A new Server Socket is created on a particular port using a Server Socket ( ) constructor.
2. The Server Socket listens for incoming connection attempts on that port using it's accept ( ) method. accept ( ) blocks until a client attempts to make a connection, at which point accept( ) returns a Socket object connecting the client and the server.
3. Depending on the type of server, either the Socket's getInputStream ( ) method, getOutputStream ( ) method, or both are called to get input and output streams that communicate with the client.
4. The server and the client interact according to an agreed-upon protocol until it is time to close the connection.
5. The server, the client, or both close the connection.
6. The server returns to for the next connection.

If step 4 is likely to take a long or indefinite amount of time, traditional Unix servers such as wu-ftpd create a new process to handle each connection so that multiple clients can be serviced at the same time. Java programs should spawn a thread to interact with the client so that the server can be ready to process the next connection sooner. A thread places a far smaller load on the server than a complete child process.

In fact, the overhead of forking too many processes is why the typical Unix FTP server can't handle more than roughly 400 connections without slowing to a crawl. On the other hand, if the protocol is simple and quick and allows the server to close the connection when it's through, then it will be more efficient for the server to process the client request immediately without spawning a thread.

Ftp Implementation

The FTP is implemented using the server sockets and socket classes. Using this sockets and standard ports which is provided in both server and client side the data's are transferred.

Normally the tcp/ip connectionless protocol uses these ports to transfer the data's from the server to client and client to server.

Generally i/o operations performed by the processors are delayed due to various non sequential hardware operations. So it takes more time to read write data's. To compensate this problem the dynamic java language provides complete solution through java threads.

Back-End Tool

Oracle 9i acts as the backend of this project. By using this Oracle 9i, a database is created to maintain the details of the users and System identity which are all configured on the LAN. In the database, we create two tables called Users and SysInfo. Using these two tables our operations are carried out.

6. Steganography & watermarking techniques implementation

The word Steganography literally means covered writing as derived from Greek and includes a vast array of methods of secret communications that conceal the very existence of the message. THE 'PERCEPTION MANAGERS' [7] [8] and their 'patriotic' paparazzi of the West seem to have shifted gears from singing paeans of technology to sowing suspicions about its possible misuse by the Al Queada, Taliban and their ilk! The word 'Steganography' should henceforth be bandied about more for its sinister implications on the security of the civilized world. In June this year, USA Today reported that the encrypted blueprints of the next terrorist attack on the U.S. and its allies may lie hidden behind the X-rated pictures on several pornographic web sites and the posted comments on sports chat rooms. A snake makes itself invisible in a bed of grass by natural subterfuge. For all visible signs one sees just a stretch of grass but not the snake hiding beneath. The word Steganography literally means covered writing as derived from Greek. It includes a vast array of methods of secret communications that conceal the very existence of the message. Invisible inks, microdots, character arrangement, digital signatures, covert channels and spread-spectrum communications and other artifacts of day-to-day use in communications have thus been converted into potent tools of Steganography.

Steganography is different from cryptography. Cryptography uses encryption to change the contents of digitized files using some known algorithm into something totally different. The same algorithm can be used to restore it to its original form. Steganography does not alter the message in any way. It simply hides it. To make detection almost impossible, encrypted messages can be hidden using Steganography.

Steganography simply takes one piece of information and hides it within another computer files (images, sound recordings, even disks) contain unused or insignificant areas of data. Steganography takes advantage of these areas, replacing them with information (encrypted mail, for instance). The files can be exchanged without anyone knowing what really lies inside them. An image of the space shuttle landing might contain a private letter to a friend. A recording of a short sentence might contain your company's plans for a secret new product. Steganography includes a vast array of techniques for hiding messages in a variety of media. Among these methods are invisible inks, music, and software, a technique referred to as writing.

In fact, it is common practice to encrypt the hidden message before placing it in the cover message. However, it should be noted that the hidden message does not be encrypted to qualify as steganography. The message itself can be in plane English and still be a hidden message. However, most steganographers like the extra layer of protection that encryption provides. If your hidden message is found, then at least make it as protected as possible.

However, steganography has a number of disadvantages as well. Unlike encryption, it generally requires a lot overhead to hide a relatively few bits of information. However, there are ways around this. Also, once a steganographic system is discovered, it is rendered useless. This problem too can be overcome if the hidden data depends on some sort of key for extraction. Digital watermarking provides a means of embedding a message in a piece of digital data without destroying its value. Images have an advantage over other pieces of digital data such as a word processed document. The content of the image can be marked without visible loss of value or dependence on specific formats. For example, a bitmap (BMP) image can be compressed to a JPEG I image. The result is an image that requires less storage space but cannot be distinguished from original. Generally, a JPEG level of 7 (70%) or higher can be applied without humanly visible degradation.

The Current Status

The major direction in steganography is the technique of hiding message in innocuous computer files such as digital picture and digitized audio. For example, the least significance bits of a bitmap graphic can be used to hide message. The message is contained in the least significant bits and changing these bits causes an almost imperceptible change in the bitmap image itself. Without a direct comparison of the original and the processed image, it is practically impossible to tell that any thing has been changed. Using these techniques, it is possible to send a secret message to someone who knows and no one else will even know that the message is there. In digitizing audio files, by encoding the message in the least significant bits of a wave file. Watermarking refers to hiding some sort of signature within an image / video / sound data file to establish traceable ownership of the data. Many projects for the development and analysis of watermarking technique for audio, image and video data are under development stage to meet certain criteria such as

Relevance and Importance of the Topic

Throughout history, people have been hiding information by employing several methods. Putting aside the examples from the world of espionage, Steganography can be very useful in real world applications. One of these could be the transmission of credit card numbers through the Internet, where ciphered data cat like a magnet for hackers. With Steganography, the existence of sensitive information id not even noticed. Another scenario for its utilization is when it is desired to maintain certain information hidden within an organization, avoiding the risk of being taken by disgruntled employees. Also, when it is desired to mange confidential information without knowledge of the secretary or the assistant; or when it is desired to send a boss, a colleague or a subordinate some information "just for your eyes". The main difference between watermarking and Steganography basically lies on the intention. Traditionally, the latter hides information, whereas watermarking extends the information and becomes an attribute of the sealed document. In Steganography, the object of communication is the hidden message, and the "packing" is only a means of sending it. In watermarking, the object of communication is the packing and the hidden message only references that packing.

The distribution of digital audio over the Internet in the MP3 format is currently a big problem. In the scenario digital watermarking may be useful to set up a controlled audio distribution and provide efficient means for copyright protection. In the field of data security, watermarking may be used for certification, authentication and conditional access. Certification is an important issue for official documents, such as identity cards or passports. Digital watermarking allows to mutually linking information on the documents. That means that some information is written twice on the document: for instance, the name of a passport owner is normally printed in clear text and is also hidden as invisible watermark in the photo of the owner. If anyone would intend to counterfeit the passport by replacing the photo, it would be possible to detect the change by scanning the passport and verifying the name hidden in the photo does not match any more the name printed on the passport.

Different techniques may be required according to the type of media (audio, image, video) and the encoding format used. In addition, each applications area may require different technologies to address the specific service requirements of that area. Another table SysInfo is used to maintain the systems that are all configured on the LAN for our paper. While we sending the files from one system to another the configured systems are selected by means of retrieving the system name and its corresponding ip address.

This is achieved through the software itself, where it has options for system configuration.

7. Conclusion

Each and every module of the paper is tested and its is verified successfully. The entire paper has been developed with almost care to give security as per the user satisfaction. It includes the following advantages:

1. Enables very secret way of communication, ie, the data transfer is not visible.
2. Complements regular encryption method
3. Much hard to break out the crypto text
4. Since the encrypted message is being embedded in the image the plaintext cannot be easily broken out.
5. Carrier image selection is left to the taste of the sender.

8. Outstanding Features & Future Inherits

The best known application that implements steganography on text hides one bite per text line and it can be easily detected. In this paper, 4 levels of security is been implemented.

Stego Archiever brings out the most sophisticated implementation of Cryptography and Steganography. Thus the Data is well secured by this software. The Data Security System that we have developed is very efficient in the environments of windows workstations.

We have not implemented the file sending over the internet. By developing servlet application for file sending this can be achieved easily. Even though the steganographic image can be send over the internet by using email applications available on the net. Since we are checking CRC code, if any hacker tries to hack the message it's very easy to find out it at the receiving end. We hope the methods used in the Stego Archiver cannot be hacked easily.

In Future this could be enhanced to work under other Operating environments like Linux, Macintosh etc.. The security limits could be upgraded with user priorities etc.

9. References

[1] A. Menezes, P. van Oorschot, and S.Vanstone, Handbook of Applied Cryptography, CRC Press, New York, 1997, p. 81-83.

[2] Neil F. Johnson and Suishil Jajodia IEEE Computer, "Seeing the unseen" Journal, February 1998: 26-34

[3] Neil F. Johnson, Stefan KAtzenbeisser, "A Survey of Steganographic Techniques", Chapter 3 in Stefan Katzenbeisser (ed) Fabien A.P. Petitcolas (ed.)

[4] Stephen Mahoney and Neil F. Johnson, workshop on Statical and Machine Learning Techniques in Computer Intrusion Detection , Audio Stegnanography and Steganlysis, Johns Hopkins University, June 11-13, 2002.

Network Intrusion Detection Using Fast K-Means

D. Saritha[1] and G. Yamuna[2]
[1]Assistant Professor; Dept of C.S.E
[2]H.O.D ,M.C.A Dept; Associate Professor
GVPCOE , Vishakapatnam

Abstract

Intrusion detection corresponds to a suite of techniques that are used to identify attacks against computers and network infrastructure. Anomaly detection is a key element of intrusion detection in which perturbations of normal behavior suggest the presence of intentionally or unintentionally induced attacks, faults, defects, etc. The K-means algorithm is by far the most widely used method for discovering clusters in data. We show how to accelerate it dramatically, while still always computing exactly the same result as the standard algorithm. The accelerated algorithm avoids unnecessary distance calculations by applying the triangle inequality in two different ways, and by keeping track of lower and upper bounds for distances between points and centers. Experiments show that the new algorithm is effective for datasets with up to 1000 dimensions, and becomes more and more effective as the number of clusters increases. For it is many times faster than the best previously known accelerated K-means method.

1. Introduction

As the cost of the information processing and Internet accessibility falls, more and more organizations are becoming vulnerable to a wide variety of cyber threats. According to a recent survey by CERT/CC [1], the rate of cyber attacks has been more than doubling every year in recent times. Therefore, it has become increasingly important to make our information systems, especially those used for critical functions in the military and commercial sectors, resistant to and tolerant of such attacks. The most widely deployed methods for detecting cyber terrorist attacks and protecting against cyber terrorism employ signature-based detection techniques. Such methods can only detect previously known attacks that have a corresponding signature, since the signature database has to be manually revised for each new type of attack that is discovered. These limitations have led to an increasing interest in intrusion detection techniques based on data mining.

Data mining based intrusion detection techniques generally fall into one of two categories; misuse detection and anomaly detection. In misuse detection, each instance in a data set is labeled as 'normal' or 'intrusive' and a learning algorithm is trained over the labeled data. These techniques are able to automatically re-train intrusion detection models on different input data that include new types of attacks, as long as they have been labeled

Appropriately. Research in misuse detection has focused mainly on classification of network intrusions using various standard data mining algorithms, rare class predictive models, and association rules and cost sensitive modeling. Unlike signature-based intrusion detection systems, models of misuse are created automatically, and can be more sophisticated and precise than manually created signatures. A key advantage of misuse detection techniques is their high degree of accuracy in detecting known attacks and their variations. Their obvious drawback is the inability to detect attacks whose instances have not yet been observed. Anomaly detection approaches, on the other hand, build models of normal data and detect deviations from the normal model in observed data. Anomaly detection applied to intrusion detection and computer security has been an active area of research since it was originally proposed by Denning. Anomaly detection algorithms have the advantage that they can detect new types of intrusions as deviations from normal usage.

The most common method for finding clusters in data used in applications is the algorithm known as k-means. K-means is considered a fast method because it is not based on computing the distances between all pairs of data points. However, the algorithm is still slow in practice for large datasets.

The number of distance computations is nke where n is the number of data points, k is the number of clusters to be found, and e is the number of iterations required. Empirically, e grows sub linearly with k, n, and the dimensionality d of the data.

The main contribution of this paper is an optimized version of the standard k-means method, with which the number of distance computations is in practice closer to n than to nke.

The optimized algorithm is based on the fact that most distance calculations in standard k-means are redundant. If a point is far away from a center, it is not necessary to calculate the exact distance between the point and the center in order to know that the point should not be assigned to this center. Conversely, if a point is much closer to one center than to any other, calculating exact distances is not necessary to know that the point should be assigned to the first center. We show below how to make these intuitions concrete.

We want the accelerated k-means algorithm to be usable wherever the standard algorithm is used. There fore, we need the accelerated algorithm to satisfy three properties. First, it should be able to start with any initial centers, so that all existing initialization methods can continue to be used. Second, given the same initial centers, it should always produce exactly the same final centers as the standard algorithm. Third, it should be able to use any black-box distance metric, so it should not rely for example on optimizations specific to Euclidean distance.

Our algorithm in fact satisfies a condition stronger than the second one above after each iteration, it produces the same set of center locations as the standard k-means method. This stronger property means that heuristics for merging or splitting centers (and for dealing with empty clusters) can be used together with the new algorithm. The third condition is important because many applications use a domain-specific distance metric. For example, clustering to identify duplicate alphanumeric records is sometimes based on alphanumeric edit distance, while clustering of protein structures is often based on an expensive distance function that first rotates and translates structures to superimpose them. Even without a domain-specific metric, recent work shows that using a non-traditional L_p norm with $0<p<1$ is beneficial when clustering in a high-dimensional space

This paper is organized as follows. Section 2 explains how to use the triangle inequality to avoid redundant distance calculations. Then Section 3 presents the new algorithm, and Section 4 discusses experimental results on six datasets of dimensionality 2 to 1000. Section 5 outlines possible improvements to the method, while Section 6 reviews related work, and Section 7 explains three open research issues.

2. Applying the triangle inequality

Our approach to accelerating k-means is based on the triangle inequality for any three points x, y and z $d(x,z)<=d(x,y)+d(y,z)$.

This is the only "black box" property that all distance metrics d possesses.

The difficulty is that the triangle inequality gives upper bounds, but we need lower bounds to avoid calculations. Let x be a point and let b and c be centers we need to know that $d(x,c)>=d(x,b)$ in order to avoid calculating $d(x,c)$ the actual value of $d(x,c)$ .The following two lemmas show how to use the triangle inequality to obtain useful lower bounds.

Lemma 1: Let x be a point and let b and c be centers. If $d(b,c)>=2d(x,b)$ then $d(x,c)>=d(x,b)$.

Proof: We know that $d(b,c)<= d(b,x)+d(x,c)$. So $d(b,c)-d(x,b)<=d(x,c)$. Consider the left-hand side: $d(b,c)-d(x,b)>=2d(x,b)-d(x,b)=d(x,b)$.so $d(x,b)<=d(x,c)$.

Lemma 2: Let x be a point and let b and c be centers. Then $d(x,c)>= \max \{0,d(x,b)-d(b,c)\}$.

Proof: We know that $d(x,b)<=d(x,c)+d(b,c)$.so $d(x,c)>=d(x,b)-d(b,c)$. Also, $d(x,c)>=0$.

Note that Lemmas 1 and 2 are true for any three points, not just for a point and two centers, and the statement of Lemma 2 can be strengthened in various ways.

We use **Lemma 1** as follows. Let x be any data point, let c be the center to which x is currently assigned, and let c′ be any other center. The lemma says that if $1/2\ d(c, c')>=d(x,c)$,then $d(x,c')>=d(x,c)$. In this case, it is not necessary to calculate $d(x, c')$.

Lemma 2 is applied as follows. Let x be any data point, let b be any center, and let b′ be the previous version of the same center. (That is, suppose the centers are numbered 1 through k, and b is center number j then b′ is center number j in the previous iteration) Suppose that in the previous iteration we knew a lower bound l′ such that $d(x, b')>= l'$. Then we can infer a lower bound l for the current iteration

$$d(x,b)>=\max\{0,d(x, b')-d(b, b')\}>=\max\{0, l'-d(b, b')\}=l.$$

Informally, if l′ is a good approximation to the previous distance between x and the jth center, and this center has moved only a small distance, then l is a good approximation to the updated distance.

The algorithm below is the first k-means variant that uses lower bounds, as far as we know. It is also the first algorithm that carries over varying information from one k-means iteration to the next. According to the authors of (Kanungo et al., 2000): "The most obvious source of inefficiency in [our] algorithm is that it passes no information from one stage to the next. Presumably in the later stages of Lloyd's algorithm, as the centers are converging to their final positions, one would expect that the vast majority of the data points have the same closest center from one stage to the next. A good algorithm would exploit this coherence to improve running time." The algorithm in this paper achieves this goal. One previous algorithm also reuses information from one k-means iteration in the next, but that method, due to does not carry over lower or upper bounds. Suppose u(x)>=d(x,c) is an upper bound on the distance between x and the center c to which x is currently assigned, and suppose l(x, c')<=d(x, c') is a lower bound on the distance between x and some other center c'. If u(x)<=l(x, c')then d(x,c)<= u(x)<=l(x, c') <= d(x, c') so it is necessary to calculate neither d(x,c) nor d(x, c'). Note that it will never be necessary in this iteration of the accelerated method to compute d(x, c'), but it may be necessary to compute d(x,c) exactly because of some other center c"for which u(x)<=l(x, c") is not true.

3. The new algorithm

Putting the observations above together, the accelerated k-means algorithm is as follows. First, pick initial centers. Set the lower bound l(x,c)=0 for each point x and center c. Assign each x to its closest initial center $c(x)=\mathrm{argmin}_c d(x,c)$, using Lemma 1 to avoid redundant distance calculations. Each time d(x,c)is computed, set l(x,c)=d(x,c).

Assign upper bounds $u(x)=\min_c d(x,c)$.

Next, repeat until convergence:

1. For all centers c and c', compute d(c, c'). For all centers c, compute $s(c)=1/2 \min_{c' \neq c} d(c, c')$. Identify all points x such that u(x)<=s(c(x)).
2. For all remaining points x and centers c such that (1)c ≠c(x) and (2)u(x)>l(x,c) and (3) u(x)>1/2d(c(x),c):

3a. If r(x) then compute d(x,c(x)) and assign r(x)=false. Otherwise, d(x,c(x))=u(x).

3b. If d(x,c(x))>l(x,c) Ord(x,c(x))>1/2d(c(x),c) then Compute d(x,c).If d(x,c)<d(x,c(x))then assign c(x)=c.

4. For each center c, let m(c)be the mean of the points assigned to c.
5. For each point x and center c, assign l(x,c)=max{l(x,c)-d(c,m(c),0} .
6. For each point x, assign u(x)= u(x)+d(m(c(x)),c(x)) r(x)=true.
7. Replace each center c by m(c).

In step (3), each time d(x,c) is calculated for any x and c,its lower bound is updated by assigning l(x,c)=d(x,c). Similarly, u(x) is updated whenever c(x) is changed or d(x,c(x))is computed. In step (3a), if r(x) is true then u(x) is out-of-date, i.e. it is possible that u(x)=d(x,c(x)) . Otherwise ,computing d(x,c(x)) is not necessary. Step (3b) repeats the checks from (ii) and (iii) in order to avoid computing d(x,c) if possible.

The fundamental reason why the algorithm above is effective in reducing the number of distance calculations is that at the start of each iteration, the upper bounds u(x)and the lower bounds l(x,c) are tight for most points x and centers c. If these bounds are tight at the start of one iteration, the updated bounds tend to be tight at the start of the next iteration, because the location of most centers changes only slightly, and hence the bounds change only slightly. The initialization step of the algorithm assigns each point to its closest center immediately. This requires relatively many distance calculations, but it leads to exact upper bounds μ(x) for all x and to exact lower bounds l(x,c)for many (x,c) pairs. An alternative initialization method is to start with each point arbitrarily assigned to one center.

The initial values ofμ(x) and l(c,x) are then based on distances calculated to this center only. With this approach, the initial number of distance calculations is only n, but μ(x) and l(c,x) are much less tight initially, so more distance calculations are required later. After each iteration each point is always assigned correctly to its closest center, regardless of how inaccurate the lower and upper bounds are at the start of the iteration. Informal experiments suggest that both initialization methods lead to about the same total number of distance calculations.

Logically, step (2) is redundant because its effect is achieved by condition (iii). Computationally, step (2) is beneficial because if it eliminates a point x from further consideration, then comparing μ(x) to l(x,c) for every c separately is not necessary. Condition (iii) inside step (3) is beneficial despite step (2), because u(x)and c(x) may change during the execution of step (3).

Step 4 computes the new location of each cluster center c. Setting m(c) to be the mean of the points assigned to c is appropriate when the distance metric in use is Euclidean distance. Otherwise, m(c) may be defined differently. For example, with k-medians the new center of each cluster is a representative member of the cluster.

4. Experimental results

This section reports the results of running the new algorithm on 2 large datasets, 1 of which are high dimensional. The datasets are described in Table 1, while Table 2 gives the results. In order to make our results easier to reproduce, we use a fixed initialization for each dataset X. The first center is initialized to be the mean of X. Subsequent centers are initialized according to the "furthest first" heuristic: each new center is argmax x€X min c€C d(x,c) where C is the set of initial centers chosen so far All algorithms that accelerate k-means incur overhead to create and update auxiliary data structures. This means that speedup compared to k-means is always less in clock time than in number of distance calculations. Our algorithm reduces the number of distance calculations so dramatically that its overhead time is often greater than the time spent on distance calculations. However, the total execution time is always much less than the time required by standard k-means.

Table 1. Datasets used in experiments.

Name	Cardinality	Dimensionality	Description
Kddcup	95413	56	KDD Cup 1998 data, un-normalized
http frequency	1000	5	http frequency observed for 10 min

Table 2. Rows labeled "standard" and "fast" give the number of distance calculations performed by the unaccelerated k-means algorithm and by the new algorithm.

		K=3	k=20	k=100
Kddcup	iterations	34	100	325
	fast	6.179e+05	3.812e+06	1.005e+07
	speedup	15.4	50.1	309
		K=2	k=3	k=4
http	iterations	14	50	150
	standard	5.732e+06	1.506e+08	2..101e+10
	fast	3.179e+05	1.712e+06	1.005e+07
	speedup	10.2.	25.1	300

Rows labeled "speedup" show how many times faster the new algorithm is, when the unit of measurement is distance calculations. A related observation is that for k>=20 we obtain a much better speedup than with the anchors method. The speedups we obtain are 8.60, 107, and 310. We conjecture that the improved speedup for k>=20 arises in part from using the actual cluster centers as adaptive "anchors," instead of using a set of anchors fixed in preprocessing. The worse speedup for k=3 remains to be explained. Another striking observation that the new method remain effective even for data with very high dimensionality

5. Limitations and extensions

During each iteration of the algorithm proposed here, the lower bounds l(x,c) are updated for all points x and centers c These updates take time, so the time complexity of the algorithm remains at least O(nk) even though the number of distance calculations is roughly O(n) only. It may be possible to avoid updating many lower bounds in most iterations, and hence to reduce the nominal complexity of the algorithm. Note that if a point x is eliminated from further consideration in step(2), then l(x,c) is not used at all. In some clustering applications,k>>d. This is the case in particular for vector quantization for image compression In main memory If the data are streamed into memory at each iteration from disk, then the l(x,c)matrix can also be streamed into memory in synchrony. Moreover, the algorithm remains beneficial even if lower bounds are not used, so condition (ii) becomes μ(x)>d(x,c), where d(x,c) is computed ,if necessary.

6. Conclusion and Future work

1. The fast K-means will accelerate the clustering by 10% and for K>=20 and higher dimensions data also it works efficiently.
2. The fast K-means clustering method first portions the training instances into k-clusters using Euclidean distance similarity.

3. On each cluster , representing a density region of normal or anomaly instances, we can build decision trees like id3 and c4.5trees.

The decision tree on each cluster refuse the decision boundaries by leaning the subgroups with in the cluster.

7. References

1. Using the Triangle inequality to Accelerate K-means (Charles elkan,Department of computer science and engineering,University of california,San Diego)
2. K-means +Id3 : A novel method for supervised Anomaly detection by cascading K-means clustering and ID3 decision tree learning methods.(shekhar R. Gaddam, vir v. Phoha, senior member, IEEE,and Kiran S.Balagani)
3. A comparative study of anomaly detection schemes in network intrusion detection(Aleksandar Lazarevic, Aysel Ozgur, levent Ertoz ,Jaideep Srivastava, vipin kumar, Department of computer science ,University of Minnesota,200 Union Street SE ,Minneapolis,MN 55455,USA)
4. R.Duda, P.Hart, and D.Stork, Pattern Classification, Second ed. Willey publishers ,Oct 2000

Secure Routing Protocols in Wired Networks

S.Venkata Raju[1], M.Venkat Dass[1], P.Premchand[1], A.Govardhan[2]
[1]Dept. of Computer Science & Engineering, Osmania University, Hyderabad, India
[2]Dept. of Computer Science & Engineering, J.N.T.U, Kukatpally, Hyderabad, India

Abstract

This paper focuses various security threats to routing protocols in wired networks. The paper also discusses the basic requirements of secure routing protocols with focus on Routing Information Protocol(RIP) .

1. Introduction

Routing protocols support the delivery of packets. It is the fundamental part of network infrastructure. Nowadays the network security is of more significance but the security concern for routing protocols has not been fully aware. For wired networks, generally the network is partitioned into two levels: intra-domain and inter-domain. Intra-domain routing involves routing within the Autonomous System (AS), and the commonly deployed routing protocols are RIP, OSPF or ISIS. Inter-domain routing handles routing between multiple Autonomous Systems. These current routing protocols are mostly designed to deal with simple network failures and can have much vulnerability facing malicious intruders. The compromise of routing function can lead to the denial of network service, the disclosure or modification of sensitive routing information, the disclosure of network traffic etc.

2. Threats to Routing Protocols

The main concern is those attacks, which are trying to improperly modify data, gain authentication, or gain authorization by inserting false packets or by modifying packets. Broadly speaking, threats to routing protocols come mainly from two sources, external and internal. External threats come from outside intruders who are non-participants in the protocol. Internal threats come from compromised protocol participants.

An outside intruder could attack a routing domain in various ways. Specific threats include

1. *Breaking the neighbor relationship*: An intelligent filter placed by an intruder on a communication link between two ISs could modify or change information in the routing updates or even intercept traffic belonging to any data session. For example, if KEEPALIVE[1][2] message are filtered out, then the neighbor relationship is terminated.
2. *Replay attack*: An intruder could passively collect routing information. Later, the intruder could retransmit "obsolete" routing information messages. If obsolete information is accepted and disseminated, a normal IS could make incorrect routing decision.
3. *Masquerading*: During the neighbor acquisition process, a outside intruder could masquerade an nonexistent or existing IS by attaching itself to communication link and illegally joining in the routing protocol domain by compromising authentication system. The threat of masquerading almost the same as that of a compromised IS.
4. *Passive Listening and traffic analysis*: The intruder could passively gather exposed routing information. Such a attack can not effect the operation of routing protocol, but it is a breach of user trust to routing the protocol. Thus, sensitive routing information should be protected. However, the confidentiality of user data is not the responsibility of routing protocol.

3. Requirements for Secure Routing Protocols

Generally speaking, to secure a routing protocol requires that important routing information be authenticated between neighboring routers. Those various kinds of attacks actually take advantage of the lack of authenticity, integrity or confidentiality. Here are the definitions of these services in the context of secure routing protocols

1. Authentication services are primarily concerned with the providing assurances about the identity of an entity. In a routing protocol context, when a router sends out a routing message, the identity of the originator of the information should be able to be validated.
2. Integrity services ensure that the data being transmitted is consistent with the data being received.
3. No-repudiation services provide irrefutable evidence that a certain event took place.
4. Confidentiality service provides privacy of routing message, which uses encryption to prevent others from knowing what the routing message is. No current routing protocol supports it.

4. Securing Routing Information Protocol (RIP)

Routing Information Protocol makes use of Distance Vector algorithm in selecting the best path to reach the destination. In a distance-vector algorithm, a router knows the length of the shortest-path from each of its neighbors to every destination in the network, and uses this information to compute its own distance and next router to each destination. Each update message sent by a router to its neighbors contains a vector with one or more entries, each of which specifies as a minimum, the distance to a given destination. So each router sends only summarized information, which is computational result based on reachability[3] information from its neighbors. Distance vector routing has its inherent problems like count to infinity problem. The nature of distance vector routing makes it more vulnerable to internal attacks. So security measures must be combined with the routing protocol to ensure correct operation.

Sequence information [6], which can be either a sequence number or timestamp, is added to each update to prevent the replay of old routing information. New sequence information is generated for each routing message. An update with old sequence information is dropped. A sequence information must be valid for the life of a given router id. The primary challenge posed by this requirement of a long life is how to prevent sequence information from wrapping around. The primary advantage of sequence numbers compared to timestamps is their significantly longer life. A sequence number can be relatively small and still provide reasonable assurance of not cycling.

A routing table update of a routing information protocol consists of one or multiple entries, each specifying a destination and a distance to the destination. By including the information about the second-to-last hop (predecessor)[4][5] in the path to a destination, the validity and integrity of the entire path from the router to the destination can by verified iteratively using information reported by the routers directly adjacent to the destination and routers immediately adjacent to each intermediate hop in the path. At all time, all the entries of a correct routing table have the property that the length of a path from a router to a destination equals to the distance from the router to the predecessor of the destination plus the length of the link between the destination and its predecessor.

The addition of predecessor information to each update provides a means of validating a link in the network, which can then be used with the routing table to authenticate the implicit path of a route.

To ensure the authenticity and integrity of the routing information exchanged between different routers, the originating router digitally signs each update it generates. In addition, to allow receiving routers to validate the signature, an IP address of the originating router must be added to each update. These signatures are used to validate a candidate path to a destination before that path is selected for use.

5. Conclusion

Above all, we have discussed the secure routing problems of wired network. Routing is the heart of network infrastructure. It controls and manages the "flow" of messages in the network. To set up connection and maintain updated network topology, routers keep exchanging messages about cost and metric. It is possible that attackers can eavesdrop, intercept, or modify these messages or even inject harmful messages into routing infrastructure. Attacker also can comprise a router and fully control it to destroy the network from inside. This kind of inside attack is more destructive. In all, the compromise of routing infrastructure can lead to the denial of service, the disclosure or modification of sensitive routing information, the revelation of network traffic, or the inaccurate accounting of network resource usage.

6. References

[1] P.Papadimitratos and Z.J. Haas, Secure Routing for Mobile Ad Hoc Networks, SCS Communication Networks and Distributed Systems Modeling and Simulation Conference (CNDS 2002), San Antonio, TX, January 27-31, 2002.

[2] J Lundberg. Routing Security in Ad Hoc Networks, Proceedings of the Helsinki University of Technology, 2000.

[3] S. Marti, T.J. Giuli, Kevin Lai and Mary Baker, Mitigating Routing Misbehavior in Mobile Ad Hoc Networks. Proceedings of MOBICOM 2000, August 2000.

[4] L. Peterson. Computer Network: A System Approach, Morgan Kaufmann Publisher, 2000.

[5] C. E. Perkins and E. M. Royer. Ad hoc on-demand distance vector routing protocol. In 2nd IEEE Workshop on Mobile Computing Systems and Applications, February 1999.

[6] K. Zhang. Efficient protocols for signing routing messages. In Proceedings of the 1998 Internet Society (ISOC) Symposium on Network and Distributed System Security, San Diego, California, March 1998.

A Summary of New Cryptographically Well-built Compression Function

A.Arul Lawrence Selvakumar[1] and C.Suresh Gnanadhas[2]
[1]Assistant Professor/CSE, The Oxford College of Engineering, Bangalore
[2]Professor/CSE, Vel Multitech SRS Engineering College, Chennai
aarul72@hotmail.com *sureshc_me@yahoo.com*

Abstract

Cryptographic hash functions are a useful building block for several cryptographic applications. The most important are certainly the protection of information authentication and digital signatures. This overview paper will discuss the definitions, describe some attacks on hash functions, and will give an overview of the existing practical constructions

1. Introduction

Hash functions are functions that map an input of arbitrary length to a string of fixed length, the hashcode. If these mappings satisfy some additional cryptographic conditions, they can be used to protect the integrity of information. Other cryptographic applications where hash functions are useful are the optimization of digital signature schemes, the protection of passphrases and the commitment to a string without revealing it.

Hash functions appeared in cryptographic literature when it was realized that encryption of information is not sufficient to protect its authenticity. The simplest example is the encryption with a block cipher in Electronic Code Book (ECB) mode, where every block is encrypted independently. It is clear that an active attacker can easily modify the order of the cipher text blocks and hence of the corresponding plaintext blocks. It will be shown that cryptographic hash functions allow for efficient constructions to protect authenticity with or without secrecy.

In a first part of this overview paper, the definitions of several types of hash functions will be given, and the basic attacks on hash functions will be discussed. Then it will be explained briefly how they can be used to protect the integrity of information. The protection of software integrity will be treated as an example. Subsequently a general model is described and an extensive overview is given of the proposed schemes. Here a distinction will be made between hash functions with an without a secret key. Finally the conclusions will be presented.

2. Definitions

In this section definitions will be given for hash functions that do not use a secret key (Manipulation Detection Code orMDC) and for hash functions that use a secret key (Message Authentication Code or MAC).

According to their properties, the class of MDC's will be further divided into one-way hash functions (OWHF) and collision resistant hash functions (CRHF).

A brief discussion of the existing terminology can avoid the confusion that is present in the literature. The term *hash functions* originates historically from computer science, where it denotes a function that compresses a string of arbitrary input to a string of fixed length. Hash functions are used to allocate as uniformly as possible storage for the records of a file. The name hash functions has also been widely adopted for cryptographic hash functions or cryptographically strong compression functions, but the result of the hash function has been given a wide variety of names in cryptographic literature: hash code, hash total, hash result, imprint, (cryptographic) checksum, compression, compressed encoding, seal, authenticator, authentication tag, finger print, test key, condensation, Message Integrity Code (MIC), message digest, etc.

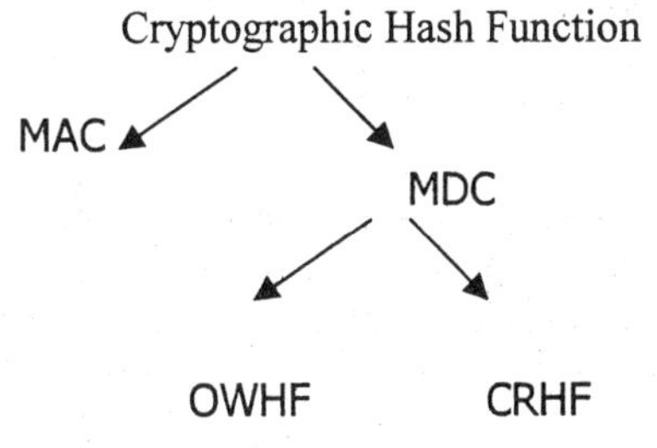

Figure 1: A taxonomy for cryptographic Hash Function

In the following the hash function will be denoted with h, and its argument, i.e., the information to be protected with X. The image of X under the hash function h will be denoted with (X) and the secret key with K. The general requirements are that the computation of the hash code is "easy" if all arguments are known. Moreover it is assumed that Kerckhoff's principle[2]is valid, which means that in the case of an MDC the description is public, and in the case of a MAC the only secret information lies in the key.

2.1 One-way hash function (OWHF)

The first informal definition of a OWHF was apparently given by R. Merkle [88, 89] and M.O. Rabin [111].

***Definition1**: A **one-way hash function** is a function h satisfying the following conditions:*
1. The argument X can be ofarbitrary length and the result h(X) has a fixed length of n bits (with $n \geq 64$).

***Definition 2:** The hash function must be one-way in the sense that given a Y in the image of h, it is **"hard"** to find a message X such that **h(X) = Y** and given X and h(X) it is **"hard"** to find a message $X^0 = X$ such that $h(X^0) = h(X)$.*

The first part of the second condition corresponds to the intuitive concept of one-wayness, namely that it is "hard" to find a preimage of a given value in the range. In the case of permutations or injective functions only this concept is relevant. The second part of this condition, namely that finding a second preimage should be hard, is a stronger condition that is relevant for most applications. The meaning of "hard" still has to be specified. In the case of "ideal security", introduced by X. Lai and J. Massey [79], producing a (second) preimage requires 2^noperations.

However, it may be that an attack requires a number of operations that is smaller than 2^n, but is still computationally infeasible.

2.2 Collision resistant hash function (CRHF)

The first formal definition of a CRHF was apparently given by I. Damg°ard [31, 32]. An informal definition was given by R. Merkle in [89].

Definition 2: **A collision resistant hash function** is a function h satisfying the following conditions:

1. The argument X can be of arbitrary length and the result h(X) has a fixed length of n bits (with $n \geq 128$).
2. The hash function must be one-way in the sense that given a Y in the image of h, it is "hard" to find a message X such that h(X) = Y and given X and h(X) it is "hard" to find a message $X^0 = X$ such that $h(X^0) = h(X)$.
3. The hash function must be collision resistant: this means that it is "hard" to find two distinct messages that hash to the same result.

Under certain conditions one can argue that the first part of the one-way property follows from the collision resistant property. Again several options are available to specify the word "hard". In the case of "ideal security" [79], producing a (second) preimage requires 2^noperations and producing a collision requires $O(2^{n/2})$ operations. This can explain why both conditions have been stated separately.

One can however also consider the case where producing a (second) preimage and a collision requires at least $O(2^{n/2})$ operations, and finally the case where one or both attacks require less than $O(2^{n/2})$ operations, but the number of operations is still computationally infeasible (e.g., if a larger value of n is selected).

2.3 Message Authentication Code (MAC)

Message Authentication Codes have been used for a long time in the banking community and are thus older than the open research in cryptology that started in the mid seventies. However, MAC's with good cryptographic properties were only introduced after the start of open research in the field.

Definition 3: A **MAC** is a function satisfying the following conditions:

1. *The argument X can be of arbitrary length and the result h (K, X) has a fixed length of n bits (with $n \geq 32 \ldots 64$).*
2. *Given h and X, it is "hard" to determine h(K, X) with a probability of success "significantly higher"than $1/2^n$. Even when a large number of pairs$\{X_i$, $h(K, X_i)\}$are known, where the $X_i$have been selected by the opponent, it is "hard" to determine the key K or to compute $h(K, X^0)$ for any $X^0 6= X_i$.This last attack is called an adaptive chosen text attack.*

Note that this last property implies that the MAC should be both one-way and collision resistant for someone who does not know the secret key K. This definition leaves open the problem whether or not a MAC should be one-way or collision resistant for someone who knows K. An example where this property could be useful is the authentication of multi-destination messages [94].

3. Methods of attack

Three elementary attacks that are independent of the specific hash function will be described. For a more extensive overview of attacks on hash functions the reader is referred to [102, 106].

In case of a random attack the opponent select a random message and hopes that the modification will remain undetected. For an ideally secure hash function, his probability of success equals $1/2^n$. The feasibility of this attack depends on the action taken in case of detection of an erroneous result, on the expected value of a successful attack and on the number of attacks that can be carried out. For most applications this implies that n = 32 bits is not sufficient. This is certainly true if an MDC is used and hence the opponent can attack several messages off-line and in parallel. In that case the hashcode should have a length of 64 bits or more.

The idea behind the **birthday attack** [126] is that for a group of 23 people the probability that at least two people have a common birthday exceeds 1/2. Intuitively one would expect that the group should be significantly larger. This can be exploited to attack a hash function in the following way: an adversary generates r_1 variations on a bogus message and $r_2$variations on a genuine message. A second possibility is that he collects a large number of messages and is able to divide them in two categories. This is the only way in the case of a MAC, where the opponent is unable to generate (message, MAC) pairs. The probability of finding a bogus message and a genuine message that hash to the same result is given by

$$1 - exp(-(r1 \cdot r2)/2^n),$$

Which is about 63 % when $r = r1 = r2 = 2^{n/2}$. The involved comparison problem does not require r^2 operations: after sorting the data, which requires O(r log r) operations, comparison is easy. If the hash function can be called as a black box, the new algorithm of J.-J. Quisquater [109], requires $\sqrt{2\pi} . 2^{n/2}$ operations and negligible storage. The conclusion is that if the hash function has to be collision resistant, n should be sufficiently large. In view of the fact that the speed of computers doubles every three years, 128 bits corresponding to 2^{64}operations is sufficient for the next 10 years, but it will be only marginally secure within 20 years.

In the case of a MAC, a third attack is relevant, namely an **exhaustive search** for the secret key K. It is a known plaintext attack, where an attacker knows M plaintext-MAC pairs for a given key and will try to determine the key by trying all possible keys. In order to determine the key uniquely, M has to be slightly larger than k/n. The expected number of trials is equal 2^{k-1}, with k the size of the key in bits.

4. Applications of cryptographic hash functions

This section aims to illustrate briefly how cryptographic hash functions can be used to protect the authenticity of information and to build digital signature schemes. In a second part the application to software protection will be discussed.

4.1 Information authentication and digital signatures

The protection of the authenticity of information includes two aspects:

- The protection of the originator of the information, or in ISO terminology [62] data origin authentication.
- The fact that the information has not been modified or in ISO terminology [62] the integrity of the information.

There are two basic methods for protecting the authenticity of information.

- The first approach is analogous to the approach of a asymmetric cipher, where the secrecy of large data quantities is based on the secrecy and authenticity of a short key. In this case the authentication of the information will also reply on the secrecy and authenticity of a key. To achieve this goal the information is compressed with a hash function and the resulting hashcode is appended to the information. The presence of this redundancy allows the receiver to make the distinction between authentic information and bogus information.
  In order to guarantee the origin of the data, a secret key that can be associated to the origin has to intervene in the process. In the case of a MAC, the secret key is involved in the compression process, while in the case of an MDC, the information and/or the hashcode will subsequently be encrypted with a secret key.
- The second approach consist of basing the authenticity (both integrity and origin authentication) of the information on the authenticity of the hashcode.

Hash functions play also an important role in digital signature schemes. A digital signature is a cryptographic technique that produces the electronic equivalent of a manual signature. This means that a digital signature can prohibit the forging of a message by anybody else but the sender. Moreover the receiver is given guarantee of the message's authenticity, in the sense that he can subsequently prove to a third party that the message is authentic even if its originator revokes it. The concept of a digital signature was suggested in 1976 by W. Diffie and M. Hellman [45]: the sender transforms the information with a secret key, and the receiver can verify the signature by applying the corresponding public key. The first practical scheme was the RSA cryptosystem [112]. Other efficient schemes include the scheme of ElGamal [46], the proposed NIST digital signature standard [51], and the schemes based on zero-knowledge techniques: Fiat-Shamir [47], Guillou-Quisquater [108], and Schnorr [117]. For a more detailed discussion the reader is referred to [95].

Most digital signature schemes can be optimized in the following way: the signature scheme is not applied to the message but to the hashcode of the message. Note that this corresponds to the second approach for authentication, i.e., replace the message by a short hashcode.

The advantages are that the signature has a fixed short length and that the computational requirements are minimized (most signature schemes are rather slow). Moreover the security level of the signature scheme can be increased. In other signature schemes, like the zero-knowledge based schemes and many theoretical constructions, a OWHF forms an integral part of the signature scheme.

Now the choice between a OWHF and a CRHF will be discussed. It is clear from the definition that a CRHF is stronger than a OWHF, which implies that using a CRHF is playing safe. On the other hand, it should be noted that designing a OWHF is easier, and that the storage for the hashcode can be halved (64 bits instead of 128 bits). A disadvantage of a OWHF is that the security level degrades proportional to the number of applications of *h:* an outsider who knows *s* hashcodes has increased his probability to find an $X^1$with a factor s. This limitation can be overcome through the use of a parameterized OWHF.

In order to understand when a CRHF is required, the following attack is considered. Assume that the has h function is not collision resistant: an attacker will thus be able to find a collision, i.e., two plain texts X and X'such that h(X) = h(X'). Subsequently he will protect the authenticity of X through h(X), and later he can substitute $X'$for X. Therefore the use of a CRHF is recommended for any application where the attacker has complete control over the argument of the hash function, which implies he can select X, or he is an insider to the system.

However, one can certainly imagine applications where this attack is not relevant. If the attacker is an outsider, he can not choose X, and will be restricted to observe X and h(X). Subsequently he will try to come up with an X'such that h(X) = h(X'). Examples of applications where a OWHF would be sufficient are the following:

1. The parties involved completely trust each other, which is trivially the case if there is only one party. One could think of someone who protects the integrity of his computer files (which he only can generate) through the calculation and storage of an MDC.
2. The computation of the h(X) involves a random component, that can not be controlled by the insider [89]: X can be randomized before applying h through encryption of X with a good block cipher using a truly random key, that is added to the resulting ciphertext [88], or through the selection of a short random prefix to X [31];h itself can be randomized through randomly choosing h from a family of functions indexed by a certain parameter.

One can conclude that the choice between a CRHF and a OWHF is application dependent.

4.2 Software protection

To illustrate the use of a MAC, MDC, and a digital signature scheme, it will be explained how these three techniques can be applied to protect the integrity of software [92].

The two parties involved in the application are the software vendor (who is also supposed to be the author of the software) and the user.

The attacker will try to modify the software: this can be a computer virus [21], a competitor or even one of the parties involved. For this application there is clearly no need for secrecy. The three approaches will be discussed together with their advantages and disadvantages.

MAC: the software vendor will use his secret key to compute the MAC for the program and append the MAC to the program. The main problem here is the distribution of the secret key to the user through a channel that protects both its secrecy and its authenticity, which induces a significant overhead. This secret key has to be protected carefully by both software vendor and user: if a compromise at one place occurs, the protection is lost. Both software vendor and user can modify the program and the corresponding MAC, and thus in the case of a dispute, a third party can not make any distinction between them. The vulnerability of the secret key implies that it is mandatory that every user shares a different key with the software vendor. The advantage of this approach is that the secret storage is independent of the number of programs to be protected, but depends on the number of users (for the software vendor) and on the number of different software vendors (for the user).

MDC: the software vendor will compute the MDC for the program. The main problem here is the distribution of the MDC to the user through a channel that protects the authenticity of the MDC. This is easier than the distribution of a secret key, but for every update of the program or for every new program a new transmission of an MDC is necessary. If the authenticity of the MDC is compromised, the protection is lost: the software vendor, the user and any third party can modify the program and the corresponding MDC. If a dispute occurs, one has to show to a judge that the value of an MDC is authentic: it is generally not possible to prove to the judge who actually modified the authentic channel and the program. The main advantage is that this approach requires no secret storage. Every program needs an authentic storage both at the user's site and at the vendor's site.

Digital signature: the software vendor will append to the program a digital signature that is computed with his secret key. The main problem here is the distribution of the corresponding public key to the user through a channel that protects its authenticity. The secrecy and authenticity of the secret key have to be protected carefully by the software vendor: if it is compromised, anyone can modify programs and update the corresponding signature.

If the authenticity of the public key is compromised, the protection is also lost: anyone can replace it with the public key corresponding to his secret key. The difference with the previous approaches is the asymmetry: only the software vendor can generate a signature, but anyone can verify it. This implies that the vendor can be held liable to a third party if the program contains a virus. The only way he can escape is by claiming that his secret key was stolen. However, if he can not repeat this type of fraud, as he will loose quickly the trust of his customers.

Every vendor has to store one secret key, while every user needs an authentic storage for the public key of every vendor.

The selection of a particular solution will depend on one hand on the number of users, vendors and programs, and on the other hand on the availability of authentic and/or secret storage and communication. The digital signature is clearly the only solution that can protect the users against a malicious software vendor.

A similar verification process can be executed when the program is loaded from disk to the Central Processing Unit. If the disk is not shared, non-repudiation is not required, but it is still attractive to use a digital signature scheme: the CPU has to know only the public key corresponding to the disk. An alternative is to provide for authentic storage of the MDC of a file that contains the MDC's of all programs.In [36] a scheme is described that combines a digital signature for checking new software with a MAC for verification at run-time.

5. An overview of MDC proposals

5.1 A general model

Before discussing a small fraction of the large number of proposals for MDC's, the general scheme for describing a hash function will be sketched. All known hash functions are based on a compression function with fixed size input; they process every message block in a similar way. This has been called an "iterated" hash function in [79]. The information is divided into t blocks X1 through X_t. If the total number of bits is no multiple of the block length, the information can be padded to the required length. The hash function can then be described as follows:

$$H_0 = IV$$
$$H_i=f(X_i,Hi-1) \qquad i=1,2,\dots t$$
$$h(X)=H_t$$

The result of the hash function is denoted with h(X) and IV is the abbreviation for Initial Value. The function f is called the round function. Two elements in this definition have an important influence on the security of a hash function: the choice of the padding rule and the choice of the IV. It is recommended that the padding rule is unambiguous (i.e., there exist no two messages that can be padded to the same message), and that it appends at the end the length of the message. The IV should be considered as part of the description of the hash function. In some cases one can deviate from this rule, but this will make the hash function less secure and may lead to trivial collisions or second preimages.

The research on hash functions has been focussed on the question: what conditions should be imposed on f to guarantee that satisfies certain conditions ? The two main results on this problem will be discussed. The first result is by X. Lai and J. Massey [79] and gives necessary and sufficient conditions for f in order to obtain an "ideally secure" hash function h.

Proposition 1 *Assume that the padding contains the length of the input string, and that the message X (without padding) contains at least 2 blocks. Then finding a second preimage for h with a fixed IV requires 2^n operations if and only if finding a second preimage for f with arbitrarily chosen H_i-1 requires 2^n operations.* A second result by I. Damg°ard [33] and independently by R. Merkle [89] states that it is sufficient for f To be a collision resistant function.

Proposition 2 *Let f be a collision resistant function mapping l to n − l bits (with n − l > 1). If an unambiguous padding rule is used, the following construction will yield a collision resistant hash function:*

$$H_1 = f(0^{l+1} \| x_1)$$
$$H_i = f(H_{i-1} \| 1 \| x_1) \quad \text{for } i = 2, 3, \dots t.$$

5.2 Hash function based on a block cipher

Two arguments can be indicated for designers of hash functions to base their schemes on existing encryption algorithms. The first argument is the minimization of the design and implementation effort: hash functions and block ciphers that are both efficient and secure are hard to design, and many examples to support this view can be found in the literature. Moreover, existing software and hardware implementations can be reused, which will decrease the cost. The major advantage however is that the trust in existing encryption algorithms can be transferred to a hash function. It is impossible to express such an advantage in economical terms, but it certainly has an impact on the selection of a hash function. It is important to note that for the time being significantly more research has been spent on the design of secure encryption algorithms compared to the effort to design hash functions. It is also not obvious at all that the limited number of design principles for encryption algorithms are also valid for hash functions.

The main disadvantage of this approach is that dedicated hash functions are likely to be more efficient. One also has to take into account that in some countries export restrictions apply to encryption algorithms but not to hash functions. Finally note that block ciphers may exhibit some weaknesses that are only important if they are used in a hashing mode. A distinction will be made between hash functions for which the size of the hashcode equals the block length of the underlying block cipher and hash functions for which the size of the hashcode is twice this length. This is motivated by the fact that most proposed block ciphers have a block length of only 64 bits, and hence an MDC with a result twice the block length is necessary to obtain a CRHF. Other proposals are based on block ciphers with a large key and on a block cipher with a fixed key. The encryption operation

E will be written as Y = E(K, X).

Here X denotes the plaintext, Y the ciphertext and K the key. The corresponding decryption operation will be denoted with X = D(K, Y). The size of the plaintext and ciphertext or the block length will be denoted with r, while the key size will be denoted with k. In the case of the well known block cipher DES, r = 64 and k = 56 [48]. It will be assumed that the reader is familiar with the basic modes of operation of a block cipher as described in [49, 66, 91]. The rate of a hash function based on a block cipher is defined as the number of encryptions to process r plaintext bits.

5.2.1 Size of hashcode equals block length

From Definition 2 it follows that in this case the hash function can only be collision resistant if the block length r is at least 128 bits. Many schemes have been proposed in this class, but the first secure scheme was not proposed until 1985. Seven years later, the author has suggested a synthetic approach: we have studied all possible schemes which use exclusive ors and with an internal memory of only 1 block. As a result, it was shown that 12 secure schemes exist, but up to a linear transformation of the variables, they correspond essentially to 2 schemes: the 1985 scheme by S Matyas, C. Meyer and J. Oseas [85]:

$f = E© (s(H_i{-}1), X_i)$

(here s() is a mapping from the ciphertext space to the key space and E ©(K, X) = E(K, X) © X), and the variant that was proposed by the author in 1989 [102] and by Miyaguchi et al. [96] for N-hash and later for any block cipher [69] $f = E ©_{(}s(H_i{-}1^{)}, X_i) © H_i{-}1$ The first scheme is currently under consideration for ISO standardization as a one-way hash function [67]. The 12 variants have slightly different properties related to weaknesses of the underlying block cipher [106]. One of those variants that is well known is the Davies-Meyer scheme [38, 125]: $f = E©_{(}X_i, H_i{-}1)$ It was also shown by the author that the security level of these hash functions is limited by min(k, r), even if the size of some internal variables is equal to max(k, r).

5.2.2 Size of hashcode equals twice block length

This type of functions has been proposed to construct collision resistant hash functions based on block ciphers with a block length of 64 bits like DES. A series of proposals attempted to double the size of the hashcode by iterating a OWHF (e.g., [73, ?] and [83]); all succumbed to a 'divide and conquer' attack [24, 55, 95]. The scheme by Zheng, Matsumoto and Imai [128] was broken in [?]. A new scheme that was broken by the author and independently by I. Damg°ard and L. Knudsen [35] is the Algorithmic Research hash function [70].

An interesting proposal was described by R. Merkle [89]. A security "proof" was given under the assumption that DES has sufficient random behaviour. However the rate of the most efficient proposal equals about 3.6. The proof for this proposal only showed a security level of 52.5 bits; however this has been improved to 56 bits in [106].

5.3 Hash functions based on modular arithmetic

These schemes are designed to use available hardware for modular arithmetic to produce digital signatures. Their security is partially based on the hardness of certain number theoretic problems and they are easily scalable. The disadvantage is that precautions have to be taken against attacks that exploit the mathematical structure like fixed points of modular exponentiation [10] (trivial examples are 0 and 1), multiplicative attacks and attacks with small numbers, for which no modular reduction occurs.

5.3.1 Schemes with a small modulus

A first type of schemes uses only a small modulus (about 32 bits). R. Jueneman proposed a first version in [71, 72], but several attacks resulted in several new versions [73, 74, 75]. The last scheme was broken by D. Coppersmith in [25].

5.3.2 Schemes with a large modulus

A second class of schemes uses a large modulus (the size of the modulus n is typically 512 bits or more). In this case the operands are elements of the ring corresponding to an RSA modulus, i.e., the product of two large primes, or of a Galois Field GF (p) or GF (2^n). For convenience these schemes will be denoted as schemes with large modulus, although this terminology applies strictly speaking only to RSA based schemes.

The latter class can be divided into practical schemes and scheme that are provably secure. In the case of an RSA modulus, one has to solve the following practical problem: the person who has generated the modulus knows its factorization, and hence he has a potential advantage over the other users of the hash function. The solution is that the modulus can be generated by a trusted third party (in that case one can not use the modulus of the user), or one can design the hash function in such a way that the advantage is limited. The most efficient schemes are based on modular squaring.

Moreover some theoretical results suggest that inverting a modular squaring without knowledge of the factorization of the modulus is a difficult problem. Again one can study all possible schemes which use a single squaring and exclusive ors and with an internal memory of only 1 block. Several schemes of this type have been evaluated in previous papers [54, 99, 100]. It can be shown [106] that the optimal scheme is of the form:

$$f = (X_i \oplus H_{i-1})^2 \bmod N$$

Most existing proposals use however the well known Cipher Block Chaining (CBC) mode:

$$f = (X_i \oplus H_{i-1})^2 \bmod N .$$

In order to avoid the vulnerabilities (one can go backwards easily), additional redundancy is added to the message. The first proposal was to fix the 64 most significant bits to 0 [38]. It was however shown in [54, 76] that this is not secure. In a new proposal, that appeared in national and international standards (the informative annex D of CCITT-X.509 [18] and the French standard ETEBAC 5 [19]) the redundancy was dispersed. D. Coppersmith showed however that one can construct two messages such that their hashcode is a multiple of each other [26, 77]. If the hash function is combined with a multiplicative signature scheme like RSA [112], one can exploit this attack to forge signatures. As a consequence, new methods for adding redundancy were specified in [58, 77, 64, 68], but these methods are still under study.

Other schemes based on squaring that are insecure are the scheme by I. Damg°ard [33] that was broken by B. den Boer [40] and the scheme by Y. Zheng, T. Matsumoto and H. Imai [128], that is vulnerable to the attack described in [54]. I. Damg°ard [34] has identified several weaknesses in an MDC (and a MAC) based on arithmetic in GF (2^{593}) [1].

Stronger schemes have been proposed that require more operations. Examples are the use of two squaring operations [54]:

$$f = \{H_{i-1} \oplus (X_i)^2\}^2 \bmod N$$

and the replacement of the squaring by a higher exponent (3 or $2^{16} + 1$) in the previous schemes. This allows to simplify the redundancy [16, 54]. One can conclude that it would be desirable to find a secure redundancy scheme for a hash function based on modular squaring and to replace the CBC mode by a more secure mode. If a slower scheme is acceptable, the exponent can be increased.

This section will be concluded with provably secure schemes. I. Damg°ard [31, 32] has suggested constructions for which finding a a collision is provably equivalent to factoring an RSA modulus or finding a discrete logarithm modulo a large prime. The construction of J.K. Gibson [53] yields a collision resistant function based on the discrete logarithm modulo a composite. Both the factoring and the discrete logrithm problem are known to be difficult number theoretic problems. The disadvantages of these schemes is that they are very inefficient.

5.4 Schemes based on knapsacks

The knapsack problem is a well known NP-complete problem. In cryptography, a special case is considered, namely given a set of n b-bit integers $\{a_1, a_2, \ldots, a_n\}$, and an s-bit integer S (with $s \approx b + \log_2 n$), find a vector X with components x_i equal to 0 or 1 such that the first application of this function was the 1978 Merkle-Hellman public key scheme [87]. Almost all schemes based on the knapsack problem have been broken [12, 44], which has given the knapsack a bad reputation. It is an open problem whether the knapsack problem is only hard in worst case, while the average instance is easy. If this would be true the knapsack problem would be useless for cryptography.

The attractivity of the problem lies in the fact that implementations in both hardware and software are much faster than schemes based on number theoretic problems. In the case of additive knapsacks, several constructions have been suggested and broken (e.g., the scheme by I. Damg°ard [33] was broken by P. Camion and J. Patarin [15]). Other results can be found in [56, 61]. It is for the time being an open problem whether a random knapsack with n = 1024 and b = 512 is hard to solve.

The first multiplicative knapsack proposed by J. Bosset [11] was broken by P. Camion [14]. An new scheme by G. Z′emor is also based on the hardness of finding short factorizations in certain groups [127]. For the suggested parameters it can be shown that two messages with the same hashcode will differ in at least 215 bits. It remains an open problem whether it is easy to find factorizations of a 'reasonable size'.

5.5 Dedicated hash functions

In this section some dedicated hash functions will be discussed, i.e., algorithms that were especially designed for hashing operations. MD2 [78] is a hash function that was published by R. Rivest of RSA Data Security Inc. in 1990. It makes use of a random 8-bit permutation and although it is software oriented, it is not too fast in software.The evaluation by the author [106] suggests that 16 rounds are sufficient, but only offer a marginal security. No other evaluations of MD2 have been published. A faster algorithm by the same designer is MD4 [113, 114]. This algorithm uses standard 32-bit logic and arithmetic operations and is very efficient in software. The number of rounds, which corresponds to the number of times a single message bit is processed, is equal to 3. It was however shown by R. Merkle in an unpublished result and by B. den Boer and A. Bosselaers [40] that omitting the third respectively the first round yields a weak scheme, which suggests that the security offered by MD4 is only marginal (although the scheme is not broken for the time being).

In consequence of these attacks, R. Rivest realized that the security level of MD4 was not as large as he intended, and he proposed in 1991 a strengthened version of MD4, namely MD5 [115, 116]. An additional argument was that although MD4 was not a very conservative design, it was being implemented fast into products. An additional round was added, and several operations were modified to make the previous attacks more difficult. It was however shown by B. den Boer and A. Bosselaers [42] that with respect to certain criteria MD5 is weaker than MD4. On January 31, 1992, NIST (National Institute for Standards and Technology, USA) published in the Federal Register a proposed Secure Hash Standard (SHS) [52] that contains the description of the Secure Hash Algorithm (SHA). This hash function is designed to work with the Digital Signature Algorithm (DSA) proposed in the Digital Signature Standard (DSS) [51]. The algorithm is clearly inspired by MD4, but it is a strengthened version. The two most remarkable changes are the increase of the size of the hashcode from 128 to 160 bits and the fact that the message words are not simply permuted but transformed with a cyclic code. Another improved version of MD4 called RIPEMD was developed in the framework of the EEC-RACE project RIPE. HAVAL was proposed by Y. Zheng, J. Pieprzyk and J. Seberry at Auscrypt'92 [129]; it is an extension of MD5. The most important properties are a variable number of rounds, a variable size of the hashcode and the use of highly nonlinear Boolean functions. This concludes the variants on MD4. N-hash is a hash function designed by S. Miyaguchi, M. Iwata and K. Ohta [96, 98]. Serious weaknesses have been identified in this scheme by B. den Boer [41] and E. Biham and A. Shamir [6]. A new version of N-hash appeared in a Japanese contribution to ISO [69]. It was shown that this scheme contains additional weaknesses [9, 106]. FFT-Hash I and II are MDC's suggested by C.P. Schnorr [118, 119]. The first version was broken independently by J. Daemen, A. Bosselaers, R. Govaerts and J. Vandewalle [?] and by T. Baritaud, H. Gilbert and M. Girault [4]. The second version was broken three weeks after its publication by S. Vaudenay [122].

R. Merkle suggested in 1989 a software oriented one-way hash function that he called Snefru [90]. It is based on large random substitution tables (2 Kbyte per pass). E. Biham and A. Shamir showed several weaknesses of Snefru [7]. A weaker attack was found independently by J. Williams [124]. As a consequence of theses attacks, it is recommended to use 6 and preferably 8 passes, possibly combined with an increased size of the hashcode. However, these measures increase the size of the substitution tables and decrease the performance. The scheme by I. Damg°ard [33] based on cellular automata has been broken in [28]. J. Daemen, J. Vandewalle and R. Govaerts subsequently proposed Cellhash, a new hash function based on a cellular automaton [28] and an improved version Subhash [30]. Both schemes are hardware oriented.

6. An overview of MAC proposals

The general model for an iterated MAC is similar as the model for an MDC. The basic difference is that the round function f and in some cases the initial value IV depend on the secret key K.In contrast with the variety of MDC proposals, very few algorithms exist. This can perhaps be explained by the fact that the existing standards are still widely accepted. The ANSI standard [3] specifies that the resulting MAC contains 32 bits. It is clear that a result of 32 bits can be sufficient if a birthday attack (cf. section 3) is not feasible and if additional protection is present against random attacks (cf. section 3), which is certainly the case in the wholesale banking environment. In other applications, this can not be guaranteed. Therefore, certain authors recommend also for a MAC a result of 128 bits [74, 75].

The most widespread method tocompute a MAC are the Cipher Block Chaining (CBC) and Cipher FeedBack (CFB) mode of DES [3, 50, 63, 65, 91]. The descriptions and standards differ because some of them select one of the two modes, suggest other padding schemes or leave open the number of output bits that is used for the MAC.

$$\mathrm{CBC} : f = E(K, H_i - 1 \;\square\; X_i)$$
$$\mathrm{CF\ B} : f = E(K, H_i - 1^{)} \square\; X_i$$

In the case of CFB it is important to encrypt the final result once more, to avoid a linear dependence of the MAC on the last plaintext block. In the case of DES, an attack based on exhaustive key search (cf. section 3) or differential attacks [8] can be thwarted by encrypting only the last block with triple DES; at the same time this can block the following chosen plaintext attack [41] (it will be described for the case` of CBC): let H and H^0 be the CBC-MAC corresponding to key K and plaintext X and X^0 respectively. The attacker appends a block The Message Authentication Algorithm (MAA) is a dedicated MAC.

It was published in 1983 by D. Davies and D. Clayden in response to a request of the UK Bankers Automated Clearing Services (BACS) [37, 39]. In 1987 it became a part of the ISO 8731 banking standard [63]. The algorithm is software oriented and has a 32-bit result, which makes it unsuitable for certain applications.

A new non-iterative MAC based on stream ciphers was proposed recently by X. Lai, R. Rueppel and J. Woollven [81]. Further study is necessary to assess its security. The DSA algorithm (Decimal Shift and Add, not to be confused with the Digital Signature Algorithm) was designed in 1980 by Sievi of the German Zentralstelle f¨ur das Chiffrierwesen, and it is used as a message authenticator for banking applications in Germany [39]. Weaknesses of this algorithm have been identified in [59, 106].

The scheme by F. Cohen [22] and its improvement by Y. Huang and F. Cohen [60] proved susceptible to an adaptive chosen message attack [103]. Attacks were also developed [5, 106] on the weaker versions of this algorithm that are implemented in the ASP integrity toolkit [23]. Finally it should be noted that several MAC algorithms exist that have not been published, such as the S.W.I.F.T authenticator and Dataseal [?]. This section will be concluded with a discussion of provably secure and efficient MAC's based on universal hash functions [17, 20, 121, ?]. The advantage is that one can prove based on information theory that an attacker can do no better than guess the MAC: the security is hence independent of the computing power of the opponent.

7. Conclusions

Cryptographic hash functions are a useful tool in the protection of information integrity. Therefore the need exist for provably secure and efficient constructions. For the time being only a limited number of provably secure constructions exist, that are very in efficient. Some theoretical results are available to support practical constructions, but most of our knowledge on practical systems is originating from trial and error procedures. Therefore it is important that new proposals are evaluated thoroughly by several independent researchers and that they are not implemented too quickly. Moreover implementations should be modular such that upgrading of the algorithm is feasible. The choice between different algorithms will also depend on the available hardware.

8. References

[1] G.B. Agnew, R.C. Mullin and S.A. Vanstone, "Common application protocols and their security characteristics,"CALMOS CA34C168 Application Notes, U.S. Patent Number 4,745,568, August 1989.

[2] S.G. Akl, "On the security of compressed encodings," Advances in Cryptology, Proceedings Crypto'83, D. Chaum, Ed., Plenum Press, New York, 1984, pp. 209–230.

[3] "American national standard for financial institution message authentication (wholesale)," X9.9-1986 (Revised), ANSI, New York.

[4] T. Baritaud, H. Gilbert and M. Girault, "FFT hashing is not collision-free," Advances in Cryptology, Proceedings Eurocrypt'92, LNCS 658, R.A. Rueppel, Ed., Springer-Verlag, 1993, pp. 35–44.

[5] I: Bellefroid and K. Beyen, "Evaluatie van de cryptografische veiligheid van anti-virus paketten (Evaluation of the security of anti-virus software – in Dutch)," ESAT Laboratorium, Katholieke Universiteit Leuven, Thesis grad. eng., 1992.

[6] E. Biham and A. Shamir, "Differential cryptanalysis of Feal and N-hash," Advances in Cryptology, Proceedings

[10] G.R. Blakley and I. Borosh, "Rivest-Shamir-Adleman public-key cryptosystems do not always conceal messages," Comp. and Maths. with Applications, Vol. 5, 1979, pp. 169–178.

[11] J. Bosset, "Contre les risques d'alt´eration, un syst`eme de certification des informations," 01 Informatique, No. 107, February 1977.

[12] E.F. Brickell and A.M. Odlyzko, "Cryptanalysis: a survey of recent results," in "Contemporary Cryptology: The Science of Information Integrity," G.J. Simmons, Ed., IEEE Press, 1991, pp. 501–540.

[13] L. Brown, J. Pieprzyk and J. Seberry, "LOKI – a cryptographic primitive for authentication and secrecy applications,"Advances in Cryptology, Proceedings Auscrypt'90, LNCS 453, J. Seberry and J. Pieprzyk, Eds., Springer-Verlag,

The Evolution of Cyber Forensics Models

Dr. P. B. Vijaya Kumar[1] and Dr P. S. Avadhani [2]

[1]Advocate, High Court of Andhra Pradesh, Hyderabad, Honourary Professor of law, University of Hyderabad and Andhra University

[2]Professor, Dept of Computer Science & Systems Engineering, College of Engineering, Andhra University, Visakhaptnam

Abstract

The rapid advancement of digital technology brought enormous speed and precession in every activity dealing with human life from welfare to warfare and from womb to tomb. As a result many a times, these machines aid in the commission of crimes or the very same machine with its data becomes the object of crime. In order to trace the culprits and prosecute the offenders, legally admissible evidence is to be gathered from a latent source, and then processed and presented before a court of law. In that context, cyber forensics assumes significance and various models have been developed over the time with varied applications. This paper addresses currently available popular cyber forensics models, its comparative study and its relative applicability to any cyber crime, ranging from simple to complex scenarios.

1. Introduction

The invention of Computers and the Internet are the cornerstones of the Information Technology Revolution, which has revolutionized the very way we think, as well as the way we act in our day-to-day life. At present, the whole world is based on digital infrastructure, in all fronts, from welfare to warfare. The entire economic activity of the globe is routed through or managed by digital means. The world's innovations and intellectual properties are being treasured in a digital form. However, notwithstanding the fact that these small electronic machines have brought enormous speed, accuracy and ease in our daily working, the digital technology has also opened up a variety of new vistas of committing and perpetrating crimes, thereby resulting in substantial /potential damage to society. A computer attached to the Internet or a major company's computer network can be a potential weapon sufficient to control, damage, and create havoc in the total environment of that organization and is highly machine critical.. The introduction of computers as a criminal tool has enhanced the criminal's ability to perform, hide or otherwise aid unlawful or unethical activity. In particular, the surge of technical adeptness by the general population, coupled with anonymity, seems to encourage crimes using computer systems since there is a small chance of being prosecuted, let alone being caught [Maher00]. Critical infrastructure comprises all computer systems that can be targets of criminal threats, industrial espionage and/or politically motivated sabotage such as the power grid, water supply, railways, nuclear energy plants and more. Attacks on such networks can cause loss of life, threaten public safety, impact national security, or create economic upheaval or environmental disaster [en08]

Cyber crime has no territorial inhibitions and any offence committed without reference to any geographical boundaries, posing challenges for its detections and also trans national legal frameworks. With the rapid advance in computer and network technology, computer-based electronic evidence has increasingly played an important role in the courtroom over the last decade. Computer forensics, a growing discipline rooted in forensic science and computer security technology, focuses on acquiring electronic evidence from computer systems to prosecute computer crimes, national security threats, and computer abuse. It has lost its mystique as a technique used solely by law enforcement and intelligence agents, and has become a popular and powerful application employed by corporations for civil disputes, employee terminations, and intellectual property proceedings. Foundations of computer forensics: A technology for the fight against computer crime. [YW05]

Cyber forensics has been defined as the use of scientifically derived and proven methods towards the preservation, collection, validation, identification, analysis, interpretation and presentation of digital evidence derived from digital sources for the purpose of facilitating or furthering the reconstruction of events found to be criminal or helping to anticipate the unauthorized actions shown to be disruptive to planned operations [GP01]. One important element of digital forensics is the credibility of the digital evidence.

Digital evidence includes computer evidence, digital audio, digital video, cell phones, digital fax machines etc. The legal settings desire evidence to have integrity, authenticity, reproductivity, non-interference and Minimization.

1.1 What is Digital Forensics

The use of scientifically derived and proven methods toward the preservation, collection, validation, identification, analysis, interpretation, documentation, and presentation of digital evidence derived from digital sources for the purpose of facilitation or furthering the reconstruction of events found to be criminal, or helping to anticipate unauthorized actions shown to be disruptive to planned operations" [Digi01].

Digital forensics has become prevalent because law enforcement recognizes that modern day life includes a variety of digital devices that can be exploited for criminal activity, not just computer systems. While computer forensics tends to focus on specific methods for extracting evidence from a particular platform, digital forensics must be modeled such that it can encompass all types of digital devices, including future digital technologies. Unfortunately, there does not exist a standard or consistent digital forensic methodology, but rather a set of procedures and tools built from the experiences of law enforcement, system administrators, and hackers. Palmer suggests that the evolution of digital forensics has proceeded from ad hoc tools and techniques, rather than from the scientific community, where many of the other traditional forensic sciences have originated. This is problematic because evidence must be obtained using methods that are proven to reliably extract and analyze evidence without bias or modification.

1.2 Need for Digital Forensics

The uses of computer forensics are wide and varied. They are not just used in law enforcement and criminal matter, computers have become an important part of our lives. Most of the time they contain important information that can turn into a piece of evidence. Technology is continually developing which means that information is the next valuable commodity. Most business stores their confidential information in computer systems which make them the target for hackers. Hacking is a possible threat. Security technologies continue develop so do criminals who are bent on cracking them. The main purpose of computer forensics is examining a computer system to find if it has been used for a criminal act. All of its contents are thoroughly analyzed to find out if it contains substantial or supportive evidence. The entire investig`ation is not as easy as it is portrayed in television shows.

Computer forensic analysts have to follow a set of procedures to be abel to comply with the standards of evidence. If they not follow legal procedures the evidence will considered inadmissible in court. Computers are used in a variety of purposes. Most often this hardware contains pertinent information. Computer forensic experts can trace emails, instant messages and computer related communication. They can examine portable storage devices that may contain evidence. They can find out when, who and what happened by acquiring and analyzing data. It can be used if a company network's security is breached. Almost all businesses nowadays store important and confidential information in their computer system. Computer forensic analysts will able to detect if someone has disclosed corporate information. In these cases they can be either accidental or intentional.

Million of dollars have been lost due to sabotage and employee theft. They can also find out if there has been a case of industrial espionage. Competition has always been stiff in any industry and with the technology today some use it to get ahead. In general cases, criminals often store or leave traces of information in their computers. It is applicable in deception cases such as counterfeiting. It has also been important in playing a part of finding evidence for phishing which is very common. Analysts are able to track down child pornography by tracing buy and sell activities online. It has played a part in many cases from corporate fraud to threats in national security. We may not know but exchanging information through the internet can also be used against us. The internet is a public place which makes it vulnerable to scams that prey on unsuspecting victims. Information now has become a valuable commodity. Criminals nowadays are able to hack into computer systems.

1.3 Qualities of a good forensic model

To summarize, a good forensic model should possess the following qualities:

(a) The ability to log anything.

(b) A provision for automated metrics, such as path length, and a tuning parameter that enables a forensic analyst to decide what to record.

(c) The ability to log data at multiple levels of abstraction, including those not explicitly part of the system being instrumented.

(d) The ability to place bounds on, and gather data about, portions of previously unknown attacks and attack methods.

(e) The ability to record information about the conditions both before (cause) and after (effect) an event has taken place.
(f) The ability to model multi-stage attacks.
(g) The ability to translate between logged data and the actual event in a one to one fashion.

2. Computer Forensics Models

2.1 Basic model by Pollitt [PM95]

Pollitt"s paper concerns mainly with admission of documentary evidence in the court of law and this model aims at comparison and mapping of the said evidence. Four distinct steps are identified precedent to the admission of any evidence into court. He identified the following steps in his model of cyber forensic.

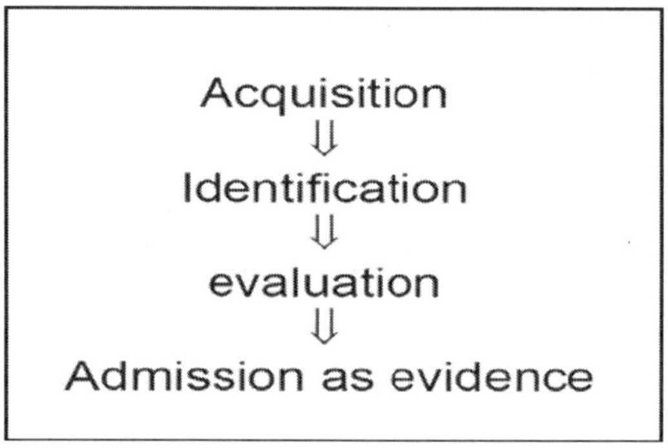

Fig. 1 Flow diagram

The admissibility of the evidence has been reflected in the knowledge management terms by Politt in the chart

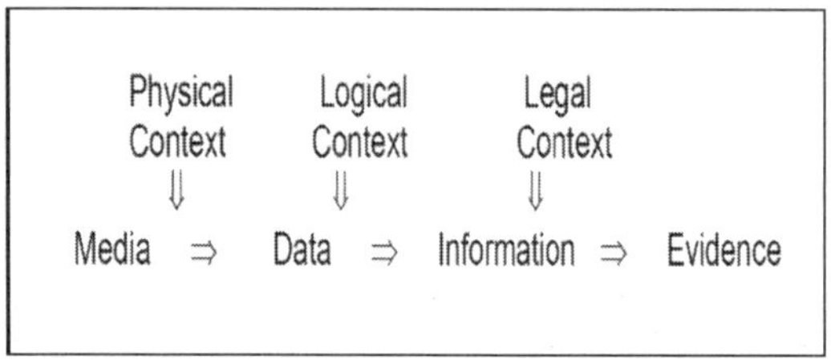

Fig. 2 Flow diagram

2.2 A Three level hierarchical model by NOBLETT [NOB 00]

This model aims at development of guidelines for computer forensic evidence by structuring a three level hierarchical model for the purpose of standardization of guide lines they were of the view that the rapid evolution of both technology and the criminal use of same suggested that a rigorous, yet flexible form of standards might be more useful than the rigid protocols usually found in traditional forensic laboratories. The model as projected is as follows suggested:

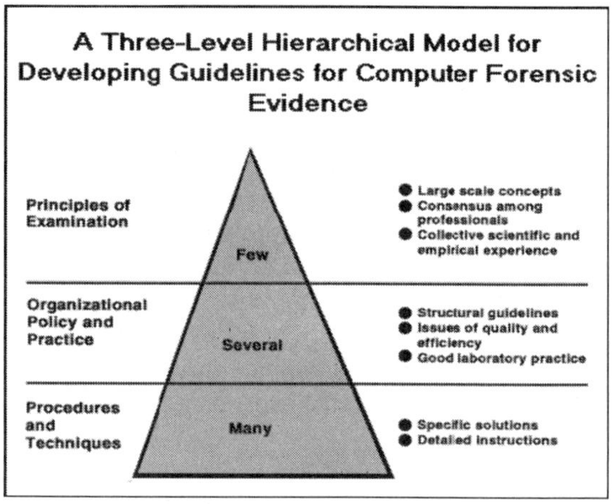

Fig. 3 A Three level hierarchical model

Identification	Preservation	Collection	Examination	Analysis	Presentation	Decision
Event/Crime Detection	Case Management	Preservation	Preservation	Preservation	Documentation	
Resolve Signture	Imaging Technologies	Approved Methods	Traceability	Traceability	Expert Testimony	
Profile Detection	Chain of Custody	Approved Software	Validation Tecniques	Statistical	Clarification	
Anomalous Detection	Time Synch.	Approved Hardware	Filtering Tecniques	Protocols	Mission Impact Statement	
Complaints		Legal Authority	Pattern Matching	Data Mining	Recommended Countermeasure	
System Monitoring		Lossless Compression	Hidden Data Discovery	Timeline	Statistical Interpretation	
Audit Analysis		Sampling	Hidden Data Extraction	Link		
Etc.		Data Reduction		Spacial		
		Recovery Techniques				

Fig. 4 Model

2.3 Enhanced DFRW Model by REITH, CARR AND GUNSCH 2002 [REITH02]

The key components of this model include the following:

(a) Identification –recognizing an incident from indicators and determining its type. This is not explicitly within the field of forensics, but significant because it impacts other steps.

(b) preparation- preparing tools, techniques, search warrants, and monitoring authorizations and management support.

(c) Approach strategy- dynamically formulating an approach based on potential impact on bystanders and the specific technology in question. The goal of the strategy should be to maximize the collection of untainted evidence while minimizing impact to the victim.

(d) Preservation-isolate, secure and preserve the state of physical and digital evidence. This includes preventing people from using the digital device or allowing other electromagnetic devices to be used within an affected radius.

(e) Collection – record the physical scene and duplicate digital evidence using standardized and accepted procedures.

(f) Examination – in-depth systematic search of evidence relating to the suspected crime. This focuses on identifying and locating potential evidence, possibly with unconventional locations. Construct detailed documentation for analysis.

(g) Analysis - determine significance, reconstruct fragments of data and draw conclusions based on evidence found. It may take several iterations of examination and analysis to support a crime theory. The distinction of analysis is that it may not require high technical ski8lls to perform and thus more people can work on this case.

(h) Presentation - summarize and provide explanation of conclusions. This should be written in a layperson's terms using abstracted terminology. All abstracted terminology should reference the specific details.

(i) Returning evidence – ensuring physical and digital property is returned to proper owner as well as determining how and what criminal evidence must be removed. Again not an explicit forensics step, however any model that seizes evidence rarely addresses this aspect.

2.3.1 Advantages of the model

- Create consistent and standardized framework for digital forensic development.
- Mechanism for applying the same framework to future digital technologies.
- Generalized methodology that judicial members can use to relate technology to non-technical observers.
- Identifies the need for specific technology-dependent tools while providing insight from previously defined tools of the same category.
- Potential for incorporating non-digital, electronic technologies within the abstraction.

2.3.2 Disadvantages of the model

- Categories may be defined as too general for practical use.
- No easy or obvious method for testing the model
- Each sub-category added to the model will make it more cumbersome to use.
- One obvious area not touched upon in our model is the chain of custody. Of course this is an important facet of any forensic or investigative work. This model assumes that a strong chain of custody will be maintained throughout the duration of the investigation. The absence of it on the model above makes no presumptions that it is not important, only that it is implied in any discussion of forensics.

2.5 Carrier and Spafford 2003

Also called a Digital investigation process model This model is based on the phases that are documented for investigating physical crime scenes. The phases are applied to a digital crime scene, where we consider the digital crime scene investigation to occur as a subset of a physical crime scene investigation. The general concepts of this model have already been published [CS03]. It is organized into the following five categories of phases,

Readiness Phases includes the operations readiness phase that trains the appropriate people and tests the tools that will be used to investigate a system. The infrastructure readiness phase configures the equipment to help ensure that the needed data exists when an incident occurs. For example, in a corporate or military environment this could include adding network monitoring tools and increasing the logging levels..

Deployment phases includes the detection and notification phase where the incident is detected by the victim or another party and the investigators are altered. For example, a network intrusion could be detected by an intrusion detection system and a contraband incident could be detected using the logs or communications of the suspect. This category of phases also includes the confirmation and authorization phase where the investigators receive authorization to conduct the investigation. In a corporate environment, this could include the incident response team doing a brief analysis of a system to confirm that it has indeed been compromised. If it is a critical system, additional permission may be needed before a full analysis can be conducted. In a law enforcement environment, the officer may need to obtain a search warrant before the investigation can progress.

Physical crime scene investigation phases: after authorization for the investigation has been granted, the physical investigation begins and the physical objects at the crime scene where a digital device exists are examined. It is in this set of phases where physical evidence will be collected that could link a person to the suspect computer activity. This set of phases includes the search for physical evidence and the reconstruction of physical events. When a physical object is found that may have digital evidence in it, a digital investigation begins. This phase will receive and correlate the analysis results from one or more digital crime scene investigations.

Digital crime scene investigation phases Includes the phases that examine the digital data for evidence. This set of phases is actually a subset of the physical crime scene investigation phases and the conclusions that are made from the digital investigation will be used in the physical investigation. An investigation occurs for each self-contained digital device. We will examine this phase in more detail in this paper. In general, this process involves the preservation of the system, the search for digital evidence, and the reconstruction of digital events.

Presentation phase after theories have been developed and tested about the events related to the incident, the results must be presented to either a corporate audience or a court of law. This phase deals with that process.

2.5 STEPHENSON 2003 [PS03]

This is also known as End –to-End digital Investigative Process (EEDI). EEDI process offers a comprehensive approach to complex digital investigations. Its primary benefit is its ability to allow an investigator to use and document a scientific approach, consistent with the Duabert tests , to solve, document and present a complex digital investigation additionally, its lends itself to future enhancements such as modeling and simulation

The basic End-to-End process consists of:

- Collecting evidence
- Analysis of individual events
- Preliminary correlation
- Event normalizing
- Event deconfliction
- Second level correlation (consider both normalized and non- normalized events)
- Timeline analysis
- Chain of evidence construction
- Corroboration (consider only non-normalized events)

2.6 Carrier 2003 [C03]

In this model Carrier outlined layers of abstraction that constitute forensic examination. For example, the content of Word document is extracted via an operating system, a file system and an application. Carrier identifies an abstraction layer as having two inputs and two outputs:

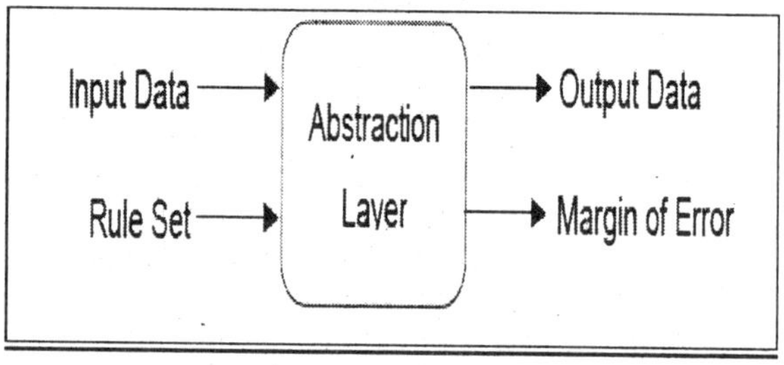

Fig. 5 Flow Diagram

This model classifies forensic tools into translation tools and presentation tools. The former reads the data, applies a set of rules and passes it to the presentation tool which then displays the information in a meaningful way. This model gives rise to analysis tool requirements

2.7 Triage process model

The computer forensics model is defined as:

Those investigating processes that are conducted within the first few hours of an investigation, that provide information used during the suspect interview and search execution phase. Due to the need for information to be obtained in a relatively short time frame, the model usually involves an on site/field analysis of the computer system(s) in question.

The foci of the model are to:

(a) find useable evidence immediately;
(b) identify victims at acute risk;
(c) guide the ongoing investigation;
(d) identify potential charges; and
(e) accurately assess the offender's danger to society.

While at the same time protecting the integrity of the evidence and/or potential evidence for further examination and analysis. Being able to conduct an examination and analysis on scene, in a short period of time and provide investigators with time sensitive leads and information provides a powerful psychological advantage to the investigative team. Suspects are psychologically more vulnerable within the first few hours of their initial contact with police, especially when this contact occurs in their place of business or dwelling. They tend to be more cooperative and open to answering questions even after being "mirandized". This cooperation can be critical in certain cases such as abductions, sexual predatory offenses etc. what is crucial to the investigator during this initial time period is the knowledge of the full extent of the crime and/or involvement of the suspect and "triggers" that further increase the suspect's willingness to talk and cooperate. These triggers may be found in the digital evidence located on the suspect's system(s) (e.g., email correspondence, digital maps, pictures, chat logs).

The CFFTPM uses phases derived from the carrier and spafford (2002) Integrated Digital Investigation Process model (IDIP) and the Digital Crime Scene Analysis (DCSA) model as developed by Rogers (2006). The phases include: planning, triage, usage/user profiles, chronology/timeline, Internet activity, and case specific evidence. These six phases constitute a high level of categorization and each phase has several sub-tasks and considerations that vary according to the specifics of the case, file system and operating system under investigation, etc. the use of higher order categories allows the process model to be generalized across various types of investigations that deal with digital evidence. The need for a general model has been identified in several studies as a core component of a practical/pragmatic approach for law enforcement investigations (ISTS, 2004;Rogers & Seigfried,2004;Stambaugh,H.,Beaupre,D., Icove,D., Baker,R., Cassaday, W., & Williams, W.,2001).

Before discussing each of the model's phases it is important that qualifications be placed around the use of the CFFTPM, as the model is not appropriate for all investigative situations.

2.8 Evidence Graph model for Network forensic Analysis by Wei Wang, Thomas E. Daniels

This model presents technique for a network forensics analysis mechanism that includes effective evidence presentation, manipulation and automated reasoning, which proposes the evidence graph as a novel graph model to facilitate the presentation and manipulation of intrusion evidence. For automated evidence analysis, this model evolved into a hierarchical reasoning framework that includes local reasoning and global reasoning. Local reasoning aims to infer the roles of suspicious hosts from local observations. Global reasoning aims to identify group of strongly correlated hosts in the attack and derive their relationships. By using the evidence graph model, they effectively integrated analyst feedback into the automated reasoning process.

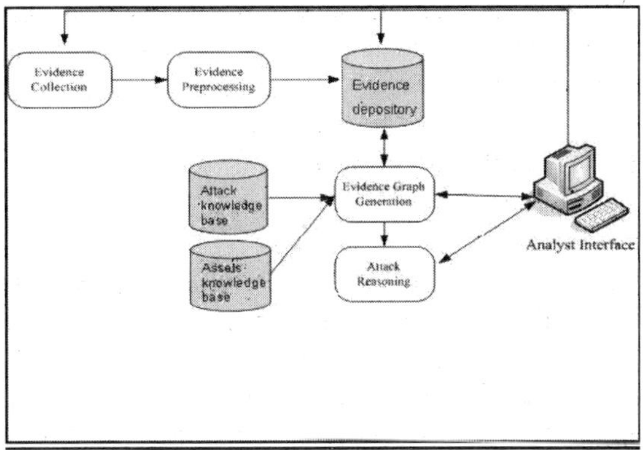

Fig. 6 Network forensics Analysis mechanism

2.9 FORZA Model by Pollitt 2004 [P04]

Mark Pollitt highlighted in DFRWS 2004 [Politt MM. Six blindmen from Indostan. Digital forensics research workshop (DFRWS); 2004] that digital forensics is not an elephant; it is a process and not just one process, but a group of tasks and processes in investigation. In fact, many digital forensics investigation processes and tasks were defined on technical implementation details Investigation procedures developed by traditional forensics scientist focused on the procedures in handling the evidence, while those developed by the technologist focused on the technical details in capturing evidence. As a result, many digital forensics practitioners simply followed technical procedures and forget about the actual purpose and core concept of digital forensics investigation. With all these technical details and complicated procedures, legal practitioners may have difficulties in applying or even understanding their processes and tasks in digital forensics investigations.

In order to break the technical barrier between information technologists, legal practitioners and investigators, and their corresponding tasks together, a technical-independent framework would be required. In this paper, he first highlighted the fundamental principle of digital forensics investigations (Reconnaissance, Reliability and Relevancy). Based on this principle, He re-visited the investigation tasks and outlined eight different roles and their responsibilities in a digital forensics investigation. For each role, He defined the sets of six key questions. They are the What (the data attributes), Why (the motivation), How (the procedures), Who (the people), Where (the location) and When (the time) questions. In fact, among all the investigation processes, there are six main questions that each practitioner would always ask.

By incorporating these sets of six questions into the Zachman's framework, a digital forensics investigation framework – FORZA is composed.

2.10 Erbacher, Christensen and Sundberg [Er06]

In this paper, Erbacher et al proposed a network forensic process that models a number of critical issues. It recognizes that network forensics is not a linear process and must have multiple feedback loops to integrate both text and visual analysis. This process is mapped as follows:

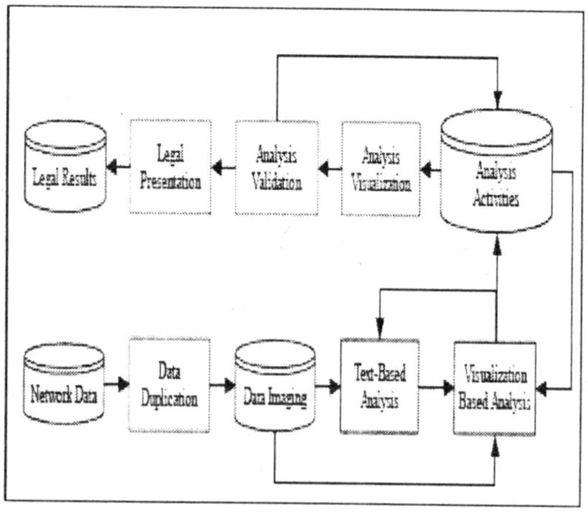

Fig. 7 Mapping

They further describe a number of problems involved in the visualization of data in both intrusion and network forensic situations. They posit that different visualization techniques will be required for different aspects of the analysis but that these, in turn, must be integrated.

2.11 Kent, Chevalier, Grance and Dang 2006 [KE06]

As part of the National Institute of Standards and Technology (NIST), they have published a Guide to Integrating Forensics into Incident Response. In it they define the basic forensic process:

- Regardless of the situation, the forensic process comprises the following basic phases:
- Collection. The first phase in the process is to identify, label, record, and acquire data from the possible sources of relevant data, while following guidelines and procedures that preserve the integrity of the data. Collection is typically performed in a timely manner because of the likelihood of losing dynamic data such as current network connections, as well as losing data from battery-powered devices (e.g., cell phones, PDAs).
- Examination. Examinations involve forensically processing large amounts of collected data using a combination of automated and manual methods to assess and extract data of particular interest, while preserving the integrity of the data.
- Analysis. The next phase of the process is to analyze the results of the examination, using legally justifiable methods and techniques, to derive useful information that addresses the questions that were the impetus for performing the collection and examination.
- Reporting. The final phase is reporting the results of the analysis, which may include describing the actions used, explaining how tools and procedures were selected, determining what other actions need to be performed (e.g., forensic examination of additional data sources, securing identified vulnerabilities, improving existing security controls), and providing recommendations for improvement to policies, guidelines, procedures, tools, and other aspects of the forensic process. The formality of the reporting step varies greatly depending on the situation.

2.13 A Computer Forensics Model Based On Danger Theory

Static methods of computer forensics relied too much on the technician's level, which show poor performance with specific circumstances surrounding environment when attack occurred, and can not extract accurate corresponding evidence and lack of convincing. So dynamic computer forensics combined with the intrusion detection, which can collect reliable evidence in real time when the system is invaded, complete the invasion of testing and the evidence of the dynamics of computer forensics, becomes research focus of computer forensics. The problems of computer network security and the problems faced by biological immune system (BIS) show pretty direct and fabulous analogy, since both of them have to maintain stability in a changing environment. Burnet proposed the famous clonal theory in 1958 [8], and built the "Self-Nonself" model. Based on "Self- Nonself", Forrest et al. proposed the negative selection algorithm (NS) in 1994 [9]. Since the "Self-Nonself" model can not explain the phenomenon of self-immune diseases, such as multiple sclerosis disease, the immune system will produce cell immune response. Matzinger proposed the danger theory [10]. The danger theory pointed out that immune system carry out not only "Self-Nonself" recognition, but also when the invasion of the "danger" accumulated to a certain degree; then it would send out a dangerous signal, which means that the immune system detected the foreign invasion antigen.

In this study, a new dynamic computer forensics model based on danger theory, referred to as Demed, is firstly proposed. Demed successfully applies the related biological immune system theory to network security technology. Compared with the presented computer forensics models, Demed can accurately calculate the real-time risk degree of the network and implement the dynamic forensics according to the network risk, which overcomes the defect of enormous amount of evidence in the existed dynamic computer forensics model and improves the quality of evidentiary information.

3. Comparative analysis

In the digital forensics investigation practices, there are over hundreds of digital forensics investigation procedures developed all over the world. Each organization tends to develop its own procedures. Some focused on the technology aspects in data acquisition, some focused on data analysis portion of the investigation (Brill and Pollitt, 2006). As many of these procedures were developed for tackling different technology used in the inspected device, when underlying technology of the target device changes, new procedures has to be developed. Among those procedures, Lee's (Lee et al., 2001), Casey's (Casey, 2003a), DFRWS (DFRWS, 2001) and Reith, Carr and Gunsch (Reith et al., 2002) procedures are the most frequently quoted procedures. They are known to be the standard procedures in digital forensics investigations. However, discrepancy still lies between them. According to Se′amus O′ Ciardhua′ in's analysis (Ciardhua′ in, 2004), the four procedures were not aligned (Table 1). Instead of difference in definition, the processes they recommend and their coverage were different. Although with Ciardhua′ in's extended model, digital forensics procedures have been extended to cover a wider prospective and area, one core issue have not been solved. That is the gap between technical aspects of digital forensics and judicial process (Losavio and Adams, 2006).

Table 1 - A comparison table between different digital forensics investigation model extracted from Séamus Ó Ciardhuáin's analysis

Term in new model	Model			
	Lee et al.	Casey	DFRWS	Reith et al.
Awareness				Identification
Authorisation				
Planning				Preparation
Notification				
Search/identification	Recognition, identification	Recognition	Identification	
Collection	Collection and preservation	Preservation, collection, documentation	Preservation, collection	Preservation, collection
Transport				
Storage				
Examination	Individualization	Classification, comparison, individualization	Examination	Examination
Hypothesis	Reconstruction	Reconstruction	Analysis	Analysis
Presentation	Reporting and presentation		Presentation	Presentation
Proof/defence			Decision	
Dissemination				

Fig. 8 Comparision of models

4. References

[1] A Computer Forensics Model Based On Danger Theory Lingxi Peng1 0-7695-3063-X/07, 2007 IEEE: DOI 10.1109/IITA.2007.57 [Li07]

[2] Kent, K., Chevalier, S., Grance, T. and Dang, H. "Guide to Integrating Forensics into Incident Response", Special Publication 800-86, Computer Security Division Information Technology Laboratory, National Institute of Standards and Technology, Gaithersburg, MD August 2006 [KE06] http://csrc.nist.gov/publications/nistpubs/800-86/SP800-86.pdf

[3] Ruibin, G., Yun C., and Gaertner, M. "Case-Relevance Information Investigation: Binding Computer Intelligence to the Current Computer Forensic Framework", International Journal of Digital Evidence Spring 2005, Volume 4, [Er06,] http://www.utica.edu/academic/institutes/ecii/publications/articles/B4A6A102-A93D-85B1-96C575D5E35F3764.pdf

[4] Pollitt, M. "Six Blind Men from Indostan", DFRWS, 2004, Baltimore, [P04] http://www.dfrws.org/2004/bios/day1/D1-Pollitt-Keynote.ppt

[5] Wei Wang and Thomas E. Daniels. Building evidence graphs for network forensics analysis. Submitted to 21st Annual Computer Security Applications Conference(ACSAC'05) [WW05]

[6] Carrier, B. "Defining Digital Forensic Examination and Analysis Tools Using Abstraction Layers", International Journal of Digital Evidence Winter 2003, Volume 1, Issue 4. [C03] http://www.utica.edu/academic/institutes/ecii/publications/articles/A04C3F91-AFBB-FC13-4A2E0F13203BA980.pdf

[7] Stephenson, P. "A Comprehensive Approach to Digital Incident Investigation" An Article Appearing in Elsevier Information Security Technical Report 2003 [PS03] http://www.emich.edu/cerns/downloads/pstephen/Comprehensive-Approach-to-Digital-Investigation.pdf

[8] Carrier, B. and Spafford, E. "Getting Physical with the Digital Investigation Process", International Journal of Digital Evidence Fall 2003, Volume 2, Issue [CS03] http://www.utica.edu/academic/institutes/ecii/publications/articles/A0AC5A7A-FB6C-325D-BF515A44FDEE7459.pdf

[9] Digital Forensic Research Workshop (DFRWS) Research Road Map, Utica, NY. (2001) http://www.dfrws.org/archive.html [DFRW01]

[10] Reith M., Carr C. and Gunsch, G. "An Examination of Digital Forensic Models", IJDE Fall 2002 Volume 1, Issue 3. [Reith02] http://www.utica.edu/academic/institutes/ecii/ijde/articles.cfm?action=article&id=A04A40DC-A6F6-F2C1-98F94F16AF57232D

[11] [N et al00] Noblett, M., Pollitt, M., Presley, L. "Recovering and Examining Computer Forensic Evidence", Forensic Science Communications, Volume 2 Number 4 2000 http://www.fbi.gov/hq/lab/fsc/backissu/oct2000/computer.htm

[12] [PM95] Pollitt, M. "Computer Forensics: an Approach to Evidence in Cyberspace", Proceedings (Vol. II, pp 487-491) of the National Information Systems Security Conference, Baltimore, MD. 1995 http://www.digitalevidencepro.com/Resources/Approach.pdf

Security Over Web Services Using Evidence Based Access Control

E. S. Shamila and Maganti Suresh Kumar
Sathyabama University, Chennai
shamiiee@rediffmail.com

Abstract

We focus on using evidence for making access control decisions in Web service. These environments create new interaction scenarios that traditional access control approaches handle poorly. Our approach views access control as the filtering of messages between communicating services. Services are known only by name, and each service makes access control decisions based on local policies and evidence it gathers about other services. We implement our evidence-based approach with a mechanism analogous to a network firewall, filtering messages going to and from a service. Our evidence-based firewall is responsible for managing evidence, laying a foundation for extensions to it that gather, trade, and evolve evidence over time.
Keywords: Web Services; Access Control; Firewall; Evidence; Security;

1. Introduction

Web services are self describing and modular business applications that expose the business logic as services over the internet through programmable interfaces and using internet protocols for the purpose of providing ways to find, subscribe and invoke those services.

1.1 Trust and Security

Trust and security in computing environments are tightly coupled in the following aspects:

1. security is viewed as one objective of trust in that only the trusted clients are allowed to access the restricted resources or services in a system,
2. security measures (e.g. cryptography) keep the trust information or evidence from being compromised during the information distribution processes among entities, and
3. security can be realized more dynamically using dynamic trust management. Therefore, trust is the prerequisite for a computing system to allow the clients wants to access the resources of a system, trust must be established between the client and the system so that the security of the system can be ensured. In this sense, trust establishment is the most critical process in trust management.

Trust establishment is mainly achieved in the following way : the system collects the trust evidence of the clients, defines the trust polices, builds up the trust levels of the clients based on the trust evidence and policies. As more evidence becomes available, the system iteratively updates the trust information including trust evidence and polices.

1.2 Access control

Access control is a mechanism that allows owners of resources to define, manage and enforce access conditions applicable to each resource.

1.2.1 An Access Control model

Access control denotes the fact of determining whether a *user* (not necessarily an human user: process, computer, etc.) is able to perform an *operation* (read, write, execute, delete, search, etc.) on an *object* (more generally: a tuple in a database, a table, an object, a file, etc.). An operation right on an object is called *permission.* An access control model define how to organize the permissions of users.

Authorization

Process of granting or denying access rights for a resource to an authenticated user. (What are you allowed to do?)

Credentials

Information that includes identification and proof of identification that is used to gain access to resources. Examples of credentials are user names and passwords, smart cards, and certificates.

1.3 Firewall

Firewalls make it possible to filter incoming and outgoing traffic that flows through your system. A firewall can use one or more sets of "rules" to inspect the network packets as they come in or go out of your network connections and either allows the traffic through or blocks it. The rules of a firewall can inspect one or more characteristics of the packets, including but not limited to the protocol type, the source or destination host address, and the source or destination port.

Firewalls can greatly enhance the security of a host or a network. They can be used to do one or more of the following things:

- To protect and insulate the applications, services and machines of your internal network from unwanted traffic coming in from the public Internet.
- To limit or disable access from hosts of the internal network to services of the public Internet.
- To support network address translation (NAT), which allows your internal network to use private IP addresses and share a single connection to the public Internet (either with a single IP address or by a shared pool of automatically assigned public addresses).

In this paper, we present an access control model that emphasizes the formation, evolution, and evaluation of evidence in making access control decisions.

2. Evidence - Based Access Model

In this section, we introduce the high-level goals of our design and provide an overview of the concepts.

The goals of our model are to:

1. Support communication between parties in different trust domains or in cases where no pre-existing trust domains exist. This goal requires that parties can name each other securely and that the model interoperates with existing access models.
2. Allow evidence associated with parties to be securely collected and evaluated for the purpose of allowing access to resources. In particular, access decisions should be based on policies that are capable of balancing security with convenience.
3. Create an ecosystem in which evidence providers can flourish. This goal requires a system for creating evidence, associating evidence with parties, and trading evidence between parties. New forms of evidence and new policies must be allowed to be introduced freely.

In our work, we separate unique identifiers from the information used to make decisions about access control. We call the identifiers entities to highlight the fact that they do not necessarily represent a user, but can uniquely name any available service. We assume that entities are uniquely defined and can provide cryptographic signatures that are sufficiently strong for the task they are being used for based on existing technology, such as a public key infrastructure.

With the traditional concept of user, identity and trust are tightly coupled. Users verify their identity by providing a password, after which, the user and the capabilities of the user are co-mingled. In our model there is no preconceived relationship between entities.

The relationship emerges locally at every service based on available evidence. While entities can be uniquely named and addressed, their names are difficult to remember, communicate, etc. To support a more convenient way to address entities and their related services, we use URIs (uniform resource identifiers), and we call an entity/URI pair a port. Messages are sent to and from ports.

A message identifies the port it comes from, the port it is being sent to, and contains the structured contents of the message. We assume that messages contain a distinguished field called action, which we interpret as the verb of the message.

In our model, a service is a container of state, with zero or more ports, that is the sender or receiver of a message, named by a port, whose behavior upon receiving a message depends on the message and the state of the service. Upon receiving a message, a service can change its state and/or send zero or more messages.

A resource is a part of a service's state that can be serialized and sent through a port in a message. A document is a resource that has been serialized, for example, into XML. We call the sender of a message requesting access to a resource a client.

A firewall is a processor, associated with a service, that processes all messages that are sent to or from the ports of the service. A service's firewall may access all the service's state.

For every message sent or received, the firewall implements the function f(message, state) that produces one of the following results:

1. the message, in whole or in part4, is delivered to or from the port,
2. the message is discarded and an error message is returned,
3. the message is silently discarded. If an error message is returned, it may contain additional information, such as the port of an evidence provider.

Firewalls manage the information needed to make access control decisions and execute the policies that determine the decisions.

Evidence is any state in a service that its firewall accesses in making an access control decision. Policies are the procedures whose evaluation results in access control decisions. While one can make the case that there is a duality between policies and evidence, for simplicity we consider only cases where policies are procedural and fixed by the entity that a firewall protects and evidence is data that is accumulated on a per-requesting-service basis. An evidence provider is a service that interacts with the environment and other services and provides data that are pertinent to firewall decisions.

3. Proposed Work

This paper considers the problem of providing access control using evidence based. One approach to access control is based on authenticating users. In this model, users are authenticated by providing a password to a central authority. Once they have established their identity, they cross the trust boundary and are granted credentials that then allow them to access resources.

By evidence, we mean any knowledge that relates to the requesting or responding service, potentially including reputation [21], recommendations, passwords, HIPs [9], CAPTCHAs [27, 28], client puzzles [10, 11, 29], biometrics [24], proximity [19], peer rating [25], credit reports, and quizzes. Evidence can conceivably be gathered, accumulated, and evolved as necessary over time. If a service needs more evidence, it can challenge the requesting service directly (e.g., by requesting a password), or it can request evidence about the requesting service from another service, an *evidence provider*.

This model captures identity in the body of collected evidence about other services that each service gathers. Access decisions are based on evidence and policies held locally by each service. Each service can have different evidence for the same requesting service, and the local evidence can be thought of as a partial view of the identity of the requesting service.

In this paper, we define a model for access control between services that filters messages between services with an evidence-based firewall (EBF). The evidence-based firewall manages the interaction between services and regulates what services have access to what resources. Figure 2 illustrates our approach, showing two communicating services that each have an EBF processing messages sent between the services. Based on access control policies and known evidence about the sender and receiver of the message, the EBF determines whether the message is allowed to be sent or received. Access control policies allow the EBF to make access control decisions based on a variety of sources, including the sender, receiver, and contents of the message.

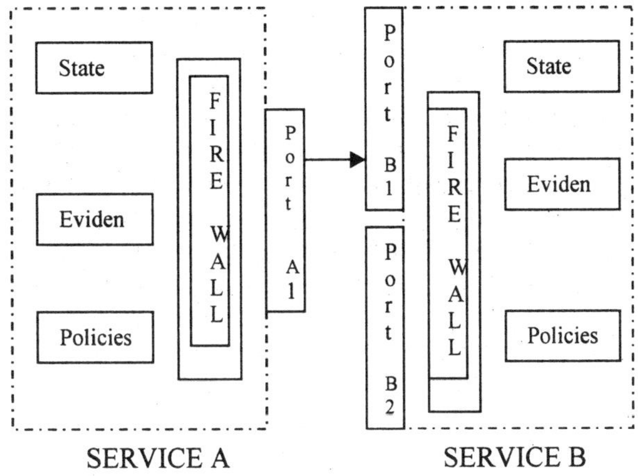

Fig. 1 Evidence-based Firewall

We base our framework on the firewall concept because it is well understood, widely used, and effective. Firewalls limit both incoming and outgoing messages, necessary to prevent access and maintain privacy in ubiquitous computing environments. Furthermore, firewalls are also used to filter data that we classify as boring or annoying.

Evidence-based access control can be used to achieve traditional centralized access control if desired. Each user would be an entity and all the resources protected by a domain would require the same evidence, for example, that a user knows a password. Nothing in our model prevents multiple services from synchronizing their policies and evidence if desired.

Beyond providing new evidence, evidence providers might also provide evidence management services, including caching, replicating, summarizing, and/or distilling it into higher order evidence.

```
boolean Access?(port sender, port receiver, action, body) {
boolean decision, error;
policy p;
evidence e;
if (sender == me) {
p = LookupPolicy(me, "out");
e = LookupEvidence(receiver);
} else {
p = LookupPolicy(me, "in");
e = LookupEvidence(sender);
}
(decision, error) = p(e, action, body);
if (error) {
if (protocol_requires_response)
Send(receiver, sender, error);
return false;
}
return decision;
}
```

Fig. 2 Access Decision Procedure

There are many ways that an access control decision can be made based on the sender, receiver, the message itself, and available evidence. We present pseudocode for a simple access control algorithm in Figure 2, which illustrates an algorithm with separate "in" and "out" policies, and uses evidence associated with the sender while making "in" decisions, and uses evidence associated with the receiver while making "out" decisions. We use such a policy organization in the scenarios that follow. While this figure depicts a Boolean policy, nothing prevents us from providing a more complex policy that allows more subtle access distinctions.

4. Related Work

There is a large body of work on the general issue of access control in a distributed environment, while less work focuses on the problems specific to web services. While some prior work has considered a general framework using evidence for access control, much of the previous work assumes a small, fixed set of evidence sources.

The work most closely related to our evidence-based access model is the dynamic trust model proposed by Xiu and Liu [30]. They also propose a service that collects trust evidence about its clients. They argue that the diversity of ubiquitous computing scenarios demands support for various forms of evidence. In subsequent work, they consider automated trust negotiation for such environments based on agents [23]. Their work differs from ours in that we separate naming from evidence, model access control as a message firewall, and emphasize creating an ecosystem for evidence services.

With our EBF approach, the main focus is on the evidence itself. With this focus, we hope to stimulate research in ways to evolve, manage, combine, and generate new evidence.

5. Summary

We describe an evidence-based access model that assumes no centralized domain, focuses on access control to non-critical data, and encourages a robust ecosystem of new evidence and policy providers. Our model binds names to evidence locally, so that every service has a potentially different view of the credentials of client services. We enforce access control by interposing a firewall on every incoming and outgoing message, allowing message filtering based on the sender, receiver, and the contents of the message. Because much data is neither dangerous or critical, relatively benign message filtering is an important part of any access control system.

6. References

[1] Oscar Almeida, Alessandro Forin, Philip Garcia, Johannes Helander, Nishith Khantal, et al. Embedded systems research at DemoFest'07. Technical Report MSR-TR-2007-94, Microsoft Research, July 2007.

[2] J. P. Anderson. Computer security technology planning study. Technical Report ESD-TR-73-51, Air Force Electronic Systems Division (ESD/AFSC), Hanscom AFB, Bedford, MA, October 1972.

[3] Ronald Ashri, Terry R. Payne, Darren Marvin, Mike Surridge, and Steve Taylor. Towards a semantic web security infrastructure. In Proceedings of Semantic Web Services 2004 Spring Symposium Series, 2004.

[4] Moritz Y. Becker, Andrew D. Gordon, and Cedric Fournet. SecPAL: Design and semantics of a decentralized authorization language. Technical Report MSR-TR-2006-120, Microsoft Research, September 2006.

[5] Blaze, Feigenbaum, and Lacy. Decentralized trust management. In RSP: 17th IEEE Computer Society Symposium on Research in Security and Privacy, 1996.

[6] Keith Brown. Managing identity: The InfoCard identity revolution. http://technet.microsoft.com, July 2006.

[7] Michael Burrows, Martin Abadi, and Roger Needham. Alogic of authentication. ACM Trans. Comput. Syst.,8(1):18{36, 1990.

[8] Kim Cameron. Introduction to the laws of identity. http://www.identityblog.com, January 2006.

[9] M. Chew and H. Baird. Ba²etext: A human interactive proof. In Proc. of SPIE-IS&T Elec. Imaging, Document Recognition and Retrieval X, pages 305{316, January 2003.

[10] Drew Dean and Adam Stubble¯eld. Using client puzzles to protect TLS. In Proceedings of the 10th USENIX Security Symposium, August 2001.

[11] Cynthia Dwork and Moni Naor. Pricing via processing or combatting junk mail. In CRYPTO '92: Proceedings of the 12th Annual International Cryptology Conference on Advances in Cryptology, pages 139{147, London, UK, 1993. Springer-Verlag.

[12] Carl M. Ellison, Bill Frantz, Butler Lampson, Ron Rivest, Brian Thomas, and Tatu Ylonen. RFC 2693: SPKI Certi¯cate Theory. The Internet Society, September 1999.

[13] Colin English, Sotirios Terzis, Waleed Wagealla, Helen Lowe, Paddy Nixon, and Andrew D. McGettrick. Trust dynamics for collaborative global computing. In WETICE, page 283, 2003.

[14] D. F. Ferraiolo, R. Sandhu, S. Gavrila, D. R. Kuhn, and R. Chandramouli. Proposed NIST standard for role-based access control. ACM Transactions on Information and System Security, 4(3):224{274, 2001.

[15] A. Forin, J. Helander, P. Pham, and J. Rajendiran. Component based invisible computing. In 3rd IEEE/IEE Real-Time Embedded Systems Workshop, 2001.

[16] Alessandro Forin, Behnam Neekzad, and Nathaniel L. Lynch. Giano: The two-headed system simulator. Technical Report MSR-TR-2006-130, Microsoft Research, September 2006.

[17] Munirul M. Haque and Sheikh Iqbal Ahamed. An omnipresent formal trust model (FTM) for pervasive computing environment. In COMPSAC, pages 49{56, 2007.

[18] Johannes Helander. Deeply embedded XML communication: towards an interoperable and seamless world. In International Conference On Embedded Software (EMSOFT'05), pages 62{67.ACM, 2005.

[19] Johannes Helander and Yong Xiong. Secure web services for low-cost devices. In ISORC, pages 130{139. IEEE Computer Society, 2005.

[20] Johannes Helander and Benjamin Zorn. Medina: Combining evidence to build trust. In Proceedings of the Workshop on Web 2.0 Security and Privacy 2007 (W2SP'07), May 2007.

[21] Audun J¿sang, Roslan Ismail, and Colin Boyd. A survey of trust and reputation systems for online service provision. Decision Support Systems, 43(2):618{644, 2007.

[22] Butler Lampson, Martin Abadi, Michael Burrows, and Edward Wobber. Authentication in distributed systems: theory and practice. SIGOPS Oper. Syst. Rev., 25(5):165{182, 1991.

[23] Zhaoyu Liu and Daoxi Xiu. Agent-based automated trust negotiation for pervasive computing. In Proceedings of the International Conference on Embedded Software and Systems (ICESS'05). IEEE, December 2005.

[24] N. K. Ratha, J. H. Connell, and R. M. Bolle. Enhancing security and privacy in biometrics-based authentication systems. IBM Sys. Journal, 40(3):614{634, 2001.

[25] Paul Resnick, Ko Kuwabara, Richard Zeckhauser, and Eric Friedman. Reputation systems. Commun. ACM, 43(12):45{48, 2000.

[26] R.S. Sandhu and P. Samarati. Access control: principle and practice. Communications Magazine, IEEE, 32(9):40{48, Sep 1994.

[27] von Ahn, Blum, Hopper, and Langford. CAPTCHA: Using hard AI problems for security. In Proceedings of EUROCRYPT, 2003.

[28] Luis von Ahn, Manuel Blum, and John Langford. Telling humans and computers apart automatically.Commun. ACM, 47(2):56{60, 2004.

[29] Brent Waters, Ari Juels, J. Alex Halderman, and Edward W. Felten. New client puzzle outsourcing techniques for dos resistance. In CCS '04, pages 246{256. ACM Press, 2004.

[30] Daoxi Xiu and Zhaoyu Liu. A dynamic trust model for pervasive computing environment.

A New Method for Identifying Monitoring Nodes Intrusion Detection Systems of Mobile Ad Hoc Network

Marjan Kuchaki Rafsanjani[1], Ali Movaghar[2], Amir Sabbagh Molahosseini
[1]Islamic Azad University Kerman Branch, Kerman, Iran
kuchaki@iauk.ac.ir
[2]Department of Computer, Engineering, Sharif University of Technology, Tehran, Iran
movaghar@sharif.edu
[3]Islamic Azad University, Science and Research Branch, Tehran, Iran
amir.sabbagh@sr.iau.ac.ir

Abstract

In this paper we consider intrusion detection systems, authentication and key management problems in Mobile Ad hoc Networks (MANET). Then, a monitoring nodes selection method with high battery power in these networks is presented. We propose a two-phase detection method. In first phase, authorized nodes are detected and in second phase, nodes with the largest battery power as monitoring nodes are considered. In most of the existing Intrusion detection systems for MANETs a detection system sits on every node, which runs all the time, which is a costly overhead for a battery powered mobile device. So, the proposed method could improve intrusion detection in the area of security.

1. Introduction

Mobile Ad hoc networks (MANETs) are wireless networks in which the mobile nodes exchange information without the help of any predefined network infrastructure. Such networks are also called spontaneous networks. Finding and maintaining communication routes in MANET is a major challenge, especially with respect to security because wireless access links makes the network more vulnerable to many attacks like passive eavesdropping, active impersonation, and denial of services. Most existing solution consists in some kind of preventing security, usually based on authentication, these preventive security services, such as intrusion detection [1].

So, routing and security are the most important problems in MANETs. For these problems various solutions and algorithms in different situations are presented, still there are certain difficulties left. In contrast with other networks which use specific nodes for supporting packet forwarding, routing, and managing the network, the MANETs operate with all the nodes of the network [2,3].

In this paper, we have presented a two phase method for the detection of authorized nodes followed by the selection of monitoring nodes in MANETs. The method is able to detect the main network functions in network layer and link layer. The first phase is based on zero knowledge technique which does not rely on the algorithms of symmetric or asymmetric encryption, digital signatures, sequence numbers, and time stamps to identify nodes. This technique is based on proofs.

2. Intrusion detection systems (IDSs)

Studies show that intrusion detection techniques just like encryption and authentication systems which are the first line of defense are not enough. As the system grows in complexity their weaknesses grow causing the network security problems to grow too. Intrusion detection can be considered as a second line of defense for network security. If an intrusion is detected then an answer for preventing intrusion or minimizing the effects can be generated [4].

There are several assumptions for developing IDS. In the first assumption, user operations and the programs are visible, and in the second assumption, normal and intrusive activities in a system behave differently. So IDS should analyze system activities and ensure whether or not an intrusion has occurred. Intrusion detection can be classified based on audit data which are host or network based. A network-based IDS, receives packets from the network and analysis it. On the other hand, host-based IDS, analyses the events taken place in application programs or the operating systems. IDS can be divided into three groups based on detection techniques; anomaly detection system, misuse detection systems and specification based detection [5,6].

3. Authentication and key management problems

The network needs the assurance that only the certified users have an access to its services and the users would have access to secure facilities in which lack of security in the network would be considered as a permanent threat for the user. The main goal is to create a session key for confidential communication, mutual authentication, and non-repudiation [7,8].

Most of the access control systems depend on public key management systems. The verification of a link between an identity and a key is established by a digital certificate. This certificate includes a public key, an identity, and other cryptography details signed by a trusted third party. In order to be used in applications, the certification of a public key is created by the Certificate Authority (CA). Security requirements are very important for CAs because they can encounter many attacks.

In conventional networks, the two main solutions of public key management are Pretty Good Privacy (PGP) and the X.509 public key infrastructure. The X.509 in comparison to PGP has a strong hierarchy. In PGP there are many central certificate repositories which are not often used. But in X.509 there is a hierarchy structure of CAs which is responsible for issuing certificates and their verifications. A node determines the verification of a certificate by using CA public key. The CA may revoke a certificate. So, it is necessary to propagate the Certificate Revocation List (CRL) periodically. Delay in propagating a CRL may cause acceptance of revoked certificates by some nodes in the network.

In Ad hoc networks, this method is difficult in practice in as much as access to a CA to get the latest CRL is not guaranteed all the time. The process of estimating the verification of a certificate in Ad hoc networks takes a lot of time and it is also difficult. It has been tried to eliminate the need for a centralized CA in key management methods for Ad hoc networks. In the first method, there is one CA with distributing parts of the secret key on several nodes [9]. One proposed public key scheme for Ad hoc networks is using the threshold cryptography and the public key technique. In this scheme, the special nodes on which parts of the secret key are distributed are determined as servers. An attacker has to attack a certain number of servers in order to get access to the secret key service. To prevent the gradual compromising of the servers, refreshing is done constantly. To establish the service, this scheme needs pre communication and coordination of the nodes. In addition, some nodes will work more than other nodes. Also, if the number of nodes in Ad hoc network is high, knowing the public key for all nodes will not be possible. In another method, a self-organized public key infrastructure was used. Hubaux et al. [3] proposed a public key distribution based on trust building scheme for Ad hoc networks. In this scheme, there are no central certificate directories for the distribution of certificates.

In Global System for Mobile (GSM) networks, Asadpour and et al. presented a new anonymity scheme for anonymous authentication of users. Anonymity can be provided to the mobile users through encrypting the real identity or assigning some kind of alias(es). Either symmetric or asymmetric cryptography can be employed for encryption [10].

In most methods of authentication and key management, there are many attacks which can target the identity of a mobile node or the encryption key that is stored or exchanged with the protocols of cryptography.

4. The detection method

The detection method that we proposed is shown in Fig. 1 and it is based on the main operations of Ad hoc networks in link and network layers of Open Systems Interconnection (OSI) Reference Model.

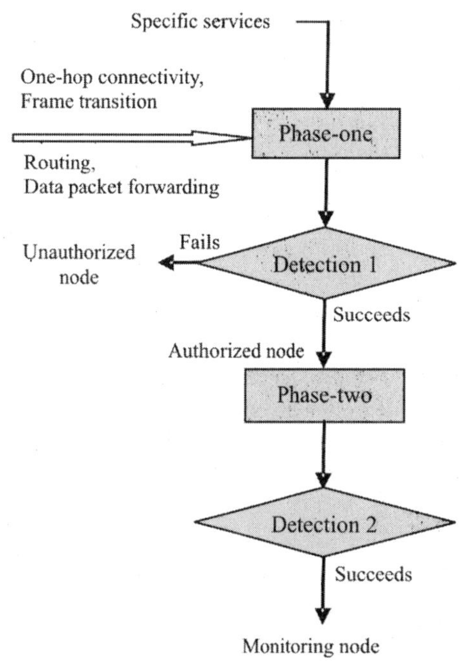

Fig. 1 The detection method of monitoring nodes in MANET

In link layer the cases of one-hop connectivity and frame transition, and in network layer, the cases of routing and data packet forwarding are considered [9,11,12]. Data link layer protocols provide the connections between neighbouring nodes and will also provide the accuracy of the transmitted frames. As routing protocols exchange routing data between nodes, as a result, they would maintain routing states in each node. Based on routing states, data packets are transmitted by mediated nodes along an established route to the destination.

The presented method includes two phases. In the first phase of the detection procedure, it is tried to detect the authorized nodes through a non-interactive zero knowledge technique. This phase of our scheme is based on first phase of Komninos and et al.'s framework [11]. Then in the second phase, from among authorized nodes, the ones which have higher battery power would be determined as monitoring nodes.

4.1 Detecting authorized nodes phase

When one or a few nodes are linked to MANET, the procedure of detecting authorized nodes begins working. Suppose B and C nodes are verified. When node X_1 enters the MANET, its authentication action is done by neighbouring nodes B and C. New routes will be built between nodes. As soon as node X_1 is verified as authorized nodes in the network, routing and transmitting packets would be done through them.

There are several suitable protocols for authentication in the MANET which can be used. Of course, it is necessary to use protocols with low complexity and non-interactive which would not produce excessive computational overhead in the network.

The interactive zero protocols are not suitable for the wireless environments because they exchange many messages and as a result the efficiency of the network decreases. The non-interactive zero knowledge protocols are proper for the MANET networks in such a way that the nodes do not need to exchange messages to verify their identities.

For example, the node x_1 can prove its identity to the nodes B and C and guarantees that discrete logarithms of $y_1=\alpha_1^{x1}$ and $y_2=\alpha_2^{x2}$ are computed with α_1 and α_2 bases and are displaced in equation (1):

$$k_1.x_1 + k_2.x_2 = b(\text{mod}\, p) \qquad (1)$$

k_1 and k_2 are integers and p is the prime number [11].

In the protocol, node X_1 first computes the y_3 and y_4 ($y_3=\alpha_3^{x3}$, $y_4=\alpha_4^{x4}$) then solves the equation (2):

$$k_1.x_3 + k_2.x_4 = 0(\text{mod}\, p) \qquad (2)$$

Then the following messages are exchanged:

$$\text{B,C} \leftarrow \text{X}_1 : y_5 = \alpha_1^{x_3}\ ,\ y_6 = \alpha_2^{x_4} \qquad (\text{M1})$$

$$\text{B,C} \rightarrow \text{X}_1 : y_7 = H(\alpha_1, \alpha_2, y_1, y_2, k_1, k_2, b, y_5, y_6) \qquad (\text{M2})$$

$$\text{B,C} \leftarrow \text{X}_1 : y_8 = x_3 - y_7.x_1(\text{mod}\, p),$$
$$y_9 = x_4 - y_7.x_2(\text{mod}\, p) \qquad (\text{M3})$$

Node X_1 sends y_5 and y_6 to the B and C nodes. As soon as these nodes receive the M1 message, compute the y_7 with a one-way hash function and send M2 message to the node X_1. Node X_1 by examining M1 validity builds the M3 message and sends y_8 and y_9 to the B and C nodes.

Node X_1 convinces nodes B and C that it knows the discrete logarithms of y_1 and y_2 with the α_1 and α_2 basis and also knows that these logarithms build a linear equation. This can be done through verifying the resulted proof of y_7, y_8, and y_9. It is easily seen that nodes B and C will be always successful in making an accurate proof by reconstructing $y_{10}=\alpha_1^{y8}.y_1^{y7}$ and $y_{11}=\alpha_2^{y9}.y_2^{y7}$, then it is examined to see whether y_7 is an equivalent to y_{12}, when $y_{12}=H(\alpha_1,\alpha_2,y_1,y_2,k_1,k_2,b,y_{10},y_{11})$, and if the equation (3) is accurate:

$$k_1.y_8 + k_2.y_9 = -y_7.b(\text{mod}\ p) \qquad (3)$$

It is seen that nodes B and C are always successful in making a reliable proof because $y_{10}=y_5$ and $y_{11}=y_6$.

$$y_{10} = \alpha_1^{y_8}.y_1^{y_7} \overset{y_8,y_1}{=} \alpha_1^{x_3-y_7.x_1}.\alpha_1^{x_1.y_7} = \alpha_1^{x_3} = y_5,$$

$$y_{11} = \alpha_2^{y_9}.y_2^{y_7} \overset{y_9,y_2}{=} \alpha_2^{x_4-y_7.x_2}.\alpha_2^{x_2.y_7} = \alpha_2^{x_4} = y_6.$$

So,

$$y_{12} = H(\alpha_1,\alpha_2,y_1,y_2,k_1,k_2,b,y_{10},y_{11})$$
$$= H(\alpha_1,\alpha_2,y_1,y_2,k_1,k_2,b,y_5,y_6) = y_7$$

In this way, nodes B and C compute y_{12} and compare it with y_7 in M2 message.

Nodes B and C, for verification, will replace the responses Y_8 and Y_9 in the equation (3):

$$k_1y_8 + k_2y_9 \overset{y_8,y_9}{=} k_1.(x_3 - y_7.x_1) + k_2.(x_1 - y_7.x_2)$$
$$= k_1.x_3 - k_1.y_7.x_1 + k_2.x_4 - k_2.y_7.x_2$$
$$= k_1.x_3 - k_2.x_4 - y_7.(k_1.x_1 + k_2.x_2)$$
$$\overset{(1),(2)}{=} -y_7.b(\text{mod}\ p)$$

Then the identity of the node X_1 is known authorized [11].

4.2 Selecting monitoring nodes phase

Since in the intrusion detection systems in MANET, the node, which has been selected to monitor, must collect and analyze all packets in the communication area. So, it uses the extra resources and energy. When the monitoring node identifies the attacker intrusion, it propagates warning messages to the neighbouring nodes. Since the bandwidth and the battery power in the MANETs are limited, there is a need for an effective method of utilizing these resources to build detecting intrusion systems. The lifetime of the network is the time that the first failure or decrease (de-charge) of the battery, which is one of the important efficiency criteria, happens to the point that the failure of one node would be able to link the network to some disconnected sub-networks and the next communication services among separated networks would stop [13].

So, in order to improve the lifetime of the network, an effective method in selecting a monitoring node is needed so that a required level of detection intrusion in MANETs would be provided. So, in the proposed method, after the authorized nodes are determined in the first phase; in the second phase, from among them, the nodes which have higher battery power would be selected as the monitoring nodes. In this phase, the mobile nodes with the highest battery power among neighbouring nodes would be selected as the monitoring nodes. Consider node i, its neighbouring nodes are the ones which are placed about one-hop from it. N^i is the set of the neighbouring nodes which include the node i too, and the P_i is the remaining battery power of node i. The node i^* is the monitoring node which is searched, for each node, according to the equation (4):

$$i^* = \arg\max_{j \in N^i} P_j \qquad (4)$$

Each node sends a periodically controlled packet including battery power value to its neighbouring nodes. So, all nodes always know their neighbouring nodes' battery power value. Then, to select the monitoring node, each node must vote.

The node which would receive at least one vote becomes a monitoring node and the monitoring sensors of the network is loaded and executed. Whenever the condition of the connectivity changes or whenever the remaining battery power of a monitoring node becomes lower than the lowest battery power among the neighbouring nodes, the process of selecting the monitoring node must be performed again (equation 5) [14].

$$P_{i^*} < \min_{j \in N^{i^*}} P_j \qquad (5)$$

In the above equation, N^{i^*} is the set of neighbouring nodes of monitoring node i*.

5. Performance measurement

The selected nodes for hosting the monitoring sensors in the network, collect all the packets in their communication area and analyze them in order to discover undesired attack patterns. The used energy by a monitoring node during an interval of Δt is computed by equation (6):

$$E = (m^t s^t + b^t) + (m^r s^r + b^r) + (m^o s^o + b^o) + (m^m s^m + b^m) \qquad (6)$$

In this equation, s^t, s^r, s^o, and s^m, respectively show the sizes of the packets in bytes in the operations of transmission, receiving, eavesdropping, and monitoring. The *m* and *b* factors are respectively the varied and constant energy costs for each operation, and are derived experimentally [15]. Since in this method, the monitoring nodes are selected according to the connectivity and the battery power, therefore, monitoring nodes change constantly. Kim and et al. [14] presented a monitoring node selection scheme for intrusion detection in mobile ad hoc network, so that selected node as the monitoring node can be an unauthorized node. The advantage of our method is that the monitoring nodes are chosen among authorized nodes.

On the other hand, in the most of the existing intrusion detection systems for MANETs, a detection system sits on every node, which runs all of the time. This intrusion detection system could be monitoring traffic in its neighbourhood, or changes in its routing table and etc. [11,16,17,18,19]. Since, a node in a MANET has limited battery power, so, selecting all of nodes to contribute in monitoring turn out to be a costly overhead.

6. Conclusions

The issue of security is very important and in order to detect intrusion in MANETs, it is necessary to identify the authentication of the participating nodes in the network. While in the intrusion detection systems in MANET, the monitoring node uses the extra resources and energy. When the monitoring node identifies the attacker intrusion, it propagates warning messages to the neighbouring nodes. Since the bandwidth and the battery power in the MANETs are limited, there is a need for an effective method of utilizing these resources to build detecting intrusion systems. Our method will improve the lifetime of the network among nodes by evenly distributing of the usage of the resources. Meanwhile the nodes that will be selected as monitoring nodes in the network will be authorized nodes.

7. References

[1] U. Kaur, R.B. Patel, "Intrusion Detection in Mobile Ad- Hoc Networks: A Mobile Agent Approach", 9th *International Conference on Information Technology (ICIT'06)*, 2006.

[2] C.M. Chlamtac, J.N. Liu, "Mobile Ad Hoc Networking: Imperatives and Challenges", *Ad Hoc Networks*, vol. 1, no.1, pp. 13-64, July, 2003.

[3] J. Hubaux, L. Buttyan, S. Capkun, "The Quest for Security in Mobile Ad Hoc Networks", *2nd ACM International Symposium on Mobile Ad Hoc Networking and Computing*, Long Beach, CA, USA, pp. 146-155, 2001.

[4] Y. Zhang, W. Lee, Y. Huang, "Intrusion Detection Techniques for Mobile Wireless Network", *Wireless Networks Journal*, vol. 9, no. 5, pp. 545-556, 2003.

[5] Y. Xiao, X. Shen, D.Z. Du, *Wireless/mobile Network Security*, Springer, 2006.

[6] M.K. Rafsanjani, A. Movaghar, F. Koroupi, "Investigating Intrusion Detection Systems in MANET and Comparing IDSs for Detecting Misbehaving Nodes", *International Conference on Applied Computer science and engineering (ICACSE\'08)*, Venice, Italy, 29-31 October, 2008 (to appear).

[7] L. Venkatraman, D.P. Agrawal, "A Novel Authentication Scheme for Ad Hoc Networks", *2nd IEEE Wireless Communications and Networking Conference*, Chicago, USA, pp. 1268-1273, 2000.

[8] E.C.H. Ngai, M.R. Lyu, R.T. Chin, "An Authentication Service Against Dishonest Users in Mobile Ad Hoc Networks", *IEEE Proceedings on Aerospace Conference*, vol. 2, pp. 1275–1285, March, 2004.

[9] L. Zhou, Z.J. Haas, "Securing Ad Hoc Networks", *IEEE Network Magazine Special Issue on Network Security*, vol. 13, no. 6, pp. 24-30, Nov./Dec, 1999.

[10] M. Asadpour, B. Sattarzadeh, A. Movaghar, "Anonymous Authentication Protocol for GSM Networks", *International Journal of Security and Networks*, vol. 3, no.1, pp. 54-62, 2008.

[11] N. Komninos, D. Vergados, C. Douligeris , "Detecting Unauthorized and Compromised Nodes in Mobile Ad Hoc Networks", *Elsevier Ad hoc networks*, vol. 5, no. 3, pp. 289-298, 2007.

[12] J. Kong, *Adaptive Security for Multi-layer Ad Hoc Networks*, Special Issue of Wireless Communications and Mobile Computing, John Wiley InterScience Press, 2002.

[13] J.H. Chang, L. Tassiulas, "Energy Conserving Routing in Wireless Ad- hoc Networks", *19th Annual Joint Conference of the IEEE Computer and Communication Societies (INFOCOM)*, pp. 22–31, 2000.

[14] H. Kim, D. Kim, S. Kim, "Life-time Enhancing Selection of Monitoring Nodes for Intrusion Detection in Mobile Ad Hoc Networks", *International journal of electronics and communications*, vol. 60, no. 3, pp. 248-250, 2006.

[15] L.M. Feeney, M. Nilsson, "Investigating The Energy Consumption of a Wireless Network Interface in an Ad Hoc Networking Environment", *INFOCOM*, pp. 1548–1557, 2001.

[16] A. Partwardhan, J. Parker, A. Joshi, M. Iorga, T. Karygiannis, "Secure Routing and Intrusion Detection in Ad hoc Networks", *3rd IEEE International Conference on Pervasive Computing and Communications*, pp: 191-199, 2005.

[17] K. Nadkarni, A. Mishra, "Intrusion Detection in MANETs - the Second Wall of Defense", *29th IEEE Industrial Electronics Society Conference*, pp: 1235–1239, 2003.

[18] S. Marti, T. J. Giuli, K. Lai, M. Baker, "Mitigating Routing Misbehavior in a Mobile Ad hoc Environment". *6th Annual ACM/IEEE International Conference on Mobile Computing and Networking*, pp: 255–265, 2000.

[19] C. Manikopoulos, L. Ling, "Architecture of the Mobile Ad hoc Network Security (MANS) System". *IEEE International Conference on Systems, Man and Cybernetics*, pp: 3122–3127, 2003.

Dynamic Resource Management and Call Admission Control in QoS Cellular Network – An Integrated Approach

Sulata Mitra
Department of Computer Science and Technology, Bengal Engineering and Science University, India
sulata@cs.becs.ac.in

Abstract

The proposed work is a dynamic resource management scheme for quality of service sensitive cellular network. It addresses the solution of three fundamental issues of cellular network maintaining a common set of information. The location update issue predicts the location probability of a user at a cell whereas the load balancing issue estimates the traffic load at each cell on the basis of location probability distribution of users as determined by the location update issue. The load balancing issue also computes the cell-wise resource requirement depending upon the estimated traffic load. Finally the resource management issue reserves the cell-wise available resource dynamically in the resource reservation pool for the processing of handoff call to keep call dropping probability below a threshold. The amount of resource in the pool depends upon the total number of channels require to process the total handoff calls in the network. The proposed scheme provides minimum call dropping probability and minimum call blocking probability at maximum bandwidth utilization. It outperforms the existing schemes in terms of bandwidth utilization and call dropping/blocking probability.

1. Introduction

Multimedia wireless environment support different type of traffic, each has its own bandwidth and quality of service (QoS) requirement. Moreover, different users have different QoS requirements. The varying bandwidth and transmission rate requirement have to be carefully considered to satisfy effectively the user demand. Consequently efficient radio resource management and call admission control strategies are the keys to quality of service requirements in such a wireless environment.

Hutchens and Singh proposed an adaptive bandwidth reservation algorithm [1] to accommodate different network topologies and therefore able to maintain the handoff dropping probability at a designated value. But the authors assume a single class of traffic, identical cells having uniform mobility and traffic conditions.

In works [2,3] an adaptive resource allocation algorithm attempts to maximize bandwidth utilization while achieving fairness using a generic algorithm. However the authors did not provide any analysis for computing the new call blocking probability or handoff call dropping probability, which are crucial to QoS provisioning.

A threshold based bandwidth reservation policy [4] for the next generation multi-class wireless cellular network assigns a threshold bandwidth to each class of traffic depending upon their QoS requirements. But the authors start from fixed channel allocation to each cell in the environment.

Hamida and Boukhatem proposed a time based bandwidth reservation scheme [5]. Each mobile station sends its position and orientation to the base station (BS) periodically, on the basis of which the BS determines the next cell of the mobile station and estimates the time for resource reservation. This scheme allows different mobile users to reserve the same resource provided there is no overlapping between their time intervals. But the scheme has huge signaling overhead.

A combination of bandwidth reservation and call admission control (CAC) mechanisms was introduced in [6,7,8]. In these schemes each BS must have some information about the number of new and handoff calls, new and handoff arrival rates and channel holding time, for each class of traffic. So these schemes have a large communication and processing overhead to maintain up-to-date information about the state of the neighboring cells.

In the schemes [9,10], a BS estimates the number of handoff calls for each class of traffic and uses this to compute the handoff call dropping probability to maintain it within a target value. But these schemes have high implementation complexity, as it needs probabilistic estimation for the potential number of handoff calls from neighboring cells.

Unlike fixed channel allocation the present resource management scheme starts with dynamic resource allocation among cells on the basis of cell-wise dynamic traffic load estimation. It maintains a resource reservation pool at each cell for the processing of handoff calls. It computes dynamically the available unused resource and the available reserved resource in the reservation pool depending upon the number of ongoing new and handoff calls respectively using dynamic available resource computation module. The CAC module is used by the proposed scheme to admit a new/handoff call request on the basis of available resource as computed by dynamic available resource computation module. Most of the previous schemes tried to maintain only the call dropping probability within limit but present scheme takes care of call dropping as well as call blocking probability by varying dynamically the available reserved resource in the pool and the available unused resource. In multimedia wireless network a mobile user may require multiple channels and different users may require different number of channels. The present scheme is able to reserve multiple channels for a single call request. So the present scheme is useful for resource management in multimedia wireless network. Moreover no attempt has been reported so far to address the three important problems in cellular network such as location update, load balancing and resource management in an integrated way.

2. Proposed integrated scheme

In the proposed scheme a wireless network with cellular architecture that supports multimedia traffic such as voice and video is considered. In this section the location update issue, load balancing issue and resource management issue of the proposed integrated scheme is considered for discussion.

2.1 Location update issue

The location update issue [11] considers an n level hierarchy of LAs. Fig.1 shows an instance of two level hierarchies of LAs (i.e. n=2). The mobile switching centre (MSC) maintains an indexed database (Fig.2) to keep the record of visiting mobile units (MUs) in the form of (MU_id,Cell_id). The data f_{Ci} under each cell C_i in the database corresponding to a particular MU identification (MU_id) indicates the frequency of locating the given MU at the cell C_i. Whenever an MU is detected at a cell C_i, the frequency associated with cell C_i corresponding to that MU is updated in the database.

2.2 Load balancing issue

In the load balancing issue, MSC uses the same database (Fig.2) to compute the cell-wise traffic load using a heuristic function for call arrival probability as discussed in section 2.2.1 and accordingly distributes the channels among cells. MSC performs such computation and assignment after each updation of the database.

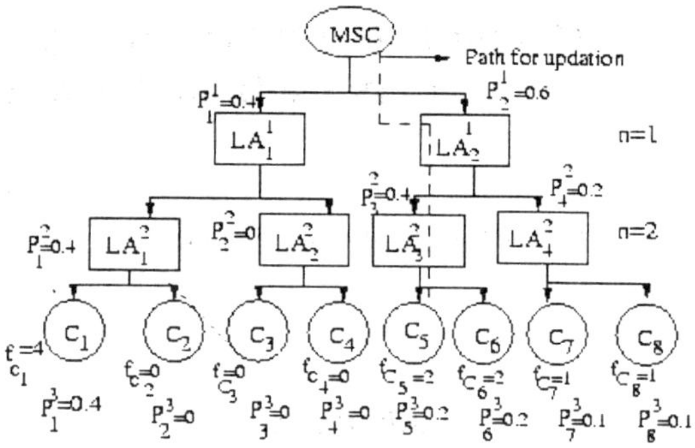

Fig. 1 An instance of two level hierarchy of LAs

MU_id
MU_id 1
MU_id 10

MU_id	C_1	C_2	C_3	C_4
1	3	4	1	4
2	1	5	2	7
5	2	1	5	1

MU_id	C_1	C_2	C_3	C_4
10	1	6	3	1
12	2	7	2	7
18	5	3	10	8

Fig. 2 Database at MSC for six MUs and four cells under MSC

2.2.1 Heuristic function for call arrival probability

The heuristic function is the call arrival probability, Q_i^3 at the leaf level node i (i.e. cell C_i). It has been defined as the ratio of number of times the various MUs are detected in the ith node after paging i.e. $\sum f_{Ci}$ to the total number of times the MUs are detected at all the cells (8 in Fig.1) in the leaf level i.e. $\sum_{i=1}^{8} \sum_{k=1}^{s1} f_{Cik}$, where s1 be the total number of MUs. Thus $Q_i^3=\sum f_{Ci}/(\sum_{i=1}^{8}\sum_{k=1}^{6} f_{Cik})$, as s1=6 in Fig.2. This function helps the MSC to compute the required number of channels CH_{Ci} of all the cells C_i under it as $CH_{Ci}=(Q_i^3)*x$, where x be the total number of available channels with MSC.

For example, in Fig.2, the total frequency of locating the six MUs in the cell C_1 is $\sum f_{Ci}=3+1+2+1+2+5=14$ whereas the total frequency of locating all the MUs in the environment within the cells C_1, C_2, C_3 and C_4 is $\sum f_{C1}+\sum f_{C2}+\sum f_{C3}+\sum f_{C4}=91$. Thus $Q_1^3=14/91$ and $CH_{C1}=14/91*x$. So, if x=13, $CH_{C1}=2$. The available bandwidth as resource at cell C_i (BW_{a_i}) is the product of CH_{Ci} and C_s, where C_s is the maximum channel capacity in Hz. So, $BW_{a\_i}=CH_{Ci}*C_s$ Hz.

2.3 Resource management issue

The resource management issue computes the total handoff calls (tot_handoff$_i$) in case of handoff call request, total handoff voice calls (voice_handoff$_i$) in case of handoff voice call request and total handoff video calls (video_handoff$_i$) in case of handoff video call request at cell C_i. It computes the total calls (tot_call$_i$) which is the sum of handoff calls and new calls at cell C_i. This issue uses dynamic resource reservation module, dynamic available resource computation module and CAC module after receiving any call request. In case of call drop, it also uses dynamic available resource variation module. The block diagram of the proposed issue is shown in Fig. 3. The function of the proposed module at cell C_i is discussed in the following sections.

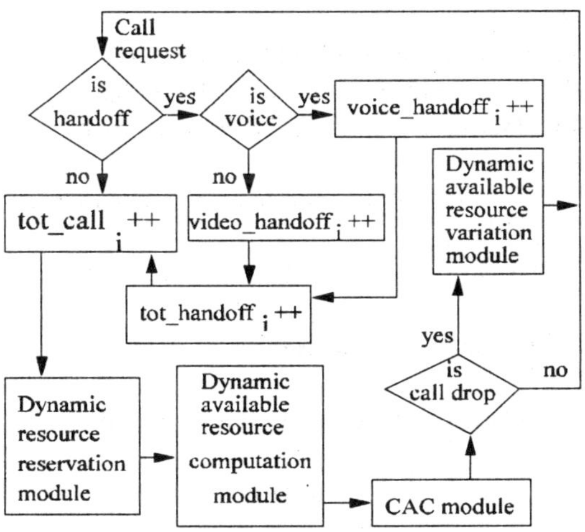

Fig. 3 Block diagram of the proposed issue

2.3.1 Dynamic resource reservation (dy_res_reser) module

The function of this module is to compute dynamically the amount of the resource in the reservation pool (BW_handoff$_i$) for the processing of handoff calls. BW_handoff$_i$ depends upon the total number of channels require for the processing of tot_handoffi at cell C_i. tot_handoff$_i$ is the sum of voice_handoff$_i$ and video_handoff$_i$. The proposed issue assumes N_{voice} as the number of channels require for the processing of a voice call and N_{video} as the number of channels require for the processing of a video call. So the total number of channels (tot_ch$_i$) require to process tot_handoff$_i$ is the sum of voice_handoff$_i$*N_{voice} and video_handoff$_i$*N_{video}. BW_handoff$_i$ is the product of tot_ch$_i$ and C_s. So the available unused bandwidth (available_BW$_{u_i}$) is the difference of BW$_{u_i}$ and BW_handoff$_i$., whereas the available reserved bandwidth in the reservation pool (available_BW$_{h_i}$) is BW_handoff$_i$.

2.3.2 Dynamic available resource computation (dy_av_res_com) module

The function of this module is to compute dynamically the available resource depending upon the ongoing new and handoff call. The ongoing new call (ongoing_new$_i$) is the sum of ongoing new voice call (ongoing_voice$_{new_i}$) and ongoing new video call (ongoing_video$_{new_i}$). The resource (ongoing_BW_voice$_{new_i}$) being used for ongoing_voice$_{new_i}$ is the product of N_{voice}, ongoing_voice$_{new_i}$ and C_s. Similarly the resource (ongoing_BW_video$_{new_i}$) being used for ongoing_video$_{new_i}$ is the product of N_{video}, ongoing_video$_{new_i}$ and C_s. Finally the resource (ongoing_BW$_{new_i}$) being used for ongoing_new$_i$ is the sum of ongoing_BW_voice$_{new_i}$ and ongoing_BW_video$_{new_i}$. So available_BW$_{u_i}$ is decreased by ongoing_BW$_{new_i}$.

The ongoing handoff call (ongoing_handoff$_i$) is the sum of ongoing handoff voice call (ongoing_voice$_{handoff_i}$) and ongoing handoff video call (ongoing_video$_{handoff_i}$). The resource (ongoing_BW_voice$_{handoff_i}$) being used for ongoing_voice$_{handoff_i}$ is the product of N_{voice}, ongoing_voice$_{handoff_i}$ and C_s. Similarly the resource (ongoing_BW_video$_{handoff_i}$) being used for ongoing_video$_{handoff_i}$ is the product of N_{video}, ongoing_video$_{handoff_i}$ and C_s. Finally the resource (ongoing_BW$_{handoff_i}$) being used for ongoing_handoff$_i$ is the sum of ongoing_BW_voice$_{handoff_i}$ and ongoing_BW_video$_{handoff_i}$. So available_BW$_{h_i}$ is decreased by ongoing_BW$_{handoff_i}$.

This module also computes the probability of resource utilization both for unused and reserved resource. The probability of unused resource utilization ($P_{BW\_u\_i}$) is the ratio of ongoing_BW$_{new_i}$ to available_BW$_{u_i}$ whereas the probability of reserved resource utilization ($P_{BW\_h\_i}$) is the ratio of ongoing_BW$_{handoff_i}$ to BW_handoff$_i$.

2.3.3 CAC module

The function of this module is to admit a call request depending upon the availability of bandwidth. This module computes the desired bandwidth (desire_BW) to process a new call in case of new call request and to process a handoff call in case of handoff call request. In case of voice call the desired bandwidth (desire_BW$_{voice}$) is the product of N_{voice} and C_s whereas in case of video call the desired bandwidth (desire_BW$_{video}$) is the product of N_{video} and C_s. A handoff call request is admitted if desire_BW is lesser than equal to available_BW_{h_i}. Otherwise it is admitted if desire_BW is lesser than equal to available_BW_{u_i}. A new call request is admitted if desire_BW is lesser than equal to available_BW_{u_i}.

If desire_BW is not available, this module computes number of call drop (call_$drop_i$) and call dropping probability (P_{drop_i}) in case of handoff call whereas number of call block (call_$block_i$) and call blocking probability (P_{block_i}) in case of new call. P_{drop_i} is the ratio of call_$drop_i$ to tot_$handoff_i$ whereas P_{block_i} is the ratio of call_$block_i$ to (tot_$call_i$-tot_$handoff_i$).

2.3.4 Dynamic available resource variation (dy_av_res_var) module

This module estimates dynamically the available reserved resource in the reservation pool and available unused resource by maintaining P_{drop_i} within a limit. If P_{drop_i} is lesser than its average ($drop_{avg}$), this module fixes P_{drop_i} to $drop_{avg}$. It computes excess call drop (excess_$drop_i$) as the product of ($drop_{avg}$-P_{drop_i}) and tot_$handoff_i$. It also computes the required excess resource (excess_BW_i) due to excess handoff call drop as the product of excess_$drop_i$, C_s and the average number of channels require for the processing of a handoff call. The average number of channels requires for the processing of a handoff call is the ratio of tot_ch_i and tot_$handoff_i$. Finally available_BW_{u_i} increases by excess_BW_i and available_BW_{h_i} decreases by excess_BW_i.

If P_{drop_i} crosses its threshold ($drop_{th}$), this module fixes P_{drop_i} to $drop_{avg}$. It computes reduce handoff call drop (reduce_$drop_i$) as the product of (P_{drop_i}-$drop_{avg}$) and tot_$handoff_i$. It also computes the required extra bandwidth (extra_BW_i) due to reduce handoff call drop as the product of reduce_$drop_i$, C_s and (tot_ch_i/tot_$handoff_i$). Finally available_BW_{u_i} decreases by extra_BW_i and available_BW_{h_i} increases by extra_BW_i. If $drop_{avg}<P_{drop\_i}<drop_{th}$, available_$BW_{u_i}$ and available_BW_{h_i} remains unchanged. Such dynamic variation of available_BW_{u_i} and available_BW_{h_i} helps to utilize any unused resource in the reservation pool for the processing of new call request, which in turn helps to reduce the call block probability of the system.

3. Simulation

In this section the simulation environment, simulation parameters and the simulation results obtained from the experiment are considered for discussion.

3.1 Simulation environments

The performance of the proposed scheme is evaluated in a cellular environment consisting of 50 cells with active users. The call arrival pattern is considered as poisson distribution with rate λ call/sec/cell. A newly generated call can appear anywhere in the cell with an equal probability. Gaussian distribution is used in the experiment to simulate the real life movement pattern of various MUs as it meets the assumption that most of the MUs are normally bound within a moderate number of cells whereas a few of them may move within a wide area containing a large number of cells. Each call life time (μ) is exponentially distributed with mean 120 seconds. The traffic load at cell C_i (L_i) is the total required average bandwidth to support all the existing call at cell C_i. It is defined as call generation rate * call bandwidth * average call lifetime. Now voice call bandwidth at cell C_i (B_{voice_i}) is the product of voice call arrival probability and desire_BW_{voice}. Again desire_BW_{voice} is the product of N_{voice} and C_s. So B_{voice_i} = (voice_new_i+voice_$handoff_i$)/tot_$call_i$ * desire_BW_{voice}.

Similarly video call bandwidth at cell C_i (B_{video_i}) is the product of video call arrival probability and desire_BW_{video}. Again desire_BW_{video} is the product of N_{video} and C_s. So

B_{video_i} = (video_new_i+video_$handoff_i$)/tot_$call_i$ * desire_BW_{video}.

$L_i = \lambda*(B_{voice\_i}+B_{video\_i})*120$

3.2 Simulation parameters

The simulation parameters are shown in Table 1.

Table 1

Parameter	Value
$drop_{avg}$	0.004, 0.009, 0.01
$drop_{th}$	0.005, 0.01, 0.02
C_s	1.36 MHz
μ	120 sec
λ	0.1-0.9
N_{voice}, N_{video}	1, 4

3.3 Simulation results

Fig. 4 shows the plot of call dropping probability (CDP) and call blocking probability (CBP) vs. traffic load for different values of $drop_{th}$. Both CDP and CBP increase with traffic load. For smaller $drop_{th}$, P_{drop_i} crosses $drop_{th}$ very frequently. So, higher bandwidth is required to reserve for the processing of handoff calls in the reservation pool, which leads to smaller unused bandwidth. So the decrease in $drop_{th}$ causes higher CBP but lower CDP.

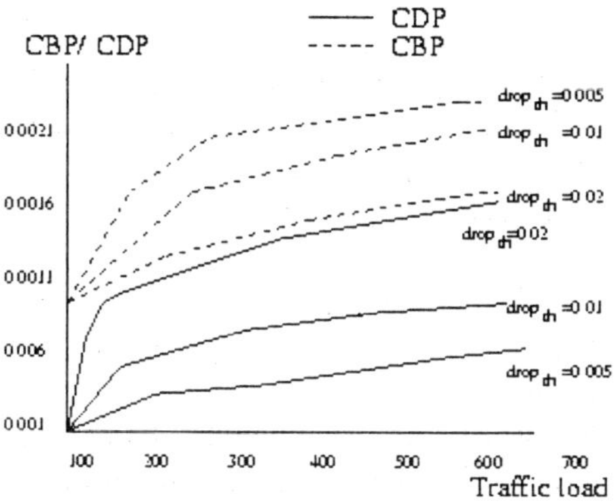

Fig. 4 CBP/CDP vs. Traffic load for different values of $drop_{th}$

Fig. 5 shows the plot of resource utilization vs. call arrival rate. Both $P_{BW\_h\_i}$ and $P_{BW\_u\_i}$ increase with call arrival rate. The amount of the resource available in the reservation pool depends upon the total number of handoff calls in the network. As a result almost the entire resource available in the reservation pool is utilized for the processing of handoff calls, which causes $P_{BW\_h\_i}$ higher than $P_{BW\_u\_i}$.

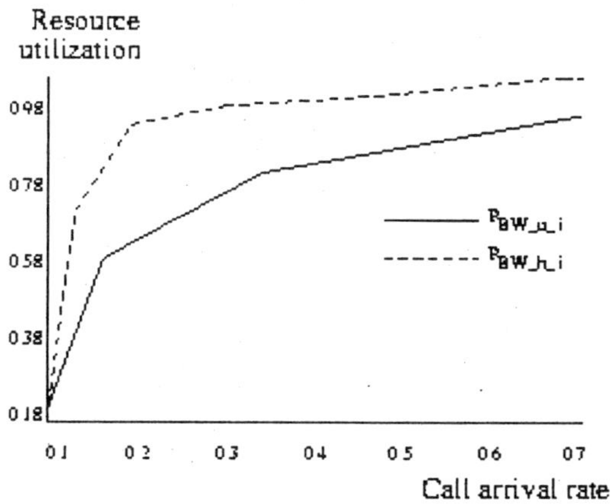

Fig. 5 Resource utilization vs. Call arrival rate

Table 2

Ref.	Traffic load	CBP
[12] Proposed scheme	6-20 100-700	0-0.35 0.0011-0.0022
Ref.	Traffic load	CDP
[12] Proposed scheme	6-20 100-700	0.02-0.12 0.001-0.0015
Ref.	λ	Bandwidth utilization
[13] Proposed scheme	0.1-0.9 0.1-0.7	0-80% 18-90%

The performance of the proposed scheme is compared with the schemes [12,13] on the basis of CBP/CDP as well as bandwidth utilization and is presented in tabular form (TABLE-2).

4. Conclusion

The proposed work is a dynamic resource management scheme for QoS cellular network. It addresses three issues of cellular network in an integrated way. The merit of the approach lies in the fact that no extra overhead such as maintenance of database etc. is needed for load balancing and resource reservation other than which is required in location update issue. The scheme is performed in each base station in a distributed manner without any central coordination. This scheme can be utilized efficiently for handover management in multimedia mobile cellular network.

The proposed scheme may be extended by considering the bit level QoS which depends on channel characteristics, receiver design and modulation channel coding. The signal overhead may be computed for the improvement of the proposed scheme. Finally in the proposed work, the allocated bandwidth per traffic class is constant during the lifetime of the transmission and is determined during the admission procedure. The effect of decreasing the allocated bandwidth may be studied to improve fairness of the system.

5. References

[1] R.Hutchens and S.Singh, "Bandwidth reservation strategies for mobility support of wireless connections with QoS guarantees", Proceedings of 25th Australasian Computer Science Conference, Conferences in Research and Practice in Information Technology, vol.4, pp.119-128, 2002.

[2] M.R.Sherif, I.W.Habib, M.Nagshineh and P.Kermani, "Adaptive allocation of resources and call admission control for wireless ATM using generic algorithms", IEEE Journal of Selected Areas in Communications, vol.18, no.2, pp.268-282, February 2000.

[3] S.Choi and K.G.Shin, "Adaptive bandwidth reservation and admission control in QoS-sensitive cellular networks", IEEE Transactions on Parallel and Distributed Systems", Special issue on Mobile computing, vol.13, no.9, pp.882-897, September 2002.

[4] N.Nasser and H.Hassanein, "Bandwidth reservation policy for multimedia wireless cellular networks and its analysis", IEEE International Conference on Communications (ICC), vol.5, pp.3030-3034, 2004.

[5] I.B.Hamida and L.Boukhatem, "A channel reservation scheme using read-time users mobility information in cellular systems", Wireless Personal Multimedia Communication, September 2005.

[6] D.Shen and C.Ji, "Admission control of Multimedia Traffic for Third Generation CDMA Network", IEEE INFOCOM, vol.3, pp.1077-1086, March 2000.

[7] H.Chen, S.Kumar and C.C.J.Kuo, "Dynamic call admission control scheme for QoS priority handoff in Multimedia Cellular Systems", IEEE WCNC, vol.1, pp.114-118, March 2002.

[8] A.Malla, M.El-Kadi, S.Olariu and P.Todorova, "A fair resource allocation protocol for multimedia wireless networks", IEEE Transactions on Parallel and Distributed Systems, vol.14, pp.63-71, January 2003.

[9] Si Wu, K.Y.Michael Wong and Bo Li, "A dynamic call admission policy with precision QoS guarantee using stochastic control for mobile wireless networks", IEEE/ACM Transactions on Networking, vol.10, no.2, pp.257-271, April 2002.

[10] S.Ganguly, B.Nath and N.Goyal, "Optimal bandwidth reservation schedule in cellular networks", IEEE INFOCOM, vol.3, pp.1591-1602, March 2003.

[11] S.DasBit, P.Raha and S.Mitra, "A probabilistic location management strategy in cellular mobile environment", IEEE TENCON, October 2002.

[12] Y.Fang and Yi Zhang, "Call Admission Control Schemes and Performance Analysis in Wireless Mobile Networks", IEEE Transactions on Vehicular Technology, vol.51, no.2, pp.371-382, March 2002.

[13] X.G.Wang et al., "A QoS-Based Bandwidth management Scheme in Heterogeneous Wireless Networks", International Journal of Simulation, vol.5, no.1-2, pp.9-17, 2004.

Implementation of an Embedded Controller to Monitor & Control Electrical/Electronic Devices Using Short Message Service

Mr.Mahendra A Sheti[1] and Dr. N. G. Bawane[2]
[1]M.E. IV Sem Embedded System & Computing G.H. Raisoni College of Engg. Nagpur (M.S.) India. Pin 440016
[2]Head Department of Computer Science & Engineering, G.H. Raisoni College of Engg
Nagpur (M.S.) India Pin 440016
mahindrra@rediffmail.com *narenbawane@rediffmail.com*

Abstract

In today's world mobile phone has become the most popular communication device, as it offers effective methods of communication to its users. The most common service provided by all network service providers is Short Message Service (SMS). As Short Message Service is cost effective way of conveying data, researchers are trying to apply this technology in the areas that are not explored by network service providers. One of such areas, that Short Message Service can be used, as a remote monitoring and controlling technology. By sending a specific SMS messages one can not only monitor and control different electrical/electronic devices from any place in the world, but also able to get alerts regarding catastrophic events.

A stand alone Embedded System (here we call it as Embedded Controller) can be developed to monitor and control the electrical/electronic devices through specific SMS. The same Embedded Controller can detect the catastrophic events like fire, earthquake, and burglary events. Implementation of such system is possible by using a programmed microcontroller, relays, and sensors like PIR sensor, Vibration sensor, Fire sensor and GSM modem which can be used to send and receive the SMS. The Programmed Embedded Controller acts as a mediator between mobile phone and electrical/electronic devices and performs the monitoring and controlling functions as well as catastrophic event detection and notification. In this paper we are presenting a design of an embedded system that will monitor and control the electric/electronic devices and will notify the catastrophic events (like Fire, burglary) by the means of SMS and will provide light when user arrives home at night.

1. Introduction

In this paper we are trying to explore the context of embedded systems and mobile communication which will make human life much easier. Imagine that you are driving from your office to your home, while driving you realized that you forgot to switch of the Air Conditioner. Now in this case you have to either go back to office or if somebody is there in office then you have to call him and tell him to switch of the Air Conditioner. If both the options are not possible for you then what? Is there any option exists that enables you to get the status of Air Conditioner, which is installed in your office and control it from the location where you are? Yes! At this situation remote monitoring and controlling comes in mind [1, 2].

The purpose behind developing Embedded Controller is to remotely monitor and control the electrical/electronic devices through SMS, which is proven to be cost effective method of data communication in recent days [3]. Such system can be helpful in not only remotely switching ON/OFF the devices but also in security or safety in industries to detect the catastrophic conditions and alerting the user through SMS message [5, 8, 4].

Before discussing the actual system let us brief out existing trends for remote monitoring and controlling.

2. Recent Trends for Remote Monitoring & Controlling

Most of the electrical/electronic devices are provided with their own remote controllers by the manufacturer but the limitation is the distance, as we are interested in controlling the devices from a long distance hence we will discuss only the technology which enables the long distance monitoring and controlling [1], [9].

After the introduction of Internet in 1990's it became a popular medium for remote communication. When researchers realized that it could become an effective medium for remote monitoring and controlling then the concept of Embedded Web Server came [6]. Embedded Web Server enabled its users to remotely monitor and control the devices over Internet [6].

But this technology is costlier as it requires an always-on connection for Embedded Web Server. Again user has to pay for the Internet access. Though Embedded Web Server can be useful for complex operations but it is really costly for simple controlling and monitoring applications [6]. Apart from the cost the factor that imposes limits on use of this technology is accessibility of Internet. Unless and until Internet accessibility is not there user cannot able to access the system.

Alternative to Internet based monitoring is making use of GSM technology, which is almost available in all the part of world even in remote locations like hill areas. GSM service is available in four frequency bands 450 MHz, 900 MHz, 1800 MHz, and 1900 MHz throughout the world. One of the unique benefits of GSM service is its capability for international roaming because of the roaming agreements established between the various GSM operators worldwide [7, 12]. Short Message Service is one of the unique features of GSM technology and can be effectively used to transmit the data from one mobile phone to another mobile phone and it was first defined as a part of GSM standard in 1985 [10].

3. Design of an Embedded Controller

As SMS technology is cheap, convenient and flexible way of conveying data as compare to Internet technology, it could be used as a cost effective and more flexible way of remote monitoring and controlling [7,10]. Hence a stand alone embedded system- "Embedded Controller" can be designed and developed to monitor and control the electrical/electronic devices through SMS with following features.

1. Remotely switch ON and OFF any electrical/electronic device by sending a specific SMS message to Embedded Controller.
2. Monitor the status of the device whether ON or OFF. For this purpose the Embedded Controller will generate a reply message to user's request including the status of the device and will send it to requested mobile phone.
3. The Embedded Controller will send alerts to the user regarding the status of the device. It is essential in cases where the device needs to be switched ON/OFF after a certain time.
4. The Embedded Controller will notify the power cut and power on conditions to the user.
5. Providing Security Lightning to deter burglars, or providing lights when user comes at home in late night for this purpose PIR sensor is used.
6. Providing Security alerts in case of catastrophic events like fire and burglary.
7. For Security purpose the already stored mobile phone numbers are allowed to use the system.
8. Any Mobile Phone with SMS feature can be used with the system.
9. Status of Device is displayed at Embedded Controller through LED's for local monitoring.
10. Atmel's AT 89C52 microcontroller is used to filter the information and perform the required functions.

3.1 System Architecture

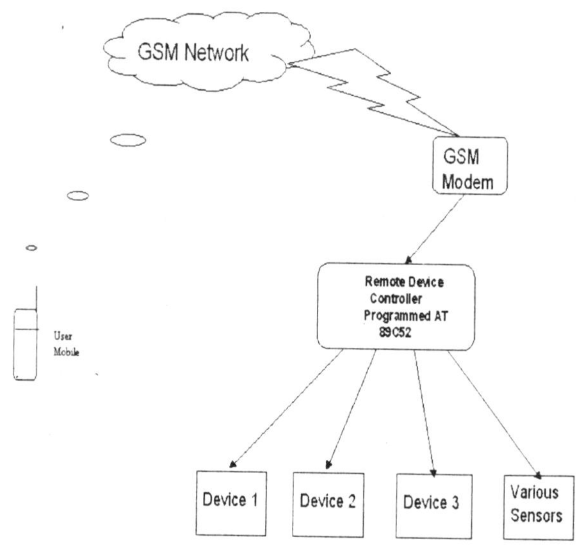

Fig. 1 System Architecture

Fig. 1 shows the system architecture of the remote monitoring and controlling system. The Embedded Controller is the heart of the system; it will perform all the system functions. As shown in figure 1 the user who is authorized to use the system is allowed to send the specific SMS message to the GSM modem, the SMS travels through GSM network to the GSM modem as in [11], the Embedded Controller periodically reads the first location of SIM (Subscriber Identity Module) which is present inside the GSM modem as in [11], as soon as Embedded Controller finds the SMS message, it start to process the SMS message and then takes necessary action and gives reply back to the user as per the software program incorporated in the ROM of microcontroller.

3.2 Hardware Design

Figure below shows the block diagram of an Embedded Controller which consists of a micro controller, GSM modem, Relays, Devices that are to be controlled, PIR sensors, ADC, Temperature sensor, Buzzer, LCD, LED's etc.

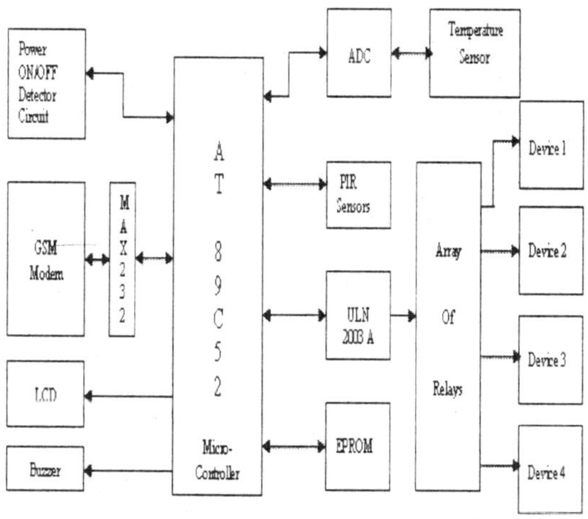

Fig. 2 Hardware Design of Embedded Controller

Here in our design we are using the following main hardware components:

- The AT 89C52 micro-controller:
  Used for processing the commands and controlling the different external devices connected as per the SMS received.
- ANALOGIC 900/1800 GSM modem:
  This GSM/GPRS terminal equipment is a powerful, compact and self-contained unit with standard connector interfaces and has an integral SIM card reader. It is used for receiving the SMS from the mobile device and then to transmit to the AT 89C52. It is also used to send SMS Reply back to user.
- A MAX232 chip:
  This converter chip is needed to convert TTL logic from a Microcontroller (TxD and RxD pins) to standard serial interfacing for GSM modem (RS232)
- ULN 2003A:
  The IC ULN 2003A is used for inductive load driving.
- RELAY:
  Used to achieve ON/OFF switching.
- PIR Sensor: A PIR Sensor is a motion detector, which detects the heat emitted naturally by humans and animals.
- ADC (Analog to Digital Converter):
  The ADC0808, data acquisition component is a monolithic CMOS device with an 8-bit analog-to-digital converter, 8-channel multiplexer and microprocessor compatible control logic.
- Temperature Sensor (LM 35):
  The LM35 series are precision integrated-circuit temperature sensors, whose output voltage is linearly proportional to the Celsius (Centigrade) temperature.
- Fire Sensor, Vibration Sensors etc can also be used.
- BUZZER:
  A buzzer is connected to one of the I/O ports of the Microcontroller. As soon as the signal about successful search is received, a logical level from the Microcontroller instructs the buzzer to go high, according to the programming, alerting the operator.
- LCD (Liquid Crystal Display):
  Use to display the various responses for crosschecking purpose.
- Power supply:
  Use to provide the power to various hardware components as per the requirement.
- LEDs:
  Used as status indicators
- Mobile Phone:
  Any mobile phone with SMS feature can be used for sending the commands (SMS).
- Control Equipment/device:
  Control Equipment is the device that can be controlled and monitored, e.g. Tube light.

3.3 Software Design

The two software modules excluding hardware module are as follows.

3.3.1 Communication Module: This module will be responsible for the communication between GSM modem and the AT 89C52 microcontroller. Major functionalities that are implemented in this module includes: Detecting connection between GSM modem and the microcontroller, Receiving data from modem, Sending data to modem etc. Additionally the status of modem, receiving/sending process, status of controlled device can be displayed on LCD.

3.3.2 Controlling Module: This module will take care of all the controlling functions. For example after extracting the particular command like "SWITCH ON FAN", the module will activate the corresponding port of the microcontroller so that the desired output can be achieved. It will also be responsible for providing the feedback to user. If catastrophic conditions are detected by the sensors then it will alert the user and will turn off the devices to avoid future danger.

4. Internal Operation of the System

The program written to achieve the desired functionality is incorporated in ROM of AT 89C52 microcontroller. For communication with GSM modem and reading, deleting, and sending the SMS messages we are using GSM AT commands [4], [11].

AT Stands for Attention. GSM AT commands are the instructions that are used to control the modem functions. AT commands are of two types Basic AT Commands & Extended AT Commands. Standard GSM AT commands used with this system are as follows:

AT+CMGR Read Message.
AT+CMGS Send Message
AT+CMGD Delete Message
AT+CMGF Select PDU mode or Text Mode

At the startup or on reset of the system, the microcontroller will first detect whether connection with GSM modem is established or not by sending the command ATE0V0 to the GSM Modem. Then after successful connection with GSM modem the AT 89C52 microcontroller reads the first location in GSM modem's SIM (subscriber identity module) card by sending AT+CMGR=1 command for an incoming SMS in each 2 seconds. The SIM is present inside the GSM modem.

The controlling of electrical/electronic devices can be accomplished by decoding the SMS received, comparing it with already stored strings in the microcontroller and accordingly providing an output on the ports of a microcontroller. This output is used to switch on/off a given electrical/electronic device.

For getting status of the device the associated pin of microcontroller is checked for active high or low signal, and as per the signal status of the device is provided to the user of the system by sending an SMS.

The program or software is loaded into AT 89C52, and then the circuit is connected to the modem. Initially the SMS received at GSM modem is transferred to the AT 89C52 with the help of a MAX 232 chip The microcontroller periodically reads the 1st memory location of the GSM modem to check either SMS has been received or not (programmed for every two second). Before implementing the control action, the microcontroller extracts the sender's number from the SMS and verifies if this number has the access to control the device or not. If the message comes from invalid number then it deletes the message and doesn't take any action. If the message comes from an authorized number then it takes the necessary action.

Generally sending and receiving of SMS occurs in two modes, Text mode and Protocol Data Unit (PDU) mode [4], [11]. Here we are using the Text Mode. In text mode the message is displayed as it is in Text. In PDU mode the entire message is given as the string of hexa-decimal numbers. The AT 89C52 microcontroller performs all the functions of system. It reads, and extracts control commands from the SMS message and processes it according to the request.

The main functions implemented using GSM AT commands are as shown below:

1. Connection to GSM Modem:
To detect whether the GSM modem is connected or not, the command ATE0V0 is sent to the GSM modem. In response to this GSM modems sends the reply as 0 or 1, which indicates the connection establishment if 1 or fail to connect if 0.
2. Deleting SMS from SIM Memory:
To delete the SMS from SIM memory the command AT+CMGD=1,0 is used which deletes the SMS messages which are present in SIM inbox. The same command is used to delete the received SMS messages after processing the message.
3. Setting SMS Mode:
To select the PDU/Text mode command
AT+CMGF=<0/1> is used
0 – indicates PDU Mode
1 – Indicates Text Mode
AT+CMGF=1 // selects text mode
4. Reading the SMS:
To read the SMS message from SIM we are sending the read command as shown bellow to GSM modem periodically (after every 2 seconds)
AT+CMGR=1
Response from modem is as follows:
+CMGR:
"RECUNREAD","9989028959","98/10/01, 18:22:11+00", This is the message
4. Processing The SMS Message:
After Reading the SMS message, the message is processed by microcontroller to extract the user's number and command as per the program written. The microcontroller does not takes any action if the received is not from a valid user & if it does not contains any command, each command is predefined in program. The matching command is only accepted and microcontroller takes the action as per the defined command.
5. Sending SMS:
Command syntax in text mode:
AT+CMGS= <da> <CR> Message is typed here <ctrl-Z / ESC >
For example to send a SMS to the mobile number 09989028959 we have to send the command in this format AT+CMGS= "09989028959"<CR> Please call me soon <ctrl-Z> the fields <CR> and <ctrl-Z> are programmed as string and used while generating the SMS message. On successful transmission GSM Modem responds with "ok" otherwise with "Error" if not transmitted

Detection of Catastrophic Events

With Embedded Controller one can use various sensors to detect the catastrophic events or some special events as shown in Fig. 2. Here we are using the PIR sensors, which enable to provide the security feature. Passive

Infra Red (PIR) is an electronic device which is commonly used to provide light and to detect motion. Whenever a suitably large (and therefore probably human) warm body moves in the field of view of the sensor, a floodlight is switched on automatically and left on for a fixed period of time - typically 30-90 seconds[13]. This can be used to deter burglars as well as providing lighting when you arrive home at night [13].

The first PIR Sensor is located at outside the door which provides light to user when he comes home in late-night & which in turn helps in deterring the burglar indicating somebody's presence. Even if burglar manage to get inside the home/office another PIR sensor detects the burglar and sends alert to user as well as to nearest police personnel for taking further actions.

The temperature sensor is set to detect a certain level of temperatures. If the temperature sensor detects the temperature greater than set point then the Embedded Controller sends an alert message to user as an indication of fire and to the fire station so that further needed action can be taken.

We can call it as an intelligent embedded system because the microcontroller is programmed in such a way that whenever the sensor detects any catastrophic event or burglary possibility then in that case it sends the notification not only to the user but also to the preventive service providers like to fire station in case of fire detection, or police station in case of burglary possibility along with the location where the event is happening, again the PIR sensor provides the light to user when he comes home late in night and stands in front of the door.

5. Conclusion

An Embedded Controller can be designed and developed to control and monitor electrical/ electronic devices through SMS using AT 89C52 microcontroller remotely using specific SMS messages. Also Embedded Controller will notifies the catastrophic events like fire, burglary by the means of SMS and provides light when user arrives home at night.

Such an Embedded Controller can be used in variety of applications [8], [14]. The Embedded Controller will be useful for the following users or systems.

A. General Public (Home users)
B. Agriculturists (Agricultural users)
C. Industries (Industrial users)
D. Electricity Board – Administrators
E. Electricity Board – Officers
F. Municipalities/ Municipal Corporations/ panchayats.

6. References

[1] Dr. Milkael Sjodin "Remote Monitoring and Control Using Mobile Phones" Newline Informations White Paper www.newlineinfo.se

[2] S. R. D. Kalingamudali, J. C. Harambearachchi, L. S. R. Kumara, J. H. S. R. De Silva,R. M. C. R. K. Rathnayaka, G. Piyasiri, W. A. N. Indika, M. M. A. S. Gunarathne, H. A. D. P. S. S. Kumara, M. R. D. B. Fernando "Remote Controlling and Monitoring System to Control Electric Circuitry through SMS using a Microcontroller",Department of Physics, University of Kelaniya", Kelaniya 11600, Sri Lanka Sri Lanka Telecom, 5th Floor, Headquarters Building, Lotus Road, Colombo 1, Sri Lanka kalinga@kln.ac.lk, jana@eng.slt.lk

[3] Guillaume Peersman and Srba Cvetkovic "The Global System for Mobile Communications Short Message Service", The University Of Hefeiled Paul Griffthsa and Hugh Spear, Dialogue Communicaions Ltd.

[4] G. Peersman, P. Griffiths, H. Spear, S. Cvetkovic and C. Smythe "A tutorial overview of the short message service within GSM", Computing & Conixol Engineering Journal Ai'kil 2000

[5] Rahul Pandhi, Mayank Kapur, Sweta Bansal, Asok Bhatacharya,"A Novel Approach to Remote Sensing and Control", Delhi University Delhi, Proceedings of the 6th WSEAS Int. Conf. on Electronics, Hardware, Wireless and Optical Communications, Corfu Island, Greece, February 16-19, 2007

[6] Eka Suwartadi, Candra Gunawan, "First Step Towards Internet Based Embedded Control System", Laboratory for control and computer systems, Department of Electrical Engineering Bandung Institute of Technology, Indonesia.

[7] Cisco Mobile Exchange Solution Guide http://www.cisco.com/univercd/cc/td/doc/product/wireless/moblwrls/cmx/mmg_sg/cmxsolgd.pdf

[8] Daniel J.S. Liml, Vishy Karri2 "Remote Monitoring and Control for Hydrogen Safety via SMS" School of Engineering, University of Tasmania Hobart, Australia jsdlim@utas.edu.au & Vishy.Karri@utas.edu.au

[9] http://en.wikipedia.org/wiki/Remote_control

[10] http://en.wikipedia.org/wiki/Short_message_service

[11] http://www.developershome.com/sms/atCommandsIntro.asp

[12] http://en.wikipedia.org/wiki/Global_System_for_Mobile_Communications

[13] http://www.reuk.co.uk/PIR-Sensor-Circuits.htm

[14] Dr. Nizar Zarka, Jyad Al-Houshi, Mohanad Akhkobek, "Temperature Control Via SMS", Communication department, Higher Institute for Applied Sciences and Technology (HIAST) P.O.Box. 31983, Damascus-Syria, Phone. +963 94954925, Fax. +963 11 2237710 e-mail. nzarka@scs-net. org

Network Management using Ant based Mobile Agents

Ms. Purnima P. Soni[1], and Prof. S. V. Gumaste[2]
[1]Student, M. E. (WCC),
[2]Asst. Professor, Dept of CSE,
G..H. Raisoni college of Engineering, University of Rashtasant tuktoji maharaj, Nagpur
purnima_456@yahoo.co.in svgumaste@gmail.com

Abstract

Network management of mobile ad hoc networks (MANETs) is still hard to achieve automatically and efficiently. In this paper, I present a framework that has the ability to perform network management tasks on MANETs using ant like mobile agents and capabilities of Ad Hoc On-Demand Distance Vector (AODV) routing protocol with a distributed topology discovery mechanism . While the main focus of the project is the framework, I present an example of mobile agents and hybrid routing protocol that are able to achieve reduced end-to-end delay and route discovery latency. Thus efficiently uses the band width.

1. Introduction

Network management is a process of the monitoring, analyzing, controlling and planning of activities and resources of a telecommunication network not only to provide services to users but also maximizing the efficiency and productivity of the network

MANET

It is Self-configuring network of mobile routers (and associated hosts) connected by wireless links. This union forms a random topology in which routers can move randomly. In MANET topology changes rapidly and unpredictably.They are of standalone fashion or connected to the larger Internet. Connectivity is in the form of random, multi-hop graphs and highly co-operative, each host is an independent router.

What are Mobile Agents?

Mobile agents are programs that can migrate from one machine to another in heterogeneous networks, at times and to places of their own choosing, hence their autonomous property (Kotz *el al*, 1997). The mobile agent can suspend its execution at an arbitrary point, jump to another machine, and resume execution there. Each agent is typically composed of the agent code, the agent execution thread along with an execution stack, and the agent data part, which corresponds to the values of the agent's global variables (Fig 1). Mobile agents are often treated as software agents but they are not always required to offer intelligent capabilities, for example reactive, pro-active, and social behaviors, which are features of existing software agent technologies. This is because these capabilities tend to be large both in scale and processing, while computational resources, which agents can use at the nodes they visit, such as processors, memory, files, and networks, are limited. That is, an intelligent and general-purpose agent is not appropriate in network management systems because no mobile agent should consume many computational resources at its destination. Also, all mobile agents must be as small as possible because the size of a moving agent seriously affects the cost of migrating it over a network. Therefore, mobile agent-based management systems should offer various small agents specialized to support particular tasks, rather than a few general-purpose agents to support various tasks. They should also select suitable agents to perform these tasks. For these reasons, mobile agents should be statically optimized for their target networks because both the cost of dynamically discovering and efficient itinerary and establishing the size of the program tend to be large. However, an agent optimized for particular networks or tasks cannot be reused in other networks or tasks. This inevitably results in a trade-off between the performance and reusability of a mobile agent.

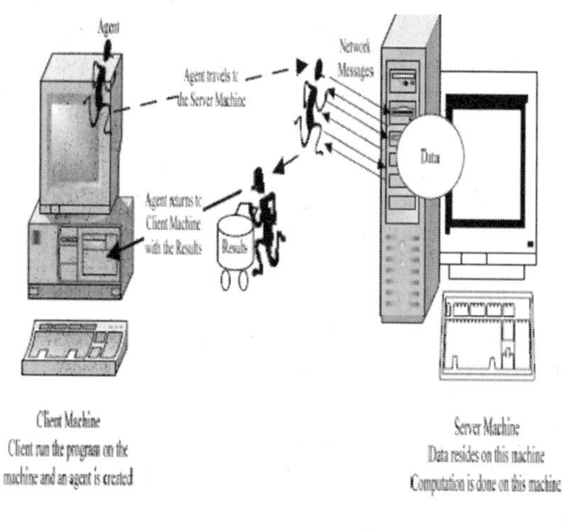

Fig. 1 A mobile agent's model

Mobile Agents as AntNET

AntNet is an innovative algorithm for packet routing in communication networks, originally proposed by M. Dorigo and G. Di Caro (1997). In AntNet, a group of mobile agents (or artificial ants) build paths between pair of nodes; exploring the network concurrently and exchanging obtained information to update the routing tables. AnNet is the design, which combines both proactive and reactive components, is based on the shortest path behavior observed in ant colonies and on the related optimization framework of *Ant Colony Optimization (ACO)* [8].

2. Related Work

AntNet: AntNet is a more recent approach to using the social insect analogy to solve routing problems in wired networks [6]. It is presented as a distributed, scalable, and responsive algorithm for routing in wired networks. The algorithm is improved upon in [7]. Each node periodically sends a forward ant packet to a random destination. The forward ant records its path as well as the time needed to arrive at each intermediate node. The timing information recorded by the forward ant, which is forwarded with the same priority as data traffic, is returned from the destination to the source by means of a high priority backward ant. Each intermediate node updates its routing tables with the information from the backward ant. Routing tables contain per destination next hop biases. In this way, faster routes are used with greater likelihood.

Ant-Colony Based Routing Algorithm: This algorithm (ARA) presents a detailed routing scheme for MANETs, including route discovery and maintenance mechanisms [5]. Route discovery is achieved by flooding forward ants to the destination while establishing reverse links to the source. A similar mechanism is employed other algorithms such as AODV. Routes are maintained primarily by data packets as they flow through the network. In the case of a route failure, an attempt is made to send the packet over an alternate link. Otherwise, it is returned to the previous hop for similar processing. A new route discovery sequence is launched if the packet is eventually returned to the source.

Routing in MANETs: Ant Colony Optimization was successfully applied also for Mobile ad-hoc Networks [2, 5, 9, 11, 13]. ARA algorithm [7, 8] maintains an entry in the routing table for each individual communication device in the network (Fig 2). 'destination address' represents the address of the sending node, 'Next hop' represents the address of the previous node, which relayed the packet to the current node, and 'Pheromone' represents the strength of the trail. Each time a packet (ant) is received by a communication device (node) the routing tables are updated. The amount of pheromone *'I ;j* for the route taken is increased with a constant value *¢'*. *'i;j := 'i;j + ¢'* (4). When operating in a dynamic network some routes may become invalid or are simply not used. In order to distinguish between optimal routes and the amount of pheromone is decreased periodically for all routes.

Destination address	Next hop	Pheromone
i	j	$\varphi_{i,j}$

Fig. 2 Routing table for MANETs

Pheromone values are decreased as below:

'i;j := (1 *¡ q*) *¢ 'i;j ; q 2* (0*;* 1] (5) The ARA routing algorithm consists of three distinct phases namely the route discovery phase, route maintenance and route failure handling. Discovery phase:-In order to communicate with other nodes the ARA protocol sends out a uniquely identifiable forward ant (FANT) (Fig. 3) that tries to establish a route to node somewhere in the network. At each node (hop) that it encounters on the way to the destination node it updates the route tables. If there is no address entry for the route taken by the FANT, the FANT senders address is noted is the 'destination addresses' the hop that relayed the packet is noted in the 'Next hop' and the pheromone value is set to default. Otherwise only the pheromone value is updated using formula 4. As soon as the FANT arrives at the destination node a uniquely identifiable backward ant is launched (BANT) (Fig. 4). The BANT traces back the route to originating FANT node by making use of the routing table entries previously made by the FANT. While tracing back the route to the BANT updates the routing tables at each hop in the same fashion the FANT did. Once the FANT originator node is reached communication between the nodes can be established. Route maintenance the individual nodes do the route maintenance by analyzing received packets and by use of pheromone formula 5. Each packet received by the node either for processing or relaying is used to update the routing table and the pheromone value by use of formula 4. A timer determines the when formula 5 is executed in order to decrease the pheromone value..

(a)

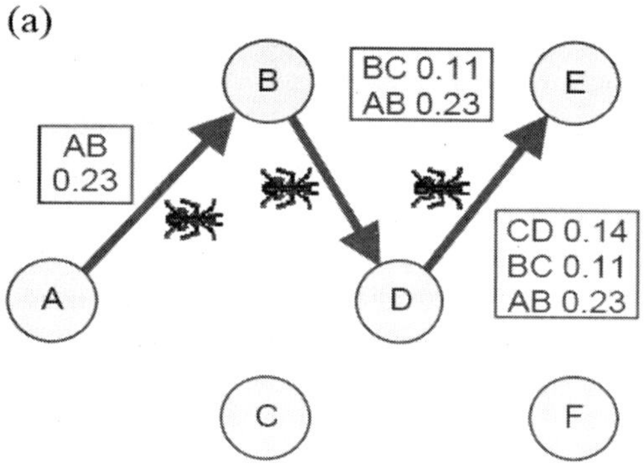

Fig. 3 AntNet – Forward Ant

(b)

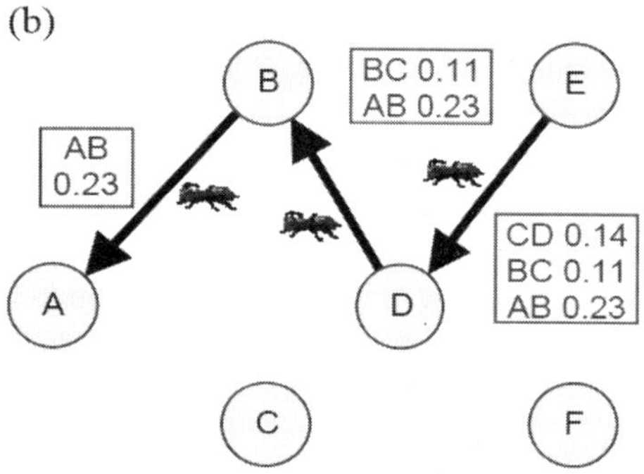

Fig. 4 AntNet – Backward Ant

Once the pheromone value for a certain route has reached zero the route can safely be discarded. Route failure The MAC (Media Access Layer) layer implemented on the NIC (Network Interface Card) of the communication device notices the ARA protocol in case of route failure by returning a ROUTE ERROR message. Once noticed by the MAC layer the ARA protocol searches the routing table for an alternative route. If no alternative route is found the packet is relayed to all the neighbors of the node who will check their routing tables for a route to the destination. If the packet cannot be relayed to the destination node the packet is send back to the destination node, each receiving hop tries to send an alternative route as described above before sending the packet back.[3] Routing system As stated in the introduction we suppose that wireless access points with computational power are available along the roads. They form a wired network with 5 the same topology as the street network. This network is communicating with the local wireless Ad-Hoc networks formed by the PDAs carried on the cars. The result is a hybrid network as in which besides communication will provide the drivers with dynamic routing.

MANET routing and ant-based routing

The specific challenges and possible applications of MANETs have made this a very popular research area, and a lot of routing algorithms have been proposed. People traditionally classify these algorithms as either *proactive* or *reactive*. In purely proactive protocols (e.g., DSDV [21]) nodes try to maintain at all times routes to all other nodes. This means that they need to keep track of all topology changes, which can become difficult if there are a lot of nodes or if they are very mobile. Therefore, reactive protocols (e.g., AODV [22] or DSR [18]) are in general more scalable (see [13]). In these protocols, nodes only gather routing information on demand: only when they have data for a certain destination they construct a path, and only when the path becomes infeasible they search a new path. In this way they greatly reduce the routing overhead, but they can suffer from oscillations in performance since they are never prepared for disruptive events. *Hybrid algorithms* like ZRP [17] have both a proactive and a reactive component, in order to try to combine the best of both worlds. Most of the algorithms are single path: at any time, they use only one path between source and destination. Multipath routing (see [20] for an overview) offers an interesting alternative in terms of link failure robustness and load balancing. Some algorithms create multiple paths at path setup time, and use the best of these until it fails, after which they switch to the second best and so on (e.g., AODV-BR [19]). A problem with this way of working is that alternative paths are often infeasible by the time they need to be used. Moreover, when only the best path is used, one looses the opportunity to spread data packets over the different paths, a practice which can improve the network throughput. The ant-based routing algorithms were ABC [23] and AntNet [14]. Both algorithms follow a similar general strategy. Nodes send ant agents out at regular intervals to randomly chosen destinations. The main aim of the ants is to sample the paths, assign a quality to them, and use this information to update the routing tables in the nodes they pass. These routing tables contain an entry for each destination and each neighbor, indicating the goodness of going over this neighbor on the way to the destination. This goodness value is called pheromone. This pheromone information is used for the routing of both ants and data packets: all packets are routed stochastically, choosing with a higher probability those links with higher pheromone values. If enough ants are sent to the different destinations, nodes keep up-to-date information about the best paths, and automatically adapt their data load spreading to this.

Working of AODV

Each mobile host in the network acts as a specialized router and routes are obtained as needed, thus making the network self-starting. Each node in the network maintains a routing table with the routing information entries to it's neighbouring nodes, and two separate counters: a node sequence number and a broadcast-id. When a node (say, source node 'S') has to communicate with another (say, destination node 'D'), it increments its broadcast-id and initiates path discovery by broadcasting a route request packet RREQ to its neighbors. The RREQ contains the following fields: – source-addr

- source-sequence to maintain freshness info about the route to the source.
- dest-addr ,– dest-sequence- specifies how fresh a route to the destination must be before it is accepted by the source.
- hop-cnt

The (source-addr, broadcase-id) pair is used to identify the RREQ uniquely. Then the dynamic route table entry establishment begins at all the nodes in the network that are on the path from S to D. As RREQ travels from node to node, it automatically sets up the reverse path from all these nodes back to the source. Each node that receives this packet records the address of the node from which it was received. This is called Reverse Path Setup. The nodes maintain this info for enough time for the RREQ to traverse the network and produce a reply to the sender and time depends on network size. If an intermediate node has a route entry for the desired destination in its routing table, it compares the destination sequence number in its routing Table with that in the RREQ. If the destination sequence number in its routing table is less than that in the RREQ, it rebroadcasts the RREQ to its neighbors. Otherwise, it unicasts a route reply packet to its neighbor from which it was received the RREQ if the same request was not processed previously (this is identified using the broadcase-id and source-addr). Once the RREP is generated, it travels back to the source, based on the reverse path that it has set in it until traveled to this node. As the RREP travels back to source, each node along this path sets a forward pointer to the node from where it is receiving the RREP and records the latest destination sequence number to the request destination. This is called Forward Path Setup. If an intermediate node receives another RREP after propagating the first RREP towards source it checks for destination sequence number of new RREP. The intermediate node updates routing information and propagates new RREP only,

- If the Destination sequence number is greater, OR
- If the new sequence number is same and hop count is small, OR

Otherwise, it just skips the new RREP. This ensures that algorithm is loop-free and only the most effective route is used [20]. Step by step explanation of Route finding process in AODV Routing Protocol:-

1. Source 'S' has to send data to destination.
2. S sends RREQ to its neighbors A, B, C.
3. B finds the path in its routing table (with destn seq-number s1 and hop count c1) and sends RREP to S.
4. C sets up reverse path.
5. 5.C forwards RREQ to its neighbors and E.
6. E sets up reverse path.
7. EforwardsRREQ to its neighbors Fand G.
8. E deletes the reverse path after a time out period as it does not receive any RREPs from F and G.
9. D finds the path (with dest seq-number s2 which is greater than s1 and hop count c1) in its routing table and sends RREPto C.
10. C receives RREP from D and sets up forward path and forwards RREP to S.
11. A sets reverse path; forwards RREQ to its neighbors; receives RREP (with path of hop count c2 which is greater than c1); sets forward path; and forwards this RREP to S.
12. S receives a path info from C (with destn seq-number s2 and hop count c1), another path info from B (with destn seq-number s1 and hop count c1), and another path info from A (with destn seq-number x which is less than s1 and s2 and hop count c2 which is less than c1).
13. S chooses path info from C (which was originated from D), giving first priority to the path with greatest destination sequence number and then second priority to the path with smallest hop count. Though path given by A is of smallest hop count, it is ignored because the destination sequence number is greater than the path from C.

3. Proposed Work

I suggest a novel routing scheme for mobile ad hoc networks (MANETs), which combines the on-demand routing capability of Ad Hoc On-Demand Distance Vector (AODV) routing protocol with a distributed topology discovery mechanism using ant-like mobile agents is. The proposed hybrid protocol reduces route discovery latency and the end-to-end delay by providing high connectivity without requiring much of the scarce network capacity.

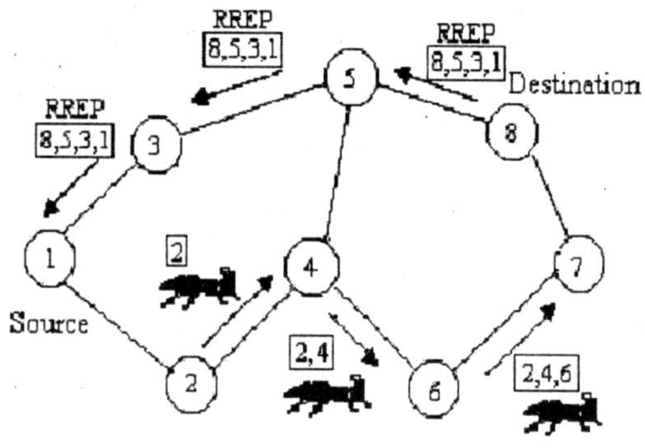

Fig. 5 Propogation of Route Replay and traversal of Ant-AODV routing protocol

On the one side the proactive routing protocols in MANETs like Destination Sequenced Distance Vector (DSDV) require to know, the topology of the entire network. Hence they are not suitable for highly dynamic networks such as MANETs, since the topology update information needs to be propagated frequently throughout the network. These frequent broadcasts limit the available network capacity for actual data communication. On the other hand, on-demand, reactive routing schemes like AODV and Dynamic Source Routing (DSR), require the actual transmission of the data to be delayed until the route is discovered. Due to this long delay a pure reactive routing protocol may not be applicable for real-time data and multimedia communication. Through extensive simulations in this paper it is proved that the proposed Ant-AODV hybrid routing technique, is able to achieve reduced end-to-end delay compared to conventional ant-based and AODV routing protocols. (Fig 5)

Mobile agents similar to ants [4,5,6,7] can be used for efficient routing in a network and discover the topology, to provide high connectivity at the nodes. However the ant-based algorithms in wireless ad hoc networks have certain drawbacks. In that the nodes depend solely on the ant agents to provide them routes to various destinations in the network. This project tries to overcome these shortcomings of ant-based routing and AODV by combining them to develop a hybrid routing scheme. The Ant-AODV hybrid routing protocol is able to reduce the end-to-end delay and route discovery latency by providing high connectivity as compared to AODV and ant-based routing schemes. The hybrid scheme also does not overload the available network capacity with control messages like the proactive protocols.

4. Conclusion and Future Work

The proposed hybrid protocol reduces route discovery latency and the end-to-end delay by providing high connectivity without requiring much of the scarce network capacity. The future work will involve adding inter agent communication and intelligence to the ant agents. This coupled with the ants providing information such as node affinity and power levels etc. to the nodes would help in taking intelligent routing decisions.

5. References

[1] C. E. Perkins and P. Bhagwat, "Highly dynamic Destination Sequenced Distance-Vector routing (DSDV) for mobile computers," in Proc. of the SIGCOMM '94 Conf. on Communications Architecture, Protocols and Applications, pp. 234-244, Aug. 1994.

[2] M. Ghanbari, D. Gavalas, D. Greenwood, M. O' Mahony, "Advanced network monitoring applications based on mobile/intelligent agent technology", Computer Communications Journal, Vol. 23, No.8, pp 720-730, 2000.

[3] A. Bieszczad, B. Pagurek, and T. White, Mobile Agents for Network Management, IEEE Communications Surveys, Vol. 1, No. 1, 1998.

[4] C. Bohoris, G. Pavlou, and H. Cruickshank, Using Mobile Agents for Network Performance Management, in Proceedings of IEEE/IFIP Network Operations and Management Symposium, pp. 637-652. April 2000.

[5] M. G¨unes, U. Sorges, I. Bouazizi, *ARA - The Ant-Colony Based Routing Algorithm for MANETs*, Proceedings of the ICPP Workshop on Ad Hoc Networks (IWAHN 2002), IEEE Computer Society Press, 2002, 79-85.

[6] G. Di Caro, M. Dorigo, *Mobile Agents for Adaptive Routing*, Technical Report, IRIDIA/97-12, Universit Libre de Bruxelles, Belgium, 1997.

[7] B. Bar´an, R. Sosa, *A New Approach for AntNet Routing*, Proceedings of the Ninth International Conference on Computer Communications and Networks, 2000.

[8] T. Maekawa, et. al. "An Ant-based Routing Protocol using Unidirectional Links for Heterogeneous Mobile Ad-Hoc Networks," in Proc. of ICWMC '06, pp. 43 - 43, July 2006.

[9] D. Gavalas, D. Greenwood, M. Ghanbari, and M. O'Mahony, An Infrastructure for Distributed and Dynamic Network Management based on Mobile Agent Technology, Proceedings of Conference on communications, pp. 1362-1366, 1999.

[10] R. Schoonderwoerd, O. Holland, J. Bruten, L. Rothkrantz, *Ant-Based Load Balancing In Telecommunications Networks, Adaptive Behavior*, 1996.

[11] A. Karmouch, Mobile Software Agents for Telecommunications, IEEE Communication Magazine.

[12] J. S. Baras and H. Mehta. A probabilistic emergent routing algorithm for mobile ad hoc networks. In *WiOpt03: Modeling and Optimization in Mobile, Ad Hoc and Wireless Networks*, 2003.

[13] J. Broch. D. Maltz, D. Johnson, Y.-C. Hu, and J. Jetcheva. A performance comparison of multi-hop wireless ad hoc network routing protocols. In *Proc. of 4th Annual ACM/IEEE Int. Conf. on Mobile Computing and Networking*, 1998.

[14] G. Di Caro and M. Dorigo. AntNet: Distributed stigmergic control for communications networks. *Journal of Arti¯cial Intelligence Research*, 9:317-365, 1998.

[15] M. GÄunes, U. Sorges, and I. Bouazizi. ARA - the ant-colony based routing algorithm for manets. In *Proc. of 2002 ICPP Workshop on Ad Hoc Networks*, 2002.

[16] S. Goss, S. Aron, J. L. Deneubourg, and J. M. Pasteels. Self-organized shortcuts in the Argentine ant. 1989

[17] Z. J. Haas. A new routing protocol for the recon¯gurable wireless networks. In *Proc. of the IEEE Int. Conf. on Universal Personal Communications*, 1997.

[18] D. B. Johnson and D. A. Maltz. *Mobile Computing*, chapter Dynamic Source Routing in Ad Hoc Wireless Networks, pages 153{181. Kluwer, 1996.

[19] S.-J. Lee and M. Gerla. Aodv-br: Backup routing in ad hoc networks. 2000. [20]S. Mueller, Multipath routing in mobile ad hoc networks: Issues and challenges. In *Performance Tools and Applications to Networked Systems*, Springer-Verlag, 2004.

[21] C. Perkins and P. Bhagwat. Highly dynamic destination sequenced distance-vector routing (DSDV) for mobile computers. In *ACM SIGCOMM'94 Conference on Communications Architectures, Protocols and Applications*, 1994.

[22] C. Perkins and E. Royer. Ad-hoc on-demand distance vector routing. In *Proc. Of 2nd IEEE Workshop on Mobile Computing Systems and Applications*, 1999.

[23] R. Schoonderwoerd, O. Holland, J. Bruten, and L. Rothkrantz. Ant-based load balancing in telecommunications networks. *Adaptive Behavior*, (2):169{207, 1996.

The Design of Mobile Agent based Intelligent System for Autonomic Network Management

Naveen Kumar Gondhi[1] and Dr. Durgesh Pant
[1]School of Computer Science and Engineering, Shri Mata Vaishno Devi University, Katra (J&K), *naveenkumargondhi@rediffmail.com,*
[2]Department of Computer Science, Kumaon University, Almorha, Uttrakhand (India)
durgesh_pant@yahoo.com

Abstract

An Intelligent System is a class of systems which attempts to codify the expert human knowledge in software systems which can mimic human actions in response to external stimuli. Network Management is a service that employs a variety of tools, applications and devices to assist human network managers in monitoring and maintaining networks. A framework for Mobile Agents based Intelligent System (MAIS) architecture is proposed to achieve Autonomic Network Management. The MAIS architecture reduces the complexity of network management at the managing entity by delegating part of the management responsibility to the managed network entities. Adding mobility and intelligence to an agent provides many advantages such as extensibility and portability.

1. Introduction

The current network connectivity has increased over the last decade. An explosive growth in the number of computers and the need to share information has triggered the development of computer networks. Moreover today's application demands a wide variety of services from the network. To provide efficient service to each application, the network must be operating efficiently at all times. Network failures cause various losses such as efficiency and productivity, and eventually manifest as monetary losses to both the clients and network access providers. The growth of the networks systems has two aspects - horizontal and vertical. Horizontal growth means the expansion of the existing network i.e. by adding more hosts to a network and vertical growth means the introduction of new technologies like ATM, FDDI etc. in the field of network system. Both these types of growth pose new challenges to network management, by giving birth to problems like congestion in networks, inefficient utilization of bandwidth etc.

Current Network Management architectures shown in Fig. 1 use the same basic structure and set of relationships. End node (managed devices) such as computer systems and other network devices, run software that enables them to send alerts when they recognize problems. Upon receiving these alerts, Network Management Station (NMS) is programmed to react by executing one, several, or a group of actions, including operator notification, event logging, system shutdown, etc. via Network Management protocol like SNMP / CMIP. Current Network Management Systems help a network operator to detect and diagnose the problems in a network.

However as the complexity of today's networks increases, there is a greater demand for the network to be self managing. A self-managing system should be capable of automatically detecting and diagnosing the network problems. A capability to repair ordinary faults would also be desirable in such systems.

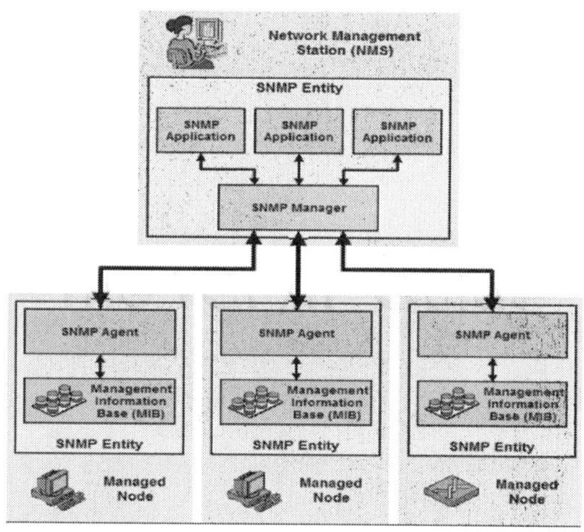

Fig. 1 Existing Network Management Architecture

The main goal of our effort is to apply expert system technology to reduce the severity of this problem and allow less experienced network operators to efficiently manage a large and complex computer network.

The rest of the paper is structured as follows. Based on the discussion in the previous section, Section 2 presents background and related work, mainly concerning the Network Management issues, Then, Proposed System Architecture and its components are described in detail in Section 3. Section 4 depicts the implementation of the System and a brief conclusion and future work are described in Section 5.

2. Related Work

The application of Artificial Intelligence (AI) and rule-based expert systems to the domain of network management is not a new concept and has been addressed by various researchers [1, 2, 3]. More recently there have been several research efforts in the diagnosis of physical systems and networks in particular by [4, 5, 6]. A real time interactive expert system is proposed [7]. and the tasks of fault isolation by formulating plans for the diagnosis process. The concept of Autonomic Computing Correlation [8, 9] is relatively a new approach for the Fault Management System in Network Management. Many attempts have been made to automate diagnosis in the networks domain [10 12]. The approach describing the Knowledge based Maintenance in Computer Networks and concepts of Artificial

Intelligence in network monitoring and diagnosis [13] are theoretically proposed and verified. The present fault identification and fault localization techniques in Network Management are also proposed [14, 15, 16]. The concept of self healing of a system during fault diagnosis has been discussed by [17, 18]. The Reference [19] describes the applications of knowledge based system for communication network management. Some new ideas are put forth for the knowledge-based system for fault localization and concept of automated knowledge acquisition [21, 22]. The Reference [23] presented the event correlation guidelines for the heterogeneous networks and. various outlines for the design of expert systems for real-time diagnosis [24] of self-correcting networks. However, most of the research has focused on building intelligence and rules for the localization of the faults [24]. But very little research [25, 26] has focused on automated corrective action in response to the diagnosed faults. This idea become the root seed of MAIS which can be viewed as a starting step in building completely autonomous systems for network management which is self-diagnostic and self-healing in nature.

3. System Architecture

In this paper, we present architecture for the Mobile Agent based Intelligent System using Expert System Technology to add intelligence capability to Network Management Solutions. The proposed Mobile Agent based Intelligent System (MAIS), a self-learning Intelligent System, integrates with PMA to build correlation rules between the reported network faults and the corresponding action initiated by the designated expert network administrator. A mobile agent is commuting software which contains the code and data to perform pre-defined management tasks at managed entities. The intelligence of a mobile agent can be used in making dynamic decisions such as finding the next destination, optimizing the travel plan, and detecting abnormal situations, as the agent travels around the network. This would help the mobile agent to increase the overall response time and efficient utilization of network resources. As shown in Figure 2, the System Architecture is composed of five main modules viz. PMA, the Network Interface Module, Monitor Module, the Network Manager Interface Module, and the Expert System Module. The *Network to be monitored* is the collection of network elements such as routers, switches, end-user devices. The detailed working on each of the module is depicted as under:-

PMA Module

PMA also known as Platform for Mobile Agent, is a platform for the development and the management of mobile agents that gives all the primitives needed for their creation, execution, communication, migration, etc. It has been entirely developed in Java. It has the complete integration and compatibility with the SNMP world. We have integrated and used classes which implement the SNMP stack. In this way, we have had the opportunity to interact with the different nodes of the network through standard Management Information Base (MIB) variables. The four basic agents identified are *Browser* Agent, *Daemon* Agent, *Messenger* Agent, *and Verifier* Agent. The *Browser* agent collects some MIB variables from a set of nodes specified by the user. The *Daemon* agent monitors a "health function" defined by the user. The two agents described before directly interact with the SNMP daemon present in the different nodes (through the Advent classes). Conversely, the *Messenger* agent, during its migration through the nodes of the network, interacts with other agents for collecting specific information produced by them. The *Verifier* agent does not perform an actual Network Management action. Its task is that of collecting important information, which might be useful for further operations of Network Management, by PMA.

Network Manager Interface Module

The main function of this interface module is to provide the human managers information, in a user-friendly manner, about network states and conditions and the expert systems' recommended actions. Also it takes directives from the user and converts them into instructions for other modules of MAIS. The interface must be able to present all the facts pertinent to the current problem and should also specify the solution in a lucid manner to the user. The user's job will be to provide a sanity check to the proposed solution

Expert System Module

The Expert System Module will analyze each scenario presented by the monitor, identify various problem symptoms, diagnose faults, isolate probable causes, and generate solutions. We have implemented Rule Based Expert System for MAIS. The core component of Expert System is the Knowledge Base where the "expertise" of the system is stored. The knowledge base is represented as a set of rules. Rules are "if-then" structures. If certain criteria are met, then the system is to take certain action. The expert system's problem solving capabilities are directly dependent on the number of rules it has in its rule-base. By increasing the number of these rules, the expert system will be able to solve many and more complicated problems.

The working database contains the rules that are directly applicable to the given problem under consideration. These are the rules that need to be "fired" – executed since their "if" clauses have been satisfied. The system updates the working memory by asserting, modifying, or retracting working memory elements. For a network application, the working memory typically contains a representation of characteristics of the network related to the current problem, including topological and state information. The Rule-Base Expert System represents knowledge about what operations to perform when the network enters an undesirable state. The Expert System Module employs heuristic techniques for finding correct responsive corrective action for faults which includes Forward Chaining and Backward Chaining. In case of Forward Chaining, the Hypothesis is taken first and the rules are verified to prove the Hypothesis whereas the process reverses in case of Backward Chaining. Given a symptom (or a set of symptoms), the heuristics initially associate the symptom(s) with particular corrective action and assert strategy (and/or tests) to adopt in diagnosis. The System Event Correlation Strategy is framed on the following patterns

If < Symptom_Patterns >

THEN< Diagonsis-Class>

Here, the <Symptom Pattern> depicts Heuristic Rule specifying various network conditions and <Diagonsis-Class> is Hypothesis showing the Corrective Action to be taken to troubleshoot the Network. The Inference Engine evaluates the Hypothesis to be TRUE if the corresponding Rules evaluates to TRUE. The following examples depict the specific network conditions as SNMP Traps and System Log Messages and the Corrective Actions executed by Expert System Module

Example # 1

Consider an environment with Cisco router 7500 and NMS station gets the following System Log (Syslog) message:

ERROR: SNMPTRAP (Chassis Alarm)

Problem Description: The operating Temperature of the networking device exceeds the threshold limit.

Corrective Action:

If String (Message (Chassis Alarm))

THEN Shut_Router (R)

The above stated Corrective Action is applied to shut down the networking device Router (R)

Example # 2

Consider Cisco 7500 router, a Cisco 5000 Catalyst Switch in a LAN Environment and the following syslog messages are logged by NMS:

Error: SNMPTRAP (E0_Router, bulk_traffic)

Problem Description The Interface E0 of Router experiencing bulk traffic i.e. no. of packets entering the interface exceeded threshold limit.

Corrective Action:

If String (Message ((Snmptrap_Bulktraffic))

Then Router(R, Increase_Queuelength) AND Switch(S, inc_time_out, inc_retry)

The correlation rule stated above is applied to try and alleviate the congestion conditions by increasing the Router Queue length, Timeout and Retry values for Packets sent over the Router and Switch Interface.

Monitor Module

The Monitor module obtains and stores all the relevant information about the network. The information about the network will be obtained from PMA. This information will come to the monitor via the Network Interface Module. The information provided by the Network Interface will consist of either general events or special traps. The general events are reports on values of the observable parameters across the managed network. These reports are generated synchronously by polling each node. The special traps are generated by nodes when some extraordinary activity takes place in the network. These events include instances of network nodes going down or coming up, and a link either failing or a new link being formed. These are generated asynchronously. After obtaining this information, the monitor makes a preliminary analysis to determine whether or not the given situation is abnormal. However it must be noted at this point that the Expert System is the final authority in determining if the current conditions are abnormal or not. For these cases all parameters are within normal ranges and do not represent any abnormal conditions. Since any network is expected to be performing normally most of the times, such a preliminary screening will serve to reduce the load on the Expert System, and consequently enhance the performance of the overall system. The cases which indicate slightly the possibility of an abnormal condition in the network will be passed on to the Expert System for further analysis.

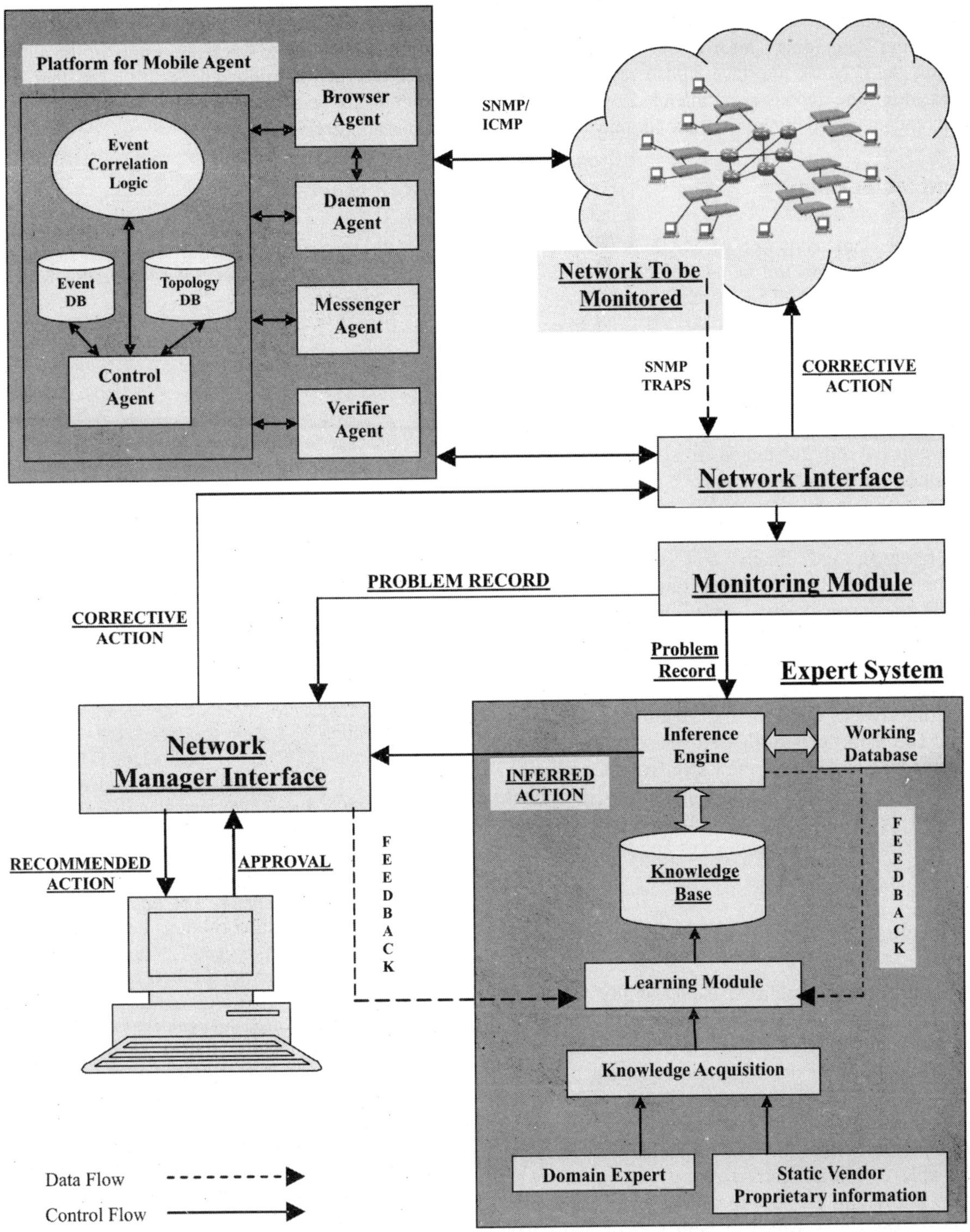

Fig. 2 Schematic Architecture of Mobile Agent based Intelligent System

Network Interface Module

The primary task for this module is to provide a seamless communication between PMA, Monitor and Network Manager Interface modules. Consequently, this module transfers network data from the PMA to the monitor and also receives control instructions from the Network Manager Interface and delivers it to the PMA. Apart from providing information to the other modules, the network interface is also responsible for implementing the actions recommended by the expert system and approved by the network administrator.

4. Implementation

A prototype implementation of MAIS is in underway and various scenarios are being framed for testing in the local test network. The Expert System Module is being developed in Visual prolog 6.0. The trial runs confirm the viability of building such a system and also its effectiveness. We selected Java as an implementation environment because it supports almost all of the required properties. Java provides a heterogeneous and distributed architecture, which is well suited for our IMA framework. Java is platform-independent since it is interpreted, so programs can easily migrate from machine to machine. Java is object-oriented, and finally and not of the least importance, delayed, dynamic binding is offered through the class loader. Only critical events of Network Management were configured by various mobile agents already stated in PMA module. The event patterns are analyzed for testing purposes and are logged into Events database and Topology database of PMA The Static pre-configured rules for the Expert System were adapted from the Cisco Event Correlation Guidelines[11] , which is a detailed document published by Cisco Inc. describing detailed event correlation scenarios for its devices and the causes for such events.

5. Conclusions and Future Work

This research paper establishes the feasibility of MAIS, which is an attempt towards building a complete Network Management Solution, one which not only has the capability of detecting and reporting network faults, but also diagnosing and executing corrective actions to resolve them, thereby completing the loop. Over a period of time, the system builds enough rules to be able to initiate corrective actions on its own, thereby alleviating the need to maintain huge IT teams within organizations which is both human and cost-intensive. Moreover, such a system serves as a tutoring tool to the new members of the IT team, by allowing them to learn from the actions taken by the experts in the team, reducing their learning curve and helping them in achieving higher levels of productivity in a relatively smaller time frame. Future work shall involve establishing contact with experts in the network management domain to enable the creation of as many rules as possible for the Expert System. Further, intelligence needs to be built into the MAIS system to enable it to track the results of the automated corrective action initiated by it, so that it can continuously evaluate the effectiveness of its own actions and improve on it.

6. References

[1] E. Hayes, D. Waterman and D. Lenat. *Building expert system.*, Addison-Wesley Publishing Company 1999.

[2] R. Davis, B. Buchanan and E. Shortliffe. Production rules as a representation for a knowledge-based consultation program. *IEEE Press* 1998.

[3] W. Denise, Irfan Khan and Ogie Richard. An artificial intelligence approach to network fault management. *IEEE, SRI International*, 1998.

[4] S. Bush and S. Kalyanaraman. Management of Active and Programmable Networks. *Journal of Network and Systems Management*. vol. 14, No. 1 pg. 1–5, March 2006.

[5] A Mcauley and R. Morera. *Fault localization and self-healing with dynamic domain configuration.* University of Delaware, Newark, de, 2002. USA.

[6] R. Hartely. CRIB: Computer fault finding through knowledge engineering, *IEEE Press Computer*, pg.76-83., March 1998.

[7] T. Marques. A Symptom-driven Expert System for Isolating and Correcting Network Faults. *IEEE Communications*, vo1.26, No.3, pg.6-13, March 1999

[8] O. Jeffrey, L. Kephart and David M. Chess. The vision of autonomic computing. *IEEE Press*, vol 36 No (1), pg. 41–52, 2003.

[9] S. Roy, B. Dave and A. McCrea. *Autonomic computing correlation for fault management system* School of Computing and Information Engineering University of Ulster Northern Ireland, 2003

[10] T. Laffey, J. Perkins and T. Nauyen. Reasoning about fault diagnosis with LES. *IEEE Expert*, pg.13-20, Spring 1996.

[11] Cisco event correlation guidelines, 2006 white paper Cisco Inc website http://www.cisco.com/cpropart/salestools/xx/pd/wr2k /tech/enm_rg.pdf.

[12] Hp open view network node manager, advance edition, 2007 hp inc. website http://openview.hp.com/nnm.

[13] D.Peacocke and S. Rabie. Knowledge based maintenance in networks. *GLOBECOM'1996*, pg.46.5.1 - 46.5.

[14] C Leckie. *Experience and trends in artificial intelligence for network monitoring and diagnosis*" Artificial Intelligence Systems Section, Telstra Research Laboratories, Victoria Australia, 1998

[15] O. Tim. *Fault identification in network management: a review and a new approach* Experimental Knowledge Laboratory, University of Massachusetts, MA, 1998

[16] M. Steindler. A survey of fault localization techniques in computer networks. Watson Research Center, Hawthorne, NY, USA, 1999.

[17] A. Kant, S. Sethi and M. Steindler. Intelligent real time network management. Proc. of 23rd Army Science Conference, Orlando, FL. 2002.

[18] A. Kant, S. Sethi and M. Steindler. Fault localization and self-healing mechanisms for FCS networks. Proc. 23rd Army Science Conference, Orlando, FL Dec. 2002.

[19] R. Doyle and A. Sastry. Application of knowledge-based network management techniques for packet radio networks. in Proceedings of *MILCOM '98*, pg.213-219, 1998.

[20] F.Monica, J. Griffen and Simon Towers. A knowledge-based system for fault localization. *Integrated Network Management II,* pg. 519-530, 1998.

[21] R.Goodman and H. Latin. Automated knowledge acquisition from network management databases. *Integrated Network Management II,* pg. 541-549, 1998.

[22] J.Jordaan and M.E. Paterok. Event correlation in heterogeneous networks using the OSI management framework. *Integrated Network Management III,* pg. 683-695, 1993.

[23] T. Mark and Paul E. Zeldin. Designing expert systems for real-time diagnosis of self-correcting networks. *IEEE Network*, pg. 43-51, Sep. 1998.

[24] P. Smyth, J. Statman, Gordon Oliver and Rodney Goodman. Combining knowledge-based techniques and simulation with applications to communications network management. *Integrated Network Management II,* pg. 505-515, 2001. .

[25] Naveen Kumar Gondhi and Durgesh Pant. Towards designing an intelligent system for resource management in mobile adhoc network. **IEEE-** International Conference on Advances in Computer Vision and Information Technology, 2007 (To Appear)

[26] Naveen Kumar Gondhi, Durgesh Pant and Neeraj Nehra. Mobile agent based expert system for distributed network management in "*Information Technology Journal*" Volume 6 pg no 891-89, 2007

A Low Cost Approach to Transfer Data in Remote Data Acquisation Systems using Cellular Phones

G. V. Ramachandra Rao[1], K. Satya Prasad[2] C. B.Rama Rao
[1]Head of ECE Setion, Govt. Polytechnic for Women, Kakinada
[2]Prof. ECE and former Principal, JNTU College of Engineering, Kakinada
[3]Associate Professor, ECE Department, National Institute Technology, Warangal

Abstract

This paper examines the feasibility of usage of cellular phones instead of GSM Modems in data transfer from remote areas. The data from remote locations is transferred using Short Message Services (SMS). S.M.S. containing data up to 160 characters (alpha numeric characters) can be sent using this system. ATMEL 89 C 52 microcontroller is programmed according to the application. The developed embedded system is useful to transfer data like (1)Air quality parameters in different locations (2) Life saving data from patients like heart rate, BP at regular intervals etc...

1. Introduction

In various data acquisition systems, data is to be collected from remote locations using transducers. The data collected in different locations is transferred through number of ways to the data processing centre. As cellular network is well developed, data transfer through cellular networks is becoming more popular. *GSM modems* are widely used in data transfer system through cellular networks. *GSM modems* are costlier than low end cell phone. To transfer data using *GSM modems* AT commands are used where as in cell phones *F Bus protocols* are used. *F Bus protocol* can be implemented using microcontroller. ATMEL 89 C 52 microcontroller and Nokia 3310 / 3315 cell phones are used to implement this work. Real time clock is generated using D S 1307. The data is received by the cell phone at the far end. The Integrated Circuit Max 232 and RS 232 protocols are used to transfer the data (received by cell phone) to the personal computer (at the receiving end).

F/M Bus Protocols

F Bus / M Bus protocols are used for serial communication in cell phones. M Bus protocol is one pin half duplex system. M Bus protocol transfers data at 9600 bps. On the other hand F Bus protocol uses one pin for transmission and one pin for reception and it is a full duplex system. F Bus protocol works at 1,15,200 bps.

To synchronize U A R T in the phone with PC or microcontroller, string '0X55' is sent or the string 'U' is sent 128 times. In the F Bus protocol the SMS in 8 bit ASCII format is packed into 7 bit GSM 3.38 format. This is fundamental difference between AT commands and F Bus protocol.

The full SMS message frame contents are as follows:

Sending Sms

The following frame will send the SMS to the number specified from byte 14 to 23.

Byte	:	00 01 02 03 04 05 06 07 08 09 10 11 12 13 14 15
Data	:	1E 00 0C 02 00 30 00 01 00 01 02 00 07 91 19 89
Byte	:	16 17 18 19 20 21 22 23 24 25 26 27 28 29 30 31
Data	:	01 50 91 41 FF 2B 2B 2B 15 00 00 00 04 0C 91 19
Byte	:	32 33 34 35 36 37 38 39 40 41 42 43 44 45 46 47
Data	:	89 01 56 80 13 00 00 00 00 A7 00 00 00 00 00 00
Byte	:	48 49 50 51 52 53 54 55
Data	:	C6 A4 B4 08 01 41 04 A0

F-Bus Frame Header

Byte 0	:	F-Bus Frame ID
Byte1	:	Destination address (Mobile phone)
Byte 2	:	Source address. (Computer)
Byte 3	:	Message Type or command 0x02 (SMS Handling)
Byte 4 & 5	:	Message length.

Short Message Service Frame Header. (SMS)

Byte 6 to 8: Start of the SMS Frame Header
Byte 9 to 11: 0x01, 0x02, 0x00 = Send SMS Message

Short Message Service Center (SMSC) (12 Bytes)

Byte 12: SMS Center number length. 0x07 is 7 bytes long.

(SMSC Number Type and SMS Center Phone Number)

Byte 13: SMSC number type

(0x81- unknown 0x91- international 0xA1- national)

Byte 14 to 23: (Octet format) SMS Center Phone Number

Transfer Protocol Data Unit (TPDU)

XXXX XXX1 = SMS transmitted from the Mobile Station (MS) to the Service Center (SC)

XXXX XXX0 = SMS transmitted from the SC to the MS.

Byte 25: Message Reference

Byte 26: Protocol ID

Byte 27: Data Coding Scheme.

Byte 28: Size of the unpacked message.

Destination's Phone Number (12 Bytes)

Byte 29: Destination's number length. Byte 30: Number type e.g. 0x81-unknown 0x91- international oxa1- national

Byte 31 to 40: Destination's Phone Number.

Validity Period (VP)

Byte 41: Validity- Period Code.

Byte 42 to 47: Service Center Time Stamp.

The Sms Message (SMS-SUBMIT)

Byte 48 to 52: This is the SMS message packed into 7 bit characters. SMS Point-to-point Character Packing.

The F-Bus Frame Ending

Byte 53: Packet sequence Number

Byte 54: Padding Byte – String requires being even

Byte 55 & 56: Even & Odd checksum Bytes

When the phone receives this frame, it acknowledges it by sending the frame shown below:

Byte: 00 01 02 03 04 05 06 07 08 09

Data: 1E 0C 00 7F 00 02 03 1C 72

The destination and source addresses are swapped as this is a frame from the phone to the PC. This message is two bytes long with the first byte representing the message type received (0x02) and the next byte, the sequence number (0x03). The last two bytes are the checksum.

After a short time the phone replies with a 'Message sent' frame shown below.

Byte: 00 01 02 03 04 05 06 07 08 09 10 11 12 13 14 15 16 17

Data: 1E 0C 00 02 00 09 01 08 00 02 64 12 00 01 44 00 3F 1E

Byte 03: Message Type = 0x02 – SMS Handing

Byte 04 & 05: Message Length = 0x0009 – 9 Bytes long

Byte 09: 0x02 = Message Sent

Byte 10 to 14: Message center stamp

The PC then acknowledges the frame

Byte: 00 01 02 03 04 05 06 07 08 09

Data: 1E 00 0C 7F 00 02 02 04 10 79

This completes the first phase of sending an SMS.

Receiving An SMS

The mobile phone can be instructed to send the received SMS, as soon as it is received, by sending it the following 'get SMS' query. However it is essential to synchronize the UART of the mobile phone.

Byte: 00 01 02 03 04 05 06 07 08 09 10 11 12 13 14 15

Data: 1E 00 0C 02 00 08 00 01 00 33 64 01 01 40 77 79

After receiving the SMS, the mobile phone sends the following frame to the computer. However, it is observed that immediately after the synchronization if the 'get SMS' query is sent then an extra frame is received before the actual message-containing frame. This extra frame contains the message center details and is discarded. The actual message-containing frame is as follows:

Byte: 00 01 02 03 04 05 06 07 08 09 10 11 12 13 14 15

Data: 1E 0C 00 02 00 59 01 08 00 10 02 10 00 07 91 16

Byte: 16 17 18 19 20 21 22 23 24 25 26 27 28

Data: 14 91 09 10 F0 00 10 19 38 04 00 00 04

Byte: 29 30 31 32 33 34 35 36 37 38 39 40 41 42 43 44

Data: 0B 91 16 04 73 08 70 F4 70 40 32 25 30 30 E8 32

Byte: 45 46 47 48 49 50 51

Data: 9B FD 06 45 00 4A 5C

F-Bus Frame Header

Byte 00 05: Hold same significance as explained in the sending of an SMS

Short Message Service Frame Header (SMS)

Byte 6 to 8: Start of SMS Frame Header 0x00, 0x01, 0x00

Byte 09: SMS Message received

Byte 10: Memory Type = SIM

Byte 11: Location where SMS message stored.

Short Message Service Center (SMSC) (12 Bytes)

Byte 12 to 23: Hold same significance as explained in the sending of an SMS

Transfer Protocol Data Unit (TPDU)

Byte 24: 0x38

Byte25: 0x04

Byte 26: Protocol ID

Byte 27: Data Coding Scheme

Byte 28: Message Length.

Sender's Phone Number (12 Bytes)

Byte 29: Sender's number length.
Byte 30: Number type e.g. 0x81-unknown 0x91-international 0xal-national
Byte 31 to 40: (Octet format) Sender's Phone Number

The Sms Message (SMS-Received)
The frame received contains the packed message from the 43rd byte onwards and the size of the message received is specified by the 28th byte. The message can be unpacked using the unpacking procedure.
This is subsequently followed by an acknowledgement, to this received frame, by the computer. The Protocol for acknowledgement frame is same for any received frame, as mentioned in the sending SMS phase.

Hard-Ware Unit Developed
It is developed as two parts:
1. Transmitter 2. Receiver.

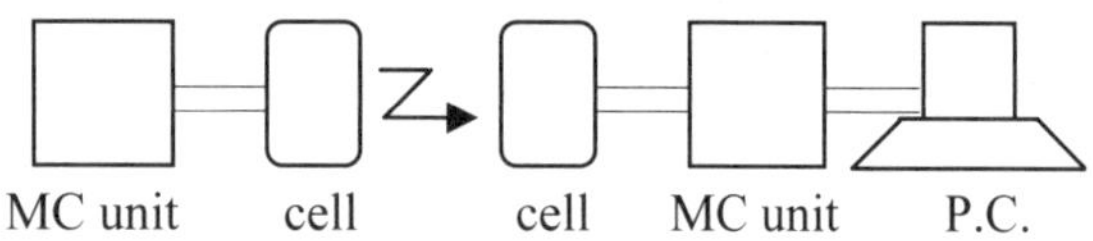

Fig.1

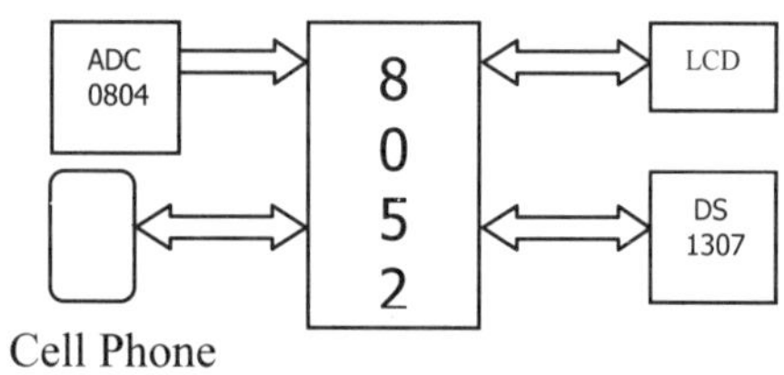

Fig. 2 Transmitter

Transmitter
Transmitter contains the following blocks.
1. ADC 0804
2. Mobile Phone
3. 8052 microcontroller
4. L C D
5. D S 1307

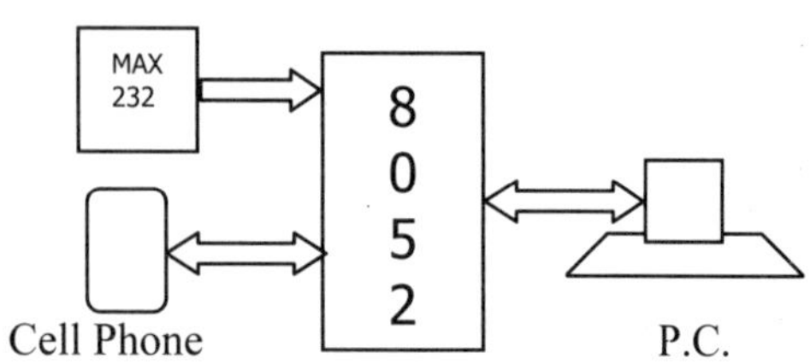

Fig. 3 Receiver

8 BIT ADC 0804 is used as data input unit to the microcontroller. Nokia 3310 is used as transmitting cell phone. D S 1307 is used to develop date and time in the message. L C D is used for verification.

1. **ADC 0804 :**
ADC 0804 is 8 bit successive approximation A / D converter. The following are few important specifications of ADC 0804.
   1. 2.5 V reference voltage
   2. Total error ± 1LSB
   3. 8 bit resolution.
2. **NOKIA 3310/3315:**
Popular cell phone model from Nokia. Serial communication pins are as shown below.

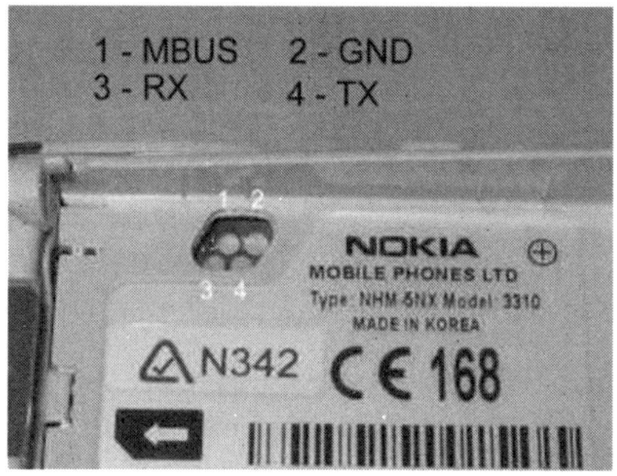

Fig. 4

3. **8052 Micro controller :**
It has been used due to the following features which are essential:
   1. 8 K Internal ROM
   2. 3 times
   3. 256 bytes on chip RAM
   4. 1,15,200 bps USART baud rate.
4. **DS 1307 :**
The following are few useful specifications.
   1. Real time clock connects seconds, minutes, hours, date of the month, month, day of the week and year.
   2. Consumes less than 500 n A in battery backup.

Programming of Micro Controller:
Details of the micro controller program developed for this system are described in the following flow charts.

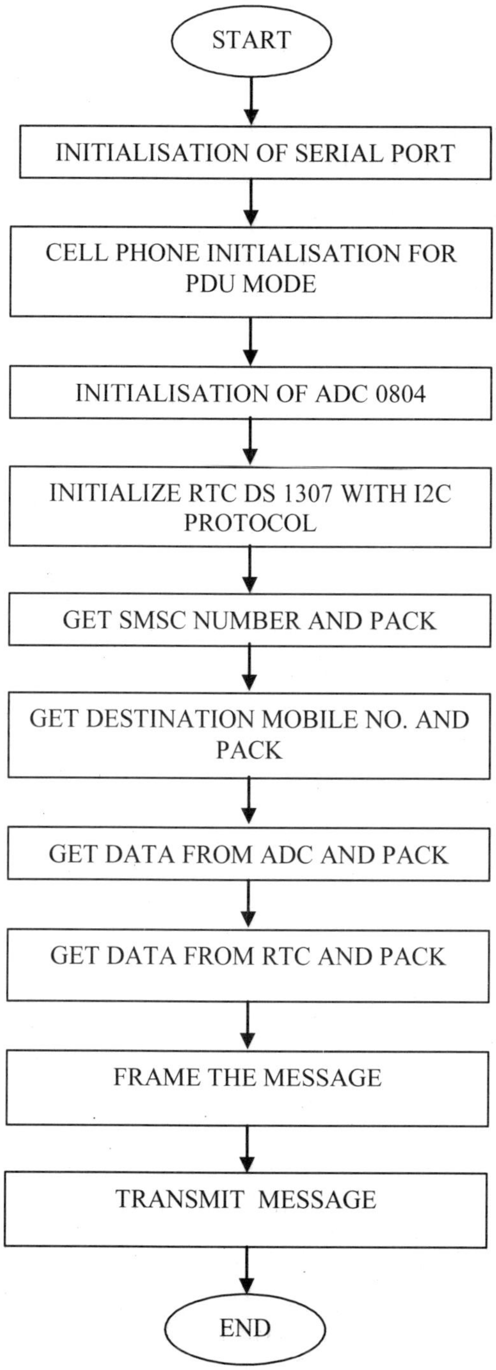

Flow Chart 1 (Transmitter)

Advantages:

1. Low cost when compared to the data transfer using GSM modems.
2. Mass production is easy.

Applications

It can be used as data transfer unit in

1. Remote air quality monitoring systems
2. Remote patient monitoring systems.
3. Pollution monitoring systems.

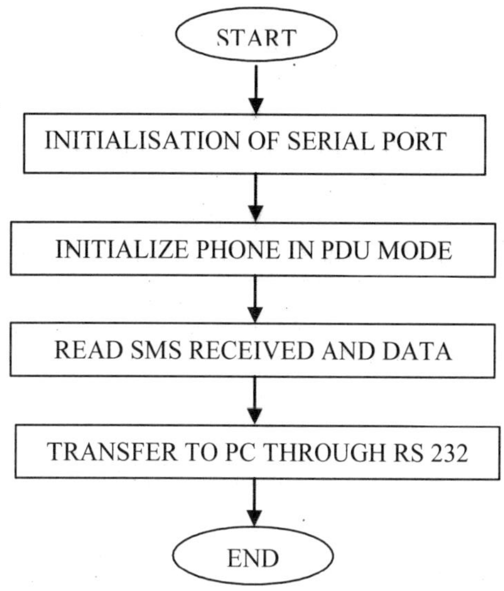

Flow Chart 2 (Receiver Programme)

Fig. 5 Hardware Developed

2. Conclusion

In this paper we discussed the use of embedded system in extending the application of cell phones to transfer data using SMS. System cost is very low including cell phone. It will cost around Rs. 2,000/-, when few transmitters are assembled in laboratory. In bulk production it will come down further. This system can be widely used in pollution monitoring systems, which in turn improves air and water quality.

3. References

[1] Peacock. W., Nokia F Bus Protocol http//www.ebededtronics.com/nokia/Fbus.html

[2] ADC 0804 Data sheets

[3] ATMEL 89 C 52 Data sheet.

[4] DS 1307 Data sheet.

[5] Mafalda Seixas, Joao Palma. Remote Alarm And Command Systems For Residential Domotics Through GSM – SMS

Self-Organized Public-Key Management for Mobile Ad Hoc Networks using Mat Lab

Dr.G.V.S.Raju[1], P. Ravi Kiran[2] G. V. Suresh
[1]Swarnandhra College of Engg &Tech.
rajugvs@rediffmail.com arkay.kakinada@gmail.com vijaysuresh.g@gmail.com

Abstract

Adhoc networks are the networks. These networks do not rely on fixed infrastructure. In such network all the networking functions are performed by the nodes in a self organized manner. Due to infrastructure less architecture security in communication is of a major concern.Adhoc networks are the evolving technology in wireless networks. This network does not rely on fixed infrastructure. In such network all the networking functions are performed by the nodes in a self organized manner. Due to infrastructure less architecture security in communication is of a major concern.

Purpose
The main objective is to develop a fully self-organized public-key management system for Adhoc networks. Aims to realize a public-key cryptographic method to perform authentication regardless of the network partitions and without any centralized services. The Security method to be realized is based on self organization among network nodes by updating information.
Keyword: *Ad-hoc networks, authentication, evaluation, simulation*

1. Introduction

Ad-hoc networks are a new paradigm of wireless communication for mobile hosts. There is nofixed infrastructure such as base stations for mobile switching. Nodes within each other's radio range communicate directly via wireless links while those which are far apart rely on other nodes to relay messages . Node mobility causes frequent changes in topology. The wireless nature of communication and lack of any security infrastructure raises several security problems The following flowchart depicts the working of any general ad-hoc network.

There are two different types of wireless nennetworks

- The easiest network topology is where each node is able to reach all the other nodes with a traditional radio relay system with a big range. There is no use of routing protocols with this kind of network because all nodes "can see" the others.
- The second kind uses also the radio relay system but each node has a smaller range, therefore one node has to use neighboring nodes to reach another node that is not within its transmission range. Then, the intermediate nodes are the routers.

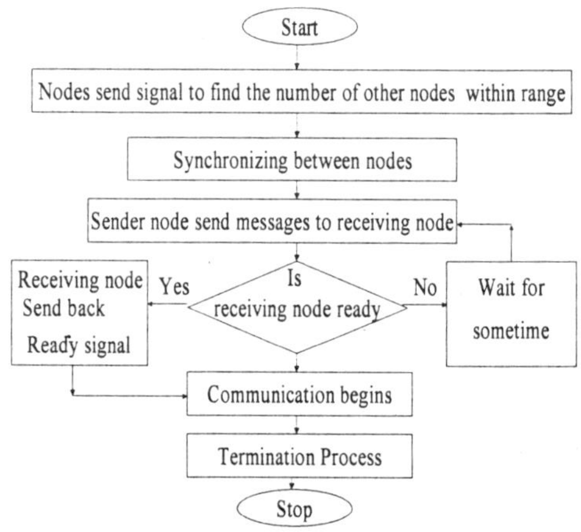

..

Fig. 1 Working of a general Ad-Hoc Network

There are five major security goals that need to be addressed in order to maintain a reliable and secure ad-hoc network environment. They are mainly

- *Confidentiality*: Protection of any information from being exposed to unintended entities. In ad-hoc networks this is more difficult to achieve because intermediates nodes (that act as routers) receive the packets for other recipients, so they can easily eavesdrop the information being routed.
- *Availability:* Services should be available whenever required. There should be an assurance of survivability despite a Denial of Service (DOS) attack. On physical and media access control layer attacker can use jamming

techniques to interfere with communication on physical channel. On network layer the attacker can disrupt the routing protocol. On higher layers, the attacker could bring down high level services e.g. key management service.

- *Authentication*: Assurance that an entity of concern or the origin of a communication is what it claims to be or from. Without which an attacker would impersonate a node, thus gaining unauthorized access to resource and sensitive information and interfering with operation of other nodes.
- *Integrity*: Message being transmitted is never altered.
- *Non-repudiation:* Ensures that sending and receiving parties can never deny ever sending or receiving the message.

Authentication

Authentication is the basis of any secure communication.

Without a robust authentication mechanism security goals are not achievable.

Authentication assures that the origin of communication is what it claims to be or from.

Without this an attacker would pretend to be another node and may gain unauthorized access to resource and secure information.

Methods of authentication

- Several methods of authentication have been proposed for ad hoc networks.
- The threshold cryptographic method is found to be the most commonly used current method

2. Threshold Cryptogrphic Method:

The Network authenticate the data transfer based on a centralized node key exchange

- The centralized node is decided based on the node coverage Probability.
- The node with maximum number of nodes as it's neighbor is declared as the head.
- All the member nodes transfer there public key to the centralized node.
- The keys are requested and recovered from this node on request.

Threshold cryptography:

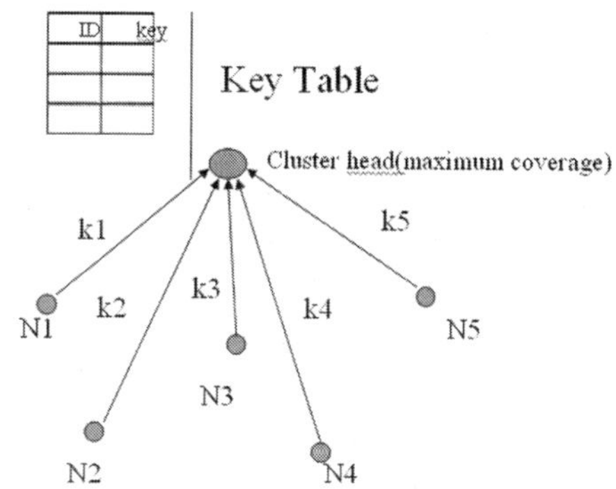

N1,N2,N3,….. Member nodes
K1,K2,K3,….. Corresponding Keys

Fig. 2 Threshold cryptography

Limitations

- Threshold based cryptography method is based on the centralized node for monitoring the keys.
- The key distribution and Authentication is completely relied on centralized node.
- Any failure in key generation may result in wrong authentication.
- All node depend on the centralized node for authentication.
- Due to key Request the communication results in delayed packet transfer rate.

Self organized cryptography

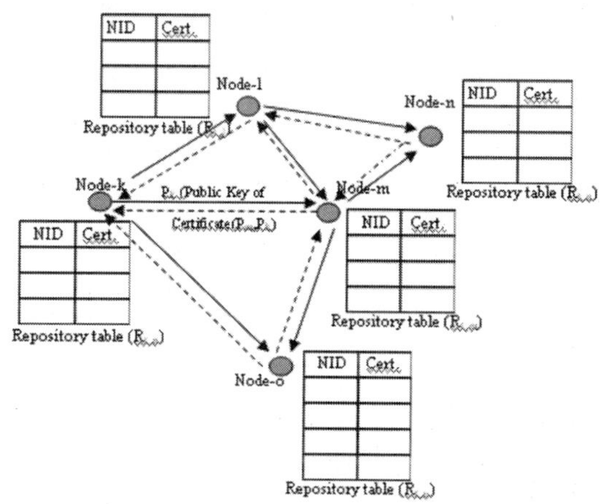

Fig. 3 Self organized cryptography

- Each node distribute it's public key to there one hop neighbor during the broadcast period.
- Each node acknowledge back to the node back with the certificate for the received node key.

- The Exchanged certificates are saved as repository tables in each node.
- The exchanged certificate gives the authentication of the key received by presenting the key of node-m's key which it received with it' s own key.
- The authentication of the key is done by the node by checking the second field of the certificate i.e it's own as received by node-n

Repository Updation

After every beacon period the network update the repository entry with the new certificates as updated entry and previous entry as Backup repository.

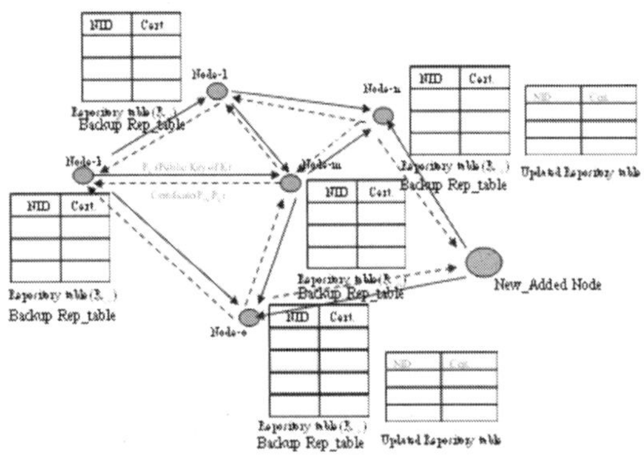

Fig. 4 Repository Updation

Advantages

The proposed self-organized public key management system is completely independent in operation. Does not relies on any centralized node for key.

The method performs certificate exchange so the authentication is most secure.

The repetitive certificates are kept as backup so the trustiness of the key is evaluated.

As the updated repository table holds only the new keys entered the resource required is very less. Each Node maintains a key table hence the key request time is completely avoided, making the communication delay minimum.

Implementation

We will consider randomly distributed nodes and create nodes and keys.

In this implementation using mat lab, we will compare the threshold cryptography method with the self organized cryptography method and calculate and plot Propagation delay , Average Packet Delivery , Repository Updation .

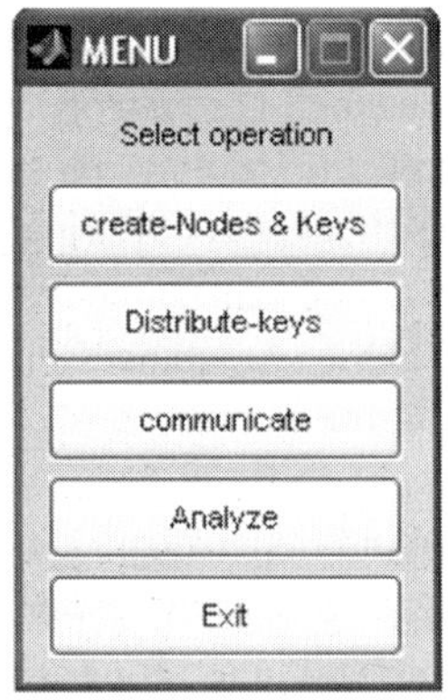

Fig. 5 Select operation

Fig. 6 Selecting cryptography method

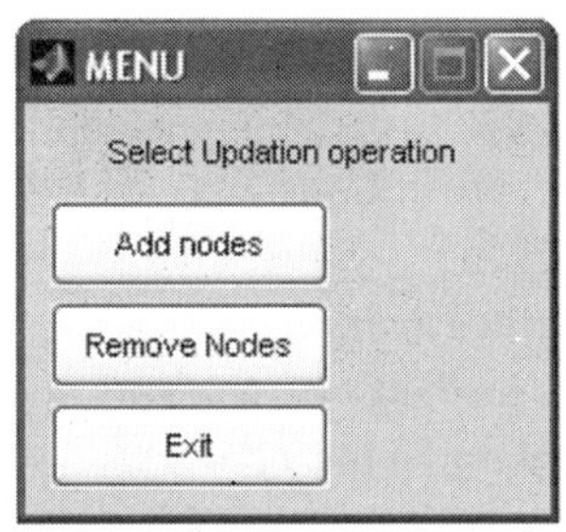

Fig. 7 Adding or removing nodes and updation

3. Results

Considered Network

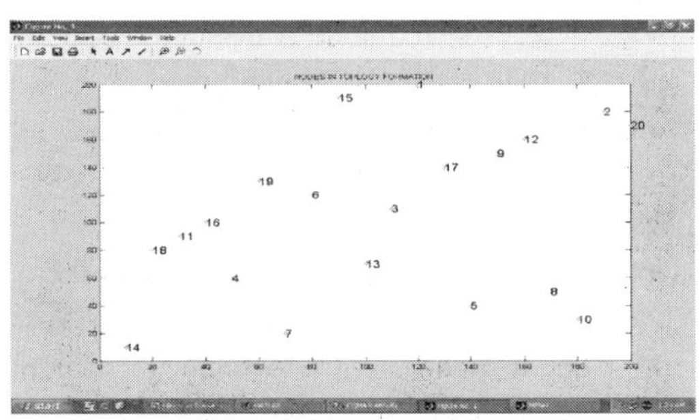

Fig. 8 Randomly distributed Nodes

Case 1 : With No Add-on nodes
Propagation delay plot

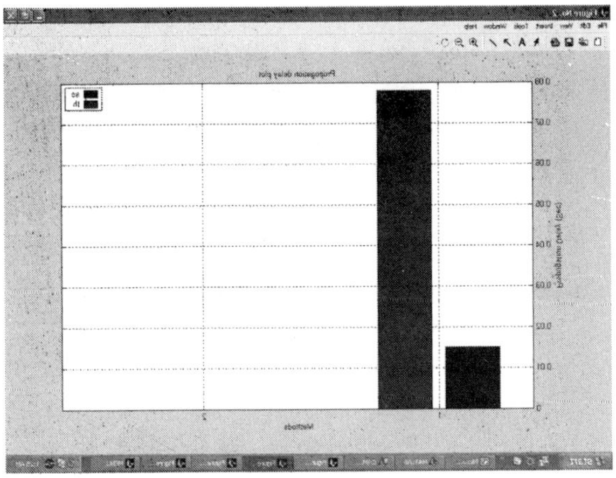

Fig. 9

Average Packet Delivery plot

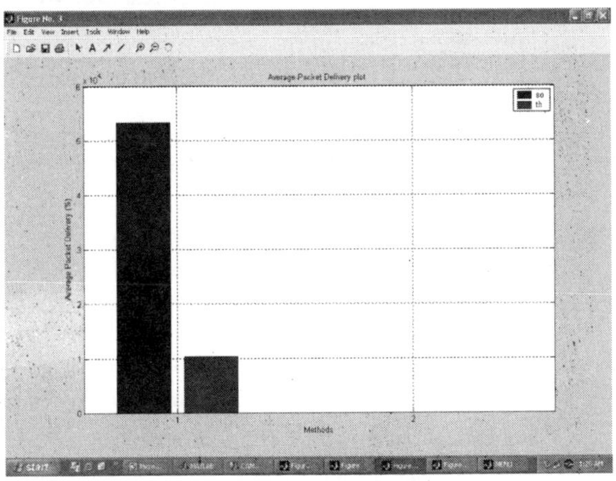

Fig. 10

Repository Updation plot

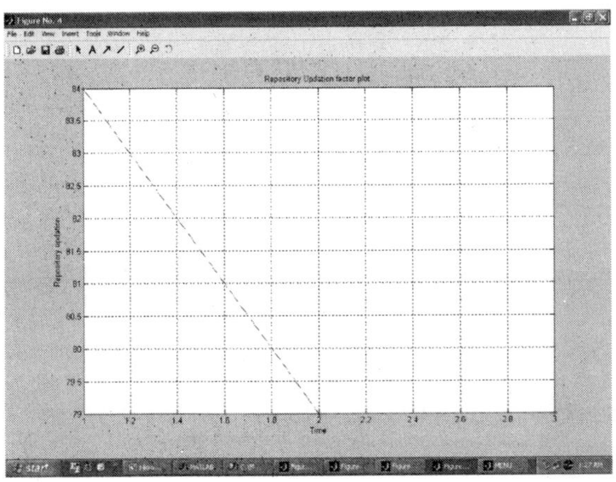

Fig. 11

Case 2: With 2 Add-on nodes
Propagation delay plot

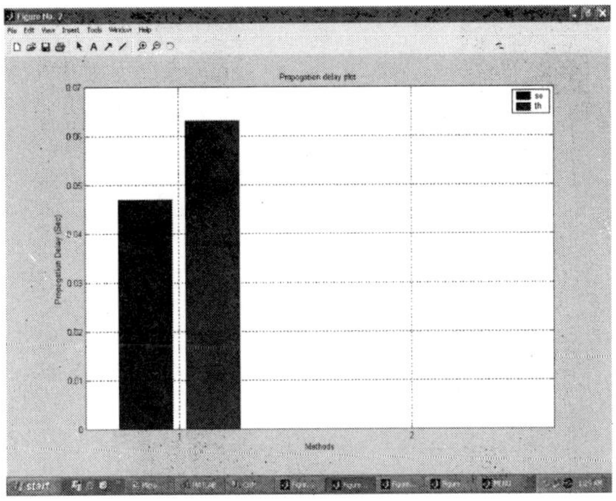

Fig. 12

Average Packet Delivery plot

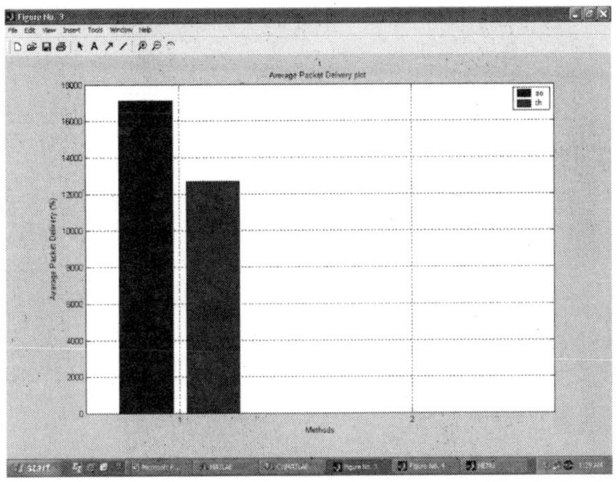

Fig. 13

Repository Updation plot

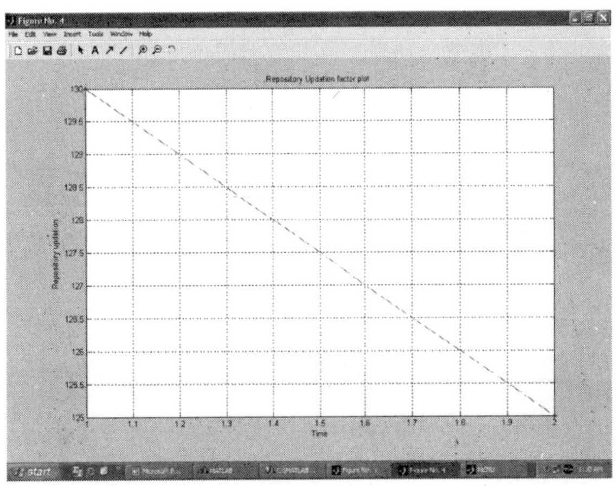

Fig. 14

Case 3: With 2 Add-on nodes, 1-remove-Node Propagation delay plot

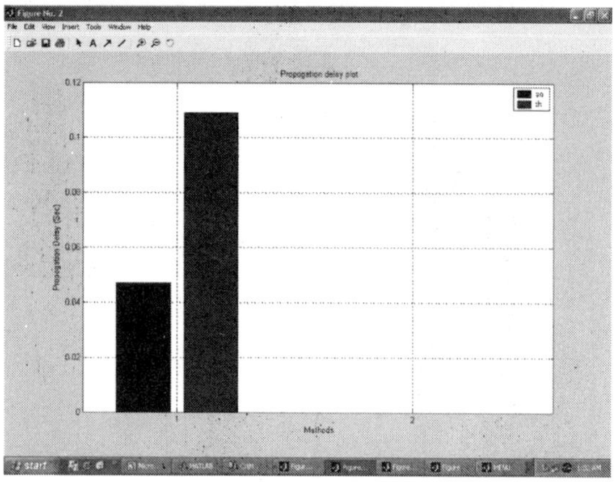

Fig. 15

Average Packet Delivery plot

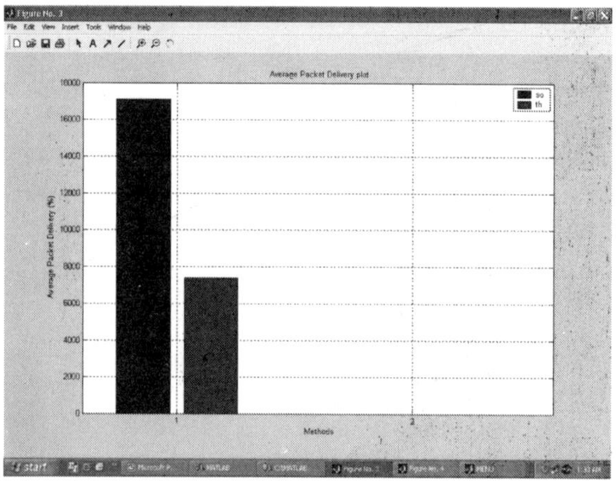

Fig. 16

Repository Updation plot

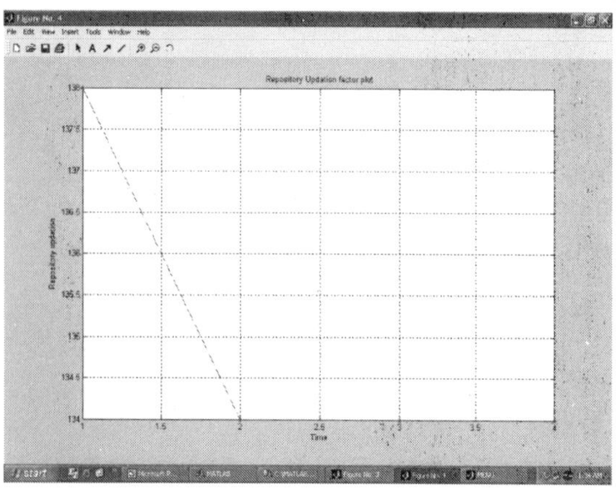

Fig. 17

3. Conclusion

- A self organized key distribution mechanism is developed for ad Hoc network.
- The proposed self key management scheme outperforms the performance of the existing threshold based cryptography.
- The repository updation factor is observed to be reduced down with more number of user, hence the proposed scheme is optimal under resource constraint systems.
- The packet delay is found to be less in self organized cryptography as compared to Threshold based cryptography.

4. References

[1] C. E. Perkins, *Ad Hoc Networking*, Addison Wesley Professional, Dec. 2000.

[2] D. B. Johnson, "Routing in Ad Hoc Networks of Mobile Hosts," in *Proceedings of the IEEE Workshop on Mobile Computing Systems and Applications*, December 2001.

[3] S. Garfinkel, "PGP: Pretty Good Privacy," *O'Reilly & Associates Inc.*, USA, 2005

[4] "PKI practices and policy framework," *ANSI X9.79*, American National Standards Institute, 2000.

[5] L. Gong, "Increasing availability and security of an authentication service," *IEEE Journal on Selected Areas in Communications*, Vol.11, No.5, Jun. 2001.

[6] Y. Frankel, P. Gemmell, P. Mackenzie and M. Yung, "Proactive RSA," *CRYPTO*, 1999

Energy Evaluation of Two Reactive Protocols under ON/OFF Source Traffic

Dhiraj Nitnaware and Ajay Verma[2]
Electronics & Telecommunication Dept., Institute of Engineering & Technology, DAVV, Indore (M.P)
dnitnaware.iet@rediffmail.com *ajayrt@rediffmail.com* •

Abstract

In Mobile Ad-hoc Network (MANET), a multi-hop wireless network, it is important to have an efficient (in terms of energy consumption and lifetime of network) routing protocols. Many routing protocols have been developed in the past. To study the existing protocols under self similar traffic, this paper concentrates on comparison of the energy consumption for two reactive protocols DSR and AODV under ON/OFF Exponential source traffic and compared with CBR source traffic. Energy consumption is evaluated as a function of pause time, speed, number of nodes, area pattern, sending rate and number of sources. The simulation is done with the help of NS-2. Two protocols have shown different behaviours in terms of energy consumption under ON/OFF source traffic with respect to CBR source traffic. This paper compares the two protocols under different scenarios.

Keywords: *Energy consumption, ON/OFF traffic, Reactive protocols, basic scenario, NS-2 simulator.*

1. Introduction

Mobile Ad-hoc Networks (MANETs) is a multi-hop wireless network in which nodes are free to move independently in any direction. It is a wireless network without any infrastructure in which nodes do not required any base station. Each node acts as a router between sender and receiver.

Energy efficient algorithm finds an important role in MANET as each node has limited battery power. In [2], the authors have compared two reactive protocols for mobile ad hoc network AODV and DSR under ON/OFF source traffic. They have selected packet delivery ratio, normalized routing overhead and average end to end delay as the performance parameters. The author of paper [3] had compared the MANET routing protocols taking energy consumption as the performance parameter.

In this paper, we have compared the energy consumption of two reactive protocols AODV and DSR under ON/OFF Exponential source traffic. The total energy consumption by each node during transmission and reception process is evaluated. The variable selected parameters are pause time, speed, number of nodes, number of sources, sending rate and area shape.

The paper is arranged as follows. Sections 2 describe two reactive routing protocols in brief. Section 3 gives the details of simulation and energy model. Simulation results are shown in section 4. Sections 5 describe our conclusion and future scope.

2. Reactive Routing Protocols

MANET routing protocols are mainly classified into two groups namely proactive and reactive protocols. Proactive protocol is a table driven routing protocol while reactive protocol is on-demand routing protocol. Here we have described the two reactive routing protocols for MANET.

2.1 Dynamic Source Routing Protocol

The Dynamic Source Routing (DSR) protocol [7] [8] finds route to destination when required. Each node in the network maintains a cache. The cache contains the route to reach the other nodes in the network. If sender wants to send data to destination then the path stored in cache is checked. If path is available then it is used. If not then the source node initiate the route construction process. In the construction phase the source flood *RouteRequest (RREQ)* packet to its neighbors. Each *RouteRequest* packet contains a sequence number which is used to prevent loop and to avoid multiple sending of *RouteRequest* packet. After receiving this packet all the nodes forward it to their neighbours provided they are not the final destination. When the request reaches the destination, the destination responds by sending *RouteReply (RREP)* packet. The path followed by *RouteReply* packet is used to send back the data packets.

2.2 Ad hoc on Demand Distance Vector Protocol

The Ad hoc On demand Distance Vector (AODV) protocol [9] uses *Hello* beacon to inform its neighbours of its presence. There is no route cache used in this protocol. AODV uses routing table to avoid loop and to distinguish between stale and fresh route. The routing table contains the sequence number and next hop information. If source has data to send, it floods the *RREQ* packet. The destination then send *RREP* packet in response to the request. If the link breaks then the route is maintained using *Route Error (RERR)* message. The *RERR* message is send by the intermediate nodes to the source informing the source node about the link break. AODV protocol uses the route discovery process like in DSR and routing table like DSDV [6].

3. Simulation Model

The simulation is done with the help of network simulator NS-2 [10] version 2.31. Here the basic scenario and the traffic model used are explained.

3.1 Basic Scenario

The network contains 50 nodes randomly distributed in a 750m X 500m area, with 30 numbers of connections. The parameters for basic scenario are listed in Table 1.

Table 1 Basic Scenario

Parameter	Value
Number of Nodes	50
Grid Area	750m x 500m
Transmission Range	250 meter
Pause Time	10 seconds
Speed	5 m/s
Seed	1000
Sending Rate	64 packets/s
Simulation Time	1000 seconds

3.1.1 CBR Traffic Model

CBR generates traffic at a deterministic rate. Packet size was set to 512 bytes at a constant rate of 32kbps.

3.1.2 Exponential Traffic Model:

It is an ON/OFF traffic with exponential distribution. Traffic generation rate is 32kbps during ON period. Average ON and OFF time are 1.5s and 0.5s respectively.

3.2 Energy Evaluation Model

We have taken the initial energy as 1000 Joules, power consumed during transmission and receptions are 1.65 W and 1.1 W respectively. Bandwidth is 2Mbps; the radio network interface card (NIC) is WaveLan from Lucent. Energy is converted in joules by multiplying power with time. The following equations are used to convert energy in joules:
Transmitted Energy

$$Tx\ Energy = (Tx\ Power*PacketSize)/2x10^6 \quad (1)$$

Receiving Energy

$$Rx\ Energy = (Rx\ Power*PacketSize)/2x10^6 \quad (2)$$

Total energy consumed by each node during transmission and reception is calculated by the following equation :

Total Energy Consumed

= Initial energy – Energy left at each node (3)

We have taken the same energy model as given by Marzoni and Cano [3]. The selected parameters behave as 2400 MHz WaveLan of IEEE 802.11. The Radio Frequency (RF) value is set at 281.8 mW which is equivalent to a radio range of 250 m. The traffic model parameters for CBR and Exponential are shown in Table 2.

Table 2 Traffic Model's Parameters

Parameter	CBR Value	Exponential Value
Data Packet Size	512 bytes	512 bytes
Sending Rate	32 kbps	32 kbps
Burst Time	NA	1.5 s
Idle Time	NA	0.5 s
Simulation Time	1000 s	1000 s

NA- Not Applicable

4. Results

The results are shown in the form of graph. Section 4.1 shows the bar graph of energy consumption due to basic scenario while the energy consumption as a function of selected parameters is given in section 4.2.

4.1 Due to Basic Scenario

Here we have evaluated

1. Energy consumed (%) during transmission and reception at MAC level (Fig. 1).
2. Energy consumed (%) due to packet type (routing/ MAC/ CBR or EXPO) during transmission and reception (Fig. 2).
3. Energy consumed (%) during transmission and reception of control packets (Fig. 3).

4. Energy consumed due to packet type (routing/ MAC) during transmission and reception of control packets (Fig. 4).

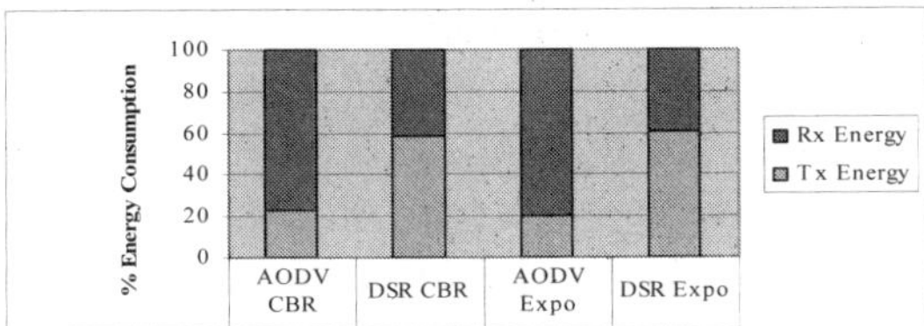

	AODV CBR	DSR CBR	AODV Expo	DSR Expo
Rx Energy	76.831315	40.962029	79.64619	39.671528
Tx Energy	23.168685	59.037971	20.35381	60.328472

Values in Percentage(%)

Fig. 1 Total energy consumption (%) in transmitting and receiving at MAC level

Fig. 1 shows the total energy in percentage at MAC level during transmitting and receiving. The energy consumption is mainly due to receiving process.

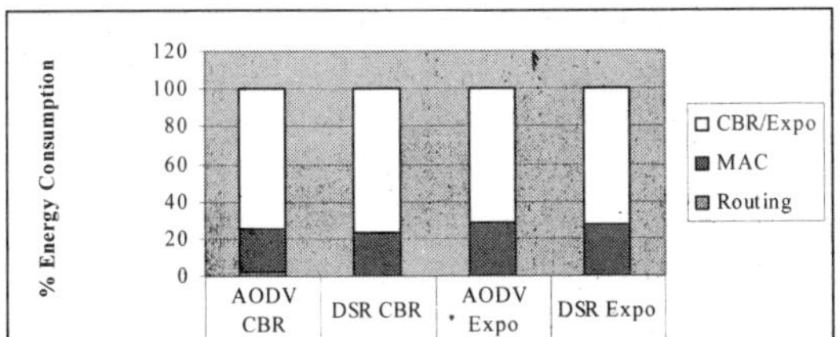

	AODV CBR	DSR CBR	AODV Expo	DSR Expo
CBR/Expo	75.196308	77.289874	71.856711	72.811489
MAC	22.517191	22.32365	28.008065	27.089991
Routing	2.286501	0.3864761	0.1352239	0.0985206

Fig. 2 Total energy consumption (%) due to packet type

Fig. 2 shows the percentage total energy consumption as a function of packet type. The result shows that MAC packets affect significantly the total energy consumption with CBR traffic as well as with Exponential traffic. Also AODV consume more energy than DSR in terms of routing packets as DSR first uses the cache and then go for route discovery.

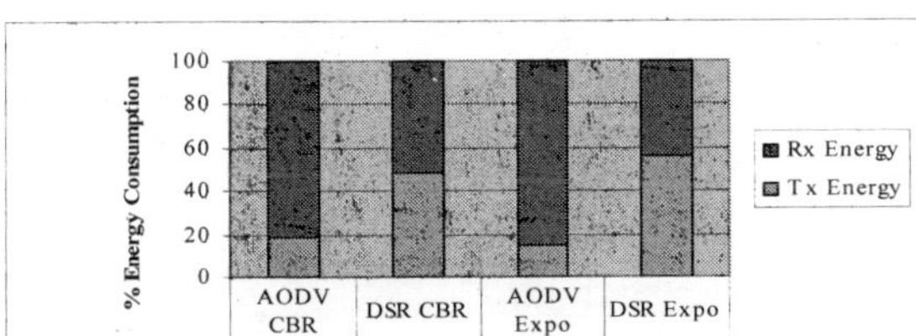

	AODV CBR	DSR CBR	AODV Expo	DSR Expo
Rx Energy	81.69404	50.99327	85.03358	44.13381
Tx Energy	18.30596	49.00673	14.96642	55.86619

Values in Percentage(%)

Fig. 3 Energy consumption (%) in transmitting and receiving control packets.

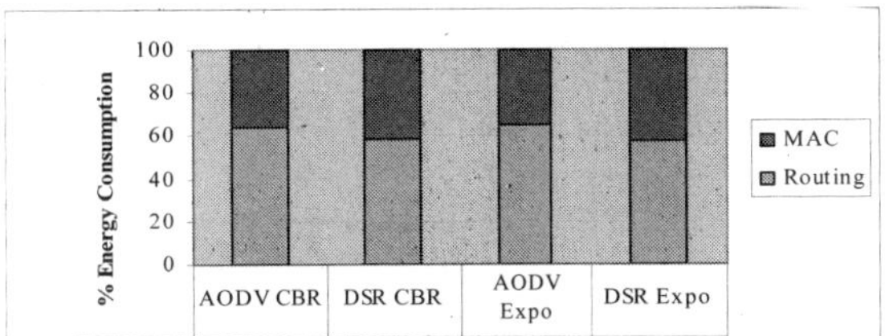

	AODV CBR	DSR CBR	AODV Expo	DSR Expo
MAC	35.395596	41.582742	35.04234	42.113135
Routing	64.604404	58.417258	64.95766	57.886865

Values in Percentage(%)

Fig. 4 Energy consumption (%) at routing and Mac levels due to control packets overhead.

Fig. 3 shows the percentage energy consumption in transmitting and receiving control packets. Route Request (RREQ), Route Reply (RREP), Route Error (RERR) are the routing control packets while Request to Send (RTS), Clear to Send (CTS) and Acknowledgement (ACK) are the MAC control packets. The result shows that the energy consumed mainly due to receiving control packets irrespective of the traffic model. Fig. 4 shows the energy consumed due to packet type. The energy consumed due to MAC control packets significantly affects the total energy for both the protocols. The result shows that DSR performed better than AODV if energy consumption only due to routing packets is considered.

4.2 Due to Selected Variable Parameters

Here we have evaluated the energy consumption for AODV and DSR by varying the selected parameters.

4.2.1 As a function of Pause Time

Fig. 5(a) shows the total energy consumed (Joules) by all the nodes used in transmission and reception as a function of pause time. Pause Time is varied as 0, 50, 250, 500, 800 and 1000 seconds. Both AODV and DSR with Exponential model consumed more energy by a factor of 5 as compared with CBR model. The result show that AODV slightly outperformed DSR at high mobility. There is a chance of link breaks at high mobility so more route discovery process is needed which is less in AODV.

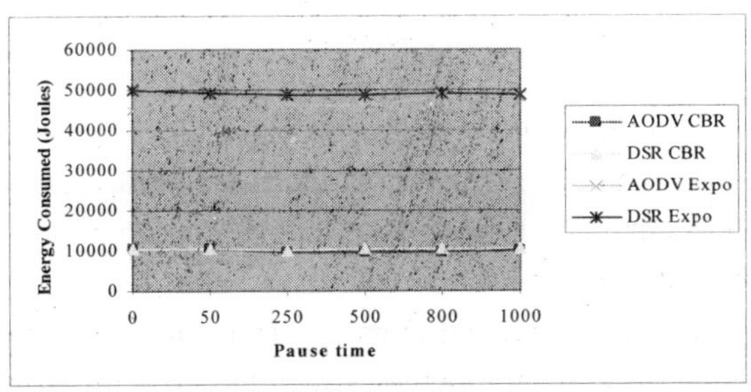

Fig. 5(a) Energy consumption Versus Pause Time

4.2.2 As a function of Speed

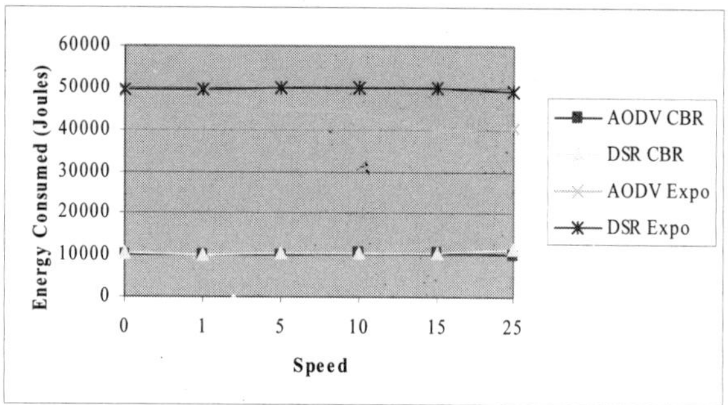

Fig. 5(b) Energy consumption Versus Speed

Fig. 5(b) shows the total energy consumed (Joules) when speed is varied as 0 m/s correspond to static network, 1 m/s – MANET on human walking, 5 m/s – MANET on cycle, 10 m/s – MANET on motor cycle, 15 m/s – MANET on car, and 25 m/s – MANET on car running on empty road. Both pause time and speed are mobility parameters. Low speed is equivalent to high mobility and vice-versa. Therefore the same result is observed here. At high speed ADOV performed better because at high speed the route cache in DSR becomes useless that results in more route discovery process as compared to AODV.

4.2.3 As a function of Source

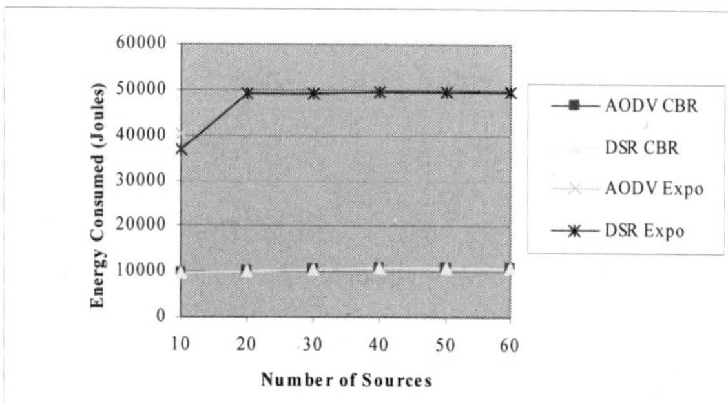

Fig. 5(c) Energy consumption Versus Number of Sources

The sources are varied between 10, 20, 30, 40, 50 and 60. The routing packet is increased with increase in the number of sources so energy consumption of both AODV and DSR increases with number of sources. The increment in energy is due to increase in routing packets that increases with the increase in the number of sources. DSR performed slightly better than AODV at less number of sources as multiple paths are available in the cache.

4.2.4 As a function of Nodes

The total energy consumed (Joules) as a function of nodes is shown in Fig. 5(d), when varying the number of nodes between 30, 40, 50, 60, 70, and 80. Both protocols show the increment in energy consumption due to increase in nodes. This is due to increase in the control packets that is received and transmitted by the nodes for discovery and maintenance process. Again AODV consumed less energy than DSR. AODV uses the routing table and learn quickly about the neighbours using *Hello* beacon.

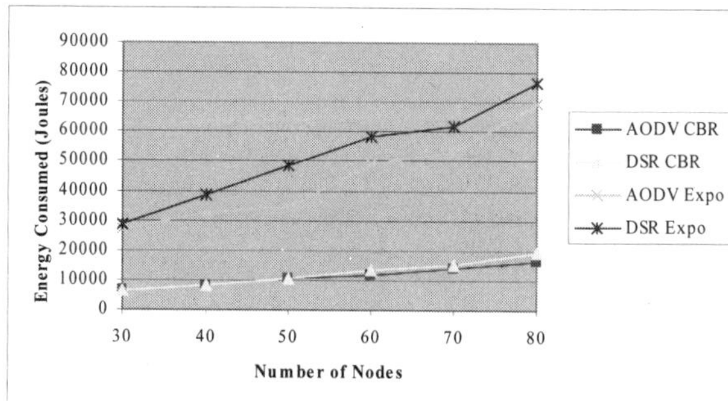

Fig. 5(d) Energy consumption Versus Number of Nodes

4.2.5 As a function of Grid Area

The selected grid areas were: 500m x 250m, 500m x 500m, 750m x 500m, 750m x 750m, 1000m x 750m and 1000m x 1000m.The result shows that AODV outperformed DSR. The routing table in AODV helps the nodes to learn about new routes that result in less route discovery than DSR.

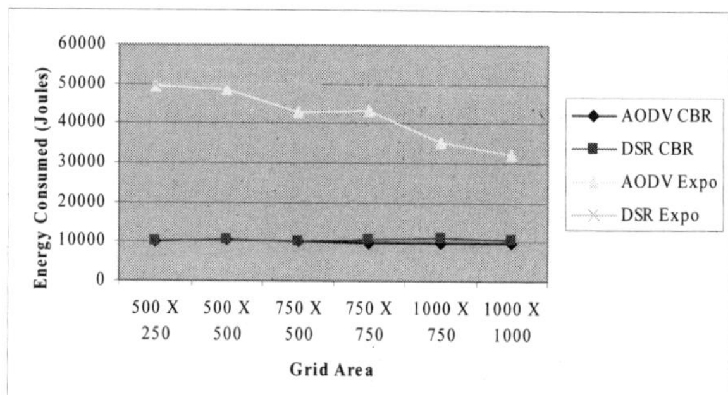

Fig. 5(e) Energy consumption Versus Grid Area

4.2.6 As a function of Sending Rate

The sending rate is varied by 16packets/s, 32packets/s, 48packets/s, 64packets/s, 80packets/s, 96packets/s. Fig. 5(f) gives the same result as in Fig. 5(c).

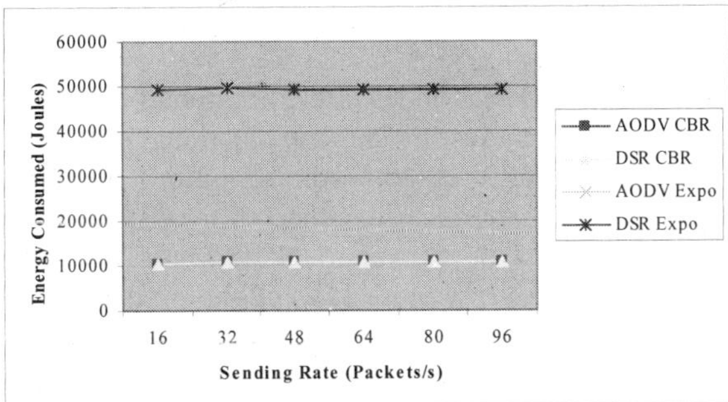

Fig. 5(f) Energy consumption Versus Sending Rate

5. Conclusion and Future Scope

From the above simulation results we have observed that:

1) AODV outperformed DSR as a function of pause time, at high speed, number of nodes, number of sources, grid area and sending rate with ON/OFF traffic model.
2) AODV and DSR show almost the same result with CBR traffic.
3) Energy consumption in both on-demand protocols is increased mainly due to the increase in the routing control packet overhead. If we reduced these routing control packets, we can reduce the energy consumption and increase the lifetime of the network

In future, energy evaluation of more existing protocols can be undertaken and evaluate them on Pareto traffic.

6. References

[1] Ahmed Al-Maashri and M. Ould-Khaoua, "Performance Analysis of MANET Routing Protocols in the Presence of Self-Similar Traffic", Proceeding 31st IEEE Conference on Local Computer Networks, pp- 801-807, 2006.

[2] Jun-Hoong and Au-Yong, "Comparison of On Demand Mobile Ad Hoc Network Routing Protocols Under ON/OFF Source Traffic Effect", Proc. of IASTED International Conference, March 29-31, Chiang Mai, Thailand.

[3] Juan Carlos Cano and Pietro Manzoni., "A Performance Comparison of Energy Consumption for Mobile Ad Hoc Network Routing Protocols", Proceeding of 8th International Symposium on Modeling, Analysis and Simulation of Computer & Telecommunication System 2000.

[4] J. Broch., "A Performance Comparison of Ad-Hoc Multi Hop Wireless Networks Routing protocols", IEEE/ACM MOBICOM, Oct 1998

[5] Humaira Ehsan and Zartash Afzal Uzmi, "Performance Comparison of Ad Hoc Wireless Network Routing Protocols", Proceeding of INMIC 2004, 8th International Multitopic Conference, pp 457-465, IEEE December 2004.

[6] Charles E. Perkins and Pravin Bhagwat, "Highly Dynamic Destination Sequenced Distance Vector Routing (DVDV) for Mobile Computers", Proceeding of ACM SIGCOMM, October 1994.

[7] David B. Johnson, Davis A. Maltz and J. Broch, "DSR for Mobile Ad Hoc Network", November 1999.

[8] David B. Johnson, Davis A. Maltz and Y.C.Hu, "DSR for Mobile Ad Hoc Network", Internet-Draft, draft-ietfmanet-drs-09.txt, July 2003.

[9] Charles E. Perkins, Elizabeth M. Royer and S. Das, "Ad-Hoc On Demand Distance Vector Routing (AODV)", draft-ietfmanet-aodv-05.txt, March 2000.

[10] Network Simulator, ns-2, http://www.isi.edu/nsnam/-ns/

[11] http://www.isi.edu/nsnam/ns/tutorial/

[12] Charles E. Perkins and Elizabeth M. Royer, Performance Comparison of Two On-Demand Routing Protocols for Ad Hoc Networks", IEEE Personal Communication, February 2001.

[13] Walter Willinger, Murad S. Taqqu, Robert Sherman and Daniel V. Wilson, "Self-Similarity through High-Variability: Statistical Analysis of Ethernet LAN Traffic at the Source Level", IEEE/ACM Transactions on Networking 5, pp. 71-86. April 1997.

Threshold Key Management for MANET

P. Sumathi
II M.E.(CSE), Adhiyamaan College of Engineering, Hosur
sumithirulogu@yahoo.co.in

Abstract

A mobile ad hoc network is a collection of mobile wireless nodes that can dynamically form a network without necessarily using any pre-existing infrastructure. Security of mobile ad hoc networks is built upon a reliable key management system to generate and distribute symmetric encryption/decryption keys for communicating parties. While central servers generate and distribute the keys in traditional wired networks, distributive key management systems are used in mobile ad hoc networks where central approaches will fail in such dynamic, high mobility networks Threshold cryptography has been proposed to provide a reliable, distributive key management for networks. In an (n, t+1) threshold system, there are n servers to provide key generation and distribution when needed for the whole network. From these n servers, any x servers ($t<x \leq n$) can co-operate and generate a key for any node. Until now, threshold cryptography has remained only a theory. No practical key management system has been proposed to use threshold cryptography that mentioned what kind of shares servers will have in common and the practical way of creating the key from these shares. . In this paper, we propose a new key management system in mobile ad hoc networks based on maximum distance separable (MDS) codes and symmetric key generation system The main idea in the proposed scheme is to use a global MDS code to generate node key chains.

Keywords: *MANET, ad hoc networks, MDS code, mobile security, symmetric key,SKGS, threshold cryptography.*

1. Introduction

An ad hoc network is a set of wireless mobile nodes that form a dynamic autonomous network without the intervention of centralized access points or base stations. MANETs consist of mobile nodes interconnected by multihop communications paths or radio links. A MANET consists of mobile platforms, known as nodes, which are free to move at any speed in any direction and organize themselves randomly. The nodes in the network function as routers, clients, and servers. These nodes are constrained in power consumption, bandwidth, and computational power.

MANETs lack central administration and prior organization, so the security concerns are different than those that exist in conventional networks. Wireless links make MANETs more susceptible to attacks. It is easier for hackers to eavesdrop and gain access to confidential information. It is also easier for them to enter or leave a wireless network because no physical connection is required. They can also directly attack the network to delete messages, inject false packets, or this method does not meet these resource limitations Unlike traditional wireless networks, ad hoc networks require no fixed infrastructure. Such networks can be very useful in scenarios where natural conditions or time constraints make it impossible to pre-deploy infrastructure. Examples of applications include battlefields, emergency services, conference rooms, and home and office. Mobile nodes in an ad hoc network have limited radio transmission range .Each node operates not only as an end system, but also as a router to forward packets on behalf of others. The nodes are free to move and organize themselves into a dynamic network.

A MANET does not require any fixed infrastructure such as base stations, and therefore, it is an attractive networking option for connecting mobile devices quickly and spontaneously to environments such as military battle fields and rescue operations.

Networks security is an important factor in constructing any network.. In traditional wired networks, central servers are available to provide security services for the users inside the network system. In Kerberos, a central server will generate the keys and distribute them securely to the nodes in the network. In MANETs, absence of fixed infrastructure creates new challenges in security measurements.

Secure mobile network necessities like privacy, authentication, integrity and non-repudiation rely on secure key management framework. For MANETs, the existence of a secure key management protocol is a prerequisite for network establishment. Central key management protocols based on trusted third party (TTP) technology works well for traditional wired networks, because all the nodes can access the TTP to retrieve the key needed for communication with any other node. In contrast, due to mobility and topology changes, mobile networks cannot rely on central approaches: only distributive key management protocols (e.g., threshold key management protocols) can operate in such mobile networks efficiently. The threshold approach for key management assigns number of nodes to be servers. Any number of these servers greater than the threshold value can co-operate to generate keys for any node in the network.

Blom proposed a distributed symmetric key generation system (SKGS) based on the key pre distribution scheme. In SKGS, a central server is responsible for the creation and distribution of nodal key chains. Nodes can derive any future key from the key chain they received from the main server. SKGS provides security against cooperative malicious attacks: to retrieve the key of the node the attacker has to compromise a minimum number of nodes (t+1), and with any number less than t+1, the attacker can not retrieve the key chain for the attacked node. The main problem in the SKGS approach is the single point of failure of the central server: if an attacker compromises the central node, all the keys it has can be retrieved, and the security of the network is exposed.

Threshold cryptography is a proposed cryptography scheme suited for mobile networks to provide robustness and defense against single point of failure in the central server. In threshold cryptography, the central server function is distributed among a group of servers. When one of these servers is compromised or fails, the rest of the group can take place of this single server. This distribution provides a co-operative security model and robustness against the single point of failure. The main drawback in threshold cryptography is the difficulty in applying the distributive function. Until now, there has been no practical security model that could use threshold cryptography efficiently. In this paper we will propose a distributed co-operative key management system to generate and deliver the keys based on SKGS and threshold cryptography.

2. Previous Work

Blom proposed a symmetric key generation system (SKGS) based on secret sharing systems. In SKGS, nodes are supplied with a relatively small amount of secret data that is used to derive all the node's keys. A central server (trusted authority) generates a global matrix G of size k x n that is known to all the nodes in the network, and a symmetric secret matrix D of size k x n. The central node calculates the key matrix for the network as $K = (D \,.\, G)^T \,.\, G$. Because D is symmetric, K will be also symmetric, for rows i and j in K, we have $K_{i,j} = K_{j,i}$. So, $K_{i,j}$ is common between the rows i, j. If row i is the key chain for node i, and row j is the key chain for node j, the element $K_{i,j}$ will be the symmetric key between them.

Because G is known by all the participant in the networks, while external nodes (malicious nodes) do not know this matrix G, the central server delivers the $_i$ th row of $(D.\, G)^T$ node i. Upon reception, node I will calculates its key chain $k_i = {}_i th$ row of $(D.G)^T .G$. This division of key generation into more than one step adds more secrecy to their key chains, and make it harder for the intruder to retrieve any information about other nodes.

Blom showed in his paper that by using SKGS scheme, at least k users have to co-operate to get any information about keys they do not have. Thus, any coalition of less than k nodes can not reveal any information about the key chain of any other node.

The problem of this approach is that it relies on a central point to do all the work, making it vulnerable as a single point of failure. Another problem arising from key request and delivery is that some nodes may not be able to reach the central server due to existence of broken links or n trustworthy routing information.

3. Proposed Approach:

The assumptions we made and the notation we will use are as follows:

- Symmetric matrix D is of size k xk.
- MDS code generator matrix G is of size k x n with $k < n$.
- Number of servers is equal to n.
- All the keys value are in GF(q).
- Any node is able to reach k server when it requests a key.
- K denotes key matrix.

In order to construct a practical key management system for MANETs, we used Blom's SKGS in conjunction with theory of threshold cryptographic systems. In addition, we also used coding theory to overcome the shortcomings of central approaches in SKGS, and to provide a practical threshold cryptographic system capable of operating in a dynamic environment.

In our proposed approach, each node will be provided with a group of keys (key chain) when it joins the network. This key chain will be used to derive all the future keys for this node such that any two nodes can calculate a symmetric keys between them based on these key chains. Key authority servers are distributed among the network in a threshold way.

There are n key authority servers with k threshold value. Generator matrix (G) for the MDS code used in our distributive key management system (with code distance d=n-k+1) will be distributed among the n key authority servers. Recall from MDS code properties that every set of k columns in G are linearly independent. Thus, it is enough to know k columns of

G to construct it . Now, any *k* servers chosen from the *n* authority servers are capable of reconstructing *G*. Each of the *n* servers in the network will be initialized with a column *r* of *G* during the network setup, such that any *k* nodes can collaborate with each other and reconstruct *G*, while any number less than this threshold value *k* will not be able to reconstruct *G*.

On the other hand, since matrix *D* is known only to the authority servers, regular nodes do not know any information about *D* except what they receive from the servers during the key generation's phase. Now, each of the *n* servers knows what is the secret matrix *D*, but knows only a part of *G*. When a node demands a key, it will initialize the key generation system, and *k* servers will be asked to communicate with. One server will be elected as a collector, and every selected server (within the *k* group) will send its share of *G* to the collector, who in turn will construct *G* and then calculate *K* which contains shares from the other servers. Since the key chain of node *i* will be row *i*, the collector will send the key chain to node *i*.

4. Maximum Distance Separable (MDS) Codes

Coding theory and its applications have long been used extensively in the communication field to provide parity checking and an error detection mechanism. In coding theory, we define "code" as a group of code words with known length, such that the mapping between the data we are going to transmit and the code words is a one-to-one function. If we have data mi of length k, by using codes, we can convert it to a code word c_i with length n, where n > k using some defined encoding scheme. The code word c_i will have n − k redundant elements. Those elements are used for parity checking and error detection purposes on the decoding side.

We define the distance d of the code C [n, k] as the number of different elements between any two code words. Singleton found that the minimum distance for code C [n, k] must satisfy $d(C) \leq n-k+1$. When Singleton bound is at maximum (i.e., $d(C) = n-k+1$), the code C[n, k] will be an MDS code.

MDS codes are a class of error control codes created to deal with the problem of communication over a noisy channel, where some of the bits of the message may be corrupted on route. Such codes are used in cryptography and coding theory applications. The MDS code satisfies the Singleton Bound requirement. The value of distance d determines the maximum error t that can be corrected using this code ($d \geq 2t+1$). We can view MDS codes as a linear independent set of vectors that form a subspace in the vector space GF (q^k) .The basis of these vectors can form the generator matrix (G) for that MDS code.

All MDS code words (i.e., the key chains for the nodes) can be generated using a carefully chosen special matrix called a generator matrix G, a [n, k]-MDS code with k rows and n columns. The relation between G and code words C can be expressed as

$$C = v. G$$

where v is the message represented as a vector and C is the code word generated for that message v.

Let C be a [n, k] linear code in GF (q^k) with minimum distance d. We can assume C to be MDS if the following properties were satisfied:

1. Generator matrix G for this code is an MDS code.
2. The code $G^{\perp}$ dual to C is an MDS code.
3. Any k columns of a generator matrix for G are linearly independent.
4. If a generator matrix for C is in standard form [I,A], then every square sub matrix of A is nonsingular.
5. Given any d(G) coordinate positions, there is a minimum weight code word whose non-zero entries are in precisely these positions.

Using matrix transformation on MDS code to generate code C from a secret symmetric matrix D, each node does not need large amounts of memory space to save all its keys. The security of MDS codes relies on the idea that all the columns of C are linearly independent and any coalition of less than k nodes can not retrieve the secret. Reed and Solomon have found an equation to generate G matrix for any MDS- [n, k, d] in GF (q^k) by using the value α which is a primitive root of GF(q).

Reed-Solomon codes are very common MDS codes in the communication world. They are famous for their optimized generator matrix G in GF(q). Using α, which is a primitive root of q (i.e., $\alpha^x \equiv 1 \mod q$, the least value of x is q-1), we define the generator matrix for Reed-Solomon codes as

$$G_{i,j} = \alpha^{(i-1)(j-1)} \mod q.$$

5. Threshold Cryptography

Threshold cryptography (TC) involves sharing of a key by multiple individuals called shareholders engaged in encryption or decryption. The objective is to have distributed architecture in a hostile environment. Other than sharing keys or working in distributed manner, TC can be implemented to redundantly split the message into n pieces such that with t or more pieces the original message can be recovered. This ensures secure message transmission between two nodes over n multiple paths.

The basic idea of threshold cryptography is to protect encryption keys by making a group of nodes (servers) to co-operate to provide fault-tolerant distribution of keys within the security model. Threshold cryptography allows one to distribute a piece of secret information (keys) among several servers in a way that meets the following two requirements:

1) no group of compromised servers (smaller than a given threshold) can figure out what the secret is, even if they cooperate.
2) when it becomes necessary that the secret information be reconstructed, any large enough number of servers (a number larger than the above threshold) can always do it.

The primary objective of sharing of a key by multiple servers (shareholders) in threshold cryptography system is to have distributed architecture in a hostile environment. Other than sharing keys or working in a distributed manner, threshold cryptography can be implemented to redundantly split the message into n pieces such that with t or more pieces the original message can be recovered. This ensures secure message transmission between two nodes over n multiple paths.

An (n, t + 1)-threshold cryptography scheme allows n parties to share the ability to perform a cryptographic operation (e.g., creating a digital signature), so that any t + 1 parties can perform this operation jointly, while it is infeasible for at most t parties to do the same operation even by collusion. In our proposed key management scheme, the n servers of the key management service share the ability to create the key chain for the node. For the service to tolerate t compromised servers, we employ an (n, t+1) threshold cryptography scheme and divide the secret symmetric matrix D. The matrix is used in conjuction of the generator matrix of the MDS code to generate the key chains for the participant nodes in the network into n shares (s1, s2, ..., sn), assigning one share to each server. We call (s1, s2, ..., sn) shares of the secret matrix D. In order for a node to have its key chain, it will ask t+1 on n shareholder to generate a partial share of the key chain. Each one of those k servers generates a partial sum for this key chain and send it to the sender, who will in turn perform the operation of complete key chain retrieval from these partial sums.

6. Conclusion and Future Work

In this paper, we proposed a distributive key management system suitable for ad hoc networks. Based on threshold cryptography and MDS codes with SKGS, the proposed system is applicable and practical. The future work will include the simulation of the proposed approach in addition to the study of the effect of dishonest nodes on the security of the proposed system.

7. References

[1] Distributive Key Management for Mobile Ad Hoc Networks, Al-Shurman, M.; Seong-Moo Yoo; Bonam Kim;

[2] R. Blom, *"Optimal class of symmetric key generation systems "*, Proc. of the EUROCRYPT 84 workshop on Advances in cryptology: theory and application of cryptographic techniques, p.335-338, December 1985, Paris, France.

[3] L. Zhou, Z. Haas *"Securing ad hoc networks "* , IEEE Network Magazine, vol. 13, no.6, 1999.

[4] S. Yamiolkoski, *"The Road to Maximum Distance Separable Codes"*, Lecture notes in projective geometry.

[5] I.S. Reed, G. Solomon, *"Polynomial codes over certain finite fields"*, Journal of the Society for Industrial and Applied Mathematics (SIAM), vol. 8, no. 2, pp. 300-304, 1960.

[6] A. Jeffrey, *"Advanced Engineering Mathematics"*, ISBN 012382592X, Academic Press Publisher, London, 2001.

[7] L. Xu, *"A general encryption scheme based on MDS code"* Proceedings of IEEE International Symposium on Information Theory, 2003.

[8] T. Matsumoto, H. Imai, *"On the Key Predistribution System: A Practical Solution to the Key Distribution Problem"*, A Conference on the Theory and Applications of Cryptographic Techniques on Advances in Cryptology, vol. 293, pp. 185-193, 1987.

[9] H. K. Kim, V. Lebedev, *"On optimal superimposed codes"*, Journal of Combinatorial Designs, Vol. 12, Issue 2, pp. 79 91, 2003.

Performance Improvement in Cluster Based Routing using Selective Unidirectional Link

Sonal A. Bhople[1], Sunita S. Barve[2] and Lata Ragha[3]
[1,2]Lecturer, Dept of Computer Engg, Lokmanya Tilak College of Engg, Mumbai
sonal.bhople@gmail.com
barve_sunita@rediffmail.com
[3]Assistant Professor, Dept of Computer Engg, Ramrao Adik Institute of Technology, Mumbai
lata.ragha@gmail.com

Abstract

A Mobile Ad hoc NETwork (MANET) is a collection of mobile nodes that dynamically form a temporary network and are capable of communicating with each other without the use of a network infrastructure or any centralized administration. Routing in wireless mobile ad-hoc networks should be efficient. Cluster Based Routing Protocol (CBRP) is one such routing protocol designed for use in mobile ad hoc networks. Most routing protocols, simply assume that all network links are bidirectional, and thus may need additional protocol actions to remove unidirectional links from route computations. Unidirectional links can presumably benefit routing by providing improved network connectivity and shorter paths. But prior work indicates that routing over unidirectional links usually causes high overheads. With this in mind the protocol proposed here makes use of selective unidirectional links so that the overhead is minimized and connectivity is improved.

1. Introduction

MANET (Mobile Ad hoc Network) consists of a dynamic set of nodes with a network set up by them with no preexisting infrastructure. So this can easily result in some conditions including difference in radio transceiver capabilities of nodes, the use of transmission range control and difference in wireless channel interference experienced by different nodes. Depending on such conditions, unidirectional links can be quite common. But the majority of the on-demand routing protocols proposed for MANET like

Ad hoc on-demand Distance Vector (AODV) [8], Dynamic Source Routing (DSR) [6] etc, assumes that all links between nodes are bidirectional. There are mainly three techniques proposed for handling unidirectional links in on-demand routing protocol: Blacklisting, Hello, ReversePathSearch. Most of them try to eliminate the unidirectional links in the network. Unidirectional links can presumably benefit routing by providing improved network connectivity and shorter paths.

Routing in wireless mobile ad-hoc networks should be dynamic and resource saving. Cluster Based Routing Protocol [4, 10] (CBRP) is one such dynamic protocol. It reduces the resource consumption by dividing the network into clusters and reducing the flooding traffic across the network. Moreover instead of considering only bidirectional links for routing unidirectional links can also be considered for inter cluster and intra cluster routing.

2. MANET

Wireless network is the network of mobile computer nodes or stations that are not physically wired. The main advantage of this is communicating with rest of the world while being mobile. The disadvantage of this is their limited bandwidth, memory, processing capabilities, open medium and less secure compared to wired devices. Two basic system models are Fixed backbone wireless system and Wireless Mobile Ad hoc Network (MANET).An ad hoc network is a collection of nodes that do not need rely on a predefined infrastructure to keep the network connected. So the functioning of Ad-hoc networks is dependent on the trust and co-operation between nodes. Nodes help each other in conveying information about the topology of the network and share the responsibility of managing the network. Hence in addition to acting as hosts, each mobile node does the function of routing and relaying messages for other mobile nodes. Routing protocols can be divided into proactive, reactive and hybrid protocols, depending on the routing topology [3].

Proactive routing protocols: In proactive protocols, the routes are discovered before usage avoiding the latency incurred in finding the route. These protocols require the nodes to maintain routing and network topology information through one or more tables. Any change in the network needs to be reflected in these tables by propagating the changes throughout the network. Examples of this class include DSDV, WRP.

Reactive routing protocols: Reactive protocols try to conserve the precious battery power of the nodes by discovering routes only when it is required. Only when there is a packet to be transferred, the route discovery protocol is initiated by the source and the route is found. Because of this nature, this class of routing protocols is also called as "Dynamic routing protocols". Examples of this class include DSR, AODV and ABR. Hybrid protocols make use of both reactive and proactive approaches. They typically offer means to switch dynamically between the reactive and proactive parts of the protocol. Examples of this class include TORA and ZRP.

MANET (Mobile Ad hoc Network) consists of a dynamic set of nodes with a network set up by them with no preexisting infrastructure. So this can easily results in some conditions including difference in radio transceiver capabilities of nodes, the use of transmission range control and difference in wireless channel interference experienced by different nodes. Depending on such conditions, unidirectional links can be quite common. But the majority of the on-demand routing protocols proposed for MANET like AODV [8], DSR [6], DSDV [9] etc, assume that all links between nodes are bidirectional. Several papers have been published answering the problems concerned with unidirectional links [1, 2, 3, 10]. In those papers there are mainly three techniques for handling unidirectional links in on-demand routing protocol: Blacklisting Hello and ReversePathSearch. Most of the protocols eliminate unidirectional links.

3. Unidirectional Links in Routing

3.1 Handling of Links

The Blacklisting technique reactively eliminates unidirectional links. Whenever a node detects a link failure, it inserts the next hop of the failed link into a "blacklist" set. Later when a node receives a RREQ from one of the nodes in its blacklist set, it discards the RREQ. So this technique just isolates the unidirectional links; it is simple and has little overhead when there are few unidirectional links. However, when many unidirectional links exist, this approach is inefficient because of iterative insertion into blacklist set. The Hello technique proactively eliminates unidirectional links by using periodic one-hop Hello packets. Each Hello packet sent by a node includes all nodes from which it can hear Hellos (i.e. its set of neighbors). If a node does not find itself in the Hello packet from another node, it marks that link as unidirectional. The advantage of this technique is that it automatically detects unidirectional links by exchanging Hello packets. But the periodic large Hello packets can be a significant overhead.

Unlike the above two techniques, ReversePathSearch technique does not explicitly remove unidirectional links. Instead, it takes a completely different approach. Each unidirectional link is viewed as a "fault" in the network and multiple paths between the nodes are discovered to perform fault tolerant routing. The basic idea is as follows. During the RREQ flood, multiple loop-free reverse paths to the source are formed at intermediate nodes and the destination. Using a distributed search procedure, multiple RREPs explore this multipath routing structure in an attempt to find one or more bidirectional paths between the source and the destination. This search procedure is somewhat similar to the well known depth first search algorithm. When RREP fails at a node, the corresponding reverse path is erased and the RREP is retried along an alternate reverse path, if one is available; when all reverse paths fail at a node during this process, the search backtracks to upstream nodes2 of that node with respect to the source and they too follow the same procedure. This continues until either one or more bidirectional paths are found at the source, or all reverse paths are explored.

3.2 Uni-directional Link Formation

Generally speaking, there are two principal reasons [1] behind the presence of unidirectional links in multihop wireless networks. First, difference in radio transmission power level (or receiver sensitivity) of the nodes give rise to unidirectional links. When two nodes (say A and B) have widely different radio transmission ranges so that node A can transmit to node B but not the other way, a unidirectional link forms from node A to node B. Nodes may naturally have different transmission ranges in a heterogeneous network where there is an inherent difference in radio capabilities. Alternatively, they may have different transmission ranges when power control algorithms are used for energy savings or topology control.

Second, difference in interference (or noise) at different nodes cause asymmetric links. Asymmetric links occur between a pair of nodes if the link quality is different in each direction. An extreme case of link asymmetry leads to unidirectional links. Nodes may experience different interference levels because of wireless channel imperfections such as multipath fading and shadowing. Hidden terminals can be another cause of wide variation in interference levels.

For Unidirectional links to be effective for routing, they should exist long enough for the routing protocol to compute routes through them and to later use such routes to forward some data. Depending on such conditions, unidirectional links can be quite common. Most of the previous work on this problem concentrated on developing routing protocols [1, 2], or techniques to allow the use of unidirectional links. But the resulting performance advantages and tradeoffs are not well understood. Utilizing unidirectional links along with bidirectional links for routing has two conceivable advantages over using only bidirectional links. First, they can improve the network connectivity. Second, they can provide better, i.e., shorter, paths. But routing using unidirectional links is complex and entails high overheads. Main difficulty comes from the asymmetric knowledge about a unidirectional link at its end nodes. A node downstream of a unidirectional link immediately knows about the incoming unidirectional link on hearing a transmission from the upstream node; but the upstream node may not know about its outgoing unidirectional link until the downstream node explicitly informs it over a multihop reverse path. Learning about the unidirectional link thus incurs higher overhead than when the link is bidirectional.

Routing protocols for ad hoc networks may deal with the possibility of unidirectional links in a number of ways [2]:

Some protocols, such as DSDV [7] or conventional distance vector routing protocols, simply do not consider the problem and thus may create routes that fail to work, causing packet losses.

Other protocols handle the presence of unidirectional links by treating all links as if they might be unidirectional; in order to avoid the problem above, but this causes extra routing overhead. Example DSR [6].

Still other protocols detect and keep track of unidirectional links as network conditions change, and then either use them for routing [9] or simply ignore them as in AODV when the likelihood that the routing protocol would encounter a unidirectional link is higher, since handling each unidirectional link requires additional mechanisms and control packet transmissions to either ignore or be able to use the link for routing.

4. Cluster Based Routing Protocol

CBRP has the following features:

Fully distributed operation.

- Less flooding traffic during the dynamic route discovery process.
- Explicit exploitation of uni-directional links that would otherwise be unused.
- Broken routes could be repaired locally without rediscovery.
- Sub-optimal routes could be shortened as they are used.

4.1 CBRP terminology [5, 10]

This section defines terms used in CBRP:

- Node ID: Node ID is a string that uniquely identifies a particular mobile node. Node IDs must be totally ordered. In CBRP, we use a node's IP address as its ID for purposes of routing and interoperability with fixed networks.
- Cluster: A cluster consists of a group of nodes with one of them elected as a cluster head. A cluster is identified by its Cluster Head ID. Clusters are either overlapping or disjoint. Each node in the network knows its corresponding Cluster Head(s) and therefore knows which cluster(s) it belongs to.
- Host Cluster: A node regards itself as in cluster X if it has a bi-directional link to the head of cluster X. In such a case, cluster X is a host cluster for this node. A node could have several host clusters.
- Cluster Head: A cluster head is elected in the cluster formation process for each cluster. Each cluster should have one and only one cluster head.

The cluster head has a bi-directional link to every node in the cluster.

A cluster head will have complete knowledge about group membership and link state information in the cluster within a bounded time once the topology within a cluster stabilizes. Conceptually, two cluster heads are not allowed to have a direct bi-directional link to each other. If such a link exists, one of the cluster head will relinquish its role as cluster head to the other.

However in CBRP, we do allow two cluster heads to be able to hear each other directly for CONTENTION_PERIOD seconds before one cluster head has to give up its cluster head status; this delay postpones any cluster re-organization, in case the two clusters are next to each other only in passing.

- Cluster Member
  All nodes within a cluster EXCEPT the cluster head are called members of this cluster.
- Gateway Node
  Any node a cluster head may use to communicate with an adjacent cluster is called a gateway node.
- HELLO message
  All nodes broadcast HELLO messages periodically every HELLO_INTERVAL seconds; a node's HELLO message contains its Neighbor Table and Cluster Adjacency Table. A node may sometimes broadcast a triggered HELLO message in response to some event that needs quick action.

4.2 Conceptual Data Structures

Neighbor Table

The neighbor table is a conceptual data structure that we employ for link status sensing and cluster formation. Each entry contains - the ID of the neighbor that it has connectivity with and - the role of the neighbor (a cluster head or a member).

- the status of that link (bi-directional or uni-directional)
- Cluster Adjacency Table

Cluster Adjacency Table
The Cluster Adjacency Table keeps information about adjacent clusters and is maintained by CBRP's Adjacent Cluster Discovery procedure.
Each entry contains:

- the ID of the neighboring cluster head
- the gateway node (a member) to reach the neighboring cluster head
- the status of the link from the gateway to the neighboring cluster head (bi-directional or uni-directional)

Two-Hop Topology Database
In CBRP, each node broadcasts its neighbor table information periodically in HELLO packets. Therefore, by examining the neighbor table from its neighbors, a node is able to gather 'complete' information about the network topology that is at most two-hops away from itself. This two-hop topology information is kept in a data structure in each node.

4.3 Cluster formation

The following states describe the clustering process depending on the current node state. These states are:
Undecided: This means the node does not belong to any cluster: this usually occurs if a new node appears in the network. Thus, if it receives a HELLO message from a cluster head and there is a bi-directional link between them it changes its state to be member of the cluster indicated by the cluster head. Otherwise it looks up in its neighbor table if it has any bi-directional links. If so, it becomes itself the cluster head of a new cluster, if not, it remains in the undecided state and tries again.
Cluster head: If a cluster head detects that it has a bi-directional link to another cluster head for a time period; it changes its state to member if the other cluster head has a lower ID. Otherwise it stays the cluster head and the other node has to change its state. This is a special case which may result in cluster re-organization (Fig. 1).
Member: If a member looses its cluster head, it looks for bi-directional links to other nodes. If it detects any, it changes its state to cluster head if it has the lowest ID, otherwise it switches to the undecided state. Each member node belongs at least to one cluster.

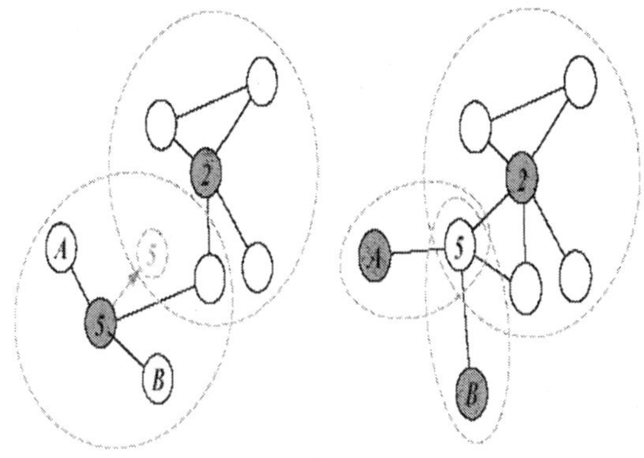

Fig. 1 When cluster head 5 moves into cluster 2 it gives up its role as cluster head according to its higher ID. Nodes A and B which lost their cluster head form new clusters. Striking for the goal to minimize cluster re-organization, the structure of the clusters should change as seldom as possible. This means "a non-cluster head never challenges the status of an existing cluster head", even if it has a lower ID.

4.4 Routing

CBRP uses two data structures to support the routing process: the cluster adjacency table (CAT) and the two-hop topology database.

The CAT stores information about neighboring clusters. This is, whether they are bi-directionally or uni-directionally linked. That means, a cluster is called

- bi-directionally linked, if there is a bi-directional link between two nodes of the clusters, or if there are at least two opposite uni-directional links between two nodes (Fig. 2)
- Uni-directionally linked, if there is just one uni-directional link between them (Fig. 2).

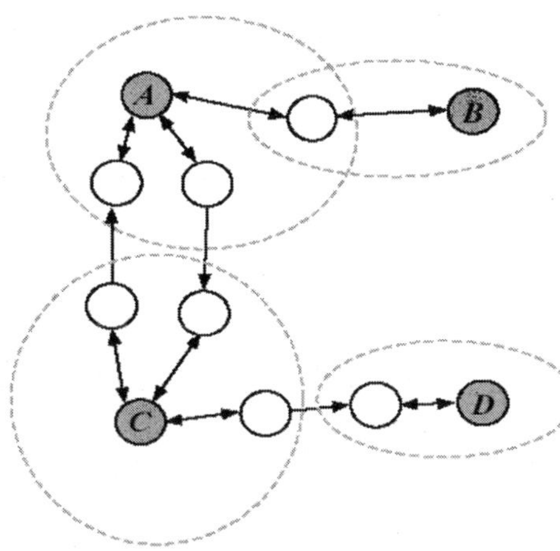

Fig. 2 Clusters A, B and A, C are bi-directionally linked, clusters C,D are uni-directionally linked

The two-hop topology database is build from the information received by HELLO messages. It contains all nodes that are at most two hops away. The routing process works in two steps. First, it discovers a route from a source node S to a destination node D, afterwards it routes the packets.

4.5 Route discovery

Route discovery is done by using source routing. In the CBRP only cluster heads are flooded with route request package (RREQ). Gateway nodes receive the RREQs as well, but without broadcasting them. They forward them to the next cluster head. This strategy reduces the network traffic.

4.6 Routing and route improvement

Due to node movement, (dis-)appearance of nodes or failures, the CBRP includes two mechanisms to improve a route: The first is Local Repair and the second is Route Shortening.

Local repair
If a connection between two node fails, the CBRP is able to repair the route. Therefore one of the following nodes of the route has to be in the two-hop topology database of the node that discovered the broken link (Fig. 4). If the node is unable to repair the route, the route has to be recalculated.

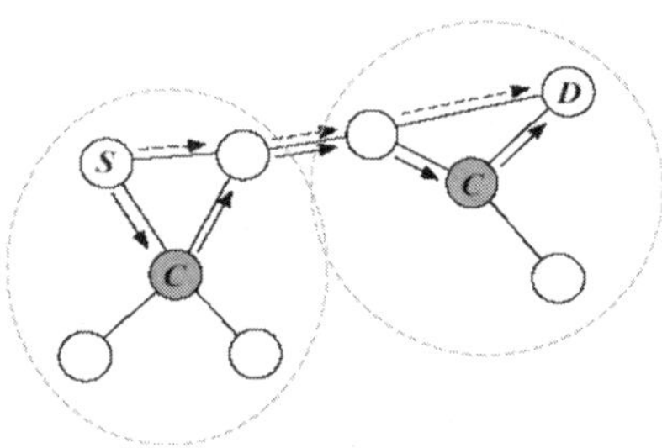

Fig. 3 The loose source route (non-dashed arrows) and the strict source route (dashed arrows) from S to D

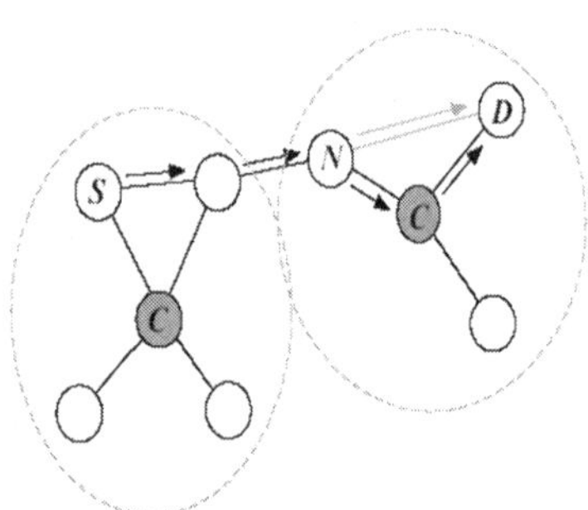

Fig. 4 The broken route between N and D (gray arrow) was repaired by using the cluster head

4.7 Route Shortening

Sometimes a node may discover a connection between itself and another succeeding node of the route that is not its direct successor or a connection between two following nodes, respectively. This can be done by examining the information stored in the two-hop topology database. If so, it shortens the route by excluding the redundant node(s) from the route (Fig. 5).

In both cases, Local Repair and Route Shortening, the destination node is informed about the changes by receiving a gratuitous route reply packet from the node that performed the changes.

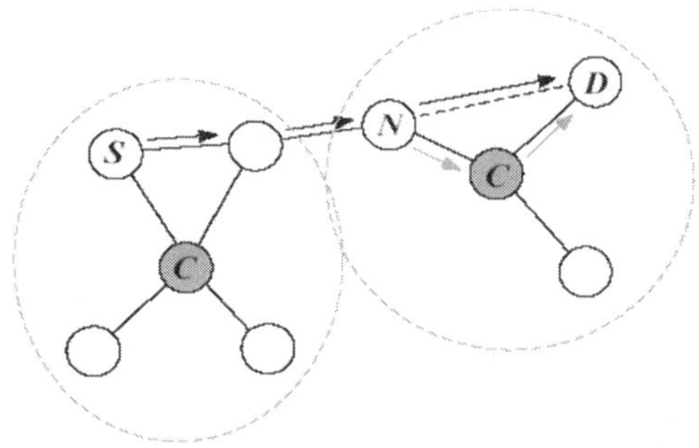

Fig. 5 Node N discovered a new connection between itself and D (dashed line) and shortened the route

5. Proposed Methodology

The proposed scheme is based on enhancing the cluster based routing protocol by utilizing selective unidirectional links for routing. This will minimize the overhead which results due to use of every unidirectional link in the network and increase reachability of nodes and connectivity of network.

The objectives are:

- Implement and evaluate the use of unidirectional links in CBRP using the cooperative neighbor technique.
- To verify optimal route (dynamic) discovery.

In Cluster Based Routing protocol (CBRP), the nodes are divided into clusters. To form the cluster the following algorithm will be used.

When a node comes up, it enters the "undecided" state, starts a timer and broadcasts a Hello message. When a cluster-head gets this hello message it responds with a triggered hello message immediately.

When the undecided node gets this message it sets its state to "member".

If the undecided node times out, then it makes itself the cluster-head of a new cluster if it has bi-directional link to some neighbor and all the nodes with bidirectional links become the cluster member.

Otherwise it remains in undecided state and repeats the procedure again.

Cluster heads are changed as infrequently as possible. A cluster-head will keep information about the members of its cluster and also maintain a cluster adjacency table that contains information about the neighboring clusters.

Each node maintains a neighbor table. For each neighbor, the neighbor table of a node contains the neighbor nodes Node ID, status of the link (uni- or bi-directional) and the state of the neighbor (cluster-head or member). To reduce the complexity unidirectional links will be considered only in inter cluster communication. This table will help to use unidirectional links in route formation.

In proposed scheme, routing will be done using source routing. It will also use route shortening. If a node detects a broken link it will use local repair and route recovery mechanism.

6. References

[1] Zhen-zhong Wang, Jian-de Lu and Jia-Jia Tang "Neighbor Monitoring Mechanism to Solve Unidirectional Link Problem in Manet" Proceedings of IEEE Third International Conference on Wireless and Mobile Communications (ICWMC'07) 2007

[2] Jorjeta G. Jetcheva and David B. Johnson. "Routing characteristics of ad hoc networks with unidirectional links". Ad Hoc Net-works, 4:303-325, 2006.

[3] Mahesh K. Marina and Samir R. Das "Routing Performance in the Presence of Unidirectional Links in Multihop Wireless Networks" MOBIHOC'02, June 911, 2002, EPFL Lausanne, Switzerland. ACM.

[4] B.Kadri, A.M'hamed, M.Feham "Secured Clustering Algorithm for Mobile Ad-hoc Networks". IJCSNS International Journal of Computer Science and Network Security, VOL. 7 No. 3, March 2007.

[5] Tim Daniel Hollerung, "The Cluster Based Routing Protocol", Mobile Adhoc Networks Based on wireless Lan project group, 2004.

[6] B. Johnson, D.A. Maltz, Y.-C. Hu, "The Dynamic Source Routing Protocol for Mobile Ad Hoc Networks", Internet-Draft, draft-ietf-manet-dsr-10.txt, July 2004,

[7] C.E. Perkins, P. Bhagwat, "Highly dynamic destination sequenced distance-vector routing (DSDV) for mobile computers", in: Proceedings of the SIGCOMM _94 Conference on Communications Architectures, Protocols and Applications, August 1994, pp. 234–244.

[8] C.E. Perkins, E.M. Royer, S.R. Das, Ad Hoc On-Demand Distance Vector (AODV) Routing, RFC 3561, July 2003.

[9] V. Ramasubramanian, R. Chandra, D. Mosse, Providing a bidirectional abstraction for unidirectional ad hoc networks, in: Proceedings of IEEE Infocom, June 2002.

[10] Mingliang Jiang, Jinyang Li, Y.C. Tay, "Cluster Based Routing Protocol" August 1999 IETF Draft, 27 pages.

Amendments and Confrontations in the Management of Resources for Mobile Grid Computing

Aditya Vidyart[1] and Divya Bhatnagar[2]
[1]Reader CSE IITM (ITM Universe) Gwalior
[2]Reader MCA MPCT Gwalior
rashi_vid@yahoo.co.in divyabbb@yahoo.co.in

Abstract

This paper provides a discussion on the Mobile Grid concept, the amendments that this implies in the Grid technology and the confrontations that have to be met in order to address the new computing paradigm, mainly focused on the aspect of resource management, which is the heart of every Grid functionality. Grid computing has recently migrated from traditional high performance and distributed computing to pervasive and utility computing based on the advanced capabilities of the wireless networks and the lightweight, thin devices. This has as result the emergence of a new computing paradigm which is the Mobile Grid.

1. Introduction

One of the most important things for understanding and grasping *Mobile Grid computing* is to have a unfailing and exact definition, or at least fortitude of what a Mobile Grid is. There are many attempts for the accurate definition of the Grid. How- ever the various approaches that have been made address in a high degree of accuracy the term Grid. The Grid can be viewed as a distributed, high performance computing and data handling infrastructure, that incorporates geographically and organization- ally dispersed, heterogeneous resources (computing systems, storage systems, instruments and other real-time data sources, human collaborators, communication systems) and provides common interfaces for all these resources, using standard, open, general-purpose protocols and interfaces [1]. However, it is also the basis and the enabling technology for pervasive and utility computing due to the ability of being open, highly heterogeneous and scalable.

The Mobile Computing is a general term relating the application of small, transferable, and wireless computing and communication devices. The devices includes Lap- tops with Wireless Local Area Networks technology, mobile phones, and Personal Digital Assistants (PDAs) with Bluetooth or Infrared Data Association (IrDA) inter- faces.

The Mobile Computing centers on the prerequisite of providing access to information, communications and services everywhere, anytime and by any available means. The technical clarification for achieving this are not always easy to implement.

In fact, mobile computing requires the creation of communication infrastructures and the modification of computer networks, operating systems, and application programs [2]. The mobility issue implies some constraints that must be addressed since they limit the capability of a moving resource in contrast to a fixed one.

Mobile Grid, in relevance to both Grid and Mobile Computing, is a full *inheritor* of Grid with the additional feature of supporting *mobile users* and *resources* in a *seamless*, *transparent*, *secure* and *efficient* way. It has the ability to deploy underlying ad-hoc networks and provide a self-configuring Grid system of mobile resources (*hosts and users*) connected by wireless links and forming arbitrary and unpredictable topologies.

2. Mobile Grid as a prerequisite

Grid is already being productively used in many scientific applications where huge amounts of data have to be processed and/or stored. Such tough applications have created, justified and diffused the concept of Grid among the scientific community. As the amount of potential Grid users is really enormous, the accumulated data processing and storage requirements are at least comparable. Wireless devices (lap- tops and PDAs), with currently limited resources (low processing power, finite battery life and constrained storage space), would benefit from the opportunity of using a considerable amount of resources made available by all the other devices connected to the network [3]. In particular, mobile users might be the future users of this new technology. Moreover, we have nomadic users who travel and work only seldom at their offices [2]. Mobile Grid enables both the mobility of the users requesting access to a fixed Grid and the resources that are themselves part of the Grid. Both cases have their own limitations and constraints that should be handled [5]. In the first case the devices of the mobile users act as interfaces to the Grid enabling job submission, monitoring and management of the activities in an 'anytime, anywhere' mode, while the Grid pro- vides them with a high reliability, performance and cost-efficiency. Physical limitations of the mobile devices make necessary the adaptation of the services that Grid can provide to the users' mobile devices.

In the second case of having mobile Grid re- sources, we should underline that the performances of current mobile devices are significantly increased. Laptops and PDAs can provide aggregated computational capability when gathered in hotspots, forming a Grid on site. This capability can ad- vantage the usage of Grid applications even in places where this would be imaginary. However, there will always be the question on why a Grid solution should be adopted in comparison to any other non-Grid Information Technology (IT) solution. Grid is not intended to be the 'panacea' to the problems related to IT domain. It is a promising emerging technology that has the ambition to provide more efficient and beneficial solution than its 'competitors' by enabling the simple 'connect and share' approach in the same manner as the current Internet search engines apply the 'connect and acquire information' concept. By this, Grids and mobile Grids can be the ideal solution for many large scale applications that are of active nature and require transparency for users. Grid will increase the job throughput and performance of the involved applications and will increase utilization rate of resources by applying efficient mechanisms for resource management in the vast amount of its resources. It will enable advanced forms of cooperative work by allowing the seamless integration of resources, data, services and ontologies.

3. Definition of mobile Grid

It is a stage that should speak to the mobility problem by means of permitting both fixed and mobile users to have access to both fixed and mobile Grid resources utilizing transparently and efficiently the underlying technologies. Mobility involves a set of issues for both users and communication/collaboration mode that will be presented shortly in the follow-up. Roaming users move around between different terminals and ask session movement (*user mobility*). For example, a user can open a session on a workstation at his office and then ask its movement to a personal computer at home. Roaming users, instead, moving around with their own wireless devices, want to continue their sessions when they cross different localities, as it happens today in cell phones telecommunications (*terminal mobility*). In both cases the middleware should hide the details of the active utilization of service components, when the session movement is required, besides it should manage all the session hand-off transparently to the user and possibly to the application components. One more kind of mobility is the *service mobility* which is meant as the ability of the infrastructure to maintain the services for a user while he is mobile. These services should be independent from the devices and from the location of the user with respect to the network he is accessing. [9] Another aspect of mobility that should be considered is the distinction between wireless networking and mobile user interfaces. In wireless networking the problem relies in the fact that the connection is highly variable both in quality and in price, and moreover that disconnections happen unexpectedly, thus constituting synchronous interaction uncertain. In case of mobile user interfaces the confrontation come from the restrictions imposed by the small device size. Small displays can only present limited amount of information, while absence of keyboard makes data entry hard [5].

It should be observed that mobility stresses the fact of the synchronous mode of communication. In a collaboration environment the most challenging aspect is to en- able a synchronous mode of co-operation between the peer entities. While asynchronous mode is easier to be implemented in unreliable and complex environments, the synchronous mode introduces a set of constraints that are by nature difficult to handle. The shared objects are no more workspaces and databases where many users act on, but moreover mechanisms have to be applied for enabling shared applications and concurrent schemes for the session handling.

4. What will get altered?

The mobile Grid will introduce amendments to the general Grid concept. New functionalities of the Grid will be required since the old ones will not make use of all the capabilities that will be available. These functionalities will involve end-to-end solutions with emphasis on Quality of Service (QoS) and security, as well as interoperability issues between the diverse technologies involved. Enhanced security policies and approaches to address large scale and heterogeneous environments will be needed. Additionally, the volatile, mobile and poor networked environments have to be ad- dressed with adaptable

QoS aspects which have to be contextualized with respect to users and their profiles.

Mobile Grids will make use of the value that many mobile users perceive due to the advanced capabilities of their mobile devices. These advanced capabilities refer to the comparison of today's mobile devices with the ones that existed in the past. Although mobile devices are subject to physical constraints due to their nature they have the ability of having computational and storage capabilities similar to PCs, high quality displays, multiple interfaces (for instance Bluetooth, Ethernet adapters, USB, Infrared) etc. This value can be converted into revenue for service providers.

This implies amendments in various business models and policy issues. Complex workflows for businesses will be needed and Virtual Organizations (VO) will be enriched with the opportunity for automatic federations and resource sharing schemes. Valuations of the diverse services and especially with respect to the Service/Sharing level agreement have to be adapted in relation to QoS aspects. Enterprises have to issue policies that will handle the conflict between public rights to their users and viable models for operation.

Moreover the fair use of Grid must be determined by reconciling rights of public access to resources and private ownership of infrastructure and resources.

In the continuation we present a short discussion on some of the most important confrontations of Mobile Grids with respect to the resource management topic. Of course many things will alter and raise their own confrontations to be addressed in this new context. Our study will focus in resource management topic which is a very critical subject for the efficient utilization of the Grid infrastructure functional entities.

5. Confrontations of Resource Management in Mobile Grids

5.1 Resource Unearthing and Choosing

The unstable and active environment of the mobile Grid makes necessary the use of hi-tech mechanisms for resource discovery and selection. The inventory of the authorized machines and resources that are available in the Grid infrastructure is continuously updated. The selection of those resources that are expected to meet the time or cost constraints imposed by the user has to be based not only on deterministic criteria but also on stochastic parameters, thus providing complex probabilistic models for the topology of the Grids and their capabilities. Some of the required parameters are resource accessibility, system workload, network performance, etc. Not to forget that the target audience of the mobile Grids is the broad spectrum of the citizens who would like to use the Grid for solving problems of their everyday life. Thus, a financial criterion of the resources used should be under consideration for the proper resource selection.

5.2 Scheduling of Jobs

Scheduling of Jobs is classified as an NP-complete problem [6] [7] due to the fact that an algorithm has to be applied that would allocate jobs to resources in an efficient and cost effective manner, so as to minimize the resource utilization gaining the maximum profit and satisfying at the same time the user constraints (Security, Quality of Service, Fault tolerance etc). In a mobile Grid environment there are many more constraints that would make the job scheduling problem more complicated. The cost of resources is in that case a metric that is subject to context parameters. Imagine what can happen in a big conference room where the aggregated performance due to the many notebooks linked in wireless hotspots can result in a very cost effective solution for "instant" high performance computing. So the optimization criteria for a job scheduling mechanism should take under consideration not only the cost and the performance of each resource, but also the current availability of resources in the context and their reliability in providing the specific resources for the execution of the job under the given QoS constraints.

5.3 Replication of job, Migration and its Monitoring

After agreeing to the earlier Job Scheduling problem, we claim that the mobile grid is an active system where environmental conditions are subject to unpredictable amendments: system or network failures, system performance degradation, addition of new machines, variations in the cost of resources, etc. In such context job migration and re-scheduling, as well as job replication and co-scheduling are both (from different perspectives) efficient ways to guarantee the completion of the jobs according to the restrictions set by the users. Job monitoring and check pointing (especially in the case of long running tasks) is difficult in active environments. Especially job monitoring is responsible for detecting alert situations that could initiate a migration and alternatively identify if a job has been completed so as to suspend/stop/cancel the execution of the other replicas.

5.4 Management of Replica for huge Data Sets

Replica management is an important issue for a number of applications that utilize huge data sets (like for instance experimental results for scientific applications, for simulations and prediction models) [8]. The complete data set of a VO may exist in one or possibly several physical locations but it is possible that no single organization has sufficient storage to hold a complete copy. Instead, the common practice is to have copies of the most relevant portions of the data set stored on local storage for faster access. Replica Management keeps track of where portions of the data set can be found by providing mappings between logical names for files and one or more copies of the files on physical storage systems. This mapping is of particular interest in mobile environments, since access to specific physical locations might be impossible. Storage devices are constantly changing their connection status and sometimes their physical location, thus imposing different schemes for accessing their data, which includes context aware information. Moreover, mobile Grids have to address the issue of not only locating a Data Base containing the relative data, but also if this location is the most suitable and reliable (with respect to avoiding a failure) to be used.

6. Conclusions

In this paper we presented a discussion on Mobile Grid definition, the basic motivation and benefits that can branch from this new technology, especially as far as it concerns collaborative engineering, industry and the everyday life of the "mobile" citizen. In the sequel it presents a set of major technical topics that influence the traditionally basic Grid Infrastructure services under the new Grid environment involving Mobile Grids. This topic indicates the necessity for research in these domains so as to enable the implementation of the new Mobile Grid environment. Moreover, the paper presented existing work and projects on worldwide level which are promising for the elaboration of thorough study in the domain. As the Grid computing seems to gain more space in the technology areas, it will be the basis for utility and pervasive computing in the forthcoming years by leveraging the mobility advantage that it will be enhanced with. The future work in this area will investigate not only issues concerning the interoperability but mainly with respect to the efficiency of mobile Grid solutions so as to enable the deployment in commercial and everyday life applications.

7. References

[1] Foster, "What is the Grid? A Three Point Checklist", GRID Today, July 20, 2002

[2] S. Gai, "Internetworking IPv6 with Cisco Routers", avail. at http://www.ip6.com

[3] D. Bruneo, M. Scarpa, A. Zaia, A. Puliafito, "Communication Paradigms for Mobile Grid Users", 3rd International Symposium on Cluster Computing and the Grid May 2003, Tokyo, Japan

[4] M. Graf, "Grid collaboration in the mobile environment." IBM. Speech at the Collaboration@work Workshop on June 25th 2003.

[5] S.-M. Park, Y.-B. Ko, and J.-H. Kim, "Disconnected Operation Service in Mobile Grid Computing," International Conference on Service Oriented Computing(ICSOC'2003), Trento, Italy, Dec 2003

[6] R. Moreno, "Job scheduling and Resource Management Techniques in Dynamic Grid Environments" 1st European Across Grids Conference, February 2003, Spain

[7] A. Abraham, R. Buyya, B. Nath, "Nature's Heuristics for Scheduling Jobs on Computational Grids", International Conference on Advanced Computing and Communications.

A Summary of Current Approaches and Future Challenges in IP Over WDM

Amitangshu Pal
Department of Computer Science and Engineering, Jadavpur University, Kolkata 700032, India
amitangshupal@yahoo.co.in

Abstract

One of the prime interests for the next generation Optical Networks is IP over WDM. Fast, accurate and efficient means for restoration are the central importance while designing IP over WDM technologies. I have first reviewed the different IP/WDM networking architecture models and their tradeoffs. Next I have presented an overview of the schemes proposed by different scholars for the improvement of fault and performance management of IP over dynamic WDM networks. I have also outlined the future research directions and challenges for improving IP over WDM technologies.
Keywords: IP over WDM, p-cycle, Deflection Routing, Sink Tree, Overlay Model, Augmented Model, Peer Model, Survivability, Link Utilization.

1. Introduction

The arrival of broadband communications has increased the necessity of high speed signals and services. Optical Wavelength division multiplexing (WDM) promises increased bandwidth based on SONET or Gigabit Ethernet. But the next generation Internet will be an Internet Protocol(IP) based on WDM network which combines gigabit and terabit IP routers with WDM switching and transmission systems so that an optimized transport network can be created. The two basic requirements for this two-layered model are: 1) dynamic bandwidth provisioning and 2) survivability against link failures.

Survivability techniques in IP over WDM networks can be classified as: survivability at the WDM layer, survivability at the IP layer, and survivability at both layers. In the WDM based approach, recovery from a failure is performed only at the bottom layer (e.g., recovering failed lightpaths in an optical transport network). This scheme has some advantages because it is simple and provides fast recovery of aggregate traffic. However, the major drawback of this scheme is that it cannot recover from failures that occur at the IP layer, such as, the failure of an IP router or its interfaces. In the survivability at the IP based scheme, failure recovery is performed only at the top layer, (e.g., recovering failed label switched paths (LSPs) in a MPLS network using fast reroute). The advantage of this scheme is that it can recover from failures that occur in both layers. The major drawbacks of this approach are its complexity and slower speed of fault recovery. So it is not obvious which layered approach is the best; each has pro and cons. Thus it is necessary to consider restoration techniques at both WDM and IP layers.

The paper is organized as follows. In section II I have discussed the three different IP over WDM network models. In section III different proposals to improve IP over WDM techniques have been discussed. Section IV states the summary of all proposals. I have concluded this paper in section V where I have also discussed the future challenges and directions to improve IP over WDM technology.

2. Different IP over WDM Models

IP and WDM layers can be combined in several different models such as Overlay Model, Augmented Model, Peer Model etc.

Overlay Model: In overlay model IP and WDM layers relate to each other in a client-server relationship. Here IP is the client layer and WDM is the server layer. The IP layer links are realized by the corresponding WDM layer connections. There are separate control and management protocols between two layers. They interact with each other by User Network Interface (UNI). The overlay Model is shown in Fig. 1.

Augmented Model:- In Augmented Model IP and WDM layers have a single addressing plane and separate routing instances. Control information is passed from one instance to another. A single signaling protocol can be used to control both IP and WDM. Border Gateway Protocol (BGP) is used to interact between two routing instances. The model is depicted in Fig. 2.

Peer Model:- In Peer Model IP and WDM network relates to each other in a peer-to-peer relationship. In this model IP routers and Optical Cross Connects belong to a single routing instance. They interact with each other using IGP with WDM extension. Peer Model is shown in Fig. 3.

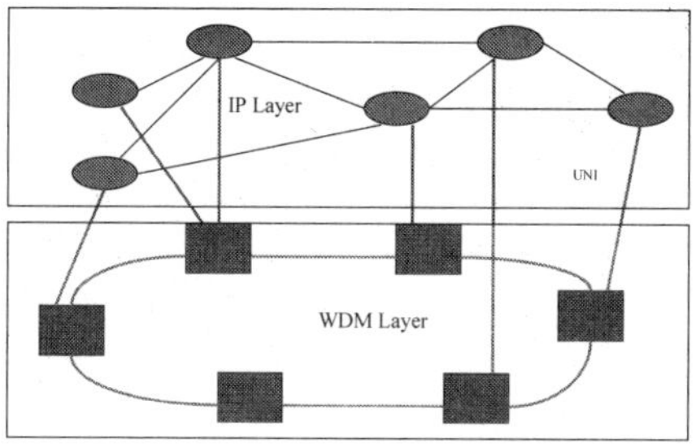

Fig. 1 Overlay IP over WDM Network Model

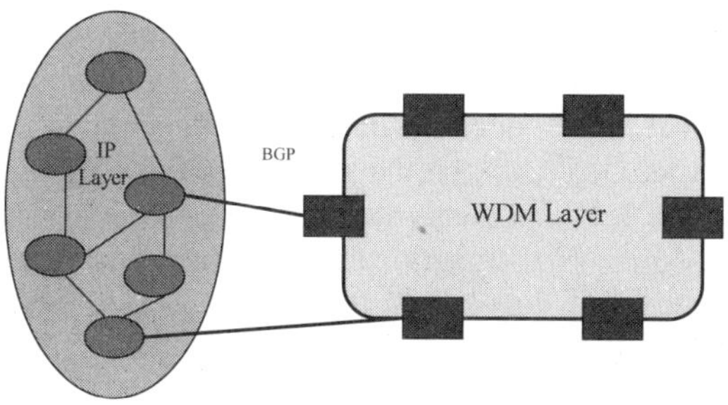

Fig. 2 Augmented IP over WDM Network Model

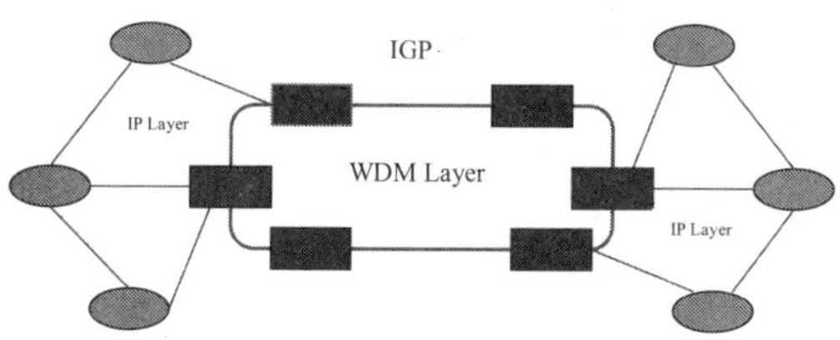

Fig. 3 Peer IP over WDM Network Model

3. Different Proposals for Network Management and Control Issues

Conventional network management discipline divides the management and control issues into five categories: fault, configuration, accounting, performance and security. In this section we will discuss different proposals put forward by the research community in the areas of IP/WDM network fault and performance management and control and critique their contributions.

Research on IP over WDM can be classified into two broad categories.

IP over reconfigurable WDM network: These approaches use the WDM layer's reconfigurability to change the IP network's virtual topology to better match the traffic demand. As representative proposals in this category I have examined the work in [1], [2] in greater detail.

IP over non reconfigurable WDM network: In this category of proposals, researchers proposed survivability scheme over WDM architecture which is non reconfigurable. Some of the proposals [3], [4], [5], [6], [7], [8] in this category are described below.

A classification of various schemes is shown in Fig. 4.

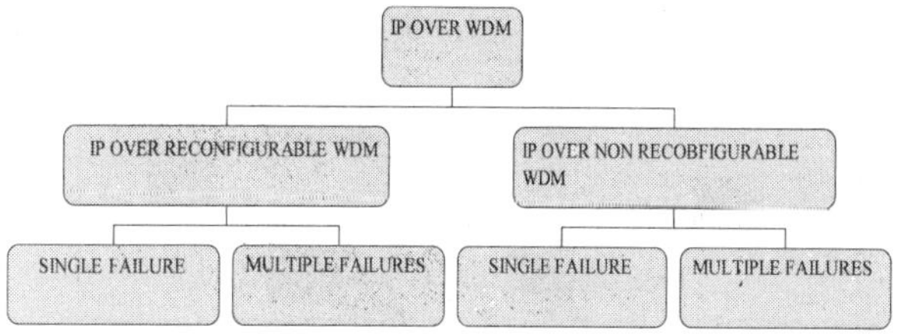

Fig. 4. Classification of various proposals for IP/WDM

IP over reconfigurable WDM network

Traffic engineering framework for reconfigurable IP/WDM networks: - In [1] the author present an innovative integrated approach for reconfigurable IP/WDM networks. Initially at low loads only shortest-cost path is used for each source to destination. As traffic load increases between a pair of router the proposed algorithm can reroute *label switched paths* (LSP) between the router pair on less loaded alternate routes. The alternate route selection process works by computing the shortest-cost-path on an auxiliary graph formed by deleting heavily loaded links of the topology. The maximum traffic that can be supported between a node pair is limited by min-cut-capacity of the IP topology. As the traffic between a router pair increases the min-cut-capacity will be saturated and no alternate paths between the router pair can be found. So the cut edges between the router pair are now all saturated with traffic and the only solution at that point is to expand the capacity of the min-cut via topology reconfiguration.

As an example consider the topology and traffic shown in Fig. 5 where the capacity of each link is 1 unit. Now under this loading no additional traffic between routers R0 and R1 can be accommodated as the remaining capacity if the R0-R1 is zero. Fig. 5(b) is the auxiliary graph obtained by removing the links loaded with 1. In this topology there is no path between R0 and R1and so no increase in traffic between routers R0 and R1 can be supported. So the reconfigurable optical layer can be used to expand min-cut capacity between the router-pair.

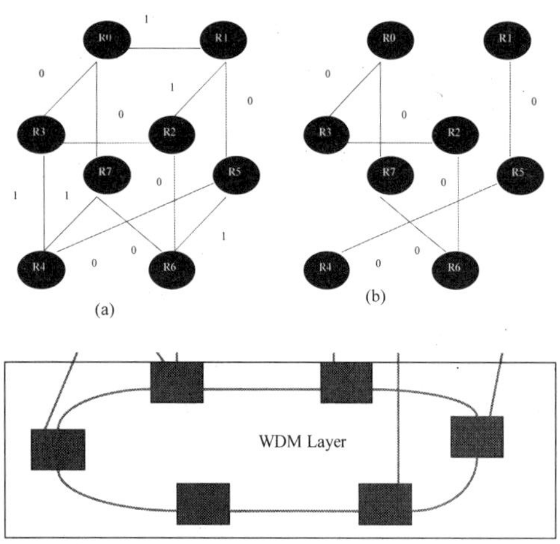

Fig. 5 Illustrative example showing network congestion and capacity exhaustion [1].

Fig. 6 shows three different topologies obtained after reconfiguration where the min-cut capacity between R0-R1 has been increased. Here additional unit of spare capacity between R0 and R1 has been created without affecting the existing traffic flow pattern. Now these three reconfigured topologies can accommodate additional unit of traffic loading between R0-R1.

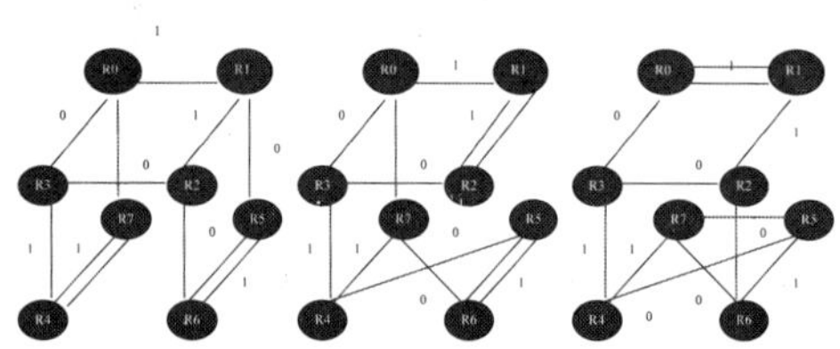

Fig. 6 Reconfigured network topologies [1]

Checking the Survivability and Piecewise Survivability by SMART algorithm: - According to [2] failure restoration at the IP layer in IP-over-WDM networks requires to map the IP topology on the WDM topology in such a way that a failure at the WDM layer leaves the IP topology connected. Such a mapping is called survivable. The authors have proposed an algorithm called SMART algorithm which searches for a survivable mapping. They have described some definitions before describing the SMART algorithm.

Contraction: Contracting an edge e€ E of a graph G = (V,E) can be obtained by deleting that edge and merging its end–nodes into a single node and is denoted by $G^C = G\downarrow e$. We can also contract a set of edges $A \subset E$, which results a contracted graph $G^C = G\downarrow A$, obtained by successively contracting the graph G on every edge of A.

Origin: Let $G^C = G \downarrow A$. G^C_{sub} is a subgraph and $G^C_{sub} \subseteq G^C$. Now $G_{sub} = \text{Origin}(G^C_{sub})$, if G_{sub} is the maximal subgraph of G that was transformed into G^C_{sub} by the contraction of A in G. For example, we can say that in Fig. 7, the vertex z€ G was transformed into the vertex u^C € G^C, however $z \neq \text{Origin}(u^C)$ because it is not the only element that was transformed into u^C by contraction. The maximal subgraph in this case is $(\{y, z\}, g) = \text{Origin}(u^C)$.

Survivability: Let $G^L = (V,E^L)$, $A \subset E^L$ and $G^C = (V^C,E^C) = G^L \downarrow A$. Take any connected subgraph $G^C_{sub} = (V^C_{sub}, B)$ of the contracted topology G^C, and let M_B be a mapping of the set B of logical links. The pair $[G^C_{sub}, M_B]$ is survivable if the failure of any single physical link $e^{\varnothing}$ does not disconnect the graph $G^C_{sub.}$ In Fig 8 let $G^L_{\{a^L,b^L,c^L\}}$ be the subgraph of G^L defined by edges a^L, b^L, c^L and their end vertices. The pair $[G^L_{\{a^L,b^L,c^L\}}, M_1]$ is survivable, because the failure of any physical link does not disconnect $G^L_{\{a^L,b^L,c^L\}}$. Similarly the pair $[G^L_{\{f^L,g^L,h^L\}}, M_1]$ is also survivable.

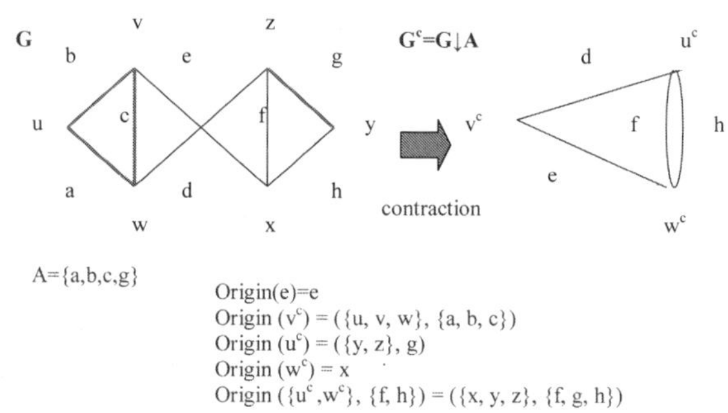

Fig. 7 Contraction of a graph *G* on a set of edges *A = {a, b, c, g}*. The origins of some elements are also shown (bottom) [2]

Piecewise Survivability: Let M_A be a mapping of a set A € E^L on the physical topology. The pair $[G^L,M_A]$ is piecewise survivable if, for every vertex v^C of the contracted logical topology $G^L \downarrow A$, the pair $[\text{Origin}(v^C),M_A]$ is survivable. In Fig 8 the pair $[G^L, M_1]$ is piecewise survivable because for vertices u^C and v^C of $G\downarrow A$, the pairs $[\text{Origin}(u^C), M_1] = [G^L_{\{a^L,b^L,c^L\}}, M_1]$ and $[\text{Origin}(v^C), M_1] = [G^L_{\{f^L,g^L,h^L\}}, M_1]$ are survivable.

The authors have presented a SMART algorithm which maps the topology part by part, gradually converging to a final solution. If SMART converges cimpletely then a survivable mapping is found, otherwise when the algorithm terminates before its complete convergence, the returned mapping is piecewise survivable and no survivable solution exists. The pseudo-code of SMART is as follows:

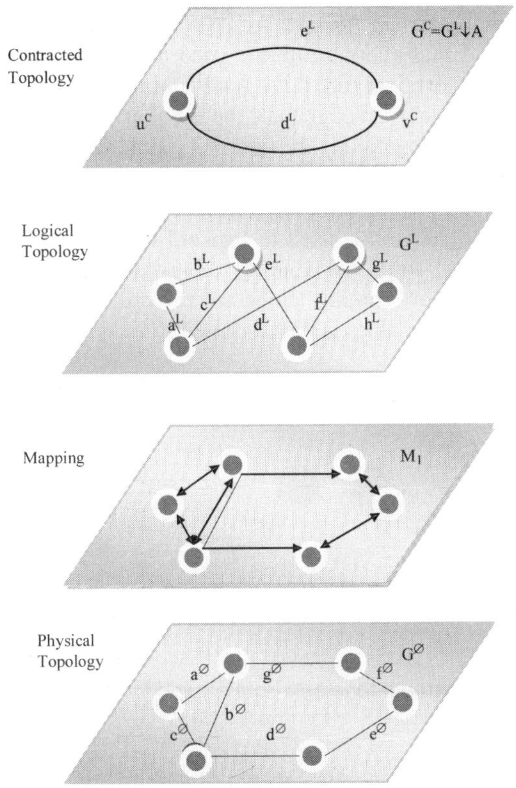

Fig. 8 Mapping of the set A={ a^L, b^L, c^L, f^L, g^L, h^L } [2]

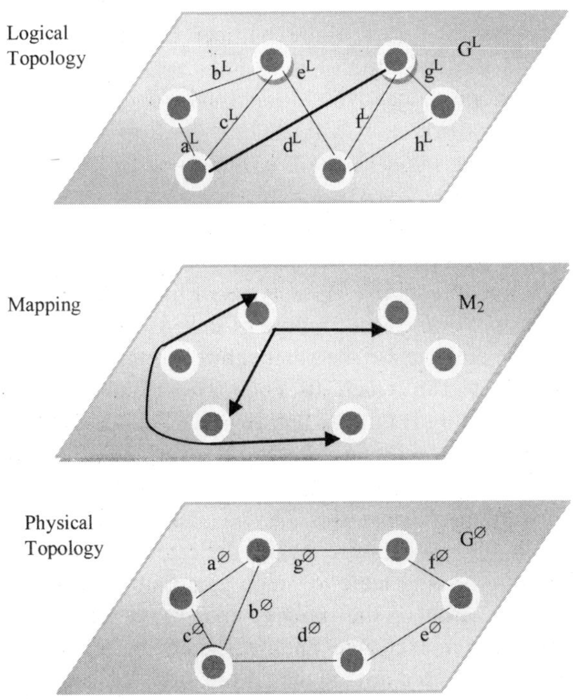

Fig. 9 Mapping of the set B={ d^L, e^L } [2]

Step 1: Begin from the full logical topology $G^C=G^L$, and an empty mapping $M_A=\emptyset$, $A=\emptyset$.
Step 2: Take some subgraph $G^C_{sub}=(V^C_{sub}, B)$ of G^C and find a mapping M_B, such that the pair $[G^C_{sub}, M_B]$ is survivable. If no such pair exists, then return M_A AND $G^C=G^L\downarrow A$, END.
Step 3: Update the mapping by merging M_A and M_B, i.e. $M_A:=M_A\cup M_B$.
Step 4: Contract G^C on B, i.e.$G^C:=G^C\downarrow B$.
Step 5: If G^C is a single node, Then return M_A, END.
Step 6: Goto Step 2.

I am illustrating the SMART algorithm by Fig 8, 9, 10. The algorithm starts with $G^C=G^L$ and $M_A=\emptyset$. Now in the first iteration for subgraph $G^L_{\{a^L,b^L,c^L\}}$ and $G^L_{\{f^L,g^L,h^L\}}$ the pairs $[G^L_{\{a^L,b^L,c^L\}}, M_1]$ and $[G^L_{\{f^L,g^L,h^L\}}, M_1]$ are survivable. So $M_A=M_1$(Step 3) and $G^C=\{u^C, v^C\}$(Step 4). In the next iteration $G^C_{sub}=G^C$ which consists of two logical links d^L and e^L. Now the pair $[G^C, M_2]$ is survivable because a single physical link failure cannot bring down both d^L and e^L at the same time, hence G^C remains connected. So $M_A=M_1\cup M_2$(Step3) and G^C is a single node and the algorithm converges and gives the survivable mapping $M_A=M_3$(Fig. 10) of the entire logical topology.

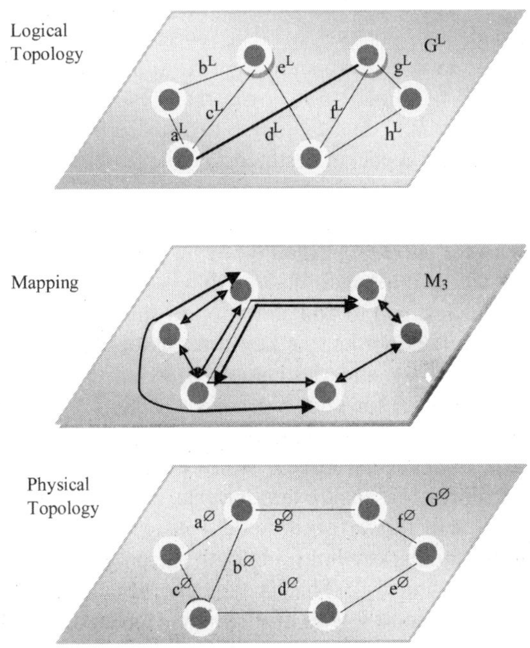

Fig. 10 Mapping of the set A∪B={ a^L, b^L, c^L, d^L, e^L, f^L, g^L, h^L } [2]

If the mapping is not survivable (i.e. piecewise survivable) then an additional logical or physical link can be introduced to repair the vulnerable areas of the network to enable a survivable mapping.

IP over non reconfigurable WDM network

Failure Insensitive Routing (FIR):- In [3] the authors present an algorithm called Failure Insensitive Routing (FIR) to compute interface-specific forwarding and backwarding tables for handling single suppressed link failures. Under FIR, when a link fails, adjacent node initiates local rerouting of packets, using the backwarding table, that were to be forwarded through the failed link. Though other nodes are not explicitly notified of the failure, they infer it from packet's flight. When a packet arrives at a node through an unusual interface (through which it would never arrive had there been no failure), the potentially failed links, referred to as key link, can be inferred and an appropriate next hop is used to avoid the failed links. For routing interface specific forwarding tables can be precornputed since inferences about key links can be made in advance. Thus under FIR, when a link fails, only nodes adjacent to it locally reroute packets to the affected destinations and all other nodes simply forward packets according to their precomputed interface specific forwarding tables without being explicitly aware of the failure. Once the failed link comes up again, forwarding resumes over the recovered link as if nothing ever happened.

For example consider Fig. 11 where each link is labeled with its weight. The corresponding routing table at node 1 is shown in Fig. 11. Suppose link 2-5 is down. When link 2-5 is down, node 2 locally reroutes packets from node 1 to node 6 to 1 instead of dropping them. When a packet destined to node 6 arrives at node 1 from node 2, node 1 can infer that some link along its shortest path to node 6 must have failed, as otherwise node 2 should never forward packets destined to node 6 to node 1. Node 2 would forward packets destined to node 6 to node 1 only if the link 2-5 or 5-6 is down i.e. the key links associated with the interface 2→1 and destination 6 are {2-5, 5-6}. So when a packet for node 6 arrives at node 1 from node 2, node 1 can infer that one or both of these links are down, in spite that node 1 is not explicitly notified of the failures. To ensure that the packet reaches node 6, node 1 will forward it to node 4 instead, avoiding the corresponding key links, i.e. both the potentially failed links 2-5 and 5-6. That is why in Fig. 11, a packet arriving at node 1 with destination 6 through neighbor node 2 is forwarded to node 4 while it is forwarded to node 2 if it arrives through the other two neighbors. Such interface specific routing makes it possible to perform local rerouting without explicit failure notification.

Improving Service Availability during link failure Transients through Alternate Routing: In [4] the authors proposed a simple alternate/deflection specific scheme activated by the routers at the time of link failures until new routes are computed. Each node computes a map for each of it's links to an alternate link and that alternate link is used to forward packets when the original link fails. As the number of links at a router is much smaller than the number of destination in the routing table, the alternate link table will be much smaller than the routing table. The link table mappings are precomputed so that when a link fails, the alternate link is used to forward the packets to the destination until the routing tables are recomputed. Once the new routing tables are forwarding along the alternate link tables is discontinued.

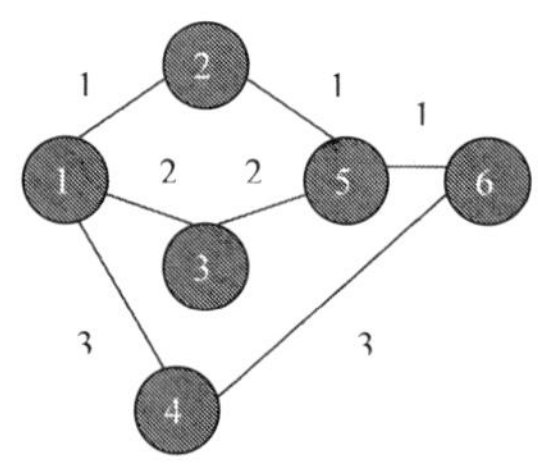

Routing Table					
Dest	2	3	4	5	6
Next hop	2	3	4	2	2

Forwarding Table					
2→1	-	3	4	3	4
3→1	2	-	4	2	2
4→1	2	3	-	2	2

Fig. 11 Sample topology, routing and forwarding tables for node 1 [3]

Authors have used the concept of sink tree to calculate the alternate link mapping. A sink tree of a node R in a network is a tree that has only the links used by all other nodes to reach R and vice versa. Obviously sink tree will not contain any loops, so each packet will be delivered within a finite number of hops. Fig. 12 shows the sink tree of R as R is assumed to be the destination node. Now in normal condition all the nodes under node A will use link A→R to reach R and all the nodes under node B will use link B→R to reach R.

The dotted edge shown in Fig. 12 is a link that allows packets to be deflected from one subtree of the sink tree to another. These types of links are known as bridges. So in case of failure of link A→R the packets will be deflected to the other subtree of the sink tree so that they can reach to node B and thus can be forwarded by B to R by link B→R. So A→B can be an alternate link for A→R. So this algorithm mainly fulfill the following goals: a) to employ normal forwarding mechanisms i.e. no source routing even when the packets are being deflected, b) to utilize existing routing table as much as possible for routing packets around the failure and c) to require no information exchange among routers before packets can be deflected around the failure.

IP layer restoration based on Virtual Protection Cycles: In [5] the author proposed a novel restoration strategy called Virtual Protection Cycles or *p-cycles* for extremely fast restoration in IP networks. In an IP router-based network, p-cycles are implemented with virtual circuit techniques to form closed logical loops that protect a number of IP links, or a node.

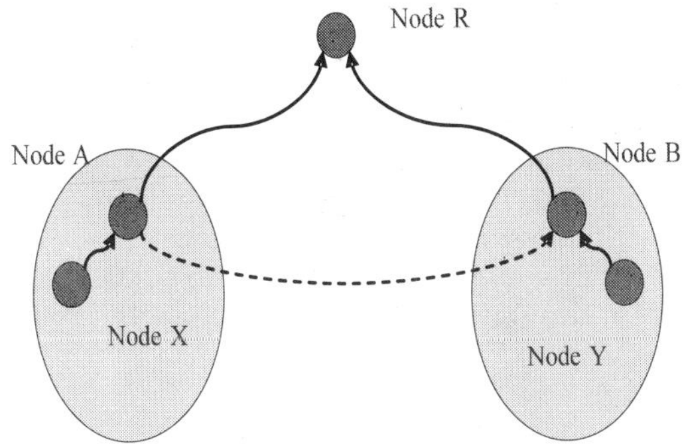

Fig. 12 Sink tree of node R in a network [4]

A. Restoration of IP Link Failures Using p Cycles

When an IP link failure has been detected, the router ports which terminate the failed link will be marked as dead and any packet whose next hop, as indicated by the normal routing table entry for the packet's destination address, would have been directed into the dead port, is instead deflected onto a p-cycle which has been assigned to protect the link.

"Deflection onto a p-cycle" occurs by *encapsulating* the original IP packet in a "p-cycle packet" and forwarded through the p-cycle to the other side of the dead link. When that packet arrives at the router on the other side of the dead link the original IP packet is removed from the encapsulating packet and continued on its prefailure route toward its final destination.

An example of this process is given in Fig. 13. The example shows a link failure, X, its associated p-cycle, and routers, A and B, which were adjacent through the link X. In Fig. 13(a), an IP packet is arrives at router A with a next hop, indicated by the routing tables, that would normally be into the failed link X. In Fig. 13(b), router A, seeing the failure, encapsulates the packet in an appropriate p-cycle packet (one available locally that is known to protect link X) and inserts it into the p-cycle. The p-cycle packets traverse all intervening routers along the p-cycle, as in Fig. 13(c), until, at Fig. 13(d), it arrives at router B, where the original IP packet is decapsulated from the p-cycle packet. Finally, at event Fig. 13(e), the IP packet is routed normally toward its final destination.

B. "Node-encircling" p -cycles for recovery from router failure

Now when a router fails the same concept of p-cycles is extended to *node-encircling p*-cycles. In node-encircling p-cycle each router in the p-cycle compares the original route cost (i.e. the cost of the route the packet would have used prior to failure) in the encapsulating p-cycle packet to the local route cost entry. If the later is less than the original route cost then it will decapsulate the original IP packet from the p-cycle packet and forward it according to the preexisting route entry for the destination. If the local routing cost is greater than or equal to the original route cost then the router just forward the packet along the p-cycle. Let us discuss this with Fig. 14 where the costs of each link are shown. In Fig. 14(a) a packet follows it's normal route to it's destination.

After the router failure the subsequent packets are encapsulated within a p-cycle packet (with original route cost of 3) and injected into the p-cycle. In 14(c) the router checks that the local cost (11) is not less than the original cost (3), so it will again forward the packet in the p-cycle. In Fig. 14(d) the router checks that the local cost (1) is less than the original cost (3), so it decapsulate the original IP packet and routes it normally. Finally in 14(e) the packet arrives at the destination.

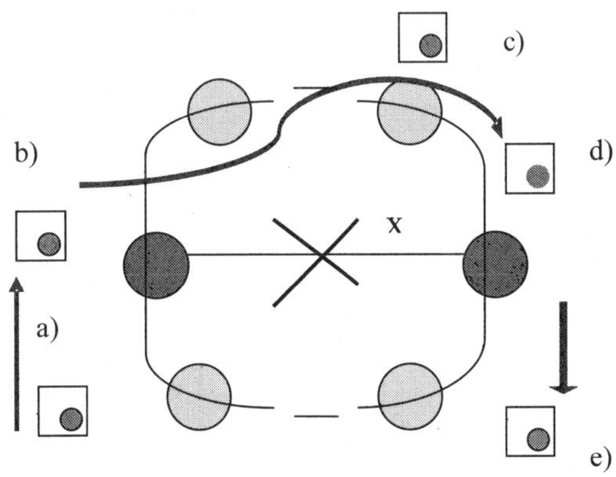

Fig. 13 p-cycle recovery of an IP packet from a link failure. [5]

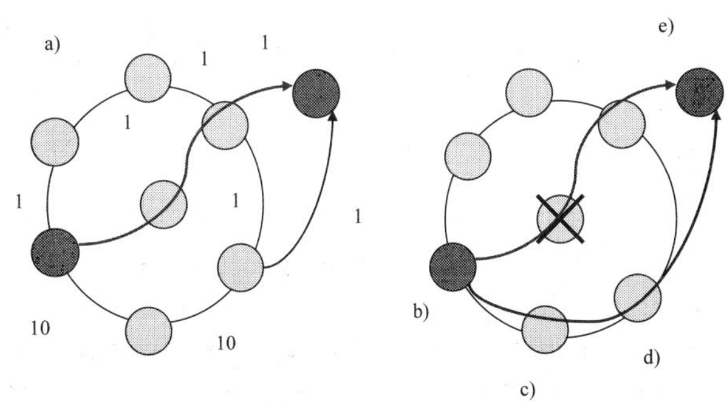

Fig. 14 p-cycle restoration for router failure. [5]

Spare Capacity allocation in IP over WDM:- In [6] the authors have presented two models of provisioning spare capacity in two-layer backbone networks using shared backup path protection. The first model captures failure propagation using overlay information between two layers for backup paths to meet diversity requirements. The second model improves bandwidth efficiency by moving spare capacity sharing from the top layer to the bottom layer. Before describing the two models some notations have been stated.

The authors have modeled the network by a directed graph of N nodes, L links, and R flows. Flow r, $1 \leq r \leq R$ has its origin/destination node pair (o(r), d(r)) and traffic demand m_r. Working and backup paths of flow r are represented by two $1 \times L$ binary row vectors $p_r = \{p_{rl}\}$ and $q_r = \{q_{rl}\}$ respectively. The l-th element in one of the vectors equals to one if and only if the corresponding path uses link l. The path link incidence matrices for working and backup paths are the collections of these vectors, forming two $R \times L$ matrices $P = \{p_{rl}\}$ and $Q = \{q_{rl}\}$ respectively. Let $M = \text{Diag}(\{m_r\}_{R\times 1})$ denote the diagonal matrix representing demand bandwidth m_r of flow r. $G = \{g_{lk}\}_{L\times K}$ is the spare provision matrix, g_{lk} is spare capacity on link l for failure k. The minimum spare capacity required on each link is denoted by the column vector $s = \{s_l\}_{L\times 1}$. $U = \{u_{rk}\}_{R\times K}$ is the flow failure incidence matrix, $u_{rk} = 1$ iff failure scenario k will affect flow r's working path.

Model A: Use of overlay information for failure propagation:

To protect against failure propagation of any single bottom-layer link failures, the overlay information H is used to derive the failure scenario matrix F as $F = F^b \times H^T$. The flow failure incidence matrix U and the spare provision matrix $G^{[A]}$ can be written as

$U = P \times F^T = P \times (F^b \times H)^T = P \times H \times F^{bT}$

and $G^{[A]} = Q^T MU = Q^T M(P \times H \times F^{bT})$

Now the objective is to minimize the total spare capacity i.e.

$\min S^{[A]} = e^T s^b = e^T H^T s$ where e is unit coloumn vector of size L.

Model B: Use of overlay information for both failure propagation and cross-layer spare capacity reservation:

In addition to using the overlay information for failure propagation, the second model computes the top-layer spare capacity sharing at the bottom layer instead of at the top layer. Since every top-layer link traverses one or more bottom-layer links, spare capacity sharing on these bottom-layer links could further minimize the total spare capacity required. The disadvantage of this model is the requirement of a method for the top layer to record and reserve spare capacity on the bottom-layer links.

As an example to illustrate this approach consider the two layer network of Fig. 15. The overlay information H for the network is given by

H = {1 0 0 0 0 0 0
0 1 0 0 0 1 0
0 1 0 0 0 0 1
0 0 1 0 0 0 0
0 0 1 0 1 0 0
0 0 0 0 1 0 0}

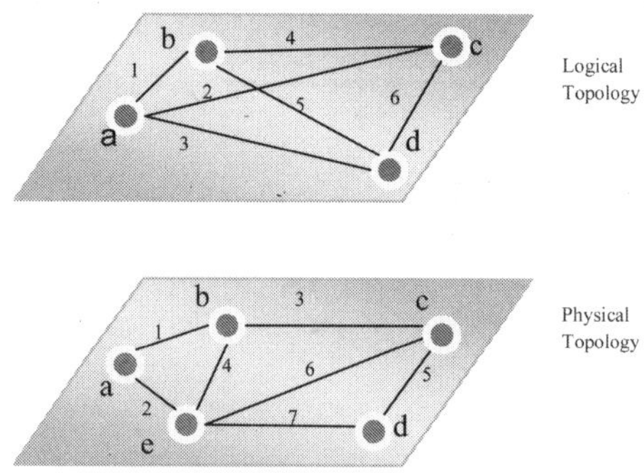

Fig.15 Illustration of Model B [6]

In the figure, two working flows a–b and c–d at the top-layer traverse the bottom-layer links 1and 5 respectively. Their backup paths are a–c–b and c–b–a–d respectively. The backup paths use the top-layer links 2 (a–c) and 3 (a–d) respectively. The bottom-layer paths of these top-layer links overlap on the bottom-layer link 2 (a–e) whose spare capacity could be shared by the backup paths. In this example, the top-layer not only uses the overlay information H to avoid failure propagation, but also shares spare capacity at the bottom layer to achieve lower redundancy.

This spare capacity sharing scheme is equivalent to: (i) converting all backup paths in Q at the top layer into ones at the bottom layer by multiplexing them with H. (ii) finding the spare capacity reserved at the bottom layer $s^b = \max((QH)^T MU) = \max(H^T G^{[A]})$.

(iii) then minimizing the objective function, the total spare capacity

$$\min S^{[B]} = e^T s^b = e^T \max(H^T G^{[A]}).$$

Since $\max(H^T G^{[A]}) \leq H^T \max(G^{[A]})$, the total spare capacity using Model B will be equal to or smaller than that in Model A i.e. $S^{[B]} \leq S^{[A]}$. Thus Model B improves bandwidth efficiency by spare capcity sharing.

Increasing the link utilization in IP over WDM: In [7] the authors have presented the two service classes that are differentiated based on their level of protection. The first class of service, called Fully Protected (FP), offers end-users a guarantee of survivability in the case of a single failure; all FP traffic is protected either by using a 1:1 or 1+1 protection scheme at the WDM layer. The second class of service, called Best Effort Protected (BEP) is not protected; instead restoration at the IP layer is provided. When a failure occurs, the network restores as much BEP traffic as possible, and the BEP traffic does not receive any specific guarantee. The BEP traffic is designed to run over the large amount of unused bandwidth that consist in today's Internet. The motivation of this approach is to give carriers a mechanism for increasing the load carried on the backbone networks without reducing the QoS received by the existing customers. They have described a Tabu Search algorithm which is stated below.

1. *Preprocessing step:* In this step the set of all pairs of disjoint paths that could be used for each logical link is generated.
2. *Initial solution:* For each logical link, randomly select one pair of disjoint physical path. Choose randomly which physical path is assigned as the working path and which is assigned as the backup path. The aggregated BEP traffic flowing on each logical link can be set either on the working path or on the backup path.
3. *Create Neighborhood:* Select a logical link at random. Keep the working path fixed and change the physical backup path. The set of all admissible backup paths for the selected logical link defines the neighborhood of the current solution.
4. *Evaluation of the current solution in the neighborhood:*

   A: Check the capacity of each solution to ensure protection requirements for the FP traffic are satisfied. If enough resources are not available on the physical paths to protect the FP traffic, the solution is discarded as infeasible.

   B: Determine the allocation of BEP traffic onto the spare bandwidth that maximizes the network load.

   C: Elect the best solution found in the neighborhood of as the new current solution.
5. *Update:* Update the Tabu List by adding the latest move used to generate the current solution.
6. *Repeat:* If the number is less than the threshold, go to step 3, else stop.

The optimization scheme needs to find a pair of disjoint fiber path for each logical link. There are typically a large number of such possible pairs. The algorithm chooses the combinations of pairs for all logical links that maximize the network wide load. Thus the amount of BEP traffic that can be added onto the network using the remaining spare capacity is determined after the demands for FP traffic has been satisfied. So the objective of this optimization scheme is to maximize the BEP traffic. But this approach may lead to a very unbalanced distribution of BEP load, giving large amounts of traffic to some connections and close to zero to others. That is why a max-min fair strategy has been adopted which starts by routing all the logical connections to logical topology using the OSPF IP routing algorithm. Then the amount of BEP traffic allocated to each connection is increased in equal increments until a logical link gets saturated. At this point, the BEP bandwidth allocated to all logical connections sharing its bottleneck is frozen. All the other connections, which do not share this bottleneck, can still receive additional BEP traffic, without impacting the bandwidth allocated to the frozen connections. Next the bandwidths of all remaining unfrozen connections are being increased in equal increments until a new logical link becomes a bottleneck. The algorithm repeats until the bandwidth of all logical connections are frozen. To illustrate this heuristic, a small example is shown in Fig 16, with three logical links (continuous lines) between four IP routers. Four logical connections (dashed lines) are routed over the logical topology. Each logical link is marked with a number that represents its capacity. Using the algorithm, the first logical link that will be saturated is (R_b, R_c). Since the bandwidth available to BEP traffic on this link is 9 units, and the link is crossed by three logical connections (C_{ad}, C_{ac} and C_{bc}), each of them will receive 3 units of BEP traffic. Next the algorithm will assign 9 units of BEP to the remaining logical connection C_{cd}. So the max-min fairness algorithm assigns the minimum amount of 3 BEP units to each logical connection and the total BEP load carried by the network is 18 units.

Improving throughput by dynamic allocation of spare capacity: -In [8] the authors have proposed an algorithm which is fulfilling the primary requirements of dynamic spare capacity allocation and survivability against failures in the WDM layer. To fulfill the first requirement they have proposed a MIN-COST algorithm which basically divides the traffic from source router to destination router in different paths, thus reducing the pressure on one path and improves bandwidth efficiency and throughput. In survivability phase they have proposed to reroute the traffic while a link in a WDM network fails so that no data loss will take place.

A. Generalities

The authors have used following notations to describe our algorithm.

- P corresponds to the physical topology,
- L corresponding to the logical topology,
- a, b, c, d, e, f, g, h are used to denote edges/links,
- p is used to denote a path. A path from vertex u to vertex v is denoted by $p_{u,v}$. Physical and

logical topologies can be represented by graphs $G^P = (V^P, E^P)$ and $G^L = (V^L, E^L)$ where V^P, V^L are the set of vertices in the physical and logical layer respectively. E^P, E^L are the set of edges in the physical and logical layer respectively. Obviously $V^L \subseteq V^P$.

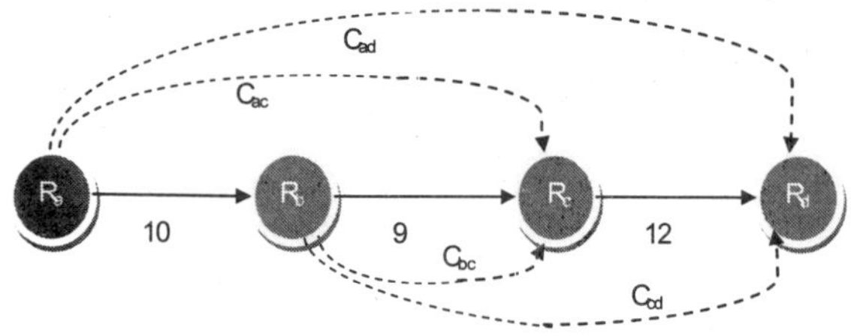

Fig. 16 Illustration of max-min fairness algorithm [7]

B. Lightpath and Mapping

A logical link e^L is mapped on a physical path p^P in such a way that p^P converts same source and destination in G^P as e^L connects G^L. The physical path p^P is called a lightpath. So failure in any physical link in p^P breaks the lightpath and brings down the logical link e^L.

A mapping M is a function $M : E^L \rightarrow p^P$ associating each logical link from the set E^L with a lightpath in the physical topology. For some particular logical edge $e^L \in E^L$, M returns a physical path $p^P = M(e^L)$.

I am illustrating the definition of mapping by Fig 17. from Fig. 17. we can get the following results. $M(f^L) = \{ d^P, b^P, g^P \}$, $M(g^L) = \{ f^P \}$, $M(h^L) = \{ e^P \}$, $M(c^L) = \{ b^P \}$, $M(b^L) = \{ a^P \}$, $M(a^L) = \{ c^P \}$, $M(d^L) = \{ b^P, g^P \}$, $M(e^L) = \{ a^P, c^P, d^P \}$.

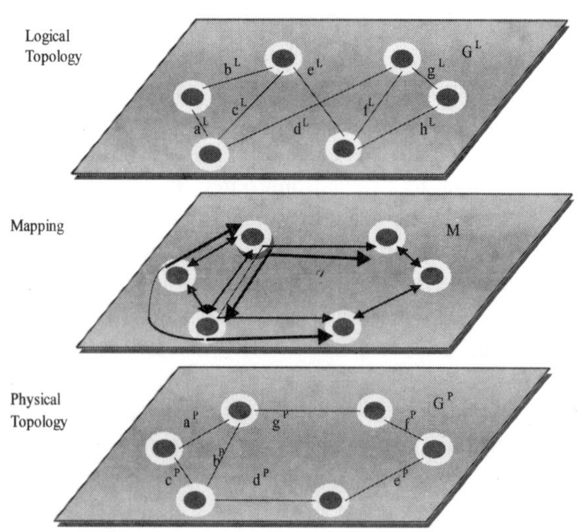

Fig. 17 Mapping of the set $A = \{ a^L, b^L, c^L, d^L, e^L, f^L, g^L, h^L \}$ [8]

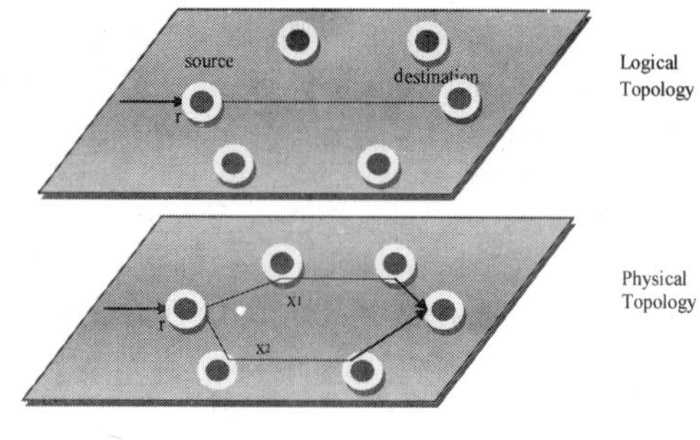

Fig.18 Distribute traffic r in two paths x_1 and x_2 [8]

C. Dynamic Allocation of Residual Bandwidth

In dynamic allocation of residual bandwidth we are dividing the traffic from source to destination (in IP layer) through different (in WDM layer) paths, thus reducing the possibility of congestion. This has been illustrated in Fig. 18.

For each logical link e^L there may be one to many mapping in the WDM layer i.e. $M(e^L) = \{ p_1^P \}, \{ p_2^P \}, \ldots\ldots\ldots, \{ p_n^P \}$ and if $p_1^P \cap p_2^P \cap \ldots\ldots\ldots \cap p_n^P = \varnothing$, then the network is survivable. On the other way if there is any link failure in any of the link of p_i^P then the traffic can be bypassed through p_j^P $j \neq i$ and j=1, 2,….., n. The authors are basically dividing the traffic of e^L in each p_i^P i=1, 2, ….., n to reduce pressure on one path. Here they have defined a function called cost function for each traffic from source to destination as

$D(x) = D_1(x_1) + D_2(x_2) + \ldots\ldots\ldots\ldots + D_n(x_n)$

$= \sum_{\text{all paths}}$(traffic in the path/residual capacity of the path)

that are used to

send r to destination

$= \sum_{i=1}^{n} (x_i^* / C_i - x_i^*)$

where x_i^* is the traffic passed through path x_i and C_i is the residual capacity of path x_i, n is the number of paths which are used to send the traffic r from source to destination.

Now the proposed scheme will minimize D(x) for each traffic. The problem can be formulated as follows

Minimize $\sum_{i=1}^{n} (x_i^* / C_i - x_i^*)$

Subject to $\sum_{i=1}^{n} x_i^* = r$

And $x_i^* \geq 0$ for i= 1, 2,….., n.

Now let in Fig. 13. there are two paths x_1 and x_2 which can be used to send r from source to destination. Now two cases may arise

Case 1: The entire traffic will be sent through x_1

Case 2: The traffic will be divided into x_1^* and x_2^* and then sent through x_1 and x_2.

In Case 1 the entire traffic has been passed through x_1 (as $C_1 > C_1$) upto which the cost function will be minimum. So we have to find a upper bound of r that can be passed through x_1. Now r will be passed through x_1 if

$D_1(r) + D_2(0) \leq D_1(x_1^*- \delta h) + D_2(\delta h)$

$\rightarrow D_1(r) - D_1(r- \delta h) \leq D_2(\delta h) - D_2(0)$

$\rightarrow [D_1(r- \delta h) - D_1(r)] / (- \delta h) \leq [D_2(\delta h) - D_2(0)] / (\delta h)$

$\rightarrow \lim_{(-\delta h)\rightarrow 0} [D_1(r- \delta h) - D_1(r)] / (- \delta h) \leq \lim_{(\delta h)\rightarrow 0} [D_2(\delta h) - D_2(0)] / (\delta h)$

$\rightarrow \partial D_1(r)/\partial x_1 \leq \partial D_2(0)/\partial x_2$

$\rightarrow C_1/ (C_1-r)^2 \leq 1/C_2$

$\rightarrow r \leq C_1 - \sqrt{C_1C_2}$

So, if $r \leq C_1 - \sqrt{C_1C_2}$ then the traffic will be passed through x_1.

In Case 2 $r > C_1 - \sqrt{C_1C_2}$ i.e. when the traffic will be passed through x_1 and x_2 ($x_1^* >0$ and $x_2^*>0$) then

$\partial D_1(x_1^*)/\partial x_1 = \partial D_2(x_2^*)/\partial x_2$

$\rightarrow C_1/ (C_1-x_1^*)^2 = C_2/ (C_2-x_2^*)^2$

$\rightarrow \sqrt{C_1}/(C_1- x_1^*) = \sqrt{C_2}/(C_2- x_2^*)$

$\rightarrow x_1^* = \sqrt{C_1}[r-(C_2- \sqrt{C_1C_2})]/[\sqrt{C_1}+ \sqrt{C_2}]$

and $x_2^* = \sqrt{C_2}[r-(C_1- \sqrt{C_1C_2})]/[\sqrt{C_1}+ \sqrt{C_2}]$

Now, if there are three paths x_1, x_2, x_3.

So, if $r \leq C_1 - \sqrt{C_1C_2}$ then the traffic will be passed through x_1.

If $r > C_1 - \sqrt{C_1C_2}$ and $r \leq C_{12} - \sqrt{C_{12}C_3}$ (where $C_{12} = C_1 + C_2$) then the traffic will be passed through x_1 and x_2 ($x_1^* >0$ and $x_2^*>0$) and

$x_1^* = \sqrt{C_1}[r-(C_2- \sqrt{C_1C_2})]/[\sqrt{C_1}+ \sqrt{C_2}]$

and $x_2^* = \sqrt{C_2}[r-(C_1- \sqrt{C_1C_2})]/[\sqrt{C_1}+ \sqrt{C_2}]$

If $r > C_{12} - \sqrt{C_{12}C_3}$ (where $C_{12} = C_1 + C_2$) then the traffic will be passed through x_1, x_2 and x_3 ($x_1^* >0$ $x_2^*>0$and $x_3^*>0$) and

$x_{12}^* = \sqrt{C_{12}}[r-(C_3- \sqrt{C_3C_{12}})]/[\sqrt{C_{12}}+ \sqrt{C_3}]$

and $x_3^* = \sqrt{C_3}[r-(C_{12}- \sqrt{C_3C_{12}})]/[\sqrt{C_{12}}+ \sqrt{C_3}]$ where $x_{12}^* = x_1^*+ x_2^*$.

In general if there are n+1 paths between the source and destination then if $r \leq C_{1n}- \sqrt{C_{1n}C_{n+1}}$ (where $C_{1n} = C_1 + C_2 +C_3+.....+C_n$) then the traffic will be passed through $x_1, x_2,........x_n$ and if $r > C_{1n} - \sqrt{C_{1n}C_{n+1}}$ then the traffic will be passed through $x_1, x_2, x_3,.....x_n$ and x_{n+1} and

$x_{1n}^* = \sqrt{C_{1n}}[r-(C_{n+1}- \sqrt{C_{n+1}C_{1n}})]/[\sqrt{C_{1n}}+ \sqrt{C_{n+1}}]$

and $x_{n+1}^* = \sqrt{C_{n+1}}[r-(C_{1n}- \sqrt{C_{n+1}C_{1n}})]/[\sqrt{C_{1n}}+ \sqrt{C_{n+1}}]$

where $x_{1n}^* = x_1^*+ x_2^*+ x_3^*+.....+ x_n^*$.

D. Survivability against failures

The authors have defined the definition of survivability as follows. A network is called N-survivable for any e^L there are N+1 disjoint paths in the physical layer i.e. for any e^L there are N+1 paths such that $\cap_{i=1}^{N+1} P_i^P= \emptyset$. So the IP topology will remain connected even after maximum N number of failures at the WDM layer.

So, for any failure in a link $e^P \in E^P$ if the path P_i^P will get disrupted then put the capacity pf $e^P= 0$ and call the MIN_COST algorithm. So all traffic will be bypassed through e^P to the destination.

4. Summary of Proposals

The different schemes reviewed in this article are summarized in Table 1.

5. Conclusion

After reviewing different schemes I have found that there has been considerable amount research activity to improve IP over WDM technology. But there are also some interesting open problems that need further attention.

Improving QoS by reducing the delay:-Multi-Protocol Label Switching (MPLS) is the technology envisaged for future backbone IP networks to overcome some of the current problems associated with the provision of IP services with Quality of Service (QoS). In particular, MPLS (i) improves the packet switching performance of routers and (ii) enables traffic engineering by introducing the possibility of source based routing (where the forwarding path from an ingress router to an egress router is not constrained by the paths of other ingress-egress pairs). A router that supports MPLS is known as a Label Switching Router (LSR). The forwarding of IP packets from ingress to egress LSRs is done by means of routing paths, called Label Switched Paths (LSPs). In the ingress LSR, incoming IP packets are labeled based on their destination and required QoS and, depending on this classification, are forwarded through the appropriate LSP towards an egress LSR. A packet traveling from ingress to egress undergoes a queuing delay in each LSR it traverses. Thus, reducing the QoS delay is an open problem in future.

Tackling the problems caused by impairments:-IP over WDM technologies have a limitation on their physical extent due to various transmission impairments (e.g. attenuation, crosstalk, dispersion, nonlinearities). So a very efficient algorithm is required to tackle with different types of impairments.

Resource sharing:-MPLS over WDM (and IP over WDM) networks are gaining significant attention due to the efficiency in resource utilization that can be achieved by jointly considering the two network layers. These networks are configured by defining lightpaths at the optical layer and the LSPs at the packet layer. Lightpaths are routed over the physical network (comprising OXCs connected through optical fibers) and LSPs are routed over the logical topology of lightpaths (the virtual optical network). Besides the OXCs, which provide wavelength switching capabilities, some nodes may also include packet switching capabilities, i.e., some OXCs may have co-located LSRs (these nodes are sometimes called

Generalized LSRs). OXCs with co-located LSRs can switch traffic demands between lightpaths, enabling increased resource sharing (i.e. having the traffic demand accommodated in a lower number of lightpaths). In fact, having all OXC sites with co-located LSRs would maximize the resource sharing gains, but this could lead to unnecessarily high network costs. So an open area of future research is to determine the minimum number and location of the core LSRs.

So these are the few problems for future research work to improve IP over WDM technology.

Table 1 Summary of proposals for IP over WDM

PROPOSALS	*OBJECTIVE*	*HANDLING SINGLE/MULTIPLE FAILURES*	*DES CRIPTION (IN BRIEF)*
WEI [1]	Implement an innovative integrated traffic engineering framework for reconfigurable IP/WDM networks	Multiple Failures	In an IP/WDM network, traffic engineering can be effected through wavelength circuit reconfiguration that adapts the IP network topology to the evolving traffic pattern. By exploring the WDM layer's reconfigurability, the IP network's virtual topology can be changed to better match the ensuing traffic demand pattern.
M.KURANT, P.THIRAN [2]	How to trace the vulnerable areas in the topology and how to strengthen them to enable a survivable mapping	Multiple Failures	Proposed an algorithm, named SMART When SMART converges completely, a survivable mapping is found. Otherwise the mapping piecewise survivable, so repair the vulnerable areas in the network by adding links.
LEE, Y.YU, NELAKUDITI, ZHANG, CHUAH[3]	Local rerouting of packets through interface specific forwarding	Single Failure	Proposed an algorithm, FIR that initiates the local rerouting of packets. When a packet arrives at a node through unusual interface, the potentially failed links, can be inferred and an appropriate next hop is used to avoid those key links.
VELLANKI, REDDY [4]	Local rerouting through alternate link tables	Single Failure	Precompute an alternate link mapping for every link. When a link fails it's alternate link is selected.
GROVER, STAMATELAKIS [5]	Describe a novel restoration strategy called *virtual protection cycles* for extremely fast restoration in IP networks	Multiple Failures	In the event of failure packets which would normally have been lost are encapsulated with a p cycle IP address and reenter the routing table, which diverts them onto a protection cycle. They travel by normal forwarding and label switching along the p cycle until they reach a node where the continuing route cost to the original destination is lower than that at p cycle entry node. Diverted packets are decapsulated at that node and follow the normal route to the destination
Y. LIU, D. TIPPER,K. VAJANAPOOM [6]	Provisioning spare capacity in two-layer backbone networks using shared backup path protection	Multiple Failures	Presented two models of provisioning spare capacity in two-layer backbone networks using shared backup path protection and compared them.
A. NUCCI, N. TAFT, P. THIRAN, H. ZANG, C. DIOT [7]	Described the two service classes(FP and BEP) that are differentiated based on their level of protection	Single Failure	Determined how to allocate the traffic such that the amount of BEP traffic that can be added on the network is maximized subject to a constraint imposing a minimally fair allocation of BEP load without impacting FP service
A. PAL, A. MUKHERJEE, M. K. NASKAR, P. DEY, A. KUNDU [8]	Fulfill the basic two requirements of IP/WDM i.e. dynamically bandwidth provisioning and survivability against multiple failures	Multiple Failures	Proposed a MIN_COST algorithm that forwards packets to destination through different paths so that the cost function will be minimum. In the event of failure, packets would reach to the destination through alternate links.

6. References

[1] John Y. Wei, "Advances in management and Control of Optical Internet", IEEE Journal of Selected Areas of Communications, Vol. 20, No. 4, May 2002, pp 768-785.

[2] M. Kurant and P. Thiran, "Survivable Routing of Mesh Topologies in IP-over-WDM Networks by Recursive Graph Contraction", IEEE Journal of Selected Areas of Communications, Vol. 25, No. 5, June 2007, pp 922-933.

[3] S. Lee et al., "Proactive vs. Reactive Approaches to Failure Resilient Routing", Proc. INFOCOM, Mar. 2004.

[4] S. Vellanki and A.L.N. Reddy, "Improving Service Availability During Link Failure Transients through Alternate Routing", Texas A & M Univ., Tech. rep. TAMU-ECE-2003-02, Feb. 2003.

[5] D. Stamatelakis and Wayne D. Grover, "IP Layer Restoration and Network Planning Based on Virtual Protection Cycles", IEEE Journal of Selected Areas of Communications, Vol. 18, No. 10, October 2000, pp 1938-1949.

[6] Y. Liu, D. Tipper and K. Vijanapoom, "Spare Capacity Allocation in Two-Layer Networks", IEEE Journal of Selected Areas of Communications, Vol. 25, No. 5, June 2007, pp 974-986.

[7] A. Nucci, N. Taft, P. Thiran, H. Zang and C. Diot, "Increasing the Link Utilization in IP over WDM Networks Using Availability as QoS", Kluwer Photonic Network Communications-special issue on Mesh Restoration, Vol 9.1, pp 55-75, January 2005.

[8] A. Pal, A. Mukherjee, M. K. Naskar, P. Dey and A. Kundu, "Dynamic Bandwidth Provisioning and Survivability in IP over WDM networks", communicated to IEEE ANTS 2008.

Protecting Web Servers from DDoS Attacks using WebSOS

M. Sankara Prasanna Kumar[1] and M. Rudra Kumar[2]
[1]M.Tech, *Assistant Professor*
sankaraprasannakumar@gmail.com
[2]M.Tech, *Associate Professor*
mrudrakumar@gmail.com
Department of Computer Science & Engineering, Annamacharya Institute of Technology & Sciences
New Bowenapalli, Rajampet, Kadapa.

Abstract

We present the WebSOS architecture, a mechanism for countering denial of service (DoS) attacks against web servers. WebSOS uses a combination of overlay networking, content based routing, and aggressive packet filtering to guarantee access to a service that is targeted by a DoS attack. Our approach requires *no modifications* to servers or browsers, and makes use of the web proxy feature and TLS client authentication supported by modern browsers.

We use a WebSOS prototype to conduct a preliminary performance evaluation both on the local area network and over the Internet using PlanetLab, a testbed for experimentation with network overlays. We determine the end-to-end latency imposed by the architecture to increase by a factor of 5 on average. We conclude that this overhead is reasonable in the context of a determined DoS attack.

Keywords: *Denial of Service, web proxies, overlay networks, packet filtering, consistent hashing, distributed hash tables*

1. Introduction

The extremely widely-used World Wide Web environment provides a rich set of targets for motivated attackers. This has been demonstrated by the large number of vulnerabilities and exploits against web servers, browsers, and applications utilizing these (*e.g.* CGI scripts). Traditional security considerations revolved around protecting the network connection's confidentiality and integrity, protecting the server from break-in, and protecting the client's private information from unintended disclosure. To that end, several protocols and mechanisms have been developed. One area that has been neglected thus far has been that of service availability in the presence of denial of service (DoS) attacks, and their distributed variants (DDoS). Such attacks can take many forms, depending on the resource the attacker is trying to exhaust. Of particular interest are *link congestion* attacks, where by attackers identify "pinch" points in the communications substrate and flood them with large volumes of traffic. An example of an obvious attack point is the location (IP address) of the destination that is to be secured, or the routers in its immediate network vicinity; sending enough attack traffic will cause the links closest to the destination to be congested and drop all other traffic.

Previous approaches that address the general network DoS problem are *reactive*: they monitor traffic at a target location, waiting for an attack to occur. After the attack is identified, typically via analysis of traffic patterns and packet headers, filters may be established in an attempt to block the offenders. The main two problems with this approach are the accuracy with which legitimate traffic can be distinguished from the DoS traffic, and the robustness of the mechanism for establishing filters deep enough in the network (away from the target) so that the effects of the attack are minimized.

We build on the *Secure Overlay Services (SOS)* architecture. Our intent is to allow legitimate users to access web servers under a congestion-based DDoS attack. We assume that there is a pre-determined subset of clients scattered throughout the wide-area network who require (and should have) access to these servers. These users prove their right to contact the web server through cryptographic means — *i.e.,* possession of a secret key. This works well in the web environment, where users are familiar with SSL and, more importantly, practically all browsers provide the necessary functionality. We should stress that WebSOS does not solve the general DoS problem (*e.g.,* the "flash crowd" phenomenon). We are interested in classes of communication where both participants are known to each other *a priori.*

In WebSOS, the portion of the network immediately surrounding the web servers to be protected aggressively filters and blocks all incoming packets from hosts that are not approved, as shown in Fig. 1. The small set of nodes that are approved at any particular time is kept secret so that attackers cannot try to impersonate them to pass through the filter. These nodes are picked from among those within a distributed set of nodes throughout the wide area network, that form a *secure overlay* dedicated to DoS protection services. Any transmissions that wish to traverse the overlay must first be validated at entry points of the overlay. Once inside the overlay, the traffic is tunneled securely for several hops along the overlay to the approved (and secret from attackers) locations, which can then forward the validated traffic through the filtering routers to the target. Thus, the two main principles behind our design are the elimination of communication pinch-points, which constitute attractive DoS targets, via a combination of filtering and overlay routing to obscure the identities of the sites whose traffic is permitted to pass through the filter, and the ability to recover from random or induced failures within the forwarding infrastructure or within the secure overlay nodes.

We use web proxies enhanced with Chord-routing functionality as the overlay nodes. A proxy local to the web browser performs the authentication between the legitimate user and the overlay network, using TLS. Traffic inside the overlay is also protected via TLS. The implementation is fairly compact, and was used to evaluate the performance of the WebSOS overlay both in a local area scenario and using the PlanetLab testbed. The results show that the end-to-end latency increases, on average, by a factor 5. We believe this is an acceptable alternative to providing no service. WebSOS can be used on an as-needed basis, without affecting performance when no DoS attack is taking place.

A. Paper Organization

The remainder of this paper is organized as follows. Section II gives an overview of Secure Overlay Services (SOS) discusses the specifics of the WebSOS architecture. Section III presents details of our prototype implementation, while Section IV contains a preliminary performance evaluation. Section V concludes the paper and discusses directions for future research.

2. The WebSOS Architecture

The goal of the WebSOS infrastructure is to distinguish between authorized and unauthorized traffic. The former is allowed to reach the destination, while the latter (or, more generally, unverified traffic) is dropped or rate-limited. Thus, at a very basic level, we need the functionality of a firewall "deep" enough in the network that the access link to the target is not congested. This imaginary firewall performs access control by using traditional protocols such as IPSec. Without WebSOS, knowledge of the target's IP address is sufficient to a moderately-provisioned attacker to saturate the target site.

Unfortunately, traditional firewalls themselves are susceptible to DoS attacks. One way to address this problem is to replicate the firewall functionality. To avoid the effects of a DoS attack against the firewall connectivity, we need to distribute these instances of the firewall across the network. In effect, we are "farming out" the expensive processing (such as cryptographic protocol handling) to a large number of nodes. However, firewalls depend on topological restrictions in the network to enforce access control policy. Since our distributed firewall has performed the access control step, it would seem obvious that all we need around the target is a router that is configured to only let through traffic forwarded to it by one of the firewalls.

However, a security system cannot depend upon the identity of these firewalls to remain secret. Thus, an attacker can launch a DoS attack with spoofed traffic purporting to originate from one of these firewalls. Notice that, given a sufficiently large group of such firewalls, we can select a very small number of these as the designated authorized forwarding stations: only traffic forwarded from these will be allowed through the filtering router, and we change this set periodically. We call these nodes *secret servlets.* All other nodes must forward traffic for the target to one of these nodes. Fig. 1 gives a high-level overview of the WebSOS architecture.

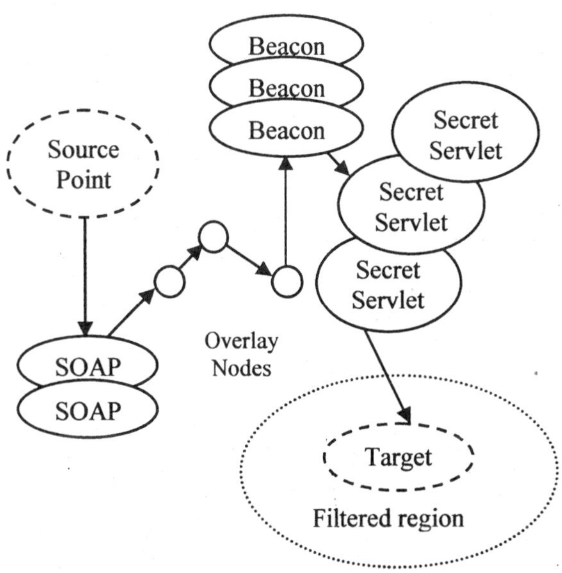

Fig. 1 Basic SOS architecture

To route traffic internally, WebSOS uses Chord, which can be viewed as a routing service that can be implemented as a network overlay. Consistent hashing is used to map an arbitrary identifier to a unique destination node that is an active member of the overlay. Each overlay node maintains a list that contains O(logN) identities of other active nodes in the overlay, where N is the number of overlay nodes. Given the destination identifier, each node knows how to choose a member in its list such that, from an arbitrarily chosen starting node, the destination node to which the identifier hashes is reached in O(logN) overlay hops. The Chord service is robust to changes in overlay membership: each node's list is adjusted to account for nodes leaving and joining the overlay such that the above stated properties continue to hold. Note that WebSOS can use any routing algorithm; we chose Chord because of our familiarity with it and its self-healing properties.

In WebSOS, the identifier to which the hash function is applied to is the IP address of the target (web server). Thus, Chord can be used to direct a packet from any node in the overlay to the node that the identifier is mapped to (or the node whose identifier is "closest" to that value), by applying the hash function to the target's IP address. This node to which Chord delivers the packet is not the target, nor is it necessarily the secret servlet. It is simply a unique node that will be eventually being reached using Chord, regardless of the starting point in the overlay. We refer to this node as the *beacon*, since it is to this node that packets destined for the target are first guided. When a packet is approved by a SOAP for forwarding over the overlay, the hash on the IP address of the target is used as the key. Chord therefore provides a robust and reliable while relatively unpredictable means of routing packets from an access point to one of several beacons.

The secret servlet can determine the beacon's identity by hashing on the target identifier (which the secret servlet knows), and then use Chord to route traffic to it. Hence, the secret servlet can inform the beacon of the secret servlet's identity. The servlets send these advertisements periodically. Should the servlet for a target change, the beacon will find out as soon as the new servlet sends an advertisement. If the old beacon for a target drops out of the overlay, Chord will route the advertisements to a node closest to the hash of the target's identifier. Such a node will know that it is the new beacon because Chord will not be able to further forward the advertisement. By providing only the beacon with the identity of the secret servlet, the packet can be delivered from any overlay entry point (we call these Secure Overlay Access Points, or SOAPs) to the target by traveling across the overlay to the beacon, then from the beacon to the secret servlet, and finally from the secret servlet (through the filter) to the target. This allows the overlay to scale for arbitrarily large numbers of overlay nodes and target sites.

A. WebSOS Overlay Nodes

We use special-purpose web proxies as the overlay nodes. These proxies implement the following functionality:

1) Receive SSL connections from other proxies; both sides are mutually authenticated using public key certificates issued by the administrator of the WebSOS overlay.
2) Proxy HTTP (or HTTPS) requests received over these SSL connections to other WebSOS nodes, again over SSL.
3) Accept SSL connections from browsers, verify the client certificate received over the SSL exchange, and proxy the HTTP or HTTPS request(s) to other overlay nodes, per item *(2)*
4) Implement the Chord routing algorithm, as discussed above. The routing table thus constructed is used to determine the next proxy to forward an HTTP/HTTPS request to, as per above.
5) Implement beacon functionality. This means that every node must maintain a table associating web server IP addresses to secret servlet IP addresses. If a proxy request for a web server in this table is received, the connection is proxied to the associated secret servlet.
6) Implement secret servlet functionality. If a request is received for a web server for which the node is a secret servlet, the connection is forwarded directly to the web server. Furthermore, allow authorized web servers to notify a WebSOS node that it is a secret servlet for that server. The node must verify the certificate presented by the server in the SSL exchange, and then notify the beacon for that target that it is the new servlet.

Notice that if the browser is doing end-to-end SSL (to the web server), the encrypted link will be super-encrypted with SSL on the link between the browser and the SOAP, and between each overlay node. We use SSL in the intermediate links to prevent an attacker from inserting traffic in the overlay through IP spoofing. We also use SSL as an admission-control mechanism to the overlay; SOAPs perform the admission control function. No special functionality is required by the proxies to perform these tasks; the user browser simply has to be supplied with the appropriate public key certificate(s) from the WebSOS administrator.

Traffic in the reverse direction (from web server to client) could also traverse the overlay, by reversing the roles of user and target. In that case, the path taken by requests and responses would be different. Alternatively, traffic from the target to the user could be sent directly (without using the overlay); this is usually not a problem, since most communication channels are full-duplex and, in the event of a DDoS attack, only the downstream portion (to the target) is congested. An additional benefit of this asymmetric approach is reduced latency, especially considering that most client/server traffic (especially in the web environment) is highly asymmetric (*i.e.,* clients receive a lot more information than they transmit). This was possible because routing decisions in SOS are made on a per-packet basis.

In WebSOS, routing decisions are made on a per-connection basis. Any subsequent requests over the same connection (when using HTTP 1.1) and any responses from the web server can take the reverse path through the overlay. While this makes the implementation simpler, it also introduces increased latency, as the bulk of the traffic will also traverse the overlay. We shall see in the next section how to avoid this problem.

B. Sequence of Operations

The sequence of operations in the WebSOS architecture consists of the following steps.

- A site (target) installs a filter on a router in its immediate vicinity and then selects a number of WebSOS nodes to act as servlets. Routers at the perimeter of the site are instructed to only allow traffic from these servlets to reach the internal of the site's network. These routers are powerful enough to do filtering (using only a small number of rules) on incoming traffic without adversely impacting their performance. In order to make guessing the identity of a secret servlet for a particular target harder for the attacker, the filtering mechanism should use packet fields with potentially high entropy. For example, only GRE packets form a particular source (the secret servlet) containing a specific 32-bit value in the GRE Key field. An attacker trying to slip attack traffic through the filter must guess both the current servlet's IP address and the correct 32-bit key.
- When an SOS node is informed that it will act as a secret servlet for a site (and after verifying the authenticity of the request, by verifying the certificate received during the SSL exchange), it will compute the key k for each of a number of well-known consistent hash functions, based on the target site's network address. Each of these keys will identify a number of overlay nodes that will act as beacons for that web server. Any traffic to the target received from the overlay will be directly forwarded to these nodes, and from there to the secret servlets.
- Having identified the beacons, the servlets or the target will contact them, notifying the beacons of the servlets' existence and association with a particular target. Beacons, after verifying the validity of the request, will store the necessary information to forward traffic for that target to the appropriate servlet.
- A source that wants to communicate with the target contacts SOAP. After authenticating and authorizing the request, the SOAP securely proxies all traffic from the source to the target via one of the beacons. The SOAP (and all subsequent hops on the overlay) can proxy the HTTP request to an appropriate beacon in a distributed fashion using Chord, by applying the appropriate hash function(s) to the target's IP address to identify the next hop on the overlay.
- Finally, the beacon proxies the request to a secret servlet that then proxies the traffic (through the filtering router) to the target.

This scheme is robust against DoS attacks because if an access point is attacked, the confirmed source point can simply choose an alternate access point to enter the overlay. Any overlay node can provide all different required functionalities (SOAP, Chord routing, beacon, secret servlet). If a node within the overlay is attacked, the node simply exits the overlay and the Chord service self-heals, providing new paths over the re-formed overlay to (potentially new sets of) beacons. Furthermore, no node is more important or sensitive than others — even beacons can be attacked and are allowed to fail. Finally, if a secret servlet's identity is discovered and the servlet is targeted as an attack point, or attacks arrive at the target with the source IP address of some secret servlet, the target can choose an alternate set of secret servlets.

3. Implementation

We have an initial implementation of WebSOS, consisting of three main modules. The components are a communications module, a SOS routing module, and an overlay routing module running on each node in the SOS overlay.

The ***communications module*** is responsible for forwarding HTTP requests and responses among the nodes in the SOS overlay. When a new proxy request (in the form of a new TCP connection) is received, the communications module calls the SOS routing module with the target's destination address to obtain the address of the next hop in the overlay. It then opens a new TCP connection to that node and relays the received HTTP request. Any traffic received in the opposite direction (*i.e.,* the HTTP responses and web content) are relayed back to the source. Authentication of the requesting node by the SOAP and internal nodes is accomplished through SSL. Authorized users and SOS overlay nodes are issued X.509 certificates signed by the WebSOS certificate authority.

Thus, when a request is issued by the browser, it is tunneled through a series of SSL-encrypted links to the target, allowing the entire transmission between the requester and target to be encrypted. These SSL connections between WebSOS nodes are dynamically established, as new requests are routed. One problem we ran into while developing the WebSOS prototype is that web browsers do not provide support for the actual proxy request to be encrypted. To solve this problem, we wrote a port forwarder that runs on the user's system, accepts plaintext proxy requests locally, and forwards them using SSL to the access point node. In the current implementation, this forwarder is a stand-alone program. Thus, to use WebSOS, an authorized user simply has to access any SOAP, download the proxy code, and set the browser's proxy settings to the local host. The downloaded proxy itself is not considered part of the WebSOS overlay and is not trusted to perform any access control decisions; it is simply a "helper" application.

The ***SOS routing module*** receives requests from the communications module and responds with the IP address of the next node in the SOS overlay to which the request should be forwarded. The module first checks whether the current node serves a specific purpose (*i.e.*, whether is it a beacon or secret servlet for that target). If the node serves no such purpose, the module calls the overlay routing module to determine the next hop in the SOS overlay and passes the reply to the communications module.

Table 1 Latency, measured in seconds, when contacting various SSL-enabled web servers directly and with different numbers of (intermediate) overlay nodes in the same LAN.

Server / nodes	Direct	1	4	7	10
Yahoo!	1.39	2.06	2.37	2.79	3.33
Verisign	3.43	4.22	5.95	6.41	9.01
CU BB	0.64	0.86	1.06	1.16	1.21
CU BB (2nd)	0.14	0.17	0.19	0.20	0.25

The ***overlay routing module*** is a general routing algorithm for overlay networks. A Chord implementation was used in our initial tests, but can be replaced with any other routing algorithm, *e.g.*, CAN. It receives queries containing a destination IP address and responds with the IP address of the next node in the overlay to which the request should be forwarded. For maintenance of its own routing table, the Chord implementation also communicates with other overlay nodes to determine their status.

4. Experimental Evaluation

In order to quantify the overhead imposed by the WebSOS architecture, we created a simple topology running on the local network (100 Mbit fully-switched Ethernet). For our local-area network overlay, we used 10 commodity PCs running Linux Redhat 7.3. We measured the time-to-completion of https requests. That is, we measured the elapsed time starting when the browser initiates the TCP connection to the destination or the first proxy, to the time all data from the remote web server have been received. We ran this test by contacting 3 different SSL-enabled sites: ***www.login.yahoo.com, www.verisign.com.*** For each of these sites we measured the time-to-completion for a different number of overlay nodes between the browser and the target (remote web server).

The browser was located in a separate network. The reason for this configuration was to introduce some latency in the first-hop connection (from the browser to the SOAP), thus simulating (albeit using a real network) an environment where the browsers have slower access links to the SOAPs, relative to the links connecting the overlay nodes themselves (which may be co-located with core routers). By locating all the overlay nodes in the same location, we effectively measure the aggregate overhead of the WebSOS nodes in the optimal performance case.

Table 1 shows the results for the case of 0 (browser contacts remote server directly), 1, 4, 7, and 10 traffic-handling overlay nodes. The times reported are in seconds, and are averaged over several HTTPS GET requests of the same page, which was not locally cached. For each GET request, a new TCP connection was initiated by the browser. The row labeled "CU BB (2nd)" shows the time-to-completion of an HTTPS GET request that uses an already-established connection through the overlay to the web server, using the HTTP 1.1 protocol.

Table 2 Latency, measured in seconds, when contacting various SSL-enabled web servers directly and with different numbers of (intermediate) overlay nodes using PlanetLab.

Server/Nodes	Direct	1	4	7	10
Yahoo!	1.39	3.15	5.53	10.65	14.36
Verisign	3.43	5.12	7.59	14.59	22.82
CU BB	0.64	1.01	1.45	3.14	5.07
CU BB (2nd)	0.14	0.23	0.28	0.57	0.72

As the table shows, WebSOS increases the end-to-end latency between the browser and the server by a factor of 2 to 3. This increase can be primarily attributed to the network stack and proxy processing overhead at each hop.

Furthermore, there is an SSL-processing overhead for the inter-overlay communications. A minor additional cryptographic overhead, relative to the direct access case, is the certificate validation that the SOAPs have to perform, to determine the client's authority to use the overlay, and the SSL connection between the proxy running on the user's machine and the SOAP. Use of cryptographic accelerators can further improve performance in that area. One further optimization is to maintain persistent SSL connections between the overlay nodes. However, this will make the task of the communication module harder, as it will have to parse HTTP requests and responses arriving over the same connection in order to make routing decisions.

Table 2 shows the same experiment using PlanetLab, a wide-area overlay network testbed. The PlanetLab nodes are distributed in academic institutions across the country, and are connected over the Internet. We deployed our WebSOS proxies PlanetLab and ran the exact same tests. Naturally, the direct-contact case remains the same. We see that the time-to completion in this scenario increases by a factor of 2 to 10, depending on the number of nodes in the overlay. In each case, the increase in latency over the local-Ethernet configuration can be directly attributed to the delay in the links between the WebSOS nodes. While the PlanetLab configuration allowed us to conduct a much more realistic performance evaluation, it also represents a worst-case deployment scenario for WebSOS: typically, we would expect WebSOS to be offered as a service by an ISP, with the (majority of) WebSOS nodes located near the core of the network. Using PlanetLab, the nodes are distributed in (admittedly well-connected) end-sites. We would expect that a more commercial-oriented deployment of WebSOS would result in a corresponding decrease in the inter-overlay delay. On the other hand, it is easier to envision end-site deployment of WebSOS, as it does not require ISP participation.

Note the latency increases with the log of the number of nodes in the overlay, since that is how many nodes, in the worst case, a connection will be relayed through before it reaches the beacon. However, the difficulty of shutting down the network for the attacker increases linearly with the number of nodes. This is directly analogous to modern cryptography: extending the length of a cryptographic key increases the work factor for legitimate users linearly, but makes a brute force attack exponentially more difficult.

Finally, while the additional overhead imposed by WebSOS can be significant, we have to consider the alternative: no web service while a DoS attack against the server is occurring. While an increase in end-to-end latency by a factor of 5 (or even 10, in the worst case) is considerable, we believe it is more than acceptable in certain environments and in the presence of a determined attack.

5. Conclusions

We presented WebSOS, an architecture that allows legitimate users to access a web server in the presence of a DoS attack. We use a combination of cryptographic protocols for authentication, packet filtering, overlay networks, and consistent hashing to provide service to authorized users trying to contact a web server under attack. Our architecture requires no changes to web servers, browsers, or existing protocols.

We evaluated the performance of WebSOS, using our prototype implementation, over both a local area network and over the Internet using PlanetLab. Our measurements show that in a realistic but worst-case deployment scenario the end-to-end communication latency between browser and server increases on the average by a factor of 5, with a worst case of 10. We also discussed various potential optimizations for improving performance. We believe that even at its current level, the overhead imposed is acceptable in many critical environments and applications.

6. References

[1] T. Dierks and C. Allen, "The TLS protocol version 1.0," RFC 2246, January 1999. [Online]. Available: ftp://ftp.isi.edu/in-notes/rfc2246.txt

[2] R. S. Sandhu and J. S. Park, "Decentralized user-role assignment for web-based intranets," in *ACM Workshop on Role-Based Access Control*, 1998, pp.1–12.[Online].Available: citeseer.nj.nec.com/sandhu98decentralized.html

[3] L. Gong and R. Schemers, "Implementing Protection Domains in the Java Development Kit 1.2," in *Proceedings of Network and Distributed System Security Symposium (NDSS)*, March 1998, pp. 125–134.

[4] D. Goldschlag, M. Reed, and P. Syverson, "Onion routing for anonymous and private internet connections," *Communications of the ACM (USA)*, vol. 42, no. 2, pp. 39–41, 1999. [Online]. Available: citeseer.nj.nec.com/goldschlag99onion.html

[5] L. Cranor, M. Langheinrich, M. Massimo, M. Presler-Marshall, and J. Reagle, "The Platform for Privacy Preferences 1.0 (P3P1.0) Specification," World Wide Web Consortium (W3C), Tech. Rep., 2002.

[6] J. Ioannidis and S. M. Bellovin, "Implementing Pushback: Router-Based Defense Against DDoS Attacks," in *Proceedings of the Network and Distributed System Security Symposium (NDSS)*, February 2002.

[7] D. Dean, M. Franklin, and A. Stubblefield, "An Algebraic Approach to IP Traceback," in *Proc. of the Network and Dsitributed System Security Symposium (NDSS)*, February 2001, pp. 3–12.

[8] S. Savage, D. Wetherall, A. Karlin, and T. Anderson, "Network Support for IP Traceback," *ACM/IEEE Transactions on Networking*, vol. 9, no. 3, pp. 226–237, June 2001.

Progress in Optical Networks

K.Aparna and S. Suryanarayana
Department of Electronics & communication, CVR college of Egineering, Hyderabad
aparna.kukunuri@yahoo.com suryam_sakhamuri@yahoo.com

Abstract

Increasing bandwidth demands, caused by growing numbers of users, increasing popularity of the Internet, multi-media services, and higher demands on quality, urge the development of ever faster networks. To meet these demands, optical techniques are being introduced in public networks but on a link-to-link basis. This paper addresses future networks that will be to a large extent alloptical. A comparison is made of the strengths and weaknesses of two multiplexing techniques: wavelength division multiplexing (WDM) and space division multiplexing (SDM). It is prompted by the fact that both SDM and WDM are viable options for the optical layer of all-optical networks. Several issues are considered: switches, singleand multi-hop operation, core and access network, and scalability.

1. Introduction

In recent years an increasing amount of research has been devoted to the development of multi-wavelength optical networks [4,13,20,21]. The goal is to exploit the capacity of optical fibres better, which is much greatér than single wavelength systems can utilise. Whereas current systems provide several hundred Mb/s to a few Gb/s, WDM systems promise capacities on the order of several Tb/s without dramatic electronic speed improvements. Thus, a new era of cheap, massive bandwidth is envisioned.

Among the challenges is to keep signals in the photonic domain. We then speak of all-optical networks. These have several advantages. One is protocol transparency, to the point that signals may be analogue or digital. WDM networks can transport these over the same fibres, at different wavelengths. An all-optical infrastructure is bit-rate independent, so it can be used at ever higher speeds, which makes it future proof.

Yet, is all-optical multi-wavelength technology really needed to provide Gb/s speeds to the user? Several factors impede the deployment of large scale all-optical networks. Also, SDM is often a good alternative for WDM, even if it does not provide high utilisation of bandwidth in the fibre.

We shall compare WDM and SDM as they are the basić options for the construction of all-optical networks. They define the lightpaths in which other multiplexing techniques: TDM, SCM, and CDMA, can be used. Those help diminish the complexity of switching but we will not look at them here. A comprehensive study of combining several switching techniques is presented in [26]. Other work on this topic can be found in [12] and [27].

To see how SDM can be competitive with WDM, consider the following points:

1. All-optical networks have physical limitations due to a.o. cross-talk, noise, wavelength alignment, non linearities [5]. These make purely all-optical networks infeasible.
2. In the access network, fibres are usually laid in large bundles. In hybrid fibre-coax (HFC) networks, e.g., typically 48 or 96 fibres. Also in other topologies fair multiplicities may be expected. It is then more natural to use separate fibres than wavelengths.
3. Wavelength reuse allows a modest number of wavelengths to serve large numbers of users: [6] shows that multi-hop networks with 8 to 32 wavelengths can serve up to hundreds of millions of users. [24] presents comparable results for smaller networks.
4. Fibre amplifiers work over a narrow wavelength range: 30 nm. However, certain WDM devices require wide wavelength spacing (about 9 nm in acoustooptic filters). This limits the number of wavelengths to 3 or 4 where amplification is needed.

The results of point 3 can also be applied to SDM networks if one exchanges wavelengths for parallel fibres. One could conclude that where fibre multiplicity is sufficient, SDM can do the same job as WDM. But if this is so, why should we use WDM?

1. WDM provides more bandwidth when there are very few fibres, e.g., in long-haul lines like the Transatlantic line [13]. Bit rates can be increased only up to a limit (about 40 Gb/s) because of dispersion. WDM is the solution to make more bandwidth available.

2. WDM allows new users or sub-networks to be connected to existing fibre networks without laying more fibres, by adding wavelengths. This makes WDM better scalable.
3. Signals must be amplified after certain distances or splitting. A single amplifier can amplify all wavelengths in the erbium window. This reduces amplifier costs for WDM.
4. As we shall see in section 2, WDM can lead to smaller or cheaper switches.

We see that SDM is a strong alternative to WDM where fibre multiplicity is sufficient. On the other hand, WDM has some inherent advantages. So, we must compare them further. For instance, what switching techniques can be used? How well do they scale? Which technique leads to a cheaper network? But also: can SDM and WDM be used together?

2. Switching Techniques

In this section we will have a look at some switch types. Fig. 1 shows a part of a network with a number of switches. In space multiplexed networks, signals are transported over separate fibres, while in the wavelength multiplexed networks they can be carried over one fibre. For simplicity, we will not look at mixtures, which could be necessitated by limits in the number of wavelengths per fibre, e.g., due to fibre amplifiers.

Obviously, in the space switched network space switches must be used. For WDM networks there are more options, which take advantage of the nature of WDM. We shall look at the use of 1′2 and 2′2 space switches and the acoustooptic tunable filter (AOTF) as basic switching elements. We will not consider packet switches because we do not expect them to become practical soon, largely because optical buffering is so difficult.

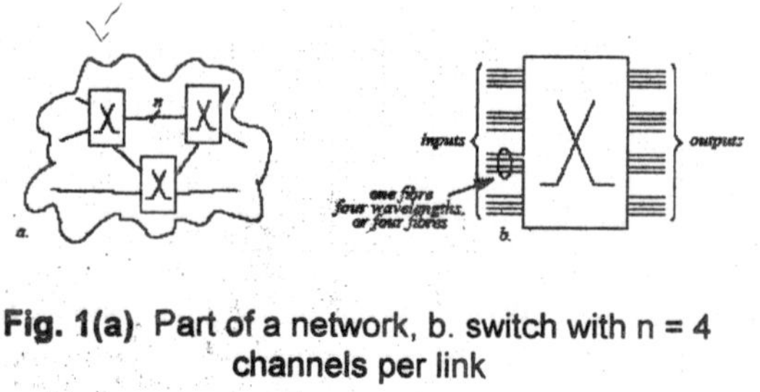

Fig. 1(a) Part of a network, b. switch with n = 4 channels per link

2.1. 1′2 and 2′2 space switches

Fig. 2.a shows two basic space switches: the 1′2 switch and the 2′2 switch. Besides the suggested states, they may also be used to broadcast (at the penalty of a power split). Various switching methods can be used in these devices, e.g., directional couplers, or Mach Zehnder interferometers. For an introduction see [13,19,27]. The various possibilities for the realisation of these switches give rise to different physical characteristics, e.g., wavelength dependency, polarisation dependency, switching speed, cross-talk, and signal loss. We will not take this into account in our discussion.

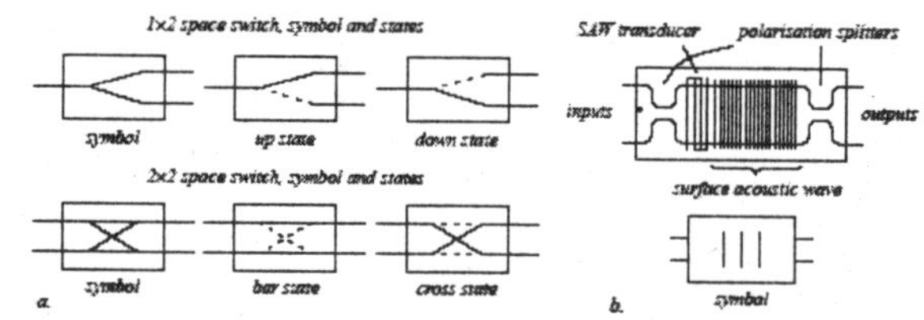

Fig. 2a Space switches and b. acoustooptic tunable filter, symbols and states

2.2. The acoustooptic tunable filter

Acoustooptic filters, shown schematically in Figure 2.b, are four-port devices with an additional control port. The normal ports are the two input and output fibres, the control port is the RF signal driving the Surface Acoustic Wave (SAW) transducer, which defines a number of superimposed gratings in the optical path. The device can be used as a tunable filter, wavelength selective splitter, combiner, or 2′2 switch. The tuning range is about 200 nm. Because of the wavelength spacing of about 9 nm, about 22 wavelengths can be resolved. The tuning time is on the order of microseconds, so AOTFs are best used for fairly long-lived connections. It is clearly too long for per-packet switching.

AOTFs can route multiple wavelengths simultaneously. The RF signal applied to the SAW transducer puts the device in cross or bar state for each wavelength individually. For our discussion, this is all we need to know. For more information, see [13]. Section 2.4 shows that these routing properties can lead to smaller switches. The number of switched wavelengths is programmed by the SAW transducer input. We shall say that AOTFs are *soft* with respect to the number of wavelengths. An AOTFbased network can easily upgrade to a larger number of wavelengths. In a space switched network this requires the installation of new equipment.

2.3. Compound switches

In the literature a great deal has been said on the construction of switches from basic switching elements. For circuit switches there are a few important issues: the number of switching elements, signal degradation, the level of blocking, and ease of routing.

A number of well-known composition methods are: the Clos method, the tree method, the Benes network, and the shuffle configuration. Of these, the Clos and tree method yield strictly non-blocking switches, the Benes network essentially non-blocking switches, and in shuffle networks it depends on the number of shuffle stages. Essentially non-blocking switches are rarely if ever used for circuit switching as existing connections may have to be rerouted. Routing decisions are complicated in shuffle networks. So, for non-blocking switches the Clos and tree methods are the best options. These can be further compared with respect to the number of switching elements and the number of elements in the signal path (signal degradation). In large switches it is unlikely that all inputs and outputs will be used simultaneously, so a non-zero level of blocking is often acceptable.

The Clos method (Fig. 3) divides an N × N switch into a column of k $\frac{N}{n}\times\frac{N}{n}$ switches and two columns of $\frac{N}{n}$ n × k switches. The condition $k \geq 2n-1$ must be met. Recursive application with $n = 2$ and $k = 3$ leads to a $2^K \times 2^K$ switch of $M_K = 32\cdot 3^{K-1} + 28\cdot 2^{K-1}$ switch elements or, in terms of N, $M_N = \frac{32}{3}\cdot N^{3/2} + 14N$. This assumes that the $n \times k$ and $k \times n$ switches are built as in Fig.3.c. The number of elements in the signal path is then bound by $2+4K \leq L_K \leq 2+6K$.

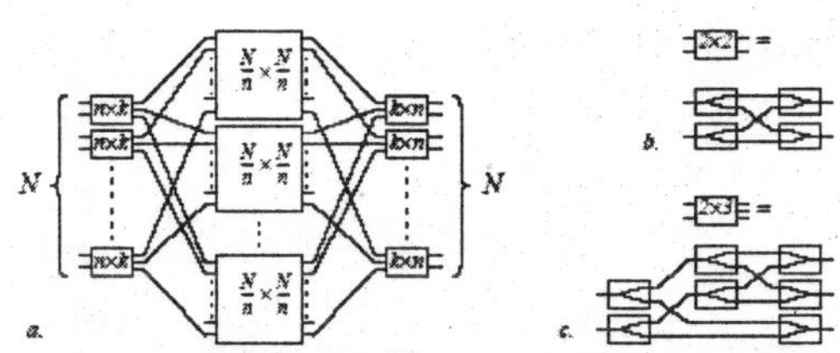

Fig. 3 Clos strictly non-blocking network

Fig. 4 shows the tree method, which leads to a shorter signal path length and, for small N, to smaller switch sizes. The switch size is given by. $M_2k = 2^{2k+1} - 2^{k+1}$. With , k = ^{2}logN, this yields $M_N = O(N^2)$. The signal path length is $L_k = 2k$.

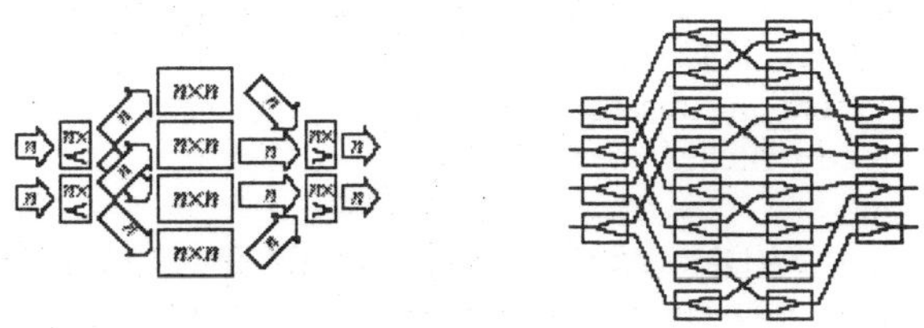

Fig. 4 Tree construction of strictly non-blocking switches and a 4 × 4 example

2.4. Wavelength switches

WDM switches can be built from space switches with multiplexers and demultiplexers, or from devices that exploit the wavelength multiplexed nature of the signals. Fig. 5 shows a four fibre, four wavelength switch using a space switch. Clearly, a full-blown 16′16 space switch is not needed: it would allow superfluous paths that could lead to conflicts. Instead, only one 4′4 space switch is needed per wavelength, as in Fig. 5.b.

Fig. 5 shows how a switch for the same number of fibres but variable number of wavelengths can be built using AOTFs. As long as the number of wavelengths can be accommodated by single AOTFs, the number of AOTFs depends only on the number of input and output

fibres. For an 8×8 switch operating at sixteen wavelengths, the space switch needs 16.80 = 1280 switch elements, while an AOTF-based switch needs 20 AOTFs, and is able to switch any number of wavelengths up to a certain maximum. This is true for all methods mentioned in Section 2.3.

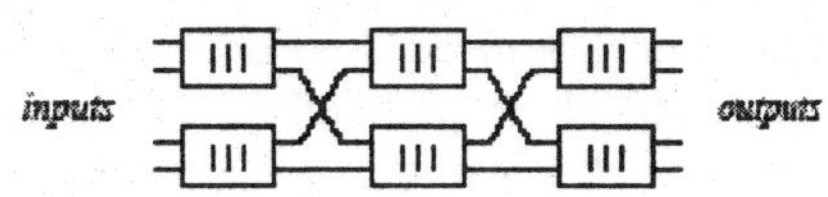

Fig. 5 Switch with four fibres, variable number of wavelengths using AOTFs

This comparison is a little unfair because AOTFs are bigger than 1×2 switches. Also, it may prove difficult to integrate several AOTFs on a chip because of their size and the power needed to drive the SAW transducers. On the other hand, a reasonable number of 1×2 elements can be integrated on chip. [14] reports a 4×4 switch using 24 such elements in tree configuration. Moreover, the crosstalk characteristics of AOTFs may be worse. Lastly, as we saw before, the use of fibre amplifiers may limit the number of wavelengths. Also, space switches can take advantage of WDM techniques by converting to wavelength multiplexed format intermediately. An example where space and wavelength multiplexing are combined can be found in [22].

From the discussion of space switches and AOTF based switches, we find:

- WDM enables switches of far fewer elements than current SDM technology allows.
- WDM networks can be "soft" w.r.t. the number of wavelengths. However, AOTFs also introduce new problems.
- They require fairly wide wavelength spacing.
- They limit either the number of wavelengths to 3 or 4, or the optical path length.
- The tuning time is fairly long.

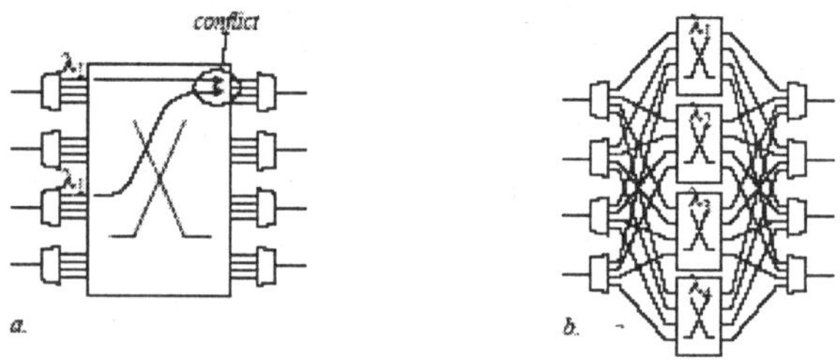

Fig. 6 Four fibre, four wavelength space switch. a. Full-blown, b. One switch for each wavelength

2.5. Wavelength conversion and wavelength reuse

In the switches discussed so far, signals stay at the same wavelength and so they will along the whole path through the network. A request for a connection over a path is blocked when no wavelength is free on all links along that path. Wavelength conversion enables a different wavelength to be used on each link, and so decreases the blocking probability. A simple way to convert wavelengths is to detect the optical signal and use the resulting signal to modulate a properly tuned laser.

Wavelength conversion also enhances wavelength reuse, that is, the use of the same wavelength in different parts of a network. Wavelength reuse and wavelength conversion together make possible the construction of networks of many more nodes than wavelengths, to the point claimed in [6] where the network size becomes virtually independent of the number of available wavelengths.

WDM networks without wavelength conversion can be mimicked by SDM networks. A WDM signal is identified by its wavelength, an SDM signal by the fibre it is on. Let us now tag each fibre in a bundle with a label. A WDM switch without wavelength conversion corresponds with an SDM switch in which signals enter and leave at fibres with the same label. Wavelength converting WDM switches are mimicked by SDM switches that can route outgoing signals on any fibre in a bundle. We shall call such SDM switches and networks label-free. Clearly, wavelength conversion is not an inherent advantage of WDM.

WDM switches with wavelength conversion and label free SDM switches must be able to route a signal from any input to any output. A WDM switch for wavelengths and input and output fibres can be built from a ´ space switch and wavelength convertors that convert to a fixed wavelength, Fig. 7. This configuration can be found in, e.g., [11,24]. A corresponding label-free SDM switch needs only the cP × cP switch.

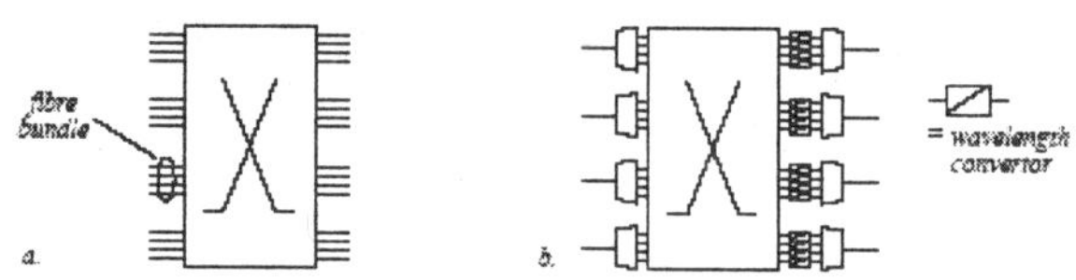

Fig. 7. a Label-free SDM switch, b. WDM switch with wavelength conversion

WDM devices can lead to smaller designs: tunable wavelength convertors allow a simplification of the space switch. Fig. 8.a shows a space switch partitioned into 4´4 switches. This is wasteful as it takes more switch elements and results in a longer signal path. However, when used in Fig. 7.b, tunable wavelength convertors make the third column unnecessary, Fig. 8.b. AOTFs lead to even smaller switches, but they need two tunable wavelength conversion stages to ensure that signals that enter or leave at the same fibre, use distinct wavelengths in the switching stage (Fig. 8.c).

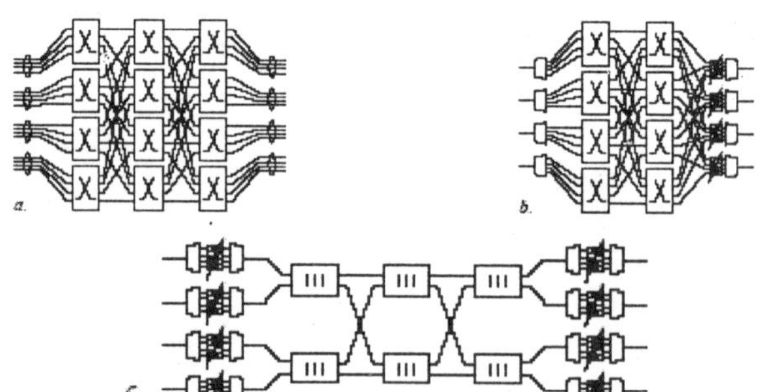

Fig. 8 (a) Label-free SDM switch built from 4 × 4 elements
b. WDM switch with tunable wavelength convertors
c. AOTF-based switch with wavelength conversion

It depends on the cost of tunable convertors whether WDM switches with wavelength conversion can be cheaper than label-free SDM switches. Section 3 shows that wavelength conversion can also be achieved in the access nodes of multi-hop networks. So, the switch size and the mode of operation (single- or multi-hop) determine whether WDM or SDM leads to cheaper switches in a network with wavelength or label conversion.

3. Single-hop and Multi-hop Routing

In contrast to single-hop systems, which route a connection directly from its source to its destination, in multihop networks a connection may exit the optical network at various intermediate nodes, where routing decisions are made, and be re-inserted in the optical network. After a number of hops, the connection reaches its destination. Multi-hop networks provide packet switching and allow lightpaths, and therefore transmission capacity, to be shared. The lightpaths form a network in its own right, called the virtual topology. For more on multi-hop routing, see [6,21]. A multi-hop network, discussed extensively in [6], with AOTFs and access nodes with ATM switching capability, is drawn in Fig. 9.

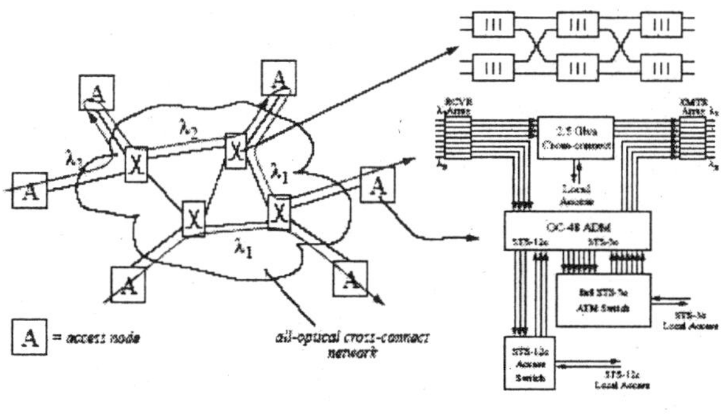

Fig. 9 A multi-hop network, with details of the optical cross-connects and the access nodes. This figure is due to [6]

The figure shows two connections, one of which is routed in three hops. The multi-hop connection uses different wavelengths on its hops. The wavelength conversion is achieved in the access nodes by electronic means. The overall blocking probability between source and destination can be much smaller than in a single-hop network. Single-hop routing is often said to scale worse than multi-hop, even with wavelength conversion. However, the results of analysis and simulations in [24] for arbitrary topology networks with fairly few nodes (up to one thousand), are not dramatically different from those for multihop networks [6], which are based on ShuffleNet. The authors of [6] expect different, but not radically different results for other virtual topologies. They express the need to develop of algorithms to construct virtual topologies that are scalable and modular, can be made to fit geographic patterns, can be adapted to changing traffic conditions, and can route around network faults.

Circuit-switched connections have the full bandwidth of the channels they use. In optical networks, this is the bandwidth of the transmission equipment on the fibre or the wavelength. Multi-hop connections occupy as many receiver-transmitter pairs as hops, and take capacity from the switches at the access nodes. They may take a longer overall route through the optical network and use up a larger portion of the network capacity than strictly necessary, depending on the efficiency of the virtual topology. The aforementioned study [6] shows that a ShuffleNet serving 100 million users requires 12 hops on average when 8 wavelengths are used. Multi-hop access nodes require routing capability and are therefore expensive (Fig. 9, due to [6]). Single-hop access nodes only need as many pairs of transmitters and receivers as the number of connections they must support.

Multi-hop networks fully regenerate signals at the access nodes. If hops can be kept within a certain length (not in long-haul links) less amplifiers are needed, and AOTFs can be used without being limited to 3 or 4 wavelengths. A hierarchical routing approach can enable this. In this= approach, the network is divided in areas. The first level routing decision is which areas to cross. The second level routes connections within an area. In single-hop networks signals stay optical, so amplification and regeneration take extra equipment.

Packet-switching is easy to do in multi-hop systems by putting packet switches in the access nodes. For singlehop routing it is much more difficult because it requires optical packet-switching. High-speed switching techniques are under development [8,9,22], but buffering is very difficult. Options include: routing packets through big coils of fibre, deflection routing [21] (or hot potato routing [28]), or routing on another wavelength. Without buffering, performance will be unacceptably low. The technology for multi-hop routing is rapidly maturing, but that for all-optical packet and ATM-cell switching, is still experimental. So, for the near term future multi-hop routing is the most attractive option for packet-switching. Because the ITU-T has specified ATM as the transmission mode for B-ISDN, multi-hop routing seems the best candidate for a future optical public network.

Although multi-hop operation is often discussed with respect to WDM, it should be clear that multi-hop routing can just as easily be implemented over SDM networks. The cost implications and control complexities are difficult to compare. Therefore, the choice for single-hop or multi-hop does not lead to a clear answer as to which of WDM and SDM should be used. On the other hand, regardless of the latter, we have seen some compelling reasons to use multi-hop routing.

4. The core network versus the access network

In this section we will examine where SDM and WDM are best used in the core and the access network. Let us first make clear what we mean by core and access network. Simply put, the core network is the network that interconnects user areas, while the access network connects the customers within a user area, which is a fairly small geographical region. The access network is a collection of small and metropolitan area networks with high connectivity and many terminals. It extends from the user terminals to a point where high traffic aggregation is reached. In telephone and ATM networks, it extends to the Local Exchange (LEX) or Transit Exchange (TEX) switch. Examples include: city neighbourhoods, business parks, corporate networks, LANs. The core network connects access networks. It is less dense and carries highly aggregated traffic. This 'definition' does not make a sharp distinction but allows us to discuss these aspects of public networks.

4.1. The core network

- The core network crosses long distances, using a lot of so-called long-haul lines. Because of attenuation in the fibre, amplification and signal regeneration are needed.
- Fibre is already employed in the core network, together with other technologies such as copper, radio links, and satellite. Fibre is commonly used with synchronous digital transmission systems: PDH, SDH, SONET. Common topologies are ring and star.
- The fibre multiplicity is usually small. The Transatlantic cable, for instance, has only two fibres.
- The topology of the core network changes as nodes and trunks are added, but this happens at a modest rate: cities, business parks, and campuses do not pop up very fast.

4.2. The access network

- The access network covers relatively small areas, up to 50 or 100 kilometres across. Link lengths may be short enough that no amplifiers and signal regenerators are needed. As suggested earlier, the right virtual topologies may make this possible. However, certain topologies bring about splitting of fibres, which necessitates amplification.
- In the access network fibre is mostly used where aggregation is high. This is because bringing fibre to the home takes enormous investments. An attractive candidate for getting fibre nearer to the home is hybrid fibre coax (HFC).
- Fibre multiplicity is bigger in the access network than in the core network because of the large number of terminals to be connected.
- The access network undergoes frequent topology changes: new terminals are added daily. Individual additions may not give rise to topology changes, but after a number of additions the network must adopt a new configuration to serve traffic flows better.
- In the access network traffic is less aggregated than in the core network. Therefore, there may be stronger traffic fluctuations that the network has to cope with.

Currently, HFC networks [18,23] are mostly disjoint from telecommunication networks, but this is rapidly changing. Many activities are going on to provide new services over HFC, like telephony [7] and data-oriented services such as video on demand and Internet. These are pursued by DAVIC and IEEE 802.14 [3,10]. HFC may play an important role in future optical networks simply because they are there. If their fibre can be included in the public network, big savings can be made on fibre installation [2]. The star, or sometimes ring of stars, topology of HFC networks reflects their aim, which is distribution of TV signals. There may be as many as 200 to 5,000 homes on a fibre. HFC is not designed for two-way communication, so that is a challenge to achieve. Work is being done to introduce interactive services in HFC networks through the use of WDM [15].

There are considerable differences between access networks. LANs and corporate networks are intended for inter-user traffic, while in blocks of homes inter-user traf- fic is much less. In the public network, therefore, the part of the access network nearest to the user needs only multiplexing capability, and switching is postponed until multiple multiplexed traffic streams come together at the LEX. In particular, the access nodes of multi-hop networks could assume the function of a LEX, so that customer premises equipment (CPE) needs only be able to multiplex and can be kept affordable.

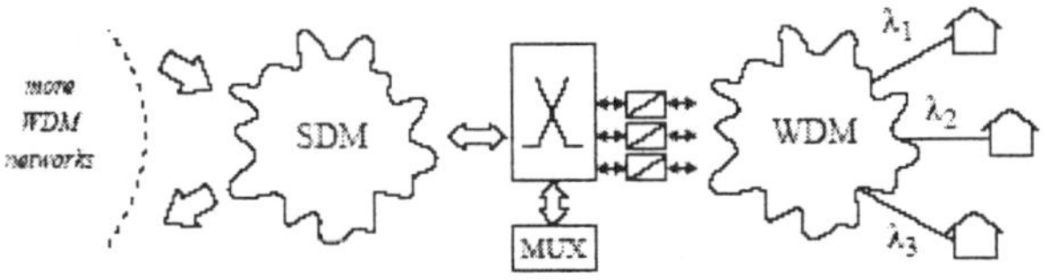

Fig. 12 De/multiplexing and wavelength conversion between SDM and WDM network

5. Conclusions

We have compared WDM and SDM for use in future optical networks. WDM enables networks with less fibres, less optical amplifiers, and less complex switches. On the other hand, in small areas where fibres are already available in bundles of high multiplicity, SDM can provide the same connectivity. Also, space switches behave better regarding signal degradation and seem to allow a higher degree of on-chip integration. The promise of WDM of enabling more bandwidth and simpler switches is therefore not decisive.

WDM offers better scalability, with respect to gradual increase of bandwidth and continuous addition of users and sub-networks. SDM is better for the distribution part of the access network. Costs impede the introduction of WDM in the customer premises at short term. Therefore, SDM will continue to play an important role in the access network.

Since the public network is expected to offer B-ISDN, public optical networks must be able to perform packet (ATM cell) switching. As this is difficult to realise in single- hop mode, the best suited routing mode is multi-hop. This also leads to better control of signal degradation. Multi-hop routing is not an entirely all-optical solution, but studies by other authors have shown that large scale all-optical networks are not feasible anyway. Last but not least, SDM and WDM can be combined in the same network, which is important for network evolution.

6. References

[1] Barry R.A., Humblet P.A., "Models of Blocking Probability in All-Optical Networks with and Without Wavelength Changers," *IEEE Journal on Selected Areas in Communications*, vol. 14, no. 5, pp. 858-867, June 1996

[2] Bell G., Gemmell J., "On-Ramp Prospects for the Information Superhighway Dream," *Communications of the ACM*, vol. 39, no. 7, pp. 55-61, July 1996

[3] Bisdikian C., et al., "MLAP: A MAC Level Access Protocol for the HFC 802.14 Network," *IEEE Communications Magazine*, pp. 114-121, March1996

[4] Brackett C.A., "Dense Wavelength Division Multiplexing Networks: Principles and Applications," *IEEE Journal on Selected Areas in Communications*, vol. 8, no. 6, Aug 1990

[5] Brackett C.A., "Obstacles on the Way to Transparent Multiwavelength Networks," *Proc. ECOC'95*, Brussels, 1995

[6] Brackett C.A., et al., "A Scalable Multiwavelength Multihop Optical Network: A Proposal for Research on All-Optical Networks" (invited paper), *IEEE Journal of Lightwave Technology*, vol. 11, no. 5/6, pp. 736-753, May/June 1993

[7] Carroll C., "Development of Integrated Cable/Telephony in the United Kingdom," *IEEE Communications Magazine*, pp. 48-60, Aug 1995

[8] Cinato P., et al., "Architectural Analysis, Feasibility Study and First Experimental Results for a Photonic ATM Switching Module to be Employed in a Large Size Switching Network," *ISS'95*, vol. 2, pp. 382-386, April 1995

[9] Cotter D., et al., "100 Gbit/s Packet Self-Routing Using All-Optical 6-Bit 'Keyword' Address Recognition," *ECOC'95*, Brussels, pp. 637-640, 1995

[10] Dail J.E., et al., "Adaptive Digital Access Protocol: A MAC Protocol for Multiservice Broadband Networks," *IEEE Communications Magazine*, pp. 104-112, March 1996

[11] Derr F., et al., "An Optical Infrastructure for Future Telecommunications Networks," *IEEE Communications Magazine*, pp. 84-88, Nov 1995

[12] Giglmayr J., "Architectural Framework for Optical Frequency Division Multiplexing Systems Based on Regular Space-Frequency Interconnections," *IEEE Journal of Lightwave Technology*, vol. 12 no. 7, pp. 1291-1306, July 1994

[13] Green P.E., "Fiber Optic Networks," Englewood Cliffs, NJ. Prentice Hall, 1993

[14] Johansson S., et al., "Optical Cross-Connect System in Broad-Band Networks: System Concept and Demonstrators Description" (invited paper), *IEEE Journal of Lightwave Technology*, vol. 11, no. 5/6, pp. 688-694, May/June 1993

[15] Koonen A.M.J., et al., "TOBASCO: An Innovative Approach for Upgrading CATV Fibre-Coax Networks for Broadband Interactive Services," CTIT Technical

A Layered Approach to Modeling Network Connectivity for Topological Analysis of Network Security

M. Sreedevi[1] and Dr. R. Seshadri[2]

[1]Research Scholar

[2]Professor and Director of Computer Center,

S.V.U, Tirupati.

srikundu@yahoo.co.in *ravalaseshadri@gmail.com*

Abstract

Topological vulnerability analysis (TVA) extends this by searching for sequences of interdependent vulnerabilities, distributed among the various network hosts. The individual vulnerabilities of hosts on a network can be combined by an attacker to gain access that would not be possible if the hosts were not interconnected. Currently available tools report vulnerabilities in isolation and in the context of individual hosts in a network.. Model checking has been applied to the analysis of this problem with some interesting initial result. However previous efforts did not take into account a realistic representation of network connectivity. This paper extends the previous model checking approach by including representations of network connectivity in the analysis model. It is TCP/IP and Ethernet centric, but the methods used could easily be extended to support alternative networking protocols. A layered approach is used to capture specific vulnerabilities that exist at different layers of TCP/IP. With this enhancement, it is possible to represent realistic networks including common network security devices.

Key Words: *Vulnerability, Network Security, Exploit, Network Connectivity*

1. Introduction

A common approach used to analyzing network security is to focus on individual vulnerabilities on each host that makes up the network. There are many products designed to assist in this process, including products that scan for vulnerabilities on a host from across a network [7] and products that run on the host being analyzed [5]. These tools can help identify known vulnerabilities on these computers and can produce reports that help security administrators identify steps to reduce the vulnerabilities that exist on each of the scanned systems. This is a reasonable approach as the reduction in vulnerability for the individual hosts on a network is bound to have a positive impact on the security of the network as a whole. However, it does not offer any insight into vulnerabilities caused by interactions of systems on a network. Previous work used a modeling approach to analyze network security based on the interactions of vulnerabilities within individual hosts and between hosts connected by the network [8]. This work applied model checking technology to analyze a simplified network security model and determine whether the network's security requirements were met or if there was a method that could be used to invalidate any of the requirements. The security requirements were encoded as assertions in the model checker. The model checker was used to determine whether any of these assertions could be proved false. In this case the model checker produced a detailed set of steps that it had used to invalidate the assertion. This set of steps constituted a potential path an attacker might follow to circumvent the security of the network.

While this work was useful for validating the model checking approach, substantial improvements are required to make it a practical tool in analyzing real-world network vulnerabilities. These include the development of automated tools to populate the model, the encoding of a large set of exploitation techniques into the model, and refinements in the model itself to allow it to more accurately represent modern computer networks. Our research center and others are actively working on these issues, but most of the work has concentrated on the first two problems. This paper specifically addresses enhancements to the model described in [8] that support a sufficiently rich representation of connectivity for real-world networks. A sophisticated depiction of network connectivity is essential to model network vulnerability. A primary means of defending against network attack is the use of firewalls and filtering routers. For a model to produce useable results, the effects of these devices must be represented. In addition, there are certain attacks that operate against the network itself as opposed to targeting a particular host on the network. These also must be represented for the model to be capable of analyzing real-world network security problems. In summary, this paper presents extensions to the previous model checking approach that provides sophisticated representation of network connectivity while not excessively increasing the state-space of the model. This is interesting because it brings us much closer to the ability to produce a tool capable of analyzing the impact that interactions of vulnerabilities have between hosts on real-world networks.

2. The Network Security Model

Our approach, which we call Topological Vulnerability Analysis (TVA), uses a state-based model of network security to discover attack paths. In this section, we provide a short description of how the model is structured.

2.1 Model Elements

There are four major elements that make up the network security model.

- A network of hosts, including the network services, components and configuration details that give rise to vulnerabilities
- Connectivity of the hosts
- Exploits, or attacks, that change the state of the model
- A list of security requirements the model should attempt to validate.

Hosts are described by their network services, components and configurations, and the current user privileges obtained by the attacker. Vulnerabilities might arise from obvious problems, such as running an outdated network service like Send mail [4]. They might also depend on general configuration details, such as operating system version, type of authentication, and password length. Our definition of vulnerability is broad. In this model, vulnerability is any system attribute that can be used as a prerequisite for an exploit. This may seem unbounded, but in reality, because there is a finite number of known exploits each with a finite number of prerequisite vulnerabilities, the total set of vulnerabilities needed by the model is finite. This is important because it allows us to bound the total number of system features we must search for to populate the analysis model.

Connectivity is modeled using a variety of techniques depending upon the TCP/IP layer that is being represented. This is an extension of the previous connectivity model, which used a simple Boolean matrix to represent connectivity. The enhancements presented in the paper allow the model to more accurately represent real-world networks, making its results more relevant. More will be said about this in the following sections. Exploits are modeled using functions that, given the right circumstances, can cause changes to the state of the model. Exploits are used by the model to affect changes to the security of the hosts under analysis. The quality and quantity of exploits encoded in the model have a direct relationship with the quality of the analysis that can be performed with the model.

Security requirements are represented by invariant statements made about the security of particular hosts on the network (e.g. an attacker can not obtain administrative access to host A).

2.2 Vulnerabilities and Exploits

Vulnerabilities and the methods necessary to exploit them form the core of the model. The technique relies on modeling the network attributes that give rise to vulnerabilities, then analyzing whether the exploits encoded into the model can take advantage of the vulnerabilities to circumvent the network's security. Vulnerabilities come from many sources and are difficult to eliminate because of several factors. For a network to be useful, it must offer services. These services are implemented in software and it is difficult to guarantee that any complex piece of software does not contain some flaws [2]. These flaws frequently translate into security vulnerabilities. In addition, simple network configuration errors can introduce exploitable security flaws.

To break into a network, it is not sufficient to know about the vulnerabilities on the network. You must also have an exploit to take advantage of these vulnerabilities. In addition, before an exploit can be used, its pre-conditions must be met. These preconditions may include the set of vulnerabilities that the exploit relies on, sufficient user rights on the target, sufficient user rights on the attacking host, and network connectivity. Results of a successful exploit could include discovering valuable information about the network, elevating user rights, defeating filters, and adding trust relationships among other possible effects. These post-conditions share a common feature; they reduce the security of the network. The concept of exploit pre-conditions and post-conditions is illustrated in Fig. 1

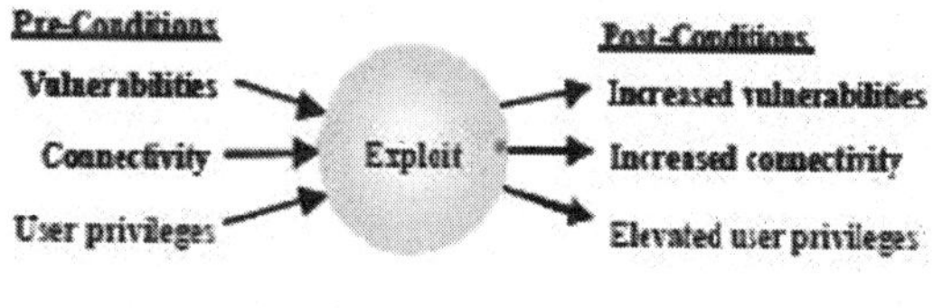

Fig. 1 Exploit Model

By successively employing exploits, an increasing number of vulnerabilities can be added to a host. Given the right set of circumstances, this may result in the complete compromise of the host. If an attacker gains control of a host, it can be used to attack other hosts on the network. It is in this fashion that an attacker can move through a network until they have achieved their final goal. This chaining of exploits to compromise multiple hosts is shown in Fig. 2.

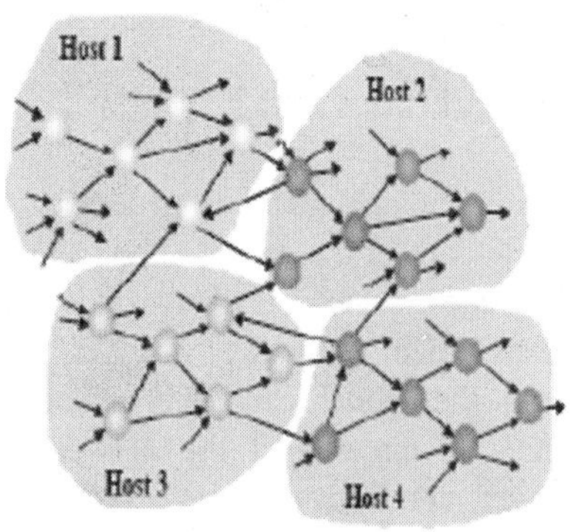

Fig. 2 A Network of Exploits

2.3. Model Checking

Initial versions of TVA relied upon model checkers to act as the analysis engine. Model checkers are attractive because they are designed to handle large state spaces [3] and they efficiently generate counterexamples that, for TVA, correspond to attack paths. Thus they provide a mechanism to avoid custom building the same capabilities into special purpose tools. They are not particularly well suited for this application, though, because the TVA model is monotonic. In it, exploits don't decrease the vulnerability of the network. They always increase it. There is never a need for the analysis engine to back track to come up with a solution. Model checkers on the other hand, must support non-monotonic and other more general problems. This requires them to be substantially more complex than TVA requires. While the work of this paper is not directly affected by the choice of the analysis engine, it is worth noting that a custom application has the potential to substantially outperform a general purpose model checker.

3. Modeling Link Layer Security

As stated previously, we use a layered approach to modeling network connectivity within TVA. These layers are derived from the structure of the TCP/IP network protocol stack. The lowest layer of the TCP/IP protocol stack is the Link layer, which provides and manages access to the network medium.

At the Link layer, communication can only occur between hosts located on the same network segment. To deliver a TCP/IP packet to a host on the segment, the destination IP address must be resolved into a Link layer address. The protocol that performs this resolution is the Address Resolution Protocol (ARP). ARP-resolved addresses therefore identify hosts that share a common network segment, and we label such connectivity LINK_ARP. This type of connectivity is the prerequisite for many network attacks such as TCP session hijacking.

Another Link layer characteristic relevant to network security is packet sniffing. Sniffing is an activity through which a privileged user can eavesdrop on network traffic. Most network traffic is transmitted unencrypted, and might include usernames and passwords for protocols such as telnet, ftp, rlogin, pop3 and others. An attacker could use this ability to capture the authentication details for a particular user, then use them to impersonate the user on the network.

The ability to sniff network traffic is affected by whether a network is switched or not. Ethernet was developed as a bus-like medium where all hosts connected to a hub shared the network bandwidth. Hubs re-broadcast all received packets to every connected host. With this scheme, all network traffic is visible to every host's network interface card (NIC) connected to the same network segment. Normally, a NIC ignores traffic that is not specifically addressed to it. However, it is possible for privileged users to put NICs in promiscuous mode, allowing them to capture all local traffic. Sniffing on a non-switched network, then, enables an attacker to capture all traffic crossing the local network, whether or not it's addressed to or fromthe attacker's machine.

Ethernet switches essentially eliminate bandwidth sharing by directing traffic to those hosts specifically addressed in the Link layer frames. This filtering process limits the usefulness of sniffing because the only network traffic that the attacker will see are packets addressed to or leaving from the sniffing host. Note that broadcast packets (packets addressed to all hosts on the same network segment) will be visible to the attacker regardless of whether the network is switched or non switched.

Fig. 3 depicts a generic ARP exploit (a) and a generic SNIFF exploit (b). Note that we show only the connectivity pre-conditions; other preconditions, such as the presence of a sniffer program or the attainment of super user access, would be required for a full TVA model. Also, the exploit post-conditions are not labeled because they depend on the exploit specifics (e.g., a password sniffing exploit would have a post-condition that indicated a password had been obtained).

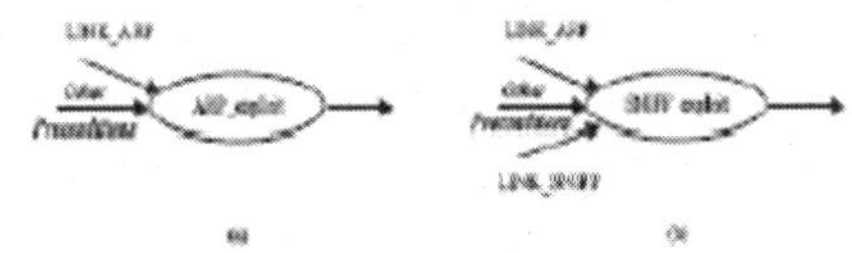

Fig. 3 Generic Link Layer Exploits

The following example shows how these exploits might map to a real network. In Fig. 4, Fred and Helen share a hub, so they can sniff each other's communications with Sheila. Because a switch separates Sheila and the hub, Sheila cannot sniff traffic between Fred and Helen. The generic ARP exploit shown in Fig. 3(a) can trigger for all three hosts, because all have LINK_ARP connectivity between them. However, the generic SNIFF exploit in Fig. 3(b) can only apply to Fred and Helen because Sheila does not have any LINK_SNIFF connectivity.

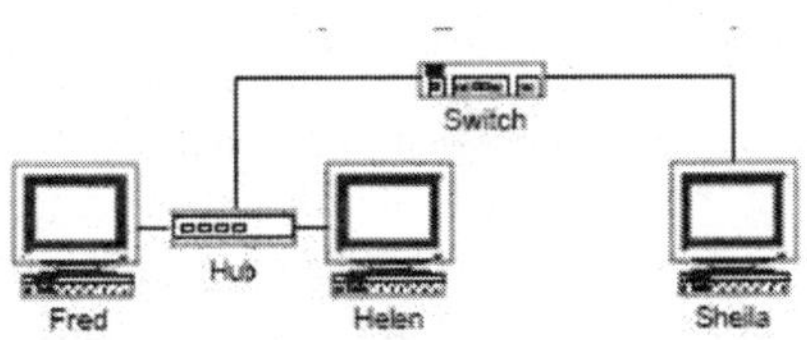

Fig. 4 Mixed Network (Switched & Non-Switched)

4. Modeling Network and Transport Layer Security

The Network layer of TCP/IP provides global addressing and routing of packets between network segments. The source and destination IP addresses of the packet are specified at this layer. The Transport layer controls the flow of data between different host services, which are addressed by a local port number. TCP/IP offers two transport protocols. The Transmission Control Protocol (TCP) is stream oriented and provides a reliable, byte oriented data flow through control functions that are largely transparent at the Application layer. The User Datagram Protocol (UDP) is record oriented and simply offers the ability to send packets between hosts, so the application must provide control functions if reliable delivery is required.

Most network services communicate via transport protocols, so their packets contain both Network layer (IP) and Transport layer (port) addresses. These address details are commonly used by firewalls to decide whether a packet should be allowed between hosts. They may restrict access based on the IP address and/or port number of either the source or destination host. Capturing this connectivity-limiting firewall behavior at both the Network and Transport layers is therefore critical in analyzing network security.

In [8], connectivity was represented with a simple Boolean matrix, which is sufficient to characterize firewall restrictions based solely on IP address. Transport layer connectivity requires a more complex representation. One possible method is to simply add dimensions to the connectivity matrix for the UDP and TCP port numbers. This may work from an analytical point of view, but it would drastically increase the size of the model to account for the 65,536 port numbers associated with each transport protocol. An easy way to reduce this is to track only the ports on a network that are actually in use. Symbolic labels can be created for each of these in-use ports and the total number of labels would dictate the size of the matrix. While this would greatly reduce the size of the connectivity matrix, it does not address an important requirement of the security analysis problem. From a security analysis perspective, raw connectivity is not the only pre-condition necessary for an attack to succeed. A vulnerability must also exist in the application that supports the network service. Such a vulnerability is usually specific to the particular application. For example, Microsoft's Internet Information Server (IIS) web server is susceptible to different attacks than the Apache web server [1, 6]. It is much more important to track the specific application details associated with the service than it is to track the port number on which the service runs. Therefore, we name Transport layer connectivity variables after the application that supports the network service (e.g., TRANS_APACHE_1_3_21). Such names can easily be extended to include patch level and other information required to delineate between different exploits' pre-conditions. By avoiding port numbers, this approach also eliminates complications associated with running services on non-standard ports. Web servers, for example, often run on ports other than 80. A port based approach would require a table to map port numbers to application details. Instead, we collapse the required connectivity information into a single, appropriately named variable as shown in Fig. 5.

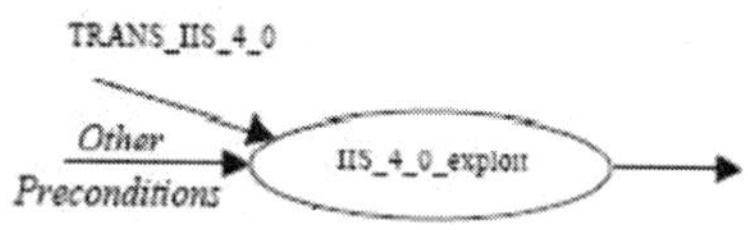

Fig. 5 Example Transport Layer Exploit

Fig. 6 shows a small but typical network where a firewall policy limits Transport layer connectivity to some public services. Specifically, external hosts (represented by Smithers) are allowed to connect to internal hosts on ports 80 and 8080 (which would allow Smithers to communicate with the Apache and IIS servers located on Homer), but connections to all other ports (including Send mail on Marge) are blocked. Homer and Marge, on the other hand, are permitted to any port on Smithers.

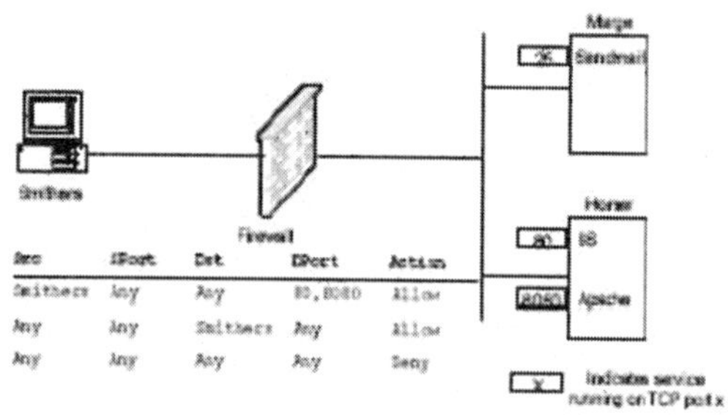

Fig. 6 Example Network with Connectivity- Limiting Firewall

As discussed earlier, the actual port numbers are irrelevant for TVA analysis. Rather, the ability of an attacker to launch an exploit is based on whether Transport layer connectivity exists to the service applications themselves. An attacker with access to Smithers, for example, might use exploits against Homer that require TRANS_IIS or TRANS_APACHE connectivity, but couldn't directly launch exploits against Marge's Send mail service because the firewall blocks access to it. Homer, though, enjoys unrestricted access to Marge. If the attacker on Smithers could first gain control of Homer by exploiting one of the directly accessible services, Marge would be indirectly reachable. Fig. 7 shows a possible exploit path from Smithers to Marge, where an IIS exploit first yields the ability to execute programs on Homer. This increase in access level, combined with Homer's Transport layer connectivity to Marge, then allows the attacker to apply a Send mail exploit against Marge. One of TVA's core capabilities is it's ability to shift the locus of attack in this way, just as a real attacker would, to work around connectivity limiting facilities such as firewall policies.

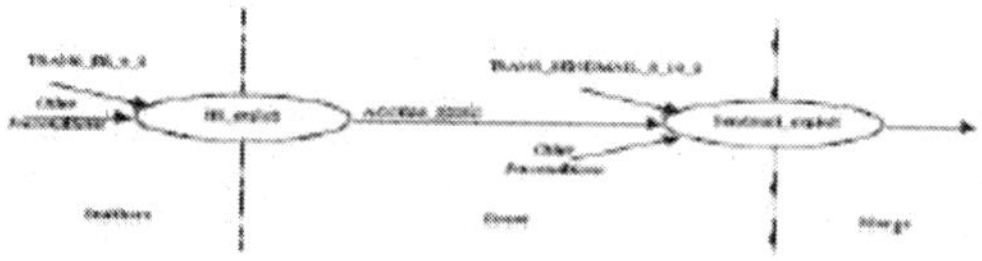

Fig. 7 Example Exploit Path

In addition to a symbolic label for each service on the network, the special symbol TRANS_UNUSED is included as a standard entry in the Transport layer definitions. This symbol refers to the collection of all ports on a system that are not currently being used by a listening service. Capturing this condition is needed to model a class of exploit called port forwarding, and results when connectivity-limiting devices permit connections to services that aren't actually running on the destination host. For example, Smithers can send packets to port 8080 on Marge even though a service isn't actually running on that port.

5. Modeling Application Layer Security

The first three layers of the TCP/IP reference model do not address all connectivity-related security issues. For example, an attacker might be able to connect with a Transport layer service, but might have to authenticate with a password to actually exploit it. TVA uses a separate Application layer to address these types of issues. Some services such as telnet establish trust relationships based on password authentication. TVA represents this with an Application layer connection, e.g.,

APP_PW_AUTH. The sample telnet exploit shown in Figure 8 includes both the TRANS_TELNET and APP_PW_AUTH connections required to exploit it. Note that TVA includes the normal operation of services such as telnet in its exploit database, and applies them just as a real attacker would if he had successfully acquired a user's password.

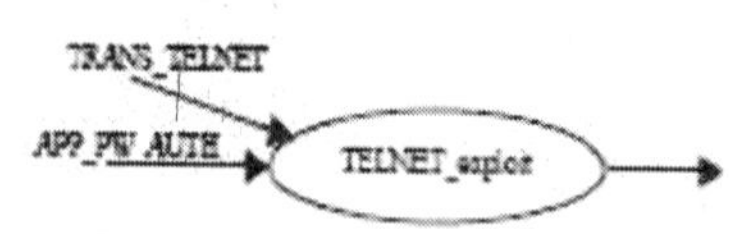

Fig. 8 Example Telnet Exploit

So far, we've presented several layers of connectivity, as they pertain to security, in the context of individual exploits. The real power of TVA, though, is its ability to chain exploits together into multi-step attack paths. The next section presents an example that highlights this capability.

6. An Example

To illustrate the ideas developed in this paper, we present a small network similar to the example in Section 4. Fig. 9 is deceptively simple in terms of the number of hosts on the network, but offers an exploit path that might not be obvious to many administrators. The firewall policy is restrictive, allowing only Secure Shell (port 22) and IIS (port 80) traffic from the attack machine (i.e., inbound). Secure Shell is allowed to both Maude and Ned, though you'll note it isn't actually running on Maude. Inbound IIS traffic is restricted to Maude, and inbound FTP traffic isn't permitted at all. Outbound traffic to the attack machine is unrestricted.

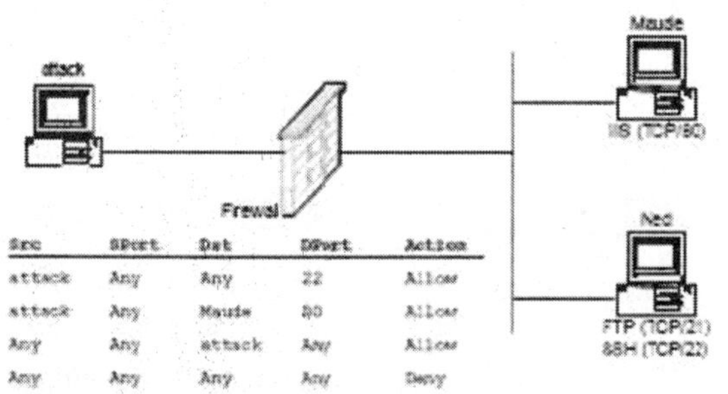

Fig. 9 Final Example

A simplified TVA connectivity matrix for this configuration is shown in Table 1. The keyword 'ANY' indicates the source host can connect to any service on the destination, and is only used to make the matrix more readable. An actual TVA model would list all connections, but for simplification we only record those to and from machines Maude and Ned.

Source \ Destination	attack	Maude	Ned
attack	ANY	TRANS_IIS TRANS_UNUSED	TRANS_SSH
Maude	ANY	ANY	TRANS_FTP TRANS_SSH
Ned	ANY	TRANS_IIS TRANS_UNUSED	ANY

Table 1 Example Connectivity Matrix

Now suppose TVA is configured with the exploits shown in Fig. 10. The input arrows represent pre-conditions that must exist on the attacking machine to trigger the exploit, and the output arrows signify post-conditions that apply to the victim machine. For example, the FTP exploit shown in (b) requires Transport layer connectivity to an FTP service and the ability to execute programs on the attacking machine as preconditions, and yields the ability to execute programs on the victim machine as a postcondition. Besides the ACCESS_EXEC post condition already mentioned, we included another condition that isn't related to connectivity in exploits (c) and (d). The PGM_PORT-FWD condition indicates that a port-forwarding program is installed on the machine. These conditions hint at other elements required in a full TVA model, and are included here to illustrate how exploit postconditions can satisfy the pre-conditions of other exploits.

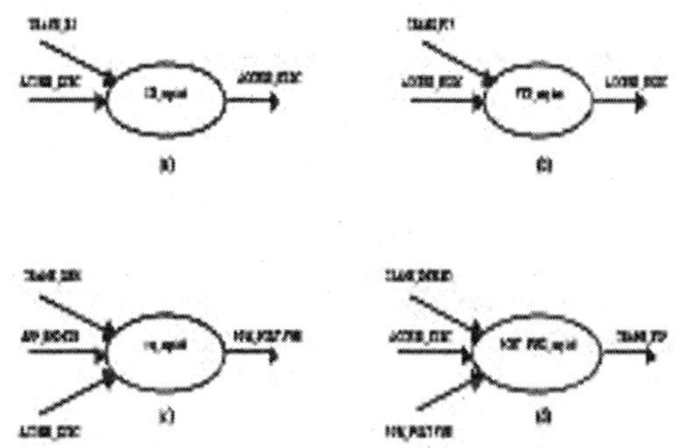

Fig. 10 Example Exploits

We set our attack goal as obtaining execute access on Ned. Assuming the attacker starts with the ability to execute programs on her own machine, the reader might compare the connectivity matrix and exploits to construct the exploit path shown in Fig. 11, which realizes the goal even though the firewall blocks access from the attack machine to Ned. The attacker has TRANS_IIS connectivity to Maude, so she can execute the IIS exploit (a), which yields execute access on Maude. The new execute access enables her to copy a port forwarding program from the attack machine using RCP_exploit (c). Although we don't show it in the diagram, an rcp client is required to actually execute RCP_exploit. An rcp client is included in the default Windows NT installation, on which the IIS web server runs. Note that all the preconditions for (c) apply to Maude because the locus of attack has transferred there. Maude is exploiting its TRANS_RSH and APP_RHOSTS connectivity to hack the attack machine and download a program! Of course, it's the attacker that really drives the process, and she must set up her machine to allow the connections. The PGM_PORT-FWD download, combined with connectivity to an unused port, then triggers the port forward exploit (c), which in turn yields TRANS_FTP connectivity to Ned. Finally, the attacker takes advantage of the indirect access to Ned to execute the FTP exploit (b), which gives her the ability to execute programs on Ned. The goal has been realized.

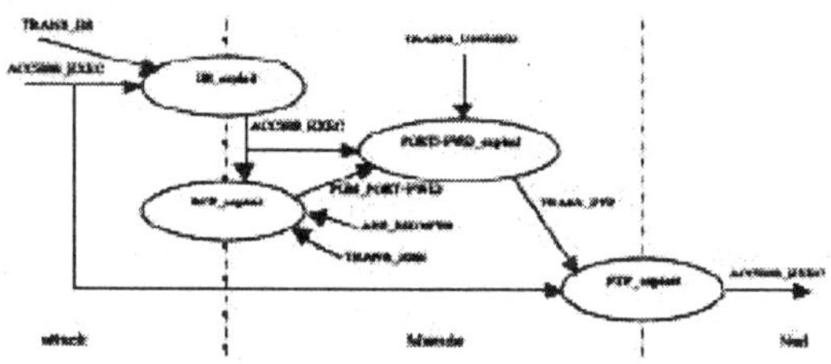

Fig. 11 Exploit Path

Manually constructing this exploit path is fairly trivial, but the complexity of a more realistic network with hundreds of machines and thousands of exploits is daunting. Fortunately, TVA automates the process so the problem becomes one of designing a network model with the flexibility to address all types of vulnerabilities and exploits.

7. Conclusion

The work presented in this paper substantially improves the ability for this analysis model to represent real-world networks. This is important because it allows the model to more closely represent the type of network connectivity issues that directly affect network security. These new enhancements were carefully designed to minimize their state-space requirements. In the small example networks that have been encoded so far, state-space issues are not much of a concern. However, when representing larger networks, the size of the state-space becomes a concern. By limiting the impact of the connectivity enhancements, larger networks are able to fit within the constraints of the current analysis tool. This is interesting because it brings us much closer to the ability to produce a tool capable of analyzing the impact that interactions of vulnerabilities have between hosts on real-world networks.

8. References

[1] Apache Web Server information and software on the web at www.apache.org.

[2] B. Beizer, "Software Testing Techniques, 2nd edition," Thomson Computer Press, 1990.

[3] J. Birch, E. Clark, K. McMillan, D. Dill, and L.J. Hwang, Symbolic Model Checking: 1020 States and Beyond, Proceedings of the ACM/SIGDA International Workshop in Formal Methods in VLSI Design, January, 1991.

[4] Coleson, Jay, An Elementary Introduction to Send mail, The SANS Institute, 2000. http://www.sans.org/infosecFAQ/unix/intro_sendmail.htm

[5] Computer Oracle and Password System (COPS) information and software on the web at ftp.cert.org/pub/tools/cops.

[6] Internet Information Server information on the web at www.microsoft.com/iis.

[7] Internet Security Systems, System Scanner information on the web at www.iss.net.

[8] Ronald W Ritchey and Paul Ammann, Using Model Checking To Analyze Network Security, 2000 IEEE

A Scalable Intrusion Detection System for Wireless Sensor Networks

Ravindara Bhatt and T.S. Lamba
Jaypee University of Information Technology, Waknaghat, Solan (H.P), India – 173 215
ravibhatt2@rediffmail.com   *tsl@juit.ac.in*

Abstract

Wireless sensor networks (WSNs) have many potential applications. In many scenarios (health care, surveillance, etc) WSNs are of interest to adversaries and they become susceptible to some types of attacks since they are deployed in open and unprotected environments and are constituted of cheap small devices. Preventive mechanisms can be applied to protect WSNs against some types of attacks. However as a second line of defense Intrusion Detection System (IDS) is necessary.

This paper describes a Scalable Intrusion Detection System (IDS) for wireless sensor networks (WSNs). Clustering sensor nodes is an effective topology control approach which increases network scalability. Distributed clustering is used and cluster heads are responsible for coordination among the nodes within their clusters. IDS for WSNs use collaborative efforts of nodes in a neighbourhood to detect a malicious node in that neighbourhood (Cluster). Also our intrusion detection system is independent of any routing protocol
Keywords: *Clustering, Intrusion detection system, Collaborative, Wireless Sensor networks.*

1. Introduction

This section first introduces the wireless sensor network (WSN), and then describes the issues in WSNs.

Wireless sensor networks have recently become new technique and popular research issues. A wireless sensor network consists of a large number of sensor nodes that have the capabilities of sensing, computing and wireless transmission.

Sensors are tiny, autonomous, electronic devices that collect data about some physical phenomena such as light, sound, etc. and are equipped with:

- a low power battery,
- sensing hardware,
- an on-board processor,
- a wireless transceiver and
- some memory

One very popular type of sensor nodes is the motes developed primarily at U.C. Berkeley and Intel (See Figure 1- Mica mote family).

Motes are low cost, small wireless devices with very constrained resources. An example of a sensor mote is the mica2dot. A typical configuration of a mote has a 4MHz, 8-bit processor, with 128KB of instruction memory, 4KB of RAM, and 512KB of external flash memory. The radio has a frequency of 433 MHz and 38.4 Kbps.

Fig. 1 Mica mote family [1]

A sensor network consists of anything from a handful to thousands of tiny wireless devices with sensors. A sensor network is a communication network of such sensors.

Sensor networks consist of large number of sensor nodes and a few base stations or sinks. The base stations are powerful compared to sensor nodes and are used to send data to some application for further processing. Packets are forwarded in smaller hops. This solves the problem of energy consumption and collisions.

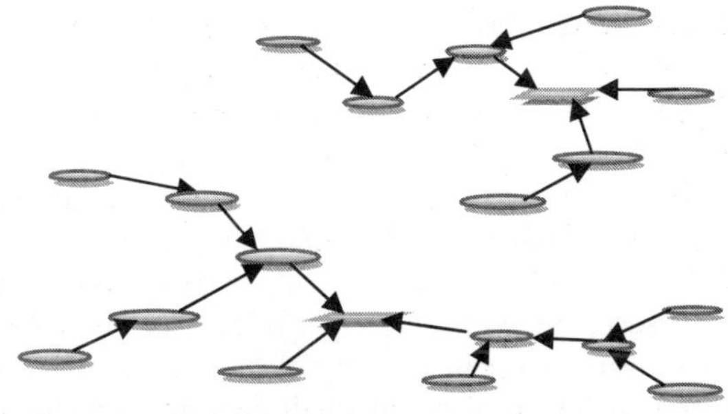

Fig. 2 A sensor network: (Oval Shaped – Sensor Nodes, Square Shaped –Base station). Sensor nodes forwards packet towards the base station.

Sensor networks are becoming widely integrated into the critical physical as well as personal infrastructures.

Sensor nodes have applications in the following areas:

- Military (monitoring, surveillance, etc.)
- Environmental monitoring (forest fire etc.)
- Health applications (telemonitoring of people health conditions, drug admin-istration, etc.)
- Smart environment
- Monitoring buildings, agriculture fields, etc.

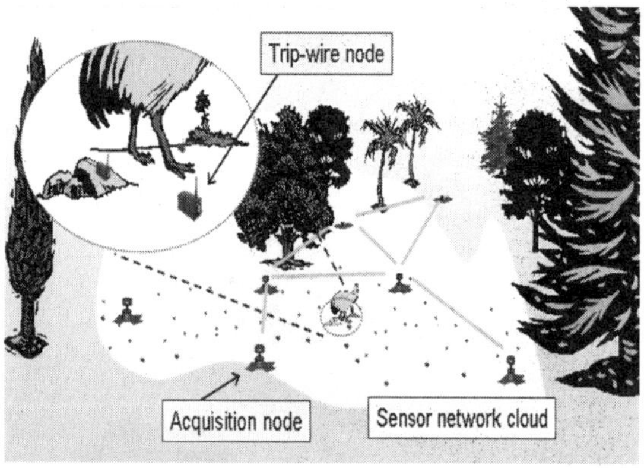

Fig. 3 Example: Habitat monitoring system [2]

Sensor networks are an upcoming network. Some of the important mechanisms for sensor networks are described in Table 1.

Table 1 Mechanisms required for Sensor Networks [3]

Sr. No.	Naming and addressing	Security associations	Securing neighbor discovery	Secure routing
Sensor Networks	YES	YES	YES	YES

The main issues for sensor networks include [3]:

- Main design criteria are to reduce the energy consumption (As sensor nodes are battery operated).
- Integrity and confidentiality of control and message data.
- Every security issue must take into account the reducing of power consumption in a network.

WSNs are of interest to adversaries and they become susceptible to some types of attacks since they are deployed in open and unprotected environments and are constituted of cheap small devices. Preventive mechanisms can be applied to protect WSNs against some types of attacks. However as a second line of defense Intrusion Detection System (IDS) are necessary.

Intrusion detection (ID) is a security technology that attempts to identify individuals who are trying to break into and misuse a system without authorization and those who have legitimate access to the system but are abusing their privileges. Our Intrusion detection system for sensor networks solves the security problem with some assumptions.

The remainder of the paper is organized as follows. Section 2 describes the related work. Section 3 describes the problem statement followed by Section 4 which is our proposed methodology. The analysis will be presented in section 5. Section 6 draws conclusions and specifies area of future work.

2. Related Work

In this section, we summarize a number of most related works.

Fang Liu et. al. [4] proposed LKE, a self-configuring scheme for location-aware key establishment that targets resource constrained sensor networks. LKE consists of four phases: Each sensor is preloaded with a bootstrap program and several system parameters during the predistribution phase, and is differentiated as either a service sensor or a worker node in the node self-configuration phase.

Ningrinla Marchang and Raja Datta [5] present two intrusion detection techniques for mobile ad-hoc networks, which use collaborative efforts of nodes in a neighbourhood to detect a malicious node in that neighbourhood. The algorithms use collaborative effort from a group of nodes for determining the malicious nodes by voting. Messages are passed between the nodes and depending on the messages received; these nodes determine suspected nodes (nodes that are suspected to be malicious).

Zhang et al. [6] developed architecture for intrusion detection which is distributive and cooperative.

Kun Sun et al. [7] propose a secure distributed cluster formation protocol to organize sensor networks into mutually disjoint cliques. The cluster structure in sensor networks can help to achieve scalability, power saving, channel access, routing, etc.

In malicious sensor network environment, our scalable intrusion detection system is successful in identifying and removing malicious node on cooperative basis.

3. Problem Statement

We first describe the network model and then give our objectives.

3. 1 Network Model

Consider a set of sensors dispersed in a field. We assume the following properties about the sensor network:

- The sensor nodes are quasi-stationary.
- Links are symmetric, i.e., two nodes SN_1 and SN_2 can communicate using the same transmission power level.
- We assume homogeneous sensors are deployed across the region and virtual grid is in place.
- Nodes are left unattended after deployment. Therefore battery recharge is not possible.
- Let the clustering process duration, $T_{CP,}$ be the time interval duration, taken by the clustering protocol to cluster the network. Let T_N, be the time between the end of T_{CP} , interval and subsequent T_{CP} interval . We assume that $T_{N} >> T_{CP.}$
- We assume secure communication among nodes.
- We assume malicious nodes do not coordinate among themselves.

Communication framework can be described as follows (Fig. 4). When a sensor receives the request for the first time:

- The receiving node joins the tree by adding the sending node as its parent and also stores the identity of the root node.
- When a sensor receives the request from a different neighbour, it discards the request as it is already part of the same tree.

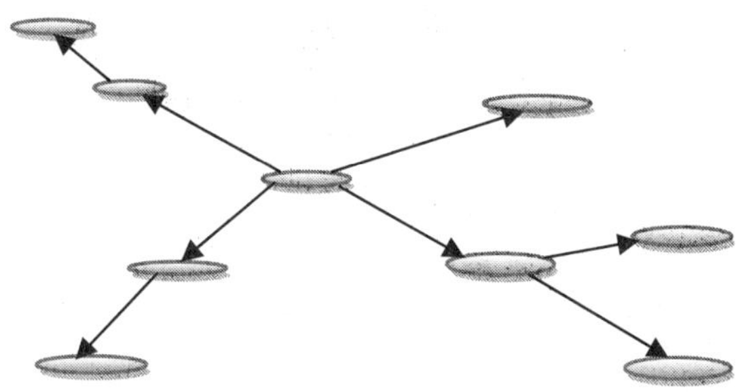

Fig. 4 Communication Framework in Sensor Networks

The problem of Scalable Intrusion Detection is then defined as follows. For a wireless sensor networks with node set V, the goal is to identify a set of cluster-heads that cover the whole network. Each and every node *v* in set V must be mapped into exactly one cluster. The clustering protocol must be completely distributed meaning each node can make its decision based on its local information.

Further collaborative efforts from all nodes can identify malicious node in each grid. This malicious node can be removed from network by all nodes.

The Intrusion detection system should be scalable. Each virtual grid is the smallest unit in our intrusion detection system. All cluster heads must communicate among themselves to share the malicious node list in the network.

4. Methodology

4. 1 Proposed Algorithm

The Scalable Intrusion Detection System for Sensor Networks:

In this section, we present the details of our protocol.

Our scalable Intrusion detection system consists of four steps. When all nodes are normal the process terminates after the first three steps. In hostile environment when inconsistency is detected, the protocol provides an extra step four to remove the identified malicious nodes from the network and restart the protocol from Step 2.

The network is divided into virtual grid. Each virtual grid will perform the following steps.

After successful execution of the protocol each grid will elect one cluster head In addition each cluster head will announce the malicious node within each virtual grid. This malicious node will be deleted from the virtual grid by all nodes.

Further all cluster head will coordinate among themselves to exchange the list of malicious nodes in network and making this intrusion detection system a scalable intrusion detection system for wireless sensor networks.

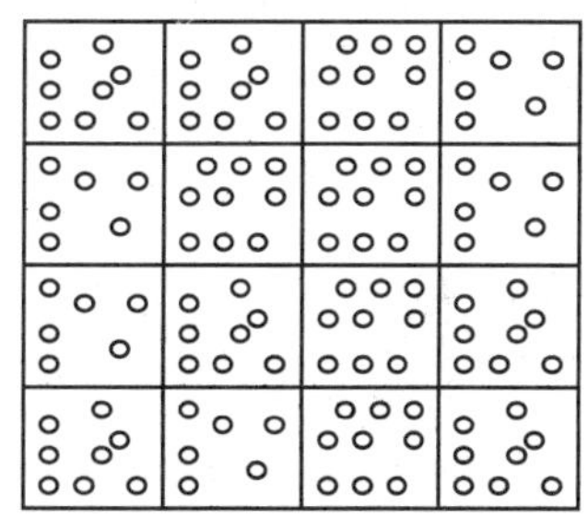

Fig. 5 The virtual square deployment region for sensor nodes.

The protocol is summarized below:

- STEP 1: Node Self-Configuration
  - o After deployment, a sensor positions itself and determines its role independently and locally. In addition each node will maintain neighbour and malicious node list. The sensor node can become either as a CANDIDATE node or as normal node based on computed score.
- STEP 2: Cluster Head (CH)Selection in each ith virtual grid
  - o In this phase, one cluster head (CH) node is elected out of k_{opt} CANDIDATE nodes present in each virtual grid. Each CANDIDATE node will broadcast a competition message with some random delay. If no competition message is

received, the CANDIDATE node announces itself as cluster head (CH). All other nodes in each grid are normal nodes.

- STEP 3: Announcement by CH in i^{th} virtual grid
  - The cluster head (CH) in each virtual grid requests for malicious node (one entry per node) from all normal nodes. All nodes forward malicious node list to their respective CH.
- STEP 4: Announcement by CH of malicious node in i^{th} virtual grid.
  - After compilation if malicious node is identified, then CH announces malicious node. The malicious node is deleted from each node neighbor list.

4. 2 Algorithm operation

1. Step 1: Node self-Configuration

After deployment, a sensor positions itself and determines its role independently and locally according to the following algorithm. A virtual grid is computed based on local information. Each sensor is aware of its location say (x, y). The home grid where sensor resides can be derived using a simple formula:

$X = \lfloor x/L \rfloor$, $Y = \lfloor y/L \rfloor$. The grid centre lies at X_0 , Y_0 . The centre can be computed as follows: $X_0 = (X + 1/2) \times L$ and $Y_0 = (Y + 1/2) \times L$. Each node can obtain a neighbour list NL_{neigh} that contain the IDs of its one hop neighbour. Each node exchanges its neighbour lists with its neighbour. Based on the neighbour matrix M_{neigh} each node computes its local clique and malicious node list [Figure 5].

The sensor node computes its distance from centre. The distance of a point from the centre is given by: $D = \sqrt{(x - X_0)^2 + (y - Y_0)^2}$. If the distance is less than some threshold, it becomes a possible cluster head (Possible_CH). Each Possible_CH node will compute their score based on the following score function: $score = w_1 RE + w_2 C$, where RE stands for node residual energy , C stands for node connectivity. And weights follow $\sum_{i=1}^{2} w_i = 1$. Nodes become CANDIDATE nodes if their score is above some threshold (say δ').

The algorithm for Step 1 is presented below.

Algorithm for Node Self Configuration:

function n = Node self Configuration
  ▶n is the selected role.
(x,y) ← self positioning
$X = \lfloor x/L \rfloor$ and $Y = \lfloor y/L \rfloor$
  ▶Get virtual grid id.
$X_0 = (X + 1/2) \times L$ and $Y_0 = (Y + 1/2) \times L$
  ▶Get grid centre
Node n exchanges its neighbour list and constructs node 1's neighbour matrix
$D = \sqrt{(x - X_0)^2 + (y - Y_0)^2}$
  ▶Distance of sensor from centre
If (D ≤ Threshold) then
$score = w_1 RE + w_2 C$
  ▶Compute score.
If (score ≥ Threshold) then
n ←CANDIDATE node
Else
n← normal node
Else
n← normal node
end function

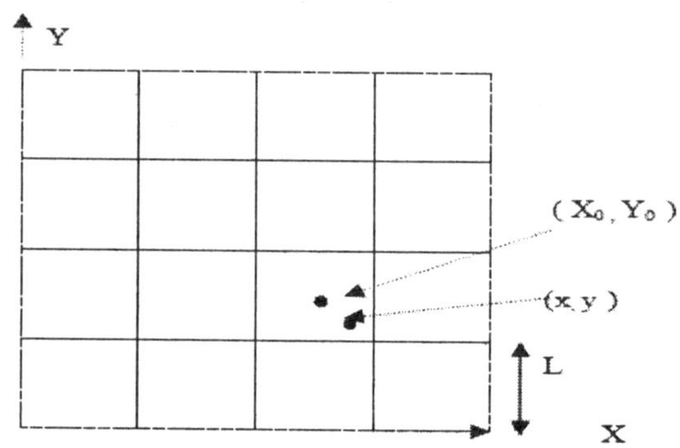

Fig. 6 A virtual grid with each grid size of L

2. Step 2: Cluster Head Selection in each virtual grid

The sensor nodes after Step 1 will be categorized as a possible cluster head (CANDIDATE NODES) or normal node based on the criteria in STEP 1.

- The CANDIDATE nodes in each virtual grid wait for random amount of time. This random time is a function of computed score and monotonically decreasing function [Figure 5].
- The possible cluster heads will now broadcast a competition message. If no competition message is received the possible cluster head announces itself as final cluster head. This is valid for each virtual grid.

  This step ensures that a cluster head is selected for every grid.

The algorithm for Step 2 is presented below.

Algorithm for Cluster head Election in each ith virtual grid.

If (CANDIDATE NODE of ith virtual grid) then
Random delay ← f (score)
  ▶Delay is monotonic decreasing function ▶of score.

If (not received competition message) then
broadcast (competition message)
▶ Succeed
CH of ith virtual grid ← CANDIDATE node of ith virtual grid
Else
normal node ← CANDIDATE node

3. Step 3: Announcement by CH in i^{th} virtual grid

The cluster head (CH) sends the request for malicious node to all normal nodes. All nodes maintain malicious node list (if any) and one entry per node are forwarded to cluster head. The cluster head compiles the result and broadcast the malicious node to all normal nodes.

The algorithm for Step 3 is presented below.

Announcement by CH in i^{th} virtual grid

If (CH) then
broadcast (request for malicious node in each virtual grid)
▶ Wait
Else
receive (request from CH)
send (malicious node entry to CH) ◀ one entry per node

4. Step 4:

After compilation if malicious node is identified, then CH announces malicious node. The malicious node is deleted from each node neighbour list.

- Malicious node is deleted from each node neighbor list

  The cluster heads for each virtual grid can communicate among themselves to exchange the malicious node list and other network parameters using secure communications.

5. Performance Analysis

Average cluster size: The average cluster size depends on the parameters of the virtual grid. The number of clusters in a network will be equal to the number of virtual grid.

Let total area of deployment is 100×100. Let virtual grid area be 10×10. We uniformly deploy 100,200,300,400 and 500 sensor nodes. The number of cluster will be equal to the number of virtual grid (100). Further the number of clusters will be independent of the number of sensors. Only increasing the sensor will increase the average cluster density [figure 6].

The number of cluster in a grid will be always constant [Fig. 7].

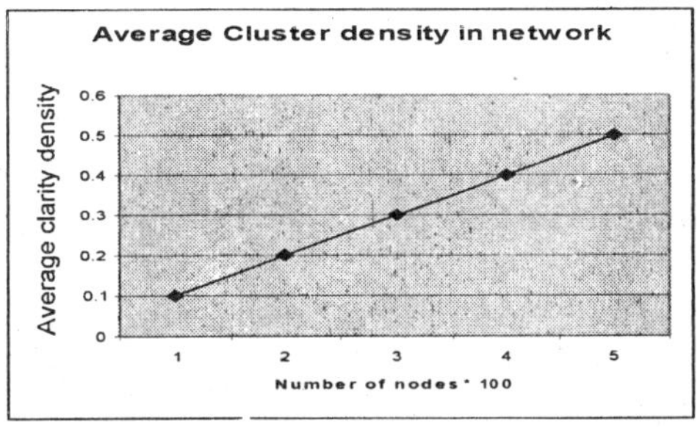

Fig. 7 Average cluster Density is uniform

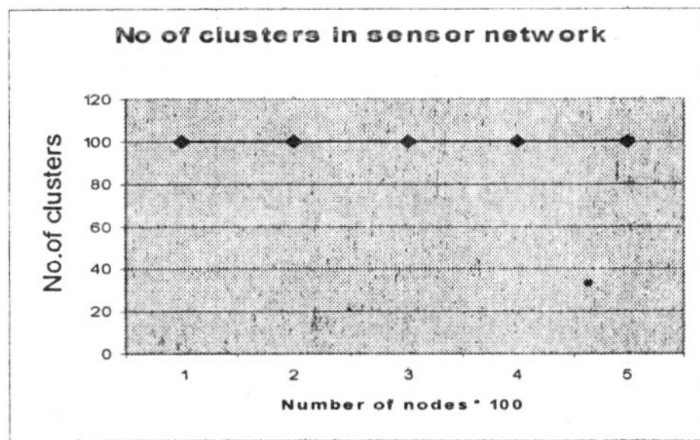

Fig. 7 Number of cluster in a sensor network.

6. Conclusion

In this scheme, sensors determine their roles and configure themselves automatically based on a pure localized algorithm. Sensors which have distance from each grid centre becomes as possible cluster heads. Based on computed score possible cluster heads can become CANDIDATE. Each virtual grid selects one CH from possible list of CANDIDATE. All other sensors are normal nodes.

The suspected nodes (votes) are sending to CH for malicious node identification. All nodes cooperate to identify and delete malicious node present in virtual grid. Further all CH can coordinate to make IDS scalable. The algorithm works in such a way that group of nodes together makes a decision.

Further our system works for non colluding malicious nodes. This work can be extended for colluding malicious nodes in wireless sensor networks.

7. References

[1] Tanya Roosta, Shiuhpyng Shieh, Shankar Sastry. Taxonomy of Security Attacks in Sensor Networks and Countermeasures.

[2] http://www-mtl.mit.edu/research/icsystems/uamps/research/sensor_net.shtml

[3] Levente Buttyan and Jean-Pierre Hubaux, "Security and cooperation in wireless networks", Cambridge University press(under print), Accessed from http://secowinet.epfl.ch

[4] Fang Liu et. al. Location-aware Key Establishment in Wireless Sensor Networks. IWCMC'06, ACM, 2006.

[5] Ningrinla Marchang, Raja Datta. Collaborative techniques for intrusion detection in mobile ad-hoc networks. Ad Hoc Networks 6, 508–523 Elsevier, 2008.

[6] Y. Zhang, W. Lee, Intrusion Detection in Wireless Ad-hoc Networks, Mobicom 2000, August 6–11, 2000, Boston, Massachusetts, USA.

[7] Kun Sun et al. Secure Distributed Cluster Formation in Wireless sensor Networks. ACSAC'06, IEEE.

Adaptive Slot Transfer TDMA Protocol for Energy-Efficient Wireless Intelligent NanoSensor Networks

Irrai Anbu .J
Department Of Information Technology, PSNA College Of Engineering and Technology, Tamil Nadu, India.
anbu.irrai@gmail.com

Abstract

ASTP is TDMA protocol that provides a contemporized and free slot structure. NanoNodes can construct, change topology and extend their planned slots during execution, based on their intelligent information. NanoNodes wake up for their scheduled slots; otherwise, they switch into power-saving sleep mode. This flexible schedule allows ASTP to be strongly adaptive and highly energy efficient. ASTP is scalable because its depth-first-search schedule minimizes buffering, and it allows communication slots to be reused by nodes outside each other's interference range. Hence, the overall scheme of ASTP provides end-to-end guarantees on data delivery (fair access, robust self-healing and throughput) while also respecting the severe energy and memory constraints of wireless sensor networks. Simulations in ns-2 show that ASTP ensures energy efficiency and is robust to network dynamics (faults such as dropped packets and nodes joining or leaving the network) under various network configurations (network topology and network density), providing an efficient solution for data-gathering applications. Unlike FlexiTP, ASTP provide more energy efficiency and network performance for Nano node in the network topology.

Keywords: Wireless NanoSensor networks, energy efficiency, quantum dots, end-to-end data delivery guarantees.

1. Introduction

WIRELESS sensor networks promises to revolutionize the way we live, work, and interact with the physical Environment. Networks in these environments including space need to be able to self-configure and, ideally, to self-calibrate, without knowledge of the network topology or sensor requirements in advance.The potential for collaborative, robust networks of microsensors has attracted a great deal of research attention. The WINS [5] and Pico Radio [6] and projects, for instance, aim to integrate sensing, processing and radio communication onto a microsensors node. Current prototypes are custom circuit boards with mostly commercial, off-the-shelf components. The Smart Dust [4] project seeks a minimum-size solution to the distributed sensing problem, choosing optical communication on coin-sized "motes." The prospect of thousands of communicating nodes has sparked research into network protocols for information flow among microsensors, such as *directed diffusion* [7].Sensor Network need to be energy aware due to limited power. The users of sensor networks need end-to-end guarantees on data delivery [3],[4]: predictable throughput for gathered data, fair access to the network for all data-gathering nodes, and robust self-healing of the network when nodes join or leave the network and when communication conditions change [5], [6], [7]. In practice, however, it has proved difficult to achieve these guarantees, because of the severe resource constraints (battery power and data memory) of sensor network nodes and the hostile environments in which they must operate [8]. In addition to minimizing network resources while maintaining end-to-end delivery guarantees, modularity in sensor network designs is important. Most sensor network protocols focus on performance while addressing issues such as scheduling, routing, data buffering, and power management at different levels [9], [10]. These observations lead to the design of a Adaptive- based TDMA Protocol (ASTP) that provides end-to-end guarantees on data delivery while also respecting the severe energy and memory constraints of wireless sensor networks. Sensor nodes serve as both gatherers and routers for the data. ASTP supports modularity through a distributed slot-structure algorithm that provides scheduling, routing, and time synchronization functions. ASTP is a TDMA-based protocol in which nodes only transmit and receive packets at their own time slot(s) and sleep until their slots turn up again. This approach conserves energy as nodes in sleep mode consume much less energy than those in idle mode [12]. ASTP nodes require minimal local buffering since the network schedule is chosen so that each node forwards messages immediately. ASTP is designed for a static ad hoc network, in which nodes may suffer temporary or permanent failure, and new nodes may be added to the network at any time, but nodes otherwise remain in (nearly) the same location. ASTP adjusts to different node topologies and densities to create an efficient self healing data delivery tree.

Furthermore, buffering and retransmission are used to recover from a small number of lost packets. The central contribution of the ASTP protocol is its synchronized and loose slot structure. Nodes can claim or remove a slot based on the current information in their lookup table (that is, schedule) without exchanging information with any other nodes in the network prior to modifying their schedules. In ASTP, it is not necessary to specify the number of slots required for the network in advance, and nodes can join or leave the network at any time. This flexible slot structure makes ASTP strongly fault tolerant and also highly energy efficient. In ASTP, initially, all nodes in a network build their data-gathering schedules. After this initial global one-off setup phase, all repair operations are local. As network density increases, the initial network setup cost and packet latency increase. Our simulations based on Mica2 Mote hardware show that ASTP is scalable for a large number of nodes (up to 400 nodes) because it sustains the low initial network setup cost and low packet latency, as well as maintains good throughput for different network densities. ASTP achieves a balance among data delivery guarantees, energy efficiency, and memory efficiency through the following schemes:

ASTP maximizes the network lifetime by putting nodes into sleep mode without disrupting the ongoing traffic and fairly distributing energy intensive operations across the network.

ASTP is scalable for large numbers of network nodes because 1) local repair is used to recover from node and communication failures, 2) nodes minimize buffered information, and 3) communication slots are reused by nodes outside each other's interference range.

ASTP provides data delivery guarantees because

1. Scheduled communication is used to minimize communication errors from radio interference and to guarantee a communication path for each node and
2. Local repair is used to recover from node and Communication faults.

The rest of the paper is organized as follows: We discuss some related work in Section 2. We describe our ASTP approach in Section 3. Section 4 describes our simulation methodology and presents our simulation results. We conclude with some discussion and present future work in Section 5.

2. Related Works

The protocol in [15] uses the base station to adjust the modulation level (bits per symbol) of each cluster head in a network based on the cluster head's feedback in order to make a good trade-off between energy consumption and transmission quality. The drawbacks of this protocol are the queuing process at cluster heads and the centralized decision making. The number of packets arriving at cluster heads is not controlled, and so, packets will be dropped if the buffer overflows, resulting in increased latency and packet loss.

Energy-efficient protocols based on CSMA [10], TDMA [20], [21], [23], [24], [25], [26], or both [27], [28], [29]. Provide focus to minimize sources of energy waste: idle listening, overhearing, collisions, and protocol overhead. ASTP is distinguished from previous protocols by providing end-to-end guarantees on data delivery within the energy and memory constraints of wireless sensor networks.

The protocol in [19] provides energy efficiency by rotating nodes in the network to act as backbone sensors, based on their residual energy. These backbone sensors are responsible for in-network data processing and packet routing, whereas the rest of nodes in the network sleep to conserve energy. This provides high energy savings for event-driven applications where nodes only report events upon their detection. In contrast to [19], ASTP is designed for periodic sensing applications, where each node has data to send at regular intervals. EAD uses CSMA/CA for data transmission, whereas ASTP eliminates RTS/CTS handshakes during data gathering, and these results in a low packet overhead. Similar to EAD, ASTP uses a forwarding-to-parent routing scheme where a tree is constructed at the initial network setup, and so, every node in the network knows where to route its packet during sensor network execution. This simple routing scheme is suitable for static sensor networks since it sustains high throughput and good energy efficiency [19].Examples of TDMA-based MAC protocols are TRAMA [24], L-MAC [20], SS-TDMA [21], and PACT [23]. TRAMA [24] organizes time into frames and uses a distributed election scheme based on traffic information at each node to determine which node can transmit at a particular slot. TRAMA uses a distributed hash function to determine a collision-free slot assignment. TRAMA builds a schedule when a node has data to send. Scheduling scheme increases queuing delays. In contrast, ASTP reduces queuing delays as schedules are assigned to nodes at the time of the initial network setup and nodes maintain this schedule throughout their lifetime. In this way, ASTP also avoids the need for a centralized scheduler. In addition, ASTP has a simpler algorithm to establish a schedule compared to TRAMA. SS-TDMA [21] is designed to operate on a regular grid topology such as rectangular, hexagonal, and triangular grids. The TDMA algorithm proposed in SS-TDMA is selfstabilizing.It tolerates faults such as nodes that are improperly initialized, slots assigned to corrupted nodes, and nodes with clock drifts. The main drawback of SS-TDMA is its constraint on the location of the nodes, which is impractical for many sensor network applications. Unlike SS-TDMA, ASTP caters to any network topology. L-MAC [20] divides time into slots with a fixed frame consisting of a control message and a data unit. The main drawback of the L-MAC scheme is that it increases the idle-listening overhead since nodes must always listen to the control sections of all slots in a frame to allow nodes to receive data and to allow new nodes to join the network anytime.

PACT [23] uses passive clustering to create a communication network of cluster heads and base stations. The role of cluster heads and base stations is rotated based on the nodes' energy level. To prolong the network lifetime, only a subset of nodes (cluster heads and base stations) are active. At the start of a TDMA frame, these active nodes get preference in claiming a sequence of communication slots. PACT rotates the role of cluster heads to amortize the overheads of the TDMA scheduler. However, this method requires the cluster heads to rebuild a schedule for all nodes within their clusters. Unlike PACT, ASTP nodes maintain a fixed schedule throughout their lifetime until the network topology changes.

3. ASTP

3.1 Protocol Overview

The main functions of ASTP are to manage

- The establishment of routes (data-gathering tree construction),
- The establishment of node schedules (time slot assignment),
- time synchronization to minimize clock drifts, and
- Local repair for a network in the event of faults (fault tolerance).

ASTP has two main phases: an initial network setup and data-gathering cycles. Fig. 1 shows the order of steps executed in a network. Users can implement any data gathering tree construction algorithm; the time slot assignment is the important feature of ASTP. Some steps within phases are carried out in parallel by the nodes, which are the neighbor schedule exchange and the fault-tolerant schedule exchange(depicted by dashed lines).Initially, ASTP builds a data gathering tree and assigns the nodes' schedules. Nodes then maintain their schedules throughout their lifetime in the network. Thus, this initial network setup is a one-off phase. During the initial network setup, ASTP uses CSMA/CA for packet transmission, and so, the nodes' receivers are always on (that is, in listening mode) and also uses a token-passing scheme. Nodes execute specific procedures only if they hold token, hence avoiding collisions. After the initial network setup finishes, nodes perform regular data-gathering tasks using their TDMA schedules.

3.2 Terminology

A first-level neighbor of a sensor node is any node (not necessarily along the tree) within its communication range. Furthermore, any node that is within the communication range of the node's first-level neighbor(s) is referred to as a second-level neighbor. For example, B's first-level (direct) neighbors are A and D. Accordingly, B's second-level neighbors are BS, C, and E. Parent refers to an immediate node that forwards a source node's packet and that is closer to the base station (in terms of hop count) compared to the node. For example, A is the parent of B, and so, B is the child of A. Ancestor refers to a router that is more than one hop away from a source node to which the source node's packet is forwarded to and which is closer to the base station (in terms of hop count). For example, BS is the ancestor of B and D, that is, B and D are descendants of BS.

3.3 Time Slot Assignment

ASTP uses a depth-first-search schedule to reduce buffering. This scheduling scheme allows data sent by a source node to be forwarded by routers to the base station in an interleaving manner. This scheme enhances reliability by preventing the loss of packets due to buffer overflow. After a data-gathering tree is constructed, the local topology is known to nodes in the network such that each node knows its parent and children (if any). The base station then generates a time slot assignment token and initiates the time slot assignment phase. The token passing is done using the depth-first-search technique. The token is passed to the child that has the lowest node ID.

The ASTP time slot assignment function consists of four main phases: data-gathering slot assignment, MFS assignment, neighbor schedule exchange, and GHS assignment. In the data-gathering slot assignment, each node in the network builds its data-gathering schedule by selecting a slot to transmit its own data and then routers on the path to the base station assign receive and forward slots for that node's data. Once a node claims a slot, it executes the neighbor schedule exchange to propagate the claimed slot to its first-level and second-level neighbors. After all nodes in the network build their data-gathering schedules, they execute the MFS assignment. Finally, the base station informs the network's highest slot to all nodes in the network through the GHS assignment. In ASTP, the slot selection always starts from slot number 2 because slot number 1 is dedicated to FTS. A node can claim a slot if the slot is not listed in its RSL, TSL, and CSL. Therefore, in selecting a slot, there is no need to know the true value of GHS. This slot selection scheme allows a slot to be reused by many nodes as long as the nodes' transmissions are not within interference range of each other, and hence, the spatial slot reuse can be maximized.

3.3.1 Data-Gathering Slot Assignment

When a node obtains the token, it allocates a transmit slot to send its own data by choosing the lowest slot number that is not listed in its RSL, TSL, and CSL fields. The node (current requestor) then informs the claimed slot to its parent (one of its first-level neighbors) by uncasting a forward_slot_request, as well as piggybacking an inform_slot_request. In this way, slots to forward the node's data to the base station are allocated. Furthermore, the inform_slot_request on the broadcast packet triggers the neighbor schedule exchange phase that will be described in Section 3.4.3. The forward_slot_request contains the claimed slot information: the slot number, the receiver's ID (parent ID), and the neighbor level counter. The requestor's first-level neighbors that receive the forward_slot_request check the intended receiver of that packet. If a neighbor node is the intended receiver of the packet, it knows that it is the parent of the current requestor and so lists the received slot number in its RSL; else, it will execute the neighbor schedule exchange. The parent then assigns the corresponding transmits slot, that is, a slot to forward the requestor's data. The corresponding transmit slot must be bigger than the received slot number and is not listed in the parent's RSL, TSL, and CSL. Afterward, the parent executes the neighbor schedule exchange and sends the forward_slot_request to the requestor's ancestor (that is, routers). The data-gathering slot assignment as explained before is repeated until the base station receives the forward slot request.The data gathering slot assignment ends when the token is returned to the base station.

3.3.2 Neighbour Schedule Exchange

The neighbor schedule exchange phase is performed through CSMA/CA communication in which a node broadcasts its claimed slot to its direct neighbors (first-level neighbors), and then, each of these direct neighbors propagate the slot information again to their direct neighbors (second-level neighbors). In this way, a slot claimed by a node is informed to all neighbors within twice the node's communication range. Since ASTP prevents nodes that are potentially within the interference range of each other to claim the same slot, collision-free traffic can be guaranteed. If during the data-gathering slot assignment or the MFS assignment phase a node receives the inform slot request in a packet, it means that the neighbor schedule exchange phase needs to be executed. The neighbor slot exchange is controlled by the neighbor level counter information in the packet, which indicates the status of a neighbor, whether it is a first-level neighbor (the neighbor level counter is equal to one) or a second-level neighbor (the neighbor level counter is equal to two). If a node receives a packet with a level counter less than or equal to two, it will include the slot in its CSL. Furthermore, if the current level counter is less than two, the node increments the level counter value and broadcasts the packet to its direct neighbors; if not, it stops the neighbor schedule exchange.

3.4 Fault Tolerance

In ASTP, nodes listen to environment activities during the FTS to allow these nodes to self configure in the event of failures without prior knowledge of the network topology. If there is a node that sends a distress signal during FTS, nodes in the network that receive this signal will reply to it and perform a local self repair. In the event that a new node is added to the network or when an existing node in the network wants to find a new parent, ASTP allows nodes in the network to adopt these faulty nodes as their children, assign schedules for these faulty nodes, and rebuild their own schedules. ASTP utilizes the existing TDMA schedule to perform a local repair, and so, a collision-free and cost-free schedule rebuilding and schedule exchange is guaranteed, which will be described later.

3.4.1 Packet Loss

ASTP handles packet loss during the initial network setup, as well as data gathering. In the initial network setup, ASTP utilizes an RTS/CTS/ACK scheme of IEEE 802.11 to handle packet loss during the depth-first-search token passing. For example, when a parent does not receive a token ACK from its child (receiver), the parent keeps retransmitting the token until it receives an ACK, for a specified period of time (user parameter). If after the time expires, the parent still receives no ACK, it proceeds with passing the token to the next child. On the other hand, if a child does not receive a token ACK from its parent (the parent probably dies) after a period of time, it will find a new parent. Since in the initial network setup phase, nodes work in CSMA/CA and they are all in listening mode, the child can broadcast a distress signal for finding a new parent. The child's neighbors that receive the signal send a reply. The child then selects the best parent based on the lowest hop count to the base station. The selected parent then updates its list of children and propagates this topology change to the base station, and so, the token passing flow in the network reflects the current network showed that nodes may lose connectivity for extended periods. In ASTP, during data-gathering cycles, nodes detect packet loss based on their RSL, that is, their scheduled receive slots. For example, when a node does not receive a packet when it expects data from its child, it will request a data retransmission from that child during the MFS. The child appends the requested data onto the data packet that will be sent in the immediate data-gathering slot in the next data gathering cycle.

3.4.2 New Nodes

In FTS, a new node sends a distress signal. Nodes that are within the communication range of the new node become neighbors and prospective parents of the new node. The new node then selects one of them as its parent, based on the lowest hop count to the base station. The selected parent allocates two slots to the new node: one data-gathering slot (that is, the parent's GHS incremented by one) and one MFS (the parent's MFS). If the parent does not have an MFS because it did not have a child before, it will assign an MFS to itself first, which is equal to the current GHS incremented by two, before allocating its MFS to the new node. Afterward, the new node's routers build the new node's data-gathering schedule by utilizing existing data-gathering slots and MFSs. The selected parent (let it be a requestor) first proposes a forward slot (that is, forward slot request) for the new node to its parent. The requestor piggybacks the proposed slot on the data packet sent in the immediate data-gathering slot. The requestor's parent then checks the proposed slot against its lookup table. If the proposed slot exists in its lookup table, a next available slot will be chosen to replace it. The approved slot will be listed in the requestor parent's RSL and also will be sent to the requestor in MFS. The requestor then claims the approved slot and lists the slot in its TSL. Afterward, the requestor's parent becomes the current requestor and proposes a forward slot to its parent. This scheme is executed by traversing the path to the base station. Note that every time a node claims a new slot, it triggers the fault-tolerant schedule exchange (executed within a data-gathering cycle), which is described in Section 3.6.4.

4. Initial Network Setup

The initial network setup cost is the energy cost for constructing a data-gathering tree, collecting neighborhood information, and building nodes' schedules. Recall that this setup cost is a one-off cost as nodes maintain their schedules throughout their lifetime in the network.

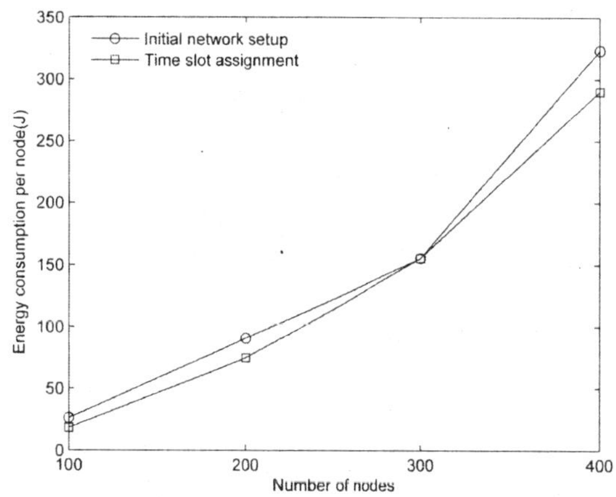

Fig.1 Initial network setup cost per node versus network density

The initial network setup cost per node is less than 0.6 percent of the node's total initial energy of 54,000 J, across various network scenarios. Thus, our simulations based on Mica2 Mote show that ASTP is scalable for up to 400 nodes since it maintains a low initial network setup cost.

5. Conclusions

ASTP is a novel TDMA-based protocol for scheduling, routing, and the application layer (time synchronization) and provides end-to-end guarantees on data delivery such as predictable throughput for gathered data, fair access to the network for all sensor nodes, and robust self healing while also respecting the severe operating constraints of wireless sensor networks. To the best of our knowledge, ASTP is the first integrated protocol for sensor networks that proposes a scheduling scheme that provides a balance among end-to-end guarantees on data delivery, energy efficiency, and memory efficiency.

ASTP implements local synchronization to minimize clock drifts among nodes: A parent synchronizes its children during a designated MFS. As the network density increases, the length of the data-gathering cycle increases. One can increase the frequency of time resynchronization within a data-gathering cycle by assigning additional MFSs in order to provide tighter time synchronization. In ASTP, nodes can continue to function accurately in the event of failure of individual nodes (for example, erroneous network link, dying node, and topology changes) by performing a local repair in the FTS. The length of FTS can be adjusted according to the application requirements. For example, users can set a very short FTS (for example, 100 ms) for a sensor network application that is deployed in a stable environment or an application that can tolerate a slow network stabilization. Through comprehensive analysis and simulation results, we substantiate our argument that ASTP is fault tolerant and energy efficient across different network configurations. Our simulation results confirm that in high contention networks, ASTP performs better than Z-MAC in terms of energy savings and network performance. The distributed and flexible slot-structure algorithm of ASTP enables nodes to modify their lookup tables during network execution. ASTP is extended for event-sensing applications. Currently, we are working on using ASTP to support wireless sensor networks under microgravity and nanowire technology for dynamic power support

6. References

[1] I.F. Akyildiz, W. Su, Y. Sankarasubramaniam, and E. Cayirci, "Wireless Sensor Networks: A Survey," Computer Networks, vol. 38, no. 4, pp. 393-422, 2002.

[2] F. Chen, F. Dressler, and A. Heindl, "End-to-End Performance Characteristics in Energy-Aware Wireless Sensor Networks," Proc. Third ACM Int'l Workshop Performance Evaluation of Wireless Ad Hoc, Sensor, and Ubiquitous Networks (PE-WASUN '06), Oct. 2006.

[3] R. Iyer and L. Kleinrock, "QoS Control for Sensor Networks," Proc. IEEE Int'l Conf. Comm. (ICC '03), May 2003.

[4] D. Chen and P.K. Varshney, "QoS Support in Wireless Sensor Networks: A Survey," Proc. Int'l Conf. Wireless Networks (ICWN '04), June 2004.

[5] L.H.A. Correia, D.F. Macedo, A.L. dos Santos, and J.M. Nogueira, "Issues on QoS Schemes in Wireless Sensor Networks," Technical Report RT.DCC.004/2005, DCC/UFMG, Apr. 2005.

[6] D. Culler, P. Dutta, C.T. Ee, R. Fonseca, J. Hui, P. Levis, J. Polastre, S. Shenker, I. Stoica, G. Tolle, and J. Zhao, "Towards a Sensor Network Architecture: Lowering the Waistline," Proc. 10th Workshop Hot Topics in Operating Systems (HotOS '05), June 2005.

[7] J. Polastre, J. Hill, and D. Culler, "Versatile Low Power Media Access for Wireless Sensor Networks," Proc. Second ACM Int'l Conf. Embedded Networked Sensor Systems (SenSys '04), Nov. 2004.

[8] M. Bhardwaj, T. Garnett, and A.P. Chandrakasan, "Upper Bounds on the Lifetime of Sensor Networks," Proc. IEEE Int'l Conf. Comm. (ICC '01), June 2001.

[9] G. Anastasi, M. Conti, M.D. Francesco, and A. Passarella, "An Adaptive and Low-Latency Power Management Protocol for Wireless Sensor Networks," Proc. Fourth ACM Int'l Workshop Mobility Management and Wireless Access (MobiWac '06), Oct. 2006.

[10] Y. Yuan, Z. Yang, Z. He, and J. He, "An Integrated Energy Aware Wireless Transmission System for QoS Provisioning in Wireless Sensor Network," to be published in, Elsevier Computer Comm., May 2005.

[11] W. Ye, J. Heidemann, and D. Estrin, "An Energy-Efficient MAC Protocol for Wireless Sensor Networks," Proc. IEEE INFOCOM '02, June 2002..

[12] A. Boukerche, X. Cheng, and J. Linus, "A Performance Evaluation of a Novel Energy-Aware Data-Centric Routing Algorithm in Wireless Sensor Networks," Wireless Networks, vol. 11, no. 5, pp. 619-635, 2005.

[13] L.F.W. van Hoesel and P.J.M. Havinga, "A Lightweight Medium Access Protocol (LMAC) for Wireless Sensor Networks," Proc. First Int'l Workshop Networked Sensing Systems (INSS '04), June 2004.

[14] S.S. Kulkarni and M.U. Arumugam, "TDMA Service for Sensor Networks," Proc. 24th Int'l Conf. Distributed Computing Systems Workshops (ICDCSW '04), Mar. 2004.

[15] G. Pei and C. Chien, "Low Power TDMA in Large Wireless Sensor Networks," Proc. IEEE Military Comm. Conf. (MILCOM '01), Oct. 2001.

[16] V. Rajendran, K. Obraczka, and J.J. Garcia-Luna-Aceves, "Energy- Efficient Collision-Free Medium Access Control for Wireless Sensor Networks," Proc. First ACM Int'l Conf. Embedded Networked Sensor Systems (SenSys '03), Mar. 2003.

[17] V. Rajendran, J.J. Garcia-Luna-Aceves, and K. Obraczka, "Energy- Efficient, Application-Aware Medium Access for Sensor Networks," Proc. Second IEEE Int'l Conf. Mobile Ad Hoc and Sensor Systems (MASS '05), Nov. 2005.

[18] S.C. Ergen and P. Varaiya, "PEDAMACS: Power Efficient and Delay Aware Medium Access Protocol for Sensor Networks," IEEE Trans. Mobile Computing, vol. 5, no. 7, pp. 920-930, July 2006.

[19] B. Hohlt, L. Doherty, and E. Brewer, "Flexible Power Scheduling for Sensor Networks," Proc. Third Int'l Symp. Information Processing in Sensor Networks (IPSN '04), Apr. 2004.

[20] N. amanathan, M. Yarvis, J. Chhabra, N. Kushalnagar, L. Krishnamurthy, and D. Estrin, "A Stream-Oriented Power Management Protocol for Low Duty Cycle Sensor Network Applications," Proc. Second IEEE Workshop Embedded Networked Sensors (EmNetS '05), May 2005.

[21] M.L. Sichitiu, "Cross-Layer Scheduling for Power Efficiency in Wireless Sensor Networks," Proc. IEEE INFOCOM '04, Mar. 2004.

[22] M. Maroti, B. Kusy, G. Simon, and A. Ledeczi, "Robust Multi-Hop Time Synchronization in Sensor Networks," Proc. Int'l Conf. Wireless Networks (ICWN '04), June 2004.

[23] A. Boukerche, I. Chatzigiannakis, and S. Nikoletseas, "Power- Efficient Data Propagation Protocols for Wireless Sensor Networks," SCS J. Simulation: Trans. Soc. For Modeling and Simulation Int'l, 2005.

[24] I. Raicu, L. Schwiebert, S. Fowler, and S.K.S. Gupta. "Local Load Balancing for Globally Efficient Routing in Wireless Sensor Networks," Int'l J. Distributed Sensor Network, 2005.

[25] G. Anastasi, A. Falchi, A. Passarella, M. Conti, and E. Gregori, "Performance Measurements of Motes Sensor Networks," Proc. Seventh ACM Int'l Symp. Modeling, Analysis and Simulation of Wireless and Mobile Systems (MSWiM '04), Oct. 2004.

[26] G. Xing, C. Lu, Y. Zhang, Q. Huang, and R. Pless, "Minimum Power Configuration in Wireless Sensor Networks," Proc. ACM MobiHoc '05, May 2005.

Dynamic Mobility Management and Vertical Handoff Algorithm for Next Generation All-IP Wireless Network

Sulata Mitra
Department of Computer Science and Technology, Bengal Engineering and Science University, India,
sulata@cs.becs.ac.in

Abstract

The present work is a dynamic mobility management and vertical handoff algorithm for next generation all-IP wireless network. The mobility management algorithm is used to provide a global roaming and internetworking facilities among different access technologies as well as seamless service negotiation including mobility, security and quality of service. The network initiated vertical handoff algorithm is used to perform load balancing, to maximize battery power life time of a mobile node, to minimize power consumption, system delay and loss of packet, and finally to maximize the throughput of the network. Results based on a detailed performance evaluation study are also presented to demonstrate the efficacy of the proposed scheme.

1. Introduction

In the next generation wireless network, a user may roam over a series of networks during his global travel. Internet browsing "on-the-move", video conferencing and file transfer are some of the new expected services in near future. Recently WLAN found its application as a low cost high speed solution to cover the hot spot whereas the cellular network has the excellence of wide coverage, seamless roaming support and better quality of service (QoS). So a possible architecture of integrating cellular/WLAN domain helps to exploit the seamless roaming support of cellular network and high data rate of WLAN.

Several integration architecture has been proposed so far. Tight coupling integration architecture (TCIA) is proposed by Jaseemuddin [2] in which the core network is exposed completely to the WLAN network which violets the security and privacy of the cellular network.

Though the loosely coupled integration architecture [3] overcomes the limitation of TCIA, but it suffers from huge signaling overhead in case of vertical handoff. Several protocols have also been proposed so far to provide seamless mobility. MIP [4] has higher signaling overhead, handover latency and location update frequency. MIPv4 [4] has shortage of globally routable IPv4 address, lack of security, high delay and packet loss. In MIPv6 [5] high signaling overhead occurs in case of large network and high mobility MNs. CIP [6] is inefficient in handling inter domain location update and thus not able to handle global reach ability perfectly. TeleMIP [7] is not suitable for large network. TLMMv4 [8] has huge signaling overhead and suffers the problem like MIPv4. TLMMv6 [9] also has huge signaling overhead. FMIPv6 [10] has huge location update cost and packet loss. F-TLMM [11] has huge computation overhead as it needs to compute the average velocity of all the MNs in a domain.

The proposed work considers the all-IP integration architecture [1] in which each node has an IP address in the dotted decimal format as considered in [1]. When a mobile node (MN) sends initial registration to a local agent (LA), LA sends an IP address [1] to MN in the form global mobility agent identification (GMA_id).mobility agent identification (MA_id).subnet agent identification (SA_id).local agent identification (LA_id).MN identification (MN_id). So MN has local care of address (LCoA) as LA_id.MN_id, subnet care of address as SA_id.LA_id.MN_id, regional care of address (RCoA) as MA_id.SA_id.LA_id.MN_id and global care of address (GCoA) as GMA_id.MA_id.SA_id.LA_id.MN_id. With this IP address, MN is able to roam across any other network without any interruption in transmission and without any change in future IP address due to handoff. No handoff registration is required from the MN which helps to reduce the overhead in terms of power consumption of the mobile unit, location update cost, delay and packet loss. The proposed scheme uses vertical handoff algorithm in case the average delay of a domain crosses a threshold. The vertical handoff from one domain to other domain reduces the congestion of the network which in turn reduces the average cost, average delay and average packet loss of the network.

2. Proposed scheme

The proposed work is a dynamic mobility management and vertical handoff algorithm for next generation wireless network.

2.1 MN route request message

A MN sends this message to its current LA for the selection of a new route. The route request message from MN_i contains 4 tuple as route identification ($r\_id=route_i$), packet size ($p\_sz=P_i$), number of packet ($n\_pac=T_i$) and data rate ($d\_r=d_i$). In case of 100000 MNs, the number of bits require to represent a MN in binary is 17. The $route_i$ is considered as identical to MN_i of MN. So the number of bits to represent $route_i$ in binary is 17. The requested packet size of each MN is assumed to be in the range 8 KB to 12 KB. So the maximum number of bits require to represent packet size in binary is 4. The number of bits require to represent the number of data packets in binary is $\log_2(T_i)$. The requested data rate of each MN can be one of the values from the set (64 kbps, 128 kbps, 256 kbps). So the maximum possible data rate is 256 kbps and the number of bits require to represent data rate in binary is 8. So for MN_i the length of route request message (rrm_bit_i) in binary is $29+\log_2(T_i)$ bits.

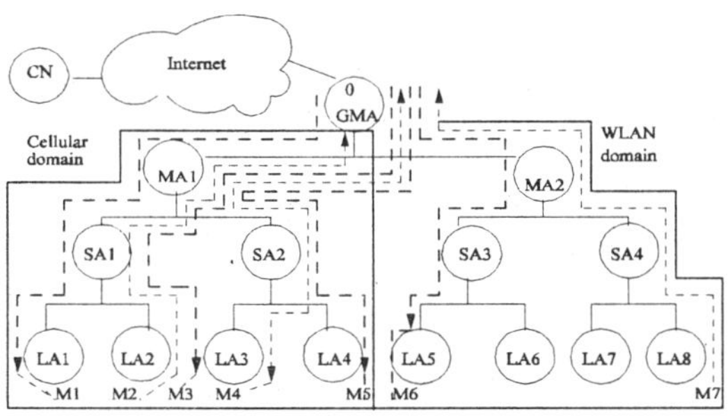

Fig.1 Existing routes in each domain

2.2 Information available at each node

The existing routes in the cellular domain and WLAN domain are shown in Fig.1. Each GMA, MA, SA and LA in Fig.1 performs the following operations for each route passing through them. The operation performed by all the nodes associated with i^{th} route is discussed below.

1. GMA of the network maintains three separate counters for each MN in the network. Let GMA maintains intra_*subnet*$_i$, inter_subnet$_i$ and inter_domain$_i$ counter to count the number of times the route selection occurs due to intra subnet, inter subnet and inter domain handoff during the transmission or reception of the entire session of ith MN (MN_i) using i^{th} route.
2. Each node in Fig.1 maintains a list of information in the memory. A record is inserted in the list after establishing i^{th} route, updated in the list in case of any intra subnet, inter subnet and inter domain handoff of MN_i, deleted from the list when route duration time corresponding to i^{th} route is over. The record in the list corresponding to i^{th} route contains route, $route_i$, T_i, P_i, d_i information. The list maintains by node 0 in Fig.1 is shown in TABLE-1. List at node 1 in Fig.1 is identical to the rows R1, R2, R3, R4 and R5 of TABLE-1. List at node 2 in Fig.1 is identical to the rows R6 and R7 of TABLE-1. List at node 11 in Fig.2 is identical to the rows R1, R2 and R3 of TABLE-1. List at node 12 in Fig.1 is identical to the rows R4 and R5 of TABLE-1. List at node 21 in Fig.1 is identical to the row R6 of TABLE-1. List at node 22 in Fig.1 is identical to the row R7 of TABLE-1. List at node 110 in Fig.1 is identical to the row R1 of TABLE-1. List at node 111 in Fig.1 is identical to the rows R2 and R3 of TABLE-1. List at node 120 in Fig.1 is identical to the row R4 of TABLE-1. List at node 121 in Fig.1 is identical to the row R5 of TABLE-1. List at node 210 in Fig.1 is identical to the row R6 of TABLE-1. List at node 221 in Fig.1 is identical to the row R7 of Table-1.

Table 1

Row	Route	r_id	n_pac	p_sz	d_r
R1	0->1->11->110->M1	M1	T1	P1	d1
R2	M2->111->11->1->0	M2	T2	P2	d2
R3	0->1->11->111->M3	M3	T3	P3	d3
R4	M4->120->12->1->0	M4	T4	P4	d4
R5	0->1->12->121->M5	M5	T5	P5	d5
R6	0->2->21->210->M6	M6	T6	P6	d6
R7	M7->221->22->2->0	M7	T7	P7	d7

3. Each node associated with i^{th} route computes route duration time ($r\_d\_time_i$) after establishing a new route or after updating an existing route. The route duration time of ith route ($r\_d\_time_i$) is computed as the ratio of (T_i*P_i) and d_i in sec in case of establishing a new route. It is computed as the ratio of $(T_i-N_i)*P_i$ and d_i in sec in case of updating an existing route where N_i is the number of data packets whose transmission or reception is already over using the existing route.

   All the nodes in both the domain monitor the status of all the existing route passing through them. If a route remains idle for a long time or route duration time is over, all the nodes associated with that route deletes the corresponding information from the list in memory.
4. All the nodes associated with a particular route maintains separate counter for the corresponding

MN. For example, GMA, MA and SA associated with i^{th} route using by MN_i maintains C_GMA_i, C_MA_i and C_SA_i counter respectively which indicates the number of packets of MN_i whose transmission or reception is already over. The GMA, MA and SA associated with i^{th} route computes the value of C_GMA_i, C_MA_i and C_SA_i easily by decreasing the value of T_i by 1 after the completion of the transmission or reception of each data packet of MN_i. So in case of intra subnet handoff of MN_i, the new route is selected for T_i-C_SA_i number of data packets and the route duration time of the new route is $(T_i-C\_SA_i)*P_i/d_i$. In case of inter subnet handoff of MN_i, the new route is selected for T_i-C_MA_i number of data packets and the route duration time is $(T_i-C\_MA_i)*P_i/d_i$. In case of inter domain handoff of MN_i the new route is selected for T_i-C_GMA_i number of data packets and the route duration time is $(T_i-C\_GMA_i)*P_i/d_i$.

5. After establishing i^{th} route and after starting transmission or reception using i^{th} route, each node associated with i^{th} route maintains two counter N_i and $count_i$ to compute the delay in i^{th} route due to congestion. At any instant of time N_i indicates how many packets has already been transmitted or received and $count_i$ indicates how much time is elapsed to transmit or receive N_i number of data packets. Now time requires to transmit or receive N_i number of data packets is $(N_i * P_i)/d_i$ sec. $Delay_i$ is the difference of $count_i$ and $(N_i*P_i)/d_i$ in sec.

3. Mobility management algorithm

Step 1: Let MN_i equal to M sends MN route request message to LA identified as B under the coverage area of SA identified as S which is in the network N1 and domain MA1. So GMA_id=N1, MA_id=MA1, SA_id=S and LA_id=B.

Step 2: GMA_id sends a message to M through MA_id, SA_id and LA_id. In response M sends a message containing the encrypted version of encryption/decryption key to home agent (HA) through LA_id, SA_id, MA_id and GMA_id. In case of valid encryption/decryption key, HA sends a positive acknowledgement to GMA_id, GMA_id sends a positive acknowledgement to LA_id through MA_id and SA_id. GMA_id also stores the encrypted message of M in memory for authentication in case of future inter domain handoff of M. The HA has the responsibility for sending binding update to CN so that CN can send the packets of MN directly to GMA and GMA delivers the packets of MN at its original destination within the network.

Step 3: In case of successful authentication a route is established as M->B->S->MA1->N1->CN in case of transmission and CN->N1->MA1->S->B->M in case of reception. The route is identified as M and all the nodes (GMA_id,MA_id,SA_id,LA_id) associated with the route inserts the record of M in the list. SA_id, MA_id, GMA_id and CN binds LCoA, SCoA, RCoA and GCoA in binding cache (BC).

Step 4: When an LA identified as B1 (i.e. LA_id=B1) detects M as a new MN within its coverage area, LA_id sends M to its parent SA identified as S (i.e. SA_id=S). SA_id searches the list for the identification number M among the existing route for transmission or reception through it. If found SA_id senses an intra subnet handoff of M from LA B to LA B1, modifies the existing route as M->B1->S->MA1->N1->CN in case of transmission and CN->N1->MA1->S->B1->M in case of reception (i.e. B1 is under the coverage area of SA identified as S which is in the network N1 and domain MA1) and the route is identified as M. SA_id binds new LCoA (LA_id.M) of M in BC. SA_id sends LCoA of M to GMA id through MA id. B1 inserts and N1, MA1, S updates the record of M by replacing the old route by the new route in the list. The node B deletes the record of M from the list as soon as the route duration time corresponding to r_id=M is over. GMA_id increases $intra\_subnet_i$ counter by 1. Otherwise go to Step 5.

Step 5: M is under the coverage area of new SA identified as S1 (i.e. SA_id=S1). SA_id sends M to MA_id. MA_id searches the list for the identification number M among the existing route for transmission or reception. If found, MA_id senses an inter subnet handoff of M from subnet S to subnet S1, modifies the existing route as M->B1->S1->MA1->N1->CN in case of transmission and CN->N1->MA1->S1->B1->M in case of reception (i.e. B1 is under the coverage area of S1 which is in the network N1 and domain MA1) and the route is identified as M. SA_id and MA_id binds new LCoA (LA_id.M) and SCoA (SA_id.LA_id.M) of M in BC. MA_id sends SCoA of M to GMA_id. S1, B1 insert and N1, MA1 update the record of M by replacing the old route by the new route in the list. The nodes S, B delete the record of M from the list as soon as route duration time corresponding to r_id=M is over. GMA_id increases $inter\_subnet_i$ counter by 1. Otherwise go to Step 6.

Step 6: M is under the coverage area of new MA identified as MA2 (i.e. MA_id=MA2). MA_id sends M to GMA_id. GMA_id searches the list for the identification number M among the existing route for transmission or reception. If found, GMA_id senses an inter domain handoff of M from domain MA1 to domain MA2, modifies the existing route as M->B1->S1->MA2->N1->CN in case of transmission and CN->N1->MA2->S1->B1->M in case of reception (i.e.B1 is under the coverage area of S1 which is in the network N1 and domain MA2) and the route is identified as M. SA_id, MA_id and GMA_id binds new LCoA (LA_id.M), SCoA (SA_id.LA_id.M) and RCoA (MA_id.SA_id.LA_id.M) of M in BC. MA2, S1, B1 insert and N1 updates the record of M by replacing the old route by the new route in the list. The nodes B, S, MA1 delete the record of M from the list as soon as route duration time corresponding to r_id=M is over. GMA_id increases $inter\_domain_i$ counter by 1. Otherwise go to Step 7.

Step 7: M is under the coverage area of new GMA identified as N2 (i.e.GMA_id=N2). So B1 is under the coverage area of GMA_id=N2, MA id=MA2, SA_id=S1 and LA_id=B1. Go to Step 2.

4. Computation of route selection time

In this section the time requires to select route for MN_i during initial registration and also during handoffs are considered for discussion. The time requires for route selection depends upon the number of wireless message requires to exchange among various nodes as discussed in section 3.

4.1 Computation of route selection time during initial registration of MN_i ($r\_s\_time_{Regis\_i}$): This is the time requires to select i^{th} route for transmission or reception of T_i number of data packets of MN_i. It depends upon the number of bits ($r\_s\_bit_{regis\_i}$) in wireless message require to exchange among various nodes to establish i^{th} route. It is the product of $r\_s\_bit_{regis\ i}$ and time/bit. $r\_s\_bit_{regis\_i}$ is computed as follows:

The number of wireless message (MN route request message) requires to exchange for the selection of ith route for MN i is 5 (M->LA_id->SA_id->MA_id->GMA_id->CN). So $r\_s\_bit_{regis\_i}=5*rrm\_bit_i$ and $r\_s\_time_{regis\ i} = r\_s\_bit_{regis\_i} * time/bit$.

4.2 Computation of route selection time during intra subnet handoff of MN_i($r\_s\_time_{intra\_sub\_i}$): This is the time requires to select i^{th} route for transmission or reception of T_i-C_SA_i number of data packets of MN_i. It depends upon the number of bit ($r\_s\_bit_{intra\_sub\_i}$) in wireless message requires to exchange among various nodes for establishing i^{th} route. It is the product of $r\_s\_bit_{intra\_sub\_i}$ and time/bit. $r\_s\_bit_{intra\_sub\_i}$ is computed as follows:

new LA_id->SA_id (send M)=1 message and 17 bits per message

SA_id->new LA_id (send MN route request message) = 1 message and $29+\log_2 T_i$ bits per message

SA_id->MA_id->GMA_id (send LCoA i.e. LA_id.MN_id)=2 message and ($\log_2 no\_of\_LA_{SA}$ + 17) bits per message

So $r\_s\_bit_{intra\_sub\_i} = 80 + \log_2 T_i + 2\log_2(no\_of\_LA_{SA})$

$r\_s\_time_{intra\ sub\ i} = r\_s\_bit_{intra\ sub\ i} * time/bit$

4.3 Computation of route selection time during inter subnet handoff of MN i($r\_s\_time_{inter\_sub\_i}$): This is the time requires to select i^{th} route for transmission or reception of T_i-C_MA_i number of data packets of MN_i. It depends upon the number of bits ($r\_s\_bit_{inter\_sub\_i}$) in wireless message requires to exchange among various nodes for establishing i^{th} route. It is the product of $r\_s\_bit_{inter\_sub\_i}$ and time/bit. $r\_s\_bit_{inter\_sub\_i}$ is computed as follows:

new LA_id->new SA_id->MA_id (send M)=2 message and 17 bits per message

MA_id->new SA_id->new LA_id (send MN route request message)=2 message and ($29 + \log_2 T_i$) bits per message

MA_id->GMA_id (send SCoA i.e. SA_id.LA_id.MN_id)=1 message and $\log_2(no\_of\_SA_{MA}) + \log_2(no\_of\_LA_{SA})$ + 17 bits per message

So $r\_s\_bit_{inter\_sub\_i} = 109 + 2\log_2(T_i) + \log_2(no\_of\_SA_{MA}) + \log_2(no\_of\_LA_{SA})$

$r\_s\_time_{inter\_sub\_i} = r\_s\_bit_{inter\_sub\_i} * time/bit$

4.4 Computation of route selection time during inter domain handoff of MN_i ($r\_s\_time_{inter\_dom\_i}$): This is the time requires to select i^{th} route for transmission or reception of T_i-C_GMA_i number of data packets of MN_i. It depends upon the number of bits ($r\_s\_bit_{inter\_dom\_i}$) in wireless message requires to exchange among various nodes for establishing i^{th} route. It is the product of $r\_s\_bit_{inter\_dom\_i}$ and time/bit. $r\_s\_bit_{inter\_dom\_i}$ is computed as follows:

new LA_id->new SA_id->new MA_id->GMA_id (send M)=3 message and 17 bits per message

GMA_id->new MA_id->new SA_id->LA_id (send MN route request message)=3 message and $29+\log_2 T_i$ bits per message

So $r\_s\_bit_{inter\_dom\_i} = 138 + 3\log_2(T_i)$.

$r\_s\_time_{inter\_dom\_i} = r\_s\_bit_{inter\_dom\_i} * time/bit$

5. Theoretical analysis

In this section the performance of the proposed scheme is analysed numerically. GMA of a network computes the parameters as discussed in the following sections.

5.1 Average cost of the network ($Cost_n$)

The cost for transmission or reception of the data packets of MN_i using i^{th} route ($Cost_i$) is the product of the number of bits require to exchange and cost/bit. Now the number of bits require to exchange (bit_i) is the sum of the number of bits to select i^{th} route, number of bits to transmit or receive using i^{th} route, number of bits require to exchange among various nodes due to handoff. Now the number of bits requires to exchange among various nodes due to handoff (h_i) is the sum of $intra\_subnet_i*r\_s\_bit_{intra\_sub\_i}$, $inter\_subnet_i*r\_s\_bit_{inter\_sub\_i}$ and $inter\_domain_i*r\_s\_bit_{inter\_dom\_i}$.

So $bit_i = r\_s\_bit_{regis\_i} + T_i*P_i + h_i$.

$Cost_i = bit_i*cost/bit$, where cost/bit is assumed as 1 unit in case of WLAN domain and 2 unit in case of cellular domain.

$Cost_n=\Sigma_{i=1}^{U} Cost_i/U$, where U=total number of MNs in the network

5.2 Average delay of the network ($Delay_n$)

The delay during transmission or reception of the data packets of MN_i using i^{th} route (D_i) is the sum of the initial route selection time, delay due to congestion and the delay due to message exchange among various nodes during handoff. Now the delay due to handoff is the product of the number of bits require to exchange among various nodes due to handoff (h_i) and time/bit.

$D_i = (h_i + r\_s\_bit_{regis\_i})*time/bit + Delay_i$.

The delay of cellular domain ($Delay_{CD}$) is $\Sigma_{i=1}^{U_{CD}} D_i$, where U_{CD} is the number of MNs in cellular domain. The delay of WLAN domain ($Delay_{WD}$) is $\Sigma_{i=1}^{U_{WD}} D_i$, where U_{WD} is the number of MNs in WLAN domain.

So $Delay_n=(Delay_{CD}+Delay_{WD})/U$. The wireless network data rate is assumed as 30 kbps as per websites:
http://www.computerworld.com/mobiletopics/mobile/technology/story/0,10801,87486,00.html
http://www.ee.latrobe.edu.au/mf/ELE52PMC/Lectures/PMC-06.ppt.

5.3 Average packet loss of the network (PL_n)

The number of loss of bits due to D_i for MN_i is d_i*D_i. The number of loss of packets due to D_i for MN_i (PL_i) is $(d_i*D_i)/P_i$. $PL_n=\Sigma_{i=1}^{U}PL_i$. The packet loss probability of the network is $\Sigma_{i=1}^{U}(PL_i/T_i)$.

5.4 Computation of remaining battery power life time for MN_i (r_i)

GMA computes the remaining battery power life time of all the MNs during their transmission or reception dynamically. For MN_i the computation of r_i by GMA after transmitting or receiving N_i number of packets is as follows:

Time of transmitting or receiving N_i number of packets of MN_i ($time_i$) using i^{th} route is the sum of transmission or reception time, $r\_s\_time_{regis\_i}$, b_i*time/bit and $Delay_i$ in sec. Now transmission or reception time is the ratio of N_i*P_i and d_i. So $time_i=(N_i*P_i)/d_i+r\_s\_time_{regis\_i}+h_i*time/bit+Delay_i$ and $r_i=life\_time - time_i$.

5.5 Average power consumption of the network (PC_n)

The power consumption of ith route using by MN_i after transmitting or receiving N_i number of data packets is computed as the product of consumption rate and $time_i$. Consumption rate (C) is equal to the ratio of initial battery power of a MN and life time in consumption/sec. C is assumed as 5 mJ/sec. So $PC_i=C*time_i$ mJ. $PC_n=(\Sigma_{i=1}^{U}PC_i)/U$.

6. Vertical handoff algorithm

GMA of a network schedules the MNs in a queue in the ascending order of their remaining battery power life time. As soon as the delay of a domain crosses a threshold (D_{th}), GMA triggers vertical handoff algorithm. If delay of cellular domain crosses its threshold, GMA triggers vertical handoff from cellular domain to WLAN domain for the MN who is at the front end of the queue due to low cost, high speed and high bandwidth of WLAN domain. The algorithm repeats these steps for other MNs from the front end of the queue till the delay of cellular domain reduces below its threshold and delay of WLAN domain increases towards its threshold. If delay of WLAN domain crosses its threshold, GMA triggers vertical handoff from WLAN domain to cellular domain for the MN who is at the rear end of the queue due to high cost and low bandwidth of cellular domain. The algorithm repeats these steps for other MNs from the rear end of the queue till the delay of WLAN domain reduces below its threshold and delay of cellular domain increases towards its threshold. GMA increases inter domain counter by 1 corresponding to each MN for which it triggers vertical handoff.

7. Simulation results

VHC computes the effective load of a domain as the product of traffic load of that domain and the percentage of total route request that will go to that domain. The traffic load of a domain is computed as the ratio of arrival rate and departure rate of service request. In the present work both the arrival rate and departure rate of service request in a domain is considered as poisson distribution. VHC computes the percentage of total request that will go to a particular domain as the ratio of the number of service request to that domain to the sum of the service request of both the domain

Fig.2, Fig.3 and Fig.4 show the plot of $Cost_n$, $Delay_n$ and PL_n vs. traffic load for two different cases. For case 1 $no\_of\_LA_{SA}$=20 and $no\_of\_SA_{MA}$ varies from 10 to 30. For case 2 $no\_of\_LA_{SA}$ varies from 10 to 30 and $no\_of\_SA_{MA}$=10. For both the cases $Cost_n$, $Delay_n$ and PL_n increase with traffic load due to increase of network congestion with traffic load.

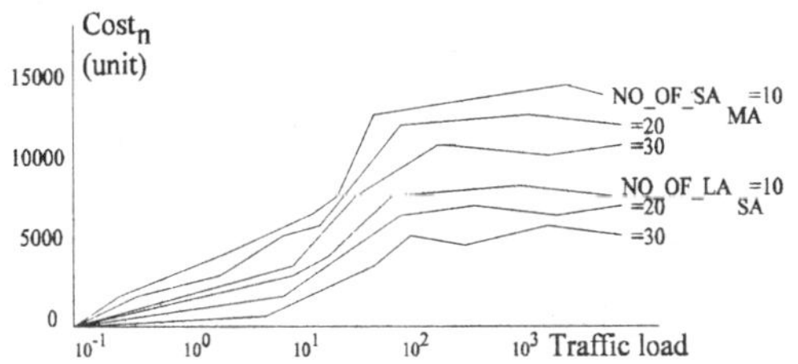

Fig. 2 $Cost_n$ vs. Traffic load

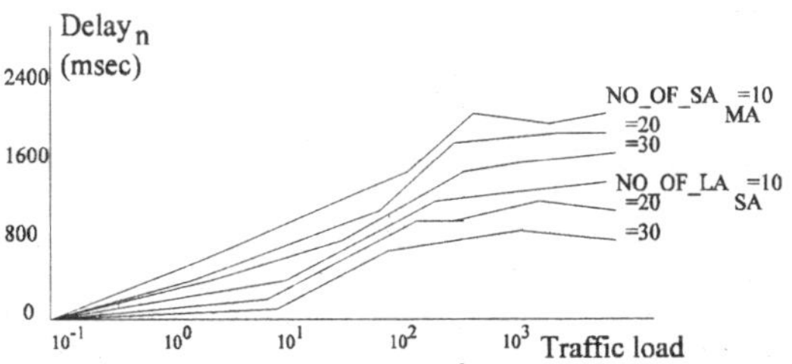

Fig. 3 $Delay_n$ vs. Traffic load

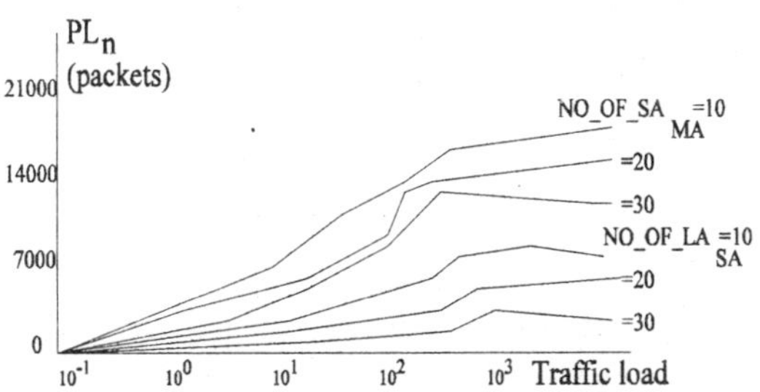

Fig. 4 PL_n vs. Traffic load

The increase in $no\_of\_SA_{MA}$ in case 1 causes the reduction in inter domain handoff but the increase in $no\_of\_LA_{SA}$ in case 2 causes the reduction both in inter subnet and inter domain handoff. As a result $Cost_n$, $Delay_n$ and PL_n are higher in case 1 than in case 2. In case the delay of the cellular domain crosses its threshold GMA triggers vertical handoff from cellular domain to WLAN domain. After such vertical handoff $Cost_n$, $Delay_n$ and PL_n reduces with traffic load. In case the delay of the WLAN domain crosses its threshold GMA triggers vertical handoff from WLAN domain to cellular domain. After such vertical handoff $Cost_n$, $Delay_n$ and PL_n increases with traffic load. Moreover the vertical handoff algorithm tries to balance the effective load of the two domains. As a result the rate of change of $Cost_n$, $Delay_n$ and PL_n lies within a limit after traffic load greater than equal to 10^2.

8. Conclusion

The proposed scheme is a mobility management protocol for next generation cellular network. The scheme provides minimum cost, delay and packet loss without any extra complexity of the mobile unit.

The performance of the scheme is evaluated considering only the data class of traffic. It can be extended by evaluating its performance in presence of other traffic classes such as voice and video in the network.

References

[1] S.Mitra, "Dynamic Mobility Management for Next Generation All-IP Wireless Network", International Conference on Communication Systems and Networks, April 2008.

[2] M.Jaseemuddin, "Architecture for Integrating UMTS and 802.11 WLAN Networks", IEEE Symposium on Computers and Communications, ISCC, pp.1-8, 2003.

[3] M.M.Buddhikot, G.Chandranmenon, S.Han, Y.Lee, S.Miller, and L.Salgarelli, "Design and Implementation of a WLAN/CDMA 2000 Interworking Architecture", IEEE Communication Magazine, pp.93-97, November 2003.

[4] C.Perkins, "IP Mobility Support", IETF RFC, 2002.

[5] D.Johnson and C.Perkins, "Mobility Support in IPv6", IETF draft,draft-ietf-mobileip-ipv6-15.txt, July 2001.

[6] A.T.Campbell, J.Gomez, C.Y.Wan, S.Kim, Z.Turanyi, and A.Valko, "Cellular IP", Internet draft, draft-ietf-mobileip-cellularip-00.txt, December 1999.

[7] A.Misra, P.Agrawal, and S.K.Das, "TeleMIP:Telecommunications-Enhanced Mobile IP Architecture for Fast Intradomain Mobility", IEEE Personal Communication, vol.7, pp.50-58, August 2000.

[8] S.Misra, M.Chakraborty, D.Saha, A.Mukherjee, B.Deb, and B.Chatterjee, "Global Mobility Management: A Three Level Architecture Wireless IP Networks", IEEE IWDC Springer LNCS 2918, pp.184-193, December 2003.

[9] I.S.Misra, S.Dey, and D.Saha, "TLMIPv6: A Next Generation Three Layer Mobile IPv6 Mobility Management Architecture", WWC 2005.

[10] G.Dommety and et al., "Fast Handovers Mobile IPv6", IETF draft, draft-ietf-mobileipfast-mipv6-03.txt, July 2001.

[11] M.Chakraborty, I.S.Misra, D.Saha, and A.Mukherjee, "A Novel Fast Handover Technique for TLMM: Three Level Mobility for Next Generation Wireless IP-based Networks", Proceedings Int. conference Indicon, 2004.

Self-Adaptive Handoff Model for 4G

Mr. Alok Singh[1] and Mr. Saurabh Singh[2]
[1,2]Student of Final Year E&TC, R.C. Patel, Shirpur
aloksingh87@gmail.com *saurabhsu30@gmail.com*

Abstract

Revolutionary drivers for 4G wireless communication include a push toward universal wireless access and ubiquitous computing through seamless personal and terminal mobility. One of the major challenges for seamless mobility is the creation of vertical hand off protocol: a handoff protocol for users that move between types of networks. Traditional operations for hand off detection policies, decision metrics, and end radio link transfer are not able to adapt to dynamic handoff criteria, or react to user inputs and changing networks availability. Nor are they able to deliver context aware services or ensure network interoperability. Thus, new techniques are needed to manage user's mobility between different types of networks.

This article presents a design mobile architecture which is seen suitable for envisioned various network architectures and technologies for 3G and beyond. Then the problem of vertical hand off is defined in the context of such a diverse network environment. We present an approach which is employed to solve and facilitate handoff in 4G. Since the phones of vogue even though having myriad applications are not interoperable, they give more work to the stations at hand off. The manipulated mobile architecture which capable of soft vertical handoff facilitated within the mobile itself along with the handoff between base stations which seams to be a self adaptive handoff model for 2G, 2.5G, 3G, B3G and most importantly 4G.

1. Introduction

The 4G wireless networks will integrate heterogeneous technologies such as wireless LAN (WLAN) and third generation (3G) cellular network because no single wireless network technology simultaneously can provide a low latency, high bandwidth, and wide area data service to a large number of mobile users.

The movement of a user within or among different types of networks can be referred as the vertical mobility. One of the major challenges for seamless service in the vertical mobility is a vertical handoff, where handoff is the process of maintaining a mobile user's active connection by changing its point of attachment. In the 4G wireless systems, seamless handoff with small latency and packet losses should be executed. Handoff latency is one of important factors that decide the quality of service (QoS) in the 4G wireless networks. In the deployment of multimedia services with real-time requirements, the handoff process can significantly degrade the QoS from the user's perspective. Since many packets can be typically lost before vertical handoff by the unstable channel condition, this article presents a design mobile architecture which is seen suitable for envisioned various network architectures and technologies for 3G and beyond.

The continuing evolution of micro electronics, telecommunication, audio-visual techniques and information services is delivering the technology to fulfill the vision of omnipresent services. Today many technologies are available that can be combined to exploit the business potential of application that work anywhere anytime in a seamless and intuitive way.

The wide spread success of wireless and mobile communication has resulted in the creation of a large variety of wireless technologies, including 2G and 3G cellular, satellite, Wi-Fi, and Bluetooth. Each technology is tailored to reach a particular market.

The advantage of these diverse networks is that they offer many choices for increasing bandwidth, accessing the internet and increasing the coverage area for the average user. Expanding services to the use and co-ordination of diverse networks creates the challenge of developing novel interoperable network protocols to manage user mobility, between different types of systems-a level of interoperability currently not available in 3G systems.

The evolutionary goals of beyond 3G (B3G) and 4G include building on packet based CDMA networks. Some goals may be forecast by emerging issues, such as spectrum efficiency, dynamic bandwidth allocation, security, quality of service (QoS) and transceiver technology.

Universal wireless access refers to the ability of the user to connect any where at any time from any network. The change in connection may be initiated by the user or by the network, transparent to the user. For instance, a user may choose to access a wireless LAN

(WLAN) to send a large a data file, but may choose a cellular network for voice call on the other hand, a network may decide to handoff a stationary data user to a WLAN user in order to increase bandwidth availability for mobile users in a 3G cellular networks. To achieve seamless mobility, network management operations must be conducted without causing degradation of services, and without need for user intervention. The movement of a user within or among different types of networks can be referred to as intersystem or vertical mobility. Handoff research has been based on evaluation of the signal strength received at the mobile node, followed by a change in access point, if needed and up dated.

2. Hand Off

Any hand off operation is a three stage process, that includes hand off decision, radio link transfer and channel assignment. Hand off decision is performed based on a perception of channel quality reflected by the received signal strength and other measurements and the availability of resources in a new cell. The base station usually measures quality of the radio link channels being used by mobile nodes in its surface area. This is done periodically so that degradation in signal strength below a prescribed threshold can be detected and hand off is initiated by the base station. Radio link transfer refers to the responsibility of the network to form links to the call at its new point of attachment. It may require hand off rerouting operations. The third handoff stage channel assignment consists of allocations of resources to the hand off at the new point of attachment.

While performing handoff, the mobile user connection may be created at the target base station before the old base station connection is released. This is soft hand off. On the other hand the new connection may be set up after the old connection is released. This is hard hand off. Also we have hand off between different networks termed as vertical handoff and handoff between same networks known as horizontal handoff. The handoff model developed here can suite any network.

2.1 Vertical Hand-Off Scenario

Today's wireless access networks consist of several overlapping tiers. The combination of 3G and WLAN technologies enable the internet access from anywhere and anytime thereby bringing benefits to both end users and service providers. A horizontal handoff is defined as a handoff between base stations (BSs) that use the same type of wireless network interface. This is the traditional definition of handoff for homogeneous cellular systems. A vertical handoff is defined as a handoff between BSs that uses different wireless network technologies such as the WLAN and the 3G cellular network. The heterogeneous networks (3G cellular network and WLAN) have some important properties. First, the network service areas are overlapped as shown in Fig. [1].

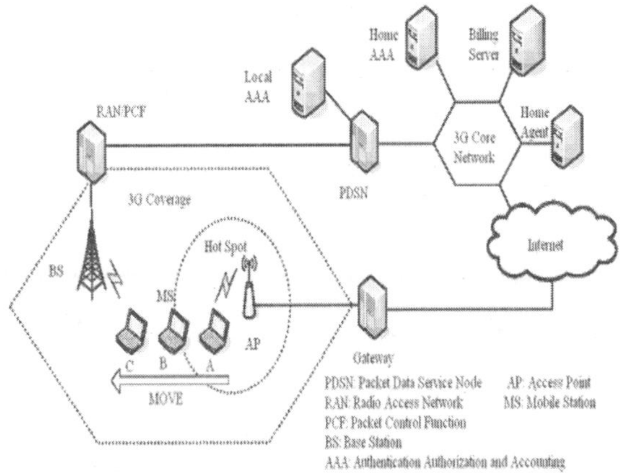

Fig. 1 Vertical Handoff Scenario

For example, the 3G cellular network acts as an umbrella network to the WLAN network. Also the different cells of the same network are overlapped. To reduce service disruption, we can utilize this overlapping by simultaneously connecting to the different networks at the boundary of one network during vertical handoff. Second, two networks may support different data rates. The WLAN can support a data rates in Mbps, while 3G cellular network can only supply tens of Kbps. In our scenario, we focus on the vertical handoff between the WLAN and the 3G cellular network. Fig. 1 shows the vertical handoff when the mobile station (MS) moves from the location A in the WLAN to the location C in the 3G cellular networks. As the MS leaves the access point (AP), the strength of the beacon signal received from the AP periodically weakens. If its strength is decreased below the threshold value, the MS tries connecting to the 3G cellular network and starts synchronizing with the system to prepare the handoff.

2.2 Dynamic GOP Structure Selection

This paper proposes a dynamic GOP structure selection method to provide seamless video streaming for vertical handoff in the heterogeneous wireless network. The proposed method dynamically changes the interval of I-pictures by using the RSSI and Ec/Io in order to reduce error propagation due to packet losses. Our proposed method finds the optimal I-picture interval (N) suitable to the network condition and determines the final N before the handoff process. Thus, after the vertical handoff the client should receive a new I-picture as soon as possible. The proposed framework is illustrated in Fig. 2.

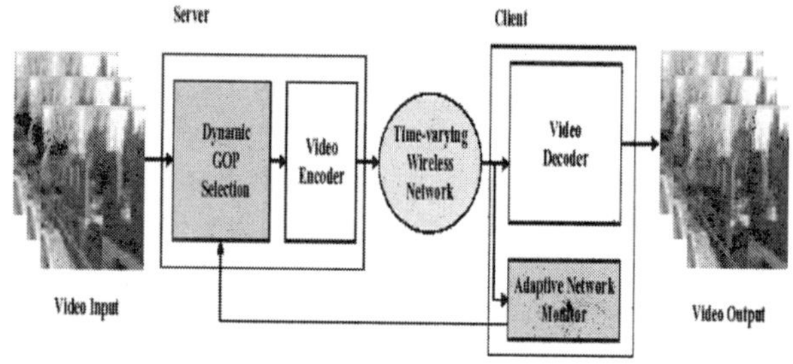

Fig. 2 Proposed framework for the dynamic GOP structure selection for the heterogeneous wireless network.

3. Comparison between 3G And 4G

3.1 Comparison between 3G and 4G in terms of parameters

Major Requirement Driving Architecture	Predominantly voice driven - data was always add on	Converged data and voice over IP
Network Architecture	Wide area cell-based	Hybrid - Integration of Wireless LAN (WiFi, Bluetooth) and wide area
Speeds	384 Kbps to 2 Mbps	20 to 100 Mbps in mobile mode
Frequency Band	Dependent on country or continent (1800-2400 MHz)	Higher frequency bands (2-8 GHz)
Bandwidth	5-20 MHz	100 MHz (or more)
Switching Design Basis	Circuit and Packet	All digital with packetized voice
Access Technologies	W-CDMA, 1xRTT, Edge	OFDM and MC-CDMA (Multi Carrier CDMA)
Forward Error Correction	Convolutional rate 1/2, 1/3	Concatenated coding scheme
Component Design	Optimized antenna design, multi-band adapters	Smarter Antennas, software multiband and wideband radios
IP	A number of air link protocols, including IP 5.0	All IP (IP6.0)

3.2 Comparison of 3G and 4G in terms of Technology

3G	4G
Back compatible to 2G.	Extend 3G capacity by one order of magnitude.
Circuit and packet switched networks.	Entirely packet switched networks.
Combination of existing & evolved equipment.	All network elements are digital.
Data rate (up to 2Mbps).	Higher bandwidth (up to 100Mbps).

4. Need for 4G

4G has sprung from a usage –driven research frame work to invent new technologies to wireless world vision. The evolution of such a wireless system (also called 'Beyond 3G 'or 'B3G') is closely linked to rapid advances in digital and component technologies. The merger of consumer electronics, computer system, telecommunication and broadcasting is leading to an information convergence that will require increasingly seamless connection. Seamless means getting over barriers of different wireless standards and bands. So future mobile devices will be capable of supporting multiple wireless standards, and operate in multi-mode, multiband fashion.

The 4G wireless communication system can be integrated with the Internet protocol (IP) backbone network to provide quality of service (QoS) support for multimedia applications. It will support dynamical scheduling, link adaptation and frequency selection as well as full roaming capabilities.

4G also mean mobile telephony at a data rate of 100Mbps globally (between any two points in the world) and 1Gbps locally.

- Need for 4 G3G performances may not be sufficient to meet needs of future high-performance applications like multi-media, full-motion video, wireless teleconferencing. We need a network technology that extends 3G capacity by an order of magnitude.
- There are multiple standards for 3G making it difficult to roam and inter operate across networks. we need global mobility and service portability
- 3G is based on primarily a wide-area concept. We need hybrid networks that utilize both wireless LAN (hot spot) concept and cell or base-station wide area network design.

5. Factors

We put forward two major factors which governs the model.

a) Numbering Scheme
b) Programming

Numbering Scheme: Here the network operator has to divide the subscriber's number into two

a) Active Subscriber Number (ASN)
b) Passive Subscriber Number (PSN)

Customer is provided an ASN by the operator and any PSN is given any subscriber. Here the distinction is in between 4-5 numbers between PSN and ASN the above distinction applies to all cellular or QLAN networks, the software program may be written on java platform. It interfaces various technology dependent functional blocks.

Whose outputs are voltage levels, the cost etc in addition a look up table consists of the PSN of all networks and their corresponding related technical information.

When a customer gets his handset burnt then one PSN number form all the networks and their corresponding technical information deducted form the look up table and put into the customer's handset.

6. Proposed Mobile Model

Even today researchers are looking in innovative point of view about the handoff feature in soft vertical handoff which facilitates 4G. We have worked out such that we give less work to the BTS, BSC, MTC etc and mould the mobile handset in order to provide more complex operations which is carried out in a simpler fashion and also flexible as compared to the present approach models (vertical handoff and other models).

Here we introduce a block which contains both hardware and software sectors as shown in fig 3 and fig 4. In the hardware sector we have a block which can be an integral part of mobile with various available chips like DSP, Microprocessors, A/D Converters Memory.

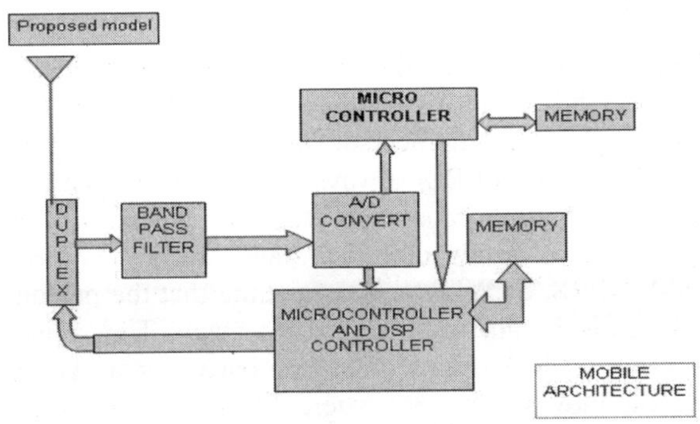

Fig. 3 Hardware of Proposed Model

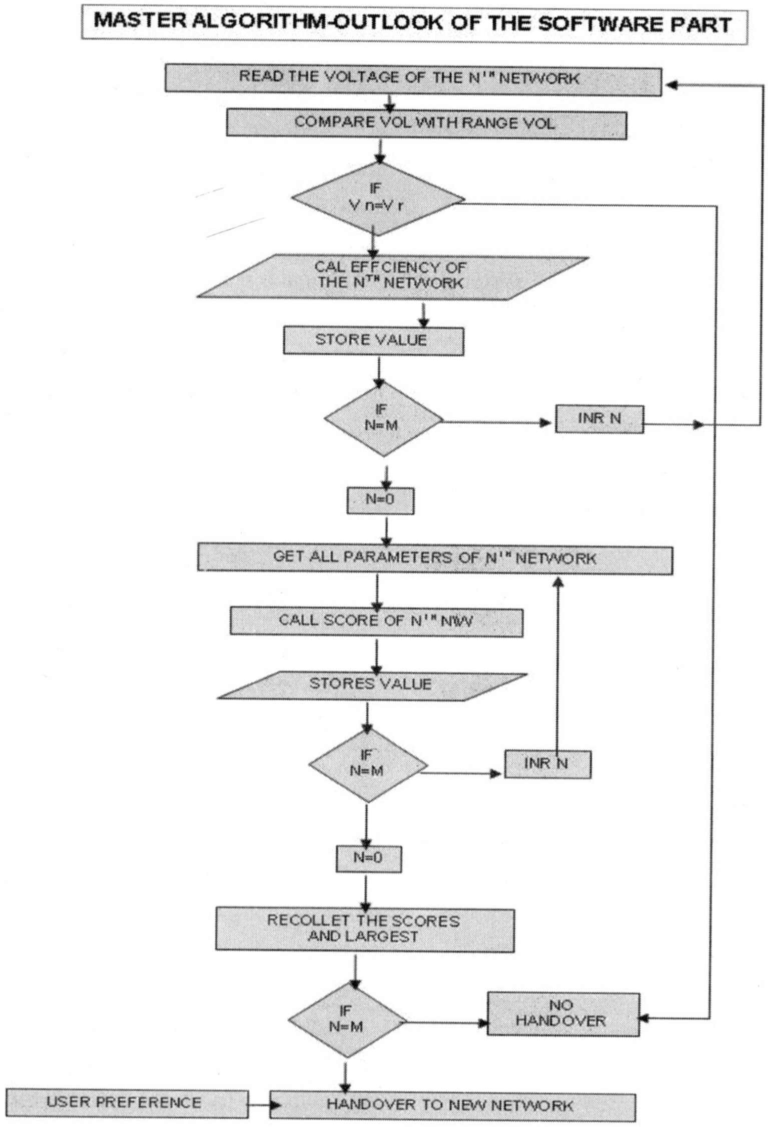

Fig. 4 Software of Proposed Model

7. How does it work

This can be explained by taking an example that the customer has burnt his handset to CDMA. When his mobile is the microprocessor along with the support with the support of DSP always keeps in track with the best network in accordance with the power of the signals, cost, bandwidth, data rate, traffic may be GSM, GPRS, or WLAN. Now assume that the person calling his friend, who is very far away. The signal power of CDMA is more in calling party's area. As he talks he moves to an area where GSM scores more in his mobile when this is observed immediately the PSN of the GSM is appended to his message signal and is transmitted. In addition the CDMA tower contacts GSM tower and also the respective MCS. Then the Handoff is done. At the initial stage of vertical handoff the soft handoff is accompanied by an adaptive decay detecting method is used here. One or two sampled signals are compared with max-min value. If it is not the required value then it can activate network switching circuit. Again the test is repeated for a period of time if signal found to decay, and then there is no effect on the switching circuit. Suppose if the signal strength increases then the switching circuit is deactivated.

Later after the radio link is established then Context Transfer takes place. So the detail of the customer is passed to the handover access point. This may facilitate in billing and message transfer between routers. Consider another case that is if a caller activates a call if he finds that there is a problem in the connection then he can directly select a priority code any start his call for this if any one network is sufficient.

8. IGPBS Packet Transmission In 4G Field Experiment

NTT DoCoMo announced it achieved 1Gbps real-time packet transmission in the downlink at the moving speed of about 20km/h in a field experiment on fourth-generation (4G) radio access. The experiment took place in Yokosuka, Kanagawa.

This is the latest achievement in DoCoMo's ongoing development of key radio access technology for 4G mobile communications. The 1Gbps real-time packet transmission was realized through Variable Spreading Factor-Spread Orthogonal Frequency Division Multiplexing (VSF-Spread OFDM) radio access and 4-by-4 Multiple-Input-Multiple-Output (MIMO) multiplexing using "adaptive selection of surviving symbol replica candidate" (ASESS) based on Maximum Likelihood Detection with QR decomposition and the M-algorithm (QRM-MLD), which was developed by DoCoMo. By using the new algorithm, DoCoMo was able to reduce the large computational complexity of the original MLD method while maintaining almost the same achievable throughput performance. Frequency spectrum efficiency, which is expressed as information bits per second per Hertz, is 10 bits per second per Hertz, about 20 times that of 3G radio networks' spectrum efficiency.

During an earlier trial, DoCoMo achieved 100Mbps and 20Mbps data rate transmission in the downlink and unlink, respectively, in outdoor environments using the same 100MHz bandwidth.

DoCoMo will continue to conduct field trials as part of its program to develop a 4G global standard in cooperation with the International Telecommunication Union Radio communication Sector. The telecommunications council of Japan's Ministry of Internal Affairs and Communications aims to see 4G services commercialized in the country by 2010.

9. 4G Applications

1. **Public Safety**
   One of the most notable advanced applications for 4G systems is location-based service. 4G location applications would be based on visualized, virtual navigation schemes that would support a remote database containing graphical representations of streets, buildings, and other physical characteristics of a large metropolitan area. This database could be accessed by a subscriber in a moving vehicle equipped with the appropriate wireless device, which would provide the platform on which would appear a virtual representation of the environment ahead. For example, one would be able to see the internal layout of a building during an emergency rescue. This type of application is sometimes referred to as "Telegeoprocessing", which is a combination of Geographical Information Systems (GIS) and Global Positioning Systems (GPS) working in concert over a high-capacity wireless mobile system. Telegeoprocessing over 4G networks will make it possible for the public safety community to have wireless operational functionality and specialized applications for everyday operations, as well as for crisis management.
2. **Virtual Navigation:** As described, a remote database contains the graphical representation of streets, buildings, and physical characteristics of a large metropolis. Blocks of this database are transmitted in rapid sequence to a vehicle, where a rendering program permits the occupants to visualize the environment ahead. They may also "virtually" see the internal layout of buildings to plan an emergency rescue, or to plan to engage hostile elements hidden in the building.
3. **Tele-Medicine:** A paramedic assisting a victim of a traffic accident in a remote location could access medical records (e.g., x-rays) and establish a video conference so that a remotely based surgeon could provide “on-scene” assistance. In such a circumstance, the paramedic could relay the victim's vital information (recorded locally) back to the hospital in real time, for review by the surgeon.
4. **Crisis-Management Applications**: These arise, for example, as a result of natural Disasters where the entire communications infrastructure is in disarray. In such circumstances, restoring communications quickly is essential. With wideband wireless mobile communications, both limited and complete communications capabilities, including Internet and video services, could be set up in a matter of hours. In comparison, it may take days or even weeks to re-establish communications capabilities when a wireline network are rendered inoperable.

9. Future Challenges

One of the most challenging issues facing deployment of 4G technologies is how to make the network architectures compatible with each other. The success of 4G systems would largely depend upon its ability to overcome the capability challenges. Some of the challenges concerning 4G architectural design issues are given below:

1. **High Usability and Global Roaming:** The end user terminals should be compatible with any technology, at any time, anywhere in the world. The basic idea is that the user should be able to take his mobile to any place, for example, from a place that uses CDMA to another place that employs GSM.
2. **Multimedia Support:** The user should be able to receive high data rate multimedia services. This demands higher bandwidth and higher data rate.
3. **Personalization:** This means that any type of person should be able to access the service. The service providers should be able to provide customized services to different type of users.
4. **Terminal Mobility:** This is one of the biggest issues the researchers are facing. Terminal mobility allows the user to roam across different geographical areas that uses different technologies. There are two important issues related to terminal mobility. One is location management where the system has to locate the position of the mobile for providing service. Another important issue is hand off management. In the traditional mobile systems only horizontal hand off has to be performed where as in 4G systems both horizontal and vertical hand off should be performed. As shown in figure 1, horizontal hand off is performed when a mobile movies from on cell to another and vertical handoff is performed when a mobile moves between two wireless systems.
5. **Security and privacy:** The existing security measures for wireless systems are inadequate for 4G systems. The existing security systems are designed for specific services. This does not provide flexibility for the users and as flexibility is one of the main concerns for 4G, new security systems has to be introduced.
6. **Fault tolerance**: As we all know, fault tolerant systems are becoming more popular throughout the world. The existing wireless system structure has a tree like topology and hence if one of the components suffers damage the whole system goes down. This is not desirable in case of 4G. Hence one of the main issues is to design a fault tolerant system for 4G.
7. **Billing System:** 3G mostly follows a flat rate billing system based where the user is charged just by a single operator for his usage according to call duration, transferred data etc. But in 4G wireless systems, the user might switch between different service providers and may use different services. In this case, it is hard for both the users and service providers to deal with separate bills. Hence the operators have to design a billing architecture that provides a single bill to the user for all the services he has used. Moreover the bill should be fair to all kinds of users.

10. Reasons to have 4G

- Support interactive multimedia services: teleconferencing, wireless Internet, etc.
- Wider bandwidths, higher bit rates.
- Global mobility and service portability.
- Low cost.
- Scalability of mobile networks.

10. 1 What's New in 4G

- Entirely packet-switched networks.
- All network elements are digital.
- Higher bandwidths to provide multimedia services at lower cost (up to 100Mbps).

11. Pros and Cons

11.1 Pros

- Integration of different networks of different technologies can be achieved.
- Mobility among networks can be achieved.
- Flexible-to parameters of any technology and network.
- Since a major part of soft vertical handoff is supported by the hardware and software module handoff is seamlessly achieved giving less work to base and control stations.
- Not much manipulation required by the user – User Friendly.

11.2 Cons

One major draw is that we require the co-operation of all networks in supporting numbering and vertical hand off. But this is seen that it can be over come by change in present software of the various stations.

12. Conclusion

4G in its evolutionary and revolutionary contexts does not allow an exact vision of the future. However if past evolution developments are a indication of the future, there is need to promote technological adaptability interoperability for the next generation of wireless communication. The article presents the design for achieving an adaptable-soft vertical handoff in a multi-network of 4G environment Possible mobile architecture which we have proposed for 3G, B3G, or 4G is a significant step towards 4G systems based on all IP networking technologies. Traditional handoff considered among the various stations requires support which can be provided by out mobile model.

13. References

[1] G. G. Savo, "Advanced Wireless Communications 4G Technologies".

[2] J. McNair and Zhu. Fang, "Vertical handoffs in fourth-generation multinetwork environments," *IEEE Wireless Communications*, vol. 11, pp. 8-15.

[3] [3] U. Varshney and R. Jain, "Issues in emerging 4G wireless networks," *IEEE Computer*, vol. 34, pp. 94-96.

[4] J. McNair and Zhu. Fang, "Vertical handoffs in fourth-generation multi-network environments,"

IP Based Address Network Management

Dr. H. V Ramakrishnan[1], Dr. Sira G Rao[2] and Nagaraja G.S.[3]
[1]Additional Rector, Dept of CSE, Dr.MGR University, Chennai-600095
[2]Professor, Dept ECE, JSSATE Bangalore-560060
[3]Assistant Professor, Dept of CSE, R.V. College of Engg, Bangalore-560059
drhvr@hotmail.com siragrao@hotmail.com nagarajgs2000@yahoo.com

Abstract

Internet Protocol addresses have been managed by using spread sheets manually instead of having automated software. IP automated management can reduce the cost of administering IP addresses. IP networks are increasing in complexity as users demand more communications features from the billions of electronic devices now deployed. This amplifies the impact of manual errors on network reliability, security, customer service, user access, and IT department productivity. There is a strong Demand for the automated protocol based address management solution which takes cares of the requirements of the organization with respect to IP address usage. The solution also needs to perform fast, secure, and reliable DNS updates so that an organization can easily reach new customers and prevent security attacks, and customers can remain confident in the company's ability to manage information.

We propose system architecture to develop automated protocol based address management software for the DHCP server. We are expected to take care of all the IP address assignment and releases by DHCP server. Apart from that we need to provide a Good GUI to view the IP address usage. Every time an IP is rejected we have to notify the Administrator of rejections by clients. We also need to maintain the History of IP address usage over some period so that any damage occurred can verify from the source.

Keywords: *IP, DHCP, DNS, GUI, Address Management.*

1. Introduction

An IP address is a unique address that certain electronic devices currently use in order to identify and communicate with each other on a computer network utilizing the Internet Protocol standard in simpler terms, a computer address. The IP address acts as a locator for one IP device to find another and interact with it. It is not intended, however, to act as an identifier that always uniquely identifies a particular device. In current practice, an IP address is not always a unique identifier, due to Technologies such as dynamic assignment and network address translation. IP addresses are managed and created by the Internet Assigned Numbers Authority (IANA). The IANA generally allocates super-blocks to Regional Internet Registries, who in turn allocate smaller blocks to Internet service providers and enterprises.

An IP address that is assigned to a client when requested, which is not permanent and keeps changing whenever the host restarts the system is known as Dynamic IP Address. Dynamic IP Addresses are most frequently assigned on LANs and broadband networks by Dynamic Host Configuration Protocol (DHCP) servers. They are used because it avoids the administrative burden of assigning specific static addresses to each device on a network. An IP address that is assigned to a client permanently, which does not change after every reboot is known as Static IP Address. Static addressing is essential in some infrastructure situations, such as finding the Domain Name Service directory host that will translate domain names to numbers (IP addresses). IP addresses are an integral part of any corporate network, and companies large and small are consuming them faster with more applications and devices than ever before. Overlooking the importance of getting a handle on IP addresses can prove disastrous.

IP addresses are one of the most critical resources that need to be managed in any network. Every networked application and device from e-mail and Web connectivity to file storage and networked printers depends on IP and requires address assignment. That presents a big enough challenge, but it's becoming an even bigger challenge as new core services like VOIP and mobile networks increase IP address assignment needs, requiring more robust allocation, classification, and tracking of addresses.

IPAM can enable administrators to eliminate network conflicts and outages, track critical assets and ensure network security by providing reports based on a wide range of parameters, including IP address status (dynamic, static, available, reserved, etc.), hostnames, MAC address, and DHCP lease data including lease date/time, time left on lease, time of last renewal, and more.

Having real-time access to IPAM data is increasingly important for any network administrator or security officer. For example, the ability to immediately access information such as IP addresses in use, when they were allocated, which devices they were assigned to, and who is using them is critical to identifying potential network abuse or security breaches by internal or foreign users. In addition, as network access control (NAC) systems become more widely deployed, IPAM plays a key role in facilitating and monitoring enforcement of policies, like validating that operating system and anti-virus software is current before assigning an IP address and granting access to the network.

2. Overview

The components of any protocol based network management are

- Domain Name System
- Dynamic Host Configuration Protocol
- Dynamic DNS Update

Domain Name System

The Domain Name System (DNS) was designed in the 1980s to handle the growing number of Internet users. The Domain Name System translates names, such as www.infoseek.com, into IP addresses that computers need to be able to communicate with each other. DNS makes using Internet applications, such as the World Wide Web, easy. The process is as if when phoning your friends and relatives you could use their names instead of having to remember their phone numbers.

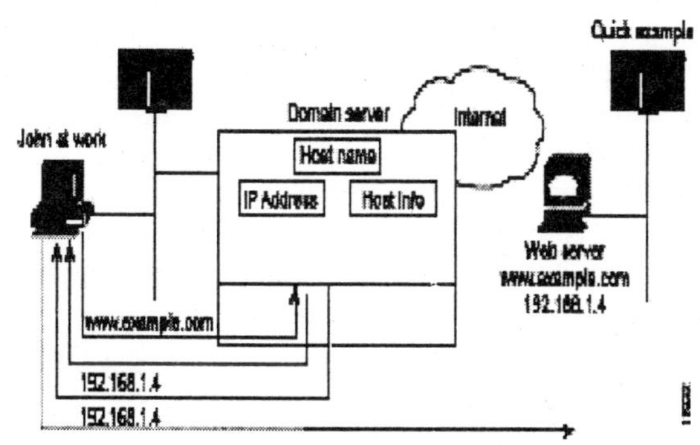

Fig. 1 Dynamic Host Configuration Protocol

All hosts that want to access the Internet must have an IP address. As Internet administrator, you must do the following for every new user and for every user whose computer has been moved to another subnet:

- Select a legal IP address
- Assign the address to the individual workstation
- Define workstation configuration parameters
- Update the DNS database, mapping the workstation name to the IP address.

These activities are time-consuming and error prone. For these reasons, the Dynamic Host Configuration Protocol (DHCP)_was created. DHCP frees you from the burden of individually assigning IP addresses. It was designed by the Internet Engineering Task Force (IETF) to reduce the amount of configuration required when using TCP/IP. DHCP allocates IP addresses to hosts and can provide all the parameters hosts require to operate and exchange information on the Internet network to which they are attached. DHCP localizes TCP/IP configuration information and manages the allocation of TCP/IP configuration information by automatically assigning IP addresses to systems configured to use DHCP. Thus, you can ensure that hosts have Internet access without having to configure each host individually.

Working of DHCP server

DHCP was designed to make TCP/IP easier to install on large networks with little user intervention required. DHCP accomplishes much of this by shifting the configuration from the individual workstation level to that of global address pools at the server level. DHCP uses a client/server model. The client software runs on the individual workstation and the server software runs on the DHCP server.

The workstation automatically requests an IP address from a DHCP server on the network.

The DHCP server offers a lease that is an IP address with all the other configuration information necessary to use the Internet. The leased IP address is not used by anyone else, and is valid only for that workstation.

Before the IP address's lease expiration time, bethpc renews its lease, extending the Expiration time. It will continue to use the lease right up to its expiration if it cannot reach the server.

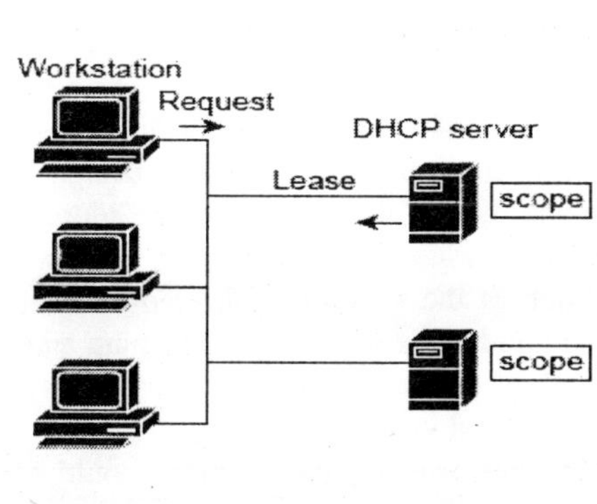

Fig. 2 Hosts Request an IP Address Protocol

As long as the DHCP server has the correct configuration information, none of the workstations or servers using DHCP will ever be configured incorrectly. Therefore, there is less chance of incurring difficult-to-trace network problems that can result from incorrectly configured workstations and servers.

Dynamic DNS Update

Although DHCP frees you from the burden of distributing IP addresses, it still requires updating of the DNS server with the names and IP addresses of the DHCP hosts. Dynamic DNS update automates the task of keeping the DNS database of names and IP addresses current. Network Registrar's dynamic DNS update allows the DHCP server to tell the corresponding DNS server when a name-to-address association has been created or changed. When a host obtains a lease for an address, Network Registrar tells DNS to add the host information. When the lease expires, or when the host gives up a lease, Network Registrar tells DNS to remove the association. In normal operation you do not have to manually reconfigure DNS, no matter how frequently clients' addresses change through the use of DHCP.

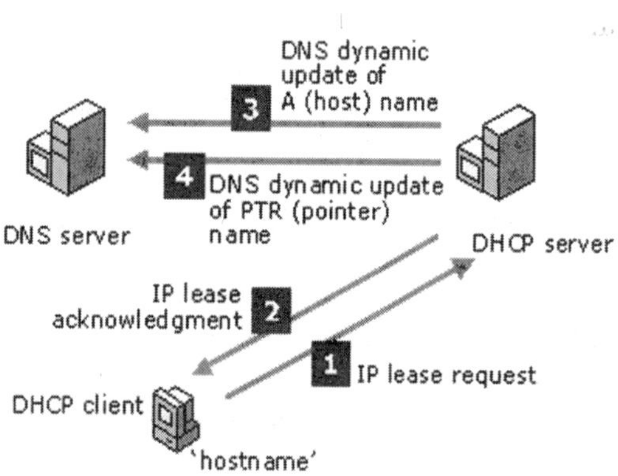

Fig. 3 Dynamic DNS Update

3. Design Considerations

There are a number of design considerations, which must be taken into account before design phase is begun. The issues that we need to address before considering a design for implementing our system are

- Each of the systems connected in the LAN should have a DHCP client running and thus the solution can be executed on any system connected in the network.
- The person using the solution should be the administrator and thus provide authentication details.
- Ipam solution uses a database to store all the required details regarding each subnet and hence requires a MYSQL database.
- The daemons keep updating all the necessary data to the database. This information retrieved and displayed to the user

Assumptions and Dependencies

Every project is completed with certain assumptions about users, technology used, output expected etc and as well dependencies on other components. These assumptions basically arise from the fact that no project irrespective of its sophistication level can work under all conditions. Other assumptions regarding operating systems, hardware requirements are also specified. Some of our assumptions and dependencies are as follows:

- The required subnets and Ip pools should already be configured.
- This solution is specific to Linux platform.
- It is being developed for a Linux OS.
- Our solution is to be integrated with the other tools.

General Constraints

General constraints specify the constraints one has developed the project under. These constraints can have significant impact on the final system being developed and the performance of the system. Constraints are limitations while developing the project including hardware specifications, user interfaces, and interoperability requirements etc.

Our application requires an already running DHCP and DNS server from which the required information is to be retrieved.

It displays all the required information to the user but doesn't allow the user to modify the information.

We require at least two systems on the network, one which is a server whereas the other is a client.

All the systems in the network must have a DHCP client.

4. Architectural Strategies

We have developed the system using the Top-Down approach. In this method, the entire system is visualized a whole, later each component of the system is split into modules, which, in the next level are further divided into sub-modules and so on. The modules which run in the backend involve PERL scripts which run as daemons. These modules keep retrieving information from the server and update them to the database. The modules which run in the front end include HTML web pages and PHP scripts to retrieve information from the database. MYSQL is being used to maintain the database.

System Architecture

The approach used in our application development is a layer-based approach, wherein we classify the system into different layers, which can perform certain operations on the given input and give us the required output.

Our application involves four layers of data processing.

- User authentication.
- GUI which is used to display the required information.
- Database used to store information.
- Daemons used to update database.

The first layer or the user authentication provides security by requesting for a username and password. The user information is then verified if it has all the privileges to see the necessary network data.

The second layer or the Graphical User Interface entails the authenticated person from viewing the requested as efficiently as possible. It also provides detailed information of the all the subnets, all the ip pools in each subnet. The web pages also provide details of individual IP's like the Mac address of the system the lease time etc.

The third layer i.e. the database layer is one which has all the information stored in it. All the necessary information for the administrator which has been retrieved is stored in this database. Any change made to data is also done here. The daemons from the lower retrieve information from the server and store them in the database.

The fourth layer or the daemons are the backend processes which are responsible for retrieving the necessary information from the server. These backend processes keep running always to check for any changes in the network in terms of host additions and deletions from the network.

Large systems are always decomposed into subsystems that provide some related set of services. The initial design process of identifying these subsystems and establishing a framework for sub-system control and communication is called architecture design. The output of this design process is a description of the software architecture.

The structure chart is depicted in figure-4. We have four main layers of execution. They are:

- The data update and storage modules
- The storage space
- The data retrieval modules
- The user interface

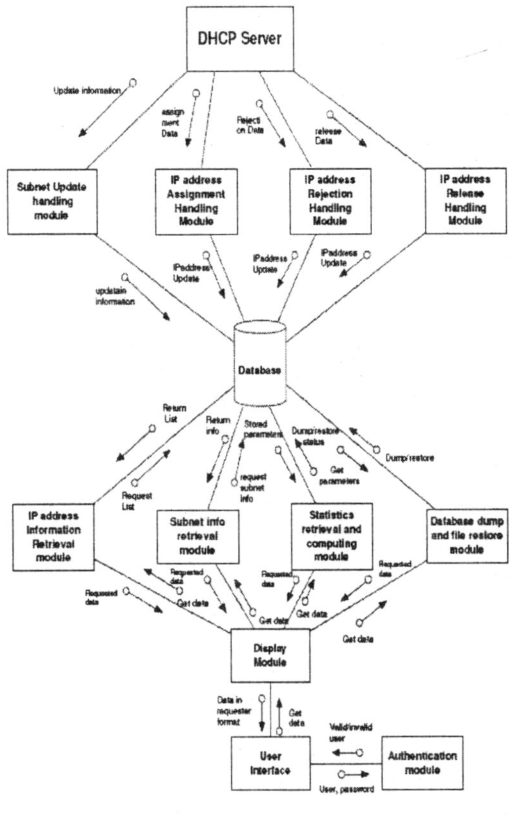

Fig. 4 Architecture Chart for Address Management

User interface: This layer supports the GUI part of the solution. All the necessary information to be displayed to the user is displayed via the web pages. Each web page gives respective information.

Data retrieval: This layer includes modules which retrieve data from the database, when requested by the user. These modules retrieve the necessary information as requested by the user.

Database: This is the storage layer where all the necessary information is stored. Mysql database is used to store all the data pertaining to the IP addresses. The storage space does not have any restrictions it only depends on the hard disk space.

Data update and storage: This is the bottom most layer which keep running in the background. These modules retrieve information from the DHCP server and store them in the database. Apart from this the modules also update the data in the database as and when there is change in the information.

5. Conclusion

We propose system architecture to develop an automated protocol address based management software solution for DHCP server. Developing an automated IPAM software solution involves keeping track of all the IP addresses assigned by the DHCP server and also keeping track of the IP addresses released or rejected by the DHCP client. Our IPAM solution keeps track of IP address usage by keeping track of assignments and releases by DHCP server, the details can only be viewed but cannot be modified. The management solution is provided with a good GUI which makes the task of maintaining the IP addresses much easier. Our solution is designed in such a way that it can be ported to any DHCP server with minimal modifications.

6. References

[1] The RFC s of IETF standard and were available at hhtp://www.ietf.org/
DNSRFC1 :http://www.ietf.org/rfc/rfc1034.txt DNS RFC1 :http://www.ietf.org/rfc/rfc1035.txtDNSRFC1 :http://www.ietf.org/rfc/rfc2131.txt

[2] Introduction to DHCP server installation and configuration at
http://www.isc.org/idex.p1?/sw/dhcp

[3] A detailed description of OMAPI and there functionality with ISC DHCP server
http://en.wikipedia.org/wiki/OMAPI

[4] An introduction to OMSHELL and explanation of working the OMAPI's
http://linuxreviews.org/man/omapi

[5] Internetworking with TCP/IP principles, protocols and architecture, Fifth edition ,Douglas E. Comer

[6] IP Routing O'reilly publication Ravi Malhotra

Reverse AARM: A novel and effective suffix based IP Address Assignment and Routing Mechanism

Prof. Monika Mangla
Sr. Lecturer, Terna Engineering College, Navi Mumbai
manglamona@gmail.com

Abstract

An explosive growth of networks in the current scenario demands for various challenges to be handled, to have an efficient and effective routing methodology and make best utilization of the networks [1]. Number of routing algorithms are available [2]; in this paper a suffix based approach for IP Address assignment and Routing Mechanism has been proposed for peer to peer tree topology based networks [3,4]. Proposed methodology stores routing information among the participating nodes in a distributed fashion. Arrangement of routing information in a distributed fashion results in minimal number of hops, thus avoids nodes being overburdened that consequently eliminates unnecessary routing; thereby limiting time complexity [5,6].

1. Introduction

Peer to peer networks have been very well-liked for applications like file sharing [7]. The most important aspect of peer to peer networks is that all the communications are symmetric and autonomous in all respects [8] [9]. Such networks have many challenging issues associated like scalability, self organization, adaptation and routing [10].

The paper here discusses the issue of routing by providing a scheme for IP Address Assignment and Routing Mechanism (AARM) ; that is able to route data packets in tree topology based peer to peer networks with minimal hopping [11].

One of the key problems in the large scale peer to peer networks is to provide an efficient algorithm for location of destination node and routing the information [12] [13]. Once destination node is located, a path is established among source and destination node, which is followed by routing the information.

Routing aids in providing a communication path between source and destination pair for hassle free delivery of information [14]. AARM strategy suggested here emphasizes on setting a communication path between pair of source and destination. Proposed methodology is armed with handling of best and worst cases in similar manner.

2. Proposed Modus Operandi: Suffix based AARM

The strength of suggested methodology lies in storing the routing information in a way so that routing information for all IP addresses sharing the same suffix lies together [15]. In this Paper, Section 3 discusses unique and orderly assignment of IP addresses while Section 4 focuses on suggested routing methodology.

3. AARM: Unique IP Address Assignment

This section deals with the unique IP addresses allocation such that all possible IP addresses are utilized, the assignment always starts from the root node.

IP Address Assignment

i. Start from root node
   Root node would consist of router that connects four LAN's in this case. Here, in the proposed methodology four LANs will be developed on the basis suffix. All IP addresses sharing the same suffix are put in same LAN. Root node would be primarily responsible for enabling data flow within WAN [16] [17].
ii. IP Address Assignment at Level 0:
   Format of IP address at this level would be as follows:

7	6	5	4	3	2	1	0
←			x		→	b	b

   where b is a bit and x is a prefix of 6 bits with value 0 (000000). According to the suffix based AARM methodology, all IP addresses with bb as 00 are put in same LAN. For the purpose of clarification only LAN 1(with suffix 00) has been detailed.
iii. IP Address Assignment at Level 1:
   Forlevel 1, bit assignment for 0th and 1st bit would remain same as in level 0. Considering that as y, move to 2nd and 3rd bit; and toggle the values from 00 to 11. Bit positions(4-7) are considered as z and x. Thus different formats at level 1 would be zbby or xbby

7 6 5 4	3	2	1 0
z	b	b	y
x	b	B	y

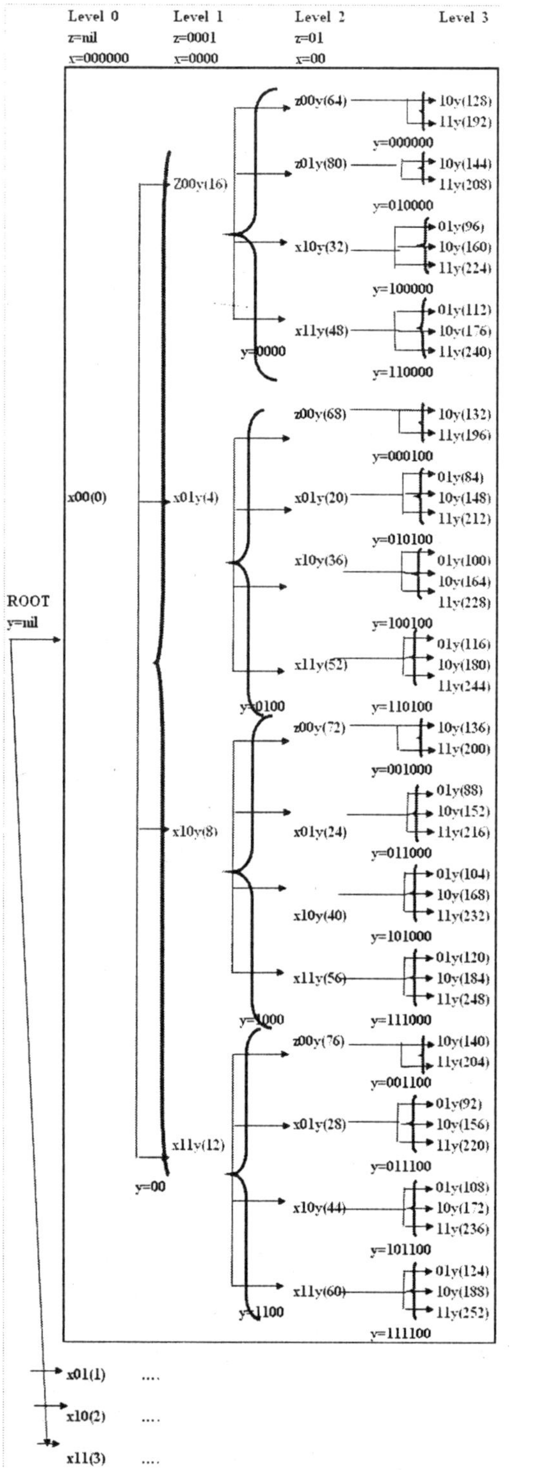

Fig. 1 Suffix based IP Address Assignment for tree topology based networks

where z and x are prefix of 4 bits, y is suffix of 2 bits. Value of z, x and y for each level has been shown in figure 1. Value of y for all siblings would remain same which in this level would be 00. z has been taken as 0001 so that duplicate IP address assignment could be avoided as if z would have been taken as 0000 the address would be similar to the address of parent i.e 0 in this case.

iv. Level 2 IP Address Assignment

Format of IP addresses at level 2 would be similar to that at level 1 but the number of bits in z and x would be reduced by 2 and that in y would be increased by 2.

7 6	5	4	3 2 1 0
z	b	b	y
x	b	b	y

Here, in the proposed approach value of y for any node at level i can be derived from bits at positions 2(i-1), 2(i-1)+1 in the IP Address of parent followed by y of parent. As shown in figure 1, values of z and x would remain same for all nodes at same level.

v. Same is applicable here as well, and the IP address format for level 3 would be as follows:

7	6	5 4 3 2 1 0
b	b	y

where b is a bit.

IP Address Assignment for one LAN connected to a router has been shown in figure 1. The numbers written along with general format of IP addresses shows the decimal equivalent of 8 bits IP address. This IP address assignment ensures that all IP addresses are diligently utilized. Proposed AARM distributes all IP addresses among four LANs on the basis of modulus value of decimal equivalent of IP address, when divided by 4.

LAN 1 consists of all IP addresses with modulus value 0. Proposed AARM methodology has significantly simplified the process of object location on the basis of how routing information has been stored within the network [18] [19]. Thus object is located by location of intermediate node that is most likely to store the routing information for the destination IP address.

Above steps can be generalized as

$z_i=6-2*i$ expect at level 0.

$x_i=6-2*i$

$y_i=2*i$

where x_i, y_i, z_i represents no. of bits in x, y ,z at i^{th} level.

4. Routing Methodology

This section discusses the reverse AARM approach for distribution of routing information so as to simplify the routing process.

In Proposed suffix based AARM routing approach, node at a level store the routing information for its immediate children and of its immediate parent. Router at root level would be storing the IP addresses of the roots of the different LAN's that are connected to it.

The AARM routing proposed here can be very well applied to 32 bits IP addresses, but for the sake of simplicity figure 1 represents IP Addresses Assignment taking only 8 bits in consideration.

Every IP address stored in routing table of a node is associated with a match bit flag M that is initially set to true for all addresses. Here matching process starts from LSB taking two bits at a time. If bits at these position matches, then process is repeated taking next two bits moving towards MSBs until the desired IP address is located.

Stepwise AARM routing algorithm used is given below:

a. First of all compare the destination IP address with the IP address of holding node. If a match is found then routing process is halted, which indicates that data packet has moved to its desired location. Else move to step b.

b. Repeat until there is only one entry in routing table of the holding node, with match flag bit set to true or if there is no IP address with match flag bit set to true, then by default data packet will be routed to the parent of the holding node.

   1. Starting from LSBs of the desired IP address take two bits (bi,bj) (initially i=1, j=0 and bi refers to the bit at position i)and compare them with bits at same position of all IP addresses; having match flag bit set to true, stored in routing table of the holding node. Matching is done by match( ) function.
      i. Match function will return true if match (both bits are matched) is found else it will return false; represented by R.
      ii. For every IP address stored in routing table, update the match flag bit M to :

      New match flag bit M= AND (previous match flag bit, value of R),

      This operation ensures that wherever match is found, match flag bit is stored as true else it will be set to false. The suggested technique ensures limited comparison while finding next hop. Current bit pair will be matched for only those entries, which were matched for previous bit pair.

   2. i= i+ 2 , j= j+2, repeat 1 for all IP addresses in routing table whose match flag is set to true.

c. Forward the data packet to the single IP address with match flag bit set to true and repeat the routing algorithm.

Using match flag bit in Reverse AARM helps in minimizing time complexity for routing as while scanning the routing table only limited entries are matched, whose match flag bit has been set to true.

Case 1: Communication among sibling nodes.

Consider communication is to set between 00011000(24) and 00101000(40) as these are sibling nodes as shown in figure 1. Routing process starts as follows:

a. Match source IP address 00011000(24) with destination IP address 00101000(40) as a whole, as there is no match so it's routing table will be scanned.

b. Routing table of source node 24 would be

00011000(24) – self
01011000(88)
10011000(152)
11011000(216)
00001000(8)-parent

As per suggested methodology for first bit pairs all entries would be set to true, as first bit pair from LSBs is same for all entries in the routing table. Again for next bit pair all flag bits will set to true. The process will be repeated with third bit pair 10 in the case, none of the entries has a match thus all flag bits will be set to false, thus packet will be forwarded to parent of the holding node, which in the case is 00001000(8)

d. Routing table of 00001000(8)-would be

00001000(8)-self
01001000(72)
00011000(24)
00101000(40)
00111000(56)
00000000(0)-Parent

Iterative matching process will result in all entries in the routing table with the flag bit set to true for first two bit pairs. While continuing with third bit pair(10 in the case) only one entry will be having flag bit set to true, thus packet will be forwarded to the same node with match flag bit as true.

e. Now, the holding node is 00101000(40) with routing table as follows:

00101000(40) – self
01101000(104)
10101000(168)
11101000(232)
00001000(8)-parent

While comparing the destination IP address with that of holding node, a match is found thus routing process is halted.

Case 2: Communication from root node to a leaf node within a LAN

Consider that the data is to move from node with IP address 00000000(0) to node 10101100(172).

a. As no match is found with holding node so process continues followed by iterative matching.
b. Routing table of source node 00000000 would be as follows:

00000000 (0)-self
00010000(16)
00000100(4)
00001000(8)
00001100(12)
Router- Parent

During iterative matching for first bit pair, each entry has a match: setting match flag bit to true for all children. While continuing with second bit pair only node 12 has a match, thus packet is forwarded to the node with IP address 12.

c. Routing table of node 12 would be as follows:

00001100(12)- self
01001100(76)
00011100(28)
00101100(44)
00111100(60)
00000000(0)-Parent

Again mo match with holding node, while comparing with entries in the routing table, iterative matching results in node 44 with flag bit set to true, thus packet would be forwarded to node 44.

d. Routing table of node 44 would be as follows:

00101100(44)-self
01101100(108)
10101100(172)
11101100(236)
00001100(12)-parent

No match with holding node, followed by iterative matching that results in node 172 with flag bit set to true. Therefore, packet is forwarded to node 172.

f. Routing table of node 172 is as follows:

10101100(172)
00101100(44)

As match is found with the holding node, routing process is halted.

Case3: Communication within two LANs

Consider that the data is to move from node 00010000(16) to node with IP address 01000011(67).

a. No match with holding node, therefore matching process starts. Routing table of source node in the case would be as follows:

00010000(16) –self
01000000(64)
01010000(80)
00100000(32)
00110000(48)
00000000(0)- parent

Iterative matching process results in no match which results in forwarding the data packet to the parent of holding node. Therefore, data packet in this case is forwarded to the node 0.

b. Routing table of node 0 is as follows:

00000000 (0)-self
00010000(16)
00000100(4)
00001000(8)
00001100(12)
Router-Parent

Again no match is found this time even for first bit pair, therefore data packet is forwarded to the parent of node i.e router in this case. Router in turn will be forwarding the data packet to node 00000011(3) which is root node of the LAN where destination node is located. Data would be forwarded to desired destination using method discussed earlier.

5. Conclusion and Future Work

As discussed in the paper, the suggested suffix based Address Assignment and Routing Mechanism surely helps in alleviating the routing performance of tree topology based Peer to Peer networks. The proposed AARM methodology is capable of reducing number of intermediate hops for data packet by selecting the best possible shortest communication path in the network; irrespective of source and destination nodes. The proposed work can be extended in the direction of application for hybrid networks.

6. References

[1] Dimitri Bertsekas ,and Robert Gallager " Data Networks", second addition, Prentice-Hall, 1992.

[2] M. Zitterbart et al., "HeaRT: High Performance Routing Table Lookup," *4th IEEE Workshop on Architecture & Implementation of High Performance Communications Subsystems*, Thessaloniki, Greece, Jun. 1997.

[3] Dimitrios Tsoumakos , Nick Roussopoulos, Analysis and comparison of P2P search methods, Proceedings of the 1st international conference on Scalable information systems, p.25-es, May 30-June 01, 2006, Hong Kong

[4] K. Sklower, "A Tree-Based Packet Routing Table for Berkeley Unix," *USENIX, Winter'91*, Dallas, TX, 1991.

[5] C. Huitema, *Routing in the Internet*, Prentice Hall, 1996.J. Moy, *OSPF: Anatomy of an Internet Routing Protocol*, 1998.

[6] B. Halabi, *Internet Routing Architectures*: New Riders Publishing, 1997.

[7] Ranganathan, K., Ripeanu, M., Sarin, A., and Foster, I. To Share or Not to Share: An Analysis of Incentives to Contribute in Collaborative File Sharing Environments. In Workshop on Economics of Peer-to-Peer Systems

[8] Philippe Golle , Kevin Leyton-Brown , Ilya Mironov, Incentives for sharing in peer-to-peer networks, Proceedings of the 3rd ACM conference on Electronic Commerce, p.264-267, October 14-17, 2001, Tampa, Florida, USA

[9] Information retrieval techniques for peer-to-peer networks, Zeinalipour-Yazti, D.; Kalogeraki, V.; Gunopulos, D. *Computing in Science & Engineering* On page(s): 20- 26, Volume: 06, Issue: 4, July-Aug. 2004

[10] An-Hsun Cheng , Yuh-Jzer Joung, Probabilistic file indexing and searching in unstructured peer-to-peer networks, Computer Networks: The International Journal of Computer and Telecommunications Networking, v.50 n.1, p.106-127, 16 January 2006

[11] M. Degermark, *et al.*, "Small Forwarding Tables for Fast Routing Lookups," *Proc.ACM SIGCOMM'97*, Cannes, France, Sept. 1997.

[12] Beverly Yang , Hector Garcia-Molina, Improving Search in Peer-to-Peer Networks, Proceedings of the 22 nd International Conference on Distributed Computing Systems (ICDCS'02), p.5, July 02-05, 2002

[13] Luca Gatani , Giuseppe Lo Re, An efficient adaptive strategy for searching in peer-to-peer networks, Multiagent and Grid Systems, v.1 n.3, p.209-224, August 2005

[14] John Risson , Tim Moors, Survey of research towards robust peer-to-peer networks: search methods, Computer Networks: The International Journal of Computer and Telecommunications Networking, v.50 n.17, p.3485-3521, 5 December 2006

[15] Ruiz-Sanchez, M.A.; Biersack, E.W. and Dabbous, "Survey and taxonomy of IP address look up algorithms, "W. *Network, IEEE* v.15 n.2, p. 8-23, Mar/Apr 2001

[16] Y. Katsube, K. Nagami, and H. Esaki, "Toshiba's Router Architecture Extensions for ATM: Overview," *IETF RFC 2098*, April 1997.

[17] S. Keshav and R. Sharma, "Issues and Trends in Router Design," *IEEE Commun. Mag.*, May 1998, pp. 144 - 151.

[18] Panayotis Antoniadis , Costas Courcoubetis, Enforcing efficient resource provisioning in peer-to-peer file sharing systems, ACM SIGOPS Operating Systems Review, v.40 n.3, July 2006

[19] John Risson , Tim Moors, Survey of research towards robust peer-to-peer networks: search methods, Computer Networks: The International Journal of Computer and Telecommunications Networking, v.50 n.17, p.3485-3521, 5 December 2006

Vehicular ad-hoc Network

Ms.Smita N.Pathak and Prof.S.A.Raut
G.H.Raisoni College of engg. Department of computer science and engg.
smita_27dec@yahoo.co.in rautsa@gmail.com

Abstract

Vehicular Communications (VC) is at the heart of both academia and car manufacturers. They are progressively paying more and more attention towards VC, that allow vehicles to connect to each other and with the roadside infrastructure to form a Vehicular Ad-hoc Network (VANET) and a key component of Intelligent Transportation Systems (ITS) is the provision of adequate network infrastructure to support vehicular communication. In this paper we present the results of classify these applications according to their distinguishing characteristics and discuss their network architecture requirements. We outline how VANET will be a better option than GPS technology. We consider the network architectural alternatives available for wireless on roads in addition with mapping of coverage.
Keywords: IEEE 802.11, Wireless Access, VANET, vehicular communication.

1. Introduction

Currently, Inter-Vehicle Communication systems (IVC) is an emerging class of wireless communication, attracting considerable attention from the research community as well as the automotive industry also enabling mobile users in their vehicles to communicate to the road and to each other. Some of the initial efforts in this field began with the development and standardization of vehicular communication technologies. That is the case of DSRC (Dedicated Short Range Communication) in North America and Japan, as well as some European projects. Vehicular communication are expected to take place in urban zones, rural zones and highways through providing some network functionalities, protocols and integration strategies for services' delivery to users. On-Board Units (OBU), that are radio devices installed on vehicles, and Road Side Units (RSU), that constitute the network infrastructure are the two basic classification of VANET and the three architectural alternatives as shown in Fig. 1.
include:

i) A pure wireless Vehicle-to-Vehicle ad hoc network (V2V) allowing standalone vehicular Communication with no infrastructure support
ii) An Infrastructure-to-Vehicle (I2V) architecture with wired backbone and wireless last hops,
iii) A hybrid architecture that exploits the fixed infrastructure using V2V communication.

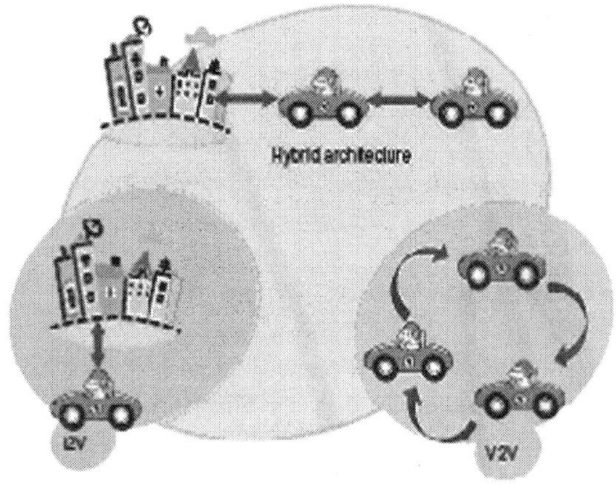

Fig.1 Vehicular communication architecture

These three architectural technologies provide a wealth of other business driven applications like road information services, and infotainment services for passengers, navigational driver assistance, (e.g. video on demand, web browsing, email access, games, file downloads, file sharing, car following). Consequently, vehicular networks offer a rich set of tools to drivers and administrators of transportation systems but, at the same time, they make possible a formidable set of abuses and attacks. Consider, for example, nodes that 'contaminate' large portions of the vehicular network with false information, or the deployment of nodes that collect VC messages, track the location and transactions of vehicles and infer sensitive information about their drivers. Worse even, vehicles and their processing and sensing equipment can be physically compromised, while any wireless-enabled device could pose a threat to the VC system. These simple examples of exploits indicate that under all circumstances VC systems must be secured. Otherwise antisocial and criminal behavior could be made easier, actually jeopardizing the benefits of the VC system deployment. A comprehensive set of security mechanisms is thus critical, and facilities and protocols that mitigate attacks are necessary.

These unique characteristics, the popularity of GPS (Global Positioning System) system, the availability of traffic data and a wide range of safety, commercial, and infotainment applications motivate new VANET characterization studies.

In this paper, we investigate the usability of providing network connectivity to mobile users in vehicles for the three architectures cited before (V2V, I2V, and hybrid).

The rest of the paper is organized as follows. First, we outline VANET over GPS in section 2, and then describe network architecture used for wireless on roads in section 3. Application construction is outlined in section 4. Section 5 concludes the paper and in section 6 there are the references.

2. VANET over GPS

Global positioning system (GPS) technology is a satellite based navigation system that sends and receives radio signals [20]. A GPS receiver acquires these signals and provides you with the information. Using GPS you can determine location velocity and time but you can not establish the communication this is possible with VANET (in both V2V & I2V architecture). VC, that allow vehicles to connect to each other and with the roadside infrastructure to form a Vehicular Ad-hoc Network (VANET and a key component of Intelligent Transportation Systems (ITS) is the provision of adequate network infrastructure to support vehicular communication. So VANET it will be actually be useful in the applications of air, sea and land. In addition in GPS system there are some errors which can affect the accuracy of GPS signal .These errors are [20]

i) Ionosphere and Troposphere Delays:-the satellite signals lows down as they passes through the atmosphere.
ii) Orbital Errors:-Inaccuracy of satellite reported location
iii) Receiver clock error:-GPS have built in clock that can have small timing errors.
iv) Number of satellites visible:-Obstruction can block signal reception causing position error or no position reading
vi) Signal multipath:-the GPS signal bounces off of objects, such as tall buildings or large rock surfaces, before it reaches to GPS receiver.

3. Network architecture used for wireless on roads

There are number of applications which focuses on wireless network on roads like;

i) Entertainment.
ii) Mobile Commerce.
iii) Remote Operation.
iv) Asset Tracking
v) Congestion Information.
vi) Real-Time Weather
vii) Road Hazard Detection.
viii) Map Generation.

These different classes of applications in the wireless network area possess different network architectural requirements. We now analyze those requirements in detail.

1. User centric

User-Centric applications are concerned with obtaining data from servers located in the fixed Internet. The quantities of data concerned can be small, such as traffic updates, or large, as in the case of pod casts or digital map updates. Quality of Service (QoS) requirements neither is nor did particularly onerous; data is downloaded in the background to the vehicle for later use, or streaming media is heavily buffer. Network conditions can therefore vary, handovers between different networks can take place, and patchy coverage is acceptable. Provided that the average throughput is sufficient to obtain the data in a reasonable time (e.g. traffic information within 5 minutes, or a connection to the streaming media source every 5 seconds), user requirements will be satisfied.

The communications paradigm in such applications is simple: data is either broadcast over a medium that the vehicle can listen to, or the system onboard the vehicle uses a ubiquitous connection such as a cellular link, or a localized one such as a WiFi hotspot to request the data. A lookup takes place for a server that is explicitly specified by name.

2. Fixed-to-mobile

Fixed-to-Mobile applications differ from User-Centric in that communication is no-longer predominantly one-way. The throughputs required vary from low in applications such as remote home-device operation, to high in the case of voice or video calling. However, whilst communication is two way, it always involves the vehicle registering itself with the service concerned, whether this is initiating each connection, or providing its identifier to a lookup service. Depending on the application, synchronous or asynchronous communications may be required, though any application with which user interaction takes place is likely to require a fixed QoS. For this to be the case a (near-) ubiquitous network is needed. Data may be encrypted such that only that vehicle can decode it. Crucially, there must exist a naming service that keeps track of how the vehicle may be contacted. Technologies such as Mobile IP become important in allowing seamless mobility. In-network proxy servers that buffer packets whilst network handovers take place and versions of transport protocols [11] that are optimized for such varying network conditions are also important.

3. Network Pull

Network-Pull applications centre on retrieving data from vehicles that act as mobile sensor-platforms. They are therefore not concerned with contacting specific vehicles by their identifiers, but instead obtaining data concerning a particular geographical area or captured during a specified period of time. Applications will generate spatio-temporal queries which the network will then translate into vehicle-specific requests. In order to achieve this, the network may be aware of the approximate locations of all vehicles, or it may broadcast queries to a particular geographic region. Privacy is therefore traded-off against the ability to obtain a richer dataset. Query languages, such as that used in the Cartel project [20], must be developed .An important consideration for a sensor data-rich network is security. Whilst data such as environmental conditions can be placed in the public domain, fleet management information will need to traverse the network in an encrypted form such that only the fleet owner can read it. Network designers must therefore ensure that query languages and location services take such data-hiding requirements into account. Privacy aspects of Network-Pull applications also influence how query languages are designed. Data suppliers will wish to decide whether information is artificially delayed or the position blurred before it is uploaded, whilst the network should also ensure that anonymity is aided by using, for example, mix zones [19].The QoS required by Network-Pull applications will depend both on the update frequency and the degree of confidence requested.. The lower the rate of Sensor-platforms traversing the area, the more time will be needed for the necessary number of readings to be amassed to provide a particular level of confidence. Also, the QoS for a particular area will be affected by the number of users competing for access to radio channels, as well as the available network technologies. Hence, designers must consider demand not from a mobile client's perspective, but rather from the view of a fixed client requesting data from multiple mobile servers.

4. Network-push

An evolution of the Network-Pull paradigm, Network-Push applications will involve vehicles supplying sensor data, and subsequently receiving the processed values. The network will now also need to provide on-demand aggregated information, and provide mechanisms for automated pushing of data to mobile clients. Middle ware using publish/subscribe message queues will need to be deployed, and QoS requirements will now also include the capacity of the message server. The network architecture for the physical and data-link layers will be similar to that used for Network-Pull. However, multicast communication will be key in ensuring efficient bandwidth utilization and transport protocols will be more geared to ensuring that "enough" (rather than all) the data transmitted is received by the client, perhaps by using fountain code. Also, vehicles requiring aggregated information from the network will have a feedback effect on what data is required to be queried from the network. Network-Push applications will produce many mobile clients, each of whom will make a specific spatiotemporal request. This will in turn make the level of network provision required vary far more dynamically.

5. Peer-centric

Peer-Centric applications will develop as processing resources on vehicles increase, and for some applications it becomes viable to bypass a central server altogether. Vehicles will communicate information between each other in order to relieve the backbone of some of the overhead of transmission to every node, similar to the route optimization technique used in the Mobile IP protocol [22]. Requests will be directed first to a geographically-local group of nodes, to ascertain whether the data required (or a subset of it) is available. If it is not, the request will then be made to the fixed network. In addition, vehicles will act as data-mules, aggregating data from fixed sensors and transferring it up a hierarchy, such as private cars uploading their data to public buses, whose routes are fixed and have a well-defined schedule [23] Peer-Centric applications will also need to cope with the entire network topology constantly changing, whereas with Network-Push only the final or initial hops were subject to such churn. Networks may require some fixed, but isolated, network nodes to provide predictable hops in the ad-hoc topology. In the case of safety-critical applications, such as intersection collision avoidance, it may be beneficial to involve a fixed node in order to provide QoS guarantees; certainly this type of application will be hardest to deploy on a network architecture which is purely ad hoc .

4. Application construction

We now move from the network requirements of applications to consider the design, development and deployment. We can consider the suitability of the possible mappings with respect to various metrics. Three metrics which are relevant to many typical applications are:

i) Total execution time: If the size of each task is known to the compiler along with the speed of the available processors, the duration of the execution of the application for a given mapping can be deduced.
ii) Quality of the result: The quality of the result of some processing is related to the number of vehicles whose data contributes to the result. A centralized configuration may process data from a larger number of vehicles than a peer-to-peer configuration.
iii) Privacy: The level to which the privacy of the originators of the data is respected is important in applications where personally-identifiable data is processed. Privacy is protected most strongly when individuals' data is mixed with others' data before the data becomes visible publicly. For typical applications, the fully centralized approach has a higher execution time than the approach which uses regional servers because there is less parallelization. On the other hand, the quality of result is better for the centralized approach. Privacy is poor in a centralized approach because an attacker observing the data arriving can see everything, but the attack must be distributed if a decentralized approach is adopted. The problem of searching for the optimal mapping throughout the space of possibilities defined by any combination of such metrics is NP-complete, so is not practical to achieve in real-time. Instead, we must settle for an approximate approach to yield a near-optimal solution. We have implemented a framework in which applications can be described in terms of constituent tasks; the network can be defined in terms of constituent processing nodes and the communication links; and the metrics against which to optimize are specified.

5. Mapping of coverage

In order for many of the applications we have described where vehicles are used as nodes for distributed processing, their levels of network connectivity must be predictable. Whilst in our vision of Connected Traffic network connectivity will be near-ubiquitous, there will still exist small areas where radio shadowing will cause connection drop-outs or educed performance, as in the cellular network today. There is therefore a need for the coverage along roads to be accurately and efficiently mapped, and these data constantly updated. Our current work therefore examines methods for the aggregation, storage, and use of coverage maps. Large amounts of data can be collected by using vehicles as sensor platforms, including data on the signal strength or throughput experienced on the various wireless interfaces that the vehicle possesses. This can be uploaded to a central server, or distributed between multiple nodes f or processing. Signal strength data, particularly from moving vehicles, has a relatively large variability, due to obstructions by other vehicles, meteorological conditions, and time-varying multi path effects. Hence, this data will have significant amounts of noise.

The objective of coverage mapping is to aggregate this large corpus of data into a much simpler form, that can be efficiently stored in a database on the vehicle, and queried in minimal time. Simple smoothing of the data is not an option, since it is crucial that large drops in signal strength are captured, but that may cover only a small area of road. We are therefore developing algorithms that will preserve significant points of the graph, whilst removing random noise. Long term time variability of signals must also be included in any model. Once a coverage map exists, vehicles can then predict what their likely network performance will be, and adjust parameters such as TCP timers, streaming media buffer sizes, and media bit rate. Handovers between different networks can be more easily anticipated, and the decision as to whether to perform route optimization in Mobile IP-based connections will be more informed. Such coverage maps are also crucial for predicting how nodes' reach ability will vary for task partitioning applications, where the throughput of the constituent communication links is a factor in

6. Proposed Work

Amongst the three architectural alternatives (V2V, I2V, Hybrid) we are focusing on I2V and hybrid architecture. As this is an issue based project we will try to develop its simulation using VB.Net and MATLAB so that communication between infrastructure and vehicle should take place. In which we will started with configuration of one RF Transmitter in MATLAB coding and one RF receiver in MATLAB coding. We will be passing vehicle License number as a parameter to get a required communication output.

7. Conclusion

In this paper we have outlined the different architectural classification of VANET and our vision for how a near ubiquitous wireless network for vehicular access will be used. The provision of wireless networks to support this wide range of uses is challenging, and requires both experimental characterizations of network deployments in urban environments and careful coverage mapping and planning help us to implement large number of corpus of data into a much simpler form, that can be efficiently stored in a database on the vehicle, and queried in minimal time. The comparison of GPS and VANET and by setting number of experiments based on network architecture will help us to analyze result and also it will help to compare other different technologies with VANET to generating value from it necessitating research into compilers and Overall, we conclude that wireless access for the road network is a challenging area.

8. References

[1] V. Bychkovsky, B. Hull, A. Miu, H. Balakrishnan, S.Madden: A measurement study of vehicular internet accessusing in situ Wi-Fi networks. MOBICOM 2006: 50-61.

[2] R. Gass, J. Scott, and C. Diot. Measurements of In-Motion 802.11 Networking. In Proc. WMCSA, Apr. 2006.

[3] J. Ott and D. Kutscher. Drive-thru internet: IEEE 802.11b for automobile users. In IEEE INFOCOM, 2004.

[4] P. Bucciol, E. Masala, N. Kawaguchi, K. Takeda, J.C. De Martin, "Performance Evaluation of H.264 Video Streaming over Inter-Vehicular 802.11 Ad Hoc Networks", Proc. Of 16th Annual IEEE International Symposium on Personal Indoor and Mobile Radio Communications (PIMRC), Berlin, Germany, Sep. 2005.

[5] J¨org Ott and Dirk Kutscher. Drive-thru Internet: IEEE 802.11b for"automobile" users. In Proceedings of IEEE INFOCOM, March 2004.

[6] Jatinder Pal Singh, Nicholas Bambos, Bhaskar Srinivasan, and Detlef Clawin. Wireless LAN performance under varied stress conditions in vehicu!ar traffic scenarios. In Proc. IEEE VTC, volume 2, Fall 2002.

[7] R. Gass, J. Scott, and C. Diot. Measurements of in-motion 802.11 networking. In Proc. IEEE WMCSA, 2006.

[8] David N. Cottingham, Ian J. Wassell, and Robert K. Harle. Performance of IEEE 802.11a in vehicular contexts. In Proc. IEEE VTC Spring, April 2007. In press.

[9] A. Aijaz, B. Bochow, F. Dtzer, A. Festag, M. Gerlach, R. Kroh andT. Leinmuller, Attacks on Inter-Vehicle Communication Systems – An Analysis. in Proceedings of the 3rd International Workshop on Intelligent Transportation (WIT 2006), March 2006

[10] F. Armknecht, A. Festag, D. Westhoff, and K. Zeng,. Cross-Layer Privacy Enhancement and Non-Repudiation in Vehicular Communication,. 4th Workshop on Mobile Ad-Hoc Networks (WMAN), March 2007

[11] M. Blum and A. Eskandarian. The Threat of Intelligent Collisions,. IT Professional, January 2004

[12] A. Baig, M. Hassan, and L. Libman. Prediction-based recovery from link outages in on-board mobile communication networks. In *Proc.IEEE GLOBECOM*, November-December 2004

[13] L. Butty'an, T. Holczer, and I. Vajda, On the effectiveness of changing pseudonyms to provide location privacy in VANETs,. In Proceedings of the Fourth European Workshop on Security and Privacy in Ad hoc and Sensor Networks (ESAS 2007), Springer LNCS 4572, Cambridge, 2007

[14] D. Chaum .Security without identification to make big brother obsolete,. Communications of the ACM, 1985

[15] O. Berthold, H. Federrath, and M. Köhntopp. Project Anonymity and Unobservability in the Internet. In CFP '00: Proceedings of the tenth conference On Computers, freedom and privacy, pages 57–65. ACM Press, 2000

[16] K. Sampigethaya, L. Huang, M. Li, R. Poovendran, K. Matsuura,and K. Sezaki.

[17] "CARAVAN: Providing Location Privacy for VANET". In Proceedings of the Embedded Securityin Cars (ESCAR) Workshop, 2005.

[18] IEEE-2007VIPER: A vehicle-to-infrastructure communication privacy enforcement protocol Paolo Cencioni Dipartimento di Informatica Università di Roma "Sapienza"Via Salaria, 113 00198 - Roma, Italy cencioni@di.uniroma1.it Roberto Di Pietro Dipartimento di Matematica Università di Roma Tre L.go S. Leonardo Murialdo, 100146 Roma, Italy dipietro@mat.uniroma3.it

[19] Alastair R. Beresford, Jonathan J. Davies, and Robert K. Harle. Privacysensitive congestion charging. In *14th International Workshop onSecurity Protocols (to appear)*, LNCS, March 2006.

[20] Bret Hull, Vladimir Bychkovsky, Yang Zhang, Kevin Chen, Michel Goraczko, Allen K. Miu, Eugene Shih, Hari Balakrishnan, and Samuel Madden. CarTel: a distributed mobile sensor computing system. In *4th ACM SenSys*, November 2006.

[21] GPS beginner's gude.

[22] D. Johnson, C. Perkins, and J. Arkko. Mobility support in IPv6.Technical Report RFC 3775, IETF, June 2004.

[23] G. Liu, B. Lee, B.Seet, C. Foh, K. Wong, and K. Lee. A routing strategy for metropolis vehicular communications. In *Proc. International Conference on Information Networking*, volume 2, pages 533–542,Feb-04

A System for Locating Users of WLAN using Statistical and Dynamic Mapping in Indoor and Outdoor Environment-LOIDS

K. Krishna Naik[1], Dr. M.N. Giri Prasad[2], Sara Tabassum[3] and K Sri Lakshmi[3]
[1]Assitant Professor, Sree Visvesvaraya Institute of Technology & Science
[2]Professor and Head Dept. of ECE, JNTU college of Engg., Pulivendula
[3]Dept. of IT, SVITS
krishnakaramtoti@yahoo.co.in purklekrishk@rediffmail.com muskan.sara@gmail.com lakshmi_kotte06@yahoo.com

Abstract

These days people using wireless networks in their day to day work. The development of wireless Local Area Networks made usage of wireless technology efficiently. The availability of portable, light weight, hand held computing devices and high speed wireless local area network enabled users to remain connected while moving in indoor or outdoor environment. Wireless local area network has a wide range of utilization while moving from one location to another location. When a user is moving from one location to another, how the other user knows about the required station inside the WLAN. For that, we designed and developed a system to locate a mobile user inside the wireless local area network with the help of RSSI. We designed four different architectures and used statistical and dynamic radio mapping of indoor and outdoor locations. These architectures are based on statistical and dynamic configuration of radio maps in indoor and outdoor environment with the help of Sniffer, a specially designed application to locate a station at that time. We found a better location of a mobile user in WLAN with the help of Pamvotis a WLAN simulator. We tested this work in indoor and outdoor environment with different locations practically.
Keywords: WLAN, AP, RSSI, RPM

1. Introduction of LOIDS

These days wireless local area networks has become very popular, when the initial IEEE802.11 is the standard for providing wireless connectivity to automatic machinery, equipment and stations that require rapid deployment, which may be portable, handheld or which may be mounted on moving vehicles within a local area. IEEE802.11 Wireless local area network is a shared-medium communication network that transmits information over wireless links for all IEEE802.11 stations in its transmission range to receive [3][4][5][10]. The main characteristic of the IEEE802.11 W-LAN's is its simplicity, scalability & robustness against failures due to its distributed nature. IEEE802.11 wireless networks can be configured into two different modes: Ad-hoc & infrastructure modes.
In Ad-hoc mode, all wireless stations within the communication range can communicate directly with each other, whereas in infrastructure mode, an Access Point is needed to connect all stations to a distribution system, each station can communicate with other through the AP.

IEEE802.11 provides the data rates upto 2 Mbps at 2.4 GHz ISM band. Later, IEEE802.11 working group published its enhanced version named IEEE802.11b that extends the data rate upto 11Mbps at this ISM band. Its high-speed version at 5 GHz UNII band (IEEE802.11a) was also defined. IEEE802.11a standard can achieve data rate of upto 54Mbps by using OFDM (Orthogonal Frequency Division Multiplexing) modulation technique at physical layer. The fundamental building block of the IEEE 802.11 architecture has the Basic Service Set (BSS). A BSS can be defined as a group of stations that are located in the same geographical area. The area covered by the BSS is also known as basic service area (BSA). Any station can establish a direct communication session with any other station in the BSS, without the requirement of channeling all traffic through a centralized AP.

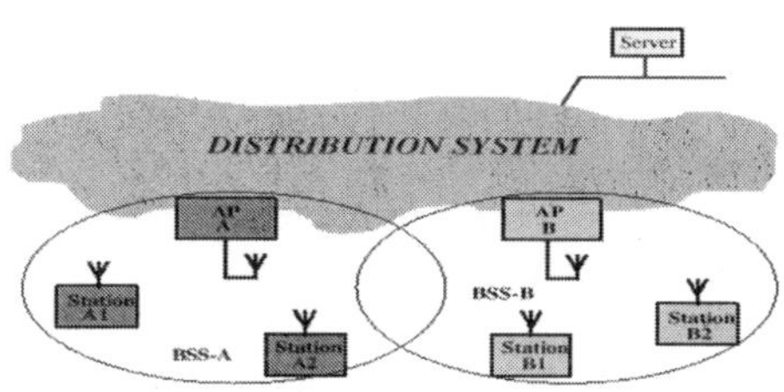

Fig. 1 An Extended Service Set

Infrastructure network is built to provide wireless users with specific services and range extensions. In the context of IEEE 802.11, infrastructure network is established using APs. AP supports geographical range extension by providing the integration points necessary for network connectivity among multiple BSSs to form an Extended Service Set (ESS). The ESS consists of multiple BSSs which are integrated together using a common distributed system as shown in the Figure-1 above. Based on this infrastructure network with location of every station in the network to provide better services must be known to the service provider. That is possible only with the help of creating a map i.e. radio map. This map is based on the geographical area of our institute. We divided this area into few blocks and placed an individual access point which covers the entire area to make the complete network. These access points forms a dynamic mapping whenever the user tries to locate the required station, where it/that is.

Here we mainly focus on the signal propagation which can generally attribute to reflection, diffraction and scattering mechanisms. The changes in furniture placement, surrounding structures and occupancy conditions seriously affect signal propagation condition in normal WLAN environment. Large scale fading and small scale fading are the two methods, which are used to explain RSSI (Received Signal Strength Indication) fluctuations. The large scale fading occurs due to the distance separation between AP (Transmitter) and wireless Sniffer (Receiver), where RSSI decreases as the distance increases. The small scale fading is given by the rapid fluctuations of the RSSI over very short distances or short time durations caused by multipath in the radio environment.

2. WLAN Location Architecture

In the existing WLAN infrastructure without using any additional hardware we can increase efficiency of the network by using suitable network location architecture. With that aspect we are developing a system architecture which estimates the accurate location of the user. Here we are proposing four types of location architectures. One is Source- Destination, another one is Client-Server, third one is Sniffer based and final one is Access Point (AP) based architectures[6][8].

Source-Destination Architecture: Source station in one area can search for any other required (destination) station in same or different network. Here a source station sends request to the nearby station that may be the destination or may be connected with the destination. The concerned station which is helping to find the location of the destination records the received signal strength indication from the destination. Based on that RSSI we can identify the location of the destination with help of radio map. The architecture of this is shown in the Figure 2.A.

Client-Server Architecture: This architecture has two phases of location estimation, the first one is offline phase and second one is real-time phase. In offline phase infrastructure mode of WLAN access point (AP) provides services to all clients in that area as an ESS. The ESS may have many APs, Client in one AP can receive signal from other or many other APs. But only one AP has to serve the client. That selection of the AP by client is based on the RSSI from other APs. In real-time phase service provided to the clients based on the request made by the respective client with the help of the location based services i.e. as client needed for service made available with that AP. The architecture of this is shown in the Figure 2.B.

Sniffer Based Architecture: It has great advantages over all other architectures because it is application based architecture. In this architecture all stations are preinstalled specially designed application which can identify the location of the system. The application software that monitors all the stations will captures all the traffic in the network. This application software is considered as a Sniffer in the network. For reading the RSSI information from WLAN we will try to connect over the network by using a WNIC (here we are using DWL and NetGare). The WNICs work like passive entities, try to send packets in the wireless medium and capable of capturing all frames transmitted in the same channel. Basically to detect and monitor the wireless medium, Sniffer has to execute two functions continuously. Firstly detecting the wireless clients and recording the available RSSI values of it and second one is measuring RSSI from one or more reference devices in order to construct the location model in the map. The architecture of this is shown in the Figure 2.C.

Access point Based Architecture: As we all are aware of WLAN that, it has two modes of operation one is Ad-Hoc mode and another is Infrastructure mode, these two modes will be used to form BSS and ESS. Here we are considering ESS to construct a specialized architecture for WLAN location determination system. In ESS basically we use an access point to connect available stations in the coverage area. Suppose any client wants to connect any remote station a client need to contact parent AP to find the location of destination station. The destination station may be available with any other AP or the same AP. In this connection to remember all the stations in the network we are placing a RADIUS server with every AP. RADIUS is a server which will keep information about all stations available with that AP if any AP sends a request asking information about any station, then that AP [1] RADIUS server sends reply to the originated AP with the available information. The architecture of this is shown in the Figure 2.D.

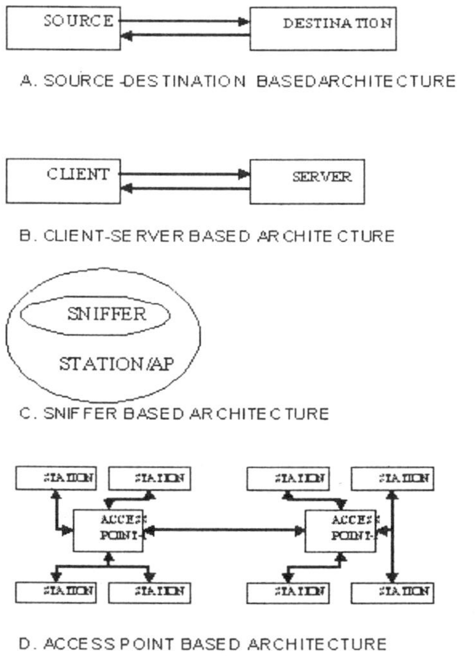

Fig. 2 Architectures for location determination

3. LOIDS- Location of Indoor and Outdoor Determination System

Our aim is to discuss and differentiate the Indoor and outdoor locations of WLAN enabled stations and providing the best services to every station in the network. This system (LOIDS) helps to find the required station in the network. A lot of efforts in preparing LOIDS include building of Radio map. There are two methods to consider one is empirical and mathematical methods. In empirical method the radio map created by involving a mobile user in different places and recording physical coordinate at each position for different APs with in the range. In mathematical method the radio map is generated by using the RSSI of RF propagation.

While describing the LOIDS in the indoor and outdoor environment let us assume the physical dimensional space L where a device is situated, a AP with Sniffer loaded at l , RSSI measured by K Sniffer given a tx device located at l for each position lεL. Here we assume L discrete and also define a signal space S with K dimensions where element of this space is a vector of dimension K in which its positions represent RSSI readings from the K different Sniffers[6][7][9]. Samples from the signal space S are denoted by s, the given RSSI vector s=(s1,s2,...sk) we are determining the position of the station by lεL., this maximizes the probability p(l/s) of a tx device to be located at l with a captured RSSI vector measured by K Sniffers. The required information is then molded into the database where the location server creates the radio propagation map (RPM), where the grid position l=(x,y) is associated to probability distribution p(s/l). The location server builds a RPM for each Sniffer I, i.e. for K Sniffers a total of K RPM s will be formed at the server. To measure the signal strength Si from a tx situated at l is given by p(s/l) according to Gaussian distribution:

$$P(s/l) = \frac{1}{\sigma(l)\sqrt{2\Pi}} \exp\left(\frac{s-\mu(l)^2}{2\sigma^2(l)}\right) \quad .....(1)$$

Here $\mu(l)$ is RSSI expected values of all stations in the network at a Sniffer loaded station and $\sigma(l)$ is the distribution standard deviation (SD). $\mu(l)$ Can be estimated by large scale propagation model,

$$\mu_{(l)}(d) = \mu_0(d_0) - 10_{n0}\log(\frac{d}{d_0}) - \alpha \quad .....(2)$$

In this equation α is attenuation caused by interferences and d distance between transmitter, receiver and Sniffer placed station. To calculate the distance d between transmitter, receiver and Sniffer placed station is

$$d = \sqrt{(|x_{SNIFFER} - x|)^2 + (|y_{SNIFFER} - y|)^2}$$

in above equation x and y are coordinates at location l. RPM can be constructed when the significant changes in RSSI occur. RSSI measurements are used between the pairs Sniffers and APs to sense whether the WLAN propagation environment has changed and when to rebuilt RPM. If RSSI follows Gaussian distribution where mean and standard deviation between the pair of Sniffers and APs the RPM can be estimated by real-time measurements between the pair of Sniffers and APs. After measuring many times the above said measurements for M consecutive RSSIs may fall outside the interval(mean and standard deviation), with that a new RPM should be formed. Another method to reconstruct the RPM is for every T seconds. If found any changes in mean and standard deviation that may not affect the RPM because, it is a pre-defined map. Here any number of users may enter into the scenario and may leave the scenario. The calculated RSSI with Sniffer s and APs may not show much difference. In radio environment no user would stay at a specific point or location, for that the dynamic formation of the RPM is more comfortable than statistical formation of RPM.

As we discussed above the statistical and dynamic location of RPM the RSSI vector s= (s1, s2, sk) we found a position lєL which maximizes the probability p (l/s). As per Bayees theorem to find position of a user in the location l is by using this formula

$$P(l/s)=\frac{P(s/l)P(l)}{P(s)}=\frac{P(s/l)P(l)}{\sum_{l'\in L}P(s/l)P(l')} \qquad \text{....(3)}$$

This is for $l\varepsilon L$ ie all possible positions in the RPM grid the sum goes through. P(s/l) indicates the probability to receive s from tx position at l P(l) is the probability a priority of finding a tx in the position l. Let a wireless transmitter situated at l and k Sniffer will calculate a vector s= (s1, s2 ...sk) and for each Sniffer P(l/s) is determined.

4. Experimental Evaluation

As we discussed in the above sections, we prepared a setup of all four types of WLAN location determination architectures (A, B, C & D architectures) in our laboratory. We used DWL and NetGear network interface card which supports IEEE802.11a/b/g standards. In the institute premises we prepared a radio map in area of 1KM range. Two modes of WLAN Ad-Hoc and Infrastructures are prepared by using DWL and NetGear NICs and APs. In this section we are discussing and showing the differences between Indoor and outdoor locations and determining the location of the user with different positions with the help of Statistical and Dynamic radio mapping. We designed radio maps manually and automatically. In manual configuration of radio maps we placed respective access points in required positions where the user of WLAN moves as we predicated. In automatic configuration of radio maps whenever the user moves in some direction, the access point available in that direction only gives the services. We formed the radio maps in indoor and outdoor locations.

Here we discussed indoor and outdoor location determination of a user in the wireless local area network, with IEEE802.11a/b/g by using DWL and NetGear NICs. The differences between a/b/g are tabulated in the table below in the table-1. A dynamic mapping of RPM is somewhat difficult than statistical mapping. In dynamic mapping Sniffer has to search and scan the channel all the time in the form of "Refresh Always" method, without which it is not possible to see who is entering the network and who is leaving the network.

Table 1 Differences between IEEE802.11a/b and IEEE802.11g

Properties	802.11a/b	802.11g
Frequency	2.4Ghz / 5Ghz	2.4 GHz
Modulation	Direct sequence spread spectrum (CCK, DQPSK, DBPSK)	Orthogonal frequency division multiplexing (64QAM, 16QAM, QPSK, BPSK)
Data rate	1,2,5.5,11Mbps	1,2,5.5,6,9, 11,12,18,18, 24,36, 48,54Mbps
Os platform	Windows Vista	Windows XP

Here Figure-3 is a Sniffer application which shows how many users are coming into the network and working in the network by Green indication as shown below, and whoever leaving the network by a Red Cross mark indication. The traffic can also be monitored by a statistics graph.

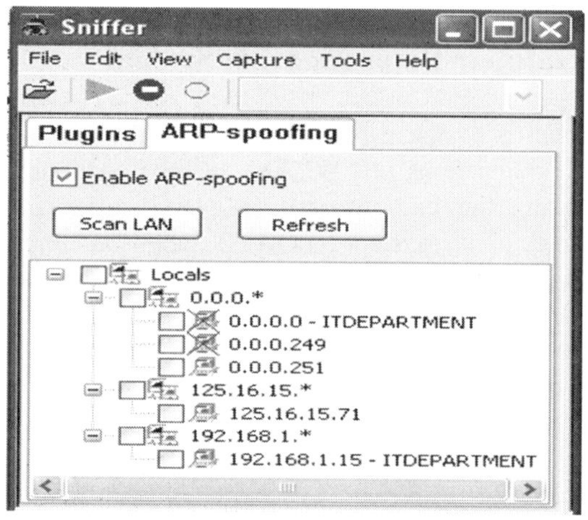

Fig. 3 Sniffer indications

After taking many iterations practically in Indoor and Outdoor locations by using IEEE802.11 a/b/g by connecting DWL and NetGear NICs at client side and server side, readings were recorded in the form of signal strength (RSSI). In indoor we found the location of the user somewhat slow when compared to the outdoor location and it is shown with the graphical notation below. One thing we can say and understood that, we cannot carry and move AP dynamically from one place to another. For that reason we are proposing a statistical radio map location by equal division area spaces as shown below. We considered all four architectures and verified by taking RSSI indications at client and server sides in both indoor and outdoor environment. Figure-5 and Figure-6 show that the performances of indoor and outdoor environment and performance of Ad-hoc and infrastructure modes differences respectively in different positions i.e.50mts, 75mts,100mts, 125mts, 150mts and so on with RSSI indications Excellent, Very good, Good and Poor .

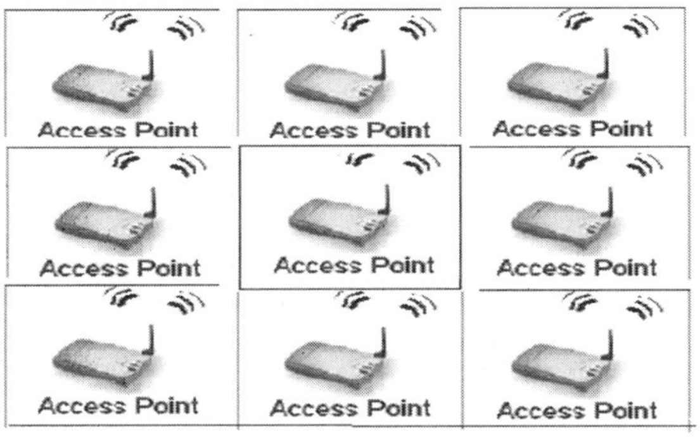

Fig. 4 A statistical radio map location by equal division area spaces

As figure-4 shown above that all the access points are place at suitable places as statistical radio maps in the required location to form the network may be in indoor or outdoor environment. Here all access points plays equal role and placement. We clearly found the location of a user in indoor and outdoor environment with Ad-hoc and Infrastructure modes of operation. An infrastructure mode shows better results than Ad-hoc mode in both environment, because in ad-hoc, mode of operation we won't use any access point. All stations plays equal role in ad-hoc mode of operation. We calculated the location of a user in indoor and outdoor environment theoretically and practically. By using Sniffer and Pamvotis applications we calculated location of a user practically. Theoretical calculations we used Bayees theorem and found the location of a user as discussed in section III. Figure-7 shows the difference between statistical and dynamic radio mapping performances. Figure shows that the statistical map shows better results then dynamic map. We conducted location finding operation in the campus lab and outside the campus to find the location of a user in indoor and outdoor environment. The performances showed in the graphical representations below.

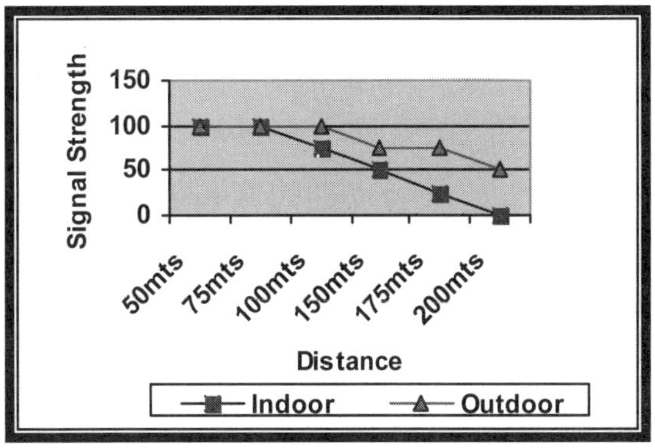

Fig. 5 Performance at Indoor and Outdoor environment

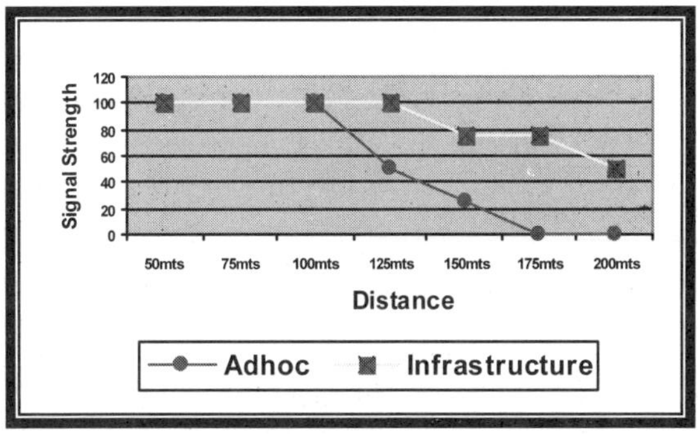

Fig. 6 Performance of Ad-hoc and Infrastructure modes

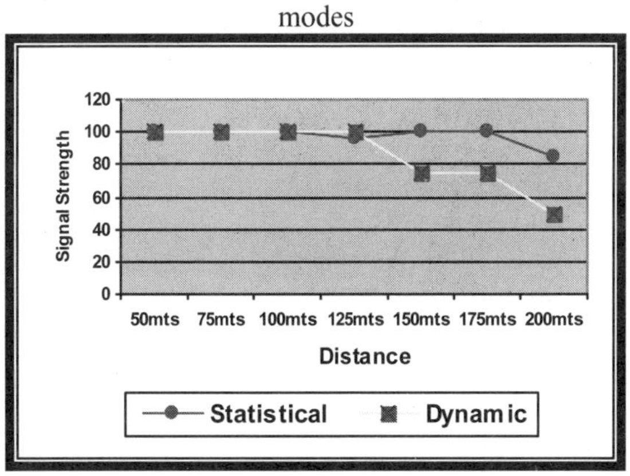

Fig. 7 Performance of Statistical and Dynamic radio mappings

5. Related and Future Work

In this work we basically concentrated to determine location of a user in the environment of indoor and outdoor environment with statistical and dynamic location mapping as it is shown in the figure-4. But we found some difficulty in finding location of a user in dynamic method because of how to locate a position to an access point in the network. At the same time we are also focused to form a radio map with equally divided area in indoor and outdoor environment as a statistical mapping. Finding an accurate position of a user, we used this statistical method by using Bayees theorem and tried to find the correct position of the user in both the indoor and outdoor environment. In future we try to design a system, based on only signal strength based location determination. We are tried to test our work by using different NIC's and with multiple locations/positions. We are also working on continuation of this work with cluster based calibration-free dynamic mapping of signal strength of a user in indoor and outdoor environment

6. Conclusions

In this paper we discussed the system LOIDS which will helps to locate and finds a user in Indoor and Outdoor environment with the help of statistical and dynamic location mapping. Here we developed four architectures and enabled WLAN strategies in those architectures in testbed. In that testbed we tested all four architectures with different places in indoor and outdoor environment. In source destination architecture, it is somewhat difficult to continue the communication path while searching the location of a user, because of if any node in the sequence or Ad-hoc network is not having next node or station, this system may not work properly. In client server based, Sniffer based and Access point based architectures we found the considerable results shown in the graphical representations in indoor and outdoor environment with Ad-hoc and Infrastructure modes of operation.

7. References

[1] Dr. M.N. Giri Prasad and K.Krishna Naik "IAPP for IEEE802.11 WLAN Range Improvements", I-Managers Journal on Software Engineering,Vol. 1 No. 4 April-June 2007.

[2] K.Krishna Naik and B.M.G.Prasad "QoS in IEEE802.11 Wireless Local Area Networks with Enhanced MAC"- I-Manager's Journal on Engineering & Technology,vol.1 No.3, February 2006.

[3] K.Krishna Naik "Antenna Design Analysis, Construction and Testing for IEEE802.11 WLAN Range Improvements"-M.Tech Thesis at IIIT-Allahabad-2004.

[4] Neeli Prasad and Anand Prasad "WLAN System and Wireless IP for next generation communication"

[5] IEEE 802.11b Wireless LAN Medium Access Control (MAC) and Physical Layer (PHY) Specifications, http://standards.ieee.org/getieee802/802.11.html

[6] Luis Felipe M.de Moraes and Bruno Astuto A. Nunes "Calibaration free WLAN location system based on dynamic mapping of signal strength" Mobiwac'06 october 2006.

[7] Paramvir Bhal and Venkata N Padmanabhan" A software system for Locating Mobile Users: Design, Evaluation and Lessons".

[8] P. Bahl, V.N. Padmanabhan, "RADAR: An In-Building RFbased User Location and Tracking System," *Proceedings of IEEE Infocom 2000, Tel Aviv, Israel,* March 2000.

[9] P. Krishnan, A.S. Krishnakumar, Wen-Hua Ju, C. Mallows, S.Ganu, "A System for LEASE: System for Location Estimation Assisted by Stationary Emitters for Indoor RF Wireless Networks", *Proceedings of IEEE Infocom 2004, Hong Kong,March 2004.*

[10] Moustafa Youssef, Ashok Agrawala, A. Udaya Shankar, "WLAN Location Determination via Clustering and Probability Distributions," *IEEE Intnl. Conf. on Pervasive Comp. andComm. (PerCom) 2003*, March 23-26, 2003.

[11] W. Stallings. *Wireless Communications and Networks*. Prentice Hall, first edition, 2002

An Efficient Fault-Tolerant Irregular Extra Group Network

Harsh Sadawarti[1] **and** P.K. Bansal[2]
[1] Prof. cum Vice Principal, Deptt. of Computer Science & Engg.,
RIMT-Institute of Engineering & Technology, Mandi Gobindgarh, Punjab, India,
harshsada@yahoo.com
[2]Principal, MIMIT, Malout, Punjab, India
pkbmimit@yahoo.com

Abstract

The Performance of a system depends directly on the time required to perform an operation and number of these operations that can be performed concurrently. High performance computing systems can be designed using parallel processing. The effectiveness of these parallel systems rests primarily on the communication network linking processors and memory modules. Hence, an interconnection network that provides the desired connectivity and performance at minimum cost is required for communication in parallel processing systems. Multistage interconnection networks provide a compromise between shared bus and crossbar networks. A new Fault-tolerant irregular interconnection network named IEGN (IRREGULAR EXTRA GROUP NETWORK) has been proposed. As the network is irregular, 50% of the requests are routed through minimum path length of 2 in comparison to the regular networks. Thus, the irregular network IEGN helps in reducing the latency or delay. In this proposed IEGN network, the network achieves significant tolerance to faults, relatively low cost and simple control scheme. IEGN is 2 fault-tolerant and robust in the presence of more than 2 faults. Routing tag has been evaluated and Routing procedure has also been discussed.

1. Introduction

A fault-tolerant IEGN of size N x N is designed by dividing N sources and N destinations into 2 disjoint partitions of N/2 sources and N/2 destinations. There are 2 independent subnetworks, and an extra one, such that a connection path between each source-destination pair can be established via any one of the subnetwork. All the 3 subnetworks are of identical type and consists of a IEGN network of size N/2 x N/2. The extra subnetwork helps to enhance fault-tolerant capability and to keep a desired level of performance even in the presence of faults. There are no particular sources and destinations associated with it, but it is for added redundancy. Each source and each destination are compared to all the 3 subnetworks via 2 x 1 multiplexers and 1 x 2 demultiplexers.

Thus an IEGN consists of (2n-2) number of stages and 3 (2^{n+1} -4) number of switches, where n = $\log_2 N/2$. further, it consists of N x 3/2 number of 2 x 1 multiplexers and an equal number of 1 x 2 demultiplexers.Each IEGN network of size N/2 x N/2 plus its associated multiplexers and demultiplexers constitute a module. These modules are denoted by M_0, M_1 .... M_k . Any module can be assumed to be extra one, but for the sake of convenience M_k is trated as extra one.

Let Si,j and D i,j denote the source i and destination j respectively, which are associated with module Mi based on the partition $0 \leq i \leq 2$ and $0 \leq j \leq (N/2 - 1)$. Also, let MUX1 , m and DEMUX1 , m represent the MUX m and DEMUX m in M1 module respectively, where $0 \leq 1 \leq 2$ and $0 \leq m \leq (N/2 -1)$.

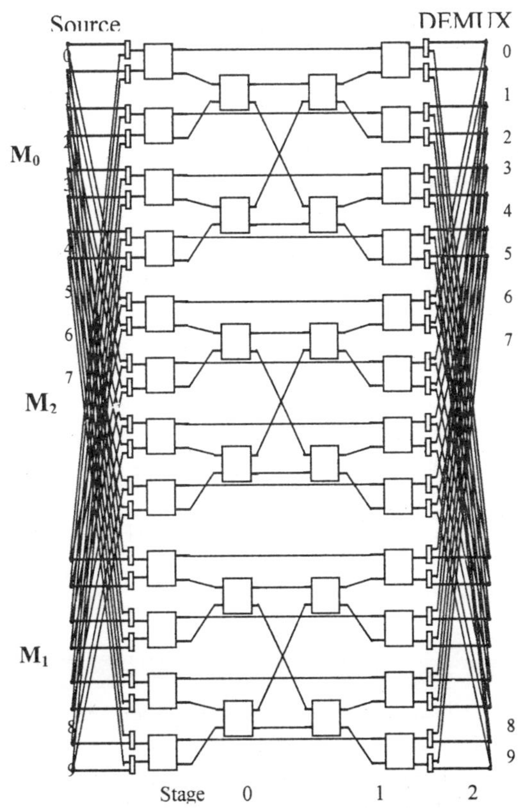

Fig. 1.1(A) Irregular Extra Group Network (IEGN)

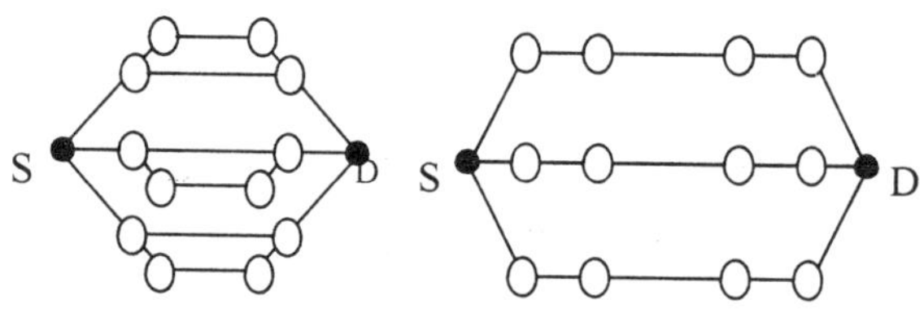

(i) (ii)

REDUNDANCY GRAPHS FOR S – D TERMINAL PAIR CONTAINING

1. ALL THE PATH LENGTH
2. THE LONGEST PATH LENGTH

Fig. 1.1(b)

The sources and destinations are connected as follows:

1. Each $S_{i,j}$ is connected to every ith input port of the 3 multiplexers from MUX $_{0,j}$ to MUX $_{2,j}$.
2. Every ith output port of the 3 demultiplexers from DEMUX $_{0,j}$ to $DEMUX_{2,j}$ is connected to each $D_{i,j}$.

   A network resulting from this construction is called IEGN. Example of IEGN network of size 16 x 16 along with its redundancy graph is illustrated in figure 1.1.

2. Routing Scheme of IEGN Network

In the following section, the routing scheme of IEGN is described.

2.1 Path Length Algorithm

For a given source-destination pair, there are multiple paths of varying path lengths in an IEGN. The number of possible paths between a source-destination pair varies from 3 to 3.(n-1), depending upon the addresses of the source and destination terminals. Path length algorithm gives the information about the various possible paths between a source-destination pair.

Let the source S and destination D be represented in binary code as :

$S = S_{i,j} = s_n , (s_{n-1} \ldots\ldots\ldots\ldots s_0)$

$D = D_{i,j} = d_n , (d_{n-1} \ldots\ldots\ldots\ldots d_0)$

In any module the path length algorithm is :

if

$[(s_{n-1} + d_{n-1}) + (s_{n-2} + d_{n-2}) + \ldots\ldots + (s_1 + d_1)]$ is zero

(+ Represents an exclusive - OR operation and + represents a logical OR operation)

then minimum path length is 2 and all paths of various lengths are possible i.e. 2,4,..........., 2n-2.

else

if

$[(s_{n-1} + d_{n-1}) + (s_{n-2} + d_{n-2}) + \ldots\ldots + (s_2 + d_2)]$ is zero

then

all paths of length equal to or greater than 4 are possible.

else

.

.

.

if

$[(s_{n-1} + d_{n-1}) + (s_{n-2} + d_{n-2}) + \ldots\ldots + (s_j + d_j)]$ is zero

(where $1 \le j \le n-1$)

then

all paths of length equal to or greater than 2j are possible.

else

path of length 2n-2 (i.e. longest path) is possible only.

2.2 Routing Tag Algorithm

Routing tag algorithm gives the information about the distributed routing control required to establish a path between any source-destination terminal pair for a given path length.

The required algorithm is given as :

if

$2 \le x < 2n-2$

(where x is the path length)

then

Routing tag = $(1.1\ldots1)_{([x/2]-1)}.0.(d_{([x/2]-1)} \ldots . d_0). d_n$

else

if

$x = 2n-2$

then

routing tag = $(1.1\ldots1)_{(n-2)}.(d_{n-1}\ldots.d_0).d_n$

Example

The functioning of routing tag algorithm is illustrated with examples for an IEGN of size 16 X 16.

Case 1 : Let the data be routed from source 0 to destination 1.

The source S and destination D are represented as :

S = 0, 000 D = 0, 001

Then $n = \log_2 N/3 = 3$

Therefore, in this case paths of lengths 2 and 4 are possible i.e x = 2 and 4.

So for x = 2 routing tag = 0.1.0 and

for x = 4 routing tag = 1.0.0.1.0

Case 2 : Let the data be routed from source 0 to destination 15.

The source S and destination D are represented as :

S = 0, 000 D = 1, 111

Therefore in this case longest path of path length 4 is only possible

i.e. x = 4.

for x = 4 the routing tag = 1.1.1.1.1

As can be seen from the Fig. 1.1, these tags give the desired destinations.

2.3 Routing Procedure

One way of selecting a module for routing in IEGN, is to use a "preferred module" for a path between a source-destination pair, which is the path always chosen first by the source. For example in figure 1.1, if a source needs to communicate with a destination $D_{i,j}$, the preferred module can be M_i i.e the source will sent a request to the corresponding MUX in M_i. If the preferred module is faulty (it is assumed that some techniques of fault diagnosis are available to detect and locate faults in the network), the source then may try a path in a module other that M_i. If that module is faulty too, the request will be submitted to an alternative module until all the 3 modules are faulty. In this way one can maintain a "desirable" performance level.

Another possible way is the "universal random" selection of a module out of the 3 available modules, selecting a module randomly with equal probability. As one of the module becomes faulty, the number of modules a source can utilize decreases. In this way, one can achieve a graceful degradation of the performance in case of faults.

Assuming that the selection of a module out of the 3 modules is already done at source, first find the minimum path length possible between a source-destination pair and then the corresponding routing tag. No tag bit is consumed at the multiplexer stage, because a multiplexer has only one output. After the multiplexer, the router in the intermediate stages of a module depends upon routing tag. With the help of routing tag and the routing procedure described above , a path is established to the proper destination.

3. Fault Tolerance of IEGN Network

Fault–tolerance of IEGN network can be analysed by defining a critical set of components. A critical set of SEs in an IEGN is defined as the set of 3 SEs, each from different modules and having the same position, such that a failure will occur if all the 3 SEs become faulty simultaneously.

The following theorem characterizes certain minimum faults that are always tolerated in an IEGN.

Theorem 1 : The fault – tolerance of IEGN is 2

Proof : In the redundancy graph of IEGN , there are 3 paths available between each source-destination pair. If the faults are such that they affect 2 or fewer modules, there exists at least one fault free module. Thus the fault-tolerance is 2.

Theorem 2 **:** IEGN has full access.

Proof : Since an IEGN provides at least 3 disjoint paths for each source-destination pair, through the 3 identical modules, and if there are 2 or fewer faulty modules, then at least one of the module is still fault free. Since every module of IEGN has full access, so IEGN has full access.

However, 3 faults can cause a failure in an IEGN. For instance, if 3 faulty components are distributed in 3 modules and the position of each faulty component in all modules is the same, then some sources and destinations become disconnected from the rest of the network. Some instances of even more than 2 faults can be tolerated ; for example , if the faulty switches are confined to 2 or less modules, then the system will still work properly.

A network is robust in the presence of 2 faults, if it can tolerate some instances of 2 faults. An IEGN is robust in the presence of more than 2 faults. The maximum number of faults it can tolerate comes from the case that only one of the module is fault free.

4. Permutation Capability of IEGN Network

Permutation is an important criterion of any MIN. For an IEGN, the goal is to maintain permutation capability in the presence of any single fault. This goal is achieved by the extra module provided in an IEGN. It is clear that the extra one can be used to replace the faulty module without increasing conflicts. So an IEGN can maintain the permutation capability as long as there are 2 fault free modules.

5. Reliability And Repairability of IEGN Network

Since an IEGN is 2 fault-tolerant so it is quite reliable as compared to other networks containing nearly same amount of hardware. The added reliability comes at the cost of the general performance of the network, because basically a stage of switches is replaced by multiplexers and demultiplexers, which are less complex. Due to the presence of 2 modules, each module connects every source to every destination, so even a single module will have the full access capability. If some faults develops in any module, then the faulty module can be simply replaced by the new one without causing a breakdown in the system. Thus, the system is on-line repairable.

6. Communication Delay In IEGN Network.

Even though parallel processing has increased computational speed, still there is scope of increasing it further by reducing the communication delay in an IN. In a module of IEGN, each source is connected to two "favourite" destinations with the minimum path length i.e. 2. Thus, the total number of output favourite memory modules/processors to which a input processor can communicate with the shortest possible path length is 4 in an IEGN. The reduced path length results in shorter communication delay and hence increased speed.

7. Conclusion

In this chapter, a new class of statically reroutable irregular fault-tolerant multistage interconnection network named IEGN network has been proposed and analyzed. The network achieves significant tolerance to faults and good performance with relatively low cost and simple control scheme. IEGN is 2 fault –tolerant and robust in the presence of more than 2 faults. Moreover, due to the presence of extra subnetwork, IEGN can maintain permutation capability when any single fault occurs. Algorithm for path length and routing have been developed. In short, IEGN network offers the following advantages :

- 2 switch fault tolerant.
- On-line repairability of faulty components.
- Significantly improved reliability and performance.
- Multiple paths of varying lengths are available between each source-destination pair.
- For a connection to a favourite memory module, the path length is only 2 irrespective of the size of the network.
- Cost-effective.

8. References

[1] Adams G.B., Aggarwal D.P. and Siegel H.I, " A Survey and Comparison of Fault-tolerant Interconnection Networks", DEEE Computers, Vol. 20, June 1987, pp. 14-27,

[2] Adams EH G.B. and Siegel H.J., " The Extra Stage Cube: A Fault Tolerant Interconnection Network for Supersystems", IEEE Transactions on Computer, 1982, pp. 443-454.

[3] Anderson G.A., Jensen E.D,, "Computer Interconnection Networks: Taxonomy, Characteristics and Examples", ACM Computing Surveys, Vol. 7, Dec. 1975, pp. 197-213

[4] Balaguruswamy. E., "Reliability Engineering", TataMc-Graw Hill, 1989.

[5] Bansal P.K., Singh K. and Joshi R.C., "Fault-Tolerant Double Tree Network", Proc. of International Conference IEEE INFOCOM 91, April, pp. 462-468

[6] Bansal P.K., Singh K. and Joshi R.C., "Routing and Path Length for a Cost-Effective Four tree Multistage Interconnection Network", International Journal of Electronics and Electrical Engineering, Vol 73, No.l, 1992, pp. 107-115.

[7] Bansal Savina and Bansal P.K., "Performance and Reliability Analysis for a Multistage Interconnection Network", presented in NSC-93 atlIT Kanpur, Dec. 1993.

[8] Bansal P.K., Singh K. and Joshi R.C., "On a Fault-Tolerant Multistage Interconnection Network", International Journal of Electronics and Electrical Engineering, Vol 20, N0.4, 1994, pp. 335-345.

[9] Booting C, Rai S. and Agarwal D.P., "Reliability • Computation' of "Multistage Interconnection Networks", IEEE Transactions on Reliability, Vol. 38, No. 1,1994, pp. 13-8-145.

[10] Duato J., Yalmanchili S. and Ni L.M., "Interconnection Networks: An 'Engineering Approach", IEEE Computer Society, 1997.

[11] Feng T.Y., "Survey of Interconnection Networks", IEEE Computers, Vol. 4, Dec. 1981, pp. 12-27.

[12] Howard J. Siegel, Wayne G. Nation, Cylde P. Kruskal and Leonard M. Napolitano, "Using the Multistage Cube Network Topology in Parallel Supercomputers", Proceedings of IEEE, Vol. 77, No, 12, Dec. 1979, pp. 1932-1953.

[13] Hwang Kai, "Advanced Parallel Processing with Super Computers", Proc. DEEE OC-75,Oct 1987, pp. 127-137.[14] Hwang Kai, and Faye A. Briggs, "Computer Architecture and Parallel Processing", Mc-GrawHill, 1998.

[14] Hwang Kai, and Faye A. Briggs, "Computer Architecture and Parallel Processing", Mc-GrawHill, 1998.

[15] Kumar V.P. and Reddy S.M., "Augmented Shuffle Exchange Multistage Interconnection Network", IEEE Computer, June 1987, pp.30-40,

[16] Lawrie D.H., "Access and Alignment of Data in an Array Processor", IEEE Transactions on Computers, VoL C-24, Dec. 1975, pp. 1145-1155.

[17] Levitt N., Green M.W. and Goldberg J., "A Study Communication Problem in the Self-Repairable Multiprocessor", Proc. AFIPS Conference, VoL 32, 1968,

[18] Liu M.T., "Distributed Loop Computer Networks"; Advances in Computers, VoL 17, 1978, pp. 163-221.

[19] Mudge T.N., Hayes J.P. and Winsor D.C, "Multiple Bus Architecture", IEEE Computers, June 1987, pp. 42-48.

[20] Patel J.H., "Performance of Prpcessor-Memory Interconnections for Multiprocessors", IEEE Transactions on Computers, Vol. 30,1981, pp. 771-780.

[21] Raghavandera C.S. and Verma A.. "INDRA: A Class of Interconnection Networks with Redundant Paths", Proc. Real-Time Systems Symposium. Dec. 1984, pp. 153-164.

[22] Sengupta Jyotsna, "On Fault-Tolerant Multistage Interconnection Networks", Ph.D, thesis. Thapar Institute of Engg. and Technology. Patiala, June 2001.

[23] Siegel H.J.and Mcmillan R.L. "Using the Augmented Data Manipulator Network in PASM", IEEE Computer, Vol. 4, No. 2, Feb. 1981.

[24] Siegel H.J., "Interconnection Network for Large Scale Parallel Processing: Theory and Case Studies", Mc-Graw Hill, 1990.

[25] Stone H.S., "Parallel Processing with Perfect Shuffle", EEE Transactions on Computers, VoL C-20,Feb. 1971, pp. 153-161.

[26] Wei S. and Lee. G. "Extra Group Network: A Cost Effective Fault-Tolerant Multistage Interconnection Network", Proceedings of 15th Annual Symposium on Computer Architecture, May 1988, pp. 108-115.

[27] Tzeng N, Yew P. and Zhu C., "A Fault-Tolerant Scheme for Multistage Interconnection Networks'V 12th International Symposium on Computer Architecture, 1985, pp. 368-375.

[28] Varma A. and Raghavandera C.S., "Fault-Tolerant Routing in Multistage Interconnection Networks", IEEE Transactions on Computers, Vol. 38, No. 3, March 1989, pp. 385-393.

[29] Wittie L.D., "Communication Structures for Large Networks of Microcomputers",

[30] IEEE Transactions on Computers, Vol. 30, April 1981, pp. 264-273

[31] Wu C. and Feng T., "On a class of Multistage Interconnection Networks" , IEEE Transactions on Computers, 1980 , pp. 696 - 702

Fault Tolerant Local Delaunay Triangulation for Ad Hoc Sensor Network

Mr. Annaji M. Kuthe, Mr. Amit R. Ukalkar, Mr, Animesh Tayal, Mrs. Madhuri A. Tayal
G. H. R. C. E. Nagpur
a_kuthe@rediffmail.com *ukalkar_amit@yahoo.co.in* *animesh_tayal@rediffmail.com*
madhuri_kalpe@rediffmail.com

Abstract

In Ad Hoc sensor network local delaunay triangulation spanner use for efficient communication in ad hoc routing. The network contains frequent node failure due to the low battery power so the local delaunay performance is degraded in resource constrained sensor networks. And geometric properties of the spanner local delaunay are last when a node failure occurs in a network. If fail node exist in the routing path then it leads to heavy packet loss. So to overcome such a problem we propose new fault tolerant local delaunay triangulation (FTLDT) which perform well at even low battery condition The FTLDelconstructs the network graph with only a subset of given wireless nodes. To evaluate the performance of FTLDel, we have done the simulation using network simulator (ns-2.28). The simulation results show that FTLDel gives better performance than LDel.

1. Introduction

The wireless nodes in ad hoc network produce a unit disk graph (UDG)[13], if all the nodes have same transmission range of one unit. Thecommunication cost over UDG is costly, as it contains the edges as large as $O(n^2)$, where n is the number of nodes in the network. To reduce the communication cost in UDG, researchers have derived several proximity subgraphs containing $O(n)$ edges. A proximity subgraph G' is called a spanner if it is a spanning subgraph of the given graph G and the length of the shortest path between any two nodes in G' is at most t times the length of the shortest path between the same nodes in graph G. Here t is called length stretch factor. Various geometric spanners were proposed for ad hoc networks. They include relative neighborhood graph (RNG) [3], Gabriel graph (GG) [3], Yao graph (Yao) [16], [18], Delaunay triangulation (Del) [17], and local Delaunay triangulation (LDel) [15], [14].

The movement of wireless nodes causes the network topology to change constantly, which makes the topology control and efficient routing in nonstatic wireless ad hoc networks difficult and challenging. Thus, we will assume that the nodes are static or can be viewed as static during a reasonable period of time. For example, the sensors in the sensor network do not move usually. We study the topology control for a static wireless network. Notice that our algorithms do not need to update the network topology when nodes are moving, as long as no link used in the final network topology is broken. In other words, although the actual physical deployment of the network topology is no longer a planar graph when nodes are moving, the logical network topology is still a planar graph, which is crucial for some routing algorithm.

WE consider a wireless ad hoc network (or sensor network) with all nodes distributed in a two-dimensional plane. Assume that all wireless nodes have distinctive identities and each static wireless node knows its position information, either through a low-power Global Position System (GPS) receiver or through some other way. For simplicity, we also assume that all wireless nodes have the same maximum transmission range and we normalize it to one unit. By one-hop broadcasting, each node u can gather the location information of all nodes within the transmission range of u. Consequently, all wireless nodes V together, define a unit-disk graph UDG(V), which has an edge uv if and only if the Euclidean distance $\|uv\|$ between u and v is less than one unit. A broadcast by a node u means u sends the message to all nodes within its transmission range. In wireless ad hoc networks, the radio signal sent out by a node u can be received by all nodes within the transmission range of u. The main communication cost in wireless networks is to send out the signal while the receiving cost of a message is neglected here. Consequently, throughout this paper, we are interested in designing a protocol with a small total number of messages sent out by all wireless nodes.

Among the existing spanners, LDel provides better communication in ad hoc routing because of its useful geometric properties. But these properties may not last for a longer time if there are node failures in the network, which are frequent in the case of sensor network, especially due to the low battery power. The node failures in the spanner cause the problems of network connectivity, network partitions, and change of spanning ratio. In addition to the violation of geometric properties of the spanner, the heavy packet loss also occur if the failed node exists in the routing path. These problems were not considered in the existing spanners, instead the researchers concentrated on the geometric properties.

In order to solve these problems, we propose a new spanner called fault tolerant local Delaunay triangulation (FTLDel), in this paper. The existence of a wireless node in the spanner FTLDel depends on the node's power level. The spanner FTLDel sustain the node failure conditions in the network without loosing their geometric properties. The heavy packet loss occurred in LDel is also recovered in FTLDel. In Section III contribution, FTLDel, is described. The simulation work and results are presented in the Section IV. The Section V presents conclusion of this paper with some new research directions.

2. Related Work

Assuming that all wireless nodes have the same and fixed transmission range of one unit, then we define a unit disk graph (UDG) [13] as a graph such that there exists an edge between two nodes if and only if the Euclidean distance between these two nodes is not more than one unit.

A t-spanner is a spanning subgraph G of a given graph H such that the length of the shortest path between any two nodes in G is bounded in graph H by a value t. In other words, a graph G is called a *t-spanner* of a UDG, if the number of nodes in G is equal to the number of nodes in UDG and $L(_{u,v})G < t\ L(_{u,v})$UDG, where $L(_{u,v})G$ represents the length of the shortest path between nodes u and v in graph G.

In this paper, we first consider several well-known proximity graphs including relative neighborhood graph, Gabriel graph and Yao graph. These graphs are sparse and can be constructed locally in an efficient way. We show that the power stretch factor of Gabriel graph is always one, and the power stretch factor of Yao graph is bounded by a constant while the power stretch factor of relative neighborhood graph could be as large as the network size minus one. Notice that all of these graphs do not have constant degrees. We further propose another sparse topology that has both constant degree and constant power stretch factor. An efficient local algorithm is presented for constructing this topology.

The sparseness implies that the average node degree is bounded by a constant. However the maximum degree could be as large as $n - 1$. The instance consists of n points lying on the unit circle centered at a node $u \in V$. Thus, each edge uv_i belongs to the $RNG(V)$, $GG(V)$ and $YG_k(V)$.

Several researchers proposed another set of routing protocols, namely, the localized routing, which selects the next node to forward the packets based on the information in the packet header and the position of its local neighbors. Bose and Morin showed that several localized routing protocols guarantee to deliver the packets if the underlying network topology is the Delaunay triangulation of all wireless nodes. They also gave a localized routing protocol based on the Delaunay triangulation such that the total distance traveled by the packet is no more than a small constant factor of the distance between the source and the destination. However, it is expensive to construct the Delaunay triangulation in a distributed manner, and routing based on it might not be possible since the Delaunay triangulation can contain links longer than one unit.

Several researchers also proposed to use some planar network topologies that can be constructed efficiently in a distributed manner. Lin et al. proposed the first localized algorithm that guarantees delivery by memorizing past traffic at nodes. Bose et al. proposed to use the Gabriel graph as the underlying structure for the FACE routing method. Subsequently, Karp et al. discussed, in detail, the medium access layer and conducted experiments with moving nodes for the Face routing method. Barrie´re et al. extended the scheme on graphs which are fuzzy unit graphs; that is, two nodes are connected if their distance is at most r, not connected if the distance is at least R, and may be connected otherwise. They showed that their algorithm works correctly if $R \leq \sqrt{2}r$. Routing, according to the right-hand rule, which guarantees delivery in planar graphs, is also used when simple greedy-based routing heuristics fail.

The Gabriel graph can be constructed with $(q + p + 1)n$ bits and is very easy to maintain when the network changes. Thus, there is a trade off between the better worst-case spanning ratio when applying the greedy routing schemes on our structure and the higher cost of constructing and maintaining it, compared to the Gabriel graph.

Previously, there were some approaches proposed to approximate the Delaunay triangulation locally. Hu [18] used the Delaunay triangulation to configure the wireless network topology such that a planar graph with a bounded node degree is computed. A major step in his method is that each node u computes all Delaunay edges whose length is no more than the transmission range. It used the Voronoi diagram of node u to compute all such Delaunay edges. However, this approach will not always work. A simple observation is that, in order to determine whether an edge uv belongs to the Delaunay triangulation, we have to check whether certain circles passing through u and v are empty (not containing wireless nodes in their interior). Obviously, in the worst case, the circumradius of such a circle could be infinity even when the edge length uv is bounded, implying that we may have to check all nodes. Due to space limit, we omit the detail of why the method in [18] will not work. Moreover, it is unknown whether Hu's structure has a constant spanning ratio.

The following parameters are the fundamental criteria for evaluation of the spanners.

1. **Bounded Degree:** Each node has bounded number neighbors in the subgraph. This is crucial since nodes have limited memory and power resources. Each node has a bounded degree. Consequently, each node needs to hold and process a constant number of neighbors. This is attractive since every wireless node has limited computational resources, storage and, more importantly, limited power.
2. **Localized Construction:** Centralized algorithms are not suitable for ad hoc networks, since it is an infrastructure-less network. Thus distributed local algorithms are desirable for maintenance of network topology, as it is easy to maintain the information of nodes within the constant number of hops. The network topology can be constructed and maintained in a localized manner due to the limited resources of the wireless nodes. Here, a distributed algorithm constructing a graph G is a localized algorithm if every node u can exactly decide all edges incident on u based only on the information of all nodes within a constant hops of u (plus a constant number of additional nodes' information if necessary). More importantly, the number of messages sent by each node shall be bounded. In addition it is anticipated that each node needs only time complexity $O(d \log d)$ to construct the underlying topology, where d is the number of one-hop neighbors.
3. **Planarity:** If a graph does not have edge crossings then it called planar graph. Many routing algorithms rely on planarity of the communication topology. The topology is a planar graph (i.e., no two edges cross each other in the graph). Some routing algorithms, such as right-hand routing and *Greedy Perimeter Stateless Routing* (GPSR) [4], require the topology be planar.
4. **Sparseness:** The sparseness of a topology reduces the channel contention of the shared media in the medium access layer. Sparseness enables most routing protocols to run efficiently.
   The topology should be a sparse graph, i.e., the total number of links in this network topology is linear with the total number of wireless nodes. This enables most of algorithms, e.g., routing algorithm based on the shortest path, to run on this topology more efficiently in term of both time and power consumption.
5. **Spanning ratio:** The distance between the nodes in the spanner should be comparable to their distance in the original network.
   The topology is a spanner of $UDG(V)$ in terms of both length and hops. Given a weighted graph G, let $d_G(u,v)$ be the weight of the shortest path connecting u and v in G. A subgraph G' is subset of G is a spanner of G if there is a positive real constant t such that, for any two nodes u and v, $d_{G'}(u,v) \leq t.d_G(u,v)$. The constant t is called the *length stretch factor* if the weight is the Euclidean length. It is called the *hops stretch factor* if the weight of a link is one. It is called the *power stretch factor* if the weight of a link is the power needed to support the communication of this link.

Several spanners have been studied recently both by computational geometry scientists and network engineers. Here we review the definitions of some of them.

The minimum Spanning tree (MST) [2] is a tree that connects all the nodes in the network and whose total edge length is minimum. MST is obviously one of the sparest possible connected subgraph, but it's stretch factor can be as large as n-1.

The edges in the nearest neighborhood graph (NNG) [6] are determined by minimum distance. More precisely for any node p, there exists an edge pq if and only if node q is the nearest neighbor of p. Although NNG incorporates a useful notation, it has the disadvantage that the resulting graph may be disconnected.

A trade-off can be made between the sparseness of the topology and the power efficiency. However, not all sparse subgraphs are good candidates for the underlying network topology. There are two sets of structures used for wireless networks: flat structures and hierarchical structures. The flat structures used previously, include the relative neighborhood graph, Gabriel graph, Yao structure, and the Delaunay triangulation. On the other hand, the hierarchical structures used typically are based on dominating set or connected dominating set, or their extensions such as d-dominating set [15].

In [4], Karp and Kung used two planar subgraphs: the relative neighborhood graph and the Gabriel graph. Bose et al. [12] proved that the length stretch factors of these two graphs are $\theta(n)$ and $(\sqrt{n})$, respectively. Recently, some researchers [16], [17] proposed to construct the wireless network topology based on Yao graph (also called θ-graph). It is known that the length stretch factor and the node outdegree of the Yao graph are bounded by some positive constants. But, as Li et al. mentioned in [17], all these three graphs cannot guarantee a bounded

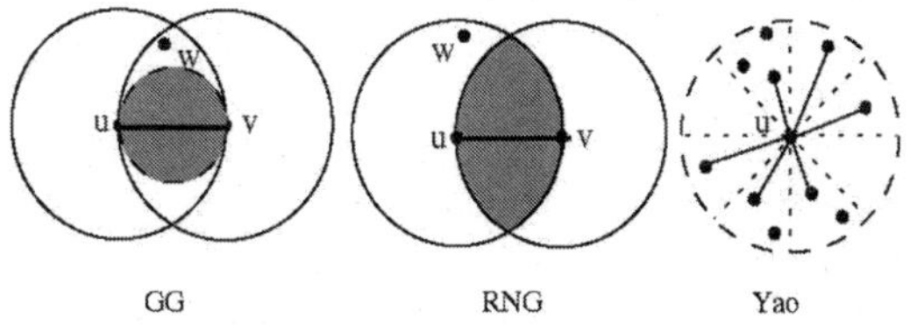

Fig. 1. GG, RNG, and Yao graphs

node degree, e.g., the node in-degree of the Yao graph could be as large as $O(n)$. In [11], [17], Li et al. further proposed to use another sparse topology, Yao and Sink, that has both a constant bounded node degree and a constant bounded length stretch factor. It is a spanner for length or power, but not for hops. It is easy to construct a configuration of a set of nodes, for example, n nodes evenly distributed on a unit segment, such that the Yao structure is not a hop spanner. In addition, all these graphs related to Yao graph are not planar graphs.

Various proximity subgraphs of the unit disk graph can be used in ad hoc wireless networks [4], [11], [16], [17], such as the *relative neighborhood graph*, the *Gabriel graph*, and the Yao graph. None of these graphs are hop-spanners. In contrast, we use a *connected dominating set* (CDS) as a virtual backbone of the wireless network and use *localized Delaunay graph* (LDel) to make the backbone planar. when an edge is included in a graph defined.

A subset of vertices in a graph *G* is an *independent set* if, for any pair of vertices, there is no edge between them. It is a *maximal independent set* if no more vertices can be added to it to generate a larger independent set. It is a *maximum independent set* (MIS) if no other independent set has more vertices.

In relative neighborhood graph (RNG) [3], the neighborhood association is determined by a lune. Formally, the lune $l_{(p,q)}$ of nodes p and q is the intersection of two circles with radius $|pq|$ and at p and q, respectively. The $|pq|$ the euclidean distance between two nodes p and q. The edge pq of spanner RNG exists if the lune $l_{(p,q)}$ does not contain any node in the network, as shown in the Fig. 1. The spanning ratio of RNG can be as large as n-1.

Delaunay triangulation (*Del*) [17] has many attractable geometric properties useful for efficient communication in ad hoc networks. A triangle *uvw* of three nodes *u*, *v*, and *w* is called Delaunay triangle if the circumcircle of three nodes does not contain any other node inside of it, as shown in the Fig. 2. The spanning ratio of Del is 2.4 [9], [10]. But constructing the spanner Del for ad hoc networks is not feasible, because the edges in Del can be larger than the transmission range. The unit Delaunay triangulation (UDel) [14] contains the edges that are both in UDG and Del. The UDel is a *t-spanner* of UDG .But, it is not known how to construct UDel for ad hoc networks. Xiang li et al. [14], [7] proposed a localized algorithm called localized Delaunay

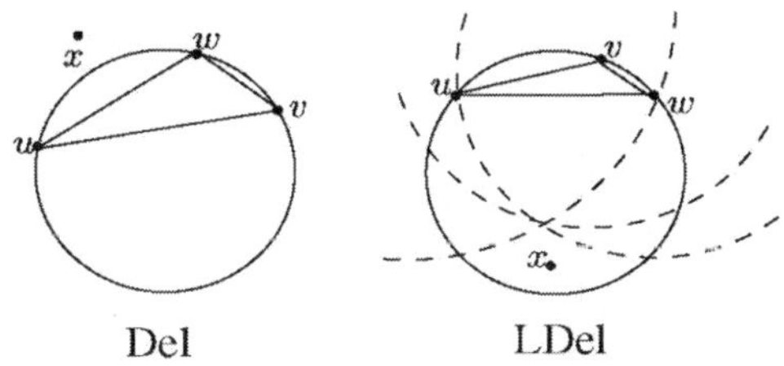

Fig. 2. Rules of Del and LDel

triangulation (LDel) with useful Delaunay properties for ad hoc networks. A triangle *uvw* of three nodes *u, v*, and *w* is called a local Delaunay triangle if the circumcircle of the three nodes does not contain any other node that is a neighbor of node *u, v,* or *w*, as shown in the Fig.2. The spanning ratio of LDel is 2.5 [14], [7].There are other set of spanners called hierarchical spanners [7], [1] which combine the node clustering algorithms with Delaunay triangulation. Several geometric routing protocols use these spanners as the underlying network topology. They include GPSR [8], FACE [5], AFR [11], GFG [5], GOAFR+ [12], and localized routing protocols [4]. The greedy routing, compass routing, and random compass routing provide guarantee delivery of packets if the underlying network topology is a Delaunay triangulation [8], [5].

3. Fault Tolerant Local Delaunay Triangulation (FTLDT)

The frequent node failures is a common phenomenon in sensor networks, which leads to the violation of geometric properties of the spanner. The main objective of our proposal FTLDel is to preserve the geometric properties of the spanner LDel on power constrained ad hoc networks, such as sensor networks. The following algorithm illustrates the construction of FTLDel.

Algorithm:

1. Each node *u* checks, if the energy-level is less than the threshold then the node *u* switches off its transmitter.
2. Each node *u* broadcasts its ID and location information through hello-packet.

3. Each node u collects 1-hop neighborhood information, $n_1(u)$ through the hello-packets sent in the step2.
4. Each node u computes $Del(n_1(u))$. Find all the Gabriel edges which will never be removed.
5. Each node u finds the consistent triangles.
6. Each node u broadcasts all the edges of consistent triangles and Gabriel edges.
7. Remove the consistent triangles which have the edge crossings with the edges sent in the previous step.

The algorithm assumes that every wireless node knows its position information through some positioning techniques such as global positioning system (GPS) and that the nodes are static. In the algorithm, each node tests whether the *energy_level* is less than the *threshold* value. If it is so, the transmitter of the node is switched off. Here, energy-level represents the current energy level of the node and the *threshold* value is the energy level at which the probability of the node failure is high in the near future. The protocol assumes that the source and destination nodes have sufficient power levels. Each node u gathers one hop neighbor information $n_1(u)$ from the broadcasted hello-packets and computes $Del(n_1(u))$. The consistent triangles and Gabriel edges are calculated. A triangle *uvw* is called consistent triangle if each node *u, v*, and *w* has *uvw* in it's $Del(n_1(u))$. The graph after the step 5 in the algorithm is not a planar graph. The step 6 and 7 are responsible to the graph planar. The resulting graph with consistent triangles and Gabriel edges is called FTLDel.

4. Simulation and Performance

The simulation work has been carried out using network simulator (ns2.28). *ns* is an object oriented simulator, written in C++, with an OTcl interpreter as a frontend. The simulator supports a class hierarchy in C++ (also called the compiled hierarchy in this document), and a similar class hierarchy within the OTcl interpreter (also called the interpreted hierarchy in this document). The two hierarchies are closely related to each other; from the user's perspective, there is a one-to-one correspondence between a class in the interpreted hierarchy and one in the compiled hierarchy. The root of this hierarchy is the class TclObject. Users create new simulator objects through the interpreter; these objects are instantiated within the interpreter, and are closely mirrored by a corresponding object in the compiled hierarchy. The interpreted class hierarchy is automatically established through methods defined in the class TclClass. user instantiated objects are mirrored through methods defined in the class TclObject. There are other hierarchies in the C++ code and OTcl scripts; these other hierarchies are not mirrored in the manner of TclObject.

The mobilenode is designed to move in a three dimensional topology. However the third dimension (Z) is not used. That is the mobilenode is assumed to move always on a flat terrain with Z always equal to 0. Thus the mobilenode has X, Y, Z(=0) co-ordinates that is continually adjusted as the node moves. There are two mechanisms to induce movement in mobilenodes. In the first method, starting position of the node and its future destinations may be set explicitly. These directives are normally included in a separate movement scenario file. which starts the mobilenode with a random position and have routined updates to change the direction and speed of the node. The destination and speed values are generated in a random fashion.

Different experiments are done to evaluate the performance of fault tolerant local Delaunay triangulation.In addition we have simulated the following six routing protocols to run on the spanners FTLDel and LDel.

1) **Greedy routing (Grdy):** Let the node b is the destination node then the current node a selects a node c as the next relay node in its transmission range such that the distance $\|cb\|$ is the smallest among its neighbors. Here the circle with the center at a represents the transmission range of node a. Please node that if there exists a node in the shaded area then the node c cannot be next relay node.
2) **Compass routing (Cmp):** Assume that the node b is the destination node. The current node a sends packet to the next relay node c which makes the smallest angle. That is, $<cab$ is the smallest among all a's neighbors.
3) **Random compass routing (RandCmp):** It is similar to the compass routing.let a and b are the current and destination nodes respectively. We compute the two nodes c and d, above and below the line ab respectively. Here the angle $<cab$ and $<dab$ are the minimum angles above and below the line ab respectively, among a's neighbors. The current node a sends packet to the destination node, by randomly selecting, either node c or node d as the next relay node.
4) **Most forward routing (MFR):** The current node a selects the next relay node c to transmit the packet to the destination node b such that the distance $\|db\|$ is the smallest among a's neighbors.

5) **Nearest neighbor routing (NN):** Let *a* and *b* be the current and destination nodes respectively.For a particular angle α, node α selects the next relay node *c* such that <*cab* ≤ *a* and *c* is the nearest neighbor of *a*.
6) **Farthest neighbor routing (FN):** In this routing protocol, for the given angle *a,* the current node *a* selects the next. relay node *c* such that <*cab* ≤ *a* and *c* is the farthest neighbor of node *a*. Here *b* is the destination node.

In the simulation model, Table I shows the simulation parameters used for all the simulations. For each node, *a* random initial energy between 15 and 45 joules is given. The threshold value considered in the simulation is 20 joules. For the connection patterns, randomly three source nodes are taken at one side of the grid where as the destination nodes are taken at the other side.

In the experimental results, we evaluate the delivery ratio of six routing protocols on two spanners, FTLDel and LDel. These delivery ratios are taken at different packet transfer rates. The delivery ratio (DR) iS the ratio of the total number of packets received successfully to the total packets sent by the source.

5. Conclusion

In this paper we studied the need of fault tolerant local Delaunay triangulation in the resource constraint based ad hoc networks, especially sensor networks. The spanner FTLDel recovers the heavy packet loss occurred in LDel without losing its geometric properties. The experimental results showed that the performance of FTLDel is better than LDel. It would be interesting to study the spanner FTLDel and its properties under mobility.

6. References

[1] Khaled Alzoubi, Xiang-Yang Li, Yu Wang, Peng-Jun Wan, and Ophir Frieder. Geometric spanners for wireless ad hoc networks. IEEE Trans. Parallel Distrib. Syst., 14(4):408-421, 2003.

[2] Dimitris Bertsimas, Garrett John. Van Ryzin, and Sloan School of Management. An asymptotic determination of the minimum spanning tree and minimum matching constants in geometrical probability. Working papers 3058-89., Massachusetts Institute of Technology (MIT), Sloan School of Management, April 2003. available at http://ideas.repec.org/p/mit/sloanp/2263.html.

[3] Prosenjit Bose, Luc Devroye, William S. Evans, and David G. Kirkpatrick. On the spanning ratio of gabriel graphs and beta-skeletons. In Latin American Theoretical INformatics, pages 479-493, 2002.

[4] Prosenjit Bose and Pat Morin. Online routing in triangulations. In Proceedings of the 10th International Symposium on Algorithms and Computation, pages 113-122, London, UK, 1999. Springer-Verlag.

[5] Prosenjit Bose, Pat Morin, Ivan Stojmenovic, and Jorge Urrutia. Routing with guaranteed delivery in ad hoc wireless networks. Wireless Networks, 7(6):609-616, 2001.

[6] Eppstein, Paterson, and Yao. On nearest neighbor graphs. GEOMETRY: Discrete and Computational Geometry, 17:263-282, 1997.

[7] Jie Gao, Leonidas J. Guibas, John Hershberger, Li Zhang, and An Zhu. Geometric spanner for routing in mobile networks. In Proceedings of the 2ndACM international symposium onMobile adhoc networking & computing, pages 45-55, New York, USA, 2001. ACM Press.

[8] Brad Karp and H. T. Kung. Gpsr: greedy perimeter stateless routing for wireless networks. In Proceedings of the 6th annual international conference on Mobile computing and networking, pages 243-254, New York, USA, 2000. ACM Press.

[9] J. Mark Keil and Carl A. Gutwin. The delauney triangulation closely approximates the complete euclidean graph. In Proceedings of the Workshop on Algorithms and Data Structures, pages 47-56, London, UK, 1989. Springer-Verlag.

[10] J. Mark Keil and Carl A. Gutwin. Classes of graphs which approximate the complete euclidean graph. Discrete Comput. Geom., 7(1):13-28, 1992.

[11] F. Kuhn, R. Wattenhofer, and A. Zollinger. Asymptotically optimal geometric mobile ad-hoc routing. In Proc. of the 6th international workshop on Discrete algorithms and methods for mobile computing and communications (Dial-M), pages 24-33. ACM Press, 2002.

[12] Fabian Kuhn, Roger Wattenhofer, Yan Zhang, and Aaron Zollinger. Geometric ad-hoc routing: of theory and practice. In Proceedings of the twenty-second annual symposium on Principles of distributed computing, pages 63-72, New York, USA, 2003. ACM Press.

[13] Fabian Kuhn and Aaron Zollinger. Ad-hoc networks beyond unit disk graphs. In DIALM-POMC, pages 69-78, 2003.

[14] X.-Y Li, G. Calinescu, and P. Wan. Distributed construction of planar spanner and routing for ad hoc wireless networks. In Proceedings of the 21st Annual Joint Conference of the IEEE Computer and Communications Societies (INFOCOM'02), volume 3, pages 1268-1277, 2002.

[15] Xiang-Yang Li, Gruia Calinescu, Peng-Jun Wan, and Yu Wang. Localized delaunay triangulation with application in ad hoc wireless networks. IEEE Transactions on Parallel and Distributed Systems, 14(10):1035-1047, 2003.

[16] Xiang-Yang Li, Peng-Jun Wan, and Yu Wang. Power efficient and sparse spanner for wireless ad hoc networks. In IEEE International Conference on Computer Communications and Networks (ICCCN01), pages 564-567, 2001.

[17] Franco P. Preparata and Michael I. Shamos. Computational geometry: An Introduction. Springer-Verlag, New York, USA, 1985.

[18] Roger Wattenhofer, Li Li, Paramvir Bahl, and Yi-Min Wang. Distributed topology control for wireless multihop ad-hoc networks. In INFOCOM, pages 1388-1397, 2001.

Issues in Cognitive Radio Network for Dynamic Spectrum Access in Wireless Networks

Sunita S. Barve[1], Sonal A. Bhople[2] and Dipali Shende[3]
[1]Lecturer, Department of Computer Engineering, Lokmanya Tilak College of Engineering, Mumbai
barve_sunita@rediffmail.com
[2]Lecturer,
Department of Computer Engineering, Lokmanya Tilak College of Engineering, Mumbai
sonal.bhople@gmail.com
[3]Lecturer,
Department of Electronics and Telecommunication Engineering, Sinhagad Institute of Technology, Pune
dipalishe@gmail.com

Abstract

In contrast to current systems where the spectrum allocation is static, future cognitive radio devices will be able to seek and use in a dynamic way the frequencies for network access; this will be done by autonomous detection of vacant bands in the radio spectrum. The limited available spectrum and the inefficiency in the spectrum usage necessitate a new communication paradigm to exploit the existing wireless spectrum opportunistically. This new networking paradigm is referred to as Dynamic Spectrum Access (DSA) and cognitive radio networks. The term Cognitive network is used throughout the paper. The novel functionalities and current research challenges of the Cognitive networks are explained in detail. More specifically, a brief overview of the cognitive radio technology is provided and the Cognitive network architecture is introduced.

1. Introduction

No one would question the fact that the demand for bandwidth or data rate capacity is dramatically rising in nower days and the near future. This can be seen with a glimpse on the enormous improvements in communication networks, e.g., the Internet. As a lot of frequency bands are already allocated in a very unflexible way, namely by selling access rights exclusively to users, it is very difficult to find free spectrum bands and to deploy new applications. Moreover, this resource is further limited by fundamental physical laws. However, measurements have shown that large parts of the spectrum lie idle during significant time periods. A fact that implies that spectrum is not really a scarce resource, but that it is used very inefficiently. In addition, a large portion of the assigned spectrum is used sporadically as illustrated in Fig. 1, where the signal strength distribution over a large portion of the wireless spectrum is shown. The spectrum usage is concentrated on certain portions of the spectrum while a significant amount of the spectrum remains unutilized [1]. According to Federal Communications

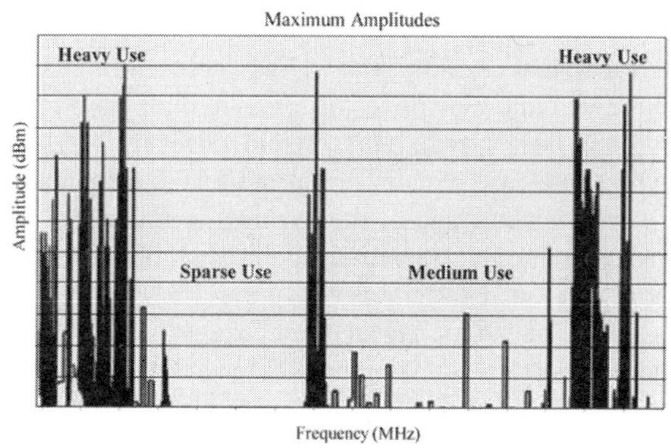

Fig. 1 Spectrum Utilization

Commission (FCC), temporal and geographical variations in the utilization of the assigned spectrum range from 15% to 85%. Although the fixed spectrum assignment policy generally served well in the past, there is a dramatic increase in the access to the limited spectrum for mobile services in the recent years. This increase is straining the effectiveness of the traditional spectrum policies. Hence, new ways have to be found in order to allow a more dynamic and flexible allocation of frequency bands. The limited available spectrum and the inefficiency in the spectrum usage necessitate a new communication paradigm to exploit the existing wireless spectrum opportunistically. Dynamic spectrum access is proposed to solve these current spectrum inefficiency problems. Dynamic Spectrum Access network program aims to implement the policy based

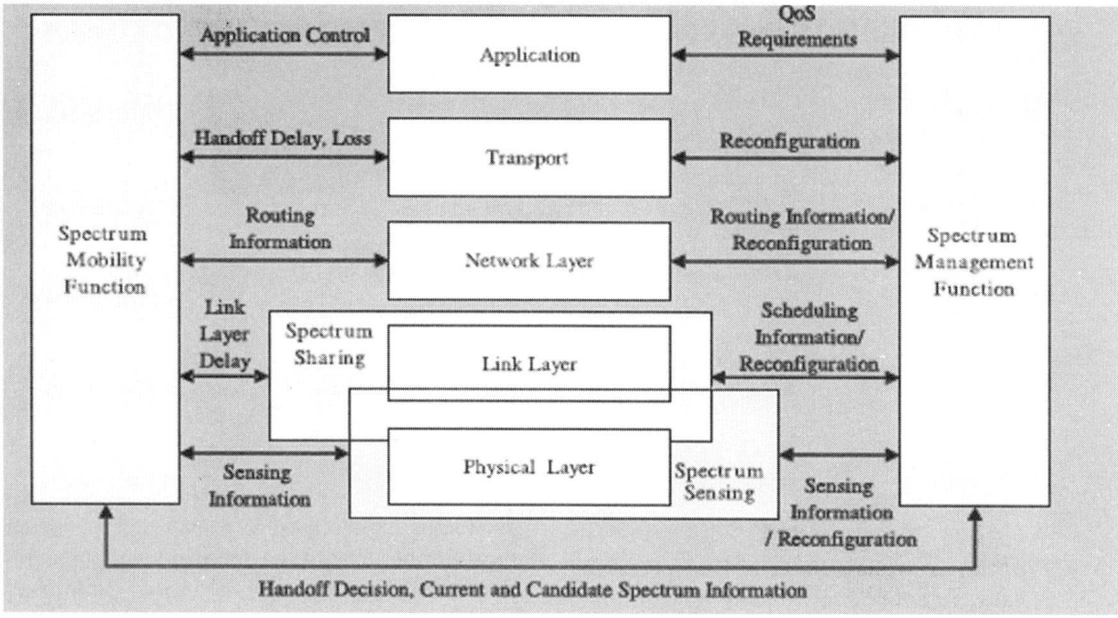

Fig. 2 Cognitive Network Communication Functionalities

Intelligent radios known as cognitive radios. cognitive radio networks, will provide high bandwidth to mobile users via heterogeneous wireless architectures and dynamic spectrum access techniques. The inefficient usage of the existing spectrum can be improved through opportunistic access to the licensed bands without interfering with the existing users [2]. Cognitive networks, however, impose several research challenges due to the broad range of available spectrum as well as diverse Quality-of-Service (QoS) requirements of applications. These heterogeneities must be captured and handled dynamically as mobile terminals roam between wireless architectures and along the available spectrum pool. The key enabling technology of Cognitive networks is the cognitive radio. Cognitive radio techniques provide the capability to use or share the spectrum in an opportunistic manner. Dynamic spectrum access techniques allow the cognitive radio to operate in the best available channel. More specifically, the cognitive radio technology will enable the users to

(1) Spectrum sensing: Determine which portions of the spectrum is available and detect the presence of licensed users when a user operates in a licensed band
(2) Spectrum management: Select the best available channel
(3) spectrum sharing: Coordinate access to this channel with other users
(4) Spectrum mobility: Vacate the channel when a licensed user is detected.

The Cognitive network communication components and their interactions are illustrated in Fig. 2. It is evident from the significant number of interactions that the Cognitive network functionalities necessitate a cross-layer design approach. More specifically, spectrum sensing and spectrum sharing cooperate with each other to enhance spectrum efficiency. In spectrum management and spectrum mobility functions, application, transport, routing, medium access and physical layer functionalities are carried out in a cooperative way, considering the dynamic nature of the underlying spectrum.

This paper presents a definition, functions and current research challenges of the Cognitive networks. In Section 2, cognitive radio network is defined. In Section 3, we provide a brief overview of the cognitive radio technology. The Cognitive network architectures on licensed band and on unlicensed band are presented in Section 4. Then, we describe the Cognitive network applications in section 5 and we conclude with section 6.

2. Cognitive Radio Network

Cognitive Radio (CR) is built using

- **Cognitive modules, and**
- **Software Defined Radio (SDR)**

SDR provides capability to dynamically change transmission parameters of the radio as well as modulation / demodulation scheme in software. Cognitive modules sense the environment (sensor modules), learn from the history (modeler), and make decisions to adjust the transmission parameters of the SDR. A network of communication devices, which are equipped with cognitive radios, is called a Cognitive Radio Network.

Cognitive radio is a paradigm for wireless communication in which either a network or a wireless node changes its transmission or reception parameters to communicate efficiently avoiding interference with licensed or unlicensed users. This alteration of parameters is based on the active monitoring of several factors in the external and internal radio environment, such as radio frequency spectrum, user behavior and network state.

A *cognitive radio* is a smart radio which has the ability to sense the external environment, learn from the history, and make intelligent decisions to adjust its transmission parameters according to the current state of environment. Cognitive radio enables dynamic spectrum sharing of the licensed bands between licensed and unlicensed devices. Cognitive Radio is observed as a novel approach, which could cope with the spectral limitations. However, there are some challenges such as the protection of the licensed users from the opportunistic usage of the unlicensed radios. Spectrum sensing and interference avoidance for cognitive radio systems are considered as very important issues.

3. Cognitive Radio

Cognitive radio technology is the key technology that enables an Cognitive network to use spectrum in a dynamic manner. The term, cognitive radio, can formally be defined as follows A ''Cognitive Radio'' is a radio that can change its transmitter parameters based on interaction with the environment in which it operates. From this definition, two main characteristics of the cognitive radio can be defined

- **Cognitive capability:** Cognitive capability refers to the ability of the radio technology to capture or sense the information from its radio environment. This capability cannot simply be realized by monitoring the power in some frequency band of interest but more sophisticated techniques are required in order to capture the temporal and spatial variations in the radio environment and avoid interference to other users. Through this capability, the portions of the spectrum that are unused at a specific time or location can be identified. Consequently, the best spectrum and appropriate operating parameters can be selected.
- **Reconfigurability:** The cognitive capability provides spectrum awareness whereas reconfigurability enables the radio to be dynamically programmed according to the radio environment. More specifically, the cognitive radio can be programmed to transmit and receive on a variety of frequencies and to use different transmission access technologies supported by its hardware design.

In cognitive radio the main focus was on the radio knowledge representation language (RKRL) and how the cognitive radio can enhance the flexibility of personal wireless services. The cognitive radio is regarded as a small part of the physical world to use and provide information from environment. The ultimate objective of the cognitive radio is to obtain the best available spectrum through cognitive capability and reconfigurability as described before. Since most of the spectrum is already assigned, the most important challenge is to

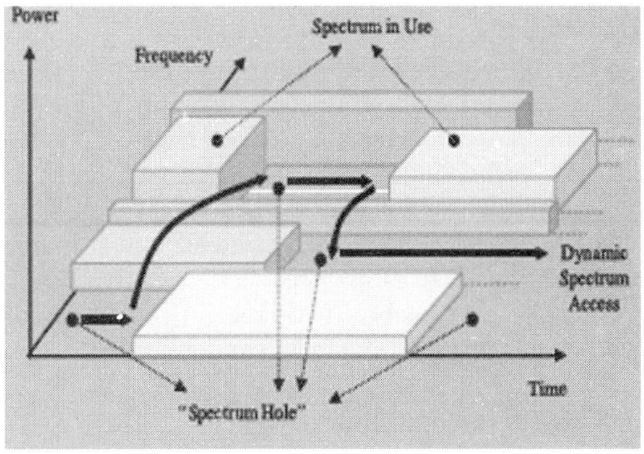

Fig. 3. Spectrum hole Concept

share the licensed spectrum without interfering with the transmission of other licensed users as illustrated in Fig. 3 [3]. The cognitive radio enables the usage of temporally unused spectrum, which is referred to as spectrum hole or white space. If this band is further used by a licensed user, the cognitive radio moves to another spectrum hole or stays in the same band, altering its transmission power level or modulation scheme to avoid interference as shown in Fig. 3. In the following subsections, we describe the physical architecture, cognitive functions and reconfigurability capabilities of the cognitive radio technology.

3.1 Physical architecture of the cognitive radio

A generic architecture of a cognitive radio transceiver is shown in Fig. 4. The main components of a cognitive radio transceiver are the radio front-end and the baseband processing unit. ach component can be reconfigured via a control bus to adapt to the time-varying RF environment. In the RF front-end, the received signal is amplified, mixed and A/D converted. In the baseband processing unit, the signal is modulated/demodulated and encoded/decoded. The baseband processing unit of a cognitive radio is essentially similar to existing transceivers. However, the novelty of the cognitive radio is the RF front-end.

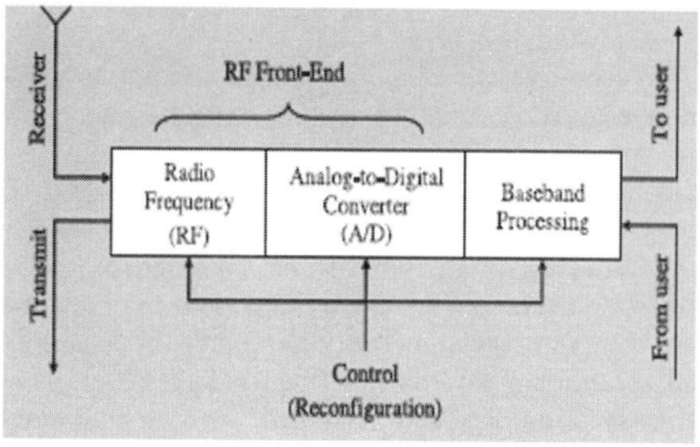

Fig. 4. Cognitive radio transceiver

The novel characteristic of cognitive radio transceiver is a wideband sensing capability of the RF front-end. This function is mainly related to RF hardware technologies such as wideband antenna, power amplifier, and adaptive filter. RF hardware for the cognitive radio should be capable of tuning to any part of a large range of frequency spectrum. Also such spectrum sensing enables real-time measurements of spectrum information from radio environment.

3.2 Cognitive capability

The cognitive capability of a cognitive radio enables real time interaction with its environment to determine appropriate communication parameters and adapt to the dynamic radio environment. The three main steps of the cognitive cycle are spectrum sensing, spectrum analysis, and spectrum decision.

1. **Spectrum sensing**: A cognitive radio monitors the available spectrum bands, captures their information, and then detects the spectrum holes.
2. **Spectrum analysis**: The characteristics of the spectrum holes that are detected through spectrum sensing are estimated.
3. **Spectrum decision**: A cognitive radio determines the data rate, the transmission mode, and the bandwidth of the transmission. Then, the appropriate spectrum band is chosen according to the spectrum characteristics and user requirements [4].

Once the operating spectrum band is determined, the communication can be performed over this spectrum band. However, since the radio environment changes over time and space, the cognitive radio should keep track of the changes of the radio environment. If the current spectrum band in use becomes unavailable, the spectrum mobility function that will be explained in Section 6, is performed to provide a seamless transmission. Any environmental change during the transmission such as primary user appearance, user movement, or traffic variation can trigger this adjustment.

3.3 Reconfigurability

Reconfigurability is the capability of adjusting operating parameters for the transmission on the fly without any modifications on the hardware components. This capability enables the cognitive radio to adapt easily to the dynamic radio environment. There are several reconfigurable parameters that can be incorporated into the cognitive radio as explained below:

- **Operating frequency:** A cognitive radio is capable of changing the operating frequency. Based on the information about the radio environment, the most suitable operating frequency can be determined and the communication can be dynamically performed on this appropriate operating frequency.
- **Modulation:** A cognitive radio should reconfigure the modulation scheme adaptive to the user requirements and channel conditions. For example, in the case of delay sensitive applications, the data rate is more important than the error rate. Thus, the modulation scheme that enables the higher spectral efficiency should be selected. Conversely, the loss-sensitive applications focus on the error rate, which necessitate modulation schemes with low bit error rate.
- **Transmission power:** Transmission power can be reconfigured within the power constraints. Power control enables dynamic transmission power configuration within the permissible power limit.
- **Communication technology:** A cognitive radio can also be used to provide interoperability among different communication systems. The transmission parameters of a cognitive radio can be reconfigured not only at the beginning of a transmission but also during the transmission.

4. The Cognitive network architecture

Existing wireless network architectures employ heterogeneity in terms of both spectrum policies and communication technologies. Moreover, some portion of the wireless spectrum is already licensed to different purposes while some bands remain unlicensed. For the development of communication protocols, a clear description of the Cognitive network architecture is essential. In this section, the

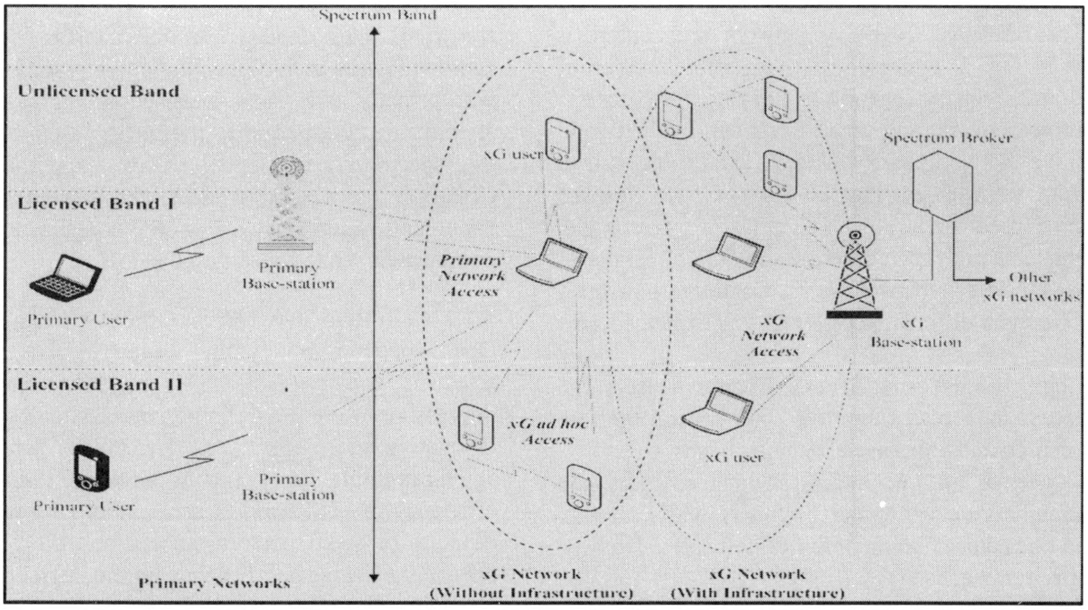

Fig. 5. Cognitive Network Architecture

Cognitive network architecture is presented such that all possible scenarios are considered. The components of the Cognitive network architecture, as shown in Fig. 5, can be classified in two groups as the primary network and the Cognitive network. The basic elements of the primary and the Cognitive network are defined as follows [5]:

1. **Primary network:** An existing network infrastructure is generally referred to as the primary network, which has an exclusive right to a certain spectrum band. Examples include the common cellular and TV broadcast networks. The components of the primary network are as follows:

- **Primary user:** Primary user (or licensed user) has a license to operate in a certain spectrum band. This access can only be controlled by the primary base-station and should not be affected by the operations of any other unlicensed users. Primary users do not need any modification or additional functions for coexistence with Cognitive base-stations and Cognitive users.
- **Primary base-station:** Primary base-station (or licensed base-station) is a fixed infrastructure network component which has a spectrum license such as base-station transceiver system (BTS) in a cellular system. In principle, the primary base-station does not have any Cognitive capability for sharing spectrum with Cognitive users. However, the primary base-station may be requested to have both legacy and Cognitive protocols for the primary network access of Cognitive users, which is explained below.

2. **Cognitive network:** Cognitive network (or cognitive radio network, Dynamic Spectrum Access network, secondary network, unlicensed network) does not have license to operate in a desired band. Hence, the spectrum access is allowed only in an opportunistic manner. Cognitive networks can be deployed both as an infrastructure network and an adhoc network as shown in Fig. 6. The components of an Cognitive network are as follows:

- **Cognitive user:** Cognitive user (or unlicensed user, cognitive radio user, secondary user) has no spectrum license. Hence, additional functionalities are required to share the licensed spectrum band.
- **Cognitive base-station:** Cognitive base-station (or unlicensed base-station, secondary base-station) is a fixed infrastructure component with Cognitive capabilities. Cognitive base-station provides single hop connection to Cognitive users without spectrum access license. Through this connection, an Cognitive user can access other networks.
- **Spectrum broker:** Spectrum broker (or scheduling server) is a central network entity that plays a role in sharing the spectrum resources among different Cognitive networks. Spectrum broker can be connected to each network and can serve as a spectrum information manager to enable coexistence of multiple Cognitive networks

The reference Cognitive network architecture is shown in Fig. 5, which consists of different types of networks: a primary network, an infrastructure based Cognitive network, and an ad-hoc Cognitive network. Cognitive networks are operated under the mixed spectrum environment that consists of both licensed and unlicensed bands. Also, Cognitive users can either communicate with each other in a multihop manner or access the base-station. Thus, in Cognitive networks, there are three different access types as explained next [6]:

- **Cognitive network access:** Cognitive users can access their own Cognitive base-station both on licensed and unlicensed spectrum bands.
- **Cognitive ad hoc access:** Cognitive users can communicate with other Cognitive users through ad hoc connection on both licensed and unlicensed spectrum bands.
- **Primary network access:** The Cognitive users can also access the primary base-station through the licensed band.

According to the reference architecture shown in Fig. 5, various functionalities are required to support the heterogeneity in Cognitive networks. In Section 4.1, we describe the Cognitive network functions to support the heterogeneity of the network environment.

4.1 Cognitive network functions

As explained before, Cognitive network can operate in both licensed and unlicensed bands. Hence, the functionalities required for Cognitive networks vary according to whether the spectrum is licensed or unlicensed [7]. Accordingly, in this section, we classify the Cognitive network operations as Cognitive network on licensed band and Cognitive network on unlicensed band. The Cognitive network functions are explained in the following sections according to this classification.

4.1.1 Cognitive network on licensed band

As shown in Fig. 1, there exist temporally unused spectrum holes in the licensed spectrum band. Hence, Cognitive networks can be deployed to exploit these spectrum holes through cognitive communication techniques, where the Cognitive network coexists with the primary network at the same location and on the same spectrum band. There are various challenges for Cognitive networks on licensed band due to the existence of the primary users. Although the main purpose of the Cognitive network is to determine the best available spectrum, Cognitive functions in the licensed band are mainly aimed at the detection of the presence of primary users. The channel capacity of the spectrum holes depends on the interference at the nearby primary users. Thus, the interference avoidance with primary users is the most important issue in this architecture. Furthermore, if primary users appear in the spectrum band occupied by Cognitive users, Cognitive users should vacate the current spectrum band and move to the new available spectrum immediately, called spectrum handoff.

4.1.2 Cognitive network on unlicensed band

Open spectrum policy that began in the industrial scientific and medical (ISM) band has caused an impressive variety of important technologies and innovative uses. However, due to the interference among multiple heterogeneous networks, the spectrum efficiency of ISM band is decreasing. Ultimately, the capacity of open spectrum access, and the quality of service they can offer, depends on the degree to which a radio can be designed to allocate spectrum efficiently. Cognitive networks can be designed for operation on unlicensed bands such that the efficiency is improved in this portion of the spectrum. Since there are no license holders, all network entities have the same right to access the spectrum bands. Multiple Cognitive networks coexist in the same area and communicate using the same portion of the spectrum. Intelligent spectrum sharing algorithms can improve the efficiency of spectrum usage and support high QoS. In this architecture, Cognitive users focus on detecting the transmissions of other Cognitive users. Unlike the licensed band operations, the spectrum handoff is not triggered by the appearance of other primary users. However, since all Cognitive users have the same right to access the spectrum, Cognitive users should compete with each other for the same unlicensed band. Thus, sophisticated spectrum sharing methods among Cognitive users are required in this architecture. If multiple Cognitive network operators reside in the same unlicensed band, fair spectrum sharing among these networks is also required.

5. Cognitive network applications

Cognitive networks can be applied to the following cases:

Leased network: The primary network can provide a leased network by allowing opportunistic access to its licensed spectrum with the agreement with a third party without sacrificing the service quality of the primary user. For example, the primary network can lease its spectrum access right to a mobile virtual network operator (MVNO). Also the primary network can provide its spectrum access rights to a regional community for the purpose of broadband access.

Cognitive mesh network: Wireless mesh networks are emerging as a cost-effective technology for providing broadband connectivity. However, as the network density increases and the applications require higher throughput, mesh networks require higher capacity to meet the requirements of the applications. Since the cognitive radio technology enables the access to larger amount of spectrum, Cognitive networks can be used for mesh networks that will be deployed in dense urban areas with the possibility of significant contention

Emergency network: Public safety and emergency networks are another area in which Cognitive networks can be implemented. In the case of natural disasters, which may temporarily disable or destroy existing communication infrastructure, emergency personnel working in the disaster areas need to establish emergency networks. Cognitive networks can enable the usage of the existing spectrum without the need for an infrastructure and by maintaining communication priority and response time.

Military network: One of the most interesting potential applications of Cognitive network is in a military radio environment. Cognitive networks can enable the military radios choose arbitrary, intermediate frequency (IF) bandwidth, modulation schemes, and coding schemes, adapting to the variable radio environment of battlefield. Also military networks have a strong need for security and protection of the communication in hostile environment. Cognitive networks could allow military personnel to perform spectrum handoff to find secure spectrum band for themselves and their allies.

6. Conclusions

xG networks are being developed to solve current wireless network problems resulting from the limited available spectrum and the inefficiency in the spectrum usage by exploiting the existing wireless spectrum opportunistically. xG networks, equipped with the intrinsic capabilities of the cognitive radio, will provide an ultimate spectrum-aware communication paradigm in wireless communications.

7. References

[1] Mohamed Ghozzi, Mischa Dohler , François Marx , Jacques Palicot, Cognitive radio: methods for the detection of free bands, *C. R. Physique 7 (2006) pp 794–804*

[2] Zhi Quan, Shuguang Cui, Ali H. Sayed, and H. Vincent Poor,Wideband Spectrum Sensing in Cognitive Radio Networks, arXiv:0802.4130v1 [cs.IT] 28 Feb 2008

[3] Yuan Yuan, Paramvir Bahl, Ranveer Chandra, Thomas Moscibroda, Yunnan Wu, Allocating Dynamic Time-Spectrum Blocks In Cognitive Radio Networks, *MobiHoc'07,* September 9–14, 2007, Montreal, Quebec, Canada.

[4] Manuj Sharma, Anirudha Sahoo, and K. D. Nayak, Channel Selection under Interference Temperature Model in Multi-hop Cognitive Mesh Networks, DYSPAN 2007

[5] T. Clancy, "Formalizing the Interference Temperature Model," *to appear in Wiley Journal on Wireless Communications and Mobile Computing 2006.*

[6] William Krenik and Anuj Batra, Cognitive Radio Techniques for Wide Area Networks, in : Proc.ACM *DAC 2005,*,pp.409-412.

[7] Danijela Cabric, Shridhar Mubaraq Mishra, Robert W. Brodersen, Implementation Issues in Spectrum Sensing for Cognitive Radios, in : Proc. IEEE 2004 pp.772-776

Intelligent Model for Agent Based Secure Web Services Discovery

V.Prasath, D. Kiran Kumar Reddy and M. Thirumaran
Dept. of Computer Science, Pondicherry Engg.College
prasathvijayan@gmail.com kirankumarpec@gmail.com thirumaran.pec@gmail.com

Abstract

Web services are becoming increasingly important in the enterprise sector and as a result, the security of web services will become paramount. A web service security requires authentication, confidentiality, integrity and Non-reputation. The Universal Description, Discovery and Integration (UDDI) registries do not have the ability to publish the security related information. However the defined web services security can only detect known threats but in the internet resources new threats has become challenging to the service provider and consumer in order to consume the services in secure way. In this paper we describe the architecture of our agent based secure workflow system that can apply security to web services environment to protect against unknown threats and vulnerabilities based on security diagnose of each transaction..

1. Introduction

Web services are relatively new technologies that allow a client to communicate with a server by sending messages using the HTTP protocol[3]. However, most organizations are still hesitating to deploy Web services in a WAN. One important reason is the security of Web services. Currently, the society of Web services have produced a series of specifications in order to enhance the security of Web services from basic WS-Security that aims at end-to-end security to WS-Trust, WSSecureConversation and WS-Secure Policy that aim at securing exchange of multiple messages in multiple trust domains with different local policies[8]. In principle, Web services can run on many geographically distributed computers, and thus raise many security-related issues[6]. We concentrate here on one key issue, providing security for web services in dynamic nature. In particular we are interested in focusing on web service security. This concept is implemented in ASWSD through the aggregation of several intelligent agents to tackle future threats, and through specialisations of intelligent agent capabilities to deal with known threats or risks. Such a mechanism is unlike a rule-based detection mechanism which can not detect unforeseen attacks.

In this paper we explain the architecture of integration of web services security with our secure workflow system and also, explain how to enhance security against future risks and threats of web service is achieved. We believe that security diagnose can be used to improve the secure web service applications. A brief description of our agent-based framework system overview is given in Section 2. In Section 3 we explain intelligent architecture for agent based secure web service discovery. In Section 4 we explain the architecture evaluation of our architecture using SAAM. An example of secure searching the web services will be illustrated in Section 5. The concluding remarks are presented in Section 6.

2. System Overview

Fig.1 shows a conceptual view of the proposed system architecture. The design of secure web services discovery is the key for web services security. The technique facilitates the security diagnose between agents[2]. Therefore it is feasible to realize the automatic system of secure web services based on the agent, Figure1 explains how to achieve automated secure web service discovery, retrieval and to update new threats.

- Automatic Web service discovery involves automatically locating the web services required by consumers. We should check results satisfy the security requirements.
- Automatic Web service execution involves an agent automatically executing an identified web service threats.
- Automatic Web service security diagnose involves execution of existing threats test case to match, if request is not return to the consumer then security diagnose will be verified for each transaction.

3. Agent Based Secure Web Services Discovery (ASWSD)

We propose a model called ASWD for secure web services discovery. Most business communication needs secure transaction over network path. Our architecture is based on the two phase access model. During the first phase services provider need to register their services should accomplish the security requirements given by the UDDI registry. In this phase UDDI has to execute web service test case to find out the provider services has threat that are vulnerable to the consumer. If security requirements fail to met, then it will inform to the web service provider to support security requirements that needs to register their service into the registry. Web service provider provides permission to UDDI that introduce new add on security features into service during registration. Web service consumers are able to retrieve web services from the UDDI registry, according to their retrieval conditions, and subsequently perform the services with required security needs. During the second phase when user sends web request to the

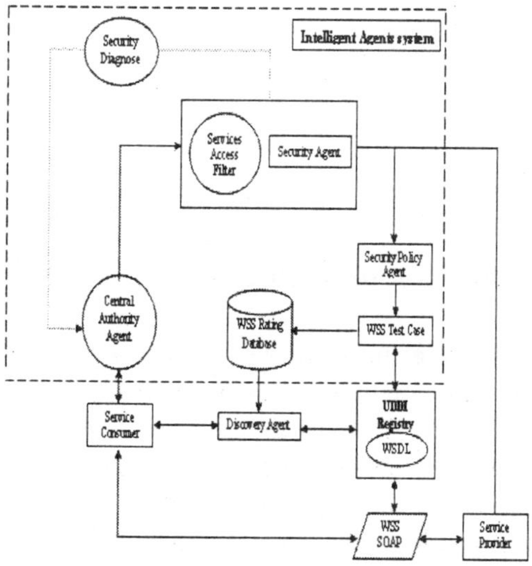

Figure 1. Architecture of ASWSD

target service with the session information in the target address, the security agent will trace the user name from the target address. Based on the current information services access filter will allow or deny the user to access the web service. For each transaction, security agent will process an information regarding new threat diagnose. Security diagnose will inform to the central authority agent to deny the access to particular transaction without required authority certificate processing .This will reduce new threats attack to the registry and provide successful access to the service consumer to avoid any misuse.

3.1 Security Policy Manager

The Security Manager describes the security requirement that service provider needs to be registering their WSDL into the registry. WSS test case(Figure 2) describe a testing methodology for web services security and outline a process that can be adopted to evaluate web services security rating. WSS Test Case can be classified according to different categories of threat faced by web services. WSS security rating should be calculated based on the specific security mechanisms that incorporated into web services, latency of the web service with and without the above WSS settings. Based on these setting non functional requirements for web services providing similar functionalities should be calculated and ranked.

3.2 Discovery Agent

A discovery agent receives service requests containing specifications for functional, security requirements from the service consumer, finds the services that meet the specified criteria, and then returns a list of services to the consumer. Discovery should be based on WSS security rating for concerned request. The list of available services will be return to the service consumer with order priority. This avoids the overhead of discovery mechanism to search secure web services over UDDI registry for consumers needs.

3.3 Security Agent

The proposal system is based on the technique of web services security threats that are faced by the consumer during transaction. It also requires for UDDI services to prevent from new threats that can affect the user transaction. It will monitor the user transaction and has to maintain the transaction database for security traffic. Any new security symptoms will be observed or existing threat has been detected then it will inform to security diagnose for further notification to the central authority agent deny the particular user transaction. Once Central Authority Agent will revised the new threat and apply to test case model with proper permission from security manager.

3.4 Security Diagnose

It need to observe and analyse the behaviour of each transaction, they also need to be able to recognise unusual or uncommon activities/conditions of both user and provider applications by analysing the previous and common transaction activities. The aggregation of components in a system can protect against unknown errors while separated functionalities of the components can only detect known errors. This concept is implemented in ASWSD through the aggregation of several intelligent agents to tackle future threats, and through specialisations of intelligent agent capabilities to deal with known threats or risks. Such a mechanism is unlike a rule-based detection mechanism which can not detect unforeseen attacks.

3.5 Web Services Access Filter

Now we describe the filtering algorithm towards the above objective.

```
Input: User request with Security Token
Output: Allow/Deny User Request against threat action

Incoming Request (Req)
{ if (Request Id is in Threat List)
  { deny the request
        if (check whether malicious user)}
        else
{verify the central authority agent certificate for access}
   }
 else if (incoming access will make load to server (dos attack) || perform malicious action against security agent test case)
{deny service temporarily and check authority}
else
{allow access to service that available in the registry}
```

Figure 2. Filtering Algorithm

3.6 Ranking and Selection Algorithm

When the discovery agent receives a discovery request, it executes Func_Match which returns a list of services that meet the functional requirements. If a security requirement has been specified then Sec_Search is executed next on the set of services and it returns a subset of services that meet the security requirements in accordance with the WSS rating scores.

```
Input: User request with specified security criteria
Output: Secure match set of services from UDDI

U (H): Select all available services that exists in UDDI
WSS (H): Select services that web security policy applied

1. for each web services WSi in U (H)
  //find services that meet functional Requirements
2. Fun_Search = Functional_Match(functional Requirements);
3. if WSS(H) requirements specified then
4. Sec_Search=Secuirty_Match(Fun_Search,WSS(H) specified);
5. if WSS(H) ratings specified then
  //select all available services in U(H) that matches with security information
6. return output of Sec_Search available services in WSSi in
   U (H)
7. else
8. return output of Sec_Search available services WSi in
  U (H)
```

Figure 3. Ranking and Selection Algorithm

4. Evaluation of Architecture

The proposed architecture is evaluated by the Software Architecture Analysis Method (SAAM). All the scenarios corresponding to each application of the agent based secure web services discovery are listed and evaluated. The steps corresponding to SAAM for evaluating the agent web services security are described as follows:

4.1 Scenario Development

The Scenarios chosen for evaluation of the architecture are given below:

Scenario1: Authentication and Access Control
Scenario2: Integration with existing security environment
Scenario3: Automated threat response
Scenario4: Ability to retrieve related domain services.
Scenario5: Language neutral

Scenario6: Support for easy up gradation
Scenario7: Support for security standards
Scenario8: Malicious attack protection
Scenario9: Data collection
Scenario10: Encrypted Data
Scenario11: Service virtualization
Scenario12: Ability to incorporate other functional behaviors that rely on secure service discovery.
Scenario 13: Fail negatively

4.2 Scenario Classification

The Scenarios are classified as direct or indirect with respect to the supportability of the scenario in the abstract architecture shown in Figure 2.

Scenario 1	Direct
Scenario 2	Indirect
Scenario 3	Indirect
Scenario 4	Direct
Scenario 5	Indirect
Scenario 6	Indirect
Scenario 7	Indirect
Scenario 8	Indirect
Scenario 9	Indirect
Scenario 10	Direct
Scenario 11	Indirect
Scenario 12	Indirect

Figure 4. Scenario Interaction

4.3 Scenario Evaluation

To evaluate the architecture based on scenarios, neglecting direct scenarios, indirect scenarios has to be considered for calculating number of components affected in architecture. Each of the indirect and direct scenarios is evaluated as follows:

Scenario 1: This scenario requires that the user should get the authentication and access rights to their request before accessing the web services that present in the registry. To provide for this central authority agent has to provide security token to the user to establish a connection to access the web services the web services instead of contacting to the UDDI registry.

Scenario 2: This scenario is supported in architecture; it can be easily integrated with other security environment

Scenario 3: This scenario needs updated web services security test case database for frequently access the new threat issues while user queries the web services.

Scenario 4: This scenario requires discovery agent component to use efficient selection algorithm to retrieve the security services from related domain based on wss rating information.

Scenario 5: The proposed architecture should support for implementation in any language.

Scenario 6: This scenario demands the proposed architecture to support for adding new components or subcomponents within a component.

Scenario 7: This scenario needs standards security format for transferring messages in secured manner, where there is possibility of getting unknown or non-standard security format.

Scenario 8: This scenario requires the architecture to possess the security properties to protect the web services and registry from serious attack. It supports protection against the latest Web Services and XML-based attacks.

Scenario 9: This scenario requires architecture to be risks assessment to protect the service from fault and failure from attacks. An audit data is crucial for identifying and diagnosing attack as well as proving compliance.

Scenario 10: This scenario reveals that if any data bit is missed or error bit is occurred in encryption of messages in communication.

Scenario 11: This scenario requires the architecture to be used in secure environment. Since it hiding details on back end resources.

Scenario 12: The interfaces provided between the components are more flexible and hence this architecture requires only minimal changes for the support of this scenario.

Scenario 13: This scenario requires the architecture to possess the security properties across all Web services traffic and must be applied in a consistent manner regardless of the different types of technologies being connected in the web service network.

4.4 Scenario Interaction

Scenario interaction is to reveal changes in components when two or more scenarios affect components in architecture. Table: 1 shows the list of scenarios which affects the component description

Table 1. Scenarios affecting the components

Components	Scenario affecting the component
Service Consumer	Scenario 2,Scenario 9
Security Diagnose	Scenario 2,Scenario 7, Scenario 9
Central Authority Agent	Scenario 1,Scenario9
Security Policy Agent	Scenario 1,Scenario 2
WSS Rating	Scenario 2
Discovery Agent	Scenario 8,Scenario 9
Service Provider	Scenario 11
Security Agent	Scenario 7, Scenario 8
WSS Test Case	Scenario 3, Scenario9, Scenario13

The figure 5 shows scenario interaction chart corresponds to table 1, in which x- axis contains components in architecture and y-axis contains scenarios which are indirectly affecting the components.

4.5 Overall Evaluation

The Software Architecture Analysis Method (SAAM) reveals that proposed architecture for agent based secure web services discovery is flexible and maintainability is also high since in scenario interaction table shows components which are not affected by more than three scenarios. Hence the proposed architecture proved it possesses high quality attributes in it.

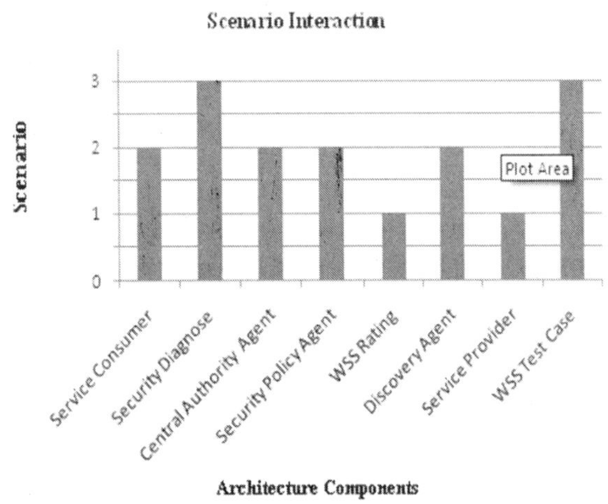

Figure 5. Scenario Interaction Chart

5. Example

In this section, we give an example that involves threat dos attack from valid user. We assumed that the consumer want to access the web services that available in the UDDI. The feature here is session based filter. In the current implementation, we do not focus on who can login and retrieve a WSDL file. This is important as well because if some attackers can easily register and get many user names, they can retrieve many valid session identities by themselves directly. We take a session based approach that each valid Web service request have to present its session identity with it. We designed a services access based filtering algorithm that can allocate the processing capability of a service among different users using the recorded session information. This filtering algorithm can guarantee that when the working load is high, the requests from DoS will be discarded, so the normal request can still come in and get processed with a reasonable response time.

6. Conclusion

With an increasing number of web services providing similar functionalities, security has become one of the most critical issues. UDDI has no way to identify the secure web services when multiple service providers are now providing similar services. We proposed an architecture called ASWSD to automate agent based secure web service discovery and retrieval for aggregation of several intelligent agents to tackle future threats, and risks for both consumer and provider that allow efficient access to web services present in the registry with dynamic nature. This paper also identifies and details an approach to web services security testing techniques and diagnose processes. It aims to standardized process for evaluating security mechanisms in web services. A discovery agent helps finding services that meet the functional and security requirements specified by the consumers. It also presents the WSS rating algorithm to match the consumer security needs based on rating attributes and top ranked services are returned to the service consumers.

7. References

[1] Kassem Saleh and Maryam Habil, "The Security Requirements Behavior Model for Trustworthy Software", International MCETECH Conference on e-Technologies 2008 pp 235 - 238.

[2] Janette Hicks, Madhusudhan Govindaraju, Weiyi Meng, "Enhancing Discovery of Web Services through Optimized Algorithms" IEEE International Conference on Granular Computing 2007 pp 685 - 698.

[3] Colin Atkinson, Philipp Bostan, Oliver Hummel and Dietmar Stoll, "A Practical Approach to Web Service Discovery and Retrieval", IEEE International Conference on Web Services (ICWS 2007).

[4] Janette Hicks, Madhusudhan Govindaraju, Weiyi Meng, "Search Algorithms for Discovery of Web Services", IEEE International Conference on Web Services (ICWS 2007).

[5] Artem Vorobiev and Jun Han, "Specifying Dynamic Security Properties of Web Service Based Systems", IEEE Computer Society 2006.

[6] Jie Xu, Erica Y. Yang, and Keith H. Bennett, "A Practical Approach to Secure Web Services", Proceedings of the Ninth IEEE International Symposium on Object and Component-Oriented Real-Time Distributed Computing 2006.

[7] Slim Trabelsi Jean-Christphe Pazzaglia Yves Roudier, "Secure Web service discovery: overcoming challenges of ubiquitous computing", Proceedings of the European Conference on Web Services (ECOWS'06).

[8] David Geer, "Taking Steps to Secure Web Services", Technology News October 2003.

[9] Tiantian Zhang, Junzhou Luo, Weining Kong "An Agent-based Web Service Searching Model", 9th International Conference on Computer Supported Cooperative Work in Design Proceedings pp 390 - 295.

A Novel Kernel Level Mechanism for Preventing Password Thefts by TSRs

Mr. A.Narayana Rao and Mr. H.Balaji
Dept of Computer science & Engg, JNTUCE, Anantapur,
narayanaraoappini@gmail.com *balajimtech.se@gmail.com*

Abstract

Terminate and Stay Resident (TSR) programs are application programs that always stay in the system once these are loaded and executed, until the system is shut down. TSR programs are highly used tools in password hacking techniques. For instance a TSR can be designed as a screen lock program that prompts the user for entering the proper password for unlocking the screen which was locked for no activity on the system for a certain period of time. Such a TSR can be invoked automatically with malicious intention before the actual screen lock program runs. This malicious TSR captures and passes the password to any malicious program in the system or stores some where for further use. Presently no standard mechanism is available for preventing all such malicious TSR programs from stealing the passwords without the knowledge of the user. Albeit some third party tools exist for this purpose at application level, these cannot prevent all types of TSRs. Further these books were designed as particular TSR specific solutions.

In this paper we propose an algorithm that can be implemented in operating system(OS) kernel for preventing all types of TSRs from stealing the system passwords. This solution needs no special software or hardware or any third party tool. Moreover the user need not know any thing about this change in the OS. The proposed solution consists of modification of keyboard device driver, inclusion of new encryption and decryption modules in the kernel modes of which the later has been implemented in Linux kernel 2.6 of SUSE 10 Linux distribution.

1. Introduction

As the deployment and usage of computer systems grow larger and larger, the security threats are also increasing. Many viruses, worms, Trojans, and other computer threats are being found day by day [7]. At the same time effective solutions are also being developed. For instance u*ntil now 12000 different attacks were found on MS Windows where as it was only 30 on Linux due to its stringent access control policies on the users.* Albeit Linux offers many security features [9], all those features are dependent on the secrecy of the root password. Because, once the root password is out no security policy or feature can prevent any attack on the system and hence all the advantages are gone. In the same manner many security policies in the system are strongly dependent on the passwords or password related mechanisms. *Hence, obviously strong and reliable password protection mechanisms are needed.*

Many password stealing mechanisms exist in the literature. Terminate and Stay Resident (TSR) [1] programs are one of the best and easiest methods of stealing the passwords. TSR programs are application programs that always stay in the system once these are loaded and executed, until the system is shut down. A TSR can be easily created to mislead the legitimate user and to capture the certain system passwords. Presently no standard mechanism is available for preventing all such TSR programs from stealing the passwords. Albeit some third party tools exist for this purpose at application level, these tool cannot prevent all types of TSRs [5]. *In this paper we proposed an algorithm that can be implemented in OS kernel for preventing all types of TSRs, which act as the screen lock programs and other programs in the same manner, from stealing the system passwords.*

The rest of the paper is organized as follows:

In section 2, the overview of the related work is given. In section 3, the proposed algorithm and its working are described. In section 4, the pros and cons of the proposed mechanism are discussed. Finally section 5 concludes the paper.

2. Related work

The TSR programs mentioned in this paper are basically a type of key loggers discussed in [3][4][6]. Key logger is a program which captures the user key strokes of the standard key board. The key strokes can be the password characters or some important user data. The key loggers that exist in the literature [3] are as follows:

2.1 Hardware key loggers

These are small inline devices placed between the keyboard and the computer. Because of their smaller size these can often go undetected for long periods of time. However, these of course require physical access to the machine. These hardware devices have the power to capture hundreds of keystrokes including banking and email username and passwords.

2.2 Software key loggers

This type of logging is accomplished by using the Windows function SetWindowsHookEx() that monitors all keystrokes. The spyware will typically come packaged as an executable file that initiates the hook function, plus a DLL file to handle the logging functions. An application that calls SetWindowsHookEx() is capable of capturing even auto complete passwords.

2.3 Kernel level key loggers

This type of key logger is at the kernel level and receives data directly from the input device (typically, a keyboard). It replaces the core software for interpreting keystrokes. It can be programmed to be virtually undetectable by taking advantage of the fact that it is executed on boot, before any user-level applications start. Since the program runs at the kernel level, one inability of this approach is that it fails to capture auto complete passwords, as this information is passed in the application layer.

Generally different solutions such as anti-key loggers, virtual key boards, and firewalls exist to defend the attacks from those key loggers. Existing solutions and their drawbacks are as follows:

a) Software anti-key loggers are good defendable tools for software key loggers but these are not suitable for kernel level key loggers, which act directly on the key board registers.
b) Kernel level anti-key loggers are suitable for both the types of key loggers but these generally encrypt each and every character typed by the user by putting more processing burden on the processor.
c) Virtual key boards (also called on-screen boards) can be used for entering passwords but these are prone to screen grabbers, which can scan every action on the screen there by estimating the passwords [4].
d) Enabling a firewall does not stop key loggers from stealing the passwords, but can possibly prevent transmission of the logged material over the net [3].

In this paper the focus has been on the design and development of the software and kernel level key loggers as the solution is developed for execution in the kernel. But it does not deal with the hardware tampering as in hardware key loggers.

3. Proposed solution

The aim of this solution is to keep the system passwords safe using symmetric encryption at the keyboard registers level even though the hacker captures them using some sort of TSR programs. The solution uses the following:

a) The mode of the operation (read/write) by the application on the password file, which stores the system passwords.
b) The data entered by the user (passwords/ ordinary data).

If the running program is screen lock program, the mode of operation is *read* and if the program is password changing application the mode is *write*. Instead of encrypting each and every character that user has typed a simple hot key mechanism is used to differentiate the critical data to ordinary data. The user has to use CTRL+ALT+P before entering the password and CTRL+ALT+Q after entering the password.

We introduce a simple and less complex symmetric encryption in the key board device driver and a pair of symmetric encryption and decryption routines in the kernel with the same key. This encryption does not affect the actual encryption that takes place on the password files.

The solution can be described in two perspectives as follows:

3.1 Legitimate user's perspective

The flow chart for the proposed mechanism in legitimate user perspective is shown in Fig. 1. The shaded portion of the diagram is the actual flow of the proposed solution. Remaining portion is the conventional flow.

a) When the user is about to enter the passwords into screen lock or password changing programs first the user will give the hot key combination CTRL+ALT+P, which informs the keyboard driver to set a flag *keyreg* and encrypt the following data before putting into the registers.
b) Now if the application uses the password file in *read* mode (screen lock program) and the flag *keyreg* is set, the corresponding password contents will be read from the password file and encrypted before comparing with the password entered by the user. The comparison results in a match as both passwords are encrypted with the same symmetric key.
c) If the application uses the password file in *write* mode (password changing program) and the flag *keyreg* is set, the entered and encrypted password will again be decrypted before writing into the file.

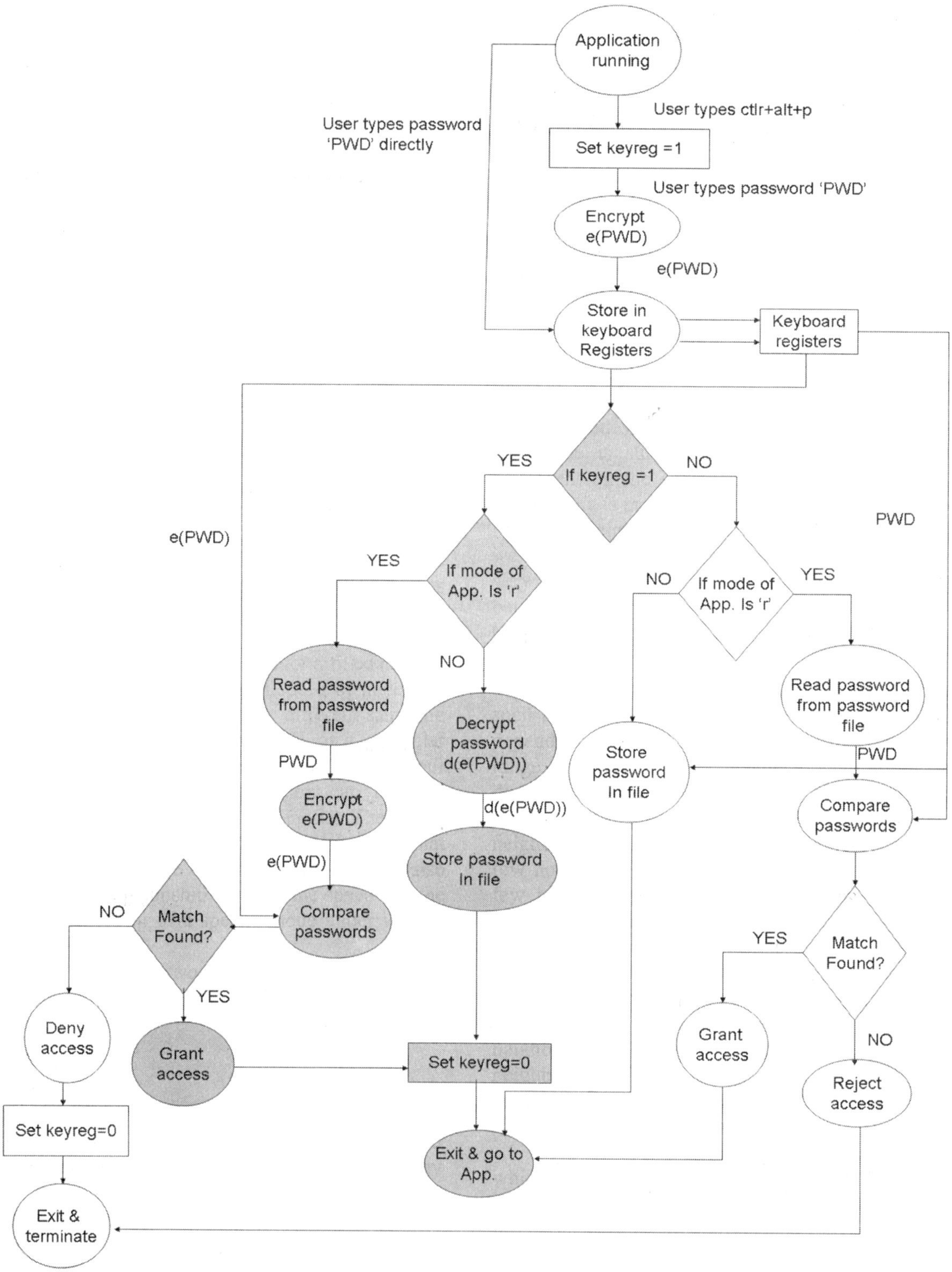

Fig. 1 Legitimate user perspective flow chart

3.2 Hacker's perspective

As the TSR program can read the passwords through the keyboard registers at its best (kernel level key logger), the hacker knows only the encrypted password. Further the hacker may or may not know the existence of the hot key mechanism. In both the cases the hacker is prevented from stealing the password. The flow chart for the proposed mechanism in hacker perspective is shown in Fig. 2. The lightly shaded portion of the diagram will be executed when the hacker tries to access the system. The thickly shaded portion of the diagram will not be executed as the hacker can not work with write access to the resources at that point of time.

a) If the hacker knows the hot key mechanism, the hacker will enter the already encrypted password after hot keys and hence it is twice encrypted for comparison with password from password file, leading to denial of access.
b) If the hacker does not know the hot key mechanism or intentionally not using the mechanism, the flag *keyreg* will not be set. Therefore even though the application is in *read* mode, as the flag is not set, the corresponding password contents of password file will not be encrypted for comparison with the entered (not encrypted) password leading to denial of access.

The following example makes the idea clear:

Suppose the password is *suresh* and for simplicity assume that the encryption is toggling the letters of even and odd positions.

a) The user entered the password after hot key combination. Now the keyboard registers will have the password as *userhs*. The hacker can read this only.
b) If the user wants to save the password into password file, the access will be *write* and hence it will be decrypted into *suresh* before writing into the file.
c) If the user is using password in the application like screen lock program, the access will be *read* and hence the password file contents, *suresh*, will be encrypted into *userhs*, which is used for comparison leading to granting access.
d) If the hacker enters the password as *userhs* without hot key combination it will be compared with the contents of the password file *suresh* without encryption leading to denial of access.
e) If the hacker enters the password with hot key mechanism, encryption will be done twice to make it *suresh*. It will be compared with *userhs* which is taken from encrypting the contents of the password file leading to denial of access.

3.3 Algorithms

3.3.1 Algorithm 1

(Part of Modified Keyboard Driver)

```
ReadScanCodes (scancode);
if ( scancode = = ' CTRL + P' )
{
        keyreg = true;
}
else
{
    if ( keyreg )
    {
        tempkeycode = Encrypt ( scancode ) ;
    }
    SetKeyRegisters ( tempkeycode );
}
```

3.3.2 Algorithm 2 (Accessing the Password File)

```
if ( mode = = 'r')
{
    if ( CheckPermission ( processid, fileid, 'r' ) )
    {
    temppassword = Read ( passwordid, fileid);
    if ( keyreg = = true )
        {
    temppassword = Encrypt ( temppassword );
    }
    }
    if ( Compare ( temppassword, userpassword ) )
    {
        PermitAccess();
    }
    else DenyAccess();
    keyreg = false;
}
if ( mode = = 'w' )
{
    temppassword = userpassword;
    if ( CkeckPermission ( processed, fileid, 'w' ) )
    {
    if(keyreg = = true)
    temppassword = Decrypt ( userpassword );
    Write ( passwordid, fileid, temppassword );
    }
    keyreg = false;
}
```

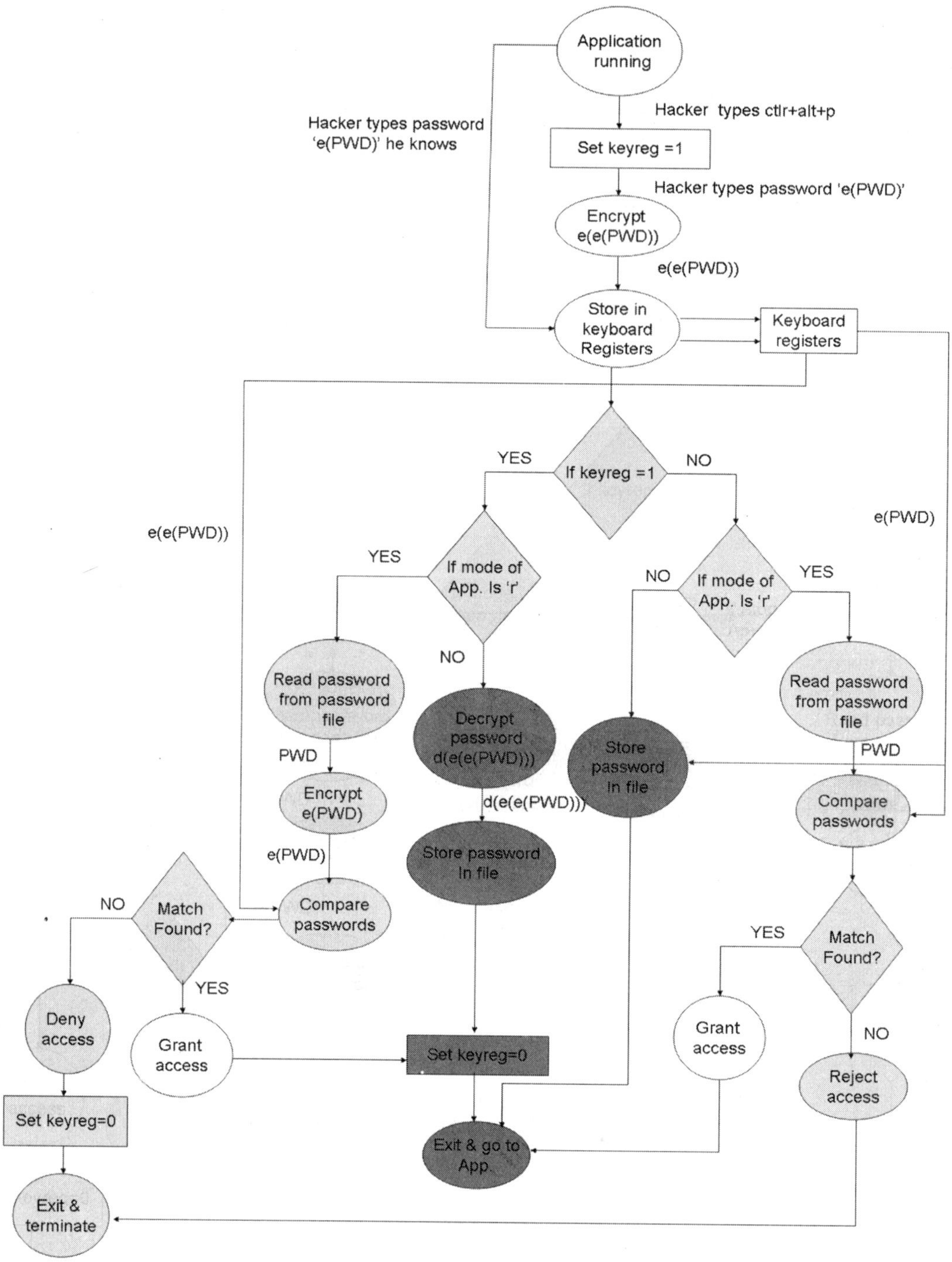

Fig. 2 Hacker perspective flow chart

4. Pros and Cons of the solution

The positive side of the solution is, it requires no special hardware or software or third party tools for designing this solution. Even the end user need not know any thing about this change except the usage of hot key combination. As the solution can be uploaded into the kernel as Dynamically Loadable Modules (DLM) [8] it is backward compatible as those modules can be loaded and removed as and when needed. By implementing this solution into open source kernel such as Linux distributions, the strength and other security features of such operating systems remains unaltered.

The other side of this solution is it has been designed only for a specific class of password thefts. Hundreds of methods exist in the literature for password thefts. And this solution can not be ported into other Operating Systems that are not open source. This method seems to be increasing the load on the processor due to another layer of encryption. But of course care has been taken so that encryption will be used only on critical data such as passwords which may not leave burden on the processor. The main drawback of this approach is it does not work with the web related passwords as they will be stored somewhere in the internet and those servers are not accessible to the host system.

5. Conclusion

A kernei level mechanism for preventing system password thefts by TSR programs has been proposed. The key idea is using one more level of encryption on the passwords at the keyboard registers to mislead the TSRs on the content of the passwords. Care has been taken to reduce the load of the encryption by using some hot key combination. Based upon the access mode of the password file and hot key combination an intelligent escape from the TSR to capture the password has been discussed. More over this approach does not require any hardware or software or any third party tool. Even the user need not know this change in the kernel.

6. References

[1] Hacking novell local area networks, Fairfax Country, http://www.textfiles.com/hacking

[2] Young, M. Yung, "Deniable Password Snatching: On the Possibility of Evasive Electronic Espionage," IEEE Symposium on Security & Privacy, pages 224-235, May 4-7, 1997.

[3] Complete details of key logging, http://en.wikipedia.org/wiki/Keystroke_logging

[4] White paper on key loggers by sachin setty, http://www.securityfocus.com

[5] Cormac Herley and Dinei Florencio, "How To Login From an Internet Caf'e Without Worrying About Keyloggers", Microsoft Research, Redmond.

[6] http://www.keylogger.org

[7] "Hacking Exposed", by S. McClure, J. Scambray, and G. Kurtz. McAfee, 5th edition, 2005.

[8] "Understanding Linux kernel", by Daniel P. Bovet, Marco Cesati, O'Reilly (3rd edition).

[9] Linux network security by Peter G. Smith, Charles River Media 2005.

DT Algorithm Agents for Mobile Robot Navigation

M. Hariharasudan
Department of Computer Science and Engineering,
Thiagarajar College of Engineering,
Madurai 625 015, Tamil Nadu, India
mhariharasudan@gmail.com

Abstract

Agent System proposed for the Mobile Robot Navigation in an indoor environment using Distance Transform Methodology (DT). The proposed algorithm guides the mobile robot to navigate with intelligence. The Software agent system has the subtasks path planning, boundary following, and obstacle avoidance developed under the simulated environment. The Hardware agent handles the subtasks motor agent and sensor Agents. The multi agent intelligently control and co ordinates the software and hardware agent during navigation. The mobile robot acquires knowledge from the environment and imparting the DT algorithmic approach during indoor navigation.

Key words: *Mobile Robot, Path Planning, Obstacle Avoidance, Multi Agent, Distance Transform Algorithm*

1. Introduction

1.1 Mobile Robot

Mobile robot devices with legs and treads capable of moving on an uneven terrain have been built but a vast majority of mobile robots are wheeled mobile robots. It have been used in industrial environments, military and security applications, handling of hazardous material, providing mobility to handicapped persons, and in planetary exploration – the most spectacular example of the last is the Mars Rover [1] of NASA. Machine learning is bound to play a significant role in the development of robotic assistants for human environments such as homes, schools, hospitals, nursing homes, and offices. In order for assistive robots to play a long-term role in people's lives, we should additionally expect the need for the robot to periodically learn new tasks and task refinements. Robots will inevitably become a part of our daily lives.

Research concerns how people will expect and want to interact with them. For example, efforts are underway in research labs around the world to put robots into homes assisting the elderly and into space working in robot astronaut teams. Robots will inevitably [2] become a part of our daily lives.

As robots move into our natural environment [3], it is easy to envision situations that afford the need for efficient task learning and collaboration. Consider working together with a robot on a maintaining a flower garden, fixing a car, or cooking a large dinner. In each of these scenarios, one would neither want to wholly relinquish control of the process nor use the robot as a simple-minded tool that needs to be guided each step of the way. The robot should rather act as a partner that can be taught a complex goal oriented procedure and then effectively collaborate with the human providing appropriate assistance in performing the learned task. Sensing of the environment and subsequent control are important features of the navigation of an autonomous mobile agent. Wall following is a popular and useful technique for mobile robot navigation in structured or known environments and has been intensively studied.

1.2 Agents

There was a requirement that intelligence be reactive to dynamic aspects of the environment, that a mobile robot operate on time scales similar to those of animals and humans, and that intelligence be able to generate robust behavior in the face of uncertain sensors, an unpredicted environment, and a changing world. None of the existing approaches at that time seemed to be able to satisfy these conditions. Some of the key realizations about the organization of intelligence were as follows: Most of what people do in their day to day lives is not problem-solving or planning, but rather it is routine activity in a relatively benign, but certainly dynamic, world. Furthermore the representations an agent [4] uses of objects in the world need not rely on a semantic correspondence with symbols that the agent possesses, but rather can be denied through interactions of the agent with the World. Agents based on these ideas have achieved Interesting performance levels and were built from combinatorial circuits plus a little timing circuitry. Recently the emergence of agent technique is used a new paradigm for software [5] development. A simple way to describe agents is they are the entities perceiving their environment and capable of acting rationally on it.

2. Multi Agent System

2.1 Multiagent

Multiagent system's (MAS) research is useful in a number of application areas. The need for automation in the decision making of mission-critical systems such as space exploration and for designing complex systems such as distributed operating systems and computer networks has accelerated the research in multiagent systems. Agents in the multiagent systems are considered to be intelligent because they posses a high degree of autonomy and can make decisions by perceiving the environment in which they reside.

Multiagent systems evolved as a methodical solution to large, complex and distributed problems [6] where single agent control is either not feasible or restricted by the amount of resources it may posses. There are also risks involved in using a centralized control system. This has led to the new conceptualization of multiple agent solutions. The requirement of multiple agents to work collectively on large problems can be visualized as modules in object-oriented programming. Each agent is assigned to a particular sub-problem from the main problem and each part of the problem is required to be as independent as possible from other parts but this is not necessary. The more independent a sub-problem becomes the more autonomous an agent must be. These independent agents need to coordinate and share information to bring about a solution to the problem

2.2 MultiAgent Architecture

Multi-Agent Systems (MAS) are becoming an important paradigm in intelligent mobile robot research. In MAS agents need to communicate with each other to complete a given task. Although an atomic agent can solve some particular problems, a complex problem typically requires multiple agents. MAS can provide distributed information, flexibility, fault-tolerance, and reusability. Various Agents with the role of mobile robot navigation to reach the destination is with the DT algorithm assistance.

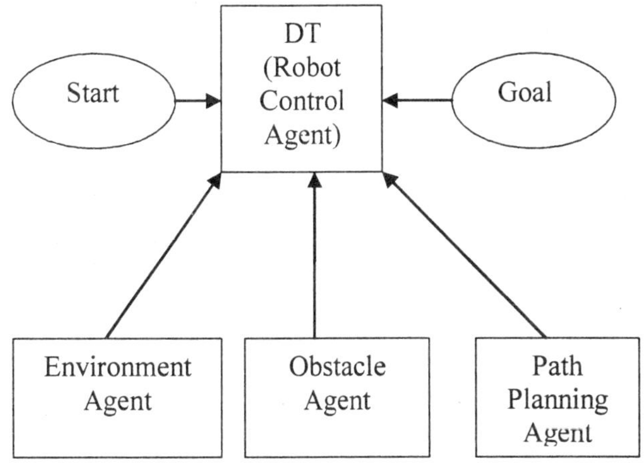

Figure 1 : Architecture for Multi Agent System – Algorithmic Approach

The Environment Agent: Provides an abstraction for dealing with objects in the robot's environment such as cone, ball, or other robots. This abstraction [7] includes operations that the robot can perform on the object, e.g., "look at." or "move to'. The Obstacle Agents or Behavior/Skill Agent: Encapsulate basic behaviors or skills: This agent is a higher level than the Hardware/Resource agent. It consists of behaviors or primitive skills needed for the robot to perform some tasks. For example avoid-obstacle, tracking-object, wander and move-to-goal. DT algorithm agent is a sequencer agent provides a sequence of actions, which may interact with one or more other atomic agents. DT Agents steps are briefed in the implementation phase. Navigation Agent / Multi-Type Agent: Combines the functionality of at least two of the atomic agent types. It provides a complicated agent that can combine the resource, behavior, environment and sequencer agents into a single agent.

3. Algorithm for Path Planning

3.1 DT Algorithm

Using distance transforms for planning paths for mobile robot applications was first reported by R.A. Jarvis and J.C. Byrne [9] . This approach considered the task of path planning to find paths from the goal location back to the start location. The path planner propagates a distance wave front through all free space grid cells in the environment from the goal cell. The distance wave front flows around obstacles and eventually through all free space in the environment. For any starting point within the environment [10] representing the initial position of the mobile robot, the shortest path to the goal [8] is traced by walking down hill via the steepest descent path. If there is no downhill path, and the start cell is on a plateau then it can be concluded that no path exists from the start cell to the goal cell i.e. the goal is unreachable. Initially all the cells are initialized to high values.

The algorithm for DT in an indoor environment is as follows:

Set Start Cell to Current Cell
Set all Cells to Not Visited
Loop
Find unvisited Neighboring cell with highest DT
If No Neighbor Cell found then
Mark as Visited and Stop at Goal
If Neighboring Cell DT <= Current Cell DT then
Mark as Visited and Stop at Goal
Set Current cell to Neighboring cell
Loop End

4. Implementation

Environment Agent created using the grid based environment with the size of 15x15. Each cell is assigned with the cost value randomly. The cost value of each cell is fixed during the task, so that other agents refers the value and take decision during navigation,. The static obstacle is considered for this implementation. The presence of obstacles in the environment will change the cost function for the particular cell. The change in the cell values of the environment agent will makes the robot agent for path selection, to reach the goal with shortest path using DT algorithm. The obstacle agent is created by setting the cell values to 0 in the specified grid location (i , j). The path planning agents have a vital role in taking the decision for the path assignment. Once the robot starts from its position, it monitors and selects the cell values for the optimum path selection. The DT algorithm guides the path planning agent during navigation. Any reachable, not reachable condition can be analyzed by this agent and perform the navigation. The Robot Agent which acts as a multiagent agent plays a major role for reaching the robot to goal position. It interacts with other agents for the current position and values, take decision accordingly. Multi agent system makes the robot agent to reach the goad with shortest path and efficient navigation in the specified environment.

The various outputs of path planning of mobile robot navigation with different conditions like, i). DT algorithm inputs considered without obstacles, ii) with obstacles, iii) goal not reachable conditions are shown in the snapshots.

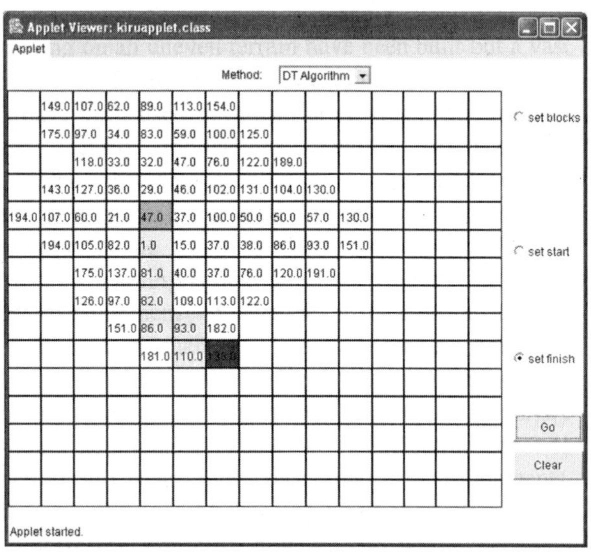

Figure 2. Distance Transform Path Planning

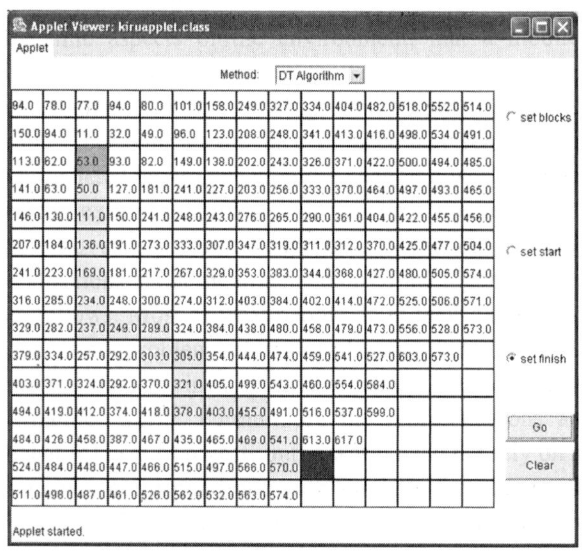

Figure 3. Without obstacles in an Environment

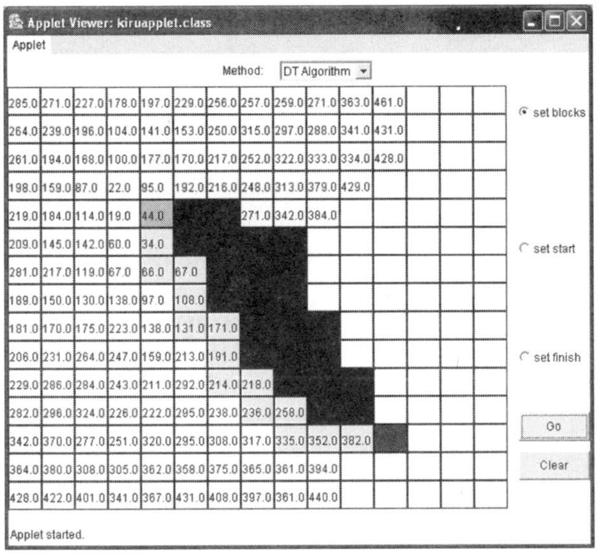

Figure 4. With obstacles in an Environment

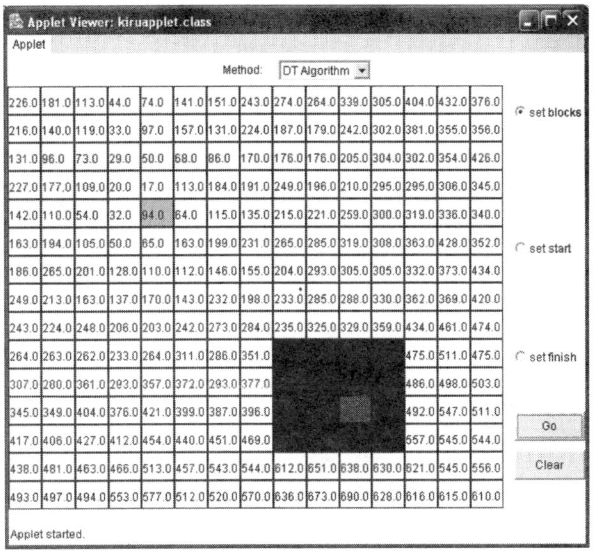

Figure 5. Wih destination not reachable in an Environment

5. Conclusion and Future Work

The mobile robot navigation in the indoor environment using multiagent system implemented using java applet. The multi agent system created using java with the simulation results will give the efficient reactive navigation. Various obstacle agents created simultaneously in the environment, will give the different navigation methods to be followed by the mobile robot to reach the goal with the intelligence added to the robot during navigation using Distance Transform Algorithm. This can be extended further in real time applications like visually challenging people for the mobility in an indoor environment and finding the efficient navigation using the multiagent system with algorithmic approach. Additional hardware agents are also included in future for the real time navigation system in the outdoor environment considering the dynamic obstacles.

6. References

[1] "Robotics – Fundamental Concepts and Analysis" - Ashitava Ghosal Oxford Press

[2] Andrea Lockerd Thomaz, Guy Hoffman, and Cynthia Breazeal "Real-Time Interactive Reinforcement Learning for Robots",Robotic Life Group, MIT Media Lab

[3] Cynthia Breazeal, Guy Hoffman, Andrea Lockerd, "Teaching and Working with Robots as a Collaboration," MIT Media Laboratory

[4] Rodney A. Brooks "The Role of Learning in Autonomous Robots," MIT Artificial Intelligence Laboratory

[5] Patrick Beaumont, Brhim Chaib-draa," Multi agent co ordination Techniques for Complex Environments", IEEE Transactions on Systems, Man and Cybernetics Part C: Applications and Reviews, Vol.37,No.3,May 2007

[6] Henry Hexmoor, Satish Gunnu Venkata. "Modeling Social Norms in Multiagent Systems", Journal of Experimental and Theoretical Artificial Intelligence,Vol. 18, No. 1, Pages 49- 71, Taylor and Francis

[7] Kanok Kusumalnukool " The Robot Self Agent for Mobile Robot" Thesis, Electrical Engineering, Vanderbilt University. Tennessee

[8] Yew Tuck Chin, Han Wang, Leng Phuan Tay, Hui Wang, , Singapore, "Vision Guided AGV using Distance Transform", Nanyang Technological University Proceedings of the 32nd ISR (International Symposium on Robotics), 19-21, April 2001

[9] A. Zelinsky1, R.A. Jarvis2, J.C. Byrne2 and S. Yuta3, " Planning Paths of Complete Coverage of an Unstructured Environment by a Mobile Robot", 1Intelligent Machine Behavior Section, Electrotechical Laboratory, Tsukuba, Japan.

[10] Lim Chee WangY, Lim Ser YongY , Marcelo H. Ang Jr, "Hybrid of Global Path Planning and Local Navigation implemented on a Mobile Robot in Indoor Environment" National University, Singapore

[11] www.mit.edu

[12] www.cs.cmu.edu

[13] www.mlab.gatech.edu/index.htm

[14] http://robotics.anu.edu.au/Groups/RSG.htmlhttp://guidance.aero.iisc.ernet.in/robotics/research.html

[15] http://www.robotics.laboratorium.dist.unige.it/corso_robotica/Projects/AE01/ArtificialEcosystem.html

EAD for Wireless Sensor Networks

Mayank Chakraverty, Mohamed Arshad Akbar and S.Vignesh
Department of Electronics and Communication Engineering
Vel's Srinivasa College of Engineering and Technology, Chennai-603103
may_ank2004@indiatimes.com *mohamedarsh@gmail.com* *vigneshreach@gmail.com*

Abstract

In this paper, we present a novel energy-data centric routing algorithm for wireless sensor networks , which we refer to as EAD . We discuss the algorithm and its implementation, and report on the performance result of several workloads using the network simulator ns2. EAD represents an efficient energy-aware distributed protocol to build a rooted broadcast tree with many leaves, and facilitate the data-centric routing in wireless micro sensor networks. The idea is to turn off the radios of all leaf nodes and let the non-leaf nodes are in charge of data aggregation and relaying tasks.The main contribution of this protocol is the introduction of the novel approach based on the low-cost backbone provisioning with in wireless sensor network in order to turn off the non backbone nodes and save energy without compromising the connectivity of the network, and there by extending the network lifetime. EAD makes no assumption on the network topology, and it is based on the residual power. We present an extensive simulation experiments to evaluate the performance of our EDA forwarding to parent routing scheme over a tree created by a single EAD execution, and compare it with the routing scheme over a regular Ad hoc On Demand Distance vector routing (AODV)protocol .last but not least ,we evaluate the performance of our proposed EAD algorithm and compare it to the low energy adaptive clustering hierarchy(LEACH protocol, a cluster based, energy-aware routing protocol specifically designed sensor networks .our results indicate clearly that EDA out performs AODV and LEACH in energy conservation, throughput, and network lifetime extension.

1. Introduction

Recent advances in wireless communication, micro sensor technology, on-board processing, radio and actuators have been a driving force to expand our ability to remotely monitor and interact with the physical world. Wireless sensor networks provide a global view of the monitored area based on local observations measured by each sensor. This sensor network usually contains thousands or millions of sensors, which are randomly and densely deployed (10 to 20 sensors per m2). Sensor networks have short transmission range (up to 10 meters) and low data rate (several bytes). Each sensor has a light weight and a low cost and they may not have a globally unique Id. Sensors are powered by battery, which is impossible to get recharged after deployment. Note that sensor networks are designed to have long operation time. However, sensors do not have unlimited resource supplies, e.g., power, CPU, memory, etc. Consequently, they are prone to failure. There by making routing schemes based on unique addresses that are originated and applied in IP networks a challenging problem for the design of reliable wireless sensor networks. There are two kinds of dominant message traffic in a sensor network: queries from the user to the network and the actual data collected from the sensor node back to the user. Each sensor acts as a power aware sensor to sense the environment and as a router to relay traffic to other sensors. In this study, the sensor nodes are assumed to be using μAMPS sensors. The radio characteristics and power utilization of these sensors were simulated in experiments using the μAMPS extensions to the Network Simulator ns-2. The amount of data generated by one sensor can be large enough to block the whole network, and a large part of these data may be useless to the end user. Thus, data is processed before they are transmitted. This is referred to as *in-network processing* during which redundant, useless and spurious data are deleted, and partial observations from different sensors are combined and aggregated. Innetwork data processing is a *must* to decrease the large volume of raw observations per sensor and to reduce the number of broadcasts. This can conserve the sensors' battery power, which to a great degree, determines the network lifetime. Within a sensor, the dominant energy consumer is the radio transceiver. For a sensor network with a short transmission range, the radio consumes almost the same amount of energy in transmit, receive and idle mode. Therefore, the only way to save energy is to completely turn off the radio. However, a sleeping sensor can't function as a relay even though it can continue sensing and it can wake up when some events are detected. Thus, we can't turn off all sensors at the same time in a sensor network. Some sensors, indeed, must be active for traffic relaying purpose. In this paper, we propose to construct a virtual backbone, which contains all active sensors, to assist the energy-aware routing scheme. All sensors not in the virtual backbone turn off their radios in order to conserve their power supply.

Backbone sensors are in charge of in-network data processing and traffic relaying. This virtual backbone can be easily reconfigured When its topology changes. Our work is motivated by SPAN, GAF and LEACH. SPAN and GAF are elaborated in the context of MANET (multi hop ad hoc wireless networks), where traffic-flow may originate from any node to any other nodes. SPAN, a topology based protocol, assumes that each node knows its 2-hop neighbors. GAF, a location-based protocol, requires that each node to be aware of its own position and the grid where it resides. LEACH, a clustering based hierarchical protocol used to save battery life, features the concept of rounds to counter the cluster-head's fatigue. Both SPAN and GAF models propose algorithms to compute a subset of nodes whose radios can be turned off with little influence on data dissemination while network lifetime can be greatly extended. Even though both SPAN and GAF are promising methods, they may not be suitable for dense micro sensor networks, due to their assumptions and the unique features of sensor networks presented above. A sensor with tens neighbors may not afford to store its 2-op neighborhoods' information as is done in the SPAN model, and it may not have information such as the position of the nodes as in the GAF model. In this paper, we propose an algorithm to compute a broad cast tree rooted at the gateway, and introduce a novel approach based on a low cost backbone provisioning within a sensor network in order to turn off the remaining nodes and save energy without compromising the connectivity. This broadcast tree spans all sensors and it has large number of leaves. All the leaf sensors turn off their radios to save power while all active sensors stay alert for traffic relaying. We map our problem to the construction of the *spanning tree with maximum number of leaves*, which is known as a NP-hard problem, since it is equivalent to minimum connected dominating set. The reduced topology by all non-leaf nodes forms the virtual backbone. We propose a novel Energy-Aware Data-centric routing heuristic, which we refer to as EAD that exhibits a low message overhead, and computes a broadcast tree approximating the optimal spanning tree with a maximum number of leaves. The novel concepts involved in EAD include the *neighboring broadcast scheduling* and the *distributed competition among neighbors*, based on residual energy. These two characteristic ensure that the resultant tree has many leaves, and sensors with a higher residual power have higher chance to be non-leaf nodes. EAD follows this energy-aware paradigm and results in a special rooted broadcast tree, which is designed intentionally for data-centric routing. Each sensor needs to broadcast messages at most twice, which will result in a large message overhead in a large-scale sensor network containing thousands or millions of sensors. To address this problem, we propose to let a subset of sensors turn off their radios before the execution of EAD. We present a heuristic, which we refer to as a topology-based scheme, in order to determine which sensors need to sleep ahead of time. The remainder of the paper is organized as follows. In Section 2, we present the network model. Section 3 outlines the basic idea of our data-centric routing scheme. In Section 4,we present our Energy-Aware Datacentric routing heuristic in full details. Section 5 reports on the simulation experiments we have carried out to evaluate the performance of EAD. Section 6 concludes the paper.

2. Network Model

In this paper, we consider wireless micro sensor networks for monitoring abnormal events.

Example applications include the habitat monitoring, the contamination transport monitoring, and the forest fire pre-warning, just to mention a few. We assume that the network contains hundreds or thousands of smart sensors deployed randomly in the target area. There exists one gateway that connects the micro sensor network to the outside distributed system such as the Internet.

The gateway is located at the boundary of the monitored area, where it is reachable by at least some sensors. We refer to each micro sensor as a data source or an event source since data in a sensor network are generated by sensors, and the gateway as a data sink or an event sink. The architecture of a micro sensor contains four components:

Sensing circuitry, digital processing, power supply, and radio transceiver. Among these four components, radio Transceiver is the dominant power consumer the energy spent for sensing and data processing is negligible. For example, the power consumed by a Berkeley mote to transmit 1 bit data is equivalent to 800 instructions .For sensors with short transmission range like mote, the energy consumed for different mode (transmit, receive and idle)are comparable , while a sleeping sensor (radio is off) consumes little energy. Thus, in order to save energy the sensor needs to completely turn off its radio. Figure 1 provides a good illustration on the energy consumption in a typical sensor.

3. Data-centric routing in micro sensor networks

In this section, we highlight the basic ideas of the data centric routing in a micro sensor network. First, let us recall that the in-network processing can significantly improve the evaluation of a novel energy-aware data-centric routing algorithm. Fig. 1. Energy consumption for a typical sensor reported in [7]. Fig. 2. An example to demonstrate data-centric routing. Label $x(y)$ at each node means the local temperature measurement is x while the aggregated value so far is y. The aggregation function is *max*.Scalability and the lifetime of micro sensor networks. Thus at each sensor, the local raw data is, first, combined with partially processed data delivered from sensors that are farther away from the sink. Then, the aggregated result is transmitted to the sensor that is closer to the sink or the sink itself for further processing. Intuitively, data is routed along a *reversed multicast tree* with the sink as the root. Data aggregation happens at each non-leaf node, which summarizes the output based on the aggregation functions (e.g., SUM, AVG, MEAN, MAX, etc.) used by the sensor nodes in the sub tree rooted at itself and transmits the aggregated data to its parent. This process is referred to as a *data-centric routing.* Fig. 2 gives an example of data-centric routing where the highest temperature needs to be reported to the user.

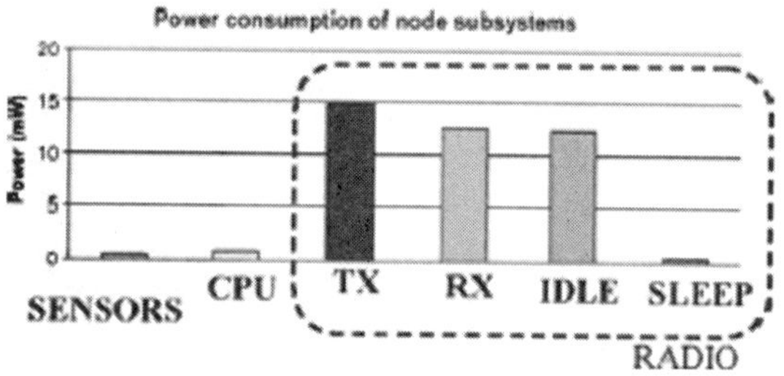

Fig. 1 Energy consumption for a typical sensor reported in [7]

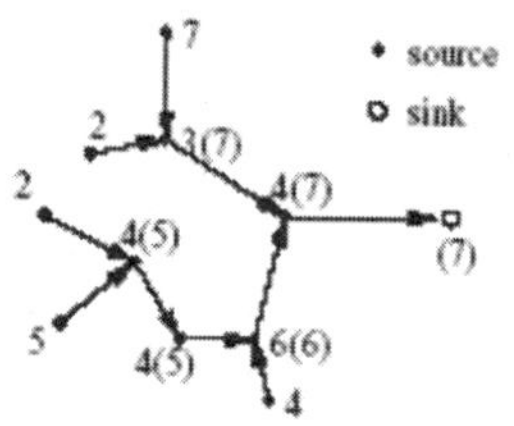

Fig. 2

Traditional network-wide routing is referred as *address centric routing.* A packet is routed based on the unique IP destination address and its data payload remains unchanged during the delivery from the source to its destination. This routing scheme does not work with micro sensor networks, mainly due to the lack of a globally unique address, and the sensor node's energy constraints. In a micro sensor network, the data are processed before their transmission. Redundant and useless data are discarded. Local data are aggregated to provide globally-effective result. It is possible that an information packet contains different values from hop to hop during the course of its transmission from a leaf to the intermediate sensors then to the sink in the tree, because each intermediate sensor may aggregate multiple packets. In this respect, micro sensor network is similar to a pure *peer-to-peer* network. For applications with frequent occurrence of queries and events, our proposed approach is extremely helpful. Actually for a dense sensor network in which each sensor has a large number of neighbors, only a few number of sensors need to be active at any time. These sensors form a virtual backbone rooted at the sink, and they are ready for a query and/or an event dissemination. In this paper, we propose a heuristic protocol to build a rooted broadcast tree with many leaves, which we refer to as EAD, and will be described in the next section.

4. EAD: A heuristic algorithm to construct a rooted broadcast tree with many leaves

In this section, we discuss the details of EAD, the heuristic algorithm we use to construct a rooted broadcast tree with many leaves, as well as the broadcast tree maintenance scheme we are proposing to use within the EAD protocol.

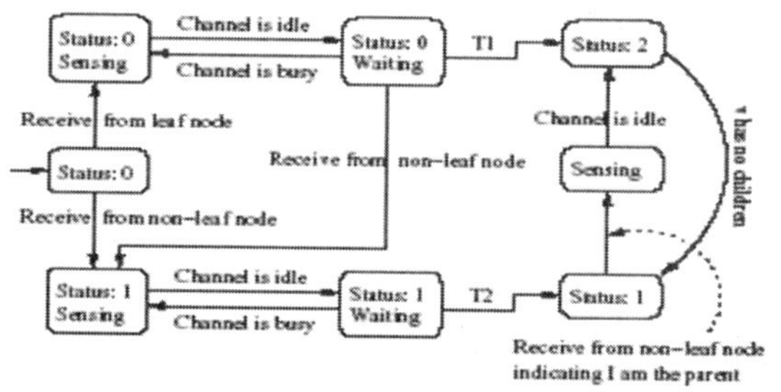

igure 3. State diagram for the proposed heuristic run by a node v other than ı sink.

Fig. 3 State diagram for the proposed beuristic run by a node v other than sink

4.1. EAD description

We assume that each sensor has its own radio transceiver on and is sensing the common channel when the network is initially deployed. We also assume that all of the sensors have the same transmission range. In other words, we only consider symmetric links. The control message contains four fields: *type, level, parent, power*. Let v be the sender of the message, and *type* v its status (0: undefined; 1: leaf node; 2: non-leaf node). *Level* v refers to the number of hops from v to the sink; Receive from leaf node Receive from non leaf node

Receive from
non leaf node
Status: 0 Sensing
Channel is busy
Channel is idle
T1
T2
Channel is idle
v has no children
Status: 0
Status: 1
Waiting
Status: 1
Sensing Channel is busy
Channel is idle
Status: 0
Waiting
Status: 2
Status: 1
Sensing
Receive from non leaf node, indicating I am the parent

Parent v is the next hop of *v* in the path to the sink; *power v* is the residual power *Ev*. If *Ev* is unavailable, we can use the difference between the expected lifetime of the battery and the total time with the radio transceiver already on. The basic outline of the heuristic is portrayed in figure 3.Initially each sensor *v* has status 0. The sink first broadcasts *msg* (2, 0, *NULL*, _), where _ indicates that the sender is the sink. When a node *v* receives *msg* (2, *levelu, parentu,Eu*) from node *u*, it becomes a leaf node, senses the channel until it is idle, and then waits for *T v*2 time. If the channel is still idle, *v* broadcasts *msg* (1, *levelu* + 1, *u, Ev*). If *v* receives *msg* (1, *levelu, parentu, Eu*) from *u*, it senses the channel until it is idle, waits for time *T v*1. If the channel is still idle, *v* broadcasts *msg* (2, *levelu* + 1, *u, Ev*). In other words, it becomes a non-leaf node. Note that a waiting sensor goes back to sensing (see figure 3) if the common channel is occupied by other sensors before it times out. If a node *v* with status 1receives *msg*(2, *levelu, v, Ew*) from *w* indicating that *v* is its parent, *v* broadcasts *msg*(2, *levelv ,parentv, Ev*) immediately after the channel is idle (No waiting!). This process continues until every sensor is either a leaf node, or a non-leaf node. A sensor with status 2 will become a leaf node if it detects that it has no children. Note that we use *T v*1 and *T v*2 to ensure that no two neighboring broadcasts are scheduled at the same time. *T v*1 and *T v*2can be computed locally. Let *Nv* be the set of 1-hop neighbors of *v*. We require *T v*1 > *maxu, Nv* {*T u*2 } to ensure that a sensor becomes a non-leaf node in the tree only when necessary. We also require that *T v*1 and *T v*2 to be monotonically decreasing functions of *Ev*, the residual power of *v*. The basic idea is to force the neighboring sensors with a higher energy to broadcast earlier than those nodes with a lower residual power. For example, we can choose *T v*1 = 2 · *t*0 + *Ev* and *T v*2 = *t*0 + *cEv*, where *t*0 is the upper bound of the propagation time between any pair of neighboring sensors, and *c* > san adjusting constant. Note that with properly selected functions for *T v*1and *T v*2, local broadcasting among neighboring sensors can be scheduled without conflict. The main features of EAD include the *scheduling of local broadcasts* by *T*1.

EVALUATION OF A NOVEL ENERGY-AWARE DATA-CENTRIC ROUTING ALGORITHM

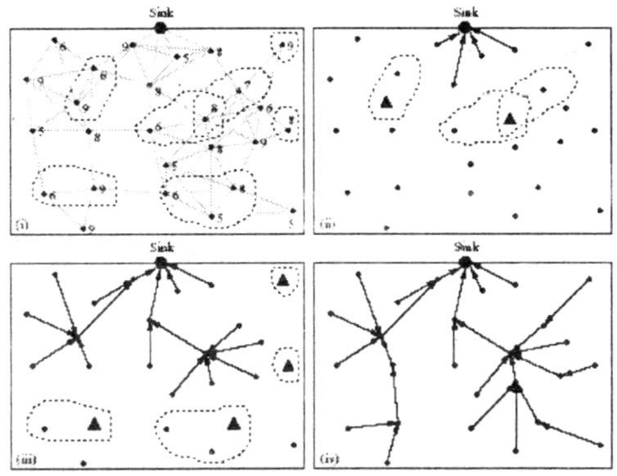

Fig. 4 An illustrative example.

The intuition behind the algorithm is stated as follows: once a sensor *u* announces its status 2 (i.e., non-leaf node) through a broadcast, all of its 1-hop neighbors with status 0 become leaf nodes. They announce their status in the reverse order of their residual power, with higher energy node in the neighborhood broadcasts earlier (for example, T *v* 2 = *t*0 + *cEv*). When the 2—hop neighbors of *u* with status0 hear these broadcasting messages, they start to compete with each other. The winners are those with a highest residual energy among all of its neighboring competitors (thus, with a smallest *T*1 among all of its neighboring competitors). Figure 4gives an illustrative example. In figure 4(i) the original sensor network topology is given. Each sensor is labeled with its residual power. The islands indicate the competing neighboring groups in (ii) and (iii). In figure 4(ii), sink broadcasts to its4 neighbors. The 2-hop neighbors form 3 neighboring groups. The sensors with highest energy in each group (replaced by triangles) win the local competition. In figure 4(iii), winners become non-leaf nodes. Each node specifies its own parent, the neighbor with the highest energy in the partial tree. Each designated parent becomes a non-leaf node, with its neighbors not in the tree joining the tree immediately after the parent announces its new status. Later, the neighbors of the winners (not in the tree) join the tree as children of its corresponding winner. The winner's 2hop neighbors (not in the tree) form four neighboring competing groups. Figure 4(iv) repeats (iii) to get the final broadcast tree with many leaves. Note that the two winners (triangles) in (iii) become leaf nodes in the final tree even though they were the winners, since they have no children. Note that EAD grows a broadcast tree from the sink. Once the algorithm terminates, all the leaf nodes can turn off their radios to save energy. These nodes may switch to "power on" periodically, or when some abnormal events are detected. Using this simple scheme, each node will broadcast at most twice. The induced graph by all of the non-leaf nodes forms the virtual backbone. Due to the broadcasting nature in a wireless network setting, the virtual backbone may have a mesh structure. But each sensor records its parent leading to the sink. The sink can restrict the broadcast of queries to nodes within the virtual backbone and the sources can send back data to the sink along the backbone.

5. LEACH: Low-Energy Adaptive Clustering Hierarchy

LEACH is a self-organizing, adaptive clustering protocol that uses randomization to distribute the energy load evenly among the sensors in the network. In LEACH, the nodes organize themselves into local clusters, with one node acting as the local base station or cluster-head. If the cluster heads were chosen a priori and fixed throughout the system lifetime, as in conventional clustering algorithms, it is easy to see that the unlucky sensors chosen to be cluster-heads would die quickly, ending the useful lifetime of all nodes belonging to those clusters. Thus LEACH includes randomized rotation of the high-energy cluster-head position such that it rotates among the various sensors in order to not drain the battery of a single sensor. In addition, LEACH performs local data fusion to "compress" the amount of data being sent from the clusters to the base station, further reducing energy dissipation and enhancing system lifetime. Sensors elect themselves to be local cluster-heads at any given time with a certain probability. These cluster head nodes broadcast their status to the other sensors in the network. Each sensor node determines to which cluster it wants to belong by choosing the cluster-head that requires the minimum communication energy2. Once all the nodes are organized into clusters, each cluster-head creates a schedule for the nodes in its cluster. This allows the radio components of each non-cluster-head node to be turned off at all times except during it's transmit time, thus minimizing the energy dissipated in the individual sensors. Once the cluster-head has all the data from the nodes in its cluster, the cluster-head node aggregates the data and then transmits the compressed data to the base station. Since the base station is far away in the scenario we are examining, this is a high energy transmission.

However, since there are only a few cluster-heads, this only affects a small number of nodes.As discussed previously, being cluster-head drains the battery of that node. In order to spread this energy usage over multiple nodes, the cluster-head nodes are not fixed; rather, this position is self-elected at different time intervals. Thus a set C of nodes might elect themselves cluster-heads at time t1, but at time t1 + d a new set C0 of nodes elect themselves as cluster-heads, as shown in Fig. 6. The decision to become a cluster-head depends on the amount of energy left at the node. In this way, nodes with more energy remaining will perform the energy-intensive functions of the network. Each node makes its decision about whether to be a cluster-head independently of the other nodes

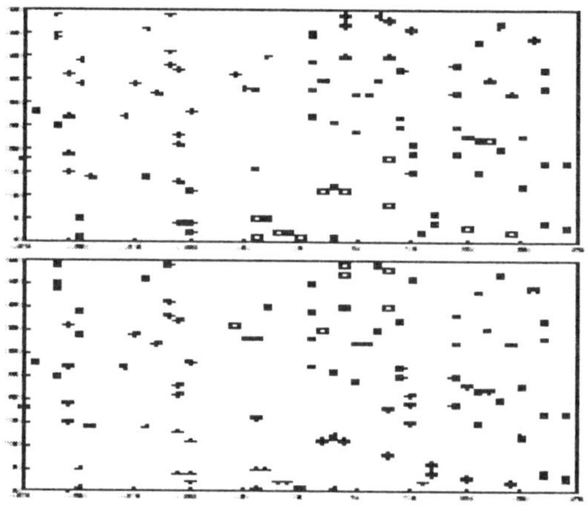

Fig. 5

This will depend on several parameters, such as the network topology and the relative costs of computation versus communication. We simulated he LEACH protocol for the random network shown in Fig. 3 using the radio parameters in Table 1 and a computation cost of 5 nJ/bit/message to fuse 2000-bit messages while varying the percentage of total nodes that are cluster heads. Figure 8 shows how the energy dissipation in the system varies as the percent of nodes that are cluster-heads is changed. Note that 0 cluster-heads and 100% cluster heads is the same as direct communication. From this plot, we find that there exists an optimal percent of nodes ^N that should be cluster-heads. If there are fewer than ^ N cluster heads, some nodes in the network have to transmit their data very far to reach the cluster-head, causing the global energy in the system to be large. If there are more than ^N cluster heads, the distance nodes have to transmit to reach the nearest cluster-head does not reduce substantially, yet there are more cluster-heads that have to transmit data the long-haul distances to the base station, and there is less compression being performed locally.

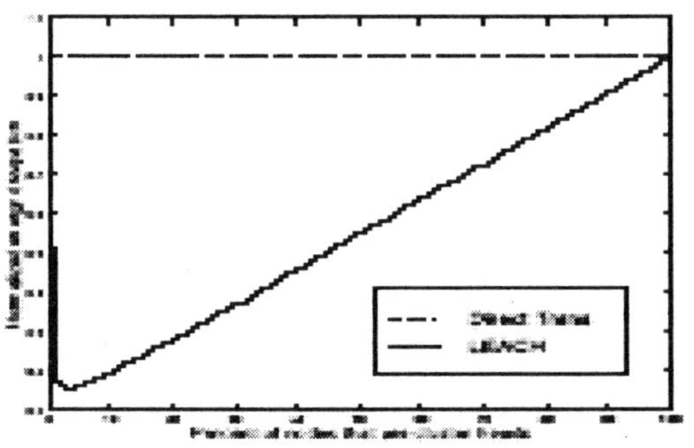

Figure 6. Normalized total system energy dissipated versus the percent of nodes that are cluster heads. Note that direct transmission is equivalent to 0 nodes being cluster heads or all the nodes being cluster heads.

6. References

[1] Wei Ye,John Heidemann and Deborah Estrin "An energy-efficient mac protocol for wireless sensor networks," in *Proceedings of the IEEE Infocom* , New York ,NY ,June 2002 ,pp. 1567-1576.

[2] T.S. Rappaport , "Wireless Communications ,Principles and Practice ," Prentice Hall ,1996.

[3] LAN-MAN Standards Committee of the IEEE Computer Society, *Wireless LAN* medium access control*(MAC) and physical layer(PHY) specification*, IEEE, New York, NY, USA, IEEE Std 802.11-1997 edition, 1997

Intelligent Robotic Control: Operated by Wireless 802.11 wi-fi System

Er. Aishwari V. Talhan[1], Prof. S. A. Raut[2] and Er. S. P. Gawate[1]
[1,3]Student, G. H Raisoni College of Engineering
[2]Asst. Professor, G. H Raisoni College of Engineering
aishtalhan@gmail.com *sitaldhote@yahoo.com* *sachingawate@gmail.com*

Abstract

Aim of this paper is the propose idea to design and create a Robotic control, which will be capable of being controlled wireless technologies. The Robot control is to incorporate two main features. First, It will have the capability of Obstacle detection which will allow the robot to roam freely, without becoming obstructed by any object within path, and secondly it will have capability to follow a path or track. The interface which is to be use to control the robot by an internet web page. Aim of this paper is to design and create a Robotic control, which will be capable of being controlled wireless technologies. The Robot control is to incorporate two main features. First, It will have the capability of Obstacle detection which will allow the robot to roam freely, without becoming obstructed by any object within path, and secondly it will have capability to follow a path or track. The interface which is to be use to control the robot by an internet.

Keywords-*embedded, robotic control*, Wireless

1. Introduction

A robot is defined as a mechanical manipulator that can be programmed according to the needs of the application by the end user, which is used to move materials or tools through planned trajectories to perform the desired task [5,6]. The Robot control is the study of controlling robots. A robot is a mechanical or virtual artificial agent. In practice, it is usually an electro-mechanical system which, by its appearance or movements, conveys a sense that it has intent or agency of its own. A robotic control is something, which has been designed and built by man, carry out processes in a much faster, more precise way. Most everyday objects were manufactured using at least one automated system or robotic device. The aim of this paper is to design and create a robotic vehicle, capable of being controlled wirelessly using 802.11 wi-fi technologies.

The robotic controls will have incorporate two main features.

The first will be the capability of Obstacle detection, which will allow the robot to roam freely, without becoming obstructed by any object within its path.

The second will be the capability to follow a line or track. The interface to be used to control the robot is to be an internet webpage

Some additions to the basic spec have been added so as to create the most advanced robot possible. Add-ons, such as live camera streaming and the ability to control the robot with a mobile phone, However the basic aim remains to design and create a robot, which can be controlled using a webpage via a Wi-fi 802.11 technology connection and which has the previously mentioned add-ons.

The paper has 4 definitive areas:

1] Literature review
2] Designing and Building the architecture
3] Programming and Networking
4] Designing and Building of Sensor Circuits
5] Additional add-ons.

The tools to develop this system,The well-known software MPLAB Simulator by microchip has been widely used in system programming and simulation of control algorithms. Since years ago, Tool to implement this system are PIC 16F877 development board and MPLAB simulator by microchip and PIC Flash programmer. [4].

2. Theory

A fast-growing area in robotics involves interaction with wirelessly. Wireless environment may provide the ideas to make robot behavior more successful and adaptive, including design of sensor hardware, vehicle morphology and control mechanisms based upon microcontroller and neural circuitry. At the same time, robots can be used as hardware models for embedding and testing thus it increases the application of robotic controls and making this approach more and more plausible and productive.

For designing and implementing the intelligent wireless robotic control the proposed review literature is given below.

2.1 Robotic System Features

After examination of the literature review basic system requirements the following list of features for the robotic system will created as certain aims or milestones to which the system should be capable of reaching. Further revisions to the list would take place depending on time required for the main features and due to the capabilities of the tools available.

Basic Features:

1]Servo Motor Driven Robot Chassis
2] Microprocessor Controlled System
3] Wireless technology
4] Obstacle Detection
5] Line Following
6] Online Webpage Interface

Desired Additional Features:

1] Live Camera Streaming
2] Mobile Phone Interface

3. Basic Overview of system

Robotic control is the hardware module which will have the microcontroller PIC 16F877. The working of this module will be basically line following and obstacle avoidance robot which will work as Robotic control. It will also work as transmitter and receiver module so that it will wireless Wi-fi 802.11 enabled control.

Second module will be Computer system from which the command could send and receive to the robotic Control like Move Forward, Reverse, Turn-Left, Turn-right etc.

These both modules will connect to each other by using Internet so that from any where the system can be work easily.

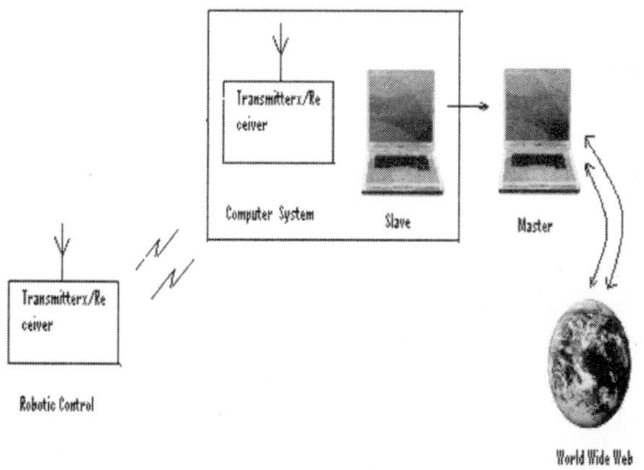

Fig. 1 Basic System Overview

4. Choosing a Microcontroller

The "Brain" for this robotic control will be its microcontroller and several GPIO will be going to connect with the brain. All parts of the system will be going to driven by the microcontroller it self.

4.1 Requirements of the chosen microcontroller

One requirement for this system, which made searching for a suitable microcontroller difficult, that is it should be capable of connecting with a wireless network. Other requirements of the desired processor is that it would have to be able to generate pulses for motors i.e. Pulse Width Modulation (PWM). Also Several GPIO pins would be required to communicate with sensors.

4.1.2 Microcontroller PIC 16F877

Due to system requirements here for this system PIC 16F877 microcontroller. PIC stands for Peripheral Interface Controller. It has wide range of application features because of its attractive features. PIC is embedded controller in real sense. Cause it provides program and use the powerful PIC microcontroller for artificial intelligence & robotics applications. Build & apply simple circuits for autonomous robot navigation with object detection & avoidance, light sensing, sonar range finding, wireless communications, remote control, and more with the PIC robotics development system.

5. The Robot

5.1. The Chassis

What was required for the desired Robot chassis to make this project simple:

1) A platform or tiered platforms with enough space for all hardware.
2) Two servo motors.

The robot chassis has the following features:

1) Sufficient space for all hardware, with two decks.
2) Two pre-calibrated servomotors.
3) Chassis is constructed using easily cut plastic, which is required for securing hardware.

For Example.

Fig. 2 Robot classics

6. The Motors

The two motors supplied with the Robot Kit are GWS Standard Modified Servos. The term modified means that they are calibrated for continuous rotation, once a supply voltage of between 4.8V and 6V. There three pin outs on the motors:

- Red – Supply Voltage (6V)
- Black – Ground
- White – PWM Signal (To control rotation of motor i.e. forward or reverse)

The speed range of the motors is between 0.23 and 0.18 sec/60o. This translates to rpm as follows:

Max speed = 1.08 sec/360o = 1 revolution takes 1.08 seconds.

60/1.08 = 55.56 rpm.

6.1 Power Supplies

The system required two power supplies that will be need for the robot. One, which will supply the motors and circuitry and the other to solely supply the PIC microcontroller hardware as embedded, microprocessor systems, can be very power consuming. The power supply to supply the motors will be of the following spec:

- 12V supply by battery
- 4HA for robot assembly

The PIC consumes relatively low amounts of power even running at 100% capacity.

- IR sensor [100mA] +
- Wireless unit [200mA]+
- DC motor [500mA + 00mA]+
- Control ckt [150mA]

1 A * 12 V + 450 mA * 5V
= 12 + 2.550 = 14.550 W

7. GPIO and Peripherals

Several GPIO would be required to have the desired functionality of the robot. GPIO would be required to send and receive signals to and from the following:

- Two PWM signals to the motors.
- Obstacle Detection sensors
- Line following sensors
- Camera

The PIC Breakout has 40 pins, which can be programmed to be an input or an output. There are also several GND pins on the board. In addition, each pin has an alternate or special function. GPIO are controlled and monitored, by programming the register banks.

7.1 PWM Signals

This use for controlling speed of dc motors.
PWM (0:1) are the "AF2" or second alternate function being output to GPIO. By default, these GPIO pins are set to be an input. This means they will have to be program to their alternate function every time they are required.

7.2. Sensor Inputs

Several GPIO pins will also be required to be program to be inputs, for reading sensor output levels. Input levels are read by the processor and are stored in a "Level Read" register bank, with one level read register for every GPIO.

8. Programming

To control the robot, the registers on the PIC need to be manipulated. This can be done using the Assembly programming in assembly language or the coding can be done in C language. Though the line of code in C language can be large code but its more familiar and more comfortable so here the coding of PIC will be in C language.

In order to write simple programs to control the motors, this would involve creating copies of the original program and changing some numbers in certain structures, in order to change the values of the desired registers.

In order to control the robot using a web page interface. CGI programming would be used. CGI is a form of Internet programming. Links from the main page would link to CGI files which output HTML and execute a program. The main page would link to CGI files which output HTML and execute a program.

9. Interfacing with the Robot

The basic system specification expects that the robot may be controlled via the Internet using a web page. Also the desired specification expects that the robot may be controlled using a mobile phone[6]. This could be done by using a WAP browser the first task will to learn how to implement a network connection between the robot and a computer and control this connection using a webpage.

10. Final Designs

The initial idea for the project is to design and build a robot, which could incorporate, line following and obstacle detection capabilities and be controlled using an 802.11 wireless network[12.13]. Here is a breakdown of the requirements of the final spec.

1]. Tank-Bot robot chassis
2] 2 RC Modified motors
3] 2 x Battery Power Supplies
4] IR Sensors for Line Following and Obstacle Detection
5] Circuitry to interface between peripherals and GPIO.

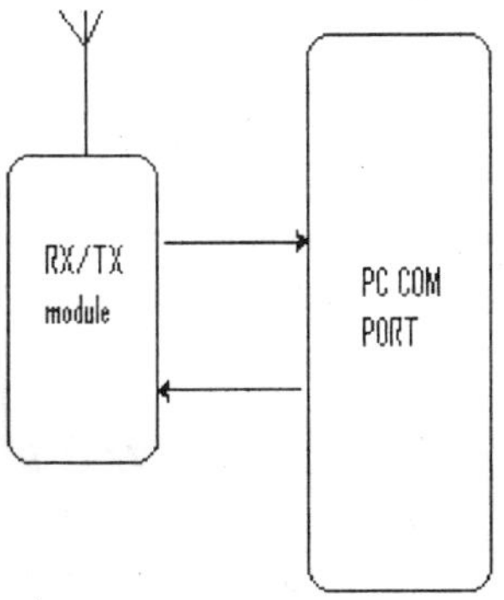

Fig. 3.1 Connections between Computers System and slave

This will be the connection between the computer system and slave as per the basic system overview. The transmitter and receiver module will be a hard ware module, which is assembled at the computer system so that it makes the computer system enabled to the 802.11 wi-fi system.

The Fig. 3.2 is showing the Robotic control, which will be completely hardware system. This hardware will be microcontroller enabled. The microcontroller which will uses the PIC 16F877. It will also include the sensor module. Sensors, which will be used here, are IR sensors, which detect the particular path/ track and it also sense the obstacles. It will also have the transmitter and receiver so that it will do the communication through 802.11 wi-fi technology. It will also have the compactor ICs.

The module of robotic control is shown in the Fig.3.2.

The initial propose idea is to design and build a robotic control which could incorporate line following and obstacle detection capabilities and be controlled using an 802.11 wi-fi wireless network. Here is a breakdown of the requirements of the final spec.

1] TankBot robot chassis
2] 2 RC Modified motors
3] 2 x Battery Power Supplies
4] PIC 16 F877 microcontroller
5] 802.11 technologies.

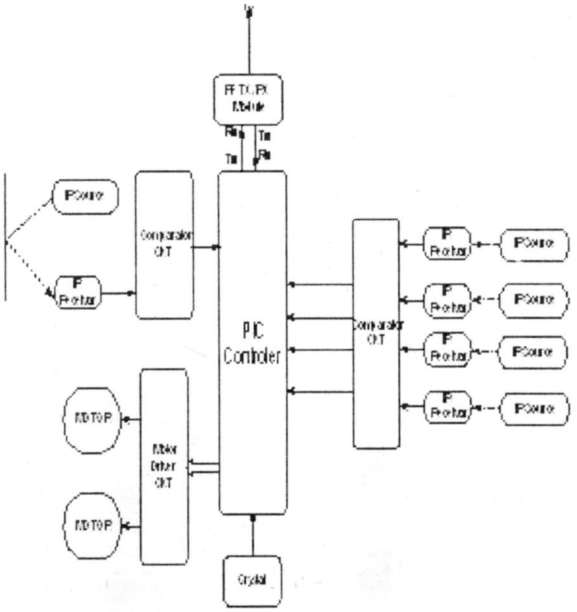

Fig. 3.2 Robotic Control

11. Conclusion

The system should meet all the requirements of the basic spec. This proposed work has to produce a reliable Robotic system control, which can be fully controlled via wireless connection to the Internet, using a Web Page as the Control Interface. After the basic requirement of this system then we can give special add-on to the systems like live camera streaming and navigation through GPS and an application to control the Robotic control through a mobile phone. However, mobile phone control is possible using a WAP browser. The robotic control is just the small module but it can be use in wide way. The more complex functions of this robot implement new technologies in the automotive industry such as Lane Detection and Cruise Control. The possibility that the Robot may be controlled via the web, from anywhere on Earth, is a very powerful asset and one which with future work can become a great marketing front for such Robotic Systems.

12. References

[1] Myke Predko, programming and customizing PIC microcontrollers Third Edition of McGraw-Hill's.

[2] Ajay Deshmukh, Microcontrollers [Theory and Applications] McGraw-Hill's companies computer Engineering series.

[3] Myke Predko. Robot builder's bonanza third edition Mc-Grow Hills.

[4] Myke predko. Myke Predko's PIC Micro Tutorial with the PIC Micro.

[5] J. Craig. Introduction to Robotics-Machanics and Control. Addision-Wesley. 1989

[6] K.H.low.hengWang.Michal Yu Wang "On the Development of a Real Time Control System by Using xPC Target: Solution to Robotic System Control" IEEE international conference on automation science and Engg.. Canada.(PP345-350).2005

[7] H. Asada and J.E. Slotine. Robot Analysisand Control. John-Wiley and Sons. 1987

[8] http://elm-an.org/works/ltc/report.html - line following.

[9] http://www.acroname.com/robotics/info/articles/sharp/sharp.html - obstacle detection.

[10] http://www.rentron.com/Micro-bot/Startup.htm

[11] "Multiple wireless switching units embedded in a switching system", http://www.freepatentsonline.com/5781854.html.

[12] www.retntron.com/pic basic/Ir-chips.htm

[13] www.rentron.com/IR_transreceiver.htm

[14] www.tedlarson.com/robots/amiebot.htm

[15] www.circuitcellur.com/liabrary/print/0404/miller165

MFL3G: An Open Source Mobile Forensics Library for Digital Analysis and Reporting of Mobile Devices for Collecting Digital Evidence An Overview from Windows Mobile OS perspective

Rizwan Ahmed
Post Graduate, Department of Computer Science and Engineering,
G. H. Raisoni Collage of Engineering, Hingna Road, Nagpur- 440016 (MS) India
rizwanmailbox@gmail.com

Abstract

Mobile phone proliferation in our societies is on the increase. Advances in semiconductor technologies related to mobile phones and the increase of computing power of mobile phones led to an increase of functionality of mobile phones while keeping the size of such devices small enough to fit in a pocket. This led mobile phones to become portable data carriers. This in turn increased the potential for data stored on mobile phone handsets to be used as evidence in civil or criminal cases. This paper examines the nature of some of the newer pieces of information that can become potential evidence on mobile phones. It also discusses some of the emerging technologies and their potential impact on mobile phone based evidence. The paper will also cover some of the inherent differences between mobile phone forensics and computer forensics. It also highlights some of the weaknesses of mobile forensic toolkits and procedures. Finally, the paper highlights the development of the proposed MFL3G forensic library for more in depth examination of Windows OS based mobile phones for collection and reporting of digital evidence.

1. Introduction

These guidelines include complete descriptions of the fonts, spacing, and related information for producing your proceedings manuscripts. Please follow them.

Mobile phone proliferation is on the increase with the worldwide cellular subscriber base reaching 4 billion by the year end of 2008 [1]. In India alone, there are 272 million mobile phone subscribers [33] which are growing at a rapid pace. India has surpassed United States of America in number of mobile subscribers to become number 2 in the world which is only next to China [34].

While mobile phones outsell personal computers three to one, mobile phone forensics still lags behind computer forensics.

2. Computer forensics v/s mobile phone forensics

Our paper [35] compares computer and mobile forensics on the following aspects:

- Reproducibility of evidence in the case of dead forensic analysis
- Connectivity options and their impact on dead and live forensic analysis
- Operating Systems (OS) and File Systems (FS)
- Hardware
- Forensic Tools and Toolkits Available

3. Mobile phone as data evidence

This section of the paper will highlight some forensic definitions, principles and best practice guidelines and how they address mobile phone forensics issues. It will also discuss some of the forensic guides that cover mobile phone forensics and mention their shortcomings.

3.1 Definition of Digital Evidence

According to the Scientific Working Group on Digital Evidence (SWGDE), Digital Evidence [18] is "information of probative value that is stored or transmitted in binary form". Therefore, according to this definition, evidence is not only limited to that found on computers but may also extend to include evidence on digital devices such as telecommunication or electronic multimedia devices. Furthermore, digital evidence is not only limited to traditional computer crimes such as hacking and intrusion, but also extends to include every crime category in which digital evidence can be found [19]. However, the Australian Standards HB171 document titled "Guidelines for the Management of IT Evidence" refers to IT Evidence as: "any information, whether subject to human intervention or otherwise, that has been extracted from a computer. IT evidence must be in a human readable form or able to be interpreted by persons who are skilled in the representation of such information with the assistance of a computer program". This definition is lacking as it does not address evidence on digital devices other than a computer [19]. The latter definition shows that not all digital evidence definitions or procedures related to them are updated to address mobile phone evidence. Even the Information Technology Act 2000 (No. 21 of 2000) is not updated to include information about mobile phone evidence [30]. This fact again can be clearly highlighted in view of two big criminal cases [31, 32] in India which involved mobile phone evidence. The following section of the paper will cover some of these definitions and procedures and highlight their shortcomings.

3.2 Principles of Electronic Evidence

According to the United Kingdom's Association of Chief Police Officers (ACPO) Good Practice Guide for Computer based Electronic Evidence, Four principles are involved with Computer-Based Electronic Evidence [20]. They are:

Principle 1: No action taken by law enforcement agencies or their agents should change data held on a computer or storage media which may subsequently be relied upon in court.

Principle 2: In exceptional circumstances, where a person finds it necessary to access original data held on a computer or on storage media, that person must be competent to do so and be able to give evidence explaining the relevance and the implications of their actions.

Principle 3: An audit trail or other record of all processes applied to computer based electronic evidence should be created and preserved. An independent third party should be able to examine those processes and achieve the same result.

Principle 4: The person in charge of the investigation (the case officer) has overall responsibility for ensuring that the law and these principles are adhered to.

When it comes to the recovery of digital Evidence, "The Guidelines for Best Practice in the Forensic Examination of Digital Technology" publication by the International Organization on Computer Evidence (IOCE) considers the following as the General Principles Applying to the Recovery of Digital Evidence [21]:

i. The general rules of evidence should be applied to all digital evidence.
ii. Upon seizing digital evidence, actions taken should not change that evidence.
iii. When it is necessary for a person to access original digital evidence that person should be suitably trained for the purpose.
iv. All activity relating to the seizure, access, storage or transfer of digital evidence must be fully documented, preserved and available for review.
v. An individual is responsible for all actions taken with respect to digital evidence whilst the digital evidence is in their possession.

As with the ACPO principles, principle 2 can not be strictly applied to evidence recovered from Smartphone devices because of their dynamic nature. Furthermore, mobile phone acquisition tools that claim to be forensically sound do not directly access the phone's memory but rather use commands provided by the phone's software and/or hardware interfaces for memory access and thus rely on the forensic soundness of such software or hardware access methods [16]. Therefore, when using such tools, the ability to extract that information in a manner that will not significantly change the mobile phone's memory is not verifiable.

3.3 Mobile Phone Evidence Guides

There are a number of guides that briefly mention potential evidence on mobile phone devices. Our paper [35] lists and compares all of them.

4. MFL3G: An Open Source Mobile forensics library

MFL3G is developed for Windows Mobile OS devices initially which later will cater to all mobile device forensic investigation.

4.1 Purpose

MFL3G is a forensic software framework to assist forensic investigators with their examinations of electronic devices. It is not a "push one button" tool automating the complete forensic analysis process. It assumes trained examiners who know how to investigate a device, but are in need of some assistance to speed up the forensic investigation process and to minimize human errors.

The framework itself does not contain specific functionality for data extraction, decoding, or reporting. It only defines a general examination workflow for investigators and offers an abstract design to developers of so called *plug-ins*. These plug-ins contain the actual investigation methods. From a user's perspective the advantage of using a framework concept is the "learn once apply everywhere" principle. A drawback of this general purpose concept is the initial effort needed to get used to the workflow. The most important reason for introducing a framework concept is to make it easy for software developers to add specific device functionality without troubling them with GUI aspects and repeating common programming tasks. By creating this we hope to stimulate developers and increase the number of automated forensic extraction methods for electronic devices.

4.2 MFL3G architecture and plug-in concept

MFL3G architecture with plug-in concept is depicted in Fig. 1.

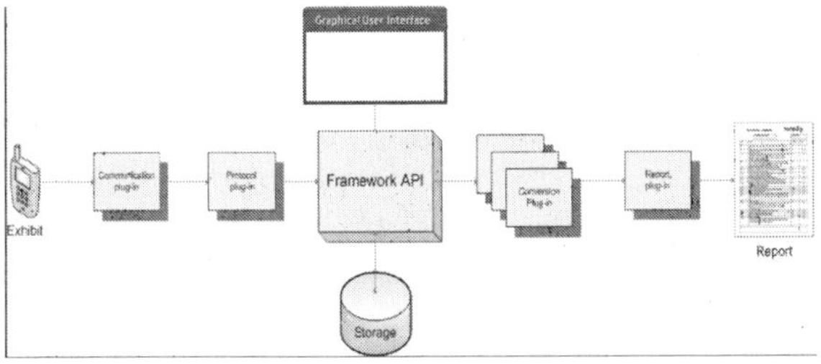

Fig. 1 MFL3G architecture

Each investigation starts with an exhibit containing data and ends with a report containing information originating from the exhibit data and/or related to the investigation process. The investigation process is modeled with four different *plug-in* categories: two for data acquisition and two for data conversion and export. A fifth *Tool* plug-in category has been defined for case-related tasks not directly linked to an exhibitor tasks which need a dedicated user interface. Investigations can be grouped into *Cases.* All data related to a case is stored in one XML formatted file.

4.3 Communication plug-ins

These plug-ins handle the lowest level of communication with devices: setting up and closing connections and sending and receiving raw data. Because of this they directly interface with the external device through a driver or other low-level piece of software. Examples of communication plug-ins are the serial communication plug-in for accessing devices via RS232, Infrared or Bluetooth, and the PC/SC communication plug-in for chip card access via the standardized PC/SC interface. Communication plug-ins can call functions from the framework API for logging and user interface purposes. Because communication plug-ins are specific to a certain type of communication and not to a device, they are not used on their own to read information from a device. Another plug-in that uses the services of a communication plug-in is required to supply the actual data that needs to be exchanged with the device to retrieve useful information from it.

4.4 Protocol plug-ins

Protocol plug-ins are the counterparts of communication plug-ins. They do not have the ability to actually connect to a device, but instead they implement a protocol and use a communication plug-in to actually send and receive information from a device, according to the protocol that they implement. Examples of protocol plug-ins are the AT_ETSI protocol plug-in for extracting data from mobile phones and the SIM protocol plug-in for extracting data from SIM chip cards. Protocol plug-ins can call functions from the framework API for logging, user interface, and storing data from exhibits purposes.

4.5 Conversion plug-ins

A conversion plug-in receives data stored by the framework, originating from exhibits, and is able to convert specific data types. Conversion plug-ins can be chained in order to support sequential decoding (onion peeling). This mechanism is supported to maximize code re-use and avoid complex software maintenance procedures. Examples of conversion plug-ins are the SIM conversion plug-in for converting low level SIM data into report-ready XML data (except for low level SMS TPDUs, they are only "peeled" out of their "SIM skin") and the SMS conversion plug-in for converting SMS PDUs not only originating from SIM cards, but from mobile phones. Conversion plug-ins can call functions from the framework API for logging and user interface purposes and are controlled through a selected *export plug-in.*

4.6 Export plug-ins

Export plug-ins send all data stored by the framework, originating from exhibits, and selected by the user, through the activated conversion plug-ins. If data is converted by a converted one. Once all data conversions have taken place, the export plug-in converts the resulting data to a plug-in specific output format, such as XML, HTML, PDF, or DOC. Most Export plug-ins will be using a template-based conversion method to allow for small changes to be made to the output format without having to recompile or rewrite an entire export plug-in. An example of an export plug-in is the XML export plug-in for generating XML and/or HTML using XSL stylesheets. Conversion plug-ins can call functions from the framework API for logging and user interface purposes (e.g. specifying a template file or an output folder for extracted multimedia data).

4.7 Tool plug-ins

The framework's tool functionality makes it possible to create additional plug-ins to perform investigation-related tasks using MFL3G's rich plug-in interface. Tool plug-ins are basically free-form; there is no strict interface they should adhere to besides the mechanism used by MFL3G to load plug-ins. This allows tool plug-ins to perform all kinds of different tasks. An example of a tool plug-in is the IMEI decoder plug-in for getting brand and type information from mobile phones.

4.8 Evidence file format

MFL3G heavily uses XML for data storage and retrieval. XML is not only used for saving and loading investigation data, but for storing output, configuration, and language data, as well as for internal data structures during conversion and export.

5. MFL3G: a retrospection

MFL3G will be a generic Forensic Software Library which will consist of general examination workflow for investigators and will offer an abstract design to developers with the use of ***plug-ins.*** These plug-ins contain the actual investigation methods. From a user's perspective the advantage of using a framework concept is the "learn once apply everywhere" principle. The most important reason for introducing a framework concept is to make it easy for software developers to add specific device functionality without troubling them with GUI aspects and repeating common programming tasks. By creating this MFL3G hopes to stimulate developers and increase the number of automated forensic extraction methods for mobile devices.

MFL3G will use **XML** as format to store information about the cases containing digital evidence. The XML format will be used so as to be platform independent and in future Webservices can be can be used to inter-operate with other Forensic tools and Libraries. The framework is being developed in Visual Studio 2008 with C#.net 3.5 and in future, it will ported to be platform independent.

MFL3G is based on the mobile forensics methods and processes listed and identified as in our paper [35]. MFL3G will be Forensic Software Library to assist forensic investigators with their examinations of electronic devices. It can not be a "push one button" tool automating the complete forensic analysis process. It assumes that trained examiners who know how to investigate a device for digital evidence, but are in need of some assistance to speed up the forensic investigation process and to minimize human errors. The Generic MFL3G library is being developed for **Windows Mobile OS based devices** to start with. This will be an ongoing project which in future will support all kind of Mobile operating systems and respective devices after customization, defining the scope of which is may be actually out of this document.

5. Concluding remarks and future work

With increased connectivity options and higher storage capacities and processing power, abuse of mobile phones can become more main stream. Mobile phones outsell personal computers and with digital crime rates rising, the mobile phone may be the next avenue for abuse for digital crime. Mobile phones with their increased connectivity options may become a source of viruses that infect computers and spread on the internet. Virus writers typically look for operating systems that are widely used. This is because they want their attacks to have the most impact. When it comes to mobile phones and their operating systems, there seems to be certain operating systems that are dominating the market which makes them a prime candidate for attacks. According to recent studies, phone virus and malware infection rates are expected to increase with newer smart phones [28, 29].

Mobile phone technology is evolving at a rapid pace. Digital forensics relating to mobile devices seems to be at a stand still or evolving slowly. This paper presented a forensic software framework for acquiring and decoding data stored in electronic devices. The current version of the framework along with the available plug-ins can already be used to assist investigators with their manual investigation tasks for Windows Mobile OS based mobile phone devices. To widen the usefulness, new functionality is needed to support more devices and enlarge the completeness of the data extraction and decoding process for supported devices. Additional work is required in the area of testing and evaluation. The core framework functionality needs extensive testing and auditing and for testing specific plug-in setups a general test protocol needs to be defined.

6. References

[1] Paul Doran, MDA (2008). 2008- the year of mobile customers, URL, http://www.themda.org/documents/PressReleases/General/_MDA_future_of_mobile_press_release_Nov07.pdf (Accessed in August 18, 2008).

[2] Canalys (2007). Smart mobile device shipments hit 118 million in 2007, up 53% on 2006, URL, http://www.canalys.com/pr/2008/r2008021.htm, (Accessed in August 18, 2008).

[3] Aljazeera (2005). Phone Dealers in al-Hariri Probe Net, URL, http://english.aljazeera.net/archive/2005/09/200841014558113928.html, (Accessed in August 18, 2008).

[4] Westtek (2008). ClearVue Suite, URL, http://www.westtek.com/smartphone/, (Accessed in August 18, 2008).

[5] Alex Manfrediz (2008). IDC Press Release. IDC Finds More of the World's Population Connecting to the Internet in New Ways and Embracing Web 2.0 Activities, URL, http://www.idc.com/getdoc.jsp?containerId=prUS21303808, (Accessed in August 18, 2008).

[6] FoneKey (2008). URL, www.FoneKey.net, http://www.youtube.com/watch?v=qW8MdpZFKUY, http://www.youtube.com/watch?v=BqJiNvQ3xp8, http://www.youtube.com/watch?v=9eAKvCKanH0, (Accessed in August 18, 2008).

[7] Ducell (2008). URL, www.DuCell.org, (Accessed in August 18, 2008).

[8] Mock, D (2002). Wireless Advances the Criminal Enterprise, URL, http://www.thefeaturearchives.com/topic/Technology/Wireless_Advances_the_Criminal_Enterprise.html, (Accessed in August 18, 2008).

[9] Ayers, R., Jansen, W., Cilleros, N., & Daniellou, R. (2007). Cell Phone Forensic Tools: An Overview and Analysis, URL, http://csrc.nist.gov/publications/nistir/nistir-7250.pdf, (Accessed in August 18, 2008).

[10] Carrier, B. D. (2006). Risks of Live Digital Forensic Analysis. *Communications of the ACM*, 49(2), 56-61. URL, http://portal.acm.org/citation.cfm?id=1113034.1113069&coll=GUIDE&dl=GUIDE, (Accessed in August 18, 2008).

[11] Jansen, W., & Ayers, R. (2004). Guidelines on PDA Forensics, URL, http://csrc.nist.gov/publications/nistir/nistir-7100-PDAForensics.pdf, (Accessed in August 18, 2008).

[12] Symbian (2008). History, URL, http://www.symbian.com/about/overview/history/history.html, (Accessed in August 18, 2008).

[13] Jansen, W., & Ayers, R. (2006). Guidelines on Cell Phone Forensics, URL, http://csrc.nist.gov/publications/nistpubs/800-101/SP800-101.pdf, (Accessed in August 18, 2008).

[14] Zheng, P., & Ni, L. M. (2006). The Rise of the Smart Phone. *IEEE Distributed Systems Online*, 7(3), art. no. 0603-o3003.

[15] Espiner, T. (2006). Mobile Phone Forensics 'Hole' Reported, URL, http://news.zdnet.co.uk/hardware/0,1000000091,39277347,00.htm, (Accessed in August 18, 2008).

[16] McCarthy, P. (2005). Forensic Analysis of Mobile Phones. Unpublished Bachelor of Computer and Information Science (Honours) Degree, University of South Australia, Adelaide.

[17] Jansen, W. (2005). Mobile Device Forensic Software Tools. Paper presented at the *Techno Forensics 2005*, Gaithersburg, MD, USA.

[18] SWGDE. (2006). SWGDE and SWGIT Digital & Multimedia Evidence Glossary, URL, http://www.swgde.org/documents/swgde2005/SWGDE%20and%20SWGIT%20Combined%20Master%20Glossary%20of%20Terms%20-July%2020..pdf, (Accessed in August 18, 2008).

[19] Ghosh, A. (2004). Guidelines for the Management of IT Evidence, URL, http://unpan1.un.org/intradoc/groups/public/documents/APCITY/UNPAN016411.pdf, (Accessed in August 18, 2008).

[20] ACPO. (2003). Good Practice Guide for Computer based Electronic Evidence, URL, http://www.acpo.police.uk/asp/policies/Data/gpg_computer_based_evidence_v3.pdf, (Accessed in August 18, 2008).

[21] IOCE. (2002). Best Practice Guidelines for Examination of Digital Evidence, URL, http://www.ioce.org/2002/Guidelines%20for%20Best%20Practices%20in%20Examination%20of%20Digital%20Evid.pdf, (Accessed in August 18, 2008).

[22] USSS. (2006). Best Practices for Seizing Electronic Evidence, URL, http://www.ustreas.gov/usss/electronic_evidence.shtml, (Accessed in August 18, 2008).

[23] NIJ. (2001).. Electronic Crime Scene Investigation: A Guide for First Responders, URL, http://www.ncjrs.gov/pdffiles1/nij/187736.pdf, (Accessed in August 18, 2008).

[24] Keizer, G. (2006). First Mobile Phone Java Trojan on the Loose, URL, http://www.crn.com.au/story.aspx?CIID=35467&r=rstory, (Accessed in August 18, 2008).

[25] CCIPS. (2002). Searching and Seizing Computers and Related Electronic Evidence Issues, URL, http://www.usdoj.gov/criminal/cybercrime/searching.html, (Accessed in August 18, 2008).

[26] Mellars, B. (2004). Forensic Examination of Moblie Phones. Digital Investigation: *The International Journal of Digital Forensics & Incident Response*, 1(4), 266-272.

[27] Becker, D. (2005). Toshiba Reports Battery Breakthrough, URL, http://news.com.com/2061-10786_3-5649141.html?tag=nl, (Accessed in August 18, 2008).

[28] Long, M. (2005). Airborne Viruses: Real Threat or Just Hype, URL, http://www.newsfactor.com/story.xhtml?story_id=12100002P4HM, (Accessed in August 18, 2008).

[29] McAfee Mobile Security Report (2008). URL, http://www.mcafee.com/mobile, (Accessed in August 18, 2008).

[30] The Information Technology Act 2000, India (2000). URL, http://www.legalserviceindia.com/cyber/itact.html, (Accessed in August 18, 2008).

[31] Yahoo News India (2008). The Arushi Murder Case: CBI says it has found the evidence. URL, http://in.news.yahoo.com/32/20080731/1053/tnl-aarushi-case-cbi-says-it-has-found-e_1.html, (Accessed in August 18, 2008).

[32] Helplinelaw (2007). Pramod Mahajan Murder Trial: SMS cannot be valid evidence, says defence. URL, http://news.helplinelaw.com/1207/echo12.php, (Accessed in August 18, 2008).

[33] India-cellular (2008). http://www.india-cellular.com/Market-Share.html (Accessed in August 18, 2008).

[34] IndustryWeek (2008). India hits #2 spot in Cellphone market. URL, http://www.industryweek.com/ReadArticle.aspx?ArticleID=16218 (Accessed in August 18, 2008).

[35] Rizwan Ahmed, R. V. Dharaskar, V. M. Thakare (2008). Mobile Forensics: the study of collecting digital evidence from mobile device. *The proceedings of International Conference of Computer Networks and Security*, pp 246-253.

Performance Analysis of Power Aware Cross Layer Routing Protocol for Manet

Rekha Patil[1] , Dr A.Damodaram[2]
[1]Assistant professor, Dept. of Computer Science and Engineering, PDA College of Engineering, Gulbarga
[2]Professor, Dept. of Computer Science and Engineering, J.N.T.University, Hyderabad
rekha.patilcse@gmail.com damodarama@gmail.com

Abstract

Mobile Ad-Hoc Networks (MANETs) are wireless networks consisting of a collection of mobile nodes with no fixed infrastructure, where some intermediate nodes should participate in forwarding data packets. So energy conservation is a critical issue in ad hoc wireless networks for node and network life. This issue is crucial in the design of new routing protocols. To design such protocols, we have to look away from the traditional minimum hop routing schemes. In this paper, we propose a power aware cross layer design to AODV. The discovery mechanism in this algorithm uses Battery Capacity of a node as a routing metric. This approach is based on intermediate nodes calculating cost based on Battery capacity .The intermediate node judges its ability to forward the RREQ packets or drop it. That is it integrates the routing decision of network layer with battery capacity estimation of MAC layer. Simulations are performed to study the performance of power aware cross layer AODV protocol using NS2.the simulation shows that the cross layer protocol improves packet delivery ratio & throughput and nodes energy consumption is reduced by routing packets using energy optimal routes. In summary our design offers a simple but efficient power aware cross layer routing protocol to support routing in AdHoc networks.

Keywords: *Mobile AdHoc networks(MANETS),cross layer design,adhoc on demand distance vector ,energy consumption.*

1. Introduction

The increasing progress of wireless local area networks (WLAN), has opened new horizons in the field of telecommunications. Among the various network architectures, the design of mobile adhoc network (MANET) has attracted a lot of attention [1],[2],[3],[4],[5]and [6] A MANET is composed of a set of mobile hosts that can communicate with one another. No base stations are supported in such an environment and mobile hosts Communicate in a multi-hop fashion. Such networks are needed in situations where temporary network connectivity is required, such as in battlefields, disaster areas, and meetings, because of their capability of handling node failures and fast topology changes. A set of ad hoc routing protocols has been proposed in the IETF's MANET [1] group to ensure the network connectivity. They operate in either proactive or reactive modes. Building such routing algorithms poses a significant technical challenge, since the devices are battery operated.

The devices need to be energy conserving so that battery life is maximized. The shortest path is the most common criteria adopted by the conventional routing protocols proposed in the MANET Working Group. The problem is that nodes along shortest paths may be used more often and exhaust their batteries faster. The consequence is that the network may become disconnected leaving disparity in the energy, and eventually disconnected sub networks. Therefore, the shortest path is not the most suitable metric to be adopted by a routing decision. Other metrics that take the power constraint into consideration for choosing the appropriate route are more useful in some scenarios (e.g. sensor networks).

Research on cross-layer design in ad-hoc networks has recently attracted a significant interest [8][9]. It is concerned with sharing information between various protocol layers. A simple cross layer design between PHY and MAC layers for power conservation based on transmission power control is proposed in [7]

In this paper we propose a simple but efficient approach based on cross layer design that rejects the paths with nodes having less battery power than the specified threshold value. we investigate by implementing needed changes in the route discovery process using cross layer approach in the well known on demand routing protocol AODV, as a case study. but this cross layer design is suitable to implement with all reactive protocols which use a route request/query packets in the route discovery phase. Using NS2, we evaluate the performance of our power aware cross layer design to AODV, which is named as Power Aware Cross Layer AODV (PACL- AODV) in mobile AdHoc networks. The rest of the paper is organized as follows.Section 2 reviews related work, section 3 presents PACL-AODV,We study performance evaluation & numerical results in section 4, finally section 5 summarizes our conclusion.

2. Related Work

Developing core protocols (at different layers, e.g.,MAC and network layers) for MANETs has been an area of extensive research in the past few years. Since most of nodes in MANETs rely on batteries, we experienced the advent of studies to address energy-constraint in MANETs.

In [12], Shu-Lin Wu et al., proposed a new mechanism to reduce power consumption while increasing channel utilization. The approach tries to adapt the power level used by a mobile host to transmit data packets as a function of the relative distance to the target node according to the strengths at which RTS/CTS packets are received. S. Singh and C. S.

Raghavendra [13] proposed the PAMAS protocol, a new channel access protocol for ad hoc networks. PAMAS uses two different channels, separate data and signaling channels. The signaling channel tells the nodes when to power off their RF devices if a packet is not being transmitted nor received. In addition, Wan et al., [14] proposed a routing solution for minimum energy broadcasting dedicated to static MANETs. Laura Feeney presented in [15] a combination of simulation and experimental results showing that energy and bandwidth are substantively different metrics and that resource utilization in routing protocols is not fully addressed by bandwidth- centric analysis. Recently, some routing protocols targeting efficient power utilization have been proposed. Recently some routing protocols to efficiently utilize energy power have been proposed. The MTPR (Minimum Total Transmission Power Routing) [16] was initially developed to minimize the total transmission power consumption of nodes participating in the acquired route. According to [17], the transmission power required is proportional to d^{α}, where d is the distance between two nodes and α between 2 and 4. This means that the MTPR prefers routes with more hops having short transmission ranges to those with fewer hops but having long transmission ranges, with the understanding that more nodes involved in forwarding packets can increase the end-to-end delay. In addition, since the MTPR does not consider the remaining power of nodes, it fails to prolong the lifetime of each host. Furthermore, since schemes trying to reduce only total transmission power do not reflect the nodes' remaining power, some other proposals, like the Min-Max Battery Cost Routing (MMBCR) [18], appeared that consider the remaining power of nodes as the metrics for acquiring routes in order to prolong the lifetime of each node. Finally, C. K. Toh [19] presented the Conditional Max-Min Battery Capacity Routing (CMMBCR) protocol, which is a hybrid protocol that tries to arbitrate between the MTPR and MMBCR. Research on cross-layer design in ad-hoc networks has recently attracted a significant interest. It is concerned with sharing information between various protocol layers. In [12] impact of routing protocols and channel conditions on the link layer ARQ is studied. A simple cross layer design between PHY and MAC layers for power conservation based on transmission power control is proposed in [13] and it has been shown that the amount of power conserved dependent on the accompanying routing protocol.

3. POWER AWARE CROSS LAYER AODV (PACL-AODV)

This section presents the new energy efficient routing algorithm. it is designed to increase the network survivability by maintaining network connectivity & to lead to a longer battery life of terminals. This is in contrast to AODV, which does not consider power but optimizes routing for lowest delay. The PACL-AODV ensures survivability of the network by establishing routes that ensure that all nodes equally deplete their battery power. It is a reactive protocol & is based on the AODV routing protocol described below.

3.1 AODV Protocol

AODV routing protocol is a reactive routing algorithm. It maintains the established routes as long as they are needed by the sources. AODV uses sequence numbers to ensure the freshness of routes.

Route Discovery: The route discovery process is initiated whenever a traffic source needs a route to a destination. Route discovery typically involves a network-wide flood of route request (RREQ) packets targeting the destination and waiting for a route reply (RREP).

1) When a node receives a RREQ packet for the first time; it sets up a reverse path to the source. If a valid route to the destination is available, then, it sends a RREP to the source on the reverse path; otherwise, it broadcasts it to the other nodes.
2) When the destination receives a RREQ, it sends a RREP to the source via the reverse path.

Route Maintenance: Route maintenance is done using route error (RERR) packets. When a link failure is detected, a RERR is sent back via separately maintained predecessor links to all sources using that failed link. Routes are erased by the RERR along its way. When a traffic source receives a RERR, it initiates a new route discovery, if the route is still needed.

3.2 PACL-AODV

Utilizing physical & Mac information for routing purpose is at the heart of cross layer design. The proposed cross layer design is based on sharing the following MAC & physical layer information

1. Transmit power
2. Full charge battery capacity
3. Remaining battery capacity of node at time t.

having access to this, the activity begins with the source node flooding the network with RREQ packets when it has data to send all nodes except the source & destination calculates their link cost C_i [6] using the following formula

$$C(\pi,t) = \sum_{i\in\pi} C_i(t) \quad (1)$$

$$C_i(t) = \rho_i \left(\frac{F_i}{E_i(t)}\right)^{\alpha} \quad (2)$$

where

ρ_i = transmit power of node i
F_i = full charge battery capacity of node i
E_i (t) = remaining battery capacity of node i at time t
α = +ve weighting factor

After computing, a node adds it to the path cost c(π,t). a node before forwarding the RREQ packet learns about its remaining battery capacity & drops the packets when it has a lower battery level than its threshold value ($E_r <= \Theta$).This gives chance for another RREQ that flows through nodes with adequate battery level to result in successful route discovery.

In our, power aware cross layer AODV implementation for simplicity we have a module called power module to which the MAC layer passes the information. The cost is computed in the power module & is made available to the network layer as shown in fig 1.

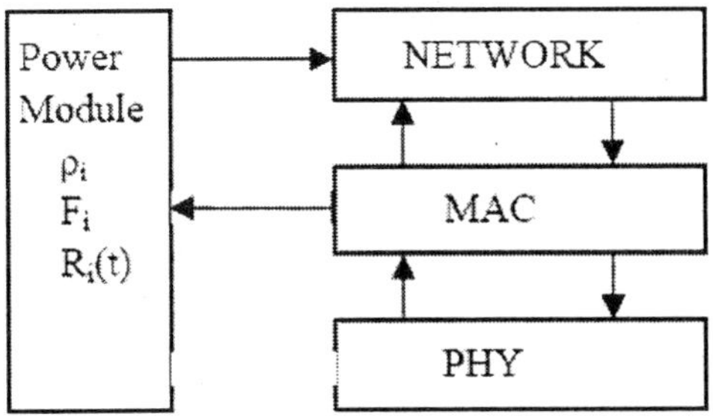

Fig.1 Information sharing in PACL-AODV

The link cost C_i is added to the path cost in the header of the RREQ packet. Hence the route discovery process of PACL- AODV performs the following steps in a node.

1. A intermediate node when receives a RREQ packet it keeps the cost in the header of that packet as min cost
2. If additional RREQ's arrive with the same destination & sequence number, the cost of the newly arrived RREQ packet is compared to the min-cost

Three cases are possible

1. If the new packet has a lower cost and if the intermediate node does not know any valid route to the destination, Min- Cost is changed to this new value and the new RREQ packet is rebroadcast;
2. If the new packet has a lower cost but the intermediate node knows a route to the destination, the node forwards (unicast) a COMPUTE_Cost message. The COMPUTE_Cost calculates this route cost;
3. Otherwise, if the new packet has a greater cost, the new RREQ packet is dropped.

When the destination receives either a RREQ or a COMPUTE_Cost message, it generates a RREP message. The RREP is routed back to the source via the reverse path. This reply message contains the cost of the selected path. The source node will select the route with the minimum cost. This PACL-AODV does not need any major modification in the basic AODV. Handling of RERR packets of basic AODV are left as they are and no other functions of routing layers including communication with Mac & network layers is changed. Only a simple computation module is incorporated that is used in decision making step to decide whether to forward or discard the RREQ packet during route discovery phase.

If there are any other parameters they can be easily included in the cross layer information sharing structure if they are needed at routing layer for effective decision on RREQ forward.

4. Evaluation & Numerical results

The performances of our algorithms are evaluated using NS2 [10]. The simulation consists of a network of 40 nodes confined in a 1000 * 1000 m^2 area. Random connections were established using CBR traffic (at 4 packets/second with a packet size of 1024 bytes). The initial battery capacity of each node is 10 units. This initial energy is progressively reduced by data transmission/reception. When it reaches zero units, the corresponding node cannot take part any more in the communication, and is regarded as died. Each node has a radio propagation range of 250 meters and channel capacity was 2 Mb/s. We consider the simple case when the transmit power is fixed. Network performance of our algorithm is compared to AODV since they are derived from it.

Graphs show the considerable performance improvement of the PACL-AODV over basic AODV.

Throughput: The measure of number of packets passing through the network in a unit of time. This metric shows the total number of bytes that have been successfully delivered to the destination nodes.

Both PACL-AODV and AODV have higher throughput when nodes move at low speeds. And when speed increases all routing protocols suffer a decrease in throughput. Higher speed causes frequent link changes and connection failures. PACL-AODV shows better throughput as it integrates cross layer decision (Graph 1).

Packet Delivery Ratio: The ratio of the data packets delivered to the destination to those generated by CBR sources. This metric illustrates the effectiveness of best effort routing protocols PACL-AODV & AODV for delivering packets to their intended destination. PACL-AODV has better PDR than the reference system (Graph 2).

Overhead: The number of routing packets transmitted per data packet delivered at the destination. Each hop wise transmission of a routing packet is counted as one transmission. The number of control packets for the routing protocol over the number of data packets sent increases with speed (Graph 3).

End-to-End Delay: This includes all possible delays caused by buffering during route discovery latency, queuing delay during other processes, transmission delay at the MAC and propagation delay. There is significant increase in time taken for packets to reach destination (End to End delay) (Graph 4).

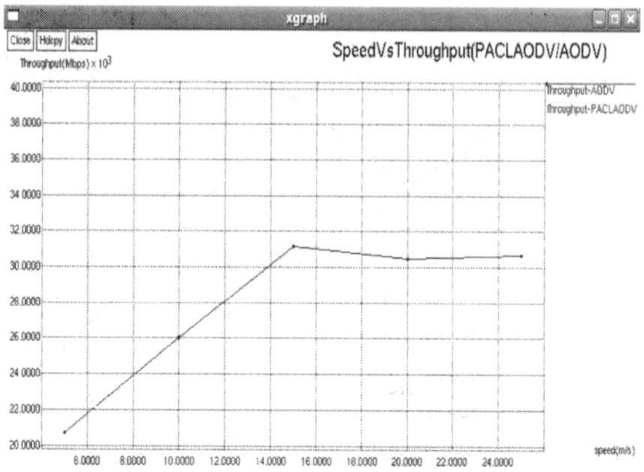

Graph 1:Speed Vs Throughput

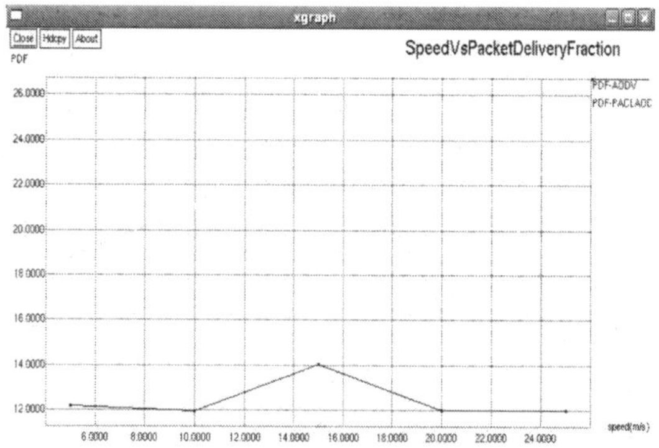

Graph 2: Speed Vs Packet Delivery Ratio.

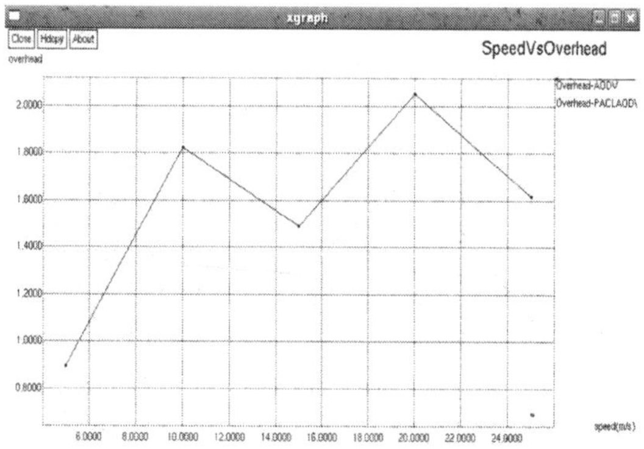

Graph 3: Speed Vs Overhead

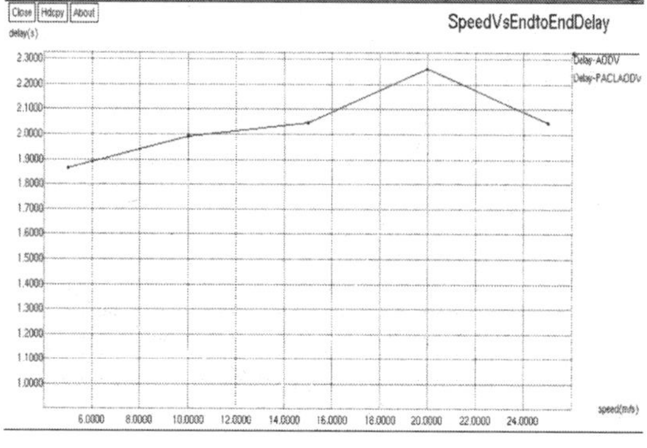

Graph 4: Speed Vs End to End Delay.

Graphs show the significant performance improvement over the reference system. At all the condition of the load the proposed algorithm works better than the reference system.

5. Conclusion

This paper proposed power aware cross layer protocol results in improved throughput, packet delivery ratio and average end-to-end delay performance. Also, significant reduced overhead, both in routing and MAC layers is achieved..PACL-AODV saves the precious lifetime of batteries of low power nodes and other network resources. The low power nodes are identified and rejected in RREQ flooding phase itself and not after facing any RREP transmission failures.

When a node has a lower battery level than its threshold value (R_r <= Θ), any request is simply dropped therefore the source will not receive a RREP message even if there exists a route between the source and destination. In our future work, we will aim to effectively address this problem with simple and efficient cross layer design.

6. References

[1] IETF MANET WG (Mobile Ad hoc NETwork), www.ietf.ora/html.charters/manet-charter.html.

[2] C. E. Perkins, E. M. Belding-Royer, and S. R. Das, "Ad hoc On-Demand Distance Vector (AODV) Routing", *IETF Internet Draft*, draft-ietf-manet-aodv-13.txt.

[3] L. Ouakil, S. Senouci, and G. Pujolle, "Performance Comparison of Ad Hoc Routing Protocols Based on Energy Consumption", *Ambience Workshop 2002*, Torino, Italy, September 2002.

[4] D. B. Johnson, D. A. Maltz, Y.–C. Hu, "The Dynamic Source Routing Protocol for Mobile Ad Hoc Networks (DSR)", *IETF Internet Draft*, draft-ietf-manet-dsr-09.txt.

[5] K. Woo, C. Yu, D. Lee, H. Y. Youn, and Ben Lee, "Non- Blocking, Localized Routing Algorithm for Balanced Energy Consumption in Mobile Ad Hoc Networks", *MASCOTS'01*, Cincinnati, Ohio, August 15-18, pp. 117-124, 2001.

[6] M. Maleki, K. Dantu, and M. Pedram, "Power-aware Source Routing in mobile ad hoc networks", *Proceedings of ISLPED '02*, Monterey, CA, pp. 72-75, August 12-14, 2002

[7] B. Ramachandran and S. Shanmugavel, " A Power Conservative Cross 1400 - AOD Layer Design for Mobile Ad hoc Networks", Information Technology Journal 4(2), pp 125-131, 2005.

[8] S. Shakkottai, T. S. Rappaport, and P. C. Karlsson, Cross- layer design for wireless networks," IEEE Communications Mag., vol. 41, pp. 74{80, Oct. 2003.

[9] Srivastava, V; Motani, M."Cross-layer design: a survey and the road ahead " Communications Magazine, IEEE Volume 43, Issue 12, Date: Dec. 2005, Pages: 112- 119

[10] Network Simulator-2. www.isi.edu/nsnam/ns/.

[11] S. Corson and J. Macker, "Mobile Ad hoc Networking (MANET): Routing Protocol Performance Issues and Evaluation Considerations," RFC 2501, January 1999.

[12] S-L. Wu, Y-C Tseng and J-P Sheu, "Intelligent Medium Access for Mobile Ad Hoc Networks with Busy Tones and Power Control," Proceedings of the International Conference on Computer Communications and Networks, 1999.

[13] S. Singh and C. S. Raghavendra, "PAMAS - Power Aware Multi-Access protocol with Signalling for Ad Hoc Networks," ACM SIGCOMM, Computer Communication Review, July, 1998.

[14] Peng-Jun Wan, Gruia Calinescu, Xiangyang Li and Ophir Frieder,"Minimum-Energy Broadcast Routing in Static Ad Hoc Wireless Netwo rks", Proceedings of IEEE INFOCOMM 2001, April, 2001.

[15] L. Feeney and M. Nilsson, "Investigating the Energy Consumption of a Wireless Network Interface in an Ad Hoc Networking Environment," In Proceedings of IEEE INFOCOM, Anchorage, AK, 2001.

[16] K.Scott and N.Bambos, "Routing and channel assignment for low power transmission in PCS," ICUPC '96, Oct., 1996.

[17] Theodore S. Rappaport, Wireless Communications: Principles and Practice, Prentice Hall, 1996.

[18] S. Singh, M.Woo, and C. S. Raghavendra, "Power-aware with Routing in Mobile Ad Hoc Networks," Proceedings of Mobicom 1998, Dallas, TX, 1998.

[19] C.-K. Toh, "Maximum Battery Life Routing to Support Ubiquitous Mobile Computing in Wireless Ad Hoc Networks," IEEE Communications Magazine, June, 2001.

[20] D.B. Johnson, D.A. Maltz, Y.C. Hu, and J.G. Jetcheva, "The Dynamic Source Routing Protocol for Mobile Ad Hoc Networks," Internet Draft, MANET Working Group, draft- ietf-manet-dsr-04.txt, November 2000,Work in progress.

Temporal Modeling of Node Mobility in a Mobile Ad hoc Network

Jyoti Prakash Singh[1], Paramartha Dutta[2]
[1]Dept of Information Technology, Academy of Technology, West Bengal, India
[2]Dept of Computer & System Sciences, Visva-Bharati University, West Bengal, India
jyotip.singh@gmail.com *paramartha.dutta@gmail.com*

Abstract

Ad hoc network consists of a set of identical nodes that move freely and independently and communicate among themselves via wireless links. The most interesting feature of this network is that that they do not require any existing infrastructure of central administration and hence it is very suitable for temporary communication links in an emergency situation. This flexibility however is achieved at a price of communication difficulty induced due to frequent topology changes. In this article we have tried to identify the system dynamics using the proven concepts of time series modeling. Here we have analyzed variation of the number of neighbor nodes of a particular node over a fixed area and for a fixed number of nodes (i) for different values of speed of nodes (ii) the transmission power and (iii) for different sampling period. The number of neighbor nodes of a particular node behaves as a random variable. Through our analysis we found that this variation can be well modeled by an autoregressive AR(p) model. The values of p are evaluated for different scenario and find that the value is in the range of 1 to 5. Moreover we also investigated the relationship between the speed and the time of measurement of a specific node under various situations.

Keywords: *ad hoc network, mobility modeling, time series analysis, autoregressive modeling.*

1. Introduction

A Multi-hop wireless networks, commonly referred to as ad hoc wireless networks do not require a fixed infrastructure because the mobile node can relay packets to another node without using base stations. The nodes are mobile and changing locations regularly. A node in MANET is moving and its neighborhood is changing constantly with time and place. The number of neighbor nodes of a node is an important information for several applications like routing, topology construction etc. The neighbor count NC of a node Ni is changing constantly. At every instant some new nodes are coming into the transmission range of Ni and some old neighbor nodes are leaving the transmission range of N_i. Say node N_i has NC_t number of nodes at t instant of time. After a small amount of time Δt seconds i.e. at $t+\Delta t$, this number has become $NC_{t+\Delta t}$. $NC_{t+\Delta t}$ is basically a function of the previous neighbor counts NC_t, $NC_{t-\Delta t}$, and so on down to some lags. The reason is that some old nodes have left, some new nodes have come into the transmission range with some old nodes still remaining. How may nodes leave and come is surely a random phenomenon but is dependent on the speed with which node N_i and its surrounding is moving, the transmission range of nodes N_i and its neighbors, and the time interval after which we are taking the readings. If the nodes are moving very slowly or almost stationary then the correlation between old and new value of Neighbor count NC will be very high. In other words, we can define $NC_{t-\Delta t}$ as a function of NC_t, $NC_{t-\Delta t}$, $NC_{t-2\Delta t}$ and so on.

$NC_{t+\Delta t} = f(NC_t, NC_{t-\Delta t}, \ldots NC_{t-p})$ for some integer p such that $1 \le p < \infty$. The autocorrelation of NC also depends on speed, sampling time, and transmission range. If the speed is low, the nodes cover a short distance during a given duration. Most nodes which were neighbor in earlier instant are expected to remain neighbor again for a fixed transmission range. Very few nodes moves out of transmission range and very few new nodes come in. If the speed is increased, during that interval, the node covers a long distance and may be out of the transmission range. Similarly, several other new nodes may come in the range of the node N_i becoming its neighbor. Since large number of nodes are leaving and joining, with very few old neighbors remaining, the correlation between the old neighbor count value NC_{old} and new neighbor count value NC_{new} does not remain as strong as it used to be if nodes were moving slowly.

The transmission range is defines the area with in which the packet sent by a node can be received correctly by another node. This area usually represented by a circle around the sending node. The radius of this circle is proportional to the square root of the power used to send the packet. If the transmission power of a node is low, i.e. the transmission range is quite small then the neighbor count will vary dramatically. The reason is that if this node moves to a dense region, momentarily its neighbor count will be very high, but a small change in location at next instant may leave this node with very less or even zero neighbors. In simple words, we can say that the autocorrelation between NC values will be very low if the transmission power (and hence transmission range) is low. The autocorrelation between NC values increases with increase in the transmission power.

The time after which readings are taken is termed as sampling time in this article. The variation in neighbor count value NC happens due to change of locations by nodes. What distance a node will cover depends on two factors (i) speed and (ii) time. Because *distance = speed X time.* Even for a moderate speed, if the sampling time is increased, several nodes move out of the range of N_i and several other nodes come in the range of N_i. Due to large number of node movement, the correlation with the previous value of NC does not remain very strong. So autocorrelation among NC decreases, as we increase the sampling time.

The rest of this paper is organized as follows. Although very few works have been done using time series modeling in ad hoc network. But what ever has been done and we can get is outlined in Section 2. Section 3 covers our proposal for using autoregressive of order p (AR (p)) model and some discussion on that. In Section 4, we present the simulation results to support our proposal of modeling the network dynamics using AR(p) model. In Section 5 describes the techniques to find the order p of AR(p) model. The forecasted values using the said model are also described in that section. Section 6 we conclude our paper devoting some lines to describe what we have done and some lines to describe how this can be more useful in future.

2. Related Works

Time series [15] modeling is drawing a lot of attention in the modeling of internet traffic, wireless sensor and ad hoc network traffic. Basu and Mukherjee [11] modeled the internet traffic using the AutoRegressive Moving Average Model of order p, and q (ARMA(p,q)) model. Using the model they forecasted the traffic which was generated by a TCP source using FDDI protocol. They also did develop a system to generate synthetic traffic which can be useful for simulation studies of internet traffic and in resource management algorithms.

Chun You and Kavitha Chandra [12] have shown by statistical tests that the aggregate TCP packet arrival process exhibits both non-stationary and nonlinear features. They derived a stationary traffic stream by filtering a subset of the applications exhibiting non-stationary features from the aggregate process. They modeled this filtered traffic process using non-linear threshold autoregressive processes. Their traffic model was found to be in good agreement with real traffic in the packet loss statistics. The model was used in the design of traffic shapers and provided a simple and accurate approach for simulating Internet data traffic patterns.

Borgne et. al. [9] used a set of Time series models to predict the sensors reading at regular interval of time by the sink node. The sink node transmits this data to every sensor. If sensor nodes find that their reading is different form the sink's prediction by a value greater than a threshold δ, then the sensors send their reading to sink. This approach has shown a great saving in communication cost in sensor networks. Banerjee et. al. [1, 2] modeled the system dynamics using birth and death model. When a node enters in the transmission range of a source node say Ni, that was treated as the birth of that the particular node in the Radio Range of the source node. Similarly when a node was going out of the transmission range, it was identified as the death from the Radio Range of the source node.

3. Our Model

As we pointed out in section 1 that the neighbor count NC of a node N_i number is changing with time and is a function of the values of NC at previous instances. In this article we have tried to identify the system dynamics [7] using the proven concepts of time series. A time series is a sequence of observations that are arranged according to the time of their outcome. By recording and analyzing the data of a time series, we can gain a better understanding of the data generating mechanism and make a prediction of future values. The main characteristic of a time series is that the data are often governed by a trend and they have cyclic components. An important part of the analysis of a Time series [15] is the selection of a suitable model (or class of models) fitting that data. Naturally, more appropriate is the model selection, better expected is the prediction. The neighbor count NC of a node Ni is a parameter varying with time and are a suitable candidate to be considered for such modeling. The relation of NC with the previous values is also supported with the corrlelogram of nodes. The plot of experimental data confirms that the autocorrelation is very high at initial lags and is constantly decreasing with higher lags. This implies that the current neighbor count NC is a function of values of NC on previous instances with a white noise whose mean is zero and variance σ^2. This behavior of data can be represented well with the help of an AR(p) model [15]. An AR(p) model can be defined as

$$r_t = \phi_0 + \phi_1 r_{t-1} + \phi_2 r_{t-2} + \cdots \phi_p r_{t-p} + a_t$$

where p is a non-negative integer and $\{a_t\}$ is assumed to be a white noise series with mean zero and variance σ^2. This model says that the past p values r_{t-i}

(i = 1,..., p) jointly determine the conditional expectation of r_t given the past data. The series, we obtained through our experiment is stationary since it fulfils the requirements of stationarity[15] which are given below.

(a) $E(r_t) = \mu$, which is a constant, and

(b) $Cov(r_t, r_{t-j}) = \gamma_j$, which only depends on j, not on time t

Since the series is stationary, the mean and the variance of this series can be given by the formulae provided that the denominator is not zero.

$$E(r_t) = \frac{\phi_0}{(1-\phi_1-\phi_2-\cdots-\phi_p)}$$

And the autocovariance are given by

$$\gamma_j = \begin{cases} \phi_1\gamma_{j-1} + \phi_2\gamma_{j-2} + \cdots\phi_p\gamma_{j-p} & for\ j=1,\ 2,\ 3...p \\ \phi_1\gamma_1 + \phi_2\gamma_2 + \cdots\phi_p\gamma_p + \sigma^2 & for\ j = 0 \end{cases}$$

The associated polynomial equation of the model, called characteristic equation, is given by

$$x^p - \phi_1 x^{p-1} - \phi_2 x^{p-2} - \cdots - \phi_p = 0$$

The other condition of stationarity is that if all the characteristic roots of this equation are less than unity in modulus, then the series $\{r_t\}$ is stationary. The characteristics equation gives an indication that the plot of the autocorrelations, called as autocorrelation function, (ACF) of AR(p) model would show a mixture of damping sine and cosine patterns and exponential decays depending on the nature of its characteristic roots. This is totally in conformity with our experimental data. One major hurdle in representing data using AR(p) model is finding the proper value of p. In our case we have used the partial autocorrelation function (PACF) to find an idea about the order of AR and then Akeike Information Criterion (AIC) is used to confirm that value of p.

3. Simulation and Results

We have used Omnet++ for node mobility simulation and Minitab is used for the analysis of the results.

3.1 Simulation Setup

The node mobility and traffic generations are simulated using Omnet++ 3.3 discrete event system simulator with 131 mobile nodes. The nodes are moving with normal (Gaussian) distribution. Assumed Gaussian distribution is used because of its simplicity and widespread use in academy circle. The analysis under different mobility models [3, 4, 5, 6, 8] are in progress. The nodes are distributed over an area of 600 X 600 m^2. The speed of the node movement is varied between 10 to 100 m/s. The transmission power is varied from 1000 m to 90000m. The actual coverage area is square root of the transmission power. The number of neighbors of each node is studied at 0.5 hr, 1 hr, 1.5 hr and 2 hr for each speed variation. No standard network protocol has been used for the total simulation. The results are then taken to Minitab version 14 for carrying out necessary statistical analysis.

3.2 Analysis under variable speed for a fixed sampling rate.

Our first experiment deals with finding the relationship between the autocorrelation of NC and speed of moving nodes. For our experiment, we have assumed that all nodes are moving with the equal speed and readings are taken after 1 sec. At low speed, NC shows a nice autocorrelation with several previous lagged values. But as the speed is increased, the nodes starts leaving and joining region rapidly and so the autocorrelation with the previous values starts diminishing.

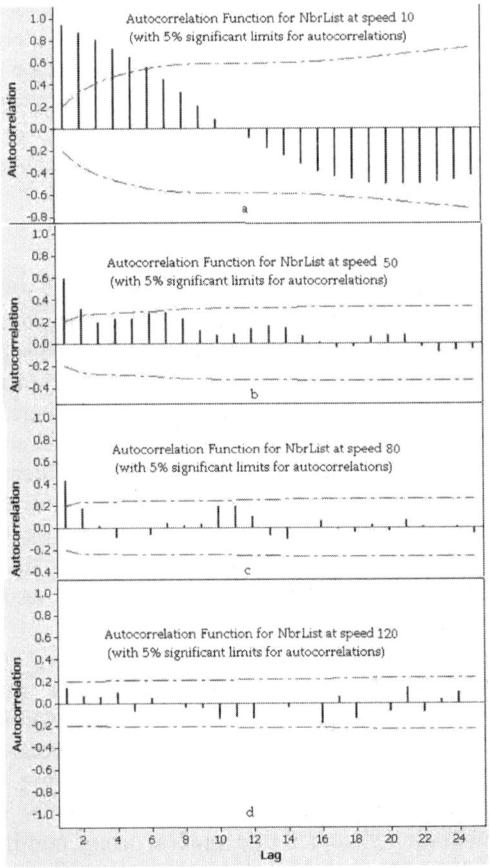

Fig. 1 Variation of autocorrelation between NC values with speed

We calculated the autocorrelations among NC data for nodes moving with the speed of 10. The speed was varied from 10 to 120 with an increment of 10. The sample is taken after 1 sec in each case. Some of the sample correlations at speed 10 m/s, 50 m/s, 80 m/s, and 120 m/s are shown in figure 1. As evident from figure 1.a that the NC values for nodes moving with the speed of 10m/s have shown nice autocorrelation with high peaks at initial lags but decreases at higher lags. But when the speed has gone to 120 m/s, then no significant autocorrelation exists as evident from figure 1.d.

3.3 Analysis under constant speed for variable sampling rate.

Our second experiment is concerned with the variation of number of neighbors with the time at which we are recording the data, called as sampling time. Since the nodes are moving very slowly at low speed, the neighborhood is also changing very slowly. In this case if we sample data very frequently, we ought to get nearly similar number of neighborhood.

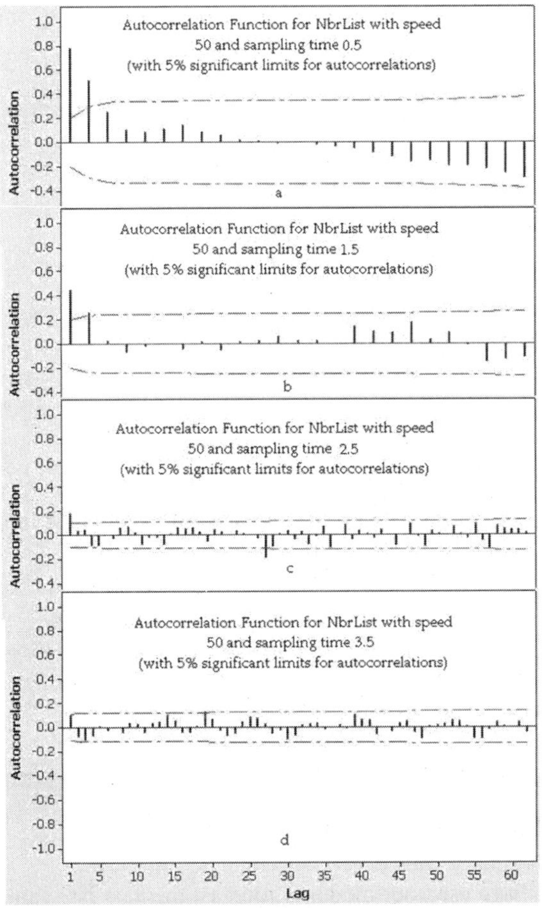

Fig. 2 Variation of autocorrelation between NC values with sampling time

For this experiment, we have sampled the network for a time period of 0.5sec to 5sec with a sampling peıiod of 0.5sec. For our data we have fixed the speed to 50m/sec and the sampling time was varied from 0.5 sec to 5 sec in increments of 0.5sec. The autocorrelation diagram ACF is shown in figure 2 for each case. With sampling time of 0.5 sec, we get an ACF which is sinusoidal in nature having higher autocorrelation value at initial lags. But for sampling time of more than 3.5, no autocorrelation value is significant enough as evident from ACF shown in figure 2.d.

3.4 Analysis under variable speed and variable sampling rate

Our next experiment was concerned with the combined effect of speed and sampling time on the autocorrelation of neighbor count NC values. The speed was varied from 10m/sec to 100m/sec in increments of 10m/sec and the sampling time was varied from 0.5sec to 5sec in increment of 0.5sec. The findings are listed in table 1.

Table 1. Changes in autocorrelation with time and speed

Speed	Sampling Time → 0.5	1	1.5	2	2.5	3	3.5	4	4.5	5
10	Y	Y	Y	Y	Y	Y	Y	Y	Y	Y
20	Y	Y	Y	Y	Y	Y	Y	Y	Y	Y
30	Y	Y	Y	Y	Y	Y	Y	Y	Y	Y
40	Y	Y	Y	Y	Y	Y	Y	Y	Y	Y
50	Y	Y	Y	Y	Y	N	N	N	N	N
60	Y	Y	Y	N	N	N	N	N	N	N
70	Y	Y	Y	N	N	N	N	N	N	N
80	Y	Y	N	N	N	N	N	N	N	N
90	Y	Y	N	N	N	N	N	N	N	N
100	Y	Y	N	N	N	N	N	N	N	N
110	Y	N	N	N	N	N	N	N	N	N
120	N	N	N	N	N	N	N	N	N	N

As evident from table 1 that the neighbor count NC data moving with speed of 10m/sec has significant autocorrelation for each sampling period i.e. from 0.5 to 5. When the speed becomes 50, the autocorrelations are significant only up to the sampling period of 3.5 but after that interval, no significant autocorrelation is found. This behavior is expected because the distance covered by a node is product of speed and time. So for a moderate speed, if the time is increased several nodes move out of range and similarly several nodes move in thereby manifesting lower autocorrelation with the values at previous lags.

3.5 Analysis under variable radio range

The radio range is determined by the transmitting power of a node. For our experiment, we have defined the range as the square root of the transmitting power. We have varied the transmitting power form 1000 to 90000. For low transmitting power, no significant autocorrelation exists between nodes because few nodes will be in the transmission range. A node moving very slowly will also change neighborhood rapidly. So no correlation exists. But as we increase the transmitting power, the autocorrelation between the nodes starts exhibiting a sinusoidal pattern with high peaks at the start as shown in figure 3. From figure 3.a, we can see that the autocorrelation is not significant for neighbor count NC data when the transmission power is 1000. It becomes significant only after the transmission power is beyond 9000.

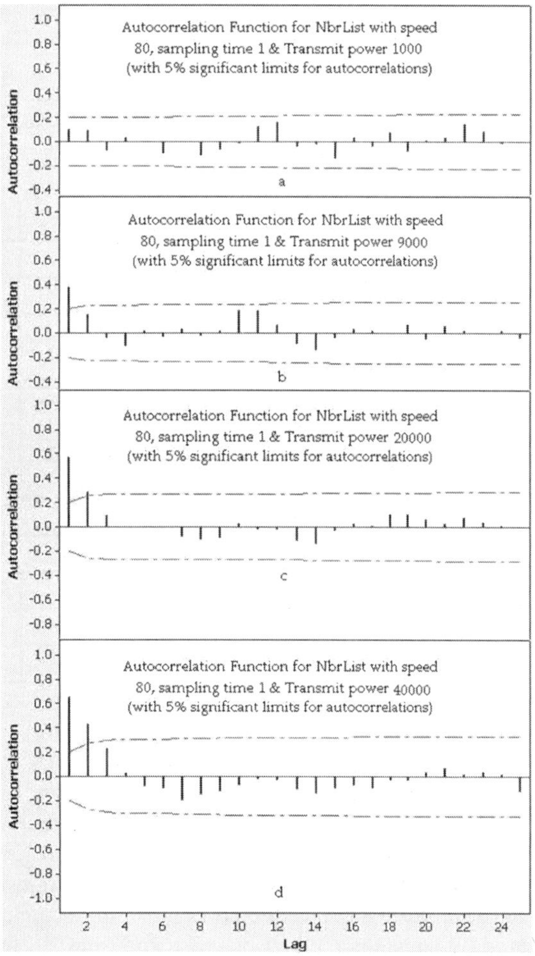

Fig. 3 Variation of autocorrelation between NC values with transmission speed

4. Results

As evident from the previous simulation that within a threshold value of speed, sampling period, and transmission power, the neighbor count NC data shows a nice autocorrelation with high peaks at initial lags and decreases at higher lags. This property of data confirms that with in that threshold, it is justified to model the neighbor count NC data with Autoregressive model. Autoregressive modeling requires the order p of the model to be specified. In the next section we outline the process of ascertaining the order of AR. The chosen AR(p) model is then used to forecast the next value of neighbor count.

4.1 Finding the order of AR

To calculate the order of AR process, we have to find the PACF, which gives us an indication of probable value of p. Then we have used AIC to confirm on that. PACF and table 2 of AIC values are given below. The PACF in figure 4 tells us that this data can be modeled with an AR(2) process. When we find the AIC values, the value is smaller for 3, but the difference is very low. So we may stick with 2 for p value.

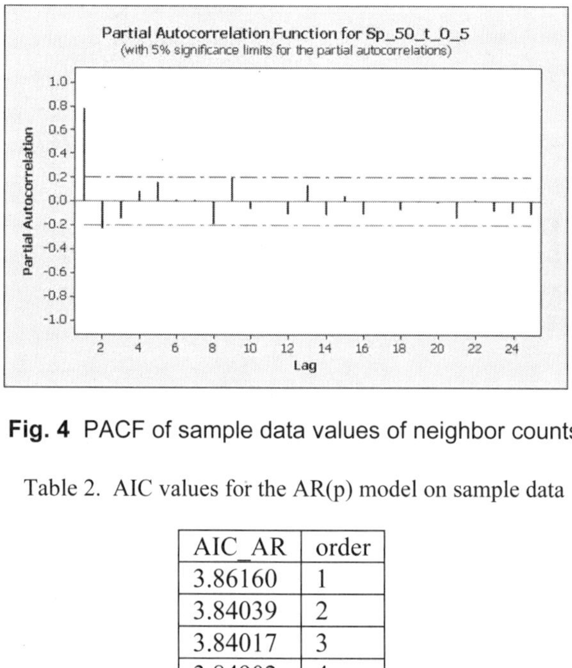

Fig. 4 PACF of sample data values of neighbor counts

Table 2. AIC values for the AR(p) model on sample data

AIC_AR	order
3.86160	1
3.84039	2
3.84017	3
3.84902	4

4.2 Forecasting with AR(2)

We have used our model to forecast the next NC value. For forecasting we have used an AR(2) model. The comparison of forecasted and original data obtained from our experiment is shown in figure 5. It is evident from the figure 5 that the actual data and the forecasted data value are very close to each other.

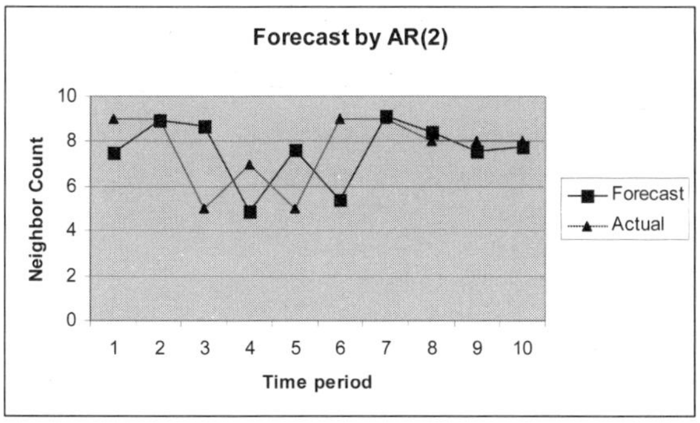

Fig. 5 Forecast value made by AR(2) model

5. Conclusion

In this paper, we have modeled the temporal neighbor distribution of a node using a popular Time series [15] model Autoregressive AR(p) model. We found through our experiment that node distribution under a threshold value of speed, range and sampling time are well correlated and can be represented by AR(p) model. But above a threshold value, the autocorrelation of node distribution does not remain significant enough. The thresholds for different parameters are also determined in this article. We have also predicated the number of neighbor nodes in future time frames and found that the prediction is close enough to the real value. These predicated values of neighbor nodes can be used for different application which relies on number of neighbor nodes like multi-path routing, topology construction, traffic prediction etc. Although, in this article we have used the predicted value of neighbor nodes but we are in the process of using it for other purpose as well.

6. References

[1] A.Banerjee, K. Majumder, P. Dutta, K. Mondal, "Implementation of the behavior and structure of the multihop mobile environment as a pushdown automata and birth-and-death based statistical model", in Proceedings of MobiComNet-2004.

[2] A. Banerjee, P. Dutta, "A Birth and Death Based Mathematical Model for Tracking Mobile Nodes in a Multihop Environment", in Proceedings of BIG-2004, June.2004.

[3] Denizhan N. Alparslan, Khosrow Sohraby, "A Generalized Random Mobility Model for Wireless Ad hoc Networks and Its Analysis: One Dimensional Case", IEEE/ACM Transactions on Networking (TON), Vol. 15, No. 3, 602-615, June 2007.

[4] Qunwei Zheng, Xiaoyah Hong, Sibabrata Ray, "Recent Advances in Mobility Modeling for Mobile Ad hoc Network Research", in Proceedings ACM Southeast Regional Conference, 70-75, 2004.

[5] Christian, Bettstetter, " Topology Properties of Ad hoc Networks with Random Waypoint Mobility", ACM SIGMOBILE Mobile Computing and Communication Review, Vol. 7, No. 3, 50-52, July 2003.

[6] Tracy Camp, Jeff Boleng, Vanessa Davies, " A Survey of Mobility Models for Ad hoc Network", Special issue on Mobile Ad hoc Networking: Research, Trends and Applications, Vol. 2, No. 5, pp. 483-502, 2002.

[7] V.R. Syrotiuk, K. Shaukat, Y.J. Kwon, M. Kreatzl, J. Arnold, " Application of a Network Dynamics Analysis Tool to Mobile Ad hoc Networks", in Proceedings of ACM, 36-43, 2006.

[8] S. Gowrishankar, T.G. Basavraju, Subir K. Sarkar, "Effect of Random Mobility Models Pattern in Mobile Ad hoc Networks", International Journal of Computer Science and Network Security, Vol. 7, No. 6, June 2007.

[9] Yann-Aël Le Borgne and Silvia Santini and Gianluca Bontempi," Adaptive Model Selection for Time Series Prediction in Wireless Sensor Networks" International Journal for Signal Processing, vol. 87, no. 12, pp 3010--3020, 2007

[10] Herbert, D., Modelo-Howard, G., Perez-Toro, C., and Bagchi, S.. Fault tolerant ARIMA-based aggregation of data in sensor networks. IEEE International Conference on Dependable Systems and Networks. 2007

[11] Basu, S. Mukherjee, A. Klivansky, S.," Time series models for internet traffic" Proceedings IEEE INFOCOM '96 Vol. 2, pp 611-620, Mar 1996

[12] Chun You and Kavitha Ch," Time series models for internet data traffic", In Proceedings of the 24th Conference on Local Computer Networks LCN 99, pp 164—171, 1999

[13] Davis, J.L.; Chandra, K.; Thompson, C.," Nonlinear time-series model for VBR video traffic", IEEE Conference on Local Computer Networks 2000 pp 678 – 683.

[14] ue Wang and Jun-jie Ma and Liang Ding and Dao-wei Bi", Robust Forecasting for Energy Efficiency of Wireless Multimedia Sensor Networks", SENSORS, Vol. 7, pp 2779-2807, 2007.

[15] J. Hamilton, Time Series Analysis, Princeton University Press, Princeton, NJ, 1994.

Traffic Aware Multipath Routing Protocol for Adhoc Networks

Sujatha P. Terdal[1] , Dr V.D Mytri[2] and Dr. A Damaodaram[3]
[1]Asst Prof, Dept. of CSE PDA College of Engineering, Gulbarga
[2]Principal, GND College of Engineering, Bidar
[3] Professor, Dept. of CSE JNTU college of Engineering, Hyderabad
suja_pst@rediffmail.com vdmytri@gmail.com damodarama@gmail.com

Abstract

Mobile Adhoc networks (MANETs) are characterized by frequent topology changes , multi-hop connectivity ,mobile nodes and scarce resources like bandwidth ,memory and power. Current unipath routing protocols for these networks incur increased control overhead due to unrealiability of wireless channel and unconstrained mobility of nodes. Multipath routing is an attractive alternative to minimize control message overhead by providing secondary path in the event of link failure of the primary path. In this paper an effort is made to improve further , the performance of the multipath routing protocol by selecting less congested alternate paths that avoids network hotspots. Simulation study is conducted using ns-2 to compare this enhanced multipath routing protocol with its unipath counterpart.

1. Introduction

MANETs are gaining increasing popularity due to wide ranging wireless applications supported on it. They can be deployed instantaneously without any infrastructure . It consists of wireless mobile nodes which can act both as a node and router. These mobile nodes are constrained by limited bandwidth and battery power . Hence routing is a challenging task. On demand routing is the most favoured routing technique in ad hoc networks. Routes are computed only when needed instead of pro-active route calculation. The source floods RREQ packet to search the destination . This method of route discovery ensures that path to destination includes only active links. But on demand routing protocols cannot satisfactorily support multimedia applications as they have stringent QOS requirements which means that these protocols should further be enhanced .

Maintaining multiple routes between source and destination has been proposed as a performance enhancement to these already existing on demand routing protocols. Whenever an ongoing data transmission fails due to link failure , source can continue with the data transmission along the next alternate route that is already computed. This avoids initiating a new route discovery process and thereby reduce control overhead. Apart from this other forms of Multipath Routing has been explored to provide load balancing , fault tolerance and higher aggregate bandwidth. Load balancing can be achieved by spreading the traffic along multiple routes. This can alleviate congestion and bottle necks. From a fault tolerance perspective, multipath routing can provide route resilence. Like any other unipath routing protocols multipath extensions of AODV & DSR compute alternate paths that are shortest paths making some areas of network more prone to congestion. To correct this we suggest a modification to route discovery phase of DSR called Traffic Aware Multipath routing protocol (TAMR) that computes alternate paths which are less congested .Our mechanism prevents concentration of data paths via a node due to shortest delay path metric.

The remainder of this paper is organized as follows. section 2 presents review of literature, section 3 explains the protocol, performance analysis by simulation is given in section 4 & 5 and section 6 concludes.

2. Review of literature

The concept of multipath routing has been used in different contexts . Traditional circuit switched telephone networks used a type of multipath routing called alternate path routing[1] .This was proposed to decrease the call blocking probability and increase overall network utilization . [2] suggests Dispersity Routing which shows initial approach to multipath routing. The application of multipath concept in MANETs is very useful keeping in view the unreliability of the wireless channel and constantly changing topology. On-Demand routing protocols for MANETs like Dynamic Source Routing (DSR) protocol and Ad Hoc On Demand Routing protocol(AODV) are extended to support multipath routing and thus solve the problems of unipath routing. [3] presents an intelligent multipath technique for the DSR protocol. This study demonstrates that multipath techniques always perform better than single path routing. Alternate paths computed by a multipath

Routing protocol may be node disjoint or link Disjoint. Split Multipath Routing proposed in [4] focuses on building and maintaining maximally disjoint paths. Multiple routes of which one is the shortest delay path are discovered on demand. Data traffic is split into multiple routes to avoid congestion and to use network resources efficiently. This scheme uses 2 routes for each session.[5] is an extension to AODV called Ad Hoc on-Demand Multipath Distance vector (AOMDV) protocol that finds loop free link disjoint paths .Primary design goal behind AOMDV is to provide efficient fault tolerance in the sense of faster and efficient recovery from route failures in dynamic networks. Simulation study conducted for AOMDV shows significant reduction in delay and overall routing performance than AODV in variety of mobility and traffic conditions.

Various studies have been performed on the use of Multipath Routing to support QOS. One such study is MP-DSR [6] where DSR is enhanced to provide routes with increased stability and reliability . Here the protocol forwards outgoing packets along multiple paths that are subject to a particular end-to-end reliability requirement. There have some work done on distributing traffic in to multiple simultaneously in ad hoc networks. Multiple Source Routing(MSR)[7] is presented as a method of distributing the traffic onto multiple paths using weighted round-robin heuristic based scheduling strategy. It uses the round trip time as the criterion to distribute the traffic.

3. Traffic Aware Multipath routing protocol (TAMR)

TAMR is a source routing protocol based on DSR. TAMR computes multiple node disjoint alternate paths that are less congested. One metric to measure the level of congestion at a node is the instantaneous transmission queue length. If a node has many packets backlogged , then choosing such a node to forward packets would obviously increase the packet latency and may even drop packets due to a limit on the queue length.

TAMR's route discovery procedure uses this congestion measurement metric to avoid selecting such congested nodes in a data path as against normal shortest path metric.

DSR's route discovery phase is modified to measure congestion and generate node disjoint paths .TAMR's source node starts with flooding of RREQ packet to discover new route in the same way as DSR. Intermediate nodes are prohibited from replying to RREQ packet by disabling the route cache so that multiple routes are generated. When this RREQ packet reaches the destination , it sends RREP packet to the source. While RREP travels to the source node transmission queue length at the each intermediate node is checked. If the length is greater than the threshold then the intermediate node will not forward the RREP packet thus avoiding busy nodes.

4. Performance Evaluation

To evaluate the performance of TAMR we compare the simulation results from our protocol against DSR.Ns-2 simulator is used.

N mobile nodes are moving in a square area of size 1500 X 300 m. Mobility model assumed is Random way point. Here initially nodes are placed in random positions inside the square.Nodes choose a random destination and move to that destination with a constant speed. Mobile nodes have a transmission range of 250 m.Channel bandwidth assumed is 2Mbps.MAC protocol used is 802.11 DCF. It allows mobile nodes to share the wireless channel in an ad hoc configuration. Transmission queue length assumed to be 60 packets. Packet size is 512 bytes. Traffic model assumed is CBR. Following metrics were considered for evaluating the performance of our protocol.
packet delivery fraction, normalized routing load and throughput.

5. Results and Analysis

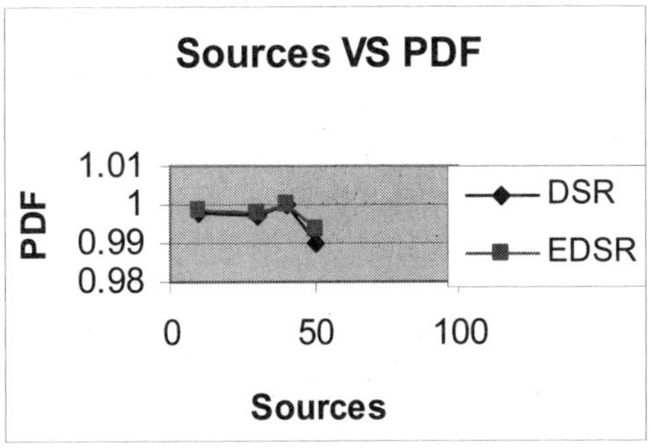

Fig.1 PDF DSR & TAMR(EDSR)

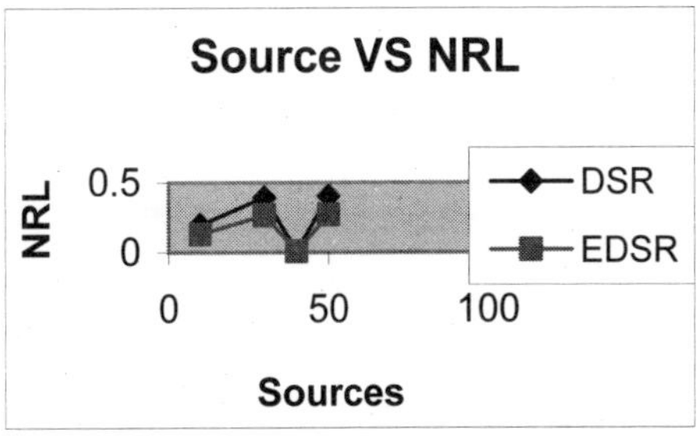

Fig. 2 NRL of DSR & TAMR(EDSR)

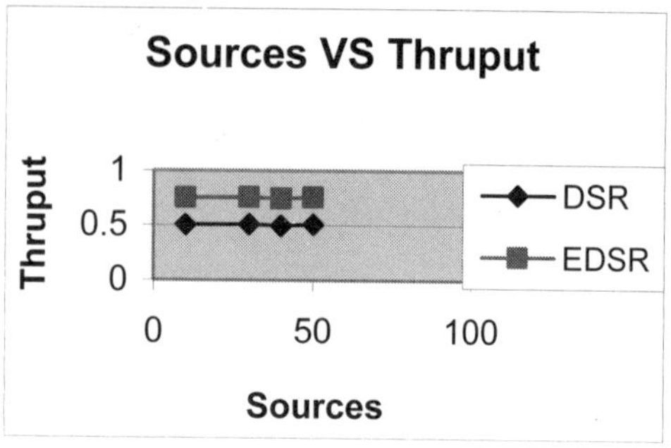

Fig. 3 Throuhgput of DSR & TAMR(EDSR)

Fig. 1 shows Packet delivery ratio achieved by this protocol which is only marginal, but shows reduction in the normalized routing overload improvement in the throughput .

6. Conclusion

This paper presents a node disjoint multipath DSR protocol (TAMR) which avoids busy nodes in its routing path. This uses transmission queue length as the congestion metric to measure congestion. This shows improved packet delivery fraction, normalized routing overload and throughput

7. References

[1] Stephen Mueller, Rose P. Tsang, Deepak Ghosal : Multipath routing in Mobile Ad hoc Networks: Issues and challenges

[2] N.F. Maxemchuk : Dispersity Routing , Proceedings of IEEE ICC '75 pp. 41.10-41.13, San Francisco, CA, USA, June 1975.

[3] Asis Nasipuri , Samir R Das: On-Demand Multipath Routing for Mobile Ad Hoc Networks.

[4] S.J. Lee , M.Gerla: Split Multipath Routing with Maximally Disjoint Paths in Ad Hoc Networks ICC 2001.

[5] Mahesh K Marina , Samir R Das: On-Demand Multiipath Distance Vector Routing for Ad Hoc Networks.

[6] Roy Leung , Jilei Liu, Edmond Poon, Ah-Lot Charles Chan, Baochun Li: MP-DSR A QOS-aware Multipath Dynamic Source Routing Protocol for Wireless Ad-Hoc Networks.

[7] L.Wang et al : Multipath Source Routing in Wireless Ad Hoc Networks Canadian Conf. Elec. Comp. Engineering Vol 1 2000, pp 479-83.

Session – 8
Applications of Science and Engineering

Advancements in Power System Protection and Control

Mr. Bhushan V. Patil[1], Mr. Kalpesh V. Joshi[2], Mr. Kiran H. Sonawane[3]
[1]Bhopal, 49, Gayatri Colony, Shirpur,
patilbhushan007@gmail.com
[2]Amravati, 7, Shivaji Nagar, Wadibhokar Road, Dhule,
kalpesh_vj@rediffmail.com
[3]Aurangabad, 16, A, Wankhedkar Nagar, Deopur, Dhule,
khsona2007@rediffmail.com

Abstract

As a consequence of deregulation, competition, and problems in securing capital outlays for expansion of the infrastructure, modern power systems are operating at ever-smaller capacity and stability margins. Traditiona lenities involved in securing adequate protection and control for the system may soon become inadequate, and the emergence of the new participants (non-utility generation, transmission, and distribution companies) requires coordinated approach and careful coordination of the new operating conditions. The paper reviews the key issues and design considerations for the present and new generation of SPS and emergency control schemes, and evaluates the strategies for their implementation.

1. Introduction

System-wide disturbances in power systems are a challenging problem for the utility industry because of the large scale and the complexity of the power system. When a major power system disturbance occurs, protection and control actions are required to stop the power system degradation, restore the system to a normal state, and minimize the impact of the disturbance. The present control actions are not designed for a fast-developing disturbance and may be too slow. Further, dynamic simulation software is applicable only for off-line analysis. The operator must therefore deal with a very complex situation and rely on heuristic solutions and policies.

The trend in power system planning utilizes tight operating margins, with less redundancy, because of new constraints placed by economical and environmental factors. At the same time, addition of non-utility generators and independent power producers, an interchange increase, an increasingly competitive environment, and introduction of FACTS devices make the power system more complex to operate and to control, and, thus, more vulnerable to a disturbance. On the other hand, the advanced measurement and communication technology in wide area monitoring and control. paradigms (fuzzy logic and neural networks) may provide better ways to detect and control an emergency. Better detection and control strategies through the concept of wide area disturbance protection offer a better Management of the disturbances and significant opportunity for higher power transfers and operating economies. Wide area disturbance protection is a concept of using system-wide information and sending selected local information to a remote location to counteract propagation of the major disturbances in the power system.

With the increased availability of sophisticated computer, communication and measurement technologies, more "intelligent" equipment can be used at the local level to improve the overall emergency response. Decentralized subsystems, that can make local decisions based on local measurements and remote information (system-wide data and emergency control policies) and/or send pre-processed information to higher hierarchical levels are an economical solution to the problem.

A major component of the system-wide disturbance protection is the ability to receive system wide information and commands via the data communication system and to send selected local information to the SCADA centre. This information should reflect the prevailing state of the power system.

2. Types of Disturbances and Remedial Measures

Phenomena which create the power system disturbance are divided into the following categories: angular stability, voltage stability, overload and power system cascading.

2.1 Angular stability

The objective of out-of-step protection as it is applied to generators and systems is to eliminate the possibility of damage to generators as a result of an out-of-step condition. In the case of the power system separation is imminent; it should take place along boundaries which will form islands with matching load and generation. Distance relays are often used to provide an out-of-step protection function, whereby they are called upon to provide blocking or tripping signals upon detecting an out-of-step condition. The most common predictive scheme to combat loss of synchronism is the Equal-Area Criterion and its variations. This method assumes that the power system behaves like a wo-machine model where one area oscillates against the rest of the system. Whenever the underlying assumption holds true, the method has potential for fast detection.

2.2 Voltage stability

Voltage stability is defined by the System Dynamic Performance Subcommittee of the IEEE Power System Engineering Committee as being the ability of a system to maintain voltage such that when load admittance is increased, load power will increase, and so that both power and voltage are controllable. Also, voltage collapse is defined as being the process by which voltage instability leads to a very low voltage profile in a significant part of the system. It is accepted that this instability is caused by the load characteristics, as opposed to the angular instability which is caused by the rotor dynamics of generators. The risk of voltage instability increases as the transmission system becomes more heavily loaded.

The typical scenario of these instabilities starts with a high system loading, followed by a relay action due to a fault, a line overload or hitting an excitation limit. Voltage instability can be alleviated by a combination of the following remedial measures means: adding reactive compensation near load centers, strengthening the transmission lines, varying the operating conditions such as voltage profile and generation dispatch, coordinating relays and controls, and load shedding. Most utilities rely on planning and operation studies to guard against voltage instability. Many utilities utilize localized voltage measurements in order to achieve load shedding as a measure against incipient voltage instability.

2.3 Overload and Power System Cascading

Outage of one or more power system elements due to the overload may result in overload of other elements in the system. If the overload is not alleviated in time, the process of power system cascading may start, leading to power system separation. When a power system separates, islands with an imbalance between generation and load are formed with a consequence of frequency deviation from the nominal value. If the imbalance cannot be handled by the generators, load or generation shedding is necessary. The separation can also be started by a special protection system or out-of-step relaying. A quick, simple, and reliable way to re-establish active power balance is to shed load by under frequency relays. There are a large variety of practices in designing load shedding schemes based on the characteristics of a particular system and the utility practices [5-6]. While the system frequency is a final result of the power deficiency, the rate of change of frequency is an instantaneous indicator of power deficiency and can enable incipient recognition of the power imbalance. However, change of the machine speed is oscillatory by nature, due to the interaction among generators. These oscillations depend on location of the sensors in the island and the response of the generators. The problems regarding the rate-of-change of frequency function are :-

- A smaller system inertia causes a larger peak-to-peak value for oscillations. For the larger peak-to-peak Values, enough time must be allowed for the relay to calculate the actual rate-of-change of frequency reliably. Measurements at load buses close to the Electrical center of the system are less susceptible to oscillations (smaller peak-to-peak values) and can be used in practical applications. Smaller system inertia causes a higher frequency of oscillations, which enables faster calculation of the actual rate-of-change of frequency. However, it causes faster rate-of-change of frequency, and, consequently, a larger frequency drop.
- Even if rate-of-change of frequency relays measure the average value throughout the network, it is difficult to set them properly, unless typical system boundaries and imbalance can be predicted. If this is the case (eg. industrial and urban systems), the rate of change of frequency relays may improve a load shedding scheme (scheme can be more selective and/or faster).
- Adaptive settings of frequency and frequency derivative relays may enable implementation of a frequency derivative function more effectively and Reliably. This will be discussed later.

3. Possible Improvement in Control and Protection

Existing protection/control systems may be improved and new protection/control systems may be developed to better adapt to prevailing system conditions during system-wide disturbance. However, even if communication links exist, systems with only local information may still need improvement since they are envisioned as fallback positions. The modern energy management system (EMS) can provide system-wide information for the network control and protection.

The EMS is supported by supervisory control and data acquisition (SCADA) software and various power system analysis tools. The increased functions and communication ability in today's SCADA systems provide the opportunity for an intelligent and adaptive control and protection system for system-wide disturbance. This in turn can make possible full utilization of the network, which will be less vulnerable to a major disturbance?

3.1 Angular stability

Out-of-step relays have to be fast and reliable. The increased utilization of transmission and generation capacity as well as the increased distance of power transmissions are some of the factors that cause an out-of step situation to develop rapidly. The interconnected nature of power systems cause large geographic areas to be affected by an out-of-step condition. The present technology of out-of-step tripping or blocking distance relays are not capable of fully dealing with the control and protection requirements of power systems. Central to the development effort of an out-of-step protection system is the investigation of the multi-area out-of-step situation.

The new generation of out-of-step relays has to utilize more measurements, both local and remote, and has to produce more outputs. The structure of the overall relaying system has to be distributed and coordinated through a central control. In order for the relaying system to manage complexity, most of the decisions have to be taken locally. The relay system is preferred to be adaptive, in order to cope with system Changes.

To deal with out-of-step prediction, it is necessary to start with a system-wide approach, find out what sets of information are crucial, how to process information with acceptable speed and accuracy.

3.2 Voltage Instability

The protection against voltage instability should also be addressed as a part of hierarchical structure. Decentralized actions are performed at substations with local signals and signals obtained from slow communication with other substations and/or central level (e.g. using SCADA data). The higher hierarchical level requires more sophisticated communication of relevant system signals and a coordination between the actions of the various substations. The recommended approach for designing the new generation of voltage instability protection is to first design a voltage instability relay with only local signals.

The limitations of local signals should be identified in order to be in a position to select appropriate communicated signals. However, a minimum set of communicated signals should always be known in order to design a reliable protection, and it requires the following:

(a) determining the algorithm for gradual reduction of the number of necessary measurement sites with minimum loss of information necessary for voltage stability monitoring, analysis, and control.

(b) development of methods (i.e. sensitivity analysis of reactive powers), which should operate *concurrent* with any existing local protection techniques, and possessing superior performance, both in terms of security and dependability?

3.3 Power System Cascading and Load Shedding Strategies

Conventional load shedding schemes without communications are not adaptive to system conditions which are different from the one used in the load shedding design. For the relays to adapt to the prevailing system conditions, their settings should change based on the available spinning reserve, total system inertia, and load characteristics. These values may be periodically determined at the central site from SCADA data and Provided to the relays using low speed communications. In addition, the actual load, which would represent an assigned percentage for shedding at each step, may be periodically calculated at a central site based on the actual load distribution. However, the system characteristics may change depending on the separation points. If the separation is controlled from a central site or can be predicted, an algorithm may calculate the settings and assign the appropriate load in coordination with switching actions. However, high speed communication may be required to and from the central location for fast-developing disturbances, such as multi-machine angular instability.

Another aspect, may be adding a correction element to a scheme. If only slow speed communications are available, a fast load shedding scheme may be implemented to stop system degradation. When adequate information is available, corrective measures may be applied. If the composite system inertia constant is known, the actual power imbalance may be calculated directly from the frequency. This detection should be fast (to avoid a large frequency drop) and done at the location close to the center of inertia. High speed communications are required to initiate load shedding at different power system locations.

Further, changes of load and generation, with frequency and in particular voltage, impact the power imbalance and calculation of the average of the frequency derivative. In addition, the power system imbalance changes after the initial disturbance due to dynamic system changes. Thus, relay settings should be based on the spinning reserve, total system inertia, and load characteristics and distribution. In conclusion, sophisticated models and/or High-speed communication may be required for accurate estimation of the amount and distribution of the load to be shed.

If communications are available, it is easier and more reliable to calculate the amount of load to shed from the switching information and the mismatch (based on data on load and generation before the separation) in the island.

To avoid disadvantages of the under frequency load shedding and difficulties with implementing the rate-of change of frequency function, the automated load shedding that will reduce overloading or prevent system instability before the system is isolated is proposed as an advantageous strategy.

3.1.1 Example: Angular Stability

An algorithm for predicting the location at which an out of- step can take place following a disturbance in a large-scale system is shown as an example of the hierarchical protection and control strategies using communications.

To implement this scheme, one needs a central computer that receives information from across the system. The sets of crucial information that require fast communications consist of: generator speeds, and changes in line status. Other information needed by the algorithm is generation and load levels. Using these sets of information, a simple and quick processing method is able to tell, with a high degree of accuracy, (1) whether an out-of-step is imminent, and (2) the boundary across which this out-of step will take place. This algorithm has been tested thoroughly using a Monte-Carlo-type approach. At each test, random values are assigned to line impedances, load, generator inertias, as well as disturbance location.

It is found that the algorithm is capable of making accurate prediction.

To illustrate how the algorithm works, consider the power system shown in Fig. 1. This system is a modified version of the IEEE 39-bus test system. In Fig. 1, each generator is marked with a circle, and each load with a square; the size of each symbol indicates relatively the power generated or consumed at the node. For example- Generator 34 supplies more MW to the grid than does Generator 38.

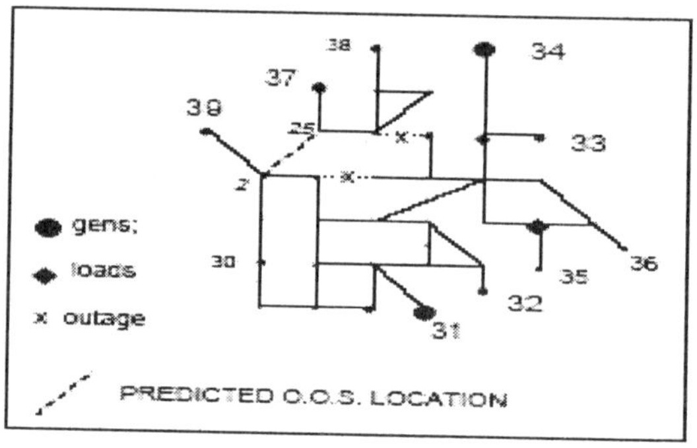

Fig. 1 Graph of the 39-bus test system

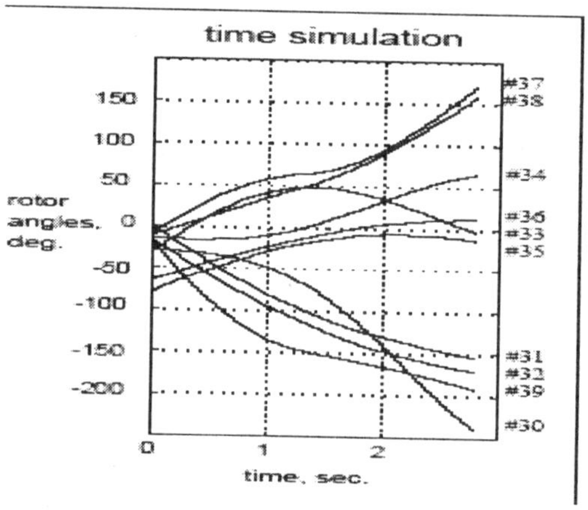

Fig. 2 Time domain simulation of the system

A disturbance is introduced to the system where two lines are simultaneously removed (each line is marked by an 'x' in Figure (1)). This information is fed to the algorithm, which predicts that an out-of-step will occur across the line 2-25. Figure. (2) reveals that the two generators 37 and 38 eventually separate from the other generators. All line angles have been checked and none but line 2-25 indicates the boundary of the out-of-step. The angle of critical line is shown in Fig. 3. This confirms the result of the algorithm.

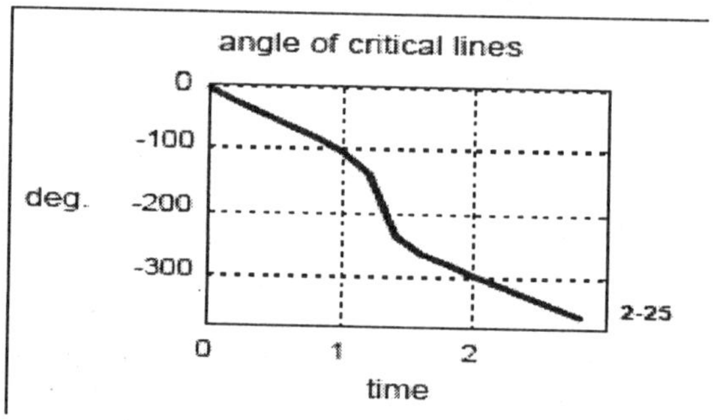

Fig. 3 Angle of critical line

Such an algorithm requires a centralized scheme and high-speed communication links across the wide

system. Decentralized scheme requires communications with a central location. According to this hierarchical scheme, each regional computer issues control actions to alleviate problems that are imminent within its jurisdiction; the coordination among regions is left to the central computer.

3.1.2 Example: TCSC Control

In this section we briefly present a method for online detection of interarea oscillations. The method does not require the topological knowledge of the system and is based on the spectral characteristics of the locally observable data. Moreover, we introduce a different approach to the power system stabilization. We apply the globally available information about the system to the adaptation of TCSC (thyristor-controlled series compensator).

The control we propose attempts to optimally adjust the line admittance on sample to sample basis in order to reduce the inter area oscillations in the power systems. We explain how such approach may combine the global system information with locally observable quantities and eventually result in the damping of inter-area modes.

4. Power System Modeling and Spectral Characteristics

We consider a generic *N*-machine, *p*-bus power system described by the following swing equation: ωΔ represent the deviation of the rotor angle and its speed relative to the synchronous reference frame, ∏ *(t)* is thc accelerating power, i.e. imbalance between the mechanical and mechanical power, ***Mi*** is the inertia constant for machine ***i***, ***B*** ω is the synchronous angular frequency, and ***Di*** is the damping factor corresponding to the machine ***i***. Swing equation can be linearized to obtain u *B x A x* Δ + Δ = Δ_where vector *x* Δ is the vector obtained by concatenating rotor angle deviation vector and rotor speed deviation vector and *u* Δ is the vector of power imbalances for each machine.

Information about possible modes of the system can now be obtained by eigen analysis of matrix **A**, and its participation factors. This however, is not the only way that the information on the oscillatory modes can be obtained. In a system subject to the impulse excitation, the oscillatory modes can be determined from the power spectral density of the system response. In other words, the modes would appear as peaks of the power spectral density function of state variable **x** calculated as: where ***F*** represents the Fourier transformation. Peaks of the power spectral density correspond to the modes of the interarea oscillations, and can be therefore determined from measurements of ***x*** over a time window, if we consider ***x*** as a time-frequency distribution. Descriptive (measurement) quantity we use is the machine speed. We think of interarea oscillations as energy exchanges between the groups of the machines, this energy exchange should be visible from the machine speed data. Moreover, the machine speed is easily measurable quantity, thus making a perfect candidate for descriptive quantity for a pattern recognition task. Algorithm we propose is following:

- Collect machine speed data.
- Perform spectrum estimation on machine speed data.
- Identify the frequencies of possible modes of interarea oscillations.
- Perform clustering on the phases of machine spectrum data at inter-area frequencies Identify inter-area groups with clusters of phases of machine spectrum data.

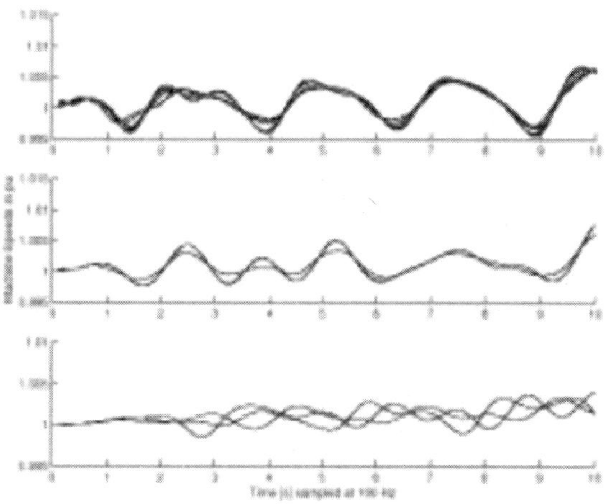

Fig. 4 Transient disturbance of the test system

Fig. (4.1) shows the machine speeds of the 16 machine 64-bus NPCC system subject to the fault on line between busses 28 and 29. The fault is cleared by tripping the line after three cycles but still divides machines in three groups thus producing the interarea oscillations. In this simulation we used the transient model for synchronous machines. It is obvious that the system is divided into three groups that oscillate against each other. In one group we have machines 1 through 8, in second machines 11 through 13 and all other machines oscillate by them.

Modal analysis of the liberalized system reveals five oscillatory modes under 1Hz: at 0.4150 Hz, at 0.5564 Hz, at 0.7326 Hz, at 0.8066 Hz, and one at 0.9825 Hz. Participation factor analysis indicates those machines most likely to oscillate at 0.415 Hz are machines 1 through 9 and 13 through 16. Machine 15 seems very prone to the mode at .5Hz, machines 10 through 13 are susceptible to the mode at 0.7326 Hz, and machines 14 through 16 are prone to oscillatory mode at 0.8066 Hz.

We use the phase angles of the power spectral density at the given mode to determine the group to which machine belongs. The phase data is summarized in Table 1. Indeed, machines 1 through 8 have the phase angle of approximately 11 degrees; machines 11, 12 and 13 have phase angles of approximately 3 degrees, while phase angles of speed spectra of other machines do not belong to any of the groups.

Table 1 Phase angles of the power spectral density at the inter area oscillation mode at 0.4 Hz.

Machine Number	Speed PSD Phase at 0.4 Hz [degrees]
1	11.6975
2	10.3086
3	10.8000
4	12.5058
5	12.1250
6	12.0467
7	12.6263
8	12.4726
9	25.6914
10	8.2753
11	3.2167
12	3.5110
13	2.7732
14	63.4004
15	144.1611
16	195.3319

We propose to use the information about groups of machines belonging to interarea modes to formulate an emergency control by modulating the admittance of the thyristor-controlled series capacitor (TCSC). The control we propose is based on the premise that we only want to enhance the stability of the system by applying the admittance adjustment control. The main control still relies on power system stabilizers, which usually perform this task very well.

We would like to use the admittance control to minimize the inter area oscillations which are exhibited as the flow of energy between machines or groups there of. We use the rate of change of machine speeds as an indication of the energy change at particular machine. In that sense, we would keep the undesirable variations of the machine velocities to their minimum, reducing the energy transfers between different groups of machines.

In turn, reduced energy exchange reduces the interarea oscillations, which is the goal of our control. While this type of control does not guarantee the stability, it does guarantee that the exponents of a system with such control will be smaller than the ones of the system without the control. This is a result of the facts that machine states are the state variables of linearized system, and that the logarithm is a monotonous function. In that sense, the system is *more* stable than the system without the control.

Moreover, proposed type of control can be computed with a cost of QR decomposition for the matrix of sensitivity coefficients and one matrix multiplication. In addition, this type of the control guarantees the minimum energy solution, i.e. minimum per-sample change of line admittances.

The stability of the control computation procedure, low computational cost, and easy parallelization of the process this algorithm very appealing for the real time applications on multiprocessor architectures.

5. Minimum Energy Control

- Various and possibly multiple faults may happen.
- All machines need to be controlled at the same time to insure the control of all interarea modes (this condition may be relaxed by adaptive tracking of the Inter area groups).
- Since all machines participating in a certain inter area mode will have similar angles and rates of change of angles (speeds), it is technically possible to use just a representative machine from a group. This may be useful in speeding up the control processing to enable Real-time control.
- Above two tasks have to be performed with minimum change of the line admittances since the TCSC devices have range typically limited to a certain percentage of the nominal line admittance, for a variety of reasons.

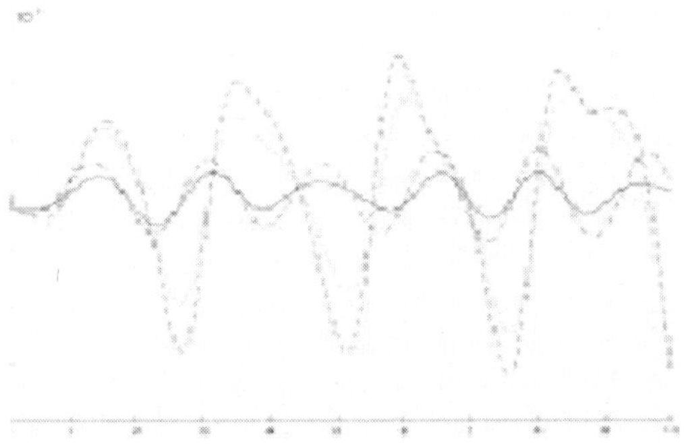

Fig. 5

The presented scenarios involve situations when no control was applied to the system under disturbance, and When group of 5 optimally selected and tuned PSS and 5 TCSC was used, both individually and together. The opportunity to speed up processing.

6. Conclusion

A large disturbance such as a sudden outage of a transmission line may trigger a sequence of events leading to machine swings, voltage problem, and eventually power outage in a large area of the system.

7. References

[1] Prabha S. Kundur, *Power System Stability And Control.*

[2] A. K. Padiyar, *Power System Dynamics.*

[3] Voltage Stability Of Power Systems, "Concepts and Analytical"

[4] A. Apostolov, D. Novosel, and D. G. Hart, "*Intelligent Protection and Control during Power System Disturbance*".

[5] Dr. V.B. Pandya, Elements *of power system protection.*

[6] Dr. Ayanger's and Prof. Tekwani's - a research Project submitted in partial fulfillments of Power system-Nirma University.

[7] www.howstuffworks.com

[8] www.ieee-explore.org

Detection and Analysis of Human Energy Field A Review

D. V. Kurmude[1], Dr. Satish Panchal[2] and Dr. J. S. Sardar[3]
[1]Sr. Lecturer in Physics, Milind College of Science, Aurangabad – 431005, India
dvkurmude@yahoo.com
[2]Dept. of Mathematics, Dr. B.A.M. University, Aurangabad – 431004, India.
[3]Director, International Meditation Centre, Nandanvan Colony, Aurangabad–431002, India.
drjanardans@gmail.com

Abstract

In this paper an attempt is made to look in to the Human Energy Field from Physics point of view. Brain activity, being electrical in nature emanates energy radiations giving rise to what is called as Aura – the human energy field. Various methods of aura detection and theories have been discussed. Analysis of Resonant Field Imaging (RFI) and Poly-contrast Interference Photography (PIP), the computer based methods to shoot; photograph human energy field is done.

1. Introduction

We often refer to the energy of a person in everyday conversation – we may get 'good vibes' from someone or be 'on the same wavelength' as them. We may feel 'energized' or 'drained' after dealing with a person.

Human Energy Field is unique constituent, just like a fingerprint. It is different for each person. However, it is far more complex than just fingerprints. Firstly, we are born with an aura, which stays with us in some sort of way for the whole of our life. As we progress through life, the situations which we are placed in and the way our spiritual growth occurs tempers the aura further.

Modern science tells us that the human organism is not just a physical structure made of molecules; but like everything else, is composed of energy fields. We are constantly changing, ebbing, and flowing, just like the sea. Scientists are working to measure these subtle changes. The human energy field is the frontier for modern research, and the development of new diagnostic and treatment systems.

In Physics, "field" refers to "a force which can cause action at a distance" The term "biofield" according to Dr. Beverly Rubik focuses on bioelectromagnetics (including bioradiation), and other biophysical fields (known and hypothesized – such as quantum field effects) that play a potential regulatory role in cellular structure and function. It is important to recognize that fields are "invisible" and are not "material." In physics, the term "energy" refers to "the capacity to do work and overcome resistance" Einstein's famous formula E=mc2 revealed the fact that mass is actually "organized energy" and that matter and energy are fundamentally interrelated. Fields of force can vary (1) in the energy they express, and (2) the information they carry. The term biofield combines aspects of both energy and information in its description.

Basic biofield science requires the careful integration of quantum physics, physics, biophysics and bioengineering, in order to obtain a comprehensive and accurate description of the phenomena. [1][2]

2. HEF Detection History

2.1 Walter Kilner

In 1911, Walter Kilner, M.D., from St. Thomas Hospital in London, reported on seeing the HEF. Looking through glass screens stained with dicyanin dye, he saw a glowing mist around the body in three distinct zones.

1. A 1/4 inch layer closest to skin;
2. A more vaporous layer, 1 inch wide, streaming perpendicularly from the body;
3. A delicate exterior luminosity with indefinite contours, about 6 inches wide.

In his work "The Human Aura" published in New York, 1965, he states that the appearance of the aura differs from person to person, depending on their physical, mental, and emotional states. Kilner actually developed a system of diagnosis based on the consistent differences he found in persons suffering a particular disease. He successfully treated many conditions, including epilepsy, liver disease, tumors, appendicitis, and hysteria.

2.2 Kirlian Photography

In 1939 in Krasnodar, near the Black Sea in Russia, Semyon Davidovich Kirlian, an electrician, and his wife, Valentina Kirlian, a teacher and journalist, became fascinated by the sight of a tiny flash of light which ocurred between the electrodes of an electrotherapy machine and the skin of a patient. Other Russian scientists had also noted this energy, but ignored it. The equipment and procedures they finally developed were to record on film this luminous energy emanating from the physical body - the HEF. They invented a new type of photography, and had more than fourteen patents. The original system photographed static images of fingers or leaves. Next, they developed a special optical instrument to observe the motion of this luminous phenomenon. Now they saw the hand as either flashing, sparkling, steadily glowing, or as diminishing particles of light. They also showed the difference in the HEF of a human being harboring a disease that had not yet manifested symptoms!

2.3 Radionics

Dr. George De La Warr & Dr. Ruth Drown built instruments to detect radiation from living tissues, and developed Radionics, a system of detection, diagnosis & healing from a distance, using the human energy field. They took photographs using the patient's hair as an antenna. These photographs showed internal diseases, like tumors and cysts inside the liver, and cancers within the brain. The study of Radionics continues today in England.

2.4 Light Emissions Studies Bio-Energetics

Dr. John Pierrakas and Eva Pierrakas have developed a system of diagnosis and treatment of psychological disorders based on visual and pendulum-derived observations of the HEF. The information from these observations combined with body psychotherapeutic methods eventually developed into Bio-Energetics. The process called *Core Energetics* was delineated in a publication "The Core Energetics Process", in 1977. Dr. Pierrakas work suggests that the light emissions from the human body are closely related to health. Dr. Richard Dobrin, Dr. John Pierrakos, and Barbara Brennan - published "Instrumental Measurements of the Human Energy Field" in 1978. They measured the light level of a wave length of around 350 nanometers in a darkroom before, during, and after there were people in that room. Results show a slight increase of light when people are in it. When someone feeling exhausted and full of despair was in the room, the light value actually fell. With a colorizer they were able to show part of the auric field, or the HEF, on black and white television.

2.5 Hiroshi Motoyama

He measured low light levels coming from people who have practiced yoga for many years. He did this with a movie camera in a darkroom. Also, he studied the strength of a sender's and a receiver's energy meridians before and after treatment. Most of the time, the sender's energy level dipped and then rose again. Also, the energy at the heart chakra of the sender or healer increased after treating a patient.

2.6 Dr. Valorie Hunt

Dr. Valorie Hunt and colleagues at UCLA, published "A Study of Structural Neuromuscular Energy Field and Emotional Approaches", which is a study of the effects of *Rolfing* on the body and the psyche. She placed electrodes on the skin to record the low millivoltage signals from the body during rolfing sessions. Rosalyn Bruyere observed the auras and recorded her observations of both the rolfer and the patient. Breyere's observations were recorded on the same tape as the electronic data. She described the color, size, and energy movements of the chakras, and auric clouds, or HEF, involved.

Scientists then mathematically analyzed the wave patterns recorded by a Fourier analysis and a sonogram frequency analysis. The wave forms and frequencies reported by Rosalyn Bruyere correlated specifically with the colors reported. When Breyere saw blue in the HEF at a specific location, the electronic measurements would always show the characteristic blue wave form and frequency in the same location. Hunt repeated this experiment with seven other aura readers. Each of the seven also saw auric colors that correlated with the same frequency wave patterns. In 1988, the results of their research showed these color and frequency correlations. Dr. Hunt says, "Throughout the centuries in which sensitives have seen and described the auric emissions, this is the first objective electronic evidence of frequency, amplitude and time, which validates their subjective observation of color discharge."

2.7 HEF Electromagnetic Field Studies

Dr. Robert Becker, at Upstate Medical School, mapped a complex electrical field on the body that was shaped like the body and the central nervous system. He named this field *"The Direct Current Control System"* in his publication of the same name in 1962. He found that this field changes shape and strength with physiological and psychological changes. Continuing his experiments through 1979, he found particles the size of electrons moving through this field.

2.8 Dr. Zheng Ronliang

At Lanzhou University in China, in "Scientific Research of Qigong", measured the Qi radiated from the human body by using a biological detector made from a leaf vein connected to a photo quantum device. He studied the Qi emissions of a Qigong master, and the energy field emanations of a clairvoyant. The energy pulses emanating from the hands of the Qigong Master are very different in nature from that of the clairvoyants. At Shanghai Atomic Nuclear Institute of Academia, Sinica, it was shown that some vital force emanations from Qigong masters seem to have a very low frequency fluctuating carrier wave. Sometimes, Qi was detected as a micro particle flow with a particle size of 60 microns in diameter, and velocity of 20-50 cm/sec.

2.9 HEF Bioplasma Studies

Russian scientists from the Bio-information Institute of A. S. Popov All-Union Scientific and Technical Society of Radio Technology and Electrical Communications, began a crash program on extra-sensory perception in 1965. They started to use the methods of physicists with their experiments on telepathy. The scientists of this Popov group later announced the discovery that living organisms emit vibrations at a frequency of 300 to 2,000 nanometers. They called this energy the biofield, or bioplasma. They showed that the biofield was stronger when people were more successful at transferring their bioenergy. These findings were confirmed at the Medical Sciences Academy in Moscow, and are supported by research in Germany, Poland, the Netherlands, and Great Britain. Since the 1950's, Dr. Victor Inyushin at Kazakh University in Russia has also done extensive research in HEF. He suggests the existence of a bioplasmic energy field composed of ions, free protons, and free electrons. He suggests that the bioplasmic energy field is a fifth state of matter. Inyushin's work shows that the bioplasmic particles are constantly renewed by chemical processes in the cells and are in constant motion. There is a balance of positive and negative particles within the bioplasma that is relatively stable. A severe shift in this balance causes a change in the health of the patients or organism. At the same time, in a healthy being, some of this energy or bioplasma is radiated into space. [1]

3. Know HEF with Computers

3.1 Resonant Field Imaging

Resonant Field Imaging is an "external electro-field imaging" technology. RFI is a passive measurement system. It causes no distortion or contamination of the Energy Field. It literally measures the identity of the detected energy according to its characteristic frequency, and makes this frequency available to the user as data in standard international scientific units.

Just feeding a frequency number to computer one can obtain the colour of the detected bio-energy, as well as the Health or Psychological Level interpretation of that colour.

Since electrical impulses from the brain are transmitted and radiate throughout the central, autonomic and parasympathetic nervous system, each area of our body to which the nerves extend radiate the brain signals which originated in the corresponding connected area of the brain. As a result, the human body becomes a macrocosm for the small scale of the complex brain, and serves as an accessible magnified window into the intricacies of the brain. The RFI system generates a detailed, full colour Brain scan image, by actually tracing the bio-energies from 40 regions of the human electro-field, back through the connecting neurological systems, and into the medically correct corresponding regions and organs of the human Brain. The RFI scan measures conditions and events in the brain indirectly, by first using the electrical field sensor to detect electromagnetic radiation originating in the brain, and then using a computer to compile the numerical data, and automatically construct a visual image of the brain.

RFI does not subject the patient to any radiation or unnatural substances which could have any side effects. Instead, it passively detects and analyses the electro-field bio-energies which naturally emanate from the Brain.

By identifying the bio-energies that are present in specific regions and organs of the brain, RFI gives a more complete picture of the events, situations and conditions in the brain. It reveals which parts of the brain are effecting each other through the exchange of energy-information, and reveals the primary function or role of each part of the brain in a system of physical or mental illness. In addition, it is able to reveal exactly how the brain is influencing health conditions, and how health conditions and the patient's psychology are physically affecting the brain. Therefore, RFI brain scans are a very interesting supplement to conventional medical technologies.

RFI and the presumption of the existence of the aura is based upon the principle that all mental activity is electromagnetic. While some medical theorists argue that mental activity is chemical, because of the chemical neurotransmitters involved, the fact is that neurotransmitters are created only when electrical impulses induce a voltage in a neuron which exceeds its firing threshold. In addition, EEG (electroencephalogram) technology shows that mental activity can be effectively analyzed and monitored entirely by electromagnetic principles. In electrical engineering, it is an established principle that all electrical currents produce surrounding electromagnetic (EM) fields. Our psychological and emotional activities are sent throughout the body as electrical impulses, radiating electromagnetic fields outside the body. Indeed, even the mere movement of atoms will produce a quantifiable electromagnetic field. This is most clearly observed in the case of charged radioisotopes, but even neutral atoms and molecules will emit a field through valence motion of the charged substructure particles. As proven by Russian Tesla technology experiments in the 1950s, this phenomenon causes prokaryotic organisms to produce an external electromagnetic field, which consists of the combined EM emissions from millions of molecules in the biological body. Most researchers in this field acknowledge that complex biological organisms such as humans also produce electro-field frequencies in much the same way, except that in addition to the molecular contribution, the nervous system plays a significant role. The nerves and nerve synapses carry electrical currents as large as 55 mV for neuron firings, and sometimes as large as 3 volts for motor impulses (to move the muscles), which radiate much larger electrical fields in accordance with electro-field physics. All of these radiating fields are the very tangible essence and ONE definition of the human Aura There is a possibility for this technology to be able to identify psychological and emotional states. First, one has a psychological perception of oneself and one's environment. This perception, being a mental process, induces characteristic electrical impulses in the brain, which can affect related parasympathetic nerves or endocrine glands (e.g., a perception of fear stimulates the adrenal glands via the brain). Since the brain is neurologically connected to the entire human body, these electrical impulses may travel throughout the central, sympathetic and parasympathetic nervous system, creating the characteristic electrical fields. The impulses may even travel through the Collagen fibres of the connective tissue as Dr Keith suggests (see references) He explains there is a continuum of liquid crystalline water-bound collagen fibres running throughout the entire body Biological activity such as autonomic responses initiate cellular and electrochemical changes, thereby creating an environment thermodynamically favourable to the conversion of metabolic kinetic energy into electromagnetic energy. Localized bio-energy forms a dynamic field that differentiates according to the neurological information that stimulated it. Since the muscles and skin is no barrier for such electromagnetic energy. [2].

3.2 Polycontrast Interference Photography

PIP a real time imaging system with software, which highlights the contrast between the interference patterns emanating from the human body 'biofield' and the standard PIP 'full spectrum' lighting environment.

Harry Oldfield invented Polycontrast Interference Photography (PIP) in the late 1980s using microchip technology. Oldfield developed a scanner that could provide a real time, moving image of the energy field. He believed that the future of diagnosis lay in finding an effective scanner that can see imbalances in the energy field rather than disease in the physical body. Oldfield thought that the human energy field might possibly interfere with photons - energy packets of light - or even what might be called "subtle energy photons" in some way. He decided that ambient (surrounding) light would be interfered with by the field both when the incident ray traveled towards the object and when the reflected ray bounced off the object.

He then devised a computer program that would analyze the different light intensities being reflected from the person or object being scanned. According to Oldfield, "We believe that we are showing up an energy interaction with light, which is giving us an insight into the energy counterpart, the etheric template on which our physical molecules are strung. On average, every atom in the human body is replaced every seven to nine years. Think of your body not as a physical structure but as a moving fountain of molecules that are constantly being replaced. So what keeps them a coherent recognizable form? We believe it to be an organizing template of energy."

PIP displays a live image on a PC monitor where the electrical signals from a video camera are graded into clearly visible colors representing a much finer gradation of light intensity than the image entering the camera. Light intensities are distinguished in a way that is impossible to the human eye.

PIP software includes a number of "filters" that allow you to change the focus and contrast of the image to help visualize areas of "pooling" or congestion (i.e., energy "blockages"). You can record video segments and "still shots". You can also play older video recordings through the software for analysis. PIP is one of the best investments a serious researcher or practitioner can make in the field of energy medicine.

To use PIP you will need a video camera (digital preferred) and tripod, a computer to view and record video images (a minimum of 400 MHz Windows 98 (or later) with 512 MB RAM, not Mac compatible at this time), a cable to connect the camera to the computer (Firewire preferred), and a full-spectrum lighting environment (floor lighting directed at the subject or an overhead light). A white background is desirable to ensure the best reflection of light.

PIP can assess and evaluate health issues; show developing and existing stresses to the body; demonstrate healing procedures; and provides an evaluation of treatment methods and systems.[3]

4. Conclusion

Our Newtonian world of solid concrete objects is surrounded and permeated by a fluid world of radiating energy. It is constantly moving and changing; an ocean of dancing, spinning, flashing particles of light, energy, and information. Our linear way of thinking, seeing, and expressing needs to expand to accommodate this new reality.

It is time for a new paradigm, or model, of science, reality, and consciousness. It is time to bridge the gaps between science and alternate science, physics and metaphysics, and the external scientific experiment and the inner personal experience. This may well begin with the unification of the concepts of mind, energy, and consciousness. Using our minds to study energy, we may simultaneously define consciousness as one and the same.

Holistic, awareness remains beyond linear time and three dimensional spaces, and therefore is not easily recognized.

Modern means of HEF detection can give safe solutions to health problems.

5. References

[1] Website: **http://www.vxm.com**

[2] Website: http://www.biofieldsciences.com

[3] Website: http://www.item-bioenergy.com/

Simulation of Digital Organisms using AI techniques to Design Controllers

S. Raja Mohamed[1], N. Rajeswaran[2], V. RamaRaju[3] and Dr T. Madhu [4]
[1]Dept of CSE/SVECW, [2]Dept of ECE/SVECW, [3]Dept of ECE/VIT and [4]Principal/GVIT
raja_delip@yahoo.com rajeswarann@gmail.com tennetimadhu@yahoo.co.in

Abstract

Real time modeling of characters/creatures is increasing day by day in developing various computer games. The real world simulation of digital organism in the virtual world is done using artificial life techniques like Co-evolution, Ecology and Learning during lifetime. Both the complex and noncomplex life techniques include for complex and non-complex digital organisms are represented by their genome through which properties like co-existence, altruism, mutation etc are tested and adapted to improve their surveillance. This paper deals with a new method to create real world AI engine that incorporates the above qualities.

1. Introduction

The realistic physical modeling of characters in games and virtual worlds is becoming a viable alternative to more traditional animation techniques. Physical modeling of characters and environments can enhance realism and allow users to interact with the virtual world much more freely. By modeling the forces and torques acting on bodies within a virtual environment, detecting and responding to collisions between bodies, respecting constraints arising from, for example, joints in articulated multi-body objects, etc., the system behaves in a believable manner in all situations, and the user can therefore be allowed to interact with it much more freely. The growing popularity of this approach is demonstrated by the appearance over the last couple of years of a number of off-the-shelf physics engines aimed at games programmers (e.g. Math Engine). While these engines handle the modeling of inanimate bodies, programmers are still left with the task of writing controllers for motile objects within the environment (e.g. cars, human characters, monsters, etc.). Writing a controller for a physically modeled character is a question of calculating the appropriate forces to apply to each body part at each point of time to achieve the desired movement (e.g. a realistic walking gait for a human character). This is generally a very hard task. Artificial life techniques can be useful in automating this task. For example, artificial evolution can generate suitable controllers for simple behaviors, given only a high level description of that behavior in terms of a fitness function. In this paper, the state of the art in evolving controllers, and also in evolving the characters' body shapes, is described. It is then suggested that current approaches will not be able to scale up to more complicated behaviors. A number of possible solutions to this problem are described. Finally, several routes for delivering this technology to the games industry are discussed.

2. Background

Several groups have employed techniques from the fields of artificial intelligence and artificial life to automate the generation of controllers for physically simulated characters. The use of genetic algorithms in this area generally falls into one of two categories: the evolution of controllers for characters with predefined, fixed body shape [1], [5]; and the evolution of both the controller and the body shape of the creature [2], [7], [8], [10], [13]. Karl Sims [10]. He used an artificial evolutionary process to generate both controllers and body shapes for creatures that could perform simple tasks such as crawling, swimming, jumping and following a target. However, the basic limitation of the model is that it cannot be used for more complex behaviors. Each creature is described by a "genome" that contains information about the body shape and controller. In Sims' work, the body shape was described by a directed graph, where each node represents an individual body part, and the connections between nodes describe how the parts are connected. Each node also describes an augmented neural network type controller for the corresponding body part. This representation provides modularity to the mapping from genotype (the description of the creature) to phenotype (the instantiation of the creature as a physical model and controller), and naturally leads to features such as duplication and recursion of body parts.

A run is started by randomly generating a population of genotypes. Each genotype in turn is translated into a physical creature, and then evaluated in a physically simulated environment for its performance at a given task. Sims used two basic environments, sea and land. The sea environment included a simplistic model of fluid drag, while the land environment included gravity, a ground plane, and frictional forces for ground contacts. A number of different criteria (or "fitness functions" in genetic algorithm jargon) were used for scoring the success of each creature in its environment. The evolutionary process can only get off the ground if the initial, randomly generated population of creatures contains at least one creature that can achieve a non-zero score on the fitness function. The more complicated the function is, the less likely this is to be the case. For example, consider an attempt to evolve a behavior whereby a reature needed to process complex visual data about the movement of another creature standing in front of it, and use this to decide whether that creature was a friend or foe. This enterprise would clearly have little chance of success if the evolutionary process was starting from scratch

The first, randomly generated population of creatures typically performed poorly at the designated task, although a few would, by chance, have some degree of success. Each creature was scared according to its performance, and when all creatures had been evaluated the population was ranked according to score. The best individuals were kept to form the basis of a new generation. This new population was filled up by adding mutated forms of these best genotypes and genetic crosses of pairs of genotypes. By repeating this process, efficient creatures evolved surprisingly quickly. Sims typically used populations of 300 individuals and the experiment for 50-100 generations. In a recent reimplementation of Sims' work, a single run of this size would take between 2-3 hours on a single 1GHz Pentium PC. Pictures and movies of a variety of creatures evolved using these systems are available online. One of the nice properties of systems such as these is that each run generally produces a very different result due to the stochastic nature of the evolutionary process. Sims only selected for high-level behaviors such as the ability to move forwards, but within the vast space of different creature designs describable with the genetic system used, there are countless forms, which can competently perform such behaviors. The evolutionary process is therefore a tool for exploring interesting regions of this immense landscape of creature designs; it is a creative machine for generating suitable and interesting forms and behaviors, not limited by the preconceptions of a human designer's imagination.

3. Proposed Models to achieve more Complex Behaviors

Researchers in the field of evolutionary robotics have considered various methods of overcoming the difficulties like selecting a non-zero fitness function, mutation etc. These generally involve either the incremental acquisition of increasingly complicated tasks [3], [9], or the decomposition of the task into a sequence of easier tasks together with some way of combining them [8]. A problem with many of these approaches is that the decomposition of the task into easier and/or incremental steps is something of an art in itself and there are no general guidelines to suggest the most appropriate way to do this sensible task. Decomposition from the designer's point of view may not be the best route by which one can evolve a complex behavior; in the worst case, it could even be a hindrance. Despite the problems described above with evolving single creatures to perform complex tasks, there are a number of alternative approaches that have shown some signs of success. Five such popular methods are given below:

3.1 Co-Evolution

Co-evolution is a very promising technique for developing complex behaviors, especially when there is a competition between two or more creatures. The idea is that rather than evolving a population against a fixed fitness function, two populations are used instead, with one evolving against the other. For example, Hillis evolved efficient number sorting algorithms by co-evolving a population of candidate algorithms against a population of numbers to be sorted [6]. As the sorting algorithms got improved, so are the population of numbers to be sorted evolved to present tougher challenges to the algorithms. Evolution in one population thereby catalyzed further evolution in the other. Sims has also used a similar technique to evolve interesting competitive behaviors in virtual creatures. In this work, rather than simulating a single creature at a time, he simulated a couple. These two creatures were opponents in a simple game where they had to fight for possession of a cube that was initially placed halfway between them. The creatures not only evolved behaviors to reach the cube quickly, but also to fend off their opponents. A wide variety of different behaviors were evolved in this way, and the resulting competitions were very engaging to watch.

3.2 Virtual Ecologies

Taking co-evolution to its logical conclusion, we could forget about defining some sort of high-level game (such as fighting for possession of a cube) altogether. Instead, we could simply concurrently simulate a large population of creatures that are competing with each other for basic resources such as food and space, and let the creatures reproduce "by themselves" according to, say, how much food they have managed to eat. That way we get away from the sort of "artificial selection" we have talked about up to now (a fitness function is really the virtual equivalent of the selection employed by livestock farmers when trying to improve a particular trait in their animals), towards a closer approximation to "natural selection". We would not be selecting for particular high-level behaviors, but rather creating a virtual ecology and letting it evolve in any way it likes. Some progress in this direction has been made [7], although because of the much larger drain on computational resources required to simulate large populations of creatures concurrently, these studies have used somewhat simplified physical simulations. As computers become increasingly powerful, as physics engines become more efficient, and, most importantly, with the opportunities for running massively parallel simulations afforded by the Internet, the size of the ecologies that can be modeled and the complexity of the physical simulation will certainly increase greatly over the coming months and years.

3.3 Lifetime Learning

The creatures' controllers improve by evolution, but they do not actually adapt whilst an individual creature is being simulated. Some recent results from evolutionary robotics suggest that combining an evolutionary algorithm with the ability of the controllers to adapt or learn over an individual creature's lifetime can lead to improved robustness and complexity of behaviors compared to evolution by itself [4]. Giving an individual creature the ability to adapt and learn during its lifetime effectively smoothes the search space over which evolution is happening, thereby helping the process to progress. It is reasonable to assume that adding these sorts of abilities to our artificial creatures will improve their ability to evolve complex behaviors just as it has done in evolutionary robotics.

3.4 Behavioral Primitives

The evolution of complex behaviors can in general be evolved by task decomposition. Rather than trying to evolve complex behaviors, another approach is to evolve a collection of primitive behaviors, and then use other, non-evolutionary techniques for combining these primitive into more complicated sequences. The task of programming a game character using this approach could now become somewhat like directing an actor in a film; the character has a certain degree of competence at autonomous behavior and the programmer/director issues high-level commands to it such as "jump from top" or "attack the target! ". Some have suggested that this is the most useful route by which this sort of technology may be harnessed by games programmers. Alternatively, rather than directing the creatures manually, other AI techniques could be used to co-ordinate the primitive behaviors to automatically generate more complex tasks [11].

3.5 User Guided Evolution

Another alternative to supplying a fixed fitness function to the genetic algorithm is to present the user with a variety of creatures from the evolving population at various intervals, and allow them to select their favorite creatures to be used as the foundation of the next generation. The user may select the creatures by any criteria they wish, and can therefore guide the path of evolution according to their own preferences without having to formally instruct the individual creatures.

4. Results and Discussion

Simulation and optimization of digital creatures was attempted by several researches. In this paper Framsticks software is used to simulate and evolve digital creatures. Framsticks virtual world is a system for simulation and optimization of three dimensional agent structures and their control systems. It allows users to perform pre-defined experiments. It is open and allows creating user-defined experiment setups, fitness functions, and neurons and is suitable for testing various research hypotheses where fast 3D simulation and evolutionary optimization is required.

The physical structure of Framsticks agents is made of parts (material points) and joints. The control system is made of neurons (including sensors and actuators) and their connections. In this work, only a subset of system features was used: physical structure was fixed (not optimized), and there was a homogeneous, fuzzy control system (ie. it was not composed of many heterogeneous neurons with changing topology). Framsticks supports multiple genetic representations and operators. These representations range from simple and direct descriptions of agents to the ones encoding developmental process in genotypes. In this work, the direct encoding was used, and special genetic operators were designed to provide mutation and crossing over of a fuzzy control system.

Licensing Characters from a Virtual Library
One possibility would be for a specialist artificial life company to develop this technology in-house, and build up a huge library, or virtual zoo, of different characters. Games companies could inspect these characters and license individual characters for specific games or other applications. This approach would be particularly appropriate for evolved body shapes as well as controllers, as characters evolved in this way often have very strange or unusual forms and behaviors.

The virtual zoo could therefore act as a source of inspiration for new types of characters, as well as a source for directly licensable characters.

Online Evolution

At the other extreme, a consumer application could be written that allows users to evolve their own creatures, and to exchange them with other users over the Internet. Alternatively, a central server could oversee a genetic algorithm in which the evaluation of individual creatures was farmed out to end-users' PCs over the Internet. This could be achieved as a background process on the PC, while the user was playing a game or it could be run as a screen-saver. Users could also be allowed to guide evolution according to their own aesthetic tastes.

Co-Evolved Characters for Combat Games

Another example application would be to co-evolve twin populations of creatures competing in some sort of contest, such as a combat game. Having co-evolved creatures in this way, by allowing evolution in one population to catalyze evolution in the other, one of the creatures in the contest could simply be replaced by a human player. The difficulty is about designing a user interface that allows the player to control the creature in a suitable way.

Co- Existence

Fig. 1(a) represents the fitness parameters of five different genotypes that are generalist population and fig1b genotypes are of specialist population type. During the fitness test of genotypes only one out of 5 remains at end of the run. Here density dependent selection acts to create multiple niches. At one extreme, organisms could specialize, adapting to one resource at the expense of their competitiveness for others. The effect of this is to partition the environment such that as many species as there are resources are potentially able to coexist. Update function is $O = (2/1+e-i\beta)$. Where O is the activation variant, i denote synaptic weights and β denotes steepness parameter of Transfer function

Altruism and Mutation

The concept of unselfishness that takes place in digital organism evolution during the course of simulation gives interesting information that kin-cheaters eliminate kin-altruists very early. Same group of creatures will not allow it's brother creature to evolve over period of time in order to survive in the world. During this phase there is no sexual contact between organism A (DNA) and B (RNA). Creatures have achieved higher mutation rate when they were tested in an open environment.

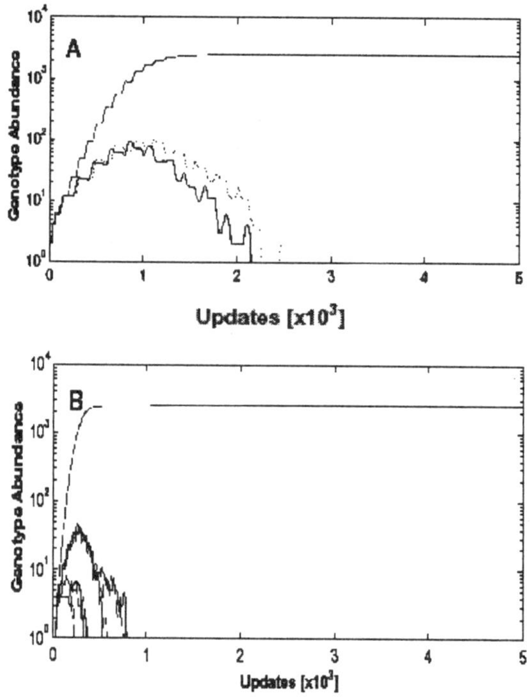

Fig. 1(a)&(b) Co-existence of genotypes during continued ecology phase with infinite resources.

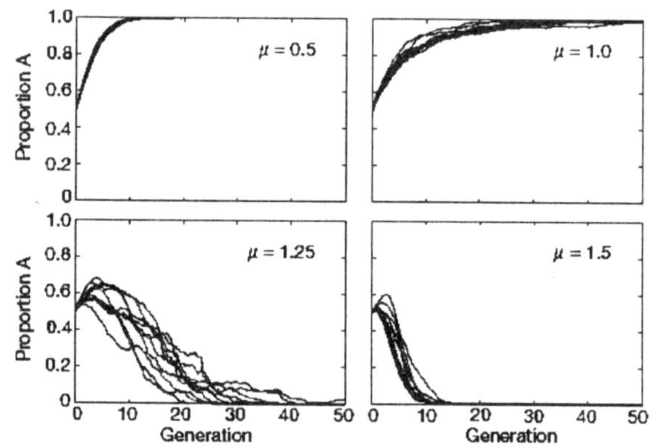

Fig. 2 Competitions for one pair of organisms at four different mutation rates.

Organism A replicates 1.96 times faster than B. Genomic mutation rate Fidelity $F = e\text{-}\mu$. Where $\mu = RL$ is the mutation rate per genome and R is the rate of error per evolving instruction sets, L is the length of the genomic sequence. To measure the actual growth rate of the population spawned from a single organism across a range of mutation rates. The decay in growth rate with increasing mutation rate was well described by

$$w(\mu) = w0 \exp(-a\mu - b\mu 2)$$

w0 is the intrinsic replication rate, a and b are robust parameters estimated by fitting data concerned to the organism groups.

Complex Creatures
(Bending, Rotating, Touching, Equilibrium)
To examine the evolutionary origin of a complex feature in much greater detail we have performed experiments with digital organisms—computer programs that self replicate, mutate and compete. Evolution will occur whenever and wherever three conditions are met: replication, variation (mutation), and differential fitness (competition). According to a case study of the genomic and phenotypic changes in a population that evolved an especially complex function, and then a functional-genomic analysis of the first genotype able to perform that function. Genetic encoding sequence of the digital organism comes with three types that are recurrent, simulated and developed. Genetic encoding .has also got information on no of points, joints, and connections in the respective organism For example in framsticks world genome is represented using the following format X[T][G][S] [-3:1,-2:1,-1:1] Where t denotes touch, G denotes gyroscope and S denotes smell all receptors or sensors mounted in one stick. Here the Brain of the system which is nothing but the neural network of that digital organism.

Table1 Rewards for performing nine one and two input logic functions

Function name	Logic operation	Computational merit
NOT	~A; ~B	2
NAND	~(A and B)	2
AND	A and B	4
OR_N	(A or ~B); (~A or B)	4
OR	A or B	8
AND_N	(A and ~B); (~A and B)	8
NOR	~A and ~B	16
XOR	(A and ~B) or (~A and B)	16
EQU	(A and B) or (~A and ~B)	32

The symbol (~) denotes negation. The reward for computational merit increases with 2n, where n is the minimum number of nand operations needed to perform the listed function. Symmetrical operations, shown separated by a semi-colon, are treated as the same function. No added benefit is obtained for performing any function multiple times. These functions include all one and two-input logic operations except ECHO, which requires no nand operations and was not rewarded. Trajectories of the two fitness components showing each genotype in the line of descent for different population. Replication efficiency which is the ratio of genome length to the energy used in an organism's lifetime and computational merit shown in log2 transformed which is the product of all the rewards obtained by the organism for logic functions performed during its lifetime.

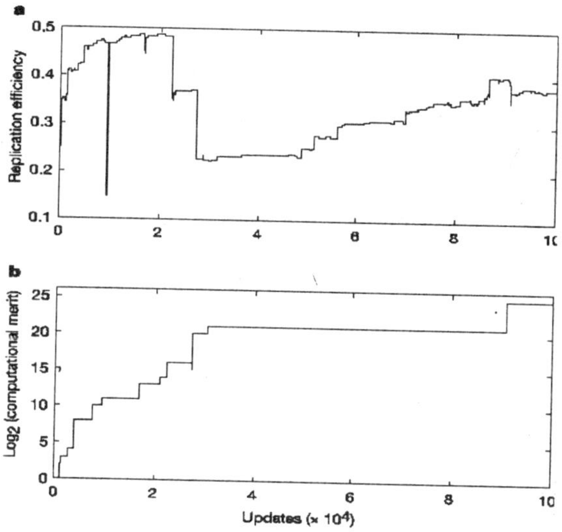

Fig. 3 Fitness function graph

5. Conclusions

With the help of artificial evolution, body shapes of characters and creatures and creating one evolved genetic algorithm and used evolutionary details to capture the complex behaviors of digital organism with difficult fitness functions. This method helps capturing the finest details/movements of various creatures. Methods suggested in this paper vindicate that effective construction of digital creatures and evolving them in an artificial environment provides sufficient information to design the physical controllers in order to emulate them in a successful way.

6. References

[1] Arnold, D. (1997). Evolution of Legged Locomotion. MSc thesis, School of Computing Science, Simon Fraser University.

[2] Bongard, J.C. & Paul, C. (2000). Investigating Morphological Symmetry and Locomotive Efficiency Using Virtual Embodied Evolution. Meyer, J.-A. et al. (eds.) From Animals to Animats: The Sixth International Conference on the Simulation of Adaptive Behavior: MIT Press.

[3] Dorigo, M. & Colombetti, M. (1997). Robot Shaping: An Experiment in Behavior Engineering. MIT Press.

[4] Floreano, D. & Urzelai, J. (1999). Evolution of Neural Controllers with Adaptive Synapses and Compact Genetic Encoding. Floreano, D. et al. (eds.) Advances in Artificial Life: Proceedings of the Fifth European Conference on Artificial Life, pp.183-194: Springer Verlag.

[5] Gritz, L. & Hahn, J. K. (1997). Genetic Programming Evolution of Controllers for 3-D Character Animation. Koza, J.R. et al. (eds.) Genetic Programming 1997: Proceedings of the Second Annual Conference, pp.139-146: Morgan Kaufmann.

[6] Hillis, W. D. (1991). Co-evolving parasites improves simulated evolution as an optimization technique. Langton, C. G. et al. (eds.), Artificial Life II, pp.313-384: Addison-Wesley.

[7] Komosinski, M. & Ulatowski, S. (1999). Framsticks: Towards a Simulation of a Nature-Like World, Creatures and Evolution. Floreano, D. et al. (eds.) Advances in Artificial Life: Proceedings of the Fifth European Conference on Artificial Life, pp.261-265: Springer Verlag.

[8] Lee, W.-P. (1997). Evolving Robots: from Simple Behaviors to Complete Systems. Ph.D. thesis. Department of Artificial Intelligence. University of Edinburgh.

[9] Perkins, S. (1998). Incremental Acquisition of Complex Visual Behaviour using Genetic Programming and Shaping. PhD thesis. Division of Informatics, University of Edinburgh.

[10] Sims, K. (1994b). Evolving Virtual Creatures. Computer Graphics (SIGGRAPH 94 Proceedings), pp.15-22: ACM SIGGRAPH.

[11] Terzopoulos, D., Tu, X. & Grzeszczuk, R. (1994). Artificial Fishes: Automomous Locomotion, Perception, Behavior, and Learning in a Simulated Physical World. Artificial Life 1, pp.327-351.

[12] Van de Panne, M. & Fiume, E. (1993). Sensor-Actuator Networks. Computer Graphics (SIGGRAPH 93 Proceedings), pp.335-342: ACM SIGGRAPH.

[13] Ventrella, J. (1999). Animated Artificial Life. Chapter 3 in Heudin, J.-C. (ed.) Virtual Worlds: Synthetic Universes, Digital Life and Complexity: Perseus Books.

Fault Prognosis for Electrical Equipment for Battery Operated Vehicle

M. Lakshmi Swarupa[1], G. TulasiRamDas[2] and P.V.RajaGopal
[1]Sr. Professor, Sadhana Institute, Balanagar
[2]Director, Academic & Planning, JNTU, Kukatpally
[3]AGM, BHEL R&D

Abstract

An electric vehicle, or BEV (Battery Electrical Vehicle), is a vehicle with one or more electric motors for propulsion. Creating diagnostic information for complex technical systems has become a very costly and challenging process. Separation of the process of creating diagnostics from the processes of design and of reliability analysis (as is the default in many companies) means that reliability analysis work is often ignored or repeated by electronicers creating diagnostics practical and theoretical problems related to the design of real time diagnostics, prognostics, & process modeling systems.

A fault detection method is presented for determining whether a fault exists with a rotating/static element of a vehicle that includes a transducer, a diagnosis sampler, and a controller. In this project, the replacement of ECU (electronic control unit) is obtained by using fault prognosis test. The controlling of the voltage and current sensing is done by microcontroller (PIC16F87xx) programming in CCS C compiler and interfacing is done to LCD.

1. Introduction to Fault Prognosis

Creating diagnostic information for complex technical systems has become a very costly and challenging process. Separation of the process of creating diagnostics from the processes of design and of reliability analysis (as is the default in many companies) means that reliability analysis work is often ignored or repeated by electronicers creating diagnostics practical and theoretical problems related to the design of real time diagnostics, prognostics, & process modeling systems.

Major algorithms for autonomous monitoring of machine health in industrial networks are proposed and relevant architectures for incorporation of intelligent prognostics within plant floor information systems are reviewed. There is currently great interest in the control of multi-agent networked systems.

A fault detection method for determining whether a fault exists with a rotating element of a vehicle that includes a transducer, a diagnosis sampler, and a controller is very simple. The transducer converts sounds to an electrical signal that includes a noise component generated from the rotating element. The diagnosis sampler provides a sample of the electrical signal to the controller, which has functional aspects such as an envelope detect, a spectrum analysis, and a fault detect.

The envelope detect detects an envelope of the electrical signal. The spectrum analysis forms spectra from the envelope of the electrical signal, where the spectra is associated with the noise component generated from the rotating element. The fault detect determines (from the formed spectra) whether the fault exists with the rotating element.

2. Importance of ECU

In automotive electronics, an **electronic control unit** (ECU), also called a control unit or control module, is an embedded system that controls one or more of the electrical subsystems in a vehicle. Some modern cars have up to 70 ECUs, including:

- Electronic Control Unit, also called Power train Control Module (PCM)
- Transmission Control Unit - TCU
- Man Machine Interface - MMI
- Door Control Unit
- Seat Control Unit
- Climate Control Unit
- Speed Control unit

Managing the increasing complexity of ECUs and number of ECUs in a vehicle has become a key challenge for OEMs.

Electronic control unit

An **electronic control unit** *(ECU)* is an electronic control unit, which controls various aspects of an internal combustion electronic's operation. The simplest ECUs control only the quantity of fuel injected into each cylinder in each electronic cycle. More advanced ECUs, found on most modern cars, also control the ignition timing, variable valve timing *(VVT)*, the level of boost maintained by the turbocharger (in turbocharged cars), and control other peripherals. ECUs determine the quantity of fuel, ignition timing and other parameters by monitoring the electronic through sensors. These can include: MAP sensor, throttle position sensor, air temperature sensor, oxygen sensor and many others. Often, this is done using a control loop (such as a PID controller).

Before the use of ECUs, most electronic parameters were fixed. The quantity of fuel per cylinder per electronic cycle was determined by a carburetor or injector pump.

Control of fuel injection

For an electronic with fuel injection, an ECU will determine the quantity of injected fuel based on a number of parameters. If the throttle pedal is pressed further down, this will open the throttle body and allow more air to be pulled into the electronic. The ECU will inject more fuel according to how much air is passing into the electronic. If the electronic has not warmed up yet, more fuel will be injected (causing the electronic to run slightly 'rich' until the electronic warms up).

Control of ignition timing

A spark ignition electronic requires a spark to initiate combustion in the combustion chamber. An ECU can adjust the exact timing of the spark (called ignition timing) to provide better power and economy. If the ECU detects knock, a condition which is potentially destructive to electronics, and "judges" it to be the result of the ignition timing being too early in the compression stroke, it will delay (retard) the timing of the spark to prevent this.

A second, more common source of knock is operating the electronic in too low of an RPM range for the "work" requirement of the moment. In this case, the knock results from the piston not being able to move downward as fast as the flame front is expanding. But, this latter mostly applies only to manual transmission equipped vehicles. The ECU controlling an automatic transmission would simply downshift the transmission were this the cause of knock.

Control of variable valve timing

Some electronics have Variable Valve Timing. In such an electronic, the ECU controls the time in the electronic cycle at which the valves open. The valves are usually opened later at higher speed than at lower speed. This can optimize the flow of air into the cylinder, increasing power and economy.

Control of starting

A relatively recent application of electronic control is the use of precisely timed injection and ignition to start an electronic without the use of a starter motor. Such a *static-start* electronic would provide the efficiency and pollution-reduction improvements of a mild hybrid-electric drive, but without the expense and complexity of an oversized starter motor.

Programmable ECUs

A special category of ECUs are those which are programmable. These units do not have a fixed behavior, but can be reprogrammed by the user.

Programmable ECUs are required where significant aftermarket modifications have been made to a vehicle's electronic. Examples include adding or changing of a turbocharger, adding or changing of an intercooler, changing of the exhaust system, and conversion to run on alternative fuel. As a consequence of these changes, the old ECU may not provide appropriate control for the new configuration. In these situations, a programmable ECU can be wired in. These can be programmed with a laptop connected using a serial or USB cable, while the electronic is running.

The programmable ECU may control the amount of fuel to be injected into each cylinder. This varies depending on the electronic's RPM and the position of the gas pedal (or the manifold air pressure). The electronic tuner can adjust this by bringing up a spreadsheet-like page on the laptop where each cell represents an intersection between a specific RPM value and a gas pedal position (or the throttle position, as it is called). In this cell, a number corresponding to the amount of fuel to be injected is entered.

By modifying these values while monitoring the exhausts using a wide band lambda probe to see if the electronic runs rich or lean, the tuner can find the optimal amount of fuel to be injected into the electronic at every different combination of RPM and throttle position. This process is often carried out at a dynamometer, giving the tuner a controlled environment to work in.

Other parameters that are often mappable are:

- **Ignition:** Defines when the spark plug should fire for a cylinder.
- **Rev limit:** Defines the maximum RPM that the electronic is allowed to rev to. After this, fuel and/or ignition is cut.
- **Water temperature correction:** Allows for additional fuel to be added when the electronic is cold (choke).
- **Transient fueling:** Tells the ECU to add a specific amount of fuel when throttle is applied.
- **Low fuel pressure modifier:** Tells the ECU to increase the injector fire time to compensate for a loss of fuel pressure.
- **Closed loop lambda:** Lets the ECU monitor a permanently installed lambda probe and modify the fueling to achieve stoichiometric (ideal) combustion.

Some of the more advanced ECUs include functionality, such as launch control, limiting the power of the electronic in first gear to avoid burnouts.

- **Waste gate control:** Sets up the behavior of a turbo waste gate, controlling boost.
- **Banked injection:** Sets up the behavior of double injectors per cylinder, used to get a finer fuel injection control and atomization over a wide RPM range.
- **Variable cam timing:** Tells the ECU how to control variable intake and exhaust cams.
- **Gear control:** Tells the ECU to cut ignition during (sequential gearbox) upshifts or blip the throttle during downshifts.

A ECU is often equipped with a data logger recording all sensors for later analysis using special software in a PC. This can be useful to track down electronic stalls, misfires or other undesired behaviors during a race by downloading the log data and looking for anomalies after the event. The data logger usually has a capacity between 0.5 and 16 megabytes. In order to communicate with the driver, an ECU can often be connected to a "data stack", which a simple dash board is presenting the driver with the current RPM, speed and other basic electronicdata.

ECU flashing

Many recent (around 1996 or newer) cars use OBD-II ECUs that are sometimes capable of having their programming changed through the OBD port. Automotive enthusiasts with modern cars take advantage of this technology when tuning their electronics. Rather than use an entire new electronic management system, one can use the appropriate software to adjust the factory equipped computer. By doing so, it is possible to retain all stock functions and wiring while using a custom tuned program. This should not be confused with "chip tuning", where the owner has ECU ROM physically replaced with a different one -- no hardware modification is (usually) involved with flashing ECUs, although special equipment is required.

Factory electronic management systems often have similar controls as aftermarket units intended for racing, such as 3-dimensional timing and fuel control maps. They generally do not have the ability to control extra ancillary devices, such as variable valve timing if the factory vehicle was a fixed

Block Diagram of Fault Prognosis

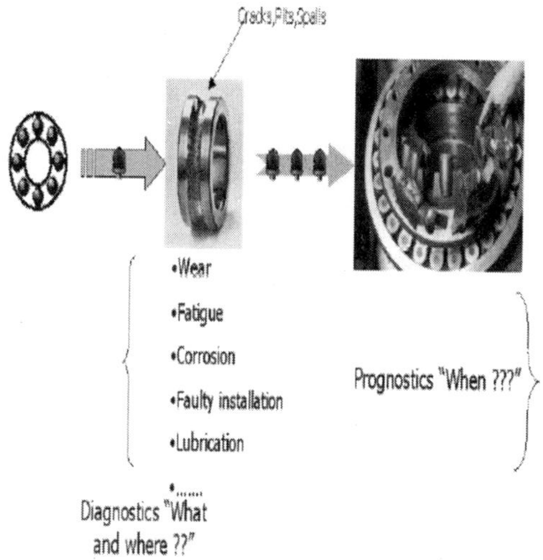

Fig. 1 Diagnostics and prognostics of rolling element bearings

3. Comparison of ECU and Fault Prognosis

In Fig (1, 2, 3, and 4) shows the diagnostics and prognostics of the rolling element bearings, which is the difference between them and a flowchart representation. Method for monitoring an apparatus, such as a marine propulsion system, and determining how various measurements of indicator parameters should be compared to reference magnitudes of those indicator parameters. In addition, the method monitors the usage time of the apparatus at various operating conditions to determine whether or not calculated reference magnitudes should be used to determine appropriate and inappropriate power spectral density profiles for various indicator parameters. Conventional maintenance strategies consist of corrective and preventive maintenance. In corrective maintenance, the system is maintained on an "as-needed" basis, usually after a major breakdown. In preventive maintenance, components are replaced based on a conservative schedule to "prevent" commonly occurring failures. Although preventive maintenance programs increase system availability, they are expensive because of frequent replacement of costly parts before the end of their life. Another disadvantage of preventive maintenance is that it is time-based. Studies have revealed that most of the equipment failures are not related to the number of hours they were operated. Hence, time-based solutions are not cost-effective. Consequently, these conventional maintenance strategies are not adequate to fulfill the needs of expensive and high availability industrial systems.

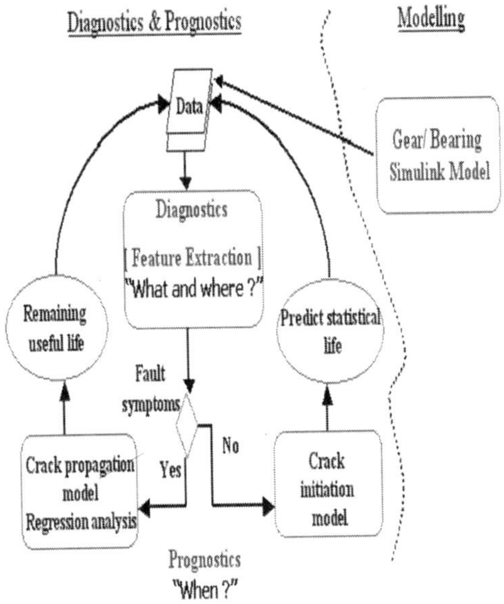

Fig. 2 Main areas of project

Condition-based predictive maintenance is an alternative that uses embedded diagnostics and prognostics to determine system's health. Failure prognosis involves forecasting of system degradation based on observed system condition. The recent advances in model-based design technology have resulted in significant time savings in product development cycle.

A number of applications of model-based design can be found in automotive, aerospace and defense industries. Because system model is simulated early in the design stage, the reliability and robustness of the system are ultimately increased. These advances facilitate the integration of model-based diagnosis and prognosis of systems, leading to condition-based maintenance and increased availability of systems. With an accurate simulation model of a system, diagnostics and prognostics can be synthesized concurrently with system design. An intelligent model-based diagnostic procedure combines quantitative and graph-based dependency models. The hybrid model-based diagnostic method not only improves the diagnostic system's accuracy and consistency of those based solely on a graph based model, but also exploits the existing validated knowledge on rule-based methods, enables rapid remote diagnosis, and responds to the challenge of increased system complexity. The hybrid model-based diagnostic process was demonstrated on an anti-lock braking system. In this project, the focus of our application is on prognosis (remaining life prediction) of an automotive suspension system. However, the solution is generic and has the potential for application in a wide range of systems.

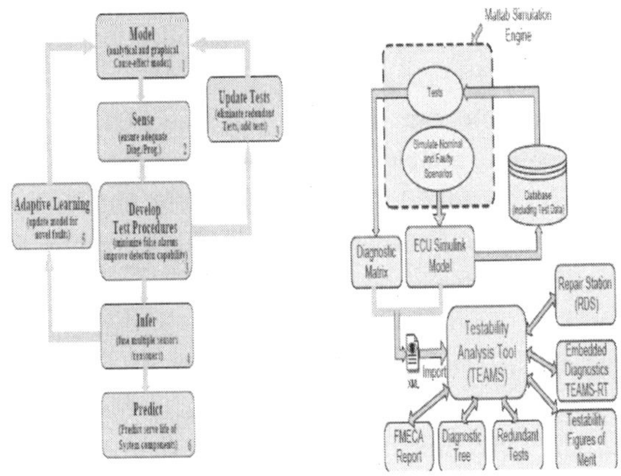

Fig. 3 (a) Intelligent diagnostic and prognostics (b) Hybrid model approach process

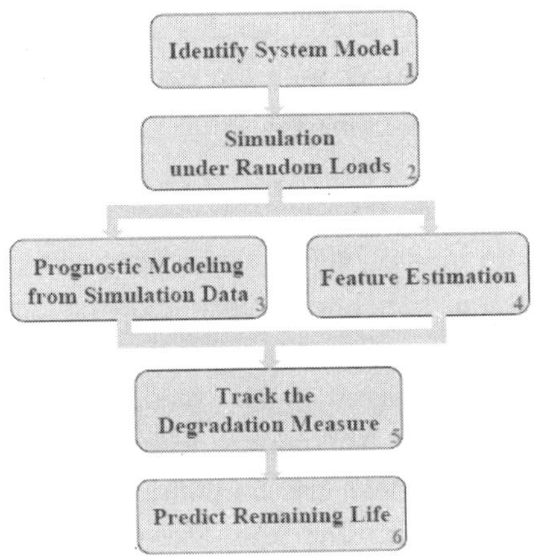

Fig. 4 Model- based prognostic process

Many industrial systems exhibit increasing wear and tear of equipment during operation. For example, an automobile has many pieces of equipment, such as the electronic, gearbox and valves that exhibit various types of performance degradation due to erosion, friction, internal damage and cracks. Prognostics are viewed as an add-on capabilities to diagnosis; they assess the current health of a system and predict its remaining life based on features that capture the gradual degradation in the operational capabilities of a system.

4. Complete Circuit

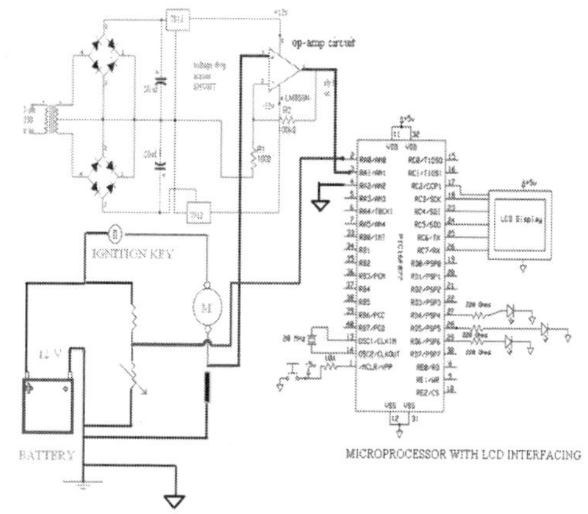

Fig. 5 Complete circuit diagram

In Fig (5) the fault prognosis test is proved for the battery and similarly can be extended to all other electrical equipments.

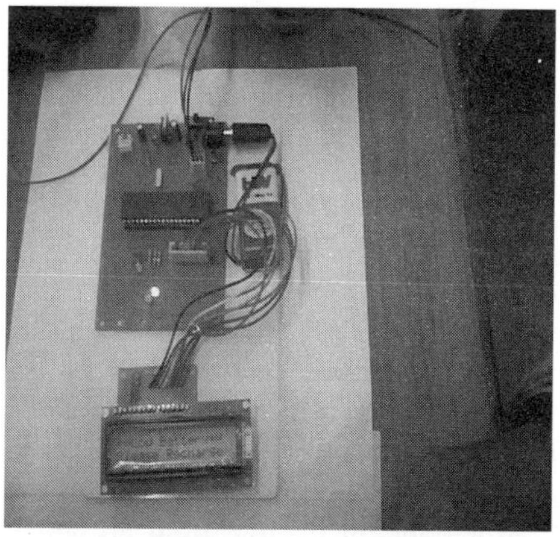

Fig. 6 Microcontroller (PIC) kit with LCD display

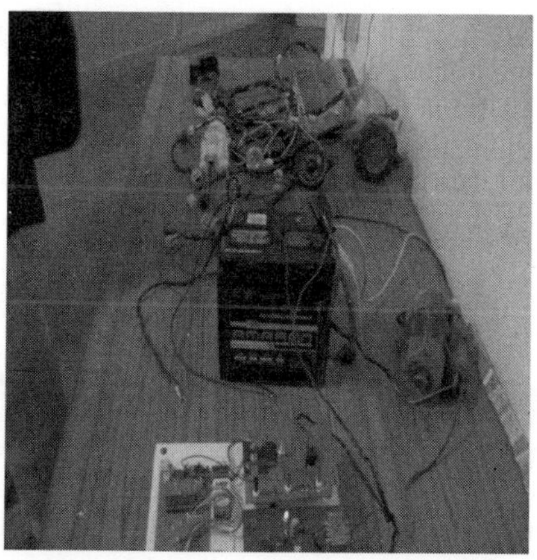

Fig. 7 Real model with electrical wiring of Maruti car with controlling by microcontroller

5. Conclusions

Automotive systems are becoming increasingly dependent on electrical components, computer control, and sensors. It has become extremely critical to detect faults in the electrical system and predict the remaining useful life of failing components. This project introduces an integrated methodology for monitoring, modeling, data processing, fault diagnosis, and failure prognosis of critical electrical components such as the battery.

The enabling technologies include signal processing, sensor selection and placement, selection and extraction of optimum condition indicators, and accurate fault diagnosis and failure prognosis algorithms that are based on both the physics of failure models and Bayesian estimation methods.

The proposed architecture is implementable on-board an Electronic Control Unit (ECU) requiring minimum computational resources. Potential benefits include reduction in maintenance costs, improved asset reliability and availability and longer life of critical components like battery in Maruti 800 vehicle. Fault prognosis programming was done in CCS software using PIC 16F87X microcontroller.

6. References

[1] **www.booksgoogle.com**

[2] **www.ieeexplore.ieee.org**

[3] **Hybrid Electric vehicles by Iqbal Hussain**

[4] **www.fuelcells.org**

[5] **www.revacars.com**

[6] **Hybrid Electric vehicles by crouise**

[7] http://www.freepatentsonline.com/ 5434019.html

[8] www.greencarcongress.com/2005/06/ degussa_and_ena.html

[9] www.siamindia.com/scripts/rules.aspx

[10] www.researchandmarkets.com/reports/ 357524/intelligent_**fault**_diagnosis_and_**prognosis**.pdf

Modeling of Direct Silicon Fusion Wafer Level Packaging

Shruti Jain[1], S. C. Sood[2] and C. C. Tripathi[3]
[1]Dept. of ECE, Jaypee University of Information Technology, Solan-173215, India
[2]Ambala College of Engineering. & Applied Research, Ambala Cantt, India
[3]University Institute of Engineering Technology, Kurukshetra University, Kurukshetra-132119 India
jain.shruti15@gmail.com *soodsu@icqmail.com*

Abstract

In this paper, we present the process for silicon-to-silicon bonding. High temperature annealing prevents the use of bonding technology for compound semiconductor materials since their dissociation temperature is usually low. The elevated temperature is the driving force for a chemical reaction at the interface resulting in the increase of Si-O-Si bonds. A model for the bonding process that is based on the structure of the adsorbed water molecules at the SiO_2 surface is discussed. We haved observed that at constant temperature the surface energy has exponential dependence on time also for fixed activation energy; the surface energy is exponential function of temperature.

Keywords: *Direct wafer bonding, activation energy, surface energy, annealing temperature.*

1. Introduction

The MEMS represents the new revolution in microelectronics. It is similar to VLSI circuits in that it allows the execution of complex functions on a size scale orders of magnitude lower and at far less power than discrete circuits [1]. In the past decades, many advances have been made in the fabrication of miniaturized mechanical structures. MEMS are characterized widely as sensors/actuators, MOEMS, Bio MEMS and RF MEMS (as shown in Fig.1.) RF MEMS is an emerging technology that promises the potential of revolutionalizing RF and microwave system implementation for the next generation of telecommunication applications [2,3]. Its low power, better RF performance, large tuning range and integration capability are the key characteristics enabling system implementation. An RF MEMS switch is one of the basic building blocks in the RF communication system. RF MEMS switches have drawn a lot of attention since they have the ability to significantly out perform their solid state counterparts improving the efficiencies of their host systems.

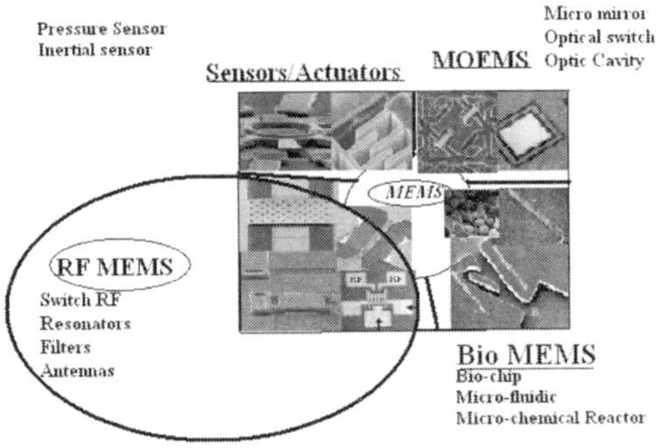

Fig. 1 Different MEMS areas.

Yet the application of this technology is hampered by the lack of production-worthy packages. There are several wafer-level packaging (WLP) techniques widely used with silicon micromachining: fusion bonding, anodic bonding, eutectic bonding, thermal compression bonding, and glass-frit bonding. Direct bonding also known as Silicon-fusion bonding is typically associated with bonding of two silicon wafers. The direct silicon bonding is independent of crystallographic structure, crystal orientation, and lattice mismatch, conductivity type or resistivity of the wafers [3, 4]. The main criteria for bonding are surface cleanliness, which should be free from all sought of contaminations, and the surface smoothness should be less than the lattice constant of the crystal. So when extremely clean and sufficiently smooth wafers are brought into contact with each other they can be reliably bonded with nearly perfect interface due to the intermolecular forces of attraction between them. So this technique has got an excellent application in depositing the silicon layer of different resistivity (epitaxy), which has lesser defects and quite cheap as compare to conventional growth of epitaxial layer [5]. In order for wafer bonding to occur at room temperature, under atmospheric pressure conditions, the surfaces to be bonded have to be mirror polished, totally dust free and hydrophilic. The latter of the three conditions implies that silanol groups (≡Si—OH) are present at the bonding interface that may form siloxane (≡Si—O—Si≡) bonds between the two surfaces accompanied by the release of water at temperatures above 500°C.

2. Experimental

The silicon wafers used in this process were 2 cm square peaces, polished N-type<111> of resistivity 40 to 60 ohms-cm and thickness 280 μm. The silicon wafers for bonding was prepared by using standard RCA solution, consisting of mixture of ammonium hydroxide (NH_4OH), hydrogen peroxide (H_2O_2) and DI water as 1:1:5 The wafer were dipped in the mixture at 70°C for 15 min and then rinsed in DI water for five min. Then the wafers were kept in ultrasonic bath for five min. and this helps in removing the particles from the surface of wafers by mechanical action. The wafers are dipped in hot HNO_3 for 15 min and then rinsed with DI water for five min. The surface thus obtained was hydrophilic in nature due to the absorption of OH ions at the surface. The wafers were then blown dry by nitrogen gas and then immediately brought in contact with each other. Then slight pressure was applied with the help of tweezer to make sure that bonding had taken place at room temperature [1, 6]. The contacting forces are believed to be caused by attraction between hydroxyl groups (—OH) and possibly some water molecules adsorbed on the two surfaces. The attraction can be significant enough to cause the spontaneous formation of hydrogen bonds across the gap between two wafers. The spontaneity in the initiation of the contacting occurs only between exceptionally flat, smooth, and clean surfaces. Once initiated, this bonding process can spread in a form of "contacting wave" throughout the entire area between two silicon wafers with speeds of several cm/s. MATLAB has been used for calculating surface energy with variation in time, temperature and activation energy.

3. Results and Discussions

Hydrogen bonding between OH groups terminated on opposite surfaces (initially via water bridging) has been recognized as the bonding mechanism of hydrophilic Si/Si, and SiO_2/SiO_2 pairs at room temperature (RT) [7, 8]. According to the following reaction the polymerization of silanol bonds is possible even at RT if the two OH groups are close neighbors such as those that are hydrogen bonded.

$$\underset{(Silanol)}{Si-OH}+OH-Si\rightarrow \underset{(Siloxane)}{Si-O-Si}+H_2O \qquad (1)$$

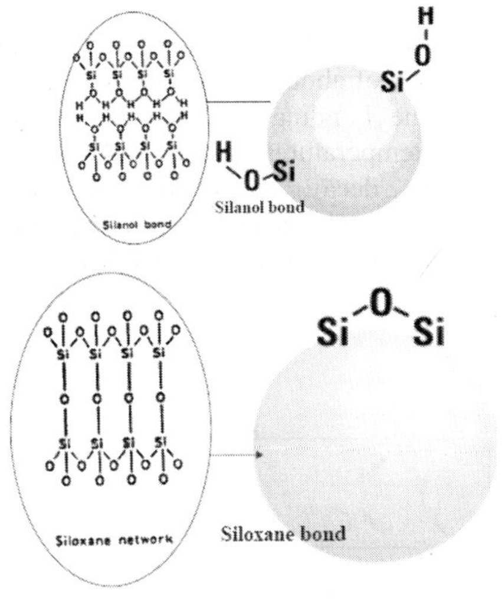

Fig. 2 Formation of Silanol bond and Siloxane bond.

The above reaction is reversible at $T<\sim 400^{\circ}C$ and is characterized by equilibrium between concentrations of OH groups and molecular water at a given temperature. The polymerization of the hydrogen bonded silanol (Si—OH) bonds between opposite bonding surfaces can occur when excess water is removed by either laterally migrating away from the bonding interface or by diffusion into the surrounding oxide. On the other hand, if excess water is present, the siloxane (Si—O—Si) bonds both on and between the mating surfaces can react with the interface water and rupture. This reaction has been termed "slow fracture effect" [7, 8]. After RT bonding water at the interface of hydrophilic Silicon wafers attacks the strained Si-O-Si bonds on both mating surfaces to form hydrogen bonded OH group pairs on each of the mating surfaces. Some of these newly generated singular OH groups are likely to interact to form hydrogen bonds between opposite wafer surfaces and result in enhanced interface energy. The percentage of OH groups forming hydrogen bonds is again a function of storage temperature as well as storage duration. For this bonding process model (similar with Stengl et al) that is based on the structure of the adsorbed water molecules at the SiO_2 surface is designed [9]. If two of the SiO_2 surfaces with adsorbed water are brought into the intimate contact, hydrogen bonds develop between the oxygen and hydrogen atoms of the adsorbed water molecules. (The specific structure is shown schematically in the upper part of Fig. 3.). If the adsorbed water molecules of the two SiO_2 surfaces are joined in the way given in Fig. 3, four of these water molecules can form a water cluster (cyclic tetramer). It is therefore energetically favorable that, after bonding, the water clusters separate forms the $SiOH$ groups and form rings around the now developing $SiOH:SiOH$

bonds. The mid portion of Fig. 3. show the product of this reaction for one bonding site. Since the tetramers have a diameter of about 4Å they cannot easily diffuse away from the bonding interface through the SiO_2 network. At temperatures above 700ºC, however, the water clusters decay and diffuse away from the interface. The single silanol bonds may now form SiOSi bonds accompanied by the release of a water monomer.

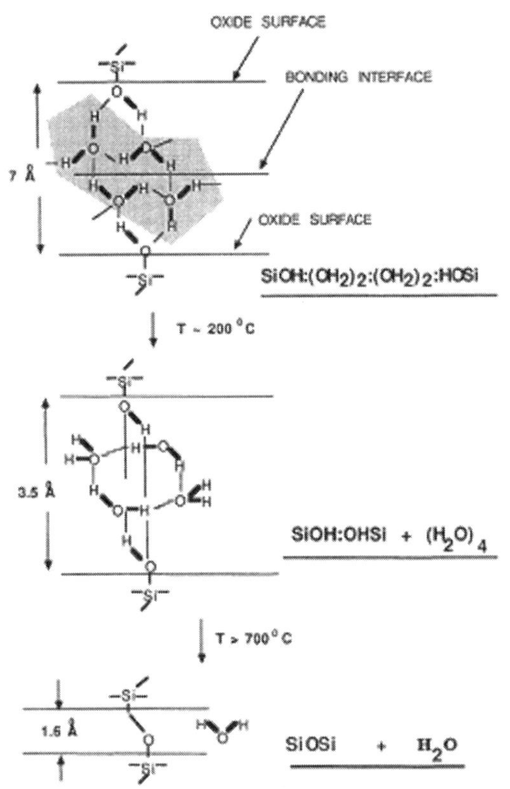

Fig. 3 Proposed model for the silicon wafer bonding process

Model accounts three step wafer bonding process [9]. Phase 1 the two wafers are joined via water clusters and the surface energy is roughly 100 erg/cm^2. In Phase 2 hydrogen bonds between silanol groups connect the wafers. The maximum surface energy in Phase 2 is 634 erg/cm^2. Above 800ºC in Phase 3 siloxane bonds develop between the two wafers, and a monomer is released during this step which diffuses away immediately from the interface. In Phase 3 the maximum bonding strength of more than 634 erg/cm^2. In a very thorough investigation, we come to know that surface energies as a function of annealing time and temperature. For convenience we choose the following abbreviations:

$$A = SiOH : \left(OH_2\right)_2 : \left(OH_2\right)_2 : OHSi$$

$$B = SiOH : SiOH \quad (2)$$

$$B^* = SiOH : SiOH + \left(H_2O\right)_4$$

The structures corresponding to A, B and B* are also shown in Fig 3. Some of the important possible reactions occurring between Phase 1and Phase 2 may then be written as

$$A \rightarrow B^* \quad (3)$$

The reaction occurring between Phase 2 and Phase 3 are

$$(H_20)_4 \rightarrow (H_20)_3 + H_20\uparrow \rightarrow (H_20)_2 + (H_20)\uparrow \rightarrow 2(H_20)\uparrow \quad (4)$$

$$B \leftrightarrow SiOSi + H_2O \quad (5)$$

$$B \xrightarrow{k_2} SiOSi + H_2O\uparrow \quad (6)$$

The activation energy for reaction (3) should be of the order of the energy per hydrogen bond that is in the range of about 50meV. The activation energy "E_a" for reaction (6) should be between 1.8 and 2.1 eV since this reaction is similar to the surface reaction involved in silicon oxidation.

k_2 in equation (6) is written as

$$k_2 = \frac{1}{\tau}\exp\left(-\frac{E_a}{kT}\right), \quad (7)$$

where k is boltzmann's constant, τ is time constant parameter or fitting parameter that may depend on mechanical properties of the interface and T the absolute temperature.

In comparison with experimental data we assume that the gain in surface energy is proportional to the number of SiOSi bonds. We then get

$$W = \left[(1960-634)\times\left(1-\exp\left(-k_2t\right)\right)+634\right]\text{erg/cm}^2 \quad (8)$$

as an expression for the bonding energy. Fig. 4. shows a data for water treated samples and eq (8) with the constant parameter τ =7ms[9] and E_a=1.8eV calculated for four different temperatures.

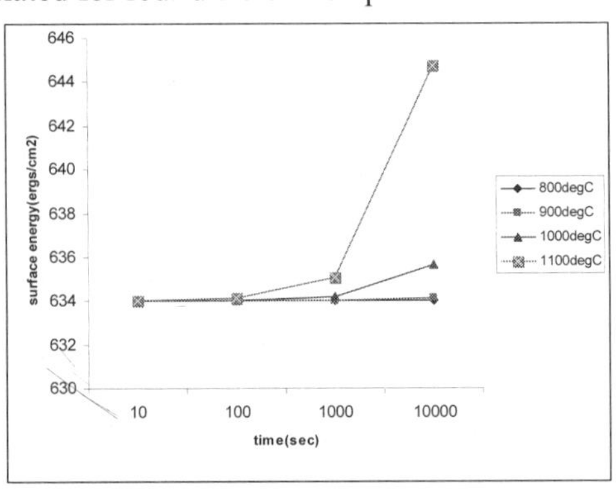

Fig. 4. Dependence of bonding strength versus annealing time calculated with E_a=1.8eV and τ =7ms

From Eq 8 we also come to know that there is exponential dependence of surface energy with temperature at constant activation energies E_a. As the E_a increases from (1.8eV-2.1eV) the surface energy decreases at higher temperature but remain constant between 800°C-900°C i.e. around 634erg/cm^2

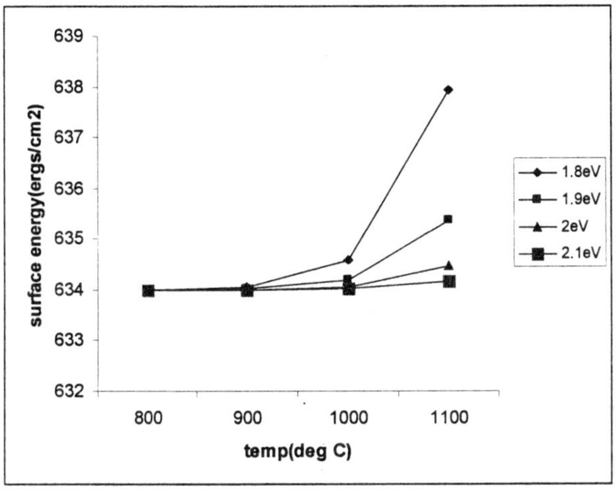

Fig. 5 Dependence of surface energy (bonding strength) versus temperature calculated with different activation energies E_a (time=1 hr and τ =7msec)

The surface energies for the different temperatures (T<800°C) do not saturate at a value of about 600erg/cm^2 with increasing annealing time. The bonding strength up to an annealing temperature of 800°C is well described by the equation

$$W_B = 630 \exp\left(\frac{-0.05eV}{kT}\right) erg/cm^2 \qquad (9)$$

In the total investigated temperature range, the surface energy may be written as:

$$W = \left(1960\, erg/cm^2 - W_B\right) \times \left[1 - \exp\left(-k_2 t\right)\right] + W_B \qquad (10)$$

This shows the exponential dependence of surface energy with temperature (T<800°C) at constant activation energy i.e. 0.05eV .For temperature T>800°C, E_a =1.8eV the surface energy remains constant i.e. around 634 erg/cm^2. Thus result indicates that the surface energy comes out to be 634 erg/cm^2 after annealing at 800°C and remains constant till 1000°C up to 10000sec (~2hrs).

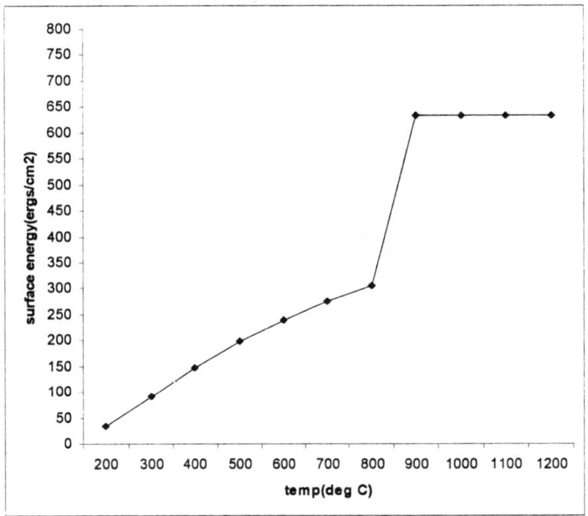

Fig. 6 Surface energy vs Temp (If temp<800°C, E_a=0.05eV and for temp>800°C, E_a=1.8eV)

4. Conclusion

The silicon-to-silicon wafer bonding has a potential bright future as it can be used to fabricate much smaller devices and now as the technology is advancing its getting smaller and more reliable. It has been found that when sufficiently smooth, properly clean and activated surfaces are brought into close contact the bonding can be achieved at room temperature. Surface roughness can be accommodated in bonding process by the presence of hydroxyl groups (Si-OH) on silicon in case of hydrophilic bonding. We have developed the quantitative model for the silicon wafer bonding reaction kinetics with mechanisms that explain the basic three-step reaction during bonding. We come to know that the percentage of OH groups forming hydrogen bonds is a function of storage temperature as well as storage duration. We have observed that at constant temperature the surface energy has exponential dependence on time also for fixed activation energy; the surface energy is exponential function of temperature. Thus result indicates that the surface energy comes out to be 634 erg/cm^2 after annealing at 800°C and remains constant till 1000°C up to 10000sec (~2hrs). Experimentally we have observed that the bonding strength achieved is comparable to that of bulk silicon that is at 800°C in 2 hrs. Results are similar to that of theoretical modeling.

5. References

[1] Madou, M.J., "Fundamentals of Micro fabrication", The Science of Miniaturization, CRC Press, and Boca Raton, FL, 2002.

[2] M.S. Giridhar, et al, "High performance MEMS based RF switches for satellite communication", Proceedings of ISSS 2005, SE-24, July 28-30, 2005.

[3] W. P. Maszara, "Silicon-on-insulator by wafer bonding: A review," *J. Electrochem. Soc.*, vol. 138, no. 1, p. 341, Jan. 1991.

[4] Kurt Petersen, et al, "Silicon Fusion Bonding for Pressure Sensor", Nova sensor, 1055 Mission Court Fremont, CA 94539 (415) 490-9100.

[5] P. W. Barth, "Silicon fusion bonding for fabrication of sensors, actuators and microstructures," *Sensors Actuators,* vol. A21 -A23, pp. 919- 926, 1990.

[6] Gandhi Sourabh K, VLSI Fabrication Principles, 2nd edition, John Wiley & Sons, 1994.

[7] Q.-Y. Tong, G. Cha, R. Gafiteanu, and U. G¨osele, "Low temperature wafer direct bonding," *J. .Microelectromech. Syst.*, vol. 3, no. 1, p. 29, Mar. 1994.

[8] M. Shimbo, K. Furukawa, K. Fukuda, and K. Tanzawa, "Silicon-to-silicon direct bonding method," J. Appl. *Phys.*, vol. 60, 2987 (1986).

[9] R. Stengl, T. Tan, and U. Gosele, "A model for the silicon wafer bonding process," *Japan. J. Appl. Phys.*, vol. 28, No. 10, pp. 1735-1741, 1989.

Designing a Low Power Sigma Delta Modulator and HRV Analysis for ECG System

T. Padma[1], M. Madhavi Latha[2], K. Jaya Kumar[3] and B. Balaji[4]
[1,3]Associate Professor, Gokaraju Rangaraju Institute of Engineering and Technology
[2]Professor, JNT University
[4]Assistant Professor, Gokaraju Rangaraju Institute of Engineering and Technology
tatipartipadma@gmail.com mkmakkena@yahoo.com jaykumar70@yahoo.com balu_802@yahoo.com

Abstract

The vital signal for monitoring and analyzing is the electrocardiography (ECG). The advancement in the electronics and its applications in medicine it is possible to transmit and process many vital signs of biological parameters. So such a widespread use of bio-electrical signal monitoring systems are already exist that can collect and analyze these individual signals. The recording and interpretation of the ECG has a long history and its important aspects of clinical evaluation of an individual cardiac status and overall health. The different biomedical signals have different amplitudes and frequencies. Creating a small sized and low cost device for the collection of several different biomedical signals is not a simple task, because multiple frequencies and amplitudes occur in one signal. The Pre-amplifier section was designed on PCB. The second order sigma-delta ADC and Filter modules were implemented using FPGA. The transmission was made using Bluetooth technology.

Keywords: *Field Programmable Gate Array (FPGA), Sigma Delta Modulator, Low Pass Filter, Decimation Filter, FIR Filter, Heart Rate Variability (HRV), Heart Rate(HR)*

1. Introduction

An ECG is a measurement of the electrical activity of the heart (cardiac) muscle as obtained from the surface of the skin. As the heart performs its function of pumping blood through the circulatory system[1]. The result of the action potentials responsible for the mechanical events within the heart is the generation of P, QRS, T and U wave sequence of electrical events.

Thus, this whole device can be deployed as a wearable component that contains all sensors, processing logic, analysis and communication equipment. A simple block diagram as shown in fig.1. Illustrates the basic architecture of the ECG system[3].

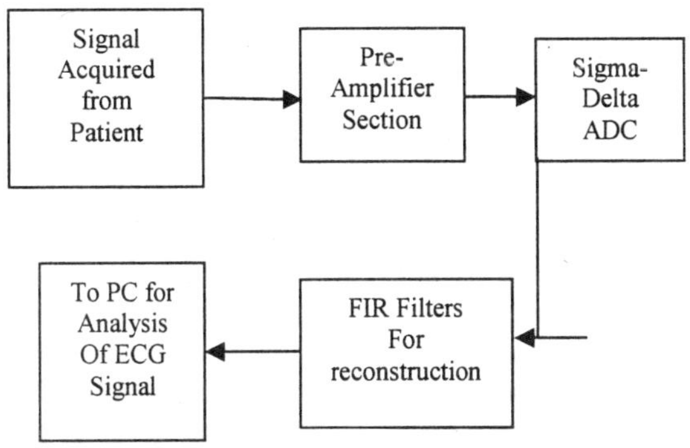

Fig. 1 Block Diagram of the ECG system

Currently biomedical instrumentation is performed with the use of discrete elements, but advances in IC technology made the creation of an integrated circuit possible. This includes the ability to mix analog and digital functions during the creation on an IC (e.g., the Analog Devices and Signal Conditioning ADC) with the help of FPGA implementation. The brief information related to all the blocks are discussed below.

2. Signal Acquired from Patient

Electrodes are used for sensing bio-electric potentials as caused by muscle and nerve cells of the patient. ECG electrodes are generally of the direct-contact type. They work as transducers converting ionic flow from the body through an electrolyte into electron current and consequentially an electric potential measurable by the front end of the ECG system. These transducers, known as bare-metal or recessed electrodes, generally consist of a metal such as silver or stainless steel, with a jelly electrolyte that contains chloride and other ions.

The front end of an ECG sensor must be able to deal with the extremely weak nature of the signal it is measuring[2]. Even the strongest ECG signal has a magnitude of less than 10mV, and furthermore the ECG signals have very low drive (very high output impedance). The requirements for a typical ECG sensor include:

- Capability to sense low amplitude signals in the range of 0.05 – 10mV
- Very high input impedance, > 5 MΩ
- Very low input leakage current, < 1 micro-Amp
- Flat frequency response of 0.05 – 150 Hz
- High Common Mode Rejection Ratio

3. Pre-Amplifier

The Pre-amplifier is extremely important to the design for several reasons. Amplification is nearly always necessary in electrophysiological applications. This is because biomedical signals have extremely low frequencies and amplitudes are in a frequency range that is prone to corruption by the 50/60Hz noise produced by power supplies. A Pre-amplifier also allows subtraction of an error signal to eliminate motion artifacts and baseline drift, other common noise sources, from biomedical signals.

The front-end for the signal acquisition system is an instrumentation amplifier. It has a very high common mode rejection ratio (CMRR) and high input impedance which is required for capturing ECG signals. The Analogue Devices AD624 was chosen for implementation in the system. The AD624 is a high-precision, low-noise, instrumentation amplifier[5] designed primarily for use with bio-electronics. Fig.2. shows the pin connections of the AD624 as integrated into the breadboard circuitry. A gain of 1000 was setup by connecting pins 3, 11 and 13.

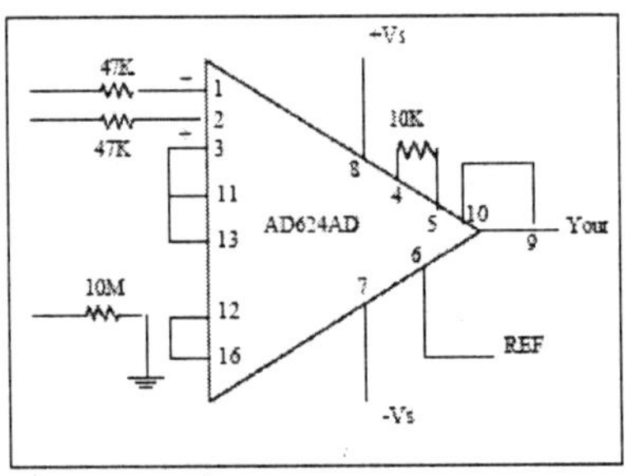

Fig. 2 AD624 Circuit Diagram

The EKG signals were amplified by the instrumentation amplifier and fed into the noise filtering circuits [4] in different stages.

Low pass filter: F_{low}= 33.33 Hz
High pass filter: F_{high}=0.33 Hz
Notch filter: F_{notch}=50Hz

4. Sigma-delta ADC

Suppressing the power consumption will be widely utilized for biomedical application. At the same time, in order to get accurate data, the simple Sigma delta modulation is first-selected to incorporate on the system chip definitely. Sigma-delta modulator has proven to be very suitable in low frequency, high performance application. One of advantages of sigma-delta ADCs is that they do not require high-precision and accurately trimmed analog components. With sigma-delta architectures, a resolution up to 16~24 bits can be reached using standard IC technologies Sigma-delta converters offer high resolution, high integration, and low cost, making them a good ADC choice for applications such as biomedical. Some of the advantages of sigma delta converters include relaxed requirements for anti-alias filters and component matching, high resolution and compatibility with digital VLSI technology

Second order sigma delta modulator consists of two integrator, 1-bit ADC, and 1-bit DAC. The power of the first integrator is the major consumption to the overall power dissipation in sigma delta modulator. The output of the sigma-delta modulator is a 1-bit data stream at the sampling rate, which can be in the megahertz range. The purpose of the digital-and-decimation filters is to extract information from this data stream and reduce the data rate to a more useful value. In a sigma-delta ADC, the digital filter averages the 1-bit data stream, improves the ADC[7]resolution, and removes quantization noise (i.e. outside the band of interest), it determines the signal bandwidth, settling time, and stop band rejection.

A sigma-delta ADC consists of a sigma-delta modulator and a digital filter, as shown in Fig.4. Sigma-delta modulator (or noise-shaper) shapes the quantization noise and push the majority of the in band noise to higher frequencies. The digital filter removes the high frequency quantization noise and down samples the high frequency to Nyquist rate.

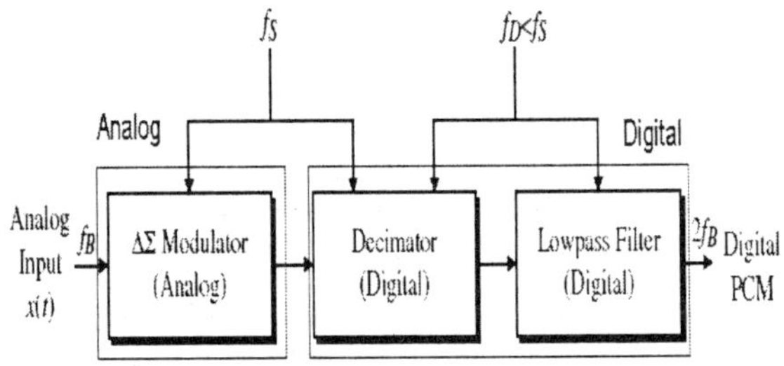

Fig. 3 Simple Block Diagram of a First Order Sigma-Delta ADC

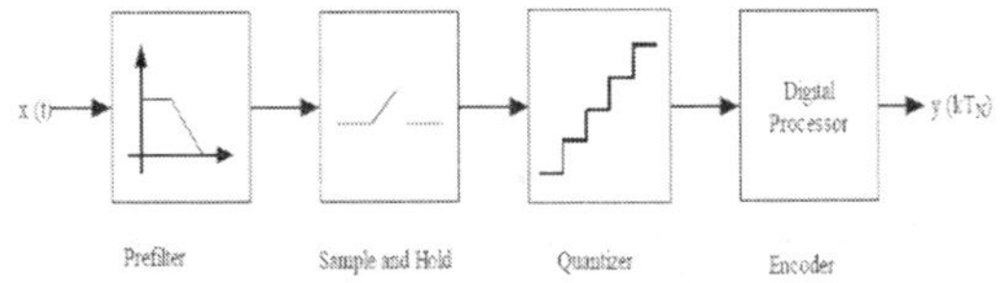

Fig. 4 Block diagram of General ADC

Most integrated circuit implementation of sigma delta ADCs use Switched Capacitor circuits because it are easily simulated, compatible with VLSI CMOS process. The model based second order Sigma Delta modulator with switched capacitor was designed using MatLab Simulink as shown in the Fig. 5 and also the simulated results are as shown in the Fig. 6 and Fig. 7. The bit loss is being represented by hysteresis curve and the frequency response is as shown in Fig. 8.

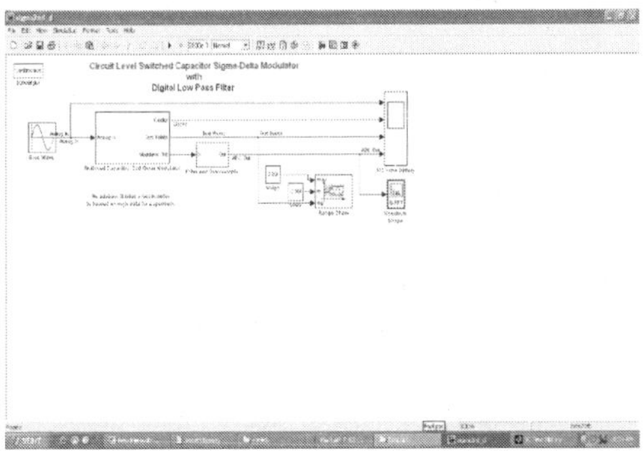

Fig. 5 Sigma Delta ADC with Switched Capacitor and Low Pass Filter Second Order

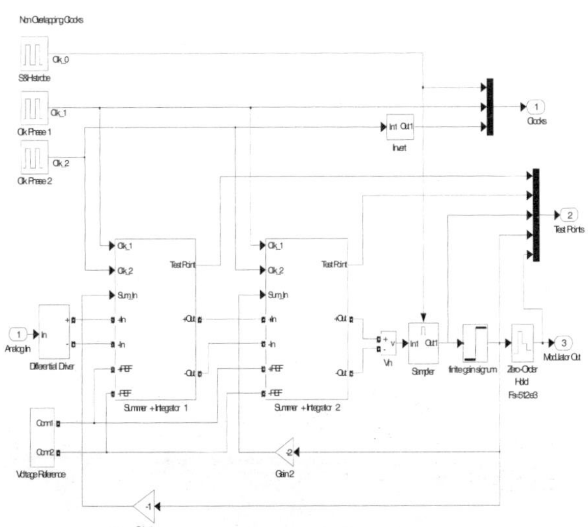

Fig. 6 Circuit Level Switched Capacitor Sigma Delta Modulator Result

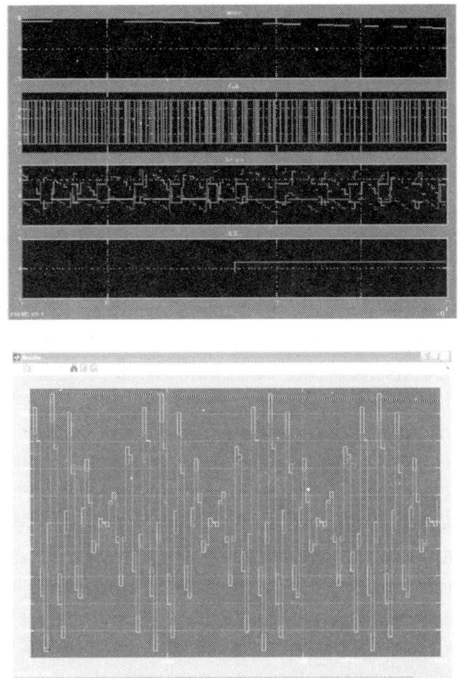

Fig. 7 Model Based Design Simulation Result

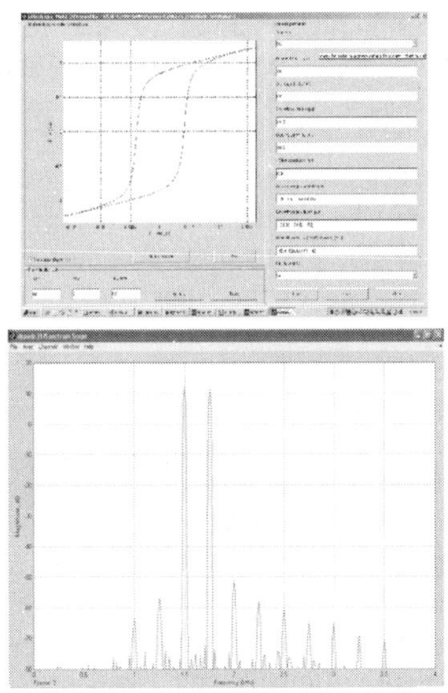

Fig. 8 Hysteresis Curve and Frequency response of Sigma Delta 2nd Order ADC

Results of Behavior Simulation

Specifications	Integrator1	Integrator2
Signal Swing	±0.8Vref	±0.5Vref
Slew rate	>40V/μs	>15V/μs
Unit Gain bandwidth	>50MHz	>20MHz
Sampling Cap	>3pF	>0.5Pf
Sampling Linearity	>18bit	>12bit

The Simulink behavior results of second order sigma delta modulator with switched capacitor is as shown in the table above which gives an detail description for the choice of second order ADC is most suitable for the biomedical applications.

5. Reconstructing the Signal and filter

The Sigma-Delta ADC output contains the original signal fed into it, but it requires some filtering before it can reconstruct the original input. This section describes how the signal can be reconstructed, as well as what filter is plan to use on the FPGA and how to choose that filter. In order to reconstruct the signal, is to simply have to remove the high frequency noise. This can be done by implementing a simple low pass filter with a cutoff frequency placed before the high frequency noise. The highest frequency in the electrophysiological signals that it will be processing is about 2 kHz. The high frequency noise in the Sigma-Delta ADC output doesn't occur until the frequency is over 10 kHz. Because of this, the cutoff frequency of the reconstruction filter was set at 5 kHz.

Since the implementation of the filter on the FPGA, it must weigh the effectiveness of the filter between the ease and feasibility of implementing it on the FPGA. A higher order filter will give us less high frequency noise and a better reconstructed signal, but it will be harder to implement and may use more resources than the FPGA has. Another issue is the quantization is, use for the filter coefficients and the output signal. Using a lower number of bits will make it easier to implement, but it will round off a significant portion of the coefficients in higher order filters and make them ineffective. Alternatively, using a higher number of bits will use more memory and be more difficult to implement, but will make higher order filters effective. Filters were analyzed by putting a 2 kHz sine wave into a Sigma-Delta ADC converter and gradually increasing the filter order and observing the output in the time domain and frequency domain. It was noted that there was a point where jagged edges stopped appearing in the filter – this was shortly before a 400th order filter. The basic block of the filter implemented with FPGA is as shown in Fig. 9.

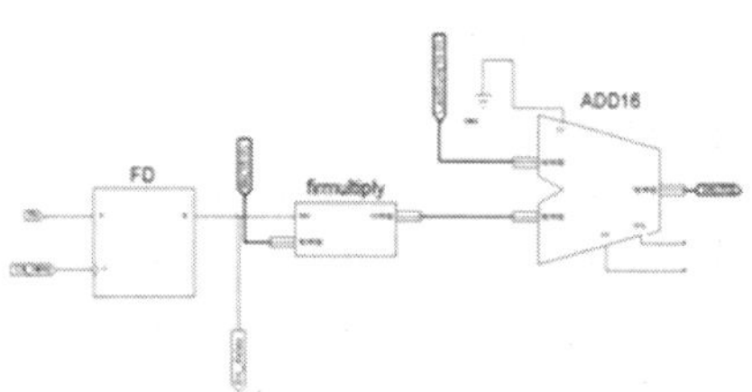

Fig. 9 Filter Block

The overall result of designing a second order sigma delta type ADC is implemented with FPGA is shown in Fig.10.

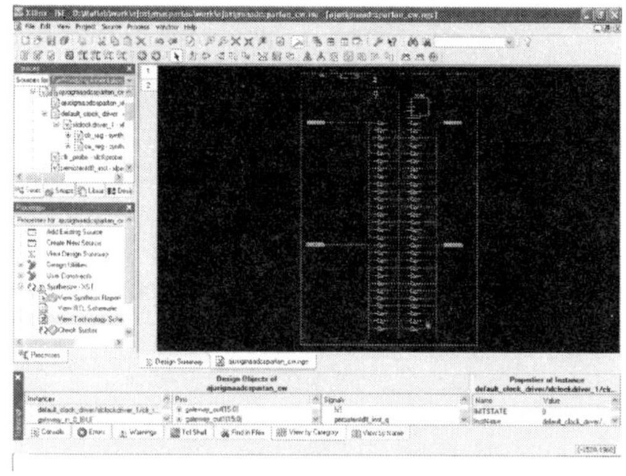

Fig. 10 Schematic Results

6. Data analysis unit

Heart rate variability (HRV), the changes in the beat-to-beat rate calculated from the electro cardiogram, is a key indicator of individual's cardiovascular condition. The Fig. 11 and Fig. 12 shows the practical implementation of the system. The variation in time period separating consecutive heart beats has come to be conventionally described as HRV

6.1 ECG Heart Rate Variability (HRV)

All parameters of HRV[4], whether in time or frequency domain are derived from ECG data. Either in time domain or frequency the first and foremost thing to do is detect the QRS peak using the peak detection algorithm.

Fig. 11 ECG Signal Acquired from the Normal Subject

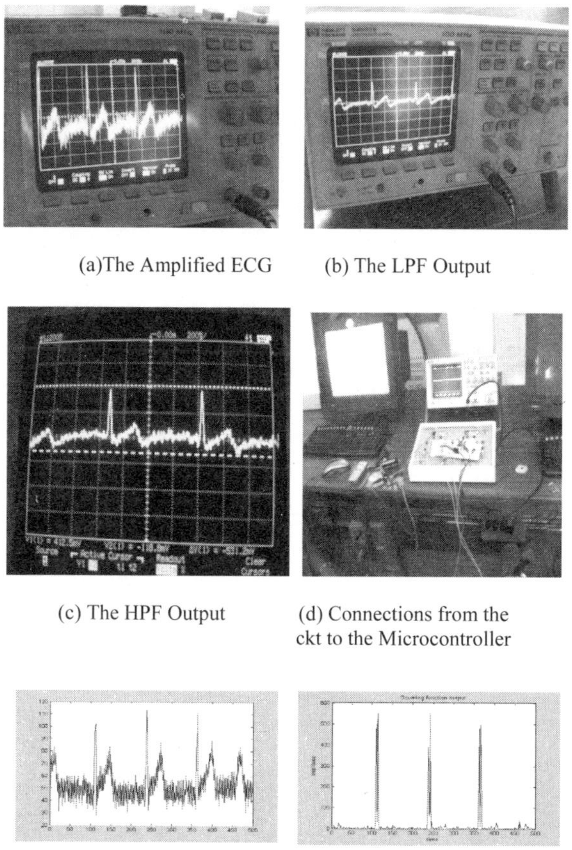

(a)The Amplified ECG (b) The LPF Output

(c) The HPF Output (d) Connections from the ckt to the Microcontroller

(e) Original Acquired Signal (f) Squared Output

Fig. 12 The out put results acquired on CRO and data acquired from MATLAB.

Series of RR intervals are obtained and analyzed either in time domain or frequency domain.

So the first thing is to implement QRS DETECTION algorithm. The various stages that are involved in the algorithm are

Step1: Low pass filter

The difference equation of this filter is given as

Y(nT)=2y(nT-T)-y (nT-2T)+x (nT)-2x (nT-6T) +x (nT-12T)

Step2: High pass filter

The difference equation for this filter is

Y (nT)=32x (nT-16T)-[y (nT-T)+x (nT)-x (nT-32T)]

Step3: Derivative function and the difference equation is: and the filter delay is about 2 samples.

Y (nT)= 0.27*(2x(nT)+x (nT-T)-x (nT-3T)-2x (nT-4T))

Step 4: Squaring this is done to remove the negatives peaks available in the signal

Y (nT)=[x (nT)]^{2}

Step 5: Window integration: Moving window integration extracts features in addition to the slope of the R wave. It is implemented with the following difference equation.

Y (nT)=(1/N)*[x (nT- (N-1) T)+x (nT- (N-2) T)+.... x (nT)]

Step 6: Thresholding: In ECG waveform the maximum amplitude is obtained at R wave. So the maximum value is selected in every cycle and the corresponding cycle is also detected.

Step 7: Heart period signal: To generate a HRV signal, first one needs to develop a heart period signal Heart Period signal is basically the signal obtained when the difference between consecutive the R peaks are taken. The signal is plotted in time i.e., the RR intervals of each beat. The heart period signal (also known as RR signal or HP signal) is obtained from those R wave peak time instants. Its graph shows the time interval between the heartbeats on a certain time instant and the previous beat

7. Future Scopes

This project can be comprehended in the future, so that it may benefit the field of medicine and technology even more greatly. A number of the future benefits are as follows:

1. The Data acquisition system, which is a now a single parameter can be extended to multi parameter monitoring.
2. Due to the size limit of RAM, the acquired signal can only be stored for approximately 2 minutes. This would like to attach a storage device, which would enable to store the data for more then six hours in the future.
3. Data transfer is currently performed through two-step process. Once all data is displayed through HyperTerminal, the result is saved as a text file, which later would be loaded into MatLab. This is a cumbersome process and then to export the data directly by using data acquisition system, provided in MatLab.

8. References

[1] Bronzino, J. D., The Biomedical Engineering Handbook, IEEE Press, 2000, pp 73-1 - 73-5.

[2] BE304 Laboratory Notes, Michigan Technological University www.biomed.mtu.edu.au/osoykan/c lasses/be304/wee k3/week3.htm

[3] Khorovets, A., "What is An Electrocardiogram?" The Internet Journal of Health, Volume 1 Number 2, 2000.

[4] Ayang-ang, C. K. B., Sison, L. G., "Electrocardiograph Pre-Filtering, QRS Detection, and Palm Display Programming for Biomedical Applications," ECE Conference, University of St. Tomas, Manila, 2001.

[5] Schamroth. C.. An Introduction to Electrocardiography. Blackwell Sci. Publishing. 7th edition. 2001.

[6] Timothy K.. Knilans. T.-C., Chou. L. S. R. , Electrocardiography in Clinical Practice Adult and Pediatric , W B Saunders: 4th edition. 1996. [7]www.datasheetcatalog.com/datasheets_pdf/A/D/6/2/AD624.shtml-14k. AD624 Instrumentation amp datasheet.

[8] Lown B, Verrier RL. Neural activity and ventricular fibrillation. N Engl J Med 1976; 294: 1165–70.

[9] Corr PB, Yamada KA, Witkowski FX. Mechanisms controlling cardiac autonomic function and their relation to arrhythmogenesis. In: Fozzard HA, Haber E, Jennings RB, Katz AN, Morgan HE. eds. The Heart and Cardiovascular System. New York: Raven Press, 1986: 1343–1403.

[10] Schwartz PJ. Priori SG. Sympathetic nervous system and cardiac arrhythmias. In: Zipes DP. Jalife J. eds. Cardiac Electrophysiology. From Cell to Bedside. Philadelphia: W.B. Saunders, 1990: 330–43.

[11] Leung SW and Zhang YT: Digitization of electrocardiogram (ECG) signals using delta-sigma modulation. IEEE Engineering in Medicine and Biology Society 1998; 4: 1964 -1966.

Fuzzy Controller for DC/DC Converter

B. Jagadish Kumar[1], Dr. Banakara Basavaraja[2] and G.Rajendar
[1]Lecturer, KITS, Warangal
[2]Principal, Dr.B.V.R.I.T, Narasapur
[3]Assistant Professor, KITS,Warangal
jagadeesh908@gmail.com banakara_36@rediffmail.com 4u.rajendar@gmail.com

Abstract

In this paper implementation of fuzzy controllers for DC-DC converters is presented. Fuzzy logic control topology is developed and implemented for different types of DC-DC converters such as the buck, the boost, the buck-boost, and the sepic converters. In this paper sudden changes in a load is considered and discussed. The fundamentals governing the design, control and performance of the DC-DC converters are also illustrated. Simulation results have been obtained by considering appropriate scaling factors associated with the input variables of the fuzzy controller.

1. Introduction

Dc-dc converters are an intriguing subject from the control point of view, due to their intrinsic non-linearity. Common control approaches, like *Voltage Control* and *Current Injected Control* (and its derivations like *Standard Control Module* and *Average Current Control) [1],* require a good knowledge of the system and accurate tuning in order to obtain desired performances. These controllers are simple to implement and easy to design, but their performances generally depend on the working point, so that the presence of parasitic elements, time-varying loads and variable supply voltages can make difficult selection of the control parameters which ensure a proper behavior in any operating conditions. Achieving large-signal stability often calls for a reduction of the useful bandwidth, so affecting converter performances. Moreover, application of these control techniques to high-order dc-dc converters, e.g. Cuk and Sepic topologies, may result in a very critical design of control parameters and difficult stabilization.

A completely different approach is offered by the Fuzzy Logic Control (FLC), which does neither require a precise mathematical modeling of the system nor complex computations [2-4]. This control technique relies on the human capability to understand systems' behavior, and is based on qualitative control rules. Thus, control design is simple, since it is only based on linguistic rules of the type: "*if the output voltage error is positive and its rate of change is negative then reduce slightly the duty-cycle",* and so on. This approach lies on the basic physical properties of the systems and it is potentially able to extend control capability even to those operating conditions where linear control techniques fail, i.e. large-signal dynamics and large parameter variations. Of course, fuzzy controllers cannot provide, in general, better small-signal response than standard regulators. However, since fuzzy control is based on heuristic rules, it makes easy application of non-linear control laws to face the non-linear nature of dc-dc converters.

The FLC approach is general, in the sense that almost the same control rules can be applied to several dc-dc converters; however, some scale factors must be tuned according to converter topology and parameters.

In our proposal, the fuzzy controller requires only sensing of one inductor current and the output voltage, and its implementation is relatively simple.

The proposed control technique was tested on Buck-Boost and Sepic converters, in order to verify the theoretical forecasts. Simulated results confirm validity of the solution.

2. Basics of Fuzzy Logic Controllers

Fuzzy Logic Control is one of the most successful applications of Fuzzy Set Theory, introduced by L.A. Zadeh in 1965 [2]. Its major features are the use of linguistic variables rather than numerical variables. *Linguistic variables,* defined as variables whose values are sentences in a natural language (such as *small* and *large),* may be represented by fuzzy sets.

A *fuzzy set* is an extension of a crisp set, where an element can only belong to a set (full membership) or not belong at all (no membership). Fuzzy sets allow *partial membership,* which means that an element may partially belong to more than one set.

A fuzzy set A is characterized by a *membership function* μ_A that assigns to each object in a given class a grade of membership to the set. Of course, the grade of membership can range from 0 (no membership) to 1 (full membership); we therefore write:

$$\mu_A: X \rightarrow [01,] \qquad (1)$$

which means that the fuzzy set A belongs to an universal set X (usually called *universe of discourse)* defined in a specific problem. A fuzzy set A is called *fuzzy singleton,* when there is only one element x_o with $\mu_A(x_o)=1$, while all the other elements have a membership grade equal to zero.

The general structure of a fuzzy logic control is represented in Fig. 2 and comprises four principal components: a *fuzzyfication interface,* which converts input data into suitable linguistic values; a *knowledge base,* which consists of a data base with the necessary linguistic definitions and the control rule set; a *decisionmaking logic* which, simulating a human decision process, infers the fuzzy control action from theknowledge of the control rules and the linguistic variable definitions; a *defuzzyfication interface,* which yields a nonfuzzy control action from an inferred fuzzy controlaction.

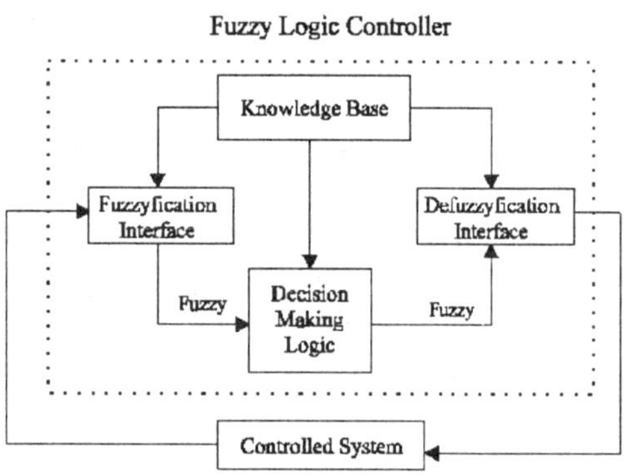

Fig. 2 Basic configuration of FLC

3. Application of Fuzzy Control To DC/DC Converters

The basic scheme of a general-purpose fuzzy controller for dc-dc converters is shown in Fig. 3. The converter is represented by a "black box", from which we only extract the terminals corresponding to input voltage u_g, output voltage u_o, one inductor current i_L and controlled switch S. As we can see, only two state variables are sensed: the output voltage and one inductor current. This latter is the inductor current for 2nd-order schemes (i.e., Buck, Boost, Buck-Boost) and the input inductor current for 4th-order schemes (i.e., Cuk and Sepic).

From these measurements, the fuzzy controller provides a signal proportional to the converter duty-cycle, which is then applied to a standard PWM modulator.

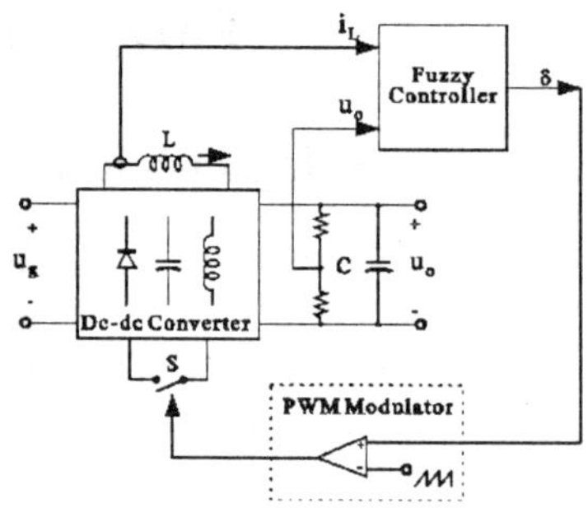

Fig. 3 Block diagram of fuzzy control scheme of dc-dc converters

A. Fuzzy controller structure

The first important step in the fuzzy controller definition is the choice of the input variables. Approaches which utilize only the output voltage and its rate of change were already presented in the literature [5-6], but they show poor dynamic

Performances. In order to improve operation we need additional information on the energy stored in the converter, i.e., an inductor current must be sensed. Accordingly, in the proposed fuzzy controller we use three input variables: output voltage error C_u, inductor current error C_i and the inductor current i_L, which is used for current limiting.

A block diagram of the fuzzy controller structure is shown in Fig. 4. While the output voltage reference is usually available as an external signal, the inductor current reference (ILRef) depends on the operating point. For this reason it is computed by means of a low-pass filter, in the assumption that the dc value of the current is automatically adjusted by the converter according to power balance condition.

The controller output variable is the switch duty-cycle, which is obtained by adding the outputs of two different fuzzy controllers: one ("Fuzzy-P") gives the proportional part 0_P of the duty-cycle as a function of C_i, C_u and i_L; the other ("Fuzzy-I") gives the increment $A0_I$, which is then integrated to provide integral term 0_I of the duty cycle 0.

This structure allows selection of indipendent control laws for the "proportional" part and the "integral" part of the duty cycle.

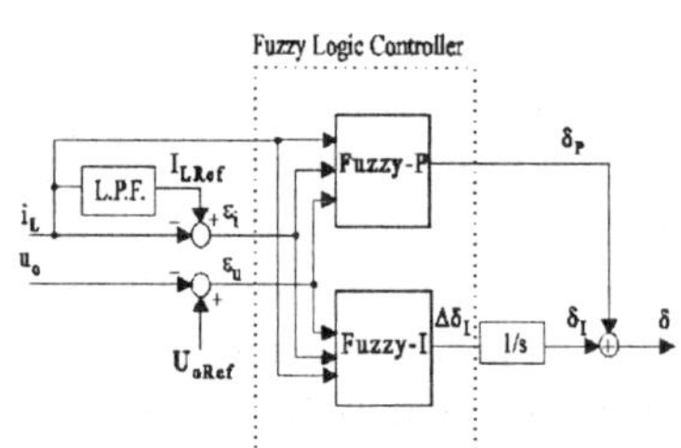

Fig. 4 Fuzzy logic controller structure.

B. Membership functions

Fuzzy sets must be defined for each input and output variable. As shown in Fig. 5, five fuzzy subsets PB (Positive Big), PS (Positive Small), ZE (Zero), NS (Negative Small), NB (Negative Big) have been chosen for input variables C_i and C_u, while only two fuzzy subsets (NORM (normal operation), LIMIT (current limit) have been selected for the input current, since the purpose is only to handle the current limit condition. For the output variables seven fuzzy subsets have been used (PB,PM,PS,ZE,NS,NM,NB), in order to smooth the control action. As shown in Fig. 5, triangular and trapezoidal shapes have been adopted for the membership functions; the value of each input and output variable is normalized in [-1,1] by using suitable scale factors.

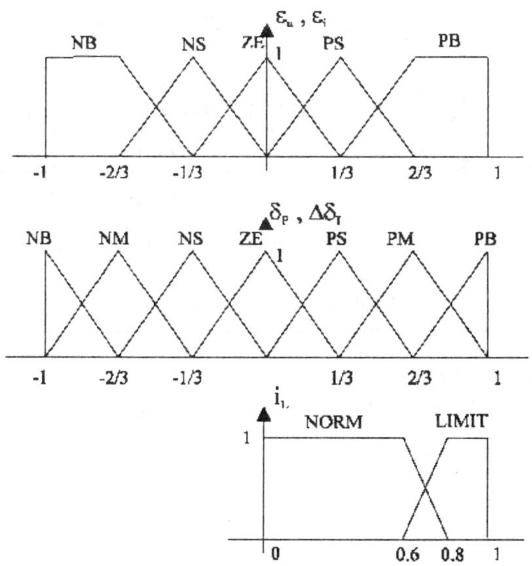

Fig. 5 Membership functions for C_i, C_u, i_L and O_P, AO_I.

C. Derivation of control rules

Fuzzy control rules are obtained from the analysis of the system behavior. In their formulation it must be considered that using different control laws depending on the operating conditions can greatly improve the converter performances in terms of dynamic response and robustness.

First, when the output voltage is far from the set point (C_u is PB or NB) the corrective action done by the controller must be strong (duty cycle close to zero or one) in order to have the dynamic response as fast as possible, obviously taking into account current limit specifications.

Second, when output voltage error approaches zero (C_u is NS, ZE, PS) the current error should be properly taken into account similarly to current-mode control, in order to ensure stability around the working point.

Finally, when the current approaches the limit value, suitable rules must be introduced in order to perform the current limit action while preventing large overshoots.

The selected control rules are described hereafter.

C1) far from the set point

When the output voltage is far from the set point (C_u is PB or NB) the corrective action must be strong: this means that 0 P should be NB (or PB), while $A0_I$ should be zero (ZE) in order to prevent continuous increase (or decrease) of integral term 0_I, that would cause overshoots.

The basic control rules are:

IF C_u is PB and i_L is NORM THEN 0_P is PB and $A0_I$ is ZE IF C_u is NB and i_L is NORM THEN 0_P is NB and $A0_I$ is ZE

which state that, far from the set point the control action is primarily determined by the output voltage error. This control strategy can be adopted provided the existence of the current limit.

C2) close to the set point

In this region the current error must be properly taken into account in order to ensure stability and speed of responce. The goal of the fuzzy controller in this region is to achieve a satisfactory dynamic performance with small sensitivity to parameter variations.

The control rules can be written according to energy balance conditions. Assuming that the inductor current is far from the limit, the following criteria hold:

i. if C_u and C_i are both zero, O_P and AO_I must be zero too (steady-state condition); in fact, in the steady state the duty cycle is determined only by the integral term, that should be kept constant.
ii. if output voltage error C_u is negative and inductor current is greater than its reference value (C_i<0), O_P and AO_I must be negative; in fact in this condition the system energy must be decreased.
iii. if output voltage error C_u is positive and inductor current is lower than its reference value (Ci<0), O_P and AO_I must be positive; in fact, in this condition the system energy must be increased.
iv. if output voltage error is positive and inductor current is greater than its reference value (or vice-versa), both O_P and AO_I must be kept to zero in order to prevent undershoot or overshoot, awaiting for a partial discharge of the inductor energy on the output capacitor before taking some control action.

According to these criteria, the rule sets shown in Table 1 and 2 are derived for O_P e AO_I. Figs. 4 and 5 give a graphical representation of Tables 1 and 2.

Table I Rule table for "Fuzzy-P", assuming that iL is NORM

$c_i \backslash c_u$	NB	NS	ZE	PS	PB
PB	NB	PS	PM	PB	PB
PS	NB	ZE	PS	PM	PB
ZE	NB	NS	ZE	PS	PB
NS	NB	NM	NS	ZE	PB
NM	NB	NB	NM	PS	PB

Table 2 Rule table for "Fuzzy-I", assuming that iL is NORM

$c_i \backslash c_u$	NB	NS	ZE	PS	PB
PB	ZE	PS	PM	PS	ZE
PS	ZE	ZE	PS	PM	ZE
ZE	ZE	NS	ZE	PS	ZE
NS	ZE	NM	NS	ZE	ZE
NB	ZE	NS	NM	NS	ZE

C3) current limit operation

Current limit operation is governed by the following strategy:

1. Current limitation is achieved by choosing the value of O_p according to the output voltage error. For example: if C_u is negative big, O_p is kept zero in order to limit the current value; instead, when C_u is approaching zero O_p must go negative, so as to avoid unwanted overshoots (e.g. at start up with light load). The fuzzy rules that implement this strategy are:

PB	*PS*	*ZE*	*NS*	*NB*
ZE	*NS*	*NB*	*NB*	*NB*

As long as the current is close to the limit value, the integral action must be disabled in order to prevent overshoots; the fuzzy rule is:

IF i_L is LIMIT THEN AO_i is ZE

2. An external action is also performed during limit operation: since the reference value of the inductor current takes a wrong value during this operation (it becomes equal to ^{I}lim),

IF i_L is LIMIT and C_u is THEN O_p is the capacitor of the low-pass filter generating the current reference is reset to zero as long as the current is close to ^{I}lim·

It is important to note that the heuristic approach described in this paragraph remains valid irrespective of converter topology.

D. Low-pass filter time costant τ.

The choice of ô can heavily affect the system behaviour. ô should be suitably higher than the switching period in order to provide a ripple-free current reference, but small enough to allow fast converter response. In practice, values close to the natural time costants of the system give the best results

6. Simulated Results

Control operation was verified by simulation. Several topologies have been tested, and results of Buck-Boost and Sepic converters are reported. The basic schemes are shown in below, respectively, their parameters being listed in Table 3.

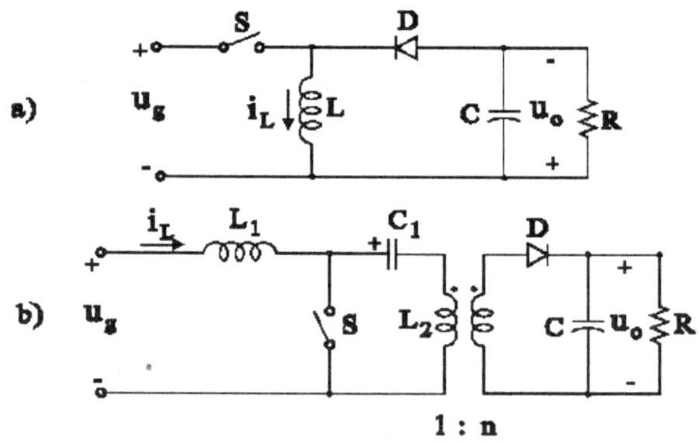

Fig. a) Buck-Boost converter; b) Sepic converter.

Table 3 Converter Parameters.

BUCK-BOOST
V_in = 12.0; %Input voltage in Volts
V_Refl = 8.0; % Reference output voltage in Volts
R_L = 6.0; %Load Resistance in Ohms
I_Ref = V_Refl/R_L ;
L_ind = 335.0e-6;
R_ind = 0.00001;
Cap = 10.0e-7;
Iz = 0.0

;SEPIC

V_in = 15.0; %Input voltage in Volts
V_Refl = 20.0; % Reference output voltage in Volts
R_L = 20.0; %Load Resistance in Ohms
I_Ref = V_Refl/R_L ;
L1 = 120.0e-8;
C1 = 47.0e-5;
Lm = 120.0e-8;
Cap = 47.0e-6

Buck-Boost.

The converter behavior in the case of step load changes from full-load to light-load and vice-versa is shown in below. Output voltage u_o and inductor current i_L behave well both in terms of overshoot and response speed. Voltage and inductor current behavior during a start up under light-load condition (worst case), followed by a step in the output voltage reference from 12V to 8V. In both cases the output voltage error is initially NB, so that a strong action is applied causing a current limit action. The overshoot on the output voltage is almost avoided at start up, while it is limited at 2% of the nominal value in the other case, in spite of a high limit current value. The robustness to wide parameter variations was also verified.

Sepic. The same rule set used for the buck-boost converter was applied to the Sepic converter. Results shows the converter behavior under fuzzy control in the case of a step load variation from full-load to light-load and vice-versa. Good performances both in terms of overshoot and response speed are achieved even in this 4-th order converter. Note that, as soon as the load is disconnected, the control opens the switch and the converter turns in discontinuon conduction mode. In this way no energy goes to the output, because the diode D is off.

Boos converter simulation results.

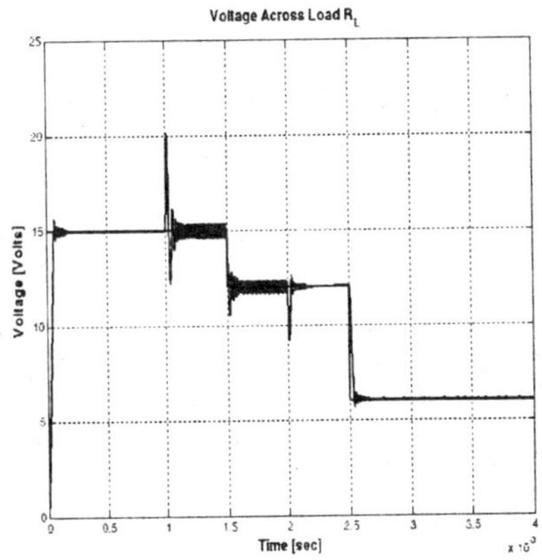

Simulated response of output voltage for buck-boost converter subject to step change in load resistance followed by output voltage variation

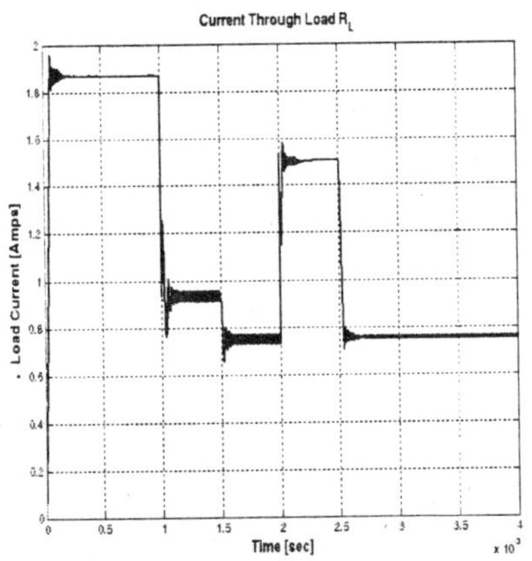

Simulated responce of Current through load resistance for buck-boost converter subject to step change in load resistance followed by output voltage variations

Sepic converter simulation results:

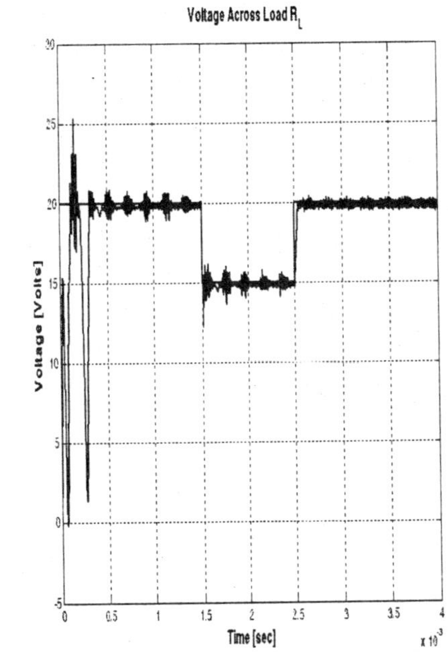

Simulated response of output voltage for sepic converter subject to step change in load resistance followed by output voltage variation

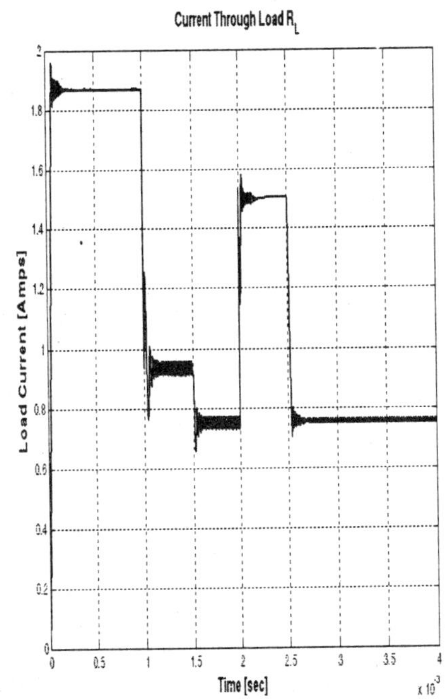

Simulated responce of Current through load resistance for sepic converter subject to step change in load resistance followed by output voltage variations

7. Conclusions

A general-purpose controller for dc-dc converters based on the fuzzy logic is presented. As compared to standard controllers, it provides improved performances in terms of overshoot limitation and sensitivity to parameter variations.

This is possible since fuzzy logic control rules can be assigned separately for the various regions of operation, resulting in effective small-signal and large-signal operation.

Simulation results of Buck-Boost and Sepic converter confirm the validity of the proposed control technique.

8. References

[1] R.Redl, N.Sokal. "Current-Mode control, five different types, used with the three basic classes of power converter: small-signal AC and large-signal DC characterization, stability requirement, and implementation of practical circuits", PESC 1985, pp.771-785.

[2] L.A. Zadeh, "Outline of a New Approach of the Analysis of Complex System and Decision Processes", IEEE Trans. on System, Man and Cybernatics, Vol. SMC-3, No.1,pp. 28-44, 1973.

[3] C.C. Lee, "Fuzzy Logic in Control System: Fuzzy Logic Controller - Part I", IEEE Trans. on System, Man and Cybernatics, vol.20, n.2, pp 404-418, March/April 1990.

[4] C.C. Lee, "Fuzzy Logic in Control System: Fuzzy Logic Controller - Part II", IEEE Trans. on System, Man and Cybernatics, vol.20, n.2, pp 404-418, March/April 1990.